Random House

LATIN-AMERICAN SPANISH

Dictionary

Random House LATIN-AMERICAN SPANISH *Dictionary*

Spanish-English
English-Spanish

David L. Gold
Doctor in Romance Philology
University of Barcelona

Random House
NEW YORK

Library of Congress Cataloging-in-Publication Data

Gold, David L.
Random House Latin-American Spanish dictionary : Spanish-English. English-Spanish / David L. Gold.
p. cm.
ISBN 0-679-45294-X
1. Spanish language—Provincialisms—Latin America—Dictionaries. 2. Spanish language—Dictionaries—English. 3. English language--Dictionaries—Spanish. I. Title.
PC4822.G65 1997
463'.21—dc20 96-27274
CIP

Random House Web address http://www.randomhouse.com/

Typeset and Printed in the United States of America
First Edition
9 8 7 6 5 4 3 2 1

New York Toronto London Sydney Auckland

Contents

Preface

Selection of Vocabulary

The aim of this dictionary is to cover as much current vocabulary as possible, as well as certain items found in standard works of Modern Spanish and English literature.

This dictionary includes items often omitted in other bilingual dictionaries—road and street signs, for example—though few things could be as frustrating (and, sometimes, as dangerous) as seeing such signs but not knowing what they mean (in this dictionary, all kinds of public notices are enclosed by the symbols « » in Spanish and by double quotation marks in English). Also, many vocabulary items consisting of more than one word have been treated here (see for instance **do** in the English-Spanish section).

For lack of space, however, not every current or useful item could be included and a selection of material was thus necessary.

Spanish Spelling and Alphabetization

On January 1, 1959, the Spanish language academies changed certain spelling rules and on April 27, 1994, they eliminated **ch** and **ll** as separate letters of the alphabet. Thus, whereas words like **chico** and **chocolate** were formerly alphabetized under their own letter (**ch**, which came between **c** and **d**) and words like **llamar** and **llegar** were formerly alphabetized under their own letter (**ll**, which came between **l** and **m**), words containing **ch** or **ll**, in whatever part of the word they may appear, are now alphabetized as they would be in English (**chico** therefore now appears under **c** and **llegar** under **l**).

Field Labels

Only essential field labels are given in this dictionary. For example, the label *medicine* or *pathology* is unnecessary at **flebitis** 'phlebitis' (in the Spanish-English section) because both the Spanish and the English words refer only to the pathological condition so called in those languages.

In contrast to that entry, we do need a label at **foca** 'seal' (in the Spanish-English section) because English **seal** has several meanings and only the zoological one is intended here. Anglophones looking up **foca** thus need the label *zoology* (hispanophones need no label because they know that **foca** is the name of an animal, hence they will correctly assume that **seal** is intended only in its zoological sense).

Spatial Labels for Spanish

Spatial variation in Spanish ranges from nil to extreme. On one hand, the words for 'flower' and 'mother-in-law', for example, are everywhere **flor** and **suegra** respectively. On the other hand, the language has many words for 'bus' and 'ballpoint pen' (see the English-Spanish section of this dictionary).

Little of what has been written on how Spanish differs from place to place is reliable. For example, the Spanish-English section of one dictionary offers **alborotos** *Central America* 'popcorn', **cabritos** *Chile* 'popcorn', and **palomitas** 'popcorn', but the English-Spanish section of the very same dictionary has **popcorn** 'alborotos' *the River Plate region and Peru*, 'cabritas', and 'palomitas de maíz'.

In the absence of trustworthy sources, spatial labels are best dispensed with, though some are given in this dictionary when I have been able to ascertain at first hand that a less than universal usage is found in a certain area.

In general, this dictionary emphasizes Spanish of the Western Hemisphere. In particular, it tries to convey some of the spatial variation that may be found from country to country within that area. Therefore, certain usages are labeled *Latin American* (if they are used in at least many Western Hemispheric countries) and others are given more restricted labels, like *Argentina* and *Mexico* (if they appear to be limited to just certain countries).

Spatial characterizations in this dictionary should be interpreted in a minimal way. For instance, *Mexican* means that the usage so labeled is found in Mexico but it says nothing about whether that usage is present or absent elsewhere (something which only further research could determine).

Subentries

If a main entry head is repeated in a subentry in exactly the same form, it is abbreviated to its first letter (for instance, at **fin** in the Spanish-English section we find **a f. de**, which stands for **a fin de**). If the main entry head appears in any other form, the full form is given in the subentry (thus, at **fin**, the subentry head **a fines de** is spelled without abbreviation).

Irregular Spanish Verbs and the Direction "See . . ."

If a Spanish verb is irregular, it has been treated in one of two ways: either its principal parts are shown (see for example the end of the entry for **caber**) or you are referred to an analogous irregular verb for guidance (see for example the end of the entry for **comparecer**, where you are directed to **conocer**). Thus, since the irregular form **conozco**, is shown at **conocer** (it being irregular in the sense that it has a **z**), you may infer that **comparecer** has the irregular form **comparezco.**

One of the consequences of the changes in Spanish spelling of January 1, 1959, is that a new kind of orthographically irregular verb has come into existence (for example **ahijar, ahincar, ahitar, ahuchar, ahumar, ahusar, cohibir, prohibir, prohijar, rehilar, rehusar, sahumar, sobrehilar,** and **trashumar**).

If "See . . . " is all you find at an entry, you are being directed to a synonym. Thus, "**descompasarse** See **descomedirse**" means that the translations of **descomedirse** are those of **descompasarse** too.

Spanish Equivalents of 'you'

Today's Spanish, when taken as a whole, has at least six equivalents of 'you': **tú, vos, usted** (abbreviated to **Vd.**), **su merced** (all of which are used in addressing one person), **ustedes** (abbreviated to **Vds.**), **vosotros, vosotras,** and **sus mercedes** (all used in addressing more than one person).

When **you** occurs in this dictionary, usually only one of those words has been chosen to translate it, though three are never used here: **su merced, sus mercedes,** because they are now limited to only a small area of the Spanish-speaking world (the Cundinamarca Savanna, in Colombia) and even there they are now obsolescent, and **vos,** because the verb forms corresponding to this pronoun often vary from country to country.

Usually, the selection of one pronoun or another in this dictionary has been arbitrary, in which case any of the others could just as easily have been chosen. For example, for **How are you?** the translation '¿Cómo está Vd.?' is offered, yet any of the other pronouns could appear instead (with, in certain cases, a different verb form, for instance '¿Cómo están Vds.?').

In certain cases, however, not all pronouns (whether actually used or just implicit) would be appropriate. For example, among the translations of **please . . .** are imperative forms of **servirse . . . .** Because **servirse** in this sense is a formal usage (found mostly in impersonal writing like application blanks), it is not found in any familiar form of the imperative. The dictionary therefore gives **¡sírvase . . . !** (where the understood subject is **usted,** a formal pronoun). It could also have given **¡sírvanse . . . !** (where the understood subject is **ustedes,** likewise a formal pronoun), but not any form in which the subject were an informal pronoun.

Masculine and Feminine, Male and Female

As women engage in more and more activities once the domain of men, a growing number of Spanish nouns formerly used only in the masculine gender are being used in the feminine too. This dictionary thus labels **nauta, paracaidista, púgil, pugilista, recluta, reservista,** and **seminarista,** for example, as both masculine and feminine (the gender to be chosen depending on the gender of the person in question). For the user's convenience, the gender of Spanish nouns is indicated not only in the Spanish-English section but also in the English-Spanish one.

Many sample Spanish phrases and sentences in this dictionary can refer to people of either gender. For example, under **wish** in the English-Spanish section the sample sentence **I wished him a Merry Christmas** is translated 'Le deseé unas Pascuas muy felices' and 'Le felicité las Pascuas'. Since they both also mean 'I wished her a Merry Christmas', the sentence could as easily have contained **her** rather than **him.** It should therefore not be inferred that every phrase or sentence referring to a male cannot refer to a female (or vice versa). In this dictionary, male and female references have been chosen randomly, hopefully in about equal number.

In other cases, a slight change is needed to turn a male reference into a female one or vice versa. For instance, **He was within an ace of being killed** (under **within,** prep., in the English-Spanish section) is rendered by 'Por poco le matan'. Changing **he** to **she** and **le** to **la** will yield a correct equivalence referring to a female. Since it would have taken up too much space to indicate those alternate equivalences, they are not given here, but with just an elementary knowledge of both languages, users of this dictionary will be able to make the necessary changes and thus have at their disposal many more sample phrases and sentences than it supplies.

A dictionary of any living language can always be improved, all the more so a dictionary of two living languages. Additions, corrections, and other suggestions will be received with thanks. They should be addressed to:

Random House Reference & Information Publishing
Random House, Inc.
201 East 50th St.
New York, NY 10022-7703
U.S.A.

To Sol Steinmetz, editorial director of Random House Reference & Information Publishing, and to his staff go my thanks for their help in seeing this dictionary into print.

D.L.G.
September
1996

The Basics of Spanish Pronunciation

Whereas the fit between English spelling and pronunciation has for centuries been less than ideal (think, for example, of the various pronunciations of **-ough,** as in **although, bough, cough,** and **slough**), the fit between today's Spanish spelling and pronunciation is quite good, thanks to the regulatory efforts of the Spanish academies.

Because of that good fit, Spanish-speakers learn to read and spell faster than English-speakers, there is no such thing as a Spanish spelling bee, and Spanish spelling is a good basis for teaching the rudiments of Spanish pronunciation. The following instructions thus take spelling as their starting point. Pronunciation is described in two ways: with phonetic symbols (enclosed in slashes or brackets) and by way of approximate comparisons with English. A wavy line separates variants (like **esnob** ~ **snob**). A stress mark (ˈ) means that the syllable following it is stressed (as in [reˈlo]). An asterisk indicates a nonexistent form (like English ***llion**). A right-facing "arrow"(>), or "greater than" sign, means 'became in Spanish' (as in English **rum** and French **rhum** > **ron** ~ **romo**).

As may be expected of a language that has been used for many centuries, over a vast area, and by diverse people, Spanish is now pronounced in various ways. Of the many current pronunciations, two are offered as most suitable for speakers of Spanish as a second language. The two standards are identical to a large extent, differing chiefly with respect to the pronunciation of **c** before **e; c** before **i; z** in any position; and, optionally, **ll** in any position.

To the extent that the two standards differ, features belonging to just one of them are labeled either *Standard 1* or *Standard 2* below.

Features labeled *Standard 1* are accepted as standard in Spain but not in the Western Hemisphere. Features labeled *Standard 2* are accepted as standard in the Western Hemisphere but not in Spain. If you speak Spanish mostly with Spaniards or mostly with people in or from the Western Hemisphere, your choice of standard will thus be straightforward. If you speak with people from both areas, you can either try to master both standards or, if you want to follow just one of them no matter to whom you speak, pick Standard 2.

In the Western Hemisphere, features labeled *Standard 1* are often either erroneously admired as being "the correct pronunciation of the language" or, quite the opposite, disdained as highfalutin (which are precisely the same reactions to British English frequently heard in English-speaking areas outside Europe). Neither standard, however, is intrinsically better than the other.

If possible, review the material given here with a speaker of Standard Spanish and hear how the sample words, phrases, and sentences are pronounced.

a is pronounced /a/, which is similar to the second vowel of the English interjection **aha!** and the vowel of the English interjection **ah,** although much shorter in duration.

See also "Diphthongs and Triphthongs" below.

b has three pronunciations. At the beginning of an utterance, after [m] (whether represented by **m** or by **n**), or after [n] (whether represented by **n** or by **m**), the letter **b** is pronounced [b], which is similar to the pronunciation of the first consonant of English **beach, broth, pebble,** etc. For example, in the sentence **Bulgaria envió a ambos embajadores en un barco japonés,** each of the four instances of **b** (and the one instance of **v**) is so pronounced.

Before /č/, /f/, /t/, /k/, /s/, /x/, or /θ/ in the same word (see **ch** [under **c**], **f, t, c, g,** and **c** respectively for interpreting those symbols), **b** is pronounced [p] (see **p** for interpreting that symbol), as in **subtítulo, absceso, subjefe,** and, in Standard 1, **subcentral.** That rule also holds before [p] in the same word (with the further result that [p] + [p] is reduced to [p]; hence the first two syllables of **subproducto,** for example, are [supro]) and for [p] before /s/ in the same word (with the further result that [ps] may be reduced to [s.] In certain words, nonpronunciation of **b** became so widespread that the only spelling now used is without that letter, for instance **ofuscar** and its derivatives (contrast English **obfuscate, obfuscation,** etc.).

At the end of a word, more than one pronunciation of **b** may be heard. For example, **club** may be [klub], [kluβ], or [klu]. Its plural (**clubs**) may be [klups], [klus], and possibly [kluβs] (unless the plural **clubes** is used, whose universal pronunciation is [kluβεs] (see the next paragraph for interpreting [β] and **e** for interpreting [ε)]. All of the foregoing holds for compounds of **club**, like **aeroclub.** In **esnob** ~ snob, the final **b** is pronounced [b].

In all other positions (for example, **habas, hablar,** and **habré**), **b** is pronounced [β] a sound absent in English, which is made by bringing the lips close together without letting them touch each other (as if you were blowing dust away or blowing out a match or candle), expelling air through the mouth, and vibrating the vocal cords. This sound is thus similar to /v/ (as in English **very** and **vowel**), except that the latter is made by making the lower lip touch the upper teeth. English-speakers should not mistake Spanish [β] for English /v/.

It follows from the foregoing that if the position of **b** in the utterance changes, its pronunciation may change. Contrast, for example, these three utterances: (1) **Bulgaria mandó embajadores a ambos países,** (2) **En Bulgaria viven unos cuantos rusos,** and (3) **Iremos a Bulgaria.** In (1), the b of **Bulgaria** is pronounced [b] because it comes at the beginning of an utterance; in (2) the same **b** is also pronounced [b] because it comes after [m] (see the instructions for **n** on its pronunciation as [m]); but in (3) the same **b** is pronounced [β] because none of the conditions for pronouncing it [b] is met.

Similarly, when the word **baba** is pronounced in isolation, the first **b** is rendered [b] and the second one [β], but in the phrase **la baba,** the first **b** is no longer at the beginning of an utterance (nor is it preceded by the sounds [m] or [n)], hence the phrase is pronounced [laβaβa].

Or, if the **b** of **club** is pronounced, it will be [β] before a vowel. So too the final letter of **esnob**, which is always pronounced.

See also **v** and, on **tranvía,** "Miscellaneous" below.

c has several pronunciations. If it is followed by **e** or **i,** the letter c is pronounced /θ/ in Standard 1 and [s] in Standard 2. The pronunciation of /θ/ in Spanish is similar to that of **th** in English **thatch, think,** etc., but made with somewhat more protrusion of the tongue. The sound [s] is similar to the pronunciation of **s** in English **say, simple,** etc., though in northern Spain [s] is often produced with the tip of the tongue higher in the mouth than in other varieties of Spanish, the result being that this sound has a hushing quality there (similar to Modern Greek /s/), which English-speakers should not mistake for /š/, which is the pronunciation of **sh** in English **shall, should,** etc.

Although Standard 1 has /θ/ for **c** before **e** or **i**, people who use that pronunciation will not be put off if they hear you pronounce the c as [s], because the latter is widespread (though not standard) in Spain. In the Western Hemisphere, c before **e** or **i** is always pronounced [s] and never /θ/. Speakers of Western Hemispheric Spanish will react to /θ/ either as "the correct pronunciation" ("though we don't use it") or as a highfalutin pronunciation (unless it comes from people who are to the manner born, i.e., many Spaniards). Thus, whereas it is desirable though not obligatory that you use Standard 1 in Spain, you would be well advised to use only Standard 2 in the Western Hemisphere, where /θ/ is bound to elicit a sharp reaction of one kind or another (as sharp as British **drawing pin, lorry,** or **trunk call** instead of **thumbtack, truck, long-distance call** would probably elicit in the United States).

Most speakers pronounce the combination **ch,** wherever it is found, as /č/, which is similar to the pronunciation of **ch** in English **child, church,** etc. Speakers who know Catalan or, at least, are aware of the Catalan pronunciation of **ch,** may pronounce this letter combination as /k/ in Catalan-origin proper nouns used in Spanish, like the family names **Escrich** and **Roch** (see the next paragraph on Spanish /k/). The letter combination **tch** (as in **catch**) is pronounced /č/ (in general, that sound at the end of a word is extremely rare, being limited to Catalan-origin proper nouns ending in **-ch** but not pronounced in Catalan fashion and to recent borrowings from English like **catch** and **punch**).

If c ends a syllable that is not the last syllable in the word and the next syllable begins with any consonant except /t/ (for instance **accionista, facsímil,** and **técnico**), you have an alternative: c may be pronounced either /k/ or /g/. Spanish /k/ is similar to the pronunciation of c in English **escape, scandal,** etc., but different from that of c in English **cape, coop,** etc. To achieve a good rendition of Spanish /k/, hold your open palm in front of your mouth and pronounce first **cape** and **coop,** then **escape** and **scandal.** When pronouncing the first two words, you felt a noticeable puff of air on your palm, but in the last two words you felt almost no puff at all. A noticeable puff of air accompanying a speech sound is called *aspiration;* sounds pronounced with aspiration are *aspirated;* and those pronounced without it are *unaspirated.* Spanish /k/ (like Spanish /p/ and /t/) is always unaspirated, wherever it occurs. Thus, you should have no trouble with Spanish **escapar** and **escándalo** because here /k/ occurs after [s] and as an English speaker you will automatically pronounce it as unaspirated (just as you would the c of the English cognates of those words: **escape** and **scandal**). It is in other positions that you have to be careful not to aspirate: **claro, crear, tocología,** etc. (contrast them with their English cognates, all of which have an aspirated /k/: **clear, create, tocology**). See **g** for interpreting [g]. Note that if **c** is followed by **c**, the next letter is always **e** or **i** (as in **accionista** and **confección**). In such cases, you have an alternative with respect to the first **c** (either /k/ or [g] is correct) and the second **c** is pronounced according to either of the instructions given above for **c** before **e** or **i**.

If **c** ends a syllable that is not the last syllable in the word and the next syllable begins with /t/, it is pronounced /k/ in most words (like **actor** and **actriz**) and in at least one you may pronounce it /k/ or not pronounce it at all (**coctel** and its plurals: **coctels** ~ **cocteles**). In the place name **Vitoria** the absence of /k/ has been universal for so long that that is now its only spelling (in contrast to the female given name **Victoria** and the common noun **victoria**).

If **c** or **k** ends the last syllable of the word, that letter is pronounced /k/ at least in **cinc** ~ **zinc, clac, copec, frac, Nueva York,** and **tictac,** whereas in **biftec, bistec,** and **coñac** many speakers do not pronounce it (likewise in the plural of the last word, **coñacs**).

In all other cases (as in **aclarar, acoplar, acreditar, capaz, chucruta, claro,** and **creer**), **c** is pronounced /k/.

See also **k, ll** (under **l**), **q, s,** and **z.**

d has several pronunciations. At the beginning of an utterance, after [n], or after /l/, this letter is pronounced [d], which is similar to the pronunciation of **d** in English **dear, dust,** etc., with this difference: in the production of Spanish [d], the tongue touches the lower edge of the upper front incisors.

When between two vowels, when preceded by a vowel and followed by **r**, or when at the end of a word and not preceded by **r** (as in **pedir, Pedro,** and **libertad**), the letter **d** is pronounced [ð], which is similar to the pronunciation of **th** in English **that, there,** etc., but less interdental than English [ð] (in the production of the Spanish sound, the tip of the tongue gently touches the lower edge of the upper incisors).

If **d** is at the end of a word and it is preceded by **r** (as in **lord, milord**), it is silent. In the plurals, no matter how they are spelled, **d** is never present, hence never pronounced: **lores, milores.**

It follows from the foregoing that if the position of **d** in the utterance changes, its pronunciation may change. Contrast, for example, these three utterances: (1) **Dinamarca mandó embajadores a doce países,** (2) **En Dinamarca viven unos cuantos americanos,** and (3) **Iremos a Dinamarca.** In (1), the **d** of **Dinamarca** is pronounced [d] because it comes at the beginning of an utterance; in (2) the same **d** is also pronounced [d] because it comes after [n]; but in (3) the same **d** is pronounced [ð] because none of the conditions for pronouncing it [d] is met. Similarly, when the word **dedo** is pronounced in isolation, the first **d** is rendered [d] (and the second one [ð]), but in the phrase **mi dedo,** the first **d** is no longer at the beginning of an utterance (nor is it preceded by [n] or /l/); hence the phrase is pronounced [miðeðo].

e has two pronunciations. The instruction given in some books that **e** is pronounced [e] when stressed and [ɛ] when unstressed does not hold true for today's Spanish and may never have been an accurate description of its pronunciation in any variety of the language.

Here are better guidelines for **e** (except when it is part of a diphthong or triphthong):

If **e** is found in a syllable ending in a consonant (see "Syllabification" below), it is pronounced [ɛ], which is similar to the pronunciation of **è** in French or to the vowel of **bet, let, met,** etc., as pronounced in Standard English, that is, with considerable lowering of the jaw. For example, **embaldosar, fresco, hablen,** and **mestizo.**

If **e** ends a syllable and the next one begins with **r, rr,** or **t,** it is pronounced [ɛ]. For instance, **pero, caballete** (the first **e**), **cerrar,** and **jinete.**

Otherwise, **e** is pronounced [e], which is similar to the pronunciation of **é** in French, that is, the jaw is lowered only minimally (the closest English comes to having a sound like [e] is probably the vowel of **ache, rake, stake,** etc.). For example, **caballete** (the second **e**), **hablé, mesa,** and **poeta. Caballete** thus has both renditions of **e**, though the plural of that word, **caballetes,** has only [ɛ], because here the last syllable ends in a consonant.

Many Spanish verbs show variation between **-ar** and **-ear,** like **bazucar** ~ **bazuquear, chapurrar** ~ **chapurrear** (**e** is optional in **Yugoeslavia** ~ **Yugoslavia** and in **yugoeslavo** ~ **yugoslavo**).

See also "Diphthongs and Triphthongs" below.

f is pronounced /f/, which is similar to the pronunciation of **f** in English **fate, feet,** etc. For example, **afectar, fecha, golf, golfo, ¡uf!.**

See also **h.**

g has several pronunciations. At the beginning of an utterance and when followed by **a, o, u,** or a consonant letter except **n** (as in **gato, goma, gusto, glaciar,** or **grave**), **g** is pronounced [g], which is similar to the pronunciation of g in English **get, go, gumption,** etc.

At the beginning of a word and when followed by **n,** the letter g is silent (as in **gnomo**). That pronunciation is in fact so widespread and reputable that a g-less spelling is now acceptable and is in fact preferred in this dictionary (see "Miscellaneous" below).

When **g** is preceded by **n** and is followed in the next syllable of the same word by **a, o, u, ü,** or a consonant letter (as in **angosto, ángulo, ungüento, englobar,** and **engrasar**), it is pronounced [g].

When **g** occurs at the end of a syllable and is preceded by **n**, it is silent, as in **bumerang.** In older borrowings from other languages, that g was systematically or sometimes omitted, as in **sterling** > **esterlina, pudding** > **pudín.**

Before **e** or **i** (as in **gemir** and **gigante**), except if it comes at the end of a word, the letter **g** is pronounced /x/, which is absent in most varieties of current English. This sound is similar to the pronunciation of **ch** in German **Bach,** that of **ch** in Israeli Hebrew **zecher,** and that of **ch** in Scots English **loch, Lochaber,** etc. Press the back of the tongue against the soft palate, expel air (as if coughing), and do not vibrate the vocal chords.

If **g** ends a syllable that is not the last syllable of the word (as in **dogma** and the first syllable of **zigzag**), this letter is pronounced [g]. In such cases, the next syllable always begins with a consonant.

Otherwise, g is pronounced [ɣ], a sound absent in English, which is made by bringing the back of the tongue close to the soft palate (without letting them touch), expelling air through the mouth, and vibrating the vocal chords. Examples are **hago** and **hígado.**

It follows from the foregoing that if the position of g in the utterance changes, its pronunciation may change. Contrast, for example, these three utterances: (1) **Grecia mandó embajadores,** (2) **En Grecia viven unos cuantos italianos,** and (3) **Iremos a Grecia.** In (1), the g of **Grecia** is pronounced [g] because it comes at the beginning of an utterance; in (2) the same **g** is also pronounced [g] because it comes after [n]; but in (3) the same g is pronounced [ɣ] because none of the conditions for pronouncing it [g] is met.

h is silent. In older Spanish, this letter was pronounced /h/ (a sound similar to the first consonant of **here, how,** and **huddle** in Standard English), which has remained in a few words in the guise of /x/ (see **g** for interpreting that symbol). In such cases, **h** has been replaced by **j** (**cante jondo** and **joder,** from older **cante hondo** and **hoder** respectively). In at least four words, both spellings remain standard: **halar** ~ **jalar, halón** ~ **jalón, holgorio** ~ **jolgorio, ¡hopo!** and **¡jopo!** (in the first variant of each pair, the **h** is not now pronounced). To at least some Spanish ears, the variants with /x/ are more emphatic or affective than those without it.

Since **h** is now silent, its presence or absence does not affect pronunciation. Thus, **Ghana** and **Lesotho,** for example, are pronounced exactly as if spelled without that letter. In some words, **h** is optional and the tendency to omit it can only be encouraged: **armonizar** ~ **harmonizar, baraúnda** ~ **barahúnda, Rodesia** ~ **Rhodesia.**

Many words that in older Spanish had **f** now have **h.** In a few instances, variants with both **f** and **h** remain in today's Spanish. They may be either full synonyms of each other or less than full synonyms (like **faz** and **haz, forma** and **horma**).

See also **g** and **w.**

i has two pronunciations. When representing a full vowel, it is pronounced [i], which is similar to the vowel of English **beet, feet, sheen,** etc., but shorter (for instance, **dicho, isla,** and **cursi**). When bearing a dieresis, this letter is likewise pronounced [i], as in **pïada** (were the dieresis absent, **ia** here would represent a diphthong).

When **i** represents part of a diphthong or a triphthong (see "Diphthongs and Triphthongs" below), it is pronounced [y], which is similar to the pronunciation of y in English **year, yes,** or **yolk.** Thus, **miel** and **tiesto** are pronounced [myɛl] and [tyɛsto].

See also **y.**

j is almost always pronounced /x/ (see **g** for interpreting that symbol). A notable exception is **reloj,** which many speakers pronounce [re'lo]. That pronunciation of **reloj** is so widespread that **reló** is an alternate spelling of the singular form, but only in informal writing. In the plural, everyone pronounces /x/ and therefore writes the **j: relojes.**

See **x.**

k, which is now found only in recent borrowings from other languages, is pronounced /k/ (see **c** for interpreting that symbol). The letter combination **ck** (as in **crack, flashback, shock, snack, stock**) is pronounced /k/.

l when not doubled is pronounced /l/, which is formed by putting the tip of the tongue against the sockets of the upper incisors, the remainder of the tongue lying flat. Spanish /l/ thus does not have the hollow sound of English /l/, in whose formation the back of the tongue rises toward the palate.

The letter combination **ll** (which always begins a syllable) has two pronunciations in Standard Spanish: /λ/ (which is similar to the pronunciation of **lli** in English **million** or that of **li** in **vermilion**) and [y], which is similar to the pronunciation of **y** in English **year, yes,** or **yolk.** Since English words like **million** and **vermilion** actually have [ly] rather than /λ/, that is, [l] ends one syllable of those English words and [y] begins the next one (whereas Spanish **ll,** except at the end of a word, always begins a syllable), English-speakers should be careful not to misinterpret /λ/ as [ly]. To achieve a good rendition of Spanish /λ/, pronounce **million** as if it did not contain **mi-**, that is, as if it were ***llion.** Good practice words are those beginning with **ll** (like **llamar, llegar,** and **llorar**) since here you are forced to pronounce /λ/ at the beginning of a syllable. See also **ñ** and "Syllabification" below.

In Spain, although /λ/ is still prestigious, it has been going out of use for decades as more and more people switch to [y] (in the unvarnished pronunciation of Madrid, for example, /λ/ has disappeared entirely). Spaniards now using /λ/ natively are mostly from northern Spain or, if not from that part of the country, they first learned [y] and later intentionally replaced that sound by the more prestigious /λ/. You may thus use either pronunciation in speaking to Spaniards, but /λ/ has a cachet in Spain that [y] lacks. Standard 1 therefore has /λ/.

In the Western Hemisphere, **ll** is pronounced /λ/, [y], /ž/, or /š/, according to area or speaker (/ž/ is similar to the pronunciation of **z** in English **azure** and of **zs** in the name **Zsa Zsa;** /š/ is similar to the pronunciation of **sh** in English **shall, should,** etc.). You may want to pick the sound your interlocutors use or, if you want to choose a SINGLE pronunciation that most speakers of Western Hemispheric Spanish will find acceptable (whatever they themselves use), take /λ/ or [y] (though /λ/ might sound a tad highfalutin to certain Spanish-speakers in the Western Hemisphere who do not use it themselves).

If you want to pick a SINGLE pronunciation of **ll** acceptable both in Spain and in the Western Hemisphere, take /λ/. However, if you do, you should also choose Standard 1 for the pronunciation of **c** before **e** or **i** and of **z** when speaking to Spaniards, since it seems that no speakers of the language in Spain who pronounce **ll** as /λ/ follow Standard 2 for those other two letters. With regard to the Western Hemisphere, since Standard 2 for those other two letters co-occurs there with all of the pronunciations of **ll** (/λ/, [y], /ž/, /š/), you have four choices, the only selection not recommended for this part of the Spanish-speaking world being Standard 1 for **c** before **e** or **i** and for **z** in all positions (whatever pronunciation of **ll** you may choose).

l is optional in **belfo ~ befo.**

m: Traditionally, Spanish does not have [m] at the end of a word when it is pronounced in isolation. Consequently, in many words borrowed from other languages ending in that sound, it was replaced by [n] (see the next section for interpreting that symbol) and the word was respelled accordingly (for example, **harén, ínterin, Jerusalén, macadán, querubín, ron, serafín**). However, a few words (all learned borrowings from Latin and recent borrowings from other languages) end in **m** (for example, **álbum, factótum, ídem, médium, memorándum, ultimátum,** and **vademécum**) and that letter also appears in the Spanish names of many places outside Spanish-speaking areas, like **Bírmingham, Búckingham, Siam,** and **Vietnam.** Both [m] and [n] are heard in such words, depending on people's ability to pronounce [m] at the end of a word (as more and more Spanish-speakers study other languages, they find it easier to produce that sound in that position) and their interest in maintaining the supposedly "correct" (i.e., non-Spanish) pronunciation of that letter. The unaffected pronunciation is [n] (and **mm** in **súmmum** is always pronounced as if it were a single **m**), but if in another form of the word the **m** is followed by a vowel, it is pronounced according to rule, i.e., [m] (as in **siamés**).

In all other positions, **m** is pronounced [m], which is similar to the pronunciation of **m** in English **make, might,** etc. For example, **amar, almirante, ambos, mayor.**

n has several pronunciations. If immediately followed by a labial consonant (represented by **b, f, m, p,** or **v**) whether in the same word or in the next one, it is pronounced [m] (as in the words **anfitrión, inmediato, anverso** or the sentences **insiste en bucear, insiste en pelear,** and **en muchos casos hay más**). Since [m] + [m] is reduced to a single [m], **en muchos casos** actually has just one [m].

It follows from the foregoing that the word **tampoco** and the phrase **tan poco** are pronounced identically, as are the word **ciempiés** and the phrase **cien pies** (each of those words is in fact derived from the corresponding phrase); **Edimburgo** and **Nuremberg** also show the replacement of [n] by [m] before a labial.

However, [n] + [m] (as in **insomne**) is not reduced.

Before /k/ or [g] (as in **aunque** and **angosto**), **n** is pronounced [ŋ], which is similar to the final consonant of **long, sing,** and **song** as pronounced in Standard English.

In all other positions (as in **Anatolia, andan** and **nombrar**), **n** is pronounced [n], which is similar to the pronunciation of **n** in English **hand, near,** etc.

Instances of [n] + [n] are reduced to a single [n], as in the words **ennegrecer, ennoblecer, perenne, sinnúmero** or a phrase like **sin número** (the word **connoto** and the phrase **con Otto** are thus pronounced identically), though an effect of the double [n] remains: the preceding **e** is pronounced [ɛ], not [e], that is, as if the first syllable ended in the first [n].

Instances of [m] + [n], however, are not reduced (as in **amnesia** and **amnistiar**).

Spanish-speakers who know Catalan or, at least, are aware of the pronunciation of **ny** in that language at the end of a word, pronounce it [n] in Catalan-origin proper nouns used in Spanish (like the family names **Capmany, Castany,** and **Fortuny**). Others pronounce it [ni].

See also **m**, "Stress," and, on **tranvía**, "Miscellaneous" below.

ñ is pronounced /ɲ/ which is similar to the pronunciation of **ny** in English **canyon** or **ni** in English **onion.** Since English words like those two actually have [ny] rather than /ɲ/ (that is, [n] ends one syllable and [y] begins the next one), English-speakers should be careful not to misinterpret /ɲ/ as [ny]. To achieve a good rendition of Spanish /ɲ/ (which always begins a syllable), pronounce **canyon** as if it did not contain **ca-**, that is, as if it were ***nyon,** or **onion** as if it were ***nion.** Good practice words are those beginning with **ñ** (like **ñiquiñaque** and **ñoño**) since here you are forced to pronounce /ɲ/ at the beginning of a syllable.

See also **ll** (under **l**).

o has two pronunciations, neither of which can easily be described with reference to English. In a syllable ending in a consonant (see "Syllabification" below), this letter is pronounced somewhat like the **o** of English **port** or **short** (for instance **pondré** and **sondear**). Otherwise (that is, when **o** ends the syllable), it is pronounced somewhat like the **o** of English **coke** or **tote** (for instance, **codo** and **lodo**). The words **costo** and **zonzo** thus contain an example of each kind of **o.** The two kinds of /o/ are similar to the closed and open /o/ of Italian.

See also "Diphthongs and Triphthongs" below.

p, where it is pronounced, stands for [p], which is similar to the pronunciation of **p** in English **space, spear, spook,** etc., but different from that of **p** in English **pike, peak, poke,** etc. To achieve a good rendition of Spanish [p], hold your open palm in front of your mouth and pronounce first **pike, peak, poke,** then **space, spear, spook.** When pronouncing the first three words, you felt a noticeable puff of air on your palm, but in the last three words you felt almost no puff at all. A noticeable puff of air accompanying a speech sound is called *aspiration;* sounds pronounced with aspiration are *aspirated;* and those pronounced without it are *unaspirated.* Spanish [p] (like Spanish /k/ and /t/) is always unaspirated, wherever it occurs. Thus, you should have no trouble with Spanish **espacio, especial, especie,** etc. because here [p] occurs after [s] and as an English-speaker you will automatically pronounce it as unaspirated (just as you would the English cognates of those words: **space, special,** and **species**). It is in other positions that you have to be careful not to aspirate: **particular, poeta, puerta,** etc. (contrast them with their English cognates, all of which have an aspirated [p]: **particular, poet, port**).

Spanish **ps** at the beginning of a word is pronounced [s]. Some pretentious Spanish-speakers may tell you that the "correct" pronunciation is [ps], but that would be as artificial as pronouncing English **psyche, psychology,** etc., in that way. In fact, nonpronunciation of **p** in the combination **ps** at the beginning of a word is so entrenched in Spanish that the preferred spelling is now **s** (this dictionary thus gives only **sicología, sicólogo,** etc. and not the older spellings **psicología, psicólogo,** etc.). See "Miscellaneous" below.

Before /t/, some speakers pronounce **p** as [p] and some do not pronounce it at all. Thus, some write **excerpta, septiembre,** etc., and some **excerta, setiembre,** etc. Although both are correct, the spelling with **p** is preferred in this dictionary (except in the first word, for which both forms are given). Whether or not one pronounces the **p** of **óptimo,** it seems that standard spelling requires that the word always be spelled with that letter.

At the end of a word, you may have an alternative: in **galop,** for example, the **p** may be pronounced [p] or be silent.

The number of instances in which **p** is silent or may be silent is small.

q is always followed by **ue** or **ui.** The sequence **que** is pronounced either [kɛ] or [ke] and **qui** is pronounced [ki] (for example, **quince**) or [ky] (for instance, **quien**) (see "Diphthongs and Triphthongs" below).

To represent the sound sequences[kwe], [kwɛ], and [kwi], Spanish has **cue, cue,** and **cui** respectively (as in **cueva, cuestión,** and **cuidar**).

Because **q** is always followed by **u**, if Spanish-speakers borrow words containing just **q** from other languages, that letter is changed to **k.** Thus, the Spanish names of Iraq and Qatar, for example, are **Irak** and **Katar.**

r has two pronunciations. At the beginning of a word or when it comes after **l, n,** or **s** (for example, **reir, alrededor, enrojecer,** and **Israel**), this letter has the same pronunciation as **rr** (see below).

If **b** ends one syllable and **r** begins the next one in the same word (see "Syllabification" below), **r** is pronounced exactly like **rr** (for example **subrayar** if syllabified **sub-ra-yar**). If **b** + **r** belong to the same syllable (for instance **bramar** and **lubricar**), **r** is pronounced with one flip of the upper front part of the tongue against the sockets of the upper incisors (for instance **subrayar** if syllabified **su-bra-yar**). See "Syllabification" below on the alternative now permitted in words beginning with the prefix **sub-**.

In all other positions, **r** is likewise pronounced with one flip of the upper front part of the tongue against the sockets of the upper incisors (for instance, **leer, para, pera, pero, tercero,** and **treinta**).

rr is pronounced with a trill (several flips) of the upper front part of the tongue against the sockets of the upper incisors (for instance, **parra, perra, perro,** and **sierra**). Thus, **para** and **parra** are different words, with different pronunciations and different meanings. The same applies to **caro** and **carro, pera** and **perra, pero** and **perro, torero** and **torrero,** and other pairs of words.

s has several pronunciations. When it represents the plural ending of nouns recently borrowed from other languages, it is silent in certain words, like **cabarets, carnets, complots, conforts, superávits, tíckets, trusts, vermuts.**

Before the letters **b, v, d, g** (but only when this letter is not followed by **e** or **i**), **l, m, n,** or **r** (whether any of those eight letters appear in the same word as **s** or they appear in the next word), you have an alternative (in both standards) if **s** is not the last letter of the word: it may be pronounced [z] (a sound similar to the pronunciation of **z** in English **zebra, zoo,** etc.) or [s] (see **c** for interpreting that symbol): **esbelto, esdrújulo, esgrimir, isla, esmalte, Israel, los baúles, los varones, los dedos, los guantes, los lagos, los maestros, los nervios, los ratones,** etc. If **s** is the last letter, only [s] is found (for instance, in the family name **Pons**).

If **s** is followed by **r** (whether in the same word or in the next one), besides the two pronunciations suggested above [s] or [z]), a third possibility is not to pronounce the **s** at all and, as a compensation, trill the **r** more. The word **Israel** (and its derivatives) thus has three pronunciations: [isrraɛl], [izrraɛl], and [irraɛl].

Otherwise, **s** is pronounced [s] (as in **ese, especial, hablas, hasta, insistir, seco**).

If **s** is followed by **h**, the foregoing paragraph applies, except in the case of Spanish words recently borrowed from other languages or words modeled on such recently borrowed words, in which **sh** constitutes a unit, to be pronounced /š/ (a sound similar to the pronunciation of **sh** in English **shall, sheet, should,** etc.). Thus, in **deshacer,** an old Spanish word not recently borrowed from another language, the instructions about **s** apply and the **h** is silent (hence the first two syllables of that word are [desa]), whereas in **riksha** and **yídish, sh** is pronounced /š/.

Spanish spelling does not distinguish the two kinds of **sh,** which you can, however, partly distinguish in this way: **sh** at the beginning or at the end of a word is of recent non-Spanish origin. If **sh** appears in the middle of a word, you have to know its origin to determine how that letter combination should be pronounced, though this rule of thumb will almost always hold: a word beginning **desh-** is likely not to be a recent borrowing from another language; rather, it probably consists of the centuries-old Spanish negating prefix **des-** and a word beginning with **h-.** Furthermore, the recent borrowings are often easily identified because of their unusual spelling (for example, it is clear that **riksha** is new).

Traditionally, no Spanish words began with **s** followed by a consonant, as a result of which Spanish-speakers either dropped **s** when borrowing non-Spanish words so beginning or, more frequently, added **e** to them: Dutch **sloeren** > **eslora**, Dutch **skiff,** English **skiff,** French **esquif,** French **skiff,** Italian **schifo,** and/or Portuguese **esquife** > **esquife**, English **sterling** > **esterlina,** Italian **strambotto** > **estrambote,** Latin **scientia** > **ciencia,** etc.

S is optional in **quizá** ~ **quizás.**

See also **b, c, t, z,** and "Syllabification" below.

t, except before **l** in the same word, is pronounced [t], which is similar to the pronunciation of **t** in English **stake, steer, stoop,** etc., but different from that of **t** in English **take, teak, took,** etc. To achieve a good rendition of Spanish /t/, hold your open palm in front of your mouth and pronounce first **take, teak, took,** then **stake, steer, stoop.** When pronouncing the first three words, you felt a noticeable puff of air on your palm, but in the last three words you felt almost no puff at all. A noticeable puff of air is called *aspiration;* sounds pronounced with aspiration are *aspirated;* and those pronounced without it are *unaspirated.* Spanish /t/ (like Spanish /k/ and /p/) is always unaspirated, wherever it occurs. Thus, you should have no trouble producing an unaspirated /t/ in Spanish **estado, estimar, estúpido,** etc. because here /t/ occurs after [s] and as an English-speaker you will automatically pronounce it as unaspirated (just as you would the English cognates of those words: **state, esteem,** and **stupid**). It is in other positions that you have to be careful not to aspirate: **tocar, tabla, Túnez,** etc. (contrast them with their English cognates, all of which have an aspirated /t/: **touch, table, Tunisia**). Furthermore, Spanish /t/ is made by touching the tip of the tongue against the upper incisors (in contrast to English /t/, in whose production the tongue touches the gums).

In three positions, **t** may not be pronounced as described above. First, before **l** or **m** in the same word (as in **atleta, aritmético,** and **ritmo**) you have an alternative: **t** may be pronounced as described or it may be pronounced [ð] (see **d** for interpreting that symbol).

Second, the **t** of the prefix **post-** is not pronounced if it is followed by any pronounced consonant letter except **r**, so much so that alternate spellings without **t** are also found and they are in fact the preferable ones, for instance, **posguerra** and posmeridiano. (but also **postergar,** etc.).

Third, **t** at the end of a word may be silent. Probably many, most, or all Spanish-speakers pronounce it in **cenit, déficit, fagot, mamut, superávit,** and **el Tíbet ~ el Tibet,** whereas in other words final **t** is silent, for instance **cabaret, carnet, complot, tícket, trust,** and **vermut,** which are pronounced as if written ***cabaré, *carné, *compló, *tique, *trus,** and ***vermú** (the plurals are pronounced identically to their singulars. In still other words you have an alternative: **confort** is pronounced either [kom'for] or [kom'fort] (the plural **conforts** has both variants too).

u has several pronunciations. In the combinations **gue, gui, que,** and **qui,** the letter **u** is silent. For example, **guedeja** [geðexa] ~ [ɣeðexa], **quedar** [keðar], and **quien** [kyɛn] (see **q** and **e** on the pronunciation of those letters).

When **u** represents part of a diphthong or a triphthong (see "Diphthongs and Triphthongs" below), it is pronounced [w], which is similar to the first sound of English **win** and **won.** Thus, **puesto** and **seudónimo,** for example, are pronounced [pwɛsto] and [sewðonimo].

If a **u** bears a dieresis, it is pronounced [w]. Thus, **lingüista** is pronounced [lingwista].

In all other cases, **u** is pronounced [u], which is similar to the vowel of English **coot** or **toot,** although in the production of the Spanish sound the lips are more rounded and the vowel is of shorter duration than in the production of the English one. For example, **ducha, hubo, u, Unamuno,** and **uno.**

v has two pronunciations. At the beginning of an utterance or after **n** (which in this position is pronounced [m]), the letter **v** is pronounced [b], which is similar to the first consonant of English **beach, broth, pebble,** etc. In all other positions, this letter is pronounced [β] (see **b** for interpreting that symbol). For example, in the sentence **¿Verdad que en el anverso de la medalla se ve un pavo real?,** the first and fifth words have [b] and the tenth and twelfth have [β].

Therefore, the instructions for pronouncing **b** and those for pronouncing **v** are identical (depending on the position of those letters in the utterance), as a consequence of which pairs of words like **baca** and **vaca** or **hube** and **uve** are homophones in today's Spanish and, as a further consequence of which, if you hear [b] or [β], you cannot tell whether it is to be represented by **b** or by **v** unless you know how to spell the word.

If people try to tell you that **b** is pronounced in one way and **v** in another in today's Spanish, tell them that is a figment of their imagination. Spelling differences (like **baca** vs. **vaca**) are misleading them into thinking they hear a difference (or believing there should be a difference) when none in fact exists. The fact that native speakers of the language less skilled in spelling often write **b** when **v** is required or vice versa is proof enough that no difference in pronunciation is made.

w, which is found only in borrowings from Germanic languages and French, has several pronunciations. In several words, it is pronounced as if it were **b** or **v** and in such cases alternate spellings with **v** are found too: **wagneriano ~ vagneriano, Westfalia ~ Vestfalia.** The forms with **v** are preferable.

In at least a few words, **w** is pronounced [w] (a sound similar to the first sound of English **win** and **won**) and for one of them an alternate spelling with **u** exists: **Malawi, Taiwán, Zimbabwe.**

In **whisky,** the letter combination **wh** is pronounced [w] by those who want to show off their knowledge of English and [gw] or [ɣw] by those who speak normally (the choice of [gw] or [ɣw] depends on the position of the word in the utterance; see the instructions for **g**).

Whereas **Trans World Airlines** is shortened to the initialism **TWA** in English, in Spanish it is shortened to the acronym **la TWA**, which is pronounced /la'tua/.

x has several pronunciations. For a time, the recommended pronunciation was [ks]. Later, [gz] in certain positions was allowed as an alternate pronunciation. Today, those instructions, especially the one calling for [ks] wherever **x** occurs, would probably result in a pronunciation no native speaker uses and which would sound artificial. The following suggestions are more realistic for our times.

If **x** occurs before a consonant (as in **experiencia, extremidad** and **mixto**), pronounce it [s]. That pronunciation is probably most frequent in words beginning with the prefix **ex-** followed by a consonant, for example **excelente,** widely pronounced [ɛsθelɛnte] or [ɛselɛnte]. In the latter pronunciation, [s] + [s] becomes a single [s], though an effect of the double [s] remains: the preceding **e** is pronounced [ɛ], not [e], that is, as if the first syllable ended in a consonant, i.e., as if it ended in the first [s].

If **x** occurs between vowels, you have an alternative in certain words (**examen** and **exiguo,** for example, may be pronounced with [ks], [gz], or [s]) but not in others (for instance, all Spanish-speakers, it seems, now pronounce **sexo** with [ks]).

At the end of a word, the pronunciation of **x** is in flux. In **ántrax, Benelux, dux, fénix, látex,** and **tórax,** [ks] seems to be most frequent if not universal today, whereas in **clímax** and **flux,** [s] may now be more frequent.

At least some exceptions to those pronunciations are heard in words of Native American origin: for example, in **México** and **mexicano,** the **x** is now always pronounced [x] (those are the spellings official and universal in Mexico; elsewhere, **Méjico, mejicano** are used); in **Xochimilco** (a Mexican place name), the **x** is always pronounced [s].

Further exceptions are certain given and family names, which are found in two variants: one preserving a now archaic spelling with **x** (like **Xavier** and **Ximénez**) and the other spelled in modern fashion with **j** (**Javier** and **Jiménez**). Here, **x** is pronounced /x/, that is, just like **j.**

y has several pronunciations. In the word **y,** it is pronounced [i] (see **i** for interpreting that symbol).

When it represents the first or last segment of a diphthong or triphthong (see "Diphthongs and Triphthongs" below), as in **ya, yegua, yunque, ley, rey, soy,** and **Paraguay,** the letter **y** is pronounced [y] (see **ll** [under **l**] for interpreting that symbol).

In certain varieties of Spanish, [y] is pronounced with more occlusion, so that it has come to be close to [ž] if not actually that sound (see **ll** [under **l**] for interpreting the latter symbol); and in still other varieties it is pronounced with so much occlusion that it has come to be close to [ǰ] if not actually that ([ǰ] is similar to the first consonant of English **Jacob, Jerusalem, Jew,** etc.). Both Standard 1 and Standard 2 have [y] rather than [ž] or [ǰ], except in the emphatic pronunciation of **yo** (as in **¡yo, y yo sólo, soy el dueño aquí!**), for which [ǰo] is a widespread rendition acceptable in both standards.

Certain family names have two spelling variants, an archaic one with **y** and one spelled in modern fashion with **i** (like **Yglesias ~ Iglesias**). Here, **y** is pronounced /i/, that is, just like **i.**

See also **n** with regard to **ny.**

z has several pronunciations. In Standard 1, you have an alternative:

(1) In all positions, pronounce it [θ] (see **c** for interpreting that symbol). Or,

(2) Before the letters **b, v, d, g, l, m, n,** or **r** (whether in the same word or in the next one), pronounce it [ð] (see **d** for interpreting that symbol) and in all other positions pronounce it [θ] (see **c** for interpreting that symbol).

In Standard 2, you have an alternative:

(3) In all positions, pronounce it [s] (see **s** for interpreting that symbol). Or,

(4) Before the letters **b, v, d, g, l, m, n,** or **r** (whether in the same word or in the next one), pronounce it [z] and in all other positions pronounce it [s] (see **s** for interpreting that symbol).

That is to say, if you pronounce **c** before **e** or **i** as [θ], you must follow instruction (1) or (2) above. If you pronounce **c** before **e** or **i** as [s], you must follow instruction (3) or (4) above.

Furthermore, if you choose to pronounce **s** as [s] before **b, v, d, g, l, m, n,** or **r,** you must pronounce **z** before any of those eight letters as [θ] (= Standard 1) or as [s] (= Standard 2); if you choose to pronounce **s** as [z], you must pronounce **z** before any of those eight letters as [ð] (= Standard 1) or [z] (= Standard 2).

Thus, in the sentence **César el hazmerreír de toda la isla,** for example, you have these choices for the **c** of the first word, the **z** of the third word, and the **s** of the seventh word:

c [θ] + z [θ] + s [s] (= Standard 1)
c [θ] + z [ð] + s [z] (= Standard 1)
c [s] + z [s] + s [s] (= Standard 2)
c [s] + z [z] + s [z] (= Standard 2)

The same restrictions apply to any individual word. Thus, **civilización,** for example, must be pronounced either [θiβiliθaθyon] (= Standard 1) or [siβilisasyon] (= Standard 2).

Diphthongs and Triphthongs

Spanish has fifteen diphthongs and six triphthongs.

Eight of the diphthongs begin with a semivowel:

ia [ya] is spelled **ya** at the beginning of a word, e.g., **desahuciar, yámbico.**

ua [wa] (e.g., **guardar**).

ie [ye] or [yɛ] is spelled **ye** at the beginning of a word, e.g., **agüero, bien, higiene, siete, yema.** The rules for choosing [e] or [ɛ] (see **e**) apply to [ye] and [yɛ] too.

ue [we] or [wɛ] is spelled **üe** after **g** that is not pronounced [x], e.g., **huelga, hueste, huevo, vergüenza.** The rules for choosing [e] or [ɛ] (see **e**) apply to [we] or [wɛ] too.

io and **yo** [yo], e.g., **soslayar, yo.** The spelling **io** at the beginning of a word is an imitation of Greek.

uo [wo] (e.g., **arduo**).

iu [yu] is spelled **yu** at the beginning of a word, e.g., **triunfo, yugo.**

ui [wi] (spelled **uy** in **muy**), e.g., **cuidar, muy.** For **uy** representing [uy], see **uy** in the next section.

Take care to pronounce diphthongs beginning with a semivowel as diphthongs and not as two syllables. Thus, whereas English **barrio** has three syllables, Spanish **barrio** has two (**ba-rrio**), pronounced [barryo].

Six of the diphthongs end in a semivowel:

ai [ay] is spelled **ay** at the end of most words; rarely, **ay** is found in the middle of a word (e.g., **aimará ~ aymará, hay, Raimundo, Seychelles**). If **ay** occurs before a vowel in the same word, it represents not a diphthong but /a/ + /y/ and each of those sounds belongs to a different syllable (thus, **aya** and **haya** for example are syllabified **a-ya** and **ha-ya**).

au [aw] (e.g., **caudillo**).

ei is almost always pronounced [ey] and is almost always spelled **ey** at the end of a word, e.g., **reina, rey.** A pronunciation exception is **reir,** which is pronounced as if spelled ***reír.** If **ey** occurs before a vowel in the same word, it represents not a diphthong but /e/ + /y/ and each of those sounds belongs to a different syllable (thus, **reyes** and **leyenda** for instance are syllabified **re-yes** and **le-yen-da**).

eu [ew] (e.g., **seudónimo**).

oi is almost always pronounced [oy] and is spelled **oy** at the end of a word (e.g., **hoy**) and in certain family names in other positions too (like **Goytisolo**). A pronunciation exception is **oir,** which is pronounced as if spelled ***oír.** If **oy** occurs before a vowel in the same word, it represents not a diphthong but /o/ + /y/ and each of those sounds belongs to a different syllable (thus, **Goya** is syllabified **Go-ya**).

uy, which always occurs at the end of a word, is almost always pronounced [uy] (as in **¡huy!, Jujuy**). The exception is **muy,** whose pronunciation is given in the previous section. If **uy** occurs before a vowel in the same word, it represents not a diphthong but /u/ + /y/ and each of those sounds belongs to a different syllable (thus, **cuyo** and **tuyas** are syllabified **cu-yo** and **tu-yas**).

The triphthongs are:

iai [yay] (e.g., **despreciáis**).

iau [yaw] (e.g., **miau**).

iei [yey] (e.g., **despreciéis**).

uai [way] (spelled **uay** at the end of a word), e.g., **evaluáis, Uruguay.**

uau [waw] (e.g., **guau**).

uei [wey] (spelled **uey** at the end of a word), e.g., **evaluéis, buey.**

Syllabification

Spanish is a consonant-vowel language, that is, syllables preferably end in a vowel (though many exceptions are found). Therefore, a single consonant and the vowel following it usually form a syllable or, expressed otherwise, a single consonant between two vowels usually goes with the following vowel (thus, **ba-jo, a-dhe-sión**). Since **ch, ll, ñ,** and **rr** represent a single consonant, the syllabification is, for example, **mu-cha-cho, ha-llar, ni-ño, ba-rrio,** and **haz-me-rreír.**

The consonant clusters **bl, cl, dl, fl, gl, pl, tl, br, cr, dr, fr, gr, pr,** and **tr** form a syllable with the following vowel, for instance, **ha-blar, a-cla-rar, a-flo-jar, a-glo-me-rar, a-pla-zar, a-tle-ta, a-bra-zar, a-cre-di-tar, a-drede, a-fran-ce-sar, a-gre-gar,** and **a-pren-der.**

When representing /š/, **sh** is not divided, whereas if a consonant letter + **h** is found in the middle of a word and the **h** is silent, the **h** begins a new syllable: **al-ha-ra-ca, clor-hi-dra-to, des-hi-dra-tar, in-hu-ma-ción.**

All other clusters of two consonants between vowels (including diphthongs and triphthongs) are usually divided, so that the first consonant belongs to the preceding syllable and the second consonant to the following syllable, for example, **a-cos-tar-se, ac-tuar, cuer-do, en-car-gar, es-la-vo, fras-co, Is-ra-el, llan-ta, per-di-ción, sol-da-du-ra,** and **der-vi-che.** Subject to that rule are also instances of double **c** or **n**, as in **per-fec-ción** and **en-ne-gre-cer.**

If a cluster of three or more consonants stands between vowels, the last two consonants are usually **bl, cl, dl, fl, gl, pl, tl, br, cr, dr, fr, gr, pr,** or **tr** and they go with the following syllable, for instance, **tem-blar, ten-dré, ex-plo-tar, tem-prano.**

If a cluster of three or more consonants stands between vowels and if the second consonant is **s**, the **s** goes with the preceding syllable, for example **ins-tan-te** and **pers-pec-ti-va.**

If one vowel follows another and they do not constitute a diphthong (see above), they belong to separate syllables, for instance, **ma-es-tro, cre-o, le-er, to-a-lla.** Accordingly, if **i** or **u** (which represent respectively [y] or [w] in diphthongs and triphthongs) represents a vowel, it belongs in a separate syllable and that fact is indicated by a stress mark. Thus, **ahínco** (three syllables: **a-hín-co**), **búho** (two syllables: **bú-ho**), **traído** (three syllables: **tra-í-do**), **prohíbo** (three syllables: **pro-hí-bo**), **Raúl** (two syllables: **Ra-úl**), **haría** (three syllables: **ha-rí-a**), **haríais** (three syllables: **ha-rí-ais**), etc.

If **y** is preceded and followed by a vowel, it forms a diphthong with the following one and therefore belongs in the following syllable, for instance, **ca-yo, tu-yo, cre-yó.** In fact, all diphthongs and triphthongs (see the list above) form syllables of their own. In contrast, identical contiguous vowels (as in **creer**) and vowels that do not form diphthongs or triphthongs (as in **leal**), as well as diphthongs or triphthongs dissolved by the stress mark (see the examples from **ahínco** to **haríais** in the previous paragraph), form separate syllables (thus, **cre-er, le-al,** etc.).

It is permissible but not obligatory to set aside the foregoing rules in the case of prefixes, which one may consider as forming syllables of their own (whether or not such would be the case if the rules were followed) or which one may, rather, subject to the rules. For example, **ab-ro-ga-ción** or **a-bro . . . , des-a-bro-char** or **de-sa . . . , ex-a-cer-ba-ción** or **e-xa . . . , sub-li-mar** or **su-bli . . .** (in each pair, the first variant reflects treatment of the prefix as a syllable in its own right, no matter what the rules would require, and the second variant shows syllabification when the rules are suspended). The same applies to solid compounds: **nos-o-tros** or **no-so-tros, vos-o-tras** or **vo-so-tras,** etc.

The foregoing paragraph not withstanding, the rules must be followed with respect to a succession of three consonant letters, the second of which is **s,** in which case **s** belongs with the preceding, not the following letter (thus, as already noted, **ins-tante, pers-pect-ti-va,** not **in-st . . . , per-sp . . .**) and with respect to prefixes if the first letter immediately following them is **h** (thus, **des-ha-cer** and **des-hi-dra-tar,** not **de-sha . . .** or **de-shi . . .**).

Stress

Most Spanish words have only one primary stress, which can be determined from the spelling according to these rules:

(1) If a word is spelled with a stress mark, stress the syllable in which it is found (like **águila, bíceps, fórceps, hablarán, Martínez**), the only exception being **ó**, which is not stressed (this is the form taken by the conjunction **o** when it appears between two Arabic numerals, the purpose of the mark being solely to prevent misinterpretation of the conjunction as the Arabic numeral for zero; thus, **6 ó 7,** for instance, means '6 or 7').

(2) If a word contains no stress mark:

[2.A] Stress the last syllable if the word ends in:

[2.A.i] a vowel letter + **y** (like **convoy, Uruguay, virrey**),

[2.A.ii] a consonant letter other than **n** or **s** (like **consentir, David, lateral**),

[2.A.iii] **n** not preceded by a vowel letter (like **Isern**),

[2.A.iv] **s** not preceded by a vowel letter (like **Fontanals, Casals**).

[2.B] Stress the next-to-last syllable if the word ends in:

[2.B.i] a vowel letter other than **y** (like **casi, habla, hable, hablo, fatuo, patria, sitio**),

[2.B.ii] a vowel letter + **n** (like **consienten, hablan**),

[2.B.iii] a vowel letter + **s** (like **consientes, hablas**).

Catalan-origin names like **Capmany, Castany, Fortuny** are stressed on the vowel immediately preceding **-y** (thus, stress [man], [tan], [tun]).

The triplets **árbitro, arbitro, arbitró; público, publico, publicó; término, termino, terminó; tráfago, trafago, trafagó;** and **válido, valido, validó** illustrate several possibilities.

Miscellaneous

It is noted above that [m] + [m], [n] + [n], [p] + [p], and [s] + [s] are respectively reduced to one [m], [p], and [s]. Since the number of instances of [s] + [s] is not the same in all varieties of Spanish, the number of reductions to [s] varies accordingly. For example, **absceso** is pronounced [apseso] only where c before e (or i) is pronounced [s] (otherwise it is rendered [apθeso]); see also **excelente** in the remarks on **x**.

Reduction of identical contiguous sounds (whether vowels or consonants) is widespread in Spanish, whether within a word or between two words. Thus, [a] + [a] is reduced to [a] both in the word **portaaviones** and in a phrase like **a ambos;** or, [ɛ] + [e] is reduced to [e] in the word **sobreexcitar** and in a phrase like **este efecto** (in this regard, [e] and [ɛ] are considered "identical"; the same holds true for the two kinds of /o/; hence reduction is found in a sentence like **escojo ocho opciones**). The spellings **guardagujas, guardalmacén, remplazar, sobrentender,** etc., are in fact used too and they are preferable. In many cases, only spellings reflecting a reduction are now found, for example, **aprensión, prensil,** and **reprensible** (contrast those forms with their English cognates: **apprehension, prehensile,** and **reprehensible**).

In certain cases, however, two contiguous sounds are pronounced separately (by some speakers) or reduced to a single, slightly longer than usual one (by other speakers), for example in **creer** and its derivatives having **ee**. When to reduce to a single vowel and when not to reduce or to reduce to a single, slightly longer vowel must be learned individually for each word.

Other simplifications preferred in this dictionary are, at the beginning of a word, **g** instead of **gn, m** instead of **mn,** and **s** instead of **ps** (see, for example, **nomo, nemotecnia,** and **seudónimo**), as well as spellings like **oscuro** and **sustituir.**

Two sounds may influence each other. **Tranvía,** for example, is pronounced [**trambia**] because the sound represented by **v** causes the **n** to be pronounced [m] and the sound represented by **n** causes the **v** to be pronounced [b].

In both standards, vowels are relatively short, though in stressed syllables and when a vowel results from a reduction of two identical vowels, they are slightly longer than usual (thus, sentences **vi a ambos** and **vi ambos,** for instance, differ slightly in the length of /a/). You need not make an effort to lengthen a vowel in a stressed syllable because that will in most cases come naturally as a result of the stress on the vowel in that syllable. In Buenos Aires Spanish, as a consequence of Italian influence, stressed syllables are noticeably longer than unstressed ones. That feature is not recommended.

English, especially British English, is a stress-timed language (it has rhythm in which stressed syllables tend to occur at regular intervals of time, regardless of the number of intervening unstressed syllables) whereas Spanish is a syllable-timed language (with rhythm in which syllables are approximately equal in duration and thus tend to follow one another at regular intervals). Consequently, speakers of English, especially British English, tend to reduce unstressed syllables (as in the British pronunciation of **momentary, pattern,** and **secretary**), whereas Spanish-speakers tend to pronounce each syllable distinctly and do not often slur over any of them. Spanish-speakers thus often react to English-accented Spanish as one in which *se comen las vocales* 'the vowels are swallowed up' and speakers of English (especially of British English) tend to react to Spanish-accented English as "overly precise" (to get an idea of the difference between stress- and syllable-timed languages, contrast American and British pronunciations of **momentary** and **secretary:** Americans pronounce each syllable of those words with more or less the same degree of distinctiveness, whereas Britishers pronounce only the first syllable distinctly and slur over the others; thus, American English is more syllable-timed and British English more stress-timed). To pronounce Spanish correctly, English-speakers should therefore give each vowel its full value.

Formerly, in the Spanish-speaking world, the pronunciation and spelling of words borrowed from other languages were routinely changed so that they conformed to Spanish norms. Thus for example, **bowline** > **bolina, coolie** > **culí, goal** > **gol, kerosene** > **kerosén, ketch** > **queche, Quaker** > **cuáquero, shilling** > **chelín, sweater** > **suéter, trolley bus** > **trolebús, volt** > **voltio, yacht** > **yate;** English and/or French **bureau** > **buró,** English **jacket** and/or French **jaquette** > **chaqué** and **chaqueta;** English **packet boat** and/or French **paquebot** > **paquebote;** English **pudding** and/or French **pudding** > **pudín;** English and/or French **restaurant** > **restaurante** ~ **restorán;** English **role** and/or French **rôle** > **rol;** English **toupée** and/or French **toupet** > **tupé;** French **bivouac** > **vivac** (which was later completely hispanized to **vivaque**), **boudin** > **budín, boulevard** > **bulevar, bourgeois** > **burgués, corset** > **corsé, meeting** > **mitin, necéssaire** > **neceser, purée** > **puré, terreplain** > **terraplén, vaudou** > **vodú;** German **Schomberg** > **chambergo;** and, from various languages, **zar** 'tsar'. Or, non-Spanish /š/ usually became /č/ (not only in **chambergo** but also in **bolchevique, chal, champán** ~ **champaña, champú, coqueluche, derviche,** and **fetiche**) or /s/ (as in **Visnú**).

Now, however, the trend is to retain non-

Spanish spellings, though not necessarily non-Spanish pronunciations, with the result that the good fit between Spanish spelling and pronunciation is in certain words absent.

After the death of Francisco Franco (1975), the non-Spanish languages of Spain, long discouraged or suppressed in various ways up to that time, gained or regained their legitimate rights, although an unfortunate consequence thereof has been the use of non-Spanish spellings in certain Spanish words referring to elements of the cultures of which those languages are the vehicle. Thus, not uncommon in today's Spanish are Catalan spellings like "Catalunya" and "Convergencia i Unió" and Basque spellings like "batzoki," "txistu," and "txistulari." The Spanish language academies recognize only **Cataluña, Convergencia y Unión, bachoqui, chistu,** and **chistulari.**

All of which is to say that from the spelling of a recent Spanish borrowing from another language you may not be able to infer its pronunciation fully. But, on the whole, the number of Spanish words in which the fit between spelling and pronunciation is less than optimal or whose pronunciation is in some way unusual is still small.

D.L.G.

Spanish Irregular Verbs

Infinitive	Present	Future	Preterit	Past Part.
andar	ando	andaré	anduve	andado
caber	quepo	cabré	cupe	cabido
caer	caigo	caeré	caí	caído
conducir	conduzco	conduciré	conduje	conducido
dar	doy	daré	di	dado
decir	digo	diré	dije	dicho
estar	estoy	estaré	estuve	estado
haber	he	habré	hube	habido
hacer	hago	haré	hice	hecho
ir	voy	iré	fui	ido
jugar	juego	jugaré	jugué	jugado
morir	muero	moriré	morí	muerto
oir	oigo	oiré	oí	oído
poder	puedo	podré	pude	podido
poner	pongo	pondré	puse	puesto
querer	quiero	querré	quise	querido
saber	sé	sabré	supe	sabido
salir	salgo	saldré	salí	salido
ser	soy	seré	fui	sido
tener	tengo	tendré	tuve	tenido
traer	traigo	traeré	traje	traído
valer	valgo	valdré	valí	valido
venir	vengo	vendré	vine	venido
ver	veo	veré	vi	visto

Las Formas del Verbo Inglés

1. Se forma la 3ª persona singular del tiempo presente exactamente al igual que el plural de los sustantivos, añadiendo **-es** o **-s** a la forma sencilla según las mismas reglas, así:

(1)	teach teaches	pass passes	wish wishes	fix fixes	buzz buzzes		
(2)	place places	change changes	judge judges	please pleases	freeze freezes		
(3a)	find finds	sell sells	clean cleans	hear hears	love loves	buy buys	know knows
(3b)	think thinks	like likes	laugh laughs	stop stops	hope hopes	meet meets	want wants
(4)	cry cries	try tries	dry dries	carry carries	deny denies		

Cinco verbos muy comunes tienen 3ª persona singular irregular:

(5)	go	do	say	have	be
	goes	does	says	has	is

2. Se forman el tiempo pasado y el participio de modo igual, añadiendo a la forma sencilla la terminación **-ed** o **-d** según las reglas que siguen:

(1) Si la forma sencilla termina en **-d** o **-t,** se le pone **-ed** como sílaba aparte:

end	fold	need	load	want	feast	wait	light
ended	folded	needed	loaded	wanted	feasted	waited	lighted

(2) Si la forma sencilla termina en cualquier otra consonante, se añade también **-ed** pero sin hacer sílaba aparte:

(2a)	bang	sail	seem	harm	earn	weigh
	banged	sailed	seemed	harmed	earned	weighed
(2b)	lunch	work	look	laugh	help	pass
	lunched	worked	looked	laughed	helped	passed

(3) Si la forma sencilla termina en **-e,** se le pone sólo **-d**:

(3a)	hate	taste	waste	guide	fade	trade
	hated	tasted	wasted	guided	faded	traded
(3b)	free	judge	rule	name	dine	scare
	freed	judged	ruled	named	dined	scared
(3c)	place	force	knife	like	hope	base
	placed	forced	knifed	liked	hoped	based

(4) Una **-y** final que sigue a cualquier consonante se cambia en **-ie** al añadir la **-d** del pasado/participio:

cry	try	dry	carry	deny
cried	tried	dried	carried	denied

3. Varios verbos muy comunes forman el tiempo pasado y el participio de manera irregular. Pertenecen a tres grupos.

(1) Los que tienen una sola forma irregular para tiempo pasado y participio, como los siguientes:

bend	bleed	bring	build	buy	catch	creep	deal
bent	bled	brought	built	bought	caught	crept	dealt
dig	feed	feel	fight	find	flee	get	hang
dug	fed	felt	fought	found	fled	got	hung
have	hear	hold	keep	lead	leave	lend	lose
had	heard	held	kept	led	left	lent	lost
make	mean	meet	say	seek	sell	send	shine
made	meant	met	said	sought	sold	sent	shone
shoot	sit	sleep	spend	stand	strike	sweep	teach
shot	sat	slept	spent	stood	struck	swept	taught

(2) Los que tienen una forma irregular para el tiempo pasado y otra forma irregular para el participio, como los siguientes:

be was been	beat beat beaten	become became become	begin began begun	bite bit bitten
blow blew blown	break broke broken	choose chose chosen	come came come	do did done
draw drew drawn	drink drank drunk	drive drove driven	eat ate eaten	fall fell fallen
fly flew flown	forget forgot forgotten	freeze froze frozen	give gave given	go went gone
grow grew grown	hide hid hidden	know knew known	ride rode ridden	ring rang rung
rise rose risen	run ran run	see saw seen	shake shook shaken	shrink shrank shrunk
sing sang sung	sink sank sunk	speak spoke spoken	steal stole stolen	swear swore sworn
swim swam swum	tear tore torn	throw threw thrown	wear wore worn	write wrote written

(3) Los que no varían del todo, la forma sencilla funcionando también como pasado/participio; entre éstos son de mayor frecuencia:

bet	burst	cast	cost	cut
hit	hurt	let	put	quit
read	set	shed	shut	slit
spit	split	spread	thrust	wet

El Plural del Sustantivo Inglés

A la forma singular se añade la terminación **-es** o **-s** de acuerdo con las reglas siguientes.

(1) Si el singular termina en **-ch, -s, -sh, -x** o **-z,** se le pone **-es** como sílaba aparte:

match	glass	dish	box	buzz
matches	glasses	dishes	boxes	buzzes

(2) Si el singular termina en **-ce, -ge, -se** o **-ze,** se le pone una **-s** que con la vocal precedente forma sílaba aparte:

face	page	house	size
faces	pages	houses	sizes

(3) Una **-y** final que sigue a cualquier consonante se cambia en **-ie** a ponérsele la **-s** del plural:

sky	city	lady	ferry	penny
skies	cities	ladies	ferries	pennies

(4) Los siguientes sustantivos comunes tienen plural irregular:

Man	woman	child	foot	mouse	goose
men	women	children	feet	mice	geese
wife	knife	life	half	leaf	deer
wives	knives	lives	halves	leaves	deer

List of Abbreviations Used in this Dictionary

a adjective
abb abbreviation
acc accusative
adv adverb
aer aeronautics
agr agriculture
anat anatomy
ant antiquated
arch architecture
archeol archeology
art. article
art art
ast astronomy
astrol astrology
aut automobiles
aux auxiliary
biol biology
bot botany
cards card games
carp carpentry
chem chemistry
com commerce
comp comparative
condit conditional
conjunc conjunction
cul culinary
dance dancing
dat dative
dim diminutive
ecc ecclesiastical
elec electricity
eng engineering
ent entomology
euphem euphemism
f feminine
fig figurative
fig inf used figuratively in informal speech or writing
fut future
gen generally; genitive
geog geography
geol geology
geom geometry
gram grammar
gym gymnastics
her heraldry
hist history
icht ichthyology
imperf imperfect
impers impersonal
ind indicative
indef art. indefinite article
inf informal
infin infinitive
insep inseparable
interj interjection, exclamation
interr interrogative
iron ironical
irr irregular
Lat. Am. Latin America
law law
ling linguistics
lit literature
m masculine
mas masonry
math mathematics
mech mechanics
med medical
met metallurgy
mf masculine or feminine
mil military
min mineralogy
mus music
myth mythology
n noun
naut nautical
nav naval
neut neuter
opt optics
orn ornithology
part participle
pers personal; person
pharm pharmacy
phil philosophy
phon phonetics
phot photography
phys physics
physiol physiology
pl plural
poet poetic
pol political
pol econ political economy
poss possessive
prep preposition
pres present
print printing
pron pronoun
psy psychology
rad radio
rw railway
s substantive, noun
sew sewing
sing singular
spirit spiritualism
sport sports
subjunc subjunctive
sup superlative
surg surgery
surv surveying
tan tanning
theat theater
theol theology
univ university
v aux auxiliary verb
vi intransitive verb
vr reflexive verb
vt transitive verb
WH Western Hemispheric Spanish
zool zoology

SPANISH-ENGLISH
Dictionary

a *f,* name of the letter A

a *prep* to; at; on; by; in, into; up to; according to; if, etc. 1. Denotes the direct complement of verb before objects representing specified persons or animals, personified nouns, pronouns referring to specific persons (**alguien, entrambos, cualquiera,** etc.), demonstrative or relative pronouns, collective nouns representing persons (**el público, la muchedumbre,** etc.), names of countries, cities, rivers, etc., except where these invariably take the def. art., e.g. **Dejé a Varsovia,** I left Warsaw, *but* **Dejé el Perú,** I left Peru. 2. Introduces indirect obj. when this is a noun governed by a verb implying motion, or an emphatic pers. pron., e.g. **Nos conviene a ti y a mí,** It suits both you and me. It is also used before indirect obj. to avoid ambiguity when there is both an indirect and direct obj. 3. Denotes the complement of verb when this is an infin., e.g. **Enseñó a pintar a María,** He taught Mary to paint. 4. Indicates direction or destination, e.g. **Vamos a Edimburgo,** We are going to Edinburgh. 5. Signifies location, or point of time when action takes place, e.g. **Vinieron a las doce.** They came at twelve o'clock. 6. Describes position of persons or things, e.g. **Se sentaron a la puerta,** They sat down at the door. **La casa queda a la derecha,** The house is on the right. 7. Denotes interval of time or place between one thing and another, e.g. **de tres a cinco de la tarde,** from three to five in the afternoon, **de calle a calle,** from street to street. 8. Expresses manner of action, e.g. **a la francesa,** in the French way, **bordado a mano,** embroidered by hand. 9. Indicates rate or price, e.g. **a cuatro pesetas la libra,** at four pesetas the lb. 10. Indicates difference or comparison, e.g. **Va mucho de querer a hacer,** There's a difference between wishing and doing. 11. Sometimes is synonymous with **hasta, según, hacia** and governs almost all parts of speech. Has many idiomatic uses. 12. Before infin. sometimes has conditional sense, e.g. **A haber sabido las noticias no lo hubiéramos hecho,** If we had heard the news we would not have done it. 13. With certain nouns, adjectives, and infinitives forms adverbial phrases, e.g. **poco a poco,** little by little, **a veces,** sometimes, **a ciegas,** blindly, etc. **¡a ver!** let's see!; *Colombia* hello! (on telephone). **A + el** becomes **al,** e.g. **al rey,** to the king. **Al** + infin. means when or on, e.g. **al marcharme yo,** when I left (on my leaving); *Lat. Am.* **al año** a year later; *Lat. Am.* **a la semana** a week later; *Lat. Am.* **al mes** a month later

abacería *f,* grocery shop

abacero (-ra) *n* grocer

ábaco *m, arch* abacus; counting frame

abad *m,* abbot

abajo *adv* under; underneath; below; down. Used immediately after noun in adverbial phrases, e.g. **cuesta a., escalera a.,** downhill, downstairs. *interj* Down with! e.g., **¡A. el rey!** Down with the king! **venirse a.,** to fall down; *fig* collapse

abalanzamiento *m,* balancing; rushing upon; dashing

abalanzar *vt* to balance; impel violently; *vr* throw oneself upon; attack, rush upon; (*with prep a*) rush into, risk. **Se abalanzó hacia ellos,** He rushed toward them

abalear *vt, Lat. Am.* to shoot at

abalorio *m,* glass bead; bead work

abanderado *m,* standardbearer; *Argentina* valedictorian

abanderizar *vt* to organize in groups; *vr* band together

abandonado *a* deserted; forlorn; helpless; indolent, careless; slovenly

abandonamiento *m,* desertion; forlornness; helplessness; carelessness; slovenliness

abandonar *vt* to forsake, desert; neglect; leave; give up; renounce; *vr* neglect oneself; grow discouraged; (*with prep a*) give oneself over to

abandono *m,* abandonment; defencelessness; forlornness; dilapidation; renunciation; neglect; slovenliness; debauchery

abanicar *vt* to fan

abanico *m,* fan; anything fan-shaped; *inf* sword; railway signal; *naut* derrick. **en a.,** fan-shaped

abaniqueo *m,* fanning; swinging, oscillation; gesticulation

abaratar *vt* to cheapen, make less expensive; *vr* fall in price

abarca *f,* leather sandal, worn chiefly in the Basque provinces

abarcador(-ra) *n* one who clasps or embraces; monopolist

abarcadura *f,* **abarcamiento** *m,* inclusion; scope

abarcar *vt* to clasp, encircle; include, comprise; undertake, attempt; monopolize

abarquillar *vt* to shape into a roll; roll; curl

abarracar(se) *vi* and *vr mil* to go into barracks

abarrancadero *m,* rough road; ravine, precipice; *fig* difficult situation

abarrancar *vt* to ditch; make a ravine; *vr* fall into a pit; stick (in the mud, etc.); get into difficulties; *naut* run aground

abarrotería *f, Mexico* grocery store, grocery, grocer's

abarrotero, -a *mf Lat. Am.* grocer

abarrotes *m pl, Lat. Am.* groceries

abastar see **abastecer**

abastecedor (-ra) *a* provisioning, supplying. *n* provider; purveyor, supplier; caterer

abastecer *vt irr* to supply, provide; purvey. See **conocer**

abastecimiento *m,* providing; supply, provision; catering; supplies

abasto *m,* provisions, food; *com* supply. *adv* plentifully, abundantly

abate *m,* abbé

abatido *a* dejected, depressed; spiritless; discouraged; crushed, humbled; *com* depreciated

abatimiento *m,* dejection, depression; humiliation; discouragement; falling; lowering; (*aer naut*) drift

abatir *vt* to knock down; overthrow; demolish; lower, take down; droop; humiliate; discourage; *naut* dismantle; *vi* (*aer naut*) drift; *vr* be despondent, despair; humble oneself; swoop down (of birds). **a. el vuelo,** to fly down

ABC *m,* ABCs (e.g. **el ABC de la física,** the ABCs of physics)

abdicación *f,* abdication

abdicar *vt* to abdicate; revoke, cancel; give up (rights, opinions)

abdomen *m,* abdomen

abdominal *a* abdominal

abecé *m,* ABCs

abecedario *m,* ABCs, alphabet; reading book, primer

abedul *m,* birch tree; birch wood

abeja *f,* bee. **a. maestra,** queen bee. **a. obrera,** worker

abejar *m,* beehive

abejero (-ra) *n* beekeeper

abejón *m,* drone; hornet

abejorro *m,* bumblebee

aberración *f,* deviation; error, lapse; (*ast phys biol*) aberration

abertura *f,* opening; aperture, gap, hole; fissure, cleft; mountain pass; naturalness, frankness

abeto *m,* yew-leaved fir

abierto *a* free, unobstructed; open, not enclosed; open, full-blown (flowers); frank, sincere. *adv* openly

abigarrado *a* variegated; varied; speckled

abigarrar *vt* to variegate; vary; speckle; fleck; spot; dapple
abigotado *a* having a thick moustache
abintestato *a law* intestate
abismal *a* abysmal
abismar *vt* to plunge into an abyss; depress, sadden; *vr* despair; be plunged in thought, be abstracted; be amazed
abismo *m*, chasm, abyss, gulf; hell
abjuración *f*, abjuration
abjurar *vt* to forswear, retract
ablactar *vt* to wean
ablandamiento *m*, softening; placating
ablandante *a* softening; placatory
ablandar *vt* to soften; appease, placate; loosen; relax; *vi* and *vr* be softened; be appeased; grow less stormy; (elements) decrease in force
ablandecer *vt irr* to soften. See **conocer**
ablución *f*, ablution
abnegación *f*, abnegation, self-sacrifice
abnegado *a* self-sacrificing
abnegarse *vr irr* to deprive oneself, sacrifice oneself. See **cegar**
abobado *a* bewildered; foolish-looking, silly
abobar *vt* to daze, bewilder; make stupid
abocado *a* full-flavoured, pleasant (of wine)
abocar *vt* to seize with the mouth; bring nearer; transfer (contents of one jug to another); *vr* meet, assemble; *vi naut* enter (a channel, port, etc.). **abocarse (con . . .),** to contact (. . .), get in touch (with . . .)
abocetado *a art* unfinished; sketchy
abochornado *a* flushed (of the face); ashamed; embarrassed
abochornar *vt* to overheat, make flushed; shame; embarrass; *vr* (plants) dry up
abofetear *vt* to slap, hit; buffet
abogacía *f*, legal profession; practice of law; advocacy
abogaderas, abogaderías *f pl Lat. Am.* hair-splitting, specious arguments, legalistics
abogado (-da) *n* lawyer
abogar *vi* to defend at law; intercede for; advocate, champion
abolengo *m*, lineage, descent, family; inheritance
abolición *f*, abolition
abolir *vt* to abolish; cancel; annul
abolladura *f*, bruise; dent; embossment
abollar *vt* to bruise; dent
abombado *a* convex; domed; *Mexico* tight (tipsy)
abombar *vt* to make convex; *inf* deafen, bewilder; *vr* begin to putrefy; get intoxicated; *Mexico* become tight, get tight (tipsy)
abominable *a* abominable
abominación *f*, abomination; loathing, detestation
abominar *vt* to abominate, loathe, detest
abonable *a* subscribable; payable
abonado (-da) *a* trustworthy, reliable; ready, prepared, inclined. *n* subscriber; season ticket holder (for concerts, etc.)
abonanzar *vi impers* to clear up, be fine (weather)
abonar *vt* to guarantee; go surety for; improve, better; manure; ratify, confirm; pay; *com* place to the credit of; *vr* subscribe, become a subscriber; take out (season tickets, etc.)
abonaré *m*, *com* due bill; promissory note, I.O.U.
abono *m*, subscription; voucher; guarantee; manure. **a. verde,** leaf mold. **en a. de,** in payment of; in support of
aboquillado *a* tipped (of cigarettes)
abordar *vt naut* to board a ship; *naut* collide, run into; accost, tackle; undertake; *vi naut* put into port
aborigen *a* aboriginal
aborígenes *m pl*, aborigines
aborrachado *a* bright red; highly colored; flushed
aborrascarse *vr* to grow stormy
aborrecedor (-ra) *a* hateful. *n* hater, loather
aborrecer *vt irr* to hate, loathe; desert offspring (animals, birds). See **conocer**
aborrecible *a* hateful, detestable
aborrecimiento *m*, hate, detestation; dislike
abortar *vt* to abort; foil (a plot); *vi med* miscarry; fail, go awry
abortivo *a* abortive
aborto *m*, abortion; miscarriage; monster; failure
abotagarse *vr* to swell up, become bloated
abotonador *m*, button-hook
abotonar *vt* to button; *vi* bud, sprout
abra *f*, cove, small bay; narrow gorge; fissure, cleft; *Argentina* clearing (in a forest)
abrasador *a* burning, flaming
abrasamiento *m*, burning; ardour, heat
abrasar *vt* to burn; dry up, parch (plants); squander, waste; shame; *vi* burn; *vr* be very hot, glow; burn with passion
abrasión *f*, abrasion
abrasivo *a* and *m*, abrasive
abrazadera *f*, clasp; clamp
abrazamiento *m*, embracing
abrazar *vt* to embrace, clasp in one's arms; follow, adopt; engage in; seize, take advantage of; comprise, include; surround; take in hand; clamp; clasp. **abrazarse a,** to clutch, hang on to
abrazo *m*, embrace
abrelatas *m*, can opener
abrevar *vt* to water cattle; irrigate, water
abreviación *f*, abbreviation, shortening; summary; hastening
abreviador *m*, abridger, condenser
abreviar *vt* to abbreviate, shorten; hasten, accelerate; condense, abridge. **a. tiempo,** to save time. **Y para a. . . . ,** And, to cut a long story short . . .
abreviatura *f*, abbreviation, contraction; shorthand
abridor *m*, opener; ear-ring (for keeping holes in ears open). **a. de guantes,** glove-stretcher. **a. de láminas,** engraving needle. **a. de latas,** can opener
abridura *f*, (act of) opening (e.g. of a trunk)
abrigada *f*, **abrigadero** *m*, sheltered place
abrigar *vt* to shelter, protect (against the cold, etc.); defend, help; hold (opinions); nurse (a hope, etc.); cover; *vr* take shelter; wrap oneself up
abrigo *m*, shelter; defence; protection; help; sheltered place; wrap, coat; *naut* haven
abril *m*, April; youth; *pl poet* years
abrillantar *vt* to cut in facets like a diamond; polish, burnish; cause to shine; *fig* improve, add lustre to
abrir *vt* to open; reveal; unlock; slide the bolt of; extend, spread out; cleave; engrave; clear (the way, etc.); begin; head, lead; separate; dig; inaugurate. *vi* unfold (flowers); expand; **en un abrir y cerrar de ojos,** in the twinkling of an eye, in the wink of an eye; *vr* open; expand; (*with con*) confide in. **a. el camino (a . . .),** to pave the way (for . . .). **abrirse camino,** to make one's way; **abrirse paso a codazos,** to elbow one's way out, (or through)
abrochador *m*, button-hook
abrochar *vt* to button; fasten, clasp; hook up (a dress, etc.); buckle; *Lat. Am.* **abrocharse (con . . .)** struggle (with . . .), wrestle (with . . .)
abrogación *f*, repeal, annulment
abrogar *vt* to repeal, annul
abrojo *m*, thistle; *bot* caltrops; thorn, prickle; *pl* submerged rocks in sea
abroncar *vt inf* to bore, annoy
abrumador *a* burdensome, crushing, oppressive; troublesome, tiresome; exhausting
abrumar *vt* to weigh down; overwhelm, oppress; weary, exhaust; *vr* grow misty
abrupto *a* steep; rough, broken (ground); rugged
absceso *m*, abscess
absentismo *m*, absenteeism
ábside *mf*, *arch* apse. *m*, *ast* apsis

absolución *f,* (*ecc* and *law*) absolution; remission, pardon
absoluta *f, mil* discharge
absolutista *mf* absolutist
absoluto *a* absolute; categorical; *inf* despotic. **en a.,** absolutely
absolver *vt irr* to absolve; acquit (of a charge). *law* **a. de la instancia,** to dismiss the case. See **mover**
absorbente *a* and *m,* absorbent
absorber *vt* to absorb; consume, use up; attract, hold (the attention, etc.); imbibe
absorción *f,* absorption
absortar *vt* to amaze, dumbfound
absorto *a* amazed, astounded; abstracted, lost in thought
abstemio *a* abstemious
abstención *f,* abstention
abstenerse *vr irr* to refrain; abstain. See **tener**
abstinencia *f,* abstinence; fasting
abstinente *a* abstemious; temperate
abstracción *f,* abstraction; preoccupation; absent-mindedness
abstracto *a* abstract. **en a.,** in the abstract
abstraer *vt irr* to abstract; consider separately; *vi* (*with de*) do without, exclude; *vr* be preoccupied; let one's thoughts wander. See **traer**
abstraído *a* retired, recluse; preoccupied; absent-minded
abstruso *a* abstruse
absurdidad *f,* absurdity; folly, nonsense
absurdo *a* ridiculous, absurd. *m,* piece of folly, nonsense
abuchear *vt vi* to boo, hoot, jeer
abuela *f,* grandmother; old woman, dame
abuelo *m,* grandfather; *gen pl* ancestor; old man; *pl* grandparents
abulia *f,* lack of will-power, abulia
abúlico *a* abulic, lacking will-power
abultado *a* bulky, large; voluminous; exaggerated
abultamiento *m,* bulkiness; enlargement, increase; mound; exaggeration
abultar *vt* to enlarge, increase; exaggerate; model in rough (sculpture); *vi* be bulky; be large
abundancia *f,* abundance, plenty
abundante *a* abundant, plentiful; abounding (in)
abundar *vi* to be plentiful, abound
aburrido *a* boring, tedious, dull; tired, weary
aburrimiento *m,* boredom, dullness; wearisomeness, tediousness
aburrir *vt* to bore; *inf* spend (time, money); (birds) desert the nest; *vr* grow bored; be weary
¡abusado! *Mexico* careful!, look out!, watch out!
abusar *vi* to abuse; exceed one's rights, go too far; (*with de*) take advantage of
abusivo *a* abusive
abuso *m,* abuse. **a. de confianza,** abuse of trust
abyección *f,* degradation, misery; abjectness, servility
abyecto *a* abject, wretched; servile
acá *adv* hither, here; at this time, now. **a. y acullá,** hither and thither. **desde ayer a.,** from yesterday until now
acabable *a* terminable, finishable; achievable
acabado *a* complete; perfect; expert, consummate; old, worn out; ill, infirm. *m,* finish
acabamiento *m,* finishing, completion; end; death, decease
acabar *vt* to end, terminate; finish; complete, perfect; kill; (*with con*) destroy, finish off; suppress; squander; *vi* end; die; be destroyed; (*with de + infin*) to have just (e.g. **Acaba de salir,** He has just gone out); *vr* end, be exhausted, run out of (e.g. **Se le acabó el dinero,** His money ran out); fade, grow weak; be destroyed. **Se les acabaron las dudas,** Their doubts were cleared up. **a. de desconcertar,** to nonplus completely; **a. de decidirse,** to come to a decision; **a. de saber,** to finally learn
acacia *f, bot* acacia
academia *f,* academy
académico (-ca) *a* academic. *n* academician. **a. de la lengua,** member of the Royal Spanish Academy
acaecer *vi irr* to happen, occur. See **conocer**
acaecimiento *m,* happening, occurrence, event
acalambrarse (muscle) to contract with cramps. **Estar acalambrado,** to have cramps
acalenturarse *vr* to grow feverish
acallar *vt* to quieten, hush; soothe, appease
acalorado *a* hot; fervent; *fig* heated
acaloramiento *m,* excitement, agitation, vehemence; ardour
acalorar *vt* to warm; aid, encourage; excite, stimulate; stir, move (to enthusiasm); inflame, rouse; tire (by exercise); *vr* grow hot; become agitated or excited; become heated (arguments)
acamar *vt* to lay flat (plants by the wind); *vr* be flattened (plants); lie down (animals); go rotten (fruit)
acampar *vi* and *vt* to encamp
acanalar *vt* to groove; striate, flute; corrugate; furrow, channel
acantilado *a* steep, precipitous; shelving (ocean-bed). *m,* cliff
acanto *m,* (*arch bot*) acanthus
acantonamiento *m,* billeting; cantonment
acantonar *vt* to billet or quarter troops
acaparador (-ra) *n* monopolist
acaparar *vt com* to monopolize, corner; seize, take possession of
acápite *m, WH* new paragraph
acaracolado *a* spiral, winding, twisting
acardenalar *vt* to bruise; *vr* be bruised; be covered with livid marks
acarear *vt* to face; face up to, meet with courage
acariciador (-ra) *a* caressing, loving. *n* fondler
acariciar *vt* to caress; brush, touch lightly; cherish, treat affectionately; toy with (a suggestion)
acarraladura *f, Lat. Am.* run (in a stocking)
acarreador (-ra) *n* carrier, carter
acarreamiento, acarreo *m,* cartage, carting; transport, carriage; occasioning
acarrear *vt* to cart, transport; occasion, bring (gen. evil). **La guerra acarreó la carestía,** The war brought scarcity
acartonado *a* shriveled; shrunken; of cardboard; *fig* forced (dialogue)
acaso *m,* chance. *adv* by chance; perhaps, perchance. **por si a.,** in case (e.g. **Por si a. venga,** In case he comes)
acatable *a* venerable, worthy
acatamiento *m,* respect; reverence; observance
acatar *vt* to treat with respect, honor, revere; observe
acatarrar *vt, Lat. Am.* to annoy, bother, pester
acatarrarse *vr* to catch a cold; *Argentina* booze up, tank up
acaudalado *a* wealthy, well-to-do
acaudalar *vt* to make money; hoard up wealth; acquire (learning, etc.)
acaudillar *vt mil* to command, lead; head (a party, etc.)
acceder *vi* (*with prep a*) to concede, grant; accede to, agree to
accesibilidad *f,* accessibility; approachableness
accesible *a* accessible; approachable
accesión *f,* agreement, acquiescence; accession; accessory; feverish attack
acceso *m,* access; paroxysm, outburst; *med* attack
accesorio *a* accessory
accesorios *m pl,* accessories; *theat* properties
accidentado *a* rough, uneven; stormy, troubled (life, etc.)
accidentar *vt* to cause (someone) an accident; *vr* be the victim of an accident; be seized by a fit
accidente *m,* chance; accident, mishap; illness, indisposition; *med* fit; *gram* accidence; *mus* accidental. **a. del**

trabajo, accident at work. **por a.,** by chance, accidentally
acción *f*, action; battle; skirmish; *mech* drive; *com* share; gesture; lawsuit; *lit* action (of play, etc.); *art* posture, pose. **a. de gracias,** thanksgiving; *com* **a. liberada,** paid-up share. **a. privilegiada,** preference share
accionar *vi* to gesture, gesticulate; *Lat. Am.* act, be active
accionista *mf com* shareholder
acechar *vt* to spy upon, watch; lie in ambush for
acecho *m*, spying upon, watch; waylaying, ambush. **al a.,** in ambush; on the watch
acechona *f*, waylaying; ambush
acecinar *vt* to salt and dry (meat); *vr* (persons) wither, dry up
acedar *vt* to make bitter, sour; embitter, displease; *vr* turn sour; wither (plants)
acefalía *f*, acephalia, headlessness
acéfalo *a* acephalous
aceitar *vt* to oil, lubricate; rub with oil
aceite *m*, olive oil; oil. **a. de hígado de bacalao,** cod-liver oil. **a. de linaza,** linseed oil. **a. de ricino,** castor-oil. **a. de trementina,** oil of turpentine
aceitera *f*, woman who sells oil; oil can; oil bottle; *pl* cruet
aceitero *m*, oil seller. *a* oil
aceitoso *a* oily
aceituna *f*, *bot* olive
aceitunado *a* olive-colored
aceitunero (-ra) *n* olive picker; olive seller. *m*, warehouse for storing olives
aceituno *m*, olive tree; *a*, *Lat. Am.* olive-colored
aceleración *f*, speed, haste; acceleration
aceleradamente *adv* hastily, swiftly
acelerador *a* accelerating. *m*, hastener; *aut* accelerator
acelerar *vt* to hasten, speed up; accelerate
acémila *f*, beast of burden, mule
acendrado *a* pure, unblemished, spotless
acendrar *vt* to refine (metals); purify, make spotless
acento *m*, accent; tone, inflection; *poet* voice, words. **a. agudo,** acute accent. **a. circunflejo,** circumflex accent. **a. grave,** grave accent. **a. ortográfico,** graphic accent, written accent. **a. tónico,** tonic accent
acentuación *f*, accentuation, stress; emphasis
acentuar *vt* to accent; stress, emphasize; *vr* become evident, become marked, be noticeable
aceña *f*, water-mill; irrigation water-wheel; chain-well
acepción *f*, meaning, significance, acceptation. **a. de personas,** partiality, preference
acepilladura *f*, sweeping, brushing; planing; wood-shaving
acepillar *vt* to sweep, brush; plane; *inf* brush up, polish up
aceptabilidad *f*, acceptability
aceptable *a* acceptable
aceptación *f*, acceptance; popularity; approval
aceptador (-ra) *a* accepting. *n* acceptor
aceptar *vt* to accept; approve; accept a challenge; *com* honor
acequia *f*, ditch, trench; irrigation channel
acera *f*, sidewalk, pavement. **a. del sol,** sunny side of the street
acerado *a* steel; steel-like; strong, tough; mordant, incisive
acerar *vt* to steel; treat (liquids) with steel; harden, make obdurate
acerbidad *f*, bitterness, acerbity, sourness; harshness, cruelty
acerbo *a* sour, tart, bitter; cruel, harsh
acerca de *adv* about, concerning
acercamiento *m*, approach
acercar *vt* to bring nearer; *vr* be near at hand, draw near; (*with prep a*) approach
acerico *m*, small cushion; pincushion
acero *m*, steel; blade, sword; *pl* bravery, spirit; *inf* good appetite. **a. inoxidable,** stainless steel
acérrimo *a sup* extremely strong, mighty; most harsh; most resolute, unflinching; very strong (taste, smell)
acerrojar *vt* to lock, padlock; bolt
acertado *a* well-aimed; fitting, suitable; wise; successful
acertar *vt irr* to hit the mark; find, come across; succeed (in), achieve; guess, find out; **No acertaba a explicármelo,** I couldn't quite understand it. **a. por chambra,** to make a lucky guess. *vi* be successful; thrive (of plants); (*with prep a + infin*) happen, occur, come to pass. *Pres. Ind.* **acierto, aciertas, acierta, aciertan.** *Pres. Subjunc.* **acierte, aciertes, acierte, acierten**
acertijo *m*, riddle
acervo *m*, pile, heap; *fig* storehouse, wealth (e.g. of words)
acetato *m*, acetate
acético *a* acetic
acetileno *m*, acetylene
achacar *vt* to attribute, impute, assign. **achacable a,** imputable to
achacoso *a* ailing, ill, sickly
achantarse *vr inf* to hide from danger; put up with, bear
achaparrado *a* stocky
achaque *m*, ailment, illness (permanent); *inf* period, menstruation; pregnancy; matter, affair; pretext; failing, bad habit. **En a. de . . . ,** Re . . . , concerning . . .
achatamiento *m*, flattening
achatar *vt* to flatten, make flat
achicado *a* childish
achicar *vt* to make smaller, diminish; drain, bail out; depreciate, belittle
achicarse *inf* to get smaller
achicharrar *vt cul* to overcook; overheat; annoy, importune
achicoria *f*, chicory
achique *m*, bailing, draining
achispado *a inf* tipsy
achubascarse *vr* to become overcast, grow stormy
achuchar *vt inf* to squeeze, hug; jostle, push against
achuchón *m*, *inf* shove, push; hug, squeeze
achulado *a inf* brazen, tough
aciago *a* unhappy, ill-omened; fateful
acíbar *m*, aloe tree; bitter aloes; sorrow, bitterness
acibarar *vt* to add bitter aloes to; embitter, sadden
acicalado *a* polished; neat; well-groomed. *m*, polishing, burnishing (of weapons)
acicalador (-ra) *a* polishing. *n* polisher. *m*, burnisher (machine)
acicalar *vt* to burnish (weapons); adorn, deck; *vr* dress oneself with care
acicate *m*, Moorish spur; incitement, stimulus
acicatear *vt* to induce, spur on. **a. la curiosidad,** arouse curiosity
acidez *f*, acidity, bitterness
acidia *f*, indolence; sluggishness
ácido *a* acid; sour; harsh. *m*, acid. **a. fénico,** carbolic acid. **a. graso,** fatty acid
acidular *vt chem* to acidulate
acídulo *a chem* acidulous
acierto *m*, good hit, bull's-eye; success; achievement; cleverness; dexterity, skill; wisdom, sense; tact
acimut *m*, *ast* azimuth
aclamación *f*, acclamation; shout of acclamation. **por a.,** unanimously
aclamador (-ra) *a* acclaiming. *n* applauder, acclaimer
aclamar *vt* to acclaim; applaud
aclaración *f*, explanation; elucidation
aclarado *m*, rinse; rinsing
aclarador, aclaratorio *a* explanatory
aclarar *vt* to clarify, purify; clear; rinse (clothes); explain; thin; *vi* clear; (sky) clear up; dawn
aclimatación *f*, acclimatization; *Lat. Am.* air-conditioning
aclimatar *vt* to acclimatize
acné *m*, acne
acobardar *vt* to intimidate, frighten
acocear *vt* to kick; *inf* insult, humiliate

acocharse *vr* to squat, crouch
acocil *m, Mexico* freshwater shrimp
acodalar *vt* to prop
acodiciar *vt* to yearn for, covet, desire
acogedizo *a* gathered haphazardly
acogedor (-ra) *a* welcoming, friendly; inviting (e.g. a chair or room); *n* protector
acoger *vt* to receive, welcome, admit; protect, harbour; *vr* take refuge; (*with prep a*) make use of, resort to; **acogerse a sagrado,** seek sanctuary
acogida *f,* reception, welcome; protection, shelter; meeting place; confluence (of waters). **tener buena a.,** to be well received
acogollar *vt* to protect, cover (plants); *vi* sprout, shoot
acogotar *vt* to fell by a blow on the neck; *inf* knock out
acolada *f,* accolade
acolitar *vi* to serve as an altar boy, serve as an altar girl
acólito *m,* acolyte
acomedido, -a *Lat. Am.* helpful, obliging
acometedor (-ra) *a* capable, enterprising; aggressive. *n* aggressor, attacker
acometer *vt* to attack furiously; undertake; take in hand; overcome (of sleep, etc.)
acometida *f,* **acometimiento** *m,* assault, onrush; undertaking
acometividad *f,* aggressiveness; *Argentina* touchiness
acomodable *a* easily arranged
acomodación *f,* adjustment; adaptation; accommodation
acomodadizo *a* accommodating, easy-going
acomodado *a* suitable; convenient; wealthy, well-off; comfort-loving; moderate, low (of price)
acomodador (-ra) *n* theater attendant, usher
acomodamiento *m,* agreement, transaction; accommodation
acomodar *vt* to arrange, adjust, accommodate; adapt; appoint; place; reconcile; employ, take on; equip, provide; lodge; *vi* suit, be convenient; *vr* compromise, agree
acomodaticio *a* accommodating
acomodo *m,* post, employment; arrangement; settlement
acompañamiento *m,* accompaniment; following, retinue; *mus* accompaniment; *theat* crowd, chorus
acompañanta *f,* chaperon; maid, servant
acompañante *m, mus* accompanist
acompañar *vt* to accompany; follow, escort; enclose (a letter, etc.); *mus* accompany
acompasado *a* rhythmic; deliberate, slow
acondicionado *a* conditioned; (*with* **bien** *or* **mal**) in good or bad condition; of good or bad quality; good- or ill-natured. **reflejo acondicionado** *med* conditioned reflex
acondicionar *vt* to prepare; mend, repair; *vr* condition oneself
acongojar *vt* to sadden, grieve; oppress
aconsejable *a* advisable
aconsejar *vt* to advise; *vr* (*with con*) consult, ask advice of
acontecedero *a* possible
acontecer *vi irr impers* to happen. See **conocer**
acontecimiento *m,* event, occurrence
acopiar *vt* to collect, amass, gather
acopio *m,* collection, store; accumulation, gathering
acopladura *f,* **acoplamiento** *m,* (*carp. mech*) joint; coupling; yoking; mating (of animals)
acoplar *vt* to join, couple; yoke; mate (animals); reconcile (opinions); *vr inf* fall in love
acoquinar *vt inf* to intimidate, terrify
acorazado *a* (*nav mil*) armoured, iron-clad. *m,* iron-clad, battleship
acorcharse *vr* to dry up, shrivel; go numb (limbs)
acordadamente *adv* by common consent, unanimously; deliberately, after due thought
acordar *vt irr* to decide unanimously; resolve; remind; tune; harmonize (colors); *vi* agree; *vr* remember; come to an agreement. **Si mal no me acuerdo,** If memory serves me right. *Pres. Ind.* **acuerdo, acuerdas, acuerda, acuerdan.** *Pres. Subjunc.* **acuerde, acuerdes, acuerde, acuerden**
acorde *a* agreed; in harmony; in agreement. *m, mus* chord; harmony
acordeón *m,* accordion; (slang) crib sheet
acordonar *vt* to lace; cordon off, surround; mill (coins)
acornear *vt* to butt, toss (bulls)
acorralamiento *m,* corralling, penning
acorralado *a* at bay, intimidated
acorralar *vt* to corral, pen; confine; corner, silence (in argument); frighten; harass
acorrer *vt* to aid, assist; *vi* run, hasten; *vr* take refuge
acortamiento *m,* shortening
acortar *vt* to shorten; *vr* be speechless, be shy. **a. las velas,** to take in sail
acosador (-ra) *a* persecuting. *n* persecutor
acosamiento *m,* persecution
acosar *vt* to persecute relentlessly; annoy, harass
acostado *a* in bed; stretched out; *her* couchant
acostar *vt irr* to lay down, stretch out; put to bed; *vi* lean, tilt; *vr* lie down; go to bed; *naut* come alongside. See **contar**
acostumbrado *a* accustomed, usual
acostumbrar *vt* to habituate, accustom; *vi* be in the habit of (e.g. **Acostumbramos ir a la playa en el verano,** We generally go to the seashore in summer); *vr* (*with prep a*) become used to
acotación *f,* noting; marginal note; stage direction; ordnance survey number
acotar *vt* to annotate; mark out boundaries; fix, establish; accept; *inf* choose; testify; fill in elevation figures (on a map); *vr* seek refuge
acotejar *vt, Lat. Am.* to arrange, put in order
acre *a* bitter, sour; harsh; biting, mordant. *m,* acre (land measure)
acrecencia *f,* **acrecentamiento** *m,* increase; addition
acrecentar *vt irr* to increase; augment; promote, prefer. See **acertar**
acrecer *vt irr* to increase; augment. See **conocer**
acreción *f,* accretion
acreditado *a* accredited, well-reputed; respected
acreditar *vt* to prove; verify; accredit; recommend; sanction, authorize; vouch for, guarantee; *com* credit
acreedor (-ra) *n* creditor; claimant. *a* deserving. **a. hipotecario,** mortgagee
acreencia *f,* debt; *com* claim
acribillar *vt* to riddle with holes; wound repeatedly; pelt; torment; *inf* pester, harass
acriminación *f,* accusation
acriminador (-ra) *a* incriminating. *n* accuser
acriminar *vt* to accuse, charge
acrimonia *f,* acrimony
acriollarse *vr, Lat. Am.* to adopt local customs, go native
acrisolar *vt* to refine, purify (metals); perfect; clarify, elucidate
acrobacia *f,* acrobatics
acróbata *mf* acrobat
acrobático *a* acrobatic
acromatópsico *a* color-blind
acróstico *a* and *m,* acrostic
acta *f,* minutes, record; certificate of election (as deputy to Cortes, etc.); *pl* deeds (of a martyr). **a. matrimonial,** marriage register
actitud *f,* attitude
activar *vt* to stimulate, make active; accelerate, hasten
actividad *f,* activity; movement, bustle. **en a.,** in action; at work
activo *a* active. *m, com* assets
acto *m,* act, deed, action; act, law; act (of a play); public ceremony; *pl* minutes (of a meeting), proceedings (of a conference). **a. continuo** *or* **a. seguido,** immediately afterwards. **a. vandálico,** act of vandalism. **los Actos de los Apóstoles,** Acts of the Apostles. **en a.,** in the act (of doing). **en el a.,** in the act; immediately

actor *m*, actor; *law* plaintiff
actriz *f*, actress
actuación *f*, operation, functioning; action; *pl* legal functions, judicial acts
actual *a* present; contemporary
actualidad *f*, present, present time; topic of interest. **actualidades,** current events. **en la a.,** at the present time
actuar *vt* to operate, set in motion; *vi* act; exercise legal functions
actuario (de seguros) *m*, actuary
acuarela *f*, water-color painting
acuarelista *mf* water-colorist
acuario *m*, aquarium; Aquarius
acuartelamiento *m*, billeting (of troops); billet, quarters
acuartelar *vt* to billet
acuático, acuátil *a* aquatic
acuatinta *f*, aquatint
acuatizar *vi*, *Lat. Am.* to land on water, touch down on water
acuchillado *a* taught by experience, schooled
acuchillar *vt* to hack, cut about; stab, put to the sword; slash (sleeves, etc.); *vr* fight with swords, daggers
acucia *f*, fervor, zeal; yearning, longing
acuciar *vt* to incite; goad; stimulate; encourage
acuciosidad *f*, eagerness, fervor, zeal
acucioso *a* eager, fervent, keen, zealous
acuclillarse *vr* to squat, crouch
acudir *vi* to go, repair (to); come; go or come to the aid of; attend, be present; **No me acude ningún ejemplo a la memoria,** No example comes to mind; resort (to), seek protection; reply, respond
acueducto *m*, aqueduct
acuerdo *m*, motion, resolution; decision; harmony, agreement; opinion, belief; remembrance; report; meeting (of members of a tribunal); *art* harmony (of colors). **de a.,** in agreement, in conformity; unanimously. **estar de a. (con),** to agree (with). **estar de acuerdo en** (+ inf.), to agree to (+ inf.) **ponerse de a.,** to come to an understanding
acuilmarse *vr Central America* to get depressed, get the blues
acuitar *vt* to distress, trouble; grieve
acumulación *f*, accumulation, collection
acumulador (-ra) *a* accumulative. *m*, accumulator, storage battery. *n* collector, accumulator
acumulamiento *m*, accumulation (act)
acumular *vt* to accumulate, amass, collect; accuse, charge with
acuñación *f*, minting, coining; wedging
acuñador (-ra) *n* coiner, stamper; wedge. *m*, coining machine
acuñar *vt* to mint, stamp, coin; wedge
acuoso *a* aqueous, watery
acurrucarse *vr* to huddle; curl up; crouch
acusación *f*, accusation; *law* charge; *law* prosecution
acusado (-da) *a* accused; prominent; well-defined; *n* accused; *law* defendant
acusador (-ra) *a* accusing. *n* accuser; *law* prosecutor
acusar *vt* to accuse; blame; denounce; *com* acknowledge receipt; *law* prosecute; *law* charge. **acusarle a uno las cuarenta,** *inf* to give someone a piece of one's mind
acusatorio *a* accusatory
acusón (-ona) *n inf* telltale, sneak, informer
acústica *f*, acoustics
acústico *a* acoustic
adagio *m*, adage; *mus* adagio
adalid *m*, chieftain; head, leader
adamado *a* effeminate; refined; genteel
adamantino *a* adamantine
adaptabilidad *f*, adaptability
adaptación *f*, adaptation
adaptar *vt* to adapt, make suitable; *vr* adapt oneself
adarme *m*, tittle, jot. **por adarmes,** in bits and pieces, in drabs and driblets
adecentar *vt* to make decent; tidy up; *vr* tidy oneself
adecuación *f*, adequacy; suitability
adecuado *a* adequate; suitable
adecuar *vt* to proportion, fit; *fig* tailor
adefesio *m*, *inf* folly, absurdity (gen. *pl*); extravagant attire; guy, sight
adelantado *a* precocious; forward, pert; fast (clocks); early (of fruit); excellent; capable, proficient. *m*, *ant* provincial governor *or* chief justice *or* captain-general (Spanish history). **por a.,** in advance
adelantamiento *m*, promotion, furtherance; progress, advancement; betterment, improvement; *ant* office of **adelantado;** anticipation
adelantar *vt* to advance, move on; hasten; forestall; overtake; move forward (the hands of clocks); improve, better; beat, excel; place in front; *vi* progress, advance; be fast (clocks); grow, develop; *vr* come forward
adelante *adv* on, forward; further on; straight ahead. **¡A.!** Onward!; Come in! **de hoy en a.,** henceforth, from today
adelanto *m*, anticipation; progress; *com* payment in advance. **el a. de la hora,** moving the clock forward
adelgazamiento *m*, loss of weight; slenderness; thinness
adelgazar *vt* to make slender or thin; *fig* split hairs; whittle, taper; *vi* grow slender or thin
ademán *m*, posture, attitude; gesture; *pl* behaviour, manners
además *adv* besides, in addition; moreover. **a. de,** as well as
adentro *adv* inside, within
adentros *m pl*, private thoughts (e.g. **Pensé para mis adentros,** I thought to myself). *Interj* **¡Adentro!** Come in!; Go in!
adepto *a* affiliated; adept, proficient
aderezamiento *m*, dressing; seasoning; embellishment
aderezar *vt* to deck, embellish; cook; *cul* season; *cul* dress; prepare; repair, mend; guide, direct; dress (cloth)
aderezo *m*, dressing, adornment; beautifying; finery, ornament; preparation; seasoning; set of jewels; horse's trappings; gum starch (for dressing cloth); equipment
adeudar *vt* to owe; be dutiable (goods); *com* debit; *vi* become related (by marriage); *vr* run into debt
adeudo *m*, debt; customs duty; *com* debit
adherencia *f*, adherence; adhesion
adherente *a* adhesive; connected, attached. *mf* adherent, follower; *m pl.* **adherentes,** accessories, requisites
adherirse *vr irr* to adhere, stick; follow; believe (in). See **herir**
adhesión *f*, adhesion; adherence
adhesivo *a* adhesive
adición *f*, addition; *Argentina* check (in a restaurant)
adicional *a* additional, extra
adicionar *vt* to add up; add to
adicto (-ta) *a* addicted, fond; joint. *n* addict; follower, disciple; *Lat. Am.* (drug) addict
adiestrador (-ra) *n* trainer, coach; guide, teacher
adiestrar *vt* to train, coach; guide, teach; lead; *vr* practise, perfect oneself
adietar *vt med* to put on a diet
adifés *adv*, *Central America* deliberately, on purpose
adinerado *a* wealthy, well-off, rich
adiós *interj* Good-bye!; Hello, God be with you! (used as greeting). *m*, farewell
aditamento *m*, addition
adive *m*, jackal
adivinación *f*, divination; guess
adivinanza *f*, divination; riddle; puzzle. **adivinanzas,** guessing games. **no estar para jugar a las a.,** to be in no mood for guessing games
adivinar *vt* to prophesy, foretell; divine, guess; solve, guess (riddles, etc.)
adivino (-na) *n* soothsayer, prophet

adjetivo *a* adjectival. *m*, adjective
adjudicación *f*, adjudication, award
adjudicador (-ra) *n* adjudicator
adjudicar *vt* to adjudge; award; *vr* appropriate
adjudicatario (-ia) *n* recipient (of a prize, etc.); grantee
adjuntar *vt* to enclose (with a letter, etc.)
adjunto *a* attached; enclosed, accompanying; assistant, deputy; adjectival. *m*, addition, supplement
administración *f*, administration; direction, control; administratorship
administrador (-ra) *a* administrative. *n* administrator. **a. de correos,** postmaster
administrar *vt* to control, manage; provide, supply; administer. **administrarse el tiempo,** to budget one's time
administrativo *a* administrative, executive
admirable *a* admirable
admirablemente *adv* admirably, excellently
admiración *f*, amazement; admiration; wonder; exclamation mark
admirador (-ra) *a* admiring. *n* admirer
admirar *vt* to admire; surprise, amaze (e.g. **Me admira su acción,** His action surprises me); to see (e.g. **Desde la colina se pueden admirar varios edificios de la ciudad,** From the hill several buildings in the city can be seen); *vr* (*with de*) be surprised at or by
admirativo *a* admiring; admirable, excellent
admisibilidad *f*, allowability, permissibility
admisible *a* admissible; permissible
admisión *f*, admission; acceptance; allowance
admitir *vt* to admit; receive, accept; tolerate, brook; allow, permit
admonición *f*, admonition, warning; reprimand
adobar *vt* to prepare; *cul* garnish; pickle (meat); cook; dress (hides)
adobo *m*, repairing; dressing (for cloth, leather); *cul* savory sauce; pickling sauce; make-up, cosmetic
adocenado *a* ordinary; narrow-minded
adoctrinar *vt* to instruct
adolecer *vi irr* to fall ill; (*with de*) suffer from (diseases, defects); *vr* be sorry for, regret. See **conocer**
adolescencia *f*, adolescence
adolescente *a* and *mf* adolescent
adonde *adv* (*interr* **a dónde**) where to, whither (e.g. **¿A dónde fuiste?** Where did you go to?)
adondequiera *adv* wherever
adopción *f*, adoption
adoptador (-ra) *a* adopting. *n* adopter
adoptar *vt* to adopt (children); make one's own, embrace (opinions); take (decisions)
adoptivo *a* adoptive
adoquín *m*, cobble-stone; *fig* blockhead
adoquinado *m*, cobbling, paving. *m*, cobbled pavement
adoquinar *vt* to pave with cobble-stones
adorable *a* adorable
adoración *f*, worship, adoration. **A. de los Reyes,** Adoration of the Magi; Epiphany
adorador (-ra) *a* adoring. *n* adorer
adorar *vt* to adore; worship; (*with en*) dote on; *vi* pray
adormecedor *a* soporific, drowsy
adormecer *vt irr* to make drowsy; soothe, lull; hush to sleep; *vr* go to sleep (limbs); fall asleep; (*with en*) persist in. See **conocer**
adormecimiento *m*, sleepiness; lulling asleep; numbness
adormitarse *vr* to doze, take a nap, snooze
adornamiento *m*, adornment, decoration
adornar *vt* to deck, beautify; decorate; trim, embellish; adorn (of virtues, etc.)
adorno *m*, decoration, adornment; ornament; trimming. **de a.,** ornamental; flowering (shrubs)
adquiridor (-ra) *a* acquiring. *n* acquirer
adquirir *vt irr* to acquire, get; achieve, obtain. *Pres. Ind.* **adquiero, adquieres, adquiere, adquieren.** *Pres. Subjunc.* **adquiera, adquieras, adquiera, adquieran**
adquisición *f*, acquirement; acquisition. **poder de a.,** purchasing power
adquisidor (-ra) *a* acquiring. *n* acquirer, obtainer
adquisitivo *a* acquisitive
adquisividad *f*, acquisitiveness
adrazo *m*, salt-water still
adrede *adv* on purpose, intentionally
adrenalina *f*, adrenaline
adscribir *vt* to ascribe, attribute; appoint (to a post, etc.)
adscripción *f*, ascription, attribution; appointment
aduana *f*, customs house, customs. **pasar por la a.,** to go through customs
aduanero *a* customs. *m*, customs officer
aducir *vt irr* to adduce, allege, cite; add. See **conducir**
adueñarse (de) *vr* to appropriate, take possession (of)
adulación *f*, adulation, flattery
adulador (-ra) *a* fawning. *n* flatterer
adular *vt* to flatter, fawn over, adulate
adulonería *f*, *Lat. Am.* flattery, fawning
adulteración *f*, adulteration; falsification
adulterador (-ra) *a* adulterant. *n* adulterator; falsifier; coiner
adulterar *vi* to commit adultery; *vt* adulterate; falsify
adulterino *a* adulterous; false
adulterio *m*, adultery
adúltero (-ra) *a* adulterous; corrupt. *n* adulterer
adulto (-ta) *a* and *n* adult
adunar *vt* to join, unite; unify, combine
adusto *a* extremely hot (of climate); grave, austere; standoffish, reserved
advenedizo *a* foreign, alien; strange, unknown; upstart; newly rich; *Lat. Am.* novice, tyro
advenimiento *m*, advent, arrival; ascension (to the throne)
advenir *vi irr* to come, arrive; happen, befall. See **venir**
adventicio *a* casual, accidental; *bot* adventitious
adverbio *m*, adverb
adversario (-ia) *n* adversary, rival; opponent
adversidad *f*, adversity, misfortune, sorrow
adverso *a* unfavorable, contrary, adverse; opposite
advertencia *f*, warning; introduction, preface; remark
advertido *a* capable, clever; experienced; expert
advertir *vt irr* to observe, notice; warn; advise; feel, be conscious of; point out, indicate; inform; discover. See **sentir**
adyacencia *f*, *Argentina* nearness, proximity
adyacente *a* adjacent, near-by, neighboring
aeración *f*, aeration
aéreo *a* aerial; airborne; airy; air; aeronautic; unsubstantial, fantastic. **correo a.,** airmail. **linea aérea** airline
aerobismo *m*, aerobics
aerodinámica *f*, aerodynamics
aeromozo, -a *mf*, *Lat. Am.* flight attendant
aeronauta *mf* aeronaut, balloonist
aeronáutica *f*, aeronautics
aeronáutico *a* aeronautic
aeropuerto *m*, airport
aeróstato *m*, dirigible
afabilidad *f*, affability, geniality, friendliness
afable *a* affable, genial, pleasant
afamado *a* famous, well-known
afamar *vt* to make famous
afán *m*, effort; manual labor; desire, anxiety **a. de mando,** thirst for power
afanar *vt* to press, urge on; filch; *vr* toil, labor; (*with por*) work hard to, try to
afanoso *a* hard, laborious; hard-working, painstaking; eager, anxious
afasia *f*, *med* aphasia
afear *vt* to make ugly; distort, deform; blame; criticize
afección *f*, fondness, affection; complaint, ailment, trouble
afectación *f*, affectation
afectado *a* affected

afectar *vt* to feign, assume; affect; move, touch; *law* encumber; *Lat. Am.* damage, hurt, injure
afectivo *a* affective
afecto *a* fond, affectionate; *law* encumbered; (*with prep a*) addicted to. *m*, emotion, sentiment; affection
afectuosidad *f*, affectionateness
afectuoso *a* affectionate, fond
afeitada *f*, shave, shaving
afeitar *vt* to shave; make up (one's face); adorn, beautify
afeite *m*, cosmetic; make-up (for the complexion)
afelpado *a* velvet-like, plushy
afeminación *f*, effeminacy; weakness, languor
afeminado *a* effeminate
afeminar *vt* to make effeminate; weaken; *vr* grow effeminate
aferradamente *adv* tenaciously, persistently, obstinately
aferramiento *m*, seizing, clutching; *naut* furling; *naut* grappling; mooring, anchoring; obstinacy
aferrar *vt* to seize, clutch; *naut* take in, furl; *naut* grapple; *vi naut* anchor; *vr* (*with con, en, a*) persist in, insist on
afestonado *a* festooned
Afganistán Afghanistan
afgano (-na) *a* and *n* Afghan
afianzamiento *m*, fastening, fixing; propping; grasping; guarantee, security
afianzar *vt* to fasten, fix; prop; consolidate (e.g. one's power); guarantee, be security for; grasp
afición *f*, propensity, inclination; fondness. **tomar a. (a),** to take a liking to
aficionado (-da) *a* amateur. *n* amateur, fan, enthusiast. **ser a a.,** to be fond of, have a liking for
aficionar *vt* to inspire liking or affection; *vr* (*with prep a*) take a liking to, grow fond of; become an enthusiast of
afijo *m*, *gram* affix
afiladera *f*, whetstone, grindstone
afilado *a* sharp, keen (of edges)
afilador *m*, grinder (of scissors, etc.); razor strop
afilalápices *m*, pencil sharpener
afilar *vt* to sharpen; grind, whet; taper; *Lat. Am.* flatter; *Lat. Am.* court, woo; *vr* grow thin; taper
afiliación *f*, affiliation
afiliar *vt* (*with prep a*) to affiliate with; *vr* (*with prep a*) become affiliated with; join, become a member of
afiligranado *a* filigree; delicate, fine; slender
afilón *m*, steel, knife sharpener; razor-strop
afín *a* nearby, contiguous; similar, related. *mf* relative by marriage
afinador *m*, tuning key; tuner (of pianos, etc.)
afinar *vt* to finish, perfect; *fig* polish, refine; tune (musical instruments); refine (metals); *vi* sing in tune; *vr* grow refined
afinidad *f*, affinity, analogy; relationship (by marriage); *chem* affinity
afirmación *f*, affirmation, statement
afirmadamente *adv* firmly
afirmar *vt* to make firm; fix, fasten; affirm; *vr* steady oneself; hold on to
afirmativa *f*, affirmative
afirmativo *a* affirmative
aflicción *f*, affliction, grief
aflictivo *a* sorrowful, grievous
afligir *vt* to sadden; afflict, trouble; *vr* lament, mourn
aflojamiento *m*, slackening; loosening; diminution
aflojar *vt* to slacken; loosen; *vi* relax, weaken; abate, diminish. **a. el paso,** to slow down
afluencia *f*, crowd, concourse; eloquence, fluency
afluente *a* fluent, eloquent. *m*, tributary (river)
afluir *vi irr* to crowd, swarm; flow (into). See **huir**
afonía *f*, *med* aphonia, loss of voice; hoarseness
afónico *a* hoarse
aforismo *m*, aphorism
aforrador (-ra) *n* one who lines jackets, etc.
aforrar *vt* to line (clothes, etc.); *vr* wrap oneself up; *inf* gormandize
afortunadamente *adv* luckily, fortunately
afortunado *a* lucky, fortunate; happy; stormy
afortunar *vt* to bring luck to, make happy
afrancesado (-da) *a* Francophile; Frenchified. *n* Francophile
afrancesamiento *m*, adoption of the French way of life; servile imitation of everything French
afrancesar *vt* to make French, gallicize; Frenchify; *vr* become a Francophile
afrenta *f*, insult, affront; disgrace
afrentar *vt* to insult; *vr* be ashamed
afrentoso *a* insulting, outrageous; disgraceful
África Africa
africanismo *m*, Africanism
africano -na *a* and *n* African
afrodisíaco *a* and *m*, aphrodisiac
afrontar *vt* to place opposite; confront; face (danger, etc.)
afuera *adv* outside, out
afueras *f pl*, suburbs, outskirts
afusilar *vt*, *Lat. Am.* to shoot
agachada *f*, crouch, duck; jerk
agachar *vt inf* bend, bow; *vr inf* crouch down; lie low, hide
agalla *f*, oak-apple; tonsil (gen. *pl*); *zool* gill; *inf* gall, cheek
agalludo, -a *a*, *Argentina* mean, stingy, tight; bold, daring
ágape *m*, agape; banquet, feast
Agar Hagar
agárico *m*, *bot* agaric
agarrada *f*, *inf* brawl, scuffle
agarradero *m*, handle; heft; *inf* influence, pull
agarrado *a inf* tight-fisted, mean
agarrar *vt* to grip, grasp; seize, take; *inf* nab (jobs); *vr* grip, hold on
agarro *m*, hold; grip, grasp
agarrotar *vt* to garrotte; tighten (ropes, etc.); press, squeeze; *vr* (limbs) go numb
agasajar *vt* to indulge, spoil, pet; receive kindly; entertain; caress
agasajo *m*, indulgence, kindness; affability, geniality; entertainment; gift, offering
agauchado *a* gaucho-like
agazapar *vt inf* to nab, catch; *vr inf* squat, crouch
agencia *f*, influence, agency
agenciar *vt* to negotiate, arrange; procure, manage
agenda *f*, notebook; agenda
agente *m*, agent. **a. de bolsa** *or* **a. de cambio,** bill broker. **a. de negocios,** business agent. **a. de policía,** police officer. **a. fiscal,** revenue officer
agerasia *f*, sickness-free old age
agestado *a* used generally with advs. **bien** *or* **mal,** well *or* ill-featured
agigantado *a* enormous, gigantic; outstanding, extraordinary
ágil *a* agile, nimble; easy to use (e.g. **un libro ágil,** a book easy to use)
agilidad *f*, agility, nimbleness
agilizar *vt* to make agile, limber; refresh one's knowledge of (e.g. **Quiero agilizar mi español,** I want to refresh my knowledge of Spanish); to enable; *vr* limber up
agitación *f*, shaking; agitation, excitement
agitador (-ra) *a* stirring; agitating. *n* agitator. *m*, stirrer, stirring rod
agitar *vt* to stir; shake; agitate, excite. **a. una cuestión,** raise a question; discuss a question
aglomeración *f*, agglomeration
aglomerar *vt* to agglomerate, amass
aglutinación *f*, agglutination
aglutinar(se) *vt* and *vr* to stick, agglutinate
agnóstico (-ca) *a* and *n* agnostic
agobiar *vt* to bow, bend down; *fig* weigh down, oppress; *vr* bend (beneath a weight)

agobio *m,* bowing, bending down; oppression, burden, weight
agolparse *vr* to rush, crowd, swarm
agonía *f,* agony, anguish
agonizante *a* dying
agonizar *vt* to attend a dying person; *inf* pester, annoy; *vi* be dying (gen. **estar agonizando**)
agorar *vt* to prophesy, foretell
agorero (-ra) *a* prophetic; ill-boding. *n* seer, augur
agostarse *vt* and *vr* to dry up, shrivel
agosto *m,* August; harvest. *inf* **hacer su a.,** to make hay while the sun shines
agotable *a* exhaustible
agotado *a* exhausted; out of print (of books)
agotador *a* exhausting; exhaustive
agotamiento *m,* exhaustion
agotar *vt* to drain off (water); empty (a glass); exhaust; run through (money); study thoroughly, examine closely (a subject)
agraciado *a* graceful; pretty
agraciar *vt* to lend grace to; make pretty; favor
agradable *a* agreeable, pleasant
agradar *vi* to be pleasing, like, please (e.g. **Me agrada su sinceridad,** I like his sincerity)
agradecer *vt irr* to be grateful for; thank for; *fig* repay, requite. See **conocer**
agradecido *a* grateful; thankful
agradecimiento *m,* gratitude; thankfulness
agrado *m,* pleasure; desire, liking; amiability, affability
agrandar *vt* to enlarge
agrario *a* agrarian
agrarismo *m, Mexico* farmers' movement, peasant movement
agravación *f,* **agravamiento** *m,* aggravation, worsening
agravador *a* aggravating; worsening; increasing
agravar *vt* to aggravate, increase; oppress (taxes, responsibilities); make worse; exaggerate; *vr* grow worse
agraviador -ra *a* offensive. *n* offender
agraviar *vt* to offend; wrong; *vr* take offence, be insulted
agravio *m,* offence, insult; wrong, injury
agraz *m,* unripened grape; verjuice; *fig* bitterness
agredir *vt* to attack
agregación *f,* association, aggregation; total, collection, aggregate
agregado *m,* aggregate; assistant; attaché; *Lat. Am.* sharecropper
agregar *vt* to add; collect, amass; appoint (to a post). **agregarse a . . . ,** to join . . . (e.g. an association)
agresión *f,* aggression
agresivo *a* aggressive
agresor (-ra) *a* and *n* aggressor
agreste *a* rural, rustic; wild; uncouth, rude
agriar *vt* to make bitter or sour; exasperate, provoke
agrícola *a* agricultural; *mf* agriculturalist, farmer
agricultura *f,* agriculture
agridulce *a* bitter-sweet
agrietarse *vr* to crack, split
agrimensor *m,* surveyor
agrimensura *f,* surveying
agrio *a* bitter, sour; rough, uneven (ground); brittle; sharp (of color contrast); unsociable; disagreeable
agronomía *f,* agronomy
agrónomo *a* agronomic. *m,* agronomist
agrupación *f,* congregation, assembly; group; crowd; crowding, grouping
agrupar *vt* to assemble, group; *vr* crowd, cluster
agrura *f,* bitterness; sourness; asperity
agua *f,* water; rain; slope of a roof; *pl* shot or watered effect on silks, etc.; medicinal waters; waves; water (of precious stones). **a. abajo,** down-stream. **a. arriba,** upstream. **a. bendita,** holy water. **a. cruda,** hard water. **a. de colonia,** eau de Cologne. **a. dulce,** fresh water. **a. fresca,** cold water. **a. nieve,** sleet. **a. oxigenada,** hydrogen peroxide. *fig inf* **estar con el a. al cuello,** to be in low water. *fig inf* **estar entre dos aguas,** to be between two fires. *naut* **hacer a.,** to leak. **Todo eso es ya a. pasada,** That's all water under the bridge
aguacate *m,* avocado
aguacero *m,* heavy rainfall, shower
aguada *f,* water supply on board ship; flood (in mines); watering station; *art* water color
aguadero *m,* (animals') watering place
aguado *a* watery; abstemious; watered
aguador (-ra) *n* water carrier, water seller; drawer (of water)
aguafiestas *mf fig inf* wet blanket
aguafuerte *f,* etching
aguaje *m,* tide, waves; sea current; water supply (on board ship); wake (of a ship)
aguamanil *m,* washstand; pitcher, ewer
aguamanos *m,* water for washing hands; pitcher
aguamarina *f,* aquamarine
aguamiel *f,* honey and water, hydromel
aguantable *a* tolerable, bearable
aguantar *vt* to bear, tolerate, endure; restrain, resist, oppose; *vr* bear in silence, keep quiet
aguante *m,* patience, endurance; resistance
aguar *vt* to water down (wine, etc.); spoil (fun, etc.); *vr* be filled with water; be flooded; become watery or thin
aguardar *vt* to await; expect; allow time to (debtors)
aguardentería *f,* liquor shop
aguardentoso *a* spirituous, containing **aguardiente;** hoarse, husky (of the voice)
aguardiente *m,* liquor. **a. de caña,** rum
aguarrás *m,* oil of turpentine
aguatinta *f,* aquatint
aguatocha *f,* pump (for water, etc.)
aguaturma *f,* Jerusalem artichoke
agudeza *f,* sharpness; keenness; distinctness; alertness, cleverness; witty sally, repartee; wit; swiftness
agudo *a* sharp; alert, clever; (*geom med*) acute; fine, keen; rapid; high-pitched; strong (of scents, etc.)
agüero *m,* omen, sign; prophecy, prediction
aguerrido *a* veteran, war-hardened
aguerrir *vt defective* to harden to war; toughen
aguijada *f,* goad, spur
aguijar *vt* to prick (with a goad); urge on, encourage (animals); incite, instigate; spur on; *vi* walk swiftly
aguijón *m,* goad; sting; thorn, prickle; spur; incitement, stimulus. **tener aguijones,** to be on pins and needles
aguijonazo *m,* prick (with a goad)
águila *f,* eagle; master mind. **a. caudal** *or* **a. real,** royal eagle. **á. o sol,** *Mexico* heads or tails
aguileña *f, bot* columbine
aguileño *a* aquiline
aguilón *m, arch* gable; boom (of a crane)
aguinaldo *m,* Christmas present; New Year's gift
aguja *f,* needle; hand, pointer; hatpin; engraver's burin; switch; *rw* point; *rw* rail; obelisk; spire; bodkin; knitting needle; crochet hook; (compass) needle. *pl bot* plumelet. **a. capotera, a. de zurcir,** darning needle. **a. de marear** *naut,* binnacle; mariner's compass. **a. de media,** knitting needle. **a. espartera,** packing needle
agujerear *vt* to perforate, make holes in
agujero *m,* hole, aperture; needle maker or seller; needle case
agujeta *f,* lace (for shoes, etc.); *pl* muscular pains, aches; tip, gratuity
agusanarse *vr* to become worm-infested
aguzadura *f,* sharpening, grinding, whetting
aguzar *vt* to sharpen; grind, whet; stimulate, encourage; urge on, incite
ahechadura *f,* chaff (of grain)
ahembrado *a* effeminate
aherrojar *vt* to put (a prisoner) in irons; oppress
aherrumbrar *vt* to give the color or taste of iron to; *vr* taste or look like iron; go rusty
ahí *adv* there; over there. **de a.,** thus, so. **por a.,** somewhere about, near at hand.
ahidalgado *a* gentlemanly; noble, generous

ahijado (-da) *n* godchild; protégé
ahijar *vt* to adopt (children); mother (animals); attribute, impute; *vi* bring forth offspring; *bot* sprout. See **prohibir**
ahincado *a* earnest, eager
ahincar *vt* to urge, press; *vr* hurry, hasten. See **prohibir**
ahínco *m*, earnestness, eagerness
ahitar *vt* to stuff with food; bore, disgust. See **prohibir**
ahíto *a* full of food; *fig* fed up. *m*, indigestion
ahogado (-da) *a* drowned; suffocated; stuffy, unventilated; stifling. *n* drowned person; victim of suffocation
ahogamiento *m*, drowning; suffocation
ahogar *vt* to drown; suffocate; put out (the fire); stifle (yawns, etc.); suppress, extinguish; tire; overwater (plants); *vr naut* sink, founder; drown; suffocate
ahogo *m*, anxiety, grief; difficulty in breathing, oppression; asthma; embarrassment; suffocation; straitened circumstances
ahondamiento *m*, in-depth treatment (e.g. **el a. de un problema,** in-depth treatment of a problem)
ahondar *vt* to deepen; excavate, dig; go into thoroughly; go deep into, penetrate; *vr* (earth) subside
ahora *adv* now; very soon; just now, a short time ago. *conjunc* whether; now. **a. bien,** well now, given that. **a. mismo,** immediately, at once. **por a.,** for the present
ahorcado (-da) *n* hanged man
ahorcar *vt* to execute by hanging, hang. *inf* **a. los hábitos,** to leave the priesthood, cease to be an ecclesiastic
ahorita *adv, Mexico* right away, right now
ahormar *vt* to adjust, shape; break in (new shoes); make (a person) see reason
ahorquillar *vt* to prop up (trees) with forks; *vr* grow forked
ahorrar *vt* to free (slaves); save, economize; avoid, eschew; *vr* avoid; remove clothing
ahorro *m*, economy, thrift; *pl* savings
ahuchar *vt* to hoard; expel, drive away
ahuciar *vt* take possession of (a house)
ahuecar *vt* to hollow out; loosen; shake out; puff out, inflate; put on a solemn voice; hoe, dig; *inf vr* puff oneself out; put on airs
ahumada *f*, smoke signal
ahumado *a* smoked; smoky
ahumar *vt* to smoke (herrings, etc.); fill with smoke; *vi* smoke, burn; *vr* be full of smoke; taste smoked; *inf* get drunk. See **desahuciar**
ahusado *a* spindle-shaped
ahuyentar *vt* to frighten off; drive away; dismiss, banish (anxiety, etc.); *vr* flee
airadamente *adv* wrathfully, angrily
airado *a* angry
airar *vt* to annoy, anger; *vr* grow annoyed
aire *m*, air; atmosphere (sometimes *pl*); breeze, wind; bearing, appearance; vanity; (horse's) gait; futility, frivolity; grace, charm; gracefulness; *mus* air; *mus* tempo. **a. popular,** popular tune. **al a. libre,** in the open air, outdoors. *inf* **beber los aires (por),** to yearn (for)
aireación *f*, airing; ventilation
airear *vt* to air; ventilate; aerate; *vr* take the air; catch a chill
airecito *m, Lat. Am.* breeze, gentle wind
airosidad *f*, gracefulness; jauntiness
airoso *a* airy, open; windy, breezy, fresh; graceful; handsome; jaunty; victorious, successful
aislacionamismo *m, pol* isolationism
aislacionista *mf pol* isolationist
aislado *a* isolated; remote; individual; single; *elec* insulated
aislador *m, phys* insulator
aislamiento *m*, isolation; *phys* insulation
aislante *a* isolating; insulating
aislar *vt* to isolate; *elec* insulate; *vr* become a recluse; become isolated
¡ajá! *interj inf* Aha! Good!
ajar *vt* to crease, crumple, spoil; humiliate; *vr* fade, wither (flowers)
ajedrecista *mf* chess player
ajedrez *m*, chess
ajenjo *m, bot* wormwood; absinthe
ajeno *a* alien; belonging to another; various, diverse; free, exempt; unsuitable; irrelevant
ajetrear *vt* to tire out, exhaust; *vr* be overtired
ajetreo *m*, exhaustion, fatigue
ají *m, Lat. Am.* chili, red pepper; chili sauce; **estar hecho un ají** to be hopping mad, be fuming
ajo *m*, garlic; *inf* make up, paint; disreputable affair, shady business; curse, oath. *inf* **revolver el a.,** to stir up trouble
ajorca *f*, bracelet; slave bangle
ajornalar *vt* to hire by the day
ajuar *m*, trousseau; household equipment
ajustado *a* exact; tight-fitting; trim
ajustador (-ra) *a* adjusting. *n* adjuster. *m*, tight-fitting jacket
ajustamiento *m*, adjustment; agreement
ajustar *vt* to adjust; fit; arrange; make an agreement about; reconcile; settle (accounts); engage, employ; retain (a barrister); regulate; tune up (a motor); *vi* fit; *vr* adapt oneself. *inf* **a. cuentas viejas,** to settle old accounts
ajuste *m*, fitting; adjustment; agreement; arrangement; *print* make-up; reconciliation; settlement; regulation; engagement, appointment
ajusticiado (-da) *n* executed person
ajusticiar *vt* to put to death
al (contraction of *a* + *el*). 1. *prep a* + *m. def. art.,* to the, e.g. **Han ido al mar,** They have gone to the sea. 2. *prep a* + *el* used as *dem. pron* to that, to the one, e.g. **Mi sombrero se parece mucho al que tiene Vd.,** My hat is very similar to the one you have. *al* + *infin.* means when, as, at the same time as, e.g. **Al llamar a la puerta la vi en el jardín,** As I was knocking at the door, I saw her in the garden
ala *f, zool* wing; row, line; brim (of a hat); eaves; (*arch aer mil bot*) wing; blade (of propeller); fin (of fish); *pl* courage. **a. del corazón,** *anat* auricle. **arrastrar el a.,** to woo, flirt with. *fig* **cortar** (*or* **quebrar**) **las alas (a),** to clip a person's wings
alabador (-ra) *n* praiser, extoller
alabanza *f*, praise; eulogy
alabar *vt* to praise; *vr* brag, boast
alabastrino *a* alabastrine, alabaster
alabastro *m*, alabaster
alacena *f*, cupboard; recess; closet; safe (for food)
alacrán *m*, scorpion
alacre *a, Mexico* agile, nimble
alacridad *f*, alacrity, eagerness; *Mexico* agility, nimbleness
alado *a* winged; feathered; *fig* soaring
alambicado *a* sparing, frugal; subtle; euphuistic
alambicar *vt* to distil; examine carefully, scrutinise; make over-subtle or euphuistic (of style)
alambique *m*, still
alambrada *f, mil* wire-entanglement
alambrado *m*, wire-netting; *mil* wire-entanglement; wire cover
alambrar *vt* to wire (fence)
alambre *m*, wire; sheep bells. **a. espinoso,** barbed wire
alambrera *f*, wire fence; wire-netting; wire cover
alambrista *mf* tight-rope walker; (Mexico) wetback
alameda *f*, poplar wood or grove; avenue of poplars
álamo *m*, poplar. **a. temblón,** aspen tree
alano *m*, mastiff
alarde *m, mil* parade; display, ostentation. **hacer a. de,** to brag about
alargamiento *m*, lengthening; stretching
alargar *vt* to lengthen; prolong; pass, hand (things); pay out (ropes, etc.); increase; *vr* go away, depart; be wordy, spread oneself; lengthen

alarido *m*, yell, shout; shriek, scream; howl; yelp; cry (of a seagull)
alarma *f*, alarm. **a. aérea,** air-raid warning
alarmante *a* alarming
alarmar *vt* to give the alarm; frighten; *vr* be alarmed
alarmista *mf* alarmist
alazán *a* sorrel-colored. *m*, sorrel horse
alazo *m*, flap or stroke of the wings
alba *f*, dawn; *ecc* alb, vestment. **al a.,** at dawn
albacea *mf* executor, executrix; testator
albanés (-esa) *a* and *n* Albanian. *m*, Albanian language
albañil *m*, mason, bricklayer
albañilería *f*, masonry; bricklaying
albarda *f*, pack-saddle; *Lat. Am.* saddle
albardilla *f*, small saddle; pad; small pillow; *arch* coping
albaricoque *m*, apricot
albaricoquero *m*, apricot tree
albarrada *f*, stone wall; mud fence
albatros *m*, albatross
albear *vi* to become white, whiten
albedrío *m*, free will; fancy, caprice
albéitar *m*, veterinary surgeon; farrier
alberca *f*, reservoir, tank; vat; artificial lake; *Lat. Am.* (swimming) pool
albergar *vt* to shelter; nourish, harbor; *vi* and *vr* take refuge or shelter; lodge
albergue *m*, shelter, refuge; den, lair; hospitality; lodging; asylum
albo *a* pure white
albóndiga *f*, forced meat ball, rissole
albor *m*, whiteness; dawnlight, dawn. **a. de la vida,** life's dawning, childhood
alborada *f*, dawn; reveille; *mil* dawn attack; *mus* aubade
alborear *vi* to grow light, dawn
albornoz *m*, burnouse
alborotado *a* impulsive; turbulent; noisy; excitable
alborotar *vt* to disturb; *vi* make a noise; be gay; *vr* riot; grow rough (sea)
alboroto *m*, noise; confusion; tumult; riot; rejoicing, gaiety
alborotos *mpl, Argentina, Central America, Peru* popcorn
alborozar *vt* to overjoy, gladden; *vr* rejoice, be glad
alborozo *m*, gladness, rejoicing, joy
albricias *f pl*, reward for bringer of good tidings. *interj* **¡A.!** Joy! Congratulations!
álbum *m*, album
albúmina *f*, albumin
albur *m*, *icht* dace; chance, risk. **al a. de,** at the risk of
alcachofa *f*, artichoke
alcahuete *m*, procurer, go-between, pimp, pander; *fig inf* protector, screen; *inf* scandalmonger
alcahuetear *vt* to procure, act as a go-between for; *vi* be a pimp or a procuress
alcaide *m*, governor of a fortress *ant*; governor of a prison
alcalde *m*, mayor; magistrate. *inf* **tener el padre a.,** to have a friend at court
alcaldesa *f*, mayoress
alcaldía *f*, office or authority of an alcalde
álcali *m*, *chem* alkali
alcalino *a* alkaline
alcance *m*, reaching, attainment; range (of firearms, etc.); scope; arm's length or reach; pursuit; stop press *or* extra edition (newspapers); *com* deficit; importance; *pl* talent; capacity. **al a. de la voz,** within call. **hombre de cortos alcances,** a limited, dull man. **poner al a. de,** to make available to; make intelligible to
alcancía *f*, money-box; coin bank, piggy bank
alcanfor *m*, camphor
alcantarilla *f*, little bridge; sewer; culvert; bed for electric cable
alcantarillado *m*, sewage system; main sewer
alcanzable *a* obtainable; attainable
alcanzadizo *a* attainable, easily reached
alcanzar *vt* to overtake; reach; range (of guns, etc.); attain, achieve; understand; *fig* equal (in attainments); live at the same time as, be contemporaneous with; be capable of, be able; *vi* reach; share, participate in; be enough
alcaparra *f*, *bot* caper; caper bush
alcaucil *m*, (in most places) wild artichoke; (in some places) cultivated artichoke
alcazaba *f*, fortress (within a walled town or city), casbah
alcázar *m*, fortress; royal residence, castle; *naut* quarter-deck
alción *m*, *orn* kingfisher
alcista *mf* speculator (on Stock Exchange)
alcoba *f*, bedroom; alcove, recess; Moorish flute
alcohol *m*, alcohol; galena; eye black (cosmetic); spirits of wine. **a. desnaturalizado,** industrial alcohol, methylated spirit. **a. metílico,** wood alcohol
alcohólico *a* alcoholic
alcoholismo *m*, alcoholism
alcor *m*, hill; slope
Alcorán *m*, Koran
alcornoque *m*, cork tree; dunderhead, dolt
alcorza *f*, *cul* icing, sugar-paste
alcorzar *vt* *cul* to ice, cover with sugar; decorate, adorn
alcurnia *f*, lineage, family, descent
alcuza *f*, oil-bottle; oil-can; cruet
aldaba *f*, door knocker; bolt, latch; *pl* protectors, influential helpers. *inf* **tener buenas aldabas,** to have plenty of pull
aldabada *f*, rap with the knocker; sudden shock
aldabeo *m*, knocking
aldea *f*, village
aldeano (-na) *a* village; country, ignorant. *n* villager; countryman, peasant
aldehído *m*, *chem* aldehyde
aleación *f*, alloy
alear *vi* to flutter, beat the wings; flap one's arms; recuperate, grow well; *vt* alloy
aleatorio *a* accidental, fortuitous
aleccionamiento *m*, teaching, training, coaching
aleccionar *vt* to teach, train, coach
aledaño *a* adjoining; border. *m*, boundary, border
alegación *f*, allegation, statement
alegar *vt* to allege, state; cite; *vi law* bring forward, adduce
alegato *m*, *law* speech (for the prosecution or defence)
alegoría *f*, allegory
alegórico *a* allegorical
alegorizar *vt* to interpret allegorically, treat as an allegory
alegrar *vt* to make happy, gladden, rejoice; adorn, beautify; stir (fires); *vr* be glad, rejoice; *inf* be merry (tipsy)
alegre *a* joyful, glad; cheerful, gay; bright (colors, etc.); pretty, attractive; *inf* risqué; *inf* flirtatious, light
alegría *f*, joy, gladness; cheerfulness, gaiety; *pl* public rejoicings
alegrón *m*, sudden unexpected joy; *inf* flash of light. *a inf* flirtatious
alejamiento *m*, placing at a distance, removal; withdrawal
Alejandría Alexandria
alejar *vt* to place at a distance, remove; withdraw; ward off (dangers, etc.); *vr* depart, go away; withdraw. **alejarse de,** to abandon (a belief, custom, superstition, etc.)
alelar *vt* to make silly or stupid
aleluya *mf*, alleluia. *m*, Eastertide. *f*, small Easter cake; *inf* daub, poor painting; *inf* doggerel; joy, rejoicing
alemán (-ana) *a* and *n* German. *m*, German language.
Alemania Germany
alentada *f*, deep breath
alentado *a* valiant, spirited; proud; *Argentina* strong, vigorous
alentador *a* encouraging, inspiring, stimulating

alentar *vi irr* to breathe; *vt* encourage, inspire; *vr* be encouraged. See **sentar**
alerce *m*, larch tree and wood
alergia *f*, allergy
alergólogo *m*, allergist
alero *m*, projecting roof; splashboard (of carriages); eaves; gable end
alerón *m*, *aer* aileron
alerta *adv* watchfully. *interj* Take care! Look out! **estar ojo a.,** to be on the watch
alerto *a* watchful, alert
aleta *f*, *dim* small wing; fin
aletargado *a* lethargic; comatose
aletargamiento *m*, lethargy
aletargar *vt* to cause lethargy; *vr* become lethargic
aletazo *m*, flapping, beating (of wings); *inf* theft
aletear *vi* to flap the wings, flutter; move the arms up and down; become convalescent
aleteo *m*, fluttering, flapping of wings; beating, palpitation (of heart)
aleve *a* See **alevoso**
alevosía *f*, *law* malice; treachery
alevoso *a law* malicious; treacherous
alfabético *a* alphabetical
alfabetización *f*, literacy work
alfabetizador *m*, literacy worker
alfabeto *m*, alphabet. **a. manual,** sign language
alfalfa *f*, *bot* lucerne
alfandoque *m*, *Lat. Am.* cheesecake; maraca
alfanje *m* cutlass; *Mexico* machete
alfar *m*, potter's workshop; pottery, earthenware
alfarería *f*, pottery shop; potter's workshop; potter's craft
alfarero *m*, potter
alfeñique *m*, *cul* icing, sugarpaste; *inf* affectation
alférez *m*, *mil* ensign; second lieutenant; lieutenant. *nav* **a. de fragata,** sub-lieutenant. *nav* **a. de navío,** lieutenant
alfil *m*, bishop (in chess)
alfiler *m*, pin; brooch with a pin; tiepin; *pl* pin-money, dress-allowance; *fig inf* **no estar uno con sus alfileres,** to have a slate loose. *inf* **vestido de veinticinco alfileres,** dressed to the nines
alfiletero *m*, needle-case
alfombra *f*, carpet; rug
alfombrado *m*, carpeting
alfombrar *vt* to carpet
alfombrilla eléctrica *f*, electric pad or blanket
alfombrista *m*, carpet merchant; layer of carpets
alforja *f*, saddle-bag; *mil* knapsack
alforza *f*, *sew* tuck; *inf* scar
alforzar *vt sew* to tuck
alga *f*, alga, seaweed
algalia *f*, civet
algarabía *f*, Arabic; *inf* gibberish; din of voices, uproar
algarada *f*, troop of horse; uproar, hubbub; outcry
algarroba *f*, *bot* carob bean
algazara *f*, Moorish war cry; rejoicing, merriment; noise, clamor
álgebra *f*, algebra; art of bone setting
algebrista *mf* bonesetter; algebraist
álgido *a* icy cold
algo *indef pron* some, something (e.g. **Se ve que hay a. que le molesta,** You can see that something is irritating him). *adv* somewhat, a bit. **en a.,** in some way
algodón *m*, cotton plant; cotton flower; cotton fabric; candy floss (UK), cotton candy (USA). **a. en rama,** cotton-wool. **a. hidró-filo,** absorbent cotton wool. **a. pólvora,** nitrocellulose
algodonal *m*, cotton plantation
alguacil *m*, policeman, constable; *ant* city governor; short-legged spider
alguien *indef pron* someone, somebody, e.g. **Dime si viene a.,** Tell me if anyone comes
algún *abb* of **alguno** bef. *m sing* noun, e.g. **a. libro**
alguno *a* (*abb* **algún** bef. *m, sing*) some, any. *indef pron* someone, somebody; *pl* some, some people. **alguno que otro,** a few
alhaja *f*, jewel; ornament; treasure, precious object; *inf* gem, excellent person (also ironic, e.g. **Es una a.,** He's a fine fellow)
alhajar *vt* to adorn with jewels, bejewel; furnish, equip
alharaca *f*, vehemence, demonstration, fuss (gen. *pl*)
alheña *f*, *bot* privet; henna
alhóndiga *f*, corn exchange; public granary
aliado (-da) *a* allied. *n* ally
alianza *f*, alliance; pact, agreement; relationship (by marriage); sum total, whole (of factors, etc.); wedding-ring
aliarse *vr* to join together, become allies; be associated
alicaído *a* drooping; *inf* weak, exhausted; discouraged, downhearted; come down in the world
alicates *m pl*, pincers, pliers
aliciente *m*, attraction, inducement
alícuota *f*, *a* aliquot; proportional. **partes alícuotas,** aliquot parts
alienación *f*, alienation
alienado *a* insane, mad
alienar *vt* See **enajenar**
alienista *mf med* alienist
aliento *m*, breathing; breath; courage, spirit; encouragement. **el posterior a.,** one's last breath. **cobrar a.,** to regain one's breath; take heart. **de un a.,** in one breath; without stopping
alifafe *m*, *inf* ailment; tumor on horse's hock
aligación *f*, binding together, alligation
aligeramiento *m*, lightening, reduction in weight
aligerar *vt* to lighten, make less heavy; quicken, hasten; ease, alleviate; moderate; shorten, abbreviate
alimaña *f*, destructive animal
alimentación *f*, nourishment; feeding
alimentar *vt* to feed; nourish; encourage, foment; assist, aid; keep, support
alimenticio *a* nourishing; feeding
alimento *m*, food, nourishment; stimulus, encouragement; *pl* alimony; allowance
alindar *vt* to mark the boundary of; beautify, adorn; *vi* border, be contiguous
alineación *f*, alignment
alinear *vt* to align, range in line; dress (troops); *vr* fall into line
aliñar *vt* to decorate, adorn; *cul* season; prepare; set (bones)
aliño *m*, decoration, ornament; preparation; condiment, seasoning; setting (bones)
aliquebrado *a* broken-winged; *inf* down in the mouth
alisador (-ra) *a* smoothing; polishing. *n* polisher
alisar *vt* to smooth; polish; sleek; plane; comb lightly
alisios *m pl*, trade winds
aliso *m*, alder tree and wood
alistador *m*, enroller
alistamiento *m*, enlistment; conscription; enrolment
alistar *vt* to enrol, list; enlist; conscript; prepare, get ready; *vr* enrol; *mil* enlist; get ready
alitranca *f*, *Chile, Peru* brake
aliviar *vt* to lighten; alleviate, mitigate; relieve; ease; quicken (one's step); hasten, speed up; steal
alivio *m*, lightening; relief; alleviation; ease
aljaba *f*, quiver (for arrows); *Lat. Am.* fuchsia
aljibe *m*, tank, cistern; watership or tanker
aljófar *m*, small irregular shaped pearl; dew-drop, rain-drop, tear drop
aljofifa *f*, floorcloth
allá *adv* there; to that place. **más a.,** farther on, beyond. Used in conjunction with phrases of time, indicates remoteness, e.g. **a. en tiempos de los Reyes Católicos,** long ago in the time of the Catholic Monarchs. **a. por 1900,** way back in 1900
allanamiento *m*, leveling, flattening; condescension,

affability; (police) raid, (police) search acceptance of a judicial finding
allanar *vt* to level, flatten; overcome (difficulties); soothe; break into (a house, etc.); give entrance to the police; *vr* collapse (buildings, etc.); abide by, adapt oneself (to); condescend, be affable. **a. el camino (a . . .),** to pave the way (for . . .)
allegado (-da) *a* near, allied; related. *n* follower, ally
allegar *vt* to gather, collect; draw nearer; *agr* reap; add; *vi* arrive
allende *adv* beyond; besides. **de a. el mar,** from beyond the sea
allí *adv* there; to that place, thereto; thereupon, then. **por a.,** through there; that way
alma *f,* soul; living person; essence, core; vivacity, animation; energy, vitality; spirit, ghost; core (of a rope). **a. de cántaro,** fool, ninny. **a. de Dios,** simple soul, kind person. **a. en pena,** soul in purgatory. **¡A. mía!** My darling! **con todo el a.,** with all my heart. **Lo siento en el a.,** I feel it deeply
almacén *m,* warehouse; store, shop
almacenaje *m,* cost of storage
almacenar *vt* to store; put in store; hoard
almacenero *m,* warehouseman, storekeeper
almacenista *mf* owner of a store; assistant, salesman (saleswoman)
almáciga *f,* mastic; tree plantation or nursery
almagre *m, min* red ocher; stain, mark
almanaque *m,* calendar, almanac
almeja *f, icht* clam
almenara *f,* beacon fire
almendra *f,* almond; kernel; crystal drop (of chandeliers, etc.); cocoon; bean (of cocoa tree, etc.). **a. garapiñada,** sugar almond
almendro *m,* almond tree
almendruco *m,* green almond
almete *m,* casque, helmet; helmeted soldier
almiar *m,* haystack, hayrick
almíbar *m,* sugar syrup; nectar
almibarado *a* syrupy; *inf* sugary
almibarar *vt* to coat with sugar; preserve (fruit) in syrup; flatter with sweet words
almidón *m,* starch
almidonado *a* starched; *fig inf* stiff, unbending; prim, starchy
almidonar *vt* to starch
alminar *m,* minaret (of mosque)
almirantazgo *m,* Admiralty; admiralship; Admiralty Court
almirante *m,* admiral
almizcle *m,* musk
almizcleño *a* musk (of scents)
almizclero *a* musky. *m, zool* musk-deer
almocafre *m, agr* hoe; trowel, dibble
almohada *f,* pillow; pillowcase; cushion. *inf* **aconsejarse** *or* **consultar con la a.,** to think over (a matter) carefully, sleep on it
almohadilla *f, dim* small cushion; lace or sewing cushion; pin cushion
almohadillado *a* cushioned; padded
almoneda *f,* auction; furniture sale
almonedear *vt* to auction; sell off (furniture)
almorranas *f pl,* hemorrhoids
almorzar *vi irr* to lunch; breakfast. See **forzar**
almuercería *f, Mexico* lunch counter, luncheonette
almuecín, almuédano *m,* muezzin
almuerzo *m,* luncheon; breakfast (not so usual)
alocado *a* feather-brained, reckless; crazy, wild
alocución *f,* allocution, address, harangue
áloe *m, bot* aloe
alojado (-da) *m,* billeted soldier. *n* lodger, guest
alojamiento *m,* lodging; dwelling; *mil* billeting; *naut* steerage; camp, encampment
alojar *vt* to lodge; billet, quarter (troops); insert, introduce; *vi* and *vr* lodge; live, dwell
alondra *f, orn* lark
alopatía *f, med* allopathy
alpaca *f,* alpaca (animal and fabric); nickel silver
alpargata *f,* sandal with hemp sole
alpargatero (-ra) *n* manufacturer or seller of alpargatas
Alpes, los the Alps
alpestre *a* Alpine; rock (of plants); mountainous, lofty
alpinismo *m,* mountaineering
alpinista *mf* mountaineer, climber
alpino *a* Alpine
alpiste *m,* bird seed
alpro *f,* (Alianza para el Progreso)
alquería *f,* farmstead
alquiladizo *a* rentable, hirable
alquilador (-ra) *n* hirer
alquilamiento *m,* See **alquiler**
alquilar *vt* to rent; hire out; hire; *vr* hire oneself out, serve on a wage basis
alquiler *m,* hiring out; renting; rental; hire; wages. **de a.,** for hire, on hire
alquimia *f,* alchemy
alquimista *mf* alchemist
alquitrán *m,* tar, pitch. **a. mineral,** coal tar
alquitranado *a* tarred. *m, naut* tarpaulin
alrededor *adv* around, round about. **a. de,** around; approximately, about (e.g. **a. de cinco dólares,** about $5)
alrededores *m pl,* environs, surrounding country
Alsacia Alsace
alsaciano (-na) *a* and *n* Alsatian
alta *f,* certificate of discharge from hospital
altanería *f,* hawking; haughtiness, disdain; superciliousness
altanero *a* soaring, high-flying (of birds); supercilious; haughty, disdainful
altar *m,* altar. **a. mayor,** high altar
altavoz *m,* loudspeaker; megaphone
altearse *vr* to rise, grow steep (of land)
alterabilidad *f,* alterability, changeability
alteración *f,* alteration, change; debasement (of coinage); agitation
alterar *vt* to change, alter; debase (coinage); disturb, agitate; *vr* grow angry; become excited
altercación, *f.* **altercado** *m,* altercation, quarrel
altercar(se) *vi* and *vr* to quarrel, dispute, altercate
alternación *f,* alternation
alternado *a* alternate
alternador *a* alternating. *m, elec* alternator
alternante *a* alternating
alternar *vt* to alternate; make one's debut as a **matador;** *vi* alternate; (*with con*) have dealings with, know
alternativa *f,* alternative, option; service performed by turns; alternation
alternativo *a* alternative
alterno *a* alternative; *bot* alternate
alteza *f,* altitude, height; sublimity, perfection; **(A.)** Highness (title)
altibajo *m,* embossed velvet; *pl inf* rough ground; *inf* vicissitudes of fortune
altillo *m,* hillock, eminence; garret, attic
altímetro *m, aer* altimeter
altiplano *m* plateau; **el A.** the High Andes, the high Andean plateau
altiplanicie *f,* plateau; highland
altisonante *a* sonorous; sublime; high-flown, pompous
altitud *f,* altitude, height
altivez *f,* arrogance, haughtiness
altivo *a* arrogant, haughty
alto *a* high; tall; difficult, arduous; sublime; deep; most serious (of crimes, etc.); dear (of price); small, early (hours). *m,* height; eminence, hill; story, floor; *mil* halt; red light (traffic light). *adv* up, above, on high; loudly. *interj* **¡A.!** *mil* Halt! *mil* **A. Mando,** High Command. **las altas horas de la noche,** the small (or early) hours. **en alta voz,** in a loud voice. **en alto,** on high; up above. **hacer alto,** to halt, stop
altozano *m,* mound, hillock; viewpoint, open space

altruismo *m,* altruism
altruista *a* altruistic. *mf* altruist
altura *f,* height; altitude; *geom* altitude or height; top, peak; sublimity; tallness
alucinación *f,* **alucinamiento,** *m,* hallucination
alucinado *m,* person suffering from hallucinations
alucinador *a* hallucinatory, deceptive
alucinar *vt* to dazzle, fascinate; deceive
alud *m,* avalanche
aludir *vi* to allude (to); refer (to), cite
alumbrado *m,* lighting; *pl* illuminati
alumbramiento *m,* lighting, supply of light; childbirth
alumbrar *vt* to light, illuminate; give sight to the blind; instruct, teach; inflict (blows); hoe vine roots; *vi* give birth to a child; *vr inf* grow tipsy
alumbre *m,* alum
aluminio *m,* aluminum
alumno (-na) *n* ward, adopted child; pupil. **a. externo,** day pupil. **a. interno,** boarder
alunizar *vi* to land on the moon
alunizaje *m,* landing on the moon, moon-landing
alusión *f,* allusion
alusivo *a* allusive, suggestive; hinting
aluvial *a* alluvial
aluvión *m,* alluvium. **de a.,** alluvial
alverjana *f, Lat. Am.* pea
alza *f,* rise (of temperature, etc.); increase (in price); front sight (of guns)
alzacuello *m,* high collar, clerical collar; neck stock
alzada *f,* horse's stature; mountain pasture; *law* appeal
alzado *a* fraudulent (of bankruptcy); fixed (of price); *Mexico* haughty, proud *m,* theft; *Lat. Am.* wild; insolent; rebellious; *arch* front elevation
alzamiento *m,* raising, lifting; higher bid (at auction); rising, rebellion; fraudulent bankruptcy
alzaprima *f,* lever; wedge; bridge (of string instruments)
alzar *vt* to raise; lift up; elevate (the Host); steal, remove; hide; gather in the harvest; build, construct; *naut* heave; *vr* rise (of temperature, mercury, price, etc.); make a fraudulent bankruptcy; *law* appeal; (*with con*) run off with, steal. *naut* **a. la vela,** to set sail
ama *f,* mistress of the house; owner; housekeeper; wet nurse. **a. de casa,** housemaker, housewife. **a. de leche,** foster-mother. **a. de llaves** *or* **a. de gobierno,** housekeeper. **a. seca,** children's nurse
amabilidad *f,* lovableness; kindness; niceness, goodness, helpfulness
amable *a* lovable; kind; nice, good, helpful
amador (-ra) *a* loving. *n* lover, admirer
amadrigar *vt* to welcome, receive well; *vr* go into a burrow or lair; go into seclusion
amaestrar *vt* to train, instruct; tame; break in (horses)
amagar *vt* and *vi* to threaten; *vt* show signs of (diseases, etc.); *vr inf* hide
amago (contra . . .), threat (to . . .), menace (to . . .)
amainar *vt naut* to take in the sails; *vi* drop (of the wind); *vi* and *vt* relax (efforts, etc.)
amaine *m,* dropping, abatement (of the wind)
amalgama *f, chem* amalgam
amalgamación *f,* amalgamation
amalgamar *vt* to amalgamate; *vr* be amalgamated
amamantamiento *m,* suckling, nursling
amamantar *vt* to suckle
amancillar *vt* to discredit, dishonor; tarnish; stain
amanecer *vi irr* to dawn; arrive *or* be somewhere *or* be doing, at dawn (e.g. **Amanecimos en el barco,** Dawn came while we were on the ship. **Amanecimos escribiendo la carta,** The day broke as we were writing the letter); appear at daybreak; begin to appear. *m,* dawn, daybreak. See **conocer**
amanerado *a* mannered; affected
amaneramiento *m,* manneredness; mannerism
amanerarse *vr* to acquire mannerisms or tricks of style; become affected
amansador (-ra) *a* soothing, calming. *n* appeaser
amansar *vt* to tame; appease, moderate; soothe, pacify; break in (horses)
amante *a* loving. *mf* lover
amanuense *mf* amanuensis, secretary, clerk
amanzanar to lay out the streets of
amañar *vt* to execute with skill; *vr* grow skilful
amaño *m,* skill, dexterity; *pl* schemes, intrigues; tools, equipment
amapola *f,* poppy
amar *vt* to love
amaranto *m, bot* amaranth
amarar *vi* to alight on the water (of hydroplanes)
amarchantarse con *vr, Lat. Am.* deal regularly with, do business with
amargar *vi* to taste or be bitter; *vt* make bitter; embitter
amargo *a* bitter; embittered; grievous, sad. *m,* bitterness; *pl* bitters
amargor *m,* **amargura,** *f,* bitter taste, bitterness; trouble, affliction, pain
amaricado *a inf* effeminate
amarillear *vi* to look yellow; turn yellow; tend to yellow
amarillento *a* yellowish, turning yellow
amarilleo *m,* yellowing
amarillez *f,* yellowness
amarillo *a* and *m,* yellow
amarilloso *a, Lat. Am.* yellowish, turning yellow
amarra *f, naut* cable, thick rope
amarradero *m, naut* mooring berth; mooring-post; hitchingpost or ring
amarraje *m, naut* mooring charge
amarrar *vt* to tie up, hitch; moor
amarre *m,* mooring; hitching
amartelar *vt* to make jealous; court, woo, make love to; *vr* be jealous; fall madly in love
amartillar *vt* to hammer, knock; cock (firearms)
amasadera *f,* kneading-trough
amasador (-ra) *a* kneading. *n* kneader
amasar *vt* to knead; massage; scheme, plot
amasia *f,* concubine
amasiato *m,* concubinage
amasijo *m, cul* dough; kneading; portion of plaster or mortar; *inf* hotchpotch, mixture; scheme, plot
amatista *f,* amethyst
amazacotado *a* heavy, dense; *fig* stodgy (of writings, etc.)
amazona *f,* Amazon; independent woman; woman rider; woman's riding habit
ambages *m pl,* maze, intricate paths; circumlocutions
ámbar *m,* amber. **a. gris,** ambergris
ambarino *a* amber
Amberes Antwerp
ambición *f,* ambition
ambicionar *vt* to long for; desire eagerly; be ambitious to
ambicioso *a* ambitious; eager, desirous
ambidextro *a* ambidextrous
ambiente *a* ambient, surrounding. *m,* air, atmosphere; environment
ambigú *m,* cold buffet; buffet (in theaters, etc.)
ambigüedad *f,* ambiguity
ambiguo *a* ambiguous
ámbito *m,* precincts; boundary, limit; compass, scope
amblar *vi* to pace (of a horse)
ambos, *a m pl,* **ambas** *a f pl,* both, e.g. **ambas casas,** both houses
ambulancia *f,* ambulance. **a. de correos,** railway post office. **a. fija,** field-hospital
ambulante *a* walking; traveling, wandering
amedrentar *vt* to frighten, scare; intimidate
ameliorar *vt* to better, improve
amelonado *a* melon-shaped; *inf* madly in love
amén *m,* amen, so be it. **a. de,** besides, in addition to. *inf* **en un decir a.,** in a trice
amenaza *f,* threat

amenazador, amenazante *a* menacing, threatening
amenazar *vt* to threaten; *vt* and *vi* presage, be pending
amenguamiento *m,* lessening, diminution; discredit; loss of prestige
amenguar *vt* to lessen, decrease; dishonor, discredit
amenidad *f,* amenity; agreeableness
amenizar *vt* to make pleasant or attractive
ameno *a* pleasant; entertaining; agreeable, delightful
América America
América del Norte North America
América del Sur South America
americana *f,* (man's) jacket
americanismo *m,* usage typical of Western-Hemisphere Spanish
americano (-na) *a* Western Hemispheric; *mf* native of the Western Hemisphere; resident of the Western Hemisphere
ameritar *vt WH* to deserve, merit
ametrallador *m,* machine-gunner
ametralladora *f,* machine-gun
amianto *m, min* amianthus, asbestos
amiba *f, zool* ameba
amicísimo *a sup.* **amigo,** most friendly
amiga *f,* woman friend; mistress, lover; dame, schoolmistress; dame school
amigabilidad *f,* friendliness, amicability
amigable *a* friendly, amicable; harmonious; suitable
amígdala *f,* tonsil
amigdalitis *f,* tonsillitis
amigo (-ga) *a* friendly; fond, addicted. *n* friend. *m,* lover. *inf* **ser muy a. de,** to be very friendly with; be very keen on or fond of
amilanado *a* cowed, spiritless
amilanar *vt* to terrify, intimidate; *vr* grow discouraged
aminorar *vt* to diminish, lessen
amistad *f,* friendship; liaison; favor; *pl* acquaintances, friends
amistar *vt* to introduce, make known to each other; bring about a reconciliation between or with
amistoso *a* friendly
amnesia *f,* amnesia
amnistía *f,* amnesty
amnistiar *vt* to concede an amnesty, pardon
amo *m,* head of the house; master; owner; overlord; overseer. **a. de huéspedes,** keeper of a boarding house. **Nuestro A.** Our Lord. *inf* **ser el a. del cotarro,** to rule the roost
amoblado *m, Central America, Mexico* furniture
amodorramiento *m,* stupor, deep sleep
amodorrarse *vr* to fall into a stupor; fall into a heavy sleep
amoladera *f,* whetstone
amolador *m,* scissors grinder; knife grinder; sharpener
amoladura *f,* grinding, whetting, sharpening
amolar *vt irr* to grind, sharpen; *inf* pester, annoy. See **colar**
amoldar *vt* to mold; adjust; *vr* adapt oneself
amonedar *vt* to coin, mint
amonestación *f,* warning; advice. **correr las amonestaciones,** to publish banns of marriage
amonestador (-ra) *a* warning, admonitory. *n* admonisher
amonestar *vt* to warn; advise; rebuke; *ecc* publish bans of marriage
amoníaco *m,* ammonia
amontillado *m,* kind of pale, dry sherry
amontonamiento *m,* accumulation; gathering, collection; piling up, heaping
amontonar *vt* to pile up, heap; gather; collect; accumulate; *vr inf* fly into a rage
amor *m,* love; beloved; willingness, pleasure; *pl* love affairs; caresses. **a. propio,** self-esteem; vanity. *inf* **con mil amores,** with great pleasure. **por a. de,** for love of; for the sake of
amoral *a* amoral
amoratado *a* livid, bluish
amorcillo *m, dim.* little love; unimportant love affair; Cupid
amordazar *vt* to muzzle; gag; prevent speaking
amorfo *a* amorphous
amorío *m, inf* wooing, love making; *pl* love affairs
amoroso *a* loving; gentle; mild, balmy
amorrar *vi inf* to hang one's head; sulk, be sullen
amortajar *vt* to wrap in a shroud; enshroud
amortiguador *m, mech* shock absorber. *aut* **a. de los muelles,** shock-absorber
amortiguamiento *m,* softening, deadening; mitigation, lessening
amortiguar *vt* to soften, deaden; absorb (shocks); moderate, mitigate; soften (colors)
amortización *f,* amortization
amortizar *vt* to amortize; recover, redeem; suppress, abolish (posts)
amoscarse *vr inf* to be piqued or annoyed; become agitated
amostazar *vt inf* to annoy; *vi* become peeved
amotinador (-ra) *a* mutinous, rebellious. *n* rebel, mutineer; rioter
amotinar *vt* to incite to rebellion; unbalance, unhinge (mind); *vr* rebel; riot; *fig* be unhinged
amovible *a* movable, removable; removable (of officials, etc.)
amovilidad *f,* movability, removability; liability to discharge or dismissal
amparador (-ra) *a* protective; sheltering. *n* protector, defender, helper; shelterer
amparar *vt* to protect, favor, help; shelter; *vr* take refuge, take shelter; defend oneself
amparo *m,* shelter, refuge; protection, favor, help; defense
amper *m, elec* ampere
amperímetro *m, elec* ammeter
amperio *m, elec* ampere
ampliable *a* amplifiable
ampliación *f,* enlargement, increase, extension; *phot* enlargement
ampliador (-ra) *a* enlarging. *n* enlarger
ampliadora *f, phot* enlarger
ampliar *vt* to extend, enlarge, increase; *phot* enlarge
amplificación *f,* extension, amplification; *phot* enlargement
amplificar *vt* to enlarge; extend; increase; amplify, expatiate upon
amplio *a* wide; extensive; roomy, ample; prolix
amplitud *f,* extension; width; spaciousness, amplitude
ampolla *f,* blister; ampoule; bubble; *elec* bulb
ampulosidad *f,* pomposity, redundancy (of style)
ampuloso *a* pompous, high-flown (style)
amputación *f,* amputation
amputar *vt* to amputate
amuchachado *a* boyish
amueblar *vt* to furnish; provide with furniture
amuinar *vt, Mexico* to anger, make angry
amuleto *m,* amulet, charm
amurallar *vt* to surround with a wall, wall
amurrarse *vr, Lat. Am.* get depressed, get the blues
amusgar *vt* and *vi* to flatten the ears (animals); *vt* screw up the eyes (to see better)
ana *f,* ell (measure)
anacardo *m,* cashew (nut)
anacoreta *mf* anchorite, hermit
anacreóntico *a* Anacreontic
anacrónico *a* anachronous
anacronismo *m,* anachronism
ánade *mf* duck
anadear *vi* to waddle (like a duck)
anadeo *m,* waddle
anadino (-na) *n* duckling
anadón *m,* drake
anáfora *f,* anaphora
anafrodisíaco *a* anaphrodisiac
anagrama *m,* anagram

analectas *f, pl* analects
anales *m, pl* annals
analfabetismo *m,* illiteracy
analfabeto (-ta) *a* and *n* illiterate
analgesia *f,* analgesia
analgésico *a* and *m, med* analgesic
análisis *m,* analysis; *gram* parsing
analista *mf* analyst
analizar *vt* to analyse
analogía *f,* analogy
analógico, análogo *a* analogous
ananás *m,* pineapple
anaquel *m,* shelf, ledge
anaranjado *a* and *m,* orange (color)
anarquía *f,* anarchy
anárquico *a* anarchical
anarquismo *m,* anarchism
anarquista *mf* anarchist
anatema *mf,* anathema
anatomía *f,* anatomy
anatómico *a* anatomical
anca *f,* croup, hindquarters of a horse
ancianidad *f,* old age; seniority; oldness
anciano (-na) *a* old; ancient. *n* old person
ancla *f,* anchor. **a. de la esperanza,** sheet anchor. **echar anclas,** to anchor
ancladero, anclaje *m,* anchorage
anclar *vi* to anchor
ancón *m,* cove, *Mexico* corner
áncora *f,* anchor; refuge, haven
ancho *a* wide, broad. *m,* width, breadth. *inf* **a mis (tus, sus,** etc.) **anchas** *or* **anchos,** at my (your, his, etc.) ease, with complete freedom
anchoa *f,* anchovy
anchura *f,* width, breadth; ease, freedom; extent
anchuroso *a* very wide; extensive; spacious
andada *f,* wandering, roving; hard bread roll; pasture; *pl* trail, tracks. *fig inf* **volver a las andadas,** to return to one's old tricks
andaderas *f pl,* go-cart (for learning to walk)
andador *a* walking; swift walking; wandering. *m,* walker; garden path; *pl* leading-strings, reins
andadura *f,* walk, gait; pace, step
Andalucía Andalusia
andaluz (-za) *a* and *n* Andalusian
andaluzada *f, inf* exaggeration, tall story
andamio *m,* scaffolding; stand, platform
andanada *f, naut* broadside; cheapest priced seat in a bullring; *inf* dressing-down, scolding
andante *a* walking, strolling; errant (of knights). *a* and *m, mus* andante
andanza *f,* happening, occurrence; *pl* doings, deeds. **buena a.,** good fortune
andar *vi irr* to walk; move; work, operate, run (machines, etc.); progress, get along (negotiations, etc.); be, feel; elapse (of time); be occupied; behave; (*with prep a*) administer (blows, etc.); (*with en*) upset, turn over (papers, etc.); ride in or on (cars, bicycles, etc.); be engaged in; (*with con*) use, handle; *vt* traverse. *m,* gait, walk. **a. por los cuarenta,** to be in one's forties. **a. con paños tibios,** not to be firm. **a. con pies de plomo,** to be extremely cautious. **a. tras,** to follow, go after; persecute; desire ardently (things). **andarse a la flor del berro,** to sow one's wild oats. *fig inf* **andarse por las ramas,** to beat about the bush. **¡Anda!** Get along with you!; Hurry up!; You don't say so! **¡Andando!** Let's get going!, Let's get a move on it! *Preterite* **anduve,** etc. *Imperf subjunc* **anduviese,** etc.
andariego *a* swift walking; wandering, vagrant
andarín (-ina) *n* good walker; professional walker
andas *f pl,* kind of stretcher; bier
andén *m,* railway platform; *Lat. Am.* sidewalk
andero *m,* bearer (of a bier)
andinismo *m, Lat. Am.* mountain climbing **andinista** *mf Lat. Am.* mountain climber
andino *a* Andean
andorrano (-na) *a* and *n* Andorran
andrajo *m,* rag, wisp of cloth, tatter
andrajoso *a* ragged, tattered
andurriales *m pl,* byways, unfrequented paths; remote places
anécdota *f,* anecdote
anecdótico *a* anecdotal
anegación *f,* drowning; flooding, inundation
anegar *vt* to drown; inundate; shipwreck; *vr* drown; be flooded
anejo *a* attached, annexed. *m,* annexed borough
anemia *f,* anemia
anémico *a* anemic
anémona, anémone *f,* anemone. **anémona de mar,** sea-anemone
anestesia *f,* anesthesia
anestesiador (-ra) *n* anesthetist
anestesiar *vt* to anesthetize
anestésico *a* and *m,* anesthetic
aneurisma *mf med* aneurism
anexar *vt* to annex
anexión *f,* annexation
anexo *a* attached, joined. *m,* annex
anfibio *a* amphibious. *m,* amphibian
anfiteatro *m,* amphitheater; operating theater; dissecting room; morgue; *theat* dress-circle
anfitrión *m, inf* host, one who entertains guests
ánfora *f,* amphora; *Lat. Am.* ballot box
angarillas *f pl,* hand barrow; table cruet; yoke and panniers
ángel *m,* angel; *Lat. Am.* (hand) microphone **á. de la guarda,** guardian angel. **estar con los ángeles,** to be in Heaven (euphem. for 'to be dead')
angelical, angélico *a* angelic; divine, excellent
angina *f, med* angina, tonsillitis. **a. de pecho,** angina pectoris
anglicanismo *m,* Anglicanism
anglicano (-na) *a* and *n* Anglican
anglicismo *m,* anglicism
anglo (-la) *a* and *n* Angle. *a* Anglo-
anglófilo (-la) *n* Anglophile
anglosajón (-ona) *a* and *n* Anglo-Saxon. *m,* Anglo-Saxon language
angostar *vi* and *vt* to narrow; tighten
angosto *a* narrow; tight
angostura *f,* narrowness; tightness; narrow pass; strait; *fig* tight corner, fix
anguila *f, icht* eel; *pl naut* slipway, slips
angula *f, icht* elver (young eel)
ángulo *m,* angle. **á. inferior izquierdo,** lower lefthand corner. **á. inferior derecho,** lower righthand corner. **á. superior izquierdo,** upper lefthand corner. **á. superior derecho,** upper righthand corner. **á. recto,** right angle
anguloso *a* angulate; angular, gaunt; cornered
angustia *f,* anguish, grief
angustiante *a* distressing
angustiar *vt* to grieve; afflict; *vr* be full of anguish
anhelación *f,* panting, hard breathing; yearning, longing
anhelar *vi* to pant, breathe with difficulty; *vi* and *vt* long for, yearn for, desire
anhélito *m,* pant, hard breathing
anhelo (de) *m,* longing (for), desire (for), yearning (for)
anheloso *a* difficult, labored (of breathing); anxious, longing
anidar *vi* to nest (birds); swell; *vt* shelter, protect; *vr* nest; dwell; nestle
anilla *f,* curtain ring; *pl* gymnastic rings
anillo *m,* finger ring; small ring; coil (of serpents and ropes). **a. de compromiso** *Mexico* engagement ring. *inf* **venir como a. al dedo,** to fit like a glove; come just at the right moment
ánima *f,* soul, spirit; soul in purgatory; bore (of firearms); *pl* prayer bell for the souls of the departed

animación *f,* liveliness, gaiety; animation, vivacity; bustle, movement
animal *m,* animal; *inf* dolt, brute. *a* animal; *inf* brutish, doltish
animalada *f, inf* stupidity, foolishness
animalidad *f,* animalism
animar *vt* to animate; encourage, incite; invigorate, enliven; make gay, cheer up; make attractive, adorn; *vr* take heart; make up one's mind; cheer up; grow gay
animismo *m,* animism
ánimo *m,* soul, spirit; courage; endurance, fortitude; will, intention; mind. **con ánimo de + inf.,** with the intention of + *ger.* **¡Á.!** Courage!
animosidad *f,* hatred, animosity, dislike
animoso *a* spirited, lively; valiant
aniñado *a* childlike, childish
aniquilable *a* destructible
aniquilación *f,* destruction, annihilation; suppression; decay
aniquilador (-ra) *a* destructive, annihilating. *n* destroyer
aniquilamiento *m,* See **aniquilación**
aniquilar *vt* to annihilate, destroy completely; *vr* waste away, decay
anís *m,* aniseed, anise; anisette (liqueur)
anisar *vt* to flavor with aniseed
anisete *m,* anisette
aniversario *a* annual. *m,* anniversary
Anjeo Anjou
ano *m,* anus
anoche *adv* last night; the previous night
anochecer *vi irr* to grow night; become dark; be in a place *or* be doing something at nightfall (e.g. **Anochecimos en Lérida,** We were in Lerida at nightfall). *vr poet* be obscured or darkened. *m,* nightfall, dusk. See **conocer**
anochecida *f,* dusk, late twilight
anodino *a med* anodyne; ineffective, useless; inoffensive. *m,* anodyne
anomalía *f,* anomaly, inconstancy, irregularity; *ast* anomaly
anómalo *a* anomalous, abnormal, unusual
anonadación, *f,* **anonadamiento** *m,* destruction, annihilation; despair, melancholy; suppression
anonadar *vt* to destroy, annihilate; suppress; *fig* overwhelm, depress; humble
anónimo *a* anonymous. *m,* anonymity; anonymous letter; unsigned literary work
anormal *a* abnormal; irregular, unusual. *mf* abnormal person
anormalidad *f,* abnormality; irregularity, inconsistency
anotación *f,* annotation; *Lat. Am.* score (in sports)
anotador (-ra) *n* annotator
anotar *vt* to annotate; note down
anquilostoma *m, med* hookworm
ánsar *m,* goose; drake
ansarino *a* goose. *m,* gosling
anseático *a* Hanseatic
ansia (de) *f,* anxiety, trouble; grief; longing (for), yearning (for); greed
ansiar *vt* to long for, yearn for; covet, desire
ansiedad *f,* anxiety, anguish, worry
ansión *f,* intense desire
ansioso *a* anxious; grievous, painful; eager, desirous; greedy
anta *f, zool* elk; obelisk
antagónico *a* antagonistic
antagonismo *m,* antagonism
antagonista *mf* antagonist, adversary
antaño *adv* last year, yesteryear; long ago
antártico *a* antarctic
ante *m, zool* elk; suede; buffalo
ante *prep* in the presence of, before; regarding, in the face of (e.g. **a. deber tan alto,** in the face of so noble a duty)
anteado *a* beige, buff-colored, fawn
anteanoche *adv* the night before last
anteayer *adv* the day before yesterday
antebrazo *m,* forearm
antecámara *f,* antechamber
antecedente *m,* antecedent. **antecedentes** *m pl* background (of a case, situation, etc.)
antecedentemente *adv* previously
anteceder *vt* to precede
antecesor (-ra) *a* previous. *n* predecessor. *m,* forebear, ancestor
antecoger *vt* to carry in front, lead before; pick too soon
antecomedor *m,* breakfast nook, breakfast room
antedata *f,* antedate
antedatar *vt* to antedate
antedicho *a* aforementioned, aforesaid
antediluviano *a* antediluvian
antelación *f,* advance, anticipation
antellevar *vt, Mexico* to knock down, run over
antemano, de *adv* in advance, beforehand
antemeridiano *a* antemeridian, forenoon
antena *f,* antenna; *rad* aerial
antenacido *a* born prematurely
antenombre *m,* title (placed before name)
anteojera *f,* horse's blinker; eyeglass case
anteojo *m,* spy-glass, small telescope; *pl* horse's blinkers; eyeglasses, glasses; spectacles; goggles
antepagar *vt* to pay in advance
antepalco *m,* vestibule of a box in a theater
antepasado *a* previous, past. *m,* ancestor (gen. *pl*)
antepecho *m,* parapet; windowsill; railing, balustrade; front (of a theater box, etc.); *naut* bulwark
antepenúltimo *a* antepenultimate, second from the last
anteponer *vt irr* to place before; prefer, favor. See **poner**
anteproyecto *m,* first sketch, preliminary work or plan
antepuerta *f,* door-curtain, portiere; *mil* anteport
anterior *a* previous, former; anterior; aforementioned, preceding
anteriormente *adv* beforehand, previously
antes *adv* before; rather, on the contrary; previously. **a. bien,** rather, sooner. **a. con a.** *or* **cuanto a.,** as soon as possible
antesala *f,* antechamber
antevíspera *f,* two days previously
antiaéreo *a* antiaircraft. *m pl.* **(cañones) antiaéreos,** A.A. guns
anticiclón *m,* anticyclone
anticipación *f,* anticipation; advance
anticipada *f,* foul thrust (in fencing, etc.)
anticipadamente *adv* in advance; prematurely
anticipado *a* in advance; premature
anticipador *a* anticipatory
anticipar *vt* to anticipate; foresee; forestall; advance (money); lend; *vr* happen before time; (*with prep a*) act in advance of, anticipate; get ahead of oneself
anticipo *m,* anticipation, advance; advance payment; sum of money lent
anticlerical *a* anticlerical
anticlímax *m,* anticlimax
anticonstitucional *a* unconstitutional
anticuado *a* antiquated, ancient
anticuario *m,* antiquarian, antique dealer
antídoto *m,* antidote
antiesclavista *a* antislavery. *mf* antislavist
antiespasmódico *a* and *m, med* antispasmodic
antiestético *a* unesthetic
antietimológico *a* non-etymological, unetymological
antifaz *m,* mask; face-covering
antiflogístico *a* and *m, med* antiphlogistic
antigramatical *a* ungrammatical
antigualla *f,* antique; ancient custom; anything out-of-date
antiguamente *adv* in time past, formerly
antiguamiento *m,* seniority

antigüedad *f*, antiquity; ancients; length of service (in an employment); *pl* antiquities
antiguo *a* ancient, very old; antique; senior (in an employment); former. *m*, senior member (of a community, etc.). *m pl*, ancients. **A. Testamento,** Old Testament. **de a.,** from ancient times. **en lo antiguo,** in ancient times; in former times, in days of yore
antillano (-na) *a* and *n* of or from the Antilles
Antillas, las the Antilles
antílope *m*, antelope
antimacasar *m*, antimacassar
antimilitarismo *m*, antimilitarism
antimilitarista *a* antimilitaristic
antimonárquico *a* antimonarchical
antimonio *m*, *met* antimony
antipalúdico *a* antimalarial
antipara *f*, screen, shield
antiparras *f pl*, *inf* spectacles, eyeglasses, glasses
antipatía *f*, antipathy
antipático *a* disagreeable; unattractive
antipatriótico *a* unpatriotic
antípoda *a* and *m*, or *f*, antipode
antiquísimo *a sup*, **antiguo,** most ancient
antisemita *a* anti-Semitic. *mf* anti-Semite
antisemitismo *m*, anti-Semitism
antiséptico *a* and *m*, antiseptic
antisifilítico *a med* anti-syphilitic
antisocial *a* antisocial
antítesis *f*, antithesis
antitético *a* antithetic, contrasted
antófago *a* anthophagous, flower-eating
antojadizo *a* capricious, fanciful, whimsical
antojarse *vr* to have a fancy for, want (e.g. **Se me antoja marcharme al campo,** I have a yen to go to the country); suspect, imagine
antojito *m*, *Mexico* typical Mexican dish (of food)
antojo *m*, caprice, fancy, whim; desire, will; *pl* birthmark
antología *f*, anthology
antólogo *m*, anthologist
antonomasia *f*, antonomasia. **por a.,** by analogy, by transference
antorcha *f*, torch, flambeau
antracita *f*, anthracite
ántrax *m*, *med* anthrax
antro *m*, cave, cavern; *anat* antrum
antropofagia *f*, cannibalism, anthropophagy
antropófago (-ga) *a* cannibalistic. *n* cannibal
antropología *f*, anthropology
antropológico *a* anthropological
antropólogo *m*, anthropologist
antropometría *f*, anthropometry
antropomorfo *a* anthropomorphous
antroposofía *f*, anthroposophy
antruejo *m*, three days of carnival before Lent
anual *a* yearly, annual
anualidad *f*, annuity
anuario *m*, directory, yearbook, handbook
anubarrado *a* covered with clouds, cloudy
anublado *a* lowering, overcast; clouded
anublar *vt* to cloud; darken, obscure; blight (plants); *vr* cloud over; become blighted or mildewed
anudar *vt* to knot; tie, fasten; join; continue; **a. amistad de,** to strike up a friendship with. **a. la corbata,** to put on one's tie, tie one's tie; *vr* grow stunted
anulable *a* annulable, voidable
anulación *f*, annulment, abrogation
anular *a* annular, ring-shaped. *vt* to annul; *math* cancel out
anuloso *a* annulate, formed of rings
anunciación *f*, *ecc* Annunciation; announcement
anunciador (-ra), *n* anunciante *mf* announcer; advertiser
anunciar *vt* to announce; publish, proclaim; advertise; foretell, presage. **Anuncian lluvia,** The forecast calls for rain
anuncio *m*, announcement; publication, proclamation; advertisement; presage, omen. **a. luminoso,** sky-sign
anverso *m*, obverse, face
anzuelo *m*, fish-hook; *cul* fritter; *inf* attraction, inducement
añadido *m*, hair-switch; make-weight
añadidura *f*, addition; make-weight, extra
añadir *vt* to add; increase
añagaza *f*, decoy bird; enticement, lure
añejo *a* very old
añicos *m pl*, fragments, small pieces. **hacer a.,** to break into fragments
añil *m*, indigo; indigo blue
año *m*, year; *pl* birthday. **a. bisiesto,** leap-year. **a. económico,** fiscal year. **A. Nuevo,** New Year. **tener (siete) años,** to be (seven) years old. **los Años Bobos,** the period from 1874 to 1898 in Spain
añoranza *f*, homesickness, loneliness; nostalgia
añorar *vi* to be homesick or lonely
añoso *a* very old, full of years
añublo *m*, mildew
aojamiento *m*, evil eye, wicked spell
aojar *vt* to bewitch, place under a spell; spoil, frustrate
aojo *m*, evil eye; magic spell
aorta *f*, *anat* aorta
aovillarse *vr* to roll oneself into a ball; curl up
apabullante *a* crushing, flattening
apacentadero *m*, grazing land, pasture
apacentamiento *m*, pasturage; grazing
apacentar *vt irr* to put out to grass; teach, instruct; satisfy (one's desires); *vr* graze (cattle). See **acertar**
apachurar *vt*, *Mexico* to press (button, etc.)
apacibilidad *f*, agreeableness; mildness; peaceableness
apacible *a* agreeable; mild; peaceable; calm, peaceful
apaciguamiento *m*, appeasement, soothing, pacification
apaciguar *vt* to appease, pacify; calm
apadrinar *vt* to act as godfather to; be best man to (at a wedding); act as a second for (in a duel); sponsor; favor
apagable *a* extinguishable
apagado *a* timid, nervous; pale (of colors); dull, lusterless
apagador (-ra) *a* quenching. *n* extinguisher. *m*, candle-snuffer; damper (of a piano)
apagaincendios *m*, ship's fire-extinguisher
apagamiento *m*, quenching, extinguishment
apagar *vt* to extinguish, put out; *fig* quench, moderate; slake (lime); *art* tone down (colors); shut off (engines)
apagarrisas *mf* crapehanger, killjoy, wet blanket
apagavelas *m*, candle-snuffer
apalabrar *vt* to make an appointment with; discuss, consider
apaleamiento *m*, beating, thrashing
apalear *vt* to beat, thrash; knock down with a stick
apandillarse *vr* to form a gang or group
apañar *vt* to take away, remove; seize; steal; dress, get ready; *inf* wrap up; patch, repair; *vr inf* grow skilful
apaño *m*, dexterity, skill; craft, guile
aparador *m*, sideboard; workshop; *ecc* credence (table); *Mexico* (shop) window
aparato *m*, apparatus; equipment, utensils; pomp, ostentation; symptoms; sign, circumstance, token. **a. digestivo,** digestive system; digestive tract. **a. fonador,** speech apparatus
aparatoso *a* showy, ostentatious. **incendio. a.,** conflagration, large fire
aparear *vt* to match, make equal; pair; mate (animals); *vr* form up in pairs
aparecer(se) *vi* and *vr irr* to appear; seem; be. See **conocer**
aparecido *m*, apparition, specter
aparejador *m*, overseer, foreman; *naut* rigger
aparejar *vt* to prepare, make ready; saddle (horses); prime, size; rig (a ship)
aparejo *m*, preparation, arrangement; harness, trap-

pings; *naut* rigging; *naut* gear; priming, sizing; *mech* tackle; *pl* equipment
aparentar *vt* to pretend, simulate
aparente *a* seeming, apparent; obvious, visible; suitable, proper
aparición *f*, appearance, arrival; apparition, phantom
apariencia *f*, appearance, looks, probability, likelihood; outward semblance; *pl theat* scenery
apartadamente *adv* apart, in private; secretly
apartadero *m*, passing place for cars; railway siding; grass verge. **a. ferroviario,** railway marshaling yard
apartado *a* distant, far off; secluded; different. *m*, post-office box; secluded room; smelting house; sorting of cattle; selection of bulls for a bullfight
apartamento *m Lat. Am.* (*except Argentina*) apartment
apartamiento *m*, separation; withdrawal, retiral; seclusion; apartment, flat; *law* withdrawal of an action
apartar *vt* to separate; remove (e.g. an obstacle), take away; *rw* shunt; dissuade; sort; *vr* obtain a divorce; *law* withdraw an action. **apartarse de la tradición,** to depart from tradition
aparte *adv* aside, on one side; separately; *theat* aside; besides; beyond. *m*, *theat* aside; paragraph; space between words. **¡Aparte!** Move to one side!
apartidario *a* non-partisan
apasionado (-da) *a* impassioned; fervent, devoted; passionate; enthusiastic. *n* admirer, lover; enthusiast
apasionamiento *m*, passion
apasionar *vt* to arouse to passion; pain; *vr* (*with por*) grow passionately fond of; become enthusiastic for
apatía *f*, apathy
apático *a* apathetic
apeadero *m*, mounting-block; halt, stopping place; wayside railway station; pied-à-terre, occasional dwelling
apear *vt* to dismount; hobble (horse); survey, map out; fell a tree; *fig* overcome (difficulties); *inf* dissuade; prop; remove, bring down; scotch (a wheel); *vr* dismount; alight, step off
apechugar *vi* to push with the breast; *inf* put up with reluctantly
apedazar *vt* to tear; break; mend, repair
apedrear *vt* to stone; stone to death; *vi impers* hail; *vr* be damaged by hail (crops)
apegarse *vr* to grow fond (of), become attached (to)
apego *m*, fondness, inclination; affection, attachment
apelación *f*, *law* appeal; *inf* doctor's consultation
apelante *a* and *mf law* appellant
apelar *vi law* to appeal; (*with prep a*) have recourse to; *vi* be of the same color (horses)
apellidar *vt* to name, call; acclaim; call to arms; *vr* be named
apellido *m*, surname; nickname; call to arms; clamor; name
apenar *vt* to grieve, afflict; cause sorrow
apenarse *vr Lat. Am.* to be ashamed
apenas *adv* scarcely; immediately, as soon as; with trouble or difficulty
apéndice *m*, appendix, supplement; *anat* appendix
apendicitis *f*, appendicitis
Apeninos, los the Apennines
apeo *m*, survey; scaffolding; prop, support
apercibimiento *m*, preparation; provision; warning; *law* summons
apercibir *vt* to prepare, furnish; warn; *law* summon
apergaminarse *vr inf* to shrivel, dry up (with old age, etc.)
aperitivo *a* aperitive. *m*, aperient; aperitive, appetiser
apertura *f*, opening; inauguration; reading (of a will)
apesadumbrar *vt* to sadden, afflict, grieve
apestar *vt* to infect with the plague; catch the plague; *fig* corrupt; *inf* pester, annoy; *vi* stink
apestoso *a* stinking, putrid
apetecer *vt irr* to want, desire; attract. See **conocer**
apetecible *a* attractive, desirable
apetencia *f*, appetite; desire
apetito *m*, appetite
apetitoso *a* appetising; tasty, savory; attractive
apiadarse *vr* (*with de*) to have compassion on, be sorry for
ápice *m*, apex; peak, summit, top; orthographic accent; iota, tittle; crux (of a problem)
apicultor (-ra) *n* apiarist, beekeeper
apicultura *f*, apiculture, beekeeping
apilar *vt* to pile, heap
apimplado, -a *a*, *Lat. Am.* boozed up, drunk
apiñado *a* crowded, serried
apiñamiento *m*, crowding; congestion
apiñar *vt* to group together, crowd; *vr* crowd
apio *m*, celery
apisonadora *f*, steam-roller; roller
apisonar *vt* to roll, stamp, flatten, ram down; tamp, pack down (e.g. tobacco in a pipe)
apizarrado *a* slate-colored
aplacable *a* appeasable, placable
aplacamiento *m*, appeasement
aplacar *vt* to appease, calm; moderate, mitigate
aplacible *a* agreeable, pleasant
aplanacalles *mf*, *Lat. Am.* idler, lay about, lazybones
aplanar *vt* to flatten, level; roll (pastry); *inf* dumbfound, overwhelm; *vr* collapse (buildings); lose heart
aplastar *vt* to flatten, squash, crush; *inf* squash flat, floor
aplaudir *vt* to applaud, clap; praise, commend, approve
aplauso *m*, applause; clapping, plaudit; approbation, commendation
aplazamiento *m*, postponement; appointment, summons
aplazar *vt* to summon, arrange a meeting; postpone; adjourn
aplicabilidad *f*, applicability
aplicable *a* applicable
aplicación *f*, application; diligence, assiduity; appliqué, ornamentation
aplicado *a* diligent, hardworking; appliqué
aplicar *vt* to apply; impute; intend, destine (for processions); *law* adjudge; *vr* engage in; apply oneself. **a. el oído,** to listen intently. **a. sanciones,** *pol* to impose sanctions
aplomado *a* self-possessed, dignified; leaden, lead-colored
aplomar *vt* and *vi* to plumb, test with a plumb-line; *vr* collapse, fall down
aplomo *m*, self-possession, dignity; sang-froid
apocado *a* spiritless, timid; base, mean
Apocalipsis *m*, Apocalypse
apocalíptico *a* apocalyptic
apocamiento *m*, timidity, pusillanimity; depression, discouragement; shyness; baseness, meanness
apocar *vt* to diminish, reduce; humiliate, scorn
apócrifo *a* fictitious, false; apocryphal. **Apócrifos,** Apocrypha
apodar *vt* to nickname
apoderado *a* authorized. *m*, attorney; deputy; proxy
apoderar *vt* to authorize; grant powers of attorney to; *vr* (*with de*) seize, take possession of
apodo *m*, nickname
apogeo *m*, *ast* apogee; *fig* zenith, peak (of fame, etc.)
apolillar *vt* to eat clothes (moths); *vr* be moth-eaten
apologista *mf* apologist
apólogo *m*, apologue, moral fable
apoltronarse *vr* to grow idle
apoplejía *f*, apoplexy
aporrear *vt* to beat, cudgel; *vr* work hard, slog away
aportación *f*, contribution; occasionment
aportar *vt* to cause, occasion; contribute; *vi naut* reach port; **El buque aportó a Nueva York,** The ship reached New York, The ship sailed into New York harbor; arrive at an unexpected place
aposentador *m*, usher; *mil* billeting officer
aposentar *vt* to lodge, give hospitality to; *vr* lodge, settle down

aposento *m*, room; suite, apartments; lodging, accommodation; *theat* box
aposición *f*, *gram* apposition
apósito *m*, poultice, external application; (medical) dressing
apostadero *m*, *naut* naval station; placing or stationing (of soldiers)
apostar *vt irr* to bet; station (soldiers); *vi* compete, rival. See **contar**
apostasía *f*, apostasy
apóstata *mf* apostate
apostilla *f*, marginal note, gloss
apóstol *m*, apostle
apostólico *a* apostolic
apóstrofe *m*, or *f*, apostrophe, hortatory exclamation
apóstrofo *m*, *gram* apostrophe
apostura *f*, neatness, spruceness
apotegma *m*, apothegm, maxim
apoteosis *f*, apotheosis
apoyar *vt* (*with en*) to lean against; rest upon; *vt* uphold, favor; confirm, bear out; droop the head (horses); second (a motion); *vi* (*with en*) rest on; lean against; *vr* (*with en*) rest on; lean against; **apoyarse de codos,** to lean on one's elbows; be upheld by; *fig* be founded on; *fig* depend on, lean on
apoyo *m*, support, prop; windowsill, sill; assistance; backing, support
apreciable *a* appreciable; estimable; important
apreciación *f*, appreciation; valuation, estimate
apreciador (-ra) *a* appreciatory. *n* appreciator
apreciar *vt* to estimate (values); appreciate; like, esteem, have a regard for
apreciativo *a* appreciative
aprecio *m*, valuation; appreciation, regard
aprehender *vt* to apprehend, catch; seize (contraband); understand, grasp
aprehensión *f*, seizure, apprehension
apremiador, apremiante *a* urgent, pressing
apremiar *vt* to hurry; urge, press; force, oblige; burden, oppress (with taxes)
apremio *m*, insistence, pressure; compulsion; demand note
aprendedor (-ra) *n* learner
aprender *vt* to learn. **a. de memoria,** to learn by heart
aprendiz (-za) *n* apprentice
aprendizaje *m*, apprenticeship. **hacer el a.,** to serve an apprenticeship
aprensión *f*, capture; fear, apprehension; suspicion, fancy; prejudice, scruple
aprensivo *a* apprehensive, nervous, fearful
apresar *vt* to nab, catch; capture (a ship); imprison; fetter
aprestar *vt* to prepare, arrange; dress (fabrics)
apresto *m*, preparation, arrangement; dressing (for cloth)
apresurar *vt* to quicken; *vr* hasten, be quick
apretado *a* difficult, dangerous; tight; crabbed (of handwriting); clustered (e.g. **casas apretadas alrededor de la sinagoga,** houses clustered around the synagogue). *inf* mean, close-fisted. *m*, small close handwriting
apretadura *f*, tightening, compression
apretar *vt irr* to tighten; compress; urge on, press; harass, vex; trouble, worry; speed up; squeeze; press (bells, gun triggers, etc.); *vi* increase, grow worse (storms, heat, etc.); pinch, hurt (shoes). **a. los pasos,** to quicken one's pace. *inf* **a. a correr,** to take to one's heels. **¡Aprieta!** *inf* Nonsense! It can't be! See **acertar**
apretón *m*, squeeze, grip, pressure; *inf* sprint, spurt; *inf* fix, pickle. **a. de manos,** handshake
apretujamiento *m*, squeezing together
apretujar *vt inf* to squeeze, hug
aprieto *m*, crowd, crush; urgency; *inf* jam, trouble, fix
aprisa *adv* quickly, in a hurry
aprisco *m*, cattle-shed; sheepfold
aprisionar *vt* to imprison; bind, fetter; tie
aprobación *f*, approbation, approval, commendation; ratification (of a bill); pass (in an examination)
aprobado *m*, pass certificate (in examinations)
aprobar *vt irr* to approve; pass (in an examination). See **contar**
aprontar *vt*, *Lat. Am.* to pay in advance, prepay
apropiación *f*, appropriation; application; adaptation
apropiado *a* appropriate, suitable, proper
apropiar *vt* to appropriate; adapt, fit; *vr* appropriate, take possession
aprovechable *a* usable, available
aprovechado *a* advantageous; assiduous, conscientious; capable; thrifty
aprovechador *a* self-seeking
aprovechamiento *m*, utilization, employment; exploitation; profitable use
aprovechar *vi* to be advantageous or useful; be beneficial; make progress (in studies, etc.); *vt* use; profit by; *vr* take advantage of, make use of. **¡Que aproveche!** May it do you good! (said to anyone eating)
aprovisionar *vt* to provision, supply
aproximación *f*, approximation; consolation prize (in a lottery)
aproximadamente *adv* approximately; nearly, almost
aproximar *vt* to bring or draw nearer; *vr* approach; be almost, be approximately; draw closer
aptitud *f*, aptitude, ability; fitness; propensity
apto *a* suitable, fitting; competent. **no apta para menores,** not suitable for children (of films, etc.)
apuesta *f*, bet, wager; competition
apuestas benéficas de fútbol football pools
apuesto *a* elegant; handsome, well set-up
apuntación *f*, noting down; note; *mus* notation
apuntador (-ra) *n* note-taker; observer. *m*, *theat* prompter; *theat* stage-manager
apuntalar *vt* to prop, prop up, underpin, bolster
apuntamiento *m*, summary; *law* indictment, minute
apuntar *vt* to aim (a gun, etc.); point to, indicate; note down; mark; sketch; sharpen; bet (at cards); fasten temporarily; *inf* mend; *theat* prompt; suggest, hint (e.g. **La fecha está apuntada en varios manuscritos,** The date is hinted at in various manuscripts); *vi* begin to appear. *inf* **a. y no dar,** to promise and do nothing
apunte *m*, abstract; note; annotation; sketch; *theat* prompt *or* prompter *or* prompt book *or* cue; stake in a card game
apuñalado *a* dagger-shaped
apuñalar *vt* to stab, attack with a dagger
apurado *a* poor, needy; dangerous; difficult; accurate, exact; hurried
apurar *vt* to purify; drain; exhaust; finish, conclude; examine closely, scrutinize (e.g. **apurar una materia,** to exhaust a subject, examine a subject thoroughly); irritate, make impatient; urge on, hasten; *vr* be anxious, fret; *Lat. Am.* hurry, hurry up
apuro *m*, difficulty, fix; poverty, want; anxiety, worry. **pasar apuros,** to have a hard time
aquejar *vt* to afflict; weary, beset, harass; *vr* complain; hurry
aquel, *a m* **aquella,** *a f* **aquellos,** *a m pl* **aquellas** *a f pl*, that, those; that or those over there (farther off than **ese**)
aquel *m*, charm, attraction, it
aquél, aquélla, aquéllos, aquéllas *dem pron m, f*, sing. and pl., that, the one, those, those ones; the former. e.g. **La casa que ve usted a lo lejos aquélla es la vivienda de mi tío,** The house that you see in the distance, that is my uncle's dwelling. **Éste no me gusta pero aquél sí,** I do not like the latter, but I like the former
aquelarre *m*, witches' sabbath
aquello *dem pron neut* that; the fact; the matter, the affair, the former (remark, idea, etc.). e.g. **Todo a. por fin acabó,** All that came to an end at last. **a. de,** the fact that
aquende *adv* on this side (rarely used)

aquí *adv* here. **de a.,** hence the fact that. **¡He a.!** Behold!
aquietar *vt* to calm, soothe
aquilatar *vt* to assay; scrutinize; examine, weigh up (persons)
aquistar *vt* to attain, acquire
ara *f,* altar; **en aras de,** in honor of; for the sake of
árabe *a* Arab, Arabic. *mf* Arab. *m,* Arabic (language)
arabesco *a* Arabic. *m, art* arabesque
Arabia Saudita Saudi Arabia
arábigo *a* Arabic. *m,* Arabic (language)
arácnido *m, zool* arachnid
arado *m,* plow
arador *a* plowing. *m,* plowman. **a. de la sarna,** *ent* scabies mite
aragonés (-esa) *a* and *n* Aragonese
araguato *m, Lat. Am.* howler monkey
arahuaco *a* and *n* Arawak, Arawakian
arancel *m,* tariff, duty, tax
arancelar to charge tuition for (e.g. **a. la universidad,** charge tuition for college studies)
arancelario *a* tariff, tax; customs
arándano *m, bot* bilberry
arandela *f,* candle-dripper; *mech* washer; wall candelabrum
araña *f,* spider; chandelier; *Lat. Am.* whore
arañacielos *m,* skyscraper
arañar *vt* to scratch; *inf* scrape together, hoard
arañazo *m,* scratch
arar *vt* to plough. **a. en el mar,** to labor in vain
arbitrador (-ra) *n* arbitrator
arbitraje *m,* arbitration; arbitrament, decision
arbitrar *vt* to judge freely; *law* arbitrate, mediate; devise; invent; marshal (money, resources, etc.); draft (a law) *vr* make shift, contrive
arbitrariedad *f,* arbitrariness
arbitrario *a* arbitral, mediatory; arbitrary, capricious
arbitrio *m,* free will; arbitration; means, way; discretion; arbitrament, judgment; *pl* rates, municipal taxes
árbitro (-ra) *a* arbitrary. *n* arbiter. *m, sport* umpire; referee
árbol *m,* tree; *mech* shaft; *naut* mast; axis of a winding stair. **a. de amor** *or* **a. de Judas,** Judas tree. **a. de la ciencia (del bien y del mal),** Tree of Knowledge (of good and evil). **a. de levas,** *mech* camshaft. **a. del pan,** breadfruit tree. *naut* **a. mayor,** mainmast. **a. motor** *mech,* drivingshaft
arbolado *a* tree-covered, wooded. *m,* copse, woodland
arboladura *f, naut* masts and spars
arbolar *vt* to hoist (flags); *naut* fit with masts; place upright; *vr* rear, prance (horses)
arboleda *f,* copse, grove, spinney
arbotante *m,* flying buttress
arbusto *m,* shrub, woody plant
arca *f,* chest; money-box, coffer; ark; *pl* (treasury) vaults. **a. caudal,** strong box. **a. de agua,** water-tower. **a. de la alianza.** *or* **a. del testamento,** Ark of the Covenant (Bible). **a. de Noé,** Noah's Ark; lumber box
arcabucero *m,* arquebusier; maker of arquebuses
arcabuz *m,* arquebus
arcada *f,* arcade; series of arches; *pl* sickness, nausea
árcade *a* and *mf* Arcadian
arcaico *a* archaic
arcaísmo *m,* archaism
arcángel *m,* archangel
arcano *a* secret. *m,* mystery, arcanum
arce *m, bot* maple tree
archifeliz *a* extremely happy, in bliss
archimillonario (-ia) *a* and *n* multimillionaire
archipiélago *m,* archipelago
Archipiélago de Colón *m,* Galapagos Islands
archivar *vt* to place in an archive; file (papers)
archivero *m,* archivist, keeper of the archives; librarian; registrar; (Mexico) file cabinet, filing cabinet
archivista *mf* archivist; file clerk, filing clerk
archivo *m,* archives
arcilla *f,* clay
arcilloso *a* clayey, like or full of clay
arcipreste *m,* archpriest
arco *m, geom* arc; *mil* bow; bow (of a stringed instrument); hoop (of casks, etc.); *arch* arch; *Lat. Am.* goal (in sports). **a. del cielo** *or* **a. de San Martín** *or* **a. iris,** rainbow. **a. voltaico,** electric arc. *mus* **para a.,** for strings
arder *vi* to burn; shine, gleam; *fig* burn (with passion, etc.); *vt* to set alight, burn
ardid *a* crafty. *m,* trick, stratagem
ardiente *a* burning; ardent, passionate; vehement; enthusiastic; flame-colored; fiery-red
ardilla *f,* squirrel; *Lat. Am.* wheeler-dealer
ardite *m,* ancient Spanish coin of little value; *fig* farthing, fig, straw. **no valer un a.,** to be not worth a straw
ardor *m,* great heat; zeal, earnestness; passion, ardor; courage
ardoroso *a* ardorous
arduo *a* arduous
área *f,* area; small plot of ground; common threshing floor; arc (surface measure)
arena *f,* sand; arena; grit, gravel. **a. movediza,** quicksand
arenal *m,* quicksand; sand pit; sandy place
arenero (-ra) *n* sand merchant. *m,* sand-box (carried by railway engines)
arenga *f,* harangue, discourse *Argentina* argument, fight, quarrel
arenilla *f,* sand (for drying writing)
arenisca *f,* sandstone
arenisco *a* sandy
arenque *m,* herring
arete *m,* earring
argamasa *f,* mortar
argayo *m,* landslide; (Asturias) **a. de nieve,** avalanche
Argel Algiers
Argelia Algeria
argelino (-na) *a* and *n* Algerian
argentado *a* silvered; silvery
argénteo *a* silver; silvery
argentífero *a* silver-yielding
argentino (-na) *a* silvery. *a* and *n* Argentinian. *m,* Argentinian gold coin
argento *m,* silver. **a. vivo,** mercury
argolla *f,* thick metal ring (for hitching, etc.); croquet (game); stocks, pillory; hoop, iron arch; *Lat. Am.* wedding ring
argonauta *m, myth* Argonaut; *zool* paper nautilus, argonaut
argucia *f,* sophism, quibble; subtlety
argüir *vt irr* to deduce, imply; prove; reveal, manifest; accuse; *vi* argue, debate; dispute, oppose. See **huir**
argumentador (-ra) *a* argumentative. *n* arguer
argumentar *vi* to argue; dispute; oppose
argumento *m,* contention, case; theme (of a book, etc.); argument, discussion
aridez *f,* aridity, dryness; drought; sterility, barrenness; dullness, lack of interest
árido *a* dry, arid; sterile, barren; uninteresting, dull
ariete *m, mil* battering ram
arisco *a* unsociable, surly; wild, shy (animals)
arista *f, bot* arista, awn, beard; pebble; edge, side
aristocracia *f,* aristocracy
aristócrata *mf* aristocrat
aristocrático *a* aristocratic
aristotélico *a* Aristotelian
aritmética *f,* arithmetic
aritmético (-ca) *a* arithmetical. *n* arithmetician
arlequín *m,* harlequin; *inf* fool, buffoon; Neapolitan ice-cream
arma *f,* weapon; *mil* arm, branch; bull's horn; *pl* troops, army; means, way; arms, coat of arms. **a. arrojadiza,** missile. **a. blanca,** steel weapon. **a. de fuego,** fire-

arm. **¡Armas al hombro!** Shoulder Arms! **armas portátiles,** small arms. *inf* **de armas tomar,** belligerent; resolute. **pasar por las armas,** *mil* to shoot. **presentar las armas,** *mil* to present arms. **ser a. de dos filos,** *fig* to cut both ways

armada *f,* navy, armada; fleet, squadron; *Argentina* lasso

armadía *f,* raft, pontoon

armador (-ra) *n* supplier, outfitter. *m,* shipowner; pirate, privateer; jacket; assembler, fitter

armadura *f,* armature, armor; frame, framework; skeleton (of a building); skeleton (of vertebrates); *phys* armature; plate armor (of persons)

armamento *m, mil* armament; arms, military equipment

armar *vt* to arm; *mech* mount; man (guns); put together, assemble; roll (a cigaret); reinforce (concrete); *inf* arrange, prepare; *inf* occasion (quarrels); *inf* outfit; *naut* equip; commission (a ship); *vr* prepare oneself, arm oneself. **a. caballero,** to knight. **a. los remos,** to ship the oars. *inf* **armarla,** to cause a row or quarrel

armario *m,* cupboard; wardrobe. **a. de luna,** wardrobe with a mirror

armatoste *m,* unwieldy piece of furniture; *fig inf* dead weight, clumsy person; snare

armazón *f,* frame, framework; ship's hulk. *m, anat* skeleton

armenio (-ia) *a* and *n* Armenian. *m,* Armenian language

armería *f,* armory; heraldry; gunsmith's craft or shop

armero *m,* gunsmith, armorer; stand for weapons. **a. mayor,** Royal Armorer

armiño *m,* ermine

armisticio *m,* armistice

armón de artillería *m,* gun-carriage

armonía *f,* harmony; friendship, concord; *mus* harmony

armónica (de boca) *f,* mouth-organ

armónico *a* harmonious. *a* and *m, mus* harmonic

armonio *m,* harmonium

armonioso *a* harmonious

armonización *f, mus* harmonization

armonizar *vt* to bring into harmony; *mus* harmonize

arnero *m, Lat. Am.* sieve

arnés *m,* armor; harness; *pl* horse trappings; *inf* equipment, tools

aro *m,* hoop; rim (of wheel, etc.); napkin-ring; croquet hoop; *bot* wild arum; child's hoop; *Lat. Am.* earring **a. de empaquetadura,** *mech* gasket

aroma *m,* aroma, fragrance; balsam; sweet-smelling herb

aromático *a* aromatic

arpa *f,* harp. **a. eolia,** Eolian harp

arpar *vt* to scratch, claw; tear, rend

arpegio *m, mus* arpeggio

arpía *f,* harpy

arpicordio *m,* harpsichord

arpista *mf* harpist, harp player

arpón *m,* harpoon

arponear *vt* to harpoon

arponero *m,* harpooner; harpoon maker

arquear *vt* to arch; bend; beat (wool); gauge (ship's capacity); *vi* retch

arqueo *m,* arching; bending, curving; *naut* tonnage; gauging (of ship's capacity); *com* examination of deposits and contents of safe

arqueología *f,* archeology

arqueológico *a* archeological

arqueólogo *m,* archeologist

arquero *m, com* cashier, treasurer; *mil* archer

arquitecto *m,* architect. **a. de jardines,** landscape gardener

arquitectura *f,* architecture

arquitrabe *m,* architrave

arrabal *m,* suburb, district; *pl* outskirts

arracada *f,* pendant-earring

arracimarse *vr* to cluster; group

arraigadamente *adv* deeply, firmly

arraigado *a* deep-rooted; firm; convinced

arraigar *vi* to take root; *vi* and *vr fig* become established, take hold; *vr* settle; take up residence

arraigo *m,* rooting; settlement, establishment; landed property

arrancaclavos *m,* nail-puller

arrancadero *m, sport* starting-point

arrancar *vt* to uproot; pull out; wrench; tear off; extirpate; obtain by threats; clear one's throat; *vt* and *vi naut* put on speed; *vi* start (a race); *inf* leave, quit; derive, originate **¡Arrancan!** And they're off! (races)

arrancarse *vr, Lat. Am.* to kick the bucket, pop off

arranque *m,* uprooting; extirpation; wrenching, pulling, seizing; stimulus (of passion); sudden impulse; *mech* start; *mech* starter. **a. automático,** self-starter

arras *f pl,* dowry; coins given by bridegroom to his bride; earnest money, token

arrasamiento *m,* demolition, destruction; leveling

arrasar *vt* to demolish, destroy; level; fill to the brim; *vi* and *vr* clear up (sky). **ojos arrasados de lágrimas,** eyes brimming with tears

arrastrado *a inf* poverty-stricken, wretched; *inf* knavish; unhappy, unfortunate

arrastrar *vt* to drag; trail; convince; haul; *vi* trail along or touch the ground; trump (at cards); *vr* crawl, creep; shuffle along; humble oneself

arrastre *m,* dragging, trailing; haulage; trumping (at cards); *Central America, Mexico,* clout, pull

¡arre! *interj* Gee up! Get along!

arrear *vt* to spur on, whip up (horses, etc.). *interj inf* **¡Arrea!** Hurry up! Get on!

arrebañar *vt* to pick clean, clear; eat or drink up

arrebatado *a* precipitate, headlong; rash; flushed, red

arrebatador *a* overwhelming; violent; bewitching, captivating; delightful

arrebatamiento *m,* abduction; seizure; fury; ecstasy

arrebatar *vt* to abduct, carry off; seize, grab; attract, charm; grip (the attention); *vr* be overcome with rage

arrebatiña *f,* grab; scuffle, scrimmage

arrebato *m,* fit (gen. of anger); ecstasy, rapture

arrebozar *vt* to muffle; envelop

arrebujarse *vr* to huddle; wrap oneself up

arrechucho *m, inf* fit of rage; sudden slight ailment

arreciar *vi* to increase in intensity; *vr* grow strong

arrecife *m,* reef (in the sea); stone-paved road

arredrar *vt* to separate, remove; force back, repel; terrify

arregazar(se) *vt* and *vr* to tuck up one's skirts

arreglado *a* regular; regulated; ordered; methodical

arreglar *vt* to regulate; arrange; adjust, put right; tidy; make up (the face); *vr* (*with prep a*) conform to; (*with con*) reach an agreement with. **Me voy a a.,** I am going to make myself presentable. *inf* **arreglárselas,** to shift for oneself

arreglo *m,* arrangement; rule; regulation; method, order; agreement; adjustment; compromise

arrellanarse *vr* to settle comfortably in one's chair; be happy in one's work

arremangar *vt* to roll up (sleeves, trousers, etc.); *vr inf* make a decision

arremango *m,* rolling or tucking up (of sleeve, etc.)

arremetedor (-ra) *n* attacker, assailant

arremeter *vt* to attack, assail; *vi* launch oneself (at); *fig* spoil the view, shock the eye

arremetida *f,* attack, assault

arremolinarse *vr* to crowd, cluster, group

arrendador (-ra) *n* landlord; renter; hirer; tenant

arrendamiento *m,* letting, renting; hiring; rental; agreement, lease

arrendar *vt irr* to let, lease; hire; rent (as a tenant); train (horses); tie up (horses); restrain; mimic, imitate. See **recomendar**

arrendatario (-ia) *a* rent, lease. *n* tenant; lessee; hirer. **a. de contribuciones,** tax farmer

arreo *m,* ornament; apparel; *pl* horse trappings; appurtenances, equipment
¡Arrepa! But look!, Hold on!, Hold your horses!, Not so fast!
arrepentimiento *m,* repentance
arrepentirse *vr irr* to repent. See **sentir**
arrestado *a* courageous, audacious, bold
arrestar *vt* to arrest, detain; *vr* be bold, dare
arresto *m,* arrest; detention; imprisonment; audacity, boldness
arriada *f,* lowering (of a boat); taking in (of sail)
arriar *vt naut* to strike (colors); take in (sail); pay out (ropes, etc.); lower (boats); flood, inundate
arriate *m,* garden border; avenue, walk; trellis (for plants)
arriba *adv* up, above; overhead; upstairs; earlier, before; upwards (with prices). *interj* **¡A.!** Up with!; Long live! **de a. abajo,** from head to foot, from one end to the other; completely, wholly
arribada *f, naut* arrival. **de a.,** emergency (port)
arribar *vi naut* to arrive; put into an emergency port; reach, arrive at; *inf* convalesce; attain; *naut* drift
arribista *mf* social climber
arriero *m,* farrier; muleteer
arriesgado *a* dangerous, risky; rash, daring
arriesgar *vt* to risk; *vr* run into danger; dare, risk
arrimado *m, Mexico* parasite
arrimar *vt* to bring or draw near; abandon (professions, etc.); lay aside, discard; *inf* administer (blows); *naut* stow (cargo); *vr* (*with prep a*) lean against, rest on; join, go with; seek the protection of. **Cada cual se arrima a su cada cual,** Birds of a feather flock together
arrimo *m,* bringing or placing near; leaning or resting against; abandonment, giving up; protection; staff, support
arrinconado *a* remote, secluded; forgotten, neglected
arrinconar *vt* to discard, lay aside; corner, besiege; set aside, dismiss; forsake; *vr* go into retirement, withdraw
arriscado *a* craggy, rugged; bold, resolute; sprightly, handsome
arriscarse *vr Lat. Am.* to dress to kill, dress to the nines
arro, arro, arro purrrr (echoic of a cat's purr)
arrobamiento *m,* ecstasy, rapture; trance
arrobar *vt* to charm, entrance; *vr* be enraptured; be in ecstasy
arrodillar *vt* to cause to kneel down; *vi* and *vr* kneel down
arrogancia *f,* arrogance; courage; majesty, pride
arrogante *a* arrogant, haughty; courageous; proud, majestic
arrogar *vt* to adopt (as a son); *vr* usurp, appropriate
arrojadizo *a* easily cast or hurled; projectile
arrojado *a* bold, determined; rash
arrojar *vt* to throw, hurl, cast; shed (light, etc.; e.g. **La cuenta arroja un total de cien dólares,** The bill shows a total of a hundred dollars); *com* show (a balance, etc.); put out (sprouts); dismiss, send away; *vr* cast oneself; (*with prep a*) hurl oneself against or upon; undertake, venture upon. **a. de sí (a),** to get rid of, dismiss
arrojo *m,* daring, intrepidity; boldness
arrollar *vt* to roll; make into a roll, roll up; defeat (the enemy); silence, confound; rock to sleep; bear along, carry off
arromar *vt* to blunt; flatten
arropar *vt* to wrap up, cover
arrostrar *vt* to confront, defy, face up to; *vr* fight hand to hand. **a. las consecuencias,** *fig* to face the music
arroyada *f,* gorge, gully; course, channel; flood
arroyo *m,* stream, brook; street gutter; road, street; *fig* flood, plenty
arroz *m,* rice
arrozal *m,* rice field
arruga *f,* wrinkle; fold, pleat; crease
arrugamiento *m,* wrinkling; fold, pleating; crumpling, creasing; corrugation
arrugar *vt* to wrinkle; pleat; corrugate; crumple, crease. **a. el ceño,** to knit one's brow, scowl
arruinamiento *m,* ruin, decay, decline
arruinar *vt* to ruin; destroy, damage severely
arrullar *vt* to bill and coo (doves); lull to sleep; *inf* whisper sweet words to, make love to
arrullo *m,* cooing of doves; lullaby
arrumaco *m, inf* embrace, caress (gen. *pl*); ornament in bad taste
arrumaje *m, naut* stowage; clouds on the horizon
arrurruz *m,* arrowroot
arsenal *m,* dockyard; arsenal; *fig* store (of information, etc.)
arsénico *m,* arsenic
arte *mf,* art; skill; ability, talent; guile, craftiness. **las bellas artes,** fine arts. *inf* **no tener a. ni parte en,** to have nothing to do with, have no part in
artefacto *m,* machine, mechanism, apparatus; device, appliance. **a. atómico,** atomic bomb
arteria *f, med* artery; main line (of communication)
artería *f,* craftiness, guile
arterial *a* arterial
artesa *f,* wooden trough; kneading bowl
artesano (-na) *n* artisan; mechanic
artesiano *a* artesian
artesón *m,* bucket, pail; *arch* curved ceiling-panel; paneled ceiling
artesonado *a arch* paneled (ceiling). *m,* paneled ceiling
ártico *a* Arctic
articulación *f,* joint, articulation; jointing; enunciation, pronunciation
articular *vt* to joint, articulate; enunciate, pronounce clearly
articulista *mf* article writer
artículo *m,* finger knuckle; heading; article; *anat* joint; *gram* article; *pl* goods, things. **a. de fondo,** leading article (in a newspaper). **a. de primera necesidad,** prime necessity, essential
artífice *mf* craftsman, artificer; author, creator; forger
artificial *a* artificial
artificio *m,* skill, art; appliance, contraption, mechanism; trick, cunning device; guile, craftiness
artificioso *a* skilful; artificial; crafty, cunning
artillería *f,* artillery. **a. de costa,** coastal guns. **a. ligera, a. montada, a. rodada** *or* **a. volante,** field artillery
artillero *m,* gunner
artimaña *f,* trick, ruse, stratagem
artista *mf* artist; performer
artístico *a* artistic
artrítico *a med* arthritic
artritis *f, med* arthritis
arveja *f, bot* vetch; *Lat. Am.* pea
arzobispo *m,* archbishop
as *m,* Roman copper coin; ace (*aer* cards, etc.)
asa *f,* handle; pretext, excuse
asadero *m, Mexico* cottage cheese
asado *m, cul* roast
asador *m, cul* roasting-spit; roaster
asadura *f, cul* chitterlings; offal
asalariar *vt* to fix a salary for
asaltador (-ra) *a* attacking. *n* assailant, attacker
asaltar *vt* to storm, besiege; assault, attack; occur to (ideas); come on suddenly (illness)
asalto *m,* storming, besieging; assault, attack; bout (in fencing, boxing, wrestling); round (in a fight)
asamblea *f,* congregation, assembly; meeting; legislative assembly; *mil* assembly (bugle call)
asambleísta *mf* member of an assembly
asar *vt cul* to roast; grill; *vr* be burning-hot; *fig* burn (with enthusiasm)
asaz *adv* sufficiently, enough; very; in abundance. *a* sufficient; many
asbesto *m,* asbestos
ascalonia *f, bot* shallot
ascendencia *f,* lineage, ancestry, origin
ascendente *a* ascending

ascender *vi irr* to ascend, climb; be promoted; (*with prep a*) amount to (bills, etc.); *vt* promote. See **entender**
ascendiente *mf* ancestor, forbear. *m*, influence, ascendancy
ascensión *f*, ascension; promotion; *ast* exaltation
ascenso *m*, ascent; promotion, preferment
ascensor *m*, lift, elevator
ascensorista *mf* elevator operator
asceta *mf* ascetic
ascético *a* ascetic
ascetismo *m*, asceticism
asco *m*, nausea; repugnance, loathing; revolting thing. *inf* **Me da a.,** It sickens me
ascua *f*, live coal, ember. **estar como una a. de oro,** to be as bright as a new pin. **estar en ascuas,** *fig* to be on pins
aseado *a* clean, tidy
asear *vt* to tidy, make neat; clean up; decorate, adorn
asechanza *f*, ambush; trick, snare, stratagem
asechar *vt* to ambush, waylay; *fig* lay snares for
asediador (-ra) *n* besieger
asediar *vt* to besiege; pester, importune
asedio *m*, siege; importunity
asegurado (-da) *a* insured. *n* insured person
asegurador (-ra) *a* insuring. *n* insurer
asegurar *vt* to fasten, make secure; pinion, grip; reassure, soothe; assert, state; *com* insure; guarantee; ensure, secure; *vr com* insure oneself; (*with de*) make sure of
asemejar *vt* to imitate, copy; make similar to; *vr* (*with prep a*) be like, be similar to
asenderear *vt* to make a pathway through; persecute, harass
asenso *m*, assent. **dar a.,** to believe, give credence (to)
asentaderas *f pl*, *inf* buttocks, seat
asentado *a* prudent, circumspect; permanent, stable
asentamiento *m*, seating; settlement, residence; prudence, judgment
asentar *vt irr* to seat; place; fasten, fix; found; plant (flags); pitch (a tent); establish, make firm; smooth; hone (razors); estimate, budget, arrange, set forth; note down; affirm, believe; *com* enter (in an account); *vi* fit (clothes); *vr* seat oneself; alight (birds); settle (liquids); *arch* settle, subside; to be located (e.g. **El edificio se asienta en una esquina,** The building is located on a corner). **a. la mano en,** to strike hard. See **acertar**
asentimiento *m*, assent; consent, approval
asentir *vi irr* to assent, agree; (*with en*) consent to. See **sentir**
aseñorado *a* refined, gentlemanly; ladylike; presumptuous
aseo *m*, cleanliness, neatness
asepsia *f*, asepsis
asequible *a* attainable; obtainable
aserción *f*, assertion
aserradero *m*, sawmill; saw-pit
aserrador (-ra) *n* sawyer
aserrar *vt irr* to saw. See **acertar**
aserrín *m*, sawdust
aserruchar *vt*, *Lat. Am.* to saw
asertivo *a* assertive
aserto *m*, assertion
asesinar *vt* to assassinate, murder
asesinato *m*, assassination, murder
asesino *mf* assassin, murderer; murderess
asesor (-ra) *n* assessor
asesorar *vt* to give advice; *vr* take legal advice; seek advice
asestar *vt* to aim (firearms); fire; deal (a blow)
aseveración *f*, assertion, statement
aseveradamente *adv* affirmatively
aseverar *vt* to affirm, assert
asfaltado *m*, asphalting; asphalt pavement
asfaltar *vt* to asphalt
asfalto *m*, asphalt
asfixia *f*, *med* asphyxia
asfixiante *a* asphyxiating
asfixiar *vt* to asphyxiate
así *adv* thus, so, in this way; like this (e.g. **en días a.,** on days like this); even if; so that, therefore. **a. a.,** middling, so-so. **a. como a.,** as well as; as soon as. **a. las cosas,** that being the case, **a. que,** as soon as, immediately; consequently, thus
asiático (-ca) *a* and *n* Asiatic
asidero *m*, hold, grasp; handle, haft; pretext, excuse
asido a wedded to (e.g. a belief)
asiduo *a* assiduous
asiento *m*, seat; place, position; site; base (of a vase, etc.); lees, sediment; indigestion; *arch* subsidence, settling; treaty, pact; contract; note, reminder; *com* entry; permanence, stability; prudence; bit (of a bridle); *pl* buttocks, seat. **estar de a.,** to be established (in a place)
asignación *f*, assignation; appropriation (of money); salary; portion, share
asignar *vt* to assign; apportion; destine, intend; appoint
asignatario, -a *mf Lat. Am.* heir, heiress, legatee
asignatura *f*, subject (of study in schools, etc.)
asilar *vt* to give shelter to, receive; put into an institution
asilo *m*, shelter, refuge; sanctuary, asylum; *fig* protection, defence; home, institution
asimetría *f*, asymmetry
asimétrico *a* asymmetrical
asimiento *m*, hold, grasp; attachment, affection
asimilación *f*, assimilation
asimilar *vt* to compare, liken; (*bot zool gram*) assimilate; *vi* resemble, be like; *fig* assimilate, digest (ideas)
asimismo *adv* similarly, likewise
asir *vt irr* to grasp, take hold of; seize; *vi* take root (plants); *vr* (*with de*) lay hold of; take advantage of; make an excuse to. *Pres. Ind.* **asgo, ases,** etc. *Pres. Subjunc.* **asga,** etc.
asirio (-ia) *a* and *n* Assyrian. *m*, Assyrian language
asistencia *f*, presence, attendance; minimal attendance required (e.g. **Los alumnos tienen que completar una a.,** Pupils must attend a certain number of classes) assistance, help; service, attendance; medical treatment; remuneration; *pl* allowance. **a. pública,** Public Assistance. **a. social,** social work
asistenta *f*, daily maid; waiting-maid
asistente *m*, assistant; *mil* orderly
asistir *vt* to accompany; assist, help; attend, treat; (*with de*) act as; *vi* (*with prep a*) be present at, attend; follow suit (in cards)
asma *f*, asthma
asmático (-ca) *a* asthmatic. *n* asthma sufferer
asnal *a* asinine; brutish, stupid
asno *m*, ass
asociación *f*, association; company, partnership; society, fellowship
asociado (-da) *n* associate; member; partner
asociar *vt* to associate; *vr* associate oneself; join together; form a partnership
asolación, *f*. **asolamiento** *m*, destruction, ruin
asolar *vt irr* to destroy, devastate, lay flat; *vr* wither; settle (liquids). See **contar**
asoldar *vt irr* to employ, engage, hire. See **contar**
asolear *vt* to expose to the sun; *vr* sun oneself; become sunburnt
asomada *f*, brief appearance; vantage point
asomar *vt* to show, allow to appear, put forth; *vi* begin to show; *vr* show oneself, appear; *inf* be flushed (with wine); (*with prep a, por*) look out of. **asomarse a la ventana,** to show oneself at, or look out of, the window
asombrar *vt* to shade, shadow; darken (a color); terrify; amaze
asombro *m*, fright, terror; amazement; wonder, marvel
asombroso *a* amazing; marvellous, wonderful
asonancia *f*, assonance; congruity, harmony

asordar *vt* to deafen
asorocharse *vr, Peru* to come down with altitude sickness, get altitude sickness
aspa *f,* cross; sail of a windmill
aspaviento *m,* exaggerated display of emotion; gesture (of horror, etc.); **hacer aspavientos,** to make a fuss
aspecto *m,* look, appearance; aspect, outlook
aspereza *f,* roughness, harshness; ruggedness, rockiness; severity, asperity
áspero *a* rough, harsh; uneven, rocky; jarring, grating; hard, severe
aspersión *f, ecc* aspersion; sprinkling
áspid *m,* asp, viper
aspiración *f,* breath; breathing; aspiration, desire; *mus* pause
aspirador (de polvo) *m,* vacuum cleaner
aspirante *m,* aspirant, novice; office-seeker; applicant
aspirar *vt* to breathe in, inhale; *gram* aspirate; (*with prep a*) aspire to, desire
aspirina *f,* aspirin
asquear *vi* and *vt* to hate, loathe
asquerosidad *f,* filthiness, loathsomeness; vileness, hatefulness
asqueroso *a* nauseating; loathsome, revolting; vile, hateful
asta *f,* lance, spear, pike; horn (of bull); antler; flagstaff; shaft. **a media a.,** at half-mast
asterisco *m,* asterisk
astigmático *a* astigmatic
astigmatismo *m,* astigmatism
astil *m,* handle, pole, shaft; bar of a balance; beam feather
astilla *f,* splinter
astillar *vt* to splinter, chip
astillero *m,* shipyard; rack for lances and pikes
astilloso *a* splintery, fragile
astracán *m,* astrakhan
astringente *a* astringent
astringir *vt* to tighten up; compress; constrain
astro *m,* heavenly body
astrolatría *f,* astrolatry, star worship
astrología *f,* astrology
astrológico *a* astrological
astrólogo (-ga) *n* astrologist
astronauta *m,* astronaut
astronomía *f,* astronomy
astronómico *a* astronomical
astrónomo *m,* astronomer
astucia *f,* astuteness, guile, craftiness
asturiano (-na) *a* and *n* Asturian
astuto *a* guileful, crafty, astute
asueto *m,* day's holiday
asumir *vt* to assume; adopt, appropriate
asunción *f,* assumption
asunto *m,* matter, theme, subject; business, affair
asustadizo *a* timid, nervous, easily frightened
asustar *vt* to frighten; **que asusta,** terribly (e.g. **Es de una ñoñería que asusta,** It's a terribly timid thing to do) *vr* be frightened
atablar *vt* to roll, flatten (earth)
atacado *a inf* hesitant; mean, stingy
atacador (-ra) *a* attacking. *n* aggressor, attacker
atacar *vt* to attack; fasten, button; fit (clothes); ram (guns); *fig* press hard, corner (persons). **a. a los nervios,** to jar on the nerves
ataché *m. Central America* (paper) clip
atadero *m,* rope, tie, cord; hook, ring, etc. (for hitching); hindrance, impediment; hitching or fastening point
atado *m,* bundle, roll
atadura *f,* tying, stringing, fastening, tie; knot; connection
atajar *vi* to take a short cut; *vt* intercept, cut off; screen off, divide; impede, stop; interrupt (people); **atajarle la palabra a uno,** to cut somebody off, interrupt *vr* be overcome (by fear, shame, etc.)
atajo *m,* short cut, quick way; cutting, abbreviation; division. *inf* **echar por el a.,** to go to the root of (a matter)
atalaya *f,* look out, watch tower; observation point. *m,* lookout
atalayar *vt* to scan, watch; spy upon
atalón *m,* atoll, coral island
atañadero: en lo atañadero a with regard to, with respect to
atañer *vi impers* to concern, affect; belong, pertain
ataque *m,* (*mil med*) attack; quarrel, fight
atar *vt* to tie; fasten; lace; stop, paralyse; *vr* get in a fix; confine oneself. **a. cabos,** to put two and two together
atardecer *vi irr impers* to grow dusk. See **conocer**
atardecer *m,* dusk, evening
atarear *vt* to set to work, assign work to; *vr* work hard
atarugar *vt* to wedge; stop up; plug; block; *inf* silence, shut up; stuff, cram; *vr fig inf* lose one's head
atasajar *vt* to cut up, jerk (beef, etc.)
atascadero *m,* deep rut, boggy place; impediment, obstacle
atascar *vt* to plug; block up; stop (a leak); hinder, obstruct; *vr* stick in the mud; be held up or delayed; *inf* get stuck in a speech
atasco *m,* obstruction, block
ataúd *m,* coffin
ataviar *vt* to deck, apparel, adorn
atavío *m,* get-up, dress, apparel; *pl* ornaments
atavismo *m,* atavism
ate *m, Mexico* kind of Turkish delight
ateísmo *m,* atheism
atejonarse *vr Mexico* to hide
atelaje *m,* team, yoke (of horses); trappings, harness; *inf* trousseau
atemperación *f,* moderation, mitigation; tempering
atemperar *vt* to moderate, mitigate; adapt, adjust; temper, cool. **atemperarse a la realidad,** to adjust to reality
Atenas Athens
atenazar *vt* to grip, grasp; torture
atención *f,* attention; solicitude, kindness; courtesy, civility; *pl* business affairs. *interj* **¡A.!** Take care! Look out!; *mil* Attention! **en a.** (**a**), taking into consideration. **estar en a.,** (patient) to be under treatment
atender *vt irr* to await, expect; take care of, look after; *vi* (*with prep a*) attend to, listen to; *vi* remember. See **entender**
ateneo *m,* atheneum. *a* Athenian
atenerse *vr irr* (*with prep a*) to abide by; resort to, rely on. See **tener**
ateniense *a* and *mf* Athenian
atentado *a* prudent, sensible; secret, silent. *m,* infringement, violation; attempt (on a person's life); crime
atentar *vt irr* to do illegally; attempt a crime; *vr* proceed cautiously; restrain oneself. See **acertar**
atento *a* attentive; courteous, civil. *adv* taking into consideration. **su atenta** (**atta**), *com* your favor
atenuación *f,* attenuation, diminution
atenuante *a* attenuating; extenuating (of circumstances)
atenuar *vt* to attenuate, diminish; extenuate
ateo (-ea) *a* atheistic. *n* atheist
aterirse *vr defective* to grow stiff with cold
aterrador *a* terrifying, dreadful
aterraje *m,* (*aer, naut*) landing
aterramiento *m,* horror, terror; terrorization; *naut* landing; ruin, demolition
aterrar *vt irr* to demolish; discourage; cover with earth; *vi* land; *vr naut* draw near to land. See **acertar**
aterrizaje *m, aer* landing. **a. forzoso,** forced landing. **campo de a.,** landing field
aterrizar *vi aer* to land, touch down
aterrorizar *vt* to terrify; terrorize
atesar *vt Lat. Am.* to tighten (up)
atesorar *vt* to hoard, treasure up
atestación *f,* attestation, affidavit

atestar *vt irr* to stuff, cram; insert; *inf* stuff with food; crowd, fill with people. See **acertar**
atestar *vt* to attest, testify
atestiguación *f*, deposition, testimony
atestiguar *vt* to testify, attest
atetar *vt* to suckle; *vi* suck
atezado *a* bronzed, sunburnt; black
ático *a* Attic; *m*, penthouse
atiesar *vt* to stiffen
atildar *vt* to place a tilde over; blame, criticize; decorate, ornament
atimia *f*, loss of status
atinado *a* pertinent, relevant
atinar *vi* to find by touch; discover by chance; guess; hit the mark
atinente a . . . concerning . . .
atingencia *f*, *Lat. Am.* connection, relationship
atingir *vt*, *Lat. Am.* to concern, relate to
atisbadura *f*, watching, spying, prying
atisbar *vt* to spy upon, watch
atisbo *m*, prying, watching; suspicion, hint
atisbón *a* penetrating (mind, vision)
atizador *m*, poker (for the fire)
atizar *vt* to poke (the fire); dowse, snuff; trim (lamps); excite, rouse; *inf* slap, wallop
atlántico *a* Atlantic. *m*, Atlantic Ocean
atleta *m*, athlete
atlético *a* athletic
atletismo *m*, athletics
atmósfera *f*, atmosphere
atmosférico *a* atmospheric
atolladero *m*, rut; mud; bog
atolón *m*, atoll, coral island
atolondrado *a* scatter-brained, flighty
atolondramiento *m*, rashness, recklessness; bewilderment
atolondrar *vt* to bewilder, confuse
atómico *a* atomic
átomo *m*, atom; speck, particle
atónito *a* amazed, astounded
atontar *vt* to confuse, daze; make stupid; stun
atormentador (-ra) *a* torturing. *n* tormentor; torturer
atormentar *vt* to torment; torture; grieve, harass
atorrante *a* and *mf* (Argentina) good-for-nothing
atracadero *m*, jetty, landingstage
atracar *vt inf* to stuff with food; *naut* tie up, moor; hold up, rob; *vi naut* moor, stop; *vr inf* guzzle, gorge
atracción *f*, attraction
atraco (a) *m*, hold up (of), ambush (of)
atracón *m*, *inf* gorge, fill; surfeit. **darse atracones de,** to gorge oneself on
atractivo *a* attractive. *m*, attraction, charm
atractriz *a* attracting; *f*, force of attraction; (fig.) lure
atraer *vt irr* to attract; charm, enchant. See **traer**
atragantarse *vr* to choke; *inf* be at a loss, dry up (in conversation)
atraíble *a* attractable, able to be attracted
atrancar *vt* to bar the door; obstruct, block; hinder; *vi inf* stride; skip (in reading)
atrapar *vt inf* grab, seize, catch; net, obtain; deceive
atrás *adv* behind, back; past; previously. **¡A.!** Back! **años a.,** years ago
atrasado *a* slow (of clocks); backward; old-fashioned; hard-up, poor. **a. mental,** retarded person
atrasar *vt* to delay, retard; fix a later date than the true one; put back (clocks). *vi* be slow (clocks); *vr* be late; be left behind
atraso *m*, delay; backwardness, dullness; slowness (clocks); lateness; *pl* arrears. **El reloj lleva cinco minutos de a.,** The watch is five minutes slow
atravesado *a* slightly squint-eyed; mongrel, crossbreed; half-caste; ill-intentioned
atravesar *vt irr* to lay across, put athwart; cross, traverse; pierce; obstruct; *naut* lie to; *vr* be among, mingle (with); interrupt; interfere, take part; quarrel; occur, arise. See **confesar**
atrayente *a* attractive
atreverse *vr* to dare, risk, venture; be overbold or insolvent
atrevido *a* bold, audacious; hazardous, dangerous; brazen, impudent
atribuible *a* attributable
atribución *f*, attribution; perquisite, attribute
atribuir *vt irr* to impute, attribute; assign, turn over to; *vr* take upon oneself, assume. See **huir**
atributo *m*, attribute, quality
atril *m*, lectern, reading desk; music stand
atrincherar *vt* to protect with entrenchments; *vr* entrench oneself
atrio *m*, atrium; hall, vestibule; *arch* parvis
atrocidad *f*, atrocity, cruelty; *inf* terrific amount; enormity, crime
atrofia *f*, atrophy
atrofiarse *vr* to atrophy
atrojarse *vr Mexico* to be stumped, be stuck (for an answer)
atronado *a* harebrained, foolish
atronar *vt irr* to deafen, stun with noise; confuse, daze. See **tronar**
atropelladamente *adv* in disorder, helter-skelter
atropellado *a* rash, foolhardy
atropellar *vt* to trample upon; thrust out of the way; knock down; disregard, violate (feelings); insult, abuse; transgress; do hastily; *vr* act rashly
atropello *m*, trampling; road accident; knocking over; upsetting; violation; outrage
atroz *a* atrocious, savage; monstrous, outrageous; *inf* terrific, enormous
atufar *vt* to irritate, vex; *vr* grow irritated; turn sour (wine, etc.)
atún *m*, tunny fish
aturdido *a* reckless, scatterbrained, silly; thoughtless; stunned
aturdimiento *m*, daze; confusion, bewilderment
aturdir *vt* to daze; confuse, bewilder; amaze; stun
atusar *vt* to trim (hair, beard); *agr* prune; smooth down (hair); *vr* dress over-carefully
audacia *f*, audacity
audaz *a* audacious, daring
audibilidad *f*, audibility
audición *f*, audition
audiencia *f*, audience, hearing; *law* audience; audience chamber
audífono *m*, hearing aid
audioteca *f*, audio library
auditor *m*, magistrate, judge
auditorio *a* auditory. *m*, audience
auge *m*, *fig* zenith, height; *ast* apogee
augusto *a* august, awesome
aula *f*, lecture or class room; *poet* palace
aullar *vi* to howl; bay
aullido *m*, howl; baying
aumentar(se) *vt vi vr* to increase, augment
aumentativo *a gram* augmentative
aumento *m*, increase; progress; enlargement; *Mexico* postscript **ir en a.,** to increase; advance, progress; prosper
aun *adv* even. **A. los que viven lejos han de oíros,** Even those who live far must hear you. **a. así** *or* **a. siendo así,** even so. **a. ayer,** only yesterday. **a. cuando,** even if. **más a.,** even more. **ni a. si,** not even if.
aún *adv* still, yet. **A. no te creen** *or* **No te creen a.,** They still don't believe you **¿A. se lo darás?** *or* **¿Se lo darás a.?** Will you still give it to her?
aunque *conjunc* although, even if, even though. It takes the Indicative referring to statement of fact and Subjunctive referring to a hypothesis, e.g. **A. vino, no lo hizo,** Although he came, he did not do it. **A. él cantase yo no iría allí,** Even though he sang (were to sing), I should not go there

aura *f,* zephyr, gentle breeze; popularity, approbation; aura. **a. epiléptica,** *med* epileptic aura
áureo *a* gold, gilt; golden
auricular *a* auricular. *m,* little finger; receiver, ear-piece (of a telephone); earphone (radio)
aurífero *a* gold-yielding, auriferous
auriga *m,* charioteer
aurora *f,* dawn; genesis, beginnings. **a. boreal,** aurora borealis, Northern Lights
auscultación *f, med* auscultation
auscultar *vt med* to auscultate
ausencia *f,* absence. **en ausencia de,** in the absence of
ausentar *vt* to send away; *vr* absent oneself
ausente *a* absent. *mf* absent person
auspicio *m,* augury, prediction; favor, patronage; *pl* auspices
austeridad *f,* austerity; mortification of the flesh
austero *a* austere, ascetic; severe, harsh; honest, upright
austral *a* southerly, austral
australiano (-na) *a* and *n* Australian
austríaco (-ca) *a* and *n* Austrian
austrófilo *a* and *n* Austrophile
autenticación *f,* authentication
autenticar *vt* to authenticate, attest; prove genuine
autenticidad *f,* authenticity
auténtico *a* authentic
autero, -a *mf, Lat. Am.* car thief
auto *m, law* sentence, decision; *theat* one-act allegory (gen. religious); *pl* proceedings. **a. de fe,** auto-da-fé. **a. de reconocimiento,** search-warrant. **a. sacramental,** one-act religious drama on theme of mystery of the Eucharist. **hacer a. de fe de,** to burn
autobiografía *f,* autobiography
autobús *m,* motor bus, bus
autocitarse *vr* to quote from one's own works
autoclave *m,* pressure cooker
autocracia *f,* autocracy
autócrata *mf* autocrat
autocrático *a* autocratic
autocrueldad *f,* self-inflicted pain
autodescubrimiento *m,* self-discovery
autodidacto *a* autodidactic; self-educated, self-taught
autódromo *m,* speedway
autógeno *a* autogenous, self-generating
autogiro *m, aer* autogyro
autografía *f,* autography
autográfico *a* autographic, in lithographic reproduction
autógrafo *a* autographical. *m,* autograph
autoinducción *f,* self-induction
autómata *m,* automaton
automático *a* automatic. *m, sew* press stud
automatismo *m,* automatism
automejoramiento *m,* self-improvement
automóvil *m,* automobile, motor car. *a* automatic
automovilismo *m,* motoring
automovilista *mf* motorist
autonombrarse *vr* to call oneself, go by the name of
autonomía *f,* autonomy
autónomo *a* autonomous
autopista *f,* motor road
autopsia *f, med* autopsy, post-mortem
autor (-ra) *n* agent, originator; author; inventor; *law* perpetrator
autoridad *f,* authority; pomp, show
autoritario *a* authoritarian; authoritative
autorización *f,* authorization
autorizado *a* approved, authorized, responsible
autorizar *vt* to authorize; *law* attest, testify; cite, prove by reference; approve; exalt
autorretratarse *vr* to have one's portrait painted, sit for one's portrait
autorretrato *m,* self-portrait
autostopista *mf* hitchhiker (Spain)
autosugestión *f,* autosuggestion
auxiliador (-ra) *a* assistant; helpful. *n* helper, assistant
auxiliar *vt* to help, aid; attend (the dying). *m, univ* lecturer. *a* assisting
auxiliaría *f, univ* lectureship
auxilio *m,* help, aid, assistance
aval *m, com* endorsement; voucher
avalar *vt* to enhance. **avalado por la tradición,** hallowed by tradition
avalentado *a* boastful, bragging
avalorar *vt* to value, estimate; put spirit into, encourage
avance *m,* advance; advance payment; balance sheet; attack
avanzada *f, mil* advance guard
avanzado *a* advanced, progressive
avanzar *vt* to advance; promote; *vi* advance; attack; grow late (time)
avanzo *m,* balance sheet; price estimate
avaricia *f,* greed, avarice
avaricioso, avariento *a* avaricious, greedy
avaro (-ra) *a* miserly; greedy. *n* miser
avasallador *a* dominating; *fig* overwhelming; enslaving
avasallar *vt* to subdue, dominate; *vr* become a vassal; surrender, yield
ave *f,* bird. **a. de paso,** migratory bird; *fig* bird of passage. **a. de rapiña,** bird of prey. **a. fría,** *orn* plover. **ave cantora,** songbird
avecinarse *vr* to be approaching (e.g. **el año que avecina,** the coming year)
avellana *f,* hazel nut
avellano *m, bot* hazel
avemaría *f,* Hail Mary (prayer); Angelus; rosary bead. *inf* **en un a.,** in a trice
avena *f,* oats; *poet* oaten pipe. **a. loca,** wild oats
avenal *m,* oatfield
avenar *vt* to drain (land); drain off (liquids)
avenencia *f,* agreement, arrangement; transaction; conformity, harmony
avenida *f,* flood, spate; avenue; abundance; way, approach (to a place)
avenido *a* (*with bien or mal*) well *or* ill-suited
avenidor (-ra) *n* arbitrator, mediator
avenir *vt irr* to reconcile; *vi* happen (used in infinitive and third singular and plural); *vr* be reconciled; agree; compromise, give way; harmonize (things); (*with con*) get on with, agree with. See **venir**
aventador *m, agr* winnower; pitchfork
aventajado *a* outstanding, talented; advantageous. *m, mil* private who enjoys extra pay
aventajar *vt* to improve, better; promote, prefer; excel; *vr* (*with prep a*) surpass, excel. **Te aventajo en diez años,** I'm ten years older than you
aventamiento *m,* winnowing
aventar *vt irr* to fan; air, ventilate; winnow; *inf* drive away, expel; *vr* be inflated; *inf* flee; smell (bad meat). See **sentar**
aventón *m, Mexico* hitch, lift, ride
aventura *f,* adventure; chance, luck; risk, danger
aventurar *vt* to risk, hazard
aventurero (-ra) *a* adventurous; unscrupulous, intriguing; undisciplined (of troops). *n* adventurer
avergonzar *vt irr* to shame; make shy, abash; *vr* be ashamed; be shy or sheepish. *Pres. Ind.* **avergüenzo, avergüenzas, avergüenza, avergüenzan.** *Pres. Subjunc.* **avergüence, avergüences, avergüence, avergüencen**
avería *f,* aviary; damage (to merchandise); loss, harm; *elec* fault; breakdown. **a. gruesa,** general average (marine insurance)
averiarse *vr* to be damaged; deteriorate; break down
averiguable *a* examinable, investigable; discoverable
averiguación *f,* inquiry, investigation; discovery
averiguar *vt* to investigate, inquire into; discover, ascertain. **¡averígüelo Vargas!** Beats me!, Search me!
averigüetas *mf, Lat. Am.* snoopers, nosy parker
averío *m,* flock of birds
aversión *f,* aversion, repugnance

avestruz *m*, ostrich
avetado *a* veined, mottled, streaked
avezar *vt* to accustom; *vr* grow accustomed (to)
aviación *f*, aviation
aviador *m*, aviator
aviar *vt* to outfit, equip; prepare, make ready; *inf* speed up; caulk (ship). *fig inf* **estar aviado,** to be in a mess
avidez *f*, avidity, greed; longing, desire
ávido *a* avid, greedy
avieso *a* twisted, crooked; ill-natured; sinister; *m Colombia* abortion
avillanado *a* countrified; gross, vulgar; boorish
avío *m*, preparation, provision; picnic lunch; money advanced (to miners or laborers); *pl inf* equipment, tools. **avíos de pesca,** fishing tackle
avión *m*, airplane; *orn* martin or swift. **a. de bombardeo,** bomber. **a. de caza,** fighter plane. **a. de combate nocturno,** night fighter. **a. de hostigamiento,** interceptor. **a. de reacción,** jet airplane. **a. de transporte,** *aer* transport. **a. en picado,** dive-bomber. **a. taxi,** air taxi. **por a.,** by airmail «**Avión**» "Airmail"
avioneta *f*, light airplane, small airplane
avisado *a* shrewd, sensible. **mal a.,** ill-advised, imprudent
avisar *vt* to inform, acquaint; warn; advise
aviso *m*, notice, announcement; warning; advice; care, caution; attention; shrewdness, prudence. **estar sobre a.,** to be on call; be on the alert
avispa *f*, wasp
avispado *a inf* smart, clever, quick; wide-awake
avispar *vt* to goad, prick; *inf* rouse, incite; *vr* be uneasy, fret
avispero *m*, wasp's nest; swarm of wasps; *fig inf* hornet's nest
avispón *m*, hornet
avistamiento *m*, sighting, spotting (e.g. of a ship)
avistar *vt* to descry, sight, spot; *vr* **avistarse con,** to interview
avituallar *vt* to victual, supply with food
avivar *vt* to enliven; stimulate, encourage; stir (fire); trim (wicks); brighten (colors); inflame; vivify, invigorate; *vi* revive, recover
avizor *m*, watcher, spy. *a* watchful, vigilant
avizorar *vt* to watch, spy upon
avutarda *f*, bustard
axila *f*, *bot* axil; *anat* axilla, armpit
axioma *m*, axiom
axiomático *a* axiomatic
¡ay! *interj* Alas! Woe is me! *m*, complaint, sigh
ayer *adv* yesterday; a short while ago; in the past. *m*, past
ayllu *m*, *Peru* Native American commune
ayo *m*, tutor
ayote *m*, *Mexico, Central America* pumpkin
ayuda *f*, help, assistance; enema; clyster; watch dog. *m*, **a. de cámara,** valet
ayudador (-ra) *a* helping, assisting. *n* helper
ayudante *m*, assistant; teaching assistant; *mil* adjutant. **a. a cátedra,** *univ* assistant lecturer. **a. de plaza,** post adjutant
ayudar *vt* to assist; help, aid; *vr* make an effort; avail oneself of another's help
ayunador (-ra) *a* fasting. *n* faster; abstainer
ayunar *vi* to fast
ayuno *m*, fast. *a* fasting; ignorant, unaware. **en a.** *or* **en ayunas,** before breakfast, fasting; *inf* ignorant, unaware
ayuntamiento *m*, meeting, assembly; municipal government; town hall; sexual union
azabache *m*, *min* jet
azada *f*, *agr* spade; hoe
azadón *m*, *agr* hoe
azafata *f*, queen's waiting-maid *ant*; flight attendant
azafate *m*, flat basket; small tray
azafrán *m*, *bot* saffron; crocus
azafranado *a* saffron-colored
azahar *m*, flower of orange, lemon or sweet lime tree
azar *m*, chance, hazard; unexpected misfortune; losing card or throw of dice
azararse *vr* to go wrong, fail (negotiations, etc.); grow nervous; become confused; blush
azaroso *a* unlucky, ill-omened; hazardous
ázimo *a* unleavened (bread)
ázoe *m*, nitrogen
azogar *vt* to silver (mirrors, etc.); slake lime; *vr* suffer from mercury poisoning; *inf* grow uneasy, be agitated
azogue *m*, *min* mercury, quick-silver; market-place
azolve *m*, silt
azoramiento *m*, alarm, terror; confusion, stupefaction; incitement
azorar *vt* to alarm, terrify; confuse, stun, dumbfound; excite, stimulate; encourage
azotacalles *mf inf* idler, street loafer
azotaina *f*, *inf* whipping, spanking
azotamiento *m*, flogging, beating, whipping
azotar *vt* to whip, beat, flog; acourge, ravage; knock against or strike repeatedly
azotazo *m*, spank
azote *m*, whip; scourge; lash, blow with a whip; spank, slap; misfortune, disaster. *inf* **azotes y galeras,** monotonous diet
azotea *f*, flat terrace roof
azotera *f*, *Lat. Am.* beating, thrashing
azozador party whip, whip
azteca *a* and *mf* Aztec
azúcar *m*, sugar. **a. blanco** *or* **a. de flor,** white sugar. **a. de pilón,** loaf sugar. **a. moreno,** brown sugar. **a. quebrado,** brown sugar. **a. y canela,** sorrel gray (of horses)
azucarado *a* sugary; sugared, sugar-coated; *inf* honeyed, flattering
azucarar *vt* to coat with sugar; sweeten; *inf* soften, mitigate; *vr* crystallize; go sugary (jam)
azucarera *f*, sugar-basin
azucarero *a* sugar-producing (e.g. province)
azucarillo *m*, *cul* bar made of white of egg and sugar for sweetening water
azucena *f*, white lily. **a. de agua,** water-lily
azuela *f*, adze
azufre *m*, sulphur
azul *a* and *m*, blue. **a. celeste,** sky blue, azure. **a. de mar** *or* **a. marino,** navy blue. **a. de ultramar,** ultramarine. **a. turquí,** indigo
azulado *a* bluish, blue
azulear *vi* to look bluish, have a blue tint
azulejo *m*, ornamental glazed tile
azurumbado *m*, *Central America* dumb, silly, stupid; boozed up, drunk
azuzar *vt* to set on (dogs); irritate, provoke; incite, urge

B

baba *f*, saliva; secretion (of snails, etc.); viscous fluid (of plants). *inf* **caérsele (a uno) la b.,** to ooze satisfaction; be dumbfounded
babador, babero *m*, bib, feeder
babear *vi* to dribble, slaver; *fig inf* slobber over, be sloppy
babel *m*, babel
babélico *a* Babelian, Babel-like confused; unintelligible
Babia, estar en to be daydreaming
babieca *mf inf* stupid person. **Babieca** *f*, the Cid's horse
Babilonia Babylon
babilónico *a* Babylonian

bable *m*, Asturian (language)
babor *m*, *naut* larboard, port
babosa *f*, slug; young onion
baboso *a* slavering; *fig inf* "sloppy"; *inf* incompetent, useless; *Lat. Am.* dumb, stupid
babucha *f*, heelless slipper, babouche
babuino *m*, *zool* baboon
baca *f*, luggage carrier (on roof of bus, etc.)
bacalao *m*, codfish
bacanales *f pl*, Bacchanalia
bacante *f*, Bacchante
bacará *m*, baccarat (card game)
baceta *f*, pool (in card games)
bache *m*, rut (in road); pothole
bacheo *m*, repairing of streets
bachiller *mf* high-school graduate *m*, *inf* babbler. *f*. **bachillera,** *inf* blue-stocking; garrulous woman
bachillerarse *vr* to graduate as a bachelor
bachillerato *m*, baccalaureate, bachelor's degree
bacho *m*, *Peru* fib, tall tale
bacía *f*, bowl; barber's circular shaving-dish; barber's trade sign
bacilar *a* bacillary
bacilo *m*, bacillus
bacterial, bacteriano *a* bacterial
bactericida *m*, bactericide
bacteriología *f*, bacteriology
bacteriológico *a* bacteriological
bacteriólogo *m*, bacteriologist
báculo *m*, staff; walking-stick; *fig* support. **b. episcopal,** bishop's crozier
badajo *m*, clapper (of a bell); chatterbox, gossip
badana *f*, cured sheepskin, chamois leather, wash-leather; sweat band; *inf* **zurrar (a uno) la b.,** to take the hide off; insult
badén *m*, channel made by rain, furrow; conduit
badulaque *m*, *inf* good-for-nothing
bagaje *m*, *mil* baggage; beast of burden, transport animal; luggage
bagatela *f*, trifle, oddment, bagatelle
bagazo *m*, oilcake, bagasse
bagual *a WH* untamed, wild; doltish, dull. *m*, untamed horse, wild horse
bahía *f*, bay, harbor
bailable *a* dance (of music). *m*, *theat* dance number
bailador (-ra) *n* dancer
bailar *vi* to dance; spin round. **b. al son que le toca,** to adapt oneself to circumstances
bailarín *a* dancing. *m*, professional dancer. **b. de cuerda, bailarín de la cuerda floja,** tightrope dancer
bailarina *f*, ballerina
baile *m*, dance; ball; ballet. **b. de máscaras, b. de trajes,** fancy-dress ball. **b. de San Vito,** St. Vitus' dance. **b. ruso,** ballet
bailotear *vi* to jig about; dance
baja *f*, drop, diminution; fall (in price, etc.); *mil* casualty; discharge. *inf* **darse de b.,** to leave an employment
bajada *f*, descent, fall; slope, incline; hollow, depression. **b. de aguas,** roof gutter
bajalato *m*, pashalik
bajamar *f*, low tide
bajamente *adv* basely, abjectly
bajar *vi* to descend; go down; get off; drop; fall, decrease; *vt* lower, take down, bring down; let down; dismount, alight; bend, droop; drop; reduce (price); *fig* lower (voices); humiliate, humble; **b. a tierra,** to step ashore; **b. la cabeza ante,** to submit to (e.g. a judgment) *vr* alight, dismount; humble oneself
bajel *m*, *naut* galley, ship
bajeza *f*, base action; meanness; *fig* humble estate, lowliness. **b. de ánimo,** timorousness
bajío *m*, *naut* shallows, shoal; depression, hollow
bajista *mf* speculator, bear (Stock Exchange)
bajo *a* low; short, not tall; downcast; under; subordinate; pale (of colors); humble (origin); base; coarse, vulgar; cheap (price); low (sounds). *m*, depth; shoal, sand bank; *mus* bass; *pl* petticoats, skirts; horses' hoofs. *adv* beneath, below. *prep* under, beneath. **b. juramento,** upon oath. **bajo relieve,** bas relief. **en voz baja,** in a low voice. **planta baja,** ground floor. **por lo b.,** in a whisper; in secret, on the sly
bajolatino *a* Low Latin
bajón *m*, *mus* bassoon; bassoon player; *fig inf* downfall
bajonista *mf* bassoon player
bala *f*, bullet, ball; bale. **b. fría,** spent bullet. **b. luminosa,** tracer bullet. **b. perdida,** stray bullet. *inf* **como una b.,** like a shot
balacear *vt*, *Central America, Mexico* to shoot (at)
balada *f*, ballad, song
baladí *a* worthless, insignificant
baladro *m*, yell, outcry, shout
baladrón *a* braggart
baladronada *f*, bravado, bragging
balagar *m*, straw rick
balance *m*, balance; swinging, oscillation; rolling, rocking (of a ship, etc.); doubt, insecurity, *com* balance; *com* balance sheet **b. de situación** *Lat. Am.* balance sheet
balancear *vi* to swing; oscillate; vacillate, hesitate; *vt* balance; *vr* balance oneself; rock or swing oneself
balanceo *m*, balancing; rocking; swinging; rolling (of a ship, etc.)
balancín *m*, swing-bar; whipple-tree; balance beam; tight-rope dancer's pole; minting-mill; yoke (for carrying pails); *pl naut* lifts
balandra *f*, *naut* sloop, cutter
balanza *f*, balance; scale; judgment; comparison. **b. de comercio,** balance of trade. **en balanzas,** in doubt or danger, in the balance
balar *vi* to bleat (sheep)
balasto *m*, *rw* ballast
balaustrada *f*, balustrade
balaustre *m*, baluster
balazo *m*, shot; bullet wound
balbuceo *m*, stammering; babbling; lisping; **balbuceos** *fig* beginnings, early stages (e.g. **los b. de la literatura yídica,** the beginnings of Yiddish literature)
balbuciente *a* stammering; babbling; lisping
balbucir *vi irr defective* to stammer; lisp; babble; read hesitantly. See **lucir**
Balcanes, los the Balkans
balcón *m*, balcony
baldaquín *m*, canopy, baldachin
baldar *vt* to cripple; impede, obstruct
balde *m*, bucket
balde (en) *adv* in vain. **de b.,** gratis, free of charge
baldear *vt naut* to wash the decks
baldío *a* untilled; fallow; useless, worthless; vagrant
baldón *m*, insult; dishonor
baldonar *vt* to insult
baldosa *f*, paving stone; tile
baldrufa *f*, top, spinning top
balduque *m*, red tape
Baleares, las Islas the Balearic Islands
baleárico *a* Balearic
balido *m*, bleat, bleating
balística *f*, ballistics
baliza *f*, *naut* buoy, beacon
balizamiento *m*, marking with beacons, marking with buoys; traffic signs and signals
ballena *f*, whale; whalebone
ballenero *a* whaling. *m*, whaler
ballesta *f*, crossbow; spring (of carriages)
ballestería *f*, archery; crossbowmen
ballestero *m*, archer; crossbowman; crossbow maker
balneario *a* pertaining to public baths; bathing; holiday; spa. *m*, watering place, spa
balompié *m*, football (game)
balón *m*, large ball; football; *chem* balloon; bundle; bale. **b. de ensayo,** *fig* feeler
baloncesto *m*, *sport* basket ball
balota *f*, ballot
balotaje *m*, balloting; run-off election

balotar *vi* to ballot
balsa *f,* pond; raft
balsadera *f,* ferry
bálsamo *m,* balm
balsero *m,* ferryman; rafter (person fleeing a country by raft, rowboat, etc.)
báltico *a* Baltic. **el Mar Báltico** the Baltic Sea
baluarte *m,* bulwark; bastion; protection, defence
bamboleante *a* swaying, swinging; *fig* tottering (e.g. empire)
bambolearse *vr* to sway; swing; totter; be shaky; stagger
bamboleo *m,* rocking; swinging; tottering; staggering; reeling
bambolla *f, inf* ostentation, swank
bambú *m,* bamboo
banal *a* banal, commonplace
banana *f,* banana
banasta *f,* big basket
banastero (-ra) *n* basket maker or dealer
banca *f,* bench; card game; stall; *com* banking
bancada *f,* rowing seat
bancal *m,* oblong garden plot; terrace
bancario *a* banking, bank
bancarrota *f,* bankruptcy. **hacer b.,** to go bankrupt
banco *m,* form, bench; rowing seat; settle; seat; *carp* bench; *com* bank; *naut* bar, shoal; school (of fish). **b. azul,** government benches in Spanish Parliament. **b. de arena,** sand-bank. **b. de descuento,** discount bank. **b. de emisión, banco emisor,** bank of issue. **b. de hielo,** iceberg. **b. de nivel,** benchmark
banda *f,* wide ribbon; sash; ribbon, insignia; strip; border; party, group; gang; flock (of birds); zone, belt; side (of ship); *mus* band; cushion (billiards); *her* bar, bend. **b. elástica,** rubber band. *naut* **dar a la b.,** to lie along
bandada *f,* flock (of birds)
bandeja *f,* tray, salver
bandera *f,* banner, flag; colors, standard. **b. de popa,** ensign. **jurar la b.,** (*mil nav*) to take the oath of allegiance
banderilla *f,* banderilla (bullfighting)
banderillear *vt* to put banderillas on bulls
banderillero *m,* man who puts banderillas on bulls
banderín *m, dim* small flag; recruiting post
banderizo *a* factious; vehement, excitable
banderola *f,* banderole, pennon; bannerole
bandido (-da) *a* and *n* outlaw, fugitive. *m,* bandit; highwayman; rogue, desperado
bando *m,* proclamation, order; faction, group, party
bandola *f, mus* pandora, pandore
bandolerismo *m,* brigandage
bandolero *m,* robber, footpad, brigand
bandolín *m,* mandolin
bandurria *f, mus* mandolin
banjo *m,* banjo
banquero *m,* banker
banqueta *f,* three-legged stool; seat; footstool; *Mexico* sidewalk
banquete *m,* banquet, feast
banquetear *vt* and *vi* to banquet
banqueteo *m,* banqueting, feasting
bañadera *f, Argentina* bathtub
bañado *m,* chamber pot; *WH* marshy land, marsh; **bañados** *pl* marsh
bañador (-ra) *a* bathing. *n* bather. *m,* bathing dress; bath, vat
bañar *vt* to bathe; coat, cover; dip; lave, wash; *fig* bathe (of sunlight, etc.). *vr* take a bath; bathe
bañera *f,* bath attendant; bathtub
bañista *mf* bather; one who takes spa waters
baño *m,* bathing; bath; bathroom; bathtub; bagnio, Turkish prison; covering, coat; *pl* mineral baths, spa. **b. de China** *Argentina* shower bath, shower **b. de mar,** sea bath. **b. de María,** double saucepan. **b. de sol,** sunbath. **casa de baños,** public baths. **cuarto de b.,** bathroom
bao *m, naut* beam
baptisterio *m,* baptistery; *ecc* font
baquelita *f,* bakelite
baqueta *f,* ramrod; *pl* drumsticks; *mil* gauntlet
bar *m,* bar; café
barahúnda *f,* See **baraúnda**
baraja *f,* pack (of cards); game of cards
barajar *vt* to shuffle (cards); jumble, mix; *vi* quarrel
baranda *f,* handrail, banister; cushion (of billiard table)
barandilla *f, dim* railing
barata *f, Mexico* bargain sale, sale
baratija *f,* (gen. *pl*) trifle, oddment
baratillo *m,* second-hand article, frippery; second-hand shop or stall; bargain counter
barato *a* cheap; easy. *m,* bargain sale. *adv* cheaply
baratura *f,* cheapness
baraúnda *f,* uproar, confusion
barba *f,* chin; beard; whiskers; fin; barb (of a feather); *m,* actor who plays old men. *f pl,* fibers of plants. **b. bien poblada,** a thick beard. **barbas de ballena,** whalebone. *fig inf* **echar a las barbas,** to throw in a person's face. **en la barba, en las barbas,** to ones face (e.g. **Me lo dijeron en las barbas.** They told me so to my face). **hacer la b.,** to shave; *inf* annoy
barbacoa *f, WH* barbecue; trellis (for climbing plants)
barbado *a* bearded. *m,* shoot; sucker; transplanted plant
barbárico *a* barbarian; barbaric
barbaridad *f,* barbarity; blunder; atrocity; outrage; *inf* huge amount. **¡Qué b.!** How awful! You don't say so!
barbarie *f,* barbarism; barbarity, cruelty
barbarismo *m,* barbarism; cruelty; barbarians
bárbaro (-ra) *a* and *n* barbarian. *a* fierce; headstrong; uncivilized. **como un b.,** like crazy (e.g. **estudiar como un b.,** to study like crazy)
barbechar *vt* to plow; leave fallow
barbecho *m, agr* fallow; first plowing
barbería *f,* barber shop
barbero *m,* barber; *Guatemala, Mexico* flatterer
barbihecho *a* fresh-shaved
barbilampiño *a* smooth-faced, beardless, clean-shaven
barbilindo *a* dandified, dappy; *m,* dandy
barbilla *f,* point of the chin; chin. **acariciar la b. (de),** to chuck under the chin
barbiquejo *m, naut* bobstay; hat-guard
barbudo *a* heavily bearded
barbulla *f, inf* babble, chatter, murmur of voices
barca *f,* small boat, bark; barge. **b. de pasaje,** ferryboat. **b. plantaminas** minelayer
barcada *f,* boat-load; ferry crossing
barcaza *f, naut* lighter; barge. **b. de desembarco,** landingcraft
barcelonés (-esa) *a* and *n* of or from Barcelona
barcino *a* ruddy (of animals); fawn and white; *inf* turncoat (of politicians)
barco *m,* boat; ship; hollow, rut. **b. barredero,** trawler. **b. siembraminas,** minelayer
barda *f,* horse armor; thatch; *carp* shingle; (Mexico) cement fence, cement wall
bardal *m,* thatched wall; mud wall
bardar *vt* to thatch
bardo *m,* poet, bard
bario *m,* barium
barítono *m,* baritone
barloventear *vi naut* to tack; ply to windward; *inf* wander about
barlovento *m, naut* windward
barnacla *m,* barnacle
barniz *m,* varnish; glaze; smattering, veneer
barnizar *vt* to varnish; glaze
barométrico *a* barometric
barómetro *m,* barometer
barón *m,* baron
baronesa *f,* baroness
barquero *m,* boatman; bargee; *ent* water-boatman

barquillero *m*, seller of wafers; waffle-iron
barquillo *m*, wafer, cornet
barquín *m*, furnace bellows
barra *f*, bar; ingot; railing (in courtroom); sandbank; fault (in cloth); lever, crossbar; (in cricket) bail; *mus* bar. **b. de jabón de afeitar,** shaving-stick. **a barras derechas,** without deceit
barrabasada *f*, *inf* wilfulness, escapade
barraca *f*, cabin, hut; stall; sideshow; *Latin Am.* barracks **b. de tiro,** shooting gallery
barracón *m*, side-show; stall
barragana *f*, concubine, mistress
barranca, *f*, **barranco** *m*, furrow, channel, rut; gorge; difficulty, fix
barrancoso *a* rutty, uneven
barredor (-ra) *n* sweeper
barredura *f*, sweeping; *pl* sweepings; rubbish
barrena *f*, borer, gimlet, drill, auger. *aer* **b. de cola,** tail-spin
barrenar *vt* to drill, bore; blast (in quarries)
barrendero (-ra) *n* sweeper, scavenger
barrenero *m*, driller; blaster
barreno *m*, blast hole; bore, drill; vanity; *Lat. Am.* mania, pet peeve
barreño *m*, earthenware bowl (for dish washing, etc.)
barrer *vt* to sweep; *fig* clear, make a clean sweep
barrera *f*, barrier; barricade; *fig* obstacle. **b. de golpe,** automatic gate (at level crossings, etc.). **b. de minas,** minefield
barriada *f*, district; quarter (of a city); *Peru* slum, shanty town
barrica *f*, cask; barrel
barricada *f*, barricade
barriga *f*, *inf* belly
barrigón, barrigudo *a* pot-bellied
barril *m*, barrel; cask; water-butt
barrilero *m*, cooper
barrio *m*, district, quarter; suburb. **barrios bajos,** slums, back streets. **el otro b.,** the other world, Eternity
barrizal *m*, muddy place; claypit
barro *m*, mud; clay; earthenware drinking vessel; *inf* money
barroco *a* baroque
barroso *a* muddy; pimpled; mud-colored
barrote *m*, thick iron bar; stave, bond
barruntar *vt* to conjecture; suspect
barrunto *m*, conjecture; indication, sign
bártulos *m pl*, household goods; *fig* means, wherewithal
barullo *m*, *inf* confusion, disorder; mob
basa *f*, base; *arch* pedestal; foundation, basis
basalto *m*, basalt
basar *vt* to base, place on a base; *fig* found, base; *vr* (*with en*) rely upon, base oneself on
basca *f*, (gen. *pl*) nausea; retching; wave of anger
báscula *f*, weighing-machine, platform-scale; weigh-bridge
base *f*, base; (*chem geom mil*) base; basis; *arch* pedestal; *mus* root. **sin b.,** baseless
básico *a* basic
Basilea Basel, Basle
basílica *f*, palace; church, basilica
basquear *vi* to retch; feel squeamish
bastante *a* sufficient, enough. *adv* sufficiently; enough; fairly; a good deal; somewhat. **Hace b. calor,** It is quite hot. **Tengo b.,** I have enough. **Tenemos b. tiempo,** We have sufficient time
bastar *vi* to suffice. **¡Basta!** Enough! No more! Stop! **¡Basta de . . . !** Enough of . . . ! **Basta decir que . . . ,** Suffice it to say that . . .
bastardía *f*, bastardy, illegitimacy; baseness, meanness
bastardilla *f*, *print* italics
bastardo (-da) *a* bastard; spurious. *n* bastard
bastear *vt sew* to baste
bastidor *m*, embroidery frame; *art* stretcher (for canvas); *theat* wing; *mech* underframe; chassis, carriage; frame (of a window). *fig* **entre bastidores,** behind the scenes
bastilla *f*, *sew* hem; bastille
bastimentar *vt* to provision; supply
bastimento *m*, supplies; provisioning
bastión *m*, bastion
basto *m*, pack-saddle; ace of clubs; clubs (cards). *a* rude; tough; *fig* unpolished, rough
bastón *m*, cane, walking-stick; rod (of office); truncheon. **b. de junquillo,** Malacca cane. **empuñar el b.,** to take control, take over. **meter el b.,** to mediate
bastonear *vt* to cane; stir with a stick
basura *f*, rubbish, refuse; dung; sweepings
basural *m*, *Lat. Am.* garbage dump
basurero *m*, dustman; dunghill, rubbish dump; kitchen middens; dust-bin
bata *f*, dressing-gown; smoking-jacket; old-fashioned dress; overall, smock
batacazo *m*, bump, noise of a fall; *pol* dark horse
batahola *f*, *inf* hurly-burly, hubbub
batalla *f*, battle; *fig* struggle, conflict; tournament; *art* battle-piece. **b. campal,** pitched battle
batallador *a* fighting, warlike
batallar *vi* to battle, fight; dispute, argue; hesitate
batallón *m*, battalion
batata *f*, sweet potato, yam
batayola *f*, *naut* rail
batea *f*, wooden tray; punt
bateador, -a *mf*, *Lat. Am.* batter
batear *vt*, *Lat. Am.* to bat
batería *f*, (*mil elec naut*) battery. **b. de cocina,** kitchen utensils. **b. de pilas secas,** dry battery. **b. de teatro,** stage lights. **b. eléctrica,** electric battery
baticola *f*, crupper
batida *f*, game drive; attack; *met* beating
batido *a* beaten (of metals); shot (of silk); trodden, worn (roads, etc.). *m*, *cul* batter; hunting party
batidor *m*, beater; scout; outrider; hair comb; *cul* whisk. **b. de oro** (*or* **de plata**), gold (*or* silver) beater
batiente *m*, jamb (of door, etc.); damper (piano); leaf (of door); place where sea beats against cliffs, etc.
batihoja *m*, gold beater; metal worker
batimiento *m*, beating
batín *m*, smoking-jacket; man's dressing-gown
batintín *m*, Chinese gong
batir *vt* to beat, slap; demolish; dismantle, take down (stall, etc.); hammer, flatten; batter; *fig* beat (of sun, etc.); stir; pound; churn; comb (hair); vanquish, defeat; coin; reconnoiter, beat; throw down or drop; *vr* fight; swoop (birds of prey). **b. palmas,** to clap, applaud
batista *f*, cambric, batiste
baturrillo *m*, hotchpotch (gen. food); *inf* farrago, medley
batuta *f*, baton, conductor's wand. **llevar la b.,** *inf* boss the show, call the music, be in charge, to rule the roost
baúl *m*, trunk; *inf* belly; *Lat. Am. also* trunk (of a car) **b. escaparate** *or* **b. mundo,** wardrobe trunk
bauprés *m*, *naut* bowsprit
bausán (-ana) *n* guy, strawman; puppet; fool, idiot; lazybones
bautismo *m*, baptism
bautista *m*, baptizer, baptist. **San Juan B.,** St. John the Baptist
bautisterio *m*, baptistery
bautizar *vt* to baptize, christen; *inf* nickname; *inf* water (wine); accidentally shower with water
bautizo *m*, baptism; christening party
baya *f*, berry
bayeta *f*, baize; flannel
bayo (-ya) *a* bay (of horses)
Bayona Bayonne
bayoneta *f*, bayonet. **b. calada,** fixed bayonet
bayonetazo *m*, bayonet thrust

baza *f*, tricks taken (playing cards). *fig inf* **meter b.**, to stick one's oar in
bazar *m*, bazaar; shop, store; department store
bazo *m*, *anat* spleen. *a* yellow-brown
bazucar, bazuquear *vt* to shake or stir (liquids)
bazuqueo *m*, shaking or stirring of liquids
be *f*, letter B. *m*, baa
beata *f*, devout woman; *inf* pious hypocrite, prude; Sister of Mercy; over-religious woman
beatería *f*, sanctimoniousness; bigotry
beatificación *f*, beatification
beatificar *vt* to make happy; sanctify; beatify
beatífico *a* beatific
beatitud *f*, blessedness, beatitude; happiness
beato (-ta) *a* happy; blessed, beatified; devout; prudish. *n* devout person; over-pious person
beba *f*, *Argentina* baby (girl)
bebé *m*, baby
bebedero *a* drinkable. *m*, drinking trough or place
bebedizo *a* drinkable. *m*, draught of medicine; love-potion; poisonous drink
bebedor (-ra) *a* drinkable. *n* drinker; toper
beber *vt* to drink; absorb; *vi* toast, drink to the health (of); tipple. *m*, drinking; drink
bebida *f*, drink; beverage; alcoholic liquor
beca *f*, academic scarf or sash; scholarship, exhibition
becado, becario *m*, exhibitioner, scholarship holder
becerra *f*, calf; *bot* snapdragon
becerro *m*, bullock; bull calf; calf-skin. **b. marino,** *zool* seal
Beda el Venerable the Venerable Bede
bedel *m*, beadle; servitor, university porter
beduino (-na) *a* and *n* Bedouin. *m*, savage, bloodthirsty man
befar *vt* to mock, ridicule
befo *a* thick-lipped; knock-kneed. *m*, animal's lip
begonia *f*, *bot* begonia
bejín *m*, *bot* puff-ball; spoilt child
bejuco *m*, rattan
beldad *f*, beauty; belle
beldar *vt agr* to winnow
Belén Bethlehem
belén *m*, nativity, manager; *inf* bedlam; *inf* gossip
belfo *a* thick-lipped
belga *a* and *mf* Belgian
Bélgica Belgium
bélgico *a* Belgian
Belgrado Belgrade
Belice Belize
belicista *adj* war, militaristic; *mf* warmonger
bélico *a* warlike, military
belicoso *a* bellicose, aggressive; warlike
beligerancia *f*, belligerency
beligerante *a* and *mf* belligerent
belitre *a inf* knavish, cunning
bellaco (-ca) *a* artful, cunning. *n* knave; *Lat. Am.* untamed horse
belladona *f*, belladonna
bellaquería *f*, roguery, knavery, cunning
bellasombra *f*, umbra tree
belleza *f*, beauty, loveliness, fairness
bello *a* beautiful
bellota *f*, acorn; carnation bud; ornamental button, knob
bemol *a* and *m*, *mus* flat. *inf* **tener bemoles,** to be thorny, be difficult
bencina *f*, benzine; petrol, gasoline, gas
bendecir *vt irr* to praise, extol; bless; dedicate, consecrate. See **decir**
bendición *f*, benediction; blessing; consecration; *pl* marriage ceremony. **b. de la mesa,** grace before meals
bendito *a* holy, blessed; fortunate; simple. **ser un b.,** to be a simpleton; be a good soul. **¡Benditos los ojos que te ven!** It's so nice to see you!
benedictino (-na) *a* and *n* Benedictine. *m*, Benedictine liqueur
beneficencia *f*, beneficence; charitable institutions
beneficiación *f*, benefaction
beneficiado (-da) *n* beneficiary. *m*, incumbent of a benefice
beneficiador (-ra) *n* benefactor
beneficiar *vt* to benefit; improve; cultivate (land); exploit (mine); purchase (directorship, etc.); sell at a loss (bonds, etc.)
beneficiario (-ia) *n* beneficiary
beneficiencia *f*, beneficence, charity
beneficio *m*, benefit; profit; cultivation (land, etc.); working (mine); *ecc* benefice; *theat* benefit
beneficioso *a* beneficial; useful
benéfico *a* beneficent; kind, helpful; charitable
benemérito *a* benemeritus, worthy, meritorious
beneplácito *m*, approbation; consent
benevolencia *f*, benevolence, goodwill
benévolo *a* benevolent, kind
Bengala Bengal
bengalí *a* and *mf* Bengali
benignidad *f*, kindness; mildness (of the weather, etc.)
benigno *a* kind; benign; mild; balmy
beodo (-da) *a* drunk, intoxicated. *n* drunkard
berbén *m*, *Mexico* scurvy
Berbería Barbary
bereber *a* and *mf* Berber
berenjena *f*, eggplant
bergante *m*, rascal, rogue
berilo *m*, beryl
Berlín Berlin
berlinés (-esa) *a* and *n* of or from Berlin
bermejear *vi* to be or look reddish
bermejo *a* reddish; red; redgold; carroty (of hair)
bermellón *m*, vermilion
bernardina *f*, lie; boast; gibberish
bernardo (-da) *a* and *n ecc* Bernardine (Order of St. Bernard)
berquelio *m*, berkelium
berrear *vi* to low, bellow; yell, squall; shriek; *vr* reveal, confess
berrido *m*, lowing, bellowing; *inf* yell
berrinche *m*, *inf* tantrum, fit, fit of sulks
berro *m*, watercress
berroqueña *f*, granite
berza *f*, cabbage
besamanos *m*, ceremony of kissing royal hand, levee; kissing fingers (in salute)
besar *vt* to kiss; *inf* brush against, touch (of things); *vr* kiss one another; *inf* bang into, knock against one another
beso *m*, kiss; knock, collision
bestia *f*, quadruped (especially horses or mules); beast. *mf inf* nasty piece of work. **b. de carga,** beast of burden. **como una b.,** like a dog (e.g. **Trabajo como una b.** I work like a dog)
bestial *a* bestial; brutal; beastly
bestialidad *f*, brutality; bestiality; beastliness
bestialismo *m*, bestiality (sexual orientation)
besuquear *vt inf* to cover with kisses; *vr inf* spoon, make love
besuqueo *m*, *inf* kissing and spooning
betabel *m*, *Mexico* beetroot
bético *a* Andalusian
betún *m*, bitumen; shoe blacking; kind of cement. **b. de Judea** *or* **b. judaico,** asphalt
bezo *m*, blubber lip; proud flesh (of a wound)
bezudo *a* thick-lipped
biberón *m*, feeding bottle
Biblia *f*, Bible
bíblico *a* biblical
bibliófilo *m*, bibliophile
bibliografía *f*, bibliography
bibliográfico *a* bibliographical
biblioteca *f*, library; book series. **b. por subscripción,** circulating library
bibliotecario (-ia) *n* librarian

bibliotecnia, bibliotecología, biblioteconomía *f,* library science
bicarbonato *m,* bicarbonate
bíceps *m,* biceps
bicherío *m, Lat. Am.* bugs, insects
bicho *m,* any small animal or reptile; quadruped; fighting bull; scarecrow, sight. **b. viviente,** *inf* living soul. **mal b.,** rogue
bicicleta *f,* bicycle, bike. **ir** (*or* **andar** *or* **montar**) **en b.,** to bicycle, bike, go by bicycle, go by bike
bicoca *f, inf* trifle, bagatelle
bicolor *a* bicolored
bidé *m,* bidet
biela *f,* axle-tree; connecting-rod; big-end
bielda *f,* pitchfork; *agr* winnowing
bien *m,* ideal goodness, perfection; benefit, advantage; welfare; *pl* property, wealth. *adv* well; willingly; happily; perfectly; easily; enough, sufficient; all right! very well! **b. que,** although. **b. de equipo,** capital good. **bienes muebles,** movables, goods and chattels. **bienes raíces,** real estate. **el B. y el Mal,** Good and Evil. **¡Está b.!** All right! **no b.,** scarcely, as soon as. **si b.,** although, even if. **¿Y b.?** And so what? Well, then; What next?
bienal *a* biennial
bienamado *a* dearly beloved
bienandante *a* prosperous; happy
bienandanza *f,* happiness, welfare; prosperity
bienaventurado *a* blessed, holy; happy; *inf* over-simple, innocent, foolish
bienaventuranza *f,* blessedness
bienestar *m,* wellbeing; ease; comfort
bienhablado *a* well-spoken; civil, polite
bienhadado *a* fortunate, happy
bienhechor (-ra) *a* kind, helpful. *n* benefactor
bienintencionado *a* well-meaning
bienio *m,* biennium, space of two years, period of two years
bienquisto *a* respected; generally esteemed
bienvenida *f,* safe or happy arrival; welcome. **dar la b.,** to welcome
bienvivir *vi* to live comfortably; live decently or uprightly
bies *m,* bias, cross; slant
bife *m Argentina* beefsteak, steak
biftec *m,* beefsteak, steak
bifurcación *f,* bifurcation; fork, branch, junction
bifurcarse *vr* to fork, branch
bigamia *f,* bigamy
bígamo (-ma) *a* bigamous. *n* bigamist
bigornia *f,* anvil
bigote *m,* moustache; *pl* whiskers
bigotudo *a* moustached, whiskered
bikini *m,* bikini
bilateral *a* bilateral
bilingüe *a* bilingual
bilioso *a* bilious
bilis *f,* bile
billar *m,* billiards; billiard table
billete *m,* note, short letter; ticket; banknote. **b. circular,** excursion ticket. **b. de abono,** season ticket. **b. de andén,** platform ticket. **b. de banco,** banknote. **b. de favor,** free ticket. **b. de ida y vuelta,** round trip ticket. **b. entero,** full fare. **b. kilométrico,** tourist ticket. **b. sencillo,** one-way. **medio b.,** half-fare
billón *m,* billion
bimestral *a* bimonthly
bimestre *a* bimonthly. *m,* two months' duration; money paid or received at two-monthly intervals
bimotor *a* two-motor. *m,* twin-engined aircraft
binario *a* binary
bincha *f, Lat. Am.* hairband
binóculo *m,* opera glasses
biofísica *f,* biophysics
biografía *f,* biography
biográfico *a* biographical
biógrafo (-fa) *n* biographer; (Chile) movie theater (e.g. **¡Vamos al biógrafo!** Let's go to the movies!)
biología *f,* biology
biológico *a* biological
biólogo *m,* biologist
biombo *m,* screen
bioquímica *f,* biochemistry
bioquímico *m,* biochemist
bipartido *a* bipartite
bípedo *a* and *m,* biped
biplano *m,* biplane
biplaza *a* two-seater
birla *f,* skittle
birlar *vt* to bowl from where the bowl stopped; *inf* knock down; snatch away; *inf* rob
birlocha *f,* child's kite
Birmania Burma
birmano (-na) *a* and *n* Burmese
birreta *f,* biretta
birrete *m,* biretta; university cap; cap
bis *adv* twice; repeat; encore. *a* duplicate; **B** (in addresses, e.g., **Calle de Alcalá 18bis,** 18b Alcalá St.)
bisabuela *f,* great-grandmother
bisabuelo *m,* great-grandfather
bisagra *f,* hinge; shoemaker's polisher
bisbís *m,* game of chance
bisbisar *vt inf* to mutter; whisper
bisbiseo *m, inf* muttering; murmuring; whispering
bisecar *vt* to bisect
bisección *f, geom* bisection
bisectriz *f,* bisector
bisel *m,* bevel, chamfer
bisiesto *a* leap and *m,* leap (year)
bisílabo *a* two-syllabled
bismuto *m,* bismuth
bisnieto (-ta) *n* great-grandchild
bisonte *m,* bison
bisoño (-ña) *a* inexperienced, raw. *n* recruit; *inf* greenhorn
bistec *m,* beef steak
bisturí *m,* surgical knife
bisunto *a* grubby, greasy
bisutería *f,* imitation jewelry
bituminoso *a* bituminous
bivalvo *a* bivalve
Bizancio Byzantium
bizantinismo *m,* Byzantinism
bizarría *f,* handsomeness; dash; verve; gallantry, courage; magnificence; liberality; whim, caprice
bizarro *a* handsome; dashing; gallant, courageous; liberal; splendid, magnificent
bizcaitarrismo *m,* doctrine of Basque autonomy; Basque autonomy movement
bizco *a* squint-eyed, cross-eyed
bizcocho *m,* biscuit; spongecake; bisque
bizma *f,* poultice. **poner bizmas,** to poultice
biznieto *n* See **bisnieto**
blanca *f,* old Spanish coin; *inf* penny; *mus* minim. **sin b.,** penniless
blanco *a* white; fair-skinned; blank, vacant; *inf* cowardly. *m,* target; blank left in writing; white person; interval. **b. de España,** whiting. **b. de la uña,** half-moon of the nail. **dar en el b.,** to hit the mark. **en b.,** blank, unused; *inf* in vain; uncomprehendingly; (of nights) sleepless
blancor, *m.* **blancura** *f,* whiteness; fairness (of skin)
blandear *vt* to moderate, soothe; brandish; *vi fig* give way, yield
blandir *vt* to brandish, wield, flourish
blando *a* soft; mild (weather); delicate; kind; peaceable; delicate, effeminate; *inf* cowardly
blandón *m,* wax taper
blandura *f,* softness; poultice; blandishment, compliment; mildness (of weather); gentleness, affability; luxury

blanquear *vt* to bleach; whitewash; whiten; *vi* appear white; show white
blanquecino *a* whitish
blanqueo *m*, whitening; whitewashing; bleaching
blanquillo *m*, *Central America, Mexico* egg; *Chile, Peru,* white peach
blanquizal *m*, pipe-clay
blasfemador (-ra) *a* blaspheming. *n* blasphemer
blasfemar *vi* to blaspheme; curse, swear
blasfemia *f*, blasphemy; insult
blasfemo (-ma) *n* blasphemer. *a* blasphemous
blasón *m*, heraldry; escutcheon; glory, honor. **una familia con antiguos blasones,** a family of ancient lineage
blasonar *vt* to blazon; *vi* boast, brag, blazon abroad
bledo *m*, blade, leaf. **no importar un b.,** not to matter a straw
blenda *f*, *min* blende
blindado *a nav* armored, ironclad
blindaje *m*, *nav* armor-plating; *mil* blindage
blindar *vt* to plate with armor, to case with steel
blofista *mf*, *Lat. Am.* bluffer
blonda *f*, blonde (of lace)
blondo *a* fair, blond, flaxen-haired
bloque *m*, block, slab
bloquear *vt* to blockade; besiege
bloqueo *m*, blockade; siege; blocking; freezing (of assets). **violar el b.,** to run the blockade
blusa *f*, blouse
boa *f*, boa, large snake. *m*, boa (fur)
boato *m*, outward show, ostentation
bobería *f*, foolishness, stupidity
bóbilis, bóbilis (de) *adv inf* free of charge; without effort
bobina *f*, bobbin, spool, reel; *elec* coil; spool (of fishing rod)
bobo (-ba) *a* stupid, idiotic; simple, innocent. *n* fool. *m*, clown, jester
boca *f*, mouth; pincers (of crustaceans); entrance or exit; mouth (of a river), gulf, inlet; orifice, opening; muzzle (of guns); cutting edge (of tools); taste (of wine, etc.). **b. abajo,** face down, prone. **b. arriba,** on one's back, face up, supine. **b. del estómago,** pit of the stomach. **b. rasgada,** large mouth. **a b.,** verbally. **a b. de jarro,** point-blank. **a pedir de b.,** just as one would wish. **de b.,** by word of mouth. *inf* **sin decir esta b. es mía,** without a word, in silence
bocacalle *f*, entrance (to a street); street junction
bocadillo *m*, narrow ribbon; sandwich
bocado *m*, mouthful. **b. de reyes,** delicacy, exquisite dish (of food); snack; bite; (horse's) bit; bridle; *pl* preserved fruit cut up
bocamanga *f*, wrist (of sleeve)
bocana *f*, *Lat. Am.* estuary
bocanada *f*, mouthful (of liquid); cloud (of smoke). **b. de aire,** gust of wind
boceto *m*, sketch; outline; rough-cast model
bocha *f*, *sport* bowl; *pl* bowls
bochorno *m*, sultry weather; heat, stuffiness; blush, hot flush; shame
bochornoso *a* sultry; shameful
bocina *f*, trumpet; megaphone; foghorn; hooter; *aut* horn; horn (of gramophone); *ast* Ursa Minor
bocio *m*, *med* goiter
bocoy *m*, hogshead; large cask
boda *f*, wedding, marriage. **bodas de oro,** fiftieth (golden) anniversary. **bodas de plata,** silver wedding anniversary
bodega *f*, wine-cellar; storeroom; stockroom; granary; *Puerto Rico* grocery store; *naut* hold (of ship)
bodegón *m*, eating-house; tavern; *art* still-life; genre picture
bofes *m pl*, lungs, lights. *inf* **echar los b.,** to work oneself to death
bofetada *f*, **bofetón** *m*, blow, slap; box on the ear
boga *f*, rowing; fashion, vogue; *mech* bogie. *mf* oarsman, rower. **estar en b.,** to be fashionable
bogador (-ra) *n* rower, oarsman
bogar *vi* to row
bogavante *m*, lobster
bogotano (-na) *a* and *n* of or from Bogotá
bohemio (-ia) *a* and *n* gipsy; bohemian; Bohemian. *m*, archer's short cloak
bohío *m*, *Lat. Am.* hut
boicotear *vt* to boycott
boicot, boicoteo *m*, boycott
boina *f*, Basque cap; beret
bola *f*, globe; ball; *sport* bowl; *arch* balloon; *inf* trick, lie; (Cuba) rumor; *Mexico* shoeshine, shine. **b. de nieves,** snowball. *inf* **dejar rodar la b.,** to let things slide
bolardo *m*, bollard
bolchevismo *m*, Bolshevism
bolea *f*, (tennis) volley; throw
bolera *f*, bowling alley
bolero *m*, bolero; dancer; *inf* top hat; *Mexico* bootblack
boleta *f*, admission ticket; billet ticket; warrant, voucher; summons, ticket, traffic ticket
boletería *f*. *Lat. Am.* ticket office, box office
boleto *m*. *Lat. Am.* ticket
boletín *m*, bulletin; admission ticket; pay warrant; *com* price list; learned periodical. **b. de noticias,** news bulletin. **b. meteorológico,** weather report
boliche *m*, jack (in bowls); cup-and-ball toy; small oven (for charcoal); dragnet; *Mexico* bowling **juego de b.,** bowls
bólido *m*, *ast* bolide, meteor
bolillo *m*, bobbin (lace making); *Mexico* roll (food)
bolina *f*, *naut* bowline; *naut* sounder; *inf* uproar, tumult
bolita *f*, pellet
boliviano(-na) *a* and *n* Bolivian. *m*, silver coin
bollo *m*, bread roll; bun; bulge, bruise (in metal); *med* lump
bollón *m*, round-headed or brass-headed nail; *bot* bud (especially vines)
bolo *m*, skittle, ninepin; pillow (for lace making); Cuban coin; *med* large pill; *fig inf* blockhead; *pl* skittles (game of)
bolsa *f*, purse; bag; footmuff; fold, pucker; pouch; exchange, stock exchange, capital, money; prize money; *med* sac; *min* pocket. **b. de estudio,** scholarship grant. **b. de trabajo,** labor exchange. **b. de valores,** stock exchange. **bajar** (*or* **subir**) **la b.,** to fall (or rise) (of stock exchange quotations). **jugar a la b.,** to speculate on the stock exchange
bolsillo *m*, pocket; purse; money
bolsista *mf* stock-broker; speculator (on the stock exchange)
bomba *f*, *mech* pump; pumping engine; bomb; *mil* shell; lamp globe; *inf* improvised verses; *inf* drinking bout. **¡B.!** Listen! Here goes! **b. de incendios,** fire-engine. **b. marina,** waterspout. **b. de mecha atrasada,** time bomb. **b. volante,** flying-bomb. **a prueba de b.,** bombproof. **arrojar bombas,** to bomb. *inf* **caer como una b.,** to be a bombshell
bombachos *a* baggy, loose-fitting; *m pl*, plus fours
bombardear *vt* to bombard; bomb; shell
bombardeo *m*, bombardment, bombing; shelling
bombardero *m*, gunner, bombardier; *aer* bomber. **b. pesado,** *aer* heavy bomber. **Servicio de b.,** Bomber Command
bombástico *a* bombastic, high sounding
bombazo *m*, bombshell; bomb crater; noise of an exploding bomb
bombear *vt* to pump; bombard, shell; praise
bombero *m*, worker of a pressure pump; fireman; mortar, howitzer
bombilla *f*, *naut* lantern; (*elec phys*) bulb; small pump; straw for drinking maté *WH*
bombillo *m*, w.c. siphon; handpump
bombo *m*, big drum or player of it; *naut* barge, ferry; ballot box; exaggerated praise
bombón *m*, bonbon, sweet
bombonera *f*, box for toffee, etc.

bonachón *a inf* genial, good-natured
bonaerense *a* and *mf* of or from the Province of Buenos Aires
Bonaira Bonaire
bonancible *a* calm (of weather, sea)
bonanza *f*, fair weather; prosperity
bondad *f*, goodness; kindness, helpfulness. **Tenga la b. de . . . ,** Be good enough to . . . , Please . . .
bondadoso *a* good, kind
bonete *m*, academic cap; *zool* reticulum (ruminants); *ecc* biretta. **gran b.,** important person. *inf* **a tente b.,** insistently
bonetero (-ra) *n* seller or maker of caps and birettas
boniato *m*, *Lat. Am.* sweet potato, yam
bonificación *f*, bonus; allowance, discount
bonísimo, ***a sup*** **bueno** extremely good
bonito *a* pretty; graceful; (ironical) fine. *m*, *icht* striped tunny
bono *m*, voucher; *com* bond, certificate. **b. postal,** postal money order. **bono del gobierno,** government bond
boñiga *f*, cow-dung, animal manure
boqueada *f*, gasp, opening of the mouth. **dar las boqueadas, estar en las últimas boqueadas,** to be at the last gasp
boquear *vi* to gasp; be dying; *inf* be at last gasp (of things); *vt* say, utter
boquera *f*, sluice (in irrigation canal)
boquerón *m*, large opening; *icht* anchovy (fish); whitebait
boquete *m*, narrow entrance, aperture; gap, breach; hole
boquiabierto *a* open-mouthed; amazed
boquiancho *a* wide-mouthed
boquiasombrado *a* gaping
boquilla *f*, *dim* small mouth; mouthpiece (of wind instruments, etc.); cigar- or cigarette-holder; gas-burner; nozzle; tip (of cigarettes)
boquirroto *a inf* loquacious, indiscreet
borbollar *vi* to bubble, foam, froth
borbollón, borbotón *m*, gushing, bubbling, welling up. **a borbollones,** in a torrent; hastily, impetuously
borbotar *vi* to gush out, well up
borda *f*, hut, cabin; *naut* gunwale
bordado *m*, embroidery
bordador (-ra) *n* embroiderer
bordar *vt* to embroider; *fig* perform perfectly
borde *m*, edge; fringe; verge; rim; mount (of a picture); brim (of a hat); side (of ship). *a* wild (of plants); illegitimate. **estar lleno hasta los bordes,** to be full to the brim
bordear *vt* to border, trim with a bordear; line (a street, e.g. **Diez mil personas bordearon las calles durante el desfile,** Ten thousand people lined the streets during the parade)
bordillo *m*, curbstone, curb.
bordo *m*, side (of ships); border, edge. **a b.,** on board
bordón *m*, pilgrim's staff; monotonous repetition; refrain; *mus* bass string; *fig* guide, stay
borgoña *m*, Burgundy wine
borgoñón (-ona) *a* and *n* Burgundian
bórico *a* boric
boricua *a*, **borinqueño, -a** *a*, *mf* Puerto Rican
borla *f*, tassel; puff (for powder). *fig* **tomar la b.,** to take one's doctorate, graduate
bornear *vt* to bend, twist; *arch* hoist into position; *vr* warp (wood)
borra *f*, yearling ewe; thickest wool; wad-stuffing; lees, sediment; fluff, dust; *inf* trash. **b. de algodón,** cottonwaste
borrachera *f*, drunkenness; orgy, carousal; *inf* blunder
borrachín (-ina) *n* tippler, toper
borrachito *a* high (on liquor), tipsy
borracho (de) *a* drunk (on), intoxicated (with); *inf* blind (with rage, etc.). *n* tippler, drunkard
borrador *m*, rough draft. **en borrador,** in the works (e.g. **Tiene dos ensayos en borrador,** She has two essays in the works). **estar en borrador,** to be in the works
borradura *f*, erasure
borrajear *vt* to scribble
borrar *vt* to erase; cross out; blot out; *fig* obliterate
borrasca *f*, storm, tempest; peril, danger; *inf* orgy
borrascosidad *f*, storminess
borrascoso *a* stormy; disordered, turbulent
borrego (-ga) *n* lamb; *inf* nincompoop, simpleton; *m pl*, fleecy clouds; white horses (waves)
borrico (-ca) *n* donkey; fool. *m*, *carp* sawing-horse
borrón *m*, blot; rough draft; defect; *fig* stigma
borroso *a* blurred, indistinct; full of dregs, muddy
boscaje *m*, grove, group of trees, thicket
Bósforo, el the Bosporus
bosque *m*, wood, forest
bosquejar *vt art* to sketch; sketch out, draft; model in rough (sculpture); outline
bosquejo *m*, outline, sketch; rough plan or idea; unfinished work. **en bosquejo,** grosso modo
bostar *m*, ox barn
bostezar *vi* to yawn
bostezo *m*, yawning; yawn
bota *f*, small wineskin; barrel, butt; boot. **b. de montar,** riding boot. **botas de campaña,** top-boots. **botas de vadear,** waders
botada, botadura *f*, launching (of a ship)
botador *m*, thrower; boating-pole; *carp* nail-puller
botafuego *m*, *mil* linstock; *inf* quick-tempered, irascible person
botalón *m*, *naut* boom. **b. de foque,** jib-boom
botana *f*, *Lat. Am.* bite (to eat), snack
botánica *f*, botany
botánico (-ca) *a* botanical. *n* botanist
botar *vt* to fling; launch (boat); *Lat. Am.* to discard, throw away, throw out *naut* shift the helm; *vi* jump; bounce, rebound; rear, prance (horses)
botarate *m*, *inf* madcap, devil-may-care
botarel, botarete *m*, *arch* abutment, buttress, flying buttress
botarga *f*, motley; harlequin
bote *m*, thrust (with lance, etc.); rearing (of horse); rebound; *aer* bump; open boat; small bottle, jar. **b. salvavidas,** lifeboat. *inf* **de b. en b.,** chockfull
botella *f*, bottle; bottleful; flask
botica *f*, chemist's shop; medicines, remedies; physic; store, shop; medicine chest
boticario *m*, apothecary, chemist
botija *f*, earthen jug; *slang* chunky person
botijo *m*, earthenware jar with spout and handle
botillería *f*, ice-cream bar
botín *m*, gaiter; buskin; booty
botiquín *m*, first-aid kit; medicine chest
botón *m*, bud; button; knob, handle; switch (electric); press button (bell); *bot* center; button (on a foil); *mech* stud
botonero (-ra) *n* button maker or seller
bóveda *f*, *arch* vault, arch; crypt; cavern. **b. celeste,** sky
boxeador *m*, boxer
boxear *vi sport* to box
boxeo *m*, *sport* boxing
boya *f*, *naut* buoy; float
boyante *a* floating; light, buoyant; prosperous
boyar *vi naut* to float
boyero *m*, cowherd
boza *f*, painter (of a boat)
bozal *m*, muzzle; nosebag; harness bells. *mf inf* greenhorn; *a* wild, untamed (horses)
bozo *m*, down which precedes beard; muzzle; headstall; lips, snout
bracero *m*, one who offers his arm (to a lady); day laborer; strong man. **de b.,** arm-in-arm
bracete *m*, small arm. **de b.,** arm-in-arm
bracmán *m*, Brahmin
braga *f*, (gen. *pl*) breeches; knickerbockers; hoist or pulley rope

bragazas *m, inf* weak-willed, fellow, soft specimen
braguero *m, med* truss
bragueta *f,* fly (of breeches)
brahmanismo *m,* Brahmanism
bramante *a* roaring. *m,* twine, pack-thread
bramar *vi* to roar; rage; *fig* howl (of the wind, etc.)
bramido *m,* bellowing; roaring; yell of rage; *fig* howling (wind, sea, etc.)
brancada *f,* drag net
branquia *f,* (gen. *pl*) *icht* gill
branquial *a* branchiate
braquicefalia *f,* brachycephaly
braquiotomía *f, surg* brachiotomy, amputation of the arms
brasa *f,* live coal. **estar como en brasas,** to be like a cat on hot bricks
brasero *m,* brazier; *Mexico* fireplace
Brasil Brazil
brasileño (-ña) *a* and *n* Brazilian
bravata *f,* bravado; threat
braveza *f,* ferocity, savageness; valor; violence, fury (of elements)
bravío *a* savage, untamed; wild (plants); uncultured
bravo *a* valiant; surly, rude; independent, strong-minded, good, excellent; savage (animals); stormy (sea); rough, rugged; violent, angry; *inf* sumptuous, magnificent.
bravura *f,* ferocity (animals); courage (persons); boastful threat
braza *f, naut* fathom; stroke (in swimming)
brazado *m,* armful
brazal *m,* armlet, brassard
brazalete *m,* bracelet; brassard
brazo *m,* arm; upper arm; front paw; *mech* arm; branch (of chandelier, etc.); bough; arm (of chair); power, courage; *pl* protectors; workmen, hands. **b. de mar,** firth, arm of the sea. **a b. partido,** in unarmed fight, man to man. **con los brazos abiertos,** welcomingly; willingly, gladly. **dar los brazos (a),** to embrace. *inf* **hecho un b. de mar,** dressed up to the nines
brea *f,* pitch, tar; sacking, canvas
brebaje *m,* beverage; unpleasant drink; *naut* draught (of beer, grog, etc.)
brecha *f, mil* breach; opening; *fig* impression (on mind). **morir en la b.,** to fight to the last ditch; die in harness
brécol *m, bot* broccoli
brega *f,* fight; quarrel; disappointment, trick. **andar a la b.,** to work hard. **dar b.,** to play a trick
bregar *vi* to fight; work hard; *fig* struggle; **bregarse con,** to tackle (a problem)
Brema Bremen
breña *f,* rough ground, bramble patch
breñal *m,* scrub, brushwood
breñoso *a* rugged, rocky
Bretaña Brittany
brete *m,* fetters, shackles; *fig* fix, squeeze, tight spot, tight squeeze (e.g. **Estoy en un brete.** I'm in a tight spot)
bretón (-ona) *a* and *n* Breton. *m,* Breton (language)
breva *f,* early fig; early acorn; *fig* advantage, "plum"; *inf* peach (girl); *inf* windfall, piece of luck; Havana cigar
breve *a* brief; concise. *m,* papal brief. *f, mus* breve. **en b.,** shortly, concisely; in a short while, soon
brevedad *f,* brevity **a la mayor brevedad** *Lat. Am.* as soon as possible
breviario *m,* breviary
brezal *m,* heath, moor
brezo *m, bot* heath
bribón (-ona) *n* rogue, ruffian. *a* knavish, dishonest; lazy
bribonada *f,* knavery, mischievous trick
bribonear *vi* to idle; play tricks, be a rogue
bribonería *f,* rascality, vagrant life
brida *f,* bridle
brigada *f, mil* brigade; *naut* division of fleet; beasts of burden. **brigada millonaria,** (Castroist Cuba) team of thirty sugarcane cutters who cut a million or more arrobas in one harvest
brillante *a* sparkling, brilliant; *fig* outstanding. *m,* diamond
brillantez *f,* brightness, luster; fame; *fig* brilliance
brillantina *f,* brilliantine
brillar *vi* to shine, sparkle, gleam, glisten; *fig* be brilliant or outstanding
brillo *m,* brilliancy, brightness, shine; fame, glory; distinction, brilliance, splendour
brincar *vi* to spring, leap, skip, frisk; *fig inf* skip, omit; *inf* grow angry; *vt* jump a child up and down
brinco *m,* leap, spring; skip, frolicking
brindar *vi* to invite, provoke (of things); (*with prep a or por*) drink the health of, toast; *vt* and *vi* give, present; offer; *vr* offer one's services
brindis *m,* toast (drink)
brío *m,* vigor; spirit, courage; gusto, verve
brioso *a* vigorous, enterprising; spirited, courageous; dashing, lively
briqueta *f,* briquette
brisa *f,* breeze; grape pressings
británico *a* British
brizna *f,* shred, paring; blade (grass); filament, fiber; string (of bean-pod, etc.); splinter, chip
briznar *vi, Lat. Am.* to drizzle
broca *f,* reel; tack (shoemaker's); *mech* drill, bit
brocado *m,* brocade. *a* brocade or embroidered like brocade
brocal *m,* puteal (of a well); mouthpiece (of wineskin); metal ring (of sword-sheath)
brocamantón *m,* large jeweled brooch
brocatel *m,* imitation brocade
brocha *f,* brush. **b. de afeitar,** shaving brush. **de b. gorda,** crudely painted. **pintor de b. gorda,** decorator
brochada *f,* stroke (of the brush)
brochado *a* brocaded, embossed
brochadura *f,* fastening, set of hooks and eyes
broche *m,* clasp, fastening; brooch; hooks and eyes; *Lat. Am.* (paper) clip
brochón *m,* whitewash brush
broma *f,* merriment; joke, jest; ship-worm. **b. literaria,** literary hoax
bromear(se) *vi* and *vr* to joke, make fun
bromista *a* joking, jesting; mischievous. *mf* genial person; prankster, tease
bromo *m,* bromine
bronca *f, inf* shindy
bronce *m,* bronze; brass; *poet* gun, bell, trumpet; bronze statue; sunburn
bronceado *a* bronzed; sunburnt. *m,* sunburn
broncear *vt* to bronze; sunburn
bronco *a* rough, coarse; brittle; (of metals); harsh (voice, musical instruments); rigid, stiff; surly
bronconeumonía *f,* bronchopneumonia
bronquial *a* bronchial
bronquio *m,* (gen. *pl*) bronchi
bronquitis *f,* bronchitis
broquel *m,* shield; *fig* protection
broquelero *m,* shield maker; quarrelsome man
broqueta *f,* skewer
brotadura *f,* budding
brotar *vi* to germinate, sprout; gush forth (water); issue forth, burst out; *fig* appear (of rash); *fig* begin to appear; *vt* to bring forth; produce (of earth)
brote *m,* bud, sprout; *fig* germ, genesis; iota, jot, atom
broza *f,* garden rubbish; debris; thicket
bruces (a *or* **de)** *adv* face downwards. **caer de b.,** to fall flat. Also with other verbs: *dar, echarse,* etc.
bruja *f,* witch; owl; *inf* hag
brujear *vi* to practise witchcraft
brujería *f,* witchcraft
brujo *m,* magician, wizard
brújula *f,* magnetic needle; compass; mariner's com-

pass. **b. de bolsillo,** pocket compass. **b. giroscópica,** gyrocompass
bruma *f*, haze; sea-mist
brumoso *a* misty, hazy
bruno *a* dark brown
bruñido *m*, polishing; burnish
bruñidor (-ra) *a* polishing. *n* burnisher. *m*, polisher (instrument)
bruñir *vt* to polish, burnish; *inf* apply make up
brusco *a* brusque, rude; blunt; sudden, unexpected; sharp (of bends)
Bruselas Brussels
bruselense *a* and *mf* of or from Brussels
brusquedad *f*, brusquerie, rudeness; bluntness; suddenness, unexpectedness; sharpness (of a bend)
brutal *a* brutal
brutalidad *f*, brutality; *fig* brutishness; viciousness
bruto *a* stupid, unreasonable; vicious; unpolished, rough. *m*, animal (gen. quadruped). **en b.,** in the rough; *com* in bulk. **diamante en b.,** an uncut diamond
bruza *f*, strong brush; scrubbing brush
Bs. As. abbrev. of Buenos Aires
bu *m*, *inf* bogey man
buba *f*, pustule; *pl* buboes
bubónico *a* bubonic
bucal *a* buccal
bucanero *m*, buccaneer
búcaro *m*, arsenican clay; jar made of arsenican clay
buceador *m*, diver
bucear *vi* to work as a diver; swim under water; *fig* investigate
bucéfalo *m*, bucephalus; *inf* fool, blockhead
buceo *m*, diving; dive; *fig* investigation
buchaca *f*, *Lat. Am.* saddlebag; billiard pocket
buche *m*, craw or crop; mouthful; wrinkle, pleat; *inf* stomach, belly. *fig inf* inmost heart
bucle *m*, ringlet, curl
bucólico *a* bucolic
budismo *m*, Buddhism
budista *a* and *mf* Buddhist
budín *m*, pudding
buen *a abb* of **bueno,** good. Used before *m*, singular nouns and infinitives used as nouns, e.g. **un b. libro,** a good book. **el b. cantar,** good singing
buenamente *adv* easily; comfortably, conveniently; willingly
buenaventura *f*, good luck; fortune told from hand
bueno (see buen) *a* good; kind; useful; convenient; pleasant; healthy; large (drink, etc.); simple, innocent; suitable; sufficient; opportune. **¡B.!** Good!; Enough!; *Mexico* Hello! (on telephone); All right! **a buenas,** willingly. **de buenas a primeras,** at first sight, from the beginning. **hacer bueno,** to prove, justify (a claim)
buey *m*, ox. **b. suelto,** *inf* freelance; bachelor
búfalo (-la) *n* buffalo
bufanda *f*, scarf
bufar *vi* to bellow; snort; *inf* snort with rage
bufete *m*, desk, writing table; lawyer's office or practice; sideboard
bufido *m*, snort; bellow
bufo *a* comic. *m*, clown, buffoon
bufón *m*, buffoon, clown; jester. *a* comical, clownish
bufonada *f*, buffoonery, clowning; raillery, taunt
bufonear(se) *vr* and *vi* to joke, jest, parody
bufonería. See **bufonada**
buhardilla *f*, garret; skylight
búho *m*, owl; *inf* hermit, unsociable person
buhonería *f*, pedling, hawking; pedler's wares
buhonero *m*, pedler
buido *a* sharp-pointed; sharp
buitre *m*, vulture
bujía *f*, candle; candlestick; *elec* candle-power; *aut* sparking plug
bula *f*, (Papal) bull
bulbo *m*, *bot* bulb. **b. dentario,** pulp (of teeth)
bulboso *a* bulbous
bulevar *m*, boulevard, promenade
bulla *f*, noise; bustle; confusion; fuss. *inf* **meter a b.,** to throw into great confusion
bullente *adj* boiling, bubbling; frothey (beer); swarming, teeming. **b. de sol,** drenched in sunlight, sundrenched
bullebulle *mf* busybody; madcap
bullicio *m*, noise, bustle; rioting; uproar
bullicioso *a* noisy, merry, boisterous; rebellious; lively, restless
bullir *vi* to boil; foam, bubble; *fig* seethe; *fig* swarm (insects); bustle; *vt* move, stir; *vr* stir, give signs of life
bulto *m*, bulk, mass, size; form of person, etc., seen indistinctly; swelling; bust, statue; bundle, package, piece of luggage; pillowcase. *fig inf* **poner de b.,** to put clearly, emphasize. **ser de b.,** to be obvious
bumerang *m*, boomerang
buñolería *f*, bun or waffle shop
buñuelo *m*, bun; waffle, fritter; *fig* botch
buque *m*, ship, vessel; capacity of ship; ship's hull. **b. barreminas,** minesweeper. **b. de guerra,** battleship, man-of-war. **b. de vapor,** steamer. **b. de vela,** sailing ship. **b. escuela,** trainingship. **b. mercante,** merchant vessel. **b. submarino,** submarine. **b. transbordador,** train-ferry
burbuja *f*, bubble
burbujear *vi* to bubble
burdel *m*, brothel; *inf* untidy, noisy place. *a* lascivious
burdo *a* coarse, tough
burgalés (-esa) *a* and *n* of or from Burgos
burgo *m*, borough, burgh
burgomaestre *m*, burgomaster
burgués (-esa) *a* and *n* bourgeois
burguesía *f*, bourgeoisie
buriel *a* dark red
buril *m*, burin, engraver's tool
burla *f*, mockery; joke, jest; trick. **b. burlando,** without effort; negligently. **de burlas,** in fun. **entre burlas y veras,** half-jokingly
burlador *a* mocking. *m*, libertine, rake; deceiver
burlar *vt* to play a trick on; deceive; disappoint; *vr* and *vi* (*with de*) make fun of,. laugh at, ridicule
burlesco *a* jocular, comic, burlesque
burlón (-ona) *a* joking; mocking, scoffing. *n* joker; scoffer
buró *m*, bureau, writing-desk; *Mexico* night table
burocracia *f*, bureaucracy
burócrata *mf* bureaucrat
burocrático *a* bureaucratic
burocratismo *m*, bureaucracy, red tape
burra *f*, she-ass; foolish, unteachable woman; painstaking, patient woman
burrajo *m*, dry stable dung used as fuel
burro *m*, ass, donkey; sawing-horse; card game
bursátil *a com* relating to the stock exchange; financial
busca *f*, search; hunting party; research; pursuit
buscado *adj* deliberate, intentional (negligence, etc.)
buscador (-ra) *n* searcher; investigator. *m*, finder (of a camera, etc.)
buscapié *m*, hint or suggestion; *fig* feeler
buscapiés *m*, squib, cracker, firecracker
buscapleitos *mf Lat. Am.* troublemaker
buscar *vt* to search, look for; pursue. **ir a b.,** to go to look for, go and get; bring, fetch
buscarruidos *mf inf* quarrel maker
buscavidas *mf inf* busybody; *inf* go-getter
buscón (-ona) *n* searcher; pickpocket, thief, swindler, rogue
buscona *f*, prostitute
busilis *m*, *inf* knotty problem, snag; **ahí está el b.,** there's the rub; core, main point
búsqueda (de) *f*, search (for)
busto *m*, *art* bust, head and shoulders
butaca *f*, armchair; *theat* orchestra stall; seat (in movies, etc.)

butifarra *f,* sausage made principally in Catalonia and the Balearic Islands; *inf* badly fitting stocking
buzo *m,* diver
buzón *m,* mailbox; letter-box; canal, channel; sluice

C

C. abbrev. of ciudadano
¡ca! *interj* Fancy! Oh no!
cabal *a* just, exact; perfect; complete; faultless. *interj* Exactly! **por sus cabales,** according to plan; perfectly
cábala *f,* cabala; divination; *inf* intrigue. **hacer cábalas,** to venture a guess
cabalgada *f,* cavalcade; foray, raid
cabalgador (-ra) *n* rider, horseman
cabalgadura *f,* riding horse; beast of burden
cabalgar *vi* to ride a horse; ride in procession
cabalístico *a* cabalistic; mysterious
caballa *f,* mackerel
caballada *f,* pack of horses; stud (of horses)
caballeresco *a* gentlemanly; knightly; chivalrous
caballería *f,* riding animal; cavalry; knightly deed or quest; any of Spanish Military Orders; knight-errantry; knighthood; chivalry; share of the spoils of war; horsemanship. **c. andante,** knight-errantry. **c. ligera,** *mil* light horse. **c. mayor,** horses, mares, mules. **c. menor,** asses, donkeys
caballeriza *f,* stable; stud of horses; staff of a stable
caballerizo *m,* head stable-groom. **c. mayor del rey,** Master of the King's Horse
caballero *m,* gentleman; cavalier; knight. **c. andante,** knight-errant. *inf* **c. de industria,** adventurer, sharper. **el C. de la Mancha,** the Knight of La Mancha. **el C. Sin Miedo y Sin Tacha,** the Seigneur de Bayart. **c. del hábito,** knight of one of the Spanish Military Orders. **c. novel,** untried knight. **armar c.,** to dub a knight
caballerosidad *f,* gentlemanliness; nobility; generosity; chivalry
caballeroso *a* gentlemanly; noble; generous; chivalrous
caballete *m,* ridge (of a roof); *mil* wooden horse; brake (for flax and hemp); *agr* furrow; easel; sawing-frame; trestle; bridge (of the nose)
caballito *m, dim* little horse; *pl* merry-go-round; automatic horse gambling game; circus equestrian act. **c. del diablo,** dragonfly
caballo *m,* horse; (chess) knight; (Spanish cards) queen; sawing-frame; *pl* cavalry. **c. balancín,** rocking horse. **c. de batalla,** war-horse; *fig* hobby-horse; forte; crux. **c. de cartón,** hobby-horse; rocking horse. **c. de carrera,** racehorse. **c. de tiro,** draft-horse. **c. de vapor,** horsepower. **c. marino,** sea-horse. **a c.,** on horseback. **A c. regalado no le mires el diente,** Never look a gift horse in the mouth. **caer bien a c.,** to have a good seat (on a horse). **ser un c. loco en una cacharrería,** to be like a bull in a china shop
cabaña *f,* hut, cabin, cottage; flock (of sheep); drove (of mules); *Argentina* cattle ranch; *art* pastoral scene; balk (billiards)
cabaret *m,* cabaret, nightclub
cabaretero *m,* nightclub owner
cabeceada *f, Lat. Am.* nod (of the head)
cabecear *vi* to nod; shake the head in disapproval; move the head from side to side; toss the head (horses); (*aer naut*) pitch; sway (of a carriage); lean; *vt* refoot (socks); head (wine)
cabeceo *m,* nod, shake (of head); (*naut aer*) pitching; lurching (of a carriage, etc.); bight (of river)
cabecera *f,* top, upper portion, head; seat of honor; bedhead; river source; capital (country or county); illustrated chapter heading; pillow; inscription, heading
cabecilla *dim f,* small head. *mf inf* hothead. *m,* rebel leader
cabellera *f,* head of long hair; hair-switch; tail (of comet)
cabello *m,* hair; head of hair; silk (of maize). *fig inf* **asirse de un c.,** to clutch at a straw
cabelludo *a* hairy; *bot* fibrous
caber *vi irr* to be room for, contain; fit into, go into (e.g. **No cabemos todos en este coche,** There isn't room for all of us in this car); happen, befall, have (e.g. **No les cupo tal suerte,** They did not have such luck—Such luck did not befall them); be possible (e.g. **Todo cabe en Dios,** All things are possible with God). **No cabe más,** There's no room for anything else; *fig* That's the limit. *fig* **no c. en sí,** to be beyond oneself (with joy, pride, etc.). **No cabe duda de que,** There's no doubt that. *Pres. Ind.* **quepo, cabes,** etc. *Fut.* **cabré,** etc. *Conditional* **cabría,** etc. *Preterite* **cupe, cupiste,** etc. *Pres. Subjunc.* **quepa, quepas,** etc. *Imperf. Subjunc.* **cupiese,** etc.
cabestrar *vt* to halter
cabestrillo *m,* sling; thin chain (for ornament). **en c.,** in a sling (e.g. **Tenía el brazo en c.,** His arm was in a sling)
cabestro *m,* halter; sling; leading ox
cabeza *f,* head; top, upper end; nail-head; brain; mind; judgment; self-control; edge (of book); peak, summit; source, origin; individual, person; head of cattle; capital city. *m,* leader, chief, head. *mech* **c. de biela,** big-end. *inf* **c. de chorlito,** scatterbrain (person). **c. de hierro,** blockhead. *mil* **c. de puente,** bridgehead. **c. de partido,** principal town of a region. **c. de turco,** scapegoat. **irse la c. (a alguien),** to feel giddy. *fig inf* **meter a uno en la c.,** to put into someone's head. *inf* **quebrarse la c.,** to rack one's brains. *inf* **quitar a uno de la c. (una cosa),** to dissuade; get an idea out of someone's head
cabezada *f,* blow with or on the head; nod; headshake; headstall; *naut* pitching. **dar cabezadas,** to nod, go to sleep
cabezal *m,* small head pillow; *surg* pad; bolster; narrow mattress; *mech* head
cabezo *m,* summit (of mountain); hill; *naut* reef
cabezón *m,* tax-register; collar-band; head-opening (of a garment)
cabezudo *a* large-headed; *inf* obstinate; *inf* heady (of wine). *m,* carnival grotesque
cabida *f,* space, capacity; extent, area
cabildear *vi* to canvass votes, lobby
cabildo *m, ecc* chapter; municipal council; meeting, or meeting place of council. **c. abierto,** town meeting
cabina *f,* cabin. **c. telefónica** phone booth
cabinero, -a *mf, Lat. Am.* flight attendant
cabizbajo *a* crestfallen; pensive, melancholy
cable *m,* cable; string (of bridge); cable's length; **c. aéreo,** overhead cable. **c. alimentario,** feed line. **c. eléctrico,** electric cable
cabo *m,* end, extremity; stump, stub; handle, shaft, haft; leader; *geog* cape; end, conclusion; *naut* rope; ply (of wool, etc.); *mil* corporal; *pl* accessories (clothes); horse's tail and mane. **c. de maestranza,** foreman. **c. de mar,** naval quartermaster. **c. furriel,** *mil* quartermaster. **al c.,** in the end. **llevar a c.,** to finish
Cabo de Hornos Cape Horn
cabotaje *m, naut* coasting trade
cabra *f,* nanny-goat; goat. **c. montesa,** wild goat
cabrerizo (-za) *a* goatish. *m,* goatherd
cabrero (-ra) *m,* goatherd; *a Argentina* bad-tempered, cantankerous
cabria *f,* winch, hoist
cabrilla *f, carp* saw-horse; *pl ast* Pleiades; burn marks

on legs from sitting too near fire; white crests (of waves)
cabrillear *vi* to foam, froth (the sea)
cabrío *a* goatish. *m*, herd of goats. **macho c.,** male goat, he-goat
cabriola *f*, fouetté (in dancing); spin in the air (acrobats); curvet (horses); caper
cabriolar *vi* to curvet; caper, skip
cabriolé *m*, cabriolet; short cape with or without sleeves
cabritilla *f*, dressed kid; lambskin, etc.
cabrito *m*, *zool* kid; *pl* toasted maize, popcorn
cabrón *m*, billy goat, buck, he-goat; *inf* complaisant husband, cuckhold; *Chile* owner or operator of a brothel
cabrona *f*, *Chile* bawd, madam
cabruno *a* goatish
cabujón *m*, *min* uncut gem; unpolished ruby; *pl* vignettes
cacahual *m*, cacao plantation
cacahuete *m*, *bot* peanut, monkey nut
cacao *m*, *bot* cacao tree; cacaonut
cacarear *vi* to crow, cackle; *vt inf* boast
cacareo *m*, crowing, cackling; *inf* boast
cacatúa *f*, cockatoo
cacera *f*, irrigation channel
cacería *f*, hunting party; hunting bag, booty; *art* hunting scene
cacerola *f*, stew-pot, casserole
cachalote *m*, sperm whale
cachano *m*, Old Nick
cachar *vt* to break in fragments; split (wood)
cacharrería *f*, crockery store
cacharro *m*, coarse earthenware vessel; *inf* decrepit, worthless object
cachazudo *a* phlegmatic, slow
cachear *vt* to search (a person) for weapons
Cachemira Kashmir
cachemira *f*, cashmere
cacheo *m*, search (of persons) for weapons
cachetada *f*, *Lat. Am.* slap (in the face)
cachete *m*, blow on the head or face with one's fist; cheek (especially fat one)
cachetero *m*, dagger
cachetina *f*, hand-to-hand fight
cachimba *f*, *Lat. Am.* pipe (for smoking)
cachiporra *f*, club, bludgeon
cachivache *m*, *inf* (gen. *pl*) trash; pots, pans, utensils
cacho *m*, small slice (gen. of bread or fruit)
cachón *m*, breaker, wave; small waterfall
cachorro (-rra) *n* puppy; cub. *m*, small pistol
cacillo *m*, ladle; basting spoon
cacique *m*, Indian chief, cacique; *inf* political "boss"
caciquismo *m*, political "bossism"
caco *m*, pickpocket, thief; *inf* poltroon
cacofonía *f*, cacophony
cacografía *f*, cacography
cacto *m*, cactus
cacumen *m*, *inf* brains, acumen
cada *a* every, each. **c. cual,** each. **c. que,** whenever; every time that. **c. y cuando que,** whenever
cadalso *m*, scaffold; platform, stand
cadáver *m*, corpse
cadavérico *a* cadaverous, ghastly
cadena *f*, chain; link, tie; *fig* bond; *fig* sequence (of events); *law* imprisonment; *arch* buttress; grand chain (dancing); **c. de montañas,** range of mountains. **c. perpetua,** life imprisonment
cadencia *f*, cadence; rhythm; *mus* measure, time; *mus* cadenza
cadencioso *a* rhythmic
cadente *a* falling, declining; decaying, dying; rhythmic
cadera *f*, hip; flank
cadete *m*, *mil* cadet
cadi *mf* caddy
Cádiz Cadiz
caducar *vi* to become senile; become invalid, be annulled; expire, lapse; *fig* be worn out
caduceo *m*, Mercury's wand
caducidad *f*, decrepitude; lapse, expiry
caduco *a* senile; decrepit; perishable; lapsed; obsolete
caduquez *f*, senility
caedizo *a* ready to fall; timid, cowardly, weak
caer *vi irr* to fall, drop; drop out or off; suit, fit, become; fail; fade (colors); *fig* drop (voice); (*with sobre*) attack, fall upon; (*with en*) fall in or on to; decay, collapse; understand; (*with preps. a, hacia*) *fig* look on to, face; (*with por, en*) *fig* fall on, occur on; *vr aer* crash; fly off (buttons, etc.). **c. de cabeza,** to fall head foremost. **c. en conflicto (con),** to come into conflict (with) **c. en las manos de uno,** to come into somebody's possession (come to be owned by somebody). **c. en gracia,** to make a good impression, arouse affection. **caerse de suyo,** to be self-evident. **c. por tierra,** (plan, etc.) to fall through. **Cayó enfermo,** He was taken ill. **cayendo y levantado,** dying *Pres. Ind.* **caigo, caes,** etc. *Pres. Part.* **cayendo.** *Preterite* **cayó cayeron.** *Pres. Subjunc.* **caiga,** etc.
café *m*, coffee (tree, berry, drink); café, coffeehouse. **c. con leche,** café au lait. **c. negro** *Lat. Am. (except Columbia)* black coffee. **c. solo** *Spain* black coffee. **c. tinto** *Colombia* black coffee
cafeína *f*, caffeine
cafetal *m*, coffee plantation
cafetera *f*, coffeepot; *Peru* cab, taxi
cafeto *m*, coffee tree
cafiche *m*, *Argentina, Chile* pimp
caficultor *m*, coffee-grower
caficultura *f*, coffee-growing
cafúa *f*, *Argentina* clink, slammer
cagadas *f pl*, droppings, dung
cagar(se) *vi vt vr* to evacuate (bowels); *vt inf* spoil, make a botch of
cagarruta *f*, dung of sheep, deer, rabbits, etc.
caída *f*, falling; fall; ruin; failure; close (of day); *fig* falling off; hanging (curtains, etc.); diminution; incline; *pl* coarse wool; *inf* repartee. **a la c. de la tarde,** at the end of the afternoon. **a la c. del sol,** at sunset
caído (-da) *a* debilitated, languid; lapsed; (of a shoulder) sloping. **los caídos,** the fallen, the dead (in war, etc.)
caimán *m*, alligator; *inf* shark, astute person
caite *m*, *Central America* sandal
caja *f*, box; safe, cash box; coffin; (of a vehicle) body; *mus* drum; case (of piano, watch, etc.); cavity; well (of a stair); *com* cash; cash-desk; cashier's office; *bot* sheath. **c. de ahorros,** savings bank. **c. de caudales,** strong-box. *print* **c. de imprenta,** type case. **c. de música,** musical box. **c. de reclutamiento,** recruiting office. **c. de velocidades,** gearbox. **c. registradora,** cash register. **c. torácica,** rib cage, thoracic cage
cajero (-ra) *m*, boxmaker; *n com* cashier; pedler **c. automático,** automatic teller, automatic teller machine, bank machine, money machine
cajetilla *f*, packet (cigarettes, etc.)
cajón *m*, chest, locker, case; drawer. **c. de municiones,** ammunition-box
cajonera *f*, *ecc* chest of drawers in sacristy; *agr* frame
cal *f*, lime. **c. muerta,** slaked lime. **c. viva,** quicklime. *fig inf* **de c. y canto,** tough, strong
cala *f*, sample slice (of fruit); *naut* hold; *surg* probe; cove, small bay; *bot* iris
calabacera *f*, *bot* pumpkin or gourd plant
calabacín *m*, kind of vegetable marrow; *inf* dolt
calabaza *f*, *bot* pumpkin (plant and fruit); gourd; *inf* dolt. **dar calabazas,** to refuse (suitor); flunk (an examinee). *inf* **llevar calabazas,** to get the sack; be jilted
calabobos *m*, *inf* drizzle
calabocero *m*, jailer
calabozo *m*, dungeon; prison cell; pruning knife

calada *f,* soaking, wetting through; flight of bird of prey; swoop. **dar una c.,** *fig inf* to dress down
calado *a* soaked, wet through. *m, sew* open-work; fretwork; *naut* draught of a ship; water level; *pl* lace. **c. hasta los huesos,** soaked to the skin; madly in love
calador *m,* one who does open or fretwork; caulking iron; borer; *surg* probe
calafate *m,* caulker
calafatear *vt naut* to caulk
calamaco *m, Mexico* kidney bean
calamar *m, zool* squid, calamary
calambre *m,* cramp. **c. del escribiente,** writer's cramp
calamidad *f,* misfortune, calamity
calamina *f, min* calamine
calamitoso *a* calamitous; unfortunate, unhappy
cálamo *m,* ancient flute; stalk (of grass); *poet* pen
calamocano *a* maudlin, tipsy
calandria *f, orn* calender, lark; *mech* calender; treadmill. *mf inf* malingerer
calaña *f,* sample; model; pattern; kind, quality; temperament; cheap fan
calar *vt* to permeate, soak through; pierce; do openwork (in cloth, paper, metal); cut a sample slice from fruit; pull (hat, etc.) well down on head; put down (an eyeshade or visor); fix (bayonets, etc.); *inf* understand (persons); *inf* guess, realize; *naut* let down; *vi naut* draw (water); *vr* be drenched, wet through; swoop (birds of prey); *inf* sneak in. *a* calcareous
calar *m,* limestone deposit or region
calatear *vt, Peru* to undress
calato, -a *a, Peru* naked, nude; broke, penniless
calavera *f,* skull. *m,* dare-devil, madcap; roué; *Mexico* taillight
calaverada *f, inf* dare-devilment, foolishness; escapade
calcañar *m,* heel (of foot)
calcar *vt* to trace (drawing); press with foot; copy servilely, imitate
calcáreo *a* calcareous
calce *m,* rim of a wheel; wedge; tyre
calcés *m, naut* masthead
calceta *f,* stocking; fetter. *inf* **hacer c.,** to knit
calcetería *f,* hosiery shop; hosiery trade
calcetero (-ra) *n* hosier; hose maker or darner
calcetín *m,* sock
calcificación *f, med* calcification
calcinación *f,* calcination
calcinar *vt* to calcine
calcio *m,* calcium
calco *m,* tracing (drawing)
calcografía *f,* chalcography
calcografiar *vt* to transfer; make chalcographies of
calcomanía *f,* transfer
calculación *f,* calculation
calculado *a* calculated
calculador *a* calculating. *m,* calculating machine, comptometer
calcular *vt* to calculate
cálculo *m,* calculation; *math* estimate; investigation; conjecture; (math med) calculus. **c. hepático,** *med* gallstone
calda *f,* heating; *pl* hot mineral baths
caldear *vt* to heat
caldeo *m,* heating
caldera *f,* cauldron; cauldron full; *WH* teapot; *eng* boiler. **c. de vapor,** steam-boiler
calderería *f,* coppersmith's trade and shop
calderero *m,* boiler maker; coppersmith; tinker
calderilla *f,* holy water stoup; any copper coin
caldero *m,* small cauldron; casserole; kettle
calderón *m,* large cauldron; *mus* rest; *mus* trill; pause
caldo *m,* broth; salad dressing; *pl agr* oil, wine, vegetable juices
calefacción *f,* heating. **c. central,** central heating
calendario *m,* calendar. **c. deportivo,** fixture card. **c. gregoriano,** Gregorian calendar
calendas *f pl,* calends. **en las c. griegas,** at the Greek calends
caléndula *f,* marigold
calentador *a* heating, warming. *m,* heater; warming-pan
calentamiento *m,* heating, warming
calentar *vt irr* to heat, warm; rev-up (an engine); hasten; *inf* spank; *vr* warm oneself; be in heat (animals); grow excited. See **acertar**
calentura *f,* fever
calenturiento *a* feverish
calera *f,* lime-pit; lime-kiln; fishing smack
calesa *f,* calash, calèche, chaise (two-wheeled carriage)
calesita *f, Lat. Am.* merry-go-round
caleta *f,* cove, creek
caletre *m, inf* discernment, head, sense
calibrar *vt* to calibrate; gauge
calibre *m, mech* gauge; bore, caliber; diameter (tubes, pipes, etc.)
calidad *f,* quality; role; character, temperament; condition, requisite; importance, gravity; personal particulars; nobility; *pl* qualities of the mind. **c. originaria,** rank and birth. **c. de oficio,** justification for action. **en c. de,** in the capacity of
cálido *a* warm, hot; warming, heating; vehement, ardent; *art* warm
calidoscopio *m,* kaleidoscope
calientalibros *mf,* bookworm (person)
calientapiés *m,* footwarmer
calientaplatos *m,* hot plate, plate-warmer
caliente *a* warm, hot; excited; *art* warm
calientito *a* piping hot
califa *m,* caliph
calificable *a* classifiable; qualifiable
calificación *f,* classification; qualification; judgment; mark, place (examinations)
calificar *vt* to class; authorize; judge (qualities); *fig* ennoble; *vr* prove noble descent
calificativo *a gram* qualifying. *m,* epithet
californio (-ia) *a* and *n* Californian
caliginoso *a* murky, dark
caligrafía *f,* calligraphy
calígrafo *m,* calligraphist
caliqueño *m,* cheroot
calistenia *f,* callisthenics
cáliz *m,* chalice; *poet* cup; *bot* calyx
caliza *f,* limestone
calizo *a* calcareous
callado *a* silent; reserved; secret
callar(se) *vi* and *vr* to say nothing, keep silent; stop speaking; stop making any sound (persons, animals, things); *vt* conceal, keep secret; omit, leave out; *inf interj* **¡Calle!** You don't say so! **Quien calla otorga,** Silence gives consent
calle *f,* street. **c. de un sentido, c. de una corrida** *Mexico* one-way street. **c. de una sola mano** *Argentina* one-way street *inf* **abrir c.,** to clear the way. *inf* **dejar en la c.,** to leave destitute. *inf* **echar a la c.,** put out of the house, to throw out of the house; make known, publish. **ponerse en la c.,** to go out
calleja, callejuela *f,* small street, alley, side street
callejear *vi* to walk the streets, wander about the streets, loaf around the streets
callejero *a* fond of gadding. *m,* street directory
callejón *m,* alley, lane. **c. sin salida,** cul-de-sac; *fig* impasse
callicida *m,* corn cure
callista *mf* chiropodist
callo *m,* corn, callosity; *med* callus; *pl* tripe
calloso *a* callous, horny
calma *f,* calm, airlessness; serenity, composure; quiet, tranquillity, peace. **c. chicha,** dead calm. **en c.,** at peace; tranquil; calm (of the sea)
calmante *a* calming, soothing. *med a* and *m,* sedative, tranquilizer

calmar *vt* to soothe, calm; moderate, mitigate; pacify; quench (thirst); *vi* grow calm; moderate; be becalmed
calmoso *a* calm, tranquil; *inf* sluggish, lazy; imperturbable
calor *m,* heat; ardor, vehemence; cordiality; *fig* heat (of battle); excitement
caloría *f, phys* calorie
calórico *a phys* caloric, thermic
calorífero *a* heat-giving. *m,* heater, radiator
calumnia *f,* calumny; *law* slander
calumniador (-ra) *a* slandering. *n* calumniator, slanderer
calumniar *vt* to calumniate; *law* slander
calumnioso *a* calumnious, slanderous
caluroso *a* hot, warm; cordial, friendly; enthusiastic; ardent, impassioned; excited
calva *f,* bald patch on head; worn place (cloth, etc.); bare spot, clearing (trees, etc.)
Calvario *m,* Calvary; *inf* series of disasters; *inf* debts
calvero *m,* clearing (in a wood); chalk or marl pit
calvicie *f,* baldness
calvo *a* bald; bare, barren (land); worn (cloth, etc.)
calza *f,* breeches (gen. *pl*); wedge; *inf* stocking. *inf* **tomar calzas,** to beat it
calzada *f,* roadway. **c. romana,** Roman road
calzado *m,* footwear, shoes
calzador *m,* shoehorn
calzadura *f,* wedging (of a wheel); act of putting on shoes; felloe of a wheel
calzar *vt* to put on shoes; wear (spurs, gloves, etc.); wedge, block (wheel); scotch (a wheel). *fig inf* **c. el coturno,** don the buskin; write in the sublime style; write a tragedy, write tragedies. **calzarse a una persona,** to have a person in one's pocket
calzón *m,* breeches (gen. *pl*). *fig inf* **ponerse los calzones,** to wear the breeches (of a woman)
calzonazos *m, inf* weak-willed, easily led fellow
calzoncillos *m pl,* drawers, pants
calzoneras *fpl, Mexico* pants buttoned down the sides
cama *f,* bed; bedstead; bedhanging; lair, form; floor (of a cart); check (of bridle) (gen. *pl*). **c. de campaña,** camp bed. **c. de matrimonio,** double bed. **c. de monja,** single bed. **c. de operaciones,** operating table. **c. turca,** settee-bed. **guardar c.,** to stay in bed
camada *f,* brood, litter; *inf* gang
camafeo *m,* cameo
camaleón *m,* chameleon; *inf* changeable person
cámara *f,* chamber; hall; house (of deputies); granary; *naut* state room; chamber (firearms, mines); *phys* camera; human excrement; *aut* inner tube. **c. acorazada,** strong-room. **c. alta,** Upper House, **c. baja** *or* **c. de los comunes,** lower house, house of commons. **c. de comercio,** chamber of commerce. **c. oscura,** (optics) dark room
camarada *mf* pal, companion, comrade
camaradería *f,* comradeship, companionship
camarera *f,* waiting-maid; waitress; chambermaid; stewardess
camarero *m,* waiter; papal chamberlain; chamberlain; steward; valet. **c. mayor,** lord chamberlain
camarilla *f,* palace or other clique, coterie; *inf* backscratch
camarín *m, theat* dressing-room; closet; boudoir; cage (of a lift); niche
camarón *m,* prawn, shrimp; tip, reward
camarote *m,* cabin; berth
cambalachear *vt inf* to barter
cambalache *m, Lat. Am.* secondhand shop; exchange
cámbaro *m,* sea-crab
cambiable *a* exchangeable; changeable
cambiante *a* exchanging; changing. *m,* sheen, luster (gen. *pl*); money changer
cambiar *vt* to exchange; convert. *vt* and *vi* change, alter; *vi* and *vr* to veer (wind). **c. de aguas,** *poet* to move (change one's residence). **c. de aire,** get a change of scenery. **c. de frente,** to face about; *fig* change front
cambio *m,* exchange; change; *com* rate of exchange; money change; *com* premium on bills of exchange. **a c. de, en c. de,** in exchange for; instead of. **en c.,** instead, on the other hand. **c. de velocidad,** *aut* gear-changing. **letra de c.,** bill of exchange. **libre c.,** free trade
cambista *mf* money changer. *m,* banker
cambullón *m, Lat. Am.* swindle
cambur *m, Venezuela* banana
camelar *vt inf* to woo; seduce
camelia *f,* camelia. **c. japonesa,** japonica
camelo *m, inf* eyewash
camellero *m,* camel keeper or driver
camello *m,* camel. **c. pardal,** giraffe
camellón *m,* furrow; drinking trough; *Mexico* island, traffic island, median strip
camilla *f,* couch; small round skirted table with brazier underneath; stretcher, litter
camillero *m, mil* stretcher-bearer
caminador *a* in the habit of walking a great deal
caminante *mf* walker, traveler
caminar *vi* to travel; walk; *fig* move on, go (inanimate things). *fig inf* **c. derecho,** to walk uprightly
caminata *f,* long, tiring walk; excursion
caminejo *m,* worn path
camino *m,* road; route; journey; way, means; **c. de hierro,** railway. **c. de mesa,** table-runner. **c. de sirga,** towpath. **c. real,** highway, main road. **de c.,** on the way, in passing. **ponerse en c.,** to set out
camión *m,* truck. **c. de volteo, c. volquete** dump truck; *Mexico* bus; truck
camionera *f, Mexico* bus station
camioneta *f,* light truck, pick-up truck; *WH* station wagon
camisa *f,* shirt, stiff shirt; thin skin (of fruit); sloughed skin of snakes; coat (of whitewash, etc.); *mech* jacket; mantle (gas). **c. de fuerza,** straitjacket. **dejar sin c.,** *inf* to leave penniless
camisería *f,* shirt shop or factory
camisero (-ra) *n* shirt maker or seller
camiseta *f,* undershirt, T-shirt. **c. de fútbol,** soccer player's jersey
camisola *f,* stiff shirt; ruffled shirt
camisón *m,* large wide shirt; night shirt
camomila *f,* chamomile
camorra *f, inf* brawl, shindy. **armar c.,** to start a row
camote *m, Lat. Am.* sweet potato
campal *a* field, country
campamento *m,* camping; *mil* encampment; camp; jamboree
campana *f,* bell; anything bell-shaped; church, parish. **c. de chimenea,** mantelpiece. **c. de hogar,** hood, shutter (of a fireplace)
campanada *f,* peal of a bell; scandal
campanario *m,* belfry, bell tower
campanear *vi* to ring bells frequently
campaneo *m,* bell-ringing; chime
campanero *m,* bell-founder; bell ringer
campanil *m,* small belfry, campanile
campanilla *f,* hand-bell; bubble; any bell-shaped flower
campante *a* outstanding; *inf* proud, satisfied
campanudo *a* bell-shaped; sonorous (of words); pompous (of speech)
campaña *f,* level country; campaign. *naut* voyage, cruise. **correr la c.,** to reconnoiter. **la C. del Desierto,** the War against the Gauchos (in Argentina)
campar *vi* to camp. *inf* **c. por sus respetos,** to stand on one's own feet
campeador *a* mighty in battle
campear *vi* to go out to graze; grow green (crops); excel; *mil* be engaged in a campaign, reconnoiter
campechano *a inf* hearty; frank; cheerful; generous
campeche *m, bot* logwood
campeón *m,* champion; advocate, defender
campeonato *m,* championship
campesinado *m,* peasantry

campesino (-na) *a* rural, rustic. *n* country dweller
campestre *a* rural
campiña *f*, expanse of cultivated land; countryside, landscape
campo *m*, country (as opposed to urban areas); field; *fig* sphere, province; (*phys her mil*) field; *art* ground; *mil* camp, army; plain ground (of silks, etc.). «**C. Abierto**», "Miscellaneous" (e.g. as the title of a section in a book catalog). **c. de aterrizaje,** *aer* landing-field. **c. de batalla,** battlefield. **c. de concentración,** concentration camp. **c. de experimentación,** testing ground. **c. de golf,** golf course. **c. de prisioneros** *mil* prison camp. **c. de tiro,** rifle-range. **c. santo,** graveyard. **c. visual,** field of vision. **a c. abierto,** in the open air. **a c. travieso,** cross-country
camuflaje *m*, camouflage
camuflar *vt* to camouflage
can *m*, dog; trigger; *arch* modillion; *ast* Dog Star
cana *f*, gray hair
Canadá Canada
canadiense *a* and *mf* Canadian
canal *m*, canal. *mf*, *geol* subterranean waterway; channel; *anat* canal, duct; defile, narrow valley; gutter; drinking trough; animal carcass. **abrir en c.,** to open up, split open
canalera *f*, roof gutter
canaleta *f*, (wooden) trough; gutter (on roof)
canalete *m*, paddle
canalización *f*, canalization; *elec* main, mains; piping, tubing
canalizar *vt* to make canals or channels; regulate waters of rivers, etc.; canalize
canalón *m*, gutter, spout; shovel hat; pantile
canalla *f*, *inf* mob, rabble. *m*, *inf* scoundrel
canallesco *a* scoundrelly, knavish; despicable
canana *f*, cartridge belt
canapé *m*, sofa
canario (-ia) *m*, canary. *a* and *n* pertaining to or native of the Canary Islands.
canasta *f*, hamper, basket; card game
canastilla *f*, small basket; layette
canastillo *m*, basket-work tray
cáncamo *m*, ring-bolt
cancamusa *f*, *inf* trick, deception
cancel *m*, draftscreen; *ecc* screen
cancela *f*, wrought-iron door
cancelación *f*, cancellation; expunging
cancelar *vt* to cancel; expunge, annul; abolish, blot out; pay off, clear (a mortgage)
cancelaría *f*, papal chancery
cancelario *m*, chancellor (universities)
cáncer *m*, cancer
cancerar *vt* to consume; weaken; mortify; *vr* suffer from cancer; become cancerous
cancerbero *m*, *myth* Cerberus; *fig* unbribable guard
canceroso *a* cancerous
cancha *f*, *sport* fronton; (tennis) court; cockpit; yard; hippodrome; widest part of a river; road; toasted maize. **estar en su cancha** *Argentina, Chile* to be in one's element. **tener cancha** *Argentina* to be experienced; *Venezuela* have charisma, charm, allure
canciller *m*, chancellor; foreign minister; assistant vice-consul
cancillería *f*, chancellorship; chancellery; foreign ministry
canción *f*, song; lyric poem; musical accompaniment; old name for any poetical composition. **volver a la misma c.,** *fig* to be always harping on the same theme
cancionero *m*, collection of songs and verses; songbook
cancionista *mf* singer; song writer
candado *m*, padlock; earring
candeal *a* white (of bread)
candela *f*, candle; horse-chestnut flower; candlestick; *inf* fire. **en c.,** *naut* vertical (of masts, etc.)
candelabro *m*, candelabrum
candelero *m*, candlestick; lamp; candle maker or seller; *naut* stanchion
candente *a* candescent, red-hot
candidatear *vi* to run (for office)
candidato (-ta) *n* candidate
candidatura *f*, candidature
candidez *f*, simplicity, ingenuousness; candidness
cándido *a* white; simple, ingenuous; candid, frank
candil *m*, oil lamp; Greek lamp; tips of stag's horns; *inf* cock of a hat
candileja *f*, oil reservoir of lamp; *pl* footlights, floats
candor *m*, extreme whiteness; sincerity, candor; simplicity, innocence
candoroso *a* candid, open; simple, honest
canela *f*, *bot* cinnamon; *fig* anything exquisitely perfect
canelo *m*, cinnamon tree. *a* cinnamon-colored
cangilón *m*, pitcher, jar; bucket (for water); dredging bucket
cangreja *f*, *naut* gaffsail. **c. de mesana,** *naut* jigger
cangrejo *m*, crab. **c. de mar,** sea-crab. **c. ermitaño,** hermit crab
canguro *m*, kangaroo
caníbal *a* and *mf* cannibal
canibalismo *m*, cannibalism
canica *f*, marble (for playing with)
canícula *f*, dog days; *ast* Dog star
caniculares *m pl* dog days
canijo *a inf* delicate, sickly; anemic, stunted
canilla *f*, long bone of leg or arm; any principal bones in bird's wing; tap, faucet; spool, reel; fault (in cloth)
canillera *f*, *Lat. Am.* cowardice; fear
canillito, -a *mf*, *Lat. Am.* newsboy, newsgirl
canino *a* canine
canje *m*, (diplomacy, *mil., com.*) exchange, substitution. **c. de prisioneros,** exchange of prisoners
canjear *vt* to exchange
cano *a* white-haired, hoary; ancient; *poet* white
canoa *f*, canoe; launch. **c. automóvil,** motor launch
canoero (-ra) *n* canoeist
canódromo *m*, dog-race track
canon *m*, rule; (*ecc print*) canon; catalog; part of the Mass; *mus* canon, catch; tax. *pl* canon law
canónico *a* canonic, canonical
canónigo *m*, canon; prebendary
canonización *f*, canonization
canonizar *vt* to canonize; extol, exalt; approve, acclaim
canonjía *f*, canonry, canonship; *inf* sinecure
canoso *a* white-haired, hoary
cansado (-da) *a* tired; weary; exhausted; decadent; tiresome; *inf* fed up. *n* bore, tedious person
cansancio *m*, fatigue, weariness
cansar *vt* to tire, weary; *agr* exhaust soil; bore; badger, annoy; *vr* be tired; grow weary
cansino *a* worn-out (of horses, etc.)
cantable *a* singable; *mus* cantabile
cantábrico (-ca) *a* and *n* Cantabrian
cantante *a* singing. *mf* professional singer
cantar *vi* to sing; twitter, chirp; extol; *inf* squeak, creak; *fig* call (cards); *inf* squeal, confess. *m*, song. **C. de los Cantares,** Song of Songs. **cantarlas claras,** to call a spade a spade
cántara *f*, pitcher, jug
cantárida *f*, Spanish fly
cántaro *m*, pitcher, jug; jugful; varying wine measure; ballot box; tax on spirits and oil
cantata *f*, cantata
cantatriz *f*, singer, prima donna
cante *m*, song; singing
cantera *f*, *min* quarry; capacity, talent
cantería *f*, stone-cutting; quarrying; building made of hewn stone
cantero *m*, stone-cutter; quarryman
cántico *m*, *ecc* canticle; *poet* poem
cantidad *f*, quantity; large part; portion; sum of money; quantity (prosody). **c. llovida,** rainfall

cantiga *or* **cántiga** *f,* old poetic form designed to be sung
cantil *m,* cliff; steep rock
cantimplora *f,* water cooler; canteen (of water); siphon
cantina *f,* wine cellar; canteen; refreshment room
cantinero *m,* sutler; owner of a canteen
canto *m,* singing; song; canto; epic or other poem; end, rim, edge; non-cutting edge (knives, swords); pebble, stone; angle (of a building). *mus* **c. llano,** plain-song. **al c. del gallo,** at cockcrow. **de c.,** on edge
cantón *m,* province, region; corner (of a street); cantonment; *her* canton, quartering
cantonera *f,* corner-piece (books, furniture, etc., as ornament); angle-iron; bracket, small shelf
cantor (-ra) *a* singing. *n* singer; song-bird
Cantórbery Canterbury
cantuja *f, Peru* underworld slang
canturía *f,* singing exercise; vocal music; monotonous song; droning; *mus* execution, technique
canturreo, *m,* **canturria** *f,* humming; droning
canturriar *vi inf* to hum, sing under one's breath
caña *f,* stalk; reed; bone of arm or leg; leg (of a trouser, stocking, boot, etc.); marrow; *bot* cane; tumbler, glass; wine measure; gallery (of mine); *pl* mock joust on horseback using **cañas** as spears. **c. de azúcar,** sugarcane. **c. de pescar,** fishing rod. **c. del timón,** tiller *naut*
cañada *f,* glen, gulch, gully, hollow, ravine, vale, cattle path; *WH* brook, cattle track
cañal *m,* cane-break; weir (for fish)
cañamazo *m,* hempen canvas; embroidery canvas; embroidered canvas
cañamelar *m,* sugar-cane plantation
cáñamo *m,* hemp; *Lat. Am.* marijuana
cañar *m,* canebrake; growth of reeds; fishgarth made of reeds
cañavalera *f,* canefield
cañaveral *m,* cane-brake; *WH* bamboo field
cañazo *m,* blow with a cane
cañería *f,* conduit; pipe; piping
cañero *m,* pipe layer
caño *m,* pipe, tube, sewer; organ pipe; jet (of water); mine gallery
cañón *m,* pipe, cylindrical tube; flue; quill (of birds); cannon; soft down; *arch* shaft (of column); stack (of a chimney). **c. antiaéreo,** A.A. gun. **c. antitanque,** anti-tank gun. **c. de escalera,** well of a staircase; *slang* terrific-looking, absolutely gorgeous (e.g. mujer cañón)
cañonazo *m,* cannon shot; roar of a cannon
cañoneo *m,* cannonade; bombardment
cañonería *f, mil* group of cannon; *mus* set of organ pipes
cañonero *m,* gunboat
cañuto *m, bot* internode; small pipe or tube; *inf* talebearer
caoba *f, bot* mahogany
caos *m,* chaos; confusion
caótico *a* chaotic
capa *f,* cloak; cape; *ecc* cope; coating; layer; cover; coat (animals); *fig* cloak, disguise; *geol* stratum. **la c. del cielo,** the canopy of heaven. *fig inf* **echar la c. al toro,** to throw one's cap over the windmill. *naut* **estarse** (*or* **ponerse) a la c.,** to lie to
capacete *m,* helmet
capacha *f* basket; *Argentina, Chile* clink, jug (jail)
capacidad *f,* capacity; extension, space; mental capacity, talent; opportunity, means; *law* capacity. **c. de compra,** buying power, purchasing power. **c. de producción,** output
capacitación *f,* qualification, (act of) qualifying; (act of) training
capacitar *vt* to capacitate, qualify, enable
capadura *f,* castration
capar *vt* to castrate, geld; *inf* diminish, reduce
caparazón *m,* caparison, horse blanket; waterproof cover; hood (of carriages); nosebag; shell (insects, crustaceans)
capataz *m,* foreman; steward; overseer
capaz *a* capacious; large, spacious; capable, competent; *law* able
capcioso *a* deceitful, artful; captious, carping
capear *vt* to steal a cape; play the bull with a cape (bullfighting); *inf* put off with excuses, deceive; *naut* lie to
capelo *m,* cardinal's hat; cardinalate
capellán *m,* chaplain; any ecclesiastic
capeo *m,* playing the bull with a cape (bullfighting)
caperuza *f,* hood, pointed cap; *arch* coping-stone
capigorrón *a inf* loafing. *m,* loafer, idler
capilar *a* capillary
capilaridad *f,* capillarity
capilla *f,* cowl, hood; chapel; *ecc* chapter; *ecc* choir. **c. ardiente,** chapelle ardente. **estar en c.,** to await execution (criminals); *inf* be in suspense, await anxiously
capillero *m,* sexton; churchwarden
capillo *m,* baby's bonnet; cocoon of silkworm; flowerbud
capirotazo *m,* box on the ear; fillip
capirote *m,* academic hood and cap; hood (falconry); tall pointed cap. **ser tonto de c.,** *inf* to be a complete fool
capitación *f,* poll-tax, capitation
capital *a* relating to the head; capital (sins, etc.); main, principal. *m,* capital, patrimony; *com* capital stock. *f,* capital (city). **c. pagado,** paid-in capital stock
capitalino, -a *Lat. Am. a* of the capital; *n* native of the capital; resident of the capital
capitalismo *m,* capitalism
capitalista *a* capitalistic. *mf* capitalist
capitalización *f,* capitalization
capitalizar *vt* to capitalize
capitán *m,* captain, skipper; chief, leader; ringleader. *aer* **c. de aviación,** group captain. **c. de fragata,** *nav* commander. **c. de puerto,** harbor master. **c. general de ejército,** field-marshal
capitana *f,* admiral's ship; *inf* captain's wife
capitanear *vt* to captain, command; *fig* guide, lead
capitanía *f,* captaincy; captainship
capitolio *m,* dignified building; *arch* acropolis; Capitol
capitulación *f,* agreement, pact; capitulation; *pl* marriage articles
capitular *a* capitulary, belonging to a Chapter. *m,* capitular, member of a Chapter. *vi* to make an agreement; capitulate; sing prayers; arrange order
capítulo *m, ecc* Chapter; meeting of town council, etc.; chapter (of book); item (in a budget); determination, decision
capó *m, aut* hood
capón *a* castrated; gelded. *m,* capon; bundle of firewood or vines
caponera *f,* coop for fattening capons; *inf* gaol; *inf* place where one lives well free of charge
capota *f, bot* head of teasel; bonnet; hood (of vehicles)
capote *m,* short, brightly colored cape (used by bullfighters); cape coat; (cards) slam; *inf* scowl
capricho *m,* caprice, fancy; strong desire
caprichoso *a* capricious; whimsical
caprichudo *a* headstrong; capricious
cápsula *f,* cartridge-case; bottlecap; (*bot med chem zool*) capsule
captar *vt* gain, attract (goodwill, attention, etc.); *mech* collect; monitor (foreign broadcasts)
captor *m,* capturer
captura *f, law* capture; seizing, arrest
capturar *vt* to capture; arrest, apprehend
capucha *f,* hood; cowl; *print* circumflex accent
capuchina *f,* Capuchin nun; *bot* nasturtium; table-lamp with an extinguisher
capucho *m,* cowl
capullo *m,* cocoon; flower bud; acorn cup; *anat* prepuce
caqui *m,* khaki; khaki color
cara *f,* face; likeness, aspect; façade, front; surface; side

(of metal, etc.); mien. **c. a c.,** face to face; frankly; openly. *inf* **c. de juez,** severe face. *inf* **c. de pascua,** smiling face. *inf* **c. de vinagre,** sour face. **c. o cruz,** heads or tails. **c. o sello** *Argentina, Chile,* heads or tails **de c.,** opposite. **hacer a dos caras,** to be deceitful, be two-faced. **hacer c. (a),** to stand up to
caraba *f, slang* 25-centimo coin
cárabe *m,* amber
carabina *f,* carbine; rifle
carabinazo *m,* report of a carbine
carabinero *m,* carabineer; customs' guard, revenue guard; customs officer, customs official
caracol *m,* snail; snail's shell; cure; *zool* cochlea; winding stair. **c. marino,** periwinkle. **¡Caracoles!** Fancy!
caracola *f,* conch shell used as a horn
caracolear *vi* to prance from side to side (horses)
carácter *m,* sign, mark; character, writing (gen. *pl*); style of writing; brand (animals); nature, temperament; character, individuality, strong-mindedness, energy, firmness; condition, state, capacity. **comedia de c.,** psychological play. **en su c. de,** as in one's capacity as. **caracteres de imprenta,** printing types
característica *f,* quality, characteristic; *math* characteristic; actress who plays the part of an old woman
característico *a* characteristic, distinctive. *m,* actor who plays roles of old men
caracterización *f,* characterization; *theat* make-up
caracterizar *vt* to characterize; confer an office, honor, dignity, on; *theat* create a character; *vr theat* to make up, dress as, a character
caraíta *a* and *mf* Karaite
¡caramba! *interj* gosh!; blast!
carámbano *m,* icicle
carambola *f,* cannon (billiards); *inf* double effect; *inf* trick, deception
caramelo *m,* caramel; toffee
caramillo *m,* flageolet; small flute, pipe; gossip, intrigue
carancho *m, Argentina* vulture; *Peru* owl
carantamaula *f, inf* hideous mask; ugly person
carapacho *m,* carapace, shell
carátula *f,* mask; *fig* dramatic art, the theater
caravana *f,* caravan, group of traders, pilgrims, etc. (especially in East); *inf* crowd of excursionists, picnickers, etc.
¡caray! *interj* blast!; gosh!
carbólico *a* carbolic
carbón *m,* coal; charcoal; black chalk, crayon. **c. bituminoso,** soft coal. **c. de coque,** coke. **c. de leña,** charcoal. **c. mineral,** coal, anthracite. **mina de c.,** coal-mine
carbonada *f, Lat. Am.* meat stew
carboncillo *m,* charcoal crayon
carbonear *vt* to turn into charcoal; *naut* coal
carboneo *m,* coaling
carbonera *f,* coal-cellar, coal-house, etc.; coal-scuttle; woman who sells charcoal or coal; charcoal burner
carbonería *f,* coal or charcoal merchant's office
carbonero *a* relating to coal or charcoal. *m,* collier; charcoal maker; coal merchant; *naut* coal-ship
carbónico *a chem* carbonic
carbonífero *a* carboniferous
carbonizar *vt* to carbonize
carbono *m, chem* carbon
carbunco *m, med* carbuncle
carbúnculo *m,* carbuncle, ruby
carburador *m,* carburetor
carcaj *m,* quiver (for arrows); *Mexico* rifle case
carcajada *f,* burst of laughter, guffaw. **reírse a carcajadas,** to roar with laughter
carcajearse *vi* to guffaw
carcamal *m, inf* dotard
cárcel *f,* prison, jail
carcelario *a* prison, jail
carcelero (-ra) *a* jail. *n* jailer
cárcola *f,* treadle (of a loom)
carcoma *f,* wood-worm; dry rot; *fig* gnawing care; spendthrift
carcomer *vt* to gnaw wood (worms); *fig* undermine (health, etc.); *vr* be worm-eaten
carda *f,* card, carding; teasel head; card brush; *inf* reprimand
cardador (-ra) *n* carder, comber
cardadura *f,* carding; carding frame
cardar *vt* to card, tease; brush up (felt, etc.)
cardenal *m,* cardinal; cardinal bird; bruise
cardenalato *m,* cardinalate, cardinalship
cardenillo *m,* verdigris; *art* verditer
cárdeno *a* livid
cardíaco *a med* cardiac
cardinal *a* principal; cardinal (point); *gram* cardinal (number)
cardiógrafo *m, med* cardiograph
cardiograma *m, med* cardiogram
cardo *m, bot* thistle
carear *vt* to confront; compare; *vi* turn towards, face; *vr* meet; come together
carecer *vi irr* to be short; lack, need (e.g. **Carece de las condiciones necesarias,** It lacks the necessary conditions). See **conocer**
carencia *f,* shortage, lack
carestía *f,* shortage, scarcity; famine; dearness, high price
careta *f,* mask; beekeeper's veil; fencing mask. *fig* **quitar la c. (a),** to unmask
carey *m, zool* shell turtle; tortoise-shell
carga *f,* loading; *elec* charging, charge; load; burden, weight; cargo; explosive charge; *fig* imposition; tax; duty, obligation. *naut* **c. de profundidad,** depth charge
cargadero *m,* place where goods are loaded or unloaded
cargado *a* loaded; heavy, sultry; strong (tea, coffee). **c. de cadenas,** (prisoner, etc.) in chains. **c. de espaldas,** round-shouldered
cargador *m,* loader; porter; dockhand; pitchfork; rammer; *mech* stoker; *elec* charger
cargamento *m, naut* cargo, freight, shipload
cargar *vt* to load; charge (guns, etc.); stoke; overburden; tax, impose; blame for, charge with; *inf* annoy, bore; *Argentina inf* to kid, tease; *com* charge, book; *mil* attack; (football) tackle; *vi* tip, slope; (*with con*) carry away; be loaded with (fruit); assume responsibility; (*with sobre*) importune, urge; lean against; *vr* turn (head, etc.); lower, grow darker (sky); (*with de*) be abundant (in or with); load oneself with
cargazón *f,* cargo; loading; heaviness; darkness (of the sky)
cargo *m,* loading; load, weight; post, office; duty, obligation; management, charge; care; *com* debit; accusation. *com* **el c. y la data,** debit and credit. **hacerse c. de,** to take charge of; understand; consider carefully. **ser en c. (a),** to be debtor (to)
cargosear *vt, Lat. Am.* to annoy, pester
cargoso, -a *a, Lat. Am.* annoying, pestering
cariancho *a inf* broadfaced
cariacontecido *a* crestfallen, disappointed; glum
cariarse *vr* to become carious
caribe *a* Caribbean. *mf* cannibal, savage
caricatura *f,* caricature
caricaturista *mf* caricaturist
caricaturizar *vt* to caricature
caricia *f,* caress
caridad *f,* charity; charitableness; alms
caries *f,* caries
carilargo *a inf* long-faced
carilla *f, dim* small face; mask; page (of a book)
carilleno *a inf* plump-faced, round-faced
carillón *m,* peal (of bells)
cariño *m,* affection; love; caress affectionately (gen. *pl*); fondness, inclination. **con c.,** affectionately
cariñoso *a* affectionate; loving; kind

carioca *a* of Rio de Janeiro; *n* native of Rio de Janeiro; resident of Rio de Janeiro
carirredondo *a inf* roundfaced
carismático *a* charismatic
caritativo *a* charitable
cariz *m*, appearance of the sky; look, face; aspect; *inf* outlook (for a business deal, etc.)
carlista *a* and *mf* Carlist
carmelita *a* and *mf* Carmelite
carmen *m*, country house and garden (Granada); song; poem
carmesí *a* crimson. *m*, crimson color; cramoisy
carmín *m*, red, carmine color; red wild rose-tree and flower
carnada *f*, bait
carnaje *m*, salted meat
carnal *a* carnal; lascivious; materialistic, worldly; related by blood
carnalidad *f*, carnality
carnaval *m*, carnival. **martes de c.,** Shrove Tuesday
carnavalesco *a* carnival
carne *f*, flesh; meat; pulpy part of fruit; carnality. **c. concentrada,** meat extract. **c. congelada,** frozen meat. **c. de gallina** *fig* gooseflesh. **c. de membrillo,** quince cheese or conserve. **c. y hueso,** *fig* flesh and blood. *inf* **cobrar carnes,** to put on weight. **poner toda la c. en el asador,** *inf* to put all one's eggs in one basket
carné de conductor *Argentina* driver's license
carnerada *f*, flock of sheep
carnerero (-ra) *n* shepherd
carnero *m*, sheep; mutton; mortuary; charnel-house; family burial vault. **c. marino,** *zool* seal
carnestolendas *f pl* three days of carnival before Ash Wednesday
carnet *m*, notebook, diary; identity card; membership card, pass. **c. de chófer,** driver's license
carnicería *f*, butcher's shop; carnage, slaughter
carnicero *a* carnivorous; inhuman, cruel. *m*, butcher
carnívoro *a* carnivorous. *m*, carnivore
carnosidad *f*, proud flesh; local fat; fatness
carnoso *a* meaty; fleshy; full of marrow; *bot* pulpy, juicy
caro *a* beloved; expensive; dear. *adv* expensively; dear
carolingio (-ia) *a* and *n* Carolingian
carótida *f*, carotid artery
carpa *f*, *icht* carp. **c. dorada,** goldfish; *Lat. Am.* tent; awning
carpanta *f*, *inf* violent hunger; *Mexico* gang
Cárpatos, los Montes the Carpathian Mountains
carpeta *f*, table or chest cover, doily; writing case; portfolio; docket, letter file
carpetazo, dar *vt* to shelve (a project, etc.)
carpintear *vi* to carpenter
carpintería *f*, carpenter's shop; carpentry
carpinteril *a* carpentering
carpintero *m*, carpenter, joiner; *theat* scene-shifter. **c. de carretas,** wheelwright. **c. de ribera,** shipwright
carraca *f*, rattle; ratchet-drill
Carrapempe *m*, Old Nick
carrascal *m*, field of pinoaks
carraspear *vi* to clear one's throat, cough
carraspera *f*, *inf* hoarseness
carrera *f*, run; race; racing; racecourse; *ast* course; high road; route; *mas* layer, course; line, row; *fig* ladder (in stockings, etc.); course; duration (of life); career, profession; conduct; girder. **c. de fondo,** long-distance race. **c. de relevos, c. de equipos,** relay race. **a c. abierta, a c. tendida,** at full speed
carrerista *mf* racing enthuriast; professional racer
carreta *f*, long, narrow two-wheeled cart; wagon; tumbril
carretada *f*, cart-load; *inf* great deal, mass
carretaje *m*, cartage; carriage, transport
carrete *m*, spool, reel, bobbin; fishing reel; *elec* coil; *phot* film spool
carretear *vt* to cart; drive a cart
carretera *f*, high road; highway
carretería *f*, number of carts; carting trade; cartwright's yard
carretero *m*, cartwright; carter, driver
carretilla *f*, wheelbarrow; hand cart; railway truck; squib. **de c.,** *inf* mechanically, without thought; (*with saber, repetir,* etc.) by rote
carretón *m*, truck, trolley; hand cart
carril *m*, wheel mark; furrow, rut; cart road, narrow road; rail (railways, etc.)
carrillera *f*, jaw (of some animals); chin strap; *pl* bonnet strings, etc.
carrillo *m*, cheek; jowl
carriola *f*, truckle bed; curricle
carro *m*, cart; cartload; car, chariot; carriage (of a typewriter, etc.); chassis; *ast* Plow, Great Bear; *Lat. Am.* automobile, auto, car; *mil* **c. blindado,** armored car. *mil* **c. de asalto,** tank. **c. de mudanzas,** moving van. **c. de regar,** watercart
carrocería *f*, place where carriages are made, sold, repaired; *aut* coachwork, body shop
carrocha *f*, eggs (of insects)
carrochar *vi* to lay eggs (insects)
carromato *m*, road wagon; covered wagon
carroña *f*, putrid flesh, carrion
carroza *f*, elegant coach; state coach; carriage; float (for tableaux, etc.); *naut* awning
carruaje *m*, carriage; any vehicle
carta *f*, letter; charter; royal order; playing card; chart, map. **c. certificada,** registered letter. **c. de amparo,** safe-conduct. **c. de crédito,** *com* letter of credit. **c. de marear,** sea chart. **c. de naturaleza,** naturalization papers. **c. de pésame,** letter of condolence. **c. de venta,** *com* bill of sale. **c. ejecutoria de hidalguía,** letters patent of nobility. **carta-poder,** letter of proxy, proxy. **cartas rusas,** (game of) consequences. **poner las cartas boca arriba,** *fig* to lay one's cards on the table
cartabón *m*, set-square; shoemaker's slide; quadrant
cartaginés (-esa) *a* and *n* Carthaginian
Cartago Carthage
cartapacio *m*, note-book; schoolbag, satchel; file, batch of papers
cartear *vi cards* to play low; *vr* to correspond by letter
cartel *m*, placard, poster; cartel; pasquinade, lampoon. **fijar carteles,** to placard
cartela *f*, tablet (for writing); slip (of paper, etc.); *arch* console, bracket
cartelera *f*, billboard
cartelero *m*, billpaster, billsticker
carteo *m*, correspondence (by letter)
cartera *f*, pocketbook; wallet; dispatch-case; portfolio; notebook; pocket flap; office of a cabinet minister; *com* shares
cartería *f*, sorting room (in a post-office)
carterista *mf* pickpocket
cartero *m*, mail carrier, postman
cartesiano (-na) *a* and *n* Cartesian
Cartesio Descartes
carteta *f*, lansquenet (card game)
cartilaginoso *a* cartilaginous
cartílago *m*, cartilage
cartilla *f*, first reading book; primer; certificate of ordination; note-book; liturgical calendar. **c. de racionamiento,** ration book
cartografía *f*, cartography
cartógrafo *m*, map maker
cartón *m*, pasteboard, cardboard; *arch* bracket; *art* cartoon, design
cartucho *m*, cartridge; paper cone
cartuja *f*, Carthusian Order or monastery
cartujano *a* Carthusian
cartujo *m*, Carthusian monk; *inf* taciturn, reserved man
cartulina *f*, Bristol board, oaktag, pasteboard, card
carúncula *f*, caruncle, comb of cock, etc.
casa *f*, house; home; household; residence, dwelling;

family house; *com* firm. **c. consistorial,** town hall. **c. cuna,** crèche. **c. de campo,** country-house. **c. de empeño,** pawnshop. **c. de huéspedes,** boarding house, lodging-house. **c. de los sustos,** haunted house (at amusement park). **c. de moneda,** mint. **c. de socorro,** First Aid Post. **c. de vecindad,** tenement. **c. mala,** house of ill repute. **c. solar** *or* **c. solariega,** family seat. **en c.,** at home (also sport usage). **poner c.,** to set up house

casaca *f,* dress coat. **volver la c.,** to become a turncoat, change one's allegiance

casación *f, law* cassation

casadero *a* marriageable

casadoro *m, Costa Rica* bus

casamiento *m,* marriage; wedding

casar *vt* to marry (of a priest); *law* repeal; *inf* marry off; join; match, harmonize; *vi* and *vr* (*with con*) to get married

casar *m,* group of houses

casca *f,* grape skin; tan (bark); shell, peel, rind

cascabel *m,* small bell (for harness, etc.). **serpiente de c.,** rattlesnake. *inf* **ser un c.,** to be feather-brained

cascabeleo *m,* jingling of bells

cascabillo *m,* husk (of cereals)

cascada *f,* cascade; waterfall

cascadura *f,* cracking, crack

cascajo *m,* gravel, shingle; *inf* broken, old things, junk; nuts

cascanueces *m,* nutcrackers

cascar *vt* to crack, split, break; *inf* beat; *fig inf* break down (of health); *vi inf* talk, chatter

cáscara *f,* shell; peel, rind; bark. *med* **c. sagrada,** cascara

cascarón *m,* eggshell; *arch* vault

cascarrabias *mf inf* spitfire

cascarriento, -a *Argentina* filthy; greasy

casco *m,* cranium; broken fragment of china, glass, etc.; crown of hat; helmet; tree of saddle; bottle; tank, pipe; barrel; *naut* hull; hoof; quarter (of fruit); *pl inf* head. **c. colonial,** sun-helmet. **c. respiratorio,** smoke-helmet

cascote *m,* rubble, ruins

caseoso *a* cheesy

caserío *m,* group of houses; country house

casero *a* home made; home bred; familiar; informa; *inf* domesticated, home-loving; domestic. *m,* landlord; caretaker; tenant

caserón *m,* large tumbledown house, mansion, hall

caseta *f,* hut; cottage; booth, stall. **c. de baños,** bathing van

casi *adv* almost, nearly. **c. c.,** very nearly

casilla *f,* hut; cabin; lodge; ticket office; pigeon-hole; *Argentina, Chile* post-office box *aer* **c. del piloto,** cockpit

casillero *m,* file cabinet, filing cabinet; locker (as in a locker room); set of pigeonholes; *sports* scoreboard; *rw* crossing guard

casino *m,* casino; club

caso *m,* happening, event; chance, hazard; occasion, opportunity; case, matter; (*med gram*) case. **en el c. de,** in a position to (e.g. **No estamos en el c. de pagar tanto dinero.** We are in no position to pay so much money). **en tal c.,** in such a case. **en todo c.,** in any case. **no hacer c. de,** to take no notice of. **venir al c.,** to be opportune

caspa *f,* dandruff; scab

¡cáspita! *interj* Amazing! Wonderful!

casquete *m,* helmet; skullcap; half wig

casquijo *m,* gravel

casquillo *m,* tip, cap, ferrule; socket; arrow-head; metal cartridge-case

casquivano *a inf* giddy, feather-brained

casta *f,* race; caste; breed (animals); kind, species, quality. **de buena c.,** pedigree (e.g. **perros de buena c.,** pedigree dogs)

castaña *f, bot* chestnut; knot, bun (of hair)

castañar *m,* chestnut plantation or grove

castañetear *vi* to play the castanets; snap one's fingers; chatter (of teeth); knock together (of knees)

castaño *a* chestnut-colored. *m,* chestnut tree; chestnut wood. **c. de Indias,** horse-chestnut tree

castañuela *f,* castanet. **tocar las castañuelas,** to play the castanets

castellán *m,* castellan

castellano (-na) *n* Castilian; Spaniard. *m,* Spanish (language); castellan. *a* Castilian; Spanish

casticismo *m,* purity (of language); Spanish spirit; traditionalism

castidad *f,* chastity

castigador *a* punishing. *m,* punisher; *inf* lady-killer

castigadora *f, inf* man-hunter

castigar *vt* to punish; chastise; chasten, advise; pain, grieve; correct, edit; decrease (expenses); *com* allow a discount

castigo *m,* punishment; emendation, correction

Castilla Castile

castillo *m,* castle; howdah. **c. de naipes,** house of cards. **c. de proa,** *naut* forecastle. **c. fuerte,** fortified castle. *inf* **hacer castillos en el aire,** to build castles in the air or in Spain

castizo *a* pure-blooded; prolific; pure (of language); typically Spanish; traditional

casto *a* chaste; pure, unsullied

castor *m, zool* beaver (animal and fur); soft, woollen cloth

castración *f,* castration, gelding

castrado *a* castrated. *m, inf* eunuch

castrador *m,* castrator, gelder

castrapo *m,* mixed Spanish and Galician spoken in Galicia, Spain

castrar *vt* to castrate, geld; prune; remove honeycomb from hives; weaken

castrense *a* military

castrista *v* and *mf* Castroite

casual *a* accidental, casual

casualidad *f,* chance, coincidence. **por c.,** by chance. **ser mucha c. que . . . ,** to be too much of a coincidence that . . .

casucha *f, inf* tumbledown hut

casuista *a* casuistic. *mf* casuist

casuística *f,* casuistry

casulla *f,* chasuble

cata *f,* tasting; taste, sample; *Lat. Am.* parrot

catabolismo *m,* catabolism

cataclismo *m,* cataclysm

catacumbas *f pl,* catacombs

catador *m,* taster, sampler

catadura *f,* tasting; look, countenance (gen. qualified)

catafalco *m,* catafalque

catalán (-ana) *a* and *n* Catalan, Catalonian. *m,* Catalan (language)

catalejo *m,* telescope

cataléptico *a* cataleptic

catálisis *f, chem* catalysis

catalítico *a* catalytic

catalogar *vt* to catalogue, list

catálogo *m,* catalogue, list

Cataluña Catalonia

cataplasma *f,* cataplasm

catapulta *f,* catapult

catar *vt* to taste, sample; see, examine; inspect; regard

catarata *f,* cataract, waterfall; *med* cataract (of the eyes)

catarral *a* catarrhal

catarro *m,* catarrh; common cold

catástrofe *f, lit* tragic climax; catastrophe

catastrófico *a* catastrophic

catavino *m,* taster (cup)

catavinos *mf,* professional wine taster; *inf* tippler, tavern haunter

cate *m, slang* flunk (failure in a course at school)

catecismo *m,* catechism

catecúmeno (-na) *n* catechumen

cátedra *f,* university chair; chair in a Spanish **instituto**;

professorship; university lecture room; subject taught by professor; reading desk, lectern; *ecc* throne; *ecc* see. **c. del espíritu santo,** pulpit. **c. de San Pedro,** Holy See
catedral *f,* and *a* cathedral
catedrático (-ca) *n* professor
categoría *f, phil* category; class, rank
categórico *a* categorical, downright
cateo *m, WH* sampling; prospecting; house search (by the police)
catequismo *m,* catechism; question and answer method of teaching
catequista *mf* catechist
catequizar *vt* to catechize; persuade, induce
caterva *f,* crowd, throng; jumble, collection
catéter *m, surg* probe; catheter
catoche *m, Lat. Am.* bad temper
catódico *a elec* cathodic
cátodo *m,* cathode
catolicidad *f,* catholicity; catholic world
catolicismo *m,* Catholicism
católico (-ca) *a* universal, catholic; infallible. *a* and *n* Catholic (by religion)
catorce *a* fourteen; fourteenth. *m,* number fourteen; fourteenth (of days of month)
catorzavo *a* fourteenth
catre *m,* camp-bed; truckle-bed; cot
Cáucaso, el the Caucasus
cauce *m,* river or stream bed; ditch, irrigation canal
cauchal *m,* rubber plantation
cauchera *f,* rubber tree
cauchero *m,* rubber planter; rubber-plantation worker
caucho *m,* caoutchouc, rubber; *Lat. Am.* tire
caución *f,* caution, precaution; surety; security
caucional *a* See **libertad**
caudal *m,* wealth, capital; flow, volume (of water); plenty, abundance (e.g. **un c. de conocimientos,** a wealth of knowledge)
caudaloso *a* carrying much water; wealthy; abundant
caudillo *m,* head, leader; chief tain. **el C.,** (title of Francisco Franco)
causa *f,* cause; reason, motive; lawsuit; *law* trial. **c. final,** *phil* final cause. **c. pública,** public welfare. **ser c. bastante para . . . ,** to be reason enough to . . .
causador (-ra) *a* motivating. *n* occasioner, originator
causalidad *f,* causality
causante *a* causative, causing. *m, law* principal; *Mexico* taxpayer
causar *vt* to cause; occasion
causticidad *f,* causticity; mordacity
cáustico *a* burning, caustic; scathing; mordant; *surg* caustic
cautela *f,* caution; astuteness, cunning
cauteloso *a* cautious; cunning
cauterio *m,* cautery
cauterización *f,* cauterization
cauterizar *vt* to cauterize
cautivar *vt* to capture; captivate, charm; attract; *vi* become a prisoner
cautiverio *m,* captivity
cautivo (-va) *a* and *n* captive
cauto *a* cautious; prudent; sly
cava *f,* digging (especially vines); wine cellar in royal palaces
cavador (-ra) *n* digger, hoer
cavadura *f,* digging, hoeing; sinking (wells)
cavar *vt* to dig, hoe; sink (wells); *vi* hollow; *fig* go deeply into a thing
caverna *f,* cavern, cave; *med* cavity (generally in the lung)
cavernícola *a* cave. **hombre c.,** cave-man
cavernoso *a* cavernous; caverned; *fig* hollow (cough, etc.); deaf
cavidad *f,* cavity; sinus; cell
cavilación *f,* caviling
cavilar *vt* to cavil; criticize
caviloso *a* captious
caz *m,* channel, canal; head-race, flume
caza *f,* hunting; hunt, chase; game. *m, aer* fighter. *aer* **c. lanzacohetes,** rocket-launching aircraft. **c. nocturno,** night fighter. *naut* **dar c.,** to pursue
cazaautógrafos *mf,* autograph hunter
cazabombardero *m, aer* fighter bomber
cazadero *m,* hunting ground
cazador *a* hunting. *m, mil* chasseur; huntsman
cazadora *f,* huntress; jacket; forage cap
cazadotes *m,* dowry hunter
cazafortunas *mf* fortune hunter
cazar *vt* to hunt, chase; *fig inf* run to earth; *fig inf* catch out; *inf* overcome by flattery
cazasubmarino *m,* submarine chaser
cazatorpedero *m, naut* torpedo-boat destroyer
cazo *m,* ladle; dipper
cazolada *f,* panful
cazoleta *f,* small pan; bowl (of pipe, etc.); sword guard; boss of a shield; pan (of a firelock)
cazuela *f,* earthenware cooking dish; stew-pot; part of theater formerly reserved for women; *theat* gallery
cazumbrón *m,* cooper
cazurro *a inf* unsociable; surly, boorish
c.c.p. abbrev. of **con copia para**
ce *f,* name of the letter C. *interj* Look! Chist! **ce por be,** in detail
cebada *f,* barley (plant and grain). **c. perlada,** pearl barley
cebadal *m,* barley field
cebadera *f,* nose-bag; barley bin
cebadero *m,* barley dealer
cebado *a* on the prowl; having tasted human flesh (animal)
cebar *vt* to feed or fatten (animals); fuel, feed (furnace, etc.); prime, charge (fire-arms, etc.); start up (machines); bait (fish hook); stimulate (passion, etc.); *vi* stick in, penetrate (nails, screws, etc.); *vr* put one's mind to; grow angry. **cebarse en vanas esperanzas,** to nurture vain hopes
cebo *m,* fodder; detonator; encouragement, food; bait
cebolla *f,* onion; onion bulb; any bulbous stem; oil bulb (of lamp). **c. escalonia,** shallot
cebollana *f,* chive
cebollero (-ra) *n* onion seller
cebolleta *f,* leek; young onion
cebollino *m,* onion seed; onion bed; chive
cebra *f,* zebra
ceca *f,* mint (for coining money); name of mosque in Cordova. **de C. en Meca,** from pillar to post, hither and thither
cecear *vi* to lisp
ceceo *m,* lisping
ceceoso *a* lisping
cecial *m,* dried fish
cecina *f,* dried salt meat
cedazo *m,* sieve, strainer
ceder *vt* to cede, give up; transfer; *vi* give in, yield; diminish, decrease (fever, storm, etc.); fail, end; happen, turn out; sag, give, stretch. **No c. la fama a,** to be no less famous than
cedro *m,* cedar tree; cedar wood. **c. dulce,** red cedar
cédula *f,* document, certificate, card. *ecc* **c. de comunión,** Communion card. **c. personal,** identity card. **c. real,** royal letters patent
céfiro *m,* west wind; *poet* zephyr
cegajoso *a* blear-eyed
cegar *vi irr* to become blind; *vt* to put out the eyes; *fig* blind; wall up, close up, stop up; infatuate. *Pres. Ind.* **ciego, ciegas, ciega, ciegan.** *Pres. Subjunc.* **ciegue, ciegues, ciegue, cieguen**
cegato *a inf* short-sighted
ceguedad, ceguera *f,* blindness; delusion; ignorance
Ceilán Ceylon
ceja *f,* eyebrow; cloud cap; mountain peak; *mus* bridge

(of stringed instruments). *fig* **quemarse las cejas,** to burn the midnight oil
cejar *vi* to go backwards; give way, hesitate
cejijunto *a* having eyebrows that almost meet, beetle-browed
cejo *m,* river mist
cejudo *a* having long thick eyebrows
celada *f,* helmet; ambush; fraud, trick
celador (-ra) *a* watchful, zealous. *n* supervisor; caretaker; guard (at a museum, etc.)
celaje *m,* sky with scudding clouds (gen. *pl*); skylight, window; promising sign, presage
celar *vt* to be zealous in discharge of duties; spy upon; watch; oversee, superintend; conceal; engrave
celda *f,* cell
celdilla *f,* cell (bees, wasps, etc.); (*zool bot*) cell; *bot* capsule
celebérrimo, *a sup* **célebre** most celebrated
celebración *f,* celebration; applause
celebrador (-ra) *n* celebrator; applauder
celebrante *a* celebrating. *m, ecc* celebrant
celebrar *vt* to celebrate; applaud; praise; venerate; hold, conduct; **c. que** + *subj,* to be happy that, be glad that. *vt* and *vi ecc* officiate; *vr* take place
célebre *a* famous
celebridad *f,* fame, celebrity; magnificence, show, pomp
celeridad *f,* celerity
celeste *a* celestial, heavenly
celestial *a* celestial, heavenly; perfect, delightful; *inf* foolish (ironical)
celestina *f,* procuress (allusion to *Tragicomedia de Calixto y Melibea*)
celibato *m,* celibacy; *inf* bachelor
célibe *a* celibate, unmarried. *mf* unmarried person
celo *m,* enthusiasm, ardor; religious zeal; devotion; jealousy; heat, rut; *pl* jealousy, suspicion. **dar celos (a),** to make jealous
celosía *f,* lattice; Venetian blind
celoso *a* zealous; jealous; suspicious
célula *f,* cell
celular *a* cellular
celuloide *f,* celluloid
celulosa *f,* cellulose
celuloso *a* cellular
cementación *f,* cementation
cementar *vt* to cement
cementerio *m,* cemetery
cemento *m,* cement
cena *f,* evening meal; supper; Last Supper
cenacho *m,* marketing bag
cenáculo *m,* cenacle
cenador *m,* diner out; arbor, pergola
cenagal *m,* quagmire; *fig* impasse
cenagoso *a* miry, muddy
cenar *vi* to dine, sup; *vt* eat for evening meal, sup off
cenceño *a* slim, thin
cencerrada *f,* noisy mock serenade given to widows or widowers on the first night of their new marriage
cencerrear *vi* to jingle; *inf* play out of tune; bang in the wind, rattle; squeak
cencerreo *m,* jingling; jangle; rattling; squeaking
cencerro *m,* cow-bell
cendal *m,* gauze; *ecc* stole; barbs of a feather
cenefa *f,* border; valance, flounce; edging
cenicero *m,* ash-pan; ash-pit; ash-tray
ceniciento *a* ash colored, ashen. **la Cenicienta,** Cinderella
cenit *m, ast* zenith; *fig* peak, summit
ceniza *f,* ash, cinders
cenotafio *m,* cenotaph
cenote *m, Central America, Mexico* cenote (deep natural well or sinkhole)
censo *m,* census; agreement for settlement of an annuity; annual ground rent; leasehold
censor *m,* censor; censorious person; *univ* proctor
censual *a* pertaining to census, annuity, rents
censualista *mf* annuitant
censura *f,* censorship; criticism; blame, reproach; scandal, gossip; *psy* censorship
censurable *a* reprehensible; censorable
censurar *vt* to judge; censure; criticize
centauro *m, myth* centaur
centavo *m,* hundredth part; cent; *Lat. Am.* centavo
centella *f,* lightning; spark; flash; *fig* spark (of anger, affection, etc.)
centellador *a* flashing
centellear *vi* to flash; twinkle; sparkle
centelleo *m,* scintillation; sparkle; flash
centén *m,* Spanish gold coin once worth 100 reals and later 25 pesetas
centena *f,* hundred
centenal, centenar *m,* hundred; centenary; rye field. **a centenares,** by the hundred, in crowds
centenario (-ia) *a* centenary. *n* centenarian. *m,* centenary
centeno *m, bot* rye
centésimo *a* and *m,* hundredth
centígrado *a* centigrade
centigramo *m,* centigram
centilitro *m,* centiliter
centímetro *m,* centimeter. **c. cúbico,** cubic centimeter, milliliter
céntimo *a* hundredth. *m,* centime (coin)
centinela *mf mil* sentry, sentinel; person on watch. **estar de c.,** to be on sentry duty; be on guard
centolla *f,* marine crab
centón *m,* patchwork quilt
central *a* central; centric. *f,* head office; central depot; mother house. **c. de fuerza,** power-house. **c. telefónica,** telephone exchange
centralilla, centralita *f,* local exchange, private exchange
centralismo *m,* centralism
centralización *f,* centralization
centralizador *a* centralizing
centralizar *vt* to centralize
centrar *vt* to center
céntrico *a* central, centric; centrally located; downtown
centrífugo *a* centrifugal
centrípeto *a* centripetal
centro *m,* center; headquarters, meeting place, club; center, hub; middle; core (of a rope); *fig* focus. *phys* **c. de gravedad,** center of gravity. **c. de mesa,** table center-piece. *anat* **centro nervioso,** nerve center
Centroamérica *f.* Central America
centroamericano (-na) *a* and *n* Central American
céntuplo *a* centuple
centuria *f,* century
ceñidamente tightly (e.g. **un argumento c. organizado,** a tightly organized plot)
ceñido *a* thrifty; wasp-waisted, slender waisted; fitting (of garments)
ceñidor *m,* girdle, belt
ceñir *vt irr* to girdle; surround; shorten, abbreviate; *vr* be moderate (speech, expenditure, etc.); conform, confine oneself (to). **ceñirse a las reglas,** to abide by the rules. *Pres. Ind.* **ciño, ciñes, ciñen.** *Pres. Part.* **ciñendo.** *Preterite* **ciñó, ciñeron.** *Pres. Subjunc.* **ciña,** etc. *Imperf. Subjunc.* **ciñese,** etc.
ceño *m,* band, hoop; frown; *fig* dark outlook
ceñudo *a* frowning
cepillar *vt* to brush; plane; smooth
cepa *f,* stump; vine-stock; root (tails, antlers, etc.); *fig* origin, trunk (of a family); *biol* strain. **de la más pura c.,** of the best quality
cepillo *m,* brush; *carp* plane; poor-box, offertory-box. **c. para los dientes,** toothbrush. **c. para ropa,** clothes-brush. **c. para el suelo,** scrubbing-brush. **c. para las uñas,** nail-brush
cepo *m,* bough; wooden stocks; snare; trap; poor-box; collecting-box

cera *f,* beeswax; wax; wax candles, etc., used at a function. *inf* **ser como una c.,** to be like wax (in the hands of)
cerador *m,* floor waxer (person)
ceradora *f,* floor waxer (machine)
cerámica *f,* ceramics; ceramic art, pottery
cerámico *a* ceramic
cerbatana *f,* blow-pipe, popgun; pea-shooter; ear-trumpet
cerca *f,* fence, wall
cerca *adv* near. **c. de,** near to; almost, nearly (e.g. **c. de las once,** nearly eleven o'clock)
cercado *m,* enclosure, fenced in place; fence
cercanía *f,* nearness, proximity; (gen. *pl*) outskirts, surroundings
cercano *a* near, neighboring; impending, early
cercar *vt* to enclose; build a wall or fence round; to lay siege to; crowd round; *mil* surround
cercenamiento (**a**) *m,* curtailment (of)
cercenar *vt* to lop off the ends, clip; curtail, diminish; abridge; whittle
cerciorar *vt* to assure, confirm; *vr* make sure
cerco *m,* ring, hoop; fence; siege; small conversational circle; spin, circling; halo (sun, moon); frame; sash (of a window). **poner c.** (**a**), to lay siege to, blockade
cerda *f,* sow; bristle
Cerdeña Sardinia
cerdo *m,* pig, hog
cerdoso *a* bristly
cereal *a* and *m,* cereal
cerebelo *m, anat* cerebellum
cerebral *a* cerebral
cerebro *m,* cerebrum; brain; intelligence
cerebro-espinal *a* cerebrospinal
ceremonia *f,* ceremony; function, display; formality. **de c.,** ceremonial; formally. **por c.,** for politeness' sake
ceremonial *a* ceremonial. *m,* ceremony; rite; protocol (rules of behavior)
ceremonioso *a* ceremonious; formal, over-courteous
cerero *m,* wax-chandler
cereza *f,* cherry
cerezal *m,* cherry orchard
cerezo *m,* cherry tree; cherry wood
cerilla *f,* wax taper; match; ear wax
cerillo *m, Mexico* match
cerner *vt irr* to sieve; watch, observe; *fig* sift, clarify; *vi* bolt (of plants); drizzle; *vr* waddle; hover; threaten (of evil, etc.). *Pres. Ind.* **cierno, ciernes, cierne, ciernen.** *Pres. Subjunc.* **cierna, ciernas, cierna, ciernan**
cernícalo *m, orn* kestrel; *inf* lout
cernidillo *m,* drizzle; teetering walk
cernido *m,* sifting, sieving; sifted flour
cerniduras *f pl,* siftings
cero *m, math* zero; naught; (tennis) love. *fig inf* **ser un c.,** to be a mere cipher
cerote *m,* cobbler's wax. *inf* fear
cerquillo *m,* tonsure; welt (of a shoe); *Lat. Am.* fringe
cerquita *adv* very near, hard by
cerradero, *m,* **cerradera** *f,* bolt staple; catch of a lock; clasp or strings of a purse
cerradizo *a* closable, lockable
cerrado *a* closed; compact; incomprehensible, obscure; overcast, cloudy; *inf* taciturn; secretive. *m,* enclosure
cerradura *f,* fastening, lock; closing, locking
cerraja *f,* lock (of a door); bolt
cerrajería *f,* locksmith's craft; locksmith's workshop or shop
cerrajero *m,* locksmith
cerramiento *m,* closing, locking up; fence; enclosure, shooting preserve; partition wall
cerrar *vt irr* to close; lock, fasten, bolt; shut up; *mech* shut off, turn off; fold up; block or stop up; seal (letters, etc.); close down; terminate; obstruct; (*with con*) attack; *vi* close; close in (of night, etc.); *vr* heal up (wounds); close (flowers); *rad* close down; crowd together; *fig* stand firm. *inf* **cerrarse la espuela,** to take a nightcap, have a last drink. **c. la marcha,** to bring up the rear. **al c. la edición,** stop press. See **acertar**
cerrazón *f,* dark, overcast sky heralding a storm
cerril *a* rough, rocky; wild, untamed (cattle, horses); *inf* boorish
cerro *m,* neck of an animal; spine, backbone; hill. *fig* **irse por los cerros de Úbeda,** to go off the track, indulge in irrelevancies
cerrojo *m,* bolt (of a door, etc.); lock (of a door, gun, etc.)
certamen *m,* contest; competition; match
certero *a* well-aimed; sure, well-timed; knowledgeable, sure
certeza, certidumbre *f,* certitude, assurance
certificación *f,* certification; certificate; affidavit
certificado *a* certified; registered. *m,* registered letter; certificate
certificar *vt* to certify; register (letter, etc.)
certificatorio *a* certifying or serving to certify
certísimo *a* learned form of the superlative of **cierto** (see **certísimo**)
certitud *f,* certitude
cervantino *a* Cervantine
cervecería *f,* brewery; ale-house
cervecero (**-ra**) *n* brewer; beer seller
cerveza *f,* beer, ale. **c. negra,** stout
cerviz *f,* cervix, nape (of neck). **doblar** (*or* **bajar**) **la c.,** to humble oneself
cesación *f,* cessation, stopping
cesante *a* dismissed; pensioned off. **declarar c.** (**a**), to dismiss (a person from a post). **estar c.,** to be out of a job
cesantía *f,* status of dismissed or retired official; retirement pension
cesar *vi* to cease, stop, end; leave an employment; desist; retire
cesáreo *a* Cesarean; imperial
cese *m,* stopping of payment for an employment
cesión *f,* cession; transfer; resignation; *law* release
cesionario (**-ia**) *n* cessionary, transferee
césped *m,* grass, sward; sod, lawn
cesta *f,* basket, hamper; *sport* racket; cradle (for a wine bottle)
cestada *f,* basketful
cestería *f,* basketmaking, basketweaving; basket factory; basket shop; basketwork
cestero (**-ra**) *n* basket maker or seller
cesto *m,* basket, hamper, skip
cesura *f,* cesura
cetorrino *m,* basking shark
cetrería *f,* falconry
cetrino *a* greenish-yellow; sallow; citrine; melancholy; reserved, aloof
cetro *m,* scepter; verge; reign
chabacanería *f,* bad taste; vulgarity
chabacano *a* vulgar, common; rude, uncouth
chacal *m, zool* jackal
cháchara *f, inf* empty chatter; verbiage
chacharear *vi* to chatter; gabble, cackle
chacharero *a inf* chattering; talkative
chacolotear *vi* to clatter, clink (loose horseshoe)
chacota *f,* merriment, mirth
chacotear *vi inf* to be merry, have fun
chacotón *a* of a boisterous humor
chacra *f, Lat. Am.* small farm, small holding
chafado *a* taken aback; disappointed
chafallar *vt inf* to mend carelessly, botch
chafandín *m,* vain fool
chafar *vt* to flatten; crumple, crease (clothes); *inf* heckle
chafarrinar *vt* to stain, mark, blot
chaflán *m,* bevel edge, chamfer
chagrén *m,* shagreen leather
chagüe *m, Central America* bog, marsh, swamp
chal *m,* shawl
chalán *m,* horse-dealer
chalana *f, naut* wherry, lighter

chalanear *vt* to bargain; indulge in sharp practice
chalar *vt* to drive mad; enamour
chaleco *m*, waistcoat; cardigan
chalequear *vt*, *Mexico* to pilfer, swipe
chalina *f*, flowing scarf, artist's bow
Chalo pet form of the male given name *Carlos* 'Charles', hence = English *Chuck; Bud, Mac* (in direct address to a male whose name one does not know)
chalote *m*, shallot
chalupa *f*, shallop; launch; canoe; long boat, ship's boat
chamar *vt inf* to palm off, barter
chamarasca *f*, brushwood, tinder
chamarilero (-ra) *n* secondhand dealer
chamarreta *f*, sheepskin jacket; *Mexico* jacket
chambergo *a* pertaining to the Chambergo regiment. *m*, broad-brimmed hat
chambón *a inf* awkward, clumsy; lucky
chambonada *f*, *inf* blunder; fluke, chance
chambra *f*, dressing-jacket, peignoir, negligee
chamicera *f*, piece of scorched earth (woodland, etc.)
chamorro *a* close-cropped, shorn (hair)
champán *m*, champagne. **c. obrero,** *humorous* cider
champaña *m*, champagne
champar *vt inf* to cast in a person's face, remind
champú *m*, shampoo
chamuscar *vt* to scorch; singe
chamusquina *f*, scorching; singeing; *inf* brawl
chanada *f*, *inf* trick, mischievous act
chancaca *f*, *Lat. Am.* syrup cake
chancada *f*, *Lat. Am.* dirty trick
chancearse *vr* to joke
chancero *a* joking, facetious
chancho, -a *mf*, *Lat. Am.* pig
chanchollada *f*, dirty trick, foul play, trick
chanchullo *m*, *inf* fraud
canciller *m*, chancellor
chancillería *f*, chancery
chancla *f*, down at heel shoe; heelless slipper
chancleta *f*, heelless slipper, babouche. *mf inf* ninny
chanclo *m*, overshoe; Wellington
chanfaina *f*, *cul* savory fricassee
chanflón *a* tough, coarse; ungainly
changador *m*. *Argentina* porter
chantaje *m*, blackmail
chantajista *mf* blackmailer
chantar *vt* to put on, clothe; *inf* tell plainly. *inf* **c. sus verdades,** to tell hometruths
chanza *f*, joke, jest
chanzoneta *f*, canzonetta; *inf* joke
¡chao! *Argentina, Chile* bye!
chapa *f*, plate, sheet; veneer; clasp; *inf* prudence, common sense; rouge. **c. de hierro,** sheet-iron. **c. de identidad,** number plate
chapado a la antigua *a* old-fashioned
chapalear *vi* to dabble in water; splash; clatter (of a horseshoe)
chapaleo *m*, dabbling, paddling; splash; clattering, clink (of a horseshoe)
chapaleteo *m*, lapping of water; splashing (of rain)
chaparrear *vi* to pour with rain
chaparrón *m*, heavy shower of rain, downpour
chapear *vt* to veneer; *vi* clatter (loose horseshoe)
chaperón *m*, hood
chapeta *f*, *dim* clasp; red flush or spot on cheek
chapetón (-ona) *n WH* recently arrived European, especially Spaniard
chapín *m*, cork-soled leather overshoe (for women) *ant*
chapino *a* and *m*, *Mexico contemptuous* Guatemalan
chapodar *vt* to prune, lop off branches; cut down, reduce
chapotear *vt* to sponge, moisten, damp; *vi* paddle, splash; dabble or trail the hands (in water)
chapoteo *m*, moistening, sponging; paddling, splashing; dabbling
chapucear *vt* to botch, do badly; bungle
chapuceramente *adv* awkwardly. **hablar el japonés c.,** to speak broken Japanese
chapucería *f*, roughness, poor workmanship; botch
chapucero *a* rough, badly finished; bungling, clumsy, awkward
chapurrado *a* broken (e.g. **hablar un italiano c.,** to speak broken Italian)
chapurrar, chapurrear *vt* to speak badly (a language); jabber; *inf* mix (drinks)
chapuz *m*, ducking, submerging; plunge; unimportant job; clumsiness
chapuzar *vt* to duck, submerge; plunge
chaqué *m*, morning coat; morning suit
chaqueta *f*, jacket; *mech* casing
chaquete *m*, backgammon
chaquetilla *f*, short jacket; coatee; blazer
chaquetón *m*, short coat. **c. de piloto,** *aer* pea-jacket
charabán *m*, charabanc
charada *f*, charade
charamusca *f*, *Lat. Am.* firewood, kindling
charanguero *a* rough, badly finished; clumsy. *m*, Andalusian boat
charca *f*, pond, pool; reservoir
charco *m*, puddle; *inf* sea
charla *f*, *inf* chatter; conversation; talk, informal lecture
charlar *vi inf* to prattle, chatter; chat, converse; give a talk (on)
charlatán (-ana) *a* loquacious, garrulous; indiscreet; fraudulent, false. *n* charlatan; chatterer
charlatanería *f*, loquacity, garrulity; quackery
charlatanismo *m*, charlatanism, quackery
charnela *f*, hinge; hinged joint
charol *m*, japan, varnish; patent leather
charolar *vt* to japan, varnish
charolista *mf*, varnisher
charpa *f*, pistol-belt; sling
charrán (-ana) *n* rogue, trickster
charranada *f*, roguery, knavery
charrería *f*, tawdriness; gaudiness
charretera *f*, *mil* epaulet; garter
charro *a* churlish, coarse; flashy, tawdry
chasca *f*, brushwood, firewood
chascar *vi* to creak, crack; clack (the tongue); swallow
chascarrillo *m*, *inf* amusing anecdote, good story
chasco *m*, trick, practical joke; disappointment. **llevarse un c.,** to meet with a disappointment
chasis *m*, *aut* chassis; *phot* plate-holder; *mech* underframe
chasquear *vt* to play a trick on; wag (one's tongue); crack (a whip, one's knuckles); break a promise, disappoint; *vi* creak, crack; meet with a disappointment
chasquido *m*, crack (of whip); creaking (of wood); click (of the tongue)
chatarra *f*, scrap iron; junk
chato *a* flat-nosed; flat
chauvinismo *m*, chauvinism
chaval *a inf* young. *m*, lad
chaveta *f*, *mech* bolt, pin, peg, cotter, key
checo (-ca) *a* and *n* Czech. Czech (language)
Chejov Chekov
chelín *m*, shilling
Chengis-Jan Genghis Khan
chepa *f*, *inf* hunch (back); hump
cheque *m*, check. **c. cruzado,** crossed check
chica *f*, girl; *inf* dear
chicana *f*, chicanery
chicano (-na) *a* and *n* Chicano, American of Mexican ancestry
chicha *f*, *Lat. Am.* corn liquor
chícharo *m*, pea
chicharrón *m*, *cul* crackling; burnt meat; *inf* sunburnt person
chichón *m*, bruise, bump
chichonera *f*, child's protective hat (something like a straw crash-helmet)
chicle *m*, chewing gum

chiclero *m*, chicle-gatherer
chico *a* little, small; young. *m*, little boy; youth; *inf* old boy, dear. **Es un buen c.,** He's a good fellow
chicoleo *m*, *inf* compliment
chicote *mf* sturdy child. *m*, *inf* cigar; *Lat. Am.* whip
chifla *f*, whistling, whistle; tanner's paring knife
chiflado *a inf* cracked, daft; crack-brained
chifladura *f*, whistling; *inf* whim, mania, hobby
chiflar *vi* to whistle; *vt* to make fun of, hiss; pare or scrape leather; *inf* swill, tipple; *vr inf* have a slate loose; be slightly mad; *inf* lose one's head over, adore
chifle *m*, whistle, whistling; decoy call (birds)
chiflón *m*, *Lat. Am.* draft (of air)
chile *m*, *bot* red pepper, chilli
chileno (**-na**) *a* and *n* Chilean
chilla *f*, *Argentina* fox
chillador *a* screaming, shrieking
chillar *vi* to scream, shriek; creak; squeak; jabber (monkeys, etc.); *art* be strident (of colors)
chillería *f*, shrieking, screaming
chillido *m*, scream, shriek; squeak (of mice, etc.); jabber (of monkeys, etc.)
chillón *a inf* screaming, yelling; strident, piercing; crude, loud (colors)
chimenea *f*, chimney; funnel; fireplace; kitchen range
chimpancé *m*, chimpanzee
china *f*, pebble; porcelain, china; Chinese silk
chinche *f*, bedbug; thumbtack, drawing-pin. *mf inf* bore
chinchona *f*, quinine
chinchorrería *f*, *inf* impertinence, tediousness; gossip
chinela *f*, mule, slipper; overshoe, patten *ant*
chinero *m*, china cupboard
chinesco *a* Chinese. **a la chinesca,** in Chinese fashion
chingana *f*, *Lat. Am.* bar
chino (**-na**) *a* and *n* Chinese. *m*, Chinese (language)
Chipre Cyprus
chiquero *m*, pigsty; stable for bulls
chiquillada *f*, childishness, puerility
chiquillería *f*, *inf* crowd of children
chiquillo (**-lla**) *n* small boy
chiquito (**-ta**) *a dim* **chico,** tiny, very small. *n* little one, small boy
chiripa *f*, (billiards) fluke; *inf* happy coincidence, stroke of luck; lucky guess
chirivía *f*, *bot* parsnip; *orn* wagtail
chirlar *vi inf* to gabble, talk loudly
chirlo *m*, knife wound, sabre cut; knife scar
chirona *f*, *inf* jail
chirriador *a* sizzling, crackling; creaking, squeaking
chirriar *vi* to sizzle, crackle; creak, squeak; squawk; *inf* croak, sing out of tune
chirrido *m*, squawk; croaking; noise of grasshoppers; squeaking; creaking, creak
¡chis! *interj* Shh! Silence!
chisme *m*, gossip, tale; *inf* small household utensil, trifle
chismear *vt* to tell tales, gossip
chismero (**-ra**), **chismoso** (**-sa**) *a* gossiping, talebearing. *n* gossip, tale bearer
chispa *f*, spark; ember; *elec* spark; tiny diamond; small particle; wit; quickwittedness; *inf* drunkenness. **c. del encendido,** ignition spark
chispazo *m*, flying out of a spark, sparking; damage done by spark; *inf* gossip, rumor
chispeante *a* sparking; sparkling; *fig* scintillating (with wit etc.)
chispear *vi* to throw out sparks, spark; sparkle, gleam; *fig* scintillate; drizzle gently
chisporrotear *vi inf* to sputter; fizz
chisposo *a* sputtering, throwing out sparks
chistar *vi* to speak, break silence (gen. used negatively)
chiste *m*, witticism, bon mot; amusing incident; joke
chistera *f*, creel (for fish); *inf* top-hat, tile
chistoso *a* joking; amusing, funny
chiticallando *adv* quietly, stealthily; *inf* on the quiet, in secret
¡chito! ¡chitón! *interj* Hush! Sh!
chiva *f*, *Colombia, Panama* bus; *Venezuela* beard, goatee; **chivas** *f*, *Venezuela* hand-me-downs
chivo *n zool* kid. **c. expiatorio,** scapegoat
chocante *a* colliding; provoking; shocking; surprising
chocar *vi* to collide; strike (against); run into; fight, clash; *vt* clink (glasses); provoke, annoy; surprise, shock. **¡Choca cinco!** Clasp five!, Gimme five!, Put it there!, Give some skin! (invitation to shake hands)
chocarrería *f*, coarse joke
chochear *vi* to be senile; *fig inf* dote (on)
chocho *a* senile; *fig inf* doting
choco *m*, small hump, hunchback
chocolate *m*, chocolate; drinking chocolate. **c. a la española,** thick chocolate. **c. a la francesa,** French drinking chocolate
chocolatería *f*, chocolate factory or shop
chocolatero (**-ra**) *a* fond of chocolate. *n* chocolate maker or seller
chófer *m*, chauffeur; driver
chompa *f*, *Lat. Am.* jumper, pullover
chonta *f*, *Lat. Am.* palm tree
chopera *f*, grove or plantation of black poplar trees
chopo *m*, *bot* black poplar; *inf* gun
choque *m*, collision; shock; jar; *med* concussion; fight; clink (of glasses); clash; *mil* skirmish
choricera *f*, sausage-making machine
choricero (**-ra**) *n* sausage maker
chorizo *m*, kind of pork sausage; counterweight
chorrear *vi* to spout, jet; drip; *fig inf* trickle, arrive slowly
chorreo *m*, drip, dripping; spouting, gushing
chorrera *f*, spout; drip; jabot, lace front
chorro *m*, jet; stream (of water, etc.); *fig* shower. **a chorros,** in a stream; in abundance, plentifully
chova *f*, rook; carrion crow; jackdaw
choza *f*, hut, cabin; cottage
chubasco *m*, squall, downpour; storm; transitory misfortune
chuchería *f*, gewgaw, trinket; savory titbit; snaring, trapping
chucruta *f*, sauerkraut
chueca *f*, round head of a bone; small ball; game like shinty; *inf* practical joke
chueco *a Mexico* bent, crooked, twisted
chufa *f*, *bot* chufa; *inf* joke, trick
chufería *f*, place where drink made of **chufas** is sold
chufla *f*, flippant remark
chufleta *f*, *inf* joke; taunt
chulada *f*, mean trick, base action; drollery
chulería *f*, drollness; attractive personality
chuleta *f*, *cul* cutlet, chop; mutton-chop; *inf* slap
chulo *a* droll, amusing; attractive. *m*, slaughterhouse worker; bullfighter's assistant; pimp; rogue
chumbera *f*, prickly pear; Indian fig
chupada *f*, sucking; suck; suction
chupado de cara, c. de mofletes *a* lantern-jawed
chupador *a* sucking. *m*, baby's comforter or dummy
chupar *vt* to suck; absorb (of plants); *fig inf* drain, rob; *vr* grow thin. **chuparse los dedos,** *inf* to lick one's lips; be delighted
chupatintas *mf*, *inf* scrivener, clerk (scornful)
churdón *m*, raspberry cane; raspberry; raspberry vinegar
churrería *f*, place where **churros** are made or sold
churrero (**-ra**) *n* maker or seller of **churros**
churrigueresco *a* Churrigueresque
churro *a* coarse (of wool). *m*, *cul* a kind of fritter eaten with chocolate, coffee, etc.
churumbela *f*, *mus* pipe; reed for drinking mate *WH*
chusco *a* droll, witty, amusing
chusma *f*, galley hands, crew; rabble, mob
chutar *vt sport* to shoot (a goal)
chuzo *m*, *mil* pike
chuzón *a* wily, suspicious, cunning
cianuro *m*, cyanide

ciar *vi* to go backwards; *naut* row backwards; *fig* make no headway (negotiations)
ciática *f*, sciatica
ciático *a* sciatic
cicatería *f*, niggardliness, avarice
cicatero *a* avaricious, niggardly, mean
cicatriz *f*, cicatrice; *fig* scar, mark, impression
cicatrizar *vt* to cicatrize, heal; *vr* scar over
cíclico *a* cyclic, cyclical
ciclismo *m*, bicycling
ciclista *mf* cyclist
ciclo *m*, cycle (of time). **c. artúrico, c. de Artús,** Arthurian Cycle. **c. de conferencias,** series of lectures
ciclón *m*, cyclone
ciclópeo *a* cyclopean
cicuta *f*, hemlock
cid *m*, great warrior, chief. **el Cid,** national hero of Spanish wars against the Moors
cidra *f*, citron
cidro *m*, citron tree
ciego *a* blind; dazed, blinded; choked up. *m*, blind man; *anat* cæcum. **a ciegas,** blindly; heedlessly
cielo *m*, sky, firmament; atmosphere; climate; paradise; Providence; bliss, glory; roof, canopy; *inf* darling. **a c. abierto,** in the open air. **parecer un c.,** to be heavenly
ciempiés *m*, centipede
cien *a* abb. **ciento,** hundred. Used always before substantives (e.g. **c. hombres,** 100 men)
ciénaga *f*, swamp; morass
ciencia *f*, science; knowledge; erudition, ability. **ciencias naturales,** natural science. **a c. cierta,** for certain, without doubt (gen. with *saber*)
cienmilésimo *a* hundred-thousandth
cieno *m*, slime, mud; silt
científico *a* scientific. *m*, scientist
ciento (cf. **cien**) *a* hundred; hundredth. *m*, hundred. **por c.,** per cent.
cierne, en in flower; *fig* in the early stages, in embryo
cierre *m*, closing, shutting; closing time of shops, etc.; fastening; fastener; clasp (of a necklace, handbag, etc.). **c. cremallera,** zip fastener. **c. metálico,** doorshutter
ciertamente *adv* certainly; undoubtedly; indeed
ciertísimo *a* everyday form of the superlative of **cierto** (see **certísimo**)
cierto *a* certain, sure; true; particular (e.g. **c. hombre,** a certain man (note no *def. art.*)). **un c. sabor,** a special flavor. **una cosa cierta,** something certain. **no, por c.,** no, certainly not. **por c.,** truly, indeed
cierva *f*, hind
ciervo *m*, stag. **c. volante,** stagbeetle
cierzo *m*, northerly wind
cifra *f*, number; figure; sum total; cipher, code; monogram; abbreviation
cifrar *vt* to write in cipher; summarize, abridge; (*with en*) be dependent on; depend on
cigarra *f*, *ent* cicada, harvest fly
cigarral *m*, (Toledo) countryhouse and garden or orchard
cigarrera *f*, woman who makes or sells cigars; cigar-cabinet; cigar-case
cigarrería *f*, *Lat. Am.* tobacco shop
cigarrillo *m*, cigarette
cigarro *m*, cigar; *Lat. Am.* cigarette
cigüeña *f*, *orn* stork; *mech* crank
ciliar *a* ciliary
cilicio *m*, hairshirt
cilindrar *vt* to roll; calendar; bore
cilindrero *m*, organ grinder
cilíndrico *a* cylindrical
cilindro *m*, cylinder; roller
cima *f*, summit; top of trees; apex; *arch* coping; head (thistle, etc.); *fig* aim, goal, end
cimbalero (**-ra**) *n* cymbalist
címbalo *m*, cymbal
cimborrio *m*, *arch* cupola; cimborium
cimbrar, cimbrear *vt* to bend; brandish; *vr* sway (in walking)
cimbreño *a* graceful, lithe, willowy
cimbreo *m*, swaying, bending
cimbrón *m*, *Lat. Am.* vibration
cimentar *vt irr* to lay foundations; refine (gold, metals, etc.); found; *fig* ground (in virtue, etc.). See **acertar**
cimera *f*, crest of helmet
cimiento *m*, foundation (of a building); bottom; groundwork; origin, base. **abrir los cimientos,** to lay the foundations
cimitarra *f*, scimitar
cinabrio *m*, cinnabar; vermilion
cinc *m*, zinc
cincel *m*, chisel; burin, engraver
cincelador (**-ra**) *n* engraver; chiseler
cincelar *vt* to chisel; carve; engrave
cincha *f*, girth of a saddle
cinchar *vt* to tighten the saddle girths
cincho *m*, belt, girdle; iron hoop
cinco *a* and *m*, five; fifth. **a las c.,** at five o'clock
cincuenta *a* and *m*, fifty; fiftieth
cincuentavo *a* fiftieth
cincuentenario *m*, fiftieth anniversary
cincuentón (**-ona**) *a* and *n* fifty years old (person)
cine, cinema *m*, cinema, movies. **c. sonoro,** sound film
cinemática *f*, *phys* kinematics
cinematografía *f*, cinematography
cinematografiar *vt* to film
cinematográfico *a* cinematographic
cinematógrafo *m*, cinematograph; cinema
cínico *a* cynical; impudent; untidy. *m*, cynic
cinismo *m*, cynicism
cinta *f*, ribbon; tape; strip; film (cinematograph). **c. métrica,** tape-measure
cintillo *m*, hatband; small ring set with gems
cinto *m*, belt, girdle. **c. de pistolas,** pistol-belt
cintoteca *f*, tape library
cintura *f*, waist; belt, girdle
cinturón *m*, large waist; belt girdle; sword-belt; that which encircles or surrounds. **c. de seguridad,** seat belt
ciprés *m*, *bot* cypress tree or wood
cipresal *m*, cypress grove
cipresino *a* cypress; cypresslike
circasiano (**-na**) *a* and *n* Circassian
circo *m*, circus; amphitheater
circón *m*, zircon
circuir *vt. irr* to surround, encircle. See **huir**
circuito *m*, periphery; contour; (*elec phys*) circuit. **corto c.,** short circuit
circulación *f*, circulation; traffic. **c. de la sangre,** circulation of the blood. **calle de gran c.,** busy street
circular *a* circular. *f*, circular. *vt* to pass round; *vi* circle; circulate; move in a circle; move about; run, travel (traffic)
circulatorio *a* circulatory
círculo *m*, circle; circumference; circuit; casino, social club
circuncidar *vt* to circumcise; modify, reduce
circuncisión *f*, circumcision
circunciso *a* circumcised
circundar *vt* to surround
circunferencia *f*, circumference
circunflejo *a* circumflex. **acento c.,** circumflex accent
circunlocución *f*, circumlocution
circunnavegación *f*, circumnavigation
circunnavegar *vt* to circumnavigate
circunscribir *vt* to circumscribe. *Past Part.* **circunscrito**
circunscripción *f*, circumscription
circunspección *f*, circumspection; seriousness, dignity
circunspecto *a* circumspect; serious, dignified
circunstancia *f*, circumstance; incident, detail; condition. **c. agravante,** aggravating circumstance. **c. atenuante,** extenuating circumstance. **bajo las circunstancias,** in the circumstances. **de circunstancias,** occasional (e.g. **poesías de circunstancias,**

occasional verse). **estar al nivel de las circunstancias,** to rise to the occasion
circunstanciado *a* circumstantiated, detailed
circunstancial *a* circumstantial; occasional (e.g. **poesías circunstanciales,** occasional verse)
circunstante *a* surrounding; present. *mf* person present, bystander
circunvecino *a* adjacent, neighboring
circunvolución *f,* circumvolution
cirial *m,* processional candlestick
cirio *m,* wax candle
cirro *m, med* scirrhus; *bot* tendril; *zool* cirrus
cirrosis *f,* cirrhosis
cirroso *a med* scirrhous; (*zool bot*) cirrose
ciruela *f,* plum; prune. **c. claudia, c. veidal,** greengage. **c. damascena,** damson
ciruelo *m,* plum tree
cirugía *f,* surgery
cirujano *m,* surgeon
cisco *m,* coal dust, slack coal; *inf* hubbub, quarrel
cisma *m,* or *f,* schism; disagreement, discord. **el C. de Occidente,** the Western Schism
cismático *a* schismatic; discordant, inharmonious
cisne *m,* swan
cisterciense *a* Cistercian
cisterna *f,* water-tank, cistern
cístico *a* cystic
cistitis *f,* cystitis
cita *f,* appointment; quotation, citation
citable *a* quotable
citación *f,* quotation; *law* summons
citar *vt* to make an appointment; cite, quote; *law* summon. **c. en comparecencia,** to summon to appear in court
cítara *f, mus* zither
citatorio *m,* summons
citerior *a* hither, nearer
citrato *m, chem* citrate
cítrico *a* citric
ciudad *f,* city; municipal body. **la c. señorial,** the Aristocratic City (Ponce, Puerto Rico)
ciudadanía *f,* citizenship
ciudadano (-na) *a* city; civic, born in or belonging to a city. *n* citizen; burgess; bourgeois. **c. de honor,** freeman (of a city)
ciudadela *f,* citadel
cívico *a* civic; patriotic; *Lat. Am.* police officer
civicultura *f,* raising of civets
civil *a* civil; civilian; polite
civilidad *f,* politeness, civility
civilización *f,* civilization
civilizador *a* civilizing
civilizar *vt* to civilize; educate; *vr* grow civilized; be educated
civismo *m,* civism; patriotism; civics
cizalla *f,* shears, shearing machine; metal filings
cizaña *f, bot* darnel, tare; vice, evil; dissension, discord (gen. with *meter* and *sembrar*)
clac *m,* opera-hat; tricorne
clamar *vi* to cry out; *fig* demand (of inanimate things); vociferate; speak solemnly
clamor *m,* outcry, shouting; shriek, complaint; knell, tolling of bells
clamorear *vt* to implore, clamor (for); *vi* toll (of bells)
clamoroso *a* noisy, clamorous
clandestino *a* clandestine, secret
clangor *m, poet* blare, bray (of trumpet)
claqué *m,* tap-dance
clara *f,* white of egg; bald patch (in fur); *inf* fair interval on a rainy day
claraboya *f,* skylight; *arch* clerestory
claramente *adv* clearly, evidently
clarear *vt* to clear; give light to; *vi* to dawn; grow light; *vr* be transparent; *inf* reveal secrets unwittingly
clarete *m,* claret (wine); claret color. *a* claret; claret-colored
claridad *f,* clearness; transparency; lightness, brightness; distinctness; clarity; good reputation, renown; plain truth, home truth (gen. *pl*)
clarificación *f,* clarification; purifying, refining
clarificar *vt* to illuminate; clarify, purify; refine (sugar, etc.)
clarín *m,* bugle; clarion; organ stop; bugler
clarinete *m,* clarinet; clarinet player
clarión *m,* white chalk, crayon
clarividencia *f,* perspicuity, clear-sightedness
clarividente *a* perspicacious, clear-sighted
claro *a* clear; light, bright; distinct; pure, clean; transparent, translucent; light (of colors); easily understood; evident, obvious; frank; cloudless; shrewd, quick-thinking; famous. *m,* skylight; space between words; break in a speech; space in procession, etc.; *art* (gen. *pl*) high lights. *interj* **¡C.!** or **¡C. está!** Of course! **a las claras,** openly, frankly
claroscuro *m,* chiaroscuro; monochrome
clase *f,* class, group; kind, sort, quality; class (school, university); lecture room; lecture, lesson; order, family. **c. dirigente,** ruling class. **c. media,** middle class. **c. social,** social class
clasicismo *m,* classicism
clasicista *a* and *mf* classicist
clásico *a* classic; notable; classical. *m,* classic
clasificación *f,* classification
clasificador (-ra) *n* classifier. **c. de billetes,** ticket-punch
clasificar *vt* to classify, arrange. **c. correspondencia,** to file letters
claudicación *f,* limping; negligence; hesitancy, weakness; backing down
claudicar *vi* to limp; be negligent; hesitate, give way
claustral *a* cloistral
claustro *m,* cloister; council, faculty, senate (of university); monastic rule
claustrofobia *f,* claustrophobia
cláusula *f,* clause. **c. de negación implícita,** contrary-to-fact clause. **c. principal,** main clause. **c. subordinada,** dependent clause, subordinate clause. **c. sustantiva,** noun clause
clausura *f,* sanctum of convent; claustration; solemn ending ceremony of tribunal, etc. **la vida de c.,** monastic or conventual life
clava *f,* club, truncheon; *naut* scupper
clavadizo *a* nail-studded (doors, etc.)
clavar *vt* to nail; fasten with nails; pierce, prick; set gems (jeweler); spike (cannon, gum); *fig* fix (eyes, attention, etc.); *inf* cheat
clave *m,* clavichord. *f,* code, key; *mus* clef; *arch* keystone; plug (telephones); **c. (de),** key to. *mus* **c. de sol,** treble clef
clavel *m, bot* carnation plant and flower
clavelito *m, bot* pink plant and flower
clavero (-ra) *n* keeper of the keys. *m,* clove tree
clavetear *vt* to stud with nails; *fig* round off (business affairs)
clavicordio *m,* clavichord
clavícula *f,* clavicle
clavija *f,* peg, pin; plug; peg of stringed instrument; axle-pin
clavo *m,* nail, spike, peg; corn (on foot); anguish. **c. de especia,** clove. **c. de herradura,** hob-nail
claymore *f,* claymore
clemátide *f, bot* clematis
clemencia *f,* mildness; clemency; mercy
clemente *a* mild; clement; merciful
cleptomanía *f,* kleptomania
cleptómano (-na) *a* and *n* kleptomaniac
clerecía *f,* clergy
clerical *a* belonging to the clergy; clerical
clericalismo *m,* clericalism
clerigalla *f,* (*contemptuous*) dog-collar men
clérigo *m,* cleric, clergyman; clerk (in Middle Ages)
clero *m,* clergy

cliente *mf* client, customer; protégé, ward
clientela *f,* patronage, protection; clientele
clima *m,* climate, clime
climatérico *a* climacteric
climático *a* climatic
climatología *f,* climatology
clímax *m,* climax
clínica *f,* clinic, nursing home; department of medicine or surgery
clínico *a* clinical
clíper *m,* (*aer* and *naut*) clipper
clisar *vt print* to cast from a mold, stereotype
clisé *m, print* stereotype plate
cloaca *f,* sewer, drain; *zool* cloaca
cloquear *vi* to go broody (hen); cluck
cloqueo *m,* cluck, clucking
cloquera *f,* broodiness (hens)
clorato *m,* chlorate
clorhídrico *a* hydrochloric
cloro *m,* chlorine
clorofila *f,* chlorophyll
cloroformizar *vt* to chloroform
cloroformo *m,* chloroform
clorosis *f,* chlorosis
cloruro *m,* chloride
club *m,* club
clueca *f,* broody hen
clueco *a* broody (hens); *inf* doddering
C.N.T. initialism of Confederación Nacional de Trabajo
coacción *f,* coercion
coactivo *a* coercive
coadjutor *m,* co-worker, assistant
coadunar *vt* to join or mingle together
coadyuvar *vt* to assist
coagulación *f,* coagulation
coagular *vt* to coagulate; clot; curdle
coágulo *m,* clot; coagulation; congealed blood
coalición *f,* coalition
coartada *f,* alibi. **probar la c.,** to prove an alibi
coartar *vt* to limit, restrict
coautor (**-ra**) *n* co-author
cobalto *m,* cobalt
cobarde *a* cowardly; irresolute. *m,* coward
cobardía *f,* cowardice
cobayo *m,* guinea-pig
cobertera *f,* lid, cover
cobertizo *m,* overhanging roof; shack, shed, hut. **c. de aeroplanos,** *aer* hangar
cobertura *f,* covering; coverlet; wrapping
cobija *f,* imbrex tile; cover; *Lat. Am.* blanket
cobijar *vt* to cover; shelter
cobra *f, zool* cobra; rope or thong for yoking oxen; retrieval (of game)
cobradero *a* that which can be collected, recoverable
cobrador *m,* collector, receiver. *a* collecting. **c. de tranvía,** tram conductor
cobranza *f,* receiving, collecting; collection of fruit or money
cobrar *vt* to collect (what is owed); charge; earn; regain, recover; feel, experience (emotions); wind, pull in (ropes, etc.); gain, acquire; retrieve (game); *vr* recuperate. **c. ánimo,** to take courage. **c. cariño (a),** to grow fond of. **c. fuerzas,** to gather strength. **c. importancia,** to gain importance. **¿Cuánto cobra Vd.?** How much do you charge?; How much do you earn?
cobre *m, min* copper; copper kitchen utensils; *pl mus* brass; *Lat. Am.* (copper) cent, centavo.
cobrizo *a* containing copper; copper-colored
cocacolonizar *vt* (United States) to gain economic control of . . . and introduce into its pop culture
cocacolonización *f,* economic domination by the United States and introduction of its pop culture
cocaína *f,* cocaine
cocción *f,* coction
coceador *a* inclined to kick; kicking (animals)
coceadura *f,* kicking
cocear *vi* to kick; *inf* kick against, oppose
cocedero *a* easily cooked
cocer *vt. irr* to boil; cook; bake (bricks, etc.); digest; *surg* suppurate; *vi* boil (of a liquid); ferment; *vr* suffer pain or inconvenience over a long period. *Pres. Ind.* **cuezo, cueces, cuece, cuecen.** *Pres. Subjunc.* **cueza, cuezas, cueza, cuezan**
cochayuyo *m, Lat. Am.* edible seaweed
coche *m,* carriage, car. **c. camas,** sleeping car. **c. -camioneta,** station wagon. **c. cerrado,** *aut* sedan. **c. de muchos caballos,** high-powered car. **c. de plaza,** hackney-carriage. **c. fúnebre,** hearse. **c. -línea,** intercity bus. *f, Ecuador* puddle
cochera *f,* coach house; tramway depot
cochero *m,* coachman; driver. *a* easily cooked
¡cochi! (call to pigs)
cochina *f,* sow
cochinería *f, inf* filthiness; mean trick
cochinilla *f,* wood louse; cochineal insect; cochineal
cochinillo *m,* sucking-pig. **c. de Indias,** guinea-pig
cochino *m,* pig; *inf* filthy person. *a* filthy
cocido *a* boiled, cooked, baked. *m,* dish of stewed meat, pork, chicken, with peas, etc.
cociente *m,* quotient
cocimiento *m,* cooking; decoction
cocina *f,* kitchen; pottage; broth; cookery. **c. de campaña,** field-kitchen. **c. económica,** cooking range
cocinar *vt* to cook; *vi inf* meddle, interfere
cocinería *f, naut* galley
cocinero (**-ra**) *n* cook, chef
cocinilla *f,* spirit-stove
coco *m, bot* coconut tree and fruit; coconut shell; grub, maggot; bogeyman; hobgoblin; *inf* grimace. *inf* **ser un c.,** to be hideously ugly
cocacolismo *n inf* economic dependence on the United States and adoption of its pop culture
cocodrilo *m,* crocodile
cócora *mf inf* bore, nosy Parker
cocotal *m,* grove of coconut palms
cocotero *m,* coconut palm
coctel *m,* cocktail
cocuyo *m,* firefly
codal *a* cubital. *m,* shoot of a vine; prop, strut; frame of a hand-saw
codazo *m,* blow or nudge of the elbow. **dar codazos,** to elbow, shoulder out of the way
codear *vi* to jostle; elbow, nudge; *vr* be on terms of equality with
codeína *f,* codeine
codelincuente *mf* partner in crime, accomplice
codera *f,* elbow rash; elbow-piece or patch
codeso *m,* laburnum
códice *m,* codex
codicia *f,* covetousness; greed
codiciar *vt* to covet
codicilo *m,* codicil
codicioso (**-sa**) *a* covetous; *inf* hardworking. *n* covetous person
codificación *f,* codification
codificar *vt* to codify, compile
código *m,* code of laws. **c. civil,** civil laws. **c. de la circulación, c. de la vía pública,** highway code, traffic code. *naut* **c. de señales,** signal code. **c. penal,** criminal laws. **c. postal,** zip code
codillo *m,* knee (of quadrupeds); shaft (of branch); bend (pipe, tube); stirrup
codo *m,* elbow; angle, bend (pipe, tube); cubit. *inf* **hablar por los codos,** to chatter
codorniz *f, orn* quail
coeducación *f,* co-education
coeficiente *m,* coefficient
coercer *vt* to restrain, coerce
coerción *f, law* coercion
coercitivo *a* coercive
coetáneo (**-ea**) *a* contemporaneous. *n* contemporary
coevo *a* coeval

coexistencia *f,* co-existence
coexistir *vi* to co-exist
cofia *f,* hairnet; coif
cofín *m,* basket
cofradía *f,* confraternity, brotherhood or sisterhood **c. de gastronomía,** eating club (US), dining society (UK)
cofre *m,* trunk, chest (for clothes); coffer
cogedor *m,* collector, gatherer; dustpan; coal-shovel
coger *vt* to seize, hold; catch; take, collect, gather; have room for; take up or occupy space; find; catch in the act; attack, surprise; reach; **c. un berrinche,** have a fit, have a tantrum. *vi* have room, fit
cogida *f,* gathering, picking; *inf* fruit harvest; toss (bull-fighting)
cogido *m,* pleat, fold; crease. **estar c. de tiempo** to be pressed for time.
cogitabundo *a* very pensive
cognación *f,* cognation; kinship
cognoscitivo *a* cognitive
cogollo *m,* heart (of lettuce, etc.); shoot; topmost branches of pine tree
cogote *m,* nape (of neck)
cogulla *f,* monk's habit
cohabitación *f,* cohabitation
cohabitar *vt* to cohabit
cohechador (-ra) *a* bribing. *n* briber
cohechar *vt* to bribe, corrupt, suborn
cohecho *m,* bribing; bribe
coherencia *f,* coherence, connection
coherente *a* coherent
cohesión *f,* cohesion
cohesivo *a* cohesive
cohete *m,* rocket
cohetero *m,* firework manufacturer
cohibir *vt* to restrain; repress. See **Prohibir**.
cohombrillo *m, dim* gherkin
cohombro *m,* cucumber
cohonestar *vt fig* to gloss over, cover up; make appear decent (actions, etc.)
cohorte *f,* cohort
coima *f, Lat. Am.* bribe
coincidencia *f,* coincidence
coincidir *vt* to coincide; (two or more people) be in the same place at the same time. **c. con que . . .** to agree that . . .
coito *m,* coitus
cojear *vi* to limp; wobble, be unsteady (of furniture); *fig inf* go wrong or astray; *inf* suffer from (vice, bad habit)
cojera *f,* lameness, limp
cojijoso *a* peevish
cojín *m,* cushion; pad; pillow (for lace-making)
cojinete *m,* small cushion; *mech* bearing. **c. de bolas,** ball-bearing
cojo *a* lame; unsteady, wobbly (of furniture, etc.)
col *f,* cabbage. **c. de Bruselas,** Brussels sprouts
cola *f,* tail; train (of gown); shank (of a button); queue; tailpiece (of a violin, etc.); appendage; glue. **c. de milano,** *carp* dovetail. **c. de pescado,** isinglass. **formar c.,** to line up, queue up
colaboración *f,* collaboration. **en c.,** joint (e.g. **obra en colaboración,** joint work)
colaboracionista *mf* collaborationist
colaborador (-ra) *n* collaborator
colaborar *vt* to collaborate
colación *f,* conferment of a degree; collation (of texts); light repast; cold supper; area of a parish
colada *f,* wash; bleaching; mountain path; *met* casting; *inf* trusty sword (allusion to name of one of the Cid's swords)
coladero *m,* colander, sieve, strainer; narrow path
colador *m,* colander
coladura *f,* straining, filtration; *inf* untruth; *inf* howler, mistake
colapso *m, med* prostration, collapse
colar *vt irr* to filter, strain; bleach; *met* cast; *vi* go through a narrow place; *inf* drink wine; *vr* thread one's way; *inf* enter by stealth, steal in; *inf* tell untruths. *Pres. Ind.* **cuelo, cuelas, cuela, cuelan.** *Pres. Subjunc.* **cuele, cueles, cuele, cuelen**
colateral *a* collateral
colcha *f,* bedspread, counterpane, quilt
colchadura *f,* quilting
colchero *m,* quilt maker
colchón *m,* mattress. **c. de muelles,** spring-mattress. **c. de viento,** air-bed
colchoneta *f,* pad, thin mattress
coleada *f,* wag of the tail
colear *vi* to wag the tail
colección *f,* collection
coleccionador (-ra) *n* collector
coleccionar *vt* to collect
coleccionista *mf* collector
colecta *f,* assessment; collection (of donations); *ecc* collect; voluntary offering
colectivero *m,* bus driver
colectividad *f,* collectivity; body of people
colectivismo *m,* collectivism
colectivista *a* collectivist
colectivo *a* collective; *Argentina* (local) bus
colector *m,* gatherer; collector; tax-collector; water-pipe; water-conduit; *elec* commutator, collector
colega *m,* colleague
colegiado *a* collegiate
colegial (-la) *a* college, collegiate. *n* student; pupil; *fig inf* novice.
colegiarse *vr* to meet as an association (professional, etc.)
colegiata *f,* college church
colegiatura *f,* scholarship, fellowship (money granted a student); tuition (fee paid by a student), tuition fee, tuition fees
colegio *m,* college; school; academy; association (professional); council, convocation; college or school buildings. **c. de abogados,** bar association. **c. de cardenales,** College of Cardinals. **c. electoral,** polling-booth. **c. militar,** military academy
colegir *vt irr* to collect, gather; deduce, infer. See **elegir**
cólera *f,* bile, anger. *m,* cholera. **montar en c.,** to fly into a rage
colérico *a* angry; choleric; suffering from cholera
colesterina *f, chem* cholesterol
coleta *f,* pigtail; queue; *inf* postscript
coletazo *m,* blow with one's tail, lash with one's tail; lash of a dying fish; *fig* last hurrah
coleto *m,* leather jerkin; *inf* body of a man
colgadero *a* able to be hung up. *m,* coat-hanger, hook
colgadizo *a* hanging. *m,* overhanging roof
colgadura *f,* hangings, drapery, tapestries. **c. de cama,** bedhangings
colgajo *m,* tatter; bunch (of grapes, etc.); *surg* skin lap
colgar *vt irr* to hang up; decorate with hangings; *inf* hang, kill; *vi* hang, be suspended; *fig* be dependent. See **contar**
colibrí *m,* hummingbird
cólico *m,* colic
colicuar *vt* to dissolve
coliflor *f,* cauliflower
coligarse *vr* to confederate, unite
colilla *f,* stub (of a cigar or cigarette)
colina *f,* hill; cabbage seed; *chem* choline
colindante *a* adjacent, contiguous
coliseo *m,* coliseum; theater
colisión *f,* collision; abrasion, bruise; *fig* clash (of ideas)
colitis *f,* colitis
collado *m,* hill, hillock
collar *m,* necklace; chain of office or honor; collar (dogs, etc.)
collera *f,* horse collar; *Chile* cuff link
collerón *m,* horse collar
colmado *a* abundant. *m,* provision shop
colmar *vt* to fill to overflowing; bestow generously, heap upon

colmena *f,* beehive
colmenero (**-ra**) *n* beekeeper
colmillo *m,* canine tooth; tusk; fang
colmilludo *a* having large canine teeth; tusked; fanged; sagacious
colmo *m,* overflow; highest point; completion, limit, end. **ser el c.,** *inf* to be the last straw. **el c. de los colmos,** the absolute limit
colocación *f,* placing, putting; situation, place; employment; *sport* placing; order, arrangement; *ling* collocation
colocar *vt* to place, put, arrange; place in employment. **c. bajo banderas,** to draft (into the armed forces). *vr* place oneself
colocho *m, Guatemala* (naturally) curly hair
colofón *m, print* colophon
colofonia *f,* solid resin (for bows of stringed instruments, etc.)
colombiano (**-na**) *a* and *n* Colombian
colombina *f,* columbine
colombofilia *f,* pigeon fancying
colonia *f,* colony; plantation
coloniaje *m, Lat. Am.* colonial period; colonial government
colonial *a* colonial
colonización *f,* colonization
colonizador (**-ra**) *a* colonizing. *n* colonizer
colonizar *vt* to colonize; settle
colono *m,* settler, colonist; farmer
coloquio *m,* colloquy, conversation, talk; colloquium
color *m,* color; dye; paint; rouge; coloring; pretext, excuse; character, individuality; *pl* natural colors. **c. estable, c. sólido,** fast color. **mudar de c.,** to change color. **de c.,** colored. **so c.,** under the pretext. **ver las cosas c. de rosa,** to see things through rose-colored glasses
colorado *a* colored. *WH* red, reddish; *inf* blue, obscene; specious
colorante *a* coloring. *m,* dyestuff; coloring (substance)
colorar *vt* to color; dye
colorear *vt* to color; pretext; *fig* whitewash, excuse; *vi* show color; be reddish; grow red, ripe (tomatoes, cherries, etc.)
colorero *m,* dyer
colorete *m,* rouge
colorido *m,* coloring, color
colorín *m,* goldfinch; bright color
colosal *a* colossal, enormous; extraordinary, excellent
coloso *m,* colossus; *fig* outstanding person or thing, giant; **el C. del Norte, el Gran C. del Norte,** (contemptuous epithet for the United States of America)
columbino *a* pertaining to a dove; dovelike; candid, innocent; purply-red
columbrar *vt* to discern in the distance, glimpse; conjecture, guess
columna *f, mil arch print* column; *fig* protection, shelter; *naut* stanchion. **c. cerrada,** *mil* etc. mass formation. **c. de los suspiros,** agony column (in a newspaper)
columnata *f,* colonnade
columpiar *vt* to swing; dangle (one's feet); *vr inf* sway in walking; swing
columpio *m,* swing
colusión *f,* collusion
colusorio *a* collusive
coma *f, gram* comma. *m, med* coma
comadre *f,* midwife; *inf* procuress, go-between; *inf* pal, gossip
comadrear *vi inf* to gossip
comadreja *f, zool* weasel
comadrón *m,* accoucheur
comadrona *f,* midwife
comandancia *f, mil* command; commandant's H.Q.
comandante *m,* commandant; commander; major; squadron-leader. *a mil* commanding. **c. en jefe,** commanding officer
comandar *vt mil* to command
comandita *f, com* sleeping partnership; private company
comando *m, mil* commando
comarca *f,* district, region
comatoso *a* comatose
comba *f,* bend, warping; jump rope, skipping-rope; camber (of road)
combadura *f,* curvature; warping; camber (of a road)
combar *vt* to bend; twist; warp; camber
combate *m,* fight, combat; mental strife; contradiction, opposition. **c. judicial,** trial by combat. **dejar fuera de c.,** (a) (boxing) to knock out
combatiente *m,* combatant, soldier
combatir *vi* to fight; *vt* attack; struggle against (winds, water, etc.); contradict, oppose; *fig* disturb, trouble (emotions)
combi *m, Mexico* minibus
combinación *f,* combination; list of words beginning with same letter; project; concurrence; underskirt, petticoat. **estar en c. (con),** to be in cahoots (with), connive (with)
combinar *vt* to combine; (*mil nav*) join forces; arrange, plan; *chem* combine; **combinar para + inf.** (two or more people) to make arrangements to + inf.
combustible *a* combustible. *m,* fuel
combustión *f,* combustion. **c. activa,** rapid combustion. **c. espontánea,** spontaneous combustion
comedero *a* edible. *m,* feeding-trough; dining-room
comedia *f,* comedy; play; theater; comic incident; *fig* play-acting, theatricalism. **c. alta,** art theater. **c. de costumbres,** comedy of manners. **c. de enredo,** play with very involved plot. *inf* **hacer la c.,** to play-act, pretend
comediante *m,* actor; *inf* dissembler.
comedianta *f,* actress
comedido *a* courteous; prudent; moderate
comedimiento *m,* courtesy; moderation; prudence
comedir *vt irr* to prepare, premeditate; *vr* restrain oneself, be moderate; offer one's services. See **pedir**
comedor *a* voracious. *m,* dining-room
comendador *m,* knight commander
comendatorio *a* commendatory (of letters)
comensal *mf* table companion
comentador (**-ra**) *n* commentator
comentar *vt* explain (document); *inf* comment
comentario (**a**) *m,* commentary (on)
comentarista *mf* commentator
comento *m,* comment; commentary
comenzante *mf* beginner, novice. *a* initial
comenzar *vt vi irr* to begin, commence. See **empezar**
comer *m,* eating; food. *vi* to eat; feed; dine. *vt* eat; *inf* enjoy an income; waste (patrimony); consume, exhaust; fade (of colors); *vr* be troubled, uneasy, remorseful. **ser de buen c.,** to have a good appetite; taste good. **tener que c.,** to be obliged to eat; have to eat; have enough to eat
comerciable *a* marketable; sociable, pleasant (of persons)
comercial *a* commercial
comerciante *a* trading. *mf* merchant, trader
comerciar *vt* to trade; have dealings (with)
comercio *m,* trade, commerce; intercourse, traffic; illicit sexual intercourse; shop, store; tradesmen; commercial quarter of town
comestible *a* edible, eatable. *m,* (gen. *pl*) provisions
cometa *m, ast* comet. *f,* kite (toy). **c. celular,** box-kite
cometedor (**-ra**) *n* perpetrator
cometer *vt* to entrust, hand over to; commit (crime, sins, etc.); *com* order
cometido *m,* charge, commission; moral obligation; function
comezón *f,* itching, irritation; hankering, longing
cómico *a* comic; funny, comical. *m,* actor; comedian. **c. de la legua,** strolling player
comida *f,* food; meal; dinner; eating. **c. corrida** *Mexico*

table d'hôte **c. de gala,** state banquet. **c. de prueba,** *med* test meal
comienzo *m,* beginning, origin
comilón (**-ona**) *a inf* gluttonous. *n* glutton
comillas *f pl, gram* inverted commas
comino *m, bot* cumin. **no valer un c.,** to be not worth a jot
comisar *vt* to confiscate, sequestrate
comisaría *f,* commissaryship; commissariat. **c. de policía,** police station
comisario *m,* deputy, agent; commissary, head of police; commissioner; *Argentina,* purser. **alto c.,** high commissioner. **c. propietario,** stockholders' representative
comisión *f,* perpetration, committal; commission; committee; *com* commission
comisionado (**-da**) *a* commissioned. *m,* commissary
comisionar *vt* to commission
comisionista *mf com* commission agent
comiso *m, law* confiscation, sequestration; contraband
comité *m,* committee
comitiva *f,* retinue, following
como *adv* like, as; in the same way; thus, accordingly; in the capacity of; so that; since. *conjunc* if (*followed by subjunc.*); because. **c. no,** unless. **¿Cómo?** How? In what way? Why? Pardon? What did you say? *interj* **¡Cómo!** What! You don't say! **¡Cómo no!** Why not! Of course! Surely! **¿Cómo que . . . ?** What do you mean that . . . ?
cómo *m,* the wherefore. **no saber el porqué ni el c.,** not to know the why or wherefore
cómoda *f,* chest of drawers
comodidad *f,* comfort; convenience; advantage; utility, interest
comodín *m,* (in cards) joker
cómodo *a* comfortable; convenient; opportune
comodón *a inf* comfort-loving; easy-going; egoistical
comodoro *m, naut* commodore
comoquiera que *adv* by any means that, anyway; whereas, given that
compacto *a* compact, dense; close (type)
compadecer *vt irr* to pity; *vr* (*with* **de**) sympathize with; pity; harmonize, agree with. See **conocer**
compadre *m, inf* pal; *Argentina* bully
compaginación *f,* joining, fixing; *print* making-up
compaginar *vt* to fit together; join, put in order; harmonize, square (e.g. **compaginé una cuenta con la otra,** I squared one account with the other); *print* make up
compañero (**-ra**) *n* companion, comrade; fellow-member; partner (games); *fig* pair, fellow, mate (things). **c. de armas,** brother-in-arms, companion-at-arms. **c. de cabina,** boothmate. **c. de exilio,** companion in exile, fellow exile. **c. de generación,** contemporary, person of the same generation. **c. de viaje,** traveling companion; *pol* fellow traveler (communist sympathizer)
compañía *f,* company; society, association; theatrical company; (*com mil*) company. **C. de Jesús,** Order of Jesus. **c. de la zarza,** guild of guards and woodcutters for autos de fe. **c. de navegación,** shipping company. **c. por acciones,** joint stock company
comparable *a* comparable
comparación *f,* comparison
comparar *vt* to compare; collate
comparativo *a* comparative
comparecencia *f,* (gen. *law*) appearance
comparecer *vi irr law* to appear (before tribunal, etc.); present oneself. See **conocer**
comparendo *m, law* summons
comparsa *f,* retinue; *theat* chorus; troop of carnival revelers dressed alike. *mf theat* supernumerary actor
comparte *mf law* partner; accomplice
compartimiento *m,* share, division; railway carriage. *naut* **c. estanco,** compartment
compartir *vt* to share out, divide; participate
compás *m,* compasses; callipers; size; compass, time; range of voice; (*naut min*) compass; *mus* time, rhythm, bar, marking time. **c. de mar,** mariner's compass. **c. de puntas,** dividers, callipers. **fuera de c.,** *mus* out of time; out of joint (of the times). *mus* **llevar el c.,** to beat time
compasar *vt* to measure with compasses; arrange or apportion accurately; *mus* put into bars
compasillo *m, mus* $\frac{4}{4}$ measure
compasivo *a* compassionate; tender-hearted
compatibilidad *f,* compatibility
compatible *a* compatible
compatriota *mf* compatriot
compeler *vt* to compel, force
compendiar *vt* to abridge, summarize
compendio *m,* compendium. **en c.,** briefly
compendioso *a* summary, condensed; compendious
compenetración *f,* co-penetration; intermingling
compenetrado (**de**) *a* thoroughly convinced (of)
compenetrarse *vr* to co-penetrate; intermingle
compensación *f,* compensating; compensation
compensar *vt* to equalize, counterbalance; compensate
compensatorio *a* compensatory; equalizing
competencia *f,* competition, contest; rivalry; competence; aptitude; *law* jurisdiction
competente *a* adequate, opportune; rightful, correct; apt, suitable; learned, competent
competer *vi irr* to belong to; devolve on; concern. See **pedir**
competición *f,* competition
competidor (**-ra**) *n* competitor
competir *vi irr* to compete, contest; be equal (to), vie (with). See **pedir**
compilación *f,* compilation
compilador (**-ra**) *n* compiler. *a* compiling
compilar *vt* to compile
compinche *mf inf* pal, chum
complacencia *f,* satisfaction, pleasure
complacer *vt irr* to oblige, humor; *vr* (*with en*) be pleased or satisfied with; delight in, like to. See **nacer**
complaciente *a* pleasing; obliging, helpful
complejidad *f,* complexity
complejo *a* complex; intricate. *m,* complex. **c. de inferioridad,** inferiority complex
complementario *a* complementary
complemento *m,* complement (all meanings)
completar *vt* to complete; perfect
completo *a* full; finished; perfect
complexión *f,* physical constitution
complexo *a* complex; intricate
complicación *f,* complication
complicar *vt* to complicate; muddle, confuse; *vr* be complicated; be muddled or confused
cómplice *mf* accomplice
complicidad *f,* complicity
complot *m, inf* conspiracy, plot, intrigue
complutense *a* native of, or belonging to, Alcalá de Henares
componedor (**-ra**) *n* repairer; arbitrator; bone-setter; *mus* composer; writer, author, compiler; *print* compositor
componenda *f,* mending, repair; *inf* settlement; compromise, arbitration; *inf* shady business
componente *a* and *m,* component
componer *vt irr* to construct, form; *mech* resolve; compose, create; *print* compose; prepare, concoct, mend, repair; settle (differences); remedy; trim; correct, adjust; *lit mus* compose; add up to, amount to; *vi* write (verses); *mus* compose; *vr* dress oneself up. **c. el semblante,** to compose one's features; *inf* **componérselas,** to fix matters, use one's wits. See **poner**
componible *a* reparable, mendable; able to be arranged or adjusted
comportamiento *m,* conduct; deportment
comportar *vt* to tolerate; *vr* behave, comport oneself
composición *f,* composition; repair; arrangement,

compromise; *print* composition; *gram* compound; *chem* constitution; *mech* resolution
compositor (-ra) *n mus* composer; *print* compositor
Compostela Compostella
compostura *f*, composition, structure; repair; neatness (of person); adulteration; arrangement, agreement; discretion, modesty
compota *f*, fruit preserve, compote; thick sauce
compotera *f*, jam or preserve dish
compra *f*, buying; marketing, shopping; purchase. **estar de compras,** *euphem* to be in the family way. **ir de compras,** to go shopping
comprable *a* purchasable
comprador (-ra) *a* purchasing. *n* purchaser; buyer; shopper
comprar *vt* to buy; bribe
comprender *vt* to encircle, surround; include, comprise, contain; understand
comprensible *a* comprehensible
comprensión *f*, comprehension, understanding
comprensivo *a* understanding; comprehensive
compresa *f*, *med* compress, swab; pack (for the face, etc.)
compresión *f*, compression; squeeze
compresivo *a* compressive
compresor *m*, compressor; *aut aer* supercharger
comprimido *m*, tablet, pill
comprimir *vt* to compress; squeeze; restrain; *vr* restrain oneself
comprobación *f*, verification; checking; proof
comprobante *a* verifying; confirmatory
comprobar *vt irr* to verify, check; confirm, prove. See **probar**
comprobatorio *a* confirmatory; verifying; testing
comprometedor *a inf* compromising; jeopardizing
comprometer *vt* to submit to arbitration; compromise; imperil, jeopardize; *vr* pledge oneself; *inf* compromise oneself
comprometido *a* awkward, embarrassing; (e.g. literature of a writer) committed, engagé
compromiso *m*, compromise, agreement, arbitration, commitment, obligation; appointment, engagement; jeopardy; difficulty
compuerta *f*, half-door, wicket, hatch; floodgate, sluice. **c. flotante,** floating dam
compuesto *a* and *past part* made-up, built-up; composite; circumspect; *bot gram* compound. *m*, composite; preparation, compound
compulsar *vt* to collate; *law* make a transcript of
compulsivo *a* compelling
compunción *f*, compunction
compungir *vt* to cause remorse or pity; *vr* repent; sympathize with, pity
computable *a* computable
computación *f*, **cómputo** *m*, calculation, computation
computador (-ra) *n* computer
computar *vt* to compute
cómputo *m*, computation; estimate
comulgar *vt* to administer Holy Communion; *vi* receive Holy Communion
comulgatorio *m*, communion rail, altar rail
común *a* general, customary, ordinary; public, communal; universal, common; vulgar, low. *m*, community, population; water-closet. **en c.,** in common; generally. **por lo c.,** generally. **sentido c.,** common sense
comuna *f*, *Lat. Am.* district
comunal *a* communal; common. *m*, commonalty
comunero *a* popular, affable, democratic. *m*, joint owner; commoner; *hist* commune
comunicable *a* communicable; communicative, sociable
comunicación *f*, communication; (telephone) call, message; letter (to the press); *mil* communiqué; *pl* lines of communication, transport
comunicado *m*, official communication, communiqué; letter (to the press)
comunicante *a* communicating
comunicar *vt* to communicate; transmit; impart, share; *vr* **comunicarse con,** (door) to open onto (e.g. **Esta puerta se comunica con el jardín.** This door opens onto the garden); communicate, converse, correspond with each other
comunicativo *a* communicative; talkative, not reserved
comunidad *f*, the common people; community; generality, majority; *pl hist* Commune
comunión *f*, communion; intercourse, fellowship; *ecc* Communion
comunismo *m*, communism
comunista *a* and *mf* communist
comunistófilo, comunistoide *a* fellow-traveling; *n* fellow traveler
comúnmente *adv* commonly, generally; frequently
con *prep* with; by means of; in the company of; towards, to; although (followed by *infin.*, but generally translated by an inflected verb, e.g. **C. ser almirante, no le gusta el mar,** Although he is an admiral, he doesn't like the sea); by (followed by *infin.* and generally translated by a gerund, e.g. **c. hacer todo esto,** by doing all this). **c. bien,** safe and sound, safely (e.g. **Llegamos con bien.** We arrived safely.) **c. cuentagotas,** sparingly; stingily. **c. que,** so, then. **c. tal que,** provided that, on condition that. **c. todo,** nevertheless. **¿Con . . . ?** Is this . . . ? (on the telephone, e.g. **¿Con el Sr. Piñangos?** Is this Mr. Piñangos?)
conato *m*, effort, endeavor; tendency; *law* attempted crime
concatenación *f*, concatenation
concavidad *f*, concavity; hollow
cóncavo *a* concave. *m*, concavity; hollow
concebible *a* conceivable
concebimiento *m*. See **concepción**
concebir *vi irr* to become pregnant; conceive, imagine; understand; *vt* conceive, acquire (affection, etc.). See **pedir**
concedente *a* conceding
conceder *vt* to confer, grant; concede; agree to
concejal *m*, councillor; alderman
concejil *a* pertaining to a municipal council; public
concejo *m*, town council; town hall; council meeting
concentración *f*, concentration
concentrado *a* concentrated; (of persons) reserved
concentrar *vt* to concentrate
concéntrico *a* concentric
concepción *f*, conception; idea, concept; *ecc* Immaculate Conception
conceptismo *m*, *lit* Concetism (cf. *Euphuism*)
conceptista *a* and *mf* concettist
concepto *m*, idea, concept; epigram; opinion. **en mi c.,** in my opinion; judgment. **por c. de,** in payment of
conceptuar *vt* to judge, take to be; believe; imagine
conceptuoso *a* witty, ingenious
concernencia *f*, respect, relation
concerniente *a* concerning
concernir *vi irr defective* to concern. See **discernir**
concertadamente *adv* methodically, orderly; by arrangement, or agreement
concertar *vt irr* to arrange, settle, adjust; bargain; conclude (business deal); harmonize; compare, correlate; tune instruments; *vi* reach an agreement. See **acertar**
concertina *f*, concertina
concertista *mf mus* performer, soloist; *mus* manager. **c. de piano,** concert pianist
concesión *f*, conceding, grant; concession; lease
concesionario *m*, *law* concessionaire, leaseholder
concho *m*, *Lat. Am.* dregs, sediment
conciencia *f*, consciousness; conscience; conscientiousness. **c. doble,** dual personality. **ancho de c.,** broadminded. **a c.,** conscientiously

concienzudo *a* of a delicate conscience, scrupulous; conscientious
concierto *m*, methodical arrangement; agreement; *mus* concert; *mus* concerto. **de c.,** by common consent
conciliable *a* reconcilable compatible
conciliábulo *m*, conclave, private meeting; secret meeting
conciliación *f*, conciliation; similarity, affinity; protection, favor
conciliador *a* conciliatory
conciliar *m*, councilor. *vt* to conciliate; *fig* reconcile (opposing theories, etc.). **c. el sueño,** to induce sleep, woo sleep. *vr* win liking (or sometimes dislike)
concilio *m*, council; *ecc* assembly; conciliary decree; findings of council
concinidad *f*, concinnity
concino *a* concinnous
concisión *f*, conciseness, brevity
conciso *a* concise
concitar *vt* to stir up, foment
conciudadano (-na) *n* fellow citizen; fellow countryman
cónclave *m*, conclave; meeting
concluir *vt irr* to conclude, finish; come to a conclusion, decide; infer, deduce; convince by reasoning; *law* close legal proceedings; *vr* expire, terminate. **c. con,** to put an end to. See **huir**
conclusión *f*, finish, end; decision; close, denouement; theory, proposition (gen. *pl*); deduction, inference; *law* close. **en c.,** in conclusion
conclusivo *a* final; conclusive
concluyente *a* concluding; convincing; conclusive
concomer *vi inf* to give a shrug, shrug one's shoulders; fidget with an itch. **c. de placer,** to itch with pleasure
concomitancia *f*, concomitance
concomitante *a* and *m*, concomitant
concordable *a* conformable
concordador (-ra) *a* peacemaking. *n* peacemaker
concordancia *f*, harmony, agreement; (*mus gram*) concord; *pl* concordance
concordar *vt irr* to bring to agreement; *vi* agree. See **acordar**
concordato *m*, concordat
concorde *a* agreeing; harmonious
concordia *f*, concord, agreement, harmony; written agreement
concreción *f*, concretion
concretar *vt* to combine, bring together; make concise; resume; *vr fig* confine oneself (to a subject) to hammer out, work out (an agreement)
concreto *a* concrete, real, not abstract. **en c.,** in definite terms; finally, to sum up
concubina *f*, concubine, mistress
concubinato *m*, concubinage
conculcación *f*, trampling, treading; violation
conculcador *m*, violator
conculcar *vt* to trample under foot, tread on; break, violate
concupiscencia *f*, concupiscence, lust; greed
concupiscente *a* concupiscent, lustful; greedy
concurrencia *f*, assembly; coincidence; attendance; help, influence
concurrido *a* crowded; busy; frequented
concurrir *vi* to coincide; contribute; meet together; agree, be of same opinion; compete (in an examination, etc.)
concurso *m*, crowd, concourse; conjunction, coincidence; help; competition; (tennis) tournament; competitive examination; invitation to offer tenders. **c. de acreedores,** creditors' meeting. **c. interno,** competitive examination for a position open to staff members only
concusión *f*, concussion; shock; extortion
concha *f*, shell; turtle-shell; prompter's box; cove, creek; anything shell-shaped. *fig* **meterse en su c.,** to retire into one's shell. *inf* **tener más conchas que un galápago,** to be very cunning
conchado *a* scaly, having a shell
condado *m*, earldom; county
condal *a* of an earl, earl's; of a count, count's; of Barcelona
conde *m*, earl; king of the gypsies
condecir (con) *vi* to agree (with)
condecoración *f*, conferment of an honor, decoration; medal
condecorar *vt* to confer a decoration or medal
condena *f*, *law* sentence; punishment; penalty
condenable *a* culpable, guilty; worthy of damnation
condenado (-da) *a* damned; wicked, harmful. *n law* convicted criminal
condenador *a* condemning; incriminating; blaming
condenar *vt law* to pronounce sentence (on), convict; condemn; disapprove; wall or block or close up. **c. a galeras,** to condemn to the gallies. *vr* blame oneself; be eternally damned
condenatorio *a* condemnatory; incriminating
condensación *f*, condensation
condensador *a* condensing. *m*, (*elec mech chem*) condenser
condensante *a* condensing
condensar *vt* to condense; thicken; abridge
condesa *f*, countess
condescendencia *f*, affability, graciousness
condescender *vi irr* to be obliging, helpful, agreeable. See **entender**
condescendiente *a* affable, gracious
condestable *m*, *hist* constable, commander-in-chief
condición *f*, condition; quality; temperament, character; (social) position; rank, family; nobility, circumstance; stipulation, condition, requirement. **estar en condiciones de,** to be in a position to. **no estar en condiciones de,** to be in no condition to
condicional *a* conditional
condicionar *vi* to come to an agreement, arrange; *vt* impose conditions
condigno *a* condign
condimentación *f*, *cul* seasoning
condimentar *vt* to flavor, season (food)
condimento *m*, condiment, flavoring
condiscípulo *m*, schoolfellow
condolencia *f*, compassion; condolence
condolerse *vr* (*with de*) to sympathize with, be sorry for. See **doler**
condonar *vt* to condone
conducción *f*. **conducencia,** *f*, transport, conveyance, carriage; guiding; direction, management; *phys* conduction; *mech* control-gear. *aut* **c. a izquierda,** left-hand drive
conducente *a* conducting, conducive
conducir *vt irr* to transport, convey, carry; *phys* conduct; guide, lead; manage, direct; *aut* drive; conduce; *vi* be suitable; *vr* behave, conduct oneself. *Pres. Ind.* **conduzco, conduces,** etc. *Preterite* **conduje, condujiste,** etc. *Pres. Subjunc.* **conduzca, conduzcas,** etc. *Imperf. Subjunc.* **condujese,** etc.
conducta *f*, transport, conveyance; management, conduct, direction; behavior
conductibilidad *f*, *phys* conductivity
conductivo *a* conductive
conducto *m*, pipe, conduit, drain, duct; *fig* channel, means; *anat* tube
conductor (-ra) *n* guide; leader; driver (vehicles); *m*, *phys* conductor. **c. de caballos,** teamster. **c. de entrada,** *rad* lead-in. **c. del calor,** heat-conductor. **c. eléctrico,** electric wire or cable
conectar *vt elec* to connect, switch on; couple; attach, join
conectivo *a* connective; (*elec mech*) connecting
conejera *f*, rabbit-warren; *inf* low dive or haunt
conejillo de Indias *m*, guineapig
conejo *m*, rabbit

conejuno *a* rabbit, rabbit-like
conejuna *f*, rabbit fur, coney
conexión *f*, connection; *elec* switching on, connection; joint; joining; *pl* friends, connections; *elec* wiring
conexo *a* connected
confabulación *f*, confabulation, conspiracy
confabular *vi* to confer; *vr* scheme, plot
confalón *m*, standard, banner
confección *f*, making; confection; making-up; concoction, remedy; ready-made garment
confeccionador (**-ra**) *n* maker (of clothes, etc.)
confeccionar *vt* to make; prepare; make up (pharmaceuticals)
confederación *f*, alliance, pact; confederacy, federation
confederarse *vr* to confederate, be allied
conferencia *f*, conference, meeting; lecture; (telephone) long-distance call (US), trunk call (UK)
conferenciante *mf* lecturer
conferencista *mf*, *Lat. Am.* lecturer
conferenciar *vi* to confer
conferir *vt irr* to grant, concede; consider, discuss; compare, correlate. See **herir**
confesable *a* acknowledgeable, avowable
confesar *vt irr* to avow, declare; acknowledge, admit; *ecc* hear confession; *vr ecc* confess. *Pres. Ind.* **confieso, confiesas, confiesa, confiesan.** *Pres. Subjunc.* **confiese, confieses, confiese, confiesen**
confesión *f*, confession
confesional *a* confessional
confesionario, confesonario, confesorio *m*, *ecc* confessional
confeso *a* confessed; converted (of Jews). *m*, *ecc* lay brother
confesor *m*, confessor
confeti *m*, confetti
confianza *f*, confidence, trust; assurance, courage; over-confidence, conceit; intimacy; familiarity. **de c.,** reliable (e.g. **persona de c.,** reliable person); informal (e.g. **reunión de c.,** informal meeting). **en c.,** in confidence, confidentially
confianzudo *a inf* overconfident
confiar *vi* (*with en*) to trust in, hope; *vt* (*with prep a* or *en*) entrust, commit to the care of; confide in
confidencia *f*, trust; confidence; confidential information
confidencial *a* confidential
confidente (**-ta**) *a* trustworthy, true. *m*, seat for two. *n* confidant(e); spy
configuración *f*, configuration, form, lie
configurar *vt* to shape
confín *m*, boundary, frontier; limit. *a* boundary
confinado *a* banished. *m*, *law* prisoner
confinar *vi* (*with con*) to be bounded by, contiguous to; *vt* banish; place in confinement
confirmación *f*, corroboration; *ecc* confirmation
confirmar *vt* to corroborate; uphold; *ecc* confirm
confiscación *f*, confiscation
confiscar *vt* to confiscate
confitar *vt* to candy, crystallize or preserve (fruit, etc.); *fig* sweeten
confite *m*, bonbon, sugared almond, etc.
confitería *f*, confectionery
confitero (**-ra**) *n* confectioner
confitura *f*, preserve, jam
conflagración *f*, conflagration, blaze; uprising, rebellion
conflicto *m*, strife, struggle; spiritual conflict; *fig* difficult situation
confluencia *f*, confluence; crowd
confluir *vi irr* to meet, flow together (rivers); run together (roads); crowd. See **huir**
conformación *f*, conformation; make-up, structure (e.g. of an organization)
conformar *vt* to fit, adjust; *vr* agree, be of the same opinion; submit, comply; to make up (e.g. **los grupos sociales que conforman este país,** the social groups who make up this country)
conforme *a* similar, alike; consistent; in agreement; long-suffering, resigned. *adv* according (to), in proportion (to)
conformidad *f*, conformity; similarity; resignation; agreement, harmony; proportion, symmetry. **de c.,** by common consent. **en c.,** according to
confort *m*, comfort
confortante *a* comforting; consoling; strengthening (of beverages)
confortar *vt* to comfort, reassure; encourage; console
confortativo *a* comforting; comfortable; strengthening, warming (of beverages); encouraging, cheering
confrontación *f*, confrontment; comparison (of texts, etc.)
confrontar *vt* to bring face to face; compare, correlate; *vi* face; (*with con*) be contiguous to, border on
confucianismo *m*, Confucianism
confundible *a* mistakable, liable to be confused
confundimiento *m*, confounding; mistaking; confusion
confundir *vt* to mix, confuse; jumble together; mistake; *fig* confound (in argument); humble; bewilder, perplex; *vr* be mixed together; mistake, confuse; be ashamed; be bewildered
confusión *f*, confusion; perplexity; shame; jumble
confuso *a* mixed, upset; jumbled; obscure; indistinct; blurred; bewildered
confutación *f*, confutation
confutar *vt* to confute
conga *f*, conga (dance; drum)
congelación *f*, freezing; congealment. **punto de c.,** freezing point
congelar *vt* to congeal; freeze
congeniar *vi* to be congenial
congénito *a* congenital
congestión *f*, *med* congestion
congestionar *vt* to congest; *vr med* be overcharged (with blood)
conglomeración *f*, conglomeration
conglomerar *vt* to conglomerate
congoja *f*, anguish, anxiety, grief
congraciarse (*con*), *vr* to ingratiate oneself (with), get into the good graces (of)
congratulación *f*, congratulation
congratular *vt* to congratulate; *vr* congratulate oneself
congratulatorio *a* congratulatory
congregación *f*, gathering, meeting, congregation; brotherhood, guild
congregar(**se**) *vt* and *vr* to meet, assemble
congresista *mf* member of a congress
congreso *m*, congress; conference, meeting; sexual intercourse
congrio *m*, conger eel
congruencia *f*, suitability, convenience; *math* congruence
congruente *a* convenient, opportune; *math* congruent
cónico *a* conical, tapering *math* conic
conífera *f*, conifer
conífero *a* coniferous
conjetura *f*, conjecture
conjetural *a* conjectural
conjeturar *vt* to conjecture surmise
conjugación *f*, conjugation
conjugar *vt* to conjugate
conjunción *f*, connection, union association; (*ast gram*) conjunction
conjuntivitis *f*, conjunctivitis
conjunto *a* united, associated adjoining; mingled, mixed (with) bound, affiliated. *m*, whole; combo, ensemble (of musicians). **c. habitacional,** housing complex, housing project
conjura, conjuración *f*, conspiracy, plot
conjurador (**-ra**) *n* conspirator, plotter; exorcist

conjurar *vi* to conspire, plot *vt* swear, take an oath; exorcise; implore, beg; ward off (danger)
conjuro *m,* plot, conspiracy, spell, incantation; entreaty
conllevar *vt* to share (troubles) bear, put up with; endure
conmemoración *f,* commemoration
conmemorar *vt* to commemorate
conmemorativo *a* commemorative
conmensurable *a* commensurable
conmigo *pers. pron* 1st pers. sing. *mf* with myself, with me
conminar *vt* to threaten
conminatorio *a* threatening
conmiseración *f,* commiseration, compassion, pity
conmoción *f,* disturbance (mind or body); upheaval, commotion. **c. eléctrica,** electric shock
conmovedor *a* moving, pitiful; stirring, thrilling
conmover *vt irr* to perturb, stir; move to pity. **c. los cimientos de,** to shake the foundations of; *vr* be emotionally moved. See **mover**
conmutable *a* commutable
conmutación *f,* commutation
conmutador *m, elec* commutator; change-over switch
conmutar *vt* to commute; *elec* switch, convert
conmutatriz *f, elec* converter
connato *a* contemporary
connatural *a* innate, inborn
connaturalizar *vt* to connaturalize
connaturalizarse (con) *vr* to become accustomed (to), become acclimated (to)
connivencia *f,* connivance
connotación *f,* connotation
connotado, -a *a, Lat. Am.* well-known
connotar *vt* to connote
cono *m,* (*geom bot*) cone. **el C. Sur,** the Southern Cone
conocedor (-ra) *n* one who knows; connoisseur; expert
conocer *vt irr* to know; understand; observe, perceive; be acquainted (with); conjecture; confess, acknowledge; know carnally; *vr* know oneself; know one another. **conocerle a uno la voz,** to recognize somebody's voice (e.g. **Le conozco la voz.** I recognize her by her voice.) **conocerle a uno en su manera de andar,** to recognize somebody by his gait, recognize somebody by his walk. *Pres. Ind.* **conozco, conoces,** etc. *Pres. Subjunc.* **conozca,** etc.
conocido (-da) *a* illustrious, distinguished. *n* acquaintance
conocimiento *m,* knowledge; understanding; intelligence; acquaintance (*not* friend); consciousness; *com* bill of lading; *pl* knowledge, learning
conque *conjunc* so, so that (e.g. **¿C. Juan se va?** So John's going away?)
conquista *f,* conquest
conquistador (-ra) *a* conquering. *n* conqueror
conquistar *vt* to conquer; *fig* captivate, win
consabido *a* aforesaid, beforementioned
consagración *f,* consecration; dedication
consagrar *vt* to consecrate; dedicate, devote; deify; *vr* (*with prep a*) dedicate oneself to, engage in
consanguíneo *a* consanguineous
consciente *a* conscious; aware; sane. *m, psy* conscious
conscripción *f,* conscription
conscripto *m,* conscript
consecución *f,* obtainment; attainment
consecuencia *f,* consequence, outcome; logical consequence, conclusion; importance; consistence (of people)
consecuente *a* consequent, resultant; consistent. **c. consigo mismo,** self-consistent *m,* consequence; *math* consequent
consecutivo *a* consecutive, successive
conseguir *vt irr* to obtain, achieve. See **seguir**
conseja *f,* story, fairy-tale; old wives' tale
consejero (-ra) *n* adviser; member of council. *m.* **c. de estado,** counselor of state
consejo *m,* advice; council, commission, board; council chamber or building. **c. de administración,** board of directors. **c. de guerra,** council of war. **c. del reino,** council of the realm. **c. privado,** privy council
consenso *m,* consensus of opinion, unanimity
consentido *a* complaisant (of husband); spoilt, over-indulged
consentimiento *m,* consent; assent
consentir *vt irr* to permit, allow; believe; tolerate, put up with; over-indulge, spoil; *vr* crack, give way (furniture, etc.). **c. en,** to consent to; to agree to. See **sentir**
conserje *m,* concierge, porter; warden or keeper (of castle, etc.)
conserjería *f,* conciergerie, porter's lodge; warden's dwelling (in castles, etc.)
conserva *f,* jam; preserve; pickles; *naut* convoy. **en c.,** preserved, tinned
conservación *f,* upkeep; preservation, maintenance; *cul* preserving; conservation. **c. refrigerada,** cold-storage
conservador (-ra) *a* keeping, preserving. *a* and *n* preserver; *pol* conservative; traditionalist. *m,* curator
conservadurismo *m,* conservatism
conservar *vt* to keep, maintain, preserve; keep up (custom, etc.); guard; *cul* preserve. **c. en buen estado,** to keep in repair
conservatorio *m,* conservatoire; academy; *Lat. Am.* greenhouse. **c. de música,** academy of music, conservatoire
considerable *a* considerable; worthy of consideration, powerful; numerous; large; important
consideración *f,* consideration, attention; reflection, thought; civility; importance. **en c. de,** considering
considerado *a* considerate; prudent; distinguished; important
considerar *vt* to consider, reflect upon; treat with consideration (persons); judge, estimate, feel (e.g. **Considero que . . .** I feel that . . .)
consigna *f, mil* watchword; left luggage office
consignador (-ra) *n com* consigner, sender
consignar *vt* to assign, lay aside; deposit; *com* consign; entrust, commit; put in writing; *law* deposit in trust; book (a suspect)
consignatario *m, law* trustee; mortgagee; *com* consignee. **c. de buques,** shipping agent
consigo *pers. pron* 3rd sing. and pl. *mf* with himself, herself, oneself, yourself, yourselves, themselves
consiguiente *a* consequent, resulting. *m,* consequence. **por c.,** in consequence
consistencia *f,* solidity; consistence, density; consistency, congruity, relevance
consistente *a* of a certain consistency; solid
consistir *vi* (*with en*) to consist in; be comprised of; be the result of
consistorio *m,* consistory; municipal council (in some Spanish towns); town hall
consola *f,* console table; piertable; *mech* bracket
cónsola *f,* radio cabinet
consolación *f,* consolation
consolador (-ra) *n* comforter, consoler
consolar *vt irr* to comfort, console. **consolarse de + inf.,** to console oneself for + *pp.* See **contar**
consolidación *f,* consolidation; stiffening
consolidar *vt* to consolidate; strengthen; combine, unite; *vr law* unite
consomé *m,* consommé
consonancia *f,* harmony; agreement
consonante *a* consonant, consistent. *m,* rhyme. *f, gram* consonant
consonantismo *m,* consonantism, consonant system
consorcio *m,* partnership; trust; intimacy, common life
consorte *mf* consort; companion, associate, partner; spouse
conspicuo *a* outstanding, distinguished; conspicuous
conspiración *f,* conspiracy

conspirador (-ra) *n* conspirator
conspirar *vi* to conspire; plot, scheme; tend, combine
constancia *f*, constancy, steadfastness; stability, steadiness; transcript (of grades); *Lat. Am. law* deposition. **c. de estudios,** transcript (of grades)
constante *a* constant; durable; *mech* steady, non-oscillating. *m*, constant
Constantinopla Constantinople
Constanza Constance (female given name and lake)
constar *vi* to be evident, be clear; (*with de*) be composed of, consist of, comprise
constelación *f*, *ast* constellation; climate
consternación *f*, dismay, alarm
consternarse *vr* to be dismayed or alarmed
constipado *m*, *med* cold; chill
constiparse *vr* to catch a cold or chill
constitución *f*, constitution; composition, make-up (e.g. **la c. del suelo,** the make-up of the soil)
constitucional *a* constitutional
constituir *vt irr* to constitute, form; found, establish; (*with en*) appoint, nominate; *fig* place in (a difficult situation, etc.); *vr* (*with en* or *por*) be appointed or authorized; be under (an obligation). See **huir**
constituyente, constitutivo *a* and *m*, constituent
constreñir *vt irr* to constrain, oblige; constrict; constipate. See **ceñir**
constricción *f*, constriction; contraction, shrinkage
construcción *f*, construction; art or process of construction; fabric, structure; *gram* construction; building, erection. **c. de caminos,** road making. **c. naval,** shipbuilding
constructor (-ra) *a* building, constructive. *n* builder; constructor
construir *vt irr* to construct; build, make; *gram* construct. See **huir**
consuelo *m*, consolation; comfort, solace; joy, delight
cónsul *m*, consul
consulado *m*, consulate. **c. general,** consulate general
consulta *f*, deliberation, consideration; advice; reference; conference, consultation
consultar *vt* to discuss, consider; seek advice, consult. **consultarlo con la almohada,** *fig* to sleep on it, think it over, mull it over
consultor (-ra) *a* consultative, advisory; consulting. *n* consultant; adviser. **c. externo,** outside consultant
consultorio *m*, *med* consulting rooms; surgery; technical information bureau
consumación *f*, consummation; completion, attainment; extinction, end
consumado *a* consummate; *inf* thorough, perfect
consumar *vt* to consummate; complete, accomplish, perfect
consumido *a inf* emaciated, wasted away; timid, spiritless
consumidor (-ra) *a* consuming. *n* consumer, user
consumir *vt* to destroy; consume, use; waste away, wear away; *ecc* take communion; *inf* grieve; *vr* be destroyed; *inf* be consumed with grief
consumo *m*, consumption; demand. **c. de combustible,** fuel consumption
contabilidad *f*, bookkeeping; accounts; accounting
contable *m*, bookkeeper
contacto *m*, contact (also *elec mil*). **en c.,** in common (e.g. **Los dos libros tienen mucho en c.** The two books have much in common.)
contado *a* few; infrequent; rare. **al c.,** *com* cash down. **por de c.,** presumably; of course, naturally
contador *a* counting. *m*, accountant; *law* auditor; counter (in banks); *elec* meter, counter; *naut* purser. **c. oficial,** *Argentina* certified public accountant. **c. público titulado,** certified public accountant
contaduría *f*, accountancy; counting house; accountant's office; auditorship; *theat* box-office; *naut* purser's office
contagiar *vt* to infect; corrupt, pervert; *vr* (*with con, de* or *por*) be infected by or through
contagio *m*, infection; contagious disease; *fig* contagion, perversion, corruption
contagioso *a* infectious; *fig* catching, contagious
contaminación *f*, contamination, pollution
contaminar *vt* to pollute, contaminate; infect; *fig* corrupt
contante *a* ready (of money)
contar *vt irr* to count; recount, tell; place to account; include, count among; *vi* calculate, compute. **contarle a uno las cuarenta,** *inf* to give someone a piece of one's mind. **c. con,** to rely upon; reckon upon. *Pres. Ind.* **cuento, cuentas, cuenta, cuentan.** *Pres. Subjunc.* **cuente, cuentes, cuente, cuenten**
contemplación *f*, meditation, contemplation; consideration
contemplar *vt* to consider, reflect upon; look at, contemplate; indulge, please
contemplativo *a ecc* contemplative; reflective, thoughtful; kind, indulgent
contemporáneo (de) *a* contemporaneous (to *or* with) *n* contemporary
contemporizar *vi* to temporize, gain time
contencioso *a* contentious, argumentative; *law* litigious
contender *vi irr* to contain; restrain, hold back; comprise; *vr* control oneself. See **entender**
contendiente *mf* contestant
contener *vt irr* to contain; include; comprise; hold back; restrain; check, repress; hold down, subdue; suppress, put down; *vr* contain oneself; keep one's temper; keep quiet; refrain. See **tener**
contenido *m*, contents. *a* contained; *fig* restrained; reserved (of persons)
contentamiento *m*, contentment
contentar *vt* to satisfy, please; *com* endorse; *vr* be pleased or satisfied
contento *a* happy; content; satisfied; pleased. *m*, pleasure; contentment. **no caber de c.,** to be overjoyed
contestación *f*, reply, answer; discussion, argument, dispute
contestar *vt* to reply, answer; confirm, attest; *vi* accord, harmonize
contexto *m*, context
contextura *f*, structure; context; physique, frame
contienda *f*, struggle, fight; quarrel, dispute; discussion
contigo *pers. pron* 2nd sing. *mf* with thee, with you
contigüidad *f*, proximity, nearness
contiguo *a* adjacent, near
continencia *f*, moderation, self-restraint; continence; chastity; containing
continental *a* continental. *m*, express messenger service; *Puerto Rico* person from the mainland United States
continente *a* continent. *m*, container; demeanor, bearing; *geog* continent; mainland
contingencia *f*, contingency; risk, danger
contingente *a* incidental; fortuitous; dependent; *m*, *mil* taskforce, contingent
continuación *f*, continuation; prolongation; sequel (of a story, etc.)
continuador (-ra) *n* continuer
continuar *vt* to continue; *vi* continue; last, remain, go on; *vr* be prolonged
continuidad *f*, continuity
continuo *a* continuous, steady, uninterrupted; persevering, tenacious; persistent, lasting, unremitting. *m*, a united whole. **de c.,** continuously
contonearse *vr* to swing the hips (in walking); strut
contorno *m*, contour, outline; (gen. *pl*) environs, surrounding district
contorsión *f*, contortion
contorsionista *mf* contortionist
contra *prep* against, counter, athwart; opposed to, hostile to; in front of, opposite; towards. *m*, opposite view or opinion. *f*, *inf* difficulty, trouble. **c. la corriente,** up-

stream. **el pro y el c.,** the pros and cons. **en c.,** in opposition, against
contraalmirante *m,* rear admiral
contraataque *m,* counterattack
contraaviso *m,* countermand
contrabajo *m,* doublebass; player of this instrument; deep bass voice
contrabalancear *vt* to counterbalance; *fig* compensate
contrabandista *a* smuggling. *mf* smuggler
contrabando *m,* contraband; smuggling
contracción *f,* contraction; shrinkage; abridgment; abbreviation
contracubierta *f,* book jacket, jacket
contradanza *f,* square dance
contradecir *vt irr* to contradict; *vr* contradict oneself. See **decir**
contradicción *f,* contradiction
contradictorio *a* contradictory
contraer *vt irr* to shrink, reduce in size, shorten; abridge; contract (matrimony, obligations); *fig* acquire (diseases, habits); *vr* shorten, contract, shrink. See **traer**
contrafuerte *m,* buttress, counterfort, abutment; *geog* spur
contrahacer *vt irr* to forge, counterfeit; mimic; imitate. See **hacer**
contrahecho *a* deformed
contralor *m,* comptroller
contraloría *f,* comptrollership, office of comptroller (position); comptroller's office (place)
contralto *m,* contralto (voice)
contraluz *f,* counterlight
contramaestre *m, naut* boatswain; overseer, superintendent, foreman
contramarcha *f,* retrogression; *mil* countermarch
contramedida *f,* counter-measure
contraorden *f,* countermand
contrapedalear *vi* to backpedal
contrapelo *a adv* the wrong way of the hair, against the grain; *inf* reluctantly, distastefully
contrapeso *m,* counterpoise, counterweight; balancing-pole (acrobats); *fig* counterbalance; makeweight
contraponer *vt irr* to compare; place opposite; oppose. See **poner**
contraproducente *a* counteractive, counterproductive, unproductive, self-deceiving; self-defeating
contrapuesto *a* opposing, divergent
contrapunto *m,* counterpoint
contrariar *vt* to counter, oppose; impede; vex, annoy
contrariedad *f,* contrariety, opposition; obstacle; vexation, trouble
contrario (-ia) *a* opposite; hostile, opposed; harmful; adverse, contrary. *n* adversary; opponent. *m,* obstacle. *f.* **contraria,** contrary, opposite. **al contrario,** on the contrary. **llevar la contraria (a),** to oppose; contradict
contrarreforma *f,* counter-Reformation
contrasentido *m,* wrong sense, opposite sense (of words); contradiction of initial premise; self-contradiction; nonsense
contraseña *f,* countersign; *mil* password
contrastar *vt* to contrast; oppose, resist; check (weights and measures); assay; *mech* calibrate, gauge; *vi* contrast
contraste *m,* contrast; opposition, difference; weights and measures inspector; dispute, clash. **en c. a,** in contrast to
contrata *f,* **contrato,** *m,* contract. **contrato de arrendamiento,** lease
contratación *f,* hiring; *com* transaction; commerce, trade
contratapa *f,* back cover (of a periodical, etc.)
contratar *vt* to contract, enter into an agreement; make a bargain (with), deal (with); hire, contract
contratiempo *m,* mishap, accident
contratista *mf* contractor
contratorpedero *m,* torpedoboat destroyer
contravención *f,* contravention; violation. **en c. a,** in violation of
contraveneno *m, med* antidote; remedy, precaution
contravenir *vt irr* to infringe, contravene. See **venir**
contraventana *f,* shutter (for windows)
contravidriera *f,* storm window
contrayente *a* contracting. *mf* contracting party (used of matrimony)
contribución *f,* contribution; tax. **c. sobre la propiedad,** property tax
contribuir *vt irr* to pay (taxes); contribute. See **huir**
contribuyente *a* contributing; contributory. *mf* contributor; taxpayer
contrición *f,* contrition
contrincante *m,* competitor, candidate (public examinations); rival, opponent
contrito *a* contrite
control *m,* control; checking. **c. de precios,** price control
controlar *vt* to control
controversia *f,* controversy
controvertir *vi* and *vt irr* to dispute, argue against, deny. See **sentir**
contumacia *f,* obstinacy; *law* contumacy
contumaz *a* stubborn; impenitent; *law* contumacious; *med* obstinate, resistant (to cure)
contumelia *f,* contumely
conturbar *vt* to perturb, make anxious, disturb; *vr* be perturbed
contuso *a* contused, bruised
convalecencia *f,* convalescence; convalescent home
convalecer *vi irr* to convalesce, get better; *fig* recover, regain (influence, etc.). See **conocer**
convaleciente *a* and *mf* convalescent
convalidar *vt* to ratify, confirm
convecino *a* nearby; neighboring
convencedor *a* convincing
convencer *vt* to convince; prove beyond doubt, demonstrate to (persons); be convincing (e.g. **No convence,** It's not convincing; He's not convincing.) *vr* be convinced
convencimiento *m,* conviction, belief, assurance
convención *f,* pact, formal agreement; harmony, conformity; convention
convencional *a* conventional (all meanings)
convencionalismo *m,* conventionality
convenido *a* agreed
conveniencia *f,* conformity, harmony, adjustment; experience, suitability, convenience; advantage; agreement, pact; post as domestic; ease, comfort; *pl* income; social conventions
conveniente *a* convenient, opportune; suitable, fitting; profitable; useful; decorous. **tener por c. + inf,** to think it fitting to + *inf,* find it appropriate to + *inf*
convenio *m,* pact, treaty; *com* agreement, contract
convenir *vi irr* to agree; assemble, congregate; belong; be suitable; *vr* agree; suit oneself. **No me conviene salir esta tarde,** It does not suit me to go out this afternoon. **Me convendría pasar un mes allí,** It would be a good idea (or a wise thing) for me to spend a month there. See **venir**
conventillo *m, Lat. Am.* tenement
convento *m,* convent; monastery; religious community
conventual *a* conventual; monastic. *m, ecc* conventual
convergencia *f,* convergence
convergir *vi* to converge; *fig* coincide (views, etc.)
conversación *f,* conversation; intercourse, company; *law* criminal conversation
conversar *vi* to converse; chat; live with others; know socially
conversión *f,* conversion; change, transformation; *com* conversion; *mil* wheel; wheeling
converso (-sa) *n* convert
convertible *a* convertible
convertir *vt irr* to change, transform; convert; reform;

vr be transformed; be converted; be reformed. See **sentir**
convexo *a* convex
convicción *f*, conviction; certitude; *law* conviction
convicto (-ta) *a* and *n law* convict
convidado (-da) *n* guest
convidar *vt* to invite (persons); encourage, provoke; entice, attract; *vr* invite oneself; offer one's services
convincente *a* convincing
convite *m*, invitation; banquet; party
convivencia *f*, coexistence, common life, life together. **c. pacífica,** peaceful coexistence
convivial *a* convivial
convivir *vi* to live together, live under the same roof
convocación *f*, convocation
convocar *vt* to convene, convoke
convoy *m*, convoy; escort; following; cruet-stand
convoyar *vt* to convoy, escort
convulsión *f*, convulsion
convulsivo *a* convulsive
conyugal *a* conjugal
cónyuge *mf* husband or (and) wife (used gen. in *pl*)
coñac *m*, brandy
coñete *a*, *Chile, Peru* mean, stingy
cooperación *f*, cooperation
cooperador (-ra) *a* cooperative. *n* cooperator, collaborator
cooperar *vt* to cooperate
cooperativa *f*, cooperative society
cooperativo *a* cooperative
coordenada *f*, coordinate
coordinación *f*, coordination
coordinar *vt* to coordinate, classify
copa *f*, wineglass, goblet; glassful; top branches (of trees); crown (of hat); *cards* heart; gill (liquid measure); *inf* drink, glass; *pl cards* hearts (in Spanish pack, goblets)
copal *m*, *Central America, Mexico* resin
copartícipe *mf* co-partner, partaker, participant
copec *m*, kopeck
Copenhague Copenhagen
copernicano *a* Copernican
copero *m*, cupbearer; sideboard; cocktail cabinet
copete *m*, lock, tress (hair); tuft, crest; forelock (horses); head, top (ice-cream, drinks); *inf* **de alto c.,** aristocratic; socially prominent
copetudo, -a *a*, *Lat. Am.* tufted, crested; haughty, stuck-up
copia *f*, abundance, plenty; copy, reproduction; transcript; imitation
copiador (-ra) *a* copying. *n* copier; transcriber. *m*, copybook
copiar *vt* to copy
copioso *a* abundant, plentiful
copla *f*, couplet; popular four-line poem; couple, pair; *pl inf* verses
coplero (-ra) *n* balladmonger; poetaster
copo *m*, cop (of a spindle); snowflake
copón *m*, large goblet; *ecc* ciborium, chalice
coprófago *a* coprophagous
copropietario (-ia) *n* coproprietor, coowner
copto (-ta) *n* Copt
cópula *f*, connection; coupling; joining; copulation
copularse *vr* to copulate
coque *m*, coke
coqueluche *f*, whooping cough
coqueta *f*, coquette, flirt
coquetear *vi* to flirt
coqueteo *m*, coquetry; flirtation
coquetería *f*, coquetry
coquetón *a* coquettish
coraje *m*, courage, valor; anger
coral *m*, coral. *f*, coral snake. *m*, *bot* coral tree; *pl* coral beads
coral *a* choral
coralina *f*, coral (polyp).
coraza *f*, cuirass; shell (of tortoise); armor-plate, armor (ships, etc.)
corazón *m*, heart; courage, spirit; love, tenderness; goodwill, benevolence; core (of a fruit); *fig* pith. **de c.,** sincerely. **tener el c. en la mano,** to wear one's heart on one's sleeve
corazonada *f*, feeling, instinct; presentiment, apprehension
corbata *f*, necktie; scarf; ribbon (insignia)
corbatería *f*, necktie shop
corbatero *m*, necktie maker; necktie dealer; tie rack
Córcega Corsica
corchea *f*, *mus* quaver
corchete *m*, *sew* hook and eye; hook
corcho *m*, *bot* cork, cork bark; stopper, cork; cork mat; bee hive
corcova *f*, hump, abnormal protuberance
corcovado (-da) *a* hunchbacked, crooked. *n* hunchback
corcovear *vi* to curvet, caper
cordaje *m*, *naut* cordage, tackling, rope
cordel *m*, cord; *naut* line. **a c.,** in a straight line
cordelería *f*, rope making; ropeyard; cordage
cordelero (-ra) *n* rope maker
cordera *f*, ewe lamb; sweet, gentle woman
corderillano, -a *a*, *Argentina, Chile* Andean
cordero *m*, lamb; dressed lambskin; peaceable, mild man; Jesus (gen. **Divino C.**)
cordial *a* warming, invigorating; affectionate, loving, friendly. *m*, *med* cordial
cordialidad *f*, cordiality, friendliness
cordillera *f*, mountain range
Córdoba Cordova
cordobán *m*, cured goatskin; Cordovan leather, Spanish leather
cordobés (-esa) *a* and *n* Cordovan
cordón *m*, cord; cordon; *ecc* rope girdle; *arch* stringcourse
cordoncillo *m*, rib (in cloth); ridge, milling (of coins); *sew* piping
cordura *f*, good sense, prudence
Corea Korea
coreografía *f*, choreography; art of dancing
coreográfico *a* choreographic
coreógrafo *m*, choreographer
corintio (-ia) *a* and *n* Corinthian
Corinto Corinth
corista *m*, *ecc* chorister. *mf theat* member of the chorus
cornada *f*, horn thrust or wound (bulls, etc.)
cornamenta *f*, horns (bulls, deer, etc.)
córnea *f*, cornea
corneja *f*, carrion or black crow
córneo *a* horny, corneous
corneta *f*, *mus* bugle; *mus* cornet; swineherd's horn; *mil* pennon. *m*, bugler; *mil* cornet. **c. de monte,** hunting horn
cornetín *m*, *dim* **corneta,** *mus* cornet; cornet player
cornezuelo *m*, *dim* little horn; *med* ergot; *bot* variety of olive
cornisa *f*, cornice
cornucopia *f*, cornucopia, horn of plenty; sconce; mirror
cornudo *a* horned. *m*, cuckold. **el C.,** the Devil
coro *m*, choir; chorus; *arch* choir. **hacer c. (a),** to listen to, support. **saber de c.,** to know by heart
corolario *m*, corollary
corona *f*, garland, wreath; halo; (*ast arch*) corona; crown (of tooth); crown (of head); tonsure; crown (coin); royal power; kingdom; triumph; reward; summit, height, peak; circlet (for candles)
coronación *f*, coronation; coping stone
coronamiento *m*, coronation; coping stone; *fig* crowning touch; *naut* taffrail
coronar *vt* to crown; crown (in draughts); complete, round off; *vr* be crowned; crown oneself; be tipped or capped
coronel *m*, colonel

coronela *f, inf* colonel's wife
coronelía *f,* colonelcy
coronilla *f, dim* small crown; crown of head; *fig inf* **estar hasta la c.,** to be fed up
coroza *f,* dunce's cap
corpiño *m,* bodice
corporación *f,* corporation, body, association
corporal *a* and *m, ecc* corporal
corporativo *a* corporate, corporative
corpóreo *a* corporeal
corporizar *vt* to embody
corpulento *a* corpulent, stout
Corpus *m,* Corpus Christi
corpúsculo *m,* corpuscle
corral *m,* yard; pen, enclosure, corral; old-time theater. **c. de madera,** timber yard. *inf* **hacer corrales,** to play truant
correa *f,* leather strap or thong; flexibility; *mech* belt, band
corrección *f,* correction; correctness; punishment; emendation. **c. de pruebas,** proofreading, proofing, reading proof
correcional *a* correctional. *m,* reformatory
correcto *a* correct; well-bred; unexceptionable, irreproachable; regular (of features)
corredera *f,* link (engines); *mech* slide; *naut* log; racecourse; *inf* procuress
corredizo *a* easy to untie; running (of knots); sliding
corredor (**-ra**) *n* runner. *m, com* broker; corridor; *inf* meddler; *inf* procurer, pimp. *a* running. **c. de bolsa,** stockbroker
corregible *a* corrigible
corregidor *m,* Spanish magistrate; *ant* mayor
corregidora *f,* wife of corregidor; mayoress
corregir *vt irr* to correct; scold, punish; moderate, counteract; *mech* adjust; *vr* mend one's ways. **c. pruebas,** to read proof. *Pres. Ind.* **corrijo, corriges, corrige, corrigen.** *Pres. Part.* **corrigiendo.** *Pres. Subjunc.* **corrija, corrijas,** etc. *Imperf. Subjunc.* **corrigiese,** etc.
correligionario (**-ia**) *n* coreligionist; fellow-supporter or believer
correlón, -ona *a Mexico, Venezuela* cowardly
correntada *f, Argentina* rapids
correo *m,* courier; mail; post-office; letters. **c. aéreo,** air-mail. **c. certificado,** registered mail. **a vuelta de c.,** by return of mail. **tren c.,** mail train
correr *vi* to run; race; sail, steam; flow; blow; flood; extend, stretch; pass (of time); fall due (salary, etc.); be current or general; (*with con*) be in charge of or responsible for; *vt* run (a horse); fasten, slide (bolts, etc.); draw (curtains); undergo, suffer; sell, auction; *inf* steal; *fig* embarrass; spread (a rumor, etc.); catch, make (bus, train, etc.); *vr* slide, glide, slip; run (of colors); *inf* spread oneself, talk too much. **c. cañas,** to participate in a mock joust using reeds as spears
correría *f,* raid, foray; excursion, trip
correspondencia *f,* relationship, connection; intercourse, communication; correspondence, letters; equivalence, exact translation
corresponder *vi* to requite, repay; be grateful; belong to, concern; devolve upon, fall to; suit, harmonize (with); fit; *vr* correspond by letters; like or love each other
correspondiente *a* suitable; proportionate; corresponding. *mf* correspondent
corresponsal *mf* correspondent (especially professional); *com* agent
corretear *vi* to wander about the streets; gad
correveidile *mf inf* tale-bearer, gossip
corrida *f,* race, run; *aer* taxying; bull fight (abb. for **c. de toros**)
corrido *a* extra, over (of weight); embarrassed; experienced
corriente *a* current, present; well-known; usual, customary; fluent (style); ordinary, average; easy. *f,* flow, stream; *fig* course (of events, etc.); *elec* current. *adv* quite, exactly. *elec* **c. alterna,** alternating current. **c. continua,** direct current. **c. de aire,** draught. **estar al c.,** to be informed (of something)
Corriente del Golfo Gulf Stream
corrillo *m,* knot, group, huddle (of people)
corro *m,* circle, group; ring (for children's games)
corroboración *f,* corroboration, confirmation
corroborar *vt* to fortify; corroborate, support
corroer *vt irr* to corrode, waste away; *fig* gnaw. See **roer**
corromper *vt* to rot; mar; spoil, ruin; seduce; corrupt (texts); bribe; *fig* contaminate, corrupt; *vi* stink; *vr* putrefy, not; be spoilt; *fig* be corrupted
corrosión *f,* corrosion
corrosivo *a* corrosive
corrugación *f,* corrugation, wrinkling
corrupción *f,* rot, putrefaction; corruption, depravity; decay; stink; bribery; falsification (of texts); corruption (of language, etc.)
corrupto *a* corrupt
corruptor (**-ra**) *n* corrupter
corsario *m,* pirate; privateer
corsé *m,* corset
corsetería *f,* corset shop or manufactory
corso (**-sa**) *a* and *n* Corsican
corta *f,* felling, cutting
cortacircuitos *m, elec* circuit breaker, cut-out; disconnecting switch
cortado *a* fitting, proportioned; disjointed (style); confused, shamefaced
cortador *m,* cutter; cutter-out (dresses, etc.); butcher
cortadura *f,* cut, wound; cutting (from periodicals); defile; *pl* clippings, cuttings
cortafrío *m,* cold chisel; *carp* hammer-head chisel
cortalápices *m,* pencil sharpener
cortante *a* cutting; sharp; piercing (of wind, etc.); trenchant; *m, Argentina* scissors *pl.*
cortapapel *m,* paper-knife
cortapisa *f,* condition, stipulation
cortaplumas *m,* penknife
cortapuros *m,* cigar cutter
cortar *vt* to cut; cut out (dresses, etc.); switch off, shut off (water, electricity, etc.); cleave, divide; cut (cards); pierce (wind, etc.); interrupt, impede; omit, cut; *fig* interrupt (conversation); decide, determine; *vr* be confused or shamefaced; curdle, turn sour (e.g. **Se cortó la leche,** The milk turned sour); split, fray; chap
cortavidrios *m,* diamond, glasscutter
cortaviento *m,* windscreen
corte *f,* court (royal); retinue; yard; *pl* Spanish parliament. *m,* cutting, cut; blade, cutting edge; cutting out, dressmaking; length, material required for garment, shoes, etc.; cut, fit; style; book edge; *arch* section; means, expedient; counting of money (in a till). **c. de caja,** counting of money (in a till). **c. trasversal,** side view
cortedad *f,* shortness, brevity; smallness; stupidity, dullness; timidity, shyness. **c. de fuerzas,** lack of strength
cortejar *vt* to accompany, escort; woo, court
cortejo *m,* courtship, wooing; suite, accompaniment; gift, present; homage, attention; *inf* lover, beau
cortés *a* polite, attentive, courteous, civil
cortesana *f,* courtesan
cortesano *a* court; courtly. *m,* courtier
cortesía *f,* politeness, courtesy; attentiveness; civility; gift, present; favor. **c. internacional,** courtesy of nations. **c. de boca mucho vale y poco cuesta.** Courtesy is worth much and costs little
corteza *f, bot* bark; *anat* cortex; skin, peel, crust; aspect, appearance; roughness. **c. terrestre,** Earth's crust, crust of the Earth. **de c.,** superficial (e.g. explanation)
cortijo *m,* farmhouse and land
cortina *f,* curtain; *fig* veil; *inf* heel taps; *mil* curtain, screen. **c. de fuego de artillería,** anti-aircraft barrage. **c. de globos de intercepción,** balloon barrage. **c. de humo,** smoke screen. **c. metálica,** metal shutter

cortinaje *m*, curtains, hangings
corto *a* short, brief; timid, bashful; concise; defective; stupid, dull; tongue-tied, inarticulate. **c. circuito,** *elec* short-circuit. **c. de alcances,** dull-witted. **c. de vista,** short-sighted
coruscar *vi* to glitter, shine
corvadura *f*, bend; curvature
corveta *f*, curvet, prancing; *a*, *Central America* bow-legged
corvetear *vi* to curvet
corzo *m*, roe-deer, fallow-deer
cosa *f*, thing. **c. rara,** strange to relate; an extraordinary thing. **como si tal c.,** as though nothing had happened. *inf* **poquita c.,** a person of no account
cosaco (-ca) *a* and *n* Cossack
coscorrón *m*, blow on the head, cuff
cosecha *f*, harvest; harvest time; reaping, gathering, lifting; yield, produce; crop, shower (of honors, etc.). **c. de vino,** vintage
cosechar *vi* and *vt* to harvest, reap
coseno *m*, cosine
coser *vt* to sew, stitch; join, unite; press together (lips, etc.). **c. a puñaladas,** to stab repeatedly
Cosme Cosmo
cosmético *a* and *m*, cosmetic
cósmico *a* cosmic
cosmografía *f*, cosmography
cosmógrafo *m*, cosmographer
cosmonave *f*, spaceship
cosmopolita *a* and *mf* cosmopolitan
cosmopolitismo *m*, cosmopolitanism
cosmos *m*, cosmos
cospel *m*, blank (from which to stamp coins); to ken; subway to ken
cosquillas *f pl*, tickling. **hacer c. (a),** to tickle
cosquillear *vt* to tickle
cosquilleo *m*, tickle, tickling
cosquilloso *a* ticklish; hypersensitive, touchy
costa *f*, cost; expense; coast; *pl law* costs. **a c. de,** by dint of; at the cost of. **a toda c.,** at all costs
Costa del Oro, la the Gold Coast
Costa de Marfil Ivory Coast
costado *m*, *anat* side; *mil* flank; side; *pl* line of descent, genealogy. *naut* **dar el c.,** to be broadside on
costal *m*, sack, bag
costanero *a* sloping; coast, coastal
costar *vi irr* to cost; cause. See **contar**
costarriqueño (-ña) *a* and *n* Costa Rican
coste *m*, cost, price
costear *vt* to pay for, defray the expense of; *naut* coast; *Argentina* pasture; *vr* pay (for itself)
costilla *f*, (*anat aer naut arch*) rib; *fig inf* better half, wife; *pl inf* back, behind
costillaje, costillar *m*, *anat* ribs; *naut* ship's frame
costoso *a* expensive, costly; valuable; dear, costly, difficult
costra *f*, crust; scab; rind (of cheese)
costumbre *f*, habit; custom
costumbrista *mf* writer on everyday life and customs. *a* (of literary work) dealing with life and customs
costura *f*, sewing; seam; needlework; *carp* joint; riveting
costurar, costurear *vi*, *Lat. Am.* to sew
costurera *f*, seamstress
costurero *m*, work-box, sewing bag
cota *f*, *surv* elevation, height; coat (of mail); quota. **c. de malla,** chain-mail
cotangente *f*, cotangent
cotejar *vt* to compare; collate
cotejo *m*, comparison; collation
cótel *m*, cocktail, drink
cotelera *f*, cocktail shaker
cotí *m*, ticking (cloth)
cotidiano *a* daily
cotizable *a* valued at; (of prices, shares) quoted
cotización *f*, *com* quotation; *com* rate. **boletín de c.,** price list (of shares, etc.)
cotizar *vt com* to quote (prices, rates)
coto *m*, enclosed ground; boundary stone; preserve, covert; hand's breadth; end, stop, limit. **c. de caza,** game preserve
cotorra *f*, small green parrot; magpie; *inf* chatterbox
cotufa *f*, earthnut; titbit; *inf* **pedir cotufas en el golfo,** to ask for the moon; **cotufas** *f pl Venezuela* popcorn
coyote *m*, coyote, prairie wolf; *Mexico* fixer (anyone who can pull strings to cut red tape or achieve something illegally); smuggler (of goods or people)
coyuntura *f*, *anat* joint; juncture, occasion
coz *f*, kick, recoil (of gun); butt (of a rifle); *inf* slap in the face, unprovoked rudeness. **dar coces,** to kick
craneal *a* cranial
cranearse *vr*, *Chile* to burn the midnight oil
cráneo *m*, cranium, skull
crápula *f*, drunkenness; depravity, immorality, debauchery
craquear *vt* to crack (petroleum)
crasitud *f*, greasiness; fatness; crassness
craso *a* fat, greasy; thick; unpardonable, crass (often with *ignorancia*). *m*, fatness; ignorance
creación *f*, creation; universe, world; foundation, establishment; appointment (dignitaries)
creador (-ra) *n* creator, originator. *m*, God. *a* creative
crear *vt* to create; found, institute, establish; make, appoint
crecer *vi irr* to grow; grow up; increase in size; grow longer; wax (moon); come in (of the tide); increase in value (money); *vr* become more sure of oneself; swell with pride; grow in authority. See **nacer**
creces *f pl*, increase, interest. **con c.,** fully, amply. **pagar con c.,** *fig* to pay with interest
crecida *f*, swollen river or stream; food; rising (of the tide)
crecido *a* grown up; considerable; abundant, plentiful; large; full; serious, important
crecidos *m pl*, widening stitches (knitting)
creciente *a* growing; rising (of the tide); crescent (moon). *m*, *her* crescent. *f*, rising of the tide; crescent moon
crecimiento *m*, growing; growth, development; increase (in value, money); waxing (of moon)
credenciales *f pl*, credentials
credibilidad *f*, credibility
crédito *m*, belief, credence; assent, acquiescence; reputation, name; favor, popularity, acceptance; *com* credit; *com* letter of credit. **créditos activos,** assets. **créditos pasivos,** liabilities. **a c.,** on credit
credo *m*, creed. *inf* **en un c.,** in a jiffy
credulidad *f*, credulity
crédulo *a* credulous
creencia *f*, belief; religion, sect, faith
creer *vt irr* to believe; think, consider, opine; think likely or probable. **¡Ya lo creo!** I should just think so! Rather! **creerse la divina garza,** *Mexico* to think one is God's gift to the world. **creerse descender del sobaco de Jesucristo,** to think one is God's gift to the world. *Pres. Part.* **creyendo.** *Preterite* **creyó, creyeron.** *Imperf. Subjunc.* **creyese,** etc.
creíble *a* credible
creído, -a *a*, *Lat. Am.* credulous, trusting
crema *f*, cream (off milk); custard mold, cream, shape; face cream; cold cream; elect, flower (of society, etc.)
cremación *f*, cremation; burning, incineration
cremallera *f*, *mech* rack, ratch; zip fastener. **colgar la c.,** to give a house-warming
crematístico *a* economic, financial
crematorio *m*, crematorium. *a* burning; cremating
cremor *m*, *chem* cream of tartar
cremoso *a* creamy
crencha *f*, parting (of the hair); each side of parting
crepitación *f*, crackling, sputtering; hissing; roar (of a fire); *med* crepitation
crepitar *vi* to crackle; sputter; hiss; roar (of a fire); *med* crepitate

crepuscular *a* twilight
crepúsculo *m*, twilight, half light
cresa *f*, maggot; cheese-mite; fly's egg
Creso Croesus
crespo *a* curly, frizzy (hair); rough (of animal's fur); curled (leaves); artificial, involved (style)
crespón *m*, crape
cresta *f*, comb (of cock, etc.); tuft, topknot (birds); plume; summit, top (of mountains); crest (of a wave); *her* crest
Creta Crete
creta *f*, chalk
cretense *a* Cretan
cretinismo *m*, cretinism
cretino (**-na**) *a* and *n* cretin
creyente *a* believing; religious. *mf* believer
cría *f*, rearing; bringing up; nursing; suckling; breeding; brood; litter
criada *f*, servant, maid
criadero *m*, *min* vein, deposit; tree nursery, plantation; breeding farm or place. *a* prolific
criado *m*, servant. *a* bred, brought up (used with *bien* or *mal*, well *or* badly brought up)
criador (**-ra**) *n* breeder, keeper, raiser. *a* creating; rearing; creative; fertile, rich
criandera *f*. *Lat. Am.* nursemaid, wet nurse
crianza *f*, feeding, suckling; lactation; manners. **buena** (or **mala**) **c., good (or bad) breeding or upbringing**
criar *vt* to create; procreate; rear, educate, bring up; feed, nurse, suckle; raise (birds, animals); inspire, give rise to. **Me crié raquítico,** I grew up delicate
criatura *f*, being, creature; man, human being; infant; small child; fetus; *fig* puppet, tool
criba *f*, sieve, cribble
cribar *vt* to sieve; riddle (earth, etc.)
crimen *m*, crime. **c. pasional,** crime of passion
criminal *a* and *m*, criminal
criminalidad *f*, guilt; crime ratio; delinquency
criminalista *mf* criminal lawyer; criminologist
criminología *f*, criminology
crin *f*, horsehair; (gen. *pl*) mane
crinolina *f*, crinoline
crío *m*, *inf* kid, brat
criollo (**-lla**) *a* and *n* creole. *a* indigenous, native
cripta *f*, crypt
criptografía *f*, cryptography
criquet *m*, *sport* cricket
crisantemo *m*, chrysanthemum
crisis *f*, crisis. **c. de desarrollo,** growing pains. **c. de vivienda,** housing shortage
crisma *m*, or *f*, chrism
crisol *m*, crucible; melting pot
crispado *a* stiffened
crispar *vt* to cause to contract or twitch; *vr* twitch. *inf* **Se me crispan los nervios,** My nerves are all on edge
cristal *m*, crystal; glass; windowpane; mirror; water. **c. tallado,** cut glass
cristalería *f*, glassware; glass manufacture; glass panes; glass and china shop
cristalino *a* crystalline. *m*, lens (of the eye)
cristalización *f*, crystallization
cristalizar *vi* to crystallize; *fig* take shape; *vt* cause to crystallize
cristalografía *f*, crystallography
cristiandad *f*, Christendom
cristianismo *m*, Christianity; Christendom
cristianizar *vt* to convert to Christianity, christianize
cristiano (**-na**) *a* and *n* Christian. *a inf* watered (of wine). *m*, *inf* Spanish (contrasted with other languages); *inf* soul, person
cristino (**-na**) *a* and *n* supporting, or follower of, Queen Regent Maria Cristina during Carlist wars
cristo *m*, Christ; crucifix. *inf* **donde C. dio las tres voces,** in the middle of nowhere
cristus *m*, Christ-cross; alphabet. **no saber el c.,** to be extremely ignorant
criterio *m*, criterion, standard; judgment, discernment; opinion. **a c. de,** in the opinion of. **según mi c.,** in my opinion
crítica (**a**) *f*, criticism (of)
criticar *vt* to criticize; censure, find fault with, blame
crítico *a* critical; censorious; dangerous, difficult; *med* critical. *m*, critic; fault-finder
criticón (**-ona**) *a* censorious, hyper-critical. *n* fault-finder
Croacia Croatia
croar *vi* (frog) to croak
croata *a* and *mf* Croatian
croché *m*, crochet work
crol *m*, crawl (swimming)
cromado *a* chromium-plated
cromático *a* chromatic
crómico *a* chromic
cromo *m*, chrome; chromium; chromolithograph
crónica *f*, chronicle; diary of events
crónico *a* chronic; inveterate
cronista *mf* chronicler
cronología *f*, chronology
cronológico *a* chronological
cronómetro *m*, stop-watch
croqueta *f*, croquette
croquis *m*, sketch, outline, drawing. **c. de nivel,** (optical) foresight
crótalo *m*, rattlesnake; snapper (kind of castanet)
cruce *m*, crossing; point of intersection; crossroads
crucero *m*, *ecc* cross-bearer; crossroads; *arch* transept; *ast* Cross; *naut* cruiser
crucificar *vt* to crucify; *fig inf* torment, torture
crucifijo *m*, crucifix
crucifixión *f*, crucifixion
crucigrama *m*, crossword puzzle
cruda *f*, *Mexico* hangover
crudelísimo *a sup* **cruel,** most cruel, exceedingly cruel
crudeza *f*, rawness, uncookedness; unripeness; rawness (silk, etc.); crudeness; harshness; *inf* boasting
crudo *a* uncooked, raw; green, unripe; indigestible; raw, natural, unbleached; harsh, cruel; cold, raw; *inf* boastful. **crudos de petróleo,** *m pl* crude oil
crueldad *f*, cruelty; harshness
cruento *a* bloody
crujía *f*, passage, corridor; *naut* midship gangway
crujidero *a* crackling; creaking; crispy; clattering; rustling; chattering
crujido *m*, creak, crack, crackling, rustle
crujir *vi* to creak, crackle, rustle
crup *m*, croup
crupié *m*, croupier
crustáceo *a* and *m*, crustacean
cruz *f*, cross; tails (of coin); withers (of animals); insignia, decoration; affliction, trouble; *ast* Southern Cross; *print* dagger, obelisk, obelus. **c. doble,** diesis, double dagger. **c. de mayo,** May cross. **c. gamada,** swastika. *inf* **¡C. y raya!** An end to this! **en c.,** in the shape of a cross. *inf* **hacerse cruces,** to be left speechless, be dumbfounded
cruza *f*, *Lat. Am.* intersection
cruzada *f*, crusade; crossroads; campaign
cruzado *a* cross; double-breasted (of coats). *m*, crusader; member of military order
cruzamiento *m*, crossing; intersection
cruzar *vt* to cross; intersect; interbreed; bestow a cross upon; *naut* cruise; *Chile, Peru* quarrel with; *vr* take part in a crusade; cross one another; coincide; *geom* intersect
cu *f*, name of the letter Q
cuaco *m*, *Lat. Am.* horse
cuacuac *m*, quack (of a duck)
cuaderna *f*, *naut* ship's frame, timber; double fours (backgammon)
cuaderno *m*, notebook, jotter, account book; *inf* card pack. *naut* **c. de bitácora,** logbook

cuadra *f*, stable; ward, dormitory; hall, large room; quarter of a mile; *Lat. Am.* block (of houses)
cuadrado *a* square; perfect, exact. *m*, square; (*carp mil math*) square; window-frame; clock (of a stocking)
cuadragésima *f*, Quadragesima
cuadragésimo *a* fortieth
cuadrángulo *m*, quadrangle
cuadrante *m*, quadrant; dial, face
cuadrar *vt* (*math carp*) to square; make square; *vi* correspond, tally; fit, be appropriate. *vr mil* stand at attention; *fig inf* dig one's heels in
cuadrática *f*, quadratic equation
cuadrático *a* quadratic
cuadratura *f*, squareness; (*math ast*) quadrature
cuadrienio *m*, space of four years
cuadriga *f*, quadriga
cuadrilátero *m*, quadrilateral; boxing ring. *a* quadrilateral
cuadrilongo *a* and *m*, oblong
cuadrilla *f*, gang; company, band, group; police patrol; quadrille (dance); matadors and their assistants (at a bull fight). **c. carrillana,** track gang
cuadrimotor *a aer* four-engined
cuadrivio *m*, quadrivium
cuadro *m*, square; picture-frame; frame (of bicycle); flowerbed; *theat* tableau, scene; spectacle, sight; board (of instruments); description (in novel, etc.); *mil* command, officers; square (of troops). **c. de distribución,** *elec* main switchboard. **c. enrejado,** play pen. **cuadro de costumbres,** word-picture of everyday life and customs. **cuadro vivo,** tableau vivant. **a cuadros,** checked, in squares
cuadrúpedo (-da) *a* and *n* quadruped
cuadruple *a* quadruple
cuadruplicar *vt* to quadruple
cuajada *f*, curd (of milk)
cuajar *m*, maw (of a ruminant)
cuajar *vt* to coagulate; curdle; *vi inf* achieve, get away with; *vr* be coagulated or curdled; *inf* be packed or chock full; get stuck (e.g. a piece of food in one's throat)
cuajarón *m*, clot (of blood, etc.)
cuajo *m*, rennet; coagulation; curdling; *anat* abomasum
cual *rel. pron* sing. *mf* and *neut. pl* **cuales,** which; who; such as (e.g. **Le detuvieron sucesos cuales suelen ocurrir,** He was detained by events such as usually happen). **a c. mas,** vying (with) (e.g. **Los dos canónigos a c. más grueso,** The two canons each fatter (vying in fatness) than the other). **c.** is used with *def. art* **el (la, lo, los, las) cual(es),** who; which, when the antecedent is a noun (e.g. **Juan saltó en el barco, el c. zarpó en seguida,** John jumped into the boat which sailed at once). **por lo c.,** for which reason. *adv* like (gen. literary or poet.). **¿cuál?** *interr. pron* (no article) which? what? e.g. **Aquí tienes dos cuadros, ¿cuál de ellos te gusta?** Here are two pictures, which one do you like? Also expresses an implicit question, e.g. **No sé cuál te guste,** I don't know which you will like. **¡cuál!** *adv interj* how! **c. . . . c.** *indef pron* some . . . some
cualesquier *a pl* of **cualquier**
cualesquiera *a pl* of **cualquiera**
cualidad *f*, quality; characteristic; talent
cualitativo *a* qualitative
cualquier *abb* **of cualquiera,** any; *pl* **cualesquier.** Only used as abb. *before* noun
cualquiera *a mf* any, e.g. **una canción c.,** any song. *pron* anybody, each, anyone whatsoever, whoever (e.g. **¡C. diría que no te gusta!** Anyone would say you don't like it!) *inf* **un c.,** a nobody
cuán *adv* how (e.g. **¡C. bello es!** How beautiful it is). Used only before *a* or *adv.* Abb. of **cuánto**
cuando *adv* when; if. *interr* **¿cuándo?** *conjunc* although; since; sometimes; *prep* during (e.g. **c. la guerra,** during the war) **c. más,** at most, at best. **c. menos,** at the least. **c. no,** if not (e.g. **Es agnóstica cuando no atea,** She's an agnostic, if not an atheist) **de c. en c.,** from time to time
cuandoquiera *adv* whenever
cuanta, teoría de la *f*, quantum theory
cuantía *f*, quantity, amount; importance, rank, distinction
cuantiar *vt* to value, estimate; tax
cuantidad *f*, quantity
cuantioso *a* large, considerable; numerous; plentiful, abundant
cuantitativo *a* quantitative
cuanto *a* as much as, all the; *pl* as many as, all the (e.g. **Te daré cuantas muñecas veas allí,** I'll give you all the dolls you see there). *a. correlative* the . . . the, as . . . as (e.g. **C. más tanto, mejor,** The more the better). **cuánto,** *a* and *pron interr* and *interj* how much; *pl* how many (e.g. **¡Cuánto tiempo sin verla!** How long without seeing her!) *pron neut* **cuanto,** as much as, all that (e.g. **Te daré c. quieras,** I shall give you all that you wish). *adv* **cuanto,** as soon as. **c. antes,** as soon as possible. **c. a** *or* **en c. a,** concerning. *adv* and *conjunc* **c. más,** all the more (e.g. **Se lo diré c. más que tenía esa intención,** I shall tell him all the more because I meant to do so). *adv* **en c.,** as soon as, immediately (e.g. **Lo haré en c. venga,** I shall do it immediately he comes). **en c. a,** with regard to. **por c.,** inasmuch, for this reason. *adv interr* **¿Cuánto?** How much? How long? *adv interj* How! How much! (e.g. **¡Cuánto me gustaría ir!** How much I should like to go!)
cuaquerismo *m*, Quakerism
cuáquero (-ra) *n* Quaker
cuarenta *a* and *m*, forty; fortieth. **esas son otras cuarenta** *Argentina, Peru* that's a different story, that's a horse of another color
cuarentena *f*, fortieth; period of forty days, months or years; Lent; quarantine
cuarentón (-ona) *n* person forty years old
cuaresma *f*, Lent
cuaresmal *a* Lenten
cuarta *f*, quarter, fourth; hand's breadth; *mus* fourth; *ast* quadrant
cuarteadura *f*, crack
cuartear *vt* to quarter, divide into quarters; cut or divide into pieces
cuartel *m*, barracks; *naut* hatch; quarter, fourth; *her* quarter; district, ward; flowerbed; *inf* house, accommodation; *mil* quarter, mercy; *mil* billet, station. *mil* **c. general,** general headquarters
cuartelada *f*, *naut* quarter; military rebellion, military uprising, mutiny
cuartelazo *m*, military rebellion, military uprising, mutiny
cuarteta *f*, quatrain
cuarteto *m*, *mus* quartet; *poet* quatrain
cuartilla *f*, sheet of paper; liquid measure; quarter of an arroba; pastern (horses)
cuarto *m*, room; quarter, fourth; point (of compass); watch (on battleships); *ast* quarter, phase; portion, quarter; joint (of meat); *pl* quarters (of animals); *inf* penny, farthing. *a* quarter, fourth. **c. creciente,** first phase (of moon). **c. de hora,** quarter of an hour. **c. doble** *Mexico* double room. **c. sencillo** *Mexico* single room. **en c.,** *print* in quarto. *inf* **no tener un c.,** to be broke
cuarzo *m*, quartz
cuasidelito *m*, *law* technical offence
cuasimodo *m*, *ecc* Low Sunday, Quasimodo
cuatrillón *m*, quadrillion
cuatrimestre *a* of four months' duration. *m*, space of four months
cuatrimotor *m*, *aer* four-engine airplane
cuatrisílabo *a* quadrisyllabic
cuatro *a* four; fourth. *m*, figure four; fourth (of days of months); playing-card with four spots; *mus* quartet. **el c. de mayo,** the fourth of May. **Son las c.,** It is four o'clock

cuatrocientos *a* four hundred; four hundredth.
cuba *f,* barrel, cask; tub, vat; *inf* pot-bellied person; *inf* drunkard, toper
cubano (**-na**) *a* and *n* Cuban
cubería *f,* cooperage
cubeta *f, dim* keg, small cask; bucket, pail; *phot* developing dish
cubicar *vt math* to cube; *geom* measure the volume of
cúbico *a* cubic
cubículo *m,* cubicle
cubierta *f,* cover; envelope; casing; deck (of ship); tire cover; book-jacket; pretext, excuse. **c. de escotilla,** *naut* companion-hatch. **c. de paseo,** promenade deck
cubierto *m,* cover, place at table; course (of a meal); table d'hôte, complete meal; roof. **un c. de doscientas pesetas,** a two hundred peseta meal
cubil *m,* lair, den (of animals)
cubilete *m, cul* mold; dice box; conjurer's cup
cubismo *m,* cubism
cubista *mf* cubist. *a* cubistic
cubo *m,* bucket, pail; *mech* socket; *math* cube; hub (of a wheel); mill-pond
cubrecama *m,* bedspread
cubrimiento *m,* covering
cubrir *vt* to cover; *mil* defend; spread over, extend over; conceal, hide; *com* cover; dissemble; *arch* roof; *vr* cover one's head; pay, meet (debts, etc.); cover or protect oneself (by insurance, etc.). *Past Part.* **cubierto**
cucaña *f,* greasy pole; *inf* snip, cinch, bargain
cucaracha *f,* cockroach
cuchara *f,* spoon; ladle; *naut* boat scoop; scoop, dipper. *fig* **meter c.,** to stick one's oar in
cucharada *f,* spoonful; ladleful
cuchí *m, Peru* hog
cúchi *a inf Venezuela* cute, sweet
cuchicheador (**-ra**) *n* whisperer
cuchichear *vi* to whisper
cuchicheo *m,* whisper; whispering; murmur
cuchillada *f,* knife thrust or wound; *pl* (in sleeves, etc.) slashes; fight, blows
cuchillero *m,* cutler
cuchillo *m,* knife; *sew* gore, gusset (gen. *pl*); authority, power; anything triangular in shape. **pasar a c.,** to put to the sword
cuclillas, en *adv* in a squatting position
cuclillo *m, orn* cuckoo; *inf* cuckold
cuco *a inf* pretty, cute; crafty, smart
Cucufo *m,* the Devil
cuculla *f,* cowl, hood
cucurucho *m,* paper cornet
cueca *f, chile* cueca (Chilean dance)
cuello *m, anat* neck; neck (of bottle, etc.); *sew* neck; collar; necklet (of fur, etc.)
cuenca *f,* socket (of eye); *geog* catchment-basin; gorge, deep valley. **c. de un río,** river-basin
cuenta *f,* count, counting; calculation; account; bead; charge, responsibility; reckoning; explanation, reason; *com* bill. **c. a cero, c. a la inversa, c. atrás,** countdown. **c. corriente,** current account. **cuentas alegres, cuentas galanas,** *inf* idle dreams, illusions. **c. pendiente,** outstanding account. *inf* **caer en la c.,** to tumble to, realize. **llevar la c.,** to reckon, keep account. **sin c.,** countless. **tener en c.,** to bear in mind
cuentacorrentista *mf* one who has a bank account
cuentagotas *m,* dropper, dropping tube
cuentakilómetros *m,* speedometer
cuentapasos *m,* pedometer
cuentista *mf* storyteller; *inf* gossip
cuento *m,* story, tale; narrative; calculation; *inf* gossip, fairytale; *math* million. **c. de viejas,** old wives' tale. *fig inf* **dejarse de cuentos,** to go straight to the point. *inf* **Va de c.,**It is told, they say
cuerda *f,* rope; cord; string; *geom* chord; *mus* string; catgut; chain (of clock); *mus* chord; vocal range. **dar c. (a),** to wind up (a watch); lead on, make talk. **de cuerdas cruzadas,** overstrung (of a piano)
cuerdo *a* sane; prudent; levelheaded
cuerno *m, anat* horn; feeler, antenna; *mus* horn; horn (of the moon). **c. de abundancia,** horn of plenty. *inf* **poner en los cuernos de la luna,** to praise to the skies
cuero *m,* hide, pelt; leather. **c. charolado,** patent leather. **en cueros,** stark naked
cuerpo *m, anat* body or trunk; flesh (as opposed to spirit); bodice; volume, book; main portion; collection; size, volume; physical appearance; corpse; group, assembly; corporation, association; *geom* solid; *chem* element; thickness, density; *mil* corps. **c. de bomberos,** fire brigade. **c. de guardia,** guardhouse. **c. de la vida,** staff of life; *inf* **dar con el c. en tierra,** to fall flat. **de c. entero,** *art* full-length (portrait). **en c.,** without a coat, lightly clad. **un c. a c.,** a clinch (in wrestling)
cuervo *m,* raven; crow
cuesco *m,* stone, seed, pip
cuesta *f,* slope, incline, gradient. **c. abajo (arriba),** down (up) hill. **a cuestas,** on one's back; having the responsibility of
cuestión *f,* problem, question; quarrel, disagreement; affair, matter; torture
cuestionable *a* doubtful, questionable
cuestionar *vt* to discuss, debate
cuestionario *m,* questionnaire
cueva *f,* cave, cavern; basement, cellar. *fig* **c. de ladrones,** den of thieves
cuévano *m,* hamper, basket
cui *m, Lat. Am.* guinea pig
cuico, -a *mf, Argentina, Chile* foreigner, outsider; *Mexico, informal* cop (police officer)
cuidado *m,* carefulness, pains; attention; charge, care, responsibility; anxiety, fear. *interj* **¡C.!** Careful! Look out! **Me tiene sin c. su opinión,** I am not interested in his (your) opinion. *inf* **estar al c. de,** to be under the direction of. **estar de c.,** to be dangerously ill
cuidadoso (de) *a* careful (about *or* with); anxious (about); concerned (with); watchful; conscientious
cuidar *vt* to care for; tend; take care of, look after; mind, be careful of; *vr* look after oneself
cuita *f,* misfortune, anxiety, trouble
cuitado *a* unfortunate, worried; timid, bashful, humble
cuitla *f, Mexico* poultry manure
culata *f, anat* haunch; butt (of fire-arms); back, rear; *aut* sump
culebra *f,* snake; *inf* trick, joke; *inf* sudden uproar. **hacer c.,** to stagger along
culebrear *vi* to wriggle; grovel; meander, wind
culí *m,* coolie
culinario *a* culinary
culminación *f,* culmination, peak; *ast* zenith
culminante *a* culminating; *fig* outstanding
culminar *vi* to culminate (in)
culo *m,* buttocks, seat; rump; anus; base, bottom. **c. de lámpara,** *arch* pendant; *print* tail-piece
culpa *f,* fault; blame. **echar la c. (a),** to blame. **por c. de,** through the fault of. **tener la c.,** to be to blame
culpabilidad *f,* guilt
culpable *a* culpable
culpado (**-da**) *n* culprit
culpar *vt* to blame, accuse; criticize, censure
cultígeno *m,* cultigen
cultismo *m,* cultism (Gongorism); learned form, learnedism, learned word
cultivación *f,* cultivation; culture
cultivador (**-ra**) *n* cultivator; planter
cultivar *vt* to cultivate; develop; exercise, practise (professions); culture (bacteriology)
cultivo *m,* cultivation; farming; culture (bacteriological)
culto *a* cultivated; educated; cultured; elegant, artificial (style). *m,* worship; cult; religion, creed; homage
cultura *f,* cultivation; culture. **de c. universitaria,** college-educated

cultural *a* cultural
cumbre *f*, peak, crest, summit; *fig* zenith, acme
cumpleaños *m*, birthday
cumplidamente *adv* fully, completely
cumplido *a* complete; thorough; long; plentiful; courteous, punctilious; fulfilled. *m*, courtesy, attention; formality. **gastar cumplidos,** to stand on ceremony; be formal
cumplimentar *vt* to congratulate; perform, carry out
cumplimentero *a* over-complimentary; *inf* gushing
cumplimiento *m*, fulfilment, performance; courtesy, formality; completion; complement
cumplir *vt* to perform, carry into effect; reach (of age); keep (promises). **c. su palabra,** to keep one's word; *vi* perform a duty; expire, fall due; serve the required term of military service; be necessary, behove; *vr* be fulfilled, come true. **por c.,** as a matter of form
cumulativo *a* cumulative
cúmulo *m*, heap, pile; great many, host, mass, myriad; (cloud) cumulus, thunderhead
cuna *f*, cradle; foundling hospital; birthplace; origin, genesis; *pl* cat's cradle (game)
cundir *vi* to extend, spread (gen. liquids); be diffused (news); expand, grow
cuneco, -a *mf Venezuela* baby of the family
cuneiforme *a* wedge-shaped, cuneiform
cunero (-ra) *n* foundling, orphan
cuña *f*, wedge; *mech* quoin. *mil* **practicar una c.,** to make a wedge
cuñada *f*, sister-in-law
cuñado *m*, brother-in-law
cuño *m*, die, stamp; *fig* impression; mark on silver, hallmark. **de viejo c.,** old-guard (e.g. socialites)
cuota *f*, quota; share; subscription; fee
cupé *m*, coupé
Cupido *m*, Cupid; philanderer
cuplé *m*, couplet; song
cupo *m*, quota; share; tax rate; *mil* contingent
cupón *m*, coupon
cúpula *f*, *arch* dome, cupola; *bot* cup
cuquería *f*, craftiness, smartness; cuteness, prettiness
cura *m*, parish priest; *inf* Roman Catholic priest. *f*, cure (e.g. **La enfermedad tiene c.,** The illness can be cured); healing; remedy. **c. de almas,** cure of souls. **primera c.,** first aid. *inf* **c. de misa y olla,** ignorant priest
curación *f*, cure, remedy; healing
curador (-ra) *n* curer, salter. *m*, (*Scots law*) curator. *a* curing; healing
curaduría *f*, *law* guardianship
curanderismo *m*, quackery, charlatanism; quack medicine
curandero (-ra) *n* quack doctor; charlatan
curar *vi* to heal, cure; (*with de*) take care of; care about, mind; *vt* cure, salt; treat medically (bandage, give medicines, etc.); cure (leather); bleach (cloth); season (timber); *fig* remedy (an evil)
curasao *m*, curaçao (drink)
curativo *a* curative
curato *m*, *ecc* parish, cure
Curazao Curaçao
cúrcuma *f*, turmeric
cureña *f*, gun-carriage
curia *f*, *law* bar; tribunal; *ecc* curia; care, attention
curiana *f*, cockroach
curiche *m*, swamp
curiosear *vi* to pry; be curious (about); meddle, be a busybody
curiosidad *f*, curiosity; inquisitiveness, meddlesomeness; neatness; carefulness, conscientiousness; curio
curioso *a* curious; inquisitive; interesting, odd; neat, clean; conscientious, careful
Curita *f*, *trademark* Band-Aid
cursado *a* experienced, versed
cursante *m*, student
cursar *vt* to frequent, visit; do repeatedly; study, attend classes, take courses (e.g. **¿En qué escuela cursan?** At what school are you studying?); expedite (public admin.)
cursi *a inf* vulgar, in bad taste; loud, crude
cursilería *f*, *inf* vulgarity, bad taste
cursillo *m*, minicourse, short course; short series of lectures
cursiva *f*, italics. **en c.,** in italics, italicized
cursivo *a* cursive
curso *m*, course, direction; duration, passage (time); progress; route; course of study; academic year; succession, series; *com* tender
curtido *m*, tanning; leather; tanned leather (gen. *pl*)
curtidor *m*, tanner
curtiduría *f*, tannery
curtimiento *m*, tanning; effect of weather on the complexion; toughening-up; hardening
curtir *vt* to tan; *fig* bronze (complexions); make hardy, harden up; *vr* be weatherbeaten; be hardy. *inf* **estar curtido en,** to be experienced in; be expert at
curul *a* **curule** *m*, seat (in parliament)
curva *f*, curve; bend. *surv* **c. de nivel,** contour line
curvatura, curvidad *f*, curvature
curvo *a* curved; bent. *m*, curve
cusma *f*, *Lat. Am.* sleeveless shirt, tunic
cúspide *f*, peak, summit; (*geom arch*) cusp
custodia *f*, custody; guardianship, care; *ecc* monstrance; custodian, keeper; guardian; guard
custodiar *vt* to watch, guard; look after, care for; *naut* convoy
custodio *a* guardian; guarding; custodial. *m*, custodian; guard. **angel c.,** guardian angel
cutama *f*, *Argentina* blanket; *Chile* bag, sack
cutáneo *a* cutaneous, skin
cúter *m*, *naut* cutter
cutícula *f*, cuticle
cutis *m*, complexion; skin (sometimes *f*)
cuyo (cuya, cuyos, cuyas) *rel pron poss* whose, of which (e.g. **el viejo cuya barba era más blanca que la nieve,** the old man whose beard was whiter than snow). *interr* **¿Cúyo?** Whose? (e.g. **¿Cúyos son estos lápices?** Whose pencils are these?) (gen. **de quién** or **de quiénes** is used rather than **cúyo**). *m*, beau, lover

D

dable *a* practicable, possible
daca Give me!
dactilografía *f*, typewriting
dactilógrafo (-fa) *n* typist
dactilología *f*, dactylology
dadista *mf*, *Mexico* gambler
dádiva *f*, gift, present
dadivoso *a* generous, liberal
dado *m*, die; *arch* dado. *conjunc* **d. que,** given that, supposing that. **cargar los dados,** to load the dice
dador (-ra) *n* giver, donor. *m*, *com* bearer; *com* drawer (of a bill of exchange)
daga *f*, dagger
daguerrotipo *m*, daguerreotype
daifa *f*, concubine
¡dale! *interj* Stop! No more about . . . !
dalia *f*, *bot* dahlia
dallar *vt* to scythe (grass)
dalle *m*, scythe
dálmata *a* and *mf* Dalmatian

dalmática *f,* dalmatic, loose tunic or vestment
dalmático (-ca) *a* and *n* Dalmatian
daltoniano *a* color-blind
daltonismo *m,* color-blindness
dama *f,* lady; noblewoman; lady-in-waiting; lady-love; mistress, concubine; queen (chess); king (checkers); *theat* **d. primera,** leading lady
damajuana *f,* demijohn
damas *f pl,* checkers (game)
damasceno (-na) *a* and *n* Damascene
Damasco Damascus
damasco *m,* damask
damasquino *a* damascened (swords, etc.)
damería *f,* prudery, affectation
damisela *f,* damsel; *inf* woman of the town
damnificar *vt* to injure
dandi *m,* dandy
dandismo *m,* dandyism
danés (-esa) *a* Danish. *n* Dane. *m,* Danish (language)
danta *f, zool* tapir
dantesco *a* Dantesque
danubiano *a* Danubian
Danubio, el the Danube
danza *f,* dance; set (of dancers); *fig inf* dirty business. **d. de arcos,** dance of the arches. **d. de cintas,** maypole dance. **d. de monos,** amusing spectacle
danzador (-ra) *n* dancer; *a* dancing
danzante (-ta) *n* dancer; *fig inf* live wire; *inf* busybody
danzar *vt* and *vi* to dance; *vi* jump up and down, rattle; *inf* interfere, meddle
danzarín (-ina) *n* good dancer; *inf* meddler; *inf* playboy
danzón *m,* Cuban dance
dañable *a* harmful; worthy of condemnation
dañado *a* evil, perverse; damned; spoiled, damaged
dañador (-ra) *a* harmful. *n* injurer, offender
dañar *vt* to hurt, harm; damage, spoil; *vr* spoil, deteriorate
dañino *a* destructive (often of animals); hurtful, harmful. **animales dañinos,** vermin, pests
daño *m,* hurt; damage; loss. *law* **daños y perjuicios,** damages. **hacerse d.,** to hurt oneself
dañoso *a* hurtful, harmful
dar *vt irr* to give; wish, express (congratulations, etc.); hand over; concede, grant; inspire; produce, yield; cause, create; sacrifice; propose, put forward; take (a walk); believe, consider; deliver (blows, etc.); administer (medicine); provide with; apply, coat with; occasion; perform (plays); propose (a toast); give forth, emit; set (norms), render (thanks, etc.); hold (banquets, etc.); proffer, hold out; *vi* to strike (clocks); (*with prep a*) overlook, look on to (e.g. **Su ventana da a la calle,** His window looks on to the street); (*with con*) find, meet (things, persons); (*with de*) fall on, fall down (e.g. **Dio de cabeza,** He fell head first. **Dio de espaldas,** He fell on his back); (*with en*) fall into, incur; insist on or persist in (doing something); acquire the habit of (e.g. **Dieron en no venir a vernos,** They took to not coming to see us); solve, guess (riddles, etc.); strike, wound, hurt (e.g. **La bala le dio en el brazo,** The bullet struck him in the arm); (*with por*) decide on (e.g. **Di por no hacerlo,** I decided not to do it). *vr* to yield, give in; (*with prep a*) engage in, devote oneself to; (*with por*) think or consider oneself (e.g. **Me di por muerto,** I gave myself up for dead). **d. alas a,** to propagate, spread (a belief). **darse a la vela,** to set sail. **darse la mano,** to shake hands. **darse por buenos,** to make up a quarrel, be friends. **darse prisa,** to hurry up, make haste. **darse uno a conocer,** to make oneself known. **darse uno por entendido,** to show that one understands; be grateful. **No se me da un bledo,** I don't care a straw. **d. abajo,** to fall down. **d. bien por mal,** to return good for evil. **d. a conocer,** to make known. **d. a entender,** to suggest, hint. **d. a luz,** to give birth; publish, issue. **d. cuenta de,** to give an account of. **d. de baja,** *mil* to muster out, discharge. **d. de comer,** to feed. **d. de sí,** to stretch, expand; produce, yield; give of itself (oneself, himself, themselves) (either in good or bad sense). **d. diente con diente,** to chatter (of teeth), shiver. **d. el pésame,** to tender condolences. **d. en cara,** *fig inf* to throw in one's face. **d. en el clavo,** *fig* to hit the mark. **d. en qué pensar,** to make suspicious, cause to think. **d. fe,** to certify, attest. **d. fiado,** to give on credit. **d. fianza,** to give security. **d. fin a,** to finish. **d. licencia,** to permit, allow. **d. los buenos días,** to wish good day or good morning. **d. mal,** to have bad luck at cards. **d. parte de,** to announce; issue a communiqué about (e.g. **Dieron parte de la pérdida del buque,** They announced the loss of the ship). **d. prestado,** to lend. **d. qué decir,** to cause a scandal. **d. qué hacer,** to cause trouble. **d. razón de,** to give an account of. **d. sobre uno,** to assault a person. **d. un abrazo,** to embrace. **d. voces,** to shriek; call out. *inf* **Donde las dan las toman,** It's only tit-for-tat. *inf* **No me da la real gana,** I darn well don't want to. *Pres. Ind.* **doy, das,** etc. *Preterite* **di, diste,** etc. *Pres. Subjunc.* **dé,** etc. *Imperf. Subjunc.* **diese,** etc.
Dardanelos, los the Dardanelles
dardo *m,* (*mil sport*) dart; *icht* dace; lampoon
dares y tomares *m, pl* give and take; *inf* back-chat. Generally used with *andar, haber* or *tener*
dársena *f, naut* dock
darviniano *a* Darwinian
darvinismo *m,* Darwinism
darvinista *mf* Darwinian
data *f,* date (calendar); *com* credit
datar *vt* to date; *vi* (*with de*) date from; *vr com* credit
dátil *m, bot* date
datilado *a* date-like or date-colored
datilera *f, bot* date-palm
dativo *m, gram* dative
dato *m,* datum; basis, fact
davídico *a* Davidic
de *f,* name of letter D. *prep* of (possessive) (e.g. **Este cuadro es de Vd.,** This picture is yours); from (place and time) (e.g. **Vengo de Madrid,** I come from Madrid. **de vez en cuando,** from time to time); with, of, from, as the result of (e.g. **Lloraban de miedo,** They were crying with fright. **Murió de un ataque del corazón,** He died from a heart attack); for, to (e.g. **Es hora de marchar,** It is time to leave); with (of characteristics) (e.g. **el señor de los lentes,** the gentleman with the eyeglasses. **el cuarto de la alfombra azul,** the room with the blue carpet); when, as (e.g. **De niños nos gustaban los juguetes,** When we were children we liked toys); by (e.g. **Es un ensayo del mismo autor,** It is an essay by the same author. **Fue amado de todos,** He was loved by all. **Es hidalgo de nacimiento,** He is a gentleman by birth). Indicates the material of which a thing is made (e.g. **La mesa es de mármol,** The table is marble). Indicates contents of a thing (e.g. **un vaso de leche,** a glass of milk). Shows manner in which an action is performed (e.g. **Lo hizo de prisa,** He did it hurriedly). Shows the use to which an article is put (e.g. **una mesa de escribir,** a writing-table. **una máquina de coser,** a sewing-machine. **un caballo de batalla,** a war-horse). Sometimes used for emphasis (e.g. **El tonto de tu secretario,** That fool of a secretary of yours). Used by Spanish married women before husband's family name (e.g. **Señora Martínez de Cabra,** Mrs. Cabra (née Martínez)). Used after many adverbs (generally of time or place) to form prepositional phrases (e.g. **detrás de,** behind. **enfrente de,** opposite to; in front of. **de acá para allá,** here and there. **de allí a poco,** shortly afterward. **de allí a pocos días,** a few days later. **de bamba,** by chance. **de cabo a rabo,** from cover to cover. **además de,** besides, etc.). Used at beginning of various adverbial phrases (e.g. **de noche,** at night. **de día,** by day. **de antemano,** previously, **la persona de mi derecha** the person at my right, etc.). Used partitively before nouns, pronouns, adjectives (e.g. **Estas historias ti-**

enen algo de verdad, These stories have some truth in them. **¿Qué hay de nuevo?** What's the news?) Forms many compound words (e.g. **deponer, denegar,** etc.). With **"uno"** means "at" (e.g. **Lo cogió de un salto,** He caught it at one bound). **de a** is used before expressions of price, weight, etc. (e.g. **un libro de a cinco pesetas,** a five-peseta book)
dea *f, poet* goddess
deán *m,* dean
debajo *adv* underneath; below
debate *m,* discussion, debate; dispute
debatible *a* debatable
debatir *vt* to discuss, debate, argue
debe *m, com* debtor
debelación *f,* conquest
debelador (-ra) *a* conquering. *n* conqueror
debelar *vt* to conquer, overthrow
deber *vt* to owe (e.g. **Le debo mil pesetas,** I owe him one thousand pesetas). Used as auxiliary verb followed by infinitive, ought to, be obliged to (e.g. **Debía haberlo hecho,** I ought to have done it. **Deberá hacerlo,** He will have to do it); be destined to (e.g. **La princesa que más tarde debió ser reina,** The princess who later was destined to be queen); be essential, must (e.g. **La cuestión debe ser resuelta,** The question must be settled); (*with de + infin.*) be probable (indicates supposition) (e.g. **Debe de tener cincuenta años,** He is probably about fifty. **Debía de sufrir del corazón,** He probably suffered from heart trouble); (preceded by a negative *with de + infin.*) be impossible (e.g. **No debe de ser verdad,** It can't be true)
deber *m,* duty, obligation; debt. **hacer su d.,** to do one's duty
debidamente *adv* justly, rightly; duly
debido *a* correct, due. **d. a,** owing to, because of
débil *a* weak; *fig* spineless; frail
debilidad *f,* weakness; feebleness
debilitación *f,* debilitation
debilitante *a* weakening
debilitar *vt* to weaken; *vr* become weak
débito *m,* debit, debt; duty
debutar *vi* to appear for the first time, make one's début
década *f,* decade
decadencia *f,* decadence, decline
decadente *a* decadent, decaying
decaer *vi irr* to fail (persons); decay, decline. See **caer**
decagramo *m,* decagram
decaimiento *m,* decadence; *med* prostration
decalaje *m, aer* stagger
decalitro *m,* decaliter
decálogo *m,* decalogue, the Ten Commandments
decámetro *m,* decameter
decampar *vi mil* to decamp
decanato *m,* deanery; *univ* dean's rooms
decano *m,* senior member; *univ* dean
decantación *f,* decantation
decantar *vt* to decant (wines); praise
decapitación *f,* decapitation
decapitar *vt* to decapitate, behead
decena *f,* ten; *mus* tenth
decenal *a* decennial
decenario *m,* decade
decencia *f,* propriety, decency; decorum, modesty
decenio *m,* decade
deceno *a* tenth
decentar *vt irr* to begin, cut (loaves, etc.); *fig* undermine (health, etc.); *vr* suffer from bedsores. See **acertar**
decente *a* decent, honest; respectable; suitable; tidy
decepción *f,* disillusionment, disappointment
dechado *m,* model, ideal; *sew* sampler; exemplar, ideal
decible *a* expressible
decidero *a* that which can be safely said
decidido *a* decided; resolute, determined
decidir *vt* to resolve, decide; *vr* make up one's mind
decidor (-ra) *a* talkative, fluent, eloquent. *n* good talker
decigramo *m,* decigram
décima *f,* tenth; tithe; ten-line stanza of eight-syllable verse
decimal *a* decimal; pertaining to tithes. **sistema d.,** metric system
decímetro *m,* decimeter
décimo *a* tenth. *m,* tenth part; tenth of a lottery ticket
decimoctavo *a* eighteenth
decimocuarto *a* fourteenth
decimonono *a* nineteenth
decimoquinto *a* fifteenth
decimoséptimo *a* and *m,* seventeenth
decimosexto *a* sixteenth
decimotercio *a* thirteenth
decir *vt irr* to say; name; indicate, show; tell. **d. bien,** to go with, suit; speak the truth; be eloquent. **d. entre** (*or* **para**) **sí,** to say to oneself. *inf* **d. nones,** to refuse. **¡Diga!** Hello! (telephone). *inf* **el que dirán,** public opinion (what will people say!). **Es d.,** That is to say. **Se dice,** It is said, people say. *Pres. Ind.* **digo, dices,** etc. *Pres. Part.* **diciendo.** *Past Part.* **dicho.** *Fut.* **diré,** etc. *Condit.* **diría,** etc. *Preterite* **dije,** etc. *Pres. Subjunc.* **diga,** etc. *Imperf. Subjunc.* **dijese,** etc.
decir *m,* saying, saw; maxim, witticism (often *pl.*)
decisión *f,* decision, resolution; *law* judgment; firmness, strength (of character)
decisivo *a* decisive
declamación *f,* declamation, oration; *theat* delivery; recitation
declamador (-ra) *a* declamatory. *n* reciter; orator
declamar *vi* to make a speech, declaim; recite
declamatorio *a* declamatory, rhetorical
declaración *f,* declaration; exposition, explanation; confession; statement; *law* deposition. **d. jurada,** affidavit, sworn statement
declaradamente *adv* avowedly
declarante *a* declaring. *mf law* deponent
declarar *vt* to declare; make clear, explain; *law* find; *vi law* give evidence; *vr* avow, confess (one's sentiments, etc.); show, reveal itself
declarativo, declaratorio *a* explanatory, declaratory
declinación *f,* fall, descent; decadence, decay; *ast* declination; *gram* declension. *inf* **no saber las declinaciones,** not to know one's ABC, be very ignorant
declinante *a* declining; sloping
declinar *vi* to slope; diminish, fall; decline, deteriorate; *fig* near the end; *vt gram* decline
declive, *m.* declividad *f,* slope, incline; gradient
decocción *f,* decoction
decoloración *f,* decoloration; decolorization
decomisar *vt* to confiscate, seize
decoración *f,* decoration; ornament, embellishment; *theat* scenery
decorado *m, theat* scenery, décor
decorador *m,* decorator
decorar *vt* to adorn, ornament; *poet* decorate, honor
decorativo *a* decorative
decoro *m,* respect, reverence; prudence, circumspection; decorum, propriety; integrity, decency; *arch* decoration
decoroso *a* decorous, honorable, decent
decrecer *vi irr* to decrease, grow less. See **conocer**
decreciente *a* decreasing
decrepitación *f, chem* decrepitation, crackling
decrepitar *vi chem* to decrepitate, crackle
decrépito *a* decrepit
decrepitud *f,* decrepitude
decretar *vt* to decree, decide; *law* give a judgment (in a suit)
decreto *m,* decree, order; judicial decree
decuplar, decuplicar *vt* to multiply by ten
décuplo *a* tenfold
decurso *m,* course, lapse (of time)
dedada *f,* thimbleful, finger; pinch
dedal *m,* thimble; finger-stall
dédalo *m,* labyrinth
dedeo *m, mus* touch

dedicación *f*, dedication (all meanings)
dedicar *vt* to dedicate; devote; consecrate; *vr* (*with prep a*) dedicate oneself to, engage in
dedicatoria *f*, dedication (of a book, etc.)
dedicatorio *a* dedicatory
dedil *m*, finger-stall
dedillo, saber al *fig* to have at one's fingertips, know perfectly
dedo *m*, finger; toe; finger's breadth. **d. anular,** third (ring) finger. **d. de en medio** *or* **del corazón,** middle finger. **d. índice,** forefinger. **d. meñique,** little finger. **d. pulgar,** thumb or big toe. *fig inf* **a dos dedos de,** within an inch of. *fig inf* **chuparse los dedos,** to smack one's lips over. *inf* **estar unidos como los dedos de la mano,** to be as thick as thieves
deducción *f*, inference, deduction; derivation; (*mus math*) progression
deduciente *a* deductive
deducir *vt irr* to deduce, infer; deduct, subtract; *law* plead, allege in pleading. See **conducir**
deductivo *a* deductive
defecación *f*, purification; defecation
defecar *vt* to clarify, purify; defecate
defección *f*, defection
defectible *a* deficient; imperfect
defecto *m*, defect, fault; imperfection
defectuoso *a* imperfect, defective
defender *vt irr* to defend, protect; maintain, uphold; forbid; hinder; *vr* defend oneself. See **entender**
defendible *a* defensible
defensa *f*, defence; protection; (hockey) pad; *law* defense; *sport* back; *pl mil* defenses; *naut* fenders. **d. química,** chemical warfare. *mil* **defensas costeras,** coastal defenses
defensiva *f*, defensive
defensivo *a* defensive. *m*, safeguard
defensor (-ra) *n* defender. *m*, *law* counsel for the defense
deferencia *f*, deference
deferente *a* deferential
deferir *vi irr* to defer, yield; *vt* delegate. *Pres. Ind.* **defiero, defieres, defiere, defieren.** *Pres. Part.* **defiriendo.** *Preterite* **defirió, defirieron.** *Pres. Subjunc.* **defiera,** etc. *Imperf. Subjunc.* **defiriese,** etc.
deficiencia *f*, defect, deficiency
deficiente *a* faulty, deficient
déficit *m*, deficit
definible *a* definable
definición *f*, definition; decision
definido *a* definite
definir *vt* to define; decide
definitivo *a* definitive. **en definitiva,** definitely; in short
deflagración *f*, sudden blaze, deflagration
deflagrador *m*, *elec* deflagrator
deflagrar *vi* to go up in flames
deformación *f*, deformation; *rad* distortion
deformado *a* deformed; misshapen
deformador (-ra) *a* disfiguring, deforming. *n* disfigurer
deformar *vt* to deform; *vr* become deformed or misshapen
deformidad *f*, deformity; gross error; vice, lapse
defraudación *f*, defrauding; deceit
defraudador (-ra) *n* defrauder
defraudar *vt* to defraud; usurp; frustrate, disappoint; impede
defuera *adv* outwardly, externally
defunción *f*, decease, death
degeneración *f*, degeneration. **d. grasienta,** fatty degeneration
degenerado (-da) *a* and *n* degenerate
degenerar *vi* to degenerate
deglución *f*, swallowing, deglutition
deglutir *vi* and *vt* to swallow
degollación *f*, decollation, throat slitting
degolladero *m*, slaughterhouse; execution block
degollador *m*, executioner
degolladura *f*, slitting of the throat
degollar *vt irr* to behead; slit the throat; *fig* destroy; (*fig theat*) murder; *inf* annoy, bore. *Pres. Ind.* **degüello, degüellas, degüella, degüellan.** *Pres. Subjunc.* **degüelle, degüelles, degüelle, degüellen**
degollina *f*, *inf* massacre
degradación *f*, degradation; humiliation, debasement; *art* gradation, shading (colors, light)
degradante *a* degrading, humiliating
degradar *vt* to degrade; humiliate; *art* grade, blend; *vr* degrade oneself
degüello *m*, decollation; havoc, destruction; haft (of swords, etc.)
degustación *f*, act of tasting or sampling
dehesa *f*, pasture, meadow
deicida *mf* deicide (person)
deicidio *m*, deicide (act)
deidad *f*, divinity; deity, idol
deificación *f*, deification
deificar *vt* to deify; overpraise
deífico *a* deific, divine
deísmo *m*, Deism
deísta *mf* deist. *a* deistic
dejación *f*, relinquishment, abandonment
dejadez *f*, slovenliness; neglect; laziness; carelessness
dejado *a* lazy; neglectful; slovenly; discouraged, depressed
dejamiento *m*, relinquishment; negligence; lowness of spirits; indifference
dejar *vt* to leave; omit, forget, allow, permit (e.g. **Déjame salir,** Let me go out); yield, produce, entrust, leave in charge; believe, consider; intend, appoint; cease, stop; forsake, desert; renounce, relinquish; bequeath; give away; *vr* neglect oneself; engage (in); lay oneself open to, allow oneself; abandon oneself (to), fling oneself (into); *fig* be depressed or languid; (*with de + infin.*) cease to (e.g. **Se dejó de hacerlo,** He stopped doing it); *vi* (*with de + adjective*) be none the less, be rather (e.g. **No deja de ser sorprendente,** It isn't any the less surprising). **d. aparte,** to omit, leave out. **d. atrás,** to overtake; *fig* leave behind, beat. **d. caer,** to let fall. **dejarse caer,** to let oneself fall; *fig inf* to let fall, utter; appear suddenly. **dejarse vencer,** to give way, allow oneself to be persuaded
dejo *m*, relinquishment; end; accent (of persons); savor, after-taste; negligence; *fig* touch, flavor
del contraction of **de + el,** (*def. art. m.*) of the (e.g. **del perro,** of the dog)
delación *f*, accusation, denunciation
delantal *m*, apron
delante *adv* before, in front, in the presence (of)
delantera *f*, front, front portion; *theat* orchestra stall, front seat; front (of garment). **tomar la d.,** to take the lead; *inf* steal a march on
delantero *a* fore, front. *m*, postilion; *sport* forward. **d. centro,** *sport* centerforward
delatable *a* impeachable; blameworthy
delatar *vt* to inform against, accuse; impeach
delator (-ra) *a* denunciatory, accusing. *n* denouncer, informer
delectación *f*, delectation, pleasure
delegación *f*, delegation; proxy
delegado (-da) *n* delegate; proxy
delegar *vt* to delegate
deleitable *a* delightful
deleitar *vt* to delight, charm, please; *vr* delight (in)
deleite *m*, delight; pleasure
deleitoso *a* delightful, pleasant
deletéreo *a* deleterious; poisonous
deletrear *vi* to spell; *fig* decipher
deletreo *m*, spelling; *fig* decipherment
deleznable *a* fragile, brittle; slippery; brief, fugitive, transitory
délfico *a* Delphic
delfín *m*, (*icht ast*) dolphin; dauphin

delfina *f,* dauphiness
Delfos Delphi
delgadez *f,* thinness; slenderness, leanness
delgado *a* slim; thin; scanty; poor (of land); sharp, perspicacious
delgaducho *a* slenderish, somewhat thin
deliberación *f,* deliberation; consideration; discussion
deliberadamente *adv* deliberately
deliberante *a* deliberative, considering
deliberar *vi* to deliberate, consider; *vt* decide after reflection; discuss
delicadez *f,* weakness; delicacy; hypersensitiveness; amiability
delicadeza *f,* delicacy; fastidiousness; refinement, subtlety; sensitiveness; consideration, tact; scrupulosity
delicado *a* courteous; tactful; fastidious; weak, delicate; fragile, perishable; delicious, tasty; exquisite; difficult, embarrassing; refined, discriminating, sensitive; scrupulous; subtle; hypersensitive, suspicious. **d. de salud,** in poor health
delicia *f,* pleasure, delight; sensual pleasure
delicioso *a* delightful, agreeable, pleasant
delimitar *vt* to delimit
delincuencia *f,* delinquency
delincuente *a* and *mf* delinquent
delineación *f,* delineation; diagram, design, plan
delineador (-ra), *n* **delineante** *m,* draftsman, designer
delineamiento *m,* delineation
delinear *vt* to delineate; sketch; describe
delinquimiento *m,* delinquency; crime
delinquir *vi irr* to commit a crime. *Pres. Ind.* **delinco.** *Pres. Subjunc.* **delinca**
deliquio *m,* faint, swoon
delirante *a* delirious
delirar *vi* to be delirious; act or speak foolishly
delirio *m,* delirium; frenzy; foolishness, nonsense. **d. de grandezas,** illusions of grandeur
delito *m,* delict, offense against the law, crime
delta *f,* fourth letter of Greek alphabet. *m,* delta (of a river)
delusorio *a* deceptive
demacración *f,* emaciation
demacrado *a* emaciated
demacrarse *vr* to become emaciated
demagogia *f,* demagogy
demagógico *a* demagogic
demagogo (-ga) *n* demagogue
demanda *f,* petition, request; collecting (for charity); collecting box; want ad; question; search; undertaking; *com* order or demand; *law* claim
demandadero (-ra) *n* convent or prison messenger; errandboy
demandado (-da) *n law* defendant; *law* respondent
demandante *mf law* plaintiff
demandar *vt* to ask, request; desire, yearn for; question; *law* claim
demarcación *f,* demarcation, limit
demarcar *vt* to fix boundaries, demarcate
demás *a* other. *adv* besides. **lo d.,** the rest. **los (las) d.,** the others. **por d.,** useless; superfluous. **por lo d.,** otherwise; for the rest
demasía *f,* excess; daring; insolence; guilt, crime. **en d.,** excessively
demasiado *a* too; too many; too much. *adv* excessively
demencia *f,* madness, insanity
demencial *a* insane
dementar *vt* to render insane; *vr* become insane
demente *a* insane, mad. *mf* lunatic
demérito *m,* demerit, fault
demeritorio *a* undeserving, without merit
demisión *f,* submission, acquiescence
democracia *f,* democracy
demócrata *mf* democrat
democrático *a* democratic
democratizar *vt* to make democratic
demoledor (-ra) *a* demolition. *n* demolisher
demoler *vt irr* to demolish, destroy, dismantle. See **moler**
demolición *f,* demolition, destruction, dismantling
demoníaco *a* devilish; possessed by a demon
demonio *m,* devil; evil spirit. *interj* **¡Demonios!** Deuce take it! *inf* **tener el d. en el cuerpo,** to be always on the move, be very energetic
demontre *m, inf* devil
demora *f,* delay; *naut* bearing; *com* demurrage
demorar *vt* to delay; *vi* stay, remain, tarry; *naut* bear
demorón, -ona *a, Lat. Am.* slow
demostrable *a* demonstrable
demostración *f,* demonstration; proof
demostrador (-ra) *a* demonstrating. *n* demonstrator
demostrar *vt irr* to demonstrate, explain; prove; teach. See **mostrar**
demostrativo *a* demonstrative. *gram* **pronombre d.,** demonstrative pronoun
demudación *f,* change; alteration
demudar *vt* to change, vary; alter, transform; *vr* change suddenly (color, facial expression, etc.); grow angry
denario *a* denary. *m,* denarius
denegación *f,* denial; refusal
denegar *vt irr* to deny, refuse. See **acertar**
dengoso *a* fastidious, finicky
dengue *m,* affectation, faddiness, fastidiousness
denigrable *a* odious
denigración *f,* slander, defamation (of character)
denigrante *a* slanderous
denigrar *vt* to slander; insult
denodado *a* valiant, daring
denominación *f,* denomination
denominador *a* denominating *m, math* denominator
denominar *vt* to name, designate
denostada *f,* insult
denostar *vt irr* to revile, insult. See **acordar**
denotar *vt* to denote, indicate
densidad *f,* density; closeness, denseness; *phys* specific gravity; obscurity
denso *a* compact, close; thick, dense; crowded; dark, confused
dentado *a* toothed; pronged; dentate
dentadura *f,* set of teeth (real or false). **d. de rumiante,** teeth like an ox. **d. postiza,** false teeth
dental *a* dental
dentar *vt irr* to provide with teeth, prongs, etc.; *vi* cut teeth. See **sentar**
dentellada *f,* gnashing or chattering of teeth; bite; toothmark
dentellar *vt* to chatter, grind, gnash (teeth)
dentellear *vt* to bite, sink the teeth into
dentera *f,* **(dar)** to set one's teeth on edge; *fig inf* make one's mouth water
dentición *f,* teething, dentition
dentífrico *m,* toothpaste
dentista *mf* dentist
dentro *adv* within, inside. **d. de poco,** soon, shortly. **por d.,** from the inside; on the inside
dentudo *a* having large teeth
denudación *f,* denudation; *geol* erosion
denudar *vt* to denude
denuedo *m,* courage, daring
denuesto *m,* insult
denuncia *f,* denunciation, accusation
denunciante *a* accusing. *mf law* denouncer
denunciar *vt* to give notice, inform; herald, presage; declare, proclaim; denounce; *law* accuse
denunciatorio *a* denunciatory
deparar *vt* to furnish, offer, present
departamental *a* departmental
departamento *m,* department; compartment (railway); branch, section; *Argentina* apartment. **d. de lactantes,** nursery (in a hospital)
departir *vi* to converse
depauperación *f,* impoverishment; *med* emaciation

depauperar *vt* to impoverish; *vr med* grow weak, become emaciated
dependencia *f,* dependence; subordination; dependency; *com* branch; firm, agency; business affair; kinship or affinity; *pl arch* offices; *com* staff; accessories
depender *vi* (*with de*) to be subordinate to; depend on; be dependent on, need
dependiente (**-ta**) *a* and *n* dependent, subordinate. *m,* employee; shop assistant
depilar *vt* to depilate
depilatorio *m,* depilatory
deplorar *vt* to deplore, lament
deponente *a* deposing; affirming. *mf* deponent. *gram* **verbo d.,** deponent verb
deponer *vt irr* to lay aside; depose, oust; affirm, testify; remove, take from its place; *law* depose; *Central America, Mexico* throw up, vomit. See **poner**
deportación *f,* deportation
deportar *vt* to exile; deport
deporte *m,* sport; *pl* games. **d. de vela,** sailing; boating
deportismo *m,* sport
deportista *a* sporting. *mf* sportsman (sportswoman)
deportivo *a* sporting
deposición *f,* affirmation, statement; *law* deposition; degradation, removal (from office, etc.)
depositador (**-ra**) *a* depositing. *n* depositor
depositar *vt* to deposit; place in safety; entrust; lay aside, put away; *vr chem* settle
depositaría *f,* depository; trusteeship; accounts office
depositario (**-ia**) *a* pertaining to a depository. *n* depositary, trustee
depósito *m,* deposit; depository; *com* depot, warehouse; *chem* deposit, sediment; tank, reservoir; *mil* depot. **d. de bencina, d. de gasolina,** gas tank; service station. **d. de municiones,** munitions dump. *com* **en d.,** in bond. **Queda hecho el d. que marca la ley,** Copyright reserved
depravación *f,* depravity
depravar *vt* to deprave, corrupt; *vr* become depraved
deprecación *f,* supplication, petition; deprecation
deprecar *vt* to supplicate, petition; deprecate
depreciación *f,* depreciation, fall in value
depreciar *vt* to depreciate, reduce the value (of)
depredación *f,* depredation, robbery
depredar *vt* to pillage
depresión *f,* depression. **d. nerviosa,** nervous breakdown
depresivo *a* depressive; humiliating
deprimir *vt* to depress, compress, press down; depreciate, belittle; *vr* be compressed
depuración *f,* cleansing, purification; *pol* purge
depurar *vt* to cleanse, purify; *pol* purge
derecha *f,* right hand; *pol* (gen. *pl*) Right. *mil* **¡D.!** Right Turn! **a la d.,** on the right
derechamente *adv* straight, directly; prudently, justly; openly, frankly
derechera *f,* direct road
derechista *mf pol* rightist
derecho *a* straight; upright; right (not left); just, reasonable; *sport* forehand. *adv* straightaway. *m,* right; law; just claim; privilege; justice, reason; exemption; right side (cloth, etc.); *pl* dues, taxes; fees. **d. a la vía,** right of way. **d. de apelación,** right to appeal. **d. de visita,** (international law) right of search. **derechos de aduana,** customhouse duties. **derechos de entrada,** import duties. **según d.,** according to law. **usar de su d.,** to exercise one's right
derechura *f,* directness, straightness; uprightness; *Lat. Am.* good luck
deriva *f,* (*naut aer*) drift, leeway
derivación *f,* origin, derivation; inference, consequence; *gram* derivation
derivar *vi* to originate; *naut* drift; *vt* conduct, lead; *gram* derive; *elec* tap
dermatología *f,* dermatology
dermatólogo *m,* dermatologist
derogación *f,* repeal, annulment; deterioration
derogar *vt* to annul, repeal; destroy, suppress
derogatorio *a law* repealing
derrama *f,* apportionment of tax
derramado *a* extravagant, wasteful
derramamiento *m,* pouring out; spilling; scattering
derramar *vt* to pour out; spill; scatter; apportion (taxes); publish abroad, spread; *vr* be scattered; overflow
derrame *m,* spilling; leakage; overflow; scattering; slope
derredor *m,* circumference. **al** (*or* **en**) **d.,** round about
derrelicto *a* abandoned; derelict. *m, naut* derelict
derrengado *a* crooked; crippled
derretimiento *m,* melting; thaw; liquefaction; *inf* burning passion
derretir *vt irr* to melt, liquefy; waste, dissipate; *vr* be very much in love; *inf* be susceptible (to love); *inf* long, be impatient. See **pedir**
derribar *vt* to demolish; knock down; fell; throw down; *aer* shoot down; throw (in wrestling); *fig* overthrow; demolish, explode (a myth); control (emotions); *vr* fall down; prostrate oneself; throw oneself down. **d. el chapeo,** *humorous* to doff one's hat
derribo *m,* demolition; debris, rubble; throw (in wrestling)
derrocadero *m,* rocky precipice
derrocar *vt* to throw down from a rock; demolish (buildings); overthrow, oust
derrochador (**-ra**) *a* wasteful, extravagant. *n* spendthrift
derrochar *vt* to waste, squander
derroche *m,* squandering
derrota *f,* road; route, path; *naut* course; *mil* defeat
derrotar *vt* to squander; destroy, harm; *mil* defeat; *vr naut* drift, lose course
derrotero *m, naut* course; *naut* ship's itinerary; number of sea charts; means to an end, course of action
derrotismo *m,* defeatism
derrotista *mf* defeatist
derruir *vt irr* to demolish (a building). See **huir**
derrumbadero *m,* precipice; risk, danger
derrumbamiento *m,* landslide; collapse, downfall
derrumbar *vt* to precipitate; *vr* throw oneself down, collapse, tumble down (buildings, etc.)
derrumbe *m,* collapse; subsidence
derviche *m,* dervish
desabarrancar *vt* to pull out of a ditch or rut; extricate (from a difficulty)
desabillé *m,* deshabille
desabor *m,* insipidity
desabotonar *vt* to unbutton; *vi* open (flowers)
desabrido *a* insipid, poor-tasting; inclement (weather); disagreeable; unsociable; homely, plain (woman)
desabrigar *vt* to uncover; leave without shelter
desabrigo *m,* want of clothing or shelter; poverty, destitution
desabrimiento *m,* insipidity; harshness, disagreeableness; melancholy, depression
desabrir *vt* to give a bad taste (to food); annoy, trouble
desabrochar *vt* to unbutton, untie; open; *vr inf* confide, open up
desacatar *vt* to behave disrespectfully (towards); lack reverence
desacato *m,* irreverence; disrespect
desacertado *a* wrong, erroneous; imprudent
desacertar *vi irr* to be wrong; act imprudently. See **acertar**
desacierto *m,* mistake, miscalculation, blunder
desacomodado *a* lacking means of subsistence; poor; unemployed (servants); troublesome
desacomodar *vt* to incommode, make uncomfortable, inconvenience; dismiss, discharge
desaconsejado *a* ill-advised
desaconsejar *vt* to advise against, dissuade
desacoplar *vt* to disconnect

desacordar *vt irr mus* to put out of tune; *vr* (*with de*) forget. See **acordar**
desacorde *a* discordant, inharmonious; *mus* out of tune
desacostumbrado *a* unaccustomed; unusual
desacostumbrar *vt* to break of a habit
desacotar *vt* to remove (fences); refuse, deny; *vi* withdraw (from agreement, etc.)
desacreditar *vt* to discredit
desacuerdo *m*, disagreement, discord; mistake; forgetfulness; swoon, loss of consciousness
desadeudar *vt* to free from debt
desadornar *vt* to denude of ornaments
desadorno *m*, lack of ornaments; bareness
desafecto *a* disaffected; hostile. *m*, disaffection
desaferrar *vt irr* to untie, unfasten; *fig* wean from; *naut* weigh anchor. See **acertar**
desafiador (-ra) *a* challenging. *n* challenger. *m*, duelist
desafiar *vt* to challenge; compete with; oppose; *Mexico* fight
desafinar *vi mus* to go out of tune; *fig inf* speak out of turn
desafío *m*, challenge; competition; duel
desaforado *a* lawless; outrageous; enormous
desaforar *vt* to infringe (laws, etc.); *vr* be disorderly
desaforrar *vt* to remove the lining of or from
desafortunado *a* unfortunate
desafuero *m*, act of injustice; outrage, excess
desagarrar *vt inf* to release, loosen; unhook
desagraciado *a* ugly, unsightly
desagraciar *vt* to disfigure, make ugly
desagradable *a* disagreeable; unpleasant
desagradar *vi* to be disagreeable, displease (e.g. **Me desagrada su voz,** I find his voice unpleasant)
desagradecer *vt irr* to be ungrateful (for). See **conocer**
desagradecido *a* ungrateful
desagradecimiento *m*, ingratitude
desagrado *m*, displeasure, dislike, dissatisfaction
desagraviar *vt* to make amends, apologize; indemnify
desagravio *m*, satisfaction, reparation; compensation
desagregar(se) *vt* and *vr* to separate
desaguadero *m*, drain, waste pipe
desaguar *vt* to drain off; dissipate; *vi* flow (into sea, etc.)
desagüe *m*, drainage; outlet, drain; catchment
desaguisado *a* outrageous, lawless. *m*, offense, insult
desahogado *a* brazen, insolent; clear, unencumbered; in comfortable circumstances
desahogar *vt* to ease, relieve; *vr* unburden oneself; recover (from illness, heat, etc.); get out of debt; speak one's mind
desahogo *m*, relief, alleviation; ease; comfort, convenience; freedom, frankness; unburdening (of one's mind). *inf* **vivir con d.,** to be comfortably off
desahuciar *vt* to banish all hope; give up, despair of the life of; put out (tenants); *Chile* dismiss
desahúcio *m*, ejection, dispossession (of tenants); *Chile* dismissal
desahumar *vt* to clear of smoke
desairado *a* unattractive, graceless, ugly; unsuccessful, crestfallen; slighted
desairar *vt* to disdain, slight, disregard; underrate (things)
desaire *m*, gracelessness, ugliness; insult, slight
desalabanza *f*, disparagement; criticism
desalabar *vt* to censure, disparage
desalación *f*, desalinization
desalado *a* anxious, precipitate, hasty
desalar *vt* to remove the salt from; take off wings; *vr* walk or run at great speed; long for, yearn
desalentar *vt irr* to make breathing difficult (work, fatigue); discourage; *vr* be depressed or sad. See **sentar**
desaliento *m*, depression, discouragement, dismay
desalinear *vt* to throw out of the straight
desaliñado *a* slovenly; slipshod
desaliñar *vt* to disarrange, make untidy, crumple
desaliño *m*, untidiness, slovenliness; negligence, carelessness
desalmado *a* soulless, conscienceless; cruel
desalmamiento *m*, inhumanity, consciencelessness; cruelty
desalmidonar *vt* to remove starch from
desalojamiento *m*, dislodgement, ejection
desalojar *vt* to dislodge, remove, eject; *vi* move out, remove
desalquilado *a* untenanted, vacant
desalquilar *vt* to leave, or cause to leave, rented premises
desalterar *vt* to soothe, calm
desamar *vt* to cease to love; hate
desamarrar *vt* to untie; separate; *naut* unmoor
desamor *m*, indifference; lack of sentiment or affection; hatred
desamotinarse *vr* to cease from rebellion; submit
desamparar *vt* to abandon, forsake; leave (a place)
desamparo *m*, desertion; need
desamueblado *a* unfurnished
desamueblar *vt* to empty of furniture
desandar lo andado *vt irr* to retrace one's steps. See **andar**
desangrar *vt med* to bleed; drain (lake, etc.); impoverish, bleed; *vr* lose much blood
desangre *m*, *Lat. Am.* bleeding, loss of blood
desanidar *vi* to leave the nest; *vt* eject, expel
desanimado *a* downhearted; (of places) dull, quiet
desanimar *vt* to discourage, depress
desanublar, *vt* **desanublarse** *vr* to clear up (weather)
desanudar *vt* to untie; disentangle
desaojar *vt* to cure of the evil eye
desapacibilidad *f*, disagreeableness, unpleasantness
desapacible *a* disagreeable; unpleasant; unsociable
desaparecer *vt irr* to cause to disappear; *vi* and *vr* disappear. See **conocer**
desaparecido *a* late (deceased); *mil* missing
desaparejar *vt* to unharness
desaparición *f*, disappearance
desapegar *vt* to unstick, undo; *vr* be indifferent, cast off a love or affection
desapego *m*, lack of affection or interest, coolness
desapercibido *a* unnoticed; unprovided, unprepared
desapestar *vt* to disinfect
desapiadado *a* merciless
desaplicación *f*, laziness, lack of application; carelessness, negligence
desaplicado *a* lazy; careless
desapoderado *a* precipitate, uncontrolled; furious, violent
desapoderar *vt* to dispossess, rob; remove from office
desapolillar *vt* to free from moths; *vr inf* take an airing
desaposentar *vt* to evict; drive away
desapreciar *vt* to scorn
desaprensivo *a* unscrupulous
desapretar(se) *vt* and *vr irr* to slacken. See **acertar**
desaprisionar *vt* to release from prison
desaprobación *f*, disapproval
desaprobar *vt irr* to disapprove; disagree with. See **probar**
desapropiamiento *m*, renunciation or transfer of property
desapropiarse *vr* to renounce or transfer (property)
desaprovechado *a* unprofitable; backward; unintelligent
desaprovechar *vt* to take no advantage of, waste; *vi fig* lose ground, lose what one has gained
desapuntar *vt* to unstitch; lose one's aim
desarbolar *vt naut* to unmast
desarenar *vt* to clear of sand
desarmador *m*, *Mexico* screwdriver
desarmar *vt* to disarm; dismantle, dismount; appease
desarme *m*, disarming; disarmament
desarraigar *vt* to pull up by root (plants); extirpate, suppress; eradicate (opinion, etc.); exile

desarraigo *m*, uprooting; extirpation; eradication; exile
desarrebujar *vt* to disentangle, uncover; explain
desarreglado *a* disarranged; untidy; intemperate, immoderate
desarreglar *vt* to disarrange
desarreglo *m*, disorder; disarrangement; irregularity
desarrendar *vt irr* to unbridle a horse; end a tenancy or lease. See **recomendar**
desarrollar *vt* to unroll; increase, develop, grow, unfold; explain (theory); *vr* develop, grow
desarrollo *m*, unrolling; development, growth; explanation
desarropar *vt* to uncover, remove the covers, etc. from
desarrugar *vt* to take out wrinkles or creases
desarticulación *f*, disarticulation
desarticular *vt* to disarticulate; *mech* disconnect
desaseado *a* dirty; unkempt, slovenly
desaseo *m*, dirtiness; slovenliness
desasimiento *m*, loosening; liberality; disinterestedness; indifference, coldness
desasir *vt irr* to loosen, undo. *vr* disengage oneself. See **asir**
desasnar *vt inf* to instruct, educate, polish
desasosegar *vt irr* to disturb, make anxious. See **cegar**
desasosiego *m*, uneasiness, disquiet
desastre *m*, disaster, calamity
desastroso *a* unfortunate, calamitous
desatacar *vt* to unfasten, undo, unbutton
desatadura *f*, untying
desatar *vt* to untie; melt, dissolve; elucidate, explain; *vr* loosen the tongue; lose self control; lose all reserve; unbosom oneself
desatascar *vt* to pull out of the mud; free from obstruction; extricate from difficulties
desataviar *vt* to strip of ornaments
desatavío *m*, carelessness in dress, slovenliness
desatención *f*, inattention, abstraction; incivility
desatender *vt irr* to pay no attention to; disregard, ignore. See **entender**
desatentado *a* imprudent, ill-advised; excessive, immoderate
desatento *a* inattentive, abstracted; discourteous
desatinado *a* foolish, imprudent, wild
desatinar *vt* to bewilder; *vi* behave foolishly; lose one's bearings
desatino *m*, folly, foolishness, imprudence, rashness; blunder, faux pas, mistake
desatracar *vi naut* to push off
desatrancar *vt* to unbar the door; remove obstacles
desaturdir *vt* to rouse (from torpor, etc.)
desautorizar *vt* to remove from authority; discredit
desavenencia *f*, disharmony, disagreement
desavenido *a* disagreeing, discordant
desavenir *vt irr* to upset. See **venir**
desaventajado *a* disadvantageous; unfavorable, inferior
desaviar *vt* to lead astray; deprive of a necessity; *vr* lose one's way
desayunador *m*, breakfast nook
desavisado *a* unaware, unprepared
desavisar *vt* to take back one's previous advice
desayunarse *vr* to have breakfast, eat breakfast
desayuno *m*, breakfast
desazón *f*, insipidity, lack of flavor; poorness (soil); anxiety, trouble; vexation
desazonar *vt* to make insipid; make anxious, worry; vex; *vr* feel out of sorts
desbancar *vt* to break the bank (gambling); supplant
desbandada *f*, dispersal, rout. **a la d.,** in confusion or disorder
desbandarse *vr* to disband, retreat in disorder; *mil* desert
desbaratado *a inf* corrupt, vicious
desbaratar *vt* to spoil, destroy; dissipate, waste; foil, thwart (a plot); *mil* rout; *vi* talk foolishly; *vr* go too far, behave badly
desbarbado *a* beardless
desbastar *vt carp* to plane, dress; polish, refine, civilize
desbocado *a* (of tools) blunt; runaway (of a horse); *inf* foul-tongued; *Lat. Am.* overflowing (its banks)
desbocar *vt* to break the spout or neck (of jars, etc.); *vi* run (into) (of streets, etc.); *vr* bolt (horses); curse, swear
desboquillar *vt* to remove or break a stem or mouthpiece
desbordamiento *m*, overflowing, flood
desbordarse *vr* to overflow; lose self-control. **d. en alabanzas para,** to heap praise on
desbravar *vt* to break in (horses, etc.); *vi* grow less savage; lose force, decrease
desbrozar *vt* to free of rubbish, clear up
descabalgadura *f*, alighting (from horses, etc.)
descabalgar *vi* to alight (from horse); *vt* dismantle (gun)
descabellado *a* disheveled; ridiculous, foolish
descabellar *vt* to disarrange, ruffle (hair)
descabezado *a* headless; rash, impetuous
descabezar *vt* to behead; cut the top off (trees, etc.); *fig inf* break the back of (work); *vi* abut, join; *vr* (*with con* or *en*) rack one's brains about
descacharrado, -a *a*, *Central America* dirty, filthy, slovenly
descalabazarse *vr inf* to rack one's brains
descalabradura *f*, head wound or scar
descalabrar *vt* to wound in the head; wound; harm
descalabro *m*, misfortune, mishap
descalzar *vt* to remove the shoes and stockings; undermine; *vr* remove one's shoes and stockings; lose a shoe (horses)
descalzo *a* barefoot
descaminar *vt* to lead astray; pervert, corrupt
descamisado (**-da**) *a inf* shirtless; ragged, poor. *n inf* down and out, outcast; vagabond
descansadero *m*, resting place
descansado *a* rested, refreshed; tranquil
descansar *vi* to rest, repose oneself; have relief (from anxiety, etc.); sleep; *agr* lie fallow; sleep in death; (*with en*) trust, have confidence in; (*with sobre*) lean on or upon; *vt* (*with sobre*) rest (a thing) on another. **¡Que en paz descanse!** May he rest in peace!
descanso *m*, rest, repose; relief (from care); landing of stairs; *mech* bench, support; *mil* stand easy
descarado *a* impudent, brazen
descararse *vr* to behave impudently
descarbonizar *vt* to decarbonize
descarga *f*, unloading; *naut* discharge of cargo; *elec* discharge; *mil* volley. **d. cerrada,** dense volley, fusillade
descargadero *m*, wharf
descargador *m*, unloader, docker; *elec* discharger
descargar *vt* to unload; *mil* fire; unload (fire-arms); *elec* discharge; rain (blows) upon; *fig* free, exonerate; *vi* disembogue (of rivers); burst (clouds); *vr* relinquish (employment); shirk responsibility; *law* clear oneself
descargo *m*, unloading; *com* acquittance; *law* answer to an impeachment
descargue *m*, unloading
descarnado *a* fleshless; scraggy; spare, lean
descarnador *m*, dental scraper; tanner's scraper
descarnar *vt* to scrape off flesh; corrode; inspire indifference to earthly things
descaro *m*, impudence
descarriar *vt* to lead astray; *vr* be lost, be separated (from others); *fig* go astray
descarrilamiento *m*, derailment
descarrilar *vi* to run off the track, be derailed
descarrío *m*, losing one's way
descartar *vt* to put aside; *vr* discard (cards); shirk, make excuses
descarte *m*, discard (cards); excuse, pretext
descascarar *vt* to peel; shell; *vr* peel off

descendencia *f,* descendants, offspring; lineage, descent
descender *vi irr* to descend; flow (liquids); (*with de*) descend from, derive from; *vt* lower, let down. See **entender**
descendiente *mf* descendant, offspring. *a* descending
descendimiento *m,* descent
descenso *m,* descent; lowering, letting down; degradation
descentralizar *vt* to decentralize
desceñir(se) *vt* and *vr irr* to ungird, remove a girdle, etc. See **ceñir**
descepar *vt* to tear up by the roots; *fig* extirpate
descercado *a* unfenced, open
descercar *vt* to pull down a wall or fence; *mil* raise a siege
descerrajar *vt* to remove the locks (of doors, etc.)
descifrable *a* decipherable
descifrador *m,* decipherer, decoder
descifrar *vt* to decipher; decode
descinchar *vt* to loosen or remove girths (of horse)
desclavar *vt* to remove nails; unnail, unfasten
descoagular *vt* to liquefy, dissolve, melt
descobijar *vt* to uncover; undress
descocado *a inf* brazen, saucy
descoco *m, inf* impudence
descogollar *vt* to prune a tree of shoots; remove hearts (of lettuces, etc.)
descolar *vt irr* to cut off or dock an animal's tail; *Mexico* slight, snub. See **colar**
descolgar *vt irr* to unhang; lower; *vr* lower oneself (by rope, etc.); come down, descend; *inf* come out (with), utter. See **volcar**
descoloramiento *m,* discoloration
descolorar *vt* to discolor; *vr* be discolored
descolorido *a* discolored; pale-colored; pallid
descollar *vi irr* to excel, be outstanding. See **degollar**
descomedido *a* excessive, disproportionate; rude
descomedimiento *m,* disrespect, lack of moderation, rudeness
descomedirse *vr irr* to be disrespectful or rude. See **pedir**
descompasarse *vr* See **descomedirse**
descomponer *vt irr* to disorder, disarrange; *chem* decompose; unsettle; *vr* go out of order; rot, putrefy; be ailing; lose one's temper. See **poner**
descomposición *f,* disorder, confusion; discomposure; *chem* decomposition; putrefaction
descompostura *f,* decomposition; slovenliness, dirtiness, untidiness; impudence, rudeness
descompuesto *a* rude, impudent; *Lat. Am.* tipsy; *Venezuela* ill, sick
descomunal *a* enormous, extraordinary
desconcertar *vt irr* to disorder, disarrange; dislocate (bones); disconcert, embarrass; *vr* disagree; be impudent. See **acertar**
desconcharse *vr* to flake off, peel
desconcierto *m,* disorder, disarrangement; dislocation; embarrassment; disagreement; impudence
desconectar *vt* to disconnect; switch off
desconfianza *f,* lack of confidence
desconfiar *vi* to lack confidence
desconformidad *f,* See **disconformidad**
desconformismo *m,* non-conformism
desconocer *vt irr* to forget; be unaware of; deny, disown; pretend ignorance; not to understand (persons, etc.). See **conocer**
desconocido (-da) *a* unknown; ungrateful. *n* stranger; ingrate
desconocimiento *m,* unawareness; ignorance; ingratitude
desconsiderado *a* inconsiderate; discourteous; rash
desconsolación *f,* affliction, trouble
desconsolar *vt irr* to afflict, make disconsolate; *vr* grieve, despair. See **colar**
desconsuelo *m,* anguish, affliction, despair
descontar *vt irr com* to make a discount; ignore, discount; take for granted, leave aside. See **contar**
descontentadizo *a* discontented, difficult to please; fastidious, finicky
descontentar *vt* to displease; *vr* be dissatisfied
descontento *m,* discontent, dissatisfaction
descontextualizar *vt* to take out of context
descontrolarse *vr* to lose control, lose control of oneself.
desconveniencia *f,* inconvenience, unsuitability, disagreement
desconvenir *vi irr* to disagree; be unsuitable, unsightly or odd (things). See **venir**
descorazonamiento *m,* depression, despair
descorazonar *vt* to tear out the heart; depress, discourage
descorchar *vt* to take the cork from cork tree; draw a cork (bottles); force, break into (safes)
descorrer *vt* to re-run (race, etc.); draw back (curtains, etc.); *vi* run, flow (liquids)
descorrimiento *m,* overflow (liquids)
descortés *a* impolite
descortesía *f,* impoliteness, discourtesy
descortezadura *f,* peeling (of bark)
descortezar *vt* to decorticate; remove crust (bread, etc.); polish, civilize
descoser *vt sew* to unpick; *vr* be unpicked; be indiscreet or tactless
descosido *a* tactless, talkative; *fig* disjointed; desultory; unsewn. *m, sew* rent, hole
descoyuntamiento *m,* dislocation (bones); irritation, bore; ache, pain
descoyuntar *vt* to dislocate (bones); bore, annoy; *vr* be dislocated
descrédito *m,* fall in value (things); discredit (persons)
descreer *vt irr* to disbelieve; depreciate, disparage (persons). See **creer**
descreído (-da) *a* unbelieving. *n* unbeliever; infidel
descremar *vt, Lat. Am.* to skim (milk)
describir *vt* to describe; outline, sketch. *Past Part.* **descrito**
descripción *f,* description; *law* inventory
descriptible *a* describable
descriptivo *a* descriptive
descuajar *vt* to liquefy; *inf* discourage; *agr* pull up by the root
descuartizar *vt* to quarter; joint (meat); *inf* carve, cut into pieces, break up
descubierto *a* bareheaded; exposed. *m,* deficit. **al d.,** openly; in the open, without shelter. **girar en d.,** to overdraw (a bank account)
descubridero *m,* viewpoint, lookout
descubridor (-ra) *n* discoverer; inventor; explorer. *m, mil* scout
descubrimiento *m,* find; discovery; revelation; newly discovered territory
descubrir *vt* to reveal; show; discover; learn; unveil (memorials, etc.); *vr* remove one's hat; show oneself, reveal one's whereabouts. *Past Part.* **descubierto**
descuello *m,* extra height; *fig* pre-eminence; arrogance
descuento *m,* reduction; *com* rebate, discount
descuidado *a* negligent; careless; untidy; unprepared
descuidar *vt* to relieve (of responsibility, etc.); distract, occupy (attention, etc.); *vi* and *vr* be careless; *vr* (*with de* or *en*) neglect
descuido *m,* carelessness, negligence; oversight, mistake; incivility; forgetfulness; shameful act
desde *prep* since, from (time or space); after (e.g. **d. hoy,** from today). **d. la ventana,** from the window. **d. allá,** from the other world. **d. aquella época,** since that time
desdecir *vi irr* (*with de*) to degenerate, be less good than; be discordant, clash; be unworthy of; *vr* unsay one's words, retract. See **decir**
desdén *m,* indifference, coldness; disdain, scorn

desdentado *a* toothless; *zool* edentate
desdentar *vt* to remove teeth
desdeñar *vt* to scorn; *vr* (*with de*) dislike, be reluctant
desdeñoso *a* disdainful, scornful
desdibujado *a* badly drawn; blurred, confused
desdicha *f,* misfortune; extreme poverty, misery. **por d.,** unfortunately
desdichado *a* unfortunate; *inf* timid, weak-kneed
desdicharse *vr* to bewail one's fate
desdinerarse una fortuna *vr* to spend a fortune
desdoblar *vt* to unfold
desdorar *vt* to remove the gilt; *fig* tarnish, sully
desdoro *m,* discredit, dishonor
deseable *a* desirable
desear *vt* to desire; yearn or long for
desecar *vt* to dry; *vr* be desiccated
desechar *vt* to reject, refuse; scorn; cast out, expel; put away (thoughts, etc.); cast off (old clothes); turn (key); give up
desecho *m,* residue, rest, remains; cast-off; scorn; *Lat. Am.* shortcut
desembalar *vt* to unpack
desembanastar *vt* to take out of a basket; *inf* unsheath (sword); *vr* break loose (animals); *inf* get out, alight
desembarazar *vt* to clear of obstruction; disembarrass, free; vacate; *vr fig* rid oneself of obstacles
desembarazo *m,* freedom, insouciance, naturalness
desembarcadero *m,* landing-stage
desembarcar *vt* to unload; *vi* disembark; alight from vehicle
desembarco *m,* disembarkation, landing; staircase landing
desembargar *vt* to free of obstacles or impediments; *law* remove an embargo
desembargo *m, law* removal of an embargo
desembarque *m,* disembarkation, landing
desembarrancar *vt* and *vi naut* to refloat
desembaular *vt* to unpack from a trunk; disinter, empty; *inf* unbosom oneself
desembocadero *m,* exit, way out; mouth (rivers, etc.)
desembocadura *f,* mouth (rivers, etc.); street opening
desembocar *vi* (*with en*) to lead to, end in; flow into (rivers)
desembolsar *vt* to take out of a purse; pay, spend
desembolso *m,* disbursement; expenditure
desemboscarse *vr* to get out of the wood; extricate oneself from an ambush
desembozar *vt* to unmuffle
desembozo *m,* uncovering of the face
desembragar *vt mech* to disengage (the clutch, etc.)
desembravecer *vt irr* to tame, domesticate. See **conocer**
desembriagar(se) *vt* and *vr* to sober up (after a drinking bout)
desembrollar *vt inf* to disentangle, unravel
desemejanza *f,* unlikeness
desemejar *vi* to be unlike; *vt* disfigure, deform
desempacar *vt* to unpack
desempapelar *vt* to unwrap, remove the paper from; remove wallpaper
desempaquetar *vt* to unpack
desemparejar *vt* to split (a pair); make unequal
desemparentado *a* without relatives
desempedrar *vt irr* to take up the flags (of a pavement). See **acertar**
desempeñar *vt* to redeem (pledges); free from debt; fulfil (obligations, etc.); take out of pawn; hold, fill (an office); extricate (from difficulties, etc.); perform, carry out; *theat* act
desempeño *m,* redemption of a pledge; fulfilment (of an obligation, etc.); performance, accomplishment; *theat* acting of a part
desempolvar *vt* to free from dust, dust
desenamorar *vt* to kill the affection of; *vr* fall out of love
desencadenar *vt* to unchain, unfetter; *fig* unleash, let loose; *vr fig* break loose
desencajamiento *m,* disjointedness, dislocation; rickētiness, broken-down appearance
desencajar *vt* to disconnect, disjoint; dislocate; *vr* be out of joint; be contorted (of the face); be tired looking
desencaje *m,* See **desencajamiento**
desencantar *vt* to disenchant
desencanto *m,* disenchantment; disillusionment
desencerrar *vt irr* to set at liberty; unlock; disclose, reveal. See **acertar**
desenchufar *vt* to disconnect, unplug (electric plugs, etc.)
desenclavijar *vt* to remove the pegs or pins; disconnect, disjoint
desencoger *vt* to unfold, spread out; *vr* grow bold
desencolerizar *vt* to placate; *vr* lose one's anger, grow calm
desenconar *vt* to reduce (inflammation); appease (anger, etc.); *vr* become calm
desencono *m,* reduction of inflammation; appeasement (of anger, etc.)
desencordelar *vt* to untie the ropes (of), unstring
desencorvar *vt* to straighten (curves, etc.)
desenfadado *a* expeditious; natural, at ease; gay; forward, bold; wide, spacious
desenfadar *vt* to appease, make anger disappear
desenfado *m,* freedom; ease; unconcern, frankness
desenfrailar *vi* to leave the cloister, become secularized; *inf* emancipate oneself
desenfrenar *vt* to unbridle (horses); *vr* give rein to one's passions, etc.; break loose (storms, etc.)
desenfreno *m,* license, lasciviousness; complete freedom from restraint
desengalanar *vt* to strip of ornaments
desenganchar *vt* to unhook; uncouple; unfasten; unharness
desengañador *a* undeceiving
desengañar *vt* to undeceive, disillusion
desengaño *m,* undeceiving, disabuse; disillusionment
desengarzar *vt* to loosen from its setting; unlink, unhook, unclasp
desengastar *vt* to remove from its setting (jewelry, etc.)
desengrasar *vt* to remove the grease from, clean; *vi inf* grow thin
desenlace *m,* loosening, untying; *lit* denouement, climax (of play, etc.)
desenlatar *vt, Lat. Am.* to open (canned food)
desenlazar *vt* to untie, unloose; *lit* unravel (a plot)
desenlosar *vt* to remove flagstones
desenmarañar *vt* to disentangle; *fig* straighten out
desenmascarar *vt* to remove the mask from; *fig* unmask
desenmudecer *vi irr* to be freed of a speech impediment; break silence, speak. See **conocer**
desenojar *vt* to soothe, appease; *vr* distract oneself, amuse oneself
desenojo *m,* relenting, abatement of anger
desenredar *vt* to disentangle; *fig* set right; straighten out; *vr* extricate oneself, get out of a difficulty
desenredo *m,* disentanglement; *lit* climax
desenroscar *vt Lat. Am.* to unscrew
desentablar *vt* to tear up planks or boards; disorder, disrupt
desentenderse *vr irr* (*with de*) to pretend to be ignorant of; take no part in. See **entender**
desenterrador *m,* disinterrer, unearther
desenterramiento *m,* disinterment; *fig* unearthing, recollection
desenterrar *vt irr* to unbury, disinter; rummage out; *fig* unearth, bring up, recall. See **acertar**
desentoldar *vt* to take away an awning; *fig* strip of ornament
desentonar *vt* to humiliate; *vi mus* be out of tune;

speak rudely; *vr* be inharmonious; raise the voice (anger, etc.), behave badly
desentono *m*, bad behavior, rudeness; *mus* discord; grating quality or harshness (of voice)
desentorpecer *vt irr* to restore feeling to (numbed limbs); free from torpor; *vr* become bright and intelligent. See **conocer**
desentramparse *vr inf* free oneself from debt
desentrañar *vt* to disembowel; *fig* unravel, penetrate; *vr* give away one's all
desentumecer *vt irr* to free from numbness (limbs); *vr* be restored to feeling (numb limbs). See **conocer**
desenvainar *vt* to unsheath; *inf* reveal, bring into the open
desenvoltura *f*, naturalness, ease, freedom; eloquence, facility (of speech); effrontery, audacity, shamelessness (especially in women)
desenvolver *vt irr* to unroll; unfold; *fig* unravel, explain; *fig* develop, work out (theories, etc.); *vr* unroll; unfold; lose one's timidity, blossom out; be over-bold; extricate oneself (from a difficulty). See **resolver**
desenvuelto *a* natural, easy; impudent, bold
deseo *m*, desire, will, wish
deseoso *a* desirous, wishful
desequilibrar(se) *vt* and *vr* to unbalance
desequilibrio *m*, lack of balance; confusion, disorder; mental instability
deserción *f*, *mil* desertion. **d. estudiantil,** school dropout
desertar *vt mil* to desert; *inf* quit
desertor *m*, *mil* deserter; *inf* quitter
deservicio *m*, disservice
desesperación *f*, desperation, despair; frenzy, violence
desesperado *a* desperate, hopeless; frenzied
desesperanza *f*, despair; hopelessness
desesperanzar *vt* to render hopeless; *vr* despair, lose hope
desesperar *vt* to make hopeless; *inf* annoy, make furious; *vr* lose hope, despair; be frenzied
desestañar *vt* to unsolder
desestimación *f*, disrespect, lack of esteem; rejection
desestimar *vt* to scorn; reject
desfachatado *a inf* impudent, brazen
desfachatez *f*, *inf* effrontery, cheek
desfalcador (-ra) *a* embezzling. *n* embezzler
desfalcar *vt* to remove a part of; embezzle
desfalco *m*, diminution, reduction; embezzlement
desfallecer *vt irr* to weaken; *vi* grow weak; faint, swoon. See **conocer**
desfallecimiento *m*, weakness, languor; depression, discouragement; faint, swoon
desfavorable *a* unfavorable; hostile, contrary
desfavorecer *vt irr* to withdraw one's favor, scorn; disfavor; oppose. See **conocer**
desfiguración *f*, deformation; disfigurement
desfigurar *vt* to deform, misshape; disfigure; *fig* disguise, mask; obscure, darken; distort, misrepresent; *vr* be disfigured (by rage, etc.)
desfijar *vt* to unfix, pull off, remove
desfiladero *m*, defile, gully
desfilar *vi* to walk in file; *inf* file out; *mil* file or march past
desfile *m*, *mil* march past; parade; walk past; procession
desflecarse (en) *vr* to disintegrate (into)
desfloración *f*, defloration
desflorar *vt* to tarnish, stain; deflower, violate; *fig* touch upon, deal lightly with
desfortalecer *vt irr mil* to dismantle a fortress. See **conocer**
desfruncir *vt* to unfold, shake out
desgaire *m*, untidiness, slovenliness; affectation of carelessness (in dress); scornful gesture. **al d.,** with an affectation of carelessness, negligently
desgajar *vt* to tear off a tree branch; break; *vr* break off; dissociate oneself (from)
desgalgar *vt* to throw headlong
desgana *f*, lack of appetite; lack of interest, indifference; reluctance
desganar *vt* to dissuade; *vr* lose one's appetite; become bored or indifferent, lose interest
desgarbado *a* slovenly, slatternly; gawky, graceless
desgarrado *a* dissolute, vicious; impudent, brazen
desgarrador *a* tearing; heart-rending
desgarrar *vt* to tear; *vr* leave, tear oneself away
desgarro *m*, tearing; rent, breach; boastfulness, impudence, effrontery; *Lat. Am.* phlegm
desgastar *vt* to corrode, wear away; spoil, corrupt; *vr* lose one's vigor, grow weak; wear away
desgaste *m*, attrition; wearing down or away; corrosion; wear and tear
desgobernado *a* uncontrolled (of persons)
desgobernar *vt irr* to upset or rise against the government; dislocate (bones); *naut* neglect the tiller; *vr* affect exaggerated movements in dancing. See **recomendar**
desgobierno *m*, misgovernment; mismanagement; maladministration; disorder, tumult
desgomar *vt* to ungum (fabrics)
desgorrarse *vr* to doff one's cap, doff one's hat
desgoznar *vt* to unhinge; *vr fig* lose one's self-control
desgracia *f*, misfortune, adversity; mishap, piece of bad luck; disgrace, disfavor; disagreeableness, brusqueness; ungraciousness. **por d.,** unhappily, unfortunately
desgraciado *a* unfortunate, unhappy; unlucky; dull, boring; disagreeable
desgraciar *vt* to displease; spoil the development (of), destroy; maim; *vr* fall out of friendship; be out of favor; turn out badly, fail; be destroyed or spoiled; be maimed
desgranar *vt agr* to thresh, flail; *vr* break (string of beads, etc.)
desgrasante *m*, grease remover
desgreñar *vt* to dishevel the hair; *vr inf* pull each other's hair, come to blows
desguarnecer *vt irr* to strip of trimming; *mil* demilitarize; *mil* disarm; dismantle; unharness. See **conocer**
desguazar *vt* to break up (ships)
deshabitado *a* uninhabited, empty
deshabitar *vt* to desert, quit, leave (a place)
deshabituar *vt* to disaccustom; *vr* lose the habit, become unaccustomed
deshacer *vt irr* to undo; destroy; *mil* rout, defeat; take to pieces; melt; pulp (paper); untie (knots, etc.); open (parcels); diminish, decrease; break in pieces, smash; *fig* obstruct, spoil; *vr* be wasted or spoiled; be full of anxiety; vanish; try or work very hard; injure oneself; be emaciated, grow extremely thin; (*with de*) part with. **d. agravios,** to right wrongs. See **hacer**
desharrapado *a* tattered, shabby
deshebillar *vt* to unbuckle
deshebrar *vt* to unravel; shred
deshecha *f*, pretense, evasion; courteous farewell; obligatory departure
deshechizar *vt* to disenchant
deshelar *vt irr* to thaw, melt. See **acertar**
desherbar *vt irr* to pull up weeds. See **acertar**
desheredar *vt* disinherit; *vr fig* lower oneself
desherrar *vt irr* to unfetter, unchain; strike off horseshoes; *vr* lose a shoe (horses). See **acertar**
desherrumbrar *vt* to remove the rust from; clean off rust from
deshidratación *f*, dehydration
deshidratar *vt* to dehydrate
deshielo *m*, thaw
deshilado *a* in single file. *m*, *sew* drawn-thread work (gen. *pl*). **a la deshilada,** *mil* in file formation; secretly
deshiladura *f*, unraveling

deshilar *vt* to unravel; *sew* draw threads; *cul* shred, grate
deshilvanado *a fig* disjointed, disconnected
deshilvanar *vt sew* to remove the tacking threads
deshincar *vt* to pull out, remove, draw out
deshinchar *vt* to remove a swelling; deflate; lessen the anger of; *vr* decrease, subside (swellings); deflate; *inf* grow humble
deshojar *vt* to strip the leaves from, strip the petals from; *Lat. Am.* husk (corn); peel (fruit)
deshollejar *vt* to skin, peel (fruit); shell (peas, etc.)
deshollinador *m*, chimney-sweep; wall-brush; chemical chimney cleaner
deshollinar *vt* to sweep chimneys; clean down walls; *inf* examine closely
deshonestidad *f*, immodesty, shamelessness; indecency
deshonesto *a* shameless, immodest; dissolute, vicious; indecent
deshonor *m*, dishonor; disgrace, insult
deshonra *f*, dishonor
deshonrabuenos *mf inf* slanderer; degenerate
deshonrador (-ra) *a* dishonorable. *n* dishonorer
deshonrar *vt* to dishonor; insult; seduce (women)
deshonroso *a* dishonorable, insulting, indecent
deshora *f*, inconvenient time. **a d.,** *or* **a deshoras,** at an inconvenient time, unseasonably; extempore
deshuesar *vt* to bone, remove the bone (from meat); stone (fruit)
deshumedecer *vt irr* to dry; *vr* become dry. See **conocer**
desidia *f*, negligence; laziness
desidioso *a* negligent; lazy
desierto *a* deserted, uninhabited, solitary. *m*, desert; wilderness
designación *f*, designation; appointment
designar *vt* to plan, intend; designate; appoint
designio *m*, intention, idea
desigual *a* unequal; uneven (ground); rough; arduous, difficult; changeable
desigualar *vt* to make unequal; *vr* prosper
desigualdad *f*, inequality; unevenness, rockiness; *fig* changeability; variability
desilusión *f*, disillusionment; disappointment
desilusionar *vt* to disillusion; *vr* become disillusioned; be undeceived
desinclinar *vt* to dissuade
desinfectante *a* and *m*, disinfectant
desinfectar *vt* to disinfect
desinflar *vt* to deflate
desinterés *m*, disinterestedness
desinteresado *a* disinterested; generous
desinteresarse *vr* to lose interest, grow indifferent
desistencia, *f*, **desistimiento** *m*, desistance, ceasing
desistir *vi* to desist; cease; *law* renounce
desjuntamiento *m*, separation; division
desjuntar(se) *vt* and *vr* to separate; divide
deslavado *a* brazen, impudent
deslavar *vt* to wash superficially; spoil by washing, take away the body of (cloth, etc.)
desleal *a* disloyal, treacherous
deslealtad *f*, disloyalty
desleír *vt irr* to dissolve; dilute. See **reír**
deslenguado *a* shameless, foulmouthed
deslenguar *vt* to remove the tongue; *vr inf* be insolent
desliar *vt* to untie, undo, unloose
desligadura *f*, untying, loosening
desligar *vt* to unfasten, unbind; *fig* solve, unravel; relieve of an obligation; *mus* play staccato; *vr* come unfastened, grow loose. **desligarse de,** to weasel out of, wiggle out of (a promise)
deslindador *m*, one who fixes boundaries or limits
deslindar *vt* to fix the boundaries (of); limit, circumscribe
deslinde *m*, demarcation, boundary
desliz *m*, slipping, slip, slide; skid; indiscretion, slip; peccadillo, trifling fault
deslizadero *m*, slippery place; chute
deslizadizo *a* slippery
deslizar *vt* to slip, slide; skid; *vr* commit an indiscretion; speak or act unwisely; escape, slip away; slip; skid
deslucido *a* fruitless, vain; stupid, clumsy, awkward; discolored; tarnished, dull; unsuccessful
deslucimiento *m*, clumsiness, gracelessness; failure, lack of success
deslucir *vt irr* to fade; discolor, stain; tarnish; spoil; sully the reputation of; *vr* do a thing badly, fail at. See **lucir**
deslumbrador *a* dazzling
deslumbramiento *m*, brilliant light, glare, dazzle; bewilderment, confusion
deslumbrar *vt* to dazzle; confuse, bewilder; *fig* daze (with magnificence)
deslustrar *vt* to dull, dim, tarnish; frost (glass); discredit, sully (reputation)
deslustre *m*, dullness, tarnish; frosting (of glass); disgrace, stigma
deslustroso *a* ugly, unsuitable, unbecoming
desmadejar *vt* to debilitate, enervate
desmalezar *vt, Lat. Am.* to clear the underbrush from; weed
desmán *m*, outrageous behavior; disaster, misfortune
desmandado *a* disobedient
desmandar *vt* to cancel, revoke (orders); withdraw (an offer). *vr* behave badly; stray
desmantelado *a* dismantled, dilapidated
desmantelamiento *m*, dismantling; dilapidation
desmantelar *vt* to dismantle; abandon, forsake
desmaña *f*, lack of dexterity, clumsiness, awkwardness
desmañado *a* clumsy, awkward, unhandy
desmayado *a* pale, faint (of colors); weak (of a voice)
desmayar *vt* to cause to faint; *vi* grow discouraged, lose heart; *vr* swoon, faint
desmayo *m*, depression, discouragement; faint, swoon
desmedido *a* disproportionate; excessive
desmedirse *vr* to misbehave, go too far
desmedrado *a* thin, emaciated; deteriorated, spoiled
desmedrar *vt* to spoil, ruin; *vi* deteriorate; decline
desmedro *m*, impairment; decline, deterioration. **en d. de,** to the detriment of
desmejora *f*, deterioration
desmejorar *vt* to spoil, impair, cause to deteriorate; *vr* deteriorate; *vi* and *vr* decline in health; lose one's beauty
desmelenar *vt* to ruffle or dishevel the hair
desmembración *f*, dismemberment
desmembrar *vt* to dismember; separate, divide
desmemoriarse *vr* to forget, lose one's memory
desmenguar *vt* to reduce, decrease; *fig* diminish
desmentida *f*, action of giving the lie to
desmentir *vt irr* to give the lie to; contradict, deny; lower oneself; behave unworthily; *vi* deviate (from right direction, etc.). See **sentir**
desmenuzar *vt* to crumble, break into small pieces; *fig* examine in detail; *vr* be broken up
desmeollar *vt* to remove the marrow of
desmerecedor *a* unworthy
desmerecer *vt irr* to become undeserving of; *vi* deteriorate; be inferior to. See **conocer**
desmesura *f*, insolence; disproportion; excess
desmesurado *a* disproportionate; excessive, enormous; insolent, uncivil
desmesurar *vt* to disarrange, disorder; *vr* be insolent
desmigajar(se) *vt* and *vr* to crumble
desmigar *vt cul* to make breadcrumbs
desmilitarizar *vt* to demilitarize
desmochar *vt* to lop off the top; pollard (trees)
desmonetización *f*, demonetization; conversion of coin into bullion

desmonetizar *vt* to convert money into bullion; demonetize; *vr* depreciate (shares, etc.)
desmontable *a* movable; sectional
desmontadura *f*, clearing; deforestation; leveling; demounting, dismounting
desmontar *vt* to clear wholly or partly of trees or shrubs; clear up (rubbish); level (ground); dismantle; dismount; uncock (firearms); *vi* and *vr* dismount (from horse, etc.)
desmonte *m*, clearing of trees and shrubs; clearing, cleared ground; timber remaining
desmoralización *f*, demoralization, corruption
desmoralizador *a* demoralizing
desmoralizar *vt* to demoralize, corrupt
desmoronamiento *m*, crumbling; decay, ruin
desmoronar *vt* to destroy, decay; crumble; *vr* crumble away, fall into ruin; decline, decay; wane, fade (power, etc.)
desmovilización *f*, demobilization
desmovilizar *vt* to demobilize
desnacificación *f*, denazification
desnatar *vt* to skim; *fig* take the cream or best
desnaturalización *f*, denaturalization
desnaturalizar *vt* to denaturalize; exile; deform, disfigure, pervert; *vr* give up one's country
desnivel *m*, unevenness; slope, drop
desnivelar(se) *vi* and *vr* to become uneven
desnudar *vt* to undress; *fig* despoil, strip, denude; *vr* undress oneself; deprive oneself
desnudez *f*, nudity; nakedness; bareness; plainness
desnudo *a* nude; ill-clad; bare, naked; clear, patent; *fig* destitute (of grace, etc.). *m*, *art* nude
desnutrición *f*, malnutrition
desobedecer *vt irr* to disobey. See **conocer**
desobediencia *f*, disobedience
desobediente *a* disobedient
desobligar *vt* to free from obligation; offend, hurt
desocupación *f*, lack of occupation; leisure
desocupado *a* idle; vacant, unoccupied
desocupar *vt* to empty; vacate; *vr* give up an employment or occupation
desodorante *a* and *m*, deodorant
desoir *vt irr* to pay no attention, pretend not to hear. See **oir**
desojar *vt* to break the eye of (needles, etc.); *vr* gaze intently
desolación *f*, destruction, desolation; affliction
desolador *a* desolate; grievous
desolar *vt irr* to lay waste, destroy; *vr* grieve, be disconsolate. See **contar**
desoldar *vt* to unsolder; *vr* become unsoldered
desolladero *m*, slaughterhouse
desollado *a inf* impertinent, barefaced. *m*, carcass
desolladura *f*, flaying, skinning; *inf* slander
desollar *vt irr* to flay, skin; harm, discredit. **d. vivo,** *inf* to extort an exorbitant price; slander. See **contar**
desopinado *a* discredited
desopinar *vt* to discredit, defame
desorden *m*, disorder, disarray; confusion; excess
desordenado *a* disordered; vicious; licentious
desordenar *vt* to disorder; confuse; *vr* go beyond the just limits; behave badly; be impertinent
desorganización *f*, disorganization
desorganizador *a* disorganizing
desorganizar *vt* to disorganize; disband
desorientación *f*, disorientation, loss of bearings; lack of method, confusion
desorientar *vt* to disorient; perplex, confuse; *vr* lose one's way; be disoriented
desovar *vi* to spawn
desove *m*, spawning; spawning season
desovillar *vt* to unwind; uncoil; uncurl; explain, clarify
despabiladeras *f pl*, snuffers
despabilado *a* alert, wide-awake; watchful, vigilant
despabiladura *f*, snuff of a candle, lamp, etc.
despabilar *vt* to snuff (a candle); trim (lamps); hasten, expedite; finish quickly; steal, rob; *fig* quicken (intelligence, etc.); *inf* kill; *vr* rouse oneself, wake up
despachador (-ra) *n* dispatcher, sender
despachar *vt* to expedite; dispatch, conclude; forward, send; attend to correspondence; sell; dismiss; *inf* serve in a shop; *inf* kill; *vi* hasten; carry letters to be signed (in offices, etc.); *vr* get rid of
despachero, -a *mf Chile* shopkeeper, storekeeper
despacho *m*, transaction, execution; study; office, room; department; booking-office; dispatch, shipment; expedient; commission, warrant; dispatch (diplomatic); telegram; telephone message. **d. particular,** private office
despachurrar *vt inf* to crush, squash; recount in a muddled fashion; *fig* squash flat, confound
despacio *adv* slowly, little by little; deliberately, leisurely. *interj* Careful! Gently now!
despacito *adv inf* very slowly
despalmador *m*, dockyard
despampanar *vt agr* to prune vines; *inf* amaze, stun, astound; *vi inf* relieve one's feelings; *vr inf* receive a serious injury (through falling)
desparpajar *vt* to spoil; *vi inf* chatter
desparpajo *m*, *inf* loquaciousness, pertness; disorder, muddle
desparramar *vt* to disperse, scatter; squander, waste (money, etc.); *vr* amuse oneself; be dissipated
despavorido *a* terrified, panicstricken
despechar *vt* to anger; make despair; *inf* wean; *vr* be angry; be in despair
despecho *m*, rancor, malice; despair. **a d. de,** in spite of
despechugar *vt* to cut off the breast (fowls); *vr inf* show the bosom
despectivo *a* contemptuous, depreciatory
despedazar *vt* to cut or break into pieces; *fig* break (heart, etc.)
despedida *f*, dismissal, discharge; seeing off (a visitor, etc.); farewell, good-by
despedir *vt irr* to throw out, emit, cast up; dismiss, discharge; see off (on a journey or after a visit); banish (from the mind); get rid of; *vr* say good-by; leave (employment). See **pedir**
despedregar *vt* to clear of stones
despegadamente *adv* uninterestedly, unconcernedly, indifferently
despegado *a inf* indifferent, unconcerned, cold
despegar *vt* to unstick; unglue; separate, detach; *vr* become estranged; come apart or unstuck; *vi aer* take off. **sin d. los labios,** without saying a word
despegue *m*, *aer* take-off
despeinar *vt* to disarrange the hair; undo the coiffure
despejado *a* lively, sprightly; logical, clear-cut; cloudless; spacious, unobstructed, clear
despejar *vt* to clear, free of obstacles; **d. el camino de,** to clear the way for; *fig* elucidate, solve; *math* find the value of; *vr* smarten up, grow gay; amuse oneself; clear up (weather, sky, etc.); improve (a patient)
despejo *m*, freeing of obstacles; smartness, gaiety; grace, elegance; perkiness; clear-sightedness, intelligence
despeluzar *vt* to disorder the hair; cause the hair to stand on end; horrify; *vr* stand on end (hair); be horrified or terrified
despeluznante *a* hair-raising, terrifying
despellejar *vt* to flay, skin; slander
despendedor (-ra) *n* spendthrift, waster
despender *vt* to spend; waste
despensa *f*, larder, pantry; store (of food); *naut* steward's room; stewardship
despensero (-ra) *n* steward; caterer; victualler; *naut* steward
despeñadero *m*, precipice, crag; dangerous undertaking, risk. *a* steep, precipitous
despeñar *vt* to precipitate, fling down from a height,

hurl down; *vr* fling oneself headlong; throw oneself into (vices, etc.)
despeño *m*, precipitation; headlong fall; *fig* collapse, ruin
despepitar *vt* to remove seeds or pips; *vr* vociferate; act wildly; *inf* desire, long (for)
desperdiciador (**-ra**) *a* squandering, wasting. *n* squanderer
desperdiciar *vt* to squander; *fig* misspend, waste
desperdicio *m*, waste; remains, leftovers (gen. *pl*)
desperdigar *vt* to separate, sever; scatter
desperecerse *vr irr* to crave, yearn (for). See **conocer**
desperezarse *vr* to stretch oneself
desperfecto *m*, imperfection, flaw; slight deterioration
despernado *a* weary, footsore
despertador (**-ra**) *a* awakening. *n* awakener. *m*, alarm clock; incentive, stimulus
despertar *vt irr* to awaken; bring to mind, recall; incite, stimulate; *vi* waken; *fig* wake up, become more intelligent. See **acertar**
despiadado *a* cruel, merciless
despicar *vt* to satisfy, content; *vr* revenge oneself
despierto *a* wide-awake, clever
despilfarrado *a* ragged, shabby; wasteful; spendthrift
despilfarrar *vt* to squander, waste
despilfarro *m*, slovenliness; waste, extravagance; mismanagement, maladministration
despintar *vt* to paint out; wash off the paint; efface, blot out; disfigure, deform; *vi* be unlike or unworthy (of); *vr* fade (colors); forget
despiojar *vt* to remove lice, delouse; *inf* rescue from misery
despique *m*, vengeance, revenge
despistar *vt* to throw off the scent; mislead
desplacer *vt irr* to displease. *m*, disgust, displeasure, sorrow. See **placer**
desplantar(**se**) *vt* and *vr* to deviate from the vertical
desplazamiento *m*, *naut* displacement
desplegadura *f*, unfolding
desplegar *vt irr* to unfold; spread open; *fig* reveal, disclose, explain; evince, display; *mil* deploy troops; *vr* unfold, open (flowers, etc.); *mil* deploy. See **cegar**
despliegue *m*, unfolding; spreading out; evincing, demonstration; *mil* deployment
desplomar *vt* to put out of the straight, cause to lean (walls, buildings); *vr* lean, tilt (buildings); topple, fall down (walls, etc.); collapse (people); be ruined
desplome *m*, collapse
desplomo *m*, tilt, cant, deviation from vertical
desplumar *vt* to remove feathers, pluck; rob, despoil
despoblación *f*, depopulation. **d. forestal,** deforestation
despoblado *m*, wilderness; deserted place
despoblar *vt* to depopulate; despoil, rob; *vr* become depopulated
despojador (**-ra**) *a* robbing, despoiling. *n* despoiler
despojar *vt* to plunder, despoil; dispossess; *vr* (*with de*) remove (garments, etc.); relinquish, give up
despojo *m*, pillaging, spoliation; booty, plunder; butcher's offal; *pl* remains, leavings; debris, rubble; corpse
despolvorear *vt* to remove dust; *fig* shake off
desposado *a* recently married; fettered, handcuffed. **los desposados,** the newlyweds
desposar *vt* to perform the marriage ceremony; *vr* become betrothed; marry
desposeer *vt* to dispossess; *vr* renounce one's possessions. See **creer**
desposeimiento *m*, dispossession
desposorio *m*, betrothal, promise of marriage; (gen. *pl*) wedding, marriage
déspota *m*, despot, tyrant
despótico *a* tyrannical
despotismo *m*, despotism
despotricarse *vr* to rave (against), rail (against)
despreciable *a* worthless, contemptible
despreciar *vt* to scorn, despise; *vr* despise oneself
despreciativo *a* contemptuous, scornful
desprecio *m*, contempt, scorn
desprender *vt* to loosen, remove, unfix; give off (gases, etc.); *vr* work loose, give way; deduce, infer; give away, deprive oneself (of)
desprendido *a* disinterested; generous
desprendimiento *m*, loosening; removal, separation; emission; indifference, lack of interest; generosity; impartiality
despreocupación *f*, fair mindedness, impartiality; lack of interest
despreocupado *a* unprejudiced, broadminded; indifferent, uninterested
despreocuparse *vr* to shake off prejudice; (*with de*) pay no attention to; set aside
desprestigiar *vt* to discredit; *vr* lose prestige; lose caste
desprestigio *m*, loss of prestige, discredit
desprevenido *a* unprepared, improvident
desproporción *f*, disproportion
desproporcionado *a* disproportionate; out of proportion
despropósito *m*, nonsense, absurdity
desproveer *vt irr* to deprive of necessities. See **creer**
despueble *m*, depopulation
después *adv* afterwards, after, next (of time and place) (e.g. **Vendrá d. de Pascua,** He will come after Easter. **Zaragoza viene d. de Madrid,** Saragossa comes after Madrid)
despuntar *vt* to blunt the point; *naut* double, sail round; *vi* show green, sprout; appear (the dawn); grow clever; *fig* stand out, excel
desquiciamiento *m*, unhinging; disconnecting; *fig* upsetting, throwing out of gear; downfall, fall from favor
desquiciar *vt* to unhinge; disconnect; *fig* throw out of gear, upset; banish from favor; *vr* become unhinged; *fig* be disordered; upset
desquitar(**se**) *vt* and *vr* to retrieve a loss; take revenge, retaliate
desquite *m*, compensation; revenge
desrielar *vt*, *Lat. Am.* to derail
destacamento *m*, *mil* detachment
destacar *vt mil* to detach; *vr* excel; be prominent; be conspicuous; *art* stand out
destajador *m*, smith's hammer
destajar *vt* to cut (cards); set forth conditions, stipulate, contract; *Lat. Am.* cut up
destajista *mf* pieceworker; jobber (worker)
destajo *m*, piecework; job. **a d.,** quickly and diligently. *inf* **hablar a d.,** to chatter, talk too much
destapar *vt* to remove the cover or lid; reveal, uncover; *vr* be uncovered; reveal oneself. **no destaparse,** to keep quiet, be mum
destartalado *a* tumble-down, rickety; poverty-stricken
destechado *a* roofless
destejar *vt* to remove tiles or slates; leave unprotected
destejer *vt* to unweave, unravel; *fig* undo, spoil
destello *m*, gleam, sparkle, brilliance; flash, beam, ray; *fig* gleam (of talent)
destemplado *a* out of tune; inharmonious; intemperate; *art* inharmonious; *inf* out of sorts, indisposed
destemplanza *f*, inclemency, rigor (weather); intemperance, excess, abuse; *inf* indisposition; lack of moderation (actions, speech)
destemplar *vt* to disturb, upset, alter; *mus* put out of tune; put to confusion; *vr* be unwell; *fig* go too far, behave badly; lose temper (metals)
destemple *m*, *mus* being out of tune; *med* indisposition; uncertainty (weather); lack of temper (metals); disturbance, disorder; intemperance, excess, confusion
desternillarse de risa to shake with laughter
desterrado (**-da**) *a* exiled. *n* exile

desterrar *vt irr* to exile; shake off the soil; *fig* discard, lay aside; extirpate (an error). See **recomendar**
destetar *vt* to wean
destete *m,* weaning
destiempo, a *adv* untimely, inopportunely
destierro *m,* banishment, exile; place of exile; remote place
destilación *f,* distillation
destilador (-ra) *n* distiller. *m,* still
destilar *vt* to distil; filter; *vi* to drip
destilatorio *a* distilling. *m,* distillery; still
destilería *f,* distillery
destinar *vt* to destine; appoint; assign
destino *m,* fate, destiny; post, appointment; destination. **con d. a,** going to, bound for
destitución *f,* destitution; discharge, dismissal
destituir *vt irr* (*with de*) to dismiss or discharge from (employment); deprive of. See **huir**
destorcer *vt irr* to untwist; straighten out; *vr naut* drift. See **torcer**
destornillado *a* reckless; *fig inf* with a screw loose
destornillador *m,* screwdriver
destornillamiento *m,* unscrewing
destornillar *vt* to unscrew; *vr* act rashly
destrenzar *vt* to unplait. **destrenzarse las cintas,** to unlace one's shoes
destreza *f,* dexterity; agility
destrón *m,* blind person's guide
destronamiento *m,* dethronement
destronar *vt* to dethrone, depose; oust
destroncamiento *m,* detruncation
destroncar *vt* to lop, detruncate (trees); dislocate, disjoint; mutilate; *fig* ruin, seriously harm; tire out; *Lat. Am.* uproot *vr* be exhausted or tired
destrozar *vt* to destroy; break in pieces, shatter; *mil* wipe out, annihilate; squander, dissipate
destrozo *m,* destruction, ruin; shattering; *mil* rout; dissipation, waste
destrozón *a* hard on wearing apparel, shoes, etc.
destrucción *f,* destruction; ruin, irreparable loss
destructible *a* destructible
destructivo *a* destructive
destructor (-ra) *a* destructive. *n* destroyer. *m, nav* destroyer
destruible *a* destructible
destruir *vt irr* to destroy, ruin, annihilate; frustrate, blast, disappoint; deprive of means of subsistence; squander, waste; *vr math* cancel. See **huir**
desuello *m,* flaying, skinning; forwardness, impertinence; extortion, fleecing. *fig inf* **¡Es un d.!** It's highway robbery!
desunión *f,* disunion, separation; *fig* discord, disharmony
desunir *vt* to disunite, separate; *fig* cause discord or disharmony
desusarse *vr* to fall into disuse, become obsolete
desuso *m,* disuse
desvaído *a* gaunt, lanky; pale, faded, dull (of colors)
desvainar *vt* to shell (peas, beans)
desvalido *a* unprotected, helpless
desvalijar *vt* to rifle (a suitcase, etc.); swindle
desvalimiento *m,* defenselessness, lack of protection; lack of favor; desertion, abandonment
desvalorización *f,* devaluation
desván *m,* garret
desvanecer *vt irr* to cause to disappear; disintegrate; make vain; remove; *vr* evaporate; faint, swoon; grow vain or conceited. See **conocer**
desvanecimiento *m,* faintness, loss of consciousness; vanity, conceit
desvarar *vt* to slip, slide; *naut* refloat
desvariar *vi* to be delirious; rave, talk wildly
desvarío *m,* foolish action, absurdity; delirium; monstrosity; whim, caprice
desvedar *vt* to raise a ban or prohibition
desvelar *vt* to keep awake; *vr* be sleepless; (*with por*) take great care over
desvelo *m,* sleeplessness, vigil; care, attention, vigilance; anxiety. **con d.,** watchfully
desvencijar *vt* to loosen, disconnect, disjoint; *vr* work loose, become disjointed
desventaja *f,* disadvantage. **estar en d.,** to be at a disadvantage
desventajoso *a* disadvantageous
desventura *f,* misfortune
desventurado *a* unfortunate; timid, faint-hearted; miserly
desvergonzado *a* shameless, brazen, impudent
desvergonzarse *vr irr* to be brazen, be impudent. See **avergonzar**
desvergüenza *f,* insolence; shamelessness
desvestir(se) *vt* and *vr irr* to undress. See **pedir**
desviación *f,* deviation, deflection
desviadero *m,* diversion; *rw* siding
desviar *vt* to divert, deflect; dissuade
desvío *m,* deviation; indifference, coldness; repugnance
desvirgar *vt* to deflower
desvirtuar *vt* to decrease in strength or merit
desvivirse *vr* (*with por*) to adore, love dearly; yearn for, be dying to; do one's best to please, (e.g. **Juan se desvive por servirme,** John does his best to help me)
detallar *vt* to tell in detail; relate
detalle *m,* detailed account; detail, particular
detallismo *m,* meticulous attention to details
detective *mf* detective
detector *m,* detector; *rad* catwhisker
detención *f,* stop, halt; delay; prolixity; arrest, detention. **con d.,** carefully, meticulously
detener *vt irr* to detain, stop; arrest; retain, keep; *vr* go slowly; tarry; halt, stop; (*with en*) pause over, stop at. See **tener**
detenido *a* timid, irresolute; miserable, mean
deterioración *f,* deterioration
deteriorar(se) *vt* and *vr* to deteriorate
determinación *f,* determination; daring; decision
determinado *a* resolute, determined
determinar *vt* to determine, limit; discern, distinguish; specify, appoint; decide, resolve; *law* define, judge; *vr* make up one's mind
determinativo *a* determining
determinismo *m,* determinism
determinista *mf* determinist. *a* deterministic
detersorio *a* and *m,* detergent
detestable *a* detestable
detestación *f,* detestation
detestar *vt* to abominate, detest
detonación *f,* detonation
detonador *m,* detonator
detonar *vi* to detonate
detractor (-ra) *a* slandering *n* detractor, slanderer
detraer *vt irr* to detract, take away; separate; slander. See **traer**
detrás *adv* behind, after (place). **por d.,** in the rear; *fig* behind one's back
detrimento *m,* detriment; moral harm. **en d. de,** to the detriment of
deuda *f,* debt; fault, offence; sin. **d. exterior,** foreign debt. **estar en d. con,** to be indebted to. **Perdónanos nuestras deudas,** Forgive us our trespasses
deudo *m,* relative, kinsman; kinship, relationship
deudor (-ra) *a* indebted. *n* debtor. **d. hipotecario,** mortgagor
devanadera *f,* bobbin, reel, spool; winder (machine)
devanador (-ra) *n* winder (person). *m,* spool, bobbin
devanar *vt* to reel, wind. *inf* **devanarse los sesos,** to rack one's brains
devanear *vi* to rave, talk nonsense

devaneo *m,* delirium; foolishness, nonsense; dissipation; love affair
devastación *f,* devastation
devastar *vt* to devastate, lay waste; *fig* destroy, ruin
develador *m,* betrayer
devengar *vt* to have a right to, earn (salary, interest, etc.)
devoción *f,* piety; affection, love; pious custom; prayer
devocionario *m,* prayer book
devolución *f,* restitution, return; its devolution
devolutivo *a law* returnable
devolver *vt irr* to restore to original state; return, give back; repay; **devolverse** *vr Lat. Am.* to come back, go back, return. See **resolver**
devorador (-ra) *a* devouring. *n* devourer
devorar *vt* to devour; destroy, consume
devoto (-ta) *a* devout, pious; devoted, fond. *n* devotee. *m,* object of devotion
día *m,* day; daylight; *pl* name or saint's day; birthday (e.g. **Hoy son los días de María,** This is Mary's saint's day (or birthday)). **d. de Año Nuevo,** New Year's Day. **d. de asueto,** day off. **d. de ayuno** or **de vigilia,** fast day. **d. del cura,** *humorous* wedding day. **d. del juicio,** Day of Judgment. **d. de los difuntos,** All Souls' Day. **d. de recibo,** at home day. **d. de Reyes,** Epiphany (when Spanish children receive their Christmas presents). **d. de trabajo** or **d. laborable,** working day. **d. por medio,** every other day. **días caniculares,** dog days. **d. por d.,** day by day. **al d.,** up to date; per day. **al otro d.,** next day. **¡Buenos días!** Good morning! Good day! **de d.,** by day. **de d. en d.,** from day to day. **de un d. a otro,** any time now, very soon. **el d. de mañana,** tomorrow, the near future. **un d. sí y otro no,** every other day. **vivir al d.,** to live up to one's income
diabético *a* diabetic
diablillo *m, dim* devilkin, imp; *inf* madcap
diablo *m,* devil; Satan; *fig* fiend. *inf* **d. cojuelo,** mischievous devil; *fig inf* imp. *inf* **Anda el d. suelto,** The Devil's abroad, there's trouble. *inf* **tener el d. en el cuerpo,** to be as clever as the Devil; be mischievous
diablura *f,* mischief, prank; devilry
diabólico *a* diabolical, devilish; *inf* fiendish, iniquitous
diaconisa *f,* deaconess
diácono *m,* deacon
diadema *f,* diadem; crown; tiara
diafanidad *f,* transparency
diáfano *a* transparent, diaphanous
diafragma *m, anat mech* diaphragm; sound-box (of a phonograph)
diagnosticar *vt med* to diagnose
diagnóstico *a* diagnostic. *m,* diagnosis. **d. precoz,** early diagnosis
diagonal *a* diagonal; oblique
diagrama *m,* diagram
diagramación *f,* layout (of a publication)
dialectal *a* dialect
dialéctica *f,* dialectic
dialéctico *a* dialectic. *m,* logician
dialecto *m,* dialect
dialogar *vi* to hold dialogue, converse; *vt* write dialogue
diálogo *m,* dialogue
diamante *m,* diamond; miner's lamp; glass-cutting diamond. **d. bruto,** rough diamond
diamantífero *a* diamond-bearing
diamantino *a* diamantine; *poet* adamant
diamantista *mf* diamond-cutter; diamond merchant
diámetro *m,* diameter
diana *f, mil* reveille; bull's-eye (of a target); the moon
¡diantre! *interj inf* the deuce!
diapasón *m, mus* tuning fork; diapason; neck (of violins, etc.). **d. normal,** tuning fork. **d. vocal,** pitch-pipe
diapositiva *f, phot* diapositive; (lantern) slide
diario *a* daily. *m,* diary; daily paper; daily expenses. **d. de navegación,** ship's log. **d. de viaje,** travel diary, trip journal
diarismo *m, Lat. Am.* journalism
diarista *mf* journalist, diarist
diarrea *f,* diarrhea
diatónico *a mus* diatonic
diatriba *f,* diatribe
diávolo *m,* diabolo (game)
dibujante *m,* sketcher; draftsman; designer
dibujar *vt art* to draw; describe, depict; *vr* appear, be revealed; be outlined, stand out
dibujo *m,* drawing; sketch, design, pattern; depiction, description. **d. a la pluma,** pen-and-ink drawing. **d. a pulso,** freehand drawing. **d. del natural,** drawing from life
dicción *f,* word; diction, language, style
diccionario *m,* dictionary
díceres *m pl WH* news
diciembre *m,* December
dictado *m,* title of honor; dictation; *pl* promptings (of heart, etc.). **escribir al d.,** to write to dictation
dictador *m,* dictator
dictadura *f,* dictatorship
dictamen *m,* judgment, opinion
dictaminar *vi* to give judgment or opinion
dictar *vt* to dictate; suggest, inspire; *Lat. Am.* give (a lecture). **dictar fallo,** to hand down a decision, render judgment
dictatorial, dictatorio *a* dictatorial
dicterio *m,* taunt, insult
dicha *f,* happiness; good fortune. **por d.,** by chance; fortunately
dicharacho *m, inf* vulgar expression, slangy expression
dicho *m,* saying, phrase, expression; witty remark; *law* declaration; *inf* insult. *a* said, aforementioned. *past part* **decir,** "said." **D. y hecho,** No sooner said than done. **Del d. al hecho hay muy gran trecho,** There's many a slip 'twixt the cup and the lip. **Lo d. d.,** The agreement stands
dichoso *a* happy; lucky; *inf* blessed, wretched, darn
didáctica *f,* didactics
didáctico *a* didactic
diecinueve *a* and *m,* nineteen
diecinuevavo *a* and *m,* nineteenth
dieciochavo *a* and *m,* eighteenth
dieciocheno *a* See **décimoctavo**
dieciocho *a* and *m,* eighteen
dieciséis *a* and *m,* sixteen
dieciseisavo *a* and *m,* sixteenth
dieciseiseno *a* See **décimosexto**
diecisiete *a* and *m,* seventeen
diecisieteavo *a* and *m,* seventeenth
diente *m,* tooth; tooth (of saw, etc.); tusk; cog (of wheel); prong (of fork); tongue (of a buckle). **d. de leche,** milk-tooth. *bot* **d. de león,** dandelion. **d. de perro,** *sew* feather-stitch. *inf* **dar d. con d.,** to chatter (teeth). *fig inf* **enseñar** (*or* **mostrar**) **los dientes,** to show one's teeth; threaten. *inf* **estar a d.,** to be famished. **hablar entre dientes,** to mutter; fume, grumble. *inf* **tener buen d.,** to have a good appetite. **traer a uno entre dientes,** to loathe someone; speak scandal of
Diepa Dieppe
diestra *f,* right hand; protection
diestro *a* right (hand); skilful, dextrous; shrewd; astute, cunning; favorable, happy. *m,* expert fencer; bullfighter; halter; bridle
dieta *f, med* diet; *inf* fast, abstinence; legislative assembly; travel allowance (gen. *pl*); day's journey of ten leagues; daily fee (gen. *pl*)
dietario *m,* household accounts' book
dietética *f,* dietetics
dietético *a* dietetic
dietista *mf* dietician
diez *a* ten; tenth. *m,* ten; decade of rosary

diezmar *vt* to tithe; decimate; punish every tenth person
diezmero (-ra) *n* tax-gatherer
diezmesino *a* ten months old
diezmillo *m, Mexico* sirloin
diezmo *m,* ten per cent tax; tithe
difamación *f,* defamation, libel
difamador (-ra) *a* libeling. *n* libeler
difamar *vt* to libel; denigrate
difamatorio *a* libelous, defamatory
diferencia *f,* unlikeness, dissimilarity; *math* difference; dissension, disagreement. **a d. de,** unlike; in contrast to
diferenciación *f,* differentiation. **d. del trabajo,** division of labor
diferencial *a* differential
diferenciar *vt* to differentiate; change the function (of); *vi* dissent, disagree; *vr* be different, differ; distinguish oneself
diferente *a* different, various
diferir *vt irr* to delay, retard; postpone; suspend, interrupt; *vi* be different. See **discernir**
difícil *a* difficult
dificultad *f,* difficulty; impediment, obstacle; objection
dificultar *vt* to raise difficulties; put obstacles in the way; *vi* think difficult (of achievements)
dificultoso *a* difficult; *inf* ugly (face, figure, etc.)
difidencia *f,* mistrust; lack of faith, doubt
difidente *a* mistrustful
difracción *f,* diffraction
difractar *vt* to diffract
difteria *f,* diphtheria
difundir *vt* to diffuse (fluids); spread, publish, divulge; *rad* broadcast
difunto (-ta) *a* and *n* deceased. *m,* corpse
difusión *f,* diffusion; prolixity; *rad* broadcasting
difusivo *a* diffusive
difuso *a* widespread, diffuse; prolix, wordy
digerible *a* digestible
digerir *vt irr* to digest; bear patiently; consider carefully; *chem* digest. See **sentir**
digestible *a* easily digested
digestivo *a* digestive
digesto *m, law* digest
digitación *f, mus* fingering
digital *a* digital. *f, bot* foxglove, digitalis
dígito *a* digital. *m,* (*ast math*) digit
dignación *f,* condescension
dignarse *vr* to deign, condescend
dignatario *m,* dignitary
dignidad *f,* dignity, stateliness; serenity, loftiness; high office or rank; high repute, honor; *ecc* dignitary
dignificar *vt* to dignify
digno *a* worthy, deserving; upright, honorable; fitting, suitable, appropriate
digresión *f,* digression
dije *m,* charm; trinket, any small piece of jewelry; *inf* person of excellent qualities, jewel
dilacerar *vt* to lacerate, tear flesh; *fig* discredit
dilación *f,* delay
dilapidación *f,* waste, dissipation, squandering
dilapidar *vt* to waste, squander
dilatación *f,* expansion; enlargement, widening; prolongation; *surg* dilatation; respite (in trouble)
dilatador *a* dilating. *m, surg* dilater
dilatar *vt* to dilate, enlarge; expand; delay, postpone; spread, publish abroad; prolong; *vr* expand; be prolix, spread oneself; *Lat. Am.* to be slow, take a long time
dilatorio *a* procrastinating, dilatory
dilección *f,* affection, love
dilema *m,* dilemma
diletantismo *m,* dilettantism
diligencia *f,* care, conscientiousness, industry; haste, briskness; diligence (coach); *inf* business, occupation. **hacer sus diligencias,** to try one's best
diligenciar *vt* to set on foot, put into motion
diligente *a* diligent, conscientious, industrious; speedy, prompt
dilucidación *f,* elucidation, clarification
dilucidar *vt* to elucidate, clarify
dilución *f,* dilution
diluir *vt irr* to dilute. See **huir**
diluviar *vi* to teem with rain
diluvio *m,* flood, inundation; *inf* very heavy rain, deluge; overabundance
dimanación *f,* emanation, source
dimanar *vi* (*with de*) to rise in (rivers); proceed from, originate in
dimensión *f,* dimension; size, extent
dimes y diretes *m pl, inf* back-chat
diminutivo *a* diminutive; diminishing; *gram* diminutive
diminuto *a* defective, incomplete; minute, very small
dimisión *f,* resignation (of office, etc.)
dimisorias *f pl, ecc* letter dimissory. *inf* **dar d. a uno,** to give a person his marching orders, dismiss
dimitente *a* resigning; retiring. *mf* resigner (of a post)
dimitir *vt* to resign (office, post, etc.)
Dinamarca Denmark
dinamarqués (-esa) *a* Danish. *n* Dane
dinámica *f,* dynamics
dinámico *a* dynamic
dinamita *f,* dynamite
dinamo *f,* dynamo
dinasta *mf* dynast
dinastía *f,* dynasty
dinástico *a* dynastic
dineral *m,* large amount of money, fortune
dinero *m,* money; Peruvian coin; wealth, fortune; currency. **d. contante, d. junto,** ready cash, **Poderoso caballero es Don D.,** Money talks
dinosauro *m,* dinosaur
dintel *m,* lintel; *Lat. Am.* threshold
diocesano *a* diocesan
diocesis *f,* diocese
Dios *m,* God; deity. **¡D. le guarde!** God keep you! **¡D. lo quiera!** God grant it! **D. mediante,** God willing (D.V.). **¡D. mío!** Good gracious! **De menos nos hizo D.,** Nothing is impossible, Never say die. *inf* **haber** (*or* **armarse**) **la de D. es Cristo,** to be the deuce of a row. **¡No lo quiera D.!** God forbid! **¡Plegue a D.!** Please God! **¡Por D.!** For goodness sake! Heavens! **¡Válgame D.!** Bless me! **¡Vaya Vd. con D.!** Goodbye! Off with you! Depart! **¡Vive D.!** By God!
diosa *f,* goddess
diploma *m,* license, bull; diploma. **d. de suficiencia,** general diploma
diplomacia *f,* diplomacy; tactfulness; *inf* astuteness
diplomarse *vr, Lat. Am.* to get one's degree, receive one's degree
diplomático *a* diplomatic; tactful; *inf* astute. *m,* diplomat. **cuerpo d.,** diplomatic corps
dipsomanía *f,* dipsomania
diptongo *m,* diphthong
diputación *f,* deputation; mission
diputado (-da) *n* deputy, delegate. **d. a Cortes,** member of the Spanish Parliament, congressman
diputar *vt* to appoint, depute; delegate; empower
dique *m,* dike; dam; dry dock; *fig* bulwark, check; **d. flotante,** floating dock
dirección *f,* direction; management, control, guidance; directorate; instruction; information; order, wish, command; editorial board; directorship, managership; (postal) address; managerial office. **d. cablegráfica,** cable address. **d. particular,** home address
directiva *f,* board, governing body
directivo *a* directive, control, ling, guiding, managing
directo *a* direct; straight
director (-ra) *a* directing, controlling. *n* director; manager; principal, head (schools, etc.); editor. **d. del ceremonial,** chief of protocol. **d. de escena,**

stagemanager. **d. espiritual,** *ecc* father confessor. **d. gerente,** managing director
directorio *a* directory, advising. *m,* directory; directorate, board of directors
dirigible *m,* airship
dirigir *vt* to direct; regulate; govern; supervise; guide; *mus* conduct; address (an envelope, etc.); keep (a shop, etc.); edit; put (a question); point (a gun); cast (a glance); *vr* go; wend one's way. **d. la palabra (a),** to speak to, address. **d. la vista a,** to look towards, look in the direction of, turn towards, turn in the direction of. **dirigirse a,** to go towards; make one's way to
dirimir *vt* to annul, make void; break, dissolve; settle (disputes, etc.)
discernimiento *m,* discernment; judgment; discrimination
discernir *vt irr* to discern, distinguish. *Pres. Ind.* **discierno, disciernes, discierne, disciernen.** *Pres. Subjunc.* **discierna, disciernas, discierna, disciernan**
disciplina *f,* discipline; system, philosophy, education; submission, obedience; subject (arts or science); *pl* scourge
disciplinante *a* disciplinary. *m,* scourge
disciplinar *vt* to train; educate; scourge, beat; discipline; *vr* scourge oneself
disciplinario *a* disciplinary
discipulado *m,* pupilship, studentship; education, teaching; discipleship; body of pupils (of a school, etc.)
discípulo (-la) *n* pupil, student; disciple, follower
disco *m,* discus; disk; phonograph record; *ast* disk. **d. de señales,** railway signal. **d. giratorio,** turntable (of a phonograph)
discóbolo *m,* discus thrower
díscolo *a* willful, unmanageable
disconformidad *f,* disagreement; disconformity
discontinuo *a* intermittent, discontinuous
discordancia *f,* discord, disagreement
discordar *vi* to be discordant; disagree; *mus* be out of tune
discorde *a* discordant; *mus* dissonant
discordia *f,* discord, disagreement
discreción *f,* discretion; circumspection; prudence, good sense; shrewdness; pithy or clever saying. **a d.,** at discretion; at will; voluntarily. *mil* **darse** (*or* **entregarse**) **a d.,** to surrender unconditionally
discrecional *a* optional, voluntary
discrepancia *f,* discrepancy; disagreement
discrepar *vi* to be discrepant; differ; disagree
discreto *a* discreet; ingenious, witty
disculpa *f,* excuse
disculpabilidad *f,* pardonableness
disculpable *a* excusable
disculpar *vt* to excuse; forgive, pardon; *vr* apologize; excuse oneself
discurrir *vi* to wander, roam; flow, run (rivers, etc.); (*with en*) consider, think about; (*with sobre*) discourse on; *vt* invent; conjecture
discursivo *a* discursive; thoughtful, reflective
discurso *m,* reasoning power; oration, discourse; consideration, reflection; speech, conversation; dissertation. **d. aceptatorio,** acceptance speech
discusión *f,* discussion
discutible *a* debatable; disputable
discutir *vt* to discuss, debate, consider
disecar *vt anat* to dissect; stuff animals; mount plants
disección *f,* dissection
disector *m,* dissector, anatomist
diseminación *f,* dissemination
diseminar *vt* to disseminate; spread
disensión *f,* dissension
disentería *f,* dysentery
disentimiento *m,* dissent
disentir *vi irr* to dissent; disagree. See **sentir**
diseñador *m,* delineator, drawer
diseñar *vt* to outline, sketch
diseño *m,* outline, sketch; plan; description
disertación *f,* dissertation
disertar *vi* (*with sobre*) to discourse on, discuss, treat of
diserto *a* eloquent
disfavor *m,* disfavor, discourtesy, slight
disforme *a* deformed; ugly; enormous
disfraz *m,* disguise; mask; fancy dress; pretence
disfrazar *vt* to disguise; dissemble, misrepresent; *vr* disguise oneself; wear fancy dress
disfrutar *vt* to enjoy (health, comfort, friendship, etc.); reap the benefit of; *vi* take pleasure in, enjoy
disfrute *m,* enjoyment, use, benefit
disgregación *f,* separation, disjunction
disgregar *vt* to separate, disjoin
disgustado *a* annoyed; discontented, dissatisfied; melancholy, depressed
disgustar *vt* to displease, dissatisfy; annoy; *fig* depress; *vr* quarrel, fall out. **Me disgusta la idea de marcharme,** I don't like the idea of going away
disgusto *m,* displeasure, dissatisfaction; discontent; annoyance; affliction, sorrow, trouble; quarrel; boredom; repugnance
disidente *a* dissenting. *mf* dissenter, nonconformist
disidir *vi* to dissent
disímil *a* dissimilar, different, unlike
disimulación *f,* dissimulation, pretence
disimulado *a* feigned, pretended
disimular *vt* to dissemble; pretend, feign; put up with, tolerate; misrepresent, misinterpret
disimulo *m,* pretence, dissimulation; tolerance, patience
disipación *f,* dispersion; dissipation, frivolity; immorality
disipado *a* spendthrift; dissipated, frivolous
disipar *vt* to disperse; squander; *vr* evaporate; vanish, fade, disappear
dislate *m,* absurdity, nonsense
dislocación *f,* dislocation
dislocar *vt* to dislocate; *vr* dislocate; sprain
disminución *f,* diminution. **ir (una cosa) en d.,** to diminish, decrease; taper, grow to a point
disminuido físico *m,* physically impaired person, physically handicapped person
disminuir *vt* and *vi irr* to diminish, decrease. See **huir**
disociación *f,* dissociation. **d. nuclear,** nuclear fission
disociar *vt* to dissociate, separate; *chem* dissociate
disoluble *a* dissoluble
disolución *f,* dissolution; immorality, laxity; disintegration; loosening, relaxation
disolutivo *a* dissolvent, solvent
disoluto *a* dissolute, vicious
disolvente *m,* dissolvent, solvent
disolver *vt irr* to loosen, undo; *chem* dissolve; separate, disintegrate; annul. See **resolver**
disonancia *f,* dissonance; disagreement; *mus* dissonant
disonante *a* dissonant; discordant, inharmonious
disonar *vi irr* to be inharmonious; disagree. See **sonar**
dísono *a* dissonant
dispar *a* unequal; unlike, different
disparadero *m,* trigger of a firearm
disparador *m,* shooter, firer; trigger (of firearms); ratchet (of watch); *a, Mexico* lavish
disparar *vt* to shoot, fire; throw or discharge with violence; *vr* run precipitately; rush (towards); bolt (horses); race (of a machine); explode, go off; *inf* go too far, misbehave; *Mexico* spend lavishly
disparatado *a* foolish; absurd, unreasonable
disparatar *vi* to act or speak foolishly
disparate *m,* foolishness, nonsense
disparidad *f,* disparity, dissimilarity
disparo *m,* shooting; explosion; racing (of an engine); discharge; foolishness
dispendio *m,* squandering, extravagance
dispendioso *a* costly, expensive
dispensa *f,* dispensation; privilege
dispensable *a* dispensable; excusable
dispensación *f,* dispensation; exemption

dispensar *vt* to grant, concede, distribute; exempt; excuse, forgive
dispensario *m*, dispensary
dispepsia *f*, dyspepsia
dispéptico (-ca) *a* and *n* dyspeptic
dispersar *vt* to disperse, scatter, separate; *mil* rout
dispersión *f*, dispersion
disperso *a* dispersed, scattered; *mil* separated from regiment
displicencia *f*, disagreeableness, coldness; hesitation, lack of enthusiasm
displicente *a* unpleasant, disagreeable; difficult, peevish
disponer *vt irr* to arrange, dispose; direct, order; decide; prepare, get ready; *vi* (*with de*) dispose of, make free with; possess; have at one's disposal; *vr* prepare oneself to die; make one's will; get ready. See **poner**
disponible *a* disposable; available
disposición *f*, arrangement; order, instruction; decision; preparation; aptitude, talent; disposal; condition of health; temperament; grace of bearing; promptitude, competence; measure, step, preliminary; *arch* plan; proviso, stipulation; symmetry. **A la d. de Vd,** I (we, he, it, etc.) am at your disposal. **hallarse en d. de hacer una cosa,** to be ready to do something. **última d.,** last will and testament
dispositivo *a* directory, advisory
dispuesto *a* ready, prepared; handsome, gallant; clever, wide-awake. **bien d.,** well-disposed; well, healthy. **mal d.,** ill-disposed; disinclined; out of sorts, indisposed
disputa *f*, dispute. **sin d.,** undoubtedly
disputar *vt* to argue, debate; dispute, question; *fig* fight for
disquisición *f*, disquisition
distancia *f*, distance; interval of time; difference, dissimilarity; unfriendliness, coolness
distanciar *vt* to separate, place farther apart
distante *a* separated; distant; far off
distar *vi* to be distant (time and place); be different, unlike
distender(se) *vt* and *vr med* to distend, swell
distinción *f*, distinction, differentiation; difference, individuality; privilege, honor; clarity, order; distinction (of bearing or mind). **a d. de,** unlike, different from
distinguible *a* distinguishable
distinguido *a* distinguished, illustrious
distinguir *vt* to distinguish, discern; differentiate; characterize; esteem, honor, respect; discriminate; see with difficulty; make out; *vr* be different; excel, distinguish oneself
distintivo *a* distinguishing; distinctive. *m*, distinguishing mark
distinto *a* different; distinct; clear
distracción *f*, distraction; abstraction, heedlessness, absentmindedness; pleasure, amusement; licentiousness
distraer *vt irr* to lead astray; distract (attention); influence for bad; amuse. *vr* be absentminded; amuse oneself. See **traer**
distraído *a* abstracted, absentminded; inattentive; licentious *Lat. Am.* slovenly
distribución *f*, distribution; (gen. *pl*) share
distribuidor (-ra) *a* distributing. *n* distributor
distribuir *vt irr* to distribute; share out, divide. See **huir**
distributivo *a* distributive
distrito *m*, district
disturbio *m*, disturbance
disuadir *vt* to dissuade
disuasión *f*, dissuasion
disuasivo *a* dissuasive
disyunción *f*, disjunction
dita *f*, *Lat. Am.* debt
ditirambo *m*, dithyramb; excessive praise
diurético *a* diuretic
diurno *a* diurnal
diva *f*, prima donna; woman singer
divagación *f*, wandering, roaming; digression
divagar *vi* to wander, roam; digress
diván *m*, divan (Turkish supreme council); divan, sofa; collection of Arabic, Persian or Turkish poems
divergencia *f*, divergence; disagreement
divergente *a* divergent; conflicting, dissentient
divergir *vi* to diverge; dissent
diversidad *f*, diversity, unlikeness, difference; variety
diversificar *vt* to differentiate; vary
diversión *f*, pastime, amusement; *mil* diversion
diverso *a* diverse, unlike; *pl* various, many
divertido *a* amusing, funny, entertaining
divertir *vt irr* to lead astray, turn aside; entertain; *mil* create a diversion. *vr* amuse oneself. See **sentir**
dividendo *m*, dividend. *com* **d. activo,** dividend
dividir *vt* to divide; distribute; stir up discord; *vr* (*with de*) part company with, leave
divieso *m*, *med* boil
divinamente *adv* divinely; excellently, admirably, perfectly
divinidad *f*, divinity, Godhead; person or thing of great beauty
divino *a* divine; excellent, admirable, superb
divisa *f*, badge, emblem; *her* motto
divisar *vt* to glimpse, descry
divisibilidad *f*, divisibility
divisible *a* divisible
división *f*, division, partition; discord; (*math mil*) division; hyphen; apportionment; district, ward
divisor (-ra) *a* dividing, separating. *m*, *math* divisor. *n* divider, separator
divisoria *f*, dividing line
divisorio *a* dividing
divorciar *vt* to divorce; separate; *vr* be divorced, be separated
divorcio *m*, divorce
divulgación *f*, spreading, publication, propagation
divulgar(se) *vt* and *vr* to spread abroad, publish
do *m*, *mus* doh, C. *poet* where
dobladillo *m*, *sew* hem; turn-up (of a trouser)
doblado *a* stocky, thickset, sturdy; rocky, rough, uneven; dissembling. *m*, garret
dobladura *f*, fold, crease; crease mark
doblamiento *m*, doubling; folding
doblar *vt* to double, multiply by two; fold, double; bend; persuade, induce; *naut* double, sail round; turn, walk round; *vi ecc* ring the passing bell; *theat* double a role; *vr* fold, double; bend; bow; stoop; allow oneself to be persuaded
doble *a* double, twofold; duplicate; insincere, false; thick (cloth); *bot* double (flowers); hardy, robust. *m*, fold, crease; *ecc* passing-bell; Spanish dance step. *adv* double, twice. *ecc* **rito d.,** full rites
doblegar *vt* to fold; bend; brandish; dissuade in favor of another proposition; *vr* submit, give way, acquiesce
doblete *a* of medium thickness. *m*, imitation jewel
doblez *m*, fold, crease; fold mark. *mf*, double dealing, treachery
doblilla *f*, twenty-real coin
doblón *m*, doubloon
doce *a* twelve. *m*, twelve; twelfth (of the month). **las d.,** twelve o'clock
docena *f*, dozen. **la d. del fraile,** baker's dozen
docente *a* teaching
dócil *a* docile; obedient; flexible, easily worked (metals, etc.)
docilidad *f*, docility; obedience; flexibility
docto *a* learned, erudite
doctor (-ra) *n* doctor; physician; teacher. *f*, *inf* bluestocking
doctorado *m*, doctorate
doctorarse *vr* to get one's doctorate
doctrina *f*, doctrine; instruction, teaching; theory, conception; *ecc* sermon
doctrinar *vt* to teach, instruct

documentación *f,* documentation; collection of documents, papers
documental *a* documental. *m,* documentary film
documentar *vt* to document
Dodecaneso, el the Dodecanese
dogal *m,* halter; noose; slipknot. *fig* **estar con el d. a la garganta,** to be in a fix
dogma *m,* dogma
dogmático *a* dogmatic
dogmatizar *vt* to teach heretical doctrines; dogmatize
dólar *m,* dollar
dolencia *f,* ailment; pain; ache
doler *vi irr* to be in pain; be reluctant; *vr* be sorry, regretful; grieve; sympathize, be compassionate; complain. *Pres. Ind.* **duelo, dueles, duele, duelen.** *Pres. Subjunc.* **duela, duelas, duela, duelan**
doliente *a* suffering; ill; afflicted, sad. *mf* sufferer, ill person. *m,* chief mourner
dolo *m,* fraud; deception; deceit; *law* premeditation
dolor *m,* pain, ache; mental suffering. **d. sordo,** dull pain
dolorido *a* painful; afflicted, sad
doloroso *a* sad, regrettable; mournful, sorrowful; pitiful; painful
doloso *a* deceitful, fraudulent
domable *a* tamable; controllable
domador (-ra) *n* subduer, controller; wild animal tamer; horsebreaker
domadura *f,* taming, breaking in; controlling (emotions)
domar *vt* to tame, break in; control, repress (emotions)
domesticable *a* tamable; domesticable
domesticar *vt* to tame; domesticate; *vr* grow tame; become domesticated
domesticidad *f,* domesticity
doméstico (-ca) *a* domestic, domesticated; tame. *n* domestic worker
domiciliar *vt* to domicile; *vr* become domiciled, settle down; *Mexico* address (a piece of mail)
domiciliario *a* domiciliary
domicilio *m,* domicile; house
dominación *f,* domination; power, authority; command (of a military position, etc.); *mil* high ground; *pl* dominions, angels
dominador *a* dominating; overbearing
dominante *a* dominating; overbearing, domineering; dominant. *f, mus* dominant
dominar *vt* to dominate; repress, subdue; *fig* master (branch of knowledge); *vi* stand out; *vr* control oneself
dómine *m, inf* teacher; pedant, know-all
domingo *m,* Sunday. **d. de Cuasimodo,** Low Sunday. **d. de Pentecostés,** Whitsuntide Sunday. **d. de Ramos,** Palm Sunday. **d. de Resurrección,** Easter Sunday
dominguero *a inf* Sunday; special, excursion (trains)
dominicano (-na) *a* and *n* Dominican; native of Santo Domingo
dominio *m,* authority, power; rule, sovereignty; dominion (country); domain
dominó *m,* domino; game of dominoes
don *m,* gift; quality, characteristic; talent. **d. de gentes,** the human touch; charm
don *m,* title of respect equivalent to English Mr. or Esquire. Used only before given name and *not* before a family name, e.g. **don Juan Martínez,** *or* **don Juan**
donación *f,* donation, gift, grant
donador (-ra) *a* donating. *n* donor
donaire *m,* discretion, wit; witticism; gracefulness, elegance
donar *vt* to bestow, give; transfer; grant
donatario *m,* recipient, grantee
doncel *m,* squire, youth not yet armed; knight; male virgin; king's page
doncella *f,* virgin, maid; maidservant; lady's maid
donde *adv* where, wherein. Sometimes used as relative pronoun "in which" (e.g. **La casa d. estaba,** The house in which I was); *Lat. Am.* at the house of, at . . .'s; to the house of, to . . .'s (e.g. **Mi tía está donde mis abuelos** My aunt is at my grandparents' **Mi tío no fue donde mis primos** My uncle did not go to my cousins') *interrog* **¿dónde? ¿A dónde va Vd.?** Where are you going to? **¿De dónde viene Vd.?** Where do you come from? **¿Por dónde se va a Madrid?** Which is the way to Madrid?
dondequiera *adv* wherever, anywhere, everywhere
donoso *a* witty; graceful
donostiarra *a* and *mf* of or from San Sebastian (N. Spain)
donosura *f,* wit; grace; dash, verve
doña *f,* feminine equivalent of **don** (e.g. **D. Catalina Palacios**)
dorado *a* golden, gilded; fortunate, happy. *m,* gilding
dorador *m,* gilder
doradura *f,* gilding
dorar *vt* to gild; make golden; *fig* gild the pill; *cul* toast lightly; *vr* become golden
dormidero *a* soporiferous, narcotic; *m, Lat. Am.* roost (of chickens)
dormilón (-ona) *a inf* sleepy. *n* sleepyhead
dormir *vi irr* to sleep; spend the night; *fig* grow calm; sleep (tops); (*with sobre*) sleep on, consider; *vt* put to sleep; *vr* go to sleep; go slow over, neglect; be dormant; go numb (limbs). **d. como un lirón,** to sleep like a top. *inf* **d. la mona,** to sleep oneself sober. **entre duerme y vela,** half-awake. *Pres. Ind.* **duermo, duermes, duerme, duermen.** *Pres. Part.* **durmiendo.** *Preterite* **durmió, durmieron.** *Pres. Subjunc.* **duerma, duermas, duerma, duerman**
dormitar *vi* to doze
dormitivo *a* and *m,* sedative
dormitorio *m,* dormitory; bedroom
dorso *m,* back; dorsum
dos *a* two. *m,* two; second (of the month). **las d.,** two o'clock. **d. a d.,** two against two. **de d. en d.,** two by two. *inf* **en un d. por tres,** in a twinkling
doscientos *a* and *m,* two hundred; two hundredth
dosel *m,* canopy; dais
dosis *f,* dose; quantity
dotación *f,* endowment; *naut* crew; staff, workers; equipment
dotar *vt* to give as dowry; endow, found; *fig* endow (with talents, etc.); equip; apportion (salary)
dote *mf,* dowry. *f,* (gen. *pl*) gifts, talents. **dotes de mando,** capacity for leadership
dracma *f,* drachma; dram
draga *f,* dredger
dragado *m,* dredging
dragaminas *m, nav* minesweeper
dragar *vt* to dredge
dragón *m,* dragon; *bot* snapdragon; *mil* dragoon; *zool* dragon, giant lizard; *ast* Draco
dragona *f,* female dragon; *mil* shoulder-strap
dragonear *vi, Lat. Am.* to boast, brag
drama *m,* play; drama. **d. lírico,** opera
dramática *f,* dramatic art
dramático *a* dramatic; vivid, unexpected, moving
dramaturgo *m,* dramatist, playwright
drenaje *m,* drainage (of land and wounds)
Dresde Dresden
dril *m,* drill, cotton cloth
droga *f,* drug; falsehood, deception; nuisance
droguería *f,* chemist's shop; drug trade
droguero (-ra) *n* chemist, druggist
dromedario *m, zool* dromedary
druida *m,* Druid
dualidad *f,* duality
ducado *m,* dukedom; duchy; ducat
ducentésimo *a* two hundredth
ducha *f,* shower-bath; douche; stripe in cloth; furrow
ducho *a* experienced, skilful

dúctil *a* ductile (metals); adaptable, docile, flexible
ductilidad *f*, ductility; adaptability
duda *f*, doubt, hesitation; problem. **sin d.,** doubtless
dudable *a* doubtful
dudar *vi* to be in doubt; *vt* doubt, disbelieve
dudoso *a* doubtful; uncertain, not probable
duela *f*, hoop, stave
duelista *mf* dueler; duelist
duelo *m*, sorrow, grief; mourning; mourners; duel; (gen. *pl*) troubles, trials. **duelos y quebrantos,** *cul* fried offal. **sin d.,** in abundance
duende *m*, imp, elf, sprite, ghost
dueña *f*, owner, proprietress, mistress; duenna; married lady *ant*
dueño *m*, owner, proprietor; master (of servants). **d. de sí mismo,** self-controlled
Duero, el the Douro
duetista *mf* duetist
dula *f*, common pasture ground or herds
dulce *a* sweet; fresh, pure; fresh, not salty; fragrant; melodious; pleasant, agreeable; tender, gentle; soft (metals). *m*, sweetmeat, bonbon. **d. de almíbar,** preserved fruit.
dulcedumbre *f*, sweetness; softness
dulcémele *m*, dulcimer
dulcera *f*, preserve dish, fruit dish
dulcería *f*, See **confitería**
dulcificar *vt* to make sweet; alleviate, sweeten
dulcinea *f*, *inf* sweetheart; ideal
dulzaina *f*, *mus* flageolet
dulzura *f*, sweetness; gentleness; pleasure; meekness; agreeableness
duna *f*, (gen. *pl*) sand dune
Dunquerque Dunkirk
dúo *m*, *mus* duet
duodécimo *a* twelfth
duodeno *a* twelfth. *m*, *anat* duodenum
duplicación *f*, duplication
duplicado *m*, duplicate
duplicar *vt* to duplicate; double
duplicidad *f*, duplicity, falseness
duplo *a* double
duque *m*, duke
duquesa *f*, duchess
duración *f*, duration; durability
duradero *a* lasting; durable
durante *adv* during
durar *vi* to continue; endure, last
dureza *f*, hardness; *med* callosity; severity, harshness
durmiente *a* sleeping. *mf* sleeper; *m*, *arch* dormant
duro *a* hard; firm, unyielding; vigorous, robust; severe, inclement; exacting, cruel; *mus* metallic, harsh; *art* crude, too sharply defined; miserly, avaricious; obstinate; self-opinionated; unbearable, intolerable; merciless, hard; harsh (style). *m*, Spanish coin worth five pesetas
dux *m*, doge

E

e *f*, letter E. *conjunc* used instead of *y* (and) before words beginning with *i* or *hi*, provided this last is not followed by a diphthong (e.g. **e invierno, e hijos,** *but* **y hierro**)
¡ea! *interj* Well!; Come on!; Let's see! (often used with **pues**)
ebanista *mf* cabinetmaker
ebanistería *f*, cabinetmaker's shop; cabinetmaking or work
ébano *m*, ebony
ebonita *f*, ebonite, vulcanite
ebrio *a* intoxicated, inebriated
ebullición *f*, boiling, ebullition
ebúrneo *a* eburnine, ivory-like
echada *f*, throw, cast; pitch; fling; length of a man
echador (-ra) *n* thrower. *m*, *inf* chucker-out
echadura *f*, sitting on eggs to hatch them; (gen. *pl*) gleanings
echamiento *m*, throw, fling; throwing, casting; expulsion; rejection
echar *vt* to throw, fling; eject, drive away; cast out, expel; put forth, sprout; emit, give forth; cut (teeth); dismiss, discharge; couple (animals); pour (liquids); place, apply; put into, fill; turn (keys, locks); impute; attribute; impose (penalty, taxes, etc.); play (game); try one's luck; distribute; publish, make known; perform (plays); (*with por*) go in direction of; (*with prep a + infin.*) begin to (**e. a andar,** to begin to walk); *vr* throw oneself down, lie down; sit on eggs (birds); abate, calm (wind); apply oneself, concentrate on; rush (towards), fling oneself (upon). **e. abajo,** to overthrow; demolish. **e. aceite al fuego,** to add fuel to the flames. **e. a perder,** to spoil, deteriorate. *naut* **e. a pique,** to sink. **e. a vuelo,** to ring (bells). **e. carnes,** to put on weight, grow fat. **e. cuentas,** to reckon up. **e. de menos,** to miss; mourn absence of. **e. de ver,** to notice. *fig* **e. en cara,** to throw in one's face, reproach. **echarla de majo,** to play the gallant. **e. las cartas al correo,** to post the letters. **e. las cartas,** to tell fortunes. **e. el pie atrás,** *fig* to climb down; *fig* back out. **e. raíces,** to take root; **e. las bases de, e. los cimientos de,** to lay the foundation of, lay the foundation for. *fig* become established. **e. rayos por la boca,** to fly into a rage. **e. suertes,** to draw lots. **echarlo todo a rodar,** to spoil everything. **e. una mano,** to lend a hand. **echar un volado** *Mexico* to toss a coin
echazón *f*, throw, cast; jetsam
eclecticismo *m*, eclecticism
ecléctico (-ca) *a* and *n* eclectic
eclesiástico *a* ecclesiastical. *m*, ecclesiastic, clergyman; Ecclesiasticus
eclipsar *vt ast* to eclipse; surpass, outvie; *vr ast* be in eclipse; disappear
eclipse *m*, *ast* eclipse; retirement, withdrawal
eco *m*, echo; verse-echo; muffled sound; slavish imitation or imitator
economato *m*, trusteeship; cooperative store
econometría *f*, econometrics
economía *f*, economy, thrift; structure, organization; poverty, shortage; saving (of time, labor, etc.); *pl* savings. **e. dirigida,** planned economy. **e. doméstica,** domestic economy. **e. política,** political economy
económico *a* economic; thrifty; avaricious; cheap
economista *mf* economist
economizar *vt* to economize; save
ecónomo *m*, trustee, guardian
ecuación *f*, (*math* and *ast*) equation. **e. personal,** personal equation
ecuador *m*, equator
ecuánime *a* calm, unruffled; impartial
ecuanimidad *f*, calmness, serenity; impartiality
ecuatorial *a* equatorial
ecuatoriano (-na) *a* and *n* Ecuadorian
ecuestre *a* equestrian
ecuménico *a* ecumenical
eczema *m*, eczema
edad *f*, age; epoch; period. **e. de piedra,** Stone Age. **e. media,** Middle Ages. **de cierta e.,** middle-aged. **ser mayor de e.,** to have attained one's majority. **ser menor de e.,** to be a minor
edecán *m*, aide-de-camp
edema *m*, edema
Edén *m*, Eden; *fig* paradise
edición *f*, edition. **e. diamante,** miniature edition. **e. príncipe,** first edition
edicto *m*, edict, decree; public notice
edificación *f*, building, construction; edification

edificador (-ra) *a* uplifting, edifying; building. *n* builder
edificante *a* building, constructing; edifying
edificar *vt* to build, construct; edify
edificio *m*, building, structure, fabric
Edimburgo Edinburgh
editar *vt* (of a publisher) to publish; edit
editor (-ra) *n* publisher; editor
editorial *a* publishing; editorial. *m*, editorial, leading article
edredón *m*, down of an eiderduck; eiderdown, quilt
eduardiano (-na) *a* and *n* Edwardian
educable *a* educable
educación *f*, upbringing; education; good breeding, good manners
educado *a* educated. **ser mal e.,** to be badly brought up; be ill-mannered
educador (-ra) *a* educating. *n* educator
educando (-da) *n* pupil
educar *vt* to educate; bring up, train, teach, develop
educativo *a* educational, educative
educción *f*, eduction; inference, deduction
educir *vt irr* to educe; infer, deduce. See **conducir**
efe *f*, name of letter F
efectismo *m*, sensationalism; striving after effect
efectista *a* (*art lit*) striking, sensational
efectivo *a* effective; real. *m*, cash. **hacer e.,** to put into effect
efecto *m*, effect, result; purpose, intent; impression; *pl* assets; goods, chattels. **efectos de escritorio,** stationery. **efectos públicos,** public securities. **en e.,** in fact, actually. **llevar a e.,** to put into effect; make effective
efectuación *f*, accomplishment, execution
efectuar *vt* to accomplish, effect; make (a payment); *vr* be effected; happen, take place
eferente *a* efferent
efervescencia *f*, effervescence; excitement, enthusiasm
efervescente *a* effervescent
Éfeso Ephesus
eficacia *f*, efficacy; effectiveness
eficaz *a* efficacious; effective
eficiencia *f*, efficiency
eficiente *a* efficient, effective
efigie *f*, effigy; image, representation, symbol
efímero *a* ephemeral; brief
eflorescencia *f*, *chem* efflorescence
efluvio *m*, effluvium; exhalation
efugio *m*, subterfuge, evasion
efusión *f*, effusion; *fig* spate (of words, etc.)
efusivo *a* effusive, expansive
Egeo, Mar Aegean Sea
égida *f*, shield; egis, protection
egipcíaco (-ca), egipcio (-ia) *a* and *n* Egyptian
Egipto Egypt
egiptólogo (-ga) *n* Egyptologist
egoísmo *m*, egoism
egoísta *a* egoistic. *mf* egoist
egolatría *f*, self-love
egotismo *m*, egotism
egotista *a* egotistical. *mf* egotist
egregio *a* distinguished, celebrated
egresado *m*, graduate (of a certain school)
egresar (de . . .) *vi*, *Lat. Am.* to go out (of . . .), leave (. . .); be graduated (from . . .)
egreso *m*, *Lat. Am.* departure, leaving; graduation
eje *m*, axis; axle-tree; shaft; pivot, fundamental idea. **e. trasero,** rear-axle
ejecución *f*, accomplishment, performance; execution, technique; death penalty
ejecutable *a* feasible, practicable
ejecutante *mf mus* executant, performer
ejecutar *vt* to discharge, perform; put to death; (*art mus*) execute; serve (a warrant, etc.); *law* seize (property)
ejecutivo *a* executive; urgent
ejecutor *m*, executor
ejecutoria *f*, letters patent of nobility; *law* judgment, sentence
ejemplar *a* exemplary. *m*, copy, specimen; precedent; example; warning
ejemplificar *vi* to exemplify
ejemplo *m*, example, precedent; illustration, instance; specimen. **dar e.,** to set an example. **por e.,** for example
ejercer *vt* to practise (a profession); perform, fulfil; exercise, use
ejercicio *m*, exercise; practice; performance; exertion, effort; *mil* exercises (gen. *pl*). **ejercicios espirituales,** spiritual exercises. **ejercicios físicos,** physical training
ejercitar *vt* to exercise; train, teach; *vr* exercise; practice
ejército *m*, army
ejote *m*, *Central America, Mexico* string bean
el *def art. m, sing* the
él *pers pron sing m*, he; it (*f*. **ella.** *neut* **ello**) (e.g. **Lo hizo él,** *He* did it). Also used with prep. (e.g. **Lo hicimos por él,** We did it for him)
elaboración *f*, elaboration, working out
elaborado *a* elaborate
elaborar *vt* to elaborate; produce, work out
elasticidad *f*, elasticity; adaptability
elástico *a* elastic; adaptable. *m*, elastic tape; elastic material
ele *f*, name of letter L
elección *f*, choice; election; selection; discrimination
electivo *a* elective
elector (-ra) *n* elector, voter. *m*, German prince *ant*
electorado *m*, electorate
electoral *a* electoral
electricidad *f*, electricity
electricista *mf* electrician
eléctrico *a* electric; electrical
electrificación *f*, electrification
electrificar *vt* to electrify
electrizar *vt* to electrify; startle; *vr* be electrified
electrocución *f*, electrocution
electrocutar *vt* to electrocute
electrodo *m*, electrode
electroimán *m*, electromagnet
electrólisis *f*, electrolysis
electrolizar *vt* to electrolyze
electromagnético *a* electromagnetic
electromotriz *a* electromotive. **fuerza e.,** electromotive force
electrón *m*, electron
electroquímica *f*, electrochemistry
electroscopio *m*, electroscope
electrotecnia *f*, electrical engineering
electroterapia *f*, *med* electrotherapy
elefante (-ta) *n* elephant
elefantíasis *f*, elephantiasis
elefantino *a* elephantine
elegancia *f*, elegance, grace; fashionableness; *lit* beauty of style
elegante *a* elegant; graceful, lovely; fashionable, stylish
elegantoso, -a *a*, *Lat. Am.* = **elegante**
elegía *f*, elegy
elegíaco *a* elegiac
elegibilidad *f*, eligibility
elegible *a* eligible
elegir *vt irr* to select, prefer; elect. *Pres. Ind.* **elijo, eliges, elige, eligen.** *Pres. Part.* **eligiendo.** *Preterite* **eligió, eligieron.** *Pres. Subj.* **elija,** etc.
elemental *a* elemental; fundamental; elementary
elemento *m*, element; component, constituent; *elec* element; *pl* rudiments. *mil* **elementos de choque,** shock troops
elenco *m*, *Lat. Am.* cast (of characters)
elevación *f*, lifting, raising; height, high ground; elevation; altitude; *fig* eminence; elevation, advancement; ecstasy; raising (of the voice)
elevado *a* sublime, lofty

elevar *vt* to raise, lift; *fig* exalt; *vr* be in ecstasy, be transported. **elevarse de categoría,** to rise in status
elfo *m*, elf
elidir *vt* (phonetics) to elide
eliminación *f*, elimination
eliminador *a* eliminatory. *m*, eliminator
eliminar *vt* to eliminate
elíptico *a* elliptic
elíseo *m*, Elysium. *a* Elysian. **campos elíseos,** Elysian fields
elocución *f*, elocution; style of speech
elocuencia *f*, eloquence
elocuente *a* eloquent
elogiador (-ra) *a* eulogistic. *n* eulogist
elogiar *vt* to eulogize, praise
elogio *m*, eulogy, praise. «**Elogio de la Locura**», "In Praise of Folly"
elote *m*, *Central America, Mexico* corn
elucidación *f*, elucidation, explanation
elucidar *vt* to elucidate, clarify
eludible *a* escapable, avoidable
eludir *vt* to elude, avoid
elusivo, -a *a*, *Lat. Am.* evasive, tricky
ella *pers. pron 3rd sing. f* she; it. See **él**
elle *f*, name of letter LL
ello *pers. pron 3rd sing. neut* that, the fact, it. **Ello es que . . . ,** The fact is that . . . **No tengo tiempo para ello,** I have no time for that
ellos, ellas *pers. pron 3rd pl. m* and *f*, they. See **él**
emaciación *f*, emaciation
emanación *f*, emanation; effluvium
emanar *vi* to emanate (from), originate (in)
emancipación *f*, emancipation; enfranchisement
emancipador (-ra) *a* emancipatory. *n* emancipator
emancipar *vt* to emancipate, free; enfranchise; *vr* emancipate oneself; become independent; free oneself
emascular *vt* to emasculate
embadurnar *vt* to smear, smudge, daub
embajada *f*, embassy; ambassadorship; embassy building; *inf* message
embajador *m*, ambassador; emissary
embajadora *f*, wife of ambassador; woman ambassador
embalador *m*, packer
embalaje *m*, packing; bale; wrapper; packing charge
embalar *vt* to pack
embaldosado *m*, tiled pavement or floor
embaldosar *vt* to tile, pave with tiles
embalsamador *a* embalming. *m*, embalmer
embalsamar *vt* to embalm; perfume
embalse *m*, dam; damming, impounding (of water)
embanastar *vt* to place in a basket; crowd, squeeze
embarazada *a f*, pregnant
embarazar *vt* to impede, hinder, embarrass; *vr* be hindered or embarrassed; be pregnant
embarazo *m*, difficulty, impediment; pregnancy; timidity, embarrassment
embarazoso *a* embarrassing; inconvenient; difficult, troublesome
embarcación *f*, ship, vessel; embarkation
embarcadero *m*, wharf, dock; quay; pier; jetty
embarcador *m*, shipper
embarcar *vt* to embark, ship; board (boat, train, etc.); *vr* embark; board
embarco *m*, embarking, embarkation
embargar *vt* to obstruct, impede; *law* seize; suspend, paralyse
embargo *m*, *law* seizure; embargo. **sin e.,** nevertheless, however
embarque *m*, loading, embarkation (goods)
embarrancar *vi naut* to run aground; *vr naut* be stuck on a reef or in the mud
embarrilar *vt* to barrel
embarullar *vt inf* to mix up, muddle; do hastily and badly
embastar *vt sew* to baste; tack
embaste *m*, *sew* basting; tacking stitch
embate *m*, beating of the waves; sudden attack; unexpected misfortune
embaucamiento *m*, trick, deception
embaucar *vt* to deceive, hoodwink
embaular *vt* to pack in a trunk; *inf* stuff with food
embazar *vt* to dye brown; hinder; amaze; *vr* be amazed; be tired or bored; be satiated
embebecer *vt irr* to entertain, amuse; engross, fascinate; *vr* be dumbfounded. See **conocer**
embebecimiento *m*, astonishment; absorption, engrossment
embeber *vt* to absorb; contain; shrink, contract; saturate; insert, introduce; incorporate; *vi* shrink; *vr* be amazed; master or absorb (a subject). **embedido en sus pensamientos,** absorbed in thought
embelecar *vt* to dupe, deceive, trick
embeleco *m*, deception, fraud
embelesar *vt* to astonish; fascinate, enchant; *vr* be astonished or fascinated
embeleso *m*, astonishment; fascination; charm
embellecer *vt irr* to embellish; *vr* beautify oneself. See **conocer**
embellecimiento *m*, beautifying, embellishment
emberizo *m*, *orn* yellow-hammer
embermejecer *vt irr* to dye red; shame, make blush; *vi* turn red or reddish; *vr* blush. See **conocer**
embestida *f*, assault, attack, onrush; *inf* importunity
embestir *vt irr* to rush upon, assault; *inf* importune, be a nuisance to; *vi fig inf* clash, be inharmonious. See **pedir**
emblema *m*, emblem; symbol; badge
emblemático *a* emblematic; symbolical
embobamiento *m*, stupefaction, amazement
embobar *vt* to entertain, fascinate; *vr* be dumbfounded
embobecer *vt irr* to make stupid. See **conocer**
embobecimiento *m*, stupefaction
embocadero *m*, narrow entrance, bottleneck; mouth of a channel
embocadura *f*, entrance by a narrow passage; *mus* mouthpiece; flavor (of wine); estuary, mouth of a river; *theat* proscenium
embocar *vt* to put in the mouth; go through a narrow passage; deceive; *inf* devour, wolf; initiate a business deal
embolador, -a *mf*, *Lat. Am.* bootblack
embolia *f*, embolism
émbolo *m*, *mech* piston, plunger
embolsar *vt* to place money in a purse; collect (a debt, etc.)
emborrachar *vt* to intoxicate; daze, stupefy; *vr* become intoxicated; run (of dyes)
emborrascarse *vr* to be furious; become stormy (weather); *fig* go downhill (business concern)
emborronar *vt* to blot; scribble, write hastily
emboscada *f*, ambuscade, ambush; intrigue, spying
emboscar *vt mil* to set an ambush; *vr* lie in ambush
embosquecer *vi irr* to become wooded. See **conocer**
embotar *vt* to blunt (cutting edge); *vi fig* weaken; *vr* become blunt
embotellado *m*, bottling; *fig* bottleneck
embotellador (-ra) *n* bottler. *f*. **embotelladora,** bottling outfit
embotellar *vt* to bottle; bottle up, prevent from escaping
embotijar *vt* to put into jars; *vr inf* be enraged
embozar *vt fig* to cloak, dissemble; muffle; *vr* muffle oneself up
embozo *m*, anything used to cover or muffle the face; pretense, pretext; facings (gen. *pl*); yashmak
embullo *m*, *Central America* noise; excitement; revelry
embragar *vt* to sling, lift; *mech* let in the clutch
embrague *m*, hoisting, slinging; *mech* clutch
embravecer *vt irr* to infuriate; *vr* be enraged; be boisterous (sea). See **conocer**
embravecimiento *m*, fury, rage
embrazadura *f*, grasping, clasping; handle, clasp

embreadura *f,* tarring
embrear *vt* to tar, paint with pitch
embriagador *a* intoxicating
embriagar *vt* to intoxicate; enrapture; *vr* become inebriated
embriaguez *f,* intoxication, inebriation; rapture
embriología *f,* embryology
embrión *m,* embryo; germ, rough idea
embrionario *a* embryonic
embrollar *vt* to entangle; embroil
embrollo *m,* tangle; falsehood; difficult situation
embromar *vt* to tease, chaff; trick, deceive; waste the time of; annoy; harm
embrujar *vt* to bewitch
embrutecer *vt irr* to make brutish or stupid; *vr* become brutish. See **conocer**
embudo *m, chem* funnel
embuste *m,* lie, fraud; *pl* trinkets
embustero (-ra) *a* deceitful, knavish. *n* liar, cheat, trickster
embutido *m,* inlaid work; *cul* sausage
embutir *vt* to inlay; stuff full, cram; *vt* and *vr inf* stuff with food
eme *f,* name of letter M
emergencia *f,* emergence; accident, emergency
emergente *a* emergent
emerger *vi* to emerge; have its source (rivers, etc.)
emérito *a* emeritus
emético *a* and *m,* emetic
emigración *f,* emigration; migration; number of emigrants
emigrado *m,* emigrant, emigré
emigrante *a* and *mf* emigrant
emigrar *vi* to emigrate; migrate
emigratorio *a* emigration
eminencia *f,* highland; importance, prominence; outstanding personality, genius; title given to cardinals
eminente *a* high, elevated; prominent, illustrious
emirato *m,* emirate
emisario (-ia) *n* emissary
emisión *f,* emission; *rad* broadcast; *com* issue (bonds, etc.); floating (of a loan)
emisor *m, elec* transmitter.
emisora *f, rad* broadcasting station
emitir *vt* to emit; *rad* broadcast; *com* issue (bonds, paper money, etc.); utter, give voice to
emoción *f,* emotion
emocional *a* emotional; emotive
emocionante *a* moving, causing emotion; thrilling
emocionar *vt* to cause emotion, move; *vr* be stirred by emotion; be thrilled
emoliente *a* and *m,* emollient
emolumento *m,* emolument (gen. *pl*)
empachado *a* awkward, clumsy
empachar *vt* to hinder, impede; disguise, dissemble; *vr* overeat, stuff; be bashful
empacho *m,* bashfulness, timidity; embarrassment, impediment; indigestion, satiety
empadronamiento *m,* census
empadronar *vt* to take the census
empalagar *vt* to cloy (of food); tire, annoy
empalagoso *a* sickly, oversweet; cloying; *fig* sugary, honeyed
empalar *vt* to impale
empalizada *f,* stockade, fencing
empalmar *vt* to dovetail; splice (ropes); clamp; *fig* combine (plans, actions, etc.); *vi* join (railroad lines); couple (railroad trains); *vr* palm (as in conjuring)
empalme *m,* connection; splicing; *fig* combination (of plans, etc.); railroad junction; continuation; palming, secreting
empanada *f,* savory turnover or pie; secret negotiations, intrigue
empanar *vt* to bread; *cul* cover with breadcrumbs; *agr* sow grain
empantanar *vt* to turn into marsh; embog; delay, embarrass
empañar *vt* to swaddle; tarnish, dim; blur; *fig* sully (fame, etc.)
empapar *vt* to saturate; absorb; impregnate; *vr* be saturated; absorb; *fig* be imbued
empapelado *m,* paperhanging; wallpaper
empapelador *m,* paperhanger
empapelar *vt* to wrap in paper; paper (a room, etc.)
empaque *m,* packing; paneling; *inf* mien, air; pomposity
empaquetador (-ra) *n* packer
empaquetar *vt* to pack; make up parcels or packages; overcrowd
emparedado (-da) *a* cloistered, reclusive. *n* recluse. *m, cul* sandwich
emparedar *vt* to shut up, immure; *vr* become a recluse
emparejar *vt* to pair, match; equalize, make level; *vi* come abreast (of); be equal
emparentar *vi irr* to become related by marriage. See **acertar**
emparrado *m,* vine arbor; vine prop; pergola
empastadura *f,* filling (of teeth)
empastar *vt* to cover with glue or paste; bind in boards (books); fill (teeth). **empastado en tela,** clothbound
empaste *m,* pasting, gluing; filling (teeth)
empatar *vt* to equal, tie with
empate *m,* tie, draw; dead heat
empavonarse *vr, Central America* to dress to the nines
empecatado *a* willful; evil-minded, wicked; incorrigible, impenitent; extremely unlucky
empecer *vt irr* to harm, damage; *vi* hinder. See **conocer**
empecinado, -a *a, Lat. Am.* pigheaded, stubborn
empedernido *a* stony-hearted, cruel
empedrado *a* dappled (horses); *fig* flecked (with clouds). *m,* paving; pavement
empedrar *vt irr* to pave with stones. See **acertar**
empegar *vt* to coat with pitch; mark with pitch (sheep)
empeine *m,* groin; instep
empellar *vt* to push, jostle
empellón *m,* hard push. *inf* **a empellones,** by pushing and shoving
empeñado *a* violent, heated (of disputes)
empeñar *vt* to pledge, leave as surety; pawn; oblige, compel; appoint as mediator; *vr* bind oneself, be under an obligation; (*with en*) insist on; persist in; *vr* intercede; mediate; *mil* begin (a battle). **empeñado en,** determined to, intent on
empeño *m,* pledge, surety; obligation, engagement; fervent desire; purpose, intention; determination, resolve; guarantor; *inf* influence, favor
empeoramiento *m,* worsening; deterioration
empeorar *vt* to make worse; *vi* and *vr* deteriorate, grow worse
empequeñecer *vt irr* to diminish, lessen; make smaller; belittle. See **conocer**
emperador *m,* emperor
emperatriz *f,* empress
emperezar *vt* to obstruct, hinder; *vr* be lazy
empernar *vt* to peg, bolt
empero *conjunc* but; nevertheless
empezar *vt irr* to begin, commence; initiate; *vi* begin. *Pres. Ind.* **empiezo, empiezas, empieza, empiezan.** *Preterite* **empecé, empezaste,** etc. *Pres. Subjunc.* **empiece, empieces, empiece, empecemos, empecéis, empiecen**
empicotar *vt* to pillory
empiezo *m, Lat. Am.* beginning
empilonar *vt, Lat. Am.* to pile up
empinado *a* steep; lofty; arrogant; exalted
empinar *vt* to raise; tip, tilt (drinking vessels); *vr* stand on tiptoe; rear, prance; tower, rise; *aer* zoom, climb steeply. *inf* **e. el codo,** to lift the elbow, tipple
empingorotado *a* important, prominent; *inf* stuck-up
empírico (-ca) *a* empiric. *n* quack, charlatan
empizarrado *m,* slate roof

empizarrar *vt* to roof with slate
emplastar *vt med* to apply plasters; make up; paint; *inf* hinder, obstruct; *vr* be smeared
emplasto *m, med* plaster; poultice; *inf* put-up job, fraud
emplazamiento *m,* placing, location; site; *law* summons; *naut* berth
emplazar *vt* to convene, arrange a meeting; *law* summon
empleado (-da) *n* employee; clerk. **e. público,** civil servant
emplear *vt* to employ; lay out, invest (money); use; *vr* be employed or occupied
empleo *m,* employment; investment, laying out (of money); occupation; post, office
emplomar *vt* to lead, solder or cover with lead; affix lead seals on or to; weight (a stick, etc.); *Argentina* fill (a tooth)
emplumar *vt* to feather; decorate with feathers; tar and feather
emplumecer *vi irr* to fledge, grow feathers. See **conocer**
empobrecer *vt irr* to impoverish; *vi* and *vr* become poor; decay. See **conocer**
empobrecimiento *m,* impoverishment
empollar *vt* to hatch; *vi* produce a brood (of bees); *inf* brood on, consider; *inf* grind, cram, swot (of students)
empollón (-ona) *n inf* plodder, grind, swot
empolvar *vt* to cover with dust; powder
emponzoñar *vt* to poison; pervert, corrupt
emporio *m,* emporium
empotrar *vt* to embed, implant; fix down
emprendedor *a* capable, efficient, enterprising
emprender *vt* to undertake; (*with prep a or con*) *inf* accost, tackle, buttonhole
empresa *f,* undertaking, task; motto, device; intention, design; management, firm; enterprise, deal
empresarial *a* entrepreneurial
empresario *m,* contractor; theatrical manager
empréstito *m,* loan
empujar *vt* to push; *fig* exert pressure, influence
empuje *m,* push; *arch* pressure; energy; power, influence
empujón *m,* violent thrust or push. *inf* **a empujones,** by pushing and shoving; intermittently
empuñar *vt* to grasp; grip; clutch
empurrarse *vr, Central America* to get angry
emu *m,* emu
emulación *f,* emulation, competition, rivalry
emulador *a* emulative
emular *vt* to emulate, rival, compete with
émulo (-la) *a* emulative, rival. *n* competitor, rival
emulsión *f,* emulsion
en *prep* in; into; on, upon; at; by. **en Madrid,** in Madrid. **en junio,** in June. **Se echó en un sillón,** He threw himself into an armchair. **Se transformó en mariposa,** It turned into a butterfly. **Hay un libro en la mesa,** There is a book on the table. **María está en casa,** Mary is at home. **en un precio muy alto,** at a very high price. **El número de candidatos ha disminuido en un treinta por ciento,** The number of candidates has decreased by thirty percent. **En** appears in a number of adverbial phrases, e.g. **en particular,** in particular, **en secreto,** in secret, **en seguida,** immediately. When it is used with a gerund, it means after, as soon as, when, e.g. **En llegando a la puerta llamó,** When he arrived at the door, he knocked. **En todas partes se cuecen habas,** That happens everywhere; It happens in the best of families
enaceitar *vt, Argentina* to oil
enagua *f,* slip, crinoline, petticoat
enajenación *f,* transference, alienation (property); abstraction, absent-mindedness. **e. mental,** lunacy
enajenar *vt* to transfer (property)
enaltecer *vt irr* to elevate, raise; exalt. See **conocer**
enamoradizo *a* susceptible, easily enamoured; fickle
enamorado *a* in love, lovesick; easily enamoured
enamorar *vt* to arouse love in; court, make love to; *vr* fall in love; (with *de*) become fond of (things)
enano (-na) *a* small, dwarf. *n* dwarf
enarbolar *vt* to hoist (flags); *vr* prance (horses); become angry
enardecer *vt irr* to kindle, stimulate (passion, quarrel, etc.); *vr* be afire (with passion); *med* be inflamed. See **conocer**
encabestrar *vt* to halter; lead, dominate
encabestrarse *vr, Lat. Am.* to dig one's heels in
encabezamiento *m,* census taking; tax register; tax assessment; heading, inscription, running head
encabezar *vt* to take the census of; put on the tax register; open a subscription list; put a heading or title to; lead, head; *vr* compound, settle by agreement (taxes, etc.)
encadenamiento *m,* fettering, chaining; connection, link, relation
encadenar *vt* to chain, fetter; *fig* link up, connect; *fig* paralyze. **encadenar el interés de,** to capture the interest of
encajar *vt* to insert, fit one thing inside another; force in; fit tightly; *inf* be opportune, fit in (often with *bien*); *vr* squeeze or crowd in; *inf* butt in, interfere
encaje *m,* fitting, insertion; socket, groove; joining; lace; inlay, mosaic
encajero, -a *mf,* lace maker; lace seller
encaladura *f,* whitewashing
encalar *vt* to whitewash
encalmado *a* calm; *com* dull
encalmarse *vr* to become calm (wind, weather)
encalvecer *vi irr* to grow bald. See **conocer**
encalladero *m, naut* sandbank, reef, shoal
encallar *vi naut* to run aground; *fig* be held up (negotiations, etc.)
encamado *a* bedridden, confined to one's bed; *m,* person confined to his bed
encamarse *vr* to go to bed (gen. illness); be laid flat (grain, etc.); crouch
encaminadura *f,* **encaminamiento** *m,* directing, forwarding, routing
encaminar *vt* to guide; direct; regulate; manage; promote, advance; *vr* (*with prep a*) make for, go in the direction of
encandecer *vt irr* to make incandescent. See **conocer**
encandilar *vt* to dazzle; mislead; *inf* poke (the fire); *vr* be bloodshot (eyes)
encanecer *vi irr* to grow gray- or white-haired; grow mold; grow old. See **conocer**
encanijar *vt* to make weak, sickly (gen. of babies); *vr* be delicate or ailing
encantado *a inf* daydreaming, abstracted; haunted; rambling (of houses)
encantador *a* captivating, bewitching, delightful. *m,* sorcerer, magician. **e. de serpientes,** snake charmer
encantamiento *m,* enchantment, spell, charm
encantar *vt* to enchant, weave a spell; delight, captivate, charm
encañada *f,* gorge, ravine
encañado *m,* trellis; pipeline
encañar *vt* to run water through a pipe; stake plants; wind thread on a spool
encañonar *vt* to run into pipes; pleat, fold
encapotarse *vr* to muffle oneself in a cloak; scowl; be overcast; lower (sky)
encapricharse *vr* to take a fancy (to); insist on having one's own way, be stubborn
encaramar *vt* to raise, lift; climb; praise, extol. **e. al poder,** to put in power (e.g. a dictator). **encaramarse por,** to climb up
encarar *vt* to place face to face; aim (at); *vt* and *vr* face; come face to face
encarcelación *f,* incarceration
encarcelar *vt* to imprison, jail; *carp* clamp
encarecer *vt irr* to raise the price; overpraise, exagger-

ate; recommend strongly; *vi* and *vr* increase in price. See **conocer**

encarecimiento *m*, increase (in price); enhancement; exaggeration. **con e.,** insistently, earnestly

encargado *m*, person in charge; manager; agent, representative. **e. de negocios,** chargé d'affaires

encargar *vt* to enjoin; commission; recommend; advise; *com* order

encargo *m*, charge, commission; order; office, employ; responsibility

encariñarse (*con*), *vi* to become fond (of)

encarnación *f*, incarnation

encarnadino *a* incarnadine

encarnado *a* incarnate; flesh-colored; red

encarnar *vi* to incarnate; pierce the flesh; *fig* leave a strong impression; *vt* symbolize, personify; *vr* mingle, blend

encarnizado *a* bloodshot (eyes); flesh-colored; bloody, cruel (gen. of battles)

encarnizamiento *m*, cruelty, fury

encarnizar *vt* to infuriate; *vr* devour flesh (animals); persecute, ill-treat

encaro *m*, stare, gaze; aim

encarrilar *vt* to set on the track or rails (vehicles); *fig* put right, set on the right track

encartamiento *m*, proscription; charter

encartar *vt* to proscribe, outlaw; place on the tax register; *law* summon, cite

encartonar *vt* to cover with cardboard; bind in boards (books)

encasar *vt surg* to set (a bone)

encasillado *m*, set of pigeonholes

encasillar *vt* to pigeonhole; file, classify

encasquetar(se) *vt* and *vr* to pull a hat well down on the head; *vr* get a fixed idea

encasquillador, -a *mf, Lat. Am.* blacksmith

encastillar *vt* to fortify with castles; *vr* retire to a castle; be headstrong, obstinate

encauzamiento *m*, channeling; *fig* direction

encauzar *vt* to channel; *fig* direct, guide

encefalitis *f*, encephalitis. **e. letárgica,** encephalitis lethargica, sleeping sickness. **enceguedor** *a* blinding, dazzling

encéfalo *m*, *anat* brain

encenagarse *vr* to wallow in mire; muddy oneself; take to vice

encendedor *a* lighting. *m*, lighter. **e. de bolsillo,** pocket lighter

encender *vt irr* to light; switch on; set fire to, kindle; arouse (emotions); inflame, incite; *vr* blush. See **entender**

encendido *a* high-colored; inflamed; ardent. *m*, *aut* ignition

encerado *a* wax-colored. *m*, oilskin; sticking plaster; blackboard; tarpaulin

enceramiento *m*, waxing

encerar *vt* to wax, varnish with wax; stain with wax; inspissate (lime)

encercar *vt, Lat. Am.* to encircle

encerotar *vt* to wax (thread)

encerrar *vt irr* to shut up, imprison; include, contain; *vr* go into seclusion. See **acertar**

encerrona *f*, *inf* voluntary retreat; *fig inf* tight corner

encespedar *vt* to cover with sod

enchilada *f*, *Mexico* rolled-up tortilla filled with meat or cheese and covered with sauce or cream

enchufar *vt* to connect tubes; *fig* combine (jobs, etc.); *elec* plug, connect

enchufe *m*, joint, fitting together (of tubes); *elec* wall socket, plug; part-time post; *inf* cushy job. **e. de reducción,** *elec* adapter

encía *f*, gum (of the mouth)

encíclica *f*, encyclical

enciclopedia *f*, encyclopedia

enciclopédico *a* encyclopedic

encierro *m*, act of closing or shutting up; prison; retreat, confinement

encima *adv* over; above; at the top; besides; (*with de*) on, on top of. **por e. de esto,** over and above this, besides this

encinta *a f*, pregnant

encintar *vt* to decorate with ribbons

enclavar *vt* to nail; pierce; embed; *inf* deceive

enclenque *a* ailing, weak; puny, anemic

enclocar *vi irr* to begin to brood (hens). See **contar**

encobar *vi* to hatch eggs

encoger *vt* to shrink, contract, recoil; discourage; *vi* shrink (wood, cloth, etc.); *vr* shrink from, recoil; be discouraged; be timid or bashful

encogimiento *m*, shrinkage; contraction; depression, discouragement; timidity; bashfulness

encoladura *f*. **encolamiento** *m*, gluing; sizing

encolerizar *vt* to anger; *vr* be angry

encomendar *vt irr* to charge with, entrust; recommend, commend; *vr* (*with prep a*) put one's trust in; send greetings to. See **acertar**

encomiar *vt* to eulogize, praise

encomienda *f*, commission, charge; knight commandership; insignia of knight commander; land formerly granted in America to *conquistadores;* recommendation, commendation; protection, defense; *pl* greetings, compliments, messages

encomio *m*, eulogy; strong recommendation

enconar *vt* to irritate, exasperate; *vr med* be inflamed; be exasperated; (*with en*) burden one's conscience with

encono *m*, rancor, resentment, ill will

encontrado *a* facing, opposite, in front; hostile, inimical, opposed (to)

encontrar *vt irr* to meet; find; *vi* meet; encounter unexpectedly; (*with con*) run into, collide with; *vr* be antagonistic; find; feel, be; differ, disagree (opinions); (*with con*) meet, come across. **e. eco,** to strike a responsive chord. **encontrarse con el cura de su pueblo,** to find someone who knows all about, meet someone who knows all about. **¿Cómo se encuentra Vd?** How are you? *Pres. Ind.* **encuentro,** etc. *Pres. Subjunc.* **encuentre,** etc.

encontrón *m*, collision, violent impact

encopetado *a* conceited, proud; of noble descent; prominent, important

encorajar *vt* to encourage, inspire, hearten; *vr* be angry

encordelar *vt* to cord, rope

encorsetar *vt* to correct

encorvadura *f*, bending, curving

encorvar *vt* to bend, curve; *vr* have a leaning toward, favor

encostrar *vt* to cover with a crust; *vr* form a crust

encrespador *m*, curling irons

encrespar *vt* to curl (hair); enrage; *vr* be curly (hair); stand on end (hair, feathers, from fright); be angry; grow rough (sea); become complicated, entangled

encrestado *a* crested; haughty, arrogant

encrestarse *vr* to stiffen the comb or crest (birds)

encrucijada *f*, crossroad, intersection; ambush

encrudecer *vt irr* to make raw-looking; annoy; *vr* be annoyed. See **conocer**

encuadernación *f*, bookbinding; binding (of a book); bookbinder's workshop. **e. en tela,** cloth binding

encuadernador (-ra) *n* bookbinder

encuadernar *vt* to bind (a book)

encuadrar *vt* to frame; fit one thing into another, insert; limit; *mil* enlist

encubar *vt* to put into casks (wine, etc.)

encubiertamente *adv* secretly; deceitfully

encubierto *a* concealed; secret

encubridor (-ra) *a* concealing, hiding. *n* hider; harborer; accomplice; receiver (of stolen goods); *law* accessory after the fact

encubrimiento *m*, hiding, concealment; *law* accessory before (after) the fact; receiving (of stolen goods)

encubrir *vt* to conceal; receive (stolen goods); *law* prosecute as an accessory. *Past. Part.* **encubierto**
encuentro *m*, collision; meeting, encounter; opposition, hostility; *mil* fight, skirmish; *arch* angle. **ir al e. de,** to go in search of. **salir al e. (de),** to go to meet; resist
encuerado, -a *a*, *Lat. Am.* naked, nude, in the buff
encuesta *f*, investigation, examination
encumbrado *a* elevated, high
encumbramiento *m*, act of elevating; height; aggrandizement, advancement
encumbrar *vt* to raise, elevate; exalt, promote; ascend, climb to the top; *vr* be proud; be lofty, tower
encurtido *m*, pickle
encurtir *vt* to pickle
ende *adv ant* there. **por e.,** therefore
endeble *a* weak, frail
endeblez *f*, weakness
endémico *a med* endemic
endemoniado *a* devil-possessed; *inf* fiendish, malevolent
endemoniar *vt* to possess with a devil; *inf* enrage
endentar *vt irr mech* to cut the cogs (of a wheel); engage, interlock (gears, wheels, etc.). See **regimentar**
endentecer *vi irr* to cut teeth. See **conocer**
enderezamiento *m*, straightening; directing, guiding; putting right, correction
enderezar *vt* to straighten; direct, guide; put right, correct; *vi* take the right road; *vr* straighten oneself; prepare to
endeudarse *vr* to contract debts; be under an obligation
endiablado *a* ugly, monstrous; *inf* fiendish
endiosar *vt* to deify; *vr* be puffed up with pride; be abstracted or lost in ecstasy
enditarse *vr*, *Lat. Am.* to go into debt
endocrino *a* endocrine
endocrinología *f*, endocrinology
endomingarse *vr* to put on one's Sunday best
endosante *m*, endorser
endosar *vt com* to endorse; transfer, pass on
endoso *m*, *com* endorsement
endrogarse *vr*, *Mexico* = **enditarse**
endulzar *vt* to sweeten; soften, mitigate
endurecer *vt irr* to harden; toughen, inure; make severe or cruel; *vr* grow hard; become hardened or robust; be harsh or cruel. **endurecerse al trabajo,** to become hardened to work. See **conocer**
endurecimiento *m*, hardness; obstinacy, tenacity
ene *f*, name of letter N
enemiga *f*, hostility, enmity
enemigo (-ga) *a* hostile. *n* enemy; antagonist. *m*, devil
enemistad *f*, enmity, hostility
enemistar *vt* to make enemies of; *vr* (*with con*) become an enemy of; cease to be friendly with
energético, -a *a*, *Lat. Am.* = **enérgico**
energía *f*, energy, vigor
enérgico *a* energetic, vigorous
energúmeno (-na) *n* energumen
enero *m*, January
enervación *f*, enervation
enervar *vt* to enervate, weaken; *fig* take the force out of (reasons, etc.)
enfadar *vt* to make angry; *vr* become angry; *Lat. Am.* to get bored
enfado *m*, anger; annoyance; trouble, toil
enfadoso *a* vexatious; troublesome, wearisome
enfaldada *f*, skirtful
enfaldar *vt* to tuck up the skirts; lop off lower branches (of trees)
enfangarse *vr* to cover oneself with mud; *inf* dirty one's hands, sully one's reputation; wallow in vice
énfasis *m*, or *f*, emphasis
enfático *a* emphatic
enfermar *vi* to fall ill; *vt* cause illness; *fig* weaken. **Enfermó del corazón,** He fell ill with heart trouble.
enfermedad *f*, illness; *fig* malady, distemper. **e. del sueño,** sleeping sickness
enfermería *f*, infirmary; hospital; first-aid station
enfermero, -a *mf* nurse
enfermizo *a* ailing, delicate; unhealthy, unwholesome
enfermo (-ma) *a* ill; *fig* corrupt, diseased; delicate, sickly. *n* patient. **e. venéreo,** person with a venereal disease
enfilar *vt* to place in line; string; *mil* enfilade
enflaquecer *vt irr* to make thin; weaken, enervate; *vi* grow thin; lose heart. See **conocer**
enflaquecimiento *m*, loss of flesh; discouragement
enfocar *vt* to focus; envisage
enfoque *m*, focus
enfoscado *a* ill-humored; immersed in business matters
enfrascar *vt* to bottle; *vr* (*with en*) plunge into, entangle oneself in (undergrowth, etc.); become engrossed or absorbed in
enfrenar *vt* to bridle; curb (a horse); restrain, repress; check
enfrente *adv* in front, opposite, facing; in opposition
enfriadero *m*, cooling place, cold cellar, root cellar
enfriamiento *m*, cooling
enfriar *vt* to cool; *fig* chill, make indifferent; *vr* grow cold; *fig* grow stormy (weather)
enfurecer *vt irr* to enrage. See **conocer**
enfurecimiento *m*, fury
enfurruñarse *vr inf* to fume, be angry; be disgruntled
engalanar *vt* to decorate, embellish. **engalanado como nunca,** dressed to the nines, dressed to kill
enganchar *vt* to hook; couple, connect; hitch, harness, yoke; *inf* seduce, hook; *mil* bribe into army; *vr* be hooked or caught on a hook; *mil* enlist
enganche *m*, hooking; coupling (of railroad trains, etc.); connection; yoke, harness; hook; *inf* enticement; *mil* enlistment; *Mexico* down payment
engañadizo *a* easily deceived, simple
engañador (-ra) *a* deceiving; deceptive. *n* deceiver, impostor
engañar *vt* to deceive; defraud, cheat; beguile, while away; hoax, humbug; *vr* be mistaken; deceive oneself. **e. como a un chino,** *inf* to pull the wool over a person's eyes. **Las apariencias engañan,** Appearances are deceptive
engañifa *f*, *inf* swindle, fraud
engaño *m*, deceit; deception, illusion; fraud; falsehood
engañoso *a* deceitful, false; fraudulent; deceptive, misleading
engarabatar *vt inf* to hook; *vr* become hooked, curved, crooked
engaratusar *vt*, *inf*, *Lat. Am.* = **engatusar**
engarce *m*, hooking; coupling; setting (of jewels)
engarzar *vt* to link, couple, enchain; hook; curl; set (jewels)
engastar *vt* to set (jewels)
engaste *m*, setting (of jewels)
engatusar *vt inf* to wheedle, coax, flatter
engendrador (-ra) *a* engendering; original. *n* begetter
engendrar *vt* to procreate; engender, produce, cause
engendro *m*, fetus; abnormal embryo; literary monstrosity
engestarse *vr*, *Mexico* to make a wry face
englobar *vt* to include, comprise, embrace
engolfarse *vr* to sail out to sea; (*with en*) *fig* be absorbed in
engomar *vt* to gum
engordar *vt* to fatten; *vi* grow fat; *inf* prosper, grow rich
engorde *m*, fattening (of stock)
engorrar *vt*, *Lat. Am.* to annoy, needle
engorro *m*, impediment, obstacle, difficulty
engorroso *a* difficult, troublesome
engranaje *m*, *mech* gearing, gear; *fig* connection, link
engrandecer *vt irr* to enlarge; augment; eulogize; promote, exalt. See **conocer**

engrandecimiento *m*, enlargement; increase; exaggeration, eulogization; advancement, promotion
engrasador *m*, greaser, lubricator; oiler
engrasar *vt* to grease; lubricate, oil; manure; stain with grease
engreimiento *m*, conceit, vanity
engreír *vt irr* to make conceited; *vr* become vain or conceited. See **reír**
engrescar(se) *vt* and *vr* to start a quarrel
engrosar *vt irr* to fatten, thicken; *fig* increase, swell; manure; *vi* put on weight, grow fat. See **contar**
engrudar *vt* to paste, glue
engrudo *m*, paste, glue
enguijarrado *a* pebbled. *m*, pebbled path
engullir *vt* to gobble, swallow
enhebrar *vt* to thread (needles); string
enhestar *vt irr* to erect; set upright; *vr* rise; rear up; straighten oneself up. See **acertar**
enhiesto *a* upright, erect
enhorabuena *f*, congratulation. *adv* well and good. **dar la e.,** to congratulate
enhoramala *adv* in an evil hour. *inf* **¡Vete e.!** Go to the devil!
enhorquetado *a* in the saddle
enigma *m*, enigma
enigmático *a* enigmatical
enjabonar *vt* to soap; *inf* soap down, flatter
enjaezar *vt* to harness (a horse)
enjalbegar *vt* to whitewash
enjambrar *vt* to hive bees; *vi* multiply, increase
enjambre *m*, swarm (of bees); crowd
enjaretado *m*, latticework
enjaular *vt* to cage; *inf* jail
enjoyar *vt* to adorn with jewels; beautify; set with precious stones
enjuagadura *f*, rinsing (the mouth); rinse water; mouthwash
enjuagar *vt* to rinse; *vr* rinse the mouth
enjuague *m*, rinse; rinsing; mouthwash; tooth mug; scheme, plan
enjugar *vt* to dry; cancel, write off; wipe, mop (perspiration, tears, etc.); *vr* grow lean
enjuiciar *vt* to submit a matter to arbitration; *law* prosecute; *law* render judgment; *law* adjudicate (a case)
enjundia *f*, animal fat or grease; *fig* substance, meat; strength, vigor; constitution, temperament
enjuto *a* dry; lean. *m pl*, brushwood; *cul* canapés, savories
enlace *m*, connection; link; tie; *chem* bond; alliance, relationship; marriage
enladrillado *m*, brick floor or pavement
enlardar *vt cul* to baste
enlazar *vt* to tie, bind; join, link; lasso; *vr* marry; be allied, related. **e. con,** to connect with (of trains); link up with
enlentecerse *vr* to decelerate, go slow, slow down
enlodar *vt* to muddy; *fig* smirch, sully
enloquecer *vt irr* to drive insane; *vi* go mad. See **conocer**
enlosado *m*, tile floor
enlosar *vt* to pave with flags
enlozar *vt*, *Lat. Am.* to enamel, glaze
enlucir *vt irr* to plaster (walls); polish (metals). See **lucir**
enlutar *vt* to put in mourning, drape with crepe; darken, obscure; sadden; *vr* go into mourning; become dark
enmaderar *vt* to panel in wood, board up
enmarañar *vt* to tangle, disorder (hair, etc.); complicate, confuse; *vr* be tangled; be sprinkled with clouds
enmaridar *vi* to become a wife
enmarillecerse *vr irr* to grow yellow. See **conocer**
enmascarar *vt* to mask; disguise, dissemble; *vr* be masked
enmasillar *vt* to putty
enmendar *vt irr* to correct, improve; reform; compensate, indemnify; *law* repeal; *vr* be improved or corrected; mend one's ways. See **acertar**
enmienda *f*, correction; reform; indemnity; compensation; amendment; *pl agr* fertilizers
enmohecer *vt irr* to rust; *vr* become moldy. See **conocer**
enmudecer *vt irr* to silence; *vi* become dumb; be silent. See **conocer**
enmugrecer *vt irr* to cover with grime; *vr* be grimy, dirty. See **conocer**
enmugrentar *vt*, *Chile* = **enmugrecer**
ennegrecer *vt irr* to dye black; make black; *vr* become black; become dark or cloudy. See **conocer**
ennoblecer *vt irr* to ennoble; enrich, embellish; adorn, befit. See **conocer**
ennoblecimiento *m*, ennoblement; enrichment
enojadizo *a* irritable, peevish
enojar *vt* to anger; annoy, irritate; *vr* be angry; rage, be rough (wind, sea)
enojo *m*, anger; resentment; vexations, troubles, trials (gen. *pl*). **con gran e. de,** much to the annoyance of
enojoso *a* annoying; troublesome, tiresome
enorgullecer *vt irr* to make proud; *vr* be proud. See **conocer**
enorme *a* enormous, huge; monstrous, heinous
enormidad *f*, hugeness; enormity; wickedness
enramar *vt* to intertwine branches; embower; *vi* branch (trees)
enrarecer *vt irr* to rarefy; *vr* become rarefied; grow rare. See **conocer**
enrarecimiento *m*, rarefaction
enredadera *f*, convolvulus. *a f*, climbing, twining (plant)
enredador (-ra) *a* mischievous, willful; intriguing, scheming; *inf* gossiping, meddlesome. *n* intriguer; *inf* meddler
enredar *vt* to catch in a net; put down nets or snares; entangle; sow discord; compromise, involve (in difficulties); *vi* be mischievous; *vr* be entangled; be involved (in difficulties)
enredo *m*, tangle; mischief, prank; intrigue, malicious falsehood; difficult situation; plot
enredoso *a* tangled; fraught with difficulties
enrejado *m*, railing, paling; trellis or latticework; *sew* openwork
enrejar *vt* to fence with a railing; cover with grating
enriquecer *vt irr* to enrich; exalt, aggrandize; *vi* grow rich; prosper, flourish. See **conocer**
enriscado *a* craggy, rocky
enristrar *vt* to couch (a lance); string (onions, etc.); *fig* surmount (difficulties); go straight to (a place)
enrojecer *vt irr* to redden; make blush; *vr* grow red; blush. See **conocer**
enroscar *vt* to twist, twine; *vr* turn (screw); twist; coil
ensaimada *f*, Spanish pastry cake
ensalada *f*, salad; hodgepodge
ensaladera *f*, salad bowl
ensalmar *vt surg* to set (bones); cure by spells
ensalmo *m*, spell, charm. **por e.,** as if by magic, rapidly
ensalzar *vt* to exalt, promote; praise
ensamblador *m*, joiner, assembler
ensambladura *f*, assemblage, joinery; joining; dovetailing
ensamblar *vt* to assemble; join, dovetail, mortise
ensanchador, -a *mf*, glove stretcher
ensanchar *vt* to widen, enlarge, extend; *sew* let out, stretch; *vr* put on airs
ensanche *m*, dilatation, widening; stretch; extension; *sew* turnings, letting out; (city) extension
ensangrentar *vt irr* to stain with blood; *vr* be bloodstained; be overhasty. See **regimentar**
ensañar *vt* to irritate, infuriate; *vr* be merciless (with vanquished)
ensartar *vt* to string (beads); thread (needles); spit, pierce; tell a string (of falsehoods)
ensayar *vt* to try out; *chem* test; *theat* rehearse; assay

ensayista *mf* essayist
ensayo *m*, test, trial; *lit* essay; assay; experiment; rehearsal. **e. general,** dress rehearsal
ensenada *f*, cove, inlet
enseñanza *f*, teaching; education; example, experience. **e. primaria,** elementary education. **e. secundaria,** secondary education. **e. superior,** higher education
enseñar *vt* to teach, instruct; train; point out; exhibit, show; *vr* become accustomed. **e. la oreja,** *fig* to show the cloven hoof
enseñorearse *vr* to take possession (of)
enseres *m pl*, household goods; utensils; equipment
ensilladero *m*, paddock
ensillar *vt* to saddle
ensimismarse *vr* to be lost in thought; *Lat. Am.* to become conceited
ensoberbecer *vt irr* to make haughty; *vr* become arrogant; grow rough (sea). See **conocer**
ensordecedor *a* deafening
ensordecer *vt irr* to deafen; *vi* become deaf; keep silent, refuse to reply. See **conocer**
ensuciar *vt* to soil, dirty; *fig* sully; *vr* be dirty; *inf* accept bribes
ensueño *m*, dream; illusion, fancy
entabicar *vt*, *Lat. Am.* to partition off
entablado *m*, stage, dais; wooden floor; planking
entablar *vt* to plank, floor with boards; board up; *surg* splint; undertake, initiate (negotiations, etc.); begin (conversations, etc.); *vr* settle (winds). **e. acción judicial,** to take legal action
entalegar *vt* to put into sacks or bags; hoard (money)
entalladura *f*, carving; sculpture; *carp* mortise, notch
entallar *vt* to carve; sculpture; engrave; notch, groove; tap (trees); fit (well or ill) at the waist
entallecer *vi irr* to sprout (plants). See **conocer**
entapizar *vt* to hang with tapestry; upholster; *fig* cover, carpet
entarimado *m*, wooden floor; dais
ente *m*, entity, being; *inf* object, individual
entechar *vt*, *Lat. Am.* to roof, to put a roof on
enteco *a* sickly, ailing, delicate
entendederas *f pl*, *inf* understanding
entendedor (-ra) *a* understanding, comprehending. *n* one who understands. **A buen e. pocas palabras,** A word to the wise is sufficient
entender *vt irr* to comprehend, understand; know; deduce, infer; intend; believe; (*with de*) be familiar with or knowledgeable about; (*with en*) have as a profession or trade; be engaged in; have authority in; *vr* understand oneself; have a reason (for behavior); understand each other; have an amatory understanding; be meant, signify; (*with con*) have an understanding with. **a mi e.,** in my opinion, as I see it. *Pres. Ind.* **entiendo, entiendes, entiende, entienden.** *Pres. Subjunc.* **entienda, entiendas, entienda, entiendan**
entendido *a* learned, knowledgeable
entendimiento *m*, understanding; mind, reason, intelligence
enteramente *adv* completely, entirely, wholly
enterar *vt* to inform, advise
entereza *f*, entirety; completeness; impartiality, integrity; fortitude, constancy; strictness, rigour
enternecer *vt irr* to soften, make tender; move to pity; *vr* be touched by compassion. See **conocer**
enternecimiento *m*, compassion, pity; tenderness
entero *a* entire; whole; robust, healthy; upright, just; constant, loyal; virgin; pure; *inf* strong, tough (cloth); *math* integral; *Lat. Am.* payment
enterrador *m*, gravedigger
enterrar *vt irr* to inter; outlive; bury, forget. See **acertar**
entibiar *vt* to make lukewarm; *fig* cool, temper
entidad *f*, entity; value, importance
entierro *m*, interment, burial; grave; funeral; buried treasure
entoldar *vt* to cover with an awning; hang with tapestry, etc., drape; cover (sky, clouds)
entomología *f*, entomology
entomológico *a* entomological
entomólogo *m*, entomologist
entonación *f*, intonation; modulation (voice); conceit
entonado *m*, haughty, conceited
entonar *vt* to modulate (voice); intone; blow (organ bellows); lead (song); *med* tone up; *art* harmonize; *vr* become conceited; *com* improve, harden (stock, etc.)
entonces *adv* then, at that time; in that case, that being so
entonelar *vt* to put in barrels or casks
entontecer *vt irr* to make stupid or foolish; *vr* become stupid. See **conocer**
entornar *vt* to leave ajar; half-close; upset, turn upside down
entorpecer *vt irr* to numb, make torpid; confuse, daze; obstruct, delay; *vr* go numb; be confused. See **conocer**
entorpecimiento *m*, numbness, torpidity; stupidity, dullness; delay, obstruction
entrada *f*, entrance; door, gate; admission; *cul* entree; admission ticket; *theat* house; takings, gate; *mil* entry; beginnings (of month, etc.); intimacy; right of entry. **entradas y salidas,** comings and goings; collusion; *com* ingoing and outgoing
entrampar *vt* to trap (animals); swindle; *fig inf* entangle (business affairs); *inf* load with debts; *vr* be bogged down; *inf* be in debt
entrante *a* incoming, entrant; next, coming (month)
entraña *f*, entrail; *pl* heart; *fig* center, core; humaneness; temperament. *inf* **no tener entrañas,** to be heartless, be without feeling
entrañable *a* intimate; dearly loved
entrar *vi* (*with en*) to enter, go into, come in; flow into; *fig* have access to; join, become a member; *fig* be taken by (fever, panic, etc.); *mil* enter; be an ingredient of; (*with por, en*) penetrate, pierce; (*with de*) embrace (professions, etc.); (*with prep a + infin*) begin to; (*with en + noun*) begin to be (e.g. **e. en calor,** begin to be hot) or begin to take part in (e.g. **e. en lucha,** begin to fight); *vt* introduce, make enter; *mil* (*with en*) occupy; *vr* (*with en*) squeeze in. **e. en apetito,** to work up an appetite, get an appetite. *inf* **no e. ni salir en,** to take no part in. *inf* **No me entra,** I don't understand it
entre *prep* between; among; to. **e. joyas,** among jewels. **E. las dos se escribió la carta,** Between them, they wrote the letter. **Dije e. mí,** I said to myself. **los días de e. semana,** weekdays. **e. tanto,** in the meanwhile.
entreabrir *vt* to leave ajar; half-open. *Past Part.* **entreabierto**
entreacto *m*, interval, entr'acte; small cigar
entrecano *a* going gray, grayish (hair)
entrecejo *m*, space between the eyebrows; frown
entrecerrar *vt*, *Lat. Am* to close halfway, half-close; leave ajar
entrecoger *vt* to intercept, catch; constrain, compel
entrecortado *a* intermittent (sounds); faltering, broken (voice)
entrecubiertas *f pl*, *naut* between decks
entredicho *m*, prohibition; *ecc* interdiction
entredós *m*, *sew* insertion
entrefino *a* middling, fairly fine
entrega *f*, handing over; delivery; *lit* part, serial; installment. **por entregas,** as a serial, serial (of stories)
entregar *vt* to hand over; deliver; surrender; *vr* give oneself up; surrender; submit; (*with prep a*) engage in, be absorbed in; (*with prep a* or *en*) give oneself over to (vice, etc.)
entreguista *mf* defeatist
entrelazar *vt* to interlace, intertwine; interweave
entrelistado *a* striped
entrelucir *vi irr* to show through, be glimpsed. See **lucir**
entremedias *adv* in between, halfway; in the meantime

entremés *m*, hors d'oeuvres (gen. *pl*); interlude, one-act farce
entremeter *vt* to place between or among; *vr* intrude; meddle, pry
entremetido (-da) *a* meddlesome. *n* busybody, meddler
entremetimiento *m*, meddlesomeness
entremezclar *vt* to intermingle
entrenador (-ra) *n* trainer; *sport* coach
entrenamiento *m*, training, exercise
entrenar(se) *vt* and *vr* to train; exercise; *sport* coach
entreoír *vt* to overhear; hear imperfectly
entrepaño *m*, *arch* panel; pier (between windows, etc.)
entrepiernas *f pl*, crotch
entresacar *vt* to choose or pick out; thin out (plants); thin (hair)
entresuelo *m*, mezzanine, entresol; ground floor
entresueño *m*, daydream
entretallar *vt* to carve in bas-relief; engrave; *sew* do openwork; intercept; *vr* connect, dovetail
entretejer *vt* to interweave; interlace; *lit* insert
entretela *f*, *sew* interlining
entretener *vt irr* to keep waiting; make more bearable; amuse, entertain; delay, postpone; maintain, upkeep; *vr* amuse oneself. See **tener**
entretenido *a* amusing, entertaining
entretenimiento *m*, amusement; pastime, diversion; upkeep, maintenance
entretiempo *m*, between seasons, spring or autumn
entreventana *f*, space between windows
entreverado *a* variegated; streaky (of bacon)
entreverar *vt* to intermingle
entrevista *f*, meeting, interview
entristecer *vt irr* to sadden; *vr* grieve. See **conocer**
entristecimiento *m*, sadness
entrometer *vt* See **entremeter**
entromparse *vt*, *Lat. Am.* to get angry
entronar *vt* See **entronizar**
entroncar *vt* to prove descent; *vi* be related, or become related (by marriage)
entronerar *vt* to pocket (in billiards)
entronizar *vt* to enthrone; exalt
entronque *m*, blood relationship, cognation; junction
entrucharse *vr*, *Mexico* to meddle into other people's business
entumecer *vt irr* to numb; *vr* go numb; swell, rise (sea, etc.). See **conocer**
enturbiar *vt* to make turbid or cloudy; confuse, disorder; *vr* become turbid; be in disorder
entusiasmar *vt* to inspire enthusiasm; *vr* be enthusiastic
entusiasmo *m*, enthusiasm
entusiasta *a* enthusiastic. *mf* enthusiast
enumeración *f*, enumeration
enumerar *vt* to enumerate
enunciación *f*, statement, declaration, enunciation
enunciar *vt* to state clearly, enunciate
envainar *vt* to sheathe
envalentonamiento *m*, boldness; braggadocio, bravado
envalentonar *vt* to make bold (gen. in a bad sense); *vr* strut, brag; take courage
envanecer *vt irr* to make vain or conceited; *vr* be vain; be conceited
envanecimiento *m*, conceit, vanity
envasador (-ra) *n* packer. *m*, funnel
envasar *vt* to bottle; barrel; sack (grain, etc.); pack in any container; pierce (with sword)
envase *m*, bottling; filling; container; packing
envejecer *vt irr* to make old, wear out; *vi* grow old. See **conocer**
envenenador (-ra) *n* poisoner
envenenamiento *m*, poisoning
envenenar *vt* to poison; corrupt, pervert; put a malicious interpretation on; embitter; *vr* take poison
envergadura *f*, wingspan
envés *m*, wrong side of anything; *inf* back. **al e.,** wrong side out
enviado *m*, messenger; envoy. **e. extraordinario,** special envoy
enviar *vt* to send, dispatch
enviciar *vt* to corrupt, make vicious; *vr* (*with con, en*) take to (drink, etc.)
envidia *f*, envy; emulation; desire (to possess)
envidiable *a* enviable
envidiar *vt* to envy, grudge; emulate
envidioso *a* envious
envilecer *vt irr* to debase; *vr* degrade oneself. See **conocer**
envinarse *vr*, *Mexico* to get drunk (on wine)
envío *m*, *com* remittance; consignment
envite *m*, stake (at cards); offer; push, shove
enviudar *vi* to become a widow or widower
envoltorio *m*, bundle
envoltura *f*, swaddling clothes; covering; wrapping
envolver *vt irr* to enfold; envelop; wrap up, parcel; *fig* contain, enshrine; swaddle, swathe; roll into a ball; confound (in argument); *mil* outflank; implicate (person). See **mover**
enyesado *m*, plastering; stucco
enyesar *vt* to plaster; *surg* apply a plaster bandage
enzarzar *vt* to fill or cover with brambles; *vr* be caught on brambles; set one person against another; get in difficulties; quarrel
eñe *f*, name of the letter Ñ
eón *m*, eon
eperlano *m*, smelt
épica *f*, epic
épico *a* epic
epicúreo (-ea) *a* epicurean; sensual, voluptuous. *n* epicure
epidemia *f*, epidemic
epidémico *a* epidemic
epifanía *f*, Epiphany, Twelfth Night
epiglotis *f*, epiglottis
epígrafe *m*, epigraph, inscription; title, motto
epigrafía *f*, epigraphy
epigrama *m*, inscription; epigram
epigramático (-ca) *a* epigrammatic. *n* epigrammatist
epilepsia *f*, epilepsy
epiléptico (-ca) *a* and *n* epileptic
epilogar *vt* to summarize, recapitulate
epílogo *m*, recapitulation; summary, digest; epilogue
episcopado *m*, episcopate; bishopric
episodio *m*, episode; digression
epistolar *a* epistolary
epitafio *m*, epitaph
epíteto *m*, epithet
epítome *m*, epitome; summary, abstract
época *f*, epoch, period; space of time. **é. de celo,** mating season. **é. de lluvias,** rainy season. **é. de secas,** dry season. **en aquella é.,** at that time
épodo *m*, *poet* epode
epopeya *f*, epic poem; *fig* epic
equidad *f*, fairness; reasonableness; equity
equidistancia *f*, equidistance
equidistante *a* equidistant
equilibrar *vt* to balance; *fig* maintain in equilibrium, counterbalance
equilibrio *m*, equilibrium; equanimity; *fig* balance
equilibrista *mf* equilibrist, tightrope walker
equino *a* equine. *m*, *arch* echinus; sea urchin
equinoccio *m*, equinox
equipaje *m*, luggage, baggage; *naut* crew
equipar *vt* to equip, furnish
equipo *m*, outfitting, furnishing; equipment; team; trousseau
equis *f*, name of the letter X
equitación *f*, horsemanship, riding
equitativo *a* equitable, just, fair
equivalencia *f*, equivalence, equality
equivalente *a* equivalent

equivaler *vi irr* to be equivalent; *geom* be equal. See **valer**
equivocación *f,* error, mistake
equivocadamente *adv* mistakenly, by mistake
equivocar *vt* to mistake; *vr* be mistaken or make a mistake. **equivocarse de medio a medio,** to be off by a long shot
equívoco *a* equivocal, ambiguous. *m,* equivocation
era *f,* era; threshing floor; vegetable or flower bed
erario *m,* public treasury, exchequer
erección *f,* raising; erection, elevation; foundation, institution
eremita *mf* hermit
erguir *vt irr* to raise; straighten; lift up; *vr* straighten up; tower; grow proud. *Pres. Ind.* **irgo** (or **yergo**), **irgues, irguen.** *Pres. Part.* **irguiendo.** *Preterite* **irguió, irguieron.** *Pres. Subjunc.* **irga** or **yerga,** etc.
erial *m,* uncultivated land
erigir *vt* to found, establish; promote, exalt. **erigirse contra,** to rise up against
erisipela *f,* erysipelas
erizado *a* standing on end (of hair); prickly, covered with bristles or quills. **e. de espinas,** bristling with thorns; covered with bristles or quills
erizar *vt* to set on end (hair); beset with difficulties; *vr* stand on end, bristle (hair, quills, etc.)
erizo *m,* hedgehog; husk (of some fruits); *inf* touch-me-not, unsociable person; *mech* sprocket wheel. **e. de mar,** sea urchin
ermita *f,* hermitage
ermitaño *m,* hermit
erogación *f, Lat. Am.* expenditure
erosión *f,* erosion
erótico *a* erotic
errabundo *a* wandering, errant, vagrant
erradamente *adv* erroneously
erradicable *a* eradicable
erradicación *f,* eradication
erradicar *vt* to eradicate
errante *a* wandering; erring; errant
errar *vi irr* to err, fail; rove, roam; wander (attention, etc.); *vr* be mistaken. *aut* **e. el encendido,** to misfire. *Pres. Ind.* **yerro, yerras, yerra, yerran.** *Pres. Subjunc.* **yerre, yerres, yerre, yerren**
errata *f,* misprint
errático *a* wandering, vagrant; *med* erratic
erre *f,* name of the letter R
erróneo *a* erroneous, mistaken
error *m,* error. **error de más,** an overestimate. **error de menos,** an underestimate
eructar *vi* to eructate, belch
eructo *m,* eructation, belching
erudición *f,* erudition
erudito *a* learned, erudite. *m,* scholar. **e. a la violeta,** pseudo-learned
erupción *f, med* rash; eruption
eruptivo *a* eruptive
es *irr 3rd pers. sing Pres. Ind.* of ser, is
esa *f, dem a* that. **ésa,** *f, dem. pron* that one; the former; the town in which you are (e.g. **Iré a é. mañana,** I shall come to your town tomorrow). Used generally in letters. See **ése**
esbeltez *f,* slenderness
esbelto *a* tall and slim and graceful, willowy
esbozar *vt* to sketch, outline
esbozo *m,* sketch; outline, rough plan, first draft
escabechar *vt* to pickle; dye (the hair, etc.); *inf* kill in anger; *inf* fail (an examination)
escabeche *m, cul* pickle; hair dye
escabechina *f, inf* heavy failure (in an examination)
escabel *m,* footstool; small backless chair; *fig* stepping-stone
escabioso *a* scabby, scabious
escabro *m,* scab, mange
escabroso *a* rough; rocky; uneven; rude, unpolished, uncivil; risqué, improper
escabullirse *vr irr* to escape; run away; slip out unnoticed. See **mullir**
escafandra *f,* diving suit, diving outfit
escala *f,* ladder; (*mus math*) scale; dial (of machines); proportion, ratio; stage, stopping place; measuring rule; *naut* port of call. **e. de toldilla,** companion ladder. *mus* **e. mayor,** major scale. **e. menor,** minor scale. *naut* **hacer e. en un puerto,** to call at a port
escalada *f,* escalade
escalafón *m,* salary scale; roll, list
escalamiento *m,* scaling, climbing; storming
escalar *vt* to scale; climb, ascend; storm, assail, enter or leave violently
escaldadura *f,* scalding; scald
escaldar *vt* to scald; make red-hot; *vr* scald or burn oneself. **Gato escaldado del agua fría huye,** Once bitten, twice shy
escalera *f,* staircase; stair. **e. abajo,** below stairs. **e. de caracol,** spiral staircase. **e. de mano,** ladder. **e. de tijera,** stepladder. **e. móvil,** escalator
escalfar *vt* to poach (eggs); burn (bread)
escalinata *f,* outside staircase or flight of steps, perron
escalofrío *m,* (gen. *pl*) shiver, shudder
escalón *m,* step, stair; rung (of a ladder); *fig* stepping-stone; grade, rank. **en escalones,** in steps
escalpar *vt* to scalp
escalpelo *m,* scalpel
escama *f, zool* scale; anything scale-shaped; flake; suspicion, resentment
escamar *vt* to scale (fish); make suspicious. *vr inf* be suspicious or disillusioned
escamondar *vt agr* to prune
escamoso *a* scaly
escamotear *vt* to make disappear; palm (in conjuring); steal
escamoteo *m,* disappearance; stealing
escampada *f, inf* clear interval on a rainy day
escampar *vi* to cease raining; clear up (of the weather, sky); stop (work, etc.)
escamujar *vt agr* to cut out superfluous wood (of trees, etc.)
escanciar *vt* to pour out wine; *vi* drink wine
escandalizar *vt* to shock, scandalize; disturb with noise; *vr* be vexed or irritated
escándalo *m,* scandal; commotion, uproar; bad example; viciousness; astonishment
escandaloso *a* disgraceful, scandalous; turbulent
escandallo *m, naut* deep-sea lead; random test
Escandinavia Scandinavia
escandinavo (-va) *a* and *n* Scandinavian
escansión *f,* scansion
escantillón *m,* template, pattern; rule
escaño *m,* bench with a back
escapada *f,* escape; escapade
escapar *vt* to spur on (a horse); *vi* escape; flee; avoid, evade; *vr* escape; leak (gas, etc.). **Se me escapó su nombre,** His name escaped me. **e. por un pelo,** to have a narrow escape
escaparate *m,* showcase, cabinet; shop window
escapatoria *f,* escape, flight; *inf* way out, loophole
escape *m,* flight; evasion; escape (gas, etc.); *aut* exhaust. **a e.,** at full speed
escápula *f,* scapula
escaque *m,* square (chessboard or checkerboard); *pl* chess
escaqueado *a* checked, worked in squares
escara *f,* scar
escarabajo *m,* beetle, scarab; *fig inf* dwarf; *pl inf* scrawl
escaramuza *f,* skirmish
escaramuzar *vi* to skirmish
escarapela *f,* cockade, rosette; brawl
escarbadientes *m,* toothpick
escarbar *vt* to scratch, scrabble (fowls); rootle, dig; rake out (the fire); inquire into
escarcha *f,* hoarfrost

escarchar *vt cul* to frost, ice; spread with frosting; *vi* freeze lightly
escarda *f*, weeding; *fig* weeding out
escardador (-ra) *n* weeder
escardar *vt* to weed; *fig* separate good from bad
escarificación *f*, scarification
escarlata *f*, scarlet; scarlet cloth
escarlatina *f*, scarlet fever
escarmentar *vt irr* to reprehend or punish severely; *vi* learn from experience, be warned. See **acertar**
escarmiento *m*, disillusionment, experience; warning; punishment, fine
escarnecedor (-ra) *a* mocking. *n* mocker
escarnecer *vt irr* to mock. See **conocer**
escarnio *m*, gibe, jeer
escarola *f*, endive; frilled ruff
escarpa *f*, steep slope, declivity; escarpment; *Mexico* pavement
escarpado *a* steep, precipitous
escarpín *m*, pump, slipper
escasear *vt* to dole out, give grudgingly; save, husband; *vi* be scarce or short; grow less
escasez *f*, meanness, frugality; want; shortage, scarcity
escaso *a* scarce; short; bare; parsimonious
escatimar *vt* to cut down, curtail
escatimoso *a* malicious, guileful
escayola *f*, plaster of Paris
escena *f*, *theat* stage; scene; scenery; theater, drama; spectacle, sight; episode, incident. **director de e.,** producer. **poner en e.,** *theat* to produce
escenario *m*, *theat* stage; scenario
escénico *a* scenic
escenografía *f*, scenography
escenógrafo (-fa) *n* scenographer, scene painter
escepticismo *m*, scepticism
escéptico (-ca) *a* sceptical. *n* sceptic
escindir *vt* to split
escisión *f*, cleavage, split; splitting; schism; disagreement
esclarecer *vt irr* to illuminate; ennoble, make illustrious; *fig* enlighten; elucidate; *vi* dawn. See **conocer**
esclarecido *a* distinguished, illustrious
esclavina *f*, short cape
esclavitud *f*, slavery; fraternity
esclavizar *vt* to enslave
esclavo (-va) *n* slave; member of a brotherhood. *a* enslaved. *f*, slave bracelet; ID bracelet
esclerosis *f*, sclerosis
esclerótica *f*, sclerotic
esclusa *f*, lock; sluice gate; weir
esclusero, -a *mf*, lock keeper
escoba *f*, broom, brush; *bot* yellow broom
escobada *f*, sweep, stroke (of a broom)
escobar *vt* to sweep with a broom
escobazo *m*, brush with a broom
escobero, -a brush maker; brush seller
escobilla *f*, brush
escocer *vi irr* to smart; *fig* sear; *vr* hurt, smart; be chafed. See **mover**
escocés (-esa) *a* Scots, Scottish. *n* Scot
Escocia Scotland
escoda *f*, claw hammer
escofina *f*, rasp, file
escoger *vt* to choose, select
escogido *a* choice, select
escolar *a* school; pupil. *m*, pupil
escolasticismo *m*, scholasticism
escolástico *a* scholastic
escoleta *f*, *Mexico* amateur band
escollera *f*, breakwater, sea wall, jetty
escollo *m*, reef; danger, risk; difficulty, obstacle
escolopendra *f*, centipede; hart's-tongue fern
escolta *f*, escort, guard
escoltar *vt* to escort; guard, conduct
escombrar *vt* to remove obstacles, free of rubbish; *fig* clean up
escombro *m*, debris, rubble, rubbish; mackerel
esconder *vt* to hide, conceal; *fig* contain, embrace; *vr* hide
escondidas, a *adv* secretly
escondite, escondrijo *m*, hiding place. **jugar al escondite,** to play hide-and-seek
escopeta *f*, shotgun. **e. de aire comprimido,** air gun, popgun. **e. de pistón,** repercussion gun. **e. de viento,** air gun
escopetazo *m*, gunshot; gunshot wound; *fig* bombshell
escopetear *vt* to shoot repeatedly
escopetero *m*, musketeer; gunsmith; man with a gun
escoplear *vt carp* to notch; chisel; gouge
escoplo *m*, chisel
escorbuto *m*, scurvy
escoria *f*, dross, slag; scoria, volcanic ash; *fig* dregs
escorial *m*, slag heap
escorpión *m*, scorpion; Scorpio
escorzo *m*, *art* foreshortening
escotado *a* low-cut (of dresses)
escotadura *a* low neck (of a dress); piece cut out of something; *theat* large trapdoor; recess
escotar *vt* to cut low in the neck (of dresses); pay one's share (of expenses)
escote *m*, low neck (of a dress); shortness (of sleeves); share (of expenses); lace yoke
escotilla *f*, *naut* hatch
escozor *m*, smart, pricking pain; irritation, prickle; heartache
escriba *m*, (*Jewish hist.*) scribe
escribanía *f*, secretaryship; notaryship; bureau, office; writing case; inkstand
escribano *m*, notary public; secretary
escribiente *mf* clerk
escribir *vt* to write; *vr* enlist; enroll; correspond by writing. *Past Part.* **escrito**
escrito *m*, writing, manuscript; literary or scientific work; *law* writ. **por e.,** in writing
escritor (-ra) *n* writer, author
escritorio *m*, escritoire; office
escritura *f*, writing; handwriting; *law* deed; literary work. **Sagrada E.,** Holy Scripture
escrófula *f*, scrofula
escrofuloso *a* scrofulous
escroto *m*, scrotum
escrúpulo *m*, scruple, qualm; conscientiousness; scruple (pharmacy)
escrupulosidad *f*, conscientiousness, scrupulousness
escrupuloso *a* scrupulous; exact, accurate
escrutador (-ra) *n* scrutinizer. *a* examining, inspecting
escrutar *vt* to scrutinize, examine; count (votes)
escrutinio *m*, scrutiny, examination; count (votes)
escuadra *f*, carpenter's square; architect's square; *nav* fleet; *aer* squadron; *mil* squad. **e. de agrimensor,** *surv* cross-staff
escuadrar *vt* (*carp* and *mas*) to square
escuadrilla *f*, squadron (airplanes, small ships)
escuadrón *m*, squadron
escualidez *f*, squalor, sordidness
escuálido *a* filthy, squalid; sordid; thin
escucha *f*, listening; peephole; *mil* sentinel
escuchar *vt* to listen; attend to, heed; *vr* like the sound of one's own voice
escudar *vt* to shield, protect
escudero *m*, squire, page; gentleman; shield maker
escudete *m*, escutcheon; shield; gusset; white water lily
escudilla *f*, bowl
escudo *m*, shield; escudo; escutcheon; protection, defense; ward (of a keyhole)
escudriñador (-ra) *a* searching; curious, prying. *n* scrutinizer; pryer
escudriñar *vt* to scrutinize; scan; investigate; pry into
escuela *f*, school; school building; style; (*lit* and *art*) school. **e. de artes y oficios,** industrial school. **e. industrial,** technical school. **e. normal,** normal school
escuelante *m*, *Mexico* schoolmaster

escueto *a* dry, bare, unadorned; simple, exact; unencumbered
escuincle *mf, Mexico* child
esculpir *vt* to sculpture; engrave
escultor (-ra) *n* sculptor
escultórico *a* sculptural
escultura *f*, sculpture; carving; modeling
escupidera *f*, spittoon
escupir *vi* to expectorate; *vt fig* spit out; cast away, throw out
escurreplatos *m*, dishrack, draining rack
escurrido *a* narrow-hipped; skintight (of skirts)
escurridor *m*, colander, sieve; dishrack; drainingboard
escurriduras *f pl*, lees, dregs
escurrir *vt* to drain to the dregs; wring, press out, drain; *vi* trickle, drip; slip, slide; *vr* slip away, edge away; escape, slip out; skid
esdrújulo *a gram* of words where the stress falls on the antepenultimate syllable
ese *f*, name of letter S; S-shaped link (in a chain). *inf* **andar haciendo eses,** to reel about drunkenly
ese *m, dem a* (*f*, **esa.** *pl* **esos, esas**) that; those. **ése,** *m, dem pron* (*f*, **ésa.** *neut* **eso.** *pl* **ésos, ésas**) that one; the former (e.g. **Me gusta éste, pero ése no me gusta,** I like this one, but I do not like that one
esencia *f*, essence, nature, character; extract; *chem* essence
esencial *a* essential
esfera *f*, *geom* sphere, globe, ball; sky; rank; face, dial; province, scope
esférico *a* spherical
esfinge *f*, sphinx
esforzado *a* valiant, courageous; spirited
esforzador *a* encouraging
esforzar *vt irr* to encourage; invigorate; *vr* make an effort. See **contar**
esfuerzo *m*, effort; courage; spirit; vigor; exertion, strain; *mech* stress. **sin e.,** effortless
esfumar *vt art* shade; *art* stump; dim; *vr* disappear
esfumino *m*, *art* stump
esgrima *f*, (art of) fencing
esgrimidor *m*, fencer, swordsman
esgrimir *vt* to fence; fend off
esguince *m*, dodging, twist; expression or gesture of repugnance; *med* sprain
eslabón *m*, link (in a chain); steel for producing fire. **e. perdido,** *fig* missing link
eslabonar *vt* to link; connect, unite
eslavo (-va) *a* Slavic. *n* Slav
eslora *f*, *naut* length (of a ship)
eslovaco (-ca) *a* Slovakian. *n* Slovak
esmaltador (-ra) *n* enameler
esmaltar *vt* to enamel; decorate, adorn
esmalte *m*, enamel; enamelwork; smalt; brilliance
esmerado *a* careful, painstaking
esmeralda *f*, emerald
esmerar *vt* to polish; *vr* (*with en*) take great pains with (or to)
esmeril *m*, emery
esmerilar *vt* to polish with emery
esmero *m*, great care, conscientiousness
esmoladera *f*, grindstone
esnob *a* snobbish. *mf* snob
eso *neut dem pron* that; the fact that; that idea, affair, etc.; about (of time) (e.g. **Vendrá a e. de las nueve,** He will come about nine o'clock). **Eso** refers to an abstraction, never to one definite object. **No me gusta e.,** I don't like that kind of thing. **e. es,** that's it. **por e.,** therefore, for that reason
esófago *m*, esophagus
esotérico *a* esoteric
espaciar *vt* to space; *print* lead; *vr* spread oneself, enlarge (upon)
espacio *m*, space; capacity; interval, duration; slowness; *print* lead
espaciosidad *f*, spaciousness; capacity
espada *f*, sword; matador; swordsman; (cards) spade. **entre la e. y la pared,** *fig* between a rock and a hard place; between undesirable alternatives.
espadachín *m*, good swordsman; bully, quarrelsome fellow
espadaña *f*, open belfry; gladiolus
espadería *f*, sword cutler's workshop or shop
espadero *m*, sword cutler
espadín *m*, small dress sword
espahi *m*, spahi
espalda *f*, *anat* back (often *pl*); *pl* rear, back portion; *mil* rear guard. **de espaldas,** with one's (its, his, etc.) back turned; on one's (its, etc.) back
espaldar *m*, backpiece of a cuirass; back (of chair); garden trellis, espalier
espaldarazo *m*, accolade
espaldera *f*, espalier, trellis
espantadizo *a* easily frightened
espantapájaros *m*, scarecrow
espantar *vt* to frighten, terrify; chase off; *vr* be amazed; be scared
espanto *m*, terror, panic; dismay; amazement; threat
espantoso *a* horrible, terrifying, awesome; amazing
España Spain
español (-la) *a* Spanish. *n* Spaniard. *m*, Spanish (language). **a la española,** in Spanish fashion
españolía *f*, Spanish colony, Spanish community (outside Spain)
españolismo *m*, love of things Spanish; Hispanism
españolizar *vt* to hispanize; *vr* adopt Spanish customs
esparadrapo *m*, court plaster
esparavel *m*, casting net
esparcimiento *m*, scattering; naturalness, frankness; geniality
esparcir *vt* to scatter, sprinkle, disperse; spread, publish abroad; entertain; *vr* be scattered; amuse oneself
espárrago *m*, asparagus
esparraguera *f*, asparagus plant; asparagus bed; asparagus dish
Esparta Sparta
espartano (-na) *a* and *n* Spartan
espartería *f*, esparto industry, esparto shop
esparto *m*, esparto grass
espasmo *m*, spasm
espasmódico *a* spasmodic
espátula *f*, spatula; palette knife
especia *f*, spice. **nuez de e.,** nutmeg
especial *a* special; particular
especialidad *f*, speciality; branch (of learning)
especialista *mf* specialist
especialización *f*, specialization
especializarse *vr* to specialize
especie *f*, class, kind; species; affair, matter, case; idea, image; news; pretext, appearance
especiería *f*, spice trade; spice shop
especiero (-ra) *n* spice merchant; spice rack
especificación *f*, specification. **e. normalizada,** standard specification
especificar *vt* to specify, particularize
específico *a* and *m*, specific patent medicine
espécimen *m*, specimen, sample
especioso *a* lovely, perfect; specious
espectacular *a* spectacular
espectáculo *m*, spectacle, sight; show, display
espectador (-ra) *n* spectator
espectral *a* spectral; faint, dim
espectro *m*, phantom, specter; *phys* spectrum
especulación *f*, conjecture; *com* speculation
especulador (-ra) *n* speculator
especular *vt* to examine, look at; (*with en*) reflect on, consider; *vi com* speculate
especulativo *a* speculative; thoughtful, meditative
espejería *f*, mirror shop or factory
espejero *m*, mirror manufacturer or seller
espejismo *m*, mirage; illusion

espejo *m*, mirror; *fig* model. **e. de cuerpo entero,** full-length mirror. **e. retrovisor,** rearview mirror
espejuelo *m*, small mirror; *min* selenite; *min* sheet of talc; *pl* lenses, eyeglasses
espeluznante *a* hair-raising
espeluznar *vt* to dishevel; untidy (hair, etc.); *vr* stand on end (hair)
espera *f*, waiting; expectation; *law* adjournment; caution, restraint; *law* respite
esperantista *mf* Esperantist
esperanto *m*, Esperanto
esperanza *f*, hope
esperanzar *vt* to inspire hope in
esperar *vt* to hope; expect; await; (*with en*) have faith in. **e. sentado,** *fig inf* to whistle for
esperma *f*, sperm, semen. **e. de ballena,** spermaceti
esperpento *m*, *inf* scarecrow, grotesque; folly, madness; fantastic dramatic composition
espesar *vt* to thicken; make closer; tighten (fabrics); *vr* thicken; grow denser or thicker
espeso *a* thick; dense; greasy, dirty
espesor *m*, thickness; density
espesura *f*, thickness; density; thicket; filth
espetar *vt cul* to spit, skewer; pierce; *inf* utter, give; *vr* be stiff or affected; *inf* push oneself in, intrude
espetera *f*, kitchen or pot rack
espetón *m*, *cul* spit; poker; large pin
espía *mf* spy. *f*, *naut* warp
espiar *vt* to spy upon, watch; *vi naut* warp
espiche *m*, sharp-pointed weapon or instrument; spit, spike
espiga *f*, *bot* spike, ear; sprig; *carp* peg; tang, shank (of sword); *carp* tenon, dowel; *naut* masthead; *her* garb
espigador (-ra) *n* gleaner
espigar *vt* to glean; *carp* tenon; *vi bot* begin to show the ear or spike; *vr bot* bolt; shoot up, grow (persons)
espigón *m*, sting; sharp point; breakwater; bearded spike (corn, etc.)
espigueo *m*, gleaning
espiguero *m*, *Mexico* granary
espín *m*, porcupine
espina *f*, thorn; prickle; splinter; fish bone; *anat* spine; suspicion, doubt
espinaca *f*, spinach
espinal *a* spinal
espinar *m*, thorn brake; *fig* awkward position. *vt* to prick, wound, hurt
espinazo *m*, backbone
espinilla *f*, shinbone; blackhead
espinoso *a* thorny; difficult, intricate
espión *m*, See **espía**
espionaje *m*, espionage; spying
espira *f*, (*geom arch*) helix; turn, twist (of winding stairs); whorl (of a shell)
espiración *f*, expiration; respiration
espiral *a* spiral. *f*, *geom* spiral; spiral watchspring
espirar *vt* to exhale, breathe out; inspire; encourage; *vi* breathe; breathe out; *poet* blow (wind)
espiritisimo *m*, spiritualism
espiritista *a* spiritualist. *mf* spiritualist
espiritoso *a* lively, active, spirited; spirituous
espíritu *m*, spirit; apparition, specter; soul; intelligence, mind; mood, temper, outlook; underlying principle, spirit; devil (gen. *pl*) vigor, ardor, vivacity; *chem* essence; *chem* spirits; turn of mind. **E. Santo,** Holy Ghost
espiritual *a* spiritual
espiritualidad *f*, spirituality
espiritualismo *m*, *phil* spiritualism
espita *f*, spigot, tap; *inf* tippler
esplender *vi poet* to shine
esplendidez *f*, liberality, abundance; splendor, pomp
espléndido *a* magnificent; liberal; resplendent (gen. *pl*)
esplendor *m*, splendor, brilliance; distinction, nobility
esplendoroso *a* splendid, brilliant, radiant
espliego *m*, lavender
esplín *m*, spleen, melancholy
espolada *f*, prick with the spur
espolear *vt* to prick with the spur; encourage, stimulate
espoleta *f*, fuse (of explosives); breastbone (of fowls); wishbone. **e. de tiempo, e. graduada,** time fuse. **e. de seguridad,** safety fuse
espolón *m*, spur (of a bird or mountain range); *naut* ram; breakwater; buttress; *naut* fender
espolvorear *vt* to sprinkle with powder
esponja *f*, sponge
esponjadura *f*, sponging
esponjar *vt* to make spongy; sponge; *vr* swell with pride; *inf* bloom with health
esponjera *f*, sponge holder
esponjosidad *f*, sponginess
esponjoso *a* spongy, porous
esponsales *m pl*, betrothal; marriage contract
espontaneidad *f*, spontaneity
espontáneo *a* spontaneous
espora *f*, spore
esporádico *a* sporadic
esportillo *m*, bass, frail
esposa *f*, wife; *pl* handcuffs
esposo *m*, husband; *pl* husband and wife
espuela *f*, spur; stimulus; (*orn bot*) spur. **e. de caballero,** larkspur
espuelar *vt*, *Lat. Am.* to spur, spur on
espulgar *vt* to delouse; examine carefully
espuma *f*, froth, foam; *cul* scum; *fig* the best of anything, flower; *fig inf* **crecer como la e.,** to flourish like weeds
espumadera *f*, skimming ladle
espumajear *vi* to foam at the mouth
espumajoso *a* frothy, foaming
espumar *vt* to skim (soup, etc.); *vi* foam; increase rapidly
espumilla *f*, *Lat. Am.* meringue
espumoso *a* frothy, foaming
espurio *a* bastard; spurious
esputo *m*, sputum
esqueje *m*, *agr* cutting
esquela *f*, note; (printed) card
esqueleto *m*, skeleton; *Mexico*, blank, form (to be filled out) *inf* skinny person; framework
esquema *f*, diagram, layout sketch; scheme, plan. **e. de una máquina,** drawing of a machine
esquemático *a* schematic; diagrammatic
esquematizar *vt* to plan, outline
esquí *m*, ski, snowshoe
esquiador, -a *mf*, skier
esquiar *vi* to ski
esquila *f*, cattle bell; small bell, hand bell; sheep shearing; (*icht bot*) squill
esquilador *a* shearing. *m*, sheep shearer
esquiladora *f*, shearing machine
esquilar *vt* to shear, clip (sheep, etc.)
esquileo *m*, shearing; shearing time or place
esquilmar *vt* to harvest; impoverish
esquilmo *m*, harvest
esquimal *a* and *mf* Eskimo
esquina *f*, corner; *Lat. Am.* corner shop; village shop
esquinado *a* having corners; *fig* difficult to approach (people)
esquirol *m*, *inf* strikebreaker, blackleg
esquisto *m*, *min* slate; shale
esquivada *f*, *Lat. Am.* evasion
esquivar *vt* to avoid; *vr* slip away, disappear; excuse oneself
esquivez *f*, unsociableness; unfriendliness, aloofness
esquivo *a* unsociable, elusive, aloof
estabilidad *f*, stability; fastness (of colors)
estabilizar *vt* to stabilize
estable *a* stable; fast (of colors)
establecer *vt irr* to establish, found, institute; decree; *vr* take up residence; open (a business firm). See **conocer**
establecimiento *m*, law, statute; foundation, institution; establishment

establero *m*, stablegroom
establo *m*, stable
estaca *f*, stake, pole; *agr* cutting; cudgel
estacada *f*, fence; *mil* palisade; place fixed for a duel
estacar *vt* to stake; fence; tie to a stake; *vr fig* be as still as a post
estación *f*, position, situation; season; station (railroad, etc.); depot; time, period; stop, halt; building, headquarters; *bot* habitat; (*surv geom ecc*) station
estacional *a* seasonal; *ast* stationary
estacionamiento *m*, stationing; *aut* parking
estacionar *vt* to station, place; *aut* park (a car); *vr* remain stationary; place oneself
estacionario *a* motionless; *ast* stationary. *m*, stationer
estacionómetro *m*, *Mexico* parking meter
estada *f*, sojourn
estadía *f*, stay, sojourn; *art* sitting (of a model)
estadio *m*, racetrack; stadium; furlong
estadista *mf*. statistician; statesman, stateswoman
estadística *f*, statistics
estadístico *a* statistical
estadizo *a* stagnant
estado *m*, state; condition; rank, position; *pol* state; profession; status; *com* statement. **e. de guerra,** state of war; martial law. **e. mayor central,** (*nav mil*) general staff. **e. tapón,** *pol* buffer state. **tomar e.,** to marry; *ecc* profess; be ordained a priest
Estados Unidos de América United States of America
estadounidense *a* United States
estafa *f*, swindle
estafador (-ra) *n* swindler
estafar *vt* to swindle
estafeta *f*, courier, messenger; branch post office; diplomatic pouch
estagnación *f*, stagnation
estalactita *f*, stalactite
estalagmita *f*, stalagmite
estallar *vi* to explode; burst; *fig* break out
estallido *m*, explosion, report; crash, crack; *fig* outbreak; *aut* **e. de un neumático,** blowout (of a tire)
estambre *m*, woolen yarn, worsted; stamen
estameña *f*, serge
estampa *f*, illustration, picture; print; aspect; printing press; track, step; *met* boss, stud
estampación *f*, stamping; printing; imprinting. **e. en seco,** tooling (of a book)
estampado *a* printed (of textiles). *m*, textile printing; printed fabric
estampar *vt* to print, stamp; leave the print (of); bestow, imprint. **e. en relieve,** to emboss. **e. en seco,** to tool (a book)
estampería *f*, print or picture shop; trade in prints
estampero *m*, print dealer, picture dealer
estampido *m*, report, bang, detonation; crash
estampilla *f*, rubber stamp; seal; *Lat. Am (except Mexico)*, (postage) stamp
estampillar *vt* to stamp, imprint
estancación *f*, stagnation
estancado *a* stagnant; blocked, held up
estancar *vt* to check, stem; set up a monopoly; *fig* hold up (negotiations, etc.); *vr* be stagnant
estancia *f*, stay, residence; dwelling; lounge, living-room; stanza; *WH* farm; ranch
estanciero *m*, *WH* farmer; rancher
estanco *a naut* watertight. *m*, monopoly; shop selling government monopoly goods; archive
estandarte *m*, standard, flag. **e. real,** royal standard
estanque *m*, tank; pool; reservoir
estanquero (-ra) *n* seller of government monopoly goods (tobacco, matches, etc.)
estante *a* present; extant; permanent. *m*, shelf; bookcase; bin (for wine)
estantería *f*, shelving; shelves, bookcase
estantigua *f*, hobgoblin, specter; *fig inf* scarecrow
estañador *m*, tinsmith
estañar *vt* to tin; solder
estaño *m*, tin
estaquilla *f*, peg, cleat
estar *vi irr* to be. Indicates: 1. Position or place (e.g. **Está a la puerta,** He is at the door). 2. State (e.g. **Las flores están marchitas,** The flowers are faded). 3. Used to form the continuous or progressive tense (e.g. **Siempre está (estaba) escribiendo,** He is (was) always writing). 4. In contrast to verb *ser*, indicates impermanency (e.g. **Está enfermo,** He is ill). 5. **Estar** forms an apparent passive where no action is implied (e.g. **El cuadro está pintado al óleo,** The picture is painted in oils). 6. Used in some impersonal expressions (e.g. **¡Bien está!** All right! **¡Claro está!** Of course! etc.). **e. de,** to be in, or on, or acting as (e.g. **e. de prisa,** to be in a hurry. **e. de capitán,** to be acting as a captain). **e. para,** to be on the point of; to be nearly; to be in the mood for. **e. para llover,** to be on the point of raining. **e. por,** to remain to be done; have a mind to (e.g. **La historia está por escribir,** The story remains to be written). **e. a mano (con . . .)** *Lat. Am.* to be even (with . . .), be quits (with . . .) **e. bien,** to be well (healthy). *mech* **e. bajo presión,** to have the steam up. *pol* **e. en el poder,** to be in office. **e. en una cuenca,** *Dominican Republic* to be broke. **¿A cómo** (*or* **A cuántos**) **estamos?** What is the date? *Pres. Ind.* **estoy, estás, está, estamos, estáis, están.** *Preterite* **estuve,** etc. *Pres. Subjunc.* **esté, estés, esté, estén.** *Imperf. Subjunc.* **estuviese,** etc.
estarcir *vt* to stencil
estatal *a* state
estática *f*, *mech* statics
estático *a* static
estatizar *vt*, *Lat. Am.* to nationalize
estatua *f*, statue
estatuaria *f*, statuary
estatuir *vt irr* to establish, order. See **huir**
estatura *f*, stature, height (of persons)
estatuto *m*, statute, law
estay *m*, *naut* stay. **e. mayor,** *naut* mainstay
este *m*, east
este *m*, *dem a* this (*f*, **esta,** *pl* **estos, estas,** these). **éste,** *m*, *dem pron* this one; the latter. (*f*, **ésta,** *neut* **esto,** *pl* **éstos, éstas,** these ones; the latter) (e.g. **Aquel cuadro no es tan hermoso como éste,** That picture is not as beautiful as this one)
estela *f*, wake, track (of a ship)
estenografía *f*, shorthand
estenordeste *m*, east-northeast
estentóreo *a* stentorian
estepa *f*, steppe, arid plain
estera *f*, matting
esterar *vt* to cover with matting; *vi inf* muffle oneself up
estercoladura *f*, manuring
estercolar *vt* to manure
estercolero *m*, manure pile; driver of a dung cart
estereoscopio *m*, stereoscope
esterería *f*, matting factory, matting shop
esterero (-ra) *n* matting maker, matting seller
estéril *a* sterile, barren; unfruitful, unproductive
esterilidad *f*, sterility; barrenness, unfruitfulness
esterilización *f*, sterilization
esterilizador *a* sterilizing. *m*, sterilizer
esterilizar *vt* to make barren; *med* sterilize
esterilla *f*, mat, matting
esterlina *a f*, sterling. **libra e.,** pound sterling
esternón *m*, sternum
estero *m*, salt marsh
estertor *m*, stertorous breathing, rattle
estesudeste *m*, east-southeast
estética *f*, aesthetics. *a* aesthete
estético *a* aesthetic *m*, aesthete
estetoscopio *m*, stethoscope
esteva *f*, plow handle
estevado *a* bandy-legged
estiaje *m*, low water level (of rivers)
estibador *m*, stevedore, dock worker

estibar *vt naut* to stow
estiércol *m,* dung; manure
estigio *a* Stygian; (*fig poet*) infernal
estigma *m,* stigma
estigmatizar *vt* to brand; stigmatize; insult
estilar *vi* to be accustomed; *vt* draw up (document)
estilete *m,* stiletto, dagger; needle, hand, pointer; *med* stylet
estilista *mf* stylist
estilística *f,* stylism, stylistics
estilizar *vt* to stylize
estilo *m,* (*art arch lit*) style, writing instrument; gnomon, pointer; manner, way; *bot* style. **por el e.,** in some such way, like that
estilográfico *a* stylographic. **pluma estilográfica,** fountain pen
estima *f,* appreciation, esteem, consideration
estimable *a* estimable
estimación *f,* valuation, estimate; regard, esteem. **e. prudente,** conservative estimate
estimar *vt* to value, estimate; esteem, judge
estimulante *m, med* stimulant. *a* stimulating
estimular *vt* to stimulate, excite; goad on, encourage, incite
estímulo *m,* stimulus; incitement, encouragement
estío *m,* summer
estipendiar *vt* to pay a stipend to
estipendiario *m,* stipendiary
estipendio *m,* stipend, pay, remuneration
estipulación *f,* stipulation; *law* clause, condition
estipular *vt* to stipulate; arrange terms; *law* covenant
estirado *a* stretched out; tight, stiff; wire-drawn (metals); stiff, pompous; parsimonious
estirador *m,* wire drawer
estirar *vt* to stretch; iron roughly (clothes); *met* wire-draw; dole out (money); *fig* stretch, go beyond the permissible; *vr* stretch oneself
estirpe *f,* race, stock, lineage
estival *a* summer
esto *dem pron neut* this, this matter, this idea, etc. Always refers to abstractions, never to a definite object. **e. de,** the matter of. **e. es,** that's it; namely. **por e.,** for this reason. **a todo e.,** meanwhile
estocada *f,* sword thrust
Estocolmo Stockholm
estofa *f, sew* quilting; kind, quality
estofado *m,* stew. *a sew* quilted; stewed
estofar *vt sew* to quilt; make a stew
estoicismo *m,* stoicism
estoico (-ca) *n* stoic. *a* stoical
estolidez *f,* idiocy
estólido (-da) *a* idiotic. *a* idiot
estomacal *a* stomach
estómago *m,* stomach
estomático *a* pertaining to the mouth, oral
estomatitis *f,* stomatitis
estonio (-ia) *a* and *n* Estonian. *m,* Estonian (language)
estopa *f,* tow; oakum
estopilla *f,* batiste, lawn; calico, cotton cloth
estopín *m, mil* quick march
estoque *m,* rapier; narrow sword
estoquear *vt* to wound or kill with a rapier
estoqueo *m,* swordplay
estorbador (-ra) *a* obstructive. *n* obstructer
estorbar *vt* to obstruct, impede; hinder
estorbo *m,* obstruction; hindrance, nuisance
estornino *m,* starling
estornudar *vi* to sneeze
estornudo *m,* sneezing; sneeze
estrabismo *m, med* strabismus, squint, cast
estrada *f,* road, highway
estrado *m,* dais
estrafalario *a inf* slovenly, untidy; *inf* eccentric, odd
estragar *vt* to corrupt, spoil, vitiate; ruin, destroy
estrago *m,* devastation, destruction, ruin, havoc
estrambólico, -a *Lat. Am.* = **estrambótico**
estrambote *m,* refrain
estrambótico *a inf* eccentric, odd, outlandish
estrangul *m, mus* mouthpiece
estrangulación *f,* strangulation; *aut* throttling
estrangulador (-ra) *a* strangling. *n* strangler. *m, aut* throttle
estrangular *vt* to strangle
estraperlista *mf* black marketeer
estraperlo *m,* black market
estratagema *f,* stratagem, trick
estrategia *f,* strategy
estratégico *a* strategic
estratego *m,* strategist
estratificación *f,* stratification
estrato *m, geol* stratum
estratosfera *f,* stratosphere
estraza *f,* rag. **papel de e.,** brown paper
estrechar *vt* to make narrower, tighten; hold tightly, clasp; compel, oblige; *vr* tighten oneself up; reduce one's expenses; *fig* tighten the bonds (of friendship, etc.). **e. la mano,** to shake hands
estrechez *f,* narrowness; tightness; scantiness; poverty, want. **e. de miras,** narrowmindedness
estrecho *a* narrow; tight; intimate, close; austere, rigid; meanspirited. *m, geog* strait
estregadera *f,* shoe scraper; scourer
estregar *vt irr* to rub, scour, scrub, scrape, scratch. See **cegar**
estrella *f,* star; fortune, fate; anything star-shaped; *fig* star. **e. de la pantalla,** movie star. **e. de mar,** starfish. **e. de rabo,** comet. **e. fugaz,** shooting star. **tener e.,** to be born under a lucky star
estrellado *a* star-shaped; full of stars, starry; shattered, broken; fried (eggs)
estrellamar *f,* starfish
estrellar *vt inf* to shatter, break into fragments; fry (eggs); *vr* be starry or sprinkled with stars; be dashed against; fail in, come up against
estrellón *m,* large, artificial star (painted or otherwise); star-like firework; *Lat. Am.* crash
estremecer *vt irr* to cause to tremble; perturb; *vr* shudder, tremble. See **conocer**
estremecimiento *m,* shudder, trembling; agitation
estrenar *vt* to use or do for the first time; inaugurate; give the first performance of (plays, etc.); *vr* do for the first time; *com* make the first sale of the day
estreno *m,* commencement, inauguration; first appearance; *theat* first performance, opening night, premiere
estrenque *m,* strong esparto rope
estrenuo *a* strong, energetic, agile
estreñimiento *m,* constipation
estreñir *vt* to constipate
estrépito *m,* clamor, din, great noise; fuss, show
estrepitoso *a* noisy, clamorous
estreptomicina *f,* streptomycin
estría *f, arch* fluting, stria
estribadero *m,* prop, support, strut
estribar *vi* (*with en*) to lean on, rest on, be supported by; *fig* be based on
estribillo *m,* refrain
estribo *m,* stirrup; footboard, step, running board (of vehicles); *arch* buttress or pier; *fig* stay, support; *anat* stapes; *mech carp* stirrup piece. **perder los estribos,** to lose patience, forget oneself
estribor *m,* starboard
estricnina *f,* strychnine
estricto *a* strict, exact; unbending, severe
estridente *a* strident, shrill
estridor *m,* strident or harsh sound; screech; creak
estro *m,* inspiration
estrofa *f,* strophe; verse, stanza
estropajo *m,* scourer, dishcloth; worthless person or thing
estropajoso *a inf* indistinct, stammering; dirty and ragged; tough (meat, etc.)
estropear *vt* to spoil, damage; ruin, undo, spoil (plans,

effects, etc.); ill-treat, maim; *vr* hurt oneself, be maimed; spoil, deteriorate
estropicio *m, inf* crash (of china, etc.)
estructura *f,* fabric, structure; *fig* construction
estructural *a* structural
estruendo *m,* din, clatter; clamor, noise; ostentation
estruendoso *a* noisy
estrujar *vt* to squeeze, crush (fruit); hold tightly, press, squeeze, bruise; *fig inf* squeeze dry
estrujón *m,* squeeze, pressure; final pressing (grapes)
estuario *m,* estuary
estucado *m,* stucco
estucar *vt* to stucco
estuco *m,* stucco; plaster
estuche *m,* case; casket, box; cover; sheath
estudiantado *m, Lat. Am.* student body, students
estudiante *mf* student
estudiantil *a inf* student
estudiantina *f,* strolling band of students playing and singing, generally in aid of charity
estudiantino *a inf* student
estudiantón *m, inf* grind
estudiar *vt* to study. **e. de,** study to be a (e.g. **e. de rabino,** study to be a rabbi); learn; *art* copy
estudio *m,* study; sketch; disquisition, dissertation; studio; diligence; *art* study; reading room, den
estudiosidad *f,* studiousness
estudioso *a* studious
estufa *f,* heating stove; hothouse; hot room (in bathhouses); drying chamber; *elec* heater
estufador *m,* stewpot or casserole
estufista *mf* stove maker or repairer, stove seller
estulto *a* foolish
estupefacción *f,* stupefaction
estupefacto *a* stupefied, stunned, amazed
estupendo *a* wonderful, marvelous
estupidez *f,* stupidity
estúpido *a* stupid
estupor *m, med* stupor; astonishment
estupro *m, law* rape
estuque *m,* stucco
estuquería *f,* stuccowork
esturión *m,* sturgeon
esvástica *f,* swastika
etapa *f, mil* field ration; *mil* halt, camp; stage, juncture. **a pequeñas etapas,** by easy stages (of a journey)
etcétera etcetera
éter *m,* ether; *poet* sky
etéreo *a* etheric; ethereal
eterizar *vt* to etherize
eternidad *f,* eternity
eternizar *vt* to drag out, prolong; eternize, perpetuate
eterno *a* eternal, everlasting; lasting, enduring
ética *f,* ethics
ético *a* ethical. *m,* moralist
etimología *f,* etymology
etimológico *a* etymological
etimologista *mf* etymologist
etimólogo *m,* etymologist
etiología *f,* etiology
etíope *a* and *mf* Ethiopian
Etiopía Ethiopia
etiqueta *f,* etiquette; label
etiquetero *a* ceremonious, stiff; prim
étnico *a* ethnic; heathen
etnografía *f,* ethnography
etnográfico *a* ethnographic
etnología *f,* ethnology
etnólogo *m,* ethnologist
etrusco (-ca) *a* and *n* Etruscan
eubolia *f,* discretion in speech
eucalipto *m,* eucalyptus
Eucaristía *f,* Eucharist
euclídeo *a* Euclidean
eufemismo *m,* euphemism
eufonía *f,* euphony
eufónico *a* euphonious
euforia *f,* resistance to disease; buoyancy, well-being
eufuismo *m,* euphuism
eugenesia *f,* eugenics
eugenésico *a* eugenic
eunuco *m,* eunuch
euritmia *f,* eurythmics
eurítmico *a* eurythmic
euro *m, poet* east wind
Europa Europe
europeizar *vt* to Europeanize
europeo (-ea) *a* and *n* European
éuscaro *a* Basque. *m,* Basque (language)
eutanasia *f,* euthanasia
evacuación *f,* evacuation
evacuar *vt* to vacate; evacuate, empty; finish, conclude (a business deal, etc.)
evadir *vt* to avoid, elude; *vr* escape; elope
evaluación *f,* valuation; estimation
evaluar *vt* to evaluate, estimate; gauge; value
evangélico *a* evangelical
evangelio *m,* Gospel; Christianity; *inf* indisputable truth
evangelista *m,* evangelist
evangelizar *vt* to evangelize
evaporación *f,* evaporation
evaporar(se) *vt* and *vr* to evaporate; disappear, vanish
evasión, evasiva *f,* subterfuge, evasion; flight, escape
evasivo *a* evasive
evento *m,* happening, event; contingency
eventual *a* possible, fortuitous; accidental (expenses); extra (emoluments)
eventualidad *f,* eventuality
evicción *f, law* eviction
evidencia *f,* proof, evidence. **ponerse en e.,** to put oneself forward
evidenciar *vt* to show, make obvious
evidente *a* obvious, evident
evitable *a* avoidable
evitación *f,* avoidance
evitar *vt* to avoid; shun, eschew
evocación *f,* evocation
evocador *a* evocative
evocar *vt* to evoke
evolución *f,* evolution; development; (*mil nav*) maneuver; change; *geom* involution
evolucionar *vi* to evolve; (*nav mil*) maneuver; change, alter
evolucionismo *m,* evolutionism
evolutivo *a* evolutional
ex *prefix* out of; from; formerly
exacción *f,* exaction; tax
exacerbación *f,* exacerbation
exacerbar *vt* to exasperate; exacerbate
exactitud *f,* exactitude; correctness; punctuality
exacto *a* exact; correct; punctual
exactor *m,* tax collector; tyrant, oppressor
exageración *f,* exaggeration
exagerador (-ra) *a* given to exaggerating. *n* exaggerater
exagerar *vt* to exaggerate
exaltación *f,* exaltation
exaltar *vt* to exalt, elevate; extol; *vr* grow excited or agitated
exalumna *f, Lat. Am.* alumna, graduate
exalumno *m, Lat. Am.* alumnus, graduate
examen *m,* inquiry; investigation, research; examination; *geol* survey. **e. parcial,** quiz (at school)
examinador (-ra) *n* examiner
examinando (-da) *n* candidate, examinee
examinar *vt* to inquire into; investigate; inspect; examine; *vr* take an examination
exangüe *a* bloodless, pale; exhausted, weak; dead
exánime *a* lifeless; spiritless, weak
exasperación *f,* exasperation
exasperador, exasperante *a* exasperating
exasperar *vt* to exasperate; irritate, annoy

excarcelar *vt* to release from jail
excavación *f,* excavation
excavador (-ra) *n* excavator. *f, mech* excavator
excavar *vt* to hollow; excavate; *agr* hoe (roots of plants)
excedente *a* exceeding; excessive; surplus
exceder *vt* to exceed; *vr* forget oneself, go too far
excelencia *f,* excellence, superiority; Excellency (title)
excelente *a* excellent; *inf* first-rate
excelso *a* lofty, high; eminent, mighty; sublime
excentricidad *f,* eccentricity
excéntrico *a* unconventional; erratic; *geom* eccentric
excepción *f,* exception
excepcional *a* exceptional
exceptuar *vt* to except
excerpta, excerta *f,* excerpt, extract
excesivo *a* excessive
exceso *m,* excess; *com* surplus; *pl* crimes, excesses. **e. de peso** *or* **e. de equipaje,** excess baggage
excisión *f,* excision
excitabilidad *f,* excitability
excitable *a* excitable, high-strung
excitación *f,* excitation; excitement
excitador *a* exciting, stimulating. *m, phys* exciter
excitar *vt* to excite, stimulate, provoke; *elec* energize; *vr* become agitated or excited
exclamación *f,* exclamation, interjection
exclamar *vi* to exclaim
excluir *vt irr* to exclude, keep out; reject, bar. See **huir**
exclusiva *f,* exclusion; special privilege, sole right
exclusive *adv* exclusively; excluded
exclusivismo *m,* exclusivism
exclusivista *a* exclusive. *mf* exclusivist
exclusivo *a* exclusive
excomulgado (-da) *a* and *n ecc* excommunicate; *inf* wicked (person)
excomulgar *vt* to excommunicate
excomunión *f,* excommunication
excoriar *vt* to flay, excoriate; *vr* graze oneself
excrecencia *f,* excrescence
excreción *f,* excretion
excremento *m,* excrement
excretar *vi* to excrete
excretorio *a* excretory
exculpación *f,* exoneration
exculpar(se) *vt* and *vr* to exonerate
excursión *f,* excursion, outing, trip; *mil* incursion
excursionarse *vr, Lat. Am.* to go on a trip, go on an outing, go on an excursion
excursionismo *m,* sightseeing; hiking
excursionista *mf* excursionist; hiker
excusa *f,* excuse
excusado *a* excused; exempt; unnecessary, superfluous; reserved, private. *m,* lavatory, toilet
excusar *vt* to excuse; avoid, ward off, prevent; exempt; *vr* excuse oneself
execración *f,* execration
execrar *vt* to execrate; denounce; loathe
exención *f,* exemption
exentar *vt* to exempt
exento *a* exempt; free, liberated; open (of buildings, etc.)
exequias *f pl,* obsequies
exfoliar *vt* to strip off; *vr* flake off
exhalación *f,* exhalation; shooting star; lightning; emanation, effluvium
exhalar *vt* to exhale, give off; *fig* give vent to
exhibición *f,* exhibition
exhibicionismo *m,* exhibitionism
exhibicionista *mf* exhibitionist
exhibir *vt* to exhibit, show
exhortación *f,* exhortation
exhortar *vt* to exhort
exhumación *f,* exhumation
exhumar *vt* to exhume, disinter
exigencia *f,* exigency; demand
exigente *a* exigent
exigir *vt* to exact, collect; need, require; demand
exigüidad *f,* exiguousness
exiguo *a* exiguous, meager
exliado, -a *Lat. Am. a* exiled, in exile; *mf* exile
eximio *a* most excellent; illustrious
eximir *vt* to exempt
existencia *f,* existence; *pl com* stock on hand
existir *vi* to exist, be; live
éxito *m,* success; result, conclusion
exitoso, -a *a, Lat. Am.* successful
éxodo *m,* Exodus; exodus, emigration. **é. rural,** rural depopulation
exoneración *f,* exoneration
exonerar *vt* to exonerate; discharge (from employment)
exorbitancia *f,* exorbitance
exorbitante *a* exorbitant, excessive
exorcismo *m,* exorcism
exorcista *m,* exorcist
exorcizar *vt* to exorcize
exordio *m,* exordium, introduction
exornar *vt* to adorn; embellish (*lit* style)
exótico *a* exotic, rare
expandir *vt* to expand
expansión *f,* expansion; recreation, hobby
expansivo *a* expansive; communicative, frank
expatriación *f,* expatriation
expatriarse *vr* to emigrate, leave one's country
expectante *a* expectant
expectativa *f,* expectancy; expectation
expectoración *f,* expectoration
expectorar *vt* to expectorate
expedición *f,* expedition; speed, promptness; *ecc* bull, dispensation; excursion; forwarding, dispatch
expediente *m, law* proceedings; file of documents; expedient, device, means; expedition, promptness; motive, reason; provision
expedir *vt irr* to expedite; forward, send, ship; issue, make out (checks, receipts, etc.); draw up (documents); dispatch, deal with. See **pedir**
expedito *a* expeditious, speedy
expeler *vt* to expel, discharge, emit
expendedor (-ra) *a* spending. *n* spender; agent; retailer; seller; *law* **e. de moneda falsa,** distributor of counterfeit money
expendeduría *f,* shop where government monopoly goods are sold (tobacco, stamps, etc.)
expender *vt* to spend (money); *com* retail; *com* sell on commission; *law* distribute counterfeit money
expendio *m, Lat. Am.* tobacco shop
expensas *f pl,* costs, charges
experiencia *f,* experience; practice, experiment
experimentación *f,* experiencing
experimentar *vt* to test, try; experience; feel
experimento *m,* experiment
experto (-ta) *a* practiced, expert. *n* expert
expiación *f,* expiation
expiar *vt* to expiate, atone for; pay the penalty of; *fig* purify
expiatorio *a* expiatory
expiración *f,* expiration
expirar *vi* to die; *fig* expire; die down; exhale, expire
explanación *f,* leveling; explanation, elucidation
explanada *f,* esplanade; *mil* glacis
explanar *vt* to level; explain
explayar *vt* to extend, enlarge; *vr* spread oneself, enlarge (upon); enjoy an outing; confide (in)
explicación *f,* explanation; elucidation
explicar *vt* to explain; expound; interpret, elucidate; *vr* explain oneself
explicativo *a* explanatory
explícito *a* explicit, clear
exploración *f,* exploration
explorador *a* exploring. *m,* explorer; prospector; boy scout; *mil* scout

explorar *vt* to explore; investigate; *med* probe
exploratorio *a* exploratory
explosión *f,* explosion; outburst, outbreak. **hacer falsas explosiones,** *mech* to misfire
explosivo *a* and *m,* explosive. **e. violento,** high explosive
explotación *f,* development, exploitation
explotar *vt* to work (mines); *fig* exploit
expoliación *f,* spoliation
expoliar *vt* to despoil
exponente *a* and *mf* exponent. *m, math* index
exponer *vt irr* to show, expose; expound, interpret; risk, jeopardize; abandon (child). See **poner**
exportación *f,* exportation; export
exportador (-ra) *a* export. *n* exporter
exportar *vt* to export
exposición *f,* exposition, demonstration; petition; exhibition; *lit* exposition; *phot* exposure; orientation, position
expósito (-ra) *a* and *n* foundling
expositor (-ra) *a* and *n* exponent. *n* exhibitor
expremijo *m,* cheese vat
exprés *a* express. *m,* messenger or delivery service; express train; transport office
expresar *vt* to express (all meanings)
expresión *f,* statement, utterance; phrase, wording; expression; presentation; manifestation; gift, present; squeezing; pressing (of fruits, etc.)
expresivo *a* expressive; affectionate
expreso *a* express; clear, obvious. *m,* courier, messenger
exprimelimones *m,* **exprimidera,** *f,* lemon squeezer
exprimidor de la ropa *m,* wringer, mangle
exprimir *vt* to squeeze, press (fruit); press, hold tightly; express, utter
expropiación *f,* expropriation
expropiar *vt* to expropriate; commandeer
expugnar *vt mil* to take by storm
expulsar *vt* to expel, eject, dismiss
expulsión *f,* expulsion
expurgar *vt* to cleanse, purify; expurgate
expurgatorio *a* expurgatory. *m, ecc* index
exquisitez *f,* exquisiteness
exquisito *a* exquisite, choice; delicate, delicious
extasiarse *vr* to fall into ecstasy; marvel (at), delight (in)
éxtasis *m,* ecstasy; rapture
extático *a* ecstatic
extemporáneo *a* untimely; inopportune, inconvenient
extender *vt irr* to spread; reach, extend; elongate; enlarge, amplify; unfold, open out, stretch; draw up (documents); make out (checks, etc.); *vr* stretch out; lie down; spread, be generalized; extend; last (of time); record; stretch, open out. **extenderse en,** to expatiate on. See **entender**
extensión *f,* extension; expanse; length; extent; duration; extension (logic)
extensivo *a* extensive, spacious; extensible
extenso *a* extensive, vast
extensor *a* extensor. *m,* chest expander
extenuación *f,* emaciation, weakness; extenuation
extenuar *vt* to exhaust, weaken; *vr* become weak
exterior *a* external; foreign (trade, etc.). *m,* outside, exterior; outward appearance
exterioridad *f,* outward appearance; outside, externality; *pl* ceremonies, forms; ostentation
exteriorizar *vt* to exteriorize, reveal
exterminador (-ra) *a* exterminating. *n* exterminator
exterminar *vt* to exterminate; devastate
exterminio *m,* extermination; devastation
externado *m,* day school
externarse *vr* to stand out
externo (-na) *a* external. *n* day
extinción *f,* extinction; extinguishment; abolition, cancellation
extinguir *vt* to extinguish; destroy
extintor *m,* fire extinguisher
extirpación *f,* extirpation
extirpador (-ra) *a* extirpating. *n* extirpator
extirpar *vt* to extirpate; *fig* eradicate
extorsión *f,* extortion
extorsionar *vt* to extort
extra *prefix* outside, without, beyond. *prep* besides. *a* extremely, most. *m, inf* extra
extracción *f,* extraction; drawing (lottery); origin, lineage; exportation
extractar *vt* to abstract, summarize
extracto *m,* abstract, summary; *chem* extract
extractor *a* extracting. *m,* extractor
extradición *f,* extradition
extraer *vt irr* to extract; draw out; export; *chem* extract. See **traer**
extranjero (-ra) *a* alien, foreign. *n* foreigner. *m,* abroad, foreign country
extrañar *vt* to exile; alienate, estrange; wonder at; miss, feel the loss of; *vr* be exiled; be estranged; be amazed (by); refuse (to do a thing)
extrañeza *f,* strangeness; estrangement; surprise
extraño *a* strange, unusual; foreign, extraneous
extraoficial *a* unofficial
extraordinario *a* extraordinary; special. *m, cul* extra course
extraterrenal, extraterreno *a, Lat. Am.* extraterrestrial, unearthly
extraterritorialidad *f,* exterritoriality
extravagancia *f,* eccentricity; queerness; folly
extravagante *a* eccentric; queer, strange; absurd
extravertido *m,* extrovert
extraviar *vt* to mislead; mislay; *vr* lose one's way; be lost (of things); *fig* go astray
extravío *m,* deviation, divergence; error; aberration, lapse
extremado *a* extreme
extremar *vt* to take to extremes; *vr* do one's best
extremaunción *f,* extreme unction
extremidad *f,* end; extremity; remotest part; edge; limit; *pl* extremities
extremista *a* and *mf* extremist
extremo *a* last, ultimate; extreme; furthest; great, exceptional; utmost. *m,* end, extreme; highest degree; extreme care; *pl* excessive emotional display
extremoso *a* immoderate, exaggerated; very affectionate
extrínseco *a* extrinsic
exuberancia *f,* abundance; exuberance
exuberante *a* abundant, copious; exuberant
exudar *vi* and *vt* to exude
exultación *f,* exultation; rejoicing
exultante *a* exultant
exultar *vi* to exult
eyaculación *f, med* ejaculation
eyacular *vt med* to ejaculate

F

fa *m, mus* fa, F
fabada *f,* dish of broad beans with pork, sausage or bacon
fábrica *f,* manufacture; making; factory, works; fabric, structure, building; creation; invention. **f. de papel,** paper mill. **marca de f.,** trademark

fabricación *f,* make; making; construction. **f. en serie,** mass production
fabricador (-ra) *a* creative, inventive. *n* fabricator; maker
fabricante *a* manufacturing. *m,* manufacturer; maker
fabricar *vt* to manufacture; make; construct, build; devise; invent, create
fabril *a* manufacturing
fabriquero *m,* manufacturer; churchwarden; charcoal burner
fábula *f,* rumor, gossip; fiction; fable; story, plot; mythology; myth; laughingstock; falsehood.
fabulista *mf* fabulist; mythologist
fabulosidad *f,* fabulousness
fabuloso *a* fabulous; fictitious; incredible, amazing
faca *f,* jackknife
facción *f,* rebellion; faction, party, band; feature (of the face) (gen. *pl*); military exploit; any routine military duty
faccionario *a* factional
faccioso (-sa) *a* factional; factious, seditious. *n* rebel
faceta *f,* facet (gems); aspect, view
facha *f, inf* countenance, look, face; guy, scarecrow. *naut* **ponerse en f.,** to lie to
fachada *f,* facade, front (of a building, ship, etc.); *inf* build, presence (of a person); frontispiece (of a book)
fachenda *f, inf* boastfulness, vanity
fachinal *m, Argentina* swamp
fachoso, -a *a, Lat. Am.* elegant, smart
facial *a* facial; intuitive
fácil *a* easy; probable; easily led; docile; of easy virtue (women). *adv* easy
facilidad *f,* easiness; facility, aptitude; ready compliance; opportunity
facilitar *vt* to facilitate, expedite; provide, deliver
facineroso *a* criminal, delinquent. *m,* criminal; villain
facistol *m, ecc* lectern; chorister's stand
facsímile *m,* facsimile
factibilidad *f,* feasibility, practicability
factible *a* feasible, practicable
facticio *a* factitious, artificial
factor *m, com* factor, agent; *math* factor; element; consideration
factoría *f,* agency; factorage; factory; merchants' trading post, especially in a foreign country
factótum *m, inf* factotum, handyman; *inf* busybody; confidential agent or deputy
factura *f, com* invoice, bill, account; *art* execution; workmanship; making
facturar *vt com* to invoice; register (luggage on a railroad)
facultad *f,* faculty; mental or physical aptitude, capability; authority, right; science, art; *univ* faculty; license
facultar *vt* to authorize, permit
facultativo *a* belonging to a faculty; optional, permissive. *m,* physician
facundia *f,* eloquence
facundo *a* eloquent
faena *f,* manual labor; mental work; business affairs (gen. *pl*)
faetón *m,* phaeton
fagocito *m,* phagocyte
fagot *m,* bassoon
fagotista *mf* bassoon player
faisán (-ana) *orn* cock (hen) pheasant
faisanera *f,* pheasantry
faja *f,* belt; sash, scarf; corset, girdle; *geog* zone; newspaper wrapper; *arch* fascia; swathing band
fajar *vt* to swathe; swaddle (a child)
fajero *m,* swaddling band
fajín *m,* ceremonial ribbon or sash worn by generals, etc.
fajina *f,* stack; brushwood; (*fort.*) fascine; *Mexico* lunch
fajo *m,* bundle, sheaf; *pl* swaddling clothes
falacia *f,* fraud, deceit; deceitfulness; fallacy
falange *f, mil* phalanx; *anat* phalange; (*Spanish pol.*) Falange
falangista *a* and *mf* Falangist
falaz *a* deceitful; fallacious
falda *f,* skirt; lap, flap, panel (of a dress); slope (of a hill); the lap; loin (of beef, etc.); brim of a hat; *pl inf* petticoats, women. **f. escocesa,** kilt. **f.-pantalón,** divided skirt, culottes.
faldellín *m,* skirt; underskirt
faldero *a* lap (dog); fond of the company of women
faldillas *f pl,* coattails
faldistorio *m,* faldstool
faldón *m,* long, flowing skirt; shirttail; coattail
falibilidad *f,* fallibility
falible *a* fallible
falla *f,* deficiency, defect; failure; *geol* displacement; bonfire (Valencia); *min* slide
fallar *vt law* to pass sentence; *vi* be deficient
fallecer *vi irr* to die; fail. See **conocer**
fallecimiento *m,* death, decease
fallido *a* frustrated; bankrupt
fallo *m, law* verdict; judgment
falsario *a* falsifying, forging, counterfeiting; deceiving, lying. *m,* falsifier, forger, counterfeiter
falseamiento *m,* falsifying; forging
falsear *vt* to falsify; forge; counterfeit; penetrate; *vi* weaken; *mus* be out of tune (strings)
falsedad *f,* falseness; falsehood
falsete *m,* spigot; *mus* falsetto voice
falsificación *f,* falsification; forgery
falsificador *a* falsifying; forging. *m,* falsifier; forger
falsificar *vt* to forge, counterfeit; falsify
falso *a* false; forged, counterfeit; treacherous, untrue, deceitful; incorrect; sham; vicious (horses). **de f.,** falsely; deceitfully
falta *f,* lack, shortage; defect; mistake; *sport* fault; shortcoming; nonappearance, absence; deficiency in legal weight of coin; *law* offense. **f. de éxito,** failure. **hacer f.,** to be necessary. **sin f.,** without fail
faltar *vi* to be lacking; fail, die; fall short; be absent from an appointment; not to fulfill one's obligations. **f. a,** to be unfaithful to, break (e.g. **Faltó a su palabra,** He broke his promise). *inf* **¡No faltaba más!** I should think not!; That's the limit!
falto *a* lacking, wanting; defective; wretched, mean, timid. **f. de personal,** short-handed
faltriquera *f,* pocket; hip pocket
falúa *f, naut* tender; longboat
falucho *m,* felucca
fama *f,* rumor, report; reputation; fame
famélico *a* ravenous
familia *f,* family; household; kindred. **ser de f.,** to run in the family
familiar *a* family; familiar; well known; unceremonious; plain, simple; colloquial (language). *m, ecc* familiar; servant; intimate friend; familiar spirit
familiaridad *f,* familiarity
familiarizar *vt* to familiarize; *vr* become familiar; accustom oneself
familiarmente *adv* familiarly
famoso *a* famous; notorious; *inf* excellent, perfect; *inf* conspicuous
fámula *f, inf* female servant
fámulo *m,* servant of a college; *inf* servant
fanal *m,* lantern (of a lighthouse); *naut* poop lantern; lantern; lamp glass
fanático (-ca) *a* fanatical. *n* fanatic; *inf* fan, enthusiast
fanatismo *m,* fanaticism
fanatizar *vt* to make fanatical; turn into a fanatic
fandango *m,* lively Andalusian dance; *Lat. Am.* rowdy party
fanega *f,* grain measure about the weight of 1.60 bushel; land measure (about $1\frac{1}{2}$ acres)
fanfarrón (-ona) *a inf* boastful, swaggering. *n* swashbuckler; boaster
fanfarronear *vi* to swagger; brag

fanfarronería *f*, bragging
fango *m*, mud, mire; degradation
fangoso *a* muddy, miry
fantasear *vi* to let one's fancy roam; boast
fantasía *f*, fancy, imagination; fantasy; caprice; fiction; *inf* presumption; *mus* fantasia
fantasma *m*, ghost, phantom; vision; image, impression; presumptuous person. *f*, *inf* scarecrow; apparition
fantasmagoría *f*, phantasmagoria
fantasmagórico *a* phantasmagoric
fantástico *a* fanciful, imaginary; fantastic, imaginative; presumptuous, conceited
fantoche *m*, puppet; *inf* yes-man, mediocrity
faquín *m*, porter, carrier
faquir *m*, fakir
farabute *mf*, *Argentina* rogue
faradio *m*, farad
faralá *m*, flounce, frill
faramallear *vi*, *Lat. Am.* to boast, brag
farándula *f*, profession of low comedian; troupe of strolling players; cunning trick
farandulero *m*, actor, strolling player. *a inf* plausible
faraón *m*, pharaoh; faro (card game)
fardel *m*, bag, knapsack; bundle
fardo *m*, bundle, bale, package
farfulla *f*, *inf* mumbling; gibbering. *mf inf* mumbler
farfullar *vt inf* to mumble; gibber; *inf* act in haste
faringe *f*, pharynx
faríngeo *a* pharyngeal
faringitis *f*, pharyngitis
farmacéutico *a* pharmaceutical. *m*, pharmacist
farmacia *f*, pharmacy
farmacología *f*, pharmacology
farmacólogo *m*, pharmacologist
faro *m*, lighthouse; beacon, guide; *aut* headlight
farol *m*, lantern, lamp; streetlamp; cresset
farola *f*, lamppost (generally with several branches); lantern
farolero *m*, lantern maker; lamplighter; lamp tender. *a inf* swaggering, braggart
fárrago *m*, hodgepodge
farruto, -a *a*, *Lat. Am.* sickly, weak
farsa *f*, old name for a play; farce; theatrical company; poor, badly constructed play; sham, trick, deception
farsante *m*, comedian; *ant* actor; *fig inf* humbug
fascinación *f*, evil eye; enchantment, fascination
fascinador (-ra) *a* bewitching; fascinating. *n* charmer
fascinante *a* fascinating
fascinar *vt* to bewitch, place under a spell; deceive, impose upon; attract, fascinate
fascismo *m*, fascism
fascista *a* and *mf* fascist
fase *f*, phase; aspect
fastidiar *vt* to disgust, bore; annoy; *vr* be bored
fastidio *m*, sickness, squeamishness; annoyance, boredom, dislike, repugnance
fastidioso *a* disgusting, sickening; annoying; boring, tiresome
fastuoso *a* ostentatious; pompous
fatal *a* fatal, mortal; predetermined, inevitable; ill-fated, unhappy, disastrous; evil
fatalidad *f*, fatality; inevitability; disaster, ill-fatedness
fatalismo *m*, fatalism
fatalista *a* fatalistic. *mf* fatalist
fatalmente *adv* inevitably, unavoidably; unhappily, unfortunately; extremely badly
fatídico *a* prophetic (gen. of evil)
fatiga *f*, fatigue; toil; difficult breathing; hardship, troubles (gen. *pl.*)
fatigar *vt* to tire; annoy; *vr* be tired
fatigoso *a* tired; tiring; tiresome, annoying
fatuidad *f*, fatuousness, inanity, foolishness; conceit; priggishness
fatuo *a* fatuous, foolish; conceited; priggish. *m*, self-satisfied fool. **fuego f.,** will-o'-the-wisp
fauces *f pl*, gullet
faul *m*, *Lat. Am.* foul
faulear *vt*, *Lat. Am.* to foul
fauna *f*, fauna
fauno *m*, faun
fausto *m*, pomp, magnificence, ostentation. *a* fortunate, happy
fautor *m*, protector, helper; accomplice. **f. de guerra,** warmonger
favonio *m*, *poet* zephyr, westerly wind
favor *m*, aid, protection, support; favor, honor, service; love favor, sign of favor. **a f. de,** in favor of; on behalf of
favorable *a* kind, helpful; favorable
favorecedor (-ra) *a* favoring, helping. *n* helper; protector
favorecer *vt irr* to aid, protect, support; favor; do a service, grant a favor. See **conocer**
favoritismo *m*, favoritism
favorito (-ta) *a* and *n* favorite
fayenza *f*, faience
faz *f*, face; external surface of a thing, side; frontage
fe *f*, faith; confidence, trust, good opinion; belief; solemn promise; assertion; certificate, attestation; faithfulness. **f. de erratas,** *print* errata. **dar f.,** *law* to testify. **de buena f.,** in good faith. **en f.,** in proof
fealdad *f*, ugliness; base action
febo *m*, Phoebus; *poet* sun
febrero *m*, February
febril *a* feverish; ardent, violent; passionate
feculento *a* starchy; dreggy
fecundación *f*, fecundation
fecundar *vt* to fertilize; fecundate
fecundidad *f*, fecundity; fertility, fruitfulness
fecundizar *vt* to fertilize; make fruitful
fecundo *a* fertile, fecund, prolific; abundant
fecha *f*, date. **a la f.,** at present, now. **hasta la f.,** up to the present (day)
fechar *vt* to date, write the date
federación *f*, federation, league
federal *a* federal. *mf* federalist
federalismo *m*, federalism
federalista *a* federal, federalist. *mf* federalist
federativo *a* federative
fehaciente *a law* authentic, attested
felicidad *f*, happiness; contentment, satisfaction; good fortune
felicitación *f*, congratulation
felicitar *vt* to congratulate; wish well; *vr* congratulate oneself
feligrés (-esa) *n* parishioner
feligresía *f*, parish
felino *a* and *m*, feline
feliz *a* happy; fortunate; skillful, felicitous (of phrases, etc.)
felón (-ona) *n* felon
felonía *f*, felony
felpa *f*, plush; *inf* drubbing, beating
felpilla *f*, chenille
felpudo *a* plush
femenino *a* feminine; female; *fig* weak
fementido *a* sly, false, treacherous, unfaithful
feminismo *m*, feminism
feminista *a* feminist. *mf* feminist
fémur *m*, femur, thigh bone
fenecer *vt irr* to conclude, finish; *vi* die; be ended. See **conocer**
fenecimiento *m*, end; death
fenicio (-ia) *a* and *n* Phoenician
fénico *a* phenic, carbolic
fénix *f*, phoenix
fenomenal *a* phenomenal; *inf* terrific
fenómeno *m*, phenomenon; *inf* something of great size
feo *a* ugly; alarming, horrid; evil. *m*, *inf* slight, insult
feraz *a* fruitful, fertile
féretro *m*, coffin; bier

feria *f,* fair, market; workday; holiday; rest
feriar *vt* to buy at a fair; bargain. *vi* cease work, take a holiday
fermentación *f,* fermentation
fermentar *vi* to ferment; be agitated; *vt* cause to ferment
fermento *m,* ferment; leaven; *chem* enzyme
ferocidad *f,* ferocity, cruelty
feroz *a* ferocious, cruel; *Lat. Am.* ugly
férreo *a* ferrous; hard, tenacious. **línea férrea,** railroad
ferrería *f,* ironworks
ferretería *f,* ironworks; ironmonger's shop; ironware, hardware
férrico *a* ferric
ferrífero *a* iron-bearing
ferrocarril *m,* railroad, railway; railroad train. **f. de cremallera,** rack railroad. **f. funicular,** funicular railway
ferroso *a* ferrous
ferroviario *a* railroad, railway. *m,* railroad employee
fértil *a* fertile; fruitful, productive
fertilidad *f,* fertility
fertilización *f,* fertilization
fertilizar *vt* to fertilize, make fruitful
férula *f,* ferule; *surg* splint; *fig* yoke, rule
fervor *m,* intense heat; fervor, devotion; zeal
fervoroso *a* fervent, zealous, devoted
festejar *vt* to feast, entertain; woo; celebrate; *vr* amuse oneself; *Mexico* to thrash
festejo *m,* feast, entertainment; courtship, wooing; *pl* public celebrations
festín *m,* private dinner or party; sumptuous banquet
festival *m,* musical festival; festival
festividad *f,* festivity; *ecc* celebration, solemnity; witticism
festivo *a* joking, witty; happy, gay; solemn, worthy of celebration. **día f.,** holiday
festón *m,* garland, wreath; festoon; border; scalloped edging
festonear *vt* to garland, festoon; border
fetal *a* fetal
fetiche *m,* fetish
fetichismo *m,* fetishism
fetidez *f,* fetidness, fetor, stink
fétido *a* stinking, fetid
feto *m,* fetus
feudal *a* feudal; despotic
feudalismo *m,* feudalism
fez *m,* fez
fiado, al *adv* on credit. **en f.,** on bail
fiador (-ra) *n* guarantor; bail. *m,* fastener, loop (of a coat, clock, etc.); safety catch, bolt. **salir f.,** to be surety (for); post bail
fiambre *m,* cold meat, cold dish; *inf* stale, out-of-date news, etc.; *inf* corpse
fiambrera *f,* lunchbox, lunchpail
fiambrería *f* delicatessen
fianza *f,* guarantee, bail; surety; security. *law* **dar f.,** to guarantee; post bail
fiar *vt* to go surety for, post bail; sell on credit; trust; confide; *vr* (*with de*) confide in; trust
fibra *f,* fiber; filament; energy, strength; *min* vein; grain (of wood)
fibroso *a* fibrous; fibroid
ficción *f,* falsehood; invention; fiction, imaginative creation; pretense
ficha *f,* chip, counter; domino; index card, filing card. **f. antropométrica,** personal particulars card
fichar *vt* to record personal particulars on a filing card; file, index
fichero *m,* filing cabinet; card catalog
fichú *m,* fichu, scarf
ficticio *a* fictitious
fidedigno *a* trustworthy, bona fide
fidelidad *f,* fidelity, honesty; loyalty; punctiliousness
fideos *m pl,* vermicelli. *m, inf* scraggy person
fiduciario *a law* fiduciary. *m, law* trustee
fiebre *f,* fever; great agitation, excitement. **f. de oro,** gold fever. **f. palúdica,** malarial fever. **f. puerperal,** puerperal fever. **f. tifoidea,** typhoid fever
fiel *a* faithful, loyal; true, exact. *m,* axis; pointer (of a scale or balance)
fieltro *m,* felt
fiera *f,* wild beast; cruel person
fiereza *f,* savageness, wildness; cruelty, fierceness; deformity
fiero *a* wild, savage; ugly; huge, enormous; horrible, alarming; haughty
fiesta *f,* merriment, gaiety; entertainment, feast; *inf* joke; festivity, celebration; public holiday; caress, cajolery (gen. *pl*); *pl* holidays. **f. fija** *ecc* immovable feast. *inf* **estar de f.,** to be making merry. **hacer f.,** to take a holiday. *inf* **Se acabó la f.,** It's all over and done with
fifiriche *a, Central America, Mexico* sickly, weak
figón *m,* eating house, diner
figulino *a* fictile, made of terra cotta
figura *f,* shape, form; face; *art* image, figure; *law* form; court card; *mus* note; *theat* character, role; (*geom gram dancing*) figure. **f. de nieve,** snowman. *naut* **f. de proa,** figurehead. *fig* **f. decorativa,** figurehead. *fig* **hacer f.,** to cut a figure
figurado *a* figurative; rhetorical
figurar *vt* to shape, mold; simulate, pretend; represent; *vi* be numbered among; cut a figure; *vr* imagine
figurilla *mf inf* ridiculous, dwarfish figure. *f, art* statuette
figurín *m,* fashion plate or model
figuroso, -a *a, Lat. Am.* flashy, loud, showy
fijación *f,* fixing; nailing; sticking, posting; attention, fixity; *chem* fixation; firmness, stability
fijador *m,* (*med phot*) fixative; setting lotion; *art* varnish. *a* fixing
fijamente *adv* firmly; attentively
fijar *vt* to fix; glue, stick; nail; make firm; settle, appoint (a date); fix, concentrate (attention, gaze); (*phot med*) fix; *vr* decide; notice (e.g. **No me había fijado,** I hadn't noticed). **f. anuncios,** to post bills
fijeza *f,* fixedness; firmness, stability; constancy, steadfastness
fijo *a* firm; fixed; stable; steadfast; permanent; exact. **de f.,** certainly, without doubt
fila *f,* line, row; *mil* rank; antipathy, hatred. **en f.,** in a line
filacteria *f,* phylactery
filamento *m,* filament
filantropía *f,* philanthropy
filantrópico *a* philanthropic
filántropo *m,* philanthropist
filarmónico *a* philharmonic
filatelia *f,* philately, stamp collecting
filatélico *a* philatelic
filatelista *mf* philatelist, stamp collector
filete *m, arch* filet; *cul* small spit; filet (of meat or fish); thread of a screw; *sew* hem
filiación *f,* filiation; affiliation, relationship; *mil* regimental register
filial *a* filial; affiliated
filibustero *m,* filibuster
filiforme *a* filamentous
filigrana *f,* filigree; watermark (of paper); *fig* delicate creation
filípica *f,* philippic
Filipinas, las the Philippines
filipino (-na) *a* and *n* Philippine
filisteo (-ea) *a* and *n* philistine
filmar *vt* to film
filo *m,* cutting edge; dividing line
filología *f,* philology
filológico *a* philological
filólogo *m,* philologist
filomela *f, poet* nightingale
filón *m, min* vein, lode; *fig* gold mine

filoso, -a *a, Lat. Am.* sharp
filosofar *vi* to philosophize
filosofía *f,* philosophy. **f. moral,** moral philosophy. **f. natural,** natural philosophy
filosófico *a* philosophic
filósofo *m,* philosopher. *a* philosophic
filoxera *f,* phylloxera
filtración *f,* filtration
filtrar *vt* to filter; *vi* filter through, percolate; *vr fig* disappear (of money, etc.)
filtro *m,* filter, strainer; love potion, philter
filudo, -a *a, Lat. Am.* = **filoso**
fin *m,* finish, end, conclusion; purpose, goal, aim; limit, extent. **a f. de,** in order to, so that. **a fines de,** toward the end of (with months, years, etc.) (e.g. **a fines de octubre,** toward the end of October). **en f.,** at last; in fine; well then! **por f.,** finally
finado (-da) *n* deceased, dead person
final *a* final. *m,* end, finish; *sport* final (gen. *pl*)
finalidad *f,* finality; purpose
finalista *mf sport* finalist
finalizar *vt* to conclude, finish; *vi* be finished; close (stock exchange)
finalmente *adv* finally
financiar *vt* to finance
financiero *a* financial. *m,* financier
finanzas *f pl,* finance
finar *vi* to die; *vr* desire, long for a thing
finca *f,* land, real estate; house property, country house, ranch
fineza *f,* fineness; excellence, goodness; kindness, expression of affection; good turn, friendly act; gift; beauty, delicacy
fingido *a* pretended; assumed; feigned; sham
fingimiento *m,* pretense; affectation, assumption
fingir *vt* to pretend, feign; imagine
finiquitar *vt* to close and pay up an account; *inf* end
finiquito *m,* closing of an account; final receipt, quittance; quietus
finito *a* finite
finlandés (-esa) *a* Finnish. *n* Finn. *m,* Finnish (language)
fino *a* fine; excellent, good; slim, slender, thin; delicate, subtle; dainty (of people); cultured, polished; constant, loving; sagacious, shrewd; *min* refined
finta *f,* feint (in fencing); menace, threat
finura *f,* fineness; excellence; delicacy; courtesy
fiordo *m,* fjord
firma *f,* signature; act of signing; *com* firm name, firm
firmamento *m,* firmament
firmante *a* signing. *mf* signatory
firmar *vt* to sign
firme *a* firm; hard; steady, solid; constant, resolute, loyal. *m,* foundation, base. *mil* **¡Firmes!** Attention! **batir de f.,** to strike hard
firmeza *f,* stability, firmness; constancy, resoluteness, loyalty
fiscal *a* fiscal. *m,* attorney general; public prosecutor; meddler. **f. de quiebras,** official receiver
fiscalizar *vt* to prosecute; pry into; meddle with; censure, criticize
fisco *m,* national treasury, exchequer, revenue
fisgar *vt* to harpoon; pry; *vi* mock, make fun of
fisgón (-ona) *a* prying; mocking. *n* pryer; mocker; eavesdropper
fisgoneo *m,* prying; eavesdropping
física *f,* physics
físico *a* physical. *m,* physicist; physician; physique
fisiología *f,* physiology
fisiológico *a* physiological
fisiólogo *m,* physiologist
fisioterapia *f,* physiotherapy
fisonomía *f,* physiognomy
fistol *m, Mexico* tie pin; crafty person, sly person
fístula *f,* pipe, conduit; *mus* pipe; *surg* fistula
fisura *f,* fissure
flaccidez *f,* flabbiness
fláccido *a* flaccid, soft, flabby
flaco *a* thin; weak, feeble; *fig* weak-minded; dispirited. *m,* failing, weakness. *inf* **hacer un f. servicio,** to do an ill turn. **estar f. de memoria,** to have a weak memory
flagelación *f,* flagellation
flagelante *m,* flagellant
flagelar *vt* to scourge; *fig* lash
flagelo *m,* whip, scourge
flagrante *a poet* refulgent; present; actual. **en f.,** in the very act, flagrante delicto
flagrar *vi poet* to blaze, be refulgent
flamante *a* resplendent; brand-new; fresh, spick-and-span
flamenco (-ca) *m, orn* flamingo. *a* and *n* Flemish. *a* Andalusian; gypsy; buxom, fresh
flan *m,* baked custard, creme caramel. **estar como un f.,** to shake like a leaf, be nervous
flanco *m,* side; *mil* flank
flanquear *vt mil* to flank
flanqueo *m, mil* outflanking
flaquear *vi* to grow weak; weaken; totter (buildings, etc.); be disheartened, flag
flaqueza *f,* weakness; thinness; faintness, feebleness; frailty, fault; loss of zeal
flato *m,* flatulence, gas
flatulento *a* flatulent, gassy
flauta *f,* flute
flautín *m,* piccolo
flautista *mf* flutist
flebitis *f,* phlebitis
flecha *f,* arrow, dart
flechar *vt* to shoot an arrow or dart; wound or kill with arrows; *inf* inspire love; *vi* bend a bow to shoot
flechazo *m,* wound with an arrow; *inf* love at first sight
flechero *m,* archer; arrow maker
fleco *m,* fringe; fringe (of hair)
fleje *m,* iron hoop (for barrels, etc.)
flema *f,* phlegm; sluggishness
flemático *a* phlegmatic; sluggish
flemón *m,* gumboil; abscess
flequetero, -a *a, Lat. Am.* dishonest, tricky
flequillo *m,* fringe (of hair)
fletamento *m,* chartering (a ship)
fletar *vt* to charter a ship; embark merchandise or people
flete *m,* freightage; cargo, freight
flexibilidad *f,* flexibility; suppleness, adaptability
flexible *a* pliant, supple; flexible, adaptable. *m, elec* flex
flirtear *vi* to flirt
flirteo *m,* flirtation
flojedad *f,* flabbiness; weakness, feebleness; laziness, negligence
flojo *a* flabby; slack, loose; weak, feeble; lazy, slothful; poor (of a literary work, etc.)
floqueado *a* fringed
flor *f,* flower; best (of anything); bloom (on fruit); virginity; grain (of leather); compliment (gen. *pl*); menstruation (gen. *pl*). **f. de especia,** mace. **f. de la edad,** prime, youth. **f. del cuclillo,** mayflower. **f. del estudiante,** French marigold. **flores de mano,** artificial flowers. **flores de oblón,** hops. **a f. de,** on the surface of, level with. **andarse en flores,** *fig* to beat about the bush. **echar flores,** to pay compliments. **en f.,** in bloom
flora *f,* flora
floral *a* floral. **juegos florales,** poetry contest
florear *vt* to adorn with flowers; *vi* execute a flourish on the guitar
florecer *vi irr* to flower, bloom; flourish, prosper; *vr* grow mold (of cheese, etc.). See **conocer**
floreciente *a* flowering; prosperous
florecimiento *m,* flowering; prosperity
floreo *m,* witty conversation; flourish (on the guitar or in fencing)
florero *m,* vase; flower pot; *art* flower piece

florescencia *f,* flowering; flowering season, florescence
floresta *f,* grove, wooded park, woodland; *fig* collector of beautiful things; anthology
florete *m,* fencing foil
floricultor (-ra) *n* floriculturist
floricultura *f,* floriculture
floridamente *adv* elegantly, with a flourish
florido *a* flowery; best, most select; florid, ornate
florilegio *m,* anthology, collection
florín *m,* florin
florista *mf* artificial-flower maker; florist; flower seller
florón *m,* large flower; *arch* fleuron; honorable deed
flota *f,* fleet of merchant ships. **f. aérea,** air force
flotación *f,* floating. *naut* **línea de f.,** water line
flotador *a* floating. *m,* float
flotamiento *m,* floating
flotante *a* floating
flotar *vi* to float on water or in air
flote *m,* floating. **a f.,** afloat; independent, solvent
flotilla *f,* flotilla; fleet of small ships. **f. aérea,** air fleet
fluctuación *f,* fluctuation; hesitation, vacillation
fluctuante *a* fluctuating
fluctuar *vi* to fluctuate; be in danger (things); vacillate, hesitate; undulate; oscillate
fluidez *f,* fluidity
flúido *a* fluid; fluent. *m,* fluid; *elec* current
fluir *vi irr* to flow. See **huir**
flujo *m,* flow, flux; rising tide. **f. de sangre,** hemorrhage
fluminense *formal a* of Rio de Janeiro; *mf* native of Rio de Janeiro; resident of Rio de Janeiro
fluorescencia *f,* fluorescence
fluorescente *a* fluorescent
flus *m, Colombia, Venezuela* suit (of clothes)
fluvial *a* fluvial
flux *m,* flush (in cards)
foca *f, zool* seal
focal *a* focal
foco *m,* focus; center; origin; source; *theat* spotlight; core (of an abscess)
fofo *a* spongy, soft; flabby
fogata *f,* bonfire
fogón *m,* fire, cooking area, kitchen range, kitchen stove; furnace of a steamboiler; vent of a firearm
fogonazo *m,* powder flash
fogonero *m,* stoker
fogosidad *f,* enthusiasm; vehemence; ardor
fogoso *a* ardent; vehement; enthusiastic
folclórico *a* pertaining to folklore
folclorista *mf* folklorist
folículo *m,* follicle
folio *m,* leaf of a book or manuscript, folio. **en f.,** in folio
follaje *m,* foliage; leafy ornamentation; crude, unnecessary decoration; verbosity
folletín *m,* feuilleton, literary article; serial story; *inf* dime novel, potboiler
folletinista *mf* pamphleteer
folleto *m,* pamphlet, leaflet
follisca *f, Lat. Am.* brawl
follón *a* lazy; caddish; craven
fomentación *f, med* fomentation, poultice
fomentador *a* fomenting. *m,* fomenter
fomentar *vt* to warm, foment; incite, instigate; *med* apply poultices
fomento *m,* heat, shelter; fuel; protection, encouragement; *med* fomentation
fonda *f,* inn; restaurant
fondeadero *m,* anchorage, anchoring ground
fondear *vt naut* to sound; search a ship; examine carefully; *vi naut* anchor; *vr, Lat. Am.* get rich
fondillos *m pl,* seat (of the trousers)
fondista *mf* owner of an inn or restaurant
fondo *m,* bottom (of a well, etc.); bed (of the sea, etc.); depth; rear, portion at the back; ground (of fabrics); background; *com* capital; *com* stock; *fig* fund (of humor, etc.); character, nature; temperament; *fig* substance, core, essence; *naut* bottom; *pl com* resources, funds. **f. de amortización,** sinking fund. **f. doble** *or* **f. secreto,** false bottom. **f. muerto, f. perdido** *or* **f. vitalicio,** life annuity. *com* **fondos inactivos,** idle capital. **a fondo,** completely, thoroughly. **artículo de f.,** editorial, lead article. *sport* **carrera de f.,** long-distance race. *naut* **irse a f.,** to sink, founder
fonética *f,* phonetics
fonético *a* phonetic
fonetista *mf* phonetician
fonógrafo *m,* phonograph
fonología *f,* phonology
fonológico *a* phonological
fontanar *m,* spring, stream
fontanería *f,* pipe laying, plumbing
fontanero *m,* pipe layer; plumber
forajido (-da) *a* fugitive, outlawed. *n* robber, fugitive
foramen *m, Lat. Am.* hole
forastero (-ra) *a* strange, foreign; alien, exotic. *n* stranger
forcejear *vi* to struggle; try, strive; oppose, contradict
forcejo *m,* struggle; endeavor; opposition, hostility
fórceps *m pl,* forceps
forense *a* forensic
forillo *m, theat* backdrop
forja *f,* forge
forjador *m,* smith, ironworker
forjar *vt* to forge; fabricate; create; counterfeit
forma *f,* shape, form; arrangement; method; style; manifestation, expression; formula, formulary; ceremonial; *print* form; manner; means, way; mold, matrix; style of handwriting. *law* **en debida f.,** in due form
formación *f,* formation; form, contour, shape; (*mil geol*) formation. **f. del censo,** census taking
formador *a* forming, shaping
formal *a* apparent, formal; serious, punctilious, steady; truthful, reliable; sedate; orderly, regular, methodical
formaldehído *m,* formaldehyde
formalidad *f,* orderliness, propriety; formality; requirement, requisite; ceremony; seriousness, sedateness; punctiliousness
formalismo *m,* formalism; bureaucracy, red tape
formalizar *vt* to put into final form; legalize; formulate, enunciate; *vr* take seriously (a joke)
formar *vt* to shape; form; educate, mold; *mil* form. **formarle causa a uno,** to bring charges against someone. *vr* develop, grow; *Mexico* get in line
formativo *a* formative
formato *m, print* format; *chem* formate
formidable *a* formidable, awe-inspiring; huge, enormous
fórmula *f,* formula; prescription; mode of expression. (*math chem*) **f. clásica,** standard formula
formular *vt* to formulate; prescribe
formulario *m, law* formulary; handbook
formulismo *m,* formulism; bureaucracy, red tape
fornicación *f,* fornication
fornicador (-ra) *a* and *n* fornicator
fornicar *vi* to fornicate
fornido *a* stalwart, muscular, strong
foro *m,* forum; law courts; law, bar, legal profession; *theat* back scenery; leasehold
forraje *m,* forage, fodder; foraging
forrajeador *m,* forager
forrajear *vt* to gather forage, go foraging
forrar *vt sew* to line; cover, encase, make a cover for
forro *m,* lining, inner covering; cover (of a book); *Argentina* condom; *Lat. Am.* fraud, swindle
fortalecedor *a* fortifying
fortalecer *vt irr* to fortify. See **conocer**
fortaleza *f,* vigor; fortitude; fortress; natural defense; *Lat. Am.* stench, stink. *aer* **f. volante,** flying fortress
fortificable *a* fortifiable

fortificación *f,* fortification
fortificador *a* fortifying
fortificar *vt* to fortify
fortísimo *a sup* **fuerte** extremely strong
fortuito *a* fortuitous, chance
fortuna *f,* fate, destiny; fortune, capital, estate; tempest. **por f.,** fortunately. **probar f.,** to try one's luck
forzado *a* forced, obliged. *m,* convict condemned to the galleys
forzador *m,* violator, seducer
forzar *vt irr* to force, break open; take by force; rape, ravish; oblige, compel. *Pres. Ind.* **fuerzo, fuerzas, fuerza, fuerzan.** *Preterite* **forcé, forzaste,** etc. *Pres. Subjunc.* **fuerce, fuerces, fuerce, forcemos, forcéis, fuercen**
forzoso *a* obligatory, unavoidable, necessary
forzudo *a* brawny, stalwart
fosa *f,* grave; socket (of a joint). **f. común,** potter's field.
fosar *vt* to undermine; dig a trench around
fosfato *m,* phosphate
fosforecer *vi irr* to phosphoresce. See **conocer**
fosforera *f,* matchbox
fosforero (-ra) *n* match seller
fosforescente *a* phosphorescent
fósforo *m,* phosphorus; match; morning star
fósil *a* and *m,* fossil; *inf* antique
foso *m,* hole, hollow, pit; trench; pit (in garages); *theat* room under the stage.
foto *f,* snapshot, photo
fotocopia *f,* photocopy
fotogénico *a* photogenic
fotograbado *m,* photogravure
fotografía *f,* photography; photograph
fotografiar *vt* to photograph
fotográfico *a* photographic
fotógrafo *m,* photographer
fotograma *m,* (cinema) shot
fotoquímica *f,* photochemistry
fotostato *m,* photostat
frac *m,* tail coat
fracasar *vi* to break, crumble, be shattered; collapse (of plans, etc.); fail; be disappointed
fracaso *m,* shattering; collapse (of plans, etc.); disaster; failure, disappointment, downfall
fracción *f,* division into parts; fraction. **f. impropia,** *math* improper fraction
fractura *f,* fracture. **f. conminuta,** compound fracture
fracturar *vt* to fracture
fragancia *f,* fragrance, perfume; renown, good name
fragante *a* fragrant; perfumed; flagrant
fragata *f,* frigate
frágil *a* fragile, brittle; perishable, frail; weak, sinful
fragilidad *f,* fragility; frailty, sinfulness
fragmentario *a* fragmentary
fragmento *m,* fragment
fragor *m,* noise, crash
fragosidad *f,* roughness, rockiness, unevenness
fragoso *a* craggy, rocky; rough; noisy, clamorous
fragua *f,* forge
fraguar *vt* to forge, work; plot, scheme; *vi* set (concrete, etc.)
fraile *m,* friar, monk. *inf* **f. de misa y olla,** ignorant friar
frailesco *a inf* pertaining to friars, friar-like
frambuesa *f,* raspberry
francachela *f, inf* binge
francés (-esa) *a* French. *n* Frenchman (-woman). *m,* French (language). **a la francesa,** in French fashion
francesilla *f, cul* French roll
Francia France
francmasón (-ona) *n* Freemason
francmasonería *f,* freemasonry
franco *a* generous, liberal; exempt; sincere, genuine, frank; duty-free; Frank; Franco (in compound words). *m,* franc (coin). **f. de porte,** post-free; prepaid
francotirador *m,* sharpshooter, franc tireur
franela *f,* flannel; *Lat. Am.* undershirt; T-shirt
frangir *vt* to divide, quarter
frangollar *vt* to scamp, skimp (work); botch, bungle
franja *f,* fringe; border, trimming; stripe. *rad* **f. undosa,** wave band
franjar *vt sew* to fringe, trim
franqueadora *f,* postage meter
franquear *vt* to exempt; make free, make a gift of; clear the way; stamp, prepay; free (slaves); *vr* fall in easily with others' plans; make confidences
franqueo *m,* exemption; bestowal, making free; postage, stamping; enfranchisement (of slaves)
franqueza *f,* exemption, freedom; generosity, liberality; sincerity, frankness
franquicia *f,* exemption from excise duties
franquista *mf* Franquist, supporter of Franco
frasco *m,* bottle, flask; powder flask or horn. **f. cuentagotas,** drop bottle
frase *f,* sentence; phrase; epigram; idiom, style. **f. hecha,** cliché
frasear *vt* to phrase
fraseología *f,* phraseology; wording
fratás *m,* plastering trowel
fraternal *a* brotherly
fraternidad *f,* fraternity, brotherhood
fraternizar *vi* to fraternize
fraterno *a* fraternal
fratricida *a* fratricidal. *mf* fratricide
fratricidio *m,* fratricide (act)
fraude *m,* fraud, deception
fraudulento *a* fraudulent
fray *m, abb* **fraile.** Always followed by a proper name (e.g. **F. Bartolomé,** Friar Bartholomew)
frazada *f,* blanket
frecuencia *f,* frequency. **f. radioeléctrica,** radiofrequency
frecuentación *f,* frequenting, visiting
frecuentador (-ra) *n* frequenter
frecuentar *vt* to frequent
frecuente *a* frequent
fregada *f, Lat. Am.* bother, hassle, nuisance
fregadero *m,* kitchen sink
fregado *m,* scrubbing; rubbing; scouring; washing; *inf* murky business
fregador *m,* kitchen sink; scrub brush; dishcloth. **f. mecánico de platos,** dishwasher
fregandera *f, Mexico* charwoman, cleaning woman
fregar *vt irr* to rub; scour; wash (dishes). See **cegar**
fregona *f,* kitchen maid
fregotear *vt inf* to clean or scour inefficiently
freiduría *f,* fried-fish shop
freír *vt irr cul* to fry. See **reír**
fréjol *m,* kidney bean
frenar *vt* to restrain, hold back; bridle, check; *mech* brake
frenesí *m,* madness, frenzy; vehemence, exaltation
frenético *a* mad, frenzied; vehement, exalted
freno *m,* bridle; *mech* brake; restraint, check. **f. de pedal,** foot brake. **f. neumático,** vacuum brake, pneumatic brake
frente *f,* brow, forehead; front portion; countenance; head; heading; beginning (of a letter, etc.). *m, mil* front. *mf* facade; front; obverse (of coins). *adv* in front, opposite. **f. a f.,** face to face. **con la f. levantada,** with head held high; proudly; insolently. **de f.,** abreast
freo *m,* strait, narrow channel
fresa *f,* strawberry plant and fruit (especially small or wild varieties); *mech* milling cutter, miller
fresadora *f,* milling machine
fresal *m,* strawberry bed
fresca *f,* cool air; fresh air; *inf* home truth
fresco *a* cool; fresh, new; recent; buxom, fresh-colored; calm, serene; *inf* impudent, cheeky, bold; thin (cloths). *m,* coolness; fresh air; *art* fresco. **al f.,** in the open air. **hacer f.,** to be cool or fresh
frescote *a inf* ruddy and corpulent

frescura *f*, coolness; freshness; pleasant verdure and fertility; *inf* cheek, nerve; piece of insolence; unconcern, indifference; calmness, serenity
fresero (-ra) *n* strawberry seller
fresno *m*, *bot* ash
fresón *m*, strawberry (large, cultivated varieties)
fresquera *f*, meat locker; cool place
fresquería *f*, *Mexico* refreshment stand
fresquista *mf* fresco painter
friable *a* brittle; friable, powdery
frialdad *f*, coldness, chilliness; *med* frigidity; indifference, lack of interest; foolishness; negligence
fríamente *adv* coldly; coolly, with indifference; dully, flatly
fricción *f*, friction
friccionar *vt* to rub; give a massage
friega *f*, friction, massage
frigidez *f*, See **frialdad**
frígido *a* frigid
frigio *a* and *n* Phrygian
frigorífico *a* refrigerative. *m*, refrigerator, cold-storage locker
frijol *m*, bean; *bot* kidney bean
frijoles refritos con queso *mpl*, *Mexico* twice fried Mexican beans with cheese
frío *a* cold; *med* frigid; indifferent, uninterested; dull, uninteresting; inefficient. *m*, coldness, chill; cold
friolera *f*, bagatelle, trifle, mere nothing
friolero *a* sensitive to cold
frisa *f*, frieze cloth
frisar *vt* to frizz, curl (cloth); scrub, rub; *vi* approach, be nearly (e.g. **Frisa en los setenta años,** He's nearly seventy)
friso *m*, frieze; dado, border
fritada *f*, *cul* fry, fried food
frito *a* fried
fritura *f*, frying; fried food
frivolidad *f*, frivolity
frivolité *m*, *sew* tatting
frívolo *a* frivolous, superficial; futile, unconvincing
fronda *f*, *bot* leaf; frond (of ferns); *pl* foliage
frondoso *a* leafy
frontera *f*, frontier; facade
fronterizo *a* frontier; facing, opposite
frontero *a* facing, opposite. *m*, (*ant mil*) frontier commander
frontispicio *m*, frontispiece; facade; *fig inf* face, dial
frontón *m*, pelota court; jai alai court; *arch* pediment; *Mexico* jai alai
frotamiento, frote *m*, rubbing, friction
frotar *vt* to rub
frotis *m*, *med* smear
fructífero *a* fruitful, fructiferous
fructuoso *a* fruitful, fertile; useful
frufrú *m*, rustle (of silk, etc.)
frugal *a* frugal; saving, economical
frugalidad *f*, frugality, abstemiousness, moderation
fruición *f*, enjoyment; fruition; satisfaction
fruir *vi irr* to enjoy what one has long desired. See **huir**
frunce *m*, *sew* shirring; gather; ruffling; tuck; pucker; wrinkle
fruncimiento *m*, wrinkling; puckering; *sew* shirring
fruncir *vt* to frown; purse (the lips); pucker; *sew* shirr, pleat, gather; reduce in size; conceal the truth; *vr* pretend to be prudish. **f. el ceño,** to knit one's brow, scowl
fruslería *f*, trifle, nothing
frustración *f*, frustration
frustrar *vt* to disappoint; frustrate, thwart
fruta *f*, fruit; *inf* consequence, result. **f. bomba** *Cuba* papaya **f. de hueso,** stone fruit. *cul* **f. de sartén,** fritter
frutal *a* fruit-bearing. *m*, fruit tree
frutar *vi* to bear fruit
frutería *f*, fruit
frutero (-ra) *a* fruit. *n* fruit seller. *m*, fruit dish; *art* painting of fruit; basket of imitation fruit
frútice *m*, bush, shrub
fruticultura *f*, fruit farming
fruto *m*, fruit; product, result; profit, proceeds; *agr* grain
fu spitting (of cats). *interj* expression of scorn. *inf* **ni f. ni fa,** neither one thing nor the other
fucsia *f*, fuchsia
fuego *m*, fire; conflagration; firing (of firearms); beacon; hearth, home; rash; ardor; heat (of an argument, etc.); *interj* **¡F.!** *mil* Fire! **fuegos artificiales,** fireworks. **a sangre y f.,** by fire and sword. *mil* **hacer f.,** to fire (a weapon). **pegar f.,** to set on fire
fuelle *m*, bellows; bag (of a bagpipe); *sew* pucker, wrinkle; hood (of a carriage, etc.); wind cloud; *inf* talebearer. **f. de pie,** foot pump
fuente *f*, stream, spring; fountain; meat dish; genesis, origin; source, headwaters; tap
fuera *adv* outside, out. *interj* get out! **f. de,** besides, in addition to. **f. de alcance,** out of reach. **f. de sí,** beside oneself (with rage, etc.). **de f.,** from the outside. **por f.,** on the outside, externally
fuereño, -a *mf*, *Mexico* foreigner
fuero *m*, municipal charter; jurisdiction; compilation of laws; legal right or privilege; *pl inf* arrogance. **los fueros de León,** the laws of León
fuerte *a* strong, resistant; robust; spirited, vigorous; hard (of diamonds, etc.); rough, uneven; impregnable; terrible, tremendous; overweight (of coins); active; efficacious, effective; expert, knowledgeable; *gram* strong; intense; loud; tough. *m*, fort; talent, strong point; *mus* forte. *adv* strongly; excessively. **tener genio f.,** to be quick-tempered
fuerza *f*, strength; power, might; force; efficacy; fortress; *sew* stiffening; *mech* power; violence; toughness, durability, solidity; potency; authority; courage; vigor; *pl fig inf* livewires, influential people. **a f. de,** by means of, by dint of. **a la f.,** forcibly. **en f. de,** because of, on account of. **por f. mayor,** by main force. **ser f.,** to be necessary
fuga *f*, flight, escape, running away; leak (gas, etc.); elopement; *mus* fugue; ardor, strength. **f. de cerebros,** brain drain
fugarse *vr* to run away; elope; escape
fugaz *a* fugitive; fleeting, brief
fugitivo (-va) *a* fugitive; runaway, escaping; transient. *n* fugitive
fulano (-na) *n* so-and-so, such a person **f., zutano, y mengano,** *inf* Tom, Dick, and Harry
fulcro *m*, fulcrum
fulgente, fúlgido *a* brilliant, shining
fulgor *m*, brilliance, brightness
fulgurar *vi* to shine, be resplendent, scintillate; flare
fulguroso *a* shining, sparkling
fulminante *a med* fulminant; fulminating; thundering. *m*, percussion cap
fulminar *vt* to fulminate (all meanings)
fulminato *m*, *chem* fulminate
fulmíneo, fulminoso *a* fulminous, pertaining to lightning
fullería *f*, cheating at play; craftiness, low guile
fullero (-ra) *a* cheating; crafty, astute. *n* cheat, cardsharper
fumadero *m*, smoking room
fumador (-ra) *a* smoking. *n* smoker. **«No fumadores»,** "Nonsmoking" (area)
fumar *vi* to smoke; *vr inf* dissipate, waste
fumarola *f*, fumarole
fumigación *f*, fumigation
fumigador (-ra) *n* fumigator
fumigar *vt* to fumigate
fumigatorio *a* fumigatory. *m*, perfume burner
fumista *mf* stove maker; stove dealer; *Argentina* joker, tease
fumistería *f*, stove factory or store
funámbulo *n* tightrope walker, acrobat

función *f*, function; working, operation; *theat* performance; activity, duty; ceremony; celebration; *math* function; *mil* battle
funcional *a* functional
funcionamiento *m*, functioning
funcionar *vi* to function, work. **«No funciona»,** "Out of order"
funcionario *m*, functionary, official; civil servant
funda *f*, case, cover, sheath; hold-all. **f. de almohada,** pillowcase
fundación *f*, foundation
fundadamente *adv* with reason, on good evidence
fundador (-ra) *n* founder, creator; originator
fundamental *a* fundamental
fundamento *m*, *mas* foundation; basis; basic principle, reason; origin, root
fundar *vt* to build, erect; base; found, institute; create, establish; *vr* (*with en*) found, base upon. **f. una compañía,** *com* to float a company
fundición *f*, foundry; smelting, founding, casting; cast iron; *print* font
fundido fotográfico *m*, composite photograph
fundidor *m*, founder, smelter.
fundir *vt* to melt; found, smelt; cast (metals); *vr* join together, unite; *elec* blow (fuses)
fúnebre *a* funeral; dismal, lugubrious, mournful
funerales *m pl*, funeral; *ecc* memorial masses
funerala, (a la) *adv mil* with reversed arms
funeraria *f*, funeral home, undertaker
funéreo *a* funereal, mournful
funestidad *f*, *Mexico* calamity, catastrophe
funesto *a* unlucky, unfortunate; mournful, melancholy, sad
fungoso *a* spongy, fungous
funicular *a* funicular
furgón *m*, wagon; van; guard's van, baggage car, luggage cart. **f. postal,** mail truck
furia *f*, *myth* fury; rage, wrath; fit of madness; raging, violence (of the elements); speed, haste
furibundo *a* frantic, furious; raging
fúrico *a* stark raving mad
furioso *a* furious, enraged; mad, insane; violent, terrible; enormous, excessive
furor *m*, fury, rage; poetic frenzy; violence; furor
furtivo *a* furtive; covert, clandestine; pirate (editions)
fusa *f*, demisemiquaver
fusco *a* dark
fuselado *a* streamlined
fuselaje *m*, fuselage
fusible *a* fusible. *m*, *elec* fuse; fuse wire
fusil *m*, rifle
fusilamiento *m*, execution by shooting
fusilar *vt* to execute by shooting; *inf* plagiarize
fusilazo *m*, rifle shot
fusión *f*, melting, liquefying; fusion, blending; mixture, union; *com* merger, amalgamation
fusionar *vt* to blend, fuse, merge; *vr com* combine, form a merger
fusta *f*, brushwood; whip
fustán *m Lat. Am.* skirt
fuste *m*, wood, timber; *poet* saddle; *fig* core, essence; importance, substance; shaft of a lance; *arch* shaft. **hombre de buen f.,** a man with a good (physical) constitution
fustigar *vt* to whip, lash; rebuke harshly
fútbol *m*, football; soccer
futbolista *mf* football player; soccer player
fútil *a* futile, ineffectual, worthless
futilidad *f*, futility, worthlessness
futura *f*, *law* reversion (of offices); *inf* fiancée
futurismo *m*, futurism
futurista *mf* futurist
futurístico *a* futuristic
futuro (-ra) *a* future. *m*, future. *n inf* betrothed

G

gabacho (-cha) *a* and *n* (*inf* scornful) Frenchman
gabán *m*, overcoat; cloak
gabardina *f*, gabardine; weatherproof coat
gabarra *f*, *naut* lighter, gabbard, barge
gabarro *m*, flaw (in cloth); knot (in stone); snag, drawback; slip, error (in accounts)
gabela *f*, duty, tax; imposition, burden
gabinete *m*, study, library; sitting room; den; *pol* cabinet; collection, museum, gallery; laboratory; boudoir; studio; display cabinet. **g. de lectura,** reading room
gablete *m*, *arch* gable
gacel, *m*. gacela *f*, gazelle
gaceta *f*, bulletin, review, record; newspaper; gazette (official Spanish government organ); *inf* newshound
gacetero (-ra) *n* newsdealer. *m*, news reporter
gacetilla *f*, news in brief, miscellany column, society news; gossip column; *inf* newshound
gacetillero *m*, paragrapher, penny-a-liner; reporter
gacha *f*, unglazed crock; *pl* pap; porridge
gaché *m*, (among the Romany) Andalusian; *inf* fellow
gacho *a* drooping, bent downward; slouch (hat); (of ears) lop; *Mexico* unpleasant
gachón *a inf* attractive, charming
gaélico *a* and *m*, Gaelic
gafar *vt* to claw; seize with a hook, hook; mend with a bracket (pottery)
gafas *f pl*, spectacles; goggles; spectacle earhooks; grapplehooks
gafete *m*, hook and eye; clasp
gaita *f*, bagpipe; hand organ; kind of clarinet; *inf* neck. **g. gallega,** bagpipe
gaitería *f*, crude, gaudy garment or ornament
gaitero *a inf* overmerry; loud, crude. *m*, piper
gajes *m pl*, salary; emoluments; perquisites
gajo *m*, branch, bough (gen. cut); little cluster (of grapes); bunch (of fruit); quarter (of oranges, etc.); prong (of forks, etc.)
gala *f*, evening or full dress; grace, wit; flower, cream, best; gala; *pl* finery; trappings; wedding presents. **de g.,** full dress. **hacer g. de,** to glory in, boast of
galactita *f*, fuller's earth
galaico *a* See **gallego**
galán *m*, handsome, well-made man; lover, wooer, gallant; *theat* leading man or one of leading male roles
galancete *m*, handsome little man; *theat* male juvenile lead
galano *a* smart, well-dressed; agreeable, pleasing; beautiful; ornamented; *fig* elegant (speech, style, etc.)
galante *a* gallant, courtly, attentive; flirtatious (of women); licentious
galanteador *a* flirtatious. *m*, philanderer; wooer
galantear *vt* to court; flirt with; make love to; *fig* procure assiduously
galanteo *m*, courtship; flirtation; love-making; wooing
galantería *f*, courtesy; attention, compliment; elegance, grace; gallantry; generosity, liberality
galanura *f*, showiness, gorgeousness; elegance, grace; prettiness
galápago *m*, freshwater tortoise; cleat
galardón *m*, reward, recompense, prize
galardonar *vt* to reward, recompense
gálata *a* and *mf* Galatian
galbana *f*, *inf* laziness, inertia
galbanoso *a inf* slothful
galdrufa *f*, top, spinning top
galeote *m*, galley slave

galera *f,* van, wagon, cart; *naut* galley; prison for women; *print* galley; *Central America, Mexico* shed. **echar a galeras,** to condemn to the galleys
galerada *f,* galley proof
galería *f,* gallery; corridor, passage; collection of paintings; *min* gallery, drift; *theat* gallery
galerna *f,* tempestuous northwest wind (gen. on Spanish north coast)
Gales Wales
galés (-esa) *a* Welsh. *n* Welshman. *m,* Welsh (language)
galga *f,* boulder, rolling stone; greyhound bitch
galgo *m,* greyhound. **g. ruso,** borzoi
Galia Gaul
gálibo *m, naut* mold; elegance
galicado *a* gallicized
galicismo *m,* gallicism
gálico *m,* syphilis. *a* gallic
Galilea Galilee
galileo (-ea) *a* and *n* Galilean
galimatías *m, inf* gibberish, nonsense
gallardear *vi* to behave with ease and grace
gallardete *m,* pennant; bunting
gallardía *f,* grace, dignity; spirit, dash; courage; liveliness
gallardo *a* handsome, upstanding; gallant; spirited; fine, noble; lively
gallear *vi inf* to put on airs; be a bully; shout, bawl (with anger, etc.); *fig inf* stand out
gallego (-ga) *a* and *n* Galician. *m,* Galician (language)
galleta *f,* biscuit; *inf* slap; anthracite, lump coal; small jar or vessel
gallina *f,* hen. *mf inf* coward. **g. ciega,** blindman's buff. *inf* **acostarse con las gallinas,** to go to bed early
gallinaza *f,* hen dung
gallinero (-ra) *n* poultry dealer. *m,* henhouse; brood of hens; *theat* gallery; babel, noisy place
gallito *m,* small cock; cock of the walk; bully
gallo *m, orn* cock; *inf* false note (in singing); *inf* boss, chief. **g. de viento,** weathercock. *inf* **alzar el g.,** to put on airs, boast. **Cada g. canta en su muladar,** Every man is boss in his own house. *inf* **Otro g. nos cantara,** Our lot (or fate) would have been very different
gallofero (-ra) *a* mendicant, vagabond. *n* beggar
galocha *f,* patten, clog; cap with earflaps
galón *m,* galloon, braid; *mil* stripe; gallon (measure)
galoneadura *f,* braiding, trimming
galonear *vt* to trim with braid
galop *m,* galop; gallopade
galopante *a* galloping (of consumption, etc.)
galopar *vi* to gallop; *mech* wobble
galope *m,* gallop. **a** or **de g.,** at the gallop; on the run, quickly. **andar a g. corto,** to canter
galopillo *m,* scullion
galopín *m,* ragamuffin, urchin; rogue, knave; *inf* clever rogue; *naut* cabin boy
galvanización *f,* galvanization
galvanizar *vt elec* to galvanize; electroplate; *fig* shock into life
gama *f, mus* scale; gamut, range; doe
gambado *a Lat. Am.* knock-kneed
gambito *m,* gambit (in chess)
gamella *f,* trough (for washing, feeding animals, etc.)
gamo *m,* buck (of the fallow deer)
gamuza *f,* chamois; chamois leather
gana *f,* appetite; wish, desire. **de buena g.,** willingly. **de mala g.,** reluctantly. **tener g. (de),** to wish, desire, want. **no tener g.,** to have no appetite, not be hungry. **No me da la g.,** I don't want (to), I won't
ganable *a* attainable; earnable
ganadería *f,* livestock; strain (of cattle); cattle raising; stock farm; cattle dealing
ganadero *m,* cattle raiser or dealer; herdsman
ganado *m,* livestock, herd; flock; hive (of bees); *inf* mob. **g. mayor,** cattle, mules, horses. **g. menor,** sheep, goats, etc. **g. moreno,** hogs, swine. **g. vacuno,** cattle
ganador (-ra) *a* winning. *n* winner
ganancia *f,* winning; gain, profit
ganancial, ganancioso *a* gainful, profitable; lucrative
ganapán *m,* laborer; porter; *inf* boor
ganar *vt* to gain; win; conquer; arrive at; earn; surpass, beat; achieve; acquire; *vi* prosper
ganchero *m,* lumberjack
ganchillo *m,* crochet hook; crochet. **hacer g.,** to crochet
gancho *m,* hook; stump (of a branch); shepherd's crook; crochet hook; *inf* trickster, pimp; *inf* scribble
ganchoso *a* hooked; bent; curved
gandujar *vt sew* to pleat, tuck, shirr
gandul (-la) *a inf* lazy. *n* lazybones, loafer
gandulería *f,* loafing, idleness
ganga *f, min* gangue, matrix; bargain, cinch
ganglio *m,* ganglion
gangoso *a* nasal; with a twang (of speech)
gangrena *f,* gangrene
gangrenarse *vr* to become gangrenous, mortify
gangrenoso *a* gangrenous
ganguear *vi* to speak nasally, or with a twang
ganoso *a* wishful, desirous, anxious
gansada *f, inf* impertinence, foolishness
ganso (-sa) *n* goose, gander; slow-moving person; yokel, bumpkin
ganzúa *f,* skeleton key; *inf* picklock, burglar; *inf* pumper, inquisitive person
gañán *m,* farm worker; day laborer; brawny fellow
gañido *m,* yowl, yelp, howl
gañir *vi irr* to yowl, yelp, howl (of dogs, etc.); crow, croak; *inf* talk hoarsely. See **mullir**
garabatear *vi* to hook, catch with hooks; scribble; *fig inf* beat around the bush
garabateo *m,* hooking; scribbling
garabato *m,* hook; *agr* weed clearer; scrawl, scribble; *inf* charm, sex appeal; pothook; boat hook; *pl* gestures, movements (with the hands)
garaje *m,* garage
garambaina *f,* tawdry finery gaudiness; *pl inf* grimaces of affectation; *inf* scribble, scrawl
garante *mf* guarantor; reference (person). *a* responsible, guaranteeing
garantía *f,* guarantee; security, pledge; *law* warranty
garantir *vt* to guarantee; warrant, vouch for
garañón *m Lat. Am.* stallion
garapiñar *vt* to ice, freeze (drinks, syrups, etc.); *cul* candy, coat with sugar
garbanzo *m,* chickpea. **g. negro,** *fig* black sheep
garbillar *vt agr* to sift; *min* riddle
garbo *m,* jaunty air; grace, elegance; frankness; generosity, liberality
garboso *a* attractive; handsome, sprightly, gay; graceful; munificent
garduña *f,* weasel; marten
garduño (-ña) *n inf* sneak thief
garete (**ir** *or* **irse al**) *naut* to be adrift
garfa *f,* claw (of a bird or animal)
garfear *vi* to catch with a hook, hook
garfio *m,* grappling iron, hook, drag hook, cramp; gaff
gargajear *vi* to expectorate
gargajo *m,* phlegm
garganta *f,* throat; gullet; instep; defile; neck, shaft, narrowest part
gargantear *vi* to warble, trill
gárgara *f,* gargling (gen. *pl*). **hacer gárgaras,** to gargle
gargarismo *m,* gargling; gargle
gárgol *a* rotten (eggs). *m,* groove, mortise
gárgola *f, arch* gargoyle; linseed
garguero *m,* windpipe; esophagus
garita *f,* sentry box; porter's lodge; hut; cabin. **g. de señales,** (railroad) signal box
garitero *m,* gambling house keeper; gambler
garito *m,* gambling house; profits of a gambling house
garra *f,* paw with claws; talon; hand; *mech* clamp, claw. *fig* **caer en las garras de,** to fall into the clutches (of)
garrafa *f,* decanter, carafe; carboy

garrapata *f, ent* tick
garrapatear *vi* to scribble
garrapaticida *m, Lat. Am.* insecticide
garrapato *m,* scribble, scrawl
garrido *a* handsome; gallant; elegant; graceful
garroba *f,* carob bean
garrocha *f,* goad. **salto a la g.,** pole jumping
garrotazo *m,* blow with a truncheon or cudgel. **dar garrotazos de ciego,** to lay about one
garrote *m,* truncheon, club; *med* tourniquet; garrote. **dar g.** (**a**), to strangle
garrotillo *m,* croup
garrucha *f,* pulley; *mech* gin block
garrulidad *f,* garrulity, loquaciousness
gárrulo *a* twittering, chirping (birds); garrulous; murmuring, babbling (wind, water, etc.)
ganuar *vi Lat. Am.* to drizzle
garza *f,* heron
garzo *a* blue (gen. of eyes)
gas *m,* gas; fumes. **g. asfixiante,** poison gas. **cámara de g.,** gasbag, gas chamber
gasa *f,* gauze. **tira de g.,** black mourning band
gasconada *f,* bravado, gasconade
gaseosa *f,* aerated water
gaseoso *a* gaseous
gasista *mf* gas fitter; gasman
gasolina *f,* gasoline, petrol
gasómetro *m,* gas meter; gasometer
gastado *a* worn; worn-out; exhausted
gastador (-ra) *a* extravagant, wasteful. *n* spendthrift. *m, mil* sapper; convict condemned to hard labor
gastar *vt* to spend (money); wear out; exhaust; ruin, destroy; display or have habitually; possess, use, wear; *vr* wear out; run down (of a battery)
gasto *m,* spending; expenditure; consumption (of gas, etc.); expense, cost, charge; wear (and tear). **g. suplementario,** extra charge
gástrico *a* gastric
gastritis *f,* gastritis
gastronomía *f,* gastronomy
gastronómico *a* gastronomic
gastrónomo (-ma) *n* gastronome
gata *f,* she-cat; wreath of mist; *inf* Madrilenian woman. **a gatas,** on all fours
gatada *f, inf* sly trick
gatear *vi* to climb like a cat; *inf* crawl on all fours; *vt inf* scratch (of a cat); steal, pinch
gatillo *m, dim* small cat; dental forceps; trigger (of gun); *inf* juvenile petty thief
gato *m,* cat; tomcat; moneybag or its contents; *mech* jack; mousetrap; *inf* cat burglar, sneak thief; *inf* Madrilenian; *carp* clamp. **g. atigrado,** tiger cat. **g. de algalia,** civet cat. **g. de Angora,** Persian cat. **g. montés,** wildcat. **g. romano,** tabby cat. **dar g. por liebre,** to serve cat for hare, to deceive; misrepresent. *inf* **Hay g. encerrado,** There's more to this than meets the eye
gatuno *a* feline
gaucho (-cha) *n* gaucho; cowboy, rider
gaveta *f,* drawer (of a desk)
gavia *f,* main topsail; *pl* topsails; crow's-nest
gavilán *m,* sparrow hawk; thistle flower; *Lat. Am.* ingrown toenail
gavilla *f,* sheaf (of corn, etc.); gang, rabble
gaviota *f,* seagull
gavota *f,* gavotte
gayo *a* gay, happy; showy, attractive. **gaya ciencia,** minstrelsy, art of poetry
gazapera *f,* rabbit warren; *inf* thieves' den; *inf* brawl
gazapo *m,* young rabbit; *inf* cunning fellow; fib, lie; slip, blunder
gazmoñería *f,* prudery, priggish affectation
gazmoño *a* hypocritical, prudish, priggish
gaznápiro (-ra) *n* ninny, simpleton
gaznate *m,* windpipe
gazpacho *m,* cold soup containing bread, onions, vinegar, olive oil, garlic, etc.
ge *f,* name of the letter G
gehena *m,* gehenna, hell
géiser *m,* geyser
gelatina *f,* gelatin. **g. incendiaria,** napalm. **g. seca,** cooking gelatin
gelatinoso *a* gelatinous
gélido *a poet* icy; very cold
gema *f,* gem; *bot* bud
gemelo (-la) *a* and *n* twin. *m pl,* field or opera glasses, binoculars; cuff links; *ast* Gemini
gemido *m,* groan, lament, moan
gemidor *a* groaning, moaning; wailing (of the wind, etc.)
gemir *vi irr* to moan, groan, lament; *fig* wail, howl. See **pedir**
gene *m,* gene
genealogía *f,* genealogy
genealógico *a* genealogical
genealogista *mf* genealogist
generación *f,* generation, reproduction; species; generation
generador *a* generative. *m, mech* generator
general *a* general; universal; widespread; common, usual. *m,* (*mil ecc*) general. **g. de división,** *mil* major general. **en** *or* **por lo g.,** generally
generalato *m,* generalship
generalidad *f,* majority, bulk; generality
generalísimo *m,* generalissimo, commander in chief
generalización *f,* generalization
generalizar *vt* to generalize; *vr* become widespread or general
generar *vt* to generate
genérico *a* generic
género *m,* kind; class; way, mode; *com* goods; species, genus; *gram* gender; cloth, material. **g. chico,** short theatrical pieces (gen. one act). **g. humano,** humankind
generosidad *f,* hereditary nobility; generosity, magnanimity; liberality, munificence; courage
generoso *a* noble (by birth); magnanimous; generous (of wine); munificent; courageous; excellent
genésico *a* genetic
génesis *m,* Genesis. *f,* beginning, origin
genial *a* of genius; highly talented; brilliant; characteristic, individual; pleasant; cheerful
genialidad *f,* genius; talent; brilliance; eccentricity, oddity
genio *m,* nature, individuality, temperament; temper; character; talent; genius; genie, spirit. **corto de g.,** unintelligent. **mal g.,** bad temper
genital *a* genital. *m,* testicle (gen. *pl*)
genitivo *a* reproductive, generative. *m, gram* genitive
Génova Genoa
gente *f,* people, a crowd; nation; army; *inf* family; followers, adherents. **g. baja,** rabble. **g. de bien,** honest folk; respectable people. **g. de paz,** friends (reply to sentinel's challenge). **g. fina,** nice, cultured people. **g. menuda,** children, small fry
gentecilla *f, dim inf* rabble; contemptible people
gentil *a* pagan, idolatrous; spirited, dashing, handsome; notable, extraordinary; graceful, charming
gentileza *f,* grace; elegance; beauty; verve, sprightliness; courtesy; show, ostentation
gentilhombre *m,* gentleman; handsome man; kind sir! **gentileshombres de cámara,** gentlemen-in-waiting
gentilicio *a* national; family
gentílico *a* pagan, idolatrous
gentilidad *f,* idolatry, paganism; heathendom
gentío *m,* crowd, throng
gentualla, gentuza *f,* canaille, rabble
genuflexión *f,* genuflection
genuino *a* pure; authentic, genuine; *Colombia* great, wonderful
geodesia *f,* geodesy
geodésico *a* geodesic
geografía *f,* geography

geográfico *a* geographical
geógrafo *m*, geographer
geología *f*, geology
geológico *a* geological
geólogo *m*, geologist
geometría *f*, geometry. **g. del espacio,** solid geometry
geométrico *a* geometrical
geranio *m*, geranium
gerencia *f*, *com* managership; manager's office; management
gerente *m*, *com* manager
germanía *f*, thieves' slang; association of thieves; sixteenth-century political brotherhood
germánico *a* germanic
germanófilo (-la) *a* and *n* germanophile
germen *m*, germ, sprout; *bot* embryo; genesis, origin
germinación *f*, germination
germinar *vi* to germinate, sprout; develop, grow
germinativo *a* germinative
gerundio *m*, *gram* gerund; *inf* pompous ass; *inf* tub-thumper
gesta *f*, heroic deed. **cantar de g.,** epic or heroic poem
gestación *f*, gestation
gestear *vi* to gesture, grimace
gesticulación *f*, gesticulation; grimace
gesticular *vi* to grimace, gesticulate. *a* gesticulatory
gestión *f*, negotiation; management, conduct; effort, exertion; measure
gestionar *vt* to negotiate; conduct; undertake; take steps to attain
gesto *m*, gesture; facial expression; grimace; face, visage
gestor (-ra) *n* manager; partner; promoter. *a* managing
Getsemaní Gethsemane
giba *f*, hump, hunchback; *inf* nuisance, inconvenience
gibón *m*, gibbon
giboso *a* hunchbacked
gibraltareño *a* Gibraltarian
gigante *a* gigantic. *m*, giant.
giganta *f*, giantess
gigantesco *a* giant, gigantic; *fig* outstanding
gigantez *f*, gigantic size
gigantón (-ona) *n* enormous giant; carnival grotesque
gimnasia *f*, gymnastics
gimnasio *m*, gymnasium; school, academy
gimnasta *mf* gymnast
gimnástico *a* gymnastic
gimotear *vi inf* to whine (often used scornfully)
gimoteo *m*, *inf* whining, whimpering
ginebra *f*, gin (drink); confusion; babble, din
ginebrés (-esa), ginebrino (-na) *a* and *n* Genevan
gineceo *m*, (*bot* and in ancient Greece) gynaecium
ginecología *f*, gynecology
ginecológico *a* gynecological
ginecólogo (-ga) *n* gynecologist
girado *m*, *com* drawee
girador *m*, *com* drawer
giralda *f*, weathercock in the shape of a person or animal; tower at Seville
girar *vi* to revolve; deal (with), concern; turn, branch (streets, etc.); *com* trade; *mech* turn on, revolve; *vt* and *vi com* draw, cash. **g. en descubierto,** *com* to overdraw
girasol *m*, sunflower
giratorio *a* revolving, gyrating; swiveling
giro *m*, revolution, turn; revolving; trend; course (of affairs); style, turn (of phrase); threat; knife gash; *com* draft, drawing; *com* line of business, speciality. **g. postal,** postal order
giroscopio *m*, gyroscope
gis *m Lat. Am.* chalk; *Mexico also* pulque
gitanería *f*, cajolery, wheedling; gypsies; gypsy saying or action
gitanesco *a* gypsy, gypsy-like
gitano (-na) *a* gypsy; gypsy-like; seductive, attractive; sly. *n* gypsy
glaciar *m*, glacier
gladiador *m*, gladiator
glándula *f*, gland
glanco *a Lat. Am.* light green
glicerina *f*, glycerin, glycerol
globo *m*, *geom* sphere; globe, world; globe (*elec gas*); balloon. **g. aerostático,** air balloon. **g. terrestre,** world; geographical globe
globular *a* globular
glóbulo *m*, globule.
globuloso *a* globulous
gloria *f*, heavenly bliss; fame, glory; delight, pleasure; magnificence, splendor; *art* apotheosis, glory. *m*, *ecc* doxology
gloriar *vt* to praise; *vr* (*with de or en*) boast about; be proud of, rejoice in
glorieta *f*, bower, arbor; open space in a garden; street square
glorificación *f*, glorification
glorificador *a* glorifying
glorificar *vt* to exalt, raise up; glorify, extol; *vr* (*with de or en*) be proud of; glory in; boast of
glorioso *a* glorious; *ecc* blessed; boastful, bragging
glosa *f*, gloss; explanation, note
glosador (-ra) *n* glossator; commentator. *a* explanatory
glosar *vt lit* to gloss
glosario *m*, glossary
glosopeda *f*, foot-and-mouth disease
glotón (-ona) *a* greedy, gluttonous. *n* glutton
glotonería *f*, gluttony, greed
glucosa *f*, glucose
glúteo *a* gluteal
glutinoso *a* glutinous
gn- For words so beginning, see spellings without **g.**
gobernación *f*, government; governor's office or building; ministry of the interior, home office (abb. for **ministerio de G.**)
gobernador (-ra) *a* governing, *n* governor
gobernalle *m*, helm
gobernante *a* governing. *m*, *inf* self-appointed director or manager
gobernar *vt irr* to govern, rule; lead, conduct; manage; steer; control; *vi* govern; *naut* obey the tiller. See **recomendar**
gobierno *m*, government (all meanings); *naut* helm; control (of machines, business, etc.)
goce *m*, enjoyment; possession
godo (da) *a* Gothic; aristocratic, noble. *n* Goth; aristocrat
gol *m*, *sport* goal
gola *f*, throat; gullet; gorget; tucker, bib
goleta *f*, schooner
golf *m*, golf. **palo de g.,** golf club
golfear *vi* to loaf
golfería *f*, loafing; vagabondage; loafers
golfo (-fa) *m*, *geog* gulf; sea, ocean. *n* ragamuffin, urchin. *m*, *inf* loafer; lounge lizard, wastrel
golilla *f*, ruff; *Lat. Am.* scarf; *m*, *inf* magistrate
gollería *f*, dainty, tidbit; *inf* affectation, persnicketiness
gollete *m*, gullet; neck (of a bottle, etc.); *mech* nozzle
golondrina *f*, *orn* swallow; *Chile* moving van. **g. de mar,** tern
golosina *f*, tidbit, delicacy; desire, caprice; pleasant useless thing
goloso *a* fond of sweet things; greedy, desirous; appetizing
golpe *m*, blow, knock; pull (at the oars); ring (of a bell); *mech* stroke; crowd; fall (of rain, etc.); mass, torrent; misfortune; shock, collision; spring lock; beating (of the heart); flap (of a pocket); *sew* passementerie; surprise; point, wit; bet. **g. de estado,** coup d'état. **g. de fortuna,** stroke of fortune. **g. de mano,** rising, insurrection. **g. en vago,** blow in the air; disappointment. **g. franco,** *sport* free kick. **de g.,** suddenly; quickly
golpeadura *f*. **golpeo** *m*, knocking, striking; beating, throbbing
golpear *vt* and *vi* to knock, strike; beat, throb
goma *f*, gum, rubber; India rubber; rubber band

gomería *f,* tire store
gomero *a* gum; rubber. *m, WH* rubber planter
gomoso *a* gummy; gum
gónada *f,* gonad
góndola *f,* gondola
gondolero *m,* gondolier
gongorino *a* gongoristic, euphuistic
gonorrea *f,* gonorrhea
gordo *a* fat, stout; greasy, oily; thick (thread, etc.). *m,* animal fat, suet. *inf* **ganar el g.,** to win first prize (in a lottery, etc.)
gordura *f,* grease, fat; stoutness, corpulence
gorgojo *m,* weevil; *fig* dwarf
gorgoritear *vi inf* to trill, quaver
gorgorito *m, inf* quaver, tremolo, trill (gen. *pl*)
gorgoteo *m,* gurgle
gorjear *vi* to trill, warble; twitter; *vr* crow (of a baby)
gorjeo *m,* trill, shake; warbling, twitter; crowing, lisping (of a child)
gorra *f,* cap; bonnet; *mil* busby; hunting cap. **vivir de g.,** *inf* to sponge
gorrión *m,* sparrow
gorrista *mf inf* parasite; sponger
gorro *m,* cap; bonnet
gorrón *m,* smooth, round pebble; *mech* pivot, gudgeon; sponger, waster. *a* parasitical
gota *f,* drop (of liquid); gout
gotear *vi* to drop, trickle, drip; leak; drizzle; give or receive in driblets
goteo *m,* trickling, dripping
gotera *f,* dripping; trickle; leak; leakage; valance
gotero *m Lat. Am.* (medicine) dropper
gótico *a* Gothic; noble, illustrious
gotoso (-sa) *a* gouty. *n* sufferer from gout
gozar *vt* to enjoy, have; take pleasure (in), delight (in); know carnally; *vi* (*with de*) enjoy; have, possess
gozne *m,* hinge
gozo *m,* enjoyment, possession; gladness, joy; *pl* couplets in honor of the Virgin Mary or a saint. *inf* **¡Mi g. en el pozo!** I'm sunk! All is lost!
gozoso *a* glad, happy. *adv* gladly; with pleasure
grabado *m,* engraver's art; engraving; illustration, picture. **g. al agua fuerte,** etching. **g. al agua tinta,** aquatint
grabador (-ra) *n* engraver
grabadura *f,* act of engraving
grabar *vt* to engrave; *fig* leave a deep impression
gracejo *m,* humor, wit; cheerfulness
gracia *f,* grace; attraction, grace; favor; kindness; jest, witticism; pardon, mercy; pleasant manner; obligingness, willingness; *pl* thanks, thank you. **gracias a,** thanks to. **¡Gracias a Dios!** Thank God! Thank goodness! **las Gracias,** the Three Graces
grácil *a* slender; small
graciosidad *f,* beauty, perfection, grace
gracioso (-sa) *a* attractive, graceful, elegant; witty, humorous; free, gratis. *n theat* comic role; *m, theat* fool
grada *f,* step, stair; gradin, seat; stand, gallery; *agr* harrow; *naut* runway; *pl* perron, flight of stairs
gradación *f,* gradation; climax
gradería *f,* flight of steps
grado *m,* step, stair; degree (of relationship); university degree; grade, class (in schools); (*fig geom phys*) degree; will, desire. **de buen g.,** willingly. **en sumo g.,** in the highest degree
graduación *f,* graduation; *mil* rank; rating (of a ship's company). **g. de oficial,** *mil* commission
graduado *a* graded; *mil* brevet. *m,* graduate
gradual *a* gradual
graduar *vt* to classify; *mil* grade; confer a degree on; measure; test; *com* standardize; *mech* calibrate; *vr* graduate, receive a degree. **g. la vista,** to test the eyes. **graduarse de oficial,** *mil* to get one's commission
gráfica *f,* graph
gráfico *a* graphic; vivid
grafito *m,* graphite
grafología *f,* graphology
grajear *vi* to caw; gurgle, burble (of infants)
grajo *m, orn* rook
grama *f Dominican Republic, Venezuela* grass, lawn
gramática *f,* grammar. *inf* **g. parda,** horse sense
gramático *a* grammatical. *m,* grammarian
gramo *m,* gram
gran *a abb* See **grande.** Used before a singular noun. big; great; grand
grana *f,* grain, seed; seed time; cochineal; kermes; red
granada *f, mil* grenade, shell; pomegranate
granadero *m,* grenadier; *inf* very tall person; *Lat. Am.* riot policeman
granadilla *f,* passionflower
granadina *f,* grenadine
granar *vi agr* to seed; run to seed
granate *m,* garnet; dark red
Gran Bretaña Great Britain
grande *a* big, large; great, illustrious; grand. *m,* great man; grandee. **en g.,** in a large size; as a whole; in style, lavishly
grandeza *f,* largeness; greatness, magnificence; grandeeship; vastness, magnitude
grandilocuencia *f,* grandiloquence
grandílocuo *a* grandiloquent
grandiosidad *f,* grandeur, greatness
grandioso *a* grandiose, magnificent
grandor *m,* size
granear *vt agr* to sow; grain (of leather)
granero *m,* granary; grain-producing country
granito *m, dim* small grain; granite; small pimple
granizar *vi* to hail, sleet; *vi* and *vt fig* shower down, deluge
granizo *m,* hail, sleet; hailstorm; *fig* shower, deluge
granja *f,* farm; farmhouse; dairy farm, dairy
granjear *vt* to trade, profit, earn; obtain, acquire; *vr* gain, win
granjería *f,* farming; agricultural profits; earnings, profits
granjero (-ra) *n* farmer
Gran Lago Salado, el the Great Salt Lake
grano *m, agr* grain; seed; bean (coffee, etc.); particle; markings, grain (of wood, etc.); pimple; grain (measure). *fig inf* **ir al g.,** to go to the root of the matter; come to the point
granuja *f,* grape pit. *m, inf* urchin, scamp; knave, rogue
granujiento *a* pimply
gránulo *m,* granule
granuloso *a* granulous
grapa *f,* cramp, dowel, clamp; block hook; *elec* cleat; staple
grasa *f,* fat; grease; oil; dripping, suet
grasiento *a* greasy; grubby, dirty
gratificación *f,* monetary reward; fee, remuneration; gratuity
gratificar *vt* to recompense; please, gratify
gratis *a* and *adv* gratis
gratitud *f,* gratitude
grato *a* pleasing, agreeable; free, gratuitous; *Lat. Am.* appreciative, grateful
gratuito *a* gratuitous, free; baseless, unfounded
grava *f,* gravel; stone chip, pebble; metal (of a road)
gravamen *m,* obligation; burden; tax
gravar *vt* to burden, weigh upon; tax
grave *a* heavy; important, momentous; grave; dignified, serious; sedate; tiresome; low-pitched, low; *gram* grave accent
gravedad *f, phys* gravity
gravitación *f, phys* gravitation; seriousness; sedateness; importance; enormity, gravity
gravitar *vi* to gravitate; lean or rest (upon)
gravoso *a* grievous, oppressive; onerous; costly
graznar *vi* to caw; cackle; quack; croak; sing stridently, screech
graznido *m,* caw; cackle; croaking; quack; screech
Grecia Greece

greco (-ca) *a* and *n* Greek
gregario *a* gregarious
gregoriano *a* Gregorian
gregüescos *m pl*, wide breeches (sixteenth and seventeenth centuries)
gremial *a* pertaining to a guild, union, or association. *m*, member of a guild, union, or association
gremio *m*, guild, corporation, union; society, association; (univ.) general council
greña *f*, tangled lock (of hair) (gen. *pl*); tangle, confused mass
gresca *f*, uproar, tumult; fight, row
grey *f*, flock, drove, herd; *ecc* flock, company; people, nation
griego (-ga) *a* and *n* Greek. *m*, Greek (language); *inf* gibberish
grieta *f*, fissure; crevice; chink; split; flaw; vein (in stone, etc.); *mech* leak
grietado *a* fissured; cracked
grifo *m*, griffin; tap; cock
grillo *m*, cricket; *bot* shoot; *pl* fetters, irons, chains; *fig* shackles
grima *f*, revulsion, horror
gringo (-ga) *n inf* foreigner (scornful)
gripe *f*, influenza; grippe
gris *a* and *m*, gray
grisú *m*, firedamp
gritador (-ra) *a* shouting. *n* shouter
gritar *vi* to shout, yell, scream; howl down; hoot
gritería *f*, shouting, yelling, clamor
grito *m*, shout, yell, shriek, scream. *inf* **poner el g. en el cielo,** to cry to high heaven, complain. **el Grito de Dolores** the Proclamation of Mexican Independence (1810)
groenlandés (-esa) *a* Greenland. *n* Greenlander
Groenlandia Greenland
grosella *f*, currant. **g. blanca,** gooseberry
grosería *f*, rudeness; roughness (of workmanship); ignorance; rusticity
grosero *a* coarse; rough; thick; unpolished, rude
grotesco *a* grotesque, absurd
grúa *f*, *mech* crane, hoist, derrick. **g. de pescante,** jib crane. **g. móvil,** traveling crane
gruesa *f*, twelve dozen, gross
grueso *a* stout, corpulent; large. *m*, bulk, body; major portion, majority; thick stroke (of a letter); thickness, density. **en g.,** in bulk
grulla *f*, *orn* crane
grumete *m*, ship's boy, cabin boy
grumo *m*, clot; heart (of vegetables); bunch, cluster; bud
gruñido *m*, grunt; growl
gruñidor *a* grunting; growling
gruñir *vi* to grunt; growl; grumble; squeak, creak (doors, etc.). *Pres. Part.* **gruñendo.** *Pres. Ind.* **gruño, gruñes,** etc.
grupa *f*, croup (of a horse); pillion (of a motorcycle)
grupera *f*, pillion (of a horse, etc.)
grupo *m*, knot, cluster; band, group; *art* group; *mech* set
gruta *f*, cavern, grotto
guacamayo *m*, macaw
guadamecí *m*, embossed decorated leather
guadaña *f*, scythe
guagua, *f Caribbean* bus
gualdo *a* yellow, golden
gualdrapa *f*, saddlecloth, trappings; *inf* tatter, rag
guante *m*, glove. **g. con puño,** gauntlet glove. **g. de boxeo,** boxing glove. **g. de cabritilla,** kid glove. **arrojar el g.,** to throw down the gauntlet; challenge, defy
guantelete *m*, gauntlet
guantería *f*, glove trade, shop, or factory
guantero (-ra) *n* glove maker or seller, glover
guapear *vi inf* to make the best of a bad job; *inf* pride oneself on being well dressed
guapeza *f*, prettiness; *inf* resolution, courage; *inf* smartness or showiness of dress; boastful act or behavior
guapo *a* pretty; handsome; *inf* daring, enterprising; *inf* smart, well-dressed, foppish; *inf* handsome. *m*, braggart, brawler; beau, lover; *inf* fine fellow, son of a gun
guaracha *f*, *Cuba, Puerto Rico* guaracha (vigorous dance in triple meter; music for this dance)
guarda *mf* keeper, guard. *f*, guarding, keeping, custodianship, preservation; guardianship; observance, fulfilment; flyleaf, end page (books); warder (of locks or keys); *mech* guard; guard (of a fan)
guardabarrera *mf* gatekeeper at a level crossing (railroad)
guardabarro *m*, mudguard
guardabosque *mf* gamekeeper
guardabrisa *m*, *aut* windshield; glass candle shield
guardacostas *m*, coast guard; *naut* revenue cutter
guardafrenos *m*, brakeman (railroad)
guardalmacén *mf* storekeeper
guardameta *mf* goalkeeper
guardamuebles *m*, furniture warehouse
guardapelo *m*, locket
guardapolvo *m*, dustcover; light overcoat; inner case of a pocket watch
guardar *vt* to keep; preserve, retain; maintain, observe; save, put aside, lay away; defend, protect; guard; *vr* (*with de*) avoid, guard against. **g. compás con,** to be in tune with. **guardarse mucho,** to think twice before. **g. silencio,** to keep silent. **¡Guarda!** Take care! **¡Guárdate del agua mansa!** Still waters run deep!
guardarropa *m*, cloakroom. *mf* cloakroom attendant; keeper of the wardrobe. *m*, wardrobe, clothes closet
guardarropía *f*, theatrical wardrobe
guardavía *m*, signalman (railroad)
guardería *f*, day nursery, day-care center
guardia *f*, guard, escort; protection; (*mil naut*) watch; regiment, body (of troops); guard (fencing). *m*, guardsman; policeman. **g. de asalto,** armed police. **g. de corps,** royal bodyguard. **g. civil,** civil guard. **g. marina,** midshipman. **g. municipal,** city police. *mil* **montar la g.,** to mount guard
guardián (-ana) *n* keeper; custodian; warden. *m*, watchman; jailer
guardilla *f*, attic, garret
guarecer *vt irr* to shelter, protect, aid; preserve, keep; cure; *vr* take shelter. See **conocer**
guarida *f*, lair, den; refuge, shelter; haunt, resort
guarismo *m*, *math* figure; number, numeral
guarnecer *vt irr* to decorate, adorn; *sew* trim, face, border; *mil* garrison; *mas* plaster. See **conocer**
guarnecido *m*, *mas* plastering
guarnición *f*, *sew* trimming, ornament, border, fringe; *mech* packing; *mil* garrison; setting (of jewels); guard (of a sword, etc.); *pl* harness; fittings
guarnir *vt naut* to reeve
guasa *f*, *inf* dullness, boringness; joke. **de g.,** jokingly
guasón *a inf* dull, tedious; humorous, jocose
guatemalteco (-ca) *a* and *n* Guatemalan
guau *m*, bowwow, bark of a dog
guayaba *f*, guava; guava jelly; *Lat. Am. also* hoax
Guayana Guiana
gubernamental *a* governmental
gubernativo *a* governmental; administrative
gubia *f*, *carp* chisel; gouge
guedeja *f*, long tress or lock of hair; forelock; lion's mane
Guernesey Guernsey
guerra *f*, war; struggle, fight; *fig* hostility. *inf* **dar g.,** to give trouble, annoy. **en g. con,** at war with. **la g. de Cuba,** the Spanish-American War
guerrear *vi* to make war, fight; oppose
guerrero (-ra) *a* war, martial; warrior; *inf* troublesome, annoying. *n* fighter. *m*, warrior, soldier
guerrillear *vi* to wage guerrilla warfare; fight as a guerrilla
guerrillero *m*, guerrilla fighter
guía *mf* guide, conductor; adviser, director. *f*, guide, aid;

guidebook; *mech* guide, slide; directory; signpost. **g. de ferrocarriles,** train schedule, railroad timetable. **g. de teléfonos,** telephone directory
guiar *vt* to guide; lead, conduct; *mech* work, control; *aut* drive; pilot; teach, direct, govern
guija *f,* pebble
guijarro *m,* smooth, round pebble; boulder; cobblestone
guijarroso *a* pebbly, cobbled
guijo *m,* gravel; granite chips; pebble
guillotina *f,* guillotine; paper-cutting machine
guillotinar *vt* to guillotine, decapitate
guinda *f,* mazard cherry; *naut* height of masts
guinea *f,* guinea
guinga *f,* gingham
guiñada *f,* wink; blink; *naut* yaw
guiñapo *m,* rag, tatter; sloven, ragamuffin
guiñar *vt* to wink; blink; *naut* yaw; *vr* wink at each other
guiño *m,* wink
guión *m,* royal standard; banner; summary; leader of a dance; *gram* hyphen; subtitle (in films). **g. mayor,** *gram* dash
guipuzcoano (-na) *a* and *n* Guipuzcoan
guirigay *m, inf* gibberish; uproar, babble
guirnalda *f,* garland, wreath
guisa *f,* way, manner; will, desire. **a g. de,** in the manner or fashion of
guisado *m, cul* stew; cooked dish
guisante *m, agr* pea; pea plant. **g. de olor,** sweetpea
guisar *vt* to cook; stew; *cul* prepare, dress; adjust, arrange
guiso *m,* cooked dish
güisquisoda *f Spain* highball
guitarra *f,* guitar
guitarrista *mf* guitar player
guito *a* vicious (horses, mules)
gula *f,* greed, gluttony
gusaniento *a* worm-eaten; maggoty
gusano *m,* worm; caterpillar; maggot; meek, downtrodden person. **g. de seda,** silkworm
gusanoso *a* wormy
gustar *vt* to taste, savor; try; *vi* be pleasing, give pleasure; like. **Me gusta el libro,** I like the book. **La película no me gustó,** I didn't like the film. **g. de,** to like, is used only when a person is the subject
gusto *m,* taste; flavor, savor; pleasure, delight; will, desire; discrimination, taste, style, fashion, manner; whim, caprice. **a g.,** to taste; according to taste. **con mucho g.,** with great pleasure. **dar g.,** to please. **de buen g.,** in good taste
gustoso *a* savory, palatable; willingly, with pleasure; pleasant, agreeable
gutapercha *f,* guttapercha
gutural *a* guttural

H

haba *f,* broad bean; bean (coffee, cocoa, etc.). **h. de las Indias,** sweetpea. **Esas son habas contadas,** That's a certainty
Habana, la Havana
habanero (-ra), habano (-na) *a* and *n* Havanese, from Havana. *m.* **habano,** Havana cigar
haber *m,* estate, property (gen. *pl*); income; *com* credit balance. **h. monedado,** specie
haber *vt irr* to have; catch, lay hands on (e.g. **El reo fue habido,** The criminal was caught). *v aux* (e.g. **Hemos escrito la carta,** We have written the letter). *v impers* to happen, take place; be. *3rd pers. sing Pres. Ind.* **ha** is replaced by **hay,** meaning there is or there are (e.g. **No hay naranjas en las tiendas,** There are no oranges in the shops). In certain weather expressions, **hay** means it is (e.g. **Hay luna,** It is moonlight). Used of expressions of time, **haber** means to elapse and **ha** (*3rd pers. sing Pres. Ind.*) has adverbial force of 'ago' (e.g. **muchos días ha,** many days ago). **h. de,** to be necessary (less strong than **h. que**) (e.g. **Hemos de verle mañana,** We must see him tomorrow. **He de hacer el papel de Manolo,** I am to play the part of Manolo). **h. que,** to be unavoidable, be essential. With this construction the form **hay** is used (e.g. **Hay que darse prisa,** We (or one) must hurry. **No hay que enojarse,** There's no need to get annoyed). **no h., más que pedir,** to leave nothing to be desired. **no h. tal,** to be no such thing. *inf* **habérselas con,** to quarrel or fall out with. **Hubo una vez . . . ,** Once upon a time . . . **¡No hay de qué!,** Don't mention it!; Not at all!; You're welcome! **No hay para que . . . ,** There's no point in. . . . **poco tiempo ha,** a little while ago. **¿Qué hay?** What's the matter?; What's new? **¿Qué hay de nuevo?** What's new? *Pres. Ind.* **he, has, ha, hemos, habéis, han.** *Fut.* **habré,** etc. *Condit.* **habría,** etc. *Preterite* **hube, hubiste, hubo, hubimos, hubisteis, hubieron.** *Pres. Subjunc.* **haya,** etc. *Imperf. Subjunc.* **hubiese,** etc.
habichuela *f,* kidney bean
hábil *a* clever; skillful; able; lawful
habilidad *f,* ability; skill; accomplishment; craftsmanship, workmanship
habilidoso *a* accomplished; able; skillful
habilitación *f,* habilitation; paymastership; equipment; furnishing
habilitado *m,* paymaster
habilitar *vt* to qualify; equip; furnish; habilitate; enable; *com* capitalize
habitabilidad *f,* habitability
habitable *a* habitable
habitación *f,* habitation, dwelling; room in a house; residence; (*bot zool*) habitat; caretaking
habitante *m,* inhabitant
habitar *vt* to inhabit, reside in
hábito *m,* attire; *ecc* habit; use, custom; skill, facility; *pl* vestments; gown, robe. **tomar el h.,** to become a monk or nun
habitual *a* habitual, usual
habituar *vt* to accustom; *vr* accustom oneself; grow used (to)
habitud *f,* habit, custom; connection, relationship
habla *f,* speech; language; dialect; discourse. **al h.,** within speaking distance
hablado *a* spoken. **bien h.,** well-spoken; courteous. **mal h.,** ill-spoken; rude
hablador (-ra) *a* talkative; gossipy; *Mexico also* boastful. *n* chatterbox; gossip
habladuría *f,* gossip; impertinent chatter
hablanchín *a inf* chattering, gossiping
hablar *vi* to speak; converse; express oneself; arrange; (*with de*) speak about, discuss; gossip about, criticize; (*with por*) intercede on behalf of; *vt* speak (a language); say, speak; *vr* speak to one another. **no hablarse,** to not be on speaking terms. **h. a gritos,** to shout. **h. alto,** to speak loudly or in strong terms. **h. bien** (*or* **mal**), to be well- (or ill-) spoken; be polite (or rude). **h. claro,** to speak frankly. **h. consigo** *or* **h. entre sí,** to talk to oneself. *inf* **h. cristiano, h. en cristiano,** to speak clearly or intelligibly; speak frankly. **hablarlo todo,** to talk too much. **h. por h.,** to talk for talking's sake. *inf* **h. por los codos,** to chatter. **h. sin ton ni son,** to speak foolishly
hablilla *f,* rumor, tittletattle, gossip
hacecillo *m,* small sheaf; small bundle; *bot* fascicle; beam (of light)
hacedero *a* feasible, practicable

hacedor *m*, maker; steward, manager; Creator
hacendado (-da) *a* landed. *n* landowner; *WH* cattle rancher
hacendista *mf* political economist
hacendoso *a* diligent, hard-working
hacer *vt irr* to make; fashion, form, construct; do, perform; cause, effect; arrange, put right; contain; accustom, harden; pack (luggage); imagine, invent, create; improve, perfect; compel, oblige; deliver (speeches); compose; earn; *math* add up to; suppose, imagine (e.g. **Sus padres hacían a María en casa,** Her parents imagined that Mary was at home); put into practice, execute; play the part of or act like (e.g. **h. el gracioso,** to play the buffoon); shed, cast (e.g. **El roble hace sombra,** The oak casts a shadow); assemble, convoke (meetings, gatherings); give off, produce (e.g. **La chimenea hace humo,** The chimney is smoking); perform (plays); (*with el, la, lo, and some nouns*) pretend to be (e.g. **Se hizo el desconocido,** He pretended to be ignorant). (**h.** followed by infin. is sometimes translated by a past participle in English (e.g. **Lo hice h.,** I had it done).) *vi* to matter, be important, signify (e.g. **Su llegada no hace nada al caso,** His arrival makes no difference to the case. **Se me hace muy poco . . . ,** It matters to me very little . . .); be fitting or suitable; concern, be pertinent; match, go with; agree, be in harmony; (*with de*) act as, discharge duties of temporarily (e.g. **h. de camarero,** to be a temporary waiter); (*with por*) try to, attempt to (e.g. **Haremos por decírselo,** We shall try to tell him). *vi impers* Used in expressions concerning: 1. the weather. 2. lapse of time. English uses the verb 'to be' in both cases, e.g.:
1. **hace buen** (*or* **mal**) **tiempo,** it is fine (or bad) weather. **hace mucho frío,** it is very cold. **hace sol,** it is sunny. **hace viento,** it is windy. **¿Qué tiempo hace?** What is the weather like?
2. **hace** + an expression of time is followed by **que** introducing a clause (e.g. **Hace dos horas que llegamos,** It is two hours since we arrived) or **hace** + an expression of time may be followed by **desde** + a noun (e.g. **Hace dos años desde aquel día,** It is two years since that day)

When an action or state that has begun in the past is still continuing in the present, the Spanish verb is in the Pres. Ind., whereas the English verb is in the Perfect (e.g. **Hace un mes que la veo todos los días,** I have been seeing her every day for a month). This rule holds good with other tenses. English Pluperfect, Future Perfect, Conditional Perfect become in Spanish Imperfect, Future, Conditional, respectively. *naut* **h. agua,** to leak. **h. aguas,** to pass water, urinate. **h. alarde de,** to boast of. **h. América,** to strike it rich. **h. el amor a,** to make love to, court, woo. **h. autoridad,** to be authoritative. **h. a todo,** to have many uses; be adaptable. **h. bancarrota,** to go bankrupt. **h. un berrinche, hacerse un berrinche,** to have a fit, have a tantrum. *fig inf* **h. buena,** to justify. **h. calceta,** to knit. **h. cara** or **frente a,** to face; resist. **h. caso,** to take notice, mind (e.g. **¡No hagas caso!** Never mind!). **h. causas,** to bring charges, institute proceedings. **h. cuentas,** to reckon up. **h. daño,** to harm. *inf* **h. de las suyas,** to behave in his usual manner or play one of his usual tricks. **h. diligencias por,** to endeavor to. **h. fiesta,** to take a holiday. **h. fuerza,** to struggle. **h. fuerza a,** *fig* to do violence to (e.g. **Hizo fuerza a sus creencias,** He did violence to his beliefs). **h. h.,** to cause to be made (e.g. **He hecho hacer un vestido,** I have had a dress made). **h. juego,** to make a set, match (e.g. **El sombrero hace juego con el traje,** The hat goes with the dress). **h. la corte (a),** to court, woo. *fig inf* **h. la vista gorda,** to turn a blind eye. **h. la vida del claustro,** to lead a cloistered existence. **h. mal,** to do wrong; be harmful (food, etc.). **h. pedazos,** to break. **h. pinos** (or **pinitos**) to totter; toddle; stagger. *aer* **h. rizos,** to loop the loop. **h. saber,** to make known; notify. **h. seguir,** to forward (letters). **h. señas,** to make signs (wave, beckon, etc.). *inf* **h. una que sea sonada,** to cause a big scandal. **¡Hágame el favor!** Please! *Pres. Ind.* **hago, haces,** etc. *Fut.* **haré,** etc. *Condit.* **haría,** etc. *Imperat.* **haz, haga, hagamos, haced, hagan.** *Preterite* **hice, hiciste, hizo, hicimos, hicisteis, hicieron.** *Pres. Subjunc.* **haga,** etc. *Imperf. Subjunc.* **hiciese,** etc.
hacerse *vr irr* to become (e.g. **Se ha hecho muy importante,** It (or he) has become very important); grow up (e.g. **Miguel se ha hecho hombre,** Michael has grown up (become a man)); develop, mature; pass oneself off as, pretend to be; (*with prep a*) become accustomed to or used to (e.g. **Me haré a este clima,** I shall grow used to this climate); withdraw or retire to (of places); (*with de or con*) provide oneself with. **h. a la vela,** to set sail. **h. a (uno),** to seem (e.g. **Eso que me cuentas se me hace increíble,** What you tell me seems incredible). *inf* **h. chiquito,** to be modest. **h. tarde,** to grow late; *fig* be too late. See **hacer**
hacia *prep* toward, near, about. **h. adelante,** forward, onward
hacienda *f*, country estate, land; property; *pl* domestic tasks; cattle. **h. pública,** public funds. **ministerio de h.,** national treasury, exchequer
hacina *f*, *agr* stack; heap, pile
hacinamiento *m*, stacking, piling; accumulation
hacinar *vt agr* to stack sheaves; accumulate, amass; pile up, heap
hacha *f*, large candle; torch; ax. **h. pequeña,** hatchet
hachazo *m*, stroke of an ax
hache *f*, name of the letter H
hachero *m*, candlestick; woodcutter, axman
hacho *m*, torch; beacon
hada *f*, fairy
hado *m*, fate; destiny
hagiografía *f*, hagiography
hagiógrafo *m*, hagiographer
Haití Haiti
haitiano (-na) *a* and *n* Haitian
halagar *vt* to caress; flatter; coax; please, delight
halago *m*, flattery; coaxing; caress; source of pleasure, delight
halagüeño *a* flattering; pleasing; caressing; hopeful, promising
halar *vt naut* to haul, tow
halcón *m*, falcon
halconero *m*, hawker, hunter
hálito *m*, breath; vapor; *poet* breeze
hallado *a* and *Past Part.* found, met. **bien h.,** welcome; happy, contented. **mal h.,** unwelcome; uneasy, discontented
hallador (-ra) *n* finder
hallar *vt* to find; meet; observe; discover; find out; *vr* be present; be, find oneself
hallazgo *m*, finding; thing found; finder's reward
halo *m*, halo
halterofilia *f*, weightlifting
hamaca *f*, hammock
hambre *f*, hunger; famine; desire, yearning. **tener h.,** to be hungry
hambriento *a* hungry; famished; *fig* starved (of affection, etc.)
Hamburgo Hamburg
hamo *m*, fishhook
hampa *f*, rogue's life; gang of rogues; underworld, slum
hangar *m*, hangar
haragán (-ana) *a* lazy, idle. *n* idler, lazybones
harapiento *a* ragged
harapo *m*, tatter, rag
haraposo *a* ragged
harén *m*, harem
harina *f*, flour; powder; farina. *inf* **ser h. de otro costal,** to be a horse of another color
harinero *a* relating to flour. *m*, flour merchant; flour bin
harinoso *a* floury, mealy; farinaceous
harmónica *f*, (*phys math*) harmonic

harmonizar *vt* to arrange (music)
harnear *vt Lat. Am.* to sieve, sift
harnero *m,* sieve
harón *a* slothful, slow; lazy, idle
harpillera *f,* sackcloth, sacking
hartar *vt* to satiate; tire, annoy; satisfy the appetite; shower (with blows, etc.)
hartazgo *m,* satiety
harto *a* satiated; tired (of), *adv* enough
hartón *a Central America, Mexico* gluttonous
hartura *f,* satiety; abundance
hasta *prep* until; as far as; down or up to. *conjunc* also, even. **h. la vista,** See you! Ciaio! Au revoir! **h. mañana,** until tomorrow
hastial *m,* gable, end wall; boor, lout
hastío *m,* loathing; distaste; nausea
hato *m,* personal clothing; herd of cattle; gang (of suspicious characters); crowd, mob; *inf* group, party. *inf* **liar el h.,** to pack up
Hawai Hawaii
hay there is; there are. See **haber**
haya *f,* beech tree; beechwood
hayal *m,* wood of beech trees, beech plantation
hayuco *m,* beech mast
haz *m,* bundle, sheaf; *mil* file; *pl* fasces. *f,* visage; surface, face. **h. de la tierra,** face of the earth. **h. de luz,** beam of light. *fig* **ser de dos haces,** to be two-faced
haz *2nd pers Imperat* **hacer**
hazaña *f,* exploit, prowess
hazañoso *a* heroic, dauntless, courageous
hazmerreír *m, inf* laughingstock
he *interj* and *adv* Hallo! Hist!; Behold! **¡Heme aquí!** Here I am. **he aquí,** here is . . .
hebilla *f,* buckle
hebra *f,* thread; fiber; flesh; *min* vein, streak; filament (textiles); grain (of wood); *pl poet* hair. *inf* **pegar la h.,** to start a conversation
hebraísmo *m,* Hebraism
hebraísta *m,* Hebraist
hebreo (-ea) *a* Hebraic, Jewish. *n* Jew. *m,* Hebrew (language)
hecatombe *f,* hecatomb; slaughter, massacre
hechicería *f,* sorcery; spell, enchantment
hechicero *a* bewitching, magic; charming, attractive
hechizar *vt* to bewitch; charm, attract, delight
hechizo *m,* magic spell; fascination, charm; delight, pleasure; *a Lat. Am.* homemade, produced locally, locally produced
hecho *a* developed, mature; accustomed, used; perfected, finished; ready-made. **h. una furia,** like a fury, very angry. **bien h.,** well-made, well-proportioned; well or rightly done
hecho *m,* deed, action; fact; happening, event. **los Hechos de los Apóstoles,** the Acts of the Apostles
hechura *f,* making, make; creation; form; figure, statue; *lit* composition; build (of body); *fig* puppet, creature; *pl* price paid for work done. **de h. sastre,** *a* tailor-made
hectárea *f,* hectare
hectógrafo *m,* hectograph
hectogramo *m,* hectogram
hectolitro *m,* hectoliter
hectovatio *m,* hectowatt
heder *vi irr* to stink; be intolerable. See **entender**
hediondez *f,* stink, stench
hediondo *a* stinking; intolerable, pestilential; obscene
hedonismo *m,* hedonism
hedonista *mf* hedonist
hegeliano *a* Hegelian
hegemonía *f,* hegemony
helada *f,* frost. **h. blanca,** hoarfrost
heladera *f,* refrigerator
helado *a* frozen; ice-cold; astounded, disdainful. *m,* iced drink; sherbet, ice cream
helamiento *m,* icing; freezing
helar *vt irr* to freeze; ice, chill; astound; discourage; *vr* become iced; freeze; become ice-cold. *v impers* to freeze. See **acertar**
helecho *m,* fern
helénico *a* Hellenic
helenismo *m,* Hellenism
helenista *mf* Hellenist
helenizar *vt* to Hellenize
hélice *f,* spiral, helical line; screw, propeller; *geom* helix; *ast* Ursa Major
helicóptero *m, aer* helicopter
helio *m,* helium
heliógrafo *m,* heliograph
helioscopio *m,* helioscope
helióstato *m,* heliostat
helioterapia *f,* heliotherapy
heliotropismo *m,* heliotropism
heliotropo *m,* heliotrope; agate
helvecio (-ia) *a* and *n* Helvetian
hembra *f,* female; *inf* woman; nut of a screw; eye of a hook. *inf* **una real h.,** a fine figure of a woman
hemiciclo *m,* hemicycle; floor (of a legislative building)
hemisférico *a* hemispherical
hemisferio *m,* hemisphere
hemofilia *f,* hemophilia.
hemoglobina *f,* hemoglobin
hemorragia *f,* hemorrhage
hemorroides *f,* hemorrhoids
henchido *a* swollen
henchimiento *m,* swelling; inflation; filling
henchir *vt irr* to fill; stuff; swell. *Pres. Ind.* **hincho, hinches, hinche, hinchen.** *Pres. Part.* **hinchiendo.** *Pres. Subjunc.* **hincha,** etc. *Imperf. Subjunc.* **hinchiese,** etc. *Imperat.* **hinche, hincha, hinchamos, henchid, hinchan**
hendedura *f,* fissure; rift
hender *vt irr* to split, crack; *fig* cleave (air, water, etc.); make one's way through. See **entender**
hendidura *f,* split, fissure, crack, chink
hendija *f, Lat. Am.* crack, crevice
henil *m,* hayloft
heno *m,* hay
hepático *a* hepatic
heráldica *f,* heraldry
heráldico *a* heraldic
heraldo *m,* herald; harbinger
herbaje *m,* herbage; pasture, grass; thick woolen cloth
herbario *m,* herbalist, botanist; herbarium. *a* herbal
herbívoro *a* herbivorous
herbolaria *f,* herbal
hercúleo *a* herculean
heredad *f,* landed property; country estate
heredar *vt* to inherit; make a deed of gift to; inherit characteristics, etc.; take as heir
heredera *f,* heiress
heredero *m,* heir; inheritor. **h. aparente,** heir apparent. **presunto h.,** heir presumptive
hereditario *a* hereditary
hereje *mf* heretic
herejía *f,* heresy
herencia *f,* inheritance; heredity; heritage
heresiarca *mf* heresiarch
herético *a* heretical
herida *f,* wound; insult; anguish. **h. contusa,** contusion. **h. penetrante,** deep wound
herir *vt irr* to wound; strike, harm; *fig* pierce (of sun's rays); *fig* pluck (strings of a musical instrument); impress (the senses); affect (the emotions); offend (gen. of words). *Pres. Part.* **hiriendo.** *Pres. Ind.* **hiero, hieres, hiere, hieren.** *Preterite* **hirió, hirieron.** *Pres. Subjunc.* **hiera, hieras, hiera, hiramos, hiráis, hieran.** *Imperf. Subjunc.* **hiriese,** etc.
hermafrodita *a* and *mf* hermaphrodite
hermafroditismo *m,* hermaphroditism
hermana *f,* sister; twin, pair (of things). **h. de leche,** foster sister. **h. política,** sister-in-law
hermanar *vt* to join; mate; harmonize; *Chile* to pair (like

socks); *vt* and *vr* be the spiritual brother of, be compatible

hermanastra *f,* stepsister

hermanastro *m,* stepbrother

hermandad *f,* brotherhood; friendship, intimacy; relationship (of one thing to another); confraternity. **Santa H.,** Spanish rural police force instituted in the fifteenth century

hermano *m,* brother; pair, twin (of things); *ecc* brother. **h. de raza,** member of the same race. **h. político,** brother-in-law

hermético *a* hermetic

hermosear *vt* to embellish, beautify, adorn

hermoso *a* beautiful; shapely; handsome; fine, wonderful (weather, view, etc.)

hermosura *f,* beauty; pleasantness, attractiveness, perfection of form; belle

hernia *f,* hernia

héroe *m,* hero

heroicidad *f,* heroism

heroico *a* heroic

heroína *f,* heroine

heroismo *m,* heroism

herpes *m pl,* or *f pl,* herpes

herrada *f,* pail

herradero *m,* branding of livestock

herrador *m,* blacksmith

herradura *f,* horseshoe

herraje *m,* ironwork; *Lat. Am.* horseshoe

herramienta *f,* tool; set of tools

herrar *vt irr* to shoe horses; brand (cattle); decorate with iron. See **acertar**

herrería *f,* forge; ironworks; blacksmith's shop; clamor, tumult, confusion

herrero *m,* smith

herrete *m,* ferrule, tag

herrumbre *f,* rust; taste of iron

herrumbroso *a* rusty

hervidero *m,* boiling, bubbling; *fig* ebullition; swarm, crowd

hervir *vi irr* to boil; foam and froth (sea); seethe (emotions); surge (crowds); (*with en*) abound in, swarm with. See **sentir**

hervor *m,* boiling; ebullition, vigor, zest; seething, agitation

hesitación *f,* hesitation, doubt, uncertainty

hesitar *vi* to hesitate, vacillate

heterodina *a f, rad* heterodyne

heterodoxia *f,* heterodoxy

heterodoxo *a* heterodox

heterogeneidad *f,* heterogeneity

heterogéneo *a* heterogeneous

hético *a* hectic, consumptive

hexagonal *a* hexagonal

hexágono *m,* hexagon

hexámetro *m,* hexameter

hez *f,* (gen. *pl* **heces**) lees, dregs

hiato *m,* hiatus

hibernal *a* wintry

hibernés *a* Hibernian

hibisco *m,* hibiscus

hibridación *f,* hybridization

hibridismo *m,* hybridism

híbrido *a* and *m,* hybrid

hidalgo (-ga) *n* noble, aristocrat. *a* noble; illustrious; generous

hidalguía *f,* nobility; generosity, nobility of spirit

hidra *f, zool* hydra; poisonous snake; *ast* Hydra

hidratar *vt chem* to hydrate

hidrato *m,* hydrate. **h. de carbono,** carbohydrate

hidráulica *f,* hydraulics

hidráulico *a* hydraulic

hidroavión *m,* flying boat

hidrocarburo *m,* hydrocarbon

hidrocéfalo *a* hydrocephalic

hidrodinámica *f,* hydrodynamics

hidroeléctrico *a* hydroelectric

hidrofobia *f,* hydrophobia; rabies

hidrógeno *m,* hydrogen

hidrografía *f,* hydrography

hidrología *f,* hydrology

hidropesía *f,* dropsy

hidrópico *a* dropsical

hidroplano *m,* seaplane

hidroquinona *f,* hydroquinone

hidroscopio *m,* hydroscope

hidrostática *f,* hydrostatics

hidroterapia *f,* hydrotherapy

hiedra *f,* ivy

hiel *f,* gall, bile, bitterness, affliction; *pl* troubles

hielo *m,* ice, frost; freezing, icing; stupefaction; indifference, coldness. *inf* **estar hecho un h.,** to be as cold as ice

hiena *f,* hyena

hierático *a* hieratical

hierba *f,* grass; small plant; herb. **h. cana,** groundsel. **mala h.,** weed

hierbabuena *f, bot* mint

hierra *f,* branding time

hierro *m,* iron; brand with hot iron; iron or steel head of a lance, etc.; instrument or shape made of iron; weapon of war. *pl* fetters. **h. colado,** cast iron. **h. dulce,** wrought iron. **h. en planchas,** sheet iron. **h. viejo,** scrap iron

hígado *m,* liver; courage; *Central America, Mexico also* nuisance

higiene *f,* hygiene; cleanliness, neatness. **h. privada,** personal hygiene. **h. pública,** public health

higiénico *a* hygienic

higo *m,* fig. **h. chumbo,** prickly pear

higrómetro *m,* hygrometer

higuera *f,* fig tree

hija *f,* daughter; native of a place; offspring

hijastro (-ra) *n* stepchild

hijo *m,* son; child; native of a place; offspring; shoot, sprout; *pl* descendants. **h. de la cuna,** foundling. **h. de leche,** foster child. **h. natural,** natural child. **h. político,** son-in-law

hijuela *f,* little daughter; small mattress; small drain; side road; accessory, subordinate thing; piece of material for widening a garment; *law* part of an inheritance; *Lat. Am.* rural property

hila *f,* row, line; gut; *surg* lint (gen. *pl*)

hilacha *f,* thread raveled from cloth; fiber, filament. **h. de vidrio,** spun glass

hilado *m,* spinning; thread, yarn

hilandería *f,* spinning; spinning mill; mill. **h. de algodón,** cotton mill

hilandero (-ra) *n* spinner

hilar *vt* to spin; reason, infer, discourse

hilaridad *f,* hilarity; quiet happiness

hilaza *f,* yarn

hilera *f,* line, file, row; fine yarn; *mil* file, rank; *met* wire drawer; *mas* course (of bricks)

hilo *m,* thread; linen; wire; mesh (spiders, silkworm's web, etc.); edge (of a blade); thin stream (of liquid); thread (of discourse)

hilván *m, sew* basting; tack

hilvanar *vt sew* to baste

himen *m,* hymen

himeneo *m,* marriage, wedding

himnario *m,* hymnal

himno *m,* hymn

hin *m,* whinny, neigh

hincapié *m,* foothold. **hacer h.,** to insist, make a stand

hincar *vt* to thrust in; drive in, sink; *vr* kneel. **h. el diente,** to bite. **h. la uña,** to scratch. **hincarse de rodillas,** to kneel down

hinchado *a* puffed up, vain; pompous, high-flown, redundant (style)

hinchar *vt* to inflate; puff out (the chest); swell (of a

river, etc.); exaggerate (events); *vr* swell; grow vain, be puffed up
hinchazón *f*, swelling; vanity, presumption; pomposity, euphuism (style)
hiniesta *f*, Spanish broom
hinojo *m*, *bot* fennel; knee. **de hinojos,** on bended knee
hipar *vi* to hiccup; pant (of dogs); be overanxious; be overtired; sob, cry
hipérbole *f*, hyperbole
hiperbólico *a* hyperbolical
hipercrítico *m*, hypercritic. *a* hypercritical
hipertrofiarse *vr* to hypertrophy
hípico *a* equine
hipnosis *f*, hypnosis
hipnótico *a* hypnotic. *m*, hypnotic drug
hipnotismo *m*, hypnotism
hipnotización *f*, hypnotization
hipnotizar *vt* to hypnotize
hipo *m*, hiccup; sob; longing, desire; dislike, disgust
hipocondría *f*, hypochondria
hipocondríaco (-ca) *a* hypochondriacal. *n* hypochondriac
hipocrático *a* Hippocratic
hipocresía *f*, hypocrisy
hipócrita *a* hypocritical. *mf* hypocrite
hipodérmico *a* hypodermic
hipódromo *m*, hippodrome, racetrack
hipopótamo *m*, hippopotamus
hipostático *a* hypostatic
hipoteca *f*, mortgage
hipotecable *a* mortgageable
hipotecar *vt* to mortgage
hipotecario *a* belonging to a mortgage
hipotenusa *f*, hypotenuse
hipótesis *f*, hypothesis
hipotético *a* hypothetical
hirsuto *a* hirsute, hairy
hirviente *a* boiling
hisca *f*, birdlime
hisopear *vt ecc* to sprinkle, asperse
hisopo *m*, *bot* hyssop; *ecc* hyssop, sprinkler; *Lat. Am. also* (paint)brush
hispánico *a* Spanish
hispanismo *m*, Hispanism
hispanista *mf* Hispanist
hispanoamericano (-na) *a* and *n* Spanish-American, Hispano-American
histeria *f*, hysteria
histérico *a* hysterical; hysteric
histerismo *m*, *med* hysteria
histología *f*, histology
histólogo *m*, histologist
historia *f*, history; narrative, story; tale; *inf* gossip (gen. *pl*); *art* historical piece. **h. natural,** natural history. **h. sagrada,** biblical history. *fig inf* **dejarse de historias,** to stop beating around the bush
historiador (-ra) *n* historian
historiar *vt* to narrate, relate; record, chronicle
histórico *a* historical; historic
historieta *f*, short story; anecdote
historiografía *f*, historiography
historiógrafo *m*, historiographer
histriónico *a* histrionic
hitlerismo *m*, Hitlerism
hito *m*, milestone; boundary mark; *fig* mark, target. **de h. en h.,** from head to foot
hocico *m*, snout; *inf* face, mug; *inf* angry gesture; *naut* prow. **meter el h.,** to stick one's nose into other people's business
hogaño *adv inf* during this year; at the present time
hogar *m*, hearth, fireplace; home, house; family life; firebox (of a locomotive)
hoguera *f*, bonfire
hoja *f*, *bot* leaf; petal; sheet (metal, paper, etc.); page (of book); blade (sharp instruments); leaf (door, window); sword. **h. de servicios,** service or professional record. **h. de tocino,** side of bacon. **h. extraordinaria,** extra, special edition (of a newspaper). **h. volante,** handbill, supplement. **volver la h.,** to turn over (pages); change one's opinion; turn the conversation
hojalata *f*, tin plate
hojalatería *f*, tinware; tin shop
hojalatero *m*, tinsmith
hojalda, hojalde *m* = **hojaldre**
hojaldre *m*, or *f*, puff pastry
hojarasca *f*, withered leaves; excessive foliage; rubbish, trash
hojear *vt* to turn the leaves of a book; skip, skim, read quickly; *vi* exfoliate
hojuela *f*, *dim* little leaf; *bot* leaflet; pancake
¡hola! *interj* Hallo! Goodness!
Holanda Holland
holandés (-esa) *a* and *n* Dutchman (-woman) *m*, Dutch (language)
holgado *a* leisured, free; loose, wide; comfortable; well-off, rich
holganza *f*, repose, leisure, ease; idleness; pleasure
holgar *vi irr* to rest; be idle; be glad; be unused or unnecessary (things). *vr* enjoy oneself, amuse oneself; be glad. See **contar**
holgazán (-ana) *a* idle. *n* idler
holgazanear *vi* to idle
holgazanería *f*, idleness, sloth
holgorio *m*, rejoicing, festivity, merriment
holgura *f*, enjoyment, merrymaking; width; comfort, ease; *mech* free play
hollar *vt irr* to trample under foot; humiliate. See **degollar**
hollejo *m*, peel, thin skin (of fruit); *agr* chaff
hollín *m*, soot
holocausto *m*, holocaust. **el H.** the Holocaust
hológrafo *m*, holograph
hombradía *f*, manliness; courage
hombre *m*, man; adult; omber (cards). *interj* **¡h.!** *inf* Old fellow! You don't say so! **¡h. al agua!** Man overboard! **h. de bien,** honest, honorable man. **h. de estado,** statesman. **h. de muchos oficios,** jack-of-all-trades. **h. de negocios,** businessman; man of affairs. **h. de pro,** worthy man; famous man. **ser muy h.,** to be a real man, be very manly
hombrera *f*, epaulette; shoulderpad
hombro *m*, shoulder. **echar al h.,** to shoulder; undertake, take the responsibility of. **encogerse de hombros,** to shrug one's shoulders; be indifferent or uninterested
hombruno *a inf* mannish (of a woman)
homenaje *m*, allegiance; homage; veneration, respect
homeópata *a* homeopathic. *mf* homeopath
homeopatía *f*, homeopathy
homérico *a* Homeric
homicida *a* murderous, homicidal. *mf* murderer (-ess)
homicidio *m*, homicide (act)
homilía *f*, homily
homogeneidad *f*, homogeneity
homogéneo *a* homogeneous
homónimo *a* homonymous. *m*, homonym
homosexual *a* and *mf* homosexual
honda *f*, sling, catapult, slingshot
hondear *vt naut* to sound, plumb; *naut* unload; *Lat. Am.* to hit with a slingshot
hondo *a* deep; low; *fig* profound; deep, intense (emotion). *m*, depth
hondón *m*, depth, recess
hondonada *f*, hollow; glen; valley
hondura *f*, depth
hondureño (-ña) *a* and *n* Honduran
honestidad *f*, honorableness; virtue; respectability; modesty; courtesy
honesto *a* honorable, virtuous; modest; honest, just
hongo *m*, fungus; toadstool; bowler hat
honor *m*, honor; fame; reputation (women); modesty (women); praise; *pl* rank, position; honors

honorable *a* honorable
honorario *a* honorary. *m,* honorarium, fee
honorífico *a* honorary; honorable
honra *f,* self-respect, honor, personal dignity; reputation; chastity and modesty (women); *pl* obsequies
honradez *f,* honesty; honorableness, integrity; respectability
honrado *a* honest; honorable
honrar *vt* to respect; honor; *vr* to be honored
honroso *a* honor-giving, honorable
¡hopa! *interj Argentina* cut it out!, stop it!
hora *f,* hour; opportune moment; *pl* book of hours. **horas hábiles,** working hours. **horas muertas,** wee hours; wasted time. **a última h.,** at the last minute. **dar la h.,** to strike the hour. **¿Qué h. es?** What time is it?
horadar *vt* to bore, pierce
horario *a* hourly. *m,* timetable; hour hand of a clock; watch
horca *f,* gibbet, gallows; *agr* pitchfork; fork; prop for trees
horcajadas (**a**) *adv* astride
horcajadura *f,* crotch
horchata *f,* drink made of chufas or crushed almonds
horda *f,* horde
horizontal *a* horizontal
horizonte *m,* horizon. **nuevos horizontes,** new opportunities
horma *f,* mold; cobbler's last; stone wall. *fig inf* **hallar la h. de su zapato,** to find what suits one; meet one's match
hormiga *f,* ant
hormigón *m,* concrete. **h. armado,** ferro-concrete
hormiguear *vi* to itch; crowd, swarm
hormiguero *m,* anthill; crowd, swarm
hormona *f,* hormone
hornero (-ra) *n* baker
horno *m,* oven; furnace; kiln; bakery. **h. alfarero,** firing oven (for pottery). **h. de cocina,** kitchen stove. **h. de cuba,** blast furnace. **h. de ladrillo,** brick kiln. **alto h.,** iron-smelting furnace
horóscopo *m,* horoscope
horquilla *f,* forked stick; hairpin; hatpin; *agr* fork; hook. **viraje en h.,** hairpin turn
horrendo *a* horrible, frightful
hórreo *m,* granary, barn
horribilidad *f,* horribleness
horribilísimo *a sup* most horrible, exceedingly horrible
horrible *a* horrible
horrífico *a* horrific
horripilante *a* hair-raising, horrifying
horrísono *a poet* horrid-sounding, terrifying
horror *m,* horror; horribleness; atrocity, enormity
horrorizar *vt* to horrify; *vr* be horrified, be terrified
horroroso *a* dreadful, horrible; horrid; *inf* hideous, most ugly
hortaliza *f,* green vegetable, garden produce
hortelano *m,* market gardener
hortensia *f,* hydrangea
horticultura *f,* horticulture
horticultural *a* horticultural
hosanna *m,* hosanna
hosco *a* dark brown; unsociable, sullen; crabbed
hospedaje *m,* lodging; board, payment
hospedar *vt* to lodge, receive as a guest; *vr* and *vi* lodge, stay
hospedería *f,* hostelry, inn; lodging
hospedero (-ra) *n* innkeeper
hospicio *m,* hospice; almshouse, workhouse; lodging; orphanage
hospital *m,* hospital; hospice. **h. de sangre,** field hospital
hospitalario *a* hospitable
hospitalidad *f,* hospitality; hospitableness; hospital
hostelero (-ra) *n* innkeeper
hostería *f,* hostelry; inn
hostia *f, ecc* wafer, Host; sacrificial victim
hostigamiento *m,* harassment. **h. sexual,** sexual harassment
hostigar *vt* to chastise; harass; tease, annoy
hostil *a* hostile
hostilidad *f,* hostility
hostilizar *vt* to commit hostile acts against; antagonize
hotel *m,* hotel; villa
hotelero (-ra) *n* hotelkeeper
hoy *adv* today; at present. **h. día** *or* **h. en día,** today. **h. por h.,** day by day; at the present time. **de h. en adelante,** from today forward
hoya *f,* hole; grave; valley, glen; bed (of a river)
hoyo *m,* hole; pockmark; grave; hollow
hoyuelo *m, dim* little hole; dimple
hoz *f,* sickle; defile
hozar *vt* to root (pigs, etc.)
hucha *f,* large chest; strongbox; savings
hueco *a* empty; hollow; vain; hollow (sound); pompous (style); spongy, soft; inflated. *m,* hollow; interval of time or place; *inf* vacancy; gap in a wall, etc.
huelga *f,* strike; leisure; lying fallow; merrymaking. **h. de brazos caídos,** sit-down strike. **h. patronal,** lock-out strike
huelguista *mf* striker
huella *f,* footprint, track; footstep; tread (of stairs); *print* impression; vestige, trace. **h. digital,** fingerprint
huérfano (-na) *n* orphan. *a* unprotected, uncared for
huero *a* addled; empty, hollow
huerta *f,* kitchen garden; orchard; irrigation land
huerto *m,* orchard; kitchen garden
hueso *m,* bone; stone (of fruit); kernel, core; drudgery; cheap, useless thing of poor quality. *inf* **no dejar un h. sano,** to tear (a person) to pieces. **tener los huesos molidos,** to be tired out; be bruised
huésped (-da) *n* guest; host; innkeeper
hueste *f,* (gen. *pl*) army on the march, host; party, supporters
huesudo *a* bony
hueva *f,* fish roe
huevera *f,* egg seller; eggcup
huevo *m,* egg. **h. duro,** hard-boiled egg. **h. estrellado,** fried egg. **h. pasado por agua,** soft-boiled egg. **huevos revueltos,** scrambled eggs
hugonote (-ta) *a* and *n* Huguenot
huida *f,* flight, escape; bolting (of a horse); outlet
huir *vi irr* to flee; fly (of time); elope; run away, bolt; (*with de*) avoid. *Pres. Part.* **huyendo.** *Pres. Ind.* **huyo, huyes, huyen.** *Preterite* **huyó, huyeron.** *Pres. Subjunc.* **huya,** etc. *Imperf. Subjunc.* **huyese,** etc.
hule *m,* oilcloth; rubber; *Central America, Mexico* rubber tree
hulla *f,* coal mine, coal, soft coal
hullera *f,* colliery, coal mine
humanidad *f,* humanity; human nature; human weakness; compassion; affability; *inf* stoutness; *pl* study of humanities
humanismo *m,* humanism
humanista *mf* humanist. *a* humanistic
humanitario *a* humanitarian
humanizar *vt* to humanize
humano *a* human; understanding, sympathetic. *m,* human being
humareda *f,* cloud of smoke
humeante *a* smoking; smoky
humear *vi* to give forth smoke; give oneself airs; *Lat. Am.* fumigate; beat, thrash
humedad *f,* humidity; dampness; moisture
humedecer *vt irr* to moisten, wet, damp; *vr* grow moist. See **conocer**
húmedo *a* humid; damp; wet
humildad *f,* humility; lowliness; humbleness
humilde *a* meek; lowly; humble
humillación *f,* humiliation
humillante *a* humiliating; debasing; mortifying

humillar *vt* to humble; humiliate; *vr* humble oneself
humo *m,* smoke; vapor, fume; vanity, airs
humor *m, med* humor; temperament, disposition; mood. **de buen h.,** good-tempered. **de mal h.,** ill-tempered
humorada *f,* humorous saying, extravagance, witticism
humorismo *m,* humor, comic sense; humorousness
humorista *mf* humorist
humorístico *a* humorous
humoso *a* smoky, reeky
hundible *a* sinkable
hundido *a* sunken (of cheeks, etc.); hollow, deep-set (of eyes)
hundimiento *m,* sinking; collapse; subsidence (of earth)
hundir *vt* to sink; oppress; confound; destroy, ruin; *vr* collapse (building); sink; *fig inf* disappear
húngaro (-ra) *a* and *n* Hungarian. *m,* Hungarian (language)
Hungría Hungary
huracán *m,* hurricane
hurañía *f,* shyness, unsociableness; diffidence; wildness (of animals, etc.)
huraño *a* shy, unsociable; diffident; wild (of animals, etc.)
hurgar *vt* to stir; poke, rake; touch; rouse, incite. *vr* pick one's nose
hurgón *m,* fire rake, poker; *inf* sword
hurgonada *f,* raking (of the fire, etc.)
hurguete *mf, Argentina* busybody, nosy parker
hurón (-ona) *n* ferret. *a* shy, unsociable
¡hurra! *interj* Hurrah!
hurtadillas (a) *adv* by stealth, secretly
hurtar *vt* to steal; encroach (sea, river); plagiarize; *vr* hide oneself
hurto *m,* theft. **coger con el h. en las manos,** *fig* to catch red-handed
husmear *vt* to sniff out; *inf* pry; *vi* smell bad (of meat)
huso *m,* spindle; bobbin
¡huy! *interj* (denoting pain or surprise) Oh!

I

ibérico *a* Iberian
ibero (-ra) *a* and *n* Iberian
íbice *m,* ibex
icnografía *f,* ichnography
icnográfico *a* ichnographical
icono *m,* icon
iconoclasta *a* iconoclastic. *mf* iconoclast
iconografía *f,* iconography
ictericia *f,* jaundice
ida *f,* setting out, departure, going; impetuous action; precipitancy; track, trail (of animals). **de i. y vuelta,** round trip (of tickets)
idea *f,* idea. *inf* **¡Qué ideas tienes!** What (odd) ideas you have!
ideal *a* ideal; perfect. *m,* model; ideal
idealidad *f,* ideality
idealismo *m,* idealism
idealista *a* idealistic. *mf* idealist
idealización *f,* idealization
idealizar *vt* to idealize
idear *vt* to imagine; devise; plan; design; draft, draw up
ideático, -a *a, Lat. Am.* eccentric
ídem *adv* idem
idéntico *a* identical
identidad *f,* identity
identificable *a* identifiable
identificación *f,* identification
identificar *vt* to identify; recognize; *vr* (*with con*) identify oneself with
ideografía *f,* ideography
ideograma *m,* ideogram, ideograph
ideología *f,* ideology. **i. racista,** racial ideology
ideológico *a* ideological
ideólogo (-ga) *n* ideologist; dreamer, planner
idílico *a* idyllic
idilio *m,* idyll
idioma *m,* language, tongue
idiomático *a* idiomatic
idiosincrasia *f,* idiosyncrasy
idiosincrásico *a* idiosyncratic
idiota *a* idiot; idiotic. *mf* idiot
idiotez *f,* idiocy
idiotismo *m, gram* idiom; ignorance
idiotizar *vt, Lat. Am.* to drive crazy, drive insane.
idólatra *a* idolatrous; adoring. *mf* idolater, heathen
idolatrar *vt* to idolize; worship, love excessively
idolatría *f,* idolatry; adoration, idolization
ídolo *m,* idol
idoneidad *f,* fitness, suitability; competence; capacity
idóneo *a* suitable; competent, fit
idus *m pl,* ides
iglesia *f,* church. **i. colegial,** collegiate church. **cumplir con la i.,** to discharge one's religious duties. **llevar a una mujer a la i.,** to lead a woman to the altar
ígneo *a* igneous
ignición *f,* ignition
ignominia *f,* ignominy, disgrace
ignominioso *a* ignominious
ignorancia *f,* ignorance. **pretender i.,** to plead ignorance
ignorante *a* ignorant; unaware, uninformed. *mf* ignoramus
ignorar *vt* to be unaware of, not to know
ignoto *a* unknown, undiscovered
igual *a* equal; level; even, smooth; very similar; alike; uniform; proportionate; unchanging; constant; indifferent; same. *mf* equal. *m, math* equal sign. **al i.,** equally. **sin i.,** peerless, without equal. **Me es completamente i.,** It's all the same to me
iguala *f,* equalizing; leveling; agreement, arrangement; cash adjustment
igualación *f,* equalization; leveling; arrangement, agreement; matching; *math* equation
igualador *a* equalizing; leveling
igualar *vt* to equalize, make equal; match; pair; level, flatten; smooth; adjust; arrange, agree upon; weigh, consider; *math* equate; *vi* be equal
igualdad *f,* equality; uniformity, harmony; evenness; smoothness; identity, sameness. **i. de ánimo,** equability, equanimity
igualitario *a* equalizing; egalitarian
igualmente *adv* equally; the same, likewise
ijada *f,* side, flank; pain in the side
ijadear *vt* to pant
ijar *m,* See **ijada**
ilación *f,* connection, reference
ilegal *a* illegal
ilegalidad *f,* illegality
ilegible *a* illegible, unreadable
ilegitimidad *f,* illegitimacy
ilegítimo *a* illegitimate; false
ileso *a* unharmed, unhurt
iletrado *a* unlettered, uncultured
Ilíada *f,* Iliad
iliberal *a* illiberal; narrow-minded
iliberalidad *f,* illiberality; narrow-mindedness
ilícito *a* illicit
ilicitud *f,* illicitness
ilimitado *a* unlimited, boundless
iliterato *a* illiterate, uncultured

ilógico *a* illogical
iluminación *f,* illumination; lighting. **i. intensiva,** floodlighting
iluminador (-ra) *a* lighting; illuminating. *n art* illuminator
iluminar *vt* to illuminate; light; *art* illuminate; enlighten; *vr. Lat. Am.* get drunk
iluminativo *a* illuminating
ilusión *f,* illusion; illusoriness; hope; dream
ilusionarse *vr* to harbor illusions
ilusivo *a* deceptive, illusive
iluso *a* deceived, deluded; dreamy; visionary
ilusorio *a* illusory; deceptive; null
ilustración *f,* illustration, picture; enlightenment; explanation; illustrated newspaper or magazine; erudition, knowledge; example, illustration
ilustrado *a* erudite, learned; knowledgeable, well-informed
ilustrador (-ra) *a* illustrative. *n* illustrator
ilustrar *vt* to explain, illustrate; enlighten, instruct; illustrate (books); make illustrious; inspire with divine light
ilustrativo *a* illustrative
ilustre *a* illustrious, distinguished
ilustrísimo *a sup* most illustrious (title of bishops, etc.)
imagen *f,* image; effigy, statue; idea; metaphor, simile. **i. nítida,** sharp image
imaginable *a* imaginable
imaginación *f,* imagination
imaginar *vi* to imagine; *vt* suppose, conjecture; discover, invent; imagine. **¡Imagínese!** Just imagine!
imaginario *a* imaginary
imaginativa *f,* imagination; common sense
imaginativo *a* imaginative
imaginería *f,* imagery
imán *m,* magnet; attraction, charm; imam
imanación *f,* magnetization
imanar *vt* to magnetize
imbécil *a* imbecile; stupid, idiotic. *mf* imbecile
imbecilidad *f,* imbecility; folly, stupidity
imberbe *a* beardless. *inf* **joven i.,** stripling
imbibición *f,* imbibing, absorption
imborrable *a* ineffaceable
imbuir *vt irr* to imbue. See **huir**
imitable *a* imitable
imitación *f,* imitation; reproduction, copy
imitado *a* imitation; imitated
imitador (-ra) *a* imitation; imitative. *n* imitator
imitar *vt* to imitate; counterfeit
imitativo *a* imitative
impacción *f,* impact
impaciencia *f,* impatience
impacientar *vt* to make impatient, annoy; *vr* grow impatient
impaciente *a* impatient
impacto *m,* impact. **i. de lleno,** direct hit
impago, -a *a Lat. Am.* remaining to be paid, still to be paid, unpaid; *m* non-payment
impalpabilidad *f,* impalpability
impalpable *a* impalpable
impar *a* odd; unpaired; single, uneven. **número impar,** odd number
imparcial *a* impartial
imparcialidad *f,* impartiality
imparisilábico *a* imparisyllabic
impartible *a* indivisible
impasibilidad *f,* impassivity, indifference
impasible *a* impassive
impavidez *f* dauntlessness; serenity in the face of danger; *Lat. Am.* cheek, cheekiness, effrontery
impávido *a* dauntless; calm, composed, imperturbable; *Lat. Am.* cheeky, fresh
impecabilidad *f,* impeccability, perfection
impecable *a* impeccable, perfect
impedido *a* disabled
impedimento *m,* obstacle; hindrance; *law* impediment
impedir *vt irr* to impede; obstruct; prevent; thwart; disable; delay; *poet* amaze. See **pedir**
impeler *vt* to push; incite; drive; urge
impender *vt* to spend money
impenetrabilidad *f,* impenetrability; imperviousness; obscurity, difficulty
impenetrable *a* impenetrable, dense; impervious; *fig* unfathomable; obscure
impenitencia *f,* impenitence
impenitente *a* impenitent
impensado *a* unexpected, unforeseen
imperante *a* ruling, dominant
imperar *vi* to rule; command
imperativo *a* commanding. *a* and *m, gram* imperative
imperatorio *a* imperial, imperatorial
imperceptible *a* imperceptible
imperdible *m,* safety pin
imperdonable *a* unpardonable, inexcusable
imperecedero *a* undying, eternal, everlasting
imperfección *f,* imperfection, inadequacy; fault, blemish; weakness
imperfecto *a* imperfect; inadequate; faulty. *a* and *m, gram* imperfect
imperial *a* imperial. *f,* upper deck of a bus or streetcar
imperialismo *m,* imperialism
imperialista *a* imperialistic. *mf* imperialist
impericia *f,* inexpertness; unskillfulness, unhandiness
imperio *m,* empire; rule, reign; command, sway; imperial dignity; arrogance, haughtiness. *fig inf* **valer un i.,** to be priceless
imperioso *a* imperious
imperito *a* inexpert; clumsy, unskilled
impermeabilidad *f,* watertightness; imperviousness; impermeability
impermeabilizar *vt* to waterproof
impermeable *a* watertight, impermeable; impervious. *m,* raincoat, mackintosh
impertérrito *a* unafraid, dauntless
impertinencia *f,* impertinence, insolence; peevishness; fancy, whim; overexactness, meticulousness; interference, intrusion
impertinente *a* impertinent; irrelevant; inopportune; officious, interfering
imperturbabilidad *f,* imperturbability
imperturbable *a* calm, imperturbable
impetrar *vt* to obtain by entreaty; implore
ímpetu *m,* impetus, momentum; speed, swiftness; violence
impetuosidad *f,* impetuosity
impetuoso *a* impetuous; precipitate
impiedad *f,* cruelty, harshness; irreligion
impío *a* impious, wicked; irreverent, irreligious
implacabilidad *f,* implacability, relentless
implacable *a* implacable
implantación *f,* inculcation, implantation
implantar *vt* to inculcate, implant (ideas, etc.)
implicación *f,* implication; contradiction (in terms); complicity
implicar *vt* to implicate; imply, infer; involve, entangle; *vi* imply contradiction (gen. with negatives)
implicatorio *a* contradictory; implicated (in crime)
implícito *a* implicit; implied
implorante *a* imploring
implorar *vt* to implore, entreat
implume *a* without feathers, unfeathered
impolítico *a* impolitic; unwise, inexpedient; tactless
imponderabilidad *f,* imponderability
imponderable *a* imponderable, immeasurable; most excellent
imponencia *f. Lat. Am.* impressiveness
imponente *a* imposing, impressive; awe-inspiring
imponer *vt irr* to exact, impressive; impose; malign, accuse falsely; instruct, acquaint; *fig* impress (with respect, etc.); invest or deposit (money); *print* impose; give, bestow (a name). *vr* assert oneself. See **poner**
imponible *a* taxable; ratable

impopular *a* unpopular
impopularidad *f,* unpopularity
importable *a* importable
importación *f, com* importation; import
importador (-ra) *a* import, importing. *n* importer
importancia *f,* importance; magnitude
importante *a* important
importar *vi* to matter; be important; concern, interest; *vt* amount to; import; include, comprise. **¡No importa!** It doesn't matter! Never mind!
importe *m,* amount; value, cost. **i. bruto,** gross or total amount. **i. líquido** *or* **neto,** net amount
importunación *f,* importuning; importunity
importunadamente *adv* importunately
importunar *vt* to importune, pester
importunidad (*also* importunación) *f,* importunity
importuno *a* importunate, inopportune, ill-timed; persistent; tedious
imposibilidad *f,* impossibility
imposibilitado *a* disabled, crippled; incapable, unable
imposibilitar *vt* to disable; render unable; make impossible
imposible *a* impossible
imposición *f,* imposition; exaction; tax, duty, tribute; *print* makeup **i. de manos,** *ecc* laying on of hands
impostor (-ra) *n* impostor
impostura *f,* swindle, imposture; aspersion, slur, imputation
impotable *a* undrinkable
impotencia *f,* impotence
impotente *a* impotent; powerless
impracticabilidad *f,* impracticability; impassability (of roads, etc.)
impracticable *a* impracticable; impossible; impassable (roads, etc.)
imprecación *f,* imprecation; curse, malediction
imprecar *vt* to imprecate, curse
impregnación *f,* impregnation, permeation, saturation
impregnar *vt* impregnate; to permeate; *vr* become impregnated
impremeditado *a* unpremeditated
imprenta *f,* printing; printing house or office; print; letterpress
impreparación *f,* unpreparedness
imprescindible *a* indispensable, essential
impresión *f,* printing; impression; effect; influence; imprint, stamp; *print* impression; print. **impresión digital,** fingerprint
impresionable *a* impressionable, susceptible
impresionante *a* imposing; moving, affecting
impresionar *vt* to impress; affect; fix in the mind; *fig* move deeply, stir; (*rad* cinema) record
impresionismo *m,* impressionism
impresionista *mf* impressionist. *a* impressionistic
impreso *m,* (gen. *pl*) printed matter
impresor *m,* printer
imprevisión *f,* lack of foresight; improvidence
imprevisto *a* unforeseen, unexpected, sudden
imprevistos *m pl,* incidental expenses
imprimación *f,* priming (of paint, etc.)
imprimar *vt* to prime (of paint)
imprimir *vt* to print; stamp; impress upon (the mind)
improbabilidad *f,* improbability
improbable *a* improbable
improbo *a* vicious, corrupt, dishonest; hard, arduous
improductivo *a* unproductive; unprofitable, fruitless
impronta *f, art* cast, mold
impronunciable *a* unpronounceable; ineffable
improperio *m,* insult, affront
impropiedad *f,* inappropriateness; unsuitableness; impropriety
impropio *a* unsuitable; inappropriate; inadequate; improper
improporcionado *a* disproportionate, out of proportion
impróvido *a* improvident, heedless
improvisación *f,* improvisation
improvisador (-ra) *n* improviser
improvisamente *adv* unexpectedly, suddenly
improvisar *vt* to improvise
improviso, improvisto *a* unexpected, unforeseen. **al** (*or* **de**) **improviso,** unexpectedly
imprudencia *f,* imprudence, rashness, indiscretion
imprudente *a* imprudent, unwise, rash
impúbero *a* below the age of puberty
impudencia *f,* impudence, impertinence
impudente *a* brazen, impudent
impudicia *f,* immodesty, brazenness
impúdico *a* immodest, brazen
impuesto *m,* tax; duty. **i. de utilidades,** income tax. **i. sucesorio,** inheritance tax
impugnable *a* impugnable, refutable
impugnación *f,* refutation; contradiction
impugnar *vt* to refute, contradict; oppose; criticize
impulsar *vt* to impel; prompt, cause; drive, operate, propel
impulsión *f,* impulse; impetus; *mech* operation, driving; propulsion
impulsivo *a* impulsive; irreflexive, precipitate
impulso *m,* stimulus, incitement; impulse, desire; *mech* drive, impulse
impulsor (-ra) *a* driving, impelling. *n* driver, operator
impune *a* unpunished
impunemente *adv* with impunity
impunidad *f,* impunity
impureza *f,* impurity; lack of chastity; obscenity, indecency
impurificar *vt* to defile; make impure; adulterate
impuro *a* impure; adulterated; polluted; immoral, unchaste
imputable *a* imputable
imputación *f,* imputation
imputador (-ra) *n* imputer, attributer
imputar *vt* to impute; attribute
inacabable *a* endless, interminable, ceaseless; wearisome
inaccesibilidad *f,* inaccessibility
inaccesible *a* inaccessible; incomprehensible
inacción *f,* inaction
inaceptable *a* unacceptable
inactividad *f,* inactivity; quiescence; idleness
inactivo *a* inactive; idle; unemployed; *naut* laid-up
inadaptable *a* inadaptable
inadecuado *a* inadequate, insufficient
inadmisible *a* inadmissible
inadvertencia *f,* inadvertence; oversight, mistake, slip
inadvertido *a* unnoticed; inattentive; inadvertent, unintentional; negligent
inafectado *a* unaffected, natural
inagotable *a* inexhaustible, unfailing; abundant
inaguantable *a* unbearable, intolerable
inajenable *a* inalienable
inalámbrica *f,* radio station
inalienable *a* inalienable
inalterable *a* unalterable
inamovibilidad *f,* immovability
inamovible *a* immovable
inanición *f,* inanition
inanimado *a* inanimate
inapagable *a* inextinguishable
inapelable *a* unappealable; irremediable, inevitable
inapetencia *f,* lack of appetite
inaplazable *a* undeferable, unable to be postponed
inaplicable *a* inapplicable
inaplicación *f,* laziness, inattention, negligence
inaplicado *a* lazy; inattentive; careless
inapreciable *a* inappreciable; invaluable
inarmónico *a* unharmonious, discordant
inarticulado *a* inarticulate
inasequible *a* unattainable; out of reach
inaudible *a* inaudible

inaudito *a* unheard of, unprecedented; extraordinary, strange
inauguración *f,* inauguration; induction; inception, commencement
inaugural *a* inaugural
inaugurar *vt* to inaugurate; induct
inaveriguable *a* unascertainable
inca *mf* Inca
incaico *a* Incan
incalculable *a* incalculable; innumerable
incalificable *a* indescribable, unclassable; vile
incandescencia *f,* incandescence, white heat
incandescente *a* incandescent
incansable *a* indefatigable; unflagging; unwearying
incapacidad *f,* incapacity; incompetence
incapacitar *vt* to incapacitate; disable
incapaz *a* incapable, incompetent; inefficient
incasable *a* unmarriageable; antimarriage
incásico, -a *a, Lat. Am.* Inca
incautarse *vr* to seize, take possession (of)
incauto *a* incautious; unwary
incendiar *vt* to set on fire, set alight
incendiario (-ia) *a* and *n* incendiary
incendiarismo *m,* incendiarism
incendio *m,* conflagration, fire; consuming passion
incensar *vt irr ecc* to cense, incense; flatter. See **acertar**
incensario *m,* incense burner, incensory
incentivo *m,* incentive; encouragement
incertidumbre *f,* uncertainty, incertitude
incesable, incesante *a* incessant, continuous
incesto *m,* incest
incestuoso *a* incestuous
incidencia *f,* incidence
incidente *a* incidental. *m,* incident, event, occurrence
incidir *vi* (*with en*) to incur, fall into (e.g. **Incidió en el pecado,** He fell into sin)
incienso *m,* incense; flattery
incierto *a* untrue, false; uncertain; unknown
incineración *f,* incineration
incinerador *m,* incinerator
incinerar *vt* incinerate, reduce to ashes
incipiente *a* incipient
incircunciso *a* uncircumcised
incisión *f,* incision
incisivo *a* sharp, keen; incisive, sarcastic, caustic
inciso *m,* clause; comma
incitación *f,* incitement; *fig* spur, stimulus
incitar *vt* to incite; stimulate, encourage
incivil *a* rude, discourteous, uncivil
incivilidad *f,* rudeness, incivility
inclasificable *a* unclassifiable
inclemencia *f,* harshness, severity; inclemency (of the weather). **a la i.,** at the mercy of the elements
inclemente *a* inclement
inclinación *f,* inclination; slope; slant; tendency, propensity; predilection, fondness; bow (in greeting); *geom* inclination
inclinar *vt* to incline, tilt, slant; bow; bend; influence; persuade; *vi* resemble; *vr* lean; stoop; tilt; tend, incline (to), view favorably (e.g. **Me inclino a creerlo,** I am inclined to believe it)
ínclito *a* famous, celebrated
incluir *vt irr* to comprise, embrace, contain; include, take into account. See **huir**
inclusa *f,* foundling home
inclusión *f,* inclusion; relationship, intercourse, friendship
inclusive *adv* including
inclusivo *a* inclusive
incluso *adv* including, inclusive. *prep* even
incoar *vt* to begin (especially lawsuits)
incobrable *a* irrecoverable; irredeemable
incógnita *f, math* X; unknown quantity; secret motive; unknown lady
incógnito *a* unknown. *m,* incognito, assumed name, disguise
incoherencia *f,* incoherence
incoherente *a* incoherent, disconnected, illogical
íncola *mf* resident, dweller, inhabitant
incoloro *a* colorless, uncolored
incólume *a* unharmed, unscathed; untouched, undamaged
incombustibilidad *f,* incombustibility
incomodar *vt* to disturb, incommode, inconvenience; annoy; *vr* disturb oneself, put oneself out; grow angry. **¡No se incomode!** Please don't move!; Please don't be angry!
incomodidad *f,* discomfort; inconvenience; trouble, upset; annoyance
incómodo *a* uncomfortable; inconvenient; troublesome, tiresome; *Argentina, Chile* fed up *m,* discomfort; inconvenience
incomparable *a* incomparable
incompartible *a* indivisible
incompasivo *a* unsympathetic, hard
incompatibilidad *f,* incompatibility
incompetencia *f,* incompetence
incompetente *a* incompetent
incomplejo, incomplexo *a* noncomplex, simple
incompleto *a* incomplete
incomponible *a* unrepairable, unmendable
incomprensibilidad *f,* incomprehensibility
incomprensible *a* incomprehensible
incomprensión *f,* incomprehension
incomunicado *a* in solitary confinement (of a prisoner)
incomunicar *vt* to sentence to solitary confinement; isolate, deprive of means of communication; *vr* become a recluse
inconcebible *a* inconceivable
inconciliable *a* irreconcilable
incondicional *a* unconditional; *Lat. Am.* fawning, servile
inconexión *f,* disconnectedness
inconexo *a* unconnected; incoherent
inconfeso *a* unconfessed
incongruencia *f,* incongruity
incongruente *a* incongruous, inappropriate
incommensurabilidad *f,* incommensurability
inconmovible *a* immovable; unflinching, unshakable
incommutable *a* unalterable, immutable, unchangeable
inconquistable *a* unconquerable; *fig* resolute, inflexible
inconsciencia *f,* unconsciousness; subconscious
inconsciente *a* unconscious, involuntary; subconscious
inconsecuencia *f,* inconsequence; inconsistency
inconsecuente *a* inconsequential; inconsistent
inconsideración *f,* thoughtlessness
inconsiderado *a* thoughtless; heedless, selfish
inconsiguiente *a* illogical, inconsistent
inconsistencia *f,* inconsistency
inconsistente *a* inconsistent
inconsolable *a* inconsolable
inconstancia *f,* inconstancy, infidelity
inconstante *a* inconstant, fickle
inconstitucional *a* unconstitutional
incontaminado *a* uncontaminated
incontestable *a* undeniable, unquestionable
incontinencia *f,* incontinence
incontinente *a* incontinent
incontrastable *a* insuperable, invincible; undeniable, unanswerable; *fig* unshakable, inconvincible
incontrovertible *a* undeniable, incontrovertible
inconvencible *a* inconvincible
inconveniencia *f,* discomfort; inconvenience; unsuitability
inconveniente *a* awkward, inconvenient; uncomfortable; inappropriate. *m,* inconvenience; obstacle, impediment; disadvantage
inconvertible *a* inconvertible

incorporación *f*, incorporation
incorporar *vt* to incorporate; cause to sit up, lift up; *vr* sit up, raise oneself; become a member, join (associations); be incorporated; blend, mix
incorporeidad *f*, incorporeity
incorpóreo *a* incorporeal; immaterial
incorrección *f*, incorrectness; indecorum, impropriety
incorrecto *a* incorrect; indecorous, unbecoming, improper
incorregible *a* incorrigible
incorrupción *f*, incorruption; purity; integrity; wholesomeness
incorrupto *a* incorrupt; pure; chaste
incredibilidad *f*, incredibility
incredulidad *f*, incredulity, scepticism
incrédulo (-la) *a* incredulous; atheistic. *n* atheist; unbeliever, sceptic
increíble *a* incredible; marvelous, extraordinary
incremento *m*, increment, increase
increpación *f*, scolding, harsh rebuke
increpar *vt* to scold, rebuke harshly
incriminante *a* incriminating
incriminar *vt* to incriminate, accuse; exaggerate (a charge, etc.)
incruento *a* bloodless, unstained with blood
incrustación *f*, incrustation; *art* inlay
incubación *f*, hatching; *med* incubation
incubadora *f*, incubator (for chickens)
incubar *vi* to sit on eggs (of hens); *vt* hatch; *med* incubate
inculcación *f*, inculcation, instillment
inculcar *vt* to press one thing against another; instill, inculcate; *vr* grow more fixed in one's views
inculpable *a* blameless, innocent
inculpar *vt* to blame; accuse
incultivable *a* uncultivatable; untillable
inculto *a* uncultivated, untilled; uncultured; uncivilized
incultura *f*, lack of cultivation; lack of culture
incumbencia *f*, obligation, moral responsibility, duty
incumbir *vi* to be incumbent on; concern
incumplimiento *m*, nonfulfilment
incurable *a* incurable; inveterate, hopeless
incuria *f*, negligence, carelessness
incurioso *a* incurious
incurrir *vi* (*with en*) to fall into (error, etc.); incur (dislike, etc.)
incursión *f*, incursion; inroad
indagación *f*, investigation, inquiry
indagador (-ra) *a* investigating, inquiring. *n* investigator
indagar *vt* to investigate, examine; inquire. **i. precios,** to inquire about prices
indebido *a* undue, immoderate improper; illegal, illicit
indecencia *f*, indecency; obscenity; impropriety
indecente *a* indecent; obscene; improper
indecible *a* unutterable, ineffable, unspeakable
indeciso *a* undecided; hesitant, irresolute; vague; noncommittal
indeclinable *a* obligatory; unavoidable; *gram* indeclinable, uninflected
indecoro *m*, impropriety, indecorum
indecoroso *a* indecorous, unbecoming; base, mean
indefectible *a* unfailing; perfect
indefectiblemente *adv* invariably
indefendible *a* indefensible
indefenso *a* unprotected, defenseless
indefinible *a* indefinable, vague; indescribable
indefinido *a* indefinite, vague; undefined; *gram* indefinite
indeleble *a* indelible
indeliberado *a* unpremeditated; unconsidered
indemme *a* unharmed, undamaged
indemnidad *f*, indemnity
indemnización *f*, compensation, indemnification; indemnity
indemnizar *vt* to indemnify, compensate
indemostrable *a* indemonstrable, incapable of demonstration
independencia *f*, independence
independiente *a* independent; self-contained
indescifrable *a* undecipherable; illegible
indestructible *a* indestructible
indeterminado *a* indeterminate; vague, doubtful, uncertain; hesitant, irresolute; *math* indeterminate
indiano (-na) *a* and *n* Indian; East Indian; West Indian. *m*, nouveau riche, one who returns rich from the Western Hemisphere
indicación *f*, indication; sign, evidence; intimation, hint
indicador *a* indicative. *m*, indicator. **i. del nivel de gasolina,** gas gauge
indicar *vt* to indicate; show; point out; simply, suggest; intimate
indicativo *a* indicative. *a* and *m*, *gram* indicative
índice *m*, index; indication, sign; library catalogue; catalogue room; hand (of a clock); pointer, needle (of instruments); gnomon (of a sundial); *math* index; forefinger. **I. expurgatorio,** the Index
indicio *m*, indication; sign; evidence. **indicios vehementes,** circumstantial evidence
índico *a* Indian
indiferencia *f*, indifference
indiferente *a* indifferent
indígena *a* native, indigenous. *mf* native
indigencia *f*, destitution, indigence; impecuniosity
indigenismo *m*, *Lat. Am.* Native American movement
indigente *a* destitute, indigent; impecunious
indigestión *f*, indigestion
indigesto *a* indigestible; *lit* muddled, confused; unsociable, brusque
indignación *f*, indignation, anger
indignado *a* indignant
indignar *vt* to anger, make indignant; *vr* grow angry
indignidad *f*, unworthiness; indignity; personal affront
indigno *a* unworthy; base, despicable
índigo *m*, indigo
indio (-ia) *a* Indian; blue. *n* Indian. *m*, indium
indirecta *f*, hint, covert suggestion, innuendo. *inf* **i. del padre Cobos,** strong hint
indirecto *a* indirect
indisciplina *f*, indiscipline
indisciplinado *a* undisciplined
indiscreción *f*, indiscretion
indiscreto *a* indiscreet
indiscutible *a* unquestionable, undeniable
indisoluble *a* indissoluble
indispensable *a* indispensable
indisponer *vt irr* to make unfit or incapable; indispose, make ill; (*with con or contra*) set against, make trouble with; *vr* be indisposed; (*with con or contra*) quarrel with. See **poner**
indisposición *f*, reluctance, disinclination; indisposition, brief illness
indistinguible *a* undistinguishable
indistinto *a* indistinct; indeterminate; vague
individual *a* individual; peculiar, characteristic. *m*, (tennis) single
individualidad *f*, individuality
individualismo *m*, individualism
individualista *a* individualistic. *mf* individualist
individuo (-ua) *a* individual; indivisible. *m*, individual; member, associate; *inf* self. *n inf* person
indivisibilidad *f*, indivisibility
indivisible *a* indivisible
indiviso *a* undivided
indócil *a* unmanageable; disobedient; brittle, unpliable (of metals)
indocilidad *f*, indocility; disobedience; brittleness (of metals)
indochino (-na) *a* and *n* Indochinese
indoeuropeo *a* Indo-European

indoísmo *m*, Hinduism
índole *f*, temperament, nature; kind, sort
indolencia *f*, idleness, indolence
indolente *a* nonpainful; indifferent, insensible; idle, indolent
indoloro *a* painless
indomable *a* untamable; invincible; indomitable; ungovernable, unmanageable
indomado *a* untamed
indómito *a* untamed; untamable; unmanageable, unruly; indomitable
indonesio (-ia) *a* and *n* Indonesian
indostanés *a* Hindustani
indostani *m*, Hindustani (language)
indubitable *a* unquestionable
inducción *f*, persuasion; *phys* induction
inducir *vt irr* to persuade, prevail upon; induce; infer, conclude. See **conducir**
inductivo, inductor *a* inductive
indudable *a* indubitable
indulgencia *f*, overkindness, tenderness; *ecc* indulgence
indulgente *a* indulgent, tender; tolerant
indultar *vt* to pardon; exempt
indulto *m*, amnesty; exemption; forgiveness; *ecc* indult
indumentaria *f*, clothing; outfit (of clothes)
industria *f*, assiduity, industriousness; pains, effort, ingenuity; industry. **i. pesada,** heavy industry. **i. cárnica,** meat industry. **i. extractivos,** mining industry
industrial *a* industrial. *m*, industrialist
industrialismo *m*, industrialism
industrialización *f*, industrialization
industriar *vt* to teach, train; *vr* find a way, manage, succeed in
industrioso *a* industrious; diligent, assiduous
inédito *a* unpublished; unedited
inefable *a* ineffable
ineficacia *f*, inefficiency; ineffectiveness
ineficaz *a* ineffective; inefficient
ineludible *a* unavoidable
ineptitud *f*, ineptitude
inepto *a* inept, incompetent; unfit, unsuitable
inequívoco *a* unequivocal
inercia *f*, inertia
inerme *a* defenseless, unprotected; (*bot zool*) unarmed
inerte *a* inert
inescrutable *a* inscrutable, unfathomable
inesperado *a* unexpected, sudden
inestabilidad *f*, instability
inestable *a* unstable
inestimable *a* inestimable
inevitable *a* inevitable
inexactitud *f*, inexactitude, inaccuracy; error, mistake
inexacto *a* inexact, inaccurate; erroneous
inexcusable *a* inexcusable, unforgivable; indispensable
inexhausto *a* inexhaustible
inexistente *a* nonexistent
inexorable *a* inexorable
inexperiencia *f*, inexperience
inexperto *a* inexperienced; inexpert
inexplicable *a* inexplicable
inexplorado *a* unexplored
inexplosible *a* inexplosive
inexpresivo *a* inexpressive; reticent
inexpugnable *a* impregnable; *fig* unshakable, firm; obstinate
inextinguible *a* inextinguishable; everlasting, perpetual
infalibilidad *f*, infallibility
infalible *a* infallible
infamación *f*, defamation
infamador (-ra) *a* slandering. *n* slanderer
infamar *vt* to defame, slander
infame *a* infamous, vile
infamia *f*, infamy; baseness, vileness
infancia *f*, infancy, babyhood; childhood
infanta *f*, female child under seven years; infanta, any Spanish royal princess; wife of a Spanish royal prince
infantado *m*, land belonging to an *infante* or *infanta*
infante *m*, male child under seven years; infante, any Spanish royal prince except an heir-apparent; infantryman. **i. de coro,** choir boy
infantería *f*, infantry
infanticida *a* infanticidal. *mf* infanticide (person)
infanticidio *m*, infanticide (act)
infantil *a* infantile, babyish; innocent, candid
infatigable *a* unwearying, indefatigable
infatuación *f*, infatuation
infatuar *vt* to infatuate; *vr* become infatuated
infausto *a* unlucky, unfortunate
infección *f*, infection
infeccioso *a* infectious
infectar *vt* to infect; corrupt, pervert; *vr* become infected; be corrupted
infecto *a* infected; corrupt, perverted; tainted
infecundidad *f*, sterility
infecundo *a* sterile, barren
infelice *a poet* unhappy, unfortunate
infelicidad *f*, unhappiness
infeliz *a* unhappy; unfortunate; *inf* simple, goodhearted
inferencia *f*, inference, connection
inferior *a* inferior; lower; second-rate; subordinate. *mf* inferior, subordinate
inferioridad *f*, inferiority
inferir *vt irr* to infer, deduce; involve, imply; occasion; inflict. See **sentir**
infernáculo *m*, hopscotch
infernal *a* infernal; devilish, fiendish; wicked, inhuman; *inf* confounded
inferno *a poet* infernal
infértil *a* infertile
infestación *f*, infestation
infestar *vt* to infest, swarm in; infect; injure, damage
infesto *a poet* harmful, dangerous
inficionar *vt* to infect; pervert, corrupt
infidelidad *f*, faithlessness, infidelity; disbelief in Christian religion; unbelievers, infidels
infidelísimo, *a sup* **infiel** most disloyal; most incorrect; most incredulous, faithless
infidencia *f*, disloyalty, faithlessness
infiel *a* unfaithful, disloyal; inaccurate, incorrect; infidel, unbelieving. *mf* infidel, nonbeliever
infierno *m*, hell; hades (gen. *pl*); *fig inf* inferno. **en el quinto i.,** very far off, at the end of the world. **en los quintos infiernos,** at the end of nowhere
infiltración *f*, infiltration; inculcation, implantation
infiltrar *vt* to infiltrate; imbue, inculcate
ínfimo *a* lowest; meanest, vilest, most base; cheapest, poorest (in quality)
infinidad *f*, infinity; infinitude; great number
infinitivo *a* and *m*, *gram* infinitive
infinito *a* infinite; endless; boundless; countless. *m*, *math* infinite. *adv* excessively, immensely
infinitud *f*, See **infinidad**
inflación *f*, inflation; distension; pride, vanity
inflacionismo *m*, inflationism
inflacionista *mf* inflationist
inflador *m*. *Lat. Am.* bicycle pump
inflamabilidad *f*, inflammability
inflamable *a* inflammable
inflamación *f*, inflammation; *eng* ignition
inflamador *a* inflammatory
inflamar *vt* to set on fire; *fig* inflame, excite; *vr* take fire; *med* become inflamed; grow hot or excited
inflamatorio *a med* inflammatory
inflar *vt* to inflate; blow up, distend; throw out (one's chest); exaggerate; make haughty or vain; *vr* be swollen or inflated; be puffed up with pride
inflexibilidad *f*, inflexibility; rigidity; immovability, constancy
inflexible *a* inflexible

inflexión *f*, bending, flexion; diffraction (optics); inflection
infligir *vt* to impose, inflict (penalties)
influencia *f*, influence; power, authority; *elec* charge
influir *vt irr* to influence; affect; (*with en*) cooperate in, assist with. See **huir**
influjo *m*, influence; flux, inflow of the tide
influyente *a* influential
información *f*, information; legal inquiry; report; research, investigation
informador (-ra) *a* informing, acquainting. *n* informant
informal *a* informal, irregular; unreliable (of persons); unconventional
informalidad *f*, irregularity; unconventionality; unreliability
informante *mf* informant
informar *vt* to inform, acquaint with; *vi law* plead; *vr* (*with de, en, or sobre*) find out about, investigate
informática *f*, information sciences
informativo *a* informative
informe *a* formless, shapeless. *m*, report, statement; information; *law* plea; *pl* data, particulars; references
infortificable *a* unfortifiable
infortuna *f*, *astrol* evil influence
infortunado *a* unfortunate
infortunio *m*, misfortune; unhappiness, adversity; mischance, ill luck
infracción *f*, transgression, infringement
infracto *a* imperturbable
infractor(-ra) *a* infringing. *n* transgressor, infringer
infrangible *a* unbreakable
infranqueable *a* insuperable, unsurmountable
infrarrojo *a* infrared
infrascrito *a* undersigned; undermentioned
infrecuente *a* infrequent
infringir *vt* to infringe, transgress, break
infructífero *a* unfruitful; worthless, useless
infructuosidad *f*, unfruitfulness; worthlessness, uselessness
infructuoso *a* fruitless; useless, worthless
infumable *a* unsmokable (of tobacco)
infundado *a* unfounded, groundless
infundio *m*, *inf* nonsense, untruth
infundir *vt* to infuse, imbue with
infusión *f*, infusion
ingeniar *vt* to devise, concoct, plan; *vr* contrive, find a way, manage
ingeniería *f*, engineering
ingeniero *m*, engineer. **i. agrónomo,** agricultural engineer. **i. de caminos, canales y puertos,** civil engineer. **i. radiotelegrafista,** radio engineer. **cuerpo de ingenieros,** royal engineers
ingenio *m*, mind; inventive capacity; imaginative talent; man of genius; talent, cleverness; ingeniousness; machine; guillotine (bookbinding)
ingeniosidad *f*, ingeniousness; witticism, clever remark
ingenioso *a* talented, clever; ingenious
ingénito *a* unengendered, unconceived; innate, inborn
ingente *a* huge, enormous
ingenuidad *f*, ingenuousness, naiveté
ingenuo *a* ingenuous, naive, artless, unaffected
Inglaterra England
ingle *f*, groin
inglés (-esa) *a* English; British. *n* Englishman; Briton. *m*, English (language); *inf* creditor. **a la inglesa,** in English fashion. **marcharse a la inglesa,** *inf* to take French leave
inglesismo *m*, Anglicism
ingobernable *a* ungovernable, unruly
ingratitud *f*, ingratitude
ingrato *a* ungrateful; irksome, thankless; disagreeable
ingrávido *a* light weight
ingrediente *m*, ingredient; *Argentina* appetizer
ingresar *vi* to return, come in (money); (*with en*) join, become a member of, enter
ingreso *m*, joining, entering, admission; *com* money received; opening, commencement; *pl* earnings, takings, revenue
ingurgitación *f*, *med* ingurgitation
ingurgitar *vt* to ingurgitate, swallow
inhábil *a* unskillful; unpracticed; incompetent, unfit; unsuitable, ill-chosen
inhabilidad *f*, unskillfulness; incompetence; unsuitability; inability
inhabilitación *f*, incapacitation; disqualification; disablement
inhabilitar *vt* to make ineligible; disqualify; incapacitate, make unfit; *vr* become ineligible; be incapacitated
inhabitable *a* uninhabitable
inhabitado *a* uninhabited, deserted
inhalación *f*, inhalation
inhalador *m*, *med* inhaler
inhalar *vt* to inhale
inhallable *a* nowhere to be found, unfindable
inhereditable *a* uninheritable
inherencia *f*, inherency
inherente *a* inherent, innate
inhestar *vt irr* to raise, lift up; erect. See **acertar**
inhibición *f*, inhibition
inhibir *vt law* to inhibit; *vr* inhibit or restrain oneself. See **prohibir**
inhibitorio *a law* inhibitory
inhonesto *a* indecent, obscene; immodest
inhospedable, inhospitalario *a* inhospitable; bleak, uninviting; exposed
inhospitalidad *f*, inhospitality
inhumación *f*, inhumation, burial
inhumadora *f*, crematory
inhumanidad *f*, inhumanity; brutality
inhumano *a* inhuman; brutal, barbarous
inhumar *vt* to bury, inter
iniciación *f*, initiation
iniciador (-ra) *a* initiating; *n* initiator
inicial *a* and *f*, initial
iniciar *vt* to initiate; admit, introduce; originate; *vr* be initiated; *ecc* take minor or first orders
iniciativa *f*, initiative
inicuo *a* iniquitous, most unjust, wicked
inimaginable *a* inconceivable
inimicísimo *a sup* **enemigo** most hostile
inimitable *a* inimitable
ininteligible *a* unintelligible
iniquidad *f*, iniquity, wickedness
injerir *vt irr* to insert, place within, introduce; interpolate; *vr* meddle. See **sentir**
injertar *vt agr* to graft
injerto *m*, *agr* graft; grafting; grafted plant, briar, or tree
injuria *f*, insult; slander; outrage; wrong, injustice; harm, damage
injuriador (-ra) *a* insulting. *n* offender, persecutor
injuriar *vt* to insult; slander; outrage; wrong, persecute; harm, damage
injurioso *a* insulting; slanderous; offensive, abusive; harmful
injusticia *f*, injustice; lack of justice; unjust action
injustificable *a* unjustifiable
injustificado *a* unjustified
injusto *a* unjust; unrighteous
inllevable *a* unbearable, intolerable
inmaculado *a* immaculate, pure
inmanejable *a* unmanageable; uncontrollable
inmanencia *f*, immanence
inmanente *a* immanent
inmarcesible, inmarchitable *a* unfading, imperishable
inmaterial *a* incorporeal; immaterial
inmaterialidad *f*, incorporeity; immateriality
inmaturo *a* immature; unripe

inmediación *f,* nearness, proximity; contact; *pl* outskirts, neighborhood, environs
inmediatamente *adv* near; immediately, at once
inmediato *a* adjoining, close, nearby; immediate, prompt
inmejorable *a* unsurpassable, unbeatable
inmemorable, inmemorial *a* immemorial
inmensidad *f,* vastness, huge extent; infinity; infinite space; immensity; huge number
inmenso *a* vast; infinite; immense; innumerable
inmensurable *a* immeasurable, incalculable
inmerecido *a* undeserved, unmerited
inmérito *a* wrongful, unjust
inmeritorio *a* unmeritorious, unpraiseworthy
inmersión *f,* immersion; dip
inmigración *f,* immigration
inmigrante *a* and *mf* immigrant
inmigrar *vi* to immigrate
inminencia *f,* imminence
inminente *a* imminent
inmiscuir *vt* to mix; *vr* meddle. May be conjugated regularly or like **huir**
inmisión *f,* inspiration
inmobiliario *a* concerning real estate
inmoble *a* immovable; motionless, immobile, stationary; *fig* unshakable, unflinching
inmoderación *f,* immoderateness, excess
inmoderado *a* immoderate; unrestrained, excessive
inmodestia *f,* immodesty
inmodesto *a* immodest
inmolación *f,* immolation
inmolador (-ra) *a* sacrificing. *n* immolator
inmolar *vt* to immolate; *fig* sacrifice, give up; *vr fig* sacrifice oneself
inmoral *a* immoral
inmoralidad *f,* immorality
inmortal *a* immortal
inmortalidad *f,* immortality
inmortalizar *vt* to immortalize
inmotivado *a* unfounded, without reason
inmoto *a* motionless, stationary
inmóvil *a* immovable, fixed; motionless; steadfast, constant
inmovilidad *f,* immovability; immobility; constancy, steadfastness
inmovilizar *vt* to immobilize
inmueble *m, law* immovable estate
inmundicia *f,* filth, nastiness; dirt; rubbish, refuse; obscenity, indecency
inmundo *a* dirty, filthy; obscene, indecent; unclean
inmune *a* exempt; *med* immune
inmunidad *f,* exemption; immunity
inmunizar *vt* to immunize
inmutabilidad *f,* immutability, changelessness; imperturbability
inmutable *a* immutable, unchangeable; imperturbable
inmutación *f,* change, alteration, difference
inmutar *vt* to change, alter, vary; *vr* change one's expression (through fear, etc.)
innato *a* innate; inherent; instinctive, inborn
innatural *a* unnatural
innavegable *a* unnavigable; unseaworthy (of ships)
innecesario *a* unnecessary
innegable *a* undeniable; indisputable, irrefutable
innoble *a* plebeian; ignoble
innocuo *a* harmless, innocuous
innovación *f,* innovation
innovador (-ra) *a* innovatory. *n* innovator
innovar *vt* to introduce innovations
innumerabilidad *f,* countless number, multitude
innumerable *a* innumerable, countless
innúmero *a* countless, innumerable
inobediencia *f,* disobedience
inobediente *a* disobedient
inobjetable *a, Lat. Am.* unobjectionable
inobservable *a* unobservable
inobservancia *f,* inobservance
inobservante *a* unobservant
inocencia *f,* innocence; simplicity, candor; harmlessness
inocentada *f, inf* naïve remark or action; fool's trap; practical joke
inocente *a* innocent; candid, simple; harmless; easily deceived
inocentón *a inf* extremely credulous and easily taken in
inocuidad *f,* innocuousness
inoculación *f,* inoculation
inoculador *m,* inoculator
inocular *vt* to inoculate; pervert, corrupt; contaminate
inodoro *a* odorless. *m,* toilet, lavatory
inofensivo *a* inoffensive, harmless
inolvidable *a* unforgettable
inoperable *a* inoperable
inopia *f,* poverty; scarcity
inopinable *a* indisputable, unquestionable
inopinado *a* unexpected, sudden
inoportunidad *f,* inopportuneness, unseasonableness; unsuitability
inoportuno *a* inopportune, untimely
inordenado *a* inordinate, immoderate, excessive
inorgánico *a* inorganic
inoxidable *a* rustless
inquebrantable *a* unbreakable; final, irrevocable
inquietador (-ra) *a* disturbing. *n* disturber
inquietar *vt* to disturb; trouble, make anxious, worry; *vr* be disquieted, worry
inquieto *a* restless; unquiet; fidgety; disturbed, anxious, worried, uneasy
inquietud *f,* restlessness; uneasiness; worry; trouble, care, anxiety
inquilinato *m,* tenancy; rent; *law* lease; (rental) rates
inquilino (-na) *n* tenant; lessee; *Chile* tenant farmer
inquina *f,* dislike, grudge
inquinar *vt* to contaminate, corrupt, infect
inquiridor (-ra) *a* inquiring, examining. *n* investigator
inquirir *vt irr* to inquire; examine, look into. See **adquirir**
inquisición *f,* inquiry, investigation; *ecc* Inquisition
inquisidor (-ra) *a* inquiring, investigating. *n* investigator. *m, ecc* inquisitor; judge
inquisitorial *a* inquisitorial
insaciabilidad *f,* insatiability
insaciable *a* insatiable
insalubre *a* unhealthy
insanable *a* incurable
insania *f,* insanity
insano *a* insane, mad
inscribir *vt* to inscribe; record; enter (a name on a list, etc.), register, enroll; engrave; *geom* inscribe. *Past Part.* **inscrito**
inscripción *f,* inscription; record, enrollment; registration; government bond
insecable *a* undryable, undrying
insecticida *a* insecticide
insecto *m,* insect
inseguridad *f,* insecurity
inseguro *a* insecure; unsafe; uncertain
insensatez *f,* folly, foolishness
insensato *a* foolish, stupid, mad
insensibilidad *f,* insensibility; imperception; callousness, hard-heartedness
insensibilizar *vt* to make insensible (to sensations)
insensible *a* insensible; imperceptive, insensitive; unconscious, senseless; imperceptible, inappreciable; callous
inseparabilidad *f,* inseparability
inseparable *a* inseparable
insepulto *a* unburied (of the dead)
inserción *f,* insertion; interpolation; grafting
insertar *vt* to insert; introduce; interpolate; *vr* (*bot zool*) become attached
inservible *a* useless; unfit; unsuitable

insidia *f,* insidiousness; snare, ambush
insidiador (-ra) *a* ensnaring. *n* schemer, ambusher
insidiar *vt* to waylay, ambush; set a trap for; scheme against
insidioso *a* insidious; treacherous; scheming, guileful
insigne *a* illustrious, famous; distinguished
insignia *f,* symbol; badge; token; banner, standard; *naut* pennant; *pl* insignia
insignificancia *f,* meaninglessness; unimportance, triviality; insignificance, insufficiency
insignificante *a* meaningless; unimportant; insignificant, small
insinuación *f,* insinuation; hint; implication; suggestion
insinuador *a* insinuating; suggestive, implicative
insinuar *vt* to insinuate; suggest, hint; *vr* ingratiate oneself; creep in
insinuativo *a* insinuative
insipidez *f,* tastelessness, insipidity; *fig* dullness
insípido *a* tasteless, insipid; dull, uninteresting, boring
insistencia *f,* insistence
insistente *a* insistent
insistir *vi* (*with en or sobre*) to lay stress upon, insist on; persist in
ínsito *a* inherent, innate
insociabilidad *f,* unsociability
insociable *a* unsociable
insolación *f,* insolation, exposure to the sun; sunstroke
insolar *vt* to expose to the sun's rays; *vr* contract sunstroke
insoldable *a* unsolderable, unable to be soldered
insolencia *f,* insolence; impudence, impertinence
insolentarse *vr* to grow insolent; be impudent
insolente *a* insolent; impudent, impertinent
insólito *a* unaccustomed; infrequent; unusual; unexpected
insolubilidad *f,* insolubility
insoluble *a* insoluble
insoluto *a* unpaid, outstanding
insolvencia *f,* insolvency
insolvente *a* insolvent
insomne *a* sleepless
insomnio *m,* insomnia
insondable *a* unfathomable, bottomless; inscrutable, secret
insoportable *a* intolerable, unbearable
insostenible *a* indefensible; arbitrary, baseless
inspección *f,* inspection; supervision; examination; inspectorship; inspector's office
inspeccionar *vt* to inspect; survey, examine. **i. una casa,** to view a house
inspector (-ra) *a* inspecting, examining. *n* supervisor. *m,* inspector; surveyor
inspiración *f,* inspiration; inhalation
inspirador (-ra) *a* inspiring. *n* inspirer
inspirar *vt* to breathe in, inhale; blow (of the wind); inspire; *vr* be inspired; (*with en*) find inspiration in, imitate
instabilidad *f,* instability; unsteadiness; shakiness; unreliability, inconstancy
instable *a* unstable
instalación *f,* plant, apparatus; erection, fitting; induction; installment, settling in
instalador (-ra) *n* fitter; one who installs (electricity, etc.)
instalar *vt* to appoint, induct; erect (a plant, etc.); install, put in; lay on; *elec* wire; *vr* install oneself, settle down
instancia *f,* instance; argument; suggestion; supplication; request; formal petition. **de primera i.,** in the first instance, firstly
instantánea *f, phot* snapshot
instantáneo *a* instantaneous
instante *a* urgent. *m,* second; instant, moment. **a cada i.,** every minute; frequently. **al i.,** at once, immediately. **por instantes,** continually; immediately
instar *vt* to press; persuade; insist upon; *vi* be urgent, press
instauración *f,* restoration; renewal; renovation; *Lat. Am.* establishment
instaurador (-ra) *a* renovating, renewing. *n* restorer, renovator
instaurar *vt* to restore; repair; renovate, renew; *Lat. Am.* establish, set up
instaurativo *a* restorative
instigación *f,* instigation, incitement
instigador (-ra) *n* instigator
instigar *vt* to instigate, incite; induce
instilación *f,* instillment, pouring drop by drop; inculcation, implantation
instilar *vt chem* instill; implant, inculcate
instintivo *a* instinctive
instinto *m,* instinct. **por i.,** by instinct, naturally
institución *f,* setting up, establishment; institution; teaching, instruction; *pl* institutes, digest
institucional *a* institutional
instituir *vt irr* to found, establish; institute; instruct, teach. See **huir**
instituto *m,* institute; secondary school. **i. de belleza,** beauty parlor, beauty salon
institutor *m,* founder, instituter; tutor
institutriz *f,* governess
instrucción *f,* teaching, instruction; knowledge, learning; education; *pl* orders; rules; instruction. **i. primaria,** primary education. **i. pública,** public education
instructivo *a* instructive
instructor (-ra) *a* instructive. *n* instructor
instruido *a* cultured, well-educated; knowledgeable
instruir *vt irr* to teach, instruct; train; inform, acquaint with; *law* formulate. See **huir**
instrumentación *f, mus* instrumentation
instrumentista *mf mus* instrumentalist; instrument maker
instrumento *m,* tool, implement; machine, apparatus; *mus* instrument; means, medium; legal document. **i. de cuerda,** string instrument. **i. de percusión,** percussion instrument. **i. de viento,** wind instrument
insuave *a* unpleasant (to the senses); rough
insubordinación *f,* insubordination, rebellion
insubordinado *a* insubordinate, unruly
insubordinar *vt* to rouse to rebellion; *vr* become insubordinate, rebel
insubsistencia *f,* instability
insubsistente *a* unstable; groundless, unfounded
insubstancial *a* insubstantial, unreal, illusory; pointless, worthless, superficial
insubstancialidad *f,* superficiality, worthlessness
insuficiencia *f,* insufficiency, shortage; incompetence, inefficiency
insuficiente *a* insufficient, scarce, inadequate
insufrible *a* insufferable, unbearable, intolerable
insular *a* insular
insulina *f,* insulin
insulsez *f,* insipidity, tastelessness; dullness; tediousness
insulso *a* insipid, tasteless; tedious; dull
insultador (-ra) *a* insulting. *n* insulter
insultante *a* insulting
insultar *vt* to insult; call names; *vr* take offense
insulto *m,* insult; sudden attack; sudden illness, fit; *Argentina* fit of fainting; *Mexico* indigestion
insumable *a* incalculable; excessive, exorbitant
insumergible *a* unsinkable
insumiso *a* rebellious
insuperable *a* insuperable
insurgente *a* insurgent, rebellious. *m,* rebel
insurrección *f,* insurrection
insurreccionar *vt* to incite to rebellion; *vr* rise in rebellion
insurrecto (-ta) *n* rebel
insustancial *a* See **insubstancial**

insustituible *a* indispensable
intacto *a* untouched; intact, uninjured; whole, entire; complete; pure
intachable *a* irreproachable; impeccable, perfect
intangibilidad *f,* intangibility
intangible *a* intangible
integración *f,* integration
integrar *vt* to integrate; *com* repay
integridad *f,* wholeness; completeness; integrity, probity, honesty; virginity
íntegro *a* integral, whole; upright, honest
integumento *m,* integument; pretense, simulation
intelectiva *f,* understanding
intelecto *m,* intellect
intelectual *a* intellectual
intelectualidad *f,* understanding, intellectuality; intelligentsia
inteligencia *f,* intelligence; intellect; mental alertness; mind; meaning, sense; experience, skill; understanding, secret agreement; information, knowledge; Intelligence, Secret Service
inteligente *a* intelligent; clever; skillful; capable, competent
inteligible *a* intelligible; understandable; able to be heard
intemperancia *f,* intemperance, lack of moderation
intemperante *a* intemperate
intemperie *f,* stormy weather. **a la i.,** at the mercy of the elements; in the open air
intempestivo *a* inopportune, ill-timed
intención *f,* intention; determination, purpose; viciousness (of animals); caution. *inf* **con segunda i.,** with a double meaning, slyly
intencionado *a* intentioned, disposed
intencional *a* intentional, designed, premeditated
intendencia *f,* management; supervision; administration; *pol* intendancy; *Argentina* mayoralty. *mil* **cuerpo de i.,** quartermaster corps, army supply corps
intendente *m,* director; manager; *pol* intendant; *Argentina* mayor. **i. de ejército,** quartermaster general
intensar *vt* to intensify
intensidad *f,* intensity; ardor; vehemence
intensificar *vt* to intensify
intensivo *a* intensive
intenso *a* intense; ardent; fervent, vehement
intentar *vt* to intend, mean; propose; try, endeavor; initiate. **i. fortuna,** to try one's luck
intento *m,* intention, determination; purpose. **de i.,** on purpose; knowingly
intentona *f, inf* foolhardy attempt
interacción *f,* interaction; reciprocal effect; *chem* reaction
intercalación *f,* interpolation; insertion
intercalar *vt* to intercalate; interpolate, include, insert
intercambiable *a* interchangeable
intercambio *m,* interchange
interceder *vi* to intercede, plead for
interceptación *f,* interception
interceptar *vt* to intercept; interrupt; hinder
intercesión *f,* intercession
intercesor (-ra) *a* interceding. *n* intercessor
intercutáneo *a* intercutaneous
interdecir *vt irr* to forbid, prohibit. See **decir**
interdicción *f,* interdiction, prohibition
interdicto *m,* interdict
interés *m,* interest; yield, profit; advantage; *com* interest; inclination, fondness; attraction, fascination; *pl* money matters. **i. compuesto,** compound interest. **intereses creados,** bonds of interest; vested interests
interesado *a* involved, concerned; biased; selfish
interesante *a* interesting
interesar(se) *vi* and *vr* to be interested; *vt com* invest; interest
interfecto (-ta) *n law* victim (of murder)
interferencia *f, phys* interference
interfoliar *vt* to interleave (of books)
ínterin *m,* interim. *adv* meanwhile, in the meantime
interinamente *adv* in the interim; provisionally
interinar *vt* to discharge (duties) provisionally, act temporarily as
interino *a* acting, provisional, temporary
interior *a* interior; inner; inside; indoor; inland; internal, domestic (policies, etc.); inward, spiritual. *m,* interior, inside; mind, soul; *pl* entrails
interiorizar *vt, Lat. Am.* to investigate closely, look into, scrutinize
interjección *f, gram* interjection, exclamation
interlinear *vt* to write between the lines; *print* lead
interlocución *f,* dialogue, conversation
interlocutorio *a law* interlocutory
intérlope *a* interloping. *mf* interloper
interludio *m,* interlude
intermediario (-ia) *a* and *n* intermediary. *m, com* middleman
intermedio *a* intermediate. *m,* interim; *theat* interval. **por i. de,** through, by the mediation of
intermisión *f,* intermission, interval
intermitencia *f,* intermittence
intermitente *a* intermittent
intermitir *vt* to interrupt, suspend, discontinue
internación *f,* going inside; penetration; taking into
internacional *a* international
internacionalismo *m,* internationalism
internacionalista *mf* internationalist
internacionalización *f,* internationalization
internado *m,* boarding school
internamiento *m,* internment
internar *vt* to take or send inland; *vi* penetrate; *vr* (*with en*) go into the interior of (a country); get into the confidence of; study deeply (a subject)
interno (-na) *a* interior; internal; inner; inside; boarding (student). *n* boarding school student; *med* intern
internuncio *m, ecc* internuncio; interlocutor; representative
interoceánico *a* interoceanic
interpaginar *vt* to interleave (of books)
interpelación *f, law* interpellation; appeal
interpelar *vt law* to interpellate; appeal to, ask protection from
interpolación *f,* interpolation, insertion; interruption
interpolador (-ra) *n* interpolator; interrupter
interpolar *vt* to interpolate; interject
interponer *vt irr* to interpose, insert, intervene; designate as an arbitrator; *vr* intervene. See **poner**
interposición *f,* interposition; intervention; mediation, arbitration
interpresa *f, mil* surprise attack
interpretación *f,* interpretation; translation
interpretador (-ra) *a* interpretative. *n* interpreter
interpretar *vt* to interpret; translate; attribute; expound, explain. **i. mal,** to misconstrue; translate wrongly
intérprete *mf* interpreter
interregno *m,* interregnum; *Lat. Am.* interim. **i. parlamentario,** parliamentary recess
interrogación *f,* interrogation, question; *gram* question mark
interrogador (-ra) *n* questioner
interrogante *a* interrogating. *m, print* question mark
interrogar *vt* to interrogate, question
interrogativo *a* interrogative
interrogatorio *m,* interrogatory
interrumpir *vt* to interrupt; hinder, obstruct; *elec* break contact
interrupción *f,* interruption; stoppage (of work); *elec* break
interruptor (-ra) *a* interrupting. *n* interrupter. *m, elec* switch, interruptor. **i. de dos direcciones,** *elec* two-way switch
intersticio *m,* interstice, crack, crevice; interval, intervening space
intervalo *m,* interval

intervención *f,* intervention; mediation, intercession; auditing (of accounts)
intervenir *vi irr* to take part (in); intervene, interfere; arbitrate, mediate; happen, occur; *vt com* audit. See **venir**
interventor (-ra) *a* intervening. *n* one who intervenes. *m,* auditor; inspector
intervocálico *a* intervocalic
intestado (-da) *a* and *n law* intestate
intestino *a* intestinal. *m,* intestine
íntima, intimación *f,* intimation, notification
intimar *vt* to intimate; inform, notify; *vr* penetrate; *vr* and *vi* become intimate or friendly
intimidación *f,* intimidation, terrorization
intimidad *f,* intimacy
intimidar *vt* to intimidate, terrorize, cow
íntimo *a* intimate; deep-seated, inward; private, personal
intitular *vt* to give a title to, entitle, call; *vr* call oneself
intolerable *a* intolerable; unbearable
intolerancia *f,* narrow-mindedness, intolerance, bigotry
intolerante *a* narrow-minded, illiberal; *med* intolerant
intonso *a* long-haired, unshorn; boorish, ignorant
intoxicación *f,* poisoning
intoxicar *vt* to poison
intraducible *a* untranslatable
intramuros *adv* within the town walls, within the city
intranquilidad *f,* disquiet, restlessness; anxiety
intranquilizador *a* disquieting, perturbing
intranquilizar *vt* to disquiet, make uneasy, worry
intranquilo *a* uneasy, anxious
intransferible *a* untransferable, not transferable
intransigencia *f,* intolerance, intransigence
intransigente *a* intolerant, intransigent
intransitable *a* impassable; unsurmountable
intransitivo *a* intransitive
intrascendente *a, Lat. Am.* unimportant
intratable *a* intractable; impassable; rough; unsociable, difficult
intrauterino *a* intrauterine
intravenoso *a* intravenous
intrepidez *f,* intrepidity, dauntlessness, gallantry
intrépido *a* intrepid, dauntless, gallant
intriga *f,* scheme, intrigue; entanglement; *lit* plot
intrigante *mf* intriguer, schemer
intrigar *vi* to intrigue, scheme, plot; **intrigarse** *Lat. Am.* to be intrigued, be puzzled
intrincación *f,* intricacy
intrincado *a* intricate
intrincar *vt* to complicate; obscure, confuse
intríngulis *m, inf* ulterior motive
intrínseco *a* intrinsic, inherent; essential
introducción *f,* introduction
introducir *vt irr* to introduce; insert; fit in; drive in; present, introduce; bring into use; cause, occasion; show in, bring in; *vr* interfere, meddle; enter. See **conducir**
introductor (-ra) *n* introducer
introito *m,* preamble, introduction; *ecc* introit; (*theat ant*) prologue
intromisión *f,* intromission; interference; *geol* intrusion
introspección *f,* introspection
introverso *a* introvert
intruso (-sa) *a* intruding, intrusive. *n* intruder
intuición *f,* intuition
intuir *vt irr* to know by intuition. See **huir**
intuitivo *a* intuitive
intuito *m,* glance, look, view
inulto *a poet* unavenged, unpunished
inundación *f,* flood; flooding; excess, superabundance
inundar *vt* to flood; swamp; *fig* inundate, overwhelm
inurbanidad *f,* discourtesy, impoliteness
inurbano *a* discourteous, uncivil, impolite
inusitado *a* unusual, unaccustomed; rare
inútil *a* useless
inutilidad *f,* uselessness
inutilizar *vt* to render useless; disable, incapacitate; spoil, damage
invadeable *a* impassable, unfordable
invadir *vt* to invade
invaginación *f,* invagination
invalidación *f,* invalidation
invalidar *vt* to invalidate
invalidez *f,* invalidity; disablement; infirmity
inválido (-da) *a* weak, infirm; invalid, null; disabled. *n* invalid; disabled soldier
invariable *a* invariable
invariación *f,* invariableness
invariante *m,* invariant
invasión *f,* invasion, encroachment, incursion
invasor (-ra) *a* invading; *med* attacking. *n* invader
invectiva *f,* invective
invencibilidad *f,* invincibility
invencible *a* invincible
invención *f,* invention, discovery; deception, fabrication, lie; creative imagination; finding (e.g. **i. de la Santa Cruz,** Invention of the Holy Cross)
invencionero (-ra) *n* inventor; schemer, deceiver
invendible *a* unsalable
inventar *vt* to invent; create; imagine; concoct, fabricate (lies, etc.)
inventariar *vt* to make an inventory of; *com* take stock of
inventario *m,* inventory; *com* stock taking
inventiva *f,* inventiveness, ingenuity; creativeness
inventivo *a* inventive
invento *m,* See **invención**
inventor (-ra) *n* inventor, discoverer; liar, storyteller
inverecundia *f,* impertinence, impudence
inverecundo *a* shameless, brazen
inverisímil *a* See **inverosímil**
invernáculo *m,* greenhouse; conservatory
invernada *f,* winter season; hibernation; *Lat. Am.* winter pasture
invernadero *m,* winter quarters; greenhouse
invernal *a* wintry; winter
invernar *vi irr* to winter; hibernate; be wintertime. See **acertar**
invernizo *a* wintry, winter
inverosímil *a* unlikely, improbable
inverosimilitud *f,* improbability
inversamente *adv* inversely
inverso *a* inverse; inverted
inversor, -a *mf, Lat. Am.* invester
invertebrado *a* and *m,* invertebrate
invertir *vt irr* to invert, transpose; reverse; *com* invest; spend (time). See **sentir**
investidura *f,* investiture
investigación *f,* investigation, examination; research; inquiry
investigador (-ra) *a* investigating. *n* investigator; researcher
investigar *vt* to investigate, examine; research on
investir *vt irr* to confer upon, decorate with; invest, appoint. See **pedir**
inveterado *a* inveterate
inviable *a* unfeasible
invicto *a* invincible; unconquered
invierno *m,* winter; rainy season
inviolabilidad *f,* inviolability. **i. parlamentaria,** parliamentary immunity
inviolable *a* inviolable; infallible
inviolado *a* inviolate
invisibilidad *f,* invisibility
invisible *a* invisible; *m, Argentina* hairpin; *Mexico* hairnet
invitación *f,* invitation
invitado (-da) *n* guest
invitar *vt* to invite; urge, request; allure, attract
invocación *f,* invocation
invocador (-ra) *n* invoker
invocar *vt* to invoke
involuntariedad *f,* involuntariness

involuntario *a* involuntary
invulnerabilidad *f,* invulnerability
invulnerable *a* invulnerable
inyección *f,* injection
inyectado *a* bloodshot (of eyes)
inyectar *vt* to inject
ipecacuana *f,* ipecac
iperita *f,* mustard gas
ir *vi irr* to go; bet (e.g. **Van cinco pesetas que no lo hace,** I bet five pesetas he doesn't do it); be different, be changed (e.g. **¡Qué diferencia va entre esto y aquello!** What a difference there is between this and that!); suit, be becoming, fit (e.g. **El vestido no te va bien,** The dress doesn't suit you); extend; lead, go in the direction of (e.g. **Este camino va a Lérida,** This road leads to Lerida); get along, do, proceed, be (e.g. **¿Cómo te va estos días?** How are you getting along these days?); come (e.g. **Ahora voy,** I'm coming now); *math* carry (e.g. **siete y van cuatro,** seven, and four to carry); *math* leave (e.g. **De quince a seis van nueve,** Six from fifteen leaves nine). With a gerund, **ir** indicates the continuance of the action, or may mean to become or to grow (e.g. **Iremos andando hacia el mar,** We shall go on walking toward the sea, or **Entre tanto iba amaneciendo,** In the meanwhile it was growing light). With a past participle, **ir** means 'to be' (e.g. **Voy encantado de lo que he visto,** I am delighted with what I have seen). With *prep a + infin,* **ir** means to prepare (to do) or to intend (to do) or to be on the point of doing (e.g. **Van a cantar la canción que te gusta,** They are going (or preparing) to sing the song you like). With *prep a + noun,* **ir** indicates destination (e.g. **Voy al cine,** I'm going to the cinema. **¿A dónde vamos?** Where are we going to?). **ir** + *con* means to go in the company of, or to do a thing in a certain manner (e.g. **Hemos de ir con cuidado,** We must go carefully). **ir** + *en* means to concern, interest (e.g. **¿Qué le va a él en este asunto?** What has this affair to do with him?). **ir** + *por* means to follow the career of, become (e.g. **Juan va por abogado,** John is going to be a lawyer). It also means to go and bring, or to go for (e.g. **Iré por agua,** I shall go and bring (or for) water). *vr* to go away, leave, depart; die; leak (of liquids); evaporate; overbalance, slip (e.g. **Se le fueron los pies,** He slipped (and lost his balance)); be worn out, grow old, deteriorate; be incontinent; *fig inf* **írsele a uno una cosa,** not to notice or not to understand a thing. *naut* **irse a pique,** to founder, sink. **Se le fueron los ojos tras María,** He couldn't keep his eyes off Mary. **i. a caballo,** to ride, go on horseback. **i. adelante,** to go on ahead, lead; *fig inf* forge ahead, go ahead. **i. al cuartel,** to go into the army. **i. a una,** to cooperate in. **i. bien** *fig inf* to go on well; be well. **i. de brazo,** to walk arm in arm. **i. de compras,** to go shopping. **i. de juerga** *inf* to go on a binge. **i. de bicicleta** *or* **en coche,** to go by bicycle or to ride (in a car or carriage). **i. por,** to do things in order, take one thing at a time. *fig inf* **i. tirando,** to carry on, manage. **¿Cómo le va?** How are things with you? How are you getting along? *inf* **no irle ni venirle a uno nada en un asunto,** to be not in the least concerned in (an affair). **¡Qué va!** Rubbish! Nothing of the sort! **¿Quién va?** *mil* Who goes there? **Vamos,** Let's go (also used as an exclamation: Good gracious! You don't say so! Well!) **Vamos a ver . . . ,** Let's see. . . . **¡Vaya!** What a . . . !; Come now! Never mind! **¡Vaya a paseo!** *or* **¡Vaya con su música a otra parte!** Take yourself off! Get out! **¡Vaya con Dios!** God keep you! Good-bye! *Pres. Ind.* **voy, vas, va, vamos, váis, van.** *Pres. Part.* **yendo.** *Preterite* **fui, fuiste, fue, fuimos, fuisteis, fueron.** *Imperf.* **iba,** etc. *Pres. Subjunc.* **vaya,** etc. *Imperf. Subjunc.* **fuese,** etc. *Imperat.* **vé**
ira *f,* wrath, anger; vengeance; raging, fury (of elements); *pl* cruelties, acts of vengeance
iracundia *f,* irascibility, irritability; anger
iracundo *a* irascible, irritable, choleric; angry; raging, tempestuous
iranio (-ia) *a* and *n* Iranian
irascibilidad *f,* irascibility; petulance
iridiscencia *f,* iridescence
iridiscente *a* iridescent
iris *m,* rainbow; *anat* iris (of the eye)
irisación *f,* irisation
irisar *vi* to be iridescent
irlandés (-esa) *a* and *n* Irishman (woman)
Irlanda Ireland
ironía *f,* irony
irónico *a* ironical
iroqués (-esa) *a* and *n* Iroquois
irracional *a* irrational; illogical, unreasonable; *math* irrational, absurd
irracionalidad *f,* irrationality, unreasonableness
irradiación *f,* radiation, irradiation
irradiar *vt* to radiate, irradiate
irrazonable *a* unreasonable
irreal *a* unreal
irrealidad *f,* unreality
irrealizable *a* unachievable, unattainable
irrebatible *a* irrefutable, evident
irreconciliable *a* irreconcilable, intransigent
irrecuperable *a* irretrievable
irredimible *a* irredeemable
irreemplazable *a* irreplaceable
irreflexión *f,* thoughtlessness; impetuosity
irreflexivo *a* thoughtless; rash, impetuous
irreformable *a* unreformable
irrefragable *a* indisputable, unquestionable
irrefrenable *a* unmanageable, uncontrollable
irrefutable *a* irrefutable
irregular *a* irregular; infrequent, rare
irregularidad *f,* irregularity; abnormality; *inf* moral lapse
irreligión *f,* irreligion
irreligiosidad *f,* impiety, godlessness
irreligioso *a* irreligious, impious
irremediable *a* irremediable
irremediablemente *adv* unavoidably; hopelessly
irremisible *a* unpardonable, inexcusable
irremunerado *a* unremunerated, gratuitous
irreparable *a* irreparable
irreprensible *a* blameless, unexceptionable
irreprochable *a* irreproachable
irresistible *a* irresistible; ravishing
irresolución *f,* vacillation, indecision
irresoluto *a* hesitant, irresolute
irrespetuoso *a* disrespectful
irresponsabilidad *f,* irresponsibility
irresponsable *a* irresponsible
irreverencia *f,* irreverence
irreverente *a* irreverent
irrevocabilidad *f,* irrevocability, finality
irrevocable *a* irrevocable
irrigación *f,* irrigation
irrigador *m,* spray, sprinkler; *med* syringe, spray
irrigar *vt* (*med agr*) to irrigate
irrisible *a* ridiculous, laughable, absurd
irrisión *f,* derision; laughingstock
irrisorio *a* ridiculous; derisive
irritabilidad *f,* irritability, petulance, irascibility
irritable *a* irritable
irritación *f, med* irritation; petulance, exasperation
irritador *a* irritating; exasperating. *m,* irritant
irritante *a* irritating; exasperating
irritar *vt* to exasperate, annoy; provoke, inflame; (*med law*) irritate
írrito *a law* null, void
irrogar *vt* to occasion (damage, harm)
irrompible *a* unbreakable
irrumpir *vi* to enter violently, break in
irrupción *f,* irruption, incursion, invasion

irruptor *a* invading, attacking
isabelino *a* Isabelline (pertaining to Spanish Queen Isabella II (reigned 1830–68)); bay (of horses)
isla *f,* island; block (of houses)
islámico *a* Islamic
islamismo *m,* Islam
islamita *a* and *mf* Muslim
islandés (-esa), islándico (-ca) *a* Icelandic. *n* Icelander. *m,* Icelandic (language)
Islandia Iceland
isleño (-ña) *a* island. *n* islander; native of the Canary Islands
isleta *f,* islet
islote *m,* barren islet
isoca *f, Argentina* caterpillar
isométrico *a* isometric
isomorfo *a* isomorphic
isotermo *a* isothermal
isótope, isótopo *m,* isotope
israelita *mf* Israelite. *a* Israeli
istmeño (-ña) *n* native of an isthmus
ístmico *a* isthmian
istmo *m,* isthmus
Istmo de Suez, el the Suez Canal
Ítaca Ithaca
Italia Italy
italianismo *m,* Italianism
italianizar *vt* to italianize
italiano (-na) *a* and *n* Italian. *m,* Italian (language)
itálico *a* italic
iteración *f,* iteration, repetition
iterar *vt* to repeat, reiterate
iterativo *a* iterative, repetitive
itinerario *a* and *m,* itinerary
izar *vt naut* to hoist
izote *m,* yucca
izquierda *f,* left, left-hand side; *pol* left. **¡I.!** *mil* Left face! **a la i.,** on the left
izquierdo *a* left, left-hand; left-handed; bent, twisted, crooked

J

jaba *f, Lat. Am.* basket; *Mexico* crate
jabalí *m,* wild boar
jabalina *f,* sow of wild boar; javelin
jabato *m,* young wild boar
jabón *m,* soap. **j. blando,** soft soap. **j. de olor** *or* **j. de tocador,** toilet soap. **j. de sastre,** French chalk, steatite
jabonadura *f,* soaping; *pl* soapsuds, lather
jabonar *vt* to soap; wash; *inf* dress down, scold
jaboncillo *m,* toilet soap; steatite
jabonera *f,* soapdish or box; soapwort
jabonería *f,* soap factory or shop
jabonoso *a* soapy
jaca *f,* pony; filly
jacal *m, Mexico* hut, shack
jácara *f,* gay, roguish ballad; song and dance
jácena *f, arch* beam, girder
jacinto *m,* hyacinth; jacinth. **j. de ceilán,** zircon. **j. occidental,** topaz. **j. oriental,** ruby
jaco *m,* short coat of mail; hack, jade
jactancia *f,* bragging, boasting
jactancioso (-sa) *a* boastful. *n* braggart
jactarse *vr* to brag, boast
jaculatoria *f,* ejaculatory prayer
jade *m, min* jade
jadeante *a* panting
jadear *vi* to pant
jadeo *m,* pant; panting; hard breathing
jaez *m,* harness (gen. *pl*); kind, sort; *pl* trappings
jaguar *m,* jaguar
jaiba *f, Lat. Am.* crab
jáibol *m, Lat. Am.* highball
jáilaif *m, Lat. Am.* high life
¡ja, ja, ja! *interj* Ha! ha! ha!
jalbegar *vt* to whitewash; make up the face
jalbegue *m,* whitewash
jalde *a* bright yellow
jalea *f,* jelly. **j. de membrillo,** quince jelly
jalear *vt* to encourage, urge on (by shouts, etc.)
jaleo *m,* act of encouraging dancers by clapping, shouting, etc.; Andalusian song and dance, *inf* uproar
jalón *m,* surveying rod
jamaicano (-na) *a* and *n* Jamaican
jamás *adv* never. **nunca j.,** never. **por siempre j.,** for always, forever
jamba *f,* jamb (of a door or window)
jambarse *vr, Lat. Am.* to overeat
jamelgo *m,* sorry nag, miserable hack
jamón *m,* ham
jamona *f, inf* plumpish middle-aged woman
jansenista *mf* and *a* Jansenist
Japón Japan
japonés (-esa) *a* and *n* Japanese. *m,* Japanese (language)
jaque *m,* check (in chess); braggart. **j. mate,** checkmate. **en j.,** at bay
jaquear *vt* to check (in chess); *mil* harass the enemy
jaqueca *f,* migraine, sick headache. *inf* **dar una j.,** to annoy
jarabe *m,* syrup. **j. tapatío,** Mexican hat dance
jarana *f,* roundhouse; *inf* revelry; fight, roughhouse; trick, deception
jarcia *f,* equipment; *naut* tackle, rigging (gen. *pl*); fishing tackle; *inf* heap, mixture, medley
jardín *m,* garden
jardinar *vt* to landscape
jardinera *f,* plant stand, jardiniere; open streetcar
jardinería *f,* gardening
jardinero (-ra) *n* gardener
jareta *f, sew* running hem; *naut* netting
jarra *f,* jar, jug. **en jarras,** arms akimbo
jarrero *m,* jug seller or manufacturer
jarrete *m,* calf (of the leg)
jarretera *f,* garter. **Orden de la J.,** Order of the Garter
jarro *m,* pitcher; jug; jar; vase
jarrón *m,* garden urn; vase
jaspe *m,* jasper
jaspeado *a* marbled, mottled; dappled; frosted (of glass)
jauja *f, fig* paradise, land of milk and honey
jaula *f,* cage; crate; miner's cage
jauría *f,* pack of hounds
jazmín *m,* jasmine. **j. amarillo,** yellow jasmine. **j. de la India,** gardenia
jefa *f,* forewoman; manager; leader, head
jefatura *f,* chieftainship; managership; leadership. **j. de policía,** police station or headquarters
jefe *m,* chief; head, leader; manager; *mil* commanding officer. *mil* **j. de estado mayor,** chief of staff. **j. del tren,** railroad guard
jengibre *m,* ginger
jeque *m,* sheik
jerarca *m,* hierarch
jerarquía *f,* hierarchy
jerárquico *a* hierarchical
jerez *m,* sherry
jerga *f,* thick frieze cloth; jargon
jergón *m,* straw or hay mattress, pallet; misfit (garments); *inf* fat, lazy person
Jericó Jericho
jerigonza *f,* jargon; gibberish
jeringa *f,* syringe
jeringar *vt* to inject; syringe; *inf* annoy

jeringuilla *f,* small syringe; mock orange
jeroglífico *a* hieroglyphic. *m,* hieroglyph
jersey *m,* jersey, sweater
Jerusalén Jerusalem
jesuita *m,* Jesuit
Jesús *m,* Jesus. *interj* Goodness!; Bless you! (said to someone after sneezing). **¡ay J.!** Alas! *inf* **en un decir J.,** in a trice
jeta *f,* hog's snout; blubber lip; *inf* face, mug
jibia *f,* cuttlefish
jícama *f, Central America* sweet turnip
jícara *f,* small cup
jicote *m, Lat. Am.* wasp
jifa *f,* meat offal
jifia *f,* swordfish
jinete *m,* horseman, rider; horse soldier, cavalryman
jip *m,* jeep
jipijapa *f,* very fine straw. **sombrero de j.,** panama hat
jira *f,* strip of cloth; picnic; tour
jirafa *f,* giraffe
jirón *m,* rag; piece of a dress, etc.; portion of a whole
jitomate, *m, Mexico* tomato. See **tomate**
jiujitsu *m,* jujitsu
jocosidad *f,* pleasantry, jocularity; joke
jocoso *a* waggish; jocose, joyous
jocundidad *f,* jocundity
jocundo *a* jocund
jofaina *f,* washbowl
jónico (-ca) *a* Ionic. *n* Ionian. *m,* (metrics) Ionic foot
Jordán Jordan (river)
jornada *f,* day's journey; journey, trip; *mil* expedition; duration of a working day; opportunity; span of life; act of a drama. **a grandes jornadas,** by forced marches, rapidly
jornal *m,* day's wages or labor
jornalear *vi* to work by the day
jornalero (-ra) *n* day laborer; wage earner
joroba *f,* hump; *inf* impertinence, nuisance
jorobado (-da) *a* humpbacked. *n* hunchback
jota *f,* name of letter J; popular Spanish dance; jot, tittle (always used negatively). **no saber j.,** to be completely ignorant
joven *a* young. *mf* young man or woman
jovenzuelo (-la) *n* youngster, boy
jovialidad *f,* joviality, cheerfulness
joya *f,* jewel; present; *arch* astragal; *fig* a jewel of a person
joyería *f,* jeweler's shop or workshop
joyero *m,* jeweler; jewel box
juanete *m,* bunion; prominent cheekbone; *naut* topgallant sail
juanetudo *a* having bunions; with prominent cheekbones
jubilación *f,* retirement; pensioning off; pension
jubilado *a* retired
jubilar *vt* to pension off; excuse from certain duties; *inf* put aside as useless (things); *vr* rejoice; retire or be pensioned off
jubileo *m,* jubilee
júbilo *m,* rejoicing, merriment. **j. de vivir,** joie de vivre
jubiloso *a* jubilant, happy
jubón *m,* doublet; bodice
judaico *a* Judaic
judaísmo *m,* Judaism
judas *m,* Judas; traitor
judería *f,* Jewry
judesmo *m,* Judezmo (Romance language of Jews)
judía *f,* Jew (female); Jewish quarter, Jewish neighborhood; haricot bean. **judías verdes,** string beans
judicatura *f,* judicature; judgeship; judiciary
judío (-ía) *a* Jewish. *n* Jew. **j. errante,** wandering Jew
juego *m,* play, sport; gambling; hand (of cards); set; suite; *mech* play, working. **j. de café,** coffee set. **j. de los cientos,** piquet. **j. de manos,** sleight of hand, conjuring. **j. de naipes,** game of cards. **j. limpio,** fair play. **j. sencillo,** single (at tennis). **j. sucio,** foul play. **juegos florales,** floral games, poetry contest. **juegos malabares,** juggling. **en j.,** in operation; at stake. **entrar en j.,** to come into play. **hacer j.,** to match. **hacer juegos malabares,** to juggle
juerga *f, inf* spree, binge. **ir de j.,** *inf* to go on a binge
jueves *m,* Thursday. **¡No es cosa del otro j.!** *inf* It's no great shakes! It's nothing to write home about!
juez *m,* judge. **j. arbitrador,** arbitrator; referee. **j. municipal,** magistrate
jugada *f,* play; playing; move, throw; *fig* bad turn
jugador (-ra) *a* gambling; playing. *n* gambler; player. **j. de manos,** conjurer
jugar *vi irr* to play; frolic; take part in a game; gamble; make a move (in a game); *mech* work; handle (a weapon); *com* intervene; *vt* play (a match); bet; handle (a weapon); risk. **j. el lance,** *fig* to play one's cards well. **j. limpio,** to play fair; *fig inf* be straightforward. **j. sucio,** to play foul. **jugarse el todo por el todo,** to stake everything. *Pres. Ind.* **juego, juegas, juega, juegan.** *Pres. Subjunc.* **juegue, juegues, juegue, jueguen**
jugarreta *f, inf* bad play; dirty trick
juglar *m,* entertainer; buffoon, juggler; minstrel
juglaresco *a* pertaining to minstrels
jugo *m,* sap; juice; *fig* essence. **j. de muñeca,** elbow grease
jugosidad *f,* juiciness, succulence; *fig* pithiness
jugoso *a* juicy, succulent; *fig* pithy
juguete *m,* toy; plaything; *fig* puppet
juguetear *vi* to frolic, gambol
jugueteo *m,* gamboling; play, dalliance
juguetería *f,* toy trade; toy shop
juguetón *a* playful
juicio *m,* judgment; wisdom, prudence; sanity, right mind; opinion; horoscope. **j. final,** Last Judgment. **j. sano,** right mind. **asentar el j.,** to settle down, become sensible. **estar fuera de j.,** to be insane. **pedir en j.,** to sue at law
juicioso *a* judicious; prudent
julepear *vt, Lat. Am.* to get scared, be terrified
julio *m,* July; *elec* joule
jumento *m,* ass; beast of burden
juncal *a* reedy; rushy; *inf* slim, lissome
juncar *m,* reedy ground
junco *m, bot* rush, reed; *naut* junk
junio *m,* June
junquillo *m,* jonquil; *arch* reed molding
junta *f,* joint; assembly, council; committee; union, association; session, sitting; entirety, whole; board, management. **j. de comercio,** board of trade. **j. directiva,** managerial board
juntamente *adv* jointly; simultaneously
juntar *vt* to join, unite (*with prep a or con*); couple; assemble; amass; leave ajar (door); *vr* (*with con*) frequent company of; meet; join; copulate
junto *a* united, together. *adv* (*with prep a*) near; *adv* together, simultaneously. **en j.,** altogether, in all
juntura *f,* joining; joint; seam; juncture
jura *f,* solemn oath; swearing
jurado *m,* jury; jury
juramentar *vt* to swear in; *vr* take an oath
juramento *m,* oath; curse, imprecation. **j. falso,** perjury, **prestar j.,** to take an oath
jurar *vt* to swear an oath; swear allegiance; *vi* curse, be profane
jurídico *a* juridical, legal
jurisconsulto *m,* jurisconsult
jurisdicción *f, law* jurisdiction; boundary; authority
jurisprudencia *f,* jurisprudence
jurista *mf* jurist
justa *f,* joust; tournament; contest
justar *vi* to joust
justicia *f,* justice; equity, right; penalty, punishment; righteousness; court of justice; *inf* death penalty, execution. **administrar j.,** to dispense justice

justiciero *a* just
justificable *a* justifiable
justificación *f,* justification, impartiality, fairness; convincing proof
justificar *vt* to justify, vindicate; adjust, regulate; prove innocent; *vr* justify oneself; prove one's innocence
justipreciar *vt* to appraise, value
justiprecio *m,* appraisement, valuation
justo *a* just; righteous, virtuous; exact, accurate; tight-fitting, close. *adv* justly; exactly; tightly
juvenil *a* young
juventud *f,* youthfulness, youth; younger generation
juzgado *m,* court of law; jurisdiction; judgeship
juzgar *vt* to judge, pass sentence on; decide, consider

K

ka *f,* name of the letter K
káiser *m,* kaiser
kan *m,* khan
kantiano *a* Kantian
Kenia Kenya
kermese *f,* kermis, festival
kerosén *m,* kerosene
kilo *prefix* meaning a thousand. *m, abb* kilogram
kilociclo *m, elec* kilocycle
kilogramo *m,* kilogram (2.17 lb.)
kilolitro *m,* kiloliter
kilometraje *m,* number of kilometers; mileage
kilométrico *a* kilometric. **billete k.,** tourist ticket
kilómetro *m,* kilometer (about $\frac{5}{8}$ mile)
kilovatio *m, elec* kilowatt
kiosco *m,* kiosk
klaxon *m, Mexico* horn

L

la *def art. f, sing* the (e.g. **la mesa,** the table). **la** is replaced by el *m, sing* before feminine nouns beginning with stressed *a* or *ha* (e.g. **el hambre,** hunger). **la** is sometimes used before names of famous women (e.g. **la Juana de Arco, la Melba** (Joan of Arc, Melba)) and is generally not translated. *pers pron acc f sing* her; it (e.g. **La veo venir,** I see her coming). *dem. pron* followed by *de,* or by *que* introducing relative clause, that of, that which, the one that, she who (e.g. **La casa está lejos de la en que escribo,** The house is far from the one in which I write). **la de** is used familiarly for Mrs. (e.g. **la de Jiménez,** Mrs. Jimenez). **la** means some, any, one, as substitution for noun already given (e.g. **Su hija lo haría si la tuviera,** Her daughter would do it if she had one)
lábaro *m,* labarum, standard
laberíntico *a* labyrinthine
laberinto *m,* labyrinth; *fig* tangle, complication; *anat* labyrinth of the ear
labia *f, inf* blarney, gab
labial *a* labial
labihendido *a* harelipped
labio *m,* lip; rim, edge. **l. leporino,** harelip. **cerrar los labios,** to close one's lips; keep silent
labor *f,* work, toil; sewing; needlework; husbandry, farming; silkworm egg; *min* working; trimming; plowing, harrowing; *Central America* small farm
laborable *a* workable; cultivable, tillable. **día l.,** workday
laborar *vt* to work; till; plow; construct; *vi* scheme, plot, plan; *Central America* work
laboratorio *m,* laboratory
laborear *vt* to work; till, cultivate; *naut* reeve
laboreo *m,* tilling, cultivation; working, development (of mines, etc.)
laboriosidad *f,* laboriousness, diligence
laborioso *a* industrious, diligent; laborious, tedious, hard
laborista *a* and *mf* belonging to the Labor Party
labra *f,* stonecutting; carving or working (metal, stone, or wood)
labrada *f,* fallow land ready for sowing
labradero *a* workable; cultivable, tillable
labrado *a* and *past part* worked; fashioned; carved; embroidered; figured, patterned. *m,* (gen. *pl*) cultivated ground
labrador *m,* laborer, worker; farmer; peasant
labradora *f,* peasant girl; farm girl
labradoresco, labradoril *a* rustic, peasant, farming
labrandera *f,* seamstress
labrantío *a* tillable, cultivable. *m,* farming
labranza *f,* tillage, cultivation; farm; farmland; farming; employment, work
labrar *vt* to work, do; carve; fashion, construct, make; *agr* cultivate, till; plow; embroider; sew; bring about, cause; *vi fig* impress deeply, leave a strong impression
labriego (-ga) *n* agricultural laborer; peasant
laca *f,* lac; lacquer, varnish; *art* lake (pigment)
lacayo *m,* groom; lackey, footman
lacear *vt sew* to trim with bows; tie, lace; snare, trap; *Lat. Am.* lasso
laceración *f,* laceration
lacerado *a* unhappy, unfortunate; leprous
lacerar *vt* to lacerate, mangle, tear; distress, wound the feelings of
lacería *f,* poverty, misery; toil, drudgery; trouble, affliction
lacero *m,* cowboy, one who uses a lasso; poacher
lacio *a* drooping, limp; withered, faded; straight (hair)
lacónico *a* laconic; concise; Laconian
lacra *f,* aftereffect, trace (of illness); vice; fault; *Lat. Am.* sore, ulcer
lacrar *vt* to impair the health; infect with an illness; injure, prejudice (the interests, etc.); seal with sealing wax
lacre *m,* sealing wax. *a* red
lacrimoso *a* tearful, lachrymose
lactancia *f,* lactation
lactar *vt* to suckle; feed with milk; *vi* take or drink milk
lácteo *a* lacteal; milky
ladear *vt* to incline; tilt; turn aside, twist; skirt, pass close to; reach by a roundabout way, go indirectly to; *vr* tilt; be in favor of, incline to; be equal to
ladeo *m,* tilt; sloping; turning aside
ladera *f,* slope, incline; hillside
ladería *f,* terrace on a hillside
ladero *a* lateral; *Argentina* helper
ladilla *f,* crab louse
ladino *a* eloquent; versatile linguistically; wily, crafty; *m,* Ladino (variety of Judezmo)
lado *m,* side; edge, margin; slope, declivity; faction, party; side, flank; face (of a coin); *fig* aspect, view; line of descent; means, way; favor, protection; *pl* helpers, protectors; advisers. **al l.,** near at hand. *inf* **dar de l. (a),** to cool off, fall out with. **dejar a un l. (una cosa),** to omit, pass over (a thing). **mirar de l.** *or* **de medio l.,** to look upon with disapproval; steal a look at

ladrar *vi* to bark; *inf* threaten without hurting
ladrido *m,* bark, barking; slander, gossip
ladrillado *m,* brick floor or pavement
ladrillar *vt* to floor or pave with bricks. *m,* brickyard; brickkiln
ladrillo *m,* brick; tile
ladrón (-ona) *a* robbing, thieving. *n* thief, robber; burglar. *m.* **l. de corazones,** ladykiller
ladronera *f,* thieves' den; thieving, pilfering; strongbox
lagar *m,* wine or olive press
lagarta *f,* female lizard; *inf* she-serpent, cunning female
lagartera *f,* lizard hole
lagartija *f,* wall lizard, small lizard
lagarto *m,* lizard; *inf* sly, artful person, fox; *inf* insignia of Spanish Military Order of Santiago
lago *m,* lake
lagotear *vi inf* to wheedle, play up to
lagotería *f,* wheedling, coaxing, flattery
lágrima *f,* tear; drop (of liquid); exudation, ozzing (from trees)
lagrimal *a* lachrymal
lagrimear *vi* to shed tears
lagrimeo *m,* weeping, crying; watering of the eyes
lagrimoso *a* tearful; watery (of eyes); sad, tragic
laguna *f,* small lake, lagoon; lacuna; gap, hiatus
lagunoso *a* boggy, marshy
laicismo *m,* secularism
laico *a* lay, secular
laja *f, Lat. Am.* flagstone, slab
lama *f,* ooze, slime. *m,* lama, Buddhist priest
lamaísmo *m,* lamaism
lambioche *a, Mexico* cringing, fawning
lameculos *mf inf* toady
lamedura *f,* licking; lapping
lamentable *a* lamentable
lamentación *f,* lamentation; lament
lamentador (-ra) *a* lamenting, wailing. *n* wailer, mourner
lamentar *vt* to mourn, lament, bewail; *vr* bemoan, bewail
lamento *m,* lament
lamentoso *a* lamenting, afflicted; lamentable
lamer *vt* to lick; pass the tongue over; touch lightly; lap
lámina *f,* sheet (of metal); lamina; engraving; illustration, picture; engraving plate
laminación *f,* lamination, rolling (of metals)
laminado *a* laminate; rolled (metals). *m,* rolling (of metals)
laminador *m,* rolling mill (for metals)
laminar *a* laminate; laminated. *vt* to roll (metals); laminate; lick
lampa *f, Chile, Peru* hoe
lámpara *f,* lamp; radiance, light, luminous body; grease spot. **l. de los mineros** *or* **l. de seguridad,** safety lamp. **l. de soldar,** blowpipe. **l. termiónica,** *rad* thermionic valve. **atizar la l.,** to trim the lamp; *inf* refill drinking glasses
lamparería *f,* lamp factory; lamp shop
lamparero (-ra), *n* **lamparista** *mf* lamplighter; lamp maker or seller
lamparilla *f,* night-light; *bot* aspen; small lamp
lamparón *m,* scrofula, king's evil; tumor (disease of horses)
lampazo *m, Lat. Am.* (floor) mop
lampiño *a* beardless, clean-shaven; smooth-faced; *bot* nonhirsute
lampista *mf* See **lamparero**
lamprea *f,* lamprey
lana *f,* wool; fleece; woolen garments or cloth; woolen trade (gen. *pl*)
lanar *a* wool; wool-bearing. **ganado l.,** sheep
lance *m,* throw, cast; casting a fishing line; catch of fish; crisis, difficult moment; *lit* episode; quarrel; move (in a game). *fig* **l. apretado,** difficult position, tight corner. **l. de fortuna,** chance, fate. **l. de honor,** affair of honor; duel
lancear *vt* to wound with a lance; lance
lancero *m, mil* lancer; *pl* lancers (dance and music)
lanceta *f,* lancet; *Lat. Am.* goad
lancha *f, naut* launch; lighter; ship's boat; small boat; flagstone. **l. bombardera** *or* **l. cañonera,** gunboat. **l. de salvamento,** ship's lifeboat. **l. escampavía,** patrol boat
lancinar *vt med* to lance
landa *f,* lande
landó *m,* landau
lanero *a* woolen. *m,* wool merchant; wool warehouse
langosta *f,* locust; lobster. **l. migratoria,** locust
langostín *m,* crayfish
languidecer *vi irr* to languish, pine. See **conocer**
languidez *f,* lassitude, inertia; languor
lánguido *a* listless, weak, languid; halfhearted; languishing, languorous
lanolina *f,* lanolin
lanosidad *f,* woolliness; down (on leaves, etc.)
lanoso, lanudo *a* woolly
lanza *f,* lance, spear; lancer; nozzle (of a hosepipe). **correr lanzas,** to joust (in a tournament). **estar con la l. en ristre,** to have the lance in rest; be prepared or ready. *inf* **ser una l.,** to be very clever
lanzabombas *m,* (*aer nav*) bomb release
lanzada *f,* lance or spear thrust
lanzadera *f,* weaver's shuttle; sewing machine shuttle. *inf* **parecer una l.,** to be constantly on the go
lanzador (-ra) *m,* batsman. *n* thrower, caster, tosser
lanzallamas *m,* flamethrower
lanzamiento *m,* throwing; cast, throw; *law* dispossession; *naut* launching
lanzaminas *m,* minelayer
lanzar *vt* to throw, cast, hurl; *naut* launch; vomit; *law* dispossess; *agr* take root; *vr* hurl oneself, rush; take (to), embark (upon)
lanzatorpedos (tubo) *m,* torpedo tube
lañar *vt* to clamp; clean fish (for salting)
lapa *f,* barnacle, limpet; *Mexico* scrounger
lapicera *f, Argentina* ballpoint (pen)
lapicero *m,* pencil holder, pencil case; mechanical pencil
lápida *f,* memorial tablet; gravestone
lapidar *vt* to stone, lapidate; throw stones at
lapidario *a* lapidary
lapislázuli *m,* lapis lazuli
lápiz *m,* graphite; pencil; crayon. **l. para los labios,** lipstick
lapizar *m,* graphite mine. *vt* to pencil
lapón (-ona) *a* Lappish. *n* Laplander. *m,* Sami (language)
lapso *m,* lapse, period, passage; slip, error, failure
laquear *vt* to lacquer, paint
lardear *vt cul* to baste
lardo *m,* lard; animal fat
lardoso *a* greasy; fat; oily
larga *f,* longest billiard cue; delay (gen. *pl*). **a la l.,** in the long run
largamente *adv* fully, at length; generously; widely, extensively; comfortably
largar *vt* to slacken, loosen; *naut* unfurl; set at liberty; *fig inf* let fly (oaths, etc.); administer (blows, etc.); *vr inf* quit, leave (in a hurry or secretly); *naut* set sail
largo *a* long; generous, liberal; abundant, plentiful; protracted; prolonged; expeditious; *pl* many long (e.g. **por largos años,** for many long years). *m, mus* largo; length. *inf* **¡L. de aquí!** Get out! **a la larga,** in length; eventually, finally; slowly; with many digressions. **a lo l.,** lengthwise; along the length (of); in the distance, far off; along, the length (of). *fig* **ponerse de l.,** to make one's debut in society; come of age
largor *m,* **largura** *f,* length
largucho, -a *a, Lat. Am.* lanky
largueza *f,* length; generosity, munificence
largura *f,* length
laringe *f,* larynx
laríngeo *a* laryngeal

laringitis *f,* laryngitis
larva *f,* larva; worm, grub; specter, phantom
las *def art. f pl,* of **la** the. *pers pron acc f pl,* of **la,** them
lascivia *f,* lasciviousness
lascivo *a* lascivious, lewd; wanton
lasitud *f,* lassitude, weariness, exhaustion
laso *a* weary, exhausted; weak; untwisted (of silk, etc.)
lástima *f,* compassion, pity; pitiful sight; complaint, lamentation. **dar l.,** to cause pity. **Es l.,** It's a pity. **tener l.** (**a** *or* **de**) **to be sorry for (persons)**
lastimador *a* harmful, injurious; painful
lastimadura *f, Lat. Am.* injury, wound
lastimar *vt* to hurt, harm, injure; pity; *fig* wound, distress; *vr* (*with de*) be sorry for or about; complain, lament
lastimero *a* pitiful; mournful; injurious, harmful
lastimoso *a* pitiful, heartbreaking; mournful
lastrar *vt* to ballast
lastre *m,* ballast; good sense, prudence
lata *f,* can, tin; tin plate; can of food. **en l.,** canned, tinned (of food). *inf* **Es una l.,** It's a bore, It's an awful nuisance
latamente *adv* extensively, at length; broadly
latente *a* latent
lateral *a* lateral
látex *m,* latex
latido *m,* yelp, bark; beat; throb; palpitation
latifundios *m pl,* latifundia (large agricultural estates)
latigazo *m,* lash; crack of a whip; sudden blow of fate; *inf* draft (of wine, etc.); harsh scolding; *naut* jerk or flapping (of sails)
látigo *m,* whip, lash; cinch, girth of a saddle
latín *m,* Latin. **bajo l.,** low Latin. *inf* **saber l.,** to know the score; be smart
latinajo *m, inf* bad Latin
latinismo *m,* Latinism
latinista *mf* Latinist
latinizar *vt* to latinize; *vi inf* use Latin phrases
latino *a* Latin; lateen sail
latinoamericano (-na) *a* and *n* Latin-American
latir *vi* to yelp, howl; bark; throb, palpitate, beat **me late que . . .** *Mexico,* I have a hunch that . . .
latitud *f,* latitude; area, extent; breadth
latitudinario *a* latitudinarian
lato *a* extensive; large; broad (of word meanings)
latón *m,* brass
latonería *f,* brassworks; brass shop
latoso *a* boring, troublesome, annoying
latrocinio *m,* larceny
latvio (-ia) *a* and *n* Latvian
laúd *m,* lute
laudable *a* praiseworthy, laudable
laudatorio *a* laudatory
laurear *vt* to crown with laurel; honor, reward
laurel *m,* bay tree. **l. cerezo,** laurel. **l. rosa,** rosebay, oleander
láureo *a* laurel
lauréola *f,* laurel wreath
lauro *m,* bay tree; glory, triumph
Lausana Lausanne
lava *f,* lava
lavable *a* washable
lavabo *m,* washstand; cloakroom, lavatory
lavada *f,* load of wash, load
lavadedos *m,* fingerbowl
lavadero *m,* washing place; laundry
lavado *m,* washing; cleaning; wash. **l. al seco,** dry cleaning
lavadura *f,* washing
lavamanos *m,* washstand; lavatory
lavamiento *m,* washing, cleansing, ablution
lavanda *f,* lavender
lavandera *f,* laundress; washerwoman
lavandería *f,* laundry
lavandero *m,* laundry; laundryman
lavaplatos *m,* dishwasher; *Chile, Mexico* (kitchen) sink
lavar *vt* to wash; *fig* wipe out, purify; paint in watercolors. **l. al seco,** to dry-clean
lavativa *f,* enema; syringe, clyster; *inf* nuisance, bore
lavatorio *m,* washing, lavation; *ecc* lavabo; lavatory, washing place; *ecc* maundy
lavazas *f pl,* dirty soapy water
laxante *a* and *m,* laxative
laxar *vt* to loosen, relax; soften
laxitud *f,* laxity
laxo *a* lax; slack
laya *f, agr* spade; kind, sort, class
layar *vt agr* to fork
lazar *vt* to lasso
lazareto *m,* leper hospital; quarantine hospital
lazarillo *m,* boy who guides a blind person
lázaro *m,* lazar, beggar
lazo *m,* bow; knot of ribbons; tie; ornamental tree; figure (in dancing); lasso; rope, bond; lace (of a shoe); *fig* trap, snare; bond, obligation; slipknot. **l. corredizo,** running knot. *fig inf* **armar l.,** to set a trap. *inf* **caer en el l.,** to fall into the trap, be deceived
le *pers pron dat m,* or *f, 3rd pers sing* to him, to her, to it, to you (e.g. **María le dio el perro,** Mary gave him (her, you) the dog). Clarity may require the addition of **a él, a ella, a usted** (e.g. **Le dio el perro a ella,** etc.). *pers pron acc m, 3rd pers sing* him (e.g. **Le mandé a casa,** I sent him home)
leal *a* loyal; faithful (animals)
lealtad *f,* loyalty; faithfulness; sincerity, truth
lebrel *m,* greyhound
lección *f,* reading; lesson; oral test; warning, example. **l. práctica,** object lesson. **dar l.,** to give a lesson. **tomar la l.,** to hear a lesson
leccionista *mf* private teacher, coach, tutor
lechas *f pl,* soft roe; milt
leche *f,* milk; milky fluid of some plants and seeds; *Lat. Am.* good luck. *inf* **estar con la l. en los labios,** to be young and inexperienced
lechera *f,* milkmaid; milk can or jug; *Lat. Am.* cow
lechería *f,* dairy; dairy shop; *Lat. Am.* meanness
lechero (-ra) *a* dairy, milk; milky; milch, milk-giving. *n* milk seller. **industria lechera,** dairy farming
lecho *m,* bed; couch; animal's bed, litter; riverbed; bottom of the sea; layer; *geol* stratum
lechón *m,* suckling pig; hog; *inf* slovenly man
lechosa *f, Dominican Republic, Venezuela,* papaya
lechoso *a* milky
lechudo, -a *a, Lat. Am.* lucky
lechuga *f,* lettuce; frill, flounce. *inf* **como una l.,** as fresh as a daisy
lechuguero (-ra) *n* lettuce seller
lechuguilla *f,* ruff; ruche
lechuguina *f, inf* affected, overdressed young woman
lechuguino *m,* lettuce plant; *inf* young blood, gallant; *inf* foppish young man
lechuza *f,* barn owl
lector (-ra) *n* reader; lecturer
lectura *f,* reading; lecture; culture, knowledge
ledo *a* happy, content
leer *vt irr* to read; explain, interpret; teach; take part in an oral test. See **creer**
lega *f, ecc* lay sister
legación *f, ecc* legateship; legation
legado *m,* legacy; legate
legajo *m,* bundle, docket; file
legal *a* legal; legitimate; upright, trustworthy
legalidad *f,* legality
legalización *f,* legalization
legalizar *vt* to legalize
legamente *adv* ignorantly, stupidly
légamo *m,* mud, slime
legamoso *a* slimy
legañoso *a* bleary-eyed
legar *vt* to bequeath; send as a legate
legatario (-ia) *n* legatee, one to whom a legacy is bequeathed

legendario *a* legendary
legibilidad *f,* legibility
legible *a* legible
legión *f,* legion
legionario *a* and *m,* legionary
legislación *f,* legislation
legislador (-ra) *a* legislative. *n* legislator
legislar *vi* to legislate
legislativo *a* legislative
legislatura *f,* legislature
legista *mf* jurist; student of law
legítima *f,* portion of a married man's estate that cannot be willed away from his wife and children
legitimación *f,* legitimation
legitimar *vt* to legitimize
legitimidad *f,* legitimacy
legítimo *a* legitimate; real, true
lego *a* lay, secular. *m,* layman
legua *f,* league (approximately 5.573 meters). **a la l., de cien leguas, desde media l.,** from afar
legumbre *f,* pulse; vegetable
leída *f, Lat. Am.* reading. **de una leída** in one reading, at one go
leído *a* well-read
leila *f,* nocturnal Moorish merrymaking or dance
lejanía *f,* distance
lejano *a* distant, remote, far off
lejía *f,* lye; bleaching solution; *inf* dressing-down, scolding
lejos *adv* far off, far, distant. *m,* perspective, view from afar; *art* background. **a lo l.,** far off, in the distance. **de** *or* **desde l.,** from afar, from a distance
lelo *a* stupid; fatuous, inane
lema *m,* chapter heading; argument, summary; motto; theme, subject
lémur *m,* lemur
lencería *f,* linen goods; linen merchant's shop; linen closet
lencero *m,* linen merchant
lene *a* smooth, soft; kind, sweet, gentle; lightweight
lengua *f, anat* tongue; mother tongue, language; clapper of a bell; information. *mf* spokes. **l. de escorpión** *or* **mala l.,** scandalmonger, backbiter. **l. de fuego,** *ecc* tongue of fire, flame. **l. del agua,** waterline, tidemark. **l. de oc,** langue d'oc. **l. de oil,** langue d'oil. **l. de tierra,** neck of land, promontory. **l. viva,** modern language. *inf* **andar en lenguas,** to be on every lip, be famous. *inf* **hacerse lenguas de,** to praise to the skies. *inf* **irse (a uno) la l.,** to be indiscreet, talk too much. **poner l.** *or* **lenguas en,** to gossip about. *inf* **tener mucha l.,** to be very talkative. **tomar l.** *or* **lenguas,** to find out about, inform oneself on
lenguado *m, icht* sole
lenguaje *m,* language; style; speech, idiom. **l. vulgar,** common speech
lengüeta *f, dim* little tongue; *mus* tongue (of wind instruments); barb (of an arrow); needle (of a balance)
lengüeterías *Lat. Am.* gossip
lenidad *f,* lenience, indulgence, mercy
lenitivo *a* lenitive; soothing. *m, med* lenitive; *fig* balm (of sorrow, etc.)
lente *m,* lens; *pl* eyeglasses. **l. de aumento,** magnifying glass
lenteja *f,* lentil; lentil plant
lentejuela *f,* sequin
lentitud *f,* lentitude; slowness, deliberation
lento *a* slow, deliberate; sluggish, heavy; *med* glutinous, adhesive
leña *f,* firewood; *inf* beating, birching. *fig* **echar l. al fuego,** to add fuel to the flame. *fig* **llevar l. al monte,** to carry coals to Newcastle
leñador (-ra) *n* woodcutter; firewood dealer
leñera *f,* woodpile; woodshed
leño *m,* wooden log; wood, timber; *poet* ship; *inf* blockhead
leñoso *a* woody, ligneous
león *m,* lion. *ast* Leo; valiant man; *Lat. Am.* puma. **l. marino,** sea lion
leona *f,* lioness; *Chile* confusion, mixup
leonera *f,* lion cage; lion's den; *inf* gambling den; *inf* lumber room; *Mexico* whore house
leonero (-ra) *n* lionkeeper; *inf* keeper of a gambling house
leonés (-esa) *a* and *n* Leonese
leopardo *m,* leopard
leperada *f, Central America, Mexico* coarse remark
lepra *f,* leprosy
leproso *a* leprous
lerdo *a* slow, lumbering (gen. horses); stupid, slow-witted, dull
les *pers pron dat 3rd pers pl mf,* to them (e.g. **Les dimos las flores,** We gave them flowers. **Les hablé del asunto,** I spoke to them about the matter)
lesbio (-ia) *a* and *n* lesbian
lesión *f,* lesion, wound; *fig* injury
lesionar *vt* to wound; *fig* injure
lesna *f,* awl
leso *a* wounded, hurt; offensive, injurious; *fig* unbalanced, perturbed (of the mind); *Lat. Am.* dumb, stupid. **crimen de lesa majestad,** crime of lèse-majesté
letal *a* lethal; deadly
letanía *f, ecc* litany
letargia *f, med* lethargy
letárgico *a* lethargic
letargo *m,* lethargy; indifference, apathy
letra *f,* letter (of alphabet); *print* type; penmanship, hand; *fig* letter, literal meaning; words (of a song); inscription; *com* bill, draft; cunning, shrewdness; *pl* learning, knowledge. **l. abierta,** *com* open credit. **l. de cambio,** *com* bill of exchange. **l. gótica,** Gothic characters. **l. itálica,** italics. **l. mayúscula,** capital letter. **l. paladial,** palatal. **facultad de letras,** faculty of arts. **La l. con sangre entra,** Learning is acquired with pain. **primeras letras,** early education, first letters
letrado *a* learned, educated; *inf* presumptuous; pedantic. *m,* lawyer
letrero *m,* label; inscription; poster, bill; sign, indicator. **l. luminoso,** illuminated sign
letrilla *f,* short poem, often set to music
letrina *f,* latrine
leva *f, naut* weighing anchor; *mil* levy, forced enrolment; tappet; *mech* lever; *mech* cam; *inf* **irse a l. y a monte,** to flee, beat it, quit
levadizo *a* able to be raised or lowered (bridges). **puente l.,** drawbridge
levadura *f,* leaven, yeast; rising (of bread)
levantada *f,* act of rising from bed
levantamiento *m,* raising, lifting; rebellion, revolt; ennoblement, elevation; settlement of accounts
levantar *vt* to raise, lift; pick up; build, construct; cancel, remove; encourage, rouse; recruit, enlist; cut (cards); leave, abandon; survey; disturb (game); produce, raise (a swelling); found, institute; increase (prices); raise (the voice); *fig* ennoble, elevate; cause, occasion; libel, accuse falsely; *vr* rise; get up; stand up; stand out, be prominent; rebel; leave one's bed after an illness. **l. bandera,** to rebel. **l. el campo,** to break camp. **levantarse del izquierdo,** *inf* to get out of bed on the wrong side
levante *m,* east; Levant; east wind
levantino (-na) *a* and *n* Levantine
levar *vt naut* to weigh anchor; *vr* set sail
leve *a* light (in weight); unimportant, trifling
levedad *f,* lightness (in weight); unimportance, levity, flippancy
leviatán *m,* leviathan
levita *m,* Levite; deacon. *f,* frock coat
levitación *f,* levitation
levítico *a* Levitical. *m,* Leviticus
levitón *m,* frock coat
léxico *m,* lexicon

lexicografía *f*, lexicography
lexicógrafo *m*, lexicographer
lexicólogo *m*, lexicologist
ley *f*, law; precept; regulation, rule; doctrine; loyalty, faithfulness; affection, love; legal standard (weights, measures, quality); ratio of gold or silver in coins, jewelry; statute, ordinance; *pl* the Law. **l. de préstamo y arriendo,** Lend-Lease Act. **ley suntuaria,** sumptuary law. *inf* **a la l.,** with care and decorum. **a l. de caballero,** on the word of a gentleman. **de buena l.,** *a* excellent; *adv* genuinely; in good faith. **de mala l.,** *a* disreputable, base; *adv* in bad faith
leyenda *f*, legend; inscription; story, tale
leyente *a* reading. *mf* reader
lezna *f*, awl
lía *f*, plaited esparto rope; *pl* lees, dregs
liar *vt* to fasten or tie up; wrap up, parcel; roll (a cigarette); *inf* entangle, embroil; *vr* take a lover, enter on a liaison. *inf* **liarlas,** to quit, sneak off; *inf* kick the bucket, die
libación *f*, libation
Líbano, el Lebanon
libar *vt* to suck; perform a libation; sip, taste; sacrifice
libelista *mf* libeler
libelo *m*, libel; *law* petition
libélula *f*, dragonfly
liberación *f*, liberation, freeing; receipt, quittance; *law* reconveyance (of mortgages)
liberador (-ra) *a* liberating, freeing. *n* liberator
liberal *a* generous, openhanded; liberal, tolerant; learned (of professions). *a* and *mf pol* liberal
liberalidad *f*, generosity, magnanimity
liberalismo *m*, liberalism
liberalizar *vt* to liberalize, make liberal
liberar *vt* to liberate
libérrimo *a sup* extremely free, most free
libertad *f*, liberty, freedom; independence; privilege, right (gen. *pl*); exemption; licentiousness; forwardness, familiarity; naturalness, ease of manner; facility, capacity; immunity. **l. caucional,** freedom on bail, release on bail. **l. de cultos,** freedom of worship; religious toleration. **l. vigilada,** *law* probation. **poner en l.,** to set at liberty; (*with de*) *fig* free from
libertador (-ra) *a* liberating, freeing. *n* liberator, deliverer
libertar *vt* to liberate, free; save, deliver; exempt
libertario (-ia) *a* anarchistic. *n* anarchist
libertinaje *m*, libertinage, licentiousness
libertino (-na) *a* debauched, licentious. *m*, libertine. *n* child of a freed slave
liberto (-ta) *n* freed slave, freedman
Libia Libya
libídine *f*, lust
libidinoso *a* libidinous, lustful
libio (-ia) *a* and *n* Libyan
libra *f*, pound (measure, coinage); *ast* Libra. **l. esterlina,** pound sterling. **l. medicinal,** pound troy
libración *f*, oscillation; *ast* libration
librador (-ra) *a* freeing, liberating. *n* deliverer, liberator. *m*, *com* drawer (of bill of exchange, etc.)
libramiento *m*, liberation, deliverance; *com* delivery; order of payment
libranza *f*, *com* draft. **l. de correos, l. postal** *Lat. Am.* (postal) money order
librar *vt* to liberate, free; protect (from misfortune); *com* draw (a draft); *com* deliver; place confidence in; issue, enact; *vi* bring forth children; *vr* (*with de*) escape from; get rid of
libre *a* free; at liberty, disengaged; unhampered, untrammeled; independent; bold, brazen; dissolute, vicious; exempt; vacant, unoccupied; unmarried; clear, free; mutinous, rebellious; isolated, remote; innocent; unharmed; *Mexico, Venezuela* taxi. **l. cambio,** free trade
librea *f*, livery
librecambio *m*, free trade
librecambista *a* free trade. *mf* free trader
librepensador (-ra) *a* freethinking. *n* freethinker
librepensamiento *m*, free thought
librera *f*, *Lat. Am.* bookcase
librería *f*, bookshop; book trade, bookselling; bookcase
librero *m*, bookseller; *Lat. Am.* bookcase. **l. anticuario,** antiquarian bookseller; rare-book dealer
libreta *f*, *cul* 1-lb. loaf; notebook; passbook, bankbook
libretista *mf* librettist
libreto *m*, libretto
librillo *m*, *dim* small book; book of cigarette papers; tub, pail; *zool* omasum
libro *m*, book; *mus* libretto; *zool* omasum. **l. copiador,** *com* letter book. **l. de actas,** minute book. **l. de caja,** *com* cash book. **l. de cheques,** checkbook. **l. de facturas,** *com* invoice book. **l. de reclamaciones,** complaint book. **l. de texto,** textbook. **l. diario,** *com* daybook. **l. mayor,** ledger. **l. talonario,** receipt book. *fig inf* **hacer l. nuevo,** to turn over a new leaf; introduce innovations
licencia *f*, permission, license; licentiousness; boldness, insolence; *univ* bachelor's degree, licentiate. **l. absoluta,** *mil* discharge. **l. de manejar** *Lat. Am.* driver's license
licenciado (-da) *a* pedantic; free, exempt; licensed. *n univ* bachelor; licentiate. *m*, discharged soldier
licenciar *vt* to allow, permit; license; dismiss, discharge; confer degree of bachelor or licentiate; *mil* discharge; *vr* become licentious; receive bachelor's degree or licentiate
licenciatura *f*, degree of licentiate or bachelor; graduation as such; licentiate course of study
licencioso *a* licentious, dissolute
liceo *m*, lyceum; *Lat. Am.* secondary school, high school
licitación *f*, bidding (at auction)
licitador *m*, bidder (at auction); *Lat. Am.* auctioneer
licitar *vt* to bid for (at auction)
lícito *a* permissible, lawful
licor *m*, liquor, alcoholic drink; liquid
licorera *f*, liqueur set; decanter
licuadora *f*, blender
licuar *vt* to liquefy
lid *f*, combat, fight; dispute, controversy. **en buena l.,** in fair fight; by fair means
líder *m*, leader; chief
lidia *f*, fighting; bullfight
lidiador (-ra) *n* combatant, fighter
lidiar *vi* to fight; *fig* struggle; (*with contra or con*) oppose, fight against; *vt* fight (a bull). **¡Cuánto tienen que l. con . . . !** *fig* What a struggle they have with . . . !
liebre *f*, hare
liendre *f*, nit
lienza *f*, narrow strip (of cloth)
lienzo *m*, linen; cotton; cambric; hemp cloth; *art* canvas
liga *f*, garter; bandage; birdlime; mixture, blend; *met* alloy; alliance, coalition; league (football, etc.)
ligación *f*, tying; binding; union
ligado *m*, *mus* legato; *mus* tie
ligadura *f*, bond, tie; binding, fastening; *fig* shackle, link; (*surg mus*) ligature; *naut* lashing
ligamento *m*, tie, bond; mixture; *anat* ligament
ligar *vt* to tie, bind; *met* alloy; join, connect; render impotent by sorcery; *mus* slur (notes); *vr* ally, join together; *fig* bind oneself. **l. cabos,** to put two and two together
ligazón *f*, fastening; union; bond
ligereza *f*, lightness (of weight); swiftness, nimbleness; fickleness; tactless remark, indiscretion
ligero *a* light (in weight); swift, nimble; light (sleep); unimportant, insignificant; easily digested (food); thin (fabrics, etc.); fickle, changeable. **l. de cascos,** frivolous, gay. **a la ligera,** lightly; quickly; without fuss. **de l.,** impetuously, thoughtlessly; easily, with ease
lignito *m*, lignite
lija *f*, dogfish; sandpaper
lijar *vt* to sandpaper
lila *f*, lilac bush and flower; lilac color. *a inf* foolish, vain

liliputiense *a* and *mf* Lilliputian
lima *f*, sweet lime, citron fruit; lime tree; file (tool); filing, polishing
limadura *f*, filing; polishing; *pl* filings
limar *vt* to file, smooth with a file; *fig* touch up, polish
limazo *m*, slime, viscosity (especially of snails, etc.)
limbo *m*, limbo; edge, hem; (*ast bot*) limb; limb (of a quadrant, etc.). *inf* **estar en el l.,** to be bewildered or abstracted
limen *m*, *poet* threshold; *psy* limen
limeño (-ña) *a* and *n* native of or belonging to Lima (Peru)
limero (-ra) *n* seller of sweet limes. *m*, sweet lime tree (citron)
limitación *f*, limitation; limit, extent, bound; district, area
limitado *a* dull-witted, limited
limitar *vt* to limit; curb, restrict; bound
límite *m*, limit, extent; boundary, border; end, confine
limítrofe *a* bordering, contiguous
limo *m*, mud, mire, slime; *Lat. Am.* lime tree
limón *m*, lemon; lemon tree
limonada *f*, lemonade. **l. seca,** lemonade powder
limonar *m*, lemon grove
limonero (-ra) *n* lemon seller. *m*, lemon tree
limosna *f*, alms
limosnear *vi* to beg, ask alms
limosnero, -a *a* charitable, generous. *a* charitable, generous. *mf* almoner; *Lat. Am.* beggar
limoso *a* slimy, muddy
limpiabarros *m*, shoe scraper
limpiabotas *m*, bootblack (person)
limpiachimeneas *m*, chimney-sweep
limpiador (-ra) *a* cleaning. *n* cleaner
limpiadura *f*, cleaning; *pl* rubbish
limpiamanos *m*, *Central America, Mexico* towel
limpiamente *adv* cleanly; dexterously, neatly; sincerely, candidly; generously, charitably
limpiametales *m*, metal polish
limpiaparabrisas *m*, windshield wiper
limpiapipas *m*, pipe cleaner
limpiar *vt* to clean; *fig* cleanse, clear; empty, free (from); *agr* thin out; *inf* steal, pinch; *inf* win (gambling); *vr* clean oneself
limpiauñas *m*, orange stick (for fingernails)
limpidez *f*, *poet* limpidity
límpido *a poet* limpid
limpieza *f*, cleanliness; cleaning; chastity; purity; altruism; uprightness, integrity; neatness, tidiness; dexterity, skill, precision; fair play
limpio *a* clean; pure, unalloyed, unmixed; neat, tidy; pure-blooded; unharmed, free. **en l.,** in substance; as a fair copy; clearly; *com* net
linaje *m*, lineage, family; offspring; kind; sort, quality
linajudo (-da) *a* highborn. *n* noble, aristocrat; one who alleges his noble descent
linaza *f*, linseed
lince *m*, lynx; *Mexico* wild cat; *fig.* fox, crafty person
linchamiento *m*, lynching
linchar *vt* to lynch
lindar *vi* to run together, be contiguous
linde *mf* limit, extent; boundary
lindero *a* bordering, contiguous. *m*, boundary. *inf* **con linderos y arrabales,** with many digressions
lindeza *f*, beauty, loveliness; witticism; *pl* (*inf ironical*) insults
lindo *a* lovely, beautiful; perfect, exquisite. *m*, *inf* fop (gen. **lindo don Diego**)
línea *f*, line; kind, class; ancestry, lineage; limit, extent; *mil* file; equator. **l. aérea,** airline. *naut* **l. de flotación,** waterline. **l. de toque,** touchline (in soccer). **l. recta,** direct line (of descent)
lineal *a* lineal; *computers* on-line
lineamento *m*, lineament
linear *a* linear. *vt* to line, mark with lines; *art* sketch
linfa *f*, *med* lymph; vaccine; *poet* water
linfático *a* lymphatic
lingote *m*, ingot; bar (of iron). **l. de fundición,** pig iron
lingüista *mf* linguist
lingüística *f*, linguistics
lingüístico *a* linguistic
linimento *m*, liniment
lino *m*, *bot* flax; linen; *poet* ship's sail, canvas
linóleo *m*, linoleum
linotipia *f*, linotype
linterna *f*, lantern; lighthouse; lamp. **l. sorda,** dark lantern
lío *m*, bundle; *inf* muddle, imbroglio; *inf* liaison, amour. *inf* **armar un l.,** to make a muddle, cause trouble. *inf* **hacerse un l.,** to get in a fix; get in a muddle
liquen *m*, lichen
liquidable *a* liquefiable
liquidación *f*, liquefaction; *com* clearance, sale; *com* settlement
liquidar *vt* to liquefy; *com* settle; *com* liquidate; finish; *vr* liquefy
liquidez *f*, liquidness
líquido *a* liquid; *com* net. *m*, liquid; *com* net profit
lira *f*, *mus* lyre; *ast* Lyra; lira (coin)
lírica *f*, lyrical verse, lyric
lírico *a* lyrical
lirio *m*, lily. **l. cárdeno,** yellow flag (iris). **l. de los valles,** lily of the valley
lirismo *m*, lyricism
lirón *m*, *zool* dormouse; *inf* sleepyhead
Lisboa Lisbon
lisiado *a* lame, crippled
lisiar *vt* to cripple, lame; *vr* be disabled; be lame
liso *a* smooth; sleek; unadorned, plain; unicolored
lisonja *f*, flattery, adulation
lisonjear *vt* to flatter; fawn upon; *fig* delight (the ear). **lisonjearse de . . . ,** to flatter oneself on . . .
lisonjero (-ra) *a* flattering; sweet, pleasant (sounds). *n* flatterer
lista *f*, strip of cloth; streak; rib; stripe; catalog, list. **l. de correos,** general delivery, poste restante. **l. de platos,** bill of fare; *Mexico* **l. de raya** payroll. **pasar l.,** to call the roll; check the list
listado *a* streaked; striped; ribbed
listo *a* clever; expeditious, diligent; ready, prepared
listón *m*, ribbon; strip (of wood)
lisura *f*, smoothness; sleekness; flatness; sincerity
lisurero, -a, *a*, *Peru* cheeky, impudent
litera *f*, litter; *naut* berth
literal *a* literal
literario *a* literary
literatear *vi* to write on literary subjects
literato (-ta) *a* literary. *n* writer, litterateur
literatura *f*, literature
litigación *f*, litigation
litigante *mf* litigant
litigar *vt* to litigate; *vi* dispute, argue
litigio *m*, lawsuit; dispute, argument
litigioso *a* litigious; quarrelsome, disputatious
litisexpensas *f pl*, *law* costs of a suit; legal expenses
litografía *f*, lithography
litografiar *vt* to lithograph
litoral *a* and *m*, littoral
litro *m*, liter; *Chile* coarse woolen cloth
Lituania Lithuania
liturgia *f*, liturgy
litúrgico *a* liturgical
liviandad *f*, lightness (of weight); fickleness; unimportance; frivolity; lewdness; act of folly, indiscretion
liviano *a* light weight; fickle; unimportant, trifling, frivolous; lascivious
lividez *f*, lividness
lívido *a* livid; *Lat. Am.* pale, pallid
liza *f*, list (at a tournament); arena
llaga *f*, ulcer; sore; grief, affliction; *fig* thorn in the flesh
llagar *vt* to ulcerate; make or produce sores; *fig* wound; *vr* be covered with sores

llama *f,* flame; ardor, vehemence; marsh; *zool* llama
llamada *f,* call; *mil* call-to-arms, call. **l. molestosa,** annoyance call, nuisance call
llamado *a* called; so-called
llamador (-ra) *n* caller. *m,* door knocker; doorbell
llamamiento *m,* calling; call; divine summons, inspiration; invocation, appeal; summons, convocation
llamar *vt* to call; invoke, call upon; summon, convoke; name; attract; *vi* knock (at a door); ring (a bell); *vr* be named, be called; *naut* veer (wind). **Se llama Pedro,** His name is Peter
llamarada *f,* flame, flash; blaze, flare (of anger, etc.)
llamativo *a* striking, showy; provocative
llamear *vi* to throw out flames, blaze
llampo *m, Lat. Am.* ore
llana *f,* mason's trowel; plain; surface of a page
llanada *f,* plain
llanamente *adv* frankly, plainly; naturally, simply; candidly, sincerely
llanero (-ra) *n* plain dweller
llaneza *f,* naturalness; candor; familiarity; simplicity (of style)
llano *a* flat, level; smooth, even; shallow (of receptacles); unaffected, homely, natural; plain (of dresses); manifest, evident; easy; straightforward, candid; informal; simple (of style). *m,* plain; level stretch of ground
llanta *f, aut* tire; rim, felloe. **l. de refacción** *Mexico* spare tire **l. de rueda,** wheel, rim
llanto *m,* weeping, flood of tears
llanura *f,* smoothness, evenness, levelness; plain
llave (de) *f,* key (to); spigot (of), faucet (of), tap (of); spanner, wrench; *elec* switch; clock winder; *mus* key, clef; *arch* keystone; *print* brace; *mech* wrench; lock (of a gun); tuning key; piston (of musical instruments); lock (in wrestling); *fig* key (of a problem or a study). **l. de transmisión,** sender (telegraphy). **l. inglesa,** monkey-wrench, spanner. **l. maestra,** master key, skeleton key. **echar la l.,** to lock. **torcer la l.,** to turn the key
llavero (-ra) *n* keeper of the keys. *m,* key ring. **l. de cárcel,** turnkey
llavín *m,* yale key, latchkey
llegada *f,* arrival, advent
llegar *vi* to arrive; last, endure; reach; achieve a purpose; be sufficient, suffice; amount (to), make; *vt* bring near, draw near; gather; *vr* come near, approach; adhere. **l. a ser,** to become. **l. a un punto muerto,** to reach a deadlock. **l. hasta . . . ,** to stretch as far as . . .
llena *f,* spate, overflow
llenar *vt* to fill; occupy (a post); satisfy, please; fulfill; satiate; pervade; fill up (a form); *vi* be full (of the moon); *vr inf* stuff, overeat; *fig inf* be fed-up
lleno *a* full; replete; abundant; complete. *m,* full moon; *theat* full house; *inf* glut, abundance; perfection. **de l., de l. en l.,** entirely, completely
llenura *f,* abundance, plenty
lleva, llevada *f,* carrying, bearing
llevadero *a* tolerable, bearable
llevar *vt* to carry, transport; charge (a price); yield, produce; carry off, take away; endure, bear; persuade; guide, take; direct; wear (clothes); carry (a handbag, etc.); introduce, present; gain, achieve; manage (a horse); pass, spend (of time); (*with past part*) have (e.g. **Llevo escrita la carta,** I have written the letter); *math* carry; (*with prep. a*) surpass, excel. **l. a cabo,** to accomplish. **l. a cuestas,** to carry on one's back; support. **l. la correspondencia,** to look after the correspondence. **l. la delantera,** to take the lead. **l. luto,** to be in mourning. **l. por delante** *Argentina, Chile* to run over (e.g., a pedesrian) **llevarse bien,** to get on well, agree
llorar *vi* to weep, cry; drip; water (eyes); *vt* lament, mourn; bewail one's troubles
lloriquear *vi* to whine, snivel
lloriqueo *m,* whining, sniveling
lloro *m,* weeping, crying; flood of tears
llorón *a* weeping; sniveling, whining. *m,* long plume. **niño llorón,** crybaby
lloroso *a* tearful; grievous, sad; sorrowful
llovedizo *a* leaky; rainy
llover *vi impers irr* to rain; come in abundance (of troubles, etc.); *vr* leak (roofs, etc.). **l. a cántaros,** to rain in torrents, rain cats and dogs. **l. sobre mojado,** to add insult to injury. **como llovido,** unexpectedly. See **mover**
llovida *f, Lat. Am.* rain, shower
llovido *m,* stowaway
llovizna *f,* drizzle, fine rain
lloviznar *vi* to drizzle
lluvia *f,* rain; rainwater; *fig* shower; rose (of watering can) *Chile, Nicaragua* shower bath, shower
lluvioso *a* rainy, showery
lo *def art. neut* the thing, part, fact, what, that which. Used before adjectives, past participles, sometimes before nouns and adverbs (e.g. **Lo barato es caro,** Cheap things are dear (in the long run).) **Lo mío es mío, pero lo tuyo es de ambos,** What's mine is mine, but what is yours belongs to both of us. **Juan siente mucho lo ocurrido,** John is very sorry for what has happened. **a lo lejos,** in the distance). **lo . . . que,** how (e.g. **No sabes lo bueno que es,** You don't know how good he is). *pers pron acc m,* or *neut* him, it; that, it (e.g. **Lo harán mañana,** They will do it tomorrow). Means some, any, one, as substitute for noun already mentioned (e.g. **Carecemos de azúcar; no lo hay,** We are short of sugar; there isn't any). **Lo cortés no quita lo valiente,** One can be courteous and still insistent
loa *f,* praise, eulogy; *theat* prologue; short dramatic piece; *ant;* dramatic eulogy
loable *a* praiseworthy
loar *vt* to praise; commend
lobero *a* wolf; wolfish
lobo (-ba) *n* wolf. *m,* (*bot anat*) lobe; *inf* drinking fit. **l. marino,** *zool* seal. *inf* **pillar un l.,** to get drunk
lóbrego *a* murky, dark; dismal; mournful, lugubrious
lobreguez *f,* obscurity, gloom, darkness
lóbulo *m,* lobe
locación *f, law* lease; agreement, contract
local *a* local. *m,* premises; place, spot, scene
localidad *f,* location; locality; place, spot; seat (in theaters, etc.)
localización *f,* localization, placing; place
localizar *vt* to localize
locamente *adv* insanely, madly; extraordinarily, extremely
loción *f,* lotion
loco (-ca) *a* insane, mad; rash, foolish, crazy; excessive, enormous; amazing; extraordinary; infatuated. *n* lunatic; rash person. *fig inf* **Es un l. de atar,** He's completely crazy!
locomoción *f,* locomotion
locomotor *a* locomotive
locomotora *f,* locomotive
locomóvil *a* and *f,* locomotive
locro *m, Lat. Am.* meat-and-vegetable stew
locuacidad *f,* loquacity
locuaz *a* loquacious
locución *f,* style of speech; phrase, idiom; *gram* locution
locuelo (-la) *n* madcap
locura *f,* insanity, lunacy; madness, fury; folly, foolishness
locutor (-ra) *n* (radio) announcer; commentator
locutorio *m,* locutory; phone booth
lodazal, lodazar *m,* muddy place; quagmire
lodo *m,* mud
lodoso *a* muddy
logarítmico *a* logarithmic
logaritmo *m,* logarithm
logia *f,* (Freemason's) lodge
lógica *f,* logic. *inf* **l. parda,** common sense
lógico (-ca) *a* logical. *n* logician

logística *f,* logistics
lograr *vt* to achieve, attain, obtain; enjoy; (*with infin*) succeed in; *vr* succeed in, achieve; reach perfection
logrear *vi* to borrow or lend at interest
logrero (-ra) *n* moneylender; monopolist, profiteer
logro *m,* achievement, attainment; profit, gain; usury, money-lending
loma *f,* knoll, hill
lombarda *f,* red cabbage
Lombardía Lombardy
lombardo (-da) *a* of or from Lombardy. *n* native of Lombardy (Italy). *m,* mortgage bank
lombriciento, -a *a, Lat. Am.* having worms, suffering from worms
lombriz *f,* earthworm, common worm. **l. intestinal,** intestinal worm. **l. solitaria,** tapeworm
lomo *m,* loin, back of a book; ridge between furrows; *pl* ribs; loins
lona *f,* canvas, sailcloth
lonchería *f, Lat. Am.* luncheonette, lunch counter, snack bar
Londres London
longanimidad *f,* longanimity, fortitude
longaniza *f, cul* pork sausage
longevidad *f,* longevity
longevo *a* long-lived
longísimo *a sup* **luengo** exceedingly long
longitud *f,* length; longitude. **l. de onda,** *rad* wavelength
lonja *f,* slice, rasher; *com* exchange; market; grocery store; woolen warehouse
lonjista *mf* provision merchant, grocer
lontananza *f,* distance (also *art*). **en l.,** in the distance, far off
loor *m,* praise
loquear *vi* to play the fool; romp
loro *m, orn* parrot
los *def art. m pl,* the (e.g. **l. sombreros,** the hats). *pers. pron acc 3rd pers m pl,* them. **Tus cigarrillos no están sobre la mesa; los tengo en mi bolsillo,** Your cigarettes are not on the table; I have them in my pocket. Means some, any, ones, as substitution for noun already stated (e.g. **Los cigarros están en la caja si los hay,** The cigars are in the box, if there are any). Used demonstratively followed by *de* or *que* introducing relative clause, those of; those which, those who; the ones that (who) (e.g. **Estaba leyendo algunos libros de los que tienes en tu cuarto,** I was reading some books from among those which you have in your room)
losa *f,* flagstone; slab; tombstone
lote *m,* lot, portion, share
lotería *f,* lottery; lotto (game); lottery office
lotero (-ra) *n* seller of lottery tickets
loto *m,* lotus; lotus flower or fruit
loza *f,* porcelain, china
lozanía *f,* luxuriance (of vegetation); vigor, lustiness; arrogance
lozano *a* luxuriant, exuberant; vigorous, lusty; arrogant
lubricación *f,* lubrication
lubricante *a* lubricant
lubricar *vt* to lubricate
lúbrico *a* slippery, smooth; lascivious, lustful
lucera *f,* skylight
lucerna *f,* large chandelier; skylight
lucero *m,* evening star; any bright star; white star (on a horse's head); brilliance, radiance; *pl poet* eyes, orbs. **l. del alba,** morning star
lucha *f,* fight; struggle; wrestling match; argument, disagreement. **l. grecorromana,** wrestling. **l. igualada,** close fight. **l. libre,** catch-as-catch-can
luchador (-ra) *n* fighter; struggler
luchar *vi* to fight hand to hand; wrestle; fight; struggle; argue
lucidez *f,* brilliance, shine; lucidity, clarity
lucido *a* splendid, brilliant; sumptuous; fine, elegant
lúcido *a poet* brilliant; lucid; clear
luciente *a* bright, shining
luciérnaga *f,* glowworm
lucimiento *m,* brilliance, luster; success, triumph; elegance; display, ostentation
lucir *vi irr* to shine, scintillate; excel, outshine; be successful; *vt* illuminate; display, show off; show; *vr* dress elegantly; be successful; excel, be brilliant. *Pres. Ind.* **luzco, luces,** etc. *Pres. Subjunc.* **luzca,** etc.
lucrativo *a* lucrative
lucro *m,* gain, profit
lucroso *a* profitable
luctuoso *a* lugubrious, mournful
lucubración *f,* lucubration
ludibrio *m,* mockery, ridicule
luego *adv* immediately; afterward, later; then; soon, presently. *conjunc* therefore. **l. que,** as soon as. **desde l.,** immediately, at once; of course, naturally; in the first place. **hasta l.,** au revoir, good-by for the present
lueguito *adv Lat. Am.* at once, right away, right now; *Central America, Chile, Mexico* near, nearby
luengo *a* long
lugar *m,* place; spot; village, town, city; region, locality; office, post; passage, text; opportunity, occasion; cause, motive; place on a list; room, space; seat. **l. común,** commonplace. **en l. de,** instead of. **en primer l.,** firstly, in the first place. **hacer l.,** to make room, make way. *law* **No ha l.,** The petition is refused. **tener l.,** to take place; have the time or opportunity (to)
lugarejo *m,* hamlet
lugareño (-ña) *a* peasant, regional. *n* villager, peasant
lugarteniente *m,* lieutenant; substitute, deputy
lúgubre *a* lugubrious, dismal, mournful
luis *m,* louis (French coin)
lujo *m,* luxury; abundance, profusion. **artículos de l.,** luxury goods
lujoso *a* luxurious; abundant, profuse
lujuria *f,* lasciviousness; excess, intemperance
lujuriante *a* luxuriant, abundant, profuse
lujurioso *a* lascivious, voluptuous
lumbago *m,* lumbago
lumbre *f,* fire; light; splendor, lustre; transom window, opening, skylight; *pl* tinderbox
lumbrera *f,* luminary; skylight; dormer window; eminent authorit; *Mexico* box (in a theater or bullring)
luminar *m,* luminary (also *fig*)
luminaria *f,* illumination; fairy lamp, small light; lamp burning before the Sacrament in Catholic churches
luminosidad *f,* luminosity
luminoso *a* luminous; bright
luna *f,* moon; mirror; satellite; sheet of plate glass. **l. creciente,** new or rising moon. **l. de miel,** honeymoon. **l. llena,** full moon. **l. menguante,** waning moon. **media l.,** crescent moon
lunado *a* half-moon, crescent
lunar *m,* beauty spot; *fig* stain, blot (on reputation, etc.); blemish, slight imperfection. *a* lunar
lunático (-ca) *a* and *n* lunatic
lunes *m,* Monday
luneta *f,* lens (of eyeglasses), *theat* orchestra stall; (*arch mil*) lunette
lupa *f,* magnifying glass
lupanar *m,* brothel
lúpulo *m, bot* hop
lusitano (-na) *a* and *n* Lusitanian
lustrador *m,* polisher; *Lat. Am.* bootblack. **l. de piso,** floor polisher
lustrar *vt* to lustrate, purify; polish, burnish; roam, journey
lustre *m,* polish, sheen, gloss; glory, luster
lustro *m,* lustrum, period of five years; chandelier
lustroso *a* shining, glossy; brilliant; glorious, noble
luterano (-na) *a* and *n* Lutheran
luto *m,* mourning; grief, affliction; *pl* mourning draperies. **estar de l.,** to be in mourning

luxación *f, surg* luxation, dislocation
luz *f,* light; glow; brightness, brilliance; information, news; *fig* luminary; day, daylight; *pl* culture, learning; windows. **luces de estacionamiento,** parking lights. **a buena l.,** in a good light; in a favorable light; after due consideration. **a primera l.,** at dawn. **dar a l.,** to publish (a book); bring forth (children); reveal. **entre dos luces,** in the dawn light; in the twilight; *inf* tipsy. **media l.,** half-light, twilight

M

maca *f,* bruise or blemish on fruit; defect, flaw; *inf* fraud, swindle
macabro *a* macabre
macadán *m,* macadam
macagua *f, orn* macaw
macanudo *a* (*inf WH*) extraordinary; enormous; robust; fine, excellent
macarrones *m pl,* macaroni; *naut* stanchions
macarrrónico *a* macaronic, recondite, stylized
macarse *vr* to go bad, rot (fruit)
maceración *f,* maceration; steeping, soaking; mortification of the flesh
macerar *vt* to macerate; steep, soak; mortify
macero *m,* mace bearer
maceta *f, dim* small mace; handle, haft (of tools); stonecutter's hammer; flowerpot; *Lat. Am.* bouquet, bunch (of flowers)
macetero *m,* flowerpot stand; *Lat. Am.* flowerpot
machaca *f,* pestle; pulverizer. *mf inf* bore, tedious person
machacador (-ra) *a* crushing, pounding. *n* beater, crusher, pounder
machacar *vt* to crush, pound; *vi* importune; harp on a subject
machacón *a* tiresome, prolix
machado *m,* hatchet, ax
machete *m* machete
machetero *m,* one who cuts sugarcane with a machete
machihembrar *vt carp* to dovetail
machina *f,* derrick, crane; pile driver
macho *m,* male; male animal (he-goat, stallion, etc.); male plant; hook (of hook and eye); screw; *met* core; tap (tool); *inf* dunderhead, fool; *arch* buttress. *a* male; stupid, ignorant; vigorous, strong. **m. cabrío,** he-goat
machucadura *f,* **machucamiento** *m,* pounding, crushing; bruising
machucar *vt* to crush, pound; bruise
machucho *a* prudent, sensible; adult, mature
macicez *f,* solidity; massiveness; thickness
macilento *a* thin, lean, emaciated
macillo *m, dim* small mace; hammer (of a piano)
macis *f, cul* mace
macizar *vt* to block up, fill up
macizo *a* massive; compact, solid; *fig* well-founded, unassailable; thick; strong. *m,* solidity, compactness; bulk, volume; flowerbed; solid tire
macrocosmo *m,* macrocosm
macuco, -a *a, Lat. Am.* crafty, cunning, sly
mácula *f,* stain, spot; *fig* blot, blemish; *inf* trick, deception; *ast* macula
macuquero *m,* unauthorized worker of abandoned mines
madeja *f,* skein, hank; lock of hair; *inf* dummy, useless person
madera *f,* wood; timber; *inf* kind, sort; *mus* wind instruments. **m. contrachapada,** plywood. **m. de construcción,** timber. **maderas de sierra,** lumber wood. *inf* **ser de mala m.,** to be a ne'er-do-well
maderada *f,* lumber wood
maderaje *m,* woodwork, timber work
maderero *m,* timber merchant; lumberjack; carpenter
madería *f,* timber yard
madero *m,* wooden beam; log, piece of lumber; ship, vessel; *inf* blockhead or insensible person
madrastra *f,* stepmother; anything unpleasant
madraza *f, inf* overindulgent mother
madre *f,* mother; matron; cause, genesis; *inf* dame, mother; riverbed; dam; womb; main sewer; chief irrigation channel. **m. de familia,** mother; housewife. **m. de leche,** wet nurse. **m. política,** mother-in-law; stepmother. *inf* **sacar de m. (a),** to provoke, irritate (a person)
madreperla *f,* mother-of-pearl
madreselva *f,* honeysuckle
madrigado *a* twice-married (women); *inf* experienced, wide-awake
madrigal *m,* madrigal
madriguera *f,* rabbit warren; burrow, den, hole, lair; haunt of thieves, etc.
madrina *f,* godmother; matron of honor or bridesmaid; sponsor; patroness; prop; stanchion
madroncillo *m,* strawberry
madroño *m,* strawberry tree; tuft, spot; tassel
madrugada *f,* dawn, daybreak; early rising. **de m.,** at dawn
madrugador (-ra) *a* early rising. *n* early riser
madrugar *vi* to get up early; gain time; anticipate, be beforehand
maduración *f,* ripening; mellowing; preparation; ripeness; maturity
madurador *a* ripening; maturing
maduramente *adv* maturely; sensibly
madurar *vt* to ripen; mature; think out; *vi* ripen; grow mature, learn wisdom
madurez *f,* ripeness; maturity; mellowness; wisdom
maduro *a* ripe; mature; mellow; adult; wise
maestra *f,* schoolmistress; teacher, instructor; queen bee; guide, model
maestral *a* referring to the grand master of one of the Spanish military orders; teaching, pedagogic. *m,* mistral (wind); cell of a queen bee
maestranza *f, Lat. Am.* machine shop
maestrear *vt* to direct, control, manage; prune vines; *vi inf* bully, domineer
maestría *f,* mastery, skill; *univ* master's degree
maestril *m,* queen cell (of bees)
maestro *a* masterly; excellent; chief, main; midship. *m,* master, expert; teacher; instructor; master craftsman; *univ* master; *mus* composer; *naut* mainmast. **m. de armas,** fencing master. **m. de capilla,** *ecc* choirmaster. **m. de obras,** building contractor; master builder. **El ejercicio hace m.,** Practice makes perfect
Magallanes, Estrecho de Straits of Magellan
magdalena *f,* madeleine (cake); magdalen, penitent. *inf* **estar hecha una M.,** to be inconsolable
magia *f,* magic
mágica *f,* magic; enchantress, sorceress
mágico *a* magic; marvelous, wonderful. *m,* magician; enchanter, wizard
magín *m, inf* imagination; head, mind
magisterio *m,* teaching profession; teaching diploma; teaching post; pedantry, pompousness. **ejercer su m. en,** to be employed as a teacher in
magistrado *m,* magistrate; magistracy
magistral *a* magistral; authoritative, magisterial; pedantic, pompous
magistratura *f,* magistracy
magnanimidad *f,* magnanimity; generosity, liberality
magnánimo *a* magnanimous, generous, noble
magnate *m,* magnate
magnavoz *m, Mexico* loudspeaker
magnesia *f,* magnesia

magnesio *m,* magnesium
magnético *a* magnetic
magnetizar *vt* to magnetize; mesmerize
magneto *m,* magneto
magnificar *vt* to magnify, enlarge; praise, extol
magnificencia *f,* magnificence, pomp, splendor
magnífico *a* magnificent; splendid, wonderful, fine; excellent
magnitud *f,* magnitude; quantity; importance
magno *a* great; famous. **Alejandro M.,** Alexander the Great
magnolia *f,* magnolia
mago *m,* magician; *pl* magi
magra *f,* rasher (of bacon, ham)
magrez, magrura *f,* leanness; scragginess
magro *a* lean; scraggy. *m, inf* lean pork
magulladura *f,* **magullamiento** *m,* bruising; bruise, contusion
magullar *vt* to bruise
magullón *m, Lat. Am.* bruise
mahometano (-na) *a* and *n* Muslim
mahonesa *f,* mayonnaise
maíz *m,* corn
maizal *m,* cornfield
maja *f,* belle
majada *f,* sheepfold; dung
majaderear *vt, Lat. Am.* to nag, pester
majadería *f,* impertinence, insolence
majadero *a* persistent, tedious. *m,* bobbin (for lace making); pestle. *n* fool, bore
majador *m,* pestle
majar *vt* to pound, crush; *inf* importune, annoy
majestad *f,* majesty (title); dignity; stateliness
majestuosidad *f,* majesty; dignity
majestuoso *a* majestic; stately; dignified
majo *a* arrogant, aggressive; gaudily attired, smart; dashing, handsome; attractive, pretty; elegant, well-dressed. *m,* beau, gallant, man about town
majuelo *m,* new vine; species of white hawthorn
mal *a abb* **malo.** Used only before *m sing* nouns (e.g. **un m. cuarto de hora,** a bad quarter of an hour). *m,* evil; damage; harm; misfortune; illness, disease; trouble (e.g. **El m. es,** The trouble is). **m. de altura,** air sickness. **m. de ojo,** evil eye. **m. de piedra,** lithiasis, stone. **m. francés,** syphilis. **el m. menor,** the lesser of two evils. *interj* **¡M. haya!** A curse upon! **echar a m.,** to scorn (things); waste, squander. **llevar a m. (una cosa),** to take (a thing) badly, complain. **No hay m. que por bien no venga,** It's an ill wind that blows no one any good, Every cloud has a silver lining. **parar en m.,** to come to a bad end
mal *adv* badly; unfavorably; wrongly; wickedly; with difficulty; scarcely, barely. **m. que bien,** willingly or unwillingly; rightly or wrongly. **de m. en peor,** from bad to worse
mala *f,* mail, post. **m. real,** royal mail
malabarista *mf* juggler
malaconsejado *a* ill-advised; imprudent
malacostumbrado *a* badly trained, spoiled; having bad habits
malandante *a* evildoing; unfortunate, miserable; poor
malandanza *f,* evildoing; misfortune, misery; poverty
malandrín *a* wicked, ill-disposed. *m,* scoundrel, miscreant
malanga *f, Central America* kind of tuber resembling a sweet potato
malaquita *f,* malachite
malaria *f,* malaria
malaventura *f,* misfortune, adversity, bad luck
malaventurado *a* unfortunate, unlucky
malayo (-ya) *a* Malay. *n* Malayan
malbaratador (-ra) *a* wasteful, spendthrift. *n* squanderer, spendthrift
malbaratar *vt* to squander, waste; sell at a loss
malcasado *a* adulterous, unfaithful
malcasar(se) *vt* and *vr* to marry badly
malcomido *a* underfed
malcontento (-ta) *a* dissatisfied, discontented; rebellious. *n* malcontent, rebel
malcriado *a* badly brought up; ill-bred; spoiled, peevish
maldad *f,* badness; depravity, wickedness
maldecidor (-ra) *a* slanderous. *n* scandalmonger, slanderer
maldecir *vt irr* to curse; *vt* and *vi* slander, backbite. See **decir**
maldiciente *a* defamatory, slanderous; cursing, reviling. *m,* slanderer; curser
maldición *f,* malediction; curse, imprecation
maldispuesto *a* indisposed, ill; reluctant
maldita *f, inf* tongue. *inf* **soltar la m.,** to say too much, go too far
maldito *a* accursed; wicked; damned; poor (of quality); *inf* not a . . .
maleabilidad *f,* malleability, flexibility
maleable *a* malleable, flexible
maleante *a* rascally, villainous. *mf* evildoer
malecón *m,* breakwater
maledicencia *f,* slander, abuse, backbiting; cursing
maleficencia *f,* wrongdoing
maleficio *m,* (magic) curse; spell; charm
maléfico *a* malefic, harmful. *m,* sorcerer
malestar *m,* indisposition, slight illness; discomfort
maleta *f,* suitcase, valise, grip; *m, inf* clumsy matador; duffer (at games, etc.). **hacer la m.,** to pack a suitcase; *inf* prepare for a journey, get ready to leave
maletero *m,* seller or maker of traveling bags; porter
maletín *m,* small suitcase or valise
malevolencia *f,* malevolence, hatred, malice
malévolo *a* malevolent, malicious
maleza *f,* weeds; undergrowth; thicket
malgastador (-ra) *a* thriftless, wasteful. *n* squanderer
malgastar *vt* to waste (time); squander, throw away (money)
malhablado *a* foul-tongued, indecent
malhadado *a* ill-fated, unhappy
malhecho *a* deformed, twisted (persons). *m,* evil deed, wrongdoing
malhechor (-ra) *n* malefactor; evildoer
malhumorado *a* ill-humored, bad-tempered
malicia *f,* wickedness, evil; malice, maliciousness; acuteness, subtlety, shrewdness; craftiness, guile; *inf* suspicion
maliciar *vt* to suspect; spoil, damage; hurt, harm
malicioso *a* malicious; vindictive; wicked; shrewd, clever; *inf* suspicious; artful
malignidad *f,* malignancy, spite, ill will
maligno *a* malignant, spiteful; wicked; *med* malignant
malintencionado *a* ill-intentioned, badly disposed
malla *f,* mesh (of a net); coat of mail; *pl theat* tights. **m. de alambre,** wire netting. **cota de m.,** coat of mail
Mallorca Majorca
malmandado *a* disobedient; reluctant, unwilling
malmaridada *f,* adultress, faithless wife
malo *a* bad; wicked; evil; injurious; harmful; illicit; licentious; ill; difficult; troublesome, annoying; *inf* mischievous; knavish; rotten, decaying. *interj* **¡M.!** That's bad!; You shouldn't have done that!; That's a bad sign! **de malas,** unluckily, unhappily. **el M.,** the Evil One, the Devil. **estar m.,** to be ill. **Lo m. es,** The trouble is, The worst of it is. **por malas o por buenas,** willy-nilly, willingly or unwillingly. **ser m.,** to be wicked; be evil; behave badly (children)
malograr *vt* to lose (time); waste, throw away (opportunities); *vr* fall through, fail; wither, fade; die early, come to an untimely end
malogro *m,* loss, waste (time, opportunity); frustration; decline, fading; untimely death
malparar *vt* to ill-treat; damage. **quedar malparado,** to get the worst of
malparir *vt med* to miscarry
malparto *m,* miscarriage; abortion
malquerencia *f,* ill will, aversion, dislike

malquistar *vt* to stir up trouble; make unpopular; estrange; *vr* make oneself disliked
malquisto *a* unpopular, disliked
malsano *a* unhealthy
malta *m,* malt
maltés (-esa) *a* and *n* Maltese
maltraer *vt irr* to ill-treat; insult. See **traer**
maltraído, -a *a, Lat. Am.* shabby
maltratamiento *m,* abuse, ill usage; damage, deterioration
maltratar *vt* to ill-treat; abuse, insult; misuse, spoil, damage
maltrato *m,* maltreatment; misuse
maltrecho *a* ill-treated, bruised; abused, insulted; damaged
maltusiano *a* Malthusian
Malucas, las the Moluccas
malucho *a inf* off-color, below par, not well
malva *f,* mallow. **m. real, m. rosa,** *or* **m. loca,** hollyhock. **ser como una m.,** *fig inf* to be a clinging vine
malvado *a* evil, malevolent, fiendish. *n* villain, fiend
malvasía *f, bot* malvasia; malmsey (wine)
malvavisco *m, bot* marshmallow
malvender *vt* to sell at a loss
malversación *f,* malversation, maladministration; misappropriation (of funds)
malversador (-ra) *n* bad or corrupt administrator
malversar *vt* to misappropriate (funds)
Malvinas, las *fpl* the Falkland Islands
mama *f, inf* mamma, mommy; breast; udder
mamá *f,* mamma
mamado, -a *a, Lat. Am.* drunk, tipsy
mamar *vt* to suck (the breast); *inf* wolf, swallow; learn from an early age; enjoy, obtain unfairly; *vr* get drunk
mamario *a* mammary
mamarracho *m, inf* scarecrow, dummy; anything grotesque looking
mameluco *m,* mameluke; *inf* ninny, fool
mamífero *a* mammalian. *m,* mammal
mamotreto *m,* notebook, memorandum; *inf* large book or bulky file of papers
mampara *f,* folding screen; screen; partition
mamparo *m,* bulkhead
mampostería *f,* masonry, stonemasonry
mampostero *m,* stonemason
maná *m,* manna
manada *f,* handful; herd, flock; group, drove, crowd
manadero *m,* herdsman, drover; spring, stream
manantial *m,* fountain, source, spring; head (of a river)
manar *vi* to flow, stream; be plentiful
manatí *m,* sea cow, manatee
mancar *vt* to injure, maim; *vi* grow calm (elements)
manceba *f,* concubine; girl
mancebía *f,* brothel; youth, young days
mancebo *m,* youth, stripling; bachelor; shop assistant
mancha *f,* spot, smear, stain; blotch; plot of ground; patch of vegetation; stigma, disgrace
manchar *vt* to stain; smear; spot; speckle; disgrace; tarnish
manchuriano (-na) *a* and *n* Manchurian
mancilla *f,* stain; slur
mancillar *vt* to stain; *fig* smirch
manco (-ca) *a* maimed, disabled; one-handed; one-armed; armless; handless; incomplete, faulty. *n* disabled person
mancomunidad *f,* association, society; community, union; commonwealth; regional legislative assembly
mancorna, *f, Colombia* cuff link **mancuerna, mancuernilla** *f, Central America* cuff link
manda *f,* offer, suggestion, proposition; legacy
mandadero (-ra) *n* convent or prison messenger; errand boy (girl)
mandado *m,* order, command; errand
mandamiento *m,* order, command; *ecc* commandment; *law* writ; *pl inf* one's five fingers
mandar *vt* to order, command; bequeath, will; send; control, drive; promise, offer; order (e.g. **Mandó hacerse un traje,** He ordered a suit to be made); *vr* walk unaided (convalescents, etc.); lead into one another (rooms, etc.); **¿Quién manda aquí?** Who is in charge here?
mandarín *m,* mandarin; *inf* bureaucrat; *Lat. Am.* bossy person, domineering person
mandarina *f,* mandarin (classical Chinese); mandarin orange
mandato *m,* mandate; command; *ecc* maundy. *pol* mandate. **cuarto m.,** fourth term (of President, Governor, etc.)
mandíbula *f,* jaw; jawbone, mandible
mandil *m,* long leather apron; apron; Freemason's apron; close-meshed fishing net; *Lat. Am.* (horse) blanket
mandilón *m, inf* coward, nincompoop
mandioca *f,* manioc, cassava; tapioca
mando *m,* authority, power; (*mil nav*) command; *eng* regulation; controls (of a machine, etc.). **m. a distancia,** remote control. *aer* **m. de dos pilotos,** dual-controlled. **mandos gemelos,** dual control. **al m. de,** under the command of; under the direction of
mandolín *m.* **mandolina** *f,* mandolin
mandón *a* domineering, bossy
mandril *m, mech* mandrel, chuck; *zool* mandrill
manear *vt* to hobble (a horse); manage, control
manecilla *f, dim* little hand; hand of a clock; *print* fist
manejable *a* manageable, controllable
manejar *vt* to handle; use, wield; control; manage, direct; ride (horses); *vr* manage to move around (after an accident, illness)
manejo *m,* handling; use, wielding; control; management, direction; horsemanship; intrigue
maneota *f,* hobble, shackle
manera *f,* manner, way, means; behavior, style (gen. *pl*); class (of people); *art* style, manner. **a la m. de,** like, in the style of. **de esa m.,** in that way; according to that, in that case. **de m. que,** so that. **en gran m.,** to a great extent. **sobre m.,** exceedingly
manga *f,* sleeve; bag; grip; handle; pipe (of a hose); strainer; waterspout; body of troops; beam, breadth of a ship; *pl* profits. **m. de viento,** whirlwind. **echar de m. a,** to make use of a person. *inf* **estar de m.,** to be in league. **tener m. ancha,** to be broad-minded. *fig inf* **traer (una cosa) en la m.,** to have (something) up one's sleeve
mangana *f,* lasso
manganilla *f,* sleight of hand; hoax, trick
mangle *m,* mangrove tree
mango *m,* handle, haft, stock; mango. **m. de cuchillo,** knife handle
mangonear *vi inf* to loaf, roam about; interfere, meddle
mangonero *a inf* meddlesome
mangosta *f,* mongoose
mangote *m, inf* long, wide sleeve; black oversleeve
manguera *f,* hose; sleeve, tube; airshaft; waterspout
manguero *m,* fireman; hoseman
manguito *m,* muff; black oversleeve; wristlet, cuff; *mech* bush, sleeve
manía *f,* mania, obsession; whim, fancy
maniabierto, -a *a, Lat. Am.* generous, giving, open-handed
maníaco (-ca) *a* maniacal; capricious, extravagant. *n* maniac
maniatar *vt* to handcuff; hobble (a cow, etc.)
maniático (-ca) *a* maniacal; capricious; faddy, fussy. *n* crank
manicomio *m,* insane asylum, mental hospital
manicura *f,* manicure
manicuro (-ra) *n* manicurist
manida *f,* lair, den; dwelling, habitation
manifestación *f,* declaration, statement; exhibition; demonstration; *ecc* exposition (of the Blessed Sacrament)
manifestante *mf* demonstrator

manifestar *vt irr* to declare, make known, state; exhibit, show; *ecc* to expose (the Blessed Sacrament). See **acertar**
manifiesto *a* obvious, evident. *m*, manifesto; *naut* manifest; *ecc* exposition of the Blessed Sacrament. **poner de m.,** to show; make public; reveal
manigua *f*, thicket, jungle (in Cuba)
manija *f*, handle, stock, haft; hand lever; clamp; tether (for horses, etc.)
manileño (ña) *a* and *n* Manilan
manilla *f*, bracelet; handcuff, manacle
maniobra *f*, operation, process; *mil* maneuver; intrigue; tackle, gear; handling, management; *naut* working of a ship; *pl* shunting (trains)
maniobrar *vi mil* to maneuver; *naut* handle, work (ships)
manipulación *f*, handling; manipulation; control, management
manipulador *a* manipulative. *m*, sending key (telegraphy)
manipular *vt* to handle; manipulate; manage, direct
manípulo *m*, maniple
maniquete *m*, black lace mitten
maniquí *m*, mannequin; dummy; *inf* puppet, weak person
manirroto (-ta) *a* wasteful, extravagant. *n* spendthrift
manivela *f*, *mech* crank, lever; *Lat. Am.* handle
manjar *m*, dish, food; pastime, recreation, pleasure. **m. blanco,** blancmange; *Lat. Am.* fudge
mano *f*, hand; coat, coating; quire (of paper); front paw (animals); elephant's trunk; side, hand; hand (of a clock); game (of cards, etc.); lead (at cards); way, means; ability; power; protection, favor; compassion; aid, help; scolding; *mus* scale; pestle; workers. *inf* editing, correction of a literary work (gen. by a person more skilled than the author). **m. de mortero,** pestle. **m. de obra,** (manual) labor. **manos muertas,** *law* mortmain. **m. sobre m.,** with folded hands; lazily, indolently. **a la m.,** at hand, nearby; within one's grasp. **a manos llenas,** in abundance, abundantly. **bajo m.,** in an underhand manner, secretly. **buenas manos,** cleverness, ability; dexterity. **de primera m.,** firsthand, new. **estar dejado de la m. de Dios,** to be very unlucky; be very foolish. **poner la m. en,** to ill-treat; slap, buffet. **Si a m. viene . . . ,** If by chance . . . **tender la m.,** to put out one's hand, shake hands. **traer entre manos,** to have on hand, be engaged in
manojo *m*, bunch, handful. **a manojos,** in handfuls; plentifully, in abundance
manolo (-la) *n* inhabitant of low quarters of Madrid noted for pride, gaiety, quarrelsomeness, and wit
manoseado *a* hackneyed
manosear *vt* to handle; paw, touch repeatedly; finger
manoseo *m*, handling; fingering; *inf* pawing, feeling
manotada *f*, slap, cuff
manotear *vt* to slap, cuff; *vi* gesticulate, gesture with the hands
manoteo *m*, gesticulation with the hands
manquedad *f*, disablement of hand or arm; lack of one of these; defect; incompleteness
mansalva (**a**) *adv* without danger
mansedumbre *f*, meekness; kindness; gentleness
mansión *f*, stay, visit; dwelling, abode; mansion
manso *a* soft, gentle; meek, mild; tame; peaceable, amiable; calm
manta *f*, blanket; horse blanket; traveling rug; *inf* hiding, thrashing. **m. de viaje,** traveling rug. *inf* **a m. de Dios,** in abundance. **dar una m.,** to toss in a blanket. *fig inf* **tirar de la m.,** to let the cat out of the bag
manteamiento *m*, tossing in a blanket
mantear *vt* to toss in a blanket
manteca *f*, lard; cooking fat; grease; *Argentina* butter. **como m.,** as mild as milk, as soft as butter
mantecada *f*, buttered toast
mantecado *m*, French ice cream
mantecoso *a* greasy
mantel *m*, tablecloth; altar cloth
mantelería *f*, table linen
mantelete *m*, (*ecc mil*) mantlet
mantener *vt irr* to maintain; keep, feed; support; continue, persevere with; uphold, affirm; keep up; *vr* support oneself; remain in a place; (*with en*) continue to uphold (views, etc.), persevere in. **mantenerse firme,** *fig* to stand one's ground. See **tener**
mantenimiento *m*, maintenance; support; sustenance, nourishment; affirmation; upkeep; livelihood
manteo *m*, tossing in a blanket; long cloak
mantequera *f*, churn; dairymaid; butter dish
mantequero *m*, dairyman; butter dish
mantequilla *f*, butter
mantero *m*, blanket seller or maker
mantilla *f*, mantilla; saddlecloth. *pl* baby's long clothes. **estar en mantillas,** to be in swaddling clothes; *fig* be in early infancy
manto *m*, cloak; cover, disguise; *zool* mantle; *min* layer
mantón *m*, shawl. **m. de Manila,** Manila shawl
mantuano (-na) *a* and *n* Mantuan
manuable *a* easy to handle or use, handy
manual *a* manual; handy, easy to use; docile, peaceable. *m*, manual, textbook; *ecc* book of ritual; notebook
manubrio *m*, handle, crank; *Lat. Am.* handlebars
manuela *f*, open carriage (Madrid)
manufactura *f*, manufacture; manufactured article; factory
manufacturar *vt* to manufacture
manufacturero *a* manufacturing
manumisión *f*, freeing (of a slave), manumission
manumitir *vt law* to free, enfranchise (slaves)
manuscrito *a* and *m*, manuscript
manutención *f*, maintenance; upkeep; protection
manzana *f*, apple; block (of houses); city square; Adam's apple; *Argentina* 2.5 acres; *Central America* 1.75 acres
manzanal *m*, apple orchard; apple tree
manzanar *m*, apple orchard
manzanilla *f*, white sherry wine; *bot* chamomile; chamomile tea; knob, ball (on furniture); pad (on an animal's foot)
manzano *m*, apple tree
maña *f*, skill, dexterity; craftiness, guile; vice, bad habit (gen. *pl*). **darse m. para,** to contrive to
mañana *f*, morning; tomorrow. *m*, future, tomorrow. *adv* tomorrow; in time to come; soon. **¡M.!** Tomorrow! Another day! Not now! (generally to beggars). **de m.,** early in the morning. **muy de m.,** very early in the morning. **pasado m.,** the day after tomorrow
mañanica *f*, early morning
mañear *vt* to arrange cleverly; *vi* behave shrewdly
mañero *a* shrewd, clever; easily worked; handy
mañoso *a* clever, skillful; crafty; vicious, with bad habits
mañuela *f*, low guile
mapa *m*, map; card. **m. en relieve,** relief map. **m. del estado mayor,** ordnance map. *inf* **no estar en el m.,** to be off the map; be most unusual (of things)
mapache *m*, raccoon
maqueta *f*, (*art arch*) model
maquiavélico *a* Machiavellian
maquiladora *f*, maquiladora (factory run by a U.S. company in Mexico to take advantage of cheap labor and lax regulation)
maquillaje *m*, makeup, cosmetics; making up (of the face)
maquillar (se) *vt* and *vr* to make up (the face, etc.)
máquina *f*, machine, mechanism; engine; apparatus; plan, scheme; machine, puppet; *inf* mansion, palace; plenty; locomotive; fantasy, product of the imagination. **m. de vapor,** steam engine. **m. de arrastre,** traction engine; tractor. **m. de coser,** sewing machine. **m. de escribir,** typewriter. **m. fotográfica,** camera. **m. de impresionar,** movie camera. **m. de imprimir,**

printing machine. **m. herramienta,** machine tool. **m. neumática,** air pump
maquinación *f,* intrigue, machination
maquinador (-ra) *n* intriguer, schemer
maquinal *a* mechanical
maquinar *vt* to intrigue, scheme, plot
maquinaria *f,* machinery; applied mechanics; mechanism
maquinista *mf* driver, enginer; mechanic; machinist; locomotive driver
mar *mf* sea; great many, abundance. **m. bonanza** *or* **m. en calma,** calm sea. **m. de fondo** *or* **m. de leva,** swell. **alta m.,** high seas. **a mares,** plentifully. **arar en el m.,** to labor in vain. *naut* **hacerse a la m.,** to put out to sea. **la m. de historias,** a great number of stories
maraña *f,* undergrowth; tangle; *fig* difficult position; intrigue; silk waste
marasmo *m, med* marasmus, atrophy; inactivity, paralysis
maravilla *f,* marvel, wonder; admiration; amazement; marigold. **a m.,** wonderfully. **a las mil maravillas,** to perfection, excellently. **por m.,** by chance; occasionally
maravillar *vt* to amaze, cause admiration; *vr* (*with de*) marvel at, admire; be amazed by
maravilloso *a* marvelous, wonderful
marbete *m,* label, tag; edge, border
marca *f,* mark, sign; brand; frontier zone, border country; standard, norm (of size); make, brand; measuring rule; *sport* record. **m. de fábrica,** brand, trademark. **m. de ley,** hallmark. **m. registrada,** registered name. **de m.,** excellent, of excellent quality
marcado *a* marked; pronounced; strong (of accents)
marcador *a* marking. *m,* marker; scoreboard; bookmark
marcar *vt* to mark; brand; embroider initials on linen; tell the time (watches); show the amount (cash register, etc.); dial (telephone); *sport* score (a goal); notice, observe; set aside, earmark; *vr naut* check the course. **m. el compás** to beat time
marcha *f,* departure; running, working; *mil* march; speed (of trains, ships, etc.); *mus* march; progress, course (of events). **m. atrás,** backing, reversing. **m. de ensayo,** trial run. **m. forzada,** *mil* forced march. **a largas marchas,** with all speed. **a toda m.,** at top speed; full speed ahead; by forced marches; *mil* **batir la m.,** to strike up a march. **en m.,** underway; working; in operation
marchamero *m,* customs official who checks and marks goods
marchamo *m,* customs mark on checked goods
marchante, -a *mf Lat. Am.* client, customer; dealer, merchant; pedlar
marchar *vi* to run; work; function; go; leave, depart; progress, proceed; *mil* march; go (clocks); *vr* leave, go away
marchitable *a* perishable, fragile
marchitar *vt* to wither, fade; blight, spoil; weaken; *vr* wither; be blighted
marchito *a* withered; faded; blighted, frustrated
marcial *a* martial; courageous, militant
marcialidad *f,* war-like spirit, militancy
marciano *a* Martian
marco *m,* mark (German coin); boundary mark; frame (of a picture, etc.). **m. de ventana,** window frame
Mar de las Indias Indian Ocean
Mar del Norte North Sea
marea *f,* tide; strand, water's edge; light breeze; drizzle; dew; street dirt. **m. creciente,** flood tide. **m. menguante,** ebb tide. **m. muerta,** neap tide
mareaje *m,* seamanship; ship's course
marear *vt* to navigate; sell; sell publicly; *inf* annoy; *vr* be seasick; feel faint; feel giddy; be damaged at sea (goods)
marejada *f,* surge, swell; high sea; tidal wave; commotion, uproar
mareo *m,* seasickness; nausea, dizziness; *inf* irritation, tediousness
mareta *f,* movement of the waves; sound, noise (of a crowd)
marfil *m,* ivory
marfileño *a* ivory; ivory-like
marfuz *a* spurned, rejected; deceitful
marga *f,* loam, marl
margarina *f,* margarine
margarita *f,* pearl; marguerite, oxeye daisy; daisy; periwinkle
margen *mf* edge, fringe, border, verge; margin (of a book); opportunity; marginal note. **dar m. para,** to provide an opportunity for; give rise to
marginal *a* marginal
margoso *a* loamy, marly
marica *f,* magpie. *m,* (*offensive*) homosexual; milksop
maricón *m,* (*offensive*) homosexual
maridable *a* marital, matrimonial
maridaje *m,* conjugal union and harmony; intimate relationship (between things)
maridar *vi* to get married; mate, live as husband and wife; *vt* unite, link, join together
marido *m,* husband
marihuana *f,* marijuana
marimacho *m, inf* mannish woman
marina *f,* coast, seashore; *art* seascape; seamanship; navy, fleet. **m. de guerra,** navy. **m. mercante,** merchant navy
marinera *f,* sailor's blouse
marinería *f,* profession of a sailor; seamanship; crew of a ship; sailors (as a class)
marinero *m,* sailor, seaman. **m. de agua dulce,** freshwater sailor (a novice). **m. práctico,** able seaman. **a la marinera,** in a seaman-like fashion
marinesco *a* seamanly
marino *a* marine, sea; seafaring; shipping. *m,* sailor, mariner
marioneta *f,* marionette, puppet
mariposa *f,* butterfly; night-light
mariposear *vi* to flutter, flit, fly about; flirt, be fickle; follow about, dance attendance on
mariquita *f, ent* ladybird; parakeet.
marisabidilla *f, inf* blue-stocking, know-it-all
mariscal *m, mil* marshal; field marshal; blacksmith
marisco *m,* shellfish
marisma *f,* bog, morass, swamp
marital *a* marital
marítimo *a* maritime, sea
marjal *m,* marshland, fen
marmita *f,* stewpot; copper, boiler; *Mexico* kettle
marmitón *m,* kitchen boy, scullion
mármol *m,* marble; work executed in marble
marmolería *f,* marble works; work executed in marble
marmolista *mf* marble cutter; dealer in marble
marmóreo *a* marble; *poet* marmoreal
marmota *f, zool* marmot; sleepyhead, dormouse
Mar Muerto Dead Sea
maroma *f,* rope, hawser; *Lat. Am.* tightrope
maromero, -a *mf, Lat. Am.* acrobat, tightrope walker; opportunist
marquesina *f,* marquee
marquetería *f,* marquetry
marrana *f,* sow; *inf* slattern, slut
marrano *m,* pig, hog; Marrano
marras (de) *adv* long ago, in the dim past
marrasquino *m,* maraschino liqueur
marro *m,* tick, tag (game)
marrón *a* maroon; brown. *m,* brown color; maroon color; quoit
marroquí *a* and *mf* Moroccan. *m,* Morocco leather
marroquín (-ina), marrueco (-ca) *a* and *n* Moroccan
Marruecos Morocco
marrullería *f,* flattery, cajolery
marrullero (-ra) *a* wheedling, flattering. *n* wheedler, cajoler

marsopa *f*, porpoise
marta *f*, sable; marten
martajar *vt*, *Lat. Am.* to grind, pound
Marte *m*, Mars
martes *m*, Tuesday. **m. de carnaval,** mardi gras
martillar *vt* to hammer; oppress
martillazo *m*, hammer blow
martilleo *m*, hammering; noise of the hammer; clink, clatter
martillero, -a *mf*, *Lat. Am.* auctioneer
martillo *m*, hammer; oppressor, tyrant; auction rooms. **a m.,** by hammering. **de m.,** wrought (of metals)
martín pescador *m*, kingfisher
martinete *m*, hammer (of a pianoforte); pile driver; drop hammer. **m. de báscula,** tilt hammer
Martinica Martinique
mártir *mf* martyr
martirio *m*, martyrdom
martirizar *vt* to martyr; torture, torment, martyrize; tease, annoy
marxismo *m*, Marxism
marzo *m*, March
mas *conjunc* but; yet
más *adv comp* more; in addition, besides; rather, preferably. *math* plus. **el (la,** etc.) **más,** *adv sup* the most, etc. **m. bien,** more; rather; preferably. **m. que,** only; but; more than; although, even if. **a lo m.,** at the most; at the worst. **a m.,** besides, in addition. **de m.,** superfluous, unnecessary, unwanted. **no . . . m. que,** only. **por m. que,** however; even if. **sin m. ni m.,** without further ado. **M. vale un mal arreglo que un buen pleito,** A bad peace is better than a good war
masa *f*, mass; dough; whole, aggregate; majority (of people); mortar. **en la m. de la sangre,** *fig* in the blood, in a person's nature
masada *f*, farmhouse and stock
masadero *m*, farmer; farm laborer
masaje *m*, massage
masajista *mf* masseur; masseuse
masato *m*, *Lat. Am.* drink made from bananas, fermented corn, yucca, etc.
mascadura *f*, chewing
mascar *vt* to chew; masticate; *inf* mumble, mutter
máscara *f*, mask; fancy dress; pretext, excuse. *mf* masquerader, reveler; *pl* masquerade. **m. para gases,** gas mask
mascarada *f*, masquerade; company of revelers
mascarero (-ra) *n* theatrical costumer, fancy-dress dealer
mascarilla *f*, death mask
mascarón *m*, large mask; *arch* gargoyle. **m. de proa,** *naut* figurehead
mascota *f*, mascot
masculinidad *f*, masculinity
masculino *a* masculine; male; manly, vigorous
mascullar *vt inf* to chew; mutter, mumble
masera *f*, kneading bowl; cloth for covering dough
masilla *f*, mastic, putty
masón (-ona) *n* Freemason
masonería *f*, freemasonry
masónico *a* masonic
masoquismo *m*, masochism
mastelero *m*, *naut* topmast
masticación *f*, mastication
masticar *vt* to masticate, eat; *inf* chew upon, consider
masticatorio *a* masticatory
mástil *m*, *naut* mast; upright, stanchion; pole (of a tent); stem, trunk; neck (of a guitar, etc.)
mastín *m*, mastiff
mastodonte *m*, mastodon
mastoides *a* mastoid
mastuerzo *m*, watercress; fool, blockhead
masturbación *f*, masturbation
masturbarse *vr* to masturbate
mata *f*, plant, shrub; stalk, sprig; grove, copse. **m. de pelo,** mat of hair
matacandelas *m*, candle snuffer
matachín *m*, mummer; butcher; *inf* swashbuckler
matadero *m*, slaughterhouse, abattoir; *Lat. Am.* brothel
matadura *f*, sore (on animals)
matafuego *m*, fire extinguisher; fireman
matalotaje *m*, ship's supplies, stores; *inf* hodgepodge
matamoros *a* swashbuckling, swaggering
matamoscas *m*, fly swatter
matanza *f*, killing, massacre, slaughter; butchery (animals); *inf* persistence, determination
matar *vt* to kill; quench (thirst); put out (fire, light); slake (lime); tarnish (metal); bevel (corners, etc.); pester, importune; suppress; compel; *art* tone down; *vr* kill oneself; be disappointed, grieve; overwork. **estar a m.,** to be at daggers drawn. **matarse por,** to try hard to; work hard for
matasanos *m*, *inf* quack (doctor); bad doctor
matasellos *m*, cancellation, postmark
mate *a* matte, unpolished, dull. *m*, checkmate (chess); maté, Paraguayan tea; gourd; vessel made from gourd, coconut, etc.
maté *m*, maté, Paraguayan tea
matemáticas *f pl*, mathematics. **m. prácticas,** applied mathematics. **m. teóricas,** pure mathematics
matemático *a* mathematical; exact. *m*, mathematician
materia *f*, matter; theme, subject matter; subject (of study); matter, stuff, substance; pus, matter; question, subject; reason, occasion. **m. colorante,** dye. **materias plásticas,** plastics. **materias primas,** raw materials. **en m. de,** concerning; in the matter of
material *a* material; dull, stupid, limited. *m*, material; ingredient; plant, factory; equipment. **m. móvil ferroviario,** rolling stock (railroads)
materialidad *f*, materiality; external appearance (of things)
materialismo *m*, materialism
materialista *a* materialistic. *mf* materialist; *Mexico* truckdriver
materializar *vt* to materialize; *vr* materialize; grow materialistic, grow less spiritual
maternidad *f*, maternity, motherhood
materno *a* maternal
matiz *m*, combination of colors; tone, hue; shade (of meaning, etc.)
matizar *vt* to combine, harmonize (colors); tint, shade; tinge (words, etc.)
matojo *m*, shrub, bush
matorral *m*, thicket, bush, undergrowth
matraca *f*, rattle; *inf* scolding, dressing-down; insistence, importunity
matraquear *vi* to make a noise with a rattle; *inf* scold
matriarcado *m*, matriarchy
matrícula *f*, list, register; matriculation; registration number (of a car, etc.). **m. de buques,** maritime register. **m. de mar,** mariner's register; maritime register
matriculación *f*, matriculation; registration
matricular *vt* to matriculate; enrol; *naut* register; *vr* matriculate; enroll, register
matrimonial *a* matrimonial
matrimonio *m*, marriage, matrimony; married couple. **m. a yuras,** secret marriage. **m. de la mano izquierda** *or* **m. morganático,** morganatic marriage. **contraer m.,** to get married
matritense *a* and *mf* Madrilenian
matriz *f*, uterus, womb; matrix, mold; *min* matrix; nut, female screw
matrona *f*, married woman; matron; midwife; female customs officer
matusalén *m*, Methuselah, very old man
matute *m*, smuggling; contraband; gambling den
matutero (-ra) *n* smuggler, contrabandist
matutino *a* matutinal, morning
maula *f*, trash; remnant; deception, fraud, trick. *mf inf* good-for-nothing; lazybones. *inf* **ser buena m.,** to be a trickster or a fraud
maulería *f*, remnant stall; trickery

maullar *vi* to meow, mew (cats)
maullido *m,* meow, cry of the cat
Mauricio, Isla de Mauritius
mauritano (-na) *a* and *n* Mauritian
mausoleo *m,* mausoleum
maxilar *a* maxillary. *m,* jaw
máxima *f,* maxim, rule, precept, principle
máxime *adv* principally, chiefly
máximo *a sup* **grande** greatest, maximum, top. *m,* maximum
maya *f,* common daisy; May queen
mayal *m,* flail
mayo *m,* May; maypole; bouquet, wreath of flowers; *pl* festivities on eve of May Day
mayólica *f,* majolica
mayonesa *f,* mayonnaise
mayor *a comp* **grande** bigger; greater; elder; main, principal; older; high (mass, etc.); *mus* major. *mf* major (of full age). *a sup* **grande. el, la, lo mayor, los (las) mayores,** the biggest, greatest; eldest; chief, principal. **por m.,** in short, briefly; *com* wholesale
mayor *m,* head, director; chief clerk; *mil* major; *pl* ancestors
mayoral *m,* head shepherd; coachman, driver; foreman, overseer, supervisor, steward
mayorazgo *m, law* entail; entailed estate; heir (to an entail); eldest son; right of primogeniture
mayordoma *f,* steward's wife; housekeeper; stewardess
mayordomo *m,* steward, superintendent; butler; major-domo, royal chief steward
mayoreo *m, Lat. Am.* wholesale
mayoría *f,* majority
mayormente *adv* chiefly; especially
mayúscula *f,* capital letter, upper-case letter
mayúsculo *a* large; capital (letters). **letra mayúscula,** capital letter, upper-case letter
maza *f,* mallet; club, bludgeon; mace; bass drum stick; pile driver; bone, stick, etc., tied to dog's tail in carnival; *inf* pedant, bore; important person, authority; *Lat. Am.* hub (of a wheel). **m. de polo,** polo mallet
mazacote *m,* concrete; roughhewn work of art; *inf* stodgy overcooked dish; bore, tedious person
mazamorra *f,* dish made of cornmeal; biscuit crumbs; broken fragments, remains
mazapán *m,* marzipan
mazmorra *f,* dungeon
mazo *m,* mallet; bundle, bunch; importunate person; clapper (of a bell); *Argentina,* deck (of cards)
mazonería *f,* stonemasonry
mazonero *m,* stonemason
mazorca *f,* spindleful; spike, ear (of corn); cocoa berry; camarilla, group
mazurca *f,* mazurka
me *pers pron acc* or *dat 1st sing mf* me; to me
meandro *m,* meandering, twisting, winding; wandering
meato *m,* meatus
mecánica *f,* mechanics; mechanism, machinery; *inf* worthless thing; mean action
mecánico *a* mechanical; power-operated; base, ill-bred. *m,* engineer; mechanic
mecanismo *m,* mechanism; works, machinery
mecanizar *vt* to mechanize
mecanografía *f,* typewriting
mecanografiar *vt* to typewrite, type
mecanográfico *a* typewriting, typing; typewritten, typed
mecanografista *mf* **mecanógrafo (-fa)** *n* typist
mecate *m, Lat. Am.* twine; coarse person
mecedor *a* rocking, swaying. *m,* swing; *Lat. Am.* rocking chair
mecedora *f,* rocking chair
mecenas *m,* Maecenas, patron
mecer *vt* to stir, mix; shake; rock; swing
mecha *f,* wick; bit, drill; fuse (of explosives); match (for cannon, etc.); fat bacon (for basting); lock of hair; skein, twist; *Lat. Am.* fright, scare
mechar *vt cul* to baste, lard
mechero *m,* gas burner; pocket lighter; socket of a candlestick
mechón *m,* tuft, skein, bundle; lock of hair; wisp
medalla *f,* medal; medallion; plaque, round panel; *inf* piece of eight (coin)
medallón *m,* large medal; medallion; locket
media *f,* stocking
mediación *f,* mediation, arbitration; intercession
mediado *a* half-full. **a mediados (del mes,** etc.**),** toward the middle (of the month, etc.)
mediador (-ra) *n* mediator, arbitrator; intercessor
medianamente *adv* moderately; passably, fairly well
medianero (-ra) *a* middle; intervening, intermediate; mediatory. *n* mediator. *m,* owner of a semidetached house or of one in a row
medianía *f,* average; medium, mediocrity; moderate wealth or means
mediano *a* medium, average; moderate; *inf* middling, passable, fair
medianoche *f,* midnight
mediante *a* mediatory. *adv* by means of, by, through
mediar *vi* to reach the middle; get halfway; elapse half a given time; intercede, mediate; arbitrate; be in between or in the middle; intervene, take part
medicación *f,* medication
medicamento *m,* medicament, medicine, remedy
medicar *vt* to medicate
medicastro *m,* unskilled physician; quack, charlatan
medicina *f,* medicine; medicament
medicinar *vt* to attend; treat (patients)
medición *f,* measuring; measurements; survey (land); scansion
médico (-ca) *a* medical. *n* doctor of medicine. **m. de cabecera,** family doctor. **m. general,** general practitioner
medida *f,* measurement; measuring stick; measure, precaution (gen. with *tomar, adoptar,* etc.); gauge; judgment, wisdom; meter; standard. **a m. que,** while, at the same time as. **tomar las medidas (a),** *fig* to take a person's measure, sum him up. **tomar sus medidas,** to take his (their) measurements; take the necessary measures. **un traje hecho a m.,** a suit made to measure
medidor *m Lat. Am.* gauge, meter. **m. de aqua** water meter. **m. de gas** gas meter
medio *a* half; middle; intermediate; halfway. *m,* half; middle; *art* medium; spiritualist medium; proceeding, measure, precaution; environment, medium; middle way, mean; *sport* halfback. **m. galope,** canter. **m. tiempo,** *sport* halftime. **a medias,** by halves; half, partly. **de por m.,** by halves; in between; in the way. **estar de por m.,** to be in the way; take part in. *inf* **quitar de en m.,** to get rid of. *inf* **quitarse de en m.,** to go away, remove oneself
mediocre *a* mediocre
mediodía *m,* noon, meridian; south
medioeval *a* medieval
mediopelo *m,* lower middle class
mediquillo *m, inf* quack; medicine man (in the Philippines)
medir *vt irr* to measure; (metrics) scan; survey (land); compare; *vr* measure one's words; act with restraint. See **pedir**
meditabundo *a* pensive, meditative, thoughtful
meditación *f,* meditation; consideration, reflection
meditador *a* meditative, thoughtful
meditar *vt* to meditate, consider, muse
meditativo *a* meditative
mediterráneo *a* mediterranean; inland, landlocked
médium *m, spirit* medium
medra *f,* progress; improvement, betterment; growth; prosperity

medrar *vi* to flourish, grow; become prosperous or improve one's position
medro *m*, improvement, progress. See **medra**
medroso *a* timid, frightened; frightful, horrible
médula *f*, marrow; *bot* pith; *fig* essence, core
medusa *f*, jellyfish
mefistofélico *a* Mephistophelian
mefítico *a* noxious, mephitic, poisonous
megáfono *m*, megaphone
megalómano (-na) *n* megalomaniac
mejicano (-na) *a* and *n* Mexican
Méjico Mexico
mejilla *f*, *anat* cheek
mejillón *m*, sea mussel
mejor *a comp* **bueno** better. *adv* better; rather; sooner; preferably. *a sup* **bueno. el, la, lo mejor; los, las mejores,** the best; most preferable. **m. que m.,** better and better. *inf* **a lo m.,** probably, in all probability. **tanto m.,** so much the better
mejora *f*, improvement; bettering; progress; higher bid (at auctions)
mejorable *a* improvable
mejoramiento *m*, betterment, improvement
mejorar *vt* to improve; better; outbid; *vi* grow better (in health); improve (weather); make progress; rally (of markets). **Mejorando lo presente,** Present company excepted
mejoría *f*, improvement, progress; betterment; superiority; advantage, profit
mejunje *m*, *inf* brew, potion, cure-all, stuff; *Lat. Am.* mess
melado *a* honey-colored. *m*, cane syrup
melancolía *f*, melancholia; sadness, depression, melancholy
melancólico *a* melancholy, sad; depressing
melaza *f*, molasses
melena *f*, long side whiskers; loose, flowing hair (in women); overlong hair (in men); lion's mane. *inf* **andar a la m.,** to start a fight or quarrel. *inf* **traer a la m.,** to drag by the hair, force
melifluo *a* mellifluous, sweet-voiced; honeyed
melindre *m*, honey fritter; affectation, scruple, fastidiousness; narrow ribbon
melindroso *a* overfastidious, affected, prudish
mella *f*, nick, notch; dent; gap; harm, damage (to reputation, etc.). **hacer m.,** *fig* to make an impression (on the mind); *mil* breach, drive a wedge
mellar *vt* to nick, notch; dent; damage
mellizo (-za) *a* and *n* twin
melocotón *m*, peach; peach tree
melocotonero *m*, peach tree
melodía *f*, melody, tune; melodiousness
melódico *a* melodic, melodious
melodioso *a* melodious, tuneful, sweet-sounding
melodrama *m*, melodrama
melodramático *a* melodramatic
melón *m*, melon
melosidad *f*, sweetness
meloso *a* honeyed; sweet; gentle; mellifluous
membrana *f*, membrane
membrete *m*, note, memorandum; note or card of invitation; superscription, heading; address (of person)
membrillo *m*, quince tree; quince; quince jelly
membrudo *a* brawny, strong, muscular
memo *a* silly, stupid
memorable *a* memorable
memorándum *m*, notebook, jotter; memorandum
memorar(se) *vt* and *vr* to remember, recall
memoria *f*, memory; remembrance, recollection; monument; memorial; report; essay, article; codicil; memorandum; record, chronicle; *pl* regards, compliments, greetings; memoirs; memoranda. *inf* **m. de grillo,** poor memory. **de m.,** by heart. **flaco de m.,** forgetful. **hacer m.,** to remember
memorial *m*, notebook; memorial, petition
memorialista *mf* secretary, amanuensis
memorioso *a* mindful, unforgetful
mena *f*, *min* ore
menaje *m*, household or school equipment or furniture
mención *f*, mention. **m. honorífica,** honorable mention. **hacer m. de,** to mention
mencionar *vt* to mention
mendacidad *f*, mendacity, untruthfulness
mendaz *a* mendacious, untruthful
mendelismo *m*, Mendelism
mendicante *a* begging; *ecc* mendicant. *mf* beggar
mendicidad *f*, mendicancy, begging
mendigar *vt* to beg for alms; entreat, supplicate
mendigo (-ga) *n* beggar
mendoso *a* mendacious, untruthful; mistaken
mendrugo *m*, crust of bread
menear *vt* to sway, move; wag; shake; manage, control, direct; *vr inf* get a move on; sway, move; wriggle
meneo *m*, swaying movement; wagging; shaking; wriggling; management, direction; *aer* bump; *inf* spanking
menester *m*, lack, shortage; necessity; occupation, employment; *pl* physical necessities; *inf* tools, implements, equipment. **haber m.,** to need, require. **ser m.,** to be necessary or requisite
menesteroso *a* indigent, poverty-stricken, needy
menestra *f*, vegetable soup; dried vegetable (gen. *pl*)
mengano (-na) *n* so-and-so (used instead of the name of the person)
mengua *f*, decrease; lack, shortage; waning (of the moon, etc.); dishonor, disgrace; poverty
menguado (-da) *a* timid, cowardly; silly, stupid; mean, avaricious. *n* coward; fool; skinflint. *m*, narrowing stitch when knitting socks
menguante *a* ebb; waning; decreasing. *f*, ebb tide; decadence, decline. **m. de la luna,** waning of the moon
menguar *vi* to decrease; decline, decay; wane; ebb; narrow (socks); *vt* diminish; disgrace, discredit
menina *f*, child attendant (on Spanish royalty)
menino *m*, Spanish royal page; little dandy
menjurje *m*, See **mejunje**
menopausia *f*, menopause
menor *a comp* less, smaller; younger, minor; *mus* minor. *m*, minor. *f*, (logic) minor. *a sup* **el, la, lo m.; los, las menores,** the least; smallest; youngest. **m. de edad,** minor (in age). **por m.,** at retail; in detail
menoría *f*, subordination, dependence; inferiority; minority (underage); childhood, youth
menorista *Lat. Am.*, *a* retail; *mf* retailer
menos *adv* less; minus; least; except. **m. de** *or* **m. que,** less than. **al m., por lo m.,** at least. **a m. que,** unless. **De m. nos hizo Dios,** Never say die, Nothing is impossible. **poco más o m.,** more or less, about
menoscabar *vt* to lessen, diminish, decrease; deteriorate, damage; disgrace, discredit
menoscabo *m*, decrease, diminishment; harm, damage, loss
menospreciable *a* despicable, contemptible
menospreciador (-ra) *a* scornful. *n* scorner, despiser
menospreciar *vt* to despise, scorn; underestimate, have a poor opinion of
menospreciativo *a* scornful, slighting, derisive
menosprecio *m*, scorn, derision; underestimation
mensaje *m*, message; official communication
mensajería *f*, carrier service; steamship line
mensajero (-ra) *n* messenger; errand boy
menso, -a *a*, *Mexico* dumb, silly, stupid
menstruación *f*, menstruation
menstruar *vi* to menstruate
mensual *a* monthly
mensualidad *f*, monthly salary, monthly payment
mensurable *a* measurable
mensurar *vt* to measure
menta *f*, menthe, mint; peppermint
mentado *a* celebrated, distinguished, famous
mental *a* mental
mentalidad *f*, mentality
mentalmente *adv* mentally

mentar *vt irr* to mention. See **sentar**
mentas *fpl, Argentina* reputation, gossip
mente *f,* mind; intelligence, understanding; will, intention
mentecatería *f,* folly, stupidity
mentecato (-ta) *a* foolish, silly; feeble-minded, simple. *n* fool, idiot
mentir *vi irr* to lie, be untruthful; deceive, mislead; falsify; *poet* belie; disagree, be incompatible; *vt* break a promise, disappoint. **m. como un bellaco,** to lie like a trooper See **sentir**
mentira *f,* lie, falsehood; error (in writing); *inf* white spot (on a fingernail); cracking (of fingerjoints). **m. oficiosa,** white lie. **Parece m.,** It seems incredible
mentiroso *a* lying, false; full of errors (literary works); deceptive
mentís *m,* giving the lie (literally, you lie); proof, demonstration (of error)
mentol *m,* menthol
mentón *m,* chin
menú *m,* menu
menudamente *adv* minutely; in detail, circumstantially
menudear *vt* to do frequently; do repeatedly; *vi* happen frequently; describe in detail; *com* sell by retail
menudencia *f,* minuteness, smallness; exactness, care, accuracy; trifle, worthless object; small matter; *pl* offal; pork sausages
menudeo *m,* repetition; description in detail; *com* retail. **al m.,** at retail
menudillos *m pl,* giblets; offal
menudo *a* minute, tiny; despicable; thin; small; vulgar; meticulous, exact; small (money). *m,* small coal; *m pl,* offal, entrails; small change (money). **a m.,** often, frequently. **por m.,** in detail, carefully; *com* in small lots
meñique *a inf* very small. *m,* little finger (in full, **dedo m.**)
meollo *m,* brain; *anat* marrow; *fig* essence, core, substance; understanding; *inf* **no tener m. (una cosa),** to be worthless, unsubstantial (things)
mequetrefe *m, inf* coxcomb, whippersnapper
meramente *adv* solely, simply, merely
mercachifle *m,* peddler; small merchant
mercadear *vi* to trade, traffic
mercadeo *m,* marketing (study of markets)
mercader *m,* dealer, merchant, trader. **m. de grueso,** wholesaler
mercadería *f,* See **mercancía**
mercado *m,* market; marketplace
mercancía *f,* goods, merchandise; commerce, trade, traffic
mercante *a* trading; commercial. *m,* merchant, dealer, trader
mercantil *a* mercantile, commercial
merced *f,* salary, remuneration; favor, benefit, kindness; will, desire, pleasure; mercy, grace; courtesy title given to untitled person (e.g. **vuestra m.,** your honor. Has now become **usted** and is universally used). **m. a,** thanks to. **estar uno a m. de,** to live at someone else's expense, be dependent on
mercenario (-ia) *n ecc* member of the Order of la Merced. *m, mil* mercenary; day laborer. *a* mercenary
mercería *f,* haberdashery, mercery
mercerizar *vt* to mercerize
mercero *m,* haberdasher, mercer
mercurio *m,* mercury, quicksilver; *ast* Mercury
merecedor *a* deserving, worthy
merecer *vt irr* to deserve, be worthy of; attain, achieve; be worth; *vi* deserve, be deserving. **m. bien de,** to deserve well of; have a claim on the gratitude of. See **conocer**
merecido *m,* due reward
merecimiento *m,* desert; merit
merendar *vi irr* to have lunch; pry into another's affairs; *vt* have (a certain food) for lunch. *inf* **merendarse (una cosa),** to obtain (a thing), have it in one's pocket. See **recomendar**
merendero *m,* lunchroom; tearoom
merengue *m, cul* meringue
meridiana *f,* daybed, chaise longue; siesta
meridiano *a* meridian. *m,* meridian. **a la meridiana,** at noon
meridional *a* meridional, southern
merienda *f,* tea, snack; lunch; *inf* hunchback. *inf* **juntar meriendas,** to join forces, combine interests
merino *a* merino. *m,* merino wool; shepherd of merino sheep
mérito *m,* merit; desert; worth, excellence. **de m.,** excellent, notable. **hacer m. de,** to mention
meritorio *a* meritorious. *m,* unpaid worker, learner
merluza *f,* hake; *inf* drinking bout. *inf* **pescar una m.,** to get drunk
merma *f,* decrease, drop; loss, waste, reduction; leakage
mermar *vi* to diminish, waste away, decrease; evaporate; leak; *vt* filch, pilfer; reduce, decrease
mermelada *f,* conserve, preserve; jam; marmalade
mero *a* mere; simple; plain
merodeador *a* marauding. *m,* marauder, raider
merodear *vi* to maraud, raid; *Mexico* make money illegally
merodeo *m,* raiding, marauding
mes *m,* month; menses, menstruation
mesa *f,* table; board, directorate; meseta, tableland; staircase landing; flat (of a sword, etc.); game of billiards. **m. de batalla,** post office sorting table. **m. de caballete,** trestle table. **m. de noche,** bedside table. **m. de tenis,** *Mexico* tennis court. **m. de tijeras,** folding table. **m. giratoria,** turntable. **alzar** (*or* **levantar**) **la m.,** to clear the table. **cubrir** (*or* **poner**) **la m.,** to set the table
mesada *f,* monthly wages, monthly payment
mesadura *f,* tearing of the hair or beard
mesarse *vr* to tear one's hair or beard
mesenterio *m,* mesentery
mesera *f Mexico* waitress
mesero *m Mexico* waiter
meseta *f,* staircase landing; plateau, tableland
mesiánico *a* Messianic
Mesías *m,* Messiah
mesilla *f,* small table; laughing admonition; landing (of a stair)
mesnada *f,* association, company, society
mesocracia *f,* mesocracy; middle class, bourgeoisie
mesón *m,* inn, tavern
mesonero (-ra) *n* innkeeper; *Venezuela* waiter, waitress
mesta *f,* ancient order of sheep farmers; *pl* confluence, meeting (of rivers)
mester *m,* craft, occupation. **m. de clerecía,** learned poetic meter of the Spanish Middle Ages. **m. de juglaría,** popular poetry and troubadour songs
mestizo *a* half-breed; hybrid; cross-breed
mesura *f,* sedateness; dignity; courtesy; moderation
mesurado *a* sedate; dignified; moderate, restrained, temperate
meta *f,* goalpost *fig* aim, end; goal; goalkeeper
metabolismo *m,* metabolism
metáfora *f,* metaphor
metafórico *a* metaphorical
metal *m,* metal; brass; timbre of the voice; state, condition; quality, substance; *her* gold or silver; *mus* brass (instruments)
metalario *m,* metalworker
metálico *a* metallic. *m,* metalworker; coin, specie; bullion
metalistería *f,* metalwork
metalizar *vt* to metallize, make metallic; *vr* become metallized; grow greedy for money
metalurgia *f,* metallurgy
metalúrgico *a* metallurgical. *m,* metallurgist
metamorfosis *f,* metamorphosis
metano *m,* methane

metatarso *m,* metatarsus
metate *m, Central America, Mexico* flat stone for grinding and pounding
metátesis *f,* metathesis
metedor (-ra) *n* placer, inserter; smuggler, contrabandist
metellón, -ona *a, Mexico* meddling, meddlesome
metempsicosis *f,* metempsychosis
metemuertos *inf* meddler, Nosy Parker
meteórico *a* meteoric
meteorito *m,* meteorite
meteoro *m,* meteor
meteorología *f,* meteorology
meteorológico *a* meteorological
meteorologista *mf* meteorologist; weather forecaster
meter *vt* to place; put; introduce, insert; stake (gambling); smuggle; cause, occasion; place close together; persuade to take part in; *sew* take in fullness; deceive, humbug; cram in, pack tightly; *naut* take in sail; *vr* interfere, butt in; meddle (with); take up, follow (occupations); be overfamiliar; disembogue, empty itself (rivers, etc.); attack with the sword; (*with prep a*) follow (occupations); become, turn (e.g. **meterse a predicar,** to turn preacher); (*with con*) pick a quarrel with. **meterse en precisiones,** to go into details. *inf* **meterse en todo,** to be very meddlesome
metesillas y sacamuertos *m,* scene shifter, stagehand
metiche *a, Mexico* = **metellón**
meticulosidad *f,* meticulosity; timorousness
meticuloso *a* meticulous, fussy; timid, nervous
metido *a* tight; crowded; crabbed (of handwriting). *m, sew* material for letting out (seams). **m. en años,** quite old (person)
metílico *a* methylic
metimiento *m,* insertion, introduction; influence, sway
metódico *a* methodical
método *m,* method
metodología *f,* methodology
metralla *f, mil* grapeshot, shrapnel
métrica *f,* metrics
métrico *a* metric; metrical
metro *m,* (verse) meter; meter (measurement); subway, underground railway
metrónomo *m,* metronome
metrópoli *f,* metropolis, capital; see of a metropolitan bishop; mother country
metropolitano *a* metropolitan. *m,* metropolitan bishop
mexicano *Lat. Am.* = **mejicano**
México *Lat. Am.* = **Méjico**
mezcla *f,* mixture; blend, combination; mixed cloth, tweed; mortar
mezclar *vt* to mix, blend, combine; *vr* mix, mingle; take part; interfere, meddle; intermarry
mezcolanza *f, inf* hodgepodge
mezquindad *f,* poverty; indigence; miserliness; paltriness; meanness, poorness
mezquino *a* needy, impoverished; miserly, stingy; small, diminutive; unhappy; mean, paltry
mezquita *f,* mosque
mi *poss pron* my. *m, mus* mi, E
mí *pers pron acc gen dat 1st pers sing* me. Used only after prepositions (e.g. **Lo hicieron por mí,** They did it for me)
miaja *f,* See **migaja**
miasma *m,* miasma
miasmático *a* miasmatic, malarious
miau *m,* meow
mica *f, min* mica; coquette, flirt
micho (-cha) *n inf* puss, pussycat
micología *f,* mycology
micra *f,* micron, thousandth part of a millimeter
micro *m, Chile, Peru* (large, express) bus; *elsewhere in Lat. Am.* minibus
microbiano *a* microbial, microbic
microbio *m,* microbe
microbiología *f,* microbiology
microbrigada *f,* team of volunteer workers (in Castroist Cuba)
microcosmo *m,* microcosm
micrófono *m,* microphone
microonda *f,* microwave
microscópico *a* microscopic
microscopio *m,* microscope
miedo *m,* fear, apprehension, terror. **m. al público,** stagefright. **tener m.,** to be afraid
miedoso *a inf* fearful, nervous
miel *f,* honey. **m. de caña,** sugarcane syrup. *inf* **quedarse a media m.,** to see one's pleasure snatched away. *inf* **ser de mieles,** to be most pleasant or agreeable
mielitis *f,* myelitis
miembro *m, anat* limb; penis; member, associate; part, portion, section; *math* member
miente *f,* thought, imagination, mind. **parar** *or* **poner mientes en,** to consider, think about. **venírsele a las mientes,** to occur to one's mind
mientras *adv* while. **m. más . . .,** the more . . . . **m. que,** while (e.g. **m. que esperaba en el jardín,** while he was waiting in the garden). **m. tanto,** in the meanwhile
miércoles *m,* Wednesday. **m. de ceniza,** Ash Wednesday
mierda *f,* (*vulgar*) shit; *inf* filth
mies *f,* cereal plant, grain; harvest time; *pl* grain fields
miga *f,* breadcrumb; crumb; *inf* essence, core; substance; bit, scrap; *pl* fried breadcrumbs. *inf* **hacer buenas** (*or* **malas**) **migas,** to get on well (*or* badly) together
migaja *f,* breadcrumb; bit, scrap; trifle, mere nothing; *pl* crumbs (from the table); remains, remnants
migajón *m,* crumb (of a loaf): *fig inf* essence, substance, core
migración *f,* migration; emigration
migraña *f,* migraine
migratorio *a* migratory
mijo *m,* millet; maize
mil *a* thousand; thousandth; many, large number. *m,* thousand; thousandth. *inf* **Son las m. y quinientas,** It's extremely late (of the hour)
miladi *f,* my lady
milagrero *a inf* miraculous
milagro *m,* miracle; marvel, wonder. **¡M.!** Amazing! Just fancy!
milagroso *a* miraculous; marvelous, wonderful
milanés (-esa) *a* and *n* Milanese
mildeu *m,* mildew
milenario *a* millenary; millennial. *m,* millenary; millennium
milésimo *a* thousandth
milicia *f,* militia; military; art of war; military profession
miliciano *a* military. *m,* militiaman
milico *m, Lat. Am., derogatory* soldier
miligramo *m,* milligram
mililitro *m,* milliliter
milímetro *m,* millimeter
militante *a* militant
militar *a* military. *m,* soldier. *vi* to fight in the army; struggle (for a cause); *fig* militate (e.g. **Las circunstancias militan en favor de** (*or* **contra**) **sus ideas,** Circumstances militate against his ideas)
militarismo *m,* militarism
militarista *a* militaristic. *mf* militarist
militarizar *vt* to militarize; make war-like
milla *f,* mile
millar *m,* thousand; vast number (gen. *pl*)
millón *m,* million
millonario (-ia) *a* and *n* millionaire
millonésimo *a* millionth
milmillonésimo *a* billionth
milpa *f, Central America, Mexico* corn field
milpero, -a *mf, Lat. Am.* corn grower

mimar *vt* to spoil, overindulge; caress, fondle
mimbre *mf* osier; willow tree. *m*, wicker
mimbrear *vi* to sway, bend
mimbrera *f*, osier; osier bed; willow
mímica *f*, mimicry; mime
mímico *a* mimic
mimo *m*, mimic, buffoon; mime; caress, expression of affection, tenderness; overindulgence
mimoso *a* affectionate, demonstrative
mina *f*, mine; excavation, mining; underground passage; lead (in a pencil); (*mil nav*) mine; *fig* gold mine. *mil* **m. terrestre,** landmine
minador *m*, excavator; *nav* minelayer; *mil* sapper
minar *vt* to excavate, mine; *fig* undermine; (*mil nav*) mine; work hard for
minarete *m*, minaret
mineraje *m*, exploitation of a mine, mining; mineral products
mineral *a* and *m*, mineral
mineralogía *f*, mineralogy
mineralógico *a* mineralogical
mineralogista *mf* mineralogist
minería *f*, mining, mineworking; mineworkers
minero *a* mining. *m*, miner, mineworker; source, origin
minga *f*, *Lat. Am.* voluntary communal labor
miniar *vt art* to illuminate
miniatura *f*, miniature
miniaturista *mf* miniaturist
mínima *f*, *mus* minim; very small thing or portion
mínimo *a sup* **pequeño** smallest; minimum; meticulous, precise. *m*, minimum; (meteorological) trough
ministerial *a* ministerial
ministerio *m*, office, post; *pol* cabinet; ministry; government office; government department.
ministrar *vt* and *vi* to fill; administer (an office); *vt* minister to; give, provide
ministro *m*, instrument, agency; minister of state, cabinet minister; clergyman, minister; minister plenipotentiary; policeman. **m. de estado,** secretary of state. **m. de gobernación,** secretary of the interior. **m. de hacienda,** treasurer. **m. de relaciones extranjeras,** foreign secretary. **primer m.** prime minister
minoración *f*, reduction, decrease
minorar *vt* to diminish, decrease
minoría *f*, minority, smaller number; minority (of age)
minoridad *f*, minority (of age)
minorista *mf*, *Lat. Am.* retailer
minucia *f*, smallness; morsel, mite; *pl* details, trifles, minutiae
minucioso *a* meticulous, precise, minute
minúsculo *a* minute, very small
minuta *f*, memorandum, minute; note; list, catalogue
minutero *m*, minute hand (of a clock)
minuto *a* minute, very small. *m*, minute
mío *m*. **mía,** *f*, (*m pl.* **míos,** *f pl.* **mías**) *poss pron* mine (e.g. **Las flores son mías,** The flowers are mine). **Mi** is used before nouns, *not* **mío.** Also used with article (e.g. **Este sombrero no es el mío,** This hat is not mine (my one)). **de mío,** by myself, without help. *inf* **¡Esta es la mía!** This is my chance!
miope *a* myopic. *mf* myopic person
miopía *f*, shortsightedness
miosota *f*, myosotis, forget-me-not
mira *f*, sight (optical instruments, guns); intention, design; *mil* watchtower; care, precaution. **andar, estar** *or* **quedar a la m.,** to be vigilant, be on the lookout
mirada *f*, look; gaze. **lanzar miradas de carnero degollado (a),** to cast sheep's eyes at
miradero *m*, object of attention, cynosure; observation post, lookout
mirador (-ra) *n* spectator. *m*, *arch* oriel; enclosed balcony; observatory
miramiento *m*, observation, gazing; scruple, consideration; precaution, care; thoughtfulness
mirar *vt* to look at, gaze at; observe, behold; watch; consider, look after; value, appreciate; concern; believe, think; (*with prep a*) overlook, look on to; face; (*with por*) care for, protect; look after, consider. **m. contra el gobierno,** *inf* to be squint-eyed. **m. de hito en hito,** to look over, stare at. **mirarse en (una cosa),** to consider (a matter) carefully
miríada *f*, myriad, huge number
mirilla *f*, peephole
miriñaque *m*, trinket, ornament; crinoline
mirlarse *vr inf* to give oneself airs
mirlo *m*, blackbird; *inf* pompous air
mirón *a* inquisitive, curious
mirra *f*, myrrh
mirto *m*, myrtle
misa *f*, (*ecc mus*) mass. **m. de difuntos,** requiem mass. **m. del gallo,** midnight mass. **m. mayor,** high mass. **m. rezada,** low mass. **como en m.,** in profound silence. **oír m.,** to attend mass
misal *m*, missal
misantropía *f*, misanthropy
misantrópico *a* misanthropic
misántropo *m*, misanthrope
miscelánea *f*, medley, assortment, miscellany
misceláneo *a* assorted, miscellaneous, mixed
miscible *a* mixable
miserable *a* miserable, unhappy; timid, pusillanimous; miserly, mean; despicable
miseria *f*, misery; poverty, destitution; avarice, miserliness; *inf* poor thing, trifle
misericordia *f*, mercy, compassion
misericordioso *a* merciful, compassionate
mísero *a inf* fond of churchgoing
misérrimo *a sup* most miserable
misión *f*, mission; vocation; commission, duty, errand
misionar *vi* to missionize, act as a missionary; *ecc* conduct a mission
misionero *m*, missioner; missionary
Misisipi, el the Mississippi
misiva *f*, missive
mismo *a* same; similar; self (e.g. **ellos mismos,** they themselves); very, same (e.g. **Ahora m. voy,** I'm going this very minute). **Me da lo m.,** It makes no difference to me. **por lo m.,** for that selfsame reason
misógamo (-ma) *n* misogamist
misógino *m*, misogynist
misterio *m*, mystery
misterioso *a* mysterious
mística *f*, **misticismo** *m*, mysticism
místico *a* mystic
mistificación *f*, mystification; mystery; deception
mistificar *vt* to mystify; deceive
Misuri, el the Missouri
mitad *f*, half; middle, center. *fig inf* **cara m.,** better half. *inf* **mentir por la m. de la barba,** to lie barefacedly
mítico *a* mythical
mitigación *f*, mitigation
mitigador (-ra) *a* mitigatory. *n* mitigator
mitigar *vt* to mitigate, moderate, alleviate; appease
mitin *m*, mass meeting
mito *m*, myth
mitología *f*, mythology
mitológico *a* mythological
mitologista, mitólogo *m*, mythologist
mitón *m*, mitten
mitra *f*, miter; bishopric; archbishopric
mitrado *a* mitred
mixto *a* mixed, blended; hybrid; composite; mongrel. *m*, mixed train (carrying freight and passengers); sulphur match
mixtura *f*, mixture, blend; compound; mixture (medicine)
¡miz, miz! puss, puss!
moabita *mf* Moabite
mobiliario *a* movable (goods). *m*, furniture
moblaje *m*, household goods and furniture
mocasín *m*, moccasin

mocedad *f,* youth, adolescence; mischief, prank. *fig inf* **correr sus mocedades,** to sow one's wild oats
mochila *f,* knapsack; nosebag; military rations for a march
mocho *a* blunted, topless, lopped; *inf* shorn, cropped. *m,* butt, butt end
mochuelo *m,* owl; *inf* difficult job
moción *f,* motion, movement; impulse, tendency; divine inspiration; motion (of a debate)
moco *m,* mucus; candle drips; snuff of a candle. *inf* **caérsele el m.,** to be very simple, be easily deceived
mocoso (-sa) *a* running of the nose, sniffling; unimportant, insignificant. *n* coxcomb, stripling; *Lat. Am.* child
moda *f,* fashion. **estar** *or* **ser de m.,** to be fashionable, be in fashion. **la última m.,** the latest fashion
modales *m pl,* manners, behavior
modalidad *f,* form, nature; *mus* modality
modelado *m, art* modeling
modelar *vt art* to model; *vr* model oneself (on), copy
modelo *m,* example, pattern; model. *mf art* life model
moderación *f,* moderation; restraint, temperance, equability
moderado *a* moderate; restrained, temperate
moderador (-ra) *a* moderating. *n* moderator
moderantismo *m,* moderate opinion; moderate political party
moderar *vt* to moderate; temper, restrain; *vr* regain one's self-control; behave with moderation
modernidad *f,* modernity
modernismo *m,* modernism
modernista *a* modernistic; modern. *mf* modernist
modernización *f,* modernization
modernizar *vt* to modernize
moderno *a* modern. *m,* modern. **a la moderna,** in modern fashion
modestia *f,* modesty
modesto *a* modest
módico *a* moderate (of prices, etc.)
modificable *a* modifiable
modificación *f,* modification
modificador, modificante *a* modifying, moderating
modificar *vt* to modify; moderate
modismo *m,* idiom, idiomatic expression
modista *mf* dressmaker; couturier; milliner
modo *m,* mode, method, style; manner, way; moderation, restraint; civility, politeness (often *pl*); *mus* mode; *gram* mood. **m. de ser,** nature, temperament. **de m. que,** so that. **de ningún m.,** not at all, by no means. **de todos modos,** in any case
modorra *f,* deep sleep, stupor
modorro *a* drowsy, heavy
modoso *a* demure; well-behaved
modulación *f,* modulation
modulador (-ra) *a* modulative. *n* modulator, *m, mus* modulator
modular *vt* and *vi* to modulate
mofa *f,* mockery, ridicule, jeering
mofador (-ra) *a* jeering. *n* scoffer, mocker
mofarse *vr* (*with de*) to make fun of, jeer at
mofeta *f,* noxious gas; damp (gas); *zool* skunk
moflete *m, inf* plump cheek
mofletudo *a* plump-cheeked
mogol (-la) *a* and *n* Mongolian.
mogote *m,* hill; pyre, stack
mohín *m,* grimace
mohína *f,* grudge, rancor; sullenness; sulkiness
mohíno *a* depressed, gloomy; sulky; black or black-nosed (of animals)
moho *m,* mold, fungoid growth; moldiness; moss. *inf* **no criar m.,** to be always on the move
mohoso *a* mossy; moldy
mojada *f,* wetting; *inf* stab; sop of bread
mojador (-ra) *n* wetter. *m,* stamp moistener
mojar *vt* to wet; moisten; *inf* stab, wound with a dagger; *vi* take part in; meddle, interfere; *vr* get wet
mojicón *m,* kind of spongecake; *inf* slap in the face
mojiganga *f,* masquerade, mummer's show; farce; funny sight, figure of fun
mojigatería *f,* hypocrisy; sanctimoniousness; prudery
mojigato (-ta) *a* hypocritical; sanctimonious; prudish. *n* hypocrite; bigot; prude
mojón *m,* boundary marker; milestone; heap. **m. kilométrico,** milestone
molar *a* molar
molde *m,* mold, matrix; *fig* model, pattern. **de m.,** printed; suitably, conveniently; perfectly. **letra de m.,** printed letters, print
moldeador (-ra) *n* molder
moldear *vt* to mold, cast
moldura *f,* molding
moldurar *vt carp* to mold
molécula *f,* molecule
molecular *a* molecular
mole *f* mass, bulk
mole de guajolote *m, Mexico* turkey served with a heavy dark sauce made of different kinds of chiles, spices, etc.
moler *vt irr* to grind, crush; tire, exhaust; ill-treat; pester, annoy. **m. a palos,** to beat black and blue. *Pres. Ind.* **muelo, mueles, muele, muelen.** *Pres. Subjunc.* **muela, muelas, muela, muelan**
molestia *f,* inconvenience, trouble; annoyance; discomfort, pain; bore, nuisance. **Es una m.,** It's a nuisance
molesto *a* inconvenient, troublesome; annoying; painful; uncomfortable; boring, tedious
molestoso, -a *a, Lat. Am.* annoying, bothersome
moletón *m,* flannelet
molicie *f,* softness, smoothness; effeminacy, weakness
molienda *f,* milling; grinding; mill; portion ground at one time; *inf* exhaustion, fatigue; *inf* nuisance
molificar *vt* to mollify, appease
molimiento *m,* milling; grinding; exhaustion, fatigue
molinera *f,* (woman) miller; miller's wife
molinero *a* mill. *m,* miller
molinillo *m,* hand mill, small grinder; mincing machine; beater. **m. de café,** coffee mill
molino *m,* mill; harum-scarum, rowdy; bore, tedious person; *inf* mouth. **m. de rueda de escalones,** treadmill. **m. de viento,** windmill
molleja *f,* gizzard
mollera *f,* crown of the head; brains, sense. *inf* **ser duro de m.,** to be obstinate; be stupid
molusco *m,* mollusk
momentáneo *a* momentary, brief; instantaneous, immediate
momento *m,* moment, minute; importance; *mech* moment. **al m.,** immediately. **a cada m.,** all the time; frequently. **por momentos,** continually; intermittently
momería *f,* mummery
momero (-ra) *n* mummer
momia *f,* mummy
momificación *f,* mummification
momificar *vt* to mummify; *vr* become mummified
mona *f,* female monkey; *inf* imitator; drinking bout; drunk. *inf* **Aunque la m. se vista de seda, m. se queda,** Breeding will tell. *inf* **ser la última m.,** to be of no account, be unimportant
monacillo *m, ecc* acolyte
monada *f,* mischievous prank; affected gesture or grimace; small, pretty thing; childish cleverness; flattery; rash act; *pl* monkey shines
monaguillo *m, ecc* acolyte
monarca *mf* monarch
monarquía *f,* monarchy
monárquico (-ca) *a* monarchic. *n* monarchist
monarquismo *m,* monarchism
monasterio *m,* monastery; convent
monástico *a* monastic
monda *f,* skinning, peeling; *agr* pruning; cleansing; *Lat. Am.* beating, thrashing
mondadientes *m,* toothpick

mondar *vt* to skin, peel; *agr* prune; cut the hair; cleanse; free of rubbish; *inf* deprive of possessions; *Lat. Am.* to beat, beat up, thrash *vr* pick one's teeth
mondo *a* simple, plain; bare; unadulterated, pure
mondongo *m, Lat. Am.* tripe
moneda *f,* coin, piece of money; coinage; *inf* wealth; cash. **m. corriente,** currency. **m. metálica,** specie. **pagar en buena m.,** to give entire satisfaction. **pagar en la misma m.,** to pay back in the same coin, return like for like. *inf* **ser m. corriente,** to be usual or very frequent
monedero *m,* coiner, minter; handbag; purse
monería *f,* mischievous trick; unimportant trifle; pretty thing; childish cleverness, pretty ways
monetario *a* monetary. *m,* collection of coins and medals
monetización *f,* monetization
monigote *m, inf* boor; grotesque, puppet
monitor *m,* monitor
monitorio *a* monitory
monja *f,* nun; *pl* sparks
monje *m,* monk
monjil *a* nun-like. *m,* nun's habit
mono *a inf* pretty, attractive; amusing, funny. *m,* monkey; person given to grimacing; rash youth; coverall. *inf* **estar de monos,** to be on bad terms
monocromo *a* monochrome; monochromatic
monóculo *m,* monocle
monogamia *f,* monogamy
monógamo *a* monogamous. *n* monogamist
monografía *f,* monograph
monograma *m,* monogram
monolítico *a* monolithic
monolito *m,* monolith
monólogo *m,* monologue
monomanía *f,* monomania
monomaníaco (-ca) *n* monomaniac
monopatín *m,* scooter
monoplano *m,* monoplane
monopolio *m,* monopoly
monopolista *mf* monopolist
monopolizar *vt* to monopolize
monoteísmo *m,* monotheism
monoteísta *mf* monotheist
monotipia *f,* monotype
monotonía *f,* monotony; monotone
monótono *a* monotonous
monroísmo *m,* Monroe doctrine
monseñor *m,* monsignor
monserga *f, inf* rigmarole; jargon
monstruo *m,* monster; freak, monstrosity; cruel person; hideous person or thing
monstruosidad *f,* monstrousness, monstrosity
monstruoso *a* monstrous, abnormal; enormous; extraordinary; atrocious, outrageous
monta *f,* mounting a horse; total; *mil* mounting signal; breeding station (horses)
montacargas *m,* hoist, lift; freight elevator
montador *m,* mounter; mounting block
montadura *f,* mounting; mount, setting (of jewels)
montaje *m,* assembling, setting up (machines); presentation (of a book); (cinema) montage
montano *a* hilly, mountainous
montante *m,* upright, stanchion; tent pole
montaña *f,* mountain; mountainous country. **montañas rusas,** roller coaster (at an amusement park)
montañés (-esa) *a* mountain. *n* mountain dweller; native of Santander
montañoso *a* mountainous; hilly
montar *vi* to ascend, climb up, get on top; mount (a horse); ride (a horse); be important; *vt* get on top of; ride (a horse); total, amount to; set up (apparatus, machinery); *naut* sail around, double; set, mount (gems); cock (firearms); fine for trespassing; wind (a clock); command (a ship); *naut* carry, be fitted with (guns, etc.). **m. a horcajadas en,** to mount astride; straddle. **montarse en cólera,** to fly into a rage
montaraz *a* mountain-dwelling; wild, savage; rude, uncivilized, uncouth. *m,* gamekeeper, forester
monte *m,* mount, hill; woodland; obstacle, impediment. **m. de piedad,** pawnshop. **m. pío,** savings fund
montenegrino (-na) *a* and *n* Montenegrin
montepío *m, Lat. Am.* pawnshop
montera *f,* cap; glass roof
montería *f,* hunt, chase; art of hunting
montero (-ra) *n* hunter, huntsman
montés *a* wild, savage, untamed
montevideano (-na) *a* and *n* Montevidean
montículo *m,* mound, hill
montón *m,* heap, pile; *inf* abundance, lot. *inf* **a, de** *or* **en m.,** all jumbled up together. **a montones,** in abundance
montonero, -a *mf* domineering, overbearing
montuoso *a* mountainous
montura *f,* riding animal, mount; horse trappings; setting up, mounting (artillery, etc.)
monumento *m,* monument; document, record; tomb
monzón *mf,* monsoon
moña *f,* doll; dressmaker's model; bow for the hair; bullfighter's black bow; baby's bonnet; *inf* drinking bout
moño *m,* bun, chignon; topknot (birds); bunch of ribbons; *pl* tawdry trimmings
moquete *m,* slap in the face
moquillo *m,* distemper (of animals)
mora *f,* blackberry; mulberry; bramble; Moorish girl, Moorish woman
morada *f,* dwelling, abode; sojourn, stay
morado *a* purple
morador (-ra) *n* dweller; sojourner
moral *a* moral, ethical. *f,* morality, ethics; morale. *m,* blackberry bush
moraleja *f,* moral, lesson
moralidad *f,* morality
moralista *mf* moralist
moralización *f,* moralization
moralizador (-ra) *a* moralizing. *n* moralizer
moralizar *vt* to reform, correct; *vi* moralize
moratoria *f,* moratorium
morbidez *f, art* morbidezza; softness
mórbido *a* morbid, diseased; *art* delicate (of flesh tones); soft
morbo *m,* illness. **m. gálico,** syphilis
morboso *a* ill; morbid, unhealthy
morcilla *f, cul* black pudding; (*inf theat*) gag
morcillero (-ra) *n* seller of black puddings; (*inf theat*) actor who gags
mordacidad *f,* corrosiveness; mordacity, sarcasm; *cul* piquancy
mordaz *a* corrosive; sarcastic, caustic, mordant; *cul* piquant
mordaza *f,* gag
mordedor *a* biting; scandalmongering
mordedura *f,* bite, biting
mordelón, -ona *mf, Central America, Mexico* given to taking bribes
morder *vt irr* to bite; nibble, nip; seize, grasp; corrode, eat away; slander; etch. *Pres. Ind.* **muerdo, muerdes, muerde, muerden.** *Pres. Subjunc.* **muerda, muerdas, muerda, muerdan**
mordida *f, Lat. Am.* bite; *Central America, Mexico also* bribe
mordiente *m,* fixative (for dyeing); mordant. *a* mordant (of acid)
mordiscar *vt* to nibble, bite gently; bite
mordisco *m,* nibble; nibbling; bite; biting; piece bitten off
morena *f,* moraine
moreno (-na) *a* dark brown; swarthy complexioned; dark (of people). *n inf* negro, mulatto
morera *f,* mulberry bush
morería *f,* Moorish quarter

morfina *f*, morphine
morfinómano (-na) *n* morphine addict
morfológico *a* morphological
morganático *a* morganatic
moribundo (-da) *a* moribund, dying. *n* dying person
morillo *m*, andiron, fire-dog
morir *vi irr* to die; fade, wither; decline, decay; disappear; yearn (for); long (to); go out (lights, fire); *vr* die; go numb (limbs); (*with por*) adore, be mad about. *inf* **m. vestido,** to die a violent death. **¡Muera!** Down with! *Past Part.* **muerto.** For other tenses see **dormir**
morisco (-ca) *a* Moorish. *n* Morisco, Moor converted to Christianity
mormón (-ona) *n* Mormon
mormonismo *m*, Mormonism
moro (-ra) *a* Moorish. *n* Moor; Mohammedan. *inf* **haber moros y cristianos,** to be the deuce of a row. *inf* **Hay moros en la costa,** The coast is not clear; There's trouble in the offing
moronga *f*, *Central America, Mexico* blood sausage
morosidad *f*, slowness, delay; sluggishness, sloth
moroso *a* slow, dilatory; sluggish, lazy
morra *f*, crown of the head
morral *m*, nose-bag; knapsack; game-bag; *inf* lout
morriña *f*, cattle plague, murrain; *inf* depression, blues; homesickness
morro *m*, anything round; hummock, hillock; round pebble; headland, cliff
morrón *m*, *Lat. Am.* hot red pepper
morsa *f*, walrus
mortaja *f*, shroud, winding sheet
mortal *a* mortal; fatal, deadly; on the point of death; great, tremendous; certain, sure. *mf* mortal
mortalidad *f*, humanity, human race; mortality, death-rate
mortandad *f*, mortality, number of deaths
mortecino *a* dead from natural causes (animals); weak; fading; dull, dead (of eyes); flickering; on the point of death or extinction
mortero *m*, mortar (for building); *mil* mortar; pounding mortar
mortífero *a* deadly, mortal
mortificación *f*, *med* gangrene; humiliation, wounding; mortification (of the flesh)
mortificar *vt med* to mortify; humiliate, wound, hurt; mortify (the flesh); *vr* become gangrenous
mortuorio *a* mortuary. *m*, funeral, obsequies
mosaico *a* and *m*, mosaic
mosca *f*, fly; *inf* nuisance; bore, pest; cash; *pl* sparks. *inf* **m. muerta,** underhanded person. *inf* **papar moscas,** to gape, be dumbfounded. *inf* **soltar la m.,** to give or spend money unwillingly
moscardón *m*, gadfly
moscatel *a* muscatel. *m*, muscatel (grapes and wine); *inf* pest, tedious person
Moscú Moscow
mosquear *vt* to drive off flies; reply crossly; whip; *vr* be exasperated; brush aside obstacles
mosquero *m*, flypaper
mosquete *m*, musket
mosquetería *f*, musketry; (*ant theat*) male members of the audience who stood at the back of the pit
mosquetero *m*, musketeer; (Spanish theater of the sixteenth and seventeenth centuries) male member of the audience who stood at the back of the pit
mosquitero *m*, mosquito net
mosquito *m*, mosquito; midge, gnat; *inf* tippler, drunkard
mostacera *f*, mustard pot
mostacho *m*, mustache, whiskers; *inf* smudge on the face
mostaza *f*, mustard plant or seed; *cul* mustard
mostela *f*, sheaf (of corn, etc.)
mosto *m*, must, unfermented wine
mostrador (-ra) *n* one who shows, exhibitor. *m*, shop counter; face of a watch
mostrar *vt irr* to show; indicate, point out; demonstrate, prove; manifest, reveal; *vr* show oneself, be (e.g. **Se mostró bondadoso,** He showed himself to be kind). *Pres. Ind.* **muestro, muestras, muestra, muestran.** *Pres. Subjunc.* **muestre, muestres, muestre, muestren**
mostrenco *a inf* stray, vagrant, homeless; *inf* dull, ignorant; *inf* fat, heavy
mota *f*, fault in cloth; mote, defect, fault; mound, hill; thread of cotton, speck of dust, etc.; fleck (of the sun, etc.); spot
mote *m*, maxim, saying; motto, device; catchword, slogan; nickname; *Lat. Am.* boiled corn
motear *vt* to speckle, dot, variegate, spot
motejar *vt* to nickname, call names, dub
motete *m*, motet
motín *m*, mutiny; riot
motivar *vt* to motivate, cause; explain one's reasons
motivo *a* motive. *m*, cause, motive; *mus* motif. **con m. de,** on account of, because of. **de m. propio,** of one's own free will
motocicleta *f*, motorcycle
motociclista *mf* motorcyclist
motor (-ra) *a* motive, driving. *m*, motor, engine. *n* (person) mover, motive force. **m. de combustión interna,** internal combustion engine. **m. de retroacción,** jet engine
motorista *mf* motorist, driver
movedizo *a* movable; insecure, unsteady; shaky; changeable, vacillating
mover *vt irr* to move; operate, drive; sway; wag; persuade, induce; excite; move (to pity, etc.); (*with prep a*) cause; *vi* sprout (plants); *vr* move. *Pres. Ind.* **muevo, mueves, mueve, mueven.** *Pres. Subjunc.* **mueva, muevas, mueva, muevan**
movible *a* movable; insecure, shaky. *m*, motive, cause, incentive
movilidad *f*, mobility; changeableness, inconstancy
movilización *f*, mobilization
movilizar *vt* to mobilize
movimiento *m*, movement; perturbation, excitement; *mus* movement; *lit* fire, spirit; *mech* motion, movement. *mil* **m. envolvente,** encircling movement
moza *f*, maid; girl; waitress. **m. de partido,** party girl, prostitute. **buena m.,** fine, upstanding young woman
mozalbete *m*, lad, stripling, boy
mozo *a* young, unmarried. *m*, boy, youth; bachelor; waiter; porter. **m. de cordel** *or* **m. de esquina,** street porter, message boy. **m. de estación,** railroad porter. **buen m.,** fine, upstanding young man
muaré *m*, moiré silk
mucama *f*, *Argentina* chambermaid
muceta *f*, *univ* hood, short cape (of a graduate's gown)
muchacha *f*, girl, lass; female servant
muchachada *f*, childish prank
muchachez *f*, boyhood; girlhood
muchachil *a* boyish; girlish
muchacho *m*, boy, youth; male servant
muchedumbre *f*, abundance, plenty; crowd, multitude; mass, mob
muchísimo *a sup* very much. *adv* very great deal, very much
mucho *a* much; plenty of; very; long (time); *pl* many, numerous. *adv* a great deal; much; very much; yes, certainly; frequently, often; very (e.g. **Me alegro m.,** I am very glad); to a great extent; long (time). **con m.,** by far, easily. **ni con m.,** nor anything like it, very far from it. **ni m. menos,** and much less. **por m. que,** however much
mucílago *m*, mucilage, gum
mucosa *f*, mucous membrane
mucoso *a* mucous
muda *f*, change, transformation; change of clothes; molting season; molt, sloughing of skin (snakes, etc.); change of voice (in boys)
mudable *a* changeable, inconstant

mudanza *f,* change; furniture removal; step, figure (in dancing); changeability, inconstancy
mudar *vt* to change; alter, transform; exchange; remove; dismiss (from employment); molt; slough the skin (snakes, etc.); change the voice (boys); *vr* alter one's behavior; change one's clothes; change one's residence, move; change one's expression; *inf* go away, depart
mudéjar *m, arch* style containing Moorish and Christian elements. *mf* Moor who remained in Spain under Christian rule
mudez *f,* dumbness; silence, muteness
mudo *a* dumb; silent, mute, quiet
mueblaje *m,* household goods and furniture
mueble *m,* piece of furniture; furnishing
mueblería *f,* furniture store or factory
mueblista *mf* furniture maker; furniture dealer
mueca *f,* grimace
muela *f,* grindstone; molar (tooth); millstone; flat-topped hill. **m. del juicio,** wisdom tooth. **dolor de muelas,** toothache
muellaje *m,* wharfage, dock dues
muelle *a* soft, smooth; voluptuous, sensuous; luxurious. *m,* spring (of a watch, etc.); wharf, quay; freight platform (railroad). **m. real,** mainspring (of a watch). **m. del volante,** hairspring.
muérdago *m,* mistletoe
muermo *m,* glanders
muerte *f,* death; destruction, annihilation; end, decline. *inf* **una m. chiquita,** a nervous shudder. **a m.,** to the death, with no quarter. **de m.,** implacably, inexorably (of hatred); very seriously (of being ill). **dar m. (a),** to kill. **estar a la m.,** to be on the point of death. **a cada m. de un obispo,** once in a blue moon
muerto (-ta) *a* dead; slaked (lime); *mech* neutral; faded, dull (colors); languid, indifferent. **m.** is used in familiar speech as *past part* **matar** (e.g. **Le ha muerto,** He has killed him). *n* corpse. *inf* **desenterrar los muertos,** to speak ill of the dead. *inf* **echarle a uno el m.,** to pass the buck. *inf* **estar m. por,** to be dying, yearning for. **ser el m.,** to be dummy (at cards)
muesca *f,* notch, mortise, groove
muestra *f,* shop sign; sample, specimen; pattern, model; demeanor; watch or clock face; sign, indication; poster, placard; *mil* muster roll. **hacer m.,** to show
muestrario *m,* sample book, collection of samples
mufla *f,* muffler (of a furnace)
mugido *m,* mooing or lowing (of cattle)
mugir *vi* to low or moo (cattle); bellow, shout; rage (elements)
mugre *f,* grease, grime, dirt
mugriento *a* grimy, greasy
muguete *m,* lily of the valley
mujer *f,* woman; wife. **m. de la vida airada** *or* **m. del partido** *or* **m. pública,** prostitute. **m. de la luna,** man in the moon. **m. de su casa,** good housewife. **tomar m.,** to take a wife
mujerero, -a *a, Lat. Am.* fond of women
mujeriego *a* womanly, feminine; (of men) dissolute, given to philandering. **cabalgar a mujeriegas,** to ride sidesaddle
mujeril *a* womanly, feminine
mula *f,* female mule; mule (heelless slipper); *Colombia* dope smuggler; *Mexico* junk, trash. *inf* **Se me fue la m.,** My tongue ran away with me
muladar *m,* refuse heap, junkpile, dunghill
mular *a* mule; mulish
mulatero *m,* mule hirer; muleteer
mulato (-ta) *a* and *n* mulatto
muleta *f,* crutch; bullfighter's red flag; support, prop
mullir *vt irr* to make soft, shake out (wool, down, etc.); *fig* prepare the way; *agr* hoe the roots (of vines, etc.). *Pres. Part.* **mullendo.** *Preterite* **mulló, mulleron.** *Imperf. Subjunc.* **mullese,** etc.
mulo *m,* mule
multa *f,* fine
multar *vt* to impose a fine on
multicolor *a* multicolored
multiforme *a* multiform
multilátero *a* multilateral
multimillonario (-ia) *a* and *n* multimillionaire
multiplicación *f,* multiplication
multiplicador (-ra) *n* multiplier. *m, math* multiplier
multiplicando *m,* multiplicand
multiplicar((se) *vt* and *vr* to multiply; reproduce
multiplicidad *f,* multiplicity
múltiplo *a* and *m,* multiple
multisecular *a* age-old, many centuries old
multitud *f,* multitude, great number; crowd; rabble, masses, mob
mundanal, mundano *a* worldly, mundane
mundial *a* world, worldwide
mundo *m,* world, universe; human race; earth; human society; world (of letters, science, etc.); secular life; *ecc* vanities of the flesh; geographical globe. **echar al m.,** to give birth to; produce, bring forth. **el Nuevo M.,** the New World, America. *inf* **medio m.,** half the earth, a great crowd. *inf* **ponerse el m. por montera,** to treat the world as one's oyster. **ser hombre del m.,** to be a man of the world. *inf* **tener m.** *or* **mucho m.,** to be very experienced, know the world. **todo el m.,** everyone. **venir al m.,** to be born. **ver m.,** to travel, see the world
mundología *f,* worldliness, experience of the world
munición *f, mil* munition; small shot. *mil* **m. de boca,** fodder and food supplies
municionero (-ra) *n* purveyor, supplier
municipal *a* municipal. *m,* policeman
municipalidad *f,* municipality
municipio *m,* municipality, town council
munificencia *f,* munificence, generosity
munífico *a* munificent, generous
muñeca *f, anat* wrist; doll; puppet; dressmaker's dummy; polishing pad; mannequin; boundary marker; *inf* flighty young woman
muñeco *m,* boy doll; puppet; *inf* playboy
muñir *vt irr* to summon, convoke; arrange, dispose. See **mullir**
muñón *m, surg* stump of an amputated limb; *mech* gudgeon
mural *a* mural
muralla *f,* town wall; rampart, fortification
murar *vt* to surround with a wall, wall in
murciélago *m, zool* bat
murga *f,* band of street musicians
murmullo *m,* whisper; whispering; rustling; purling, lapping, splashing; mumbling, muttering
murmuración *f,* slander, backbiting, gossip
murmurador (-ra) *a* gossiping, slanderous. *n* gossip, backbiter
murmurar *vi* to rustle (leaves, etc.); purl, lap, splash (water); whisper; mumble, mutter; *vi* and *vt inf* slander, backbite
murmurio *m,* rustling; lapping (of water); whispering; murmur; *inf* slander
muro *m,* wall; defensive wall, rampart
musaraña *f, zool* shrew; any small animal; *inf* ridiculous effigy, guy. *inf* **mirar a las musarañas,** to be absent-minded
muscular *a* muscular
musculatura *f,* musculature
músculo *m,* muscle; strength, brawn
musculoso *a* muscular; strong, brawny
muselina *f,* muslin
museo *m,* museum. **m. de pintura,** art gallery, picture gallery
musgo *m,* moss
musgoso *a* mossy, moss-grown
música *f,* music; melody, harmony; musical performance; musical composition; group of musicians; sheet music. *inf* **m. celestial,** vain words, moonshine. *inf* **m.**

ratonera, badly played music. *inf* **¡Vaya con su m. a otra parte!** Get out! Go to hell!
musical *a* musical
músico (-ca) *a* music. *n* musician. **m. ambulante,** strolling musician. **m. mayor,** bandleader
musitar *vi* to mutter, mumble
muslo *m,* thigh
mustango *m, Lat. Am.* mustang
mustio *a* sad, disheartened, depressed; faded, withered; *Mexico* hypocritical
musulmán (-ana) *a* and *n* Muslim
mutabilidad *f,* mutability, changeability
mutación *f,* change, mutation; sudden change in the weather; *theat* change of scene
mutilación *f,* mutilation; damage; defacement
mutilar *vt* to mutilate; spoil, deface, damage; cut short; reduce
mutis *m, theat* exit. **hacer m.** *theat* to exit; keep quiet, say nothing
mutismo *m,* mutism, dumbness; silence, speechlessness
mutualidad *f,* reciprocity, mutuality, interdependence; principle of mutual aid; mutual aid society
mutualismo *m,* mutualism, organized mutual aid
mutualista *mf* member of a mutual aid society
mutuante *mf com* lender
mutuo *a* reciprocal, mutual, interdependent
muy *adv* very; very much; much. Used to form absolute superlative (e.g. **m. rápidamente,** very quickly). Can modify adjectives, nouns used adjectivally, adverbs, participles (e.g. **María es m. mujer,** Mary is very much a woman (very womanly)). **m. temprano,** very early. **M. señor mío,** Dear Sir (in letters)

N

naba *f,* swede, turnip
nabar *m,* turnip field
nabo *m,* turnip; turnip root; any root stem; *naut* mast; stock (of a horse's tail)
nácar *m,* mother-of-pearl
nacarado, nacáreo *a* nacreous, mother-of-pearl
nacer *vi irr* to be born; rise (rivers, etc.); sprout; grow (plumage, fur, leaves, etc.); descend (lineage); appear (stars, etc.); originate; *fig* issue forth; appear suddenly; (*with prep a* or *para*) be destined for, have a natural leaning toward. **n. con pajitas de oro en la cuna,** to be born with a silver spoon in one's mouth. *vr* grow; sprout; *sew* split at the seams. *Pres. Ind.* **nazco, naces,** etc. *Pres. Subjunc.* **nazca,** etc.
nacido *a* and *past part* born; suitable, fit. *m,* (gen. *pl*) the living and the dead. **bien n.,** noble, well-born; well-bred. **mal n.,** base-born; ill-bred
naciente *a* growing; nascent. *m,* east
nacimiento *m,* birth; source (of rivers, etc.); birthplace; origin; lineage; *ast* rising; nativity crib, manger. **de n.,** from birth; by birth; born
nación *f,* nation; country; *inf* birth
nacional *a* national; native. *mf* citizen, national
nacionalidad *f,* nationality
nacionalismo *m,* nationalism
nacionalista *a* and *mf* nationalist
nacionalización *f,* naturalization; nationalization; acclimatization
nacionalizar *vt* to naturalize; nationalize
nacionalsindicalismo *m,* national syndicalism
nacionalsocialismo *m,* national socialism, nazism
nada *f,* void, nothingness. *pron indef* nothing. *adv* by no means. **casi n.,** very little, practically nothing. **¡De n.!** Not at all! Don't mention it! You're welcome! **No vale para n.,** He (it, she) is of no use
nadaderas *f pl,* water wings (for swimming)
nadador (-ra) *n* swimmer. *a* swimming
nadar *vi* to swim; float; have an abundance (of); *inf* be too large (of garments, etc.). **n. y guardar la ropa,** *fig* to sit on the fence
nadería *f,* trifle
nadie *pron indef* no one. *m, fig* a nobody
nadir *m,* nadir
nado *a* by swimming; afloat
nafta *f,* naphtha; *Argentina* gas, gasoline
naftalina *f,* naphthalene
naipe *m,* playing card; pack of cards
naire *m,* elephant keeper or trainer
nalga *f,* (gen. *pl*) buttock(s)
nana *f, inf* grandma; lullaby; *Mexico* wet nurse; nurserymaid
nao *f,* ship
napoleónico *a* Napoleonic
Nápoles Naples
napolitano (-na) *a* and *n* Neapolitan
naranja *f,* orange. **n. dulce,** blood orange. **n. mandarina,** tangerine. *inf* **media n.,** better half
naranjada *f,* orangeade
naranjal *m,* orange grove
naranjero (-ra) *n* orange seller
naranjo *m,* orange tree; *inf* lout, blockhead
narciso *m,* narcissus; dandy, fop. **n. trompón,** daffodil
narcótico *a* and *m,* narcotic
narcotizar *vt* to narcotize
narcotraficante *mf* drug dealer
nardo *m,* tuberose, spikenard, nard
narigudo *a* large-nosed; nose-shaped
nariz *f,* nose; nostril; snout; nozzle; sense of smell; bouquet (of wine). **n. perfilada,** well-shaped nose. **n. respingona,** snub nose. *inf* **meter las narices,** to meddle, interfere
narración *f,* narration, account
narrador (-ra) *a* narrative. *n* narrator
narrar *vt* to narrate, tell, relate
narrativa *f,* narrative; account; narrative skill
narrativo, narratorio *a* narrative
nata *f,* cream; *fig* the flower, elite; *pl* whipped cream with sugar
natación *f,* swimming. **n. a la marinera,** trudgen stroke
natal *a* natal; native. *m,* birth; birthday
natalicio *a* natal. *a* and *m,* birthday
natalidad *f,* birth rate
natatorio *a* swimming. *m,* swimming pool
natillas *f pl,* custard
natividad *f,* nativity; birth; Christmas
nativo *a* indigenous; native; innate
nato *a* born; inherent; ex officio
natura *f,* nature; *mus* major scale
natural *a* natural; native; indigenous; spontaneous; sincere, candid; physical; usual, ordinary; *mus* natural; unadulterated, pure; *her* proper. *mf* native, citizen. *m,* temperament; disposition; instinct (of animals); natural inclination. **al n.,** naturally, without art. **del n.,** *art* from life
naturaleza *f,* nature; character; disposition; instinct; temperament; nationality, origin; naturalization; kind, class; constitution, physique. **n. humana,** humankind. **n. muerta,** *art* still life
naturalidad *f,* naturalness; nationality
naturalista *mf* naturalist
naturalización *f,* naturalization; acclimatization
naturalizar *vt* to naturalize; acclimatize; *vr* become naturalized; become acclimatized
naturalmente *adv* naturally; of course
naturismo *m,* nature cure
naufragar *vi* to be shipwrecked; fail, be unsuccessful

naufragio *m,* shipwreck; disaster, loss
náufrago (-ga) *n* shipwrecked person. *m,* shark
náusea *f,* nausea (*pl* more usual); repugnance
nauseabundo, nauseoso *a* nauseous; nauseating, repugnant
nauta *mf* mariner
náutica *f,* navigation; yachting; seamanship
náutico *a* nautical
navaja *f,* razor; clasp knife; boar tusk; sting; *inf* slanderous tongue. **n. de afeitar,** (shaving) razor
navajada *f,* slash with a razor
navajero *m,* razor case
naval *a* naval
Navarra Navarre
navarro (-ra) *a* and *n* Navarrese
nave *f,* ship; *arch* nave. **n. aérea,** airship. *arch* **n. lateral,** aisle. **n. principal,** *arch* nave
navegable *a* navigable
navegación *f,* navigation; sea voyage
navegante *a* voyaging; navigating. *m,* navigator
navegar *vi* to navigate; sail; fly
navidad *f,* nativity; Christmas; *pl* Christmastime
naviero *a* shipping. *m,* ship owner
navío *m,* warship; ship. **n. de transporte,** transport. **n. de tres puentes,** three-decker
náyade *f,* naiad, water nymph
nazareno (-na) *a* and *n* Nazarene; Christian
Nazaret Nazareth
nazismo *m,* nazism
neblina *f,* fog; mist
nebulosidad *f,* nebulousness; cloudiness
nebuloso *a* foggy; misty; cloudy; somber, melancholy; confused, nebulous
necedad *f,* silliness
necesario *a* necessary; unavoidable
neceser *m,* dressing case. *sew* **n. de costura,** workbox
necesidad *f,* necessity; poverty, want; shortage, need; emergency. **de n.,** necessarily
necesitado (-da) *a* needy, poor. *n* poor person
necesitar *vt* to necessitate; compel, oblige; *vi* be necessary, need
necio *a* stupid; senseless; unreasonable
necrología *f,* necrology, obituary
necromancía *f,* necromancy
neerlandés *a* Dutch
nefando *a* iniquitous
nefario *a* nefarious
nefasto *a* disastrous, ill-omened
nefrítico *a* nephritic
nefritis *f,* nephritis
negable *a* deniable
negación *f,* negation; privation; negative; nay; *gram* negative particle; *law* traverse
negado *a* inept, unfitted; stupid
negar *vt irr* to deny; refuse; prohibit; disclaim; dissemble; disown; *law* traverse; *vr* refuse, avoid; decline (to receive visitors). See **acertar**
negativa *f,* denial; refusal; *phot* negative
negativo *a* negative
negligencia *f,* negligence; omission; carelessness; forgetfulness
negligente *a* negligent; careless; neglectful
negociable *a* negotiable
negociación *f,* negotiation; business affair, deal
negociado *m,* department, section (of a ministry, etc.); business; *Chile* shop, store; *elsewhere in Lat. Am.* shady deal
negociante *m,* businessman. *a* negotiating; trading
negociar *vi* to trade, traffic; negotiate
negocio *m,* occupation; trade; business; employment; transaction; *Argentina* shop, store; *pl* business affairs. **hombre de negocios,** businessman
negra *f,* black girl, black woman; *inf* honey, *WH* sweetheart
negrecer *vi irr* to become black. See **conocer**
negrero (-ra) *n* slave trader
negro *a* black; dark; melancholy; disastrous; *her* sable. *m,* black; black (color). **n. de humo,** lampblack
negrura *f,* blackness
negruzco *a* blackish
neme *m, Colombia* asphalt
nemotécnica *f,* mnemonics
nene (-na) *n inf* baby; darling
nenúfar *m,* white water lily
neo *m,* neon
neófito (-ta) *n* neophyte
neologismo *m,* neologism
neoyorquino (-na) *a* New York. *n* New Yorker
nepotismo *m,* nepotism
Neptuno *m, ast* Neptune; *poet* sea
nervio *m,* nerve; sinew; *bot* vein; vigor; *mus* string. **n. ciático,** sciatic nerve
nervioso *a* nervous; overwrought, agitated; vigorous; neural; sinewy; jerky (of style, etc.)
nervosidad *f,* nervousness; nervosity; flexibility (metals); jerkiness (of style, etc.); force, efficacy
nervudo *a* strong-nerved, vigorous
nesga *f, sew* gore
neto *a* neat; clean; pure; *com* net. *m, arch* dado
neumático *a* pneumatic. *m,* rubber tire
neumococo *m,* pneumococcus
neurálgico *a* neuralgic
neurastenia *f,* neurasthenia
neurasténico (-ca) *a* and *n* neurasthenic
neurología *f,* neurology
neurólogo *m,* neurologist
neurosis *f,* neurosis. **n. de guerra,** war neurosis; shell shock
neurótico (-ca) *a* and *n* neurotic
neutral *a* neutral; indifferent
neutralidad *f,* neutrality; impartiality, indifference
neutralizar *vt* to neutralize; counteract, mitigate
neutro *a* neuter; *chem* neutral; *mech* neuter; sexless
nevada *f,* snowfall
nevado *m, Lat. Am.* snow-capped mountain
nevar *vi irr impers* to snow. *Pres. Ind:* **nieva.** *Pres. Subjunc.* **nieve**
nevazón *f, Lat. Am.* blizzard, snowstorm
nevera *f,* refrigerator; icehouse
nevero *m,* ice-cream man; iceman
nevisca *f,* light snowfall
nevoso *a* snowy
nexo *m,* nexus; connection, union
ni *conjunc* neither, nor. **ni bien ni mal,** neither good nor bad. **ni siquiera,** not even. **¡Ni crea!, ¡Ni creas!** Nonsense!
niara *f,* haystack, rick
nicaragüeño (-ña) *a* and *n* Nicaraguan
nicho *m,* niche; recess (in a wall)
nicotina *f,* nicotine
nidada *f,* nest full of eggs; brood, clutch
nidal *m,* nest; nest egg; haunt; cause, foundation
nido *m,* nest; den; hole; dwelling; haunt. **n. de ametralladoras,** *mil* pillbox
niebla *f,* fog; mist; cloud; mildew; haze
nieto (-ta) *n* grandchild; descendant
nieve *f,* snow; whiteness. **deportes de n.,** winter sports
nigromancia *f,* necromancy
nigromante *m,* necromancer
nihilismo *m,* nihilism
nihilista *mf* nihilist
Nilo, el the Nile
nimbo *m,* halo, nimbus
nimiedad *f,* prolixity; *inf* fussiness; fastidiousness, delicacy
nimio *a* prolix; *inf* fussy; fastidious; *inf* parsimonious
ninfa *f,* nymph; *ent* chrysalis
ningún *a abb* of **ninguno.** Used before *m, sing* nouns only. **De n. modo,** In no way! Certainly not!
niña *f,* girl. **n. del ojo,** pupil (of the eye). **n. de los ojos,** apple of one's eye, darling
niñada *f,* childishness, foolish act

niñera *f,* nursemaid
niñería *f,* childish act; trifle; childishness, folly
niñez *f,* childhood; beginning, early days; *fig* cradle
niño (-ña) *a* childish; young; inexperienced; imprudent. *n* child; young or inexperienced person. **n. de la doctrina,** charity child. **n. terrible,** enfant terrible. **desde n.,** from childhood
nipón (-ona) *a* and *n* Japanese
níquel *m, chem* nickel
niquelar *vt* to chrome-plate
niquelera *f, Colombia* purse, change purse
nirvana *m,* nirvana
níspero *m,* medlar tree; medlar
níspola *f,* medlar
nitidez *f,* brightness, neatness, cleanliness
nítido *a* bright, neat, clean (often *poet.*)
nitrato *m,* nitrate
nítrico *a* nitric
nitrógeno *m,* nitrogen
nivel *m,* level; levelness. **n. de albañil,** plummet. **n. de burbuja,** spirit level. **a n.,** on the level. **estar al n. de las circunstancias,** to rise to the occasion; save the day
nivelación *f,* leveling
nivelador (-ra) *a* leveling. *n* leveler
nivelar *vt* to level; *fig* make equal
níveo *a* snowy; snow-white
no *adv* no; not. **no bien,** no sooner. **no sea que,** unless. **no tal,** no such thing
noble *a* noble, illustrious; generous; outstanding, excellent; aristocratic. *mf* nobleman (-woman)
nobleza *f,* nobility
noche *f,* night; darkness; confusion, obscurity. *inf* **n. toledana,** restless night. **¡Buenas noches!** Good night! **de n.,** by night. **esta n.,** tonight
nochebuena *f,* Christmas Eve
nochebueno *m,* yule log; Christmas cake
nocherniego *a* night, nocturnal
nochote *m, Mexico* cactus beer
noción *f,* notion, idea; *pl* elementary knowledge
nocividad *f,* noxiousness
nocivo *a* noxious
nocturno *a* nocturnal; melancholy. *m, mus* nocturne
nodriza *f,* wet nurse
nogal *m,* walnut tree; walnut wood
nómada *a* nomadic
nomadismo *m,* nomadism
nombradia *f,* renown
nombramiento *m,* naming; appointment; nomination
nombrar *vt* to name; nominate; appoint; mention (in dispatches, etc.)
nombre *m,* name; title; reputation; proxy; *gram* noun; *mil* password. **n. de pila,** Christian name. **por n.,** called; by name. **Su n. anda puesto en el cuerno de la Luna,** He (she) is praised to the skies
nomenclatura *f,* nomenclature
nómina *f,* list, register; payroll; amulet
nominación *f,* nomination, appointment
nominador (-ra) *a* nominating. *n* nominator
nominal *a* nominal
nominalismo *m,* nominalism
nominalista *a* nominalistic. *mf* nominalist
nomo *m,* gnome
nóstico (-ca) *a* and *n* gnostic
non *a* odd (of numbers)
nonada *f,* nothing, practically nothing
nonagenario (-ia) *a* and *n* nonagenarian
nonagésimo *a* ninetieth
nones *m, pl* certainly not, definitely not, nope
nopal *m,* nopal, prickly pear tree
noque *m,* tanner's vat
noquear *vt* (*boxing*) to knock out, K.O.
norabuena *f,* congratulation
nordeste *m,* northeast
nórdico (-ca) *a* and *n* Nordic
noria *f,* water well; chain pump; *inf* hard, monotonous work
norma *f,* square (used by builders, etc.); *fig* norm, standard, model
normal *a* normal, usual; standard, average. *f,* normal school, teacher's college (also **escuela n.**)
normalidad *f,* normality
normalista *mf* student at a teacher's college
normalización *f,* normalization; standardization
normalizar *vt* to make normal; standardize
Normandía Normandy
normando (-da) *a* Norman. *n* Northman; Norman
nornordeste *m,* northnortheast
nornorueste *m,* northnorthwest
noroeste *m,* northwest
norte *m,* north pole; north; north wind; polestar; *fig* guide
norteamericano (-na) *a* and *n* North American; (*U.S.A.*) American
norteño *a* northerly, northern
Noruega Norway
noruego (-ga) *a* and *n* Norwegian. *m,* Norwegian (language)
nos *pers pron pl mf acc* and *dat* (direct and indirect object) of **nosotros,** us; to us (e.g. **Nos lo dio,** He gave it to us)
nosotros, nosotras *pers pron pl mf* we; us. Also used with preposition (e.g. **Lo hicieron por nosotros,** They did it for us)
nostalgia *f,* nostalgia
nostálgico *a* nostalgic; melancholy; homesick
nota *f,* mark, sign; annotation, comment; *mus* note; memorandum; *com* bill, account; criticism, imputation; mark (in exams); repute, renown; note (diplomatic)
notabilidad *f,* notability
notable *a* notable, remarkable; outstanding, prominent; with distinction (examination mark). *m pl,* notabilities
notación *f,* (*mus math*) notation; annotation
notar *vt* to mark, indicate; observe, notice; note down; annotate; dictate, read out; criticize, reproach; discredit
notaría *f,* profession of a notary; notary's office
notarial *a* notarial
notario *m,* notary public
noticia *f,* rudiment, elementary knowledge; information; news (gen. *pl*); *pl* knowledge. **atrasado de noticias,** *fig* behind the times
noticiar *vt* to inform, give notice
noticiario *m,* news bulletin, newsreel.
noticiero *m,* newspaper
noticioso *a* informed; learned; newsy
notificación *f, law* notification. **n. de reclutamiento,** draft notice
notificar *vt* to notify officially; inform; warn
noto *a* known. *m,* south wind
notoriedad *f,* notoriety, publicity; flagrancy; fame, renown
notorio *a* well-known; notorious, obvious; flagrant
novatada *f, inf* ragging (of a freshman); blunder
novato (-ta) *a* new, inexperienced. *n* novice, beginner
novecientos *a* and *m,* nine hundred
novedad *f,* newness, novelty; change, alteration; latest news; surprise; *pl* novelties. **sin n.,** no change; all well (or as usual); safely, without incident
novel *a* new; inexperienced
novela *f,* novel; tale; falsehood. **n. caballista,** western, cowboy story. **n. por entregas,** serial (story)
novelero (-ra) *a* fond of novelty and change; fond of novels; fickle. *n* newshound, gossip
novelesco *a* novelistic; imaginary
novelista *mf* novelist
novelística *f,* art of novel writing
novena *f, ecc* novena, religious services spread over nine days
noveno *a* and *m,* ninth

noventa *a* and *m*, ninety; ninetieth
novia *f*, bride; fiancée
noviar con *vi*, *Argentina* to court, woo
noviazgo *m*, engagement, betrothal
noviciado *m*, novitiate; training, apprenticeship
novicio (-ia) *n ecc* novice; beginner, apprentice; unassuming person
noviembre *m*, November
novillada *f*, herd of young bulls; bullock baiting
novillo *m*, bullock. **hacer novillos,** to play truant
novilunio *m*, new moon
novio *m*, bridegroom; fiancé; novice, beginner
novísimo *a sup* **nuevo** newest; latest, most recent
nubada *f*, cloudburst, rainstorm; abundance, plenty
nubarrón *m*, dense, lowering cloud, storm cloud
nube *f*, cloud; *fig* screen, impediment. **n. de verano,** summer cloud; passing annoyance
nublado *a* cloudy; overcast. *m*, storm cloud; menace, threat; multitude, crowd
nublarse *vr* to cloud over
nubloso *a* cloudy; unfortunate, unhappy
nuca *f*, nape
núcleo *m*, kernel; stone, pip (of fruit); nucleus; *fig* core, essence
nudillo *m*, knuckle; *mas* plug
nudo *m*, knot; (*bot med*) node; joint; *naut* knot; *fig* bond, tie; *fig* crux, knotty point. **n. al revés,** granny knot. **n. de comunicaciones,** communication center. **n. de marino,** reef knot. **n. de tejedor,** sheet bend (knot). **n. en la garganta,** *fig* lump in the throat (from emotion)
nudoso *a* knotted, knotty; gnarled
nuera *f*, daughter-in-law
nuestro, nuestra *poss pron 1st pers pl mf* our; ours. **los nuestros,** our friends, supporters, party, profession, etc.
nueva *f*, news
Nueva Caledonia New Caledonia
Nueva Escocia Nova Scotia
Nueva Gales del Sur New South Wales
nuevamente *adv* again
Nueva Orleans New Orleans
Nueva York New York
Nueva Zelanda, Nueva Zelandia New Zealand
nueve *a* nine; ninth. *m*, number nine; ninth (of the month) (e.g. **el nueve de marzo,** March 9th). **a las nueve,** at nine o'clock
nuevo *a* new; fresh; newly arrived; inexperienced; unused, scarcely worn. **de n.,** again. **¿Qué hay de n.?** What's the news? What's new?
Nuevo México *m* New Mexico
nuez *f*, walnut; *anat* Adam's apple. **n. moscada,** nutmeg
nulidad *f*, nullity; incompetence, ineptitude; worthlessness
nulo *a* null, void; incapable; worthless
numen *m*, divinity; inspiration
numeración *f*, calculation; numbering
numerador *m*, numerator
numerar *vt* to number; enumerate; calculate
numerario *a* numerary. *m*, cash
numérico *a* numerical
número *m*, number; figure; numeral; size (of gloves, etc.); quantity; issue, copy; rhythm; *gram* number; item (of a program); *pl ecc* Numbers. **n. del distrito postal,** ZIP code. **n. quebrado,** *math* fraction. **sin n.,** numberless
numeroso *a* numerous; harmonious
numismática *f*, numismatics
nunca *adv* never. **n. jamás,** nevermore. **N. digas «De esta agua no beberé!»** Never say "Never!"
nuncio *m*, messenger; papal nuncio; *fig* harbinger
nupcial *a* nuptial
nupcialidad *f*, marriage rate
nupcias *f pl*, nuptials, marriage
nutria *f*, otter, nutria
nutrición *f*, nourishment; nutrition
nutrido *a* abundant; numerous
nutrimento *m*, nutriment; nourishment; nutrition; *fig* food, encouragement
nutrir *vt* to nourish; encourage; *fig* fill
nutritivo *a* nourishing, nutritive

ñácara *f*, *Central America* sore, ulcer
ñaña *f*, *Lat. Am.* wet nurse; nursemaid; elder sister
ñaques *m pl*, odds and ends, rubbish
ñiquiñaque *m*, *inf* good-for-nothing, wastrel; *inf* trash
ñoco, -a *a*, *Lat. Am.* one-handed; missing a finger
ñoñería *f*, *inf* drivel; folly, stupidity
ñoño (-ña) *a inf* sentimental; foolish, idiotic. *n* fool.

o *f*, letter O. *conjunc* or, either. **o** becomes **u** before words beginning with **o** or **ho** (e.g. **gloria u honor**)
oasis *m*, oasis; *fig* refuge, haven
obcecación *f*, blindness; obstinacy; obsession
obcecar *vt* to blind; obsess; *fig* dazzle; darken
obduración *f*, obstinacy, stubbornness, obduracy
obedecer *vt irr* to obey; *fig* respond; bend, yield (metals, etc.); *vi* result (from), arise (from). See **conocer**
obedecimiento *m*, **obediencia** *f*, obedience
obediente *a* obedient; docile
obelisco *m*, obelisk
obertura *f*, *mus* overture
obesidad *f*, obesity
obeso *a* obese
óbice *m*, obstacle, impediment
obispado *m*, bishopric
obispo *m*, bishop. **o. sufragáneo,** suffragan bishop
óbito *m*, death, demise
obituario *m*, obituary; obituary column
objeción *f*, objection
objetar *vt* to object to, oppose
objetivar *vt* to view objectively
objetividad *f*, objectivity
objetivo *a* objective. *m*, *opt* eyepiece; object finder; aim, goal
objeto *m*, object; subject, theme; purpose; aim, goal. **sin o.,** without object; aimlessly
oblicuidad *f*, obliqueness
oblicuo *a* slanting, oblique
obligación *f*, obligation; *com* bond; *com* debenture; *pl* responsibilities; *com* liabilities
obligacionista *mf com* bond holder, debenture holder
obligado *m*, contractor (to a borough, etc.); *mus* obbligato
obligar *vt* to compel, oblige, constrain; lay under an obligation; *law* mortgage; *vr* bind oneself, promise
obligatorio *a* obligatory
oblongo *a* oblong
oboe *m*, oboe; oboe player, oboist
óbolo *m*, obol, ancient Greek coin
obra *f*, work; anything made; literary, artistic, scientific production; structure, construction; repair, alteration

(to buildings, etc.); means, influence, power; labor, or time spent; action, behavior. **o. de caridad,** charitable act. **o. maestra,** masterpiece. **obras públicas,** public works. **poner por o.,** to put into effect; to set to work on. **o. de,** about, approximately
obrar *vt* to work; make, do; execute, perform; affect; construct, build; *vi* be, exist (things); act, behave. **o. mal,** to behave badly, do wrong
obrero (-ra) *a* working. *n* worker; *pl* workers
obscenidad *f,* obscenity
obsceno *a* obscene
obsequiar *vt* to entertain, be attentive (to); give presents (to); court, make love to. **Me obsequia con un reloj,** He is presenting me with a watch
obsequio *m,* attention; gift; deference. **en o. de,** as a tribute to
obsequioso *a* obliging, courteous, attentive
observable *a* observable
observación *f,* observation; remark
observador (-ra) *a* observing. *n* observer
observancia *f,* observance; respect, reverence
observar *vt* to notice; inspect, examine; fulfill; remark; watch, spy upon; *ast* observe
observatorio *m,* observatory
obsesión *f,* obsession
obsesionar *vt* to obsess
obseso *a* obsessed
obsidiana *f,* obsidian
obsolecer *vi* to obsolesce, become obsolete
obsoleto *a* obsolete
obstáculo *m,* impediment; obstacle
obstante, no *adv* in spite of; nevertheless
obstar *vi* to impede, hinder
obstetra *mf* obstetrician
obstetricia *f,* obstetrics
obstinación *f,* obstinacy
obstinado *a* obstinate, stubborn
obstinarse *vr* (*with en*) to persist in, insist on, be stubborn about
obstinaz *a* obstinate
obstrucción *f,* obstruction
obstruccionar *vt, Lat. Am.* to obstruct, stonewall
obstruccionismo *m,* obstructionism, stonewalling
obstruccionista *mf* obstructionist
obstruir *vt irr* to obstruct; block; hinder; *vr* become choked or stopped up (pipes, etc.). See **huir**
obtención *f,* obtainment; attainment, realization
obtener *vt irr* to obtain; attain; maintain, preserve. See **tener**
obturador *m,* stopper; shutter (of a camera)
obturar *vt* to stopper, plug; block, obstruct
obtuso *a* blunt, dull; (*geom* and *fig*) obtuse
obús *m,* howitzer; *mil* shell
obviar *vt* to obviate
obvio *a* obvious, evident, apparent
oca *f,* goose
ocasión *f,* occasion; opportunity; motive, cause; danger, risk; *inf* **asir la o. por la melena,** to take time by the forelock. **de o.,** second-hand
ocasional *a* chance, fortuitous; occasional
ocasionar *vt* to cause, occasion; excite, provoke; risk, endanger
ocaso *m,* sunset; west; dusk; decadence, decline
occidental *a* Western
occidente *m,* West, Occident
occiso *a* murdered; killed
oceánico *a* oceanic
océano *m,* ocean; immensity, abundance
oceanografía *f,* oceanography
ocelote *m,* ocelot
ochava *f,* eighth; *ecc* octave
ochavo *m, ant* small Spanish copper coin
ochenta *a* and *m,* eighty; eightieth
ochentón (-ona) *n* octogenarian
ocho *a* eight; eighth. *m,* figure eight; playing card with eight pips; eight; eighth day (of the month). **las o.,** eight o'clock
ochocientos *a* and *m,* eight hundred; eight-hundredth
ocio *m,* leisure, idleness; *pl* pastimes; leisure time
ociosidad *f,* idleness, laziness; leisure
ocioso (-sa) *a* idle; useless, worthless; unprofitable, fruitless. *n* idle fellow
ocozoal *m, Mexico* rattlesnake
ocre *m,* ocher
octágono *m,* octagon
octava *f,* octave
octaviano *a* Octavian
octavo *a* eighth. *m,* eighth. **en o.,** in octavo
octeto *m,* octet
octogenario (-ia) *a* and *n* octogenarian
octogésimo *a* eightieth
octubre *m,* October
óctuple *a* octuple, eightfold
ocular *a* ocular. *m,* eyepiece
oculista *mf* oculist
ocultación *f,* hiding, concealment
ocultamente *adv* secretly
ocultar *vt* to hide, conceal; disguise; keep secret
ocultismo *m,* occultism
oculto *a* hidden; secret; occult. **en o.,** secretly, quietly
ocupación *f,* occupancy; occupation, pursuit; employment, office, trade
ocupado *a* occupied; busy
ocupante *m,* occupant
ocupar *vt* to take possession of; obtain or hold (job); occupy, fill; inhabit; employ; hinder, embarrass; hold the attention (of); *vr* (*with en*) be engaged in, be occupied with; (*with con*) concentrate on (a business affair, etc.)
ocurrencia *f,* occurrence, incident; bright idea; witty remark
ocurrir *vi* to anticipate; happen, take place; occur, strike (ideas)
oda *f,* ode
odalisca *f,* odalisk
odiar *vt* to hate; *Chile* annoy, irk
odio *m,* hatred; malevolence
odioso *a* hateful, odious; *Argentina, Chile, Peru* annoying, irksome
odisea *f,* odyssey
odontología *f,* odontology
odontólogo *m,* odontologist
odorífero *a* odoriferous, fragrant
odre *m,* goatskin, wineskin; *inf* wine bibber
oesnorueste *m,* westnorthwest
oessudueste *m,* westsouthwest
oeste *m,* west
ofender *vt* to ill-treat, hurt; offend, insult; anger, annoy; *vr* be offended
ofendido *a* offended; resentful
ofensa *f,* injury, harm; offense, crime
ofensiva *f, mil* offensive. **tomar la o.,** to take the offensive
ofensivo *a* offensive
ofensor (-ra) *n* offender
oferta *f,* offer; gift; proposal; *com* tender. **o. y demanda,** supply and demand
oficial *a* official. *m,* official; officer; clerk; executioner; worker
oficiala *f,* trained female worker
oficialidad *f,* officialdom; officers
oficiar *vt ecc* to celebrate or serve (mass); communicate officially, inform; *inf* (*with de*) act as
oficina *f,* workshop; office; pharmaceutical laboratory; *pl* cellars, basement (of a house)
oficinesco *a* bureaucratic, red-tape
oficinista *mf* clerk, office employee, office worker
oficio *m,* occupation, employment; office, function, capacity; craft; operation; trade, business; official communication; office, bureau; *ecc* office. **Santo O.,** Holy Office. *fig* **buenos oficios,** good offices

oficiosidad *f*, diligence, conscientiousness; helpfulness, friendliness; officiousness
oficioso *a* conscientious; helpful, useful; officious; meddlesome; unofficial, informal
ofrecer *vt irr* to offer; present; exhibit; consecrate, dedicate; *vr* occur, suggest itself; volunteer. **¿Qué se le ofrece?** What do you require? What would you like? See **conocer**
ofrecimiento *m*, offer, offering
ofrenda *f*, *ecc* offering; gift, present
oftalmología *f*, ophthalmology
oftalmólogo *m*, oculist, ophthalmologist
ofuscación *f*. **ofuscamiento** *m*, obfuscation, dazzle, dimness of sight; mental confusion, bewilderment
ofuscar *vt* to dazzle, daze; dim, obfuscate; confuse, bewilder
ogro *m*, ogre
ohmio *m*, ohm
oídas, de *adv* by hearsay
oído *m*, sense of hearing; ear. **de o.,** by ear. **decir al o.,** to whisper in a person's ear. *mus* **duro de o.,** hard of hearing; having a bad ear (for music). **estar sordo de un o.,** to be deaf in one ear
oidor *m*, hearer; judge, *ant* magistrate
oir *vt irr* to hear; give ear to, listen; understand. *Pres. Part.* **oyendo.** *Pres. Ind.* **oigo, oyes, oye, oyen.** *Preterite* **oyó, oyeron.** *Pres. Subjunc.* **oiga,** etc. *Imperf. Subjunc.* **oyese,** etc.
oíslo *mf inf* better half
ojal *m*, buttonhole; slit, hole
¡ojalá! *interj* If only that were so! God grant!
ojeada *f*, glance
ojear *vt* to look at, stare at; bewitch; scare, startle
ojera *f*, dark shadow (under the eye); eye bath .
ojeriza *f*, ill-will, spite
ojeroso *a* having dark shadows under the eyes, wan, haggard
ojete *m*, eyelet
ojinegro *a* black-eyed
ojiva *f*, ogive
ojo *m*, eye; hole; slit; socket; keyhole; eye (of a needle); span (of a bridge); core (of a corn); attention, care; mesh; spring, stream; well (of a staircase); *pl* darling. **¡Ojo!** Take care! **o. avizor,** sharp watch; lynx eye. **Ojos que no ven, corazón que no siente,** Out of sight, out of mind. **o. saltón,** prominent, bulging eye. **o. vivo,** bright eye. **a o. de buen cubero,** at a guess. **a ojos vistas,** visibly; patently
ojota *f*, *Chile*, sandal
ola *f*, billow; wave (atmospheric)
ole *m*, Andalusian dance
¡olé! *interj* Bravo!
oleada *f*, big wave, breaker; swell (of the sea); *fig* surge (of a crowd)
oleaginoso *a* oleaginous
oleaje *m*, swell, surge, billowing
olear *vt* to administer extreme unction
óleo *m*, oil; *ecc* holy oil (gen. *pl*). **al ó.,** in oils
oleoducto *m*, oil pipeline
oler *vt irr* to smell; guess, discover; pry, smell out; *vi* smell; (*with prep a*) smell of; smack of, be reminiscent of. *Pres. Ind.* **huelo, hueles, huele, huelen.** *Pres. Subjunc.* **huela, huelas, huela, huelan**
olfatear *vt* to sniff, snuff, smell; *inf* pry into
olfativo, olfatorio *a* olfactory
olfato *m*, sense of smell; shrewdness
olfatorio *a* olfactory
oliente (mal) *a* evil-smelling
oligárquico *a* oligarchic
olímpico *a* Olympic; Olympian
olisco, -a *a*, *Lat. Am.* spoiled, tainted (meat)
oliva *f*, olive tree; olive; barn owl; peace
olivar *m*, olive grove
olivo *m*, olive tree
olmeda *f*, **olmedo** *m*, elm grove
olmo *m*, elm tree
olor *m*, odor, scent, smell; hope, promise; suspicion, hint; reputation. **o. de santidad,** odor of sanctity
oloroso *a* fragrant, perfumed
olvidadizo *a* forgetful
olvidar(se) *vt* and *vr* to forget; neglect, desert. **Se me olvidó el libro,** I forgot the book. **Me olvidé de lo pasado,** I forgot the past
olvido *m*, forgetfulness; indifference, neglect; oblivion
olla *f*, stew pot; Spanish stew; whirlpool. **o. podrida,** rich Spanish stew containing bacon, fowl, meat, vegetables, ham, etc. **las ollas de Egipto,** the fleshpots of Egypt
ombligo *m*, navel; *fig* core, center
ominoso *a* ominous
omisión *f*, omission; carelessness, negligence; neglect
omiso *a* omitted; remiss; careless. **hacer caso o. de,** to set aside, ignore
omitir *vt* to omit
ómnibus *m*, bus
omnímodo *a* all-embracing
omnipotencia *f*, omnipotence
omnipotente *a* omnipotent, all-powerful
omnisciencia *f*, omniscience
omniscio *a* omniscient
omnívoro *a* omnivorous
omoplato *m*, scapula, shoulder blade
once *a* eleven; eleventh. *m*, eleven; eleventh (of the month). **las o.,** eleven o'clock
onceno *a* eleventh
onda *f*, wave; *fig* flicker (of flames); *sew* scallop; *phys* wave; ripple; *pl* waves (in hair). *rad* **o. corta,** short wave. **o. etérea,** ether wave. **o. sonora,** sound wave
ondeado *a* undulating; wavy; scalloped
ondeante *a* waving; flowing
ondear *vi* to wave; ripple; undulate; roll (of the sea); float, flutter, stream; *sew* scallop; *vr* swing, sway
ondeo *m*, waving; undulation
ondulación *f*, undulation; wave; wriggling; twisting. **o. permanente,** permanent wave, perm
ondulado *a* wavy; undulating; scalloped
ondular *vi* to writhe, squirm, wriggle; twist; coil; *vt* wave (in hair)
oneroso *a* onerous, heavy; troublesome
ónice *m*, onyx
onomástico *a* onomastic. **día o.,** saint's day
onomatopeya *f*, onomatopoeia
onza *f*, ounce. **por onzas,** by ounces; sparingly
onzavo *a* and *m*, eleventh
opacidad *f*, opacity; obscurity; gloom
opaco *a* opaque; dark; gloomy, sad
opalino *a* opaline
ópalo *m*, opal
opción *f*, option; choice, selection; *law* option
ópera *f*, opera
operación *f*, *surg* operation; execution, performance; *com* transaction
operar *vt surg* to operate; *vi* act, have an effect; operate, control; *com* transact
operario (-ia) *n* worker, hand; operator; mechanic
opereta *f*, operetta, light opera
opinar *vi* to have or form an opinion, think; judge, consider
opinión *f*, opinion, view; reputation
opio *m*, opium. **fumadero de o.,** opium den
opíparo *a* magnificent, sumptuous (banquets, etc.)
oponer *vt irr* to oppose; resist, withstand; protest against; *vr* oppose; be contrary or hostile (to); face, be opposite; object (to), set oneself against; compete (in public exams.). See **poner**
oporto *m*, port (wine)
oportunidad *f*, opportunity, occasion
oportunismo *m*, opportunism
oportunista *a* and *mf* opportunist
oportuno *a* opportune, timely
oposición *f*, opposition; resistance; antagonism; public competitive exam for a post; (*ast pol*) opposition

opositor (-ra) *n* opponent; competitor
opresión *f,* oppression; hardship; pressure. **o. de pecho,** difficulty in breathing
opresor (-ra) *a* oppressive. *n* oppressor
oprimir *vt* to oppress; treat harshly; press, crush; choke
oprobio *m,* opprobrium
optar *vt* to take possession of; (*with por*) choose
óptica *f, phys* optics; peepshow
óptico *a* optic, optical. *m,* optician
optimismo *m,* optimism
optimista *mf* optimist. *a* optimistic
óptimo *a sup* **bueno** best, optimal, optimum
opugnar *vt* to resist violently; *mil* assault, attack; impugn, challenge
opulencia *f,* opulence, riches; excess, superabundance
opulento *a* opulent, rich
opúsculo *m,* monograph, opuscule
oquedad *f,* hollow, cavity; superficiality, banality
ora *adv* now
oración *f,* oration, speech; prayer; *gram* sentence
oráculo *m,* oracle
orador (-ra) *n* orator; speech maker. *m,* preacher
oral *a* oral; verbal; buccal
orangután *m,* orangutan
orar *vi* to harangue, make an oration; pray; *vt* request, beg
orate *mf* lunatic
oratoria *f,* oratory, eloquence
oratorio *a* oratorical. *m,* oratory, chapel; *mus* oratorio
orbe *m,* sphere; orb; world
órbita *f, ast* orbit; *fig* sphere; *anat* orbit, eye socket
Órcades, las the Orkneys
ordalía *f,* (medieval hist.) ordeal
orden *mf* order, mode of arrangement; succession, sequence; group; system; orderliness, neatness; coherence, plan; *ecc* order, brotherhood; (*zool bot*) group, class; *arch* order; *math* degree. *f,* precept, command; *com* order; *pl ecc* ordination. (*mil naut*) **o. de batalla,** battle array. **o. de caballería,** order of knighthood. **o. del día,** order of the day. *ecc* **dar órdenes,** to ordain. **en o.,** in order; with regard (to). **por su o.,** in its turn; successively
ordenación *f,* order, orderly arrangement, disposition; ordinance, precept; *ecc* ordination
ordenador *m Spain* computer
ordenamiento *m,* ordaining; ordinance; edict
ordenancista *mf mil* martinet; disciplinarian
ordenanza *f,* order, method; command, instruction; ordinance, regulation (gen. *pl*). *m, mil* orderly
ordenar *vt* to put in order, arrange; command, give instructions to; decree; direct, regulate; *ecc* ordain; *vr* (*with de*) *ecc* be ordained as
ordeñadero *m,* milk pail
ordeñar *vt* to milk
ordinal *a* ordinal. *m,* ordinal number
ordinariez *f,* rudeness, uncouthness; vulgarity
ordinario *a* ordinary, usual; vulgar, coarse, uncultured; rude; commonplace, average, mediocre. *m, ecc* ordinary; carrier; courier. **de o.,** usually, ordinarily
orear *vt* to ventilate; *vr* dry; air; take the air
orégano *m,* wild marjoram
oreja *f,* external ear; lug; tab, flap; tongue (of a shoe). *inf* **con las orejas caídas,** down in the mouth, depressed
orejera *f,* earflap; mold board (of a plow)
orejudo *a* large- or long-eared
oreo *m,* zephyr; ventilation; airing
orfanato *m,* orphanage, orphan asylum
orfandad *f,* orphanhood; defenselessness, lack of protection
orfebre *mf* gold- or silversmith
orfebrería *f,* gold- or silverwork
orfeón *m,* choral society
organdí *m,* organdy
orgánico *a* organic; harmonious; *fig* organized
organillero(-ra) *n* organ grinder
organillo *m,* barrel organ
organismo *m,* organism; organization, association
organista *mf* organist
organización *f,* organization; order, arrangement
organizador (-ra) *a* organizing. *n* organizer
organizar *vt* to organize; regulate; constitute
órgano *m, mus* organ; (*anat bot*) organ; means, agency. **o. de manubrio,** barrel organ
orgasmo *m,* orgasm
orgía *f,* orgy
orgullo *m,* pride; arrogance
orgulloso *a* proud; haughty
orientación *f,* orientation; exposure, prospect; bearings
oriental *a* Oriental, Eastern. *mf* Oriental; *Argentina* Uruguayan
orientalismo *m,* Orientalism
orientalista *mf* Orientalist
orientar *vt* to orientate; *vr* find one's bearings; familiarize oneself (with)
oriente *m,* Orient, the East; luster (of pearls); youth, childhood; origin, source
orificio *m,* orifice; hole
oriflama *f,* oriflamme; standard, flag
origen *m,* origin, source, root; stock, extraction; reason, genesis. **dar o. a,** to give rise to. **país de o.,** native land
original *a* original; earliest, primitive; new, first-hand; novel, fresh; inventive, creative; eccentric; quaint. *m,* original manuscript; original; sitter (for portraits); eccentric
originalidad *f,* originality
originar *vt* to cause, originate; invent; *vr* spring from, originate (in)
originario *a* original, primary; primitive; native (of)
orilla *f,* limit, edge; hem, border; selvage; shore, margin; bank (of a river, etc.); sidewalk; brink, edge. **a la o.,** on the brink; nearly
orillar *vt* to settle, arrange, conclude; *vi* reach the shore or bank; *sew* leave a hem; *sew* border; leave a selvage on cloth
orillo *m,* selvage (of cloth)
orín *m,* rust; *pl* urine
orinal *m,* chamber pot, urinal
orinar *vi* to urinate
oriundo *a* native (of); derived (from)
orla *f,* border, fringe; selvage (of cloth, garments); ornamental border (on diplomas, etc.)
orlar *vt* to border; edge, trim
ornamentación *f,* ornamentation
ornamental *a* ornamental
ornamentar *vt* to ornament; embellish
ornamento *m,* ornament; decoration; gift, virtue, talent; *pl ecc* vestments
ornar *vt* to ornament, adorn, embellish
ornato *m,* decoration, ornament
ornitología *f,* ornithology
ornitológico *a* ornithological
ornitólogo *m,* ornithologist
oro *m,* gold; gold coins or jewelery; *fig* riches; *pl* diamonds (cards). **o. batido,** gold leaf. **o. en polvo,** gold dust. *fig* **como un o.,** shining with cleanliness. **el as de oros,** the ace of diamonds
orondo *a* hollow; *inf* pompous; *inf* swollen, spongy
oropel *m,* brass foil; showy, cheap thing; trinket; tinsel
orquesta *f,* orchestra
orquestación *f,* orchestration
orquestal *a* orchestral
orquestar *vt* to orchestrate
orquídea *f,* orchid
ortega *f, orn* grouse
ortiga *f, bot* nettle
orto *m,* rising (of sun, stars)
ortodoxia *f,* orthodoxy
ortodoxo *a* orthodox
ortografía *f,* orthography
ortográfico *a* orthographical
ortopedia *f,* orthopedics

ortopédico (-ca) *a* orthopedic. *n* orthopedist
ortopedista *mf* orthopedist
oruga *f*, caterpillar
orzuelo *m*, *med* sty; trap (for wild animals)
os *pers pron 2nd pl mf dat* and *acc* of **vos** and **vosotros** you, to you
osa *f*, she-bear; *ast* **O. mayor,** Big Bear; **O. menor,** Little Bear
osadía *f*, boldness, audacity
osado *a* daring, bold
osamenta *f*, skeleton; bones (of a skeleton)
osar *vi* to dare; risk, venture
osario *m*, charnel house, ossuary
oscilación *f*, oscillation
oscilante *a* oscillating
oscilar *vi* to oscillate, sway; hesitate, vacillate
ósculo *m*, kiss, osculation
oscurantismo *m*, obscurantism
oscurantista *a* and *mf* obscurantist
oscurear *Mexico* = **oscurecer**
oscurecer *vt irr* to darken; *fig* tarnish, dim, sully; confuse, bewilder; express obscurely; *art* shade; *vn* grow dark; *vr* cloud over (sky); *inf* disappear (things, gen. by theft). See **conocer**
oscuridad *f*, darkness; gloom, blackness; humbleness; obscurity, abstruseness
oscuro *a* dark; humble, unknown; abstruse, involved; obscure; uncertain, dangerous. **a oscuras,** in the dark; ignorant
óseo *a* osseous
osera *f*, bear's den
osezno *m*, bear cub
osificación *f*, ossification
osificarse *vr* to ossify
ósmosis *f*, osmosis
oso *m*, bear. **o. blanco,** polar bear
ostensible *a* ostensible; obvious
ostensión *f*, show, display, manifestation
ostensivo *a* ostensive
ostentación *f*, manifestation; ostentation
ostentar *vt* to exhibit, show; boast, show off
ostentoso *a* magnificent, showy, ostentatious
osteópata *mf* osteopath
osteopatía *f*, osteopathy
ostión, *m*, *Mexico* oyster
ostra *f*, oyster. **vivero de ostras,** oyster bed
ostracismo *m*, ostracism
otear *vt* to observe; look on at
otero *m*, hill, height, eminence
otología *f*, otology
otólogo *m*, otologist
otomana *f*, ottoman, couch
otomano *a* Ottoman
otoñal *a* autumnal, autumn, fall
otoño *m*, autumn, fall
otorgamiento *m*, granting; consent, approval; license, award
otorgar *vt* to grant; concede, approve; *law* grant, stipulate, execute
otro (-ra) *a* other, another. *n* another one
otrosí *adv* besides, moreover
ovación *f*, ovation, triumph; applause
ovacionar *vt* to applaud
oval *a* oval
óvalo *m*, oval
ovario *m*, ovary
oveja *f*, ewe
overol *m Lat. Am.* overalls
ovillar *vi* to wind thread into a ball; *vr* curl up; huddle
ovillo *m*, ball, bobbin (of thread); tangled heap (of things)
ovíparo *a* oviparous
OVNI *m*, UFO
ovulación *f*, ovulation
óvulo *m*, ovule
oxidación *f*, oxidation
oxidar *vt* oxidize; *vr* become oxidized
óxido *m*, oxide. **ó. de carbono,** carbon monoxide. **ó. de cinc,** zinc oxide
oxígeno *m*, oxygen
oyente *mf* hearer; *pl* audience
ozono *m*, ozone

P

pabellón *m*, pavilion; colors, flag; bell tent. **p. británico,** Union Jack. **p. de reposo,** rest home. **en p.,** stacked (of arms)
pábulo *m*, food; *fig* pabulum
pacedero *a agr* grazing, meadow
pacer *vi irr agr* to graze; *vt* nibble away; eat away. See **nacer**
paciencia *f*, patience
paciente *a* patient; long-suffering; complacent. *mf med* patient
pacienzudo *a* extremely patient or long-suffering
pacificación *f*, pacification; serenity, peace of mind
pacificador (-ra) *a* peace making; pacifying. *n* peace maker
pacificar *vt* to pacify; *vi* make peace; *vr* grow quiet, become calm (sea, etc.)
pacífico *a* pacific, meek, mild; peace-loving, peaceful. **el Océano P.,** the Pacific Ocean
pacifismo *m*, pacifism
pacifista *a* and *mf* pacifist
pacotilla *f*, goods. *inf* **hacer su p.,** to make one's packet or fortune. **ser de p.,** to be poor stuff; be jerry-built (of houses)
pactar *vt* to stipulate, arrange; contract
pacto *m*, agreement, contract; pact
padecer *vt irr* to suffer; feel keenly; experience, undergo; tolerate. **p. desnudez,** to go unclothed. **p. hambre,** to go hungry. See **conocer**
padecimiento *m*, suffering
padrastro *m*, stepfather; cruel father; *fig* impediment, obstacle; hangnail
padrazo *m*, *inf* indulgent father
padre *m*, father; stallion; head (of the family, etc.); *ecc* father; genesis, source; author, creator; *pl* parents; ancestors. **p. adoptivo,** foster father. **p. de familia,** paterfamilias. **P. Eterno,** Eternal Father. **p. nuestro,** Lord's Prayer. **P. Santo,** Holy Father, the Pope
padrear *vi* to take after one's father; *zool* reproduce, breed
padrejón *m*, *Argentina* stallion
padrino *m*, godfather; sponsor; second (in duels, etc.); patron; best man
padrón *m*, census; pattern, model; memorial stone
paella *f*, *cul* savory rice dish of shellfish, chicken, and meat
paga *f*, payment; amends, restitution; pay; payment of fine; reciprocity (in love, etc.)
pagadero *a* payable. *m*, date and place when payment is due
pagador (-ra) *n* payer. *m*, teller; wages clerk; paymaster
pagaduría *f*, pay office
paganismo *m*, paganism; heathenism
pagano (-na) *a* and *n* pagan; heathen
pagar *vt* to pay; make restitution, expiate; return, requite (love, etc.); *vr* (*with de*) become fond of; be proud of. **p. adelantado,** to prepay. *com* **p. al contado,** to pay cash. **p. la casa,** to pay the rent (for one's residence)
pagaré *m*, *com* promissory note, I.O.U.

página *f,* page (of a book); episode, occurrence
paginación *f,* pagination
paginar *vt* to paginate
pago *m,* payment; recompense, reward; region of vineyards, olive groves, etc.; *Argentina* area, region
paguro *m,* hermit crab
pailebote *m,* schooner
país *m,* country, nation; region; *art* landscape. **del p.,** typical of the country of origin (gen. of food)
paisaje *m,* countryside; landscape, scenery
paisajista, paisista *mf* landscape painter
paisano (-na) *n* compatriot; peasant; civilian
Países Bajos, los the Low Countries, the Netherlands
paja *f,* straw; chaff; trash; *fig* padding. **ver la p. en el ojo del vecino y no la viga en el nuestro,** to see the mote in our neighbor's eye and not the beam in our own
pajar *m,* barn
pájara *f,* hen (bird); kite (toy); *inf* jay; prostitute. **p. pinta,** game of forfeits
pajarear *vt* to snare birds; loaf, idle about
pajarera *f,* aviary
pajarero *m,* bird catcher or seller. *a inf* frivolous, giddy; *inf* gaudy (colors); *Lat. Am.* skittish (horse)
pajarita *f,* bow tie
pájaro *m,* bird. **p. bobo,** penguin. **p. carpintero,** woodpecker. *fig inf* **p. gordo,** big gun. **p. mosca,** hummingbird
pajarota *f, inf* canard, false report
paje *m,* page; *naut* cabin boy
pajera *f,* hayloft
pajizo *a* made of straw; covered or thatched with straw; strawcolored
pala *f,* paddle; blade (of an oar); shovel; spade; baker's peel (long-handled shovel); cutting edge of a spade, hoe, etc.; *sport* racket; vamp, upper (of a shoe); pelota or jai alai racket; tanner's knife; *inf* guile, cunning; cleverness, dexterity. **p. de hélice,** propeller blade. **p. para pescado,** fish server. *inf* **corta p.,** ignoramus; blockhead
palabra *f,* word; power of speech; eloquence; offer, promise; *pl* magic formula, spell. **p. de clave,** code word. **p. de matrimonio,** promise of marriage. **p. de rey,** inviolable promise. **palabras cruzadas,** crossword puzzle. **bajo p. de,** under promise of. **cuatro palabras,** a few words; short conversation. **de p.,** verbally, by word of mouth. **dirigir la p. a,** to address, speak to. **faltar a su p.,** to break one's promise. **llevar la p.,** to be spokesperson. **medias palabras,** half-words; hint, insinuation. **su p. empeñada,** one's solemn word. **tener la p.,** to have the right to speak (in meetings, etc.) (e.g. **El señor Martínez tiene la p.,** Mr. Martinez has the floor)
palabrería *f,* verbosity, wordiness
palabrota *f, inf* coarse language; long word
palaciego (-ga) *a* pertaining to palaces; *fig* courtesan. *n* courtier
palacio *m,* palace; mansion
palada *f,* shovelful, spadeful; oar stroke
paladar *m, anat* palate; taste; discernment, sensibility
paladear *vt* to taste with pleasure, savor; enjoy, relish
paladín *m,* paladin
paladino *a* public, clear, open
palafrén *m,* palfrey
palafrenero *m,* groom; stablehand
palanca *f, mech* lever; handle; bar; (high) diving board. **p. de arranque,** starting gear. **p. de cambio de velocidad,** gear-changing lever. **p. de mando,** control stick
palangana *f,* washbasin
palanganear *vi, Lat. Am.* to show off
palanganero *m,* washstand
palanqueta *f, dim* small lever; jimmy
palastro *m,* sheet iron or steel
palatinado *m,* Palatinate
palatino *a* palatine
palatizar *vt* to palatilize
palazón *f,* woodwork
palco *m, theat* box; stand, raised platform, enclosure. **p. de platea,** orchestra
palenque *m,* enclosure; stand; platform; palisade
paleografía *f,* paleography
paleógrafo *m,* paleographer
paleolítico *a* paleolithic
paleología *f,* paleology
paleontología *f,* paleontology
palestra *f,* tilt yard
paleta *f, dim* little shovel; trowel; *art* palette; fireplace shovel; mason's trowel; *anat* shoulder blade; blade (of a propeller, ventilator, etc.); *chem* spatula
paliacate *m, Mexico* kerchief
paliación *f,* palliation; excuse
paliar *vt* to dissemble, excuse; palliate, mitigate
paliativo *a* palliative; extenuating
palidecer *vi irr* to turn pale. See **conocer**
palidez *f,* pallor, paleness
pálido *a* pale, pallid
paliducho *a* somewhat pale, palish; sallow
palillo *m, dim* small stick; toothpick; bobbin (for lace-making); drumstick; *fig* chatter; *pl* castanets
palimpsesto *m,* palimpsest
palinodia *f, lit* palinode. **cantar la p.,** to eat one's words, recant
palio *m,* Greek mantle; cape; *ecc* pallium; canopy, awning
palique *m, inf* chat. **estar de p.,** to be having a chat
paliquear *vi* to chat
paliza *f,* caning, beating
palizada *f,* paling, fence; palisade, stockade. **p. de tablas,** hoarding
palma *f,* palm tree; palm leaf; date palm; palm (of the hand); hand; triumph. **llevarse la p.,** to bear away the palm; take the cake
palmada *f,* slap; *pl* hand-clapping
palmado *a* web (of feet); palmy
palmar *a* palmaceous; palmar; clear, obvious. *m,* palm grove
palmatoria *f,* ferule, ruler; candlestick
palmear *vi* to clap hands
palmera *f,* palm tree
palmeta *f,* ferrule, ruler
palmetazo *m,* slap on the hand with a ruler; *fig* slap in the face
palmo *m,* span; hand's breadth. **p. a p.,** inch by inch, piecemeal
palmotear *vt* to applaud; clap
palo *m,* stick; rod; pole; timber, wood; wooden log; *naut* mast; blow with a stick; execution by hanging; suit (of playing cards); fruit stalk; *her* pale. **p. de Campeche,** logwood. **p. de hule,** rubber tree. **p. de rosa,** tulipwood. *naut* **p. mayor,** mainmast. *naut* **a p. seco,** under bare poles. **de tal p., tal astilla,** a chip off the old block; like father like son. **estar del mismo p.,** to be of the same mind, agree
paloma *f,* dove; pigeon; gentle person; *pl naut* white horses. **p. buchona,** pouter pigeon. **p. mensajera,** carrier pigeon. **p. torcaz,** wood pigeon
palomar *m,* dovecote; pigeon loft
palomero (-ra) *n* pigeon fancier; pigeon dealer
palomino *m,* young pigeon
palomo *m,* male pigeon; wood pigeon
palotes *m pl,* drumsticks; pothooks (in writing)
palpabilidad *f,* palpability
palpable *a* palpable, tangible
palpación *f, med* palpation
palpar *vt* to palpate, examine by touch; grope, walk by touch; *fig* see clearly
palpitación *f,* beating (of a heart); *med* palpitation; convulsive movement
palpitante *a* palpitating; quivering; beating; (of a question) burning

palpitar *vi* to beat (heart); throb, palpitate; shudder, move convulsively; *fig* manifest itself (passions, etc.)
me palpita que . . . *Argentina,* I have a hunch that . . .
palpo *m,* palp, feeler
palta *f, Lat. Am.* avocado (pear)
palúdico *a* marshy, swampy; malarial
paludismo *m,* malaria; paludism
palurdo (-da) *a inf* gross, rude, boorish. *n* boor
palustre *m,* mason's trowel. *a* marshy, swampy
pamela *f,* wide-brimmed straw sailor (woman's hat)
pamema *f, inf* unimportant trifle; *inf* caress
pampa *f,* pampa, treeless plain
pamplina *f, inf* nonsense, rubbish
pan *m,* bread; loaf; *cul* piecrust; *fig* food; wheat; gold leaf; *pl* cereals. **p. ázimo,** unleavened bread. **p. de oro,** gold leaf. **llamar al p. p. y al vino vino,** to call a spade a spade. **venderse como p. bendito,** to sell like hot cakes
pana *f,* velveteen, velours
panacea *f,* panacea; cure-all
panadería *f,* bakery trade or shop; bakery
panadero (-ra) *n* baker. *m pl,* Spanish dance
panadizo *m, med* whitlow; *inf* ailing person, crock
panal *m,* honeycomb; wasp's nest
Panamá Panama
panamá *m, Lat. Am.* Panama hat
panameño (-ña) *a* and *n* Panamanian
panamericanismo *m,* pan-Americanism
panarra *m, inf* simpleton
páncreas *m,* pancreas
pancreático *a* pancreatic
panda *f,* gallery of a cloister. *mf zool* panda
pandémico *a* pandemic
pandemonio *m,* pandemonium
pandereta *f,* tambourine
pandero *m,* tambourine; *inf* windbag
pandilla *f,* league, group; gang (of burglars, etc.); party, crowd, band
pane *f,* breakdown
panecillo *m, dim* roll (of bread)
panegírico *a* and *m,* panegyric
panel *m,* panel
panetela *f,* panada
pánfilo (-la) *a* sluggish, phlegmatic, slow-moving. *n* sluggard
panfleto *m,* pamphlet
paniaguado *m,* servant; favorite, protégé
pánico *a* and *m,* panic
panoja *f, bot* panicle; *bot* ear, beard, awn
panoli *a inf* doltish, stupid
panorama *m,* panorama; view
panorámico *a* panoramic
pantalón *m,* pant, trouser (gen. *pl*); knickers. **p. de corte,** striped trousers. **pantalones bombachos,** plus fours
pantalla *f,* lampshade; face screen; movie screen; shade, reflector
pantano *m,* marsh, swamp; impediment; artificial pool
pantanoso *a* marshy, swampy; *fig* awkward, full of pitfalls
panteísmo *m,* pantheism
panteón *m,* pantheon; *Mexico* cemetery
pantera *f,* panther; *Venezuela* jaguar, ocelot
pantomima *f,* pantomime; mime
pantorrilla *f,* calf (of the leg)
pantuflo *m,* house slipper
panza *f,* paunch, stomach; belly (of jugs, etc.). *inf* **un cielo de p. de burra,** a dark gray sky. **p. mojada** *Mexico* wetback
panzudo *a* paunchy
pañal *m,* diaper; shirttail; *pl* long clothes, swaddling clothes; infancy
pañería *f,* drapery stores; drapery
pañero (-ra) *n* draper
paño *m,* woolen material; cloth, fabric; drapery, hanging; tapestry; linen, bandage; tarnish or other mark; *naut* canvas; *sew* breadth, width (of cloth); panel (in a dress); floor cloth, duster; livid mark on the face; *pl* garments. **p. de lágrimas,** consoler, sympathizer. **p. mortuorio,** pall (on a coffin). **paños menores,** underwear. **p. verde,** gambling table. **al p.,** *theat* from the wings, from without. *inf* **poner el p. al púlpito,** to hold forth, spread oneself
pañoleta *f,* kerchief, triangular scarf; fichu
pañuelo *m,* kerchief; handkerchief
papa *m,* pope; *inf* papa, daddy. *f, inf* potato; stupid rumor; nonsense; *pl* pap; *cul* sop; food
papá *m, inf* papa, daddy
papada *f,* double chin; dewlap
papado *m,* papacy
papagayo *m,* parrot
papal *m, Lat. Am.* potato field
papamoscas *m, orn* flycatcher; *inf* simpleton
papanatas *m, inf* simpleton
papar *vt* to sip, take soft food; *inf* eat; neglect, be careless about
paparrucha *f, inf* stupid rumor; nonsense
papel *m,* paper; document; manuscript; *theat* role, part; pamphlet; sheet of paper; paper, monograph, essay; guise, role; *theat* character. **p. carbón, p. carbónico,** carbon paper. **p. celofán,** cellophane. **p. cuadriculado,** graph paper, cartridge paper. **p. de calcar,** carbon paper; tracing paper. **p. de escribir,** writing paper. **p. de estaño,** tinfoil. **p. de estraza,** brown paper. **p. de fumar,** cigarette paper. **p. de lija,** emery- or sandpaper. **p. de paja de arroz,** rice paper. **p. de seda,** tissue paper. **p. de tornasol,** litmus paper. **p. del estado,** government bonds. **p. higiénico,** toilet paper. **p. moneda,** paper money. **p. pintado,** wallpaper. **p. secante,** blotting paper. **p. sellado,** official stamped paper. **hacer buen (mal) p.,** to do well (badly). **hacer el p. (de),** *theat* to act the part (of); feign, pretend
papelear *vi* to turn over papers, search among them; *inf* cut a dash
papeleo *m,* bureacracy, red tape
papelera *f,* mass of papers; desk (for keeping papers)
papelería *f,* heap of papers; stationer's shop; stationery
papelero (-ra) *a* paper, stationery. *n* paper maker; stationer
papeleta *f,* slip or scrap of paper
papelista *mf* paper maker; stationer; paperhanger
papelucho *m,* old or dirty piece of paper; trash, worthless writing; *inf* rag (newspaper)
papera *f,* mumps
papilla *f,* pap; guile, wiliness
papillote *m,* curl-paper
papiro *m,* papyrus
papo *m,* dewlap; gizzard (of a bird); goiter. **p. de cardo,** thistledown
paquebote *m, naut* packet; mail boat; liner
paquete *m,* packet; parcel, package
paquidermo *m,* pachyderm
par *a* equal; alike; corresponding. *m,* pair, couple; team (of oxen, mules); peer (title); rafter (of a roof); *mech* torque, couple; *elec* cell. *f,* par. **a la p.,** jointly; simultaneously; *com* at par. **a pares,** two by two. **de p. en p.,** wide-open (doors, etc.). **sin p.,** peerless, excellent
para *prep* in order to; for; to; for the sake of (e.g. **Lo hice p. ella,** I did it for her sake); enough to (gen. with *bastante,* etc.); in the direction of, toward; about to, on the point of (e.g. **Está p. salir,** He is on the point of going out). Expresses:
1. *Purpose* (e.g. **La educan p. bailarina,** They are bringing her up to be a dancer. **Lo dije p. ver lo que harías,** I said it to (in order to) see what you would do)
2. *Destination* (e.g. **Salió p. Londres,** He left for London)
3. *Use* (e.g. **seda p. medias,** silk for stockings. **un vaso p. flores,** a vase for flowers)

4. *An appointed time* (e.g. **Lo pagaré p. Navidad,** I will pay it at Christmas)
p. con, toward (a person) (e.g. **Ha obrado muy bien p. con mi hermano,** He has behaved very well toward my brother)
p. coneretar, to be exact, to wit
p. que, in order to, so that (e.g. **Lo puse en la mesa p. que lo vieses,** I put it on the table so that you would see it)
¿P. qué? Why? For what reason?
p. siempre, forever. **decir p. sí,** to say to oneself. **sin qué ni p. qué,** without rhyme or reason
parábola *f,* parable; *geom* parabola
parabrisas *m,* windshield
paracaídas *m,* parachute
paracaidista *mf* parachutist
parachoques *m, aut* bumper; buffer (railroad)
parada *f,* stopping, halting; stop; stoppage, suspension; halt; *mil* review; interval, pause; cattle stall; dam; gambling stakes; parry (in fencing); relay (of horses). **p. de coches,** taxi rank. **p. de tranvía,** streetcar stop. **p. discrecional,** request stop (buses, etc.)
paradear (con . . .) *vi, Argentina* to brag (about . . .)
paradero *m,* railroad station; stopping place; end, conclusion; whereabouts
paradisíaco *a* paradisaical
parado *a* still; indolent, lazy; unoccupied, leisured; silent, reserved; timid; unemployed
paradoja *f,* paradox
paradójico *a* paradoxical
parador *m,* inn, tavern, hostelry
parafina *f,* paraffin
parafrasear *vt* to paraphrase
paráfrasis *f,* paraphrase
paraguas *m,* umbrella
paraguayo (-ya) *a* and *n* Paraguayan
paragüería *f,* umbrella shop
paragüero (-ra) *n* umbrella maker, umbrella seller. *m,* umbrella stand
paraíso *m,* paradise; garden of Eden; heaven; (*inf theat*) gallery, gods
paraje *m,* place, locality, spot; state, condition
paralela *f, mil* parallel; *pl* parallel bars (for gymnastic exercises)
paralelismo *m,* parallelism
paralelo *a* parallel; analogous; similar. *m,* parallel, similarity; *geog* parallel
parálisis *f,* paralysis
paralítico (-ca) *a* and *n* paralytic
paralización *f,* paralysis; cessation; *com* dullness, quietness
paralizar *vt* to paralyze; stop
paramento *m,* ornament; trappings (of a horse); face (of a wall); facing (of a building). **paramentos sacerdotales,** liturgical vestments or ornaments
páramo *m,* paramo, treeless plain; desert, wilderness
parangón *m,* comparison; similarity
parangonar *vt* to compare
paraninfo *m, arch* paranymph, university hall; best man (weddings); messenger of good
paranoico *m,* paranoiac
parapetarse *vr* to shelter behind a parapet; take refuge behind
parapeto *m,* parapet
parapoco *mf inf* ninny, numskull
parar *vi* to stop, halt; end, finish; lodge; come into the hands of; *vt* stop; detain; prepare; bet, stake; point (hunting dogs); parry (fencing); *vr* halt; be interrupted; *Lat. Am.* to get up, stand up. **p. mientes en,** to notice; consider. **sin p.,** immediately, at once; without stopping
pararrayos *m,* lightning conductor
parasitario, parasítico *a* parasitic
parásito *m,* parasite; *fig* sponger; *pl rad* interference. *a* parasitic
parasitología *f,* parasitology
parasol *m,* sunshade; *bot* umbel
paratifoidea *f,* paratyphoid
parca *f,* Fate; *poet* death. **las Parcas,** the Three Fates
parcela *f,* plot, parcel (of land); atom, particle
parchar *vt, Lat. Am.* to mend, patch, patch up
parche *m, med* plaster; *aut* patch; drum; drumhead, parchment of drum; patch, mend
parcial *a* partial, incomplete; biased, prejudiced; factional, party; participatory
parcialidad *f,* partiality, bias, prejudice; party, faction, group; intimacy, friendship
parco *a* scarce, scanty; temperate, moderate; frugal
parcómetro *m Lat. Am.* (*except Argentina and Mexico*) parking meter
pardo *a* brown; gray, drab, dun-colored; cloudy, dark; husky (voices). *m,* leopard
pardusco *a* grayish; fawn-colored
parear *vt* to pair, match; put in pairs; compare
parecer *vi irr* to appear; look, seem; turn up (be found). *impers* believe, think (e.g. **me parece,** it seems to me, I think, my opinion is); *vr* look alike, resemble one another. See **conocer**
parecer *m,* opinion, belief; appearance, looks
parecido *a* (*with bien or mal*) good- or bad-looking. *m,* resemblance
pared *f,* wall; partition wall; side, face. **p. maestra,** main wall. **p. medianera,** party wall. **Las paredes oyen,** The walls have ears. *inf* **pegado a la p.,** confused, taken aback
pareja *f,* pair; dance partner; couple. **p. desparejada,** mismatched pair. **parejas mixtas,** mixed doubles (in tennis). **correr parejas** *or* **correr a las parejas,** to be equal; go together, happen simultaneously; be on a par
parejo *a* equal; similar; smooth, flat; even, regular
parentela *f,* relatives, kindred; parentage
parentesco *m,* kinship; relationship; affinity; *inf* connection, link
paréntesis *m,* parenthesis; digression. **entre p.,** incidentally
paresa *f,* peeress
paria *mf* pariah; outcast
parida *a f,* newly delivered of a child
paridad *f,* parity; analogy, similarity
pariente (-ta) *n* relative, relation; *inf* husband (wife)
parihuela *f,* wheelbarrow; stretcher
parir *vt* to give birth to; *fig* bring forth; reveal, publish; *vi* lay eggs
París Paris
parisiense *a* and *mf* Parisian
parla *f,* speech; loquaciousness, eloquence; verbiage
parlamentar *vi* to converse; discuss (contracts, etc.); *mil* parley
parlamentario *a* parliamentarian. *m,* member of parliament
parlamentarismo *m,* parliamentarianism
parlamento *m,* legislative assembly; parliament; discourse, speech; *theat* long speech; *mil* parley
parlanchín *a inf* talkative, chattering, loquacious
parlar *vt* and *vi* to speak freely or easily; chatter; reveal, speak indiscreetly; babble (of streams, etc.)
parlero *a* talkative; gossiping, indiscreet; talking (birds); *fig* expressive (eyes, etc.); prattling, babbling (brook, etc.)
parlotear *vi inf* to chatter, gossip
parloteo *m,* chattering, gossip
parnaso *m,* Parnassus; anthology of verse
paro *m, inf* work stoppage; lockout; *orn* tit. **p. forzoso,** unemployment
parodia *f,* parody
parodiar *vt* to parody
parodista *mf* parodist
parótida *f,* parotid gland; parotitis, mumps
parotiditis *f,* parotitis, mumps
paroxismo *m, med* paroxysm; frenzy, ecstasy, fit
parpadear *vi* to blink
parpadeo *m,* blinking

párpado *m,* eyelid
parque *m,* park; depot, park; paddock, pen. **p. de atracciones,** pleasure ground. **p. de** (*or* **para**) **automóviles,** car park, parking lot
parquear *vt, vi, Lat. Am.* to park
parquedad *f,* scarcity; moderation, temperance; parsimony, frugality
parquímetro *m Spain, Venezuela* parking meter
parra *f,* vine. **hoja de p.,** *fig* fig leaf
párrafo *m,* paragraph; *gram* paragraph sign. **p. aparte,** new paragraph. **echar un p.,** to chat, gossip
parranda *f, inf* binge; strolling band of musicians. **ir de p.,** to go on a binge
parricida *mf* parricide (person)
parricidio *m,* parricide (act)
parrilla *f, cul* griller, broiler; grill, gridiron; *eng* grate. *cul* **a la p.,** grilled
párroco *m,* parish priest; parson
parroquia *f,* parish church; parish; clergy of a parish; clientele, customers
parroquial *a* parochial
parroquiano (-na) *a* parochial. *n* parishioner; client, customer
parsimonia *f,* frugality, thrift; prudence, moderation
parsimonioso *a* parsimonious
parte *f,* part; share; place; portion; side, faction; *law* party; *theat* part, role. *m,* communication, message; telegraph or telephone message; (*mil nav*) communiqué. *f pl,* parts, talents. **p. actora,** *law* prosecution. **p. de la oración,** part of speech. **partes litigantes,** *law* contending parties. **dar p.,** to notify; (*mil naut*) report; give a share (in a transaction). **de algún tiempo a esta p.,** for some time past. **de p. de,** in the name of, from. **en p.,** partly. **por todas partes,** on all sides, everywhere. **ser p. a** *or* **ser p. para que,** to contribute to. **tener de su p.** (**a**), to count on the favor of. **la quinta p.,** one-fifth, etc.
partear *vt* to assist in childbirth
partera *f,* midwife
partero *m,* accoucheur
partición *f,* partition, distribution; (*aer naut*) accommodation
participación *f,* participation; notice, warning; announcement (of an engagement, etc.); *com* share
participante *a* and *mf* participant
participar *vi* to participate, take part (in), share; *vt* inform; announce (an engagement, etc.)
partícipe *a* sharing. *mf* participant
participio *m,* participle
partícula *f,* particle, grain; *gram* particle
particular *a* private; peculiar; special, particular; unusual; individual. *mf* private individual. *m,* matter, subject. **en p.,** especially; privately
particularidad *f,* individuality; speciality; rareness, unusualness; detail, circumstance; intimacy, friendship
particularizar *vt* to detail, particularize; single out, choose; *vr* (*with en*) be characterized by
partida *f,* departure; entry, record (of birth, etc.); certificate (of marriage, etc.); *com* item; *com* lot, allowance; *mil* guerrilla; armed band; expedition, excursion; game (of cards, etc.); rubber (at bridge, etc.); *inf* conduct, behavior; place, locality; death. *com* **p. doble,** double entry. **Las siete Partidas,** code of Spanish laws compiled by Alfonso X (1252–84)
partidarismo *m,* partisanship
partidario (-ia) *a* partisan. *n* adherent, disciple. *m,* partisan, guerrilla
partido *m,* party, group, faction; profit; *sport* match; team; agreement, pact. **p. conservador,** *pol* conservative party. **p. obrero** *or* **p. laborista,** *pol* labor party. **buen p.,** *fig* good match, catch. **sacar p. de,** to take advantage of, make the most of. **tomar p.,** to enlist; join, become a supporter (of)
partidor *m,* divider, apportioner; cleaver, chopper; hewer
partir *vt* to divide; split; crack, break; separate; *math* divide; *vi* go, depart; start (from). **p. como el rayo,** be off like a flash. *vr* disagree, become divided; leave, depart
partitura *f, mus* score
parto *m,* parturition, birth; newborn child; *fig* creation, offspring; important event
parturienta *a f,* parturient
parva *f,* light breakfast; threshed or unthreshed grain; heap, mass
parvedad *f,* smallness; scarcity; light breakfast (taken on fast days)
parvo *a* little, small
párvulo (-la) *n* child. *a* small; innocent, simple; lowly, humble
pasa *f,* raisin; *naut* channel; passage, flight (of birds). **p. de Corinto,** currant
pasacalle *m, mus* lively march
pasada *f,* passing, passage; money sufficient to live on; passage, corridor. **dar p.,** to let pass, put up with. *inf* **mala p.,** bad turn, dirty trick
pasadera *f,* steppingstone
pasadero *a* passable, traversable; fair (health); tolerable, passable. *m,* steppingstone
pasadizo *m,* narrow corridor or passage; alley, narrow street; *naut* alleyway
pasado *m,* past; *pl* ancestors. **Lo p., p.,** What's past is past. **p. de moda,** out of fashion, unfashionable
pasador *m,* bolt, fastener; *mech* pin, coupler; pin (of brooches, etc.); colander; *naut* marlin spike; shirt stud
pasajaretas *m,* bodkin
pasaje *m,* passing; passage; fare; passage money; *naut* complement of passengers; channel, strait; (*mus lit*) passage; *mus* modulation, transition (of voice); voyage; passage; covered way; road; *Lat. Am.* dead-end street
pasajero (-ra) *a* crowded public (thoroughfare); transitory, fugitive; passing; temporary. *n* passenger
pasamanería *f,* passementerie work, industry or shop
pasamano *m,* passementerie; banister, handrail; *naut* gangway
pasante *a her* passant. *m,* student teacher; articled clerk; apprentice; student. **p. de pluma,** law clerk
pasaporte *m,* passport; license, permission. **dar el p.** (**a**), *inf* to give the sack (to)
pasar *vt* to pass; carry, transport; cross over; send; go beyond, overstep; run through, pierce; upset; overtake; transfer; suffer, undergo; sieve; study; dry (grapes, etc.); smuggle; surpass; omit; swallow (food); approve; dissemble; transform; spend (time); *vi* pass; be transferred; be infectious; have enough to live on; cease; last; die; pass away; pass (at cards); be transformed; be current (money); be salable (goods); (*with prep a + infin*) begin to; (*with por*) pass as; have a reputation as; visit; (*with sin*) do without. *impers* happen, occur. *vr* end; go over to another party; forget; go stale or bad; *fig* go too far, overstep the mark; permeate. **p. contrato,** to draw up a contract; sign a contract. **p. la voz,** to pass the word along. **p. por alto** (**de**), to omit, overlook. **p. de largo,** to go by without stopping. **pasarse de listo,** to be too clever. **¡No pases cuidado!** Don't worry!
pasarela *f,* gangplank
pasatiempo *m,* pastime, hobby, amusement
pasavante *m, naut* safe conduct; navicert
pascua *f,* Passover; Easter; Christmas; Twelfth Night; Pentecost; *pl* twelve days of Christmas. **P. florida,** Easter Sunday. **dar las pascuas,** to wish a merry Christmas. **¡Felices pascuas!** Merry Christmas!
pascual *a* paschal
pase *m,* pass (with the hands and in football, etc.); safe conduct; free pass; thrust (in fencing)
paseante *mf* stroller, promenader, passerby
pasear *vt* to take a walk; parade up and down, display; *vi* take a walk; go for a drive; go for a ride (on horseback, etc.); stroll up and down; *vr* touch upon lightly, pass over; loaf, be idle; drift; float

paseo *m*, walk, stroll; drive; outing, expedition; promenade; boulevard. **p. a caballo,** ride on horseback
pasiega *f*, wet nurse
pasillo *m*, gallery; corridor; lobby; railway corridor; *sew* basting stitch
pasión *f*, suffering; passivity; passion; desire; *ecc* passion. **con p.,** passionately
pasionaria *f*, passionflower
pasividad *f*, passivity
pasivo *a* passive; inactive; *com* sleeping (partner); *gram* passive. *m*, *com* liabilities
pasmar *vt* to freeze to death (plants); dumbfound, amaze, stun; chill; *vr* be stunned or amazed
pasmo *m*, amazement, astonishment; wonder, marvel; *med* tetanus, lockjaw
pasmoso *a* astounding, amazing; wonderful
paso *a* dried (of fruit)
paso *m*, step; pace; passage, passing; way; footstep; progress, advancement; passage (in a book); *sew* tacking stitch; occurrence, event; *theat* short play; gait, walk; strait, channel; migratory flight (birds); *mech* pitch; event or scene from the Passion; armed combat; death; *Lat. Am.* ford. *pl* measures, steps. *adv* softly, in a low voice; gently. **p. a nivel,** level crossing. **p. a p.,** step by step. **p. doble,** quick march; Spanish dance. **p. volante,** (gymnastics) giant stride. **a cada p.,** at every step; often. **al p.,** without stopping; on the way, in passing. **ceder el p.,** to allow to pass. **de p.,** in passing; incidentally. **llevar el p.,** to keep in step. **marcar el p.,** to mark time. **salir al p. (a),** to waylay, confront; oppose. **seguir los pasos (a),** to follow; spy upon
paspa *f*, *Peru* chapped skin
paspadura *f*, *Argentina* = **paspa**
pasparse *vr*, *Lat. Am.* to chap, crack
pasquín *m*, **pasquinada** *f*, pasquinade, lampoon
pasta *f*, *cul* dough; paste; pastry; piecrust; batter; *cul* noodle paste; paper pulp; board (bookbinding). **ser de buena p.,** to be good-natured
pastar *vt* to take to pasture; *vi* graze, pasture
pastel *m*, cake; *art* pastel; pie; *inf* plot, secret understanding; cheating (at cards); *print* pie; *inf* fat, stocky person
pastelear *vi inf* to indulge in shady business (especially in politics)
pastelería *f*, cake bakery; cake shop; confectioner's art; confectionery
pastelero (-ra) *n* confectioner, pastry cook; *fig inf* spineless person, jellyfish
pastelillo *m*, *cul* turnover
pastelón *m*, meat or game pie
pasteurización *f*, pasteurization
pasteurizar *vt* to pasteurize
pastilla *f*, tablet, cake; lozenge; pastille, drop; tread (of a tire)
pasto *m*, grazing land, pasture; fodder; *fig* fuel, food; spiritual food. **a p.,** in plenty, abundantly. **de p.,** of daily use
pastor (-ra) *n* shepherd. *m*, *ecc* pastor
pastoral *a* rustic, country; *ecc* pastoral, *f*, pastoral poem; *ecc* pastoral letter
pastorear *vt* to graze, put to grass; *ecc* have charge of souls
pastorela *f*, pastoral
pastoreo *m*, pasturage, grazing
pastoril *a* shepherd, pastoral
pastoso *a* doughy; mealy; pasty; mellow
pata *f*, paw and leg (animals); foot (of table, etc.); duck; *inf* leg. **p. de gallo,** blunder; crow's-foot, wrinkle. **meter la p.,** to interfere, put one's foot in it. *inf* **tener mala p.,** to be unlucky
patada *f*, kick, stamp; *inf* step, pace
patagón (-ona) *a* and *n* Patagonian
patalear *vi* to stamp (with the feet)
pataleo *m*, kicking; stamping
pataleta *f*, *inf* convulsion; feigned hysterics
patán *m*, *inf* yokel; boor, churl
patanería *f*, *inf* boorishness, churlishness
patarata *f*, trash, useless thing; extravagant courtesy
patata *f*, potato
patatal, patatar *m*, potato patch
patatús *m*, *inf* petty worry; mishap; *med* stroke, fit
patear *vt inf* to stamp; *fig* walk on, treat badly; *vi inf* stamp the feet; be furiously angry; (*golf*) putt
patena *f*, engraved medal worn by country women; *ecc* paten
patentar *vt* to issue a patent; take out a patent, patent
patente *a* obvious, patent; *f*, patent; warrant, commission; letters patent. **p. de invención,** patent. **p. de sanidad,** clean bill of health
patentizar *vt* to make evident
paternidad *f*, paternity
paterno *a* paternal
patético *a* pitiable; pathetic, moving
patiabierto *a inf* knock-kneed
patibulario *a* heartrending, harrowing
patíbulo *m*, scaffold
paticojo *a inf* lame; wobbly; unsteady
patilla *f*, side whisker (gen. *pl*); *pl* old Nick, the Devil
patín *m*, skate; runner (of a sled); (*aer* and of vehicles) skid; *mech* shoe. **p. del diablo,** scooter. **p. de ruedas,** roller skate
patinador (-ra) *n* skater
patinaje *m*, skating; skidding (of planes and vehicles)
patinar *vi* to skate; slip, lose one's footing; skid (vehicles and planes)
patinazo *m*, skid (of a vehicle)
patinete *m*, child's scooter
patio *m*, courtyard; *theat* pit; *Mexico* shunting yard
patitieso *a inf* paralyzed in the hands or feet; open-mouthed, amazed; stiff, unbending, proud
patituerto *a* crooked-legged; pigeon-toed; *inf* lop-sided
patizambo *a* knock-kneed
pato *m*, duck; *inf* **pagar el p.,** to be a scapegoat
patógeno *a* pathogenic
patojo *a* waddling
patología *f*, pathology
patológico *a* pathological
patólogo *m*, pathologist
patoso *a fig* heavy, pedestrian, tedious
patraña *f*, nonsense, rubbish, fairy tale
patria *f*, motherland, native country; native place. **p. chica,** native region
patriarca *m*, patriarch
patriarcado *m*, patriarchy
patriarcal *a* patriarchal
patricio (-ia) *a* and *n* patrician
patrimonio *m*, patrimony
patriota *mf* patriot
patriótico *a* patriotic
patriotismo *m*, patriotism
patrocinar *vt* to protect, defend; favor, sponsor; patronize
patrocinio *m*, protection, defense; sponsorship; patronage
patrón (-ona) *n* patron, sponsor; patron saint; landlord; employer. *m*, coxswain; *naut* master, skipper; pattern, model; standard. **p. de oro,** gold standard
patronato *m*, patronage, protection; employers' association; charitable foundation. **p. de turismo,** tourist bureau
patronímico *a* and *m*, patronymic
patrono (-na) *n* protector; sponsor; patron; patron saint; employer
patrulla *f*, *mil* patrol; group, band
patrullar *vi mil* patrol; march about
patudo *a inf* large-footed
paulatinamente *adv* slowly, by degrees
pauperismo *m*, destitution, pauperism
pausa *f*, pause, interruption; delay; *mus* rest; *mus* pause. **a pausas,** intermittently
pausado *a* deliberate, slow. *adv* slowly, deliberately

pausar *vi* to pause
pauta *f*, standard, norm, design; *fig* guide, model
pava *f*, *Argentina* kettle; *Venezuela* broad-brimmed straw hat, *inf* bad luck
pavada *f*, flock of turkeys
pavana *f*, pavane, stately dance
pavero (-ra) *a* vain; strutting. *n* turkey keeper or vendor. *m*, broad-brimmed Andalusian hat; *mf*, *Chile, Peru* practical joker
pavimentación *f*, paving, flagging
pavimento *m*, pavement
pavo (-va) *n orn* turkey. **p. real,** peacock. *inf* **pelar la pava,** to serenade, court
pavón *m*, *orn* peacock; peacock butterfly; preservative paint (for steel, etc.); gunmetal
pavonear *vi* to strut, peacock (also *vr*); *inf* hoodwink, dazzle
pavor *m*, terror, panic
pavoroso *a* fearful, awesome, dreadful
payador *m*, *Argentina, Chile* gaucho minstrel
payasada *f*, clowning, practical joke; clown's patter
payasear *vi*, *Lat. Am.* to clown around
payaso *m*, clown
paz *f*, peace; harmony, concord; peaceableness. **¡P. sea en esta casa!** Peace be upon this house! (salutation). **estar en p.,** to be at peace; be quits, be even. **poner** (*or* **meter**) **p.,** to make peace (between dissentients). **venir de p.,** to come with peaceful intentions
pazguato (-ta) *n* simpleton, booby
pe *f*, name of the letter P. *inf* **de pe a pa,** from A to Z, from beginning to end
peaje *m*, toll (on bridges, roads, etc.)
peatón *m*, pedestrian; walker; country postman
pebete *m*, joss stick; fuse; *inf* stench
peca *f*, mole, freckle
pecado *m*, sin; fault; excess; defect; *inf* the Devil. **p. capital,** mortal sin
pecador *a* sinful. *m*, sinner. **¡P. de mí!** Poor me!
pecadora *f*, sinner; *inf* prostitute
pecaminoso *a* sinful
pecar *vi* to sin; trespass, transgress; (*with de*) be too . . . (e.g. **El libro peca de largo,** The book is too long)
peceño *a* pitch-black (horses, etc.); tasting of pitch
pecera *f*, goldfish bowl; aquarium
pechera *f*, shirt front; chest protector; bib, tucker; shirt frill; *inf* bosom
pecho *m*, *anat* chest; breast; bosom; mind, conscience; courage, endurance; *mus* quality (of voice); incline, slope. **p. arriba,** uphill. **abrir su p. a** (*or* **con**), to unbosom oneself to. **dar el p.** (**a**), to suckle. **de pechos,** leaning on. **echar el p. al agua,** *fig* to embark courageously upon. **tomar a pechos** (**una cosa**), to take (a thing) very seriously; take to heart
pechuga *f*, breast (of a bird); *inf* breast, bosom; slope, incline
pécora *f*, sheep, head of sheep; wily woman, serpent
pecoso *a* freckled; spotted (with warts)
pecuario *a agr* stock; cattle
peculiar *a* peculiar, individual
peculiaridad *f*, peculiarity
peculio *m*, private money or property
pecunia *f*, *inf* cash
pedagogía *f*, education, pedagogy
pedagogo *m*, schoolmaster; educationalist; *fig* mentor
pedal *m*, *mech* treadle, lever, *mus* pedal; *mus* sustained harmony. *aut* **p. de embrague,** clutch pedal
pedalear *vi* to pedal
pedante *a* pedantic. *mf* pedant
pedantería *f*, pedantry
pedazo *m*, bit, piece; lump; fragment, portion. *inf* **p. del alma, p. del corazón, p. de las entrañas,** loved one, dear one. **a pedazos** *or* **en pedazos,** in pieces, in bits. **hacer pedazos,** to break into fragments
pedernal *m*, flint; anything very hard
pedestal *m*, pedestal; base; stand; *fig* foundation
pedestre *a* pedestrian; dull, uninspired
pediatra *mf* pediatrician
pedicuro *m*, chiropodist
pedido *m*, *com* order; request, petition
pedigüeño *a* importunate, insistent
pedimento *m*, petition, demand; *law* claim; *law* motion
pedir *vt irr* to ask, request; *com* order; demand; necessitate; desire; ask in marriage. **p. aventón** *Mexico* to hitch a ride **p. en juicio,** *law* to bring an action against. *inf* **pedírselo** (**a uno**) **el cuerpo,** to desire (something) ardently. **a p. de boca,** according to one's wish. *Pres. Part.* **pidiendo.** *Pres. Ind.* **pido, pides, pide, piden.** *Preterite* **pidió, pidieron.** *Pres. Subjunc.* **pida,** etc. *Imperf. Subjunc.* **pidiese,** etc.
pedo *m*, fart
pedómetro *m*, pedometer
pedrada *f*, casting a stone; blow with a stone; innuendo
pedrea *f*, stone throwing; fight with stones; shower of hailstones
pedregal *m*, stony ground, rocky ground
pedregoso *a* stony
pedrera *f*, stone quarry
pedrería *f*, precious stones
pedrisco *m*, hailstone; shower of stones; pile of stones
pedrusco *m*, *inf* rough, unpolished stone
pega *f*, sticking; cementing; joining; pitch; varnish; *inf* joke; beating; *orn* magpie
pegadizo *a* sticky, gummy, adhesive; detachable, removable; *fig* clinging, importunate (of people)
pegado *m*, sticking plaster; patch
pegajoso *a* sticky, gluey; viscid; contagious, catching; *inf* oily, unctuous; *fig inf* cadging, sponging
pegar *vt* to stick; cement; join, fasten; press (against); infect with (diseases); hit, strike; give (a shout, jump, etc.); patch; *vi* spread, catch (fire, etc.); *fig* make an impression, have influence; be opportune; *vr cul* stick, burn; meddle; become enthusiastic about; take root in the mind. **p. un tiro** (**a**), to shoot
pegote *m*, sticking plaster; *fig inf* sponger; *inf* patch
peinado *m*, hairdressing or style; headdress. *a inf* effeminate, overelegant (men); overcareful (style). **un p. al agua,** a finger wave
peinador (-ra) *m*, peignoir, dressing gown; *Lat. Am.* dressing table. *n* hairdresser
peinadura *f*, brushing or combing of hair; *pl* hair combings
peinar *vt* to comb, dress the hair; card (wool); cut away (rock)
peine *m*, comb; *mech* hackle, reed; instep; *inf* crafty person
peinería *f*, comb factory or shop
peinero *m*, comb manufacturer or seller
peineta *f*, high comb (for mantillas, etc.)
peladilla *f*, sugared almond; smooth, small pebble
pelado *a* plucked; bare, unadorned; needy, poor; hairless; skinned; peeled; without shell; treeless
peladura *f*, peeling; shelling; skinning; plucking (feathers)
pelafustán *m*, *inf* good-for-nothing, scamp
pelagatos *m*, *inf* miserable wretch
pelágico *a* pelagian, oceanic
pelagra *f*, pellagra
pelaje *m*, fur, wool
pelamesa *f*, brawl, fight; lock, tuft (of hair)
pelapatatas *m*, potato peeler
pelar *vt* to tear out or cut the hair; pluck; skin; peel; shell; rob, fleece; *vr* lose one's hair
peldaño *m*, step, stair, tread, rung
pelea *f*, battle; quarrel, dispute; fight (among animals); effort, exertion; *fig* struggle
peleador *a* fighting; quarrelsome, aggressive
pelear *vi* to fight; quarrel; struggle, strive. **p. como perro y gato,** to fight like cat and mouse. *vr* come to blows; fall out, become enemies
pelechar *vi* to get a new coat (of animals); grow new feathers (of birds); *inf* prosper, flourish; grow well
pelele *m*, effigy; *inf* nincompoop

peletería *f*, furrier; fur shop
peletero *m*, furrier; skinner
peliagudo *a* long-haired (animals); *inf* complicated, difficult; wily, downy
pelícano *m*, pelican
pelicorto *a* short-haired
película *f*, film. **p. fotográfica,** roll of film. **p. sonora,** sound film
peligrar *vi* to be in danger
peligro *m*, danger, peril. **correr p.** *or* **estar en p.,** to be in danger
peligroso *a* dangerous, perilous, risky
pelilargo *a* long-haired
pelirrojo *a* red-haired
pelleja *f*, hide, skin (of animals); sheepskin
pellejo *m*, hide; pelt; skin; wineskin; *inf* drunkard; peel, skin (of fruit)
pelliza *f*, fur or fur-trimmed coat
pellizcar *vt* to pinch, tweak, nip; pilfer
pellizco *m*, pinch, nip, tweak; pilfering, pinching; bit, pinch
pelmazo *m*, squashed mass; *inf* idler, sluggard; *inf* bore
pelo *m*, hair; down (on birds and fruit); fiber, filament; hair trigger (firearms); hairspring (watches); kiss (in billiards); nap (of cloth), grain (of wood); flaw (in gems); raw silk. **p. chino,** *Mexico* (naturally) curly hair **p. de camello,** camel's hair. **a p.,** in the nude; without a hat; opportunely. **en p.,** bareback (of horses). **hacerse el p.,** to do one's hair; have one's hair cut. *inf* **no tener p. de tonto,** to be smart, clever. *inf* **no tener pelos en la lengua,** to be outspoken. *inf* **tomar el p. (a),** to pull a person's leg. **venir a p.,** to be apposite; come opportunely
pelón *a* hairless; *fig inf* broke, fleeced
pelonería *f*, *inf* poverty, misery
pelota *f*, ball; ball game. **p. base,** baseball. **p. vasca,** pelota. **en p.,** stark naked
pelotari *m*, professional pelota player
pelotazo *m*, knock or blow with a ball
pelotear *vt* to audit accounts; *vi* play ball; throw, cast; quarrel; argue
pelotera *f*, *inf* brawl
pelotón *m*, big ball; lump of hair; crowd, multitude; *mil* platoon. **p. de ejecución,** firing squad
peltre *m*, pewter
peluca *f*, wig; periwig; *inf* scolding
peludo *a* hairy. *m*, long-haired rug
peluquería *f*, hairdressing establishment; hairdressing trade
peluquero (-ra) *n* hairdresser; barber
peluquín *m*, small wig
pelusa *f*, down, soft hair; fluff, nap
pena *f*, punishment, penalty; grief; pain, suffering; difficulty, trouble; mourning veil; hardship; anxiety; embarrassment; tail feather. **p. capital** *or* **p. de la vida,** capital punishment. **a duras penas,** with great difficulty. **so p. de,** under penalty of. **valer** (*or* **merecer**) **la p.,** to be worth while
penable *a* punishable
penacho *m*, topknot, crest (of birds); plume, panache; *inf* pride, arrogance
penado (-da) *a* difficult, laborious; painful, troubled, afflicted. *n* convict
penal *a* penal; punitive
penalidad *f*, trouble, labor, difficulty; *law* penalty
penar *vt* to penalize; punish; *vi* suffer; undergo purgatorial pains; *vr* suffer anguish. **p. por,** to long for
penca *f*, *bot* fleshy leaf; lash, strap, cat-o'-nine-tails
penco *m*, *inf* wretched nag
pendejo *m*, pubic hair; *inf* coward; jerk
pendencia *f*, fight; quarrel
pendenciar *vi* to fight; quarrel
pendenciero *a* quarrelsome, aggressive
pender *vi* to hang; depend; be pending
pendiente *a* pending; hanging; *com* outstanding. *m*, earring; pendant. *f*, slope, incline; gradient
péndola *f*, feather, plume; quill pen; pendulum (of a clock)
pendolista *mf* calligrapher
pendón *m*, pennon, banner; *bot* shoot; *inf* lanky, slatternly woman; *pl* reins
péndulo *a* pendulous, hanging. *m*, pendulum
pene *m*, penis
peneque, *m*, *Mexico* roll of maize dough filled with cheese
penetrabilidad *f*, penetrability
penetración *f*, penetration; understanding, perspicuity; sagacity, shrewdness
penetrador *a* penetrating, perspicacious; sagacious, acute
penetrante *a* penetrating; deep; piercing (of sounds); acute, shrewd
penetrar *vt* to penetrate; permeate; master, comprehend; (*with en*) enter
penetrativo *a* piercing
penicilina *f*, penicillin
península *f*, peninsula. **la P.** the Iberian Peninsula
Península Ibérica, la the Iberian Peninsula
penique *m*, penny
penitencia *f*, penitence, repentance; penance
penitencial *a* penitential
penitenciaría *f*, penitentiary
penitente *a* penitent, repentant. *mf* penitent
penoso *a* laborious, difficult; grievous; painful; troublesome; *inf* foppish; *Lat. Am.* shy, timid
pensado *a* premeditated, deliberate. **de p.,** intentionally. **mal p.,** malicious, evil-minded
pensador *a* thinking; pensive. *m*, thinker
pensamiento *m*, mind; thought; idea; suspicion, doubt; heartsease pansy; maxim; intention, project
pensar *vt irr* to think; purpose, intend; (*with en, sobre*) reflect upon; think about; *vt* feed (animals). **p. entre sí, p. para consigo** *or* **p. para sí,** to think to oneself. See **acertar**
pensativo *a* reflective, pensive
pensil *a* hanging. *m*, hanging garden; delightful garden
pensión *f*, pension, allowance; boarding house, private hotel; scholarship grant; cost of board; trouble, drudgery
pensionado (-da) *a* pensioned; retired. *n* scholarship holder. *m*, boarding school
pensionar *vt* to pension, grant a pension to; charge a pension on
pensionista *mf* pensioner; boarder
pentágono *m*, pentagon. *a* pentagonal
pentámetro *m*, pentameter
Pentateuco *m*, Pentateuch
Pentecostés *m*, Pentecost, Whitsuntide
penúltimo *a* next to the last, penultimate
penuria *f*, scarcity; want, penury
peña *f*, crag, rock; boulder; group of friends; club. **ser una p.,** to be stony-hearted
peñasco *m*, craggy peak
peñascoso *a* craggy, rocky
peñón *m*, rock; cliff; peak
peón *m*, pedestrian; laborer; *South America* farmhand; top (toy); piece (chess, checkers); *mech* axle; infantryman. **p. caminero,** road mender. **p. de ajedrez,** pawn (in chess)
peonada *f*, day's manual labor; gang of laborers
peonar *vi*, *Argentina* to do manual labor
peonía *f*, peony
peonza *f*, top; teetotum
peor *a comp* **malo** worse. *adv comp* **mal,** worse. *a sup* **el (la, lo) peor; los (las) peores,** the worst. **p. que p.,** worse and worse. **tanto p.,** so much the worse
pepino *m*, cucumber plant; cucumber; *fig* pin, straw
pepita *f*, *min* nugget; pip, seed (of fruit)
péptico *a* peptic
pequeñez *f*, littleness, smallness; pettiness; childhood; infancy; trifle, insignificant thing; meanness, baseness

pequeño *a* little, small; petty; very young; short, brief; humble, lowly
pequero, -a *mf, Argentina* cardsharp
pera *f,* pear; goatee; *fig* plum, sinecure
peral *m,* pear tree; pearwood
perca *f, icht* perch
percal *m,* percale, calico
percalina *f,* percaline, binding cloth
percance *m,* perquisite, attribute (gen. *pl*); disaster, mischance
percebe *m,* (gen. *pl*) goose barnacle
percentaje *m,* percentage
percepción *f,* perception; idea, conception
perceptible *a* perceptible
perceptivo *a* perceptive
perceptor (-ra) *a* perceptive. *n* observer
percha *f,* stake, pole; coat hanger; perch (for birds); rack (for hay); hall stand, coat and hat stand, coatrack
perchero *m,* hall stand; clothes rack; row of perches (for fowl, etc.)
percibir *vt* to collect, draw, receive; perceive; understand, grasp
percibo *m,* perceiving; collecting, drawing, receiving
percolador *m,* percolator (coffee)
percusión *f,* percussion; shock, vibration
percusor *m,* hammer (of a firearm)
percutir *vt* to percuss, strike
perdedor (-ra) *a* losing. *n* loser
perder *vt* to lose; throw away, squander; spoil, destroy; *vi* fade (of colors); *vr* lose one's way, be lost; be confused or perplexed; be shipwrecked; take to vice, become dissolute; be spoiled or destroyed; disappear; love madly. **p. la chaveta (por),** to go out of one's head (for), be wild (about). **p. la ocasión,** to let the chance slip. **p. los estribos,** to lose patience. **p. terreno,** to lose ground. **perderse de vista,** to be lost to sight. **echarse a p.,** to spoil, be damaged. See **entender**
perdición *f,* loss; perdition, ruin; damnation; depravity, viciousness
pérdida *f,* loss; waste. **p. cuantiosa,** heavy losses
perdidamente *adv* ardently, desperately; uselessly
perdigón *m,* young partridge; decoy partridge; hailstone, pellet, shot
perdigonada *f,* volley of hailstone; hailstone wound
perdiguero (-ra) *n* game dealer; setter, retriever
perdiz *f,* partridge. **p. blanca,** ptarmigan
perdón *m,* pardon, forgiveness; remission. **con p.,** with your permission; excuse me
perdonable *a* pardonable, excusable
perdonar *vt* to pardon, forgive; remit, excuse; exempt; waste, lose; give up (a privilege)
perdonavidas *m, inf* bully, braggart
perdulario *a* careless, negligent; slovenly; vicious, depraved
perdurable *a* perpetual, everlasting; enduring, lasting
perdurar *vi* to last, endure
perecedero *a* brief, fugitive, transient; perishable. *m, inf* poverty, want
perecer *vi irr* to end, finish; perish, die; suffer (damage, grief, etc.); be destitute; *vr* (*with por*) long for, crave; desire ardently. See **conocer**
peregrinación *f,* journey, peregrination; pilgrimage
peregrinamente *adv* rarely, not often; beautifully, perfectly
peregrinar *vi* to journey, travel; make a pilgrimage
peregrino (-na) *a* and *n* pilgrim. *a* migratory (birds); rare, unusual; extraordinary, strange; beautiful, perfect
perejil *m,* parsley; *inf* ornament or apparel (gen. *pl*); *pl* honors, titles
perengano (-na) *n* so-and-so, such a one
perenne *a* incessant, constant; *bot* perennial
perennidad *f,* perpetuity
perentoriedad *f,* peremptoriness; urgency
perentorio *a* peremptory; conclusive, decisive; urgent, pressing
pereza *f,* laziness; languor, inertia; slowness, deliberateness
perezoso *a* lazy; languid; slothful; slow, deliberate. *m, zool* sloth
perfección *f,* perfection; perfecting, perfect thing, virtue, grace
perfeccionamiento *m,* perfecting; progress, improvement
perfeccionar *vt* to perfect; complete
perfectamente *adv* perfectly; quite, entirely
perfecto *a* perfect; excellent, very good; complete; whole; *gram* perfect
perfidia *f,* perfidy, treachery
pérfido *a* perfidious, treacherous
perfil *m,* ornament, decoration; outline, contour; profile; section (of metal); fine stroke (of letters); *pl* finishing touches; politeness, attention, courtesy. **de p.,** in profile; sideways
perfilado *a* long, elongated (of faces, etc.)
perfilar *vt* to draw in profile; outline; *vr* place oneself sideways, show one's profile; *inf* dress up, titivate
perforación *f,* perforation, boring; hole
perforador *a* perforating, boring. *m, mech* drill
perforar *vt* to perforate, pierce; bore, drill, make a hole in
perfumador (-ra) *a* perfuming. *n* perfumer. *m,* perfume burner
perfumar *vt* to perfume; *vi* give off perfume
perfume *m,* perfume; scent, fragrance
perfumería *f,* scent factory; perfumery; perfume shop
perfumista *mf* perfumer
perfunctorio *a* perfunctory
pergamino *m,* parchment, vellum; document; diploma; *pl* aristocratic descent
pericardio *m,* pericardium
pericia *f,* expertness; skilled workmanship
pericial *a* expert, skillful
perico *m,* parakeet; giant asparagus
periferia *f,* periphery
periférico *a* peripheral
perifollos *m pl, inf* frills, flounces, finery
perifrástico *a* periphrastic
perilla *f,* pear-shaped ornament; goatee; imperial. **p. de la oreja,** lobe of the ear. **venir de p.,** to be most opportune
perillán *m, inf* rascal, rogue
perímetro *m,* perimeter; precincts
perínclito *a* distinguished, illustrious; heroic
perineo *m,* perineum
perinola *f,* top, teetotum
periodicidad *f,* periodicity
periódico *a* periodic. *m,* newspaper; periodical publication
periodicucho *m,* rag (bad newspaper)
periodismo *m,* journalism
periodista *mf* journalist
periodístico *a* journalistic
período *m,* period; *phys* cycle; menstruation period; *gram* clause; age, era
periostio *m,* periosteum
peripatético *a* peripatetic
peripecia *f,* sudden change of fortune, vicissitude
peripuesto *a inf* overelegant, spruce, too well-dressed; smart
periquete *m, inf* jiffy, trice
periquito *m,* parakeet; budgerigar
periscopio *m,* periscope
perito (-ta) *a* expert; skillful, experienced. *n* expert
peritoneo *m,* peritoneum
perjudicador (-ra) *a* injurious, prejudicial. *n* injurer
perjudicar *vt* to harm, damage, injure; prejudice
perjudicial *a* injurious, noxious, harmful; prejudicial
perjuicio *m,* injury, damage; harm; *law* prejudice
perjurador (-ra) *n* perjurer

perjurar *vi* to perjure oneself, commit perjury; swear, curse
perjurio *m,* perjury
perjuro (-ra) *a* perjured, forsworn. *n* perjurer
perla *f,* pearl; *arch* bead; *fig* treasure, jewel, dear. **de perlas,** excellent; exactly right
perlero *a* pearl
perlesía *f,* paralysis; palsy
perlino *a* pearly, pearl-colored
permanecer *vi irr* to stay, remain. **p. en posición de firme,** to stand at attention. See **conocer**
permanencia *f,* stay, sojourn; permanence
permanente *a* permanent; lasting, enduring
permeabilidad *f,* permeability
permisible *a* permissible, allowable
permisivo *a* permissive
permiso *m,* permission, leave; permit; (*mil* etc.) pass. **¡Con p.!** Excuse me!; Allow me!
permitir *vt* to permit, allow
permuta *f,* exchange
permutación *f,* permutation, interchange
permutar *vt* to exchange
pernear *vi* to kick; *inf* bustle; fret, be impatient
pernetas, en *adv* barelegged
perniciosidad *f,* perniciousness
pernicioso *a* pernicious
pernil *m, anat* hock; ham; leg of pork; leg (of trousers)
pernio *m,* hinge (of doors, windows)
perniquebrar *vt irr* to break the legs of. See **quebrar**
perno *m,* bolt, pin, spike
pernoctar *vi* to spend the night (away from home)
pero *conjunc* but. *m, inf* defect; difficulty, snag
perogrullada *f, inf* truism
perol *m, cul* pan
peroné *m,* fibula
peronista *a, mf* Peronist
peroración *f,* peroration
perorar *vi* to make a speech; *inf* speak pompously; ask insistently
peróxido *m,* peroxide
perpendicular *a* perpendicular. *f,* perpendicular
perpetración *f,* perpetration
perpetrar *vt* to perpetrate
perpetua *f, bot* immortelle, everlasting
perpetuación *f,* perpetuation
perpetuar *vt* to perpetuate; *vr* last, endure
perpetuidad *f,* perpetuity
perpetuo *a* everlasting; lifelong
perplejidad *f,* perplexity, bewilderment, doubt
perplejo *a* perplexed, bewildered, doubtful
perquirir *vt irr* to search carefully. See **adquirir**
perra *f,* bitch; *inf* sot, drunkard; tantrums. **p. chica,** five-cent coin. **p. gorda,** ten-cent coin
perrada *f,* pack of dogs; *inf* dirty trick
perramus *m, Argentina* raincoat
perrengue *m, inf* short-tempered person
perrera *f,* dog kennel; useless toil; *inf* tantrums
perrería *f,* pack of dogs; *inf* dirty trick; fit of anger
perrero *m,* dog fancier; kennel worker
perro *m,* dog. **p. caliente** hot dog. **p. danés,** Great Dane. **p. de aguas,** poodle; spaniel. **p. de casta,** thoroughbred dog. **p. de lanas** poodle. **p. de muestra,** pointer. **p. de presa,** bulldog. **p. de San Bernardo,** St. Bernard (dog). **p. de Terranova,** Newfoundland (dog). **p. del hortelano,** dog in the manger. **p. dogo** bulldog. **p. esquimal** husky. **p. faldero,** lap dog. **p. lobo,** wolfhound. **p. pachón,** dachshund. **p. pastor alemán** *or* **p. policía,** German shepherd. **p. pequinés,** Pekingese. **p. perdiguero,** retriever. **p. pomerano,** spitz, Pomeranian (dog). **p. sabueso español,** spaniel. **p. zorrero,** foxhound. *inf* **A p. viejo no hay tus tus,** You can't fool an old dog. **vivir como perros y gatos,** *inf* to live like cat and dog
persa *a* and *mf* Persian. *m,* Persian (language)
persecución *f,* pursuit; persecution; annoyance, importuning
perseguidor (-ra) *a* pursuing; tormenting. *n* pursuer; tormentor, persecutor
perseguimiento *m,* pursuit
perseguir *vi irr* to pursue; persecute, torment; importune. See **seguir**
perseverancia *f,* perseverance
perseverante *a* persevering; constant
perseverar *vi* to persevere; last, endure
persiana *f,* Venetian blind; flowered silk material
pérsico *a* Persian. *m,* peach tree; peach
persignar *vt* to sign; make the sign of the cross over; *vr* cross oneself
persistencia *f,* persistence
persistente *a* persistent
persistir *vi* to persist
persona *f,* person; personage; character (in a play, etc.); (*gram ecc*) person. **de p. a p.,** in private, face to face
personaje *m,* important person, personage; character (in a play, etc.)
personal *a* personal. *m,* staff, personnel
personalidad *f,* personality
personalismo *m,* personality; personal question
personalizar *vt* to become personal, be offensive
personalmente *adv* personally
personarse *vr* to present oneself, call, appear
personificación *f,* personification
personificar *vt* to personify
perspectiva *f,* perspective; view; outlook; aspect, appearance. **p. aérea,** bird's-eye view
perspicacia *f,* perspicacity, shrewdness
perspicaz *a* perspicacious, clear-sighted
perspicuidad *f,* perspicuity
perspicuo *a* lucid, clear
persuadir *vt* to persuade
persuasible *a* persuadable
persuasión *f,* persuasion; belief, conviction, opinion
persuasiva *f,* persuasiveness
persuasivo *a* persuasive
pertenecer *vi irr* to belong; relate, concern. See **conocer**
perteneciente *a* belonging (to), pertaining (to)
pertenencia *f,* ownership, proprietorship; property, accessory
pértiga *f,* long rod; pole. **salto de p.,** pole vaulting
pertinacia *f,* pertinacity, doggedness
pertinaz *a* pertinacious, stubborn, dogged
pertinencia *f,* relevance, appropriateness
pertinente *a* relevant, apposite; appropriate
pertrechar *vt* to supply, equip; prepare, make ready
pertrechos *m pl, mil* armaments, stores; equipment, appliances
perturbación *f,* disturbance; agitation
perturbador (-ra) *a* disturbing. *n* disturber; heckler
perturbar *vt* to disturb; agitate
Perú *m* Peru
peruano (-na) *a* and *n* Peruvian
perversidad *f,* wickedness, depravity
perversión *f,* perversion; wickedness, evil
perversivo *a* perversive
perverso *a* wicked, iniquitous, depraved
pervertir *vt irr* to pervert, corrupt; distort. See **sentir**
pesa *f,* weight; clock weight; gymnast's weight. **pesas y medidas,** weights and measures
pesacartas *m,* letter scale, letter balance
pesada *f,* weighing
pesadez *f,* heaviness; obesity; tediousness, tiresomeness; slowness; fatigue
pesadilla *f,* nightmare
pesado *a* heavy; obese; deep (of sleep); oppressive (of weather); slow; unwieldy; tedious; impertinent; dull, boring; offensive
pesadumbre *f,* heaviness; grief, sorrow; trouble, anxiety
pésame *m,* expression of condolence. **dar el p.,** to present one's condolences

pesantez *f,* weight, heaviness; seriousness, gravity
pesar *m,* grief, sorrow; remorse. **a p. de,** in spite of
pesar *vi* to weigh; be heavy; be important; grieve, cause regret (e.g. **Me pesa mucho,** I am very sorry); influence, affect; *vt* weigh; consider. **Mal que me** (**te,** etc.) **pese . . . ,** Much as I regret . . .
pesaroso *a* regretful, remorseful; sorrowful
pesca *f,* fishery; angling, fishing; catch of fish. **p. a la rastra,** trawling. **p. deportiva** sport fishing. **p. mayor,** deep-sea fishing
pescadería *f,* fishery; fish store; fish market
pescadilla *f, icht* whiting
pescado *m,* fish (out of the water); salt cod
pescador (-ra) *n* fisherman; angler
pescante *m,* driving seat; coach box; jib (of a crane)
pescar *vt* to fish; *inf* catch in the act; acquire. **p. a la rastra,** to trawl
pescozón *m,* slap on the neck or head
pescuezo *m,* neck; throat; haughtiness, arrogance. **torcer el p.,** to wring the neck (of chickens, etc.)
pesebre *m,* manger, stable; feeding trough
pesero *m, Mexico* jitney, jitney taxi
pésimamente *adv* extremely badly
pesimismo *m,* pessimism
pesimista *a* pessimistic. *mf* pessimist
pésimo *a sup* **malo** extremely bad
peso *m,* weighing; weight; heaviness; gravity; importance; influence; load; peso (money); scale, balance. **p. bruto,** gross weight. **p. de joyería,** troy weight. **p. específico,** *phys* specific gravity. **p. pluma,** (*boxing*) featherweight
pespunte *m,* backstitch
pesquera *f,* fishing ground, fishery
pesquería *f,* fishing, angling; fisherman's trade; fishing ground, fishery
pesquero *a* fishing (of boats, etc.)
pesquisa *f,* investigation, examination; search
pesquisar *vt* to investigate, look into; search
pestaña *f,* eyelash; *sew* edging, fringe; ear, lug; *naut* fluke
pestañear *vi* to wink; blink; flutter one's eyelashes
pestañeo *m,* winking; blinking
peste *f,* plague, pestilence; nauseous smell; epidemic; pest; vice; *Chile* smallpox; *pl* oaths, curses. **p. bubónica,** bubonic plague. **p. roja** syphilis. **p. de las abejas,** foul brood. **echar pestes,** to swear; fume
pestífero *a* noxious
pestilencia *f,* plague, pestilence
pestilente *a* pestilential
pestillo *m,* latch; lock bolt. **p. de golpe,** safety latch
petaca *f,* cigarette or cigar case; tobacco pouch; *Mexico* suitcase.
pétalo *m,* petal
petardista *mf* swindler, impostor
petardo *m,* detonator; torpedo; firecracker; fraud
petición *f,* petition, request
peticionar *vt, Lat. Am.* to petition
peticionario (-ia) *n* petitioner. *a* petitionary
petimetra *f,* stylish and affected young woman
petimetre *m,* fop
petirrojo *m,* robin
petitorio *a* petitionary. *m, inf* importunity
peto *m,* breastplate; front (of a shirt); bib
pétreo *a* petrous
petrificación *f,* petrifaction
petrificar *vt* to petrify; *vr* become petrified
petrografía *f,* petrology
petróleo *m,* petroleum; oil, mineral oil. **p. bruto,** crude oil. **p. de lámpara,** kerosene
petrolero (-ra) *a* oil, petroleum. *n* petroleum seller; incendiarist. *m,* oil tanker
petrolífero *a* oil-bearing
petulancia *f,* insolence; vanity
petulante *a* insolent; vain
pez *m,* fish; *pl* Pisces. *f, chem* pitch. **p. sierra,** swordfish
pezón *m, bot* stalk; nipple; axle pivot; point (of land, etc.)
pezuña *f,* cloven hoof (of cows, pigs, etc.)
piada *f,* chirping, twittering
piadoso *a* compassionate; kind, pitiful; pious, religious
piafar *vi* to stamp, paw the ground (horses)
pianista *mf* piano maker; piano dealer; pianist
piano *m,* pianoforte. **p. de cola,** grand piano. **p. de media cola,** baby grand. **p. vertical,** upright piano
piante *a* chirping, twittering
piar *vi* to chirp, twitter
piara *f,* herd of swine; pack (of horses, etc.)
pibe, -a *mf, Argentina* kid, child
pica *f, mil* pike; bullfighter's goad; pike soldier; stonecutter's hammer. **a p. seca,** in vain. **pasar por las picas,** to suffer hardship. **poner una p. en Flandes,** to triumph over great difficulties
picacho *m,* peak, summit
picada *f,* prick; bite; peck; *aer* dive
picadero *m,* riding school; paddock (of a racetrack)
picado *a sew* pinked. *m, cul* hash
picador *m,* horse trainer; meat chopper; horseman armed with a goad (bullfights)
picadura *f,* puncture; prick; sting; *sew* pinking; peck (of birds); cut tobacco; black tobacco; beginning of caries in teeth
picajoso *a* hypersensitive, touchy, peevish
picamaderos *m,* woodpecker
picanear *vt, Lat. Am.* to goad on, spur on
picante *a* piquant; mordant; hot, highly seasoned. *m,* mordancy; pungency
picantería *f, Lat. Am.* restaurant specializing in spicy foods
picapleitos *m, inf* shady lawyer, pettifogger
picaporte *m,* latch, door catch; door knocker
picar *vt* to prick; sting; peck; bite; chop fine; mince; nibble (of fishing); irritate (the skin); *sew* pink; burn (the tongue); eat (grapes); goad; spur; stipple (walls); stimulate, encourage; split, cleave; *mil* harass; vex; *mus* play staccato; *vi* burn (of the sun); smart (of cuts, etc.); eat sparingly; *aut* knock; (*with en*) knock at (doors, etc.); *vr* be moth-eaten; go rotten (fruit, etc.); grow choppy (of the sea); be piqued; boast
picardear *vi* to play the rogue; behave mischievously
picardía *f,* knavery, roguery; mischievousness; practical joke; wantonness
picaresco *a* roguish, picaresque, knavish
pícaro (-ra) *a* knavish; base, vile; astute; mischievous. *n* rogue
picatoste *m,* kind of fritter
picaza *f,* magpie
picazo *m,* blow with a pike or anything pointed; peck, tap with a beak (of birds); sting
picazón *f,* itch, irritation; annoyance
pícea *f, bot* spruce
píceo *a* piscine, fish-like
pichincha *f, Argentina* bargain
pichón (-ona) *m,* male pigeon. *n inf* darling
pico *m,* beak (of birds); peak; woodpecker; odd amount (e.g. **treinta y p.,** thirty-odd); sharp point; spout (of a jug, etc.); *inf* mouth; blarney, gab. **p. de cigüeña,** crane's-bill. **p. de oro,** silver-tongued orator
picor *m,* burning sensation in the mouth; smarting; itching, irritation
picoso *a* pitted, marked by smallpox; *Mexico* hot, spicy (food)
picota *f,* pillory; peak; spire
picotazo *m,* peck; dab; sting, bite
picotear *vt* to peck (of a bird); *vi* toss the head (of horses); *inf* chatter senselessly; *vr inf* slang each other
picotero *a inf* chattering, talkative; indiscreet
pictórico *a* pictorial
picudo *a* pointed, peaked; having a spout; *inf* chattering; *Mexico* clever, crafty, sly
pie *m,* foot; stand, support; stem (of a glass, etc.); stan-

dard (of a lamp); *bot* trunk, stem; sapling; lees, sediment; *theat* cue; foot (measure); custom; (metrics) foot; motive, cause; pretext; (metrics) meter. **p. de cabra,** crowbar. **p. de imprenta,** printer's mark, printer's imprint. **p. de piña,** clubfoot. **p. de rey,** caliper. **p. palmado,** webfoot. **al p. de la letra,** punctiliously. *inf* **andar con pies de plomo,** to walk warily. **a p.,** on foot. **a p. firme,** without budging; steadfastly. *inf* **buscar tres pies al gato,** to look for something that isn't there; twist a person's words. **de a p.,** on foot. **en p. de guerra,** on a wartime footing. *inf* **poner pies en polvorosa,** to quit

piedad *f,* piety; pity, compassion; *art* pietà

piedra *f,* stone; tablet; *med* gravel. **p. de amolar,** whetstone, grindstone. **p. angular,** cornerstone (also *fig*). **p. caliza,** limestone. **p. clave,** keystone. **p. de construcción,** building stone; child's block. **p. de toque,** touchstone, test. **p. filosofal,** philosopher's stone. **p. fundamental,** foundation stone. **p. miliaria,** milestone. **p. mortuoria,** tombstone. *fig inf* **no dejar p. sin remover,** to leave no stone unturned. **no dejar p. sobre p.,** to demolish, destroy completely

piel *f,* skin; fur; hide; leather; peel (of some fruits); rind (of bacon). **p. de gallina,** *fig* goose flesh. **p. de rata,** horse blanket. **p. de Rusia,** Russian leather.

piélago *m,* high seas; sea, ocean; glut, superabundance

pienso *m, agr* fodder

pierna *f, anat* leg; *mech* shank; leg of a compass. *inf* **a p. suelta,** at one's ease. **en piernas,** barelegged

pietista *a* pietistic. *mf* pietist

pieza *f,* portion; piece; component part; room; *theat* play; roll (of cloth); piece (in chess, etc.); coin; piece (of music). **p. de recambio** *or* **p. de repuesto,** spare part. **p. de recibo,** reception room. *inf* **quedarse en una p.,** to be struck dumb

pífano *m,* fife; fife player, fifer

pigmentación *f,* pigmentation

pigmento *m,* pigment

pignoración *f,* hypothecation; pawning; mortgage

pignorar *vt* to hypothecate; pawn; mortgage

pigre *a* lazy; negligent, careless

pigricia *f,* laziness; negligence *Chile, Peru* trifle

pijama *m,* pajamas

pila *f,* trough, basin; heap, pile; *elec* battery; *ecc* parish; pier, pile; *phys* cell. **p. atómica,** atomic pile. **p. bautismal,** *ecc* font

pilar *m,* fountain basin; milestone; pillar

pilastra *f,* pier, pile; pilaster

pilche *m, Lat. Am.* calabash, gourd

píldora *f, med* pill; *inf* disagreeable news

pileta (de natación) *f, Argentina,* (swimming) pool

pillador (-ra) *a* pillaging, plundering. *n* plunderer

pillaje *m,* pillaging, looting; robbery, theft

pillar *vt* to pillage; steal, rob; seize, snatch; *inf* surprise, find out (in a lie, etc.). **pillarse el dedo,** to get one's finger caught (in a door, etc.)

pillastre *m, inf* rogue, ragamuffin

pillería *f, inf* gang of rogues; *inf* rogue's trick

pillo *m,* rogue, knave

pilón *m,* fountain basin; pestle; loaf sugar; pylon; *Mexico, Venezuela* gratuity, tip

pilongo *a* thin, lean

píloro *m,* pylorus

pilotaje *m,* pilotage; piling, pilework. **examen de p.,** flying test

pilotar *vt* to pilot

pilote *m, eng* pile

pilotear *vt* to pilot

piloto *m,* pilot; mate (in merchant ships). **p. de pruebas,** test pilo

pilsen *m, Chile* beer

pimentero *m,* pepper plant; pepper shaker

pimentón *m,* red pepper, cayenne

pimienta *f,* pepper. **p. húngara,** paprika. *inf* **ser como una p.,** to be sharp as a needle

pimiento *m,* pimento; capsicum; red pepper; pepper plant. **p. de cornetilla,** chili pepper

pimpollo *m,* sapling; sprout, shoot; rosebud

pina *f,* conical stone; felloe (of a wheel)

pinacoteca *f,* art gallery, picture gallery

pináculo *m,* pinnacle, summit; climax, culmination; *arch* finial

pinar *m,* pinewood

pincel *m,* paintbrush; artist, painter; painting technique. **p. para las cejas,** eyebrow pencil

pincelada *f,* brushstroke. **dar la última p.,** to add the finishing touch

pincelero (-ra) *n* seller or maker of paintbrushes; brush box

pinchadura *f,* prick, puncture, piercing; sting; nipping, biting

pinchar *vt* to prick; puncture; pierce; sting; nip, bite. **no p. ni cortar,** to be ineffective (of persons)

pinchazo *m,* prick; puncture; sting; incitement

pinche *m,* scullion, kitchen boy; *Argentina* minor office clerk; *a, Mexico* damn

pineda *f,* pinewood

pingajo *m, inf* tatter, rag

pingajoso *a inf* tattered, ragged

pingo *m, inf* tatter, rag; *pl inf* cheap clothes

pingüe *a* fat, greasy; fertile, rich

pingüino *m,* penguin

pino *a* steep. *m, bot* pine, deal; *poet* ship. **p. de tea,** pitch pine. **p. silvestre,** red fir

pinta *f,* spot; marking; mark; fleck; look, appearance; pint (measure); drop, drip; spot ball (in billiards)

pintamonas *mf inf* dauber

pintar *vt* to paint; describe, picture; exaggerate; *vi* show, manifest itself; *vr* make up (one's face). *inf* **pintarse solo para,** to be very good at, excel at

pintiparado *a* most similar, very alike; fitting, apposite

pintiparar *vt inf* to compare

pintor (-ra) *n* painter, artist. **p. callejero,** sidewalk artist, pavement artist. **p. de brocha gorda,** house painter

pintoresco *a* picturesque, quaint, pretty

pintorrear *vt inf* to daub, paint badly

pintura *f,* painting; paint, pigment; picture, painting; description. **p. a la aguada,** watercolor painting. **p. al fresco,** fresco. **p. al látex,** latex paint. **p. al óleo,** oil painting. **p. al pastel,** pastel drawing

pinturería *f,* paint store

pinturero *a inf* affected, conceited; dandified, overdressed

pinza *f,* clamp. **p. de la ropa,** clothes peg

pinzas *f pl,* pincers; pliers; tweezers; forceps. **p. hemostáticas,** arterial forceps

piña *f,* pineapple; cluster, knot (of people, etc.); pinecone

piñón *m,* pine nut; *mech* pinion, chain wheel

pío *a* pious; compassionate; good; piebald. *m,* chirping, cheep; *inf* longing

piocha *f, Lat. Am.* pickax

piojo *m,* louse

piojoso *a* lousy; avaricious, stingy

piola *f, Lat. Am.* cord, string; rope; tether

pionero *m,* pioneer

piorrea *f,* pyorrhea

pipa *f,* barrel, cask; tobacco pipe; pip (of fruits)

pipar *vi* to smoke a pipe

pipeta *f,* pipette

pipiar *vi* to chirp, twitter

pique *m,* pique, resentment. **a p. de,** on the verge of, about to. **echar a p.,** *naut* to sink; destroy. **irse a p.,** to sink, founder

piqueta *f,* pick, mattock; mason's hammer

piquete *m,* puncture, small wound; *mil* picket; pole, stake; small hole (in garments); picket (in strikes)

pira *f,* funeral pyre; bonfire

piragua *f,* piragua, canoe

pirámide *f,* pyramid

piraña *f* piranha
pirarse *vr inf* to slip away
pirata *a* piratical *mf* pirate; savage, cruel person
piratear *vi* to play the pirate
piratería *f*, piracy; plunder, robbery
pirático *a* piratical
pirca *f*, *Lat. Am.* dry-stone wall
pirenaico, pirineo *a* Pyrenean
pirético *a* pyretic
piriforme *a* pear-shaped
Pirineos, los the Pyrenees
piropear *vt inf* to pay compliments to
piropo *m*, carbuncle; *inf* compliment. **echar piropos,** to pay compliments
pirotécnico *a* pyrotechnical. *m*, pyrotechnist
pirrarse *vr inf* to desire ardently
pírrico *a* Pyrrhic
pirueta *f*, pirouette, twirl
pisada *f*, treading, stepping; footprint, footstep; stepping on a person's foot. **seguir las pisadas de alguien,** *fig* to follow in someone's footsteps, imitate someone
pisano (-na) *a* and *n* Pisan
pisapapeles *m*, paperweight
pisar *vt* to tread upon; trample upon; crush; *mus* press (strings); trespass upon; *vr*, *Argentina* to be mistaken
pisaverde *m*, *inf* fop, dandy
piscicultura *f*, pisciculture, fish farming
piscina *f*, fishpond; swimming pool; *ecc* piscina
piscolabis *m*, *inf* snack, light meal
piso *m*, treading, trampling; story, floor; flooring; apartment. **p. bajo,** ground floor
pisón *m*, rammer, ram
pisotear *vt* to trample; crush under foot; tread on; step on; humiliate, treat inconsiderately
pisoteo *m*, trampling under foot; treading
pista *f*, track, trail (of animals); circus ring; racetrack, racecourse. **p. de patinar,** skating rink. **p. de vuelo,** *aer* landing field. *inf* **seguir la p. a,** to spy upon
pistacho *m*, pistachio
pistar *va* to pestle, pound
pistero *m*, feeding cup
pistilo *m*, pistil
pisto, *m*, *Central America, slang* dough (money)
pistola *f*, pistol. **p. ametralladora,** machine gun.
pistolera *f*, holster; pistol case
pistolero *m*, gangster
pistoletazo *m*, pistol shot; pistol wound
pistón *m*, *mus* piston; *mil* percussion cap; *mech* piston
pitada *f*, blast on a whistle, whistling; impertinence
pitagórico (-ca) *a* and *n* Pythagorean
pitanza *f*, alms, charity; *inf* daily food; pittance, scanty remuneration
pitar *vi* to play the whistle; *vt* pay (debts); smoke; give alms to
pitido *m*, blast on a whistle; whistling (of birds)
pitillera *f*, cigarette case; female cigarette maker
pito *m*, whistle; *mus* fife. *inf* **Cuando pitos flautas, cuando flautas pitos,** It's always the unexpected that happens. *inf* **no valer un p.,** to be not worth a straw
pitoflero (-ra) *n* mediocre performer (gen. on a wind instrument); *inf* talebearer, gossip
pitón *m*, *zool* python; nascent horn (of goats, etc.); spout; protuberance; *bot* sprout
pitonisa *f*, *myth* pythoness; witch, enchantress
pitorrearse *vr* to ridicule, mock
pituitario *a* pituitary
pituso *a* small and amusing (of children)
pivote *m*, pivot, swivel, gudgeon
piyama *m*, pajamas
pizarra *f*, slate; blackboard
pizarral *m*. **pizarrería** *f*, slate quarry
pizarrín *m*, slate pencil
pizca *f*, *inf* atom, speck, crumb; jot, whit. **¡Ni p.!** Not a scrap!
pizpireta *a f*, *inf* coquettish; smart; dressed up
placa *f*, plate, disk; *art* plaque; *phot* plate; star (insignia). **p. recordatorio,** commemorative plaque
placabilidad *f*, placability, appeasability
pláceme *m*, congratulation
placentero *a* agreeable, pleasant
placer *vt irr* to please, give pleasure to, gratify. *m*, *naut* reef, sandbank; pleasure; wish, desire; permission, consent; entertainment, diversion. **a p.,** at one's convenience; at leisure. *Pres. Ind.* **plazco, places,** etc. *Preterite* **plugo, pluguieron.** *Pres. Subjunc.* **plazca,** etc. *Imperf. Subjunc.* **pluguiese,** etc.
placibilidad *f*, agreeableness, pleasantness
placible *a* agreeable, pleasant
placidez *f*, placidity, calmness, serenity
plácido *a* placid, calm, serene
placiente *a* pleasing, attractive
plácito *m*, decision, judgment, opinion
plafón *m*, ceiling light; *arch* panel
plaga *f*, plague; disaster, calamity; epidemic; glut; pest; grief
plagar *vt* (*with de*) to infect with; *vr* (*with de*) be covered with; be overrun by; be infested with
plagiar *vt* to plagiarize, copy; kidnap, hold for ransom
plagiario (-ia) *n* plagiarist; *Lat. Am.* kidnapper
plagio *m*, plagiary; kidnapping
plan *m*, plan; scheme; plane. **p. quinquenal,** five-year plan
plana *f*, sheet, page; mason's trowel; plain. **p. mayor,** (*mil nav*) staff
planadora *f*, steamroller
plancha *f*, sheet, slab, plate; flatiron; horizontal suspension (in gymnastics); *naut* gangway, gangplank; *inf* howler
planchado *m*, ironing; ironing to be done or already finished
planchador (-ra) *n* ironer
planchar *vt* to iron, press with an iron
planchear *vt* to plate (with metal)
planeador *m*, *aer* glider
planear *vt* to plan out; make plans for; *vi aer* glide
planeo *m*, *aer* glide
planeta *m*, planet
planetario *a* planetary. *m*, planetarium
planicie *f*, levelness, evenness; plain
planilla *f*, *Lat. Am.* application, application form, blank; payroll; list; ballot
plano *a* flat, level; plane. *m*, *geom* plane; plan, map; *aer* aileron, wing
planta *f*, *bot* plant; sole (of the foot); plantation; layout, plan; position of the feet (in dancing, fencing); scheme, project. **p. baja,** ground floor. **p. vivaz,** perennial plant. *inf* **buena p.,** good appearance
plantación *f*, planting; plantation, nursery
plantador (-ra) *n* planter. *m*, *agr* dibble. *f*. **plantadora,** mechanical planter
plantar *vt* to plant; erect; place; found, set up; pose (a problem); raise (a question, etc.); *inf* leave in the lurch; *vr* take up one's position; jib (of horses); oppose
planteamiento *m*, execution; putting into practice; planning; statement (of problems)
plantel *m*, nursery garden; training school, nursery
plantilla *f*, young plant; insole (of shoes); *mech* template, jig
plantío *m*, plantation, afforestation; planting. *a* planted or ready for planting (ground)
plantón *m*, plant or sapling ready for transplanting; *bot* cutting; doorkeeper, porter. **dar un p. (a),** to keep (a person) waiting a long time
plañidero *a* mournful, piteous, anguished
plañido *m*, lament, weeping, wailing
plañir *vi* and *vt irr* to lament, wail, weep. See **tañer**
plasma *m*, plasma
plasmar *vt* to mold, throw (pottery)
plástica *f*, art of clay modeling; plastic
plástico *a* plastic; flexible, malleable, soft

plata *f,* silver; silver (coins); *Lat. Am.,* money; white. **p. labrada,** silverware
plataforma *f,* platform; running board (of a train); *rw* turntable
platal *m, Lat. Am.* wealth
plátano *m,* banana tree, banana; plantain; plane tree
platea *f, theat* pit. **butaca de p.,** pit stall
plateado *a* silvered; silver-plated; silvery
plateador *m,* plater
platear *vt* to electroplate, silver
platería *f,* silversmith's art or trade; silversmith's shop or workshop
platero *m,* silversmith; jeweler
plática *f,* conversation; exhortation, sermon; address, discourse
platicar *vt* and *vi* to converse (about)
platija *f,* plaice
platillo *m,* saucer; kitty (in card games); pan (of a scale); *pl* cymbals
platinado *m,* plating
platino *m,* platinum
platívolo *m,* flying saucer
plato *m,* plate; dish; *cul* course, dish; pan (of a scale). **p. sopero,** soup plate. **p. trinchero,** meat dish. *inf* **comer en un mismo p.,** to be on intimate terms. **nada entre dos platos,** much ado about nothing
platónico *a* Platonic
platonismo *m,* Platonism
platudo, -a *mf,* rich, wealthy, well-heeled
plausible *a* plausible, reasonable; commendable
playa *f,* beach, seashore, strand
plaza *f,* square (in a town, etc.); marketplace; fortified town; space; duration; employment, post.; *com* market. **p. de armas,** garrison town; military camp. **p. de toros,** bullring. **p. fuerte,** strong place, fortress. **sentar p.,** to enlist in the army
plazo *m,* term, duration; expiration of term, date of payment; installment. **a plazos,** *com* by installments, on the installment system
plazoleta *f,* small square (in gardens, etc.)
pleamar *f, naut* high water
plebe *f,* common people; rabble, mob
plebeyo (-ya) *a* plebeian. *n* commoner, plebeian
plebiscito *m,* plebiscite
plectro *m,* plectrum
plegable *a* foldable
plegadera *f,* folder; folding knife; paper folder
plegadizo *a* folding; collapsible; jointed
plegado *m,* pleating; folding
plegador *a* folding. *m,* folding machine
plegadura *f,* folding, doubling; fold, pleat
plegar *vt irr* to fold; pleat; *sew* gather; *vr* submit, give in. See **acertar**
plegaria *f,* fervent prayer
pleitear *vt* to go to court about; indulge in litigation
pleitista *a* quarrelsome, litigious
pleito *m,* action, lawsuit; dispute, quarrel; litigation. **p. de familia,** family squabble. **ver el p.,** *law* to try a case
plenamente *adv* fully, entirely
plenario *a* full, complete; *law* plenary
plenilunio *m,* full moon
plenipotencia *f,* full powers (diplomatic, etc.)
plenipotenciario *a* and *m,* plenipotentiary
plenitud *f,* fullness, completeness; plenitude, abundance
pleno *a* full. *m,* general meeting
pleonasmo *m, gram* pleonasm
pleonástico *a* pleonastic
pleuresía *f,* pleurisy
plexo *m,* plexus
pliego *m,* sheet (of paper); letter, packet of papers
pliegue *m,* fold, pleat; *sew* gather
plinto *m, arch* plinth (of a column); baseboard
plisar *vt* to pleat; fold
plomada *f,* plummet; sounding lead; plumb, lead
plomería *f,* plumbing; plumbing business; lead roofing
plomero *m,* plumber
plomizo *a* lead-like; lead-colored, gray
plomo *m,* lead (metal); plummet; bullet; *inf* bore, tedious person
pluma *f,* feather; pen; plumage; quill; penmanship; writer; writing profession. **p. estilográfica,** fountain pen. **a vuela p.,** as the pen writes, written in a hurry
plumado *a* feathered
pluma fuente *f, Lat. Am.* fountain pen
plumaje *m,* plumage, feathers; plume
plúmbeo *a* plumbeous, leaden
plúmeo *a* feathered, plumed
plumero *m,* feather duster; plume, feather; plumage
plumón *m,* down; feather bed *Lat. Am.* felt-tipped pen
plumoso *a* feathered
plural *a* and *m,* plural
pluralidad *f,* plurality; multitude, number
pluralizar *vt* to pluralize
plurilingüe *a* multilingual
pluscuamperfecto *m,* pluperfect
plusmarquista *mf sport* recordholder
plutocracia *f,* plutocracy
plutócrata *mf* plutocrat
plutocrático *a* plutocratic
pluviómetro *m,* rain gauge
poblacho *m,* miserable town or village
población *f,* peopling; population; town
poblado *m,* inhabited place; town; village
poblador (-ra) *a* populating. *n* colonist, settler
poblar *vt irr* to colonize; people, populate; breed fast; stock, supply; *vr* put forth leaves (of trees). See **contar**
pobre *a* poor; indigent, needy; mediocre; unfortunate; humble, meek. *mf* beggar, pauper, needy person. *inf* **ser p. de solemnidad,** to be down and out
pobrero *m, ecc* distributor of alms
pobretería *f,* poverty; needy people
pobretón *a* extremely needy
pobreza *f,* poverty, need; shortage; timidity; *min* baseness; poorness (of soil, etc.)
pocero *m,* well digger
pocilga *f,* pigsty; *inf* filthy place
poción *f,* potion, drink; mixture, dose
poco *a* little, scanty; *pl* few. *m,* small amount, a little. *adv* little; shortly, in a little while. **p. a p.,** by degrees, little by little; slowly. **p. más o menos,** more or less, approximately. **por p.,** almost, nearly (always used with the present tense, e.g. **Por p. me caigo,** I almost fell). **tener en p. (a),** to have a poor opinion of; undervalue
poda *f, agr* pruning; pruning season
podadera *f,* pruning knife
podar *vt agr* to prune, trim
poder *m,* power; authority, jurisdiction; *law* power of attorney; strength; ability; proxy; efficacy; possession; *pl* authority; power of attorney. **los poderes constituidos,** the established authorities; the powers that be. **p. de adquisición,** purchasing power. **casarse por poderes,** to be married by proxy
poder *vt irr* to be able to (e.g. **Podemos comprar estas naranjas,** We can (are able to) buy these oranges). **Dice que la calamidad podía haberse evitado,** He says that the disaster could have been averted). **p.** also expresses possibility (e.g. **Pueden haber ido a la ciudad,** They may have gone to the city. **¡Qué distinta pudo haber sido su vida!** How different his life might have been!). *impers* be possible. **a más no p.,** of necessity, without being able to help it; to the utmost. **no p. con,** to be unable to control or manage. **no p. hacer más,** to have no alternative, have to; be unable to do more. **no p. menos de,** to be obliged to, have no alternative but. **no p. contener su emoción,** to be overcome with emotion. **no p. ver a,** to hate (persons). *impers* **Puede que venga esta tarde,** He may come (perhaps he will come) this afternoon. *Pres. Part.* **pudiendo.** *Pres. Ind.* **puedo, puedes, puede, pueden.** *Fut.* **podré,** etc. *Condit.* **podría,** etc. *Preterite*

pude, pudiste, etc. *Pres. Subjunc.* **pueda, puedas, pueda, puedan.** *Imperf. Subjunc.* **pudiese,** etc.
poderío *m,* power, authority; sway, rule; dominion; wealth
poderoso *a* powerful; opulent; effective, efficacious; mighty, magnificent
podredumbre *f,* decay; pus; *fig* canker, anguish
podredura, podrición *f,* putrefaction; decay
podrido *a* rotten; putrid; corrupt; decayed
podrir *vt* See **pudrir**
poema *m,* poem. **p. sinfónico,** tone poem
poesía *f,* poetry, verse; lyric, poem
poeta *m,* poet
poetastro *m,* poetaster
poética *f,* poetics
poético *a* poetical
poetisa *f,* poetess
poetizar *vi* to write verses; *vt* poeticize
polaco (-ca) *a* Polish. *n* Pole. *m,* Polish (language)
polainas *f pl,* leggings, puttees, gaiters
polar *a* polar
polaridad *f,* polarity; polarization
polarización *f,* polarization
polarizar *vt* to polarize
polca *f,* polka
polea *f,* pulley; *naut* block
polémica *f,* polemic, controversy, dispute
polémico *a* polemical
polemista *mf* disputant, controversialist
polen *m,* pollen
polichinela *m,* Punchinello
policía *f,* police; government, polity, administration; civility, courtesy; cleanliness, tidiness. *m,* policeman. **p. urbana,** city police
policíaco *a* police; detective
policial *a* police; *m, Lat. Am.* police officer
policromo *a* polychrome
poliedro *m,* polyhedron
polifacético *a* many-sided
polifonía *f,* polyphony
polifónico *a* polyphonic
poligamia *f,* polygamy
polígamo (-ma) *a* polygamous. *n* polygamist
poligloto (-ta) *n* polyglot. *f,* polyglot Bible
polígono *a* polygonal. *m,* polygon
polilla *f,* moth; moth grub; destroyer, ravager
polimorfismo *m, chem* polymorphism
polimorfo *a* polymorphous
Polinesia Polynesia
polinesio (-ia) *a* and *n* Polynesian
polinización *f,* pollination
poliomielitis *f,* poliomyelitis, polio
pólipo *m, zool* polyp; octopus; *med* polyp
polisílabo *a* polysyllabic. *m,* polysyllable
polista *mf* polo player
politécnico *a* polytechnic
politeísmo *m,* polytheism
politeísta *a* polytheistic. *mf* polytheist
política *f,* politics; civility, courtesy; diplomacy; tact; policy
politicastro *m,* corrupt politician
político *a* political; civil, courteous; in-law, by marriage (relationships). *m,* politician
politiquear *vi inf* to dabble in politics, talk politics
politizarse *vr* to enter the political arena
póliza *f, com* policy; *com* draft; share certificate; revenue stamp; admission ticket; lampoon. **p. a prima fija,** fixed-premium policy. **p. de seguros,** insurance policy. **p. dotal,** endowment policy
polizón *m,* loafer, tramp; stowaway; bustle (of a dress)
polla *f,* pullet; *inf* flapper, young woman
pollada *f,* brood, hatch (especially of chickens)
pollastro (-ra) *n* pullet.
pollera *f,* female poultry breeder or seller; chicken coop; go-cart; *Argentina, Chile* skirt
pollería *f,* poultry market or shop
pollero *n* poultry breeder; poulterer. *m,* hen coop; *Lat. Am.* gambler
pollino (-na) *n* young ass; donkey
pollo *m,* chicken; *inf* youth, stripling; *fig inf* downy bird. *inf* **p. pera,** young blood, lad. **sacar pollos,** to hatch chickens
polo *m,* pole (all meanings); *fig* support; popular Andalusian song; *sport* polo. **de p. a p.,** from pole to pole
polonés (-esa) *a* Polish. *n* Pole
Polonia Poland
poltrón *a* lazy, idle
poltronear *vi* to loaf about
poltronería *f,* idleness, laziness
polución *f, med* ejaculation
polvareda *f,* dust cloud; storm, agitation
polvera *f,* powder bowl; powder puff; powder compact
polvillo *m, Lat. Am.* blight
polvo *m,* dust; powder; pinch (of snuff, etc.); *pl* face or dusting powder. **Se hizo como por polvos de la madre celestina,** It was done as if by magic. *inf* **limpio de p. y paja,** gratis, for nothing; net (of profit)
pólvora *f,* gunpowder; bad temper. **p. de algodón,** guncotton.
polvorear *vt* to powder, dust with powder
polvoriento *a* dusty; powdery, covered with powder
polvorín *m,* very fine powder; powder magazine; powder flask
polvoroso *a* dusty; covered with powder
pomada *f,* pomade; salve, ointment
pomar *m,* orchard (especially an apple orchard)
pómez *f,* pumice stone (**piedra p.**)
pomo *m, bot* pome; pomander; nosegay; pommel, hilt (of a sword); handle; rose (of watering can)
pomología *f,* pomology, art of fruit growing
pompa *f,* pomp, splendor; ceremonial procession; air bubble; peacock's outspread tail; *naut* pump; billowing of clothes in the wind
Pompeya Pompeii
pomposidad *f,* pomposity
pomposo *a* stately, ostentatious, magnificent; inflated, pompous; florid, bombastic
pómulo *m,* cheekbone
ponchada *f Lat. Am.* great deal, large amount
ponche *m,* punch, toddy
ponchera *f,* punch bowl
poncho *a* lazy, negligent. *m,* military cloak; poncho, cape
ponderación *f,* weighing; reflection, consideration; exaggeration
ponderador *a* reflective, deliberate; exaggerated
ponderar *vt* to weigh; consider, ponder; exaggerate; overpraise
ponderosidad *f,* heaviness; ponderousness, dullness
ponderoso *a* heavy; ponderous; circumspect
ponedero *a* egg-laying (of hens). *m,* nest
ponencia *f,* clause, section; office of referee or arbitrator; report, referendum
poner *vt irr* to place, put; arrange; set (the table); bet, stake; appoint (to an office); call, name; lay (eggs); set down (in writing); calculate, count; suppose; leave to a person's judgment; risk; contribute; prepare; need, take; cause, inspire (emotions); make, cause; adapt; add; cause to become (angry, etc.); insult; praise; (*with prep a + infin*) begin to. **p. a contribución,** to lay under contribution, turn to account, utilize. **ponerle el cascabel al gato** *or* **el collar al gato,** to bell the cat. **p. los cuernos (a),** to cuckold. **p. al corriente,** to bring up to date, inform. **p. a prueba,** to test. **p. casa,** to set up house. *inf* **p. colorado a,** to make blush. **p. coto a,** to put a stop to, check. **p. en comparación,** to compare. **p. conato en,** to put a great deal of effort into. **p. en cotejo,** to collate. **p. en limpio,** to make a fair copy (of). **p. en marcha,** to start, set in motion. **p. en práctica,** to put into effect. **p. por caso,** to take as an example (e.g. **Pongamos por caso . . .** For example, . . .). **p. por encima (de),** to prefer. *vr* to place

oneself; become; put on (garments, etc.); dirty or stain oneself; set (of the sun, stars); oppose; deck oneself, dress oneself up; arrive; (*with prep a + infin*) begin to. **ponerse al corriente,** to bring oneself up to date. **ponerse bien,** to improve; get better (in health). **ponerse colorado,** to blush, flush. **p. una base racional a la fe,** to give faith a rational foundation. **p. los cimientos de,** lay the foundation of, lay the foundations for. **p. una conferencia,** to make a long-distance call. *Pres. Ind.* **pongo, pones,** etc. *Fut.* **pondré,** etc. *Condit.* **pondría,** etc. *Imperat.* **pon.** *Past Part.* **puesto.** *Preterite* **puse, pusiste,** etc. *Pres. Subjunc.* **ponga,** etc. *Imperf. Subjunc.* **pusiese,** etc.

pongo *m Bolivia, Peru* Native American serf

pongueaje *m* **Bolivia, Peru** Native American serfdom

ponientada *f,* steady west wind

poniente *m,* west; west wind

pontazgo *m,* bridge toll

pontear *vt* to bridge; make bridges

pontificado *m,* pontificate, papacy

pontífice *m,* pontifex; pope, pontiff; archbishop; bishop

pontón *m, mil* pontoon; hulk used as a prison, hospital, store, etc.; wooden bridge

pontonero *m,* pontoneer, military engineer

ponzoña *f,* poison, venom

ponzoñoso *a* poisonous, venomous; noxious; harmful

popa *f, naut* stern, poop. **en p.,** abaft, astern, aft

popelina *f,* poplin

popote *m, Mexico* (drinking) straw

populachería *f,* cheap popularity with the rabble

populachero *a* mob, vulgar

populacho *m,* mob, rabble

popular *a* popular

popularidad *f,* popularity

popularizar *vt* to popularize; *vr* grow popular

populoso *a* populous, crowded

popurrí *m, cul* stew; potpourri; miscellany

poquedad *f,* paucity, scarcity; timidity, cowardice; trifle, mere nothing

poquísimo *a sup* **poco** very little

poquito *m,* very little

por *prep* for; by; through, along; during; because, as (e.g. **Lo desecharon p. viejo,** They threw it away because it was old); however (e.g. **p. bonito que sea,** however pretty it is); during; in order to (e.g. **Lo hice p. no ofenderla,** I did it in order not to offend her); toward, in favor of, for; for the sake of; on account of, by reason of (e.g. **No pudo venir p. estar enfermo,** He could not come on account of his illness); via, by (e.g. **p. correo aéreo,** by airmail); as for (e.g. **P. mí, lo rechazo,** As for me, I refuse it. **p. mi cuenta,** to my way of thinking; on my own); in exchange for (e.g. **Me vendió dos libros p. seis dólares,** He sold me two books for six dollars); in the name of; as a substitute for, instead of (e.g. **Hace mi trabajo p. mí,** He is doing my work for me); per. **Por** has several uses: 1. Introduces the agent after a passive (e.g. **La novela fue escrita p. él,** The novel was written by him). 2. Expresses movement through, along or about (e.g. **Andaban p. la calle,** They were walking along (or down) the street). 3. Denotes time at or during which an action occurs (e.g. **Ocurrió p. entonces un acontecimiento de importancia,** About that time an important event occurred). 4. Expresses rate or proportion (e.g. **seis por ciento,** six percent). 5. With certain verbs, means 'to be' and expresses vague futurity (e.g. **El libro queda p. escribir,** The book remains to be written). **p. cortesía,** by courtesy, out of politeness. **p. cortesía de,** by courtesy of. **p. escrito,** in writing. **p. fas or p. nefas,** by fair means or foul; at any cost. **p. mucho que,** however great, however much; in spite of, notwithstanding. **¿P. qué?** Why? **p. si acaso,** in case, if by chance. **estar p.,** to be about to; be inclined to. **P. un clavo se pierde la herradura,** For want of a nail, the shoe was lost.

porcelana *f,* porcelain, china; chinaware

porcentaje *m,* percentage

porche *m,* porch, portico

porcino *a* porcine. *m,* young pig; bruise

porción *f,* portion; *com* share; *inf* crowd; allowance, pittance

porcionista *mf* shareholder; sharer; boarding school student

pordiosear *vi* to ask alms, beg

pordioseo *m,* asking alms, begging

pordiosero (-ra) *a* begging. *n* beggar

porfía *f,* obstinacy; importunity; tenacity. **a p.,** in competition

porfiadamente *adv* obstinately

porfiado *a* obstinate, obdurate, persistent

porfiar *vi* to be obstinate, insist; persist

pórfido *m,* porphyry

pormenor *m,* particular, detail (gen. *pl*); secondary matter

pormenorizar *vt* to describe in detail

pornografía *f,* pornography

pornográfico *a* pornographic, obscene

poro *m,* pore; *Lat. Am. also* leek

porongo *m, Lat. Am.* calabash, gourd

porosidad *f,* porosity, permeability

poroso *a* porous, leaky

poroto *m, Lat. Am.* bean; *Chile* child, kid

porque *conjunc* because, for; in order that

porqué *m,* reason, wherefore, why; *inf* money. **el cómo y el p.,** the why and the wherefore

porquería *f, inf* filth, nastiness; dirty trick; rudeness, gross act; trifle, thing of no account

porquerizo, porquero *m,* swineherd

porra *f,* club, bludgeon; last player (in children's games); *inf* vanity, boastfulness; bore, tedious person

porrada *f,* blow with a club; buffet, knock, fall; *inf* folly; glut, abundance

porrazo *m,* blow with a club; buffet, knock, fall

porrear *vi inf* to insist, harp on

porrería *f, inf* folly; obduracy, persistence

porreta *f,* green leaves of leeks, onions, and cereals. *inf* **en p.,** stark-naked

porrino *m,* seed of a leek; young leek plant

porrón *m,* winebottle with a spout; earthenware jug

porsiacaso *m, Argentina, Venezuela* knapsack

portaaviones *m,* aircraft carrier

portachuelo *m,* defile, narrow mountain pass

portada *f,* front, facade; frontispiece, title page; portal, doorway

portado (bien *or* **mal)** *a* well- or ill-dressed or behaved

portador (-ra) *n* carrier. *m, com* bearer; *mech* carrier

portaestandarte *m,* standard-bearer

portafolio *m,* portfolio; *Lat. Am. also* briefcase

portafusil *m,* rifle sling

portal *m,* entrance, porch; portico; city gate

portalámpara *f,* lamp holder; *elec* socket

portalibros *m,* bookstrap

portalón *m,* gangway

portamanteo *m,* traveling bag

portamonedas *m,* pocketbook; handbag, purse

portanuevas *mf* bringer of news, newsmonger

portaobjetos *m,* stage (of a microscope)

portaplumas *m,* pen holder

portar *vt* to retrieve (of dogs); carry (arms); *vr* behave (well or badly); bear oneself, act; be well, or ill (in health)

portátil *a* portable

portavoz *m,* megaphone; spokesman, mouthpiece

portazgo *m,* toll; tollbooth

portazguero *m,* toll collector

portazo *m,* bang of the door; slamming the door in a person's face

porte *m,* transport; *com* carriage; postage; freight, transport cost; porterage; behavior, conduct; bearing, looks; capacity, volume; size, dimension; nobility (of descent); *naut* tonnage. **p. pagado,** charges prepaid

porteador *m,* carrier; porter; carter

portear *vt* to carry, transport; *vr* migrate (of birds)
portento *m,* marvel, prodigy, portent
portentoso *a* marvelous, portentous
porteño, -a *a* of Buenos Aires; native of Buenos Aires; resident of Buenos Aires
porteo *m,* porterage, cartage
portería *f,* porter's lodge; porter's employment; *sport* goal
portero (-ra) *n* doorman, doorkeeper; porter; concierge; janitor; *sport* goalkeeper. **p. eléctrico,** door buzzer
portezuela *f, dim* small door; carriage door; pocket flap
pórtico *m,* portico, piazza; porch; vestibule, hall
portillo *m,* breach, opening; defile, narrow pass; *fig* loophole
portón *m,* hall door, inner door; *Chile* back door
portorriqueño (-ña) *a* and *n* Puerto Rican
portuario *a* dock, port
portugués (-esa) *a* and *n* Portuguese. *m,* Portuguese (language)
portuguesada *f,* exaggeration
porvenir *m,* future time
¡porvida! *interj* By the saints! By the Almighty!
pos *prefix* after; behind. Also *adv* **en p.,** with the same meanings
posa *f,* tolling bell; *pl* buttocks
posada *f,* dwelling; inn, tavern; lodging; hospitality
posaderas *f pl,* buttocks
posadero (-ra) *n* innkeeper; boardinghouse keeper
posar *vi* to lodge, live; rest; alight, perch; *vt* set down (a burden); *vr* settle (liquids); (*with en or sobre*) perch upon
posdata *f,* P.S., postscript
pose *f, phot* time exposure; *inf* pose
poseedor (-ra) *n* possessor, holder
poseer *vt irr* to own, possess; know (a language, etc.); *vr* restrain oneself. **estar poseído por,** to be possessed by (passion, etc.); be thoroughly convinced of. See **creer**
posesión *f,* ownership, occupancy; possession; property, territory (often *pl*)
posesionarse *vr* to take possession; lay hold (of)
poseso *a* possessed of an evil spirit
posesor (-ra) *n* owner, possessor
posfecha *f,* postdate
posguerra *f,* postwar period
posibilidad *f,* possibility; probability; opportunity, means, chance; *pl* property, wealth
posibilitar *vt* to make possible, facilitate
posible *a* possible. *m pl,* property, personal wealth. **hacer lo p.** *or* **hacer todo lo p.,** to do everything possible; do one's best
posición *f,* placing; position; situation; status
positivamente *adv* positively, definitely
positivismo *m,* positivism
positivista *a* positivistic. *mf* positivist
positivo *a* positive; certain, definite; (*math elec*) plus; true, real
pósito *m,* public granary; cooperative association
posma *f, inf* sluggishness, sloth
poso *m,* sediment; lees, dregs; repose, quietness
posponer *vt irr* (*with prep a*) to place after; make subordinate to; value less than. See **poner**
posta *f,* post horse; stage, post; stake (cards)
postal *a* postal. *f,* postcard, postal card
poste *m,* post, stake
postema *f,* tumor, abscess; bore, tedious person
postergación *f,* delay; delaying; relegation; disregard of seniority (in promotion)
postergar *vt* to delay; disregard a senior claim to promotion
posteridad *f,* descendants; posterity
posterior *a* back, rear; hind; subsequent
posteriormente *adv* later, subsequently
postigo *m,* secret door; grating, hatch; postern; shutter (of a window)
postillón *m,* postilion
postizo *a* false, artificial, not natural. *m,* switch of false hair
postor *m,* bidder (at an auction)
postración *f,* prostration; exhaustion; depression, distress
postrar *vt* to cast down, demolish; prostrate, exhaust; *vr* kneel down; be prostrated or exhausted
postre *a* last (in order). *m, cul* dessert. **a la p.,** at last, finally
postrero *a* last (in order); rearmost, hindmost
postrimeramente *adv* lastly, finally
postrimería *f, ecc* last period of life
postulación *f,* entreaty, request
postulado *m,* assumption; supposition; working hypothesis; *geom* postulate
postulante (-ta) *n ecc* postulant, applicant, candidate
postular *vt* to postulate; *Lat. Am.* nominate
póstumo *a* posthumous
postura *f,* posture, bearing; laying (of an egg); bid (at an auction); position; agreement, pact; bet, stake; planting; transplanted tree. **p. de vida,** way of life
potable *a* drinkable. **agua p.,** drinking water
potación *f,* potation, drink
potaje *m,* stew, potage; dried vegetables; mixed drink; hotchpotch
potasa *f,* potash
potasio *m,* potassium
pote *m,* pot; jar; flowerpot; *cul* cauldron; *cul* stew
potencia *f,* power; potency; *mech* performance, capacity; strength, force; *math* power; rule, dominion
potencial *a* potential
potentado *m,* potentate
potente *a* potent; powerful; *inf* enormous
potestad *f,* authority, power; podesta, Italian magistrate; potentate; *math* power; *pl* angelic powers
potestativo *a law* facultative
potingue *m, inf* brew; mixture; lotion; medicine; filthy place, pigsty
poto *m, Lat. Am.* calabash, gourd; backside
potra *f,* filly
potrear *vt inf* to tease, annoy
potro *m,* colt, foal; rack (for torture); vaulting horse. **p. mesteño,** mustang
poyo *m,* stone seat
pozal *m,* pail, bucket
pozo *m,* well; shaft (in a mine). *aut* **p. colector,** crankcase
pozole, *m, Mexico* stew of pork, corn, chile, etc.
práctica *f,* practice; custom, habit; method; exercise
practicabilidad *f,* feasibility
practicable *a* feasible, practicable
prácticamente *adv* practically, in practice
practicante *m,* medical practitioner; medical student; *med* intern; first-aid practitioner
practicar *vt* to execute, perform; practice; make
práctico *a* practical; experienced, expert; workable. *m, naut* pilot
pradeño *a* meadow, prairie
pradera *f,* meadow, field; lawn
pradería *f,* meadowland, prairie
prado *m,* meadow; grassland; field; lawn; walk (in cities)
Praga Prague
pragmatista *a* pragmatic. *mf* pragmatist
pravedad *f,* wickedness, immorality, depravity
pravo *a* wicked, immoral, depraved
pre *m, mil* daily pay. *prep insep* pre-
preámbulo *m,* preamble, preface; importunate digression
prebenda *f, ecc* prebend, benefice; *inf* sinecure
preboste *m,* provost
precario *a* precarious, uncertain, insecure
precaución *f,* precaution, safeguard
precaucionarse *vr* to take precautions, safeguard oneself
precautelar *vt* to forewarn; take precautions

precaver *vt* to prevent, avoid; *vr* (*with de or contra*) guard against
precavido *a* cautious, forewarned
precedencia *f*, priority, precedence; superiority; preference, precedence
precedente *a* preceding. *m*, antecedent; precedent
preceder *vt* to precede; have precedence over, be superior to
preceptivo *a* preceptive; didactic
precepto *m*, precept; order, injunction; rule, commandment. **de p.,** obligatory
preceptor (-ra) *n* teacher, instructor, tutor, preceptor
preces *f pl, ecc* prayers; entreaties
preciado *a* excellent, esteemed, precious; boastful
preciar *vt* to esteem, value; valuate, price; *vr* boast
precintar *vt* to seal; rope, string, tie up
precinto *m*, sealing; roping, tying up; strap
precio *m*, price, cost; recompense, reward; premium; rate; reputation, importance; esteem. **p. de tasa,** controlled price
preciosidad *f*, preciousness; exquisiteness, fineness; richness; wittiness; *inf* loveliness, beauty; thing of beauty
precioso *a* precious; exquisite, fine, rare; rich; witty; *inf* lovely, delicious, attractive
preciosuna *f, Lat. Am.* thing of beauty
precipicio *m*, precipice; heavy fall; ruin, disaster
precipitación *f*, precipitancy, haste; rashness; *chem* precipitation
precipitadamente *adv* precipitately, in haste; rashly, foolishly
precipitado *a* precipitate; rash, thoughtless. *m, chem* precipitate
precipitar *vt* to precipitate, hurl headlong; hasten; *chem* precipitate; *vr* hurl oneself headlong; hasten, rush
precipitoso *a* precipitous; rash, heedless
precisamente *adv* exactly, precisely, just; necessarily. **Y p. en aquel instante llegó,** And just at that moment he arrived
precisar *vt* to fix, arrange; set forth, draw up, state; compel, force, oblige
precisión *f*, accuracy, precision; necessity, conciseness, clarity; compulsion, obligation
preciso *a* necessary, unavoidable; concise, clear; precise, exact
precitado *a* aforementioned
preclaro *a* illustrious, distinguished, celebrated
precocidad *f*, precocity
precognición *f*, foreknowledge
precolombino, -a *a* pre-Columbian
preconcebido *a* preconceived
preconcepto *m*, preconceived idea, preconceived notion
preconizar *vt* to eulogize, praise publicly
preconocer *vt irr* to know beforehand; foresee. See **conocer**
precoz *a* precocious
precursor (-ra) *a* precursory; preceding, previous. *n* precursor
predecesor (-ra) *n* predecessor
predecir *vt irr* to foretell, prophesy. See **decir**
predestinación *f*, predestination
predestinado (-da) *a* predestined; foreordained. *n* one of the predestined
predestinar *vt* to predestine, foreordain
predeterminar *vt* to predetermine
prédica *f, inf* (contemptuous) sermon
predicación *f*, preaching; homily, sermon
predicadera *f*, pulpit; *pl inf* talent for preaching
predicador (-ra) *a* preaching. *n* preacher
predicamento *m*, predicament; reputation
predicar *vt* to publish; manifest; preach; *vi* overpraise; *inf* lecture, scold. **p. en el desierto,** to preach to the wind
predicción *f*, prediction, prophecy
predilección *f*, predilection, preference, partiality
predilecto *a* favorite, preferred
predisponer *vt irr* to predispose. See **poner**
predisposición *f*, predisposition; tendency, prejudice
predominación *f*, predominance
predominante *a* predominant; prevailing
predominar *vi* and *vt* to predominate; prevail; tower above; overlook
predominio *m*, predominance, ascendancy, preponderance
preeminencia *f*, preeminence
preeminente *a* preeminent
preexistencia *f*, preexistence
preexistente *a* preexistent
preexistir *vi* to preexist, exist before
prefacio *m*, introduction, preface, prologue; *ecc* preface
prefecto *m*, prefect
prefectura *f*, prefecture
preferencia *f*, preference; superiority. **de p.,** preferred, favorite; preferably
preferente *a* preferable; preferential; preferred (of stock)
preferible *a* preferable
preferir *vt irr* to prefer; excel, exceed. *Pres. Part.* **prefiriendo.** *Pres. Ind.* **prefiero, prefieres, prefiere, prefieren.** *Preterite* **prefirió, prefirieron.** *Pres. Subjunc.* **prefiera, prefieras, prefiera, prefieran.** *Imperf. Subjunc.* **prefiriese,** etc.
prefijar *vt* to prefix
prefijo *m*, prefix
prefinir *vt* to fix a time limit for
prefulgente *a* brilliant, shining, resplendent
pregón *m*, public proclamation; marriage banns
pregonar *vt* to proclaim publicly; cry one's wares; publish abroad; eulogize, praise; proscribe, outlaw. **p. a los cuatro vientos,** *inf* to shout from the rooftops
pregonería *f*, office of the town crier
pregonero *m*, town crier
preguerra *f*, prewar period
pregunta *f*, question; *com* inquiry; questionnaire, interrogation. *inf* **andar** (*or* **estar**) **a la cuarta p.,** to be very hard up, be on the rocks. **hacer una p.,** to ask a question
preguntador (-ra) *a* questioning; inquisitive. *n* questioner; inquisitive person
preguntar *vt* to question, ask; (*with por*) inquire for; *vr* ask oneself, wonder
prehistoria *f*, prehistory
prehistórico *a* prehistoric
prejuicio *m*, prejudice
prejuzgar *vt* to prejudge, judge hastily
prelacía *f*, prelacy
prelación *f*, preference
prelado *m*, prelate
preliminar *a* preliminary, prefatory. *m*, preliminary
preludiar *vi* and *vt mus* to play a prelude (to); *vt* prepare, initiate
preludio *m*, introduction, prologue; *mus* prelude; *mus* overture
prematuro *a* premature, untimely; unseasonable; immature, unripe
premeditación *f*, premeditation
premeditar *vt* to premeditate, plan in advance
premiador (-ra) *a* rewarding. *n* rewarder
premiar *vt* to reward, requite
premio *m*, prize; reward; premium; *com* interest. **p. en metálico,** cash prize. *inf* **p. gordo,** first prize (in a lottery)
premioso *a* tight; troublesome, annoying; stern, strict; slow-moving; burdensome, hard; labored (of speech or style)
premisa *f*, premise; sign, indication
premonitorio *a* premonitory
premura *f*, urgency, haste
prenda *f*, pledge; token, sign; jewel; article of clothing; talent, gift; loved one; *pl* game of forfeits
prendador (-ra) *n* pledger

prendamiento *m*, pawning
prendar *vt* to pawn; charm, delight; *vr* (*with de*) take a liking to
prender *vt* to seize; arrest; capture, catch. *vi* take root (plants); catch fire; be infectious
prendería *f*, second-hand shop
prendero (-ra) *n* second-hand dealer
prendimiento *m*, seizure, capture; arrest
prenombre *m*, given name, praenomen
prensa *f*, press; printing press; newspapers, the press. **dar a la p.,** to publish
prensado *m*, **prensadura** *f*, pressing; flattening; squeezing
prensar *vt* to press; squeeze
prensil *a* prehensile
preñado *a* pregnant; bulging, sagging (walls, etc.); swollen. *m*, pregnancy
preñez *f*, pregnancy; suspense
preocupación *f*, anxiety, preoccupation; prejudice
preocupadamente *adv* preoccupiedly, absentmindedly; with prejudice
preocupar *vt* to preoccupy; make anxious; bias, prejudice; *vr* be anxious; be prejudiced
preordinar *vt ecc* to predestine
preparación *f*, preparation; treatment; compound, specific
preparado *a* ready, prepared. *m*, preparation, patent food, etc.
preparar *vt* to prepare; *vr* prepare oneself; qualify
preparativo *a* preparatory. *m*, preparation
preparatorio *a* preparatory
preponderancia *f*, preponderance
preponderante *a* preponderant; dominant
preponderar *vi* to preponderate; dominate; outweigh
preponer *vt irr* to put before. See **poner**
preposición *f*, preposition
prepósito *m*, chairman, head, president; *ecc* provost
prepucio *m*, prepuce, foreskin
prerrogativa *f*, prerogative
presa *f*, hold, grasp; seizure, capture; booty; dam; lock (on rivers, canals); weir; ditch, trench; embankment; slice, bit. **hacer p.,** to seize; take advantage of (circumstances)
presagiar *vt* to prophesy, presage, bode
presagio *m*, presage, sign; presentiment, foreboding
présbita *a* long-sighted, farsighted
presbiterado *m*, priesthood; holy orders
presbiteriano (-na) *a* and *n* Presbyterian
presbítero *m*, priest
presciencia *f*, prescience, foresight
presciente *a* prescient, farsighted
prescindible *a* nonessential, able to be dispensed with
prescindir *vi* (*with de*) to pass over, omit; do without. **Prescindiendo de esto . . . ,** Leaving this aside. . . .
prescribir *vt* to prescribe, order
prescripción *f*, prescription
presea *f*, jewel, object of value
presencia *f*, presence, attendance; appearance, looks; ostentation. **p. de ánimo,** presence of mind
presenciar *vt* to be present at; witness, behold
presentación *f*, presentation; introduction; *Lat. Am. also* petition
presentar *vt* to show; present, make a gift of; introduce (persons); *vr* occur; present oneself; offer one's services
presente *a* present. *m*, gift; present time. *law* **Por estas presentes . . . ,** By these presents . . . . **tener p.,** to remember
presentimiento *m*, presentiment, apprehension
presentir *vt irr* to have a presentiment of. See **sentir**
preservación *f*, preservation, protection, saving
preservar *vt* to preserve, protect, save
preservativo *a* preservative. *m*, preservative, safeguard, protection
presidencia *f*, presidency; chairmanship; presidential seat or residence
presidencial *a* presidential
presidenta *f*, female president; president's wife; chairwoman
presidente *m*, president; chairman; head, director; presiding judge
presidiar *vt* to garrison
presidiario *m*, convict
presidio *m*, garrison; garrison town; fortress; penitentiary; imprisonment; *law* hard labor; assistance, protection
presidir *vt* to preside over; act as chairperson for; influence, determine
presilla *f*, loop, shank, noose; press stud; *Mexico* epaulet
presión *f*, pressure
preso (-sa) *n* prisoner, captive; convict
prestación *f*, lending, loan. **p. vecinal,** corvée
prestador (-ra) *a* lending, loan. *n* lender
prestamente *adv* expeditiously, promptly
prestamista *mf* moneylender; pawnbroker
préstamo *m*, loan; lending. **casa de préstamos,** pawnshop
prestar *vt* to lend; assist; pay (attention); give; *Lat. Am.* to borrow; *vi* be useful; give, expand; *vr* be suitable; lend itself; offer oneself. **tomar prestado,** to borrow
prestatario (-ia) *n* money borrower, debtor
preste *m*, celebrant of high mass. **el p. Juan,** title of Prester John
presteza *f*, speed; promptness, dispatch
prestidigitación *f*, prestidigitation
prestidigitador (-ra) *n* juggler, conjurer
prestigio *m*, magic spell, sorcery; trick, illusion (of conjurers, etc.); influence, prestige
prestigioso *a* illusory; influential
presto *a* quick, speedy; prompt, ready. *m*, pressure cooker. *adv* immediately; soon; quickly. **de p.,** speedily
presumido *a* conceited, vain; presumptuous
presumir *vt* to suppose, presume; *vi* be conceited
presunción *f*, supposition, presumption; vanity, presumptuousness
presuntivo *a* presumptive
presuntuosidad *f*, presumptuousness
presuntuoso *a* presumptuous, vain
presuponer *vt irr* to presuppose, assume; budget, estimate. See **poner**
presuposición *f*, presupposition
presupuesto *m*, motive, reason; supposition, assumption; estimate; *com* tender; national budget
presuroso *a* swift, speedy
pretencioso *a* pretentious, vain
pretender *vt* to seek, solicit; claim; apply for; attempt, try; woo, court
pretendiente (-ta) *n* pretender; candidate; petitioner; suitor
pretensión *f*, pretension; claim; *pl* ambitions
pretérito *a* past. *m*, preterite
pretextar *vt* to allege as a pretext or excuse
pretexto *m*, pretext, excuse
prevalecer *vi irr* to prevail; be dominant; take root (plants). See **conocer**
prevaleciente *a* prevailing; prevalent
prevaricador (-ra) *n* prevaricator
prevaricar *vi* to prevaricate
prevención *f*, prevention; precaution; prejudice; police station; *mil* guard room; foresight, prevision; preparation. **de p.,** as a precaution
prevenido *a* prepared; cautious, forewarned
prevenir *vt irr* to prepare; prevent, avoid; warn; prejudice; occur, happen; *fig* overcome (obstacles); *vr* be ready; be forewarned. See **venir**
preventivo *a* preventive
prever *vt irr* to foresee, forecast, anticipate. See **ver**
previamente *adv* previously, in advance
previo *a* previous, advance
previsión *f*, forecast; foresight, prevision, prescience. **p. social,** social insurance
previsor *a* farsighted, provident

prieto *a* almost black, blackish; tight; mean, avaricious; *Lat. Am.* dark-skinned, swarthy
prima *f, ecc* prime; *com* premium; female cousin
primacía *f,* supremacy, preeminence; primacy; primateship
primada *f, inf* act of sponging on, taking advantage of
primado *m,* primate; primateship
primario *a* primary. *m,* professor who gives the first lecture of the day
primavera *f,* springtime; primrose; figured silk material; beautifully colored thing; youth; prime
primaveral *a* spring, spring-like
primeramente *adv* first; in the first place
primerizo (-za) *n* novice; beginner; apprentice; firstborn
primero *a* first; former; excellent, first-rate. *adv* first; in the first place. **primera enseñanza,** primary education. **primera materia,** raw material. **primer plano,** *art* foreground. **primera cura,** first aid. **de buenas a primeras,** all at once, suddenly
primicia *f,* first fruits; offering of first fruits; *pl* first effects
primitivo *a* original, early; primitive
primo (-ma) *a* first; excellent, fine. *n* cousin; *inf* simpleton; *inf* pigeon, dupe. **p. carnal,** first cousin. *inf* **hacer el p.,** to be a dupe. *inf* **ser prima hermana de,** to be the twin of (of things)
primogénito (-ta) *a* and *n* firstborn
primogenitura *f,* primogeniture
primor *m,* exquisite care; beauty, loveliness; thing of beauty
primoroso *a* beautiful; exquisitely done; dexterous, skillful
princesa *f,* princess
principado *m,* principality; princedom; superiority, preeminence
principal *a* chief, principal; illustrious; fundamental, first. *m,* head, principal (of a firm); *com* capital, principal; first floor
principalmente *adv* principally, chiefly
príncipe *m,* leader; prince. **p. de Asturias,** prince of Asturias. **p. de la sangre,** prince of the blood royal
principesco *a* princely
principiante (-ta) *n* beginner, novice; apprentice
principiar *vt* to begin, commence
principio *m,* beginning; principle; genesis, origin; rudiment; axiom; constituent. **al p.,** at first. **a principios,** at the beginning (of the month, year, etc.). **en p.,** in principle
pringar *vt cul* to soak in fat; stain with grease; *inf* wound; take part in a business deal; slander; *vr inf* appropriate, misuse (funds, etc.)
pringo *m, Lat. Am.* drop (of a liquid)
pringoso *a* greasy
pringue *mf,* animal fat, lard; grease spot
priora *f,* prioress
prioridad *f,* priority
prisa *f,* haste, speed; skirmish, foray. **a toda p.,** with all speed. **correr p.,** to be urgent. **dar p.,** to hasten, speed up. **darse** (*or* **estar de**) **p.,** to hurry
prisión *f,* prison, jail; seizure; captivity, imprisonment; *fig* bond; obstacle, shackle; *pl* fetters
prisonero (-ra) *n* prisoner; *fig* victim (of passion, etc.)
prisma *m,* prism
prismáticos *m pl,* field glasses
pristino *a* pristine
privación *f,* privation; lack, shortage; deprivation; degradation
privada *f,* toilet, privy, water closet
privadamente *adv* privately; individually, separately
privado *a* private; individual, personal. *m,* favorite; confidant
privar *vt* to deprive; dismiss (from office); interdict, forbid; *vi* prevail, be in favor; *vr* swoon; deprive oneself
privilegiar *vt* to privilege; bestow a favor on
privilegio *m,* privilege; prerogative; concession; copyright; patent
pro *mf* advantage, benefit. **el p. y el contra,** the pros and cons. **en p.,** in favor
proa *f,* prow, bow
probabilidad *f,* probability
probable *a* probable; likely; provable
probación *f,* proof, test; novitiate, probation
probado *a* tried, tested, proved
probar *vt irr* to prove; test; taste; try on (clothes); *vi* suit; (*with prep a + infin*) try to. **p. fortuna,** to try one's luck. *Pres. Ind.* **pruebo, pruebas, prueba, prueban.** *Pres. Subjunc.* **pruebe, pruebes, prueben**
probatorio *a* probationary
probidad *f,* probity, trustworthiness, honesty
problema *m,* problem
problemático *a* problematical, uncertain
probo *a* honest, trustworthy
procacidad *f,* insolence, pertness
procaz *a* insolent, pert, brazen
procedencia *f,* origin, source; parentage, descent; port of sailing or call
procedente *a* arriving or coming from
proceder *vi* to proceed; behave; originate, arise; continue, go on; act. *law* **p. contra,** to proceed against (a person)
procedimiento *m,* proceeding, advancement; procedure; legal practice; process
proceloso *a* tempestuous
prócer *a* exalted, eminent; lofty. *m,* exalted personage
procesado (-da) *n* defendant
procesamiento *m,* suing, suit; indictment
procesar *vt law* to proceed against, sue
procesión *f,* proceeding, emanating; procession; *inf* train, string. **andar** (*or* **ir**) **por dentro la p.,** to feel keenly without betraying one's emotion
proceso *m,* process; progress, advancement; lapse of time; lawsuit
proclama *f,* proclamation; announcement; publication of marriage banns
proclamación *f,* proclamation; acclaim, applause
proclamar *vt* to proclaim; acclaim; publish abroad; reveal, show
proclividad *f,* proclivity, tendency
procomún *m,* social or public welfare
procreación *f,* procreation
procreador (-ra) *a* procreative. *n* procreator
procrear *vt* to procreate, beget, engender
procuración *f,* procurement; assiduity, care; *law* power of attorney; *law* attorneyship
procurador (-ra) *m,* proxy; *law* attorney; proctor. *n* procurer
procurar *vt* to try, attempt; procure, get; exercise the profession of a lawyer
prodigalidad *f,* prodigality, lavishness; waste, extravagance
prodigar *vt* to waste, squander; lavish, bestow freely; *vr* make oneself cheap
prodigio *m,* marvel, wonder; prodigy; monster; miracle
prodigiosidad *f,* prodigiousness
prodigioso *a* wonderful; prodigious; monstrous; miraculous
pródigo (-ga) *a* wasteful, extravagant; lavish, generous. *n* spendthrift, wastrel, prodigal
producción *f,* production; output, yield; generation (of heat, etc.); crop
producir *vt irr* to produce; generate; yield, give; cause, occasion; publish; *vr* explain oneself; arise, appear, be produced. **p. efecto,** to have effect; take effect. See **conducir**
productividad *f,* productivity
productivo *a* productive; fertile; profitable
producto *m,* produce; product; profit; yield, gain; *math* product. *chem* **p. derivado,** by-product
productor (-ra) *a* productive. *n* producer
proemio *m,* prologue, preface, introduction

proeza *f*, prowess, gallantry; skill; *Lat. Am.* boast
profanación *f*, profanation
profanador (-ra) *n* profaner, transgressor
profanar *vt* to profane
profanidad *f*, profanity
profano *a* profane; dissolute; pleasure-loving, worldly; immodest; lay, ignorant
profecía *f*, prophecy; *ecc* Book of the Prophets; opinion, view
proferir *vt irr* to utter, pronounce. See **herir**
profesar *vt* to exercise, practice (professions); *ecc* profess; believe in; teach
profesión *f*, profession; trade, occupation; avowal, admission
profesional *a* professional
profesionalismo *m*, professionalism
profeso (-sa) *a ecc* professed. *n* professed monk
profesor (-ra) *n* teacher; professor
profesorado *m*, teaching staff; teaching profession; professorship; professorate
profeta *m*, prophet; seer
profético *a* prophetic
profetisa *f*, prophetess
profetizar *vt* to prophesy; imagine, suppose
proficiente *a* proficient
profiláctico *a* and *m*, prophylactic
prófugo (-ga) *a* and *n* fugitive from justice. *m*, *mil* one who evades military service
profundamente *adv* profoundly; acutely, deeply
profundidad *f*, depth; profundity, obscurity; *geom* depth; concavity; intensity (of feeling); vastness (of knowledge, etc.)
profundizar *vt* to deepen; hollow out; *fig* go into deeply, fathom
profundo *a* deep; low; *fig* intense, acute; abstruse, profound; *fig* vast, extensive; high. *m*, depth, profundity; *poet* ocean, the deep; *poet* hell
profuso *a* profuse, abundant; extravagant, wasteful
progenie *f*, descendants
prognosis *f*, prognosis; forecast
programa *m*, program; edict, public notice; plan, scheme; *univ* calendar; syllabus; timetable
progresar *vt* and *vi* to make progress; progress, advance
progresión *f*, progression; advancement, progress
progresista *a pol* progressive. *mf* progressive
progresivo *a* progressive; advancing
progreso *m*, progress, advancement; growth; improvement, development
prohibente *a* prohibitory, prohibitive
prohibición *f*, forbidding, prohibition
prohibicionista *mf* prohibitionist. *a* prohibitionist
prohibir *vt* to forbid, prohibit. **«Prohibido el paso,»** "No thoroughfare"
prohibitivo, prohibitorio *a* prohibitive
prohijador (-ra) *n* adopter (of a child)
prohijamiento *m*, child adoption; fathering (of a bill, etc.)
prohijar *vt* to adopt (children, ideas); *fig* father
prohombre *m*, master of a guild; respected, well-liked man
prójimo *m*, fellow man, brother, neighbor.
prole *f*, progeny, young offspring
proletariado *m*, proletariat
proletario *a* poor; common, vulgar. *m*, plebeian; pauper; proletarian
prolífico *a* prolific; abundant, fertile
prolijidad *f*, verbosity, prolixity; nicety, scruple; importunity, tediousness
prolijo *a* verbose, prolix; fussy, fastidious; tedious, importunate; *Argentina* indefatigable, untiring
prologar *vt* to prologue; provide with a preface
prólogo *m*, preface; prologue; introduction
prolongación *f*, lengthening; prolongation, protraction; extension
prolongado *a* prolonged; oblong, long
prolongar *vt* to lengthen; *geom* produce; prolong, spin out
promediar *vt* to distribute or divide into two equal portions; average; *vi* arbitrate; place oneself between two people; reach half-time
promedio *m*, average; middle, center
promesa *f*, promise; augury, favorable sign
prometedor (-ra) *a* promising. *n* promiser
prometer *vt* to promise; attest, certify; *vi* promise well, look hopeful; *vr* devote oneself to service of God; anticipate confidently, expect; become engaged (marriage). *inf* **prometérselas muy felices,** to have high hopes
prometido (-da) *n* betrothed. *m*, promise
prometimiento *m*, promise; promising
prominencia *f*, prominence, protuberance; eminence, hill
prominente *a* prominent, protuberant; eminent, elevated
promiscuar *vi* to eat meat and fish on fast days
promiscuidad *f*, promiscuity; ambiguity
promiscuo *a* indiscriminate, haphazard, promiscuous; ambiguous
promisión *f*, promise
promisorio *a* promissory
promoción *f*, promotion; batch, class, year (of recruits, students, etc.)
promontorio *m*, headland; promontory; cumbersome object
promotor (-ra) *a* promotive. *n* promoter; supporter
promover *vt irr* to promote, further, advance; promote (a person). **p. un proceso (a),** to bring a suit (against). See **mover**
promulgación *f*, promulgation
promulgar *vt* to publish officially, proclaim; promulgate. *law* **p. sentencia,** to pass judgment
pronombre *m*, pronoun
pronosticación *f*, prognostication; presage
pronosticar *vt* to prognosticate, forecast; presage
pronóstico *m*, omen, prediction; almanac; prognosis; sign, indication. **p. del tiempo,** weather forecast
prontitud *f*, quickness, promptness; quick-wittedness; *fig* sharpness, liveliness; celerity, dispatch
pronto *a* quick, speedy; prompt; ready, prepared. *m*, *inf* sudden decision. *adv* immediately; with all speed; soon. **de p.,** suddenly; without thinking. **por lo p.,** temporarily, provisionally
prontuario *m*, compendium, handbook; summary
pronunciación *f*, pronunciation
pronunciamiento *m*, military uprising; political manifesto; *law* pronouncement of sentence
pronunciar *vt* to pronounce, articulate; decide, determine; *law* pronounce judgment; give or make (a speech)
propagación *f*, propagation; dissemination; transmission
propagador *a* propagative. *m*, propagator
propaganda *f*, propaganda organization; propaganda
propagandista *mf* propagandist
propagar *vt* to reproduce; propagate, disseminate; *vr* reproduce, multiply; propagate, spread
propalar *vt* to disseminate, spread abroad
propasarse *vr* to go too far, forget oneself; overstep one's authority
propender *vi* to be inclined, have a leaning toward
propensión *f*, propensity, inclination; tendency
propenso *a* inclined, disposed; liable
propiamente *adv* properly, suitably
propiciación *f*, propitiation
propiciador (-ra) *a* propitiatory. *n* propitiator
propiciar *vt* to propitiate, appease
propiciatorio *a* propitiatory
propicio *a* propitious, auspicious; kind, favorable
propiedad *f*, estate, property; ownership; landed property; attribute, quality, property; *art* resemblance, naturalness
propietario (-ia) *a* proprietary. *n* proprietor, owner

propina *f*, gratuity, tip. *inf* **de p.,** in addition, extra
propinar *vt* to treat to a drink; administer (medicine); *inf* give (slaps, etc.)
propincuidad *f*, propinquity, proximity
propincuo *a* near, contiguous, adjacent
propio *a* own, one's own; typical, characteristic; individual, peculiar; suitable, apt; natural, real; same. *m*, messenger; *pl* public lands
proponente *a* proposing. *m*, proposer; *com* tenderer
proponer *vt irr* to propose, suggest; make a proposition; propose (for a post, office, etc.); *math* state; *vr* intend, purpose. **proponerse para un empleo,** to apply for a post. See **poner**
proporción *f*, proportion; chance, opportunity; size; *math* proportion
proporcionado *a* fit, suitable; proportionate; symmetrical
proporcional *a* proportional
proporcionar *vt* to allot, proportion; supply, provide, give; adapt
proposición *f*, proposition; motion (in a debate)
propósito *m*, proposal; intention, aim; subject, question, matter. **a p.,** suitable, apropos; by the way, incidentally. **de p.,** with the intention, proposing. **fuera de p.,** irrelevant
propuesta *f*, proposal, tender
propugnar *vt* to defend, protect
propulsar *vt* to repulse, throw back; propel, drive
propulsión *f*, repulse; propulsion
propulsor *a* driving, propelling. *m*, propeller
prorrata *f*, quota, share, apportionment. **a p.,** in proportion
prorratear *vt* to apportion, distribute proportionately, prorate
prorrogación *f*, prorogation, adjournment; extension (of time); renewal (of a lease, etc.)
prorrogar *vt* to extend, prolong; defer, suspend, prorogue; renew (leases, etc.)
prorrumpir *vt* (*with en*) to burst out; utter, give vent to, burst into
prosa *f*, prose; prosaism, prosaic style; *inf* dull verbosity; monotony, tediousness; *Lat. Am.* pomposity
prosaico *a* prosaic; prosy; monotonous, tedious; matter-of-fact
prosapia *f*, family, lineage, descent
proscenio *m*, proscenium
proscribir *vt* to proscribe, outlaw; forbid, prohibit. *Past Part.* **proscrito**
proscripción *f*, proscription
proscrito (-ta) *n* outlaw, exile
prosecución *f*, prosecution, performance; pursuit
proseguir *vt irr* to continue, proceed with. See **pedir**
proselitismo *m*, proselytism
prosélito *m*, convert, proselyte
prosificar *vt* to turn verse into prose
prosista *mf* prose writer
prosodia *f*, prosody
prospecto *m*, prospectus
prosperar *vt* to prosper; protect; *vi* flourish, prosper
prosperidad *f*, prosperity; wealth; success
próspero *a* favorable, propitious, fortunate; prosperous
próstata *f*, prostate
prostitución *f*, prostitution
prostituir *vt irr* to prostitute; *vr* become a prostitute; sell oneself, debase oneself. See **huir**
prostituta *f*, prostitute
protagonista *mf* hero or heroine, principal character; leading figure, protagonist
protección *f*, protection, defense; favor, aid
proteccionismo *m*, protectionism
proteccionista *mf* protectionist
protector *a* protective. *m*, protector; guard
protectorado *m*, protectorate
protectriz *f*, protectress
proteger *vt* to protect, defend; favor, assist
protegido (-da) *n* protégé
proteico *a* protean
proteína *f*, protein
protervia *f*, depravity, perversity
protervo *a* depraved, perverse
protesta, protestación *f*, protest; protestation, declaration
protestante *a* and *mf* Protestant
protestantismo *m*, Protestantism
protestar *vt* to declare, attest; (*with contra*) protest against; (*with de*) affirm vigorously
protesto *m*, *com* protest; objection
protocolizar *vt* to protocol, draw up
protocolo *m*, protocol
prototipo *m*, model, prototype
protuberancia *f*, protuberance, projection, swelling
provecto *a* ancient, venerable; mature, experienced
provecho *m*, gain, benefit; profit; advantage; progress, proficiency. **¡Buen p.!** Enjoy your food! Enjoy your meal! **ser de p.,** to be advantageous or useful
provechoso *a* beneficial; profitable; advantageous; useful
proveedor (-ra) *n* provider; purveyor, supplier
proveer *vt irr* to provide; furnish; supply; confer (an honor or office); transact, arrange. **p. de,** to furnish or supply with; fit with. See **creer**
provenir *vi irr* (*with de*) to originate in, proceed from. See **venir**
provenzal *a* and *mf* Provençal. *m*, Provençal (language)
proverbio *m*, proverb; omen; *pl* Book of Proverbs
providencia *f*, precaution, foresight; provision, furnishing; measure, preparation. **la Divina P.,** Providence
providencial *a* providential
próvido *a* provident, thrifty, careful; kind, favorable
provincia *f*, province; *fig* sphere
provincial *a* provincial. *m*, *ecc* provincial
provincialismo *m*, provincialism
provinciano (-na) *a* provincial. *n* provincial, rustic, countryman; native of Biscay
provisión *f*, stock, store; provision; supply; food supply (gen. *pl*); catering; means, way
provisional *a* temporary, provisional
provisor *m*, purveyor, supplier; *ecc* vicar general
provisorio, -a *a*, *Lat. Am.* = **provisional**
provocación *f*, provocation
provocador (-ra) *a* provocative. *n* provoker; instigator
provocar *vt* to provoke; incite; irritate; help, assist; *inf* vomit; *Lat. Am.* **¿te provoca ir al cine?** Would you like to go to the movies?
provocativo *a* provocative
próximamente *adv* proximately; soon; approximately
proximidad *f*, nearness, proximity (in time or space)
próximo *a* near, neighboring; next; not distant (of time)
proyección *f*, projection (all meanings)
proyectante *a* projecting, jutting
proyectar *vt* to throw, cast; plan, contrive; design; project; *vr* jut out; be cast (a shadow, etc.)
proyectil *m*, projectile
proyectista *mf* planner
proyecto *a* placed in perspective. *m*, project, plan, scheme; planning; intention, idea
proyector (-ra) *n* designer, planner. *m*, searchlight; spotlight; projector
prudencia *f*, prudence, sagacity, caution; moderation
prudencial *a* prudent, discreet; safe
prudente *a* prudent, cautious; provident
prueba *f*, proof; test; testing; trial; fitting (of garments); sample; taste; *law* evidence; (*phot print*) proof. *law* **p. de indicios** *or* **p. indiciaria,** circumstantial evidence. *phot* **p. negativa,** negative. *com* **a p.,** on approval; on trial; up to standard, perfect. **a p. de,** proof against (water, etc.). **poner a p.,** to put to the test, try out
prurito *m*, pruritus; desire, longing

ps- For words so beginning (e.g. *psicología, psiquiatría*), see spellings without **p**
púa *f*, prong; tooth (of a comb); quill (of a porcupine); *agr* graft; plectrum (for playing the mandolin, etc.); anxiety, grief; pine needle; *inf* crafty person
púber *a* pubescent
pubertad *f*, puberty
púbico *a* pubic
publicación *f*, publication; announcement, proclamation; revelation; publishing of marriage banns
publicador (-ra) *a* publishing. *n* publisher; announcer
publicar *vt* to publish; reveal; announce, proclaim; publish (marriage banns)
publicidad *f*, publicity; advertising, propaganda
publicista *mf* publicist; publicity agent
público *a* well-known, universal; common, general; public. *m*, public; audience; gathering, attendance. **dar al p.** *or* **sacar al p.,** to publish
pucherazo *m*, *inf* electoral fraud, vote-fixing
puchero *m*, *cul* kind of stew; stew pot; *inf* daily food; puckering of the face preceding tears
pudicia *f*, modesty; bashfulness; chastity
púdico *a* modest; bashful; chaste
pudiente *a* rich, wealthy; powerful
pudín *m*, pudding
pudor *m*, modesty; bashfulness, shyness
pudoroso *a* modest; shy
pudrir *vt* to rot, putrefy; irritate, worry, provoke; *vi* rot in the grave; *vr* rot; be consumed with anxiety
puebla *f*, town; population; gardener's seed setting
pueblada *f*, *Lat. Am.* riot; rebellion, revolt, uprising
pueblo *m*, town; village, hamlet; people, population, inhabitants; common people; working classes; nation
puente *mf* bridge; *mus* bridge (of stringed instruments); *naut* bridge; *carp* crossbeam, transom. **p. colgante,** suspension bridge. **p. levadizo,** drawbridge. **hacer p. de plata (a),** to remove obstacles for, make plain sailing
puerco *m*, pig; wild boar. *a* filthy; rough, rude; low, mean. **p. espín** *or* **p. espino,** porcupine. **p. marino,** dolphin. **p. montés** *or* **p. salvaje,** wild boar
puericultura *f*, child care
pueril *a* childish, puerile; foolish, silly; trivial
puerilidad *f*, puerility; foolishness; triviality
puerro *m*, leek
puerta *f*, door; gate; goal (football, soccer, hockey); means, way. **p. batiente,** swinging door. **p. caediza,** trapdoor. **p. corrediza,** sliding door. **p. de servicio,** tradesman's entrance. **p. falsa** *or* **p. secreta,** secret door; side door. **p. trasera,** back door. **a p. cerrada,** in camera; in secret. *inf* **dar con la p. en las narices (de),** to slam the door in a person's face; offend, insult. **llamar a la p.,** to knock at the door; be on the verge of happening. **tomar la p.,** to depart, go away
puerto *m*, harbor; port; defile, narrow pass; refuge, haven. **p. fluvial,** river port. **p. franco,** free port. **tomar p.,** to put into port; take refuge
Puerto Rico *m* Puerto Rico
puertorriqueño, -a *a* and *mf* Puerto Rican
pues *conjunc* then; since, as; for, because; well. *adv* yes, certainly. *conjunc* **p. que,** since, as
puesta *f*, *ast* setting, sinking; stake (in gambling). **p. al día,** aggiornamento, updating; modernization. **p. de largo,** coming of age; coming-out party. **p. del sol,** sunset
puesto *m*, post, job; booth, stall; beat, pitch; place, position; state, condition; *mil* encampment, barracks; office, position. **p. de los testigos,** witness box. **p. de mando,** command, position of authority.
puesto *a* (*with bien* or *mal*) well-or badly dressed. *conjunc* **p. que,** since, as; although
púgil *mf* pugilist, boxer
pugilato *m*, boxing; boxing match
pugilista *mf* boxer
pugna *f*, fight, struggle; rivalry, conflict
pugnante *a* hostile, conflicting, rival
pugnar *vi* to fight; quarrel; (*with con, contra*) struggle against, oppose; (*with por, para*) strive to
pugnaz *a* pugnacious
puja *f*, outbidding (at an auction); higher bid; push, thrust
pujador (-ra) *n* bidder or outbidder (at an auction)
pujante *a* strong, powerful, vigorous
pujanza *f*, strength, vigor
pujar *vt* to push on; bid or outbid (at an auction); *vi* stutter; hesitate, falter; *inf* show signs of weeping
pujo *m*, irresistible impulse; desire; will; purpose, intention
pulcritud *f*, beauty, loveliness, delicacy; fastidiousness, subtlety
pulcro *a* beautiful, lovely; delicate, fine; fastidious, subtle
pulga *f*, flea; small top (toy). **el juego de la p.,** tiddlywinks. *inf* **tener malas pulgas,** to be irritable
pulgada *f*, inch
pulgar *m*, thumb
pulgón *m*, aphid, greenfly
pulgoso *a* full of fleas
pulguiento *a*, *Lat. Am.* = **pulgoso**
pulidez *f*, elegance, fineness; polish, smoothness; neatness
pulido *a* elegant, fine; polished, smooth; neat
pulidor *m*, polisher (machine)
pulimentar *vt* to polish, burnish
pulir *vt* to polish, burnish; give the finishing touch to; beautify, decorate; *fig* polish up, civilize; *vr* beautify oneself; become polished and polite
pulmón *m*, lung
pulmonar *a* pulmonary
pulmonía *f*, pneumonia
pulpa *f*, fleshy part of fruit; *anat* pulp; wood pulp
pulpejo *m*, *anat* fleshy part, fat portion (of thumbs, etc.)
pulpería *f*, *WH* grocery, grocery store, general store; bar, tavern
púlpito *m*, pulpit
pulpo *m*, octopus. *inf* **poner como un p.,** to beat to a pulp
pulposo *a* pulpy, pulpous
pulquérrimo *a sup* **pulcro** most lovely, most exquisite
pulsación *f*, pulsation; throb, beat
pulsar *vt* to touch, feel; take the pulse of; *fig* explore (a possibility); *vi* beat (the heart, etc.)
pulsera *f*, bracelet; wrist bandage. **p. de pedida,** betrothal bracelet
pulso *m*, pulse; steadiness of hand; tact, diplomacy, circumspection. **a p.,** freehand (drawing). **tomar a p. (una cosa),** to try a thing's weight. **tomar el p. (a),** to take a person's pulse
pulular *vi* to pullulate, sprout; abound, be plentiful; swarm, teem; multiply (of insects)
pulverización *f*, pulverization; atomization
pulverizador *m*, atomizer, sprayer; scent spray
pulverizar *vt* to pulverize, grind, make into powder; atomize; spray
pulla *f*, lewd remark; strong hint; witty comment
¡pum! *interj* Bang! Thump!
pundonor *m*, (**punto de honor**) point of honor, sense of honor
pundonoroso *a* careful of one's honor; honorable, punctilious
pungir *vt* to prick, pierce; revive an old sorrow; *fig* wound, sting (passions)
punible *a* punishable
punitivo *a* punitive, punitory
punta *f*, sharp end, point; butt (of a cigarette); end, point, tip; cape, headland; trace, touch, suspicion; nib (of a pen); pointing (pointer dogs); *her* point; *pl* point lace. **p. de París,** wire nail. **p. seca,** drypoint, engraving needle. **sacar p.,** to sharpen; *inf* twist (a remark)
puntación *f*, dotting, placing dots over (letters)
puntada *f*, *sew* stitch; innuendo, hint

puntal *m, naut* draft, depth; stanchion, prop, brace, pile; *fig* basis, foundation; *Lat. Am.* bite (to eat), snack
puntapié *m,* kick
punteado *m,* plucking the strings of a guitar, etc.; sewing
puntear *vt* to make dots; *mus* pluck the strings of; play the guitar; sew; *art* stipple; *vi naut* tack
puntera *f,* mend in the toe of a stocking; toe cap; new piece on the toe of shoe; *inf* kick
puntería *f,* aiming (of a firearm); aim, sight (of a firearm); marksmanship
puntero *a* of a good aim, having a straight eye. *m,* pointer, wand; stonecutter's chisel
puntiagudo *a* pointed, sharp-pointed
puntilla *f,* narrow lace edging; headless nail, wire nail; brad, tack. **de puntillas,** on tiptoe
puntilloso *a* punctilious; overfastidious, fussy
punto *m.;* dot; point; pen nib; gun sight; *sew* stitch; dropped stitch, hole; weaving stitch, mesh; *gram* full stop, period; hole (in belts for adjustment); place, spot; point, mark; subject matter; *mech* cog; degree, extent; taxi stand; instant; infinitesimal amount; opportunity, chance; vacation, recess; aim, goal; point of honor. **p. de congelación,** freezing point. **p. de ebullición,** boiling point. **p. de fuga,** vanishing point. **p. de fusión,** melting point. **p. de partida,** starting point. **p. de vista,** point of view. **p. final,** *gram* period, full stop. **p. interrogante,** question mark. **p. menos,** a little less. **p. y coma,** semicolon. **p. cardinal,** cardinal point. **p. suspensivo,** *gram* ellipsis point, suspension point, leader, dot. **a p.,** in readiness; immediately. **en p.,** sharp, prompt (e.g. **a las seis en p.,** at six o'clock sharp)
puntoso *a* many-pointed
puntuación *f,* punctuation; *sport* score
puntual *a* punctual; punctilious; certain, indubitable; suitable, convenient
puntualidad *f,* punctuality; punctiliousness; certainty; exactitude, accuracy
puntualizar *vt* to describe in detail; give the finishing touch to, perfect; impress on the mind
puntualmente *adv* punctually; carefully, diligently; exactly
puntuar *vt* to punctuate
puntudo *a, Lat. Am.* = **puntiagudo**
punzada *f,* prick, sting; puncture, piercing; sudden pain, twinge, stitch; *fig* anguish, pain
punzar *vt* to pierce, puncture; prick; punch, perforate; *vi* revive, make itself felt (pain or sorrow)
punzón *m,* awl; punch; die; engraver's burin
puñado *m,* handful; a few, some, a small quantity. **a puñados,** in handfuls; liberally, lavishly
puñal *m,* dagger
puñalada *f,* dagger thrust; stab, wound; *fig* unexpected blow (of fate). **p. por la espalda,** stab in the back
puñetazo *m,* blow with the fist
puño *m,* fist; handful; cuff (of a sleeve); wristband; handle, head, haft; hilt (of a sword); *pl inf* guts, courage. **p. de amura,** *naut* tack. **p. de un manillar,** handlebar grip. *inf* **meter en un p.,** to overawe. *inf* **ser como un p.,** to be tightfisted; be small (in stature)
pupila *f,* female child ward; *anat* pupil; *inf* cleverness, talent
pupilaje *m,* pupilage, minority; boarding house, guesthouse; boarding school; price of board residence; dependence, bondage
pupilo (-la) *n* ward, minor; boarder; boarding school student; *Lat. Am.* prostitute, whore
pupitre *m,* desk, school desk
puquío *m Lat. Am.* spring (of water)
puramente *adv* purely; simply, solely; *law* unconditionally, without reservation
puré *m,* purée, thick soup
pureza *f,* purity; perfection, excellence; chastity; disinterestedness, genuineness; clearness
purga *f,* laxative, purge; waste product
purgación *f,* purging; menstruation; gonorrhea
purgante *a* purgative. *m,* purge, cathartic
purgar *vt* to cleanse, purify; expiate, atone for; (*med law*) purge; suffer purgatorial pains; clarify, refine; *vr* rid oneself, purge oneself
purgativo *a* purgative
purgatorio *m,* purgatory. *a* purgatorial
puridad *f,* purity; secrecy, privacy. **en p.,** openly, without dissembling; secretly, in private
purificación *f,* purification; cleansing
purificador (-ra) *a* purifying; cleansing. *n* purifier; cleanser
purificar *vt* to purify; cleanse; *vr* be purified
purificatorio *a* purificatory
Purísima (la) *f,* the Most Blessed Virgin
purista *mf* purist
puritano (-na) *a* puritanical. *n* Puritan
puro *a* pure; undiluted; unalloyed; unmixed; disinterested, honest; virgin; absolute, sheer; mere, simple. *m,* cigar. **de p.,** by sheer . . . , by dint of
púrpura *f,* purple; *poet* blood; purpura; *her* purpure; purple (cloth); dignity of an emperor, cardinal, consul
purpurear *vi* to look like purple; be tinged with purple
purpurina *f Lat. Am.* metallic paint
purulencia *f,* purulence
purulento *a* purulent
pus *m,* pus, matter
pusilánime *a* pusillanimous, timid, cowardly
pústula *f,* pustule
putativo *a* putative
putrefacción *f,* putrefaction; rottenness, putrescence
puto, -a *mf* prostitute
putrefacto *a* rotten, decayed
pútrido *a* putrid, rotten
puya *f,* goad
puyar *vt Lat. Am.* to jab, prick, stick; *fig* needle
puyazo *m,* prick with a goad

Q

que *pron. rel* all genders sing. and pl. who; which; that; whom; when (e.g. **Un poema en que habla de su juventud,** A poem in which he speaks of his youth. **El libro que tengo aquí,** The book (that) I have here. **No es oro todo lo que reluce,** All that glitters is not gold. **Un día que nos vimos,** One day when we met. *interr* **¿qué?** what? *interj* what a ———! what! how! (e.g. **¿Qué hay?** What's the matter? **¡Qué día más hermoso!** What a lovely day! **¿qué de . . . ?** how many? **¿qué tal?** how? *inf* **¿Qué tal estás hoy?** How are you today? **¿qué tanto?** how much?) **¿a qué?** why? for what reason? (e.g. **¿A qué negarlo?** Why deny it?). *conjunc* that (e.g. **Me dijo que vendría,** He said (that) he would come). Means 'so that,' 'that,' 'for,' in commands (e.g. **Mandó que le trajesen el libro,** He ordered that they bring him the book (He ordered them to bring him the book)). Note that the translation of **que** is often omitted in English.

In compound tenses where the participle is placed first, **que** means 'when' (e.g. **llegado que hube,** when I had arrived). In comparisons, **que** means 'than' (e.g. **más joven que yo,** younger than I).

With subjunctives and expressing commands or wishes, **que** means 'let' (e.g. **¡Que venga!** Let him come!) Preceding a subjunctive, **que** is generally translated by 'to' (e.g. **Quiero, que venga** *or* **que llueva,** I

want him to come *or* I want it to rain). Also means 'may' (e.g. **¡Que lo pase bien!** May you enjoy yourself! (I hope you . . .)). **es** (**era**) **que,** the fact is (was) that . . . **que . . . que,** whether . . . or . . .
quebrada *f,* mountain gorge, ravine; *com* bankruptcy; *Lat. Am.* brook, stream
quebradizo *a* brittle, fragile; ailing, infirm; delicate, frail
quebrado (-da) *m, math* fraction; *n com* bankrupt. *a* rough, uneven (ground); *med* ruptured; bankrupt; ailing, broken-down
quebradura *f,* snap, breaking; gap, crevice; hernia
quebraja *f,* split, crack; flaw (in wood, metal, etc.)
quebrantahuesos *m,* sea eagle, osprey; *inf* bore, tedious person
quebrantamiento *m,* crushing; splitting, cleaving; fracture, rupture; profanation, desecration; burglary; violation, breaking, infringement; fatigue; *law* annulment; exhaustion
quebrantanueces *m,* nutcrackers
quebrantaolas *m,* breakwater
quebrantar *vt* to break, shatter; crush, pound; transgress, infringe; break out, force; tone down, soften; moderate, lessen; bore, exhaust; move to pity; *inf* break in (horses); profane; overcome (difficulties); assuage, placate; *law* revoke (wills); *vr* be shaken or bruised, suffer from aftereffects
quebranto *m,* breaking, shattering; crushing, pounding; infringement; breaking out (from prison); weakness, exhaustion; compassion, pity; loss, damage; pain, suffering
quebrar *vt irr* to break, shatter; crush; impede, hinder; make pale (color, gen. of complexion); mitigate, moderate; bend, twist; overcome (difficulties); *vi* break off (a friendship); weaken, give way; go bankrupt; *vr med* suffer from hernia; be interrupted (of mountain ranges). **quebrarse los ojos,** to strain one's eyes. *Pres. Ind.* **quiebro, quiebras, quiebra, quiebran.** *Pres. Subjunc.* **quiebre, quiebres, quiebre, quiebren**
queda *f,* curfew; curfew bell
quedada *f,* stay, sojourn
quedar *vi* to stay, sojourn; remain; be left over; (*with por + infin.*) remain to be (e.g. **Queda por escribir,** It remains to be written); (*with por*) be won by or be knocked down to; be, remain in a place; end, cease; (*with en*) reach an agreement (e.g. **Quedamos en no ir,** We have decided not to go). **q. en esta alternativa . . . ,** to face this alternative: . . . . *vr* remain; abate (wind); grow calm (sea); (*with con*) keep, retain possession of. **q. bien o mal,** to behave well or badly, come off well or badly (in business affairs, etc.). **quedarse muerto,** to be astounded
quedo *a* still, motionless; quiet, tranquil. *adv* in a low voice; quietly, noiselessly. **de q.,** slowly, gradually. *interj* **¡Q.!** Quiet!
quehacer *m,* odd job; task; business (gen. *pl*)
queja *f,* lamentation, grief; complaint, grudge; quarrel
quejarse *vr* to lament; complain, grumble; *law* lodge an accusation (against)
quejido *m,* complaint, moan
quejoso *a* querulous, complaining
quejumbre *f,* complaint, whine; querulousness
quejumbroso *a* complaining, grumbling
quelite *m, Central America, Mexico* vegetables
quema *f,* burn; burning; fire, conflagration
quemadero *a* burnable. *m,* stake (for burning people)
quemado *m,* burned patch of forest; *inf* anything burned or burning
quemador (-ra) *m,* jet, burner. *n* incendiary
quemadura *f,* burn; scald; burning
quemajoso *a* smarting, burning, pricking
quemar *vt* to burn; dry up, parch; scorch; tan, bronze; scald; throw away, sell at a loss; *vi* burn, be excessively hot; *vr* be very hot; be dried up with the heat; burn with (passions); *inf* be near the attainment of a desired end. **quemarse las cejas,** to burn the midnight oil, study too hard
quemazón *f,* burning; conflagration; intense heat; *inf* smarting; *inf* hurtful remark; *inf* vexation, soreness
quena *f* kind of Native American flute
querella *f,* complaint; quarrel, fight
querellarse *vr* to complain; lament, bemoan; *law* lodge an accusation; *law* contest a will
querelloso *a* complaining, grumbling, querulous
querencia *f,* love, affection; homing instinct; lair; natural inclination or desire
querer *vt irr* to desire, wish; want, will; attempt, endeavor; (*with a*) love. *impers* be on the point of. **q. decir,** to mean. **¿Qué quiere decir esto?** What does this mean? **sin q.,** unintentionally. See **entender**
querer *m,* affection, love
querido (-da) *n* lover; beloved; darling. *a* dear
querub, querube *poet* **querubín** *m,* cherub
querúbico *a* cherubic
quesadillas, *fpl, Mexico* maize dough with beans or cheese fried like a turnover
quesera *f,* dairymaid; dairy; cheese vat; cheese board; cheese dish
quesería *f,* dairy; cheese shop; season for making cheese
queso *m,* cheese. **q. de bola,** Dutch cheese. **q. rallado,** grated cheese
quetzal *m,* quetzal (monetary unit of Guatemala)
quevedos *m pl,* glasses, eyeglasses; pince-nez
¡quia! *interj inf* You don't say so!
quianti *m,* chianti
quicial *m,* doorjamb
quicio *m,* threshold; hinge; *mech* bushing. **fuera de q.,** out of order; unhinged. **sacar de q.,** to displace (things); annoy, irritate; drive crazy
quiebra *f,* breach, crack; rut, fissure; loss; bankruptcy
quiebro *m,* twisting of the body, dodging; *mus* trill
quien *rel pron mf pl* **quienes.** *interr* **quién, quiénes** who; whom; he (she, etc.) who, anyone who, whoever; which; whichever (e.g. **mis padres a quienes respeto,** my parents whom I respect. **Quien te quiere te hará llorar,** Whoever (he, those, who) love(s) you will make you weep. **¿Quién está a la puerta?** Who is at the door? **¿De quién es?** Whose is it? To whom does it belong?). *indef pron* one (*pl* some)
quienquiera *indef pron mf pl* **quienesquiera,** whosoever, whichever, whomsoever
quietador (-ra) *a* tranquilizing, soothing. *n* soother
quieto *a* quiet, still; peaceful, tranquil; virtuous, respectable
quietud *f,* stillness, repose; peacefulness; rest, quietness
quif *m,* hashish, marijuana
quijada *f,* jawbone, jaw; *mech* jaw
quijo *m,* ore (gold or silver)
quijotada *f,* quixotic action, quixotism
quijote *m,* cuisse; thigh guard; quixotic person
quijotesco *a* quixotic
quilate *m,* carat; degree of excellence (gen. *pl*). *inf* **por quilates,** in small bits, parsimoniously
quilla *f, naut* keel; breastbone (of birds)
quillotrar *vt inf* to encourage, incite; woo, make love to; consider; *vr inf* fall in love; dress up; whine, complain
quillotro *m, inf* incentive; indication, sign; love affair; puzzle, knotty point; compliment; dressing up
quimera *f,* chimera; fancy, vision; quarrel, dispute
quimérico *a* chimerical, fanciful
quimerista *mf* dreamer, visionary; quarreler, disputant
química *f,* chemistry
químico *a* chemical. *m,* chemist. **productos químicos,** chemicals
quimono *m,* kimono
quina *f,* cinchona; quinine; *pl* Arms of Portugal. *inf* **tragar q.,** to suffer in patience, put up with
quinario *m, Argentina* mud hut

quincalla *f*, cheap jewelery; fancy goods
quincallería *f*, cheap jewelery shop; hardware factory or industry; cheap jewelry; fancy goods
quince *a* and *m*, fifteen; fifteenth
quinceañero *f*, sweet sixteen party, sweet sixteen (in Spanish-speaking areas, held at age fifteen)
quincena *f*, fortnight, two weeks; bimonthly pay; *mus* fifteenth
quincenal *a* fortnightly; lasting a fortnight, lasting two weeks
quinceno *a* fifteenth
quincuagenario *a* quinquagenarian
quincuagésimo *a* fiftieth
quindécimo *a* fifteenth
quinientos *a* five hundred; five-hundredth. *m*, five hundred
quinina *f*, quinine
quinqué *m*, oil lamp, student's lamp, table lamp; perspicuity, talent
quinquenio *m*, period of five years, lustrum
quinta *f*, country house; *mus* fifth; conscripting men into army by drawing lots; *mil* draft
quintaesencia *f*, quintessence
quintal *m*, hundredweight
quintar *vt* to draw one out of every five; draw lots for conscription into the army; *vi* reach the fifth (day, etc., gen. of the moon)
quintería *f*, farm
quintero *m*, farmer; farmworker
quinteto *m*, quintet
Quintín, San. armarse (*or* **haber**) **la de San Q.** to quarrel, make trouble; be a row
quinto *a* fifth. *m*, one-fifth; *mil* conscript; duty of twenty percent; *law* fifth part of an estate. **quinta columna,** fifth column. **quinta esencia,** quintessence
quintuplicar *vt* to quintuplicate
quíntuplo *a* fivefold, quintuple
quiñón *m*, share of land owned jointly, share of the profits
quiosco *m*, kiosk, stand; pavilion, pagoda. **q. de música,** bandstand
quipo *m* quipu (Native American rope writing in Peru)
quiquiriquí *m*, cock-a-doodle-doo; *fig inf* cock of the walk
quiromancia *f*, chiromancy, palmistry
quiromántico (-ca) *n* chiromancer, palmist
quirúrgico *a* surgical
quirurgo *m*, surgeon
quisicosa *f*, *inf* riddle, puzzle, enigma
quisquilla *f*, trifle, quibble, scruple; prawn, shrimp
quisquilloso *a* quibbling, overscrupulous, fastidious; hypersensitive; irascible, touchy
quistarse *vr* to make oneself well-liked or loved
quiste *m*, *med* cyst
quita *f*, *law* discharge (of part of a debt)
quitaesmalte *m*, nail polish remover (for fingernails)
quitamanchas *mf*, dry cleaner, clothes cleaner
quitamotas *mf inf* flatterer, adulator
quitanieve *m*, snowplow
quitanza *f*, quittance; quietus
quitapesares *m*, *inf* consolation, solace, comfort
quitar *vt* to remove; take off or away; clear (the table); rob, steal; prevent, impede; parry (in fencing); separate; redeem (pledges); forbid; annul, repeal (laws, etc.); free from (obligations); *vr* shed, take off, remove; get rid of; leave, quit. **quitarse de encima (a),** to get rid of someone or something. **q. el polvo,** to dust. **de quita y pon,** detachable, removable; adjustable
quitasol *m*, parasol, sunshade
quitasueño *m*, *inf* sleep banisher, anxiety
quite *m*, hindering, impeding; obstruction; parry (in fencing). **estar al q.,** to be ready to protect someone
quizá, quizás *adv* perhaps. **q. y sin q.,** without doubt, certainly

R

rabadán *m*, head shepherd or herdsman
rabadilla *f*, rump, croup
rábano *m*, radish. **r. picante,** horseradish
rabel *m*, *mus* rebec; *inf* backside, seat
rabera *f*, tail-end; chaff, siftings
rabí *m*, rabbi
rabia *f*, rabies, hydrophobia; anger, fury. *inf* **tener r. (a),** to hate
rabiar *vi* to suffer from hydrophobia; groan with pain; be furious; (*with por*) yearn for, desire. **a r.,** excessively
rabieta *f*, *inf* tantrum
rabínico *a* rabbinical
rabinismo *m*, rabbinism
rabino *m*, rabbi. **gran r.,** chief rabbi
rabioso *a* rabid; furious, angry; vehement. **perro r.,** mad dog
rabo *m*, tail; *bot* stalk; *inf* train (of a dress); shank (of a button). **r. del ojo,** corner of the eye. *fig inf* **ir r. entre piernas,** to have one's tail between one's legs
rabón *a* tailless, docked; bobtailed
rabonear *vi*, *Lat. Am.* to play hookey
rabudo *a* big-tailed
racimo *m*, bunch (of grapes or other fruits); cluster; raceme
raciocinar *vi* to reason
raciocinio *m*, reasoning; ratiocination; discourse, speech
ración *f*, ration; portion (in a restaurant); meal allowance; *ecc* prebendary. *inf* **r. de hambre,** starvation diet; pittance, starvation wages
racional *a* reasonable, logical; rational
racionalidad *f*, reasonableness; rationality
racionalismo *m*, rationalism
racionalista *a* and *mf* rationalist. *a* rationalistic
racionalización *f*, rationalization
racionamiento *m*, rationing. *f*. **cartilla de r.,** ration book
racionar *vt* to ration
rada *f*, bay, cove; *naut* road, roadstead
radar *m*, radar
radiación *f*, radiation; *rad* broadcasting
radiactividad *f*, radioactivity
radiactivo *a* radioactive
radiador *m*, radiator (for heating); *aut* radiator
radial *a* radial
radiante *a phys* radiating; brilliant, shining; *fig* beaming (with satisfaction)
radiar *vi phys* to radiate; *vt* broadcast (by radio); *Lat. Am.* to cross off, delete, erase
radical *a* radical; fundamental; *pol* radical. *m*, *gram* root; (*math chem*) radical. *mf pol* radical
radicalismo *m*, radicalism
radicar(se) *vi* and *vr* to take root. **r. una solicitud,**file an application, submit an application. *vi* be (in a place)
radio *m*, (*geom anat*) radius; radium. *f*, radio
radioaficionado (-da) *n* radio amateur; *inf* ham, wireless fan or enthusiast
radioaudición *f*, radio broadcast
radiocomunicación *f*, radio transmission
radiodifundir *vt rad* to broadcast
radiodifusión, radioemisión *f*, *rad* broadcast; broadcasting
radiodifusora *f*, *Lat. Am.* = **radioemisora**
radioemisora *f*, radio station; (radio) transmitter
radioescucha *mf* radio listener
radiofotografía *f*, radiophotography; x-ray photograph. **tomar una r. de,** to x-ray
radiofrecuencia *f*, radiofrequency

radiografía *f*, radiography
radiografiar *vt* to x-ray, radiograph
radiografista *mf* radiographer
radiograma *m*, radiogram, cable
radiolocación *f*, radiolocation
radiología *f*, radiology
radiólogo *mf* radiologist
radiometría *f*, radiometry
radiómetro *m*, radiometer
radiorreceptor *m*, receiver, wireless set
radioscopia *f*, radioscopy
radioyente *mf* radio listener
radiotelefonía *f*, radiotelephony
radiotelegrafía *f*, radiotelegraphy
radiotelegráfico *a* radiotelegraphic, wireless
radiotelegrafista *mf* wireless operator
radiotelegrama *m*, radiogram, radiotelegram
radioterapia *f*, radiotherapy, radiotherapeutics
radiotransmisor *m*, (radio) transmitter
raedera *f*, scraper
raedor *a* scraping; abrasive
raedura *f*, scraping; rubbing; fraying
raer *vt irr* to scrape; abrade; fray; *fig* extirpate. See **caer**
ráfaga *f*, gust or blast of wind; light cloud; flash (of light)
rafe *m*, eaves
rafia *f*, raffia
raicear *vi*, *Lat. Am.* to take root
raído *a* frayed, threadbare; brazen, barefaced
raíz *f*, root. **r. amarga,** horseradish. **r. cuadrada (cúbica),** square (cubed) root. **r. pivotante,** tap root. **r. fuerte,** *Mexico* horseradish **a r.,** close to the root, closely. **a r. de,** as a result of; after. **de r.,** from the root, entirely. **echar raíces,** to take root
raja *f*, split, crack; chip, splinter (of wood); slice (of fruit, etc.)
rajadura *f*, splitting; crack, split, crevice; *geol* break
rajar *vt* to crack, split; slice; *vi inf* boast; chatter; *vr* crack, split; *inf* take back one's words
ralea *f*, kind, quality; (*inf* scornful) race, lineage
ralear *vi* to grow thin (cloth, etc.); behave true to type (gen. in a bad sense)
rallador *m*, *cul* grater
rallar *vt cul* to grate; *inf* bother, annoy
rallo *m*, *cul* grater; rasp
ralo *a* sparse, thin
rama *f*, bough, branch; *fig* branch (of family). *fig inf* **andarse por las ramas,** to beat around the bush. **en r.,** *com* raw; unbound (of books)
ramaje *m*, thickness of branches, denseness of foliage
ramal *m*, strand (of rope); halter; branch line (of a railroad); fork (of a road, etc.); ramification, division
ramalazo *m*, blow with a rope; mark left by this; bruise
rambla *f*, bed, channel, course; avenue, boulevard (in Catalonia)
ramera *f*, whore
ramificación *f*, ramification; *anat* bifurcation
ramificarse *vr* to branch, fork; *fig* spread
ramillete *m*, bouquet; table centerpiece; *bot* cluster
ramo *m*, *bot* branch; twig, spray; bouquet, bunch; wreath; *fig* branch (of learning, etc.); *com* line (of business); *fig* touch, slight attack. **Domingo de Ramos,** Palm Sunday
ramoso *a* branchy, thick with branches
rampa *f*, gradient, incline; *mil* ramp; launching site
ramplón *a* stout, heavy (of shoes); coarse; vulgar; bombastic
rana *f*, frog. **r. de San Antonio,** tree frog
ranchero *m*, *mil* cook; small farmer; *WH* rancher
rancho *m*, mess, rations; settlement, camp; hut, cabin; *inf* group, huddle; *WH* ranch; *naut* gang. **hacer r.,** *inf* to make room
rancidez *f*, rancidness; staleness; rankness; antiquity
ranciedad *f*, rancidness; antiquity, oldness; mustiness
rancio *a* rancid, rank; mellow (of wine); ancient; traditional; musty
rancotán *adv*, *Lat. Am.* in cash
rango *m*, grade, class; range; (*mil nav* and social) rank; file, line
ranura *f*, groove; rabbet; slot, notch
rapacidad *f*, rapacity, avidity, greed
rapador *a* scraping. *m*, *inf* barber
rapapolvo *m*, *inf* severe scolding, dressing-down
rapar(se) *vt* and *vr* to shave; *vt* crop, cut close (hair); *inf* steal, pinch
rapaz *a* rapacious. *m*, young boy. **ave r.,** bird of prey
rapaza *f*, young girl
rape *m*, *inf* hasty shave or haircut. **al r.,** close-cropped
rapidez *f*, speed, swiftness, rapidity
rápido *a* quick, swift; express (trains). *m*, torrent, rapid; express train
rapiña *f*, robbery, plundering, sacking
rapiñar *vt inf* to steal, pinch
raposa *f*, vixen, fox; *inf* wily person
raposo *m*, (male) fox
raposear *vi* to behave like a fox
rapsodia *f*, rhapsody
raptar *vt* to abduct; rob
rapto *m*, abduction, rape; snatching, seizing; ecstasy, trance; *med* loss of consciousness
raptor *m*, kidnapper, abductor
raquero *a* pirate. *m*, wrecker; pickpocket, dock rat
raqueta *f*, racket (tennis, badminton, squash rackets); croupier's rake. **r. de nieve,** snowshoe
raquianestesia *f*, spinal anesthesia
raquítico *a med* rachitic; small, minute; weak, feeble; rickety
raquitismo *m*, rickets
rarefacer(se) *vt* and *vr irr* to rarefy. See **satisfacer**
rareza *f*, rareness, unusualness; eccentricity, whim; oddity, curio
raridad *f*, rarity; thinness; scarcity
raro *a* rare, unusual, uncommon; notable, outstanding; odd, eccentric, queer; rarefied (gases, etc.). **rara vez,** seldom. **lo r. de,** the strange thing about (e.g. **Lo r. del caso es . . . ,** the strange thing about the case is . . .)
ras *m*, level. **a r.,** flush (with), nearly touching
rasa *f*, worn place in cloth; clearing, glade
rasar *vt* to level with a strickle; graze, brush, touch lightly; *vr* grow clear (of the sky, etc.)
rascacielos *m*, skyscraper
rascador *m*, scraper; ornamental hairpin
rascadura *f*, scraping; scratching
rascar *vt* to scratch; claw; scrape; twang (a guitar, etc.). *inf* **¡Que se rasque!** Let him put up with it! Let him lump it!
rascatripas *m*, *inf* caterwauler, squeaker (of violinists, etc.)
rascón *a* sour, tart
rasgado, -a *a*, *Lat. Am.* outspoken
rasgadura *f*, tearing; tear, rip, rent
rasgar(se) *vt* and *vr* to tear, rip; *vt* strum the guitar
rasgo *m*, flourish (of the pen); felicitous expression; characteristic, quality; *Lat. Am.* irrigation channel; *pl* features (of the face)
rasgón *m*, rip, tear
rasguear *vt* to strum, twang (the guitar); *vi* write with a flourish
rasgueo *m*, flourish (on a guitar); scratch (of a pen)
rasguñar *vt* to scratch, scrape; claw; *art* sketch
rasguño *m*, scratch; *art* sketch, outline
raso *a* flat; free of obstacles; glossy; clear (sky, etc.); plain; undistinguished; backless (chairs). *m*, satin. **al r.,** in the open air
raspa *f*, *bot* beard (of cereals); fishbone; bunch of grapes; *bot* husk; *carp* scraper
raspador *m*, eraser; scraper, rasp
raspadura *f*, scraping; erasing; shavings, filings; *Lat. Am.* brown sugar
raspar *vt* to scrape; erase; rob, steal; burn, bite (wine, etc.); *Lat. Am.* scold; *inf* to fail (student), fire (employee)
rastra *f*, trace, sign; sled; string of onions, etc.; anything

dragging; *agr* harrow; *agr* rake. **a la r.,** dragging; reluctantly. **pescar a la r.,** to trawl
rastreador *m, naut* minesweeper. *a* dragging
rastrear *vt* to trace, trail; drag, trawl; surmise, conjecture, investigate; *vi agr* rake; fly low
rastreo *m,* dragging (of lakes, etc.)
rastrero *a* dragging, trailing; low-flying; servile, abject; *bot* creeping. *m,* slaughterhouse employee
rastrillador (-ra) *n* raker; hackler
rastrilladora *f,* mechanical harrow
rastrillaje *m,* raking
rastrillar *vt* to rake; dress, comb (flax)
rastrillo *m, agr* rake; hackle; portcullis; *agr* rack
rastro *m, agr* rake; track, trail; wholesale meat market; slaughterhouse; trace, vestige; second-hand market (in Madrid)
rastrojo *m,* stubble; stubble field
rasura *f,* shaving
rasurar(se) *vt* and *vr* to shave
rata *f,* rat. *m, inf* pickpocket. **r. almizclera,** muskrat. *inf* **más pobre que las ratas,** poorer than a church mouse
rataplán *m,* rub-a-dub-dub, beating of a drum
ratear *vt* to rebate pro rata; apportion; thieve on a small scale, filch; *vi* crawl, creep
ratería *f,* filching, petty theft, picking pockets; meanness, parsimony
ratero (-ra) *n* pilferer, petty thief, pickpocket
ratificación *f,* ratification
ratificador (-ra) *n* ratifier
ratificar *vt* to ratify
ratificatorio *a* ratifying, confirmatory
rato *m,* short interval of time, while. **buen (mal) r.,** pleasant (unpleasant) time. **r. perdido,** leisure moment. **a ratos,** sometimes, occasionally. **de r. en r.,** from time to time. **pasar el r.,** *inf* to while away the time
ratón (-ona) *n* mouse
ratonera *f,* mousetrap; mousehole; mouse nest; *Lat. Am.* hovel. *fig* **caer en la r.,** to fall into a trap
ratonero, ratonesco, ratonil *a* mousy
rauco *a poet* hoarse
raudal *m,* torrent, cascade; *fig* flood, abundance
raudo *a* swift, rapid
ravioles *m pl,* ravioli
raya *f,* stripe, streak; limit, end; part (of the hair); boundary; *gram* dash; score (some games). *m, icht* ray. **pasar de r.,** to go too far; misbehave
rayadillo *m,* striped cotton
rayano *a* neighboring; border; almost identical, very similar
rayar *vt* to draw lines; streak; stripe; cross out; underline; rifle (a gun); *vi* verge (on), border (on); appear (of dawn, daylight); excel; be similar. **Raya en los catorce años,** He is about fourteen
rayo *m, phys* beam, ray; thunderbolt; flash of lightning; spoke; quick-witted person; capable, energetic person; sudden pain; disaster, catastrophe. **r. de sol,** sunbeam. **r. catódico,** cathode ray. **r. x,** x-ray. *fig* **echar rayos,** to breathe forth fury
rayón *m,* rayon
raza *f,* race; breed; lineage, family; kind, class; crack, crevice. **de r.,** purebred
razón *f,* reason; reasoning; word, expression; speech, argument; motive, cause; order, method; justice, equity; right, authority; explanation; *math* ratio, proportion. **r. de estado,** raison d'état, reasons of state. *com* **r. social,** firm, trade name. **a r. de,** at a rate of. **dar la r. (a),** to agree with. **estar puesto en r.,** to stand to reason. **tener r.,** to be in the right
razonable *a* reasonable; moderate
razonador (-ra) *n* reasoner
razonamiento *m,* reasoning
razonar *vi* to reason; speak; *vt* attest, confirm
razzia *f,* foray; pillaging, sacking; police raid
re *m, mus* re, D
reabsorción *f,* reabsorption
reacción *f,* reaction. **r. de Bayardo,** quick reaction of someone always ready to help those in distress
reaccionar *vi* to react
reaccionario (-ia) *a* and *n* reactionary
reaccionarismo *m,* reactionism
reacio *a* recalcitrant
reactivo *m,* reagent. *a* reactive; reacting
readmisión *f,* readmission
readmitir *vt* to readmit
reajustar *vt* to readjust
real *a* actual, real; kingly; royal; royalist; *fig* regal; *inf* fine, handsome. *m,* silver coin, real; *m pl,* encampment, camp. **alzar el r.,** *mil* to strike camp. **asentar el r.,** *mil* to encamp. **r. decreto,** royal decree. **sitio r.,** royal residence. **un r., sobre otro,** *inf* cash in full
realce *m,* raised or embossed work; renown, glory; *art* high light
realeza *f,* royalty, royal majesty
realidad *f,* reality; sincerity, truth. **en r.,** in fact, actually
realismo *m,* realism; regalism; royalism
realista *a* realistic; royalist. *mf* realist; royalist; regalist
realizable *a* realizable; practicable
realización *f,* realization; performance, execution
realizar *vt* to perform, execute, carry out; *com* realize. **r. beneficio,** to make a profit
realmente *adv* really, truly; actually
realzar *vt* to heighten, raise; emboss; exalt; enhance; *art* intensify (colors, etc.)
reanimar *vt* to reanimate; revive, restore, resuscitate; encourage
reanudación *f,* resumption, renewal
reanudar *vt* to resume, continue
reaparecer *vi irr* to reappear. See **conocer**
reaparición *f,* reappearance
rearmamento *m,* rearmament
rearmar *vi* to rearm
reasegurador *m,* underwriter
reasegurar *vt* to reinsure, underwrite
reaseguro *m,* reinsurance, underwriting
reasunción *f,* reassumption; resumption
reata *f,* string of horses or mules. **de r.,** in single file; *inf* blindly, unquestioningly; *inf* at once
rebaja *f,* diminution; *com* discount, rebate; remission
rebajar *vt* to lower; curtail, lessen; remit; *com* reduce in price; *mech* file; *elec* step down; humble, humiliate; *vr* cringe, humble oneself
rebajo *m,* reduction (in price, etc.); rabbet
rebanada *f,* slice, piece (of bread, etc.)
rebanar *vt* to cut into slices; split
rebaño *m,* flock, drove, herd; *ecc* flock
rebasar *vt* to exceed, go beyond; *mil* bypass
rebate *m,* altercation, dispute, quarrel
rebatiña *f,* grab; scrimmage. **andar a la r.,** to scuffle
rebatir *vt* to repulse, repel; fight again; fight hard; oppose, resist; *com* deduct; refuse, reject
rebato *m,* alarm, tocsin; *mil* surprise attack; panic, dismay
rebeca *f,* cardigan, jersey
rebeco *m, zool* chamois
rebelarse *vr* to mutiny, rebel; oppose, resist
rebelde *a* mutinous, rebellious; wilful, disobedient; stubborn. *mf* rebel
rebeldía *f,* rebelliousness; willfulness; stubbornness; *law* nonappearance
rebelión *f,* insurrection, revolt
rebenque *m, Lat. Am.* whip
rebién *adv* very well, extremely well
rebisabuelo (-la) *n.* See **tatarabuelo**
reblandecer *vt irr* to soften; *vr* become soft. See **conocer**
reblandecimiento *m,* softening; *med* flabbiness
reborde *m,* rim, edge; *mech* flange. **r. de acera,** curb
rebordear *vt* to flange

rebosar *vi* to overflow, run over; *fig* abound in; express one's feelings
rebotar *vi* to rebound; clinch (nails, etc.); refuse; *vr* change color; *inf* be vexed
rebote *m*, rebounding; rebound
rebotica *f*, back room of a pharmacy; back of a shop
rebozar *vt* to muffle up; coat with batter
rebozo *m*, muffling up, hiding the face; head shawl; pretense, excuse. *fig* **sin r.,** openly
rebueno *a inf* extremely good, fine
rebullicio *m*, uproar, clamor
rebullir *vi* to stir, show signs of movement; *fig* swarm, seethe
rebusca *f*, close search; gleaning; remains
rebuscado *a* affected, unnatural (of style)
rebuscar *vt* to search for; glean
rebuznar *vi* to bray
recadero (-ra) *n* messenger, errand boy
recado *m*, message; greeting, note; gift, present; daily marketing; outfit, implements; precaution, safeguard
recaer *vi irr* to fall again; *med* relapse; lapse, backslide; devolve, fall upon. See **caer**
recaída *f*, falling again; *med* relapse; lapse
recalar *vt* to impregnate; *naut* call at (a port), come within sight of land
recalcada *f*, pressing down, squeezing; emphasis; *naut* list
recalcar *vt* to press down; squeeze; pack tight; stress, emphasize; *vi naut* list; *vr inf* say over and over, savor one's words
recalcitrante *a* obdurate, recalcitrant
recalentador *m*, *mech* superheater
recalentar *vt irr* to overheat; superheat; reheat. See **sentar**
recamado *m*, raised embroidery
recámara *f*, dressing room; explosives chamber; breech of a gun; *inf* caution
recamarera *f*, *Mexico* chambermaid
recambio *m*, spare, spare part; *com* re-exchange
recantación *f*, retraction, recantation
recapacitar *vi* to search one's memory; think over
recapitulación *f*, summary, résumé
recapitular *vt* to recapitulate, summarize
recargar *vt* to recharge; load again; reaccuse; overcharge; overdress or overdecorate; *vr med* become more feverish. **r. acumuladores,** to recharge batteries
recargo *m*, charge; new load; *law* new accusation; overcharge, extra cost; *med* temperature increase
recatado *a* prudent, discreet, circumspect; modest, shy
recatar *vt* to hide, conceal; *vr* be prudent or cautious
recato *m*, caution, prudence; modesty, shyness, reserve
recauchutar *vt* to retread (tires)
recaudación *f*, collecting; collection (of taxes, etc.); tax collector's office
recaudador *m*, tax collector
recaudar *vt* to collect, recover (taxes, debts, etc.); deposit, place in custody
recaudo *m*, collecting; collection (of taxes, etc.); precaution, safeguard; *law* surety; *Lat. Am.* daily supply of vegetables
recelar *vt* to suspect, fear, mistrust; *vr* (*with de*) be afraid or suspicious of
recelo *m*, suspicion, mistrust, doubt, fear
receloso *a* suspicious, distrustful, doubtful
recepción *f*, receiving, reception; admission, acceptance; reception, party; *law* cross-examination
receptáculo *m*, receptacle, container; *fig* refuge; *bot* receptacle
receptador (-ra) *n* receiver (of stolen goods); accomplice
receptivo *a* receptive
receptor (-ra) *a* receiving. *n* recipient. *m*, *elec* receiver; wireless set. **r. de galena,** crystal set. **r. telefónico,** telephone receiver
receta *f*, *med* prescription; *cul* recipe
recetar *vt med* to prescribe; *inf* demand
rechapear *vt* to replate
rechazar *vt* to repulse; resist; refuse; oppose, deny (the truth of); contradict
rechazo *m*, recoil; rebound; refusal
rechinamiento, rechino *m*, squeaking, creaking; gnashing (of teeth)
rechinar *vi* to squeak, creak; gnash (teeth); chatter (teeth); do with a bad grace
rechoncho *a* squat, stocky, thickset
reciamente *adv* hard; strongly, firmly, vigorously
recibí *m*, *com* receipt
recibidor (-ra) *a* receiving. *n* recipient. *m*, reception room
recibimiento *m*, reception; welcome, greeting; reception room, waiting room; hall, vestibule
recibir *vt* to obtain, receive; support, bear; suffer, experience (attack, injury); approve; accept, receive; entertain; stand up to (attack); *vr* (*with de*) graduate as, take office as
recibo *m*, reception; *com* receipt; reception room, waiting room; hall, vestibule. *com* **acusar r.,** to acknowledge receipt
recidiva *f*, *med* relapse
recién *adv* recently, newly. Shortened form of **reciente** before a past participle (e.g. **r. llegado,** newly arrived)
reciente *a* recent; new; fresh
recinto *m*, precincts; neighborhood; premises, place
recio *a* strong; robust; bulky, thick; rough, uncouth; grievous, hard; severe (weather); impetuous, precipitate
recipiente *a* receiving. *m*, receptacle, container, vessel
reciprocar *vt* to reciprocate
reciprocidad *f*, reciprocity; reciprocation
recíproco *a* reciprocal
recitación *f*, recitation
recitado *m*, recitative
recitador (-ra) *n* elocutionist, reciter
recitar *vt* to recite, declaim
reclamación *f*, reclamation; objection, opposition; *com* claim
reclamar *vi* to oppose, object to; *poet* resound; *vt* call repeatedly; *com* claim; decoy (birds)
reclamo *m*, decoy bird; enticement, allurement; *law* reclamation; advertisement. **objeto de r.,** advertising sample. **venta de r.,** bargain sale
reclinación *f*, reclining; leaning
reclinatorio *m*, couch; prie-dieu
recluir *vt irr* to immure, shut up; detain, arrest. See **huir**
reclusión *f*, confinement, seclusion; prison
recluso (-sa) *n* recluse
recluta *f*, recruiting. *mf mil* recruit
reclutador *m*, recruiting office
reclutamiento *m*, recruiting
reclutar *vt* to enlist recruits, recruit; *Argentina* round up
recobrar *vt* to recover, regain; *vr* recuperate; regain consciousness
recobro *m*, recovery; *mech* pick-up
recocer *vt irr* to reboil; recook; overboil; overcook; anneal (metals); *vr fig* be tormented (by emotion), be all burned up. See **cocer**
recodo *m*, bend, turn, loop
recogedor *a* sheltering. *m*, *agr* gleaner
recoger *vt* to gather, pick; pick up; retake; collect (letters from a mailbox, etc.); amass; shrink, narrow; keep; hoard; shelter; reap, pick; *vr* withdraw, retire; go home; go to bed; retrench, economize; give oneself to meditation
recogida *f*, collection (of letters from a mailbox); withdrawal; retirement; harvest
recogido *a* recluse; cloistered, confined
recogimiento *m*, gathering, picking; collection, accumulation; seclusion; shelter; women's reformatory
recolección *f*, summary, résumé; harvest; collection (of taxes, etc.); *ecc* convent of a reformed order; mystic ecstasy

recoleto *a ecc* reformed (of religious orders); recluse
recomendable *a* commendable, recommendable
recomendación *f,* recommendation (all meanings)
recomendar *vt irr* to recommend (all meanings); entrust, commend. *Pres. Ind.* **recomiendo, recomiendas, recomienda, recomiendan.** *Pres. Subjunc.* **recomiende, recomiendes, recomiende, recomienden**
recompensa *f,* compensation; recompense, reward
recompensar *vt* to compensate; requite; reward, recompense
recomposición *f,* recomposition
recomprar *vt* to repurchase
reconcentrar *vt* to concentrate; dissemble; *vr* withdraw into oneself, meditate
reconciliable *a* reconcilable
reconciliación *f,* reconciliation
reconciliador (-ra) *a* reconciliatory. *n* reconciler
reconciliar *vt* to reconcile; *ecc* reconsecrate; *ecc* hear a short confession; *vr* become reconciled; *ecc* make an additional confession
recondicionar *vt* to rebuild, overhaul, recondition
recóndito *a* recondite
reconocer *vt irr* to examine, inspect; recognize; admit, acknowledge; own, confess; search; *pol* recognize; *mil* reconnoiter; (*with por*) adopt as (a son, etc.); recognize as; *vr* be seen, show; acknowledge, confess; know oneself. **Bien se reconoce que no está aquí,** It's easy to see he's not here. See **conocer**
reconocido *a* grateful
reconocimiento *m,* examination, inspection; recognition; acknowledgement, admission; search; *mil* reconnoitering; adoption; gratitude
reconquista *f,* reconquest
reconquistar *vt* to reconquer; *fig* recover, win back
reconstitución *f,* reconstitution
reconstituir *vt irr* to reconstitute. See **huir**
reconstituyente *m, med* tonic
reconstrucción *f,* reconstruction
reconstruir *vt irr* to reconstruct, rebuild; recreate. See **huir**
reconvención *f,* rebuke, reproof; recrimination; *law* countercharge
reconversión *f,* reconversion
recopilación *f,* summary, compendium; collection (of writings); digest (of laws)
recopilador *m,* compiler
recopilar *vt* to compile, collect
recordar *vt irr* to cause to remember, remind; remember; *vi* remember; awake. See **acordar**
recordatorio *m,* reminder. *a* commemorative (e.g. a plaque)
recorrer *vt* to travel over; pass through; wander around; examine, inspect; read hastily; overhaul, renovate
recorrido *m,* journey, run; *mech* stroke; overhaul. **r. de despegue,** *aer* take-off run
recortado *a bot* jagged, incised. *m,* paper cutout
recortar *vt* to clip, trim, pare; cut out; *art* outline; *vr* stand out (against), be outlined (against)
recorte *m,* clipping, paring; cutting; cutout; *art* outline; *pl* snippets, clippings. **r. de periódico,** newspaper cutting, newspaper clipping
recostar *vt irr* (*with en or contra*) to lean, rest against; *vr* (*with en or contra*) lean against, rest on; lean back; recline. See **contar**
recreación *f,* recreation, hobby
recrear *vt* to entertain, amuse; *vr* amuse oneself; delight (in), enjoy
recreo *m,* recreation, hobby; playtime, recess (in schools); place of amusement. **salón de r.,** recreation room
recriminación *f,* recrimination
recriminador *a* recriminatory
recriminar *vt* to recriminate
recrudecer(se) *vi* and *vr irr* to recur, return. See **conocer**
recrudescencia *f,* recrudescence, recurrence
rectángulo *m,* rectangle. *a* rectangular
rectificable *a* rectifiable
rectificación *f,* rectification; *mech* grinding
rectificador *m,* rectifier
rectificar *vt* to rectify; *mech* grind; *vr* mend one's ways; *mil* **r. el frente,** to straighten the line
rectilíneo *a* rectilinear
rectitud *f,* straightness; rectitude, integrity; exactness; righteousness
recto *a* straight; upright; erect; literal (meaning); just, fair; single-breasted (of coats); *m,* right angle; rectum
rector (-ra) *n* director; principal, headmaster. *m, ecc* rector
rectorado *m,* principalship, headmaster- (mistress-) ship, directorship; *ecc* rectorship
rectoría *f,* rectorate, rectorship
recua *f,* drove of beasts of burden; *inf* string or line (of things)
recubrir *vt* to re-cover; coat; plate. *Past Part.* **recubierto**
recuento *m,* calculation; recount; inventory
recuerdo *m,* memory, remembrance; memento; *pl* greetings, regards
reculada *f,* drawing back; recoil
recular *vi* to recoil, draw back; *inf* go back on, give up
recuperable *a* recoverable, recuperable
recuperación *f,* recovery, recuperation; *chem* recovery
recurrente *a* recurrent
recurrir *vi* to recur; (*with prep a*) have recourse to; appeal to
recurso *m,* recourse, resort; choice, option; reversion; petition; *law* appeal; *pl* means of livelihood; *fig* way out, last hope
recusar *vt* to refuse; challenge the authority (of)
red *f,* net; network; hairnet; railing, grating; *fig* snare; system (of communications, etc.); *fig* combination (of events, etc.); *elec* mains. **r. de arrastre,** trawl net. *fig inf* **caer en la r.,** to fall into the trap
redacción *f,* phrasing; editorial office; editing; editorial board
redactar *vt* to write, phrase; draw up; edit
redactor (-ra) *a* editorial. *n* editor
redada *f,* cast (of a fishing net); haul, catch
redecilla *f, dim* small net; netting; hairnet
redención *f,* redemption; ransom; deliverance, salvation; redeeming, paying off (a mortgage, etc.)
redentor (-ra) *a* redeeming, redemptive. *n* redeemer
redificar *vt* to rebuild
redifusión *f, rad* relay
redil *m,* sheepfold
redimible *a* redeemable
redimir *vt* to ransom; redeem, buy back; pay off (a mortgage, etc.); deliver, free; *ecc* redeem
reditar *vt* to reprint, reissue
rédito *m, com* income, revenue, interest, profit
redoblamiento *m,* redoubling; bending back (of nails, etc.); rolling (of a drum)
redoblar *vt* to redouble; repeat; bend back (nails, etc.); *vi* roll (a drum)
redoble *m,* doubling; redoubling; repetition; roll (of a drum)
redoma *f,* flask, vial
redomado *a* astute, crafty, sly; complete, perfect
redonda *f,* district; pasture ground; *naut* square sail; *mus* semibreve. **a la r.,** around
redondear *vt* to make round; round; free (from debt, etc.); *vr* acquire a fortune; clear oneself (of debts, etc.)
redondel *m,* traffic circle, rotary, roundabout
redondez *f,* roundness
redondo *a* round; circular; unequivocal, plain. *m,* round, circle; *inf* cash
reducción *f,* reduction; *mil* defeat, conquest; decrease; *com* rebate; (*math chem*) reduction
reducir *vt irr* to reduce; decrease, cut down; break up;

art scale down; *elec* step down; subdue; (*chem math surg*) reduce; exchange; divide into small fragments; persuade; *vr* be obliged to, have to; live moderately. See **conducir**
redundancia *f*, redundance
redundante *a* redundant
redundar *vi* to overflow; be excessive or superfluous; (*with en*) redound to
reduplicación *f*, reduplication
reduplicar *vt* to reduplicate
ree For words so beginning (e.g. *reeditar, reexportar*), see spellings with one **e**
refacción *f*, refection, light meal; compensation, reparation
refaccionar *vt, Lat. Am.* to fix, repair
refajo *m*, skirt, underskirt; *Colombia* mild drink consisting of champagne, soda and beer
refección *f*, refection, light meal
refectorio *m*, refectory
referencia *f*, report, account; allusion; regard, relation; *com* reference (gen. *pl*); consideration
referente *a* concerning, related (to)
referir *vt irr* to narrate; describe; direct, guide; relate, refer, concern; *vr* allude (to); refer (to); concern. See **sentir**
refinación *f*, refining
refinado *a* refined; polished, cultured; crafty
refinador *m*, refiner
refinamiento *m*, refinement, subtlety, care
refinar *vt* to refine, purify; polish, perfect
refinería *f*, refinery
reflector *a* reflecting. *m*, reflector; searchlight; shade (for lamps, etc.)
reflejar *vi phys* to reflect; *vt* consider; show, mirror; *vr fig* be reflected, be seen
reflejo *m*, reflection; image; glare. *a* reflex; considered, judicious
reflexión *f*, *phys* reflection; consideration, thought
reflexionar *vt* (*with en or sobre*) to consider, reflect upon
reflexivo *a phys* reflective; thoughtful
reflorecer *vi irr* to flower again; return to favor (ideas, etc.). See **conocer**
reflujo *m*, reflux, refluence; ebb tide
refocilar *vt* to warm up, brace up; give pleasure to; *vr* enjoy oneself
reforma *f*, reform; improvement; reformation; *hist* Reformation
reformación *f*, reform, improvement
reformador (-ra) *a* reformatory, reforming. *n* reformer
reformar *vt* to remake; reshape; repair, mend, restore; improve, correct; *ecc* reform; reorganize; *vr* mend one's ways, improve; control oneself
reformatorio *m*, reformatory. *a* reforming, reformatory
reformista *mf* reformist, reformer. *a* reformatory
reforzador *m*, *phot* reinforcing bath; *elec* booster
reforzamiento *m*, stiffening, reinforcing
reforzar *vt irr* to reinforce, strengthen, stiffen; encourage, inspirit. See **forzar**
refractar *vt* to refract
refractario *a* stubborn; (*phys chem*) refractory; unmanageable, unruly; fireproof
refrán *m*, proverb
refranero *m*, collection of proverbs
refregamiento *m*, rubbing; scrubbing, scouring
refregar *vt irr* to rub; scrub, scour; *fig inf* rub in, insist on. See **cegar**
refrenamiento *m*, curbing; control, restraint
refrenar *vt* to curb, check (horses); control, restrain
refrendar *vt* to countersign, endorse, legalize
refrescante *a* refreshing, cooling
refrescar *vt* to cool, chill; repeat; *fig* brush up, revise; *vi* be rested or refreshed; grow cooler; take the air; freshen (wind); take a cool drink; *vr* grow cooler; take the air; take a cool drink
refresco *m*, refreshment; cool drink; *Lat. Am.* soft drink, soda, pop
refresquería *f, Lat. Am.* refreshment stand
refriega *f*, affray, scuffle, rough-and-tumble
refrigeración *f*, refrigeration
refrigerador *m*, refrigerator
refrigerante *a* refrigerative; chilling; cooling. *m*, cooling chamber, cooler
refrigerar *vt* to chill; cool; freeze, refrigerate; refresh
refrigerio *m*, coolness; consolation; refreshment, food
refringente *a phys* refringent
refuerzo *m*, reinforcement, strengthening; aid, help
refugiado (-da) *a* and *n* refugee
refugiar *vt* to protect, shelter; *vr* take refuge
refugio *m*, refuge, shelter, protection; traffic island. **r. antiaéreo,** air raid shelter. **r. para peatones,** traffic island
refulgencia *f*, resplendence, splendor, brilliance
refulgente *a* resplendent, refulgent, dazzling
refulgir *vi* to shine, be dazzling
refundición *f*, recasting (of metals); adaptation; rehash, refurbishing
refundir *vt* to recast (metals); include, comprise; adapt; rehash, refurbish; *vi fig* promote, contribute to
refunfuñador *a* grumbling, fuming
refunfuñar *vi* to grumble, growl, fume
refunfuño *m*, grumble, fuming; snort
refutable *a* refutable
refutación *f*, refutation
refutar *vt* to refute
regadera *f*, watering can; irrigation canal; sprinkler; *Lat. Am.* shower bath, shower
regadío *m*, irrigated land; irrigation, watering. *a* irrigated
regajal, regajo *m*, pool, puddle; stream, brook
regalado *a* delicate, highly bred; luxurious, delightful
regalar *vt* to make a gift of, give; caress, fondle; indulge, cherish; entertain, regale; *vr* live in luxury
regalía *f*, royal privilege; right, exemption; perquisite, emolument
regaliz *m*, **regaliza** *f*, licorice
regalo *m*, gift, present; satisfaction, pleasure; entertainment, regalement; luxury, comfort
regalón *a inf* pampered
regalonear *vt, Lat. Am.* to pamper, spoil
regañadientes, a *adv* unwillingly, grumblingly
regañar *vi* to snarl (dogs); crack (skin of fruits); grumble, mutter; *inf* quarrel; *vt inf* scold
regaño *m*, angry look or gesture; *inf* scolding
regañón (-ona) *a inf* grumbling, complaining; scolding. *n inf* grumbler
regar *vt irr* to water, sprinkle with water; flow through, irrigate; spray; *fig* shower (with), strew. See **cegar**
regata *f*, regatta; small irrigation channel (for gardens, etc.)
regate *m*, twist of the body, sidestep; dribbling; (in soccer); *inf* dodging, evasion
regatear *vt* to haggle over, beat down (prices); resell, retail; dribble (a ball); *fig inf* dodge, avoid; *vi* bargain, haggle; *naut* take part in a regatta, race
regateo *m*, haggling, bargaining
regatero (-ra) *a* retail. *n* retailer
regatón (-ona) *m*, ferrule, tip. *a* haggling, bargaining. *n* haggler; retailer
regatonear *vt* to resell at retail
regazo *m*, lap, knees; *fig* heart, bosom
regeneración *f*, regeneration
regenerador (-ra) *n* regenerator. *a* regenerative, reforming
regenerar *vt* to regenerate, reform
regenta *f*, wife of the president of a court of session
regentar *vt* to fill temporarily (offices); rule, govern; manage, run (businesses)
regente *a* ruling. *mf* regent. *m*, president of a court of session; manager
regicidio *m*, regicide (act)

regidor *a* ruling, governing. *m*, magistrate, alderman
régimen *m*, administration, management; regime; (*med gram*) regimen; *mech* rating
regimentación *f*, regimentation
regimentar *vt irr* to form into regiments; regiment. *Pres. Ind.* **regimiento, regimientas, regimienta, regimientan.** *Pres. Subjunc.* **regimiente, regimientes, regimiente, regimienten**
regimiento *m*, *mil* regiment; administration, rule; *Lat. Am.* crowd (of people)
regio *a* royal; magnificent, regal. **¡regio!** great!, wonderful!
región *f*, region, country; area, tract, space. **r. industrial,** industrial area
regionalismo *m*, regionalism
regionalista *mf* regionalist. *a* regional
regir *vt irr* to govern, rule; administer, conduct; *gram* govern; *vi* be in force (laws, etc.); work, function; *naut* obey the helm. See **pedir**
registrador *a* recording. *m*, registrar, keeper of records; recorder. **caja (registradora),** (cash) register
registrar *vt* to examine, inspect; search; copy, record; mark the place (in a book); observe, note; (of thermometers, etc.) record, show; look on to (houses, etc.); *vr* register (hotels, etc.)
registro *m*, search; registration, entry; record; recording; reading (of a thermometer, etc.); *mech* damper; registry; register (book); *mus* range, compass (voice); *mus* register (organ); (*mech print*) register; bookmark. **r. civil,** register of births, marriages, and deaths
regla *f*, ruler, measuring stick; rule, principle, guide, precept; system, policy; *med* period; moderation; method, order. **r. de cálculo,** slide rule. **r. T,** T-square. **en r.,** in due form. **por r.,** general, generally, as a rule
reglamentación *f*, regulation; rules and regulations
reglamentar *vt* to regulate
reglamento *m*, bylaw; regulation, ordinance
reglar *vt* to rule (lines); regulate; govern; control; *vr* restrain oneself, mend one's ways
regocijar *vt* to cheer, delight; *vr* enjoy oneself, rejoice
regocijo *m*, happiness, joy; cheer, merriment
regordete *a inf* chubby
regresar *vi* to return
regresión *f*, return; retrogression; regression
regreso *m*, return
reguera *f*, irrigation channel, ditch
regulación *f*, regulation; *mech* control, timing
regulador *m*, *mech* governor, regulator. *a* regulating, controlling
regular *vt* to adjust, regulate; *mech* govern. *a* methodical, ordered; moderate; average, medium; (*ecc mil geom gram*) regular; so-so, not bad; probable. **por lo r.,** generally
regularidad *f*, regularity
regularización *f*, regularization; regulation
regularizar *vt* to regularize; regulate
regurgitar *vi* to regurgitate
rehabilitación *f*, rehabilitation
rehabilitar *vt* to rehabilitate; *vr* rehabilitate oneself
rehacer *vt irr* to remake; repair, mend; *vr* recover one's strength; control one's emotions; *mil* rally. See **hacer**
rehén *m*, hostage (gen. *pl*); *mil* pledge, security
rehenchir *vt irr* to restuff; refill, recharge. See **henchir**
reherir *vt irr* to repulse. See **herir**
rehilar *vt* to spin too much or twist the yarn; *vi* totter, stagger; whizz (arrows, etc.). See **prohibir**
rehuir *vt irr* to withdraw; avoid; reject. See **huir**
rehusar *vt* to refuse, reject. See **desahuciar**
reimponer *vt irr* to reimpose. See **poner**
reimportación *f*, reimportation
reimpresión *f*, reprint
reimprimir *vt* to reprint
reina *f*, queen; queen (in chess); queen bee; peerless beauty, belle
reinado *m*, reign; heyday, fashion
reinante *a* reigning; prevalent
reinar *vi* to reign; influence; endure, prevail
reincidencia *f*, relapse (into crime, etc.), recidivism
reincidente *mf* backslider
reincidir *vi* to relapse (into crime, etc.)
reincorporar *vt* to reincorporate; *vr* join again, become a member again
reingresar *vi* to reenter
reingreso *m*, reentry
reino *m*, kingdom
reinstalación *f*, reinstatement
reinstalar *vt* to reinstate; *vr* be reinstalled
reintegración *f*, reintegration
reintegrar *vt* to reintegrate; *vr* be reinstated, recuperate, recover
reir *vi irr* to laugh; sneer, jeer; *fig* smile (nature); *vt* laugh at; *vr inf* (*with de*) scorn. **reírse a carcajadas,** to shout with laughter. *Pres. Part.* **riendo.** *Pres. Ind.* **río, ríes, ríe, ríen.** *Preterite* **rió, rieron.** *Pres. Subjunc.* **ría,** etc. *Imperf. Subjunc.* **riese,** etc.
reiteración *f*, reiteration, repetition
reiteradamente *adv* repeatedly, reiteratively
reiterar *vt* to reiterate, repeat
reivindicación *f*, *law* recovery
reivindicar *vt law* to recover
reja *f*, colter, plowshare; plowing, tilling; grating, grille; *Lat. Am.* jail, prison
rejado *m*, railing, grating
rejilla *f*, grating; grille, lattice; luggage rack (in a train); cane (for chairs, seats, etc.); wire mesh; small brazier; *elec* grid; *mech* grate
rejo *m*, *Lat. Am.* whip
rejuntar *vt* to point (a wall)
rejuvenecer *vt irr* to rejuvenate; *fig* revive; bring up to date; *vi* and *vr* be rejuvenated, grow young again, rejuvenesce. See **conocer**
rejuvenecimiento *m*, rejuvenation
relación *f*, relation; connection (of ideas); report, statement; narrative, account; *math* ratio; *law* brief; intercourse, association, dealings (gen. *pl*); list; analogy, relation. **tener relaciones con,** to have dealings with; be engaged or betrothed to; woo, court
relacionar *vt* to recount, narrate, report; connect, relate; *vr* be connected
relajación *f*, relaxation; recreation; laxity, dissoluteness
relajar *vt* to relax; recreate, amuse; make less rigorous; *law* remit; *vr* become relaxed; be dissolute, lax, or vicious
relamer *vt* to lick again; *vr* lick one's lips; *fig* overpaint, make up too much; ooze satisfaction, brag
relamido *a* overdressed; affected
relámpago *m*, lightning; flash, gleam; streak of lightning (of quick persons or things); flash of wit, witticism
relampaguear *vi* to lighten (of lightning); flash, gleam
relapso *a* relapsed, lapsed (into error, vice)
relatar *vt* to relate, narrate, report
relatividad *f*, relativeness; *phys* relativity
relativo *a* relevant, pertinent; relative, comparative; *gram* relative
relato *m*, narration, account, report
relator (-ra) *a* narrating. *n* narrator. *m*, *law* reporter
relavar *vt* to rewash, wash again
relección *f*, reelection
releer *vt irr* to reread; revise. See **creer**
relegación *f*, relegation
relegar *vt* to banish; relegate, set aside
relegir *vt irr* to reelect. See **elegir**
relente *m*, night dew, dampness; *inf* cheek, impudence
relevación *f*, *art* relief; release; remission, exemption
relevar *vt art* to work in relief; emboss; relieve, free; dismiss; excuse, pardon; aid, succor; *fig* aggrandize; *mil* relieve; *vi* carve in relief
relevo *m*, relay; *mil* relief
relieve *m*, *art* relief; *pl* leftovers, remains (of food). **alto r.,** high relief. **bajo r.,** low relief
religar *vt* to retie, fasten again; fasten more securely; solder

religión *f*, religion; creed, faith, philosophy; devotion, religious practice. **r. reformada,** Protestantism. **entrar en r.,** *ecc* to profess
religiosidad *f*, religiosity; religiousness; conscientiousness, punctiliousness
religioso (-sa) *a* religious; punctilious, conscientious; moderate. *n* religious
relinchar *vi* to whinny, neigh
reliquia *f*, residue (gen. *pl*); *ecc* relic; vestige, remnant, memento; permanent disability or ailment
rellanar *vt* to make level again; *vr* stretch oneself at full length
rellano *m*, landing (of a staircase); level stretch (of ground)
rellenar *vt* to refill, replenish; fill up; *mas* plug, point; *cul* stuff; *inf* cram with food (gen. *vr*)
relleno *m*, *cul* stuffing; replenishing; filling; *fig* padding (of speeches, etc.)
reloj *m*, clock; watch. **r. de arena,** hourglass. **r. de bolsillo,** watch. **r. de la muerte,** deathwatch beetle. **r. de péndulo,** grandfather clock. **r. de pulsera,** wristwatch. **r. de repetición,** repeater. **r. de sol** *or* **r. solar,** sundial
relojera *f*, clock stand; watch case
relojería *f*, watch or clock making; jeweler, watch maker's shop
relojero (-ra) *n* watch maker, watch repairer
reluciente *a* shining, sparkling; shiny
relucir *vi irr* to glitter, sparkle, gleam; *fig* shine, excel. See **lucir**
reluctante *a* unruly, refractory, disobedient
relumbrante *a* resplendent, dazzling
relumbrar *vi* to be resplendent, shine, glitter
remachar *vt* to rivet; *fig* clinch
remache *m*, riveting; rivet
remaduro, -a *a*, *Lat. Am.* overripe
remanente *m*, remains, residue
remanso *m*, backwater; stagnant water; sloth, dilatoriness
remar *vi* to row, paddle, scull; toil, strive
rematadamente *adv* completely, entirely, absolutely
rematado *a* beyond hope, extremely ill; utterly lost; *law* convicted
rematar *vt* to end, finish; finish off, kill; knock down at auction; *sew* finish; *vi* end; *vr* be ruined or spoiled
remate *m*, end, conclusion; extremity; *arch* coping; *arch* terminal; highest bid; auction. **de r.,** utterly hopeless
rematista *mf*, *Lat. Am.* auctioneer
rembarcar *vt* to reembark, reship
rembolsable *a* repayable
rembolsar *vt* to recover (money); refund, return (money)
rembolso *m*, repayment. **contra r.,** cash on delivery, C.O.D.
remedar *vt* to copy, imitate; mimic
remediador (-ra) *a* remedying. *n* benefactor, helper
remediar *vt* to remedy; aid, help; save from danger; prevent (trouble)
remedio *m*, remedy; emendation, correction; help; refuge, protection; *med* remedy. **No hay más r.,** There's nothing else to do, It's the only way open. **no tener más r.,** to be unable to help (doing something), be obliged to
remedo *m*, imitation; poor copy
remembranza *f*, remembrance, memory
rememorar *vt* to remember, recall to mind
remendar *vt irr* to mend, patch; darn; repair; correct. See **recomendar**
remendón (-ona) *n* cobbler; mender of old clothes
remero (-ra) *n* oarsman, rower; sculler
remesa *f*, remittance; consignment, shipment
remesar(se) *vt* and *vr* to pluck out (hair); *vt com* remit; consign
remezón *m*, *Lat. Am.* (earth) tremor
remiendo *m*, *sew* patch; mend, darn; emendation; *inf* insignia of one of the Spanish military orders. **a remiendos,** *inf* piecemeal
remilgarse *vr* to preen oneself, be overdressed
remilgo *m*, affectation; mannerism; prudery, squeamishness
reminiscencia *f*, reminiscence; memory, recollection
remirado *a* wary, cautious, prudent, circumspect
remirar *vt* to revise, go over again; *vr* take great care over; behold with pleasure
remisión *f*, sending; remission; pardon, forgiveness; foregoing, relinquishment; abatement, diminution; *lit* reference, allusion
remise *m*, *Argentina* limousine, hired taxi
remiso *a* timid, spiritless; languid, slow
remitente *mf* sender. *a* sending
remitir *vt* to remit, send; pardon, forgive; defer, postpone; abate, diminish; relinquish, forgo; *lit* refer; *vr* remit, submit, consult; refer (to), cite
remo *m*, oar, scull, paddle; arm or leg (of men or animals, gen. *pl*); wing (gen. *pl*); hard, continuous toil; galleys. **al r.,** by dint of rowing; *inf* struggling with hardships
remojar *vt* to soak, steep; celebrate by drinking
remojo *m*, soaking, steeping
remolacha *f*, beet
remolcador *m*, *naut* tow, tug. *a naut* towing
remolcar *vt* (*naut aut*) to tow; *fig* press into service, use
remoler *vi*, *Lat. Am.* to live it up, live the life of Riley
remolinar *vi* to spin, whirl, eddy; *vr* throng, swarm
remolino *m*, whirlwind; eddy, swirl; whirlpool; crowd, throng, swarm; disturbance, riot
remolonear *vi inf* to loiter, lag; avoid work; be lax or dilatory
remolque *m*, towage, towing; towline; barge; *aut* trailer. **a r.,** on tow
remonta *f*, resoling (of shoes); leather gusset (of riding breeches); *mil* remount
remontar *vt* to scare off (game); *mil* supply with fresh horses; resole (shoes); *fig* rise to great heights (of oratory, etc.); *vr* soar (of birds); (*with prep a*) date from, go back to; originate in
remoquete *m*, blow with the fist; witticism; *inf* flirtation, courtship
rémora *f*, *icht* remora; delay, hindrance
remorder *vt irr* to bite again or repeatedly; *fig* gnaw, nag, cause uneasiness or remorse; *vr* show one's feelings. See **morder**
remordimiento *m*, remorse
remoto *a* distant, remote; unlikely, improbable
remover *vt irr* to remove, move; stir; turn over; dismiss, discharge. See **mover**
remozar *vt* to cause to appear young; freshen up, bring up to date; *vr* look young
remplazar *vt* to replace; exchange, substitute; succeed, take the place of
remplazo *m*, replacement; exchange, substitute; successor; *mil* replacement
remuda *f*, replacement, exchange
remudar *vt* to replace
remuneración *f*, remuneration; reward
remunerador (-ra) *a* remunerative, recompensing. *n* remunerator
remunerar *vt* to recompense, reward
remusgar *vi* to suspect, imagine
renacentista *a* renaissance
renacer *vi irr* to be reborn. See **nacer**
renacimiento *m*, rebirth; Renaissance
renacuajo *m*, tadpole; *mech* frog; *inf* twerp
rencarcelar *vt* to reimprison
rencarnación *f*, reincarnation
rencarnar(se) *vi* and *vr* to be reincarnated
rencilla *f*, grudge, grievance, resentment
rencilloso *a* peevish, easily offended, touchy
rencor *m*, rancor, spite, old grudge. **guardar r.,** to bear malice
rencoroso *a* rancorous, malicious, spiteful

rencuadernar *vt* to rebind (books)
rencuentro *m*, collision; *mil* encounter, clash
rendición *f*, surrender; yield, profit
rendido *a* submissive, obsequious
rendija *f*, crevice, cleft, crack, fissure
rendimiento *m*, weariness, fatigue; submissiveness, obsequiousness; yield, profit; *mech* efficiency
rendir *vt irr mil* to cause to surrender; defeat; overcome, conquer; give back, return; yield, provide; tire, exhaust; vomit; pay, render; *vr* be exhausted, be worn out; surrender. *mil* **r. el puesto,** to retire from or give up a post. See **pedir**
renegado (-da) *n* renegade, apostate; turncoat; *inf* malignant person. *a* renegade
renegador (-ra) *n* blasphemer; foul-mouthed person
renegar *vt irr* to deny, disown; loathe, hate; *vi* (*with de*) apostatize; blaspheme; *inf* curse. See **cegar**
renganchar(se) *vt* and *vr mil* to reenlist
renganche *m*, *mil* reenlistment
renglón *m*, *print* line; *pl* writing, composition
renguear *vi*, *Lat. Am.* to limp
renguera *f*, *Lat. Am.* limp
reniego *m*, blasphemy; *inf* foul language, cursing
renitencia *f*, repugnance
renombrado *a* illustrious, famous
renombre *m*, surname; renown, reputation, fame
renovable *a* renewable, replaceable
renovación *f*, replacement; renewal; renovation; transformation, reform
renovador (-ra) *n* reformer; renovator. *a* renovating; reforming
renovar *vt irr* to renew; renovate; replace; exchange; reiterate, repeat. See **contar**
renta *f*, yield, profit; income; revenue; government securities; rent; tax
rentar *vt* to yield, produce an income
rentero (-ra) *n* tenant farmer. *m*, one who farms out land
rentista *mf* financier; bondholder; person who lives on a private income, rentier
rentístico *a* revenue, financial
renuente *a* refractory, willful
renuevo *m*, *bot* shoot; renewal
renuncia, renunciación *f*, renunciation; resignation; abandonment, relinquishment
renunciar *vt* to renounce; refuse; scorn; abandon, relinquish; resign; revoke (at cards). **r. a,** to give up
renuncio *m*, revoke (cards); *inf* falsehood
reñidamente *adv* strongly, stubbornly, fiercely
reñir *vi irr* to quarrel, dispute; fight; be on bad terms, fall out; *vt* scold; fight (battles, etc.). See **ceñir**
reo *mf* criminal; offender, guilty party; *law* defendant
reojo *m*, (**mirar de**) to look out of the corner of the eye; *fig* look askance
reorganizador (-ra) *a* reorganizing. *n* reorganizer
reóstato *m*, rheostat
repantigarse *vr* to stretch out one's legs, make oneself comfortable
reparable *a* remediable, reparable; worthy of note
reparación *f*, repair, mending; reparation, satisfaction; indemnity, compensation
reparada *f*, shying (of horses)
reparador *a* repairing, mending; faultfinding; restoring; satisfying, compensating
reparar *vt* to repair; restore; consider; correct, remedy; atone for, expiate; indemnify; hold up, detain; protect, guard; (*with en*) notice; *Lat. Am.* to ape, imitate, mimic; *vi* halt, be detained; *vr* control oneself
reparo *m*, repair; restoration; remedy; note, reflection; warning; doubt, scruple; guard, protection; parry (at fencing)
repartición *f*, distribution
repartidero *a* distributable
repartidor (-ra) *a* distributing. *n* distributor; tax assessor
repartimiento *m*, distribution, allotment; assessment
repartir *vt* to distribute; share out; allot; deal (cards); assess; *com* deliver
reparto *m*, distribution; assessment; delivery (of letters, etc.); *theat* cast; deal (at cards); *Lat. Am.* building site, construction site
repasador *m*, *Lat. Am.* dish cloth, dishrag
repasar *vt* to pass by again; peruse, reexamine; brush up, revise; skim, glance over; mend, repair (garments); edit, revise; hone
repaso *m*, second passage through; reexamination, perusal; revision, editing; brushing up, revision; repair, mending; *inf* dressing-down, scolding
repatriación *f*, repatriation
repatriado (-da) *n* repatriate
repatriar *vt* to repatriate; *vi* and *vr* return to one's own country
repecho *m*, steep slope. **a r.,** uphill
repelar *vt* to pull by the hair; put through its paces (of a horse); clip, cut; remove, diminish
repeler *vt* to repel, throw back; reject, refute
repelo *m*, anything against the grain; *inf* skirmish; reluctance, repugnance
repente *m*, *inf* sudden or unexpected movement. **de r.,** suddenly
repentino *a* sudden, unexpected
repentizar *vi mus* to sight-read
repercusión *f*, repercussion; vibration
repercutir *vi* to recoil, rebound; *vr* reverberate; reecho; *fig* have repercussions; *vt med* repel
repertorio *m*, repertory
repesar *vt* to reweigh, weigh again
repetición *f*, repetition; *art* replica, copy; repeater (in clocks); recital
repetidamente *adv* repeatedly
repetir *vt irr* to repeat, do over again; reiterate; *art* copy, make a replica of; recite. See **pedir**
repicar *vt* to chop, mince; peal (of bells); prick again; *vr* pride oneself (on), boast
repique *m*, chopping, mincing; peal, pealing (of bells); disagreement, grievance
repisa *f*, *arch* bracket; ledge; shelf. **r. de chimenea,** mantelpiece
replantar *vt* to replant; transplant
repleción *f*, repletion, satiety
replegar *vt irr* to refold, fold many times; *vr mil* retreat in good order. See **cegar**
repleto *a* replete
réplica *f*, reply, answer; replica
replicar *vi* to contradict, dispute; answer, reply. **¡No me repliques!** *inf* Don't answer back!
repliegue *m*, double fold, crease; doubling, folding; *mil* withdrawal
repoblación *f*, repeopling, repopulation
repoblar *vt* to repeople, repopulate
repollo *m*, white cabbage; heart (of lettuce, etc.)
reponer *vt irr* to replace; reinstate; restore; reply; *vr* recover, regain (possessions); grow well again; grow calm. See **poner**
reportación *f*, serenity, moderation
reportaje *m*, journalistic report
reportar *vt* to restrain, moderate; achieve, obtain; carry; bring; *vr* control oneself
reporte *m*, report, news; rumor
reporterismo *m*, newspaper reporting
reportero (-ra) *a* news, report. *n* reporter
reposado *a* quiet, peaceful, tranquil
reposar *vi* to rest, repose oneself; sleep, doze; lie in the grave; settle (liquids); rest (on)
reposición *f*, replacement; restoration; renewal; recovery (of health); *theat* revival
repositorio *m*, repository
reposo *m*, rest, repose; peace, tranquility; sleep
repostada *f*, *Lat. Am.* cheeky reply, saucy retort
repostería *f*, confectioner's shop; pantry; butler's pantry
repostero *m*, confectioner, pastry cook

repreguntar *vt* to cross-examine
reprender *vt* to scold, reprimand, rebuke
reprensible *a* reprehensible, censurable
reprensión *f*, scolding, reprimand, rebuke
represa *f*, damming, holding back (water); dam, lock; restraining, controlling
represalia *f*, reprisal (gen. *pl*); retaliation
represar *vt* to dam, harness (water); *naut* retake, recapture; *fig* restrain, control
representación *f*, representation; *theat* performance; authority; dignity; *com* agency; portrait, image; depiction, expression; petition
representador *a* representative
representante *a* representative. *mf* representative; actor; performer
representar *vt* to represent; *theat* perform; depict, express; describe, portray; *vr* imagine, picture to oneself
representativo *a* representative
represión *f*, repression; recapture
represivo *a* repressive
reprimenda *f*, rebuke, reprimand
reprimir *vt* to repress, restrain, control; *vr* restrain oneself
reprobación *f*, censure; reprobation
reprobar *vt irr* to reprove; censure; fail (in an exam). See **probar**
réprobo (-ba) *n* reprobate
reprochar *vt* to reproach
reproche *m*, reproaching; rebuke, reproach
reproducción *f*, reproduction. **r. a gran escala,** large-scale model
reproducir *vt irr* to reproduce. See **conducir**
reproductor (-ra) *a* reproductive. *n* breeding animal
reps *m*, rep (fabric)
reptil *a* reptilian; crawling. *m*, reptile
república *f*, republic; state, commonwealth. **la r. de las letras,** the republic of letters
República Dominicana Dominican Republic
República Malgache Republic of Madagascar
republicanismo *m*, republicanism
republicano (-na) *a* and *n* republican
repudiación *f*, repudiation
repudiar *vt* to cast off (a wife); repudiate, renounce
repuesto *a* retired, hidden. *m*, stock, provision; serving table; pantry; stake (at cards, etc.). **de r.,** spare, extra
repugnancia *f*, inconsistency, contradiction; aversion, dislike; reluctance; repugnance
repugnante *a* repugnant, loathsome
repugnar *vt* to contradict, be inconsistent with; hate, be averse to (e.g. **La idea me repugna,** I hate the idea)
repujado *m*, repoussé work
repujar *vt* to work in repoussé
repulir *vt* to repolish, reburnish; *vt* and *vr* make up too much, overdress
repulsa *f*, snub, rebuff; rejection; repulse
repulsar *vt* to decline, reject; repulse; deny, refuse; rebuff
repulsión *f*, repulsion; rebuff; aversion, dislike
repulsivo *a* repellent
repunta *f*, headland, cape; *fig* first sign; *inf* disgust; caprice; fight
reputación *f*, reputation
reputar *vt* to believe, consider (e.g. **Le reputo por honrado,** I believe him to be an honorable man); appreciate, esteem
requebrar *vt irr* to break into smaller pieces; make love to, woo; compliment, flatter. See **quebrar**
requemado *a* sunburned; brown
requemar *vt* to burn again; overcook; dry up, parch (of plants, etc.); burn (the mouth) (of spicy foods, etc.); *vr fig* suffer inwardly
requerimiento *m*, requirement, demand; *law* summons
requerir *vt irr* to inform, notify; examine; need, necessitate; require; summon; woo; persuade. See **sentir**
requesón *m*, cream cheese; curd
requetebién *adv inf* exceedingly well
requiebro *m*, compliment, expression of love; wooing, flirtation
requintar *vt*, *Lat. Am.* to tighten
requisa *f*, inspection, visitation; *mil* requisitionin; *Lat. Am.* confiscation
requisar *vt mil* to requisition
requisito *m*, requisite
res *f*, animal, beast; head of cattle; *Lat. Am.* steak
resabiar *vt* to make vicious, cause bad habits; *vr* contract bad habits or vices; be discontented; relish
resabio *m*, disagreeable aftertaste; bad habit, vice
resaca *f*, surf, undertow, surge; *com* redraft
resacar *vt* to distil
resalado *a inf* very witty; most attractive
resaltar *vi* to rebound; project, jut out; grow loose, fall out; *fig* stand out, be prominent
resalto *m*, rebound; projection
resarcir *vt* to compensate, indemnify
resbaladizo *a* slippery; difficult, delicate (of a situation)
resbalar *vi* to slip; slide; skid; err, fall into sin
resbalón *m*, slip; slide; skid; temptation, error
rescatador (-ra) *n* ransomer; rescuer
rescatar *vt* to ransom; redeem, buy back; barter; free, rescue; *fig* redeem (time, etc.)
rescate *m*, ransom; redemption; barter; amount of ransom
rescindir *vt* to annul, repeal, rescind
rescoldo *m*, ember, cinder; scruple, qualm, doubt
resentimiento *m*, deterioration, impairment; animosity, resentment
resentirse *vr irr* to deteriorate, be impaired; be hurt or offended. See **sentir**
reseña *f*, *mil* review; short description; review (of a book)
reseñar *vt mil* to review; describe briefly, outline
reserva *f*, store, stock; exception, qualification; reticence; restraint, moderation; (*ecc law*) reservation; (*mil naut*) reserve. **sin r.,** frankly, without reserve
reservación *f*, reservation; scruple
reservado *a* reserved, reticent; prudent, moderate; kept, reserved. *m*, reserved compartment; private apartment, private garden, etc.
reservar *vt* to keep, hold; postpone; reserve (rooms, etc.); exempt; keep secret; withhold (information); *ecc* reserve; *vr* await a better opportunity; be cautious
reservista *a* (*mil nav*) reserved. *mf* reservist
resfriado *m*, *med* cold, chill
resfriar *vt* to chill; *fig* cool, moderate; *vi* grow cold; *vr* catch a cold; *fig* cool off (of love, etc.)
resguardar *vt* to protect; shelter; *vr* take refuge; (*with de*) guard against; (*with con*) shelter by
resguardo *m*, protection, guard; *com* guarantee, security; *com* voucher; preservation; vigilance (to prevent smuggling, etc.); contraband guards
residencia *f*, stay, residence; home, domicile; *ecc* residence
residencial *a* residential; resident, residentiary
residente *a* resident. *mf* inhabitant. *m*, resident, minister resident (diplomatic)
residir *vi* to live, inhabit; reside officially; be found, be, exist
residuo *m*, residuum, remainder; *math* remainder; *chem* residue
resignación *f*, resignation; fortitude, submission
resignar *vt* to resign, relinquish; *vr* submit, resign oneself
resina *f*, resin
resistencia *f*, resistance, opposition; endurance; (*phys mech psy*) resistance
resistente *a* resistant; tough; hardy (of plants)
resistir *vi* to resist, oppose; reject; *vt* endure, bear; resist; *vr* fight, resist
resolución *f*, decision; boldness, daring; determination, resolution; decree
resoluto *a* resolute, bold; brief, concise; able, expert

resolver *vt irr* to determine, decide; summarize; solve; dissolve; analyze; (*phys med*) resolve; *vr* decide, determine; be reduced to, become; *med* resolve. *Pres. Ind.* **resuelvo, resuelves, resuelve, resuelven.** *Past Part.* **resuelto.** *Pres. Subjunc.* **resuelva, resuelvas, resuelva, resuelvan**
resollar *vi irr* to breathe; pant. See **degollar**
resonancia *f,* resonance, sonority, ring; fame, reputation
resonante *a* resonant; resounding
resonar *vi irr* to resound, echo. See **tronar**
resoplido, resoplo *m,* heavy breathing, pant, snort
resorber *vt* to reabsorb
resorción *f,* reabsorption
resorte *m, mech* spring; elasticity; *fig* means, instrument; *Lat. Am.* rubber band
respaldo *m,* back (of chairs, etc.); reverse side (of a piece of paper)
respectivo *a* respective
respecto *m,* relation, regard, reference. **con r. a,** *or* **r. a,** with regard to, with respect to, concerning
respetabilidad *f,* respectability; worthiness
respetable *a* worthy of respect; respectable; *fig* considerable, large
respetar *vt* to respect, revere
respeto *m,* respect, honor; consideration, reason. **de r.,** spare, extra; special, ceremonial
respetuoso *a* venerable, worthy of honor; respectful, courteous
respingar *vi* to flinch, wince, kick; *inf* be uneven, rise (hem of garments); *inf* do (a thing) grumblingly
respingo *m,* wincing; jerk, shake; *inf* gesture of reluctance or dislike
respiración *f,* breathing, respiration; ventilation
respiradero *m,* ventilator; air hole, vent; rest, breathing space
respirador *a* breathing; respiratory. *m,* respirator
respirar *vi* to breathe; exhale, give off; take courage; have a breathing space, rest; *inf* speak. **sin r.,** continuously, without stopping for breath
respiratorio *a* respiratory
respiro *m,* breathing; breathing space, respite
resplandecer *vi irr* to glitter, gleam; shine, excel. See **conocer**
resplandeciente *a* glittering, resplendent, shining
resplandor *m,* radiance, brilliance; glitter, gleam; majesty, splendor
responder *vt* to reply; satisfy, answer; *vi* reecho; requite, return; produce, provide; *fig* answer, have the desired effect; *com* (*with de*) answer for, guarantee; *com* correspond
respondón *a inf* pert, impudent, cheeky, given to answering back
responsabilidad *f,* responsibility
responsable *a* responsible
responso *m, ecc* response, responsory
respuesta *f,* answer, reply; response; refutation; repartee
resquebradura *f,* fissure, crevice, crack
resquebrajarse *vr* to crack, split
resquemar *vt* to bite, sting (of hot dishes)
resquicio *m,* crack, chink, slit; opportunity; *Lat. Am.* sign, trace, vestige
resta *f, math* subtraction; *math* remainder
restablecer *vt irr* to reestablish; restore; *vr* recover one's health; reestablish oneself. See **conocer**
restablecimiento *m,* reestablishment; restoration
restañar *vt* to re-tin; staunch
restar *vt math* to subtract; deduct; return (a ball); *vi* remain. **No me resta más que decir adiós,** It only remains for me to say good-by
restauración *f,* restoration; renovation
restaurante *m,* restaurant
restaurantero *m,* restaurant operator; restaurant owner; restaurateur
restaurar *vt* to recover, recuperate; renovate, repair; restore
restaurativo *a* and *m,* restorative
restinga *f,* sandbank, bar
restitución *f,* restitution
restituible *a* returnable, replaceable
restituir *vt irr* to return, give back; restore; reestablish; *vr* return to one's place of departure. See **huir**
resto *m,* rest, balance; *math* remainder; *pl* remains
restorán *m,* restaurant
restricción *f,* limitation, restriction
restrictivo *a* restrictive; restraining
restringir *vt* to limit, restrict; contract
resucitar *vt* to raise from the dead; *fig inf* revive; *vi* resuscitate
resuelto *a* audacious, daring; resolute, capable
resuello *m,* breathing; panting, hard breathing
resulta *f,* consequence, result; decision, resolution; vacant post. **de resultas de,** as the result of; in consequence of
resultado *m,* result, consequence, outcome
resultar *vi* to result, follow; turn out, happen; result (in); *inf* turn out well. **El vestido no me resulta,** The dress isn't a success on me
resumen *m,* summary. **en r.,** in short
resumir *vt* to summarize, abridge; sum up, recapitulate; *vr* be contained, be included
resurgimiento *m,* resurgence, revival
resurgir *vi* to reappear, rise again, revive; resuscitate
resurrección *f,* resurrection
retablo *m, arch* altarpiece, retable; frieze; series of pictures
retador, -a *mf, Lat. Am.* challenger
retaguardia *f,* rear guard. **a r.,** in the rear. **picar la r.,** to harass the rear guard
retajar *vt* to cut in the round; circumcise
retal *m,* clipping, filing, shaving; remnant
retama *f, bot* broom. **r. común** *or* **r. de olor,** Spanish broom. **r. de escobas,** common broom
retar *vt* to challenge; *inf* reproach, accuse
retardación *f,* retardment
retardar *vt* to retard, delay
retardo *m,* delay, retardment
retazo *m,* remnant, cutting; excerpt, fragment
retemblar *vi* to quiver, tremble constantly
retemplar *vt, Lat. Am.* to cheer up
retén *m,* stock, reserve, provision; *mil* reserve
retención *f,* retention
retener *vt irr* to keep, retain; recollect, remember; keep back; *law* detain; deduct. See **tener**
retenidamente *adv* retentively
retentiva *f,* retentiveness, memory
retentivo *a* retentive
reticencia *f,* reticence
reticente *a* reticent
retículo *m,* reticulum, network; *phys* reticle
retina *f,* retina
retintín *m,* ringing; tinkling; *inf* sarcastic tone
retiñir *vi* to tinkle, clink; jingle
retirada *f,* withdrawal; retirement; seclusion, refuge; *mil* retreat
retirado *a* remote, secluded; *mil* retired
retirar *vt* to withdraw; remove; repel, throw back; hide, put aside; *vr* withdraw; retire; *mil* retreat
retiro *m,* withdrawal; removal; seclusion, privacy; *mil* retreat; retirement; *ecc* retreat. **dar el r. (a),** to place on the retired list
reto *m,* challenge; threat
retocar *vt* to touch again or repeatedly; *phot* retouch; restore (pictures); *fig* put the finishing touch to
retoñar *vi* to sprout, shoot; *fig* revive, resuscitate
retoño *m,* sprout, shoot
retoque *m,* frequent touching; finishing touch; touch, slight attack
retorcer *vt irr* to twist; contort; confound with one's own argument; misconstrue, distort; *vr* contort; writhe. See **torcer**
retórica *f,* rhetoric; *pl inf* quibbling

retórico (-ca) *a* rhetorical. *n* rhetorician
retornar *vt* to return, give back; turn, twist; turn back; *vi* and *vr* return, go back
retorno *m*, return, going back; recompense, repayment; exchange; return journey
retorsión *f*, twisting, writhing; *fig* misconstruction
retortijón *m*, twisting, curling. **r. de tripas,** stomachache
retozar *vi* to skip, frisk, frolic, gambol; romp; *fig* be aroused (passions)
retozón *a* frolicsome
retracción *f*, drawing back, retraction
retractación *f*, retractation, recantation
retractar *vt* to retract, recant, withdraw
retráctil *a* retractile
retraer *vt irr* to bring back again; dissuade; buy back, redeem; *vr* take refuge; retire; withdraw; go into seclusion. See **traer**
retraído *a* fugitive, refugee; retired, solitary; timid, nervous, unsociable
retraimiento *m*, withdrawal; seclusion, privacy; refuge, asylum, sanctuary; timidity, unsociability
retranca *f*, *Lat. Am.* brake
retrancar *vt*, *Lat. Am.* to brake
retrasar *vt* to postpone, delay; turn back (the clock); *vi* be slow (of clocks); *vr* be behind time, be late; be backward (persons)
retraso *m*, lateness; delay, dilatoriness; loss of time (clocks); setting back (of the clock) (e.g. **El reloj lleva cinco minutos de r.,** The clock is five minutes slow)
retratar *vt* to paint or draw the portrait of; portray, describe; photograph; copy, imitate
retratería *f*, *Lat. Am.* photographer's studio
retratista *mf* portrait painter; photographer; portrayer
retrato *m*, portrait; portrayal; *fig* image, likeness
retrechería *f*, *inf* craftiness, evasiveness
retrete *m*, toilet, water closet
retribución *f*, recompense, reward
retribuir *vt irr* to recompense, reward. See **huir**
retroactivo *a* retroactive
retroceder *vi* to withdraw, move back, draw back; recede
retroceso *m*, retrocedence, withdrawal; *med* retrogression
retrogradación *f*, retrogression
retrógrado *a* retrogressive, retrograde; *pol* reactionary
retronar *vi irr* to bang, thunder, resound with noise. See **tronar**
retrospectivo *a* retrospective
retrotraer *vt irr* to antedate. See **traer**
retruécano *m*, antithesis; play on words, pun
retumbante *a* resounding; pompous, high-flown
retumbar *vi* to resound, echo, reverberate; roll (of thunder); roar (of a cannon)
retumbo *m*, reverberation, echo; rumble; roll (of thunder); roar (of a cannon, etc.)
reuma *m*, rheumatism
reumático *a* rheumatic
reumatismo *m*, rheumatism
reunión *f*, reunion, union; meeting; assembly, gathering
reunir *vt* to reunite; unite; join; gather, assemble; *vr* meet, assemble; unite
revacunación *f*, revaccination
revacunar *vt* to revaccinate
revalidación *f*, ratification, confirmation
revalidar *vt* to ratify, confirm; *vr* pass a final examination
revejido *a* prematurely old
revelación *f*, revelation; *phot* developing
revelador *a* revealing. *m*, *phot* developer
revelar *vt* to reveal; *phot* develop
revendedor (-ra) *a* reselling, retail. *n* retailer
revender *vt* to resell; retail (goods)
reventa *f*, resale; retail
reventar *vi irr* to burst, explode; break in foam (waves); burst forth; *fig* burst (with impatience, etc.); *inf* explode (with anger, etc.); *vt* break, crush; *fig* wear out, exhaust; *inf* irritate, vex; *vr* burst; *fig* be exhausted. See **sentar**
reventón *a* bursting. *m*, explosion, bursting; steep hill; hole, fix, difficulty; uphill work, heavy toil
rever *vt irr* to look at again, revise; *law* retry. See **ver**
reverberación *f*, reflection (of light); reverberation, resounding
reverberar *vi* to reflect; resound, reverberate
reverbero *m*, reverberation; reflector; *Lat. Am.* small stove
reverdecer *vi irr* to grow green again; revive, acquire new vigor. See **conocer**
reverencia *f*, respect, veneration; bow; curtsy; *ecc* reverence (title)
reverencial *a* reverential, respectful
reverenciar *vt* to revere; honor; respect
reverendo *a* reverend; venerable; *inf* overprudent
reversión *f*, reversion
reverso *m*, wrong side, back; reverse side (of coins)
reverter *vi irr* to overflow. See **entender**
revertir *vi law* to revert
revés *m*, wrong side, back, reverse; cuff, slap; backhand (in ballgames); check, setback, reverse; disaster, misfortune. **al r.,** on the contrary; wrong side out. **de r.,** from left to right, counterclockwise
revesado *a* complicated, difficult; willful
revestimiento *m*, *mas* lining, coating
revestir *vt irr* to dress; *mas* coat, line; *fig* cover, clothe; *vr* be dressed or dress oneself; *fig* be captivated (by an idea); become haughty or full of oneself; rise to the occasion, develop qualities necessary. See **pedir**
reviejo *a* very old. *m*, dead branch (of trees)
revisar *vt* to revise; examine
revisión *f*, revision; reexamination; *law* retrial
revisor *a* revising, examining. *m*, reviser; ticket inspector
revista *f*, reexamination, revision; review, periodical; *theat* revue; reinspection; review (of a book, etc.); *law* new trial; *mil* review. **pasar r.,** to inspect; review
revivificación *f*, revivification
revivificar *vt* to revivify, revive
revivir *vi* to resuscitate; revive
revocación *f*, revocation, cancellation, annulment
revocar *vt* to revoke, annul; dissuade; repel, throw back; wash (walls); *law* discharge
revolcadero *m*, bathing place (of animals)
revolcar *vt irr* to knock down, trample underfoot; lay flat (in an argument); *vr* wallow; dig one's heels in, be obstinate. See **volcar**
revolotear *vi* to flutter, fly around; twirl; *vt* hurl, toss
revoltillo *m*, jumble, hodgepodge; confusion, tangle; *Venezuela* scrambled eggs
revoltoso *a* rebellious; mischievous, willful; intricate
revoltura *f*, *Mexico* dish of eggs and vegetables
revolución *f*, turn, revolution; rebellion, uprising; revolution
revolucionar *vt* to revolutionize
revolucionario (-ia) *a* and *n* revolutionary
revolver *vt irr* to turn over; turn upside down; wrap up; revolve; stir; reflect upon, consider; upset, cause disharmony; search through, disorder (papers, etc.); *vr* move from side to side; change (in the weather). See **resolver**
revólver *m*, revolver
revoque *m*, *mas* washing, whitewash; plastering
revuelco *m*, wallowing
revuelo *m*, second flight (of birds); irregular course of flight; disturbance, upset
revuelta *f*, second turn or revolution; revolt, rebellion; quarrel, fight; turning point; change of direction, turn; change (of opinions, posts, etc.)
revueltamente *adv* in confusion, higgledy-piggledy
revulsión *f*, revulsion
rexaminación *f*, reexamination

rexaminar *vt* to reexamine
rexpedir *vt* to forward, send on
rexportación *f*, reexport
rexportar *vt com* to reexport
rey *m*, king (in cards, chess); queen bee; *inf* swineherd; *fig* king, chief. *her* **r. de armas,** king-of-arms. **reyes magos,** magi. **día de Reyes,** Twelfth Night. **servir al r.,** to fight for the king
reyerta *f*, quarrel, row, rumpus
reyezuelo *m*, kinglet, petty king; golden-crested wren
rezagar *vt* to leave behind; postpone, delay; *vr* lag behind, straggle
rezar *vt* to pray, say prayers; say mass; *inf* state, say; *vi* pray; *inf* fume, grumble. **El edicto reza así,** The edict runs like this, The edict reads like this
rezo *m*, prayer; devotions
rezongar *vi* to grouse, grumble
rezumar(se) *vr* and *vi* to percolate, ooze through; *inf* leak out, be known
ría *f*, estuary, river mouth, firth
riachuelo *m*, rivulet, stream
riada *f*, flood. *aer* **r. de acero,** rain of flak
ribaldería *f*, ribaldry
ribaldo *a* ribald. *m*, knave
ribazo *m*, slope, incline
ribera *f*, bank, margin, shore, strand; *Lat. Am.* slum
ribereño (-ña) *a* and *n* riparian
ribero *m*, embankment, wall
ribete *m*, binding, border, trimming; stripe; increase, addition; dramatic touch, exaggeration; *pl* indications, signs
ribetear *vt sew* to bind, trim, edge
ricacho (-cha) *n inf* newly rich person, nouveau riche
ricahembra *f*, lady; daughter or wife of a Spanish noble *ant*
ricamente *adv* richly, opulently; beautifully, splendidly; luxuriously
ricino *m*, castor oil plant
rico *a* wealthy, rich; abundant; magnificent, splendid; delicious. **r. como Creso,** rich as Croesus
ricohombre *m*, nobleman *ant*
ricura *f*, *inf* richness, wealth
ridiculez *f*, absurd action or remark; ridiculousness; affectation; folly
ridiculizar *vt* to ridicule, poke fun at
ridículo *a* ridiculous, absurd; grotesque; preposterous, outrageous. *m*, reticule
riego *m*, watering, spraying; irrigation
riel *m*, ingot; rail (of a train or streetcar)
rielar *vi* to glimmer, glisten; glitter; shimmer
rienda *f*, rein (gen. *pl*); restraint; *pl* administration, government. **a r. suelta,** swiftly; without restraint
riesgo *m*, risk, danger
riesgoso, -a *a*, *Lat. Am.* dangerous, risky
rifa *f*, raffle; quarrel, disagreement
rifar *vt* to raffle; *vi* quarrel, fall out
rifle *m*, rifle
rigidez *f*, stiffness; rigidity; harshness
rígido *a* stiff; rigid; inflexible; severe, harsh
rigor *m*, severity, sternness; rigor; hardness; inflexibility; *med* rigor. **en r.,** strictly speaking. **ser de r.,** to be essential, be indispensable
rigorista *mf* martinet
riguroso *a* rigorous; harsh, cruel; austere, rigid; strict, exact, scrupulous
rijoso *a* quarrelsome; lascivious
rima *f*, rhyme, rime; heap; *pl* lyrics
rimador (-ra) *a* rhyming, rimer. *n* rhymer, rimer
rimar *vi* to compose verses; *vi* and *vt* rhyme, rime
rimbombo *m*, reverberation (of a sound)
rimero *m*, heap, pile
Rin, el the Rhine
rincón *m*, corner, angle; retreat, hiding place; *inf* home, nest, nook
rinconada *f*, corner, angle
rinconera *f*, corner cupboard; corner table
ringlera *f*, file, line, row
ringlero *m*, guiding line for writing
ringorrangos *m pl*, *inf* exaggerated flourishes in writing; *inf* unnecessary frills or ornaments
ringueletear *vi*, *Lat. Am.* to wander through the streets
rinoceronte *m*, rhinoceros
riñón *m*, kidney; *fig* center, heart; *pl anat* back
río *m*, river; *fig* stream, flood
rioja *m*, red wine from Rioja
rioplatense *a* of the River Plate area; *mf* native of the River Plate area; resident of the River Plate area
ripio *m*, remains, rest; debris, rubbish; *lit* padding; verbiage, prolixity. **no perder r.,** to lose no occasion or opportunity
riqueza *f*, riches, wealth; abundance; richness, magnificence
risa *f*, laugh; laughter; cause of amusement, joke
risco *m*, crag
riscoso *a* craggy
risible *a* laughable
risoles *m pl*, rissoles
risotada *f*, loud laugh
ristra *f*, string (of onions, etc.); file, line, row
risueño *a* smiling; cheerful; pleasant, agreeable; favorable, hopeful
rítmico *a* rhythmic
ritmo *m*, rhythm
rito *m*, rite
ritualismo *m*, ritualism
ritualista *mf* ritualist
rivalidad *f*, rivalry, competition; hostility
rivalizar *vi* to compete, rival
rizado *m*, curling; pleating, crimping; rippling, ruffling
rizar *vt* to curl (hair); ripple, ruffle (of water); pleat, crimp; *vr* be naturally wavy (of hair)
rizo *m*, curl, ringlet; cut velvet. *aer* **hacer el r.,** to loop the loop; *naut* to take in reefs
rizoso *a* naturally curly or wavy (hair)
robador (-ra) *a* robbing. *n* robber, thief. *m*, abductor
robar *vt* to rob; abduct; wash away, eat away (rivers, sea); remove honey from the hive; draw (in cards, dominoes); *fig* capture (love, etc.)
roblar *vt* to reinforce, strengthen; clinch
roble *m*, oak tree; oak; *fig* bulwark, tower of strength
robledo *m*, oak grove
roblón *m*, rivet
robo *m*, theft, robbery; booty
robustecer *vt irr* to strengthen. See **conocer**
robustez *f*, strength, robustness
robusto *a* vigorous, robust, hearty, strong
roca *f*, rock; *fig* tower of strength
roce *m*, rubbing, brushing, touching, friction; social intercourse
rociada *f*, dewing; sprinkling; dew-wet grass given as medicine to horses and mules; *fig* shower; general slander; harsh rebuke
rociar *vi* to fall as dew; drizzle; *vt* sprinkle, spray; *fig* shower (with)
rocín *m*, sorry nag; hack; *inf* ignoramus, boor
rocinante *m*, poor nag (alluding to Don Quixote's horse)
rocío *m*, dew; dewdrop; drizzle, light shower; *fig* sprinkling, spray
rocoso *a* rocky
rodaballo *m*, turbot; *inf* crafty man
rodada *f*, wheel mark or track
rodado *a* dappled (of horses)
rodaje *m*, wheeling; shooting (of a film)
rodante *a* rolling
rodar *vi* to roll; revolve, turn; run on wheels; wander, roam; be moved about; be plentiful, abound; happen successively; (*with por*) fall down, roll down
rodear *vi* to walk around; go by a roundabout way; *fig* beat around the bush; *vt* encircle, surround; besiege; *WH* round up (cattle)
rodela *f*, round shield; buckler

rodeno *a* red (of rocks, earth, etc.)
rodeo *m*, encirclement; indirect and longer way; trick to evade pursuit; *WH* rodeo, roundup; stockyard, cattle enclosure; *fig* beating around the bush; evasive reply
rodera *f*, rail, track, line; cart rut or track
rodilla *f*, knee; floor cloth. **de rodillas,** on one's knees. **ponerse de rodillas,** *or* **hincar las rodillas,** to kneel down
rodillazo *m*, push with the knee
rodillera *f*, kneecap, kneepad; mend at the knee of garments; bagginess of trouser knees
rodillo *m*, roller; traction engine; *print* inking roller; garden roller. **r. de pastas,** *cul* rolling pin
rododendro *m*, rhododendron
rodrigón *m*, stake, prop (for plants); *inf* old retainer who serves as a ladies' escort
roedor *a* gnawing; *fig* nagging; biting. *a* and *m*, rodent
roedura *f*, biting, gnawing; corrosion
roer *vt irr* to gnaw, nibble, eat; corrode, wear away; trouble, afflict. *Pres. Ind.* **roigo, roes,** etc. *Preterite* **royó, royeron.** *Imperf. Subjunc.* **royese,** etc.
rogación *f*, request, supplication, entreaty; *ecc* rogation
rogador (-ra) *a* requesting; beseeching. *n* suppliant
rogar *vt irr* to request; beseech, beg. See **contar**
rogativo *a* supplicatory, petitioning
roído *a* gnawed, eaten; *inf* miserable, stingy
rojal *a* red (of soil, etc.). *m*, red earth
rojear *vi* to appear red; be reddish
rojete *m*, rouge
rojez *f*, redness
rojizo *a* reddish
rojo *a* red; fair; red-gold (of hair); *pol* radical, red
rol *m*, roll, list
roldana *f*, pulley wheel
rollizo *a* round; plump, sturdy. *m*, log
rollo *m*, roll; *cul* rolling pin; log; town cross or pillar; anything rolled (paper, etc.); twist (of tobacco)
Roma Rome
romance *a* and *m*, romance (language). *m*, Spanish; ballad; romance of chivalry; *pl fig* fairy tales, excuses. **en buen r.,** *fig* in plain words
romancear *vt* to translate from Latin into the spoken language; translate into Spanish; paraphrase the Spanish to assist translation; *Lat. Am.* to flirt
romancero (-ra) *n* balladeer. *m*, collection of ballads
romancista *mf* romancist
románico *a arch* Romanesque
romanista *mf* expert in Roman law or Romance languages and literature
romanizar *vt* to romanize; *vr* become romanized
romano (-na) *a* and *n* Roman. **a la romana,** in the Roman way. **cabello a la romana,** *inf* bobbed hair
romanticismo *m*, romanticism
romántico (-ca) *a* romantic; emotional; fanciful. *n* romantic; romanticist
rombo *m*, rhombus
romería *f*, pilgrimage; excursion, picnic (made on a saint's day)
romero (-ra) *m*, rosemary. *n* pilgrim
romo *a* blunt, dull, unsharpened; flat (of noses); *m*. *Lat. Am.* rum
rompecabezas *m*, bludgeon; knuckleduster; *inf* teaser, puzzle, riddle; jigsaw puzzle
rompeimágenes *mf* iconoclast
rompeolas *m*, jetty, breakwater
romper *vt* to break; shatter, break into fragments; spoil, ruin; break up, plow; *fig* cut, divide (of water, etc.); *fig* end, break; interrupt; infringe, break; *vi* break; break (of waves); sprout, flower; (*with prep a*) begin to. **Rompió a hablar,** He broke into speech. *Past Part.* **roto**
rompiente *a* breaking. *m*, reef, shoal
rompimiento *m*, break, rupture; crack, split; breakage; infringement; plowing up; *fig* dividing (water, etc.); spoiling, ruining; opening (of buds, etc.)
ron *m*, rum
roncar *vi* to snore; *fig* roar, howl (of the sea, wind, etc.); *inf* brag
roncear *vi* to be dilatory or unwilling; *inf* flatter, cajole; *naut* lag behind, sail slowly
roncero *a* dilatory, slow; grumbling, complaining; cajoling, flattering; *Lat. Am.* sly
roncha *f*, wheal; bruise, bump; *inf* money lost through trickery; thin, round slice
ronco *a* hoarse, husky
ronda *f*, round, beat, patrol; serenading party; *inf* round (of drinks)
rondador *m*, watchman; roundsman; serenader; night wanderer
rondalla *f*, tale, fairy tale
rondar *vi* to patrol, police; walk the streets by night; serenade; *vt* haunt; hover about; *inf* overcome (of sleep, etc.)
ronquear *vi* to be hoarse
ronquera *f*, hoarseness
ronquido *m*, snore; hoarse sound
ronronear *vi* to purr (of cats)
ronzal *m*, halter
ronzar *vt* to munch, crack with the teeth
roña *f*, mange (in sheep); grime, filth; mold; moral corruption; *inf* stinginess; *inf* trick, deception
roñería *f*, *inf* meanness, stinginess
roñoso *a* scabby; filthy; rusty; *inf* mean, stingy
ropa *f*, fabric, material, stuff; clothes, wearing apparel; garment, outfit; robe (of office). **r. blanca,** underclothes; (domestic) linen. **r. hecha,** ready-made clothing. **r. talar,** long gown; cassock
ropaje *m*, clothes, garments; vestments; drapery; *fig* form, outline
ropavejería *f*, old-clothes shop
ropavejero (-ra) *n* old-clothes dealer
ropería *f*, clothier's shop or trade; wardrobe; cloakroom
ropero (-ra) *n* clothier; keeper of the wardrobe. *m*, wardrobe; charitable organization
ropilla *f*, doublet
ropón *m*, a loose-fitting gown generally worn over clothes
roque *m*, rook (in chess)
roqueño *a* rocky; hard as rock
roquete *m*, *ecc* rochet; barb of a lance
rorro *m*, *inf* infant, baby
rosa *f*, rose; anything rose-shaped; artificial rose; red spot on the body; *arch* rose window; *pl* rosettes. *m*, rose color. **r. de los vientos,** mariner's compass. **r. laurel,** oleander
rosado *a* rose-colored; rose; rosé (wines)
rosal *m*, rose tree. **r. de tallo,** standard rose tree
rosaleda, rosalera *f*, rose garden
rosario *m*, rosary; *fig* string; chain pump; *inf* backbone
rosbif *m*, roast beef
rosca *f*, screw and nut; *cul* twist (of bread or cake); spiral
roscado *a* twisted, spiral
rosear *vi* to turn to rose, become rose-colored
róseo *a* rose-colored
roseta *f*, *dim* small rose; rosette; rose of a watering can; rosette copper; *pl* toasted maize. **r. de fiebre,** rush of fever
rosetón *m*, large rosette; *arch* rose window
rosicler *m*, rose-pink (first flush of dawn)
rosillo *a* light red; roan (of horses)
rosmaro *m*, manatee, sea cow
roso *a* bald, worn; red
rosquete *m*, *Lat. Am.* bun
rosquilla *f*, ring-shaped cake
rosquillero (-ra) *n* seller of rosquillas
rostrituerto *a inf* wry-faced (from sadness or anger)
rostro *m*, bird's beak; face, visage. **conocer de r.,** to know by sight. **dar en r.,** *fig* to throw in one's face
rota *f*, *mil* defeat; *ecc* Rota; *bot* rattan
rotación *f*, rotation. **r. de cultivos,** rotation of crops
rotativa *f*, rotary printing press
rotativo *a* rotary

rotatorio *a* rotatory
rotisería *f, Lat. Am.* steakhouse; grillroom
roto *a* shabby, ragged; vicious, debauched
rotograbado *m,* rotogravure
rotonda *f,* rotunda
rótula *f,* rotula, patella
rotular *vt* to label; give a title or heading to
rótulo *m,* title; poster, placard; label
rotundamente *adv* tersely, roundly, plainly
rotundidad *f,* rotundity; roundness; finality (of words, etc.)
rotundo *a* round; rotund; sonorous; final, plain (of words, etc.)
rotura *f,* breaking, shattering; plowing up; breakage; rupture
roturar *vt agr* to break up, plow up
roya *f,* rust, mildew; tobacco
roza *f, agr* clearing (of weeds, etc.); ground ready for sowing. **de r. abierta,** open cast (of mining)
rozador *m, Lat. Am.* machete
rozadura *f,* rubbing, friction; abrasion, chafing
rozagante *a* long and elaborate (dresses); upstanding; handsome; strapping, fine
rozamiento *m,* grazing, brushing, rubbing; discord, disharmony, disagreement; *mech* friction
rozar *vt agr* to clear of weeds; crop, nibble; scrape; brush against, touch; *vi* brush, rub, touch; *vr* have dealings with, know; stammer; be like, resemble
rúa *f,* village street; highway
ruar *vi* to walk or ride through the streets; parade through the streets flirting with the ladies
rubeola *f,* rubella
rubí *m,* ruby; jewel (of a watch)
rubia *f, bot* madder; blonde (girl, woman)
rubicundez *f,* rubicundity, ruddiness, redness
rubicundo *a* red-gold; ruddy-complexioned; reddish
rubio *a* red-gold, gold; fair, blond
rubor *m,* blush, flush; bashfulness
ruborizarse *vr* to blush; be shamefaced
ruboroso *a* shamefaced; blushing
rúbrica *f,* rubric; personal mark, flourish added to one's signature
rubricar *vt* to sign and seal; sign with an X or other symbol; sign with a flourish
rubro *a* red
rucio *a* fawn, light-gray (of animals); *inf* going gray, gray-haired
rudamente *adv* rudely, abruptly, churlishly; roughly
rudeza *f,* roughness; rudeness, uncouthness; stupidity
rudimentario *a* rudimentary
rudimento *m,* embryo; *pl* rudiments
rudo *a* rough; unfinished; uncouth, boorish, rude; stupid
rueca *f,* distaff (in spinning); spinning wheel; curve, twist
rueda *f,* wheel; group, circle; spread of a peacock's tail; roller, castor; round piece or slice; turn, chance; succession (of events); wheel (used for torture). **r. libre,** freewheeling. *inf* **hacer la r. (a),** to flatter, make a fuss of
ruedero *m,* wheelwright
ruedo *m,* turning, rotation; circumference; lined hem of a cassock; circuit
ruego *m,* request, entreaty
rufián *m,* ruffian; pimp
rufo *a* fair; red-haired; curly-haired
rugido *m,* roaring, roar; creaking; gnashing; rumbling
rugir *vi* to roar; squeak, creak; gnash (the teeth)
ruibarbo *m,* rhubarb
ruido *m,* noise, din; disturbance; rumor. **hacer** (*or* **meter**) **r.,** to cause a sensation. *inf* **ser más el r. que las nueces,** to be much ado about nothing
ruidoso *a* noisy; notable
ruin *a* base, vile; despicable; mean; puny
ruina *f,* ruin, downfall; financial ruin; fall, decline; *pl* ruins
ruinar *vt* to ruin
ruindad *f,* baseness; meanness; pettiness, unworthiness; mean trick, despicable action
ruinoso *a* half-ruined; ruinous; useless, worthless
ruiseñor *m,* nightingale
ruleta *f,* roulette
rumano (-na) *a* and *n* Romanian. *m,* Romanian (language)
rumba *f* rumba; *Lat. Am.* party (celebration)
rumbo *m, naut* course, way, route; direction; *inf* swank; *Lat. Am.* party (celebration) **con r. a,** headed for, in the direction of. **hacer r. a,** to sail for; make for
rumboso *a inf* pompous, dignified; open-handed, generous
rumia *f,* rumination; cud
rumiante *a* and *mf zool* ruminant. *a inf* reflective, meditative
rumiar *vt zool* to ruminate; *inf* reflect upon, chew on; *inf* fume, rage
rumor *m,* noise; rumor; murmur, babble; dull sound
rúnico *a* runic
runrunearse *v impers* to be rumored
rupia *f,* rupee
ruptura *f, fig* rupture; *surg* hernia
rural *a* rustic, rural
ruralmente *adv* rurally
Rusia Russia
rusificar *vt* to russianize
ruso (-sa) *a* and *n* Russian. *m,* Russian (language)
rusticación *f,* rustication
rusticar *vi* to rusticate
rusticidad *f,* rusticity; boorishness, coarseness
rústico *a* rustic, country; boorish, uncouth. *m,* countryman; yokel; peasant. **en rústica,** in paper covers (of books)
ruta *f,* route; *fig* way. **r. de evitación,** bypass, detour
ruteno (-na) *a* and *n* Ruthenian. *m,* Ruthenian (language)
rutilante *a poet* sparkling, glowing
rutilar *vi poet* to gleam, sparkle
rutina *f,* routine
rutinario *a* routine
rutinero (-ra) *a* routinistic. *n* routinist

S

sábado *m,* Saturday; Jewish sabbath. **s. de gloria,** Easter Saturday
sábalo *m, icht* shad
sabana *f,* savannah
sábana *f,* bed sheet; altar cloth. *inf* **pegársele (a uno) las sábanas,** to be tied to the bed, get up late
sabandija *f,* any unpleasant insect or reptile; *fig* vermin
sabanero (-ra) *n* savannah dweller. *a* savannah
sabanilla *f,* small piece of linen (kerchief, towel, etc.); altar cloth
sabañón *m,* chilblain
sabatario *a* sabbatarian
sabático *a* sabbatical
sabatino *a* Saturday, Sabbath
sabedor *a* aware; knowledgeable, knowing
sabelotodo *mf inf* know-it-all
saber *m,* learning; wisdom
saber *vt irr* to know; be able to, know how; *vi* know; be shrewd, be well aware of; (*with prep a*) taste of; be like or similar to. **s. al dedillo,** *fig* to have at one's finger-

tips. **a s.,** viz., namely. *inf* **no s. cuántas son cinco,** not to know how many beans make five. **no s. dónde meterse,** to be overcome by shame; have the jitters. **No sé cuántos,** I don't know how many. **No sé quién,** I don't know who (which person). **No sé qué,** I don't know what. **un no sé qué,** a certain something; a touch (of). **¡Quién sabe!** Who knows!; Time will tell. *Pres. Ind.* **sé, sabes,** etc. *Fut.* **sabré,** etc. *Condit.* **sabría,** etc. *Preterite* **supe,** etc. *Pres. Subjunc.* **sepa,** etc. *Imperf. Subjunc.* **supiese,** etc.

sabiamente *adv* wisely, prudently

sabidillo (-lla) *a* and *n inf* know-it-all

sabiduría *f,* prudence, wisdom; erudition, learning; knowledge, awareness. **Libro de la S. de Salomón,** Book of Wisdom

sabiendas, a *adv* knowingly, consciously

sabihondo (-da) *n inf* know-it-all

sabio (-ia) *a* wise; learned, erudite; prudent, sagacious; knowing (of animals); performing (of animals). *n* wise person; scholar, erudite person

sablazo *m,* saber thrust or wound; *inf* sponging, taking advantage of. **dar un s. (a),** *inf* to sponge on; touch for money

sable *m,* saber; *her* sable; *inf* talent for sponging on people. *a her* sable

sablear *vi inf* to touch for invitations, loans, etc.; cadge

sablista *mf inf* sponger, cadger

saboneta *f,* hunting case watch, hunter

sabor *m,* taste, flavor; impression, effect. **a s.,** to taste; at pleasure

saboreamiento *m,* savoring; relishing, enjoyment

saborear *vt* to flavor, season; relish, savor; appreciate, enjoy; *vr* relish, savor; enjoy

saboreo *m,* tasting; savoring; relishing

sabotaje *m,* sabotage

saboteador *m,* saboteur

Saboya Savoy

saboyano (-na) *a* and *n* Savoyard

sabroso *a* tasty, savory, well-seasoned; delightful, delicious; *inf* piquant, racy; *Lat. Am.* garrulous, talkative

sabueso *m,* cocker spaniel. **s. de artois,** hound

sabuloso *a* sandy

saburra *f,* fur (on the tongue)

saca *f,* drawing out, removing; export, transport, shipping; removal, extraction; legal copy (of a document). **estar de s.,** to be on sale; *inf* be marriageable (of women)

sacabocados *m,* punch (tool); *inf* cinch, easy matter

sacabotas *m,* bootjack

sacabrocas *m,* tack puller

sacabuche *m, mus* sackbut; sackbut player; *inf* insignificant little man; *naut* hand pump

sacacorchos *m,* corkscrew

sacacuartos *m, inf* catchpenny

sacada *f,* territory cut off from a province

sacadineros *m, inf* catchpenny

sacamanchas *mf.* See **quitamanchas**

sacamantas *m, inf* tax collector

sacamiento *m,* removing, taking out

sacamuelas *mf* dentist; charlatan, quack; *inf* windbag

sacapotras *m, inf* unskilled surgeon

sacar *vt* to draw out; extract; pull out; take out; remove; dispossess, turn out; free from, relieve; examine, investigate; extort (the truth); extract (sugar, etc.); win (prizes, games); copy; discover, find out; elect by ballot; obtain, achieve; exclude; show, exhibit; quote, mention; produce, invent; manufacture; note down; put forth; unsheath (swords); bowl (in cricket); serve (in tennis). **s. a bailar,** to invite to dance. **s. a luz,** to publish, print; reveal, bring out. **s. a paseo,** to take for a walk. **s. de pila,** to be a godfather or godmother to. **s. en claro** *or* **s. en limpio,** to copy; conclude, infer, gather. **sacarse en conclusión que . . . ,** the conclusion is that . . .

sacarificar *vt* to saccharify

sacarina *f,* saccharine

sacasillas *mf, inf theat* stagehand

sacerdocio *m,* priesthood

sacerdotal *a* priestly

sacerdote *m,* priest

sacerdotisa *f,* priestess. **sumo s.,** high priestess

saciable *a* satiable

sachar *vt* to weed

sacho *m,* weeder

saciar *vt* to satisfy; satiate; *vr* be satiated

saciedad *f,* satiety, surfeit

saco *m,* handbag; sack, bag; sackful; sack coat; *biol* sac; *mil* sack, plundering. **s. de noche,** dressing case, weekend case. *inf* **no echar en s. roto,** not to forget, to remember

sacramentalmente *adv* sacramentally; in confession

sacramentar *vt* to consecrate; administer the Blessed Sacrament; hide, conceal

sacramentario (-ia) *n* sacramentalist; sacramentarian

sacramento *m,* sacrament; *ecc* Host; *ecc* mystery. **s. del altar,** Eucharist. **con todos los sacramentos,** with all the sacraments; done in order, complete with all formalities. **recibir los sacramentos,** to receive the last sacraments

sacratísimo *a* most sacred

sacrificadero *m,* place of sacrifice

sacrificador (-ra) *a* sacrificing. *n* sacrificer

sacrificar *vt* to sacrifice; slaughter; *vr* consecrate oneself to God; sacrifice oneself; devote or dedicate oneself (to)

sacrificio *m,* sacrifice; offering, dedication; surrendering, forgoing; compliance, submission. **s. del altar,** sacrifice of the mass

sacrilegio *m,* sacrilege

sacrílego *a* sacrilegious

sacristán *m,* sacristan; sexton; hoop (for dresses). *inf* **s. de amén,** yes-man. *inf* **ser gran s.,** to be very crafty

sacristana *f,* wife of a sacristan or sexton; nun in charge of a convent sacristy

sacristanía *f,* office of a sacristan or sexton

sacristía *f,* sacristy; vestry; office of a sacristan or sexton

sacro *a* sacred; *anat* sacral

sacrosanto *a* sacrosanct

sacudida *f,* shake, shaking; jerk, jar, jolt; twitch, pull; *aer* bump

sacudido *a* unsociable; difficult, wayward; determined, bold

sacudidor (-ra) *a* shaking; jerking. *n* shaker. *m,* carpet beater; duster

sacudidura *f,* shaking (especially to remove dust); jerking

sacudimiento *m,* shake, shaking; jerk; twitch, pull; jolt

sacudir *vt* to shake; flap, wave; jerk, twitch; beat, bang; shake off; *vr* shake off, avoid

sadismo *m,* sadism

sadista *mf* sadist

sadístico *a* sadistic

saduceo (-ea) *a* Sadducean. *n* Sadducee

saeta *f,* arrow, dart; clock hand, watch hand; magnetic needle; short sung expression of religious ecstasy; *ast* Sagitta

saetada *f,* **saetazo** *m,* arrow wound

saetera *f,* loophole; small window

saetero *a* arrow, arrow-like. *m,* archer, bowman

safado, -a *a, Lat. Am.* cheeky, impudent, saucy

saga *f,* saga

sagacidad *f,* sagacity

sagaz *a* sagacious, shrewd; farseeing; quick on the scent (dogs)

sagital *a* arrow-shaped

sagitario *m,* archer; *ast* Sagittarius

sagrado *a* sacred; holy; sacrosanct, venerable; accursed, detestable. *m,* sanctuary, refuge; haven

sagrario *m,* sanctuary; sacrarium

sagú *m,* sago

Sáhara, el the Sahara

sahornarse *vr* to chafe, grow sore

sahorno *m,* chafing, abrasion

sahumado *a* improved, rendered more excellent; perfumed; fumigated
sahumador *m*, perfumer; fumigating vessel
sahumar *vt* to perfume; fumigate. See **desahuciar**
sahumerio *m*, perfuming; fumigation; fume, smoke
saín *m*, fat, grease; sardine oil (for lamps); grease spot (on clothes)
sainar *vt* to fatten up (animals)
sainete *m*, *cul* sauce; *theat* one-act parody or burlesque; farce; delicacy, tidbit; delicate taste (of food)
sainetero *m*, writer of sainetes
sainetesco *a* pertaining to sainetes; burlesque, satirical
sajar *vt surg* to scarify
Sajonia Saxony
sajón (-ona) *a* and *n* Saxon
sal *f*, salt; wit; grace, gracefulness. **s. de cocina,** common kitchen salt. **s. de la Higuera,** Epsom salts. **s. gema,** rock salt. **s. marina,** sea salt. **sales inglesas,** smelling salts. *inf* **estar hecho de s.,** to be full of wit. *inf* **hacerse s. y agua,** to melt away, disappear (of riches, etc.)
sala *f*, drawing room; large room, hall; *law* courtroom; *law* bench; **s. de apelación,** court of appeal. **s. de hospital,** hospital ward. **s. de justicia,** court of justice. **s. de lectura,** reading room. *law* **guardar s.,** to respect the court
salacidad *f*, lewdness, salaciousness
saladero *m*, salting or curing place; *WH* meat packing factory
saladillo *m*, salt pork
salado *a* salty, briny; brackish; witty; attractive, amusing
salador (-ra) *a* salting, curing. *n* salter, curer. *m*, curing place
saladura *f*, salting, curing
salamandra *f*, salamander; fire sprite
salar *vt* to salt; season with salt; oversalt; cure, pickle (meat, etc.); *m*, *Lat. Am.* salt marsh
salario *m*, salary
salaz *a* lewd, lecherous
salazón *f*, salting, curing; salt meat or fish trade
salazonero *a* salting, curing
salchicha *f*, sausage
salchichería *f*, sausage shop
salchichero (-ra) *n* sausage maker, sausage seller
salchichón *m*, *cul* salami, kind of sausage
saldar *vt com* to settle, pay in full; sell out cheap; balance
saldista *mf* remnant buyer
saldo *m*, *com* balance; closing of an account; bargain sale. **s. acreedor,** credit balance. **s. deudor,** debit balance. **s. líquido,** net balance
salero *m*, saltshaker, saltcellar; salt storage warehouse; *inf* wit
saleta *f*, *dim* small hall; royal antechamber; court of appeal
salida *f*, going out; leaving; departure; sailing; exit, way out; projection, protrusion; *fig* escape, way out; outcome, result; witty remark; *mil* sally; *com* outlay, expense; *com* opening, sale, salability; environs, outskirts; *Argentina* bathrobe **s. de dólares,** dollar drain. **s. de tono,** *inf* an impertinent remark. **dar s.,** *com* to enter on the credit side
salidero *a* fond of going out; *m*, exit, way out
salidizo *m*, *arch* projection. *a* projecting
saliente *a* outgoing; salient, projecting. *m*, east; projection; salient. **s. continental,** continental shelf
salina *f*, salt mine; saltworks
salinero *m*, salt merchant; salter; salt worker
salino *a* saline. *m*, *med* saline
salir *vi irr* to go out; depart, leave; succeed in getting out; escape; appear (of the sun, etc.); sprout, show green; fade, come out (of stains); project, stand out; grow, develop; turn out, result; happen, take place; cost; sail; end (of seasons, time); lead off, start (some games); be published (books); do (well or badly), succeed or fail; appear, show oneself; be drawn, win (lottery tickets); balance, come out right (accounts); be elected; become; give up (posts); lead to (of streets, etc.); *naut* overtake; (*with prep a*) guarantee, be surety for; resemble, be like; (*with con*) utter, come out with; commit, do inopportunely; succeed in, achieve (e.g. **Salió con la suya,** He got his own way); (*with de*) originate in; break away from (traditions, conventions); get rid of; (*with por*) stand up for, protect; go surety for, guarantee. *vr* leak; boil over; overflow; (*with con*) achieve, get; (*with de*) *fig* break away from. *theat* **s. a la escena,** to enter, come on to the stage. **s. de,** to recover from (an illness). **no acabar de s. de,** to not be completely recovered from. **s. del apuro,** to get out of trouble. **s. de estampía,** to stampede (of animals). **s. pitando,** *inf* to get out in a hurry. **Esta idea no salió de Juan,** This wasn't John's idea. **salga lo que saliere,** *inf* come what may. . . . *Pres. Ind.* **salgo, sales,** etc. *Fut.* **saldré,** etc. *Condit.* **saldría,** etc. *Pres. Subjunc.* **salga,** etc.
salitral *a* nitrous. *m*, saltpeter bed
salitre *m*, saltpeter
salitrería *f*, saltpeter works
salitrero *n* saltpeter worker or dealer
saliva *f*, saliva. *inf* **tragar s.,** to put up with; be unable to speak through emotion
salivación *f*, salivation
salival *a* salivary
salivar *vi* to salivate; spit
salmantino (-na) *a* and *n* Salamanca
salmear *vi* to intone psalms
salmista *mf* psalmist; psalmodist, psalm chanter
salmo *m*, psalm
salmodia *f*, psalmody; *inf* drone; psalter
salmodiar *vi* to chant psalms; *vt* drone
salmón *m*, salmon
salmonado *a* salmon-like
salmonera *f*, salmon net
salmonete *m*, red mullet
salmuera *f*, brine
salobre *a* salt, salty; brackish
salobridad *f*, saltiness
salomar *vi naut* to sing chanteys
salón *m*, drawing room; large room or hall; reception room; salon, reception, social gathering. **s. de muestras,** showroom
saloncillo *m*, *dim* small room; *theat* greenroom; rest room
salpicadura *f*, sprinkling, spattering, splashing
salpicar *vt* to sprinkle, scatter; bespatter, splash
salpicón *m*, *cul* kind of salmagundi; *inf* hodgepodge; spattering
salpimentar *vt irr* to season with pepper and salt; sprinkle; *fig* leaven, enliven (a speech, etc.). See **regimentar**
salpresar *vt* to preserve in salt, salt
salpullido *m*, rash, skin eruption
salsa *f*, sauce; gravy. **s. mahonesa** *or* **s. mayonesa,** mayonnaise sauce. **s. mayordoma,** sauce maître d'hôtel
salsera *f*, sauce boat, gravy boat
saltabanco *m*, mountebank; street entertainer, juggler
saltabarrancos *mf inf* madcap, harum-scarum
saltable *a* jumpable
saltadero *m*, jumping ground; fountain, jet
saltador (-ra) *a* jumping. *n* jumper; acrobat. *m*, jump rope, skip rope
saltamontes *m*, grasshopper
saltaojos *m*, peony
saltaparedes *mf inf* madcap, romp
saltar *vi* to jump, leap, spring; prance; frisk, gambol; rebound; blow up; burst, break asunder; pop (of corks); fly off, come off (buttons, etc.); gush out, shoot up (liquids); break apart, be shattered; be obvious, stand out; come to mind, suggest itself; show anger; *fig* let slip, come out with (remarks); *vt* leap or jump over; poke out (eyes); cover (the female); omit, pass over; blow

up, explode. **s. a la cuerda,** to jump rope, play with a skip rope. **s. a la vista,** to be obvious, leap to the eye. **s. diciendo,** *inf* to come out with, say
saltarín (-ina) *a* dancing. *n* dancer
saltatriz *f,* ballet dancer, female acrobat
saltatumbas *m,* (*inf* contemptuous) cleric who makes his living off funerals
salteador *m,* highwayman
salteamiento *m,* highway robbery, holdup; assault, attack
saltear *vt* to hold up and rob; assault, attack; jump from one thing to another, do intermittently; forestall; surprise, amaze
salterio *m,* psaltery
saltimbanco, saltimbanqui *m, inf.* See **saltabanco**
salto *m,* jump, leap, bound; leapfrog (game); precipice, ravine; waterfall; assault; important promotion; omission (of words). **s. de agua,** waterfall. **s. de cama,** peignoir, bathrobe. **s. de campana,** overturning. *inf* **s. de mal año,** sudden improvement in circumstances. **s. de mata,** flight, escape. **s. mortal,** leap of death; somersault. **s. de pie,** spillway. **dar un s.,** to leap. **en un s.,** at one jump; swiftly
saltón *a* jumping, leaping; prominent (teeth, eyes). *m,* grasshopper
salubérrimo *a sup* **salubre** most healthy
salubre *a* salubrious, healthful
salubridad *f,* healthfulness
salud *f,* health; salvation; welfare, well-being; *ecc* state of grace; *pl* civilities, greetings. **¡S. y pesetas!** Here's to your good health and prosperity! (on drinking). **gastar s.,** to enjoy good health. *inf* **vender** (*or* **verter**) **s.,** to look full of health
saludable *a* healthy, wholesome
saludador (-ra) *a* greeting, saluting. *n* greeter. *m,* charlatan, quack
saludar *vt* to greet, salute; hail (as king, etc.); send greetings to; bow; *mil* fire a salute
saludo *m,* greeting, salutation; bow; (*mil nav*) salute
salutación *f,* greeting, salutation; Ave Maria
salutífero *a* salubrious
salva *f,* salutation, greeting; (*mil nav*) salvo, volley; salute (of guns); salver; ordeal (to establish innocence); solemn assurance, oath; sampling, tasting (of food, drink). **s. de veintiún cañonazos,** twenty-one–gun salute
salvación *f,* liberation, deliverance; salvation
salvado *m,* bran
salvador (-ra) *a* saving, redeeming. *n* deliverer. *m,* redeemer
salvadoreño (-ña) *a* and *n* Salvadorean
salvaguardia *m,* guard, watch. *f,* safeguard; protection, defense; safe conduct, passport
salvajada *f,* savagery, brutal action
salvaje *a* wild (plants, animals); rough, uncultivated; uncultured, uncivilized. *mf* savage
salvajismo *m,* savagery
salvamano, a *adv* safely
salvamente *adv* safely, securely
salvamento *m,* salvation; deliverance, security, safety; place of safety; salvage
salvante *adv inf* except, save
salvar *vt* to save; *ecc* redeem; avoid (difficulty, danger); exclude, except; leap, jump; pass over, clear; *law* prove innocent; *naut* salve. **s. la diferencia,** to bridge the gap. *vi* taste, sample (food, drink); *vr* be saved from danger; *ecc* be redeemed
salvavidas *m,* life belt; safety belt; life preserver; traffic island
¡salve! *interj poet* hail!; Hail Mary, Salve Regina
salvedad *f,* qualification, reservation
salvia *f, bot* sage
salvilla *f,* salver
salvo *a* safe, unharmed; excepting, omitting. *adv* except. **a s.,** safely, without harm. **a su s.,** to his (her, their) satisfaction; at his (her, etc.) pleasure. **dejar a s.,** to exclude, leave aside. **en s.,** in safety
salvoconducto *m,* safe conduct, pass
sallar *vt* to weed
samarita *a* and *mf* **samaritano (-na)** *a* and *n* Samaritan
samba *f* samba
sambenito *m,* penitent's gown (Inquisition); disgrace, dishonor
sambubia *f, Mexico* pineapple drink
Samotracia Samothrace
samotracio (-ia) *a* and *n* Samothracian
samoyedo (-da) *n* Samoyed
san *a abb* of **santo.** Used before masculine singular names of saints except **Santos Tomás** (*or* **Tomé**), **Domingo, Toribio**
sanable *a* curable
sanador (-ra) *a* healing, curing. *n* healer
sanalotodo *m, inf* cure-all, universal remedy
sanar *vt* to cure, heal; *vi* recover, get well; heal
sanatorio *m,* sanatorium; convalescent home
sanción *f,* authorization, consent; sanction; penalty
sancionable *a* sanctionable
sancionar *vt* to authorize, approve; sanction
sancochar *vt cul* to parboil, half-cook
sancocho *m,* parboiled meat
sandalia *f,* sandal
sándalo *m,* sandalwood
sandez *f,* foolishness, stupidity; folly
sandía *f,* watermelon
sandio *a* foolish, inane
sandunga *f, inf* attractiveness, winsomeness, grace; *Lat. Am.* carousing
sandunguero *a inf* attractive, appealing, winsome
saneado *a* unencumbered, nontaxable, free
saneamiento *m,* guarantee, security; indemnity; stabilization (of currency); drainage
sanear *vt com* to guarantee, secure; indemnify; stabilize (currency); drain (land, etc.)
Sanedrín *m,* Sanhedrin
sangradera *f,* lancet; channel, sluice, drain
sangrador *m,* phlebotomist; outlet, drainage
sangradura *f,* inner bend of the arm; *surg* bleeding; draining off
sangrar *vt surg* to bleed; drain off; *inf* extort money, bleed; *print* indent; draw off resin (from pines, etc.); *vi* bleed; *vr* bleed; have oneself bled; run (of colors)
sangre *f,* blood; lineage, family. **s. fría,** sang-froid. **a s. fría,** in cold blood, premeditated. **a s. y fuego,** by fire and sword, without quarter. *inf* **bullir la s.,** to have youthful blood in one's veins. **llevar en la s.,** *fig* to be in the blood. **subírsele la s. a la cabeza,** to grow excited. *fig inf* **tener s. de horchata,** to have milk and water in one's veins
sangría *f, surg* bloodletting; resin cut (on pines, etc.)
sangriento *a* bloody, bloodstained; bloodthirsty, cruel; mortal (insults, etc.); *poet* blood-colored
sangüesa *f,* raspberry
sanguijuela *f,* leech; *fig inf* sponger
sanguinaria *f,* bloodstone
sanguinario *a* vengeful, bloody, cruel
sanguíneo *a* blood; sanguineous; sanguine, fresh-complexioned; blood-colored
sanguinolento *a.* See **sangriento**
sanidad *f,* safety, security; healthiness; health department. **s. interior,** Public Health. **S. militar,** army medical corps
sanitario *a* sanitary, hygienic. *m, mil* medical officer
sano *a* healthy; safe, secure; healthful, wholesome; unhurt, unharmed; upright, honest; sincere; *inf* entire, undamaged; sane. **s. y salvo,** safe and sound. *inf* **cortar por lo s.,** to cut one's losses
San Pablo São Paulo
sánscrito *a* and *m,* Sanscrit
santa *f,* female saint
santamente *adv* in a saintly manner; simply

santero (-ra) *a* given to image worship. *n* accomplice (of a burglar); caretaker (of a hermitage); beggar
¡Santiago! *interj* St. James! (Spanish war cry). *m,* attack, assault
santiamén *m, inf* trice, twinkling
santidad *f,* sanctity; saintliness; godliness. **Su S.,** His Holiness
santificación *f,* sanctification
santificador (-ra) *a* sanctifying. *n* sanctifier
santificar *vt* to sanctify, make holy; consecrate; dedicate; keep (feast days)
santiguada *f,* crossing oneself; rough treatment, harsh reproof
santiguar *vt* to make the sign of the cross over; *inf* beat, rain blows on; *vr* cross oneself; *inf* be dumbfounded
santísimo *a sup* most saintly, most holy
santo *a* holy; saintly; saint (see **san**); consecrated; inviolate, sacred; *inf* simple, sincere, ingenuous. *m,* saint; image of a saint; saint's day, name day (of a person); *mil* password. **Santa Hermandad,** Holy Brotherhood (former name of the Spanish rural police force). **S. Oficio,** Holy Office, Inquisition. **S. y bueno,** Well and good, All right! *inf* **alzarse con el s. y la limosna,** to take the lot, make off with everything. **llegar y besar el s.,** to do in a trice. *inf* **No es s. de mi devoción,** I'm not very keen on him. *inf* **todo el s. día,** the whole blessed day
santón *m,* dervish, santon. *inf* hypocrite, sham saint
santoral *m,* book of saints; calendar of saints; choir book
santuario *m,* sanctuary
santurrón (-ona) *a* sanctimonious; hypocritical; prudish. *n* hypocrite
santurronería *f,* sanctimoniousness
saña *f,* fury, blind rage; lust for revenge, cruelty
sañoso, sañudo *a* furious, blind with rage; cruel
sapidez *f,* flavor, sapidity
sápido *a* tasty, savory
sapiencia *f,* wisdom; knowledge; erudition
sapino *m,* fir (tree)
sapo *m,* toad
saque *m, sport* serve, service; service or bowling line; *sport* server; *sport* bowler; bowling (in cricket)
saqueador (-ra) *a* looting, pillaging. *n* pillager, plunderer
saquear *vt* to pillage, plunder, sack
saqueo *m,* plundering, pillage, sacking
sarampión *m,* measles
sarao *m,* soirée, evening party
sarape, *m, Mexico* woolen shawl or blanket worn by males
sarasa *m,* (*inf* and contemptuous) pansy, faggot
sarcasmo *m,* sarcasm
sarcástico *a* sarcastic
sarcia *f,* load, cargo
sarcófago *m,* sarcophagus
sarda *f,* mackerel
sardana *f,* traditional Catalonian dance
sardina *f,* sardine. **s. arenque,** herring. **como sardinas en banasta,** *fig* packed like sardines
sardinal *m,* sardine net
sardinero (-ra) *a* sardine. *n* sardine seller or dealer. *m,* famous district of Santander
sardineta *f,* sprat; small sardine; *mil* chevron
sardónico *a* sardonic
sarga *f,* (silk) serge; willow
sargenta *f,* sergeant's wife; *inf* mannish, overbearing woman
sargentear *vt* to be in charge as a sergeant; command, captain; *inf* boss
sargento *m,* sergeant
sarita *f. Peru* straw hat
sarmentoso *a* vine-like; twining
sarmiento *m,* vine shoot
sarna *f,* scabies. **s. perruna,** mange. **más viejo que la s.,** *inf* older than the plague
sarnoso *a* itchy; mangy
sarraceno (-na) *a* Saracen. *n* Saracen; Moor
sarracina *f,* scuffle
sarrillo *m,* death rattle, rale; arum lily
sarro *m,* furry encrustation, scale; film; tartar (on teeth)
sarta *f,* string, link (of pearls, etc.); file, line
sartén *f,* frying pan. **tener la s. por el mango,** *inf* to be top dog
sastra *f,* female tailor; tailor's wife
sastre *m,* tailor. **ser buen s.,** *inf* to be an expert (in)
sastrería *f,* tailoring; tailor's shop
Satanás *m,* Satan; devil
satánico *a* satanic
satélite *m,* satellite; follower, admirer, sycophant
satén *m,* sateen
satinar *vt* to calender; glaze; satin (paper)
sátira *f,* satire
satírico *a* satiric
satirizar *vi* to write satires; *vt* satirize
sátiro *m,* satyr; *theat* indecent play
satisfacción *f,* settlement, payment; atonement, expiation; satisfaction; gratification; amends; complacency, conceit; contentment; apology. **tomar s.,** to avenge oneself
satisfacer *vt irr* to pay, settle; atone for, expiate; gratify; quench; fulfill, observe; compensate, indemnify; discharge, meet; convince, persuade; allay, relieve; reward; explain; answer, satisfy; *vr* avenge oneself; satisfy oneself. *Pres. Ind.* **satisfago, satisfaces,** etc. *Fut.* **satisfaré,** etc. *Condit.* **satisfaría,** etc. *Preterite* **satisfice,** etc. *Past Part.* **satisfecho.** *Pres. Subjunc.* **satisfaga,** etc. *Imperf. Subjunc.* **satisficiese,** etc.
satisfactorio *a* satisfactory
satisfecho *a* self-satisfied, complacent; happy, contented
sátrapa *m,* satrap; *inf* cunning fellow
saturación *f,* saturation
saturar *vt* to satiate, fill; saturate
saturnino *a* saturnine, melancholy, morose
saturnismo *m,* saturnism, lead poisoning
Saturno *m,* Saturn
sauce *m,* willow. **s. llorón,** weeping willow
saúco *m,* elder tree
saurio *a* and *m,* saurian
savia *f,* sap; energy, zest
sáxeo *a* stone, stony
saxófono *or* **saxofón** *m,* saxophone
saya *f,* skirt; long tunic
sayal *m,* thick woolen material
sayo *m,* loose smock; *inf* any garment. **cortar un s. (a),** *inf* to gossip behind a person's back
sayón *m,* executioner; *inf* hideous-looking man
sazón *f,* ripeness, maturity; season; perfection, excellence; opportunity; taste, flavor; seasoning. **a la s.,** at that time, then. **en s.,** in season; opportunely
sazonador (-ra) *a* seasoning. *n* seasoner
sazonar *vt cul* to season; mature; *vr* mature, ripen
se *object pron reflexive 3rd sing* and *pl mf* 1. Used as accusative (direct object) himself, herself, yourself, themselves, yourselves (e.g. **Juan se ha cortado,** John has cut himself). 2. Used as dative or indirect object to himself, at himself, herself, themselves, etc. (e.g. **María se mira al espejo,** Mary looks at herself in the mirror). Reciprocity is also expressed by reflexive (e.g. **No se hablan,** They do not speak to one another). When a direct object pron. (accusative) and an indirect object pron., both in the 3rd pers. (sing. or pl.), are used together, the indirect object pron. becomes **se** (instead of **le** or **les**) (e.g. **Se lo doy,** I give it to him). Many Spanish reflexive verbs have English equivalents that are not reflexive (e.g. **desayunarse,** to breakfast, **arrepentirse,** to repent, **quejarse,** to complain). Some intransitive (neuter) verbs have a modified meaning when used reflexively (e.g. **marcharse,** to go away, **dormirse,** to fall asleep). The passive may be formed by using **se** + 3rd pers. sing. of verb (e.g. **se dice,** it is

said, people say). A number of impersonal phrases are also formed in this way (e.g. «**Se alquila,**» "To Let," «**Se vende,**» "For Sale"). The imperative is used in the same way (e.g. **Véase la página dos,** See page two)

sebáceo *a* sebaceous
sebo *m,* tallow; candle grease; fat, grease
seboso *a* tallowy; fat, greasy
seca *f,* drought; *naut* unsubmerged sandbank
secadero *m,* drying place, drying room
secadora *f,* dryer, drying machine, clothesdryer. **s. de cabello,** hairdryer
secafirmas *m,* blotting pad
secamente *adv* tersely, brusquely, curtly; dryly
secamiento *m,* drying
secano *m,* nonirrigated land; *naut* unsubmerged sandbank; anything very dry
secante *a* drying. *a* and *f, geom* secant. **papel s.,** blotting paper
secar *vt* to dry; desiccate; annoy, bore; *vr* dry; dry up (of streams, etc.); wilt, fade (of plants); become parched; grow thin, become emaciated; be very thirsty; become hard-hearted
sección *f,* act of cutting; section, part, portion; *geom mil* section. **s. cónica,** conic section. **s. de amenidades,** entertainment section (of a newspaper). **s. de reserva,** *mil* reserve list
seccionar *vt* to divide into sections, section
seccionario *a* sectional
secesión *f,* secession
secesionista *a* and *mf* secessionist
seco *a* dry; dried up, parched; faded, wilted; dead (plants); dried (fruits); thin, emaciated; unadorned; barren, arid; brusque, curt; severe, strict; indifferent, unenthusiastic; sharp (sounds); dry (wines). **a secas,** only; solely; simply, just. **en s.,** on dry land; curtly. *inf* **dejar s. (a),** to dumbfound, petrify
secreción *f,* segregation, separation; *med* secretion
secreta *f, law* secret trial or investigation; *ecc* secret(s); toilet, water closet
secretar *vt med* to secrete
secretaría *f,* secretaryship; secretary's office, secretariat
secretario (-ia) *n* secretary; amanuensis, clerk. *m,* actuary; registrar. **s. de asuntos exteriores** *or* **s. de asuntos extranjeros,** foreign secretary. **s. particular,** private secretary
secretear *vi inf* to whisper, have secrets
secreteo *m, inf* whispering, exchanging of secrets
secreto *m,* secret; secrecy, silence; confidential information; mystery; secret drawer. *a* secret; private, confidential. **en s.,** in secret, confidentially. **s. a voces,** open secret
secta *f,* sect
sectario (-ia) *a* and *n* sectarian. *n* fanatical believer
sectarismo *m,* sectarianism
sector *m,* sector
secuaz *mf* follower, disciple
secuela *f,* sequel, result
secuencia *f, ecc* sequence; (cinema) sequence
secuestrador (-ra) *a* sequestrating. *n* sequestrator
secuestrar *vt* to sequester; kidnap
secuestro *m,* sequestration; kidnapping; *surg* sequestrum
secular *a* secular, lay; centennial; age-old, ancient; *ecc* secular
secularización *f,* secularization
secularizar *vt* to secularize; *vr* become secularized
secundar *vt* to second, aid
secundario *a* secondary; accessory, subordinate; *geol* mesozoic
sed *f,* thirst; desire, yearning, appetite. **apagar** (*or* **matar**) **la s.,** to quench one's thirst. **tener s.,** to be thirsty
seda *f,* silk; bristle (boar, etc.). **s. cordelada,** twist silk. **s. ocal,** floss silk. **s. vegetal** *or* **s. artificial,** artificial silk. *inf* **como una s.,** as smooth as silk; sweet-tempered; achieved without any trouble
sedación *f,* calming, soothing
sedal *m,* fish line
sedar *vt* to soothe, calm
sedativo *a* and *m, med* sedative
sede *f, ecc* see; bishop's throne; *fig* seat (of government, etc.); Holy See (also **Santa S.**)
sedentario *a* sedentary
sedeño *a* silky; silken, made of silk
sedería *f,* silk goods; silks; silk shop
sedero (-ra) *a* silk. *n* silk weaver or worker; silk merchant
sedición *f,* sedition
sedicioso *a* seditious
sediento *a* thirsty; parched, dry (land); eager (for), desirous (of)
sedimentación *f,* sedimentation
sedimentar *vt* to leave a sediment; *vr* settle, form a sediment
sedimento *m,* sediment; dregs, lees; scale (on boilers)
sedoso *a* silky, silk-like
seducción *f,* seduction; temptation, blandishment, wile; charm, allurement
seducir *vt irr* to seduce; tempt, lead astray; charm, attract; corrupt, bribe. See **conducir**
seductivo *a* tempting; seductive, charming
seductor (-ra) *a* tempting; charming. *n* seducer; charming person
sefardí *mf* Iberian Jew or Jewess; *pl* Sephardim. *a* Sephardic
segadera *f,* sickle
segador *m,* reaper, harvester
segadora *f,* mowing machine, harvester; woman harvester
segar *vt irr* to scythe, cut down; reap, harvest; mow. See **cegar**
seglar *a* secular, lay. *mf* layman
segmento *m,* segment; *geom* segment. **s. de émbolo,** piston ring
segoviano (-na) *a* and *n* Segovian
segregación *f,* segregation
segregar *vt* to segregate, separate; *med* secrete
seguida *f,* continuation, prolongation. **de s.,** continuously; immediately. **en s.,** at once, immediately
seguidamente *adv* continuously; immediately
seguidilla *f,* popular Spanish tune and dance and verse sung to them; *inf* diarrhea
seguido *a* continuous, successive; direct, straight
seguidor (-ra) *a* following. *n* follower, disciple
seguimiento *m,* following, pursuit; continuation, resumption
seguir *vt irr* to follow; go after, pursue; prosecute, execute; continue, go on; accompany, go with; exercise (a profession); subscribe to, believe in; agree with; persecute; pester, annoy; imitate; *law* institute (a suit); handle, manage; *vr* result, follow as a consequence; follow in order, happen by turn; originate. *Pres. Part.* **siguiendo.** *Pres. Ind.* **sigo, sigues, sigue, siguen.** *Pres. Subjunc.* **siga,** etc. *Imperf. Subjunc.* **siguiese**
según *adv* according to; as. **s. parece,** as it seems. **s. y como,** as, according to
segunda *f, mus* second
segundar *vt* to repeat, do again; *vi* be second, follow the first
segundero *a agr* of the second flowering or fruiting. *m,* second hand (of a watch)
segundo *a* second. *m,* second in command, deputy head; *ast geom* second. **segunda intención,** double meaning. **segunda velocidad,** *aut* second gear. **de segunda mano,** second-hand. **sin s.,** without peer or equal
segundogénito (-ta) *a* and *n* secondborn
segundón *m,* second son; any son but the eldest
segurador *m,* surety, security (person)
seguramente *adv* securely, safely; surely, of course, naturally
seguridad *f,* security; safety; certainty; trustworthiness;

com surety; *Mexico* clasp, lock (of a suitcase, trunk, etc) **con toda s.,** with complete safety, surely, absolutely. **de s.,** *a* safety
seguro *a* secure; safe; certain, sure; firm, fixed; reliable, trustworthy; unfailing. *m,* certainty; haven, place of safety; *com* insurance; permit; *mech* ratchet. **s. contra incendio, accidentes, robo,** fire, accident, burglary insurance. **s. sobre la vida,** life insurance. **de s.,** surely, certainly. **en s.,** in safety. **s. social** *Lat. Am.* social security
seis *a* six; sixth. *m,* six; sixth (of the month); playing card or domino with six spots. **Son las s.,** It is six o'clock
seiscientos *a* six hundred; six-hundredth. *m,* six hundred
selección *f,* selection, choice. **s. natural,** natural selection
seleccionar *vt* to select, choose
selectivo *a* selective
selecto *a* choice, select, excellent
sellado *m, Argentina* postage
sellador (-ra) *a* sealing, stamping. *n* sealer, stamper
selladura *f,* sealing, stamping
sellar *vt* to seal; stamp; end, conclude; close
sello *m,* seal; stamp. **s. fiscal,** stamp duty. **s. postal,** postage stamp. **s. y cruz** *Colombia,* heads or tails
selva *f,* forest, wood; jungle
Selva Negra, la the Black Forest
selvático *a* sylvan, wood, forest; wild
selvoso *a* wooded, sylvan
semafórico *a* semaphoric
semáforo *m,* semaphore, traffic light.
semana *f,* week; week's salary. **S. Mayor** *or* **S. Santa,** Holy Week. **entre s.,** during the week, on weekdays; weekdays
semanal *a* weekly; of a week's duration
semanario *a* weekly. *m,* weekly periodical
semanero, -a *a* employed by the week; paid by the week; person employed by the week; person paid by the week
semántica *f,* semantics
semántico *a* semantic
semblante *m,* facial expression, countenance; face; appearance, look, aspect. **componer el s.,** to pull oneself together, straighten one's face. **mudar de s.,** to change color, change one's expression; alter (of circumstances)
semblanza *f,* biographical sketch. **s. literaria,** short literary biography
sembradera *f,* sowing machine
sembradío *a agr* ready for sowing
sembrado *m,* sown land
sembrador (-ra) *a* sowing. *n* sower
sembradura *f, agr* sowing
sembrar *vt irr agr* to sow; scatter, sprinkle; spread, disseminate. See **sentar**
semeja *f,* resemblance, similarity; indication, sign (gen. *pl*)
semejante *a* like, similar; such a; *math* similar. *m,* similarity, imitation. *mf* fellow man
semejanza *f,* similarity, likeness. **a s. de,** in the likeness of; like
semejar(se) *vi* and *vr* to resemble
semen *m,* semen; *bot* seed
semental *a agr* seed; breeding (of male animals). *m,* stallion
sementar *vt agr* to sow
sementera *f, agr* sowing; sown land; seedbed; seedtime; *fig* hotbed, nursery, genesis
sementero *m,* seed bag; seed bed
semestral *a* biannual, half-yearly; lasting six months
semestre *a* biannual. *m,* half-year, period of six months; six months' salary; semester
semicírculo *m,* semicircle
semidifunto *a* half-dead
semidormido *a* half-asleep
semilla *f, bot* seed; *fig* germ, genesis
semillero *m,* seedbed; nursery; *fig* hotbed, origin
seminario *m,* seedbed; nursery; genesis, origin; seminary; tutorial. **s. conciliar,** theological seminary
seminarista *mf* seminarist
semiótica *f, med* symptomatology; semiotics
semita *mf* Semite. *a* Semitic
semítico *a* Semitic
semitismo *m,* Semitism
semitono *m, mus* semitone
semitransparente *a* semitransparent
semivivo *a* half-alive
sémola *f,* semolina
sempiterna *f,* everlasting flower; thick woolen material
sempiterno *a* eternal
sen *m,* senna
Sena, el the Seine
sena *f, bot* senna; six-spotted die
senado *m,* senate; senate house; any grave assembly
senador *m,* senator
senaduría *f,* senatorship
senario *a* senary
senatorio *a* senatorial
sencillez *f,* simplicity; naturalness; easiness; ingenuousness, candor
sencillo *a* simple; unmixed; natural; thin, light (fabric); easy; ingenuous, candid; unadorned, plain; single; sincere
senda *f,* path, footpath; way; means
senderear *vt* to conduct along a path; make a pathway; *vi* attain by tortuous means
sendero *m,* footpath, path
sendos, sendas *a m,* and *f pl,* one each (e.g. **Les dio sendos lápices,** He gave them each a pencil)
senectud *f,* old age
senescal *m,* seneschal
senil *a* senile
senilidad *f,* senility
seno *m,* hollow; hole; concavity; bosom, breast; chest; uterus, womb; any internal cavity of the body; bay, cove; lap (of a woman); interior (of anything), heart; gulf; *math* sine; *anat* sinus
sensación *f,* sensation
sensacional *a* sensational
sensacionalista *a* sensationalist
sensatez *f,* prudence, good sense
sensato *a* prudent, wise
sensibilidad *f,* sensibility
sensibilizar *vt phot* to sensitize
sensible *a* sensible, sensitive; tender, feeling; perceptible; noticeable, definite; sensitive; sad, regrettable
sensiblemente *adv* appreciably; perceptibly; painfully, sadly
sensiblería *f,* sentimentality, sentimentalism
sensiblero *a* oversentimental
sensitiva *f,* sensitive plant, mimosa
sensitivo *a* sensuous; sensitive, sensible
sensorio *a* sensory. *m,* sensorium
sensual *a* sensual; sensitive, sensible; carnal, voluptuous
sensualidad *f,* sensuality; sensualism
sensualismo *m,* sensualism; *phil* sensationalism
sensualista *mf phil* sensationalist; sensualist
sentadera *f, Lat. Am.* seat (of a chair)
sentadero *m,* resting place, improvised seat
sentado *a* prudent, circumspect
sentar *vt irr* to seat; *vi inf* suit, agree with (e.g. **No me sienta este clima (este plato),** This climate (dish) doesn't suit me); fit, become; *inf* please, satisfy, be agreeable to; *vr* sit down; *inf* leave a mark on the skin. *Pres. Ind.* **siento, sientas, sienta, sientan.** *Pres. Subjunc.* **siente, sientes, siente, sienten**
sentencia *f,* opinion, belief; maxim; *law* verdict, sentence; decision, judgment. *law* **fulminar** (*or* **pronunciar**) **la s.,** to pass sentence
sentenciador *a law* sentencing

sentenciar *vt law* to sentence; *inf* destine, intend
sentencioso *a* sententious
sentidamente *adv* feelingly; sadly, regretfully
sentido *m,* sense (hearing, seeing, touch, smell, taste); understanding, sense; meaning, interpretation, signification; perception, discrimination; judgment; direction, way. *a* and *past part* felt; expressive; hypersensitive, touchy. **s. común,** common sense. **costar un s.,** *fig inf* to cost a fortune. **perder el s.,** to lose consciousness
sentimental *a* emotional; sentimental; romantic
sentimentalismo *m,* emotional quality; sentimentalism
sentimiento *m,* feeling, sentiment; sensation, impression; grief, sorrow. **Le acompaño a usted en su s.,** I sympathize with you in your sorrow (bereavement)
sentina *f,* well (of a ship); *naut* bilge; cesspool; sink of iniquity
sentir *vt irr* to feel, experience; hear; appreciate; grieve, regret; believe, consider; envisage, foresee; *vr* complain; suffer; think or consider oneself; crack; feel, be; go rotten, decay (gen. with *estar + past part.*). *m,* view, opinion; feeling. **sin s.,** without feeling; without noticing. *Pres. Part.* **sintiendo.** *Pres. Ind.* **siento, sientes, siente, sienten.** *Preterite* **sintió, sintieron.** *Pres. Subjunc.* **sienta, sientas, sienta, sintamos, sintáis, sientan.** *Imperf. Subjunc.* **sintiese,** etc.
seña *f,* sign, mark; gesture; *mil* password; signal; *pl* address, domicile. **s. mortal,** definite or unmistakable sign. **dar señas,** to show signs, manifest. **hablar por señas,** to converse by signs
señal *f,* mark, sign; boundary stone; landmark; scar; signal; trace, vestige; indication, symptom, token; symbol, sign; image, representation; prodigy, marvel; deposit, advance payment. **s. de aterrizaje,** *aer* landing signal. **s. de niebla,** fog signal. **señales horarias,** *rad* time signal. **en s.,** as a sign, in proof of. **s. luminosa de la circulación,** traffic light, traffic robot
señaladamente *adv* especially, particularly, notably
señalado *a* famous, distinguished; important, notable
señalador *m, Argentina* bookmark
señalamiento *m,* marking; pointing out; appointment, designation
señalar *vt* to mark; indicate, point out; fix, arrange; wound; signal; stamp; appoint (to office); *vr* excel
señero *a* solitary, isolated
señor *a inf* gentlemanly. *m,* owner, master; mister, esquire; **(S.)** the Lord; lord, sire. **s. de horca y cuchillo,** feudal lord, lord of life and death
señora *f,* lady; owner, mistress; madam; wife. **s. de compañía,** chaperon; lady companion. **Nuestra S.,** Our Lady
señorear *vt* to control, run, manage; master; domineer; appropriate, seize; dominate, overlook; restrain (emotions); *vr* behave with dignity
señoría *f,* lordship (title and person); lordship, jurisdiction; area, territory; control, restraint
señoría *f,* dignity, sedateness; self-control
señorial *a* manorial; noble, dignified, lordly
señoril *a* lordly, noble, aristocratic
señorío *m,* lordship; jurisdiction, dominion
señorita *f,* young lady; miss; *inf* mistress of the house
señorito *m,* young gentleman; *inf* master of the house; master (address); *inf* young man about town
señuelo *m,* decoy; bait; allurement, attraction. **caer en el s.,** *fig inf* to fall into the trap
sepancuantos *m, inf* scolding, rebuke; spanking
separación *f,* separation
separado *a* separate
separador (-ra) *a* separating. *n* separator. *m,* filter. **s. de aceite,** oil filter
separar *vt* to separate; divide; dismiss (from a post); lay aside; *vr* retire, resign; separate
separatismo *m,* separatism
separatista *a* and *mf* separatist
septeno *a.* See **séptimo**
septentrión *m, ast* Great Bear; north
septentrional *a* north; northern
septeto *m,* septet
septicemia *f,* septicemia
séptico *a* septic
septiembre *m,* September
septillo *m, mus* septuplet
séptima *f, mus* seventh
séptimo *a* and *m,* seventh
septuagenario (-ia) *a* and *n* septuagenarian
septuagésimo *a* seventieth; septuagesimal. *m,* seventieth
séptuplo *a* sevenfold
sepulcral *a* sepulchral
sepulcro *m,* sepulcher
sepultador (-ra) *a* burying. *n* gravedigger; burier
sepultar *vt* to inter, bury; hide, cover up
sepultura *f,* interment; grave; tomb
sepulturero *m,* gravedigger
sequedad *f,* dryness, barrenness; acerbity, sharpness
sequía *f,* drought
séquito *m,* following, suite, retinue; general approval, popularity
ser *m,* essence, nature; being; existence, life. **El S. Supremo,** The Supreme Being, God
ser *vi irr* to be (e.g. **El sombrero es azul,** The hat is blue). **Ser** may agree with either subject or complement, though when latter is *pl* the verb tends to be so too (e.g. **Son las once, (horas),** It is eleven o'clock. **Cien libras son poco dinero,** A hundred pounds is a small amount). If verbal complement is pers. pron., **ser** agrees with it both in number and person (e.g. **Son ellos,** It is they. **Soy yo,** It is I). In impers. phrases the pron. is not expressed (e.g. **Es difícil,** It is difficult. **Es sorprendente,** It is surprising). **ser** means to exist (e.g. **Pienso luego soy,** I think, therefore I am). **ser** (also **ser de** with nouns or obj. prons.) means to belong to, be the property of (e.g. **Este gato es mío,** This cat is mine. **El libro es de Juan,** The book belongs to John). Signifies to happen, occur (e.g. **¿Cómo fue eso?** How did that happen?). Means to be suitable or fitting (e.g. **Este vestido no es para una señora mayor,** This dress is not suitable for an elderly lady). Expresses price, to be worth (e.g. **¿A cuánto es la libra?** How much is it a pound?; How much is the pound (sterling) worth?). Means to be a member of, belong to (e.g. **Es de la Academia Española,** He is a member of the Spanish Academy). Means to be of use, be useful for (e.g. **Esta casa no es para una familia numerosa,** This house is no use for a large family). **Ser** expresses nationality (e.g. **Son francesas,** They are French. **Somos de Londres,** We are from London). *Auxiliary verb* used to form passive tense (e.g. **Esta historia ha sido leída por muchos,** This story has been read by many. **Fueron mandados al Japón,** They were sent to Japan. **s. de ver,** to be worth seeing. **s. para poco,** to be of little use, amount to little. **s. testigo de,** to witness. **¡Cómo es eso!** How can that be! Surely not! **¡Cómo ha de s.!** How should it be!; One must resign oneself. **Érase una vez** *or* **que érase,** Once upon a time. **es a saber,** viz., that is to say. **un sí es no es,** a touch of, a suspicion of). *Pres. Part.* **siendo.** *Pres. Ind.* **soy, eres, es, somos, sois, son.** *Fut.* **seré,** etc. *Condit.* **sería,** etc. *Preterite* **fui, fuiste, fue, fuimos, fuisteis, fueron.** *Imperf.* **era,** etc. *Past Part.* **sido.** *Pres. Subjunc.* **sea,** etc. *Imperf. Subjunc.* **fuese,** etc. *Imperat.* **sé**
sera *f,* large frail
seráfico *a* seraphic
serafín *m,* seraphim
serbal *m,* service tree
serena *f,* serenade; *inf* dew
serenar *vt* to calm; soothe; clear; *vr* grow calm; clear up (weather); clear (liquids); be soothed or pacified
serenata *f,* serenade

serenidad *f,* serenity, composure, tranquility; Serene Highness (title)
sereno *a* cloudless, fair; composed, serene. *m,* dew; night watchman
sericultor *m,* silk cultivator, sericulturist
sericultura *f,* silk culture
serie *f,* series, sequence, succession; *math* progression; (*biol elec*) series; break (in billiards)
seriedad *f,* seriousness, earnestness; gravity; austerity; sternness; importance; sincerity; solemnity
serigrafía *f,* silkscreen printing
serio *a* serious, earnest; grave; austere; stern; important; sincere, genuine; solemn. **en s.,** seriously
sermón *m,* sermon; scolding. **dar un s.,** to give a sermon; scold
sermonar *vi* to preach
sermonear *vi* to preach sermons; *vt* scold
sermoneo *m, inf* scolding
seroja *f,* withered leaves; brushwood
serpear *vi* to wind, twist; wriggle, squirm; coil
serpenteado *a* winding
serpentear *vi* to wind, twist, meander; stagger along; wriggle; coil; *aer* yaw
serpenteo *m,* winding, twisting; wriggling; coiling; *aer* yaw
serpentín *m, chem* worm; coil (in industry); *min* serpentine
serpentina *f, min* serpentine; paper streamer
serpentino *a* serpentine; *poet* winding, sinuous
serpiente *f,* snake, serpent; Satan, the Devil; *ast* Serpent. **s. de anteojos,** cobra. **s. de cascabel,** rattlesnake
serpollo *m, bot* shoot, new branch; sprout; sucker
serrado *a* serrate
serrallo *m,* harem, seraglio; brothel
serranía *f,* mountainous territory
serrano (-na) *a* mountain, highland. *n* highlander, mountain dweller
serruchar *vt, Lat. Am.* to saw, saw off
serrucho *m,* handsaw. **s. de calar,** fretsaw
Servia Serbia
servible *a* serviceable; useful
servicial *a* useful, serviceable; obliging, obsequious
servicio *m,* service; domestic service; cult, devotion; care, attendance; military service; set, service; department, section; present of money; cover (cutlery, etc., at table); domestic staff, servants. **s. informativo,** news service. **s. nocturno permanente,** all-night service. **hacer un flaco s. (a),** *inf* to do someone an ill turn. **prestar servicios,** to render service, serve
servidor (-ra) *n* servant, domestic; name by which one refers to oneself (e.g. **Un s. lo hará con mucho gusto,** I (your servant) will do it with much pleasure). *m,* wooer, lover; bowler (in cricket). **los servidores de una ametralladora,** the crew (of a gun). **Quedo de Vd. atento y seguro s.,** I remain your obedient servant (in letters), Yours faithfully
servidumbre *f,* serfdom; servitude; servants, domestic staff; obligation, duty; enslavement (by passions); right of way; use, service
servil *a* servile; humble
servilismo *m,* servility; abjectness; absolutism (Spanish history)
servilleta *f,* table napkin. **s. higiénica,** sanitary napkin
servilletero *m,* napkin ring
servio (-ia) *a* and *n* Serbian
servir *vi irr* to be employed (by), be in the service (of); serve (as), perform the duties (of); be of use; wait (on), be subject to. *mil* serve in the armed forces; wait at table; be suitable or favorable; *sport* serve; perform a service; follow the lead (cards); (*with de*) act as, be a deputy for; be a substitute for; *vt* serve; worship; do a favor to; woo, court; serve (food, drink); *vr* be pleased or willing, deign; help oneself to (food); (*with de*) make use of. **no s. para nada,** to be good for nothing, be useless. **No sirves para tales cosas,** You are no good at this sort of thing. **Para s. a Vd,** At your service. **¡Sírvase de . . . !** (followed by infin.), Please! **s. de,** to serve as (e.g. **s. de base a,** to serve as a basis for). See **pedir**
sésamo *m,* sesame
sesenta *a* and *m,* sixty; sixtieth
sesentavo *a* and *m,* sixtieth
sesentón (-ona) *n inf* person of sixty
sesga *f, sew* gore
sesgadamente *adv* on the slant; askew; obliquely
sesgado *a* oblique, slanting
sesgar *vt sew* to cut on the bias; slant, slope; place askew, twist to one side
sesgo *a* slanting, oblique; serious-faced. *m,* slope, slant, obliquity; compromise, middle way. **al s.,** on the slant
sesión *f,* session, meeting; conference, consultation; *law* sitting; term. **abrir la s.,** to open the meeting. **levantar la s.,** to adjourn the meeting
seso *m,* brain; prudence; *pl* brains. **perder el s.,** to go mad; *fig* lose one's head
sestear *vi* to take an afternoon nap; rest; settle
sesteo *m, Lat. Am.* nap, siesta
sesudez *f,* prudence, shrewdness
sesudo *a* sensible, prudent
seta *f,* mushroom. **s. venenosa,** poisonous toadstool
setal *m,* mushroom bed, patch, or field
setecientos *a* and *m,* seven hundred; seven-hundredth
setenta *a* and *m,* seventy; seventieth
setentavo *a* and *m,* seventieth
setentón (-ona) *n* septuagenarian
seter *m,* setter (dog)
setiembre *m.* See **septiembre**
seto *m,* fence; hedge
seudo *a* pseudo
seudónimo *m,* pseudonym
severamente *adv* severely, harshly
severidad *f,* severity; harshness; strictness, rigor; austerity, seriousness
severo *a* severe; harsh; strict, rigid, scrupulous, exact; austere, serious
sevillanas *f pl,* Sevillian dance and its music
sevillano (-na) *a* and *n* of or from Seville, Sevillian
sexagenario (-ia) *n* sexagenarian
sexagésimo *a* sixtieth
sexo *m,* sex; (sexual) organ
sexología *f,* sexology
sexólogo (-ga) *n* sexologist
sexta *f, ecc* sext; *mus* sixth
sexteto *m,* sextet
sexto *a* sixth
sextuplicación *f,* multiplication by six
sextuplicar *vt* to multiply by six, sextuple
séxtuplo *a* sixfold
sexualidad *f,* sexuality
si *m, mus* B, seventh note of the scale. *conjunc* if; whether; even if, although. In conditional clause, **si,** meaning if, is followed by indicative tense unless statement be contrary to fact (e.g. **Si pierdes el tren, volverás a casa,** If you miss your train you will return home, *but* **Si hubieran venido habríamos ido al campo,** If they had come (but they didn't) we would have gone to the country). **Si** is used at the beginning of a clause to make expressions of doubt, desire, or affirmation more emphatic (e.g. **¡Si lo sabrá él, con toda su experiencia!** Of course he knows it, with all his experience. **¿Si será falsa la noticia?** Can the news be false?) **Si** also means whether (e.g. **Me preguntaron si era médico o militar,** They asked me whether I was a doctor or a soldier). Sometimes means even if, although (e.g. **Si viniesen no lo harían,** Even if they came they would not do it. **como si,** as if. **por si acaso,** in case, in the event of. **si bien,** although.
sí *pers pron reflexive 3rd pers m,* and *f, sing* and *pl* himself, herself, itself, themselves. Always used with prep. (e.g. **para sí,** for himself, herself, etc. **de por sí,** separately, on its own. **decir para sí,** to say to oneself)

sí *adv* yes. **sí** *or* **sí que** is frequently used to emphasize a verb generally in contrast to a previous negative (e.g. **Ellos no lo harán, pero yo sí,** They won't do it but I will). Often translated by 'did' (e.g. **No lo vi todo, pero lo que sí vi,** I didn't see it all, but what I did see . . .). *m,* assent; yes; consent. **dar el sí,** to say yes; agree; accept an offer of marriage
siamés (-esa) *a* and *n* Siamese. *m,* Thai (language)
sibarita *a* sybaritic. *mf* sybarite
sibarítico *a* sybaritic; sensual
sibaritismo *m,* sybaritism
siberiano (-na) *a* and *n* Siberian
sibila *f,* sibyl
sibilante *a* sibilant
sibilino *a* sibylline
sicario *m,* paid assassin
Sicilia Sicily
siciliano (-na) *a* and *n* Sicilian
sicoanálisis *m,* psychoanalysis
sicoanalista *mf* psychoanalyst
sicoanalizar *vt* to psychoanalyze
sicofanta, sicofante *m,* sycophant
sicología *f,* psychology
sicológico *a* psychological
sicólogo (-ga) *n* psychologist
sicomoro *m,* sycamore
sicopático *a* psychopathic
sicosis *f, med* psychosis
sicoterapia *f,* psychotherapy
SIDA *m,* AIDS
sideral, sidéreo *a* sidereal
sidra *f,* cider
siega *f,* reaping, harvesting; harvest time; harvest, crop
siembra *f, agr* sowing; seedtime; sown field
siempre *adv* always. **s. que,** provided that; whenever. **para s.,** forever. **por s. jamás,** for always, for ever and ever
siempreviva *f, bot* everlasting flower. **s. mayor,** houseleek
sien *f, anat* temple
sierpe *f,* serpent, snake; anything that wriggles; kite (toy); *bot* sucker; hideous person
sierra *f, carp* saw; ridge of mountains; sawfish; slope; hillside. **s. de cerrojero,** hacksaw. **s. de cinta,** handsaw
siervo (-va) *n* slave; servant; serf
siesta *f,* noonday heat; afternoon nap
siete *a* seven; seventh. *m,* seven; seventh (days of the month); playing card with seven spots; number seven. **las s.,** seven o'clock. *inf* **más que s.,** more than somewhat, extremely
sietemesino (-na) *n* seven-month-old child; *fig inf* young cock
sífilis *f,* syphilis
sifilítico (-ca) *a* and *n* syphilitic
sifón *m,* siphon; siphon bottle; soda water; *mech* trap
sigilar *vt* to seal; hide, conceal
sigilo *m,* seal; secrecy, concealment; silence, reserve
sigiloso *a* secret, silent
sigla *f,* acronym
siglo *m,* century; long time, age; social intercourse, society, world. **s. de oro,** golden age. **en** *or* **por los siglos de los siglos,** for ever and ever
signar *vt* to sign; make the sign of the cross over; *vr* cross oneself
signatario (-ia) *a* and *n* signatory
signatura *f, print* signature; mark, sign; *mus* signature
significación *f,* **significado** *m,* meaning; importance, significance
significante *a* significant
significar *vt* to signify, indicate; mean; publish, make known; *vi* represent, mean; be worth
significativo *a* significant
signo *m,* sign, indication, token; sign, character; *math* symbol; sign of the zodiac; *mus* sign; *med* symptom; *ecc* gesture of benediction; destiny, fate
siguemepollo *m, inf* streamer
siguiente *a* following; next, subsequent. **el día s.,** the next day
sílaba *f,* syllable
silabario *m,* speller, spelling book
silabear *vi* and *vt* to pronounce by syllables, syllabize
silabeo *m,* pronouncing syllable by syllable, syllabication
silábico *a* syllabic
sílabo *m,* syllabus, list
silba *f,* hissing (as a sign of disapproval)
silbador (-ra) *a* whistling; hissing. *n* whistler; one who hisses
silbar *vi* to whistle; whizz, rush through the air; *vi* and *vt theat* hiss
silbato *m,* whistle; air hole
silbido, silbo *m,* whistle, whistling; hiss, hissing
silenciador *m,* (*aut* firearms) silencer
silenciar *vt* to silence; keep secret
silenciario *a* vowed to perpetual silence
silencio *m,* silence; noiselessness, quietness; omission, disregard; *mus* rest. **en s.,** in silence; quietly; uncomplainingly. **pasar en s. (una cosa),** to pass over (something) in silence, omit. **s. de muerte,** deathly silence
silencioso *a* silent; noiseless; tranquil, quiet. *m,* (*aut* firearms) silencer
sílfide *f,* **silfo** *m,* sylph
silicato *m, chem* silicate
sílice *f, chem* silica
silla *f,* chair; riding saddle; *mech* rest, saddle; *ecc* see. **s. de manos,** sedan chair. **s. de montar,** riding saddle. **s. de posta,** post chaise. **s. de ruedas,** wheelchair. **s. de tijera,** deck chair; campstool. **s. giratoria,** swivel chair. **s. poltrona,** easy chair. *inf* **pegársele la s.,** to overstay one's welcome
sillar *m,* ashlar, quarry stone; horseback
sillería *f,* set of chairs; pew, choir stalls; chair factory; shop where chairs are sold; chair making; *mas* ashlar masonry
sillero (-ra) *n* chair maker or seller; saddler
silleta *f,* bedpan; fireman's lift
silletero *m,* runner, sedan chair carrier
sillín *m,* light riding saddle; seat, saddle (of bicycles, etc.)
sillón *m,* armchair; sidesaddle; *Lat. Am.* rocking chair. **s.-cama,** reclining chair. **s. de mimbres,** cane chair
silo *m, agr* silo; dark cavern, dark cave
silogismo *m,* syllogism
silogístico *a* syllogistic
silueta *f,* silhouette; figure
silúrico *a* silurian
siluro *m,* catfish; *nav* self-propelling torpedo
silva *f,* literary miscellany; metrical form
silvestre *a bot* wild; sylvan; uncultivated; savage
silvicultor *m,* forester
silvicultura *f,* forestry
sima *f,* abyss, chasm
simbiosis *f,* symbiosis
simbólico *a* symbolical
simbolismo *m,* symbolism
simbolista *mf* symbolist
simbolización *f,* symbolization
simbolizar *vt* to symbolize, represent
símbolo *m,* symbol. **s. de la fe,** *ecc* Creed
simetría *f,* symmetry
simétrico *a* symmetric; symmetrical
simetrizar *vt* to make symmetrical
símico *a* simian
simiente *f,* seed; semen; germ, genesis, origin
simiesco *a* apish, ape-like
símil *a* similar. *m,* comparison; simile
similar *a* similar
similitud *f,* similarity
simio (-ia) *n* ape

simón *m,* horse cab; cabdriver
simonía *f,* simony
simpatía *f,* liking, understanding, affection; fellow feeling; sympathy
simpático *a* friendly, nice, decent, congenial; sympathetic. **gran s.,** *anat* sympathetic
simpatizar *vi* to get on well, be congenial
simple *a* simple; single, not double; insipid; easy; plain, unadorned; stupid, silly; pure, unmixed; easily deceived, simple; naïve, ingenuous; mere; mild, meek. *mf* simpleton; fool
simpleza *f,* foolishness, stupidity; simplicity
simplicidad *f,* simplicity; candour, ingenuousness
simplicísimo *a sup* most simple, exceedingly simple
simplificable *a* simplifiable
simplificación *f,* simplification, simplifying
simplificador *a* simplifying
simplificar *vt* to simplify
simplista *mf* herbalist
simulación *f,* pretense, simulation
simulacro *m,* image, simulacrum; vision, fancy; *mil* mock battle
simuladamente *adv* pretendedly
simulador (-ra) *a* feigned. *n* dissembler
simular *vt* to feign, pretend
simultanear *vt* to perform simultaneously
simultaneidad *f,* simultaneousness
simultáneo *a* simultaneous
simún *m,* sandstorm
sin *prep* without (e.g. **Lo hizo s. hablar,** He did it without speaking). **s. embargo,** nevertheless. **s. fin,** endless. **s. hilos,** radio, wireless
sinagoga *f,* synagogue
sinapismo *m, med* mustard plaster; *inf* pest, bore
sincerarse *vr* to justify oneself; vindicate one's actions
sinceridad *f,* sincerity
sincero *a* sincere
síncopa *f, mus* syncopation; *gram* syncope
sincopar *vt* to syncopate; abbreviate
síncope *m,* syncope
sincrónico *a* synchronous
sincronismo *m,* synchronism
sincronizar *vt* to synchronize; *rad* tune in
sindéresis *f,* discretion, good sense
sindicación *f,* syndication
sindicado *m,* syndicate
sindical *a* syndical
sindicalismo *m,* syndicalism, trade unionism
sindicalista *mf* syndicalist, trade unionist. *a* syndicalistic, trade unionist
sindicar *vt* to accuse, charge; censure; syndicate
sindicato *m,* syndicate; trade union. **s. gremial,** trade union. **S. Internacional de Trabajadoras de la Aguja,** International Ladies' Garment Workers' Union
sindicatura *f,* (official) receivership
síndico *m, com* receiver, trustee
síndrome *m,* syndrome. **síndrome de inmunidad deficiente adquirida** acquired immunity deficiency syndrome
sinecura *f,* sinecure
sinergia *f,* synergy
sinfín *m,* countless number
sinfonía *f,* symphony
sinfónico *a* symphonic
sinfonista *mf* composer of symphonies, player in a symphony orchestra
sinfonola *f,* jukebox
singladura *f, naut* day's sailing; nautical twenty-four hours (beginning at midday)
singlar *vi naut* to sail a given course
singular *a* singular, single; individual; extraordinary, remarkable. *a* and *m, gram* singular
singularidad *f,* individuality, peculiarity; strangeness, remarkableness; oddness, eccentricity
singularizar *vt* to particularize, single out; *gram* make singular, singularize; *vr* distinguish oneself, stand out; be distinguished (by)
sinhueso *f, inf* tongue (organ of speech)
siniestra *f,* left, lefthand
siniestro *a* left (side); vicious, perverse; sinister; unlucky. *m,* viciousness, depravity (gen. *pl*); shipwreck, sinking; disaster, catastrophe; *com* damage, loss
sinnúmero *m,* countless number
sino *m,* fate, destiny. *conjunc* but; except (e.g. **No lo hicieron ellos s. yo,** They didn't do it, I did. **no . . . s.,** not . . . , but); only (e.g. **No sólo lo dijo él s. ella,** Not only he said it, but she did too)
sínodo *m,* (*ecc ast*) synod; council
sinología *f,* sinology
sinólogo *m,* sinologist
sinonimia *f,* synonymy
sinónimo *a* synonymous. *m,* synonym
sinopsis *f,* synopsis
sinóptico *a* synoptic
sinrazón *f,* injustice, wrong
sinsabor *m,* unpleasantness, trouble; grief, anxiety
sintáctico *a* syntactic
sintaxis *f,* syntax
síntesis *f,* synthesis
sintético *a* synthetic
sintetizar *vt* to synthesize
síntoma *m,* symptom
sintomático *a* symptomatic
sintomatología *f,* symptomatology
sintonización *f, rad* tuning in
sintonizador *m, rad* tuner
sintonizar *vt rad* to tune in
sinuosidad *f,* sinuosity
sinuoso *a* sinuous, winding
sinvergüenza *mf* rascal, knave, rogue
sinvergüenzada *f, Lat. Am.* dirty thing (to do)
Sión Zion
sionismo *m,* Zionism
sionista *a* and *mf* Zionist
siquiatra *m,* psychiatrist
siquiatría *f,* psychiatry
síquico *a* psychic
siquiera *conjunc* although, even if. **s. . . . s.,** whether . . . or. *adv* at least; even (e.g. **Hay que pedir mucho para tener s. la mitad,** One must ask a great deal to get even half). **ni s.,** not even (e.g. **No había nadie, ni s. un perro,** There was no one, not even a dog)
Siracusa Syracuse
siracusano (-na) *a* and *n* Syracusan
sirena *f,* mermaid, siren; siren; foghorn
sirga *f,* towline
sirgar *vt naut* to track, tow
Siria Syria
sirio (-ia) *a* and *n* Syrian. *m,* Sirius
siroco *m,* sirocco
sirte *f,* sandbank, submerged rock
sirvienta *f,* female servant
sirviente *a* serving. *m,* servant
sisa *f,* pilfering; *sew* dart. **s. dorada,** gold lacquer
sisador (-ra) *n* filcher, pilferer
sisar *vt* to pilfer, filch, steal; *sew* take in, make darts in
sisear *vi* and *vt* to hiss (disapproval); sizzle
sísmico *a* seismic
sismógrafo *m,* seismograph
sismología *f,* seismology
sismológico *a* seismological
sismómetro *m,* seismometer
sistema *m,* system. **s. ferroviario,** railroad system. **s. métrico,** metric system
sistemático *a* systematic
sistematización *f,* systematization
sistematizar *vt* to systematize
sístole *f,* systole
sitiador *a* besieging. *m,* besieger
sitiar *vt mil* to lay siege to; surround, besiege
sitio *m,* place, spot; room, space; site; locality; *mil* siege,

blockade; *Lat. Am.* taxi stand **No hay s.,** There's no room

sito *past part* situated, located

situación *f,* situation; position; circumstances; condition, state; location

situado *past part* situated, placed. *m,* income, interest

situar *vt* to situate, locate, place; assign funds; *vr* place oneself

smoking *m,* tuxedo, tux, dinner jacket

snobismo *m,* snobbery

so *prep* under (used only with **color, pena, pretexto, capa**) (e.g. **so color de,** under the pretext of). *interj* **¡So!** Whoa! (to horses); *Lat. Am.* Hush!

soba *f,* rubbing; kneading; massaging; drubbing, beating; handling, touching

sobacal *a* underarm, axillary

sobaco *m,* armpit; *bot* axil

sobajar *vt* to squeeze, press

sobaquera *f, sew* armhole; dress shield

sobar *vt* to rub; knead; massage; beat, thrash; handle, touch, paw (persons); soften

soberanear *vi* to tyrannize, domineer

soberanía *f,* sovereignty; dominance, sway, rule; dignity, majesty

soberano (-na) *a* sovereign; superb; regal, majestic. *n* ruler, lord. *m,* sovereign (coin)

soberbia *f,* arrogance, haughtiness; conceit, presumption; ostentation, pomp; rage, anger

soberbio *a* haughty, arrogant; conceited; superb, magnificent; lofty, soaring; spirited (of horses)

sobón *a inf* overdemonstrative, mushy; *inf* lazy

sobordo *m, naut* manifest, freight list

sobornación *f,* bribing; bribery

sobornador (-ra) *a* bribing. *n* briber

sobornar *vt* to bribe

soborno *m,* bribing; bribe; inducement

sobra *f,* excess, surplus; insult, outrage; *pl* leftovers (from a meal); remains, residue; rubbish, trash. **de s.,** in abundance; in excess, surplus; unnecessary, superfluous; too well

sobradamente *adv* abundantly; in excess

sobrado *a* excessive; brazen, bold; wealthy, rich. *m,* garret

sobrante *a* surplus, leftover, remaining. *m,* remainder, surplus, excess

sobrar *vt* to exceed; have too much of (e.g. **Me sobran mantas,** I have too many blankets); *vi* be superfluous; remain, be left. *inf* **Aquí sobro yo,** I am in the way here, My presence is superfluous

sobrasada *f,* spicy sausage

sobre *prep* upon, on; above, over; concerning, about; apart from, besides; about (e.g. **s. las nueve,** at about nine o'clock) (indicates approximation); toward; after. *m,* envelope; address, superscription. **s. cero,** above freezing (Fahrenheit); above zero (Centigrade). **s. el nivel del mar,** above sea level. **s. manera,** excessively, extremely. **s. todo,** especially

sobreabundancia *f,* superabundance, excess

sobreabundante *a* superabundant

sobreabundar *vi* to be superabundant

sobreagudo *a* and *m, mus* treble (pitch)

sobrealiento *m,* heavy, painful breathing

sobrealimentación *f,* overfeeding; *aut* supercharge

sobrealimentar *vt aut* to supercharge

sobreasar *vt* to roast or cook again

sobrecama *f,* bedspread, quilt

sobrecarga *f,* overload; rope, etc., for securing bales and packs; additional trouble or anxiety

sobrecargar *vt* to overload; weigh down; *sew* oversew, fell

sobrecargo *m, naut* purser; flight attendant

sobrecarta *f,* envelope (for a letter)

sobreceja *f,* brow, lower forehead; frown

sobrecejo *m,* frown

sobrecielo *m,* canopy

sobrecoger *vt* to take by surprise; *vr* be frightened or apprehensive

sobrecogimiento *m,* fright, apprehension

sobrecomida *f,* dessert

sobrecoser *vt sew* to oversew, whip

sobrecrecer *vi irr* to grow too much. See **conocer**

sobrecubierta *f,* second lid or cover; dust jacket (of a book); *naut* upper deck

sobrecuello *m,* overcollar; loose collar

sobredicho *a* aforementioned, aforesaid

sobredorar *vt* to gild (metals); make excuses for

sobreedificar *vt* to build upon or above

sobreexcitar *vt* to overexcite

sobrefaz *f,* surface, exterior

sobreganar *vt* to make an excess profit

sobreguarda *m,* head guard; extra or second guard

sobreherido *a* lightly wounded

sobrehilar *vt* to oversew or overcast. See **prohibir**

sobrehumano *a* superhuman

sobrellenar *vt* to fill full

sobrellevar *vt* to help in the carrying of a burden; endure, bear; make excuses for, overlook; help

sobremesa *f,* tablecloth; after-dinner conversation. **de s.,** *fig* at the dinner table

sobrenadar *vi* to float

sobrenatural *a* supernatural; extraordinary, singular

sobrenombre *m,* additional surname; nickname

sobrentender *vt irr* to take for granted, understand as a matter of course; *vr* go without saying. See **entender**

sobrepaga *f,* overpayment; extra pay

sobreparto *m,* time after parturition; afterbirth

sobrepasar *vt* to exceed; outdo, excel

sobrepelliz *f,* surplice

sobreponer *vt irr* to place over; overlap; *vr* rise above (circumstances); dominate (persons). See **poner**

sobreprecio *m,* extra charge, rise in price

sobreproducción *f,* overproduction

sobrepuerta *f,* curtain pelmet; door curtain

sobrepujar *vt* to excel, surpass, outdo

sobrequilla *f,* keelson

sobrerrealista *a* and *mf* surrealist

sobrerrealismo *m,* surrealism

sobresaliente *a* overhanging; projecting; distinctive, outstanding; excellent, remarkable. *m,* "excellent" (mark in examinations). *mf theat* understudy

sobresalir *vi irr* to overhang, project; stand out; be conspicuous or noticeable; excel; distinguish oneself. See **salir**

sobresaltar *vt* to assail, rush upon; startle, frighten suddenly; *vi art* stand out, be striking; *vr* be startled or frightened

sobresalto *m,* sudden attack; unexpected shock; agitation; sudden fear. **de s.,** unexpectedly

sobresanar *vi* to heal superficially but not deeply; conceal, dissemble

sobrescribir *vt* to label; address, superscribe. *Past Part.* **sobrescrito**

sobrescrito *m,* address, superscription

sobresello *m,* second seal

sobrestante *m,* overseer; supervisor; foreman; inspector

sobresueldo *m,* additional salary, bonus

sobresuelo *m,* second flooring

sobretarde *f,* early evening, late afternoon

sobretodo *m,* overcoat

sobrevenida *f,* sudden arrival

sobrevenir *vi irr* occur, take place; supervene. See **venir**

sobrevidriera *f,* storm window; wire-mesh window guard

sobrevienta *f,* gust of wind; fury, violence; shock, surprise. **a s.,** suddenly

sobreviviente *a* surviving. *mf* survivor

sobrevivir *vi* to survive

sobriedad *f,* sobriety, moderation

sobrina *f,* niece

sobrino *m*, nephew
sobrio *a* sober, moderate, temperate
socaliña *f*, cunning, craft
socaliñero (-ra) *a* cunning. *n* trickster
socalzar *vt mas* to underpin
socapa *f*, blind, pretext. **a s.,** secretly; cautiously
socarra *f*, scorching, singeing; craftiness
socarrón *a* cunning, deceitful; malicious, sly (of humor, etc.)
socarronería *f*, cunning, craftiness; slyness (of humor, etc.); knavish action
socava *f*, undermining; *agr* hoeing round tree roots
socavar *vt* to undermine
sociabilidad *f*, sociability
sociable *a* sociable; social
social *a* social
socialdemócrata *a* and *mf* social democrat
socialismo *m*, socialism
socialista *mf* socialist. *a* socialistic
socialización *f*, socialization
socializar *vt* to socialize
sociedad *f*, society; association; *com* partnership; *com* company. *com* **s. anónima,** incorporated company, limited company. **S. de las Naciones,** League of Nations. **s. de socorros mutuos,** mutual aid society. **s. en comandita,** private company
socio (-ia) *n* associate, partner; member. **s. comanditario,** *com* silent partner
sociología *f*, sociology
sociológico *a* sociological
sociólogo (-ga) *n* sociologist
socolor *m*, pretext. *adv* (also **so c.**) under pretext
socollada *f*, *naut* flapping (of sails); pitching (of a ship)
socorredor (-ra) *a* aiding, succoring. *n* helper
socorrer *vt* to aid, succor, assist; pay on account
socorrido *a* helpful, generous, prompt to assist; well-equipped, well-furnished; well-supplied
socorro *m*, aid, help, assistance; payment on account; *mil* relief (provisions or arms)
socrático *a* socratic
sodio *m*, sodium
sodomía *f*, sodomy
sodomita *mf* sodomite. *a* sodomitic
soez *a* base, vile; vulgar
sofá *m*, sofa, couch
sofaldar *vt* to tuck up the skirts; disclose, reveal
sofisma *m*, sophism, fallacy
sofista *a* sophistic. *mf* sophist, quibbler
sofistería *f*, sophistry
sofístico *a* sophistic, fallacious
soflama *f*, thin flame; glow; flush, blush; specious promise, deception
soflamar *vt* to shame, make blush; promise with intent to deceive, swindle; *vr cul* burn
sofocación *f*, suffocation, smothering; shame; anger
sofocador, sofocante *a* suffocating; stifling
sofocar *vt* to suffocate, smother; extinguish; dominate, oppress; pester, importune; shame, make blush, make angry; agitate; *vr* be ashamed; be angry
sofocleo *a* Sophoclean
sofoco *m*, mortification, chagrin; shame; anger; suffocation, smothering; hot flush
sofreír *vt irr* to fry lightly. See **reír**
sofrenada *f*, sudden check, pulling up short (of horses); harsh scolding; moral restraint
sofrenar *vt* to pull up, check suddenly (horses); scold harshly; restrain, repress (emotions)
soga *f*, rope; land measure (varies in length). *m*, *inf* rogue, knave
soguería *f*, rope making; rope walk; rope shop; ropes
soguero *m*, rope maker or seller
soja *f*, soybean
sojuzgador (-ra) *a* conquering, oppressive. *n* conqueror, oppressor
sojuzgar *vt* to conquer, oppress, subdue
sol *m*, sun; sunlight; day; Peruvian coin; *mus* G, fifth note of the scale, sol. **de s. a s.,** from sunrise to sunset. **hacer s.,** to be sunny. **morir uno sin s. sin luz y sin moscas,** *inf* to die abandoned by all. **no dejar a s. ni a sombra,** *inf* to follow everywhere; pester constantly. **tomar el s.,** to bask in the sun
solado *m*, paving; tile floor
solador *m*, tiler
solamente *adv* only; exclusively; merely, solely. **s. que,** only that; nothing but
solana *f*, sunny corner; Solarium
solanera *f*, sunburn; sunny spot
solapa *f*, lapel; excuse, pretext. **de s.,** *inf* secretly
solapado *a* cunning, sly
solapar *vt sew* to provide with lapels; *sew* cause to overlap; dissemble; *vi sew* overlap
solapo *m*, lapel; *inf* slap, buffet. **a s.,** *inf* secretly, slyly
solar *vt irr* to pave; sole (shoes). *m*, family seat, manor house; building site; lineage, family. *a* solar. See **colar**
solariego *a* memorial; of an old and noble family
solas, a *adv* alone, in private
solaz *m*, consolation; pleasure; relief, relaxation. **a s.,** enjoyably, pleasantly
solazar *vt* to solace, comfort; amuse, entertain; rest; *vr* be comforted; find pleasure (in)
soldada *f*, salary, wages, emoluments; (*nav mil*) pay
soldadesca *f*, soldiering, military profession; troops. **a la s.,** in a soldier-like way
soldadesco *a* military, soldier
soldado *m*, soldier; defender, partisan. **s. raso,** *mil* private
soldador *m*, solderer, welder; soldering iron
soldadura *f*, welding, soldering; correction, emendation
soldar *vt irr* to weld; mend by welding; correct, put right; *mil* wipe out, liquidate. See **contar**
solecismo *m*, solecism
soledad *f*, solitude; loneliness; homesickness; *pl* melancholy Andalusian song and dance (also *f pl.* **soleares**)
solemne *a* solemn; magnificent; formal; serious, grave, important; pompous; *inf* downright, complete
solemnidad *f*, solemnity; magnificence; formality; gravity, seriousness; solemn ceremony; religious ceremony; legal formality
solemnización *f*, solemnization
solemnizar *vt* to solemnize, celebrate; extol
soler *vi irr defective* to be in the habit, be used; happen frequently (e.g. **Solía hacerlo los lunes,** I generally did it on Mondays. **Suele llover mucho aquí,** It rains a great deal here). See **moler**
solercia *f*, shrewdness, ability, astuteness
solevantado *a* agitated; restless
solevantar *vt* to raise, push up; incite to rebellion. **s. con gatos,** *mech* to jack up
solfa *f*, *mus* sol-fa
solfear *vt mus* to sing in sol-fa; *inf* spank, buffet; *inf* scold
solfeo *m*, *mus* sol-fa; *inf* spanking, drubbing
solicitación *f*, request; application; solicitation; wooing; search (for a post); attraction, inducement
solicitador (-ra) *a* soliciting. *n* solicitor. *m*, agent; applicant
solicitante *mf* applicant, candidate
solicitar *vt* to solicit; request; apply for; make love to, court; seek (posts, etc.); try to, attempt to; manage (business affairs); *phys* attract; appeal to
solícito *a* solicitous; conscientious; careful
solicitud *f*, diligence, conscientiousness; solicitude; request; application; appeal, entreaty; petition; *com* demand. **a s.,** on request
solidaridad *f*, solidarity
solidario *a law* jointly responsible or liable
solideo *m*, *ecc* small skullcap
solidez *f*, solidity; *fig* force, weight (of arguments, etc.)
solidificación *f*, solidification
solidificar(se) *vt* and *vr* to solidify
sólido *a* compact, solid; thick; fast or lasting (of colors);

indisputable, convincing. *m*, (*geom phys*) solid; solidus (ancient coin)
soliloquiar *vi inf* to soliloquize, talk to oneself
soliloquio *m*, soliloquy
solio *m*, throne
solista *mf* soloist
solitario (-ia) *a* abandoned, deserted; solitary; secluded; solitude-loving. *n* recluse. *m*, solitaire diamond; hermit; solitaire (card game). **hacer solitarios,** to play solitaire (card game)
sólito *a* accustomed, wonted; customary, habitual
soliviantar *vt* to rouse, incite, excite
soliviar *vt* to help to lift up; *vr* half get up, raise oneself
sollastre *m*, scullion; brazen rogue
sollozante *a* sobbing
sollozar *vi* to sob
sollozo *m*, sob
solo *a* sole, only; alone; lonely; deserted, forsaken. *m*, solo performance; (cards) solo; solitaire (card game). **a solas,** alone; without help, unaided
sólo *or* **solo** *adv* only; merely, solely; exclusively
solomillo *m*, sirloin; filet (of meat)
solsticio *m*, solstice. **s. hiemal,** winter solstice. **s. vernal,** summer solstice
soltar *vt irr* to loosen; let go; disengage; untie; release; let drop; let out (a laugh, etc.); solve; *inf* utter; turn on (taps); set free; *vr* work loose; grow skillful; (*with prep. a + infin.*) begin to do (something). See **contar**
soltera *f*, spinster
soltería *f*, bachelorhood; spinsterhood
soltero *a* unmarried, single. *m*, bachelor
solterón *m*, confirmed bachelor
solterona *f*, confirmed old maid
soltura *f*, loosening; untying; freedom from restraint; ease, independence; impudence; immorality, viciousness; facility of speech; *law* release
solubilidad *f*, solubility
soluble *a* soluble, dissolvable; solvable
solución *f*, dissolution, loosening; (*math chem*) solution; answer, solution; payment, satisfaction; *lit* climax; conclusion, end (of negotiations)
solucionar *vt* to solve, find a solution for
solvencia *f*, *com* solvency
solventar *vt* to pay or settle accounts; solve (problems, difficulties)
solvente *a com* solvent
somático *a* somatic, corporeal
sombra *f*, shadow; shade; darkness, dimness; specter, phantom; defense, refuge, protection; resemblance, likeness; defect; *inf* luck; gaiety, charm; trace, vestige; *art* shading, shadow. **sombras chinescas,** shadow show. **a la s.,** in the shade; *inf* in jail. **hacer s.,** to shade; *fig* stand in the light, be an obstacle; protect. **ni por s.,** by no means; without warning. **no tener s. de,** to have not a trace of . . . . **tener buena s.,** *inf* to be witty or amusing and agreeable. **tener mala s.,** *inf* to bring bad luck, exert an evil influence upon; be dull and disagreeable
sombrear *vt* to shadow, shade; *art* shade; *vi* begin to show (of mustaches, beards)
sombrerera *f*, milliner; hatbox
sombrerería *f*, hat shop or trade; hat factory
sombrerero *m*, hatter; hat manufacturer
sombrerete *m*, *mech* bonnet, cap; cowl
sombrero *m*, hat; *mech* cap, cowl; sounding board; head (of mushrooms, toadstools). **s. calañés,** Andalusian hat. **s. chambergo,** broad-brimmed plumed hat. **s. de canal** *or* **teja,** shovel hat (worn by clergymen). **s. de copa,** top hat. **s. de jipijapa,** Panama hat. **s. de pelo** *Lat. Am.* top hat. **s. de tres picos,** three-cornered hat, cocked hat. **s. flexible,** soft felt hat. **s. hongo,** bowler (hat)
sombría *f*, shady spot
sombrilla *f*, sunshade
sombrío *a* dark; shadowy; overcast; *art* shaded; gloomy, melancholy
someramente *adv* superficially; briefly, summarily
somero *a* superficial, shallow; summary, rudimentary, brief
someter *vt* to put down, defeat; submit, place before; subject. **s. a votación,** to put to a vote. *vr* yield, surrender; (*with prep a*) undergo
sometimiento *m*, defeat; submission (to arbitration, etc.); subjection
somnambulismo *m*, somnambulism, sleepwalking
somnámbulo (-la) *a* somnambulistic. *n* somnambulist
somnífero *a* soporiferous
somnílocuo *a* somniloquous, sleeptalking
somnolencia *f*, somnolence
son *m*, sound; rumor; reason, motive; means, way; guise, manner. **al s. de,** to the sound of; to the music of. **en s. de,** in the manner of, as, like, under pretext of
sonadera *f*, nose blowing
sonado *a* famous; much admired or talked of. **hacer una que sea sonada,** *inf* to cause a great scandal; do something noteworthy
sonaja *f*, metal jingles on a tambourine; baby's rattle
sonajero *m*, baby's rattle
sonar *vi irr* to sound; be quoted, be mentioned; ring; *inf* be familiar, remember (e.g. **No me suena el nombre,** I don't remember the name); (*with prep a*) be reminiscent of; *vt* sound; ring; play on; clink; *vr* be rumored, be reported; blow one's nose. *Pres. Ind.* **sueno, suenas, suena, suenan.** *Pres. Subjunc.* **suene, suenes, suene, suenen**
sonata *f*, sonata
sonda *f*, *naut* taking of soundings, heaving the lead; sound, plummet, lead; dragrope; probe, sound
sondar *vt naut* to take soundings; probe; *inf* sound, try to find out; bore, drill
sondeable *a* fathomable
sondeo *m*, *naut* sounding; *min* drilling; probing
sonetear, sonetizar *vi* to write sonnets
sonetista *mf* sonneteer
soneto *m*, sonnet
sonido *m*, sound; literal meaning; rumor, report
sonochar *vi* to keep watch in the early hours of the night
sonoridad *f*, sonorousness
sonoro *a* sounding; resonant, loud; sonorous
sonreir, sonereírse *vi* and *vr irr* to smile; *vi* look pleasant (landscape, etc.); look favorable (of circumstances). **sonreir tras la barba,** to laugh to oneself. See **reir**
sonriente *a* smiling
sonrisa *f*, smile
sonrojar *vt* to cause to blush; *vr* blush
sonrosado *a* rosy, rose-colored, pink
sonrosar *vt* to make rose-colored; *vr* blush, flush
sonroseo *m*, blush, flush
sonsaca *f*, removal by stealth; pilfering; enticement; *fig* pumping (of a person for information)
sonsacar *vt* to remove by stealth; steal, pilfer; entice away; *fig* pump (a person for information), draw out
sonsonete *m*, rhythmic tapping or drumming; monotonous sound (gen. unpleasant); sarcastic tone of voice
soñador (-ra) *a* dreamy, sleepy. *n* dreamer
soñar *vt* to dream; imagine, conjure up; (*with con*) dream of; (*with prep a*) fear (of persons)
soñoliento *a* sleepy, drowsy; soothing; slow, leisurely
¡Soo! *interj* Whoa! (command to horses, etc.)
sopa *f*, sop, piece of bread; soup. **s. boba,** beggar's portion; life of ease at others' expense. **andar a la s.,** to beg one's way. **hecho una s.,** *inf* wet through
sopapo *m*, chuck under the chin; *inf* slap; valve
sopera *f*, soup tureen
sopero *m*, soup plate, soup bowl. *a* fond of soup
sopesar *vt* to try the weight of
sopetón *m*, blow, cuff. **de s.,** suddenly
soplada *f*, puff of wind
soplado *a inf* overelegant; haughty, stiff. *m*, fissure, chasm

soplador (-ra) *a* instigatory. *m*, blower, fan. *n* instigator; blower
soplar *vi* to blow; *vt* blow; blow away; inflate, blow up; filch, steal; instigate, inspire; accuse; fan; prompt, help out; *vr inf* eat and drink too much; *inf* be puffed up, grow haughty. *interj* **¡Sopla!** *inf* You don't say so!
soplete *m*, blowpipe
soplo *m*, blow; blowing; instant, trice; *inf* hint, tip; *inf* accusation; *inf* tale-bearer; puff, breath (of wind)
soplón (-ona) *a inf* tale-bearing, backbiting. *n* talebearer. *m*, *aut* scavenger
soponcio *m*, *inf* fainting fit
sopor *m*, stupor; deep sleep
soporífero *a* soporiferous
soportable *a* bearable
soportador (-ra) *a* supporting. *n* supporter
soportal *m*, portico
soportar *vt* to bear; carry, support; put up with, tolerate
soporte *m*, rest, support; *mech* bearing; *mech* bracket, support; backup (of a computer file)
sorbedor (-ra) *a* supping, sipping. *n* sipper
sorber *vt* to suck; imbibe; swallow; *fig* absorb eagerly (ideas); sip
sorbete *m*, sherbet, iced drink; French ice cream
sorbo *m*, sucking; imbibition; swallow; sip; mouthful, gulp
sordamente *adv* secretly, quietly
sordera *f*, deafness
sórdido *a* dirty, squalid; mean, niggardly; sordid
sordina *f*, *mus* sordine, mute; *mus* damper. **a la s.,** on the quiet, in secret
sordo *a* deaf; silent, quiet; dull, muted (of sounds); insensible, inanimate; obdurate, uncompliant. **a la sorda** *or* **a lo s.** *or* **a sordas,** in silence, quietly
sordomudez *f*, deaf-muteness, deaf-mutism
sordomudo (-da) *a* and *n* deaf-mute
sorna *f*, slowness, sluggishness; craftiness, guile, knavery; malice
soroche *m*, *Peru* altitude sickness, mountain sickness
sorprendente *a* surprising, amazing
sorprender *vt* to surprise, amaze
sorpresa *f*, surprise; amazement; shock
sorpresivo, -a *a*, *Lat. Am.* sudden, unexpected; surprising
sortear *vt* to raffle; draw lots for; avoid artfully (difficulties, etc.); fight (bulls)
sorteo *m*, raffle; casting lots
sortero (-ra) *n* sorcerer; holder of a draw ticket
sortija *f*, ring (for a finger); ring (for a curtain, etc.); curl
sortilegio *m*, sorcery, magic
sortílego (-ga) *a* magic. *n* sorcerer, fortuneteller
sosa *f*, sodium carbonate, soda ash. **s. cáustica,** sodium-hydroxide, caustic soda, soda
sosegado *a* tranquil, peaceful, calm
sosegador (-ra) *a* soothing, calming. *n* appeaser, soother
sosegar *vt irr* to soothe, quiet; reassure; appease, moderate; *vi* grow still; rest, sleep; *vr* grow quiet; calm down, be appeased; grow still. See **cegar**
sosería *f*, insipidness; lack of wit, dullness; stupidity
sosia *m*, double, exact likeness (of persons)
sosiego *m*, calm; peace, tranquility
soslayar *vt* to slant, place in an oblique position; *fig* go around (a difficulty)
soslayo *a* slanting. **al s.,** obliquely, on the slant; askance
soso *a* saltless, insipid; dull, uninteresting; heavy (of people)
sospecha *f*, suspicion
sospechar *vt* and *vi* to suspect
sospechoso *a* suspicious. *m*, suspect
sostén *m*, support; *mech* stand, support; brassiere, bra, bustier; steadiness (of a ship)
sostenedor (-ra) *a* supporting. *n* supporter
sostener *vt irr* to support; defend, uphold; bear, tolerate; help, aid; maintain, support. **s. una conversación,** to carry on a conversation. See **tener**
sostenido *a mus* sostenuto, sustained. *a* and *m*, *mus* sharp
sostenimiento *m*, support; defense; toleration, endurance; maintenance, sustenance
sota *f*, jack, knave (in cards); *inf* baggage, hussy. *m*, foreman, supervisor. *prep* deputy, substitute (e.g. **sotamontero,** deputy huntsman)
sotabanco *m*, attic, garret
sotana *f*, gown, cassock, robe
sótano *m*, basement, cellar
sotavento *m*, leeward. **a s.,** on the lee
sotechado *m*, hut, shed
soterrar *vt irr* to bury in the ground; hide, conceal. See **acertar**
sotileza *f*, fine cord for fishing (in Santander province)
soto *m*, thicket, grove, copse
soviético *a* soviet
sovietismo *m*, sovietism
sovietizar *vt* to sovietize
sovoz, a *adv* in a low voice
su, sus *poss pron 3rd pers mf sing* and *pl* his, her, its, one's, your, their
suasorio *a* suasive, persuasive
suave *a* soft, smooth; sweet; pleasant, harmonious, quiet; slow, gentle; meek; delicate, subtle
suavidad *f*, softness, smoothness; sweetness; pleasantness; quietness; gentleness; meekness; delicacy
suavizador *a* softening, smoothing; soothing, quietening. *m*, razor strop
suavizar *vt* to soften; smooth; strop (a razor); moderate, temper; *mech* steady; quieten; ease
subalpino *a* subalpine
subalternar *vt* to put down, subdue
subalterno *a* subordinate. *m*, subordinate; *mil* subaltern
subarrendar *vt irr* to sublet. See **recomendar**
subarrendatario (-ia) *n* sublessee
subarriendo *m*, sublease, sublet
subasta *f*, auction sale. **sacar a pública s.,** to sell by auction
subastar *vt* to auction
subcentral *f*, substation
subclase *f*, subclass
subcolector *m*, assistant collector
subcomisión *f*, subcommittee
subconsciencia *f*, subconscious
subcutáneo *a* subcutaneous
subdelegar *vt* to subdelegate
subdirector (-ra) *n* deputy, assistant director
súbdito (-ta) *a* dependent, subject. *n* subject (of a state)
subdividir *vt* to subdivide
subdominante *f*, *mus* subdominant
subgénero *m*, subgenus
subgobernador *m*, deputy governor, lieutenant governor
subibaja *f*, seesaw, teetertotter
subida *f*, ascension, ascent; upgrade; rise; carrying up; raising (of a theater curtain)
subidero *m*, uphill road; mounting block; way up (to a higher level)
subido *a* strong (of scents); deep (of colors); expensive, high-priced; best, finest
subidor *m*, porter, carrier; elevator
subintendente *m*, deputy or assistant intendant
subir *vi* to ascend, climb, go up; mount; rise; *com* amount (to), reach; prosper, advance, be promoted; grow more acute (of illnesses); intensify; *mus* raise the pitch (of an instrument or voice); *vt* ascend, climb; pick up, take up; raise up; place higher; build up, make taller; straighten up, place in a vertical position; increase, raise (in price or value); *vr* ascend, climb. **s. a caballo,** to mount a horse. **subirse a la cabeza,** *inf* to go to one's head (of alcohol, etc.)
subitáneo *a* sudden
súbito *a* unexpected, unforeseen; sudden; precipitate, impulsive. *adv* suddenly (also **de s.**)

subjefe *m,* deputy chief, second in command
subjetividad *f,* subjectivity
subjetivismo *m,* subjectivism
subjetivo *a* subjective
subjuntivo *a* and *m,* subjunctive
sublevación *f,* **sublevamiento** *m,* rebellion, mutiny, uprising
sublevar *vt* to rouse to rebellion; excite (indignation, etc.); *vr* rebel
sublimación *f,* sublimation
sublimado *m, chem* sublimate
sublimar *vt* to exalt, raise up; *chem* sublimate
sublime *a* sublime
sublimidad *f,* sublimity, majesty, nobility
submarino *a* submarine. *m,* submarine. **s. de bolsillo** *or* **s. enano,** midget submarine
suboficial *m, mil* subaltern; *nav* petty officer
subordinación *f,* dependence, subordination
subordinado (-da) *a* and *n* subordinate
subordinar *vt* to subordinate
subprefecto *m,* subprefect
subproducto *m,* by-product
subrayar *vt* to underline; emphasize
subrepción *f,* underhand dealing; *law* subreption
subrepticio *a* surreptitious; clandestine
subrogación *f,* surrogation
subrogar *vt law* to surrogate, elect as a substitute
subs—For words so beginning not found here, see **sus-**
subsanar *vt* to make excuses for; remedy, put right; indemnify
subscriptor (-ra) *n* subscriber
subsección *f,* subsection
subsecretaría *f,* assistant secretaryship; assistant secretary's office
subsecretario (-ia) *n* assistant secretary
subsecuente *a* subsequent
subsidiario *a* subsidized; subsidiary
subsidio *m,* subsidy
subsiguiente *a* subsequent; next
subsistencia *f,* permanence; stability; subsistence, maintenance; livelihood
subsistir *vi* to last, endure; subsist, live; make a livelihood
subsuelo *m,* subsoil, substratum
subte *m, Argentina, informal* subway
subteniente *m, mil* second lieutenant
subterfugio *m,* subterfuge, trick
subterráneo *a* underground, subterranean. *m,* subterranean place
subtítulo *m,* subtitle; caption
subtropical *a* subtropical
suburbano (-na) *a* suburban. *n* suburbanite
suburbio *m,* suburb
subvención *f,* subsidy, subvention, grant
subvencionar *vt* to subsidize
subvenir *vt irr* to help, succor; subsidize. See **venir**
subversivo *a* subversive
subvertir *vt irr* to subvert, overturn, ruin. See **sentir**
subyugación *f,* subjugation
subyugador (-ra) *a* subjugating. *n* conqueror
subyugar *vt* to subjugate, overcome
succión *f,* suction
suceder *vi* to follow, come after; inherit, succeed. *impers* happen, occur
sucedido *m, inf* event, occurrence
sucesión *f,* succession; series; offspring, descendants; *law* estate
sucesivo *a* successive. **en lo s.,** in future
suceso *m,* happening, occurrence; course (of time); outcome, result
sucesor (-ra) *a* succeeding. *n* successor
suciedad *f,* dirt; filth, nastiness; obscenity
sucinto *a* succinct, brief, concise
sucio *a* dirty, unclean; stained; easily soiled; *fig* sullied, spotted; obscene; dirty (of colors); *fig* tainted, infected. **jugar s.,** *sport* to play in an unsporting manner
suco *m,* juice
sucoso *a* juicy
sucre *m* sucre (monetary unit of Ecuador)
suculencia *f,* succulence; juiciness
suculento *a* succulent; juicy
sucumbir *vi* to yield, give in; die, succumb; lose a lawsuit
sucursal *a* branch. *f, com* branch (of a firm)
sud *m,* south (gen. **sur**). Used in combinations like **sudamericano**
sudadero *m,* horse blanket; sudatorium, sweating bath
sudafricano (-na) *a* and *n* South African
Sudamérica *f* South America
sudamericano (-na) *a* and *n* South American
sudante *a* sweating, perspiring
sudar *vi* and *vt* to perspire, sweat; ooze; *vi inf* toil; *vt* bathe in sweat; *inf* give reluctantly. **s. frío,** to break out in a cold sweat. **s. la gota gorda,** *fig inf* to be in a stew
sudario *m,* shroud
sudeste *m,* southeast; southeast wind
sudexpreso *m,* southern express
sudoeste *m,* southwest; southwest wind
sudor *m,* sweat, perspiration; toil; juice, moisture, sap, gum
sudoroso *a* sweaty
sudsudeste *m,* southsoutheast
sudsudoeste *m,* southsouthwest
Suecia Sweden
sueco (-ca) *a* Swedish. *n* Swede. *m,* Swedish (language)
suegra *f,* mother-in-law
suegro *m,* father-in-law
suela *f,* sole (of a shoe); *icht* sole; tanned leather; base. **no llegarle a uno a la s. del zapato,** *inf* to be not fit to hold a candle to.
sueldo *m,* salary, wages; *ant* Spanish coin. **a s.,** for a salary, salaried
suelo *m,* ground, earth; soil; bottom, base; sediment, dregs; site, plot; floor; flooring; story; land, territory; hoof (of horses); earth, world; *pl* chaff of grain. **s. natal,** native land; **besar el s.,** *inf* to fall flat. **dar consigo en el s.,** to fall down. **dar en el s. con,** to throw down; damage, spoil. *inf* **estar (una cosa) por los suelos,** to be dirt cheap
suelta *f,* loosening, unfastening; hobble (for horses); relay of oxen. **dar s. a,** to let loose, allow to go out for a time
sueltista *mf, Lat. Am.* freelance journalist, stringer
suelto *a* swift; competent, efficient; odd, separate; licentious; flowing, easy (style); loose, unbound. *m,* single copy (of a newspaper); loose change; newspaper paragraph
sueño *m,* dream; sleep; drowsiness, desire for sleep; vision, fancy. **s. pesado,** deep sleep. **conciliar el s.,** to court sleep. **echar un s.,** *inf* to take a nap. **en sueños,** in a dream; while asleep. **entre sueños,** between sleeping and waking. **¡Ni por sueño!** *inf* Certainly not! I wouldn't dream of it!
suero *m,* serum. **s. de la leche,** whey
suerte *f,* chance, luck; good luck; destiny, fate; condition, state; kind, species, sort; way, manner; bullfighter's maneuver; parcel of land. **de s. que,** so that; as a result. **echar suertes,** to draw lots. **tener buena s.,** to be lucky
sueste *m,* southeast; sou'wester (cap); *Lat. Am.* southeast wind
suéter *m,* sweater
suficiencia *f,* sufficiency; talent, aptitude; pedantry. **a s.,** enough
suficiente *a* sufficient, enough; suitable
sufijo *m,* suffix
sufragar *vt* to assist, aid; favor; pay, defray
sufragio *m,* aid, assistance; *ecc* suffragium, pious offering; vote; suffrage
sufragista *f,* suffragette
sufrible *a* bearable, endurable

sufrido *a* long-suffering, resigned; complaisant (of husbands); dirt-resistant (colors)
sufrimiento *m*, suffering, pain; affliction; tolerance
sufrir *vt* to suffer, undergo, experience; bear, endure; tolerate, put up with; allow, permit; resist, oppose; expiate; *vi* suffer
sugerir *vt irr* to suggest. See **sentir**
sugestión *f*, suggestion
sugestionable *a* easily influenced, open to suggestion
sugestionador *a* suggestive
sugestionar *vt* to suggest hypnotically; dominate, influence
sugestivo *a* suggestive, stimulating
suicida *a* suicidal, fatal. *mf* suicide (person)
suicidarse *vr* to commit suicide
suicidio *m*, suicide (act)
Suiza Switzerland
suiza *f*, row, rumpus, scrap
suizo (-za) *a* and *n* Swiss
sujeción *f*, subjection, domination; fastening, fixture; obedience, conformity
sujetador *m*, clamp; clip
sujetar *vt* to fasten, fix; hold down; grasp, clutch; subdue; *vr* (*with prep a*) conform to, obey. **s. con alfileres,** to pin up. **s. con tornillos,** to screw down
sujeto *a* liable, subject. *m*, topic, subject; person, individual; *gram phil* subject
sulfatar *vt* to sulphate
sulfato *m*, sulphate
sulfurar *vt* to sulphurate; *vr* grow irritated, become angry
sulfúrico *a* sulphuric
sulfuro *m*, sulphide
sulfuroso *a* sulphurous
sultán *m*, sultan
sultana *f*, sultana
suma *f*, total; amount, sum; *math* addition; summary, digest; computation. **en s.,** in brief, in short, finally
sumador (-ra) *n* summarizer; computator, adder
sumamente *adv* extremely, most
sumar *vt* to sum up, summarize; *math* add up
sumaria *f*, written indictment
sumariamente *adv* concisely, in brief; *law* summarily
sumario *a* brief, concise, abridged; *law* summary. *m*, summary, résumé, digest
sumergible *a* sinkable; submergible. *m*, submarine
sumergir *vt* to dip, immerse; sink, submerge; *fig* overwhelm (with grief, etc.); *vr* sink; dive; be submerged
sumersión *f*, immersion, dive, submersion
sumidero *m*, cesspool; drain; sink; pit, gully
suministración *f*. See **suministro**
suministrador (-ra) *n* purveyor
suministrar *vt* to purvey, supply, provide
suministro *m*, purveyance; provision; supply
sumir *vt* to sink; submerge; *ecc* consummate; *fig* overwhelm (with grief, etc.); *vr* fall in, become sunken (of cheeks, etc.); sink; be submerged; *Lat. Am.* cower, cringe
sumisión *f*, submission, obedience; *com* estimate, tender
sumiso *a* submissive, docile
sumista *mf* quick reckoner, computator. *m*, condenser, summarizer, abridger
sumo *a* supreme; high; tremendous, extraordinary. **a lo s.,** at the most; even if, although. **en s. grado,** in the highest degree
suntuosidad *f*, magnificence, luxury
suntuoso *a* magnificent, luxurious, sumptuous
supeditación *f*, subjection
supeditar *vt* to oppress; overcome, conquer; subordinate
superabundancia *f*, superabundance, excess; glut
superabundante *a* superabundant, excessive
superádito *a* superadded
superar *vt* to overcome, conquer; surpass; do better than
superávit *m*, *com* balance, surplus
superchería *f*, trickery, guile
superchero *a* guileful, wily
superconsciencia *f*, higher consciousness
supereminencia *f*, supereminence, greatest eminence
supereminente *a* supereminent
superentender *vt irr* to supervise, superintend. See **entender**
supererogación *f*, supererogation
superestructura *f*, superstructure
superficial *a* surface, shallow; superficial, rudimentary; futile
superficialidad *f*, superficiality; futility; shallowness
superficie *f*, area; surface; outside, exterior. **s. de rodadura,** tire tread
superfino *a* superfine
superfluidad *f*, superfluity
superfluo *a* superfluous, redundant
superfortaleza volante *f*, *aer* superfortress
superhombre *m*, superman
superintendencia *f*, supervision; superintendentship; higher administration
superintendente *mf* superintendent; supervisor
superior *a* higher, upper; excellent, fine; superior; higher (education, etc.). *m*, head, director; superior
superiora *f*, mother superior
superioridad *f*, superiority
superlativo *a* and *m*, superlative
superno *a* supreme
supernumerario (-ia) *a* and *n* supernumerary
superposición *f*, superposition
superproducción *f*, overproduction; superproduction
superrealismo *m*, surrealism
superrealista *a* surrealist
superstición *f*, superstition
supersticioso *a* superstitious
supervención *f*, *law* supervention
supervigilancia *f*, *Lat. Am.* supervision
supervivencia *f*, survival
superviviente *a* surviving. *mf* survivor
supino *a* supine; foolish, stupid. *m*, *gram* supine
suplantación *f*, supplanting
suplantador (-ra) *a* supplanting. *n* supplanter
suplantar *vt* to forge, alter (documents); supplant
suplefaltas *mf inf* scapegoat
suplementario *a* supplementary, additional
suplemento *m*, supplement; supply, supplying; newspaper supplement; *geom* supplement
suplente *m*, substitute, proxy; *fig* makeweight
súplica *f*, supplication, prayer; request
suplicación *f*, entreaty, supplication; *law* petition
suplicante *a* supplicatory; *law* petitioning. *mf* supplicator; *law* petitioner
suplicar *vt* to beg, supplicate; request; *law* appeal
suplicio *m*, torment, torture; execution; place of torture or execution; affliction, anguish. **último s.,** capital punishment
suplir *vt* to supply, furnish; substitute, take the place of; overlook, forgive
suponer *vt irr* to suppose, take for granted; simulate; comprise, include; *vi* carry weight, wield authority. See **poner**
suposición *f*, supposition; conjecture, assumption; distinction, talent, importance; falsity, falsehood
supositorio *m*, suppository
suprasensible *a* supersensible
supremacía *f*, supremacy
supremo *a* supreme; matchless, incomparable; last
supresión *f*, suppression; destruction, eradication; omission
suprimir *vt* to suppress; destroy, eradicate; omit, leave out. **s. una calle al tráfico,** to close a street to traffic, ban traffic from a street

supuesto *a* supposed; so-called; reputed. *m*, supposition, hypothesis. **por s.,** presumably; doubtless
supurar *vi* to suppurate
suputar *vt* to calculate, compute
sur *m*, south; south wind
surcador *m*, plowman
surcar *vt* to plow furrows; furrow, line; cut, cleave (water, etc.)
surco *m*, furrow; wrinkle, line; groove, channel; rut
surgidero *m*, *naut* road, roadstead
surgir *vi* to spout, gush, spurt; *naut* anchor; appear, show itself; come forth, turn up
surrealismo *m*, surrealism
surrealista *a* and *mf* surrealist
surtida *f*, hidden exit; false door; *naut* slipway
surtidero *m*, outlet, drain; jet, fountain
surtido *a* mixed, assorted. *m*, variety, assortment; stock, range. **de s.,** in everyday use
surtidor (-ra) *n* purveyor, supplier. *m*, fountain, jet. **s. de gasolina,** gasoline pump, gas pump
surtimiento *m*, assortment; stock
surtir *vt* to provide, supply, furnish; *vi* spurt, gush
surto *a* calm, reposeful; *naut* anchored
susceptibilidad *f*, susceptibility
susceptible *a* susceptible, open to; touchy, oversensitive
suscitar *vt* to cause, originate; provoke, incite; *vr* arise, take place
suscribir *vt* to sign; agree to; *vr* subscribe, contribute; take out a subscription (to a periodical, etc.). *Past Part.* **suscrito**
suscripción *f*, subscription; agreement, accession
susodicho *a* aforesaid
suspender *vt* to suspend, hang up; postpone, defer, stop; amaze, dumbfound; suspend (from employment); fail (an exam); adjourn (meetings); *vr* rear (of horses)
suspensión *f*, suspension; postponement, stoppage, deferment; amazement; failure (in an exam); adjournment (of a meeting); springs (of a car). *com* **s. de pagos,** suspension of payments. **con mala s.,** badly sprung (of a car)
suspensivo *a* suspensive
suspensivos *m, pl* suspension points, ellipsis points
suspenso *a* amazed, bewildered. *m*, failure slip (in an exam). **en s.,** in suspense
suspensor *m*, *Lat. Am.* suspender (for pants)
suspicacia *f*, suspiciousness; mistrust, uneasiness
suspicaz *a* suspicious, mistrustful
suspirado *a* eagerly desired, longed for
suspirar *vt* and *vi* to sigh. **s. por,** to long for
suspiro *m*, sigh; breath; glass whistle; *mus* brief pause, pause sign. **último s.,** *inf* last kick, end
suspirón *a* given to sighing
sustancia *f*, substance, juice, extract, essence; *fig* core, pith; *fig* meat; wealth, estate; worth, importance; nutritive part; *inf* common sense. *anat* **s. gris,** gray matter. **en s.,** in short
sustanciación *f*, substantiation
sustancial *a* substantial, real; important, essential; nutritive; solid
sustanciar *vt* to substantiate; summarize, extract, abridge
sustancioso *a* substantial; nutritive
sustantivo *a* and *m*, *gram* substantive, noun
sustentable *a* arguable, defensible
sustentación *f*, maintenance; defense
sustentar *vt* to sustain, keep; support, bear; nourish, feed; uphold, advocate. **s. un ciclo de conferencias,** to give a series of lectures
sustento *m*, maintenance, preservation; nourishment, sustenance; support
sustitución *f*, substitution
sustituible *a* substitutive, replaceable
sustituir *vt irr* to substitute. See **huir**
sustitutivo *a* substitutive
sustituto (-ta) *n* substitute
susto *m*, fright, shock; apprehension. **dar un s. (a),** to scare
sustracción *f*, subtraction
sustraer *vt irr* to remove, separate; rob, steal; *math* subtract; *vr* depart, remove oneself; avoid. See **traer**
sustrato *m*, substratum
susurrador (-ra) *a* whispering; murmuring; rustling. *n* whisperer
susurrante *a* whispering; murmuring; rustling
susurrar *vi* to whisper; murmur; rustle; babble, purl, prattle (of water); *vi* and *vr* be whispered abroad
susurro *m*, whispering, whisper; murmur; rustle; lapping
sutil *a* fine, thin; penetrating, subtle, keen
sutileza, sutilidad *f*, fineness, thinness; subtlety, penetration. **sutileza de manos,** dexterity; light-fingeredness; sleight of hand
sutilizaciones *f, pl* casuistry, hairsplitting, quibbling
sutilizar *vt* to make thin, refine; *fig* finish, perfect; *fig* split hairs, make subtle distinctions
sutura *f*, suture
suyo, suya *m*, and *f*, *pl* **suyos, suyas,** *poss pron* and *a 3rd pers* his; hers; its; yours; theirs; of his, of hers, etc. (e.g. **Este libro es suyo,** This book is his (hers, yours, theirs). **Este libro es uno de los suyos,** This book is one of his (hers, etc.). (**suyo** is often used with def. art. **el, la,** etc.) **los suyos,** his (hers, yours, etc.) family, following, adherents, etc. **de suyo,** of its very nature, of itself; spontaneously. **salirse con la suya,** to get one's own way. *inf* **ver la suyo,** to see one's opportunity

T

tabacal *m*, tobacco plantation
tabacalero (-ra) *a* tobacco. *n* tobacco merchant; tobacco planter
tabaco *m*, tobacco plant, tobacco leaf; tobacco; cigar. **t. de pipa,** pipe tobacco. **t. flojo,** mild tobacco. **t. rubio,** Virginia tobacco
tabalear(se) *vt* and *vr* to rock, sway, swing; *vi* drum with the fingers
tabaleo *m*, swaying, rocking; drumming with the fingers
tabanco *m*, market stall
tábano *m*, *ent* horsefly
tabanque *m*, potter's wheel
tabaque *m*, small osier basket (for fruit, sewing, etc.); large tack
tabaquera *f*, tobacco jar, tobacco tin; bowl of pipe tobacco; tobacco pouch; snuffbox
tabaquería *f*, tobacconist's shop
tabaquero (-ra) *n* tobacco grower; tobacco merchant; tobacco factory worker; tobacconist
tabaquismo *m*, nicotinism, nicotine poisoning
tabaquista *mf* tobacco expert; heavy smoker
tabardillo *m*, fever. **t. de tripas,** typhoid. **t. pintado,** typhus
tabardo *m*, tabard
taberna *f*, public house, tavern
tabernáculo *m*, tabernacle
tabernario *a* public house, tavern; low, vulgar
tabernera *f*, publican's wife; barmaid
tabernero *m*, publican; barman, drawer
tabicar *vt* to wall or board up; hide, cover up
tabique *m*, partition wall, inside wall; thin wall
tabla *f*, plank of wood, board; *met* plate; slab; flat side, face (of wood); *sew* box pleat; table (of contents, etc.);

art panel; vegetable garden; butcher's slab; butcher's stall; *pl* tablets (for writing); (*math* etc.) tables; stalemate (chess, checkers); draw (in an election); *theat* boards, stage. **t. de armonía,** sounding board (of musical instruments). **t. de lavar,** washboard. **t. de materias,** table of contents. **t. de multiplicación,** multiplication table. **t. rasa,** clean sheet (of paper, etc.); complete ignorance. **T. Redonda,** Round Table (of King Arthur). **escapar** *or* **salvarse en una t.,** to have a narrow escape, escape in the nick of time

tablacho *m,* sluice gate. **echar el t.,** *inf* to interrupt the flow of someone's remarks

tablado *m,* flooring; platform; *theat* stage; scaffold, gibbet. **sacar al t.,** to produce, put on the stage; to make known, publish

tablazón *f,* planks, boards; flooring; *naut* deck planks or sheathing

tablear *vt* to saw into planks; *sew* make box pleats in; hammer iron into sheets

tablero *m,* board (of wood); paneling, boarding; slab; shop counter; board (checkers, chess). **t. de instrumentos,** dashboard; instrument panel

tableta *f,* tablet; pastille, lozenge

tablilla *f,* small board; tablet; bulletin board, notice board

tablón *m,* thick plank; wooden beam; *inf* drinking bout

tabú *m,* taboo

tabuco *m,* miserable little room; hovel

taburete *m,* stool; tabouret

tacañería *f,* miserliness, niggardliness; craftiness

tacaño *a* miserly, niggardly; crafty

tacha *f,* imperfection, defect; spot, stain; fault; large tack. **poner t.,** to criticize, object to

tachable *a* censurable, blameworthy

tachar *vt* to criticize, blame; cross out, erase; charge, accuse

tacho de basura *m, Argentina* garbage can

tachón *m,* round-headed ornamental nail; *sew* gold or silver studs, trimming; crossing out, erasure

tachonar *vt* to stud with round-headed nails; *sew* trim with gold or silver studs or trimming

tachoso *a* imperfect, defective, faulty; spotted, stained

tachuela *f, carp* tack

tácito *a* silent, unexpressed; tacit, implied

taciturnidad *f,* taciturnity; reserve; melancholy

taciturno *a* taciturn; reserved; dismal, gloomy, melancholy

taco *m,* stopper, plug; billiard cue; rammer; wad, wadding (in a gun); pop gun; taco (filled tortilla); tear-off calendar; *Argentina,* heel (of a shoe) *inf* snack; obscenity, oath. **t. de papel,** writing tablet

tacón *m,* heel (of a shoe)

taconear *vi* to stamp with one's heels; walk heavily on one's heels; walk arrogantly

taconeo *m,* drumming or stamping of one's heels (gen. in dancing)

táctica *f,* method, technique; *mil* tactics; policy, way, means

táctico *a* tactical. *m, mil* tactician

táctil *a* tactile

tacto *m,* sense of touch; touch, feel; touching; skill; tact

tafetán *m,* taffeta; *pl* flags, standards. **t. de heridas** *or* **t. inglés,** court plaster

tafilete *m,* morocco leather

tahalí *m,* sword shoulder belt

tahona *f,* horse mill; bakery; baker's shop

tahonero (-ra) *n* miller; baker

tahúr *m,* gambler; cardsharper

tahurería *f,* gambling den; gambling; cheating at cards

Tailandia Thailand

taimado *a* knavish, crafty; obstinate, headstrong

taimería *f,* cunning, craftiness

taita *m,* daddy

taja *f,* cut, cutting; slice; washboard

tajada *f,* slice; strip, portion; steak, filet; *inf* cough; drinking bout; hoarseness

tajadera *f,* cheese knife; chisel; *pl* sluice gate

tajado *a* steep, sheer (of cliffs, etc.)

tajadura *f,* cutting, dividing, dissection

tajar *vt* to cut, chop; sharpen, trim (quill pens)

tajea *f,* culvert; aqueduct; drain; watercourse

tajear *vt, Lat. Am.* to cut up

Tajo, el the Tagus

tajo *m,* cut, incision; task; cutting (in a mountain, etc.); cut, thrust (of sword); executioner's block; chopping board; washboard; steep cliff, precipice

tajón *m,* butcher block; chopping board

tal *a pl* **tales,** such; said (e.g. **el t. Don Juan,** the said Don Juan). **tal** is always used before nouns and (except when meaning 'the said') without def. art. **un t.,** a certain (e.g. **un t. hombre,** a certain man). *pron* some, some people; someone; such a thing. *adv* so, thus. **t. para cual,** two of a kind, a well-matched pair; tit for tat. **con t. que,** *conjunc* on condition that, provided that. **No hay t.,** There is no such thing. *inf* **¿Qué t.?** How are you? What's the news? What's new?

tala *f,* felling or cutting down (of trees); cropping of grass (ruminants)

talabarte *m,* sword belt

talabartería *f,* saddlery

talador (-ra) *a* felling, cutting; destructive. *n* feller, cutter; destroyer

taladrar *vt* to drill, bore, gouge holes; pierce, perforate; punch (a ticket); assail or hurt the ear (sounds); *fig* go into deeply (a subject)

taladro *m,* drill, gimlet, gouge; drill hole, bore; puncher (for tickets, etc.)

tálamo *m,* marriage bed; (*bot anat*) thalamus

talán *m,* peal, tolling (of a bell)

talanquera *f,* barricade; parapet, fence, wall; refuge, asylum; safety, security

talante *m,* mode of execution, technique; personal appearance, mien; disposition, temperament; wish, desire; aspect, appearance. **de buen (mal) t.,** willingly (unwillingly)

talar *a* full-length, long (of gowns, robes, etc.)

talar *vt* to fell, chop down (trees); ravage, lay waste; prune (gen. olive trees)

talco *m, min* talc; sequin, tinsel

talcualillo *a inf* not too bad, fairly good; slightly better (of health)

taled *m,* prayer shawl, tales, tallit

talega *f,* sack, bag; sackful; money bag; *pl inf* cash wealth

talego *m,* narrow sack; *inf* dumpy person

talento *m,* talent (Greek coin); talent, gift, quality; intelligence, understanding; cleverness

talentoso *a* talented

talero *m, Argentina* whip

talión *m,* (**ley de**) law of retaliation

talismán *m,* talisman

talla *f,* carving (especially wood); cutting (of gems); reward for apprehension of a criminal; ransom; stature, height, size; height measuring rod

tallado *a* **bien** (or **mal**), well (or badly) carved; well (or badly) proportioned, of a good (or bad) figure

tallado *m,* carving

tallador *m,* metal engraver; die sinker

tallar *vt art* to carve; engrave; cut (gems); value, estimate; measure height (of persons)

tallarín *m,* (gen. *pl*) *cul* noodle

talle *m,* figure, physique; waist; fit (of clothes); appearance, aspect. *inf* **largo de t.,** long-waisted; long drawn out, overlong. **tener buen t.,** to have a good figure

tallecer *vi irr bot* to sprout, shoot. See **conocer**

taller *m,* workshop; factory; mill; workroom, atelier; industrial school; school of arts and crafts; studio

tallista *mf* engraver; wood carver; sculptor

tallo *m, bot* stalk; shoot; slice of preserved fruit; cabbage. **t. rastrero,** *bot* runner

talludo *a* long-stalked; lanky, overgrown; no longer young, aging (of women); habit-ridden

talmúdico *a* Talmudic
talón *m*, heel; heel (of a shoe); *com* counterfoil; luggage receipt; *com* sight draft; coupon; heel (of a violin bow). *inf* **apretar los talones,** to take to one's heels. *inf* **pisarle (a uno) los talones,** to follow on a person's heels; rival successfully
talonada *f*, dig in with the spurs
talonario *m*, stub book
tamaño *a comp* so big; so small (e.g. **La conocí tamaña,** I knew her when she was so high) (indicating her size with a gesture)); so great, so large (e.g. **tamaña empresa,** so great an undertaking). *m*, size
tamarindo *m*, tamarind
tambaleante *a* tottering, rickety; staggering
tambalear(se) *vi* and *vr* to totter, sway, shake; reel, stagger
tambaleo *m*, swaying; tottering; rocking; shaking; staggering, reeling
tambarillo *m*, chest with an arched lid
también *adv* also, too; in addition, as well
tambor *m*, *mus* drum; drummer; embroidery frame; *mech* drum, cylinder; roaster (for coffee, chestnuts, etc.). **t. mayor,** drum major. **a t.** (*or* **con t.**) **batiente,** with drums beating; triumphantly, with colors flying
tamborear *vi* to totter, sway; stagger, reel
tamboreo *m*, tottering, swaying; staggering, reeling
tamboril *m*, tabor
tamborilada *f*, *inf* slap on the back or face; *inf* fall on the bottom
tamborilear *vi* to play the tabor; *vt* eulogize, extol
tamborilero *m*, tabor player
tamborín *m*, tabor
Támesis, el the Thames
tamiz *m*, sieve
tamizar *vt* to sieve
tamo *m*, fluff; chaff
tampoco *adv* neither, not . . . either, nor . . . either; no more (e.g. **No lo ha hecho María t.,** Mary hasn't done it either)
tampón *m*, stamp moistener; *surg* tampon
tan *adv abb* **tanto** so, as. Used before adjectives and adverbs, excepting **más, mejor, menos, peor,** which need **tanto. t. . . . como,** as . . . as. **t. siquiera,** even (see **siquiera**). **t. sólo,** only, solely (e.g. **No vengo t. sólo para saludarte,** I do not come merely to greet you). **qué . . . t.,** what a . . . (e.g. **¡Qué día t. hermoso!** What a lovely day!)
tanda *f*, turn; opportunity; task; shift, relay; game (of billiards); bad habit; collection, batch, group; round (of a game); (*dance*) set
tándem *m*, tandem
tandeo *m*, allowance of irrigation water, turn for using water
Tangañica Tanganyika
tangente *a* and *f*, *geom* tangent
Tánger Tangier
tangerino (-na) *a* and *n* of or from Tangier, Tangerine
tanque *m*, *mil* tank; cistern, tank, reservoir; ladle, dipper
tanteador *m*, *sport* scorer, marker; scoreboard
tantear *vt* to measure, compare; consider fully; test, try out; *fig* probe, pump (persons); estimate roughly; *art* sketch, block in; *vt* and *vi sport* keep the score of
tanteo *m*, measurement, comparison; test; rough estimate; *sport* score
tanto *a* so much; as much; very great; as great; *pl* **tantos,** so many; as many (e.g. **Tienen tantas flores como nosotros,** They have as many flowers as we). In comparisons **tanto** is used before **más, mejor, menos, peor,** but generally **tan** is used before adjectives and adverbs (e.g. **¡Tanto peor!** So much the worse!). *pron dem* that (e.g. **por lo t.,** therefore, on that account). *m*, so much, a certain amount; copy of a document; man, piece (in games); point (score in games); *com* rate (e.g. **el t. por ciento,** the percentage, the rate); *pl* approximation, odd (e.g. **Llegaron cien hombres y tantos,** A hundred-odd men arrived). *adv* so much; as much; so, in such a way. **t. . . . como,** the same as, as much as. **t. . . . cuanto,** as much as. **t. más,** the more. **t. menos,** the less (e.g. **Cuanto más (menos) dinero tiene t. más (menos) quiere,** The more (less) money he has, the more (less) he wants). **t. más (menos) . . . cuanto que,** all the more (less) . . . because. **algún t.,** a certain amount, somewhat. **al t. de (una cosa),** aware of, acquainted with (a thing). **en t.** *or* **entre t.,** meanwhile. **las tantas,** *inf* late hour, wee hours. **No es para t.,** *inf* It's not as bad as that, there's no need to make such a fuss; he (she, it) isn't equal to it. **otro t.,** the same, as much; as much more. **un t.,** a bit, somewhat
tañedor (-ra) *n mus* player
tañer *vt irr mus* to play; *vi* sway, swing. **t. la occisa,** to sound the death (in hunting). *Pres. Part.* **tañendo.** *Preterite* **tañó, tañeron.** *Imperf. Subjunc.* **tañese,** etc.
tañido *m*, tune, sound, note; toll, peal; ring
taoísmo *m*, Taoism
taoísta *mf* Taoist
tapa *f*, lid; cover; cover (of books)
tapaboca *m*, blow on the mouth; *f*, scarf, muffler; *inf* remark that silences someone
tapada *f*, veiled woman, one whose face is hidden
tapadera *f*, loose lid, top, cover
tapadero *m*, stopper
tapado *m*, *Argentina* coat, overcoat
tapador (-ra) *a* covering. *n* coverer. *m*, stopper; lid; cover
tapagujeros *m*, *inf* unskilled mason or bricklayer; *fig inf* stopgap (person)
tapar *vt* to cover; cover with a lid; muffle up, veil; hide, keep secret; close up, stop up
taparrabo *m*, loincloth; swimming trunks
tapete *m*, rug; tablecover. *inf* **t. verde,** gaming table. *fig* **estar sobre el t.,** to be on the carpet, be under consideration
tapia *f*, adobe; mud wall; fence. *inf* **más sordo que una t.,** as deaf as a post
tapiar *vt* to wall up; put a fence around, fence in
tapicería *f*, set of tapestries; tapestry work; art of tapestry making; upholstery; tapestry storehouse or shop
tapicero *m*, tapestry weaver or maker; upholsterer; carpet layer; furnisher
tapioca *f*, tapioca
tapisca *f Central America, Mexico* corn harvest
tapiz *m*, tapestry; carpet
tapizar *vt* to cover with tapestry; cover, clothe; upholster; carpet; hang with tapestry; furnish with hangings or drapes
tapón *m*, stopper; cork (of a bottle); plug; *surg* tampon
taponar *vt* to stopper, cork; plug; *surg* tampon; *mil* seal off
tapujarse *vr* to wrap oneself up, muffle oneself
tapujo *m*, scarf, muffler, face covering; disguise; *inf* pretense, subterfuge
taquera *f*, rack (for billiard cues)
taquería *f*, taco stand
taquigrafía *f*, shorthand
taquigrafiar *vt* to write in shorthand
taquigráfico *a* shorthand
taquígrafo (-fa) *n* shorthand writer, stenographer
taquilla *f*, booking office; box office; grille, window (in banks, etc.); rolltop desk, cupboard for papers; *theat* takings, cash
taquillero (-ra) *n* booking office clerk
tara *f*, tally stick; *com* tare
taracea *f*, inlaid work, marquetry
taracear *vt* to inlay
tarambana *mf inf* madcap
tarántula *f*, tarantula
tararear *vt* to hum a tune
tarareo *m*, humming, singing under one's breath
tarasca *f*, figure of a dragon (carried in Corpus Christi processions); *inf* hag, trollop
tarascada *f*, bite, nip; *inf* insolent reply

tarascar *vt* to bite; wound with the teeth
tardanza *f,* delay, tardiness; slowness
tardar *vi* to delay; be tardy, arrive late; take a long time. **a más t.,** at the latest
tarde *f,* afternoon. *adv* late. **¡Buenas tardes!** Good afternoon! **de t. en t.,** from time to time, sometimes. **hacerse t.,** to grow late. **Más vale t. que nunca,** Better late than never
tardecer *vi impers irr* to grow dusk. See **conocer**
tardecica, tardecita *f,* dusk, late afternoon
tardíamente *adv* late; too late
tardío *a* late; backward; behind; slow, deliberate
tardo *a* slow, slothful, tardy; late; dilatory; stupid, slow-witted; badly spoken, inarticulate
tarea *f,* task, work
tarifa *f,* price list; tariff
tarifar *vt* to put a tariff on
tarima *f,* stand, raised platform
tarín barín *adv inf* more or less, about
tarja *f,* large shield; ancient coin; tally stick. *inf* **beber sobre t.,** to drink on credit
tarjar *vt* to reckon by tally; *Lat. Am.* cross out, erase
tarjeta *f,* buckler, small shield; *arch* tablet bearing an inscription; title (of maps and charts); visiting card; invitation (card). **t. de visita,** visiting card. **t. postal,** postcard, postal card
tarquín *m,* mud, mire
tárraga *f,* old Spanish dance
tarro *m,* jar, pot; *Lat. Am.* top hat
tarso *m, anat* tarsus, ankle; *zool* hock; *orn* shank
tarta *f,* cake pan; cake; tart
tártago *m,* spurge; *inf* misfortune, disappointment
tartajear *vi* to stammer; stutter
tartajeo *m,* stammering; stutter
tartajoso (-sa) *a* stammering; stuttering. *n* stutterer
tartalear *vi inf* to stagger, totter; be speechless, be dumbfounded
tartamudear *vi* to stammer, stutter
tartamudeo *m.* **tartamudez** *f,* stammering; stuttering
tartamudo (-da) *n* stammerer
tartán *m,* tartan
tartana *f, naut* tartan; covered two-wheeled carriage
tartáreo *a poet* infernal, hellish
tártaro (-ra) *m,* cream of tartar; tartar (on teeth); *poet* hell, hades. *a* and *n* Tartar
tartufo *m,* hypocrite
tarugo *m,* thick wooden peg; stopper; wooden block; *a Lat. Am.* dumb, stupid
tasa *f,* assessment, valuation; valuation certificate; fixed price; standard rate; measure, rule
tasación *f,* valuation; assessment
tasador *m,* public assessor; valuer
tasajo *m,* salt meat; piece of meat
tasar *vt* to value; price; fix remuneration; tax; regulate; rate; dole out sparingly
tasca *f,* gambling den; tavern
tascar *vt* to dress (hemp, etc.); graze, crop the grass
tasquera *f, inf* quarrel, row, rumpus
tasquil *m,* wood splinter, chip
tata *m, inf WH* daddy
tatarabuela *f,* great-great-grandmother
tatarabuelo *m,* great-great-grandfather
tataradeudo (-da) *n* very old relative; ancestor
tataranieta *f,* great-great-granddaughter
tataranieto *m,* great-great-grandson
tatas, andar a *vt* to walk on all fours
¡tate! *interj* Stop!; Be careful!; Go slowly!; Now I understand!, Of course!
tatuaje *m,* tattooing
tatuar *vt* to tattoo
taumaturgia *f,* thaumaturgy, wonder-working
taumaturgo *m,* thaumaturge, magician
taurino *a* taurine; pertaining to bullfights
Tauro *m,* Taurus
tauromaquia *f,* bullfighting, tauromachy
tautología *f,* tautology
taxi *m,* taxi
taxidermia *f,* taxidermy
taxidermista *mf* taxidermist
taxista *m,* taxi driver
taxonomía *f,* taxonomy
taz a taz *adv* in exchange, without payment; even
taza *f,* cup; cupful; basin (of a fountain)
tazar(se) *vt* and *vr* to fray (of cloth)
tazón *m,* large cup; bowl
te *f,* name of the letter T. *mf* dat. and acc. of *pers pron 2nd pers sing* thee; you; to thee, to you. Never used with a preposition
té *m,* tea
tea *f,* torch; firebrand
teatral *a* theatrical
teatralidad *f,* theatricality
teatro *m,* theater; stage; dramatic works; dramatic art; drama, plays. **t. de variedades,** music hall. **t. por horas,** theater where short, one-act plays are staged hourly
teca *f,* teak
techado *m,* ceiling; roof
techador *m,* roofer
techar *vt* to roof
techo *m,* roof; ceiling; dwelling, habitation
techumbre *f,* ceiling; roof
tecla *f,* key (of keyed instruments); typewriter, linotype, or calculating machine key; *fig* difficult or delicate point. *inf* **dar en la t.,** to hit on the right way of doing a thing
teclado *m,* keyboard
tecleado *m, mus* fingering
teclear *vi* to finger the keyboard; run one's fingers over the keyboard; *inf* drum or tap with the fingers; *vt* tap (the keys, etc.); *inf* try out various schemes
tecleo *m,* fingering the keys; *inf* drumming with the fingers; scheme, means
técnica *f,* technique
tecnicismo *m,* technical jargon; technicality, technical term
técnico *a* technical. *m,* technician
tecnicolor *m,* technicolor
tecnología *f,* technology
tecnológico *a* technological
tecnólogo *m,* technologist
tecolote *m, Central America, Mexico* owl; *Mexico* cop (police officer)
tedero *m,* torch seller; torch holder
tedio *m,* tedium, boredom, ennui
tedioso *a* tedious, boring
teísmo *m,* theism
teísta *a* theistic. *mf* theist
teja *f,* tile, slate. *inf* **de tejas abajo,** in the normal way; in the world of men. **de tejas arriba,** in a supernatural way; in heaven
tejadillo *m,* roof (of a vehicle)
tejado *m,* roof
tejano, -a *a* and *ms* Texan. **tejanos** jeans
tejar *m,* tile works. *vt* to roof with tiles
Tejas *m* Texas
tejavana *f,* penthouse, open shed
tejedor (-ra) *a* weaving; *inf* scheming. *n* weaver; *inf* schemer
tejedura *f,* weaving; fabric; texture
tejeduría *f,* art of weaving; weaving shed or mill
tejemaneje *m, inf* cleverness, knack
tejer *vt* to weave; plait; spin a cocoon; arrange, regulate; concoct, hatch (schemes); wind in and out (in dancing)
tejero *m,* tile manufacturer
tejido *m,* texture, weaving; textile; *anat* tissue; fabric, material
tejo *m,* quoit, discus; metal disk; yew tree
tejón *m, zool* badger
tela *f,* fabric, material, cloth; membrane; film (on liquids); spiderweb, cobweb; inner skin (of fruit, vegetables); film over the eye; matter, subject; scheme, plot.

t. metálica, wire gauze. **en t. de juicio,** under consideration, in doubt. **llegarle a uno a las telas del corazón,** to hurt deeply, cut to the quick
telar *m*, loom, weaving machine; *theat* gridiron
telaraña *f*, cobweb; mere trifle, bagatelle. *inf* **mirar las telarañas,** to be absent-minded
telarañoso *a* cobwebby
telecomunicación *f*, telecommunication
telefonear *vt* to telephone, call
telefonía *f*, telephony. **t. sin hilos,** wireless telephony, broadcasting
telefónico *a* telephonic
telefonista *mf* telephone operator
teléfono *m*, telephone. **t. automático,** dial telephone. **llamar por t. (a),** to telephone, call, ring up
telefundir *vt* to telecast
telegrafía *f*, telegraphy. **t. sin hilos,** wireless telegraphy
telegrafiar *vt* to telegraph
telegráfico *a* telegraphic
telegrafista *mf* telegraph operator
telégrafo *m*, telegraph. **t. sin hilos,** wireless telegraph. *inf* **hacer telégrafos,** to talk by signs
telegrama *m*, telegram
telemetría *f*, telemetry
telémetro *m*, telemeter, rangefinder
teleología *f*, teleology
telepatía *f*, telepathy
telepático *a* telepathic
telescópico *a* telescopic
telescopio *m*, telescope
telespectador *m*, TV viewer, member of the television audience
teletipo *m*, teleprinter
televisión *f*, television
telilla *f*, film (on liquids); thin fabric
telón *m*, *theat* curtain; drop scene. **t. contra incendios, t. de seguridad,** *theat* safety curtain. **t. de boca,** drop curtain. **t. de foro,** drop scene
tema *m*, theme, subject; *mus* motif, theme; thesis, argument. *f*, obstinacy; obsession, mania; hostility, grudge, rancor
temático *a* thematic; pigheaded, obstinate
temblador (-ra) *a* trembling, shaking. *n* Quaker
temblante *a* shaking; quivering. *m*, bracelet
temblar *vi irr* to tremble, shake; wave, quiver; shiver with fear. See **acertar**
temblequear, tembletear *vi inf* tremble; shake with fear
temblón *a inf* trembling, shaking. *m*, *inf* aspen
temblor *m*, shake, trembling, shiver. **temblor (de tierra)** earthquake
tembloroso, tembloso *a* trembling, shaking, shivering, quivering
temedero *a* fearsome, dread
temedor (-ra) *a* fearful. *n* fearer, dreader
temer *vt* to fear, dread; suspect, imagine; *vi* be afraid
temerario *a* reckless, impetuous; thoughtless, hasty
temeridad *f*, recklessness, impetuosity, temerity; thoughtlessness; act of folly; rash judgment
temerón *a inf* swaggering, bombastic
temeroso *a* frightening, dread; fearful, timid; afraid, suspicious
temible *a* dread, awesome
temor *m*, fear
temoso *a* obstinate, headstrong
témpano *m*, tabor; drumhead; block, flat piece; side of bacon. **t. de hielo,** iceberg, ice floe
temperación *f*, tempering
temperamento *m*, temperament, nature; compromise, agreement
temperar *vt* to temper; *Lat. Am.* spend the summer
temperatura *f*, temperature
temperie *f*, weather conditions
tempestad *f*, storm
tempestividad *f*, opportuneness, seasonableness
tempestivo *a* opportune, seasonable
tempestuoso *a* stormy
templa *f*, tempera; *pl anat* temples
templado *a* moderate; temperate (of regions); lukewarm; *mus* in tune; restrained (of style); *inf* brave, long-suffering. **estar bien** (*or* **mal**) **templado,** *inf* to be well (or badly) tuned (of musical instruments); be in a good (*or* bad) temper; be good- (*or* ill-) natured
templador (-ra) *n* tuner. *m*, tuning key
templadura *f*, tuning; tempering
templanza *f*, moderation; sobriety; mildness of climate
templar *vt* to tune; *met* temper; moderate; warm; allay, appease; anneal; *art* harmonize, blend; *naut* trim the sails; *vr* control oneself, be moderate; *vi* grow warm
temple *m*, weather conditions; temperature; temper (of metals, etc.); nature, disposition; bravery; mean, average; *mus* tuning. **al t.,** in tempera
templete *m*, *dim* shrine; niche (for statues); kiosk, pavilion
templo *m*, temple
temporada *f*, space of time, season, while. **de t.,** seasonal; temporary. **estar de t.,** to be out of town, on holiday
temporal *a* temporal; temporary; secular, lay; transient, fugitive. *m*, storm, tempest; rainy period; seasonal laborer
temporalidad *f*, secular character; temporality secular possession (gen. *pl*)
temporáneo, temporario *a* temporary, impermanent, fleeting
témporas *f pl*, Ember days
temporejar *vt naut* to lie to in a storm
temporero *a* temporary (of work)
temporizar *vi* to while away the time; temporize
tempranal *a* early fruiting
tempranear *vi*, *Lat. Am.* to get up early
tempranero *a* early
temprano *a* early. *adv* in the early hours; prematurely, too soon
temulento *a* intoxicated, drunken
ten con ten *m*, *inf* tact, diplomacy
tenacear *vi* to insist, be obstinate
tenacidad *f*, adhesiveness; resistance, toughness; obstinacy, tenacity
tenacillas *f pl*, *dim* small tongs; candle snuffers; sugar tongs; curling irons; tweezers
tenaz *a* adhesive; hard, resistant, unyielding; tenacious, obstinate
tenaza *f*, claw (of a lobster, etc.); *pl* tongs; pincers; pliers; dental forceps
tenazada *f*, seizing with tongs; strong bite, snap; rattle of tongs
tenazón (a or **de)** *adv* without taking aim, wildly; unexpectedly
tención *f*, retention, holding; grip
tendal *m*, awning; sheet for catching olives; *Lat. Am.* heap, lot, pile, large amount, large number
tendedero *m*, drying ground
tendedura *f*, laying out; stretching
tendencia *f*, tendency
tendencioso *a* tendentious, biased
tender *vt irr* to hang out; unfold, spread out; extend, hold out; *mas* plaster; *vi* tend, incline; *vr* lie down at full length; place one's cards on the table; gallop hard (of horses). See **entender**
tendero (-ra) *n* shopkeeper; retailer. *m*, tent maker
tendido *m*, row of seats in a bullfight arena; clothes hung out to dry; clear sky; *mas* plaster
tendón *m*, tendon
tenducha *f*, *inf* wretched little shop
tenebroso *a* dark, gloomy
tenedero *m*, *naut* anchoring ground, anchorage
tenedor *m*, table fork; possessor, retainer; *com* holder; payee. **t. de libros,** bookkeeper
teneduría *f*, employment of a bookkeeper. **t. de libros,** bookkeeping

tenencia *f*, possession; tenancy, occupation; lieutenancy

tener *vt irr* to have; hold; grasp; possess, own; uphold, maintain; contain; include; hold fast, grip; stop; keep (promises); lodge, accommodate; (*with en*) value, estimate (e.g. **Le tengo en poco,** I have a poor opinion of him); (*with para*) be of the opinion that (e.g. **tengo para mí,** my opinion is); (*with por*) believe, consider; *vi* be wealthy; *vr* steady oneself; hold on to; lean (on); rest (on); defend oneself; uphold; rely on; (*with por*) consider oneself as. **tener** is used to express: 1. *Age* (e.g. **¿Cuántos años tiene Vd?** How old are you?). 2. *Possession* (e.g. **Tenemos muchos sombreros,** We have a great many hats). 3. *Measurements* (e.g. **El cuarto tiene dieciocho metros de largo,** The room is eighteen meters long). Translated by 'be' when describing some physical and mental states (e.g. **Tenemos miedo,** We are afraid. **Tengo sueño,** I am sleepy. **Tienen frío (calor),** They are cold (hot)). Used as *auxiliary verb* replacing **haber** in compound tenses of transitive verbs (e.g. **Tengo escritas las cartas,** I have written the letters). **t. a bien,** to think fit, please, judge convenient. **t. algo en cuenta a uno,** to hold something against someone. **t. a menos de hacer (una cosa),** to scorn to do (a thing). **t. cruda,** to have a hangover. **t. curiosidad por,** to be curious about. **t. curiosidad por que** + *subj* to be interested that. **t. en aprecio,** to appreciate, esteem, value. **t. en cuenta,** to bear in mind. **t. en menos (a),** to despise (a person). **t. gana,** to want, wish; feel disposed; have an appetite. **t. lugar,** to take place, occur. **t. muchas partes cruzadas,** to be well-traveled. **t. mucho colegio** to be well-educated. **t. muy en cuenta,** to certainly bear in mind. **t. poco colegio,** to have had little education. **t. presente,** to remember. **t. que,** to have to (e.g. **tengo que hacerlo,** I must do it). **t. que ver (con),** to have something to do (with), be related to. **no tenerlas todas consigo,** *inf* to have the jitters. *Pres. Ind.* **tengo, tienes, tiene, tenemos, tenéis, tienen.** *Preterite* **tuve,** etc. *Fut.* **tendré,** etc. *Condit.* **tendría,** etc. *Pres. Subjunc.* **tenga,** etc. *Imperf. Subjunc.* **tuviese,** etc.

tenguerengue, en *adv inf* rickety, insecure

tenia *f*, tapeworm; *arch* fillet, narrow molding

teniente *a* owning, holding; unripe (of fruit); *inf* slightly deaf; stingy, mean. *m*, deputy, substitute; *mil* first lieutenant, lieutenant. **t. coronel,** lieutenant colonel. **t. de navío,** naval lieutenant. **t. general,** *mil* lieutenant general. **t. general de aviación,** air marshal

tenis *m*, tennis

tenor *m*, import, contents (of a letter, etc.); constitution, composition; *mus* tenor

tenorio *m*, rake, Don Juan, philanderer

tensar *vt* to tighten; tense

tensión *f*, tautness; tension; strain, stress; *elec* tension

tenso *a* taut; tight; tense

tentación *f*, temptation; attraction, inducement

tentáculo *m*, tentacle; feeler

tentadero *m*, yard for trying out young bulls for bullfighting

tentador (-ra) *a* tempting; attractive. *n* tempter. *m*, the Devil

tentalear *vt* to examine by touch

tentar *vt irr* to touch, feel; examine by touch; incite, encourage; try, endeavor; test; tempt; *surg* probe. See **sentar**

tentativa *f*, endeavor, attempt; preliminary exam (at some univs.)

tentativo *a* tentative, experimental

tentemozo *m*, support, prop; tumbler (toy)

tentempié *m*, *inf* snack, bite

tenue *a* thin; slender, delicate; trivial, worthless, insignificant; pale; faint

tenuidad *f*, slenderness; delicacy; triviality, insignificance; paleness; faintness

teñidura *f*, dyeing, staining

teñir *vt irr* to dye; *art* darken; color, tinge; *vr* be dyed; be tinged or colored. See **ceñir**

teocracia *f*, theocracy

teocrático *a* theocratic

teodolito *m*, theodolite

teologal *a* theological

teología *f*, theology, divinity

teológico *a* theological

teologizar *vi* to theologize

teólogo *a* theological. *m*, theologian, divine; student of theology

teorema *m*, theorem

teoría *f*, theory

teórica *f*, theory

teórico *a* theoretical, speculative. *m*, theorist

teorizar *vt* to consider theoretically, theorize about

teoso *a* resinous, gummy

teosofía *f*, theosophy

teosófico *a* theosophical

teósofo *m*, theosophist

tepe *m*, sod, cut turf

tequila *f*. *Mexico* tequila, maguey brandy

terapeuta *mf* therapeutist

terapéutica *f*, therapeutics

terapéutico *a* therapeutic

terapia *f*, therapy

teratología *f*, teratology

tercena *f*, warehouse for storing government monopoly goods (tobacco, etc.)

tercenista *mf* person in charge of a tercena

tercer *a abb* of **tercero** third. Used before *m*, *sing* nouns

tercera *f*, procuress; *mus* third

tercería *f*, arbitration, mediation; temporary occupation of a fortress, etc.

tercero (-ra) *a* third; mediatory. *n* third; mediator. *m*, pimp; *ecc* tertiary; tithes collector; third person. **¡A la tercera va la vencida!** Third time lucky!

terceto *m*, tercet, triplet

tercia *f*, one-third; *ecc* tierce, third hour; storehouse for tithes. **tercias reales,** royal share of ecclesiastical tithes

terciana *f*, tertian fever

terciar *vt* to slant; sling sideways; divide into three; equalize weight (on beasts of burden); plow or dig for the third time; *agr* prune; *vr* be opportune, come at the right time. *vi* mediate, arbitrate; make up a number (for cards, etc.); reach the third day (of the moon); take part, participate

tercio *a* third. *m*, one-third; *mil* infantry regiment; *ant*, body of foreign volunteers; fishermen's association; *pl* brawny limbs of a man. **hacer t.,** to take part in; make up the number of. **hacer buen** (*or* **mal**) **t. a alguien,** to do someone a good (*or* bad) turn

terciopelo *m*, velvet; velveteen

terco *a* pigheaded, obstinate; hard, tough

tergiversación *f*, tergiversation, vacillation

tergiversar *vt* to tergiversate, shuffle, vacillate

termal *a* thermal

termas *f pl*, thermal springs, hot mineral baths; thermal

térmico *a* thermic

terminable *a* terminable

terminación *f*, conclusion, termination; end, finish; ending of a word; *gram* termination

terminador (-ra) *a* concluding. *n* finisher

terminal *a* terminal; final. *m*, *elec* terminal. **t. de carga,** cargo terminal

terminante *a* conclusive, definite; categorical

terminar *vt* to end, conclude; complete; *vr* and *vi* end

término *m*, limit, end; term, expression; boundary marker; district, suburb; space, period; state, condition; boundary; object, aim; appearance, demeanor, behavior (gen. *pl*); completion; *mus* tone; (*math law logic*) term. **t. medio,** *math* average; medium; compromise, middle way. **correr el t.,** to lapse (of time). **en primer t.,** *art* in the foreground. **medios términos,** evasions, excuses. **primer t.,** (cinema) closeup

terminología *f,* terminology
termita *f,* thermite. *m,* termite
termodinámica *f,* thermodynamics
termoeléctrico *a* thermoelectric
termómetro *m,* thermometer
Termópilas Thermopylae
termos *m,* thermos, vacuum bottle
termoscopio *m,* thermoscope
termóstato *m,* thermostat
termostático *a* thermostatic
terna *f,* triad, trio; set of dice
ternario *a* ternal, ternary
terne *a inf* bullying, braggartly; persistent, obstinate; robust. *mf* bully
ternera *f,* female calf; veal
ternero *m,* male calf
terneza *f,* tenderness, kindness; softness; softheartedness; endearment, caress, compliment (gen. *pl*)
ternilla *f,* cartilage, gristle
ternísimo *a sup* **tierno** most tender
terno *m,* triad; suit of clothes, three-piece suit; oath, curse
ternura *f,* softness; softheartedness; tenderness, kindness, sweetness
terquedad, terquería, terqueza *f,* obstinacy, obduracy
terracota *f,* terra cotta
terrado *m,* flat roof
Terranova Newfoundland
terraplén *m,* embankment; *mil* terreplein
terraplenar *vt* to fill up with earth; fill in (a hollow); make into an embankment; terrace
terrateniente *mf* landowner
terraza *f,* terrace; flat roof; flower border (of a garden)
terrazgo *m,* tillable land; rent for farming land
terregoso *a* lumpy, full of clods (of soil)
terremoto *m,* earthquake
terrenal *a* terrestrial
terreno *a* terrestrial. *m,* ground, land; *fig* sphere; region; soil; plot of land. **ganar t.,** *fig* to win ground, make progress. **medir el t.,** *fig* to feel one's way
térreo *a* earthy
terrero *a* earthly; low-flying, almost touching the ground; humble. *m,* flat roof; pile or mound of earth; deposit of earth, alluvium; target; mineral refuse
terrestre *a* terrestrial, earthly
terrezuela *f,* poor soil
terribilidad *f,* terribleness, horribleness; rudeness
terribilísimo *a sup* most terrible
terrible *a* terrible, horrible; rude, unsociable, ill-humored; enormous, huge
terrífico *a* terrible, frightful
territorial *a* territorial
territorialidad *f,* territoriality
territorio *m,* territory; jurisdiction. **t. bajo mandato,** mandated territory
terrizo *a* earthen
terrón *m,* clod (of earth); lump; *pl* lands, landed property. **t. de azúcar,** lump of sugar
terrorismo *m,* terrorism
terrorista *mf* terrorist
terrosidad *f,* earthiness
terroso *a* earthy; earthen
terruño *m,* plot of ground; native earth; country; soil
terso *a* smooth, shiny, glossy; *lit* elegant, polished (style)
tersura *f,* smoothness, glossiness; elegance (of style)
tertulia *f,* regular social meeting (gen. in cafés); conversational group; party; part of Spanish cafés set apart for players of chess, etc. **hacer t.,** to meet for conversation
tertuliano (-na) *n* **tertuliante,** *mf* **tertulio (-ia),** *n* member of a tertulia
terzuelo *m,* third, third part
Tesalia Thessaly
tesar *vt naut* to make taut; *vi* step backward, back (oxen)
tesela *f,* tessera, square used in mosaic work
teselado *a* tessellated
tesina *f,* master's essay, thesis
tesis *f,* thesis
teso *a* tight, taut, tense. *m,* hilltop; bulge, lump
tesón *m,* persistence, obstinacy, tenacity
tesonería *f,* stubbornness, obstinacy
tesorería *f,* treasury; treasuryship
tesorero (-ra) *n* treasurer
tesoro *m,* treasure; public treasury; hoard; *fig* gem, excellent person; thesaurus. **t. de duende,** fairy gold
tespíades *f pl,* the muses
testa *f,* head; face, front; *inf* sense, acumen. **t. coronada,** crowned head
testación *f,* erasure, crossing out
testado *a* testate
testador (-ra) *n* testator
testaferro *m, fig* figurehead, proxy
testamentar *vt* to bequeath
testamentaria *f,* execution of a will; *law* estate; executors' meeting
testamentario *a* testamental, testamentary
testamento *m, law* will; testament. **Antiguo T.,** Old Testament. **ordenar** (*or* **otorgar**) **su t.,** to make one's will
testar *vi* to make a will; *vt* erase, cross out
testarada *f,* a blow with the head; pigheadedness, stubbornness
testarrón *a inf* pigheaded
testarudez *f,* obstinacy, obduracy
testarudo *a* stubborn, obstinate
testera *f,* front, face; front seat (in a vehicle); upper half of an animal's face; tester, canopy
testículo *m,* testicle
testificación *f,* testification
testificar *vt* to testify; affirm, assert; attest, prove
testigo *mf* witness. *m,* proof, evidence. *law* **t. de cargo,** witness for the prosecution. *law* **t. de descargo,** witness for the defense. **t. de vista,** eyewitness. *law* **hacer testigos,** to bring forward witnesses
testimonial *a* confirmatory, proven
testimoniar *vt* to attest, confirm, bear witness to
testimoniero (-ra) *a* slanderous; hypocritical. *n* slanderer, hypocrite
testimonio *m,* testimony, proof; slander; affidavit
testuz *m,* front of the head (of some animals); nape (of animals)
teta *f,* mammary gland, breast; teat, dug, udder. **dar la t.** (**a**), to suckle
tétano, tétanos *m,* tetanus
tetera *f,* teapot; teakettle; *Lat. Am.* (feeding) bottle
tetilla *f, dim* rudimentary teat or nipple; nipple (of a nursing bottle)
tétrico *a* gloomy; somber
teutón (-ona) *n* Teuton. *a* Teutonic
teutónico *a* Teutonic
textil *a* and *m,* textile
texto *m,* text; quotation, citation; textbook
textorio *a* textile
textual *a* textual
textualista *mf* textualist
textura *f,* texture; weaving; structure (of a novel, etc.); animal structure
tez *f,* complexion, skin
ti *pers pron 2nd sing mf dat acc abl* thee, you. Always used with prep. (e.g. **por ti,** by thee (you))
tía *f,* aunt; *inf* wife, mother, dame; *inf* coarse creature. **t. abuela,** grandaunt, great-aunt. *inf* **quedarse para t.,** to be left an old maid
tianguis *m, Central America, Mexico* open-air market
tiara *f,* ancient Persian headdress; papal tiara; coronet; dignity and power of the papacy
tiberino *a* Tiberine
tibetano (-na) *a* and *n* Tibetan. *m,* Tibetan (language)
tibia *f,* flute; tibia
tibieza *f,* tepidity; indifference, lack of enthusiasm
tibio *a* tepid, warm; indifferent, unenthusiastic

tiburón *m*, shark
ticket *m*, ticket; pass, membership card
tico, -a *mf inf* Costa Rican
tictac *m*, ticktock (of a clock)
tiempo *m*, time; season; epoch, period; chance, opportunity; leisure, free time; weather; *mus* tempo; *gram* tense; *naut* storm. **t. ha,** many years ago, long ago. **t. medio** *or* **medio t.,** *sport* halftime. **abrir el t.,** to clear up (of the weather). **ajustar los tiempos,** to fix the date (chronology). **a largo t.,** after a long time. **andando el t.,** in the course of time. **a su t.,** in due course, at the proper time. **a t.,** in time, at the right time. **a un t.,** simultaneously, at the same time. **cargarse el t.,** to cloud over (of the sky). **con t.,** in advance, with time; in time. **correr el t.,** to pass, move on (of time). **de t. en t.,** from time to time. **engañar** (*or* **entretener**) **el t.,** to kill time, while away the hours. *inf* **en t., de Maricastaña** *or* **del rey Perico,** long, long ago. **fuera de t.,** unseasonably, inopportunely; out of season. **ganar t.,** to gain time; *inf* hurry. **hacer t.,** to wait, cool one's heels; *fig* mark time. **perder el t.,** to waste time; misspend or lose time. **sentarse el t.,** to clear up (of the weather). **tomarse t.** (**para**), to postpone, take time for (or to)
tienda *f*, tent; *naut* awning, canopy; shop, store. **t. de abarrotes** *Lat. Am.* grocery store, grocery, grocer's **t. de antigüedades,** antique shop. **t. de campaña,** bell tent, pavilion. **t. oxígena,** oxygen tent
tienta *f*, astuteness; cleverness; *surg* probe; trying out young bulls for the bullring. **a tientas,** by touch, gropingly
tientaparedes *mf* one who gropes one's way
tiento *m*, touching, feeling; touch, feel; blind person's cane; tightrope walker's pole; manual control, steady hand; caution, care, tact; *mus* preliminary flourish; *inf* slap buffet; tentacle. **a t.,** by touch; unsurely, gropingly
tierno *a* soft; tender; kind; sweet; delicate; softhearted; fresh, recent; affectionate
tierra *f*, world, planet; earth; soil; ground; cultivated ground, land; homeland, native land; region; district, territory. **t. adentro,** inland. **t. de batán,** fuller's earth. **t. de Promisión,** Promised Land. **t. de Siena,** sienna. **besar la t.,** *inf* to fall down. **dar en t. con,** to throw down; demolish. **echar en t.,** *naut* to put ashore, land. **echar por t.,** *fig* to overthrow, destroy. **echar t. a,** *fig* to bury, forget. *inf* **la t. de María Santísima,** Andalusia. **por t.,** overland. **saltar en t.,** to land, disembark. **venir** (*or* **venirse**) **a t.,** to fall down, topple over
Tierra Santa Holy Land
tieso *a* hard, rigid, stiff; healthy, robust; taut; spirited, courageous; obstinate, stiff-necked; distant, formal. *adv* firmly, strongly
tiesto *m*, flowerpot; broken piece of earthenware
tiesura *f*, hardness, rigidity, stiffness; physical fitness; courageousness; obstinacy; formality, stiffness
tifoidea *f*, typhoid
tifón *m*, typhoon
tifus *m*, typhus. **t. exantemático,** trench fever
tigre *m*, tiger; ferocious person; *Lat. Am.* jaguar
tijera *f*, scissors (gen. *pl*); any scissor-shaped instrument; shears; drainage channel; carpenter's horse; scandalmonger, gossip
tijeretada *f*, cut or snip with scissors
tijeretear *vt* to cut with scissors; *inf* interfere arbitrarily
tijereteo *m*, scissor cut; click of the scissors
tila *f*, lime tree or flower; linden tree or flower; infusion made of lime flowers
tildar *vt* to cross out, erase; stigmatize; place a tilde over a letter
tilde *mf*, bad reputation; tilde; *f*, jot, iota
tilín *m*, tinkle, peal (of a bell)
tillar *vt* to lay wood floors
tilo *m*, lime tree
timador (-ra) *n inf* swindler, sharper, cheat
timar *vt* to swindle, cheat, deceive; *vr inf* exchange looks or winks
timba *f*, *inf* casino, gambling den; game of chance
timbal *m*, kettledrum
timbalero *m*, kettledrum player
timbrador *m*, stamper; stamping machine; rubber stamp
timbrar *vt* to stamp; place the crest over a coat of arms
timbre *m*, postage stamp; heraldic crest; excise stamp; bell, push-button; *mus* timbre; noble deed; personal merit; *Mexico* (postage) stamp; *Lat. Am.* description (of a person or goods)
timidez *f*, timidity, nervousness
tímido *a* timid, nervous
timo *m*, *inf* swindling, trick; thymus
timón *m*, *naut* helm; rudder; management, direction; stick of a rocket. **t. de dirección,** *aer* tailfin
timonear *vi naut* to steer
timonel, timonero *m*, helmsman, coxswain
timorato *a* godfearing; timid, vacillating
tímpano *m*, *anat* eardrum, tympanum; *mus* kettledrum; *arch* tympanum; *print* tympan
tina *f*, vat; flour bin; large earthenware jar; wooden tub; bath
tinaco *m*, *Mexico* (water) tank
tinada *f*, woodpile; cow shed
tinaja *f*, large earthenware jar; jarful
tinajero *m*, seller of earthenware jars
tinelo *m*, servants' hall
tinerfeño (-ña) *a* and *n* of or from Tenerife
tinglado *m*, overhanging roof; open shed; penthouse; intrigue
tiniebla *f*, gloom, darkness (gen. *pl*); *pl* profound ignorance; confusion of mind; *ecc* tenebrae
tino *m*, skilled sense of touch; good eye, accurate aim; judgment, shrewdness; vat. **sacar de t.** (**a**), to bewilder, confuse; irritate, exasperate. **sin t.,** without limit, excessively
tinta *f*, color, tint; ink; staining, dyeing; dye, stain; *pl* shades, colors; *art* mixed colors ready for painting. **t. china,** India ink. **t. simpática,** invisible ink. **recargar las tintas,** *fig* to overpaint, lay the colors on too thick. *inf* **saber de buena t.** (**una cosa**), to learn (a thing) from a reliable source
tintar *vt* to dye; color, tinge, stain
tinte *m*, dyeing, staining; color; dye; stain; dye house; pretext, disguise
tintero *m*, inkwell. *inf* **dejar** (*or* **quedársele a uno**) **en el t.,** to forget, omit (to say, write)
tintín *m*, ring, peal; clink; chink
tintinar *vi* to ring, tinkle; clink; jingle
tintineo *m*, ringing, tinkling; clinking; jingle
tinto *a* red (of wine). *m*, red wine; dark red
tintorera *f*, *Lat. Am.* shark
tintorería *f*, dyeing industry; dyeing and dry-cleaning shop
tintorero (-ra) *n* dyer; dry cleaner
tintura *f*, dyeing, staining; color, tint; dye; stain; tincture; smattering, slight knowledge
tinturar *vt* to dye; color, tinge, stain; give a superficial notion of
tiña *f*, ringworm; *inf* meanness, stinginess
tiñoso *a* mangy; afflicted with ringworm; *inf* mean, stingy
tiñuela *f*, shipworm
tío *m*, uncle; gaffer; fellow, chap; fool; stepfather; father-in-law. **t. abuelo,** granduncle, great-uncle
tiovivo *m*, merry-go-round
típico *a* typical
tiple *m*, soprano or treble voice. *mf* soprano
tipo *m*, model, pattern; type; print, type; species, group (of animals, etc.); *inf* guy, chap
tipografía *f*, typography
tipográfico *a* typographical
tipógrafo *m*, typographer
típula *f*, daddy-longlegs

tiquismiquis *m pl,* ridiculous scruples; affected courtesies. *a inf* faddy, fussy
tira *f,* strip, band, ribbon; stripe, rib. **t. cómica,** comic strip
tirabotas *m,* buttonhook
tirabuzón *m,* corkscrew; ringlet, curl; hair curler
tirada *f,* throwing; drawing, pulling; cast, throw; distance, space; *print* edition, issue; circulation (of a newspaper, etc.); stroke (in golf); lapse, interval (of time). **t. aparte,** reprint (of an article, etc.)
tiradero *m,* shooting butt
tirado *a inf* dirt-cheap. *m,* wire drawing
tirador (-ra) *n* thrower, caster; drawer, puller; marksman. *m,* handle, knob; *mech* trigger; bell rope, bell pull; *print* pressman. **t. de bota,** boot tag. **t. de gomas,** catapult. **t. de oro,** gold wire drawer
tiralíneas *m,* ruling pen
tiramiento *m,* pulling; stretching
tiramira *f,* long, narrow mountain range; long line of persons or things; distance
tiranía *f,* tyranny, despotism
tiranicida *mf* tyrannicide (person)
tiranicidio *m,* tyrannicide (act)
tiránico *a* tyrannical
tiranización *f,* tyranny, tyrannization
tiranizar *vt* to tyrannize over
tirano (-na) *a* tyrannous, tyrannical; *fig* overwhelming, dominating. *n* tyrant
tirante *a* taut; tense, strained. *m,* trace (of a harness); shoulderstrap; suspender (gen. *pl*); *arch* tie
tirantez *f,* tautness; tension, strain; straight distance between two points. **estado de t.,** *pol* strained relations
tiranuelo *m,* petty tyrant
tirar *vt* to throw, cast; fling, aim, toss; throw down, overthrow; pull; draw; discharge, shoot; stretch, pull out; rule, draw (lines); squander, waste; *print* print; *vi* attract; pull; (*with prep a*) turn to, turn in the direction of; incline, tend to; incline toward, have a tinge of (colors); try, aspire to; (*with de*) wield, unsheath, draw out (firearms, arms); *vr* cast oneself, precipitate oneself; throw oneself on. *inf* **ir tirando,** to carry on, get along somehow
tirilla *f, sew* shirt neckband
tiritaña *f,* thin silk material; *inf* mere nothing, trifle
tiritar *vi* to shiver with cold
tiritón *m,* shiver, shudder
Tiro Tyre
tiro *m,* throwing; throw, cast; toss, fling; try (in football); shooting; piece of artillery; report, shot (of a gun); discharge (firearms); shooting range or gallery; team (of horses); range (of firearms, etc.); hoisting cable; flight (of stairs); *min* shaft; *inf* trick; robbery, theft; innuendo, insinuation; grave harm or injury; *pl* sword belt. **t. de pichón,** pigeon shooting. **t. par,** four-in-hand. **a t.,** within firing range; within reach. **de tiros largos,** *inf* in full regalia
tirocinio *m,* apprenticeship
tiroideo *a* thyroid
tiroides *f,* thyroid gland
Tirol, el the Tyrol
tirón *m,* novice, beginner; pull, tug, heave. **de un t.,** with one tug; at one stroke, at one blow
tiroriro *m, inf* sound of a wind instrument; *pl inf* wind instruments
tirotearse *vr mil* to exchange fire; indulge in repartee
tiroteo *m,* shooting, exchange of shots; crackle (of rifle fire)
Tirreno, el Mar the Tyrrhenian Sea
tirria *f, inf* hostility, grudge, dislike
tirulato *a* dumbfounded, stupefied
tisana *f,* tisane
tísico (-ca) *a* tuberculous. *n* sufferer from tuberculosis, consumptive
tisis *f,* tuberculosis
tisú *m,* silver or gold tissue
titánico *a* titanesque; colossal, huge
títere *m,* puppet; *fig inf* dummy, grotesque; *inf* fool; obsession, fixed idea; *pl inf* circus; Punch and Judy show. *inf* **echar los títeres a rodar,** to upset the whole show; quarrel, fall out with. *inf* **no dejar t. con cabeza,** to destroy entirely, smash up completely; leave no one
titerero (-ra), titiritero (-ra), *n* **titerista** *mf* puppet showman; acrobat; juggler
tití *m,* marmoset
titilación *f,* quiver, tremor; twinkling, winking, gleam
titilador, titilante *a* quivering, trembling; twinkling
titilar *vi* to quiver, tremble; twinkle
titiritaina *f, inf* muffled strains of musical instruments; merrymaking, uproar
titiritar *vi* to tremble, shiver, shudder
titiritero (-ra) *n* puppet master; acrobat
titubear *vi* to totter, sway, rock; stutter, stammer; toddle; hesitate, vacillate
titubeo *m,* tottering, swaying; stuttering; hesitation
titulado *m,* titled person; one who holds an academic title
titular *a* titular. *vt* to entitle, call; *vi* obtain a title (of nobility); *vr* style oneself, call oneself
título *m,* title; heading; inscription; pretext, excuse; diploma, certificate; claim, right; noble title and its owner; section, clause; (univ.) degree; *com* stock certificate, bond; *com* title; caption; qualification, right, merit; basis of a claim or privilege; *pl com* securities, stocks. **t. de la columna,** *print* running title. **títulos de propiedad,** title deeds. **t. del reino,** title of nobility. **a t.,** under pretext
tiza *f,* chalk; whiting; calcined stag's antler
tiznar *vt* to make sooty; dirty, stain, begrime; *fig* sully, tarnish
tizne *m,* (sometimes *f*) soot; charcoal; stain (on one's honor, etc.); *agr* blight
tizón *m,* firebrand; *agr* blight; *fig* stain (on one's honor, etc.)
tizona *f, inf* sword (by allusion to name of that of the Cid)
tizonear *vi* to poke or rake the fire
toalla *f,* towel. **t. continua,** roller towel. **t. rusa,** Turkish towel
toallero *m,* towel rail
tobillera *f, inf* girl, flapper
tobillo *m,* ankle
tobogán *m,* toboggan; chute (in apartment buildings or amusement parks)
toca *f,* headdress; toque; wimple; coif
tocable *a* touchable
tocado *a fig* touched, half-crazy. *m,* headdress; coiffure, hairdressing
tocador (-ra) *n mus* player. *m,* dressing table; kerchief; boudoir; cloakroom; dressing room; dressing case
tocamiento *m,* touching, feeling; touch; *fig* inspiration
tocante *a* touching. **t. a,** concerning, with regard to
tocar *vt* to touch, feel; *mus* play; knock, rap; summon; ring, peal; brush against; discover by experience; persuade, inspire; mention, touch upon; *naut* touch bottom; *art* retouch, touch up. *vi* belong; stop (at), touch at; be one's turn; concern, interest; be one's lot; adjoin, be near to; be opportune; be allied or closely related to; find the scent (of dogs). **t. en un puerto,** *naut* to touch at a port. **Ahora me toca a mí,** Now it's my turn. **Es un problema que me toca de cerca,** It is a problem that touches me very nearly. **a toca teja,** *inf* in ready cash
tocayo (-ya) *n* namesake
tochedad *f,* boorishness, loutishness
tocho *a* boorish, loutish, countrified. *m,* iron bar
tocinería *f,* pork butcher's shop
tocinero *m,* pork butcher
tocino *m,* bacon; salt pork
tocología *f,* tokology, obstetrics
tocón *m,* stump (of a tree or an amputated limb)
todavía *adv* still; even; nevertheless; yet. **No han**

venido t., They have not come yet. **Queda mucho que hacer t.,** There is still much to be done.
todo *a* all; whole, entire; every, each. *m*, whole, entirety; whole word (in charades); all; *pl* all; everyone. *adv* wholly, entirely. **t. lo posible,** everything possible; all one can, one's best. **t. lo que,** all that which. **ante t.,** in the first place; especially, particularly. **así y t.,** nevertheless. **a t. esto,** in the meanwhile. **con t.** *or* **con t. esto** *or* **con t. y esto,** nevertheless, in spite of this. **del t.,** wholly, completely. **jugar el t. por el t.,** to risk everything on the outcome. **sobre t.,** especially. **y t.,** in addition, as well. **Todos somos hijos de Adán y Eva, sino que nos diferencia la lana y la seda,** We are all equal, but some of us are more equal than others
todopoderoso *a* all-powerful, almighty. *m*, the Almighty, God
toga *f*, toga; robe, gown
Tokio Tokyo
tolda *f* canvas; tent; shelter
toldadura *f*, awning; canopy; hanging, curtain
toldillo *m*, covered litter or sedan chair; *WH* mosquito net
toldo *m*, awning; canopy; pomp, show
tole *m*, outcry, uproar, tumult
toledano (-na) *a* and *n* Toledan
tolerable *a* bearable, tolerable
tolerancia *f*, tolerance, forbearance; permission
tolerante *a* tolerant, broad-minded
tolerantismo *m*, religious toleration
tolerar *vt* to put up with, bear, tolerate; overlook, allow, forgive
tolla *f*, marsh, bog
tollina *f*, *inf* spanking, whipping
tolmo *m*, tor
tolondro *a* stupid, heedless, reckless. *m*, bump, bruise
tolonés (-esa) *a* and *n* of or from Toulon
tolva *f*, chute (for grain, etc.)
toma *f*, taking; receiving; conquest, capture; dose (of medicine)
tomada *f*, taking; take; capture
tomadero *m*, handle, haft
tomadura *f*, taking; receiving; dose (of medicine). *inf* **t. de pelo,** leg-pull, joke
tomar *vt* to take; pick up; conquer; eat; drink; adopt, employ; contract (habits); engage (employees); rent; understand; steal; remove; buy; suffer; *fig* overcome (by laughter, sleep, etc.); choose; possess physically; *vi* (*with por*) go in the direction of; *vr* grow rusty; go moldy; (*with con*) quarrel with. **t. a chacota,** to take as a joke. **t. a pechos,** to take to heart. **t. el fresco,** to take the air. **tomarla con,** to contradict, oppose; bear a grudge. **t. la delantera,** to take the lead; excel, beat. **t. las de Villadiego,** *inf* to quit, show one's heels. **t. por su cuenta,** to undertake, take charge of; take upon oneself. **t. su desquite con,** to get even with. **Más vale un toma que dos te daré,** A little help is worth a lot of promises. **¡Toma!** *inf* Fancy! You don't say!; Of course! There's nothing new about that!
tomatal *m*, tomato bed, tomato patch; *Lat. Am.* tomato plant
tomate *m*, tomato; tomato plant; *Mexico* small green tomato; *inf* hole, potato (in stockings, etc.)
tomatera *f*, tomato plant
tomatero (-ra) *n* tomato seller
tómbola *f*, raffle (gen. for charity); jumble sale
tomillo *m*, thyme
tomo *m*, volume, book; importance, worth
ton *m*, *abb* **tono. sin t. ni son,** *inf* without rhyme or reason
tonada *f*, words of a song and its tune
tonadilla *f*, *dim* short song; comic song; *theat* musical interlude *ant*
tonadillero (-ra) *n* composer or singer of tonadillas
tonal *a* tonal
tonalidad *f*, tonality
tonar *vi poet* to thunder or lightning
tonel *m*, barrel; cask; butt
tonelada *f*, ton
tonelería *f*, cooperage; collection or stock of casks and barrels
tonelero *m*, cooper
tonga, tongada *f*, layer, stratum; *inf* task
tónica *f*, *mus* keynote
tónico *a* tonic. *m*, *med* tonic; pick-me-up
tonificador, tonificante *a* strengthening, invigorating tonic
tonillo *m*, *dim* monotonous singsong voice; regional accent
tonina *f*, tuna; dolphin
tono *m*, inflection, modulation; (*mus med art*) tone; pitch, resonance; energy, strength; style; manner, behavior; *mus* key; mode of speech. **bajar el t.,** *fig inf* to change one's tune. *inf* **darse t.,** to put on side, give oneself airs. **de buen (mal) t.,** in good (bad) taste
tonsila *f*, tonsil
tonsilitis *f*, tonsillitis
tonsura *f*, shearing; hair cutting; *ecc* tonsure
tonsurar *vt* to shear, clip; cut the hair off; *ecc* tonsure
tontaina *mf inf* ninny, fool
tontear *vi* to behave foolishly; play the fool
tontería *f*, foolishness, stupidity; piece of folly; trifle, bagatelle
tontiloco *a inf* crazy, daft
tontillo *m*, dress bustle; hoop (for dresses)
tontivano *a* vain, conceited
tonto (-ta) *a* silly, stupid, simple; foolish, absurd. *n* fool, idiot. *m*, short coat, stroller. **t. de capirote,** *inf* an utter fool. **a tontas y a locas,** without rhyme or reason, topsy-turvy. **volver t. (a),** *fig inf* to drive crazy
topacio *m*, topaz
topar *vt* (*with con*) to run into, collide with, hit; meet unexpectedly; come across, find; *vi* butt (of horned animals); take a bet (in cards); consist in (of obstacles); meet with (difficulties); *inf* be successful
tope *m*, projection, part that juts out; obstacle, impediment; collision, bump; crux, difficult point; quarrel, fight; *mech* stop; *naut* masthead; *rw* buffer; *Mexico* speed bump. **hasta el t.,** completely full, full to the brim
topera *f*, molehill
topetada *f*, butt (of horned animals); *inf* knock, bang
topetar *vt* and *vi* to butt (of horned animals); *vt* meet, run into
topetón *m*, butt; collision, impact, bump; blow on the head
tópico *a* topical. *m*, topic, theme
topo *m*, *zool* mole; *inf* clumsy or shortsighted person; dolt, ninny
topografía *f*, topography
topográfico *a* topographical
topógrafo *m*, topographer
toque *m*, touch, touching; pealing, ringing (of bells); crux, essence; test, proof; touchstone; *met* assay; warning; *inf* tap (on the shoulder, etc.); *art* touch. **t. de luz,** *art* light (in a picture). **t. de obscuro,** *art* shade (in a picture). **t. de queda,** curfew. **t. de tambor,** beating of a drum. **dar un t. a,** *inf* to put to the test; pump (for information)
toquero (-ra) *n* manufacturer of headdresses
toquetear *vt* to keep touching, handle repeatedly
toquilla *f*, hatband, hat trimming; kerchief; small shawl
torácico *a* thoracic
toral *a* principal, chief, main
tórax *m*, thorax
torbellino *m*, whirlwind; spate of things; *inf* madcap
torcedero *a* twisted, crooked
torcedor *a* twisting. *m*, twister; cause of continual anxiety
torcedura *f*, twisting; sprain, wrench
torcer *vt irr* to twist; bend; turn, bear (of roads, etc.); slant, slope, incline; misconstrue, pervert; dissuade; wrench, sprain (muscles); corrupt (justice). **t. el gesto,** to make a wry face. *vr* turn sour (of wine, milk); *fig* go

astray; turn out badly (of negotiations). *Pres. Ind.* **tuerzo, tuerces,** etc. *Pres. Subjunc.* **tuerza, tuerzas, tuerza, tuerzan**
torcida *f,* wick (of lamps, etc.)
torcido *a* bent, crooked, sloping, inclined; curved; dishonest, tortuous. *m,* silk twist
torcijón *m,* stomachache
torcimiento *m,* twisting; twist, turn; circumlocution; digression
tordo *a* piebald, black-and-white. *m, orn* thrush. **t. de campanario** *or* **t. de Castilla,** starling
toreador *m,* bullfighter
torear *vi* and *vt* to fight bulls; *vt* ridicule; exasperate, provoke; *inf* string along, deceive
toreo *m,* bullfighting
torera *f,* bullfighter's jacket
torero *a inf* bullfighting. *m,* bullfighter
torete *m, dim* small bull; *inf* problem, difficult question; engrossing topic of conversation
toril *m,* pen for fighting bulls
torio *m,* thorium
tormenta *f,* storm; misfortune, calamity; indignation, agitation
tormento *m,* torment; torture; pain; anxiety, anguish. **dar t.** (**a**)**,** to torture; inflict pain (on)
tormentoso *a* stormy, tempestuous; *naut* pitching, rolling
torna *f,* return; restitution; backwater
tornaboda *f,* day after a wedding; rejoicings of this day
tornada *f,* return home; return visit, revisit; *poet* envoy
tornadizo (-za) *a inf* changeable. *n* turncoat
tornamiento *m,* return; change, transformation
tornar *vt* to return, give back; change, transform; *vi* return, go back; continue
tornasol *m,* sunflower; sheen, changing light; *chem* litmus
tornasolado *a* shot (of silk, etc.)
tornasolar *vt* to look iridescent; change the color of, cause to appear variegated
tornátil *a* turned (in a lathe); inconstant, changeable; *poet* spinning, revolving
tornatrás *mf* half-caste
tornaviaje *m,* return journey
tornavoz *m,* soundboard, sounding board
torneador *m,* turner; jouster, fighter in a tournament
tornear *vt sport* to put a spin on (balls); turn in a lathe; *vi* turn around, spin; fight in a tournament; turn over in the mind
torneo *m,* tournament
tornería *f,* turnery
tornero *m,* turner; lathe maker; convent messenger
tornillero *m,* (*inf mil*) deserter
tornillo *m,* screw; (*inf mil*) desertion
torniquete *m,* turnstile; tourniquet. **dar t.** (**a**)**,** to pervert, misinterpret (meanings)
torniscón *m, inf* slap, buffet, blow; pinch
torno *m,* lathe; turntable (of a convent, etc.); turn, rotation; windlass; dumbwaiter; axletree; spinning wheel; bend, loop (in a river). **en t.,** round about, around; in exchange
toro *m,* bull; Taurus; *pl* bullfight. *inf* **t. corrido,** tough nut to crack, wise guy. *inf* **Ciertos son los toros,** So it's true (gen. of bad news)
toronja *f,* grapefruit
toroso *a* strong, vigorous, robust
torpe *a* heavy, slow, encumbered; torpid; clumsy, unskilled; stupid, dull-witted; obscene, indecent; base, infamous; ugly
torpedeamiento *m,* torpedoing, sinking
torpedear *vt* to torpedo
torpedeo *m,* torpedoing
torpedero *m,* torpedo boat
torpedo *m, icht* torpedo fish, electric ray; torpedo; sports car. **t. automóvil,** self-propelling torpedo
torpeza *f,* slowness, heaviness; torpidity; stupidity; lack of skill, clumsiness; indecency; ugliness; baseness, infamy
tórpido *a* torpid
torrar *vt* to toast, brown
torre *f,* tower; belfry, steeple; turret; rook (in chess); *naut* gun turret; stack, pile (of chairs, etc.); country house with a garden. **t. del tráfico,** traffic light. **t. de viento,** castle in the air, castle in Spain
torrefacción *f,* toasting (of coffee, etc.)
torrencial *a* torrential, rushing
torrente *m,* torrent; *fig* spate, rush; crowd
torrentoso, -a *a, Lat. Am.* = **torrencial**
torreón *m,* large fortified tower
torrero *m,* lighthouse keeper; gardener
torreznero (-ra) *n inf* lazybones, idler
torrezno *m,* rasher of bacon
tórrido *a* torrid
torsión *f,* twisting, torsion
torta *f,* cake; pastry, tart; *inf* slap. **t. de reyes,** traditional Twelfth Night cake
tortada *f,* meat pie, game pie
tortedad *f,* twistedness, crookedness
tortera *f,* cake pan; baking dish; whorl (of a spindle)
tortícolis *m,* crick (in the neck)
tortilla *f,* omelet; *Central America, Mexico* tortilla (corn pancake) **t. a la española,** potato omelet. **hacer t.,** to smash to atoms. **Se volvió la t.,** *inf* The tables are turned
tortillero, -a *mf Central America, Mexico* tortilla vendor
tórtola *f,* turtledove
tórtolo *m,* male turtledove; *inf* devoted lover
tortuga *f,* turtle; tortoise. **a paso de t.,** at a snail's pace
tortuosidad *f,* tortuousness; winding; indirectness; deceitfulness
tortuoso *a* tortuous; winding; disingenuous, deceitful
tortura *f,* twistedness; torture, torment; anguish, grief. **una t. china,** excruciating torture
torturador *a* torturing, tormenting
torturar *vt* to torture
torva *f,* squall of rain or snow
torzal *m,* sewing silk; twist, plait
tos *f,* cough. **t. ferina,** whooping cough
tosco *a* rough, unpolished; coarse; boorish, uncouth
toser *vi* to cough
tósigo *m,* poison, venom; anguish; affliction
tosigoso *a* poisoned, venomous
tosquedad *f,* roughness, lack of polish; coarseness; boorishness, uncouthness
tostada *f, cul* toast
tostadera *f,* toasting fork
tostado *a* golden brown, tanned. *m,* roasting (of coffee, etc.)
tostador (-ra) *n* toaster (of peanuts, etc.). *m,* toaster (utensil); coffee or peanut roaster
tostadura *f,* toasting; roasting (of coffee, etc.)
tostón *m,* buttered toast; anything overtoasted; roast pig; *inf* nuisance, bore
total *a* total, entire, whole; general. *m,* total. *adv* in short; so, therefore
totalidad *f,* whole; aggregate, entirety
totalitario *a* totalitarian
tótem *m,* totem
toxicidad *f,* toxicity
tóxico *a* toxic. *m,* toxic substance
toxicología *f,* toxicology
toxicológico *a* toxicological
tozo *a* dwarfish, small
tozudez *f,* obstinacy
tozudo *a* obstinate, obdurate
tozuelo *m,* scruff, fat nape (of animals)
traba *f,* setting (of a saw's teeth); tether (for horses); difficulty, obstacle; fastening; bond, tie; shackle; *law* distraint
trabacuenta *f,* mistake in accounts; argument, difference of opinion

trabajado *a* and *past part* wrought; fashioned; labored, exhausted, weary
trabajador (-ra) *a* working; conscientious. *n* worker
trabajar *vi* to work; function; stand the strain, resist (of machines, etc.); exert oneself, strive; toil, labor; operate, work; produce, yield (the earth fruits, etc.); *vt* work; till, cultivate; exercise (a horse); worry, annoy, weary; operate, drive; *vr* make every effort, work hard
trabajo *m*, work; toil, labor; operation, working; difficulty, obstacle; literary work; hardship, trouble; process; *pl* poverty; hardship. **t. a destajo,** piecework. **t. al ralenti,** go-slow tactics. **trabajos forzados** (*or* **forzosos**), *law* hard labor. **pasar trabajos,** to undergo hardships
trabajosamente *adv* painstakingly
trabajoso *a* difficult, hard; ailing, delicate; needy; afflicted
trabalenguas *m, inf* tongue twister, jawbreaker
trabamiento *m*, joining, fastening; uniting; initiation, commencement; shackling; hobbling (of horses)
trabar *vt* to join, unite, fasten; grasp, seize; set the teeth (of a saw); thicken; begin, initiate; hobble (of horses); reconcile, bring together, harmonize; shackle; *law* distrain; *vr* speak with an impediment; stutter, hesitate. **t. amistad,** to make friends. **t. conversación,** to get into conversation. **Se me trabó la lengua,** I began to stutter
trabazón *f*, join, union, fastening; connection; thickness, consistency
trabilla *f*, vest strap; dropped stitch (in knitting)
trabuca *f*, squib, Chinese firecracker, riprap
trabucar *vt* to turn upside down, upset; confuse, bewilder; mix up, confuse (news, etc.); pronounce or write incorrectly
trabucazo *m*, shot or report of a blunderbuss; *inf* calamity, unexpected misfortune
trabuco *m*, *mil* catapult; blunderbuss
trabuquete *m*, catapult
tracalada *f*, *Lat. Am.* crowd (of people); lot (large amount)
tracamundana *f*, *inf* barter, exchange of trash; hubbub, uproar
tracción *f*, pulling; traction
tracoma *f*, trachoma
tracto *m*, tract, area, expanse; lapse of time
tractor *m*, tractor. **t. de orugas,** caterpillar tractor
tractorista *mf* driver of a tractor, tractor driver
tradición *f*, tradition
tradicional *a* traditional
tradicionalismo *m*, traditionalism
tradicionalista *a* traditionalistic. *mf* traditionalist
traducción *f*, translation; interpretation, explanation
traducible *a* translatable
traducir *vt irr* to translate; interpret, explain; express. See **conducir**
traductor (-ra) *n* translator; interpreter
traedizo *a* portable, movable
traer *vt irr* to bring; attract; cause, occasion; wear, have on; quote, cite (as proof); compel, force; persuade; conduct, lead (persons); be engaged in; *vr* dress (well *or* badly). **t. consigo,** to bring with it; have or carry or bring with one. **t. entre manos,** to have on hand. *Pres. Ind.* **traigo, traes,** etc. *Pres. Part.* **trayendo.** *Preterite* **traje, trajiste,** etc. *Pres. Subjunc.* **traiga,** etc. *Imperf. Subjunc.* **trajese,** etc.
trafagador *m*, dealer, trafficker, merchant
tráfago *m*, traffic, trade; toil, drudgery
trafalmejas *a inf* rowdy, crazy, *mf inf* rowdy
traficante *mf* dealer, merchant, trader
traficar *vi* to trade; travel
tráfico *m*, traffic; trade, commerce
tragaderas *f pl*, throat, gullet. *inf* **tener buenas t.,** to be very credulous; be tolerant (of evil)
tragadero *m*, throat, gullet; sink, drain; hole, plug
tragador (-ra) *n* glutton, guzzler
tragahombres *mf inf* braggart, bully
trágala *m*, (**trágala tú, servilón**), title of Spanish Liberal song aimed at Absolutists; *inf* take that!
tragaleguas *mf inf* fast walker
tragaluz *m*, skylight; fan light
tragantón (-ona) *a inf* guzzling, greedy. *n* glutton
tragantona *f*, *inf* spread, large meal; swallowing with difficulty; *fig inf* hard pill to swallow
tragaperras *m*, *inf* vending machine, catchpenny
tragar *vt* to swallow; eat ravenously, devour; engulf, swallow up; believe, take in; tolerate, put up with; dissemble; consume, absorb
tragedia *f*, tragedy
trágico (-ca) *a* tragic. *n* tragedian; writer of tragedies
tragicomedia *f*, tragicomedy
tragicómico *a* tragicomic
trago *m*, swallow, gulp, draft; *fig inf* bitter pill. **a tragos,** *inf* little by little, slowly
tragón (-ona) *a inf* greedy, gluttonous. *n* glutton
tragonear *vt inf* to devour, eat avidly
traición *f*, treason, treachery. **a t.,** treacherously
traicionar *vt* to betray
traicionero (-ra) *a* treacherous. *n* traitor
traída *f*, conduction. **t. de aguas,** water supply
traidor (-ra) *a* treacherous. *n* traitor
traílla *f*, lead, leash (for animals)
traje *m*, dress, apparel; outfit, costume; suit. **t. de americana,** lounge suit. **t. de ceremonia** *or* **t. de etiqueta,** full-dress uniform; evening dress (men). **t. de luces,** bullfighter's gala outfit. **t. de montar,** riding habit. **t. de noche,** evening dress (women). **t. paisano,** civilian dress; lounge suit
trajín *m*, carriage, transport; busyness, moving around; bustle; clatter
trajinar *vt* to carry, transport; *Argentina* cheat, swindle; *vi* be busy, go about one's business
tralla *f*, rope, cord; lash (of a whip); whip
trama *f*, woof, texture (of cloth); twisted silk; intrigue, scheme; *lit* plot; olive flower
tramar *vt* to weave; prepare, hatch (plots); *fig* prepare the way for; *vi* flower (of trees, especially olive)
tramitación *f*, transaction, conduct; procedure, method
tramitar *vt* to transact, conduct, settle
trámite *m*, transit; negotiation, phase of a business deal; requirement, condition
tramo *m*, plot of ground; flight of stairs, staircase; stretch, expanse, reach, tract
tramontana *f*, north wind; arrogance, haughtiness
tramontano *a* ultramontane, from beyond the mountains
tramontar *vi* to cross the mountains; sink behind the mountains (of the sun); *vr* run away, escape
tramoya *f*, *theat* stage machinery; trick, deception, hoax
tramoyista *mf* stage carpenter; stagehand; sceneshifter; trickster, impostor, swindler
trampa *f*, trap, snare; trapdoor; flap of a shop counter; trouser fly; trick, swindle; overdue debt. *fig inf* **caer en la t.,** to fall into the trap. *inf* **coger en la t.,** to catch in a trap; catch in the act
trampal *m*, bog, marsh
trampantojo *m*, *inf* optical illusion, swindle
trampeador *a inf* swindling. *n* trickster, swindler
trampear *vi inf* to obtain money on false pretenses; struggle on (against illness, etc.); keep oneself alive, make shift; *vt* defraud, swindle
trampolín *m*, springboard; diving board; *fig* jumping-off place
tramposo (-sa) *n* debtor; cardsharper; swindler
tranca *f*, thick stick, cudgel; bar (of a window, etc.)
trancada *f*, stride
trancar *vt* to bar the door; *vi inf* oppose, resist; *vr, Lat. Am.* be constipated
trancazo *m*, blow with a stick; influenza, flu
trance *m*, crisis, difficult juncture; danger, peril. **t. de**

armas, armed combat. **a todo t.,** at all costs, without hesitation
tranco *m,* stride; threshold. *inf* **en dos trancos,** in a trice
tranquera *f,* stockade, palisade
tranquilar *vt com* to check off
tranquilidad *f,* tranquility, peace, quietness; composure, serenity
tranquilizador *a* tranquilizing, soothing
tranquilizar *vt* to calm, quiet; soothe
tranquilo *a* tranquil, quiet, peaceful; serene, composed
tranquiza *f, Mexico* beating, thrashing
transacción *f,* compromise, arrangement; transaction, negotiation, deal
transalpino *a* transalpine
transandino *a* transandean
transatlántico *a* transatlantic. *m,* (transatlantic) liner
transbordar *vt* to transship; transfer, remove goods from one vehicle to another
transbordo *m,* transshipment, transshipping; transfer, removal
transcendencia *f* See **trascendencia**
transcendental *a.* See **trascendental**
transcribir *vt* to transcribe; copy. *Past Part.* **transcrito**
transcripción *f,* transcription; copy, transcript
transcurrir *vi* to elapse, pass (time)
transcurso *m,* passage, lapse, course (of time)
transepto *m,* transept
transeúnte *a* transient, temporary. *mf* passerby; visitor, sojourner
transferencia *f,* transfer (from one place to another); *law* conveyance, transference. **t. bancaria,** bank draft
transferidor (-ra) *a* transferring. *n* transferrer; *law* transferor
transferir *vt irr* to transfer, move from one place to another; *law* convey (property, etc.); postpone. See **sentir**
transfiguración *f,* transfiguration
transfigurar *vt* to transfigure
transfijo *a* transfixed
transfixión *f,* transfixion
transformable *a* transformable
transformación *f,* transformation
transformador *a* transformative. *m, elec* transformer
transformar *vt* to transform; reform (persons); *vr* be transformed; reform, mend one's ways
transfregar *vt irr* to rub, scrub. See **cegar**
transfretar *vt naut* to cross the sea; *vi* spread
tránsfuga *mf* **tránsfugo** *m,* fugitive; political turncoat
transfundir *vt* to transfuse, pour from one vessel to another; imbue, transmit
transfusor *a* transfusive
transgredir *vt* to transgress, infringe
transgresión *f,* infringement, violation, transgression
transgresor (-ra) *a* infringing. *n* transgressor, violator
transición *f,* transition, change
transido *a* exhausted, worn-out, spent; niggardly, mean
transigencia *f,* tolerance, forbearance, indulgence
transigente *a* tolerant, forbearing
transigir *vi* to be tolerant; be broad-minded. *vt* put up with, tolerate
transitable *a* passable, traversable
transitar *vi* to cross, pass through; travel
transitivo *a* transitive
tránsito *m,* passage, crossing; transit; stopping place; transition, change; gallery of a cloister; *ecc* holy death. **de t.,** temporarily; in transit (of goods). **hacer tránsitos,** to break one's journey, stop
transitorio *a* transitory, fugitive, fleeting
translimitación *f,* trespass; bad behavior; armed intervention in a neighboring state
translimitar *vt* to overstep the boundaries (of a state, etc.); overstep the limits (of decency, etc.)
translucidez *f,* translucence, semitransparency
translúcido *a* translucent, semitransparent
transmarino *a* transmarine
transmigración *f,* transmigration
transmigrar *vi* to migrate; transmigrate (of the soul)
transmisión *f,* transmission. **t. del pensamiento,** thought transference
transmisor *a* transmitting. *m, elec* transmitter, sender
transmitir *vt* to transmit; *mech* drive
transmutable *a* transmutable
transmutación *f,* transmutation, transformation, change
transmutar *vt* to transmute, transform, change
transoceánico *a* transoceanic
transpacífico *a* transpacific
transparencia *f,* transparency; obviousness
transparentarse *vr* to be transparent; show through; *fig* reveal, give away (secrets)
transparente *a* transparent; translucent; evident, obvious. *m,* windowshade, blind
transpiración *f,* transpiration; perspiration
transpirar *vi* to perspire; transpire
transponer *vt irr* to move, transfer; transplant; transpose; *vr* hide behind; sink behind the horizon (of the sun, stars); be half-asleep. See **poner**
transportable *a* transportable
transportación *f.* See **transporte**
transportador (-ra) *a* transport. *n* transporter. *m, geom* protractor
transportamiento *m.* See **transporte**
transportar *vt* to transport; *mus* transpose; carry; *vr fig* be carried away by (anger, rapture)
transporte *m,* transport, carriage; cartage; *naut* transport; strong emotion, transport, ecstasy
transposición *f,* transposition
transpositivo *a* transpositive
transubstanciación *f,* transubstantiation
transubstanciar *vt* to transubstantiate, transmute
transversal, transverso *a* transverse
tranvía *m,* street railway; streetcar. **t. de sangre,** horse-drawn streetcar.
tranviario *a* streetcar. *m,* streetcar employee
trapacear *vi* to cheat, swindle
trapacete *m, com* daybook
trapacista *mf* trickster, swindler, knave
trapajoso *a* ragged, shabby, tattered
trápala *f,* noise, confusion, hubbub; noise of horse's hoofs, gallop; *inf* trick, swindle; prattling, babbling. *mf inf* babbler, prattler; trickster
trapalear *vi* to walk noisily, tramp; *inf* chatter, babble
trapatiesta *f, inf* brawl, row, quarrel
trapaza *f,* hoax, swindle
trapeador *m, Lat. Am.* (floor) mop
trapear *vt, Lat. Am.* to mop (the floor)
trapecio *m,* trapeze; *geom* trapezium, trapezoid
trapería *f,* old-clothes shop; old clothes, rags, trash, frippery
trapero (-ra) *n* old-clothes seller; rag merchant; rag-picker
trapezoide *m,* trapezium, trapezoid
trapichear *vi inf* to make shift, endeavor
trapiento *a* ragged, shabby
trapillo *m, inf* poverty-stricken lover; nest egg, savings. *inf* **de t.,** in a state of undress, in néglié
trapío *m, inf* spirit of a fighting bull; verve, dash, independent air (of women)
trapisonda *f, inf* uproar, brawl; hubbub, bustle; snare, fix
trapisondear *vi inf* to be given to brawling; scheme, intrigue
trapisondista *mf* brawler; schemer, trickster
trapo *m,* rag; *naut* canvas; bullfighter's cape; *pl* garments, bits and pieces. *inf* **poner como un t. (a),** to dress down, scold. *inf* **soltar el t.,** to burst out crying or laughing
trapujo *m, inf* trick; subterfuge

traque *m*, report, bang (of a rocket, etc.); fuse (of a firework)
tráquea *f*, trachea
traqueotomía *f*, tracheotomy
traquetear *vi* to crack, bang, go off with a report; rattle; jolt (of trains, etc.). *vt* shake, stir; *inf* paw, handle too much
traqueteo *m*, banging (of fireworks); creaking; rattling; jolting (of trains, etc.)
traquido *m*, report (of a gun); crack (of a whip); creak
tras *prep* after; behind; following, in pursuit of; trans- (in compounds). *m, inf* buttock; sound of a blow, bang, bump. **t. t.,** knocking (at a door); banging
trasalcoba *f*, dressing room
trasbarrás *m*, bang, bump, noise
trasbocar *vt, Lat. Am.* to vomit
trascendencia *f*, transcendence, excellence; consequence, result
trascendental *a* transcendental; important, far-reaching
trascender *vi irr* to spread to, influence; become known, leak out; exhale a scent; *vt* investigate, discover. See **entender**
trascocina *f*, back kitchen
trascolar *vt irr* to filter, strain; cross over, traverse. See **colar**
trascordarse *vr irr* to mix up, make a muddle of, forget. See **acordar**
trasechar *vt* to ambush, waylay
trasegar *vt irr* to upset, turn upside down; transfer, move from one place to another; empty, pour out, upset (liquids). See **cegar**
traseñalar *vt* to re-mark, mark again
trasera *f*, rear, back, rear portion
trasero *a* rear, back. *m*, hindquarters, rump; buttocks, seat; *pl inf* ancestors
trasgo *m*, imp, sprite, puck
trashumante *a* nomadic (of flocks)
trashumar *vi* to go from winter to summer pasture (or vice versa) (of flocks)
trasiego *m*, emptying, pouring out, upsetting (of liquids); decanting (of wines)
traslación *f*, removal, transfer; alteration (of the date for a meeting); metaphor
trasladable *a* removable, movable, transferable
trasladar *vt* to remove, transfer; move from one place to another; alter (the date of a meeting); translate; copy, transcribe; *vr* remove (from a place)
traslado *m*, removal; transfer; transcription
traslapar *vt* to cover, overlap
traslapo *m*, overlap, overlapping
traslucirse *vr irr* to be transparent or translucent; shine through; come out (of secrets); infer, gather. See **lucir**
traslumbramiento *m*, dazzle, glare, brilliance
traslumbrar *vt* to dazzle; *vr* flicker, glimmer; fade quickly, disappear
trasluz *m*, reflected light. **al t.,** against the light
trasminar *vt* to undermine, excavate; *vi* percolate, ooze; penetrate, spread
trasnochada *f*, previous night, last night; night's vigil; sleepless night; *mil* night attack
trasnochado *a* stale, old; weary; hackneyed; drawn, pinched
trasnochador (-ra) *n* one who watches by night or stays up all night; *inf* night owl, reveler
trasnochar *vi* to stay up all night; watch through the night; spend the night; *vt* sleep on, leave for the following day
trasnoche, trasnocho *m, inf* night out; night vigil
trasoir *vt irr* to hear incorrectly, misunderstand. See **oir**
trasojado *a* haggard, tired-eyed
trasoñar *vt irr* to imagine, mistake a dream for reality. See **contar**
traspalar *vt* to fork (grain); shovel; transfer, move
trasparencia *f*. See **transparencia**
traspasar *vt* to transfer, move; cross; *law* convey, make over to; pierce; transgress, flout; exceed one's authority; *fig* go too far; reexamine, go over again; give intolerable pain (of illness, grief). **se traspasa,** to be disposed of (houses, etc.)
traspaso *m*, transport, transfer; *law* conveyance; property transferred; price agreed upon
traspatio *m, Lat. Am.* backyard
traspié *m*, slip, catching of the foot, stumble; heel of the foot. **dar traspiés,** *inf* to blunder
trasplantación *f*, **trasplante** *m*, transplantation; emigration
trasplantar *vt agr* to transplant; *vr* emigrate
trasplante *m*, planting out
traspuesta *f*, transposition; back quarters; rear (of a house); back yard
traspunte *m*, *theat* prompter
traspuntín *m*, *aut* folding seat
trasquilar *vt* to cut the hair unevenly; shear (sheep); *inf* cut down, diminish
trasquilón *m*, cropping (of hair); shearing; *inf* money stolen by pilfering
trastada *f*, *inf* dirty trick, mean act
traste *m*, fret (of stringed instruments); tasting cup. **dar al t. con,** to spoil, upset, damage. *inf* **sin trastes,** topsy-turvy, without method
trastear *vt* to play well (on the mandolin, etc.); *inf* manage tactfully; *vi* move around, change (furniture, etc.); discuss excitedly
trastejar *vt* to repair the roof; renew slates; overhaul
trastienda *f*, back of a shop; room behind a shop; *inf* wariness, caution
trasto *m*, piece of furniture; (household) utensil; lumber, useless furniture; *theat* wing or set piece; *inf* useless person, ne'er-do-well; oddment, thing; *pl* implements, equipment
trastornable *a* easily overturned or upset; easily agitated
trastornar *vt* to turn upside down; perturb, disturb; *fig* overpower (of scents, etc.); disorder, upset; dissuade; make mad; derange the mind
trastorno *m*, upset; perturbation, anxiety; disorder; mental derangement; confusion (of the senses)
trastrabillar *vi* to stumble, slip; totter, sway; hesitate; stutter, be tongue-tied
trastrás *m*, *inf* last but one (in games)
trastrocamiento *m*, alteration, change; disarrangement
trastrocar *vt irr* to alter, change, disarrange; change the order of. See **contar**
trasudar *vt* to perspire
trasudor *m*, light perspiration
trasuntar *vt* to copy, transcribe; summarize
trasunto *m*, copy, transcript; imitation
trasver *vt irr* to see through or between, glimpse; see incorrectly. See **ver**
trasverter *vi irr* to overflow. See **entender**
trata *f*, slave trade. **t. de blancas,** white slave traffic
tratable *a* easily accessible, sociable, unpretentious
tratadista *mf* writer of a treatise; expert, writer on special subjects
tratado *m*, pact, agreement; treaty; treatise
tratador (-ra) *n* arbitrator
tratamiento *m*, treatment; courtesy title; address, style; *med* treatment; process
tratante *m*, merchant, dealer
tratar *vt* to handle, use; conduct, manage; have dealings with, meet, know (e.g. **Yo no le trato,** I don't know him); behave well or badly toward; care for, treat; discuss, deal with (e.g. **¿De qué trata el libro?** What is the book about?); propose, suggest; *chem* treat; (*with de*) address as, call; *vi* have amorous relations; (*with de*) try to, endeavor to; (*with en*) trade in; *vr* look after oneself, treat oneself; conduct oneself
trato *m*, use, handling; management; conduct, behavior; manner, demeanor; appellation, title; commerce,

traffic; dealings, intercourse; treatment; agreement, arrangement. **t. colectivo,** collective bargaining
traumático *a* traumatic
traumatismo *m,* traumatism
través *m,* slant, slope; mishap; (*mil arch*) traverse. **a t.** *or* **al t.,** across; through. **de t.,** athwart; through
travesaño *m,* crossbar; bolster; rung (of a ladder); *carp* traverse
travesear *vi* to run about, romp, be mischievous; lead a vicious life; speak wittily; move ceaselessly (of water, etc.)
travesía *f,* crossing; traverse; crossroad; side road or street; distance, space; sea crossing; crosswise position; stretch of road within a town
travestido *a* disguised, dressed up
travesura *f,* romping, frolic; mischief; prank; quick-wittedness
traviesa *f,* sleeping car, sleeper (railroad); *arch* rafter; distance between two points
travieso *a* transverse, crosswise; mischievous, willful; debauched; clever, subtle; ever-moving (of streams, etc.)
trayecto *m,* run, distance, journey; stretch, expanse, tract; fare stage
trayectoria *f,* trajectory; journey
traza *f,* plan, design, draft; scheme, project; idea, proposal; aspect, appearance; means, manner. **Hombre pobre todo es trazas,** A poor man is full of schemes (for bettering himself)
trazado *m,* designing, drawing; design, draft, model, plan; course, direction (of a canal, etc.)
trazador (-ra) *n* draftsman, designer; planner, schemer
trazar *vt* to plan, draft, design; make a drawing of; trace; describe; map out, arrange
trazo *m,* line, stroke; outline, contour, form, line; *art* fold in drapery; stroke of the pen
trebejar *vi* to frolic, skip, play
trebejo *m,* chessman, chess piece; utensil, article (gen. *pl*); plaything
trébol *m,* clover
trece *a* and *m,* thirteen, thirteenth. *m,* thirteenth (day of the month)
trecemesino *a* thirteen months old
trecho *m,* distance, space; interval (of time). **a trechos,** at intervals. **de t. en t.,** from time to time
trefe *a* pliable, flexible; light; spurious (of coins)
tregua *f,* truce, respite, rest. **dar treguas,** to afford relief, give a respite; give time
treinta *a* and *m,* thirty; thirtieth. *m,* thirtieth (day of the month)
treintavo *a* thirtieth
treintena *f,* thirtieth (part)
tremebundo *a* fearsome, dread
tremedal *m,* bog; quagmire
tremendo *a* fearful, formidable; awesome; *inf* tremendous, enormous
trementina *f,* turpentine
tremolar *vt* and *vi* to wave, fly (of banners); *fig* make a show of
tremolina *f,* noise of the wind; *inf* hubbub, confusion
trémulo *a* trembling, tremulous
tren *m,* supply, provision; outfit; equipment; pomp, show; railroad train; following, train; *Mexico also* streetcar, trolley car, trolley **t. ascendente,** up train (from coast to interior). *inf* **t. botijo,** excursion train. **t. con coches corridos,** corridor train. **t. correo,** mail train. **t. descendente,** down train (from interior to coast). **t. mixto,** train carrying passengers and freight. **t. ómnibus,** accommodation train, slow, stopping train. **t. rápido,** express
trencilla *f,* braid, trimming
trencillar *vt* to trim with braid, braid
trenza *f,* plait, braid; plait of hair; bread twist; *Lat. Am.* string (of onions). **en t.,** in plaits, plaited (of hair)
trenzadera *f,* linen tape
trenzar *vt* to plait, braid; *vi* curvet, prance *Lat. Am.* **trenzarse (en . . .)** get involved (in . . .), e.g. **trenzarse en una disputa** get involved in a dispute
trepa *f,* perforation, boring, piercing; climbing; creeping; *inf* half-somersault; grain, surface (of wood); craftiness, slyness; deception, fraud; beating, drubbing
trepador *a* climbing; crawling; *bot* creeping, climbing. *m,* climbing place
trepanación *f,* trepanning
trepanar *vt* to trepan
trepante *a* creeping; *bot* twining, climbing
trepar *vi* to climb, ascend; *bot* climb or creep; bore, perforate
trepatrepa *m,* jungle gym, monkey bars
trepidación *f,* trepidation, dread; vibration; jarring; shaking
trepidar *vi* to shiver, shudder; vibrate; shake; jar; *Lat. Am.* hesitate
trépido *a* shuddering, shivering; vibrating
tres *a* three; third. *m,* figure three; third (day of the month); three (of playing cards); trio. *inf* **como t. y dos son cinco,** as sure as two and two make four
trescientos *a* and *m,* three hundred; three-hundredth
tresillo *m,* omber (card game); *mus* triplet
tresnal *m,* *agr* stook, cock, sheaf
treta *f,* scheme; trick, hoax; feint (in fencing)
trezavo *a* thirteenth
tría *f,* selection, choice; worn place (in cloth)
triangulación *f,* triangulation
triángulo *a* triangular. *m,* (*geom mus*) triangle. **t. acutángulo,** acute triangle. **t. obtusángulo,** obtuse triangle. **t. rectángulo,** right-angled triangle
triar *vt* to select, pick out; *vi* fly in and out of the hive (of bees); *vr* grow threadbare, become worn
tribu *f,* tribe; species, family
tribulación *f,* tribulation, suffering
tribuna *f,* tribune; platform, rostrum, pulpit; spectators' gallery; stand. **t. de la prensa,** press gallery. **t. del jurado,** jury box. **t. del órgano,** organ loft
tribunado *m,* tribunate
tribunal *m,* law court; *law* bench; judgment seat; tribunal; board of examiners. **t. de menores,** children's court, juvenile court. *naut* **t. de presas,** prize court. **t. de primera instancia,** *law* petty sessions. **t. militar,** court-martial
tribuno *m,* tribune; political speaker
tributar *vt* to pay taxes; offer, render (thanks, homage, etc.)
tributario (-ia) *a* tributary; tax-paying, contributive. *n* taxpayer. *m,* tributary (of a river)
tributo *m,* contribution; tax; tribute, homage; census
tricenal *a* of thirty years' duration; occurring every thirty years
tricentésimo *a* three-hundredth
triciclo *m,* tricycle
tricolor *a* three-colored
tricorne *a poet* three-cornered, three-horned
tricornio *a* three-cornered. *m,* three-cornered hat
tricotomía *f,* trichotomy, division into three
tricromía *f,* three-color process
tridente *a* tridentate, three-pronged. *m,* trident
trienal *a* triennial
trienio *m,* space of three years
trifásico *a* three-phase
trifolio *m,* trefoil
trigal *m,* wheat field
trigésimo *a* thirtieth
trigo *m,* wheat plant; ear of wheat; wheat field (gen. *pl*); wealth, money. **t. sarraceno,** buckwheat. **t. tremés** *or* **t. trechel** *or* **t. tremesino** *or* **t. de marzo,** summer wheat
trigonometría *f,* trigonometry
trigueño *a* brunette, dark
triguero *a* wheat; wheat-growing. *m,* grain sieve; grain merchant
trilátero *a* three-sided, trilateral
trilingüe *a* trilingual

trilla *f,* red mullet; *agr* harrow; threshing; threshing season
trillado *a* frequented, trodden, worn (of paths); hackneyed
trilladora *f,* threshing machine
trillar *vt* to thresh; *inf* frequent; ill-treat
trillo *m,* threshing machine; harrow
trillón *m,* trillion
trilogía *f,* trilogy
trimestral *a* quarterly; terminal (in schools, etc.)
trimestre *a* quarterly; terminal. *m,* quarter, three months; term (in schools, etc.); quarterly payment; quarterly rent
trinado *m, mus* trill; twittering, shrilling (of birds)
trinar *vi mus* to trill; twitter, shrill; *inf* get in a temper, be furious
trincapiñones *m, inf* scatterbrained youth
trincar *vt* to fasten securely; tie tightly; pinion; *naut* lash, make fast; cut up, chop; *inf* tipple; *vi naut* sail close to the wind
trincha *f,* vest strap
trinchante *m,* table carver; carving fork; stonecutter's hammer
trinchar *vt* to carve (at table); *inf* decide, dispose
trinche *m Mexico* pitchfork; *elsewhere in Lat. Am.* fork
trinchera *f, mil* trench; cutting (for roads, etc.); trench coat
trinchero *m,* platter, trencher; serving table, side table
trineo *m,* sledge, sleigh
trinidad *f,* trinity
trinitaria *f, bot* heartsease
trinitario (-ia) *a* and *n ecc* Trinitarian
trino *a* triune; ternary. *m, mus* trill
trinomio *m,* trinomial
trinquete *m, naut* mainmast; mainsail; *sport* rackets; *mech* ratchet
trinquis *m, inf* draft, drink
trío *m,* trio
tripa *f,* entrail, gut; *inf* belly; inside (of some fruits). **hacer de tripas corazón,** *inf* to take heart, buck up. **revolver las tripas (a),** *fig inf* to make one sick
tripartición *f,* tripartition
tripartito *a* tripartite
tripicallos *m pl, cul* tripe
triple *a* triple; three-ply (of yarn)
triplicación *f,* trebling
triplicar *vt* to treble
trípode *m,* (sometimes *f*) three-legged stool or table; tripod; trivet
tríptico *m,* triptych
triptongo *m,* triphthong
tripulación *f,* crew (ships and aircraft)
tripulante *m,* crew member
tripular *vt* to provide with a crew, man; equip, furnish; serve in, work as the crew of
trique *m,* crack, creak. *inf* **a cada t.,** at every moment
triquiñuela *f, inf* evasion, subterfuge
triquitraque *m,* tap, rap; crack; firework
tris *m,* crack, noise of glass, etc., cracking; *inf* instant, trice. **estar en un t. (de),** to be on the verge (of), within an inch (of)
trisar *vt* to crack, break, splinter (of glass); *vi* chirp, twitter (especially of swallows)
trisca *f,* cracking, crushing, crackling (of nuts, etc.); noise, tumult
triscar *vi* to make a noise with the feet; gambol, frolic; creak, crack; *vt* blend, mingle; set the teeth of a saw
trisecar *vt* to trisect
trisemanal *a* three times weekly; every three weeks
trisílabo *a* trisyllabic
trismo *m,* lockjaw, trismus
triste *a* unhappy, sorrowful; melancholy, gloomy; sad; piteous, unfortunate; useless, worthless; *m, Lat. Am.* sad love song
tristeza, tristura *f,* unhappiness; melancholy, gloom; sadness; piteousness
tritón *m,* merman
triturar *vt* to crumble, crush; chew; masticate; ill-treat, bruise; refute, contradict
triunfada *f,* trumping (at cards)
triunfador (-ra) *a* triumphant. *n* victor
triunfal *a* triumphal
triunfante *a* triumphant
triunfar *vi* to triumph; be victorious, win; trump (at cards); spend ostentatiously
triunfo *m,* triumph; victory; trump card; success; booty, spoils of war; conquest
trivial *a* well-known, hackneyed; frequented, trodden; commonplace, mediocre; trivial, unimportant
trivialidad *f,* banality, triteness; mediocrity; triviality
trivio *m,* road junction
triza *f,* fragment, bit; *naut* rope. **hacer trizas,** to smash to bits
trizar *vt* to smash up, destroy
trocable *a* exchangeable
trocada, a la *adv* contrariwise; in exchange
trocador (-ra) *n* exchanger
trocar *vt irr* to exchange; vomit; distort, misconstrue, mistake; *vr* change, alter one's behavior; change places with another; be transferred. See **contar**
trocha *f,* short cut; trail, path, track
trochemoche, a *adv inf* without rhyme or reason, pell-mell
trocear *vt* to divide into pieces
trofeo *m,* trophy; victory; military booty
troglodita *a* and *mf* troglodyte. *m, fig* savage, barbarian. *mf* glutton
troj *f,* granary
trojero *m,* granary keeper
trola *f, inf* lie, nonsense, hoax
trole *m,* trolley
trolebús *m,* trolley car
trolero *a inf* deceiving, lying
tromba *f,* waterspout
trombón *m,* trombone; trombone player. **¡Trombones y platillos!** Great Scot!
trombosis *f,* thrombosis
trompa *f,* elephant's trunk; *mus* horn; proboscis (of insects); waterspout; humming top. **t. de Falopio,** fallopian tube
trompada *f, inf* bang, bump; blow, buffet, slap; collision
trompazo *m,* heavy blow, knock, bang
trompear *vi* to play with a top; *vt* knock about
trompero *m,* top maker. *a* deceiving, swindling
trompeta *f,* trumpet; bugle. *m,* trumpeter; bugler; *inf* ninny. **t. de amor,** sunflower
trompetada *f, inf* stupid remark, piece of nonsense
trompetazo *m,* bray of a trumpet; bugle blast; *inf* stupid remark
trompetear *vi inf* to play the trumpet or bugle
trompeteo *m,* trumpeting, trumpet call; sound of the bugle
trompetería *f,* collection of trumpets; metal organ pipes
trompetero *m,* trumpet or bugle maker or player
trompetilla *f, dim* little trumpet; ear trumpet
trompicar *vt* to make stumble, trip. *vi* stumble, trip up
trompicón *m,* stumble
trompo *m,* humming or spinning top; *inf* dolt, idiot
tronada *f,* thunderstorm
tronado *a* worn-out; threadbare, old; poor, poverty-stricken; down at the heels
tronar *v impers irr* to thunder; *vi* growl, roar (of guns); *inf* go bankrupt, be ruined; *inf* protest against, attack; *Central America, Mexico* execute, shoot; (*with con*) quarrel with. *Pres. Ind.* **trueno, truenas, truena, truenan.** *Pres. Subjunc.* **truene, truenes, truene, truenen**
troncal *a* trunk; main, principal
troncha *f, Lat. Am.* piece; slice
tronchar *vt* to break off, lop off (branches)
troncho *m, bot* stem, stalk, branch

tronco *m, anat bot* trunk; main body or line (of communications); trunk line; common origin, stock; *inf* blockhead, dolt; callous person. *fig* **estar hecho un t.,** to lie like a log; sleep like a log
tronera *f, naut* porthole; embrasure; slit window; pocket of a billiards table. *mf inf* madcap, harum-scarum
tronido *m,* roll of thunder
trono *m,* throne; *ecc* tabernacle; shrine; kingly might; *pl* thrones, hierarchy of angels
tronzador *m,* two-handled saw
tronzar *vt* to smash, break into bits; *sew* pleat; exhaust, overtire
tropa *f,* crowd (of people); troops, military; *mil* call to arms; *pl* army. **t. de línea,** regiment of the line. **tropas de asalto,** storm troopers. **tropas de refresco,** fresh troops. **en t.,** in a crowd; in groups
tropel *m,* rush, surge (of crowds, etc.); bustle, confusion; crowd, multitude; heap, jumble (of things). **en t.,** in a rush; in a crowd
tropelía *f,* rush, dash; violence; outrage
tropezar *vi irr* to stumble, slip; (*with con*) meet unexpectedly or accidentally come up against, be faced with (difficulties); quarrel with or oppose; fall into (bad habits). See **empezar**
tropezón *m,* stumbling, slipping; stumbling block, obstacle. **a tropezones,** *inf* stumblingly; by fits and starts
tropical *a* tropical
trópicos *m pl,* tropics
tropiezo *m,* stumble; stumbling block, obstacle; hitch; impediment; slip, peccadillo, fault; difficulty, embarrassment; fight, skirmish; quarrel
tropo *m,* trope, figure of speech
troquel *m,* die, mold
trotaconventos *f, inf* go-between, procuress
trotamundos *mf, inf* globetrotter
trotar *vi* to trot; *inf* hurry, get a move on
trote *m,* trot; toil, drudgery. **t. corto,** jog-trot. **al t.,** with all speed
trotón (-ona) *a* trotting. *m,* horse. *f,* chaperone
trova *f,* verse; song, lay, ballad; love song
trovador (-ra) *m,* troubadour, minstrel. *n* poet
trovadoresco *a* pertaining to minstrels, troubadour
trovar *vi* to compose verses; write ballads; misconstrue, misinterpret
Troya Troy
troyano (-na) *a* and *n* Trojan
trozo *m,* part, fragment; piece, portion; *lit* selection. **t. de abordaje,** *nav* landing party
trucha *f,* trout. **t. asalmonada,** salmon trout
truchuela *f,* small trout; salt cod
truco *m,* trick, deception
truculencia *f,* harshness, cruelty, truculence
truculento *a* fierce, harsh, truculent
trueco *m,* exchange. **a t. de,** in exchange for; on condition that
trueno *m,* thunder; report, noise (of firearms); *inf* rake, scapegrace
trueque *m,* exchange. **a.** (*or* **en**) **t.,** in exchange
trufa *f, bot* truffle; nonsense, idle talk
trufar *vt cul* to stuff with truffles; *vi inf* lie, tell fibs
truhán (-ana) *a* knavish, roguish, comic. *n* knave, rogue; clown, buffoon
truhanear *vi* to be a trickster, behave like a knave; play the clown
truhanería *f,* knavery, act of a rogue; clowning, buffoonery; collection of rogues
truhanesco *a* knavish, scoundrelly; clownish
trujal *m,* oil or grape press; oil mill; vat for soap making
trujar *vt* to partition off
trulla *f,* uproar, tumult; crowd, throng
truncar *vt* to shorten, truncate; decapitate, mutilate; omit, cut out (words, etc.); curtail, abridge; mutilate, deform (texts, etc.)
truque *m,* card game; kind of hopscotch
trusa *f, Cuba,* bathing suit
trust *m, com* trust
tú *pers pron 2nd sing mf* thou, you. **tratar de t.** (**a**)**,** to address familiarly; be on intimate terms with
tu *poss pron mf* thy, your. Used only before nouns
tuberculina *f,* tuberculin
tubérculo *m,* (*zool med*) tubercle; *bot* tubercle, tuber
tuberculoso *a* tubercular, tuberculous
tubería *f,* piping, tubing; pipe system; pipe factory
tuberosa *f,* tuberose
tuberoso *a* tuberous
tubo *m,* pipe, tube; lamp chimney; flue; *anat* duct, canal. **t. acústico,** speaking tube. **t. de ensayo,** test tube. **t. de escape,** exhaust pipe. **t. lanzatorpedos,** torpedo tube. **t. termiónico,** *rad* thermionic valve
tubular *a* tubular
tucán, tucano *m* toucan
tudesco *a* German
tueco *m,* stump (of a tree); wormhole (in wood)
tuerca *f,* nut (of a screw)
tuerto *a* one-eyed. *m, law* tort; *pl* afterpains. **a t.,** unjustly
tueste *m,* toasting
tuétano *m,* marrow. *inf* **hasta los tuétanos,** to the depths of one's being
tufillas *mf inf* easily irritated person
tufo *m,* strong smell, poisonous vapor; *inf* stink; side, airs, conceit (often *pl*); lock of hair over the ears
tugurio *m,* shepherd's hut; miserable little room; *inf* haunt, low dive
tul *m,* tulle
tulipa *f,* small tulip; lampshade
tulipán *m,* tulip
tullido *a* partially paralyzed; maimed, crippled
tullir *vt irr* to maim, cripple; paralyze; *vr* become paralyzed; be crippled. See **mullir**
tumba *f,* tomb; tumble, overbalancing; somersault; Catherine wheel
tumbar *vt* to knock down; kill, drop; *inf* overpower, overcome (of odors, wine). *vi* fall down; *naut* run aground; *vr inf* lie down, stretch oneself out
tumbo *m,* tumble, overbalancing; undulation (of ground); rise and fall of sea waves; imminent danger; book containing deeds and privileges of monasteries and churches
tumbón *a inf* crafty, sly; idle, lazy. *m,* trunk with an arched lid
tumefacción *f,* swelling
tumefacto, túmido *a* swollen
tumor *m,* tumor
túmulo *m,* tumulus; catafalque; mound of earth
tumulto *m,* riot, uprising; tumult, commotion, disturbance
tumultuario, tumultuoso *a* noisy, tumultuous, confused
tuna *f,* prickly pear tree or fruit; vagrant life; strolling student musicians (playing to raise money for charity)
tunante *a* rascally, roguish. *mf* rascal, scoundrel
tunantuelo (-la) *n inf* imp, little rascal
tunda *f,* shearing of cloth; *inf* sound beating, hiding
tundear *vt* to beat, drub, buffet
tundidora *f,* woman who shears cloth; cloth-shearing machine; lawn mower
tundir *vt* to shear (cloth); mow (grass); *inf* beat, wallop
tunecino (-na) *a* and *n* Tunisian
túnel *m,* tunnel
túnica *f,* tunic, chiton; tunicle; robe
tuno (-na) *a* knavish, rascally. *n* rascal, scoundrel
tupé *m,* forelock (of a horse); toupee; *inf* cheek, nerve
tupición *f, Lat. Am.* blockage, obstruction; cold (in the head)
tupido *a* thick, dense; obtuse, dull, stupid; *Lat. Am.* blocked up, obstructed
tupir *vt* to thicken, make dense; press tightly; *vr* stuff oneself with food or drink
turba *f,* crowd, multitude; peat

turbación *f,* disturbance; upset; perturbation; bewilderment, confusion; embarrassment
turbador (-ra) *a* disturbing, upsetting. *n* disturber, upsetter
turbamulta *f, inf* mob, rabble
turbante *a* upsetting, perturbing. *m,* turban
turbar *vt* to disturb, upset; make turbid, muddy; bewilder, confuse; embarrass
turbera *f,* peat bog
turbiedad *f,* muddiness (of liquids); obscurity
turbina *f,* turbine
turbio *a* turbid, muddy; troublous; turbulent, disturbed; obscure, confused (style); indistinct, blurred, *m pl,* lees, sediment (of oil)
turbión *m,* brief storm, squall; *fig* shower, rush
turbulencia *f,* turbidity, muddiness; turbulence, commotion; disturbance, confusion
turbulento *a* muddy, turbid; turbulent, disturbed; confused
turca *f, inf* drinking bout
turco (-ca) *a* Turkish. *n* Turk. *m,* Turkish (language)
turgencia *f,* swelling, turgidity
turgente *a med* turgescent; *poet* turgid, prominent, swollen
turismo *m,* touring, tourist industry. **coche de t.,** touring car
turista *mf* tourist
turno *m,* turn. **por t.,** in turn
turquesa *f,* turquoise
Turquía Turkey
turrón *m,* kind of nougat; almond paste; *inf* soft job, sinecure; civil service job
turulato *a inf* dumbfounded, speechless, inarticulate
¡tus! *interj* word for calling dogs. **sin decir t. ni mus,** *inf* without saying anything
tusa *f, Central America* corncob; whore; *Argentina* mane (of a horse)
tutear *vt* to address as tú (instead of the formal usted); treat familiarly
tutela *f,* guardianship; tutelage; protection, defense
tuteo *m,* the use in speaking to a person of the familiar tú instead of the formal usted
tutor (-ra) *n* guardian. *m,* stake (for plants); protector, defender
tutoría *f.* See **tutela**
tuyo, tuya, tuyos, tuyas *poss pron 2nd sing* and *pl mf* thine, yours. Used sometimes with def. art. (e.g. **Este sombrero es el tuyo,** This hat is yours)

U

u *f,* letter U. *conjunc* Used instead of **o** or before words beginning with **o** or **ho** (e.g. **fragante u oloroso**)
ubérrimo *a sup* most fruitful; very abundant
ubicación *f,* situation, position, location
ubicar *vt* to place, situate; *vi* and *vr* be situated
ubicuidad *f,* ubiquity
ubicuo *a* omnipresent; ubiquitous
ubre *f,* udder
Ucrania Ukraine
ucranio (-ia) *a* and *n* Ukrainian
ucelele *m,* ukulele
¡uf! *interj* ugh!
ufanarse *vr* to pride oneself, put on airs
ufanía *f,* pride, conceit
ufano *a* conceited, vain; satisfied, pleased; expeditious, masterly
ujier *m,* usher
úlcera *f,* ulcer
ulcerar(se) *vt* and *vr* to ulcerate
ulceroso *a* ulcerous
ulpo *m, Chile, Peru* corn gruel
ulterior *a* farther, ulterior; subsequent
ulteriormente *adv* subsequently, later
ultimación *f,* ending, finishing
ultimar *vt* to end, conclude
ultimátum *m,* ultimatum
último *a* last; farthermost; ultimate; top; final, definitive; most valuable, best; latter; recent. **«Última Hora.»** "Stop Press." **a última hora,** *fig* at the eleventh hour. **en estos últimos años,** in recent years. **a últimos de mes,** towards the end of the month. **el ú. piso,** the top floor. **por ú.,** finally. *inf* **estar en las últimas,** to be at the end, be finishing
ultra, *adv* besides; (with words like *mar*) beyond; (as prefix) excessively
ultrajar *vt* to insult; scorn, despise
ultraje *m,* insult, outrage
ultrajoso *a* offensive, insulting, abusive
ultramar *m,* overseas, abroad
ultramarino *a* oversea; ultramarine. *m,* foreign produce (gen. *pl*)
ultramontano *a* ultramontane
ultrarrojo *a* infrared
ultratumba *adv* beyond the grave
ultravioleta *a* ultraviolet
úlula *f,* screech owl
ululación *f,* screech, howl; hoot of an owl
ulular *vi* to howl, shriek, screech; hoot (of an owl)
ululato *m,* ululation
umbilical *a* umbilical
umbral *m,* threshold; *fig* starting point; *arch* lintel. **atravesar** (*or* **pisar**) **los umbrales,** to cross the threshold
umbría *f,* shady place
umbrío *a* shady, dark
umbroso *a* shady
un *abb* of **uno, a,** one. Used before *m, sing f,* **una,** *indef art.* a, an; a; one
unánime *a* unanimous
unanimidad *f,* unanimity. **por u.,** unanimously
unción *f,* anointing; *ecc* Extreme Unction; unction, fervor
uncir *vt* to yoke
undécimo *a* eleventh
undísono *a poet* sounding, sonorous (waves, etc.)
undoso *a* wavy, rippling
undulación *f,* undulation; *phys* wave
undular *vi* to undulate; wriggle; float, wave (flags, etc.)
undulatorio *a* undulatory
ungimiento *m,* anointment
ungir *vt* to anoint
ungüento *m,* ointment; lotion; *fig* balm, unguent
unicelular *a* unicellular
único *a* unique; sole, solitary, only. **Lo ú. que se puede hacer es . . .,** The only thing one can do is . . .
unicolor *a* of one color
unicornio *m,* unicorn
unidad *f,* unity; unit; (*math mil*) unit. **u. de bagaje,** piece of baggage. (of drama) **u. de lugar,** unity of place. **u. de tiempo,** unity of time
unidamente *adv* jointly; harmoniously
unificación *f,* unification
unificar(se) *vt* and *vr* to unify, unite
uniformación *f,* standardization
uniformar *vt* to make uniform, standardize; put into uniform; *vr* become uniform
uniforme *a* uniform; same, similar. *m,* uniform
uniformidad *f,* uniformity
unigénito *a* only-begotten. *m,* Christ
unilateral *a* one-sided, unilateral
unión *f,* union; correspondence, conformity; agreement; marriage; alliance, federation; composition,

mixture; combination; proximity, nearness; (mystic) union
unionista *mf pol* unionist
Unión Soviética Soviet Union
unir *vt* to unite, join; mix, combine; bind, fasten; connect, couple; bring together; marry; *fig* harmonize, conciliate; *vr* join together, unite; be combined; marry; (*with prep a* or *con*) be near to; associate with
unísono *a* unisonant. **al u.,** in unison; unanimously
unitario (-ia) *a* and *n* Unitarian
universal *a* universal; well-informed; widespread
universalidad *f*, universality
universalizar *vt* to make universal, generalize
universidad *f*, university; universality; universe
universitario *a* university
universo *a* universal. *m*, universe
uno (*f*, **una**) *a* a, one; single, only; same; *pl* some; about, nearly. *m*, one (number). **Tiene unos doce años,** He is about twelve. **unas pocas manzanas,** a few apples. *pron* someone; one thing, same thing; *pl* some people. **No sabe uno qué creer,** One doesn't know what to believe. **Unos dicen que no, otros que sí,** Some (people) say no, others yes. **Juan no tiene libros y le voy a dar uno,** John has no books and I am going to give him one. **Todo es uno,** It's all the same. **u. a u.,** one by one. **u. que otro,** a few. **u. y otro,** both. **unos cuantos,** a few, some. **Es la una,** It is one o'clock
untar *vt* to anoint; grease, oil; *inf* bribe; *vr* smear oneself with grease or similar thing; *fig inf* line one's pockets. **u. el carro,** *fig* to grease the wheels
unto *m*, grease; animal fat; *fig* balm; *Chile* shoe polish
untuoso *a* fat, greasy
uña *f*, nail (of fingers or toes); hoof, trotter, claw; stinging tail of scorpion; thorn; stump of tree branch; *naut* fluke; *fig inf* light fingers (gen. *pl*). **afilarse las uñas,** to sharpen one's claws, prepare for trouble. **comerse las uñas,** to bite one's nails. **caer en las uñas de,** to fall into the clutches of. **hincar la u. (en),** to stick the claws into; to defraud, overcharge. **ser u. y carne,** to be devoted friends
uñarada *f*, scratch with nails
uñero *m*, ingrowing nail, ingrown nail
¡upa! *interj* Up you get! Up you go! Upsy daisy! (gen. to children)
uranio *m*, uranium
urbanidad *f*, civility, good manners, urbanity
urbanismo *m*, town planning; housing scheme
urbanización *f*, urbanization
urbanizar *vt* to civilize, polish; urbanize
urbano *a* urban, city; urbane
urbe *f*, city, metropolis
urbícola *mf* city dweller
urdemalas *mf*, schemer, intriguer
urdidera *f*, warping-frame
urdimbre *f*, warp; scheming, plotting
urdir *vt* to warp; weave; scheme, intrigue
uréter *m*, ureter
uretra *f*, urethra
urgencia *f*, urgency; necessity; compulsion
urgente *a* urgent
urgir *vi* to be urgent; be valid, be in force (laws)
urinario *a* urinary. *m*, urinal
urna *f*, urn; ballot box; glass case
urraca *f*, magpie
Uruguáy *m* Uruguay
uruguayo (-ya) *a* and *n* Uruguayan
usado *a* worn out; accustomed, efficient. *com* **al u.,** in the usual form. **ropa usada,** second-hand clothing, worn clothing
usanza *f*, custom, usage
usar *vt* to use; wear, make use of; follow (trade, occupation); *vi* be accustomed
usina *f*, *Argentina* power plant
uso *m*, use; custom; fashion; habit; wear and tear. **al u.,** according to custom. **al u. de,** in the manner of
usted *mf* you. *pl* **ustedes.** Often abbreviated to **Vd, V, Vds, VV** or **Ud, Uds**
usual *a* usual; general, customary; sociable
usufructo *m*, *law* usufruct; life-interest; profit
usura *f*, usury; profiteering. **pagar con u.,** to pay back a thousandfold
usurario *a* usurious
usurear *vi* to lend or borrow with usury; profiteer, make excess profits
usurero (-ra) *n* usurer; profiteer
usurpación *f*, usurpation
usurpador (-ra) *a* usurping. *n* usurper
usurpar *vt* to usurp
utensilio *m*, utensil; tool, implement (gen. *pl*)
uterino *a* uterine
útero *m*, uterus
útil *a* useful; profitable; *law* lawful (of days, etc.). *m*, usefulness, profit; *pl* **útiles,** utensils, tools
utilidad *f*, utility; usefulness; profit
utilitario *a* utilitarian
utilitarismo *m*, utilitarianism
utilizable *a* utilizable
utilización *f*, utilization
utilizar *vt* to utilize
utillaje *m*, machinery
utópico *a* Utopian
uva *f*, grape. **u. espina,** kind of gooseberry. **u. moscatel,** muscatel grape. *inf* **hecho una u.,** dead-drunk
uvero (-ra) *a* pertaining or relating to grapes, grape. *n* grape seller
uxoricidio *m*, uxoricide (act)
uxorio *a* uxorious

V

v *f*, letter V. **v doble** *or* **doble v,** letter W. **V** *or* **Vd, VV,** *abbs* **vuestra(s) merced(es),** *mf sing* and *pl* you
vaca *f*, cow. **v. de San Antón,** *ent* ladybug
vacación *f*, vacation, holiday (gen. *pl*); vacancy; act of vacating (employment). **vacaciones retribuídas,** paid vacation
vacada *f*, herd of cows
vacancia *f*, vacancy
vacante *a* vacant. *f*, vacancy
vacar *vi* to be vacant; take a holiday; retire temporarily; (*with prep a*) dedicate oneself to, engage in
vaciadero *m*, rubbish dump; sewer, drain
vaciado *m*, plaster cast; *arch* excavation
vaciamiento *m*, emptying; molding, casting; depletion
vaciar *vt* to empty; drain, drink; mold, cast; *arch* excavate; hone; copy; *vi* flow (into) (rivers); *vr inf* blurt out
vaciedad *f*, emptiness; foolishness, inanity
vacilación *f*, swaying; tottering; staggering; hesitation, perplexity
vacilada *Mexico, f* joke, trick (played on someone)
vacilante *a* swaying; tottering; staggering; hesitating, vacillating
vacilar *vi* to sway; totter; stagger; flicker; hesitate
vacío *a* empty, void; fruitless, vain; unoccupied, vacant, deserted; imperfect; hollow, empty; conceited, immature. *m*, hollow; *anat* flank; vacancy; shortage; *phys* vacuum. **v. de aire,** airpocket. **de v.,** unloaded (carts, etc.). **en v.,** in vacuo. *inf* **hacer el v. (a),** to send to Coventry
vacuidad *f*, emptiness; vacuity
vacuna *f*, cowpox; vaccine. **v. antivariolosa,** smallpox vaccine
vacunación *f*, vaccination
vacunar *vt* to vaccinate; inoculate

vacuno *a* bovine
vacuo *a* empty; vacant. *m*, void; vacuum
vadeable *a* fordable (rivers, etc.); *fig* surmountable
vadear *vt* to ford, wade; *fig* overcome (obstacles); *fig* sound, find out the opinion (of); *vr* behave
vademécum *m*, vade mecum; school satchel
vado *m*, ford; expedient, help
vagabundear *vi* to wander, roam, loiter
vagabundeo *m*, vagabondage
vagabundo (-da) *a* roving, wandering; vagrant. *n* tramp, vagabond
vagamundear *vi*. See **vagabundear**
vagancia *f*, vagrancy
vagar *m*, leisure; interval, pause. *vi* be idle or at leisure; wander, roam
vagido *m*, cry, wail (infants)
vago (-ga) *a* vagrant, idle; vague; *art* indefinite, blurred. *n* idler. *m*, tramp; loafer. **en v.,** unsuccessfully, vainly
vagón *m*, wagon; (railway) coach. **v. comedor,** dining car
vagoneta *f*, open truck (railways, mines, etc.)
vaguear *vi* to roam, wander; loaf
vaguedad *f*, vagueness; vague remark
vaharada *f*, whiff, exhalation
vahído *m*, vertigo, dizzy spell
vaho *m*, vapor, fume
vaina *f*, scabbard; *bot* sheath, pod; case (scissors, etc.); *Colombia* hassle. **¡Qué vaina!** What a hassle!
vainilla *f*, *bot* vanilla; *sew* drawn-thread work
vaivén *m*, swing, sway, seesaw; instability, fluctuation
vajilla *f*, china; dinner service
val *m*, *abb* **valle**
Valdepeñas *m*, red wine from Valdepeñas
vale *m*, *com* bond, I.O.U., promissory note; voucher; valediction; *Lat. Am.* buddy, pal
valedero *a* valid, binding
valedor (-ra) *n* protector, sponsor
valencia *f*, valency
valenciano (-na) *a* and *n* Valencian
valentía *f*, bravery; heroic deed; boast; (*art lit*) dash, imagination, fire; superhuman effort
valentón *a* boastful, blustering
valer *vt irr* to protect; defend; produce (income, etc.); cost; *vi* be worth; deserve; have power or authority; be of importance or worth; be a protection; be current (money); be valid; *vr* (*with de*) make use of. *m*, value, worth. **v. la pena,** to be worthwhile. **v. tanto como cualquiera,** to be as good as the next guy, be as good as the next fellow. **¡Válgame Dios!** Heavens! Bless me! **Más vale así,** It's better thus. **Vale más ser cola de león que cabeza de ratón.** Better a big frog in a small puddle than a small frog in a big puddle. *Pres. Ind.* **valgo, vales,** etc. *Fut.* **valdré,** etc. *Condit.* **valdría,** etc. *Pres. Subjunc.* **valga,** etc.
valeriana *f*, valerian
valeroso *a* active, energetic; courageous; powerful
valetudinario *a* valetudinarian
valía *f*, value, price; influence, worth; faction, party. **a las valías,** at the highest price
validación *f*, validation; force, soundness
validar *vt* to make strong; validate
validez *f*, validity
valido *a* favorite, esteemed. *m*, court favorite; prime minister
válido *a* firm, sound, valid; strong, robust
valiente *a* strong, robust; courageous; active; excellent; excessive, enormous (gen. *iron*); boastful
valija *f*, valise, suitcase, grip; mail bag; mail
valimiento *m*, value; favor; protection, influence
valioso *a* valuable; powerful; wealthy
valisoletano (-na) *a* and *n* of or from Valladolid
valla *f*, barricade, paling; stockade; *fig* obstacle. **v. publicitaria,** billboard
vallado *m*, stockade; enclosure; *Mexico* deep ditch
valle *m*, valley; vale; river-basin
valor *m*, worth, value; price; courage; validity; power; yield, income; insolence; *pl com* securities
valoración *f*, valuation; appraisement
válorar *vt* to value; appraise
valorización *f*, valuation
valquiria *f*, Valkyrie
vals *m*, waltz
valsar *vi* to waltz
valuación *f*. See **valoración**
valuar *vt* to value; appraise; assess
valva *f*, *zool* valve
válvula *f*, *mech* valve. *aut* **v. de cámara (del neumático),** tire-valve. **v. de seguridad,** safety-valve
vampiro *m*, vampire; *fig* bloodsucker
vanagloria *f*, vaingloriousness, conceit
vanagloriarse *vr* to be conceited
vanaglorioso (-sa) *a* conceited. *n* boaster
vanamente *adv* vainly; without foundation; superstitiously; arrogantly
vandálico *a* Vandal
vandalismo *m*, vandalism; destructiveness
vándalo (-la) *a* and *n* Vandal
vanguardia *f*, vanguard; *pl* outerworks. **a v.,** in the forefront
vanidad *f*, vanity; ostentation; empty words; illusion. *inf* **ajar la v. de,** to take (a person) down a peg
vanidoso (-sa) *a* vain; ostentatious. *n* conceited person
vano *a* vain; hollow, empty; useless, ineffectual; unsubstantial, illusory. *m*, span (bridge). **v. único,** single span. **en v.,** uselessly, in vain
vapor *m*, steam, vapor; fainting fit; steamboat; *pl* hysterics. **v. de ruedas, v. de paleta,** paddle steamer. **v. volandero,** tramp steamer. **al v.,** full steam ahead; *inf* with all speed
vaporable *a* vaporizable
vaporación *f*, evaporation
vaporización *f*, vaporization
vaporizador *m*, vaporizer; spray, sprayer
vaporizar *vt* to vaporize; spray
vaporoso *a* vaporous; ethereal; gauzy
vapulación *f*, **vapulamiento** *m*, whipping
vapular *vt* to whip
vapuleo *m*, whipping, spanking
vaquería *f*, herd of cattle; dairy; dairy farm
vaquero (-ra) *n* cowboy; **vaqueros,** *m, pl* jeans
vaquilla *f*, heifer
vara *f*, staff; rod; wand (of authority); vara (2.8 feet); shaft (of cart). **v. de aforar,** water gauge
varada *f*, *naut* running aground
varadero *m*, shipyard
varar *vi naut* to run aground; *fig* be held up (negotiations, etc.); *vt naut* put in dry dock
varear *vt* to knock down (fruit from tree); beat (with a rod); measure with a rod; sell by the rod; *vr* grow thin
variabilidad *f*, variableness
variable *a* variable; changeable, inconsistent
variación *f*, variation
variado *a* varied; variegated
variante *a* varying. *f*, variant; discrepancy
variar *vt* to vary; change; *vi* change; be different
varice *f*, varix
varicela *f*, chicken pox
varicoso *a* varicose
variedad *f*, variety; change; inconstancy, instability; alteration; variation; *biol* variety
varilla *f*, *dim* rod; rib (fan, umbrella). **v. de virtudes,** conjurer's wand. *mech* **v. percusora,** tappet rod
vario *a* different, diverse; inconstant, changeable; variegated; *pl* some, a few
variopinto *a* motley
varón *m*, male; man
varonil *a* male; manly
Varsovia Warsaw
varsoviano (-na) *a* and *n* of or from Warsaw
vasallaje *m*, vassalage; dependence; tribute money

vasallo (-lla) *n* vassal. *a* vassal; dependent
vasco (-ca), vascongado (-da) *a* and *n* Basque
vascuence *m,* Basque (language); *inf* gibberish
vaselina *f,* vaseline
vasija *f,* vessel, receptacle, jar
vaso *m,* receptacle; glass, tankard, mug; glassful; (*naut anat bot*) vessel; garden-urn; vase
vástago *m,* stem, shoot; offspring, descendant; piston rod
vastedad *f,* extensiveness, largeness, vastness
vasto *a* vast, extensive
vate *m,* bard; seer
vaticano *a* and *m,* Vatican
vaticinar *vt* to prophesy, foretell
vaticinio *m,* prediction
vatímetro *m,* water meter
vatio *m,* watt. **v. hora,** watt hour
ve *f,* name of the letter V. **v. doble** *or* **doble v.,** name of the letter W
vecinal *a* neighboring, adjacent
vecindad *f,* neighborhood; *Lat. Am.* slum. **buena v.,** good neighborliness. **hacer mala v.,** to be a nuisance to one's neighbors
vecindario *m,* neighborhood; population of a district
vecino (-na) *a* neighboring; near; similar. *n* neighbor; citizen; inhabitant
vector *m,* carrier (of disease)
veda *f,* close season; prohibition
vedamiento *m,* prohibition
vedar *vt* to forbid; prevent
vedija *f,* tangled lock of hair; piece of matted wool; curl (of smoke)
veedor (-ra) *a* prying. *n* busy-body. *m,* inspector; overseer
vega *f,* fertile lowland plain; meadow
vegada *f.* See **vez**
vegetable *a* and *m,* vegetable
vegetación *f,* vegetation
vegetal *a* vegetal; plant. *m,* vegetable, plant
vegetar *vi* to flourish, grow (plants); *fig* vegetate
vegetarianismo *m,* vegetarianism
vegetariano (-na) *a* and *n* vegetarian
vegetativo *a* vegetative
vehemencia *f,* vehemence
vehemente *a* vehement; vivid
vehículo *m,* vehicle; means, instrument
veinte *a* and *m,* twenty; twentieth
veintena *f,* a score
veinticinco *a* and *m,* twenty-five; twenty-fifth
veinticuatro *a* and *m,* twenty-four; twenty-fourth
veintidós *a* and *m,* twenty-two; twenty-second
veintinueve *a* and *m,* twenty-nine; twenty-ninth
veintiocho *a* and *m,* twenty-eight; twenty-eighth
veintiséis *a* and *m,* twenty-six; twenty-sixth
veintisiete *a* and *m,* twenty-seven; twenty-seventh
veintitrés *a* and *m,* twenty-three; twenty-third
veintiuno *a* and *m,* twenty-one; twenty-first. Abbreviates to **veintiún** before a noun (even if one or more adjectives intervene)
vejación *f,* ill-treatment, persecution
vejamen *m,* irritation, provocation; taunt; lampoon
vejar *vt* to ill-treat, persecute; plague
vejatorio *a* vexing, annoying
vejete *m, inf* silly old man
vejez *f,* oldness; old age; platitude. **vejeces,** *pl* ailments of old age. *inf* **a la v., viruelas,** the older the madder
vejiga *f,* bladder; blister. **v. natatoria,** float (of a fish)
vela *f,* vigil; watch; pilgrimage; sentinel, watchman; candle; *naut* sail; awning; night work, overtime. **v. de cangreja,** boom sail. **v. de mesana,** mizzen sail. **v. de trinquete,** foresail. **v. latina,** lateen sail. **a toda v.,** with all speed. **alzar velas,** to hoist sail. **en v.,** wakeful, without sleep. *inf* **estar entre dos velas,** to be tipsy
velación *f,* vigil; watch; marriage ceremony of veiling (gen. *pl*)
velada *f,* vigil; watch; evening party
velado *a* veiled; dim; (of voice) thick, indistinct
velador (-ra) *a* watchful; vigilant. *m,* candlestick; small round table; *Mexico* lampshade. *n* watcher, guard
velar *vi* to watch, be wakeful; work overtime or at night; *ecc* watch; *fig* (*with por*) watch over, defend; *vt* veil; conceal; *phot* blur; (*with prep a*) wake (corpse); sit with (patient at night)
veleidad *f,* velleity; fickleness
veleidoso *a* inconstant, changeable
velero (-ra) *m,* sailing ship; sailmaker. *n* candlemaker
veleta *f,* weathercock; float, quill (fishing). *mf* changeable person
velís *m, Mexico* suitcase.
vello *m,* down, soft hair
vellocino *m,* wool; fleece
vellón *m,* fleece; copper and silver alloy formerly used in sense of 'sterling'; *ant* copper coin
vellosidad *f,* downiness, hairiness
velloso *a* downy, hairy
velludo *a* hairy, downy. *m,* plush, velvet
velo *m,* veil; curtain; *ecc* humeral veil; excuse, pretext; *zool* velum. **v. del paladar,** soft palate. **correr el v.,** to disclose a secret. **tomar el v.,** to take the veil, become a nun
velocidad *f,* speed; *mech* velocity. *aer* **v. ascensional,** rate of climb. *mech* **v. del choque,** speed of impact. **en gran v.,** by passenger train. **en pequeña v.,** by goods train
velocímetro *m, Mexico* speedometer
velódromo *m,* velodrome
velón *m,* oil lamp
velorio *m, Lat. Am.* (funeral) wake; dull party
veloz *a* swift; quick-thinking or acting
vena *f,* (*bot anat*) vein; streak, veining (in wood or stone); *min* seam; underground spring; inspiration. **estar de v.,** to be in the mood; be inspired
venablo *m,* javelin
venado *m,* venison; deer
venal *a* venous; saleable; venal
venalidad *f,* saleableness; venality
vencedor (-ra) *a* conquering. *n* conqueror
vencer *vt* to conquer; defeat; overcome, rise above; outdo, excel; restrain, control (emotions); convince, persuade; *vi* succeed, triumph; *com* fall due, mature; *com* expire; *vr* control oneself; twist, incline; *Argentina* wear out
vencible *a* conquerable; superable
vencimiento *m,* defeat; conquest, victory; bend, twist (of things); *com* expiration; *com* maturity (of a bill)
venda *f,* bandage; fillet. **tener una v. en los ojos,** to be blind (to the truth)
vendaje *m,* bandage
vendar *vt* to bandage; *fig* blind (generally passions)
vendaval *m,* strong wind
vendedor (-ra) *a* selling. *n* seller
vender *vt* to sell; betray; *vr* sell oneself; be sold; risk all (for someone); *fig* give away (secret); (*with por*) sell under false pretences. **v. al contado,** to sell for cash. **v. al por mayor,** to sell wholesale. **v. al por menor,** to sell retail. **venderse caro,** to be unsociable
vendí *m, com* certificate of sale
vendible *a* purchasable; saleable
vendimia *f,* vintage; profit, fruits
vendimiar *vt* to harvest the grapes; take advantage of; *inf* kill
veneno *m,* poison; venom; danger (to health or soul); evil passion
venenoso *a* poisonous, venomous
venera *f,* scallop-shell (pilgrim's badge); badge, decoration
veneración *f,* respect, veneration
venerador (-ra) *a* venerating. *n* venerator, respector
venerar *vt* to venerate; worship
venéreo *a* venereal

venero *m*, spring of water; horary line on sundial; origin, genesis; *min* bed
venezolano (-na) *a* and *n* Venezuelan
vengador (-ra) *a* avenging. *n* avenger
venganza *f*, revenge
vengar *vt* to avenge; *vr* avenge oneself
vengativo *a* vindictive
venia *f*, pardon, forgiveness; permission; inclination of head (in greeting); *law* license issued to minors to manage their own estate
venial *a* venial
venialidad *f*, veniality
venida *f*, arrival, coming; return; attack (fencing); precipitancy
venidero *a* future
venideros *m pl*, successors; posterity
venir *vi irr* to come; arrive; turn up (at cards); fit, suit; consent, agree; *agr* grow; follow, come after, succeed; result, originate; occur (to the mind); feel, experience; (*with prep a + infin.*) happen finally, come to pass; (*with en*) decide, resolve; *vr* ferment. **v. a menos,** to deteriorate, decline; come upon evil days. **v. a pelo,** to come opportunely, be just right. **v. a ser,** to become. **venirse abajo,** to fall, collapse. **¿A qué viene este viaje?** What is the purpose of this journey? **el mes que viene,** next month. **El vestido te viene muy ancho,** The dress is too wide for you. **Me vino la idea de marcharme,** It occurred to me to leave. **en lo por venir,** in the future. *Pres. Ind.* **vengo, vienes, viene, venimos, venís, vienen.** *Pres. Part.* **viniendo.** *Fut.* **vendré,** etc. *Condit.* **vendría,** etc. *Preterite* **vine, viniste, vino, vinimos, vinisteis, vinieron.** *Pres. Subjunc.* **venga,** etc. *Imperf. Subjunc.* **viniese,** etc.
venta *f*, selling; sale; inn; *inf* wilderness; *pl com* turnover. **v. pública,** auction. **a la v.,** on sale. **la V. de la Mesilla,** the Gadsden Purchase
ventada *f*, gust of wind
ventaja *f*, advantage; profit
ventajoso *a* advantageous; *Lat. Am.* unscrupulous
ventana *f*, window. **v. de guillotina,** sash window. **v. salediza,** bay window. **echar algo por la v.,** to waste a thing
ventanal *m*, large window
ventanilla *f*, small window (as in railway compartments); grill (ticket office, bank, etc.); nostril
ventarrón *m*, high wind
ventear *v impers* to blow (of the wind); *vt* sniff air (animals); air, dry; investigate; *Lat. Am.* brand (an animal); *vr* be spoiled by air (tobacco, etc.)
ventero (-ra) *n* innkeeper
ventilación *f*, ventilation; ventilator; current of air
ventilador *m*, ventilating fan; ventilator
ventilar *vt* to ventilate; shake, winnow; air; discuss
ventisca *f*, snowstorm
ventiscar, ventisquear *v impers* to snow with a high wind
ventisquero *m*, glacier; snowfield, snowdrift; snowstorm
ventolera *f*, gust of wind; *inf* boastfulness; whim, caprice
ventolina *f*, *Lat. Am.* sudden gust (of wind)
ventor (-ra) *n* pointer (dog)
ventosa *f*, vent (pipes, etc.); *zool* sucker; *surg* cupping glass
ventoso *a* windy; flatulent
ventrículo *m*, ventricle
ventrílocuo (-ua) *a* ventriloquial. *n* ventriloquist
ventriloquia *f*, ventriloquism
ventrudo *a* big-bellied
ventura *f*, happiness; chance, hazard; risk, danger. **a la v.,** at a venture. **buena v.,** good luck. **por v.,** perhaps; by chance; fortunately
venturoso *a* fortunate
Venus *m*, Venus. *f*, beautiful woman, beauty
ver *vt irr* to see; witness, behold; visit; inspect, examine; consider; observe; know, understand; *Lat. Am.* look at, watch (television, etc.) (*with de + infin.*) try to; *vr* be seen; show oneself, appear; experience, find oneself; exchange visits; meet. **v. mundo,** to travel. **V. y creer,** Seeing is believing. **A mi v.,** In my opinion. **¡A v.!** Let's see!; Wait and see! **no tener nada que v. con,** to have no connection with, nothing to do with. **Veremos,** Time will tell. **Verse en la casa,** to be a stay-at-home. **Ya se ve,** Of course, Naturally. *Pres. Ind.* **veo, ves,** etc. *Imperf.* **veía,** etc. *Past Part.* **visto.** *Pres. Subjunc.* **vea,** etc. *Imperf. Subjunc.* **viese,** etc.
vera *f*, edge; border; shore. **a la v.,** on the edge, on the verge
veracidad *f*, truthfulness, veracity
veranadero *m*, summer pasture
veraneante *mf* summer resident, summer vacationist, holiday-maker
veranear *vi* to spend the summer
veraneo *m*, summer vacation, summer holidays, summering
veraniego *a* summer; light, unimportant
verano *m*, summer; dry season *WH*
veras *f pl*, reality, truth; fervor, earnestness. **de v.,** really; in earnest
veraz *a* truthful, veracious
verbal *a* verbal; oral
verbena *f*, *bot* verbena, vervain; fair held on eve of a saint's day
verbigracia *adv* for instance. *m*, example
verbo *m*, word; vow; *gram* verb. **v. activo** *or* **v. transitivo,** active or transitive verb. **v. auxiliar,** auxiliary verb. **v. intransitivo** *or* **v. neutro,** intransitive or neuter verb. **v. reflexivo** *or* **v. recíproco,** reflexive verb
verbosidad *f*, verbosity
verboso *a* verbose, prolix
verdad *f*, truth, veracity; reality. **a la v.,** indeed; without doubt. **en v.,** in truth; indeed. **cantar cuatro verdades a alguien,** to tell someone a few home truths. **la pura v.,** the plain truth
verdadero *a* true; real; sincere; truthful
verdal *a* green. **ciruela v.,** greengage
verde *a* green; unripe; fresh (vegetables); youthful; immature, undeveloped; obscene, dissolute. *m*, green (color); verdure, foliage
verdear *vi* to look green; be greenish; grow green
verdecer *vi irr* to grow green, be verdant. See **conocer**
verdegay *a* and *m*, bright green
verdemar *a* and *m*, sea-green
verdín *m*, verdure; mold; verdigris
verdinegro *a* dark green
verdor *m*, verdure; greenness; strength; youth (also *pl*)
verdoso *a* greenish
verdugo *m*, hangman, executioner; wale, mark; shoot of tree; switch; whip; *fig* scourge; tyrant
verdulera *f*, greengrocer; market woman; *inf* harridan
verdulería *f*, greengrocer's shop
verdulero *m*, greengrocer
verdura *f*, verdure; green garden produce, vegetables (gen. *pl*); *art* foliage; obscenity
verecundo *a* bashful
vereda *f*, footpath; sheep track; *Argentina, Chile, Peru* sidewalk
veredicto *m*, *law* verdict; judgment, considered opinion
verga *f*, steel bow of crossbow; *naut* yard; *inf* penis
vergajo *m*, rod (for punishment)
vergel *m*, orchard
vergonzoso (-sa) *a* shameful; bashful, shamefaced. *n* shy person
vergüenza *f*, shame; self-respect; bashfulness, timidity; shameful act; public punishment
vericueto *m*, narrow, stony path
verídico *a* veracious; true, exact
verificación *f*, verification, checking; *law* **v. de un testamento,** probate
verificador (-ra) *a* verifying, checking. *n* inspector, checker

verificar *vt* to prove; verify; *vr* take place, happen; check; come true. *elec* **v. las conexiones,** to check the connections
verisímil *a* credible, probable
verisimilitud *f,* credibility
verismo *m,* realism; truthfulness
verja *f,* grating, grill; railing
vermífugo *a* and *m,* vermifuge
vermut *m,* vermouth
vernáculo *a* native, vernacular
vernal *a* vernal
veronés (-esa) *a* and *n* Veronese
verónica *f, bot* speedwell; veronica (bullfighting)
verosímil *a* credible, probable
verosimilitud *f,* verisimilitude, probability
verraco *m,* boar
verruga *f, med* wart; *inf* bore; defect
versar *vi* to revolve; (*with sobre*) concern, deal with (book, etc.); *vr* become versed (in)
versátil *a zool* versatile; changeable; fickle
versatilidad *f, zool* versatility; changeableness; fickleness
versículo *m,* versicle; verse (of the Bible)
versificación *f,* versification
versificador (-ra) *n* versifier
versificar *vi* to write verses; *vt* put into verse, versify
versión *f,* translation; version; account
verso *m,* poetry, verse; stanza; line (of a poem). **v. suelto,** blank verse
vertebrado *a* and *m, zool* vertebrate
vertedor *m,* drain, sewer; chute
verter *vt irr* to pour, spill; empty; translate; *vi* flow. See **entender**
vertical *a* and *f,* vertical
verticalidad *f,* verticality
vértice *m,* vertex
vertiente *a* emptying. *mf,* slope, incline; watershed; *Lat. Am. also* spring (of water)
vertiginoso *a* giddy; vertiginous
vértigo *m,* giddiness, faintness
vesícula *f,* blister; (*anat bot*) vesicle
vespertino *a* evening
vestíbulo *m,* hall, vestibule foyer
vestido *m,* dress; clothes; *Panama, Peru* suit
vestidura *f,* garment; *pl* vestments
vestigio *m,* footprint; trace, mark; remains; *fig* vestige
vestir *vt irr* to clothe, dress; adorn; embellish (ideas); *fig* disguise (truth); simulate, pretend; *vi* be dressed; *vr* dress oneself; *fig* be covered. See **pedir**
vestuario *m,* clothing, dress; *theat* wardrobe or dressing room; *ecc* vestry; *mil* uniform
Vesubio Vesuvius
veta *f,* vein; stripe, rib (fabric)
veterano (-na) *a* and *n* veteran
veterinaria *f,* veterinary science
veterinario *a* veterinary. *m,* veterinary surgeon
veto *m,* veto; prohibition
vetustez *f,* antiquity, oldness
vetusto *a* ancient, very old
vez *f,* time, occasion; turn; *pl* proxy, deputy, substitute. **a la v.,** simultaneously. **alguna v.,** sometime. **a su v.,** in its (her, his, their) turn. **a veces,** sometimes. **de una v.,** at the one time. **de v. en cuando,** from time to time. **en v. de,** instead of. **hacer las veces de,** to be a substitute for. **otra v.,** again. **Su cuarto es dos veces más grande que éste,** His room is twice as large as this one
vía *f,* way; road; railway track or gauge; *anat* tract; (mystic) way; route; conduct; *pl* procedure. **v. ancha,** broad gauge (railway). **v. angosta,** narrow gauge. **v. de agua,** *naut* leak. *law* **v. ejecutiva,** seizure, attachment. **v. férrea,** railway. **v. láctea,** Milky Way. **v. muerta,** railway siding. **v. principal,** main line. **v. pública,** public thoroughfare. **v. romana,** Roman road. **v. secundaria,** *rw* side line. **por v. aérea,** by air, by airplane
viabilidad *f,* viability
viable *a* viable; practicable; workable; passable
viaducto *m,* viaduct
viajante *mf* traveling salesman, commercial traveler
viajar *vi* to travel, journey, voyage
viaje *m,* journey; voyage; water-supply; travel journal; *naut* **v. de ensayo,** trial trip. **v. redondo,** circular tour. **¡Buen v.!** Have a good trip! Bon voyage!
viajero (-ra) *a* traveling. *n* traveler; passenger
vianda *f,* viand, victual (gen. *pl*); meal
viático *m, ecc* viaticum; provisions for a journey
víbora *f,* viper; *Lat. Am.* poisonous snake
viborezno *m,* young viper
vibración *f,* vibration; jar, jolt; thrill
vibrante *a* shaking; vibrant; thrilling
vibrar *vt* to shake, oscillate; *vi* vibrate; jar, jolt; quiver, thrill
vibratorio *a* vibratory, vibrative
vicaría *f,* vicarage; vestry
vicario *a* vicarious. *m,* vicar; curate; deputy
vicecónsul *m,* vice-consul
viceconsulado *m,* vice-consulate
vicepresidente (-ta) *n* vice president
vicesecretario (-ia) *n* assistant secretary
viciar *vt* to corrupt; adulterate; forge; annul; interpret maliciously, misconstrue; *vr* become vicious
vicio *m,* vice; defect; error, fraud; bad habit; excess, exaggerated desire; viciousness (animals); overgrowth (plants); peevishness (children). **tener el v. de,** to have the bad habit of. **el v. del juego,** fondness for gambling
vicioso *a* vicious; vigorous, overgrown; abundant; *inf* spoilt (children)
vicisitud *f,* vicissitude
víctima *f,* victim
victimar *vt, Lat. Am.* to murder
victimario, -a *mf, Lat. Am.* killer, murderer
¡víctor! *interj* Victor!; Long live!; Hurrah!
victoria *f,* victory, triumph; victoria
victoriano (-na) *a* and *n* Victorian
victorioso *a* victorious
vicuña *f* vicuna
vid *f,* vine
vida *f,* life; livelihood; human being; biography; vivacity. **v. airada,** dissolute life. **la v. allende la muerte,** life after death. **de por v.,** for life. **darse buena v.,** to live comfortably; enjoy one's life. **dar mala v.,** to ill-treat. **en la v.,** in life; never. **ganarse la v.,** to make one's living
vidente *m,* clairvoyant; seer
videograbación *f,* videotape
vidriar *vt* to glaze (earthenware)
vidriera *f,* glass window (gen. stained or colored)
vidriero *m,* glazier. *a* made of glass
vidrio *m,* glass; anything made of glass; fragile thing; touchy person. **v. inastillable,** safety-glass. **v. jaspeado,** frosted glass. **v. pintado** *or* **v. de color,** stainedglass. **v. plano,** plate glass. **v. soplado,** blown glass
vidrioso *a* brittle; slippery; fragile; hypersensitive; *fig* glazed (eyes)
vieja *f,* old woman
viejo *a* old; ancient; former; old-fashioned; worn out. *m,* old man
Viena Vienna
vienés (-esa) *a* and *n* Viennese
viento *m,* wind; scent (of game, etc.); guy (rope); upheaval; vanity. **v. en popa,** *naut* following wind; without a hitch, prosperously. **vientos alisios,** tradewinds. **v. terral,** land wind. **a los cuatro vientos,** in all directions. **contra v. y marea,** *fig* against all obstacles. **correr malos vientos,** to be unfavorable (of circumstances). **refrescar el v.,** to stiffen (of the breeze)
vientre *m,* stomach; belly; vitals; *law* venter
viernes *m,* Friday. **V. Santo,** Good Friday
viga *f,* beam, rafter; girder; joist; mill beam. **v. maestra,** main beam or girder

vigente *a* valid; in force (laws, customs)
vigésimo *a* twentieth
vigía *f*, watch tower; (gen. *m*) look-out, watch
vigilancia *f*, watchfulness, vigilance; watch patrol
vigilante *a* watchful. *m*, watcher; watchman. **v. escolar,** truant officer
vigilar *vi* to watch over; supervise
vigilia *f*, vigil; wakefulness; night study; *ecc* vigil, eve; wake; *mil* watch. **día de v.,** fast-day
vigor *m*, strength; activity; vigor, efficiency; validity
vigorizar *vt* to invigorate; exhilarate; encourage
vigoroso *a* strong, vigorous
vihuela *f*, lute
vil *a* vile, infamous; base; despicable; untrustworthy
vileza *f*, baseness; vileness, infamy
vilipendiar *vt* to revile
vilipendio *m*, vilification; contempt
villa *f*, villa; country house; town. **v. miseria** *Argentina* slum
villancico *m*, carol
villanesco *a* peasant; rustic, country
villanía *f*, humbleness of birth; vileness; villainy
villano (-na) *n* peasant. *a* rustic, country; boorish; base
vilo, en *adv* hanging in the air; *fig* in suspense
vilorta *f*, hoop; *mech* washer
vilote *mf*, *Lat. Am.* chicken, coward
vinagre *m*, vinegar
vinagrera *f*, vinegar bottle; table cruet; *Lat. Am.* heartburn
vinagreta *f*, vinegar sauce
vinagroso *a* vinegary; *inf* bad-tempered, acid
vinatero (-ra) *n* wine merchant. *a* wine
vincapervinca *f*, *bot* periwinkle
vinculación *f*, *law* entail
vincular *vt law* to entail; *fig* base; *vr* perpetuate. *a law* entail
vínculo *m*, tie, bond; *law* entail
vindicación *f*, vindication; justification; excuse
vindicador (-ra) *n* vindicator. *a* vindicative
vindicar *vt* to avenge; vindicate; justify; excuse
vindicativo *a* avenging; vindicatory
vinería *f*, *Lat. Am.* wineshop
vinícola *a* wine-growing; wine
vinicultor (-ra) *n* wine grower, viniculturalist
vinicultura *f*, wine-growing, viniculture
vinificación *f*, vinification
vinillo *m*, thin, weak wine
vino *m*, wine; fermented fruit juice. **v. de Oporto,** port wine. **v. generoso,** well-matured wine. **v. tinto,** red wine
vinoso *a* vinous; fond of wine
viña *f*, vineyard
viñador *m*, vineyard-keeper; vine-cultivator
viñedo *m*, vineyard
viñeta *f*, vignette
viola *f*, *mus* viola; *bot* viola, pansy. *mf* viola player
violación *f*, violation; infringement
violado *a* violet
violador (-ra) *n* violator. *m*, seducer
violar *vt* to violate; infringe; rape; spoil, harm
violencia *f*, violence; outrage; rape
violentar *vt* to force; falsify, misinterpret; force an entrance; *vr* force oneself
violento *a* violent; repugnant; impetuous, hasty-tempered; unnatural, false; unreasonable
violeta *f*, *bot* violet. *m*, violet color. **v. de febrero,** snowdrop
violín *m*, violin
violinista *mf* violinist
violón *m*, double-bass, bass viol; double-bass player
violoncelista *mf* cellist
violoncelo *m*, cello
viperino *a* viperine; venomous, evil
vira *f*, welt (of a shoe); dart
viraje *m*, *aut* change of direction; bend, turn
virar *vt naut* to put about; *phot* tone; *vi naut* tack; *aut* change direction. **v. de bordo,** *naut* to lay off
virgen *mf* virgin. *f*, *ast* Virgo
virginal *a* virginal; pure, unspotted
virginidad *f*, virginity
virgulilla *f*, comma; cedilla; accent; apostrophe; fine line
viril *a* manly, virile. *m*, clear glass screen
virilidad *f*, virility
virote *m*, arrow; shaft; *inf* young blood; *Mexico* roll (bread)
virreina *f*, vicereine
virreinato *m*, viceroyship
virrey *m*, viceroy
virtual *a* virtual; implicit
virtualidad *f*, virtuality
virtualmente *adv* virtually; tacitly
virtud *f*, virtue; power; strength, courage; efficacy. **en v. de,** in virtue of
virtuosidad *f*, virtuosity
virtuoso *a* virtuous; powerful, efficacious. *m*, virtuoso, artist
viruela *f*, smallpox (gen. *pl*)
virulencia *f*, virulence
virulento *a* virulent
virus *m*, virus
viruta *f*, wood-shaving
vis cómica *f*, the comic spirit
visa *f*, *Lat. Am.* visa
visado *m*, *Spain* visa
visaje *m*, grimace
visar *vt* to visa; endorse
viscosidad *f*, viscosity
viscoso *a* viscous, sticky
visera *f*, visor; eye-shade; peak (of a cap)
visibilidad *f*, visibility
visillo *m*, window-blind
visión *f*, seeing, sight; queer sight; vision; hallucination; *inf* scarecrow, sight
visionario (-ia) *a* and *n* visionary
visir *m*, vizier. **gran v.,** grand vizier
visita *f*, visit; visitor; inspection. **v. de cumplido,** formal call. **v. de sanidad,** health inspection. **hacer una v.,** to pay a call
visitación *f*, visitation; visit
visitador (-ra) *n* regular visitor. *m*, inspector. *a* visiting; inspecting
visitar *vt* to visit; inspect; *med* attend; *ecc* examine. **v. los monumentos,** to see the sights, go sightseeing
visiteo *m*, receiving or paying of visits
vislumbrar *vt* to glimpse; surmise, conjecture
vislumbre *f*, glimmer, glimpse; surmise, glimmering (gen. *pl*); semblance, appearance
viso *m*, view point, elevation; glare; shimmer, gleam; colored slip under transparent dress; semblance. **de v.,** prominent (persons)
visón *m*, mink
víspera *f*, eve; *ecc* day before festival; prelude, preliminary. *pl ecc* vespers. **en vísperas de,** on the eve of
vista *f*, vision, sight; view; eyes; eyesight; meeting, interview; *law* hearing (of a case); apparition; picture of a view; clear idea; connection (of things); proposition, intention; glance; *pl* window, door, skylight, opening for light. **v. corta,** short sight. **v. de lince,** sharp eyes. **a primera v.,** at first sight. **a v. de,** in sight of; in the presence of. **conocer de v.,** to know by sight. **dar una v.,** to take a look. **doble v.,** second sight; clairvoyance. **en v. de,** in view of, considering. **estar a la v.,** to be evident. *inf* **hacer la v. gorda,** to turn a blind eye. **¡Hasta la v.!** Good-bye! **perder de v. (a),** to lose sight of
vistazo *m*, glance. **echar un v.,** to cast a glance
visto *past part irr* **ver.** *law* whereas. **bien v.,** approved. **mal v.,** disapproved. **V. Bueno (V^o^ B^o^)** Approved, Passed. **v. que,** since, inasmuch as
vistoso *a* showy, gaudy; beautiful

visual *a* visual
vital *a* vital; essential
vitalicio *a* lifelong. *m,* life-insurance
vitalidad *f,* vitality
vitamina *f,* vitamin
vitando *a* odious; bad; vital
vitela *f,* vellum
vitícola *a* viticultural. *mf* viticulturist
viticultura *f,* viticulture
¡vítor! *interj* Victor!; Hurrah!; Long live!
vitorear *vt* to cheer; applaud, acclaim
vítreo *a* glassy, vitreous
vitrificar(se) *vt* and *vr* to vitrify
vitrina *f,* show-case; display cabinet; *Argentina, Chile, Venezuela* (shop) window
vitriólico *a* vitriolic
vitriolo *m,* vitriol
vitualla *f,* (gen. *pl*) victuals, provisions
vituperable *a* blameworthy, vituperable
vituperador (-ra) *a* vituperative. *n* vituperator
vituperar *vt* to censure, blame, vituperate
vituperio *m,* vituperation
viuda *f,* widow
viudedad *f,* widow's pension
viudez *f,* widowhood, widowerhood
viudita *f,* young widow
viudo *m,* widower
¡viva! *interj* Long live!; Hurrah!
vivacidad *f,* vivacity, gaiety; ardor, warmth; brightness
vivamente *adv* quickly, lively
vivandera *f,* vivandiere
vivandero *m,* sutler
vivaque *m,* bivouac
vivaquear *vi* to bivouac
vivar *m,* warren; aquarium; breeding ground; well (of a fishing boat); *vt, Lat. Am.* to cheer, shout hurrah (for . . .)
vivaracho *a inf* sprightly, cheery, lively
vivaz *a* vigorous; quick-witted; sprightly; *bot* perennial; vivid, bright
víveres *m pl,* provisions; *mil* stores
vivero *m, bot* nursery; vivarium; small marsh
viveza *f,* quickness, briskness; vehemence; perspicuity; witticism; resemblance; brightness (eyes, colors); thoughtless word or act
vividero *a* habitable
vívido *a poet* vivid
vividor (-ra) *a* frugal, thrifty; dissolute. *n* liver; long-liver; libertine, rake
vivienda *f,* dwelling
viviente *a* living
vivificación *f,* vivification
vivificante *a* vivifying
vivificar *vt* to vivify; comfort
vivir *vi* to be alive, live; last, endure; (*with en*) inhabit. *m,* life. **¿Quién vive?** *mil* Who goes there? **v. a costillas ajenas,** to live at someone else's expense, live off someone else
vivisección *f,* vivisection
vivo *a* alive; intense, strong; bright; *mil* active; subtle, ingenious; precipitate; *fig* lasting, enduring; diligent; hasty; persuasive, expressive. *m,* edge. **al v., a lo v.,** to the life; vividly
vizcaíno (-na) *a* and *n* Biscayan
Vizcaya, el Golfo de the Bay of Biscay
vizconde *m,* viscount
vizcondesa *f,* viscountess
vocablo *m,* word
vocabulario *m,* vocabulary
vocación *f,* vocation; trade, profession
vocal *a* vocal; oral. *f, gram* vowel. *mf* voting member
vocalización *f,* vocalization
vocalizar *vi* to vocalize
voceador, -a *mf, Lat. Am.* newsvendor
vocear *vi* to cry out, shout; *vt* proclaim; call for; acclaim
vocerío *m,* shouting; clamor, outcry
vociferación *f,* vociferation, outcry
vociferar *vt* to boast (of); *vi* shout, vociferate
vocinglería *f,* clamor; babble, chatter
vocinglero *a* vociferous; prattling, babbling
vodca *m,* vodka
volada *f,* short flight; *Mexico* flat tire, flat. *mech* **v. de grúa,** jib
voladura *f,* explosion; blasting
volandas (en), volandillas (en) *adv* in the air, as though flying; *inf* in a trice
volante *a* flying; wandering, restless. *m,* frill, flounce; screen; fan (of a windmill); *mech* flywheel; *mech* balance wheel (watches); coiner's stamp mill; shuttlecock. *aut* **v. de dirección,** steering-wheel
volantón (-ona) *n* fledgeling
volar *vi irr* to fly (birds, insects, aviation); float in the air; hurry; disappear suddenly; burst, explode; jut out (buttresses, etc.); cleave (air) (arrows, etc.); *fig* spread (rumors); *vt* explode; blast; anger. See **contar**
volatería *f,* fowling; fowls; poultry; flock of birds; *fig* crowd (of ideas)
volátil *a* volatile; inconstant
volatilizar *vt* to volatilize
volatinero (-ra) *n* tight-rope walker, acrobat
volcán *m,* volcano; violent passion. **v. extinto,** extinct volcano
volcánico *a* volcanic
volcar *vt irr* to overturn, capsize; make dizzy; cause a change (of opinion); annoy; *vi* overturn. *Pres. Ind.* **vuelco, vuelcas, vuelca, vuelcan.** *Preterite* **volqué, volcaste,** etc. *Pres. Subjunc.* **vuelque, vuelques, vuelque, vuelquen**
volear *vt* to strike in the air, volley; *agr* sow broadcast
voleo *m,* volley (tennis, etc.); high kick; straight punch
volframio *m,* wolfram, tungsten
volición *f,* volition
volquete *m,* tip-cart
voltaico *a* voltaic
voltaje *m,* voltage
voltario *a* versatile; capricious, headstrong
volteador (-ra) *n* acrobat
voltear *vt* to whirl, turn; overturn; change place (of); *arch* construct an arch or vault; *vi* revolve; tumble, twirl (acrobats)
volteo *m,* turning, revolution; whirl; overturning; twirling; *elec* voltage
voltereta *f,* somersault
volteriano *a* Voltairian
voltímetro *m,* voltmeter
voltio *m,* volt
volubilidad *f,* inconstancy, fickleness
voluble *a* easily turned; inconstant, changeable; *bot* twining
volumen *m,* bulk, size; volume, book
voluminoso *a* voluminous, bulky
voluntad *f,* will, volition; wish; decree; free will; intention; affection; free choice; consent. **a v.,** at will; by choice. **de buena v.,** of good will; willingly, with pleasure. **de su propia v.,** of one's own free will. **mala v.,** hostility, ill-will
voluntario (-ia) *a* voluntary; strong-willed. *n* volunteer
voluntarioso *a* self-willed
voluptuosidad *f,* voluptuousness
voluptuoso *a* voluptuous
volver *vt irr* to turn; turn over; return; pay back; direct, aim; translate; restore; change, alter; close (doors, etc.); vomit; reflect, reverberate; *vi* come back; continue (speech, etc.); bend, turn (roads); (*with prep a + infin.*) do something again (e.g. **v. a leer,** to read over again); (*with por + noun*) protect; *vr* become; go sour; turn. **v. a las filas,** *mil* to reduce to the ranks. **v. en sí,** to regain consciousness. **v. la cabeza,** to turn one's head. **volverse atrás,** *fig* to back out. **volverse loco,** to go mad. See **resolver**

vomitar *vt* to vomit; *fig* vomit forth; *fig* spit out (curses, etc.); *inf* burst into confidences
vomitivo *a* and *m*, emetic
vómito *m*, vomit
voracidad *f*, voracity
vorágine *f*, vortex, whirlpool
voraz *a* voracious; *Mexico* bold
vórtice *m*, whirlpool; *fig* vortex
vortiginoso *a* vortical
vos *pers pron 2nd pers sing* and *pl* you.
vosear *vt* to use the pronoun *vos*; address (someone) as *vos*
vosotros, vosotras *pers pron 2nd pers pl mf* you
votación *f*, voting
votador (-ra) *n* voter; swearer
votar *vi* and *vt* to vote; make a vow; curse, swear. **v. una proposición de confianza,** to pass a vote of confidence
votivo *a* votive
voto *m*, vote; vow; voter; prayer; curse; desire; opinion. **v. de calidad,** casting vote. **v. de confianza,** vote of confidence
voz *f*, voice; sound, noise; cry, shout (gen. *pl*); word; expression; *mus* singer or voice; *gram* mood; vote; rumor; instruction, order. **v. común,** general opinion. **a voces,** in a shout, loudly. **llevar la v. cantante,** *inf* to have the chief say
vuelco *m*, overturning
vuelo *m*, flight; wing; *sew* skirt-fullness; ruffle, frill; *arch* buttress. **v. a ciegas,** *aer* blind flying. **v. de distancia,** long-distance flight. **v. de patrulla,** patrol or reconnaissance flight. **v. de reconocimento,** reconnaissance flight. **v. nocturno,** *aer* night flying. **v. sin parar,** non-stop flight. **al v.,** on the wing; in passing; quickly. **alzar** (*or* **levantar**) **el v.,** to take flight
vuelta *f*, revolution, turn; bend, curve; return; restitution; recompense; repetition; wrong side; beating; *sew* facing, cuff; change (money); conning (lessons, etc.); stroll, walk; change; vault, ceiling; *sport* round; *mech* **vueltas por minuto,** revolutions per minute. **a v. de correo,** by return mail, by return of post. **a la v.,** on returning; overleaf. **dar la v.,** to turn round, make a détour. **dar una v.,** to take a stroll. **dar vueltas,** to revolve; search (for); consider. **media v.,** half turn
vuelto *m*, *Lat. Am.* change (money returned)
vuestro, vuestra, vuestros, vuestras *poss pron 2nd pl mf* your, yours
vulcanizar *vt* to vulcanize
vulgar *a* popular; general, common; vernacular; mediocre
vulgaridad *f*, vulgarity
vulgarismo *m*, vulgarism
vulgarización *f*, vulgarization; popularization
vulgarizar *vt* to vulgarize; popularize; translate into the vernacular; *vr* grow vulgar
vulgata *f*, Vulgate
vulgo *m*, mob
vulnerabilidad *f*, vulnerability
vulnerable *a* vulnerable
vulpeja *f*, vixen
vulpino *a* vulpine; crafty

wagneriano *a* Wagnerian
wáter *m*, toilet, water-closet
whisky *m*, whiskey

xenofobia *f*, xenophobia, hatred of foreigners
xilófago *a* xylophagous, wood-boring. *m*, wood-borer
xilófono *m*, xylophone
xilografía *f*, xylography

y *conjunc* and. See **e**
ya *adv* already; formerly; soon; now; finally; immediately; well, yes, quite. Used of past, present and future time, and in various idiomatic ways. **Ha venido ya,** He has already come. **¡Ya caerá!** His time will come!, He will get his comeuppance! **Ya vendrá,** He will come soon. **¡Ya voy!** Coming! **¡Ya lo creo!** Of course!; I should think so! **¡Ya!** Quite!; I understand. **ya no,** no longer. **ya que,** since
yacaré *m*, *Lat. Am.* alligator
yacente *a* recumbent, reclining (statues, etc.)
yacer *vi irr* to be lying at full length; lie (in the grave); be situated, be; lie (with), sleep (with); graze by night. *Pres. Ind.* **yazgo** *or* **yazco, yaces,** etc. *Pres. Subjunc.* **yazga** *or* **yazca,** etc.
yacija *f*, bed; couch; tomb
yacimiento *m*, *geol* bed, deposit
yacio *m*, india-rubber tree
yaguré *m*, *Lat. Am.* skunk
yak *m*, yak
yanqui *a* and *mf contemptuous and offensive* North American (gen. U.S.A.)
yarda *f*, yard (English measure)
yate *m*, *naut* yacht
ye *f*, name of the letter Y
yegua *f*, mare
yelmo *m*, helmet
yema *f*, bud; yolk (of egg); sweetmeat; *fig* best of anything. **y. del dedo,** finger-tip
yerba mate *m* mate (drink)
yermo *a* uninhabited, deserted; uncultivated. *m*, wilderness, desert
yerno *m*, son-in-law
yerro *m*, error; mistake; fault
yerto *a* stiff, rigid
yesca *f*, tinder; fuel, stimulus
yeso *m*, gypsum, calcium sulphate; plaster; plaster cast
yesquero *m*, *Lat. Am.* (cigaret) lighter
yídish *n* and *a* Yiddish
yip *m* jeep
yo *pers pron 1st sing mf* I. **el yo,** the ego
yodo *m*, iodine
yuca *f*, yucca
yucateco (-ca) *a* and *n* Yucatecan
yugo *m*, yoke; nuptial tie; oppression; *naut* transom; *fig* **sacudir el y.,** to throw off the yoke
yugular *a anat* jugular. *m*, jugular vein
Yukón, el the Yukon
yunque *m*, anvil; patient, undaunted person; hard worker; *anat* incus

yunta *f*, yoke (of oxen, etc.)
yute *m*, jute fiber or fabric
yuxtaponer *vt irr* to juxtapose. See **poner**
yuxtaposición *f*, juxtaposition

Z

zabarcera *f*, vegetable seller
zaborda *f*, **zabordamiento** *m*, *naut* grounding, stranding
zabordar *vi naut* to run aground, strand
zacatín *m*, street or square where clothes are sold
zafadura *f*, *Lat. Am.* dislocation, sprain
zafar *vt* to embellish, garnish, adorn; *naut* lighten (a ship); *vr* escape, hide oneself; (*with de*) excuse oneself, avoid; get rid of
zafarrancho *m*, *naut* clearing the decks; *inf* damage; *inf* scuffle
zafiedad *f*, rudeness, ignorance, boorishness
zafio *a* rude, unlettered, boorish
zafiro *m*, sapphire
zafra *f*, olive oil container; sugar crop or factory; *min* waste
zaga *f*, rear. *m*, last player. **en z.,** behind. *inf* **no quedarse en z.,** not to be left behind; be not inferior
zagal *m*, youth; strong, handsome lad; young shepherd; full skirt
zagala *f*, maiden, girl; young shepherdess
zagual *m*, paddle
zaguán *m*, entrance hall; vestibule
zaguero *a* loitering, straggling. *m*, *sport* back
zahareño *a* untamable, wild (birds); unsociable, disdainful
zaherimiento *m*, upbraiding; nagging
zaherir *vt irr* to upbraid, reprehend; nag. See **herir**
zahína *f*, *bot* sorghum
zahón *m*, leather apron (worn by cowboys)
zahorí *m*, soothsayer; waterfinder; sagacious person
zahúrda *f*, pigsty
zaino *a* treacherous; vicious (horses); chestnut (horses); black (cows)
zalagarda *f*, ambush; skirmish; snare, trap; *inf* trick, ruse; *inf* mock battle
zalamería *f*, adulation, flattery
zalamero (-ra) *a* wheedling, flattering. *n* flatterer
zalea *f*, sheepskin
zalear *vt* to shake; frighten away (dogs)
zalema *f*, salaam
zamacuco *m*, *inf* oaf, dolt; *inf* drinking bout
zamarra *f*, sheepskin jacket
zamarrear *vt* to worry, shake (prey); *fig inf* beat up; *inf* floor, confound
zambo *a* knock-kneed
zambomba *f*, rustic drum
zambuco *m*, *inf* concealment (especially of cards)
zambullida *f*, plunge, submersion; thrust (in fencing)
zambullir *vt* to plunge in water, submerge; *vr* dive; hide oneself, cover oneself
zampar *vt* to conceal (one thing in another); eat greedily; (*with en*) arrive suddenly
zampatortas *mf inf* glutton
zampoña *f*, rustic flute; *inf* unimportant work
zanahoria *f*, carrot
zanca *f*, long leg (birds); *inf* long thin leg; *arch* stringboard (of stairs)
zancada *f*, swift stride
zancadilla *f*, trip (wrestling); *inf* trick, deceit. **echar la z. (a),** to trip up
zancajear *vi* to stride about
zancajo *m*, heel-bone; torn heel (stocking, shoe); *inf* ill-shaped person. *inf* **no llegarle al z.,** to be immensely inferior to someone
zancajoso *a* flatfooted; slovenly
zanco *m*, stilt. *fig inf* **andar** (*or* **estar**) **en zancos,** to have gone up in the world
zancudo *a* long-legged
zangandungo (-ga) *n inf* loafer
zanganear *vi inf* to loaf
zángano *m*, *ent* drone; *inf* idler, parasite
zangolotear *vt inf* to shake violently; *vi* fuss about, bustle; *vr* rattle (windows, etc.)
zangoloteo *m*, shaking; rattling
zanguango *m*, *inf* lazybones
zanja *f*, trench, ditch; drain; furrow
zanjar *vt* to excavate; *fig* remove (obstacles)
Zanzíbar Zanzibar
zapa *f*, shovel, spade; *mil* sap; sandpaper
zapador *m*, *mil* sapper
zapapico *m*, pick-ax; mattock
zapaquilda *f*, *inf* she-cat
zapar *vi mil* to sap
zaparrastrar *vi inf* to trail along the floor (dresses)
zapata *f*, half-boot; piece of leather used to stop creaking of a hinge; *arch* lintel; (*naut mech*) shoe
zapatazo *m*, blow with a shoe; fall, thud; stamping (horses); flap (of sail)
zapateado *m*, dance in which rhythmic drumming of heels plays important part
zapatear *vt* to hit with a shoe; stamp feet; drum heels (in dancing); *inf* ill-treat; thump ground (rabbits); *vi* stamp (horses); *naut* flap (sails); *vr fig* stand one's ground
zapateo *m*, stamping; rhythmic drumming of heels
zapatera *f*, cobbler's wife; woman who makes or sells shoes
zapatería *f*, shoemaking; shoe shop
zapatero *m*, shoemaker; shoe seller. **z. remendón,** cobbler
zapateta *f*, caper, leap
zapatilla *f*, slipper; trotter, hoof
zapato *m*, shoe. **z. de hule** *Mexico*, galosh, rubber
zapatón *m*, *Lat. Am.* galosh, overshoe
¡zape! *interj inf* shoo! Used for frightening away cats; exclamation of surprise or warning
zapear *vt* to scare away cats; *inf* frighten off
zaque *m*, leather bottle, wineskin; *inf* drunkard, sot
zaquizamí *m*, garret; dirty little house or room
zar *m*, tsar
zarabanda *f*, saraband; *inf* racket, row
zaragata *f*, *inf* fight, brawl
Zaragoza Saragossa
zaragozano (-na) *a* and *n* Saragossan
zaragüelles *m*, *pl* wide pleated breeches
zaranda *f*, sieve, strainer, colander
zarandajas *f*, *pl inf* odds and ends
zarandar *vt* to sieve (grapes, grain); strain; *inf* pick out the best; *vr inf* move quickly
zarandillo *m*, small sieve, strainer; *inf* a live wire, energetic person; Spanish dance
zaraza *f*, chintz
zarcillo *m*, earring; *bot* tendril; *agr* trowel
zarco *a* light blue (generally eyes or water)
zarpa *f*, *naut* weighing anchor; paw
zarpada *f*, blow with a paw
zarpar *vt* and *vi naut* to weigh anchor, sail
zarza *f*, *bot* bramble, blackberry bush
zarzal *m*, bramble patch
zarzamora *f*, blackberry
zarzaparrilla *f*, sarsaparilla
zarzo *m*, hurdle; wattle
zarzoso *a* brambly
zarzuela *f*, comic opera; musical comedy
zarzuelista *mf* writer or composer of comic operas
¡zas! *m*, sound of a bang or blow

zascandil *m, inf* busybody
zatara *f,* raft
zeda *f,* name of the letter Z
zedilla *f,* cedilla
zenit *m.* See **cenit**
zepelín *m,* Zeppelin
zeta *f.* See **zeda**
zigzag *m,* zigzag
zigzaguear *vi* to zigzag
zinc *m,* zinc
zipizape *m, inf* row, quarrel
zoca *f,* square
zócalo *m, arch* socle; *Mexico* main square
Zócalo, el *m,* the Main Square (of Mexico City)
zoclo *m,* clog, sabot
zoco *m,* square; market; clog, sabot
zodiaco *m,* zodiac
zona *f,* girdle, band; strip (of land); zone; *med* shingles. **z. de depresión,** air pocket. **z. templada,** temperate zone. **z. tórrida,** torrid zone
zonal *a* zonal
zoncear *vi, Lat. Am.* to behave stupidly
zonzo, -a *a, Lat. Am.* silly, stupid
zoología *f,* zoology
zoológico *a* zoological
zoólogo *m,* zoologist
zopenco *a inf* oafish
zopo *a* maimed, deformed (hands, feet)
zoquete *m, carp* block; dowel; hunk of bread; *inf* short, ugly man; *inf* dunderhead
zorcico *m,* Basque song and dance
zorra *f,* vixen; fox; *inf* cunning person; *inf* prostitute; *inf* drinking bout; truck, dray
zorrera *f,* foxhole
zorrería *f,* foxiness; *inf* cunning
zorro *m,* fox; fox-skin; *inf* knave
zóster *f, med* shingles
zote *a* dull, ignorant
zozobra *f, naut* foundering, capsizing; anxiety
zozobrar *vi naut* to founder, sink; *naut* plunge, shiver; be anxious, vacillate
zueco *m,* sabot, clog
zulú *a* and *mf* Zulu
zumaque *m, bot* sumach tree; *inf* wine
zumba *f,* cow bell; jest
zumbar *vi* to buzz, hum; ring (of the ears); whizz; twang (of a guitar, etc.); *fig inf* be on the brink
zumbido *m,* buzzing, humming; ringing (in the ears); whizz; twanging (of a guitar, etc.); *inf* slap, blow
zumbón *a* waggish, jocose
zumo *m,* sap; juice; profit, advantage
zumoso *a* succulent, juicy
zupia *f,* wine lees; cloudy wine; *fig* dregs
zurcido *m, sew* darn; mend
zurcidor (-ra) *n* darner, mender. **z. de voluntades,** *humorous* pimp
zurcidura *f,* darning; mending; darn
zurcir *vt* to darn; mend, repair; join; *fig* concoct, weave
zurdo *a* left-handed
zurra *f, tan* currying; *inf* spanking; *inf* quarrel
zurrador *m, tan* currier, dresser
zurrapa *f,* (gen. *pl*) sediment, lees, dregs
zurrar *vt* to curry (leather); *inf* spank; *inf* dress down, scold
zurriagazo *m,* lash with a whip; *fig* blow of fate
zurriago *m,* whip
zurribanda *f, inf* whipping; fight, quarrel
zurriburri *m, inf* ragamuffin; mob; uproar
zurrido *m, inf* blow; dull noise
zurrir *vi* to have a confused sound, hum, rattle
zurrón *m,* shepherd's pouch; leather bag; *bot* husk
zutano (-na) *n inf* so-and-so, such a one

ENGLISH-SPANISH
Dictionary

A

a *n* (letter) a, *f*; *mus* la, *m*. **symphony in A major,** sinfonía en la mayor, *f*. **A1,** de primera clase; de primera calidad, excelente

a, an *indef art*. (one) un, *m*; una, *f*; (with weights, quantities) el, *m*; la, *f*; (with weeks, months, years, etc.) por, al, *m*; a la, *f*. The indef. art. is omitted in Spanish before nouns expressing nationality, profession, rank, and generally before a noun in apposition. It is omitted also before certain words such as **mil, ciento, otro, semejante, medio,** etc. Not translated in book titles, e.g., **A History of Spain,** Historia de España. *prep* a. In phrases such as **to go hunting,** ir a cazar. As prefix, see **abed, ashore,** etc. **Madrid, a Spanish city,** Madrid, ciudad de España. **three times a month,** tres veces al mes. **ten dollars an hour,** diez dólares por hora. **thirty miles an hour,** treinta millas por hora. **a certain Mrs. Brown,** una tal Sra. Brown. **a thousand soldiers,** mil soldados. **half an hour later,** media hora después

aback *adv naut* en facha; *fig* sorprendido, desconcertado. **to take a.,** desconcertar, coger desprevenido (a)

abacus *n* ábaco, *m*

abaft *adv naut* hacia la popa, en popa; atrás

abandon *vt* abandonar; dejar; desertar, desamparar; renunciar; entregar. *n* entusiasmo, fervor, *m*; naturalidad, *f*. **to a. oneself to,** (despair, vice, etc.) entregarse a

abandoned *a* entregado a los vicios, vicioso

abandonment *n* abandono, *m*; renunciación, *f*; deserción, *f*

abase *vt* humillar; degradar; abatir

abasement *n* humillación, degradación, *f*; abatimiento, *m*

abash *vt* avergonzar; confundir, desconcertar

abashed *a* avergonzado, confuso, consternado

abate *vt* disminuir, reducir; (a price) rebajar; (suppress) suprimir, abolir; (remit) condonar, remitir; (annul) anular; (moderate) moderar; (of pride, etc.) humillar; (of pain) aliviar. *vi* disminuir; moderarse; (of the wind and *fig*) amainar; cesar; apaciguarse, calmarse

abatement *n* disminución, *f*; reducción, *f*; mitigación, *f*; (of price) rebaja, *f*; supresión, *f*; remisión, *f*; (annulment) anulación, *f*; (of pride) humillación, *f*; (of the wind and of enthusiasm, etc.) amaine, *m*; (of pain, etc.) alivio, *m*

abattoir *n* matadero, *m*

abbey *n* abadía, *f*

abbreviate *vt* abreviar; condensar, resumir

abbreviation *n* abreviación, *f*; resumen, *m*, condensación, *f*; (of a word) abreviatura, *f*

abdicate *vt* renunciar; (a throne) abdicar

abdication *n* renuncia, *f*; abdicación, *f*

abdomen *n* abdomen, *m*

abdominal *a* abdominal

abduct *vt* raptar, secuestrar

abduction *n* rapto, *m*; (*anat phil*) abducción, *f*

abductor *n anat* abductor, *m*; raptor, *m*

aberration *n* aberración (also *ast phys biol*), *f*

abet *vt* ayudar, apoyar, favorecer; incitar, alentar; (in bad sense) ser cómplice de

abetment *n* ayuda, *f*, apoyo, *m*; instigación, *f*

abettor *n* instigador (-ra); cómplice, *mf*

abeyance *n* suspensión, *f*; expectativa, esperanza, *f*. **in a.,** en suspenso; vacante; latente

abhor *vt* detestar, odiar, aborrecer; repugnar

abhorrence *n* detestación, *f*, odio, aborrecimiento, *m*; repugnancia, *f*

abhorrent *a* detestable, odioso, aborrecible; repugnante

abide *vi* morar, quedar. *vt* aguardar; *inf* aguantar, sufrir. **to a. by,** atenerse a, cumplir; sostener

abiding *a* permanente, constante, perenne

ability *n* habilidad, facultad, *f*, poder, *m*; talento, *m*, capacidad, *f*. **to the best of my a.,** lo mejor que yo pueda

abject *a* abyecto, miserable; despreciable, vil; servil

abjure *vt* abjurar; renunciar; retractar

ablaze *adv* en llamas, ardiendo. *a* brillante; (with, of anger, etc.) dominado por

able *a* capaz (de); (clever) hábil; competente; en estado (de); *law* apto legalmente, capaz; bueno, excelente. **to be a. to,** poder; ser capaz de; (know how) saber. **a.-bodied,** fuerte, fornido. **a.-bodied seaman,** marinero práctico, *m*

abloom *adv* en flor

ablution *n* ablución, *f*

ably *adv* hábilmente; competentemente

abnegation *n* abnegación, *f*

abnormal *a* anormal; irregular

abnormality *n* anormalidad, *f*; irregularidad, *f*

abnormally *adv* anormalmente; demasiado

aboard *adv* a bordo. *prep* a bordo de. **to go a.,** embarcarse, ir a bordo. **All a.!** ¡Viajeros a bordo!; (a train) ¡Viajeros al tren!

abode *n* morada, habitación, *f*; residencia, *f*; (stay) estancia, *f*

abolish *vt* abolir, suprimir, anular

abolition *n* abolición, supresión, *f*; anulación, *f*

abolitionist *n* abolicionista, *mf*

abominable *a* abominable, aborrecible; repugnante, execrable; *inf* horrible

abominably *adv* abominablemente

abominate *vt* abominar, aborrecer, detestar

abomination *n* abominación, *f*; aborrecimiento, *m*; horror, *m*

aboriginal *a* aborigen; primitivo

aborigines *n pl* aborígenes, *m pl*

abort *vi* abortar, malparir; *fig* malograrse

abortion *n* aborto, *Columbia* avieso *m*; *fig* fracaso, malogro, *m*

abortive *a* abortivo

abound *vi* abundar (en)

about *adv* (around) alrededor; (round about) a la redonda, en torno; (all over) por todas partes; (up and down) acá y acullá; por aquí, por ahí; en alguna parte; por aquí; (in circumference) en circunferencia; (almost) casi, aproximadamente; (by turns) por turnos, en rotación. *prep* alrededor de; en torno; por; (near to) cerca de; (on one's person) sobre; (on the subject of) sobre; (concerning) acerca de; (over) por, a causa de; en; (of) de; (with time by the clock) a eso de, sobre; (towards) hacia; (engaged in) ocupado en; (on the point of) a punto de. **a. here,** por aquí. **a. nothing,** por nada. **a. supper time,** hacia la hora de cenar. **a. three o'clock,** a eso de las tres. **A. turn!** ¡Media vuelta! (a la izquierda or a la derecha). **He wandered a. the streets,** Vagaba por las calles. **somewhere a.,** en alguna parte. **to be a. to,** estar para, estar a punto de. **to bring a.,** ocasionar. **to come a.,** suceder. **to know a.,** saber de. **to set a.,** empezar, iniciar; (a person) acometer. **What are you thinking a.?** ¿En qué piensas?

above *adv* arriba; en lo alto; encima; (superior) superior; (earlier) antes; (higher up on a page, etc.) más arriba; (in heaven) en el cielo. *prep* encima de; por encima de; sobre; (beyond) fuera de; fuera del alcance de; (superior to) superior a; (more than) más de; (too proud to) demasiado orgulloso para; (too good to) demasiado bueno para; (in addition to) además de, en adición a; (with degrees of temperature) sobre. *a* anterior; (with past participles) antes. **from a.,** desde arriba. **a. all,** sobre todo. **over and a.,** además de. **a. board,** *adv* abiertamente, con las cartas boca arriba. *a*

franco y abierto. **a. mentioned,** supradicho, susodicho, antes citado
abrasion *n* abrasión, *f*; rozadura, *f*; *geol* denudación, *f*
abrasive *a* abrasivo. *n* substancia abrasiva, *f*, abrasivo, *m*
abreast *adv* de frente, al lado uno de otro; *naut* por el través. **to keep a. of the times,** mantenerse al dia. **to ride six a.,** cabalgar a seis de frente. **a. with,** al nivel de, a la altura de
abridge *vt* abreviar; resumir, condensar, compendiar; disminuir; reducir
abridgment *n* abreviación, *f*; resumen, *m*, sinopsis, *f*; disminución, *f*; reducción, *f*
abroad *adv* (out) fuera, afuera; (gone out) salido; ausente; (everywhere) en todas partes; (in foreign lands) en el extranjero. **to go a.,** salir de casa, echarse a la calle; ir al extranjero; (of rumors, etc.) propagarse, rumorearse
abrogation *n* abrogación, anulación, *f*
abrupt *a* (precipitous) escarpado, precipitado, abrupto; (unexpected) repentino, inesperado; (of persons) brusco, descortés; (of style) seco
abruptly *adv* bruscamente; repentinamente
abruptness *n* precipitación, *f*; brusquedad, *f*
abscess *n* absceso, *m*
abscond *vi* evadirse; huir, escaparse; (with money) desfalcar
absence *n* ausencia, *f*; alejamiento, *m*; (of mind) abstracción, *f*, ensimismamiento, *m*; (lack) falta, *f*. **leave of a.,** permiso para ausentarse, *m*; *mil* licencia, *f*, permiso, *m*
absent *a* ausente; alejado (de); (in mind) abstraído, ensimismado, distraído. *vt* ausentarse; alejarse. **the a.,** los ausentes. **a.-mindedness,** ensimismamiento, *m*, abstracción, *f*
absentee *n* ausente, *mf*
absenteeism *n* absentismo, *m*
absently *adv* distraídamente
absinthe *n* ajenjo, *m*
absolute *a* absoluto; perfecto; puro; (unconditional) incondicional; (downright) categórico; completo; (true) verdadero; (unlimited) ilimitado. **the a.,** lo absoluto
absolutely *adv* absolutamente; enteramente, completamente; realmente, categóricamente
absolution *n* (*ecc law*) absolución, *f*
absolutism *n* absolutismo, despotismo, *m*
absolutist *n* absolutista, *mf*
absolve *vt* absolver; (free) exentar, eximir; librar; exculpar
absorb *vt* absorber; (drink) beber; (use) gastar; (of shocks) amortiguar; (*fig* digest) asimilar; (engross) ocupar (el pensamiento, etc.). **to be absorbed in,** *fig* enfrascarse en, engolfarse en, estar entregado a
absorbent *a* and *n* absorbente, *m*. **a. cotton,** algodón hidrófilo, *m*
absorbing *a* absorbente; *fig* sumamente interesante
absorption *n* absorción, *f*; (*fig* digestion) asimilación, *f*; (engrossment) enfrascamiento, *m*, preocupación, abstracción, *f*
abstain *vi* abstenerse (de); evitar
abstemious *a* abstemio, abstinente; sobrio; moderado
abstention *n* abstención, *f*; abstinencia, *f*; privación, *f*
abstinence *n* abstinencia, *f*. **day of a.,** día de ayuno, *m*
abstinent *a* abstinente; sobrio
abstract *a* abstracto. *n* extracto, resumen, *m*; abstracción, *f*. *vt* abstraer; separar; extraer; (précis) resumir; (steal) substraer. **in the a.,** en abstracto
abstracted *a* distraído, desatento, absorto, ensimismado
abstraction *n* abstracción, *f*; (of mind) preocupación, desatención, *f*; (stealing) substracción, *f*
abstruse *a* abstruso, ininteligible; obscuro; recóndito
absurd *a* absurdo, grotesco; ridículo, disparatado; cómico
absurdity *n* absurdidad, ridiculez, *f*; disparate, *m*, tontería, *f*
abundance *n* abundancia, copia, *f*; muchedumbre (de), multitud (de), *f*; riqueza, *f*; prosperidad, *f*
abundant *a* abundante, copioso; rico. **to be a. in,** abundar en
abundantly *adv* en abundancia, abundantemente
abuse *n* abuso, *m*; (bad language) insulto, *m*, injuria, *f*. *vt* (ill-use) maltratar; (misuse) abusar (de); (revile) insultar, injuriar; (deceive) engañar
abuser *n* abusador (-ra); injuriador (-ra); (defamer) denigrante, *mf*
abusive *a* abusivo; (scurrilous) insultante, injurioso, ofensivo
abusively *adv* insolentemente, ofensivamente
abut (on) *vi* lindar con; terminar en; estar adosado a
abysmal *a* abismal
abyss *n* abismo, *m*, sima, *f*; (hell) infierno, *m*
acacia *n* acacia, *f*
academic *a* académico
academician *n* académico, miembro de la Academia, *m*
academy *n* academia, *f*; conservatorio, *m*; (school) colegio, *m*; (of riding, etc.) escuela, *f*. **A. of Music,** Conservatorio de Música, *m*
accede *vi* (to a throne) ascender (al trono); tomar posesión (de); (join) hacerse miembro (de); aceptar; (agree) acceder (a), consentir (en), convenir (en)
accelerate *vt* acelerar; apresurar; (shorten) abreviar
acceleration *n* aceleración, *f*
accelerator *n* (of a vehicle) acelerador, *m*
accent *n* acento (all meanings), *m*. *vt* acentuar
accentuate *vt* acentuar; dar énfasis a
accept *vt* aceptar; (believe) creer; recibir; admitir; (welcome) acoger
acceptability *n* aceptabilidad, *f*; mérito, *m*
acceptable *a* aceptable; admisible; agradable; (welcome) bien acogido
acceptably *adv* aceptablemente; agradablemente
acceptance *n* aceptación, *f*. **a. speech** discurso aceptatorio; (approval) aprobación, *f*; (welcome) buena acogida, *f*; *com* aceptación, *f*
access *n* acceso, *m*; entrada, *f*; (way) camino, *m*; *med* ataque, *m*; (fit) transporte, *m*; (advance) avance, *m*. **easy of a.,** accesible; fácil de encontrar
accessibility *n* accesibilidad, *f*
accessible *a* accesible; asequible
accession *n* (to the throne, etc.) advenimiento, *m*; aumento, *m*; (acquisition) adición, *f*; adquisición, *f*; *law* accesión, *f*
accessory *a* accesorio; secundario; suplementario, adicional. *n* accesorio, *m*; *law* cómplice, *mf*. **a. before the fact,** instigador (-ra). **a. after the fact,** encubridor (-ra)
accident *n* accidente, *m*; (chance) casualidad, *f*; (mishap) contratiempo, *m*. **by a.,** por casualidad, accidentalmente. **a. insurance,** seguro contra accidentes, *m*
accidental *a* accidental, casual, fortuito. *n mus* accidente, *m*
accidentally *adv* accidentalmente; por casualidad; sin querer
acclaim *vt* aclamar; proclamar; vitorear, aplaudir
acclamation *n* aclamación, *f*; aplauso, vítor, *m*
acclimatization *n* aclimatación, *f*
acclimatize *vt* aclimatar
accolade *n* acolada, *f*, espaldarazo, *m*
accommodate *vt* acomodar; ajustar; adaptar; (reconcile) reconciliar; (provide) proveer, proporcionar; (oblige) complacer; (fit) poner, instalar; (lodge) hospedar; (lend) prestar; (hold) tener espacio para, contener; (give a seat to) dar un sitio a. **to a. oneself to,** adaptarse a
accommodating *a* acomodadizo; (obliging) servicial
accommodation *n* acomodación, *f*; ajuste, *m*; adaptación, *f*; (arrangement) arreglo, *m*; (reconciliation) reconciliación, *f*; (lodging) alojamiento, *m*; (*aer naut*) partición, *f*; (space, room or seat) sitio, *m*; (loan) préstamo, *m*. **We found the accommodations good in**

this hotel, Estuvimos muy bien en este hotel. **a. ladder,** escalera real, *f*
accompaniment *n* acompañamiento, *m*
accompanist *n* acompañante (-ta)
accompany *vt* acompañar
accompanying *a* anexo *n* acompañamiento, *m*
accomplice *n* cómplice, comparte, *mf*
accomplish *vt* llevar a cabo, efectuar; terminar; (fulfil) cumplir; perfeccionar; (achieve) conseguir, lograr
accomplished *a* consumado; perfecto; culto; (talented) talentoso
accomplishment *n* efectuación, *f;* realización, *f,* logro, *m;* (fulfilment) cumplimiento, *m;* (gift) prenda, *f,* talento, *m; pl* **accomplishments,** partes, dotes, *f pl;* conocimientos, *m pl*
accord *n* acuerdo, *m;* unión, *f;* consentimiento, *m;* concierto, *m,* concordia, *f;* voluntad, *f. vt* otorgar, conceder. *vi* estar de acuerdo (con); armonizar (con). **of one's own a.,** espontáneamente. **with one a.,** unánimemente
accordance *n* acuerdo, *m,* conformidad, *f;* arreglo, *m.* **in a. with,** de acuerdo con, según, con arreglo a
according *adv* según, conforme. **a. as,** conforme a, a medida que. **a. to,** según
accordingly *adv* en consecuencia, por consiguiente; pues
accordion *n* acordeón, *m.* **to a.-pleat,** *vt* plisar
accost *vt* abordar, acercarse a; dirigirse a, hablar
account *vt* (judge) considerar, creer, juzgar, tener por. *vi* (for) explicar; (understand) comprender; (be responsible) responder de, dar razón de; justificar
account *n* (bill) cuenta, *f;* factura, *f;* (narrative) narración, relación, *f;* (description) descripción, *f;* historia, *f;* versión, *f;* (list) enumeración, *f;* (reason) motivo, *m,* causa, *f;* (importance) importancia, *f;* (weight) peso, *m;* (news) noticias, *f pl;* (advantage) provecho, *m,* ventaja, *f.* **by all accounts,** según lo que se oye, según voz pública. **current a.,** cuenta corriente, *f.* **outstanding a.,** cuenta pendiente, *f.* **on a.,** a cuenta. **on a. of,** a causa de, por motivo de. **on no a.,** de ninguna manera. **on that a.,** por lo tanto. **to be of no a.,** ser insignificante; ser de poca importancia; *inf* ser la última mona. **to give an a.,** contar, hacer una relación (de). **to give an a. of oneself,** explicarse. **to keep a.,** llevar la cuenta. **to settle accounts,** ajustar cuentas. **to take into a.,** considerar. **to turn to a.,** sacar provecho de. **a. book,** libro de cuentas, *m*
accountability *n* responsabilidad, *f*
accountable *a* responsable
accountancy *n* contabilidad, *f*
accountant *n* contador, *m.* **chartered a.,** contador autorizado, *m.* **accountant's office,** contaduría, *f*
accouterment *n* atavío, *m;* equipo, *m*
accredit *vt* acreditar
accretion *n* acrecentamiento, aumento, *m; law* accesión, *f*
accrue *vi* resultar (de), proceder (de); originarse (en); aumentar
accumulate *vt* acumular; amontonar, atesorar. *vi* acumularse; aumentarse, crecer
accumulation *n* acumulación, *f;* amontonamiento, *m*
accumulative *a* acumulador; adquisitivo, ahorrador
accumulator *n elec* acumulador, *m*
accuracy *n* exactitud, correción
accurate *a* exacto, correcto, fiel; (of persons) exacto, minucioso; (of apparatus) de precisión
accurately *adv* con exactitud, correctamente; con precisión
accursed *a* maldito.
accusation *n* acusación, *f.* **to lodge an a.,** querellarse ante el juez
accusatory *a* acusatorio
accuse *vt* acusar
accused *n law* acusado (-da)
accuser *n* acusador (-ra)
accustom *vt* acostumbrar (a), habituar (a)
accustomed *a* acostumbrado, usual; general; característico
ace *n* as, *m; fig* pelo, *m.* **to be within an ace of,** estar a dos dedos de
acerbity *n* acerbidad, *f; fig* aspereza, *f;* severidad, *f;* sequedad, *f*
acetate *n* acetato, *m*
acetic *a* acético
acetylene *n* acetileno, *m.* **a. lamp,** lámpara de acetileno, *f*
ache *n* dolor, *m;* pena, *f. vi* doler. **My head aches,** Me duele la cabeza, Tengo dolor de cabeza
achievable *a* alcanzable, asequible; factible
achieve *vt* conseguir, lograr; (reach) alcanzar; (obtain) obtener, ganar
achievement *n* logro, *m,* realización, *f;* obtención, *f;* (deed) hazaña, *f;* (work) obra, *f;* (success) éxito, *m;* (discovery) descubrimiento, *m;* (victory) victoria, *f*
aching *n* dolor, *m;* pena, angustia, *f. a* doliente; afligido
achromatic *a* acromático
achromic *a* acrómico
acid *a* and *n* ácido, *m.* **fatty a.,** ácido graso, *m*
acidify *vt* acidificar
acidity *n* acidez, *f*
acidosis *n med* acidismo, *m*
acknowledge *vt* reconocer; confesar; (reply to) contestar a; (appreciate) agradecer. **to a. receipt,** *com* acusar recibo
acknowledgment *n* reconocimiento, *m;* confesión, *f;* (appreciation) agradecimiento, *m;* (reward) recompensa, *f;* (of a letter) acuse de recibo, *m*
acme *n* cumbre, *f; fig* auge, apogeo, *m*
acne *n* acné, *m*
acolyte *n* acólito, monacillo (male) *m,* acólita, monacilla *f,* (female)
acorn *n* bellota, *f.* **a. cup,** capullo de bellota, *m.* **a.-shaped,** en forma de bellota, abellotado
acoustic *a* acústico
acoustics *n pl* acústica, *f*
acquaint *vt* dar a conocer, comunicar, informar (de), dar parte (de); familiarizar (con). **to be acquainted with,** conocer; saber. **to make oneself acquainted with,** familiarizarse con; entablar amistad con
acquaintance *n* conocimiento, *m;* (person) conocido (-da); *pl* **acquaintances,** amistades, *f pl.* **to make their a.,** conocer (a), llegar a conocer (a)
acquiesce *vi* asentir (en), consentir (a)
acquiescence *n* acquiescencia, *f,* consentimiento, *m*
acquiescent *a* conforme; resignado
acquire *vt* adquirir, obtener; (diseases, habits) contraer; ganar; (learn) aprender
Acquired Immune Deficiency Syndrome *n* el síndrome de Inmunodeficiencia Adquirida, *m*
acquirement *n* adquisición, *f;* (learning) conocimiento, *m;* (talent) talento, *m*
acquirer *n* adquisidor (-ra)
acquisition *n* adquisición, *f*
acquisitive *a* adquisitivo
acquit *vt* (a debt) pagar; exonerar; *law* absolver; (a duty) cumplir. **to a. oneself well (badly),** portarse bien (mal); salir bien (mal)
acquittal *n* (of a debt) pago, *m; law* absolución, *f;* (of a duty) cumplimiento, *m*
acquittance *n* descargo, *m;* quitanza, *f*
acre *n* (measure) acre, *m; pl* **acres,** terrenos, campos, *m pl.* **1.75 acres** *Central America* manzana *f.* **2.5 acres** *Argentina* manzana *f*
acreage *n* acres, *m pl*
acrid *a* acre
acrimonious *a* acrimonioso, áspero; mordaz, sarcástico
acrimony *n* acrimonia, acritud, *f;* sarcasmo, *m*
acrobat *n* acróbata. *Lat. Am. also* maromero (-ra) *mf*
acrobatic *a* acrobático
acrobatics *n pl* acrobacia, *f*
acronym *n* sigla, *f*
acropolis *n* acrópolis, *f*

across *adv* a través, de través, transversalmente; (on the other side) al otro lado; de una parte a otra; (of the arms, etc.) cruzados, *m pl. prep* a través de; al otro lado de; (upon) sobre; por. **He went a. the road,** Cruzó la calle. **to run a.,** correr por; tropezar con; dar con. **a. country,** a campo travieso. **a. the way,** en frente
acrostic *n* (poema) acróstico, *m, a* acróstico
act *n* acción, obra, *f,* hecho, *m;* acto, *m; law* ley, *f; theat* acto, *m.* **in the act,** en el acto. **in the act (of doing),** en acto de (hacer algo). **in the very act,** en flagrante. **the Acts of the Apostles,** los Actos de los Apóstoles. **act of God,** fuerza mayor, *f.* **act of indemnity,** bill de indemnidad, *m*
act *vt* (a play) representar, hacer; (a part) desempeñar, hacer (un papel); (pretend) simular, fingir. *vi* obrar, actuar, *Lat. Am.* accionar; (behave) portarse, conducirse; (function) funcionar; producir su efecto; (feign) fingir; (as a profession) ser actor. **to act as,** hacer de; cumplir las funciones de. **to act as a second,** (in a duel) apadrinar. **to act for,** representar; ser el representante de. **to act upon,** obrar sobre; afectar; influir en
acting *n* (of a play) representación (de una comedia), *f;* (of an actor) interpretación (de un papel), *f;* (as a hobby) el hacer comedia; (dramatic art) arte dramática, *f. a* interino, suplente; comanditario. **He is a. captain,** Está de capitán. **a. partner,** socio (-ia) comanditario (-ia)
action *n* acción, *f;* función, *f;* operación, *f;* (movement) movimiento, *m;* (effect) efecto, *m;* influencia, *f; law* proceso, *m; mil* batalla, acción, *f; lit* acción, *f.* **in a.,** en actividad; en operación; *mil* en el campo de batalla. **man of a.,** hombre de acción, *m.* **to be killed in a.,** morir en el campo de batalla. **to bring an a. against,** pedir en juicio, entablar un pleito contra. **to put into a.,** hacer funcionar; introducir. **to take a.,** tomar medidas (para). **to take a. against,** prevenirse contra; *law* proceder contra
actionable *a* procesable, punible
active *a* activo; ágil; diligente; *mil* vivo; enérgico; *gram* activo. **be a.** *Lat. Am.* accionar. **to make a.,** activar, estimular
activity *n* actividad, *f*
actor *n* actor, *m;* (in comedy) comediante, *m*
actress *n* actriz, *f;* (in comedy) comediante, *f*
actual *a* actual, existente; real, verdadero
actuality *n* realidad, *f*
actually *adv* en efecto, realmente, en realidad
actuary *n* actuario de seguros, *m*
actuate *vt* mover, animar, excitar
acumen *n* cacumen, *m,* agudeza, sagacidad, *f*
acute *a* agudo; (shrewd) perspicaz; (of a situation) crítico. **a. accent,** acento agudo, *m.* **a.-angled,** acutángulo
acutely *adv* agudamente; (deeply) profundamente
acuteness *n* agudeza, *f;* (shrewdness) perspicacia, penetración, *f*
ad *n* anuncio, *m.* See **advertisement**
adage *n* refrán, proverbio, decir, *m*
Adam *n* Adán, *m.* **Adam's apple,** nuez de la garganta, *f*
adamant *a* firme, duro, inexorable
adamantine *a* adamantino
adapt *vt* adaptar; ajustar, acomodar; aplicar; (a play, etc.) refundir, arreglar; *mus* arreglar
adaptability *n* adaptabilidad, *f*
adaptable *a* adaptable
adaptation *n* adaptación, *f;* (of a play, etc.) refundición, *f;* (*mus* etc.) arreglo, *m*
adapter *n* (of a play, etc.) refundidor (-ra); *elec* enchufe de reducción, *m*
add *vt* añadir; juntar; (up) sumar. **add insult to injury,** al mojado echarle agua, añadir a una ofensa otra mayor. **to add to,** añadir a; (increase) aumentar, acrecentar. **to add up,** sumar. **to add up to,** subir a; (mean) querer decir.
adder *n* víbora, serpiente, *f*
addict *n* adicto (-ta). **to a. oneself to,** dedicarse a, entregarse a
addicted *a* aficionado (a), amigo (de), dado (a); adicto (a)
addiction *n* afición, propensión, *f;* adicción, *f*
addition *n* añadidura, *f; math* adición, suma, *f.* **in a. (to),** además (de), también
additional *a* adicional
addled *a* huero, podrido; *fig* confuso
address *n* (on a letter) sobrescrito, *m;* (of a person) dirección, *f,* señas, *f pl;* (speech) discurso, *m;* (petition) memorial, *m,* petición, *f;* (dedication) dedicatoria, *f;* (invocation) invocación, *f;* (deportment) presencia, *f;* (tact) diplomacia, habilidad, *f; pl* **addresses,** corte, *f. vt* (a ball) golpear; (a letter) dirigir, poner el sobrescrito a, *Mexico* domiciliar; (words, prayers) dirigir (a); hablar, hacer un discurso. **to a. oneself to a task,** dedicarse a (or entregarse a or emprender) una tarea. **to deliver an a.,** pronunciar un discurso. **to pay one's addresses to,** cortejar, hacer la corte (a), galantear
addressee *n* destinatario (-ia)
adduce *vt* aducir, alegar; aportar
Aden Adén *m*
adenoids *n pl* amígdalas, *f pl*
adept *a* adepto, versado, consumado. *n* adepto, *m*
adequacy *n* adecuación, *f;* suficiencia, *f;* competencia, *f*
adequate *a* adecuado; proporcionado; suficiente; competente; a la altura (de)
adequately *adv* adecuadamente
adhere *vi* adherirse; pegarse; ser fiel (a); persistir (en)
adherence *n fig* adhesión, *f*
adherent *n* partidario (-ia)
adhesion *n* adherencia, *f;* (to a party, etc.) adhesión, *f*
adhesive *a* adhesivo; (sticky) pegajoso. **a. tape,** esparadrapo, *m; elec* cinta aisladora adherente, *f*
adipose *a* adiposo
adjacent *a* próximo, contiguo, adyacente, vecino
adjective *n* adjetivo, *m*
adjoin *vt* estar contiguo a, lindar con; juntar. *vi* colindar
adjoining *a* vecino, de al lado, adyacente; cercano
adjourn *vt* aplazar, diferir; (a meeting, etc.) suspender, levantar. *vi* retirarse. **The debate was adjourned,** Se suspendió el debate. **to a. a meeting,** levantar la sesión
adjournment *n* aplazamiento, *m;* (of a meeting) suspensión (de la sesión), *f*
adjudicate *vt* adjudicar; *law* declarar; juzgar. *vi* ejercer las funciones del juez; fallar, dictar sentencia
adjudication *n* adjudicación, *f; law* fallo, *m,* sentencia, *f;* (of bankruptcy) declaración (de quiebra), *f;* concesión, *f,* otorgamiento, *m*
adjudicator *n* adjudicador (-ra)
adjunct *n* atributo, *m;* accesorio, *m;* adjunto, *m; gram* adjunto, *m*
adjure *vt* conjurar; rogar encarecidamente
adjust *vt* ajustar; regular; arreglar; (correct) corregir; adaptar
adjustable *a* ajustable; regulable; desmontable; de quita y pon
adjustment *n* ajuste, *m;* regulación, *f;* arreglo, *m;* (correction) corrección, *f;* adaptación, *f; com* prorrateo, *m*
adjutant *n mil* ayudante, *m*
administer *vt* administrar; (laws) aplicar; (blows, etc.) dar; (an office) ejercer; (govern) regir, gobernar; (provide) suministrar; (an oath) tomar; (justice) hacer; (the sacraments) administrar; (with to) contribuir a. **to a. an oath,** tomar juramento (a)
administration *n* administración, *f;* (government) gobierno, *m;* dirección, *f;* (of laws) aplicación, *f;* distribución, *f*
administrative *a* administrativo; gubernativo
administrator *n* administrador, *m*
administratrix *n* administradora, *f*
admirable *a* admirable
admirably *adv* admirablemente
admiral *n* almirante, *m.* **A. of the Fleet,** almirante supremo, *m.* **admiral's ship,** capitana, *f*

admiration *n* admiración, *f*
admire *vt* sentir admiración por; (love) amar; (like) gustar; (respect) respetar
admirer *n* admirador (-ra); (amateur) aficionado (-da), apasionado (-da); (partisan) satélite, *m;* (lover) enamorado, amante, *m*
admiring *a* admirativo, de admiración
admissible *a* admisible; aceptable; lícito, permitido
admission *n* admisión, *f;* recepción, *f;* entrada, *f;* confesión, *f,* reconocimiento, *m.* **No a.!** Entrada prohibida. **right of a.,** derecho de entrada, *m.* **A. free,** Entrada libre. **a. ticket,** entrada, *f*
admit *vt* admitir; recibir; dejar entrar; hacer entrar, introducir; (hold) contener; (concede) conceder; (acknowledge) reconocer, confesar. **to a. of,** permitir; sufrir
admittance *n* admisión, *f;* entrada, *f.* **No a.!** Prohibida la entrada. **to gain a.,** lograr entrar
admittedly *adv* según opinión general; sin duda
admonish *vt* (advise) aconsejar; amonestar, advertir; (reprimand) reprender
admonition *n* amonestación, *f;* advertencia, *f;* admonición, *f*
admonitory *a* amonestador
ad nauseam *adv* hasta la saciedad
ado *n* (noise) ruido, *m;* (trouble) trabajo, *m,* dificultad, *f;* (fuss) barahúnda, *f.* **much ado about nothing,** mucho ruido y pocas nueces, nada entre dos platos. **without more ado,** sin más ni más
adolescence *n* adolescencia, *f*
adolescent *a* and *n* adolescente, *mf*
adopt *vt* adoptar. **a. local customs** *Lat. Am.* acriollarse
adopted *a* adoptivo
adoption *n* adopción, *f;* (choice) elección, *f*
adoptive *a* adoptivo
adorable *a* adorable
adoration *n* adoración, *f.* **A. of the Magi,** Adoración de los Reyes, *f*
adore *vt* adorar
adorer *n* adorador (-ra); amante, *m*
adoringly *adv* con adoración
adorn *vt* adornar, embellecer; (*fig* of persons) adornar con su presencia
adornment *n* adorno, *m;* ornamento, *m;* embellecimiento, *m*
adrenalin *n* adrenalina, *f*
Adriatic, the el (Mar) Adriático, *m*
adrift *a* and *adv* a merced de las olas; a la ventura. **to turn a.,** *inf* poner de patitas en la calle
adroit *a* hábil
adulate *vt* adular
adulation *n* adulación, *f*
adulatory *a* adulador
adult *a* and *n* adulto (-ta)
adult education *n* educación de los adultos, *f*
adulterate *vt* adulterar; falsificar; contaminar. *a* adulterado; falsificado; impuro
adulteration *n* adulteración, *f;* falsificación, *f;* impureza, *f;* contaminación, *f*
adulterer *n* adúltero, *m*
adulteress *n* adúltera, *f*
adulterous *a* adúltero
adultery *n* adulterio, *m.* **to commit a.,** cometer adulterio, adulterar
advance *n* avance, *m;* (progress) progreso, adelantamiento, *m;* (improvement) mejora, *f;* (of shares) alza, *f;* (of price) subida, *f;* (loan) préstamo, *m;* (in rank) ascenso, *m; pl* **advances,** (overtures) avances, *m pl;* (proposals) propuestas, *f pl;* (of love) requerimientos amorosos, *m pl.* **in a.,** de antemano, con anticipación, con tiempo, previamente; (of money) por adelantado. **a. guard,** *mil* avanzada, *f.* **a. payment,** anticipo, *m,* paga por adelantado, *f*
advance *vt* avanzar; (suggest) sugerir, proponer; (encourage) fomentar; (a person) ascender; (improve) mejorar; (of events, dates) adelantar; (of prices, stocks) hacer subir; (money) anticipar; (of steps) tomar. *vi* avanzar; (progress) progresar; (in rank, studies, etc.) adelantar; (of prices) subir
advanced *a* avanzado; (developed) desarrollado; (mentally, of children) precoz; (course) superior. **a. research,** investigaciones superiores. **a. standing,** equivalencias, *f pl.* **a. views,** ideas avanzadas, *f pl*
advancement *n* adelantamiento, *m;* progreso, *m;* (encouragement) fomento, *m;* (in employment) promoción, *f;* prosperidad, *f*
advancing *a* que avanza; (of years) que pasan
advantage *n* ventaja, *f;* superioridad, *f;* (benefit) provecho, beneficio, *m;* interés, *m;* ocasión favorable, oportunidad, *f;* (tennis) ventaja, *f.* **to have the a. of,** tener la ventaja de. **to show to a.,** embellecer, realzar; aumentar la belleza (etc.) de. **to take a. of,** sacar ventaja de, aprovecharse de; (deceive) engañar. **to take a. of the slightest pretext,** asirse de un cabello
advantageous *a* ventajoso, provechoso. **to be a.,** ser de provecho
advent *n* advenimiento, *m,* llegada, *f; ecc* Adviento, *m*
adventitious *a* adventicio (all uses)
adventure *n* aventura, *f;* riesgo, *m;* (chance) casualidad, *f; com* especulación, *f, vt* aventurar, arriesgar. *vi* arriesgarse, osar
adventurer *n* aventurero, *m;* (one living by his wits) caballero de industria, *m;* (in commerce) especulador, *m*
adventuresome *a* de aventura
adventuress *n* aventurera, *f*
adventurous *a* aventurero; osado, audaz; (dangerous) peligroso, arriesgado
adverb *n* adverbio, *m*
adversary *n* adversario (-ia)
adverse *a* adverso; hostil (a); malo; desfavorable; (opposite) opuesto
adversity *n* adversidad, *f*
advertise *vt* anunciar. *vi* poner un anuncio; (oneself) llamar la atención
advertisement *n* anuncio, *m;* (poster) cartel, *m;* (to attract attention) reclamo, *m.* **to put an a. in the paper,** poner un anuncio en el periódico. **a. hoarding,** cartelera, *f*
advertiser *n* anunciante, *mf*
advertising *n* anuncios, *m pl;* publicidad, propaganda, *f;* medios publicitarios, *m pl*
advice *n* consejo, *m;* (warning) advertencia, amonestación, *f;* (news) noticia, *f,* aviso, *m; com* comunicación, *f;* (belief) parecer, *m,* opinión, *f.* **piece of a.,** consejo, *m.* **to follow the a. of,** seguir los consejos de. **to give a.,** dar consejos
advisability *n* conveniencia, *f;* prudencia, *f*
advisable *a* conveniente, aconsejable; prudente
advise *vt* aconsejar; (inform) avisar, informar
advised *a* avisado; premeditado. **ill-a.,** mal aconsejado; imprudente. **well-a.,** bien aconsejado; prudente
adviser *n* consejero (-ra)
advisory *a* asesor, consultivo, consultativo
advocacy *n* defensa, *f;* apología, *f;* abogacía, intercesión, *f*
advocate *n law* abogado (-da); defensor (-ra); (champion) campeón, *m. vt* abogar, defender; sostener, apoyar; recomendar
adze *n* azuela, *f*
Aegean, the el (Mar) Egeo, *m*
aegis *n* égida, *f;* protección, *f*
aerated *a* aerado; (of lemonade, etc.) gaseoso. **a. waters,** aguas gaseosas, *f pl*
aeration *n* aeración, *f*
aerial *a* aéreo, de aire; etéreo; fantástico. *n* (radio) antena, *f.* **indoor a.,** antena interior, *f*
aerobics *n* aerobismo *m*
aerodynamics *n* aerodinámica, *f*
aeronaut *n* aeronauta, *mf*
aeronautical *a* aeronáutico
aeronautics *n* aeronáutica, *f*
afar *adv* a lo lejos, en la distancia. **from a.,** desde lejos

affability *n* afabilidad, condescendencia, urbanidad, *f*
affable *a* afable, condescendiente
affably *adv* afablemente
affair *n* asunto, *m*, cosa, *f*; cuestión, *f*; (business) negocio, *m*; (*fam* applied to a machine, carriage, etc.) artefacto, *m*; (of the heart) amorío, *m*. **a. of honour,** lance de honor, *m*
affect *vt* afectar; influir; *med* atacar; (move) impresionar, conmover; enternecer; (harm) perjudicar; (frequent) frecuentar; (like) gustar de; (love) amar; (wear) vestir; (use) gastar, usar; (feign) aparentar; (boast) hacer alarde de
affectation *n* afectación, *f*
affected *a* afectado; influido; *med* atacado; (moved) conmovido, impresionado; enternecido; (inclined) dispuesto, inclinado; (artificial) artificioso; amanerado, afectado; (of style) rebuscado, artificial
affecting *a* conmovedor, emocionante
affection *n* afecto, cariño, *m*; amor, *m*; apego, *m*; simpatía, *f*; (emotion) emoción, *f*, sentimiento, *m*; *med* afección, enfermedad, *f*
affectionate *a* afectuoso, cariñoso; mimoso; (tender) tierno; expresivo
affectionately *adv* afectuosamente. **Yours a.,** tu cariñoso . . . , tu . . . , que te quiere
affective *a* afectivo
affidavit *n* declaración jurada, declaración jurídica *f*, atestiguación, *f*
affiliate *vt* afiliar; adoptar; *law* imputar; *law* legitimar
affiliation *n* afiliación, *f*; adopción, *f*; legitimación de un hijo, *f*
affinity *n* afinidad, *f*
affirm *vt* afirmar, aseverar, declarar; confirmar. *vi law* declarar ante un juez
affirmation *n* afirmación, aserción, *f*; confirmación, *f*; *law* declaración, deposición, *f*
affirmative *a* afirmativo. *n* afirmativa, *f*
affix *vt* fijar; pegar; añadir; (seal, one's signature) poner. *n gram* afijo, *m*
afflict *vt* afligir, atormentar, aquejar
affliction *n* aflicción, *f*; tribulación, pesadumbre, *f*; calamidad, *f*; miseria, *f*; (ailment) achaque, *m*
affluence *n* afluencia, *f*; abundancia, *f*; riqueza, *f*; opulencia, *f*
affluent *a* abundante; rico; opulento
afflux *n* afluencia, *f*; *med* aflujo, *m*
afford *vt* dar, proporcionar; producir; ofrecer; (bear) soportar; poder con; (financially) tener medios para; permitirse el lujo de; (be able) poder. **I could not a. to pay so much,** No puedo (podía) pagar tanto
afforest *vt* convertir en bosque
afforestation *n* conversión en bosque, *f*; plantación de un bosque, *f*
affray *n* riña, refriega, *f*
affront *n* afrenta, *f*, insulto, agravio, *m*. *vt* insultar, ultrajar, afrentar; (offend) ofender
Afghan *a* and *n* afgano (-na)
Afghanistan Afganistán, *m*
afield *adv* en el campo; lejos. **to go far a.,** ir muy lejos
afire *adv* en fuego, en llamas; *fig* ardiendo
aflame *adv* en llamas; *fig* encendido
afloat *adv* a flote; *naut* a bordo; (solvent) solvente; en circulación; (floating) flotante; (swamped) inundado; (in full swing) en marcha, en movimiento
afoot *adv* a pie; en marcha, en movimiento; en preparación. **to set a.,** iniciar, poner en marcha
aforementioned *a* antedicho, ya mencionado
aforesaid *a* consabido, dicho, susodicho
afraid *a* espantado; temeroso, miedoso. **I'm a. that . . . ,** Me temo que. . . . **to be a.,** tener miedo. **to make a.,** dar miedo (a)
afresh *adv* de nuevo, otra vez
African *a* and *n* africano (-na)
aft *adv* en popa; a popa. **fore and aft,** de proa a popa
after *prep* (of place) detrás de; (of time) después de; (behind) en pos de; (following) tras; (in spite of) a pesar de; (in consequence of) después de, a consecuencia de; (in accordance with) según; (in the style of) al estilo de, en imitación de. *adv* (later) después, más tarde; (subsequently) después (que); (when) cuando. *a* futuro, venidero. **day a. day,** día tras día. **on the day a.,** al día siguiente. **soon a.,** poco después. **to look a.,** cuidar de. **to go a.,** ir a buscar; seguir. **the day a. tomorrow,** pasado mañana. **What are you a.?** ¿Qué buscas? **a. all,** después de todo. **a. the manner of,** a la moda de, según la moda de; al estilo de. **a.-dinner conversation,** conversación de sobremesa, *f*. **a. glow,** resplandor crepuscular, reflejo del sol poniente en el cielo, *m*. **a. life,** vida futura, *f*. **a. pains,** dolores de sobreparto, *m pl*. **a. taste,** dejo, resabio, *m*
afterbirth *n* placenta, *f*
aftermath *n* consecuencias, *f pl*, resultado, *m*
afternoon *n* tarde, *f*. **Good a.!** ¡Buenas tardes! **a. nap,** siesta, *f*. **a. tea,** el té de las cinco
afterthought *n* reflexión tardía, *f*; segunda intención, *f*. **to have an a.,** pensar en segundo lugar
afterwards *adv* después; más tarde
again *adv* (once more) otra vez, de neuvo; por segunda vez, dos veces; (on the other hand) por otra parte; (moreover) además; (likewise) también; (returned) de vuelta. Sometimes translated by prefix **re** in verbs. **as much a.,** otro tanto. **never a.,** nunca más. **not a.,** no más. **now and a.,** de vez en cuando. **to do a.,** volver a hacer, hacer de nuevo. **a. and a.,** repetidas veces
against *prep* (facing) enfrente de; contra; (in preparation for) para; (contrary to) contrario a; (opposed to) opuesto a; (near) cerca de. **to be a.,** oponer; estar enfrente de. **a. the grain,** a contrapelo
agate *n* ágata, *f*; heliotropo, *m*
age *n* edad, *f*; (generation) generación, *f*; (epoch) siglo, período, *m*; época, *f*; (old age) vejez, *f*; (majority) mayoría de edad, *f*, *vi* envejecer. **at any age,** a cualquier edad. **the golden age,** la edad de oro; (in literature, etc.) el siglo de oro. **from age to age,** por los siglos de los siglos. **to be of age,** ser mayor de edad. **to be under age,** ser menor de edad. **to come of age,** llegar a la mayoría de edad. **She is six years of age,** Ella tiene seis años. **age-old,** secular
aged *a* de la edad de; (old) anciano, viejo. **a girl a. four,** una niña de cuatro años
ageless *a* siempre joven; eterno
agency *n* órgano, *m*, fuerza, *f*; acción, *f*; influencia, *f*; intervención, *f*; mediación, *f*; *com* agencia, *f*. **through the a. of,** por la mediación (or influencia) de
agenda *n* agenda, *f*
agent *n* agente, *m*; *com* representante, *mf*; *law* apoderado (-da). **business a.,** agente de negocios, *m*
agglomerate *vt* and *vi* aglomerar(se)
agglomeration *n* aglomeración, *f*
agglutinate *vt* and *vi* aglutinar(se)
aggrandize *vt* engrandecer
aggrandizement *n* engrandecimiento, *m*
aggravate *vt* agravar, hacer peor; intensificar; (annoy) irritar, exasperar
aggravating *a* agravante, agravador; (tiresome) molesto; (annoying) irritante. **a. circumstance,** circunstancia agravante, *f*
aggravation *n* agravación, *f*, intensificación, *f*; (annoyance) irritación, *f*
aggregate *a* total. *n* agregado, conjunto, *m*. **in the a.,** en conjunto
aggression *n* agresión, *f*
aggressive *a* agresivo
aggressiveness *n* carácter agresivo, *m*, belicosidad, *f*
aggressor *a* and *n* agresor (-ra)
aggrieved *a* afligido; ofendido; lastimero
aghast *a* horrorizado, espantado; (amazed) estupefacto
agile *a* ágil; ligero, *Mexico* alacre; vivo
agility *n* agilidad, *f*; ligereza, *f*, *Mexico* alacridad
agitate *vt* agitar; excitar; inquietar, perturbar; discutir. **to a. for,** luchar por; excitar la opinión pública en favor de

agitating *a* agitador
agitation *n* agitación, *f;* perturbación, *f;* discusión, *f*
agitator *n* agitador (-ra); (apparatus) agitador, *m*
aglow *a* and *adv* brillante, fulgente; encendido
agnostic *a* and *n* agnóstico (-ca)
agnosticism *n* agnosticismo, *m*
ago *adv* hace. **a short while ago,** hace poco. **How long ago?** ¿Cuánto tiempo hace? **long ago,** hace mucho. **many years ago,** hace muchos años. **I last saw him ten years ago,** La última vez que le vi fue hace diez años
agog *a* agitado; ansioso; excitado; impaciente; curioso. *adv* con agitación; con ansia; con curiosidad
agonize *vt* atormentar. *vi* sufrir intensamente; retorcerse de dolor
agonizing *a* (of pain) intenso, atormentador
agonizingly *adv* dolorosamente
agony *n* agonía, *f;* angustia, *f;* paroxismo, *m.* **a. column,** columna de los suspiros, *f*
agrarian *a* agrario
agree *vi* estar de acuerdo. **Do you a. or disagree?** ¿Coincides o discrepas?; convenir (en); acordar; ponerse de acuerdo, entenderse; (suit) sentar bien, probar; (consent) consentir (en); *gram* concordar, (get on well) llevarse bien; (correspond) estar conforme (con). **to a. to,** convenir en, consentir en. **to a. with,** estar de acuerdo con, apoyar; dar la razón a; (suit) sentar bien; *gram* concordar
agreeable *a* agradable; afable, amable; (pleasant) ameno, grato; conforme; dispuesto a (hacer algo); conveniente
agreeableness *n* (of persons) afabilidad, amabilidad, *f;* amenidad, *f;* deleite, *m;* conformidad, *f*
agreeably *adv* agradablemente; de acuerdo (con), conforme (a)
agreed *a* convenido, acordado; (approved) aprobado. *interj* ¡convenido! ¡de acuerdo!
agreement *n* acuerdo, *m;* pacto, *m;* acomodamiento, concierto, *m;* contrato, *m; com* convenio, *m;* conformidad, *f;* consentimiento, *m; gram* concordancia, *f.* **in a.,** conforme. **in a. with,** de acuerdo con; según. **to reach an a.,** ponerse de acuerdo
agricultural *a* agrícola. **a. engineer,** ingeniero agrónomo, *m.* **a. laborer,** labriego, *m.* **a. show,** exposición agrícola, *f*
agriculturalist *n* agrícola, *mf*
agriculture *n* agricultura, *f*
agronomist *n* agrónomo, *m*
agronomy *n* agronomía, *f*
aground *adv naut* varado, encallado. **running a.,** varada, *f.* **to run a.,** varar
ague *n* fiebre intermitente, *f; fig* escalofrío, *m*
ah! *interj* ¡ah! ¡ay!
aha! *interj* ¡ajá!
ahead *adv* delante; enfrente; al frente (de); a la cabeza (de); adelante; hacia delante; *naut* por la proa. **Go a.!** ¡Adelante! **It is straight a.,** Está directamente enfrente. **to go straight a.,** ir hacia delante; seguir (haciendo algo)
ahoy! *interj* ¡ah del barco!
aid *n* ayuda, *f;* socorro, auxilio, *m;* subsidio, *m, vt* ayudar; socorrer, auxiliar. **in aid of,** pro, en beneficio de. **first aid,** primera cura, *f.* **first aid post,** puesto de socorro, *m.* **to come or go to the aid of,** acudir en defensa de
aide-de-camp *n* edecán, *m*
AIDS *n* el SIDA, *m*
ail *vt* afligir, doler; pasar. *vi* estar indispuesto (or enfermo). **What ails you?** *inf* ¿Qué te pasa?
ailing *a* enfermizo, enclenque, achacoso
ailment *n* enfermedad, *f,* achaque, *m*
aim *n* (of firearms) puntería, *f;* (mark) blanco, *m; fig* objeto, fin, *m; fig* intención, *f,* propósito, *m, vt* (a gun) apuntar; dirigir; (throw) lanzar; (a blow) asestar. *vi* apuntar (a); (a remark at) decir por; aspirar (a); intentar, proponerse. **Is your remark aimed at me?** ¿Lo dices por mí? **to aim high,** apuntar alto; *inf* picar alto. **to miss one's aim,** errar el tiro. **to take aim,** apuntar. **with the aim of,** con objeto de, a fin de
aimless *a* **aimlessly,** *adv* sin objeto, a la ventura
air *n* aire, *m,* (all meanings). **by air,** en avión; (of mail) por avión; (of goods) por vía aérea. **in the air,** al aire; al aire libre; (as though flying) en volandas. **in the open air,** al aire libre, al fresco, a la intemperie. **to be on the air,** *rad* hablar por radio. **to give oneself airs,** darse tono, tener humos. **to take the air,** tomar el fresco; despegar. **air balloon,** globo aerostático, *m;* (toy) globo, *m.* **air-base,** base aérea, *f.* **air-bed,** colchón de viento, *m.* **air-borne (to become),** levantar el vuelo, despegar. **air-brake,** *mech* freno neumático, *m.* **air-chamber,** cámara de aire, *f.* **air chief marshal,** general del ejército del aire, *m.* **air-cock,** válvula de escape de aire, *f.* **air commodore,** general de brigada de aviación, *m.* **air conditioning,** purificación de aire, *f. Lat. Am.* aclimatión, **air-cooled,** enfriado por aire. **air crash,** accidente de aviación, *m.* **air current,** corriente de aire, *f.* **air-cushion,** almohadilla neumática, *f.* **air-field,** campo de aviación, *m.* **air fleet,** flotilla aérea, *f.* **air force,** fuerza aérea, flota aérea, *f.* **air-gun,** escopeta de viento, *f.* **air-hole,** respiradero, *m.* **air-hostess,** azafata, *f.* **air-lift,** puente aéreo, *m.* **air-liner,** avión de pasajeros, *m.* **airline** linea aérea, aerolínea, *f.* **airmail,** correo aéreo, *m.* **by airmail,** por avión. **air marshal,** teniente general de aviación, *m.* **air-pocket,** bolsa (or vacío, *m*) de aire, *f.* **air pollution** contaminación atmosférica, *f.* **air pump,** bomba neumática, *f.* **air raid,** bombardeo aéreo, *m.* **air-raid shelter,** refugio antiaéreo, *m.* **air-raid warning,** alarma aérea, *f.* **air-route,** vía aérea, *f.* **air-screw,** hélice de avión, *f.* **air-shaft,** respiradero de mina, *m.* **air shuttle,** puente aéreo, *m.* **air squadron,** escuadrilla aérea, *f.* **air stream,** chorro de aire, *m.* **air taxi,** avión taxi, *m.* **air-tight,** herméticamente cerrado. **air valve,** válvula de aire, *f.* **air vice-marshal,** general de división de aviación, *m*
air *vt* airear, orear; secar al aire; ventilar; *fig* sacar a lucir, emitir; *fig* ostentar
aircraft *n* aparato, avión, *m.* **a. barrage,** cortina de fuego de artillería, *f.* **a.-carrier,** porta-aviones, *m.* **a. factory,** fábrica de aeroplanos, *f*
airily *adv* ligeramente, sin preocuparse; alegremente
airiness *n* airosidad, *f;* ventilación, *f;* situación airosa, *f;* (lightness) ligereza, *f;* alegría, *f;* frivolidad, *f*
airing *n* aireación, *f;* ventilación, *f;* secamiento, *m;* (walk) vuelta, *f,* paseo, *m.* **to take an a.,** dar una vuelta
airless *a* sin aire; falto de ventilación; sofocante
airman *n* aviador, *m*
airplane *n* aeroplano, avión, *m.* **jet-propelled a.,** aeroplano de reacción, *m.* **model a.,** aeroplano en miniatura, *m*
airport *n* aeropuerto, *m*
airsick *a* mareado en el aire, mareado
airway *n* vía aérea, *f*
airwoman *n* aviadora, *f*
airy *a* aéreo; (breezy) airoso; ligero; vaporoso; alegre; (vain) vano; (flippant) frívolo
aisle *n* nave lateral, ala, *f*
ajar *a* entreabierto, entornado. **to leave a.,** dejar entreabierto, entornar
akimbo *adv* en jarras. **with arms a.,** con los brazos en jarras
akin *a* consanguíneo, emparentado; análogo, relacionado; semejante
alabaster *n* alabastro, *m, a* alabastrino
alacrity *n* alacridad, *f*
alarm *n* alarma, *f,* toque de alarma, *m;* (tocsin) rebato, *m;* sobresalto, *m,* alarma, *f. vt* alarmar; *mil* dar la alarma (a); asustar. **to give the a.,** dar la alarma. **a. bell,** timbre de alarma, *m.* **a. clock,** despertador, *m.* **a. signal,** señal de alarma, *f*
alarming *a* alarmante

alarmingly *adv* de un modo alarmante; espantosamente
alarmist *n* alarmista, *mf*
alas! *interj* ¡ay!
alb *n* alba, *f*
Albanian *a* and *n* albanés (-esa); (language) albanés, *m*
albatross *n* albatros, *m*
albeit *conjunc* aunque, si bien; sin embargo
albinism *n* albinismo, *m*
albino *a* albino
album *n* álbum, *m*
albumin *n* albúmina, *f*
alchemist *n* alquimista, *m*
alchemy *n* alquimia, *f*
alcohol *n* alcohol, *m*. **industrial a.,** alcohol desnaturalizado, *m*. **wood a.,** alcohol metílico, alcohol de madera, *m*
alcoholic *a* alcohólico
alcoholism *n* alcoholismo, *m*
alcoholize *vt* alcoholizar
alcove *n* alcoba, *f*; nicho, *m*
alder *n* (tree and wood) aliso, *m*
alderman *n* concejal, *m*
ale *n* cerveza, *f*. **ale-house,** cervecería, *f*
alert *a* alerto; vigilante; despierto; vivo. *n* sirena, *f*. **to be on the a.,** estar sobre aviso; estar vigilante
alertly *adv* alertamente
alertness *n* vigilancia, *f*; viveza, *f*; prontitud, *f*
Alexandria Alejandría, *f*
alga *n* alga, *f*
algebra *n* álgebra, *f*
algebraic *a* algebraico
Algeria Argelia, *f*
Algerian *a* and *n* argelino (-na)
Algiers Argel, *m*
alias *adv* alias, por otro nombre. *n* nombre falso, seudónimo, *m*
alibi *n law* coartada, *f*. **to prove an a.,** probar la coartada
alien *a* ajeno; (foreign) extranjero; extraño; contrario. *n* extranjero (-ra). **a. to,** ajeno a; repugnante a. **Aliens Department,** Sección de Extranjeros, *f*
alienable *a* enajenable
alienate *vt* alejar, hacer indiferente; (property) enajenar, traspasar
alienation *n* desvío, *m*; enajenación, *f*; traspaso, *m*; enajenación mental, *f*
alight *vi* apearse (de), bajar (de); desmontar (de); (of birds, etc.) posarse (sobre)
alight *a* encendido, iluminado; en llamas
align *vt* alinear
alignment *n* alineación, *f*
alike *a* semejante; igual. *adv* del mismo modo; igualmente
alimentary *a* nutritivo; alimenticio. **a. canal,** tubo digestivo, *m*
alimentation *n* alimentación, *f*
alimony *n law* alimentos, *m pl*, pensión alimenticia, *f*
alive *a* viviente; vivo; del mundo; (busy) animado, concurrido; (aware) sensible; (alert) lleno de vida, enérgico, despierto. **He is still a.,** Aún vive. **He is the best man a.,** Es el mejor hombre que existe, Es el mejor hombre del mundo. **half-a.,** semivivo. **while a.,** en vida. **a. to,** consciente de, sensible de. **a. with,** plagado de, lleno de
alkali *n* álcali, *m*
alkaline *a* alcalino
alkaloid *n* alcaloide, *m*
all *a* todo, *m*; toda, *f*; todos, *m pl*; todas, *f pl*; (in games) iguales. *adv* enteramente, completamente; del todo; absolutamente. **after all,** después de todo; sin embargo. **at all,** nada; de ninguna manera; en absoluto. **fifteen all,** (tennis) quince iguales. **for good and all,** para siempre. **if that's all,** si no es más que eso. **in all,** en conjunto. **It is all one to me,** Me da igual. **not at all,** de ningún modo, nada de eso; nada; (never) jamás; (as a polite formula) No hay de qué. **once for all,** una vez por todas; por última vez. **That is all,** Eso es todo. **all along,** (of time) siempre, todo el tiempo; (of place) a lo largo de, de un extremo a otro de. **all but,** (almost) casi, por poco; (except) todo menos. **all joking aside,** fuera de burla. **all of them,** todos ellos, *m pl*; todas ellas, *f pl*. **All right!** ¡Bien! ¡Está bien! ¡Entendido! **all that,** todo eso; (as much as) cuanto. **all that which,** todo lo que. **all those who,** todos los que, *m pl*; todas las que, *f pl*. **all the more,** cuanto más. **all the same,** sin embargo, a pesar de todo. **all the worse,** tanto peor
all *n* todo, *m*; todos, *m pl*; todas, *f pl*; (everyone, all men) todo el mundo. **to lose one's all,** perder todo lo que se tiene. **All is lost,** Todo se ha perdido. **all told,** en conjunto
all (*in compounds*) **all-absorbing,** que todo lo absorbe; sumamente interesante. **all-bountiful,** de suma bondad. **all-conquering,** invicto. **all-consuming,** que todo lo consume; irresistible; ardiente. **all-enduring,** resignado a todo. **All Fools' Day,** Día de los Inocentes, *m*, (December 28). **all-fours,** a cuatro patas; a gatas. **to go on all fours,** andar a gatas. **All hail!** ¡Salud! ¡Bienvenido! **all-important,** sumamente importante. **all-in insurance,** seguro contra todo riesgo, *m*. **all-in wrestling,** lucha libre, *f*. **all-loving,** de un amor infinito. **all-merciful,** de una compasión infinita, sumamente misericordioso. **all-powerful,** omnipotente, todo poderoso. **all-round,** completo, cabal; universal. **an all-round athlete,** un atleta completo. **All Souls' Day,** Día de las Ánimas, Día de los difuntos, *m*. **all-wise,** omnisciο
allay *vt* calmar; (relieve) aliviar; apaciguar
allaying *n* alivio, *m*; apaciguamiento, *m*
allegation *n* alegación, *f*
allege *vt* afirmar, declarar; alegar
allegiance *n* lealtad, *f*; fidelidad, *f*; obediencia, *f*
allegorical *a* alegórico
allegory *n* alegoría, *f*
alleluia *n* aleluya, *mf*
allergic *a* alérgico
allergist *n* alergólogo, *m*
allergy *n* alergia, *f*
alleviate *vt* aliviar
alleviation *n* alivio, *m*; mitigación, *f*
alley *n* callejuela, *f*, callejón, *m*; avenida, *f*; (skittle a.) pista de bolos, *f*. **a.-way,** *naut* pasadizo, *m*
alliance *n* alianza, *f*; parentesco, *m*
allied *a* aliado; allegado
alligator *n* caimán, *m*. **a. pear,** avocado, *Mexico* aquacate *m*
alliteration *n* aliteración, *f*
allocate *vt* asignar, destinar; distribuir, repartir
allocation *n* asignación, *f*; distribución, *f*, repartimiento, *m*
allotment *n* repartimiento, *m*, distribución, *f*; porción, *f*; lote, *m*; parcela de tierra, huerta, *f*
allow *vt* permitir; autorizar; dejar; tolerar, sufrir; (provide) dar; conceder, otorgar; (acknowledge) admitir; confesar; (discount) descontar; (a pension) hacer; deducir. **to a. for,** tener en cuenta; ser indulgente con; deducir; dejar (espacio, etc.) para
allowable *a* admisible, permisible; lícito, legítimo
allowance *n* ración, *f*; (discount) descuento, *m*; pensión, *f*; concesión, *f*; excusa, *f*; (subsidy) subsidio, *m*; (bonus) abono, *m*; (monthly) mesada, *f*. **to make a. for,** tener presente; hacer excusas para, ser indulgente con
alloy *n* aleación, *f*; liga, *f*; mezcla, *f*. *vt* alear, ligar; mezclar
allspice *n* guindilla de Indias, *f*
all-star game *n* juego de estrellas, *m*
allude *vi* aludir (a), referirse (a)
allure *vt* convidar, provocar; atraer; seducir, fascinar
allurement *n* (snare) añagaza, *f*; atracción, *f*; tentación, seducción, *f*

alluring *a* atractivo, seductor, tentador; (promising) halagüeño
allusion *n* alusión, referencia, *f*; insinuación, *f*
allusive *a* alusivo
ally *n* aliado (-da), allegado (-da); asociado (-da); (state) aliado, *m*. *vt* unir. **to become allies,** aliarse
almanac *n* almanaque, *m*
almighty *a* omnipotente
almond *n* almendra, *f*; (tree) almendro, *m*. **bitter a.,** almendra amarga, *f*. **green a.,** almendruco, *m*. **milk of almonds,** horchata de almendras, *f*; (for the hands) loción de almendras, *f*. **sugar a.,** almendra garapiñada, *f*. **a.-eyed,** con, or de, ojos rasgados. **a. paste,** pasta de almendras, *f*. **a.-shaped,** en forma de almendra, almendrado
almoner *n* limosnero (-ra) *mf*
almost *adv* casi; por poco
alms *n* limosna, *f*. **to ask a.,** pedir limosna, mendigar. **to give a.,** dar limosna. **a.-box,** cepillo de limosna, *m*
almsgiving *n* caridad, *f*
aloe *n* áloe, *m*; *pl* **aloes,** *med* acíbar, *m*
aloft *adv* arriba, en alto
alone *a* solo; solitario. *adv* a solas, sin compañía; solamente; únicamente. **to leave a.,** dejar solo; dejar en paz
along *adv* adelante; a lo largo; todo el tiempo. *prep* a lo largo de; por; al lado (de); en compañía (de). **Come a.!** ¡Ven! **all a.,** todo el tiempo, desde el principio; a lo largo de. **a. with,** junto con; en compañía de
alongside *adv* al lado; *naut* al costado. *prep* junto a, al lado de; *naut* al costado de. **to bring a.,** *naut* abarloar. **to come a.,** *naut* acostarse
aloof *adv* a distancia; lejos. *a* altanero, esquivo; reservado. **to keep a.,** mantenerse alejado
aloofness *n* alejamiento, *m*; esquivez, *f*; reserva, *f*
aloud *adv* en alta voz, alto
alpaca *n* alpaca, *f*
alphabet *n* alfabeto, *m*; abecedario, *m*
alphabetical *a* alfabético
Alpine *a* alpestre, alpino
Alps, the los Alpes, *m*
already *adv* ya; previamente
Alsatian *a* and *n* alsaciano (-na†. **A. dog,** perro policía, perro pastor alemán, perro lobo, *m*
also *adv* también, igualmente, además
altar *n* altar, *m*. **high a.,** altar mayor, *m*. **to lead a woman to the a.,** llevar a una mujer a la iglesia. **a.-cloth,** mantel del altar, *m*. **a.-piece,** retablo, *m*. **a.-rail,** mesa del altar, *f*
altar boy *n* acólito, monaguillo, *m*
altar girl *n* acólita, monaguilla, *f*
altar server *n* acólito, monaguillo, *m* (male), acólita, monaguilla, *f* (female)
alter *vt* cambiar; alterar; modificar; corregir; transformar; (clothes) arreglar. *vi* cambiar
alterable *a* alterable
alteration *n* cambio, *m*, alteración, *f*; modificación, *f*; correción, *f*; innovación, *f*; (to buildings, etc.) reforma, *f*; renovación, *f*; arreglo, *m*
altercation *n* altercación, *f*
alternate *a* alternativo; (*bot* and of rhymes) alterno. *vt* and *vi* alternar
alternately *adv* alternativamente; por turno
alternating *a* alternador. **a. current,** *elec* corriente alterna, *f*
alternation *n* alternación, *f*; (of time) transcurso, *m*; turno, *m*
alternative *n* alternativa, *f*, *a* alternativo, alterno. **to have no a. but,** no poder menos de
alternatively *adv* alternativamente
alternator *n elec* alternador, *m*
although *conjunc* aunque, bien que; si bien; no obstante, a pesar de
altimeter *n aer* altímetro, *m*
altitude *n* altitud, elevación, *f*; altura, *f*
alto *n* (voice) contralto, *m*; (singer) contralto, *mf*; viola, *f*
altogether *adv* completamente; del todo; en conjunto
alto-relievo *n* alto relieve, *m*
altruism *n* altruísmo, *m*
altruist *n* altruista, *mf*
aluminum *n* aluminio, *m*
aluminum foil *n* hoja de aluminio, *f*
alumnus *n Lat. Am.* exalumno *m*.
alumna *n Lat. Am.* exalumna *f*
always *adv* siempre
amalgam *n* amalgama, *f*; mezcla, *f*
amalgamate *vt* amalgamar; combinar, unir. *vi* amalgamarse; combinarse, unirse
amalgamation *n* amalgamación, *f*; combinación, *f*; mezcla, *f*
amanuensis *n* amanuense, *mf*; secretario (-ia)
amass *vt* acumular, amontonar
amateur *a* and *n* aficionado (-da), (sports) no profesional. **a. theatricals,** función de aficionados, *f* **a. band** *Mexico* escoleta *f*
amateurish *a* no profesional; de aficionado; superficial; (clumsy) torpe
amatory *a* amatorio
amaze *vt* asombrar, sorprender; pasmar; confundir
amazed *a* asombrado; sorprendido; admirado; asustado
amazement *n* asombro, pasmo, *m*; sorpresa, *f*; (wonderment) admiración, *f*; estupor, *m*
amazing *a* asombroso, pasmoso; sorprendente
amazingly *adv* asombrosamente
Amazon *n* amazona, *f*
Amazon River, the el (Río de las) Amazonas, *m*
ambassador *n* embajador, *m*
ambassadress *n* embajadora, *f*
amber *n* ámbar, *m*, *a* ambarino
ambidextrous *a* ambidextro
ambiguity *n* ambigüedad, *f*
ambiguous *a* ambiguo, equivoco
ambition *n* ambición, *f*
ambitious *a* ambicioso. **to be a. to,** ambicionar
amble *n* (of a horse) paso de andadura, *m*; paso lento, *m*. *vi* (of a horse) andar a paso de andadura; andar lentamente
ambulance *n* ambulancia, *f*. **a. corps,** cuerpo de sanidad, *m*. **a. man,** sanitario, *m*
ambulatory *n* paseo, *m*; claustro, *m*, *a* ambulante
ambush *n* acecho, *m*, asechanza, *f*; *mil* emboscada, *f*. *vt* acechar, asechar; *mil* emboscar; sorprender. **to be in a.,** emboscarse, estar en acecho
amelioration *n* mejora, *f*
amen *n* amén, *m*
amenable *a* sujeto (a); responsable; dócil; fácil de convencer, dispuesto a ser razonable; dispuesto a escuchar. **to make a. to reason,** hacer razonable
amend *vt* enmendar; modificar. *vi* reformarse
amendment *n* enmienda, *f*; modificación, *f*
amends *n pl* reparación, *f*; satisfacción, *f*; compensación, *f*. **to make a.,** dar satisfacción
amenity *n* amenidad, *f*
America América, *f*
American *n* americano (-na); (U.S.A.) norteamericano (-na). *a* americano, de América; norteamericano, de los Estados Unidos. **Central A.,** *a* and *n* centroamericano (-na). **A. bar,** bar americano, *m*
Americanism *n* americanismo, *m*
Americanize *vt* americanizar
amethyst *n* amatista, *f*
amiability *n* amabilidad, afabilidad, cordialidad, *f*
amiable *a* amable, afable, cordial
amiably *adv* amablemente, con afabilidad
amianthus *n* amianto, *m*
amicable *a* amigable, amistoso
amice *n* amito, *m*
amid, amidst *prep* en medio de; entre; rodeado por
amidships *adv* en el centro del buque, en medio del navío
amiss *adv* mal; de más; (ill) indispuesto, enfermo;

(inopportunely) inoportunamente. *a* malo. **It would not come a.,** No vendría mal. **to take a.,** llevar a mal
ammeter *n elec* amperímetro, *m*
ammonia *n* amoníaco, *m*
ammoniacal *a* amoniacal
ammunition *n* munición, *f*. **a. box,** cajón de municiones, *m*
amnesia *n* amnesia, *f*
amnesty *n* amnistía, *f*. **to concede an a. to,** amnistiar
amok (to run a.) atacar a ciegas
among *prep* en medio de; entre; con
amoral *a* amoral
amorality *n* amoralidad, *f*
amorous *a* amoroso; (tender) tierno
amorousness *n* erotismo, *m*; galantería, *f*
amorphous *a* amorfo
amortization *n* amorcización, *f*
amortize *vt* amortizar
amount *n* importe, *m*, suma, *f*; cantidad, *f*, *vi* (to) subir a, ascender a, llegar a; valer; reducirse a. **gross a.,** importe bruto, *m*. **net a.,** importe líquido, importe neto, *m*. **It amounts to the same thing, then,** Es igual entonces, Viene a ser lo mismo pues. **What he says amounts to this,** Lo que dice se reduce a esto
amperage *n* amperaje, *m*
ampere *n* amper, amperio, *m*
amphibian *n* anfibio, *m*
amphibious *a* anfibio
amphitheater *n* anfiteatro, *m*
amphora *n* ánfora, *f*
ample *a* amplio; abundante; extenso, vasto; (sufficient) bastante, suficiente
amplification *n* amplificación, *f*
amplifier *n* amplificador, *m*
amplify *vt* amplificar; aumentar, ampliar
amplitude *n* amplitud, *f*; abundancia, *f*; extensión, *f*
amply *adv* ampliamente; abundantemente; suficientemente
amputate *vt* amputar
amputation *n* amputación, *f*
amulet *n* amuleto, *m*
amuse *vt* divertir, entretener, distraer. **to a. oneself,** divertirse; pasarlo bien
amusement *n* diversión, *f*, entretenimiento, *m*; (hobby) pasatiempo, *m*. **a. park,** parque de atracciones, *m*
amusing *a* divertido, entretenido; (of people) salado
amusingly *adv* de un modo divertido, entretenidamente
an. See **a**
Anabaptism *n* anabaptismo, *m*
Anabaptist *n* anabaptista, *mf*
anachronism *n* anacronismo, *m*
anachronistic *a* anacrónico
anagram *n* anagrama, *m*
analects *n pl* analectas, *f pl*
analgesia *n* analgesia, *f*
analgesic *a* and *n* analgésico, *m*.
analogous *a* análogo
analogy *n* analogía, *f*
analyse *vt* analizar
analysis *n* análisis, *m*
analyst *n* analista, *mf*
analytical *a* analítico
anaphora *n* anáfora, *f*
anaphrodisiac *a* anafrodisíaco
anarchic *a* anárquico
anarchism *n* anarquismo, *m*
anarchist *n* anarquista, *mf*
anarchy *n* anarquía, *f*
anastigmatic *a* anastigmático
anathema *n* anatema, *mf*
anathematize *vt* anatematizar
anatomic *a* anatómico
anatomically *adv* anatómicamente; físicamente
anatomist *n* anatomista, *mf*
anatomy *n* anatomía, *f*
ancestor *n* antepasado, abuelo, *m*
ancestral *a* de sus antepasados; de familia; hereditario. **a. home,** casa solariega, *f*
ancestry *n* antepasados, *m pl*; linaje, abolengo, *m*; estirpe, *f*; nacimiento, *m*; origen, *m*
anchor *n* ancla, *f*. *fig* áncora, *f*. *vt* sujetar con el ancla. *vi* anclar, echar anclas, fondear. **at a.,** al ancla. **drag a.,** ancla flotante, ancla de arrastre, *f*. **sheet a.,** ancla de la esperanza, *f*; *fig* ancla de salvación, *f*. **to drop a.,** anclar. **to ride at a.,** estar al ancla. **to weigh a.,** levar el ancla
anchorage *n* anclaje, *m*; ancladero, fondeadero, *m*; derechos de anclaje, *m pl*
anchovy *n* anchoa, *f*, boquerón, *m*
ancient *a* anciano; antiguo. *n pl* **ancients,** los antiguos. **from a. times,** de antiguo. **most a.,** antiquísimo
and *conjunc* y; (before stressed i or hi) e; (after some verbs and before infin.) de, a; que; (with) con; (often not translated before infins.). **Better and better,** Mejor que mejor. **I shall try and do it,** Trataré de hacerlo. **to come and see,** venir a ver. **We shall try and speak to him,** Procuraremos hablar con él
Andalusia Andalucía, *f*
Andalusian *a* andaluz. *n* andaluz (-za). **A. hat,** sombrero calañés, *m*
Andean *a* andino (-na), *Argentina, Chile also* corderillano (-na)
Andes, the los Andes, *f*
andiron *n* morillo, *m*
Andorran *a* and *n* andorrano (-na)
androgynous *a* andrógino
anecdotal *a* anecdótico
anecdote *n* anécdota, *f*
anemia *n* anemia, *f*
anemic *a* anémico
anemometer *n* anemómetro, *m*
anemone *n* anémona, anémone, *f*
aneroid *a* aneroide. *n* barómetro aneroide, *m*
anesthesia *n* anestesia, *f*
anesthetic *a* and *n* anestésico, *m*.
anesthetist *n* anestesiador (-ra)
anesthetize *vt* anestesiar
aneurism *n* aneurisma, *mf*
angel *n* ángel, *m*
angelic *a* angélico
angelica *n* angélica, *f*
anger *n* cólera, ira, *f*, enojo, *m*, *vt* enojar, encolerizar; hacer rabiar, *Mexico* amuinar
angina *n* angina, *f*. **a. pectoris,** angina de pecho, *f*
angle *n* ángulo, *m*; rincón, *m*; esquina, *f*; (of a roof) caballette, *m*; *fig* punto de vista, *m*, *vi* pescar con caña. **at an a.,** a un lado. **a.-iron,** hierro angular, *m*. **to a. for,** pescar; *fig* procurar obtener
Angle *a* and *n* anglo (-la)
angler *n* pescador (-ra) de caña
Anglican *a* and *n* anglicano (-na)
Anglicanism *n* anglicanismo, *m*
Anglicism *n* anglicismo, inglesismo, *m*
Anglicize *vt* inglesar
angling *n* pesca con caña, *f*
Anglo- (in compounds) anglo-. **A.-American,** *a* and *n* angloamericano (-na). **A.-Indian,** *a* and *n* angloindio (-ia). **A.-Saxon,** *a* and *n* anglosajón (-ona); (language) anglosajón, *m*
anglomania *n* anglomanía, *f*
anglophile *n* anglófilo (-la)
anglophobia *n* anglofobia, *f*
angora *n* angora, *f*. **a. cat,** gato de angora, *m*. **a. rabbit,** conejo de angora, *m*
angrily *adv* airadamente
angry *a* (of persons) enfadado, enojado, airado; (of waves, etc.) furioso; *med* inflamado; (red) rojo; (scowling) cenudo; (dark) obscuro. **to be a.,** estar enojado. **to get angry, to grow a.,** enojarse, enfadarse, *Lat. Am.*

entromparse; (of waves) encresparse; (of the sky) obscurecerse. **to make a.,** enojar
anguish *n* agonía, *f,* dolor, *m;* angustia, *f. vt* angustiar
angular *a* angular; (of features, etc.) anguloso
angularity *n* angulosidad, *f*
anhydrous *a* anhidro
aniline *n* anilina, *f*
animal *a* and *n* animal *m.* **a. fat,** grasa animal, *f.* **a. kingdom,** reino animal, *m.* **a. spirits,** *phil* espíritus animales, *m pl;* brío, *m,* energía, *f*
animalism *n* animalidad, *f;* sensualidad, *f*
animate *vt* animar; inspirar. *a* animado; viviente
animated *a* animado; vivo, lleno de vida
animation *n* animación, *f;* vivacidad, *f;* calor, fuego, *m*
animism *n* animismo, *m*
animosity *n* animosidad, hostilidad, *f*
aniseed *n* anís, *m*
anisette *n* (liqueur) anisete, *m*
ankle *n* tobillo, *m.* **a. bone,** hueso del tobillo, *m.* **a. sock,** calcetín corto, *m*
anklet *n* brazalete para el tobillo, *m;* (support) tobillera, *f*
annals *n pl* anales, *m pl*
anneal *vt* (metals) recocer; (glass) templar; (with oil) atemperar
annex *vt* unir, juntar; anexar. *n* anexo, *m*
annexation *n* anexión, *f*
annihilate *vt* aniquilar
annihilation *n* aniquilación,
anniversary *a* and *n* aniversario, *m.*
annotate *vt* anotar, acotar, comentar, hacer anotaciones a
annotation *n* anotación, *f;* nota, *f*
annotator *n* anotador (-ra), comentador (-ra)
announce *vt* proclamar; declarar; publicar; anunciar
announcement *n* proclama, *f;* declaración, *f;* publicación, *f;* anuncio, *m;* (of a betrothal) participación, *f*
announcer *n* anunciador (-ra); (radio or TV) locutor (-ra)
annoy *vt* exasperar, irritar, disgustar; molestar, incomodar, *Lat. Am.* acatarrar, cargosear, engorrar
annoyance *n* disgusto, *m,* exasperación, *f;* molestia, *f,* fastidio, *m*
annoying *a* enojoso, molesto, fastidioso, *Lat. Am.* cargoso
annual *a* anual. *n* anuario, *m;* calendario, *m;* planta anual, *f*
annually *adv* anualmente, cada año
annuitant *n* censualista, *mf*
annuity *n* anualidad, pensión vitalicia, *f*
annul *vt* anular
annulment *n* anulación, *f*
annunciation *n* anunciación, *f.* **the A.,** la Anunciación
anodyne *a* and *n* anodino, *m*
anoint *vt* untar; (before death) olear; (a king, etc.) ungir
anointing *n* unción, *f*
anomalous *a* anómalo
anomaly *n* anomalía, *f*
anonymity *n* anónimo, *m*
anonymous *a* anónimo. **a. letter,** anónimo, *m*
another *a* otro; (different) distinto. *n* otro, *m;* otra, *f.* **For one thing . . . and for a.,** En primer lugar . . . y además (y por otra cosa). **one after a.,** uno después de otro. **They love one a.,** Ellos se aman. **They sent it from one to a.,** Lo mandaron de uno a otro
answer *n* contestación, respuesta, *f;* (refutation) refutación, *f;* (pert reply) réplica, *f;* (solution) solución, *f; math* resultado, *m; law* contestación a la demanda, *f*
answer *vt* responder, contestar; (a letter, etc.) contestar a; (refute) refutar; (reply pertly) replicar; (write) escribir; (return) devolver; (suit) servir; (a bell, etc.) acudir a; (the door) abrir. *vi* contestar; (succeed) tener éxito; dar resultado. **to a. by return,** contestar a vuelta de correo, **to a. back,** replicar. **to a. for,** ser responsable por; ser responsable de; (speak for) hablar por; (guarantee) garantizar, responder de
answerable *a* responsable; refutable; (adequate) adecuado. **to make a. for,** hacer responsable de
answering machine *n* contestador telefónico, contestador, *m*
ant *n* hormiga, *f.* **ant-eater,** oso hormiguero, *m.* **ant-hill,** hormiguero, *m*
antagonism *n* antagonismo, *m,* hostilidad, oposición, *f*
antagonist *n* antagonista, *mf*
antagonistic *a* antagónico, hostil
antagonize *vt* contender; hacer hostil (a)
antarctic *a* antártico. *n* polo antártico, *m*
antecedent *a* and *n* antecedente, *m.*
antechamber *n* antecámara, antesala, *f*
antedate *vt* antedatar; anticipar
antediluvian *a* antediluviano
antelope *n* antílope, *m*
antenna *n* antena, *f*
anterior *a* anterior
anthem *n* antífona, *f*
anthologist *n* antólogo, *m*
anthology *n* antología, floresta, *f*
anthracite *n* antracita, *f,* carbón mineral, *m*
anthrax *n* ántrax, *m*
anthropological *a* antropológico
anthropologist *n* antropólogo, *m*
anthropology *n* antropología, *f*
anti-aircraft *a* antiaéreo. **A.A. gun,** cañon antiaéreo, *m*
antibody *n* anticuerpo, *m*
antic *n* travesura, *f*
Antichrist *n* Anticristo, *m*
anticipate *vt* (foresee) prever; anticipar; adelantarse a; (hope) esperar; (frustrate) frustrar; (enjoy) disfrutar con anticipación de
anticipation *n* anticipación, *f;* adelantamiento, *m;* esperanza, expectación, *f.* **in a. of,** en espera de
anticipatory *a* anticipador
anticlerical *a* anticlerical
anticlericalism *n* anticlericalismo, *m*
anticlimax *n* anticlímax, *m*
antidote *n* antídoto, contraveneno, *m*
antifreeze *n* anticongelante, *m*
Antilles, the las Antillas, *f*
antimony *n* antimonio, *m*
antipathetic *a* antipático
antipathy *n* antipatía, *f*
antipode *n pl* antípodas, *mf pl*
antiquarian *a* anticuario
antiquary *n* anticuario, *m*
antiquated *a* anticuado
antique *a* antiguo. *n* antigüedad, antigualla, *f.* **a. dealer,** anticuario, *m.* **a. shop,** tienda de antigüedades, *f*
antiquity *n* antigüedad, *f;* ancianidad, *f*
antireligious *a* antirreligioso
antirepublican *a* antirrepublicano
anti-Semitic *a* antisemita
anti-Semitism *n* antisemitismo, *m*
antiseptic *a* and *n* antiséptico, *m*
antisocial *a* antisocial
antithesis *n* antítesis, *f*
antithetic *a* antitético
antitoxin *n* antitoxina, *f*
antler *n* asta, *f*
antonym *n* contrario, *m*
antrum *n* antro, *m*
Antwerp Amberes, *m*
anus *n* ano, *m*
anvil *n* yunque, *m,* bigornia, *f*
anxiety *n* inquietud, intranquilidad, *f;* preocupación, *f;* ansiedad, *f;* curiosidad, *f;* impaciencia, *f;* (wish) deseo, afán, *m*
anxious *a* inquieto, intranquilo; preocupado; ansioso; impaciente; deseoso. **to be a.,** estar inquieto; apurarse. **to be a. to,** ansiar, tener deseos de. **to make a.,** preocupar, inquietar, intranquilizar

anxiously *adv* con inquietud; ansiosamente; impacientemente

any *a* cualquiera; (before the noun only) cualquier; (some) algún, *m;* alguna, *f;* (every) todo; (expressing condition or with interrogatives or negatives, following the noun) alguno, *m;* alguna, *f,* (is often not translated in a partitive sense, e.g. **Have you any butter?** ¿Tienes mantequilla?) *pron* algo; (with the relevant noun) algún, etc.; lo, *m,* and *neut;* la, *f;* los, *m pl;* las, *f pl.* **He hasn't any pity,** No tiene piedad alguna. **at any rate,** de todos modos; por lo menos. **If there is any,** Si lo (la, etc.) hay. **in any case,** venga lo que venga. **not any,** ninguno, *m;* ninguna, *f.* **Whether any of them . . . ,** Si alguno de ellos . . . **any further,** más lejos. **any longer,** más largo; (of time) más tiempo. **any more,** nada más; nunca más

anybody *n* and *pron* (someone) alguien; cualquiera, *mf;* (everyone) todo el mundo; (with a negative) nadie; (of importance) persona de importancia, *f.* **hardly a.,** casi nadie

anyhow *adv* de cualquier modo; (with a negative) de ningún modo; de cualquier manera; (at least) por lo menos, en todo caso; (carelessly) sin cuidado

anyone *n.* See **anybody**

anything *n* algo, *m,* alguna cosa, *f;* (negative) nada; cualquier cosa, *f;* todo (lo que). **a. but,** todo menos

anyway *adv* de todos modos, con todo; venga lo que venga; (anyhow) de cualquier modo

anywhere *adv* en todas partes, dondequiera; en cualquier parte; (after a negative) en (or a) ninguna parte

A.O.B. (any other business) asuntos varios (on an agenda)

aorta *n* aorta, *f*

apart *adv* aparte; a un lado; separadamente; separado (de); apartado (de). **a. from,** aparte de, dejando a un lado. **to keep a.,** mantener aislado; distinguir (entre). **to take a.,** desarmar. **wide a.,** muy distante

apartment *n* cuarto, *m,* habitación, *f;* (flat) piso, *Argentina* departamento, *elsewhere in Lat. Am.* apartamento *m*

apathetic *a* apático; indiferente

apathy *n* apatía, *f;* indiferencia, *f*

ape *n* simio, *m*

Apennines, the los Apeninos, *m*

aperitive *a* and *n* aperitivo, *m.*

aperture *n* abertura, *f;* agujero, *m;* orificio, *m*

apex *n* ápice, *m*

aphasia *n* afasia, *f*

aphorism *n* aforismo, *m*

aphrodisiac *a* and *n* afrodisíaco, *m*

apiary *n* colmenar, *m*

apiece *adv* cada uno; por persona

apish *a* simiesco, de simio; (affected) afectado; (foolish) tonto

aplomb *n* confianza en sí, *f,* aplomo, *m*

apocalypse *n* Apocalipsis, *m*

apocalyptic *a* apocalíptico

apocopate *vt* apocopar

Apocrypha *n* libros apócrifos, *m pl*

apocryphal *a* apócrifo

apogee *n* apogeo, *m*

apologetic *a* apologético

apologist *n* apologista, *mf*

apologize *vi* presentar sus excusas; disculparse, excusarse; (regret) sentir

apology *n* excusa, disculpa, *f;* defensa, apología, *f;* (makeshift) substituto, *m*

apoplectic *a* and *n* apoplético (-ca)

apoplexy *n* apoplegía, *f*

apostasy *n* apostasía, *f*

apostate *n* apóstata, *mf,* renegado (-da)

apostatize *vi* apostatar, renegar

apostle *n* apóstol, *m.* **Apostles' Creed,** el Credo de los Apóstoles

apostolic *a* apostólico

apostrophe *n* apóstrofe, *mf;* (punctuation mark) apóstrofo, *m*

Apothecaries weight peso de boticario, *m*

apothegm *n* apotegma, *m*

apotheosis *n* apoteosis, *f*

appal *vt* horrorizar, espantar, aterrar

appalling *a* espantoso, horrible

apparatus *n* aparato, *m;* máquina, *f;* instrumentos, *m pl*

apparel *n* ropa, *f;* vestiduras, *f pl;* ornamento, *m. vt* vestir

apparent *a* aparente; visible; evidente, manifiesto; (of heirs) presunto. **to become a.,** manifestarse

apparently *adv* al parecer, aparentemente

apparition *n* aparición, *f,* fantasma, espectro, *m*

appeal *n* súplica, *f;* llamamiento, *m;* (charm) atracción, *f,* encanto, *m; law* apelación, alzada, *f. vi* (to) suplicar (a); hacer llamamiento (a); poner por testigo (a); recurrir a; llamar la atención de; interesar (a); (attract) atraer, encantar; *law* apelar. **It doesn't a. to him,** No le atrae, No le gusta. **to allow an a.,** revocar una sentencia apelada. **without a.,** inapelable

appealing *a* suplicante; atrayente

appealingly *adv* de un modo suplicante

appear *vi* (of persons and things) aparecer; (seem) parecer; (before a judge) comparecer, presentarse (ante el juez); (of books) publicarse; (of lawyers) representar; (of the dawn) rayar; (of the sun, etc.) salir; (show itself) manifestarse. **to cause to a.,** hacer presentarse; (show) hacer ver; (prove) demonstrar, probar

appearance *n* aparición, *f;* (show, semblance or look, aspect) apariencia, *f;* presencia, *f;* aspecto, *m;* (in court of law) comparecencia, *f;* (of a book) publicación, *f;* (arrival) llegada, *f;* (view) perspectiva, *f;* (ghost) aparición, *f,* fantasma, *m.* **first a.,** (of an actor, etc.) debut, *m;* (of a play) estreno, *m.* **to all appearances,** según las apariencias. **to make one's first a.,** aparecer por primera vez; *theat* debutar. **Appearances are deceptive,** Las apariencias engañan

appease *vt* apaciguar, aplacar, pacificar; satisfacer

appeasement *n* apaciguamiento, aplacamiento, *m,* pacificación, *f;* satisfacción, *f*

appellant *a* and *n law* apelante, *mf*

appellation *n* nombre, *m;* título, *m*

append *vt* añadir; (a seal) poner; (enclose) incluir, anexar

appendage *n* accesorio, *m;* (*bot zool*) apéndice, *m*

appendicitis *n* apendicitis, *f*

appendix *n* apéndice, *m*

appertain *vi* pertenecer (a)

appetite *n* apetito, *m; fig* hambre, *f;* deseo, *m.* **to have a bad a.,** no tener apetito, estar desganado. **to have a good a.,** tener buen apetito. **to whet the a.,** abrir el apetito

appetizer *n* aperitivo, *Argentina* ingrediente *m*

appetizing *a* apetitoso

applaud *vt* and *vi* aplaudir; aclamar, ovacionar; celebrar

applause *n* aplauso, *m;* ovación, *f;* aprobación, alabanza, *f*

apple *n* manzana, *f.* **the a. of one's eye,** la niña de los ojos. **a. orchard,** manzanar, *m.* **a. sauce,** compota de manzanas, *f.* **a. tart,** pastel de manzanas, *m.* **a. tree,** manzano, *m*

appliance *n* aparato, *m;* instrumento, *m;* utensilio, *m;* máquina, *f*

applicability *n* aplicabilidad, *f*

applicable *a* aplicable

applicant *n* candidato, *m;* aspirante, *m;* solicitante, *mf*

application *n* aplicación, *f;* solicitud, *f;* petición, *f;* empleo, *m.* **on a.,** a solicitar

appliqué *a* aplicado. *n* aplicación, *f*

apply *vt* aplicar; (use) emplear; (place) poner; (give) dar; (the brakes) frenar; *vi* ser aplicable; ser a propósito; dirigirse (a); acudir (a); (for a post) proponerse para. **a. for,** solicitar, pedir; (a post) proponerse para. **a. for admission (to . . .),** solicitar el ingreso (en . . .). **a. oneself to,** ponerse a; dedicarse a, consagrarse a

appoint *vt* (prescribe) prescribir, ordenar; señalar; asignar; (furnish) amueblar; equipar; (create) crear, esta-

blecer; (to a post) nombrar, designar; (manage) gobernar; organizar. **at the appointed hour,** a la hora señalada. **well-appointed,** bien amueblado; bien equipado
appointive *a* por nombramiento
appointment *n* (assignation) cita, *f;* (to a post) nombramiento, *m;* (post, office) cargo, *m;* creación, *f.* **By Royal A.,** Proveedor de la Real Casa. **to make an a. with,** citar
apportion *vt* dividir; distribuir; prorratear; (taxes) derramar
apportionment *n* repartimiento, *m,* distribución, *f;* división, *f;* prorrateo, *m*
apposite *a* a propósito, pertinente, oportuno; justo
appositeness *n* pertinencia, oportunidad, *f*
appraisal *n* valoración, valuación, *f;* estimación, *f*
appraise *vt* valorar, tasar; estimar
appreciable *a* apreciable, perceptible
appreciably *adv* sensiblemente
appreciate *vt* (understand) darse cuenta de, comprender; estimar; apreciar; (distinguish) distinguir. *vi* encarecer, aumentar en valor; (of shares) subir, estar en alza
appreciation *n* (understanding) comprensión, *f;* apreciación, *f;* (recognition, etc.) aprecio, reconocimiento, *m;* (in value) aumento (en valor), *m;* subida de precio, *f*
appreciative *a* apreciativo
appreciatively *adv* con aprecio
appreciator *n* apreciador (-ra)
apprehend *vt* aprehender, prender; comprender, aprehender; (fear) temer
apprehension *n* aprehensión, comprensión, *f;* (fear) aprensión, *f;* (seizure) aprehensión, presa, *f*
apprehensive *a* aprehensivo; (fearful) aprensivo
apprehensiveness *n* aprehensión, *f;* (fear) aprensión, *f,* temor, *m*
apprentice *n* aprendiz (-za). **to bind a.,** poner de aprendiz
apprenticeship *n* aprendizaje, *m.* **to serve an a.,** hacer el aprendizaje
apprise *vt* dar parte (de), informar (de)
approach *vt* acercarse a; aproximarse a; (pull, etc. nearer) acercar, aproximar; (resemble) parecerse a, ser semejante a; (speak to) hablar con; entablar negociaciones con. *vi* acercarse, aproximarse. *n* acercamiento, *m;* (arrival) llegada, *f;* aproximación, *f;* (of night, etc.) avance, *m;* (entrance) entrada, *f;* avenida, *f;* vía, *f;* (step) paso, *m;* (to a subject) punto de vista (sobre), concepto (de), *m;* (introduction) introducción, *f; pl* **approaches,** (environs) alrededores, *m pl,* inmediaciones, *f pl;* (seas) mares, *m pl;* (overtures) avances, *m pl*
approachable *a* accesible
approaching *a* venidero, próximo, cercano
approbation *n* asentimiento, *m;* aprobación, *f*
appropriate *a* apropiado; conveniente; *vt* adueñarse de, tomar posesión de, apropiar
appropriately *adv* propiamente; convenientemente; justamente
appropriateness *n* conveniencia, *f;* justicia, *f*
appropriation *n* apropiación, *f;* aplicación, *f;* empleo, *m*
approval *n* aprobación, *f;* consentimiento, *m.* **on a.,** a prueba
approve *vt* aprobar; confirmar; (sanction) autorizar, sancionar; ratificar; estar contento (de); (oneself) demostrarse. *vi* aprobar
approved *a* aprobado; bien visto; (on documents) Visto Bueno (V° B°)
approximate *a* aproximado. *vt* acercar. *vi* aproximarse (a)
approximately *adv* aproximadamente, poco más o menos
approximation *n* aproximación, *f*
appurtenance *n* accesorio, *m,* pertenencia, *f*
apricot *n* albaricoque, *m.* **a. tree,** albaricoquero, *m*
April *n* abril, *m, a* abrileño. **A. Fool's Day,** el 1° de abril; (in Spain) el Día de los Inocentes (December 28)
apron *n* delantal, *m;* (of artisans and freemasons) mandil, *m.* **to be tied to a mother's a.-strings,** estar cosido a las faldas de su madre. **a.-stage,** proscenio, *m.* **a.-string,** cinta del delantal, *f*
apse *n* ábside, *mf*
apt *a* apto, listo; propenso (a), inclinado (a); expuesto (a); (suitable) apropiado, oportuno
aptitude *n* aptitud, disposición, facilidad, *f*
aptly *adv* apropiadamente; justamente, bien
aquamarine *n* aguamarina, *f*
aquarelle *n* acuarela, *f*
aquarellist *n* acuarelista, *mf*
aquarium *n* acuario, *m*
Aquarius *n* Acuario, *m*
aquatic *a* acuático
aquatint *n* acuatinta, *f*
aqueduct *n* acueducto, *m*
aqueous *a* ácueo, acuoso
aquiline *a* aguileño
Arab *a* árabe. *n* árabe, *mf*
arabesque *n* arabesco, *m*
Arabian *a* árabe, arábigo. **The A. Nights,** Las Mil y Una Noches
Arabic *a* arábigo. *n* (language) arábigo, árabe, *m*
Arabist *n* arabista, *mf*
arable *a* cultivable, labrantío
Aragonese *a* and *n* aragonés (-esa)
arbiter *n* árbitro (-ra), arbitrador (-ra)
arbitrariness *n* arbitrariedad, *f*
arbitrary *a* arbitrario
arbitrate *vi* arbitrar, juzgar como árbitro; someter al arbitraje
arbitration *n* arbitraje, *m*
arbitrator. See **arbiter**
arbour *n* glorieta, *f,* emparrado, *m*
arc *n* arco, *m.* **arc-light,** lámpara de arco, *f*
arcade *n* arcada, *f;* galería, *f;* pasaje, *m*
arch *n* arco, *m;* (vault) bóveda, *f. vt* abovedar; arquear; encorvar
arch *a* (roguish) socarrón; (coy) coquetón
arch- *prefix* archi-
archaic *a* arcaico
archaism *n* arcaísmo, *m*
archangel *n* arcángel, *m*
archbishop *n* arzobispo, *m*
archenemy *n* mayor enemigo (-ga); Demonio, *m*
archeological *a* arqueológico
archeologist *n* arqueólogo, *m*
archeology *n* arqueología, *f*
archer *n* flechero, saltero, *m; mil* arquero, *m*
archery *n* ballestería, *f*
archery range *n* campo de tiro con arco, *m*
archfiend *n* demonio, *m*
arching *n* arqueo, *m*
archipelago *n* archipiélago, *m*
architect *n* arquitecto, *m*
architectural *n* arquitectónico
architecturally *adv* arquitectónicamente; desde el punto de vista arquitectónico
architecture *n* arquitectura, *f*
archive *n* archivo, *m*
archivist *n* archivero, *m*
archness *n* coquetería, *f;* malicia, *f*
archway *n* arcada, *f,* pasaje abovedado, *m;* arco, *m*
arctic *a* ártico; muy frío. **A. Circle,** Círculo ártico, *m*
ardent *a* ardiente; apasionado, vehemente; fogoso
ardently *adv* ardientemente; con vehemencia, apasionadamente
ardor *n* ardor, *m*
arduous *a* arduo, difícil
arduousness *n* dificultad, arduidad, *f*
are *pl* of present indicative of **be.** See **be. There are,** Hay
area *n* área, *f;* superficie, *f;* (extent) extensión, *f;* es-

pacio, *m*; región, *f*; (of a house) patio, *m*; (of a concert hall, etc.) sala, *f*

area code *n* característica, *f*, (Chile), código territorial (Spain), prefijo (Spain), código interurbano, código (Argentina), *m*

arena *n* arena, *f*

argent *n poet* blancura, *f*; *her* argén, *m*

Argentinian *a* and *n* argentino (-na)

argonaut *n* (*zool* and *myth*) argonauta, *m*

argot *n* jerga, *f*; (thieves') germanía, *f*

arguable *a* discutible

argue *vt* discutir; persuadir; (prove) demostrar. *vi* argüir, discutir; sostener. **to a. against,** hablar en contra de, oponer

arguing *n* razonamiento, *m*; argumentación, *f*; discusión, *f*

argument *n* argumento, *m*, *Argentina* arenga *f*

argumentative *a* argumentador; contencioso

arid *a* árido, seco

aridity *n* aridez, *f*

Aries *n* Aries, *m*

arise *vi* levantarse; (appear) surgir, aparecer; ofrecerse, presentarse; (of sound) hacerse oír; provenir (de); proceder (de); (result) hacerse sentir; (rebel) sublevarse

aristocracy *n* aristocracia, *f*

aristocrat *n* aristócrata, *mf*

aristocratic *a* aristocrático

Aristotelian *a* aristotélico

arithmetic *n* aritmética, *f*

arithmetical *a* aritmético

ark *n* arca, *f*. **Noah's ark,** arca de Noé, *f*. **Ark of the Covenant,** arca de la alianza, *f*

arm *n* (*anat geog mech* of a chair, a cross, and *fig*) brazo, *m*; (lever) palanca, *f*; (of a tree) rama, *f*, brazo, *m*; (sleeve) manga, *f*; *naut* cabo de una verga, *m*; (weapon) arma, *f*; (of army, navy, etc.) ramo, *m pl*. **arms,** *her* armas, *f pl*, escudo, *m*. **in arms,** en brazos; armado; en oposición. **To arms!** ¡A las armas! **to keep at arm's length,** guardar las distancias; tratar fríamente. **to lay down arms,** rendir las armas. **to present arms,** presentar las armas. **to receive with open arms,** recibir con los brazos abiertos. **to take up arms,** alzarse en armas, empuñar las armas. **under arms,** sobre las armas. **with folded arms,** con los brazos cruzados. **arm in arm,** del bracete, de bracero. **arm of the sea,** brazo de mar, *m*. **arm-rest,** brazo, *m*

arm *vt* armar; proveer (de); (*fig* fortify) fortificar. *vi* armarse

armada *n* armada, *f*

armament *n* armamento, *m*

armchair *n* sillón, *m*, silla poltrona, *f*

armed *a* armado

Armenian *a* and *n* armenio (-ia); (language) armenio, *m*

armful *n* brazado, *m*

armhole *n* sobaquera, *f*

arming *n* armamento, *m*

armistice *n* armisticio, *m*

armless *a* sin brazos

armor *n* armadura, *f*; (for ships, etc.) blindaje, *m*. *vt* blindar, acorazar. **(to) a.-plate,** *vt* blindar. *n* coraza, plancha blindada, *f*

armored *a* blindado, acorazado. **a. car,** carro blindado, *m*. **a. cruiser,** crucero acorazado, *m*

armory *n* armería, *f*

army *n* ejército, *m*; multitud, muchedumbre, *f*. **to be in the a.,** ser del ejército. **to go into the a.,** alistarse. **a. corps,** cuerpo del ejército, *m*. **a. estimates,** presupuesto del ejército, *m*. **a. list,** escalofón del ejército, *m*. **A. Medical Corps,** Sanidad Militar, *f*. **A. Supply Corps,** Cuerpo de Intendencia, *m*

aroma *n* aroma, *m*

aromatic *a* aromático

around *prep* alrededor de; por todas partes de; cerca de; (with words like corner) a la vuelta de. *adv* alrededor; a la redonda, en torno; por todas partes; de un lado para otro

arouse *vt* despertar; excitar. **a. (someone's) suspicions,** despertar las sospechas (de fulano)

arpeggio *n* arpegio, *m*

arraign *vt* acusar; *law* procesar

arraignment *n* acusación, *f*; *law* procesamiento, *m*

arrange *vt* arregular; acomodar; poner en orden, clasificar, *Lat. Am.* acotejar; (place) colocar; (order) ordenar, disponer; (contrive) agenciar; organizar; preparar; *mus* adaptar; (of differences) concertar, ajustar. *vi* convenir, concertarse; arreglar; hacer preparativos

arrangement *n* arreglo, *m*; clasificación, *f*; disposición, *f*; (agreement) acuerdo, *m*; *mus* adaptación, *f*; *pl* **arrangements,** preparativos, *m pl*

array *n* (of troops) orden de batalla, *mf*; formación, *f*; colección, *f*; (dress) atavío, *m*, *vt* poner en orden de batalla; formar (las tropas, etc.); ataviar, adornar

arrears *n pl* atrasos, *m pl*. **in a.,** atrasado

arrest *vt* detener, impedir; (the attention) atraer; (capture) arrestar, prender; (judgment) suspender. *n* (stop) interrupción, parada, *f*; (hindrance) estorbo, *m*; (detention) arresto, *m*, detención, *f*; (of a judgment) suspensión, *f*. **under a.,** bajo arresto

arresting *a* que llama la atención, notable, muy interesante; asombroso, chocador

arrival *n* llegada, venida, *f*, advenimiento, *m*; *naut* arribada, *f*; entrada, *f*; el, *m*, (la, *f*), que llega. **on a.,** al llegar, a la llegada. **the new arrivals,** los recién llegados

arrive *vi* llegar; aparecer; (happen) suceder; *naut* arribar; entrar. **to a. at,** (a place or conclusion) llegar a

arrogance *n* arrogancia altivez, soberbia, *f*

arrogant *a* altivo, arrogante, soberbio

arrogate *vt* arrogar

arrow *n* saeta, flecha, *f*. **a.-head,** punta de flecha, *f*. **a.-shaped,** en forma de flecha, sagital. **a. wound,** flechazo, saetazo, *m*

arsenal *n* arsenal, *m*

arsenic *n* arsénico, *m*

arson *n* incendio premeditado, *m*

art *n* arte, *mf*; (cleverness) habilidad, *f*; (cunning) artificio, *m*. **Faculty of Arts,** Facultad de Letras, *f*. **fine arts,** bellas artes, *f pl*. **art exhibition,** exposición de pinturas, *f*. **art gallery,** museo de pinturas, *m*. **art school,** colegio de arte, *m*

arterial *a* arterial; (of roads) de primera clase. **a. forceps,** pinzas hemostáticas, *f pl*

artery *n* artería, *f*

artesian *a* artesiano

artful *a* habil, ingenioso; (crafty) astuto

artfully *adv* ingeniosamente; con astucia

artfulness *n* habilidad, ingeniosidad, *f*; astucia, maña, *f*

arthritic *a* artrítico

arthritis *n* artritis, *f*

artichoke *n* alcachofa, *f*. **Jerusalem a.,** aguaturma, *f*

article *n* artículo, *m*; (object) objeto, *m*, cosa, *f*; *pl* **articles,** escritura, *f*; contrato, *m*; estatutos, *m pl*. *vt* escriturar; contratar. **leading a.,** artículo de fondo, *m*. **articles of apprenticeship,** contrato de aprendizaje, *m*. **articles of association,** estatutos de asociación, *m pl*. **articles of war,** código militar, *m*

articulate *vt* articular; pronunciar, articular. *vi* estar unido por articulación; articular. *a* articulado; claro; expresivo

articulation *n* articulación, *f*, (all meanings)

artifice *n* artificio, *m*; arte, *m*, or *f*, habilidad, *f*

artificial *a* artificial; falso, fingido; afectado. **a. flowers,** flores de mano, *f pl*. **a. silk,** seda artificial, seda vegetal, *f*

artificiality *n* artificialidad, *f*; falsedad, *f*; afectación, *f*

artificially *adv* artificialmente; con afectación

artillery *n* artillería, *f*. **field a.,** artillería volante (or ligera or montada), *f*. **a. practice,** ejercicio de cañón, *m*

artilleryman *n* artillero, *m*

artisan *n* artesano (-na)

artist *n* artista, *mf*; (painter) pintor (-ra)
artiste *n* artista, *mf*
artistic *a* artístico
artistically *adv* artísticamente
artistry *n* habilidad artística, *f*, arte, *mf*
artless *a* natural; sencillo, cándido, inocente
artlessly *adv* con naturalidad; con inocencia
artlessness *n* naturalidad, *f*; sencillez, candidez, inocencia, *f*
art museum *n* museo de arte, *m*
Aryan *a* ario
as *adv conjunc rel pron* como; así como; (followed by infin.) de; (in comparisons) tan . . . como; (while) mientras; a medida que; (when) cuando, al (followed by infin.); (since) puesto que, visto que; (because) porque; (although) aunque; por; (according to) según; en; (in order that) para (que). **as a rule,** por regla general. **Once as he was walking,** Una vez mientras andaba. **as . . . as,** tan . . . como. **as far as,** hasta; en cuanto a. **as from,** desde. **as good as,** tan bueno como. **as if,** como si. **as it were,** por decirlo así, en cierto modo. **as many,** otros tantos (e.g. **six embassies in as many countries,** seis embajadas en otros tantos países). **as many as,** tanto . . . como; todos los que. **as soon as,** en cuanto, luego que, así que. **as soon as possible,** cuanto antes, *Lat. Am.* a la mayor brevedad posible. **as sure as can be,** sin duda alguna. **as to,** en cuanto a. **as usual,** como de costumbre. **as well,** también. **as well as,** (besides) además de; tan bien como. **as yet,** todavía.
asbestos *n* asbesto, amianto, *m*
ascend *vt* and *vi* subir; (on, in) subir a; ascender; (rise) elevarse; (a river) remontar. **to a. the stairs,** subir las escaleras. **to a. the pulpit,** subir al púlpito. **to a. the throne,** subir al trono
ascendancy *n* ascendiente, influjo, *m*
ascendant *n* elevación, *f*. *a* ascendente; predominante. **to be in the a.,** *fig* ir en aumento; predominar
ascending *a* ascendente
ascension *n* subida, ascension, *f*; (of the throne) advenimiento (al trono), *m*. **The A.,** La Ascensión
ascent *n* subida, *f*, ascenso, *m*; elevación, *f*; (slope) cuesta, pendiente, *f*
ascertain *vt* averiguar, descubrir
ascertainable *a* averiguable, descubrible
ascertainment *n* averiguación, *f*
ascetic *a* ascético. *n* asceta, *mf*
asceticism *n* ascetismo, *m*
ascribable *a* imputable, atribuible
ascribe *vt* atribuir, adscribir, imputar
ascription *n* atribución, adscripción, *f*
asepsis *n* asepsia, *f*
aseptic *a* aséptico
asexual *a* asexual
ash *n* ceniza, *f*; cenizas, *f pl*; (tree and wood) fresno, *m*; *pl* **ashes,** cenizas, *f pl*; restos mortales, *m pl*. **mountain ash,** serbal, *m*. **ash-bin,** basurero, *m*. **ash-coloured,** ceniciento. **ash grove,** fresneda, *f*. **ashtray,** cenicero, *m*. **Ash Wednesday,** miércoles de ceniza, *m*
ashamed *a* avergonzado. **to be a. (of),** avergonzarse (de), *Mexico* apenarse (de). **to be a. of oneself,** avergonzarse, tener vergüenza de sí mismo
ashen *a* ceniciento; (of ash wood) de fresno; pálido como un muerto
ashlar *n* sillar, *m*
ashore *adv* a tierra; en tierra. **to go** or **put a.,** desembarcar
Asiatic *a* and *n* asiático (-ca)
aside *adv* a un lado; aparte. *n theat* aparte, *m*. **to set a.,** poner a un lado; (omit) dejar aparte; descontar; abandonar; (a judgment) anular. **to take a.,** llevar aparte
asinine *a* asnal
ask *vt* (a question; enquire) preguntar; (request; demand) pedir; (beg) rogar; (invite) invitar. **to ask a question,** hacer una pregunta. **to ask about,** preguntar acerca de. **to ask after,** preguntar por. **to ask down,** invitar a bajar; invitar a visitar (a alguíen). **to ask for,** pedir; preguntar por. **ask for the moon,** pedir cotofas en el golfo. **to ask in,** invitar (a alguien) a entrar
askance *adv* al (or de) soslayo, de reojo; con recelo
askew *adv* oblicuamente; al lado; a un lado; sesgadamente
aslant *prep* a través de
asleep *a* and *adv* dormido. **to be a.,** estar dormido. **to fall a.,** dormirse
asparagus *n* espárrago, *m*. **a. bed,** esparraguera, *f*
aspect *n* aspecto, *m*; vista, *f*; apariencia, *f*, semblante, *m*. **to have a southern a.,** dar (mirar) al sur
asperity *n* aspereza, *f*
aspersion *n ecc* aspersión, *f*; calumnia, *f*; insinuación, *f*
asphalt *n* asfalto, *m*, *vt* asfaltar
asphyxia *n* asfixia, *f*
asphyxiate *vt* asfixiar
asphyxiating *a* asfixiante
aspirant *n* aspirante, candidato, *m*
aspirate *vt* aspirar. *n* letra aspirada, *f*
aspiration *n* aspiración, ambición, *f*; deseo, anhelo, *m*; *gram* aspiración, *f*
aspire *vi* aspirar (a), pretender, ambicionar; alzarse
aspirin *n* aspirina, *f*
ass *n* asno, *m*
assail *vt* atacar, acometer, arremeter
assailable *a* atacable
assailant *n* asaltador (-ra)
assassin *n* asesino, *mf*
assassinate *vt* asesinar
assassination *n* asesinato, *m*
assault *n* asalto, *m*; acometida, embestida, *f*; *fig* ataque, *m*. *vt* asaltar; acometer, embestir; atacar. **to take by a.,** tomar por asalto
assay *n* ensayo, *m*, *vt* ensayar, aquilatar
assayer *n* ensayador, *m*
assaying *n* ensaye, *m*
assemblage *n* reunión, *f*; (of a machine) montaje, *m*; (of people) muchedumbre, *f*, concurso, *m*; (of things) colección, *f*, grupo, *m*
assemble *vt* (persons) reunir, convocar; (things and persons) juntar; (a machine, etc.) armar, ensamblar. *vi* reunirse, congregarse; acudir
assembly *n* asamblea, *f*; reunión, *f*; *ecc* concilio, *m*. **a. line,** cadena de montaje, línea de montaje, *f*. **a. room,** sala de reuniones, *f*; sala de baile, *f*
assent *n* asentimiento, consentimiento, *m*; aprobación, *f*; (parliamentary, *law*) sanción, *f*. *vi* asentir (a), consentir (en); aprobar
assert *vt* mantener, defender; declarar, afirmar; hacer valer, reclamar. **to a. oneself,** imponerse, hacerse sentir; hacer valer sus derechos
assertion *n* aserción, afirmación, *f*; defensa, *f*; reclamación, *f*
assertive *a* afirmativo; dogmático
assess *vt* tasar, valorar; fijar, señalar; repartir (contribuciones, etc.)
assessment *n* tasación, *f*; fijación, *f*; repartimiento, *m*
assessor *n law* asesor (-ra); (of taxes) repartidor (-ra); (valuer) tasador, *m*. **public a.,** tasador, *m*
asset *n* ventaja, *f*; adquisición, *f*; cualidad, *f*; *pl* **assets,** fondos, *m pl*; *com* activo, *m*, créditos activos, *m pl*
assiduity *n* asiduidad, *f*
assiduous *a* asiduo
assiduously *adv* asiduamente, con asiduidad
assign *vt law* ceder; señalar, asignar; (appoint) destinar; fijar; atribuir, imputar. *n* cesionario (-ia)
assignation *n* asignación, *f*; cita, *f*; *law* cesión, *f*
assignment *n law* cesión, *f*; escritura de cesión, *f*; atribución, *f*; parte, porción, *f*
assimilable *a* asimilable
assimilate *vt* asimilar; incorporarse. *vi* mezclarse
assimilation *n* asimilación, *f*; incorporación, *f*
assimilative *a* asimilativo

assist *vt* ayudar; auxiliar, socorrer; (uphold) apoyar; (further) promover, fomentar. *vi* (be present) asistir (a)
assistance *n* ayuda, *f;* auxilio, socorro, *m;* apoyo, *m;* (furtherance) fomento, *m.* **public a.,** asistencia pública, *f*
assistant *n* ayudante, *m; ecc* asistente, *m;* (in a shop) dependiente (-ta); colaborador (-ra); (university) auxiliar, *m;* sub-. **a. secretary,** subsecretario (-ia). **a. secretaryship,** subsecretaría, *f*
associate *n* asociado (-da); miembro, *m;* socio (-ia); compañero (-ra), amigo (-ga); colega, *m;* colaborador (-ra); (confederate) cómplice, *mf a* asociado; auxiliar. *vt* asociar; unir, juntar. **to a. oneself with,** asociarse con; asociarse a. **to a. with,** frecuentar la compañía de, ir con
association *n* asociación, *f;* unión, *f;* sociedad, *f;* compañía, corporación, *f;* (connection) relación, *f.* **a. football,** fútbol, *m*
assonance *n* asonancia, *f*
assort *vt* clasificar; mezclar
assorted *a* surtido, mezclado. **They are a well-a. pair,** Son una pareja bien avenida
assortment *n* clasificación, *f,* arreglo, *m;* surtido, *m,* mezcla, *f*
assuage *vt* mitigar; suavizar; calmar; aliviar
assume *vt* asumir; tomar; apropiarse; (wear) revestir; (suppose) suponer; poner por caso
assumed *a* fingido, falso; supuesto
assumption *n* asunción, *f;* apropiación, arrogación, *f;* suposición, *f.* **Feast of the A.,** Fiesta de la Asunción, *f*
assurance *n* garantía, *f;* promesa, *f;* confianza, seguridad, *f;* (in a good sense) aplomo, *m,* naturalidad, *f;* (in a bad sense) presunción frescura, *f,* descaro, *m; com* seguro, *m*
assure *vt* asegurar
assured *a* aseguardo; seguro
assuredly *adv* seguramente
asterisk *n* asterisco, *m*
astern *adv* a popa; de popa; en popa; atrás
asthma *n* asma, *f*
asthmatic *a* asmático
astigmatic *a* astigmático
astigmatism *n* astigmatismo, *m*
astir *adv* en movimiento; (out of bed) levantado; excitado
astonish *vt* sorprender, asombrar
astonished *a* atónito, estupefacto
astonishing *a* sorprendente, asombroso
astonishment *n* asombro, *m,* sorpresa, estupefacción, *f*
astound *vt* aturdir, pasmar. **to be astounded,** *inf* quedarse muerto
astounding *a* asombroso
astray *adv* desviado, extraviado; por el mal camino. **to go a.,** errar el camino, perderse; *fig* descarriarse
astride *adv* a horcajadas. *prep* a horcajadas sobre; a ambos lados de
astringent *a* astringente
astrologer *n* astrólogo (-ga)
astrological *a* astrológico
astrology *n* astrología, *f*
astronaut *n* astronauta, *mf*
astronomer *n* astrónomo, *m*
astronomical *a* astronómico
astronomy *n* astronomía, *f*
astrophysics *n* astrofísica, *f*
astute *a* astuto, sagaz; (with knave, etc.) redomado, pícaro
astuteness *n* astucia, sagacidad, *f*
asunder *adv* en dos; separadamente; lejos uno de otro
asylum *n* asilo, *m;* (for the insane) manicomio, *m*
asymmetrical *a* asimétrico
asymmetry *n* asimetría, *f*
at *prep* a; en casa de; en; de; con; por; (before) delante de. Sometimes forms part of verb, e.g. **to aim at,** apuntar. **to look at,** mirar. May be translated by using pres. part., e.g. **They were at play,** Estaban jugando. **at a bound,** de un salto. **at peace,** en paz. **at the doctor's,** en casa del médico. **at the crack of dawn,** al rayar el alba, al romper el alba. **at the head,** a la cabeza. **John is at Brighton,** Juan está en Brighton. **at the house of . . . , at . . .'s** en casa de, *Lat. Am. also* donde (e.g., **My cousin is at my grandmother's** Mi primo está en casa de mi abuela, Mi primo está donde mi abuela) **at first,** al principio. **at last,** por fin. **at no time,** jamás. **at once,** en seguida. **at most,** a lo más. **at one go** *Lat. Am.* de una leída. **at all events,** en todo caso. **What is he getting at?** ¿Qué quiere saber? **at home,** en casa. **at-home day,** día de recibo, *m*
atavism *n* atavismo, *m*
atavistic *a* atávico
atheism *n* ateísmo, *m*
atheist *n* ateo (-ea)
atheistic *a* ateo
Athens Atenas, *f*
athlete *n* atleta, *m*
athletic *a* atlético
athletics *n* atletismo, *m*
athwart *adv* de través. *prep* al través de; contra
Atlantic *a* and *n* atlántico *m.* **A. Charter,** Carta del Atlántico, *f.* **A. liner,** transatlántico, *m*
Atlantis Atlántida, *f*
atlas *n* atlas, *m*
atmosphere *n* aire, *m;* atmósfera, *f; fig* ambiente, *m*
atmospheric *a* atmosférico
atmospherics *n pl* perturbaciones eléctricas atmosféricas, *f pl*
atoll *n* atolón, *m*
atom *n* átomo, *m.* **splitting of the a.,** escisión del átomo, *f*
atomic *a* atómico. **a. bomb,** bomba atómica, *f.* **a. pile,** pila atómica, *f.* **a. theory,** teoría atómica, *f*
atomize *vt* pulverizar
atomizer *n* pulverizador, *m*
atone *vi* (for) expiar
atonement *n* expiación, *f*
atonic *a* átono, atónico
atrocious *a* atroz; horrible
atrocity *n* atrocidad, *f*
atrophy *n* atrofia, *f, vi* atrofiarse
attach *vt* (*law* of goods) embargar; (*law* of persons) arrestar; (fix) fijar; (tie) atar; (join) juntar; (stick) pegar; (connect) conectar; (hook) enganchar; (with a brooch, etc.) prender; (blame, etc.) imputar; (importance, etc.) dar, conceder; (assign) asignar; (attract) atraer; (enclose) adjuntar, incluir. *vi* pertenecer (a), ser indivisible (de). **to a. oneself to,** pegarse a; adherirse a, asociarse con; acompañar; hacerse inseparable de
attaché *n* agregado, *m.* **a. case,** maletín, *m*
attachment *n* (*law* of goods) embargo, *m,* vía ejecutiva, *f;* (*law* of persons) arresto, *m;* unión, *f;* conexión, *f;* (hooking) enganche, *m;* (with a brooch, etc.) prendimiento, *m;* (tying) atadura, *f;* (fixing) fijación, *f;* (affection) apego, cariño, *m;* (friendship) amistad, *f*
attack *n* ataque, *m; mil* ofensiva, *f;* (access) acceso, *m. vt* atacar
attacker *n* atacador (-ra), asaltador (-ra)
attain *vt* alcanzar, conseguir, lograr. *vi* llegar a; alcanzar
attainable *a* asequible, realizable; accesible
attainment *n* consecución, obtención, *f;* logro, *m; pl* **attainments,** prendas, dotes, *f pl*
attempt *vt* (try) procurar, tratar de, intentar; ensayar; querer; *law* hacer una tentativa (de), atentar. *n* tentativa, prueba, *f;* esfuerzo, ensayo, *m;* (criminal) atentado, *m,* tentativa, *f*
attend *vi* prestar atención (a); escuchar; (look after) cuidar (de); (serve) servir; (accompany) acompañar; (await) esperar. *vt* (be present) asistir (a); (of a doctor) visitar; (accompany) acompañar; (bring) acarrear, traer; (follow) seguir. **to be attended with,** traer consigo, acarrear
attendance *n* asistencia, presencia, *f;* (those present) público, *m,* concurrencia, *f;* servicio, *m;* (train) acom-

pañamiento, *m*; *med* asistencia, *f*, tratamiento médico, *m*. **to be in a.,** acompañar (a)
attendant *a* que acompaña; que sigue; concomitante. *n* criado (-da); (keeper) guardián (-ana); (nurse) enfermero (-ra); (in a cloakroom) guardarropa, *f*; (in a theater) acomodador (-ra); (on a train) mozo, *m*; (waiter) camarero, *m*; (at baths) bañero (-ra)
attention *n* atención, *f*; cuidado, *m*. **A.!** ¡Atención!; *mil* ¡Firmes! **to pay a.,** prestar atención. **to stand to a.,** cuadrarse, permanecer en posición de firmes
attentive *a* atento; solícito; cortés, obsequioso
attentively *adv* con atención, atentamente; solícitamente
attentiveness *n* cuidado, *m*; cortesía, *f*
attenuate *vt* atenuar
attenuating *a* atenuante. **a. circumstance,** circunstancia atenuante, *f*
attenuation *n* atenuación, *f*
attest *vt* atestar. *vi* atestiguar, deponer, dar fe
attestation *n* atestación, deposición, *f*; (certificate) certificado, *m*, fe, *f*
attic *n* buhardilla, guardilla, *f*, desván, sotabanco, *m*
Attic *a* ático
attire *n* atavío, *m*; (dress) traje, *m*; (finery) galas, *f pl*. *vt* ataviar, vestir; engalanar
attitude *n* actitud, *f*; postura, *f*; posición, *f*
attorney *n* (solicitor) abogado (-da); (agent) apoderado (-da); (public) procurador, *m*. **power of a.,** poderes, *m pl* procuración, *f*. **A.-general,** fiscal, *m*
attract *vt* atraer; (charm) seducir, cautivar, apetecer; (invite) convidar; (goodwill, etc.) captar
attraction *n* atracción, *f*; atractivo, aliciente, encanto, *m*
attractive *a* atrayente; atractivo, seductivo; apetecible; encantador
attractively *adv* atractivamente
attributable *a* imputable, atribuible
attribute *vt* atribuir (a), achacar (a), imputar (a). *n* atributo, *m*
attribution *n* atribución, imputación, *f*; atributo, *m*
attrition *n* atrición, *f*
auburn *a* castaño, rojizo
auction *n* subasta, almoneda, *f*; venta pública, pública subasta, *f*. *vt* subastar. **to put up to a.,** sacar a pública subasta
auctioneer *n* subastador (-ra), *Lat. Am. also* licitador (-ra)
audacious *a* atrevido, audaz, osado, temerario; (shameless) descarado, impudente
audaciously *adv* osadamente; descaradamente
audacity *n* audacia, osadía, temeridad, *f*, atrevimiento, *m*; (shamelessness) descaro, *m*, desvergüenza, *f*
audibility *n* audibilidad, perceptibilidad, *f*
audible *a* audible, oíble
audibly *adv* en forma audible, perceptiblemente, en alta voz
audience *n* (interview and *law*) audiencia, *f*; oyentes, *m pl*, auditorio, público, *m*. **to give a.,** dar audiencia. **a. chamber,** sala de recepción, *f*
audiofrequency *n* audiofrecuencia, *f*
audit *vt* intervenir, examinar (cuentas). *n* intervención, *f*, ajuste (de cuentas), *m*
audition *n* audición, *f*
auditor *n* (hearer) oyente, *mf*; interventor, contador, *m*
auditorium *n* sala de espectáculos, *f*
auditory *a* auditivo, auditorio
Augean *a* de Augeas; muy sucio
auger *n* taladro, *m*
aught *n* algo. **For a. I know,** Por lo que yo sepa
augment *vt* aumentar, acrecentar. *vi* aumentarse, acrecentarse
augmentation *n* aumento, acrecentamiento, *m*; añadidura, *f*
augmentative *a* aumentativo
augur *n* agorero (-ra). *vt* and *vi* presagiar, anunciar; pronosticar, agorar
augury *n* predicción, *f*; agüero, presagio, pronóstico, *m*
August *n* agosto, *m*
august *a* augusto
Augustan *a* (of Roman emperor) augustal. **A. Age,** siglo de Augusto, *m*
Augustinian *a* and *n ecc* agustino (-na)
aunt *n* tía, *f*. **great-a.,** tía abuela, *f*. **A. Sally,** el pim, pam, pum
aura *n* exhalación, *f*; influencia psíquica, *f*; *med* aura, *f*
aural *a* auricular. **a. surgeon,** otólogo, *m*
auricle *n* (of the heart) aurícula, ala del corazón, *f*; oreja, *f*, pabellón de la oreja, *m*
aurora *n* aurora, *f*. **a. borealis,** aurora boreal, *f*
auspice *n* auspicio, *m*
auspicious *a* propicio, favorable, feliz
auspiciously *adv* prósperamente, felizmente
auspiciousness *n* buenos auspicios, *m pl*; felicidad, *f*
austere *a* severo, austero, adusto; ascético; (of style) desnudo
austerity *n* austeridad, severidad, *f*; ascetismo, *m*; (of style) desnudez, *f*
Australian *a* and *n* australiano (-na)
Austrian *a* and *n* austríaco (-ca)
authentic *a* auténtico
authenticate *vt* autenticar
authentication *n* autenticación, *f*
authenticity *n* autenticidad, *f*
author *n* autor, *m*
authoress *n* autora, *f*
author index *n* índice de autores, *m*
authoritarian *a* autoritario
authoritative *a* autoritario
authority *n* autoridad, *f*; poder, *m*. **to have on the best a.,** tener de muy buena fuente
authorization *n* autorización, *f*
authorize *vt* autorizar
authorship *n* profesión de autor, *f*; paternidad (literaria), *f*; origen, *m*
auto *n* = **automobile**
autobiographical *a* autobiográfico
autobiography *n* autobiografía, *f*
autocracy *n* autocracia, *f*
autocrat *n* autócrata, *mf*
autocratic *a* autocrático
autograph *n* autógrafo, *m*
autography *n* autografía, *f*
automatic *a* automático. **a. gate,** (at level crossings, etc.) barrera de golpe, *f*. **a. machine,** máquina automática, *f*; *inf* tragaperras, *m*. **a. pencil,** lapicero, *m*
automatically *adv* automáticamente
automatism *n* automatismo, *m*
automaton *n* autómata, *m*
automobile *n* automóvil, coche, *Lat. Am.* carro *m*
autonomous *a* autónomo
autonomy *n* autonomía, *f*
autopsy *n* autopsia, *f*
autosuggestion *n* autosugestión, *f*
autumn *n* otoño, *m*
autumnal *a* otoñal, de otoño
auxiliary *a* auxiliar. *n* auxiliador, *m*
avail *vi* servir; valer; importar. *vt* aprovechar. **to a. oneself of,** valerse de, aprovecharse de. **to no a.,** en balde
availability *n* utilidad, *f*; disponibilidad, *f*; provecho, *m*; (validity) validez, *f*
available *a* útil; disponible; aprovechable; válido
avalanche *n* alud, lurte, *m*
avarice *n* avaricia, *f*
avaricious *a* avaro, avaricioso
ave *interj* ¡ave! *n* avemaría, *f*; despedida, *f*
avenge *vt* vengar; vindicar. **to a. oneself for,** vengarse de
avenger *n* vengador (-ra)
avenging *a* vengador
avenue *n* avenida, *f*
aver *vt* afirmar, asegurar
average *n* promedio, término medio, *m*; (marine insur-

ance) avería, *f*, *a* de promedio; típico; corriente; normal. *vt* hallar el término medio (de); prorratear, proporcionar; ser por término medio. **general a.,** (marine insurance) avería gruesa, *f*. **on the a.,** por término medio
averse *a* opuesto (a); desinclinado (a); enemigo (de); repugnante. **to be a. to,** no gustar de; oponerse a; estar desinclinado a; ser enemigo de; repugnar
aversion *n* aversión, *f*; repugnancia, *f*
avert *vt* apartar; (avoid) evitar
aviary *n* avería, pajarera, *f*
aviation *n* aviación, *f*
aviator *n* aviador (-ra)
avid *a* ávido
avidity *n* avidez, *f*
avidly *adv* ávidamente, con avidez
avocado *n* aguacate
avocation *n* pasatiempo, *m*, distracción, *f*; ocupación, *f*; profesión, *f*
avoid *vt* evitar; (pursuit) evadir, eludir; guardarse (de), rehuir; *law* anular
avoidable *a* evitable, eludible
avoidance *n* evitación, *f*
avow *vt* confesar; declarar
avowal *n* confesión, admisión, *f*
avowedly *adv* por confesión propia
avuncular *a* avuncular
await *vt* aguardar, esperar
awake *vt* despertar. *vi* despertarse. *a* despierto; vigilante; consciente (de); atento (a)
awakening *n* despertamiento, *m*
award *n* sentencia, decisión, *f*; adjudicación, *f*; (prize) premio, *m*. *vt* adjudicar; otorgar, conceder. **She was awarded a professorship in Greek,** Ganó unas oposiciones para una cátedra de griego
aware *a* consciente, sabedor. **to be well a. of,** saber muy bien. **to make a. of,** hacer saber
awash *adv* a flor de agua
away *adv* a distancia, a lo lejos, lejos; (absent) ausente; (out) fuera; (unceasingly) sin parar, continuamente; (wholly) completamente; (visibly) a ojos vistas. In verbs of motion **a.** is rendered by the reflexive, e.g. **to go a.,** marcharse. Sometimes not translated, e.g. **to take a.,** quitar. *interj* ¡fuera de aquí! ¡márchese Vd.!; ¡vámonos! ¡adelante! **nine miles a.,** a nueve millas de distancia. **a. in the distance,** allá a lo lejos. **She sang a.,** Ella seguía cantando
awe *n* temor reverente, *m*; horror, *m*; respeto, *m*; reverencia, *f*, *vt* intimidar, aterrar; infundir respeto (a). **to stand in awe of,** tener respeto (a), reverenciar
awesome *a* pavoroso, temible, aterrador; terrible; (august) augusto; (imposing) imponente
awestruck *a* espantado, aterrado
awful *a* terrible, pavoroso; horrible; temible; atroz; *inf* enorme. **How a.!** *inf* ¡Qué barbaridad!
awfully *adv* terriblemente; horriblemente; *inf* muy
awfulness *n* lo terrible; lo horrible; atrocidad, *f*; (of a crime, etc.) enormidad, *f*
awkward *a* difícil; peligroso; delicado; embarazoso; (of time, etc.) inconveniente, inoportuno; (of things) incómodo; (clumsy) torpe, desmañado; desagradable; (ungraceful) sin gracia. **the a. age,** la edad difícil
awkwardly *adv* torpemente; incómodamente; mal; con dificultad; sin gracia. **He is a. placed,** Se encuentra en una situación difícil
awkwardness *n* dificultad, *f*; peligro, *m*; delicadeza, *f*; inconveniencia, inoportunidad, *f*; (clumsiness) torpeza, desmaña, *f*; (ungracefulness) falta de gracia, *f*
awl *n* lezna, *f*, punzón, *m*
awning *n* toldo, palio, *m*, *Lat. Am.* carpa *f*; *naut* toldilla, *f*
awry *adv* a un lado; oblicuamente; *fig* mal. *a* torcido; *fig* descarriado
ax *n* hacha, *f*
axiom *n* axioma, *m*
axiomatic *a* axiomático
axis *n* eje, *m*; *zool* axis, *m*. **A. power,** nacíon del Eje
axle *n* eje, *m*; peón, árbol (de una rueda), *m*. **back a.,** eje trasero, *m*. **differential a.,** eje diferencial, *m*. **front a.,** eje delantero, *m*
ay *interj* sí. *n* voto afirmativo, *m*
azalea *n* azalea, *f*
Aztec *a* and *n* azteca, *mf*
azure *n* azul celeste, *m*

B

b *n* (letter) be, *f*; *mus* si, *m*
baa *n* balido, be, *m*, *vi* balar, dar balidos
babble *n* (chatter) charla, *f*; (of a child) gorjeo, *m*; (confused sound) vocinglería, barbulla, *f*, rumor, *m*; (of water) murmullo, susurro, *m*. *vi* charlar; (of children) gorjearse; (incoherently) balbucir; (water) murmurar, susurrar; (a secret) descubrir
babbler *n* charlatán (-ana)
babbling *n* garrulería, locuacidad, *f*; (incoherent speech) balbuceo, *m*. (of water) murmullo, *m*. *a* gárrulo, locuaz; balbuciente; murmurante
babel *n* babel, *m*
baboon *n* babuino, *m*
baby *n* bebé, crío, *m*; niño (-ña) de pecho; *fig* gran bebé, *m*; niño mimado, *m*, *a* infantil. **b. blue,** azul claro, *m*. **b. doll,** muñeca bebé, *f*. **b. girl** *Argentina* beba *f* **b. grand piano,** piano de media cola, *m*. **b. of the family** *Venezuela* cuneco (-ca) *mf*
baby carriage *n* coche de niños, *m*
baby-faced *a* con mejillas mofletudas
babyhood *n* infancia, niñez, *f*
babyish *a* infantil, aniñado, pueril
babysitter *n* cuidaniños, *mf*
baccalaureate *n* bachillerato, *m*
baccarat *n* bacará, *m*
bachelor *n* soltero, célibe, *m*; (of a university) licenciado, bachiller, *m*; (as a title) caballero, *m*. **confirmed b.,** solterón, *m*. **degree of b.,** licenciatura, *f*. **to receive the degree of b.,** licenciarse, bachillerarse
bachelorhood *n* soltería, *f*, celibato, *m*
bacillus *n* bacilo, *m*
back *n* *anat* espalda, *f*; (of an animal) lomo, espinazo, *m*; (reins, loins) riñones, *m pl*; (of chairs, sofas) respaldo, *m*; (of a book) lomo, *m*; (back, bottom) fondo, *m*; parte posterior, parte de atrás, *f*; (of a hand, brush and many other things) dorso, *m*; (of a coin) reverso, *m*; el otro lado de alguna cosa; (in football, hockey) defensa, *m*; *theat* foro, *m*; (of fire-arms) culata, *f*; (of a knife) canto, *m*; (upper portion) parte superior, *f*. *a* posterior, trasero; de atrás; (remote) alejado, apartado; inferior; (overdue; past; out of date) atrasado; (earlier) anterior; *anat* dorsal. **at the b.,** detrás; en el fondo; en la última fila. **at the b. of one's mind,** por sus adentros, en el fondo del pensamiento. **behind one's b.,** a espaldas de uno, en ausencia de uno. **half-b.,** medio, *m*. **on one's b.,** boca arriba; a cuestas. **to see the b. of,** *inf* ver por última vez, desembarazarse de. **to turn one's b. on,** volver la espalda (a). **with one's b. to the engine,** de espaldas a la máquina. **b. to b.,** espalda con espalda
back *vt* empujar hacia atrás; (a vehicle) dar marcha atrás; hacer retroceder; (line) reforzar; (support) apoyar; (sign) endosar; (bind) forrar; (bet on) apostar a; (a sail) fachear. *vi* retroceder; dar marchar atrás; (of the wind) girar; (with on to) dar sobre, dominar; (with down) abandonar (una pretensión, etc.). **to b. out,** salir, marcharse; volverse atrás; (retract) desdecirse
back *adv* detrás; atrás; otra vez, de nuevo; (returned) de vuelta; a alguna distancia; (at home) en casa. *interj*

¡atrás! **A few weeks b.,** Hace unas semanas, Unas semanas atrás. **It stands b. from the road,** Está a alguna distancia del camino. **to go b. to,** (of families, etc.) remontar a. **to come b.,** regresar. **to come b. again,** regresar de nuevo, regresar por segunda vez
back axle *n* eje trasero, *m*
backbite *vt* cortar (a uno) un sayo, desollarle (a uno) vivo, murmurar de
backbiter *n* mala lengua, *f*, murmurador (-ra)
backbiting *n* murmuración, detracción, maledicencia, *f*, *a* murmurador, detractor
backbone *n* espinazo, *m*, columna vertebral, *f*. **to the b.,** hasta la médula
backchat *n* dimes y diretes, *m pl*; insolencia, *f*. **to indulge in b.-c.,** andar en dimes y diretes
back door *n* puerta trasera, puerta de servicio, *f*
backed *a* (lined) forrado; (in compounds; of persons) de espalda; (of chairs) de respaldo
backer *n* (better) apostador, *m*; protector (-ra, -triz)
backfire *n* contrafuego *m*, falsa explosión, *f*
backgammon *n* chaquete, *m*
back garden *n* jardín de atrás, *m*
background *n* fondo, *m*; *art* último término, *m*. **in the b.,** en el fondo; *art* en último término; *fig* en las sombras; alejado, a distancia
backhand *n sport* revés, *m*
backhanded *a* de revés, dado con el revés de la mano; *fig* ambiguo, equívoco
backing *n* forro, *m*; (lining) refuerzo, *m*; (of a vehicle) marcha atrás, *f*; retroceso, *m*; (betting) el apostar (a); (wagers) apuestas, *f pl*; (*fig* support) apoyo, *m*, ayuda, *f*; garantía, *f*
backlog *n com* rezago de pedidos, *m*
back number *n* (of a periodical) número atrasado, *m*
back pedal *vi* contrapedalear.
back premises *n* parte trasera (de una casa, etc.), *f*
backroom *n* cuarto interior, *m*, habitación trasera, *f*. **b. boy,** investigador ocupado en trabajos secretos para el gobierno, *m*
back seat *n* asiento trasero, *m*; fondo, *m*. **to take a b.-s.,** permanecer en el fondo, ceder el paso
back shop *n* trastienda, *f*
backside *n* trasero, *m*, posaderas, nalgas, *f pl*
backslide *vi* recaer, reincidir
backslider *n* (in religion or politics) apóstata, *mf*; reincidente, *mf*
backsliding *n* apostasía, *f*; reincidencia, *f*
backstage *n* foro, fondo del escenario, *m*, *adv* hacia el foro; detrás de bastidores
backstaircase *n* escalera de servicio, *f*; escalera secreta, *f*
backstairs *n* escalera de servicio, *f*; *fig* vías secretas, *f pl*, *a* de cocina; *fig* secreto
backstitch *n sew* pespunte, *m*, *vt* and *vi* pespuntar
back street *n* calle secundaria, callejuela, *f*; *pl* **back streets,** barrios bajos, *m pl*
backstroke *n* reculada, *f*; *sport* revés, *m*
back tooth *n* muela, *f*
back view *n* vista de detrás, *f*
backward *a* hacia atrás; vuelto hacia atrás; (in development) atrasado, poco avanzado; lento; negligente; (shy) modesto; (late) tardío; atrasado; retrógrado; (dull) torpe; retrospectivo. *adv* hacia atrás; atrás; al revés; (of falling) de espaldas; (of time) al pasado. **to go b. and forward,** ir y venir. **b. and forward,** de acá para allá
backwardness *n* atraso, *m*; lentitud, *f*; negligencia, *f*; modestia, *f*; (lateness) tardanza, *f*; atraso, *m*; (dullness) torpeza, *f*; falta de progreso, *f*
backwards *adv*. See **backward**
backwash *n* agua de rechazo, *f*
backwater *n* remanso, *m*
back wheel *n* rueda trasera, *f*, *vi* contrapedalear
backwoods *n* monte, *m*, selva, *f*
back yard *n* corral, *m*
bacon *n* tocino, *m*
bacteria *n* bacteria, *f*
bacterial *a* bacterial, bacteriano
bactericide *n* bactericida, *m*
bacteriological *a* bacteriológico
bacteriologist *n* bacteriólogo, *m*
bacteriology *n* bacteriología, *f*
bad *a* malo; (wicked) perverso; (ill) enfermo, malo (with estar); (naughty; undutiful) malo (with ser); (of coins) falso; (of debts) incobrable; (rotten) podrido; (harmful) nocivo; (dangerous) peligroso; (of pains, a cold) fuerte; intenso; (of a shot) errado; (mistaken) equivocado; (unfortunate) desgraciado. *n* el mal, lo malo; (persons) los malos. **extremely bad,** pésimo. **from bad to worse,** de mal en peor. **It's too bad!** ¡Esto es demasiado! **to go bad,** (fruit) macarse; (food) estropearse. **bad habit,** mala costumbre, *f*, vicio, *m*. **to have the bad habit of,** tener el vicio de. **bad temper,** malhumor, mal genio, *Lat. Am.* catoche *m*. **bad-tempered,** malhumorado, *Argentina* cabrero. **bad turn,** flaco servicio, *m*, mala pasada, *f*
badge *n* insignia, *f*; (decoration) condecoración, *f*; símbolo, emblema, *m*; (mark) marca, *f*
badger *n* tejón, *m*, *vt* cansar, molestar
Bad Lands (of Nebraska and South Dakota) Tierras malas *f pl*; (of Argentina) la Travesía, *f*
badly *adv* mal. **extremely b.,** pésimamente. **to want something b.,** necesitar algo con urgencia. **b. done,** mal hecho. **b. disposed,** malintencionado
badminton *n* el juego del volante, *m*
badness *n* maldad, *f*; mala calidad, *f*; lo malo
bad-smelling *a* maloliente
baffle *vt* desconcertar; (bewilder) tener perplejo (a); contrariar, frustrar; (obstruct) impedir; (avoid) evitar. **to b. description,** no haber palabras para describir
baffling *a* desconcertante; difícil; confuso; perturbador; (of people) enigmático
bag *n* saco, *m*; talega, *f*; (hand) bolsa, *f*, saco (de mano), *m*; (for tools) capacho, *m*; (for sewing) costurero, *m*; (of bagpipes) fuelle, *m*; (saddle) alforja, *f*; (briefcase) cartera, *f*; (suitcase) maleta, *f*; (under the eye) ojera, *f*; (game shot) caza, *f*. *vt* entalegar; coger, cazar; matar; tomar. *vi* (of garments) arrugarse. **to clear out bag and baggage,** liar el petate. **a bag of bones,** (person) un manojo de huesos. **bag wig,** peluquín, *m*
bagatelle *n* bagatela, friolera, *f*; (game) billar romano, *m*
bagful *n* saco, *m*; bolsa, *f*
baggage *n* equipaje, *m*; *mil* bagaje, *m*; (madcap) pícara, *f*; (jade) mujerzuela, *f*. **b. master,** (railway) factor, *m*. **b. car,** furgón de equipajes, *m*
baggage rack *n* (of automobile) portaequipajes, *m*
baggy *a* (creased, of trousers) con rodilleras, arrugado; (wide) bombacho
bagpipe *n* gaita, *f*
bagpiper *n* gaitero, *m*
Bahamas, the las Islas Bahamas, las Islas Lucayas, *f*
bail *n law* fianza, caución, *f*; (person) fiador (-ra); (cricket) travesaño, *m*, barra, *f*. *vt law* poner en libertad bajo fianza; salir fiador (por); (a boat) achicar. **on b.,** en fiado. **to go b.,** dar fianza, fiar.
bailiff *n law* agente ejecutivo, *m*; alguacil, *m*; mayordomo, *m*; capataz, *m*
bait *n* cebo, *m*; anzuelo, *m*; (fodder) pienso, *m*, *vt* cebar; (feed) dar pienso (a); azuzar; atormentar; (attract) atraer
baiting *n* cebadura, *f*; combate, *m*; tormenta, *f*
bake *vt* cocer; hacer (pan, etc.). **I like to bake cakes,** Me gusta hacer pasteles; *fig* endurecer. *vi* cocerse
bakelite *n* bakelita, *f*
baker *n* panadero, hornero, *m*. **a baker's dozen,** la docena del fraile
bakery *n* panadería, *f*
baking *n* cocimiento, *m*, cocción, *f*; (batch) hornada, *f*; el hacer (pan, etc.) *a inf* abrasador. **b.-dish,** tortera, *f*. **b.-powder,** levadura química, *f*
balance *n* balanza, *f*; equilibrio, *m*; *com* balance, saldo,

m; (in a bank) saldo (a favor del cuentacorrentista), *m*; *math* resto, *m*; *ast* Libra, *f*; (pendulum) péndola, *f*; (counterweight) contrapeso, *m*. **credit b.,** saldo acreedor, *m*. **debit b.,** saldo deudor, *m*. **net b.,** saldo líquido, *m*. **to lose one's b.,** perder el equilibrio. **to strike a b.,** hacer balance. **b. of power,** equilibrio político, *m*. **b. of trade,** balanza de comercio, *f*. **b.-sheet,** balance, avanzo, *Lat. Am.* balance de situación, *m*. **b. wheel,** (of watches) volante, *m*

balance *vt* balancear, abalanzar; contrapesar; (accounts) saldar; equilibrar; comparar; considerar, examinar. *vi* balancearse; ser de igual peso; equilibrarse; (accounts) saldarse

balance of trade *n* balanza comercial, *f*

balancing *n* balanceo, *m*; *com* balance, *m*. **b.-pole,** balancín, *m*

balconied *a* con balcones, que tiene balcones

balcony *n* balcón, *m*; galería, *f*; *theat* anfiteatro, *m*

bald *a* calvo; (of style) seco, pobre; *fig* desnudo, árido, pelado; sin adorno; (simple) sencillo. **to grow b.,** ponerse calvo, encalvecer

balderdash *n* galimatías, *m*, jerigonza, *f*; disparate, *m*

baldly *adv* secamente; sencillamente

baldness *n* calvicie, *f*; (of style) sequedad, pobreza, *f*; (bareness) desnudez, aridez, *f*

bale *n* (bundle) fardo, *m*; (of cotton, paper, etc.) bala, *f*

Balearic Islands, the las Islas Baleares, *f*

baleful *a* malicioso, siniestro, maligno

balk *n* obstáculo, *m*; (beam) viga, *f*; (billiards) cabaña, *f*. *vt* frustrar; impedir. *vi* resistirse, rehusar

Balkans, the los Balcanes, *m*

ball *n* globo, *m*, esfera, *f*; (plaything) pelota, *f*; (as in billiards, cricket, croquet) bola, *f*; (in football, basket-ball) balón, *m*; (shot) bala, *f*; (of wool, etc.) ovillo, *m*; (of the eye) globo (del ojo), *m*; (of the thumb) yema (del pulgar), *f*; (of the foot) planta (del pie), *f*; (dance) baile, *m*. *vi* apelotonarse. **red b.,** (in billiards) mingo, *m*. **to play b.,** jugar a la pelota. **to roll oneself into a b.,** aovillarse, hacerse un ovillo. **b.-and-socket joint,** articulación esférica, *f*. **b.-bearing,** cojinete de bolas, *m*

ballad *n* romance, *m*; (song) balada, *f*

ballast *n* (*naut* and *fig*) lastre, *m*; *rw* balasto, *m*. *vt* lastrar; llenar de balasto

ballerina *n* bailarina, *f*

ballet *n* baile ruso, ballet, *m*; baile, *m*. **b. master,** director de ballet, *m*

ballistics *n* balística, *f*

balloon *n* globo aerostático, *m*; *chem* balón, *m*; (toy) globo, *m*; *arch* bola, *f*. **captive b.,** globo cautivo, *m*. **b. barrage,** cortina de globos de intercepción, *f*. **b.-tyre,** neumático balón, *m*

balloonist *n* aeronauta, *mf*

ballot *n* votación, *f*; papeleta para votar, cédula de votación, *f*. *vi* votar, balotar. **b. box,** urna electoral, *f*

ballpoint, ballpoint pen *n* biro *m* (Argentina), birome *m* (Argentina, Uruguay), bolígrafo *m* (Spain), bolilápiz *m* (Mexico), esfero *m* (Colombia), esferográfica *f* (Colombia), estenógrafo *m* (Cuba), lapicera *f* (Argentina), lapicero *m* (Central America, Colombia), lápiz de bolilla *m* (Paraguay, Peru), lápiz de pasta *m* (Chile), pluma esférica *f* (Spain), pluma esferográfica *f* (Spain), plumilla *f* (Venezuela), polígrafo *m* (Spain), punto bola, punto-bola, puntobola *f* (Bolivia), pluma de bola *f*, pluma atómica *f*

ballroom *n* salón de baile, *m*; salón de fiestas, *m*

ballroom dancing *n* baile de salón, *m*

balm *n* bálsamo, *m*; *fig* ungüento, *m*

balminess *n* fragancia, *f*; aroma, *m*; (gentleness) suavidad, *f*

balmy *a* balsámico; fragante; aromático; (soft) suave; (soothing) calmante

balsam *n* bálsamo, *m*

Baltic, the el (Mar) Báltico, *m*

balustrade *n* balaustrada, barandilla, *f*, antepecho, *m*

bamboo *n* bambú, *m*

bamboozle *vt* engatusar, embaucar

bamboozler *n* embaucador (-ra)

ban *n* interdicción, *f*; prohibición, *f*; bando, *m*. *vt* prohibir; proscribir

banal *a* banal, vulgar, trivial

banality *n* banalidad, vulgaridad, trivialidad, *f*

banana *n* (tree and fruit) plátano, *m*; (fruit) banana, *f*, *Venezuela* cambur *m* **b. plantation,** platanar, *m*

band *n* lista, tira, *f*; zona, *f*; (black mourning) tira de gasa, *f*; (sash) faja, *f*; (ribbon) banda; cinta, *f*; (bandage) venda, *f*; *mech* correa, *f*; *arch* listón, *m*; *mus* banda, *f*; (group) pandilla, *f*, grupo, *m*. *vt* congregar, reunir. *vi* reunirse, asociarse. **b.-saw,** sierra de cinta, *f*

bandage *n* venda, *f*, vendaje, *m*, *vt* vendar, poner un vendaje en (limbs, etc. or persons)

bandaging *n* vendaje, *m*

banderol *n* banderola, *f*

bandit *n* bandido, bandolero, *m*

bandmaster *n* músico mayor, *m*; director de orquesta, *m*

bandsman *n* músico, *m*

bandstand *n* quiosco de música, *m*

bandy *vt* cambiar, trocar; pasar de uno a otro

bandy-legged *a* estevado zanquituerto

bane *n* (poison) veneno, *m*; perdición, ruina, *f*; (nuisance) plaga, *f*

baneful *a* pernicioso, funesto; dañino; maligno

banefully *adv* funestamente; malignamente

bang *n* golpe, golpazo, *m*; (of an explosive, fire-arm) estallido, *m*, detonación, *f*; (of a firework) traque, *m*; (of a door) portazo, *m*; (with the fist) puñetazo, *m*; (noise) ruido, *m*; (fringe) flequillo, *m*. *vt* golpear; (beat) sacudir; (throw) lanzar, arrojar con violencia; (a door, etc.) cerrar de golpe, cerrar con violencia. *vi* golpear; estallar; (thunder) retronar; (in the wind) cencerrear. *interj* ¡pum! ¡zas!

banging *n* golpeadura, *f*; sacudidura, *f*; detonación, *f*; ruido, *m*

bangle *n* (slave b.) esclava, *f*; pulsera, *f*; brazalete, *m*; (for ankles) ajorca, *f*

banish *vt* desterrar; apartar; (from the mind) despedir, ahuyentar; (suppress) suprimir

banishment *n* destierro, *m*; expulsión, *f*; relegación, *f*; (suppression) supresión, *f*

banister *n* baranda, *f*, pasamano, *m*

banjo *n* banjo, *m*

banjoist *n* tocador (-ra) de banjo

bank *n* (of rivers, etc.) ribera, orilla, *f*, margen, *m*; (of clouds) banda, capa, *f*; (of sand, fog, snow) banco, *m*; (embankment) terraplén, *m*; *com* banco, *m*; (gaming) banca, *f*; (for foreign exchange) casa de cambio, *f*. **b. account,** cuenta corriente, *f*. **b. book,** libreta de banco, *f*. **b. clerk,** empleado del banco, *m*. **b. holiday,** fiesta oficial, *f*, **b.-note,** billete de banco, *m*. **b. stock,** acciones de un banco, *f pl*

bank *vt* estancar, represar; amontonar; poner (dinero) en un banco, depositar en un banco. *vi* tener cuenta corriente en un banco; (gaming) tener la banca; ser banquero; *aer* inclinarse al virar

banker *n* banquero, *m*, (also at cards); (money-changer) cambista, *mf*

banking *n com* banca, *f*; *aer* vuelo inclinado, *m*, *a com* bancario. **b. house,** casa de banca, *f*

bankrupt *a* insolvente, quebrado. *n* quebrado (-da). **to go b.,** declararse en quiebra, hacer bancarrota

bankruptcy *n* bancarrota, quiebra, *f*; *fig* pobreza, decadencia, *f*. **fraudulent b.,** quiebra fraudulenta, *f*. **b. court,** tribunal de quiebras, *m*

banner *n* bandera, *f*

banns *n pl* amonestaciones, *f pl*. **to forbid the b.,** impedir las amonestaciones. **to publish the b.,** decir las amonestaciones

banquet *n* banquete, *m*, *vt* and *vi* banquetear

banqueting *a* de banquetes. **b. hall,** sala de banquetes, *f*

bantam *n* gallina enana, *f*. **b. weight,** (*sport*) *a* de peso gallo. *n* peso gallo, *m*

banter *vt* and *vi* tomar el pelo (a). *n* chistes, *m pl*, burlas, *f pl*
baptism *n* bautismo, *m*; *fig* bautizo, *m*
baptist *n* bautista, *m*. **St. John the B.,** San Juan Bautista
baptistry *n* baptisterio, bautisterio, *m*
baptize *vt* bautizar
baptizing *n* bautizo, *m*
bar *n* barra, *f*; (of chocolate, soap) pastilla, *f*; *her* banda, *f*; (on a window) reja, *f*; (of a door) tranca, *f*, barrote, *m*; (bar lever) palanca, *f*; (of a balance) astil, *m*; *mus* barra, *f*; (in the sea, etc.) banco, alfaque, *m*; (barrier) barrera, *f*; (barrister's profession) foro, *m*, curia, *f*; *fig* tribunal, *m*; (in a court) barra, *f*; *fig* impedimento, *m*; (of light) rayo, *m*; (stripe) raya, *f*; (for refreshments) bar, *m*, *Lat. Am.* chingana *f* mostrador del bar, *m*. *vt* atrancar, abarrotar; impedir, obstruir; prohibir; exceptuar, excluir; (streak) rayar. **the b.,** el cuerpo de abogados. **to be called to the b.,** ser recibido como abogado en los tribunales. **b.-tender,** camarero del bar, *m*
bar association *n* colegio de abogados, *m*
barb *n* púa, *f*; (of an arrow, fish-hook, etc.) lengüeta, *f*; (of a lance) roquete, *m*; (of fish) barbilla, *f*; (of a feather) barba, *f*; (horse) caballo berberisco, *m*. *vt* proveer de púas; armar de lengüetas
Barbados Isla de Barbados, *f*
barbarian *a* bárbaro, barbárico. *n* bárbaro (-ra)
barbaric *a* barbárico, salvaje
barbarism *n* barbarismo, salvajismo, *m*; crueldad, *f*; (of style) barbarismo, *m*
barbarity *n* barbaridad, ferocidad, *f*
barbarous *a* feroz, cruel, salvaje; inculto
barbarously *adv* bárbaramente, cruelmente
barbarousness *n* barbaridad, *f*; crueldad, ferocidad, *f*
Barbary Berbería, *f*
barbecue *n* barbacoa, *f*
barbed wire *n* alambre de púas, alambre espinoso, *m*
barber *n* barbero, *m*. **barber shop,** barbería, *f*
Barcelona (of or from) *a* and *n* barcelonés (-esa)
bard *n* bardo, vate, *m*
bare *a* desnudo; descubierto; vacío; (mere) mero, solo; (worn) raído; pelado, raso; (unadorned) sencillo; (unsheathed) desnudo; (arid) árido; (curt) seco; (unprotected) desabrigado; pobre. *vt* desnudar; descubrir; revelar. **He bared his head,** Se descubrió. **to lay b.,** dejar al desnudo; revelar
bareback *a* que monta en pelo. *adv* en pelo
barefaced *a* descarado, desvergonzado, cínico
barefoot *a* descalzo
bareheaded *a* sin sombrero, descubierto
barelegged *a* en pernetas, en piernas
barely *adv* apenas; escasamente; meramente, solamente
bareness *n* desnudez, *f*; desadorno, *m*; (aridity) aridez, *f*; pobreza, *f*
bargain *n* contrato, *m*; pacto, acuerdo, *m*; (purchase) ganga, *f*. *vi* negociar; (haggle) regatear; (expect) esperar. **into the b.,** de añadidura, también. **It is a b.,** Es una ganga; Trato hecho. **to get the best of the b.,** salir ganando. **to strike a b.,** cerrar un trato. **b. counter,** sección de saldos, *f*. **b. sale,** venta de saldos, *Mexico* barata *f*
bargainer *n* negociador (-ra); regatón (-ona)
bargaining *n* negociación, gestión, *f*; (haggling) regateo, *m*
barge *n* (for freight) barcaza, gabarra, *f*; falúa, *f*; lancha, *f*. *vi* (into) tropezar con; dar empujones
baritone *n* barítono, *m*
barium *n chem* bario, *m*
bark *n* (of a tree) corteza, *f*; (quinine) quina, *f*; (boat, *poet*) barca, *f*; *naut* buque de tres palos, *m*; (of a dog) ladrido, *m*; (of a fox) aullido, *m*; (of a gun) ruido, *m*. *vi* (of a dog) ladrar; (of a fox) aullar; (of a gun) tronar
barking *n* ladrido, *m*; (of stags) rebramo, *m*; (of foxes) aullidos, *m pl*; (of guns) trueno, *m*
barley *n* cebada, *f*, *a* de cebada. **pearl b.,** cebada perlada, *f*. **b.-bin,** cebadera, *f*. **b. dealer,** cebadero, *m*. **b. field,** cebadal, *m*. **b.-water,** hordiate, *m*
barm *n* (froth on beer) giste, *m*; (leaven) levadura, *f*
barmaid *n* moza de bar, camarera, *f*
barn *n* pajar, granero, hórreo, *m*. **b.-owl,** lechuza, *f*
barnacle *n* lapa, *f*, barnacla, *m*
barometer *n* barómetro, *m*
barometric *a* barométrico
baron *n* barón, *m*
baroness *n* baronesa, *f*
Baron Munchausen el Barón de la Castaña
baroque *a* barroco. **the b.,** lo barroco
barracks *n mil* cuartel, *m*, caserna, *Lat. Am.* barraca *f*, *vt* acuartelar
barrage *n* presa de contención, *f*; *mil* cortina de fuego, *f*; (barrier) barrera, *f*; (of questions) lluvia, *f*. **b. balloon,** globo de intercepción, *m*
barrel *n* barril, *m*; tonel, *m*, cuba, *f*; (of a gun) cañón, *m*; *mech* cilindro, *m*; (of an animal) cuerpo, *m*. *vt* embarrilar, entonelar. **b.-organ,** organillo, órgano de manubrio, *m*
barrelled *a* embarrilado; (of guns, generally in compounds) de . . . cañones. **double-b. gun,** escopeta de dos cañones, *f*
barren *a* estéril; (of ground) árido; (fruitless) infructuoso
barrenness *n* esterilidad, *f*; aridez, sequedad, *f*; (fruitlessness) inutilidad, *f*
barrens *n* yermo, *m sing*, yerma, *f sing*
barricade *n* barricada, *f*; barrera, *f*, *vt* cerrar con barricadas; obstruir
barricading *n* el cerrar con barricadas; la defensa con barricadas (de)
barrier *n* barrera, *f*; impedimento, *m*; (for customs duties) portazgo, *m*
barring *prep* salvo, excepto, con la excepción de, menos
barrister *n* abogado (-da)
barrow *n* carretón, *m*; carretilla, *f*; (tumulus) túmulo, *m*
barter *n* cambio, trueque, *m*; tráfico, *m*, *vt* and *vi* cambiar, trocar; traficar
barterer *n* traficante, *mf*
basal *a* básico, fundamental
basalt *n* basalto, *m*
base *a* bajo, vil, ruin; soez; indigno; impuro; (of metals) de mala ley. *n* base, *f*; fundamento, *m*; pie, *m*; *arch* pedestal, *m*; (*mil chem geom*) base, *f*; (of a vase) asiento, *m*, *vt* basar; fundar. **b. action,** bajeza, *f*. **b. line,** *sport* línea de base, *f*. **b. metal,** metal común, *m*
baseball *n* pelota base, *f*
baseless *a* sin base; sin fundamento; insostenible
basely *adv* bajamente, vilmente
basement *n* sótano, *m*
baseness *n* bajeza, vileza, ruindad, *f*
bashful *a* vergonzoso, ruboroso; tímido, corto; (unsociable) huraño, esquivo
bashfully *adv* vergonzosamente; tímidamente
bashfulness *n* vergüenza, *f*, rubor, *m*; encogimiento, *m*, timidez, cortedad, *f*; (unsociableness) hurañía, esquivez, *f*
basic *a* básico; fundamental
basic commodity *n* artículo básico, producto primario, *m*
basil (sweet) *n bot* albahaca, *f*
basilica *n* basílica, *f*
basilisk *n* basilisco, *m*
basin *n* vasija, *f*; (for washing) jofaina, *f*; (barber's) bacía, *f*; (of a fountain) taza, *f*; *anat* bacinete, *m*; (of a harbor) concha, *f*; (of a river) cuenca, *f*; (in the earth) hoya, *f*; (dock) dársena, *f*
basis *n* base, *f*; fundamento, *m*; elemento principal, *m*
bask *vi* calentarse; (in the sun) tomar el sol
basket *n* cesta, *f*; canasta, capacha, *Lat. Am.* jaba *f*; (frail) espuerta, *f*. **flat b.,** azafate, *m*. **large b.,** banasta, *f*. **b. with a lid,** excusabaraja, *f*. **b. ball,** baloncesto, *m*. **b. maker** or **dealer,** banastero, cestero, *m*. **b. work** or

shop or **factory,** cestería, *f.* **b. work chair,** sillón de mimbres, *m*
basketful *n* cesta, cestada, *f*
Basque *a* and *n* vasco (-ca), vascongado (-da). *n* (language) vascuence, *m*
Basque Provinces, the las Provincias Vascongadas
bas-relief *n* bajo relieve, *m*
bass *n mus* bajo, *m*; (for tying) esparto, *m*, *a mus* bajo. **double b.,** contrabajo, *m.* **figured b.,** bajo cifrado, *m.* **b. clef,** clave de fa, *f.* **b. string,** bordón, *m.* **b. voice,** voz baja, *f*
bassinet *n* cochecito de niño, *m*
bassoon *n mus* bajón, fagot, *m*
bassoonist *n* bajonista, fagotista, *mf*
bastard *n* bastardo (-da), hijo (-ja) natural. *a* bastardo, ilegítimo; espurio
baste *vt sew* bastear, hilvanar, embastar; *cul* enlardar, lardear
basting *n sew* embaste, *m*; *cul* lardeamiento, *m.* **b. spoon,** cacillo, *m.* **b. stitch,** pasillo, *m*
bastion *n* bastión, baluarte, *m.* **to fortify with bastions,** abastionar
bastioned *a* abastionado, con bastiones
bat *n zool* murciélago, *m*; (in cricket) paleta, *f*; (in table tennis) pala, *f.* *vi* (cricket) golpear con la paleta. See **without**
batch *n* (of loaves, etc.) hornada, *f*; lote, *m*; (of recruits) promoción, *f*
bath *n* baño, *m*; (room) cuarto de baño, *m*; (vat) bañador, *m*; (for swimming) piscina cubierta, *f*; (in the open air) piscina al aire libre, *f*; *phot* baño, *m*, solución, *f.* *vt* bañar, lavar. **hot mineral baths,** termas, *f pl.* **Order of the B.,** Orden del Baño, *f.* **public baths,** casa de baños, *f.* **reinforcing b.,** *phot* reforzador, *m.* **to take a b.,** bañarse, tomar un baño. **b.-chair,** cochecillo de inválido, *m.* **b.-robe,** bata de baño, *f*, albornoz, *m.* **b. room,** cuarto de baño, *m.* **b. towel,** toalla del baño, *f.* **b. tub,** bañera, *f*, baño, *m*, *Argentina* bañadera *f*
bathe *vt* bañar, lavar; (of light, etc.) bañar, envolver. *vi* bañarse. *n* baño, *m.* **to go for a b.,** ir a bañarse
bather *n* bañista, *mf*; bañador (-ra)
bathing *a* de baño; balneario, *n* baño, *m.* **b. cap,** gorro de baño, *m.* **b. dress,** traje de baño, *m.* **b. gown,** albornoz, *m*, bata de baño, *f.* **b. machine,** caseta de baños, *f.* **b.-pool,** piscina, *f.* **b.-resort,** estación balnearia, *f.* **b.-shoes,** calzado de baño, *m*
bathos *n* paso de lo sublime a lo ridículo, *m*; anticlímax, *m*
batiste *n*; batista, *f*
baton *n* bastón de mando, *m*; *mus* batuta, *f*; (policeman's) porra, *f*
battalion *n* batallón, *m*
batten *vi* engordar (de); medrar, prosperar. **to b. down,** cerrar las escotillas
batter *n cul* batido, *m*; pasta, *f*; *sport* lanzador, *m.* *vt* apalear, golpear; (demolish) derribar, demoler; (with artillery) cañonear; batir. **to coat with b.,** rebozar. **to b. down,** derribar
battering ram *n* ariete, *m*
battery *n* (*mil nav*) batería, *f*; *elec* pila, batería, *f*; *law* agresión, *f.* **dry b.,** batería de pilas, *f.* **storage b.,** acumulador, *m.* **b. cell,** pila de batería eléctrica, *f*
battle *n* batalla, *f*; pelea, *f*, combate, *m*; (struggle) lucha, *f.* *vi* batallar, pelear; luchar. **b.-array,** orden de batalla, *f.* **b.-axe,** hacha de combate, *f.* **b.-cruiser,** acorazado, *m.* **b.-field,** campo de batalla, *m.* **b.-front,** frente de combate, *m.* **b.-piece,** *art* batalla, *f.* **b.-ship,** buque de guerra, *m*
battledore (and shuttlecock) *n* raqueta (y volante), *f*
battlement *n* almenaje, *m*; muralla almenada, *f*
bauble *n* (trifle) chuchería, fruslería, *f*; (fool's) cetro de bufón, *m*
bauxite *n* bauxita, *f*
Bavaria Baviera, *f*
Bavarian *a* and *n* bávaro (-ra)
bawdy *a* obsceno, indecente, escabroso
bawl *vi* chillar, vocear
bawling *n* vocerío, *m*, chillidos, *m pl*
bay *n geog* bahía, *f*; (small) abra, *f*; *bot* laurel, *m*; (horse) bayo, *m*; (howl) aullido, *m*; *arch* abertura, *f*; *rw* andén, *m.* *a* (of horses) bayo, isabelino. *vi* aullar. **at bay,** en jaque, acorralado. **sick-bay,** enfermería, *f.* **to keep at bay,** tener a distancia; tener alejado; entretener. **bay rum,** ron de malagueta, *m.* **bay window,** ventana salediza, *f*
baying *n* aullido, *m*
bayonet *n* bayoneta, *f*, *vt* herir o matar con bayoneta. **fixed b.,** bayoneta calada, *f.* **b. charge,** carga de bayoneta, *f.* **b. thrust,** bayonetazo, *m*
Bayonne Bayona, *f*
bazaar *n* bazar, *m*
be *vi* ser; (of position, place, state, temporariness) estar; (exist) existir; (in impersonal expressions) haber; (of expressions concerning the weather and time) hacer; (remain) quedar; (leave alone) dejar; (do) hacer; (of one's health) estar; (of feeling cold, hot, afraid, etc. and of years of one's age) tener; (live) vivir; (belong) ser (de), pertenecer (a); (matter, concern) importar (a); (happen) ocurrir, suceder; (find oneself) hallarse, encontrarse, estar; (arrive) llegar (a); (cost) costar; (be worth) valer; (celebrate, hold) celebrarse, tener lugar; (forming continuous tense with present participle active or passive) estar; (with past participle forming passive) ser (this construction is often replaced by reflexive form when no ambiguity is entailed); (with infinitive expressing duty, intention) haber de; (must) tener que. **He is a soldier (doctor, etc.),** Es soldado (médico, etc.). **He is on guard,** Está de guardia. **They were at the door (in the house, etc.),** Estaban a la puerta (en la casa, etc.). **I am writing a letter,** Estoy escribiendo una carta (but this form is often replaced by a simple tense, e.g. escribo . . .). **It remains to be written,** Queda por escribir. **What is to be done?** ¿Qué hay que hacer? **Woe is me!** ¡Ay de mí! **to be hot (cold),** (of things) estar caliente (frío); (of weather) hacer calor (frío); (of persons) tener calor (frío). **How is John? He is well,** ¿Cómo está Juan? Está bien de salud. **It is daylight,** Es de día. **It is cloudy,** Está nublado. **She is 10,** Tiene diez años. **They are afraid,** Tienen miedo. **I am to go there tomorrow,** He de ir allí mañana. **What is to be will be,** Lo que tiene que ser será. **If John were to come we could go into the country,** Si viniera Juan podríamos ir al campo. **Be that as it may,** Sea como sea. **It is seven years since we saw him,** Hace siete años que no le vemos. **We have been here for three years,** Hace tres años que estamos aqui, Llevamos tres años aquí. **There is** or **there are,** Hay. **There will be many people,** Habrá mucha gente. **There were many people,** Había mucha gente. **There are many people,** Hay mucha gente. **It is three miles to the next village,** Estamos a tres millas del pueblo próximo. **So be it!** Así sea. **Your pen is not to be seen,** Tu pluma no se ve. **It is to be hoped that . . . ,** Se espera que . . . ; ¡Ojalá que . . . ! **The door is open,** La puerta está abierta. **The door was opened by Mary,** La puerta fue abierta por María. **He was accused of being a fascist,** Lo acusaron de fascista. **to be about to,** estar por; (of a more imminent action) estar para, estar a punto de. **to be in,** estar dentro; estar en casa. **to be off,** marcharse, irse. **Be off!** ¡Márchate! ¡Vete!; ¡Fuera! **to be out,** estar fuera; haber salido; no estar en casa; (of a light, etc.) estar apagado. **to be up,** estar levantado. **to be up to,** proyectar, traer entre manos; urdir, maquinar
beach *n* playa, *f*; costa, *f.* *vt* (a boat) encallar en la costa. **b. shoes,** playeras, *f pl.* **b. suit,** vestido de playa, *m*
beach club *n* club de playa, *m*
beacon *n* (lighthouse) faro, *m*; (buoy) baliza, *f*, fanal, *m*; (watch-tower) atalaya, *f*; *fig* guía, *f.* *vt* iluminar. **b. fire,** almenara, *f*
bead *n* cuenta, *f*; (of glass) abalorio, *m*; (drop) gota, *f*; *arch* perla, *f*; (bubble) burbuja, *f*; (foam) espuma,

f; pl **beads,** rosario, *m, vt* adornar con abalorios. **to tell one's beads,** rezar el rosario. **b. work,** abalorio, *m*

beading *n* abalorio, *m; arch* friso, listón, *m*

beadle *n* bedel, *m*

beadleship *n* bedelía, *f*

beagle *n* perro sabueso, *m*

beak *n* pico, *m;* punta, *f; naut* espolón, *m.* **to tap with the b.,** picotear

beaked *a* que tiene pico; (in compounds) de . . . pico

beaker *n* copa, *f; chem* vaso de precipitado, *m*

beam *n arch* madero, *m,* viga, *f;* (width of a ship) manga, *f;* (of a balance) palanca, *f;* (of a plough) cama, *f;* (of light) rayo, destello, *m; phys* rayo, *m;* (smile) sonrisa brillante, *f; pl* **beams,** (of a building) envigado, *m;* (of a ship) baos, *m pl.* **main b.,** *arch* viga maestra, *f.* **on her b.-ends,** de costado; *fig* arruinado; en la miseria. **b. feather,** astil, *m.* **b. of light,** rayo de luz, haz de luz, *m*

beam *vt* lanzar, emitir; difundir. *vi* brillar, fulgurar, destellar; estar radiante, estar rebosando de alegría

beaming *a* brillante; radiante

bean *n* haba, *f;* judía, alubia, *f;* (of coffee) grano, *m.* **broad b.,** haba, *f.* **French, haricot, kidney b.,** judía, *f.* **string b.,** judía verde, *f.* **b. field,** habar, *m*

bear *n zool* oso, *m;* (she-bear) osa, *f;* (Stock Exchange) bajista, *mf.* **Great B.,** *ast* Osa Mayor, *f,* Septentrión, *m.* **Little B.,** *ast* Osa Menor, *f.* **polar b.,** oso blanco, *m.* **b.-cub,** osezno, *m.* **bear's den,** osera, *f.* **b.-garden,** patio de osos, *m; inf* merienda de negros, *f.* **b.-hunting,** caza de osos, *f.* **b.-like,** osuno. **b.-pit,** recinto de los osos, *m*

bear *vt* and *vi* (carry) llevar; (show) ostentar; (company, etc.) hacer; (profess) profesar; (of spite, etc. and of relation) guardar; (have) tener; (fruit) dar; (give birth to) parir; (support) sostener; (endure) aguantar; (suffer) padecer, sufrir; (tolerate) tolerar, sufrir; (a strain, an operation, etc.) resistir; (lean on) apoyarse en; (experience) experimentar; (produce) producir, dar; (enjoy) disfrutar de; (use) usar; (impel) empujar; (occupy, hold) ocupar; (go) dirigirse. **It was suddenly borne in on them that . . . ,** De pronto vieron claro que . . . **I cannot b. any more,** No puedo más. **We cannot b. him,** No le aguantamos, No le sufrimos. **His language won't b. repeating,** Su lenguaje no puede repetirse. **to bring to b.,** ejercer (presión, etc.). **to b. a grudge,** guardar rencor (a), tener ojeriza (a). **to b. arms,** llevar armas; servir en el ejército o la milicia. **to b. company,** hacer compañía (a), acompañar (a). **to b. in mind,** tener en cuenta, tener presente; acordarse de. **to b. oneself,** conducirse, portarse. **to b. to the right,** ir hacia la derecha. **to b. witness,** atestiguar. **to b. false witness,** levantar falso testimonio. **to b. away,** llevarse; ganar. **to b. down,** hundir; derribar; bajar. **to b. down on,** avanzar rápidamente hacia; correr hacia; *naut* arribar sobre; (attack) caer sobre. **to b. in,** llevar adentro. **to b. off,** llevarse; ganar; *naut* apartarse de la costa. **to b. on, upon,** apoyarse en; (refer to) referirse a. **to b. out,** llevar fuera; confirmar; apoyar; justificar. **to b. up,** llevar arriba; llevar a la cumbre (de); sostener; (recover) cobrar ánimo; (against) resistir; hacer frente a. **to b. with,** soportar; sufrir; aguantar; llevar con paciencia; ser indulgente con

bearable *a* soportable; aguantable; tolerable

beard *n* barba, *f;* (of cereals) raspa, arista, *f, vt* desafiar. **thick b.,** barba bien poblada, *f*

bearded *a* con barba, barbudo

beardless *a* barbilampiño, desbarbado, imberbe, lampiño

bearer *n* llevador (-ra), portador (-ra); (of a bier) andero, *m; com* dador, portador, *m.* **good b.,** *agr* árbol fructífero, *m.* **to b.,** *com* al portador

bearing *n* porte, *m;* postura, *f;* presencia, *f;* conducta, *f;* aspecto, *m;* relación, *f;* (meaning) significación, *f; naut* demora, orientación, *f; mech* cojinete, soporte, *m;* (endurance) tolerancia, *f; pl* **bearings,** (way) camino, *m; her* escudo de armas, *m.* **to get one's bearings,** orientarse; encontrar el camino. **to lose one's bearings,** desorientarse; perderse. **to have a b. on,** tener relación con; tener que ver con; influir en

bearish *a* osuno; rudo, áspero

bearskin *n* piel de oso, *f;* birretina, *f*

beast *n* animal, bruto, *m;* cuadrúpedo, *m;* (cattle) res, *f;* bestia, *f.* **wild b.,** fiera, *f.* **b. of burden,** acémila, bestia de carga, *f.* **b. of prey,** animal de rapiña, *m*

beastliness *n* bestialidad, brutalidad, *f;* obscenidad, *f*

beastly *a* bestial, brutal; obsceno; *inf* horrible

beat *n* latido, *m,* pulsación, *f;* golpe, *m;* (of a drum) toque (de tambor), *m;* (of a clock) tictac, *m;* sonido repetido, *m;* vibración, *f*

beat *vt* and *vi* batir; golpear; (thrash) pegar, dar una paliza (a), *Lat. Am.* humear; (to remove dust, etc.) sacudir; (shake) agitar; (the wings) aletear; (hunting) batir; (excel) exceder, superar; ganar; (defeat) vencer; (of the rain, etc.) azotar; (a drum) tocar; (of the sun) batir, dar (en); (throb) latir, palpitar, pulsar. **to b. about the bush,** andarse por las ramas. **to stop beating about the bush,** dejarse de historias. **to b. a retreat,** *mil* emprender la retirada; huir. **to b. black and blue,** moler a palos. **to b. hollow,** vencer completamente; ganar fácilmente; aventajar con mucho. **to b. it,** *inf* escaparse corriendo. **to b. time,** *mus* llevar el compás; triunfar sobre la vejez. **to b. to it,** *inf* tomar la delantera. **to b. against,** golpear contra; chocar contra. **to b. back,** rechazar; (sobs, etc.) ahogar; reprimir. **to b. down,** (prices) regatear; (of the sun) caer de plomo, caer de plano; reducir; suprimir; destruir. **to b. off,** rechazar; echar a un lado. **to b. out,** hacer salir; (metals) batir; (a tune) llevar el compás (de). **to b. up,** *cul* batir; (a mattress) mullir; asaltar; maltratar

beaten *a* (of paths) trillado; (conquered) vencido; (of metals) batido; (dejected) deprimido; (trite) trivial, vulgar

beater *n* batidor, *m;* (for carpets) sacudidor (de alfombras), *m; cul* batidor, *m*

beatific *a* beatífico

beatification *n* beatificación, *f*

beatify *vt* beatificar

beating *n* batimiento, *m;* vencimiento, *m;* (thrashing) paliza, *f., Lat. Am. also* azotera, *f.;* (of the heart, etc.) palpitación, *f,* latido, *m;* (of metals) batida, *f;* (of a drum) rataplán, toque de tambor, *m;* (of waves) embate, *m;* (of wings) aleteo, aletazo, *m*

beatitude *n* beatitud, *f*

beau *n* galán, *m;* (fop) petimetre, *m*

beautiful *a* bello, lindo, hermoso; magnífico; excelente; exquisito; elegante; encantador, delicioso

beautifully *adv* bellamente; (richly) ricamente; admirablemente; magníficamente; elegantemente

beautify *vt* embellecer; hermosear; adornar. **to b. oneself,** arreglarse, ponerse elegante

beautifying *n* embellecimiento, *m;* adorno, *m*

beauty *n* belleza, hermosura, lindeza, *f;* magnificencia, *f;* excelencia, *f;* elegancia, *f;* encanto, *m;* (belle) beldad, Venus, *f.* **to lose one's b.,** desmejorarse, perder su hermosura. **b. contest,** concurso de belleza, *m.* **b. parlor,** salón de belleza, instituto de belleza, *m.* **b. sleep,** el primer sueño de la noche. **b. spot,** lunar, *m;* lunar postizo, *m;* (place) sitio hermoso, *m.* **b. treatment,** masaje facial, *m*

beaver *n* castor, *m;* (hat) sombrero de copa, *m;* (of helmet) babera, *f*

because *conjunc* porque. **b. of,** debido a, a causa de

beckon *vt* and *vi* hacer señas (a); llamar por señas, llamar con la mano

become *vi* volverse; llegar a ser, venir a ser; convertirse en; ponerse; hacerse; (befit) convenir; (suit) ir bien (a), favorecer. **He became red,** Se enrojeció. **The hat becomes you,** El sombrero te va bien. **He became king,** Llegó a ser rey. **What has b. of her?** ¿Qué es de ella?; (Where is she?) ¿Qué se ha hecho de ella? **b. binding,** adquirir carácter de compromiso

becoming *a* propio; correcto; decoroso; (suitable) conveniente; (of dress) que favorece, que va bien. **This dress is b. to you,** Este vestido te favorece

becomingly *adv* decorosamente

bed *n* cama, *f*, lecho, *m*; (of sea) fondo, *m*; (of river) cauce, *m*; *geol* yacimiento, *m*; (in a garden) cuadro, macizo (de jardín), *m*; (of a machine) asiento, *m*; (of a building) cimiento, *m*; *fig* fundamento, *m*, base, *f*, *vt* (plants) plantar; (fix) fijar, poner. **double bed,** cama de matrimonio, *f*. **single bed,** cama de monja, *f*. **in bed,** en cama. **to be gone to bed,** haber ido a la cama. **to be in bed,** estar acostado. **to get into bed,** meterse en cama. **to get out of bed,** levantarse de la cama. **to go to bed,** acostarse, ir a la cama. **to make the beds,** hacer las camas. **to put to bed,** acostar. **to stay in bed,** quedarse en cama, guardar cama. **bed-bug,** chinche, *f*. **bed-clothes,** ropa de cama, *f*. **bed-cover,** cubrecama, colcha, *f*. **bed-head,** cabecera, *f*. **bed-pan,** silleta, *f*. **bed-sore,** úlcera de decúbito, *f*

bedaub, bedazzle. See **daub, dazzle**

bedchamber *n* dormitorio, *m*, alcoba, *f*

bedded *a* con . . . cama(s). **a double-b. room,** un cuarto con dos camas; un cuarto con cama de matrimonio

bedding *n* ropa de cama, *f*; cama para el ganado, *f*

bedeck *vt* embellecer, adornar, engalanar

bedfellow *n* compañero de almohada, compañero de cama

bedlam *n* belén, manicomio, *m*; *fig* babel, *m*

bedraggled *a* mojado y sucio

bedridden *a* postrado en cama, inválido

bedrock *n* lecho de roca, *m*; *fig* principios fundamentales, fundamentos, *m pl*

bedroom *n* cuarto de dormir, dormitorio, *m*, habitación, *f*

bedside *n* lado de cama, *m*; cabecera, *f*. **b. manner,** mano izquierda, diplomacia, *f*. **b.-table,** mesa de noche, *f*

bedspread *n* colcha, cubrecama, sobrecama, *f*

bedstead *n* cama, *f*

bedtime *n* hora de acostarse, *f*

bee *n* abeja, *f*; (meeting) reunión, *f*, *a* abejuno. **queen bee,** rey, *m*, abeja maestra, *f*. **to have a bee in one's bonnet,** tener una manía (or idea fija). **to make a bee-line for,** ir directamente a. **bee-eater,** *orn* abejaruco, *m*. **bee hive,** colmena, *f*; abejar, *m*. **bee-keeper,** apicultor (-ra), colmenero (-ra), abejero (-ra). **bee's wax,** cera de abeja, *f*

beech *n* haya, *f*. **plantation of b. trees,** hayal, *m*. **b.-nut,** hayuco, *m*

beef *n* carne de vaca, *f*; (flesh) carne, *f*; (strength) fuerza, *f*. **roast b.,** rosbif, *m*. **b.-tea,** caldo, *m*

beefsteak *n* biftec, bistec, *Argentina* bife *m*

beer *n* cerveza, *f*. **b. barrel,** barril de cerveza, *m*. **b.-house,** cervecería, *f*. **b. mug,** jarro para la cerveza, *m*

beery *a* de cerveza; (tipsy) achispado

beet *n* remolacha, *f*. *Mexico* betabel *m* **b. sugar,** azúcar de remolacha, *Mexico* azúcar de betabel *m*

beetle *n* escarabajo, *m*. **b.-browed,** cejijunto

beetroot *n* remolacha, *f*, *Mexico* betabel *m*

befall *vi* acontecer, suceder, ocurrir. *vt* ocurrir (a), acontecer (a)

befit *vt* convenir (a), ser digno de

befitting *a* conveniente, apropiado; digno; oportuno

before *adv* delante; al frente; (of time), antes, anteriormente; (of order) antes; (already) ya. *prep* delante de; en frente de; (of time, order) ante; (in the presence of) ante, en presencia de; (rather than) antes de. **b. going,** antes de marcharse. **B. I did it,** Antes de que lo hiciera; Antes de hacerlo. **as never b.,** como nunca. **b. long,** en breve, dentro de poco. **b.-mentioned,** antes citado. **b. the mast,** al pie del mástil, e.g. **two years b. the mast,** dos años al pie del mástil.

beforehand *adv* previamente, de antemano

befoul *vt* ensuciar; *fig* manchar, difamar

befriend *vt* proteger, ayudar, favorecer, amparar

beg *vt* pedir, implorar, suplicar. *vi* mendigar, pordiosear; vivir de limosna. **I beg to propose,** Me permito proponer; Tengo el gusto de proponer; (the health of) Brindo a la salud de. **I beg your pardon!** ¡Vd. dispense!; (when passing in front of anyone, etc.) Con permiso; (in conversation for repetition of a word) ¿Cómo? **to beg the question,** dar por sentado lo mismo que se trata de probar. **His conduct begs description,** No hay palabras para su comportamiento

beget *vt* procrear, engendrar; causar; suscitar

begetter *n* procreador (-ra); creador (-ra)

begetting *n* procreación, *f*; origen, *m*, causa, *f*

beggar *n* mendigo (-ga), pordiosero (-ra), *Lat. Am. also* llimosnero (-ra). **beggars can't be choosers,** a falta de pan, se conforma con tortillas (Mexico); *vt* empobrecer; arruinar. **to b. description,** no haber palabras para describir

beggarliness *n* mendicidad, *f*; pobreza, *f*

beggarly *a* miserable, pobre

beggary *n* miseria, pobreza, *f*

begging *a* mendicante, pordiosero. *n* mendicidad, *f*, pordioseo, *m*. **to go b.,** andar mendigando. **b. letter,** carta pidiendo dinero, *f*

begin *vt* and *vi* empezar; comenzar; iniciar; (a conversation) entablar; (open) abrir; inaugurar; tener su principio; nacer. **to b. to,** empezar a; (start on) ponerse a; (with laughing, etc.) romper a. **to b. with,** empezar por; para empezar, en primer lugar

beginner *n* principiante (-ta); (novice) novato (-ta); iniciador (-ra); autor (-ra)

beginning *n* principio, comienzo, *Lat. Am.* empiezo. *m*; origen, *m*. **at the b.,** al principio; (of the month) a principios (de). **from the b. to the end,** desde el principio hasta el fin, *inf* de pe a pa. **in the b.,** al principio. **to make a b.,** comenzar, empezar

begone *interj* ¡fuera! ¡márchate! ¡vete!

begonia *n* begonia, *f*

begrudge *vt* envidiar

beguile *vt* engañar; defraudar; (time) entretener; (charm) encantar, embelesar

beguilement *n* engaño, *m*; (of time) entretenimiento, *m*; (charm) encanto, *m*

beguilingly *adv* encantadoramente

behalf *n* (preceded by on or upon) por; (from) de parte (de); a favor (de); en defensa (de)

behave *vi* (oneself) conducirse, portarse; (act) obrar, proceder. **to b. badly,** portarse mal; obrar mal. **B.!** ¡Pórtate bien!

behavior *n* conducta, *f*; comportamiento, *m*; proceder, *m*; (manner) modales, *m pl*; *biol* reacción, *f*

behaviorism *n psy* behaviorismo, *m*

behead *vt* decapitar, descabezar

beheading *n* decapitación, *f*

behest *n* precepto, mandato, *m*

behind *adv* detrás; por detrás; atrás; hacia atrás; en pos; (of time and order) después; (late and in arrears) con retraso; (old-fashioned) atrasado. *prep* detrás de; por detrás de; inferior a; menos avanzado que. *n inf* trasero, *m*. **from b.,** por detrás. **to be b. time,** retrasarse; llegar tarde. **b. the back of,** a espaldas de. **b. the scenes,** entre bastidores. **b. the times,** *fig* atrasado de noticias; pasado de moda. **the ideology b. the French Revolution,** la ideología que informó la Revolución Francesa.

behindhand *a* (out of date) atrasado; (late) tardío; *adv* con retraso

behold *vt* ver, mirar, contemplar; presenciar. *interj* ¡he aquí! ¡mira!

beholden *a* obligado, agradecido

beholder *n* espectador (-ra). **the beholders,** los que lo presenciaban

beholding *n* contemplación, vista, *f*

behove *vt* incumbir, tocar, corresponder

beige *n* beige, color arena, *m*

being *n* existencia, *f*; operación, *f*; ser, *m*; (spirit) alma, *f*, espíritu, *m*; esencia, *f*. **human b.,** ser humano, *m*,

alma viviente, *f*. **for the time b.,** por ahora, por el momento
bejewel *vt* enjoyar, adornar con joyas
belabor *vt* apalear, golpear
belated *a* tardío
belay *vt* amarrar
belch *n* eructo, *m*; detonación, *f*; (of a volcano) erupción, *f*. *vi* eructar. *vt* vomitar; (curses, etc.) escupir; despedir, arrojar
belching *n* eructación, *f*; (of smoke, etc.) vómito, *m*, emisión, *f*
beleaguer *vt* sitiar
belfry *n* campanario, *m*
Belgian *a* and *n* belga, *mf*
Belgium Bélgica, *f*
Belgrade Belgrado, *m*
belie *vt* desmentir, contradecir; defraudar
belief *n* creencia, *f*; fe, *f*; opinión, *f*, parecer, *m*; (trust) confianza, *f*. **in the b. that,** creyendo que, en la creencia de que
believable *a* creíble
believe *vt* and *vi* creer; opinar, ser de la opinión, parecer (a uno); confiar, tener confianza. **I b. not,** Creo que no, Me parece que no. **I b. so,** Creo que sí, Me parece que sí. **to make (a person) b.,** hacer (a uno) creer. **to b. in,** creer en; confiar en, tener confianza en
believer *n* persona que cree, *f*; creyente, *mf*
belittle *vt* achicar; conceder poca importancia a
bell *n* campana, *f*; (hand-bell) campanilla, *f*; (small, round) cascabel, *m*; (on cows, etc.) cencerro, *m*, esquila, *f*; (electric, push, or bicycle) timbre, *m*; (jester's) cascabeles, *m pl*; (cry of stag) bramido, *m*. *vt* poner un cascabel (a). *vi* (stags) bramar, roncar. **To bear away the b.,** *fig* llevarse la palma. **to ring the b.,** tocar el timbre; agitar la campanilla. **to ring the bells,** tocar las campanas. **to b. the cat,** ponerle el cascabel al gato, ponerle el collar al gato. **b.-boy,** botones, mozo de hotel, *m*. **b.-clapper,** badajo, *m*. **b.-flower,** campanilla, *f*. **b.-founder,** campanero, *m*. **b.-mouthed,** abocinado. **b.-pull,** tirador de campanilla, *m*. **b.-ringer,** campanero, *m*. **b.-shaped,** campanudo. **b.-tent,** pabellón, *m*. **b. tower,** campanario, *m*
belladonna *n* belladona, *f*
belle *n* beldad, *f*
belles-lettres *n pl* bellas letras, *f pl*
bellicose *a* belicoso, agresivo
bellicosity *n* belicosidad, *f*
belligerency *n* beligerancia, *f*
belligerent *a* beligerante; belicoso, guerrero. *n* beligerante, *mf*
bellow *n* (shout) grito, *m*; rugido, bramido, *m*; (of guns) trueno, *m*. *vi* gritar, vociferar; rugir, bramar; tronar
bellowing *n*. See **bellow**
bellows *n* fuelle, *m*
belly *n* vientre, *m*, barriga, *f*; (of a jug, etc.) panza, *f*; estómago, *m*; (womb) seno, *m*. *vt* hinchar. *vi* hincharse
belong *vi* pertenecer (a); tocar (a), incumbir (a); (to a place) ser de; residir en
belongings *n pl* efectos, *m pl*; posesiones, *f pl*; (luggage) equipaje, *m*
beloved *a* muy amado, muy querido. *n* querido (-da)
below *adv* abajo; (under) debajo; (further on) más abajo; (in hell) en el infierno; (in this world) en este mundo, aquí abajo. *prep* bajo; (underneath) debajo de; (after) después de; (unworthy of) indigno de; inferior a. **The valley lay b. us,** El valle se extendía a nuestros pies. **b. zero,** bajo cero
belt *n* cinturón, *m*; (of a horse) cincha, *f*; (corset) faja, *f*; *geog* zona, *f*; (of a machine) correa (de transmisión), *f*
beltway *n* anillo periférico, *m*
belvedere *n* mirador, *m*
bemoan *vt* deplorar, lamentar
bemoaning *n* lamentación, *f*
bemuse *vt* confundir, desconcertar
bench *n* banco, *m*; (with a back) escaño, *m*; mesa de trabajo, *f*; (carpenter's, shoemaker's, in a boat, in parliament) banco, *m*; (judges) tribunal, *m*
bend *n* corvadura, curva, vuelta, *f*; (in a river, street) recodo, *m*; (on a road) codo viraje, *m*; (of the knee) corva, *f*; (in a pipe) codo, *m*; *naut* nudo, *m*; *her* banda, *f*. **sheet b.,** (knot) nudo de tejedor, *m*
bend *vt* encorvar; doblegar; torcer; (the head) bajar; (the body) inclinar; (steps) dirigir, encaminar; (the mind) aplicarse, dedicarse. *vi* encorvarse; doblegarse; torcerse; (arch) arquear; inclinarse. **to b. the knee,** arrodillarse. **on bended knee,** de rodillas. **to b. back,** *vt* redoblar. *vi* redoblarse; inclinarse hacia atrás. **to b. down,** agacharse; inclinarse. **to b. forward,** inclinarse hacia delante. **to b. over,** inclinarse encima de
bendable *a* que puede doblarse; plegadizo; flexible
bending *n* doblamiento, *m*; flexión, *f*; inclinación, *f*. *a* doblado; inclinado
beneath *adv* abajo; debajo; (at one's feet) a los pies de uno. *prep* bajo; debajo de; al pie de; (unworthy, inferior) indigno. **He married b. him,** Se casó fuera de su clase
Benedictine *a* benedictino. *n* benedictino, *m*; (liqueur) benedictino, *m*
benediction *n* bendición, *f*; gracia divina, merced, *f*
benefaction *n* beneficiación, *f*; buena obra, *f*; beneficio, favor, *m*
benefactor *n* bienhechor, *m*; protector, *m*; patrono, *m*; fundador, *m*
benefactress *n* bienhechora, *f*; protectora, *f*; patrona, *f*; fundadora, *f*
benefice *n* beneficio eclesiástico, *m*, prebenda, *f*
beneficence *n* beneficiencia, caridad, *f*, buenas obras, *f pl*
beneficent *a* benéfico, caritativo
beneficial *a* beneficioso; provechoso, útil
beneficiary *n* beneficiado (-da), beneficiario (-ia)
benefit *n* beneficio, bien, *m*; provecho, *m*, utilidad, *f*; (favor) favor, *m*; *theat* beneficio, *m*; (help) ayuda, *f*, servicio, *m*. *vt* beneficiar; aprovechar; (improve) mejorar. *vi* (with by) sacar provecho de; ganar. **for the b. of,** para; en pro de, a favor de. **b. society,** sociedad benéfica, *f*
benevolence *n* benevolencia, bondad, *f*; liberalidad, *f*; caridad, *f*; favor, *m*
benevolent *a* benévolo; bondadoso; caritativo. **b. society,** sociedad de beneficencia, *f*
benevolently *adv* benignamente, con benevolencia
Bengal Bengala, *f*
benighted *a* sorprendido por la noche; *fig* ignorante
benign, benignant *a* benigno
bent *n* talento, *m*; inclinación, afición, *f*, *a* torcido, *Mexico* chueco; encorvado; resuelto
benumb. See **numb**
benzine *n* bencina, *f*
bequeath *vt* legar, dejar (en el testamento); transmitir
bequest *n* legado, *m*
Berber *a* and *n* bereber, *mf*
bereave *vt* privar (de), quitar; arrebatar; afligir. **the bereaved parents,** los padres afligidos
bereavement *n* privación, *f*; (by death) pérdida, *f*; aflicción, *f*
bereft *a* privado (de); desamparado; indefenso. **utterly b.,** completamente solo
beret *n* boina, *f*
Berlin *a* and *n* (of or from) berlinés (-esa). *n* (carriage) berlina, *f*
Bermudas, the, *m* las Islas Bermudas
Bernard *n* Bernardo, *m*. **St. B. dog,** perro de San Bernardo, *m*
Berne Berna, *f*
berry *n* baya, *f*; (of coffee, etc.) fruto, *m*, *vi* dar bayas; coger bayas
berth *n* (bed) litera, *f*; (cabin) camarote, *m*; (anchorage) anclaje, fondeadero, *m*; (job) empleo, *m*, *vt* (a ship) fondear. **to give a wide b. to,** *naut* ponerse a resguardo de; apartarse mucho de; evitar

beseech *vt* suplicar, rogar, implorar; (ask for) pedir con ahinco
beseeching *a* suplicante, implorante. *n* súplica, *f*; ruego, *m*
beseechingly *adv* suplicantemente
beset *vt* atacar, acosar; aquejar, acosar, perseguir. **beset by personal misfortune,** acosado por las desgracias personales; (block) obstruir; (surround) rodear, cercar
besetting *a* usual, frecuente; obsesionante
beside, besides *prep* al lado de; cerca de; (compared with) en comparación de, comparado con; (in addition) además de; aparte de; excepto. *adv* además, también. **to be beside oneself,** estar fuera de sí
besiege *vt* sitiar; (assail) asaltar, asediar; (surround) rodear; importunar
besieged *n* sitiado (-da)
besieger *n* sitiador, *m*
besieging *a* sitiador. *n* sitio, asalto, *m*; asedio, *m*, importunación, *f*
besmear *vt* embadurnar, ensuciar
besotted *a* estúpido; embrutecido; atontado
bespangled *a* adornado con lentejuelas; brillante (con); (studded) salpicado (de)
bespatter *vt* manchar; derramar; salpicar
bespeak *vt* reservar; (goods) encargar; (signify) demostrar, indicar, significar; *poet* hablar
besprinkle *vt* rociar
best *a sup* of **good** and **well,** mejor; el (la) mejor, *m, f.*, los (las) mejores, *m pl, f pl. adv* mejor; el mejor; (most) más. **as b. I can,** como mejor pueda. **at the b.,** cuando más, en el mejor caso. **He did it for the b.,** Lo hizo con la mejor intención. **the b.,** lo mejor. **to be at one's b.,** brillar; lucirse. **to do one's b.,** hacer todo lo posible. **to get the b. of,** llevar la mejor parte de; triunfar de (or sobre). **to make the b. of,** sacar el mayor provecho de. **The next b. thing to do is . . . ,** Lo mejor que queda ahora por hacer es . . . **b. man,** padrino de boda, *m*. **to be b. man to,** apadrinar, ser padrino de. **b. seller,** libro que se vende más, libro favorito, *m*
bestial *a* bestial
bestiality *n* bestialidad, *f*
bestir (oneself) *vr* menearse, moverse; preocuparse; (hurry) darse prisa
bestow *vt* (place) poner; (with upon) conferir, conceder, otorgar; (a present) regalar
bestowal *n* puesta, *f*; otorgamiento, *m*, concesión, *f*; (of a present) regalo, *m*, dádiva, *f*
bestride *vt* montar a horcajadas en; poner una pierna en cada lado de; cruzar de un tranco
bestseller *n* campeón de venta, éxito editorial, triunfo de librería, *m*
bet *n* apuesta, postura, *f*, *vi* apostar; (gamble) jugar. **What do you bet?** ¿Qué apuesta Vd.?
betake (oneself) *vr* acudir (a); darse (a); marcharse
bethink (oneself) *vr* pensar, reflexionar; (remember) recordar, hacer memoria; ocurrirse
Bethlehem Belén, *m*
betimes *adv* pronto; de buena hora, temprano; con tiempo
betoken *vt* presagiar, prometer; indicar
betray *vt* traicionar; revelar, descubrir; (a woman) seducir; (show) dejar ver
betrayal *n* traición, *f*; (of confidence) abuso (de confianza), *m*; (of a woman) seducción, *f*
betrayer *n* traidor (-ra)
betroth *vt* desposar(se) con, prometer(se). **to be betrothed to,** estar desposado con
betrothal *n* desposorio, *m*, esponsales, *m pl*; (duration) noviazgo, *m*
betrothed *n* desposado (-da), futuro (-ra)
better *a comp* of **good,** mejor; superior. *adv* mejor; más. *vt* mejorar; exceder. *n* apostador (-ra). **He has bettered himself,** Ha mejorado su situación. **It is b. to . . . ,** Es mejor . . . , Vale más . . . (followed by infin.). **little b.,** poco mejor; algo mejor; poco más. **much b.,** mucho mejor. **our betters,** nuestros superiores. **so much the b.,** tanto mejor. **the b. to,** para mejor. **to be b.,** ser mejor; (of health) estar mejor. **to get b.,** mejorar. **to get the b. of,** triunfar sobre, vencer. **b. half,** *inf* media naranja, *f*. **b. off,** mejor situado, más acomodado
betterment *n* mejora, *f*, mejoramiento, *m*; adelantamiento, avance, *m*
betting *n* apuesta, *f*
bettor *n* apostador (-ra)
between *prep* entre; en medio de; de. **the break b. Mr. X and Mrs. Y,** el rompimiento del Sr. X y la Sra. Y. *adv* en medio; entre los dos. **far b.,** a grandes intervalos. **b. now and then,** desde ahora hasta entonces. **b. one thing and another,** entre una cosa y otra. **b. ourselves,** entre nosotros
bevel *n* bisel, *m*, *vt* abiselar
beverage *n* brebaje, *m*, bebida, *f*
bevy *n* grupo, *m*; (of birds) bandada, *f*; (of roes) manada, *f*
bewail *vt* lamentar, llorar
bewailing *n* lamentación, *f*
beware *vi* guardarse (de); cuidar (de); desconfiar (de). *interj* ¡cuidado! ¡atención! **B. of imitations!** ¡Desconfiad de las imitaciones!
bewilder *vt* aturdir, abobar; dejar perplejo (a); confundir
bewildered *a* aturdido, abobado; perplejo; confuso
bewildering *a* incomprensible; complicado
bewilderment *n* aturdimiento, *m*; perplejidad, *f*; confusión, *f*
bewitch *vt* hechizar; fascinar, encantar
bewitching *a* encantador, hechicero, fascinante. *n* embrujamiento, encantamiento, *m*
bewitchingly *adv* de un modo encantador
bewitchment *n*. See **bewitching**
beyond *prep* más allá de; más lejos que; (behind) tras, detrás de; (of time) después de; *fig* fuera del alcance de; (without) fuera de; (above) encima de; (not including) aparte. *adv* más allá; más lejos; detrás. **b. doubt,** fuera de duda. **b. question,** indiscutible. **b. the sea,** allende el mar. **That is b. me,** Eso es demasiado para mí; Eso no está en mi mano; Eso está fuera de mi alcance. **the back of b.,** donde Cristo dio las tres voces, las quimbambas. **the B.,** la otra vida
Bhután Bután, *m*
bias *n* sesgo, bies, través, *m*; *fig* prejuicio, *m*; parcialidad, *f*, *vt* influir; predisponer. **to cut on the b.,** cortar al sesgo
biassed *a* parcial; tendencioso
bib *n* babero, *m*; pechera, *f*, *vi* beber mucho, empinar el codo
Bible *n* Biblia, *f*
biblical *a* bíblico. **b. history,** historia sagrada, *f*
bibliographer *n* bibliógrafo (-fa)
bibliographical *a* bibliográfico
bibliography *n* bibliografía, *f*
bibliophile *n* bibliófilo, *m*
bibulous *a* bebedor, borrachín
bicarbonate *n* bicarbonato, *m*
bicentenary *n* segundo centenario, *m*
biceps *n* bíceps, *m*
bicker *vi* disputar, altercar; (of stream, etc.) murmurar, susurrar; (of flame) bailar, centellear
bickering *n* altercado, argumento, *m*
bicycle *n* bicicleta, *f*, *vi* andar en bicicleta, ir de bicicleta
bicycle pump *Lat. Am.* inflador *m*
bicycling *n* ciclismo, *m*
bicyclist *n* biciclista, *mf*
bid *n* (at auction) postura, *f*; (bridge) puja, *f*; oferta, *f*, *vt* mandar, ordenar, invitar a; (at an auction) pujar, licitar. **to make a bid for,** (attempt) hacer un esfuerzo para; procurar. **to bid fair,** prometer; dar indicios de; dar esperanzas de. **to bid goodbye to,** decir adios (a), despedirse de. **to bid welcome,** dar la bienvenida (a)
biddable *a* obediente, dócil; manso

bidder *n* postor, *m*, pujador (-ra). **the highest b.,** el mejor postor
bidding *n* (order) orden, *f*; instrucción, *f*; invitación, *f*; (at an auction) postura, licitación, *f*. **to do a person's b.,** hacer lo que se le manda
bide *vt* aguardar, esperar. **to b. by,** (fulfil) cumplir con
bidet *n* bidé, *m*
biennial *a* bianual, bienal
bier *n* andas, *f pl*; féretro, ataúd, *m*
bifocal *a* bifocal
bifurcate *vt* and *vi* bifurcar(se)
bifurcation *n* bifurcación, *f*
big *a* grande; grueso; (grown up) mayor; (tall) alto; voluminoso; (vast) extenso, vasto; (full) lleno (de); (with young) preñada; importante. **to talk big,** echarla de importante. **big-boned,** huesudo. **big-end,** *aut* biela, *f*. **big game,** caza mayor, *f*. **big gun,** *inf* pájaro gordo, *m*
bigamist *n* bígamo (-ma)
bigamous *a* bígamo
bigamy *n* bigamia, *f*
bight *n* (in a rope) vuelta (de un cabo), *f*; (bay) ensenada, *f*
bigness *n* grandor, *m*; gran tamaño, *m*; altura, *f*; (tallness of a person) gran talle, *m*; (vastness) extensión, *f*; importancia, *f*
bigot *n* fanático (-ca)
bigoted *a* fanático, intolerante
bigotry *n* fanatismo, *m*, intolerancia, *f*
bikini *n* bikini, *m*
bilberry *n* arándano, *m*
bile *n* bilis, hiel, *f*; mal humor, *m*, cólera, *f*
bilge *n naut* pantoque, *m*, sentina, *f*. **b. water,** agua de pantoque, *f*
bilingual *a* bilingüe
bilious *a* bilioso
bill *n* (parliamentary) proyecto de ley, *m*; *law* escrito, *m*; *com* cuenta, *f*; (poster) cartel, *m*; (program) programa, *m*; (cast) repertorio, *m*; (bank note) billete de banco, *m*; (of a bird) pico, *m*; (for pruning) podadera, *f*. **due b.,** *com* abonaré, *m*. **Post no bills!** Se prohíbe fijar carteles. **b. of exchange,** letra de cambio, *f*. **b. of fare,** lista de platos, *f*; *fig* programa, *m*. **b. of health,** patente de sanidad, *f*. **b. of lading,** conocimiento de embarque, *m*. **b. of rights,** declaración de derechos, *f*. **b. of sale,** contrato de venta, *m*, carta de venta, *f*. **b.-broker,** agente de bolsa, agente de cambio, *m*. **b.-poster,** fijador de carteles, cartelero, *m*
bill *vt* anunciar; publicar; poner en el programa; fijar carteles en. **to b. and coo,** (doves) arrullar; *inf* besuquearse
billboard, *n* tablero publicitario, *m*
billed *a* (in compounds) de pico
billet *n* alojamiento, *m*; (of wood) pedazo (de leña), *m*; (job) empleo, destino, *m*, *vt* alojar (en or con)
billeting *n* alojamiento, *m*. **b. officer,** *mil* aposentador, *m*; oficial encargado de encontrar alojamiento, *m*
billiards *n pl* billar, *m*. **billiard ball,** bola de billar, *f*. **billiard cue,** taco, *m*. **billiard cushion,** baranda de la mesa de billar, *f*. **billiard marker,** marcador, *m*. **billiard match,** partida de billar, *f*. **billiard player,** jugador (-ra) de billar. **billiard pocket** *Lat. Am.* buchaca *f*. **billiard room,** sala de billar, *f*. **billiard table,** mesa de billar, *f*
billing *n* facturación, *f*
billion *n* billón, *m*; (U.S.A. and France) mil millones, *m pl*
billionth *a* billonésimo; (U.S.A. and France) milmillonésimo
bill of particulars *n* relación detallada, *f*
billow *n* oleada, *f*; *poet* ola, *f*; *fig* onda, *f*. *vi* hincharse, encresparse; ondular
billowy *a* ondulante, ondeante
bimonthly *a* bimestral
bin *n* hucha, *f*, arcón, *m*; recipiente, *m*; depósito, *m*; cajón, *m*; (for wine) estante, *m*
binary *a* binario
bind *vt* atar; unir, ligar; amarrar; (in sheaves) agavillar; (bandage) vendar; sujetar; fijar; aprisionar; (a book) encuadernar; *sew* ribetear; (oblige) obligar; comprometer; (constipate) estreñir; contratar (como aprendiz). **I feel bound to,** Me siento obligado a. **to b. over,** obligar a comparecer ante el juez
binder *n* encuadernador (-ra); *agr* agavilladora, *f*
binding *a* válido, valedero; obligatorio; **become b.,** adquirir carácter de compromiso; *med* constrictivo. *n* atadura, ligación, *f*; (of books) encuadernación, *f*; *sew* ribete, *m*
binge *n* parranda, juerga, *f*. **to go on the b.,** ir de parranda, ir de picos pardos, ir de juerga
binnacle *n naut* bitácora, *f*
binocular *a* binocular. *n pl* **binoculars,** binóculos, gemelos, *m pl*
binomial *a* and *n* binomio *m*.
biochemist *n* bioquímico, *m*
biochemistry *n* bioquímica, *f*
biographer *n* biógrafo (-fa)
biographical *a* biográfico
biography *n* biografía, vida, *f*
biological *a* biológico
biologist *n* biólogo, *m*
biology *n* biología, *f*
bipartite *a* bipartido
biped *n* bípedo, *m*, *a* bípedo, bípede
birch *n bot* abedul, *m*; (rod) vara, *f*. *a* de abedul. *vt* pegar con una vara, dar una paliza (a)
bird *n* pájaro, *m*; ave, *f*. **Birds of a feather flock together,** Cada cual se arrima a su cada cual. **hen b.,** pájara, *f*. **b.-call,** voz del pájaro, *f*, canto del ave, *m*. **b. catcher or vendor,** pajarero, *m*. **bird's-eye view,** vista de pájaro, perspectiva aérea, *f*. **b.-fancier,** aficionado (-da) a las aves; criador (-ra) de pájaros. **b.-like,** como un pájaro; de pájaro. **b.-lime,** liga, *f*. **to go b.-nesting,** ir a coger nidos de pájaros. **b. of paradise,** ave del paraíso, *f*. **b. of passage,** ave de paso, *f*. **b. of prey,** ave rapaz, *f*. **b.-seed,** alpiste, *m*
birth *n* nacimiento, *m*; (act of) parto, *m*; origen, *m*; (childhood) infancia, *f*; (family) linaje, *m*, familia, *f*; *fig* creación, *f*. **from b.,** de nacimiento. **to give b. to,** dar a luz, echar al mundo, parir. **b. certificate,** partida de nacimiento, certificación de nacimiento, *f*. **b. control,** anticoncepcionismo, *m*, regulación de la fecundidad, *f*. **b.-mark,** antojos, *m pl*. **b.-place,** lugar de nacimiento, *m*. **b.-rate,** natalidad, *f*
birthday *n* cumpleaños, *m*
birthright *n* derecho de nacimiento, *m*; herencia, *f*
Biscayan *a* and *n* vizcaíno (-na)
Biscay, the Bay of el Golfo de Vizcaya, *m*
biscuit *n* galleta, *f*; bizcocho, *m*. **b. box or maker,** galletero, *m*. **b.-like,** abizcochado
bisect *vt* dividir en dos partes iguales; *geom* bisecar
bisexual *a* bisexual
bishop *n* obispo, *m*; (in chess) alfil, *m*. **bishop's crozier,** báculo episcopal, cayado, *m*
bismuth *n* bismuto, *m*
bison *n* bisonte, *m*
bisque *n* porcelana blanca, *f*, bizcocho, *m*
bistoury *n* bisturí, *m*
bit *n* pedazo, *m*; (of grass, etc.) brizna, *f*; (moment) instante, *m*; (quantity) cantidad, *f*; (of a drill) mecha, *f*; (part) parte, *f*; (passage) trozo, *m*; (horse's) bocado, *m*; *inf* miga, *f*. **a bit,** un tanto, algo, un poco. **in bits,** en pedazos. **Not a bit!** ¡Nada!; ¡Ni pizca!; ¡Claro que no! **bit by bit,** poco a poco, gradualmente. **to give someone a bit of one's mind,** contarle cuatro verdades. **to take the bit between one's teeth,** desbocarse; *fig* rebelarse. **Wait a bit!** ¡Espera un momento!
bitch *n* (female dog) perra, *f*; (fox) zorra, *f*; (wolf) loba, *f*
bite *n* mordedura, *f*; mordisco, *m*; (mouthful, snack) bocado, *m*, *Lat. Am.* botana *f* (of fish and insects) picada, *f*; (hold) asimiento, *m*; (sting, pain) picadura, *f*; (pungency) resquemor, *m*; (offer) oferta, *f*; (*fig* mor-

dancy) mordacidad, acritud, *f*. *vt* and *vi* morder; (gnaw) roer; (of fish, insects) picar; (of hot dishes) resquemar; (of acids) corroer; (deceive) engañar, defraudar; (of wheels, etc.) agarrar; (hurt, wound) herir. **to b. one's tongue,** morderse la lengua. **to b. the dust,** caer al suelo

biting *a* (stinging) picante; (mordant) mordaz, acre; (of winds, etc.) penetrante; satírico. *n* mordedura, *f*; roedura, *f*

bitter *a* amargo; (sour) agrio, ácido; (of winds) penetrante; (of cold) intenso; cruel. **to the b. end,** hasta la muerte; hasta el último extremo. **b.-sweet,** agridulce

bitterly *adv* amargamente; intensamente; cruelmente

bitterness *n* amargura, *f*; (sourness) acidez, *f*; (of cold) intensidad, *f*; crueldad, *f*

bitters *n pl* (drink) bíter, *m*, angostura, *f*

bitumen *n* betún, *m*

bivouac *n mil* vivaque, *m*, *vi* vivaquear

bizarre *a* raro, extravagante; grotesco

black *a* negro; obscuro; (sad) triste, melancólico; funesto; (wicked) malo, perverso; (sullen) malhumorado. *n* (color) negro, *m*; (mourning) luto, *m*; (negro) negro, *m*; (negress) negra, *f*; (stain) mancha, *f*; (dirt) tizne, *m*. *vt* ennegrecer; tiznar. **in b. and white,** por escrito. **to look on the b. side,** verlo todo negro. **b. art,** nigromancia, *f*. **b.-currant,** grosella negra, *f*. **b.-eyed,** ojinegro, con ojos negros. **b.-haired,** pelinegro, de pelo negro. **b.-lead,** plombagina, *f*. **b.-list,** lista negra, *f*. **b.-market,** estraperlo, mercado negro, *m*. **b.-marketeer,** estraperlista, *mf* **b.-out,** oscurecimiento, apagamiento, *m*. **b.-pudding,** morcilla, *f*. **b. sheep,** oveja negra, *f*; *fig* oveja descarriada, *f*; (of a family) garbanzo negro, *m*. **b.-water fever,** melanuria, *f*

blackberry *n* mora, zarzamora, *f*; (bush) zarza, *f*, moral, *m*

blackbird *n* mirlo, *m*

blackboard *n* encerado, *m*, pizarra, *f*

black coffee *Spain* café solo, *Colombia* café tinto, *elsewhere in Lat. Am.* café negro *m*

blacken *vt* ennegrecer; tiznar; *fig* manchar, desacreditar. *vi* ennegrecerse

black eye *n* ojo como un tomate, ojo morado, *m*

blackguard *n* tipo de cuidado, perdido, *m*

blackhead *n* espinilla, *f*

blacking *n* betún, *m*

blackish *a* negruzco

blackmail *n* chantaje, *m*, *vt* hacer víctima de un chantaje; arrancar dinero por chantaje (a)

blackmailer *n* chantajista, *mf*

blackness *n* negrura, *f*; obscuridad, *f*; (wickedness) maldad, perversidad, *f*

blacksmith *n* herrero (-ra) *mf*, *Lat. Am.* also encasquillador (-ra) *mf*. **blacksmith's forge,** herrería, *f*

bladder *n anat* vejiga, *f*; ampolla, *f*; (of sea-plants) vesícula, *f*; (of fish) vejiga natatoria, *f*

blade *n* (leaf) hoja, *f*; (of grass, etc.) brizna, *f*; (of sharp instruments) hoja, *f*; (of oar) pala, *f*; (of propeller) paleta, ala, *f*

bladed *a* de . . . hojas. **a two-b. knife,** un cuchillo de dos hojas

blame *n* culpa, *f*; responsabilidad, *f*; censura, *f*. *vt* culpar, echar la culpa (a); tachar, censurar, criticar; acusar. **You are to b. for this,** Vd. tiene la culpa de esto

blameless *a* inculpable; inocente; intachable; elegante

blamelessness *n* inculpabilidad, inocencia, *f*; elegancia, *f*

blameworthy *a* culpable, digno de censura, vituperable

blanch *vt cul* mondar; hacer palidecer. *vi* palidecer, perder el color

blanching *n* palidecimiento, *m*; *cul* mondadura, *f*

blancmange *n* manjar blanco, *m*

bland *a* afable, cortés; dulce, agradable

blandish *vt* adular, halagar, acariciar

blandishment *n* adulación, *f*, halago, *m*, caricia, *f*

blandness *n* afabilidad, urbanidad, *f*; dulzura, *f*

blank *a* en blanco; (empty) vacío; desocupado; pálido; (confused) confuso, desconcertado; (expressionless) sin expresión; (of verse) suelto; sin adorno. *n* blanco, hueco, *m*; papel en blanco, *m*; laguna, *f*; (form to be filled out) hoja *f*, *Mexico* esqueleto *m* **b. cartridge,** cartucho para salvas, cartucho de fogueo, *m*. **b. verse,** verso suelto, *m*

blanket *n* manta, frazada, *Lat. Am.* cobija *f*; (of a horse) sudadero, *Lat. Am.* mandil *m*; *fig* capa, *f*. *vt* cubrir con una manta. **to toss in a b.,** mantear. **wet b.,** aguafiestas, *mf*. **b. maker or seller,** mantero, *m*. **b. vote,** voto colectivo, *m*

blanketing *n* manteamiento, *m*

blankly *adv* con indiferencia; sin comprender; (flatly) categóricamente

blankness *n* confusión, *f*, desconcierto, *m*; (emptiness) vaciedad, *f*; indiferencia, *f*; incomprensión, *f*

blare *n* sonido de la trompeta o del clarín, *poet* clangor, *m*; (of a car horn) ruido, *m*. *vi* sonar

blarney *n* labia, *f*. *vt* lisonjear

blaspheme *vi* blasfemar. *vt* renegar de, maldecir

blasphemer *n* blasfemador (-ra), blasfemo (-ma)

blasphemous *a* blasfemo, blasfematorio

blasphemy *n* blasfemia, *f*

blast *n* (of wind) ráfaga (de viento), *f*; (of a trumpet, etc.) trompetazo, son, *m*; (of a whistle) pitido, *m*; (draft) soplo, *m*; explosión, *f*; *fig* influencia maligna, *f*. *vt* (rock) barrenar, hacer saltar; (wither) marchitar, secar; *fig* destruir; (curse) maldecir. **in full b.,** en plena marcha. **b.-furnace,** alto horno, horno de cuba, *m*. **b. hole,** barreno, *m*

blaster *n* barrenero, *m*

blasting *n* (of rock) voladura, *f*; (withering) marchitamiento, *m*; *fig* destrucción, ruina, *f*; (cursing) maldiciones, *f pl*. **a.** destructor; *fig* funesto. **b. charge,** carga explosiva, *f*

blatant *a* ruidoso; agresivo; llamativo; (boastful) fanfarrón

blaze *n* llama, *f*; fuego, *m*; conflagración, *f*; luz brillante, *f*; (of anger, etc.) acceso, *m*. *vi* llamear, encenderse en llamas; brillar, resplandecer. **a b. of colour,** una masa de color. **Go to blazes!** ¡Vete al infierno!

blazon *n her* blasón, *m*; *fig* proclamación, *f*, *vt* blasonar; adornar; proclamar

bleach *n* lejía, *f*. *vt* blanquear; descolorar. *vi* ponerse blanco; descolorarse

bleaching *n* blanqueo, *m*. **b. powder,** hipoclorito de cal, *m*

bleak *a* yermo, desierto; frío; expuesto; (sad) triste; severo

bleakness *n* situación expuesta, *f*; desnudez, *f*; frío, *m*; (sadness) tristeza, *f*; severidad, *f*

bleary-eyed *a* legañoso, cegajoso

bleat *n* balido, *m*, *vt* and *vi* balar, dar balidos

bleating *a* balador, que bala. *n* balido, *m*

bleed *vi* sangrar, echar sangre; sufrir. *vt* sangrar; arrancar dinero a

bleeding *n* hemorragia, *f*; sangría, *f*, *Lat. Am.* desangre *m*

blemish *n* imperfección, *f*, defecto, *m*; (on fruit) maca, *f*; (stain) mancha, *f*; deshonra, *f*

blend *n* mezcla, mixtura, *f*; combinación, *f*; fusión, *f*. *vt* mezclar; combinar. *vi* mezclarse; combinarse

blende *n min* blenda, *f*

blending *n* mezcla, *f*; fusión, *f*

bless *vt* bendecir; consagrar; (praise) alabar, glorificar; hacer feliz (a). **B. me!** ¡Válgame Dios!

blessed *a* bendito; *ecc* beato, bienaventurado; (dear) querido; feliz; *inf* maldito

blessedness *n* felicidad, *f*; bienaventuranza, *f*

blessing *n* bendición, *f*; (grace) bendición de la mesa, *f*; (mercy) merced, gracia, *f*; favor, *m*; (good) bien, *m*. **He gave them his b.,** Les echó su bendición

Bless you! (to someone who has sneezed) ¡Jesús!

blight *n agr* tizne, tizón, *m*; (of cereals) añublo, *m*;

(mould) roña, *f;* (greenfly) pulgón, *m; fig* influencia maligna, *f;* (frustration) desengaño, *m;* (spoil-sport) aguafiestas, *mf vt* atizonar; anublar; (wither) marchitar, secar; *fig* frustrar, destruir; malograr

blighter *n* bribón, *m*

blind *a* ciego; (secret) secreto; (of a door, etc.) falso; (closed) cerrado, sin salida; (unaware) ignorante; sin apreciación (de). **to be b.,** ser ciego; *fig* tener una venda en los ojos. **to be b. in one eye,** ser tuerto. **to turn a b. eye,** hacer la vista gorda. **b. alley,** callejón sin salida, *m.* **b. as a bat,** más ciego que un topo. **b. flying,** *aer* vuelo a ciegas, *m.* **b. man,** ciego, hombre ciego, *m.* **b. obedience,** obediencia ciega, *f.* **b. side,** (of persons) lado débil, *m.* **b. woman,** ciega, mujer ciega, *f*

blind *vt* cegar; poner una venda en los ojos (de); (dazzle) deslumbrar; hacer cerrar los ojos a; hacer ignorar

blind *n* persiana, *f;* (Venetian) celosía, *f;* (deception) pretexto, *m;* velo, *m*

blindfold *vt* vendar los ojos (a); *fig* poner una venda en los ojos (de). *a* and *adv* con los ojos vendados; a ciegas; con los ojos cerrados

blindly *adv* ciegamente; a ciegas; ignorantemente

blindman's buff *n* gallina ciega, *f*

blindness *n* ceguedad, *f;* ofuscación, *f;* ignorancia, *f*

blink *n* parpadeo, *m,* guiñada, *f;* (of light) destello, *m;* reflejo, *m; vi* parpadear, pestañear; (of lights) destellar

blinkers *n pl* anteojeras, *f pl*

bliss *n* felicidad, *f;* deleite, placer, *m; ecc* gloria, *f*

blissful *a* feliz

blissfulness *n.* See **bliss**

blister *n med* vesícula, *f;* ampolla, *f;* (bubble) burbuja, *f. vt* ampollar; *fig* herir

blithe *a* alegre

blithely *adv* alegremente

blitheness *n* alegría, *f*

blitzkrieg *n* blitzkrieg, *m,* guerra relámpago, *f*

blizzard *n* ventisca, nevasca, *f*

bloated *a* abotagado, hinchado; orgulloso; indecente

bloater *n* arenque ahumado, *m*

blob *n* masa, *f;* mancha, *f;* gota, *f*

block *n* bloque, *m;* (log) leño, *m; naut* polea, *f;* (for beheading and of a butcher) tajo, *m;* (for mounting) apeadero, *m;* (of shares, etc.) lote, *m;* (of houses) manzana, *Lat. Am.* cuadra *f;* (jam) atasco, *m;* (obstruction) obstrucción, *f;* (for hats) forma, *f.* **A chip off the old b.,** De tal palo tal astilla. **b. and tackle,** *naut* polea con aparejo. **b.-hook,** grapa, *f.* **b.-house,** *mil* blocao, *m*

block *vt* bloquear; cerrar (el paso); (stop up) atarugar, atascar; (a wheel) calzar; (a bill, etc.) obstruir; (hats) poner en forma. **to b. the way,** cerrar el paso.

blockade *n* bloqueo, *m, vt* bloquear. **to run the b.,** violar el bloqueo

blockhead *n* leño, zoquete, imbécil, *m*

blond(e) *a* (of hair) rubio; (of complexion) de tez blanca. *n* hombre rubio, *m;* (woman) rubia, mujer rubia, *f.* **peroxide b.,** rubia oxigenada, *f.* **b. lace,** blondina, *f*

blood *n* sangre, *f;* (relationship) parentesco, *m;* (family) linaje, *m,* prosapia, *f;* (life) vida, *f;* (sap) savia, *f;* jugo, *m;* (horse) caballo de pura raza, *m;* (dandy) galán, *m. vt* sangrar. **bad b.,** mala sangre, *f;* odio, *m;* mala leche, *f.* **blue b.,** sangre azul, *f.* **in cold b.,** a sangre fría, *f.* **My b. is up,** Se me enciende la sangre. **My b. runs cold,** Se me hiela la sangre. **to be in the b.,** llevar en la sangre. **b.-bank,** banco de sangre, *m.* **b.-bath,** matanza, *f.* **b.-colored,** de color de sangre, sanguíneo. **b.-feud,** venganza de sangre, *f.* **b.-guilt,** culpabilidad de homicidio, *m.* **b.-heat,** calor de sangre, *m.* **b.-letting,** sangría, *f.* **b. orange,** naranja dulce, *f.* **b.-plasma,** plasma sanguíneo, *m.* **b.-poisoning,** septicemia, *f;* infección, *f.* **b.-pressure,** presión sanguínea, *f.* **b. purity,** limpieza de sangre, *f.* **b.-red,** rojo como la sangre. **b.-relation,** pariente (-ta) consanguíneo(a). **b.-relationship,** consanguinidad, *f.* **b.-stain,** mancha de sangre, *f.* **b.-stained,** ensangrentado, manchado de sangre. **b.-stone,** sanguinaria, *f.* **b.-sucker,** sanguijuela, *f; fig* vampiro, *m;* (usurer) avaro (-ra). **b.-vessel,** vaso sanguíneo, *m*

blooded *a* de sangre . . . ; de casta . . .

bloodhound *n* sabueso, *m*

bloodily *adv* sangrientamente; cruentamente; con ferocidad, cruelmente

bloodiness *n* estado sangriento, *m;* crueldad, ferocidad, *f*

bloodless *a* exangüe; pálido; incruento; anémico; indiferente

bloodshed *n* efusión de sangre, *f;* matanza, carnicería, *f*

bloodshot *a* (of the eye) inyectado

bloodthirstiness *n* sed de sangre, *f*

bloodthirsty *a* sanguinario, carnicero

bloody *a* sangriento; (of battles) encarnizado; (cruel) sanguinario, cruel

bloom *n* flor, *f;* florecimiento, *m;* (on fruit) flor, *f;* (prime) lozanía, *f;* (on the cheeks) color sano, *m. vi* florecer. **in b.,** en flor

blooming *a* florido; en flor; fresco; lozano; brillante

blossom *n* flor, *f. vi* florecer. **to b. out into,** hacerse, llegar a ser; (wear) lucir; (buy) comprarse

blossomed *a* con flores, de flores

blossoming *n* floración, *f*

blot *n* borrón, *m;* mancha, *f. vt* manchar; (erase) tachar; (dry) secar. **to b. out,** borrar; destruir; secar con papel secante

blotch *n* (on the skin, or stain) mancha, *f*

blotter *n com* libro borrador, *m;* teleta, *f*

blotting paper *n* papel secante, *m*

blouse *n* blusa, *f*

blow *n* golpe, *m;* bofetada, *f;* (with the fist) puñetazo, *m;* (with the elbow) codazo, *m;* (with a club) porrazo, *m;* (with a whip) latigazo, *m;* (blossoming) floración, *f;* (disaster) desastre, *m,* tragedia, *f.* **to come to blows,** venirse a las manos. **at a b.,** con un solo golpe; de una vez. **We are going for a b.,** Vamos a tomar el fresco. **b. below the belt,** golpe bajo, *m.* **b. in the air,** golpe en vago, *m.* **b. of fate,** latigazo de la fortuna, *m*

blow *vi* (of wind) soplar (el viento), hacer viento, correr aire; (pant) jadear, echar resoplidos; (of fuses) fundirse. *vt* (wind instruments) tocar; soplar; (inflate) inflar; (swell) hinchar. **to b. a kiss,** tirar un beso. **to b. one's nose,** sonarse las narices. **to b. away,** disipar; ahuyentar; llevar (el viento). **to b. down,** echar por tierra, derribar (el viento). **to b. in,** llevar adentro, hacer entrar (el viento); (windows, etc.) quebrar (el viento). **to b. off,** quitar (el viento). **to b. open,** abrir (el viento). **to b. out,** hacer salir (el viento); llevar afuera (el viento); (a light) matar de un soplo, apagar soplando. **to b. over,** pasar por (el viento); soplar por; disiparse; olvidarse. **to b. up,** (inflate) inflar; (the fire) avivar (el fuego); (explode) volar; (swell) hinchar

blowing *n* soplo, *m;* violencia, *f;* (blossoming) florecimiento, *m.* **b. up,** voleo, *m;* explosión, *f*

blow-up *n* (photograph) fotografía ampliada, *f*

blowzy *a* desaliñado

blubber *vi* gimotear; berrear. *n* (of the whale) grasa de ballena, *f.* **b.-lip,** bezo, *m.* **b.-lipped,** bezudo

bludgeon *n* cachiporra, porpa, *f;* garrote, *m;* estaca, *f. vt* golpear con una porra, dar garrotazos (a)

blue *a* azul; (with bruises) amoratado; (sad) deprimido, melancólico; (obscene) verde; (dark) sombrío; (traditionalist) conservador. *n* azul, *m;* (sky) cielo, *m;* (for clothes) añil de lavandera, *m; pl* **blues,** melancolía, depresión, *f;* (homesickness) morriña, *f. vt* (laundry) añilar. **to look b.,** parecer deprimido; (of prospects, etc.) ser poco halagüeño. **b. black,** azul negro, *m;* (of hair) azabache, *m.* **b.-bottle,** *ent* moscón, *m.* **b.-eyed,** con ojos azules. **b. gum,** eucalipto, *m.* **B. Peter,** bandera de salida, *f.* **b. print,** fotocopia, *f;* plan, *m*

bluebell *n* campanilla, *f*

bluestocking *n* marisabidilla, doctora, *f*

bluff *a* (of cliffs, etc.) escarpado; (of persons) franco, campechano, brusco

bluffer *n Lat. Am.* blofista *mf*
bluffness *n* franqueza, brusquedad, *f*
bluish *a* azulado
bluishness *n* color azulado, *m*
blunder *n* desacierto, desatino, *m*; equivocación, *f*; (in a translation, etc.) falta, *f*. *vi* tropezar (con); desacertar; equivocarse; *inf* meter la pata. *vt* manejar mal; estropear
blunderer *n* desatinado (-da)
blundering *a* desacertado; equivocado; imprudente *n*. See **blunder**
blunt *a* romo, embotado; obtuso; (abrupt) brusco; franco; descortés; (plain) claro. *vt* enromar, embotar; (the point) despuntar; *fig* hacer indiferente; (pain) mitigar
bluntly *adv* sin filo; sin punta; bruscamente, francamente; claramente
bluntness *n* embotamiento, *m*; *fig* brusquedad, franqueza, *f*; claridad, *f*
blur *n* borrón, *m*; mancha, *f*; imagen indistinta, *f*. *vt* borrar; manchar; *phot* velar
blurred *a* borroso; indistinto; turbio
blurt (out) *vt* proferir bruscamente; revelar sin querer
blush *n* rubor, *m*; rojo, *m*. *vi* enrojecerse, ruborizarse, ponerse colorado; avergonzarse (por)
blushing *a* ruboroso; púdico
bluster *vi* (of the wind) soplar con furia; (of waves) encresparse, embravecerse; (of persons) bravear, fanfarronear. *n* furia, violencia, *f*; tumulto, *m*; fanfarronería, *f*
blustering *a* (of wind) violento, fuerte; (of waves) tumultuoso; (of people) fanfarrón, valentón
boar *n* verraco, *m*; (wild) jabalí, *m*
board *n* tabla, *f*; (for notices) tablón, *m*; (b. residence) pensión, *f*; (table) mesa, *f*; (food) comida, *f*; (for chess, checkers) tablero, *m*; (sign) letrero, *m*; (of instruments) cuadro, *m*; (bookbinding) cartón, *m*; *naut* bordo, *m*; (committee) junta, dirección, *f*; tribunal, *m*; *pl* boards *theat* tablas, *f pl*. **above b.,** abiertamente, sin disimulo. **free on b.,** (f.o.b.) franco a bordo. **in boards,** (of books) encartonado. **managerial b.,** junta directiva, *f*. **on b.,** a bordo. **on the boards,** *theat* en las tablas. **to go on b.,** ir a bordo. **b. and lodging,** pensión completa, casa y comida, *f*. **b. of directors,** consejo de administración, *m*. **b. of examiners,** tribunal de exámenes, *m*. **b. of trade,** junta de comercio, *f*; ministerio de comercio, *m*
board *vt carp* entablar, enmaderar; embarcar en; (*nav* a ship) abordar; (lodge) alojar, tomar a pensión
boarder *n* huésped (-da); (at school) pensionista, *mf* alumno (-na) interno (-na)
boarding *n* entablado, *m*; (planking) tablazón, *f*; (of a ship) abordaje, *m*; (of a train) subida (al tren), *f*. **b.-house,** casa de huéspedes, pensión, *f*. **b.-school,** pensionado, *m*
boarding gate *n* puerta de embarque, *f*
boast *n* jactancia, *f*; ostentación, *f*; (honor) gloria, *f*. *vi* jactarse, vanagloriarse, *Lat. Am.* dragonear, *Argentina* faramallear; alabarse; ostentar. **to b. about,** jactarse de; hacer gala de; gloriarse en
boaster *n* vanaglorioso (-sa), jactancioso (-sa)
boastful *a* vanaglorioso, jactancioso; ostentador
boastfulness *n* vanagloria, jactancia, *f*; fanfarronería, *f*; ostentación, *f*
boasting *n* alardeo, *m*; fanfarronería, *f*
boat *n* barco, *m*; bote, *m*; (in a fun fair) columpio, *m*, lancha, *f*; (for sauce or gravy) salsera, *f*. *vi* ir en barco; (row) remar; navegar. **to b. down,** bajar en barco. **to b. up,** subir en barco. **b. building,** construcción de barcos, *f*. **b. club,** club náutico, *m*. **b. crew,** tripulación de un barco, *f*. **b.-hook,** bichero, garabato, *m*. **b.-house,** cobertizo de las lanchas, *m*. **b.-load,** barcada, *f*. **b.-race,** regata, *f*. **b.-scoop,** achicador, *m*. **b.-shaped,** en forma de barco. **b.-train,** tren que enlaza con un vapor, *m*
boating *n* pasear en bote, *m*; manejo de un bote, *m*; (rowing) remo, *m*. **b.-pole,** botador, *m*
boatman *n* barquero, *m*
boatswain *n* contramaestre, *m*. **boatswain's mate,** segundo contramaestre, *m*
bob *n* (curtsey) reverencia, *f*; (woman's hair) pelo a la romana, *m*; (of bells) toque (de campana), *m*. *vi* saltar; moverse. *vt* cortar corto. **long bob,** (hair) melena, *f*. **to bob up,** ponerse de pie; surgir. **to bob up and down,** subir y bajar; bailar. **bob-tail,** rabo corto, *m*. **bob-tailed,** rabón
Bob (pet form of *Robert*) Beto (Mexico)
bobbin *n* carrete, huso, *m*; (of wool, etc.) ovillo, *m*; (of looms, sewing machines) bobina, *f*; (in lace-making) bolillo, palillo, *m*
bobsleigh *n* trineo doble, *m*
bode *vt* presagiar, prometer. **to b. ill,** prometer mal. **to b. well,** prometer bien
bodice *n* corpiño, *m*
bodied *a* (in compounds) de cuerpo-
bodiless *a* incorpóreo
bodily *a* del cuerpo; físico; corpóreo; real; material; (of fear) de su persona. *adv* corporalmente; en persona, personalmente; en conjunto, enteramente; en una pieza
boding *a* ominoso, amenazador. *n* presagio, *m*; agüero, *m*
body *n anat* cuerpo, *m*; (trunk) tronco, *m*; (corpse) cadáver, *m*; (of a vehicle) caja, *f*; (of a motor-car) carrocería, *f*; (of a ship) casco, *m*; (of a church) nave, *f*; (centre) centro, *m*; (of a book, persons, consistency and *ast*) cuerpo, *m*; (person) persona, *f*; corporación, *f*; grupo, *m*; (of an army) grueso (de ejercito), *m*; organismo, *m*. **in a b.,** en masa, juntos (juntas); en corporación. **to have enough to keep b. and soul together,** tener de que vivir. **b.-snatcher,** junta cadáveres *mf* ladrón de cadáveres, *m*. **b.-snatching,** robo de cadáveres, *m*
bodyguard *n* guardia de corps, *f*; guardia, *f*; (escort) escolta, *f*
body language *n* el lenguaje del cuerpo, *m*
bog *n* pantano, marjal, *m*, marisma, *f*, *Central America* chagüe *m*
bogey *n* duende, *m*; (to frighten children) coco, *m*; (nightmare) pesadilla, *f*
boggy *a* pantanoso, fangoso
bogus *a* postizo, falso
Bohemian *a* and *n* bohemio (-ia)
boil *vi* bullir, hervir; (cook) cocer. *vt* hervir; cocer. *n* ebullición, *f*; *med* divieso, *m*. **to b. away,** consumirse hirviendo; *chem* evaporar a seco. **to b. over,** rebosar
boiler *n cul* marmita, olla, *f*; (of a furnace) caldera, *f*. **double-b.,** baño de María, *m*. **steam-b.,** caldera de vapor, *f*. **b.-maker,** calderero, *m*. **b. room,** cámara de la caldera, *f*. **b.-suit,** mono, *m*
boiling *n* ebullición, *f*, hervor, *m*; (cooking) cocción, *f*, *a* hirviente. **b. point,** punto de ebullición, *m*
boisterous *a* (of persons) exuberante, impetuoso; (stormy) tempestuoso, borrascoso; violento
boisterously *adv* impetuosamente, ruidosamente; tempestuosamente; con violencia
boisterousness *n* exuberancia, impetuosidad, *f*; violencia, *f*; tempestuosidad, borrascosidad, *f*
bold *a* intrépido, audaz, *Argentina* agullud(o) (determined) resuelto; (forward) atrevido; (showy) llamativo; (clear) claro. **b.-faced,** descarado, desvergonzado. **b.-faced type,** letra negra, *f*
boldly *adv* intrépidamente; descaradamente; resueltamente; claramente
boldness *n* intrepidez, valentía, *f*; resolución, *f*; (forwardness) osadía, *f*, descaro, atrevimiento, *m*; claridad, *f*
Bolivian *a* and *n* boliviano (-na)
Bolshevik *a* and *n* bolchevique, *mf*
Bolshevist *n* bolchevista, *mf*
bolster *n* travesaño, *m*. *vt* apuntalar; *fig* apoyar
bolt *n* pasador, cerrojo, *m*; (pin) perno, *m*; (knocker)

aldaba, *f*; (roll) rollo, *m*; (flight) huida, *f*; (of a cross-bow) flecha, *f*; (from the blue) rayo, *m*. *adv* (upright) recto como una flecha; enhiesto; rígido. **b. and nut,** perno y tuerca, *m*

bolt *vt* echar el cerrojo (a); empernar; (*fam* eat) zampar. *vi* huir; (horses) desbocarse, dispararse; (plants) cerner. **to b. down,** cerrar con cerrojo. **to b. in,** entrar corriendo, entrar de repente. **to b. off,** marcharse corriendo. **to b. out,** *vi* salir de golpe. *vt* cerrar fuera

bolus *n* bolo, *m*

bomb *n* bomba, *f*, *vt* bombardear. **to be a b.-shell,** *fig* caer como una bomba. **b.-carrier,** portabombas, *m*. **b. crater,** bombazo, *m*. **b.-release,** (*aer nav*) lanzabombas, *m*. **b.-sight,** mira de avión de bombardeo, *f*

bombard *vt* bombardear, bombear; *fig* llover (preguntas, etc.) sobre

bombardier *n* bombardero, *m*

bombardment *n* bombardeo, *m*

bombast *n* ampulosidad, pomposidad, *f*

bombastic *a* bombástico, altisonante, pomposo

bomber *n* avión de bombardeo, bombardero, *m*. **dive b.,** bombardero en picado, *m*. **heavy b.,** bombardero pesado, *m*. **light b.,** bombardero ligero, *m*. **b. command,** servicio de bombardero, *m*

bombproof *a* a prueba de bomba

bonafide *a* fidedigno

bonbon *n* bombón, confite, dulce, *m*. **b. box,** bombonera, *f*

bond *n* lazo, vínculo, *m*; *chem* enlace, *m*; (financial) obligación, *f*; (security) fianza, *f*; (Customs) depósito, *m*; *pl* **bonds,** cadenas, *f pl*, *a* esclavo. **in b.,** en depósito. **bonds of interest,** intereses creados, *m pl*. **b.-holder,** obligacionista, *mf*

bondage *n* esclavitud, *f*; servidumbre, *f*; cautiverio, *m*; prisión, *f*

bone *n* hueso, *m*; (of fish) espina (de pez), *f*; (whale b.) ballena, *f*; *pl* **bones,** cuerpo, *m*, *vt* deshuesar; poner ballenas (a or en). **to be all skin and bones,** estar en los huesos. **to have a b. to pick with,** tener que arreglar las cuentas con. **b.-ash,** cendra, *f*

boned *a* (in compounds) de huesos; deshuesado, sin hueso

boner *n* gazapo, *m*, patochada, plancha, *f*

bonfire *n* fogata, hoguera, *f*

Bonn Bonn, *f*

bonnet *n* capota, *f*; (of babies) gorra, *f*; (of men) boina, *f*; (of chimney and of machines) sombrerete, *m*

bonny *a* sano; hermoso; (fat) gordo

bonus *n* paga extraordinaria, bonificación, *f*; sobresueldo, *m*; (of food, etc.) ración extraordinaria, *f*

bon vivant *n* alegre, vividor, *m*

bon voyage *interj* ¡buen viaje! ¡feliz viaje!

bony *a* huesudo; (of fish-bones) lleno de espinas; óseo

booby *n* pazguato, bobo, *m*. **b.-prize,** último premio, *m*. **b.-trap,** trampa, *f*; *mil* mina, *f*

book *n* libro, *m*; volumen, tomo, *m*; (of an opera) libreto, *m*, *vt* anotar en un libro; apuntar; (seats) tomar (localidades); (tickets) sacar (billetes); (of the issuing clerk) dar; (reserve) reservar; inscribir; consignar (a suspect); (engage) contratar; (invite) comprometer. **to turn the pages of a b.,** hojear un libro. **b.-ends,** sostén para libros, sujetalibros, *m*. **b.-keeper,** tenedor de libros, *m*. **b.-keeping,** teneduría de libros, *f*. **b.-maker,** apostador de profesión, *m*. **b. of reference,** libro de consulta, *m*. **b.-plate,** exlibris, *m*. **b.-post,** tarifa de impresos, *f*. **b.-shop,** librería, *f*. **b.-trade,** venta de libros, *f*; comercio de libros, *m*

bookbinder *n* encuadernador (-ra) de libros

bookbinding *n* encuadernación de libros, *f*

bookcase *n* armario de libros, *Lat. Am.* librero *m*

booking *n* (of rooms, etc.) reservación, *f*; (of tickets) toma, *f*; *com* asiento, *m*; (engagement) contratación, *f*. **b.-clerk,** vendedor (-ra) de billetes. **b.-office,** despacho de billetes, *m*; taquilla, *f*

bookish *a* aficionado a los libros; docto, erudito

bookishness *n* afición a los libros, *f*; erudición, *f*

bookmark *n* marcador, *m*

bookseller *n* librero, *m*

bookselling *n* venta de libros, *f*; comercio de libros, *m*

bookshelf *n* estante para libros, *m*

bookstall *n* puesto de libros, *m*

bookstrap *n* portalibros, *m*

bookworm *n* polilla que roe los libros, *f*; *fig* ratón de biblioteca, *m*

boom *n naut* botavara, *f*; (of a crane) aguilón, *m*; (noise) ruido, *m*; (of the sea) bramido, *m*; (thunder) trueno, *m*; (in a port) cadena de puerto, *f*; *com* actividad, *f*; (*fig* peak) auge, *m*, *vi* sonar; bramar; tronar; *com* subir; ser famoso. **b. sail,** vela de cangreja, *f*

boomerang *n* bumerang, *m*

boon *n* favor, *m*, merced, *f*; bien, *m*, ventaja, *f*; don, *m*; privilegio, *m*, *a* (of friends) intimo

boor *n* monigote, patán, palurdo, *m*

boorish *a* rudo, zafio, rústico, cerril

boorishness *n* zafiedad, patanería, tosquedad, *f*

boost *vt elec* aumentar la fuerza de; *inf* empujar; subir; (advertise) dar bombo (a)

boot *n* bota, *f*; (of a car) compartimiento para equipaje, *m*. **button-boots,** botas de botones, *f pl*. **riding-boots,** botas de montar, *f pl*. **to b.,** además, de añadidura. **b.-maker,** zapatero, *m*. **b.-tag,** tirador de bota, *m*. **b.-tree,** horma de bota, *f*

bootblack *n* limpiabotas, *Mexico* bolero (-ra), *elsewhere in Lat. Am.* embolador (-ra), lustrador (-ra) *mf*

booted *a* con botas, calzado con botas; (in compounds) de botas . . .

bootee *n* botín, *m*

booth *n* puesto, *m*, barraca, *f*

bootlace *n* cordón para zapatos, *m*

bootlegger *n* contrabandista de alcohol, *m*

boots *n* mozo de hotel, botones, *m*

booze *vi* emborracharse. **b. up** *Argentina* acatarrarse *n* alcohol, *m*; borrachera, *f*

boozed up *Lat. Am.* apimplado (-da), *Argentina* acatarrado (-da), *Central America* azurumbado (-da)

boozer *n* borracho (-cha)

boracic *a* bórico. *n* ácido bórico, *m*

borax *n* bórax, *m*

Bordeaux *a* and *n* (of or from) bordelés (-esa). *n* (wine) vino de Burdeos, *m*

bordello *n* burdel, *m*

border *n* borde, *m*; (of a lake, etc.) orilla, *f*; (edge) margen, *m*; (of a diploma, etc.) orla, *f*; *sew* ribete, *m*, orla, *f*; (fringe) franja, *f*; (garden) arriate, *m*; (territory) frontera, *f*; límite, confín, *m*. *vt sew* orlar, ribetear; ornar (de); (of land) lindar con. **to b. on,** (of land) tocar, lindar con; (approach) rayar en. **b. country,** región fronteriza, *f*

borderer *n* habitante de una zona fronteriza, *m*; escocés (-esa) de la frontera con Inglaterra

borderland *n* zona fronteriza, *f*; lindes, *m pl*

borderline *n* frontera, *f*; límite, *m*; margen, *m*, *a* fronterizo; lindero; (uncertain) dudoso, incierto

bore *n* taladro, barreno, *m*; perforación, *f*; (hole) agujero, *m*; (of guns) calibre, *m*; (wave) oleada, *f*; (nuisance) fastidio, *m*; (dullness) aburrimiento, tedio, *m*; (person) pelmazo, *m*, machaca, *mf vt* taladrar, barrenar, horadar; perforar; hacer un agujero (en); (exhaust) aburrir; fastidiar. **It's a b.,** Es una lata. **to be bored,** aburrirse, fastidiarse

boredom *n* aburrimiento, *m*; tedio, hastío, *m*

boring *a* aburrido, pesado, tedioso; molesto, fastidioso. *n* taladro, *m*; horadación, *f*; sondeo, *m*; perforación, *f*

born *a* nacido; (by birth) de nacimiento; (b. to be) destinado a; natural (de). **He was b. in 1870.** Nació en 1870. **to be b.,** nacer, venir al mundo. **to be b. again,** renacer, volver a nacer. **well-b.,** bien nacido. **b. with a silver spoon in one's mouth,** Nacido de pie, Nacido un domingo

-borne trasmitido por . . . (e.g. **anthropod-b.,** trasmitido por los antrópodos)

borough *n* burgo, *m;* villa, *f;* ciudad, *f.* **b. surveyor,** arquitecto municipal, *m*
borrow *vt* pedir prestado; apropiarse, adoptar; copiar; (arithmetic) restar; (a book from a library) tomar prestado. **May I b. your pencil?** ¿Quieres prestarme tu lápiz?
borrower *n* el (la) que pide o toma prestado
borrowing *n* el pedir prestado, acto de pedir prestado, *m*
Bosnian *a* bosnio
bosom *n* pecho, *m;* (heart) corazón, *m;* (of the earth, etc.) seno, *m.* **b. friend,** amigo (-ga) del alma, amigo (-ga) íntimo (-ma)
Bosphorus, the el Bósforo, *m*
boss *n* (of a shield) corcova saliente, *f;* tachón, *m; arch* pinjante, *m. inf* amo, *m;* jefe, *m. vt* mandar; dominar. **political b.,** cacique, *m*
bossism *n* caudillaje, *m*
bossy *a* mandón, autoritario. **b. person** *Lat. Am.* mandarín *m*
botanical *a* botánico. **b. garden,** jardín botánico, *m*
botanist *n* botánico (-ca)
botany *n* botánica, *f*
botch *n* (clumsy work) chapucería, *f;* remiendo, *m. vt* chapucear, chafallar; (patch) remendar
both *a* and *pron* ambos, *m pl;* ambas, *f pl;* los dos, *m pl;* las dos, *f pl, adv* tan(to) . . . como; (and) y; a la vez, al mismo tiempo. **It appealed both to the young and the old,** Gustó tanto a los jóvenes como a los viejos. **b. of you,** ustedes dos, vosotros dos, vosotras dos. **b. pretty and useful,** bonito y útil a la vez
bother *n* molestia, *f,* fastidio, *m;* (worry) preocupación, *f;* dificultad, *f;* (fuss) alboroto, *m, Lat. Am.* fregada *f. vt* molestar, fastidiar, *Lat. Am.* acatarrar; preocupar. *vi* preocuparse
bottle *n* botella, *f;* (smaller) frasco, *m;* (babies) biberón, *m;* (for water) cantimplora, *f, vt* embotellar, envasar, enfrascar. **to b. up,** (liquids, capital, armies, navies) embotellar; (feelings) refrenar. **to bring up on the b.,** criar con biberón. **b.-green,** verde botella, *m.* **b.-neck,** (in an industry) embotellado, *m;* (in traffic) atascadero, *m.* **b.-washer,** fregaplatos, *mf;* (machine) máquina para limpiar botellas, *f*
bottle cap *n* corchalata, *f*
bottled *a* en botella; (of fruit, vegetables) conservado
bottleful *n* botella, *f*
bottler *n* embotellador (-ra)
bottling *n* embotellado, *m;* envase, *m.* **b. outfit,** embotelladora, *f;* (for fruit, etc.) aparato para conservar frutas o legumbres, *m*
bottom *n* base, *f;* (deepest part) fondo, *m;* (last place) último lugar, *m;* fundamento, *m;* (of a chair) asiento, *m;* (of a page, table, mountain, etc.) pie, *m;* (posterior) culo, *m;* (of a river) lecho, *m;* (of the sea) fondo, *m;* (of a ship) casco, *m;* (of a skirt) orilla, *f;* (truth) realidad, verdad, *f;* (basis) origen, *m,* causa, *f.* **at b.,** en realidad. **at the b.,** en el fondo. **false b.,** fondo doble, fondo secreto, *m.* **to be at the b. of,** ocupar el último lugar en; ser el causante de. **to get to the b. of,** descubrir la verdad de; profundizar en, analizar. **to sink to the b.,** (of ships) irse a pique
bottomed *a* (in compounds) de fondo . . .
bottomless *a* sin fondo; (of chairs, etc.) sin asiento; (unfathomable) insondable
boudoir *n* tocador, gabinete de señora, *m*
bough *n* rama, *f,* brazo (de un árbol) *m*
boulder *n* roca, peña, *f;* canto rodado, *m;* bloque de roca, *m*
boulevard *n* bulevar, *m*
bounce *n* bote, rebote, *m;* salto, *m;* (boasting) fanfarronería, *f, vi* rebotar; saltar, brincar. *vt* hacer botar o saltar
bouncing *a* (healthy) sano, robusto; vigoroso, fuerte
bound *n* límite, *m;* (jump) salto, brinco, *m, vt* limitar, confinar. *vi* saltar, brincar; (bounce) botar. **within bounds,** dentro del límite. **b. for,** con destino a; (of ships) con rumbo a
boundary *n* límite, lindero, término, *m;* frontera, *f;* raya, *f.* **b. stone,** mojón, *m*
bounden *a* obligatorio, forzoso; indispensable
boundless *a* sin límites, infinito; inmenso
bounteous, bountiful *a* dadivoso, generoso; bondadoso
bountifulness *n* munificencia, dadivosidad, generosidad, *f*
bounty *n* generosidad, munificencia, *f;* don, *m;* (subsidy) subvención, *f*
bouquet *n* ramo, ramillete (de flores), *m, Lat. Am. also* maceta *f;* perfume, *m;* (of wine) nariz, *f*
Bourbon *a* borbónico. *n* Borbón (-ona)
bourgeois *a* and *n* burgués (-esa)
bourgeoisie *n* burguesía, mesocracia, *f*
bout *n* turno, *m;* (in fencing, boxing, wrestling) asalto, *m;* (of illness, coughing) ataque, *m;* (fight) lucha, *f,* combate, *m;* (of drinking) borrachera, *f*
bovine *a* bovino, vacuno
bow *n* (weapon) arco, *m;* (of a saddle) arzón (de silla), *m; mus* arco, *m;* (knot) lazo, *m;* (greeting) saludo, *m;* reverencia, inclinación, *f;* (of a boat) proa, *f.* **to tie a bow,** hacer un lazo. **bow and arrows,** arco y flechas, *m.* **bow-legged,** patizambo, *Central America* corveta, *f,* **bow window,** ventana saliente, *f*
bow *vi* inclinarse; hacer una reverencia, saludar; (remove the hat) descubrirse; *fig* inclinarse (ante); (submit) someterse (a), reconocer; agobiarse; *mus* manejar el arco. *vt* (usher in) introducir en, conducir a; doblar; inclinar. **to bow down (to),** humillarse ante; obedecer; (worship) reverenciar, adorar. **to bow out,** despedir con una inclinación del cuerpo
bowel *n* intestino, *m; pl* **bowels,** *fig* seno, *m,* entrañas, *f pl*
bower *n* (arbor) enramada, *f;* glorieta, *f;* (boudoir) tocador de señora, *m*
bowing *n mus* arqueada, *f;* saludo, *m, a* (of acquaintance) superficial
bowl *n* receptáculo, *m;* (of a fountain) taza, *f;* (of a pipe) cazoleta, *f;* (barber's) bacía, *f;* (for washing) jofaina, *f;* (for punch) ponchera, *f;* (goblet) copa, *f;* (for soup) escudilla, *f;* (for fruit) frutero, *m;* (of a spoon) paleta, *f;* (ball) boliche, *m. vt* tirar; (in cricket) sacar; (a hoop) jugar con; (in ninepins) tumbar con una bola. **to b. along,** recorrer; ir en coche o carruaje (por). **to b. over,** *fig* dejar consternado (a), desconcertar
bowler *n* (in cricket) servidor, *m;* (hat) sombrero hongo, *m;* (skittle player) jugador de bolos, *m*
bowling *n* (in cricket) saque, *m;* (skittles) (juego de) bolos, *m;* (juego de) boliche, *m.* **b. alley,** bolera, pista de bolos, *f,* salón de boliche, *m.* **b.-green,** bolera en cesped, *f*
bowls *n* juego de boliche, *m*
bowsprit *n* bauprés, *m*
bowstring *n* cuerda de arco, *f*
bow tie *n* pajarita, *f*
bow-wow *n* guau, *m*
box *n* caja, *f;* (case) estuche, *m;* (luggage) baúl, *m,* maleta, *f;* (for a hat) sombrerera, *f; bot* boj, *m; theat* palco, *m, Mexico* lumbrera, *f;* (for a sentry, signalman, etc.) garita, casilla, *f;* (on a carriage) pescante, *m;* (blow) cachete, *m,* bofetada, *f;* (for a horse) vagón, *m.* **post office box,** apartado de correos, *m.* **box-kite,** cometa celular, *f.* **box-maker,** cajero, *m.* **box office,** taquilla, *f, Lat. Am.* boletería *f.* **box-pleat,** *sew* tabla, *f*
box *vt* encajonar, meter en una caja. *vi* boxear. **to box the ears of,** calentar las orejas de. **to box up,** encerrar
boxer *n sport* boxeador, pugilista, *m*
boxing *n* encajonamiento, *m;* envase, *m; sport* boxeo, pugilato, *m.* **B. Day,** Día de San Esteban, *m,* (A Spanish child receives its Christmas presents on the Día de Reyes (Twelfth Night).) **b.-gloves,** guantes de boxeo, *m pl.* **b.-ring,** cuadrilátero de boxeo, *m*
box-office success *n* éxito de taquilla, *m*

boy *n* muchacho, niño, rapaz, *m*; (older) chico, joven, *m*. **new boy,** nuevo alumno, *m*. **old boy,** (of a school) antiguo alumno, *m*; (*fam* address) chico. **small boy,** chiquillo, pequeño, crío, *m*. **b. doll,** muñeco, *m*. **boy scout,** muchacho explorador, *m*
boycott *vt* boicotear. *n* boicot, *m*
boyhood *n* muchachez, mocedad, *f*; (childhood) niñez, *f*
boyish *a* muchachil; pueril; de niñez
brace *n* (prop) puntal, barrote, *m*; abrazadera, *f*; *carp* berbiquí, *m*; viento, tirante, *m*; freno (for the teeth), *m*, (pair) par, *m*; *pl* **braces,** tirantes, *m pl*. *vt* apuntalar; asegurar; *carp* ensamblar; *naut* bracear; (trousers) tirar; *fig* fortalecer, refrescar
bracelet *n* pulsera, *f*, brazalete, *m*, ajorca, *f*
bracing *a* (of air, etc.) fortificante, tónico; estimulador
bracken *n* helecho, *m*
bracket *n* consola, *f*; *arch* repisa, *f*; soporte, *m*; (on furniture, etc.) cantonera, *f*; *print* paréntesis angular, *m*; (for a light) brazo (de alumbrado), *m*. *vt print* poner entre paréntesis; juntar. **in brackets,** entre paréntesis. **They were bracketed equal,** Fueron juzgados iguales
brackish *a* salobre
brag *vi* jactarse, fanfarronear, *Lat. Am.* dragonear, *Argentina* faramallear *n* jactancia, *f*. **to b. about,** hacer alarde de
braggart *a* baladrón, jactancioso. *n* jactancioso, fanfarrón, *m*
bragging *n* jactancia, *f*
Brahmin *n* brahmán, *m*
Brahminism *n* brahmanismo, *m*
braid *n* trencilla, *f*, cordoncillo, *m*; (for trimming) galón, *m*; (plait) trenza, *f*. *vt* (hair) trenzar; (trim) galonear; acordonar, trencillar
brain *n* cerebro, *m*; entendimiento, *m*, inteligencia, *f*; talento, *m*; (common sense) sentido común, *m*; *pl* **brains,** sesos, *m pl*, (animal and human); cacumen, *m*. *vt* romper la crisma (a). **to blow one's brains out,** levantarse la tapa de los sesos. **to rack one's brains,** devanarse los sesos. **Brains Trust,** masa cefálica, *f*; consorcio de inteligencias, *m*. **b.-box,** cráneo, *m*. **b.-fever,** fiebre cerebal, *f*. **b.-storm,** crisis nerviosa, *f*. **b.-wave,** idea luminosa, *f*. **b.-work,** trabajo intelectual, *m*
brainchild *n* engendro, *m*
brain drain *n* fuga de cerebros, *f*
brained *a* de cabeza, de cerebro
brainless *a* sin seso; tonto
brainy *a* sesudo, inteligente, talentudo
braise *vt cul* asar
brake *n* (of vehicles and *fig*) freno, *m*, *Chile, Peru* alitranca *f* (flax and hemp) caballete, *m*; (carriage) break, *m*; (thicket) matorral, *m*. *vt* (vehicles) frenar; (hemp, etc.) rastrillar. **foot-b.,** freno de pedal, *m*. **hand-b.,** freno de mano, *m*. **to b. hard,** frenar de repente. **to release the b.,** quitar el freno
bramble *n* zarza, *f*. **b. patch,** breña, *f*, zarzal, *m*
brambly *a* zarzoso
bran *n* salvado, *m*
branch *n* (of a tree, a family) rama, *f*; (of flowers, of learning) ramo, *m*; (of a river) tributario, afluente, *m*; (of roads, railways) ramal, *m*; (of a firm) sucursal, dependencia, *f*. *a* sucursal, dependiente; (of roads, railways) secundario. *vi* echar ramas; bifurcarse, dividirse; ramificarse. **to b. off,** bifurcarse, ramificarse. **to b. out,** extenderse; emprender cosas nuevas
branched *a* con ramas; *bot* ramoso; (of candlesticks) de . . . brazos
branchiness *n* ramaje, *m*, frondosidad, *f*
branching *n* ramificación, *f*; división, *f*. **b. off,** bifurcación, *f*
brand *n* tizón, *m*; (torch) tea, *f*; (on cattle, etc.) hierro, *m*; (trademark) marca de fábrica, *f*; marca, *f*; (stigma) estigma, *m*. *vt* marcar con el hierro, herrar; marcar; estigmatizar, tildar. **b.-new,** flamante
branding *n* (of livestock) herradero, *m*; (of slaves, criminals) estigmatización, *f*; difamación, *f*. **b.-iron,** hierro de marcar, *m*
brandish *vt* blandir
brandy *n* coñac, *m*
brass *n* latón, *m*; *mus* metal, *m*; (tablet) placa conmemorativa, *f*; *inf* dinero, *m*. **the b.,** *mus* el metal. **b. band,** banda de instrumentos de viento, *f*. **b.-neck,** *inf* cara dura, *f*. **b. works** or **shop,** latonería, *f*
brassiere *n* sostén, *m*
brat *n* crío, *m*
bravado *n* bravata, *f*
brave *a* valiente, animoso, intrépido; espléndido, magnífico; bizarro. *n* valiente, *m*. *vt* desafiar, provocar; arrostrar
bravely *adv* valientemente; espléndidamente; bizarramente
bravery *n* valentía, *f*, valor, *m*, intrepidez, *f*, coraje, *m*; esplendidez, suntuosidad, *f*; bizarría, *f*
bravo *n* bandido, *m*; asesino pagado, *m*, *interj* ¡bravo! ¡ole!
bravura *n* bravura, *f*
brawl *n* camorra, reyerta, pelotera, *Lat. Am.* follisca *f*. *vi* alborotar; (of streams) murmurar. **to start a b.,** armar camorra
brawler *n* camorrista, *mf*
brawling *n* alboroto, *m*, vocinglería, *f*; (of streams) murmullo, *m*
brawn *n cul* embutido, *m*; músculo, *m*; (strength) fuerza, *f*
brawny *a* membrudo, musculoso, forzudo
bray *n* rebuzno, *m*; (of trumpets) clangor, *m*, *vi* rebuznar; sonar
brazen *a* de latón; (of voice) bronca; desvergonzado, descarado
brazier *n* (fire) brasero, *m*; latonero, *m*
Brazil el Brasil, *m*
Brazilian *a* and *n* brasileño (-ña)
Brazil nut *n* nuez del Brasil, *f*
breach *n* violación, contravención, *f*; (gap) abertura, *f*; *mil* brecha, *f*. *vt mil* hacer brecha (en); (in a line of defence) hacer mella (en). **b. of confidence,** abuso de confianza, *m*. **b. of promise,** incumplimiento de la palabra de casamiento, *m*. **b. of the peace,** alteración del orden público, *f*, quebrantamiento de la paz, *m*
bread *n* pan, *m*. **to earn one's b. and butter,** ganarse el pan. **brown b.,** pan moreno, *m*. **unleavened b.,** pan ázimo, *m*. **b. and butter,** pan con mantequilla, *m*; *fig* sustento diario, *m*. **b.-basket,** cesta de pan, *f*; *inf* estómago, *m*. **b.-bin,** caja del pan, *f*. **b.-crumb,** miga, *f*; migaja, *f*. **b.-knife,** cuchillo para cortar el pan, *m*. **b. poultice,** cataplasma de miga de pan, *f*. **b.-winner,** ganador (-ra) de pan, trabajador (-ra)
breadfruit tree *n* árbol del pan, *m*
breadth *n* anchura, *f*; latitud, *f*; liberalidad, *f*; *sew* ancho de una tela, *m*
breadthways *adv* a lo ancho
break *n* rotura, *f*; (opening) abertura, *f*; *geol* rajadura, *f*; (fissure) grieta, *f*; solución de continuidad, *f*; interrupción, *f*; (billiards) serie, *f*; (change) cambio, *m*; (in a boy's voice) muda (de la voz), *f*; (blank) vacío, *m*; (in the market) baja, *f*; intervalo, *m*; descanso, *m*; pausa, *f*; (truce) tregua, *f*; (clearing) clara, *f*; *mus* quiebra (de la voz), *f*; (carriage) break, *m*; (*fam* folly) disparate, *m*. **with a b. in one's voice,** con voz entrecortada. **b. of day,** aurora, alba, *f*. **at the b. of day,** al despuntar el alba
break *vt* romper; quebrar; quebrantar, fracturar; (breach) abrir brecha en; (in two) partir, dividir; (into pieces) hacer pedazos, despedazar; (into small pieces) desmenuzar; (into crumbs) desmigajar; (destroy) destrozar; (a blow) parar; (a law) infringir, violar; (the bank in gambling) quebrar; (a journey, etc.) interrumpir; (of a habit) desacostumbrar, hacer perder el vicio de; (a promise) no cumplir, faltar a; (a record) superar; (plow ground) roturar; (spoil) estropear; arruinar; *com* ir a la quiebra; (an official) degradar; (an animal)

domar, amansar; (*fig* crush) subyugar; (betray) traicionar; (*fig* of silence, a spell, a lance, peace, the ranks) romper; (cushion) amortiguar; (lessen) mitigar; (disclose) revelar; *elec* interrumpir. **to b. one's promise,** faltar a su palabra. **to b. the ice,** *fig* romper el hielo. **to b. asunder,** romper en dos (partes); dividir. **to b. down,** derribar; echar abajo; destruir; (suppress) suprimir; subyugar; abolir; disolver. **to b. in,** (animals) domar, amaestrar; (persons) disciplinar; (new shoes) ahormar, romper. **to b. in two,** partir; dividir en dos; (split) hender. **to b. off,** separar, quitar; (a branch) desgajar; *fig* romper; interrumpir; cesar. **to b. open,** forzar, abrir a la fuerza. **to b. up,** hacer pedazos; (scatter) poner en fuga, dispersar; hacer levantar la sesión; (the ground) roturar; (parliament) disolver; (a ship) desguazar, deshacer (un buque)

break *vi* romperse; quebrarse; quebrantarse; (of beads) desgranarse; (burst) reventar, estallar; (of abscesses) abrirse; (of a boy's voice) mudar; (*fig* and of clouds, etc.) romperse; desaparecer; (of the dawn) despuntar (el alba), amanecer; (sprout) brotar; (of a ball) torcerse; (of fine weather) terminar; (change) cambiar; (of a storm) estallar. **to b. loose,** desasirse; *fig* desencadenarse. **to b. away,** escaparse, fugarse; (from a habit) romper con, independizarse de (another country); disiparse. **to b. down,** (of machinery, cars) averiarse; (fail) frustrarse, malograrse; (weep) deshacerse en lágrimas; (lose one's grip) perder la confianza en sí; (in health) sufrir una crisis de salud. **The car broke down,** El auto tuvo una avería. **to b. in,** (of burglars) forzar la entrada; irrumpir (en), penetrar (en); exclamar. **to b. in on,** sorprender; entrar de sopetón; invadir; interrumpir; caer sobre; molestar. **to b. into,** (force) forzar; (utter) romper a, prorrumpir en; empezar (a); pasar de repente a; (of time, etc.) ocupar; hacer perder. **to b. off,** (of speech) interrumpirse; cesar; (detach) desprenderse, separarse; (of branches) desgajarse. **to b. out,** huir, escaparse; *fig* estallar; aparecer; declararse; (of fire) tomar fuego; derramarse; (of an eruption) salir. **to b. over,** derramarse por; bañar. **to b. through,** abrirse paso (por); abrirse salida (por); atravesar; *fig* penetrar; (of the sun, etc.) romper (por). **to b. up,** (depart) separarse; (of meetings) levantarse la sesión; dispersarse; (smash) hacerse pedazos; disolverse; (of a school) cerrarse, empezar las vacaciones; (melt) fundir; desbandarse; (of a camp) levantar (el campo); (grow old) hacerse viejo; (be ill) estar agotado. **to b. with,** romper con; cesar; reñir con

breakable *a* quebradizo, frágil

breakage *n* rompimiento, quebrantamiento, *m*; cosa rota, *f*; fractura, *f*

breakdown *n* accidente, *m*; (of a machine) avería, *f*; *aut* pane, *f*; (failure) fracaso, *m*, falta de éxito, *f*; deterioración, *f*; (in health) crisis de salud, *f*. **b. gang,** pelotón de reparaciones, *m*

breaker *n* oleada, *f*

breakfast *n* desayuno, *m*. *vi* desayunar(se), tomar el desayuno. **to have a good b.,** desayunar bien. **b.-cup,** tazón, *m*. **b.-time,** hora del desayuno, *f*

breaking *n* rompimiento, *m*; quebrantamiento, *m*; fractura, *f*; ruptura, *f*; (in two) división, *f*; (into pieces) despedazamiento, *m*; (into small pieces) desmenuzamiento, *m*; (destruction) destrozo, *m*; (of a blow) parada, *f*; (of a law, etc.) violación, *f*; (of one's word) no cumplimiento, *m*; (of a journey, of sleep, etc.) interrupción, *f*; (escape) escape, *m*, huida, *f*; (of an animal) domadura, *f*; (of a boy's voice) muda (de la voz), *f*; (of news) revelación, *f*. **b. down,** demolición, *f*; (of negotiations) suspensión, *f*. **b. in,** irrupción, *f*; (of an animal) domadura, *f*; (training) entrenamiento, *m*. **b. open,** forzamiento, *m*; quebranto, *m*. **b. out,** huida, *f*, escape, *m*; *fig* estallido, *m*; aparición, *f*; declaración, *f*; (scattering) derramamiento, *m*; (of a rash) erupción, *f*. **b. up,** dispersión, *f*; disolución, *f*; fin, *m*; ruina, *f*; (of a school) cierre, *m*; (change in weather) cambio, *m*; (of a meeting) levantamiento (de una sesión), *m*; (of the earth) roturación, *f*

breakneck *a* rápido, veloz, precipitado

breakwater *n* malecón, rompeolas, *m*

bream *n icht* sargo, *m*. **sea-b.,** besugo, *m*

breast *n* pecho, *m*; (of birds) pechuga, *f*; (of female animals) teta, mama, *f*; (heart) corazón, *m*, *vt* (the waves) cortar (las olas); luchar con; *fig* arrostrar, hacer frente a. **b.-bone,** esternón, *m*. **b. high,** alto hasta el pecho. **b.-pin,** alfiler de pecho, *m*. **b.-pocket,** bolsillo de pecho, *m*. **b.-stroke,** estilo pecho, *m*

breast cancer *n* el cáncer del seno, *m*

breasted *a* de pecho . . .; de pechuga . . .; de tetas . . . **a double-b. jacket,** una chaqueta cruzada. **a single-b. jacket,** una chaqueta

breastwork *n mil* parapeto, *m*

breath *n* aliento, *m*; suspiro, *m*; (phonetics) aspiración, *f*; (breeze) soplo (de aire), *m*; (of scandal, etc.) murmurio, *m*; (fragrance) perfume, *m*, fragancia, *f*; (life) vida, *f*. **in a b.,** de un aliento. **in the same b.,** sin respirar. **out of b.,** sin aliento. **under one's b.,** por lo bajo, entre dientes. **to draw b.,** tomar aliento. **to get one's b. back,** cobrar aliento. **to hold one's b.,** contener el aliento. **to take one's b. away,** *fig* dejar consternado (a)

breathable *a* respirable

breathe *vi* respirar; vivir; (of air, etc.) soplar; (take the air) tomar el fresco; (rest) tomar aliento. *vt* respirar; exhalar; dar aire (a); (whisper) murmurar; (convey) expresar, revelar; (infuse) infundir. **to b. forth fury,** echar rayos. **to b. hard,** jadear. **to b. one's last,** exhalar el último suspiro. **to b. in,** inspirar

breathing *n* respiración, *f*; (of the air, etc.) soplo, *m*; (phonetics) aspiración, *f*. *a* que respira; viviente. **hard** or **heavy b.,** jadeo, resuello, resoplido, *m*. **b.-space,** *fig* respiro, *m*

breathless *a* jadeante, sin aliento; (dead) muerto; (sultry) sin un soplo de aire; intenso, profundo; (of haste) precipitado

breathlessly *adv* anhelosamente; con expectación

breathlessness *n* falta de aliento, *f*; respiración difícil, *f*; (death) muerte, *f*; (of weather) falta de aire, *f*

bred *a* criado. **ill (well) b.,** mal (bien) criado. **pure-b.,** de raza

breech *n anat* trasero, *m*; (of fire-arms) recámara, *f*

breeches *n* calzones, *m pl*; pantalones, *m pl*. **riding-b.,** pantalones de montar, *m pl*. **to wear the b.,** *fig* ponerse los calzones

breed *n* casta, raza, *f*; tipo, *m*; clase, *f*, *vt* procrear; engendrar, crear; (bring up) educar; criar. *vi* reproducirse; sacar cría; multiplicarse. **to b. in-and-in,** procrear sin mezclar razas

breeder *n* criador (-ra); animal reproductor, *m*

breeding *n* reproducción, *f*; cría, *f*; (upbringing) crianza, *f*; educación, *f*; instrucción, *f*; producción, *f*; creación, *f*, *a* de cría; (of male animals) semental; prolífico. **bad b.,** mala crianza, *f*. **good b.,** buena crianza, *f*. **cross b.,** cruzamiento de razas, *m*. **B. will out,** Aunque la mona se vista de seda, mona se queda. **b. farm,** criadero, *m*

breeze *n* brisa, *f*, vientecillo, *m*, soplo de aire, *m*, *Lat. Am.* airecito *m*; (argument) altercación, *f*, argumento, *m*; (of coke) cisco de coque, *m*. **fresh b.,** brisa fresca, *f*. **light b.,** brisa floja, *f*. **strong b.,** viento fuerte, viento muy fresco, *m*

breezy *a* con brisa, fresco; expuesto a la brisa; oreado; (of manner) animado, jovial

brethren *n pl* hermanos, *m pl*

Breton *a* and *n* bretón (-ona). *n* (language) bretón, *m*

brevet *n mil* graduación honoraria, *f*; nombramiento honorario, *m*. *vt mil* graduar

breviary *n* breviario, *m*

brevity *n* brevedad, *f*; concisión, *f*

brew *n* mezcla, *f*; brebaje, *m*. *vt* hacer (cerveza, té, etc.); preparar, mezclar; *fig* urdir, tramar. *vi* prepararse; urdirse; (storm) gestarse.

brewer *n* cervecero (-ra)
brewery *n* cervecería, fábrica de cerveza, *f*
brewing *n* elaboración de cerveza, *f*
briar *n* (wild rose) rosal silvestre, *m*; (heather) brezo, *m*. **b. pipe,** pipa de brezo, *f*
bribable *a* sobornable
bribe *n* soborno, cohecho, *m*, *Lat. Am.* coima *f vt* sobornar, cohechar. **to take bribes,** dejarse sobornar
briber *n* cohechador (-ra)
bribery *n* soborno, *m*
brick *n* ladrillo, *m*; (for children) piedra de construcción, *f*; bloque, *m*; *inf* buen chico, *m*, joya, *f*, *a* de ladrillo. *vt* enladrillar. **b.-floor,** ladrillado, *m*; **b.-kiln,** horno de ladrillo, *m*. **b.-maker,** ladrillero, *m*. **b.-yard,** ladrillar, *m*
bricklayer *n* albañil, *m*
bricklaying *n* albañilería, *f*
brickwork *n* masonería, *f*
bridal *a* nupcial; de la boda; de la novia. **b. bed,** tálamo, *m*. **b. cake,** torta de la boda, *f*. **b. shop,** tienda para novias, *f*. **b. shower,** despedida de soltera, despedida de soltería, *f*. **b. song,** epitalamio, *m*. **b. veil,** velo de la novia, velo nupcial, *m*. **b. wreath,** corona de azahar, *f*
bride *n* novia, desposada, *f*; (after marriage) recién casada, *f*
bridegroom *n* novio, *m*; (after marriage) recién casado, *m*
bridesmaid *n* madrina de boda, *f*; niña encargada de sostener la cola de la novia, *f*
bridge *n* (engineering, *mus naut*) puente, *m*; lomo (de la nariz), *m*; (game) bridge, *m*, *vt* construir un puente (sobre), pontear; (obstacles) salvar; evitar; (fill in) ocupar, llenar. **auction b.,** bridge por subasta, *m*. **contract b.,** bridge por contrato, *m*. **suspension-b.,** puente colgante, *m*. **b. toll,** pontazgo, *m*
bridgehead *n* cabeza de puente, *f*
bridle *n* brida, *f*; freno, *m*. *vt* embridar, enfrenar; *fig* reprimir. *vi* (of horses) levantar la cabeza; (of persons) erguirse; hacer un gesto despreciativo. **snaffle b.,** bridón, *m*. **b. path,** camino de herradura, *m*
brief *a* breve, corto; conciso; lacónico, seco; rápido; fugaz, pasajero. *n* (papal) breve, *m*; *law* relación, *f*; escrito, *m*. *vt* (a barrister) instruir. **to hold a b. for,** defender, abogar por. **b.-case,** portapapeles, *m*; cartera (grande), *f*
briefly *adv* brevemente; en pocas palabras; sucintamente; (tersely) secamente
brier *n* rosal silvestre, *m*; zarza, *f*
brigade *n mil* brigada, *f*; cuerpo, *m*; asociación, *f*
brigadier *n* brigadier, *m*
brigand *n* bandolero, bandido, *m*
brigandage *n* bandolerismo, *m*
bright *a* brillante, reluciente; vivo; cristalino; subido; claro; optimista; alegre; inteligente; (quick-witted) agudo; ilustre; (smiling) risueño; (of future, etc.) halagüeño. **to be as b. as a new pin,** estar como una ascua de oro. **b. blue,** azul subido, *m*. **b.-eyed,** con ojos vivos, con ojos chispeantes, ojialegre
Bright's disease *n* enfermedad de Bright, glomerulonefritis, *f*
brighten *vt* hacer brillar; (polish) pulir; (make happy) alegrar; (improve) mejorar. *vi* (of the weather) aclarar, despejarse (el cielo); sentirse más feliz; mejorar
brightly *adv* brillantemente; alegremente
brightness *n* brillo, *m*; claridad, *f*; esplendor, *m*; (of colors) brillantez, *f*; vivacidad, *f*; inteligencia, *f*; agudeza de ingenio, *f*
brilliance *n* fulgor, brillo, *m*, refulgencia, *f*; esplendor, *m*; lustre, *m*; talento, *m*; brillantez, gloria, *f*
brilliant *a* brillante. *n* (gem) brillante, *m*. **to be b.,** (in conversation, etc.) brillar; (be clever) ser brillante
brilliantine *n* brillantina, *f*
brim *n* (of a glass, etc.) borde, *m*; (of a hat) ala, *f*; margen, *m*, orilla, *f*. **to be full to the b.,** estar lleno hasta los bordes; *fig* rebosar. **eyes brimming with tears,** ojos arrasados de lágrimas
brimful *a* hasta el borde (or los bordes); *fig* rebosante
brimless *a* (of hats) sin ala
brimmed *a* (of hats) con ala
brimstone *n* azufre, *m*
brindled *a* atigrado, abigarrado
brine *n* salmuera, *f*; mar, *m*; *poet* lágrimas, *f pl*
bring *vt* traer; llevar; transportar; (take a person or drive a vehicle) conducir; *fig* acarrear, traer; causar, ocasionar; producir; crear; (induce) persuadir; hacer (ver, etc.); (be worth) valer; (sell for) vender por; *law* entablar (un pleito, etc.): (before a judge) hacer comparecer (ante); (present) presentar; (attract) atraer; (place) poner. **to b. home,** llevar a casa; *fig* hacer ver, hacer sentir; demostrar; (a crime) probar contra. **to b. near,** acercar. **to b. about,** efectuar, poner por obra; causar, ocasionar; (achieve) lograr, conseguir. **to b. again,** traer otra vez, llevar de nuevo. **to b. away,** llevarse. **to b. back,** devolver; traer; (of memories) recordar. **to b. down,** llevar abajo, bajar; (of persons) hacer bajar; (humble) humillar; hacer caer; (of prices) hacer bajar; arruinar; destruir. **to b. down the house,** *theat* hacer venirse el teatro abajo. **to b. forth,** (give birth to) dar a luz; producir; causar; sacar a luz. **to b. forward,** hacer adelantarse; empujar hacia adelante; *fig* avanzar; (allege) alegar; *com* llevar a nueva cuenta; presentar, producir. **brought forward,** *com* suma y sigue. **to b. in,** (things) llevar adentro; (persons) hacer entrar; introducir; aparecer con, presentarse con; (meals) servir; producir; declarar; (a verdict) dictar (sentencia de), fallar. **to b. into being,** poner en práctica; dar origen (a). **to b. off,** (a ship) poner a flote; (rescue) salvar, rescatar; (carry out) efectuar, poner en práctica; (achieve) conseguir, lograr. **B. me the glass off the table,** Tráeme el vaso que hay en la mesa. **to b. on,** causar, inducir; acarrear; iniciar. **He brought a book on to the stage,** Entró en escena llevando un libro (or con un libro). **to b. out,** sacar; poner afuera; (a person) hacer salir; publicar; (a play) poner en escena; sacar a luz; (an idea, jewels, etc.) sacar a relucir; revelar; demostrar; hacer aparecer; (a girl in society) poner de largo (a). **to b. over,** llevar al otro lado; hacer venir; traer; conducir; hacer cruzar; (convert) convertir. **to b. round,** traer; llevar; (from a swoon) sacar de un desmayo; curar; persuadir; conciliar. **to b. through,** hacer atravesar; llevar a través de; ayudar a salir (de un apuro); (an illness) curar de. **to b. to,** traer a; llevar a; (from a swoon) hacer volver en sí; *naut* ponerse a la capa. **He cannot b. himself to,** No puede persuadirse a. **to b. together,** reunir; (things) juntar, amontonar; reconciliar, poner en paz. **to b. under,** someter; sojuzgar; incluir. **to b. up,** llevar arriba, subir; (a person) hacer subir; hacer avanzar; (a price) hacer subir; ir (a); andar; (breed) criar; (educate) educar, criar; (in a discussion) hacer notar; vomitar. **to b. up the rear,** ir al fin (de); *mil* ir a la retaguardia. **well** (or **badly**) **brought up,** bien (o mal) educado. **to b. upon oneself,** buscarse, incurrir (en). **to b. up-to-date,** poner al día; refrescar; rejuvenecer
bringing *n* acción de llevar o traer, *f*; conducción, *f*; transporte, *m*. **b. forth,** producción, *f*. **b. in,** introducción, *f*. **b. out,** producción, *f*; publicación, *f*; (of a girl in society) puesta de largo, *f*. **b. under,** reducción, *f*; subyugación, *f*. **b. up,** educación, crianza, *f*
brink *n* borde, margen, *m*; (of water) orilla, *f*; *fig* margen, *m*. **on the b.,** al margen; a la orilla. **to be on the b. of,** (doing something) estar para, estar a punto de
briny *a* salado
briquette *n* briqueta, *f*, aglomerado de carbón, *m*
brisk *a* activo; vivo; animado; rápido, acelerado; enérgico
brisket *n* falda, *f*
briskly *adv* vivamente; enérgicamente; aprisa
briskness *n* actividad, *f*; viveza, *f*; animación, *f*; rapidez, *f*; energía, *f*
bristle *n* cerda, seda, *f*, *vi* erizarse
bristling *n* sardina noruega, .

bristly *a* erizado, cerdoso; espinoso; hirsuto
Bristol board *n* cartulina, *f*
British *a* británico. **the B.,** el pueblo británico; los ingleses
British Commonwealth, the la Mancomunidad Británica, *f*
Briton *n* inglés (-esa). **ancient B.,** britano (-na)
Brittany Bretaña, *f*
brittle *a* frágil, quebradizo, deleznable, friable
brittleness *n* fragilidad, friabilidad, *f*
broach *n cul* espetón, asador, *m*. *vt* espitar (un barril); abrir; *fig* introducir
broad *a* ancho; grande; (extensive) vasto, extenso; **a b. confession,** una confesión amplia; (full) pleno; (of accents) marcado; (of words) lato; (clear) claro; (of the mind) liberal, tolerante; (of humor, etc.) grosero; (general) general, comprensivo. **in b. daylight,** en pleno día. **b.-brimmed,** de ala ancha. **b.-faced,** cariancho. **b.-minded,** tolerante, liberal, ancho de conciencia, abierto al mundo. **b.-mindedness,** tolerancia, liberalidad, *f*. **to be b.-minded,** ser tolerante, tener manga ancha. **b.-shouldered,** ancho de espaldas
broadcast *n agr* siembra al vuelo, *f*; *rad* radiodifusión, radiotransmisión, emisión, *f*, *a* radiado. *adv* por todas partes; extensamente. *vt agr* sembrar a vuelo; *rad* radiodifundir, radiar, transmitir por radio; (news, etc.) diseminar
broadcaster *n* (lecturer) conferenciante, *mf*; radiodifusor (-ra); (announcer) locutor (-ra)
broadcasting *n* radiación, radiodifución, *f*; radio, *f*. **b.-station,** estación de radio, emisora, *f*. **b.-studio,** estudio de emisión, *m*
broaden *vt* ampliar, ensanchar. *vi* ampliarse, ensancharse
broad-leaved *a* frondoso
broadly *adv* anchamente; con marcado acento dialectal; de una manera general
broadness *n* anchura, *f*; extensión, vastedad, *f*; tolerancia, *f*; liberalidad, *f*; grosería, *f*; (of accent) acento marcado, *m*
broadside *n* (of a ship) costado, *m*; (of guns) andanada, *f*; *fig* batería, *f*; *print* cara de un pliego, *f*. **to be b. on,** dar el costado
brocade *a* and *n* brocado *m*.. *vt* decorar con brocado. **imitation b.,** brocatel, *m*
brocaded *a* decorado con brocado; de brocado
broccoli *n* bróculi, brécol, *m*
brochure *n* folleto, *m*
brogue *n* acento, *m*; acento irlandés, *m*; (shoe) zapato grueso, *m*
broil *vt* emparrillar, asar. *vi* asarse
broke *a* quebrado; (penniless) *Peru* calato
broken *a* roto; quebrado; (spiritless) abatido, desalentado; (infirm) agotado, debilitado; (ruined) arruinado; (of ground) desigual, escabroso; (of a language) chapucero; (spoilt) estropeado; imperfecto; incompleto; (loose) suelto; (of a horse, etc.) domado; (of the weather) variable; (of sleep) interrumpido; (of the heart, of shoes, etc.) roto; (of the voice, sobs, sighs) entrecortado; (of the voice through old age, etc.) cascada; (incoherent) incoherente. **b.-down,** (tired) rendido, agotado; arruinado; (not working) estropeado. **b.-hearted,** roto el corazón, angustiado. **b.-winged,** aliquebrado. **I speak broken Spanish,** Hablo el español chapuceramente
brokenly *adv* (of the voice) con voz entrecortada; a ratos; interrumpidamente
brokenness *n* interrupción, *f*; (of the ground) desigualdad, *f*; (of speech) imperfección, *f*
broker *n* corredor, *m*; (stock) corredor de bolsa, *m*
brokerage *n* corretaje, *m*
bromide *n* bromuro, *m*
bromine *n* bromo, *m*
bronchi *n pl* bronquios, *m pl*
bronchitis *n* bronquitis, *f*
broncopneumonia *n* bronconeumonía, *f*
Brontosaurus *n* brontosauro, *m*
bronze *n* bronce, *m*; objeto de bronce, *m*, *a* de bronce. *vt* broncear. **B. Age,** Edad de Bronce, *f*
brooch *n* broche, *m*; alfiler de pecho, *m*
brood *n* (of birds) nidada, *f*; (of chickens) pollada, *f*; (other animals) cría, *f*; prole, *f*, *vi* empollar. **to b. over,** meditar sobre, rumiar; (of mountains, etc.) dominar
broody *a* (of hens) clueca, *f*
brook *n* arroyo, riachuelo, *m*, *vt* tolerar, sufrir, permitir
broom *n* escoba, *f*; *bot* retama, *f*; hiniesta, *f*. **common b.,** retama de escobas, *f*. **Spanish b.,** retama común, retama de olor, hiniesta, *f*. **b.-handle,** palo de escoba, *m*
broomstick *n* palo de escoba, *m*
broth *n* caldo, *m*
brothel *n* burdel, lupanar, *m*, casa de trato, *f*
brother *n* hermano, *m*; (colleague) colega, *m*; *inf* compañero, *m*. **foster-b.,** hermano de leche, *m*. **half-b.,** medio hermano, *m*. **step-b.,** hermanastro, *m*. **b.-in-law,** hermano político, cuñado, *m*. **b.-officer,** compañero de promoción, *m*
brotherhood *n* fraternidad, *f*; *ecc* cofradía, *f*; hermandad, *f*
brotherliness *n* fraternidad, *f*
brotherly *a* fraterno
brow *n* frente, *f*; ceja, *f*; (of a hill) cresta, cumbre, *f*; (edge) borde, *m*. **to knit one's b.,** fruncir el ceño
browbeat *vt* intimidar, amenazar
browbeating *n* intimidación, *f*
brown *a* castaño; (gallicism often used of shoes, etc.) marrón; pardo; (of complexion, eyes, hair) moreno; (dark brown) bruno; (blackish) negruzco; (toasted) tostado; (burnt) quemado. *n* color moreno, *m*; color pardo, *m*; castaño, *m*; (from the sun) bronce, *m*. *vt* (toast) tostar; (a person) volver moreno, broncear; (meat) asar. *vi* tostarse; volverse moreno, broncearse; asarse. **b. bear,** oso pardo, *m*. **b. owl,** autillo, *m*. **b. paper,** papel de estraza, *m*. **b. study,** ensimismamiento, *m*, meditación, *f*. **b. sugar,** azúcar moreno (or quebrado), *m*
brownie *n* duende benévolo, *m*
brownish *a* morenucho; que tira a castaño o a bruno; parduzco; trigueño
brownness *n* color moreno, *m*
browse *vi* pacer; (through a publication) hojear (un libro)
browsing *n* apacentamiento, *m*; hojeo (de un libro), *m*; lectura, *f*, estudio, *m*
Bruges Brujas, *f*
bruise *n* cardenal, *m*. *Lat. Am.* magullón *m*; abolladura, *f*; (in metal) bollo, *m*; (on fruit) maca, *f*. *vt* acardenalar, magullar; abollar; (fruit) macar
bruising *n* magullamiento, *m*; (of metal) abolladura, *f*; (crushing) machacadura, *f*; (boxing) boxeo, pugilato, *m*
brunette *n* trigueña, morena, *f*
brunt *n* peso, *m*; golpe, *m*; choque, *m*; esfuerzo, *m*. **to bear the b.,** soportar el peso; sufrir el choque; *inf* pagar el pato
brush *n* cepillo, *m*; (broom) escoba, *f*; (for whitewashing, etc.) brocha, *f*; (for painting) pincel, *m*; (of a fox) cola (de zorro), *f*; (undergrowth) breñal, matorral, *m*; (fight) escaramuza, *f*; (argument) altercación, *f*. **scrubbing-b.,** cepillo para fregar, *m*. **shoe-b.,** cepillo para limpiar los zapatos, *m*. **stroke of the b.,** brochada, *f*; pincelada, *f*. **whitewash-b.,** brochón, *m*. **b. maker** or **seller,** escobero (-ra); pincelero (-ra)
brush *vt* cepillar; (sweep) barrer; frotar; (touch) rozar; (touch lightly) acariciar. **to b. against,** rozar, tocar. **to b. aside,** echar a un lado; *fig* no hacer caso de; ignorar. **to b. off,** sacudir(se); quitar(se); (sweep) barrer. **to b. up,** cepillar; (wool) cardar; (tidy) asear; (a subject) refrescar, repasar
brushing *n* acepilladura, *f*; (sweeping) barredura, *f*; (touching) roce, rozamiento, *m*; (of hair) peinadura, *f*
brushwood *n* enjutos, *m pl*, chamarasca, *f*; matorral, *m*

brusque *a* brusco, seco
brusquely *adv* secamente
brusqueness *n* brusquedad, *f*
Brussels *a* bruselense; de Bruselas. **B. lace,** encaje de Bruselas, *m*
Brussels sprouts *n pl* bretones, *m pl*
brutal *a* bestial, brutal; salvaje, inhumano
brutality *n* brutalidad, bestialidad, *f*; barbaridad, ferocidad, *f*
brutalize *vt* embrutecer
brutally *adv* brutalmente
brute *n* bruto, animal, *m*; salvaje, bárbaro, *m*. **b. force,** la fuerza bruta
brutish *a* bruto; sensual, bestial; grosero; salvaje; estúpido; ignorante. **to become b.,** embrutecerse
bubble *n* burbuja, *f*; borbollón, *m*, *vi* burbujear; borbollar, bullir, hervir
bubbling *n* burbujeo, *m*; hervidero, *m*; (of brooks) murmullo, *m*, *a* burbujeante; hirviente; (of brooks) parlero; (of wine) espumoso, efervescente
bubonic *a* bubónico. **b. plague,** peste bubónica, *f*
buccaneer *n* corsario, *m*; aventurero, *m*
Bucharest Bucarest, *m*
buck *n zool* gamo, *m*; (male) macho, *m*; (fop) galán, petimetre, *m*, *vi* (of a horse) caracolear; fanfarronear. **to pass the b.,** *inf* echarle a uno el muerto. **b.-rabbit,** conejo, *m*. **to b. up,** hacer de tripas corazón
bucket *n* cubo, balde, *m*, cubeta, *f*
buckle *n* hebilla, *f*. *vt* enhebillar, abrochar con hebilla. *vi* doblarse. **to b. to,** ponerse a hacer algo con ahinco
buckled *a* con hebillas
buckler *n* broquel, *m*, rodela, tarjeta, *f*
buckram *n* bocací, *m*
buckshot *n* perdigón, *m*
buckskin *n* ante, *m*
buckwheat *n* alforfón, trigo sarraceno, *m*
bucolic *a* bucólico, pastoril
bud *n* brote, *m*; botón, capullo, *m*; (of vines) bollón, *m*; (of vegetables) gema, *f*. *vi* brotar, germinar. *vt* injertar de escudete
Buddhism *n* budismo, *m*
Buddhist *n* budista, *mf*
budding *n* brotadura, *f*; (of roses, etc) injerto de escudete, *m*; *fig* germen, *m*
budge *vi* moverse, menearse. *vt* mover
budget *n* presupuesto, *m*; (of news, etc.) colección, *f*. *vi* presuponer
Buenos Aires (of or from the province of) *a* and *n* bonaerense, *mf*
buff *n* color de ante, *m*; piel de ante, *f*. **b.-colored,** anteado. **in the buff = naked, nude**
buffalo *n* búfalo, *f*
buffer *n* (railway) parachoques, *m*; (of cars) amortiguador, *m*. **b. state,** estado tapón, *m*
buffet *n* bofetón, *m*; bofetada, *f*; bar, *m*. *vt* abofetear; golpear; luchar con las olas
buffoon *n* bufón, *m*
buffoonery *n* bufonería, *f*
bug *n* chinche, *f*. **bugs** *Lat. Am.* bicherío *m*
bugbear *n* pesadilla, *f*
bugle *n* corneta, trompeta, *f*; (bead) abalorio, *m*. **b. blast,** trompetazo, *m*
bugler *n* trompetero, *m*
build *vt* edificar; (engines, ships, organs, etc.) construir; (a nest and *fig*) hacer; (have built) hacer, edificar; crear; formar; fundar. *n* estructura, *f*; (of the body) hechura, *f*; talle, *m*. **to b. castles in Spain,** hacer castillos en el aire. **built-up area,** zona urbana, *f*. **to b. up,** construir, levantar; (block) tapar; (business, reputation) establecer, crear. **to b. upon,** *fig* contar con, confiar en; esperar de
builder *n* constructor, *m*; maestro de obras, *m*; (laborer) albañil, *m*; creador (-ra), fundador (-ra); arquitecto, *m*
building *n* edificación, *f*; construcción, *f*; edificio, *m*; fundación, *f*; creación, *f*. **b. contractor,** maestro de obras, *m*. **b. material,** material de construcción, *m*. **b. site,** solar, terreno, *m*. **b. timber,** madera de construcción, *f*
built-in *a* empotrado. **b. closet,** armario empotrado, *m*
bulb *n bot* bulbo, *m*; (*elec phys*) bombilla, *f*; (of an oil lamp) cebolla, *f*
bulbous *a* bulboso
Bulgarian *a* and *n* búlgaro (-ra)
bulge *n* bulto, *m*; hinchazón, *f*; protuberancia, *f*; *mil* bolsa (en el frente), *f*. *vi* hincharse; estar lleno (de)
bulging *a* lleno (de); con bultos; hinchado (de)
bulk *n* volumen, tamaño, *m*; bulto, *m*; (larger part) grueso, *m*; mayor parte, *f*; (of people) mayoría, *f*; (of a ship) capacidad, *f*. **in b.,** *com* en bruto, en grueso. **to b. large,** tener mucha importancia
bulkhead *n naut* mamparo, *m*
bulkiness *n* abultamiento, *m*; volumen, tamaño, *m*
bulky *a* voluminoso, grande, grueso
bull *n* toro, *m*; *ast* Tauro, *m*; (of some animals) macho, *m*; (Stock Exchange) alcista, *mf*; (of the Pope) bula (del Papa), *f*. **a b. in a china shop,** un caballo loco en una cacharrería. **to fight bulls,** torear. **b.-calf,** ternero, *m*. **bull's eye,** blanco, *m*; acierto, *m*. **b. fight,** corrida de toros, *f*. **b. fighter's gala uniform,** traje de luces, *m*. **b.-ring,** plaza de toros, *f*
bulldog *n* perro dogo, perro de presa, *m*
bulldozer *n* (excavator) tozodora, *f*
bullet *n* bala, *f*. **spent b.,** bala fría, *f*. **stray b.,** bala perdida, *f*. **b.-proof,** a prueba de bala, blindado
bulletin *n* boletín, *m*
bulletin board *n* tablero de anuncios, tablero de avisos, tablón, *m*
bulletproof vest *n* chaleco blindado, *m*
bullfighter *n* torero, *m* (on foot), toreador, *m* (on horseback)
bullfinch *n* pinzón real, *m*
bullion *n com* metálico, *m*; oro (or plata) en barras, *m*, *f*.
bullock *n* becerro, *m*; buey, *m*
bullpen *n* toril, *m* (bullfighting); calentador, *m* (baseball)
bully *n* valentón, perdonavidas, gallito, *m*; rufián, *Argentina* compadre *m*. *vt* intimidar; tratar mal. **b. beef,** vaca en lata, *f*
bulrush *n* anea, *f*
bulwark *n* baluarte, *m*; *naut* antepecho, *m*
bumblebee *n* abejorro, *m*
bump *n* golpe, *m*; ruido, *m*; choque, *m*; (bruise) chichón, *m*, roncha, *f*; *aer* sacudida, *f*, meneo, *m*. *vi* (into, against) tropezar con; (along) saltar en. *vt* chocar (contra)
bumper *n* copa llena hasta los bordes, *f*, vaso lleno, *m*; (of a car) parachoques, *m*. **a b. harvest,** una cosecha abundante
bumpkin *n* patán, villano, *m*
bumptious *a* fatuo, presuntuoso, presumido
bumpy *n* (of surface) desigual, escabroso; (of a vehicle) incómodo, con mala suspensión
bun *n* buñuelo, bollo, *m*; (hair) moño, *m*
bunch *n* (of fruit) racimo, *m*; manojo, *m*; (of flowers) ramo, *m*, *Lat. Am. also* maceta *f*; (tuft) penacho, *m*; (gang) pandilla, *f*, *vi* arracimarse, agruparse
bundle *n* atado, lío, *m*; (of papers) legajo, *m*; (of sticks) haz, *m*; (sheaf) fajo, *m*; (package) paquete, *m*; fardo, hatillo, *m*; (roll) rollo, *m*, *vt* atar, liar; envolver; empaquetar; (stuff) meter, introducir. **to b. in,** meter dentro (de). **to b. out,** despachar sin ceremonia, poner de patitas en la calle
bung *n* tapón, tarugo, *m*, *vt* atarugar
bungalow *n* casa de un solo piso, *f*
bungle *vt* estropear; hacer mal. *n* equivocación, *f*, yerro, *m*; cosa (o obra) mal hecha, *f*
bungling *a* chapucero, torpe
bunion *n* juanete (del pie), *m*
bunk *n* litera, *f*, *vi inf* poner pies en polvorosa, pirarse
bunker *n naut* pañol, *m*; (for coal) carbonera, *f*; (golf) hoya de arena, *f*
bunkum *n* patrañas, *f pl*

bunting *n* gallardete, *m*
buoy *n* boya, baliza, *f*, *vt* boyar; abalizar; *fig* sostener. **light b.,** boya luminosa, *f*
buoyancy *n* flotación, *f*; *fig* optimismo, *m*, alegría, *f*
buoyant *a* boyante; ligero
burden *n* carga, *f*, peso, *m*; (of a ship) tonelaje, *m*, capacidad, *f*; (of a song) estribillo, *m*; (gist) esencia, *f*. *vt* cargar. **to be a b. on,** pesar sobre
burdensome *a* pesado, oneroso, gravoso; abrumador
burdensomeness *n* pesadez, *f*; agobio, *m*
bureau *n* buró, secreter, *m*; escritorio, *m*; (office) dirección, oficina, *f*; departamento, *m*
bureaucracy *n* burocracia, *f*
bureaucrat *n* burócrata, *mf*; *inf* mandarín, *m*
bureaucratic *a* burocrático
burgher *n* ciudadano (-na), vecino (-na)
burglar *n* ladrón de casas, escalador, *m*. **cat b.,** gato, *m*. **b. alarm,** alarma contra ladrones, *f*. **b. insurance,** seguro contra robo, *m*
burglary *n* robo nocturno de una casa, *m*
burgle *vi* robar una casa de noche. *vt* robar
burgundy *n* vino de Borgoña, borgoña, *m*
burial *n* entierro, *m*. **b.-ground,** campo santo, cementerio, *m*. **b. service,** misa de difuntos, *f*. **b. society,** sociedad de entierros, *f*
burlap *n* arpillera, *f*
burlesque *a* burlesco. *n* parodia. *f*. *vt* parodiar
burliness *n* corpulencia, *f*
burly *a* corpulento, fornido
burn *vt* quemar; calcinar; (bricks) cocer; cauterizar; (the tongue) picar; (dry up) secar; (the skin by sun or wind) tostar. *vi* quemar; arder; *fig* abrasarse (en). **b. at the stake,** *vt* quemar en la hoguera. **to b. to ashes,** reducir a cenizas. **to b. away,** consumir(se). **to b. oneself,** quemarse. **to b. the midnight oil** *Chile* cranearse **to b. up,** quemar del todo, consumir. **to b. with,** *fig* abrasarse en
burn *n* quemadura, *f*; (stream) arroyo, *m*
burnable *a* combustible
burner *n* quemador (-ra); mechero, *m*
burning *n* quema, *f*; incendio, *m*; fuego, *m*; (inflammation) inflamación, *f*; (pain) quemazón, *f*; abrasamiento, *m*. *a* en llamas; ardiente; intenso; (notorious) notorio, escandaloso; abrasador; palpitante. **b. question,** cuestión palpitante, *f*
burnish *n* bruñido, *m*; lustre, brillo, *m*, *vt* bruñir; pulir, pulimentar, dar brillo a; (weapons) acicalar. *vi* tomar lustre
burnisher *n* bruñidor, acicalador, *m*
burnishing *n* bruñido, *m*; pulimento, *m*; (of weapons) acicalado, *m*
burr *n bot* cáliz de flor con espinas, *m*; *mech* rebaba, *f*; sonido fuerte de la erre, *m*
burrow *n* madriguera, *f*, vivar, *m*; (for rabbits) conejera, *f*. *vt* amadrigar; minar
bursar *n* tesorero, *m*; becario, *m*
bursary *n* tesorería, *f*; beca, *f*
burst *n* estallido, *m*, explosión, *f*; (in a pipe) avería, *f*, (fit) acceso, *m*; transporte, *m*; (effort) esfuerzo, *m*; (expanse) extensión, *f*, panorama, *m*. **b. of applause,** salva de aplausos, *f*
burst *vi* estallar; reventar; quebrarse; romperse; (overflow) desbordar; (of seams) nacerse; derramarse (por); (into laughter) romper a; (into tears) deshacerse en. *vt* quebrar; romper; hacer estallar. **to b. upon the view,** aparecer de pronto. **to b. into,** irrumpir en; (exclamations, etc.) prorrumpir en. **to b. into tears,** romper a llorar, deshacerse en lágrimas. **to b. open,** abrir con violencia; forzar
bursting *n* estallido, *m*; quebrantamiento, *m*; (overflowing) desbordamiento, *m*
bury *vt* enterrar, sepultar; sumergir; (hide) esconder, ocultar; (forget) echar tierra a
bus *n* (regular city bus) autobús *m* (Colombia, Spain, Venezuela), camión *m* (Mexico), camioneta *f* (Guatemala), casadoro *m* (Costa Rica), chiva *f* (Colombia, Panama, informal), colectivo *m* (Argentina, Bolivia), flota *f* (Colombia, informal), góndola *f* (Chile), guagua *f* (Canary Islands, Cuba), micro *m* (Chile), ómnibus *m* (Peru), omnibús *m* (Uruguay); (interurban bus), aerobús *m* (Venezuela), autobús (Argentina, Chile, Spain, Uruguay), camión, camión de primera clase *m* (Mexico), interprovincial *m* (Peru), pullmán *m* (Mexico; (interurban jitney bus) colectivo *m* (Colombia); (minibus) micro *m* (Colombia, Peru), liebre (Chile, informal) **double-decker bus,** ómnibus de dos pisos, *m*. **to travel by bus,** ir en autobús. **bus station,** estación de autobuses, *Mexico* camionera, *f*
busby *n* birretina, gorra de húsar, *f*
bush *n* arbusto, matojo, *m*; (undergrowth) maleza, *f*; tierra virgen, *f*; *mech* manguito, *m*
bushel *n* medida de áridos, *f*, (In England 8 gallons or 36.37 liters)
bushiness *n* espesura, *f*; densidad, *f*
bushy *a* lleno de arbustos; denso; espeso; grueso; (eyebrows, etc.) poblado
busily *adv* diligentemente, solícitamente; afanosamente, laboriosamente. **He was b. occupied in . . . ,** Estaba muy ocupado en . . .
business *n* ocupación, *f*; quehaceres, *m pl*; (matter) asunto, *m*, cosa, *f*; empleo, oficio, *m*; *com* negocio(s), *m*, *pl*.; casa comercial, *f*; (trade) comercio, *m*; (clients, connection) clientela, *f*; (right) derecho, *m*; *theat* juego escénico, *m*, pantomima, *f*. **He had no b. to do that,** No tenía derecho a hacer eso. **Mind your own b.!** ¡No te metas donde no te llaman! **on b.,** por negocios. **to be in b. for oneself,** tener negocios por su propia cuenta. **to mean b.,** hacer algo en serio; estar resuelto. **to send about his b.,** mandar a paseo (a). **to set up in b.,** establecer un negocio. **b. affairs,** negocios, *m pl*. **b. agent,** agente de negocios, *m*. **b. hours,** horas de trabajo, *f pl*. **b.-like,** formal, práctico, sistemático. **b. man,** hombre de negocios, negociante, *m*
business administration *n* administración de empresas, *f*
bust *n art* busto, bulto, *m*; pecho, *m*. **b. bodice,** sostén, *m*
bustard *n* avutarda, *f*
bustle *n* actividad, animación, *f*; confusión, *f*; (of a dress) polizón, tontillo, *m*. *vi* menearse, darse prisa. *vt* dar prisa (a)
bustling *a* activo; ocupado, atareado; animado; bullicioso, ruidoso
busy *a* ocupado; atareado; activo, diligente; (of places) animado, bullicioso; (of streets) de gran circulación; (officious) entremetido. **to b. oneself,** ocuparse (en, con); dedicarse (a), entregarse (a); (interfere) entremeterse (con). **to be b.,** estar ocupado; estar atareado, tener mucho que hacer. **b.-body,** bullebulle, *mf*, entremetido (-da), chismoso (-sa), *Argentina* hurguete *mf*
busyness *n* ocupación, *f*; laboriosidad, *f*; actividad, *f*
but *conjunc prep adv* pero; sino; (only) solamente; (except) menos; excepto; (almost) casi; que no; si no; (that) que; (nevertheless) sin embargo, empero, no obstante; (without) sin, sin que; (of time recently passed) no más que, tan recientemente. *n* pero, *m*. **He cannot choose but go,** No puede hacer otra cosa que marcharse. **to do nothing but . . . ,** hacer únicamente . . . , no hacer más que . . . **but for,** a no ser por. **but yesterday,** solamente ayer. **but then (or but yet),** pero
butcher *n* carnicero, *m*. *vt* matar reses; hacer una carnicería en. **butcher's boy,** mozo del carnicero, *m*. **butcher's shop,** carnicería, *f*
butchery *n* carnicería, *f*; matanza, *f*
butler *n* mayordomo, *m*. **butler's pantry,** despensa, repostería, *f*
butt *n* (cask) tonel, *m*, pipa, *f*; (for water) barril, *m*; (of a cigarette, etc.) colilla, *f*; (of fire-arms) culata, *f*; (han-

dle) mango, cabo, *m*; (billiards) mocho, *m*; (earthwork) terrero, *m*; (*fig* object) objeto (de), *m*; (of bulls, etc.) topetada, *f*; *pl* **butts,** campo de tiro, *m*; (target) blanco, *m*. *vt* (toss) topar, acornear; (meet) tropezar (con). **to b. in,** *inf* entrometerse, meter baza; encajarse

butter *n* mantequilla, *f*, *vt* untar con mantequilla. **b.-dish,** mantequera, *f*. **b.-fingers,** torpe, *m*. **b.-knife,** cuchillo para mantequilla, *m*. **b.-milk,** suero de mantequilla, *m*. **b.-print,** molde para mantequilla, *m*. **b.-sauce,** mantequilla fundida, *f*

buttercup *n* ranúnculo, botón de oro, *m*

butterfly *n* mariposa, *f*

butterscotch *n* dulce de azúcar y mantequilla, *m*

buttocks *n pl* nalgas, posaderas, *f pl*

button *n* botón, *m*; *pl* **buttons,** botones, paje, *m*. *vt* abotonar, abrochar. *vi* abotonarse, abrocharse. **to press the b.,** apretar el botón. **b.-hook,** abotonador, *m*

buttonhole *n* ojal, *m*; flor que se lleva en el ojal, *f*. *vt sew* hacer ojales; (embroidery) hacer el festón; *inf* importunar

buttoning *n* abrochamiento, *m*

buttress *n* estribo, macho, contrafuerte, *m*; *fig* apoyo, sostén, *m*. *vt* afianzar, estribar; *fig* apoyar, sostener. **flying-b.,** arbotante, *m*

buxom *a* (of a woman) fresca, guapetona, frescachona

buxomness *n* frescura, *f*

buy *vt* comprar; obtener; (achieve) lograr; (bribe) sobornar. **to buy on credit,** comprar al fiado. **to buy back,** comprar de nuevo; redimir; (ransom) rescatar. **to buy for,** (a price) comprar por; (purpose or destination) comprar para. **to buy in,** (at an auction) comprar por cuenta del dueño. **to buy off,** librarse de uno con dinero. **to buy out,** (of a business) comprar la parte de un socio. **to buy up,** comprar todo, acaparar

buyable *a* comprable, que se puede comprar

buyer *n* comprador (-ra)

buying *n* compra, *f*. **b. back,** rescate, *m*. **b. up,** acaparamiento, *m*

buying power *n* capacidad de compra, *f*, valor adquisitivo, *m*

buzz *n* zumbido, *m*; (whisper) susurro, murmullo, *m*; (of a bell) sonido (del timbre), *m*, *vi* zumbar; susurrar

buzzer *n* zumbadar, *m*; sirena, *f*; (bell) timbre, *m*

buzzing *a* zumbador, que zumba, *n*. See **buzz**

by *prep* por; de; en; a; con; (of place) cerca de, al lado de; (according to) según, de acuerdo con; (in front of, past) delante (de); (at the latest) antes de, al más tardar; (expressing agency) por; (by means of) mediante; (through, along) por; (upon) sobre; (for) para; (under) bajo. **He will be here by Wednesday,** Estará aquí para el miércoles; (not later than) Estará aquí antes del miércoles (or el miércoles al más tardar). **How did he come by it?** ¿Cómo llegó a su poder? **He will come by train,** Vendrá en tren. **I know her by sight,** La conozco de vista. **There are three children by the first marriage,** Hay tres niños del primer matrimonio. **He goes by the name of Pérez,** Se le conoce por (or bajo) el nombre de Pérez. **six feet by eight,** seis pies por ocho. **They called her by her name,** La llamaron por su nombre. **two by two,** dos por dos. **The picture was painted by Cézanne,** El cuadro fue pintado por Cézanne. **drop by drop,** gota a gota. **by a great deal,** con mucho. **by all means,** naturalmente; de todos modos; cueste lo que cueste. **by chance,** por ventura. **by day (night),** de día (noche). **by daylight,** a la luz del día. **by doing it,** con hacerlo. **by myself,** solo; sin ayuda. **"By Appointment"** «Cita Previa». **by chance or by mischance,** por ventura o por desdicha. **an hour away by car,** a una hora de automóvil. **music by Brahms,** música de Brahms. **pull by the hair,** tirar por el pelo. **take by the hand,** llevar de la mano.

by *adv* (near) cerca; (before) delante; al lado; a un lado; aparte; (of time) pasado. **to put by,** (keep) guardar; (throw away) desechar; (accumulate) acumular; (put out of the way) arrinconar. **to pass by,** pasar; pasar delante (de). **by and by,** luego, pronto; más tarde. **by now,** ya, antes de ahora. **by the way,** entre paréntesis, a propósito; de paso; al lado del camino. **by-election,** elección parcial, *f*. **by-law,** reglamento, *m*. **by-pass,** ruta de evitación, *f*, desvío, *m*; (*mech elec*) derivación, *f*. *vi* desviarse de; *mil* rebasar. **by-product,** derivado, *m*; *chem* producto derivado, *m*; *fig* consecuencia, *f*; resultado, *m*

bye *n* (in cricket) meta, *f*. **by the bye,** a propósito, entre paréntesis

bye! *interj*. *Argentina, Chile* ¡chao!

bygone *a* pasado. **Let bygones be bygones,** Lo pasado pasado

byplay *n* pantomima, *f*, gestos, *m pl*; *theat* juego escénico, *m*, escena muda, *f*

bystander *n* espectador (-ra); *pl* **bystanders,** los circunstantes

bystreet *n* callejuela, *f*; calle pobre, *f*

byway *n* camino desviado, *m*; *fig* senda indirecta, *f*; *pl* **byways,** andurriales, *m pl*

byword *n* proverbio, *m*; objeto de burla o escándalo, *m*

Byzantine Empire, the el Imperio Bizantino, *m*

Byzantium Bizancio, *m*

C

c *n* (letter) c, *f*; *mus* do, *m*

cab *n* (horse-drawn) simón, *m*; (taxi) coche de alquiler, *m*; (of a locomotive) cabina del conductor, *f*. **cab-rank,** punto de coches, *m*

cabala *n* cábala, *f*

cabaret *n* cabaret, *m*; taberna, *f*

cabbage *n* col, berza, *f*. **red c.,** lombarda, *f*. **c. butterfly,** mariposa de col, *f*

cabin *n* cabaña, choza, *f*; *naut* camarote, *m*; (railway) garita, *f*; *aer* cabina, *f*. **c. boy,** grumete, galopín, mozo de cámara, *m*. **c. trunk,** baúl mundo, *m*

cabinet *n* (piece of furniture) vitrina, *f*; colección, exposición, *f*; *pol* gabinete, *m*; (of a radio) cónsola, *f*. **c.-maker,** ebanista, *m*. **c.-making,** ebanistería, *f*. **c. meeting,** consejo de ministros, *m*. **c. minister,** ministro, *m*

cable *n* amarra, maroma, *f*; cable, *m*; cable(grama), *m*, *vt* cablegrafiar. **electric c.,** cable eléctrico, *m*. **overhead c.,** cable aéreo, *m*

cabman *n* cochero de punto, simón, *m*

caboose *n naut* cocina, *f*

cache *n* escondite, escondrijo, *m*

cackle *vi* (of a hen) cacarear; (of a goose) graznar; (of humans) chacharear. *n* cacareo, *m*; graznido, *m*; cháchara, *f*

cacophony *n* cacofonía, *f*

cactus *n* cacto, *m*

cad *n* sinvergüenza, *m*; tipo de cuidado, *m*

cadaverous *a* cadavérico

caddish *a* mal educado, grosero

caddy *n* (for tea) cajita para té, *f*; (golf) cadi, *mf*

cadence *n* cadencia, *f*

cadet *n* hermano menor, *m*; *mil* cadete, *m*

cadge *vi* sablear. *vt* dar un sablazo (a)

cadger *n* sablista, *mf*; mendigo, *m*; (loafer) golfo, *m*

Cadiz Cádiz, *m*

cadmium *n* cadmio, *m*

café *n* café, *m*

cafeteria *n* bar automático, *m*

caffeine *n* cafeína, *f*

cage *n* (animal's, bird's) jaula, *f*; (of a lift) camarín, *m*; (for transporting miners) jaula, *f*. *vt* enjaular; encerrar

Cain, to raise armar lo de Dios es Cristo
cairn *n* montón de piedras, *m*
Cairo el Cairo, *m*
cajole *vt* lisonjear; engatusar, embromar; instar
cajolery *n* zalamerías, *f pl;* marrullería, *f,* engatusamiento, *m*
cake *n cul* pastel, *m,* torta, *f;* (of chocolate, etc.) pastilla, *f. vt* and *vi* cuajar; formar costra; (with mud) enlodar. **to sell like hot cakes,** venderse como pan bendito. **to take the c.,** llevarse la palma. **c. of soap,** pastilla de jabón, *f.* **c.-shop,** pastelería, *f*
calamine *n* calamina, *f*
calamitous *a* calamitoso, desastroso
calamity *n* calamidad, *f;* desastre, *m, Mexico also* funestidad *f*
calash *n* (carriage) calesa, carretela, *f;* (hood) capota, *f*
calcium *n* calcio, *m*
calculate *vt* calcular; adaptar. **to c. on,** contar con
calculated *a* premeditado. **to be c. to,** conducir a; ser a propósito para
calculatedly *adv* calculadamente
calculating *n* cálculo, *m, a* calculador; (of persons) interesado; (shrewd) perspicaz; atento. **c. machine,** máquina de calcular, *f,* calculador, *m*
calculation *n* cálculo, *m;* calculación, *f*
calculus *n* cálculo, *m*
calendar *n* calendario, *m;* almanaque, *m;* (university, etc.) programa, *m*
calender *n* calandria, *f, vt* calandrar, cilindrar
calf *n* becerro (-rra), ternero (-ra); (young of other animals) hijuelo, *m;* (of the leg) pantorrilla, *f;* (leather) cuero de becerro, *m;* piel, *f.* **calf's-foot,** pie de ternera, *m.* **c. love,** amor de muchachos, *m*
calibrate *vt* calibrar
calibre *n* calibre, *m*
calico *n* indiana, *f;* percal, *m.* **c.-printer,** fabricante de estampados, *m*
Californian *a* californio. *n* californio (-ia)
caliph *n* califa, *m*
calk. See **caulk**
call *n* llamada, *f;* (shout) grito, *m;* (of a bird) canto, *m;* (signal) señal, *f;* (visit) visita, *f;* (by a ship) escala, *f; mil* toque, *m;* (need) necesidad, *f;* (of religion, etc.) vocación, *f;* invitación, *f;* (demand) demanda, *f;* exigencia, *f.* **They came at my c.,** Acudieron a mi llamada. **c. to arms,** llamada, llamada a filas, *f.* **port of c.,** puerto de escala, *m.* **telephone c.,** llamada telefónica, *f.* **to pay a c.,** hacer una visita. **within c.,** al alcance de la voz. **c.-box,** cabina del teléfono, *f.* **c.-boy,** ayudante del traspunte, *m*
call *vi* llamar; gritar, dar voces; (visit) visitar, hacer una visita (a); venir; (stop) parar; (of a ship) hacer escala. *vt* llamar; (a meeting, etc.) convocar; (awaken) despertar, llamar; (say) decir; (appoint) nombrar; (at cards) declarar. **She is called Dorothy,** Se llama Dorotea. **Madrid calling!** ¡Aquí Radio Madrid! **Will you c. me at eight o'clock, please?** Haga el favor de despertarme (llamarme) a las ocho. **to c. at a port,** hacer escala en un puerto. **to c. a halt,** hacer alto. **to c. a strike,** declarar una huelga. **to c. names,** vituperar, injuriar. **to c. to account,** pedir cuentas (a). **to c. to arms,** tocar el arma; alarmar. **to c. to mind,** acordarse (de), recordar. **to c. to witness,** hacer testigo (de). **to c. back,** *vt* llamar; hacer volver; (unsay) desdecir. *vi* (return) volver; venir a buscar; ir a buscar. **I called back for the parcel,** Volví a buscar el paquete. **to c. for,** pedir a gritos; llamar; (demand) pedir; exigir; (collect a person) pasar a buscar; (parcels, etc.) ir (or venir) a recoger. **He called for help,** Pidió socorro a gritos. **to c. forth,** producir; provocar; inspirar; revelar; (bring together) reunir. **to c. in,** hacer entrar; invitar; (a specialist, etc.) llamar; (worn coin) retirar de la circulación; recoger. **to c. in question,** poner en duda. **to c. off,** (dogs, etc.) llamar; (a strike) cancelar; parar; terminar; (a person) disuadir (de); (postpone) aplazar; suspender; (refrain) desistir (de). **to c. on,** (visit) hacer una visita (a), ir a ver, visitar; (of a doctor) visitar; (a person to do something) recurrir (a); (for a speech) invitar (a hablar); (invoke) invocar. **I shall now c. on Mr. Martínez,** Doy la palabra al señor Martínez. **to c. out,** *vt* hacer salir; provocar; inspirar; (challenge) desafiar, retar. *vi* gritar. **c. the roll,** pasar lista. **to c. over,** (names) pasar lista (de). **to c. up,** hacer subir; (to the army) llamar a filas (a); (telephone) llamar por teléfono (a); (memories) evocar. **to c. upon.** See **to c. on**
caller *n* visita, *f*
calligraphist *n* calígrafo, *m*
calligraphy *n* caligrafía, *f*
calling *n* llamamiento, *m;* (occupation) profesión, *f;* empleo, *m;* vocación, *f;* (of a meeting) convocación, *f*
callipers *n pl* compás de puntas, pie de rey, *m*
callisthenics *n pl* calistenia, *f*
callosity *n* callosidad, *f*
callous *a* (of skin) calloso; *fig* insensible, duro, inhumano
callously *adv* sin piedad
callousness *n* falta de piedad, inhumanidad, dureza, *f*
callow *a* (of birds) implume; (inexperienced) bisoño, inexperto, novato
callus *n* callo, *m*
calm *n* calma, *f;* paz, tranquilidad, *f;* sosiego, *m;* serenidad, *f. a* (of the sea) en calma; tranquilo; sereno; sosegado. *vt* calmar; tranquilizar; apaciguar. *vi* calmarse; tranquilizarse; sosegarse. **dead c.,** calma chicha, *f*
calming *a* calmante
calmly *adv* tranquilamente, sosegadamente; con calma
calmness *n* calma, tranquilidad, *f;* ecuanimidad, serenidad, *f*
caloric *a* calórico
calorie *n* caloría, *f*
calumniation *n* calumnia, *f*
calumniator *n* calumniador (-ra)
calumny *n* calumnia, *f*
calvary *n* calvario, *m*
calve *vi* (of a cow, etc.) parir
Calvinism *n* calvinismo, *m*
Calvinist *n* calvinista, *mf*
Calvinistic *a* calvinista
calyx *n* cáliz, *m*
cam *n mech* leva, *f.* **camshaft,** árbol de levas, *m*
camaraderie *n* compañerismo, *m*
camber *n* comba(dura), *f*
cambric *n* batista, *f*
camel *n* camello (-lla). **c.-driver,** camellero, *m.* **camel's hair,** pelo de camello, *m*
camellia *n* camelia, *f*
cameo *n* camafeo, *m*
camera *n phot* máquina fotográfica, *f.* **folding c.,** máquina fotográfica plegable, *f.* **in c.,** a puerta cerrada. **c. obscura,** cámara obscura, *f*
Cameroons, the el Camerón, los Camerones, *m*
camouflage *n* camuflaje, *m, vt* camuflar
camp *n* campamento, *m;* campo, *m; fig* vida de cuartel, *f;* (for school children, etc.) colonia, *f;* (party) partido, *m. vi* acampar; vivir en tiendas de campaña. **to break c.,** levantar el campo. **c.-bed,** cama de campaña, *f.* **c.-stool,** silla de campaña, *f*
campaign *n* campaña, *f. vi* hacer una campaña
campaigner *n* veterano, *m;* propagandista, *mf*
campaigning *n* campañas, *f pl*
camphor *n* alcanfor, *m*
camphorated *a* alcanforado
campus *n* recinto, *m* (Puerto Rico), ciudad universitaria, *f*
can *v auxil* poder; (know how to) saber. **You can go to the village when you like,** Puedes ir al pueblo cuando quieras. **I cannot allow that,** No puedo permitir eso. **What can they mean?** ¿Qué quieren decir? **If only things could have been different!** ¡Si solamente las cosas hubiesen sido distintas! **Can you**

come to dinner on Saturday? ¿Puede Vd. venir a cenar el sábado? **I can come later if you like,** Puedo (or Podría) venir más tarde si Vd. quiere. **Mary can** (knows how to) **play the piano,** María sabe tocar el piano **You can't eat your cake and have it too.** No hay rosa sin espinas
can *n* lata, *f*; (for carrying sandwiches, etc.) fiambrera, *f*. *vt* conservar en latas. **canopener,** abrelatas, *m*
Canada el Canadá, *m*
Canadian *a* canadiense. *n* canadiense, *mf*
canaille *n* gentualla, gentuza, *f*
canal *n* canal, *m*
canalization *n* canalización, *f*
canalize *vt* canalizar
canary *n* canario (-ia); color de canario, *m*; vino de Canarias, *m*. **roller c.,** canario de raza flauta, *m*. **c.-seed,** alpiste, *m*
Canary Islands, the las Islas Canarias, *m*
cancel *vt* cancelar; revocar; borrar; anular. **to c. out,** *math* anular
cancellation *n* cancelación, *f*; revocación, *f*; anulación, *f*
cancer *n med* cáncer, *m*; *ast* Cáncer, *m*
cancerous *a* canceroso. **to become c.,** cancerarse
candelabrum *n* candelabro, *m*
candescent *a* candente
candid *a* franco; sincero. **If I am to be c.,** Si he de decir la verdad, Si he de ser franco
candidate *n* candidato (-ta); aspirante, *m*
candidature *n* candidatura, *f*
candidly *adv* francamente; sinceramente
candidness *n* franqueza, *f*; sinceridad, *f*
candied *a* (of peel, etc.) almibarado, garapiñado
candle *n* vela, candela, *f*. **wax c.,** cirio, *m*. **You cannot hold a c. to him,** No llegas a la suela de su zapato, Ni llegas a sus pies, Ni le llegas a los pies. **The game is not worth the c.,** La cosa no vale la pena. **to burn the c. at both ends,** consumir la vida. **c.-grease,** sebo, *m*. **c.-light,** luz de las velas, *f*; luz artificial, *f*. **c.-maker,** candelero, *m*. **c.-power,** *elec* potencia luminosa, bujía, *f*. **c.-snuffer,** apagavelas, matacandelas, *m*
Candlemas *n* candelaria, *f*
candlestick *n* candelero, *m*, palmatoria, *f*; (processional) cirial, *m*
candor *n* franqueza, *f*; sinceridad, *f*; candor, *m*
candy *n* caramelo, bombón, *m*, *vt* garapiñar, almibarar
candytuft *n* carraspique, *m*
cane *n bot* caña, *f*; (for chair seats, etc.) rejilla, *f*; (walking stick) bastón, *m*; (for punishment) vara, *f*. *vt* apalear, pegar. **sugar-c.,** caña de azúcar, *f*. **c.-break,** cañaveral, *m*. **c. chair,** sillón de mimbres, *m*. **c.-sugar,** azúcar de caña, *m*. **c.-syrup,** miel de caña, *f*
canine *a* canino. *n* (tooth) diente canino, *m*
caning *n* paliza, *f*
canister *n* bote, *m*, cajita, *f*
canker *n* úlcera, *f*; (in trees) cancro, *m*; *fig* cáncer, *m*, *vt* roer; *fig* corromper
canned *a* en lata
cannibal *n* caníbal, *mf* antropófago (-ga). *a* caníbal, antropófago
cannibalism *n* canibalismo, *m*, antropofagía, *f*
canning *n* conservación en latas, *f*. **c. factory,** fábrica de conservas alimenticias, *f*
cannon *n* (fire-arm) cañón, *m*; (billiards) carambola, *f*, *vi* carambolear. **to c. into,** chocar con. **c.-ball,** bala de cañón, *f*. **c.-shot,** cañonazo, *m*
cannonade *n* cañoneo, *m*
canny *a* cuerdo, sagaz
canoe *n* canoa, *f*; piragua, *f*, *vi* ir en canoa
canoeist *n* canoero (-ra)
canon *n* (*ecc mus print*) canón, *m*; (dignitary) canónigo, *m*; (criterion) criterio, *m*. **c. law,** derecho canónico, *m*
canonical *a* canónico
canonization *n* canonización, *f*
canonize *vt* canonizar
canopy *n* dosel, toldo, *m*; palio, *m*; *fig* capa, bóveda, *f*. **the c. of heaven,** la capa (or bóveda) del cielo
cant *vt* inclinar; ladear. *vi* inclinarse; (be a hypocrite) camandulear. *n* (slope) inclinación, *f*, sesgo, desplomo, *m*; (hypocrisy) gazmoñería, *f*
Cantabrian *a* cantábrico
cantankerous *a* irritable, intratable, malhumorado, *Argentina* cabrero
cantankerousness *n* mal humor, *m*, irritabilidad, *f*
cantata *n* cantata, *f*
canteen *n* cantina, *f*; (water bottle) cantimplora, *f*. **c. of cutlery,** juego de cubiertos, *m*
canter *n* medio galope, *m*, *vi* andar a galope corto
canticle *n* cántico, *m*
canting *a* hipócrita
canto *n* canto, *m*
canton *n* (province and *her*) cantón, *m*, *vt* (of soldiers) acantonar
cantonment *n* acantonamiento, cantón, *m*
cantor *n ecc* chantre, *m*
canvas *n* lona, *f*; *art* lienzo, *m*; *naut* vela, *f*, paño, *m*. **under c.,** en tiendas de campaña; (of ships) a toda vela
canvass *vt* (votes, etc.) solicitar
canvasser *n* solicitador (-ra) (de votos, etc.)
canvassing *n* solicitación (de votos, etc.), *f*
canyon *n* cañón, *m*
canzonet *n* chanzoneta, *f*
cap *n* gorra, *f*; (with a peak) montera, *f*; (type of military headgear with brim at front) quépis, *m*; (cardinal's) birrete, *m*; *univ* bonete, *m*; (pointed) caperuza, *f*; (woman's old-fashioned) cofia, *f*; (jester's) gorro de bufón, *m*; (on a bottle) cápsula, tapa, *f*. *vt univ* conferir el grado (a). **cap and bells,** gorro de bufón, *m*. **cap and gown,** birrete y muceta, toga y birrete, toga y bonete. **to throw one's cap over the windmill,** echar la capa al toro. **to cap it all,** ser el colmo
capability *n* capacidad, *f*; aptitud, *f*
capable *a* capaz; competente; (of improvement) susceptible; (full of initiative) emprendedor
capably *adv* competentemente
capacious *a* espacioso; grande; extenso
capaciousness *n* capacidad, *f*; amplitud, *f*
capacitate *vt* capacitar
capacity *n* capacidad, *f*; calidad, *f*; aptitud, *f*. **in one's c. as,** en calidad de. **seating c.,** número de asientos, *m*; (in aircraft) número de plazas, *m*
caparison *n* caparazón, *m*
cape *n* (cloak) capa, *f*; (short) capotillo, *m*, capeta, *f*; (fur) cuello, *m*; *geog* cabo, promontorio, *m*. **c. coat,** capote, *m*
Cape Horn Cabo de Hornos, *m*
caper *vi* (gambol) brincar, saltar; cabriolar, corcovear; (play) juguetear. *n* travesura, *f*; zapateta, *f*; cabriola, *f*; (whim) capricho, *m*; *bot* alcaparra, *f*. **to c. about,** dar saltos, brincar; juguetear
capillarity *n* capilaridad, *f*
capillary *a* capilar. *n* vaso capilar, *m*
capital *a* capital; mortal; de muerte; de vida; principal; (of letters) mayúscula; (very good) excelente; (of the capital city) *Lat. Am.* capitalino *n* (city) capital, *f*; (letter) (letra) mayúscula, *f*; *com* capital, *m*; *arch* capitel, chapitel, *m*. **floating c.,** capital fluctuante, *m*. **idle c.,** fondos inactivos, *m pl*. **c. punishment,** pena de muerte, pena capital, pena de la vida, *f*. **C.!** ¡Estupendo! ¡Excelente! **to make c. out of,** aprovecharse de, sacar ventaja de
capitalism *n* capitalismo, *m*
capitalist *n* capitalista, *mf*
capitalistic *a* capitalista
capitalization *n* capitalización, *f*
capitalize *vt* capitalizar
capitally *adv* estupendamente
capitation *n* capitación, *f*
Capitol *n* Capitolio, *m*
capitulate *vi* capitular
capitulation *n* capitulación, *f*

capon *n* capón, *m*
caprice *n* capricho, *m*
capricious *a* caprichoso
capriciousness *n* carácter inconstante, *m*; lo caprichoso
Capricorn *n* Capricornio, *m*
capsize *vt naut* hacer zozobrar; volcar. *vi naut* zozobrar; volcarse
capsizing *n naut* zozobra, *f*; vuelco, *m*
capsule *n* (*bot med chem zool*) cápsula, *f*
captain *n* (*mil nav aer* and *sport*) capitán, *m*, *vt* capitanear. **to c. a team,** ser el capitán de un equipo. **group c.,** *aer* capitán de aviación, *m*
captaincy *n* capitanía, *f*
caption *n* (arrest) arresto, *m*; (heading) encabezamiento, título, pie, *m*; (cinema) subtítulo, *m*
captious *a* capcioso, caviloso
captivate *vt* cautivar, seducir
captivating *a* encantador, seductor
captive *a* cautivo, *n* cautivo (-va), prisionero (-ra), preso (-sa). **c. balloon,** globo cautivo, globo de observación, *m*
captivity *n* cautiverio, *m*
captor *n* el, *m*, (*f*, la) que hace prisionero (-ra)
capture *n* captura, *f*; presa, toma, *f*; *law* captura, *f*. *vt* prender, capturar; tomar
car *n* (chariot) carro, *m*; (tram) tranvía, *m*; (motor) automóvil, coche, *Lat. Am.* carro *m*; (on a train) coche vagón, *m*. **sleeping car,** coche camas, *m*. **car park,** parque de automóviles, *m*
carabineer *n* carabinero, *m*
carafe *n* garrafa, *f*
caramel *n* caramelo, *m*; azúcar quemado, *m*
carapace *n* carapacho, *m*
carat *n* quilate, *m*
caravan *n* caravana, *f*; coche de gitanos, *m*; coche habitación, *m*
caraway *n* alcaravea, *f*
carbarn *n* encierro, *m* (Mexico), cochera, cochera de tranvías, *f*, cobertizo, cobertizo para tranvías, *m*
carbide *n* carburo, *m*
carbine *n* carabina, *f*
carbohydrate *n* hidrato de carbono, *m*
carbolic *a* carbólico. **c. acid,** ácido fénico, *m*
carbon *n* carbono, *m*. **c. copy,** copia en papel carbón, *f*. **c. dioxide,** anhídrido carbónico, *m*. **c. monoxide,** óxide de carbono, *m*. **c. paper,** papel carbón, papel de calcar, *m*
carbonate *n* carbonato, *m*
carbonated *a* (beverage) carbónico (formal), con gas (informal)
carbonic *a* carbónico
carbonization *n* carbonización, *f*
carbonize *vt* carbonizar
carboy *n* damajuana, garrafa, *f*
carbuncle *n med* carbunco, *m*; (stone) carbúnculo, *m*
carburetor *n* carburador, *m*
carcass *n* (animal) res muerta, *f*; (corpse) cadáver, *m*; (body) cuerpo, *m*; (of a ship) casco, *m*
carcinoma *n* carcinoma, *m*
card *n* (playing) naipe, *m*; (pasteboard) cartulina, *f*; (visiting, postal, etc.) tarjeta, *f*; (index) ficha, *f*; (for wool, etc.) carda, *f*. *vt* (wool, etc.) cardar. **I still have a c. up my sleeve,** Me queda todavía un recurso. **to lay one's cards on the table,** poner las cartas boca arriba. **to play one's cards well,** *fig* jugar el lance. **admission c.,** billete de entrada, *m*. **post c.,** tarjeta postal, *f*. **visiting c.,** tarjeta de visita, *f*. **c.-case,** tarjetero, *m*. **c.-index,** fichero, *m*. *vt* poner en el fichero. **c.-sharper,** fullero, *m*. **c.-table,** mesa de juego, *f*. **c. trick,** juego de manos con cartas, *m*
cardboard *n* cartón, *m*, *a* de cartón
cardiac *a* cardíaco
cardigan *n* rebeca, chaqueta de punto, *f*
cardinal *a* cardinal. *n* cardenal, *m*. **c. number,** número cardinal, *m*. **c. points,** puntos cardinales, *m pl*
cardinalate *n* cardenalato, *m*
carding *n* (of wool, etc.) cardadura, *f*. **c. machine,** carda mecánica, *f*
cardiogram *n* cardiograma, *m*
care *n* cuidado, *m*; atención, *f*; inquietud, ansia, *f*; (charge) cargo, *m*. *vi* preocuparse; tener interés; (suffer) sufrir. **I don't c.,** Me es igual; No me importa. **I don't c. a straw,** No se me da un bledo. **They don't c. for eggs,** No les gustan los huevos. **We don't c. what his opinion is,** Su opinión nos tiene sin cuidado (or no nos importa). **to c. for,** cuidar, mirar por; (love) querer (a); (like) gustar. **Take c.!** ¡Cuidado! ¡Ojo! **Take c. not to spoil it!** ¡Ten cuidado que no lo estropees! **Would you c. to . . . ?** ¿Le gustaría . . . ? ¿Tendría inconveniente en . . . ? **c. of,** (on a letter, etc.) en casa de. **c.-free,** *a* libre de cuidados
careen *vt* carenar. *vi* dar a la banda
careening *n* carena, *f*
career *n* carrera, *f*; curso, *m*. *vi* correr a carrera tendida; galopar
careful *a* cuidadoso (de); atento (a); prudente. **Careful!, Be careful!** ¡Cuidado! **to be c.,** tener cuidado
carefully *adv* con cuidado. **drive c.,** manejar con cuidado; cuidadosamente; prudentemente; atentamente
carefulness *n* cuidado, *m*; atención, *f*; prudencia, *f*
careless *a* sin cuidado; indiferente (a); insensible (a); negligente; (of mistakes, etc.) de (or por) negligencia
carelessly *adv* indiferentemente; negligentemente; descuidadamente
carelessness *n* indiferencia, *f*; negligencia, *f*; descuido, *m*; omisión, *f*
caress *n* caricia, *f*, *vt* acariciar
caressing *a* acariciador
caretaker *n* (of museums, etc.) guardián (-ana); (of flats, etc.) portero (-ra)
careworn *a* devorado de inquietud, ansioso
cargo *n* cargamento, *m*, carga, *f*. **c.-boat,** barco de carga, *m*
Caribbean *a* caribe
Caribbean Sea, the el Mar Caribe, *m*
caricature *n* caricatura, *f*, *vt* caricaturizar
caricaturist *n* caricaturista, *mf*
caries *n* caries, *f*
carious *a* cariado. **to become c.,** cariarse
Carmelite *a* carmelita. *n* carmelita, *mf*
carmine *n* carmín, *m*, *a* de carmín
carnage *n* carnicería, *f*
carnal *a* carnal; sensual
carnality *n* carnalidad, *f*
carnally *adv* carnalmente
carnation *n* clavel, *m*
carnival *n* carnaval, *m*, *a* de carnaval, carnavalesco
carnivore *n* carnívoro, *m*
carnivorous *a* carnívoro
carol *n* villancico, *m*; canto, *m*. *vi* cantar alegremente; (of birds) trinar, gorjear
Carolingian *a* carolingio
carotid *n* carótida, *f*
carousal *n* borrachera, *f*; holgorio, *m*, jarana, *f*
carouse *vi* emborracharse. *n* borrachera, orgía, *f*
carp *n* carpa, *f*, *vi* criticar, censurar
Carpathian Mountains, the los Montes Carpotes, *m*
carpel *n* carpelo, *m*
carpenter *n* carpintero, *m*, *vi* carpintear. **carpenter's bench,** banco de carpintero, *m*. **carpenter's shop,** carpintería, *f*
carpentry *n* carpintería, *f*
carpet *n* alfombra, *f*; *fig* tapete, *m*. *vt* cubrir de una alfombra, alfombrar; entapizar. **to be on the c.,** estar sobre el tapete. **c.-beater,** sacudidor de alfombras, *m*. **c. merchant,** alfombrista, *m*. **c. slippers,** zapatillas de fieltro, *f pl*. **c.-sweeper,** aspirador de polvo, *m*
carpeting *n* alfombrado, *m*
carping *a* capcioso, criticón
carriage *n* (carrying) transporte, porte, *m*; (deport-

ment) porte, continente, *m*, presencia, *f*; (vehicle) carruaje, *m*; carroza, *f*; coche, *m*; (railway) departamento, *m*; (chassis) chasis, bastidor, *m*; (of a typewriter, etc.) carro, *m*. **hackney c.,** coche de plaza, *m*. **c. and pair,** carroza de dos caballos, *f*. **c. door,** portezuela, *f*. **c.-forward,** porte debido. **c.-free,** franco de porte. **c.-paid,** porte pagado

carrier *n* el, *m*, (*f*, la) que lleva; portador (-ra); *com* mensajero, *m*; (on a car, bicycle) portaequipajes, *m*; (of a disease) vector, *m*; (aircraft) porta-aviones, *m*. **c.-pigeon,** paloma mensajera, *f*

carrion *n* carroña, *f*. **c.-crow,** chova, *f*

carrot *n* zanahoria, *f*

carry *vt* llevar; transportar; traer; conducir; (*mil* of arms) portar; (have with one) tener consigo; (an enemy position) tomar, ganar; (a motion) aprobar; (oneself) portarse; (one's point, etc.) ganar; (in the mind) retener; (conviction) convencer; (involve) implicar; (influence) influir; (send) despachar, enviar; (contain) incluir, comprender. *vi* (of the voice, etc.) alcanzar, llegar. **The noise of the guns carried a long way,** El ruido de los cañones se oía desde muy lejos. **to fetch and c.,** traer y llevar. **to c. all before one,** vencer todos los obstáculos. **to c. into effect,** poner en efecto. **to c. one's audience with one,** captar (or cautivar) su auditorio. **to c. oneself well,** tener buena presencia. **to c. on one's back,** llevar a cuestas. **to c. the day,** quedar victorioso, quedar señor del campo. **to c. weight,** *fig* ser de peso. **to c. along,** llevar; (drag) arrastrar; conducir; acarrear. **to c. away,** llevar; llevarse, llevar consigo; (kidnap) robar, secuestrar; (of emotions) dominar; (by enthusiasm) entusiasmar; (inspire) inspirar. **to c. forward,** llevar a cabo; avanzar; fomentar; (bookkeeping) pasar a cuenta nueva. **to c. off,** (things) llevarse; (persons) llevar consigo (a); (abduct or steal) robar; (kill) matar; (a prize) ganar. **to c. (a thing) off well,** llevar la mejor parte, salir vencedor. **to c. on,** *vt* (a discussion, etc.) seguir, continuar. **c. on a conversation,** llevar una conversación; mantener; (a business, etc.) tener; dirigir. *vi* ir tirando; seguir trabajando. **to c. out,** realizar, llevar a cabo; hacer, ejecutar, efectuar; (a promise) cumplir. **to c. through,** llevar a cabo

carrying *n* transporte, *m*; (of a motion) adopción, *f*

cart *n* carro, *m*. *vt* acarrear; llevar. **c.-horse,** caballo de tiro, *m*. **c.-load,** carretada, *f*, carro, *m*. **c.-wheel,** rueda de carro, *f*; (somersault) voltereta, *f*

cartage *n* carretaje, transporte, porte, *m*

carte blanche *n* carta blanca, *f*

cartel *n* cartel, *m*

carter *n* carretero, *m*

Cartesian *a* cartesiano. *n* cartesiano (-na)

Carthage Cartago, *m*

Carthaginian *a* cartaginés. *n* cartaginés (-esa)

car thief *Lat. Am.* autero (-ra) *mf*

cartilage *n* cartílago, *m*

cartilaginous *a* cartilaginoso

cartographer *n* cartógrafo, *m*

cartography *n* cartografía, *f*

cartomancy *n* cartomancia, *f*

carton *n* caja de cartón, *f*

cartoon *n* (design for tapestry, etc.) cartón, *m*; caricatura, *f*

cartoonist *n* caricaturista, *mf*

cartridge *n* cartucho, *m*. **blank c.,** cartucho sin bala, *m*. **c.-belt,** cartuchera, canana, *f*. **c.-case,** cápsula de proyectil, *f*

carve *vt* tallar, labrar; grabar; cortar; (meat, etc.) trinchar; (a career, etc.) hacer, forjarse

carver *n* tallador, *m*; (at table) trinchador, *m*; (implement) trinchante, *m*

carving *n* talla, *f*; (design) tallado, *m*. **c.-knife,** trinchante, *m*

cascade *n* cascada, catarata, *f*, salto de agua, *m*; *fig* chorro, *m*. *vi* chorrear

case *n* caso, *m*; *law* proceso, *m*, causa, *f*; *gram* caso, *m*; *med* caso, *m*; enfermo (-ma); (box) caja, *f*; (for scissors, etc.) vaina, *f*; (for a cushion, etc.) funda, *f*; (for jewels, manicure implements, etc.) estuche, *m*; (of a piano, watch and *print*) caja, *f*; (for documents) carpeta, *f*; (glass) vitrina, *f*; (for a book) sobrecubierta, *f*; (dressing) neceser, *m*. *vt* cubrir; forrar; resguardar. **packing-c.,** caja de embalaje, *f*. **c. of goods,** caja de mercancías, *f*; bulto, *m*. **in any c.,** en todo caso; venga lo que venga. **in c.,** por si acaso. **in c. of emergency,** en caso de urgencia. **in such a c.,** en tal caso. **in the c. of,** en el caso de; respecto a. **lower c.,** *print* caja baja, *f*. **upper c.,** *print* caja alta, *f*. **c.-hardened,** (of iron) templado; *fig* endurecido, indiferente

case closed! ¡asunto concluido!

casement window *n* ventana, *f*

cash *n* efectivo, metálico, *m*; dinero contante, *m*; *inf* dinero, *m*; *com* caja, *f*. *vt* cobrar; pagar, hacer efectivo. **hard or ready c.,** dinero contante, *m*. **to pay c.,** pagar al contado. **c. on delivery,** (C.O.D.) contra reembolso. **c. on hand,** efectivo en caja, *m*. **c.-book,** libro de caja, *m*. **c.-box,** caja, *f*. **c.-desk,** caja, *f*. **c. down,** pago al contado, *m*. **c. prize,** premio en metálico, *m*. **c.-register,** caja registradora, *f*

cashew *n* anacardo, *m*

cashier *n* cajero (-ra). *vt* degradar. **cashier's desk,** caja, *f*

cash machine *n* cajero automático, *m*

cashmere *n* cachemira, *f*

casino *n* casino, *m*

cask *n* pipa, barrica, *f*, tonel, *m*; cuba, *f*

casket *n* cajita, arquilla, *f*, cofrecito, *m*

Caspian Sea, the el (Mar) Caspio, *m*

casserole *n* cacerola, *f*

cassock *n* sotana, *f*

cast *vt* arrojar, tirar; (in fishing, the anchor, dice, darts, lots, a net, glances, blame, etc.) echar; (skin) mudar; (lose) perder; (a shadow, etc.) proyectar; (a vote) dar; (mold) vaciar; (accounts) echar, calcular; (a horoscope) hacer; (the parts in a play) repartir; (an actor for a part) dar el papel de; (metals) colar, fundir. **the shadow c. by the wall,** la sombra proyectada por el muro. **to c. anchor,** echar anclas, anclar. **to c. in one's lot with,** compartir la suerte de. **to c. something in a person's teeth,** echar en cara (a). **to c. lots,** echar suertes. **to c. about,** meditar, considerar; imaginar; (devise) inventar. **to c. aside,** desechar; poner a un lado; abandonar. **to c. away,** tirar lejos; desechar; (money) derrochar, malgastar. **to be c. away,** *naut* naufragar. **to c. down,** (overthrow) derribar, destruir; (eyes) bajar; (depress) desanimar, deprimir; (humiliate) humillar. **to be c. down,** estar deprimido. **c. iron,** *n* hierro colado, hierro fundido, *m*. **c.-iron,** *a* de hierro colado; *fig* inflexible. **to c. off,** quitarse; desechar; (a wife) repudiar; (desert) abandonar; (free oneself) librarse (de). **c.-off,** *n* desecho, *m*. **c.-off clothing,** ropa de desecho, *f*. **to c. out,** echar fuera; hacer salir; excluir. **to c. up,** echar; vomitar; (a sum) sumar; (something at a person) reprochar

cast *n* (of dice, fishing-line) echada, *f*; (of a net) redada, *f*; (worm) molde, *m*; (of a play) reparto, *Lat. Am.* elenco *m*; (of mind) inclinación, *f*; (in the eye) defecto en la mirada, *m*; (of colour) matiz, tinte, *m*. **c. of features,** facciones, *f pl*, fisonomía, *f*. **plaster c.,** vaciado, *m*

castanets *n pl* castañuelas, *f pl*

castaway *n* náufrago (-ga); *fig* perdido (-da)

caste *n* casta, *f*; clase social, *f*. **to lose c.,** desprestigiarse

castigate *vt* castigar

Castile Castilla, *f*

Castilian *a* castellano. *n* castellano (-na); (language) castellano, *m*

casting *n* lanzamiento, *m*; (of metals) fundición, colada, *f*; obra de fundición, *f*. **c.-net,** esparavel, *m*. **c.-vote,** voto de calidad, *m*

castle *n* castillo, *m*; (in chess) torre, *f*, roque, *m*. **to build castles in Spain,** hacer castillos en el aire

castor *n zool* castor, *m*; (for sugar) azucarero, *m*; (cruet)

convoy, *m*; (on chairs, etc.) ruedecilla, roldana, *f*. **c.-oil,** aceite de ricino, *m*. **c.-sugar,** azúcar en polvo, *m*
castrate *vt* castrar, capar
castration *n* castración, capadura, *f*
casual *a* fortuito, accidental; ligero, superficial; *inf* despreocupado. **c. worker,** jornalero, *m*
casually *adv* por casualidad; de paso; negligentemente
casualness *n inf* negligencia, despreocupación, *f*
casualty *n* víctima, *f*; herido, *m*; *mil* baja, *f*; *pl* **casualties,** heridos, *m pl*; muertos, *m pl*. **c.-list,** lista de víctimas, *f*; *mil* lista de bajas, *f*
casuist *n* casuista, *mf*
casuistry *n* casuística, *f*
cat *n* gato (-ta). **She is an old cat,** Ella es una vieja chismosa. **to be like a cat on hot bricks,** estar como en brasas, **to let the cat out of the bag,** tirar de la manta. **to lead a cat-and-dog life,** vivir como perros y gatos. **cat's-cradle,** (game) cunas, *f pl*. **cat's paw,** (person) hombre de paja, *m*; *naut* bocanada de viento, *f*. **cat o' nine tails,** gato de siete colas, *m*, penca, *f*. **catwhisker,** *rad* detector, *m*
cataclysm *n* cataclismo, *m*
catacombs *n pl* catacumbas, *f pl*
catafalque *n* catafalco, *m*
Catalan *a* catalán (-ana). *n* catalán; (language) catalán, *m*
catalepsy *n* catalepsia, *f*
catalogue *n* catálogo, *m*, *vt* catalogar
catalysis *n* catálisis, *f*
cat-and-mouse *n* el juego de ratón, *m*
catapult *n mil* catapulta, *f*; *aer* catapulta (para lanzar aviones), *f*; (toy) tirador de gomas, *m*. *vt* tirar con una catapulta (or con un tirador de gomas); (throw) lanzar
cataract *n* catarata, cascada, *f*, salto de agua, *m*; (of the eye) catarata, *f*
catarrh *n* catarro, *m*; constipado, resfriado, *m*
catastrophe *n* catástrofe, *f*, desastre, *m*, *Mexico also* funestidad; (in drama) desenlace, *m*
catastrophic *a* catastrófico
catcall *n* silbido, *m*
catch *vt* coger; agarrar, asir; (capture) prender, haber; (a disease) contraer; (habit) tomar; (on a hook, etc.) enganchar; (surprise) sorprender; (understand) comprender; (hear) oír; (with blows, etc.) dar. *vi* (of a lock) encajarse; (become entangled) engancharse; (of a fire) encenderse. **to c. a glimpse of,** ver por un instante (a); alcanzar a ver, entrever. **to c. at,** asir; agarrarse (a); echar mano de; procurar asir; alargar la mano hacia; (an idea, etc.) adoptar con entusiasmo. **to c. on,** (be popular) tener éxito; (understand) comprender. **to c. out,** coger en el acto; coger en un error; *sport* coger. **to c. up,** coger; interrumpir. **to c. up with,** (a person) alcanzar; (news) ponerse al corriente de
catch *n* presa, *f*; (of fish) redada, pesca, *f*; (of a window, etc.) cerradura, *f*; (latch) pestillo, *m*; (trick) trampa, *f*; *mus* canon, *m*. **a good c.,** (matrimonial) un buen partido. **to have a c. in one's voice,** hablar con voz entrecortada. **c.-as-c.-can,** lucha libre, *f*
catching *a* contagioso
catchment *n* desagüe, *m*
catchword *n* reclamo, *m*; (theater cue) pie, apunte, *m*; (slogan) mote, *m*
catchy *a* atractivo. **It's a c. tune,** Es una canción que se pega
catechism *n* catequismo, *m*
categorical *a* categórico
category *n* categoría, *f*
cater *vi* proveer, abastecer. **to c. for all tastes,** atender a todos los gustos
caterer *n* despensero (-ra)
catering *n* provisión, *f*
caterpillar *n* oruga, *Argentina* isoca *f*. **c. tractor,** tractor de orugas, *m*
caterwaul *vi* (of a cat) maullar
caterwauler *n* (violinist, etc.) rascatripas, *m*
caterwauling *n* maullidos, *m pl*; música ratonera, *f*
catfish *n* siluro, *m*
catgut *n surg* catgut, *m*; *mus* cuerda, *f*
catharsis *n med* purga, *f*; *fig* catarsis, *f*
cathedral *n* catedral, *f*
Catherine wheel *n arch* rosa, *f*; (firework) rueda de Santa Catalina, *f*; (somersault) tumba, *f*
catheter *n* catéter, *m*
cathode *n* cátodo, *m*. **c. rays,** rayos catódicos, *m pl*. **c. ray tube,** tubo de rayos catódicos, *m*
cathodic *a* catódico
catholic *a* católico
Catholicism *n* catolicismo, *m*
catkin *n* amento, *m*. **male c.,** amento macho, *m*
catlike *a* de gato; gatuno
cattle *n* ganado vacuno, *m*; ganado, *m*; animales, *m pl*. **c.-dealer,** ganadero, *m*. **c.-lifter,** hurtador de ganado, *m*. **c.-pen,** corral, *m*. **c.-raiser,** criador de ganado, *m*. **c.-raising,** ganadería, *f*. **c.-ranch,** hacienda de ganado, estancia, *Argentina* cabaña *f*. **c.-show,** exposición de ganado, *f*. **c.-truck,** vagón de ferrocarril para ganado, *m*
cattle rustler *n* abigeo, cuatrero, ladrón de ganado, *m*
cattle rustling *n* abigeato, *m*
catty *a* gatuno; malicioso, chismoso
Caucasian *a* and *n* caucáseo (-ea)
cauldron *n* caldera, *f*
cauliflower *n* coliflor, *f*
caulk *vt* calafatear
caulker *n* calafate, *m*
caulking *n* calafateado, *m*. **c. iron,** calador, *m*
causality *n* causalidad, *f*
causative *a* causante
cause *n* causa, *f*; (reason) motivo, *m*, razón, *f*; (lawsuit) proceso, *m*. *vt* causar; ocasionar, suscitar; (oblige) hacer, obligar (a). **final c.,** *phil* causa final, *f*. **to have good c. for,** tener buen motivo para
causeway *n* dique, *m*; acera, *f*
caustic *a* cáustico; *fig* mordaz. **c. soda,** sosa cáustica, *f*
caustically *adv* mordazmente, con sarcasmo
causticity *n* causticidad, *f*
cauterization *n* cauterización, *f*
cauterize *vt* cauterizar
cautery *n* cauterio, *m*
caution *n* prudencia, cautela, *f*; (warning) amonestación, *f*; aviso, *m*. *vt* amonestar. **to proceed with c.,** ir con prudencia; ir despacio
"Caution" (road sign) «Precaución»
cautionary *a* (of tales) de escarmiento
cautious *a* cauteloso, cauto; prudente, circunspecto
cautiously *adv* cautamente; prudentemente. **to go c.,** *inf* ir con pies de plomo
cavalcade *n* cabalgata, *f*
cavalier *n* jinete, *m*; caballero, *m*; galán, *m*, *a* arrogante, altanero
cavalry *n* caballería, *f*. **c.-man,** jinete, soldado de a caballo, *m*
cave *n* cueva, caverna, *f*. **to c. in,** hundirse; desplomarse; *fig* rendirse. **c.-man,** hombre cavernícola, *m*
cavern *n* caverna, *f*
cavernous *a* cavernoso
caviar *n* caviar, *m*
cavil *vi* cavilar
cavity *n* cavidad, *f*; hoyo, *m*; hueco, *m*; (in a lung) caverna, *f*
cavy *n* cobayo (-ya), conejillo (-lla) de las Indias
caw *n* graznido, *m*, *vi* graznar, grajear
cawing *n* graznidos, *m pl*
cayenne *n* pimentón, *m*
cease *vi* cesar (de), dejar de; parar. *vt* cesar de; parar de; (payments, etc.) suspender; discontinuar. **C. fire!** ¡Cesar fuego!
ceaseless *a* incesante,continuo, sin cesar
ceaselessly *adv* sin cesar, incesantemente
ceasing *n* cesación, *f*. **without c.,** sin cesar

cedar *n* (tree and wood) cedro, *m*. **red c.,** cedro dulce, *m*
cede *vt* ceder, traspasar; (admit) conceder
cedilla *n* zedilla, *f*
ceiling *n* techo, *m*; *aer* altura máxima, *f*. **c. price,** máximo precio, *m*
celebrant *n ecc* celebrante, *m*
celebrate *vt* celebrar; solemnizar. **Their marriage was celebrated in the autumn,** Su casamiento se solemnizó en el otoño
celebrated *a* célebre, famoso
celebration *n* celebración, *f*; festividad, *f*
celebrity *n* celebridad, *f*
celerity *n* celeridad, *f*
celery *n* apio, *m*
celestial *a* celestial
celibacy *n* celibato, *m*
celibate *a* célibe. *n* célibe, *mf*
cell *n* celda, *f*; (*bot biol*) célula, *f*; (bees, wasps) celdilla, *f*; *elec* elemento, *m*
cellar *n* sótano, *m*; (wine) bodega, *f*
cellist *n* violoncelista, *mf*
cello *n* violoncelo, *m*
cellophane *n* (papel) celofán, *m*
cellular *a* celular, celuloso
cellule *n* célula, *f*
celluloid *n* celuloide, *f*
cellulose *n* celulosa, *f*
Celt *n* celta, *mf*
Celtic *a* celta
cement *n* cemento, *m*, *vt* cementar
cemetery *n* cementerio, *m*
cenotaph *n* cenotafio, *m*
cenote *n* cenote *m*
cense *vt* incensar
censer *n* incensario, *m*
censor *n* censor, *m*, *vt* censurar. **banned by the c.,** prohibido por la censura
censorious *a* severo; crítico
censoriousness *n* severidad, propensión a censurar, *f*
censorship *n* censura, *f*
censure *vt* censurar, culpar, criticar
census *n* censo, *m*. **to take the c.,** formar el censo, levantar el censo, tomar el censo, empadronar
census-taking *n* la formación del censo, la formación de los censos, *f*, el levantamiento del censo, el levantamientos de los censos, *m*
cent *n* (coin) centavo, *Lat. Am.* cobre (of copper) *m*. **per c.,** por ciento. **not to have a c., not to have a c. to one's name,** no tener donde caer muerto
centaur *n* centauro, *m*
centavo *n* centavo, *Lat. Am.* cobre (of copper) *m*
centenarian *a* and *n* centenario (-ia)
centenary *n* centenario, *m*, *a* centenario
center *n* centro, *m*; medio, *m*. *a* central; centro. *vt* centrar; concentrar (en). **nervous centers,** centros nerviosos, *m pl*. **c.-forward,** *sport* delantero centro, *m*. **c.-half,** *sport* medio centro, *m*. **c. of gravity,** centro de gravedad, *m*. **c.-piece,** centro, *m*
centerfold *n* páginas centrales, *f pl*
centigrade *a* centígrado
centigram *n* centigramo, *m*
centiliter *n* centilitro, *m*
centime *n* céntimo, *m*
centimeter *n* centímetro, *m*. **cubic c.,** centímetro cúbico, *m*
centipede *n* ciempiés, *m*
central *a* central; céntrico. **The house is very c.,** La casa es muy céntrica. **C. America** *n* Centroamérica *f* **C. American,** *a* and *n* centroamericano (-na). **c. depot,** central, *f*. **c. heating,** calefacción central, *f*
centralism *n* centralismo, *m*
centralist *n* centralista, *mf*
centralization *n* centralización, *f*
centralize *vt* centralizar
centrally *adv* centralmente; céntricamente
centric *a* céntrico; central
centrifugal *a* centrífugo
centripetal *a* centrípeto
centuple *a* céntuplo
centuplicate *vt* centuplicar
centurion *n* centurión, *m*
century *n* siglo, *m*, centuria, *f*
ceramic *a* cerámico
ceramics *n* cerámica, *f*
cereal *a* cereal. *n* cereal, *m*
cerebellum *n* cerebelo, *m*
cerebral *a* cerebral
cerebrospinal *a* cerebroespinal
cerebrum *n* cerebro, *m*
ceremonial *a* ceremonial; de ceremonia. *n* ceremonial, *m*
ceremonially *adv* ceremonialmente; con ceremonia
ceremonious *a* ceremonioso
ceremoniously *adv* ceremoniosamente
ceremoniousness *n* ceremonia, formalidad, *f*
ceremony *n* ceremonia, *f*. **to stand on c.,** gastar cumplidos. **without c.,** sin cumplidos
cerise *a* de color cereza
certain *a* (sure) seguro; cierto; (unerring) certero. **a c. man,** cierto hombre. **I am c. that . . . ,** Estoy seguro de que . . . **to know for c.,** saber con toda seguridad, saber a ciencia cierta. **to make c. of,** asegurarse de
certainly *adv* seguramente; ciertamente; (as a reply) sin duda; naturalmente. **c. not,** no, por cierto; claro que no
certainty *n* certidumbre, *f*; seguridad, *f*; convicción, *f*. **of a c.,** seguramente
certificate *n* certificado, *m*; fe, *f*; partida, *f*; *com* bono, título, *m*; diploma, *m*. *vt* certificar. **birth c.,** partida de nacimiento, *f*. **death c.,** partida de defunción, *f*. **marriage c.,** partida de casamiento, *f*
certificated *a* (of teachers, etc.) con título
certify *vt* certificar; atestiguar; declarar
certitude *n* certeza, certidumbre, *f*
Cerulean *a* cerúleo
Cervantine *a* cervantino
cervix *n anat* cerviz, *f*
Cesarean *a* cesáreo
cessation *n* cesación, *f*
cession *n* cesión, *f*
cessionary *n* cesionario (-ia)
cesspool *n* sumidero, *m*
cetacean *a* cetáceo. *n* cetáceo, *m*
Ceylon Ceilán, *m*
cf. cfr.
chafe *vt* (rub) frotar; (make sore) escocer, rozar. *vi* raerse, desgastarse; escocerse; *fig* impacientarse; *fig* irritarse, enojarse
chaff *n* (of grain) ahechadura, *f*; (in a general sense and *fig*) paja, *f*; tomadura de pelo, burla, *f*. *vt* (a person) tomar el pelo (a), burlarse de
chaffinch *n* pinzón, *m*
chafing *n* frotación, *f*; (soreness) excoriación, *f*; *fig* impaciencia, *f*. **c.-dish,** escalfador, *m*
chagrin *n* mortificación, decepción, *f*, disgusto, *m*, *vt* mortificar
chain *n* cadena, *f*, *vt* encadenar. **c. of mountains,** cadena de montañas, cordillera, *f*. **c.-gang,** cadena de presidiarios, *f*. **c.-mail,** cota de malla, *f*. **c.-stitch,** cadeneta, *f*. **c.-stores,** empresa con sucursales, *f*. **in chains,** cargado de cadenas (e.g., **prisoners in chains,** prisioneros cargados de cadenas)
chair *n* silla, *f*; *univ* cátedra, *f*; (of a meeting) presidencia, *f*. *vt* llevar en hombros (a). **C.!** ¡Orden! **easy-c.,** (silla) poltrona, *f*. **to be in the c.,** ocupar la presidencia; presidir. **to take a c.,** sentarse, tomar asiento. **to take the c.,** presidir. **swivel-c.,** silla giratoria, *f*. **wheel-c.,** silla de ruedas, *f*. **c.-back,** respaldo de una silla, *m*
chairman *n* presidente (-ta). **to act as c.,** presidir
chairmanship *n* presidencia, *f*

chaise longue *n* meridiana, tumbona, *f*
Chaldea Caldea, *f*
Chaldean *a* caldeo
chalet *n* chalet, *m*
chalice *n* cáliz, *m*
chalk *n* creta, *f;* (for writing, etc.) tiza, *f,* yeso, *m. vt* marcar con tiza; dibujar con tiza. **to c. up,** apuntar. **not by a long c.,** no con mucho
chalky *a* cretáceo; cubierto de yeso; (of the complexion) pálido
challenge *n* provocación, *f;* (of a sentry) quién vive, *m;* (to a duel, etc.) desafío, reto, *m; law* recusación, *f;* concurso, *m. vt* (of a sentry) dar el quién vive (a); desafiar; provocar; *law* recusar
challenger *n* desafiador (-ra)
challenging *a* desafiador, provocador
chamber *n* cuarto, *m;* sala, *f;* (bed-) dormitorio, *m,* alcoba, *f;* cámara, *f; mech* cilindro, *m;* (in a gun) cámara, *f.* **c. concert,** concierto de música de cámara, *m.* **c.-maid,** camarera, *f.* **c. music,** música de cámara, *f.* **c. of commerce,** cámara de comercio, *f.* **c.-pot,** orinal, *m*
chamberlain *n* camarero, *m.* **court c.,** chambelán, *m.* **Lord C.,** camarero mayor, *m*
chameleon *n* camaleón, *m*
chamfer *n* chaflán, bisel, *m*
chamois *n* gamuza, *f,* rebeco, *m.* **c. leather,** piel de gamuza, *f*
chamomile *n* camomila, manzanilla, *f*
champ *vt* mascar; morder. *vi fig* impacientarse
champagne *n* (vino de) champaña, *m*
champion *n* campeón, *m;* defensor (-ra)
championship *n* campeonato, *m;* (of a cause) defensa, *f*
chance *n* casualidad, *f;* suerte, fortuna, *f;* posibilidad, *f;* probabilidad, *f;* esperanza, *f;* (opportunity) ocasión, oportunidad, *f. a* fortuito; accidental. *vi impers* suceder, acontecer. *vt inf* arriesgar; probar. **by c.,** por casualidad; por ventura. **if by c.,** si acaso. **If it chances that . . . ,** Si sucede que; Si a mano viene que . . . **The chances are that . . . ,** Las probabilidades son que . . . **There is no c.,** No hay posibilidad; No hay esperanza. **to let the c. slip,** perder la ocasión. **to take a c.,** aventurarse, arriesgarse. **to c. to do,** hacer algo por casualidad. **to c. upon,** encontrar por casualidad.
chancel *n* antealtar, entrecoro, *m*
chancellery *n* cancillería, *f*
chancellor *n* canciller, *m; univ* cancelario, *m.* **C. of the Exchequer,** Ministro de Hacienda, *m*
chancellorship *n* cancillería, *f*
chancery *n* chancillería, *f;* (papal) cancelaría, *f*
chandelier *n* araña de luces, *f*
chandler *n* velero, *m*
change *vt* cambiar; transformar; modificar; (clothes) mudarse (de); (one thing for another) trocar; sustituir (por). *vi* cambiar; (clothes) mudarse. **All c.!** ¡Cambio de tren! **to c. a check,** cambiar un cheque. **to c. color,** cambiar de color; (of persons) mudar de color. **to c. countenance,** demudarse. **to c. front,** *fig* cambiar de frente. **to c. hands,** (of shops, etc.) cambiar de dueño. **to c. one's clothes,** cambiar de ropa, mudarse de ropa. **to c. one's mind,** cambiar de opinión. **to c. one's tune,** cambiar de tono. **to c. the subject,** cambiar de conversación. **to c. trains,** cambiar de trenes
change *n* cambio, *m;* transformación, *f;* modificación, *f;* variedad, *f;* (of clothes, feathers) muda, *f;* (*theat* of scene) mutación, *f;* (money) cambio, *m;* (small coins) suelto, *m;* (stock) bolsa, *f;* lonja, *f;* vicisitud, *f;* (of bells) toque (de campanas), *m.* **for a c.,** para cambiar, como un cambio; para variar. **small c.,** suelto, *m,* moneda suelta, *f.* **c. for the better,** cambio para mejor, *m.* **c. for the worse,** cambio para peor, *m.* **c. of clothes,** cambio de ropa, *m;* **c. of front,** *fig* cambio de frente, *m.* **c. of heart,** cambio de sentimientos, *m;* conversión, *f.* **c. of life,** menopausia, *f.* **c.-over,** cambio, *m*
changeability *n* mutabilidad, *f;* inconstancia, volubilidad, *f*
changeable *a* voluble; variable; cambiable
changeless *a* immutable; constante
changeling *n* niño (-ña) cambiado (-da) por otro
changing *a* cambiante. **c.-room,** vestuario, *m*
channel *n* (of a river, etc.) cauce, *m;* canal, *m;* (irrigation) acequia, *f;* (strait) estrecho, *m; fig* conducto, *m;* (furrow) surco, *m,* estría, *f;* (of information, etc.) medio, *m. vt* acanalar; (furrow) surcar; (conduct) encauzar
chant *n* canto llano, *m;* salmo, *m. vt* salmodiar; cantar; recitar
chantey *n* saloma, *f*
chaos *n* caos, *m*
chaotic *a* caótico, desordenado
chaotically *adv* en desorden
chap *vt* agrietar. *vi* agrietarse. *n inf* chico, *m*
chapbook *n* librito de cordel, *m*
chapel *n* capilla, *f;* templo disidente, *m*
chaperon *n* dama de compañía, señora de compañía, dueña, *f, vt* acompañar
chaplain *n* capellán, *m*
chaplaincy *n* capellanía, *f*
chaplet *n* guirnalda, *f;* rosario, *m;* (necklace) collar, *m*
chapter *n* (in a book) capítulo, *m; ecc* cabildo, capítulo, *m.* **a c. of accidents,** una serie de desgracias. **c. house,** sala capitular, *f*
char *vt* (a house, etc.) fregar, hacer la limpieza de; (of fire) carbonizar. *n inf* fregona, asistenta, *f*
character *n* carácter, *m;* (of a play) personaje, *m;* (role) papel, *m;* (eccentric) tipo, *m.* **Gothic characters,** caracteres góticos, *m pl.* **in c.,** característico; apropiado. **in the c. of,** en el papel de. **out of c.,** nada característico; no apropiado. **principal c.,** protagonista, *mf.* **c. actor,** actor de carácter, *m.* **c. actress,** actriz de carácter
characteristic *a* característico, típico. *n* característica, peculiaridad, *f,* rasgo, *m*
characterization *n* caracterización, *f*
characterize *vt* caracterizar
characterless *a* sin carácter; insípido, soso
charade *n* charada, *f*
charcoal *n* carbón de leña, *m;* (for blacking the face, etc.) tizne, *m; art* carboncillo, *m.* **c. burner,** carbonera, *f.* **c. crayon,** carboncillo, *m.* **c. drawing,** dibujo al carbón, *m*
charge *vt* cargar; (enjoin) encargar; (accuse) acusar (de); (with price) cobrar; (with a mission, etc.) encomendar, confiar; *mil* acometer, atacar. *vi mil* atacar; (a price) cobrar, pedir. **How much do you c.?** ¿Cuánto cobra Vd.? **to c. with a crime,** acusar de un crimen
charge *n* (load) carga, *f;* (price) precio, *m;* gasto, *m;* (on an estate, etc.) derechos, *m pl;* (task) encargo, *m;* (office or responsibility) cargo, *m;* (guardianship) tutela, *f;* (care) cuidado, *m;* exhortación, *f; law* acusación, *f; mil* ataque, *m.* **He is in c. of . . . ,** Está encargado de . . . ; Es responsable de . . . **The diamonds are in the c. of . . . ,** Los diamantes están a cargo de. **depth c.,** carga de profundidad, *f.* **extra c.,** gasto suplementario, *m;* (on a train) suplemento, *m.* **free of c.,** gratis. **c. for admittance,** entrada, *f.* **to bring a c. against,** acusar de. **to give (someone) in c.,** entregar (una persona) a la policía. **to take c. of,** encargarse de
chargé d'affaires *n* encargado de negocios, *m*
charger *n* caballo de guerra, corcel, *m*
chariness *n* cautela, *f*
chariot *n* carro, *m*
charioteer *n* auriga, *m*
charitable *a* caritativo, limosnero; benéfico
charitableness *n* caridad, *f*
charity *n* caridad, *f;* beneficencia, *f;* (alms) limosna, *f.* **c. child,** niño (-ña) de la doctrina
charlatan *n* charlatán (-ana); (quack) curandero, *m*
charlatanism *n* charlatanismo, *m;* curanderismo, *m*

charm *n* hechizo, *m*; ensalmo, *m*; (amulet) amuleto, *m*; (trinket) dije, *m*; (general sense) encanto, atractivo, *m*. *vt* encantar, hechizar, fascinar
charming *a* encantador; atractivo, seductor, fascinador
charm school *n* academia de buenos modales, *f*
chart *n naut* carta de marear, *f*; (graph) gráfica, *f*. *vt* poner en una carta
charter *n* carta, *f*; (of a city, etc.) fuero, *m*; cédula, *f*. *vt* (a ship) fletar; (hire) alquilar. **royal c.,** cédula real, *f*
Chartism *n* el cartismo, *m*
chartist *n* cartista, *mf*
charwoman *n* fregona, asistenta; mujer de hacer faenas, *Mexico* fregandera *f*
chary *a* cauteloso; desinclinado; frugal
chase *n* caza, *f*; seguimiento, *m*. *vt* cazar; dar caza (a); perseguir; (drive off) ahuyentar; *fig* disipar, hacer desaparecer; (engrave) cincelar. **to give c. to,** dar caza (a). **to go on a wild goose c.,** buscar pan de trastrigo
chasm *n* sima, *f*, precipicio, *m*; *fig* abismo, *m*
chassis *n* chasis, *m*
chaste *a* casto
chasten *vt* castigar; corregir; humillar, mortificar
chastened *a* sumiso, dócil
chastise *vt* castigar
chastisement *n* castigo, *m*
chastity *n* castidad, *f*
chat *vi* charlar, conversar. *n* conversación, charla, *f*. **They are having a c.,** Están charlando, Están de palique
chattels *n pl* bienes muebles, efectos, *m pl*
chatter *vi* charlar; hablar por los codos, chacharear; (of water) murmurar; (of birds) piar; (of monkeys, etc.) chillar; (of teeth) rechinar; (of a person's teeth) dar diente con diente. *n* charla, *f*; cháchara, parla, *f*; (of water) murmurio, *m*; (of birds) gorjeo, *m*; (of monkeys, etc.) chillidos, *m pl*
chatterbox *n* badajo, *m*, cotorra, *f*
chatterer *n* hablador (-ra)
chattering *n* charla, cháchara, *f*; (of teeth) rechinamiento, *m*, *a* gárrulo, chacharero, locuaz
chauffeur *n* chófer, *m*
cheap *a* barato; (of works of art) cursi. *adv* barato. **dirt c.,** baratísimo. **to be dirt c.,** estar por los suelos. **to hold** (something) **c.,** tener en poco, estimar en poco
cheapen *vt* disminuir el valor de; reducir el precio de
cheaply *adv* barato; a bajo precio
cheapness *n* baratura, *f*; precio módico, *m*; mal gusto, *m*, vulgaridad, *f*
cheat *n* engaño, fraude, *m*, estafa, *f*; (person) fullero (-ra), trampista, *mf* embustero (-ra). *vt* engañar; defraudar; (at cards) hacer trampas. **He cheated me out of my property,** Me defraudó de mi propiedad
cheating *n* engaño, *m*; fraude, *m*; (at cards) fullerías, *f pl*
check *n* (chess) jaque, *m*; revés, *m*; impedimento, *m*; contratiempo, *m*; (of a bridle) cama, *f*; (control) freno, *m*; control, *m*; (checking) verificación, *f*; (ticket) papeleta, *f*; (counterfoil) talón, *m*; (square) cuadro, *m*; (bill) cuenta, *f*, *Argentina* adición *f*; (bank) cheque, *m*. *vt* (chess) jaquear; (hamper) refrenar; detener; contrarrestar; (test) verificar. *vi* detenerse. **to c. off,** marcar. **to c. oneself,** detenerse; contenerse. **to c. up,** comprobar. **crossed c.,** cheque cruzado, *m*. **c. book,** libro de cheques, *m*
checked *a* (cloth) a cuadros
checker *vt* escaquear; (variegate) motear, salpicar; diversificar. **a checkered career,** una vida accidentada
checking *n* represión, *f*; control, *m*; verificación, *f*; comprobación, *f*
checkmate *n* mate, jaque, mate, *m*. *vt* dar mate (a); (plans, etc.) frustrar
checks and balances *n pl* frenos y contrapesos, *m pl*
cheek *n* mejilla, *f*; *inf* descaro, *m*; insolencia, *Lat. Am.* impavidez *f*. **They have plenty of c.,** Tienen mucha cara dura. **c. by jowl,** cara a cara; al lado de. **c.-bone,** pómulo, *m*
cheekiness *n* cara dura, insolencia, *Lat. Am.* impavidez *f*
cheeky *a* insolente, descarado, *Lat. Am.* impávido, *Peru* lisurero; (pert) respondón
cheer *n* alegría, *f*, regocijo, *m*; vítor, *m*; aplauso, *m*. *vt* animar; alegrar, regocijar; vitorear, aplaudir. **to be of good c.,** estar alegre; ser feliz. **C. up!** ¡Ánimo! **to c. up,** animarse, cobrar ánimo
cheerful *a* alegre; jovial; de buen humor. **It is a c. room,** Es un cuarto alegre
cheerfully *adv* alegremente; (willingly) con mucho gusto, de buena gana
cheerfulness *n* alegría, *f*; jovialidad, *f*; buen humor, *m*
cheering *n* vítores, *m pl*, aclamaciones, *f pl*, *a* animador
cheerleader *n* porro, *m*
cheerless *a* triste; sin alegría; (dank) obscuro, lóbrego
cheese *n* queso, *m*. **cream c.,** queso de nata, *m*. **grated c.,** queso rallado, *m*. **c.-dish,** quesera, *f*. **c.-mite,** cresa, *f*. **c.-paring,** *n* corteza de queso, *f*. *a inf* tacaño. **c.-vat,** quesera, *f*
cheesecake *m Lat. Am.* alfandoque *m*
cheesy *a* caseoso
chemical *a* químico. **c. warfare,** defensa química, *f*
chemicals *n pl* productos químicos, *m pl*
chemise *n* camisa (de mujer), *f*
chemist *n* químico, *m*. **chemist's shop,** farmacia, *f*; droguería, *f*
chemistry *n* química, *f*
cherish *vt* amar, querer; (a hope, etc.) abrigar, acariciar
cherry *n* (fruit) cereza, *f*; (tree and wood) cerezo, *m*. **c. brandy,** aguardiente de cerezas, *m*. **c. orchard,** cerezal, *m*
cherub *n* querub(e), querubín, *m*
cherubic *a* querúbico
chess *n* ajedrez, *m*. **c.-board,** tablero de ajedrez, *m*
chessman *n* pieza de ajedrez, *f*
chest *n* arca, *f*, cofre, *m*; cajón, *m*; *anat* pecho, *m*. **to throw out one's c.,** inflar el pecho. **c.-expander,** extensor, *m*. **c. of drawers,** cómoda, *f*
chested *a* (in compounds) de pecho . . .
chestnut *n* (tree) castaño, *m*; (fruit) castaña, *f*; (color) castaño, color castaño, *m*; (horse) caballo castaño, *m*; (joke) chiste del tiempo de Maricastaña, *m*, *a* castaño. **horse-c. tree,** castaño de Indias, *m*
chevron *n her* cabrio, *m*; (*mil* etc.) sardineta, *f*
chew *vt* mascar, mascullar; (ponder) masticar
chewing *n* masticación, *f*. **c.-gum,** chicle, *m*
chianti *n* (wine) quianti, *m*
chiaroscuro *n* claroscuro, *m*
chic *n* chic, *m*, elegancia, *f*
chicanery *n* sofistería, *f*
chicken *n* pollo, *m*. **c.-hearted,** medroso, cobarde, timorato. **c.-pox,** varicela, *f*
chickenwire *n* alambrillo, *m*
chickpea *n* garbanzo, *m*
chickweed *n* pamplina, *f*
chicory *n* achicoria, *f*
chide *vt* reprender, reñir
chidingly *adv* en tono de reprensión
chief *n* jefe, *m*, *a* principal; primero; en jefe; mayor. **c.-of-staff,** jefe de estado mayor, *m*
chiefly *adv* principalmente; sobre todo
chieftain *n* caudillo, *m*; (of a clan) cabeza, jefe, *m*
chiffon *n* chifón, *m*, gasa, *f*
chiffonier *n* cómoda, *f*
chignon *n* moño, *m*
child *n* niño (-ña); hijo (-ja). *Mexico* escuincle *mf* **from a c.,** desde niño, desde la niñez. **with c.,** encinta, embarazada. **How many children have you?** ¿Cuántos hijos tiene Vd.? **child's play,** juegos infantiles, *m pl*; *fig* niñerías, *f pl*. **c. welfare,** puericultura, *f*
childbirth *n* parto, *m*
childhood *n* niñez, infancia, *f*. **from his c.,** desde su niñez, desde niño
childish *a* de niño; aniñado; pueril; fútil. **to grow c.,** chochear

childishly *adv* como un niño
childishness *n* puerilidad, *f*; futilidad, *f*
child labor *n* trabajo de menores, trabajo infantil, *m*
childless *a* sin hijos; sin niños
childlike *a* de niño, aniñado; pueril
children. See **child**
Chilean *a* and *n* chileno (-na)
chili *n* chile, pimento de cornetilla, *Lat. Am.* ají *m*. **c. sauce** *Lat. Am.* ají *m*
chill *n* frío, *m*; (of fear, etc.) estremecimiento, *m*; (illness) resfriado, *m*; (unfriendliness) frialdad, frigidez, *f*, *a* frío; (unfriendly) frígido. *vt* enfriar; helar; (with fear, etc.) dar escalofríos (de); (discourage) desalentar. *vi* tener frío; tener escalofríos. **to take the c. off,** templar, calentar un poco
chilliness *n* frío, *m*; (unfriendliness) frialdad, frigidez, *f*
chilly *a* frío; (sensitive to cold) friolero; (of politeness, etc.) glacial, frígido
chime *n* juego de campanas, *m*; repique, campaneo, *m*; armonía, *f*. *vi* (of bells) repicar; *fig* armonizar. **to c. the hour,** dar la hora
chimera *n* quimera, *f*
chimerical *a* quimérico
chimney *n* chimenea, *f*; (of a lamp) tubo (de lámpara), *m*. **c.-corner,** rincón de chimenea, *m*. **c.-pot,** sombrerete de chimenea, *m*. **c.-stack,** chimenea, *f*. **c.-sweep,** limpiador de chimeneas, deshollinador, *m*
chimpanzee *n* chimpancé, *m*
chin *n* barbilla, barba, *f*, mentón, *m*. **c.-rest,** mentonera, *f*. **c.-strap,** barboquejo, *m*; venda para la barbilla, *f*
china *n* china, porcelana, *f*; loza, *f*. *a* de porcelana; de loza. **c. cabinet,** chinero, *m*
chinchilla *n* (animal and fur) chinchilla, *f*
Chinese *a* and *n* chino (-na); (language) chino, *m*. **C. lantern,** farolillo de papel, *m*. **C. white,** óxido blanco de cinc, *m*
chink *n* resquicio, *m*, grieta, hendidura, *f*; (clink) retintín, tintineo, *m*. *vi* tintinar
chintz *n* zaraza, *f*
chip *n* astilla, *f*; (counter) ficha, *f*. *vt* picar; cincelar. **a c. off the old block,** de tal palo tal astilla. **c. potatoes,** patatas fritas, *f pl*
chiromancy *n* quiromancia, *f*
chiropodist *n* pedicuro, *m*, callista, *mf*
chiropody *n* pedicura, *f*
chiropractor *n* quiropráctico, *m*
chirp *vi* piar, gorjear. *n* pío, gorjeo, *m*
chirping *n* pïada, *f*, *a* gárrulo, piante
chisel *n* escoplo, cincel, *m*, *vt* cincelar. **cold c.,** cortafrío, *m*
chitchat *n* charla, *f*
chitterlings *n* asadura, *f*
chivalrous *a* caballeroso
chivalry *n* caballería, *f*; caballerosidad, *f*. **novel of c.,** novela de caballería, *f*
chive *n bot* cebollana, *f*, cebollino, *m*
chloral *n* cloral, *m*
chlorate *n* clorato, *m*
chloride *n* cloruro, *m*
chlorine *n* cloro, *m*
chloroform *n* cloroformo, *m*, *vt* cloroformizar
chlorophyll *n* clorófila, *f*
chock-full *a* lleno de bote en bote
chocolate *n* chocolate, *m*, *a* de chocolate. **thick drinking-c.,** chocolate a la española, *m*. **thin drinking-c.,** chocolate a la francesa, *m*. **c. shop,** chocolatería, *f*
choice *n* selección, *f*; preferencia, *f*; elección, *f*; opción, *f*; alternativa, *f*; lo más escogido. *a* escogido, selecto; excelente. **for c.,** con preferencia
choir *n* coro, *m*. **c.-boy,** niño del coro, *m*. **c.-master,** maestro de capilla, *m*
choke *vi* ahogarse; atragantarse; obstruirse. *vt* ahogar; estrangular. **to c. with laughter,** ahogarse de risa. **to c. back,** (words) tragar. **to c. off,** (a person) disuadir (de); quitarse de encima(a). **to c. up,** obstruir, cerrar, obturar; (hide) cubrir, tapar
choking *a* asfixiante, sofocante. *n* ahogamiento, *m*, sofocación, *f*
cholera *n* cólera, *m*
choleric *a* colérico
cholesterol *n* colesterina, *f*
choline *n* colina, *f*
choose *vt* escoger; elegir; optar por; (wish) querer, gustar. **They will do it when they c.,** Lo harán cuando les parezca bien. **If you c.,** Si Vd. quiere; Si Vd. gusta. **He was chosen as Mayor,** Fue elegido alcalde. **There is nothing to c. between them,** No hay diferencia entre ellos; Tanto vale el uno como el otro. **You cannot c. but love her,** No puedes menos de quererla
choosing *n* selección, *f*; (for an office, etc.) elección, *f*
chop *vt* cortar; (mince) picar; (split) hender, partir. *n* (meat) chuleta, *f*; (jaw) quijada, *f*. **to c. about, round,** (of the wind) girar, virar. **to c. down,** (trees) talar. **to c. off,** separar; cortar; tajar. **to c. up,** cortar en pedazos
chopper *n* hacha, *f*
choppy *a* picado, agitado
chopstick *n* palillo chino, *m*
choragus *n* corega, corego, *m*
choral *a* coral
chord *n* cuerda, *f*; *mus* acorde, *m*; **the right c.,** *fig* la cuerda sensible
choreographer *n* coreógrafo, *m*
choreographic *a* coreográfico
choreography *n* coreografía, *f*
chorister *n* corista, *m*
chorus *n* coro, *m*; (in revues) comparsa, *f*, acompañamiento, *m*; (of a song) refrán, *m*. **to sing in c.,** cantar a coro. **c. girl,** corista, *f*
chosen *a* escogido; elegido. **the c.,** los elegidos
chrestomathy *n* crestomatía, *f*
Christ *n* Cristo, Jesucristo, *m*
christen *vt* bautizar
Christendom *n* cristianismo, *m*, cristiandad, *f*
christening *n* bautizo, *m*, *a* bautismal, de bautizo
christian *a* cristiano. *n* cristiano (-na). **c. name,** nombre de pila, *m*
christianity *n* cristianismo, *m*
Christmas *n* Navidad, *f*. **A Merry C.!** ¡Felices Pascuas (de Navidad)! **Father C.,** Padre Noel, *m*; (Sp. equivalent) Los Reyes Magos. **C. box,** regalo de Navidad, *m*. **C. card,** felicitación de Navidad, *f*. **C. carol,** villancico de Navidad, *m*. **C. Day,** día de Navidad, *m*. **C. Eve,** Nochebuena, *f*. **C.-tide,** Navidades, *f pl*. **C. tree,** árbol de Navidad, *m*
Christopher Columbus Cristóbal Colón, *m*
chromate *n* cromato, *m*
chromatic *a* cromático
chrome *n* cromo, *m*. **c. yellow,** amarillo de cromo, *m*
chromic *a* crómico
chromium *n* cromo, *m*. **c.-plated,** cromado
chromosome *n* cromosoma, *m*
chronic *a* crónico; inveterado
chronicle *n* crónica, *f*, *vt* narrar
chronicler *n* cronista, *mf*
chronological *a* cronológico. **in c. order,** por orden cronológico
chronology *n* cronología, *f*
chronometer *n* cronómetro, *m*
chrysalis *n* crisálida, *f*
chrysanthemum *n* crisantemo, *m*
chubbiness *n* gordura, *f*
chubby *a* regordete, gordito. **c.-cheeked,** mofletudo
chuck *vt* (throw) lanzar, arrojar; (discontinue) abandonar, dejar. *n* (in a lathe) mandril, *m*. **to c. under the chin,** acariciar la barbilla (a). **to c. away,** derrochar; malgastar, perder. **to c. out,** echar, poner en la calle
chuckle *vi* reír entre dientes. *n* risa ahogada, *f*; risita, *f*
chum *n* compinche, camarada, *mf*. **to c. up with,** ser camarada de
chunk *n* pedazo, trozo, *m*
church *n* iglesia, *f*; (Protestant) templo, *m*, *vt* (a woman) purificar. **poor as a c. mouse,** más pobre que las ratas.

the C. of England, la iglesia anglicana. **to go to c.,** ir a misa; ir al templo. **c. music,** música sagrada, *f*
churchyard *n* cementerio, *m*
churl *n* patán, *m*
churlish *a* grosero, cazurro; (mean) tacaño, ruin
churn *n* mantequera, *f.* *vt* (cream) batir; *fig* azotar, agitar
chute *n* (for grain, etc.) manga de tolva, *f;* vertedor, *m;* (in flats and fun fairs) tobogán, deslizadero, *m*
ciborium *n* (chalice) copón, *m;* (tabernacle) sagrario, *m; arch* ciborio, *m*
cicada *n* cigarra, *f*
cicatrice *n* cicatriz, *f*
cicatrization *n* cicatrización, *f*
cicatrize *vt* cicatrizar. *vi* cicatrizarse
cider *n* sidra, *f*
cigar *n* cigarro, *m.* **c.-box,** cigarrera, *f.* **c.-case,** petaca, cigarrera, *f.* **c.-cutter,** corta-puros, *m*
cigarette *n* cigarrillo, pitillo, *Lat. Am.* cigarro *m.* **c.-butt,** colilla, *f.* **c.-case,** pitillera, *f.* **c.-holder,** boquilla, *f.* **c.-lighter,** encendedor de cigarrillos, *m.* **c.-paper,** papel de fumar, *m*
cinch *n* (of a saddle) cincha, *f; inf* ganga, *f; inf* seguridad, *f.* **c.-strap,** látigo, *m*
cinchona *n* quina, cinchona, *f*
cinder *n* ceniza, *f;* carbonilla, *f.* **red-hot c.,** rescoldo, *m.* **c.-track,** pista de ceniza, *f*
cinema, cinematograph *n* cine, cinematógrafo, *m*
cinematographic *a* cinematográfico
cinematography *n* cinematografía, *f*
cinemogul *n* magnate del cine, *mf*
cinnamon *n* (spice) canela, *f;* (tree) canelo, *m;* color de canela, *m*
cipher *n math* cero, *m; fig* nulidad, *f;* (code) cifra, *f;* monograma, *m.* **to be a mere c.,** ser un cero
Circassian *a* circasiano. *n* circasiano (-na)
circle *n* círculo, *m;* (revolution) vuelta, *f;* (group) grupo; *m;* (club, etc.) centro, *m;* (cycle) ciclo, *m.* *vt* dar vueltas alrededor de; rodear; ceñir; (on an application, examination, etc.) encerrar en un círculo. *vi* dar vueltas; (aircraft) volar en círculo; (of a hawk, etc.) cernerse. **dress-c.,** *theat* anfiteatro, *m.* **the family c.,** el círculo de la familia. **to come full c.,** dar la vuelta. **upper c.,** *theat* segundo piso, *m.* **vicious c.,** círculo vicioso, *m*
circlet *n* (of flowers, etc.) corona, *f;* (ring) anillo, *m*
circuit *n* circuito, *m;* (tour) gira, *f;* (revolution) vuelta, *f;* (radius) radio, *m.* **short c.,** corto circuito, *m.* **c.-breaker,** corta-circuitos, *m*
circuit court of appeals *n* tribunal colegial de circuito, *m*
circuitous *a* indirecto; tortuoso
circuitously *adv* indirectamente
circular *a* circular; redondo. *n* carta circular, *f;* circular, *f.* **c. tour,** viaje redondo, *m*
circularize *vt* enviar circulares (a)
circulate *vi* circular. *vt* hacer circular; poner en circulación; (news, etc.) divulgar, diseminar
circulating library *n* biblioteca por subscripción, *f*
circulation *n* circulación, *f;* (of a newspaper, etc.) tirada, circulación, *f.* **c. of the blood,** circulación de la sangre, *f*
circulatory *a* circulatorio
circumcise *vt* circuncidar
circumcised *a* circunciso
circumcision *n* circuncisión, *f*
circumference *n* circunferencia, *f*
circumflex *a* circunflejo. **c. accent,** acento circunflejo, *m,* (informal) capucha, *f*
circumlocution *n* circumlocución, *f*
circumnavigate *vt* circunnavegar
circumnavigation *n* circunnavegación, *f*
circumscribe *vt* circunscribir; *fig* limitar
circumscribed *a* circunscripto; *fig* limitado
circumscription *n* circunscripción, *f; fig* limitación, restricción, *f*
circumspect *a* circunspecto; discreto, correcto; prudente
circumspection *n* circunspección, *f;* prudencia, *f*
circumspectly *adv* con circunspección; prudentemente
circumstance *n* circunstancia, *f;* detalle, *m.* **aggravating c.,** circunstancia agravante, *f.* **attenuating c.,** circunstancia atenuante, *f.* **in the circumstances,** en las circunstancias. **in easy circumstances,** en buena posición, acomodado. **Do you know what his circumstances are?** ¿Sabes cuál es su situación económica? **under the circumstances,** bajo las circunstancias
circumstantial *a* circunstancial; detallado. **c. evidence,** prueba de indicios, *f*
circumvent *vt* frustrar; impedir
circumvention *n* frustración, *f*
circumvolution *n* circunvolución, *f*
circus *n* circo, *m;* plaza redonda, *f;* (traffic) redondel, *m*
cirrhosis *n* cirrosis, *f*
cirrus *n* (all meanings) cirro, *m*
cistern *n* tanque, *m;* cisterna, *f,* aljibe, *m*
citadel *n* ciudadela, *f*
citation *n law* citación, *f;* cita, *f*
citation dictionary *n* diccionario de autoridades, *m*
cite *vt* citar
citizen *n* ciudadano (-na); vecino (-na); natural, *mf.* **fellow c.,** conciudadano, *m;* compatriota, *mf*
citizenship *n* ciudadanía, *f*
citrate *n* citrato, *m*
citric *a* cítrico
citrine *a* cetrino
citron *n* (fruit) cidra, *f;* (tree) cidro, *m*
city *n* ciudad, *f, a* municipal
city-state *n* ciudad-estado, *f,* (plural: ciudades-estado)
civet *n* algalia, *f*
civic *a* cívico; municipal
civics *n* civismo, *m*
civil *a* civil; doméstico; (polite) cortés, atento; (obliging) servicial. **C. Aeronautics Board,** Dirección general de aeronáutica civil, *f.* **c. defense,** defensa pasiva, *f.* **c. engineer,** ingeniero de caminos, canales y puertos, *m.* **C. Service,** cuerpo de empleados del Estado, *m*
civilian *a* civil. *n* ciudadano (-na). **c. dress,** traje paisano, *m*
civility *n* civilidad, cortesía, *f*
civilization *n* civilización, *f*
civilize *vt* civilizar
civilized *a* civilizado
civilizing *a* civilizador
civilly *adv* civilmente, cortésmente
clack *n* golpeo, ruido sordo, *m*
clad *a* vestido
claim *vt* reclamar; pretender exigir; *law* demandar; (assert) afirmar. *vi law* pedir en juicio. *n* reclamación, *f;* pretensión, *f; law* demanda, *f;* (in a gold-field, etc.) concesión, *f;* (right) derecho, *m.* **to lay c. to,** pretender a; exigir. **to put in a c. for,** reclamar
claimant *n law* demandante, *mf;* pretendiente (-ta); *com* acreedor (-ra)
clairvoyance *n* doble vista, *f*
clairvoyant *n* vidente, *m*
clam *n* almeja, chirla, *f*
clamber *vi* trepar, encaramarse. *n* subida difícil, *f*
clamminess *n* viscosidad, humedad, *f*
clammy *a* viscoso; húmedo, mojado
clamor *n* clamor, estruendo, *m;* gritería, vocería, *f.* *vi* gritar, vociferar. **to c. against,** protestar contra. **to c. for,** pedir a voces
clamorous *a* clamoroso, ruidoso, estrepitoso
clamp *n* grapa, *f;* abrazadera, *f; carp* tornillo, *m;* (pile) montón, *m.* *vt* empalmar; sujetar, lañar
clan *n* clan, *m;* familia, *f;* partido, grupo, *m*
clandestine *a* clandestino, furtivo
clandestinely *adv* en secreto, clandestinamente
clang *vi* sonar; (of a gate, etc.) rechinar. *vt* hacer sonar. *n* sonido metálico, *m;* estruendo, *m*

clank *vi* dar un ruido metálico; crujir. *vt* hacer sonar; (glasses) hacer chocar. *n* ruido metálico, *m*; el crujir
clannish *a* exclusivista
clansman *n* miembro de un clan, *m*
clap *vt* (hands) batir; (spurs, etc.) poner rápidamente; (one's hat on) encasquetarse (el sombrero); (shut) cerrar apresuradamente. *vi* aplaudir. *n* (of the hands) palmada, *f*; (of thunder) trueno, *m*; (noise) ruido, *m*. **to c. eyes on,** echar la vista encima de. **to c. someone on the back,** dar una palmada en la espalda (a). **to c. the hands,** batir las palmas
clapper *n* (of a bell) badajo, *m*
clapping *n* aplausos, *m pl*
claque *n* claque, *f*
claret *n* clarete, *m*
clarification *n* clarificación, *f*; elucidación, *f*
clarify *vt* clarificar; elucidar, aclarar
clarinet *n* clarinete, *m*
clarinettist *n* clarinete, *m*
clarion *n* clarín, *m*
clarity *n* claridad, *f*; lucidez, *f*
clash *vi* chocar; encontrarse; (of events) coincidir; (of opinions, etc.) oponerse, estar en desacuerdo; (of colors) desentonar, chocar. *n* estruendo, fragor, *m*; choque, *m*; *mil* encuentro, *m*; (of opinions, etc.) desacuerdo, *m*; disputa, *f*
clasp *vt* (a brooch, etc.) abrochar, enganchar; (embrace) abrazar; (of plants, etc.) ceñir. *n* (brooch) broche, *m*; (of a belt) hebilla, *f*; (of a necklace, handbag, book) cierre, *m*; (for the hair) pasador, *m*. **to c. someone in one's arms,** tomar en los brazos (a), abrazar. **c.-knife,** navaja, *f*
class *n* clase, *f*; (kind) especie, *f*; (of exhibits, etc.) categoría, *f*. *vt* clasificar. **in a c. by itself,** único en su línea. **the lower classes,** las clases bajas. **the middle classes,** la clase media. **the upper classes,** la clase alta. **c.-mate,** condiscípulo (-la). **c.-room,** sala de clase, *f*, salón de clase, *f*. **c. war,** lucha de clases, *f*
classic *a* clásico. *n* clásico, *m*
classical *a* clásico
classicist *a* and *n* clasicista, *mf*
classifiable *a* clasificable
classification *n* clasificación, *f*
classified *a* (secreto) reservado, secreto; (advertisement) por palabras
classified advertisement *n* anuncio por palabras, *m*
classify *vt* clasificar
clatter *vi* hacer ruido; (knock) golpear; (of loose horseshoes) chacolotear. *vt* hacer ruido con; chocar (una cosa contra otra). *n* ruido, *m*; (hammering) martilleo, *m*; (of horseshoes) chacoloteo, *m*; (of a crowd) estruendo, *m*, bulla, *f*. **John clattered along the street,** Los pasos de Juan resonaban por la calle
clause *n gram* cláusula, *f*; *law* condición, estipulación, cláusula, *f*
claustrophobia *n* claustrofobia, *f*
clavichord *n* clavicordio, *m*
clavicle *n* clavícula, *f*
claw *n* garra, *f*; (of a lobster, etc.) tenaza, *f*; (hook) garfio, gancho, *m*. *vt* arañar, clavar las uñas en; (tear) desgarrar. **c.-hammer,** martillo de orejas, *m*
clay *n* arcilla, *f*; barro, *m*; (pipe) pipa de barro, *f*. **c.-pit,** barrizal, *m*
clayey *a* arcilloso
clean *a* limpio; puro, casto. *adv* limpio; completamente; exactamente. **to make a c. sweep (of),** no dejar títere con cabeza. **to make a c. breast of,** confesar sin tormento, no quedarse con nada en el pecho. **to show a c. pair of heels,** tomar las de Villadiego. **c. bill of health,** patente de sanidad, *m*. **c.-cut,** bien definido; claro. **c.-limbed,** bien proporcionado, gallardo. **c.-shaven,** lampiño; sin barba, bien afeitado
clean *vt* limpiar; (streets) barrer; (a floor) fregar; (dry-clean) lavar al seco. **to c. one's hands (teeth),** limpiarse las manos (los dientes). **to c. up,** limpiar; (tidy) asear; poner en orden
cleaner *n* limpiador (-ra); (charwoman) fregona, *f*; (stain remover) sacamanchas, *m*; (drycleaner, person) tintorero (-ra)
cleaning *n* limpieza, *f*, *a* de limpiar. **dry-c.,** lavado al seco, *m*. **c. rag,** trapo de limpiar, *m*. **c. woman** *Mexico* fregandera
cleanliness *n* limpieza, *f*; aseo, *m*
cleanse *vt* limpiar; lavar; purgar; purificar
cleansing *n* limpieza, *f*; lavamiento, *m*; purgación, *f*; purificación, *f*
clear *a* claro; (of the sky) sereno, despejado; transparente; (free (from)) libre (de); (open) abierto; (of profit, etc.) neto; (of thoughts, etc.) lúcido; (apparent) evidente; explícito; (of images) distinto; absoluto; (whole) entero, completo. **c. majority,** mayoría absoluta, *f*. **c. profit,** beneficio neto, *m*. **c.-cut,** bien definido. **c.-headed,** perspicaz; inteligente. **c.-sighted,** clarividente
clear *vt* aclarar; despejar; limpiar; librar (de); quitar; (one's throat) carraspear; (*com* stock) liquidar; (of a charge) absolver; (one's character) vindicar; (avoid, miss) evitar; (jump) salvar, saltar; (a court, etc.) desocupar; (a debt) satisfacer; (an account) saldar; (a mortgage) cancelar; (win) ganar; hacer un beneficio de; (through customs) despachar en la aduana. *vi* (of sky, etc.) serenarse; escampar; (of wine, etc.) aclararse; despacharse en la aduana. **to c. the table,** levantar la mesa, levantar los manteles. **to c. the underbrush from** *Lat. Am.* desmalezar. **to c. the way,** abrir calle; *fig* abrir paso. **to c. away,** *vt* quitar; disipar. *vi* disiparse. **to c. off,** *vt* (finish) terminar; (debts) pagar; (discharge) despedir. *vi* (of rain) despejarse, escampar; marcharse. **to c. out,** *vt* limpiar; (a drain, etc.) desatascar; vaciar; echar. *vi* marcharse, escabullirse. **C. out!** ¡Fuera! **c. the decks,** hacer zafarrancho. **c. the decks for action,** hacer zafarrancho. **to c. up,** *vt* poner en orden; (a mystery, etc.) aclarar, resolver, *vi* (of weather) serenarse, escampar, despejarse
clearance *n* (of trees, etc.) desmonte, *m*; eliminación, *f*; expulsión, *f*; *mech* espacio muerto, *m*; despacho de aduana, *m*. **to make a c. of,** deshacerse de. **c. sale,** liquidación, venta de saldos, *f*
clearing *n* (in a wood) claro, *m*, *Argentina* abra *f*; desmonte, *m*; (*com* of goods) liquidación, *f*; (of one's character) vindicación, *f*. **c.-house,** casa de compensación, *f*
clearness *n* claridad, *f*
cleavage *n* hendimiento, *m*; (in views, etc.) escisión, *f*
cleave *vt* partir; abrir; (air, water, etc.) surcar, hender. *vi* partirse; (stick) pegarse, adherirse
cleaver *n* partidor, *m*; hacha, *f*
clef *n* clave, *f*. **treble c.,** clave de sol, *f*
cleft *n* hendedura, fisura, rendija, abertura, *f*. **c.-palate,** paladar hendido, *m*
clematis *n* clemátide, *f*
clemency *n* (of weather) benignidad, *f*; (of character, etc.) clemencia, *f*
clement *a* (of weather) benigno; (of character, etc.) clemente, benévolo
clench *vt* agarrar; (teeth, etc.) apretar; (a bargain) cerrar, concluir
clergy *n* clero, *m*, clérigos, *m pl*
clergyman *n* clérigo, *m*
cleric *n* eclesiástico, *m*
clerical *a* clerical; de oficina. **c. error,** error de oficina, *m*. **c. work,** trabajo de oficina, *m*
clericalism *n* clericalismo, *m*
clerk *n* (clergyman) clérigo, *m*; (in an office) oficinista, escribiente, *m*; oficial, *m*; secretario, *m*
clerkship *n* puesto de oficinista, *m*; escribanía, *f*; secretaría, *f*
clever *a* listo, inteligente; ingenioso; hábil; (dexterous) diestro
cleverly *adv* hábilmente; diestramente, con destreza
cleverness *n* talento, *m*; inteligencia, *f*; habilidad, *f*; (dexterity) destreza, *f*

cliché *n* frase hecha, frase de cajón, *f*
click *vi* (of the tongue) dar un chasquido; (of a bolt, etc.) cerrarse a golpe; hacer tictac. *vt* (one's tongue) chascar; (a bolt, etc.) cerrar a golpe. *n* golpe seco, *m*; tictac, *m*; (of the tongue) chasquido, *m*. **to c. one's heels together,** hacer chocar los talones
client *n* cliente, *mf*; (customer) parroquiano (-na), *Lat. Am. also* marchante (-ta) *mf*
clientele *n* clientela, *f*
cliff *n* acantilado, *m*, roca, escarpa, *f*
cliff dweller *n* hombre de la roca, hombre de las rocas, *m*, mujer de la roca, mujer de las rocas, *f*
climate *n* clima, *m*
climatic *a* climático
climatology *n* climatología, *f*
climax *n* culminación, *f*; (rhetoric) clímax, *m*; gradación, *f*; punto más alto, apogeo, cenit, *m*; (of a play, etc.) desenlace, *m*
climb *vt* and *vi* trepar; escalar; montar; subir; ascender. **rate of c.,** *aer* velocidad ascensional, *f*. **to c. down,** bajar; *fig* echar el pie atrás. **to c. over,** (obstacles) salvar. **to c. up,** encaramarse por; subir por; montar
climber *n* alpinista, *mf*; (plant) trepadera, enredadera, *f*; (social) arribista, *mf*
clinch *vt* (nails, etc.) remachar, rebotar; (a bargain, etc.) cerrar; (an argument, etc.) remachar. *n* (wrestling) cuerpo a cuerpo, *m*
cling *vi* pegarse (a); agarrarse (a); (of scents) pegarse; (follow) seguir. **They clung together for an instant,** Quedaron abrazados un instante
clinging *a* tenaz; (of plants, etc.) trepador; (of persons) manso, dócil. **to be a c. vine,** *inf* ser una malva
clinic *n* clínica, *f*
clinical *a* clínico.
clink *vi* retiñir; (of glasses) chocarse. *vt* hacer sonar; (glasses) chocar. *n* retintín, *m*; (of a hammer) martilleo, *m*; sonido metálico, *m*; (of glasses) choque, *m*; (jail) *Argentina, Chile* capacha *f*
clip *vt* (grasp) agarrar; (sheep, etc.) esquilar; (trim) recortar, cercenar; (prune) podar; (a ticket) taladrar. *n* pinza, *f*; (paper-clip) sujetapapeles, *Central America* ataché, *elsewhere in Lat. Am.* broche *m*; *mech* grapa, escarpia, *f*; (for ornament) sujetador, *m*. **to c. a person's wings,** *fig* cortar (or quebrar) las alas (a)
clipper *n* (person) esquilador (-ra); (*naut* and *aer*) clíper, *m*; *pl* **clippers,** tenazas de cortar, *f pl*; (for pruning) podaderas, *f pl*; (punch) taladro, *m*
clipping *n* (of sheep, etc.) esquileo, *m*; (of a newspaper, etc.) recorte, *m*
clique *n* camarilla, *f*
cliquish *a* exclusivista
cloak *n* capa, *f*; manto, *m*; *fig* velo, *m*. *vt* encapotar; embozar; (conceal) ocultar, encubrir. **c. and sword play,** comedia de capa y espada, *f*. **c.-room,** guardarropa, *m*; (ladies') tocador, *m*; (on a station) consigna, *f*
clock *n* reloj, *m*; (of a stocking) cuadrado, *m*. **It is six o'clock,** Son las seis. **c.-face,** esfera de reloj, *f*. **c.-maker,** relojero, *m*. **c.-making,** relojería, *f*. **c.-work,** aparato de relojería, *m*. **to go like c.-work,** ir como un reloj. **c.-work train,** tren de cuerda, *m*
clockwise *a* and *adv* en el sentido de las agujas del reloj; de derecha a izquierda
clod *n* (of earth) terrón, *m*; (corpse) tierra, *f*; (person) zoquete, *m*. **c.-hopper,** patán, *m*
clog *n* (shoe) zueco, zoclo, *m*; (obstacle) estorbo, obstáculo, *m*. *vt* embarazar; estorbar, impedir; (block) obturar, cerrar; *fig* paralizar
cloister *n* claustro, *m*; convento, *m*. *vt* enclaustrar
cloistered *a* enclaustrado; retirado, aislado
close *a* estrecho; (of a prisoner) incomunicado; (reticent) reservado; (niggardly) tacaño, avaro; (scarce) escaso; (of friends) íntimo; (equal) igual; (lacking space) apretado; (dense) denso; (thick) tupido; compacto; (of a copy, etc.) fiel, exacto; (thorough) concienzudo; (careful) cuidadoso; (attentive) atento; (to the roots) a raíz; (of shaving) bueno; (of weather) pesado, sofocante; (of rooms) mal ventilado. **at c. quarters,** de cerca. **It is c. to eight o'clock,** Son casi las ocho. **to press c.,** perseguir de cerca; fatigar. **c. at hand, c. by,** cerca; al lado; a mano. **c.-cropped,** (of hair) al rape. **c. fight,** lucha igualada, *f*. **c.-fisted,** tacaño, apretado. **c.-fitting,** ajustado, ceñido al cuerpo; pequeño. **c. season,** veda, *f*. **c.-up,** *n* (cinema) primer plano, *m*
close *n* (end) fin, *m*, conclusión, *f*; (of day) caída, *f*; *mus* cadencia, *f*; (enclosure) cercado, *m*; (square) plazoleta, *f*; (alley) callejón, *m*; (of a cathedral) patio, *m*. **at the c. of day,** a la caída de la tarde. **to bring to a c.,** terminar; llevar a cabo. **to draw to a c.,** tocar a su fin; estar terminando
close *vt* cerrar; (end) concluir, terminar; poner fin a. *vi* cerrar(se); (of a wound) cicatrizarse, cerrarse; (end) terminar(se), acabar, concluir. **to c. the ranks,** cerrar filas. **to c. about,** (surround) rodear, cercar; (envelop) envolver. **to c. down,** *vt* cerrar. *vi* cerrar; *rad* cerrarse. **to c. halfway** entrecerrar **to c. in,** (surround) cercar; (of night) cerrar; caer; (envelop) envolver; (of length of days) acortarse. **to c. in on,** cercar. **to c. round,** envolver; (of water) tragar. **to c. up,** *vt* cerrar; cerrar completamente; obstruir. *vi* (of persons) acercarse; (of a wound) cicatrizarse; cerrarse
closed *a* cerrado. **"Road C.,"** Paso Cerrado. **to have a c. mind,** ser cerrado de mollera; sufrir de estrechez de miras
closely *adv* estrechamente; de cerca; (carefully) cuidadosamente; (exactly) exactamente; (attentively) con atención, atentamente
closeness *n* estrechez, *f*; densidad, *f*; (nearness) proximidad, *f*; (of a copy, etc.) fidelidad, exactitud, *f*; (stuffiness), falta de aire, *f*; (of friendship) intimidad, *f*; (stinginess) tacañería, *f*; (reserve) reserva.
closet *n* camarín, *m*; (cupboard) alacena, *f*; (water) excusado, *m*
closing *n* cerramiento, *m*; (of an account) saldo, *m*. **c. time,** cierre, *m*, hora de cerrar, *f*
closure *n* conclusión, *f*; *pol* clausura, *f*
clot *n* coágulo, grumo, *m*. *vt* coagular. *vi* coagularse, cuajarse
cloth *n* tela, *f*; paño, *m*; (table) mantel, *m*; (clergy) clero, *m*. **She cleaned the books with a c.,** Ella limpió los libros con un paño. **in c.,** (of books) en tela
clothe *vt* vestir; cubrir; (with authority, etc.) revestir. **to c. oneself,** vestirse
clothes *n pl* vestidos, *m pl*, ropa, *f*. **a suit of c.,** un traje. **old c. shop,** ropavejería, *f*. **c.-basket,** cesta de la colada, *f*. **c.-brush,** cepillo para ropa, *m*. **c.-hanger,** percha, *f*. **c.-horse,** enjugador, *m*. **c.-line,** cuerda de la ropa, *f*. **c.-peg,** pinza de la ropa, *f*. **c.-prop,** palo para sostener la cuerda de la colada, *m*
clothier *n* ropero, *m*. **clothier's shop,** ropería, *f*
clothing *n* vestidos, *m pl*, ropa, *f*. **article of c.,** prenda de vestir, *f*
clotted *a* grumoso
cloud *n* nube, *f*. *vt* anublar, oscurecer; empañar; (blot out) borrar. *vi* anublarse. **to be under a c.,** estar bajo sospecha. **summer c.,** nube de verano, *f*. **storm-c.,** nubarrón, *m*. **c.-burst,** nubada, *f*, chaparrón, *m*. **c.-capped,** coronado de nubes
cloudiness *n* nebulosidad, *f*; obscuridad, *f*; (of liquids) turbiedad, *f*
cloudless *a* sin nubes, despejado; sereno, claro
cloudy *a* nublado, nubloso; obscuro; (of liquids) turbio
clout *n* *Central America, Mexico* arranque *m*
clove *n* clavo de especia, *m*; (of garlic) diente de ajo, *m*. **c.-tree,** clavero, *m*
cloven *a* hendido. **to show the c. hoof,** enseñar la oreja. **c. hoof,** pezuña, *f*
clover *n* trébol, *m*. **to be in c.,** nadar en la abundancia
clown *n* patán, *m*; bufón, tonto, *m*; (in a circus) payaso, *m*. *vi* hacer el tonto, hacer el payaso
clowning *n* payasada, *f*
clownish *a* grosero; palurdo, zafio; bufón
cloy *vt* empalagar

cloying *a* empalagoso
club *n* porra, cachiporra, clava, *f;* (gymnastic) maza, *f;* (hockey) bastón de hockey, *m;* (golf) palo de golf, *m;* (in cards) basto, *m;* (social) club, *m. vt* golpear. **to c. together,** asociarse, unirse. **We clubbed together to buy him a present,** Entre todos le compramos un regalo. **c.-house,** club, *m*
clubfoot *n* pie calcáneo, pie contrahecho, pie de piña, pie equino, pie talo, pie zambo, *m*
clubman *n* miembro de un club, *m*
cluck *vi* cloquear. *n* cloqueo, *m*
clucking *n* cloqueo, *m*
clue *n* indicio, *m;* (to a problem) clave, *f;* (of a crossword) indicación, *f;* idea, *f*
clump *n* bloque, pedazo, *m;* (of trees) grupo, *m;* (of feet) ruido, *m*
clumsily *adv* torpemente; pesadamente
clumsiness *n* torpeza, *f;* falta de maña, *f;* pesadez, *f*
clumsy *a* torpe; desmañado; chapucero, sin arte; (lumbering) pesado; (in shape) disforme
cluster *n* (of currants, etc.) racimo, *m;* (of flowers) ramillete, *m;* grupo, *m. vi* arracimarse; agruparse. **They clustered round him,** Se agrupaban a su alrededor
clutch *vt* agarrar; sujetar, apretar. *n mech* embrague, *m;* (of eggs) nidada, *f; fig* garras, *f pl.* **to fall into the clutches of,** caer en las garras de. **to make a c. at,** procurar agarrar. **to throw in the c.,** *mech* embragar. **to throw out the c.,** *mech* desembragar. **c. pedal,** pedal de embrague, *m*
clutter *n* desorden, *m,* confusión, *f, vt* desordenar
coach *n* carroza, *f;* charabán, *m; rw* vagón, coche, *m;* (hackney) coche de alquiler, *m; sport* entrenador, *m;* (tutor) profesor particular, *m. vt sport* entrenar; (teach) preparar, dar lecciones particulares (a). **through c.,** coche directo, *m.* **c.-box,** pescante, *m.* **c.-house,** cochera, *f*
coaching *n sport* entrenamiento, *m;* lecciones particulares, *f pl*
coachman *n* cochero, *m*
coagulate *vi* coagularse. *vt* coagular, cuajar
coagulation *n* coagulación, *f*
coal *n* carbón, *m;* pedazo de carbón, *m;* (burning) brasa, *f. vi* carbonear, hacer carbón. *vt* proveer de carbón; carbonear. **to carry coals to Newcastle,** llevar leña al monte, elevar aqua al mar. **to haul a person over the coals,** reprender a alguien. **c.-barge,** (barco) carbonero, *m.* **c.-black,** negro como el azabache. **c.-cellar, house,** carbonera, *f.* **c.-dust,** cisco, *m.* **c.-field,** yacimiento de carbón, *m.* **c.-gas,** gas de hulla, *m.* **c.-heaver,** cargador de carbón, *m.* **c.-merchant,** carbonero, *m.* **c.-mine,** mina de carbón, *f.* **c.-miner,** minero de carbón, *m.* **c.-scuttle,** carbonera, *f.* **c.-tar,** alquitrán mineral, *m*
coalesce *vi* fundirse; unirse; incorporarse
coalescence *n* fusión, *f;* unión, *f;* incorporación, *f*
coalition *n* coalición, *f*
coarse *a* (in texture) basto, burdo; tosco; (gross) grosero; vulgar. **c.-grained,** de fibra gruesa; (of persons) vulgar, poco fino. **c. woolen cloth** *Chile* litro *m*
coarsen *vt* (of persons) embrutecer. *vi* embrutecerse; (of the skin) curtirse
coarseness *n* basteza, *f;* tosquedad, *f;* (of persons) grosería, indelicadeza, *f;* vulgaridad, *f*
coast *n* costa, *f;* litoral, *m. vi* costear; deslizarse en un tobogán; dejar muerto el motor. **The c. is not clear,** Hay moros en la costa. **c.-guard,** guardacostas, *m.* **c.-line,** litoral, *m*
coastal *a* costanero, costero. **c. defences,** defensas costeras, *f pl*
coaster *n naut* barco costanero, barco de cabotaje, *m*
coasting *n naut* cabotaje, *m*
coat *n* abrigo, *m;* gabán, *m;* chaqueta, *f;* (animal's) capa, *f;* (of paint) mano, *f. vt* recubrir; (with paint, etc.) dar una mano de. **fur c.,** abrigo de pieles, *m.* **sports c.,** Americana sport, *f.* **c. of arms,** escudo de armas, *m.* **c. of mail,** cota de malla, *f.* **c.-hanger,** percha, *f*
coating *n* (of paint, etc.) capa, mano, *f*
co-author *n* coautor, *m*
coax *vt* instar; halagar, engatusar, *Lat. Am. also* engaratusar; persuadir (a)
coaxing *n* ruegos, *m pl;* mimos, *m pl,* caricias, *f pl;* persuasión, *f. a* mimoso, zalamero; persuasivo
cob *n* (horse) jaca, *f;* (lump) pedazo, *m;* (swan) cisne macho, *m*
cobalt *n* cobalto, *m.* **c. blue,** azul cobalto, *m*
cobble *n* (stone) guijarro, *m, vt* (with stones) empedrar con guijarros; (shoes) remendar
cobbler *n* zapatero remendón, *m.* **cobbler's last,** horma, *f.* **cobbler's wax,** cerote, *m*
cobblestone *n* guijarro, *m,* piedra, *f*
cobelligerent *n* cobeligerante, *mf*
cobra *n* cobra, serpiente de anteojos, *f*
cobweb *n* telaraña, *f*
cobwebby *a* cubierto de telarañas; transparente; de gasa
cocaine *n* cocaína, *f*
coccyx *n* cóccix, *m, inf* rabadilla, *f*
cochlea *n* caracol (del oído), *m*
cock *n* gallo, *m;* (male) macho, *m;* (tap) grifo, *m,* espita, *f;* (of a gun) martillo, *m;* (weather-vane) veleta, *f;* (of hay) montón, *m. vt* (a gun) amartillar; (a hat) ladear; (raise) erguir, enderezar. **a cocked hat,** un sombrero de tres picos. **at half c.,** (of a gun) desamartillada *f.*. **He cocked his head,** Erguió la cabeza. **The dog cocked its ears,** El perro aguzó las orejas. **to c. one's eye at,** lanzar una mirada (a). **c.-a-doodle-doo,** quiquiriquí, *m.* **c.-a-hoop,** triunfante, jubiloso; arrogante. **c.-crow,** canto del gallo, *m.* **c.-fight,** riña de gallos, *f.* **c.-of-the-walk,** gallito, *m.* **c.-sure,** pagado de sí mismo; completamente convencido
cockerel *n* gallo joven, gallito, *m*
cocker spaniel *n* cóquer, *m*
cockle *n* (bivalve) bucarda, *f. vi* arrugarse; (warp) torcerse; doblarse. **c.-shell,** (pilgrims') concha, *f;* (boat) cascarón de nuez, *m*
Cockney *a* londinense, de Londres. *n* londinense, *mf*
cockpit *n* gallería, *f; aer* casilla del piloto, *f; fig* arena, *f*
cockroach *n* cucaracha, *f*
cockscomb *n* cresta de gallo, *f*
cocktail *n* (drink) cótel, coctel, *m.* **to shake a c.,** mezclar un coctel. **c. party,** coctel *m.* **c. shaker,** cotelera, *f*
cocky *a* fatuo, presuntuoso
cocoa *n* cacao, *m*
coconut *n* coco, *m; inf* cabeza, *f.* **c. milk,** agua de coco, *f.* **c. shy,** pim, pam, pum, *m.* **c. tree,** cocotero, *m*
cocoon *n* capullo, *m*
cod *n* bacalao, *m.* **cod-liver oil,** aceite de hígado de bacalao, *m*
coddle *vt* criar con mimo, mimar, consentir
code *n* código, *m;* clave, *f;* (secret) cifra, *f. vt* poner en cifra. **signal c.,** *naut* código de señales, *m.* **c. word,** palabra de clave, *f*
codeine *n* codeína, *f*
codex *n* códice, *m*
codicil *n* codicilio, *m*
codification *n* codificación, *f*
codify *vt* codificar
coeducation *n* coeducación, *f*
coefficient *n* coeficiente, *m*
coequality *n* coigualdad, *f*
coerce *vt* forzar, obligar; constreñir
coercion *n* coerción, coacción, *f*
coercive *a* coercitivo, coactivo
coeval *a* coevo
coexist *vi* coexistir
coexistence *n* coexistencia, *f*
coffee *n* café, *m.* **black c.,** café solo, *m.* **white c.,** café con leche, *m.* **c.-bean,** grano de café, *m.* **c.-cup,** taza para café, *f.* **c.-house,** café, *m.* **c.-mill,** molinillo de

café, *m.* **c.-plantation,** cafetal, *m.* **c.-pot,** cafetera, *f.* **c.-set,** juego de café, *m.* **c.-tree,** cafeto, *m*
coffer *n* cofre, *m;* arca, caja, *f*
coffin *n* ataúd, féretro, *m;* caja, *f*
cog *n mech* diente (de rueda), *m*
cogency *n* fuerza, *f*
cogent *a* convincente, fuerte; urgente
cogitate *vi* pensar, considerar, meditar
cogitation *n* reflexión, meditación, consideración, *f*
cognac *n* coñac, *m*
cognate *a* (of stock) consanguíneo; afín; análogo; semejante
cognition *n* cognición, *f*
cognitive *a* cognoscitivo
cognizance *n* conocimiento, *m;* jurisdicción, *f*
cogwheel *n* rueda dentada, *f*
cohabit *vi* cohabitar
cohabitation *n* cohabitación, *f*
coheir *n* coheredero, *m*
coheiress *n* coheredera, *f*
cohere *vi* pegarse, adherirse; unirse
coherent *a* coherente; consecuente
cohesion *n* cohesión, *f;* coherencia, *f*
cohort *n* cohorte, *f*
coif *n* cofia, *f;* toca, *f*
coiffure *n* peinado, *m;* tocado, *m*
coil *vt* arrollar; (*naut* of ropes) adujar. *vi* arrollarse; enroscarse; serpentear. *n* rollo, *m;* (of a serpent and ropes) anillo, *m;* (of hair) trenza, *f; elec* carrete, *m.* **coil of smoke,** nube de humo, *f.* **to c. up,** hacerse un ovillo
coiling *n* arrollamiento, *m;* serpenteo, *m*
coin *n* moneda, *f; inf* dinero, *m. vt* acuñar; (a new word) inventar. **to pay back in the same c.,** pagar en la misma moneda
coinage *n* acuñación, *f;* moneda, *f;* sistema monetario, *m;* invención, *f;* (new word) neologismo, *m*
coincide *vi* coincidir (con); estar conforme, estar de acuerdo
coincidence *n* coincidencia, *f;* (chance) casualidad, *f*
coiner *n* acuñador de moneda, *m;* monedero falso, *m;* (of phrases, etc.) inventor, *m*
coitus *n* coito, *m*
coke *n* (carbón de) coque, *m*
colander *n* colador, *m*
cold *a* frío. *n* frío, *m; med* catarro, constipado, *m.* **I am c.,** Tengo frío. **It is c.,** Está frío; (weather) Hace frío. **to catch a c.,** acatarrarse, resfriarse. **to grow c.,** enfriarse; (of the weather) empezar a hacer frío. **in c. blood,** a sangre fría. **c.-blooded,** (fishes, etc.) de sangre fría; (chilly, of persons) friolero; (pitiless) insensible, sin piedad; (of actions) a sangre fría, premeditado. **c.-chisel,** cortafrío, *m.* **c. cream,** crema (para el cutis), *f.* **c.-hearted,** seco, insensible. **c.-shoulder,** *n* frialdad, *f. vt* tratar con frialdad (a). **c.-storage,** conservación refrigerada, *f*
coldly *adv* fríamente
coldness *n* frío, *m;* (of one's reception, etc.) frialdad, *f;* (of heart) inhumanidad, *f*
coleopterous *a* coleóptero
colic *n* cólico, *m*
coliseum *n* coliseo, *m*
colitis *n* colitis, *f*
collaborate *vi* colaborar (con)
collaboration *n* colaboración, *f*
collaborationist *n* colaboracionista, *mf*
collaborator *n* colaborador (-ra); (quisling) colaboracionista, *mf*
collapse *n* derrumbamiento, *m;* desplome, *m; med* colapso, *m;* (of buildings and *fig*) hundimiento, *m;* (of plans) frustración, *f;* (failure) fracaso, *m. vi* derrumbarse; (of buildings, etc.) hundirse, venirse abajo; (of persons, fall) desplomarse; *med* sufrir colapso; (of plans, etc.) frustrarse, venirse abajo. **George came to us after the c. of France,** Jorge vino a quedarse con nosotros después del hundimiento de Francia
collapsible *a* plegable
collar *n* (of a garment and of fur) cuello, *m;* (of a dog, etc., and necklace) collar, *m. vt* (seize) agarrar. **detachable c.,** cuello suelto, *m.* **high c.,** alzacuello, *m.* **c.-bone,** clavícula, *f*
collate *vt* cotejar; (to a benefice) colacionar
collateral *a* colateral
collation *n* colación, *f*
colleague *n* colega, *m;* compañero (-ra)
collect *vt* (assemble) reunir; (catch) coger; acumular; (call for) pasar a buscar, ir (or venir) a buscar; (pick up) recoger; (taxes, etc.) recaudar; coleccionar; (one's strength, etc. and debts, etc.) cobrar; (letters) recoger. *vi* reunirse, congregarse; acumularse. *n ecc* colecta, *f.* **to c. oneself,** reponerse
collected *a* (of persons) seguro de sí.
collection *n* reunión, *f;* (of data, etc.) acumulación, *f;* (of pictures, stamps, etc.) colección, *f;* (of a debt, etc.) cobranza, *f;* (of taxes, etc.) recaudación, *f;* (from a mail box) recogida, *f;* (of laws, etc.) compilación, *f; ecc* ofertorio, *m;* (of donations) colecta, *f*
collection agency *n* agencia de cobros de cuentas, *f*
collective *a* colectivo. **c. bargaining,** regateo colectivo, trato colectivo, *m*
collectivism *n* colectivismo, *m*
collector *n* (of pictures, etc.) coleccionador (-ra), coleccionista, *mf;* cobrador, *m; elec* colector, *m*
college *n* colegio, *m;* escuela, *f;* universidad, *f.* **C. of Cardinals,** Colegio de Cardenales, *m*
collegiate *a* colegial, colegiado. **c. church,** iglesia colegial, *f*
collide *vi* chocar (contra), topar (con); estar en conflicto (con). **c. head-on,** chocar frontalmente
collie *n* perro de pastor escocés, *m*
collier *n* minero de carbón, *m;* (barco) carbonero, *m*
collision *n* choque, *m,* colisión, *f;* (of interests, etc.) antagonismo, conflicto, *m.* **to come into c. with,** chocar con
Cologne Colonia, *f*
colloid *a* coloide. *n* coloide, *m*
colloquial *a* familiar
colloquialism *n* expresión familiar, *f*
colloquially *adv* en lenguaje familiar; familiarmente
colloquy *n* coloquio, *m*
collusion *n* colusión, *f.* **to be in c.,** *law* coludir; conspirar, estar de manga
Colombia Colombia, *f*
Colombian *a* colombiano. *n* colombiano (-na)
colon *n anat* colon, *m;* (punctuation) dos puntos, *m pl*
colonel *n* coronel, *m*
colonial *a* colonial. *n* habitante de las colonias, *m.* **c. government** *Lat. Am.* coloniaje *m* **C. Office,** Ministerio de Asuntos Coloniales, *m.* **c. period** *Lat. Am.* coloniaje *m*
colonist *n* colono, *m;* colonizador (-ra)
colonization *n* colonización, *f*
colonize *vt* colonizar. *vi* establecerse en una colonia
colonizer *n* colonizador (-ra)
colonizing *n* colonización, *f, a* colonizador
colonnade *n* columnata, *f*
colony *n* colonia, *f*
color *n* color, *m;* colorido, *m;* tinta, *f;* materia colorante, *f; pl* **colors,** insignia, *f;* bandera, *f,* estandarte, *m; naut* pabellón, *m. vt* colorar; pintar; iluminar; (influence) influir, afectar. *vi* colorarse; ruborizarse; encenderse. **fast c.,** color estable, color sólido, *m.* **regimental colors,** bandera del regimiento, *f.* **with colors flying,** con tambor batiente, a banderas desplegadas. **to be off c.,** estar malucho, estar indispuesto. **to change c.,** (of persons) mudar de color, mudar de semblante. **to give c. to,** (a story, etc.) hacer verosímil. **to lay the colors on too thick,** recargar las tintas. **to pass with flying colors,** salir triunfante. **under c. of,** so color de, a pretexto de. **c.-blind,** daltoniano. **c.-blindness,** daltonismo, *m*
Colorado beetle *n* escarabajo de la patata, *m*

colored *a* colorado; de color
coloring *n* (substance) colorante, *m*; (act of) coloración, *f*; *art* colorido, *m*; (of complexion) colores, *m pl*
colorist *n* colorista, *mf*
colorless *a* sin color, incoloro; *fig* insípido
colossal *a* colosal, gigantesco; enorme; *inf* estupendo
colossus *n* coloso, *m*
colt *n* potro, *m*; (boy) muchacho alegre, *m*
colter *n* reja, reja del arado, *f*
colt's-foot *n bot* fárfara, *f*
columbine *n bot* aguileña, *f*; (in pantomime) Colombina, *f*
column *n* columna, *f*. **Fifth c.,** quinta columna, *f*
columned *a* con columnas
columnist *n* periodista, *m*
coma *n* coma, *m*
comatose *a* comatoso
comb *n* peine, *m*; (for flax) carda, *f*; (curry) almohaza, *f*; (of cock) cresta, carúncula, *f*; (of a wave) cima, cresta, *f*; (honey) panal, *m*, *vt* (hair) peinar; (flax) rastrillar, cardar. **c. and brush,** cepillo y peine. **high c.,** peineta, *f*. **to c. one's hair,** peinarse
combat *vt* luchar contra, combatir, resistir. *vi* combatir, pelear. *n* combate, *m*; lucha, batalla, *f*. **in single c.,** cuerpo a cuerpo
combatant *n* combatiente, *m*, *a* combatiente
combative *a* belicoso, pugnaz
combination *n* combinación, *f*; mezcla, *f*; unión, *f*; asociación, *f*; *pl* **combinations.** camisa pantalón, *f*. **c. lock,** cerradura de combinación, *f*
combine *vt* combinar; reunir, juntar; *chem* combinar. *vi* combinarse; asociarse (con); *com* fusionarse. *n* asociación, *f*; *com* monopolio, *m*
combustible *a* combustible. *n* combustible, *m*
combustion *n* combustión, *f*. **rapid c.,** combustión rápida, *f*. **spontaneous c.,** combustión espontánea, *f*
come *vi* venir; llegar; avanzar; acercarse; (happen) suceder, acontecer; (result) resultar; (find oneself) encontrarse, hallarse; (become) llegar a ser; (begin to) ponerse (a), empezar (a). **Coming!** ¡Voy! ¡Allá voy! **C., c.!** ¡Vamos! ¡No es para tanto! ¡Ánimo! **I am ready whatever comes,** Estoy preparado venga lo que venga. **He comes of a good family,** Es (Viene) de buena familia. **I came to know him well,** Llegué a conocerle bien. **I don't know what came over me,** No sé lo que me pasó. **When I came to consider it,** Cuando me puse a considerarlo. **The bill comes to six thousand pesetas,** La cuenta sale a seis mil pesetas. **He comes up before the judge tomorrow,** Ha de comparecer ante el juez mañana. **What you say comes to this,** Lo que dice Vd. se reduce a esto. **What is the world coming to?** ¿A dónde va parar el mundo? **It does not c. within my scope,** No está dentro de mi alcance. **to c. apart,** deshacerse; romperse; dividirse. **to c. home to,** *fig* impresionar mucho, tocar en lo más íntimo; hacer comprender (a). **to c. into bloom,** empezar a tener flores, florecer. **to c. into one's head,** venir a las mientes. **to c. into the world,** venir al mundo. **to c. near,** acercarse; aproximarse, estar próximo. **to c. next,** venir después; suceder luego. **to c. to an end,** terminar, acabarse. **to c. to blows,** venir a las manos. **to c. to grief,** salir mal parado; (of schemes, etc.) malograrse. **to c. to hand,** venir a mano; (of letters) llegar a las manos (de). **to c. to life,** despertar; animarse; resucitarse. **to c. to nothing,** frustrarse; no quedar en nada. **to c. to pass,** suceder; realizarse. **to c. to terms,** ponerse de acuerdo. **to c. true,** cumplirse, verificarse. **to c. about,** suceder, acontecer, tener lugar; (of the wind) girar. **to c. across,** dar con, encontrar por casualidad; tropezar con. **to c. after,** (a situation) solicitar; (follow) seguir (a); venir más tarde (que); (succeed) suceder. **to c. again,** volver. **to c. along,** caminar (por); andar (por); (arrive) llegar. **C. along!** ¡Ven! ¡Vamos! ¡Andamos! **to c. at,** alcanzar; (attack) embestir, atacar; (gain) obtener, adquirir. **to c. away,** irse, marcharse; (break) deshacerse. **to c. back,** volver, regresar, *Lat. Am.* devolverse **c.-back,** *n inf* respuesta, *f*; contraataque, *m*. **to c. before,** llegar antes; preceder (a). **to c. between,** interponerse (entre), intervenir. **to c. by,** pasar por, pasar junto a; (acquire) obtener, adquirir; (achieve) conseguir. **to c. down,** bajar, descender; (in the world) venir a menos; (be demolished) demolerse; (collapse) derrumbarse, hundirse; (of prices) bajar; (of traditions, etc.) llegar e.g. **This work has c. down to us in two fifteenth-century manuscripts** Esta obra nos ha llegado en dos manuscritos del siglo quince; (fall) caer. **c.-down,** *n* caída, *f*; frustración, *f*; desengaño, *m*; desprestigio, *m*; pérdida de posición, *f*. **to c. down on a person,** cantar la cartilla (a). **to c. down with altitude sickness** *Peru* asorocharse **to c. forward,** avanzar, adelantarse; (offer) ofrecerse; presentarse. **to c. in,** entrar; (of money) ingresar; (of trains, etc.) llegar; (of the tide) crecer; (of the new year) empezar; (of fashion) ponerse de moda; (be useful) servir (para). **C. in!** ¡Adelante! ¡Pase Vd.! **to c. into,** (a scheme) asociarse con; (property) heredar; (the mind) presentarse a la imaginación, ocurrirse (a). **to c. off,** (happen) tener lugar; realizarse, efectuarse; (be successful) tener éxito; (break off) separarse (de); romperse. **to c. off well,** tener éxito; (of persons) salir bien. **c. off the press,** salir de prensas. **to c. on,** avanzar; (of actors) salir a la escena; (progress) hacer progresos; (develop) desarrollarse; (of pain, etc.) acometer (a); (arrive) llegar; (of a lawsuit) verse. **C. on!** ¡Vamos! ¡En marcha! **to c. out,** salir; (of stars) nacer; (of buds, etc.) brotar; (of the moon, etc.) asomarse; (of stains) borrarse, salir; (of a book) ver la luz, publicarse; (of secrets) divulgarse, saberse; (of a girl, in society) ponerse de largo; (on strike) declararse en huelga; (of fashions, etc.) aparecer. **to c. out with,** (a remark) soltar; (oaths, etc.) prorrumpir (en); (disclose) revelar, hacer público. **to c. round,** (to see someone) venir a ver (a); (coax) engatusar; (after a faint, etc.) volver en sí; (after illness) reponerse; (to another's point of view) aceptar, compartir. **to c. through,** pasar por; (trials, etc.) subir; salir de; (of liquids) salirse. **to c. to,** volver en sí. **to c. together,** reunirse, juntarse; venir juntos; unirse. **to c. under,** venir (or estar) bajo la jurisdicción de; (the influence of) estar dominado por; (figure among) figurar entre, estar comprendido en. **to c. up,** subir; (of sun, moon) salir; (of plants) brotar; (of problems, etc.) surgir; (in conversation) discutirse; (before a court) comparecer. **to c. up to,** (equal) igualar, ser igual (a); rivalizar con; (in height) llegar hasta. **He came up to them in the street,** Les abordó (or se les acercó) en la calle. **We have c. up against many difficulties,** Hemos tropezado con muchas dificultades. **This novel does not c. up to his last,** Esta última novela no es tan buena como la anterior. **The party did not c. up to their expectations,** La reunión no fue tan divertida como esperaban. **to c. up with,** (a person) alcanzar (a). **to c. upon,** encontrar, hallar; tropezar con; encontrar por casualidad. **to c. upon evil days,** venir a menos
comedian *n* actor cómico, comediante, *m*
comedy *n* comedia, *f*. **c. of manners,** comedia de costumbres, *f*
comeliness *n* hermosura, *f*
comely *a* hermoso
comer *n* el, *m*, (*f*, la) que viene. **all comers,** todo el mundo. **first c.,** primer (-ra) venido (-da)
comet *n* cometa, *m*
comfort *vt* consolar, confortar; (encourage) animar; (reassure) alegrar. *n* consuelo, *m*; satisfacción, *f*; comodidad, *f*; bienestar, *m*. **He lives in great c.,** Vive con mucha comodidad. **c.-loving,** comodón
comfortable *a* cómodo; (with income) suficiente; (consoling) consolador. **to make oneself c.,** ponerse cómodo
comfortably *adv* cómodamente; suficientemente; fácil-

mente; con facilidad; (well) bien. **He is c. off,** Está bien de dinero
comforter *n* consolador (-ra); (baby's) chupador, *m;* (scarf) bufanda, *f*
comforting *a* consolador
comfortless *a* incómodo, sin comodidad; desconsolador; (of persons) inconsolable, desconsolado
comic *a* cómico; bufo; satírico. *n* cómico, *m; pl* **comics,** (printed) historietas cómicas, *f pl.* **c. opera,** ópera cómicas, *f.* **c. paper,** periódico satírico, *m*
comical *a* cómico; divertido, gracioso
coming *a* (with year, etc.) próximo, que viene; (promising) de porvenir; (approaching) que se acerca. *n* venida, *f;* llegada, *f;* advenimiento, *m.* **c.-out party,** puesta de largo, *f.* **comings and goings,** entradas y salidas, *f pl*
comma *n* coma, *f.* **inverted commas,** comillas, *f pl*
command *vt* mandar, ordenar; (silence, respect, etc.) imponer; (an army, fleet, etc.) comandar; capitanear; (one's emotions) dominar; (have at one's disposal) disponer de; (a military position, view) dominar; (sympathy, etc.) despertar, merecer; (of price) venderse por. *vi* mandar. *n* orden, *f;* (*mil nav*) mando, *m;* (of an army, etc.) comandancia, *f;* (of one's emotions, etc.) dominio, *m;* (of a military position, etc.) dominación, *f;* disposición, *f.* **By Royal C.,** Por Real Orden; (of shops, etc.) Proveedor de la Real Casa. **The house commands lovely views of the mountains,** La casa tiene hermosas vistas de las montañas. **word of c.,** orden, *f.* **Yours to c.,** A la disposición de Vd.
commandant *n* comandante, *m*
commandeer *vt* (conscript) reclutar; *mil* requisar; expropiar
commander *n mil* comandante, *m; nav* capitán de fragata, *m;* (of order of Knighthood) comendador, *m.* **c.-in-chief,** generalísimo, *m.* **C. of the Faithful,** Comendador de los creyentes, *m*
commanding *a mil* comandante; imponente; (of manner) imperioso; dominante. **c. officer,** comandante en jefe, *m*
commandment *n* precepto, mandamiento, *m.* **the Ten Commandments,** los diez mandamientos
commando *n mil* comando, *m*
commemorate *vt* conmemorar
commemoration *n* conmemoración, *f*
commemorative *a* conmemorativo
commence *vt* comenzar, empezar, principiar. *vi* comenzar. **He commenced to eat,** Empezó a comer
commencement *n* principio, comienzo, *m*
commend *vt* (entrust) encomendar; recomendar; alabar
commendable *a* loable; recomendable
commendation *n* aprobación, alabanza, *f,* aplauso, *m*
commendatory *a* (of letters) comendatorio
commensurable *a* conmensurable
commensurate *a* proporcionado (a); conforme (a)
comment *n* observación, *f;* (on a work) comento, *m;* explicación, nota, *f. vi* hacer una observación (sobre); (a work) comentar, anotar. **to c. unfavorably on,** criticar
commentary *n* comentario, *m;* (on a person, etc.) comentos, *m pl,* observaciones, *f pl*
commentator *n* comentador (-ra); (of a work) comentarista, *mf*
commerce *n* comercio, *m;* negocios, *m pl;* (social) trato, *m*
commercial *a* comercial; mercantil. **c. traveler,** viajante, *mf*
commercialism *n* mercantilismo, *m*
commercialize *vt* hacer objeto de comercio
commercially *adv* comercialmente
commingle *vt* mezclar. *vi* mezclarse
commiserate *vi* compadecerse (de), apiadarse (de)
commiseration *n* conmiseración, compasión, *f*
commissariat *n* comisaría, *f; inf* despensa, *f*
commissary *n* comisario, *m*
commission *n* comisión, *f; mil* graduación de oficial, *f. vt* comisionar; (a ship) poner en servicio activo, armar; (appoint) nombrar. **in c.,** en servicio, activo. **out of c.,** (of ships) inutilizado; inservible. **c. agent,** comisionista, *mf* **to gain one's c.,** *mil* graduarse de oficial. **to put out of c.,** retirar del servicio; poner fuera de combate; estropear
commissionaire *n* portero, *m*
commissioned *a* comisionado. **c. officer,** oficial, *m*
commissioner *n* comisario, *m.* **High C.,** alto comisario, *m.* **c. for oaths,** notario, *m.* **c. of police,** jefe de policía, *m*
commit *vt* entregar (a); (a crime) cometer; (to prison) encarcelar; (for trial) remitir. **to c. oneself,** comprometerse. **to c. to memory,** aprender de memoria. **to c. to writing,** poner por escrito
commitment *n* (financial, etc.) obligación, responsabilidad, *f;* compromiso, *m*
committal *n* (of an offence) comisión, *f;* (placing, entrusting) entrega, *f;* (to prison) encarcelamiento, *m;* (legal procedure) auto de prisión, *m*
committee *n* comité, *m;* comisión, junta, *f;* consejo, *m.* **They decided in c.,** Tomaron la resolución en comité. **c. of management,** consejo de administración, *m*
commodious *a* espacioso, grande
commodiousness *n* espaciosidad, *f*
commodity *n* artículo, *m,* mercancía, *f*
commodore *n nav* jefe de escuadra, *m;* comodoro, *m*
common *a* común; general, corriente; universal; vulgar; (disparaging) cursi; (elementary) elemental. *n* pastos comunes, *m pl.* **He is not a c. man,** No es un hombre cualquiera; No es un hombre vulgar. **in c.,** en común. **the c. man,** el hombre medio. **the c. people,** el pueblo. **c. sense,** sentido común, *m.* **c. soldier,** soldado raso, *m.* **c. speech,** lenguaje vulgar, *m.* **c. usage,** uso corriente, *m*
commoner *n* plebeyo (-ya)
commonly *adv* comúnmente, por lo general
commonness *n* frecuencia, *f;* vulgaridad, *f*
commonplace *n* lugar común, *m;* trivialidad, *f. a* trivial
commons *n* el pueblo; (House of) Cámara de los Comunes, *f;* (food) provisiones, *f pl.* **to be on short c.,** comer mal, estar mal alimentado
Commonwealth *n* estado, *m;* república, *f;* comunidad (de naciones), *f;* mancomunidad, *f.* **the Commonwealth of Puerto Rico,** el Estado Libre Asociado de Puerto Rico, *m*
commotion *n* confusión, *f;* conmoción, perturbación, *f;* tumulto, *m*
communal *a* comunal
commune *n* comuna, *f;* comunión, *f, vi* conversar (con). **to c. with oneself,** hablar consigo
communicable *a* comunicable
communicant *n ecc* comulgante, *mf;* (of information) informante, *mf*
communicate *vt* comunicar; (diseases) transmitir. *vi* comunicarse (con); *ecc* comulgar
communication *n* comunicación, *f.* **lines of c.,** comunicaciones, *f pl.* **to get into c. with,** ponerse en comunicación con. **c.-cord,** (in a railway carriage) timbre de alarma, *m*
communicative *a* comunicativo; expansivo
communicativeness *n* carácter expansivo, *m;* locuacidad, *f*
communion *n* comunión, *f.* **Holy c.,** comunión, *f.* **to take c.,** comulgar. **c. card,** cédula de comunión, *f.* **c. cup,** cáliz, *f.* **c. table,** sagrada mesa, *f;* altar, *m*
communiqué *n* comunicación, parte, *f.* **to issue a c.,** dar parte
communism *n* comunismo, *m*
communist *n* comunista, *mf a* comunista
community *n* comunidad, *f.* **the c.,** la nación; el público. **c. center,** centro social, *m*
commutation *n* conmutación, *f;* reducción, *f*
commute *vt* conmutar; reducir
compact *n* (pact) acuerdo, pacto, *m;* (powder) polvo-

rera, *f.* *a* compacto; firme; sólido; apretado, cerrado; (of persons) bien hecho; (of style) conciso, sucinto
compactness *n* compacidad, *f;* (of style) concisión, *f*
companion *n* compañero (-ra); camarada, *mf;* (of an Order) caballero, *m,* (or dama, *f*). *vt* acompañar. **lady c.,** señora de compañía, *f.* **c.-hatch,** cubierta de escotilla, *f.* **c.-ladder,** escala de toldilla, *f*
companionable *a* sociable, amistoso
companionably *adv* sociablemente, amistosamente
companionship *n* compañía, *f;* compañerismo, *m*
company *n* (*com mil* etc.) compañía, *f;* (ship's) tripulación, *f.* **I will keep you c.,** Te haré compañía. **to part c. with,** separarse de. **Present c. excepted!** ¡Mejorando lo presente! **They are not very good c.,** No son muy divertidos
company store *n* tienda de raya, *f* (Mexico)
comparable *a* comparable
comparably *adv* comparablemente
comparative *a* comparativo; relativo
comparatively *adv* comparativamente; relativamente
compare *vt* comparar. *vi* compararse; poder compararse. ser comparable. **beyond c.,** sin comparación; sin igual. **to c. favorably with,** no perder por comparación con. **to c. notes,** cambiar impresiones
comparison *n* comparación, *f.* **in c. with,** comparado con
compartment *n* compartimiento, *m; rw* departamento, *m*
compass *n* circuito, *m;* límites, *m pl;* alcance, *m;* (of a voice) gama, *f; naut* brújula, *f; pl* **compasses,** compás, *m. vt* (achieve) conseguir; (plan) idear, **mariner's c.,** compás de mar. *m,* rosa de los vientos, *f.* **pocket c.,** brújula de bolsillo, *f.* **to c. about,** cercar, rodear
compassion *n* compasión, *f.* **to have c. on,** apiadarse de, compadecerse de
compassionate *a* compasivo, piadoso. **c. leave,** permiso, *m*
compassionately *adv* compasivamente, con piedad
compatibility *n* compatibilidad, *f*
compatible *a* compatible, conciliable
compatriot *n* compatriota, *mf*
compel *vt* obligar (a), forzar (a); exigir; imponer. **His attitude compels respect,** Su actitud impone el respeto
compelling *a* compulsivo
compendious *a* compendioso, sucinto
compendium *n* compendio, *m;* resumen, *m*
compensate *vt* compensar; (reward) recompensar; (for loss, etc.) indemnizar. **to c. for,** compensar; indemnizar contra
compensation *n* compensación, *f;* (reward) recompensa, *f;* (for loss, etc.) indemnización, *f*
compensatory *a* compensatorio
compete *vi* competir (con); rivalizar; ser rivales; (in a competition) concurrir
competence *n* aptitud, *f;* capacidad, *f;* competencia, *f*
competent *a* competente; capaz
competently *adv* competentemente
competition *n* competencia, competición, rivalidad, *f;* emulación, *f;* (contest, etc.) concurso, *m.* **spirit of c.,** espíritu de competencia, *m*
competitive *a* competidor; de competición. **c. examination,** oposición, *f*
competitor *n* competidor (-ra)
compilation *n* compilación, *f*
compile *vt* compilar
compiler *n* compilador (-ra)
complacence *n* complacencia, satisfacción, *f;* contento de sí mismo, *m*
complacent *a* satisfecho; pagado de sí mismo
complacently *adv* con satisfacción
complain *vi* quejarse; lamentarse; *law* querellarse. **He complains about everything,** Se queja de todo
complainant *n law* demandante, *mf*
complaint *n* queja, *f;* lamento, *m; law* demanda, *f;* (illness) enfermedad, *f.* **to lodge a c. (against),** quejarse (de)
complaisance *n* afabilidad, cortesía, *f*
complaisant *a* complaciente, cortés, afable; (of husbands) consentido, sufrido
complement *n* complemento, *m;* total, número completo, *m. vt* completar
complementary *a* complementario
complete *a* entero; completo; perfecto; acabado. *vt* completar; acabar; (happiness, etc.) coronar, poner el último toque (a); (years) cumplir; (forms) llenar
completely *adv* completamente, enteramente
completeness *n* entereza, *f;* totalidad, *f*
completion *n* terminación, *f,* fin, *m*
complex *a* complejo. *n* complejo, *m.* **inferiority c.,** complejo de inferioridad, *m*
complexion *n* tez, *f,* cutis, *m; fig* carácter, *m*
complexity *n* complejidad, *f*
compliance *n* condescendencia, *f;* (subservience) sumisión, *f;* obediencia, *f.* **in c. with,** de acuerdo con, en conformidad con
compliant *a* condescendiente; sumiso, dócil; obediente
complicate *vt* complicar
complicated *a* complejo; complicado; enredado
complication *n* complicación, *f*
complicity *n* complicidad, *f.* **c. in a crime,** complicidad en un crimen
compliment *n* cumplido, *m,* cortesía, *f;* requiebro, *inf* piropo, *m;* favor, *m;* honor, *m;* (greeting) saludo, *m;* (congratulation) felicitación, *f. vt* cumplimentar; requebrar; (flatter) adular, lisonjear; (congratulate) felicitar. **They did him the c. of reading his book,** Le hicieron el honor de leer su libro. **to pay compliments,** hacer cumplidos; *inf* echar piropos
complimentary *a* lisonjero; galante. **c. ticket,** billete gratuito, *m*
comply *vi* (with) cumplir, obedecer; conformarse (con); consentir
component *a* componente. *n* componente, *m*
comport *vt* **(oneself),** comportarse
comportment *n* comportamiento, *m,* conducta, *f*
compose *vt* (all meanings) componer. **to c. oneself,** serenarse, calmarse. **to c. one's features,** componer el semblante
composed *a* sereno, tranquilo, sosegado
composer *n* compositor (-ra)
composite *a* compuesto; mixto. *n* compuesto, *m; bot* planta compuesta, *f*
composition *n* (all meanings) composición, *f*
compositor *n print* cajista, *mf*
composure *n* tranquilidad, serenidad, calma, *f;* sangre fría, *f,* aplomo, *m*
compote *n* compota, *f*
compound *vt* mezclar, componer; concertar. *a* compuesto. *n* compuesto, *m;* mixtura, *f.* **c. interest,** interés compuesto, *m*
comprehend *vt* comprender
comprehensible *a* comprensible
comprehensibly *adv* comprensiblemente
comprehension *n* comprensión, *f*
comprehensive *a* comprensivo
comprehensiveness *n* alcance, *m,* extensión, *f*
compress *vt* comprimir; condensar; reducir, abreviar. *n* compresa, *f*
compression *n* compresión, *f*
compressor *n* compresor, *m*
comprise *vt* comprender, abarcar, incluir
compromise *n* compromiso, *m,* transacción, *f;* componenda, *f. vt* (settle) componer, arreglar; (jeopardize) arriesgar; comprometer. *vi* transigir. **to c. oneself,** comprometerse
compromising *a* comprometedor
comptometer *n* calculador, *m*
compulsion *n* compulsión, fuerza, *f.* **under c.,** a la fuerza

compulsory *a* obligatorio. **c. measures,** medidas obligatorias, *f pl.* **c. powers,** poderes absolutos, *m pl*
compunction *n* compunción, *f,* remordimiento, *m;* escrúpulo, *m.* **without c.,** sin escrúpulo
computable *a* calculable
computation *n* computación, *f,* cómputo, *m*
compute *vt* computar, calcular.
computer *m* computador, *m* (Western Hemisphere), ordenador, *m* (Spain)
computer center *n* centro calculador, centro de computación, *m*
comrade *n* camarada, *mf* compañero (-ra)
comradeship *n* compañerismo, *m*
con *vt* estudiar; leer con atención; *naut* gobernar (el buque)
concatenation *n* concatenación, *f*
concave *a* cóncavo
conceal *vt* esconder, ocultar; (the truth, etc.) encubrir, callar; disimular
concealed *a* oculto; escondido; disimulado. **c. lighting,** iluminación indirecta, *f.* **c. turning,** (on a road) viraje oculto, *m*
concealment *n* ocultación, *f;* encubrimiento, *m;* (place of) escondite, *m;* secreto, *m*
concede *vt* conceder
conceit *n* presunción, vanidad, fatuidad, *f,* envanecimiento, *m.* **to have a good c. of oneself,** estar pagado de sí mismo
conceited *a* presumido, fatuo, vanidoso. **to become c.** *Lat. Am.* ensimismarse
conceivable *a* concebible, imaginable
conceivably *adv* posiblemente
conceive *vt* concebir; (affection, etc.) tomar; (an idea, etc.) formar; (plan) formular, idear. *vi* concebir; (understand) comprender; (suppose) imaginar, suponer
concentrate *vt* concentrar. *vi* concentrarse; (on, upon) dedicarse (a), entregarse (a); prestar atención (a), concentrar atención (en)
concentrated *a* concentrado
concentration *n* concentración, *f.* **c. camp,** campo de concentración, *m*
concentric *a* concéntrico
concept *n* concepto, *m*
conception *n* concepción, *f;* conocimiento, *m;* idea, *f,* concepto, *m.* **to have not the remotest c. of,** no tener la menor idea de
conceptualism *n* conceptualismo, *m*
concern *vt* tocar, tener que vercon, importar, concernir; interesar; referirse (a); tratar (de); (trouble) preocupar, inquietar; (take part in) ocuparse (de or con). *n* asunto, *m,* cosa, *f;* (share) interés, *m;* (anxiety) inquietud, *f;* solicitud, *f;* (business) casa comercial, firma, *f.* **as concerns . . . ,** en cuanto a . . . , respecto a . . . **It concerns the date of the next meeting,** Es cuestión de la fecha de la próxima reunión. **It is no c. of yours,** No tiene nada que ver contigo. **The book is concerned with the adventures of two boys,** El libro trata de las aventuras de dos muchachos
concerned *a* ocupado (en); afectado; (in a crime) implicado (en); (troubled) preocupado; inquieto, agitado
concerning *prep* tocante a, con respecto a, referente a, sobre
concert *n* acuerdo, concierto, *m,* armonía, *f; mus* concierto, *m, vt* concertar, acordar. **in c. with,** de acuerdo con. **c. hall,** sala de conciertos, *f*
concerted *a* concertado
concertina *n* concertina, *f*
concerto *n* concierto, *m*
concession *n* concesión, *f;* privilegio, *m*
concessionaire *n* concesionario, *m*
concierge *n* conserje, *m*
conciliate *vt* conciliar
conciliation *n* conciliación, *f*
conciliatory *a* conciliador
concise *a* conciso, breve, sucinto
concisely *adv* concisamente
concision *n* concisión, *f*
conclave *n* conciliábulo, *m;* (of cardinals) conclave, *m*
conclude *vt* concluir. *vi* concluirse
conclusion *n* conclusión, *f.* **in c.,** en conclusión, para terminar. **to come to the c. that . . . ,** concluir que . . .
conclusive *a* conclusivo, concluyente, decisivo
conclusively *adv* concluyentemente
conclusiveness *n* carácter decisivo, *m,* lo concluyente
concoct *vt* confeccionar; inventar
concoction *n* confección, *f;* mezcla, *f;* invención, *f;* (of a plot) maquinación, *f*
concomitant *a* concomitante. *n* concomitante, *m*
concord *n* concordia, buena inteligencia, armonía, *f;* (*mus gram*) concordancia, *f;* (of sounds) armonía, *f*
concordance *n* concordia, armonía, *f;* (book) concordancias, *f pl*
concordat *n* concordato, *m*
concourse *n* concurrencia, muchedumbre, *f*
concrete *a* concreto; de hormigón. *n* hormigón, *m. vt* concretar; cubrir de hormigón. **reinforced c.,** hormigón armado, *m*
concretion *n* concreción, *f*
concubine *n* concubina, manceba, *f*
concur *vi* coincidir, concurrir; estar de acuerdo, convenir (en)
concurrence *n* (agreement) acuerdo, consentimiento, *m,* aprobación, *f*
concurrent *a* concurrente; unánime; coincidente
concurrently *adv* concurrentemente
concussion *n* concusión, *f; med* concusión cerebral, *f*
condemn *vt* condenar; censurar, culpar; (forfeit) confiscar. **condemned cell,** celda de los condenados a muerte, *f*
condemnation *n* condenación, *f;* censura, *f*
condensation *n* condensación, *f*
condense *vt* condensar. *vi* condensarse
condenser *n* (*elec mech chem*) condensador, *m*
condescend *vi* dignarse; (in a bad sense) consentir (en); (with affability) condescender
condescending *a* condescendiente
condescendingly *adv* con condescendencia
condescension *n* condescendencia, *f;* afabilidad, *f*
condign *a* condigno
condiment *n* condimento, *m*
condition *n* condición, *f;* estado, *m; pl* **conditions,** condiciones, *f pl;* circunstancias, *f pl.* **on c. that,** con tal que; siempre que, dado que. **to be in no c. to,** no estar en condiciones de. **to change one's c.,** cambiar de estado. **to keep oneself in c.,** mantenerse en buena forma
conditional *a* condicional. **to be c. on,** depender de
conditionally *adv* condicionalmente
conditioned *a* acondicionado. **c. reflex,** reflejo acondicionado, *m*
condole *vi* condolerse (de); (on a bereavement) dar el pésame
condolence *n* condolencia, *f.* **to present one's condolences,** dar el pésame
condom *n* condón, *m, Argentina* forro, *m*
condone *vt* condonar, perdonar
conduce *vi* contribuir, conducir
conducive *a* que contribuye, conducente; favorable
conduct *n* conducta, *f. vt* conducir; guiar; *mus* dirigir; (oneself) portarse, conducirse; *phys* conducir. *vi mus* dirigir (una orquesta, etc.); *phys* ser conductor. **conducted tour,** excursión acompañada, *f;* viaje acompañado, *m*
conduction *n* conducción, *f*
conductive *a* conductivo
conductivity *n* conductibilidad, *f*
conductor *n* (guide) guía, *mf;* (of an orchestra) director, *m;* (on a tram, etc.) cobrador, *m; phys* conductor, *m*
conduit *n* conducto, *m;* cañería, *f;* canal, *m*
cone *n* (*bot geom* etc.) cono, *m*
confabulation *n* confabulación, *f*

confection *n* confección, *f*, *vt* confeccionar
confectioner *n* confitero (-ra); pastelero (-ra)
confectionery *n* confitería, pastelería, repostería, *f*
confederate *a* confederado; aliado. *n* confederado, *m*; (in crime) cómplice, *mf*. *vt* confederar. *vi* confederarse; aliarse
confederation *n* confederación, *f*
confer *vt* conceder, conferir; (an honor, etc.) otorgar, investir (con). *vi* consultar (con); deliberar, considerar
conference *n* conferencia, consulta, *f*; conversación, *f*
conferment *n* otorgamiento, *m*; concesión, *f*
confess *vt* confesar, reconocer; *inf* admitir; (of a priest) confesar; (of a penitent) confesarse. *vi* hacer una confesión; (one's sins) confesarse. **I c. that I was surprised,** No puedo negar que me sorprendió
confessed *a* confesado, declarado
confession *n* confesión, *f*; reconocimiento, *m*; declaración, *f*; religión, *f*; (creed) credo, *m*. **to go to c.,** confesarse. **to hear a c.,** confesar (a)
confessional *n* confesionario, *m*
confessor *n* confesor, *m*
confetti *n pl* confeti, papel picado *m*, serpentina, *f*
confidant *n* confidente, *m*
confidante *n* confidenta, *f*
confide *vi* confiar (a or en). *vt* confiar
confidence *n* confianza, *f*; seguridad, *f*; (revelation) confidencia, *f*. **in c.,** en confianza. **over-c.,** presunción, *f*. **to have c. in,** tener confianza en. **c. man,** caballero de industria, estafador, *m*. **c. trick,** timo, *m*
confident *a* confiado; seguro; (conceited) presumido
confidential *a* confidencial; de confianza. **c. clerk,** empleado (-da) de confianza. **c. letter,** carta confidencial, *f*
confidentially *adv* en confianza, confidencialmente
confidently *adv* confiadamente
confiding *a* confiado
confidingly *adv* con confianza
configuration *n* configuración, *f*
confine *vt* limitar; (imprison) encerrar. **confined space,** espacio limitado, *m*. **to be confined,** (of a woman) estar de parto, parir. **to be confined to one's room,** no poder dejar su cuarto. **to c. oneself to,** limitarse a
confinement *n* encierro, *m*, prisión, *f*; reclusión, *f*; (of a woman) parto, *m*. **to suffer solitary c.,** estar incomunicado
confines *n pl* límites, *m pl*; confines, *m pl*; fronteras, *f pl*
confirm *vt* confirmar; corroborar; *ecc* confirmar
confirmation *n* confirmación, *f*; (of a treaty) ratificación, *f*; *ecc* confirmación, *f*
confirmatory *a* confirmatorio
confirmed *a* inveterado
confiscate *vt* confiscar
confiscation *n* confiscación, *f*
conflagration *n* conflagración, *f*, incendio, *m*
conflict *n* conflicto, *m*; lucha, *f*. *vi* estar opuesto (a), estar en contradicción (con)
conflicting *a* opuesto; incompatible; (of evidence) contradictorio
confluence *n* confluencia, *f*
conform *vt* ajustar, conformar. *vi* ajustarse (a), amoldarse (a); conformarse (a); adaptarse (a)
conformation *n* conformación, *f*
conformity *n* conformidad, *f*. **in c. with,** en conformidad con, con arreglo a
confound *vt* confundir. **C. it!** ¡Demonio!
confounded *a* perplejo; *inf* maldito
confraternity *n* cofradía, hermandad, *f*
confront *vt* hacer frente (a), afrontar; salir al paso; confrontar
Confucianism *n* el confucianismo, *m*
confuse *vt* turbar, aturdir; confundir (con); (the issue) obscurecer; (disconcert) desconcertar, dejar confuso (a); dejar perplejo (a). **You have confused one thing with another,** Has confundido una cosa con otra. **My mind was confused,** Mis ideas eran confusas; Tenía la cabeza trastornada
confused *a* confuso
confusing *a* turbador; desconcertante. **It is all very c.,** Todo ello es muy difícil de comprender
confusion *n* confusión, *f*. **covered with c.,** confuso, avergonzado. **to be in c.,** estar confuso; estar en desorden
confute *vt* (a person) confundir; (by evidence) refutar, confutar
congeal *vt* congelar; (blood) coagular. *vi* congelarse, helarse; coagularse
congealment *n* congelación, *f*; (of blood) coagulación, *f*
congenial *a* (of persons) simpático; propicio, favorable; agradable
congenital *a* congénito
congest *vt* atestar; amontonar; *med* congestionar
congested *a med* congestionado; (of places) atestado de gente; de mayor población; concurrido. **c. area,** área de mayor densidad de población, *f*
congestion *n med* congestión, *f*; densidad del tráfico, *f*; mayor densidad de población, *f*
conglomerate *a* conglomerado. *n* conglomerado, *m*
conglomeration *n* conglomeración, *f*
congratulate *vt* felicitar, dar la enhorabuena (a); congratular
congratulation *n* felicitación, enhorabuena, *f*; congratulación, *f*
congratulatory *a* de felicitación, congratulatorio
congregate *vi* congregarse, reunirse, juntarse
congregation *n* congregación, *f*; asamblea, reunión, *f*; (in a church) fieles, *m pl*; (parishioners) feligreses, *m pl*
congress *n* congreso, *m*. **C.-man,** miembro del Congreso, *m*
conical *a* cónico
conifer *n* conífera, *f*
coniferous *a* conífero
conjectural *a* conjetural
conjecture *n* conjetura, *f*, *vt* conjeturar
conjoint *a* asociado, conjunto
conjointly *adv* juntamente, en común
conjugal *a* conyugal
conjugate *vt* conjugar. *vi* conjugarse
conjugation *n* conjugación, *f*
conjunction *n* conjunción, *f*. **in c. with,** de acuerdo con
conjunctive *a* conjuntivo. *n* conjunción, *f*
conjunctivitis *n* conjuntivitis, *f*
conjure *vt* (implore) rogar, suplicar. *vi* (juggle) hacer juegos de manos. **a name to c. with,** un nombre todopoderoso. **to c. up,** (spirits) conjurar; *fig* evocar
conjurer, conjuror *n* (magician) nigromante, *m*; prestidigitador, *m*. **conjuror's wand,** varilla de virtudes, *f*
conjuring *n* prestidigitación, *f*, juegos de manos, *m pl*. **c. trick,** juego de manos, *m*. **c. up,** evocación, *f*
connect *vt* juntar, unir; (relate) relacionar; asociar; (*elec* and *mech*) conectar. *vi* juntarse, unirse; relacionarse; asociarse; (of events) encadenarse; (of trains) enlazar. **This train connects with the Madrid express,** Este tren enlaza con el expreso de Madrid. **They are connected with the Borgia family,** Están emparentados con los Borgia, Son parientes de los Borgia
connected *a* conexo; (coherent) coherente; relacionado; asociado; (in a crime) implicado; (by marriage, etc.) emparentado
connectedly *adv* coherentemente
connecting *a* que une; (*mech* and *elec*) conectivo; (of doors, etc.) comunicante. **c.-link,** *mech* varilla de conexión, *f*; *fig* lazo, *m*. **c.-rod,** biela, *f*
connection, connexion *n* conexión, *f*; unión, *f*; (of ideas) relación, *f*; (junction) empalme, *m*; (of trains, boats) enlace, *m*; (intimacy) intimidad, *f*; (relative) pariente, *m*; (of a firm, etc.) clientela, *f*; *elec* conexión, *f*. **in**

c. with, con referencia a; en asociación con. **in this c.,** respecto a esto
conning tower *n* torre de mando, *f*
connivance *n* consentimiento, *m*; complicidad, *f*
connive (at) *vi* hacer la vista gorda, ser cómplice (en)
connotation *n* connotación, *f*
connote *vt* connotar
connubial *a* conyugal
conquer *vt* conquistar; vencer. *vi* triunfar
conquering *a* conquistador, vencedor; triunfante, victorioso
conqueror *n* conquistador, *m*; vencedor, *m*
conquest *n* conquista, *f*. **to make a c. of,** conquistar
consanguineous *a* consanguíneo
consanguinity *n* consanguinidad, *f*
conscience *n* conciencia, *f*. **in all c.,** en verdad. **with a clear c.,** con la conciencia limpia. **c.-stricken,** lleno de remordimientos
conscienceless *a* desalmado, falto de conciencia
conscientious *a* concienzudo; diligente. **c. objector,** objetor de conciencia, *m*
conscientiously *adv* concienzudamente
conscientiousness *n* conciencia, diligencia, *f*; rectitud, *f*
conscious *a* consciente. *n psy* consciente, *m*. **to become c.,** (after unconsciousness) volver en sí. **to become c. of,** darse cuenta de
consciously *adv* conscientemente, a sabiendas
consciousness *n* conciencia, *f*; conocimiento, sentido, *m*. **to lose c.,** perder el conocimiento, perder el sentido. **to recover c.,** recobrar el sentido, volver en sí
conscript *n* conscripto, *m*, *a* conscripto. *vt* reclutar
conscription *n* conscripción, *f*
consecrate *vt* consagrar; bendecir
consecration *n* consagración, *f*; dedicación, *f*
consecutive *a* consecutivo
consecutively *adv* consecutivamente
consensus *n* consenso, *m*, unanimidad, *f*. **c. of opinion,** opinión general, *f*
consent *vi* consentir. *n* consentimiento, *m*; permiso, *m*, aquiescencia, *f*. **by common c.,** de común acuerdo
consequence *n* consecuencia, *f*; resultado, *m*; importancia, *f*, **in c.,** por consiguiente. **in c. of,** de resultas de. **of no c.,** sin importancia
consequences *n* (game) cartas rusas, *f pl*
consequent *a* consecuente, consiguiente
consequential *a* consecuente; (of persons) fatuo, engreído
consequently *adv* por consiguiente, en consecuencia
conservation *n* conservación, *f*. **c. of energy,** conservación de energía, *f*
conservatism *n* conservadurismo, *m*
conservative *a* preservativo; conservador. *n* conservador (-ra). **c. party,** partido conservador, *m*
conservatoire *n* conservatorio de música, *m*
conservatory *n* invernáculo, invernadero, *m*
conserve *vt* conservar
consider *vt* considerar, pensar meditar; tomar en cuenta; examinar; (deem) juzgar; (believe) creer, estar convencido de (que); (of persons) considerar. **all things considered,** considerando todos los puntos, después de considerarlo todo
considerable *a* considerable
considerably *adv* considerablemente
considerate *a* considerado, solícito
considerately *adv* con consideración, solícitamente
consideration *n* consideración, *f*; reflexión, deliberación, *f*; remuneración, *f*. **out of c. for,** en consideración de; por consideración a. **to take into c.,** tomar en cuenta, tomar en consideración
considered *a* considerado
considering *prep* en consideración de, considerando, en vista de
consign *vt* consignar; *fig* enviar. **to c. to oblivion,** sepultar en el olvido
consignee *n* consignatorio, *m*
consignment *n* consignación, *f*; envío, *m*
consignor *n* consignador, *m*
consist *vi* consistir (en); ser compatible (con). **to c. of,** componerse de, consistir de
consistence, consistency *n* consistencia, *f*; compatibilidad, *f*; lógica, *f*; (of persons) consecuencia, *f*
consistent *a* compatible; lógico; (of persons) consecuente
consistently *adv* conformemente (a); consecuentemente
consolation *n* consuelo, *m*, consolación, *f*
console *vt* consolar; confortar. *n arch* cartela, *f*. **c. table,** consola, *f*
consolidate *vt* consolidar. *vi* consolidarse
consolidation *n* consolidación, *f*
consoling *a* consolador; confortador
consols *n pl* (títulos) consolidados, *m pl*
consonance *n* consonancia, *f*
consonant *a* consonante
consort *n* consorte, *mf*. **to c. with,** frecuentar la compañía de; ir con; acompañar (a). **prince c.,** príncipe consorte, *m*
conspicuous *a* conspicuo; prominente; notable. **to be c.,** destacarse; llamar la atención. **to make oneself c.,** ponerse en evidencia, llamar la atención
conspicuously *adv* visiblemente; muy en evidencia
conspiracy *n* conspiración, *f*; complot, *m*
conspirator *n* conspirador (-ra)
conspire *vi* conspirar
constable *n* agente de policía, *m*; (historical) condestable, *m*. **chief c.,** jefe de policía, *m*
constabulary *n* policía, *f*
constancy *n* constancia, *f*
constant *a* constante; incesante. *n* constante, *m*
Constantinople Constantinopla, *f*
constantly *adv* constantemente
constellation *n* constelación, *f*
consternation *n* consternación, *f*; espanto, terror, *m*
constipate *vt* estreñir
constipation *n* estreñimiento, *m*, constipación de vientre, *f*
constituency *n* distrito electoral, *m*
constituent *a* constituyente. *n* constituyente, *m*; componente, *m*; elector (-ra)
constitute *vt* constituir; nombrar; autorizar
constitution *n* constitución, *f*
constitutional *a* constitucional
constitutionally *adv* constitucionalmente
constrain *vt* obligar, forzar. **I felt constrained to help them,** Me sentí obligado a ayudarles
constrained *a* (of smiles, etc.) forzado; (of silences) violento; (of persons) avergonzado
constraint *n* fuerza, compulsión, *f*; (of atmosphere) tensión, *f*; (reserve) reserva, *f*; vergüenza, *f*
constrict *vt* apretar, estrechar
constriction *n* constricción, *f*
construct *vt* edificar; construir
construction *n* construcción, *f*; interpretación, *f*. **to put a wrong c. on,** interpretar mal
constructional *a* construccional
constructive *a* constructor
constructor *n* constructor, *m*
construe *vt* construir; (translate) traducir; *fig* interpretar
consul *n* cónsul, *m*
consular *a* consular
consular fees *n pl* derechos consulares, *m pl*
consulate *n* consulado, *m*. **c. general,** consulado general, *m*
consult *vt* consultar. *vi* consultar (con), aconsejarse (con)
consultant *n* (*med* and other uses) especialista, *m*
consultation *n* consulta, *f*
consultative *a* consultativo

consulting *a* consultor. **c. hours,** horas de consulta, *f pl.* **c. rooms,** consultorio, *m*
consume *vt* consumir; (eat) comerse, tragarse. *vi* consumirse. **to be consumed by envy,** estar consumido por la envidia. **to be consumed by thirst,** estar muerto de sed
consumer *n* consumidor (-ra)
consummate *a* consumido, perfecto. *vt* consumar
consummation *n* consumación, *f*
consumption *n* consumo, *m*; gasto, *m*; *med* tuberculosis, *f.* **fuel c.,** consumo de combustible, *m*
consumptive *a* destructivo; *med* tísico, hético. *n* tísico (-ca)
contact *n* contacto, *m*, *vt* ponerse en contacto con. **to be in c. with,** estar en contacto con
contagion *n* contagio, *m*
contagious *a* contagioso
contain *vt* contener; incluir; *geom* encerrar; (arithmetic) ser divisible por; (oneself) dominarse. **I could not c. myself,** No pude dominarme
container *n* recipiente, *m*; envase, *m*; (box) caja, *f*
contaminate *vt* contaminar; corromper
contamination *n* contaminación, *f*
contemplate *vt* contemplar; meditar, considerar; (plan) tener intención de, pensar, proponerse
contemplation *n* contemplación, *f*; meditación, *f*; expectación, esperanza, *f*; (plan) proyecto, *m*. **to have something in c.,** proyectar algo
contemplative *a* contemplativo
contemplatively *adv* contemplativamente; atentamente
contemporaneous *a* contemporáneo
contemporary *a* contemporáneo; (of persons) coetáneo; (of events, etc.) actual. *n* contemporáneo (-ea)
contempt *n* desprecio, menosprecio, *m*; desdén, *m*. **c. of court,** falta de respeto a la sala, *f*
contempt of court *n* rebeldía a la corte, *f*
contempt of law *n* rebeldía a la ley, *f*
contemptible *a* menospreciable, despreciable; vil
contemptibly *adv* vilmente
contemptuous *a* desdeñoso; despectivo; de desprecio. **to be c. of,** desdeñar; menospreciar, tener en poco (a)
contemptuously *adv* con desprecio, desdeñosamente
contend *vi* contender; (affirm) sostener, mantener. **He contended that . . . ,** Sostuvo que . . . ; **contending party,** *law* parte litigante, *f*
content *n* contenido, *m*; capacidad, *f*; (emotion) contento, *m*; satisfacción, *f*. *a* contento; satisfecho (de). *vt* contentar; satisfacer. **to one's heart's c.,** a pedir de boca; a gusto de uno; cuanto quisiera
contented *a* satisfecho, contento
contentedly *adv* con satisfacción, contentamente
contention *n* disputa, controversia, discusión, *f*; argumento, *m*, opinión, *f*
contentious *a* contencioso
contentment *n* contentamiento, *m*; contento, *m*
contest *vt* disputar; (a suit) defender; (a match, an election, etc.) disputar. *n* disputa, *f*; combate, *m*, lucha, *f*; (competition) concurso, *m*
contestant *n* contendiente, *mf*
context *n* contexto, *m*
contiguity *n* contigüidad, *f*
contiguous *a* contiguo, lindero, adyacente
continence *n* continencia, *f*
continent *a* continente. *n* continente, *m*
continental *a* continental
continental shelf *n* plataforma continental, *f*
contingency *n* contingencia, *f*
contingent *a* contingente. *n mil* contingente, *m*. **to be c. on,** (of events) depender de
continual *a* continuo
continually *adv* continuamente
continuance *n* continuación, *f*
continuation *n* continuación, *f*; prolongación, *f*
continue *vi* continuar; seguir; prolongarse; durar. *vt* continuar; seguir; proseguir; perpetuar; (in an office) retener. **to be continued,** se continuará, continuará, seguirá
continuer *n* continuador (-ra)
continuity *n* continuidad, *f*
continuous *a* continuo. **c. performance,** sesión continua, *f*
continuously *adv* de continuo, continuamente
contort *vt* retorcer
contortion *n* contorsión, *f*
contortionist *n* contorsionista, *m*
contour *n* contorno, *m*; curva de nivel, *f*. **c. map,** mapa con curvas de nivel, *m*
contraband *n* contrabando, *m*
contrabandist *n* contrabandista, *mf*
contrabass *n* contrabajo, *m*
contraception *n* anticoncepción, *f*
contraceptive *n* anticonceptivo, *m*
contract *n* pacto, *m*; (*com* and *law*) contrato, *m*; (betrothal) esponsales, *m pl*; (marriage) capitulaciones, *f pl*; (cards) "Bridge," *m*. *vt* contraer; (acquire) adquirir, contraer; (a marriage, etc.) contraer; (be betrothed to) desposarse con; (by formal contract) contratar; pactar. *vi* (shrink) contraerse, encogerse; comprometerse por contrato. **breach of c.,** no cumplimiento de contrato, *m*. **c. party,** (of matrimony) contrayente, *mf*
contractile *a* contráctil
contraction *n* contracción, *f* (act or process); forma contracta, *f* (like *isn't* or *can't*)
contractor *n* contratista, *mf*
contradict *vt* contradecir; desmentir
contradiction *n* contradicción, *f*; negación, *f*
contradictory *a* contradictorio; opuesto (a), contrario (a)
contralto *n* (voice) contralto, *m*; (woman) contralto, *f*
contraption *n inf* artefacto, *m*
contrapuntal *a mus* de contrapunto
contrariness *n inf* testarudez, terquedad, *f*
contrariwise *adv* al contrario; al revés
contrary *a* contrario; opuesto (a); desfavorable, poco propicio; (of persons) difícil, terco. *n* contraria, *f*; (logic) contrario, *m*, *adv* en contra, contrariamente. **on the c.,** al contrario. **to be c.,** (of persons) llevar la contraria
contrast *n* contraste, *m*. *vt* contrastar (con). *vi* contrastar (con), hacer contraste (con)
contravene *vt* contravenir; atacar, oponerse (a)
contravention *n* contravención, *f*
contribute *vt* contribuir; (an article) escribir
contribution *n* contribución, *f*; (to a review, etc.) artículo, *m*
contributor *n* contribuyente, *mf*; (to a journal) colaborador (-ra)
contributory *a* contribuyente
contrite *a* penitente, arrepentido, contrito
contritely *adv* contritamente
contrition *n* contrición, penitencia, *f*, arrepentimiento, *m*
contrivance *n* invención, *f*; (scheme) treta, idea, estratagema, *f*; (machine) aparato, mecanismo, artefacto, *m*
contrive *vt* inventar; idear, proyectar. *vi* (succeed in) lograr, conseguir; (manage) arreglárselas
control *n* autoridad, *f*; dominio, *m*; gobierno, *m*; dirección, *f*; regulación, *f*; (restraint) freno, *m*; (*biol* and *spirit*) control, *m*; (of a vehicle) conducción, *f*; manejo, *m*, manipulación, *f*; *pl* **controls,** *mech* mando, *m*. *vt* dirigir, regir; regular; usar, manejar, manipular; controlar; (dominate) dominar; (curb) refrenar, reprimir; (command) mandar. **He lost c. of the car,** Perdió el mando (or control) del automóvil. **out of c.,** fuera de mando, fuera de control. **remote c.,** mando a distancia, *m*. **to c. oneself,** dominarse, contenerse. **to lose c. of oneself,** no lograr dominarse, perder el control. **c. stick,** *aer* palanca de mando, *f*. **c. tower,** *aer* torre de mando, *f*

controller *n* interventor, *m*; (device) regulador, *m*
controlling *n* See **control.** *a* regulador
controversial *a* debatible, discutible
controversy *n* controversia, *f*; argumento, *m*; altercación, disputa, *f*
contumacious *a* contumaz
contumacy *n* contumacia, *f*
contumely *n* contumelia, *f*
contusion *n* herida contusa, *f*
conundrum *n* acertijo, rompecabezas, *m*; problema, *m*
convalesce *vi* convalecer, estar convaleciente
convalescence *n* convalecencia, *f*
convalescent *a* convaleciente. *n* convaleciente, *mf*. **c. home,** casa de convalecencia, *f*
convene *vt* (a meeting) convocar; (person) citar. *vi* reunirse
convenience *n* conveniencia, *f*; (comfort) comodidad, *f*; utilidad, *f*; (advantage) ventaja, *f*; (public) retretes, *m pl*. **at one's c.,** cuando le sea conveniente a uno. **to make a c. of,** abusar de. **with all modern conveniences,** con todo el confort moderno
convenient *a* conveniente; apropiado; cómodo. **I shall make it c. to see him at 6 p.m.,** Arreglaré mis asuntos para verle a las seis
conveniently *adv* cómodamente; oportunamente; sin inconveniente
convent *n* convento, *m*
convention *n* convención, *f*
conventional *a* convencional
conventual *a* conventual. *n* conventual, *m*
converge *vi* convergir
convergence *n* convergencia, *f*
convergent *a* convergente
conversance *n* familiaridad, *f*, conocimiento, *m*
conversant *a* familiar, versado, conocedor. **c. with,** versado en
conversation *n* conversación, *f*. **to engage in c. with,** entablar conversación con
conversational *a* de conversación; (talkative) locuaz
conversationally *adv* en tono familiar; familiarmente; en conversación
converse *vi* conversar. **to c. by signs,** hablar por señas
conversely *adv* recíprocamente
conversion *n* conversión, *f*
convert *vt* convertir; transformar. *n* converso (-sa). **to become a c.,** convertirse
convertible *a* convertible; transformable
convex *a* convexo
convey *vt* transportar; conducir, llevar; (a meaning, etc.) comunicar, dar a entender; expresar; *law* traspasar
conveyance *n* transporte, *m*; conducción, *f*; medio de transporte, *m*; vehículo, *m*; carruaje, *m*; (of property) traspaso, *m*; (document) escritura de traspaso, *f*. **public c.,** coche de alquiler, *m*; ómnibus, *m*
convict *n* convicto, *m*; presidiario, *m*. *vt law* condenar; culpar. **c. settlement,** colonia penal, *f*
conviction *n* (of a prisoner) condenación, *f*; (belief) convencimiento, *m*, convicción, *f*
convince *vt* convencer
convincing *a* convincente
convivial *a* convivial
conviviality *n* jovialidad, *f*
convocation *n* convocación, *f*
convoke *vt* convocar
convolution *n* circunvolución, *f*; espira, *f*
convoy *vt* convoyar, escoltar. *n* convoy, *m*. **to sail in a c.,** navegar en convoy
convulse *vt* agitar; sacudir; estremecer. **to be convulsed with laughter,** desternillarse de risa, morirse de risa
convulsion *n* convulsión, *f*; conmoción, *f*
convulsive *a* convulsivo
coo *vi* arrullar; (of infants) gorjearse. *n* arrullo, *m*
cooing *n* arrullo, *m*
cook *n* cocinero (-ra). *vt* guisar, cocer, cocinar; (falsify) falsear
cooker *n* cocina, *f*. **gas c.,** cocina de gas, *f*
cookery *n* cocina, *f*. **c.-book,** libro de cocina, *m*
cooking *n* arte de guisar, *m*, or *f*; cocina, *f*; (of accounts, etc.) falsificación, *f*. **c. range,** cocina económica, *f*. **c.-stove,** cocina, *f*. **c. utensils,** batería de cocina, *f*
cool *a* fresco; bastante frío; (not ardent and of receptions, etc.) frío; (calm) sereno, imperturbable. *n* fresco, *m*. *vi* enfriarse; (of love, etc.) resfriarse; (of the weather) refrescar; (of persons) refrescarse. *vt* refrescar; enfriar. **to grow cooler,** (of weather) refrescarse; (of persons) tener menos calor. **It is c.,** Hace fresco. **to be as c. as a cucumber,** tener sangre fría. **c. drink,** bebida fría, *f*. **c.-headed,** sereno, imperturbable
coolie *n* culí, *m*
cooling *n* enfriamiento, *m*, *a* refrescante
coolly *adv* frescamente; fríamente, con frialdad; imperturbablemente; (impudently) descaradamente
coolness *n* frescura, *f*; (of a welcome, etc.) frialdad, *f*; (sangfroid) sangre fría, serenidad, *f*; aplomo, *m*
coop *n* gallinero, *m*; caponera, *f*, *vt* enjaular; encerrar. **to keep** (someone) **cooped up,** tener encerrado (a)
cooper *n* tonelero, barrilero, *m*, *vt* hacer barriles
cooperate *vi* cooperar; colaborar
cooperation *n* cooperación, *f*
cooperative *a* cooperativo. **c. society,** cooperativa, *f*
coopt *vt* elegir por votación
coordinate *vt* coordinar. *n math* coordenada, *f*. *a* coordenado
coordination *n* coordinación, *f*
coot *n* fúlica, *f*
cop *n* (police officer) polizonte, *mf*, *Ecuador*, chapa, *Mexico* cuico (-ca)
copartner *n* copartícipe, *mf*; socio (-ia)
cope *n ecc* capa, *f*; (of heaven) dosel, *m*, bóveda, *f*. **to c. with,** contender con; (a difficulty) hacer cara a, arrostrar
copeck *n* copec, *m*
Copenhagen Copenhague, *m*
copier *n* copiador (-ra)
coping *n arch* albardilla, *f*. **c.-stone,** teja cumbrera, *f*; *fig* coronamiento, *m*
copious *a* copioso, abundante
copiously *adv* en abundancia
copiousness *n* abundancia, *f*
copper *n* cobre, *m*; (coin) calderilla, *f*; (vessel) caldera, *f*. *a* de cobre. **c.-colored,** cobrizo. **c.-smith,** calderero, *m*. **c.-sulphate,** sulfato de cobre, *m*
copperplate *n* lámina de cobre, *f*; grabado en cobre, *m*
coppery *a* cobrizo
coppice *n* soto, bosquecillo, *m*. **c. with standards,** monte medio, *m*
coproprietor *n* copropietario, *m*
copse *n* arboleda, *f*, bosquecillo, *m*
copulate *vi* copularse
copulation *n* cópula, *f*
copy *n* copia, *f*; (of a book) ejemplar, *m*; (of a paper) número, *m*; manuscrito, *m*; (subject-matter) material, *m*. *vt* copiar; imitar; tomar como modelo (a). **rough c.,** borrador, *m*. **c.-book,** cuaderno de escritura, *m*
copy editor *n* redactor de textos, *m*
copying *n* imitación, *f*; transcripción, *f*. **c. ink,** tinta de copiar, *f*
copyist *n* copiador (-ra); (plagiarist) copiante, *mf*
copyright *n* derechos de autor, *m pl*; propiedad literaria, *f*. *a* protegido por los derechos de autor. *vt* registrar como propiedad literaria. **C. reserved,** Derechos reservados, Queda hecho el depósito que marca la ley
copywriter *n* escritor de anuncios, *m*
coquet *vi* coquetear; *fig* jugar (con)
coquetry *n* coquetería, *f*
coquette *n* coqueta, *f*
coquettish *a* coquetón; atractivo
coral *n* coral, *m*; (polyp) coralina, *f*. *a* de coral, coralino.

white c., madrépora, *f.* **c. beads,** corales, *m pl.* **c.-island,** atalón, *m.* **c.-reef,** escollo de coral, *m.* **c. snake,** coral, *f*

corbel *n arch* ménsula, *f*

cord *n* cuerda, *f;* cordel, *m;* cordón, *m. vt* encordelar. **spinal c.,** médula espinal, *f.* **umbilical c.,** cordón umbilical, *m*

cordial *a* cordial; sincero, fervoroso. *n* cordial, *m*

cordiality *n* cordialidad, *f*

cordon *n* cordón, *m;* cinto, *m.* **to c. off,** acordonar

Cordova Córdoba, *f*

cordovan *a* cordobés. *n* (leather) cordobán, *m*

corduroy *n* pana de cordoncillo, *f*

core *n* (of a fruit) corazón, *m;* (of a rope) alma, *f,* centro, *m;* (of an abscess) foco, *m;* (of a corn) ojo, *m; fig* núcleo, *m;* esencia, *f;* lo esencial

coreligionist *n* correligionario (-ia)

corespondent *n* cómplice en un caso de divorcio, *mf*

Corinth Corinto, *m*

Corinthian *a* corintio. *n* corintio (-ia)

cork *n* corcho, *m;* (of a bottle) tapón, *m, a* de corcho. *vt* tapar con corcho, taponar; (wine) encorchar; (the face) tiznar con corcho quemado. **pop of a c.,** taponazo, *m.* **to draw a c.,** descorchar. **c.-jacket,** chaleco salvavidas, *m.* **c. tree,** alcornoque, *m*

corkscrew *n* sacacorchos, *m*

cormorant *n* cormorán, *m*

corn *n* grano, cereal, *m;* (wheat) trigo, *m;* (maize) maíz, *m;* (single seed) grano, *m;* (on the foot, etc.) callo, *m.* **Indian c.,** maíz, *m.* **c. cure,** callicida, *m.* **c.-exchange,** bolsa de granos, *f.* **c.-field,** campo de trigo, *m.* **c.-flower,** aciano, *m.* **c. liquor** *Lat. Am.* chicha *f*

cornea *n* córnea, *f*

corner *n* ángulo, *m;* (of a street or building) esquina, *f;* (of a room) rincón, *Mexico* ancón *m; aut* viraje, *m; com* monopolio, *m;* (of the eye) rabo, *m;* (Assoc. football) "corner," *m. vt* arrinconar; acorralar; *com* acaparar. **the four corners of the earth,** las cinco partes del mundo. **a tight c.,** un lance apretado, un apuro. **to drive into a c.,** *fig* poner entre la espada y la pared. **to look out of the c. of the eye,** mirar de reojo. **to turn the c.,** doblar la esquina; *fig* pasar la crisis. **c.-cupboard,** rinconera, *f.* **c. seat,** asiento del rincón, *m.* **c. shop** *Lat. Am.* esquina *f* **c.-stone,** piedra angular, *f.*

cornered *a* (of a person) acorralado, en aprieto; (of hats) de . . . picos. **three-c. hat,** sombrero de tres picos, *m*

cornet *n* (musical instrument) corneta, *f; mil* corneta, *m;* (paper) cucurucho, *m.* **c. player,** cornetín, *m*

cornflour *n* harina de maíz, *f*

cornice *n* cornisa, *f*

Cornish *a* de Cornualles

cornucopia *n* cornucopia, *f*

corollary *n* corolario, *m*

corona *n* (*ast arch*) corona, *f*

coronation *n* coronación, *f*

coroner *n* juez de guardia, *mf,* médico forense, *m*

coronet *n* (of a peer, etc.) corona, *f;* tiara, *f;* guirnalda, *f*

corporal *a* corporal, *n mil* cabo, *m;* (altar-cloth) corporal, *m.* **c. punishment,** castigo corporal, *m*

corporate *a* corporativo

corporation *n* corporación, *f;* concejo, cabildo municipal, *m;* (*com* U.S.A.) sociedad anónima, *f*

corporeal *a* corpóreo

corps *n* cuerpo, *m*

corpse *n* cadáver, *m*

corpulence *n* gordura, obesidad, *f*

corpulent *a* corpulento, grueso, gordo

corpus *n* cuerpo, *m.* **C. Christi,** Corpus, *m.* **c. delicti,** cuerpo del delito, *m*

corpuscle *n* corpúsculo, *m*

correct *a* correcto; exacto, justo. *vt* corregir; rectificar; amonestar, reprender

correction *n* corrección, *f;* rectificación, *f*

corrective *a* correctivo. *n* correctivo, *m*

correctness *n* corrección, *f;* exactitud, *f;* justicia, *f*

correlate *vt* poner en correlación. *vi* tener correlación

correlation *n* correlación, *f*

correspond *vi* corresponder (a); (by letter) escribirse, corresponderse

correspondence *n* correspondencia, *f; com* correo, *m.* **c. course,** curso por correspondencia, *m*

correspondent *n* correspondiente, *mf;* (*com* and journalist) corresponsal, *mf.* **special c.,** corresponsal extraordinario, *m*

corresponding *a* correspondiente. **c. member,** miembro correspondiente, *m*

corridor *n* corredor, pasillo, *m;* (railway) pasillo, *m; pol* corredor, *m.* **c. train,** tren con coches corridos, *m*

corroborate *vt* corroborar, confirmar

corroboration *n* corroboración, confirmación, *f*

corroborative *a* corroborativo, confirmatorio

corrode *vt* corroer, morder; *fig* roer

corrosion *n* corrosión, *f*

corrosive *a* corrosivo; mordaz

corrugate *vt* arrugar. *vi* arrugarse

corrugated *a* arrugado; ondulado. **c. iron,** chapa canaleta, *f*

corrugation *n* corrugación, *f,* arrugamiento, *m*

corrupt *a* corrompido; vicioso, desmoralizado. *vt* corromper. *vi* corromperse

corrupter *n* corruptor (-ra)

corruption *n* corrupción, *f*

corsage *n* corpiño, *m*

corset *n* corsé, *m, vt* encorsetar. **c. shop,** corsetería, *f*

Corsica Córcega, *f*

Corsican *a* corso. *n* corso (-sa)

cortege *n* séquito, acompañamiento, *m;* desfile, *m*

cortex *n bot anat* corteza, *f*

cortisone *n* (drug) cortisona, *f*

Corunna La Coruña, *f*

coruscation *n* brillo, *m*

corvette *n* corbeta, *f*

cosignatory *n* cosignatario (-ia)

cosine *n* coseno, *m*

cosiness *n* comodidad, *f*

cosmetic *a* cosmético. *n* afeite, cosmético, *m*

cosmic *a* cósmico

cosmographer *n* cosmógrafo, *m*

cosmography *n* cosmografía, *f*

cosmopolitan *a* cosmopolita. *n* cosmopolita, *mf*

cosmopolitanism *n* cosmopolitismo, *m*

cosmos *n* cosmos, universo, *m*

Cossack *a* cosaco. *n* cosaco (-ca)

cosset *vt* mimar, consentir

cost *vi* costar. *n* costa, *f,* coste, precio, *m; fig* costa, *f; pl* **costs,** *law* costas, *f pl.* **at all costs,** cueste lo que cueste, a toda costa. **to my c.,** a mi costa. **c. of living,** coste de la vida, *m.* **to c. a fortune,** costar un sentido

Costa-Rican *a* costarriqueño. *n* costarriqueño (-ña)

coster *n* vendedor (-ra) ambulante

costliness *n* alto precio, *m;* suntuosidad, *f*

costly *a* costoso; suntuoso, magnífico

costume *n* traje, *m;* (fancy-dress) disfraz, *m;* (tailored) traje sastre, *m;* **"Costume,"** (among credits in films and plays) «Vestuario»

costumier *n* modista, *mf;* sastre, *m*

cot *n* (hut) choza, cabaña, *f;* (child's) camita, *f*

coterie *n* círculo, grupo, *m;* (clique) camarilla, *f*

cotillion *n* cotillón, *m*

cottage *n* cabaña, choza, *f;* casita, *f,* hotelito, *m;* torre, villa, *f* **c. cheese** *Mexico* asadero *m*

cotter *n* chaveta, llave, *f*

cotton *n* algodón, *m, a* de algodón. **I don't c. to the idea at all,** No me gusta nada la idea; La idea no me seduce. **sewing-c.,** hilo de coser, *m.* **c. goods,** géneros de algodón, *m pl.* **c. mill,** hilandería de algodón, algodonería, *f.* **c. plantation,** algodonal, *m.* **c.-seed oil,** aceite de semilla de algodón, *m.* **c.-spinner,** hilandero

(-ra) de algodón. **c.-wool,** algodón en rama, *m.* **c.-yarn,** hilo de algodón, *m*
cottony *a* algodonoso
couch *n* sofá, canapé, *m;* (bed) lecho, *m;* (lair) cama, *f. vt* (lay down) acostar, echar; (a lance) enristrar; (express) expresar, redactar. *vi* acostarse; (crouch) agacharse; estar en acecho
cough *vi* toser. *n* tos, *f.* **to c. up,** escupir, expectorar. **c.-drop,** pastilla para la tos, *f*
coughing *n* tos, *f*
could. See **can**
council *n* consejo, *m;* junta, *f; ecc* concilio, *m.* **Privy C.,** consejo privado, *m.* **C. of the Realm,** Concejo del Reino, *m.* **to hold c.,** celebrar un consejo; aconsejarse (con); consultarse. **town c.,** ayuntamiento, *m.* **c. chamber,** sala consistorial, *f;* sala de actos, *f.* **c. houses,** casas baratas, *f pl.* **c. of war,** consejo de guerra, *m*
councilor *n* concejal, *m;* miembro de la junta, *m*
counsel *n* consultación, *f;* deliberación, *f;* consejo, *m; law* abogado, *m. vt* aconsejar. **a c. of perfection,** un ideal imposible. **to keep one's own c.,** no decir nada, callarse, guardar silencio. **to take c. with,** consultar (a), aconsejarse con
counselor *n* consejero, *m.* **c. of state,** consejero de estado, *m*
count *vt* contar; calcular; (consider) creer, considerar. *vi* contar. *n* cuenta, *f;* (of votes) escrutinio, *m; law* capítulo, *m.* **John simply doesn't c.,** Juan no cuenta para nada. **Erudition alone counts for very little,** La mera erudición sirve para muy poco. **to keep c. of,** tener cuenta de. **to lose c. of,** perder cuenta de. **to c. on,** contar con; (doing something) esperar. **to c. up,** contar
count *n* (title) conde, *m*
countenance *n* semblante, *m;* expresión de la cara, *f;* aspecto, *m;* (favor) apoyo, *m,* ayuda, *f. vt* autorizar, aprobar; apoyar, ayudar. **to put (a person) out of c.,** desconcertar (a)
counter *n* (in a bank) contador, *m;* (in a shop) mostrador, *m;* (in games) ficha, *f, adv* contra, al contrario; al revés. *a* opuesto (a), contrario (a). *vt* parar; contestar. **to run c. to my inclinations,** oponerse a mis deseos. **to c. with the left,** (boxing) contestar con la izquierda. **c.-attack,** contraataque, *m.* **c.-attraction,** atracción contraria, *f.* **c.-offensive,** contraofensiva, *f.* **c.-reformation,** contrarreforma, *f.* **c.-revolution,** contrarevolución, *f*
counteract *vt* neutralizar; frustrar
counterbalance *n* contrapeso, *m, vt* contrabalancear; compensar, igualar
counterblast *n* denunciación, *f;* respuesta, *f*
countercharge *n* recriminación, *f. vt* recriminar; *law* reconvenir
counterfeit *a* falso, espurio; fingido. *n* falsificación, *f;* imitación, *f;* moneda falsa, *f;* (person) impostor (-ra). *vt* imitar; (pretend) fingir; (coins, handwriting, etc.) falsificar
counterfeiter *n* falsario (-ia)
counterfoil *n* talón, *m*
countermand *vt* contramandar; (an order) revocar, cancelar. *n* contraorden, *f;* revocación, *f*
countermarch *n* contramarcha, *f*
countermeasure *n* contramedida, *f*
counterpane *n* sobrecama, colcha, *f*
counterpart *n* contraparte, *f;* (of a document) duplicado, *m*
counterplot *n* contratreta, *f*
counterpoint *n mus* contrapunto, *m*
counterpoise *n* contrapeso, *m;* equilibrio, *m, vt* contrabalancear, contrapesar
countersign *n* contraseña, *f, vt* refrendar
countess *n* condesa, *f*
counting *n* cuenta, *f;* numeración, *f;* (of votes) escrutinio, *m.* **c.-house,** contaduría, *f*
countless *a* innumerable. **a c. number,** un sinfín, un sinnúmero
countrified *a* rústico, campesino
country *n* país, *m;* (fatherland) patria, *f;* región, campiña, tierra, *f;* (as opposed to town) campo, *m. a* del campo; campesino, campestre, rústico. **He lives in the c.,** Vive en el campo. **c. club,** club campestre, *m.* **c. cousin,** provinciano (-na). **c.-dance,** baile campestre, *m.* **c. gentleman,** hacendado, *m.* **c. girl,** campesina, *f;* aldeana, *f.* **c.-house,** finca, *f;* casa de campo, *f.* **c. life,** vida del campo, *f.* **c.-seat,** finca, *f*
countryman *n* campesino, *m;* hombre del campo, *m;* compatriota, *m*
countryside *n* campo, *m;* campiña, *f*
countrywoman *n* campesina, *f;* compatriota, *f*
county *n* condado, *m;* provincia, *f.* **c. council,** diputación provincial, *f.* **c. town,** cabeza de partido, *f;* ciudad provincial, *f*
county seat *n* cabecera municipal, cabeza de partido, *f*
coup *n* golpe, *m.* **c. d'état,** golpe de estado, *m*
coupe *n* cupé, *m*
couple *n* par, *m;* (in a dance, etc.) pareja, *f. vt* enganchar, acoplar; (in marriage) casar; (animals) aparear; (ideas) asociar; (names) juntar. **the young (married) c.,** el matrimonio joven
couplet *n* copla, *f*
coupling *n* enganche, acoplamiento, *m;* (of railway carriages) enganche, *m;* (of ideas) asociación, *f*
coupon *n* talón, *m;* cupón, *m*
courage *n* valor, *m.* **C.!** ¡Ánimo! **to muster up c.,** cobrar ánimo
courageous *a* valiente
courageously *adv* valientemente
courier *n* correo, *m,* estafeta, *f;* (guide) guía, *m;* (newspaper) estafeta, *f*
course *n* curso, *m;* (of time) transcurso, *m;* (of events) marcha, *f;* (of a river, etc.) cauce, *m;* (of stars) carrera, *f,* curso, *m;* (of a ship) derrota, *f,* rumbo, *m;* (way) camino, *m,* ruta, *f;* (of conduct) línea de conducta, *f;* actitud, *f;* (of study) curso, *m;* (of a meal) plato, *m;* (of an illness) desarrollo, *m; med* tratamiento, *m.* **He took it as a matter of c.,** Lo tomó sin darle importancia. **in due c.,** a su tiempo debido. **in the c. of time,** andando el tiempo, en el transcurso de los años. **of c.,** claro está; naturalmente. **Are you coming tomorrow? Of c.!** ¿Vienes mañana? ¡Ya lo creo! **the best c. to take,** lo mejor que se puede hacer, el mejor plantamiento, *m*
course *vt* cazar, perseguir; *poet* correr por, cruzar. *vi* (of blood, etc.) correr; cazar
court *n* (yard) patio, *m;* (tennis) campo de tenis, *m;* (fives, racquets) cancha, *f;* (royal) corte, *f;* (of justice) tribunal, *m;* (following) séquito, acompañamiento, *m. vt* hacer la corte (a); cortejar, pretender; solicitar; (sleep) conciliar. **to pay c. to,** (a woman) galantear, pretender; (a person) hacer la rueda (a), *Lat. Am.* afilar. **to respect the c.,** *law* guardar sala. **c. of appeal,** sala de apelación, *f.* **c. of justice,** sala de justicia, *f;* tribunal de justicia, *m.* **supreme c.,** tribunal supremo, *m.* **c.-card,** figura, *f.* **c.-dress,** traje de corte, *m.* **c. house,** palacio de justicia, *m.* **c. jester,** bufón, *m.* **c.-martial,** tribunal militar, *m.* **c.-plaster,** tafetán inglés, tafetán de heridas, *m.* **c.-room,** sala de justicia, *f*
courteous *a* cortés
courteousness *n* cortesía, *f*
courtesy *n* cortesía, *f;* favor, *m,* merced, *f;* permiso, *m*
courtier *n* cortesano, palaciego, *m*
courtliness *n* cortesía, urbanidad, *f;* dignidad, *f;* elegancia, *f*
courtly *a* cortés, galante; digno; elegante
courtship *n* noviazgo, *m;* galanteo, *m*
courtyard *n* patio, *m*
cousin *n* primo (-ma). **first c.,** primo (-ma) carnal. **second c.,** primo (-ma) segundo (-da)
cove *n* cala, abra, ensenada, *f,* ancón *m*
covenant *n* contrato, *m;* estipulación, *f;* pacto, *m;* alianza, *f. vt* prometer; estipular

Coventry, to send to, hacer el vacío (a)
cover *vt* cubrir; abrigar; (dissemble) disimular; (a distance) recorrer; (comprise) comprender, abarcar; (with confusion, etc.) llenar (de); (with a revolver, etc.) amenazar (con); (an overdraft, etc.) garantizar; (of stallions) cubrir; (of a hen and eggs) empollar; (a story, journalism) investigar. *n* cubierta, *f*; (for a chair, umbrella, etc.) funda, *f*; (of a saucepan, jar, etc.) tapa, *f*; (dish-cover) tapadera, *f*; (of a book) cubierta, tapa, *f*; (of a letter) sobre, *m*; (shelter) abrigo, *m*; protección, *f*; (undergrowth) maleza, *f*; *fig* velo, manto, *m*; (pretence) pretexto, *m*; *com* garantía, *f*. **outer c.,** (of tire) cubierta de neumático, *f*. **to c. oneself with glory,** cubrirse de gloria. **to c. up,** cubrir completamente; (with clothes) arropar; (wrap up) envolver. **to c. with a revolver,** amenazar con un revólver. **to read a book from c. to c.,** leer un libro del principio al fin. **to take c.,** refugiarse, tomar abrigo. **under c.,** bajo tejado; al abrigo
cover charge *n* consumo mínimo, precio del cubierto, *m*
covering *n* cubrimiento, *m*; cubierta, *f*; envoltura, *f*; capa, *f*, abrigo, *m*. **c. letter,** carta adjunta, *f*
coverlet *n* colcha, sobrecama, *f*
covert *n* guarida, *f*. *a* oculto; furtivo
covertly *adv* secretamente, furtivamente
covet *vt* codiciar; ambicionar, suspirar por
covetous *a* codicioso; ávido; ambicioso
covetously *adv* codiciosamente; ávidamente
covetousness *n* codicia, avaricia, *f*; avidez, *f*; ambición, *f*
cow *vt* intimidar, acobardar
cow *n* vaca, *Lat. Am. also* lechera *f*; (of other animals) hembra, *f*. **c.-bell,** cencerro, *m*, zumba, *f*. **c.-catcher,** *aut* salvavidas, *m*. **c.-hide,** cuero, cuero de vaca, zurriago, *m*; penca, *f*. **c.-house,** establo, *m*, boyera, *f*. **c.-pox,** vacuna, *f*
coward *n* cobarde, *m*, *a* cobarde
cowardice *n* cobardía, *Argentina* canillera, *f*
cowardly *a* cobarde, *Mexico, Venezuela* correlón
cowboy *n* vaquero, *m*; gaucho, "cowboy," *m*
cower *vi* no saber dónde meterse; temblar, acobardarse
cowherd *n* vaquero, boyero, *m*
cowl *n* capucha, *f*; (of a chimney) sombrerete, *m*
coworker *n* colaborador (-ra)
cowshed *n* establo, *m*
cowslip *n* prímula, *f*
cox *n* timonel, *m*
coxcomb *n* (of a jester) gorra de bufón, *f*; mequetrefe, *m*
coxswain *n* patrón, *m*; (of a rowboat) timonel, *m*
coy *a* modoso, tímido; coquetón
coyly *adv* tímidamente; con coquetería
coyness *n* timidez, modestia, *f*; coquetería, *f*
cozy *a* cómodo; agradable; caliente. **You are very c. here,** Estás muy bien aquí
crab *n* (sea) cangrejo de mar, cámbaro, *m*, *Lat. Am. also* jaiba *m*; (river) cangrejo, *m*; *ast* Cáncer, *m*. *vt* (thwart) frustrar. **hermit c.,** cangrejo ermitaño, *m*. **c.-apple,** manzana silvestre, *f*. **c.-louse,** ladilla, *f*
crabbed *a* áspero, hosco, desabrido, arisco; (of handwriting) apretado, metido
crack *vt* hender; quebrantar, romper; (nuts) cascar; (a whip and fingers) chasquear; (a bottle of wine) abrir. *vi* (of earth, skin, etc.) agrietarse; romperse, quebrarse; (of the voice) romper; (of the male voice) mudar. *n* hendedura, rendija, *f*; quebraja, *f*; (of a whip) chasquido, *m*; (of a rifle) estallido, *m*; (blow) golpe, garrotazo, *m*, *a* excelente, de primera categoría; estupendo. **to c. a joke,** decir un chiste. **to c. up,** *vt* dar bombo (a), alabar. *vi* (in health) quebrantarse; (airplane) cuartearse, estrellarse. **c.-brained,** chiflado; estúpido, loco
cracked *a* grietado; (of a bell, etc.) hendido; (of the voice) cascada; (of a person) chiflado
cracker *n* (firework) petardo, *m*; buscapiés, *m*
crackle *vi* (of burning wood, etc.) crepitar; (rustle) crujir; (of rifle fire) tirotear. *n* crepitación, *f*; crujido, *m*; (of rifle fire) tiroteo, *m*
crackling *n*. See **crackle;** *cul* chicharrón, *m*
Cracow Cracovia, *f*
cradle *n* cuña, *f*; *fig* niñez, infancia, *f*; (for a limb) arco de protección, *m*; (for winebottle) cesta, *f*. *vt* mecer. **c.-song,** canción de cuna, *f*
craft *n* (guile) astucia, *f*; (skill) habilidad, *f*; arte, *mf*; (occupation) oficio manual, *m*; profesión, *f*; (guild) gremio, *m*; (boat) barco, *m*, embarcación, *f*
craftily *adv* astutamente
craftiness *n* astucia, *f*
craftsman *n* artífice, *m*; arte sano, *m*; artista, *m*
craftsmanship *n* arte, *m*, or *f*; habilidad, *f*; artificio, *m*
crafty *a* astuto, taimado, *Lat. Am.* macuco. **c. person** *Mexico* fistol *m*
crag *n* peña, *f*, risco, despeñadero, *m*
cragginess *n* escabrosidad, aspereza, fragosidad, *f*
craggy *a* escabroso, escarpado, peñascoso, riscoso
cram *vt* henchir; atestar; (one's mouth) llenar (de); (poultry) cebar; (a pupil) preparar para un examen; (a subject) empollar. *vi* (with food) atracarse. **The room was crammed with people,** La sala estaba atestada de gente
cramp *n* *med* calambre, *m*; (numbness) entumecimiento, *m*; (rivet) grapa, *f*. *vt* dar calambre (a); (numb) entumecer; (fasten) lañar; (*fig* hamper) estorbar. **to c. someone's style,** cortar los vuelos (a). **writer's c.,** calambre del escribiente, *m*
cramped *a* (of space) apretado, estrecho; (of writing) menuda
cranberry *n* arándano, *m*
crane *n* *orn* grulla, *f*; (machine) grúa, *f*. **jib c.,** grúa de pescante, *f*. **travelling c.,** grúa móvil, *f*. **to c. one's neck,** estirar el cuello. **crane's bill,** pico de cigüeña, *m*
cranium *n* cráneo, *m*
crank *n* (handle) manivela, *f*; (person) maniático (-ca). *vt* poner en marcha (un motor) con la manivela
crankiness *n* (crossness) irritabilidad, *f*, mal humor, *m*; (eccentricity) excentricidad, *f*
cranky *a* (cross) irritable, malhumorado; (eccentric) chiflado, maniático, excéntrico
cranny *n* hendedura, grieta, *f*
crape *n* crespón, *m*
crash *vi* caer estrepitosamente; romperse; estallarse; (of aircraft, cars) estrellarse; *fig* hundirse, arruinarse. *n* estrépito, estruendo, *m*; estallido, *m*; (of aircraft) accidente de aviación, *m*; (car) accidente, *m*, (or choque, *m*) de automóviles; (financial) ruina, *f*; *fig* hundimiento, *m*. **to c. into,** estrellarse contra, chocar con. **c. helmet,** casco, *m*. **c.-landing,** aterrizaje violento, *m*
crass *a* craso
crassness *n* estupidez, *f*
crate *n* (box) caja de embalaje, *f*; (basket) canasto, *m*, banasta, *Mexico* jaba *f*
crater *n* cráter, *m*
cravat *n* corbata, *f*
crave *vt* suplicar, implorar. **to c. for,** perecer por, suspirar por, anhelar
craven *a* cobarde, pusilánime. *n* poltrón, cobarde, *m*
craving *n* deseo vehemente, *m*, sed, *f*
crawfish *n* cangrejo de río, *m*; cigala, *f*
crawl *vi* arrastrarse; andar a gatas; andar a paso de tortuga; (abase oneself) humillarse; (be full of) abundar (en). *n* paso de tortuga, *m*; (swimming) arrastne *m*
crayfish *n* cangrejo de río, *m*; cigala, *f*
crayon *n* carbón, *m*; pastel, *m*; (pencil) lápiz de color, *m*. *vt* dibujar con pastel, etc. **c. drawing,** dibujo al carbón, *m*
craze *vt* enloquecer, volver loco (a). *n* manía, *f*, capricho, entusiasmo, *m*; (fashion) moda, *f*
crazily *adv* locamente
craziness *n* locura, *f*
crazy *a* loco; chiflado; (of structure) dilapidado. **He is c. about music,** Está loco por la música. **to be com-**

pletely c., (of persons) ser un loco de atar; ser completamente loco. **to drive c.,** volver loco (a)
creak *vi* (of shoes, chairs, etc.) crujir; (of gates, etc.) rechinar, chirriar. *n* crujido, *m*; chirrido, *m*
creaking *n*. See **creak**
creaky *a* crujiente, que cruje; chirriador
cream *n* crema, *f*; nata, *f*; *fig* flor, nata, *f*. *a* de nata. **whipped c.,** nata batida, *f*. **c. cake,** pastel de nata, *m*. **c.-cheese,** queso de nata, *m*. **c.-colored,** de color crema. **c.-jug,** jarro para crema, *m*. **c. of tartar,** cremor, tártaro, *m*
creamery *n* lechería, *f*
creamy *a* cremoso
crease *n* (wrinkle) arruga, *f*; (fold) pliegue, *m*; (in trousers) raya, *f*; (in cricket) línea de la meta, *f*. *vt* (wrinkle) arrugar; (fold) plegar; (trousers) poner la raya en. *vi* arrugarse
create *vt* crear; (appoint) nombrar; (produce) suscitar, producir
creation *n* creación, *f*; establecimiento, *m*; (appointment) nombramiento, *m*
creative *a* creador; de la creación
creativeness *n* facultad creativa, inventiva, *f*
creator *n* creador (-ra)
creature *n* criatura, *f*; animal, *m*. **c. comforts,** bienestar material, *m*
creche *n* casa cuna, *f*
credence *n* crédito, *m*, fe, creencia, *f*; *ecc* credencia, *f*. **to give c. to,** dar crédito (a), creer
credentials *n pl* credenciales, *f pl*
credibility *n* credibilidad, verosimilitud, *f*
credible *a* creíble, verosímil; (of persons) digno de confianza
credibly *adv* creíblemente
credit *n* crédito, *m*; reputación, *f*; honor, *m*; (*com* and banking) crédito, *m*; (in bookkeeping) data, *f*. *vt* dar fe (a), dar crédito (a); creer; atribuir; (bookkeeping) acreditar. **It does them c.,** Les hace honor. **on c.,** a crédito, al fiado. **open c.,** *com* letra abierta, *f*. **to give on c.,** dar fiado. **c. balance,** haber, *m*
creditable *a* loable, honroso, digno de alabanza
creditably *adv* honrosamente
creditor *n* acreedor (-ra); (bookkeeping) haber, *m*
credulity *n* credulidad, *f*
credulous *a* crédulo, *Lat. Am.* creído
credulously *adv* con credulidad, crédulamente
creed *n* credo, *m*
creek *n* caleta, abra, *f*
creel *n* (for fish) cesta de pescador, *f*
creep *vi* arrastrarse; (of plants and birds) trepar; (of infants) andar a gatas; (totter) hacer pinitos; (slip) deslizarse; (cringe) lisonjear, rebajarse; (of one's flesh) sentir hormigueo. **to c. about on tiptoe,** andar de puntillas. **to c. into a person's favor,** insinuarse en el favor de. **to c. in,** entrar sin ser notado (en); deslizarse en. **to c. on,** (of time) avanzar lentamente; (of old age, etc.) acercarse insensiblemente. **to c. out,** salir sin hacer ruido; escurrirse. **to c. up,** trepar por; subir a gatas
creeper *n bot* enredadera, *f*; *orn* trepador, *m*; *zool* reptil, *m*
creeping *a bot* trepante; *zool* trepador; (servile) rastrero
cremate *vt* incinerar
cremation *n* cremación, *f*
crematorium *n* crematorio, *m*; horno de incineración, *m*, inhumadora, *f*
creole *a* criollo. *n* criollo (-lla)
creolize *vt* acriollar
crescent *n* media luna, *f*; *her* creciente, *m*; calle en forma de semicírculo, *f*. *a* en forma de media luna; *poet* creciente
cress *n bot* berro, *m*
crest *n* (of a cock, etc.) cresta, *f*; (plume) penacho, *m*; (of a helmet) cimera, *f*; (of a hill) cumbre, cima, *f*; (of a wave) cresta, *f*. **family c.,** blasón, escudo, *m*
crested *a Lat. Am.* copetudo (-da)
crestfallen *a* cabizbajo, cariacontecido
cretan *a* cretense. *n* cretense, *mf*
cretin *n* cretino (-na)
crevasse *n* grieta en un ventisquero, *f*
crevice *n* intersticio, *m*, rendija, grieta, *f*
crew *n* (of ships, boats, aircraft) tripulación, *f*; (of a gun) servidores de una ametralladora, *m pl*; (gang) pandilla, cuadrilla, *f*
crib *n* pesebre, *m*; (child's) camita de niño, *f*; (plagiary) plagio, *m*. *vt* (plagiarize) plagiar; (steal) hurtar
crick *n* (in the neck) tortícolis, *m*
cricket *n ent* grillo, *m*; (game) cricquet, *m*. **c. ball,** pelota de cricquet, *f*. **c. bat,** paleta de cricquet, *f*. **c. ground,** campo de cricquet, *m*. **c. match,** partido de cricquet, *m*
cricketer *n* jugador de cricquet, *m*
crier *n* (town) pregonero, *m*
crime *n* crimen, *m*; ofensa, *f*, delito, *m*
Crimea, the la Crimea, *f*
Crimean War, the la guerra de Crimea, la guerra de Oriente, *f*
criminal *a* criminal. *n* criminal, *m*; reo, *mf* **C. Investigation Department,** (nearest equivalent) policía secreta, *f*. **c. laws,** código penal, *m*
criminally *adv* criminalmente
criminologist *n* criminalista, *m*
criminology *n* criminología, *f*
crimp *vt* (hair) rizar
crimson *n* carmesí, *m*. *a* de carmesí. *vt* teñir de carmesí. *vi* enrojecerse
cringe *vi* temblar; asustarse, acobardarse; inclinarse (ante)
cringing *a* servil, humilde; adulador, *Mexico also* lambioche
crinkle *vi* arrugarse; rizarse. *vt* arrugar. *n* arruga, *f*
crinoline *n* crinolina, *f*, miriñaque, guardainfante, *m*
cripple *n* tullido (-da); cojo (-ja). *vt* lisiar, tullir, estropear; *fig* paralizar
crisis *n* crisis, *f*
crisp *a* (of hair and of leaves) crespo; (fresh) fresco; (stiff) tieso; (of style) nervioso, vigoroso; (of manner) decidido; (of repartee) chispeante; (of tone) incisivo
crisscross *vt* (a body of water or land) surcar
criterion *n* criterio, *m*
critic *n* crítico, *m*; censor, *m*
critical *a* crítico
criticism *n* crítica, *f*
criticize *vt* criticar; censurar
critique *n* crítica, *f*
croak *vi* (of frogs) croar; (of ravens) graznar; (of persons) lamentarse, gruñir
croaking *n* canto de la rana, *m*; graznido, *m*
Croat *a* croata. *n* croata, *mf*
Croatia Crocia, *f*
crochet *n* ganchillo, *m*, *vi* hacer ganchillo. *vt* hacer (algo) de ganchillo. **c. hook,** aguja de gancho, *f*, ganchillo, *m*. **c. work,** croché, ganchillo, *m*
crockery *n* loza, *f*, cacharros, *m pl*. **c. store,** cacharrería, *f*
crocodile *n* cocodrilo, *m*. **c. tears,** lágrimas de cocodrilo, *f pl*
crocus *n* azafrán, *m*
croft *n* campillo, *m*; (farm) heredad, *f*
crofter *n* colono, *m*
crone *n* bruja, *f*
crony *n* compinche, *mf*
crook *n* curva, *f*; (staff) cayado, *m*; (swindler) caballero de industria, estafador, *m*, *vt* doblar, encorvar
crooked *a* curvo; encorvado; torcido, *Mexico* chueco; ladeado; (deformed) contrahecho; (of paths, etc.) tortuoso; (dishonest) torcido, tortuoso
crookedly *adv* torcidamente; de través
crookedness *n* encorvadura, *f*; tortuosidad, *f*; sinuosidad, *f*
croon *vt* and *vi* canturrear; cantar
crooner *n* cantante, *mf*

crop *n* (of birds) buche, *m*; (whip) látigo, *m*, fusta, *f*; (handle) mango, *m*; (harvest) cosecha, *f*; (of the hair) cortadura, *f*. *vt* cortar; (nibble) rozar; (hair) rapar. **Eton c.,** pelo a la garçonne, *m*. **to c. up,** aparecer, surgir
crop rotation *n* la rotación de cultivos, *f*
croquet *n* juego de la argolla, juego de croquet, *m*
croquette *n cul* croqueta, *f*
crosier *n* báculo, cayado del obispo, *m*
cross *n* cruz, *f*; *biol* cruzamiento, *m*; (*sew* bias) bies, *m*. **in the shape of a c.,** en cruz. **the Red C.,** la Cruz Roja. **c.-bearer,** *ecc* crucero, *m*
cross *vt* cruzar; atravesar; pasar por; (a check and animals) cruzar; (thwart) contrariar. **It did not c. my mind,** No se me ocurrió. **Our letters must have crossed,** Nuestras cartas deben haberse cruzado. **to c. oneself,** *ecc* persignarse. **to c. out,** tachar, rayar. **to c. over,** *vt* atravesar, cruzar. *vi* ir al otro lado
cross *a* transversal; cruzado; oblicuo; (contrary) opuesto (a); (bad-tempered) malhumorado. **c.-breed,** *a* mestizo, atravesado. **c.-country,** *a* a campo travieso. **c.-examination,** *law* repregunta, *f*, contrainterrogatorio, *m*. **c.-examine,** *vt law* repreguntar; interrogar. **c.-eyed,** bizco. **c.-fire,** *mil* fuego cruzado, *m sing* fuegos cruzados, *m pl*; *fig* tiroteo, *m*. **c.-grained,** (of wood) vetisesgado; (of persons) áspero, intratable, desabrido. **c.-legged,** con las piernas cruzadas. **c.-purpose,** despropósito, *m*. **at c.-purposes,** a despropósito. **c.-question,** *vt law* repreguntar; interrogar. **c. reference,** contrarreferencia, *f*. **c. section,** sección transversal, *f*. **c.-stitch,** punto cruzado, *m*. **c.-word puzzle,** crucigrama, *m*
crossbar *n* travesaño, *m*
crossbeam *n* viga transversal, *f*
crossbench *a* atravesado
crossbred *a* cruzado, mestizo; híbrido
crossbreed *n* mestizo (-za); híbrido, *m*
crossing *n* cruzamiento, *m*; (of the sea) travesía, *f*; (intersection) cruce, *m*; paso, *m*. **level c.,** paso a nivel, *m*. **pedestrian c.,** paso para peatones, *m*. **c.-sweeper,** barrendero, *m*
crossly *adv* con mal humor, con displicencia, irritablemente
crossness *n* irritabilidad, *f*, mal humor, *m*
crossroad *n* travesía, *f*; cruce, *m*; *pl* **crossroads,** cruce, cruce de caminos, *m sing* encrucijada, *f sing*
crosswise *adv* en cruz; a través
crotch *n* (of a tree) bifurcación, *f*; *anat* horcajadura, *f*; (of breeches) entrepiernas, *f pl*
crotchet *n mus* semínima, *f*; (fad) capricho, *m*; extravagancia, excentricidad, *f*
crotchety *a* caprichoso; raro, excéntrico; difícil
crouch *vi* acurrucarse, agacharse, acuclillarse
croup *n* (disease) crup, garrotillo, *m*; (of a horse) grupa, anca, *f*
croupier *n* coime, crupié, *m*
crow *n orn* cuervo, *m*; *orn* grajo, *m*; (of a cock) canto del gallo, cacareo, *m*; (of an infant) gorjeo, *m*. *vi* (of a cock) cantar, cacarear; (of an infant) gorjearse. **as the c. flies,** en línea recta. **to c. over,** gallear, cantar victoria. **crow's-foot,** pata de gallo, *f*. **crow's-nest,** *naut* gavias, *f pl*
crowbar *n* alzaprima, palanca, *f*
crowd *n* multitud, muchedumbre, *f*; concurso, *m*; vulgo, *m*; (majority) mayoría, *f*; *theat* acompañamiento, *m*. *vi* reunirse, congregarse; agolparse, remolinarse, apiñarse. *vt* (fill) llenar; atestar. **in a c.,** en tropel. **So many ideas crowded in on me,** Se me ocurrieron tantas ideas a la vez. **to follow the c.,** seguir la multitud; *fig* ir con la mayoría. **to c. in,** entrar en tropel. **to c. round,** cercar, agruparse alrededor de. **to c. together,** apiñarse. **to c. up,** subir en masa, subir en tropel
crowded *a* lleno; atestado, apiñado; (weighed down) agobiado; (of hours, etc.) lleno
crowing *n* cacareo, canto del gallo, *m*; (of an infant) gorjeos, *m pl*; (boasting) jactancia, *f*
crown *n* corona, *f*; (of the head) coronilla, corona, *f*; (of a hat) copa, *f*; *arch* coronamiento, *m*. *vt* coronar. **c. prince,** príncipe heredero, *m*
crowning *n* coronamiento, *m*; *arch* remate, *m*, *a* final; supremo
crozier *n*. See **crosier**
crucial *a* decisivo, crítico; difícil
crucible *n* crisol, *m*
crucifix *n* crucifijo, *m*
crucifixion *n* crucifixión, *f*
cruciform *a* cruciforme
crucify *vt* crucificar
crude *a* crudo; (of colors) chillón, llamativo; (uncivilized) cerril, inculto; (vulgar) cursi; (of truth, etc.) desnudo
crudity *n* crudeza, *f*
cruel *a* cruel
cruelty *n* crueldad, *f*
cruet *n* ánfora, vinagrera, *f*; (stand) angarillas, *f pl*, convoy, *m*
cruise *vi* cruzar, navegar; (of cars) correr. *n* viaje por mar, *m*
cruiser *n* crucero, *m*
crumb *n* miga, *f*; (spongy part of bread) migaja, *f*. *vt* (bread) desmigajar; desmenuzar. **c. brush,** recogemigas, *m*
crumble *vt* desmigajar, desmenuzar. *vi* desmoronarse, desmigajarse; *fig* hundirse, derrumbarse; *fig* desaparecer
crumbling *n* (of buildings, etc.) desmoronamiento, *m*; *fig* destrucción, *f*
crumple *vt* arrugar, ajar. *vi* arrugarse. **to c. up,** *vt* (crush) estrujar; (persons) dejar aplastado. *vi* (collapse) hundirse, derrumbarse; (of persons) desplomarse; (despair) desalentarse
crunch *vt* mascar; hacer crujir. *vi* crujir
crupper *n* baticola, *f*
crusade *n* cruzada, *f*
crusader *n* cruzado, *m*
crush *vt* aplastar; (to powder) moler, triturar; (grapes, etc.) exprimir; (crease) arrugar; (opposition, etc.) vencer; (annihilate) aniquilar, destruir; (abash) humillar, confundir; (hope, etc.) matar; (of sorrow, etc.) agobiar. **We all crushed into his diningroom,** Fuimos en tropel a su comedor. **to c. up,** machacar, moler; (paper, etc.) estrujar
crushing *a* (of defeats and replies) aplastante; (of sorrow, etc.) abrumador
crust *n* (of bread, pie) corteza, *f*; (scab) costra, *f*; (of the earth, snow) capa, *f*. *vt* encostrar. *vi* encostrarse. **c. of bread,** mendrugo de pan, *m*
crustacean *a* crustáceo. *n* crustáceo, *m*
crustily *adv* irritablemente, malhumoradamente
crustiness *n* mal humor, *m*, aspereza, *f*
crusty *a* costroso; (of persons) malhumorado, irritable; áspero
crutch *n* muleta, *f*; (fork) horquilla, *f*; (crotch) horcajadura, *f*
crux *n* problema, *m*; (knotty point) nudo, *m*
cry *vi* (weep) llorar; (shout) gritar; (exclaim) exclamar. *vt* (one's wares) pregonar. *n* grito, *m*. **to cry for help,** pedir socorro a voces. **to cry to high heaven,** poner el grito en el cielo. **to cry one's eyes out,** llorar a mares. **to cry down,** desacreditar. **to cry off,** desdecirse; volverse atrás. **to cry out,** *vt* gritar. *vi* dar gritos; gritar; *fig* clamar. **cry-baby,** niño (-ña) llorón (-ona)
crying *a* urgente; notorio. *n* gritos, *m pl*; (weeping) llanto, *m*, lamentaciones, *f pl*; (tears) lágrimas, *f pl*
crypt *n* cripta, *f*
cryptic *a* secreto, oculto
cryptography *n* criptografía, *f*
crystal *n* cristal, *m*. **c. set,** *rad* receptor de galena, *m*
crystal ball *n* bola de cristal, esfera de cristal, *f*
crystalline *a* cristalino
crystallization *n* cristalización, *f*
crystallize *vt* and *vi* cristalizar

crystallography *n* cristalografía, *f*
cub *n* cachorro (-rra)
Cuban *a* cubano. *n* cubano (-na)
cubbyhole *n* refugio, *m*; garita, *f*; cuarto pequeño, *m*; chiribitil, *m*
cube *n* cubo, *m*; (of sugar) terrón, *m*. *vt* cubicar. **c. root,** raíz cúbica, *f*
cubic *a* cúbico
cubicle *n* cubículo, *m*
cubism *n* cubismo, *m*
cuckold *n* cornudo, *m*
cuckoo *n* cuclillo, *m*; (cry) cucú, *m*. **c.-clock,** reloj de cuclillo, *m*
cucumber *n* cohombro *m*
cud *n* rumia, *f*. **to chew the cud,** rumiar
cuddle *vt* abrazar. *n* abrazo, *m*. **to c. up together,** estar abrazados
cudgel *n* porra, estaca, tranca, *f*, *vt* aporrear, apalear. **to c. one's brains,** devanarse los sesos. **to take up the cudgels for,** salir en defensa de
cue *n theat* pie, *m*; (lead) táctica, *f*; (hint) indicación, *f*; (of hair) coleta, *f*; (billiard) taco (de billar), *m*. **to take one's cue from,** tomar como modelo (a); seguir el ejemplo de
cueca *n* cueca *f*
cuff *vt* abofetear. *n* (blow) bofetón, *m*; (of sleeve) puño, *m*, bocamanga, valenciana, *f*.
cufflink *n* gemelo *m*, *Central America* mancuerna, mancuernilla *f*, *Chile* collera *f*, *Colombia* mancorna *f*
cuisine *n* cocina, *f*
cul-de-sac *n* callejón sin salida, *m*
culinary *a* culinario
cullender *n* colador, *m*
culminate *vi* culminar (en), terminar (en). **culminating point,** punto culminante, *m*
culmination *n* culminación, *f*; *fig* apogeo, punto culminante, *m*
culpability *n* culpabilidad, *f*
culpable *a* culpable
culpably *adv* culpablemente
culprit *n* culpado (-da)
cult *n* culto, *m*
cultivable *a* cultivable, labradero
cultivate *vt* cultivar
cultivated *a* cultivado; (of persons) culto, fino
cultivation *n* cultivación, *f*; (of the land) cultivo, *m*; (of persons, etc.) cultura, *f*
cultivator *n* cultivador (-ra); (machine) cultivador, *m*
cultural *a* cultural
culture *n* cultura, *f*; (bacteriology) cultivo, *m*, *vt* (bacteriology) cultivar
cultured *a* culto
culvert *n* alcantarilla, *f*
cumbersome *a* pesado; incómodo
cumulative *a* cumulativo
cumulus *n* cúmulo, *m*
cuneiform *a* cuneiforme
cunning *a* astuto, taimado, *Lat. Am.* macuco *n* (skill) habilidad, *f*; astucia, *f*
cup *n* taza, *f*; (*ecc* and *bot*) cáliz, *m*; *sport* copa, *f*; (hollow) hoyo, *m*, hondonada, *f*. **c.-final,** *sport* final de la copa, *m*. **c.-tie,** *sport* partido eliminatorio, *m*
cup-and-ball *n* boliche, *m*
cupboard *n* armario, *m*; (in the wall) alacena, *f*. **c. love,** amor interesado, *m*
cupful *n* taza, *f*
cupidity *n* avaricia, codicia, *f*
cup of sorrow *n* ramito de amargura, *m*
cupola *n* cúpula, *f*
cur *n* perro mestizo, *m*; canalla, *m*
curable *a* curable
curableness *n* curabilidad, *f*
curative *a* curativo, terapéutico
curator *n* (of a museum) director, *m*; (Scots law) curador, *m*
curb *n* (of a bridle) barbada, *f*; *fig* freno, *m*; (stone) bordillo, *m*, guarnición, *f*. *vt* (a horse) enfrenar; *fig* refrenar, reprimir; (limit) limitar
curd *n* requesón, *m*; cuajada, *f*
curdle *vi* coagularse; (of blood) helarse. *vt* coagular; (blood) helar
cure *n* cura, *f*; *ecc* curato, *m*. *vt* curar; (salt) salar; *fig* remediar. **to take a c.,** tomar una cura. **c.-all,** panacea, *f*. **c. of souls,** cura de almas, *f*
curer *n* (of fish, etc.) salador, *m*; (of evils, etc.) remediador, *m*
curfew *n* toque de queda, *m*
curing *n* curación, *f*; (salting) saladura, *f*
curio *n* curiosidad, antigüedad, *f*
curiosity *n* curiosidad, *f*
curious *a* (all meanings) curioso
curiously *adv* curiosamente
curl *n* (of hair) rizo, bucle, *m*; (of smoke) penacho, *m*. *vt* rizar. *vi* rizarse; *sport* jugar al curling. **in c.,** rizado. **to c. one's lip,** hacer una mueca de desdén. **to c. up,** *vt* arrollar; *fig* dejar fuera de combate (a). *vi* hacerse un ovillo, enroscarse; (of leaves) abarquillarse; *fig* desplomarse; desanimarse. **c.-paper,** papillote, *m*
curlew *n orn* zarapito, *m*
curling *n* (game) curling, *m*, *a* rizado. **c.-tongs,** encrespador, *m*
curly *a* rizado, crespo
curmudgeon *n* erizo, misántropo, cara de viernes, *m*
currant *n* (dry) pasa de Corinto, *f*; (fresh) grosella, *f*. **black c.,** grosella negra, *f*; (bush) grosellero negro, *m*. **c.-bush,** grosellero, *m*
currency *n* uso corriente, *m*; moneda corriente, *f*, dinero, *m*; dinero en circulación, *m*; valor corriente, *m*; estimación, *f*
current *a* corriente; presente, de actualidad; (of money) en circulación. *n* (of water, etc., *fig elec*) corriente, *f*. **alternating c.,** *elec* corriente alterna, *f*. **direct c.,** *elec* corriente continua, *f*. **the c. number of a magazine,** el último número de una revista. **c. events,** actualidades, *f pl*
currently *adv* corrientemente, generalmente
curricle *n* carriola, *f*
curriculum *n* plan de estudios, *m*; curso, *m*
curriculum vitae *n* hoja de vida, *f*
curry *vt* (leather) zurrar; (a horse) almohazar; *cul* condimentar con cari. **to c. favor with,** insinuarse en el favor de. **c.-comb,** almohaza, *f*
curse *n* maldición, *f*; blasfemia, *f*; (ruin) azote, castigo, *m*. *vt* maldecir; (afflict) castigar. *vi* blasfemar, echar pestes
cursed *a* maldito; abominable, odioso
cursing *n* maldición, *f*; blasfemias, *f pl*
cursorily *adv* rápidamente; de prisa; superficialmente
cursory *a* rápido; apresurado; superficial
curt *a* seco, brusco; corto
curtail *vt* abreviar; reducir; disminuir
curtailment *n* abreviación, *f*; reducción, *f*; disminución, *f*
curtain *n* cortina, *f*; *theat* telón, *m*. *vt* poner cortinas (a) **drop c.,** telón de boca, *m*. **iron c.,** *pol* telón de acero, *m*. **to c. off,** separar por cortinas. **c.-lecture,** reprimenda conyugal, *f*. **c.-raiser,** entremés, *m*. **c.-ring,** anilla, *f*
curtly *adv* secamente, bruscamente
curtness *n* brusquedad, sequedad, *f*
curtsey *n* reverencia, cortesía, *f*, *vi* hacer una reverencia
curvature *n* curvatura, *f*
curve *n* curva, *f*; *mech* codo, *m*; (*aut* of a road) viraje, *m*. *vt* encorvar, torcer. *vi* encorvarse, torcerse; (of a road) hacer un viraje.
curved *a* curvo
curvet *n* corveta, cabriola, *f*, *vi* corvetear, corcovear, cabriolar
curvilinear *a* curvilíneo
cushion *n* almohada, *f*; cojín, *m*; (billiards) banda, *f*; (of fingers, etc.) pulpejo, *m*. *vt* proveer de almohadas; (a shock) amortiguar; suavizar
custard *n* flan, *m*, natillas, *f pl*

custodian *n* custodio, *m;* guardián, *m;* (of a museum, etc.) director, *m*
custody *n* custodia, *f;* guarda, *f;* prisión, *f.* **in safe c.,** en lugar seguro. **to take** (a person) **into c.,** arrestar
custom *n* costumbre, *f;* uso, *m; com* parroquia, clientela, *f;* (sales) ventas, *f pl; pl* **Customs,** aduana, *f.* **to go through the Customs,** pasar por la aduana. **Customs duty,** derechos de aduana, *m pl.* **Customs officer,** aduanero, *m.* **c.-house,** aduana, *f*
customarily *adv* habitualmente, por lo general
customary *a* acostumbrado, usual, habitual
customer *n* cliente, *mf* parroquiano (-na), *Lat. Am. also.* marchante (-ta). **He is a queer c.,** Es un tipo raro
customs barrier *n* barrera aduanera, barrera arancelaria, *f*
cut *vt* cortar; (diamonds) tallar; (hay, etc.) segar; (carve) labrar, tallar; (engrave) grabar; (a lecture, etc.) no asistir a; (cards) destajar, cortar; (*fig* wound) herir; (reduce) reducir; abreviar; (teeth) echar; (of lines) cruzar. *vi* cortar; cortar bien; (*fam* go) marcharse a prisa y corriendo. **I must get my hair cut,** He de hacerme cortar el pelo. **That cuts both ways,** Es una arma de dos filos. **His opinion cuts no ice,** Su opinión no cuenta. **Mary cut him dead,** María hizo como si no le reconociera. **to cut a caper,** dar saltos; hacer cabriolas. **to cut a person short,** echar el tablacho (a). **to cut and run,** poner los pies en polvorosa. **to cut for deal,** (cards) cortar para ver quién da las cartas. **to cut short,** (a career) terminar. **to cut to the quick,** herir en lo más vivo. **to cut across,** cortar al través; (fields, etc.) atravesar; tomar por un atajo. **to cut away,** *vt* quitar. *vi inf* poner pies en polvorosa. **to cut down,** derribar; (by the sword) acuchillar; (by death, etc.) segar, malograr; (expenses, etc.) reducir; (abbreviate) cortar, abreviar. **to cut off,** cortar, separar; amputar; (on a telephone) cortar la comunicación; (gas, water, etc.) cortar; (supply of food, etc.) interrumpir; (of death) llevarse. **to cut off with a shilling,** desheredar (a). **to cut out,** (dresses, etc.) cortar; (oust) suplantar. **He is not cut out for medicine,** No tiene la disposición para la medicina. **to cut up,** trinchar, cortar en pequeños trozos, *Lat. Am.* destajar; (afflict) entristecer, afligir. **to cut up rough,** *inf* ponerse furioso
cut *a* cortado. **well-cut features,** facciones regulares, *f pl.* **cut and dried opinion,** opinión hecha, idea fija, *f;* ideas cerradas, *f pl.* **cut glass,** cristal tallado, *m*
cut *n* corte, *m;* (with a whip) latigazo, *m;* (with a sword) cuchillada, *f;* (with a sharp instrument) tajo, *m;* cortadura, *f;* (in prices, etc.) reducción, *f;* (engraving) grabado, *m;* clisé, *m;* (of cards) corte, *m.* **short cut,** atajo, *m.* **the cut of a coat,** el corte de un abrigo. **to give** (someone) **the cut direct,** pasar cerca de (una persona) sin saludarle. **cut-out,** *n* (paper) recortado, *m; elec* cortacircuitos, *m.* **cut-throat,** *n* asesino, *m*
cutaneous *a* cutáneo
cute *a* cuco, listo; mono
cuteness *n* cuquería, inteligencia, *f;* monería, *f*
cuticle *n* cutícula, *f*
cutlass *n* alfanje *m*
cutler *n* cuchillero, *m*
cutlery *n* cuchillería, *f*
cutlet *n* chuleta, *f*
cutter *n* cortador, *m; naut* cúter, *m;* escampavía, *f*
cutting *n* corte, *m;* (of diamonds) talla, *f;* (in a mountain, etc.) tajo, *m; agr* plantón, *m;* (of cloth) retazo, *m;* (newspaper) recorte, *m. a* cortante; (of remarks) mordaz. **newspaper c.,** recorte de periódico. **c. down,** (of trees) tala, *f;* reducción, *f*
cuttingly *adv* mordazmente, con malicia.
cuttlefish *n* jibia, *f*
cyanide *n* cianuro, *m*
cycle *n* ciclo, *m;* período, *m;* (bicycle) bicicleta, *f. vi* ir en bicicleta
cyclic *a* cíclico
cycling *n* ciclismo, *m*
cyclist *n* ciclista, *mf*
cyclone *n* ciclón, *m*
Cyclopean *a* ciclópeo
Cyclopean task *n* obra ciclópea, *f*
cygnet *n* pollo del cisne, *m*
cylinder *n* cilindro, *m; mech* tambor, *m.* **c. head,** culata, *f*
cylindrical *a* cilíndrico
cymbal *n* címbalo, platillo, *m*
cymbalist *n* cimbalero (-ra)
cynic *n* cínico, *m*
cynical *a* cínico
cynicism *n* cinismo, *m*
cynosure *n ast* Osa Menor, *f;* blanco, *m*
cypress *n* (tree and wood) ciprés, *m.* **c. grove,** cipresal, *m*
Cypriot *a* chipriota. *n* chipriota, *mf*
Cyprus Isla de Chipre, *f*
cyst *n* quiste, *m*
cystic *a* cístico
Czech *a* checo. *n* checo (-ca); (language) checo, *m*
Czechoslovak *n* checoslovaco (-ca)
Czechoslovakia Checoslovaquia, *f*
Czechoslovakian *a* checoslovaco

D

d *n* (letter) de, *f; mus* re, *m*
dab *vt* golpear suavemente, tocar; (sponge) esponjar; (moisten) mojar. *n* golpecito, golpe blando, *m;* (small piece) pedazo pequeño, *m;* (blob) borrón, *m;* (peck) picotazo, *m; inf* experto (-ta). **to dab at one's eyes,** secarse los ojos
dabble *vt* mojar (en). *vi* chapotear; (engage in) entretenerse en; (meddle in) meterse en; (speculate in) especular en. **to d. in politics,** meterse en política
dabbler *n* aficionado (-da)
dace *n* dardo, albur, *m*
dachshund *n* perro pachón, *m*
daddy *n* papaíto, *m.* **d.-longlegs,** típula, *f*
daffodil *n* narciso trompón, *m*
daft *a* bobo, tonto, chiflado; loco
dagger *n* daga, *f,* puñal, *m; print* cruz, *f.* **to be at daggers drawn,** estar a matar. **to look daggers (at),** lanzar miradas de odio (hacia), mirar echando chispas. **d. thrust,** puñalada, *f*
daguerreotype *n* daguerrotipo, *m*
dahlia *n* dalia, *f*
daily *a* diario, de todos los días; cotidiano. *adv* diariamente, cada día, todos los días; cotidianamente. *n* (paper) diario, *m.* **d. bread,** pan cotidiano, pan de cada día, *m.* **d. help,** (person) asistenta, *f.* **d. pay,** jornal, *m; mil* pre, *m*
daintily *adv* delicadamente; elegantemente; con primor
daintiness *n* delicadeza, *f;* elegancia, *f;* (beauty) primor, *m*
dainty *a* delicado; elegante; primoroso, exquisito; (fastidious) melindroso, difícil. *n* bocado exquisito, *m,* golosina, *f*
dairy *n* lechería, *f.* **d. cattle,** vacas lecheras, *f pl.* **d.-farm,** granja, *f.* **d.-farmer,** granjero (-ra). **d.-farming,** industria lechera, *f*
dairymaid *n* lechera, *f*
dairyman *n* lechero, *m*
dais *n* estrado, *m*
daisy *n* margarita, *f*
dale *n* valle, *m*
dalliance *n* (delay) tardanza, *f;* (play) jugueteo, *m;* diversiones, *f pl;* (caresses) caricias, *f pl,* abrazos, *m pl*

dally *vi* tardar, perder el tiempo; entretenerse, divertirse; (make love) holgar (con); (with an idea) entretenerse con, jugar con
Dalmatian *a* dalmático, dálmata. *n* dálmata, *mf.* **D. dog,** perro dálmata, *m*
dalmatic *n* dalmática, *f*
daltonism *n* daltonismo, *m*
dam *n* (of animals) madre, *f;* (of a river, etc.) presa, *f,* embalse, *m;* (mole) dique, *m;* pared de retención, *f. vt* represar, embalsar; cerrar; (restrain) contener, reprimir
damage *n* daño, perjuicio, *m;* mal, *m;* avería, *f;* pérdida, *f;* (*fam* price) precio, *m; pl* **damages,** *law* daños y perjuicios, *m pl. vt* dañar, perjudicar, *Lat. Am.* afectar; estropear; deteriorar; (reputation, etc.) comprometer
damageable *a* que puede ser dañado; frágil
damaging *a* perjudicial; comprometedor
damascene *vt* damasquinar
Damascus Damasio, *m*
damask *n* (cloth) damasco, *m;* (steel) acero damasquino, *m. a* de damasco; damasquino. *vt* (metals) damasquinar; (cloth) adamascar. **d.-like,** adamascado. **d. rose,** rosa de Damasco, *f*
dame *n* dama, señora, *f; inf* madre, *f;* (schoolmistress) amiga, *f.* **to attend a d. school,** ir a la amiga
damming *n* embalse, *m,* represa, *f;* retención, *f;* represión, *f*
damn *vt* condenar al infierno; maldecir; vituperar. **D. it!** ¡Maldito sea!
damnable *a* detestable, infame; *inf* horrible
damnably *adv* abominablemente; *inf* horriblemente
damnation *n* condenación, perdición, *f;* maldición, *f;* vituperación, *f*
damned *a* condenado; maldito; detestable, odioso
damning *a* que condena; irresistible
damp *a* húmedo. *n* humedad, *f;* (mist) niebla, *f;* exhalación, *f;* (gas) mofeta, *f; fig* tristeza, depresión, *f. vt* humedecer, mojar; apagar, amortiguar; (depress) deprimir, entristecer; (stifle) ahogar; (lessen) moderar; (trouble) turbar. **d.-proof,** impermeable
damper *n* (of a chimney) registro de humos, *m;* (of a piano) batiente, *m;* (for stamps) mojador, *m;* (gloom) depresión, tristeza, *f;* (restraint) freno, *m*
dampish *a* algo húmedo
dampness *n* humedad, *f*
damsel *n* chica, muchacha, *f;* damisela, *f*
damson *n* ciruela damascena, *f.* **d. tree,** ciruelo damasceno, *m*
dance *n* danza, *f;* baile, *m. vi* bailar, danzar; saltar, brincar. *vt* bailar; hacer saltar. **to d. attendance on,** servir humildemente; hacer la rueda (a). **to lead someone a d.,** hacer bailar. **d. band,** orquestina, *f;* orquesta de jazz, *f.* **d. floor,** pista de baile, *f.* **d. hall,** salón de baile, *m.* **d. music,** música bailable, *f.* **d.-number,** (in a theater) bailable, *m.* **d. of death,** danza de la muerte, *f*
dancer *n* bailarín (-ina); danzador (-ra), bailador (-ra); *pl* **dancers,** (partners) parejas de baile, *f pl*
dancing *n* baile, *m,* danza, *f.* **d.-girl,** bailarina, *f;* (Indian) bayadera, *f.* **d.-master,** maestro de baile, *m.* **d. school,** academia de baile, *f.* **d. slipper,** zapatilla de baile, *f*
dandelion *n* diente de león, *m*
dandle *vt* mecer, hacer saltar sobre las rodillas, hacer bailar
dandruff *n* caspa, *f*
dandy *n* dandi, petimetre, barbilindo, *m*
Dane *n* danés (-esa). **Great D.,** perro danés, *m*
danger *n* peligro, *m;* riesgo, *m.* **out of d.,** fuera de peligro. **to be in d.,** correr peligro, peligrar, estar en peligro
dangerous *a* peligroso; arriesgado; nocivo
dangerously *adv* peligrosamente
dangerousness *n* peligro, *m*
dangle *vi* colgar, pender. *vt* dejar colgar; oscilar; (show) mostrar
Danish *a* danés, de Dinamarca. *n* (language) danés, *m*
dank *a* húmedo
dankness *n* humedad, *f*
Danube, the el (Río) Danubio, *m*
dapper *a* apuesto, aseado; activo, vivaz
dapple *vt* motear, salpicar, manchar. **d.-grey,** *a* rucio
dappled *a* (of horses) rodado, empedrado
Dardanelles, the los Dardanelos, *m*
dare *vi* atreverse, osar. *vt* arriesgar; desafiar, provocar; hacer frente a, arrostrar. *n* reto, *m.* **I d. say!** ¡Ya lo creo! ¡No lo dudo! **I d. say that . . . ,** No me sorprendería que . . . ; Supongo que . . . **d.-devil,** calavera, *m;* atrevido (-da), valeroso (-sa)
daring *a* intrépido, audaz; atrevido, *Argentina* agalludo (dangerous) arriesgado, peligroso. *n* audacia, osadia, *f,* atrevimiento, *m;* peligro, *m*
daringly *adv* atrevidamente
dark *a* oscuro; (of complexion, etc.) moreno; negro; lóbrego; (of colours) oscuro; misterioso; enigmático; secreto, escondido; (sad) funesto, triste; (evil) malo, malévolo; (ignorant) ignorante, supersticioso. *n* oscuridad, *f;* (shade) sombra, *f;* ignorancia, *f.* **after d.,** *a* nocturno. *adv* después del anochecer. **in the d.,** a oscuras; de noche; *fig* **be in the d.,** quedarse en la luna. **to become d.,** oscurecerse; (cloud over) anublarse; (become night) anochecer. **to keep d.,** *vt* tener secreto. *vi* esconderse. **d. ages,** los siglos de la ignorancia y de la superstición. **d.-eyed,** de ojos negros, ojinegro. **d. horse,** caballo desconocido, *m; pol* batacazo, *m.* **d. lantern,** linterna sorda, *f.* **d. room,** cuarto oscuro, *m; phot* laboratorio fotográfico, *m;* (optics) cámara oscura, *f*
darken *vt* obscurecer; sombrear; (of color) hacer más oscuro; (sadden) entristecer. *vi* obscurecerse; (of the sky) anublarse; (of the face with emotion) inmutarse.
darkening *n* oscurecimiento, *m*
darkly *adv* oscuramente; misteriosamente; con malevolencia; secretamente; (archaic) indistintamente
darkness *n* oscuridad, *f,* tinieblas, *f pl;* sombra, *f;* (of color) oscuro, *m;* (of the complexion) color moreno, *m;* (of eyes, hair) negrura, *f;* (night) noche, *f;* (ignorance) ignorancia, *f;* (privacy) secreto, *m.* **Prince of d.,** el príncipe de las tinieblas
darling *a* querido, amado; (greatest) mayor. *n* querido (-da); (favorite) el predilecto, la predilecta, el favorito, la favorita. **My d.!** ¡Amor mío! ¡Vida mía! ¡Pichoncito mío!
darn *vt* zurcir, remendar. *n* zurcido, remiendo, *m*
darner *n* zurcidor (-ra); (implement) huevo de zurcir, *m*
darning *n* zurcidura, *f;* zurcido, recosido, *m.* **d.-needle,** aguja de zurcir, *f.* **d. wool,** lana de zurcir, *f*
dart *n* dardo, *m;* movimiento rápido, *m;* avance rápido, *m; sew* sisa, *f. vi* lanzarse, abalanzarse (sobre); volar; correr, avanzar rápidamente. *vt* lanzar, arrojar; dirigir. **to make darts in,** *sew* sisar
Darwinian *a* darviniano. *n* darvinista, *mf*
Darwinism *n* darvinismo, *m*
dash *n* (spirit) fogosidad, *f,* brío, *m;* energía, *f;* (impact) choque, golpe, *m;* (mixture) mezcla, *f;* (of a liquid) gota, *f;* (of the pen) rasgo, *m;* (attack) ataque, *m;* avance rápido, *m;* (a little) algo, un poco (de); *gram* raya, *f;* (show) ostentación, *f.* **He made a d. for the door,** Se precipitó a la puerta, Corrió hacia la puerta. **to cut a d.,** hacer gran papel. **d.-board,** tablero de instrumentos, *m*
dash *vt* arrojar con violencia; (break) quebrar, estrellar; (sprinkle) rociar (con), salpicar (con); (mix) mezclar; (knock) golpear; (disappoint) frustrar, destruir; (confound) confundir; (depress) desanimar. *vi* (rush) precipitarse; quebrarse, estrellarse; chocar (contra); (of waves) romperse. **to d. to pieces,** hacer añicos, estrellar. **to d. along,** avanzar rápidamente; correr. **to d. away,** *vi* marcharse apresuradamente. *vt* apartar bruscamente. **to d. down,** *vi* bajar aprisa. *vt* derribar; (overturn) volcar; (throw) tirar. **to d. off,** *vi* marcharse

rápidamente. *vt* hacer apresuradamente; (a letter, etc.) escribir de prisa; (sketch) bosquejar rápidamente. **to d. out,** *vi* salir precipitadamente; lanzarse a la calle. *vt* (erase) borrar; hacer saltar. **to d. through,** atravesar rápidamente; hacer de prisa. **to d. up,** llegar a prisa; (sprout) saltar

dashing *a* valiente; (spirited) fogoso, gallardo; majo, brillante. *n* choque, *m*; (breaking) quebrantamiento, *m*; (of the waves) embate, *m*

dastardly *a* cobarde

data *n pl* datos, *m pl*

data processing *n* elaboración electrónica de datos, *f*, recuento de datos, *m*

date *n* fecha, *f*; (period) época, *f*; (term) plazo, *m*; (duration) duración, *f*; (appointment) cita, *f*; *bot* dátil, *m*. *vt* fechar, datar; poner fecha a; asignar. *vi* datar (de), remontar (a). **out of d.,** anticuado; pasado de moda; (of persons) atrasado de noticias. **to be up to d.,** ser nuevo; ser de última moda; (of persons) estar al día. **to bring up to d.,** renovar; (of persons) poner al corriente. **to fix the d.,** señalar el día; (chronologically) ajustar los tiempos. **to d.,** hasta la fecha. **under d. (of),** con fecha (de). **up to d.,** hasta hoy, hasta ahora. **What is the d.?** ¿Qué fecha es? ¿A cómo estamos hoy? ¿A cuántos estamos hoy? **d. palm,** datilera, *f*

date of expiry *n* fecha de caducidad, *f*

daub *vt* barrar, embadurnar; manchar, ensuciar; untar; (paint) pintorrear. *n* embadurnamiento, *m*; (picture) aleluya, *f*

dauber *n* chafalmejas, pintamonas, *mf* pintor (-ra) de brocha gorda

daughter *n* hija, *f*. **adopted d.,** hija adoptiva, *f*. **little d.,** hijuela, *f*. **d.-in-law,** nuera, *f*

daughterly *a* de hija

daunt *vt* intimidar, acobardar; dar miedo (a), espantar; (dishearten) desanimar

dauntless *a* impávido, intrépido

dauphin *n* delfín, *m*

dawdle *vi* perder el tiempo; haraganear, gandulear

dawdler *n* gandul (-la)

dawdling *a* perezoso, lento

dawn *n* alba, madrugada, primera luz, *f*; *fig* aurora, *f*. *vi* amanecer, alborear, romper el dia; (appear) mostrarse, asomar. **at d.,** a primera luz, al amanecer, de madrugada, al alba. **It had not dawned on me,** No me había ocurrido

day *n* día, *m*; luz del día, *f*; (day's work) jornada, *f*; (battle) batalla, *f*; (victory) victoria, *f*; *pl* **days,** (time) tiempos, *m pl*, época, *f*; (life) vida, *f*; (years) años, *m pl*, *a* diario. **all day long,** durante todo el día. **any day,** cualquier día. **by day,** de día. **by the day,** al día. **every day,** todos los días, cada día. **every other day,** un día sí y otro no, cada dos días. **from this day forward,** desde hoy en adelante. **from day to day,** de día en día. **Good day!** ¡Buenos días! **in these days,** en estos días. **in olden days,** en la antigüedad; *inf* en tiempos de Maricastaña. **in the days of,** en los tiempos de; durante los años de; durante la vida de. **next day,** el día siguiente. **(on) the next day,** al día siguiente, al otro día. **one of these days,** un día de éstos. **some fine day,** el mejor día, de un día a otro. **the day after tomorrow,** pasado mañana. **the day before yesterday,** anteayer. **the day before,** la víspera. **to win the day,** ganar el día, salir victorioso. **day after day,** cada día, día tras día. **day by day,** día por día. **day in, day out,** sin cesar, día tras día. **day-book,** *com* libro diario, *m*. **day's holiday,** día de asueto, *m*; día libre, *m*. **day laborer,** jornalero, *m*. **day nursery,** guardería de niños, *f*. **day-pupil,** alumno (-na) externo (-na). **day-school,** externado, *m*. **day shift,** turno de día, *m*. **day-star,** lucero del alba, *m*. **day ticket,** billete de excursión, *m*

daybreak *n* alba, *f*, amanecer, *m*. **at d.,** al romper el día, al amanecer

daydream *n* ensueño, *m*; ilusión, *f*; fantasía, visión, *f*. *vi lit* soñar despierto, dejar volar sus pensamientos; *fig* hacerse ilusiones

daydreamer *n* soñador (-ra); visionario (-ia)

daylight *n* luz del día, *f*, día, *m*; (contrasted with artificial light) luz natural, *f*. **in broad d.,** a plena calle, a plena luz, en plena luz del día. **It's d. robbery!** ¡Es un desuello! **d.-saving,** hora de verano, *f*

daytime *n* día, *m*. **in the d.,** durante el día

daze *vt* aturdir, confundir; (dazzle) deslumbrar. *n* aturdimiento, *m*, confusión, *f*; perplejidad, *f*

dazzle *vt* (camouflage) disfrazar; deslumbrar, ofuscar. *n* deslumbramiento, *m*; brillo, *m*, refulgencia, *f*

dazzling *a* deslumbrador; brillante

deacon *n* diácono, *m*

deaconess *n* diaconisa, *f*

dead *a* and *past part* muerto; inanimado; (withered) marchito; (deep) profundo; (unconscious) inerte; inmóvil; insensible; (numb) entumecido; (complete) absoluto, completo; (sure) certero, excelente; (useless) inútil; (of color and human character) apagado; sin espíritu; inactivo; (of eyes) mortecino; (of sound) sordo, opaco; (of villages, etc.) desierto, despoblado; (quiet) silencioso; (empty) vacío; (monotonous) monótono; (of fire) apagado; (with weight, language) muerto; *elec* interrumpido; *law* muerto civilmente. *adv* completamente, enteramente; del todo; directamente; exactamente; profundamente. **the d.,** los muertos. **in the d. of night,** en las altas horas de la noche. **to be d.,** estar muerto; haber muerto. **to be d. against,** estar completamente opuesto a. **to drop d.,** caer muerto; morir de repente. **to go d. slow,** ir muy lentamente. **to rise from the d.,** resucitar. **to sham d.,** hacer la mortecina, fingirse muerto. **to speak ill of the d.,** hablar mal de los muertos; *inf* desenterrar los muertos. **d. ball,** pelota fuera de juego, *f*. **d.-beat,** muerto de cansancio. **d. body,** cadáver, cuerpo muerto, *m*. **d. calm,** calma profunda, *f*; *naut* calma chicha, *f*. **d. certainty,** seguridad completa, *f*. **d.-drunk,** hecho una uva. **d. end,** callejón sin salida, *m*. **d. heat,** empate, *m*. **d. language,** lengua muerta, *f*. **d.-letter,** letra muerta, *f*; carta devuelta o no reclamada, *f*. **d.-lock,** punto muerto, *m*. **to reach a d.-lock,** llegar a un punto muerto. **d. march,** marcha fúnebre, *f*. **d. season,** temporada de calma, *f*. **d. set,** empeñado (en). **d. shot,** (person) tirador (-ra) certero (-ra) (shot) tiro certero, *m*. **d. silence,** silencio profundo, *m*. **d. stop,** parada en seco, *f*. **d. tired,** rendido. **d. weight,** peso muerto, *m*. **d. wood,** leña seca, *f*; material inútil, *m*

deaden *vt* amortiguar; (of pain) calmar; (remove) quitar; (of colours) apagar

deadening *n* amortiguamiento, *m*

deadliness *n* carácter mortal, *m*; implacabilidad, *f*

deadly *a* mortal; implacable; *inf* insoportable. *adv* mortalmente. **He was d. pale,** Estaba pálido como un muerto. **the seven d. sins,** los siete pecados mortales. **d. nightshade,** belladona, *f*

deadness *n* falta de vida, *f*; inercia, *f*; marchitez, *f*; (numbness) entumecimiento, *m*; desanimación, *f*; parálisis, *f*

Dead Sea, the el mar Muerto, *m*

Dead Sea Scrolls, the los rollos del mar Muerto, *m pl*

deaf *a* sordo. **d. people,** los sordos. **to be d.,** ser sordo; padecer sordera. **to be as d. as a post,** ser más sordo que una tapia. **to become d.,** ensordecer, volverse sordo. **to fall on d. ears,** caer en saco roto. **to turn a d. ear,** hacerse el sordo. **d. aid,** audífono, *m*. **d.-and-dumb,** sordomudo. **d.-and-dumb alphabet,** alfabeto manual, abecedario manual, *m*. **d.-mute,** sordomudo (-da). **d.-mutism,** sordomudez, *f*

deafen *vt* asordar, ensordecer

deafening *a* ensordecedor

deafly *adv* sordamente

deafness *n* sordera, *f*

deal *n* (transaction) negocio, trato, *m*; (at cards) reparto, *m*; (wood) pino, *m*; (plank) tablón de pino, *m*. **a d., a**

great **d.,** mucho. **a very great d.,** muchísimo. **to conclude a d.,** cerrar un trato
deal *vt* repartir; (a blow) asestar, dar; (cards) dar; (justice) dispensar. **to d. a blow at,** asestar un golpe; *fig* herir (en); *fig* destruir de un golpe. **to d. in,** comerciar en, traficar en; ocuparse en; meterse en. **to d. out,** dispensar. **to d. with,** (buy from) comprar de; tener relaciones con, tratar; entenderse con; portarse con; (of affairs) ocuparse en, arreglar, dirigir; (contend) luchar con; (discuss) discutir, tratar de; (of books) versar sobre. **d. regularly with** *Lat. Am.* amarchantarse con
dealer *n* traficante, *mf* mercader, *m*, *Lat. Am.* marchante (-ta); (at cards) el que da las cartas
dealing *n* conducta, *f*; proceder, *m*; trato, *m*; tráfico, *m*; *pl* **dealings,** relaciones, *f pl*; transacciones, *f pl*
dean *n ecc* deán, *m*; *univ* decano, *m*
dear *a* (beloved) querido, amado; (charming) encantador, simpático; (in letters) estimado, querido; (favorite) predilecto; (expensive) caro. *n* querido (-da); persona querida, *f*, bien amado (-da). *adv* caro. **Oh d.!** ¡Dios mío! ¡Ay!
dearly *adv* tiernamente, entrañablemente; caro
dearness *n* cariño, afecto, *m*, ternura, *f*; (of price) precio alto, *m*
dearth *n* carestía, *f*; (of news, etc.) escasez, *f*
death *n* muerte, *f*; (*law* and in announcements) fallecimiento, *m*, defunción, *f*. **to be at death's door,** estar a la muerte. **to put to d.,** ajusticiar. **to the d.,** a muerte. **untimely d.,** muerte repentina, *f*; malogro, *m*. **death's head,** calavera, *f*. **d. certificate,** partida de defunción, *f*. **d.-duties,** derechos de herencia, *m pl*. **d.-like,** cadavérico. **d.-mask,** mascarilla, *f*. **d. penalty,** pena de muerte, *f*. **d.-rate,** mortalidad, *f*. **d.-rattle,** sarrillo, *m*. **d.-trap,** lugar peligroso, *m*; *fig* trampa, *f*. **d.-warrant,** sentencia de muerte, *f*. **d.-watch bettle,** reloj de la muerte, *m*
deathbed *n* lecho mortuorio, lecho de muerte, *m*. **on one's d.,** en su lecho de muerte
deathblow *n* golpe mortal, *m*
deathly *a* mortal
death toll *n* (of a bell) doble, toque de difuntos, *m*; (casualties) número de muertos, saldo de muertos, *m*
debacle *n fig* ruina, *f*
debar *vt* excluir, privar
debase *vt* degradar, humillar, envilecer; (the coinage) alterar (la moneda)
debasement *n* degradación, humillación, *f*, envilecimiento, *m*; (of the coinage) alteración (de la moneda), *f*
debasing *a* degradante, humillante
debatable *a* discutible
debate *n* debate, *m*; discusión, *f*; disputa, *f*. *vt* and *vi* debatir; discutir; disputar; considerar
debater *n* discutidor (-ra); orador (-ra).
debating *n* discusión, *f*; argumentación, *f*
debauch *vt* corromper, pervertir; (a woman) seducir, violar. *n* libertinaje, *m*; borrachera, *f*
debauched *a* vicioso, licencioso
debauchee *n* libertino, vicioso, *m*
debauchery *n* libertinaje, mal vivir, *m*, viciosidad, licencia, *f*
debenture *n* obligación, *f*. **d. holder,** obligacionista, *mf*
debilitate *vt* debilitar
debilitating *a* debilitante
debilitation *n* debilitación, *f*
debility *n* debilidad, *f*
debit *n* débito, cargo, *m*; saldo deudor, *m*; "debe" de una cuenta, *m*. *vt* adeudar. **d. and credit,** el cargo y la data. **d. balance,** saldo deudor, *m*
debonair *a* gallardo, gentil, donairoso; alegre
debonairly *adv* gallardamente; alegremente
débris *n* escombros, desechos, *m pl*; ruinas, *f pl*; *geol* despojos, *m pl*
debt *n* deuda, *Lat. Am. also* dita *f*. **a bad d.,** una deuda incobrable. **to be in the d. of,** ser en cargo a; deber dinero a; *fig* sentirse bajo una obligación. **to get into d.,** adeudarse, contraer deudas, *Mexico* endrogarse, *elsewhere in Lat. Am.* enditarse
debtor *n* deudor (-ra); *com* debe, *m*
debunk *vt* demoler
debut *n* (of a debutante) puesta de largo, *f*; (of a play, etc.) estreno, *m*. **to make one's d.,** ponerse de largo, presentarse en sociedad
debutante *n* debutante, *f*
decade *n* década, *f*, decenio, *m*; (of the rosary) decena, *f*
decadence *n* decadencia, *f*
decadent *a* decadente
decagramme *n* decagramo, *m*
decaliter *n* decalitro, *m*
decalogue *n* decálogo, *m*
decametre *n* decámetro, *m*
decamp *vi mil* decampar; escaparse, fugarse
decant *vt* decantar
decanter *n* garrafa, *f*
decapitate *vt* decapitar, descabezar
decapitation *n* decapitación, *f*
decarbonization *n* descarburación, *f*
decarbonize *vt* descarbonizar
decay *vi* (rot) pudrirse; degenerar; marchitarse; (of teeth) cariarse; (crumble) desmoronarse, caer en ruinas; decaer, declinar; (come down in the world) venir a menos, arruinarse. *n* pudrición, putrefacción, *f*; (of teeth) caries, *f*; (withering) marchitez, *f*; degeneración, *f*; desmoronamiento, *m*; ruina, *f*; (oldness) vejez, *f*; decadencia, declinación, *f*; (fall) caída, *f*
decease *n* fallecimiento, *m*, defunción, *f*, *vi* fallecer
deceased *n* finado (-da), difunto (-ta). *a* difunto
deceit *n* engaño, fraude, *m*; duplicidad, *f*
deceitful *a* engañoso, falso; embustero, mentiroso; ilusorio
deceitfully *adv* engañosamente
deceitfulness *n* falsedad, duplicidad, *f*
deceivable *a* fácil a engañar, engañadizo
deceive *vt* engañar; (disappoint) decepcionar, desilusionar; frustrar. **If my memory does not d. me,** Si la memoria no me engaña, Si mal no me acuerdo
deceiver *n* engañador (-ra); seductor, *m*
deceiving *a* engañador
December *n* diciembre, *m*
decency *n* decoro, *m*, decencia, *f*; pudor, *m*, modestia, *f*; conveniencias, *f pl*; *inf* bondad, *f*; (manners) cortesía, *f*, buenos modales, *m pl*
decennial *a* decenal
decent *a* decente; decoroso, honesto; púdico; (likable) simpático; (of things) bastante bueno; (honorable) honrado
decently *adv* decentemente
decentralization *n* descentralización, *f*
decentralize *vt* descentralizar
deception *n* engaño, *m*; ilusión, *f*
deceptive *a* engañoso, mentiroso, ilusorio
deceptively *adv* engañosamente
decide *vt* decidir; *law* determinar. *vi* decidir, resolver; acordar, quedar en; juzgar; *law* dictar sentencia, fallar
decided *a* decidido; (downright) categórico, inequívoco; resuelto; positivo; definitivo
decidedly *adv* decididamente; categóricamente; definitivamente
deciduous *a bot* caedizo
decigram *n* decigramo, *m*
decimal *a* decimal. **d. fraction,** fracción decimal, *f*. **d. point,** punto decimal, *m*. **d. system,** sistema métrico, *m*
decimate *vt* diezmar
decimation *n* gran mortandad, *f*; matanza, *f*
decimeter *n* decímetro, *m*
decipher *vt* descifrar; deletrear
decipherable *a* descifrable

decipherer *n* descifrador, *m*
decipherment *n* el descifrar; deletreo, *m*
decision *n* decisión, determinación, *f*; *law* sentencia, *f*, fallo, *m*; (agreement) acuerdo, *m*; (of character) firmeza, resolución, *f*
decisive *a* decísivo; terminante, conclusivo; crítico
decisively *adv* decisivamente
decisiveness *n* carácter decisivo, *m*; firmeza, resolución, *f*; decisión, *f*
deck *n* cubierta, *f*; (of cards) baraja (de naipes), *f*. *vt* adornar, ataviar; decorar. **between decks,** entrecubiertas, *fpl*. **lower d.,** cubierta, *f*. **promenade d.,** cubierta de paseo, *f*. **upper d.,** cubierta superior, *f*. **d.-cabin,** camarote de cubierta, *m*. **d.-chair,** silla de cubierta, silla de tijera, silla extensible, *f*. **d.-hand,** marinero, estibador, *m*
decked *a* ornado, ataviado; engalanado; *naut* de . . . puentes
declaim *vt* recitar. *vi* perorar, declamar
declamation *n* declamación, *f*
declamatory *a* declamatorio
declaration *n* declaración, *f*; manifiesto, *m*; proclamación, *f*
declaratory *a* declaratorio, declarativo
declare *vt* declarar; proclamar; afirmar; manifestar; confesar. *vi* declarar; *law* deponer, testificar. **to d. war (on)** declarar la guerra (a)
declaredly *adv* declaradamente, explícitamente, abiertamente
declension *n* declinación, *f*
declination *n* declinación, *f*
decline *n* declinación, decadencia, *f*; disminución, *f*; debilitación, *f*; (of the day) caída, *f*; (of stocks, shares) depresión, *f*; (illness) consunción, *f*; (*fig* setting) ocaso, *m*, *vi* declinar; inclinarse; decaer; disminuir; debilitarse; (refuse) negarse (a). *vt* (refuse) rechazar, rehusar; *gram* declinar; (avoid) evitar
declining *a* declinante. **in one's d. years,** en sus últimos años
declivity *n* cuesta, pendiente, *f*, declive, *m*
declutch *vi* desembragar
decoction *n* decocción, *f*
decode *vt* descifrar
decoder *n* descifrador, *m*
décolletee *a* escotado
decolouration *n* decoloración, *f*
decompose *vt* descomponer. *vi* descomponerse
decomposition *n* descomposición, *f*
decompressor *n* decompresor, *m*
decontaminate *vt* descontaminar
decontamination *n* descontaminación, *f*
decontrol *vt* suprimir las restricciones sobre
decorate *vt* adornar (con), embellecer; (by painting, etc.) decorar, pintar; (honor) investir (con), condecorar
decoration *n* decoración, *f*; *theat* decorado, *m*; (honor) condecoración, *f*; ornamento, *m*
decorative *a* decorativo
decorator *n* decorador, *m*; (interior) adornista, *m*
decorous *a* decoroso, decente; correcto
decorum *n* decoro, *m*; corrección, *f*
decoy *n* señuelo, *m*; añagaza, *f*; (trap) lazo, *m*, trampa, *f*; *fig* añagaza, *f*. *vt* (birds) reclamar, atraer con señuelo; *fig* tentar (con), seducir (con). **d. bird,** pájaro de reclamo, *m*
decrease *n* disminución, *f*; baja, *f*; reducción, *f*; (of the moon, waters) mengua, *f*, *vi* decrecer, disminuir; bajar; menguar. *vt* disminuir; reducir
decreasingly *adv* de menos en menos
decree *n* decreto, *m*; edicto, *m*. *vi* and *vt* decretar, mandar
decrepit *a* decrépito
decry *vt* desacreditar, rebajar
dedicate *vt* dedicar; consagrar; destinar; aplicar; (a book, etc.) dedicar. **to d. oneself to,** dedicarse a, consagrarse a, entregarse a
dedication *n* dedicación, *f*; consagración, *f*; (of a book, etc.) dedicatoria, *f*
dedicatory *a* dedicatorio
deduce *vt* derivar; deducir, inferir
deduct *vt* deducir; descontar
deduction *n* deducción, *f*; descuento, *m*
deductive *a* deductivo
deed *n* acción, *f*; hecho, acto, *m*; hazaña, *f*; (reality) realidad, *f*; *law* escritura, *f*; *law* contrato, *m*. **d. of gift,** escritura de donación, *f*
deem *vt* juzgar, creer, estimar
deep *a* profundo; (wide) ancho; (low) bajo; (thick) espeso; (of colours) subido; (of sounds) grave, profundo; (immersed (in)) absorto (en); (of the mind) penetrante; (secret) secreto; (intense) intenso, hondo; (cunning) astuto, artero; (dark) oscuro; (of mourning) riguroso. *n poet* piélago, mar, *m*; profundidad, *f*; abismo, *m*, *adv* profundamente; a una gran profundidad. **to be in d. waters,** *fig* estar con el agua al cuello. **to be three feet d.,** tener tres pies de profundidad. **to be d. in,** estar absorto en; (of debt) estar cargado de. **three d.,** tres de fondo. **d. into the night,** hasta las altas horas de la noche. **d.-felt,** hondamente sentido. **d. mourning,** luto riguroso, *m*. **d.-rooted,** arraigado. **d.-sea fishing,** pesca mayor, *f*. **d.-sea lead,** escandallo, *m*. **d.-seated,** intimo, profundo; arraigado. **d.-set,** hundido
deepen *vt* profundizar, ahondar; (broaden) ensanchar; (intensify) intensificar; (increase) aumentar; (of colors) aumentar el tono de, intensificar. *vi* hacerse más profundo, hacerse más hondo; intensificarse; aumentarse; (of sound) hacerse más grave
deeply *adv* profundamente; intensamente; fuertemente
deepness *n* (cunning) astucia, *f*; see **depth**
deer *n* ciervo (-va), venado, *m*, *a* cervuno. **d.-hound,** galgo de cazar venados, *m*. **d.-skin,** piel de venado, *f*. **d.-stalking,** caza del ciervo, *f*
deface *vt* desfigurar, mutilar; estropear; (erase) borrar
defacement *n* desfiguración, mutilación, *f*; afeamiento, *m*; borradura, *f*
defamation *n* difamación, denigración, *f*
defamatory *a* difamatorio, denigrante
defame *vt* difamar, denigrar, calumniar
default *n* omisión, *f*, descuido, *m*; falta, *f*; ausencia, *f*; *law* rebeldía, *f*. *vi* dejar de cumplir; faltar; no pagar. *vt law* condenar en rebeldía. **in d. of,** en la ausencia de
defaulter *n* el, *m*, (*f*, la) que no cumple sus obligaciones; delincuente, *mf*; desfalcador (-ra); *law* rebelde, *mf*
defeat *vt* vencer, derrotar; frustrar; (reject) rechazar; (elude) evitar; *fig* vencer, triunfar sobre. *n* derrota, *f*; vencimiento, *m*; frustración, *f*; rechazamiento, *m*. **to d. one's own ends,** defraudar sus intenciones
defeatism *n* derrotismo, *m*
defeatist *n* derrotista, *mf*
defecate *vt* defecar
defecation *n* defecación, *f*
defect *n* defecto, *m*; imperfección, *f*; falta, *f*
defection *n* defección, *f*; deserción, *f*; (from a religion) apostasía, *f*
defective *a* defectuoso; *gram* defectivo; falto; imperfecto; (mentally) anormal. *n* persona anormal, *f*, anormal, *m*
defectiveness *n* imperfección, *f*; deficiencia, *f*; defecto, *m*
defend *vt* defender; proteger; preservar; sostener; (a thesis) sustentar
defendant *n law* acusado (-da), procesado (-da), demandado (-da)
defender *n* defensor (-ra); (of a thesis) sustentante, *mf*
defense *n* defensa, *f*; justificación, *f*; *pl* **defenses,** defensas, *fpl*; obras de fortificación, *fpl*. **for the d.,** (of witnesses) de descargo; (of counsel) para la defensa. **in d. of,** en defensa de. **in one's own d.,** en su propia defensa. **d. in depth,** *mil* defensa en fondo, *f*

defenseless *a* indefenso, sin defensa
defenselessness *n* incapacidad de defenderse, *f;* debilidad, *f,* desvalimiento, *m*
defensible *a* defendible; justificable
defensive *a* defensivo. *n* defensiva, *f.* **to be on the d.,** estar a la defensiva
defensively *adv* defensivamente
defer *vt* (postpone) diferir, aplazar; suspender. *vi* (yield) deferir, ceder; (delay) tardar, aguardar. **deferred payment,** pago a plazos, *m*
deference *n* deferencia, *f,* respeto, *m;* consideración, *f*
deferential *a* deferente, respetuoso
deferment *n* aplazamiento, *m;* suspensión, *f*
defiance *n* desafío, *m;* provocación, *f;* oposición, *f;* insolencia, *f.* **in d. of,** en contra de
defiant *a* provocativo; insolente
defiantly *adv* de un aire provocativo; insolentemente
deficiency *n* falta, deficiencia, *f;* imperfección, *f;* defecto, *m;* omisión, *f;* (scarcity) carestía, *f;* (in accounts) déficit, *m*
deficient *a* deficiente; falto, incompleto; imperfecto; pobre; defectuoso; (not clever at) débil (en); (mentally) anormal. **to be d. in,** carecer de; ser pobre en
deficit *n* déficit, *m;* descubierto, *m*
defile *n* desfiladero, *m. vt* contaminar; profanar; manchar; deshonrar. *vi mil* desfilar
defilement *n* contaminación, *f;* corrupción, *f;* profanación, *f*
definable *a* definible
define *vt* definir; (throw into relief) destacar; fijar; *law* determinar
definite *a* definido; positivo; categórico; exacto; concreto. **d. article,** artículo definido, *m*
definitely *adv* positivamente; claramente. **definitely not!** ¡definitivamente no!
definiteness *n* carácter definido, *m;* exactitud, *f;* lo categórico
definition *n* definición, *f*
definitive *a* definitivo
deflate *vt* desinflar. *vi* desinflarse, deshincharse
deflation *n* desinflación, *f*
deflect *vt* desviar; apartar. *vi* desviarse; apartarse
deflection *n* desviación, *f;* apartamiento, *m*
defloration *n* desfloración, *f*
deflower *vt* desflorar
deforestation *n* desforestación, desmontadura, despoblación forestal, *f*
deform *vt* deformar, desfigurar; afear
deformation *n* deformación, *f*
deformed *a* deformado; contrahecho
deformity *n* deformidad, *f*
defraud *vt* defraudar
defrauder *n* defraudador (-ra)
defrauding *n* defraudación, *f*
defray *vt* sufragar, costear, pagar
defrayal *n* pago, *m*
defrost *vt* deshelar
deft *a* diestro; hábil
deftly *adv* con destreza; hábilmente
deftness *n* destreza, *f;* habilidad, *f*
defunct *a* and *n* difunto (-ta)
defy *vt* desafiar; (face) arrostrar; (violate) contravenir
degeneracy *n* degeneración, *f;* depravación, degradación, *f*
degenerate *a* and *n* degenerado (-da). *vi* degenerar
degeneration *n* degeneración, *f*
degradation *n* degradación, *f;* abyección, *f*
degrade *vt* degradar; envilecer, deshonrar
degrading *a* degradante
degree *n* grado, *m;* punto, *m;* clase social, *f.* **by degrees,** poco a poco, gradualmente, **five degrees below zero,** cinco grados bajo cero. **in the highest d.,** en sumo grado, en grado superlativo. **to a certain d.,** hasta cierto punto. **to receive a d.,** graduarse
degree-granting institution *n* plantel habilitado para expedir títulos, *m*
dehydrate *vt* deshidratar
dehydration *n* deshidratación, *f*
de-ice *vt* deshelar
deification *n* deificación, *f*
deify *vt* deificar, endiosar
deign *vi* dignarse. *vt* conceder
deism *n* deísmo, *m*
deist *n* deísta, *mf*
deity *n* deidad, divinidad, *f;* dios, *m*
dejected *a* abatido, desanimado, deprimido
dejectedly *adv* tristemente, abatidamente
dejection *n* abatimiento, desaliento, *m,* melancolía, *f*
delay *n* retraso, *m,* dilación, tardanza, demora, *f. vt* retrasar, demorar; (a person) entretener; (postpone) aplazar; (obstruct) impedir. *vi* tardar; entretenerse. **without more d.,** sin más tardar
delectable *a* deleitoso, delicioso
delectably *adv* deliciosamente
delectation *n* delectación, *f,* deleite, *m*
delegacy *n* delegación, *f*
delegate *n* delegado (-da). *vt* delegar, diputar
delegation *n* delegación, *f*
delete *vt* suprimir, borrar
deleterious *a* deletéreo
deletion *n* supresión, borradura, *f*
deliberate *a* premeditado, intencionado; (slow) pausado, lento. *vi* and *vt* deliberar, discurrir, considerar
deliberately *adv* (intentionally) con premeditación, a sabiendas, *Central America* adifés; (slowly) pausadamente, lentamente
deliberation *n* reflexión, deliberación, consideración, *f;* (slowness) lentitud, pausa, *f*
deliberative *a* deliberativo, de liberante
delicacy *n* delicadeza, *f;* fragilidad, *f;* suavidad, *f;* sensibilidad, *f;* escrupulosidad, *f;* (of health) debilidad, delicadez, *f;* (difficulty) dificultad, *f;* (food) manjar exquisito, *m,* golosina, *f*
delicate *a* delicado; fino; frágil; suave; exquisito; delicado (de salud); (of situations) difícil
delicatessen *n* (store) fiambrería, *f*
delicious *a* delicioso
deliciously *adv* deliciosamente
deliciousness *n* deleite, *m,* lo delicioso; excelencia, *f;* delicias, *f pl*
delict *n* delito, *m*
delictive *a* delictivo
delight *n* deleite, regocijo, *m;* encanto, *m,* delicia, *f;* placer, gozo, *m. vt* deleitar, encantar; halagar. *vi* deleitarse, complacerse. **to be delighted with,** estar encantado con. **to d. in,** deleitarse en, complacerse en; tomar placer en
delightful *a* delicioso, precioso, encantador
delightfully *adv* deliciosamente
delimit *vt* delimitar
delimitation *n* delimitación, *f*
delineate *vt* delinear, diseñar; *fig* pintar, describir
delineation *n* delineación, *f;* retrato, *m;* *fig* descripción, *f*
delineator *n* diseñador, *m*
delinquency *n* delincuencia, *f;* criminalidad, *f;* culpa, *f;* delito, *m*
delinquent *a* delincuente. *n* delincuente, *mf*
deliquescence *n* delicuescencia, *f*
deliquescent *a* delicuescente
delirious *a* delirante; desvariado; *inf* loco. **to be d.,** delirar, desvariar
delirium *n* delirio, desvarío, *m.* **d. tremens,** delírium tremens, *m*
deliver *vt* librar (de); salvar (de); (distribute) repartir; (hand over) entregar; (recite) recitar, decir; (a speech) pronunciar; comunicar; (send) despachar, expedir; (a blow) asestar; (give) dar; (bring) traer; (battle, a lecture) dar; (a woman, of a doctor) asistir en el parto (a); (a child) traer al mundo; (a judgment) pronunciar. **to be delivered (of a child),** dar a luz. **to d. oneself up,** entregarse. **delivered free,** porte pagado.

deliverance *n* libramiento, rescate, *m*; redención, salvación, *f*; (of a judgment) pronuncia, *f*
deliverer *n* libertador (-ra); salvador (-ra); (distributor) repartidor (-ra); entregador (-ra)
delivery *n* (distribution) reparto, *m*, distribución, *f*; entrega, *f*; *law* cesión, *f*; (of a judgment) pronuncia, *f*; (of a speech) pronunciación, *f*; (manner of speaking) declamación, *f*; dicción, *f*; (of a child) parto, *m*. **on d.,** al entregarse. **The letter came by the first d.,** La carta llegó en el primer reparto. **d. man,** mozo de reparto, *m*. **d. note,** nota de entrega, *f*. **d. van,** camión de reparto, *m*
delivery truck *n* camioneta de reparto, furgoneta, *f*, sedán de reparto, *m*
dell *n* hondonada, *f*; pequeño valle, *m*
delouse *vt* despiojar, espulgar
Delphi Delfos, *m*
delta *n* (Greek letter) delta, *f*; (of a river) delta, *m*
delude *vt* engañar; ilusionar. **to d. oneself,** engañarse
deluded *a* iluso, engañado, ciego
deluge *n* diluvio, *m*. *vt* diluviar; inundar (con)
delusion *n* engaño, *m*, ceguedad, *f*; error, *m*; ilusión, *f*
delve *vt* and *vi* cavar; *fig* ahondar (en), penetrar (en), investigar
demagogic *a* demagógico
demagogue *n* demagogo (-ga)
demagogy *n* demagogia, *f*
demand *n* exigencia, *f*; *com* demanda, *f*; petición, *f*; *pol econ* consumo, *m*. *vt* exigir; requerir; pedir; (claim) reclamar. **in d.,** en demanda. **on d.,** al solicitarse. **to be in d.,** ser popular. **d. note,** apremio, *m*
demanding *a* exigente
demarcate *vt* demarcar
demarcation *n* demarcación, *f*
demean (oneself) *vr* degradarse, rebajarse
demeanor *n* conducta, *f*; continente, porte, aire, *m*; (manners) modales, *m pl*
demented *a* demente, loco
demerit *n* demérito, *m*
demi *prefix* semi; casi. **d.-tasse,** taza cafetera, jícara, *f*
demigod *n* semidios, *m*
demigoddess *n* semidiosa, *f*
demijohn *n* damajuana, *f*
demilitarize *vt* desmilitarizar
demise *n law* traslación de dominio, *f*; sucesión de la corona, *f*; (death) óbito, fallecimiento, *m*
demisemiquaver *n* fusa, *f*
demobilization *n* desmovilización, *f*
demobilize *vt* desmovilizar
democracy *n* democracia, *f*
democrat *n* demócrata, *mf*
democratic *a* democrático. **to make d.,** democratizar
demolish *vt* demoler, derribar; *fig* destruir; (eat) engullir, devorar
demolisher *n* demoledor, *m*; *fig* destructor (-ra)
demolition *n* demolición, *f*; derribo, *m*, *a* demoledor; de demolición. **d. squad,** pelotón de demolición, *m*
demon *n* demonio, diablo, *m*
demonetization *n* desmonetización, *f*
demonetize *vt* desmonetizar
demoniacal *a* demoníaco
demonology *n* demonología, *f*
demonstrable *a* demonstrable
demonstrably *adv* demostrablemente
demonstrate *vt* demostrar; mostrar, probar. *vi* hacer una demostración
demonstration *n* demostración, *f*; manifestación, *f*
demonstrative *a* demostrativo; (of persons) expresivo, mimoso. **d. pronoun,** pronombre demostrativo, *m*
demonstrator *n* demostrador (-ra)
demoralization *n* desmoralización, *f*
demoralize *vt* desmoralizar
demoralizing *a* desmoralizador
demur *vi* dudar, vacilar; objetar, protestar; poner dificultades. *n* objeción, protesta, *f*
demure *a* serio, modoso recatado; púdico; de una coquetería disimulada
demurely *adv* modestamente; con recato; con coquetería disimulada
demureness *n* seriedad, *f*, recato, *m*; modestia fingida, coquetería disimulada, *f*
demy *n* papel marquilla, *m*; becario de Magdalen College, Oxford, *m*
den *n* madriguera, guardia, *f*; (of thieves) cueva, *f*; (in a zoo) cercado, recinto, *m*; (study) gabinete, *m*; (squalid room) cuartucho, *m*
denaturalization *n* desnaturalización, *f*
denaturalize *vt* desnaturalizar
denial *n* negación, *f*; rechazo, *m*; contradicción, *f*; negativa, *f*
denizen *n* habitante, *m*; ciudadano (-na)
Denmark Dinamarca, *f*
denominate *vt* denominar, nombrar
denomination *n* denominación, *f*; secta, *f*; clase, *f*
denominational *a* sectario
denominator *n math* denominador, *m*
denote *vt* denotar, indicar; significar
dénouement *n* desenlace, desenredo, *m*; solución, *f*
denounce *vt* denunciar; delatar, acusar
denouncer *n* denunciante, *mf* delator (-ra)
dense *a* denso; espeso, compacto; tupido; impenetrable; *inf* estúpido
densely *adv* densamente; espesamente. **d. populated,** con gran densidad de población
density *n* densidad, *f*; espesor, *m*; consistencia, *f*; *inf* estupidez, *f*
dent *n* mella, *f*; (in metal) abolladura, *f*, *vt* mellar; abollar
dental *a* dental. *n* letra dental, *f*. **d. forceps,** gatillo, *m*. **d. mechanic,** mecánico dentista, *m*. **d. surgeon,** odontólogo, *m*
dental floss *n* seda dental, *f*
dentifrice *n* dentífrico, *m*
dentist *n* dentista, *mf*; odontólogo, *m*
dentistry *n* odontología, *f*
dentition *n* dentición, *f*
denture *n* dentadura, *f*
denudation *n* denudación, *f*
denude *vt* denudar, despojar, privar (de)
denunciation *n* denuncia, *f*; acusación, delación, *f*
denunciatory *a* denunciatorio
Denver boot *n* cepo, *m*
deny *vt* negar; desmentir; rehusar; rechazar; renegar (de); (give up) renunciar, sacrificar. **to d. oneself,** privarse (de); sacrificar; negarse
deodorant *a* and *n* desodorante *m*.
deodorize *vt* desinfectar, destruir el olor de
depart *vi* marcharse, irse, partir; (of trains, etc., and meaning go out) salir; (deviate) desviarse (de), apartarse (de); (go away) alejarse; (leave) dejar; (disappear) desaparecer; (alter) cambiar; (die) morir
departed *a* (past) pasado; desaparecido; (dead) difunto, muerto. *n* difunto (-ta)
department *n* departamento, *m*; sección, *f*; (of learning) ramo, *m*; (in France) distrito administrativo, *m*. **d. store,** grandes tiendas, *f pl*, (Argentina), grandes almacenes, *m pl*
departmental *a* departamental
departure *n* partida, ida, *f Lat. Am.* egreso *m*; (going out, and of trains, etc.) salida, *f*; (deviation) desviación, el apartarse. **d. from the rules,** el apartarse de las reglas), *f*; (disappearance) desaparición, *f*; (change) cambio, *m*; (giving up) renuncia, *f*; (death) muerte, *f*. **to take one's d.,** marcharse
depend *vi* depender. **to d. on,** depender de; (rest on) apoyarse en; (count on) contar con; (trust) fiarse de; tener confianza en, estar seguro de. **That depends!** ¡Eso depende!
dependable *a* digno de confianza; seguro
dependence, dependency *n* dependencia, *f*; subordinación, *f*; (trust) confianza, *f*

dependent *a* dependiente; subordinado; condicional. *n* dependiente, *m*. **to be d. on,** depender de
depict *vt* representar; pintar; dibujar; *fig* describir, retratar
depiction *n* representación, *f*; pintura, *f*; dibujo, *m*; *fig* descripción, *f*
depilate *vt* depilar
depilatory *a* and *n* depilatorio *m*.
deplete *vt* agotar; disipar
depletion *n* agotamiento, *m*
deplorable *a* lamentable, deplorable
deplorably *adv* lamentablemente
deplore *vt* deplorar, lamentar
deploy *vt* desplegar. *vi* desplegarse. *n* despliegue, *m*
deployment *n* despliegue, *m*
deponent *n law* declarante, deponente, *mf a* deponente. **d. verb,** verbo deponente, *m*
depopulate *vt* despoblar
depopulation *n* despoblación, *f*
deport *vt* deportar
deportation *n* deportación, *f*
deportment *n* comportamiento, *m*; porte, aire, *m*; conducta, *f*
depose *vt* destronar; (give evidence) testificar, declarar
deposit *n* depósito, *m*; *geol* yacimiento, filón, *m*; sedimento, *m*. *vt* depositar. **to leave a d.,** dejar un depósito. **d. account,** cuenta corriente, *f*
deposition *n* deposición, *f*; *law* testimonio, *m*, declaración, *Lat. Am.* contancia *f*; (from the Cross) descendimiento, *m*, (de la Cruz)
depositor *n* depositador (-ra)
depository *n* depositaría, *f*, almacén, *m*; (of knowledge, etc.) pozo, *m*
depot *n* almacén, *m*; (military headquarters) depósito, *m*; (for army vehicles, etc.) parque, *m*; (for buses, etc.) estación, *f*
depravation *n* depravación, *f*
depraved *a* depravado, perverso, vicioso
depravity *n* corrupción, maldad, perversión, *f*
deprecate *vt* desaprobar, criticar; lamentar, deplorar
deprecatingly *adv* con desaprobación, críticamente
deprecation *n* deprecación, *f*; desaprobación, crítica, *f*
deprecatory *a* deprecativo; de desaprobación, de crítica
depreciate *vt* depreciar, rebajar; *fig* tener en poco, menospreciar. *vi* depreciarse, deteriorarse; bajar de precio
depreciatingly *adv* con desprecio
depreciation *n* (in value) amortización, depreciación, *f*; *fig* desprecio, *m*
depreciatory *a fig* despectivo, despreciativo
depredation *n* depredación, *f*
depress *vt* deprimir; (weaken) debilitar; (humble) humillar; (dispirit) abatir, entristecer; (trade) desanimar, paralizar
depressed *a* deprimido, desalentado, melancólico, triste; (of an area) necesitado
depressing *a* melancólico, triste; pesimista
depressingly *adv* con tristeza; con pesimismo
depression *n* depresión, *f*; (hollow) hoyo, *m*; (sadness) desaliento, abatimiento, *m*, melancolía, *f*; (in prices) baja, *f*; (in trade) desanimación, parálisis, *f*; *ast* depresión, *f*
deprivation *n* privación, *f*; pérdida, *f*
deprive *vt* privar (de), despojar (de); defraudar (de); *ecc* destituir (de)
depth *n* profundidad, *f*; (thickness) espesor, *m*; fondo, *m*; (of night, winter, the country) medio, *m*; (of sound) gravedad, *f*; (of colour, feeling) intensidad, *f*; (abstruseness) dificultad, *f*; (sagacity) sagacidad, *f*; *pl* **depths,** profundidades, *f pl*; abismo, *m*; lo más hondo; lo más íntimo. **to be 4 feet in d.,** tener cuatro pies de profundidad. **to the depths of one's being,** hasta lo más íntimo de su ser; hasta los tuétanos. **d. charge,** carga de profundidad, *f*
deputation *n* deputación, delegación, *f*
deputize (for) *vi* desempeñar las funciones de, substituir
deputy *n* (substitute) lugarteniente, *m*; (agent) representante, *m*; apoderado, *m*; (parliamentary) diputado, *m*; (in compounds) sub, vice. **d.-governor,** subgobernador, *m*. **d.-head,** subjefe, *m*; (of a school) subdirector (-ra)
derail *vt* (hacer) descarrilar, *Lat. Am.* desrielar
derailment *n* descarrilamiento, *m*
derange *vt* desordenar; desorganizar; turbar; (mentally) trastornar, hacer perder el juicio (a)
derangement *n* desorden, *m*; turbación, *f*; (mental) trastorno, *m*, locura, *f*
derby *n* carrera del Derby, *f*; (hat) sombrero hongo, *m*
deregulate *vt* desregular
deregulation *n* desregulación, *f*
derelict *a* abandonado, derrelicto. *n* derrelicto, *m*
dereliction *n* abandono, *m*; omisión, negligencia, *f*; descuido, *m*
deride *vt* burlarse de, mofarse de; ridiculizar
derision *n* irrisión, *f*, menosprecio, *m*
derisive *a* irrisorio; irónico
derisively *adv* irrisoriamente; con ironía, irónicamente
derivation *n* derivación, *f*
derivative *a* derivativo. *n* derivado, *m*
derive *vt* derivar; obtener; extraer; *fig* sacar, hallar. *vi* (from) derivar de; proceder de; remontar a
dermatitis *n* dermatitis, *f*
dermatologist *n* dermatólogo, *m*
dermatology *n* dermatología, *f*
derogatory *a* despectivo, despreciativo; deshonroso
derrick *n* grúa, machina, *f*; abanico, *m*
descant *n mus* discante, *m*. *vi mus* discantar; discurrir (sobre), disertar (sobre)
descend *vi* descender, bajar; (be inherited) pasar a; (fall) caer; (of the sun) ponerse. *vt* bajar. **to d. from,** descender de. **to d. to,** (lower oneself) rebajarse; (consider) venir a, considerar. **to d. upon,** caer sobre; (arrive unexpectedly) llegar inesperadamente, invadir
descendant *n* descendiente, *mf*; *pl* **descendants,** descendencia, *f*
descent *n* descenso, *m*; bajada, *f*; (slope) pendiente, cuesta, *f*; (attack) invasión, *f*, ataque, *m*; (lineage) descendencia, alcurnia, procedencia, *f*; (inheritance) herencia, *f*; transmisión, *f*. **D. from the Cross,** Descendimiento de la Cruz, *m*
describable *a* descriptible
describe *vt* describir; pintar
description *n* descripción, *f*
descriptive *a* descriptivo
descry *vt* divisar, descubrir; *poet* ver
Desdemona Desdémona, *f*
desecrate *vt* profanar
desecration *n* profanación, *f*
desert *vt* abandonar; dejar; (*mil* etc.) desertar. *vi* desertar. *a* solitario; inhabitado; desierto; *fig* árido. *n* desierto, *m*; soledad, *f*; (merit) mérito, *m*. **to receive one's deserts,** llevar su merecido
deserted *a* abandonado; desierto; solitario; inhabitado, despoblado
deserter *n* desertor, *m*
desertion *n* abandono, *m*, deserción, *f*; (*mil* etc.) deserción, *f*
deserve *vt* and *vi* merecer
deservedly *adv* merecidamente
deserving *a* merecedor; meritorio. **to be d. of,** merecer
desiccate *vt* desecar. *vi* desecarse
design *n* proyecto, *m*; plan, *m*; intención, *f*, propósito, *m*; objeto, *m*; modelo, *m*; (pattern) diseño, dibujo, *m*; arte del dibujo, *mf*. *vt* idear; proyectar; (destine) destinar, dedicar; diseñar, dibujar, delinear; planear. **by d.,** expresamente, intencionalmente
designate *vt* señalar; designar; (appoint) nombrar. *a* electo
designation *n* designación, *f*; nombramiento, *m*
designedly *adv* de propósito

designer *n* inventor (-ra), autor (-ra); delineador (-ra); dibujante, *mf*; (of public works, etc.) proyectista, *mf*
designing *a* intrigante, astuto
desirability *n* lo deseable; conveniencia, *f*; ventaja, *f*
desirable *a* deseable; conveniente; ventajoso; agradable; apetecible
desire *vt* desear; querer; ansiar, ambicionar; (request) rogar, pedir; (order) mandar. *n* deseo, *m*; ansia, aspiración, *f*; ambición, *f*; impulso, *m*; (will) voluntad, *f*. **to d. ardently,** perecerse por; suspirar por
desirous *a* deseoso (de); ambicioso (de); ansioso (de); impaciente (a); curioso (de)
desist *vi* desistir; dejar (de)
desk *n* pupitre, *m*; escritorio, buró, *m*; mesa de trabajo, *f*; (cashier's) caja, *f*; (teacher's, lecturer's; pulpit) cátedra, *f*
desolate *a* solitario; desierto; deshabitado; abandonado; arruinado; árido; (afflicted) desolado, angustiado. *vt* desolar; despoblar
desolation *n* desolación, *f*; aflicción, angustia, *f*, desconsuelo, *m*
despair *n* desesperación, *f*, *vi* perder toda esperanza. **His life is despaired of,** Se ha perdido la esperanza de salvarle (la vida). **to be in d.,** estar desesperado
despairing *a* desesperado
despairingly *adv* sin esperanza
desperate *a* desesperado; sin esperanza; irremediable; furioso; violento; (dangerous) arriesgado, peligroso; terrible
desperately *adv* desesperadamente; furiosamente; terriblemente
desperation *n* desesperación, *f*; furia, violencia, *f*
despicable *a* vil, despreciable; insignificante
despise *vt* despreciar; desdeñar
despiser *n* menospreciador (-ra)
despite *prep* a pesar de
despoil *vt* despojar, desnudar
despoiler *n* despojador (-ra)
despoliation *n* despojo, *m*
despondency *n* abatimiento, desaliento, *m*, desesperación, *f*
despondent *a* abatido, desanimado, deprimido
despondently *adv* con desaliento
despot *n* déspota, *m*
despotic *a* despótico
despotism *n* despotismo, *m*
dessert *n* postre, *m*, *a* de postre. **d. plate,** plato para postre, *m*. **d.-spoon,** cuchara de postre, *f*
destination *n* destinación, *f*
destine *vt* destinar; dedicar; predestinar
destiny *n* destino, *m*
destitute *a* indigente, menesteroso; desnudo (de); privado (de); desprovisto (de), falto (de); desamparado
destitution *n* destitución, indigencia, miseria, *f*; privación, falta, *f*; desamparo, *m*
destroy *vt* destruir; demoler; deshacer; (kill) matar; exterminar; (finish) acabar con
destroyer *n* destructor (-ra); *nav* destructor, cazatorpedero, *m*
destructible *a* destructible, destruible
destruction *n* destrucción, *f*; demolición, *f*; ruina, *f*; pérdida, *f*; muerte, *f*; exterminio, *m*; perdición, *f*
destructive *a* destructivo, destructor; (of animals) dañino. **d. animal,** animal dañino, *m*, alimaña, *f*
destructiveness *n* destructividad, *f*; instinto destructor, *m*
desultory *a* inconexo; sin método, descosido; irregular
detach *vt* separar, desprender; (unstick) despegar; *mil* destacar
detachable *a* separable, de quita y pon
detached *a* suelto, separado; (*fig* with outlook, etc.) imparcial; indiferente, despegado. **d. house,** hotelito, *m*
detachment *n* separación, *f*; *mil* destacamento, *m*; (*fig* of mind) imparcialidad, *f*; independencia (de espíritu, etc.), *f*; indiferencia, *f*
detail *n* detalle, *m*; pormenor, *m*, particularidad, *f*; circunstancia, *f*; *mil* destacamento, *m*. *vt* detallar; particularizar, referir con pormenores; *mil* destacar. **in d.,** detalladamente; al por menor; *inf* ce por be. **to go into details,** entrar en detalles
detain *vt* detener; (arrest) arrestar, prender; (withhold) retener; (prevent) impedir
detect *vt* descubrir; averiguar; (discern) discernir, percibir; *elec* detectar
detectable *a* perceptible
detection *n* descubrimiento, *m*; averiguación, *f*; percepción, *f*
detective *n* detective, *m*, *a* de detectives, policíaco. **d. novel,** novela policíaca, *f*
detector *n* descubridor, *m*; *elec* detector, *m*; *mech* indicador, *m*
detention *n* detención, *f*; (arrest) arresto, *m*; (confinement) encierro, *m*
deter *vt* desanimar, desalentar; acobardar; (dissuade) disuadir; (prevent) impedir
detergent *a* detersorio. *n* detersorio, *m*
deteriorate *vt* deteriorar. *vi* deteriorarse; empeorar
deterioration *n* deterioración, *f*; empeoramiento, *m*
determinable *a* determinable
determination *n* determinación, *f*; definición, *f*; resolución, decisión, *f*; *law* fallo, *m*; *med* congestión, *f*
determine *vt* determinar; definir; decidir, resolver; concluir; (fix) señalar; *law* sentenciar. *vi* resolverse, decidirse; (insist (on)) empeñarse en, insistir en
determined *a* determinado; resuelto, decidido; (of price) fijo
determining *a* determinante
determinism *n* determinismo, *m*
deterministic *a* determinista
deterrent *a* disuasivo. *n* freno, *m*. **to act as a d.,** servir como un freno
deterrent capability *n* poder de disuasión, *m*
detest *vt* detestar, abominar, aborrecer
detestable *a* detestable, aborrecible, abominable
detestation *n* detestación, abominación, *f*, aborrecimiento, *m*
dethrone *vt* destronar
detonate *vt* hacer detonar. *vi* detonar, estallar
detonation *n* detonación, *f*
detonator *n* detonador, *m*; señal detonante, *f*
detour *n* rodeo, *m*; desvío, *m*, desviación, *f*
detract *vt* quitar; (diminish) disminuir; (slander) detraer, denigrar
detraction *n* detracción, denigración, *f*
detractor *n* detractor (-ra); infamador (-ra)
detriment *n* detrimento, *m*; perjuicio, *m*; daño, *m*
detrimental *a* perjudicial
deuce *n* (dice, cards) dos, *m*; (tennis) "dos," *m*. **The d.!** ¡Diantre! **to be the d. of a row,** haber moros y cristianos. **D. take it!** ¡Demonios!
Deuteronomy *n* Deuteronomio, *m*
devaluation *n* desvalorización, *f*
devalue *vt* rebajar el valor de
devastate *vt* devastar, asolar
devastation *n* devastación, *f*
develop *vt* desarrollar; (make progress) avanzar, fomentar; perfeccionar; *phot* revelar. *vi* desarrollarse; crecer; avanzar, progresar; evolucionar
developer *n phot* revelador, *m*
development *n* desarrollo, *m*; evolución, *f*; progreso, avance, *m*; (encouragement) fomento, *m*; (event) acontecimiento, suceso, *m*; (product) producto, *m*; (working) explotación, *f*; *phot* revelación, *f*
deviate *vi* desviarse (de); (disagree) disentir (de)
deviation *n* desviación, *f*
device *n* (contrivance) aparato, artefacto, mecanismo, *m*; (invention) invento, *m*; (trick) expediente, artificio, *m*; (scheme) proyecto, *m*; (design) dibujo, emblema, *m*; (motto) divisa, leyenda, *f*; *pl* **devices,** placeres, caprichos, *m pl*
devil *n* diablo, Satanás, *m*; demonio, *m*; (printer's)

aprendiz de impresor, *m*. **Go to the d.!** ¡Vete enhoramala! **He is a poor d.,** Es un pobre diablo. **little d.,** diablillo, *m*. **The devil's abroad,** Anda el diablo suelto. **The d. take it!** ¡Lléveselo el diablo! **to play the d. with,** arruinar por completo. **What the d.!** ¡Qué diablos! **d.-possessed,** endemoniado
devilish *a* diabólico, demoníaco; infernal
devilry *n* diablura, *f*; magia, *f*; demonología, *f*; (wickedness) maldad, *f*; crueldad, *f*
devious *a* desviado; tortuoso
deviousness *n* tortuosidad, *f*
devise *vt* idear, inventar; fabricar; *law* legar
deviser *n* inventor (-ra)
devitalize *vt* restar vitalidad, privar de vitalidad
devoid *a* desprovisto (de), privado (de); libre (de), exento (de)
devolve *vt* traspasar, transmitir. *vi* (on, upon) incumbir (a), corresponder (a), tocar (a)
devote *vt* dedicar; consagrar. **to d. oneself to,** darse a, dedicarse a; consagrarse a
devoted *a* fervoroso, apasionado; (faithful) fiel, leal
devotedly *adv* con devoción
devotee *n* devoto (-ta), admirador (-ra); aficionado (-da)
devotion *n* devoción, *f*; dedicación, *f*; (zeal) celo, *m*; afición, *f*; (loyalty) lealtad, *f*; *pl* **devotions,** rezos, *m pl*, oraciones, *f pl*
devotional *a* devoto, religioso, de devoción. **devotional literature,** literatura de devoción, *f*
devour *vt* devorar; consumir
devourer *n* devorador (-ra)
devouring *a* devorador; absorbente
devout *a* devoto, piadoso, practicante (e.g., **a d. Catholic,** un católico practicante)
devoutly *adv* piadosamente
devoutness *n* piedad, devoción, *f*
dew *n* rocío, sereno, relente, *m*; *fig* rocío, *m*. *vt* rociar; humedecer; (refresh) refrescar. **d.-drop,** aljófar, *m*, gota de rocío, *f*
dewlap *n* papada, *f*, papo, *m*
dewy *a* rociado, lleno de rocío; húmedo; (of eyes) lustroso
dexterity *n* destreza, *f*
dextrine *n* dextrina, *f*
dextrose *n* dextrosa, glucosa, *f*
dextrous *a* diestro; hábil, listo
diabetes *n* diabetes, *f*
diabetic *a* diabético
diabolical *a* diabólico
diadem *n* diadema, *f*
diagnose *vt* diagnosticar
diagnosis *n* diagnóstico, *m*, diagnosis, *f*
diagnostician *n* diagnóstico, *m*
diagonal *n* diagonal, *f*
diagram *n* diagrama, *m*; esquema, *f*; gráfico, *m*
diagrammatic *a* esquemático
dial *n* (sundial) reloj de sol, *m*; (of clocks, gas-meter) esfera, *f*; (of machines) indicador, *m*; (of a wireless set) cuadrante graduado, *m*; (of a telephone) marcador, disco, *m*. *vt* (a telephone number) marcar. **d. telephone,** teléfono automático, *m*
dialect *n* dialecto, *m*, habla, *f*. *a* dialectal
dialectic *a* dialéctico
dialectics *n* dialéctica, *f*
dialogue *n* diálogo, *m*. **to hold a d.,** dialogar
dialysis *n* diálisis, *f*
diameter *n* diámetro, *m*
diametrical *a* diametral
diamond *n* diamante, *m*; brillante, *m*; (tool) cortavidrios, *m*; (cards) oros (de baraja), *m pl*. **rough d.,** diamante bruto, *m*. **d.-bearing,** diamantífero. **d. cutter,** diamantista, *mf* **d. cutting,** talla de diamantes, *f*. **d. edition,** edición diamante, *f*. **d.-like,** adiamantado. **d. wedding,** bodas de diamante, *f pl*
diapason *n* diapasón, *m*
diaper *n* lienzo adamascado, *m*; (baby's) pañal, *m*; (woman's) servilleta higiénica, *f*
diaphanous *a* diáfano, transparente
diaphragm *n* diafragma, *m*
diarist *n* diarista, *mf*
diarrhea *n* diarrea, *f*
diary *n* diario, *m*
diastase *n* diastasa, *f*
diastole *n* diástole, *f*
diatribe *n* diatriba, denunciación violenta, *f*
dibble *n* plantador, *m*. *vt* and *vi* plantar con plantador
dice *n pl* dados, *m pl*. **to load the d.,** cargar los dados
dicky *n* (front) pechera postiza, *f*; (seat) trasera, *f*; (apron) delantal, *m*. **d. seat,** *inf* ahí te pudras, *m*
dictaphone *n* dictáfono, *m*
dictate *vt* dictar; mandar. *n* (order) dictamen, *m*; *fig* dictado, *m*
dictation *n* dictado, *m*. **to write from d.,** escribir al dictado
dictator *n* dictador, *m*
dictatorial *a* dictatorial, dictatorio, imperioso
dictatorship *n* dictadura, *f*
diction *n* dicción, *f*
dictionary *n* diccionario, *m*
dictum *n* dictamen, *m*; (saying) sentencia, *f*; *law* fallo, *m*
didactic *a* didáctico
die *vi* morir; fallecer, finar; (wither) marchitarse; (disappear) desvanecerse, desaparecer; (of light) palidecer; extinguirse; (end) cesar; (desire) ansiar, perecerse (por). **Never say die!** ¡Mientras hay vida, hay esperanza! **to die early,** morir temprano; malograrse. **to die a violent death,** tener una muerte violenta, *inf* morir vestido. **to die from natural causes,** morir por causas naturales; *inf* morir en la cama. **to die hard,** luchar contra la muerte; tardar en morir; tardar en desaparecer. **to die of a broken heart,** morir con el corazón destrozado, morir de pena. **to die away,** desaparecer gradualmente; extinguirse poco a poco; dejar de oírse poco a poco; cesar; pasar. **to die down,** extinguirse gradualmente; palidecer; dejar de oírse; desaparecer; (of the wind) amainar; perder su fuerza. **to die out,** desaparecer; olvidarse; dejar de existir; pasarse de moda
die *n* dado, *m*; *fig* suerte, *f*; (stamp) cuño, troquel, *m*; *arch* cubo, *m*. **The die is cast,** La suerte está echada. **die-sinker,** grabador en hueco, *m*
diehard *n* valiente, *m*; tradicionalista empedernido, *m*; partidario (-ia) entusiasta
Dieppe Diepa, *f*
dieresis *n* diéresis, crema, *f*
diesel *a* Diesel. **d. engine,** motor Diesel, *m*
diet *n* dieta, *f*, régimen dietario, *m*; (assembly) dieta, *f*. *vi* estar a dieta, hacer régimen
dietetic *a* dietético
dietetics *n* dietética, *f*
dietician *n* dietista, *mf*
differ *vi* diferenciarse; (contradict) contradecir; (disagree) no estar de acuerdo; disentir
difference *n* diferencia, *f*; disparidad, *f*; contraste, *m*; (of opinion) disensión, *f*; controversia, disputa, *f*. **to make no d.,** no hacer diferencia alguna; no afectar; dar lo mismo, no importar
different *a* distinto; diferente; vario, diverso
differential *a* diferencial. **d. calculus,** cálculo diferencial, *m*
differentiate *vt* diferenciar, distinguir. *vi* diferenciarse, distinguirse
differentiation *n* diferenciación, *f*
differently *adv* diferentemente
difficult *a* difícil. **to make d.,** dificultar
difficulty *n* dificultad, *f*. **d. in breathing,** opresión de pecho, *f*
diffidence *n* modestia, timidez, *f*; huraño, *f*; falta de confianza en sí mismo, *f*
diffident *a* modesto, tímido; huraño; sin confianza en sí mismo

diffidently *adv* tímidamente; vergonzosamente
diffract *vt* difractar
diffraction *n* difracción, *f*
diffractive *a* difrangente
diffuse *vt* difundir. *a* difuso; (long-winded) prolijo
diffuseness *n* difusión, *f*; prolijidad, *f*
diffusion *n* difusión, *f*; esparcimiento, *m*; diseminación, *f*
diffusive *a* difusivo
dig *vt* and *vi* cavar; excavar; (of animals) escarbar; (mine) zapar, minar; (into a subject) ahondar (en); (with the spurs) aguijonear, dar con las espuelas; (poke) clavar. **to dig one's heels in** *Lat. Am.* encabestrarse **to dig in,** enterrarse; *mil* abrir trincheras; *inf* arreglarse las cosas. **to dig out,** excavar; sacar cavando, sacar con azadón; extraer. **to dig up,** desenterrar; descubrir
digest *vt* clasificar; codificar; (food, also *chem.* and *fig.* tolerate and think over) digerir; (of knowledge and territory) asimilar. *vi* digerir. *n* compendio, resumen, *m*; *law* digesto, *m*; recopilación, *f*. **This food is easy to d.,** Este alimento es fácil de digerir; Este alimento es muy ligero
digestibility *n* digestibilidad, *f*
digestible *a* digerible, digestible
digestion *n* digestión, *f*; (of ideas) asimilación, *f*; *chem* digestión, *f*
digestive *a* digestivo
digger *n* cavador (-ra)
digging *n* cavadura, *f*; excavación, *f*; *pl* **diggings,** minas, *f pl*; excavaciones, *f pl*; *inf* alojamiento, *m*, posada, *f*
digit *n* dígito, *m*
digital *a* digital, dígito
digitalin *n* digitalina, *f*
digitalis *n* digital, *f*
dignified *a* serio, grave; majestuoso; (worthy) digno; solemne; altivo; noble
dignify *vt* dignificar, honrar; exaltar; dar dignidad (a); ennoblecer
dignitary *n* dignatario, *m*; dignidad, *f*
dignity *n* dignidad, *f*; (rank) rango, *m*; (post) cargo, puesto, *m*; (honor) honra, *f*; (stateliness) majestad, *f*; mesura, seriedad, *f*; (haughtiness) altivez, *f*; (nobility) nobleza, *f*. **to stand on one's d.,** darse importancia
digress *vi* divagar
digression *n* digresión, divagación, *f*
dike *n* dique, *m*; (ditch) acequia, *f*; canal, *m*; (embankment) zanja, *f*, *vt* represar
dilapidated *a* arruinado, destartalado; (of fortune) dilapidado; (of persons, families) venido a menos; (shabby) raído
dilapidation *n* deterioración, *f*; ruina, *f*, estado ruinoso, *m*
dilatation *n* dilatación, *f*; ensanche, *m*
dilate *vt* dilatar; ensanchar. *vi* dilatarse. **to d. upon,** extenderse sobre, dilatarse en
dilator *n* dilatador, *m*
dilatoriness *n* tardanza, *f*; (slowness) lentitud, *f*
dilatory *a* dilatorio, tardo; (slow) lento
dilemma *n* dilema, *m*
dilettante *n* diletante, *m*; aficionado (-da)
dilettantism *n* diletantismo, *m*
diligence *n* diligencia, *f*; asiduidad, *f*; (care) cuidado, *m*; (coach) diligencia, *f*
diligent *a* diligente, asiduo, aplicado, industrioso; (painstaking) concienzudo
dilute *vt* diluir; *fig* adulterar. *a* diluido
dilution *n* dilución, *f*; *fig* adulteración, *f*
diluvian *a* diluviano
dim *a* (of light) apagado, débil, tenue; (of sight) turbio; (dark) sombrío, oscuro; (blurred, etc.) empañado; indistinto, confuso. *vt* obscurecer; empañar; (dazzle) ofuscar; (eclipse) eclipsar; reducir la intensidad (de una luz); (of memories) borrar. **dim intelligence,** de brumoso seso
dimension *n* dimensión, *f*; (size) tamaño, *m*; (scope) extensión, *f*, alcance, *m*
dimensional *a* dimensional
diminish *vt* disminuir; reducir; debilitar, atenuar. *vi* disminuir; reducirse; debilitarse, atenuarse
diminishing *a* menguante
diminution *n* disminución, *f*; reducción, *f*; atenuación, *f*
diminutive *a* diminutivo. *n* diminutivo, *m*
diminutiveness *n* pequeñez, *f*
dimly *adv* obscuramente; vagamente; indistintamente. **dimly lit,** apenas alumbrado
dimness *n* oscuridad, *f*; deslustre, *m*; (of light) tenuidad (de la luz), *f*; confusión, *f*
dimple *n* hoyuelo, *m*
dimpled *a* con hoyuelos, que tiene hoyuelos
din *n* estrépito, estruendo, ruido, *m*; algarabía, barahúnda, *f*, *vt* ensordecer
dine *vi* (in the evening) cenar; (at midday) comer. *vt* convidar a cenar or a comer. **to d. out,** cenar or comer fuera
diner *n* (on a train) coche comedor, coche restaurante, *m*; cenador, *m*; comedor, *m*
ding-dong *n* tintín, *m*
dinghy *n* lancha, *f*; canoa, *f*, bote, *m*. **rubber d.,** canoa de goma, *f*
dinginess *n* deslustre, *m*; suciedad, *f*; oscuridad, *f*; (of a person) desaseo, *m*
dingy *a* deslucido, empañado; sucio; oscuro; (of persons) desaseado
dining car *n* coche comedor, vagón restaurante, *m*
dining room *n* comedor, *m*; refectorio, *m*
dining table *n* mesa del comedor, *f*
dinner *n* (in the evening) cena, *f*; (at midday) comida, *f*. **over the d. table,** de sobremesa. **d.-jacket,** smoking, *m*. **d. party,** cena, *f*. **d. plate,** plato, *m*. **d. roll,** panecillo, *m*. **d. service,** vajilla, *f*
dinosaur *n* dinosauro, *m*
dint (by d. of) a fuerza de, a costa de
diocesan *a* diocesano
diocese *n* diócesis, *f*
Dionysus Thrax Dionisio el Tracio, *m*
dioxide *n* dióxido, *m*
dip *n* inmersión, *f*; baño, *m*; (in the ground) declive, *m*; (in the road) columpio, *m*, depresión, *f*; (slope) pendiente, *f*; (candle) vela de sebo, *f*; (of the horizon) depresión (del horizonte), *f*; (of the needle) inclinación (de la aguja), *f*. *vt* sumergir; bañar; (put) poner. *vi* inclinarse hacia abajo. **to dip into a book,** hojear un libro. **to dip the colors,** saludar con la bandera. **to dip the headlights,** bajar los faros
diphtheria *n* difteria, *f*
diphthong *n* diptongo, *m*
diploma *n* diploma, *m*
diplomacy *n* diplomacia, *f*; tacto, *m*
diploma mill *n* fábrica de títulos académicos, *f*
diplomat *n* diplomático, *m*
diplomatic *a* diplomático. **d. bag,** valija diplomática, *f*. **d. corps,** cuerpo diplomático, *m*
diplomatically *adv* diplomáticamente
dipper *n* (ladle) cazo, *m*; *ast* Osa Mayor, *f*
dipsomania *n* dipsomanía, *f*
dipsomaniac *n* dipsómano (-na)
diptych *n* diptica, *f*
dire *a* espantoso, horrible; cruel; funesto
direct *a* directo; claro, inequívoco; (of descent) recto; (of electric current) continuo; exacto. *adv* directamente. *vt* dirigir; (command) ordenar, encargar; dar instrucciones. **d. action,** acción directa, *f*. **d. current,** corriente continua, *f*. **d. line,** línea directa, *f*; (of descent) línea recta, *f*. **d. object,** acusativo, *m*. **d. speech,** oración directa, *f*
direct dialing *n* discado directo, *m*
direction *n* dirección, *f*; rumbo, *m*; instrucción, *f*; (on a letter) sobrescrito, *m*; señas, *f pl*. **in the d. of,** en la dirección de; hacia; *naut* con rumbo a. **in all direc-**

tions, por todas partes; a los cuatro vientos. **to go in the d. of,** ir en la dirección de; tomar por. **Directions for use,** Direcciones para el uso. **d. indicator, d. signal,** (on car) indicador de dirección, *m*
directive *a* directivo, director
directly *adv* directamente; inmediatamente, en seguida
directness *n* derechura, *f*
director *n* director (-triz, -ora), **managing d.,** director gerente, *m*
directorate *n* directorio, *m*, junta directiva, *f*; cargo de director, *m*
directory *n* directorio, *m*, guía, *f*. **telephone d.,** guía de teléfonos, *f*
dirge *n* endecha, *f*, lamento, *m*; canto fúnebre, *m*
dirt *n* mugre, suciedad, *f*; (mud) lodo, *m*; (earth) tierra, *f*; (dust) polvo, *m*; *fig* inmundicia, *f*. **d.-cheap,** sumamente barato. **to be d. cheap,** (of goods) estar por los suelos. **d.-track,** pista de ceniza, *f*. **d.-track racing,** carreras en pista de ceniza, *f pl*
dirtiness *n* suicedad, *f*; (untidiness) desaseo, *m*; sordidez, *f*; (meanness) bajeza, *f*
dirty *a* sucio, *Central America* descacharrado; (untidy) desaseado; (muddy) enlodado; (dusty) polvoriento; (of weather) borrascoso; (sordid) sórdido; (base, mean) vil; (indecent) indecente, verde, obsceno. *vt* ensuciar. **d. trick,** mala pasada, *Lat. Am.* chancada *f*
disability *n* incapacidad, *f*; impotencia, *f*; desventaja, *f*
disable *vt* (cripple) estropear, tullir; hacer incapaz (de), incapacitar; imposibilitar; (destroy) destruir; *law* incapacitar legalmente
disabled *a* inválido; impedido, lisiado; (in the hand) manco; incapacitado; (of ships, etc.) fuera de servicio, estropeado. **d. soldier,** inválido, *m*
disablement *n* (physical) invalidez, *f*; inhabilitación, *f*; *law* impedimento, *m*
disabuse *vt* desengañar, sacar de un error
disadvantage *n* desventaja, *f*. **to be under the d. of,** sufrir la desventaja de
disadvantaged *a* (financially) de escasos recursos
disadvantageous *a* desventajoso
disaffected *a* desafecto
disaffection *n* desafecto, descontento, *m*
disagree *vi* no estar de acuerdo; diferir; (quarrel) reñir; (not share the opinion of) no estar de la opinión (de); (of food, etc.) sentar mal; no probar. **The meat disagreed with me,** La carne me sentó mal
disagreeable *a* desagradable; repugnante; (of persons) antipático, displicente
disagreeableness *n* lo desagradable; (of persons) displicencia, *f*
disagreeably *adv* desagradablemente; con displicencia
disagreement *n* desacuerdo, *m*; diferencia, *f*; desavenencia, *f*; discordia, *f*; (quarrel) riña, disputa, *f*; discrepancia, *f*
disallow *vt* negar; rechazar
disappear *vi* desaparecer. **to cause to d.,** hacer desaparecer
disappearance *n* desaparición, *f*
disappoint *vt* desilusionar; frustrar; (hopes) defraudar; (deprive) privar de; (annoy) contrariar; (break a promise) faltar (a la palabra)
disappointedly *adv* con desilusión, con desengaño
disappointing *a* desengañador; pobre; triste; poco halagüeño
disappointment *n* desengaño, *m*, decepción, *f*; frustración, *f*; desilusión, *f*; (vexation) contrariedad, *f*; contratiempo, *m*. **to suffer a d.,** sufrir un desengaño; *inf* llevarse un chasco
disapproval *n* desaprobación, *f*
disapprove *vt* desaprobar
disapproving *a* de desaprobación, severo
disapprovingly *adv* con desaprobación
disarm *vt* desarmar. *vi* desarmarse; deponer las armas
disarmament *n* desarme, *m*
disarrange *vt* desarreglar; descomponer, desajustar; (hair) despeinar
disarrangement *n* desarreglo, *m*; desajuste, *m*; desorden, *m*
disarray *n* desorden, desarreglo, *m*; confusión, *f*. *vt* desordenar, desarreglar
disarticulate *vt* desarticular
disarticulation *n* desarticulación, *f*
disaster *n* desastre, *m*; catástrofe, *m*; infortunio, *m*
disastrous *a* desastroso; funesto, trágico
disastrously *adv* desastrosamente
disastrousness *n* carácter desastroso, *m*
disavow *vt* repudiar; retractar
disavowal *n* repudiación, *f*
disband *vt* licenciar. *vi* desbandarse, dispersarse
disbelief *n* incredulidad, *f*; desconfianza, *f*
disbelieve *vt* and *vi* descreer, no creer; desconfiar (de)
disburse *vt* desembolsar, pagar
disbursement *n* desembolso, *m*
disc *n* disco, *m*
discard *vt* desechar, arrinconar, *Lat. Am.* botar; despedir; (at cards) descartar. *n* (at cards) descarte, *m*
discern *vt* discernir, distinguir, percibir
discerner *n* discernidor (-ra)
discernible *a* distinguible, perceptible
discerning *a* perspicaz, discernidor
discernment *n* discernimiento, *m*
discharge *vt* descargar; (a gun) disparar, tirar; (an arrow) lanzar; *elec* descargar; emitir; (dismiss) destituir, despedir; arrojar; *mil* licenciar; (exempt) dispensar (de); (exonerate) absolver, exonerar; (free) dar libertad (a); (from hospital) dar de baja (a); *law* revocar; (perform) cumplir, ejecutar; (pay) pagar, saldar; (of an abscess, etc.) supurar.
discharge *n* (of firearms) disparo, tiro, *m*; (of artillery) descarga, *f*; (of goods, cargo) descargue, *m*; *elec* descarga, *f*; (from a wound, etc.) pus, *m*, supuración, *f*; (from the intestine) flujo, *m*; (of a debt) pago, m.; *com* descargo, *m*; (receipt) carta de pago, quitanza, *f*; *mil* licencia absoluta, *f*; (dismissal) despedida, destitución, *f*; (exoneration) exoneración, *f*; (freeing) liberación, *f*; (from hospital) baja, *f*; (performance) cumplimiento, *m*; ejecución, *f*
disciple *n* discípulo (-la)
disciplinarian *n* disciplinario (-ia)
disciplinary *a* disciplinario
discipline *n* disciplina, *f*, *vt* disciplinar
disclaim *vt* renunciar (a); (repudiate) rechazar, repudiar
disclaimer *n law* renunciación, *f*; repudiación, *f*
disclose *vt* descubrir, revelar
disclosure *n* descubrimiento, *m*, revelación, *f*
discolor *vt* descolorar. *vi* descolorarse
discoloration *n* descoloramiento, *m*
discomfit *vt* desconcertar
discomfiture *n* desconcierto, *m*
discomfort *n* falta de comodidades, *f*; incomodidad, *f*; malestar, *m*; molestia, *f*; inquietud, *f*; dolor, *m*
discomposure *n* confusión, agitación, inquietud, *f*
disconcert *vt* desconcertar, turbar; (of plans, etc.) frustrar
disconnect *vt* separar; (of railway engines, etc.) desacoplar; desconectar; (of electric plugs) desenchufar
disconnected *a* inconexo; incoherente, deshilvanado
disconnectedness *n* inconexión, *f*; incoherencia, *f*
disconsolate *a* desconsolado, triste
disconsolately *adv* desconsoladamente, tristemente
disconsolateness *n* desconsuelo, *m*
discontent *n* descontento, disgusto, *m*, *vt* descontentar, desagradar
discontented *a* descontentadizo, descontento, disgustado
discontinuance *n* descontinuación, cesación, *f*; interrupción, *f*
discontinue *vt* descontinuar; cesar; interrumpir; (of payments, etc.) suspender. *vi* cesar
discontinuous *a* descontinuo; interrumpido; intermitente

discord *n* discordia, *f*; *mus* disonancia, *f*, desentono, *m*
discordant *a* discorde, poco armonioso; incongruo; *mus* disonante, desentonado. **to be d.,** discordar; ser incongruo; *mus* disonar
discount *n* descuento, *m*; rebaja, *f*. *vt* descontar; rebajar; balancear; (disconsider) desechar. **at a d.,** al descuento; bajo la par; fácil de obtener; superfluo; *fig* en disfavor, en descrédito. **rate of d.,** tipo de descuento, *m*. **d. for cash,** descuento por venta al contado, *m*
discourage *vt* desalentar, desanimar; oponerse a; disuadir; frustrar
discouragement *n* desaliento, *m*; desaprobación, oposición, *f*; disuasión, *f*; (obstacle) estorbo, *m*
discouraging *a* poco animador, que ofrece pocas esperanzas; (with prospect, etc.) nada halagüeño
discourse *n* discurso, *m*; plática, *f*; (treatise) disertación, *f*. *vi* (converse) platicar, conversar; (with on, upon) disertar sobre, discurrir sobre; tratar de
discourteous *a* descortés, desconsiderado
discourtesy *n* descortesía, *f*
discover *vt* descubrir; (see) ver; (realize) darse cuenta de; (show) manifestar; revelar
discoverable *a* que se puede descubrir; averiguable; distinguible, perceptible
discoverer *n* descubridor (-ra); revelador (-ra)
discovery *n* descubrimiento, *m*; revelación, *f*
discredit *n* descrédito, *m*; des honra, *f*; duda, *f*. *vt* dudar (de), no creer (en); desacreditar; deshonrar
discreditable *a* deshonroso, ignominioso, vergonzoso
discreet *a* discreto; prudente, circunspecto
discreetly *adv* discretamente; prudentemente
discrepancy *n* discrepancia, diferencia, *f*; contradicción, *f*
discrepant *a* discrepante; contradictorio, inconsistente
discretion *n* discreción, *f*; prudencia, circunspección, *f*; juicio, *m*; voluntad, *f*. **at d.,** a discreción. **at one's own d.,** a voluntad (de uno). **years of d.,** edad de discreción, *f*
discriminate *vi* distinguir (entre); hacer una distinción (en favor de or en perjuicio de). *vt* distinguir
discriminating *a* discerniente, que sabe distinguir, juicioso; culto; diferencial
discrimination *n* discernimiento, *m*; gusto, *m*; distinción, *f*; discriminación, *f*
discursive *a* discursivo; digresivo
discus *n* disco, *m*. **d. thrower,** discóbolo, *m*
discuss *vt* discutir; hablar de; debatir; (deal with) tratar; (*fam* a dish) probar; (a bottle of wine) vaciar
discussion *n* discusión, *f*; debate, *m*
disdain *n* desdén, *m*; altivez, *f*. *vt* desdeñar, desairar, despreciar. **to d. to,** desdeñarse de
disdainful *a* desdeñoso; altivo
disdainfully *adv* desdeñosamente
disease *n* enfermedad, *f*; *fig* mal, *m*. **infectious d.,** enfermedad contagiosa, *f*
diseased *a* enfermo; (of fruit, etc.) malo
disembark *vt* and *vi* desembarcar
disembarkation *n* desembarque, *m*; *mil* desembarco (de tropas), *m*
disembodied *a* incorpóreo
disembowel *vt* desentrañar, destripar
disenchant *vt* desencantar; deschechizar; desilusionar
disenchantment *n* desencanto, *m*; desilusión, *f*
disengage *vt* desasir; soltar; (gears) desembragar; (uncouple) desacoplar; (free) librar
disengaged *a* (free) libre
disentangle *vt* (undo) desatar, desanudar; separar; (of threads, etc., and *fig*) desenredar, desenmarañar. *vi* desenredarse
disentanglement *n* desatadura, *f*; separación, *f*; desenredo, *m*
disestablish *vt* separar (la Iglesia del Estado)
disestablishment *n* separación (de la Iglesia del Estado), *f*
disfavor *n* disfavor, *m*; (disapproval) desaprobación, *f*. *vt* desaprobar
disfigure *vt* desfigurar, afear; deformar; (mar) estropear
disfigurement *n* desfiguración, *f*; deformidad, *f*; defecto, *m*
disfranchise *vt* privar de los derechos civiles (a)
disfranchisement *n* privación de los derechos civiles, privación del derecho de votar, *f*
disgorge *vt* and *vi* vomitar; (of a river) desembocar (en); hacer restitución (de lo robado)
disgrace *n* vergüenza, ignominia, *f*; deshonra, *f*; (insult) afrenta, *f*; (scandal) escándalo, *m*; disfavor, *m*. *vt* deshonrar; despedir con ignominia. **in d.,** fuera de favor; desacreditado; (of children and animals) castigado
disgraceful *a* deshonroso; ignominioso; escandaloso
disgracefully *adv* escandalosamente
disgracefulness *n* ignominia, vergüenza, *f*; deshonra, *f*
disgruntled *a* refunfuñador, enfurruñado, malhumorado
disguise *n* disfraz, *m*; (mask) máscara, *f*. *vt* disfrazar; cubrir, tapar; (*fig* conceal) ocultar. **in d.,** disfrazado
disgust *n* repugnancia, aversión, *f*; aborrecimiento, *m*; asco, *m*. *vt* repugnar, inspirar aversión; disgustar; dar asco (a)
disgusted *a* asqueado; disgustado; furioso; (bored) aburrido
disgusting *a* repugnante; odioso, horrible; asqueroso
dish *n* (for meat, vegetables, fruit, etc.) fuente, *f*; (food) plato, *m*; *pl* **dishes,** platos, *m pl*, vajilla, *f*. *vt* servir; *inf* frustrar. **cooked d.,** guiso, *m*. **special d. for today,** plato del día, *m*. **to wash the dishes,** fregar los platos. **d.-cloth,** (for washing) fregador, *m*; (for drying) paño de los platos, *m*. **d.-cover,** cubre-platos, *m*. **d.-rack,** escurre-platos, *m*. **d.-washer,** lavaplatos, lavavajillas, *m*. **d.-water,** agua de lavar los platos, *f*
disharmony *n* falta de armonía, *f*; (disagreement) discordia, desavenencia, *f*; incongruencia, *f*; *mus* disonancia, *f*
dishearten *vt* desalentar, desanimar; desesperar; disuadir (de)
disheveled *a* despeinado, desgreñado; (untidy) desaseado
dishonest *a* falto de honradez, tramposo; fraudulento; falso, desleal, *Lat. Am. also* flequetero
dishonestly *adv* de mala fe, sin honradez; fraudulentamente; deslealmente
dishonesty *n* falta de honradez, falta de integridad, *f*; fraude, *m*; falsedad, deslealtad, *f*
dishonor *n* deshonra, *f*, *vt* deshonrar; *com* no pagar, o no aceptar, un giro
dishonorable *a* deshonroso
dishonorer *n* deshonrador (-ra); profanador (-ra)
disillusion *vt* desengañar, desilusionar
disillusionment *n* desilusión, *f*, desengaño, desencanto, *m*
disinclination *n* aversión, *f*
disincline *vt* desinclinar
disinfect *vt* desinfectar
disinfectant *a* and *n* desinfectante *m*.
disinfection *n* desinfección, *f*
disingenuous *a* tortuoso, doble, falso, insincero
disinherit *vt* desheredar
disinheritance *n* desheredación, *f*
disintegrate *vt* despedazar, disgregar. *vi* disgregarse; desmoronarse
disintegration *n* disgregración, *f*; disolución, *f*; desmoronamiento, *m*
disinter *vt* desenterrar
disinterested *a* desinteresado
disinterestedness *n* desinterés, *m*
disinterment *n* desenterramiento, *m*
disjointed *a* dislocado; desarticulado; incoherente, inconexo; (of a speech, etc.) descosido
disjointedness *n* descoyuntamiento, desencajamiento, *m*; incoherencia, *f*
disk *n* disco, *m*
dislike *n* aversión, *f*; antipatía, *f*; (hostility) animosidad,

f. vt desagradar, no gustar; repugnar. **I d. the house,** No me gusta la casa. **I d. them,** No me gustan
dislocate *vt* dislocar, descoyuntar; *fig* interrumpir
dislocation *n* dislocación, *f*, descoyuntamiento, *m*; *fig* interrupción, *f*
dislodge *vt* desalojar
dislodgement *n* desalojamiento, *m*
disloyal *a* desleal, infiel, falso
disloyalty *n* deslealtad, infidelidad, falsedad, *f*
dismal *a* lóbrego, sombrío; lúgubre; funesto; triste
dismantle *vt* (a ship or fort) desmantelar; (a machine) desmontar; (a house, etc.) desamueblar
dismantling *n* desmantelamiento, *m*
dismay *n* desmayo, desaliento, *m*; consternación, *f*; espanto, terror, *m*. *vt* desanimar; consternar; espantar, horrorizar
dismember *vt* desmembrar
dismemberment *n* desmembración, *f*
dismiss *vt* (from a job) despedir (de); (from an official position) destituir (de) *Chile* desahuciar (de); (bid good-bye to) despedirse de; (after military parade) dar la orden de romper filas; (thoughts) apartar de sí; ahuyentar; (discard) desechar, descartar; (omit) pasar por alto de; (disregard) rechazar; (a parliament, etc.) disolver; (a law case) absolver de la instancia. **to d. in a few words,** tratar someramente; hablar brevemente de
dismissal *n* despedida, *f*; (from an official post) destitución, *f*, *Chile* desahúcio *m*; apartamiento, *m*; (discard) descarte, *m*; (of a parliament, etc.) disolución, *f*
dismount *vi* apearse, desmontar, echar pie a tierra; bajar. *vt* desmontar; (dismantle) desarmar
disobedience *n* desobediencia, *f*
disobedient *a* desobediente
disobey *vt* and *vi* desobedecer
disobliging *a* poco servicial
disobligingly *adv* descortésmente
disorder *n* desorden, *m*; confusión, *f*; (unrest) perturbación del orden público, *f*, motín, *m*; (disease) enfermedad, *f*; (mental) enajenación mental, *f*; trastorno, *m*. *vt* desordenar, desarreglar; (of health) perjudicar; (the mind) trastornar. **in d.,** en desorden, desarreglado; (helter-skelter) atropelladamente
disordered *a* en desorden; irregular, desordenado; (of the mind and bodily organs) trastornado; (ill) enfermo; (confused) confuso
disorganization *n* desorganización, *f*
disorganize *vt* desorganizar
disorientate *vt* desorientar
disorientation *n* desorientación, *f*
disown *vt* repudiar; negar; renegar de
disparage *vt* menospreciar; desacreditar; denigrar; (spoil) perjudicar; (scorn) despreciar
disparagement *n* menosprecio, *m*; denigración, *f*; desprecio, *m*
disparagingly *adv* con desprecio
disparity *n* disparidad, *f*
dispassionate *a* desapasionado, sereno; imparcial; moderado
dispassionately *adv* con imparcialidad; serenamente; con moderación
dispatch *n* despacho, *m*; *com* envío, *m*; (message) mensaje, *m*; (communiqué) parte, *f*; (cable) telegrama, *m*; (promptness) prontitud, presteza, *f*; (execution) ejecución, muerte, *f*. *vt* despachar; enviar, remitir; (*fam* kill) despachar. **d.-case,** cartera, *f*. **d.-rider,** mensajero motociclista, *m*
dispel *vt* disipar
dispensable *a* dispensable
dispensary *n* dispensario, *m*
dispensation *n* dispensación, *f*; (of the Pope, etc.) dispensa, *f*; (decree) ley, *f*, decreto, *m*; (of justice) administración, *f*
dispense *vt* dispensar; (of justice) administrar. **to d. with,** pasar sin, prescindir de
dispenser *n* dispensador (-ra); administrador (-ra)
dispersal *n* dispersión, *f*; disipación, *f*; esparcimiento, *m*
disperse *vt* dispersar; disipar; esparcir. *vi* dispersarse disiparse
dispirited *a* abatido, desanimado, deprimido; lánguido
dispiritedly *adv* desanimadamente, con desaliento; lánguidamente
displace *vt* desalojar; cambiar de situación; (of liquids) desplazar; (oust) quitar el puesto (a), destituir
displacement *n* desalojamiento, *m*; cambio de situación, *m*; (of liquid) desplazamiento, *m*; (from a post) destitución, *f*
display *n* exhibición, *f*; ostentación, *f*; presentación, *f*; (development) desarrollo, *m*; manifestación, *f*; (naval or military) maniobras, *f pl*; espectáculo, *m*; (pomp) pompa, *f*; fausto, *m*. *vt* exhibir; mostrar, manifestar; ostentar; (unfold) desplegar, extender; (develop) desarrollar. **d. cabinet,** vitrina, *f*
displease *vt* desagradar; ofender; enojar
displeasing *a* desagradable
displeasure *n* desagrado, *m*; disgusto, *m*; disfavor, *m*; indignación, *f*; enojo, *m*; (grief) angustia, *f*
disport *vi* (**oneself**), divertirse, entretenerse, recrearse; retozar, jugar
disposal *n* disposición, *f*; (transfer) cesión, enajenación, *f*; (sale) venta, *f*; (gift) donación, *f*. **I am at your d.,** Estoy a la disposición de Vd. **the d. of the troops,** la disposición de las tropas
dispose *vt* disponer; inclinar. *vi* disponer. **to d. of,** disponer de; (finish) terminar, concluir; (get rid of) deshacerse de; (give away) regalar; (sell) vender; (transfer) ceder; (of houses, etc.) traspasar; (kill) matar; (send) enviar; (use) servirse de; (refute) refutar. **"To be disposed of,"** (a business, etc.) «Se traspasa»
disposed *a* (in compounds) intencionado, dispuesto. **well-d.,** bien intencionado
disposition *n* disposición, *f*; (temperament) naturaleza, índole, *f*, temperamento, carácter, *m*; (humor) humor, *m*
dispossess *vt* desposeer (de); privar (de); desahuciar
dispossession *n* desposeimiento, *m*; desahúcio, *m*
disproportion *n* desproporción, *f*
disproportionate *a* desproporcionado
disproportionately *adv* desproporcionadamente
disprovable *a* refutable
disprove *vt* refutar
disputable *a* disputable; discutible
disputant *n* disputador (-ra)
dispute *n* disputa, controversia, *f*; altercación, *f*; discusión, *f*; debate, *m*. *vt* and *vi* disputar. **beyond d.,** *a* incontestable. *adv* incontestablemente; fuera de duda
disqualification *n* incapacidad, *f*; inhabilitación, *f*; impedimento, *m*; *sport* descalificación, *f*
disqualify *vt* incapacitar; inhabilitar; *sport* descalificar
disquiet *n* desasosiego, *m*; intranquilidad, inquietud, agitación, *f*. *vt* desasosegar, intranquilizar, perturbar, agitar
disquieting *a* intranquilizador, perturbador
disquisition *n* disquisición, *f*
disregard *n* indiferencia, *f*; omisión, *f*; descuido, *m*; (scorn) desdén, *m*. *vt* no hacer caso de, desatender; omitir; desconocer; descuidar; despreciar
disregardful *a* indiferente; negligente; desatento; desdeñoso
disrepair *n* deterioro, mal estado, *m*
disreputable *a* de mala fama; (shameful) vergonzoso, vil; (compromising) comprometedor; de mal aspecto, horrible; ruin
disreputably *adv* ruinmente; vergonzosamente
disrepute *n* disfavor, *m*; mala fama, *f*; deshonra, *f*; descrédito, *m*. **to come into d.,** caer en disfavor; perder su reputación
disrespect *n* falta de respeto, *f*; irreverencia, *f*
disrespectful *a* irrespetuoso, irreverente
disrobe *vt* desnudar. *vi* desnudarse
disrupt *vt* quebrar; desorganizar; interrumpir; separar

disruption *n* quebrantamiento, *m*; desorganización, *f*; interrupción, *f*; separación, *f*
dissatisfaction *n* descontento, desagrado, disgusto, *m*
dissatisfied *a* descontentado, malcontento, no satisfecho
dissect *vt* disecar; *fig* analizar
dissecting table *n* mesa de disección, *f*
dissection *n* disección, *f*; análisis, *m*
dissector *n* disector, *m*; *fig* analizador (-ra)
dissemble *vt* and *vi* disimular, fingir
dissembler *n* hipócrita, *mf*; disimulador (-ra)
disseminate *vt* diseminar; propagar, sembrar
dissemination *n* diseminación, *f*; propagación, *f*
dissension *n* disensión, *f*; disidencia, *f*
dissent *n* disentimiento, *m*, *vi* disentir, disidir
dissenter *n* disidente, *mf*
dissentient *a* disidente, divergente. **without one d. voice,** unánimemente
dissertation *n* disertación, *f*
disservice *n* deservicio, *m*
dissimilar *a* disímil, desemejante, diferente
dissimilarity *n* desemejanza, diferencia, disparidad, *f*
dissimulation *n* disimulación, *f*, disimulo, *m*
dissipate *vt* disipar; dispersar; (waste) derrochar, desperdiciar. *vi* disiparse; dispersarse; (vanish) desvanecerse; (of persons) ser disoluto
dissipated *a* (of persons) disipado, disoluto, vicioso
dissipation *n* disipación, *f*; (waste) derroche, *m*; libertinaje, *m*
dissociate *vt* disociar
dissociation *n* disociación, *f*
dissoluble *a* disoluble
dissolute *a* disoluto, vicioso, licencioso
dissoluteness *n* disolución, inmoralidad, *f*
dissolution *n* disolución, *f*; separación, *f*; muerte, *f*
dissolvable *a* soluble
dissolve *vt* disolver; derretir; (of parliament) prorrogar; (a marriage, etc.) anular; *fig* disipar. *vi* disolverse; derretirse; (vanish) desvanecerse, disiparse, evaporarse. **to d. into tears,** deshacerse en lágrimas
dissolvent *a* disolutivo. *n* disolvente, *m*
dissonance *n* disonancia, *f*; *fig* discordia, falta de armonía, *f*
dissonant *n* disonancia, *f*, *a* disonante
dissuade *vt* disuadir (de), apartar (de)
dissuasion *n* disuasión, *f*
distaff *n* rueca, *f*
distance *n* distancia, *f*; lontananza, *f*; lejanía, *f*; trecho, *m*; (of time) intervalo, *m*; (difference) diferencia, *f*. **at a d.,** a alguna distancia; lejos; (from afar) desde lejos. **from a d.,** desde (or de) lejos. **in the d.,** a lo lejos, en lontananza. **to keep at a d.,** mantener lejos; guardar las distancias (con). **to keep one's d.,** mantenerse a distancia; no intimarse, guardar las distancias. **What is the d. from London to Madrid?** ¿Qué distancia hay desde Londres a Madrid?
distant *a* distante; lejano; remoto; (of manner) frío, reservado; (slight) ligero; (of references, etc.) indirecto. **He is a d. relation,** Es un pariente lejano. **They are always rather d. with her,** La tratan siempre con bastante frialdad
distantly *adv* a distancia; a lo lejos; desde lejos; remotamente; (of manner) con frialdad; (slightly) ligeramente
distaste *n* aversión, repugnancia, *f*; disgusto, hastío, *m*
distasteful *a* desagradable
distemper *n* enfermedad, *f*; (in animals) moquillo, *m*; *fig* mal, *m*; (for walls) pintura al temple, *f*. *vt* desordenar, perturbar; (walls) pintar al temple
distend *vt* ensanchar; dilatar; inflar, henchir; *med* distender. *vi* ensancharse, etc.
distension *n* dilatación, *f*; inflación, *f*; henchimíento, *m*; *med* distensión, *f*
distil *vt* destilar; extraer. *vi* destilar; exudar
distillation *n* destilación, *f*; extracción, *f*; exudación, *f*
distiller *n* destilador (-ra)
distillery *n* destilería, *f*, destilatorio, *m*
distinct *a* distinto; diferente; claro; notable, evidente
distinction *n* distinción, *f*
distinctive *a* distintivo; característico
distinctive feature *n ling* rasgo pertinente, *m*
distinctly *adv* claramente; distintamente
distinctness *n* claridad, *f*; distinción, *f*; carácter distintivo, *m*
distinguish *vt* distinguir; discernir; caracterizar; (honor) honrar. *vi* distinguir, diferenciar
distinguishable *a* distinguible; perceptible, discernible
distinguished *a* distinguido; eminente; famoso, ilustre, egregio
distinguishing *a* distintivo
distort *vt* (twist) torcer; deformar; falsear; pervertir
distorting mirror *n* (at fairs) espejo de la risa, *m*; espejo deformador, *m*
distortion *n* deformación, *f*; torcimiento, *m*; contorsión, *f*; perversión, *f*; *rad* deformación, *f*
distract *vt* distraer; interrumpir; perturbar; (turn aside) desviar, apartar; (madden) enloquecer, volver loco (a)
distracted *a* aturdido; demente, loco
distractedly *adv* locamente; perdidamente
distraction *n* distracción, *f*; (amusement) diversion, *f*, pasatiempo, *m*; (bewilderment) confusión, *f*, aturdimiento, *m*; (madness) locura, *f*; frenesí, *m*. **to drive to d.,** trastornar, sacar de quicio.
distrain *vi* embargar
distraint *n* embargo, *m*
distraught *a* aturdido; desesperado; enloquecido
distress *n* dolor, *m*, aflicción, *f*; pena, *f*; miseria, penuria, *f*; (exhaustion) fatiga, *f*, cansancio, *m*; (pain) dolor, *m*; (misfortune) desdicha, *f*; apuro, *m*; (danger) peligro, *m*; *law* embargo, *m*. *vt* afligir, dar pena (a), llenar de angustia; cansar, fatigar; (pain) doler
distressed *a* afligido; necesitado, pobre
distressing *a* congojoso, doloroso, penoso
distributable *a* repartible
distribute *vt* (of justice, etc.) administrar; distribuir; repartir
distribution *n* (of justice) administración, *f*; distribución, *f*; reparto, *m*
distributive *a* distributivo
distributor *n* distribuidor (-ra); repartidor (-ra). **d. of false money,** expendedor (-ra) de moneda falsa
district *n* distrito, *m*; comarca, *f*; (of a town) barrio, *m*; (judicial) partido judicial, *m*, *Lat. Am.* comuna *f*; jurisdicción, *f*; región, zona, *f*
distrust *n* desconfianza, *f*; recelo, *m*, sospecha, *f*. *vt* desconfiar de, sospechar
distrustful *a* desconfiado, receloso, suspicaz
distrustfully *adv* desconfiadamente, con recelo
disturb *vt* perturbar; interrumpir; incomodar; (make anxious) inquietar; (alter) cambiar; (disarrange) desordenar, desarreglar. **to d. the peace,** perturbar el orden público
disturbance *n* perturbación, *f*; disturbio, *m*, conmoción, *f*; incomodidad, *f*; agitación, *f*; confusión, *f*; tumulto, *m*; desorden, *m*; *rad* parásitos, *m pl*
disturber *n* perturbador (-ra)
disturbing *a* perturbador; inquietador; conmovedor, impresionante, emocionante
disunion *n* desunión, *f*; discordia, *f*
disunite *vt* desunir; separar, dividir. *vi* separarse
disuse *n* desuso, *m*. *vt* desusar; desacostumbrar. **to fall into d.,** caer en desuso
ditch *n* zanja, *f*; (for defense, etc.) foso, *m*; (irrigation) acequia, *f*. *vt* zanjar; abarrancar. **to die in the last d.,** morir en la brecha
ditto *adv* ídem; también
ditty *n* canción, cantinela, *f*
diuretic *a* diurético
divan *n* diván, *m*
dive *n* buceo, *m*; *aer* picada, *f*, *vi* bucear; sumergirse (en); *aer* volar en picado; penetrar (en); (into a book) enfrascarse en. **to d. out,** salir precipitadamente. **to**

d.-bomb, bombardear en picado. **d.-bomber,** avión en picado, *m.* **d.-bombing,** bombardeo en picado, *m*
diver *n* buceador, *m;* buzo, *m;* (bird) somorgujo, *m*
diverge *vi* divergir
divergence *n* divergencia, *f*
divergent *a* divergente
diverse *a* diverso, vario
diversify *vt* diversificar
diversion *n* diversión, *f;* entretenimiento, *m,* recreación, *f;* pasatiempo, *m;* placer, *m; mil* diversión, *f*
diversity *n* diversidad, variedad, *f*
divert *vt* desviar; (amuse) divertir, entretener
diverting *a* divertido, entretenido
divide *vt* dividir; partir; separar; (cut) cortar; (share) repartir, distribuir; (hair) hacer la raya (del pelo); (of voting) provocar una votación. *vi* dividirse; separarse; (of roads, etc.) bifurcarse; (of voting) votar. **divided skirt,** *n* falda pantalón, *f*
dividend *n* dividendo, *m.* **d. warrant,** cupón de dividendo, *m*
dividers *n pl* compás de puntas, *m*
dividing *a* divisorio, divisor
divination *n* adivinación, *f*
divine *a* divino; sublime; *inf* estupendo. *n* teólogo, *m. vt* (foretell) vaticinar, pronosticar; presentir; (guess) adivinar
diving *n* buceo, *m; aer* picado, *m.* **d.-bell,** campana de bucear, *f.* **d.-board,** (low) trampolín, *m;* (high) palanca, *f.* **d.-suit,** escafandra, *f*
divining rod *n* vara divinatoria, *f*
divinity *n* divinidad, *f;* teología, *f*
divisibility *n* divisibilidad, *f*
divisible *a* divisible
division *n* división, *f;* separación, *f;* (distribution) repartimiento, *m;* (*mil math*) división, *f;* sección, *f;* grupo, *m;* (voting) votación, *f;* (discord) discordia, desunión, *f.* **without a d.,** por unanimidad, sin votar
divisor *n math* divisor, *m*
divorce *n* divorcio, *m. vt* divorciarse de; *fig* divorciar, separar. **to file a petition of d.,** poner una petición de divorcio
divorcee *n* (wife) divorciada, *f;* (husband) divorciado, *m*
divulge *vt* divulgar, revelar
dizzily *adv* vertiginosamente
dizziness *n* vértigo, *m;* mareo, *m;* (bewilderment) aturdimiento, *m,* confusión, *f*
dizzy *a* vertiginoso; mareado; confuso, perplejo, aturdido
do *vt* hacer; ejecutar; (one's duty, etc.) cumplir con; concluir; (cause) causar; (homage) rendir; (commit) cometer; (arrange) arreglar; (cook) cocer, guisar; (roast) asar; (*fam* cheat) engañar; (suit) convenir; (suffice) bastar; (act) hacer el papel (de); (*fam* treat) tratar (bien o mal); (learn) aprender; (exhaust) agotar; (walk) andar; (travel, journey) recorrer; (translate) traducir; (prepare) preparar. *vi* hacer; (behave) conducirse; (of health) estar (bien o mal); (act) obrar; (get on) ir; (be suitable, suit) convenir; (suffice) bastar; (of plants) florecer; (cook) cocerse; (last) durar. **Don't!** ¡No lo hagas! ¡Quieto! ¡Calla! **How do you do?** ¿Cómo está Vd.? ¡Buenos días! **Have done!** ¡Acaba de una vez! **It will do you good,** Te conviene; Te hará bien; Te sentará bien. **It will do you no harm,** No te perjudicará; No te hará daño. **I could do with one,** Me gustaría (tener) uno; (of drinks) Me bebería uno con mucho gusto. **That will do,** Eso basta; Se puede servirse de eso; Está bien así; (leave it alone) ¡Déjate de eso! (be quiet!) ¡No digas más! ¡Cállate! **That won't do,** Eso no es bastante; Eso no sirve; Eso no se hace así; Eso no se hace. **That will never do,** Eso no servirá; Eso no puede ser. **This will do,** (when buying an article) Me quedaré con éste; Me serviré de esto; Esto basta; Esto será suficiente; (is all right) Está bien así. **Thy will be done!** ¡Hágase tu voluntad! **to be doing,** estar haciendo; estar ocupado en (or con) hacer; (of food) estar cocinando. **to be done for,** estar perdido; estar muerto. **to do better,** hacer mejor (que); (mend one's ways) enmendarse, corregirse; (improve) mejorar, hacer progresos; (in health) encontrarse mejor. **to do business with** *Lat. Am.* amarchantarse con. **to do nothing,** no hacer nada. **to do reverence,** rendir homenaje; inclinarse. **to do to death,** matar; asesinar; ejecutar. **to do violence to,** *fig* hacer fuerza a. **to do well,** hacer bien; obrar bien; (be successful) tener éxito; hacer buena impresión; (prosperous) tener una buena posición. **to do wonders,** hacer maravillas. **to have done with,** renunciar (a); dejar de usar; dejar de hacer, cesar; concluir, terminar; no tener más que ver con; (forsake) abandonar; (a person) romper con. **to have nothing to do,** no tener nada que hacer. **to have nothing to do with,** no tener nada que ver con; (of people) no tratar; (end a friendship) romper su amistad con, dejar de ver. **well done,** bien hecho; (of food) bien guisado; (of meat) bien asado. **What is to be done?** ¿Qué hay que hacer? ¿Qué se puede hacer? **What is to do?** ¿Qué pasa? ¿Qué hay? **When he had done speaking,** Cuando hubo terminado de hablar. **to do again,** hacer de nuevo, volver a hacer, rehacer; repetir. **He will not do it again,** No lo hará más. **to do away with,** quitar; eliminar; suprimir; hacer desaparecer; poner fin a; hacer cesar; destruir; matar. **to do by,** tratar (a), portarse con. **to do for,** arruinar; matar; (suffice) bastar para; ser a propósito para, servir para; (look after) cuidar; (as a housekeeper) dirigir la casa para. **to do out,** (a room) limpiar. **to do out of,** quitar; privar de; (steal) robar. **to do up,** (tie) atar; (fold) enrollar, plegar; envolver; (parcel) empaquetar; (arrange) arreglar; decorar; poner en orden; poner como nuevo; (iron) planchar; (launder) lavar y planchar; (tire) fatigar. **to do with,** (of people) tratar; (of things) tener que ver con; (put up with) poder con; poder sufrir. **to do without,** prescindir de; pasarse sin
do as an auxiliary verb is not translated in Spanish, e.g. **I do believe,** creo. **Do not do that,** no hagas eso. **I did not know,** no sabía
When it is used for emphasis, **do** is translated by **sí, ciertamente, claro** and similar words, e.g.:
She did not know, but he did, Ella no lo sabía pero él sí
You do paint well, Pintas muy bien por cierto
Do come this time, No dejes de venir esta vez
docile *a* dócil
dock *n* dique, *m,* dársena, *f;* (wharf) muelle, *m;* (in a law court) banquillo de los acusados, *m; bot* romaza, *f. vt* (a tail) descolar; cortar, cercenar; reducir; (money) descontar; (a ship) poner en dique. *vi* entrar en dársena, entrar en dique, entrar en muelle. **dry-d.,** dique seco, *m.* **floating-d.,** dique flotante, *m.* **d.-dues,** muellaje, *m.* **d. rat,** (thief) raquero, *m*
docker *n* estibador, descargador del muelle, *m*
docket *n* (bundle) legajo, *m;* extracto, *m;* minuta, *f;* (label) etiqueta, *f,* marbete, *m*
dockyard *n* arsenal, astillero, *m*
doctor *n* doctor (-ra); (medical practitioner) médico (-ca), asistir; (repair) reparar, componer; adulterar; mezclar drogas con; falsificar. *vi* ejercer la medicina. **family d.,** médico de cabecera, *m.* **to graduate as a d.,** doctorarse. **d. of divinity, laws, medicine,** doctor (-ra) en teología, en derecho, en medicina, *m*
doctoral *a* doctoral
doctorate *n* doctorado, *m*
doctrinaire *a* and *n* doctrinario (-ia)
doctrinal *a* doctrinal
doctrine *n* doctrina, *f*
document *n* documento, *m. vt* documentar; probar con documentos. **d.-case,** carpeta, *f*
documentary *a* documental; escrito, auténtico. **d. film,** película documental, *f*
documentation *n* documentación, *f*
Dodecanese, the el Dodecaneso, *m*
dodge *n* esguince, regate, *m;* evasiva, *f;* (trick) es-

tratagema, *m*, maniobra, *f*; artefacto, *m*. *vt* esquivar, evadir
doe *n* gama, *f*. **doe rabbit,** coneja, *f*
doer *n* hacedor (-ra); autor (-ra)
doeskin *n* ante, *m*, piel de gama, *f*
doff *vt* quitar; (of hats, etc.) quitarse; desnudarse de
dog *n* perro, *m*; (male) macho, *m*; (andiron) morillo, *m*; *ast* Can Mayor (or Menor), Sirio, *m*. *vt* perseguir; seguir los pasos de; espiar. **You can't deceive an old dog,** A perro viejo no hay tus tus. **to go to the dogs,** ir a las carreras de galgos; *fig* ir cuesta abajo. **mongrel dog,** perro mestizo, *m*. **thoroughbred dog,** perro de raza pura, *m*. **dog-collar,** collar de perro, *m*; *ecc* alzacuello, *m*. **dog-days,** días caniculares, *m pl*, canícula, *f*. **dog-eared** (of books) con las puntas de las hojas dobladas. **dog-fight,** lucha de perros, *f*; combate aéreo, *m*. **dog-fish,** lija, *f*, cazón, *m*. **dog in the manger,** el perro del hortelano. **dog-kennel,** perrera, *f*. **dog-latin,** bajo latín, *m*. **dog license,** matrícula de perros, *f*. **dog-racing,** carrera de galgos, *f*. **dog-rose,** escaramujo, *m*. **dog show,** exposición canina, *f*. **dog-tooth,** *arch* diente de perro, *m*. **dog-vane,** *naut* cataviento, *m*
doge *n* dux, *m*
dogged *a* persistente, tenaz, pertinaz, obstinado
doggedly *adv* tenazmente
doggedness *n* pertinacia, tenacidad, terquedad, persistencia, *f*
doggerel *n* malos versos, *m pl*; aleluyas, coplas de ciego, *f pl*, *a* malo, irregular
dogma *n* dogma, *m*
dogmatic *a* dogmático
dogmatize *vt* and *vi* dogmatizar; mostrarse dogmático
doh *n mus* do, *m*
doily *n* carpeta, *f*, pañito de adorno, *m*
doings *n pl* acciones, *f pl*; (deeds) hechos, *m pl*; (behavior) conducta, *f*; (happenings) acontecimientos, *m pl*; (works) obras, *f pl*; (things) cosas, *f pl*
doldrums *n pl* calmas ecuatoriales, *f pl*
dole *n* limosna, *f*; porción, *f*. **to d. out,** repartir; distribuir en porciones pequeñas; racionar; dar contra la voluntad de uno.
doleful *a* triste, lúgubre, melancólico; doloroso
dolefulness *n* tristeza, melancolía, *f*; dolor, *m*
doll *n* muñeca, *f*
dollar *n* dólar, *m*
dolly *n* muñeca, *f*; (for clothes) moza, *f*. **d.-tub,** cubo para la colada, *m*
dolman *n* dormán, *m*
dolphin *n* delfín, *m*
dolt *n* cabeza de alcornoque, *mf*, zamacuco, *m*
domain *n* territorio, *m*; heredad, posesión, propiedad, *f*; (empire) dominio, *m*
dome *n* cúpula, *f*; bóveda, *f*; (palace) palacio, *m*
domestic *a* doméstico; familiar; (home-loving) casero; (of animals) doméstico; (national) interior, nacional. *n* doméstico, sirviente, *m*; criada, *f*. **d. economy,** economía doméstica, *f*
domesticate *vt* domesticar
domesticated *a* (of animals) domesticado; (of persons) casero
domestication *n* domesticación, *f*
domesticity *n* domesticidad, *f*
domicile *n* domicilio, *m*, *vt* domiciliar
domiciliary *a* domiciliario
dominant *a* dominante; imperante. *n mus* dominante, *f*. **to be d.,** prevalecer
dominate *vt* and *vi* dominar
domination *n* dominación, *f*
domineer *vi* dominar, tiranizar. **to d. over,** mandar en
domineering *a* dominante, mandón, tiránico. **d. person** *Lat. Am.* mandarín *m*
Dominican *a* dominicano. *n* dominicano, *m*
Dominican Republic, the la República Dominicana, *f*
dominion *n* dominio, *m*; autoridad, soberanía, *f*; imperio, *m*; *pl* **dominions,** *ecc* dominaciones, *f pl*
Dominions, the los Dominios, *m*
domino *n* dominó, *m*. **to go d.,** nacer domino
don *n* (Spanish and Italian title) don, *m*; señor, *m*. *vt* ponerse, vestirse
donation *n* donación, dádiva, *f*; contribución, *f*
done *a* and *past part* hecho; (of food) cocido; (roasted) asado; (tired) rendido; (*fam* deceived) engañado. **Well d.!** ¡Bien hecho! **d. for,** arruinado; muerto; perdido; vencido; (spoilt) estropeado
donkey *n* borrico (-ca), burro (-rra). **d.-engine,** máquina auxiliar, *f*
donor *n* donador (-ra); dador (-ra)
doodle *v* borrajear, garabatear, hacer garabatos
doom *n* condena, *f*; (fate) suerte, *f*; (judgment) destino, *m*; ruina, *f*; juicio, *m*. *vt* sentenciar; condenar
doomsday *n* día del juicio final, *m*
door *n* puerta, *f*; entrada, *f*. **front d.,** puerta de entrada, *f*. **next d.,** la casa vecina; la puerta de al lado, la puerta vecina. **next d. neighbor,** vecino (-na) de al lado. **out of doors,** al aire libre; en la calle. **to knock at the d.,** llamar a la puerta. **to slam the d. in a person's face,** dar con la puerta en las narices de alguien. **d.-bell,** timbre (non-electric, campanilla, *f*) de llamada, *m*. **d.-jamb,** quicial, *m*. **d. keeper,** portero, *m*. **d.-knob,** tirador, *m*. **d.-knocker,** manija, *f*; picaporte, *m*, aldaba, *f*. **d.-plate,** placa, *f*. **d.-shutter,** cierre metálico, *m*. **d.-step,** peldaño de la puerta, *m*; umbral, *m*. **d.-way,** portal, *m*
dope *n* drogas, *f pl*, narcóticos, *m pl*; (news) información, *f*. **d. fiend,** morfinómano (-na)
dope-pusher *n* narcotraficante, *mf*
Doric *a* dórico
dormant *a* durmiente; latente; secreto; inactivo. **to go d.,** dormirse
dormer window *n* lumbrera, *f*
dormitory *n* dormitorio, *m*
dormouse *n* lirón, *m*
dorsal *a* dorsal
dory *n* (fish) dorado, *m*
dose, dosage *n*; dosis, *f*
dossier *n* documentación, *f*
dot *n* punto, *m*; *mus* puntillo, *m*; *pl* **dots,** *gram* puntos suspensivos, *m pl*. *vt* poner punto (a una letra); (scatter) salpicar. **on the dot,** (of time) en punto. **to dot one's i's,** poner los puntos sobre las íes
dotage *n* senectud, chochera, *f*
dotard *n* viejo chocho, *m*; vieja chocha, *f*; *inf* carcamal, *m*
dote *vi* chochear. **to d. on,** adorar en, idolatrar
doting *a* chocho
double *a* and *adv* doble; dos veces; (in a pair) en par; en dos; doblemente; (deceitful) doble, de dos caras, falso; ambiguo. *n* doble, *m*; duplicado, *m*; *theat* contrafigura, *f*; *pl* **doubles,** (tennis) dobles, *m pl*, juego doble, *m*. *vt* doblar; duplicar; (fold) doblegar; (the fist) cerrar (el puño); (*theat* and *naut*) doblar. *vi* doblarse; (dodge) volverse atrás, hacer un rodeo, dar una vuelta; esquivarse. **to d. up,** *vt* envolver; arrollar; (a person) doblar. *vi* doblegarse; arrollarse; (collapse) desplomarse. **at the d.,** corriendo. **He was doubled up with pain,** El dolor le hacía retorcerse. **mixed doubles,** parejas mixtas, *f pl*; dobles mixtos, *m pl*. **double two,** (telephone) dos dos. **with a d. meaning,** con segunda intención. **d.-barrelled,** de dos cañones. **d.-bass,** contrabajo, *m*. **d. bed,** cama de matrimonio, *f*. **d.-bedded,** con cama de matrimonio; con dos camas. **d.-breasted,** cruzado. **d.-chin,** papada, *f*. **d.-dealing,** duplicidad, *f*. **d.-edged,** de doble filo. **d.-entry,** *com* partida doble, *f*. **d.-faced,** de dos caras. **d.-jointed,** con articulaciones dobles
double room *Mexico* cuarto doble *m*
double-spaced *a* a doble espacio, a dos espacios
doublet *n* (garment) jubón, justillo, *m*; pareja, *f*, par, *m*
doubling *n* doblamiento, *m*; doblez, plegadura, *f*; duplicación, *f*; (dodging) evasiva, *f*, esguince, *m*
doubloon *n* doblón, *m*
doubly *adv* doblemente; con duplicidad

doubt *n* duda, *f*; incertidumbre, *f*; sospecha, *f*. *vt* and *vi* dudar; sospechar; titubear, hesitar; temer. **beyond all d.,** fuera de duda. **no d.,** sin duda. **There is no d. that,** No hay duda de que, No cabe duda de que. **When in d. . . . ,** En caso de duda . . .
doubter *n* incrédulo (-la)
doubtful *a* dudoso; incierto; perplejo; ambiguo; (of places) sospechoso
doubtfully *adv* dudosamente; inciertamente; irresolutamente; ambiguamente
doubtfulness *n* duda, incertidumbre, *f*; ambigüedad, *f*
doubtless *adv* sin duda, por supuesto; probablemente
douche *n* ducha, *f*, *vt* duchar
dough *n* pasta, masa, *f*; (money) lana, *f*
dour *a* huraño, adusto, austero
dourly *adv* severamente
douse *vt* zambullir; (a sail) recoger; *inf* apagar
dove *n* paloma, *f*. **d.-cote,** palomar, *m*
dovetail *n carp* cola de milano, *f*, *vt carp* machihembrar, empalmar; *fig* encajar
dowager *n* viuda, *f*; matrona, *f*. **d. countess,** condesa viuda, *f*
dowager empress *n* emperatriz viuda, *f*
dowdiness *n* desaliño, desaseo, *m*; falta de elegancia, *f*
dowdy *a* desaliñado, desaseado; poco elegante. *n* mujer poco elegante, *f*
dowel *n* espiga, clavija, *f*, zoquete, *m*, *vt* enclavijar
down *n* (of a bird) plumón, *m*; (on a peach, etc.) pelusilla, *f*; (hair) vello, *m*; (before the beard) bozo, *m*; (of a thistle, etc.) vilano, *m*. **ups and downs,** vicisitudes, *f pl*
down *a* pendiente; (of trains, etc.) descendente. *adv* abajo; hacia abajo; (lowered) bajado; (of the eyes) bajos; (on the ground) en tierra, por tierra; (stretched out) tendido a lo largo; (depressed) triste, abatido; (ill) enfermo; (fallen) caído; (of the wind) cesado; (closed) cerrado; (exhausted) agotado; *com* al contado; (of temperature) más bajo. *prep* abajo de; abajo; en la dirección de; (along) a lo largo de; por. **"Down"** (on elevators) «Para bajar». *interj* ¡Abajo!; ¡A tierra! **He went d. the hill,** Bajaba la colina. **He is d. now,** Ha bajado ahora; Está abajo ahora; Está derribado ahora. **The sun has gone d.,** Se ha puesto el sol. **His stock has gone d.,** *fig inf* Ha caído en disfavor. **Prices have come d.,** Los precios han bajado. **Their numbers have gone d.,** Sus números han disminuido. **to be d. and out,** estar completamente arruinado, ser pobre de solemnidad. **to boil d.,** reducir hirviendo. **to come d. in the world,** venir a menos. **while I was going d. the river,** mientras iba río abajo, mientras bajaba al río. **d. below,** allá abajo; abajo; en el piso de abajo. **D. on your knees!** ¡De rodillas! **d. to,** hasta. **d. spout,** tubo de bajada, *m*. **D. with!** ¡Abajo! ¡Muera! **d.-stream,** agua abajo. **d. train,** tren descendente, *m*
down *vt* derribar; vencer. **to d. tools,** declararse en huelga
downcast *a* bajo; cabizbajo, deprimido, abatido
downfall *n* caída, *f*; derrumbamiento, *m*; (failure) fracaso, *m*; (*fig* ruin) decadencia, ruina, *f*
downhearted *a* descorazonado, alicaído, desalentado
downhill *adv* cuesta abajo, hacia abajo. *a* en declive, inclinado. **to go d.,** ir cuesta abajo
downiness *n* vellosidad, *f*
downpayment *n Mexico* enganche *m*
downpour *n* chubasco (Mexico), aguacero, chaparrón, *m*
downright *a* franco, sincero; categórico, terminante; absoluto. *adv* muy; completamente
downstairs *adv* escalera abajo; al piso de abajo; en el piso bajo; abajo. *a* del piso de abajo. *n* planta baja, *f*; piso de abajo, *m*. **to go d.,** bajar la escalera; ir al piso de abajo
downtrodden *a* oprimido, esclavizado
downward *a* descendente; inclinado. *adv* hacia abajo
downy *a* velloso; (*fam* of persons) con más conchas que un galápago
dowry *n* dote, *mf*. **to give as a d.,** dotar
dowse *vt*. See **douse**
doze *vi* dormitar. *n* sueño ligero, *m*
dozen *n* docena, *f*
drab *a* pardo, parduzco, grisáceo; *fig* gris, monótono. *n* (slut) pazpuerca, *f*; (prostitute) ramera, *f*
drachma *n* dracma, *f*
draft *n* (detachment) destacamento, *m*; *com* giro, *m*, letra de cambio, *f*; (for the army, navy) conscripción, leva, *f*; (outline) bosquejo, *m*; proyecto, *m*; borrador, *m*. *vt* (detach) destacar; (recruit) reclutar; (outline) bosquejar, delinear; (draw up) redactar; proyectar
draft card *n* cartilla (Mexico), libreta de enrolamiento (Argentina), *m*
draft dodger *n* emboscado, prófugo, *m*
drafting *n* (*mil nav*) reclutamiento, *m*; (of a bill, etc.) redacción, *f*; (wording) términos, *m pl*
draftsman *n* dibujante, *m*; delineante, *m*; redactor, *m*
drag *n* (for dredging) draga, *f*; (harrow) rastrillo, *m*; (break) freno, *m*; (obstacle) estorbo, *m*; *aer* sonda, *f*. *vt* arrastrar; (fishing nets) rastrear; (harrow) rastrillar. *vi* (of the anchor) garrar; arrastrarse por el suelo; (of time) pasar lentamente; ir más despacio (que); (of interest) decaer, disminuir. **d.-hook,** garfio, *m*. **d.-net,** brancada, *f*
dragging *n* arrastre, *m*; (of lakes, etc.) rastreo, *m*, *a* rastrero; cansado
draggled *a* mojado y sucio
dragon *n* dragón, *m*. **d.-fly,** libélula, *f*, caballito del diablo, *m*
dragoon *n mil* dragón, *m*, *vt* someter a una disciplina rigurosa; obligar a la fuerza (a)
drain *n* desaguadero, *m*; (sewer) cloaca, alcantarilla, *f*; sumidero, *m*; *agr* acequia, *f*. *vt* desaguar; sanear; (lakes, etc.) desangrar; secar; (bail) achicar; (empty and drink) vaciar; (swallow) tragar; (*fig* of sorrow, etc.) apurar; (despoil) despojar; (deprive) privar (de); (impoverish) empobrecer; (exhaust) agotar. *vi* desaguarse; vaciarse; (with off) escurrirse. **to be well drained,** tener buen drenaje. **to d. the sump,** vaciar la culata. **to d. away,** vaciar. **d.-pipe,** tubo de desagüe, *m*
drainage *n* (of land) drenaje, *m*; desagüe, *m*; (of wounds) drenaje, *m*; (sewage) aguas del alcantarillado, *f pl*. **main d.,** drenaje municipal, *m*
draining *a* de desagüe; de drenaje. **d.-board,** escurridor, *m*
drake *n* ánade macho, *m*
dram *n* dracma, *f*; (of liquor) trago, *m*
drama *n* drama, *m*
dramatic *a* dramático
dramatically *adv* dramáticamente
dramatis personae *n pl* personajes, *m pl*
dramatist *n* dramaturgo, *m*
dramatization *n* versión escénica, *f*; descripción dramática, *f*; (of emotions) dramatización, *f*
dramatize *vt* dramatizar
drape *vt* colgar, cubrir; vestir
draper *n* pañero (-ra)
drapery *n* colgaduras, *f pl*; ropaje, *m*, ropas, *f pl*; pañería, *f*
drastic *a* drástico; enérgico, fuerte; **a drastic measure,** una medida avanzada, *f*
draught *n* (act of drawing) tiro, *m*; (of liquid) trago, *m*; (glass) vaso, *m*; (of a ship) calado, *m*; (of air) corriente de aire, *f*, *Lat. Am.* chiflón *m*; (party) destacamento, *m*; *n pl* **draughts,** (game) damas, *f pl*. *vt* see **draft. on d.,** (of beer, etc.) por vaso. **d. horse,** caballo de tiro, *m*. **d. screen,** cancel, *m*
draughtboard *n* tablero de damas, *m*
draughtsman *n* dibujante, *m*; delineante, *m*; redactor, *m*; (piece in game) peón, *m*
draughtsmanship *n* arte del dibujo lineal, *mf*; redacción (de un proyecto de ley), *f*
draughty *a* que tiene corriente de aire; expuesto a los vientos. **This room is d.,** Hay corriente de aire en esta habitación

draw *vt* tirar; arrastrar; traer; (pluck) arrancar; (attract) atraer; (extract) extraer; sacar; hacer salir; (unsheath) desenvainar; (a bow-string) tender; (cards, dominoes) tomar, robar; (threads) deshilar; (disembowel) destripar; (a check, etc.) girar, librar; (of a ship) calar; (of lines) hacer (rayas); (curtains) correr; (to draw curtains back) descorrer; (salary, money) cobrar, percibir; (obtain) obtener; (persuade) persuadir, inducir; (inhale) respirar; (a sigh) dar; (win) ganar; (a conclusion) deducir, inferir; (a distinction) hacer formular; *sport* empatar; (a number, etc.) sortear; (suck) chupar; (tighten) estirar; (lengthen) alargar; (comfort, etc.) tomar; (inspiration) inspirarse en; (obtain money) procurarse (recursos); (withdraw funds) retirar; (write) escribir; (draw) dibujar; (trace) trazar; (provoke) provocar. **to be drawn,** (of tickets in a lottery and cards) salir. **to d. lots,** echar suertes. **to d. water,** sacar agua. **to d. along,** arrastrar; conducir. **to d. aside,** tomar a un lado, tomar aparte; quitar de en medio, poner a un lado; (curtains) descorrer. **to d. away,** (remove) quitar; (a person) llevarse (a); apartar. **to d. back,** hacer recular; hacer retirarse; hacer volverse atrás; (curtains) descorrer. **to d. down,** hacer bajar; tirar a lo largo de (or por); bajar; (attract) atraer. **to d. forth,** hacer salir; hacer avanzar; tirar hacia adelante; conducir; (develop) desarrollar; sacar; hacer aparecer; (comment, etc.) suscitar. **to d. in,** tirar hacia adentro; sacar; acercar; atraer. **to d. off,** sacar; retirar; quitar; (water from pipes, etc.) vaciar; *print* tirar; (turn aside) desviar. **to d. on,** (of apparel) ponerse; (boots) calzarse; (occasion) ocasionar. **to d. out,** sacar fuera; hacer salir; tirar (de); (extract) extraer; (trace) trazar; (a person) hacer hablar. **to d. over,** poner encima de; arrastrar por; hacer acercarse (a), tirar hacia; atraer; persuadir. **d. prestige (from),** cobrar prestigio (de). **to d. round,** poner alrededor de. **to d. together,** reunir; acercar. **to d. up,** tirar hacia arriba; subir; sacar; extraer; (raise) levantar, alzar; (bring) traer; (bring near) acercar; (order) ordenar; *mil* formar; (a document) redactar; formular. **to d. oneself up,** erguirse

draw *vi* tirar; (shrink) encogerse; (wrinkle) arrugarse; (of chimneys, etc.) tirar; (a picture) dibujar; *sport* empatar; (move) moverse; avanzar, adelantarse; (of a ship) calar; (a sword) desnudar (la espada); (lots) echar suertes; (attract people) atraer gente; *com* girar. **to d. aside,** ponerse a un lado; retirarse. **to d. back,** retroceder, recular; retirarse; vacilar. **to d. in,** retirarse; (of days) hacerse corto; (of dusk) caer. **to d. off,** alejarse; apartarse, retirarse. **to d. on,** (approach) acercarse; avanzar; *com* girar contra; inspirarse en. **to d. out,** hacerse largo; (of a vehicle) ponerse en marcha, empezar a andar. **to d. round,** ponerse alrededor; reunirse alrededor. **to d. together,** reunirse. **to d. up,** parar.

draw *n* tirada, *f*; (of lotteries) sorteo, *m*; *sport* empate, *m*; atracción, *f*; (*fig* feeler) tanteo, *m*. **to be a big d.,** ser una gran atracción

drawback *n* desventaja, *f*, inconveniente, *m*

drawbridge *n* puente levadizo, *m*

drawee *n com* girado, *m*

drawer *n* tirador (-ra); (of water) aguador (-ra); extractor (-ra); (in a public-house) mozo de taberna, *m*; (designer) diseñador, *m*; (sketcher) dibujante, *mf*; *com* girador, *m*; (receptacle) cajón, *m*; *pl* **drawers,** (men's) calzoncillos, *m pl*; (women's) pantalones, *m pl*

drawing *n* (pulling) tiro, *m*; atracción, *f*; (extraction) extracción, *f*; saca, *f*; (in raffles, etc. and of lots) sorteo, *m*; (of money) percibo, *m*; *com* giro, *m*; (sketch) dibujo, *m*; (plan) esquema, *f*. **free-hand d.,** dibujo a pulso, *m*. **d. from life,** dibujo del natural, *m*. **d.-board,** tablero de dibujo, *m*. **d.-paper,** papel para dibujar, *m*. **d.-pin,** chinche, *f*. **d.-room,** salón, *m*

drawl *vi* hablar arrastrando las palabras

drawn *past part* See **draw.** *a* (tired) ojeroso, con ojeras, con un aspecto de cansancio; (with pain) desencajado. **long d. out,** demasiado largo. **d. sword,** espada desnuda, *f*. **d.-thread work,** deshilados, *m pl*

dread *n* pavor, temor, terror, espanto, *m*; trepidación, *f*, miedo, *m*. *a* temible, espantoso, terrible; augusto. *vt* temer. *vi* tener miedo, temer. **in d. of,** con miedo de, con terror de

dreader *n* el, *m*, (*f*, la) que teme, temedor (-ra)

dreadful *a* terrible, pavoroso, espantoso, horroroso; formidable; augusto

dreadfully *adv* terriblemente, horriblemente

dreadfulness *n* horror, *m*

dream *n* sueño, *m*; ilusión, *f*; ensueño, *m*; fantasía, *f*. *vt* and *vi* soñar; imaginar. **He dreamed away the hours,** Pasaba las horas soñando. **I wouldn't d. of it!** ¡Ni por sueño! **in a d.,** en sueños; (waking) como en sueños; mecánicamente. **Sweet dreams!** ¡Duerme bien! **to d. of,** soñar con

dreamer *n* soñador (-ra); visionario (-ia)

dreamily *adv* como en sueños; soñolientamente; vagamente

dreaming *n* sueños, *m pl*

dreamland *n* reino de los sueños, *m*

dreamy *a* soñador; soñoliento; fantástico; (empty) vació

dreariness *n* tristeza, *f*; melancolía, *f*; lobreguez, *f*

dreary *a* triste; melancólico; lóbrego

dredge *vt* dragar; (with sugar, etc.) espolvorear

dredger *n* draga, *f*; (for sugar) azucarera, *f*; (for flour) harinero, *m*

dredging *n* dragado, *m*; (sprinkling) salpicadura, *f*. **d. bucket,** cangilón, *m*

dregs *n pl* heces, *f pl*, posos, *m pl*, *Lat. Am.* concho *m* **to drain to the d.,** vaciar hasta las heces

drench *vt* mojar, calar. **He is drenched to the skin,** Está calado hasta los huesos

Dresden *n* Dresde, *f*. **D. china,** loza de Dresde, *f*

dress *vt* (with clothes) vestir; (arrange) arreglar; (the hair) peinar(se); (a wound) curar; (hides); adobar; (cloth) aprestar; (flax) rastrillar; (stone) labrar; (wood) desbastar; (prune) podar; (a garden) cultivar; (manure) abonar; *cul* aderezar; preparar; (season) condimentar; (a table) poner; (adorn) ataviar, adornar; revestir; (a dead body) amortajar. *vi* vestirse; ataviarse; (of troops) alinearse. **all dressed up and nowhere to go,** compuesta y sin novio. **dress to kill, dress to the nines** *Lat. Am.* arriscarse, *Central America* empavonarse **dressed up to the nines,** vestido de veinticinco alfileres. **Left (Right) d.!** ¡A la izquierda (A la derecha) alinearse! **to d. down,** (scold) poner como un trapo (a), dar una calada (a). **to d. up,** *vt* ataviar; (disguise) disfrazar. *vi* ponerse muy elegante; disfrazarse

dress *n* (in general) el vestir; (clothes) ropa, *f*; (frock) vestido, traje, *m*; (uniform) uniforme, *m*; (*fig* covering) hábitos, *m pl*; (appearance) aspecto, *m*; forma, *f*. **full d.,** (uniform) uniforme de gala, *m*; (civilian, man's) traje de etiqueta, *m*; (woman's) traje de gala, *m*. **morning d.,** (man's) traje de paisano, *m*; (woman's) vestido de todos los dias, *m*; (man's formal dress) chaqué, *m*. **ready-made d.,** traje hecho, *m*. **d. allowance,** alfileres, *m pl*. **d.-circle,** anfiteatro, *m*. **d.-coat,** frac, *m*. **d. protector,** sobaquera, *f*. **d. rehearsal,** ensayo general, *m*. **d. shirt,** camisa de pechera dura, *f*. **d. suit,** (with white tie) traje de frac, *m*; (with black tie) smoking, *m*. **d. sword,** espada de gala, *f*. **d. tie,** corbata de smoking (or de frac), *f*

dresser *n* el que adereza; (of wounds) practicante (de hospital), *m*; (valet) ayuda de cámara, *m*; (maid) doncella, *f*; (of skins) adobador de pieles, *m*; (furniture) aparador, *m*; (in the kitchen) armario de la cocina, *m*

dressing *n* el vestir(se); aderezamiento, *m*; (for cloth) apresto, *m*; (of leather) adobo, *m*; (of wood) desbaste, *m*; (of stone) labrado, *m*; (manuring) estercoladura, *f*; (sauce) salsa, *f*; (seasoning) condimentación, *f*; (of a wound) cura, *f*; (bandage) apósito, *m*, vendaje, *m*. **d.-case,** neceser, saco de noche, *m*. **d.-down,** *inf* rapapolvo, *m*. **d.-gown,** (woman's) salto de cama, quimono, *m;* (man's) batín, *m.* **d.-jacket,** chambra, *f,* peinador, *m.* **d.-room,** *theat* camarín, *m;* (in a house) trasalcoba, recámara, *f.* **d.-station,** puesto de socorro, *m.* **d.-table,** tocador, *m,* mesa de tocador, *f*

dressmaker *n* modista, *mf*

dressmaking *n* confección de vestidos, *f;* arte de la modista, *mf*

dribble *vi* gotear; (slaver) babear. *vt* (in football) regatear. *n* (in football) regate, *m*

dried *a* seco; (of fruit) paso. **d. up,** (withered) marchito; (of people) enjuto. **d. fish,** cecial, *m.* **d. meat,** cecina, *f*

drift *n* (in a ship or airplane's course) deriva, *f;* (of a current) velocidad, *f;* (tendency) tendencia, *f;* (meaning) significación, *f;* (heap) montón, *m;* (aim) objeto, propósito, fin, *m; min* galería, *f;* (of dust, etc.) nube, *f;* (shower) lluvia, *f;* (impulsion) impulso, *m;* violencia, *f. vi* flotar, ir arrastrado por la corriente; amontonarse; *naut* derivar; *aer* abatir. *vt* llevar; amontonar. **drifts of sand,** arena movediza, *f.* **to d. into,** (war, etc.) entrar sin querer en; (habits) dar en la flor de; (a room, etc.) deslizarse en. **d.-wood,** madera de deriva, *f*

drill *n* (instrument) taladro, perforador, *m,* barrena, *f;* ejercicio, *m,* educación física, *f; mil* instrucción militar, *f;* (cloth) dril, *m; agr* sembradora mecánica, *f;* (for seeds) hilera, *f;* (discipline) disciplina, *f;* (teaching) instrucción, *f. vt* taladrar, barrenar; enseñar el ejercicio (a); enseñar la instrucción; disciplinar; (seed) sembrar en hileras. *vi* hacer el ejercicio; hacer la instrucción militar. **d. ground,** (in a barracks) patio de un cuartel, *m;* (in a school) patio de recreo, *m.* **d.-sergeant,** sargento instructor, *m*

drilling *n* (boring) perforación, *f,* barrenamiento, *m;* (of seeds) sembradura en hileras, *f;* ejercicios, *m pl;* (maneuvers) maniobras, *f pl*

drink *n* bebida, *f;* (glass of wine, etc.) copita, *f;* (of water, etc.) vaso, *m. vt* beber; tomar; (empty) vaciar. *vi* beber. **to d. the health of,** beber a la salud de, brindar por. **to give someone a d.,** dar a beber. **Would you like a d.?** ¿Quieres tomar algo? **to d. in,** absorber. **to d. off, up,** beber de un trago

drinkable *a* potable, bebedero

drinker *n* bebedor (-ra)

drinking *n* acción de beber, *f;* el beber, *m;* (alcoholism) bebida, *f. a* que bebe; aficionado a la bebida; (of things) para beber; (drinkable) potable; (tavern) de taberna. **d.-fountain,** fuente pública para beber agua, *f.* **d. place,** bebedero, *m;* bar, *m.* **d.-song,** canción de taberna, *f.* **d.-trough,** abrevadero, *m;* **d.-water,** agua potable, *f*

drip *vi* and *vt* chorrear, gotear; caer gota a gota; escurrir; destilar; chorrear. *n* goteo, *m;* gota, *f; arch* goterón, *m*

dripping *n* goteo, *m;* chorreo, *m;* (fat) grasa, *f, a* que gotea; mojado; que chorrea agua. **d.-pan,** grasera, *f*

drive *vt* empujar; arrojar; conducir; (grouse, etc.) batir; (a ball) golpear; (a nail, etc.) clavar; (oblige) compeler, forzar a; (a horse, plough, etc.) manejar; (*mech* work) mover; (cause to work, of machines) hacer funcionar; (a tunnel, etc.) abrir, construir; (a bargain, etc.) hacer; (cause) impulsar, hacer; (mad, etc.) volver. *vi* lanzarse; (of rain) azotar; (a vehicle) conducir; (in a vehicle) ir en (coche, etc.). **to let d. at,** (aim) asestar. **to d. a wedge,** hacer mella. **to d. home an argument,** convencer; hacer convincente. **What is he driving at?** ¿Qué se propone?; ¿Qué quiere?; ¿Qué quiere decir con sus indirectas? ¿A dónde quiere llegar con esto? **to d. along,** ir en coche o carruaje por; pasearse en coche o carruaje; conducir un auto, etc., por. **to d. away,** *vt* echar; (chase) cazar; (flies, etc.) sacudirse, espantar; (care, etc.) ahuyentar; (of persons) apartar, alejar. *vi* (depart) marcharse (en coche, etc.). **to d. back,** *vt* rechazar; (a ball) devolver. *vi* volver (en auto, etc.); (arrive) llegar. **to d. crazy,d. insane** enloquecer, *Lat. Am. also* idiotizar; **to d. down,** hacer bajar; arrojar hacia abajo; (in a vehicle) bajar (por). **to d. in, into,** *vt* hacer entrar; (of teeth, etc.) hincar; (nails) clavar; *fig* introducir. *vt* entrar (en coche, carruaje); llegar (en coche, etc.). **to d. off,** See **away. to d. off the stage,** hacer dejar la escena, silbar. **to d. on,** *vt* empujar; hacer avanzar; (attack) atacar. *vi* seguir su marcha; seguir avanzando; emprender la marcha. **to d. out,** *vt* expulsar; hacer salir; (chase) cazar. *vi* salir (en coche, etc.). **to d. up,** *vi* illegar (en coche, etc.); parar. **to d. up to,** avanzar hasta, llegar hasta; conducir (el coche, etc.) hasta

drive *n* paseo (en coche, etc.), *m;* (avenue) avenida, *f;* (distance) trayecto, *m;* (journey) viaje, *m; mech* acción, *f;* conducción, *f; m; mil* ataque, *m;* (of a person) energía, *f;* campaña vigorosa, *f;* impulso, *m.* **left (right) hand d.,** conducción a la izquierda (derecha). **to take a d.,** dar un paseo en (auto, etc.). **to take for a d.,** llevar a paseo en (auto, etc.)

drive-in *n* autocine, autocinema, *m*

drivel *n* vaciedades, patrañas, *f pl,* disparates, *m pl, vi* decir disparates, chochear

driver *n* conductor (-ra); chófer, *m;* (of an engine) maquinista, *m;* (of a cart) carretero, *m;* (of a coach, carriage) cochero, *m;* (of cattle, etc.) ganadero, *m;* (golf) conductor, *m*

driver's license *Spain* carné de chofer, *Argentina* carné de conductor, *m, elsewhere in Lat. Am.* licencia de manejar, *f*

"Driveway" «Vado Permante», «Paso de Carruajes»

driving *n* conducción, *f;* modo de conducir, *m;* paseo (en coche, etc.), *m;* impulsión, *f. a* de conducir; de chófer; para choferes; motor; propulsor; impulsor; de transmisión; *fig* impulsor; (violent) violento, impetuoso. **to go d.,** ir de paseo (en auto o carruaje). **d. mirror,** espejo retrovisor, *m.* **d. seat,** asiento del conductor, *m;* (of an old-fashioned coach, etc.) pescante, *m.* **d.-shaft,** *mech* árbol motor, *m.* **d. test,** examen para choferes, *m.* **d.-wheel,** volante, *m;* rueda motriz, *f.* **d.-whip,** látigo, *m*

drizzle *n* llovizna, *f, vi* lloviznar, *Lat. Am.* briznar

droll *a* chusco, gracioso. *n* bufón, *m*

drone *n* abejón, *m; fig* zángano, *m;* (hum) zumbido, *m;* (of a song, voice) salmodia, *f, vt* and *vi* (hum) zumbar; (of a song, voice) salmodiar; (idle) zanganear

droop *vi* inclinarse; colgar; caer; (wither) marchitarse; (fade) consumirse; (pine) desanimarse. *vt* bajar; dejar caer. *n* caída, *f;* inclinación, *f*

drooping *a* caído; debilitado; lánguido; (of ears) gacho; (depressed) alicaído, deprimido

drop *n* gota, *f;* (tear) lágrima, *f;* (for the ear) pendiente, *m;* (sweet) pastilla, *f;* (of a chandelier) almendra, *f;* (fall) caída, *f;* (in price, etc.) baja, *f;* (slope) pendiente, cuesta, *f.* **by drops,** a gotas. **d. bottle,** frasco cuentagotas, *m.* **d.-curtain,** telón de boca, *m.* **d.-hammer,** martinete, *m.* **d.-head coupé,** cupé descapotable, *m.* **d.-scene,** telón de foro, *m*

drop *vt* verter a gotas; destilar; (sprinkle) salpicar, rociar; dejar caer; soltar; (lower) bajar; (of clothes, etc.) desprenderse de, quitar; (lose) perder; (a letter in a mailbox) echar; (leave) dejar; (give up) renunciar (a); desistir (de); abandonar; (kill) tumbar; (a hint) soltar; (a curtsey) hacer. *vi* gotear, caer en gotas, destilar; (descend) bajar, descender; caer muerto; caer desmayado; (sleep) dormirse; (fall) caer; (of the wind) amainar; (of prices, temperature) bajar. **to let the matter d.,** poner fin a una cuestión. **to d. a line,** poner unas líneas. **to d. anchor,** anclar. **to d. behind,** quedarse atrás. **to d. down,** caer (a tierra). **to d. in,** entrar al pasar. **d. in on somebody,** pasarse por casa de fulano, pasarse por el despacho de (etc.). **to d. off,** separarse (de); disminuir; (sleep) quedar dormido; (die) morir de repente. **to d. out,** separarse; (from a race, etc.) retirarse (de); quedarse atrás; desaparecer; ausentarse, apartarse; (decrease) disminuir; decaer. **He has dropped out of my life,** Le he perdido de vista. **to d. through,** caer por; frustrarse; no dar resultado

dropping *n* gotera, *f;* gotas, *f pl;* (fall) caída, *f; pl* **droppings** (of a candle) moco, *m;* (dung) cagadas, *f pl.* **Con-**

stant d. wears away the stone, La gotera cava la piedra
dropsy *n* hidropesía, *f*
dross *n* escoria, *f*; (rubbish) basura, *f*
drought *n* aridez, *f*; (thirst) sed, *f*; (dry season) sequía, *f*
drove *n* manada, *f*, hato, *m*; (of sheep) rebaño, *m*; (crowd) muchedumbre, *f*
drown *vi* ahogarse. *vt* ahogar; sumergir; inundar; (*fig* of cries, sorrow, etc.) ahogar
drowning *n* ahogamiento, *m*; sumersión, *f*; inundación, *f*. *a* que se ahoga
drowse *vi* adormecerse
drowsily *adv* soñolientamente
drowsiness *n* somnolencia, *f*; sueño, *m*; (laziness) indolencia, pereza, *f*
drowsy *a* soñoliento; adormecedor, soporífero; (heavy) amodorrado. **to grow d.,** adormecerse. **to make d.,** adormecer
drubbing *n* tunda, zurra, felpa, *f*
drudgery *n* trabajo arduo, *m*, faena monótona, *f*
drug *n* droga, *f*; medicamento, *m*; narcótico, *m*. *vt* mezclar con drogas; administrar drogas (a); narcotizar. *vi* tomar drogas. **d. trade,** comercio de drogas, *m*. **d. traffic,** contrabando de drogas, narcotráfico *m*
drug addict *n* toxicómano, *Lat. Am.* adicto *m*
drug addiction *n* toxicomanía, *f*
druggist *n* droguero (-ra)
drum *n* tambor, *m*; (of the ear) tímpano (del oído), *m*; (cylinder) cilindro, *m*; (box) caja, *f*; *arch* cuerpo de columna, *m*. **bass d.,** bombo, *m*. **with drums beating,** con tambor batiente. **d.-head,** parche (del tambor), *m*. **d.-head service,** misa de campaña, *f*. **d.-major,** tambor mayor, *m*
drum *vt* and *vi* tocar el tambor; (with the fingers) tabalear, teclear; (with the heels) zapatear; (into a person's head) machacar. **to d. out,** *mil* expulsar a tambor batiente
drummer *n* tambor, *m*
drumming *n* ruido del tambor, *m*; (of the heels) taconeo, *m*; (of the fingers) tabaleo, tecleo, *m*
drumstick *n* palillo (de tambor), *m*
drunk *a* borracho, ebrio, *Lat. Am. also* iluminado, *Central America* azunumbaso *n* borracho, *m*. **to be d.,** estar borracho. **to get d.,** emborracharse, *Lat. Am. also* iluminarse; *inf* pillar un lobo, (on wine) *Mexico* envinarse. **to make d.,** emborrachar
drunkard *n* borracho (-cha)
drunken *a* borracho, ebrio
drunkenness *n* embriaguez, borrachera, ebriedad, *f*
dry *vi* secarse. *vt* secar; desaguar; (wipe) enjugar. **to dry one's tears,** enjugarse las lágrimas; *fig* secarse las lágrimas. **to dry up,** secarse; (of persons) acecinarse; (with old age) apergaminarse; (of ideas, etc.) agotarse; (be quiet) callarse
dry *a* seco; árido; estéril; (thirsty) sediento; (of wine) seco; (U.S.A.) prohibicionista; (squeezed) exprimido; (of toast) sin mantequilla; (*fig* chilly) aburrido; (sarcastic) sarcástico; (of humour) agudo. **on dry land,** en seco. **dry battery,** pila seca, *f*. **to dry-clean,** lavar al seco. **dry-cleaner,** tintorero (-ra). **dry-cleaning,** lavado al seco, *m*. **dry-cleaning shop,** tintorería, *f*. **dry goods,** lencería, *f*. **dry land,** tierra firme, *f*. **dry measure,** medida para áridos, *f*. **dry-nurse,** ama seca, *f*. **dry-point,** punta seca, *f*. **dry-rot,** carcoma, *f*. **dry-shod,** con los pies secos
drying *n* secamiento, *m*; desecación, *f*, *a* secante; seco; para secar. **d. ground,** tendedero, *m*. **d. machine,** secadora, *f*; (for the hair) secadora de cabello, *f*. **d. room,** secadero, *m*
dryly *adv* secamente
dryness *n* sequedad, *f*; aridez, *f*; (of humour) agudeza, *f*
dual *a* doble; *gram* dual. **d. control,** mandos gemelos, *m pl*. **d. personality,** conciencia doble, *f*
dualism *n* dualismo, *m*
duality *n* dualidad, *f*
dub *vt* (a knight) armar caballero; (call) apellidar; (nickname) motejar, apodar
dubbing *n* (of films) doblaje, *m*
dubious *a* dudoso, incierto; indeciso; problemático; ambiguo
dubiously *adv* dudosamente
dubiousness *n* carácter dudoso, *m*; incertidumbre, *f*; ambigüedad, *f*
Dublin Dublín, *f*
Dubliner *n* dublinés (-esa)
ducat *n* ducado, *m*
duchess *n* duquesa, *f*
duchy *n* ducado, *m*
duck *n* pato (-ta), ánade, *mf*; *sport* cero, *m*; (darling) vida mía, querida, *f*; (jerk) agachada, *f*; (under the water) chapuz, *m*; (material) dril, *m*; *mil* auto anfibio, *m*; *pl* **ducks,** pantalones de dril, *m pl*. *vi* agacharse; (under water) chapuzarse. *vt* zabullir, sumergir; bajar, inclinar
ducking *n* chapuz, *m*. **d.-stool,** silla de chapuzar, *f*
duckling *n* anadino (-na)
duct *n* conducto, canal, *m*; *bot* tubo, *m*
ductile *a* dúctil
ductility *n* ductilidad, *f*
ductless *a* sin tubos
due *a* debido; (payable) pagadero; (fallen due) vencido; (fitting) propio; (expected) esperado. *n* impuesto, *m*; derecho, *m*. **in due form,** en regla. **in its due time,** a su tiempo debido. **to fall due,** vencerse. **due bill,** *com* abonaré, *m*. **due west,** poniente derecho, *m*
duel *n* duelo, lance de honor, *m*; *fig* lucha, *f*. **to fight a d.,** batirse en duelo
dueling *n* el (batirse en) duelo
duelist *n* duelista, *m*
duenna *n* dueña, *f*
duet *n* dúo, *m*
duettist *n* duetista, *mf*
duffer *n* estúpido (-da); ganso, *m*; (at games, etc.) maleta, *m*
dug *n* teta, *f*
dugout *n* trinchera, *f*
duke *n* duque, *m*
dukedom *n* ducado, *m*
dulcet *a* dulce
dulcimer *n* dulcémele, *m*
dull *a* (stupid) lerdo, estúpido, obtuso; (boring, tedious) aburrido; (of pain, sounds) sordo; (of colors and eyes) apagado; (of light, beams, etc.) sombrío; (not polished) mate; (pale) pálido; (insipid) insípido, insulso; (of people) soso, poco interesante; (dreary, sad) triste; (gray) gris; (of mirrors, etc.) empañado; (of weather) anublado; (of hearing) duro; (slow) lento; lánguido; insensible; (blunt) romo; *com* encalmado, inactivo. **to find life d.,** encontrar la vida aburrida. **d. of hearing,** duro de oído, algo sordo. **d. pain,** dolor sordo, *m*. **d. season,** temporada de calma, *f*. **d.-eyed,** con ojos apagados. **d.-witted,** lerdo
dull *vt* (make stupid) entontecer; (lessen) mitigar; (weaken) debilitar; (pain) calmar, aliviar; (sadden) entristecer; (blunt) embotar; (spoil) estropear; (a mirror, etc.) empañar; (a polished surface) hacer mate, deslustrar; (of enthusiasm, etc.) enfriar; (tire) fatigar; (obstruct) impedir
dullness *n* (stupidity) estupidez, *f*; (boredom) aburrimiento, *m*; (heaviness) pesadez, *f*; (drowsiness) somnolencia, *f*; (insipidity) insipidez, insulsez, *f*; (of literary style) prosaísmo, *m*; (of persons) sosería, *f*; (of a surface) deslustre, *m*; (laziness) pereza, languidez, *f*; (slowness) lentitud, *f*; (tiredness) cansancio, *m*; (sadness) tristeza, *f*; (bluntness) embotamiento, *m*; (of hearing) dureza, *f*; *com* desanimación, *f*
dully *adv* (stupidly) estúpidamente; sin comprender; (insipidly) insípidamente; (not brightly) sin brillo; (slowly) lentamente; (sadly) tristemente; (tiredly) con cansancio; (of sound) sordamente

duly *adv* debidamente; puntualmente
dumb *a* mudo; callado; silencioso; *inf* tonto, estúpido, *Lat. Am. also* baboso, *Central America* azurumbado. **to become d.,** enmudecer. **to strike d.,** dejar sin habla. **d.-bell,** barra con pesas, *f.* **d. show,** pantomima, *f.* **d. waiter,** bufete, *m*
dumbfound *vt* dejar sin habla; confundir; pasmar
dumbness *n* mudez, *f,* mutismo, *m;* silencio, *m*
dummy *n* (tailor's, etc.) maniquí, *m;* (puppet) títere, *m;* cabeza para pelucas, *f;* (figurehead) hombre de paja, testaferro, *m;* (baby's) chupador, *m;* (at cards) el muerto. *a* fingido. **to be d.,** (at cards) ser el muerto
dump *n* depósito, *m;* vaciadero, *m. vt* depositar; (goods on a market) inundar (con)
dumping *n* depósito, *m;* vaciamiento, *m;* (of goods on a market) inundación, *f.* **"D. prohibited,"** «Se prohibe arrojar la basura»
dumps *n* murria, *f*
dun *vt* apremiar, importunar
dun-colored *a* pardo
dunce *n* asno, bobo, zoquete, *m.* **dunce's cap,** coroza, *f*
dunderhead *n* cabeza de alcornoque, zoquete, *m*
dune *n* duna, *f*
dung *n* estiércol, *m;* (of rabbits, mice, deer, sheep, goats) cagarruta, *f;* (of cows) boñiga, *f;* (of hens) gallinaza, *f.* **d.-cart,** carro de basura, *m*
dungarees *n* mono, *m,* pantalones-vaquero, *m pl*
dungeon *n* mazmorra, *f,* calabozo, *m*
dunghill *n* muladar, *m*
duodenum *n* duodeno, *m*
dupe *n* víctima, *f;* tonto (-ta). *vt* embelecar, engañar. **to be a d.,** *inf* hacer el primo
duplicate *a* duplicado, doble. *n* duplicado, *m;* copia, *f, vt* duplicar
duplication *n* duplicación, *f*
duplicator *n* copiador, *m*
duplicity *n* duplicidad, *f*
durability *n* duración, *f.* **This is a cloth of great d.,** Este es un paño que dura mucho, Este es un paño muy duradero
durable *a* duradero
duration *n* duración, *f*
duress *n* compulsión, *f;* (prison) prisión, *f*
during *prep* durante
dusk *n* atardecer, anochecer, *m;* (twilight) crepúsculo, *m;* (darkness) oscuridad, *f.* **at d.,** al atardecer, a la caída de la tarde
dusky *a* (swarthy) moreno; (black) negro; (dim, dark) oscuro; (of colors) sucio
dust *n* polvo, *m;* (cloud of dust) polvareda, *f;* (ashes) cenizas, *f pl;* (of coal) cisco, *m;* (sweepings) barreduras, *f pl;* (of grain) tamo, *m. vt* desempolvar, quitar (or sacudir) el polvo de; (cover with dust) polvorear; (scatter) salpicar; (sweep) barrer; (clean) limpiar. **d.-bin,** basurero, *m.* **d.-cart,** carro de la basura, *m.* **d. cloud,** polvareda, *f.* **d. jacket,** (books) sobrecubierta, *f.* **d.-pan,** recogedor de basura, *m.* **d.-sheet,** guardapolvo, *m.* **d. storm,** vendaval de polvo, *m*
duster *n* el, *m,* que quita el polvo; paño (para quitar el polvo), *m;* (of feathers) plumero, *m*
dustiness *n* empolvoramiento, *m;* estado polvoriento, *m*
dusting *n* limpieza, *f;* (sweeping) barredura, *f;* (powder) polvos antisépticos, *m pl*
dustman *n* basurero, *m*
dusty *a* polvoriento, polvoroso, empolvado; del color del polvo; (of colours) sucio. **It is very d.,** Hay mucho polvo. **to get d.,** llenarse (or cubrirse) de polvo
Dutch *a* holandés. **the D.,** los holandeses. **double D.,** griego, galimatías, *m.* **D. cheese,** queso de bola, *m.* **D. courage,** coraje falso, *m.* **D. woman,** holandesa, *f*
Dutchman *n* holandés, *m*
dutiable *a* sujeto a derechos de aduana
dutiful *a* que cumple con sus deberes; obediente, sumiso; respetuoso; excelente, muy bueno
dutifully *adv* obedientemente; respetuosamente
dutifulness *n* obediencia, docilidad, *f;* respeto, *m*
duty *n* deber, *m;* obligación, *f;* (greetings) respetos, *m pl;* (charge, burden) carga, *f;* (tax) derecho, impuesto, *m; mil* servicio, *m;* (guard) guardia, *f.* **off d.,** libre. **on d.,** de servicio. **to be on sentry d.,** estar de guardia. **to do d. as,** servir como. **to do one's d.,** hacer (or cumplir con) su deber. **to pay d. on,** pagar derechos de aduana sobre. **d.-free,** franco de derechos
dwarf *a* enano. *n* enano (-na). *vt* impedir el crecimiento de; empequeñecer
dwarfish *a* enano
dwell *vi* vivir, habitar; (with on, upon) (think about) meditar sobre, pensar en; (deal with) tratar de; hablar largamente de; (insist on) insister en; apoyarse en, hacer hincapié en; (pause over) detenerse en
dweller *n* habitante, *mf;* (more poetic) morador (-ra)
dwelling *n* vivienda, *f;* (abode) morada, habitación, *f;* residencia, *f;* casa, *f;* (domicile) domicilio, *m.* **d.-house,** casa, *f*
dwindle *vi* disminuirse; consumirse; (decay) decaer; (degenerate) degenerar. **to d. to,** reducirse a
dwindling *n* disminución, *f*
dye *vt* teñir, colorar. *vi* teñirse. *n* tinte, *m;* (colour) color, *m.* **fast dye,** tinte estable, *m.* **dye-house,** tintorería, *f.* **dye-stuff,** materia colorante, *f.* **dye-works,** tintorería, *f*
dyed-in-the-wool *a* de pies a cabeza
dyeing *n* teñidura, tintura, *f;* (as a trade) tintorería, *f.* **d. and dry-cleaning shop,** tintorería, *f*
dyer *n* tintorero (-ra)
dyestuff *n* materia colorante, materia de tinte, materia tintórea, *f*
dying *a* moribundo, agonizante; de la muerte; (of light) mortecino; (last) último; supremo; (languishing) lánguido; (deathbed) hecho en su lecho mortuorio. **to be d.,** estar agonizando; (of light) fenecer. **to be d. for,** estar muerto por
dynamic *a* dinámico
dynamics *n* dinámica, *f*
dynamite *n* dinamita, *f*
dynamo *n* dinamo, *f*
dynastic *a* dinástico
dynasty *n* dinastía, *f*
dysentery *n* disentería, *f*
dyspepsia *n* dispepsia, *f*
dyspeptic *a* dispéptico. *n* dispéptico (-ca)

E

e *n* (letter) e, *f; mus* mi, *m*
each *a* cada (invariable), todo. *pron* cada uno, *m;* cada una, *f.* **e. of them,** cada uno de ellos. **They help e. other,** Se ayudan mutuamente, Se ayudan entre sí. **to love e. other,** amarse
eager *a* impaciente; ansioso, deseoso; ambicioso
eagerly *adv* con impaciencia; con ansia; ambiciosamente
eagerness *n* impaciencia, *f;* ansia, *f,* deseo, *m;* (promptness) alacridad, *f;* (zeal) fervor, *m*
eagle *n* águila, *f.* **royal e.,** águila caudal, águila real, *f.* **e.-eyed,** con ojos de lince, de ojo avizor. **have the eyes of an e.,** tener ojos de lince, tener vista de lince
ear *n* (outer ear) oreja, *f;* (inner ear and sense of hearing) oído, *m; bot* espiga, panoja, *f.* **to begin to show the ear,** (grain) espigar. **to be all ears,** ser todo oídos.

to give ear, dar oído. **to have a good ear,** tener buen oído. **to play by ear,** tocar de oído. **to turn a deaf ear,** hacerse el sordo. **ear-ache,** dolor de oídos, *m*. **ear-drum,** tímpano (del oído), *m*. **ear-flap,** orejera, *f*. **ear-phone, ear-piece,** auricular, *m*. **ear-piercing,** penetrante, agudo. **ear-shot,** alcance del oído, *m*. **to be within ear-shot,** estar al alcance del oído. **ear-trumpet,** trompetilla, *f*. **ear wax,** cerilla, *f*

eared *a* con orejas; de orejas; *bot* con espigas

earl *n* conde, *m*

earldom *n* condado, *m*

earlier, earliest *a comp* and *sup* más temprano; más primitivo; más antiguo; (first, of time) primero. *adv* más temprano; más pronto; antes

earliness *n* lo temprano; antigüedad, *f*, lo primitivo; (precocity) precocidad, *f*. **The e. of his arrival,** Su llegada de buena hora

early *a* temprano; primitivo; (of fruit, etc.) temprano, adelantado; (movement) primero (e.g. **early Romanticism,** el primer romanticismo); (person) de la primera época (e.g. **the early Cervantes,** Cervantes de la primera época); (work) un primer (e.g. **an early work of Unamuno's,** una primera obra de Unamuno); (advanced) avanzado; (precocious) precoz; (first, of time) primero; (in the morning) matutino; (near) próximo; cercano; (premature) prematuro; (of child's age) tierno; joven. **in the e. hours,** en las primeras horas; en las altas horas (de la noche). **e. age,** edad temprana, tierna edad, *f*. **e.-fruiting,** *agr* tempranal. **e. riser,** madrugador (-ra). **e.-rising,** *a* madrugador. **e. years,** primeros años, años de la niñez, *m pl*

early *adv* temprano; al principio (de); en los primeros días (de); desde los primeros días (de); (in the month, year) a principios (de); (in time) a tiempo; (in the day) de buena hora; (soon) pronto; (among the first) entre los primeros (de). **as e. as possible,** lo más temprano posible; lo más pronto posible. **to be e.,** llegar antes de tiempo; llegar de buena hora. **to get up e.,** madrugar. **to go to bed e.,** acostarse temprano. **too e.,** demasiado temprano. **e. in the morning,** de madrugada

earmark *vt* marcar; *fig* destinar, reservar

earn *vt* ganar; obtener, adquirir; (deserve) merecer

earnable *a* ganable

earnest *a* serio; fervoroso; diligente; sincero. **to be in e. about something,** tomarlo en serio; ser sincero (en). **e. money,** arras, *f pl*

earnestly *adv* seriamente; fervorosamente; con diligencia; sinceramente, de buena fe

earnestness *n* seriedad, *f*; fervor, celo, *m*; diligencia, *f*; sinceridad, buena fe, *f*

earnings *n pl com* ingresos, *m pl*; (salary) salario, *m*; estipendio, *m*; (of a workman) jornal, *m*

earring *n* pendiente, arete, *Lat. Am. also* aro *m*

earth *n* tierra, *f*; (of a badger, etc.) madriguera, *f*; *rad* tierra, *f*. *vt* cubrir con tierra; *rad* conectar con tierra. **clod of e.,** terrón, *m*. **half the e.,** *inf* medio mundo, *m*. **on e.,** en este mundo, sobre la tierra

earthen *a* terrizo, terroso; (of mud) de barro

earthenware *n* alfar, *m*, *a* de loza, de barro

earthiness *n* terrosidad, *f*

earthly *a* terrestre, terrenal; de la tierra; (fleshly) carnal; (worldly) mundano; material. **There is not an e. chance,** No hay la más mínima posibilidad

earthquake *n* terremoto, temblor de tierra, *m*

earth tremor movimiento sísmico, *m*

earthwork *n* terraplén, *m*

earthworm *n* gusano de tierra, *m*

earthy *a* térreo, terroso

earwig *n* tijereta, *f*

ease *n* bienestar, *m*; tranquilidad, *f*; descanso, *m*; (leisure) ocio, *m*; (comfortableness) comodidad, *f*; (freedom from embarrassment) naturalidad, *f*, desembarazo, desenfado, *m*; (from pain) alivio, *m*; (simplicity) facilidad, *f*. *vt* (widen) ensanchar; aflojar; (pain) aliviar; (lighten) aligerar; (moderate) moderar; (soften) suavizar; (free) librar; (one's mind) tranquilizar. **in my moments of e.,** en mis ocios, en mis momentos de ocio. **Stand at e.!** *mil* ¡En su lugar descansen! **to be at e.,** estar a sus anchas; encontrarse bien; comportarse con toda naturalidad. **with e.,** fácilmente. **to e. off,** *vt* (*naut* cables, sails) arriar. *vi* sentirse menos, cesar

easel *n* caballete (de pintor) *m*

easily *adv* fácilmente. **The engine runs e.,** El motor marcha bien

easiness *n* facilidad, *f*; sencillez, *f*; (of manner) desembarazo, *m*, naturalidad, *f*

east *n* este, *m*; oriente, *m*, (of countries) Oriente, *m*; Levante, *m*. *a* del este; del oriente; (of countries) de Oriente, oriental; levantino. **e. North e.,** estenordeste, *m*. **e. South e.,** estesudeste, *m*. **e. wind,** viento del este, *m*

Easter *n* Pascua de Resurrección, *f*. **E. egg,** huevo de Pascua, *m*. **E. Saturday,** sábado de gloria, *m*. **E. Sunday,** domingo de Pascua, *m*

easterly *a* del este; al este. *adv* hacia el este

eastern *a* del este; de Oriente; oriental. *n* oriental, *mf*

easternmost *a* situado más al este

East Indies Indias Orientales, *f pl*

eastward *adv* hacia el este, hacia oriente

easy *a* fácil; sencillo; (comfortable) cómodo; (free from pain) aliviado; *com* flojo; (well-off) acomodado, holgado; (calm) tranquilo; tolerante; natural; afable, condescendiente; (of virtue, women) fácil. *adv* con calma; despacio. **I must make myself e. about,** he de tranquilizarme sobre. **Stand e.!** ¡En su lugar descansen! **to take it e.,** tomarlo con calma. **e.-chair,** (silla) poltrona, *f*. **easy come, easy go,** lo que por agua, agua (Mexico and Colombia), los dineros del sacristán cantando vienen y cantando se van (Spain). **e.-going,** acomodadizo; indolente; (morally) de manga ancha; (casual) descuidado

eat *vt* comer; (meals, soup, refreshments) tomar; (with a good, bad appetite) hacer; consumir; (corrode) corroer; desgastar. *vi* comer; (*fam* of food) ser de buen (or mal) comer. **to eat one's breakfast (lunch),** tomar el desayuno, desayunar (almorzar). **to eat one's words,** retractarse. **to eat away,** comer; consumir; corroer. **to eat into,** (of chemicals) morder; (a fortune) consumir; gastar. **eat out of s.b.'s hand,** comer de la mano de fulano, comer en la mano de fulano. **to eat up,** devorar (also *fig*)

eatable *a* comestible, comedero. *n pl* **eatables,** comestibles, *m pl*

eater *n* el, *m*, (*f*, la) que come

eating *n* el comer; comida, *f*. **e. and drinking,** el comer y beber. **e.-house,** casa de comidas, *f*

eau de cologne *n* agua de Colonia, *f*

eaves *n* rafe, alero, *m*. **under the e.,** debajo del alero

eavesdrop *vi* escuchar a las puertas; fisgonear, espiar

eavesdropper *n* fisgón (-ona)

eavesdropping *n* fisgoneo, *m*

ebb *n* (of the tide) reflujo, *m*; menguante, *f*; *fig* declinación, *f*; *fig* decadencia, *f*; (of life) vejez, *f*. *vi* (of tide) menguar; declinar; decaer. **to ebb and flow,** fluir y refluir. **to ebb away from,** dejar; dejar aislado. **ebb-tide,** marea menguante, *f*

ebonite *n* ebonita, *f*

ebony *n* ébano, *m*

ebullience *n* efervescencia, exuberancia, *f*

ebullient *a* efervescente, exuberante

ebullition *n* (boiling) ebullición, *f*, hervor, *m*; *fig* efervescencia, *f*, estallido, *m*

eccentric *a geom* excéntrico; raro, original; extravagante, excéntrico, *Lat. Am.* ideático. *n* persona excéntrica, *f*, original, *m*

eccentrically *adv* excéntricamente

eccentricity *n geom* excentricidad, *f*; rareza, extravagancia, excentricidad, *f*

Ecclesiastes *n* Eclesiastés, *m*

ecclesiastic *a* eclesiástico. *n* eclesiástico, clérigo, *m*

ecclesiastically *adv* eclesiásticamente
echo *n* eco, *m*; reverberación, resonancia, *f*. *vt* repercutir; *fig* repetir. *vi* resonar, retumbar, reverberar
echoing *a* retumbante. *n* eco, *m*
eclectic *a* and *n* ecléctico (-ca)
eclecticism *n* eclecticismo, *m*
eclipse *n ast* eclipse, *m*, *vt* eclipsar, hacer eclipse a. **to be in e.,** estar en eclipse
ecliptic *n ast* eclíptica, *f*, *a* eclíptico
eclog *n* égloga, *f*
economic *a* económico
economical *a* económico
economics *n* economía política, *f*
economist *n* economista, *mf*
economize *vt* economizar, ahorrar. *vi* hacer economías
economy *n* economía, *f*. **domestic e.,** economía doméstica, *f*. **political e.,** economía política, *f*
ecstasy *n* éxtasis, arrebato, *m*; transporte, *m*. **to be in e.,** estar en éxtasis
ecstatic *a* extático
Ecuador el Ecuador
Ecuadorian *a* and *n* ecuatoriano (-na)
ecumenical *a* ecuménico
eczema *n* eczema, *f*
eddy *n* remolino, *m*, *vi* remolinar; *fig* remolinear
edelweiss *n* inmortal de las nieves, *f*
edema *n med* edema, *m*
Eden *n* Edén, *m*
edge *n* (of sharp instruments) filo, *m*; (of a skate) cuchilla, *f*; margen, *mf*; (shore) orilla, *f*; (of two surfaces) arista, *f*; (of books) borde, *m*; (of a coin) canto, *m*; (of a chair, a precipice, a forest, a curb, etc.) borde, *m*; (extreme) extremidad, *f*. **on e.,** de canto; *fig* ansioso. **to be on e.,** *fig* tener los nervios en punta. **to set on e.,** poner de canto; (of teeth) dar dentera
edge *vt* (sharpen) afilar; *sew* ribetear; orlar; poner un borde (a); (cut) cortar. **to e. away,** escurrirse. **to e. into,** *vt* insinuarse. *vi* deslizarse en. **to e. out,** salir poco a poco
edged *a* afilado, cortante; (in compounds) de . . . filos; (bordered) bordeado; (of books) de bordes . . .
edgeways *adv* de lado; de canto. **He couldn't get a word in e.,** No pudo meter baza en la conversación
edging *n* borde, *m*; ribete, *m*
edibility *n* el ser comestible
edible *a* comestible
edict *n* edicto, *m*
edification *n* edificación, *f*
edifice *n* edificio, *m*
edify *vt* edificar
edifying *a* edificante, edificador, de edificación
Edinburgh Edinburgo, *m*
Edipus complex *n* complejo de Edipo, *m*
edit *vt* editar; (a newspaper, journal) ser director de; (prepare for press) redactar; (correct) corregir
editing *n* trabajo editorial, *m*; redacción, *f*; dirección, *f*; corrección, *f*
edition *n* edición, *f*; *print* tirada, *f*. **first e.,** edición príncipe, *f*. **miniature e.,** edición diamante, *f*
editor *n* (of a book) editor, *m*; (of a newspaper, journal) director, *m*
editorial *a* de redacción; editorial. *n* editorial, artículo de fondo, *m*. **e. staff,** redacción, *f*
editorial board consejo de redacción, *m*
editorship *n* dirección (de un periódico, de una revista), *f*
editress *n* (of a paper, journal) directora, *f*; editora, *f*
educability *n* educabilidad, *f*
educable *a* educable
educate *vt* educar; formar; (accustom) acostumbrar
educated *a* culto
education *n* educación, *f*; enseñanza, *f*; pedagogía, *f*. **chair of e.,** cátedra de pedagogía, *f*. **early e.,** primeras letras, *f pl*. **higher e.,** enseñanza superior, *f*
educational *a* educativo; pedagógico; instructivo
educationalist *n* pedagogo, *m*
educative *a* educativo
educator *n* educador (-ra)
educe *vt* educir; deducir; *chem* extraer
eduction *n* educción, *f*
Edwardian *a* and *n* eduardiano (-na)
eel *n* anguila, *f*. **electric eel,** gimnoto, *m*. **eel-basket,** nasa para anguilas, *f*
eerily *adv* fantásticamente; de modo sobrenatural
eeriness *n* ambiente de misterio, *m*; efecto misterioso, *m*
eerie *a* misterioso, fantástico; sobrenatural; lúgubre
efface *vt* borrar, destruir; quitar. **to e. oneself,** retirarse; permanecer en el fondo
effacement *n* borradura, *f*
effect *n* efecto, *m*; impresión, *f*; (result) resultado, *m*, consecuencia, *f*, (meaning) substancia, *f*, significado, *m*; *pl* **effects,** efectos, bienes, *m pl*. *vt* efectuar; producir. **in e.,** en efecto, efectivamente. **of no e.,** inútil. **striving after e.,** efectismo, *m*. **to feel the effects of,** sentir los efectos de; padecer las consecuencias de. **to put into e.,** poner en práctica; hacer efectivo. **to take e.,** producir efecto; ponerse en vigor
effective *a* eficaz; (striking) de mucho efecto, poderoso, vistoso. **to make e.,** llevar a efecto
effectively *adv* eficazmente; (strikingly) con gran efecto; efectivamente, en efecto
effectiveness *n* eficacia, *f*; efecto, *m*
effectuate *vt* efectuar
effeminacy *n* afeminación, *f*
effeminate *a* afeminado, adamado. **to make e.,** afeminar
efferent *a* eferente
effervesce *vi* estar efervescente, hervir
effervescence *n* efervescencia, *f*
effervescent *a* efervescente
effete *a* gastado; estéril; decadente
effeteness *n* decadencia, *f*; esterilidad, *f*
efficacious *a* eficaz
efficacy *n* eficacia, *f*
efficiency *n* eficiencia, *f*; buen estado, *m*; habilidad, *f*; *mech* rendimiento, *m*
efficient *a* (e.g. medicine) eficaz; eficiente; (person) competente, capaz
efficiently *adv* eficientemente; eficazmente; competentemente
effigy *n* efigie, imagen, *f*
efflorescence *n chem* eflorescencia, *f*; *bot* florescencia, *f*
effluvium *n* efluvio, *m*
effort *n* esfuerzo, *m*. **to make an e.,** hacer un esfuerzo. **make every effort to,** hacer lo posible por + *inf*; empeñar sus máximos esfuerzos en el sentido de + *inf*
effortless *a* sin esfuerzo
effrontery *n* descaro, *m*, insolencia, *f*
effulgence *n* esplendor, fulgor, *m*
effulgent *a* fulgente, resplandeciente
effusion *n* efusión, *f*
effusive *a* efusivo, expansivo
egg *n* huevo, *m*. **to egg on,** incitar (a). **boiled egg,** huevo cocido, *m*. **fried egg,** huevo frito, *m*. **hard egg,** huevo duro, *m*. **poached egg,** huevo escalfado, *m*. **scrambled egg,** huevos revueltos, *m pl*. **soft egg,** huevo pasado por agua, *m*. **to lay eggs,** poner huevos. **to put all one's eggs in one basket,** *fig* poner toda la carne en el asador. **egg-cup,** huevera, *f*. **egg dealer,** vendedor (-ra) de huevos. **egg flip,** huevo batido con ron, *m*. **eggplant,** berenjena, *f*. **egg-shaped,** aovado. **egg-shell,** cascarón, *m*, cáscara de huevo, *f*. **egg-shell china,** loza muy fina, *f*. **egg-spoon,** cucharita para comer huevos, *f*. **egg-whisk,** batidor de huevos, *m*
ego *n* yo
egoism *n* egoísmo, *m*
egoist *n* egoísta, *mf*
egoistic *a* egoísta
egoistically *adv* egoístamente
egotism *n* egotismo, *m*, egolatría, *f*
egotist *n* egotista, *mf*
egotistic *a* egotista

egregious *a* notorio
egress *n* salida, *f*
Egypt Egipto, *m*
Egyptian *a* egipcio. *n* egipcio (-ia); cigarrillo egipcio, *m*
Egyptologist *n* egiptólogo (-ga)
Egyptology *n* egiptología, *f*
eh? *interj* ¿eh? ¿qué?
eider *n orn* pato de flojel, *m*
eiderdown edredón, *m*
eight *a* and *n* ocho *m*. **He is e. years old,** Tiene ocho años. **It is e. o'clock,** Son las ocho. **e.-day clock,** reloj con cuerda para ocho dias, *m*. **e. hundred,** *a* and *n* ochocientos *m*.. **e.-syllabled,** octosilábico
eighteen *a* and *n* diez y ocho, *m*.
eighteenth *a* décimoctavo; (of the month) (el) diez y ocho, dieciocho; (of monarchs) diez y ocho. *n* décimoctava parte, *f*. **Louis the E.,** Luis diez y ocho
eightfold *a* óctuple
eighth *a* octavo, *m*; (of the month) (el) ocho; (of monarchs) octavo. *n* octavo, *m*
eighthly *adv* en octavo lugar
eightieth *a* octogésimo
eighty *a* and *n* ochenta, *m*.
either *a* and *pron* uno u otro, cualquiera de los dos; ambos (-as). *conjunc* o (becomes **u** before words beginning with **o** or **ho**). *adv* tampoco. **I do not like e.,** No me gusta ni el uno ni el otro (ni la una ni la otra). **e. . . . or,** o . . . o
ejaculate *vt* exclamar, lanzar; *med* eyacular
ejaculation *n* exclamación, *f*; *med* eyaculación, *f*
ejaculatory *a* jaculatorio
eject *vt* echar, expulsar; *law* desahuciar; (emit) despedir, emitir
ejection *n* echamiento, *m*, expulsión, *f*; *law* desahúcio, *m*; (emission) emisión, *f*
eke (out) *vt* aumentar, añadir a
elaborate *a* elaborado; primoroso; elegante; complicado; (detailed) detallado; (of meals) de muchos platos; (of courtesy, etc.) estudiado. *vt* elaborar; amplificar
elaborately *adv* primorosamente; elegantemente; complicadamente; con muchos detalles
elaborateness *n* primor, *m*; elegancia, *f*; complicación, *f*; (care) cuidado, *m*; minuciosidad, *f*
elaboration *n* elaboración, *f*
elapse *vi* transcurrir, andar, pasar
elastic *a* elástico. *n* elástico, *m*. **e. band,** anillo de goma, *m*; cinta de goma, *f*. **e. girdle,** faja elástica, *f*
elasticity *n* elasticidad, *f*
elate *vt* alegrar; animar
elatedly *adv* alegremente; triunfalmente
elation *n* alegría, *f*, júbilo, *m*; triunfo, *m*
elbow *n* codo, *m*; ángulo, *m*; (of a chair) brazo, *m*. *vt* codear, dar codazos (a). **at one's e.,** a la mano. **nudge with the e.,** codazo, *m*. **to be out at e.,** enseñar los codos, tener los codos raídos; ser harapiento. **to e. one's way,** abrirse paso a codazos. **e.-chair,** silla de brazos, *f*. **e.-grease,** jugo de muñeca, *m*. **e.-piece** or **patch,** codera, *f*. **e. room,** libertad de movimiento, *f*
elder *a comp* mayor. *n* persona mayor, *f*; señor mayor, *m*; (among Jews and in early Christian Church) anciano, *m*; *bot* saúco, *m*
elderly *a* mayor
eldest *a sup* old (el, la, etc.) mayor. **e. daughter,** hija mayor, *f*. **e. son,** hijo mayor, *m*
elect *vt* elegir. *a* elegido; predestinado. *n* electo, *m*; elegido, *m*
election *n theol* predestinación, *f*; elección, *f*. **by-e.,** elección parcial, *f*
electioneer *vi* solicitar votos; distribuir propaganda electoral
electioneering *n* solicitación de votos, *f*; propaganda electoral, *f*
elective *a* electivo. *n* (subject at school) materia optativa, *f*
elector *n* elector (-ra); (prince) elector, *m*
electoral *a* electoral. **e. register,** lista electoral, *f*
electoral college colegio de compromisarios, *m*
electorate *n* electorado, *m*
electric, electrical *a* eléctrico; *fig* vivo, instantáneo. **e. arc,** arco voltaico, *m*. **e. engineer,** ingeniero electricista, *m*. **electric fan,** (Spain) ventilador, (Western Hemisphere) ventilador eléctrico, *m*. **e. fire,** estufa eléctrica, *f*. **e. immersion heater,** calentador de agua eléctrico, *m*. **e. light,** luz eléctrica, *f*. **e. pad,** alfombrilla eléctrica, *f*. **e. shock,** conmoción eléctrica, *f*. **e. washing-machine,** lavadora eléctrica, *f*. **e. wire** or **cable,** conductor eléctrico, *m*
electrically *adv* por electricidad
electrician *n* electricista, *mf*
electricity *n* electricidad, *f*
electrification *n* electrificación, *f*
electrify *vt* electrificar; *fig* electrizar
electro *prefix* (in compounds) electro. **e.-chemistry,** electroquímica, *f*. **e.-dynamics,** electrodinámica, *f*. **e.-magnet,** electroimán, *m*. **e.-magnetic,** electromagnético. **e.-plate,** *vt* galvanizar, platear. *n* artículo galvanizado, *m*. **e.-therapy,** electroterapia, *f*
electrocute *vt* electrocutar
electrocution *n* electrocución, *f*
electrode *n* electrodo, *m*
electrolysis *n* electrólisis, *f*
electrolyte *n* electrólito, *m*
electrolyze *vt* electrolizar
electrometer *n* electrómetro, *m*
electromotive *a* electromotriz. **e. force,** fuerza electromotriz, *f*
electron *n* electrón, *m*
electroscope *n* electroscopio, *m*
elegance *n* elegancia, *f*
elegant *a* elegante; bello
elegantly *adv* elegantemente, con elegancia
elegiac *a* elegíaco
elegy *n* elegía, *f*
element *n* elemento, *m*; factor, *m*; ingrediente, *m*; *elec* par, elemento, *m*; *chem, phys* cuerpo simple, *m*; *pl* **elements,** rudimentos, *m pl*, nociones, *f pl*; (weather) intemperie, *f*; (Eucharist) el pan y el vino. **to be in one's e.,** estar en su elemento
elemental *a* elemental; rudimentario, lo elemental
elementariness *n* el carácter, elemental
elementary *a* elemental; rudimentario; primario. **e. education,** enseñanza primaria, *f*
elephant *n* elefante (-ta). **e. keeper** or **trainer,** naire, *m*
elephantiasis *n* elefantíasis, *f*
elephantine *a* elefantino
elevate *vt* (the Host) alzar; elevar; (the eyes, the voice) levantar; (honor) enaltecer
elevated *a* noble, elevado, sublime; edificante; (drunk) achispado
elevation *n* elevación, *f*; enaltecimiento, *m*; (of style, thought) nobleza, sublimidad, *f*; (hill) eminencia, altura, *f*
elevator *n* (lift) ascensor, *m*; (for grain, etc.) montacargas, *m*
elevator shaft caja, *f*, hueco pozo, *m*
eleven *a* once. *n* once, *m*. **It is e. o'clock,** Son las once
eleventh *a* onceno, undécimo; (of month) (el) once; (of monarchs) once. *n* onzavo, *m*; undécima parte, *f*. **at the e. hour,** *fig* a última hora. **Louis the E.,** Luis once (XI)
elf *n* elfo, duende, *m*; (child) trasgo, *m*; (dwarf) enano, *m*
elfin *a* de duendes; de hada
elicit *vt* sacar; hacer contestar; hacer confesar; descubrir
elicitation *n* descubrimiento, *m*
elide *vt* elidir
eligibility *n* elegibilidad, *f*
eligible *a* elegible; deseable
eliminate *vt* eliminar; quitar
elimination *n* eliminación, *f*

eliminatory *a* eliminador
elision *n* elisión, *f*
elite *n* nata, flor, *f*
elixir *n* elixir, *m*
Elizabethan *a* de la época de la Reina Isabel I de Inglaterra
elk *n* ante, *m*
ell *n* (measure) ana, *f*
ellipse *n geom* elipse, *f*; óvalo, *m*
ellipsis *n gram* elipsis, *f*
elliptic *a geom, gram* elíptico
elm *n* olmo, *m*. **e. grove,** olmeda, *f*
elocution *n* elocución, *f*; (art of elocution) declamación, *f*
elocutionist *n* recitador (-ra), declamador (-ra)
elongate *vt* alargar; extender. *vi* alargarse; extenderse. *a* alargado; (of face) perfilado
elongation *n* alargamiento, *m*; prolongación, *f*; extensión, *f*
elope *vi* evadirse, huir; fugarse (con un amante)
elopement *n* fuga, *f*
eloquence *n* elocuencia, *f*
eloquent *a* elocuente
eloquently *adv* elocuentemente
else *adv* (besides) más; (instead) otra cosa, más; (otherwise) si no, de otro modo. **anyone e.,** (cualquier) otra persona; alguien más. **Anything e.?** ¿Algo más? **everyone e.,** todos los demás. **everything e.,** todo lo demás. **nobody e.,** ningún otro, nadie más. **nothing e.,** nada más. **or e.,** o bien, de otro modo; si no. **someone e.,** otra persona, otro. **somewhere e.,** en otra parte. **There's nothing e. to do,** No hay nada más que hacer; No hay más remedio
elsewhere *adv* a, or en, otra parte
elucidate *vt* elucidar, aclarar
elucidation *n* elucidación, aclaración, *f*
elucidatory *a* aclaratorio
elude *vt* eludir, evitar
elusive *a* (of persons) esquivo; fugaz; difícil de comprender
elusiveness *n* esquivez, *f*; fugacidad, *f*
Elysian *a* elíseo. **E. Fields,** campos elíseos, *m pl*
Elysium *n* elíseo, *m*
emaciate *vt* extenuar, demacrar, enflaquecer
emaciated *a* extenuado, demacrado. **to become e.,** demacrarse
emaciation *n* demacración, emaciación, *f*; *med* depauperación, *f*
emanate *vi* emanar (de), proceder (de)
emanation *n* emanación, *f*; exhalación, *f*
emancipate *vt* emancipar
emancipated *a* emancipado
emancipation *n* emancipación, *f*
emancipator *n* emancipador (-ra), libertador (-ra)
emancipatory *a* emancipador
emasculate *a* afeminado. *vt* emascular; *fig* afeminar; mutilar
emasculation *n* emasculación, *f*
embalm *vt* embalsamar; *fig* conservar el recuerdo de; perfumar
embalmer *n* embalsamador, *m*
embalmment *n* embalsamamiento, *m*
embankment *n* declive, *m*; ribera, *f*; terraplén, *m*; dique, *m*; (quay) muelle, *m*
embargo *n* embargo, *m*, *vt* embargar. **to put an e. on,** embargar. **to remove an e.,** sacar de embargo
embark *vi* embarcarse; lanzarse (a). *vt* embarcar
embarkation *n* (of persons) embarcación, *f*; (of goods) embarque, *m*
embarrass *vt* impedir; (financially) apurar; (perplex) tener perplejo; (worry) preocupar; (confuse) desconcertar, turbar; (annoy) molestar
embarrassed *a* turbado
embarrassing *a* embarazoso; desconcertante; molesto
embarrassingly *adv* de un modo desconcertante; demasiado
embarrassment *n* impedimento, *m*; (financial) apuro, *m*; (obligation) compromiso, *m*; (perplexity) perplejidad, *f*; (worry) preocupación, *f*; (confusion) turbación, *f*
embassy *n* embajada, *f*
embattled *a* en orden de batalla; *her* almenado
embed *vt* empotrar, enclavar; fijar
embellish *vt* embellecer; adornar
embellishment *n* embellecimiento, *m*; adorno, *m*
ember *n* rescoldo, *m*. **E. days,** témporas, *f pl*
embezzle *vt* desfalcar
embezzlement *n* desfalco, *m*
embezzler *n* desfalcador (-ra)
embitter *vt fig* amargar; envenenar
embittering *a* amargo
embitterment *n* amargura, *f*
emblazon *vt* blasonar; *fig* ensalzar
emblem *n* emblema, *m*
emblematic *a* emblemático
embodiment *n* incarnación, *f*; expresión, *f*; personificación, *f*; símbolo, *m*; síntesis, *f*
embody *vt* encarnar; expresar; personificar; incorporar; contener; formular; sintetizar. **to be embodied in,** quedar plasmado en
embolden *vt* animar, dar valor (a)
embolism *n med* embolia, *f*
emboss *vt* repujar, abollonar; estampar en relieve
embossment *n* abolladura, *f*; relieve, *m*
embrace *n* abrazo, *m*. *vt* abrazar, dar un abrazo (a); (*fig.* seize) aprovechar; (accept) aceptar; adoptar; (engage in) dedicarse a; (comprise) incluir, abarcar; (comprehend) comprender. **They embraced,** Se abrazaron
embroider *vt* bordar; embellecer; (a tale, etc.) exagerar; *vi* hacer bordado
embroiderer *n* bordador (-ra)
embroidery *n* bordado, *m*; labor, *f*. **e.-frame,** bastidor, *m*. **e. silk,** hilo de bordar, *m*
embroil *vt* enredar, embrollar; desordenar
embryo *n* embrión, *m*; *fig* germen, *m*. *a* embrionario
embryology *n* embriología, *f*
embryonic *a* embrionario
emend *vt* enmendar; corregir
emendation *n* enmienda, *f*; corrección, *f*
emerald *n* esmeralda, *f*, *a* de color de esmeralda. **e. green,** verde esmeralda, *m*
emerge *vt* emerger; surgir; *fig* salir; aparecer
emergence *n* emergencia, *f*; salida, *f*; aparición, *f*
emergency *n* urgencia, *f*; necesidad, *f*; emergencia, *f*; aprieto, *m*. **e. exit,** salida de urgencia, *f*. **e. port,** *naut* puerto de arribada, *m*
emergent *a* emergente; que sale; naciente
emery *n* esmeril, *m*. **to polish with e.,** esmerilar. **e.-paper,** papel de lija, *m*
emetic *a* and *n* emético, vomitivo, *m*.
emigrant *a* emigrante. *n* emigrante, *mf* emigrado, *m*
emigrate *vi* emigrar; *inf* trasladarse
emigration *n* emigración, *f*. **e. officer,** oficial de emigración, *m*
eminence *n* (hill) elevación, prominencia, *f*; eminencia (also as title), *f*; distinción, *f*
eminent *a* distinguido, eminente; famoso, ilustre; notable; conspicuo
eminently *adv* eminentemente
emir *n* amir, *m*
emissary *n* emisario (-ia); embajador (-ra); agente, *m*
emission *n* emisión, *f*
emit *vt* despedir; exhalar; emitir
emollient *a* emoliente, lenitivo. *n* emoliente, *m*
emolument *n* emolumento, *m*
emotion *n* emoción, *f*. **to cause e.,** emocionar
emotional *a* emocional, sentimental; emocionante
emotionalism *n* sentimentalismo, *m*
emotionalize *vt* considerar bajo un punto de vista sentimental
emotionally *adv* con emoción, sentimentalmente
emotionless *a* sin emoción

emotive *a* emotivo
emperor *n* emperador, *m*
emphasis (on) *n* énfasis (en), *mf*; insistencia especial (en), especial atención (a), *f*; accentuación, *f*
emphasize *vt* subrayar, dar énfasis a, poner de relieve, hacer resaltar, dar importancia a; acentuar; insistir en, hacer hincapié (en)
emphatic *a* enfático
emphatically *adv* con énfasis
empire *n* imperio, *m*
empiric *a* empírico
empiricism *n* empirismo, *m*
employ *n* empleo, *m*; servicio, *m*. *vt* emplear; ocupar; tomar; servirse de, usar. **How do you e. yourself?** ¿Cómo te ocupas? ¿Cómo pasas el tiempo?
employable *a* empleable; utilizable
employee *n* empleado (-da)
employer *n* el, *m*, (*f*, la) que emplea; dueño (-ña), amo (-a); patrón (-ona)
employment *n* empleo, *m*; uso, *m*; ocupación, *f*; aprovechamiento, *m*; (post) puesto, cargo, *m*; (situation) colocación, *f*. **e. exchange,** bolsa de trabajo, *f*
emporium *n* emporio, *m*; (store) almacén, *m*
empower *vt* autorizar; permitir; ayudar (a); dar el poder (para)
empress *n* emperatriz, *f*
emptiness *n* vaciedad, *f*; futilidad, *f*; vacuidad, *f*; (verbosity) palabrería, *f*
empty *a* vacío; (of a house, etc.) deshabitado, desocupado; (deserted) desierto; (vain) vano, inútil; frívolo; (hungry) hambriento. *n* envase vacío, *m*. *vt* vaciar; descargar. *vi* vaciarse; (river, etc.) desembocar, venir a morir en. **e.-handed,** con las manos vacías. **e.-headed,** casquivano
emptying *n* vaciamiento, *m*; abandono, *m*; *pl* **emptyings,** heces de la cerveza, *f pl*
emu *n* emu, *m*
emulate *vt* emular
emulation *n* emulación, *f*
emulative *a* emulador
emulsify *vt* emulsionar
emulsion *n* emulsión, *f*
emulsive *a* emulsivo
enable *vt* (to) hacer capaz (de); ayudar (a); autorizar (para); permitir (de)
enact *vt law* promulgar; decretar; (a part) hacer, desempeñar (un papel); (a play) representar; (happen) ocurrir, tener lugar
enaction *n law* promulgación, *f*
enamel *n* esmalte, *m*, *vt* esmaltar
enameler *n* esmaltador (-ra)
enameling *n* esmaltadura, *f*
enamor *vt* enamorar. **to be enamored of,** estar enamorado de; estar aficionado a
encamp *vt* and *vi* acampar
encampment *n* campamento, *m*
encase *vt* encajar; encerrar; (line) forrar
encasement *n* encaje, *m*; encierro, *m*
encephalitis *n* encefalitis, *f*. **e. lethargica,** encefalitis letárgica, *f*
enchant *vt* encantar, hechizar; fascinar, embelesar, deleitar
enchanter *n* encantador, *m*
enchanting *a* encantador, fascinador
enchantment *n* encantamiento, *m*; fascinación, *f*, encanto, deleite, *m*
enchantress *n* bruja, *f*; *fig* mujer seductora, *f*
encircle *vt* cercar; rodear; dar la vuelta (a)
enclose *vt* cercar; meter dentro de; encerrar; (with a letter, etc.) incluir, adjuntar
enclosed *a* (of letters) adjunto
enclosure *n* cercamiento, *m*; cercado, *m*; recinto, *m*; (wall) tapia, cerca, *f*; (with a letter) contenido adjunto, *m*
encomium *n* encomio, *m*
encompass *vt* cercar, rodear
encore *n* repetición, *f*, *interj* ¡bis!
encounter *n* encuentro, *m*; combate, *m*; conflicto, *m*; lucha, *f*. *vt* encontrar; atacar; tropezar con
encourage *vt* animar; alentar; estimular; incitar; ayudar; (approve) aprobar; (foster) fomentar
encouragement *n* ánimos, *m pl*; estímulo, incentivo, *m*; ayuda, *f*; (approval) aprobación, *f*; (promotion) fomento, *m*
encourager *n* instigador (-ra); ayudador (-ra); aprobador (-ra); fomentador (-ra)
encouraging *a* alentador; estimulante; fomentador; (favorable) halagüeño, favorable
encouragingly *adv* de un modo alentador; con aprobación
encroach *vi* usurpar; abusar (de); invadir; robar; (of sea, river) hurtar
encroaching *a* usurpador; invadiente
encroachment *n* usurpación, *f*; abuso, *m*; invasión, *f*
encrust *vt* encostrar; incrustar
encumber *vt* impedir, estorbar; llenar; (burden) cargar; (mortgage) hipotecar; (overwhelm) agobiar
encumbrance *n* impedimento, estorbo, *m*; gravamen, *m*; carga, *f*; (mortgage) hipoteca, *f*
encyclical *n* encíclica, *f*
encyclopedia *n* enciclopedia, *f*
encyclopedic *a* enciclopédico
encyclopedist *n* enciclopedista, *m*
end *n* fin, *m*; extremidad, *f*; extremo, *m*; conclusión, *f*; (point) punta, *f*; cabo, *m*; (district) barrio, *m*; cabeza, *f*; (death) muerte, *f*; (aim) objeto, intento, *m*; (purpose) propósito, *m*; (issue) resultado, *m*; (bit) fragmento, pedazo, *m*; (of a word) terminación, *f*. *vi* terminar; acabar; concluir; cesar; (in) terminar en; resultar en; (with) terminar con. *vt* terminar; acabar, dar fin a. **at an end,** terminado. **at the end,** al cabo (de); al extremo (de). **end of quotation,** fin de cita, final de la cita, *m*. **from end to end,** de un extremo a otro; de un cabo a otro. **in the end,** por fin, finalmente. **on end,** de pie, de cabeza, derecho; de punta; (of hair) erizado. **no end of,** un sinnúmero de. **to make both ends meet,** pasar con lo que se tiene. **to make an end of,** acabar con. **to put an end to,** poner fin a. **to the end that,** a fin de que, para que; con objeto de. **toward the end of,** (months, years, etc.) a fines de, a últimos de; hacia el fin de. **two hours on end,** dos horas seguidas. **end-paper,** guarda, *f*
endanger *vt* arriesgar, poner en peligro
endear *vt* hacer querer
endearing *a* que inspira cariño; atrayente; cariñoso
endearment *n* cariño, amor, *m*; caricia, terneza, *f*; palabra de cariño, *f*
endeavor *vi* procurar, intentar, hacer un esfuerzo. *n* esfuerzo, *m*, tentativa, *f*
endemic *a med* endémico
ending *n* fin, *m*; conclusión, *f*; *gram* terminación, *f*; cesación, *f*; (climax) desenlace, *m*
endive *n bot* escarola, *f*
endless *a* eterno; inacabable; infinito; sin fin; interminable; incesante
endlessly *adv* sin fin; incesantemente; sin parar
endlessness *n* eternidad, *f*; infinidad, *f*; continuidad, *f*
endocrine *a* endocrino. *n* secreción interna, *f*
endocrinology *n* endocrinología, *f*
end-of-season *a* por final de temporada (e.g., **end-of-season reductions,** rebajos por final de temporada, *m pl*. **end-of-season sale,** liquidación por final de temporada, *f*)
endogenous *a* endógeno
endorse *vt com* endosar; garantizar; (uphold) apoyar; confirmar
endorsee *n* endosatario (-ia)
endorsement *n com* endoso, *m*; aval, *m*, garantía, *f*; corroboración, confirmación, *f*
endorser *n com* endosante, *m*
endow *vt* dotar; fundar; crear
endowment *n* dotación, *f*; fundación, *f*; creación, *f*;

(mental) inteligencia, *f;* cualidad, *f,* don, *m.* **e. policy,** póliza dotal, *f*
endurable *a* sufrible, soportable; tolerable
endurance *n* aguante, *m;* resistencia, *f;* sufrimiento, *m;* tolerancia, *f;* paciencia, *f;* (lastingness) duración, continuación, *f.* **beyond e.,** intolerable, inaguantable. **e. test,** prueba de resistencia, *f*
endure *vt* soportar; tolerar, aguantar; sufrir; resistir. *vi* sufrir; (last) durar, continuar
enduring *a* permanente, perdurable; continuo; constante
enduringness *n* (lastingness) permanencia, *f;* paciencia, *f;* aguante, *m*
enema *n* lavativa, enema, *f*
enemy *n* enemigo (-ga); adversario (-ia); (in war) enemigo, *m. a* del enemigo, enemigo. **to be one's own e.,** ser enemigo de sí mismo. **to become an e. of,** enemistarse con; hacerse enemigo de, volverse hostil a
energetic *a* enérgico
energy *n* energía, fuerza, *f,* vigor, *m*
enervate *vt* enervar; debilitar. *a* enervado
enervation *n* enervación, *f;* debilitación, *f*
enfeeble *vt* debilitar
enfeeblement *n* debilitación, *f,* desfallecimiento, *m*
enfold *vt* envolver; abrazar
enforce *vt* (a law) poner en vigor; (impose) imponer a la fuerza; hacer cumplir; conseguir por fuerza; (demonstrate) demostrar
enforcement *n* (of a law) ejecución (de una ley), *f;* imposición a la fuerza, *f;* observación forzosa, *f*
enfranchise *vt* emancipar; conceder derechos civiles (a)
enfranchisement *n* emancipación, *f;* concesión de derechos civiles, *f*
engage *vt* empeñar; contratar; tomar en alquiler; tomar a su servicio; (seats, etc.) reservar; (occupy) ocupar; (attention) atraer; (in) aplicarse a, dedicarse a; *mil* combatir con, librar batalla con; atacar; (of wheels) endentar con. *vi* obligarse; dedicarse (a); tomar parte (en); (bet) apostar; *mil* librar batalla; (fight) venir a las manos. **to be engaged in,** traer entre manos, ocuparse en. **to become engaged,** prometerse. **Number engaged!** (telephone) ¡Están comunicando!
engaged *a* ocupado; (betrothed) prometido; reservado
engagement *n* obligación, *f;* compromiso, *m;* (date) cita, *f;* (betrothal) palabra de casamiento, *f;* (battle) combate, *m,* batalla, *f.* **I have an e. at two o'clock.** Tengo una cita a las dos
engagement gift regalo de esponsales, *m*
engaging *a* simpático, atractivo
engagingly *adv* de un modo encantador
engender *vt fig* engendrar; excitar
engine *n* máquina, *f;* motor, *m;* (locomotive) locomotora, *f;* (pump) bomba, *f.* **to sit with one's back to the e.,** estar sentado de espaldas a la máquina (or locomotora). **e. builder,** constructor de máquinas, *m.* **e. driver,** maquinista, *mf.* **e. room,** cuarto de máquinas, *m.* **e. works,** taller de maquinaria, *m*
engineer *n* ingeniero, *m;* mecánico, *m. vt fig* gestionar, arreglar. **civil e.,** ingeniero de caminos, canales y puertos, *m.* **Royal Engineers,** Cuerpo de Ingenieros, *m*
engineering *n* ingeniería, *f; fig* manejo, *m. a* de ingeniería
England Inglaterra, *f*
English *a* inglés. *n* (language) inglés, *m.* **in E. fashion,** a la inglesa. **to speak E.,** hablar inglés. **to speak plain E.,** hablar sin rodeos; hablar en cristiano. **E. Church,** iglesia anglicana, *f.* **E.-teacher,** maestro (-ra) de inglés. **English-translator,** traductor al inglés, *m*
English Channel, the el Canal de la Mancha
Englishman *n* inglés, *m*
Englishwoman *n* inglesa, *f*
engrain *vt* inculcar
engrave *vt* grabar; esculpir, cincelar; *fig* grabar
engraver *n* grabador (-ra); (tool) cincel, *m*
engraving *n* grabadura, *f;* (picture) grabado, *m.* **e. needle,** punta seca, *f*
engross *vt* (a document) poner en limpio; redactar; (absorb) absorber
engrossing *a* absorbente
engulf *vt* hundir, sumir, sumergir
enhance *vt* realzar; intensificar; aumentar; mejorar
enhancement *n* realce, *m;* intensificación, *f;* aumento, *m;* mejoría, *f*
enigma *n* enigma, *m*
enigmatic *a* enigmático
enjoin *vt* imponer; ordenar, mandar; encargar
enjoy *vt* disfrutar; gustar de; gozar de; poseer, tener. **to e. oneself,** recrearse, regocijarse; (amuse oneself) divertirse; entretenerse; pasarlo bien. **Did you e. yourself?** ¿Lo pasaste bien?
enjoyable *a* agradable; divertido, entretenido
enjoyableness *n* lo agradable; lo divertido
enjoyably *adv* de un modo muy agradable
enjoyer *n* el, *m,* (*f,* la) que disfruta; poseedor (-ra); (amateur) aficionado (-da)
enjoyment *n* posesión, *f;* goce, disfruto, *m;* (pleasure) placer, *m;* aprovechamiento, *m;* utilización, *f;* (satisfaction) satisfacción, *f*
enlarge *vt* agrandar; aumentar; ensanchar; extender; *phot* ampliar; dilatar; (the mind, etc.) ensanchar. *vi* agrandarse; ensancharse; aumentarse; extenderse. **an enlarged heart,** dilatación del corazón, *f.* **to e. upon,** tratar detalladamente, explayarse en
enlargement *n* engrandecimiento, *m;* ensanchamiento, *m; phot* ampliación, *f; med* dilatación, *f;* aumento, *m;* amplificación, *f;* (of a town, etc.) ensanche, *m*
enlarger *n phot* ampliadora, *f*
enlighten *vt* iluminar; aclarar; informar
enlightened *a* culto; ilustrado; inteligente
enlightening *a* instructivo
enlightenment *n* ilustración, *f;* cultura, civilización, *f*
enlist *vt mil* reclutar; alistar; obtener, conseguir. *vi mil* sentar plaza, sentar plaza de soldado; engancharse; alistarse
enlistment *n mil* enganche, *m;* reclutamiento, *m;* alistamiento, *m*
enliven *vt* animar; avivar; alegrar
enmity *n* enemistad, enemiga, hostilidad, *f*
ennoble *vt* ennoblecer; ilustrar
ennui *n* tedio, *m;* aburrimiento, *m*
enormity *n* enormidad, *f;* gravedad, *f;* atrocidad, *f*
enormous *a* enorme, colosal
enormously *adv* enormemente
enormousness *n* enormidad, *f*
enough *a* bastante, suficiente. *n* lo bastante, lo suficiente. *adv* bastante; suficientemente. *interj* ¡bastante! ¡basta! **to be e.,** ser suficiente; bastar. **two are enough,** con dos tenemos bastante, con dos tengo bastante
enquire. See **inquire**
enrage *vt* enfurecer, hacer furioso; *inf* hacer rabiar
enraged *a* furioso
enrapture *vt* entusiasmar, extasiar; (intoxicate) embriagar; (charm) encantar, deleitar
enrich *vt* enriquecer; (adorn) adornar, embellecer; (the land) fertilizar
enrichment *n* enriquecimiento, *m;* embellecimiento, *m;* (of the land) abono, *m*
enroll *vt* alistar; matricular; inscribir; (perpetuate) inmortalizar
enrollment *n* alistamiento, *m;* inscripción, *f*
ensconce *vt* acomodar, colocar; ocultar
ensemble *n* conjunto, *m*
enshrine *vt* poner en sagrario; guardar con cuidado; *fig* guardar como una reliquia
enshroud *vt* amortajar; envolver; esconder
ensign *n* (badge) insignia, *f;* (flag) enseña, bandera, *f;* pabellón, *m;* bandera de popa, *f; mil* alférez, *m;* (U.S.A. navy) subteniente, *m*
enslave *vt* esclavizar; *fig* dominar
enslavement *n* esclavitud, *f*

ensue *vt* conseguir. *vi* resultar; suceder, sobrevenir
ensuing *a* (next) próximo; (resulting) resultante
ensure *vt* asegurar; estar seguro de que; garantizar
entail *vt* traer consigo, acarrear; *law* vincular; *n law* vinculación, *f*; herencia, *f*
entangle *vt* enredar; coger; *fig* embrollar
entanglement *n* enredo, *m*; complicación, *f*; intriga, *f*; (*mil* of wire) alambrada, *f*
entangling *a* enmarañador (e.g., **entangling alliances,** alianzas enmarañadoras, *f pl*)
enter *vt* entrar en; penetrar; (of thoughts) ocurrirse; (join) ingresar en; entrar en; (become a member of) hacerse miembro de; (enroll) alistarse; (a university) matricularse; (inscribe) inscribir, poner en la lista; (note) anotar, apuntar; (a protest) hacer constar; (make) hacer; formular. *vi* entrar; *theat* salir (a la escena); penetrar; *com* anotarse. **to e. for,** *vt* inscribir. *vi* inscribirse, tomar parte en. **to e. into,** entrar en; formar parte de; (conversation) entablar (conversación); (negotiations) iniciar; considerar; (another's emotion) acompañar en; (an agreement, etc.) hacer; (sign) firmar; (bind oneself) obligarse a, comprometerse a; tomar parte en; (undertake) emprender; empezar; adoptar. **to e. up,** anotar; poner en la lista; registrar. **to e. upon,** comenzar, emprender; tomar posesión de; encargarse de, asumir; inaugurar, dar principio a
enteric *a* entérico
enteritis *n* enteritis, *f*
enterprise *n* empresa, *f*; aventura, *f*; (spirit) iniciativa, *f*, empuje, *m*
enterprising *a* emprendedor, acometedor; de mucha iniciativa
entertain *vt* (an idea, etc.) acariciar, abrigar; considerar; (as a guest) agasajar, obsequiar; recibir en casa; (amuse) divertir, entretener. *vi* ser hospitalario; tener invitados en casa; dar fiestas
entertaining *a* entretenido, divertido
entertainingly *adv* entretenidamente; (witty) graciosamente
entertainment *n* convite, *m*; fiesta, *f*; reunión, *f*; banquete, *m*; (hospitality) hospitalidad, *f*; (amusement) diversión, *f*, entretenimiento, *m*; espectáculo, *m*; función, *f*; concierto, *m*
enthrall *vt* seducir, atraer, encantar; absorber, captar la atención
enthralling *a* absorbente; atrayente, halagüeño
enthrallment *n* absorción, *f*; atracción, *f*
enthrone *vt* entronizar
enthronement *n* entronización, *f*
enthusiasm *n* entusiasmo, *m*
enthusiast *n* entusiasta, *mf*
enthusiastic *a* entusiasta. **to make e.,** entusiasmar. **to be e.,** entusiasmarse
enthusiastically *adv* con entusiasmo
entice *vt* tentar, inducir; atraer, seducir
enticement *n* tentación, *f*; atractivo, *m*
enticing *a* seduciente, atrayente; halagüeño
entire *a* entero; completo; intacto; absoluto; perfecto; íntegro; total
entirely *adv* enteramente; completamente; integralmente; totalmente
entirety *n* totalidad, *f*; integridad, *f*; todo, *m*
entitle *vt* (designate) intitular; dar derecho (a); autorizar. **to be entitled to,** tener derecho a
entity *n* entidad, *f*; ente, ser, *m*
entombment *n* sepultura, *f*, entierro, *m*
entomological *a* entomológico
entomologist *n* entomólogo, *m*
entomology *n* entomología, *f*
entourage *n* séquito, *m*; (environment) medio ambiente, *m*
entr'acte *n* entreacto, *m*
entrails *n* entrañas, tripas, *f pl*, intestinos, *m pl*
entrain *vi* tomar el tren, subir al tren
entrance *n* entrada, *f*; *theat* salida (a la escena), *f*; (into a profession, etc.) ingreso, *m*; alistamiento, *m*; (beginning) principio, *m*; (door) puerta, *f*; (porch) portal, *m*; (of a cave) boca, *f*. **e. fee,** cuota de entrada, *f*. **e. hall,** zaguán, *m*. **e. money,** entrada, *f*
entrance *vt fig* encantar, fascinar; ecstasiar
entrancing *a* encantador
entreat *vt* suplicar, implorar, rogar
entreating *a* suplicante, implorante
entreatingly *adv* de un modo suplicante; insistentemente
entreaty *n* súplica, instancia, *f*, ruego, *m*
entree *n* entrada, *f*
entrench *vt* atrincherar
entrenchment *n* atrincheramiento, *m*; *mil* parapeto, *m*; (encroachment) invasión, *f*
entresol *n* entresuelo, *m*
entrust *vt* confiar a (or en), encomendar a; encargar
entry *n* entrada, *f*; (passage) callejuela, *f*; (note) inscripción, apuntación, *f*; *com* partida, *f*; (registration) registro, *m*. **double e.,** *com* partida doble, *f*. **single e.,** *com* partida simple, *f*
entwine *vt* entrelazar, entretejer
enumerate *vt* enumerar
enumeration *n* enumeración, *f*
enumerative *a* enumerativo
enunciate *vt* enunciar; articular
enunciation *n* enunciación, *f*; articulación, *f*
envelop *vt* envolver, cubrir
envelope *n* sobre, *m*
envelopment *n* envolvimiento, *m*; cubierta, *f*
enviable *a* envidiable
envious *a* envidioso. **an e. look,** una mirada de envidia
enviously *adv* con envidia
environment *n* medio ambiente, *m*
environs *n* inmediaciones, *f pl*, alrededores, *m pl*
envisage *vt* hacer frente a; contemplar; imaginar
envoy *n* enviado, *m*; mensajero (-ra)
envy *n* envidia, *f*, *vt* envidiar
enzyme *n* fermento, *m*, enzima, *f*
eon *n* eón, *m*
epaulette *n* hombrera, *f*
ephemeral *a* efímero; *fig* fugaz, pasajero
Ephesus Efiso, *m*
Ephraim Efraín, *m*
Ephraimite *n* and *adj* efraíta, *mf*
epic *a* épico. *n* epopeya, *f*
epicenter *n* epicentro, *m*
epicure *n* epicúreo (-ea)
epicurean *a* epicúreo
Epicureanism *n* epicureísmo, *m*
epidemic *n* epidemia, *f*; plaga, *f*, *a* epidémico
epidermis *n* epidermis, *f*
epiglottis *n* epiglotis, *f*
epigram *n* epigrama, *m*
epigrammatic *a* epigramático
epigraph *n* epígrafe, *m*
epigraphy *n* epigrafía, *f*
epilepsy *n* epilepsia, alferecía, *f*
epileptic *a* and *n* epiléptico (-ca). **e. fit,** ataque epiléptico, *m*. **e. aura,** aura epiléptica, *f*
epilog *n* epílogo, *m*
epiphany *n* epifanía, *f*
Epirus Epiro, *m*
episcopacy *n* episcopado, *m*
episcopal *a* episcopal
episcopalianism *n* episcopalismo, *m*
episode *n* suceso, incidente, *m*; *lit* episodio, *m*
episodic *a* episódico
epistle *n* epístola, *f*
epistolary *a* epistolar
epitaph *n* epitafio, *m*
epithet *n* epíteto, *m*
epitome *n* epítome, *m*
epitomize *vt* resumir, abreviar
epoch *n* época, edad, *f*
epode *n* épodo, *m*
Epsom salts *n* sal de la Higuera, *f*

equability *n* igualdad (de ánimo), ecuanimidad, *f;* uniformidad, *f*
equable *a* igual, ecuánime; uniforme
equably *adv* con ecuanimidad; igualmente; uniformemente
equal *a* igual; uniforme; imparcial; equitativo, justo. *n* igual, *mf. vt* ser igual a; equivaler a; igualar; *sport* empatar. **to be e. to,** (of persons) ser capaz de; servir para; atreverse a; (circumstances) estar al nivel de; sentirse con fuerzas para. **without e.,** sin igual; (of beauty, etc.) sin par. **e. sign,** *math* igual, *m*
equality *n* igualdad, *f;* uniformidad, *f*
equalization *n* igualación, *f*
equalize *vt* igualar
equalizing *a* igualador; compensador
equally *adv* igualmente; imparcialmente
equanimity *n* ecuanimidad, *f*
equation *n* ecuación, *f*
equator *n* ecuador, *m*
equatorial *a* ecuatorial
equerry *n* caballerizo del rey, *m*
equestrian *a* ecuestre
equiangular *a* equiángulo
equidistance *n* equidistancia, *f*
equidistant *a* equidistante
equilateral *a* equilátero
equilibrist *n* equilibrista, *mf*
equilibrium *n* equilibrio, *m*
equine *a* equino; hípico; de caballo
equinoctial *a* equinoccial. **e. gale,** tempestad equinoccial, *f*
equinox *n* equinoccio, *m*
equip *vt* proveer; pertrechar; equipar
equipage *n* (train) séquito, tren, *m;* (carriage) carruaje, *m*
equipment *n* habilitación, *f;* equipo, *m;* pertrechos, *m pl;* material, *m;* aparatos, *m pl;* armamento, *m*
equitable *a* equitativo, justo
equitableness *n* equidad, justicia, *f*
equitably *adv* equitativamente, con justicia
equity *n* equidad, *f;* imparcialidad, justicia, *f*
equivalence *n* equivalencia, *f*
equivalent *a* and *n* equivalente, *m.* **to be e. to,** equivaler a
equivocal *a* equívoco, ambiguo
equivocally *adv* equivocadamente
equivocate *vi* usar frases equívocas, emplear equívocos, tergiversar
equivocation *n* equívoco, *m*
era *n* época, era, *f*
eradiation *n* irradiación, *f*
eradicable *a* erradicable
eradicate *vt* erradicar; destruir, extirpar; suprimir
eradication *n* erradicación, *f;* destrucción, *f;* supresión, *f*
erasable *a* borrable
erase *vt* borrar; tachar
eraser *n* goma de borrar, *f.* **ink e.,** goma para tinta, *f*
erasure *n* borradura, *f;* tachón, *m*
ere *conjunc* antes de (que), antes de. *prep* antes de
erect *a* (upright) derecho; erguido; vertical; (uplifted) levantado; (standing) de pie; (firm) firme, resuelto; (alert) vigilante. *vt* (build) edificar, construir; instalar; (raise) alzar; convertir
erectile *a* eréctil
erection *n* erección, *f;* construcción, edificación, *f;* (building) edificio, *m;* (structure) estructura, *f;* instalación, *f;* (assembling) montaje, *m*
erectly *adv* derecho
erectness *n* derechura, *f*
erg *n phys* ergio, *m*
ermine *n* armiño, *m, a* de armiño
erode *vt* corroer; comer; *geol* denudar
erosion *n* erosión, *f*
Erostrato Eróstrato
erotic *a* erótico
err *vi* desviarse; errar; desacertar; pecar
errand *n* mensaje, recado, *m;* encargo, *m;* misión, *f.* **e.-boy,** mandadero, mensajero, motril, mozo, recadero, *m*
errant *a* errante; (of knights) andante
erratic *a* (of conduct) excéntrico, irresponsable; (of thoughts, etc.) errante; *med* errático
erratum *n* errata, *f*
erring *a* extraviado; pecaminoso
erroneous *a* erróneo; falso; injusto
erroneously *adv* erróneamente; falsamente; injustamente
erroneousness *n* falsedad, *f*
error *n* error, *m;* equivocación, *f,* desacierto, *m;* (sin) pecado, *m.* **in e.,** por equivocación
erudite *a* erudito; sabio
erudition *n* erudición, *f*
erupt *vi* entrar en erupción, estar en erupción; *fig* salir con fuerza
eruption *n* erupción, *f*
erysipelas *n* erisipela, *f*
escalade *n* escalada, *f, vt* escalar
escalator *n* escalera automática, escalera eléctrica, escalera mecánica, escalera móvil, escalera rodante, *f*
escapable *a* evitable, eludible
escapade *n* escapada, *f;* aventura, *f*
escape *n* huida, fuga, *f;* evasión, evitación, *f;* (leak) escape, *m; fig* salida, *f. vt* eludir, evitar; (of cries, groans, etc.) dar, salir de. *vi* huir, fugarse, escapar; (slip away) escurrirse; librarse; salvarse; (leak) escaparse. **His name escapes me,** Se me escapa (or se me olvida) su nombre. **to e. notice,** pasar inadvertido. **to have a narrow e.,** salvarse en una tabla. **to e. from,** escaparse de; librarse de; huir de
escape clause *n* cláusula de salvaguardia, *f*
escaping *a* fugitivo
escarpment *n* escarpa, *f*
eschew *vt* evitar
eschewal *n* evitación, *f*
escort *n mil* escolta, *f;* (of ships) convoy, *m;* acompañamiento, *m;* acompañante, *m. vt mil* escoltar; (of ships) convoyar; acompañar
escritoire *n* escritorio, *m*
escudo *n* escudo, *m*
escutcheon *n* escudo, blasón, *m*
Eskimo *a* and *n* esquimal *mf*
esoteric *a* esotérico
esparto *n* esparto, *m*
especial *a* especial; particular
especially *adv* especialmente; ante todo; en particular
Esperantist *n* esperantista, *mf*
Esperanto *n* esperanto, *m*
espionage *n* espionaje, *m*
esplanade *n mil* explanada, *f;* bulevar, paseo, *m*
espousal *n* desposorio, *m; fig* adhesión (a una causa), *f*
espouse *vt* desposar; (a cause) abrazar; defender
espy *vt* divisar, ver, observar
esquire *n* escudero, *m;* (landowner) hacendado, *m;* (as a title) don (before given name)
essay *n* tentativa, *f; lit* ensayo, *m, vt* probar; procurar; (on an examination) tema, *m.* **essay question,** tema, *m*
essayist *n* ensayista, *mf*
essence *n* esencia, *f*
essential *a* esencial; indispensable, imprescindible; intrínseco. *n* artículo de primera necesidad, *m;* elemento necesario, *m*
essentially *adv* esencialmente
establish *vt* establecer; fundar; crear; erigir, *Lat. Am. also* instaurar; (constitute) constituir; (order) disponer; (prove) demostrar, probar; (take root, settle) arraigarse
established *a* establecido; arraigado; (proved) demostrado; bien conocido; (author) consagrado; (of churches) oficial
establishment *n* establecimiento, *m;* fundación, *f;* creación, *f, Lat. Am. also* instauración; institución, *f;*

(building) erección, *f*; arraigo, *m*; (house) casa, *f*; (church) iglesia oficial, *f*; demostración, *f*; reconocimiento, *m*

estate *n* estado, *m*; clase, *f*; condición, *f*; (land) propiedad, finca, *f*; fortuna, *f*; (inheritance) heredad, *f*, patrimonio, *m*; *law* bienes, *m pl*. **personal e.,** bienes muebles, *m pl*; fortuna personal, *f*. **third e.,** estado llano, *m*. **e. agent,** agente de fincas, *m*; agente de casas, *m*

esteem *n* estima, *f*, aprecio, *m*; consideración, *f*, *vt* estimar, apreciar; creer, juzgar

ester *n chem* éster, *m*

esthete *n* estético, *m*

esthetic *a* estético

esthetically *adv* estéticamente

esthetics *n* estética, *f*

estimable *a* apreciable, estimable

estimableness *n* estimabilidad, *f*

estimate *n* estimación, tasa, *f*; cálculos, *m pl*; apreciación, *f*; opinión, *f*; *pl* **estimates,** presupuesto, *m*. *vt* (value) avalorar, tasar; calcular, computar; considerar. *vi* hacer un presupuesto

estimation *n* opinión, *f*; cálculo, cómputo, *m*; (esteem) aprecio, *m*, estima, *f*

estrange *vt* enajenar; ofender

estrangement *n* enajenación, alienación, *f*

estuary *n* estuario, *m*, ría, *f*

etcetera etcétera. (Used as noun, *f*)

etch *vt* grabar al agua fuerte

etcher *n* grabador (-ra) al agua fuerte

etching *n* aguafuerte, *f*; grabado al agua fuerte, *m*. **e. needle,** punta seca, aguja de grabador, *f*

eternal *a* eterno; incesante. *n* (E.) el Eterno

eternally *adv* eternamente

eternity *n* eternidad, *f*

eternize *vt* eternizar

ether *n* éter, *m*

ethereal *a* etéreo; vaporoso, aéreo

etheric *a* etéreo

etherize *vt* eterizar

ethical *a* ético, moral; *n* droga de ordenanza, *f*

ethics *n* ética, *f*; (filosofía) moral, *f*

Ethiopia Etiopia, *f*

ethnic *a* étnico

ethnographic *a* etnográfico

ethnography *n* etnografía, *f*

ethnologist *n* etnólogo, *m*

ethnology *n* etnología, *f*

ethyl *n chem* etilo, *m*

ethylene *n chem* etileno, *m*

etiquette *n* etiqueta, *f*

Eton coat *n* chaquetilla, *f*

Eton collar *n* cuello de colegial, *m*

Etna, Mount el Etna

Etruscan *a* and *n* etrusco (-ca)

etymological *a* etimológico

etymologist *n* etimólogo, *m*, etimologista, *mf*

etymology *n* etimología, *f*

eucalyptus *n* eucalipto, *m*

Eucharist *n* Eucaristía, *f*

eucharistic *a* eucarístico

eugenic *a* eugenésico

eugenics *n* eugenesia, *f*

eulogist *n* elogiador (-ra), loador (-ra)

eulogistic *a* elogiador

eulogize *vt* elogiar, alabar, encomiar

eulogy *n* elogio, encomio, *m*; alabanza, *f*; panegírico, *m*

eunuch *n* eunuco, *m*

euphemism *n* eufemismo, *m*

euphonious *a* eufónico

euphony *n* eufonía, *f*

euphuistic *a* alambicado, gongorino

Eurasian *a* and *n* eurasio (-ia)

eurhythmic *a* eurítmico

eurhythmics *n* euritmia, *f*

European *a* and *n* europeo (-ea)

europeanize *vt* europeanizar

euthanasia *n* eutanasia, *f*

evacuate *vt* evacuar

evacuation *n* evacuación, *f*

evade *vt* evadir, eludir; evitar, esquivar; rehuir

evaluate *vt* evaluar, estimar; calcular

evaluation *n* evaluación, estimación, *f*

evanescent *a* transitorio, fugaz, pasajero

evangelical *a* evangélico

evangelicalism *n* evangelismo, *m*

evangelist *n* evangelista, *m*

evangelize *vt* evangelizar

evaporate *vi* evaporarse; desvanecerse. *vt* evaporar

evaporation *n* evaporación, *f*; desvanecimiento, *m*

evaporative *a* evaporatorio

evasion *n* (escape) fuga, *f*; evasión, *f*; evasiva, *f*, efugio, *m*, *Lat. Am.* esquivada, *f*

evasive *a* evasivo, ambiguo

evasively *adv* evasivamente

evasiveness *n* carácter evasivo, *m*

eve *n* víspera, *f*; *ecc* vigilia, *f*. **on the eve of,** la víspera de; *fig* en vísperas de

even *a* (flat) llano; (smooth) liso; igual; (level with) al mismo nivel (de); uniforme; (of numbers) par; (approximate, of sums) redondo; rítmico; invariable, constante; (of temper) apacible; (just) imparcial; (monotonous) monótono, igual; (paid) pagado; (*com* of date) mismo. **to get e. with,** pagar en la misma moneda, vengarse de. **to be e. (with . . .)** (be quits) *Lat. Am.* estar a mano (con . . .)

even *adv* siquiera; aun; hasta; (also) también. **not e.,** ni siquiera. **e. as,** así como, del mismo modo que. **e. if,** aun cuando, si bien. **e. now,** aun ahora; ahora mismo. **e. so,** aun así; (nevertheless) sin embargo. **e. though,** aunque; suponiendo que

even *vt* igualar; (level) allanar, nivelar; (accounts) desquitar; compensar; hacer uniforme

evening *n* tarde, *f*, atardecer, *m*; noche, *f*; *fig* fin, *m*, *a* vespertino, de la tarde. **Good e.!** ¡Buenas tardes! ¡Buenas noches! **in the e.,** al atardecer. **tomorrow e.,** mañana por la tarde. **yesterday e.,** ayer por la tarde. **e. class,** clase nocturna, *f*. **e. dress,** (women) traje de noche, *m*; (men) traje de etiqueta, *m*. **e. meal,** cena, *f*. **e. paper,** periódico (or diario) de la noche, *m*. **evening primrose,** hierba del asno, onagra, *f*. **e. star,** estrella vespertina, estrella de la tarde, *f*; (Venus) lucero de la tarde, *m*

evenly *adv* igualmente; (on a level) a nivel; uniformemente; imparcialmente; (of speech) con suavidad

evenness *n* igualdad, *f*; (smoothness) lisura, *f*; uniformidad, *f*; imparcialidad, *f*; (of temper) ecuanimidad, serenidad, *f*

evensong *n* vísperas, *f pl*

event *n* incidente, suceso, acontecimiento, *m*; (result) consecuencia, *f*; resultado, *m*; caso, *m*; (athletics) prueba, *f*; (race) carrera, *f*. **at all events,** de todas maneras. **in such an e.,** en tal caso. **in the e. of,** en el caso de

eventful *a* lleno de acontecimientos; accidentado; memorable

eventual *a* eventual; final, último

eventuality *n* eventualidad, *f*

eventually *adv* a la larga, al fin

ever *adv* siempre; (at any time) jamás; alguna vez; nunca; (even) siquiera; (very) muy; (in any way) en modo alguno. **As fast as e. he can,** Lo más aprisa que pueda. **Be it e. so big,** Por grande que sea. **Did you e.!** ¡Habráse visto! ¡Qué cosa! **for e.,** para siempre. **for e. and e.,** para siempre jamás; (mostly ecclesiastical) por los siglos de los siglos; eternamente. **He is e. so nice,** Es muy simpático. **Hardly e.,** casi nunca. **I don't think I have e. been there,** No creo que haya estado nunca allí. **if e.,** si alguna vez; (rarely) raramente. **nor . . . e.,** ni nunca. **not . . . e.,** nunca. **e. after,** desde entonces; (afterward) después. **e. and anon,** de vez en cuando. **e. so little,** siquiera un poco; muy poco

evergreen *a* siempre verde. *n* planta vivaz, *f.* **e. oak,** encina, *f*
everlasting *a* eterno, perpetuo; (of colors) estable; incesante. **e. flower,** perpetua, *f*
evermore *adv* eternamente
every *a* todo; cada (invariable); todos los, *m pl;* todas las, *f pl.* **e. day,** todos los días, cada día. **e. now and then,** de cuando en cuando. **e. other day,** cada dos días
everybody *n* todo el mundo, *m;* todos, *m pl;* todas, *f pl;* cada uno, *m;* cada una, *f*
everyday *a* diario, cotidiano; corriente, de cada día, usual
everything *n* todo, *m;* (e. that, which) todo lo (que). **e. possible,** todo lo posible
everywhere *adv* por todas partes
evict *vt* desahuciar; expulsar
eviction *n* evicción, *f,* desahúcio, *m;* expulsión, *f*
evidence *n law* testimonio, *m,* deposición, *f;* indicios, *m pl;* evidencia, *f;* prueba, *f;* hecho, *m, vt* patentizar, probar. **to give e.,** dar testimonio, deponer
evident *a* evidente, patente, manifiesto; claro. **to be e.,** ser patente, estar a la vista
evidently *adv* evidentemente; claramente
evil *a* malo; malvado, perverso; de maldad; (unfortunate) aciago; de infortunio; (of spirits) diabólico, malo. *n* mal, *m;* maldad, perversidad, *f;* (misfortune) desgracia, *f.* **the E. one,** el Malo. **e.-doer,** malhechor (-ra). **e. eye,** mal de ojo, aojo, *m.* **e.-minded,** mal pensado; malintencionado. **e.-speaking,** maledicencia, calumnia, *f.* **e. spirit,** demonio, espíritu malo, *m*
evince *vt* evidenciar; mostrar
eviscerate *vt* destripar, desentrañar
evocation *n* evocación, *f*
evocative *a* evocador
evoke *vt* evocar
evolution *n* evolución, *f;* desarrollo, *m;* (*nav, mil*) maniobra, *f; math* extracción de una raíz, *f;* (revolution) revolución, vuelta, *f*
evolutionism *n* evolucionismo, *m*
evolutive *a* evolutivo
evolve *vi* evolucionar; desarrollarse. *vt* producir por evolución; desarrollar; pensar
ewe *n* oveja, *f.* **ewe lamb,** cordera, *f*
ewer *n* aguamanil, *m*
exacerbate *vt* exacerbar; agravar, empeorar
exacerbation *n* exacerbación, *f;* agravación, *f*
exact *a* exacto; fiel; metódico; estricto. *vt* exigir
exacting *a* exigente; severo, estricto; (hard) agotador, arduo
exaction *n* exigencia, *f;* extorsión, exacción, *f*
exactly *adv* exactamente; precisamente
exactness *n* exactitud, *f*
exaggerate *vt* exagerar; acentuar. *vi* exagerar
exaggerated *a* exagerado
exaggeration *n* exageración, *f*
exaggerator *n* exagerador (-ra)
exalt *vt* exaltar; enaltecer, elevar; (praise) glorificar, magnificar; (intensify) realzar; intensificar
exaltation *n* exaltación, elevación, *f;* alegría, *f,* júbilo, *m;* (ecstasy) éxtasis, arrobamiento, *m;* (of the Cross) exaltación, *f*
exalted *a* exaltado, eminente
exaltedness *n* exaltación, *f*
examination *n* examen, *m;* inspección, *f;* investigación, *f; law* interrogatorio, *m;* prueba, *f.* **to sit an e.,** examinarse. **written e.,** prueba escrita, *f*
examine *vt* examinar; inspeccionar; investigar; *law* interrogar; (search) reconocer; (by touch) tentar; observar; analizar. **to e. into,** examinar; considerar detenidamente; ahondar en
examinee *n* examinando (-da)
examiner *n* examinador (-ra); inspector (-ra)
examinership *n* cargo de examinador, *m*
examining *a* que examina; de examen; *law* interrogante
example *n* ejemplo, *m;* ilustración, *f;* (parallel) ejemplar, *m;* (warning) escarmiento, *m.* **for e.,** por ejemplo. **to set an e.,** dar ejemplo, dar el ejemplo.
exasperate *vt* exasperar, irritar; (increase) aumentar; (worsen) agravar
exasperating *a* exasperante, irritante, provocador
exasperation *n* exasperación, irritación, *f;* (worsening) agravación, *f;* enojo, *m*
excavate *vt* excavar; (hollow) vaciar
excavation *n* excavación, *f; arch* vaciado, *m*
excavator *n* excavador (-ra); (machine) excavadora, *f*
exceed *vt* exceder; (excel) superar, aventajar; (one's hopes, etc.) sobrepujar. *vi* excederse. **e. all expectations,** exceder a toda ponderación. **to e. one's rights,** abusar de sus derechos, ir demasiado lejos
exceedingly *adv* sumamente, extremadamente; sobre manera
excel *vt* aventajar, superar; vencer. *vi* sobresalir; distinguirse, señalarse; ser superior
excellence *n* excelencia, *f;* superioridad, *f;* perfección, *f;* mérito, *m;* buena calidad, *f*
excellency *n* (title) Excelencia, *f.* **Your E.,** Su Excelencia
excellent *a* excelente; superior; perfecto; magnífico; (in examinations) sobresaliente
excellently *adv* excelentemente; perfectamente; magníficamente
except *vt* exceptuar; omitir
except, excepting *prep* excepto, con excepción de; exceptuando; menos; salvo; fuera de. *conjunc* a menos que. **except for,** si no fuese por; con excepción de; fuera de
exception *n* excepción, *f;* objeción, protesta, *f.* **to make an e.,** hacer una excepción. **to take e. to,** protestar contra; tachar, criticar; desaprobar
exceptional *a* excepcional
excerpt *n* excerpta, *f,* extracto, *m, vt* extraer
excess *n* exceso, *m;* superabundancia, *f;* demasía, *f; com* superávit, *m.* **in e.,** en exceso, de sobra. **in e. of,** en exceso de; arriba de. **to e.,** excesivamente, demasiado. **e. fare,** suplemento, *m.* **e. luggage,** exceso de equipaje, *m;* (overweight) exceso de peso, *m*
excessive *a* excesivo; superabundante; inmoderado, desmesurado; exagerado
excessively *adv* excesivamente; exageradamente
excessiveness *n* exceso, *m;* superabundancia, *f;* exageración, *f*
exchange *n* cambio, trueque, *m;* (of prisoners) canje, *m;* (financial) cambio, *m;* (building) bolsa, lonja, *f;* (telephone) oficina central de teléfonos, *f. vt* cambiar (for, por); trocar; (replace) reemplazar; (prisoners) canjear; (of blows) darse; (pass from, into) pasar de . . . a. *vi* hacer un cambio. **in e. for,** en cambio de, a trueque de; por. **to e. greetings,** saludarse; cambiar saludos. **They exchanged looks,** Se miraron. **What is the rate of e.?** ¿Cuál es el tipo de cambio? **e. of prisoners,** canje de prisioneros, *m*
exchangeable *a* cambiable; trocable
exchequer *n* (public finance) Hacienda pública, *f;* tesorería, *f;* (funds) fondos, *m pl.* **Chancellor of the E.,** Ministro de Hacienda, *m*
excise *n* contribución indirecta, *f;* (customs and e.) Aduana, *f. vt* (cut) cortar, extirpar; imponer una contribución indirecta. **e. duty,** derecho de aduana, *m*
excise tax arbitrios, *m pl*
excision *n* excisión, *f;* extirpación, *f*
excitability *n* excitabilidad, *f*
excitable *a* excitable
excitation *n* excitación, *f*
excite *vt* emocionar; conmover; agitar; excitar; suscitar, provocar; incitar, instigar; (attention, interest) despertar; estimular. **to become excited,** emocionarse; exaltarse; (annoyed) acalorarse; (upset) agitarse
excitedly *adv* con emoción; acaloradamente; agitadamente
excitement *n* conmoción, *f;* agitación, *f, Central America* embullo *m;* (annoyance) acaloramiento, *m;* emoción, *f;*

estímulo, *m;* instigación, *f,* fomento, *m;* (amusement) placer, *m*
exciting *a* emocionante; conmovedor; agitador; muy interesante
exclaim *vt* and *vi* exclamar. **to e. against,** clamar contra
exclamation *n* exclamación, *f.* **e. mark,** punto de exclamación, *m*
exclamatory *a* exclamatorio
exclude *vt* excluir; exceptuar; evitar; (refuse) rechazar
exclusion *n* exclusión, *f;* exceptuación, *f;* eliminación, *f*
exclusive *a* exclusivo; (snobbish) exclusivista. **e. of,** no incluido; aparte de
exclusively *adv* exclusivamente; únicamente
exclusiveness *n* carácter exclusivo, *m*
exclusivism *n* exclusivismo, *m*
exclusivist *n* exclusivista, *mf*
excommunicate *vt* excomulgar. *a* excomulgado
excommunication *n* excomunión, *f*
excrement *n* excremento, *m*
excrescence *n* excrecencia, *f*
excrescent *a* que forma excrecencia; superfluo
excrete *vt* excretar
excretion *n* excreción, *f*
excretory *a* excretorio
excruciating *a* atormentador, angustioso; (of pain) agudísimo
excursion *n* excursión, *f;* expedición, *f;* (digression) digresión, *f.* **e. ticket,** billete de excursión, *m.* **e. train,** tren de excursionistas, *m*
excursionist *n* excursionista, *mf;* turista, *mf*
excusable *a* disculpable, excusable
excusably *adv* excusablemente
excuse *n* excusa, *f;* disculpa, *f;* pretexto, *m;* justificación, defensa, *f.* **to give as an e.,** pretextar
excuse *vt* disculpar, excusar; dispensar (de); librar (de); (forgive) perdonar; (defend) justificar, defender; (minimize) paiar; (oneself) disculparse. **E. me!** ¡Con permiso!; ¡Perdone Vd.!; ¡Dispense Vd.!
execrable *a* execrable, abominable
execrate *vt* execrar, abominar. *vi* maldecir
execration *n* execración, abominación, *f;* maldición, *f*
execute *vt* (perform) ejecutar, poner en efecto, realizar; (*art, mus*) ejecutar; (part in a play) hacer, desempeñar; (fulfil) cumplir; *law* otorgar (un documento); (kill) ajusticiar
execution *n* efectuación, realización, *f;* (*art, mus*) ejecución, *f;* (of part in a play) desempeño (de un papel), *m;* (fulfilment) cumplimiento, *m; law* otorgamiento (de un documento), *m;* (killing) suplicio, *m,* ejecución de la pena de muerte, *f;* (*law* seizure) ejecución, *f*
executioner *n* verdugo, *m*
executive *a* ejecutivo; administrativo. *n* poder ejecutivo, *m*
executor *n* administrador testamentario, *m*
executrix *n* administradora testamentaria, *f*
exegesis *n* exégesis, *f*
exegetical *a* exegético
exemplary *a* ejemplar
exemplification *n* ejemplificación, ilustración, demostración, *f*
exemplify *vt* ejemplificar; ilustrar, demostrar
exempt *vt* exentar, eximir; librar; dispensar, excusar. *a* exento; libre; excusado; inmune
exemption *n* exención, *f;* libertad, *f;* inmunidad, *f*
exercise *n* ejercicio, *m;* uso, *m;* (essay) ensayo, *m; pl* **exercises,** (on land or sea) maniobras, *f pl. vt* ejercer; usar, emplear; (train) ejercitar, entrenar; adiestrar; pasear, dar un paseo; (worry) preocupar. *vi* hacer ejercicio; ejercitarse; adiestrarse. **spiritual exercises,** ejercicios espirituales, *m pl.* **to take e. in the open air,** tomar ejercicio al aire libre. **to write an e.,** escribir un ejercicio. **e. book,** cuaderno de ejercicios, *m*
exert *vt* hacer uso de, emplear, ejercer, poner en juego; (deploy) desplegar. **to e. oneself,** hacer un esfuerzo (para); esforzarse (de); trabajar mucho; tratar (de); apurarse, tomarse mucha molestia; preocuparse
exertion *n* esfuerzo, *m;* uso, *m;* (exercise) ejercicio, *m;* (good offices) diligencias, gestiones, *f pl;* buenos oficios, *m pl*
exhalation *n* exhalación, *f;* efluvio, *m;* vapor, *m;* humo, *m*
exhale *vt* exhalar; emitir, despedir. *vi* evaporarse; disiparse
exhaust *vt* agotar; (empty) vaciar; (end) acabar; apurar; consumir; (tire) rendir, cansar mucho; (weaken) debilitar; (a subject) tratar detalladamente. *n mech* escape, *m;* emisión de vapor, *f;* vapor de escape, *m.* **e. pipe,** tubo de escape, *m*
exhaustible *a* agotable
exhausting *a* cansado, agotador
exhaustion *n* agotamiento, *m;* rendimiento, cansancio, *m;* lasitud, *f;* postración, *f*
exhaustive *a* completo; minucioso
exhaustively *adv* detenidamente; detalladamente; minuciosamente
exhaustiveness *n* lo completo; minuciosidad, *f*
exhibit *vt* exhibir; manifestar, ostentar; revelar, descubrir; presentar. *vi* exhibir, ser expositor. *n* objeto exhibido, *m; law* prueba, *f*
exhibition *n* exposición, *f;* (performance) función, *f;* espectáculo, *m;* exhibición, *f;* (showing) manifestación, *f;* (grant) bolsa de estudio, beca, *f*
exhibitionism *n* exhibicionismo, *m*
exhibitionist *n* exhibicionista, *mf*
exhibitor *n* expositor (-ra)
exhilarate *vt* alegrar, alborozar
exhilarating *a* alegre; estimulador; vigorizador, tonificante
exhilaration *n* alegría, *f,* alborozo, regocijo, *m*
exhort *vt* and *vi* exhortar
exhortation *n* exhortación, *f*
exhumation *n* exhumación, *f*
exhume *vt* exhumar
exigence *n* exigencia, *f;* urgencia, *f;* (need) necesidad, *f*
exigent *a* exigente; urgente
exiguous *a* exiguo
exiguousness *n* exigüidad, *f*
exile *n* destierro, *m;* (person) desterrado (-da), *Lat. Am.* exiliado (-da) *mf vt* desterrar, *Lat. Am.* exiliar
exist *vi* existir
existence *n* existencia, *f;* (being) ser, *m;* (life) vida, *f.* **to bring into e.,** causar; producir
existentialism *n* existencialismo, *m*
existing *a* existente
exit *n* salida, *f;* partida, *f;* (death) muerte, *f; theat* mutis, *m. vi theat* hacer mutis. **to make one's e.,** salir; marcharse; irse; morir; *theat* hacer mutis
exodus *n* éxodo, *m;* salida, *f;* emigración, *f;* (Old Testament) Éxodo, *m*
exonerate *vt* exonerar
exoneration *n* exoneración, *f*
exorbitance *n* exorbitancia, *f*
exorbitant *a* exorbitante
exorcism *n* exorcismo, *m*
exorcist *n* exorcista, *m*
exorcize *vt* exorcizar, conjurar
exotic *a* exótico. *n* planta exótica, *f; fig* flor de estufa, *f*
expand *vt* extender; abrir; (wings, etc.) desplegar; (the chest, etc.) expandir; dilatar; (amplify) ampliar; (an edition) ampliar, aumentar; (develop) desarrollar; *fig* ensanchar; (increase) aumentar. *vi* dilatarse; hincharse; abrirse; extenderse; *fig* ensancharse; (increase) aumentarse
expanse *n* extensión, *f*
expansibility *n phys* expansibilidad, *f;* dilatabilidad, *f*
expansible *a phys* expansible; dilatable
expansion *n* expansión, *f;* extensión, *f;* dilatación, *f;* (amplification) ampliación, *f;* (development) desarrollo, *m; fig* ensanchamiento, *m;* (increase) aumento, *m*
expansionism *n* expansionismo, *m*

expansive *a* expansivo; (of persons) efusivo, expresivo, comunicativo, afable
expansiveness *n* expansibilidad, *f*; (of persons) afabilidad, *f*
expatiate (upon) *vi* extenderse en
expatiation *n* discurso, *m*; digresión, *f*
expatriation *n* expatriación, *f*
expect *vt* esperar; (await) aguardar; (suppose) suponer; (demand) exigir; (count on) contar con. *vi* creer
expectance *n* expectación, *f*; esperanza, *f*
expectant *a* expectante; (hopeful) esperanzudo; (pregnant) embarazada
expectantly *adv* con expectación
expectation *n* expectación, *f*; (hope) esperanza, expectativa, *f*; probabilidad, *f*
expectorate *vt* expectorar. *vi* escupir
expectoration *n* expectoración, *f*
expedience *n* conveniencia, *f*; oportunidad, *f*; aptitud, *f*; (self-interest) egoísmo, *m*
expedient *a* conveniente; oportuno; apto; prudente; político. *n* expediente, recurso, medio, *m*
expedite *vt* acelerar; facilitar; (send off) despachar
expedition *n* expedición, *f*; (haste) celeridad, diligencia, *f*
expeditionary *a* expedicionario. **e. force,** fuerza expedicionaria, *f*
expeditious *a* expedito, pronto
expeditiously *adv* expeditamente, prontamente
expeditiousness *n* prontitud, *f*
expel *vt* expeler, expulsar; echar, arrojar; despedir
expend *vt* gastar, expender; (time) perder
expenditure *n* gasto, desembolso, *m*, *Lat. Am.* erogación *f*; (of time) pérdida, *f*
expense *n* gasto, *m*; pérdida, *f*; costa, *f*; *pl* **expenses,** expensas, *f pl*, gastos, *m pl*. **at the e. of,** a costa de. **to be put to great e.,** tener que gastar mucho. **to pay one's expenses,** pagar sus gastos
expensive *a* costoso; caro
expensively *adv* costosamente
expensiveness *n* lo costoso; costa, *f*
experience *n* experiencia, *f*. *vt* experimentar; sentir; sufrir. **by e.,** por experiencia
experienced *a* experimentado; experto; hábil; (lived) vivido
experiment *n* experimento, *m*; prueba, *f*; ensayo, *m*, tentativa, *f*, *vi* experimentar; hacer una prueba
experimental *a* experimental; tentativo
experimentally *adv* experimentalmente; por experiencia
expert *a* experto; perito; hábil; (finished) acabado. *n* experto, *m*, especialista, *mf*
expertly *adv* expertamente; hábilmente
expertness *n* pericia, *f*; maestría, *f*; habilidad, *f*; (knowledge) conocimiento, *m*
expiable *a* que se puede expiar
expiate *vt* expiar; reparar
expiation *n* expiación, *f*
expiatory *a* expiatorio
expiration *n* (breathing out) espiración, *f*; (ending) expiración, *f*; terminación, *f*; *com* vencimiento, *m*; (death) muerte, *f*
expiration date fecha de caducidad, *f*
expire *vi* (exhale) espirar; (die) morir, dar el último suspiro; (of fire, light) extinguirse; (end) expirar; terminar; *com* vencer
expiry *n* terminación, *f*; expiración, *f*; *com* vencimiento, *m*
explain *vt* explicar; aclarar; demostrar; exponer; (justify) justificar, defender. *vi* explicarse. **to e. away,** explicar; justificar
explainable *a* explicable
explanation *n* explicación, *f*; aclaración, *f*
explanatory *a* explicativo; aclaratorio
expletive *a* expletivo. *n* interjección, *f*
explicable *a* explicable
explicit *a* explícito
explode *vi* estallar; detonar; reventar. *vt* hacer estallar; (a mine) hacer saltar; (a belief, etc.) hacer abandonar; desechar
exploit *n* hazaña, proeza, *f*; aventura, *f*. *vt* explotar
exploitation *n* explotación, *f*
exploiter *n* explotador (-ra)
exploration *n* exploración, *f*
exploratory *a* exploratorio
explore *vt* explorar; examinar; averiguar; investigar; (*med surg*) explorar
explorer *n* explorador (-ra)
explosion *n* explosión, *f*; estallido, *m*, detonación, *f*
explosive *a* and *n* explosivo, *m*. **high e.,** explosivo violento, *m*. **explosives chamber,** recámara, *f*
explosiveness *n* propiedad explosiva, *f*; lo explosivo; violencia, *f*
exponent *a* and *n* exponente, *mf*
export *n* exportación, *f*, *vt* exportar. **e. licence,** permiso de exportación, *m*. **e. trade,** comercio de exportación, *m*
exportation *n* exportación, *f*
exporter *n* exportador (-ra)
expose *vt* exponer; arriesgar; (exhibit) exhibir, (unmask) desenmascarar; descubrir; revelar; *phot* exponer; (ridicule) ridiculizar
exposed *a* descubierto; no abrigado; expuesto, peligroso
exposition *n* explicación, interpretación, *f*; declaración, *f*; (exhibition) exposición, *f*
expostulate *vi* protestar, **to e. with,** reprochar; reconvenir
expostulation *n* protesta, *f*; reconvención, *f*
exposure *n* exposición, *f*; (aspect) orientación, *f*; (scandal) revelación, *f*, escándalo, *m*; peligro, *m*; exposición al frío or al calor, *f*
expound *vt* exponer, explicar; comentar
expounder *n* intérprete, *mf*; comentador (-ra)
express *a* (clear) categórico, explícito, claro; expreso; (exact) exacto; (quick) rápido. *n* (messenger, post) expreso, *m*; (train) (tren) expreso, (tren) rápido, *m*; (goods) exprés, *m*. *vt* expresar; (a letter, etc.) mandar por expreso
expressible *a* decible
expression *n* expresión, *f*
expressionless *a* sin expresión
expressive *a* expresivo; que expresa
expropriate *vt* expropiar
expropriation *n* expropiación, *f*
expulsion *n* expulsión, *f*
expunge *vt* borrar; testar; omitir
expunging *n* borradura, *f*; testación, *f*; omisión, *f*
expurgate *vt* expurgar
expurgation *n* expurgación, *f*
expurgator *n* expurgador, *m*
expurgatory *a* expurgatorio
exquisite *a* exquisito, precioso, primoroso; excelente; (acute) agudo, intenso; (keen) vivo. *n* elegante, petimetre, *m*
exquisitely *adv* primorosamente, pulcramente; a la perfección
exquisiteness *n* primor. *m*; pulcritud, perfección, *f*; excelencia, *f*; (of pain) intensidad, *f*; (keenness) viveza, *f*
ex-serviceman *n* excombatiente, antiguo soldado, *m*
extant *a* estante; existente; viviente
extempore *a* improvisado
extemporize *vt* and *vi* improvisar
extend *vt* extender; (hold out) tender, alargar; (lengthen) prolongar; (a period of time) prorrogar, diferir; (make larger) ensanchar; (increase) aumentar; dilatar; ampliar; (offer) ofrecer; *vi* extenderse; dilatarse; continuar; (give) dar de sí, estirarse; (last) prolongarse, durar; (become known) propagarse
extensible *a* extensible
extension *n* extensión, *f*; expansión, *f*; (increase) aumento, *m*; prolongación, *f*; ampliación, *f*; *com* prórroga, *f*; (telephone number) extensión, *f*, interno, *m*

extension cord *n* cordón de extensión, *m*; ladrón *m*, (Mexico; slang)
extensive *a* extenso, ancho, vasto; grande, considerable; (comprehensive) comprensivo
extensively *adv* extensamente; generalmente
extensiveness *n* extensión, *f*; amplitud, *f*
extensor *n anat* extensor, *m*
extent *n* extensión, *f*; (degree) punto, *m*; (limit) límite, *m*. **to a great e.,** en gran parte; considerablemente. **to some e.,** hasta cierto punto. **to the full e.,** en toda su extensión; completamente. **to what e.?** ¿hasta qué punto?
extenuate *vt* atenuar, desminuir, mitigar, paliar
extenuating *a* atenuante
extenuation *n* atenuación, mitigación, *f*
exterior *a* exterior, externo; de fuera; (foreign) extranjero. *n* exterior, *m*; aspecto, *m*; forma, *f*
exterminate *vt* exterminar
extermination *n* exterminio, *m*
exterminator *n* exterminador (-ra)
exterminatory *a* exterminador
external *a* externo, exterior; (foreign) extranjero. *n pl* **externals,** apariencias, *f pl*; aspecto exterior, *m*; comportamiento, *m*
externally *adv* exteriormente
exterritorial *a* extraterritorial
exterritoriality *n* extraterritorialidad, *f*
extinct *a* extinto; (of light, fire) extinguido; suprimido
extinction *n* extinción, *f*
extinguish *vt* extinguir; apagar; *fig* eclipsar
extinguishable *a* apagable
extinguisher *n* apagador (-ra); (for fires) extintor, *m*; (snuffer) matacandelas, *m*
extinguishment *n* apagamiento, *m*; extinción, *f*; abolición, *f*; (destruction) aniquilamiento, *m*
extirpate *vt* extirpar
extirpation *n* extirpación, *f*
extol *vt* elogiar, encomiar, alabar; cantar
extoller *n* alabador (-ra)
extort *vt* arrancar, sacar por fuerza; exigir por amenazas
extortion *n* extorsión, *f*; exacción, *f*
extortionate *a* injusto; opresivo; (of price) exorbitante, excesivo
extra *a* and *adv* adicional; extraordinario; suplementario; (spare) de repuesto. *prefix* (in compounds) extra. *n* extra, *m*; suplemento, *m*; (of a paper) hoja extraordinaria, *f*; (actor) supernumerario (-ia). **e. charge,** gasto suplementario, *m*; (on the railway, etc.) suplemento, *m*. **e.-mural,** *a* de extramuros.
extract *vt* sacar; (*chem math*) extraer; extractar; (obtain) obtener. *n chem* extracto, *m*; (excerpt) cita, *f*
extraction *n* saca, *f*; extracción, *f*; obtención, *f*
extradite *vt* entregar por extradición
extradition *n* extradición, *f*
extraneous *a* extraño; (irrelevant) ajeno (a)
extraordinarily *adv* extraordinariamente, singularmente
extraordinariness *n* lo extraordinario; singularidad, *f*; (queerness) rareza, *f*
extraordinary *a* extraordinario; singular; (queer) raro, excéntrico; (incredible) increíble
extraterrestrial *a Lat. Am.* extraterrenal
extravagance *n* (in spending) prodigalidad, *f*, derroche, *m*; (of dress, speech) extravagancia, *f*; (foolishness) disparate, *m*; (luxury) lujo, *m*
extravagant *a* extravagante; (queer) extraño, raro; (wasteful) pródigo; (of persons) gastador, manirroto; (of price) exorbitante; excesivo
extravagantly *adv* extravagantemente; de un modo extraño; pródigamente; profusamente; excesivamente
extreme *a* extremo. *n* extremo, *m*. **in e.,** extremamente, en extremo, en sumo grado. **to carry to extremes,** llevar a extremos; **E. Unction,** Extremaunción, *f*
extremely *adv* sumamente; *inf* muy
extremism *n* extremismo, *m*
extremist *a* and *n* extremista, *mf*
extremity *n* extremidad, *f*; (point) punta, *f*; necesidad, *f*; *pl* **extremities,** *anat* extremidades, *f pl*; (measures) medidas extremas, *f pl*
extricate *vt* desenredar; librar; sacar
extrication *n* liberación, *f*
extrinsic *a* extrínseco
extrovert *n psy* extravertido, *m*
exuberance *n* exuberancia, *f*
exuberant *a* exuberante
exudation *n* exudación, *f*
exude *vt* exudar; rezumar; sudar. *vi* exudar; rezumarse
exult *vi* exultar; alegrarse
exultant *a* exultante, triunfante
exultantly *adv* con exultación; triunfalmente
exultation *n* exultación, *f*; triunfo, *m*
eye *n* ojo, *m*; (sight) vista, *f*; (look) mirada, *f*; atención, *f*; (opinion) opinión, *f*, juicio, *m*; (of a needle, of cheese) ojo, *m*; (of a hook) corcheta, *f*; *bot* yema, *f*; (of a potato) grillo, *m*. *vt* ojear; fijar los ojos en; examinar, mirar detenidamente. **bright eyes,** ojos vivos, *m pl*. **prominent eyes,** ojos saltones, *m pl*. **He couldn't keep his eyes off Mary,** Se le fueron los ojos tras María. **as far as the eye can reach,** hasta donde alcanza la vista. **before one's eyes,** a la vista de uno, ante los ojos de uno. **in my (etc.) eyes,** *fig* según creo yo, en mi opinión. **in the twinkling of an eye,** en un abrir y cerrar de ojos. **with an eye to,** pensando en. **with my own eyes,** con mis propios ojos. **with the naked eye,** con la simple vista. **to keep an eye on,** vigilar. **to make eyes at,** guiñar el ojo; mirar con ojos de enamorado. **to have one's eyes opened,** *fig* caérsele la venda. **eye-bath,** ojera, *f*. **eye-opener,** revelación, sorpresa, *f*. **eye-pencil,** pincel para las cejas, *m*. **eye-piece,** objetivo, ocular, *m*. **eye-shade,** visera, *f*. **eye-tooth,** colmillo, *m*. **eye-witness,** testigo ocular, testigo de vista, testigo presencial, *mf*
eyeball *n* globo ocular, *m*
eyebrow *n* ceja, *f*
eye care atención de la vista, *f*
eyed *a* que tiene ojos; (in compounds) de ojos . . ., con ojos . . .; con los ojos; (of a needle) con el ojo . . . **She is a blue-eyed child,** Es una niña de ojos azules
eyeglass *n* lente, *m*
eyelash *n* pestaña, *f*
eyeless *a* sin ojos
eyelet *n* ojete, *m*
eyelid *n* párpado, *m*
eyesight *n* vista, *f*
eyewash *n* colirio, *m*; *inf* camelo, *m*. **That's all e.!** ¡Eso es un camelo!
eyrie *n* nido (of any bird of prey), nido de águila (eagle's) *m*

F

f *n* (letter) efe, *f*; *mus* fa, *m*. **f sharp,** fa sostenido, *m*
fa *n mus* fa, *m*
fable *n* fábula, leyenda, historia, *f*, apólogo, cuento, *m*; (untruth) invención, mentira, *f*
fabled *a* celebrado, famoso
fabric *n* obra, fábrica, *f*; estructura, construcción, *f*; (making) manufactura, *f*; (cloth) tejido, paño, *m*; textura, *f*
fabricate *vt* fabricar, construir; (invent) fingir, inventar
fabrication *n* fabricación, manufactura, *f*; construcción, *f*; (lie) invención, ficción, *f*
fabulist *n* fabulista, *mf*

fabulous *a* fabuloso
façade *n* fachada, frente, *f*
face *n* superficie, *f*; (of persons) cara, *f*, rostro, *m*; (look) semblante, aire, *m*; (of coins) anverso, *m*; (grimace) mueca, *f*, gesto, *m*; (dial) esfera, *f*; (of gems) faceta, *f*; (of a wall) paramento, *m*; (front) fachada, frente, *f*; (effrontery) cara dura, *f*, descaro, *m*. **in the f. of,** ante; en presencia de. *mil* **Left f.!** ¡Izquierda! **on the f. of it,** juzgando por las apariencias. **to bring f. to f.,** confrontar (con). **to laugh in a person's f.,** reírse a la cara (de). **to make a f.,** hacer muecas. **to my f.,** en mi cara, en mis barbas. **to put a good f. on,** *fig* poner (or hacer) buena cara a. **to set one's f. against,** oponerse resueltamente a. **to straighten one's f.,** componer el semblante. **to throw in one's f.,** *fig* dar en rostro, dar en cara. **to wash one's f.,** lavarse la cara. **f. card,** figura (de la baraja), *f*. **f.-cloth,** paño para lavar la cara, *m*. **f. downward,** boca abajo. **f. lift,** operación estética facial, *f*. **f. of the waters,** faz de las aguas, *f*. **f. powder,** polvos de arroz, *m pl*. **f. to f.,** cara a cara, de persona a persona; frente a frente. **f. value,** significado literal, *m*; *com* valor nominal, *m*
face *vt* mirar hacia; confrontar, hacer cara (a); (of buildings, etc.) mirar a, caer a (or hacia); *fig* arrostrar, enfrentarse con; *sew* guarnecer, aforrar. *vi* estar orientado. **to f. the facts,** enfrentarse con la realidad. **to f. the music,** *fig* arrostrar las consecuencias. **to f. about,** volver la espalda; *mil* dar una vuelta, cambiar de frente. **to f. up to,** *fig* hacer cara a
faced *a* con cara . . . , de cara . . . ; *sew* forrado (de). **to be two-f.,** *fig* ser de dos haces
facer *n* puñetazo en la cara, *m*; *fig* dificultad insuperable, *f*, problema muy grande, *m*
facet *n* faceta, *f*
facetious *a* chancero, chistoso, jocoso
facetiousness *n* jocosidad, festividad, *f*
facial *a* facial. **f. expression,** expresión de la cara, *f*, semblante, *m*
facile *a* (frivolous) ligero (e.g., a deduction or inference)
facilitate *vt* facilitar
facilitation *n* facilitación, *f*
facility *n* facilidad, *f*; habilidad, destreza, *f*
facing *n sew* vuelta, *f*; (of a building) paramento, *m*; (of lumber) chapa *f*; encaramiento, *m*
facsimile *n* facsímile, *m*
fact *n* (event) hecho, suceso, *m*; (datum) dato, *m*; realidad, verdad, *f*. **as a matter of f.,** en realidad. **in f.,** en efecto, en realidad. **I know as a f.,** Tengo por cierto. **The f. is . . . ,** La verdad es (que) . . . **the f. that,** el hecho de que
fact-finding informador (e.g. **send s.b. on a fact-finding mission,** enviar a fulano en misión informadora)
faction *n* facción, *f*, partido, bando, *m*; (tumult) alboroto, *m*
factional *a* partidario
factious *a* faccioso, sedicioso
factiousness *n* espíritu de facción, *m*; rebeldía, *f*
factitious *a* falso; artificial
factor *n* (fact) factor, elemento, *m*; consideración, *f*; *math* factor, *m*; *com* agente, factor, *m*
factory *n* fábrica, manufactura, *f*; taller, *m*. **F. Act,** ley de trabajadores industriales, *f*. **f. hand,** operario (-ia)
factotum *n* factótum, *m*
factual *a* basado en hechos, objetivo
faculty *n* facultad, *f*; (talent) habilidad, *f*, talento, *m*; (university division) facultad, *f*; (teachers as a group) claustro de profesores, claustro, profesorado, *m*; (authorization) privilegio, *m*, autoridad, *f*
fad *n* capricho, *m*, chifladura, *f*, dengue, *m*
faddiness *n* manías, *f pl*, excentricidad, *f*
faddist *n* chiflado (-da)
faddy *a* caprichoso, dengoso, difícil, excéntrico
fade *vi* (of plants) marchitarse, secarse; (of color) palidecer, descolorarse; (vanish) disiparse, desaparecer; (of persons) desmejorarse; (of stains) salir. *vt* descolorar. **to f. away,** desvanecer; (of persons) consumirse. **f.-out,** *n* (cinema) desaparecimiento gradual, *m*
faded *a* (of plants) seco, marchito, mustio; (of colors) descolorado, pálido; (of people) desmejorado
fadeless *a* de colores resistentes; eterno, no olvidado; siempre joven
fading *a* que palidece; (of flowers) medio marchito; (of light) mortecino, pálido; decadente. *n* desaparecimiento, *m*, marchitez, *f*; decadencia, *f*
fag *n inf* pitillo, *m*. **f.-end,** fin, *m*; restos, *m pl*, sobras, *f pl*; (of a cigarette) colilla, *f*; (*offensive*) maricón. *vi* trabajar mucho. *vt* fatigar mucho; hacer trabajar.
faggot *n* haz (or gavilla) de leña, *f*
faience *n* fayenza, *f*
fail *vi* faltar; fracasar, malograrse; no tener éxito, salir mal; (of strength) decaer, acabarse; (be short of) carecer (de); *com* hacer bancarrota, suspender pagos. *vt* abandonar; (disappoint) decepcionar, engañar; (in exams) suspender. **Do not f. to see her,** No dejes de verla. **He failed to do his duty,** Faltó a su deber
fail *n* **without f.,** sin falta
failing *n* falta, *f*; (shortcoming) vicio, flaco, *m*, debilidad, *f*; malogro, fracaso, *m*; decadencia, *f*
failure *n* fracaso, *m*; falta de éxito, *f*; (in exams) suspensión, *f*; (of power) no funcionamiento, *m*; omisión, *f*, descuido, *m*; *com* quiebra, bancarrota, *f*; (decay) decadencia, *f*. **on f. of,** al fracasar; bajo pena de
fain *a* deseoso, muy contento. **He was f. to . . . ,** Se sintió obligado a . . . ; Quería
faint *a* débil; (dim) indistinto, vago, borroso; (of colors) pálido, desmayado; (weak) lánguido, desfallecido; (slight) superficial, rudimentario. *vi* perder el sentido, desmayarse. *n* desmayo, *m*. **to be f. with hunger,** estar muerto de hambre. **to cause to f.,** hacer desmayar. **f.-hearted,** pusilánime, medroso. **f.-heartedness,** pusilanimidad, *f*
faintly *adv* débilmente; en voz débil; indistintamente
faintness *n* languidez, debilidad, *f*; (swoon) desmayo, *m*; lo indistinto; lo borroso.
fair *n* feria, *f*; (sale) mercado, *m*; (exhibition) exposición, *f*
fair *a* (beautiful) hermoso, lindo, bello; (of hair) rubio; (of skin) blanco; (clear, fresh) limpio, claro; (good) bueno; (favorable) favorable, propicio, próspero; (of weather) despejado, sereno; (just) imparcial; (straightforward) honrado, recto, justo; (passable) regular, mediano; (of writing) legible; (proper) conveniente. *adv* honradamente; (politely) cortésmente; exactamente. **by f. means,** por medios honrados. **It's not f.!** ¡No hay derecho! **to become f.,** (of weather) serenarse. **to give a f. trial,** juzgar imparcialmente; dar una buena oportunidad; *law* procesar imparcialmente. **to make a f. copy,** poner en limpio. **f.-haired,** de pelo rubio, rubio. **f. one,** una beldad, *f*. **f. play,** *sport* juego limpio, *m*; proceder leal, *m*. **f.-skinned,** de tez blanca, rubio. **f.-weather,** buen tiempo, *m*, bonanza, *f*. **f.-weather friends,** amigos de los dias prósperos, *m pl*
fairing *n Brit* regalo de feria, *m*. **to give fairings,** feriar
fairly *adv* (justly) con imparcialidad; (moderately) bastante; totalmente, enteramente. **f. good,** bastante bueno; regular
fairness *n* belleza, hermosura, *f*; (of skin) blancura, *f*; (justness) imparcialidad, *f*; (reasonableness) justicia, equidad, *f*; (of hair) color rubio, oro, *m*
fairway *n naut* canalizo, paso, *m*; (golf) terreno sin obstáculos, *m*
fairy *n* hada, *f*, duende, *m*, *a* de hada, de duendes; *fig* delicado. **f.-gold,** tesoro de duendes, *m*; **f.-light,** lucecillo, *m*; luminaria, *f*. **f.-like,** aduendado, como una hada. **f.-ring,** círculo mágico, *m*. **f.-tale,** cuento de hadas, *m*; patraña, *f*, cuento de viejas, *m*
fairyland *n* país de las hadas, *m*
faith *n* fe, *f*; confianza, *f*; (doctrine) creencia, religión, filosofía, *f*; (honor) palabra, *f*. **in good f.,** de buena fe.

to break f., faltar a la palabra dada. **f.-healing,** curanderismo, *m*
faithful *a* fiel, leal; (accurate) exacto; (trustworthy) veraz. **the f.,** los creyentes
faithfully *adv* fielmente, lealmente; (accurately) con exactitud. **Yours f.,** Queda de Vd. su att. s.s.
faithfulness *n* fidelidad, lealtad, *f;* (accuracy) exactitud, *f*
faithless *a* infiel, desleal, pérfido.
faithlessness *n* infidelidad, deslealtad, traición, *f*
fake *vt* imitar, falsificar. *n* imitación, falsificación, *f.* **to f. up,** inventar
Falangist *a* and *n* falangista *mf*
falcon *n* halcón, *m.* **f. gentle,** *orn* neblí, *m*
falconry *n* cetrería, *f*
Falkland Islands, the *pl* las Malvinas, *fpl*
fall *n* caída, *f;* (of temperature, mercury) baja, *f;* (of water) salto de agua, *m,* catarata, cascada, *f;* (in value) depreciación, *f;* (in price and Stock Exchange) baja, *f;* (descent) bajada, *f;* (autumn) otoño, *m;* (declivity) declinación, *f,* declive, desnivel, *m;* (ruin) ruina, *f;* destrucción, *f;* (of night, etc.) caída (de la noche), *f;* (of snow) nevada, *f;* (of rain) golpe, *m;* (*theat* of curtain) caída, bajada, *f;* (surrender) capitulación, rendición, *f;* (of earth) desprendimiento de tierras, *m;* (of the tide) reflujo, *m*
fall *vi* caer; (of mercury, temperature) bajar; (collapse) desplomarse, hundirse, derrumbarse; (die) caer muerto; (descend) descender; (*theat* of the curtain) bajar, caer; (of a river into the sea, etc.) desembocar, desaguar; (of hair, draperies) caer; (decrease) disminuir; (of spirits) ponerse triste, sentirse deprimido; (sin) caer; (come upon) sobrevenir; (of dusk, etc.) caer, llegar; (strike, touch) tocar; (as a share) tocar en suerte; (as a duty, responsibility) tocar, corresponder; (of seasons) caer en; (of words from the lips) caer de (los labios); (say) decir, pronunciar palabras; (of exclamations) escaparse; (become) venir a ser; (happen) suceder; (be) ser. **fallen upon evil days,** venido a menos. **His face fell,** Puso una cara de desengaño. **Christmas falls on a Thursday this year,** Navidad cae en jueves este año. **to let f.,** dejar caer. **to f. a-** (followed by verb) empezar a. **He fell a-crying,** Empezó a llorar. **to f. again,** volver a caer, recaer. **to f. among,** caer entre. **to f. astern,** quedarse atrás. **to f. away,** (leave) abandonar, dejar; (grow thin) enflaquecer; marchitarse; (crumble) desmoronarse. **to f. back,** retroceder, volver hacia atrás. **to f. back upon,** recurrir a; *mil* replegarse hacia. **to f. backward,** caer de espaldas, caer hacia atrás. **to f. behind,** quedarse atrás. **to f. down,** venirse a tierra; venirse abajo, dar consigo en el suelo, caer. **to f. due,** vencer. **to f. flat,** caer de bruces; (be unsuccessful) no tener éxito. **to f. in,** caer en; (collapse) desplomarse; *mil* alinearse; (expire) vencer. **to f. into,** caer en. **to f. in with,** tropezar con; reunirse con, juntarse con; (agree) convenir en; **to f. off,** caer de; (of leaves, etc.) desprenderse de, separarse de; (abandon) abandonar; (diminish) disminuir. **to f. on,** caer de (e.g. **to f. on one's back,** caer de espaldas); (of seasons) caer en; (attack) echarse encima de, atacar. **to f. out,** (of a window, etc.) caer por; (happen) acontecer, suceder; (quarrel) pelearse, reñir; *mil* romper filas. **to f. out with,** reñir con. **to f. over,** volcar, caer; (stumble) tropezar con. **to f. short,** faltar; carecer, ser deficiente; (fail) malograrse, no llegar a sus expectaciones; (of shooting) errar el tiro. **to f. through,** caer por; (fail) malograrse, fracasar. **to f. to,** empezar a, ponerse a; (be incumbent on) tocar a, corresponder a; (attack) atacar. **to f. under,** caer debajo; caer bajo; sucumbir, perecer; (incur) incurrir en, merecer. **to f. upon,** (attack) caer sobre, acometer; acaecer, tener lugar; (be incumbent) tocar a
fallacious *a* falaz, engañoso, ilusorio
fallaciousness *n* falacia, *f,* engaño, *m*
fallacy *n* error, *m,* ilusión, *f*
fallen *a* caído; arruinado; degradado. **f. angel,** ángel caído, *m.* **f. woman,** perdida, mujer caída, *f*
fallibility *n* falibilidad, *f*
fallible *a* falible
falling *a* que cae, cayente. *n* caída, *f;* (of mercury, temperature) baja, *f;* (crumbling) desmoronamiento, *m;* (collapse) hundimiento, derrumbamiento, *m;* (of tide) reflujo, *m;* (of waterlevel) bajada, *f;* (in value) depreciación, *f;* (of prices and Stock Exchange) baja, *f;* (diminishment) disminución, *f;* (in level of earth) declinación, *f;* (*com* expiry) vencimiento, *m;* (*theat* of curtain) bajada, caída, *f.* **f. away,** (crumbling) desmoronamiento, *m;* desprendimiento de tierras, *m;* (desertion) deserción, *f,* abandono, *m.* **f. back,** retirada, *f,* retroceso, *m.* **f. down,** caída, *f;* derrumbamiento, *m.* **f. due,** vencimiento, *m.* **f. in,** hundimiento, *m;* (crumbling) desmoronamiento, *m.* **f. off,** caída de, *f;* (disappearance) desaparición, *f;* (diminution) disminución, *f;* (deterioration) deterioración, *f.* **f. out,** caída por, *f;* disensión, *f.* **f. short,** falta, *f;* carácter inferior, *m;* frustración, *f.* **f. star,** estrella fugaz, *f*
fallout caída radiactiva, llovizna radiactiva, precipitación radiactiva, *f*
fallow *a* (of color) leonado; *agr* barbechado; descuidado. *n* barbecho, *m.* *vt* barbechar. **to leave f.,** dejar en barbecho. **f. deer,** corzo (-za)
false *a* incorrecto, erróneo, equivocado; falso; (unfounded) infundado; (disloyal) infiel, traidor, desleal; (not real) postizo; artificial; de imitación; *mus* desafinado; (pretended) fingido; engañoso, mentiroso. **to play a person f.,** traicionar (a). **f. bottom,** fondo doble, *m;* **f. claim,** pretensión infundada, *f.* **f. door,** surtida, *f.* **f.-hearted,** pérfido, desleal. **f. teeth,** dientes postizos, *m pl,* dentadura postiza, *f*
falsehood *n* mentira, *f*
falseness *n* falsedad, *f;* (disloyalty) duplicidad, perfidia, traición, *f*
falsetto *n* falsete, *m,* voz de cabeza, *f*
falsification *n* falsificación, *f;* (of texts) corrupción, *f*
falsifier *n* falsificador (-ra)
falsify *vt* falsear, falsificar; (disappoint) defraudar, frustrar, contrariar
falter *vi* (physically) titubear; (of speech) balbucir, tartamudear; (of action) vacilar. **to f. out,** balbucir; hablar con voz entrecortada; decir con vacilación
faltering *a* titubeante; (of speech) entrecortado; vacilante. *n* temblor, *m;* vacilación, *f*
falteringly *adv* (of speech) balbuciente, en una voz temblorosa; con dificultad, vacilantemente
fame *n* fama, *f;* reputación, *f;* (renown) celebridad, *f,* renombre, *m.* **of ill f.,** de mala fama
famed *a* reputado; renombrado, célebre, famoso
familiar *a* íntimo, familiar; afable, amistoso; (ill-bred) insolente, demasiado familiar; (usual) corriente, usual, común; conocido. *n* amigo (-ga) íntimo (-ma); *ecc* familiar, *m;* demonio familiar, *m.* **to be f. with,** (a subject) estar versado en, conocer muy bien; (a person) tratar con familiaridad. **to become f. with,** acostumbrarse a; familiarizarse con; (a person) hacerse íntimo de
familiarity *n* intimidad, familiaridad, confianza, *f;* (friendliness) afabilidad, *f;* (over-familiarity) insolencia, demasiada familiaridad, *f;* (with a subject) conocimiento (de), *m,* experiencia (de), *f*
familiarize *vt* familiarizar, acostumbrar, habituar. *vr* familiarizarse
familiarly *adv* familiarmente; amistosamente
family *n* familia, *f;* (lineage) linaje, abolengo, *m;* (*bot zool*) familia, *f;* (of languages) grupo, *m.* *a* de familia; familiar; casero. **f. doctor,** médico de cabecera, *m.* **f. life,** vida de familia, *f;* hogar, *m.* **f. man,** padre de familia, *m.* **f. name,** apellido, *m.* **f. seat,** casa solar, *f.* **f. tree,** árbol genealógico, *m*
family quarrel disputa de familia, *f*
famine *n* hambre, *f;* carestía, escasez, *f*
famish *vt* matar de hambre. *vi* morirse de hambre

famished *a* hambriento
famous *a* famoso, célebre, renombrado; insigne, distinguido; *inf* excelente
famously *adv inf* muy bien, excelentemente
fan *n* abanico, *m*; *agr* aventador, *m*; *mech* ventilador, *m*; (on a windmill) volante, *m*; (amateur) aficionado (-da); (admirer) admirador (-ra); *arch* abanico, *m*. *vt* abanicar; *agr* aventar; ventilar. **fan oneself,** hacerse viento. **tap with a f.,** abanicazo, golpecito con el abanico, *m*. **f.-belt,** *mech* correa de transmisión del ventilador, *f*. **f.-light,** tragaluz, *m*. **f. maker** or **seller,** abaniquero (-ra). **f.-shaped,** en abanico, abanicado, en forma de abanico
fanatic *a* and *n* fanático (-ca)
fanaticism *n* fanatismo, *m*
fanaticize *vt* fanatizar
fancied *a* imaginario
fancier *n* aficionado (-da); (of animals) criador (-ra)
fanciful *a* romántico, caprichoso; fantástico
fancifulness *n* extravagancia, *f*; romanticismo, *m*
fancy *n* fantasía, imaginación, *f*; (idea) idea, *f*, ensueño, *m*; (caprice) capricho, antojo, *m*; (liking) afecto, cariño, *m*; gusto, *m*, afición, *f*; (wish) deseo, *m*; (fantasy) quimera, *f*, *a* imaginario; elegante, ornado; *com* de capricho, de fantasía; fantástico, extravagante. *vt* imaginar, figurarse; (like) gustar de; aficionarse a; antojarse. **I have a f. for . . . ,** Se me antoja. . . . **Just f.!** ¡Toma! ¡Quia! ¡Parece mentira! **to take a f. to,** (things) tomar afición a; (people) tomar cariño (a). **f.-dress,** disfraz, *m*. **f.-dress ball,** baile de trajes, *m*
fancy goods *n pl* artículos suntuarios *m pl*
fane *n* templo, *m*
fanfare *n* tocata de trompetas, *f*
fang *n* colmillo, *m*; raíz de un diente, *f*
fanged *a* que tiene colmillos; (of teeth) acolmillado
fangless *a* sin colmillos
fanner *n* abanicador (-ra); *agr* aventador, *m*
fanning *n* abaniqueo, *m*; *agr* avienta, *f*
fantastic *a* fantástico; extravagante
fantastically *adv* fantásticamente; extravagantemente
fantasy *n* imaginación, *f*; fantasía, quimera, visión, *f*; creación imaginativa, *f*
far *adv* lejos; a lo lejos; (much, greatly) mucho, en alto grado; (very) muy; (mostly) en gran parte. *a* lejano, distante; (farther) ulterior. **as far as,** tan lejos como; (up to, until) hasta; en cuanto, por lo que, según que. (e.g. **As far as we know,** Por lo que nosotros sepamos. **As far as we are concerned,** En cuanto a nosotros toca). **by far,** con mucho. **from far and near,** de todas partes. **from far off,** desde lejos. **He read far into the night,** Leyó hasta las altas horas de la noche. **how far?** ¿a qué distancia?; (to what extent) ¿hasta qué punto? ¿hasta dónde? **How far is it to . . . ?** ¿Qué distancia hay a . . . ? **in so far as,** en tanto que. **on the far side,** al lado opuesto; al otro extremo. **so far,** tan lejos; (till now) hasta ahora. **to go far,** ir lejos. **far away,** *a* distante, remoto, lejano; *fig* abstraído. *adv* muy lejos. **far beyond,** mucho más allá. **far-fetched,** increíble, improbable. **far-off,** *a* distante. *adv* a lo lejos, en lontananza. **far-reaching,** de gran alcance. **far-sighted,** sagaz, presciente, previsor. **far-sightedness,** sagacidad, previsión, *f*
farce *n* farsa, *f*. *vt cul* embutir, rellenar
farcical *a* burlesco, cómico, sainetesco; absurdo, grotesco, ridículo
fare *n* (price) pasaje, precio del billete, *m*; (traveler) viajero (-ra), pasajero (-ra); (food) comida, *f*. *vi* pasarlo (e.g. **to f. well,** pasarlo bien). **bill of f.,** menú, *m*. **full f.,** billete entero, *m*. **f. stage,** trayecto, *m*
farewell *n* despedida, *f*, adiós, *m*. *a* de despedida. *interj* ¡adiós! ¡quede Vd. con Dios! **to bid f. to,** despedirse de
farewell address *n* discurso de despedida *m*
farflung de gran alcance, extenso, vasto; (empire) dilatado
farina *n* harina (de cereales), *f*; *chem* fécula, *f*, almidón, *m*; *bot* polen, *m*
farm *n* granja, hacienda, quintería, finca, chacra, *f*, cortijo, *m*. *vt* cultivar, labrar (la tierra); (taxes) arrendar. *vi* ser granjero. **to f. out,** (taxes) dar en arriendo. **f. girl,** labradora, *f*. **f. house,** alquería, casa de labranza, granja, *f*. **f. laborer,** labriego, peón, *m*. **f. yard,** corral de una granja, *m*
farmer *n* granjero, hacendado, quintero, *m*, agrícola, *mf*; (small) colono, labrador, *m*; (of taxes) arrendatario, *m*
farmers' movement *Mexico* agrarismo *m*
farmhand gañán, mozo, mozo de granja, peón *m*
farming *n* labranza, *f*, cultivo, *m*; agricultura, labor agrícola, *f*; (of taxes) arriendo, *m*. *a* de labranza, labradoril; agrícola
faro *n* (card game) faraón, *m*
farouche *a* huraño, esquivo
farrago *n* fárrago, *m*, mezcla, *f*
farrier *n* herrador, *m*
farther *adv* más lejos; (beyond) más adelante; (besides) además. *a* ulterior; más distante. **at the f. end,** al otro extremo; en el fondo. **f. on,** más adelante; más allá
farthest *adv* más lejos. *a* más lejano, más distante; extremo
farthing *n* cuarto, *m*; *fig* ardite, maravedí, *m*. **He hasn't a brass f.,** No tiene dos maravedís
fasces *n pl* fasces, *f pl*
fascinate *vt* fascinar; encantar, hechizar, seducir
fascinating *a* fascinador; encantador, seduciente
fascination *n* fascinación, *f*; encanto, hechizo, *m*
Fascism *n* fascismo, *m*
Fascist *a* and *n* fascista *mf*
fashion *n* (form) forma, hechura, *f*; (way) modo, *m*; (custom) costumbre, *f*, uso, *m*; (vogue) moda, *f*; (high life) alta sociedad, *f*; (tone) buen tono, *m*. *vt* hacer, labrar; inventar. **in Spanish f.,** a la española, al uso de España. **the latest f.,** la última moda. **to be in f.,** estar de moda. **to go out of f.,** dejar de ser de moda, perder la popularidad. **f. book,** revista de modas, *f*. **f. plate,** figurín, *m*
fashionable *a* de moda; elegante; de buen tono. **to be f.,** estar en boga, ser de moda. **f. world,** mundo elegante, mundo de sociedad, *m*
fashionableness *n* buen tono, *m*; elegancia, *f*
fashionably *adv* a la moda, elegantemente
fashion show desfile de modas, *m*, exhibición de modas, *f*
fast *a* (firm) firme; (secure) seguro; (strong) fuerte; (fixed) fijo; (closed) cerrado; (of boats) amarrado; (tight) apretado; (of colors) estable; (of trains) rápido; (of sleep) profundo; (of friends) leal, seguro; (quick) rápido, veloz; (of a watch) adelantado; (dissipated) disoluto. *adv* firmemente, seguramente; (quickly) rápidamente; (of sleep) profundamente; (tightly) estrechamente, apretadamente; (of rain) (llover) a cántaros; (ceaselessly) continuamente; (often) frecuentemente; (entirely) completamente. **to be f.,** (clocks) adelantar. **to make f.,** *naut* amarrar, trincar. **f. asleep,** profundamente dormido. **f. color,** color estable, color sólido, *m*
fast *n* ayuno, *m*, *vi* ayunar. **to break one's f.,** romper el ayuno. **f.-day,** día de ayuno, día de vigilia, *m*
fasten *vt* (tie) atar; (fix) fijar; sujetar; (stick) pegar; (a door) cerrar; (bolt) echar el cerrojo; *naut* trincar; (together) juntar, unir; (with buttons, hooks, etc.) abrochar; (on, upon) fijar en; *fig* imputar (a). *vi* fijarse; pegarse; (upon) agarrarse a, asir. **to f. one's eyes on,** fijar los ojos en. **to f. up,** cerrar; atar; (nail) clavar
fastener *n* (bolt) pasador, *m*; (for bags, jewelery, etc.) cierre, *m*; (buckle) hebilla, *f*; (of a coat, etc.) tiador, *m*; (of a book, file) sujetador, *m*; (lock) cerrojo, *m*. **paper-f.,** sujetador de papeles, *m*. **patent-f.,** botón automático, *m*
fastening *n* atadura, *f*; sujeción, *f*, afianzamiento, *m*; (together) union, *f*; (of a garment) brochadura, *f*; (of a handbag) cierre, *m*

fastidious *a* dengoso, melindroso, desdeñoso; (sensitive) sensitivo, delicado; (critical) discerniente, crítico
fastidiously *adv* melindrosamente
fastidiousness *n* dengues, melindres, *m pl*, nimiedad, *f*, desdén, *m*; sensibilidad, delicadeza, *f*; sentido crítico, *m*
fasting *n* ayuno, *m*. *a* and *part* de ayuno; en ayunas
fastness *n* firmeza, solidez, *f*; (stronghold) fortaleza, *f*; (retreat) refugio, *m*; (speed) velocidad, rapidez, *f*; (dissipation) disipación, *f*, libertinaje, *m*
fat *a* (stout) gordo, grueso; mantecoso, graso, seboso; (greasy) grasiento; (rich) fértil, pingüe; (productive) lucrativo. *n* (stoutness) gordura, *f*; (for cooking) manteca, *f*; (lard) lardo, *m*; (of animal or meat) grasa, *f*; sebo, saín, *m*; *fig* riqueza, *f*; *fig* fertilidad, *f*. **to grow fat,** engordarse, ponerse grueso
fatal *a* fatal, mortal; funesto
fatalism *n* fatalismo, *m*
fatalist *n* fatalista, *mf*
fatalistic *a* fatalista
fatality *n* fatalidad, *f*; infortunio, *m*, calamidad, *f*; muerte, *f*
fatally *adv* mortalmente, fatalmente; inevitablemente
fate *n* destino, sino, hado, *m*, providencia, *f*; fortuna, suerte, *f*; destrucción, ruina, *f*; muerte, *f*. **the Three Fates,** las Parcas
fated *a* fatal, destinado; predestinado
fateful *a* decisivo, fatal; aciago, ominoso
father *n* padre, *m*. *vt* prohijar, adoptar; (on or upon) atribuir (a), imputar (a). **Eternal F.,** Padre Eterno, *m*. **Holy F.,** Padre Santo, *m*. **indulgent f.,** padre indulgente, padrazo, *m*. **Like f. like son,** De tal palo tal astilla. **f. confessor,** *ecc* director espiritual, *m*. **f.-in-law,** suegro, *m*
fatherhood *n* paternidad, *f*
fatherland *n* patria, madre patria, *f*
fatherless *a* sin padre, huérfano de padre
fatherliness *n* amor paternal, *m*; sentimiento paternal, *m*
fatherly *a* paternal, de padre
fathom *n naut* braza, *f*. *vt* sondear; *fig* profundizar, tantear; (a mystery) desentrañar
fathomless *a* insondable; *fig* incomprensible, impenetrable
fatigue *n* fatiga, *f*, cansancio, *m*; *mil* faena, *f*; *mech* pérdida de resistencia, *f*. *vt* fatigar, cansar. **to be fatigued,** estar cansado, cansarse, fatigarse. **f. party,** *mil* pelotón de castigo, *m*
fatiguing *a* fatigoso
fatness *n* (stoutness) gordura, carnosidad, *f*; grasa, *f*, gordo, *m*; (richness) fertilidad, *f*; lo lucrativo
fatten *vt* engordar; (animals) cebar, sainar; (land) abonar, fertilizar. *vi* ponerse grueso, echar carnes
fatty *a* untoso, grasiento; *chem* graso. **f. acid,** ácido graso, *m*. **f. degeneration,** degeneración grasienta, *f*
fatuity *n* fatuidad, necedad, *f*
fatuous *a* fatuo, necio, lelo
faucet *n* canilla, llave, *f*, grifo, *m*
fault *n* defecto, *m*, imperfección, *f*; (blame) culpa, *f*; (mistake) falta, *f*, error, *m*; (in cloth) canilla, barra, *f*; *geol* falla, quiebra, *f*; *elec* avería, *f*; *sport* falta, *f*, *vi sport* cometer una falta. **to a f.,** excesivamente. **to be at f.,** (to blame) tener la culpa; (mistaken) estar equivocado; (puzzled) estar perplejo; (of dogs) perder el rastro. **to find f.,** tachar, culpar, criticar. **Whose f. is it?** ¿Quién tiene la culpa?
faultfinder *n* criticón (-ona)
faultiness *n* defectuosidad, imperfección, *f*
faultless *a* sin faltas; perfecto, sin tacha; impecable
faulty *a* defectuoso, imperfecto
fauna *n* fauna, *f*
favor *n* favor, *m*; (protection) amistad, protección, *f*, amparo, *m*; (permission) permiso, *m*, licencia, *f*; (kindness) merced, gracia, *f*; (gift) obsequio, *m*; (favoritism) favoritismo, *m*, preferencia, *f*; (benefit) beneficio, *m*; (badge) colores, *m pl*; *com* grata, atenta, *f*. *vt* favorecer, apoyar; mirar con favor, mostrar parcialidad (hacia); (suit) favorecer; (be advantageous) ser propicio (a); (contribute to) contribuir a, ayudar; (resemble) parecerse (a). **Circumstances f. the idea,** Las circunstancias son propicias a la idea, Las circunstancias militan en pro de la idea. **I f. the teaching of modern languages,** Soy partidario de la enseñanza de lenguas vivas. **in f. of,** a favor de, en pro de. **in the f. of,** en el favor de. **out of f.,** fuera de favor; (not fashionable) fuera de moda. **to count on the f. of,** tener de su parte (a), contar con el apoyo de. **to do a f.,** hacer un favor. **to enjoy the f. of,** gozar del favor de. **to fall out of f.,** caer en desgracia; (go out of fashion) pasar de moda. **to grow in f.,** aumentar en favor
favorable *a* favorable; propicio, próspero
favorableness *n* lo favorable; lo propicio; benignidad, benevolencia, *f*
favored *a* favorecido; predilecto; (in compounds) parecido, encarado
favoring *a* favorecedor, propicio
favorite *a* favorito; predilecto, preferido. *n* favorito (-ta). **court f.,** valido, privado, *m*; (mistress) querida (de un rey), *f*; (lover) amante (de una reina), *m*. **to be a f.,** ser favorito
favoritism *n* favoritismo, *m*
fawn *n zool* cervato, *m*; (color) color de cervato, color de ante, *m*. *a* de color de cervato, anteado, pardo; (of animals) rucio, pardo. *vt* and *vi* parir la cierva. *vi* acariciar; (on, upon) adular, lisonjear
fawning *n* adulación, *Lat. Am.* adulonería *f*, *a* adulador, lisonjero, *Lat. Am. also* incondicional, *Mexico* lambioche
fear *n* miedo, temor, *m*, *Argentina* canillera *f*; (apprehension) ansiedad, aprensión, *f*, recelo, *m*; (respect) veneración, *f*. *vt* temer; recelar; (respect) reverenciar. *vi* tener miedo; estar receloso, estar con cuidado. **for f. of,** por miedo de. **for f. that,** por temor de que, por miedo de que. **from f.,** por miedo. **There is no f. of . . .,** No hay miedo de (que) . . .
fearer *n* temedor (-ra), el (la) que teme
fearful *a* miedoso, aprensivo, receloso; (cowardly) tímido, pusilánime; (terrible) horrible, espantoso, pavoroso; *inf* tremendo, enorme
fearfully *adv* con miedo; tímidamente; (terribly) horriblemente; *inf* enormemente
fearfulness *n* temor, miedo, *m*; (horribleness) lo horrible
fearless *a* sin miedo, intrépido, audaz
fearlessness *n* intrepidez, valentía, *f*
fearsome *a* temible, horrible, espantoso
feasibility *n* practicabilidad, posibilidad, *f*
feasible *a* factible, hacedero, practicable, ejecutable
feast *n ecc* fiesta, *f*; banquete, *m*; *fig* abundancia, *f*, *vi* regalarse. *vt* festejar, agasajar; (delight) recrear, deleitar. **immovable f.,** *ecc* fiesta fija, *f*. **movable f.,** fiesta movible, *f*. **f. day,** día de fiesta, *m*, festividad, *f*
feasting *n* banquetes, *m pl*; fiestas, *f pl*
feat *n* hazaña, proeza, *f*, hecho, *m*
feather *n* pluma, *f*; (of the tail) pena, *f*; *pl* **feathers,** plumaje, *m*; plumas, *f pl*. *vt* emplumar; adornar con plumas; (rowing) poner casi horizontal la pala del remo. **to f. one's nest,** *inf* hacer su agosto. **f.-bed,** plumón, colchón de plumas, *m*. **f.-brained,** casquivano, alocado, aturdido. **f.-duster,** plumero, *m*. **f.-stitch,** *sew* diente de perro, *m*. **f. weight,** (boxing) peso pluma, *m*
feathered *a* plumado, plumoso; adornado con plumas; (winged) alado
feathery *a* plumoso; como plumas
feature *n* rasgo, *m*, característica, *f*; (cinema) número de programa, *m*; *pl* **features** (of the face) facciones, *f pl*. *vt* dar importancia (a); (cinema) presentar. **f. film,** documentaria, *f*
febrile *a* febril
February *n* febrero, *m*
fecal *a* fecal
feces *n* heces, *f pl*; excremento, *m*
fecund *a* fecundo, fértil

fecundate *vt* fecundar
fecundity *n* fecundidad, fertilidad, *f*
federal *a* federal, federalista
federalism *n* federalismo, *m*
federalist *n* federalista, federal, *mf*
federate *vt* confederar. *vi* confederarse. *a* confederado
federation *n* confederación, federación, *f;* liga, unión, asociación, *f*
fed up *a Argentina, Chile* incomódo
fee *n* (feudal law) feudo, *m;* (homage) homenaje, *m;* (duty) derecho, *m;* (professional) honorario, estipendio, *m;* (to a servant) gratificación, *f;* (entrance, university, etc.) cuota, *f;* (payment) paga, *f*
feeble *a* débil; lánguido; enfermizo; (of light, etc.) tenue; *fig* flojo. **to grow f.,** debilitarse; disminuir. **f.-minded,** anormal
feebleness *n* debilidad, *f; fig* flojedad, *f*
feebly *adv* débilmente; lánguidamente
feed *n* alimento, *m;* (meal) comida, *f;* (of animals) pienso, forraje, *m; mech* alimentación, *f. vt* alimentar; dar de comer (a); (animals) cebar; *mech* alimentar; mantener; *fig* nutrir. *vi* comer, alimentarse; (graze) pastar. **to be fed up,** *inf* estar hasta la coronilla, estar harto. **to f. on,** alimentarse de; *fig* nutrirse de. **f. pipe,** tubo de alimentación, *m*
feedback retrocomunicación, *f*
feeder *n* el, *m,* (*f,* la) que da de comer a; (eater) comedor (-ra); (of a river) tributario, afluente, *m;* (bib) babero, *m; mech* alimentador, *m;* (cup for invalids) pistero, *m*
feeding *n* alimentación, *f, a* alimenticio, de alimentación. **f.-bottle,** biberón, *m.* **f.-cup,** pistero, *m.* **f.-trough,** pesebre, *m*
feel *n* (touch) tacto, *m;* (feeling) sensación, *f;* (instinct) instinto, *m,* percepción innata, *f*
feel *vt* (touch) tocar, tentar, palpar; (experience) sentir, experimentar; (understand) comprender; (believe) creer; (be conscious of) estar consciente de; (the pulse) tomar; examinar. *vi* sentir, ser sensible; sentirse, encontrarse; (to the touch) ser . . . al tacto, estar. **How do you f.?** ¿Cómo se siente Vd.? **I f. cold,** Tengo frío. **I f. for you,** Lo siento en el alma; Estoy muy consciente de ello. **I f. strongly that . . .,** Estoy convencido de que . . . **I f. that it is a difficult question,** Me parece una cuestión difícil. **It feels like rain,** Creo que va a llover. **to f. at home,** sentirse a sus anchas, sentirse como en su casa. **to f. hungry (thirsty),** tener hambre (sed). **to f. one's way,** andar a tientas; *fig* medir el terreno. **to f. soft,** ser blando al tacto. **to make itself felt,** hacerse sentir. **Your hands f. cold,** Tus manos están frías
feeler *n* (of insects) palpo, *m,* antena, *f;* tentáculo, *m; fig* tentativa, *f,* balón de ensayo, *m*
feeling *n* (touch) tacto, *m;* (sensation) sensación, *f;* (sentiment) sentimiento, *m;* emoción, *f;* (premonition) corazonada, intuición, premonición, *f;* (tenderness) ternura, *f;* (perception) sensibilidad, percepción, *f;* (passion) pasión, *f;* (belief) opinión, *f,* sentir, *m. a* sensible; tierno; (compassionate) compasivo; apasionado; (moving) conmovedor
feelingly *adv* con emoción; (strongly) enérgicamente, vivamente; (understandingly) comprensivamente
feign *vt* fingir; (invent) inventar, imaginar; simular; (allege) pretextar; (dissemble) disimular. *vi* disimular
feint *n* artificio, engaño, *m;* (in fencing) treta, finta, *f. vi* hacer finta
feldspar *n min* feldespato, *m*
felicitate *vt* felicitar, congratular, dar el parabién (a)
felicitation *n* felicitación, *f,* parabién, *m*
felicitous *a* feliz, dichoso, afortunado; (of phrases, etc.) feliz, acertado; oportuno
felicity *n* felicidad, dicha, *f*
feline *a* felino, gatuno, de gato. *n* felino, *m*
fell *n* (skin) piel, *f;* (upland) altura, cuesta de montaña, *f. a* cruel, feroz; (unhappy) aciago, funesto. *vt* talar, cortar; (knock down) derribar; *sew* sobrecoser
feller *n* talador, leñador, *m*
felling *n* corta, tala, *f*
fellow *n* compañero (-ra); (equal) igual, *mf;* (in crime) cómplice, *mf;* (man) hombre, *m;* (boy, youth) chico, *m;* (colleague) colega, *m;* (of a society) miembro, *m;* (of a pair of objects) pareja, *f; inf* tipo, chico, *m.* **He's a good f.,** Es un buen chico. **How are you, old f.?** ¡Hombre! ¿Cómo estás? **f.-citizen,** conciudadano (-na). **f.-countryman,** compatriota, *m;* paisano (-na). **f.-creature,** semejante, *mf* **f.-feeling,** simpatía, comprensión mutua, *f.* **f.-member,** compañero (-ra); colega, *m.* **f.-passenger,** compañero (-ra) de viaje. **f.-prisoner,** compañero (-ra) de prisión. **f.-student,** condiscípulo (-la). **f.-worker,** compañero (-ra) de trabajo; (collaborator) colaborador (-ra); (colleague) colega, *m*
fellowship *n* coparticipación, *f;* (companionship) compañerismo, *m;* (brotherhood) comunidad, confraternidad, *f;* (society) asociación, *f;* (grant) beca, *f;* (of a university) colegiatura, *f*
felon *n* reo, criminal, *mf;* felón (-ona); malvado (-da); (swelling) panadizo, *m*
felonious *a* criminal; pérfido, traidor
felony *n* felonía, *f*
felt *n* fieltro, *m.* **a f. hat,** un sombrero de fieltro
female *n* hembra, *f, a* femenino. (**f.** is often rendered in Sp. by the feminine ending of the noun, e.g. **a f. cat,** una gata; **a f. friend,** una amiga.) **This is a f. animal,** Este animal es una hembra. **f. screw,** hembra de tornillo, tuerca, *f*
feminine *a* femenino; mujeril, afeminado. **in the f. gender,** en el género femenino
feminism *n* feminismo, *m*
feminist *n* feminista, *mf*
feministic *a* feminista
femur *n anat* fémur, *m*
fen *n* marjal, pantano, *m*
fence *n* cerca, *f;* (of stakes) estacada, palizada, *f;* (hedge) seto, *m;* (fencing) esgrima, *f; mech* guía, *f; inf* comprador (-ra) de efectos robados. *vi* esgrimir; *fig* defenderse; *inf* recibir efectos robados. *vt* cercar; estacar; *fig* defender; proteger. **to sit on the f.,** *fig* estar a ver venir
fencer *n* esgrimidor, *m*
fencing *n* esgrima, *f;* palizada, empalizada, *f.* **f. mask,** careta, *f.* **f. master,** maestro de esgrima, maestro de armas, *m.* **f. match,** asalto de esgrima, *m*
fencesitter bailarín de la cuerda flaja, *m*
fend (off) *vt* parar; defenderse de, guardarse de. *vi* (for) mantener, cuidar de. **to f. for oneself,** ganarse la vida; defenderse
fender *n* (round hearth) guardafuegos, *m; naut* espolón, *m,* defensas, *f pl; aut* parachoques, *m*
fennel *n bot* hinojo, *m*
ferment *n* fermento, *m;* fermentación, *f; fig* agitación, conmoción, efervescencia *f. vt* hacer fermentar; *fig* agitar, excitar. *vi* fermentar, estar en fermentación; *fig* hervirse, agitarse, excitarse
fermentation *n* fermentación, *f*
fern *n* helecho, *m*
ferny *a* cubierto de helechos
ferocious *a* feroz, bravo, salvaje
ferocity *n* ferocidad, braveza, fiereza, *f*
ferreous *a* férreo
ferret *n zool* hurón (-ona); **to f. out,** cazar con hurones; (discover) husmear, descubrir
Ferris wheel *n* estrella giratoria, gran rueda, novia, rueda de feria, *f*
ferroconcrete *n* hormigón armado, *m*
ferrous *a* ferroso
ferruginous *a* ferruginoso; aherrumbrado, rojizo
ferrule *n* herrete, regatón, *m,* contera, *f;* garrucha de tornillos, *f*
ferry *n* barca de transporte, *f;* barca de pasaje, *f,* transbordador, *m. vt* transportar de una a otra orilla, llevar en barca. *vi* cruzar un río en barca. **ferry across** *vt* transbordar. **F.-Command,** servicio de entrega y transporte de aeroplanos, *m*

ferryman *n* barquero, *m*
fertile *a* fértil, fecundo; (rich) pingüe; *fig* prolífico, abundante
Fertile Crescent, the el Creciente Fértil *m*
fertility *n* fertilidad, fecundidad, *f*
fertilization *n biol* fecundación, *f*; *agr* fertilización, *f*, abono, *m*
fertilize *vt biol* fecundar; *agr* fertilizar, abonar
fertilizer *n* abono, *m*
ferule *n* palmatoria, palmeta, férula, *f*
fervent *a* ardiente; fervoroso, intenso; (enthusiastic) entusiasta, apasionado
fervently *adv* con fervor, con vehemencia
fervor *n* ardor, fervor, *m*, pasión, *f*; (enthusiasm) entusiasmo, celo, *m*; vehemencia, *f*
festal *a* de fiesta; alegre, festivo, regocijado
fester *vi* ulcerarse, enconarse; *fig* inflamarse, amargarse. *vt* ulcerar
festival *a* de fiesta. *n* festividad, *f*; *ecc* fiesta, *f*; (musical, etc.) festival, *m*
festive *a* de fiesta; festivo, alegre
festivity *n* festividad, fiesta, *f*; (merriment) alegría, *f*, júbilo, *m*
festoon *n* festón, *m*, guirnalda, *f*. *vt* festonear
festschrift *n* libro de homenaje, libro jubilar, *m*
fetal *a* fetal
fetch *vt* traer; ir a buscar; ir por; llevar; (conduct) conducir; (of tears) hacer derramar lágrimas, hacer saltársele las lágrimas; (blood) hacer correr la sangre; (produce, draw) sacar; (a blow, a sigh) dar; (acquire) conseguir; (charm) fascinar; (of price) venderse por. **to go and f.,** ir a buscar. **to f. and carry,** *vt* (news) divulgar, publicar. *vi* estar ocupado en oficios humildes, trajinar. **to f. away,** llevarse; ir a buscar; venir a buscar. **to f. back,** devolver; (of persons) traer (a casa, etc.); traer otra vez. **to f. down,** bajar, llevar abajo; hacer bajar. **to f. in,** hacer entrar; (place inside) poner adentro; (persons and things) llevar adentro. **to f. out,** hacer salir; (bring out things) sacar; (put out) poner afuera; (an idea, etc.) sacar a relucir. **to f. up,** (a parcel, etc.) subir; (a person) hacer subir; llevar arriba
fete *n* fiesta, *f*
fetid *a* fétido, hediondo
fetidness *n* fetidez, *f*, hedor, *m*
fetish *n* fetiche, *m*
fetishism *n* fetichismo, *m*
fetter *n* grillete, *m*; *pl* **fetters,** grillos, *m pl*, cadenas, *f pl*; prisión, cárcel, *f*. *vt* encadenar, atar
fettle *n* condición, *f*, estado, *m*
fetus *n* feto, *m*
feud *n* enemistad, riña, *f*; (feudal law) feudo, *m*
feudal *a* feudal. **f. lord,** señor feudal, señor de horca y cuchillo, *m*
feudalism *n* feudalismo, *m*
feudatory *a* and *n* feudatario (-ia)
fever *n* fiebre, *f*; calentura, *f*; (enthusiasm) pasión, afición, *f*. **to be in a f.,** tener fiebre; (agitated) estar muy agitado. **to be in a f. to,** estar muy impaciente de. **puerperal f.,** fiebre puerperal, *f*. **tertian f.,** fiebre terciana, *f*. **yellow f.,** fiebre amarilla, *f*
feverish *a* febril; *fig* ardiente, febril, vehemente. **to grow f.,** empezar a tener fiebre, acalenturarse
feverishness *n* calentura, *f*; (impatience) impaciencia, *f*
few *a* and *n* pocos, *m pl*; pocas, *f pl*; algunos, *m pl*; algunas, *f pl*; (few in number) número pequeño (de), *m*. **a good f.,** bastantes, *mf pl*. **not a f.,** no pocos, *m pl*, (pocas, *f pl*). **the f.,** la minoría, *f*. **f. and far between,** raramente, en raras ocasiones; pocos y contados
fewer *a comp* menos. **The f. the better,** Cuantos menos mejor
fewest *a sup* (el) menos, *m*; el menor número (de), *m*; (el) menos posible de, *m*
fewness *n* corto número, *m*
fiancé(e) *n* novio (-ia); desposado (-da), prometido (-da)
fiasco *n* fiasco, mal éxito, fracaso, malogro, *m*
fiat *n* fiat, mandato, *m*, orden, *f*
fib *n* mentirilla, *f*, *Peru* bacho *m vt*, decir mentirillas, mentir
fibber *n* embustero (-ra), mentiroso (-sa)
fiber *n* fibra, *f*; filamento, *m*, hebra, *f*; (of grass, etc.) brizna, *f*; *fig* naturaleza, *f*
fibroid *a* fibroso. *n* fibroma, *m*
fibrous *a* fibroso
fibula *n anat* peroné, *m*
fichu *n* pañoleta, *f*, fichú, *m*
fickle *a* inconstante; mudable; (of persons) liviano, ligero, voluble
fickleness *n* inconstancia, *f*; mudanza, *f*; liviandad, ligereza, veleidad, volubilidad, *f*
fiction *n* ficción, *f*; invención, *f*; literatura narrativa, *f*; novelas, *f pl*. **legal f.,** ficción legal, ficción de derecho, *f*
fictitious *a* ficticio; imaginario; fingido
fictitiousness *n* carácter ficticio, *m*; falsedad, *f*
fiddle *n* violín, *m*. *vt* tocar . . . en el violín. *vi* tocar el violín; (fidget) jugar; perder el tiempo. **to play second f.,** tocar el segundo violín; *fig* ser plato de segunda mesa
fiddler *n* violinista, *mf*
fiddling *a* insignificante, trivial, frívolo
fidelity *n* fidelidad, *f*
fidget *vi* estar nervioso, estar inquieto; impacientarse; trajinar; (with) jugar con. *vt* molestar; impacientar
fidgetiness *n* inquietud, nerviosidad, *f*
fidgety *a* inquieto, nervioso. **to be f.,** tener hormiguillo
fiduciary *a* fiduciario. *n* fideicomisario (-ia)
fief *n* feudo, *m*
field *n* campo, *m*; (meadow) prado, *m*, pradera, *f*; (sown field) sembrado, *m*; (*phys, her*) campo, *m*; (of ice) banco, *m*; *min* yacimiento, *m*; (background) fondo, *m*; (campaign) campaña, *f*; (battle) batalla, lucha, *f*; (space) espacio, *m*; (of knowledge, etc.) especialidad, esfera, *f*; (hunting) caza, *f*; *sport* campo, *m*; (competitors) todos los competidores en una carrera, etc.; (horses in a race) el campo. *a* campal, pradeño; de campo; de los campos. *vt sport* parar y devolver la pelota. **in the f.,** *mil* en el campo de batalla, en campaña. **magnetic f.,** campo magnético, *m*. **to take the f.,** entrar en campaña. **f.-artillery,** artillería ligera, artillería montada, *f*. **f.-day,** (holiday) día de asueto, *m*; (day out) día en el campo, *m*; *mil* día de maniobras, *m*. **f.-glasses,** anteojos, gemelos, *m pl*. **f.-hospital,** hospital de sangre, *m*; ambulancia fija, *f*. **f.-kitchen,** cocina de campaña, *f*. **f.-marshal,** capitán general de ejército, *m*. **f.-mouse,** ratón silvestre, *m*. **f. of battle,** campo de batalla, *m*. **f. of vision,** campo visual, *m*. **f.-telegraph,** telégrafo de campaña, *m*
fielder *n* (baseball) jardinero (-ra)
field work prácticas de campo, *f pl*
fiend *n* diablo, demonio, *m*; malvado (-da); (addict) adicto (-ta). **morphia f.,** morfinómano (-ma)
fiendish *a* diabólico, infernal; malvado, cruel, malévolo
fiendishness *n* perversidad, crueldad, *f*
fierce *a* salvaje, feroz, cruel; (of the elements) violento, furioso; (intense) intenso, vehemente
fiercely *adv* ferozmente; violentamente, con furia; intensamente, con vehemencia
fierceness *n* ferocidad, fiereza, *f*; violencia, furia, *f*; intensidad, vehemencia, *f*
fieriness *n* ardor, *m*; (flames) las llamas, *f pl*; (redness) rojez, *f*; (irritability) ferocidad, irritabilidad, *f*; (vehemence) pasión, vehemencia, *f*; (of horses) fogosidad, *f*
fiery *a* ardiente; (red) rojo; (irritable) feroz, colérico, irritable; (vehement) apasionado, vehemente; (of horses) fogoso
fife *n mus* pífano, pito, *m*
fifteen *a* and *n* quince *m*.; (of age) quince años, *m pl*
fifteenth *a* and *n* décimoquinto *m*.; (part) quinzavo, *m*, décimoquinta parte, *f*; (of the month) (el) quince, *m*; (of monarchs) quince; *mus* quincena, *f*
fifth *a* quinto; (of monarchs) quinto; (of the month)

(el) cinco. *n* quinto, *m*; (part) quinto, *m*, quinta parte, *f*; *mus* quinta, *f*. **Charles V,** Carlos quinto. **f. column,** quinta columna, *f*

fifthly *adv* en quinto lugar

fiftieth *a* quincuagésimo; (part) quincuagésima parte, *f*, cincuentavo, *m*

fifty *a* and *n* cincuenta *m*.; (of age) cincuenta años, *m pl*

fiftyfold *a* and *adv* cincuenta veces

fig *n* higo, *m*; (tree) higuera, *f*; *fig* bledo, ardite, *m*. **green fig,** higo, *m*, breva, *f*. **I don't care a fig,** No se me da un higo. **to be not worth a fig,** no valer un ardite. **fig-leaf,** hoja de higuera, *f*; *fig* hoja de parra, *f*

fight *n* lucha, pelea, *f*, combate, *m*; batalla, *f*; (struggle) lucha, *f*; (quarrel) riña, pelea, *Argentina* arenga *f*; (conflict) conflicto, *m*; (valor) coraje, brío, *m*. **hand-to-hand** *f*, cachetina, *f*. **in fair f.,** en buena lid. **to have a f.,** tener una pelea. **to show f.,** mostrarse agresivo

fight *vt* luchar contra, batirse con; (a battle) dar (batalla); (oppose) oponer, *Mexico* desafiar; (defend) defender, pelear por; hacer batirse. *vi* luchar, batirse, pelear; (with words) disputar; (struggle) luchar; (make war) hacer la guerra; (in a tournament) tornear. **to f. one's way,** abrirse paso con las armas. **to f. against,** luchar contra. **to f. off,** librarse de; sacudirse. **to f. with,** luchar con; pelear con; reñir con

fighter *n* luchador (-ra); combatiente, *m*; guerrero, *m*; duelista, *m*; (boxer) boxeador, *m*; *aer* (avión de) caza, *m*. **night f.,** *aer* (avión de) caza nocturno, *m*. **f.-bomber,** *aer* caza bombardero, *m*. **F. Command,** *aer* servicio de aviones de caza, *m*

fighting *n* lucha, *f*, combate, *m*; el pelear; (boxing) boxeo, *m*, *a* combatiente; (bellicose) agresivo, belicoso. **f.-man,** combatiente, guerrero, *m*

figment *n* ficción, invención, *f*

figurative *a* figurado, metafórico; figurativo; simbólico

figuratively *adv* en sentido figurativo; metafóricamente

figure *n* figura, *f*; forma, *f*; (statue) estatua, figura, *f*; (of a person) silueta, *f*; talle, *m*; (number) cifra, *f*, número, *m*; (quantity) cantidad, *f*; (price) precio, *m*; *geom, gram, dance* (skating) figura, *f*; (appearance) presencia, *f*, aire, *m*; (picture) imagen, *m*; (on fabric) diseño, *m*; *mus* cifra, *f*; *pl* **figures,** aritmética, *f*, matemáticas, *f pl*. *vt* figurar; (imagine) figurarse, imaginar; *mus* cifrar. *vi* figurar, hacer un papel; (calculate) calcular, hacer cuentas. **to f. out,** calcular; (a problem, etc.) resolver. **a fine f. of a woman,** *inf* una real hembra. **lay f.,** maniquí, *m*. **to be good at figures,** estar fuerte en matemáticas. **to cut a f.,** *fig* hacer figura. **to have a good f.,** tener buen talle. **f. of speech,** figura retórica, figura de dicción *f*; (manner of speaking) metáfora *f*. **f. dance,** baile de figuras, *m*, contradanza, *f*. **f.-head,** *naut* mascarón, *m*, (or figura, *f*) de proa; *fig* figura decorativa, *f*

figured *a* estampado, con diseños, labrado

figurine *n* figurilla, *f*

filament *n* filamento, *m*; hebra, *f*

filbert *n* avellana, *f*; (tree) avellano, *m*

filch *vt* sisar, ratear

filching *n* sisa, *f*

file *n* (line) fila, hilera, sarta, línea, *f*; *mil* fila, *f*; (tool) lima, *f*; (rasp) escofina, *f*; (list) lista, *f*, catálogo, *m*; (for documents) carpeta, *f*, cartapacio, *m*; (bundle of papers) legajo, *m*; (for bills, letters, etc.) clasificador, *m*; archivo, *m*; (in an archives) expediente *m*. **in a f.,** en fila; en cola

file *vt* hacer marchar en fila; (smooth) limar; (literary work) pulir; (classify) clasificar; (note particulars) fichar; (keep) guardar; (a petition, etc.) presentar, registrar. *vi* marchar en fila. **to f. in,** entrar en fila. **to f. off,** desfilar. **to file a brief,** presentar un escrito. **to f. letters,** clasificar correspondencia. **to f. past,** *mil* desfilar

filial *a* filial

filiation *n* filiación, *f*

filibuster *n* filibustero, pirata, *m*

filigree *n* filigrana, *f*, *a* afiligranado

filing *n* (with a tool) limadura, *f*; clasificación, *f*; (of a petition, etc.) presentación, *f*, registro, *m*; *pl* **filings,** limaduras, *f pl*, retales, *m pl*. **f.-cabinet,** fichero, *m*. **f.-card,** ficha, *f*

fill *vt* llenar; (stuff) rellenar; (appoint to a post) proveer; (occupy a post) desempeñar; (imbue) henchir; (saturate) saturar; (occupy) ocupar; (a tooth) empastar, *Argentina* emplomar; (fulfil) cumplir; (charge, fuel) cargar; (with food) hartar. *vi* llenarse. **fill an order,** servir un pedido. **fill a prescription,** surtir una receta. **to f. the chair,** ocupar la presidencia; (university) ocupar la cátedra. **to f. the place of,** ocupar el lugar de; substituir; suplir. **It will be difficult to find someone to f. his place,** Será difícil de encontrar uno que haga lo que hizo él. **to f. to the brim,** llenar hasta los bordes. **to f. in, f. out,** (a form) llenar (or completar) (una hoja); (insert) insertar, añadir; (a hollow) terraplenar. **to f. out,** *vt* hinchar. *vi* hincharse; echar carnes; (of the face) redondearse. **to f. up,** colmar, llenar hasta los bordes; (an office) proveer; (block) macizar; (a form) completar, llenar

fillet *n* venda, cinta, *f*; (of meat or fish) filete, *m*; (of meat) solomillo, *m*; *arch* filete, *m*. *vt* atar con una venda o cinta; *cul* cortar en filetes

filling *n* envase, *m*; (swelling) henchimiento, *m*; (of a tooth) empastadura, *f*; (in or up, of forms, etc.) llenar, *m*. **f. station,** depósito de gasolina, *m*

fillip *n* capirotazo, *m*; (stimulus) estímulo, *m*; (trifle) bagatela, *f*. *vt* and *vi* dar un capirotazo (a); *vt* estimular, incitar

filly *n* jaca, potra, *f*

film *n* (on liquids) tela, *f*; membrana, *f*; (coating) capa ligera, *f*; (on eyes) tela, *f*; (cinema) película, cinta, *f*; *phot* película, *f*; *fig* velo, *m*; nube, *f*, *vi* cubrirse de un velo, etc. *vt* cubrir de un velo, etc.; filmar, fotografiar para el cine. **roll f.,** película fotográfica, *f*. **silent f.,** película muda, *f*. **talking f.,** película sonora, *f*. **to shoot a f.,** hacer una película. **to take part in a f.,** actuar, or tomar parte, en una película. **f. pack,** película en paquetes *f*. **f. star,** estrella de la pantalla (or del cine), *f*

film industry industria fílmica, *f*

filminess *n* transparencia, diafanidad, *f*

filmy *a* transparente, diáfano

filter *n* filtro, *m*. *vt* filtrar. *vi* infiltrarse; (*fig* of news) trascender, divulgarse. **f.-bed,** filtro, *m*. **f.-paper,** papel filtro, *m*

filth *n* inmundicia, suciedad, *f*; *fig* corrupción, *f*; *fig* obscenidad, *f*

filthiness *n* suciedad, *f*; escualidez, *f*; *fig* asquerosidad, *f*; *fig* obscenidad, *f*

filthy *a* inmundo, sucio; escuálido, *Argentina* cascarriento, *Central America* descacharrado; *fig* asqueroso; *fig* obsceno

filtrate *n* filtrado, *m*, *vt* filtrar

filtration *n* filtración, *f*

fin *n* (of fish) aleta, ala, *f*; (of whale) barba, *f*; *aer* aleta, *f*

final *a* último, final; (conclusive) conclusivo, decisivo, terminante. *n sport* finales, *m pl*; *univ* último examen, *m*. **f. blow,** *fig* golpe decisivo, *m*. **f. cause,** *phil* causa final, *f*

finale *n* final, *m*

finalist *n* finalista, *mf*

finality *n* finalidad, *f*; (decision) determinación, resolución, decisión, *f*

finally *adv* por fin, finalmente, por último, a la postre; (irrevocably) irrevocablemente

finance *n* hacienda pública, *f*, asuntos económicos, *m pl*; finanzas, *f pl*. *vt* financiar

financial *a* financiero, monetario. **f. year,** año económico, *m*

financially *adv* del punto de vista financiero

financier *n* financiero, *m*

find *vt* encontrar, hallar; (discover) descubrir, dar con; (invent) inventar, crear; (supply) facilitar, proporcionar; (provide) proveer; (instruct) instruir; *law* declarar. *vi law* fallar, dar sentencia. *n* hallazgo, *m*; descubrimiento, *m.* **I found him out a long time ago,** *fig* Hace tiempo que me di cuenta de cómo era él. **I found it possible to go out,** Me fue posible salir. **The judge found them guilty,** El juez les declaró culpables. **to f. a verdict,** *law* dar sentencia, fallar. **to f. one's way,** encontrar el camino. **to f. oneself,** hallarse, verse, encontrarse. **to f. out,** averiguar, descubrir. **to f. out about,** informarse sobre (or de)

finder *n* hallador (-ra); (inventor) inventor (-ra), descubridor (-ra); (telescope, camera) buscador, *m*

finding *n* hallazgo, *m*; (discovery) descubrimiento, *m*; *law* fallo, *m*, sentencia, *f*

fine *n* multa, *f*; (end) fin, *m*. **in f.,** en fin, en resumen

fine *vt* multar, cargar una multa de

fine *a* (thin) delgado; (sharp) agudo; (delicate) fino, delicado; (minute) menudo; (refined) refinado, puro; (healthy) saludable; (of weather) bueno; magnífico; (beautiful) hermoso, lindo; excelente; (perfect) perfecto; (good) bueno; elegante; (showy) ostentoso, vistoso; (handsome) guapo; (subtle) sutil; (acute) agudo; (noble) noble; (eminent, accomplished) distinguido, eminente; (polished) pulido; (affected) afectado; (clear) claro; (transparent) transparente, diáfano. *adv* muy bien. **a f. upstanding young man,** un buen mozo. **a f. upstanding young woman,** una real moza. **He's a f. fellow,** (ironically) Es una buena pieza. **That is all very f. but . . . ,** Todo eso está muy bien pero. . . . **to become f.,** (weather) mejorar

finely *adv* finamente; menudamente; elegantemente; (ironically) lindamente

fineness *n* (thinness) delgadez, *f*; (excellence) excelencia, *f*; delicadeza, *f*; (softness) suavidad, *f*; elegancia, *f*; (subtlety) sutileza, *f*; (acuteness) agudeza, *f*; (perfection) perfección, *f*; (nobility) nobleza, *f*; (beauty) hermosura, *f*

finery *n* galas, *f pl*, atavíos magníficos, *m pl*; adornos, *m pl*; primor, *m*, belleza, *f*

finesse *n* sutileza, diplomacia, *f*; estratagema, artificio, *m*; (cunning) astucia, *f*, *vi* valerse de estratagemas y artificios

finger *n* dedo, *m*; (of a clock, etc.) manecilla, *f*; (measurement) dedada, *f*; *fig* mano, *f*. *vt* manosear, tocar; (soil) ensuciar con los dedos; (steal) sisar; (*mus* a keyed instrument) teclear, (a stringed instrument) tocar. **first f.,** dedo indice, *m*. **fourth f.,** dedo anular, *m*. **little f.,** dedo meñique, *m*. **second f.,** dedo de en medio, dedo del corazón, *m*. **to burn one's fingers,** quemarse los dedos; *fig* cogerse los dedos. **to have at one's f.-tips,** *fig* saber al dedillo. **f.-board,** (of piano) teclado, *m*; (of stringed instruments) diapasón, *m*. **f.-bowl,** lavadedos, lavafrutas, *m*. **finger's breadth,** dedo, *m*. **f.-mark,** huella digital, *f*. **f.-nail,** uña del dedo, *f*. **f.-print,** impresión digital, *f*. **f.-stall,** dedil, *m*. **f.-tip,** punta del dedo, yema del dedo, *f*. **f.-wave,** peinado al agua, *m*

fingered *a* (in compounds) con dedos, que tiene los dedos . . .

fingering *n* (touching) manoseo, *m*; *mus* digitación, *f*; (*mus* the keys) tecleo, *m*; (wool) estambre, *m*

finial *n* pináculo, *m*

finicky *a* (of persons) dengoso, remilgado; (of things) nimio

finish *n* fin, *m*, conclusión, terminación, *f*; (final touch) última mano, *f*; perfección, *f*; (of an article) acabado, *m*; *sport* llegada, (*horse race*) meta, *f*. *vt* terminar, acabar, concluir; llevar a cabo, poner fin a; (perfect) perfeccionar; (put finishing touch to) dar la última mano a; (kill) matar; (exhaust) agotar, rendir; (overcome) vencer. *vi* acabar; concluirse. **to f. off,** acabar, terminar; (kill) matar, acabar con; (destroy) destruir. **to f. up,** acabar; (eat) comer; (drink) beber

finishable *a* acabable

finished *a* acabado, terminado, completo; perfecto; (careful) cuidadoso

finished goods *n pl* bienes terminados, *m pl*

finisher *n* terminador (-ra), acabador (-ra); pulidor (-ra); (final blow) golpe de gracia, *m*

finishing *a* concluyente. *n* terminación, *f*, fin, *m*; perfección, *f*; (last touch) última mano, *f*. **to put the f. touch,** dar la última pincelada

finite *a* finito

Finland Finlandia, *f*

Finn *n* finlandés (-esa)

Finnish *a* finlandés. *n* (language) finlandés, *m*

fir *n* abeto, sapino, pino, *m*. **red fir,** pino silvestre, *m*. **fir-cone,** piña de abeto, *f*. **fir grove,** abetal, *m*

fire *n* fuego, *m*; (conflagration) incendio, *m*; (on the hearth) lumbre, *f*, fuego, *m*; *fig* ardor, *m*, pasión, *f*; (shooting) fuego, tiro, *m*. **by f. and sword,** a sangre y fuego. **by the f.,** cerca del fuego; (in a house) al lado de la chimenea. **long-range f.,** *mil* fuego de largo alcance, *m*. **short-range f.,** *mil* fuego de corto alcance, *m*. **on f.,** en fuego, ardiendo, en llamas; *fig* impaciente; *fig* lleno de pasión. **to be between two fires,** *fig* estar entre dos aguas. **to make a f.,** encender un fuego. **to miss f.,** no dar en el blanco, errar el tiro. **to open f.,** *mil* hacer una descarga. **to set on f.,** prender fuego a, incendiar. **to take f.,** encenderse. **under f.,** bajo fuego. **f.-alarm,** alarma de incendios, *f*. **f.-arm,** arma de fuego, *f*. **f.-box,** hogar, *m*. **f.-brand,** tea, *f*. **f.-brigade,** cuerpo de bomberos, *m*. **f.-damp,** aire detonante, grisú, *m*, mofeta, *f*. **f.-dog,** morillo, *m*. **f.-drill,** (firefighters') instrucción de bomberos, *f*, (others') simulacro de incendio, *m*. **f.-engine,** autobomba, bomba, de incendios, *f*. **f.-escape,** escalera de incendios, *f*. **f.-extinguisher,** apagador de incendio, extintor, matafuego, *m*. **f.-guard,** vigilante de incendios, *m*; alambrera, *f*. **f.-hose,** manguera de incendios, *f*. **f.-insurance,** seguro contra incendios, *m*. **f.-irons,** badil *m*. y tenazas *f pl*. **f.-lighter,** encendedor, *m*. **f.-screen,** pantalla, *f*. **f.-ship,** brulote, *m*. **f.-shovel,** badil, *m*, paleta, *f*. **f.-spotter,** vigilante de incendios, *m*. **f.-sprite,** salamandra, *f*. **f.-watching,** servicio de vigilancia de incendios, *m*

fire *vt* incendiar, prender (or pegar) fuego a; quemar; (bricks) cocer; (fire-arms) disparar; (cauterize) cauterizar; (*fig* stimulate) estimular, excitar; (inspire) inspirar; (*inf* of questions) disparar; (*inf* sack) despedir. *vi* encenderse; (shoot) hacer fuego, disparar (un tiro); (*inf* away) disparar; (up) enojarse. **to f. a salute,** disparar un saludo. *mil* **F.!** ¡Fuego!

firecracker *n* buscapiés *m*

fire department *n* parque de bomberos, servicis de bomberos, servicio de incendios, parque de bombas (Puerto Rico), *m*

firefly *n* cocuyo, *m*

fireman *n* bombero, *m*; (of an engine, etc.) fogonero, *m*. **fireman's lift,** silleta, *f*

fireplace *n* chimenea francesa, chimenea, *f*, *Mexico* brasero *m*; (hearth) hogar, *m*

fireproof *a* a prueba de incendios; incombustible

firer *n* disparador, *m*

firewood *n* leña, *Lat. Am.* charamusca *f*. **f. dealer,** leñador (-ra), vendedor (-ra) de leña

firework *n* fuego artificial, *m*

firing *n* (of fire-arms) disparo, *m*; (burning) incendio, *m*, quema, *f*; (of bricks, etc.) cocimiento, *m*; (of pottery) cocción, *f*; (cauterization) cauterización, *f*; (fuel) combustible, *m*; (*inf* sacking) despedida, *f*. **within f. range,** a tiro. **f.-line,** línea de fuego, *f*. **f.-oven,** (pottery) horno alfarero, *m*. **f.-squad,** pelotón de ejecución, *m*

firm *a* firme; (strong) fuerte; (secure) seguro; sólido; (resolute) inflexible, resoluto; severo; (steady) constante; (persistent) tenaz. *n com* casa (de comercio), empresa, *f*; razón social, *f*

firmament *n* firmamento, *m*

firmly *adv* firmemente; inflexiblemente; constantemente

firmness *n* firmeza, *f*; solidez, *f*; inflexibilidad, resolución, *f*; severidad, *f*; constancia, *f*; tenacidad, *f*

first *a* primero (primer before *m sing* nouns); (of monarchs) primero; (of dates) (el) primero. *n* primero, *m*; (beginning) principio, *m*. *adv* primero, en primer lugar; (before, of time) antes; (for the first time) por primera vez; (at the beginning) al principio; (ahead) adelante. **at f.,** al principio. **from the very f.,** desde el primer momento. **to appear for the f. time,** aparecer (or presentarse) por primera vez; *theat* debutar. **to go f.,** ir delante de todos, ir a la cabeza; ir adelante. **f. and foremost,** en primer lugar; ante todo. **f.-aid,** primera cura, *f*. **f.-aid post,** casa de socorro, *f*. **f.-aider,** practicante, *m*. **f.-born,** *a* and *n* primogénito (-ta). **f.-class,** *a* de primera clase; *fig* excelente. **f.-cousin,** primo (-ma) carnal, primo (-ma) hermano (-na). **f. edition,** edición príncipe, *f*. **f. floor,** primer piso, *m*. **f. fruits,** frutos primerizos, *m pl*; *fig* primicias, *f pl*. **f.-hand,** *a* original, de primera mano. **f. letters,** primeras letras, *f pl*. **f. night,** *theat* estreno, *m*. **f. of all,** primero, ante todo. **f.-rate,** *a* de primera clase

firstly *adv* en primer lugar, primero

firth *n* ría, *f*

fiscal *a* and *n* fiscal *m*.. **f. year,** año económico, *m*

fish *n* pez, *m*; (out of the water) pescado, *m*; *inf* tipo, indivíduo, *m*. *vt* pescar; (out) sacar. *vi* pescar; *fig* buscar. **fried f.,** pescado frito, *m*. **He is a queer f.,** Es un tipo muy raro. **to be neither f. nor fowl,** no ser ni carne ni pescado. **to feel like a f. out of water,** sentirse fuera de su ambiente. **to f. in troubled waters,** A río revuelto ganancia de pescadores. **f.-eating,** *a* ictiófago. **f.-fork,** tenedor de pescado, *m*. **f.-glue,** cola de pescado, *f*. **f.-hook,** anzuelo, *m*. **f.-knife,** cuchillo de pescado, *m*. **f.-like,** de pez; como un pez, parecido a un pez. **f. roe,** hueva, *f*. **f.-server,** pala para pescado, *f*

fishbone *n* espina de pescado, raspa de pescado, *f*

fisherman *n* pescador, *m*

fishery *n* pesquería, *f*

fishing *n* pesca, *f*, *a* de pescar. **to go f.,** ir de pesca. **f.-boat,** bote de pesca, *m*. **f.-floats,** levas, *f pl*. **f.-line,** sedal, *m*. **f.-net,** red de pesca, *f*. **f.-reel,** carretel, carrete, *m*. **f.-rod,** caña de pescar, *f*. **f.-tackle,** aparejo de pesca, *m*. **f. village,** pueblo de pescadores, *m*

fishmeal harina de pescado, *f*

fishmonger *n* pescadero (-ra).

fishpond *n* vivero, *m*, piscina, *f*

fishwife *n* pescadora, *f*

fishy *a* de pescado; (of eyes, etc.) de pez, como un pez; (in smell) que huele a pescado; *inf* sospechoso; (of stories) inverosímil

fissure *n* grieta, hendidura, rendija, *f*; (*anat, geol*) fisura, *f*

fissured *a* hendido

fist *n* puño, *m*; *print* manecilla, *f*; (handwriting) letra, *f*. **with clenched fists,** a puño cerrado

fisticuff *n* puñetazo, *m*; *pl* **fisticuffs,** agarrada, riña, *f*

fit *n* espasmo, paroxismo, *m*; ataque, *m*; (impulse) acceso, arranque, *m*; (whim) capricho, *m*; (of a garment) corte, *m*; (adjustment) ajuste, encaje, *m*. **by fits and starts,** a tropezones, espasmódicamente. **fit of fainting** *Argentina, Venezuela* insuilto *m*

fit *a* a propósito (para), bueno (para); (opportune) oportuno; (proper) conveniente; apto; (decent) decente; (worthy) digno; (ready) preparado, listo; (adequate) adecuado; (capable) capaz, en estado (de); (appropriate) apropiado; (just) justo. **It is not in a fit state to be used,** No está en condiciones para usarse. **to be not fit for,** no servir para; (through ill-health) no tener bastante salud para. **to think fit,** creer (or juzgar) conveniente. **fit for use,** usable. **fit to eat,** comestible

fit *vt* ajustar, acomodar, encajar; adaptar (a); (furnish) proveer (de), surtir (con); (of tailor, dressmaker) entallar, probar; (of shoemaker) calzar; (of garments, shoes) ir (bien o mal); (prepare) preparar; (go with) ser apropiado (a); (adapt itself to) adaptarse a. *vi* ajustarse, acomodarse, encajarse; adaptarse; (clothes) ir (bien o mal). **to fit in,** *vt* encajar; incluir. *vi* encajarse; caber; adaptarse. **to fit out,** equipar; proveer (de); preparar. **to fit up,** montar, instalar; proveer (de). **to fit with,** proveer de

fitful *a* intermitente; espasmódico; caprichoso

fitfully *adv* por intervalos, a ratos; caprichosamente

fitly *adv* adecuadamente; justamente; apropiadamente

fitment *n* equipo, *m*; instalación, *f*; (of bookcase, etc.) sección, *f*; (furniture) pieza, *f*, mueble, *m*

fitness *n* conveniencia, *f*; aptitud, capacidad, *f*; oportunidad, *f*; salud, *f*; (good health) vigor, *m*

fitted *a* (of clothes) ajustado

fitter *n* ajustador, *m*; (mechanic) armador, mecánico, *m*; (tailoring) cortador, *m*; (dressmaking) probador (-ra)

fitting *n* encaje, ajuste, *m*; adaptación, *f*; (of a garment) prueba, *f*; (size) medida, *f*; (installation) instalación, *f*; **pl. fittings,** guarniciones, *f pl*; instalaciones, *f pl*; accesorios, *m pl*. *a* conveniente, justo; apropiado; adecuado; (worthy) digno; (of coats, etc.) ajustado. **f. room,** cuarto de pruebas, *m*. **f. in,** encaje, *m*. **f. out,** equipo, *m*. **f. up,** arreglo, *m*; (of machines) montaje, *m*; (of a house) mueblaje, *m*

five *a* and *n* cinco *m*.; (of the clock) las cinco, *f pl*; (of age) cinco años, *m pl*. **to be f.,** tener cinco años. **f. feet deep,** de cinco pies de profundidad. **f. feet high,** cinco pies de altura. **f.-finger exercises,** ejercicios de piano, *m pl*. **F.-Year Plan,** Plan Quinquenal, *m*

fivefold *a* quíntuplo

fix *n* aprieto, apuro, *m*; callejón sin salida, *m*. *vt* fijar; sujetar, afianzar; (bayonets) calar; (with nails) clavar; (*phot, chem, med*) fijar; (decide) establecer; (a date) señalar; (eyes, attention) clavar; (on the mind) grabar, estampar; (one's hopes) poner; (base) basar, fundar; (*inf* put right) arreglar, componer. *vi* fijarse; establecerse; determinarse. **to get in a fix,** hacerse un lío. **to fix a price,** fijar un precio. **to fix on, upon,** elegir, escoger; decidir, determinar. **to fix up,** arreglar; decidir; organizar; (differences) olvidar (sus disensiones)

fixation *n* obsesión, idea fija, *f*; (scientific) fijación, *f*

fixative *n* (*med, phot*) fijador, *m*; (dyeing) mordiente, *m*. *a* que fija

fixed *a* fijo; inmóvil; permanente; (of ideas) inflexible. **f. bayonet,** bayoneta calada, *f*. **f. price,** precio fijo, *m*. **f. star,** estrella fija, *f*

fixedly *adv* fijamente; resueltamente; firmemente

fixing *n* fijación, *f*; afianzamiento, *m*; arreglo, *m*; (of a date) señalamiento, *m*. **f. bath,** *phot* baño fijador, *m*

fixity *n* permanencia, *f*; inmovilidad, *f*; invariabilidad, *f*; firmeza, *f*

fixture *n* instalación, *f*; accesorio fijo, *m*; *sport* partido, *m*; *inf* permanencia, *f*. **f. card,** *sport* calendario deportivo, *m*

fizz *n* espuma, *f*; chisporroteo, *m*. *inf* champaña, *m*. *vi* (liquids) espumear; (sputter) chisporrotear

fizzle *n* (failure) fiasco, fracaso, *m*. *vi* chisporrotear; (out) apagarse; (fail) fracasar, no tener éxito

fjord *n* fiordo, *m*

flabbergast *vt* dejar con la boca abierta, dejar de una pieza

flabbiness, flaccidity *n* flaccidez, flojedad, *f*; *med* reblandecimiento, *m*; (of character) debilidad, flaqueza del ánimo, *f*

flabby, flaccid *a* fláccido, flojo; *fig* débil

flag *n* bandera, *f*; pabellón, estandarte, *m*; (small) banderola, *f*; (iris) (yellow) cala, *f*, (purple) lirio cárdeno, *m*; (stone) losa, *f*. **to dip the f.,** saludar con la bandera. **to hoist the f.,** izar la bandera. **to strike the f.,** bajar la bandera; (in defeat) rendir la bandera. **f. bearer,** portaestandarte, abanderado, *m*. **f.-day,** día de la banderita, *m*; (in U.S.A.) día de la bandera, *m*. **f.-officer,** almirante, *m*; vicealmirante, *m*; jefe de escuadra, *m*. **f. of truce,** bandera blanca, bandera de paz, *f*

flag *vi* flaquear, debilitarse; languidecer; (wither) marchitarse; decaer, disminuir. *vt* adornar con banderas; (signal) hacer señales con una bandera; (for a race, etc.) marcar con banderas; (with stones) enlosar, embaldosar.

flagellant *n* flagelante, *m*
flagellate *vt* flagelar
flagellation *n* flagelación, *f*
flageolet *n mus* caramillo, *m*, chirimía, *f*. **f. player,** chirimía, *m*
flagging *n* pavimentación, *f*; (floor) enlosado, *m*. *a* lánguido, flojo
flagon *n* frasco, *m*; botella, *f*
flagrancy *n* escándalo, *m*, notoriedad, *f*
flagrant *a* escandaloso, notorio
flagship *n* capitana, *f*
flagstaff *n* asta de bandera, *f*
flagstone *n* losa, lancha, *Lat. Am.* laja *f*
flail *n* mayal, *m*
flair *n* instinto natural, *m*, comprensión innata, *f*; habilidad natural, *f*
flak *n* cortina (or barrera) antiaérea, *f*
flake *n* escama, *f*; laminilla, hojuela, *f*; (of snow) copo, *m*; (of fire) chispa, *f*. *vt* cubrir con escamas, etc.; exfoliar; (crumble) hacer migas de, desmigajar. *vi* escamarse; (off) exfoliarse; caer en copos
flaky *a* escamoso; en laminillas; (of pastry) hojaldrado. **f. pastry,** hojaldre, *f*
flamboyance *n* extravagancia, *f*, *lit* ampulosidad, *f*
flamboyant *a arch* flamígero; extravagante, llamativo, rimbombante; (of style) ampuloso. **f. gothic,** gótico florido, *m*
flame *n* llama, *f*; *fig* fuego, *m*. *inf* amorío, *m*, *vi* flamear, llamear; arder, abrasarse; (shine) brillar; (up, *fig*) inflamarse; acalorarse. **f.-colored,** de color de llama, anaranjado. **f.-thrower,** lanzallamas, *m*
flaming *a* llameante; abrasador; (of colors) llamativo, chillón; (of feelings) ardiente, fervoroso, apasionado
flamingo *n orn* flamenco, *m*
Flanders flandes, *m*
flange *n mech* reborde, *m*, *vt* rebordear
flank *n* (of animal) ijada, *f*; (human) costado, *m*; (of hill, etc.) lado, *m*, falda, *f*; *mil* flanco, *m*. *a* (*mil nav*) por el flanco. *vt* lindar con, estar contiguo a; (*mil, nav*) flanquear. *vi* estar al lado de; tocar a, lindar con.
flannel *n* franela, *f*, *a* de franela
flannelette *n* moletón, *m*
flap *n* golpe, *m*; (of a sail) zapatazo, *m*, sacudida, *f*; (of a pocket) cartera, tapa, *f*; (of skin) colgajo, *m*; (of a shoe, etc.) oreja, *f*; (of a shirt, etc.) falda, *f*; (of a hat) ala, *f*; (of trousers) bragueta, *f*; (rever) solapa, *f*; (of a counter) trampa, *f*; (of a table) hoja plegadiza, *f*; (of the wings) aletazo, *m*; (of w.c.) tapa, *f*. *vt* sacudir, golpear, batir; agitar; (the tail) menear. *vi* agitarse; (of wings) aletear; (of sails) zapatear, sacudirse; colgar. **f.-eared,** de orejas grandes y gachas
flapjack *n cul* torta de sartén, *f*; (for powder) polvorera, *f*
flapper *n inf* polla, tobillera, chica "topolino," *f*
flapping *n* batimiento, *m*; (waving) ondulación, *f*; (of sails) zapatazo, *m*; (of wings) aleteo, *m*
flare *n* fulgor, *m*, llama, *f*; hacha, *f*; *aer* cohete de señales, *m*; *sew* vuelo, *m*. *vi* relampaguear, fulgurar; brillar; (of a lamp) llamear; (up) encolerizarse, salirse de tino; (of epidemic) declararse; (war, etc.) desencadenarse
flash *n* relámpago, centelleo, *m*, ráfaga de luz, *f*; brillo, *m*; (from a gun) fuego, fogonazo, *m*; (of wit, genius) rasgo, *m*; (of joy, etc.) acceso, *m*. *vi* relampaguear, fulgurar, centellear; brillar; cruzar rápidamente, pasar como un relámpago. *vt* hacer relampaguear; hacer brillar; (a look, etc.) dar; lanzar; (light) encender; (powder) quemar; transmitir señales por heliógrafo; *inf* sacar a relucir, enseñar. **shoulder-f.,** *mil* emblema, *m*. **to be gone like a f.,** desaparecer como un relámpago. **to f. out,** brillar, centellear. **f. of lightning,** relámpago, rayo, *m*. **f. of wit,** agudeza, *f*, rasgo de ingenio, *m*
flashback *n* episodio intercalado, *m*, retrospección, *f*
flashily *adv* llamativamente, con mal gusto
flashing *n* centelleo, *m*, llamarada, *f*. *a* centellador, relampagueante; brillante; chispeante
flashlight *n* luz de magnesio, *f*; (torch) lamparilla eléctrica, *f*, rayo, *m* (Mexico); **f. photograph,** magnesio, *m*
flashy *a* llamativo, de mal gusto, charro, *Lat. Am.* figuroso; frívolo, superficial
flask *n* frasco, *m*, redoma, botella, *f*; (for powder) frasco, *m*; (vacuum) termos, *m*
flat *a* llano; (smooth) liso; (lying) tendido, tumbado; (flattened) aplastado; (destroyed) arrasado; (stretched out) extendido; (of nose, face) chato, romo; (of tire) desinflado; (uniform) uniforme; (depressed) desanimado; (uninteresting) monótono; (boring) aburrido; *com* paralizado; (downright) categórico; absoluto; (net) neto; *mus* bemol; (of boats) de fondo plano. *adv* See **flatly.** *n* planicie, *f*; (of a sword) hoja, *f*; (of the hand) palma, *f*; (land) llanura, *f*; (apartment) piso, *m*; *mus* bemol, *m*. **to fall f.,** caer de bruces; *fig* no tener éxito. **to make f.,** allanar. **to sing f.,** desafinar. **f. boat,** barco de fondo plano, *m*. **f.-footed,** de pies achatados; *fig* pedestre. **f.-iron,** plancha, *f*. **f. roof,** azotea, *f*
flatly *adv* de plano; a nivel; (plainly) llanamente, netamente; (dully) indiferentemente; (categorically) categóricamente
flatness *n* planicie, *f*; llanura, *f*; (smoothness) lisura, *f*; (evenness) igualdad, *f*; (uninterestingness) insulsez, insipidez, *f*; aburrimiento, *m*; (depression) desaliento, abatimiento, *m*
flatten *vt* aplanar, allanar; aplastar; (smooth) alisar; (even) igualar; (destroy) derribar, arrasar, destruir; (dismay) desconcertar; (out) extender. *vi* aplanarse, allanarse; aplastarse
flattening *n* achatamiento, *m*, allanamiento, *m*; aplastamiento, *m*; igualación, *f*
flatter *vt* adular, lisonjear, halagar, engatusar, *Lat. Am. also* afilar, engaratusar; (of a dress, photograph, etc.) favorecer, (please the senses) regalar, deleitar; (oneself) felicitarse
flatterer *n* adulador (-ra), lisonjero (-ra), *Guatemala* barbero (-ra) *mf*
flattering *a* adulador, lisonjero; (promising) halagüeño; favoreciente; deleitoso
flattery *n* adulación, *Lat. Am.* adulonería *f*
flat tire llanta desinflada, *f*
flatulence *n* flatulencia, *f*
flatulent *a* flatulento
flaunt *vi* (flutter) ondear; pavonearse. *vt* desplegar; ostentar, sacar a relucir; enseñar
flaunting *n* ostentación, *f*; alarde, *m*. *a* ostentoso; magnífico; (fluttering) ondeante
flautist *n* flautista, *mf*
flavor *n* sabor, gusto, *m*; *cul* condimento, *m*; *fig* dejo, *m*. *vt cul* sazonar, condimentar; dar un gusto (de), hacer saborear (a); *fig* dar un dejo (de)
flavored *a* (in compounds) de sabor . . . ; sazonado; que tiene sabor de . . .
flavoring *n cul* condimento, *m*; *fig* sabor, dejo, *m*
flavorless *a* insípido, soso, sin sabor
flaw *n* desperfecto, *m*, imperfección, *f*; (crack) grieta, hendedura, *f*; (in wood, metals) quebraja, *f*; (in gems) pelo, *m*; (in fruit) maca, *f*; (in cloth) gabarro, *m*; *fig* defecto, error, *m*; (wind) ráfaga de viento, *f*
flawless *a* sin defecto; perfecto; impecable
flax *n* lino, *m*. **to dress f.,** rastrillar lino. **f.-comb,** rastrillo, *m*. **f. field,** linar, *m*
flaxen *a* de lino; (fair) rubio, blondo. **f.-haired,** de pelo rubio
flay *vt* desollar; (criticize) despellejar
flaying *n* desuello, *m*, desolladura, *f*
flea *n* pulga, *f*. **f. bite,** picada de pulga, *f*
fleck *n* pinta, mancha, *f*, lunar, *m*; (of sun) mota, *f*; (speck) partícula, *f*; (freckle) peca, *f*. *vt* abigarrar; manchar; (dapple) salpicar, motear
fledged *a* emplumecido, plumado; alado; *fig* maduro
fledgeling *n* volantón, *m*; *fig* niño (-ña); *fig* novato (-ta)

flee *vi* huir, fugarse, escapar; (vanish) desaparecer; (avoid) evitar, huir de. *vt* abandonar
fleece *n* vellón, *m*; lana, *f*; toisón, *m*. *vt* esquilar; *fig inf* pelar. **Order of the Golden F.,** Orden del Toisón de Oro, *f*
fleecy *a* lanudo, lanar; (white) blanquecino; (of clouds) borreguero. **f. clouds,** borregos, *m pl*
fleet *n* (navy) armada, *f*; escuadra, flota, *f*; *fig* serie, *f*, *a* alado, rápido, veloz. **F. Air Arm,** Aviación Naval, *f*. **f.-footed,** ligero de pies
fleeting *a* fugaz, momentáneo, efímero, pasajero
flesh *n* carne, *f*; (mankind) género humano, *m*, humanidad, *f*; (of fruit) pulpa, *f*. **a man of f. and blood,** un hombre de carne y hueso. **of one's own f. and blood,** de la misma sangre de uno. **to make one's f. creep,** dar carne de gallina (a). **f.-coloured,** encarnado, de color de carne. **f.-eating,** carnívoro. **f. wound,** herida superficial, *f*
fleshiness *n* carnosidad, gordura, *f*
fleshpot *n* marmita, *f*; *fig* olla, *f*. **the fleshpots of Egypt,** las ollas de Egipto
fleshy *a* carnoso, grueso; (of fruit) pulposo; suculento
fleur-de-lis *n* flor de lis, *f*
flex *n elec* flexible, *m*, *vt* doblar. *vi* doblarse
flexibility *n* flexibilidad, *f*; (of style) plasticidad, *f*; docilidad, *f*
flexible *a* flexible; dúctil, maleable; (of style) plástico; of) voice) quebradizo; adaptable; dócil
flexion *n* flexión, *f*; *gram* inflexión, *f*; *gram* flexión, *f*
flexor *n anat* músculo flexor, *m*
flick *n* golpecito, toque, *m*; (of the finger) capirotazo, *m*; *inf* cine, *m*, *vt* dar un golpecito a; dar ligeramente con un látigo; sacudir. **flick one's wrist** hacer girar la muñeca **to f. over the pages of,** hojear
flicker *n* estremecimiento, temblor, *m*; fluctuación, *f*; (of bird) aleteo, *m*; (of flame) onda (de una llama), *f*; (of eyelashes) pestañeo, *m*; (of a smile) indicio, *f*, *vi* agitarse; (of flags) ondear; vacilar
flickering *a* tenue; vacilante
flier *n* volador (-ra); aviador (-ra); piloto, *m*; fugitivo (-va)
flight *n* vuelo, *m*; (of bird of prey) colada, *f*; (flock of birds) bandada, *f*; (migration) migración, *f*; (of time) transcurso, *m*; (of imagination, etc.) arranque, *m*; (volley) lluvia, *f*; (of aeroplanes) escuadrilla (de aviones), *f*; (of stairs) tramo, tiro, *m*; (staircase) escalera, *f*; (of locks on canal, etc.) ramal, *m*; (escape) huida, fuga, *f*. **long-distance f.,** *aer* vuelo de distancia, *m*. **non-stop f.,** *aer* vuelo sin parar, *m*. **reconnaissance f.,** *aer* vuelo de reconocimiento, vuelo de patrulla, *m*. **test f.,** *aer* vuelo de pruebas, *m*. **to put to f.,** ahuyentar, poner en fuga. **to take f.,** alzar el vuelo. **f.-lieutenant,** teniente aviador, *m*. **f.-sergeant,** sargento aviador, *m*
flight attendant sobrecargo, *Lat. Am.* aeromozo (-za), cabinero (-ra) *mf*
flightiness *n* frivolidad, veleidad, ligereza, *f*
flighty *a* frívolo, inconstante, veleidoso
flimsiness *n* falta de solidez, endeblez, *f*; fragilidad, *f*; (of arguments) futilidad, *f*
flimsy *a* endeble; frágil; fútil, insubstancial
flinch *vi* echarse atrás, retirarse (ante); vacilar, titubear. **without flinching,** sin vacilar; sin quejarse
fling *vt* arrojar, echar, tirar; lanzar; (scatter) derramar; (oneself) echarse; (oneself upon) echarse encima; *fig* confiar en. *vi* lanzarse; marcharse precipitadamente; saltar. *n* tiro, *m*; (of dice, etc.) echada, *f*; (gibe) sarcasmo, *m*, burla, chufleta, *f*; (of horse) respingo, brinco, *m*; baile escocés, *m*. **in full f.,** en plena operación; en progreso. **to have one's f.,** darse un verde, correrla. **to f. away,** *vt* desechar; (waste) desperdiciar, malgastar, perder. *vi* marcharse enfadado; marcharse rápidamente. **to f. back,** (a ball) devolver; (the head) echar atrás. **to f. down,** tirar al suelo; arrojar; derribar. **to f. off,** *vt* rechazar; apartar; (a garment, etc.) quitar. *vi* marcharse sin más ni más. **to f. oneself down,** tumbarse, echarse; despeñarse (por). **to f. oneself headlong,** despeñarse. **to f. open,** abrir violentamente, abrir de repente. **to f. out,** *vt* echar a la fuerza; (a hand) alargar, extender. *vi* salir apresuradamente. **to f. over,** (upset) volcar; arrojar por; abandonar. **to f. up,** lanzar al aire; levantar, erguir; renunciar (a), abandonar; dejar
flint *n* pedernal, *m*; (for producing fire) piedra de encendedor, *f*
flinty *a* pedernalino; *fig* endurecido
flippancy *n* levedad, ligereza, *f*; frivolidad, *f*; impertinencia, *f*
flippant *a* poco serio, ligero; frívolo; impertinente
flipper *n* aleta, *f*
flirt *n* (man) coquetón, castigador, *m*; (woman) coqueta, castigadora, *f*. *vt* (shake) sacudir; (move) agitar; (wave) menear. *vi* flirtear, coquetear; (toy with) jugar con; divertirse con
flirtation *n* flirteo, amorío, *m*
flirtatious *a* (of men) galanteador, castigador; (of women) coqueta
flit *vi* revolotear, mariposear; (move silently) deslizarse, pasar silenciosamente; (depart) irse, marcharse; mudarse por los aires. **to f. about,** ir y venir silenciosamente. **to f. past,** pasar como una sombra
flitch *n* (of bacon) hoja de tocino, *f*
float *n* masa flotante, *f*; (raft) balsa, *f*; *mech* flotador, *m*; (of fishing rod or net) corcho, *m*; (of fish) vejiga natatoria, *f*; (for swimming) nadadera, calabaza, *f*; (for tableaux) carroza, *f*; *pl* **floats,** *theat* candilejas, *f pl*. *vi* flotar; (flags, hair, etc.) ondear; (wander) vagar; *naut* boyar. *vt* poner a flote; hacer flotar; (a grounded ship) desencallar; (*com* a company) fundar; (a loan, etc.) emitir, poner en circulación; (launch a ship) botar; (flood) inundar
floating *n* flotación, *f*, flote, *m*; *com* fundación (de una compañía), *f*; (of a loan) emisión, *f*; (of a ship) botadura, *f*. *a* flotante; boyante; *com* en circulación, flotante; fluctuante, variable. **f. capital,** capital fluctuante, *m*. **f. debt,** deuda flotante, *f*. **f. dock,** dique flotante, *m*. **f. light,** buque faro, *m*. **f. population,** población flotante, *f*. **f. rib,** costilla flotante, *f*
flock *n* rebaño, *m*, manada, *f*; (of birds) bandada, *f*; *fig* grey, *f*; (crowd) multitud, muchedumbre, *f*; (parishioners) congregación, *f*; (of wool or cotton) vedija (de lana or de algodón), *f*; *pl* **flocks,** (for stuffing) borra, *f*. *vi* concurrirse, reunirse, congregarse; ir en tropel, acudir; (birds) volar en bandada. **f.-bed,** colchón de borra, *m*
floe *n* banco de hielo, *m*
flog *vt* azotar; castigar
flogging *n* azotamiento, vapuleo, *m*
flood *n* inundación, *f*; (Bible) diluvio, *m*; (of the tide) flujo, *m*; *fig* torrente, *m*; (abundance) copia, abundancia, *f*; (fit) paroxismo, *m*. *vt* inundar; sumergir; (of tears) mojar. *vi* desbordar. **f. lighting,** iluminación intensiva, *f*
floodgate *n* compuerta (de esclusa), *f*
flooding *n* inundación, *f*; desbordamiento, *m*; *med* hemorragia uterina, *f*
floodtide *n* marea creciente, *f*
floor *n* suelo, piso, *m*; (wooden) entarimado, *m*; (story) piso, *m*; (of a cart) cama, *f*; *agr* era, *f*. *vt* entablar; echar al suelo, derribar; *fig* desconcertar, confundir. **on the f.,** en el suelo. **on the ground f.,** en el piso bajo. **to take the f.,** *fig* tener la palabra. **f. mop** *Lat. Am.* lampazo *m*. **f.-polisher,** lustrador de piso, *m*
flooring *n* tablado, *m*, tablazón, *f*; piso, *m*
flop *n* golpe, *m*; ruido sordo, *m*; (splash) chapoteo, *m*; *inf* fiasco, *m*. *vi* dejarse caer
flora *n* flora, *f*
floral *a* floral. **f. games,** juegos florales, *m pl*
Florence Florencia, *f*
Florentine *a* and *n* florentino (-na)
florescence *n* florescencia, *f*
florid *a* florido; demasiado ornado, cursi, llamativo; (of complexion) rubicundo

floridness *n* floridez, *f*, estilo florido, *m*; demasiada ornamentación, vulgaridad, *f*, mal gusto, *m*; (of complexion) rubicundez, *f*
florin *n* florín, *m*
florist *n* florista, *mf*
floss *n* seda floja, filoseda, *f*; (of maize) penacho, *m*; (of a cocoon) cadarzo, *m*. **f. silk,** seda floja, *f*
flotilla *n* flotilla, *f*
flotsam *n* pecio, *m*
flounce *n* volante, *m*, *vi* saltar de impaciencia. **to f. out,** salir airadamente
flounder *n* (nearest equivalent) *icht* platija, *f*; tumbo, *m*. *vi* tropezar; revolcarse; andar dificultosamente
flour *n* harina, *f*, *vt* enharinar. **f.-bin,** tina, *f*, harinero, *m*. **f. merchant,** harinero, *m*
flourish *n* movimiento, *m*; gesto, saludo, *m*; (of a pen) plumada, *f*; (on the guitar, in fencing) floreo, *m*; preludio, *m*; (fanfare) tocata (de trompetas), *f*; (of a signature) rúbrica, *f*; (in rhetoric) floreo, *m*. *vi* (of plants) vegetar; (prosper) prosperar, medrar; florecer; (of the guitar, in fencing) florear; *mus* preludiar; (with a pen) hacer plumadas (or rasgos de pluma); (of a signature) firmar con rúbrica; (sound a fanfare) hacer una tocata (de trompetas). *vt* agitar en el aire, blandir
flourishing *a* (of plants) lozano; floreciente; (prosperous) próspero; (happy) feliz
flourmill *n* molino de harina, *m*, fábrica de harina, *f*, molina harinero, *m*
floury *a* harinoso
flout *vt* burlarse de; despreciar, no hacer caso de
flow *n* flujo, *m*; corriente, *f*; chorro, *m*; (of water) caudal, *m*; (output) producción total, cantidad, *f*; (of the tide) flujo (de la marea), *m*; (of words) facilidad, *f*. *vi* fluir, manar; correr; (of the tide) crecer (la marea); (pass) pasar, correr; (result) resultar (de), provenir (de); (of hair, drapery) caer, ondular; (abound) abundar (en). **to f. away,** escaparse, salir. **to f. back,** refluir. **to f. down,** descender, fluir hacia abajo; (of tears) correr por. **to f. from,** dimanar de; manar de; *fig* provenir de. **to f. in,** llegar en abundancia. **to f. into,** (rivers) desaguar en, desembocar en. **to f. over,** derramarse por. **to f. through,** fluir por; atravesar; (water) regar. **to f. together,** (rivers) confluir
flower *n* flor, *f*; (best) flor y nata, crema, *f*. *vi* florecer. **in f.,** en flor. **No flowers by request,** (for a funeral) No flores por deseo del finado. **f.-bud,** capullo, *m*. **f.-garden,** jardín, *m*. **f. girl,** florista, vendedora de flores, *f*. **f. market,** mercado de flores, *m*. **f.-piece,** florero, *m*. **f. pot,** tiesto, *m*, maceta, *f*, *Lat. Am.* macetero *m*. **f. show,** exposición de flores, *f*. **f. vase,** florero, *m*
flowerbed *n* cuadro, macizo, *m*
flower car coche portacoronas, *m*
flowered *a* (in compounds) con flores; con dibujos de flores
floweriness *n* abundancia de flores, *f*; (of style) floridez, *f*, estilo florido, *m*
flowering *n* florecimiento, *m*. *a* floreciente; con flores; (of shrubs) de adorno. **f. season,** época de la floración, *f*
flowery *a* florido
flowing *n* flujo, *m*; derrame, *m*. *a* fluente, corriente; (of tide) creciente; (waving) ondeante; suelto; (of style) flúido
flow of capital corriente de capital, *f*
fluctuate *vi* fluctuar, vacilar; variar
fluctuating *a* fluctuante, vacilante; variable; (hesitating) irresoluto, dudoso
fluctuation *n* fluctuación, *f*; cambio, *m*, variación, *f*; (hesitancy) indecisión, vacilación, *f*
flue *n* (of a chimney) cañón, *m*; (of a boiler) tubo, *m*
fluency *n* fluidez, *f*
fluent *a* flúido; fácil
fluently *adv* corrientemente, con facilidad, de corrido
fluff *n* borra, pelusa, *f*, tamo, *m*
fluffy *a* velloso; (feathered) plumoso; (woolly) lanudo; (of hair) encrespado
fluid *n* flúido, líquido, *m*, *a* flúido
fluidity *n* fluidez, *f*
fluke *n* (in billiards) chiripa, *f*; *naut* uña, *f*; *inf* carambola, chiripa, chambonada, *f*. **by a f.,** de carambola, por suerte. **f.-worm,** duela del hígado, *f*
flunkey *n* lacayo, *m*; *fig* adulador, *m*
fluorescence *n* fluorescencia, *f*
fluorescent *a* fluorescente
fluorine *n chem* flúor, *m*
fluorite *n* fluorita, *f*
flurry *n* (of wind) ráfaga, *f*; (squall) chubasco, *m*; agitación, *f*; conmoción, *f*. *vt* agitar
flush *n* rubor, *m*; (in the sky) arrebol, rojo, color de rosa, *m*; emoción, *f*, acceso, *m*; sensación, *f*; (at cards) flux, *m*; vigor, *m*; (flowering) floración, *f*; abundancia, *f*; (of youth, etc.) frescura, *f*. *a* (level) igual, parejo; abundante; (generous) pródigo, liberal; (rich) adinerado. *vi* ruborizarse, enrojecerse, ponerse colorado; (flood) inundarse, llenarse (de agua, etc.); (of sky) arrebolarse. *vt* inundar, limpiar con un chorro de agua, etc., lavar; (of blood) circular por; (redden) enrojecer; (make blush) hacer ruborizarse; (exhilarate) excitar, animar; (inflame) inflamar, encender; (make level) igualar, nivelar. **f. with,** a ras de
flushing *n* rojez, *f*; (cleansing) limpieza, lavadura, *f*; (flooding) inundación, *f*
fluster *n* agitación, confusión, *f*, aturdimiento, *m*. *vt* agitar, poner nervioso (a), aturdir; (oneself) preocuparse. *vi* agitarse; estar nervioso, estar perplejo; (with drink) estar entre dos velas
flute *n* flauta, *f*; *arch* estría, *f*; (organ-stop) flautado, *m*. *vi* tocar la flauta, flautear; tener la voz flauteada. *vt* tocar (una pieza) en la flauta; (groove) encanutar, acanalar, estriar. **f. player,** flautista, *mf*
fluted *a* (grooved) acanalado
fluting *n mus* son de la flauta, *m*; (of birds) trinado, *m*; *arch* estría, *f*; *sew* rizado, *m*
flutter *n* (of wings) aleteo, *m*; (of leaves, etc.) murmurio, *m*; (of eyelashes) pestañeo, *m*; (of flags, etc.) ondeo, *m*, ondulación, *f*; (excitement) agitación, *f*; (stir) sensación, *f*; (gamble) jugada, *f*. *vi* (of birds) aletear; revolotear; (of butterflies) mariposear; (of flags) ondear; palpitar; (of persons) estar agitado. *vt* agitar; (the eyelashes) pestañear; (agitate) agitar, alarmar
fluttering *n* mariposeo, *m*; revoloteo, *m*; (of birds) aleteo, *m*; (of leaves, etc.) murmurio, *m*; (of flags, etc.) ondeo, *m*, ondulación, *f*; (of eyelashes) pestañeo, *m*
fluvial *a* fluvial
flux *n* flujo, *m*
fly *n* (insect) mosca, *f*; (on a fishhook) mosca artificial, *f*; (carriage) calesín, *m*; (of breeches) bragueta, *f*; *theat* bambalina, *f*; (of a tent) toldo, *m*; (flight) vuelo, *m*; (of a flag) vuelo, *m*. **fly-blown,** manchado por las moscas. **fly-by-night,** trasnochador (-ra). **fly-catcher,** *orn* papamoscas, *m*; matamoscas, *m*. **fly-fishing,** pesca con moscas artificiales, *f*. **fly-leaf,** guarda (de un libro), *f*. **fly-paper,** papel matamoscas, *m*. **fly-swatter,** matamoscas, *m*. **fly-wheel,** *mech* volante, *m*
fly *vi* volar; (flutter) ondear; (jump) saltar; (rush) lanzarse, precipitarse; (pass away) pasar volando, volar; (run off) marcharse a todo correr; (escape) huir, escapar; (seek refuge) refugiarse; (to the head, of intoxicants) subirse; (vanish) desaparecer. *vt* hacer volar; hacer ondear, enarbolar; (an airplane) pilotar, dirigir; (flee from) huir de; evitar. **to let fly (at),** descargar, tirar; *fig* saltar la sinhueso. **to fly about,** volar en torno de; revolotear. **to fly at,** lanzarse sobre; acometer, asaltar. **to fly away,** emprender el vuelo. **to fly back,** volar hacia el punto de partida; (of doors, etc.) abrir, or cerrar, de repente. **to fly down,** volar abajo. **to fly in,** volar dentro de; volar adentro; (of airplanes) llegar (el avión). **to fly in pieces,** hacerse pedazos. **to fly into a rage,** montarse en cólera. **to fly low,** rastrear; *aer* volar a poca altura. **to fly off,** emprender el vuelo; (hasten) marcharse volando; (of buttons, etc.) saltar (de), separarse (de). **to fly open,** abrirse de repente.

to fly over, volar por, volar por encima de. **to fly upwards,** volar hacia arriba; subir
flying *n* vuelo, *m. a* volante, volador; que vuela; de volar; volátil; (hasty) rápido; (flowing) ondeante, ondulante. **to shoot f.,** tirar al vuelo. **with f. colors,** con banderas desplegadas, triunfante. **f.-boat,** hidroavión, *m.* **f.-buttress,** botarel, arbotante, *m.* **f.-column,** *mil* cuerpo volante, *m.* **f.-fish,** (pez) volador, *m.* **f.-fortress,** *aer* fortaleza volante, *f.* **f.-officer,** oficial de aviación, *m.* **f.-sickness,** mal de altura, *m.* **f.-squad,** escuadra ligera, *f.* **f.-test,** *aer* examen de pilotaje, *m*
foal *n* potro (-ra). *vi* and *vt* parir una yegua
foam *n* espuma, *f. vi* espumar; (of horses, etc.) echar espumarajos. **to f. and froth,** (of the sea) hervir. **f. at the mouth,** echar espuma por la boca.
foam rubber *n* caucho esponjoso, *m,* espuma de caucho, *f,* espuma sintética, *f*
foamy *a* espumoso
fob *n* bolsillo del reloj, *m;* faltriquera pequeña, *f. vt* (off) engañar con
focal *a* focal
focus *n* foco, *m;* centro, *m. vt* enfocar; concentrar. *vi* convergir. **in f.,** en foco
fodder *n agr* pienso, forraje, *m. vt* dar forraje (a)
foe *n* enemigo, *m*
fog *n* neblina, niebla, *f; fig* confusión, *f; fig* perplejidad, *f, vt* obscurecer; *phot* velar; *fig* ofuscar. *vi* hacerse nebuloso; *phot* velarse. **fog-signal,** señal de niebla, *f*
fogbound *a* rodeado de niebla; detenido por la niebla
fogey *n* obscurantista, *m.* **He is an old f.,** Es un señor chapado a la antigua
fogginess *n* oscuridad, neblina, *f*
foggy *a* nebuloso; *phot* velado. **It is f.,** Hay niebla
foghorn *n* sirena, *f;* bocina, *f*
foible *n* flaco, *m,* debilidad, *f*
foil *n* (sword) florete, *m;* (coat) hoja, *f;* (of a mirror) azogado, *m. vt* frustrar. **f. a plot,** desbaratar un complot. **She makes a good f. for her sister's beauty,** Hace resaltar la belleza de su hermana
foiling *n* frustración, *f*
foist *vt* imponer; insertar, incluir; engañar (con)
fold *n* doblez, *f,* pliegue, *m;* arruga, *f; sew* cogido, *m;* (for sheep) redil, aprisco, *m; fig* iglesia, congregación de los fieles, *f;* (in compounds) vez, *f. vt* doblar, plegar, doblegar; (the arms) cruzar (los brazos); (embrace) abrazar; (wrap) envolver; (clasp) entrelazar; (sheep) meter en redil, encerrar. *vi* doblarse, plegarse; cerrarse
folder *n* doblador (-ra); plegadera, *f*
folding *n* plegadura, *f,* doblamiento, *m;* (of sheep) encerramiento, *m, a* plegadizo. **f.-door,** puerta plegadiza, *f.* **f.-machine,** plegador, *m.* **f.-seat,** *aut* traspuntín, *m.* **f.-table,** mesa de tijeras, *f;* mesa plegadiza, *f*
foliage *n* follaje, *m,* frondas, *f pl.* **thick f.,** frondosidad, *f*
folio *n* folio, *m;* (a volume) infolio, *m. a* de infolio. *vt* foliar
folk *n* (nation) pueblo, *m,* nación, *f;* gente, *f; pl* **folks,** *inf* familia, *f;* parientes, *m pl.* **f.-dance,** danza popular, *f*
folklore *n* folclore, *m,* tradiciones folclóricas, *f pl*
folklorist *n* folclorista, *mf*
folksong *n* canción popular, *f;* romance, *m;* copla, *f*
folktale *n* conseja, *f,* cuento popular, *m*
follicle *n* (*anat, bot*) folículo, *m*
follow *vt* seguir; (pursue) perseguir; (hunt) cazar; (adopt) adoptar; (understand) comprender; (notice) observar. *vi* ir, or venir, detrás; (of time) venir después; (gen. impers.) seguir, resultar; seguirse. **as follows,** como sigue. **I shall f. your advice,** Seguiré tus consejos. **to f. on the heels of,** *fig* pisar los talones (a). **to f. suit,** (at cards) asistir, jugar el mismo palo; *fig* imitar. **to f. up,** proseguir; continuar; (pursue) perseguir; (enhance) reforzar. **f.-me-lads,** *inf* siguemepollo, *m*
follower *n* seguidor (-ra); adherente, secuaz, *mf;* (imitator) imitador (-ra); (lover) novio, *m; pl* **followers,** acompañamiento, séquito, *m*
following *n* séquito, acompañamiento, *m,* comitiva, *f;* partidarios, *m pl,* adherentes, *mf pl. a* siguiente; próximo. **f. wind,** viento en popa, *m*
folly *n* locura, extravagancia, absurdidad, tontería, *f,* disparate, *m*
foment *vt* (poultice) fomentar; provocar, incitar, instigar; (assist) fomentar, proteger, promover
fomentation *n med* fomentación, *f;* provocación, instigación, *f;* fomento, *m,* protección, *f*
fomenter *n* fomentador (-ra), instigador (-ra)
fond *a* (credulous) vano, crédulo, vacío; (doting) demasiado indulgente; (loving) cariñoso, tierno, afectuoso; (addicted to) aficionado a, adicto a, amigo de. **to be f. of,** (things) tener afición a, estar aficionado de; (people) tener cariño (a). **to grow f. of,** (things) aficionarse a; (people) tomar cariño (a)
fondle *vt* mimar, acariciar; jugar (con.)
fondly *adv* (vainly) vanamente, sin razón; cariñosamente, tiernamente
fondness *n* cariño, afecto, *m;* (for things) afición, inclinación, *f;* gusto, *m*
font *n* pila bautismal, *f; poet* fuente, *f; print* fundición, *f*
food *n* alimento, *m;* comida, *f,* el comer; (of animals) pasto, *m; fig* pábulo, *m;* materia, *f.* **She gave him f.** Le dio de comer. **You have given me f. for thought,** Me has dado en qué pensar. **f.-card,** cartilla de racionamiento, **food, clothing, and shelter** comida, abrigo y vivienda, *f.* **F. Ministry,** Ministerio de Alimentación, *m.* **f. value,** valor nutritivo, *m.* **food poisoning,** intoxicación alimenticia, *f*
foodstuffs *n pl* comestibles, víveres, *m pl*
fool *n* tonto (-ta), mentecato (-ta), majadero (ra) necio (-ia); (jester) bufón, *m;* (butt of jest) hazmerreír, *m;* víctima, *f; cul* compota de frutas con crema, *f, vi* tontear, hacer tonterías. *vt* poner en ridiculo (a); (deceive) engañar, embaucar; (with) jugar con. **to make a f. of oneself,** ponerse en ridículo. **to f. about,** *vi* perder el tiempo, vagabundear. **to f. away,** malgastar, malbaratar. **fool's bauble,** cetro de bufón, *m.* **fool's cap,** gorro de bufón, *m*
foolhardiness *n* temeridad, *f*
foolhardy *a* temerario, atrevido
fooling *n* payasada, bufonada, *f;* (deceiving) engaño, *m,* burla, *f*
foolish *a* imprudente; estúpido, tonto; ridículo, absurdo; imbécil
foolishly *adv* imprudentemente; tontamente; imbécilmente
foolishness *n* imprudencia, *f;* estupidez, tontería, *f,* disparate, *m;* ridiculez, *f;* imbecilidad, *f*
foolproof *a* (of utensils, etc.) con garantía absoluta
foolscap *n* (nearest equivalent) papel de barba, *m*
fool's gold *n* pirita amarilla, *f,* sulfuro de hierro *m*
foot *n* pie, *m;* (of animals, furniture) pata, *f;* (of bed, sofa, grave, ladder, page, etc.) pie, *m;* (hoof) pezuña, *f;* (metric unit and measure) pie, *m; mil* infantería, *f;* (base) base, *f;* (step) paso, *m. a mil* de a pie; a pie. *vi* ir a pie; venir a pie; bailar. *vt* hollar; (account) pagar (una cuenta); (stockings) poner pie (a). **on f.,** a pie; (of soldiers) de a pie; (in progress) en marcha. **to go on f.,** ir a pie, andar. **to put one's best f. forward,** apretar el paso; *fig* hacer de su mejor. **to put one's f. down,** poner pies en pared, pararle fulano el alto. **to put one's f. in it,** meter la pata. **to rise to one's feet,** ponerse de pie. **to set f. on,** pisar, hollar. **to set on f.,** poner en pie; *fig* poner en marcha. **to trample under f.,** pisotear. **f.-and-mouth disease,** glosopeda, *f.* **f.-brake,** freno de pedal, *m.* **f.-pump,** fuelle de pie, *m.* **f.-rule,** (nearest equivalent) doble decímetro, *m.* **f.-soldier,** soldado de a pie, infante, *m*
football *n* (game) fútbol, *m;* (ball) pelota de fútbol, *f.* **f. field,** campo de fútbol, *m.* **f. match,** partida de fútbol, *f.* **f. pools,** apuestas de fútbol, *f pl;* (in Spain) apuestas benéficas de fútbol, *f pl*
footballer *n* fútbolista, *m*
footbath *n* baño de pies, *m*

footbridge *n* puente para peatones, *m*
footed *a* con pies; de pies . . . ; de patas . . .
footfall *n* pisada, *f*, paso, *m*
foothills *n pl* faldas de la montaña, *f pl*
foothold *n* hincapié, *m*; posición establecida, *f*
footing *n* hincapié, *m*; posición firme, *f*; condiciones, *f pl*; relaciones, *f pl*. **on a peacetime f.,** en pie de paz. **to be on an equal f.,** estar en pie de igualdad, estar en iguales condiciones. **to miss one's f.,** resbalar
footlights *n pl* canilejas, candilejas, *f pl*. **to get across the f.,** hacer contacto con el público
footman *n* lacayo, *m*
footnote *n* llamada a pie de página, nota a pie de página, *f*
footpath *n* senda, vereda, *f*, sendero, *m*
footprint *n* huella, pisada, *f*, vestigio, *m*
footsore *a* con los pies lastimados
footstep *n* paso, *m*; (trace) pisada, huella, *f*. **to follow in the footsteps of,** *fig* seguir las pisadas de
footstool *n* escabel, banquito, *m*
footwarmer *n* calientapiés, *m*
footwear *n* calzado, *m*
fop *n* petimetre, *m*
foppery *n* afectación en el vestir, *f*; vanidad, *f*
foppish *a* presumido, afectado; elegante
for *prep* (expressing exchange, price or penalty of, instead of, in support or favor of, on account of) por; (expressing destination, purpose, result) para; (during) durante, por; (for the sake of) para; (because of) a causa de; (in spite of) a pesar de; (as) como; (with) de; (in favor of) en favor de; (in election campaign) con (e.g., "Ecuadorians for Martínez!" ¡Ecuatorianos con Martínez!) (toward) hacia; (that) que, para que (with *subjunc*); a, (before) antes de; (searching for) en busca de; (bound for) con rumbo a; (regarding) en cuanto a; (until) hasta. What's for dinner? ¿Qué hay de comida? **center for . . .** centro de . . . (e.g., **Center for Applied Linguistics,** Centro de Lingüística Aplicada). **He is in business for himself,** Tiene negocios por su propia cuenta. **It is raining too hard for you to go there,** Llueve demasiado para que vayas allí. **It is not for him to decide,** No le toca a él decidirlo. **Were it not for . . . ,** Si no fuese por . . . **She has not been to see me for a week,** Hace una semana que no viene a verme. **It is impossible for them to go out,** Les es imposible salir. **but for all that,** pero con todo. **for ever,** por (or para) siempre. **for fear that,** por miedo de que. **for myself,** en cuanto a mí, personalmente. **for the present,** por ahora. **for what reason?** ¿para qué? ¿por cuál motivo? **for brevity's sake, for the sake of brevity,** por causa de la brevedad
for *conjunc* porque; visto que, pues, puesto que, en efecto, ya que
forage *n* forraje, *m*. *vt* and *vi* forrajear. **to f. for,** buscar. **f. cap,** gorra de cuartel, *f*
forager *n* forrajeador, *m*
foraging *n* forraje, *m*
forasmuch as *conjunc* puesto que, como que, ya que
foray *n* correría, cabalgada, *f*; saqueo, *m*
forbear *vt* and *vi* dejar (de), guardarse (de); abstenerse de; evitar; reprimirse (de); rehusarse (de); (cease) cesar (de); (be patient) ser paciente; ser tolerante
forbearance *n* abstención, *f*; tolerancia, transigencia, *f*; indulgencia, *f*; paciencia, *f*
forbearing *a* tolerance, transigente; generoso, magnánimo; paciente
forbid *vt* prohibir, defender (de); impedir. **I f. you to do it,** Te prohibo hacerlo. **The game is forbidden,** El juego está prohibido. **They have forbidden me to . . . ,** Me han defendido de . . . **Heaven f.!** ¡Dios no lo quiera!
forbidden *a* prohibido; ilícito. **f. fruit,** fruto prohibido, *m*
forbidding *a* repugnante, horrible; antipático, desagradable; (dismal) lúgubre; (threatening) amenazador. *n* prohibición, *f*
force *n* fuerza, *f*; violencia, *f*; vigor, *m*; (efficacy) eficacia, *f*; (validity) validez, *f*; (power) poder, *m*; (motive) motivo, *m*, razón, *f*; (weight) peso, *m*, importancia, *f*; (police) policía, *f*; *pl* **forces,** *mil* fuerzas, tropas, *f pl*. **by main f.,** por fuerza mayor. **in f.,** vigente, en vigor. **to be in f.,** estar vigente
force *vt* forzar; (compel) obligar, constreñir, precisar; (ravish) violar; *cul* rellenar; (impose) imponer; (plants) forzar; (the pace) apresurar; (cause) hacer; (a lock, etc.) forzar. **to f. oneself into,** entrar a la fuerza en; (a garment) ponerse con dificultad; imponerse a la fuerza. **to f. oneself to,** esforzarse a. **to f. the pace,** forzar el paso. **to f. away,** ahuyentar. **to f. back,** hacer retroceder; rechazar; (a sigh, etc.) ahogar. **to f. down,** hacer bajar, obligar a bajar; (make swallow) hacer tragar; (of airplanes) hacer tomar tierra. **to f. in,** introducir a la fuerza; obligar a entrar. **to f. into,** meter a la fuerza; obligar a entrar (en). **to f. on, upon,** imponer. **to f. open,** abrir a la fuerza; (a lock) romper, forzar. **to f. out,** hacer salir; empujar hacia fuera; (words) pronunciar con dificultad. **to f. up,** obligar a subir; hacer subir; hacer vomitar
forced *a* forzado; forzoso; afectado. **f. landing,** *aer* aterrizaje forzoso, *m*. **f. march,** *mil* marcha forzada, *f*
forceful *a* See **forcible**
forcemeat *n* picadillo, *m*; relleno, *m*. **f. ball,** albóndiga, *f*
forceps *n pl* fórceps, *m pl*; pinzas, *f pl*. **arterial f.,** pinzas hemostáticas, *f pl*
forcible *a* fuerte; a la fuerza; violento; enérgico, vigoroso; poderoso; *lit* vívido, gráfico, vehemente. **f. feeding,** alimentación forzosa, *f*
forcibleness *n* fuerza, *f*; vigor, *m*, energía, *f*; vehemencia, *f*
forcibly *adv* a la fuerza
forcing *n* forzamiento, *m*; compulsión, *f*. **f. frame,** semillero, *m*, especie de invernadero, *f*
ford *n* esguazo, vado, *m*. *vt* esguazar, vadear
fordable *a* esguazable, vadeable
fore *a* delantero; *naut* de proa. *adv* delante; *naut* de proa. **f.-and-aft,** *naut* de popa a proa.
forearm *n* antebrazo, *m*. *vt* armar de antemano; preparar
forebear *n* antecesor, *m*, ascendiente, *mf*
forebode *vt* presagiar, augurar, anunciar; presentir
foreboding *n* presagio, augurio, *m*; presentimiento, *m*, corazonada, *f*
forecast *n* pronóstico, *m*; proyecto, plan, *m*, *vt* pronosticar; proyectar. **weather f.,** pronóstico del tiempo, *m*
forecastle *n naut* castillo de proa, *m*
foreclose *vt* excluir; impedir; vender por orden judicial; anticipar el resultado de; decidir de antemano
foreclosure *n* venta por orden judicial, *f*; juicio hipotecario, *m*
foredoom *vt* predestinar
forefather *n* antepasado, antecesor, *m*
forefinger *n* índice, dedo índice, *m*
forefoot *n* pata delantera, *f*
forefront *n* delantera, primera línea, *f*; frente, *m*; vanguardia, *f*. **in the f.,** en la vanguardia; en el frente
foregoing *a* precedente, anterior
foregone *a* decidido de antemano; previsto
foreground *n* primer plano, primer término, frente, *m*. **in the f.,** *art* en primer término
forehand *a* derecho. **f. stroke,** golpe derecho, *m*
forehead *n* frente, *f*
foreign *a* extranjero; extraño; exótico; exterior; (alien) ajeno. **f. affairs,** asuntos extranjeros, *m pl*. **f. body,** cuerpo extraño, *m*. **f. debt,** deuda exterior, *f*. **F. Legion,** tercio extranjero, *m*. **F. Office,** Ministerio de Relaciones Extranjeras, *m*. **f. parts,** extranjero, *m*. **f. policy,** política internacional, *f*. **F. Secretary,** Secretario de Asuntos Extranjeros, Secretario de Asuntos Exteriores, Ministro de Relaciones Extranjeras, *m*. **f. trade,** comercio con el extranjero, *m*

foreigner *n* extranjero (-ra), *Argentina, Chile also* cuico (-ca), *Mexico also* fuereño (-ña) *mf*
foreignness *n* extranjerismo, *m;* (strangeness) extrañeza, *f;* lo exótico
foreknowledge *n* presciencia, precognición, *f*
foreland *n* promontorio, cabo, *m*
foreleg *n* pata delantera, *f*
forelock *n* guedeja, vedeja, *f;* (of a horse) copete, tupé, *m.* **to take time by the f.,** asir la ocasión por la melena
foreman *n* (of jury) presidente (del jurado), *m;* (of a farm) mayoral, *m;* (in a works) capataz, *m*
foremost *a* delantero; de primera fila; más importante. *adv* en primer lugar; en primera fila
forensic *a* forense, legal. **f. medicine,** medicina legal, *f*
foreordained *a* predestinado
forerunner *n* precursor (-ra), predecessor (-ra); (presage) anuncio, presagio, *m*
foresee *vt* prever, anticipar
foreseeing *a* presciente, sagaz
foreseer *n* previsor (-ra)
foreshadow *vt* anunciar, prefigurar; simbolizar; hacer sentir.
foreshorten *vt art* escorzar
foreshortening *n art* escorzo, *m*
foresight *n* presciencia, *f;* previsión, prudencia, *f;* (of gun) punto de mira, *m;* (optical) croquis de nivel, *m*
forest *n* bosque, *m,* selva, *f. vt* arbolar
forestall *vt* anticipar, saltear; prevenir; *com* acaparar
forestalling *n* anticipación, *f*
forestation *n* repoblación forestal, *f*
forester *n* silvicultor, guardamonte, ingeniero forestal, *m;* habitante de los bosques, *m*
forest fire incendio forestal, *m*
forestry *n* silvicultura, *f*
foresworn *a* perjuro
foretaste *n* muestra, *f;* presagio, *m. vt* gustar con anticipación
foretell *vt* predecir, profetizar; anunciar, presagiar
foreteller *n* profeta, *m;* presagio, *m*
foretelling *n* profecía, predicción, *f*
forethought *n* presciencia, previsión, *f;* prevención, *f*
forewarn *vt* prevenir
forewarning *n* presagio, *m*
forewoman *n* encargada, *f;* primera oficiala, *f*
foreword *n* prefacio, *m,* introducción, *f*
forfeit *n* pérdida, *f;* (fine) multa, *f;* (in games) prenda, *f;* (of rights, goods, etc.) confiscación, *f. a* confiscado. *vt* perder; perder el derecho o el título de
forfeiture *n* pérdida, *f;* confiscación, *f;* secuestro, *m*
forge *n* fragua, *f;* (smithy) herrería, *f. vt* and *vi* fraguar, forjar; (fabricate) inventar, fabricar; falsificar; (advance) avanzar lentamente. **to f. ahead,** abrirse camino; avanzar
forged *a* (of iron) forjado; (of checks, etc.) falso, falsificado
forger *n* falsificador (-ra), falsario (-ia); (creator) artífice, *mf*
forgery *n* falsificación, *f*
forget *vt* olvidar; descuidar. *vi* olvidarse. **to f. about,** olvidarse de, desacordarse de. **to f. oneself,** olvidarse de sí mismo; propasarse; (in anger) perder los estribos
forgetful *a* olvidadizo; descuidado, negligente
forgetfulness *n* olvido, *m;* descuido, *m;* falta de memoria, *f*
forging *n* fraguado, *m;* falsificación, *f*
forgivable *a* perdonable, excusable
forgive *vt* perdonar, disculpar, condonar; (debts) remitir
forgiveness *n* perdón, *m;* condonación, *f;* (remission) remisión, *f*
forgiving *a* misericordioso, clemente, dispuesto a perdonar
forgo *vt* renunciar, sacrificar, privarse de; abandonar, ceder
forgoing *n* renunciación, *f,* sacrificio, *m;* cesión, *f*
"For Immediate Occupancy" «De Ocupación Inmediata»
fork *n agr* horca, horquilla, *f;* (table fork) tenedor, *m;* bifurcación, *f;* (of rivers) confluencia, *f;* (of branches) horcadura, *f;* (of legs) horcajadura, *f;* (for supporting trees, etc.) horca, *f; mus* diapasón normal, *m. vt* hacinar con horca. *vi* bifurcarse; ramificarse
forked *a* bifurcado, hendido, ahorquillado. **f. lightning,** relámpago, *m.* **f. tail,** cola hendida, *f*
forlorn *a* abandonado, desamparado, desesperado. **f. hope,** aventura desesperada, *f*
forlornness *n* desamparo, *m,* miseria, *f;* desolación, *f,* desconsuelo, *m*
form *n* forma, *f;* figura, *f;* (shadowy) bulto, *m;* (formality) formalidad, *f;* ceremonia, *f; ecc* rito, *m;* método, *m;* regla, *f;* (in a school) clase, *f;* (lair) cama, *f;* (seat) banco, *m;* (system) sistema, *m;* (ghost) espectro, *m;* aparición, *f;* (to fill out) documento, *m;* hoja, *f, Mexico* esqueleto *m;* (state) condición, *f; lit* construcción, forma, *f.* **It is a matter of f.,** Es una pura formalidad. **in due f.,** en debida forma, en regla. **in the usual f.,** *com* al usado. **It is not good f.,** No es de buena educación
form *vt* formar; (a habit) contraer; (an idea) hacerse (una idea). *vi* formarse. **to f. fours,** *mil* formar a cuatro
formal *a* esencial; formal; ceremonioso, solemne; (of person) etiquetero, formalista. **f. call,** visita de cumplido, *f*
formaldehyde *n* formaldehído. *m*
formalism *n* formalismo, *m*
formality *n* formalidad, *f;* ceremonia, solemnidad, *f*
formally *adv* formalmente
format *n* formato, *m*
formation *n* formación, *f;* disposición, *f,* arreglo, *m;* organización, *f;* (*mil, geol*) formación, *f*
formative *a* formativo
forme *n print* forma, *f,* molde, *m*
former *a* primero; antiguo; anterior; pasado. **in f. times,** antes, antiguamente. **the f.,** ése, aquél, *m;* ésa, aquélla, *f;* aquéllos, *m pl;* aquéllas, *f pl*
former *n* formador (-ra); creador (-ra), autor (-ra)
formerly *adv* antiguamente, antes
formidable *a* formidable; terrible, espantoso
formless *a* informe
formlessness *n* falta de forma, *f*
formula *n* fórmula, *f.* **standard f.,** (*math, chem*) fórmula clásica, *f*
formulate *vt* formular
fornicate *vi* fornicar
fornication *n* fornicación, *f*
fornicator *n* fornicador (-ra)
forsake *vt* dejar, desertar; abandonar, desamparar; separarse de; (of birds, the nest) aborrecer; (one's faith) renegar de
forsaker *n* el, *m,* (la, *f*) que abandona; desertor, *m;* renegado (-da)
"For Sale" «Se Vende»
forsooth *adv* ciertamente, claro está
forswear *vt* abjurar; renunciar a. **to f. oneself,** perjurarse
forswearing *n* abjuración, *f;* renuncia, *f;* perjurio, *m*
fort *n* fortaleza, *f,* fuerte, *m*
forte *n* fuerte, *m. a mus* fuerte
forth *adv* (on) adelante, hacia adelante; (out) fuera; (in time) en adelante, en lo consecutivo; (show) a la vista. **and so f.,** y así en lo sucesivo; etcétera
forthcoming *a* próximo; futuro; en preparación
forthwith *adv* en seguida, sin tardanza
fortieth *a* cuadragésimo; cuarenta. *n* cuarentavo, *m*
fortifiable *a* fortificable
fortification *n* fortificación, *f*
fortify *vt* fortificar; fortalecer; confirmar; *fig* proveer (de)
fortitude *n* aguante, *m,* fortaleza, *f,* estoicismo, *m*
fortnight *n* quince días, *m pl,* dos semanas, *f pl;* quincena, *f.* **a f. ago,** hace quince días. **a f. tomorrow,**

mañana en quince. **in a f.,** dentro de quince días; al cabo de quince días. **once a f.,** cada quince días
fortnightly *a* quincenal. *adv* cada dos semanas, dos veces al mes. *n* revista quincenal, *f*
fortress *n* fortaleza, plaza fuerte, *f*
fortuitous *a* fortuito, accidental
fortuitously *adv* accidentalmente
fortuity *n* casualidad, *f*; accidente, *m*
fortunate *a* dichoso, feliz; afortunado; próspero. **to be f.,** (of persons) tener suerte
fortunately *adv* afortunadamente, por dicha, felizmente
fortune *n* suerte, fortuna, *f*, destino, *m*; (money) caudal, *m*, fortuna, *f*; bienes, *m pl*; buena ventura, *f*. **good f.,** buena fortuna, dicha, *f*. **ill f.,** mala suerte, *f*. **to cost a f.,** costar un sentido. **to make one's f.,** enriquecerse; *inf* hacer su pacotilla. to tell fortunes, echar las cartas. **f. hunter,** buscador de dotes, cazador de dotes, cazador de fortunas, aventurero, *m*. **f.-teller,** adivinadora, *f*; echadora de cartas, *f*. **f.-telling,** buenaventura, *f*
forty *a* and *n* cuarenta, *m*. **He is turned f.,** Ha cumplido los cuarenta. **person of f.,** cuarentón (-ona). **She is f.,** Tiene cuarenta años
forum *n* foro, tribuna *f*, (e.g., **to serve as a forum for discussion,** servir de tribuna de discusión)
forward *a* avanzado; adelantado; (of position) delantero; (ready) preparado; (eager) pronto, listo, impaciente; activo, emprendedor; (of persons, fruit, etc.) precoz; (pert) insolente, desenvuelto, atrevido. *adv* adelante; hacia adelante; (of time) en adelante; (farther on) más allá; hacia el frente; en primera linea. *vt* ayudar, promover; adelantar; (letters) hacer seguir; *com* expedir, remitir; (a parcel) despachar; (hasten) apresurar; (plants) hacer crecer. *n sport* delantero, *m*. **center-f.,** *sport* delantero centro, *m*. **from this time f.,** de hoy en adelante. **Please f.,** ¡Haga seguir! **putting f. of the clock,** el adelanto de la hora. **to carry f.,** *com* pasar a cuenta nueva. **to go f.,** adelantarse; estar en marcha, estar en preparación. **f. line,** *sport* delantera, *f*. **F.!** ¡Adelante!
forwarder *n* promotor (-ra); *com* remitente, *m*
forwarding *n* fomento, *m*, promoción, *f*; *com* expedición, *f*, envío, *m*
forwardness *n* progreso, adelantamiento, *m*; (haste) apresuramiento, *m*; (of persons, fruit, etc.) precocidad, *f*; (pertness) desenvoltura, insolencia, frescura, *f*, descaro, *m*; (eagerness) impaciencia, *f*
fossil *a* and *n* fósil, *m*.
fossilization *n* fosilización, *f*
fossilize *vt* fosilizar; petrificar. *vi* fosilizarse
foster *vt* provocar, promover, suscitar; (favor) favorecer, ser propicio a. **f.-brother,** hermano de leche, *m*. **f.-child,** hijo (-ja) de leche. **f.-father,** padre adoptivo, *m*. **f.-mother,** ama de leche, *f*. **f.-sister,** hermana de leche, *f*
foul *a* sucio, asqueroso, puerco; (evil-smelling) hediondo, fétido; (of air) viciado; impuro; (language) ofensivo; (coarse) indecente, obsceno; (harmful) nocivo, dañino; (wicked) malvado; infame; vil; (unfair) injusto; *sport* sucio; (ugly) feo; (entangled) enredado; (with corrections) lleno de erratas; (choked) atascado; (of weather) borrascoso, tempestuoso; malo, desagradable; (repulsive) repugnante. *n sport* juego sucio, *Lat. Am.* faul *m*. *vt* ensuciar; *naut* chocar, abordar; (block) atascar; (the anchor) enredar; *Lat. Am. sports* faulear; (dishonor) deshonrar. *vi* atascarse; (anchor) enredarse; *naut* chocar. **to fall f. of,** *naut* abordar (un buque); *fig* habérselas con. **by fair means or f.,** a las buenas o a las malas. **f. breath,** aliento fétido, aliento corrompido, *m*. **f. brood,** peste de las abejas, *f*. **f. language,** palabras ofensivas, *f pl*; lenguaje obsceno, *m*. **f. play,** juego sucio, *m*. **f. weather,** mal tiempo, tiempo borrascoso, *m*
found *vt* fundar; (metal, glass) fundir; (create, etc.) establecer
foundation *n* fundación, *f*; establecimiento, *m*; creación, *f*; *arch* cimiento, embasamiento, *m*; (basis) base, *f*; (cause) causa, *f*, origen, principio, *m*; (endowment) dotación, *f*; *sew* refuerzo, *m*. **to lay the f.,** poner las fundaciones. **f. stone,** piedra angular, *f*; *fig* primera piedra, *f*. **to lay the f. stone,** poner la piedra angular
founder *n* fundador (-ra); (of metals) fundidor, *m*. *vt* (a ship) hacer zozobrar. *vi* zozobrar, irse a pique; *fig* fracasar
foundering *n naut* zozobra, *f*
founding *n* fundación, *f*; establecimiento, *m*; (of metals) fundición, *f*
foundling *n* hijo (-ja) de la cuna, expósito (-ta). **f. hospital** or **home,** casa de cuna, casa de expósitos, inclusa, *f*
foundress *n* fundadora, *f*
foundry *n* fundición, *f*
fountain *n* fuente, *f*; (spring) manantial, *m*; (jet) chorro, *m*; (artificial) fuente, *f*, surtidero, *m*; (source) origen, principio, *m*. **f.-head,** fuente, *f*. **Fountain of Youth,** Fuente de la juventud, Fuente de Juvencio, *f*. **f. pen,** pluma estilográfica, *f*
four *a* and *n* cuatro, *m*. **It is f. o'clock,** Son las cuatro. **She is f.,** Tiene cuatro años. **on all fours,** a gatas. **f.-course,** (of meals) de cuatro platos. **f.-engined,** cuadrimotor. **f.-engined plane,** cuadrimotor, *m*. **f.-footed,** cuadrúpedo. **f.-horse,** de cuatro caballos. **f. hundred,** cuatrocientos. **f.-inhand,** tiro par, *m*. **f.-part,** (of a song) a cuatro voces. **f.-wheel brakes,** freno en las cuatro ruedas, *m*
fourfold *a* cuádruple
fourposter *n* cama de matrimonio, *f*
fourscore *a* and *n* ochenta, *m*.
foursome *n* partido de cuatro personas, *m*
fourteen *a* and *n* catorce, *m*. **He is f.,** Tiene catorce años
fourteenth *a* and *n* décimocuarto *m*.; (of the month) (el) catorce, *m*; (of monarchs) catorce. **April f.,** El 14 (catorce) de abril
fourth *a* cuarto; (of the month) el cuatro; (of monarchs) cuarto. *n* (fourth part) cuarta parte, *f*; *mus* cuarta, *f*. **f. dimension,** cuarta dimensión, *f*. **f. term,** (U.S.A. *pol*) cuarto mandato, *m*
fourthly *adv* en cuarto lugar
fowl *n* gallo. *m*; gallina, *f*; (chicken) pollo, *m*; (bird) ave, *f*; (barndoor f.) ave de corral, *f*. *vi* cazar aves. **f.-house or run,** gallinero, *m*
fox *n* zorro, *m*; (vixen) zorra, raposa, *Argentina* chilla *f*; *fig* zorro, taimado, *m*. *vi* disimular. *vt* (books) descolorar. **f.-brush,** cola de raposa, *f*. **f.-earth,** zorrera, *f*. **f.-hunting,** caza de zorras, *f*. **f. terrier,** fox-térrier, *m*
foxglove *n* digital, dedalera, *f*
foxhound *n* perro zorrero, *m*
foxiness *n* zorrería, astucia, *f*
foxtrot *n* foxtrot, *m*
foxy *a* de zorro; zorrero, astuto
foyer *n* foyer, salón de descanso, *m*
fraction *n math* fracción, *f*, número quebrado, *m*; pequeña parte, *f*; fragmento, *m*. **improper f.,** *math* fracción impropia, *f*. **proper f.,** *math* fracción propia, *f*
fractional *a* fraccionario
fractious *a* malhumorado, enojadizo
fractiousness *n* mal humor, *m*
fracture *n surg* fractura, *f*. *vt* fracturar. **compound f.,** fractura conminuta, *f*
fragile *a* frágil, quebradizo; (of persons) delicado
fragility *n* fragilidad, *f*
fragment *n* fragmento, *m*; trozo, pedazo, *m*. **to break into fragments,** hacer pedazos, hacer añicos
fragmentary *a* fragmentario
fragrance *n* fragancia, *f*, buen olor, perfume, aroma, *m*
fragrant *a* fragante, oloroso. **to make f.,** perfumar
frail *a* frágil, quebradizo; débil, endeble. *n* capacho, *m*, espuerta, *f*
frailty *n* fragilidad, *f*; debilidad, *f*
frame *n* constitución, *f*; sistema, *m*; organización, *f*; (of the body) figura, *f*, talle, *m*; (of window, picture) marco, *m*; (of machine, building) armadura, *f*; (of a bi-

cycle) cuadro (de bicicleta), *m; agr* cajonera, *f;* (embroidery) bastidor (para bordar), *m;* (skeleton) esqueleto, *m; lit* composición, construcción, *f;* (of spectacles) armadura, *f;* (of mind) disposición (de ánimo), *f;* humor, *m. vt* formar; construir; arreglar; ajustar; (a picture) enmarcar; componer, hacer; (draw up) redactar; (think up) idear, inventar; (words) articular, pronunciar. **f. a constitution,** elaborar una constitución
framer *n* fabricante de marcos, *m;* autor (-ra), creador (-ra), inventor (-ra)
framework *n* armadura, armazón, *f,* esqueleto, *m;* organización, *f;* (basis) base, *f*
franc *n* (coin) franco, *m*
franchise *n* (exemption) franquicia, *f;* privilegio, *m;* (vote) derecho de sufragio, *m;* (citizenship) derecho político, *m*
France Francia, *f*
Franche-Comté Franco-Condado, *m*
Franciscan *a* and *n* franciscano (-na)
Franco- (in compounds) franco- . . . *a* (Spanish *pol*—referring to General Franco) franquista
Francophile *a* and *n* afrancesado (-da)
Frank *n* franco (-ca), galo (-la)
frank *a* franco, cándido, sincero; abierto. *vt* franquear
frankincense *n* incienso, *m*
frankly *adv* francamente; sinceramente; cara a cara; sin rodeos, claramente; abiertamente. **to speak f.,** hablar claro, hablar sin rodeos
frankness *n* franqueza, *f;* sinceridad, *f,* candor, *m*
frantic *a* frenético, furioso, loco. **He drives me f.,** Me vuelve loco
fraternal *a* fraterno, fraternal
fraternity *n* fraternidad, hermandad, *f*
fraternization *n* fraternización, *f*
fraternize *vi* fraternizar
fratricidal *a* fratricida
fratricide *n* (person) fratricida, *mf;* (action) fratricidio, *m*
fraud *n* fraude, *m;* engaño, embuste, *Argentina also* forro *m;* (person) farsante, *m,* embustero (-ra)
fraudulence *n* fraudulencia, fraude, *f*
fraudulent *a* fraudulento
fraught *a* (with) cargado de; lleno de, preñado de
fray *n* refriega, riña, *f;* combate, *m,* batalla, *f;* (rubbing) raedura, *f. vt* raer, tazar. *vi* tazarse, deshilarse
frayed *a* raído
fraying *n* raedura, deshiladura, *f*
freak *n* monstruo, *m;* fenómeno, *m;* (whim) capricho, *m*
freakish *a* monstruoso; caprichoso; extravagante; raro, singular
freakishness *n* carácter caprichoso, *m;* extravagancia, *f;* rareza, extrañeza, *f*
freckle *n* peca, *f. vi* tener pecas; salir pecas (a la cara, etc.)
freckled *a* pecoso, con pecas
free *a* (in most senses) libre; independiente; emancipado; desembarazado; abierto; limpio (de); franco; (voluntary) voluntario; (self-governing) autónomo, independiente; accesible; (disengaged) desocupado; (vacant) vacío; (exempt) exento (de); (immune) immune (de); ajeno; gratuito; (loose) suelto; (generous) generoso, liberal; (vicious) disoluto, licencioso; (bold) atrevido; (impudent) insolente, demasiado familiar. *adv* gratis, gratuitamente. **There are two f. seats in the train,** Hay dos asientos libres en el tren. **to get f.,** libertarse. **to make f. with,** tomarse libertades con; usar como si fuera suyo. **to set f.,** poner en libertad. **f. agent,** libre albedrió, *m.* **f. and easy,** familiar, sin ceremonia. **f. gift,** *com* objeto de reclamo, *m.* **f.-hand drawing,** dibujo a pulso, *m.* **f. kick,** *sport* golpe franco, *m.* **f. love,** amor libre, *m.* **f. play,** rienda suelta, *f; mech* holgura, *f.* **f. port,** puerto franco, *m.* **f. speech,** libertad de palabra, *f.* **f. thought,** libre pensamiento, *m.* **f. ticket,** *theat* billete de favor, *m.* **f. trade,** *a* librecambista. *n* librecambio, *m.* **f. trader,** librecambista, *mf.* **f. verse,** verso libre, verso suelto, *m.* **f.-wheeling,** desenfrenado, libre. **f. will,** propia voluntad, *f;* (theology) libre albedrío, *m*
free *vt* libertar, poner en libertad (a); librar (de); (slave) salvar; emancipar; exentar; (of obstacles, difficulties) desembarazar; **to f. from,** libertar de; librar de; (clean) limpiar de
freebooter *n* pirata, filibustero, *m*
freeborn *a* nacido libre, libre por herencia
freedman *n* liberto, *m*
freedom *n* libertad, *f;* independencia, *f;* exención, *f;* inmunidad, *f;* soltura, facilidad, *f,* franqueza, *f;* (over-familiarity) insolencia, *f;* (boldness) audacia, intrepidez, *f;* (of customs) licencia, *f.* **to receive the f. of a city,** ser recibido como ciudadano de honor. **f. of speech,** libertad de palabra, *f.* **f. of the press,** libertad de la prensa, *f.* **f. of worship,** libertad de cultos, *f*
freehold *n* feudo franco, *m*
freeing *n* liberación, *f;* emancipación, *f;* salvación, *f;* (from obstruction) desembarazo, *m;* limpieza, *f*
freelance *n mil* soldado libre, *m; pol* independiente, *m;* aventurero (-ra). **f. journalist,** periodista libre, *m*
freely *adv* libremente; francamente; generosamente; sin reserva
freeman *n* hombre libre, *m;* (of a city) ciudadano de honor, *m*
freemason *n* francmasón, *m.* **freemason's lodge,** logia masónica, *f*
freemasonry *n* francmasonería, masonería, *f*
freethinker *n* librepensador (-ra)
freeze *vt* helar; (meat, etc.) congelar; *fig* helar. *vi* helarse; congelarse; (*impers,* of the weather) helar. **to f. to death,** morir de frío
freezing *n* hielo, *m;* congelación, *f. a* glacial; congelante, frigorífico. **f. mixture,** mezcla frigorífica, *f.* **f. of assets,** bloqueo de los depósitos bancarios, *m.* **f.-point,** punto de congelación, *m.* **above f.-point,** sobre cero. **below f.-point,** bajo cero
freight *n* flete, *m;* porte, *m. vt* fletar
freighter *n* fletador, *m;* (ship) buque de carga, *m*
French *a* francés. *n* (language) francés, *m;* (people) los franceses, *m pl.* **in F. fashion,** a la francesa. **to take F. leave,** despedirse a la inglesa. **What is the F. for "hat"?** ¿Cómo se dice «sombrero» en francés? **F. spoken,** Se habla francés. **F. bean,** judía, *f.* **F. chalk,** jabón de sastre, *m.* **F. horn,** trompa, *f.* **F. lesson,** lección de francés, *f.* **F. marigold,** flor del estudiante, *f.* **F. polish,** barniz de muebles, *m.* **F. poodle,** perro (-rra) de aguas. **F. roll,** panecillo, *m.* **F. window,** puerta ventana, *f*
Frenchify *vt* afrancesar
Frenchman *n* francés, *m.* **a young F.,** un joven francés
Frenchwoman *n* francesa, mujer francesa, *f.* **a young F.,** una joven francesa, una muchacha francesa, *f*
frenzied *a* frenético
frenzy *n* frenesí, delirio, paroxismo, *m*
frequency *n* frecuencia, *f.* **high f.,** alta frecuencia, *f.* **low f.,** baja frecuencia, *f*
frequent *a* frecuente; (usual) común, corriente. *vt* frecuentar
frequentation *n* frecuentación, *f*
frequenter *n* frecuentador (-ra)
frequently *adv* frecuentemente, con frecuencia, muchas veces; comúnmente
fresco *n art* fresco, *m,* pintura al fresco, *f. vt* pintar al fresco
fresh *a* fresco; nuevo; reciente; (newly arrived) recién llegado; (inexperienced) inexperto, bisoño; (of water, not salt) dulce; puro; (healthy) sano; (brisk) vigoroso, enérgico; (vivid) vivo, vívido; (bright) brillante; (cheeky) fresco, *Lat. Am.* impávido. *adv* neuvamente, recién (with past participle). **He came to us f. from school,** Vino a nosotros recién salido de su colegio. **We are going to take the f. air,** Vamos a tomar el fresco. **The milk is not f.,** La leche no está fresca. **f.-complexioned,** de buenos colores. **f. news,** noticias nuevas, *f pl.* **f. troops,** tropas nuevas, *f pl,* (reinforce-

ments) tropas de refuerzo, *f pl.* **f. water,** agua fresca, *f;* (not salt) agua dulce, *f.* **f.-water shrimp** *Mexico* acocil *m.* **f. wind,** viento fresco, *m*
freshen *vt* refrescar; (remove salt) desalar. *vi* (wind) refrescar. **to f. up,** renovar; refrescar; (of dress, etc.) arreglar
freshly *adv* nuevamente; recientemente
freshness *n* frescura, *f;* (newness) novedad, *f;* (vividness, brightness) intensidad, *f;* pureza, *f;* (beauty) lozanía, hermosura, *f;* (cheek) frescura, *f,* descaro, *m*
freshwater *n* agua dulce, *f.* **f. sailor,** marinero de agua dulce, *m*
fret *n* agitación, *f;* ansiedad, preocupación, *f; arch* greca, *f;* (of stringed instrument) traste, *m. vt* roer; (of a horse) bocezar; (corrode) desgastar, corroer; (of the wind, etc.) rizar; (worry) tener preocupado (a); irritar, enojar; (lose) perder; (oneself) apurarse, consumirse; *arch* calar. *vi* torturarse, preocuparse, inquietarse; (complain) quejarse; (mourn) lamentarse, estar triste
fretful *a* mal humorado, mohíno, quejoso, irritable
fretfully *adv* irritablemente, con mal humor
fretwork *n* calado, *m*
Freudian *a* freudiano
friar *n* fraile, *m.* **Black f.,** dominicano, *m.* **Gray f.,** franciscano, *m.* **White f.,** carmelita, *m.* **f.-like,** frailesco
friction *n* frote, frotamiento, roce, *m; phys* rozamiento, *m;* fricción, *f.* **to give a f.,** friccionar, dar fricciones (a). **f. gearing,** engranaje de fricción, *m.* **f. glove,** guante de fricciones, *m*
Friday *n* viernes, *m.* **Good F.,** Viernes Santo, *m*
fried *a* frito. **f. egg,** huevo frito, *m*
friend *n* amigo (-ga); (acquaintance) conocido (-da); (Quaker) cuáquero (-ra); (follower) adherente, *m;* partidario (-ia); (ally) aliado (-da); *pl* **friends,** amistades, *f pl;* amigos, *m pl.* **a f. of yours,** un amigo tuyo, uno de tus amigos. **to make friends,** hacer amigos; (become friends) hacerse amigos; (after a quarrel) hacer las paces. **Friends!** (to sentinel) ¡Gente de paz!
friendless *a* sin amigos; desamparado
friendliness *n* amabilidad, afabilidad, cordialidad, amigabilidad, *f*
friendly *a* amistoso, amigable, amigo; afable, acogedor, simpático; propicio, favorable. **to be f. with,** ser amigo de. **f. society,** sociedad de socorros, *f*
friendship *n* amistad, intimidad, *f*
frieze *n* friso, *m;* (cloth) frisa, jerga, *f*
frigate *n nav* fragata, *f*
fright *n* terror, susto, *m;* (guy) espantajo, *m. vt* asustar. **to have a f.,** tener un susto. **to take f.,** asustarse
frighten *vt* espantar, dar un susto (a), alarmar, asustar; horrorizar; (overawe) acobardar. **to be frightened out of one's wits,** estar muerto de miedo. **to f. away,** ahuyentar, espantar
frightened *a* miedoso, tímido, medroso, nervioso
frightening *a* que da miedo; alarmante, amedrentador; horrible
frightful *a* horrible, espantoso, horroroso; *inf* tremendo, enorme
frightfully *adv* horrorosamente; *inf* enormemente
frigid *a* frío; helado; *med* impotente
frigidity *n* frialdad, frigidez, *f; med* impotencia, *f*
frigidly *adv* fríamente
frill *n sew* volante, *m;* (jabot) chorrera, *f;* (round a bird's neck) collarín de plumas, *m;* (of paper) frunce, *m. vt* alechugar; fruncir
fringe *n* fleco, *m,* franja, *f, Lat. Am.* cerquillo *f;* (of hair) flequillo, *m;* (edge) borde, *m,* margen, *mf. vt* guarnecer con fleco, franjar; adornar; (grow by) crecer al margen (de)
Frisian *a* and *n* frisón (-ona); (language) frisón, *m*
frisk *vi* retozar, brincar
friskiness *n* viveza, agilidad, *f*
frisky *a* retozón, juguetón
fritter *n cul* fruta de sartén, *f. vt* (away) malgastar, desperdiciar; perder
frivolity *n* frivolidad, ligereza, *f;* futilidad, *f*
frivolous *a* frívolo, ligero, liviano; (futile) trivial, fútil
frizz *vt* (cloth) frisar; (hair) rizar
frizzy *a* (of hair) crespo, rizado
fro *adv* hacia atrás. **movement to and fro,** vaivén, *m.* **to and fro,** de un lado a otro. **to go to and fro,** ir y venir
frock *n* vestido, *m;* (of a monk) hábito, *m;* (of priest) sotana, *f.* **f.-coat,** levita, *f*
frog *n* rana, *f.* **to have a f. in the throat,** padecer carraspera
frolic *n* (play) juego, *m;* (mischief) travesura, *f;* (folly) locura, extravagancia, *f;* (joke) chanza, *f;* (amusement) diversión, *f;* (wild party) holgorio, *m,* parranda, *f. vi* retozar, juguetear; divertirse
frolicsome *a* retozón, juguetón
from *prep* de; desde; (according to) según; (in the name of, on behalf of) de parte de; (through, by) por; (beginning on) a contar de; (with) con; **F.** (on envelope) Remite, Remitente. **He is coming here f. the dentist's,** Vendrá aquí desde casa del dentista. **Give him this message f. me,** Dale este recado de mi parte. **Judging f. his appearance,** Juzgando por su apariencia. **prices f. five hundred pesetas upward,** precios desde quinientos pesetas en adelante. **f. what I hear,** según mi información, según lo que oigo. **f. above,** desde arriba. **f. among,** de entre. **f. afar,** de lejos, desde lejos. **f. time to time,** de cuando en cuando, de vez en cuando
frond *n bot* fronda, *f*
front *n* frente, *f;* cara, *f; mil* frente, *m;* (battle line) línea de combate, *f;* (of a building) fachada, *f;* (of shirt) pechera, *f;* (at the seaside) playa, *f;* (promenade) paseo de la playa, *m;* (forefront) primera línea, *f;* (forepart) parte delantera, *f; theat* auditorio, *m;* (organization) organización de fachada, *f;* (impudence) descaro, *m, a* delantero; anterior; de frente; primero. *adv* hacia delante. *vi* mirar a, dar a; hacer frente a. **in f.,** en frente. **in f. of,** en frente de; (in the presence of) delante de, en la presencia de. **to face f.,** hacer frente. **to put on a bold f.,** hacer de tripas corazón. **f. door,** puerta de entrada, puerta principal, *f.* **f. line,** *mil* línea del frente, *f;* primera línea, *f.* **f. seat,** (at an entertainment, etc.) delantera, *f.* **f. organization** organización de fachada *f.* **f. tooth,** diente incisivo, *m.* **f. view,** vista de frente, *f;* vista de cerca, *f*
frontage *n* (of a building) fachada, *f;* (site) terreno de . . . metros de fachada, *m*
frontal *a mil* de frente; *anat* frontal
frontier *n* frontera, *f; fig* límite, *m. a* fronterizo
frontispiece *n* (of a building) frontispicio, *m,* fachada, *f;* (of a book) portada, *f*
frost *n* escarcha, *f;* helada, *f. vt* helar; *cul* escarchar; (glass) deslustrar; *fig* escarchar. *vi* helar. **f.-bitten,** helado
frostbite *n* efectos del frío, *m pl*
frosted *a* escarchado; helado; (of glass) deslustrado, opaco; *cul* escarchado
frostily *adv fig* glacialmente, con frialdad.
frostiness *n;* frío glacial, *m*
frosting *n* escarcha, *f;* (of glass) deslustre, *m; cul* cobertura, escarcha, *f*
frosty *a* helado; de hielo; (of hair) canoso; *fig* glacial, frío. **It was f. last night,** Anoche heló
froth *n* espuma, *f; fig* frivolidad, vanidad, *f, vi* espumar, hacer espuma; echar espuma. *vt* hacer espumar; hacer echar espuma
frothiness *n* espumosidad, *f; fig* frivolidad, superficialidad, vaciedad, *f*
frothy *a* espumoso, espumajoso; *fig* frívolo, superficial
frown *n* ceño, *m;* cara de juez, expresión severa, *f;* desaprobación, *f;* (of fortune) revés, golpe, *m. vi* fruncir el ceño. **to f. at, on, upon,** mirar con desaprobación, ver con malos ojos; ser enemigo de; desaprobar
frowning *a* ceñudo; severo; amenazador
frowningly *adv* severamente

frowsiness *n* mal olor, *m*; (dirtiness) suciedad, *f*; (untidiness) desaliño, desaseo, *m*
frowsy *a* fétido, mal oliente; mal ventilado; (dirty) sucio; (untidy) desaliñado, desaseado
frozen *a* helado; cubierto de hielo; congelado; (*geog* and *fig*) glacial. **to be f. up,** estar helado. **f. meat,** carne congelada, *f*
frugal *a* económico; frugal; sobrio
frugality *n* economía, *f*; frugalidad, sobriedad, *f*
fruit *n* (in general sense) fruto, *m*; (off a tree or bush) fruta, *f*; *fig* fruto, *m*; resultado, *m*, consecuencia, *f*. *vi* frutar, dar fruto. **bottled f.,** fruta en almíbar, *f*. **candied f.,** fruta azucarada, *f*. **dried f.,** fruta seca, *f*. **first fruits,** primicias, *f pl*. **soft f.,** frutas blandas, *f pl*. **stone f.,** fruta de hueso, *f*. **f.-bearing,** frutal. **f.-cake,** pastel de fruta, *m*. **f.-dish,** frutero, *m*. **f. farming,** fruticultura, *f*. **f.-knife,** cuchillo de postres, *m*. **f. shop,** frutería, *f*. **f. tree,** frutal, *m*
fruiterer *n* frutero (-ra)
fruitful *a* fructuoso, fértil; prolífico, fecundo; provechoso
fruitfulness *n* fertilidad, *f*; fecundidad, *f*; provecho, *m*
fruition *n* fruición, *f*
fruitless *a* infructuoso, estéril; inútil
fruitlessness *n* infructuosidad, esterilidad, *f*; inutilidad, *f*
fruity *a* de fruta; (wines) vinoso; (of voice) melodioso
frump *n* estantigua, *f*
frumpish *a* estrafalario; fuera de moda
frustrate *vt* frustrar; defraudar; malograr; destruir; anular
frustration *n* frustración, *f*; defraudación, *f*; malogro, *m*; destrucción, *f*; desengaño, *m*
fry *n cul* fritada, *f*. *vt* freír. *vi* freírse. **small fry,** *inf* gente menuda, *f*
frying *n* fritura, *f*, el freír. **to fall out of the f.-pan into the fire,** ir de mal en peor, andar de zocos en colodros, ir de Guatemala en Guatapeor. **f.-pan,** sartén, *f*
fuchsia *n* fuscia, *Lat. Am.* aljaba *f*
fuddle *vt* atontar, aturdir; embriagar, emborrachar
fudge *n* patraña, tontería, *f*, disparate, *m*; (food) *Lat. Am.* manjar *m*. *interj* ¡qué disparate! ¡qué va!
fuel *n* combustible, *m*; *fig* cebo, pábulo, *m*. *vt* cebar, echar combustible en. *vi* tomar combustible. **to add f. to the flame,** echar leña al fuego. **f. consumption,** consumo de combustible, *m*. **f.-oil,** aceite combustible, aceite de quemar, *m*. **f.-tank,** depósito de combustible, *m*
fueling *n* aprovisionamiento de combustible, *m*
fugitive *a* fugitivo; pasajero, perecedero; transitorio, efímero, fugaz. *n* fugitivo (-va); (from justice) prófugo (-ga); *mil* desertor, *m*; (refugee) refugiado (-da)
fugue *n mus* fuga, *f*
fulcrum *n mech* fulcro, *m*
fulfil *vt* cumplir; (satisfy) satisfacer; (observe) observar; guardar. **to be fulfilled,** cumplirse, realizarse
fulfilment *n* cumplimiento, *m*; desempeño, ejercicio, *m*; (satisfaction) satisfacción, realización, *f*; (observance) observancia, *f*
full *a* lleno; colmado; todo; pleno; (crowded) atestado; (replete) harto; abundante; (intent on) preocupado con, pensando en; (loose) amplio; (plentiful) copioso; (occupied) ocupado; completo; (resonant) sonoro; (mature) maduro; puro; perfecto; (satiated) saciado (de); (of the moon, sails) lleno; (weighed down) agobiado, abrumado; (detailed) detallado; (with uniform, etc.) de gala; (with years, etc.) cumplido. *n* colmo, *m*; totalidad, *f*. *adv* muy; completamente, totalmente. **f. many a flower,** muchas flores. **at f. gallop,** a galope tendido. **at f. speed,** a todo correr; a toda velocidad. **His hands are f.,** Sus manos están llenas. **The moon was at the f.,** La luna estaba llena. **in f.,** por completo; sin abreviaciones; integralmente. **in f. swing,** en plena actividad. **in f. vigor,** en pleno vigor. **to the f.,** completamente; hasta la última gota; a la perfección. **to be f. to the brim,** estar lleno hasta el tope. **f.-blooded,** sanguíneo; de pura raza; *fig* viril, vigoroso; *fig* apasionado. **f.-blown,** en plena flor, abierto. **f. dress,** *a* de gala. *n* traje de etiqueta, traje de ceremonia, *m*. **f.-face,** de cara. **f.-flavored,** (wine) abocado. **f.-grown,** adulto; completamente desarrollado. **f.-length,** de cuerpo entero. **f. moon,** luna llena, *f*; plenilunio, *m*. **f. name,** nombre y apellidos, *m*. **f. powers,** plenos poderes, *m pl*. **f. scale,** tamaño natural, *m*. **f. scope,** carta blanca, *f*; toda clase de facilidades. **f. steam ahead,** a todo vapor. **f. stop,** *gram* punto final, *m*
full-color *a* a todo color. **full-color plates,** láminas a todo color
fuller *n* batanero, *m*. **fuller's earth,** tierra de batán, galactita, *f*
fulling *n* abatanadura, *f*. **f.-mill,** batán, *m*
fullness *n* abundancia, *f*; plenitud, *f*; (repletion) hartura, *f*; (of clothes) amplitud, *f*; (stoutness) gordura, *f*; (swelling) hinchazón, *f*. **She wrote with great f. of all that she had seen,** Describía muy detalladamente todo lo que había visto. **in the f. of time,** andando el tiempo
full-page *a* a toda plana. **full-page advertisement,** anuncio a toda plana.
full-time *a* de tiempo completo
fully *adv* plenamente; enteramente. **It is f. six years since . . . ,** Hace seis años bien cumplidos que . . . **It is f. 9 o'clock,** Son las nueve bien sonadas. **f. dressed,** completamente vestido
fulminant *a med* fulminante
fulminate *n chem* fulminato, *m*. *vi* estallar; fulminar. *vt* volar; fulminar
fulminous *a* fulmíneo, fulminoso
fulsome *a* servil; insincero, hipócrita; asqueroso, repugnante
fumble *vi* (grope) ir a tientas; procurar hacer algo; chapucear (con); (for a word) titubear
fumbling *n* hesitación, *f*; tacto incierto, *m*. *a* incierto; vacilante
fumblingly *adv* de manera incierta; a tientas
fume *n* vaho, humo, gas, *m*; emanación, *f*; mal olor, *m*, fetidez, *f*; *fig* vapor, *m*; (state of mind) agitación, *f*; frenesí, *m*. *vi* humear; refunfuñar, echar pestes, *Lat. Am.* estar hecho un ají
fumigate *vt* fumigar, *Lat. Am. also* humear; sahumar, perfumar; desinfectar
fumigation *n* fumigación, *f*; sahumerio, *m*
fumigator *n* fumigador (-ra); (apparatus) fumigador, *m*
fumigatory *a* fumigatorio
fuming *n* refunfuño, *m*. *a* refunfuñador
fumy *a* humoso
fun *n* diversión, *f*, entretenimiento, *m*; (joke) chanza, broma, *f*. **for fun,** para divertirse; en chanza. **in fun,** de burlas. **to have fun,** divertirse. **to poke fun at,** burlarse de, mofarse de, ridiculizar
function *n* función, *f*. *vi* funcionar
functional *a* funcional
functionary *n* funcionario, *m*. *a* funcional
functioning *n* funcionamiento, *m*
fund *n* fondo, *m*; *pl* **funds,** fondos, *m pl*; *inf* dinero, *m*. **public funds,** fondos públicos, *m pl*. **sinking f.,** fondo de amortización, *m*
fundamental *a* fundamental, básico; esencial. *n* fundamento, *m*
fundamentally *adv* fundamentalmente, básicamente; esencialmente
funeral *a* funeral, fúnebre, funerario. *n* funerales, *m pl*; entierro, *m*. **to attend the f. (of),** asistir a los funerales (de). **f. feast,** banquetes fúnebres, *m pl*. **f. director, f. furnisher,** director de pompas fúnebres, *m*. **f. procession,** cortejo fúnebre, *m*. **f. pyre,** pira funeraria, *f*. **f. service,** misa de difuntos, *f*
funereal *a* fúnebre, lúgubre
fungicide *n* anticriptógamo, *m*
fungous *a* fungoso
fungus *n* hongo, *m*

funicular *a* funicular. **f. railway,** ferrocarril funicular, *m*

funnel *n chem* embudo, *m*; *naut* chimenea, *f*; (of a chimney) cañón (de chimenea), *m*. **f.-shaped,** en forma de embudo

funnily *adv* de un modo raro

funniness *n* lo divertido; rareza, extrañeza, *f*

funny *a* cómico, gracioso; divertido; (strange) extraño, raro; (mysterious) misterioso. **It struck me as f.,** (amused me) Me hizo gracia; (seemed strange) Me pareció raro. **f.-bone,** hueso de la alegría, *m*

fur *n* piel, *f*; depósito, sarro, *m*; (on tongue) saburra, *f*. *a* hecho de pieles. *vt* forrar, or adornar, or cubrir, con pieles; depositar sarro sobre; (the tongue) ensuciarse la lengua. *vi* estar forrado, or adornado, or cubierto, con pieles; formarse incrustaciones; (of the tongue) tener la lengua sucia. **fur cap,** gorra de pieles, *f*. **fur cape,** cuello de piel, *m*; capa de pieles, *f*. **fur trade,** peletería, *f*

furbish *vt* pulir; renovar; limpiar

furious *a* furioso. **to become f.,** ponerse furioso, enfurecerse

furiously *adv* furiosamente, con furia

furiousness *n* furia, *f*

furl *vt* plegar; enrollar; *naut* aferrar

furlong *n* estadio, *m*

furlough *n mil* permiso, *m*. *vt* conceder un permiso (a). **on f.,** de permiso

furnace *n* horno, *m*; (of steam boiler) fogón, *m*; (for central heating) caldera de calefacción central, *f*; (for smelting) cubilote, *m*

furnish *vt* proveer (de), equipar (de), suplir (de); amueblar; (an opportunity) proporcionar; producir

furnished *a* amueblado, con muebles. **f. house,** casa amueblada, *f*

furnisher *n* decorador, *m*; proveedor (-ra)

furnishing *n* provisión, *f*, equipo, *m*; *pl* **furnishings,** accesorios, *m pl*; mobiliario, mueblaje, *m*

furniture *n* mobiliario, mueblaje, *Central America, Mexico* amoblado *m*; ajuar, equipo, *m*; avíos, *m pl*; *naut* aparejo, *m*. **a piece of f.,** un mueble. **to empty of f.,** desamueblar, quitar los muebles (de). **f. dealer** or **maker,** mueblista, *mf*. **f. factory,** mueblería, *f*. **f. polish,** crema para muebles, *f*. **f. mover,** transportador de muebles, *m*; (packer) embalador, *m*. **f. repository,** guardamuebles, *m*. **f. van,** carro de mudanzas, *m*

furor *n* furor, *m*

furred *a* forrado or cubierto or adornado de piel; (of the tongue) sucia

furrier *n* peletero, *m*. **furrier's shop,** peletería, *f*

furrow *n* surco, *m*; *carp* muesca, *f*; *arch* estría, *f*; (wrinkle) arruga, *f*. *vt* surcar

furry *a* cubierto de piel; parecido a una piel; hecho de pieles

further *a* ulterior, más distante; (other) otro; opuesto; adicional, más. *adv* más lejos; más allá; además; también; por añadidura. *vt* promover, fomentar; ayudar. **on the f. side,** al otro lado. **till f. orders,** hasta nueva orden. **f. on,** más adelante; más allá

furtherance *n* fomento, *m*, promoción, *f*; progreso, avance, *m*

furthermore *adv* además, por añadidura

furthest *a* (el, la, lo) más lejano or más distante; extremo. *adv* más lejos

furtive *a* furtivo

furtively *adv* furtivamente, a hurtadillas. **to look at f.,** mirar de reojo

fury *n* furor, enfurecimiento, *m*, rabia, *f*; violencia, *f*; frenesí, arrebato, *m*; furia, *f*. **like a f.,** hecho una furia. **to breathe forth f.,** echar rayos

fuse *n* (of explosives) espoleta, mecha, *f*; *elec* fusible, *m*. *vt* (metals) fundir; fusionar, mezclar. *vi* (metals) fundirse; mezclarse. **safety-f.,** espoleta de seguridad, *f*. **time-f.,** espoleta de tiempo, *f*. **to blow a f.,** fundir un fusible. **f. box,** caja de fusibles, *f*. **f. wire,** fusible, *m*

fuselage *n aer* fuselaje, *m*

fusible *a* fusible

fusillade *n* descarga cerrada, *f*

fusion *n* fusión, *f*; unión, *f*; (melting) fundición, *f*

fuss *n* agitación, *f*; (bustle) conmoción, bulla, *f*; bullicio, *m*. *vi* agitarse, preocuparse. *vt* poner nervioso. **There's no need to make such a f.,** No es para tanto. **to make a f. of,** (a person) hacer la rueda (a), ser muy atento (a); (spoil) mimar mucho (a). **to f. about,** andar de acá para allá

fussily *adv* nerviosamente; de un aire importante

fussy *a* meticuloso, nimio; nervioso; (of style) florido, hinchado; (of dress) demasiado adornado

fustigate *vt* fustigar

fusty *a* (moldy) mohoso; mal ventilado; mal oliente; (of views, etc.) pasado de moda

futile *a* fútil, superficial, frívolo; inútil

futility *n* futilidad, superficialidad, frivolidad, *f*; (action) tontería, estupidez, *f*

future *a* futuro, venidero. *n* futuro, porvenir, *m*. **in the f.,** en adelante, en lo venidero, en lo sucesivo. **for f. reference,** para información futura. **f. perfect tense,** *gram* futuro perfecto, *m*. **f. tense,** *gram* futuro, *m*

futurism *n* futurismo, *m*

futurist *n* futurista, *mf*

futuristic *a* futurístico

fuzz *n* tamo, *m*, pelusa, *f*. **f.-ball,** *bot* bejín, *m*

fuzzy *a* crespo rizado; velloso

g *n* (letter) ge, *f*; *mus* sol, *m*. **G clef,** clave de sol, *f*

gab *n inf* labia, *f*. **to have the gift of the gab,** tener mucha labia

gabardine *n* gabardina, *f*

gabble *vi* chacharear, garlar; hablar indistintamente; (of goose and some birds) graznar. *vt* decir indistintamente; decir rápidamente; (a language) chapurrear; mascullar. *n* cháchara, *f*; vocerío, *m*; (of goose and some birds) graznido, *m*

gabbler *n* charlatán (-ana), chacharero (-ra)

gabbling *n* See **gabble**

gable *n arch* gablete, hastial, *m*. **g.-end,** alero, *m*

gad *vi* corretear, callejear. **to gad about,** correr por todos lados; divertirse.

gadabout *n* azotacalles, *mf*; gandul (-la), vagabundo (-da)

gadding *a* callejero; vagabundo. *n* vagancia, *f*; vida errante, *f*; gandulería, *f*

gadfly *n ent* tábano, *m*; *inf* moscardón, *m*

gadget *n* accesorio, *m*; aparato, *m*; chuchería, *f*

Gadsden Purchase la Venta de la Meseta, *f*

Gael *n* escocés (-esa) del norte; celta, *mf*

Gaelic *a* gaélico. *n* gaélico, *m*

gaff *n* (hook) garfio, *m*; *naut* pico de cangrejo, *m*; *theat* teatrucho, *m*

gaffer *n* viejo, tío, abuelo, *m*

gag *n* mordaza, *f*; *theat* morcilla, *f*. *vt* amordazar; *fig* hacer callar. *vi theat* meter morcillas

gage *n* prenda, fianza, *f*; (symbol of challenge) guante, *m*; (challenge) desafío, *m*. See **gauge**

gagging *n* amordazamiento, *m*

gaggle *n* (cry) graznido, *m*; (of geese) manada (de ocas), *f*. *vi* graznar; cacarear

gaiety *n* alegría, *f*; animación, vivacidad, *f*; (entertainment) diversión, festividad, *f*

gaily *adv* alegremente

gain *n* ganancia, *f*; provecho, beneficio, *m*; (increase) aumento, *m*; (riches) riqueza, *f*. *vt* ganar; (acquire) conseguir; adquirir; obtener; conquistar, captar; (friends) hacerse; (reach) llegar a, alcanzar. *vi* ganar; (improve) mejorar; (of a watch) adelantarse. **What have they gained by going to Canada?** ¿Qué han logrado con marcharse al Canadá? **to g. ground,** *fig* ganar terreno. **to g. momentum** adquirir velocidad **to g. time,** ganar tiempo. **to g. on, upon,** acercarse a; (overtake) alcanzar; (outstrip) dejar atrás, pasar; (of sea) invadir; (of habits) imponerse

gainful *a* ganancioso, lucrativo; ventajoso

gainfully *adv* ventajosamente; lucrativamente

gainsay *vt* contradecir; oponer; negar

gainsaying *n* contradicción, *f;* oposición, *f;* negación, *f*

gait *n* porte, andar, *m;* paso, *m,* andadura, *f*

gaiter *n* polaina, *f;* (spat) botín, *m*

gala *n* gala, fiesta, *f.* **g.-day.** día de fiesta, *m.* **g.-dress,** traje de gala, *m*

galaxy *n ast* vía láctea, *f; fig* constelación, *f;* grupo brillante, *m*

gale *n* vendaval, ventarrón, *m;* (storm) temporal, *m;* tempestad, *f*

Galician *a* and *n* gallego (-ga).

Galilean *a* and *n* galileo (-ea)

Galilee Galilea, *f*

gall *n* (on horses) matadura, *f;* (abrasion) rozadura, *f;* hiel, bilis, *f; fig* hiel, amargura, *f;* rencor, *m;* (American slang) descaro, *m,* impertinencia, *f; bot* agalla, *f. vt* rozar; *fig* mortificar, herir. **g.-apple,** agalla, *f.* **g.-bladder,** vejiga de la hiel, *f.* **g.-stone,** cálculo hepático, *m*

gallant *a* hermoso; (imposing) imponente, majestuoso; (brave) valiente, gallardo, valeroso, intrépido; (chivalrous) caballeroso; noble; (attentive to ladies, or amorous) galante. *n* galán, *m. vt* galantear, cortejar

gallantly *adv* (bravely) valientemente; caballerosamente; cortésmente; galantemente

gallantry *n* (bravery) valentía, *f,* valor, *m;* heroísmo, *m,* proeza, *f;* (chivalry) caballerosidad, *f;* (toward women, or amorousness) galantería, *f*

galleon *n* galeón, *m*

gallery *n* galería, *f;* pasillo, *m;* (of a cloister) tránsito, *m;* (cloister) claustro, *m;* (for spectators) tribuna, *f; theat* paraíso, gallinero, *m;* (theater audience) galería, *f;* (of portraits, etc.) galería, colección, *f;* (*min, mil*) galería, *f;* (building) museo, *m.* **art g.,** museo de pinturas, *m*

galley *n* (*naut, print*) galera, *f;* (kitchen) cocina, *f;* (rowboat) falúa de capitán, *f.* **to condemn to the galleys,** echar a galeras. **wooden g.,** *print* galerín, *m.* **g.-proof,** galerada, *f.* **g.-slave,** galeote, *m*

Gallic *a* gálico, galicano; francés

gallicism *n* galicismo, *m*

galling *a fig* irritante; mortificante

gallivant *vi* callejear, corretear; divertirse; ir de parranda

gallon *n* galón, *m*

galloon *n* galón, *m,* trencilla, *f*

gallop *n* galope, *m. vi* galopar; ir aprisa. *vt* hacer galopar, **at full g.,** a rienda suelta, a galope tendido. **to g. back,** volver a galope. **to g. down,** bajar a galope. **to g. off,** marcharse galopando; alejarse corriendo. **to g. past,** desfilar a galope ante. **to g. through,** cruzar a galope. **to g. up,** *vt* subir a galope. *vi* llegar a galope

gallopade *n* (dance) galop, *m*

galloping *n* galope, *m;* galopada, *f. a* que va a galope; *med* galopante. **g. consumption,** tisis galopante, *f*

gallows *n* patíbulo, *m,* horca, *f;* (framework) montante, *m.* **g.-bird,** criminal digno de la horca, *m*

galop *n* galop, *m*

galore *adv* a granel, en abundancia (e.g. **sunshine galore,** sol a granel)

galosh *n* chanclo, *m*

galvanic *a elec* galvánico; espasmódico

galvanize *vt* galvanizar

gambit *n* (chess) gambito, *m; fig* táctica, *f*

gamble *n* juego de azar, *m;* jugada, *f;* aventura, *f; com* especulación, *f. vi* jugar por dinero; especular; (with) *fig* aventurar, arriesgar. **to g. on the Stock Exchange,** jugar en la bolsa. **to g. away,** perder al juego

gambler *n* jugador (-ra), *Mexico* dadista *mf*

gambling *n* juego, *m. a* jugador; de juego. **g.-den,** casa de juego, *f,* garito, *m*

gambol *n* salto, brinco, retozo, *m;* cabriola, *f;* juego, *m. vi* saltar, brincar, retozar; juguetear

game *n* juego, *m;* (match) partido, *m;* (jest) chanza, *f;* (trick) trampa, *f;* (birds, hares, etc.) caza menor, *f;* (tigers, lions, etc.) caza mayor, *f;* (flesh of game) caza, *f; pl* **games,** deportes, *m pl. a* de caza; (courageous) valiente, animoso, brioso; resuelto. *vi* jugar por dinero. **He is g. for anything,** Se atreve a todo. **big g. hunting,** caza mayor, *f.* **head of g.,** pieza de caza, *f.* **It is a g. at which two can play,** Donde las dan las toman. **The g. is not worth the candle,** La cosa no vale la pena. **The g. is up,** *fig* El proyecto se ha frustrado. **to make g. of,** (things) burlarse de; (persons) tomar el pelo a; mofarse de. **to play the g.,** *fig* jugar limpio. **to g. away,** perder al juego. **g. of cards,** juego de naipes, *m.* **g. of chance,** juego de azar, *m.* **g.-bag,** morral, *m.* **g. drive,** batida de caza, *f.* **g.-laws,** leyes de caza, *f pl.* **g.-licence,** licencia de caza, *f.* **g.-pie,** tortada, *f.* **g. preserve,** coto de caza, *m*

gamekeeper *n* guardabosque, *m*

gamely *adv* valientemente

gameness *n* valentía, resolución, fortaleza, *f*

gamete *n* gameto, *m*

gaming *n* juego, *m, a* de juego. **g.-house,** garito, *m.* **g.-table,** mesa de juego, *f; fig* juego, *m*

gammon *n* (of bacon) jamón, *m. vt* curar (jamón)

gamut *n* gama, *f*

gander *n* ganso, *m*

gang *n* cuadrilla, pandilla, *Mexico* carpanta *f;* (squad) pelotón, *m;* (of workers) brigada, cuadrilla, *f;* group, *m.* **g.-plank,** plancha, *f*

ganglion *n* ganglio, *m; fig* centro, *m*

gangrene *n* gangrena, *f. vt* gangrenar. *vi* gangrenarse

gangrenous *a* gangrenoso

gangster *n* pistolero, gángster, *m*

gangway *n* pasillo, *m; naut* plancha, *f,* pasamano, *m;* (opening in ship's side) portalón, *m.* **midship g.,** crujía, *f*

gap *n* brecha, *f;* abertura, *f;* (hole) boquete, *m;* (pass) desfiladero, paso, *m;* (ravine) hondonada, barranca, *f;* (blank) laguna, *f,* vacío, *m;* (crack) intersticio, *m,* hendedura, *f,* resquicio, *m.* **to fill a gap,** llenar un boquete; llenar un vacío

gape *vi* estar con la boca abierta, papar moscas. **to g. at,** mirar con la boca abierta

gaping *n* huelgo, *m;* abertura, *f, a* que bosteza; boquiabierto; abierto

garage *n* garaje, *m. vt* poner (un coche, etc.) en un garaje. **g. owner,** garajista, *mf*

garb *n* traje, vestido, *m;* uniforme, *m; her* espiga, *f. vt* vestir, ataviar

garbage *n* basura, inmundicia, *f*

garbage can basurero, tarro de la basura, *m*

garbage dump *Lat. Am.* basural *m*

garble *vt* falsear, mutilar, pervertir

garden *n* jardín, *m;* huerto, *m;* (fertile region) huerta, *f. a* de jardín. *vi* trabajar en el jardín, cultivar un huerto. **g. city,** ciudad jardín, *f.* **g.-frame,** semillero, *m.* **g. mold,** tierra vegetal, *f.* **g.-party,** fiesta de jardín, *f.* **g.-plot,** parterre, *m.* **g. produce,** hortalizas, legumbres, *f pl.* **g. roller,** rodillo, *m.* **g.-seat,** banco de jardín, *m.* **g. urn,** jarrón, *m*

gardener *n* jardinero, *m*

gardenia *n* gardenia, *f,* jazmín de la India, *m*

gardening *n* jardinería, *f;* horticultura, *f. a* de jardinería

gargantuan *a* gargantuesco; tremendo, enorme

gargle *n* (liquid) gargarismo, *m;* gárgaras, *f pl. vi* hacer gárgaras, gargarizar

gargling *n* gargarismo, *m*

gargoyle *n* gárgola, *f*

garish *a* cursi, llamativo, charro, chillón

garishness *n* cursería, ostentación, *f*, lo llamativo
garland *n* guirnalda, *f*; corona, *f*; (anthology) florilegio, *m*; *arch* festón, *m*. *vt* enguirnaldar
garlic *n* ajo, *m*
garment *n* prenda de vestir, *f*; traje, vestido, *m*; *fig* vestidura, *f*; (*fig* cloak) capa, *f*
garner *n* granero, *m*; tesoro, *m*; colección, *f*. *vt* atesorar, guardar
garnet *n* granate, *m*
garnish *n cul* aderezo, *m*; adorno, *m*. *vt cul* aderezar; embellecer, adornar
garnishing *n*. See **garnish**
garret *n* guardilla, buhardilla, *f*, desván, *m*
garrison *n* guarnición, *f*, presidio, *m*. *vt* guarnecer, presidiar. **g. town,** plaza de armas, *f*
garrotte *n* garrote, *m*. *vt* agarrotar, dar garrote (a)
garrulity *n* garrulidad, locuacidad, charlatanería, *f*
garrulous *a* gárrulo, locuaz, charlatán
garter *n* liga, *f*; (G.) Jarretera, *f*, *vt* atar con liga; investir con la Jarretera. **Order of the G.,** Orden de la Jarretera, *f*
gas *n* gas, *m*; *fig, inf* palabrería, *f*; (petrol) bencina, *f*, *a* de gas; con gas; para gases. *vt* asfixiar con gas; *mil* atacar con gas; saturar de gas. **gas attack,** ataque con gases asfixiantes, *m*. **gas-bag,** bolsa de gas, *f*; *inf* charlatán (-ana). **gas-burner,** mechero de gas, *m*. **gas-chamber,** cámara de gas, *f*. **gas detector,** detector de gases, *m*. **gas-fire,** estufa de gas, *f*. **gas-fitter,** gasista, *m*. **gas-fittings,** lámparas de gas, *f pl*. **gas-light,** luz de gas, *f*; mechero de gas, *m*. **gas-main,** cañería maestra de gas, *f*. **gas-man,** gasista, *m*. **gas-mantle,** camiseta incandescente, *f*. **gas-mask,** máscara para gases, *f*. **gas-meter,** contador de gas, *m*. **gas-pipes,** cañerías (or tuberías) de gas, *f pl*. **gas-ring,** fogón de gas, *m*. **gas-shell,** obús de gases asfixiantes, *m*. **gas-stove,** cocina de gas, *f*. **gas warfare,** guerra química, *f*. **gas-works,** fábrica de gas, *f*
Gascon *a* and *n* gascón (-ona)
Gascony Gascuña, *f*
gaseous *a* gaseoso
gash *n* cuchillada, *f*; herida extensa, *f*. *vt* acuchillar; herir extensamente
gasket *n* aro de empaquetadura, *m*
gasoline *n* gasolina, *f*; bencina, *f*
gasp *n* boqueada, *f*. *vi* boquear. **to be at the last g.,** estar agonizando. **to g. for breath,** luchar por respirar. **to g. out,** decir anhelante, decir con voz entrecortada
gastric *a* gástrico
gastritis *n* gastritis, *f*
gastronome *n* gastrónomo (-ma)
gastronomic *a* gastronómico
gastronomy *n* gastronomía, *f*
gate *n* puerta, *f*; cancela, verja, *f*; entrada, *f*; (of a lock, etc.) compuerta, *f*; (across a road, etc.) barrera, *f*; (money) entrada, *f*; *fig* puerta, *f*. **automatic g.,** (at level crossings, etc.) barrera de golpe, *f*. **to g.-crash,** asistir sin invitación. **g.-keeper,** portero, *m*; guardabarrera, *mf* **g.-money,** entrada, *f*. **g.-post,** soporte de la puerta, *m*
gateway *n* entrada, *f*; puerta, *f*; paso, *m*; vestíbulo, *m*; *fig* puerta, *f*
gather *vt* (assemble) reunir; (amass) acumular, amontonar; (acquire) obtener, adquirir; hacer una colección (de); cobrar; (harvest) cosechar, recolectar; (pick up) recoger; (pluck) coger; (infer) sacar en limpio, aprender; *sew* fruncir; (the brows) fruncir (el ceño). *vi* reunirse, congregarse; amontonarse; (threaten) amenazar; (sadden) amargar; (*fig* hover over) cernerse (sobre); (increase) aumentar, crecer; (be covered) cubrirse; (fester) supurar. *n sew* frunce, pliegue, *m*. **to g. breath,** tomar aliento. **to g. speed,** ganar velocidad. **to g. strength,** cobrar fuerzas. **I g. from Mary that they are going abroad,** Según lo que me ha dicho María, van al extranjero. **to g. in,** juntar; reunir; (harvest) cosechar; coger. **to g. together,** *vt* reunir. *vi* reunirse. **to g. up,** recoger; coger; tomar; (one's limbs) encoger. **to g. up the threads,** *fig* recoger los hilos.
gatherer *n* cogedor, colector, *m*; (harvester) segador, *m*; (of grapes) vendimiador (-ra); (of taxes) recaudador, *m*
gathering *n* cogedura, *f*; (fruit, etc.) recolección, *f*; (of taxes) recaudación, *f*; amontonamiento, *m*; colección, *f*; *med* absceso, *m*; *sew* fruncimiento, *m*; (assembly) reunión, asamblea, *f*; (crowd) concurrencia, muchedumbre, *f*
gathers *n sew* fruncidos, pliegues, *m pl*
gauche *a* torpe, huraño
gaudily *adv* ostentosamente; brillantemente
gaudiness *n* ostentación, *f*; brillantez, *f*
gaudy *a* llamativo, vistoso, brillante, ostentoso
gauge *n* (of gun) calibre, *m*; (railway) entrevía, *f*; (for measuring) indicator, *m*; regla de medir, *f*; *naut* calado, *m*; *fig* medida, *f*; (test) indicación, *f*; (model) norma, *f*. *vt* calibrar; medir; estimar; (ship's capacity) arquear; (judge) juzgar; (size up) tomar la medida (de); *fig* interpretar; *sew* fruncir; (liquor) aforar. **broad (narrow) g. railway,** ferrocarril de vía ancha (estrecha), *m*. **pressure g.,** manómetro, *m*. **water g.,** indicador del nivel de agua, *m*
gauging *n* medida, *f*; (of ship's capacity) arqueo, *m*; (of liquor) aforamiento, *m*; *fig* apreciación, *f*; interpretación, *f*
Gaul Galia, *f*
gaunt *a* anguloso, huesudo, desvaído; (of houses, etc.) lúgubre
gauntlet *n* guante de manopla, *m*; (part of armor) manopla, *f*, guantelete, *m*. **to throw down the g.,** echar el guante, desafiar
gauntness *n* angulosidad, flaqueza, *f*
gauze *n* gasa, *f*; (mist) bruma, *f*. **wire-g.,** tela metálica, *f*
gauziness *n* diafanidad, *f*
gauzy *a* diáfano; de gasa
gavotte *n* gavota, *f*
gawkiness *n* torpeza, desmaña, *f*
gawky *a* anguloso, desgarbado, torpe
gay *a* alegre; festivo, animado; ligero de cascos, disipado; homosexual; (of colors) brillante, llamativo
Gaza Strip la franja de Gaza, *f*
gaze *n* mirada, *f*; mirada fija, *f*. *vi* mirar; mirar fijamente, contemplar
gazelle *n* gacel (-la)
gazer *n* espectador (-ra)
gazette *n* gaceta, *f*. *vt* publicar en la gaceta.
gazing *n* contemplación, *f*, *a* contemplador; que presencia, que asiste a
gear *n* (apparel) atavíos, *m pl*; (harness) guarniciones, *f pl*, arneses, *m pl*; (tackle) utensilios, *m pl*, herramientas, *f pl*; *naut* aparejo, *m*; *mech* engranaje, *m*; juego, *m*, marcha, *f*. *vt* aparejar, enjaezar; *mech* poner en marcha, hacer funcionar. *vi mech* engranar, endentar. **low g.,** pimera velocidad, *f*. **neutral g.,** punto muerto, *m*. **reverse g.,** marcha atrás, *f*. **second g.,** segunda velocidad, *f*. **three-speed g.,** cambio de marchas de tres velocidades, *m*. **top g.,** tercera (or cuarta—according to gear-box) velocidad, *f*. **to change g.,** cambiar de marcha, cambiar de velocidad. **to throw out of g.,** *fig* desquiciar. **g.-box,** caja de velocidades, *f*. **g.-changing,** cambio de velocidad, *m*. **g.-changing lever,** palanca de cambio de velocidad, palanca de cambio de marchas, *f*
gearing *n* engranaje, *m*
gee up *interj* ¡arre!
gehenna *n* gehena, *m*
geisha *n* geisha, *f*
gelatine *n* gelatina, *f*. **cooking g.,** gelatina seca, *f*
gelatinous *a* gelatinoso
geld *vt* capar, castrar
gelder *n* castrador, *m*
gelding *n* castración, capadura, *f*; caballo castrado, *m*; animal castrado, *m*
gelid *a* gélido, helado; *fig* frío, frígido

gem *n* piedra preciosa, *f;* joya, alhaja, *f; fig* joya, *f. vt* adornar con piedras preciosos; enjoyar
Gemini *n* (los) Gemelos
gender *n gram* género, *m;* sexo, *m*
gene *n biol* gene, *m*
genealogical *a* genealógico. **g. tree,** árbol genealógico, *m*
genealogist *n* genealogista, *mf*
genealogy *n* genealogía, *f*
general *a* general; universal; común; corriente; (usual) acostumbrado, usual; del público, público. *n* lo general; (*mil, ecc*) general, *m; inf* criada para todo, *f.* **in g.,** por lo general, en general, generalmente. **to become g.,** generalizarse. **to make g.,** generalizar, hacer general. **g. average,** (marine insurance) avería gruesa, *f.* **g. election,** elección general, *f.* **g. meeting,** pleno, mitin general, *m.* **g. opinion,** voz común, opinión general, *f.* **G. Post Office,** Oficina Central de Correos, *f.* **g. practitioner,** médico (-ca) general. **g. public,** público, *m.* **the general reader** el lector de tipo general *m*
generalissimo *n* generalísimo, *m*
generality *n* generalidad, *f*
generalization *n* generalización, *f*
generalize *vt* and *vi* generalizar
generally *adv* en general, por regla general, por lo general, generalmente; comúnmente, por lo común
generalship *n mil* generalato, *m;* (strategy) táctica, estrategia, *f;* dirección, jefatura, *f*
generate *vt* (beget) engendrar, procrear; (*phys, chem*) generar; *fig* producir, crear
generation *n* procreación, *f;* generación, *f; fig* producción, creación, *f.* **the younger g.,** los jóvenes
generative *a* generador
generator *n mech* generador, *m;* dínamo, *f*
generic *a* genérico
generosity *n* generosidad, *f;* liberalidad, *f*
generous *a* generoso; liberal, dadivoso, limosnero, *Lat. Am.* maniabierto; magnánimo; (plentiful) abundante; (of wines) generoso
generously *adv* generosamente; abundantemente
genesis *n* principio, origen, *m;* (G.) Génesis, *m*
genetic *a* genético
genetics *n* genética, *f*
Geneva Ginebra, *f*
genial *a* (of climate) agradable, bueno; (of persons) afable, bondadoso; de buen humor, bonachón
geniality *n* afabilidad, bondad, *f;* buen humor, *m*
genially *adv* afablemente
genie *n* genio, *m*
genital *a* genital, sexual. *n pl* **genitals,** genitales, *m pl*
genitive *a* and *n gram* genitivo *m.*
genius *n* genio, *m;* carácter, *m,* índole, *f;* ingenio, *m; inf* talento, *m*
Genoa Genova, *f*
Genoese *a* and *n* genovés (-esa)
genre *n* género, *m.* **g. painting,** cuadro de género, *m*
genteel *a* fino; (affected) remilgado, melindroso; de buen tono; de buena educación
gentile *a* and *n* gentil, *mf*
gentility *n* aristocracia, *f;* respetabilidad, *f*
gentle *a* noble, bien nacido, de buena familia; amable; suave; ligero; dulce; (docile) manso, dócil; (affectionate) cariñoso; bondadoso; sufrido, paciente; cortés; pacífico, tolerante. **He was a man of g. birth,** Era un hombre bien nacido. **"G. reader,"** «Querido lector». **g. wind** *Lat. Am.* airecito *m*
gentlefolk *n pl* gente de bien, gente fina, *f;* gente de buena familia, *f*
gentleman *n* caballero, señor, *m;* gentilhombre, *m.* **Ladies and gentlemen,** Señoras y caballeros, Señores. **young g.,** señorito, *m.* **to be a perfect g.,** ser un caballero perfecto. **g.-inwaiting,** gentilhombre de la cámara, *m*
gentlemanliness *n* caballerosidad, *f*
gentlemanly *a* caballeroso
gentleness *n* amabilidad, *f;* suavidad, *f;* dulzura, *f;* mansedumbre, docilidad, *f;* bondad, *f;* paciencia, *f;* cortesía, *f;* tolerancia, *f*
gentlewoman *n* dama, *f;* dama de servicio, *f*
gently *adv* suavemente; dulcemente; silenciosamente, sin ruido; (slowly) despacio, poco a poco. **g. born,** bien nacido
gentry *n* pequeña aristocracia, alta clase media, *f;* (disparaging) gentle, *f*
genuflect *vi* doblar la rodilla
genuflexion *n* genuflexión, *f*
genuine *a* puro; genuino; verdadero; real; sincero; auténtico
genuinely *adv* genuinamente; verdaderamente; realmente; sinceramente
genuineness *n* pureza, *f;* autenticidad, *f;* verdad, *f;* sinceridad, *f*
genus *n* género, *m*
geodesic *a* geodésico
geodesy *n* geodesia, *f*
geographer *n* geógrafo, *m*
geographical *a* geográfico
geographically *adv* geográficamente; desde el punto de vista geográfico
geography *n* geografía, *f*
geological *a* geológico
geologically *adv* geológicamente; desde el punto de vista geológico
geologist *n* geólogo, *m*
geologize *vi* estudiar la geología. *vt* estudiar desde un punto de vista geológico
geology *n* geología, *f*
geometric *a* geométrico
geometry *n* geometría, *f*
geophysics *n* geofísica, *f*
Georgian *a geog* georgiano; del principio del siglo diez y nueve
georgic *n* geórgica, *f*
geotropism *n* geotropismo, *m*
geranium *n* geranio, *m*
germ *n* embrión, germen, *m;* microbio, bacilo, *m; fig* germen, *m.* **g.-cell,** célula germinal, *f*
German *a* alemán; germánico. *n* alemán (-ana); (language) alemán, *m;* germano (-na), germánico (-ca). **Sudeten G.,** alemán (-ana) sudete. **G. measles,** rubeola, *f.* **G. silver** alpaca, *f,* melchor *m,* plata alemana *f*
germander *n bot* camedrio, *m*
germane *a* pertinente (a), a propósito (a)
Germanic *a* germánico. *n* (language) germánico, *m*
Germanization *n* germanización, *f*
Germanize *vt* germanizar. *vi* germanizarse
Germanophile *n* germanófilo (-la)
Germany Alemania, *f*
germicidal *a* bactericida
germicide *n* desinfectante, *m*
germinal *a* germinal. *n* (G.) germinal, *m*
germinate *vi* germinar, brotar. *vt* hacer germinar
germination *n* germinación, *f*
germinative *a* germinativo
gerund *n* gerundio, *m*
gerundive *n* gerundio adjetivado, *m*
Gestapo *n* Gestapo, *f*
gestation *n* gestación, *f*
gesticulate *vi* gesticular, hacer gestos; accionar. *vt* expresar por gestos
gesticulation *n* gesticulación, *f*
gesticulatory *a* gesticular
gesture *n* movimiento, *m;* gesticulación, *f;* (of the face) gesto, *m,* mueca, *f;* ademán, *m,* acción, *f. vi* gesticular. *vt* decir por gestos; acompañar con gestos
get *vt* (obtain) obtener; (acquire) adquirir; (buy) comprar; (take) tomar; (receive) recibir; (gain, win) ganar; (hit) acertar, dar; (place) poner; (achieve) alcanzar, lograr; (make) hacer; (call) llamar; (understand) comprender; (catch) coger; (procreate) procrear, engendrar; (induce) persuadir; (invite) convidar, invitar; (cause) hacer; (with have and past part.) tener;

(with have and past part. followed by infin.) tener que; (followed by noun and past part.) hacer; (fetch) buscar, ir a buscar; (order) mandar, disponer; (procure) procurar; (bring) traer; (money) hacer; (a reputation, etc.) hacerse; (a prize, an advantage) llevar; (learn) aprender; (be) ser. *vi* (become) hacerse; ponerse; venir a ser; (old) envejecerse; (angry) montar (en cólera), enojarse; (arrive) llegar a; (attain) alcanzar; (accomplish) conseguir, lograr; (drunk) emborracharse; (hurt) hacerse daño; (wet) mojarse; (cool) enfriarse; (money) hacer (dinero); (of health) ponerse; (find oneself) hallarse, encontrarse; (late) hacerse (tarde); (dark) empezar a caer (la noche), empezar a caer (la noche), empezar a oscurecer; (put oneself) meterse; (grow, be) estar; (on to or on top of) montar sobre, subir a. **He has got run over,** Ha sido atropellado. **It gets on my nerves,** Se me pone los nervios en punta. **Let's get it over!** ¡Vamos a concluir de una vez! **How do you get on with her?** ¿Cómo te va con ella? **She must be getting on for twenty,** Tendrá alrededor de veinte años. **to get a suit made,** mandar hacerse un traje. **to get altitude sickness** *Peru* asorocharse **to get better,** (in health) mejorar de salud; hacer progresos adelantar. **to get dark,** obscurecer. **to get depressed** *Lat. Am.* amurrarse **to get into conversation with,** trabar conversación con. **to get into bad company,** frecuentar malas compañías. **to get into the habit of,** acostumbrarse a. **to get married,** casarse. **to get near,** acercarse. **to get one's own way,** salir con la suya. **to get oneself up as,** disfrazarse de. **to get out in a hurry,** salir apresuradamente; marcharse rápidamente, *inf* salir pitando. **to get out of the way,** quitarse de en medio, apartarse. **to get rid of,** desembarazarse de, librarse de; salir de; perder. **to have got,** poseer; tener; padecer. **Get on!** ¡Adelante!; (to a horse) ¡Arre!; (continue) ¡Sigue! **Get out!** ¡Fuera! ¡Largo de aquí! ¡Sal! **to get the blues = to get depressed. Get up!** ¡Levántate!; (to a horse) ¡Arre! **to get about,** moverse mucho; andar mucho; (attend to business affairs) ir a sus negocios; (travel) viajar; (get up from sick bed) levantarse; (go out) salir; (be known) saberse, divulgarse, hacerse público. **to get above,** subir a un nivel más alto (de). **to get across,** *vi* cruzar, atravesar. *vt* hacer cruzar. **to get along,** *vi* (depart) marcharse; (continue) seguir, vivir; (manage) ir, ir tirando. *vt* llevar; traer; hacer andar por. **How are you getting along?** ¿Cómo le va? **I am getting along all right, thank you,** Voy tirando, gracias. **to get along without,** pasarse sin. **to get angry** *vi Central America* empurrarse **to get at,** (remove) sacar; (find) encontrar; (reach) llegar a; alcanzar; (discover) descubrir; (allude to) aludir a; (understand) comprender. **to get away,** *vi* dejar (un lugar); marcharse, irse; (escape) escaparse. *vt* ayudar a marcharse; ayudar a escaparse. **to get away with,** llevarse, marcharse con; *inf* salir con la suya. **to get back,** *vi* regresar, volver; (get home) volver a casa; (be back) estar de vuelta. *vt* (recover) recobrar; (receive) recibir; (find again) hallar de nuevo. **to get depressed** *Central America* acuilmarse **to get down,** *vi* bajar, descender. *vt* bajar; (take off a hook) descolgar; (swallow) tragar; (note) anotar; escribir. **to get down on all fours,** ponerse en cuatro patas. **to get down to,** ponerse a (estudiar, trabajar, etc.). **to get in,** *vi* entrar en; lograr entrar en; (slip in) colarse en; (of political party) entrar en el poder; (of a club) hacerse socio de; (return) regresar; (home) volver a casa; (find oneself) hallarse, estar; (a habit) adquirir. *vt* hacer entrar en; (a club, etc.) hacer socio de; (a word) decir. **to get in line** *Mexico* formarse **to get into.** See **to get in. to get off,** *vt* apearse de; bajar de; (send) enviar; (from punishment) librar; (bid goodbye) despedirse de; (remove) quitar, sacar. *vi* apearse; bajar; (from punishment) librarse; (leave) ponerse en camino, marcharse. **to get on,** *vi* (wear) tener puesto; (progress) hacer progresos, adelantar; (prosper) medrar, prosperar; (succeed) tener éxito; avanzar; seguir el camino; (agree) avenirse. *vt* (push) empujar; (place) poner; (cause) hacer; (clothes) ponerse; (mount) subir a. **to get open,** abrir. **to get out,** *vt* hacer salir; sacar; (publish) publicar; divulgar. *vi* salir; escapar; **to get out of a jam,** salir de un paso; (descend) bajar (de). **to get over,** (cross) atravesar, cruzar; (an illness, grief, etc.) reponerse, reponerse de; (excuse) perdonar; (surmount) superar; (ground) recorrer. **to get round,** (a person) persuadir; (surround) rodear; (avoid) evitar; (difficulties) superar, vencer. **to g. one's degree** *Lat. Am.* diplomarse. **to get through,** pasar por; (time) pasar, entretener; (money) gastar; (finish) terminar, acabar; (pierce or enter) penetrar; (communicate) comunicar (con); (difficulties) vencer; (an exam) aprobar. **to get the blues** *Central America* acuilmarse **to get to,** llegar a; encontrar; (begin) empezar. **to get together,** *vt* reunir, juntar. *vi* reunirse, juntarse. **to get under,** ponerse debajo de; (control) dominar. **to get up,** *vt* (raise) alzar, levantar; (carry up things) subir; hacer subir; organizar; preparar; (learn) aprender; (linen) blanquear, colar; (ascend) subir; hacer; (dress) ataviar; (steam) generar; (a play) ensayar, poner en escena. *vi* levantarse; (on a horse) montar a caballo; (of the wind) refrescarse; (of the fire) avivarse; (of the sea) embravecerse. **to get up to,** llegar a; alcanzar

get-at-able *a* accesible

getting *n* adquisición, *f*; (of money) ganancia, *f*. **g. up,** preparación, *f*; organización, *f*; (of a play) representación (de una comedia), puesta en escena, *f*

get-up *n* atavío, *m*; (of a book, etc.) aspecto, *m*

gewgaw *n* chuchería, *f*

geyser *n* géiser, *m*; (for heating water) calentador (de agua), *m*

ghastliness *n* horror, *m*; palidez mortal, *f*; aspecto miserable, *m*; (boringness) tedio, aburrimiento, *m*; lo desagradable

ghastly *a* horrible; de una palidez mortal; cadavérico; (boring) aburrido; muy desagradable

ghetto *n* gueto *m*

ghost *n* fantasma, espectro, aparecido, *m*; (spirit) alma, *f*, espíritu, *m*; (shadow) sombra. *f*; (writer) mercenario, *m*. **Holy G.,** Espíritu Santo, *m*. **to give up the g.,** entregar el alma; perder la esperanza, desesperarse. **to look like a g.,** parecer un fantasma

ghostliness *n* espiritualidad, *f*; lo misterioso; palidez, *f*; tenuidad, *f*

ghostly *a* espiritual; espectral; misterioso; pálido; vaporoso, tenue; indistinto

ghost town *n* pueblo-fantasma, *m*

ghost word *n* palabra-fantasma, *f*

ghoul *n* vampiro, *m*

ghoulish *a* insano; cruel; sádico

giant *n* gigante, *m*; *fig* coloso, *m*, *a* gigantesco; de gigantes; de los gigantes. **g.-killer,** matador de gigantes, *m*. **g.-stride,** (gymnastics) paso volante, *m*

gibber *vi* hablar incoherentemente, hablar entre dientes; farfullar, hablar atropelladamente; decir disparates

gibberish *n* galimatías, *m*; jerigonza, *f*, griego, *m*

gibbet *n* horca, *f*, patíbulo, *m*. **to die on the g.,** morir ahorcado

gibbon *n zool* gibón, *m*

gibe *n* improperio, escarnio, *m*, burla, mofa, *f*. *vi* criticar. **to g. at,** burlarse de, ridiculizar, mofarse de

gibing *a* burlón, mofador. *n* mofas, burlas, *f pl*

gibingly *adv* burlonamente, con sorna

giblets *n* menudillos, *m pl*

giddily *adv* vertiginosamente; frívolamente, atolondradamente

giddiness *n* vértigo, *m*; atolondramiento, *m*; inconstancia, *f*; frivolidad, ligereza de cascos, *f*

giddy *a* vertiginoso; mareado; atolondrado, casquivano, frívolo; inconstante. **She felt very g.,** Se sintió muy mareada. **to make g.,** dar vértigo (a), marear

gift *n* regalo, *m*, dádiva, *f;* (quality) don, talento, *m;* prenda, *f;* poder, *m; law* donación, *f;* (offering) ofrenda, oblación, *f. vt* dotar. **deed of g.,** *law* escritura de donación, *f.* **in the g. of,** en el poder de, en las manos de. **I wouldn't have it as a g.,** No lo tomaría ni regalado. **Never look a g. horse in the mouth,** A caballo regalado no se le mira el diente. **g. of tongues,** don de las lenguas, genio de las lenguas, *m*

gifted *a* talentoso

gig *n* (carriage) carrocín, *m;* (boat) falúa, lancha, *f;* (for wool) máquina de cardar paño, *f;* (harpoon) arpón, *m*

gigantic *a* gigantesco; colosal, enorme

giggle *vi* reírse sin motivo; reírse disimuladamente. *n* risa disimulada, *f*

giggling *n* risa estúpida, *f;* risa nerviosa, *f*

gigolo *n* gigolo, mantenido, jinetero (Cuba), *m*

gild *vt* dorar; (metals) sobredorar; embellecer. **to g. the pill,** dorar la píldora

gilder *n* dorador, *m*

gilding *n* dorado, *m*, doradura, *f;* embellecimiento, *m*

Gileadite *n* and *a* galaadita, *mf*

gill *n* (of fish) agalla, branquia, *f;* (ravine) barranco, *m;* (measure) cierta medida de líquidos, *f,* ($\frac{1}{8}$ litro)

gilt *n* dorado, *m;* pan de oro, *m;* relumbrón, *m; fig* encanto, *m, a* dorado, áureo. **g.-edged,** (of books) con los bordes dorados. **g.-edged security,** papel del Estado, *m;* valores de toda confianza, *m pl*

gimcrack *n* chuchería, *f. a* de baratillo, cursi; mal hecho

gimlet *n* barrena, *f,* taladro, *m*

gin *n* (drink) ginebra, *f;* (snare) trampa, *f. vt* (snare) coger con trampa. **g. block,** *mech* garrucha, *f*

ginger *n* jengibre, *m; inf* energía, *f,* brío, *m, a* rojo. *vt* sazonar con jengibre; *inf* animar, estimular. **g.-beer,** gaseosa, *f*

gingerly *adv* con gran cuidado; delicadamente

gingham *n* guinga, *f*

gingivitis *n* gingivitis, *f*

gipsy *n.* See **gypsy**

giraffe *n* jirafa, *f*

gird *vt* ceñir; (invest) investir; (surround) cercar, rodear; (put on) revestir. **to g. oneself for the fray,** prepararse para la lucha

girder *n* viga, jácena, *f.* **main g.,** viga maestra, *f*

girdle *n* (belt) cinturón, *m;* (corset) faja, *f;* circunferencia, *f;* zona, *f. vt* ceñir; *fig* cercar, rodear

girl *n* niña, *f;* chica, muchacha, *f;* (maidservant) criada, muchacha, *f;* (young lady) señorita, *f.* **a young g.,** una jovencita; (a little older) una joven. **old g.,** (of a school) antigua alumna, *f; inf* vieja, *f;* (*inf* affectionate) chica, *f.* **g. friend,** amiguita, *f.* **g. guide, girl scout,** exploradora, *f.* **girls' school,** colegio de niñas, colegio de señoritas, *m*

girlhood *n* niñez, *f;* juventud, *f*

girlish *a* de niña, de muchacha; (of boys) afeminado; joven

girth *n* (of horse, etc.) cincha, *f;* circunferencia, *f;* (of person) talle, *m;* (obesity) corpulencia, obesidad, *f*

gist *n* esencia, substancia, *f,* importe, *m*

give *vt* dar; (a present) regalar; (infect) contagiar; (impart) comunicar; (grant) otorgar; (allow, concede) conceder; (assign) asignar, señalar; (appoint) nombrar; (a toast) brindar (a la salud de); (a party, ball, etc.) dar; (a bill) presentar; (wish) desear; (punish) castigar; (pay) pagar; (hand over) entregar; (names at baptism) imponer; (produce) producir; dar; (cause) causar; (of judicial sentences) condenar a; (evoke) proporcionar; (provoke) provocar; (devote) dedicar, consagrar; (sacrifice) sacrificar; (evidence, an account, orders, a lesson, a performance, a concert) dar; (a cry, shout) lanzar, proferir; (a laugh) soltar; (describe) describir; (paint) pintar; (write) escribir; (offer) ofrecer; (show) mostrar; (transmit) transmitir; (heed, pain) hacer; (a speech) pronunciar, hacer; (award, adjudge) adjudicar; (ear) prestar (oído (a)). *vi* dar; ser dadivoso, mostrarse generoso; (give in) ceder; (be elastic) dar de sí; ablandarse; (collapse) hundirse. **G. them my best wishes!** ¡Dales mis mejores recuerdos! **G. us a song!** ¡Cántanos algo! **I can g. him a lift in my car,** Puedo ofrecerle un asiento en mi auto. **I g. you my word,** Os doy mi palabra. **to g. a good account of oneself,** defenderse bien; hacer bien; salir bien. **to g. a person a piece of one's mind,** contarle cuatro verdades. **to g. chase,** dar caza (a). **to g. it to a person,** poner a uno como nuevo; reprender; (beat) pegar, dar de palos. **to g. of itself,** dar de sí. **to g. rise to,** dar lugar a, ocasionar, causar. **to g. way,** no poder resistir; (break) romperse; (yield) ceder; (collapse) hundirse; (retreat) retroceder. **to g. way to,** (retreat before) retirarse ante; (abandon oneself to) entregarse a, abandonarse a. **to g. away,** enajenar; dar; regalar; (sell cheaply) vender a un precio muy bajo; (get rid of) deshacerse de; (sacrifice) sacrificar; (a secret) revelar; (betray) traicionar; (expose) descubrir; (tell) contar; (a bride) conducir al altar. **He gave himself away,** Reveló su pensamiento sin querer. **to g. back,** *vt* devolver; restituir. *vi* retirarse, cejar. **to g. forth,** divulgar, publicar; (scatter) derramar; (emit) emitir, despedir; (smoke, rays) echar. **to g. in,** *vt* entregar; presentar. *vi* darse por vencido. **to g. in to,** (agree with) asentir en, consentir en; rendirse ante. **Mary always gives in to George,** María hace siempre lo que Jorge quiere. **to g. off,** (of odors, etc.) emitir, exhalar, despedir. **to g. out,** *vt* (distribute) distribuir, repartir; (allocate) asignar; (publish) publicar; (announce) anunciar; (reveal) divulgar; (allege) afirmar, hacer saber; (emit) emitir. *vi* (be exhausted) agotarse; (end) acabarse; (be lacking) faltar. **to g. over,** *vt* entregar; (transfer) traspasar; cesar de. *vi* cesar. **to g. up,** entregar; ceder; (renounce) renunciar (a); (sacrifice) sacrificar; (abandon) abandonar; (cease) dejar de; (as lost) dar por perdido; (of a patient) desahuciar; (a post) dimitir de; (return) devolver, restituir; (a problem) renunciar (a resolver un problema); (lose hope) perder la esperanza; (give in) darse por vencido. **I had given you up,** (didn't expect you), Creí que no ibas a venir. **to g. oneself up to,** entregarse a; dedicarse a; *mil* rendirse a. **to g. up one's seat,** ceder su sitio (or asiento). **to g. upon,** (overlook) dar sobre

give *n* elasticidad, *f;* el dar de sí; (concession) concesión, *f.* **g. and take,** concesiones mutuas, *f pl.* **g. away,** *inf* revelación indiscreta, *f*

given *a* dado; especificado; convenido; (with to) dado a, adicto a. **in a g. time,** en un tiempo dado. **g. that,** dado que

giver *n* dador (-ra); donador (-ra)

giving *a* = **generous**

gizzard *n* molleja, *f.* **It sticks in my g.,** *inf* No lo puedo tragar

glacial *a* glacial

glacier *n* glaciar, *m*

glad *a* feliz, alegre; contento, satisfecho; *inf* elegante. **to be g.,** alegrarse, estar contento; estar satisfecho. **to give the g. eye,** hacer ojos

gladden *vt* alegrar, regocijar

glade *n* claro, *m;* rasa, *f*

gladiator *n* gladiador, *m*

gladiolus *n bot* gladíolo, gladio, *m;* espadaña, *f*

gladly *adv* alegremente; con mucho gusto, gustoso, de buena gana

gladness *n* alegría, felicidad, *f,* contento, *m;* placer, *m*

glamorous *a* exótico; garboso

glamour *n* encanto, *m,* fascinación, *f;* garbo, *m.* **g. girl,** belleza exótica, *f*

glance *n* (of a projectile) desviación, *f;* (of light) vislumbre, *m;* relumbrón, centelleo, *m;* (look) vistazo, *m,* ojeada, *f;* mirada, *f, vi* desviarse; relumbrar, centellear, brillar; (with at) ojear, echar un vistazo a, lanzar miradas a; (a book) hojear; mirar; mirar de reojo; *fig* indicar brevemente. **at a g.,** con un vistazo; en seguida. **at the first g.,** a primera vista. **to g. off,** desviarse (al chocar). **to g. over,** repasar, echar un vistazo a; (a book) hojear

glancing *a* (of a blow) que roza

gland *n* (*anat, bot*) glándula, *f*; (in the neck) ganglio, *m*. **to have swollen glands,** tener inflamación de los ganglios
glandular *a* glandular
glare *n* brillo, fulgor, *m*; luminosidad, *f*; reflejo, *m*; (look) mirada feroz, *f*. *vi* relumbrar, centellear; (stare) mirar con ferocidad, mirar fijamente
glaring *a* deslumbrante, brillante; (of colors) chillón, llamativo; (of looks) de mirada feroz; (flagrant) notorio, evidente
glaringly *adv* brillantemente; con mirada feroz; notoriamente
glass *n* vidrio, *m*; cristal, *m*; (glassware) artículos de vidrio, *m pl*; cristalería, *f*; (for drinking) vaso, *m*, copa, *f*; (pane) cristal, *m*; (mirror) espejo, *m*; (telescope) telescopio, *m*; catalejo, *m*; (barometer) barómetro, *m*; (hour-glass) reloj de arena, *m*; (of a watch) vidrio (de reloj), *m*; *pl* **glasses,** (binoculars) anteojos, *m pl*; (spectacles) gafas, lentes, *m pl*; (opera glasses) gemelos de teatro, *m pl*, *a* de vidrio; de cristal. *vt* vidriar. **John wears glasses,** Juan lleva gafas. **The g. is falling (rising),** El barómetro baja (sube). **to clink glasses,** trincar las copas. **to look in the g.,** mirarse en el espejo. **clear g.,** vidrio trasparente, *m*. **cut g.,** cristal tallado, *m*. **frosted g.,** vidrio jaspeado, *m*. **plate-g.,** vidrio plano, *m*; **safety g.,** vidrio inastillable, *m*. **stained g.,** vidrio de color, vidrio pintado, *m*. **under g.,** bajo vidrio; en invernáculo. **g. bead,** abalorio, *m*; cuenta de vidrio, *f*. **g.-blower,** soplador de vidrio, *m*. **g.-blowing,** el soplar de vidrio. **g. case,** escaparate, *m*. **g.-cloth,** paño para vasos, *m*. **g. eye,** ojo de cristal, *m*. **g. paper,** papel de vidrio, *m*. **g. roof,** techo de cristal, *m*. **g. window,** vidriera, *f*
glasscutter *n* cortador de vidrio, *m*
glassful *n* contenido de un vaso, *m*; vaso, vaso lleno, *m*, copa, *f*
glasshouse *n* fábrica de vidrio, *f*; vidriería, *f*; invernáculo, invernadero, *m*, estufa, *f*
glassware *n* cristalería, *f*
glassy *a* vitreo; (of eyes) vidrioso; *fig* cristalino; (smooth) liso, raso
glaucous *a* de color verdemar; *bot* glauco
glaze *n* barniz, *m*: lustre, brillo, *m*. *vt* poner vidrios (a); vidriar; barnizar; (paper, leather, etc.) satinar. *vi* (of eyes) vidriarse, ponerse vidrioso
glazier *n* vidriero, *m*
glazing *n* vidriado, *m*; barnizado, *m*; satinado, *m*; (material) barniz, *m*
gleam *n* rayo, destello, *m*; (of color) viso, *m*, mancha, *f*; *fig* rayo, *m*; (in the eye) chispa, *f*. *vi* relucir, centellear, resplandecer; brillar; reflejar la luz; *fig* brillar. **g. of hope,** rayo de esperanza, *m*
gleaming *a* reluciente, centelleante; brillante. *n* see **gleam**
glean *vt* espigar, rebuscar; recoger. *vi* espigar
gleaner *n* espigador, *m*; recogedor (-ra)
gleaning *n* espigueo, *m*; rebusca, recolección, *f*; *pl* **gleanings,** fragmentos, *m pl*
glee *n* alegría, *f*, júbilo, alborozo, *m*; *mus* canción para voces solas, *f*
gleeful *a* alegre, jubiloso, gozoso
gleefully *adv* alegremente, con júbilo
glen *n* cañada, *f*, cañón, *m*, hondonada, *f*
glib *a* locuaz, voluble; (easy) fácil
glibness *n* locuacidad, volubilidad, *f*; (easiness) facilidad, *f*
glide *n* deslizamiento, *m*; *aer* planeo, *m*. *vi* deslizarse; resbalar; *aer* planear. **to g. away,** escurrirse; desaparecer silenciosamente
glider *n aer* deslizador, planeador, *m*
gliding *n aer* vuelo sin motor, *m*
glimmer *n* luz trémula, luz débil, *f*, tenue resplandor, *m*; vislumbre, *m*. *vi* brillar con luz trémula, rielar *fig*; tener vislumbres (de)
glimpse *n* vistazo, *m*; vislumbre, *m*; indicio, *m*; impresión, *f*; vista, *f*. *vt* entrever, divisar; tener una vista (de); ver por un instante; vislumbrar
glint *n* tenue resplandor, *m*; lustre, *m*; centelleo, *m*; reflejo, *m*; (in the eye) chispa, *f*. *vi* relucir, destellar, rutilar; reflejar
glisten *vi* brillar, relucir
glistening *a* coruscante; brillante, reluciente
glitter *n* brillo, resplandor, *m*, rutilación, *f*. *vi* brillar, resplandecer, relucir; rutilar. **All that glitters is not gold,** Todo lo que reluce no es oro
glittering *a* reluciente, resplandeciente; *fig* brillante
gloat (over) *vi* recrearse en, gozarse en, deleitarse en
globe *n* globo, *m*; esfera, *f*; (for fish) pecera, *f*; (for gas, electric light) globo, *m*. **geographical g.,** globo terrestre, *m*. **g.-trotter,** trotamundos, *mf*
globular *a* globular, esférico
globule *n* glóbulo, *m*
gloom *n* obscuridad, *f*; lobreguez, *f*, tinieblas, *f pl*; *fig* melancolía, tristeza, *f*; taciturnidad, *f*. *vi fig* ponerse melancólico; ser taciturno
gloomily *adv* obscuramente; *fig* tristemente; taciturnamente
gloomy *a* obscuro; sombrío, lóbrego; melancólico, triste; taciturno; (of prospects, etc.) poco halagüeño, nada atrayente
glorification *n* glorificación, *f*
glorify *vt* glorificar; exaltar; alabar
glorious *a* glorioso; espléndido, magnífico; insigne; *inf* estupendo
glory *n* gloria, *f*; esplendor, *m*, magnificencia, *f*; *art* gloria, *f*. *vi* recrearse, gozarse; glorificarse, jactarse. **to be in one's g.,** estar en la gloria. **to g. in,** hacer gala de, glorificarse en
gloss *n* (sheen) lustre, brillo, *m*; *fig* apariencia, *f*; (note) glose, *m*; (excuse) disculpa, *f*. *vt* pulir; glosar. **to g. over,** (faults) disculpar, excusar
glossary *n* glosario, *m*
glossiness *n* lustre, *m*, tersura, *f*; brillo, *m*
glossy *a* lustroso, terso; brillante; (of hair) liso
glottis *n anat* glotis, *f*
glottal stop *n* choque glótica, golpe de glotis, *m*
glove *n* guante. **evening gloves,** guantes largos, *m pl*. **to be hand in g. with,** juntar diestra con diestra. **to fit like a g.,** sentar como un guante. **to put on one's gloves,** ponerse los guantes. **g. shop,** guantería, *f*. **g.-stretcher,** ensanchador (-ra) de guantes, abridor (-ra) de guantes *mf*
glove compartment gaveta, guantera, *f*, guantero, portaguantes *m*
glove-compartment light luz de portaguantes, *f*
glover *n* guantero (-ra)
glow *n* incandescencia, *f*; claridad, *f*; luz difusa, *f*; (heat) calor, *m*; (of color) intensidad, *f*; color vivo, *m*; (enthusiasm) ardor, entusiasmo, *m*; (redness) rojez, *f*; (in the sky) arrebol, *m*; (of pleasure, etc.) sentimiento de placer, *m*; sensación de bienestar, *f*. *vi* estar incandescente; arder; abrasarse; sentir entusiasmo; mostrarse rojo; experimentar un sentimiento de placer o una sensación de bienestar. **to g. with health,** estar rebosando de salud. **g.-worm,** luciérnaga, *f*
glower *n* ceño, *m*; mirada amenazadora, *f*. *vi* poner cara de pocos amigos, mirar airadamente; tener los ojos puestos (en)
glowing *a* candente, incandescente; ardiente; entusiasta; satisfecho; intenso; (bright) vivo; (red) encendido; (with health) rebosante de salud. *n* see **glow**
glowingly *adv* encendidamente; *fig* con entusiasmo
glucose *n* glucosa, *f*
glue *n* engrudo, *m*, cola, *f*. *vt* encolar, engrudar; pegar; *fig* fijar, poner. **He kept his eyes glued on them,** Tenía los ojos fijados (or pegados) en ellos. **g.-pot,** pote de cola, *m*
gluey *a* gomoso; pegajoso, viscoso
glueyness *n* viscosidad, *f*
gluing *n* encoladura, *f*
glum *a* deprimido, taciturno, sombrío

glumly *adv* taciturnamente
glut *n* superabundancia, *f*, exceso, *m*. *vt* (satiate) hartar; *fig* saciar; (the market) inundar
gluteal *a* glúteo
glutinous *a* glutinoso, pegajoso, viscoso
glutton *n* glotón (-ona); *fig* ávido (-da)
gluttonous *a* glotón, comilón
gluttony *n* glotonería, gula, *f*
glycerine *n* glicerina, *f*
gnarled *a* nudoso; (of human beings) curtido
gnash *vt* rechinar, crujir (los dientes)
gnashing *n* rechinamiento (de dientes), *m*
gnat *n* mosquito, *m*
gnaw *vt* roer; morder; (of wood by worms) carcomer; *fig* roer
gnawing *n* roedura, *f*; mordedura, *f*, *a* roedor; mordedor
gnome *n* nomo, *m*
gnostic *a* and *n* nóstico (-ca)
gnosticism *n* nosticismo, *m*
go *vi* ir; (depart) irse, marcharse; (go toward) dirigirse a, encaminarse a; (lead to, of roads, etc.) conducir a, ir a; (vanish) desaparecer; (leave) dejar, salir de; (lose) perder; (pass) pasar; (of time) transcurrir, pasar; (be removed) quitarse; (be prohibited) prohibirse; (fall) caer; (collapse) hundirse; (be torn off) desprenderse; desgajarse; *mech* funcionar, trabajar, andar; (sound) sonar; (of the heart) palpitar, latir; (follow) seguir; (gesture) hacer un gesto; (be stated) decirse, afirmarse; (live) vivir; (wear) llevar; (turn out) salir, resultar; (improve) mejorar; (prosper) prosperar; (turn, become) ponerse; volverse; (to sleep) dormirse; (into a faint) desmayarse; (decay) echarse a perder, estropearse; (turn sour) agriarse; (become, adopt views, etc.) hacerse; (be sold) venderse; (be decided); decidirse, ser decidido; (have) tener; (by will) pasar; (belong) pertenecer; (receive) recibir; (have its place) estar; (put) ponerse; (going plus infin.) ir a; (die) morir, irse; (do a journey, a given distance) hacer; (a pace, step) dar; (take) tomar; (escape) escaparse, (contribute) contribuir (a); (harmonize) armonizar (con); (be current) ser válido; (be) ser; (of a document, etc., run) rezar, decir; (attend) asistir a; (be broken) estar roto; (be worn) estar raído; (be granted) darse, otorgarse. **It's gone five,** Ya dieron las cinco. **It's time to be going,** Es hora de marcharse. **Let's go!** ¡Vamos! **These two colours go well together,** Estos colores armonizan bien. **Well, how goes it?** Bueno, ¿qué tal? ¿Cómo te va? **Who goes there?** *mil* ¿Quién va? **to go and fetch,** ir a buscar. **to let go,** soltar; dejar ir. **to go one's way,** seguir su camino. **to go wrong,** salir mal, fracasar; (sin) descarriarse. **"Go!"** (traffic sign) «¡Siga!» **Go on!** ¡Adelante!; (continue) ¡Siga!; *inf* ¡Qué va! **to go about,** dar la vuelta a; rodear; recorrer; (undertake) emprender, hacer; intentar; (of news, etc.) circular; *naut* virar de bordo. **Go about your business!** ¡Métete en lo que to importa! **to go abroad,** ir al extranjero; salir a la calle; publicarse, divulgarse. **to go across,** cruzar, atravesar; pasar. **to go after,** andar tras; seguir; (seek) ir a buscar; (persecute) perseguir. **to go again,** ir de nuevo; (be present) asistir otra vez; volver. **to go against,** ir contra; militar contra; oponerse a; ser desfavorable a. **to go ahead,** adelantar, avanzar; progresar; prosperar; (lead) ir a la cabeza (de), conducir; *naut* marchar hacia adelante. **to go along,** andar por; recorrer; (depart) irse, marcharse. **go apartment-hunting,** ir en busca de piso. **to go along with,** acompañar (a). **to go aside,** quitarse de en medio; apartarse, retirarse. **to go astray,** perderse; extraviarse, descarriarse. **to go at,** atacar, acometer; (undertake) emprender; empezar a. **to go at it again,** *inf* volver a la carga. **to go away,** irse, marcharse; ausentarse; alejarse; desaparecer. **to go away with,** marcharse con; (an object) llevarse. **to go back,** volver, regresar, *Lat. Am.* devolverse; (retreat) retroceder, volverse atrás; (in history) remontarse a. **to go back on,** (a promise, etc.) faltar a; (retract) retractarse; (betray) traicionar. **to go backwards,** retroceder, cejar; desandar lo andado; *fig* deteriorar, empeorar. **to go backwards and forwards,** ir y venir; oscilar. **to go before,** (lead) ir a la cabeza de, conducir; anteceder; proceder; (a judge, etc.) comparecer ante. **to go behind,** ir detrás de; esconderse detrás de; seguir; (evidence, etc.) mirar más allá de. **to go between,** ponerse entre; interponerse; (as a mediator) mediar; (insert) intercalarse; (travel) ir entre; llevar cartas entre, ser mensajero de. **to go beyond,** ir más allá; exceder. **to go by,** pasar por; pasar cerca de, pasar junto a; ir por; (of time) transcurrir, pasar; (follow) seguir; guiarse por, atenerse a; (judge by) juzgar por; (a name) pasar por; tomar el nombre de. **to go down,** bajar, descender; (of the sun) ponerse; (sink) hundirse; sumergirse; (fall) caer; (be remembered) ser recordado; (believe) tragar; ser creído. **to go down again,** bajar de nuevo; volver a caer. **go Dutch,** ir a escote, ir a la gringa, ir a la par, ir a limón. **to go far,** ir lejos; influir mucho (en); impresionar mucho; (contribute) contribuir (a). **to go for,** (seek) ir en busca de; procurar tener; (attack) echarse encima de, atacar. **to go for a ride (by car, bicycle, on horseback),** dar un paseo (en coche, en bicicleta, a caballo). **to go forth,** salir; publicarse. **to go forward,** adelantar, avanzar; progresar; continuar; (happen) tener lugar. **to go from,** dejar, abandonar; separarse de, apartarse de; marcharse de. **to go in,** entrar en; (a railway carriage, etc.) subir a; (compete) concurrir. **to go in again,** volver a entrar en, entrar de nuevo en. **to go in and out,** entrar y salir; ir y venir. **to go in for,** entrar a buscar; dedicarse a, entregarse a; (buy) comprarse; tomar parte en; (an examination) tomar (un examen); (for a competition) entrar en (un concurso); (try) ensayar; arriesgar. **to go into,** entrar en; examinar; investigar; ocuparse con. **to go native** *Lat. Am.* acriollarse. **to go near,** acercarse a. **to go off,** marcharse; (explode) estallar; (of fire-arms) dispararse; (of the voice, etc.) perder (la voz, etc.); (run away) huir, fugarse. **to go off badly,** salir mal, fracasar, no tener éxito. **to go off well,** salir bien, tener éxito. **to go on,** subirse a; continuar; durar; avanzar; proseguir su marcha; progresar; prosperar; *theat* entrar en escena; (of clothes) ponerse; (rely on) apoyarse en. **to go on an excursion, go on an outing, go on a trip** *Lat. Am.* excursionarse. **Don't go on like that,** No seas así, No te pongas así. **This glove will not go on me,** No puedo ponerme este guante. **to be gone on a person,** *inf* estar loco por. **I went on to say . . . ,** Después dije; Continuando mi discurso dije . . . **It was going on for six o'clock when . . .** Serían alrededor de las seis cuando . . . **He is going on for fifty,** Raya en los cincuenta años. **to go on foot,** ir a pie. **to go on with,** continuar con; empezar. **to go out,** salir; (descend) bajar; (of fires, lights) extinguirse, apagarse; (of fashion, etc.) pasar (de); (the tide) menguar; (retire) retirarse; (in society) frecuentar la alta sociedad; (die) morir; (arouse) excitar. **to go out of** salir de, *Lat. Am. also* egresar de. **to go out of fashion,** pasar de moda. **to go out of one's way (to),** dejar su camino (para); (lose oneself) perder el camino, extraviarse; (take trouble) desvivirse (por), tomarse molestia (para). **to go over,** cruzar; pasar por encima; (to another party or to the other side) pasarse a; (read) repasar; examinar. **to go past,** pasar; pasar en frente de. **to go round,** dar la vuelta a; (revolve) girar: (surround) rodear; (of news, etc.) divulgarse; (be enough) ser suficiente para todos. **to go through,** ir por, pasar por; recorrer; (pierce) penetrar, atravesar; (examine) examinar; (suffer) padecer, sufrir; (experience) experimentar; (live) vivir; (of time) pasar; (of money) malgastar, derrochar. **to go through with,** llevar a cabo; terminar. **to go to,** ir a, encaminarse a; (a person) acercarse a, dirigirse a; (help, be useful) servir para; (be meant for) destinarse a; (rise of price) subir a; (find) encontrar; (of a bid) subir una apuesta hasta. **to go to**

war, declarar la guerra. **to go together,** ir juntos (juntas). **to go toward,** encaminarse hacia; ir hacia; (help) ayudar a. **to go under,** pasar por debajo de; (sink) hundirse; (fail) fracasar; (be bankrupt) arruinarse, declarare en quiebra; (the name of) hacerse pasar por. **to go up,** subir; ir arriba; (a tree) trepar; (a ladder, etc.) subir; (a river) ir río arriba; (to town) ir a; (explode) estallar. **to go up and down,** subir y bajar; oscilar; ir de una parte a otra. **to go upon,** subirse a; (rely on) apoyarse en; obrar según; emprender. **to go upstairs,** ir arriba; (to another story, as in a flat) subir al otro piso; subir la escalera. **to go up to,** acercarse a; (of a bid) subir una apuesta hasta. **to go with,** acompañar; (agree with) estar de acuerdo con; (of principles) seguir, ser fiel a; (harmonize) armonizar con; (be suitable to) ir bien con; convenir a; (*inf* get along) ir. **to go without,** marcharse sin; (lack) pasarse sin. **It goes without saying that . . .,** Huelga decir que **Where are you going with this?** (What do you mean?) ¿A dónde quieres llegar con esto?

go *n* (fashion) moda, boga, *f;* (happening) suceso, *m;* (fix) apuro, *m;* (energy) energía, *f,* empuje, brío, *m;* (turn) turno, *m;* (attempt) tentativa, *f;* (action) movimiento, *m,* acción, *f;* (bargain) acuerdo, *m.* **It's a go!** (agreed) ¡Trato hecho! ¡Acordado! ¡Entendidos! ¡Entendidas! **It is all the go,** Hace furor, Es la gran moda. **It is no go,** No puede ser, Es imposible. **Now it's my go,** Ahora me toca a mí, Ahora es mi turno. **on the go,** en movimiento; entre manos; ocupado. **to have a go,** probar suerte; procurar, tratar de; tener un turno

goad *n* garrocha, aguijada, *f,* aguijón, *m, Lat. Am.* lanceta *f; fig* acicate, estímulo, *m. vt* aguijar, picar; *fig* incitar, estimular, empujar. **prick with a g.,** aguijonazo, *m*

go-ahead *a* emprendedor: progresivo

goal *n* (posts in football, etc.) meta, portería, *f, Lat. Am.* arco, *m;* (score) gol, *m;* (in racing) meta, *f;* (destination) destinación, *f; fig* ambición, *f;* (purpose, objective) fin, objeto, *m.* **to score a g.,** marcar un gol. **g.-keeper,** guardameta, *m,* portero (-ra). **g.-post,** palo de la portería, *m*

goat *n* cabra, *f; ast* capricornio, *m.* **he-g.,** cabrón, *m.* **young g.,** cabrito, *m,* chivo (-va). **g.-herd,** cabrero, *m.* **g. skin,** piel de cabra, *f;* (wineskin) odre, *m*

goatee *n* pera, perilla, *f*

goatish *a* cabruno; de cabra; lascivo

gobble *vt* and *vi* engullir, tragar. *vi* (of turkey) gluglutear. *n* glugluteo, *m,* voz del pavo, *f*

go-between *n* trotaconventos, *f;* alcahuete, *m;* (mediator) medianero (-ra)

goblet *n* copa, *f*

goblin *n* trasgo, duende, *m*

go-by, to give the evitar; pasar por alto de; omitir

go-cart *n* andaderas, *f pl;* pollera, *f;* cochecito de niño, *m*

god *n* dios, *m; pl* **gods,** dioses, *m pl;* (in a theater) público del paraíso, *m;* paraíso, *m.* **By God!** ¡Vive Dios! **For God's sake,** ¡Por el amor de Dios!; ¡Por Dios! **Please God,** ¡Plegue a Dios! **Thank God!** ¡Gracias a Dios! **God Bless You!** (to someone who has sneezed) ¡Jesús! **God forbid!** ¡No lo quiera Dios! **God grant it!** ¡Dios lo quiera! **God keep you!** ¡Dios le guarde! ¡Vaya Vd. con Dios! **God willing,** Dios mediante. **My father, God rest his soul, was . . .,** Mi padre, que Dios perdone, era . . .

godchild *n* ahijado (-da)

goddess *n* diosa, *f; poet* dea, *f*

godfather *n* padrino, *m.* **to be a g. to,** ser padrino de, sacar de pila (a)

godfearing *a* timorato, temeroso de Dios; religioso

godforsaken *a* dejado de la mano de Dios; (of places) remoto, solitario

Godhead *n* divinidad, *f*

godkin diosecillo, *m*

godless *a* impío, irreligioso; sin Dios

godlessness *n* impiedad, irreligiosidad, *f*

godlet diosecilla, *m*

godlike *a* divino

godliness *n* piedad, *f;* santidad, *f*

godling diosecillo, *m*

godly *a* devoto, piadoso, religioso

godmother *n* madrina, *f.* **fairy g.,** hada madrina, *f.* **to be a g. to,** ser madrina de

godparent *n* padrino, *m;* madrina, *f pl.* **godparents,** padrinos, *m pl*

godsend *n* bien, *m;* buena suerte, *f;* fortuna, *f*

go-getter *n* buscavidas, *mf*

goggle *n* mirada fija, *f; pl* **goggles,** anteojos, *m pl,* gafas, *f pl;* (of a horse) anteojeras, *f pl. vi* mirar fijamente; salirse a uno los ojos de la cabeza. **g.-eyed,** de ojos saltones. **g.-eyes,** ojos saltones, *m pl*

going *n* ida, *f;* (departure) partida, marcha, *f;* salida, *f;* (pace) paso, *m;* (speed) velocidad, *f.* **It was heavy g.,** El avance era lento; El progreso era lento; (of parties, etc.) Era aburrido. **The g. was difficult on those mountainous roads,** El conducir (or el ir or el andar) era difícil en aquellos caminos de montaña. **g. back,** vuelta, *f,* regreso, *m.* **g. down,** bajada, *f,* descenso, *m;* (of the sun, etc.) puesta, *f.* **g. forward,** avance, *m;* progreso, *m.* **g. in,** entrada, *f.* **g. in and out,** idas y venidas, *f pl.* **g. out,** salida, *f;* (of a fire, light) apagamiento, *m*

going *a* and *pres part* que va, yendo; que funciona. **G., g., gone** (at an auction) A la una, a las dos, a las tres. **goings-on,** (tricks) trapujos, *m pl;* (conduct) conducta, *f.* **g. concern,** empresa próspera, *f.* **g. to,** con destino a

going-away present *n* regalo de despedida, *m*

goiter *n* bocio, *m*

gold *n* oro, *m;* color de oro, *m. a* de oro; áureo. **All that glitters is not g.,** No es oro todo lo que reluce. **cloth of g.,** tela de oro, *f.* **dull g.,** oro mate, *m.* **light g.,** oro pálido, *m.* **old g.,** oro viejo, *m.* **g.-beater,** batidor de oro, *m.* **g.-digger,** minero de oro, *m;* (woman) aventurera, *f.* **g. dust,** oro en polvo, *m.* **g.-fever,** fiebre de oro, *f.* **g. lace,** galón de oro, *m.* **g. lacquer,** sisa dorada, *f.* **g. leaf,** pan de oro, oro batido, *m.* **g.-mine,** mina de oro, *f.* **g. piece,** moneda de oro, *f.* **g. plate,** vajilla de oro, *f.* **g. standard,** patrón oro, *m.* **g.-thread,** hilo de oro, *m.* **g.-yielding,** *a* aurífero

golden *a* de oro; dorado; áureo; amarillo; *fig* feliz; excelente. **to become g.,** dorarse. **g. age,** edad de oro, *f.* **g.-crested wren,** abadejo, *m.* **g. hair,** cabellos dorados (or de oro), *m pl.* **G. Legend,** leyenda áurea, *f.* **g. mean,** justo medio, *m.* **g. rose,** rosa de oro, *f.* **g. rule,** regla áurea, *f.* **g. syrup,** jarabe de arce, *m.* **g. voice,** voz de oro, *f.* **g. wedding,** bodas de oro, *f pl*

goldfinch *n* jilguero, *m*

goldfish *n* carpa dorada, *f.* **g. bowl,** pecera, *f*

goldrush carrera de oro, *f*

goldsmith *n* orfebre, oribe, orífice, *m*

golf *n* golf, *m.* **g.-club,** (stick) palo de golf, *m;* (organization) club de golf, *m.* **g.-course,** campo de golf, *m*

golfer *n* jugador (-ra) de golf

gonad *n* gonada, *f*

gondola *n* góndola, *f*

gondolier *n* gondolero, *m*

gone *a* and *past part* ido; (lost) perdido; (ruined) arruinado; (dead) muerto; (past) pasado; (disappeared) desaparecido; (fainted) desmayado; (suppressed) suprimido; (pregnant) encinta; (drunk) borracho; (ended) terminado; (exhausted) agotado; (ill) enfermo. **far g.,** avanzado; (in years) de edad avanzada; (of illness) cerca de la muerte, muy enfermo; (in love) loco de amor; (drunk) muy borracho. **It is all g.,** No hay más. **It is g. seven o'clock,** Son las siete y pico, Son las siete ya

gong *n* gong, *m;* (Chinese) batintín, *m*

gonorrhea *n* gonorrea, *f*

good *a* bueno (before *m sing* nouns) buen; agradable; afortunado; (appropriate) apropiado, oportuno; (beneficial) provechoso, ventajoso; (wholesome) sano, saludable; (suitable) apto; (useful) útil; (kind) bondadoso; (much) mucho; (obliging) amable; (virtuous) virtuoso; (skilled) experto; (fresh) fresco; (genuine) genuino, legítimo; verdadero. *adv* bien. *interj* ¡bueno! ¡bien! **a g. deal,** mucho. **a g. many,** bastantes. **a g. turn,** un favor. **a g. way,** (distance) un buen trecho; mucho. **a g. while,** un buen rato. **as g. as,** tan bueno como. **Be so g. as to . . . !** Haga el favor de, Tenga Vd. la bondad de (followed by infin.). **fairly g.,** *a* bastante bueno. *adv* bastante bien. **I'm g. for another five miles,** Tengo fuerzas para cinco millas más. **It was g. of you to do it,** Vd. fue muy amable de hacerlo, Vd. tuvo mucha bondad de hacerlo. **to be no g. at this sort of thing,** no servir para tales cosas. **to have a g. time,** pasarlo bien. **to make g.,** reparar; indemnizar; (accomplish) llevar a cabo, poner en práctica; justificar; (a promise) cumplir. **very g.,** *a* muy bueno. *adv* muy bien. **g.-feeling,** buena voluntad, *f.* **g.-fellowship,** compañerismo, *m;* buena compañía, *f.* **g.-for-nothing,** *n* papanatas, badulaque, *m.* **to be g.-for-nothing,** no servir para nada. **g. luck,** buena suerte, *Lat. Am. also* derechura, leche *f.* **g. manners,** buenos modales, *m pl;* buena crianza, educación, *f.* **g. nature,** buen natural, *m;* buen humor, *m.* **g.-natured,** de buen natural; de buen humor, bonachón. **g. offices,** buenos oficios, *m pl.* **g.-tempered,** de buen humor

good *n* bien, *m;* provecho, *m;* utilidad, *f; pl* **goods.** See separate entry. **I am saying this for your g.,** Lo digo para tu bien. **Much g. may it do you!** ¡Buen provecho te haga! **for g. and all,** para siempre jamás. **It is no g.,** Es inútil; No vale la pena. **the g.,** el bien; (people) los buenos. **They have gone for g.,** Se han marchado para no volver. **to do one g.,** hacer bien a uno; mejorar; ser provechoso (a uno); (suit) sentar bien (a uno). **What is the g. of . . . ?** ¿Para qué sirve . . . ?; ¿Qué vale . . . ? **g. and evil,** el bien y el mal

good-bye *interj* ¡adiós! *n* adiós, *m,* despedida, *f.* **to bid g.-b.,** decir adiós. **G.-b. for the present!** ¡Hasta la vista! ¡Hasta luego! **G.-b. until tomorrow, then,** Hasta mañana pues, adiós, Hasta mañana entonces

goodness *n* bondad, *f;* (of quality) buena calidad, *f;* (of persons) amabilidad, benevolencia, *f;* (essence) esencia, substancia, *f;* bien, *m:* excelencia, *f; interj* ¡Jesús! ¡Dios mío! **For g. sake!** ¡Por Dios! **I wish to g. that,** ¡Ojalá que . . . !

goods *n pl* bienes, efectos, *m pl;* artículos, *m pl; com* mercancías, *f pl,* géneros, *m pl.* **by g.-train,** en pequeña velocidad. **stolen g.,** objetos robados, *m pl.* **g. lift,** montacargas, *m.* **g. office,** depósito de mercancías, *m.* **g. station,** estación de carga, *f.* **g.-train,** tren de mercancías, *m.* **g. van,** furgón, *m.* **g. wagon,** vagon de mercancías, *m*

good-smelling *a* oloroso

goodwill *n* benevolencia, *f;* buena voluntad, *f;* (of a business) clientela, *f*

goose *n* oca, *f,* ganso (-sa); plancha de sastre, *f. a* de oca. **g.-flesh,** *fig* carne de gallina, *f.* **g. girl,** ansarera, *f.* **g.-step,** paso de oca, *m*

gooseberry *n* uva espina, *f*

Gordian *a* gordiano. **G. knot,** nudo gordiano, *m*

gore *n* sangre, *f; sew* sesga, nesga, *f. vt* acornear; desgarrar; herir (con arma blanca)

gorge *n* (valley) cañón, barranco, *m;* (heavy meal) comilona, *f,* atracón, *m. vt* engullir, tragar. *vi* hartarse, atracarse

gorgeous *a* magnífico; espléndido, suntuoso; *inf* maravilloso, estupendo

gorgeously *adv* magníficamente

gorgeousness *n* magnificencia, *f;* suntuosidad, *f,* esplendor, *m*

gorilla *n* gorila, *m*

gormandize *vi* glotonear

gormandizer *n* glotón (-ona)

gorse *n* tojo, *m,* aulaga, *f*

gory *a* ensangrentado; sangriento

gosh *interj* ¡caray! ¡caramba!

goshawk *n orn* azor, *m*

gosling *n* ansarino, *m*

gospel *n* evangelio, *m;* doctrina, *f.* **The G. according to St. Mark,** El Evangelio según San Marcos. **to believe as g. truth,** creer como si fuese el evangelio. **to preach the G.,** predicar el evangelio

gossamer *n* hilo de araña, *m,* red de araña, telaraña, *f;* (filmy material) gasa, *f;* hilo finísimo, *m, a* de gasa; sutil, delgado, fino

gossip *n* murmurador (-ra), chismoso (-sa), hablador (-ra); (scandal) chisme, *m, Lat. Am. also* lengüeterías *fpl;* habladuría, murmuración, *f;* (obsolete, of a woman) comadre, *f;* (talk) charla, *f. vi* charlar, conversar; (in bad sense) murmurar, chismear; criticar. **to g. about,** charlar de; poner lenguas en, cortar un sayo (a); hablar mal de. **g. column,** gacetilla, *f*

gossiping *a* charlatán, hablador; chismoso, murmurador. *n* See **gossip**

Goth *n* godo (-da); bárbaro (-ra)

Gothic *a art* gótico; (of race) godo; bárbaro. *n* (language) gótico, *m;* arquitectura gótica, *f.* **G. characters,** letra gótica, *f*

gouge *n* gubia, *f. vt* escoplear. **to g. out,** vaciar; sacar

gourd *n* calabaza, *f*

gourmand *n* glotón, *m*

gourmet *n* gastrónomo, *m*

gout *n med* gota, *f*

gouty *a* gotoso

govern *vt* gobernar; regir; (guide) guiar; dominar; domar, refrenar; *gram* regir; (regulate) regular

governable *a* gobernable; manejable; dócil

governess *n* institutriz, *f;* (in a school) maestra, *f*

governing *a* gubernante; director; (with principle, etc.) directivo. *n* See **government**

government *n* gobierno, *m;* dirección, *f;* autoridad, *f.* **g. bond,** bono del gobierno, *m.* **g. house,** palacio del gobernador, *m.* **g. office,** oficina del gobierno, *f.* **g. stock,** papel del Estado, *m*

governmental *a* gubernamental, gubernativo.

Government Printing Office Talleres Gráficos de la Nación, *m pl*

governor *n* gobernador (-ra); vocal de la junta de gobierno, *mf;* (of a prison) director (-ra) (de una prisión); *mech* regulador, *m.* **g.-general,** gobernador general, *m*

governorship *n* gobierno, *m;* dirección, *f*

gown *n* toga, *f;* (cassock) sotana, *f;* (dressing-g.) bata, *f;* (for sleeping) camisa de noche, *f;* (bathing-wrap) albornoz, *m;* (dress) vestido, traje, *m*

Goyesque *a* goyesco

grab *n* asimiento, *m,* presa, *f; mech* gancho, *m. vt* arrebatar, asir, agarrar; *fig* alzarse con, tomar

grabber *n* cogedor (-ra); codicioso (-sa)

grace *n* elegancia, *f;* simetría, armonía, *f;* gracia, gentileza, *f,* donaire, *m;* encanto, *m;* (goodness) bondad, *f;* gracia, *f;* merced, *f,* favor, *m;* (period of time) plazo, *m;* (privilege) privilegio, *m; theol* gracia divina, *f;* (at table) bendición de la mesa, *f;* (as a title) excelentísimo, (to an archbishop) ilustrísimo. *vt* adornar; favorecer; honrar. **airs and graces,** humos, *m pl.* **the Three Graces,** las Gracias. **three days' g.,** plazo de tres dias, *m.* **to get into a person's good graces,** congraciarse con; caer en gracia con. **to say g.,** bendecir la mesa. **with a bad g.,** a regañadientes. **with a good g.,** de buena gana. **g.-note,** *mus* nota de adorno, *f*

graceful *a* airoso, gentil, gracioso; elegante; bonito

gracefully *adv* airosamente, gentilmente; con gracia; elegantemente

gracefulness. See **grace**

graceless *a* réprobo; dejado de la mano de Dios; sin gracia

gracious *a* (merciful) piadoso, clemente; (urbane) afable, condescendiente, agradable. **Good g.!** ¡Vamos!, ¡Dios mío!

graciously *adv* afablemente; con benevolencia. **to be g. pleased,** tener a bien

graciousness *n* amabilidad, afabilidad, condescendencia, *f*

gradate *vt* graduar; *art* degradar

gradation *n* graduación, *f; mus* gradación, *f;* paso gradual, *m;* serie, *f*
grade *n* grado, *m;* (quality) calidad, clase, *f;* (in a school) clase, *f;* (gradient) pendiente, *f,* declive, *m. vt* graduar, clasificar; (cattle breeding) cruzar. **down g.,** cuesta abajo. **up g.,** cuesta arriba. **highest g.,** *n* primera clase, *f. a* de primera clase; de calidad excelente
gradient *n* declive, *m.* cuesta, pendiente, *f*
gradual *a* gradual. *n ecc* gradual, *m*
gradually *adv* gradualmente; poco a poco
graduate *n* licenciado (-da), *Lat. Am.* exalumno (na) *mf a* graduado. *vt* graduar. *vi* graduarse; (as a doctor) doctorarse. **to g. as,** recibirse de. **be graduated from . . .** *Lat. Am.* egresar de . . .
graduation *n* graduación, *f, Lat. Am.* egreso *m*
graft *n bot* injerto, *m; surg* injerto de piel, *m;* (swindle) estafa, *f;* (bribery) soborno, *m. vt bot* injertar; *surg* injertar un trozo de piel; *fig* injerir
grafting *n bot* injerto, *m; surg* injerto de piel, *m; fig* inserción, *f*
grain *n* (corn) grano, *m;* (cereal) cereal, *m,* or *f;* (seed, weight) grano, *m;* (trace) pizca, *f;* (of wood, etc.) hila, *m,* fibra, hebra, veta, *f;* (of leather) flor, *f;* (texture) textura, *f. vt* granear; granular; (wood, marble, etc.) vetear. **against the g.,** a contrapelo. **g. lands,** mieses, *f pl*
gram *n* gramo, *m*
grammar *n* gramática, *f.* **g. school,** instituto de segunda enseñanza, *m*
grammarian *n* gramático, *m*
grammatical *a* gramático
grammatically *adv* gramaticalmente, como la gramática lo quiere. (e.g., **She now speaks Catalan g.,** Ahora habla el catalán como la gramática lo quiere)
grammaticalness *n* corrección gramatical, *f*
gramophone *n* gramófono, *m.*
granary *n* granero, hórreo, *m,* troj, *f, Mexico* espiguero *m.* **g. keeper,** trojero, *m*
grand *a* magnífico, soberbio; imponente; (of dress) espléndido, vistoso; (of people) distinguido, importante; aristocrático; (proud) orgulloso; (of style) elevado, sublime; (morally) noble; augusto; (main) principal; (full) completo; *inf* estupendo, magnífico; (with duke, etc.) gran. *n* piano de cola, *m.* **g.-aunt,** tía abuela, *f.* **g. cross,** gran cruz, *f.* **g. duchess,** gran duquesa, *f.* **g. duke,** gran duque, *m.* **g. lodge,** (of freemasons) Gran Oriente, *m.* **g. master,** gran maestre, *m.* **g.-nephew,** resobrino, *m.* **g.-niece,** resobrina, *f.* **g. opera,** ópera, *f.* **g. piano,** piano de cola, *m.* **g.-stand,** tribuna, *f.* **g.-uncle,** tío abuelo, *m.* **g. vizier,** gran visir, *m*
grandchild *n* nieto (-ta). **great-g.,** bisnieto (-ta). **great-great-g.,** tataranieto (-ta)
granddaughter *n* nieta, *f.* **great-g.,** bisnieta, *f.* **great-great-g.,** tataranieta, *f*
grandee *n* grande (de España, grande de Portugal), *m*
grandeur *n* magnificencia, *f;* grandiosidad, *f;* magnitud, grandeza, *f;* (pomp) pompa, *f,* fausto, *m*
grandfather *n* abuelo, *m.* **great-g.,** bisabuelo, *m.* **great-great-g.,** tatarabuelo, *m*
grandfather's clock reloj de péndulo, *m*
grandfatherly *a* de abuelo
grandiloquence *n* grandilocuencia, *f*
grandiloquent *a* grandílocuo
grandiose *a* grandioso, sublime; impresionante; imponente; (in a bad sense) extravagante: (of style) bombástico, hinchado
grand jury *n* jurado de acusación, jurado de jucio, *m*
grandmother *n* abuela, *f.* **great-g.,** bisabuela, *f.* **great-great-g.,** tatarabuela, *f*
grandness *n* magnificencia, *f;* aristocracia, *f;* (pride) orgullo, *m;* grandiosidad, *f;* (of style) sublimidad, *f;* (of character) nobleza, *f*
grandparent *n* abuelo, *m;* abuela, *f; pl* **grandparents,** abuelos, *m pl.* **great-grand-parents,** bisabuelos, *m pl.* **great-great-grandparents,** tatarabuelos, *m pl*
grandson *n* nieto, *m.* **great-g.,** bisnieto, *m.* **great-great-g.,** tataranieto, *m*
grange *n* granja, *f;* casa de campo, *f*
granite *n* granito, *m*
granny *n* abuelita, nana, *f;* abuela, *f.* **g. knot,** nudo al revés, *m*
grant *n* concesión, *f;* otorgamiento, *m;* donación, *f;* privilegio, *m;* (for study) beca, bolsa de estudio, *f;* (transfer) traspaso, *m,* cesión, *f. vt* conceder; (bestow) otorgar, dar; donar; (agree to) acceder a, asentir en; permitir; (transfer) traspasar; (assume) suponer. **to g. a degree,** expedir un título. **to g. a motion,** dar por entrada a una moción. **to take for granted,** descontar; dar por hecho, dar por sentado. **God g. it!** ¡Dios lo quiera! **granted that,** dado que
grantee *n* cesionario (-ia), adjudicatorio (-ia)
grantor *n* cesionista, *mf;* otorgador (-ra)
granulated *a* granulado
granule *n* gránulo, *m*
granulous *a* granuloso
grape *n* uva, *f.* **bunch of grapes,** racimo de uvas, *m.* **muscatel g.,** uva moscatel, *f.* **sour grapes,** uvas agrias, *f pl;* (phrase) ¡están verdes! **g.-fruit,** toronja, *f.* **g. gatherer,** vendimiador (-ra). **g. harvest,** vendimia, *f.* **g. juice,** mosto, *m.* **g.-shot,** metralla, *f.* **g. stone,** granuja, *f.* **g.-sugar,** glucosa, *f.* **g.-vine,** vid, parra, *f*
graph *n* gráfica, *f;* diagrama, *m*
graphic *a* gráfico
graphite *n* grafito, *m*
graphology *n* grafología, *f*
grapple *n naut* rezón, arpeo, *m;* lucha a brazo partido, *f. vt naut* aferrar; asir, agarrar. *vi naut* aferrarse. **to g. with,** luchar a brazo partido (con); *fig* luchar con
grappling *n naut* aferramiento, *m;* lucha cuerpo a cuerpo, *f;* (with a problem) lucha con, *f*
grasp *n* agarro, *m;* (reach) alcance, *m;* (of a hand) apretón, *m;* (power) garras, *f pl,* poder, *m;* (understanding) comprensión, *f;* inteligencia, capacidad intelectual, *f. vt* agarrar, asir; empuñar; abrazar; *fig* comprender, alcanzar; (a hand) estrechar. *vi* agarrarse. **within one's g.,** al alcance de uno. **to g. at,** asirse de
grasping *n* asimiento, *m;* (understanding) comprensión, *f, a* codicioso, tacaño, mezquino
graspingness *n* codicia, *f*
grass *n* hierba, *f;* (pasture) pasto, herbaje, *m;* (sward) césped, *m. vt* cubrir de hierba; sembrar de hierba; apacentar. **to hear the g. grow,** sentir crecer la hierba. **to let the g. grow,** *fig* dejar crecer la hierba. **to turn out to g.,** echar al pasto. **g.-blade,** brizna de hierba, *f.* **g.-green,** *a* and *n* verde como la hierba *m..* **g.-grown,** cubierto de hierba. **g.-land,** pradera, *f.* **g.-snake,** culebra *f.* **g. widow,** mujer cuyo marido está ausente
grasshopper *n* saltamontes, *m.* **grasshopper's chirp,** chirrido (del saltamontes), *m*
grassy *a* parecido a la hierba, como la hierba; cubierto de hierba; de hierba
grate *n* parrilla, *f;* (grating) reja, *f. vt* raspar, raer; *cul* rallar; (make a noise) hacer rechinar. *vi* rozar; rechinar, chirriar. **to g. on, upon,** (of sounds) irritar, molestar; chocar con. **to g. on the ear,** herir el oído
grateful *a* agradecido, reconocido; (pleasant) agradable, grato
gratefully *adv* agradecidamente; gratamente
gratefulness *n* agradecimiento, *m,* gratitud, *f;* (pleasantness) agrado, *m*
grater *n cul* rallador, *m*
gratification *n* satisfacción, *f;* (pleasure) placer, gusto, *m*
gratified *a* satisfecho, contento
gratify *vt* satisfacer; (please) gratificar, agradar
gratifying *a* satisfactorio, agradable
grating *n* reja, *f;* rejilla, *f; naut* jareta, *f;* (optics) retículo, *m;* (sound) rechinamiento, chirrido, *m. a* rechinante, chirriador; áspero
gratis *a* and *adv* gratis
gratitude *n* agradecimiento, *m,* gratitud, *f*
gratuitous *a* gratuito
gratuitousness *n* gratuidad, *f*

gratuity *n* gratificación, propina, *f*
grave *n* (hole) sepultura, fosa, *f;* (monument) tumba, *f,* sepulcro, *m; fig* muerte, *f.* **g.-digger,** enterrador, sepulturero, *m*
grave *a* grave; importante; serio; sobrio; (anxious) preocupado; (of accent) grave. *n* (grave accent) acento grave, *m*
gravel *n* grava, *f;* cascajo, casquijo, *m; med* arenillas, *f pl,* cálculo, *m*
gravely *adv* gravemente; seriamente
Graves' disease *n* bocio exoftálmico, *m*
gravestone *n* lápida mortuoria, *f*
graveyard *n* camposanto, cementerio, *m*
gravitate *vi* gravitar; tender
gravitation *n* gravitación, *f;* tendencia, *f*
gravitational *a* de gravitación, gravitacional, gravitatorio
gravitational pull *n* atracción gravitatoria, *f*
gravity *n phys* gravedad, *f;* seriedad, *f;* solemnidad, *f;* gravedad, *f;* (weight) peso, *m;* importancia, *f;* (enormity) enormidad, *f;* (danger) peligro, *m.* **center of g.,** centro de gravedad, *m.* **law of g.,** ley de la gravedad, *f.* **specific g.,** peso específico, *m*
gravy *n* salsa, *f;* jugo (de la carne), *m.* **g.-boat,** salsera, *f*
gray *a* gris; (of animals) rucio. *n* color gris, gris, *m;* caballo gris, *m.* **His hair is turning g.,** El pelo se le vuelve gris. **g.-haired,** de pelo gris. **g. matter,** materia gris, *f;* cacumen, *m.* **g. mullet,** *icht* mújol, *m.* **g. squirrel,** gris, *m.* **g. wolf,** lobo gris, *m*
grayish *a* grisáceo, agrisado; (of hair) entrecano
grayness *n* color gris, gris, *m; fig* monotonía, *f*
graze *n* abrasión, *f;* (brush) roce, *m, vi* pacer, apacentarse. *vt* pastorear, apacentar; (brush) rozar
grazing *n agr* apacentamiento, pastoreo, *m;* (brushing) rozadura, *f. a* que pace, herbívoro; (of land) pacedero. **g. land,** pasto, *m*
grease *n* grasa, *f;* (dirt) mugre, *f;* (of a candle) sebo, *m,* cera, *f. vt* engrasar; manchar con grasa; *fig inf* untar. **to g. the wheels,** *fig* untar el carro. **g.-box,** *mech* caja de sebo, *f.* **g.-gun,** engrasador de compresión, *m.* **g.-paint,** afeites de actor (or de actriz), *m pl.* **g.-proof paper,** papel impermeable, *m.* **g. spot,** lámpara, mancha de grasa, *f,* saín, *m*
greaser *n* engrasador, *m*
greasiness *n* graseza, *f;* lo aceitoso; untuosidad, *f*
greasing *n* engrasado, *m*
greasy *a* grasiento; (oily) aceitoso; (grubby) mugriento, bisunto, *Argentina* cascarriento; *fig* lisonjero. **g. pole,** cucaña, *f*
great *a* gran; grande; enorme; vasto; (much) mucho; (famous) famoso, ilustre; noble, sublime; (intimate) íntimo; importante; principal; poderoso; magnífico, impresionante; *inf* famoso, estupendo; (of time) largo; (clever) fuerte. **Alexander the G.,** Alejandro Magno. **the G. Mogul,** el Gran Mogul. **a g. deal,** mucho. **a g. man,** un grande hombre, un hombre famoso. **a g. many,** muchos (muchas). **He lived to a g. age,** Vivió hasta una edad avanzada. **so g.,** tan grande, tamaño. **the g.,** los grandes hombres. **g. on,** aficionado a. **g.-aunt,** tía abuela, *f.* **g.-grandchild,** etc. See **grandchild,** etc. **g.-hearted,** valeroso; magnánimo, generoso. **g. power,** gran poder, *m.* **G. War,** Gran Guerra, *f.* **the Great Schism,** el Gran Cisma, *m*
greater *a* comp. of **great,** mayor; más grande. **to make g.,** agrandar. **G. London,** el Gran Londres, *m*
greatest *a* sup. of **great,** más grande; mayor; máximo; más famoso; sumo
greatly *adv* mucho; con mucho; (very) muy; noblemente
greatness *n* grandeza, *f;* grandiosidad, *f;* extensión, vastedad, *f;* importancia, *f;* poder, *m;* majestad, *f;* esplendor, *m;* (intensity) intensidad, *f;* (enormity) enormidad, *f*
Greco- *prefix* (in compounds) greco-, greco
greed *n* (cupidity) codicia, rapacidad, avaricia, *f;* avidez, ansia, *f;* (of food) gula, glotonería, *f*
greedily *adv* codiciosamente; con avidez; (of eating) vorazmente
greedy *a* (for food) glotón; codicioso; ambicioso; ávido; deseoso
Greece Grecia, *f*
Greek *a* and *n* griego (-ga); (language) griego, *m.* **It's all G. to me,** Para mí es como si fuese en latín, Me es chino. **G. tunic,** peplo, *m*
green *a* verde; (inexpert) inexperto, bisoño; (recent) nuevo, reciente; (fresh) fresco; (of complexion) pálido, descolorido; (flowery) floreciente; (vigorous) lozano; (young) joven; (unripe) verde; (credulous) crédulo; (raw) crudo; (of wood, vegetables) verde. *n* verde, color verde, *m;* (vegetables) verdura, *f;* (meadow) prado, *m;* (turf) césped, *m;* (grass) hierba, *f;* (bowling) campo de juego, *m. vt* teñir (or pintar) de verde. **bright g.,** *n* verdegay, verde claro, *m.* **dark g.,** *n* verdinegro, *m.* **light g.,** *n* verde pálido, *m.* **to grow** or **look g.,** verdear. **g.-eyed,** de ojos verdes. **g. peas,** guisantes, *m pl.* **g. table,** tapete verde, *m*
greenery *n* follaje, *m;* verdura, *f*
greengrocery *n* verdulería, *f*
greenhorn *n* bisoño (-ña); papanatas, *m*
greenhouse *n* invernáculo, invernadero, *Lat. Am.* conservatorio *m*
greenish *a* verdoso. **g.-yellow,** cetrino
Greenland Groenlandia, *f*
Greenlander *n* groenlandés (-esa)
greenness *a* lo verde; verdor, *m,* verdura, *f;* (inexperience) falta de experiencia, *f;* (vigor) vigor, *m,* lozanía, *f;* (newness) novedad, *f;* (of wood, fruit) falta de madurez, *f*
greenroom *n theat* saloncillo, *m*
greenstuff *n* hortalizas, legumbres, *f pl*
greet *vt* saludar; recibir; (express pleasure) dar la bienvenida (a)
greeting *n* salutación, *f,* saludo, *m;* recepción, *f;* (welcome) bienvenida, *f; pl* **greetings,** recuerdos, *m pl*
gregarious *a* gregario
gregariousness *n* gregarismo, *m*
Gregorian *a* gregoriano
grenade *n* granada, bomba, *f.* **hand-g.,** bomba de mano, *f*
grey See **gray**
greyhound *n* galgo, lebrel, *m.* **g. bitch,** galga, *f;* **g. racing,** carreras de galgos, *f pl*
grid *n* (of electric power) red, *f;* rejilla, *f;* (for water, etc.) alcantarilla, *f*
gridiron *n cul* parrilla, *f;* (of electric power) red, *f; theat* telar, *m*
grief *n* angustia, pena, aflicción, *f;* dolor, suplicio, *m.* **to come to g.,** pasarlo mal, tener un desastre
grievance *n* injusticia, *f;* motivo de queja, *m*
grieve *vt* entristecer, afligir, angustiar; atormentar. *vi* entristecerse, afligirse, acongojarse. **to g. for,** lamentar: echar de menos
grievous *a* (heavy) oneroso, gravoso; opresivo; doloroso, penoso; lamentable; cruel. **g. error,** error lamentable
grievousness *n* (weight) peso, *m;* carácter opresivo, *m;* dolor, *m,* aflicción, *f;* enormidad, *f;* crueldad, *f*
griffin *n* grifo, *m;* (*fig* chaperon) carabina, *f;* (dog) grifón, *m*
grill *n cul* parrilla, *f;* (grating) rejilla, *f;* (before a window) reja, *f;* (food) asado a la parrilla, *m. vt cul* asar a la parrilla; (burn) quemar; (question) interrogar; (torture) torturar. *vi cul* asarse a la parrilla; (be burnt) quemarse. **g.-room,** parrilla, *f*
grille *n* reja, *f;* rejilla, *f;* (screen) verja, *f*
grilled *a cul* a la parrilla; con rejilla
griller *n cul* parrilla, *f*
grim *a* (fierce) feroz, salvaje; (severe) severo, ceñudo, adusto; inflexible; (frightful) horrible
grimace *n* mueca, *f,* gesto, mohín, visaje, *m, vi* hacer muecas
grime *n* mugre, *f;* suciedad, *f.* **to cover with g.,** enmugrecer

grimly *adv* severamente; sin sonreír; inflexiblemente; (without retreating) sin cejar; (frightfully) horriblemente; de un modo espantoso

grimness *n* (ferocity) ferocidad, *f;* (severity) severidad, *f;* inflexibilidad, *f;* (frightfulness) horror, *m,* lo espantoso

grimy *a* mugriento, sucio

grin *n* sonrisa grande, *f;* sonrisa burlona, *f;* (grimace) mueca, *f. vi* sonreír mostrando los dientes; sonreír bonachonamente; sonreír de un modo burlón

grind *vt* (to powder) pulverizar; moler; (break up) quebrantar; (oppress) agobiar, oprimir; (sharpen) afilar, amolar; (a barrel-organ) tocar (un manubrio); (the teeth) crujir, rechinar (los dientes); (into) reducir a; (*inf* teach) empollar. *vi* moler; *fig inf* trabajar laboriosamente. *n fig inf* trabajo pesado, *m; n fig inf* estudiantón, *m*

grinder *n* (of scissors, etc.) afilador, *m;* (of an organ) organillero; (mill-stone) piedra de moler, *f;* (molar) muela, *f*

grinding *a* (tedious) cansado, aburrido; opresivo; (of pain) incesante. *n* pulverización, *f;* amoladura, *f;* (of grain) molienda, *f;* (polishing) pulimento, bruñido, *m;* (oppression) opresión, *f;* (of teeth) rechinamiento, *m*

grindstone *n* amoladera, afiladera, piedra de amolar, *f.* **to have one's nose to the g.,** batir el yunque

grinning *a* sonriente; riente; (mocking) burlón

grip *n* asimiento, agarro, *m;* (claws, clutches) garras, *f pl;* (hand) mano, *f;* (of shaking hands) apretón de manos, *m;* (of a weapon, etc.) empuñadura, *f;* (reach) alcance, *m;* (understanding) comprensión, *f;* (control) dominio, *m;* (bag) portamanteo, *m;* maleta, *f. vt* asir, agarrar; (of wheels) agarrarse; *mech* morder; (a sword, etc.) empuñar; (pinch) pellizcar; (surround) cercar; (understand) comprender; (press; to grip the hand and *fig* the heart) apretar; (fill) llenar; (the attention) atraer, llamar; (sway, hold) dominar

gripe *n* (*inf* pain) retortijón (de tripas), *m*

grisly *a* espantoso; repugnante

grist *n* molienda, *f.* **Everything is g. to their mill,** Sacan partido de todo

gristle *n* cartílago, *m,* ternilla, *f*

gristly *a* cartilaginoso

grit *n* cascajo, *m;* polvo, *m; fig* firmeza (de carácter), *f;* (courage) valor, *m;* (endurance) aguante, *m*

gritty *a* arenoso, arenisco

grizzled *a* (of hair, etc.) gris; canoso; grisáceo

grizzly bear *n* oso (-sa) pardo (-da)

groan *n* gemido, *m. vi* gemir; (creak) crujir. **to g. out,** decir (or contar) entre gemidos. **to g. under,** sufrir bajo, gemir bajo; (of weight) crujir bajo

groaning *n* gemidos, *m pl. a* que gime, gemidor; (under a weight) crujiente

grocer *n* abacero (-ra) vendedor (-ra) de comestibles, *Lat. Am.* abarrotero (-ra). **grocer's shop,** tienda de comestibles, bodega, *f, Mexico* abarrotería, *f*

grocery *n* tienda de comestibles, tienda de ultramarinos, abarrotería, lonja, bodega, *f,* negocio de comestibles, *m; pl* **groceries,** provisiones, *f pl,* comestibles, *m pl, Lat. Am.* abarrotes *mpl*

groin *n anat* ingle, *f*

groom *n* (in a royal household) gentilhombre, *m;* lacayo, *m;* mozo de caballos, *m;* (of a bride) novio, *m. vt* (a horse) cuidar; (oneself) arreglarse. **She is always well groomed,** Está siempre muy bien arreglada

groomsman *n* padrino de boda, *m*

groove *n* ranura, muesca, *f;* estría, *f;* surco, *m; fig* rutina, *f. vt* entallar; estriar

grooved *a* con ranura; estriado

grope *vi* andar a tientas; (with for) buscar a tientas; procurar, encontrar, buscar. **to g. one's way toward,** avanzar a tientas hacia; *fig* avanzar poco a poco hacia

gropingly *adv* a tientas; irresolutamente

gross *n com* gruesa, *f;* totalidad, *f, a* grueso; denso, espeso; (unrefined) grosero; (great) grande; (crass) craso; total; *com* bruto; (tremendous) enorme. **in g.,** en grueso. **g. amount,** total, *m; com* importe bruto, *m.* **g. weight,** peso bruto, *m*

grossly *adv* groseramente; (much) enormemente

grossness *n* gordura, *f;* (vulgarity) grosería, *f;* obscenidad, *f;* (enormity) enormidad, *f*

grotesque *a* grotesco; extravagante, estrambótico; ridículo. *n* grotesco, *m*

grotesqueness *n* lo grotesco; ridiculez, *f*

grotto *n* gruta, *f*

ground *n* suelo, *m;* (of water and *naut*) fondo, *m;* (earth) tierra, *f; fig* terreno, *m;* (strata) capa, *f; sport* campo, *m;* (parade) plaza (de armas), *f;* (background) fondo, *m;* (basis) base, *f,* fundamento, *m;* (reason) causa, *f;* motivo, *m;* (excuse) pretexto, *m; pl* **grounds,** jardines, *m pl,* parque, *m;* (sediment) sedimento, *m,* heces, *f pl;* (reason) causa, *f. vi naut* varar, encallar. *vt* poner en tierra; *naut* hacer varar; *elec* conectar con tierra; (base) fundar (en), basar (en); (teach) enseñar los rudimentos (de). *a* molido; en polvo; (of floors, stories) bajo; (of glass) deslustrado; *bot* terrestre. **common g.,** tierra comunal, *f; fig* tierra común, *f.* **He is on his own g.,** Está en terreno propio. **It fell to the g.,** Cayó al suelo; *fig* Fracasó. **It is on the g.,** Está en el suelo. **It suits me to the g.,** Me viene de perilla. **to break fresh g.,** *fig* tratar problemas nuevos. **to be well grounded in,** conocer bien los elementos (or rudimentos) de. **to cover g.,** cubrir terreno; recorrer; (in discussion) tocar muchos puntos. **to cut the g. from beneath one's feet,** hacer perder la iniciativa (a). **to give g.,** retroceder; perder terreno. **to raze to the g.,** echar por tierra, arrasar. **to stand one's g.,** resistir el ataque; no darse por vencido; *fig* mantenerse firme, mantenerse en sus trece. **to win g.,** ganar terreno. **g. coffee,** café molido, *m.* **g.-color,** (of paint) primera capa, *f;* (color de) fondo, *m;* **g.-floor,** piso bajo, *m.* **g. glass,** vidrio deslustrado, *m.* **g.-ivy,** hiedra terrestre, *f.* **g. nut,** cacahuete, *m.* **g.-plan,** *arch* planta, *f.* **g.-rent,** censo, *m.* **g.-sheet,** tela impermeable, *f;* **g. staff,** *aer* personal del aeropuerto, *m.* **g.-swell,** mar de fondo, *m*

grounded *a* fundado. **The airplanes are g.,** Los aviones están sin volar. **His suspicions are well g.,** Tiene motivos para sus sospechas

grounding *n naut* encalladura, *f;* (teaching) instrucción en los rudimentos, *f*

groundless *a* sin fundamento, inmotivado, sin causa, sin motivo

groundwork *n* fundamento, *m;* base, *f;* principio, *m*

group *n* grupo, *m. vt* agrupar. *vi* agruparse. **g. captain,** coronel de aviación, *m*

grouping *n* agrupación, *f*

grouse *n orn* ortega, *f. vi* rezongar, refunfuñar

grove *n* soto, boscaje, *m;* arboleda, *f*

grovel *vi* arrastrarse; *fig* humillarse

groveling *a fig* servil; ruin

grow *vi* crecer; (increase) aumentar; (become) hacerse; empezar a; llegar a; (turn) volverse, ponerse; (flourish) progresar, adelantar; (develop) desarrollarse; (extend) extenderse. *vt* cultivar; dejar crecer. **I grew to fear it,** Llegué a temerlo. **to g. cold,** ponerse frío; enfriarse; (of weather) empezar a hacer frío. **to g. fat,** engordar. **to g. hard,** ponerse duro; *fig* endurecerse. **to g. hot,** ponerse caliente; calentarse; (of weather) empezar a hacer calor. **to g. like Topsy,** crecer a la buena de Dios. **to g. old,** envejecer. **to g. tall,** crecer mucho; ser alto. **to g. again,** crecer de nuevo. **to g. into,** hacerse, llegar a ser; venir a ser. **to g. out of,** brotar de; originarse en; (a habit) desacostumbrarse poco a poco. **He is growing out of his clothes,** La ropa se le hace pequeña. **to g. up,** (of persons) hacerse hombre (mujer); desarrollarse; (of a custom, etc.) imponerse. **to g. on, upon,** crecer sobre; llegar a dominar; (make think) hacer creer, empezar a pensar; (of a habit) arraigar en

grower *n* cultivador (-ra)

growing *n* crecimiento, *m;* desarrollo, *m;* (increase) aumento, *m;* (of flowers, etc.) cultivación, *f. a* creciente
growing pains *n pl* crisis de desarrollo, *f*
growl *n* gruñido, *m;* reverberación, *f;* trueno, *m. vi* gruñir; (of guns) tronar; (of thunder) reverberar. **to g. out,** decir gruñendo
grown *a* crecido; maduro; adulto. **a g. up,** una persona mayor. **to be full-g.,** estar completamente desarrollado; haber llegado a la madurez. **g. over with,** cubierto de
growth *n* crecimiento, *m;* (development) desarrollo, *m;* (progress) progreso, adelanto, *m;* (increase) aumento, *m;* (cultivation) cultivo, *m;* (vegetation) vegetación, *f; med* tumor, *m.* **He has a week's g. on his chin,** Tiene una barba de una semana
grub *n* larva, *f,* gusano, *m. vt* (with up, out) desarraigar; cavar; desmalezar; *fig inf* buscar
grubbiness *n* suciedad, *f;* (untidiness) desaliño, *m*
grubby *a* lleno de gusanos; sucio; bisunto; desaliñado
grudge *n* motivo de rencor, *m;* rencor, resentimiento, *m,* ojeriza, *f;* mala voluntad, *f;* aversión, *f. vt* envidiar. **to bear a g.,** tener ojeriza
grudging *a* (niggardly) mezquino; envidioso; poco generoso; de mala gana; nada afable
grudgingly *adv* de mala gana, contra su voluntad; con rencor; a regañadientes
gruel *n* gachas, *f pl*
gruesome *a* pavoroso, horrible; macabro
gruff *a* (of the voice) bronco, grave, áspero; (of manner) brusco, malhumorado
gruffly *adv* en una voz bronca (or áspera); bruscamente, con impaciencia, malhumoradamente
gruffness *n* aspereza, bronquedad, *f;* brusquedad, sequedad, impaciencia, *f,* mal humor, *m*
grumble *n* ruido sordo, trueno, *m;* estruendo, *m;* (complaint) refunfuño, rezongo, *m. vi* tronar; refunfuñar, rezongar; hablar entre dientes; quejarse; protestar (contra). *vt* decir refunfuñando
grumbler *n* murmurador (-ra), refunfuñador (-ra)
grumbling *a* gruñón, refunfuñador; regañón; descontento. *n* See **grumble**
grumblingly *adv* a regañadientes, refunfuñando
grumpiness *n* mal humor, *m,* irritabilidad, *f*
grumpy *a* malhumorado, irritable
grunt *n* gruñido, *m. vi* gruñir
grunting *a* gruñidor
guarantee *n law* persona de quien otra sale fiadora, *f;* garantía, *f;* abono, *m. vt* garantizar; responder de; abonar; (assure) asegurar, acreditar
guarantor *n* garante, *mf*
guard *n* (watchfulness) vigilancia, *f;* (in fencing) guardia, *f;* (of a sword) guarnición, *f;* (sentry) centinela, *m;* (soldier) guardia, *m;* (body of soldiers) guardia, *f;* (escort) escolta, *f;* (keeper) guardián, *m;* (protection) protección, defensa, *f;* (of a train) jefe de tren, *m. vt* guardar; proteger, defender; vigilar; (escort) escoltar. **to g. against,** guardarse de. **the changing of the g.,** el relevo de la guardia. **to be on g.,** *mil* estar de guardia; (in fencing) estar en guardia. **to be on one's g.,** estar prevenido, estar alerta. **to be off one's g.,** estar desprevenido. **to mount g.,** *mil* montar la guardia; vigilar. **guard's van,** furgón de equipajes, *m.* **g.-house,** cuerpo de guardia, *m;* prisión militar, *f*
guarded *a* (reticent) reservado, circunspecto, prudente, discreto
guardedly *adv* prudentemente, con circunspección, discretamente
guardian *n* protector (-ra); guardián (-ana); *law* tutor, *m. a* que guarda; tutelar. **g. angel,** ángel de la guarda, ángel custodio, *m;* deidad tutelar, *f*
guardianship *n* protección, *f;* patronato, *m; law* curaduría, tutela, *f*
guardsman *n* guardia, *m*
Guatemalan *a* and *n* guatemalteco (-ca)
guava *n bot* guayaba, *f*
Guernsey Guenesy, *m*
guerrilla *n* guerrilla, *f;* (soldier) guerrillero, *m. a* de guerrilla. **g. warfare,** guerra de guerrillas, *f*
guess *n* adivinación, *f;* estimación, *f;* conjetura, *f;* sospecha, *f. vt* and *vi* adivinar; conjeturar; sospechar; imaginar; (suppose) suponer, creer; calcular. **to g. at,** formar una opinión sobre; imaginar. **a rough g.,** estimación aproximada, *f.* **at a g.,** a poco más o menos, a ojo de buen cubero. **g.-work,** conjeturas, suposiciones, *f pl*
guest *n* (at a meal) convidado (-da), invitado (-da); (at a hotel, etc.) cliente (-da); (houseguest) *Lat. Am.* alojado *biol* parásito, *m.* **g.-room,** alcoba de respeto, alcoba de honor, alcoba de huéspedes, *f,* cuarto de amigos, cuarto para invitados, *m*
guffaw *n* carcajada, *f. vi* reírse a carcajadas, soltar el trapo
Guiana Guayana, *f*
guidance *n* dirección, *f;* gobierno, *m;* (advice) consejos, *m pl;* inspiración, *f*
guide *n* (person) guía, *mf;* (girl g.) exploradora, *f;* (book and *fig*) guía, *f;* mentor, *m;* modelo, *m;* (inspiration) norte, *m; mech* guía, *f. vt* guiar; conducir; encaminar; dirigir; (govern) gobernar. **g.-book,** guía (de turistas), *f.* **g.-post,** poste indicador, *m*
guided tour *n* visita explicada, visita programada, *f*
guideline *lit* falsarregla, falsilla, *f; fig* pauta, *f*
guiding *a* que guía; directivo; decisivo. *n* See **guidance**
guild *n* gremio, *m. a* gremial. **g. member,** gremial, *m*
guilder *n* (coin) florín holandés, *m*
guile *n* astucia, superchería, maña, *f*
guileful *a* astuto
guileless *a* cándido, sin malicia, inocente
guilelessly *adv* inocentemente
guilelessness *n* inocencia, candidez, *f*
guillotine *n* guillotina, *f. vt* guillotinar
guilt *n* culpabilidad, *f;* crimen, *m;* (sin) pecado, *m*
guilt complex complejo de culpa, *m*
guiltily *adv* culpablemente; como si fuese culpable
guiltless *a* libre de culpa, inocente; puro; ignorante
guilty *a* culpable; delincuente; criminal. **to find g.,** encontrar culpable. **to plead g.,** confesarse culpable. **g. party,** culpable, *m*
Guinea Guinea, *f*
guinea *n* guinea, *f.* **g.-fowl,** gallina de Guinea, *f.* **g.-pig,** conejillo de Indias, cobayo, *m*
guise *n* manera, guisa, *f;* (garb) traje, *m;* máscara, *f; fig* pretexto, *m.* **under the g. of,** bajo el pretexto de; bajo la apariencia de
guitar *n* guitarra, *f*
guitarist *n* guitarrista, *mf*
gulf *n* golfo, *m;* abismo, *m*
Gulf Stream, the la Corriente del Golfo
gull *n orn* gaviota, *f;* (dupe) primo, *m. vt* engañar, timar, defraudar
gullet *n* esófago, *m;* garganta, *f*
gullibility *n* credulidad, *f*
gullible *a* crédulo
gully *n* hondonada, barranca, *f;* (gutter) arroyo, *m*
gulp *n* trago, sorbo, *m. vt* engullir, tragar; (repress) ahogar; (believe) tragar. **to g. up,** vomitar
gum *n* (of the mouth) encía, *f;* goma, *f. vt* engomar; pegar con goma. **gum arabic,** goma arábiga, *f.* **gum boots,** botas de goma, *f.* **gum-resin,** gomorresina, *f.* **gum starch,** aderezo, *m.* **gum tree,** eucalipto, *m*
gummy *a* gomoso
gumption *n* sentido común, seso, *m*
gun *n* arma de fuego, *f;* (handgun) fusil, *m;* (sporting g.) escopeta, *f;* (pistol) pistola, *f,* revólver, *m;* (cannon) cañón, *m;* (firing) cañonazo, *m.* **big gun,** *inf* pájaro gordo, *m.* **heavy gun,** cañón de grueso calibre, *m.* **gun-barrel,** cañón de escopeta, *m.* **gun-carriage,** cureña, *f.* **gun-cotton,** pólvora de algodón, *f.* **gun-fire,** cañonazos, *m pl,* fuego, *m.* **gun-metal,** bronce de cañón, *m;* pavón, *m.* **gun-room,** armería, *f;* (on a ship) polvorín, *m.* **gun-running,** contrabanda de armas, *f.* **gun-turret,** torre, *f.* **gun wound,** balazo, *m*

gunboat *n* cañonero, *m*, lancha bombardera, *f*
gunflint *n* piedra de escopeta, *f*
gunman *n* escopetero, armero, *m*; bandido armado, *m*; gángster, apache, *m*
gunner *n* artillero, *m*; escopetero, *m*
gun permit *n* licencia de armas, *f*, permiso de armas, *m*
gunpowder *n* pólvora, *f*
gunshot *n* escopetazo, *m*; tiro de fusil, *m*
gunsmith *n* escopetero, armero, *m*
gunwale *n naut* regala, borda, *f*
gurgle *n* murmullo, murmurio, gorgoteo, *m*; gluglú, *m*; (of a baby) gorjeo, *m*. *vi* murmurar; hacer gluglú; (of babies) gorjear
gurgling *a* murmurante; (of babies) gorjeador. *n* See **gurgle**
gush *n* chorro, *m*; (of words) torrente, *m*; (of emotion) efusión, *f*. *vi* chorrear, borbotar; surtir, surgir. **to g. out,** saltar, brotar a borbotones, salir a borbollones, salira borbotones. **to g. over,** *fig* hablar con efusión de
gushing *a* hirviente; (of people) efusivo, extremoso, empalagoso
gusset *n sew* escudete, *m*
gust *n* (of wind) ráfaga, bocanada (de aire), *f*; *fig* arrebato, acceso, *m*
gusto *n* brío, *m*; entusiasmo, *m*
gusty *a* borrascoso
gut *n* intestino, *m*, tripa, *f*; (catgut) cuerda de tripa, *f*; *naut* estrecho, *m*; *pl* **guts,** tripas, *f pl*; (content) meollo, *m*, substancia, *f*; (stamina) aguante, espíritu, *m*. *vt* (of fish, etc.) destripar; (plunder) saquear; destruir por completo; quemar completamente
gutta-percha *n* gutapercha, *f*
gutter *n* canal, *m*; (of a street) arroyo (de la calle), *m*; (ditch) zanja, *f*; *fig* hampa, *f*. *vt* surcar. *vi* gotear; (of a candle) cerotear, gotear la cera. **g. spout,** canalón, *m*
guttersnipe *n* golfillo, *m*, niño (-ña) del hampa
guttural *a* gutural. *n* letra gutural, *f*
guy *n* (rope) viento, *m*; *naut* guía, *f*; (effigy) mamarracho, *m*; (scarecrow) espantajo, *m*, *vt* sujetar con vientos o guías; burlarse de
guzzle *vt* tragar, engullir. *vi* atracarse, engullir; emborracharse. *n* comilón, *m*; borrachera, *f*
guzzler *n* tragador (-ra); borracho (-cha)
gymnasium *n* gimnasio, *m*
gymnast *n* gimnasta, *mf*
gymnastic *a* gimnástico. **g. rings,** anillas, *f pl*
gymnastics *n* gimnasia, *f*
gynecological *a* ginecológico
gynecologist *n* ginecólogo (-ga)
gynecology *n* ginecología, *f*
gypsum *n* yeso, *m*
gypsy *n* gitano (-na). *a* gitano, gitanesco; (music) flamenco
gyrate *vi* girar, rodar
gyration *n* giro, *m*, vuelta, *f*
gyratory *a* giratorio
gyro-compass *n* brújula giroscópica, *f*
gyroscope *n phys* giroscopio, *m*

H

h *n* (letter) hache, *f*
ha *interj* ¡ah!
haberdasher *n* mercero, *m*
haberdashery *n* mercería, *f*
habiliment *n* vestidura, *f*; *pl* **habiliments,** indumentaria, *f*
habilitate *vt* habilitar
habilitation *n* habilitación, *f*
habit *n* costumbre, *f*, hábito, *m*; (temperament) temperamento, carácter, *m*; (use) uso, *m*; (of body) complexión, constitución, *f*; *ecc* hábito, *m*. **to be in the h. of,** soler, acostumbrar, estar acostumbrado a. **to have bad habits,** estar malacostumbrado. **to have the bad h. of,** tener el vicio (or la mala costumbre) de. **to contract the h. of,** contraer la costumbre de. **h. maker,** sastre de trajes de montar, *m*
habitable *a* habitable, vividero
habitat *n* (*bot, zool*) medio, *m*, habitación, *f*
habitation *n* habitación, *f*
habit-forming *a* enviciador, que crea vicio
habitual *a* habitual, acostumbrado, usual; constante; común
habitually *adv* habitualmente; constantemente; comúnmente
habituate *vt* habituar, acostumbrar
habituation *n* habituación, *f*
habitué *n* parroquiano (-na); veterano (-na)
hack *n* caballo de alquiler, *m*; rocín, jaco, *m*; (writer) escritor mercenario, *m*. *vt* acuchillar; tajar, cortar. *vi* cortar. **to h. to pieces,** cortar en pedazos; pasar a cuchillo
hacking *a* (of coughs) seco
hackle *n* (for flax, hemp) rastrillo, *m*
hackney carriage *n* coche de plaza, coche de alquiler, *m*
hackneyed *a* gastado, trillado, muy usado, repetido, resobado
hacksaw *n* sierra de cerrajero, sierra para metal, *f*
hackwork *n* trabajo de rutina, *m*
haddock *n* merlango, *m*, pescadilla, *f*
Hades *n* Hades, *m*; *inf* el infierno, *m*
haft *n* mango, tomadero, *m*, manija, *f*; puño, *m*
hag *n* bruja, *f*
haggard *a* ojeroso, trasnochado, trasojado
haggardly *adv* ansiosamente
haggardness *n* aspecto ojeroso, *m*
haggle *vi* regatear; vacilar
haggling *n* regateo, *m*, *a* regatón
hagiographer *n* hagiógrafo, *m*
hagiography *n* hagiografía, *f*
ha, ha! *interj* ¡ja, ja!
hail *n* (salutation) saludo, *m*; (shout) grito, *m*; aclamación, *f*; (frozen rain) granizo, *m*; (of blows) lluvia, *f*. *interj* ¡salve! *vt* saludar; llamar; aclamar; *fig* lanzar, echar. *vi* (hailstones) granizar; (blows, etc.) llover. **to h. from,** proceder de, ser natural de. **within h.,** al habla. **H. Mary,** Salve Regina, Avemaría, *f*
hailstone *n* granizo, pedrisco, *m*
hailstorm *n* granizada, *f*
hair *n* (single h.) cabello, *m*; (*zool, bot*) pelo, *m*; (of horse's mane) crin, *f*; (head of h.) cabellera, mata de pelo, *f*, pelo, *m*; (superfluous) vello, *m*; (fiber) fibra, *f*, filamento, *m*; (on the pen) raspa, *f*, pelo, *m*; *fig* pelo, *m*. **lock of h.,** bucle, rizo, *m*; mecha, *f*. **to dress one's h.,** peinarse. **to have one's h. cut,** hacerse cortar el pelo. **to part the h.,** hacer(se) la raya del pelo. **to put up one's h.,** hacerse el moño; (to "come out") ponerse de largo. **to tear one's h.,** mesarse los cabellos. **h. combings,** peinaduras, *f pl*. **h.-curler,** tirabuzón, *m*. **h. dryer,** secadora de cabello, *f*. **h. dye,** tinte para el pelo, *m*. **h.-net,** redecilla, *f*, *Mexico* invisible *m*. **h.-oil,** brillantina, *f*. **h.-raising,** horripilante, espeluznante. **h.-ribbon,** cinta para el pelo, *f*. **h.-shirt,** cilicio, *m*. **h. slide,** pasador, *m*. **h.-splitting,** sofistería, argucia, *f*; mez quinas argucias, quis quillas, *f pl*. **h.-spring,** muelle del volante, *m*. **h.-switch,** añadido, *m*. **h.-trigger,** pelo de una pistola, *m*
hairband *m Lat. Am.* bincha *f*
hairbreadth *n* pelo, *m*. **to have a h. escape,** escapar por un pelo.
hairbrush *n* cepillo para el cabello, *m*
hairdresser *n* peluquero (-ra), peinadora, *f*

hairdressing *n* peinado, *m*. **h. establishment** or **trade,** peluquería, *f*
haired *a* peludo, con pelo; (in compounds) de pelo . . .
hairless *a* sin pelo; calvo
hairlike *a* filiforme
hairpin *n* horquilla, *f*, *Argentina* invisible *m*. **h. bend,** viraje en horquilla, *m*
hairsplitting arguments *Lat. Am.* abogaderas, abogaderías *fpl*
hairy *a* peludo; velloso; *bot* hirsuto
Haiti Haití, *m*
Haitian *a* and *n* haitiano (-na)
hake *n* merluza, *f*
halcyon *n* alción, martín pescador, *m*. *a fig* feliz, sereno, tranquilo
hale *a* fuerte, sano, robusto. *vt* hacer comparecer
half *n* mitad, *f*; (school term) trimestre, *m*. *a* medio; semi. *adv* a medias; mitad; (almost) casi; insuficientemente; imperfectamente. **I don't h. like it,** No me gusta nada. **It is h.-past two,** Son las dos y media. **an hour and a h.,** una hora y media. **better h.,** *inf* media naranja, cara mitad, *f*. **by halves,** a medias. **in h.,** en dos mitades. **one h.,** la mitad. **to go halves,** ir a medias. **to h. close,** entornar. **to h. open,** entreabrir. **h. a bottle,** media botella, *f*. **h. a crown,** media corona, *f*. **h.-alive,** semivivo. **h. an hour,** media hora, *f*. **h.-and-h.,** mitad y mitad; en partes iguales. **h.-asleep,** semidormido, medio dormido. **h.-awake,** medio despierto, entre duerme y vela. **h.-back,** *sport* medio, *m*. **h.-baked,** medio cocido, crudo; *fig* poco maduro. **h.-binding,** encuadernación en media pasta, *f*. **h.-breed,** *a* mestizo. *n* cruce, *m*. **h.-brother,** hermanastro, hermano de padre, hermano de madre, *m*. **h.-caste,** mestizo. **h. circle,** semicírculo, *m*. **h.-closed,** entreabierto; medio cerrado. **h.-dead,** medio muerto; más muerto que vivo. **h.-done,** hecho a medias, sin acabar. **h.-dozen,** media docena, *f*. **h.-dressed,** medio desnudo. **h. fare,** medio billete, *m*. **h.-full,** medio lleno. **h.-hearted,** débil, poco eficaz, lánguido; indiferente, sin entusiasmo. **h.-heartedness,** debilidad, *f*; indiferencia, *f*. **h.-holiday,** media fiesta, *f*. **h.-hourly,** cada media hora. **h.-length,** (portrait) de medio cuerpo. **h.-length coat,** abrigo de tres cuartos, *m*. **h.-light,** media luz, *f*. **h.-mast,** a media asta. **h.-measure,** medida poco eficaz, *f*. **h.-moon,** *n* media luna, *f*; *ast* semilunio, *m*; (of a nail) blanco (de la uña), *m*. **h.-mourning,** medio luto, *m*. **h.-pay,** media paga, *f*. **h.-price,** a mitad de precio. **h.-seas-over,** *inf* entre dos velas. **h.-sister,** hermanastra, hermana de padre, hermana de madre, *f*. **h.-time,** *sport* media parte, *f*, medio tiempo, *m*. **h.-tone,** de medio tono. **h.-tone illustration,** fotograbado a media tinta, *m*. **h.-truth,** verdad a medias, *f*. **h.-turn,** media vuelta, *f*. **h.-way,** a medio camino; medio. **h.-witted,** medio loco, tonto, imbécil. **h.-year,** medio año, *m*. **h.-yearly,** semestral
half close *vt* entrecerrar
half title anteportada, falsa portada, portadilla, preportada, *f*
halibut *n* halibut, *m*; (genus) hipogloso, *m*
halitosis *n* halitosis, *f*
hall *n* (mansion) mansión, casa de campo, *f*, caserón, *m*; (public building) edificio, *m*, casa (de); (town h.) casa del ayuntamiento, *f*; (room) sala, *f*; (entrance) vestíbulo, *m*; (dining room) comedor, *m*; (of residence for students) residencia, *f*. **h. door,** portón, *m*, puerta del vestíbulo, *f*. **h. porter,** conserje, *m*. **h.-stand,** perchero, *m*
hallelujah *n* aleluya, *f*
hallmark *n* marca de ley, *f*; *fig* señal, *f*; indicio, *m*. *vt* poner la marca de ley sobre; *fig* sellar
halloo *vt* (hounds) azuzar; perseguir dando voces; (call) llamar
hallow *vt* santificar; reverenciar; (consecrate) consagrar
Halloween *n* la víspera de Todos los Santos, *f*
hallucination *n* alucinación, ilusión, *f*; visión, *f*; fantasma, *m*
hallucinatory *a* alucinador
halo *n* halo, nimbo, *m*
halogen *n chem* halógeno, *m*
halt *n mil* alto, *m*; cesación, *f*; interrupción, *f*; (on a railway) apeadero, *m*; (for trams, buses) parada, *f*. *vt* parar, detener. *vi* pararse, detenerse; *mil* hacer alto; cesar; interrumpirse; (in speech) titubear; (of verse) estar cojo; (doubt) dudar; (limp) cojear. **H.!** *mil* ¡Alto!
halter *n* ronzal, cabestro, *m*; (for hanging) dogal, *m*. *vt* encabestrar, cabestrar
halting *n* parada, *f*; interrupción, *f*. *a* (of gait) cojo; incierto; vacilante; (of speech) titubeante
halve *vt* partir (or dividir) en dos mitades
ham *n* jamón, *m*; *anat* pernil, *m*; (radio-operator) radioaficionado, *m*
Hamburg Hamburgo, *m*
hamlet *n* aldea, *f*, pueblecito, *m*
hammer *n* martillo, *m*; (stone cutter's) maceta, *f*; (mason's) piqueta, *f*; (of fire-arms) percusor, *m*; (of piano) macillo, *m*. *vt* amartillar, martillar, batir. **to throw the h.,** lanzar el martillo. **under the h.,** en subasta, al remate. **h. blow,** martillazo, *m*
hammering *n* martilleo, martillazo, *m*. **by h.,** a martillo
hammock *n* hamaca, *f*; *naut* coy, *m*
hamper *n* banasta, canasta, *f*, cesto grande, *m*. *vt* estorbar, dificultar, impedir; *fig* embarazar
hamster *n zool* hámster, *m*, marmota de Alemania, rata del trigo, *f*
hand *n* mano, *f*; (of animal) pata, mano, *f*; (worker) operario (-ia); obrero (-ra); (skill) habilidad, *f*; (side) mano, *f*, lado, *m*; (measure) palmo, *m*; (of a clock) manecilla, *f*; (of instruments) aguja, *f*; (applause) aplauso, *m*; (power) poder, *m*; las manos; (at cards) mano, *f*; (card player) jugador, *m*; (signature) firma, *f*; (handwriting) letra, escritura, *f*; (influence) influencia, parte, mano, *f*. **old h.,** veterano; perro viejo. **at h.,** a mano, al lado, cerca. **have at hand,** tener a la mano. **at the hands of,** de manos de. **by h.,** a mano; (on the bottle) con biberón. **from h. to h.,** de mano a mano. **in h.,** entre manos; (of money) de contado. **in the hands of,** *fig* en el poder de. **"Hands wanted,"** «Se desean trabajadores.» **h. over h.,** mano sobre mano. **hand's breadth,** palmo, *m*. **Hands off!** ¡Fuera las manos! **Hands up!** ¡Manos arriba! **lost with all hands,** (of a ship) perdido con toda su tripulación. **off one's hands,** despachado; (of a daughter) casada. **on all hands,** por todas partes. **on h.,** entre manos; (of goods) existente; (present) presente. **on one's hands,** a cargo de uno. **on the one h.,** por un lado; a un lado. **on the other h.,** por otra parte; en cambio. **out of h.,** luego, inmediatamente; revoltoso. **to come to h.,** venir a mano; (of letters) llegar a las manos (de). **to get one's h. in,** ejercitarse. **to have a h. in,** tener parte en; intervenir en. **to have no h. in,** no tener arte ni parte en. **to have on h.,** traer entre manos. **to have the upper h.,** tener la sartén por el mango, llevar la ventaja. **to hold one's h.,** abstenerse; detenerse. **to hold hands,** cogerse de las manos. **to lay hands on,** tocar; poner mano en; echar manos a. **to set one's h. to,** emprender; (sign) firmar. **to shake hands,** estrechar la mano. **to stretch out one's hands,** tender las manos. **to take one's hands off,** no tocar. **with folded hands,** mano sobre mano. **with his hands behind his back,** con las manos en la espalda. **h.-in-h.,** cogidos (cogidas) de las manos. **h.-lever,** manija, *f*. **h.-loom,** telar de mano, *m*. **h. luggage,** equipaje de mano, *m*. **h.-made,** hecho a mano. **h.-mill,** molinillo, *m*. **h.-pump,** *n naut* sacabuche, *m*. **h. rail,** pasamano, *m*, baranda, balustrada, *f*. **h.-sewn,** cosido a mano. **h.-to-h.,** de mano en mano; (of a fight) a brazo partido, cuerpo a cuerpo. **h.-to-h. fight,** cachetina, *f*. **h.-to-mouth,** precario. **to live from h.-to-mouth,** vivir de día en día
hand *vt* dar; entregar; alargar. **to h. down,** bajar; (a

person) ayudar a bajar; transmitir. **to h. in,** entregar; (a person) ayudar a entrar; (one's resignation) dimitir; (send) mandar, enviar. **to h. on,** transmitir. **to h. out,** *vt* distribuir; (a person) ayudar a salir; (from a vehicle) ayudar a bajar. *vi inf* pagar. **to h. over,** *vt* entregar. *vi mil* traspasar los poderes (a). **to h. round,** pasar de mano en mano; pasar; ofrecer. **to h. up,** subir; (a person) ayudar a subir

handbag *n* bolso, saco, monedero, *m*

handbill *n* anuncio, *m*

handbook *n* manual, compendio, tratado, *m*; anuario, *m*; (guide) guía, *f*

handbreadth *n* palmo, *m*

handcart *n* carretilla de mano, *f*, carretón, *m*

handcuff *n* esposa, *f*, grillo, *m*, (gen. *pl*). *vt* poner las esposas (a), maniatar

handed *a* (in compounds) que tiene manos; de manos . . . ; con las manos . . . **four-h.,** *sport* de cuatro personas. **one-h.,** manco

handful *n* puño, puñado, manojo, *m*. **to be a h.,** *inf* tener el diablo en el cuerpo. **in handfuls,** a manojos

handgrip *n* apretón de manos, *m*

handicap *n* desventaja, *f*; obstáculo, *m*; *sport* handicap, *m*; ventaja, *f*. *vt fig* perjudicar, impedir, dificultar. **the handicapped,** los lisiados, *m pl*

handicraft *n* mano de obra, *f*; (skill) destreza manual, *f*,

handiwork *n* mano de obra, *f*; trabajo manual, *m*; obra, *f*; (deed) acción, *f*, hecho, *m*

handkerchief *n* pañuelo, *m*

handle *n* mango, puño, *m*, *Lat. Am. also* manivela *f*; (lever) palanca, *f*; (of baskets, dishes, jugs) asa, *f*; (of doors, windows, drawers) pomo, *m*, (of a car door) picaporte *m*; (to one's name) designación, *f*; título, *m*; (excuse) pretexto, *m*. *vt* (touch) tocar; manejar, manipular; (treat) tratar; **h. with kid gloves,** tratar con guantes de seda; (deal in) comerciar en; tomar; (paw) manosear; (direct) dirigir; (control) gobernar; (pilot) pilotar; (a theme) explicar, tratar de. **h.-bar grip,** puño de un manillar, *m*

handlebars *npl Spain* guia *fsg*, manillar *msg*, *Lat. Am.* manubrio *msg*

handless *a* sin manos; manco; *fig* torpe

handling *n* manejo, *m*; manipulación, *f*; (treatment) trato, *m*, relaciones (con), *f pl*; (thumbing) manosco, *m*; interpretación, *f*; *art* tratamiento, *m*, técnica, *f*

handmaid *n* sirvienta, criada, *f*; *fig* mayordomo, *m*

handsaw *n* sierra de mano, *f*, serrucho, *m*

handshake *n* apretón de manos, *m*

handsome *a* (generous) generoso; magnánimo; considerable; hermoso, bello; elegante; (of people) guapo, distinguido; excelente; (flattering) halagüeño. **He was a very h. man,** Era un hombre muy guapo

handsomely *adv* generosamente; con magnanimidad; elegantemente; bien

handsomeness *n* generosidad, *f*; magnanimidad, *f*; hermosura, *f*; elegancia, *f*; distinción, *f*

handspring *n* voltereta sobre las manos, *f*

handwork *n* obra hecha a mano, *f*, trabajo a mano, *m*; (needlework) labor de aguja, *f*

handworked *a* hecho a mano; (embroidered) bordado

handwriting *n* caligrafía, letra, escritura, *f*. **the h. on the wall,** la mano que escribía en la pared, *f*

handy *a* (of persons) diestro, mañoso, hábil; (of things) conveniente; útil; (near) cercano, a mano. *adv* cerca. **h.-man,** hombre de muchos oficios, *m*; factótum, *m*

hang *vt* colgar; suspender; (execute) ahorcar; (the head) bajar; dejar caer; (upholster) entapizar; (with wallpaper) empapelar; (drape) poner colgaduras en; (place) poner; (cover) cubrir. *vi* colgar, pender; estar suspendido; (be executed) ser ahorcado; (of garments) caer. *n* (of garments) caída, *f*; (of a machine) mecanismo, *m*; (meaning) sentido, *m*, significación, *f*. **to h. by a thread,** pender de un hilo. **to h. in the balance,** estar en la balanza. **to h. fire,** estar (una cosa) en suspenso. **to h. loose,** caer suelto; (clothes) venir ancho. **to h. about,** (surround) rodear, pegarse a; (frequent) frecuentar; (haunt) rondar; (be imminent) ser inminente, amenazar; (embrace) abrazar. **to h. back,** retroceder; quedarse atrás; *fig* vacilar, titubear. **to h. down,** colgar, pender; estar caído; caerse. **to h. on,** seguir agarrado (a); apoyarse en; *fig* persistir; (a person's words) estar pendiente de, beber; (remain) quedarse. **to h. out,** *vt* tender. *vi* (lean out) asomarse (por); (*inf* live) habitar. **to h. over,** colgar por encima; (brood) cernerse sobre; (lean over) inclinarse sobre; quedarse cerca de; (overhang) sobresalir; (overarch) abovedar; (threaten) amenazar. **to h. together,** (of persons) permanecer unidos; (of things) tener cohesión; (be consistent) ser lógico, ser consistente. **to h. up,** colgar; suspender; *fig* dejar pendiente, interrumpir. **to h. upon,** apoyarse en; (a person's words) beber las palabras de uno

hangar *n* cobertizo; *aer* hangar, *m*

hanger *n* colgadero, *m*; percha *f*. **h.-on,** parásito, *m*; dependiente, *m*

hanging *n* colgamiento, *m*; (killing) ahorcamiento, *m*; *pl* **hangings,** colgaduras, *f pl*, cortinajes, *m pl*. *a* pendiente colgante; péndulo; (of gardens) pensil. **It's not a h. matter,** No es una cuestión de vida y muerte. **h. bridge,** puente colgante, *m*. **h. committee,** junta (de una exposición,) *f*. **h. lamp,** lámpara de techo, *f*

hangman *n* verdugo, *m*

hangnail *n* padrastro, *m*

hangover *n* (after drinking) resaca, cruda (Mexico), *f*

hank *n* madeja, *f*

hanker *vi* (with after) ansiar, ambicionar; (with for) anhelar, suspirar por, desear con vehemencia

hankering *n* ambición, *f*; deseo vehemente, *m*

hanky-panky *n* superchería, *f*; engaño, *m*

hap *n* casualidad, suerte, *f*; suceso fortuito, *m*

haphazard *n* casualidad, *f*. *a* fortuito, casual

hapless *a* desgraciado, desdichado

haplessness *n* desgracia, desdicha, *f*

happen *vi* suceder, acontecer, ocurrir, pasar; (to be found, be) hallarse por casualidad; (take place) tener lugar, verificarse; (arise) sobrevenir. **Do you know what has happened to . . .?** ¿Sabes qué se ha hecho de . . .? **as if nothing had happened,** como si no hubiese pasado nada. **He turned up as if nothing had happened,** Se presentó como si tal cosa. **How did it h.?** ¿Cómo fue esto? **If they h. to see you,** Si acaso te vean. **I happened to be in London,** Me hallaba por casualidad en Londres. **It won't h. again,** No volverá a suceder. **whatever happens,** venga lo que venga

happening *n* suceso, acontecimiento, hecho, *m*, ocurrencia, *f*

happily *adv* felizmente; por suerte

happiness *n* felicidad, dicha, *f*; alegría, *f*, regocijo, *m*

happy *a* (lucky) afortunado; (felicitous) feliz, oportuno; feliz, dichoso; alegre, regocijado. **to be h.,** estar contento, ser feliz. **to be h. about,** alegrarse de. **to make h.,** hacer feliz, alegrar. **h.-go-lucky,** irresponsable, descuidado

harangue *n* arenga, *f*. *vt* arengar. *vi* pronunciar una arenga

harass *vt* hostigar, acosar; atormentar; preocupar; *mil* picar. **to h. the rear-guard,** picar la retaguardia

harbinger *n fig* precursor, heraldo, *m*; presagio, anuncio, *m*. *vt* anunciar, presagiar

harbor *n* puerto, *m*; (bay) bahía, *f*; (haven) asilo, refugio, *m*. *vt* dar refugio (a), albergar, acoger; (cherish) abrigar, acariciar; (conceal) esconder. **inner h.,** puerto, *m*. **outer h.,** rada del puerto, *f*. **to put into h.,** entrar en el puerto. **h. bar,** barra del puerto, *f*. **h.-dues,** derechos de puerto, *m pl*. **h.-master,** capitán de puerto, contramaestre de puerto, *m*

harborer *n* amparador (-ra), protector (-ra); (criminal) encubridor (-ra)

hard *a* duro; (firm) firme; difícil; laborioso, agotador; violento; poderoso; arduo; fuerte, recio; vigoroso, robusto; insensible, inflexible; cruel; (of weather) inclemente, severo; (unjust) injusto, opresivo; (stiff) tieso; (of water) cruda; (of wood) brava. *adv* duro; duramente; con ahínco; con fuerza; de firme; difícilmente; (of gazing) fijamente; severamente; (firmly) firmemente; vigorosamente; (of raining) a cántaros, mucho; (quickly) rápidamente; excesivamente; (much) mucho; (of bearing misfortune) a pechos; (attentively) atentamente; (heavily) pesadamente; (badly) mal; (closely) de cerca, inmediatamente. **It was a h. blow,** Fue un golpe recio. **to be h. put to,** encontrar difícil. **to go h.,** endurecerse. **to go h. with,** irle mal a uno. **to have a h. time,** pasar apuros, pasarlo mal. **to look h. at,** mirar atentamente, examinar detenidamente; mirar fijamente. **to be a h. drinker,** ser un bebedor empedernido. **h. and fast rule,** regla inalterable, *f.* **h.-bitten,** de carácter duro. **a h.-boiled egg,** un huevo duro. **h. breathing,** resuello, *m.* **h. by,** muy cerca. **h. cash,** efectivo, *m.* **h.-earned,** difícilmente conseguido; ganado con el sudor de la frente. **h.-featured,** de facciones duras. **h.-fisted,** tacaño. **h.-fought,** arduo, reñido. **h.-headed,** práctico, perspicaz. **h.-hearted,** duro de corazón, insensible. **h.-heartedness,** insensibilidad, *f.* **h. labor,** *law* trabajos forzados, *m pl,* presidio, *m.* **h.-mouthed,** (of horses) boquiduro. **h. of hearing,** duro de oído. **h.-up,** apurado. **to be very h.-up,** ser muy pobre; *inf* estar a la cuarta pregunta. **h.-wearing,** duradero; sufrido. **h.-won,** See **h.-earned. h.-working,** trabajador, hacendoso, diligente

harden *vt* endurecer; (metal) templar; robustecer; (to war) aguerrir; (make callous) hacer insensible. *vi* endurecerse; hacerse duro; templarse; robustecerse; (of shares) entonarse

hardening *n* endurecimiento, *m;* (of metal) temple, *m.* **h. of the arteries,** arteriosclerosis, *f*

hardiness *n* vigor, *m,* fuerza, robustez, *f;* audacia, *f*

hardly *adv* duramente; difícilmente; (badly) mal; severamente; (scarcely) apenas, casi. **h. ever,** casi nunca

hardness *n* dureza, *f;* severidad, *f;* inhumanidad, insensibilidad, *f;* (stiffness) tiesura, *f;* (difficulty) dificultad, *f;* (of water) crudeza, *f;* (of hearing) dureza de oído, *f*

hardship *n* penas, *f pl,* trabajos, *m pl;* infortunio, *m,* desdicha, *f;* (suffering) sufrimiento, *m;* (affliction) aflicción, *f;* (privation) privación, *f.* **to undergo h.,** pasar trabajos

hardware *n* ferretería, *f*

hardwood *n* madera brava, *f*

hardy *a* audaz, intrépido; (strong) fuerte, robusto; *bot* resistente

hare *n* liebre, *f.* **young h.,** lebrato, *m.* **h. and hounds,** rally paper, *m,* caza de papelitos, *f.* **h.-brained,** casquivano, atronado, con cabeza de chorlito. **hare's foot,** mano de gato, *f.* **h.-lip,** labio leporino, *m.* **h.-lipped,** labihendido

harebell *n* campanilla, campánula, *f*

harem *n* harén, serrallo, *m*

haricot *n* (green bean) judia, *f;* (dried bean) alubia, *f*

hark *vt* escuchar; oír. **to h. back,** volver al punto de partida; volver a la misma canción

harlequin *n* arlequín, *m*

harlequinade *n* arlequinada, *f*

harlot *n* ramera, prostituta, meretriz, *f*

harlotry *n* prostitución, *f*

harm *n* mal, *m;* daño, *m;* perjuicio, *m;* (danger) peligro, *m;* (detriment) menoscabo, *m;* (misfortune) desgracia, *f, vt* hacer mal (a); dañar, hacer daño (a); perjudicar. **And there's no h. in that,** Y en eso no hay mal. **to keep out of harm's way,** evitar el peligro; guardarse del mal

harmful *a* malo; dañino, perjudicial, nocivo; (dangerous) peligroso. **to be h.,** (of food, etc.) hacer mal (a); (of pests) ser dañino; (of behavior, etc.) perjudicar

harmfulness *n* lo malo; perniciosidad, *f;* daño, *m;* peligro, *m*

harmless *a* innocuo; inofensivo; inocente

harmlessness *n* innocuidad, *f;* inocencia, *f*

harmonic *n* (*phys math*) harmónica, *f; mus* armónico, *m, a mus* armónico

harmonica *n* armónica, *f*

harmonics *n* armonía, *f;* (tones) armónicos, *m pl*

harmonious *a* armonioso

harmoniously *adv* armoniosamente; *fig* en armonía

harmoniousness *n* armonía, *f*

harmonium *n* armonio, *m*

harmonization *n* armonización, *f*

harmonize *vt* armonizar. *vi* armonizarse, estar en armonía

harmony *n* armonía, *f; fig* paz, *f,* buenas relaciones, *f pl;* música, *f.* **to live in h.,** vivir en paz

harness *n* guarniciones, *f pl,* jaeces, *m pl;* (armor) arnés, *m. vt* enjaezar; (yoke) enganchar; (water) represar. **to die in h.,** *fig* morir en la brecha. **h. maker,** guarnicionero, *m.* **h. room,** guadarnés, *m*

harp *n* arpa, *f.* **to h. on,** volver a la misma canción, volver a repetir

harpist *n* arpista, *mf*

harpoon *n* arpón, *m. vt* arponear

harpooner *n* arponero, *m*

harpsichord *n* arpicordio, *m*

harpy *n* arpía, *f*

harridan *n* bruja, *f*

harrow *n agr* rastra, *f,* escarificador, *m. vt agr* escarificar; *fig* lastimar, atormentar

harrowing *a* patibulario, conmovedor, atormentador, angustioso

harry *vt* devastar, asolar; (persons) robar; perseguir; (worry) atormentar; (annoy) molestar

harsh *a* áspero; (of voice) ronco; (of sound) discordante; (of colors) áspero; duro; chillón; severo, duro; (of features) duro; (of taste) ácido, acerbo

harshly *adv* severamente

harshness *n* (roughness) aspereza, *f;* (of voice) ronquedad, aspereza, *f;* (of sound) disonancia, *f;* (of colors) aspereza, *f;* severidad, *f;* dureza, *f;* (of taste) acidez, *f*

harum-scarum *n* tronera, saltabarrancos, *mf* molino, *m, a* irresponsable

harvest *n* cosecha, siega, *f;* recolección, *f; fig* producto, fruto, *m. vt* cosechar; recoger. **h. festival,** fiesta de la cosecha, *f*

harvester *n* segador, *m,* cosechero (-ra); (machine) segadora, *f*

hash *n cul* picado, *m. vt cul* picar

hashish *n* hachich, hachís, quif, *m*

hasp *n* pasador, *m;* sujetador, *m*

hassock *n* cojín, *m*

hassle *n Lat. Am.* fregada *f*

haste *n* prisa, rapidez, *f;* precipitación, *f;* urgencia, *f. vt* dar prisa (a); acelerar; precipitar. *vi* darse prisa; acelerarse; precipitarse. **in h.,** de prisa, aprisa. **to be in h.,** estar de prisa, llevar prisa. **in great h.,** muy aprisa, aprisa y corriendo, precipitadamente; con mucha prisa. **More h. less speed,** (Spanish equivalent. Words said by Charles III of Spain to his valet) ¡Vísteme despacio que voy de prisa!

hasten *vt* acelerar, apresurar; precipitar. *vi* darse prisa, apresurarse; moverse con rapidez; correr. **to h. one's steps,** apretar el paso. **to h. away,** marcharse rápidamente. **to h. back,** regresar apresuradamente. **to h. down,** bajar rápidamente. **to h. on,** seguir el camino sin descansar; seguir rápidamente. **to h. out,** salir rápidamente. **to h. towards,** ir rápidamente hacia; correr hacia. **to h. up,** subir aprisa, correr hacia arriba; darse prisa

hastily *adv* de prisa, rápidamente; con precipitación, precipitadamente; (angrily) impacientemente, airadamente; (thoughtlessly) sin reflexión

hastiness *n* rapidez, *f;* precipitación, *f;* (anger) impaciencia, irritación, *f*

hasty *a* rápido, apresurado; precipitado; (superficial)

superficial, ligero; (ill-considered) desconsiderado, imprudente; (angry) impaciente, irritable; violento, apasionado

hat *n* sombrero, *m*. **to pass round the h.,** pasar el platillo. **Andalusian h.,** sombrero calañés, *m*. **bowler h.,** sombrero hongo, *m*. **broad-brimmed h.,** sombrero chambergo, *m*. **Panama h.,** sombrero de jipijapa, *m*. **picture h.,** pamela, *f*. **shovel h.,** sombrero de teja, *m*. **soft felt h.,** sombrero flexible, *m*. **straw h.,** sombrero de paja, *m*. **three-cornered h.,** sombrero de tres picos, *m*. **top-h.,** sombrero de copa, *m*. **h. shop** or **trade,** sombrerería, *f*

hatband *n* cinta de sombrero, *f*, cintillo, *m*

hatbox *n* sombrerera, *f*

hatbrush *n* cepillo para sombreros, *m*

hatch *n* (wicket) compuerta, *f*; (trap-door) puerta caediza, *f*; *naut* escotilla, *f*; compuerta de esclusa, *f*; (of chickens) pollada, *f*; (of birds) nidada, *f*. *vt* (birds) empollar; incubar, encobar; *fig* tramar, urdir. *vi* empollarse, salir del cascarón; incubarse; *fig* madurarse. **to h. a plot,** urdir un complot, conspirar. **to h. chickens,** sacar pollos

hatchet *n* hacha pequeña, *f*, machado, *m*. **to bury the h.,** hacer la paz. **h.-faced,** de cara de cuchillo

hatching *n* incubación, *f*; (of a plot) maquinación, *f*

hatchway *n naut* escotilla, *f*

hate *n* odio, aborrecimiento, *m*, aversión, *f*; abominación, *f*. *vt* odiar, aborrecer, detestar; repugnar; saber mal, sentir. **I h. to trouble you,** Me sabe mal molestarle, Siento mucho molestarle. **to h. the sight of,** *inf* no poder ver (a)

hateful *a* odioso, aborrecible; repugnante

hatefulness *n* odiosidad, *f*, lo odioso; maldad, *f*

hater *n* aborrecedor (-ra). **to be a good h.,** saber odiar

hatful *n* un sombrero lleno (de)

hatless *a* sin sombrero, descubierto

hatpin *n* horquilla de sombrero, *f*

hatred *n* odio, aborrecimiento, *m*, detestación, *f*; aversión, enemistad, *f*

hatstand *n* perchera, *f*

hatter *n* sombrerero, *m*. **as mad as a h.,** loco como una cabra

haughtiness *n* altanería, arrogancia, altivez, soberbia, *f*, orgullo, *m*

haughty *a* altanero, arrogante, altivo, orgulloso *Lat. Am.* copetudo, *Mexico also* alzado

haul *n* (pull) tirón, *m*; (of fish) redada, *f*; (booty) botín, *m*. *vt* arrastrar, tirar de; *naut* halar. **to h. at, upon,** (ropes, etc.) aflojar, soltar, arriar. **to h. down,** (flags, sails) arriar

haulage *n* transporte, acarreo, *m*; coste de transporte, *m*. **h. contractor,** contratista de transporte, *m*

haunch *n* anca, culata, *f*; (of meat) pierna, *f*. **h.-bone,** hueso ilíaco, *m*

haunt *n* punto de reunión, lugar frecuentado (por), *m*; (lair) cubil, nido, *m*, guarida, *f*. *vt* frecuentar; rondar; (of ideas) perseguir; (of ghosts) aparecer, visitar. **It is a h. of thieves,** Es una cueva de ladrones

haunted *a* (by spirits) encantado

haunter *n* frecuentador (-ra); (ghost) fantasma, espectro, *m*

haunting *n* frecuentación, *f*; aparición de un espectro, *f*. *a* persistente

hautboy *n* oboe, *m*

hauteur *n* altivez, *f*

Havana la Habana, *f*. *n* (cigar) habano, *m*. (native) habanero (-ra), habano (-na)

have *vt* tener; poseer; (suffer) padecer; (spend) pasar; (eat or drink) tomar; (eat) comer; (a cigarette) fumar; (a bath, etc.) tomar; (a walk, a ride) dar; (cause to be done) mandar (hacer), hacer (hacer); (deceive) engañar; (defeat) vencer; (catch) coger; (say) decir; (allow) permitir; (tolerate) tolerar, sufrir; (obtain) lograr, conseguir; (wish) querer; (know) saber; (realize) realizar; (buy) comprar; (acquire) adquirir. As an auxiliary verb, haber (e.g. **I h. done it,** Lo he hecho, etc.). **As fate would h. it,** Según quiso la suerte. **Do you h. to go?** ¿Tiene Vd. que marcharse? **H. him come here,** Hazle venir aquí. **I h. been had,** Me han engañado. **I h. a good mind to . . .,** Tengo ganas de . . . **I had all my books stolen,** Me robaron todos los libros. **You had better go,** Es mejor que te vayas. **I had rather,** Preferiría, Me gustaría más bien. **I h. had a suit made,** Mandé hacerme un traje, Hice hacerme un traje. **I would not h. had it otherwise,** No lo hubiese querido de otra manera. **I will not h. it,** No lo quiero; No quiero tomarlo; (object) No lo permitiré. **If we had known,** Si lo hubiésemos sabido. **It has to do with the sun,** Está relacionado con el sol, Tiene que ver con el sol. **Have a good trip!** ¡Buen viaje!, ¡Feliz viaje! **What are you going to h.?** ¿Qué quiere Vd. tomar? **Will you h. some jam?** ¿Quiere Vd. mermelada? **to h. breakfast,** desayunar. **to h. dinner, supper,** cenar. **to h. lunch,** almorzar. **to h. for tea,** invitar a tomar el té; (of food) merendar. **to h. tea,** tomar el té. **to h. it out with,** habérselas con. **to h. just,** acabar de. **I h. just done it,** Acabo de hacerlo. **to h. on hand,** traer entre manos. **to h. one's eye on,** no perder de vista (a), vigilar. **to h. one's tail between one's legs,** ir rabo entre piernas. **to h. to,** tener que; deber. **It has to be so,** Tiene que ser así. **to h. too much of,** sobrar, tener demasiado de. **He has too much time,** Le sobra tiempo. **to h. about one,** tener (or llevar) consigo. **to h. back,** aceptar; recibir. **to h. down,** hacer bajar. **She had her hair down,** El pelo le caía por las espaldas. **to h. in,** hacer entrar. **to h. on,** vestir, llevar puesto; (engagements) tener (compromisos). **to h. out,** hacer salir; llevar a paseo; llevar fuera; (have removed) hacerse sacar; quitar. **to h. up,** (persons) hacer subir; (things) subir; *law* llevar a (ante) los tribunales. **to h. with one,** tener consigo. **I h. her with me,** La tengo conmigo, Ella me acompaña

haven *n* puerto, *m*, abra, *f*; *fig* oasis, abrigo, refugio, *m*

haversack *n* mochila, *f*, morral, *m*

havoc *n* destrucción, ruina, *f*; *fig* estrago, *m*. **to wreak h. among,** destruir; *fig* hacer estragos entre (or en)

Hawaii Hawai, *m*

Hawaiian *a* and *n* hawaiano; *n* (language) hawaiano, *m*

hawk *n* halcón, *m*; gavilán, milano, *m*. *vi* cazar con halcón. *vt* vender mercancías por las calles; *fig* difundir. **h.-eyed,** de ojos de lince. **h.-nosed,** de nariz aguileña

hawker *n* halconero, *m*; (vendor) buhonero, *m*, vendedor (-ra) ambulante

hawking *n* caza con halcones, cetrería, *f*; (expectorating) gargajeo, *m*; (selling) buhonería, *f*

hawser *n* maroma, *f*, calabrote, *m*

hawthorn *n* espino, *m*. **white h.,** espino blanco, *m*

hay *n* heno, *m*. **to make hay while the sun shines,** hacer su agosto. **hay fever,** fiebre del heno, *f*. **hayfork,** horca, *f*

hayloft *n* henil, *m*

haymaker *n* segador (-ra); (machine) segadora, *f*

haymaking *n* recolección del heno, *f*

haystack *n* almiar, *m*, niara, *f*

hazard *n* azar, *m*, suerte, *f*; riesgo, peligro, *m*; (game) juego de azar, *m*. *vt* arriesgar, aventurar. **at all hazards,** a todo riesgo

hazardous *a* azaroso, arriesgado, peligroso

haze *n* bruma, *f*; confusión, *f*

hazel *n* avellano, *m*. **h.-nut,** avellana, *f*

hazy *a* brumoso, calinoso; confuso

he *pers. pron* él. *n* (of humans) varón, *m*; (of animals) macho, *m*. **he who,** el que, quien. **he-goat,** macho cabrío, *m*. **he-man,** todo un hombre, hombre cabal, *m*

head *vt* golpear con la cabeza; encabezar; (lead) capitanear; (direct) dirigir, guiar; (wine) cabecear. *vi* estar a la cabeza de; dirigirse a. **headed for,** con rumbo a, en dirección a. **to h. off,** interceptar; desviar; *fig* distraer

head *n anat* cabeza, *f*; (upper portion) parte superior, *f*; (of a coin) cara, *f*; (hair) cabellera, *f*; (individual) persona, *f*; (of cattle) res, *f*; (of a mountain) cumbre, *f*; (of a ladder) último peldaño, *m*; (of toadstools) sombrero, *m*; (of trees) copa, *f*; (of a stick) puño, *m*; (of a cylinder) culata, *f*; (of a river, etc.) manantial, origen, *m*; (of a bed) cabecera, *f*; (of nails, pins) cabeza, *f*; (froth) espuma, *f*; (flower) flor, *f*; (leaves) hojas, *f pl*; (first place) primer puesto, *m*; (of game, fish) pieza, *f*; (of a page, column) cabeza, *f*; (cape) cabo, *m*; (of an arrow, dart, lance) punta, *f*; (front) frente, *m*; (leader) jefe, cabeza, *m*; (chief) director (-ra), superior (-ra); presidente (-ta); (of a school) director (-ra); (of a cask) fondo, *m*; *mech* cabezal, *m*; (of an ax) filo, *m*; (of a bridge) cabeza, *f*; (of a jetty, pier) punta, *f*; (of a ship) proa, *f*; (of a flower) cabezuela, *f*; (of asparagus) punta, *f*; (of a table) cabeza, *f*; (of the family) jefe, cabeza, *m*; (seat of honor) cabecera, *f*; (title) título, *m*; (aspect) punto de vista, *m*; (division) capítulo, *m*; (management, direction) dirección, *f*; (talent) talento, *m*, cabeza, *f*; (intelligence) inteligencia, *f*. *a* principal; primero; en jefe. **at the h. of,** a la cabeza de. **crowned h.,** testa coronada, *f*. **from h. to foot,** de pies a cabeza; de hito en hito; de arriba abajo. **He took it into his h. to . . .,** Se le ocurrió de . . . **This story has neither h. nor tail,** Este cuento no tiene pies ni cabeza. **with h. held high,** con la frente levantada. **to come to a h.,** llegar a la crisis; llegar al punto decisivo. **to get an idea out of a person's h.,** quitar una idea a uno de la cabeza. **to keep one's h.,** *fig* conservar la sangre fría, no perder la cabeza. **to lose one's h.,** *fig* perder la cabeza. **to put into a person's h.,** *fig* meter (a uno) en la cabeza. **to run one's h. against,** golpear la cabeza contra. **h. first,** de cabeza. **h. of cattle,** res, *f*. **h. office,** central, *f*. **h. of hair,** cabellera, *f*; mata de pelo, *f*. **h.-on,** de cabeza. **h.-on collision,** choque de frente, *m*. **h. opening,** (of a garment) cabezón, *m*. **heads or tails,** cara o cruz (Spain), águila o sol (Mexico), cruz o sello (Argentina, Chile). **h. over heels,** de patas arriba. **h. over heels in love,** calado hasta los huesos. **h.-dress,** tocado, *m*; peinado, *m*; sombrero, *m*. **h. voice,** voz de cabeza, *f*. **h. waiter,** encargado de comedor, jefe de camareros, *m*

headache *n* dolor de cabeza, *m*; *fig* quebradero de cabeza, *m*

headboard *n* cabecera (de una cama), *f*

headed *a* con cabeza . . .; que tiene la cabeza . . .; de cabeza . . .; (of an article) intitulado. **large h.,** cabezudo

header *n* caída de cabeza, *f*; salto de cabeza, *m*

headgear *n* tocado, *m*; sombrero, gorro, *m*

head-hunting *n* la caza de cabezas, *f*

heading *n naut* el poner la proa en dirección (a); el guiar en dirección (a); (of a book, etc.) título, encabezamiento, *m*; (soccer) golpe de cabeza, *m*. **to come under the h. of,** estar incluido entre; clasificarse bajo

headland *n* cabo, promontorio, *m*

headlight *n aut* faro, *m*; (*rw, naut*) farol, *m*. **to dip the headlights,** bajar los faros. **to switch on the headlights,** encender los faros (or los faroles)

headline *n* (of a newspaper) titular, *m*; (to a chapter) título de la columna, *m*

headlong *a* precipitado; despeñado. *adv* de cabeza; precipitadamente. **to fall h.,** caer de cabeza

headman *n* cacique, cabecilla, *m*; (foreman) capataz, contramaestre, *m*

headmaster *n* director de colegio, rector, *m*

headmistress *n* directora de colegio, rectora, *f*

head-on collision *n* choque frontal, *m*

head nurse enfermero-jefe, *m*

headphones *n pl* auriculares, *m pl*

headquarters *n mil* cuartel general, *m*; oficina central, *f*; jefatura, *f*; centro, *m*

headrest *n* respaldo, *m*; apoyo para la cabeza, *m*

headstone *n* piedra mortuoria, *f*

headstrong *a* impetuoso, terco, testarudo

headway *n* marcha, *f*; *fig* progreso, avance, *m*. **to make h.,** avanzar; *fig* hacer progresos; *fig* prosperar

headwind *n* viento en contra, *m*

heady *a* apasionado, violento; impetuoso, precipitado; (obstinate) terco; (of alcohol) encabezado; *fig* embriagador

heal *vt* curar, sanar; (flesh) cicatrizar. *vi* curar, sanar; cicatrizarse; (superficially) sobresanar

healable *a* curable

healer *n* sanador (-ra), curador (-ra); curandero, *m*

healing *a* curador, sanador; médico. *n* curación, *f*; cura, *f*, remedio, *m*

health *n* salud, *f*; higiene, sanidad, *f*. **Here's to your very good h.!** ¡Salud y pesetas! **He is in good h.,** Disfruta de buena salud. **to drink a person's h.,** beber a la salud de. **to enjoy good h.,** gozar de buena salud. **to look full of h.,** vender salud. **h.-giving,** saludable. **h. inspection,** visita de sanidad, *f*. **h. officer,** inspector de sanidad, *m*. **h. resort,** balneario, *m*

healthiness *n* buena salud, *f*; sanidad, salubridad, *f*

healthy *a* sano; con buena salud; (healthful) saludable. **to be h.,** tener buena salud

heap *n* montón, *m*; rima, pila, *f*, acervo, *m*; (of people) muchedumbre, *f*, tropel, *m*. *vt* amontonar; apilar; colmar. **in heaps,** a montones. **We have heaps of time,** Nos sobra tiempo, Tenemos tiempo de sobra. **to h. together,** juntar, mezclar. **to h. up, upon,** colmar; amontonar; *agr* hacinar; *fig* acumular

hear *vt* oír; (listen) escuchar; (attend) asistir a; (give audience) dar audiencia (a); (a lawsuit) ver (un pleito); (speak) hablar; (be aware of, feel) sentir. *vi* oír; tener noticias; (learn) enterarse de; (allow) permitir. **H.! H.!** ¡Muy bien! ¡Bravo! **I have heard it said that . . .** He oído decir que . . . **Let me h. from you!** ¡Mándame noticias tuyas! **They were never heard of again,** No se volvió a saber de ellos, No se supo más de ellos. **to h. about,** oír de; (know) saber de, tener noticias de; recibir información sobre. **to h. from,** ser informado por; tener noticias de: recibir carta de. **to h. of,** enterarse de, saber; recibir información sobre; (allow) permitir

hearer *n* oyente, *mf*

hearing *n* (sense of) oído, *m*; alcance del oído, *m*; presencia, *f*; audición, *f*; *law* vista (de una causa) *f*. **It was said in my h.,** Fue dicho en mi presencia. **out of h.,** fuera del alcance del oído. **within h.,** al alcance del oído. **have a h. problem,** ser parcialmente sordo

hearing aid acústica, aparato auditivo, aparato acústico, audífono, *m*

hearsay *n* fama, *f*, rumor, *m*. **by h.,** de oídas

hearse *n* coche fúnebre, *m*

heart *n* corazón, *m*; (feelings) entrañas, *f pl*; (of the earth, etc.) seno, corazón, *m*; (of lettuce, etc.) cogollo, repollo, *m*; (suit in cards) copas, *f pl*; *bot* médula, *f*; (soul) alma, *f*; (courage) valor, *m*; ánimo, *m*. **at h.,** en el fondo, esencialmente. **by h.,** de memoria. **from the h.,** con toda sinceridad, de todo corazón. **He is a man after my own h.,** Es un hombre de los que me gustan. **I have no h. to do it,** No tengo valor de hacerlo. **in the h. of the country,** en medio del campo. **to break one's h.,** partirse el corazón. **to have one's h. in one's mouth,** tener el alma en un hilo, estar muerto de miedo. **to have no h.,** *fig* no tener entrañas. **to lose h.,** desanimarse, descorazonarse. **to set one's h. on,** poner el corazón en. **to take h.,** cobrar ánimo; *inf* hacer de tripas corazón. **to take to h.,** tomar a pechos. **to wear one's h. on one's sleeve,** tener el corazón en la mano. **with all my h.,** con toda el alma. **h.-ache,** angustia, pena, *f*. **h.-beat,** latido del corazón, *m*. **h.-breaker,** (woman) coqueta, *f*; (man) ladrón de corazones, *m*. **h. disease,** enfermedad del corazón, enfermedad cardíaca, *f*. **h. failure,** colapso cardíaco, *m*. **h.-rending,** desgarrador, angustioso. **h.-searching,** examen de conciencia, *m*. **h.-shaped,** acorazonado, en forma de corazón. **h.-strings,** fibras del corazón, *f pl*. **h.-to-h. talk,** conversación íntima, *f*. **h.-whole,** libre de afectos

heartbreaking *a* desgarrador, angustioso, doloroso, lastimoso

heartbroken *a* acongojado, afligido, transido de dolor

heartburn *n* acidez del estómago, acedia, pirosis, rescoldera, *f*

heartburning *n* rencor, *m*, animosidad, envidia, *f*

hearted *a* de corazón . . . que tiene el corazón . . . **kind-h.,** de buen corazón, bondadoso
hearten *vt* alentar, animar
heartfelt *a* hondo; de todo corazón, sincero; más expresivo
hearth *n* hogar, *m*; chimenea, *f*; *fig* hogar, *m*
heartily *adv* cordialmente; sinceramente; enérgicamente; con entusiasmo; (of eating) con buen apetito; (very) muy, completamente. **I am h. sick of it all,** *inf* Estoy harto hasta los dientes
heartiness *n* cordialidad, *f*; sinceridad, *f*; energía, *f*, vigor, *m*; vehemencia, *f*; entusiasmo, *m*; (of appetite) buen diente, buen apetito, *m*
heartless *a* sin corazón, sin piedad, despiadado, inhumano, cruel
heartlessness *n* falta de corazón, inhumanidad, crueldad, *f*
hearty *a* cordial; sincero; enérgico; vigoroso; robusto; (frank) campechano; (of appetite) voraz; bueno; (big) grande
heat *n* calor, *m*; (in animals) celo, *m*; (of an action) calor, *m*; *fig* vehemencia, fogosidad, *f*; *fig* fuego, *m*; (passion) ardor, *m*, pasión, *f*; (of a race) carrera eliminatoria, *f*. *vt* calentar; (excite) conmover, acalorar, excitar; (annoy) irritar. *vi* calentarse. **dead h.,** empate, *m*. **in h.,** en celo. **in the h. of the moment,** en el calor del momento. **to become heated,** *fig* acalorarse, exaltarse. **white h.,** candencia, incandescencia, *f*. **h. lightning,** fucilazo, *m*. **h. spot,** pápula, *f*; terminación sensible, *f*. **h. stroke,** insolación, *f*. **h. wave,** onda de calor, *f*
heated *a* calentado; caliente; excitado; apasionado
heatedly *adv* con vehemencia, con pasión
heater *n* calentador, *m*; calorífero, *m*; (stove) estufa, *f*; (for plates) calientaplatos, *m*. **water-h.,** calentador de agua, *m*
heath *n* brezal, *m*; yermo, páramo, *m*; *bot* brezo, *m*
heathen *n* pagano (-na); idólatra, *mf*; ateo (-ea), descreído (-da). *a* pagano; ateo; bárbaro
heathenism *n* paganismo, *m*; idolatría, *f*; ateísmo, *m*
heather *n* brezo, *m*
heating *n* calefacción, *f*, *a* calentador; (of drinks) fortificante. **central h.,** calefacción central, *f*
heave *vt* alzar, levantar; *naut* izar; (the anchor, etc.) virar; (throw) arrojar, lanzar; elevar; (extract) extraer; (emit) dar, exhalar. *vi* subir y bajar; palpitar; agitarse. *n* tirón, *m*; (of the sea) vaivén, *m*. **to h. in sight,** aparecer, surgir. **to h. out sail,** *naut* desenvergar. **to h. the lead,** *naut* escandallar. **to h. to,** *naut* estarse a la capa
heaven *n* cielo, *m*; firmamento, *m*; paraíso, *m*. **Heavens!** ¡Cielos! ¡Por Dios! **Thank H.!** ¡Gracias a Dios! **h.-born,** celeste. **h.-sent,** *fig* providencial
heavenliness *n* carácter celestial, *m*; delicia, *f*
heavenly *a* celeste, celestial; divino; *fig* delicioso. **h. body,** astro, *m*
heavily *adv* pesadamente; torpemente; penosamente; (slowly) lentamente; severamente; excesivamente; (of sighing) hondamente; (sadly) tristemente; (of rain, etc.) reciamente, fuertemente; (of wind) con violencia. **He fell h.,** Cayó de plomo. **to lie h. upon,** pesar mucho sobre. **to rain h.,** llover mucho, diluviar
heaviness *n* peso, *m*; (lethargy) torpor, letargo, *m*; sueño, *m*, languidez, *f*; (clumsiness) torpeza, *f*; (severity) severidad, *f*; importancia, responsabilidad, *f*; dificultad, *f*; (gravity) gravedad, *f*; tristeza, melancolía, *f*; (boredom) sosería, insulsez, *f*; (of style) monotonía, ponderosidad, *f*
heaving *n* levantamiento, *m*; (of the anchor, etc.) virada, *f*; (of the sea) vaivén, *m*; (of the breast) palpitación, *f*
heavy *a* pesado; torpe; sin gracia; (slow) lento; (thick) grueso; (strong) fuerte; (hard) duro; grave; difícil; oneroso; responsable, importante; (oppresive) opresivo; penoso; grande; (sad) triste, melancólico; (of the sky) anublado; (of food) indigesto; (tedious) aburrido, soso; (pompous) pomposo; (of roads) malo; (of scents) fuerte, penetrante; (of sleep, weather) pesado; (weary) rendido; (charged with) cargado de; (of a meal) grande, abundante; (violent) violento; (of a cold, etc.) malo; (drowsy) soñoliento; (torpid) tórpido; (of rain, snow, hail) fuerte, recio; (of firing) intenso; (of sighs) profundo; (of soil) recio, de mucha miga; (*phys chem*) pesado. **to be h.,** pesar mucho. **How h. are you?** ¿Cuánto pesa Vd.? **h.-armed,** pesado; armado hasta los dientes. **h.-eyed,** con ojeras. **h. guns,** artillería pesada, *f*. **h.-handed,** de manos torpes; *fig* tiránico, opresivo. **h.-hearted,** triste, apesadumbrado. **h. industry,** la gran industria, la industria pesada, *f*. **h.-laden,** muy cargado. **h. losses,** *mil* pérdidas cuantiosas, *f pl*. **h.weight,** *sport* peso pesado, *m*
Hebraic *a* hebraico, hebreo, judaico
Hebraism *n* judaísmo, hebraísmo, *m*
Hebraist *n* hebraísta, *m*
Hebrew *n* hebreo (-ea), judío (-ía): (language) hebreo, *m*
Hebrides, the las Hébridas
hecatomb *n* hecatombe, *f*
heckle *vt fig* interrumpir, importunar con preguntas
heckler *n* perturbador (-ra)
heckling *n* interrupción, *f*
hectare *n* hectárea, *f*
hectic *a* (consumptive) hético; (feverish) febril; *fig inf* agitado
hectogram *n* hectogramo, *m*
hectoliter *n* hectolitro, *m*
hector *vt* intimidar, amenazar
hectoring *a* imperioso; amenazador
hectowatt *n elec* hectovatio, *m*
hedge *n* seto, *m*; barrera, *f*. *vt* cercar con un seto; rodear. *vi fig* titubear, vacilar. **h.-hopping,** *aer* vuelo a ras de tierra, *m*. **h.-sparrow,** acentor de bosque, *m*
hedgehog *n* erizo, *m*. **h. position,** *mil* puesto fuerte, *m*
hedonism *n* hedonismo, *m*
hedonist *n* hedonista, *mf*
heed *n* atención, *f*, cuidado, *m*. *vt* atender; observar, considerar; escuchar. *vi* hacer caso
heedful *a* atento; cuidadoso
heedless *a* desatento; descuidado, negligente; distraído
heedlessly *adv* sin hacer caso; negligentemente; distraídamente
heedlessness *n* desatención, distracción, *f*; descuido, *m*; negligencia, *f*; inconsideración, *f*
heel *n anat* talón, calcañar, *m*; (of shoe) tacón, *m*; (of a violin, etc., bow) talón, *m*; (remains) restos, *m pl*. *vt* poner tacón a; poner talón a; *naut* hacer zozobrar. *vi naut* zozobrar. **rubber h.,** tacón de goma, *m*. **She let him cool his heels for half an hour,** le dio un plantón de media hora. **to follow on a person's heels,** pisarle (a uno) los talones. **to be down at h.,** (of shoes) estar gastados los tacones; estar desaseado. **to take to one's heels,** apretar a correr, poner pies en polvorosa. **to turn on one's h.,** dar media vuelta. **h.-bone,** zancajo, *m*. **h.-piece,** talón, *m*
heeltap *n* tapa de tacón, *f*; escurridura, *f*
heft *vt* sopesar, tomar al peso
hegemony *n* hegemonía, *f*
heifer *n* ternera, vaquilla, *f*
heigh *interj* (calling attention) ¡oye! ¡ioiga! **h.-ho!** ¡ay!
height *n* altura, *f*; elevación, *f*; altitud, *f*; (stature) estatura, *f*; (high ground) cerro, *m*, colina, *f*; (sublimity) sublimidad, excelencia, *f*; colmo, *m*; (zenith) auge, *m*, cumbre, *f*
heighten *vt* hacer más alto; (enhance) realzar; (exaggerate) exagerar; (perfect) perfeccionar; (intensify) intensificar
heightening *n* elevación, *f*; (enhancement) realce, *m*; (exaggeration) exageración, *f*; (perfection) perfección, *f*; (intensification) intensificación, *f*
heinous *a* atroz, nefando, horrible.
heinousness *n* atrocidad, enormidad, *f*
heir *n* heredero, *Lat. Am.* asignatario *m*. **h. apparent,**

heredero aparente, *m.* **h.-at-law,** heredero forzoso, *m.* **h. presumptive,** presunto heredero, *m*
heiress *n* heredera, *Lat. Am.* asignataria *f*
heirloom *n* reliquia de familia, *f; fig* herencia, *f*
helicopter *n* helicóptero, *m*
helium *n chem* helio, *m*
helix *n geom* hélice, *m;* (*arch geom*) espira, *f*
hell *n* infierno, *m.* **h.-fire,** fuego del infierno, *m,* llamas del infierno, *f pl*
Hellenic *a* helénico
Hellenism *n* helenismo, *m*
Hellenist *n* helenista, *mf*
Hellenize *vt* helenizar
hellish *a* infernal; *inf* horrible, detestable
hello *interj* ¡hola!; (on telephoning someone) ¡oiga! ¡alo!; (answering telephone) *Spain* ¡diga!, ¡alo!, *Colombia* ¡a ver!, *Mexico* ¡bueno!
helm *n* caña del timón, *f;* timón, gobernalle, *m.* **to obey the h.,** obedecer el timón. **to take the h.,** gobernar el timón; ponerse a pilotar
helmet *n* casco, *m;* (in olden days) yelmo, capacete, *m;* (sun) casco colonial, *m*
helminthic *a* helmíntico, vermífugo
helmsman *n* timonero, *m*
help *n* ayuda, *f;* auxilio, socorro, *m;* (protection) favor, *m,* protección, *f;* (remedy) remedio, *m;* (cooperation) cooperación, *f,* concurso, *m;* (domestic) criada, *f.* **A little h. is worth a lot of sympathy,** Más vale un toma que dos te daré. **There's no h. for it,** No hay más remedio. **to call for h.,** pedir socorro a gritos. **without h.,** a solas, sin la ayuda de nadie
help *vt* ayudar; socorrer, auxiliar; (favor) favorecer; (mitigate) aliviar; (contribute to) contribuir a, facilitar; (avoid) evitar. *vi* ayudar. **He cannot h. worrying,** No puede menos de preocuparse. **God h. you!** ¡Dios te ampare! **So h. me God!** ¡Así Dios me salve! **to h. one another,** ayudarse mutuamente, ayudarse los unos a los otros. **to h. oneself,** (to food) servirse. **to h. down, off,** ayudar a bajar; ayudar a apearse. **to h. in,** ayudar a entrar. **to h. along, forward, on,** avanzar, fomentar, promover; contribuir a. **Shall I h. you on with the dress?** ¿Quieres que te ayude a ponerte el vestido? **to h. out,** ayudar a salir; (from a vehicle) ayudar a bajar; (of a difficulty, etc.) sacar; suplir la falta de; ayudar. **to h. over,** ayudar a cruzar; (a difficulty) ayudar a salir (de un apuro); ayudar a vencer (un obstáculo, etc.); (a period) ayudar a pasar. **to h. to,** contribuir a, ayudar en; (food) servir. **to h. up,** ayudar a subir; ayudar a levantarse, levantar
helper *n* auxiliador (-ra); asistente (-ta); (protector) favorecedor (-ra); bienhechor (-ra), *Argentina also* ladero *m;* (colleague) colega, *m;* (co-worker) colaborador (-ra). **He thanked all his helpers,** Dio las gracias a todos los que le habían ayudado
helpful *a* útil, provechoso; (obliging) servicial, atento, *Lat. Am.* acomedido; (favorable) favorable; (healthy) saludable
helpfulness *n* utilidad, *f;* bondad, *f*
helping *n* ayuda, *f;* (of food) porción, ración, *f,* plato, *m.* **Won't you have a second h.?** ¿No quiere usted servirse más (or otra vez)? ¿No quiere usted repetir? **to lend a h. hand (to),** prestar ayuda (a)
helpless *a* desamparado, abandonado; (through infirmity) imposibilitado; impotente, sin fuerzas (para); (shiftless) incompetente, inútil
helplessness *n* desamparo, *m;* invalidez, debilidad, *f;* impotencia, *f;* incompetencia, *f*
helter-skelter *adv* atropelladamente; en desorden. *n* barahunda, *f*
hem *n sew* dobladillo, filete, *m,* bastilla, *f;* (edge) orilla, *f. interj* ¡ejem! *vt* hacer dobladillo en, dobladillar. *vi* (cough) fingir toser. **false hem,** *sew* dobladillo falso, *m.* **running hem,** *sew* jareta, *f.* **to hem and haw,** tartamudear; vacilar. **to hem in,** cercar, sitiar
hemisphere *n* hemisferio, *m*
hemispherical *a* hemisférico, semiesférico
hemlock *n bot* cicuta, *f*
hemoglobin *n chem* hemoglobina, *f*
hemophilia *n med* hemofilia, *f*
hemorrhage *n* hemorragia, *f,* flujo de sangre, *m*
hemorrhoids *n pl med* hemorroides, *f*
hemp *n* cáñamo, *m.* **h. cloth,** lienzo, *m.* **h.-seed,** cañamón, *m*
hemstitch *n* vainica, *f. vt* hacer vainica en
hen *n* gallina, *f;* (female bird) hembra, *f.* **the hen pheasant,** la hembra del faisán. **hen bird,** pájara, *f.* **hen-coop** or **house,** gallinero, *m.* **hen party,** *inf* reunión de mujeres, *f.* **hen-roost,** nidal, ponedero, *m*
hence *adv* (of place) de aquí; (of time) de ahora, de aquí a, al cabo de, en; (therefore) por eso, por lo tanto, por consiguiente. *interj* ¡fuera! ¡fuera de aquí! **I shall come to see you a month h.,** Vendré a verte en un mes (or al cabo de un mes). **ten years h.,** de aquí a diez años. **h. the fact that . . . ,** de aquí que. . . . **H. it happens that . . . ,** Por eso sucede que . . .
henceforth *adv* desde aquí en adelante, de hoy en adelante
henchman *n* escudero, *m;* satélite, secuaz, *m*
henna *n* alheña, *f*
henpecked *a* gobernado por su mujer, que se deja mandar por su mujer
her *pers pron direct object* la; (with prepositions) ella. *pers. pron indirect object* le, a ella. *poss a* su, *mf;* sus, *mf pl,* de ella. **I saw her on Wednesday,** La vi el miércoles. **The message is for her,** El recado es para ella. **It is her book,** Es su libro, Es el libro de ella
herald *n* heraldo, *m;* presagio, anuncio, *m. vt* proclamar; anunciar, presagiar
heraldic *a* heráldico
heraldry *n* heráldica, *f*
herb *n* hierba, *f*
herbaceous *a* herbáceo
herbage *n* herbaje, *m;* pasto, *m*
herbal *a* herbario. *n* herbolaria, *f*
herbalist *n* herbario, *m,* simplista, *mf*
herbarium *n* herbario, *m*
herbivorous *a* herbívoro
herby *a* herbáceo
Herculean *a* hercúleo
herd *n* manada, *f;* (of cattle) hato, *m;* (race) raza, *f;* (*fig* contemptuous) populacho, *m,* masa, *f. vt* reunir en manadas; reunir en hatos; (sheep) reunir en rebaños; guiar las manadas, etc. *vi* ir en manadas, hatos o rebaños; asociarse, reunirse. **h.-instinct,** instinto gregario, *m;* instinto de las masas, *m*
herdsman *n* ganadero, pastor, manadero, *m;* (head herdsman) rabadán, *m*
here *adv* aquí; (at roll-call) ¡presente!; acá; an este punto; ahora. *n* presente, *m.* **And h. he looked at me,** Y a este punto me miró. **Come h.!** ¡Ven acá! **in h.,** aquí dentro. **h. below,** aquí abajo, en la tierra. **h. and there,** aquí y allá. **h., there and everywhere,** en todas partes. **H. I am,** Heme aquí. **h. is . . . ,** he aquí. . . . **H. they are,** Aquí los tienes, Aquí están. **Here's to you!** (on drinking) ¡Salud y pesetas! ¡A tu salud!
hereabouts *adv* por aquí cerca
hereafter *adv* en lo futuro; desde ahora; en adelante. *n* futuro, *m.* **the H.,** la otra vida
hereat *adv* en esto
hereby *adv* por esto, por las presentes
hereditarily *adv* hereditariamente, por herencia
hereditary *a* hereditario
heredity *n* herencia, *f*
herein *adv* en esto; aquí dentro; incluso
hereinafter *adv* después, más abajo, más adelante, en adelante, en lo sucesivo
hereinbefore *adv* en la anterior, en lo arriba citado, en lo antes mencianado, en lo precedente.
hereof *adv* de esto
heresy *n* herejía, *f*
heretic *n* hereje, *mf*
heretical *a* herético

hereunder *adv* abajo
hereupon *adv* en esto, en seguida
herewith *adv* junto con esto, con esto; ahora, en esta ocasión
heritage *n* herencia, *f*
hermaphrodite *a* and *n* hermafrodita, *mf*
hermetic *a* hermético
hermit *n* ermitaño, *m*. **h. crab,** paguro, cangrejo ermitaño, *m*
hernia *n* hernia, *f*
hero *n* héroe, *m*. **h.-worship,** culto a los héroes, *m*
heroic *a* heroico, épico
heroin *n chem* heroína, *f*
heroine *n* heroína, *f*
heroism *n* heroísmo, *m*
heron *n* garza, *f*
herpes *n pl* herpes, *mf pl*
herring *n* arenque, *m*
hers *poss pron 3rd sing* (el) suyo, *m*; (la) suya, *f*; (los) suyos, *m pl*; (las) suyas, *f pl*; de ella. **This book is h.,** Este libro es suyo, Este libro es de ella. **This book is h., not mine,** Este libro es el suyo no el mío. **a sister of h.,** una de sus hermanas, una hermana suya
herself *pron* sí misma, sí; ella misma; (with reflexive verb) se. **She has done it by h.,** Lo ha hecho por sí misma. **She h. told me so,** Ella misma me lo dijo. **She is by h.,** Está a solas, Está sola
hesitancy. See **hesitation**
hesitant *a* indeciso, vacilante, irresoluto. **to be h.,** mostrarse irresoluto
hesitate *vi* vacilar, dudar; titubear. **I do not h. to say . . . ,** No vacilo en decir . . . **He hesitated over his reply,** Tardaba en dar su respuesta
hesitatingly *adv* irresolutamente; titubeando
hesitation *n* vacilación, hesitación, *f*; irresolución, indecisión, *f*; (reluctance) aversión, repugnancia, *f*; titubeo, *m*
heterodox *a* heterodoxo
heterodoxy *n* heterodoxia, *f*
heterogeneity *n* heterogeneidad, *f*
heterogeneous *a* heterogéneo
hew *vt* cortar, tajar; (trees) talar; (a career, etc.) hacerse
hewer *n* partidor, talador, *m*
hexagon *n* hexágono, *m*
hey *interj* ¡he! ¡oye!
heyday *n* apogeo, colmo, *m*; buenos tiempos, *m pl*; reinado, *m*; pleno vigor, *m*
hi *interj* ¡oye! ¡hola!
hiatus *n* hiato, *m*; laguna, *f*, vacío, *m*
hibernate *vi* invernar
hibernation *n* invernada, *f*
hibiscus *n bot* hibisco, *m*
hiccough *n* hipo, *m*. *vi* hipar. *vt* decir con hipo
hidden *a* escondido, secreto, oculto
hide *n* piel, *f*; pellejo, cuero, *m*
hide *vt* esconder, ocultar; (cover) cubrir, tapar; (dissemble) disimular; (meaning) obscurecer. *vi* esconderse; ocultarse, *Mexico* atejonarse; refugiarse. **to h. from each other,** esconderse el uno del otro. **h.-and-seek,** escondite, dormirlas, *m*
hidebound *a fig* muy conservador, reaccionario, de ideas muy tradicionales
hideous *a* horrible, repulsivo, horroroso; repugnante, odioso
hideously *adv* horriblemente. **to be h. ugly,** (of people) ser más feo que Picio
hideousness *n* fealdad, horribilidad, *f*; repugnancia, *f*
hiding *n* ocultación, *f*; encubrimiento, *m*; refugio, *m*; *inf* paliza, tunda, *f*. **h.-place,** escondite, escondrijo, *m*
hie *vi* apresurarse, ir a prisa
hierarch *n* jerarca, *m*
hierarchical *a* jerárquico
hierarchy *n* jerarquía, *f*
hieroglyph *n* jeroglífico, *m*
higgledy-piggledy *adv* revueltamente, en confusión; en montón, en desorden
high *a* alto; elevado; (with altar, Mass, street, festival) mayor; grande; eminente; aristocrático; (of shooting) fijante; (of quality) superior; excelente; (haughty) orgulloso; (solemn) solemne; (good) bueno; noble; supremo; sumo; (of price) subido; *mus* agudo; (of the sea) tempestuoso, borrascoso; (of wind and explosives) violento, fuerte; (of polish) brillante; (with speed) grande; (with tension, frequency) alto; (with number, etc.) importante, grande; (with colors) subido; (of food) pasado; (angry) enojado, airado; (of cheek bones) saliente, prominente; (well-seasoned) picante; (flattering) lisonjero. *adv* alto; hacia arriba; arriba; (deeply) profundamente; fuertemente; con violencia; (of price) a un precio elevado; (luxuriously) lujosamente; *mus* agudo. **a room 12 ft. h.,** un cuarto de doce pies de altura. **I knew her when she was so h.,** La conocí tamaña. **It is h. time he came,** Ya es hora de que viniese. **on h.,** en alto, arriba; en los cielos. **h. altar,** altar mayor, *m*. **h. and dry,** en la playa, varado; *fig* en seco. **h. and low,** de arriba abajo; por todas partes. **h.-born,** aristocrático, de alta alcurnia. **h.-bred,** (of people) de buena familia; (of animals) de buena raza. **h.-class,** de buena clase; de alta calidad. **h. collar,** alzacuello, *m*. **h. colored,** de colores vivos; *fig* exagerado. **h. command,** (*mil, nav*) alto mando, *m*. **h. court,** tribunal supremo, *m*. **h. day,** día festivo, *m*. **h. explosive,** explosivo violento, *m*. **h.-flown,** hinchado, retumbante, altisonante. **h. frequency,** alta frecuencia, *f*. **h.-handed,** arbitrario, dominador, despótico. **h.-heeled,** *a* de tacón alto. **h. jump,** salto de altura, *m*. **h. land,** tierras altas, *f pl*; eminencia, *f*. **h. life** *Lat. Am.* jáilaif *m*. **h. light,** *art* realce, *m*; acontecimiento de más interés, *m*; momento culminante, *m*. **h. mass,** misa mayor, *f*. **h.-minded,** de nobles pensamientos; arrogante. **h.-necked,** con cuello alto. **h.-pitched,** de tono alto, agudo. **h.-powered,** de alta potencia. **h.-powered car,** coche de muchos caballos, *m*. **h. precision,** suma precisión, *f*. **h. pressure,** *n* alta presión, *f*; *fig* urgencia, *f*; *n* de alta presión; *fig* urgente. **h.-priced,** caro. **h. priest,** sumo pontífice, sumo sacerdote, alto sacerdote, *m*. **h. relief,** alto relieve, *m*. **h. road,** carretera mayor, *f*. **h. school,** instituto de segunda enseñanza, instituto, colegio, liceo, *m*; colegio, liceo, instituto, *m*, escuela secundaria, secundaria, *f*. **h. sea,** marejada, *f*. **h. seas,** alta mar, *f*. **h.-seasoned,** picante. **h. society,** alta sociedad, *f*. **h.-sounding,** altisonante, bombástico. **h.-speed,** de alta velocidad. **h.-spirited,** brioso; alegre. **h.-strung,** nervioso, excitable, sensitivo. **h. tension,** alta tensión, *f*. **h. tide,** marea alta, *f*. **h.-toned,** *mus* agudo; *inf* de alto copete; aristocrático. **h. treason,** alta traición, *f*. **h. water,** marea alta, pleamar, *f*. **h.-water mark,** límite de la marea, *m*; *fig* colmo, *m*; apogeo, *m*
High Andes, the el Altiplano *m*
highball *m Spain* qüisquisoda *f*, *Lat. Am.* jáibol *m*
highbrow *a* and *n* intelectual, *mf*
high-ceilinged *a* alto de techo
higher *a comp* of **high,** más alto; más elevado; superior. **on a h. plane,** en un nivel más alto. **h. education,** enseñanza superior, *f*. **h. mathematics,** la alta matemática, *f*. **h. criticism,** la alta crítica. **h. up,** más arriba. **h. up the river,** río arriba
highest *a superl* of **high,** el más alto; la más alta; los más altos; las más altas; sumo, supremo; excelente. **h. common factor,** *math* máximo común divisor, *m*. **h. references,** (of cook, gardener, etc.) informes inmejorables, *m pl*; *com* referencias excelentes, *f pl*
highland *n* altiplanicie, *f*; montañas, *f pl*, distrito montañoso, *m*. *a* montañoso
highlight *vtr* dar relieve a, destacar
highly *adv* altamente; mucho; muy; extremadamente; grandemente; bien; favorablemente; con lisonja, lisonjeramente. **h. seasoned,** picante. **h. strung,** nervioso, excitable
highness *n* altura, *f*; elevación, *f*; excelencia, *f*; nobleza,

f; (title) Alteza, *f.* **His Royal H., Her Royal Highness,** Su Alteza Real
high-ranking *a* de alta jerarquía, de alto rango
highway *n* camino real, *m*, carretera, *f.* **h. code,** código de la via pública (or de la circulación), *m.* **h. robbery,** salteamiento de caminos, atraco, *m*
highwayman *n* salteador de caminos, *m*
highways and byways caminos y veredas
hike *vi* ir de excursión. *n* marcha con equipo, *f*
hiker *n* excursionista, *mf*
hiking *n* excursionismo, *m;* marcha con equipo, *f*
hilarious *a* alegre
hilarity *n* hilaridad, *f*
hill *n* colina, *f*, cerro, otero, *m;* monte, *m*, montaña, *f;* (pile) montón, *m.* **h.-side,** falda de montaña, ladera de una colina, *f.* **h.-top,** cumbre de una colina, *f*
hilliness *n* montuosidad, *f*, lo montañoso
hillman *n* montañés, *m*
hillock *n* altozano, montículo, collado, *m*
hilly *a* montañoso
hilt *n* puño, *m*, empuñadura, *f*
him *pers pron 3rd sing direct object* le, lo; (with prep.) él; *indirect object* le, a él; (with a direct obj. in 3rd person) se. **I gave him the magazine,** Le di la revista. **I gave it to him,** Se lo di a él. **This is for him,** Esto es para él
Himalayas, the los Himalayas, *m pl*
Himalayan *a* himalayo
himself *pron* sí, sí mismo; él mismo; (reflexive) se. **He did it by h.,** Lo hizo por sí mismo. For more examples see **herself**
hind *n* corza, cierva, *f. a* trasero, posterior. **h.-quarters,** cuarto trasero, *m;* (of a horse) ancas, *f pl*
hinder *a* trasero, posterior
hinder *vt* impedir, estorbar; embarazar, dificultar; interrumpir. *vi* ser un obstáculo; formar un obstáculo
hinderer *n* estorbador (-ra); interruptor (-ra)
hindmost *a* posterior, postrero, último
hindrance *n* obstáculo, estorbo, impedimento, *m;* perjuicio, *m;* interrupción, *f*
Hindu *a* hindú, *mf*
Hinduism *n* indoísmo, *m*
Hindustani *a* indostanés. *n* (language) indostani, *m*
hinge *n* gozne, pernio, *m*, bisagra, *f;* articulación, *f; fig* eje, *m. vi* moverse (or abrirse) sobre goznes; *fig* depender (de). *vt* engoznar
hinged *a* con goznes
hint *n* indirecta, insinuación, sugestión, *f;* (advice) consejo, *m. vt* dar a entender, decir con medias palabras, insinuar, sugerir. *vi* insinuar. **to take the h.,** darse por aludido
hinterland *n* interior (de un país), *m*
hip *n anat* cadera, *f; bot* fruto del rosal silvestre, *m.* **h.-bath,** baño de asiento, *m.* **h.-bone,** hueso ilíaco, *m.* **h.-joint,** articulación de la cadera, *f.* **h.-pocket,** faltriquera, *f*
hipped *a* de caderas
hippodrome *n* hipódromo, *m*
hippopotamus *n* hipopótamo, *m*
hire *n* alquiler, arriendo, *m;* salario, *m. vt* alquilar, arrendar; tomar en arriendo; (person) contratar; tomar a su servicio. **to h. out,** alquilar. **for** or **on h.,** de alquiler. **h.-purchase,** compra a plazos, *f*
hireling *n* mercenario, *m*
hirer *n* alquilador (-ra), arrendador (-ra)
hirsute *a* hirsuto. **non-h.** *bot* lampiño
his *poss pron 3rd sing* (el) suyo, *m;* (la) suya, *f;* (los) suyos, *m pl;* (las) suyas, *f pl;* de él. *poss a* su, *mf;* sus, *mf pl;* de él. **his handkerchiefs,** sus pañuelos. **his mother,** su madre, la madre de él. **a sister of his,** una de sus hermanas, una hermana suya. See **hers** for more examples.
Hispanism *n* hispanismo, *m*
Hispanist *n* hispanista, *mf*
hispanize *vt* españolizar
Hispano-American *a* hispano-americano
hiss *n* silbido, *m;* (sputter) chisporroteo, *m. vi* silbar
hissing *n* silbido, *m;* chisporroteo, *m. a* silbante
hist *interj* ¡chist!
histologist *n* histólogo, *m*
histology *n* histología, *f*
historian *n* historiador (-ra)
historic *a* histórico
historical *a* histórico. **h. truth,** verdad histórica, *f*
historically *adv* históricamente
historiographer *n* historiógrafo, *m*
historiography *n* historiografía, *f*
history *n* historia, *f.* **Biblical h.,** historia sagrada, *f.* **natural h.,** historia natural, *f*
histrionic *a* histriónico
hit *n* golpe, *m; aer* impacto, *m;* (success) éxito, *m;* (piece of luck) buena suerte, *f;* (satire) sátira, *f. vt* golpear; (buffet) abofetear, pegar; (find) dar con, tropezar con; (attain) acertar; (guess) adivinar; (attract) atraer; (deal) lanzar, dar; (wound) herir, hacer daño (a). **The sun hits me right in the eyes,** El sol me da en la cabeza. **direct hit,** *aer* impacto de lleno, *m.* **lucky hit,** acierto, *m.* **to hit a straight left,** (boxing) lanzar un directo con la izquierda. **to hit the mark,** dar en el blanco; *fig* dar en el clavo. **hit or miss,** acierto o error. **to hit against,** dar contra, estrellar contra. **to hit back,** defenderse; devolver golpe por golpe. **to hit off,** imitar; (a likeness) coger. **to hit out,** abofetear; *fig* atacar; golpear (la pelota) fuera. **to hit upon,** dar con; tropezar con; encontrar por casualidad; (remember) acordarse de
hitch *n* (jerk) sacudida, *f;* nudo fácil de soltar, *m; fig* obstáculo, *m; fig* dificultad, *f;* (lift, ride) *Mexico* aventón *m* **give s.b. a hitch,** levantar a fulano. *vt* sacudir; (a chair, etc.) arrastrar, empujar; amarrar, enganchar; atar. *vi* (along a seat, etc.) correrse (en); (get entangled) enredarse, cogerse; (rub) rascarse. **without a h.,** sin dificultad alguna, viento en popa; (smoothly) a pedir de boca. **to h. up,** sacudir, dar una sacudida (a)
hitchhike *vi* ir a dedo (Argentina), pedir aventón (Mexico), pedir botella (Cuba), hacer autostop, ir por autostop (Spain)
hither *adv* acá, hacia acá; *a* citerior, más cercano. **h. and thither,** acá y aculla allá
hitherto *adv* hasta ahora, hasta el presente
Hitlerian *a* hitleriano, nacista
Hitlerism *n* hitlerismo, nacismo, *m*
hive *n* (for bees) colmena, *f;* (swarm) enjambre, *m; fig* centro, *m. vt* (bees) enjambrar. **h. of industry,** centro de industria
hoard *n* acumulación, *f;* provisión, *f;* tesoro, *m. vt* acumular, amasar, amontonar; guardar
hoarder *n* acaparador (-ra)
hoarding *n* amontonamiento, *m;* acaparamiento, *m;* (fence) empalizada, cerca, *f;* palizada de tablas, *f*
hoarfrost *n* escarcha, helada blanca, *f*
hoariness *n* (of the hair) canicie, *f;* blancura, *f;* (antiquity) vejez, vetustez, *f*
hoarse *a* ronco; discordante. **to be h.,** tener la voz ronca. **to grow h.,** enronquecerse
hoarsely *adv* roncamente
hoarseness *n* ronquera, *f; inf* carraspera, *f*
hoary *a* (of the hair) canoso; blanco; (old) vetusto, antiguo, viejo
hoax *n* estafa, *f*, engaño, *m;* broma pesada, *f;* burla, *f. vt* estafar, engañar; burlar
hoaxer *n* burlador (-ra); estafador (-ra)
hob *n* repisa interior del hogar, *f*
hobble *n* (gait) cojera, *f;* traba, maniota, *f. vi* cojear. *vt* manear. **h. skirt,** falda muy estrecha, *f*
hobby *n* pasatiempo, *m*, recreación, *f;* manía, afición, *f.* **h.-horse,** caballo de cartón, *m; fig* caballo de batalla, *m*
hobgoblin *n* trasgo, duende, *m*
hobnail *n* clavo de herradura, clavo de botas, *m*
hobnailed *a* (of boots) con clavos
hobnob *vi* codearse, tratar con familiaridad
hock *n anat* pernil, *m;* (wine) vino del Rin, *m*

hockey *n* chueca, *m.* **h. ball,** bola, pelota de chueca, *f.* **h. stick,** bastón de chueca, *m*

hocus-pocus *n* juego de pasa pasa, *m;* engaño, *m,* treta, *f*

hod *n* cuezo, *m*

hodgepodge See **hotchpotch**

hoe *n* azadón, *m, Chile, Peru* lampa *f. vt* azadonar; sachar

hoeing *n* cavadura con azadón, *f;* sachadura, *f*

hog *n* cerdo, puerco, *Peru* cuchí *m.* **to go the whole hog,** ir al extremo. **hogskin,** piel de cerdo, *f*

hoggish *a* porcuno; (greedy) comilón, tragón; (selfish) egoísta

hoist *n* levantamiento, *m;* (lift) montacargas, *m;* (winch) cabria, *f;* (crane) grúa, *f. vt* levantar, alzar; (flags) enarbolar; suspender; *naut* izar

hoity-toity *a* picajoso, quisquilloso; presuntuoso

hold *n* asimiento, agarro, *m,* presa, *f;* asidero, *m; fig* autoridad, *f,* poder, *m; fig* comprensión, *f;* (of a ship) cala, bodega, *f.* **to loose one's h.,** aflojar su presa. **to lose one's h.,** perder su presa. **to seize h. of,** asirse de, echar mano de. **h.-all,** funda, *f.* **h.-up,** (robbery) atraco, robo a mano armada, *m;* (in traffic) atasco (or obstáculo) en el tráfico, *m;* (in work) parada, cesación (de trabajo), *f*

hold *vt* tener; asir, agarrar; coger; retener; (embrace) abrazar; (a post) ocupar; (a meeting, etc.) celebrar; (bear weight of) aguantar, soportar; (own) poseer; *mil* ocupar, defender; (contain) contener; (have in store) reservar; tener capacidad para; (retain) retener; (believe) creer, sostener; (consider) opinar, tener para (mí, etc.); juzgar; (restrain) detener; contener; (of attention, etc.) mantener; (maneuvers) hacer; (observe) guardar. *vi* resistir, aguantar; (be valid) ser válido; regir; (apply) aplicarse; (last) continuar, seguir. *interj* ¡tente! ¡para! **The room won't h. more,** En este cuarto no caben más. **They h. him in great respect,** Le tienen mucho respeto. **The theory does not h. water,** La teoría es falsa, La teoría no es lógica. **to h. one's own,** defenderse, mantenerse en sus trece. **to h. one's breath,** contener la respiración. **to h. one's tongue,** callarse. **to h. sway,** mandar; reinar. **to h. tightly,** agarrar fuertemente; (clasp) estrechar. **H. the line!** (telephone) ¡Aguarde un momento! **to h. back,** *vt* detener; contener; retener; esconder; abstenerse de entregar. *vi* quedarse atrás; vacilar, dudar; tardar en. **to h. by,** seguir; basarse en, apoyarse en. **to h. down,** sujetar; (oppress) oprimir. **to h. fast,** *vt* sujetar fuertemente. *vi* mantenerse firme; *fig* estar agarrado (a). **to h. forth,** *vt* ofrecer; expresar. *vi* hacer un discurso, perorar. **to h. in,** *vt* contener; retener. *vi* contenerse. **to h. off,** *vt* apartar, alejar. *vi* apartarse, alejarse, mantenerse alejado. **to h. on,** seguir, persistir en; aguantar. **to h. out,** *vt* alargar, extender; ofrecer. *vi* aguantar; durar, resistir. **to h. over,** tener suspendido sobre; (postpone) aplazar; *fig* amenazar con. **to h. to,** agarrarse a; atenerse a. **to h. together,** *vt* unir; juntar. *vi* mantenerse juntos. **to h. up,** *vt* (display) mostrar, enseñar; levantar; sostener, soportar; (rob) atracar, saltear; (delay) atrasar; (stop) interrumpir, parar. *vi* mantenerse en pie; (of weather) seguir bueno. **The train has been held up by fog,** El tren viene con retraso a causa de la niebla

holder *n* el *m,* (*f,* la) que tiene; poseedor (-ra); *com* tenedor (-ra); inquilino (-na); propietario (-ia); (support) soporte, *m;* mango, *m;* asa, *f;* (in compounds) porta . . .

holding *n* tención, *f;* posesión, *f;* propiedad, *f;* (leasing) arrendamiento, *m;* (celebration) solemnización, *f;* (of a meeting) el celebrar, el tener; *pl* **holdings,** *com* valores habidos, *m pl*

holding company *n* compañía de cartera, *f*

hole *n* hoyo, *m, Lat. Am. also* foramen *m;* boquete, *m;* agujero, *m;* cavidad, *f;* (hollow) depresión, *f,* hueco, *m;* orificio, *m;* (tear) roto, desgarro, *m;* (eyelet) punto, *m;* (in cheese) ojo, *m;* (in stocking) rotura, *f,* punto, *m;* (lair) madriguera, *f;* (nest) nido, *m;* (golf) hoyo, *m;* (fix) aprieto, *m. vt* agujerear; excavar; (bore) taladrar; *sport* meter la pelota (en). **to h. out,** (golf) meter la pelota en el hoyo. **h.-and-corner,** *a inf* bajo mano, secreto

hole-puncher *n* agujereadora, *f*

holiday *n* día feriado, *m;* día de fiesta, día festivo, *m;* vacación, *f. a* festivo, alegre; de vacación; de vacaciones; de excursión; (summer) veraniego. **day's h.,** día de asueto, *m.* **to take a h.,** tomar una vacación; hacer fiesta. **h. camp,** colonia veraniega, *f.* **h.-maker,** excursionista, turista, *mf;* (in the summer) veraneante, *mf* **holidays with pay,** vacaciones retribuidas, *f pl*

holiness *n* santidad, *f*

Holland Holanda, *f*

holland *n* lienzo crudo. *a* holandés. **H. gin,** ginebra holandesa, *f*

hollow *a* hueco; cóncavo; (empty) vacío; (of eyes, etc.) hundido; (of sound) sordo; (of a cough) cavernoso; (echoing) retumbante; (*fig* unreal) vacío, falso; insincero. *adv* vacío; *inf* completamente. *n* hueco, *m;* concavidad, *f;* (hole) hoyo, *m;* cavidad, *f;* (valley) hondanada, *f,* barranco, *m;* (groove) ranura, *f;* (depression) depresión, *f;* (in the back) curvadura, *f. vt* excavar, ahuecar; vaciar. **h.-cheeked,** con las mejillas hundidas. **h.-eyed,** con los ojos hundidos, de ojos hundidos

hollowness *n* concavidad, *f;* (falseness) falsedad, *f;* insinceridad, *f*

holly *n* acebo, agrifolio, *m*

holocaust *n* holocausto, *m*

holograph *n* hológrafo, *m*

holster *n* pistolera, *f*

holy *a* santo; sagrado; (blessed) bendito. **most h.,** *a* santísimo. **to make h.,** santificar. **H. Father,** Padre Santo, el Papa, *m.* **H. Ghost,** Espíritu Santo, *m.* **H. Office,** Santo Oficio, *m,* Inquisición, *f.* **H. Orders,** órdenes sagradas, *f pl.* **h. places,** santos lugares, *m pl.* **H. Scripture,** Sagrada Escritura, *f.* **H. See,** Cátedra de San Pedro, *f.* **h. water,** agua bendita, *f.* **H. Souls,** las Ánimas Benditas. **h. water stoup,** acetre, *m.* **H. Week,** Semana Santa, *f*

Holy Land, the la Tierra Santa, *f.*

homage *n* homenaje, *m;* culto, *m;* reverencia, *f.* **to pay h.,** rendir homenaje

home *n* casa, *f;* hogar, *m;* domicilio, *m,* residencia, *f;* (institution) asilo, *m;* (haven) refugio, *m;* (habitation) morada, *f;* (country of origin) país de origen, *m;* (native land) patria, *f;* (environment) ambiente natural, *m; sport* meta, *f. a* casero, doméstico; nativo; nacional, del país; indígena. *adv* a casa, hacia casa; (in one's country) en su patria; (returned) de vuelta; (of the feelings) al corazón, al alma; (to the limit) al límite. **at h.,** en casa; *fig* en su elemento; (of games) en campo propio; de recibo. **at-h. day,** día de recibo, *m.* **He shot the bolt h.,** Echó el cerrojo. **one's long h.,** su última morada. **to be at h.,** estar en casa; estar de recibo. **to be away from h.,** estar fuera de casa; estar ausente. **to bring h.,** traer (or llevar) a casa; hacer ver; convencer; llegar al alma; (a crime) probar (contra). **to go h.,** volver a casa; volver a la patria; (be effective) hacer su efecto; (move) herir en lo más vivo. **to make oneself at h.,** ponerse a sus anchas, sentirse como en casa de uno. **Please make yourself at home!** ¡Ha tomado posesión de su casa! **to strike h.,** dar en el blanco; herir; (hit) golpear; herir en lo más vivo; hacerse sentir. **h. affairs,** asuntos domésticos, *m pl,* (Ministry of) Gobernación, *f.* **h.-bred,** criado en el país. **h.-brewed,** fermentado en el país; fermentado en casa. **h.-coming,** regreso al hogar, *m.* **h. counties,** condados alrededor de Londres, *m pl.* **H. Defense,** defensa nacional, *f.* **h. farm,** residencia del propietario de una finca, *f.* **h. for the aged,** asilo de ancianos, *m.* **h. front,** frente doméstico, *m.* **H. Guard,** milicia nacional, *f.* **h. life,** vida de familia, *f.* **h.-made** casero, de fabricación casera, hecho en casa. **H. Office,** Ministerio de Gobernación, *m.* **H. Rule,** autonomía, *f.* **H. Secretary,** Ministro de Gobernación, *m.* **h. stretch,** último trecho (de una

carrera), *m*. **h. truth,** verdad, *inf* fresca, *f*. **to tell someone a few h. truths,** contarle cuatro verdades
homeless *a* sin casa; sin hogar. **the h.,** los sin techo
homeliness *n* comodidad, *f*; sencillez, *f*; (ugliness) fealdad, *f*
homely *a* doméstico; familiar; (unpretentious) sencillo; llano; (ugly) feo; desabrido
homeopath *n* homeópata, *mf*
homeopathic *a* homeópata
homeopathy *n* homeopatía, *f*
Homeric *a* homérico
homesick *a* nostálgico. **to be h.,** tener morriña
homesickness *n* nostalgia, añoranza, morriña, *f*
homespun *a* tejido en casa; hecho en casa; basto, grueso
homestead *n* hacienda, *f*; casa solariega, *f*; casa, *f*
homeward *adv* hacia casa, en dirección al hogar; de vuelta; hacia la patria. **h.-bound,** en dirección a casa; (of ships) con rumbo al puerto de origen; (of other traffic) de vuelta
homicidal *a* homicida
homicide *n* (act) homicidio, *m*; (person) homicida, *mf*
homily *n ecc* homilía, *f*; sermón, *m*
homing pigeon *n* palomo (-ma) mensajero (-ra)
homogeneity *n* homogeneidad, *f*
homogeneous *a* homogéneo
homologous *a* homólogo
homonym *n* homónimo, *m*
homonymous *a* homónimo
homosexual *a* and *n* homosexual, *mf*
Honduran *a* and *n* hondureño (-ña)
hone *n* piedra de afilar, *f*. *vt* afilar, vaciar
honest *a* honrado; decente, honesto; (chaste) casto; (loyal) sincero, leal; (frank) franco; imparcial. **an h. man,** un hombre de buena fe, un hombre honrado, un hombre decente
honesty *n* honradez, *f*; honestidad, *f*; (chastity) castidad, *f*; sinceridad, *f*; rectitud, imparcialidad, *f*
honey *n* miel, *f*. **h.-bee,** abeja obrera, *f*. **h.-colored,** melado. **h.-pot,** jarro de miel, *m*. **h.-tongued,** melifluo; de pico de oro
honeycomb *n* panal, *m*
honeycombed *a* apanalado
honeydew *n* mielada, *f*; *fig* ambrosia, *f*
honeyed *a* de miel; *fig* meloso, adulador
honeymoon *n* luna de miel, *f*; viaje de novios, viaje nupcial, *m*. *vi* hacer un viaje nupcial
honeysuckle *n* madreselva, *f*
honor *n* honor, *m*; honra, *f*; honradez, rectitud, integridad, *f*; *pl* **honors,** honores, *m pl*; condecoraciones, *f pl*; (last h.) honras, pompas fúnebres, *f pl*. *vt* honrar; (God) glorificar; (decorate) condecorar, laurear; (respect) respetar; reverenciar; *com* aceptar; (a toast) beber. **On my h.,** A fe mía. **point of h.,** punto de honor, pundonor, *m*. **word of h.,** palabra de honor, *f*. **Your H.,** (to a judge) Excelentísimo Señor Juez
honorable *a* honorable; glorioso; digno; ilustre; (sensitive of honor) pundonoroso
honorable mention *n* accésit, *m*
honorableness *n* honradez, *f*
honorably *adv* honorablemente; dignamente
honorarium *n* honorario, *m*
honorary *a* honorario, honorífico. **h. member,** socio (-ia) honorario (-ia). **h. mention,** mención honorífica, *f*
hood *n* capucha, caperuza, *f*; (folding, of vehicles) capota, cubierta, cubierta del motor *f*; (of a carriage) caparazón, fuelle, *m*; (of a car) capó, *m*, (university) muceta, *f*; (of a fireplace) campana (de hogar), *f*; (cowl of chimney) sombrerete (de chimenea), *m*. *vt* cubrir con capucha; cubrir; (the eyes) ocultar, cubrir, velar
hooded *a* con capucha
hoodwink *vt* vendar (los ojos); *fig* engañar, embaucar, burlar
hoof *n* casco, *m*; (cloven) pezuña, *f*
hoofed *a* ungulado
hoof it ir a golpe de calcetín
hook *n* gancho, garfio, *m*; (boat-) bichero, *m*; (fish-) anzuelo, *m*; (on a dress) corchete, *m*; (hanger) colgadero, *m*; (claw) garra, *f*. *vt* enganchar; (a dress) abrochar; (fish) pescar, coger; (nab) atrapar, pescar. **by h. or by crook,** a tuertas o a derechas. **left h.,** (boxing) izquierdo, *m*. **right h.,** (boxing) derecho, *m*. **to catch oneself on a h.,** engancharse. **h. and eye,** los corchetes. **h.-nosed,** con nariz de gancho, con nariz aguileña. **h.-up,** *rad* circuito, *m*; transmisión en circuito, *f*
hooked *a* con ganchos; corvo, ganchoso
hooking *n* enganche, *m*; (of a dress) abrochamiento, *m*; (of fish and *inf*) pesca, *f*
hookworm *n* anquilostoma, *m*
hooligan *n* rufián, *m*
hoop *n* aro, arco, *m*; (of a skirt) miriñaque, *m*; (croquet) argolla, *f*; (toy) aro, *m*; círculo, *m*. *vt* poner aros a; *fig* rodear
hoot *n* (of owls) ululación, *f*, grito, *m*; (whistle) silbido, *m*; ruido, clamor, *m*. *vi* (of owls) ulular, gritar; silbar; *aut* avisar con la bocina. **to h. off the stage,** hacer abandonar la escena. **to h. down,** silbar
hooting *n* See **hoot**
hop *n* salto, brinco, *m*; *bot* lúpulo, *m*; *bot* flores de oblón, *f pl*; (dance) baile, *m*. *vi* saltar con un pie; andar dando brincos; saltar; (limp) cojear; recoger lúpulo; (of plant) dar lúpulo. *vt* saltar. **hop-garden,** huerto de lúpulo, *m*. **hop-kiln,** horno para secar lúpulo, *m*. **hop-picker,** recolector (-ra) de lúpulo. **hop-picking,** recolección de lúpulos, *f*
hope *n* esperanza, *f*; (faith) confianza, *f*; (expectation) anticipación, expectación, *f*; (probability) probabilidad, *f*; (illusion) ilusión, *f*; sueño, *m*. *vi* esperar. **to live in h. that,** vivir con la esperanza de que. **to lose h.,** desesperarse. **to h. against h.,** esperar sin motivo, esperar lo imposible. **to h. for,** desear. **to h. in,** confiar en
hopeful *a* lleno de esperanzas, confiado; optimista; (*fig*) risueño. *n inf* la esperanza de la casa. **to look h.,** *fig* prometer bien
hopefully *adv* con esperanza
hopefulness *n* optimismo, *m*; *fig* aspecto prometedor, *m*
hopeless *a* desesperado, sin esperanza; irremediable; (of situations) imposible; (of disease) incurable. **to be h.,** (lose hope) desesperarse; (have no remedy) ser irremediable; (of disease) no tener cura. **to make h.,** hacer perder la esperanza, desesperar; dejar sin remedio; (a situation) hacer imposible; (an illness) hacer imposible de curar
hopelessly *adv* sin esperanza; sin remedio; imposiblemente; incurablemente
hopelessness *n* desesperación, *f*; (of an illness) imposibilidad de curar, *f*; lo irremediable; imposibilidad, *f*
hopping mad *Lat. Am.* hecho un ají
hopscotch *n* infernáculo, *m*, rayuela, *f*
horal, horary *a* horario
horde *n* horda, *f*
horizon *n* horizonte, *m*
horizontal *a* horizontal. **h. suspension,** (gymnastics) plancha, *f*
horizontality *n* horizontalidad, *f*
horizontally *adv* horizontalmente
hormone *n* hormona, *f*
horn *n* (of bull, etc.) cuerno, *m*; (antler) asta, *f*; (of an insect) antena, *f*; (of a snail) tentáculo, *m*; *mus* cuerno, *m*; trompa, *f*; (of motor and phonograph) bocina, *f*, *Mexico* kláxon *m*; (of moon) cuerno (de la luna), *m*. **article made of h.,** objeto de cuerno, *m*. **on the horns of a dilemma,** entre la espada y la pared. **h. of plenty,** cuerno de abundancia, *m*; cornucopia, *f*. **h.-rimmed spectacles,** anteojos de concha, *m pl*. **h. thrust,** cornada, *f*
horned *a* cornudo; (antlered) enastado
hornet *n* avispón, abejón, *m*
horny *a* córneo; calloso; duro. **h.-handed,** con manos callosas

horoscope *n* horóscopo, *m*
horrible *a* horrible, repugnante, espantoso; (of price) enorme; *inf* horrible
horribleness *n* horribilidad, *f*, horror, *m*, lo espantoso
horribly *adv* horriblemente
horrid *a* horroroso; desagradable
horridness *n* horror, *m*; lo desagradable
horrific *a* horrífico, horrendo
horrify *vt* horrorizar; escandalizar
horrifying *a* horroroso, horripilante
horror *n* horror, *m*. **h.-stricken,** horrorizado
hors d'œuvres *n pl* entremeses, *m pl*
horse *n* caballo, *m*, *Lat. Am.* cuaco *m*; (cavalry) caballería, *f*; (frame) caballete, *m*; (gymnastics and as punishment) potro, *m*. *a* caballar, caballuno. *vt* montar a caballo. **pack of horses,** caballada, *f*. **to ride a h.,** cabalgar, montar a caballo. **H. Artillery,** artillería montada, *f*. **h. blanket,** manta para caballos, *f*; sudadero *m*, *Lat. Am.* mandil *m*. **h.-block,** montador, *m*. **h.-box,** vagón para caballos, *m*. **h.-breaker,** domador de caballos, *m*. **h.-cab,** simón, *m*. **h.-chestnut,** castaña pilonga, *f*. **h.-chestnut flower,** candela, *f*. **h.-collar,** collera, *f*, collerón *m*. **h.-dealer,** chalán, *m*. **h.-doctor,** veterinario, *m*. **h.-flesh,** carne de caballo, *f*. **h.-fly,** tábano, *m*. **H. Guards,** guardias montadas, *f pl*. **h.-latitudes,** calmas de Cáncer, *f pl*. **h.-laugh,** carcajada, *f*. **h.-master,** maestro de equitación, *m*. **h. meat,** carne de caballo, *f*. **h. pistol,** pistola de arzón, *f*. **h.-play,** payasada, *f*. **h.-power,** caballo de vapor, *m*; potencia, *f*. **a twelve-h.p. car,** un coche de doce caballos. **h.-race,** carrera de caballos, *f*. **h.-radish,** rábano picante, raíz amarga, *m*. **h.-sense,** sentido común, *m*, gramática parda, *f*. **h. show,** exposición de caballos, feria equina *f*; concurso de caballos, *m*. **h.-trainer,** entrenador de caballos, *m*. **h. tram,** tranvía de sangre, *m*. **h. trappings,** monturas, *f pl*. **That's a horse of a different color** Es harina de otro costal, *Argentina, Peru* Esas son otras cuarenta
horseback *n* lomo de caballo, *m*. **on h.,** a caballo. **to ride on h.,** ir a caballo
horseman *n* jinete, cabalgador, *m*
horsemanship *n* equitación, *f*, manejo del caballo, *m*
horseshoe *n* herradura, *f*. **h. arch,** arco de herradura, arco morisco, *m*
horsewoman *n* amazona, *f*
horticultural *a* horticultural. **h. show,** exposición de flores, *f*
horticulturalist *n* horticultor (-ra)
horticulture *n* horticultura, *f*
hosanna *n* hosanna, *m*
hose *n* (tube) manga, *f*; (breeches) calzón, *m*; (stockings) medias, *f pl*; (socks) calcetines, *m pl*. **h. man,** manguero, *m*. **h.-pipe,** manga de riego, manguera, *f*
hosier *n* calcetero (-ra)
hosiery *n* calcetería, *f*. **h. trade,** calcetería, *f*
hospice *n* hospicio, *m*; asilo, refugio, *m*
hospitable *a* hospitalario
hospitableness *n* hospitalidad, *f*
hospital *n* hospital, *m*; (school) colegio, *m*. **h. nurse,** enfermera, *f*. **h. ship,** buque hospital, *m*
hospital bed cama hospitalaria, *f*
hospitality *n* hospitalidad, *f*
host *n* huésped, convidador, (of radio or tv program) presentador, *m*; (at an inn) patrón, mesonero, *m*; (army) ejército, *m*; (crowd) multitud, muchedumbre, *f*; *ecc* hostia, *f*; *pl* **hosts,** huestes, *f pl*. **h.-plant,** planta huésped, *f*
hostage *n* rehén, *m*; *fig* prenda, *f*
host country *n* (of an organization) país-sede, *m*
hostel *n* hostería, *f*; club, *m*; residencia de estudiantes, *f*
hostelry *n* hospedería, *f*; parador, mesón, *m*
hostess *n* ama de la casa, *f*; la que recibe a los invitados; la que convída; (of an inn) patrona, mesonera, *f*
hostile *a* enemigo; hostil, contrario (a); (of circumstances, etc.) desfavorable
hostility *n* enemistad, *f*, antagonismo, *m*, mala voluntad, *f*; hostilidad, guerra, *f*. **suspension of hostilities,** suspensión de hostilidades, *f*
hot *a* caliente; (of a day, etc.) caluroso; (piquant) picante; ardiente; vehemente, impetuoso; violento; impaciente; colérico; entusiasta; lleno de deseo; *art* intenso; (great) grande, mucho; (vigorous) enérgico. **You are getting very hot now,** *inf* (in a game, etc.) Te estás quemando. **It is hot,** Está caliente; (of weather) Hace calor. **to grow hot,** calentarse; *fig* acalorarse; (of weather) empezar a hacer calor. **to make hot,** calentar; dar calor (a); *inf* dar vergüenza. **hot-blooded,** de sangre caliente; apasionado; colérico. **hot-foot,** aprisa, apresuradamente. **hot-headed,** impetuoso. **hot-plate,** *elec* calientaplatos, *m*. **hot springs,** termas, *f pl*. **hot-tempered,** colérico, irascible. **hot water,** agua caliente, *f*. **hot-water bottle,** bolsa de goma, *f*. **hot-water pipes,** las cañerías del agua caliente
hotbed *n* semillero, vivero, *m*; *fig* semillero, foco, *m*
hotchpotch *n* potaje, *m*; *fig* mezcolanza, *f*, fárrago, *m*
hotel *n* hotel, *m*. **h.-keeper,** hotelero (-ra)
hothead *n* exaltado (-da), fanático (-ca)
hothouse *n* invernáculo, *m*, estufa, *f*. **h. plant,** *fig* planta de estufa, *f*
hotly *adv* calurosamente; con vehemencia; coléricamente
hough *n zool* pernil, *m*; (in man) corva, *f*
hound *n* perro de caza, sabueso de artois, *m*; perro, *m*; *inf* canalla, *m*. *vt* cazar con perros; *fig* perseguir; *fig* incitar. **master of hounds,** montero, *m*. **pack of hounds,** jauría, *f*
hour *n* hora, *f*; momento, *m*; ocasión, oportunidad, *f pl*. **hours,** horas, *f pl*. **after hours,** fuera de horas. **at the eleventh h.,** en el último minuto. **by the h.,** por horas; horas enteras. **small hours,** altas horas de la noche, *inf* las tantas, *f pl*. **to keep late hours,** acostarse tarde. **to strike the h.,** dar la hora. **h.-glass,** reloj de arena, *m*. **h.-hand,** horario, *m*. **h. of death,** hora suprema, hora de la muerte, *f*
hourly *a* cada hora; por hora; continuo. *adv* a cada hora; de un momento a otro
house *n* casa, *f*; (home) hogar, *m*; (lineage) familia, *f*, abolengo, *m*; (*threat.*) sala, *f*, teatro, *m*; *com* casa comercial, *f*; (takings) entrada, *f*; (audience) público, *m*; (of Lords, Commons) cámara, *f*; (college) colegio, *m*; (parliament) parlamento, *m*; (building) edificio, *m*. *a* de casa; de la casa; doméstico. *vt* dar vivienda (a); alojar, recibir (or tener) en casa de uno; (store) poner, guardar. **The cottage will not h. them all,** No habrá bastante lugar para todos ellos en la cabaña, No cabrán todos en la cabaña. **country-h.,** finca, *f*; casa de campo, *f*. **full h.,** casa llena, *f*; *theat* lleno, *m*. **to bring down the h.,** *theat* hacer venirse el teatro abajo. **to keep h.,** llevar la casa; ser ama de casa. **to keep open h.,** tener mesa puesta, ser hospitalario. **to set up h.,** poner casa. **h. of cards,** castillo de naipes, *m*. **H. of Commons,** Cámara de los Comunes, *f*. **H. of Lords,** Cámara de los Lores, *f*. **h.-agent,** agente de casas, *m*. **h.-boat,** barco-habitación, *m*, casa flotante, *f*. **h.-dog,** perro de guardia, *m*; perro de casa, *m*. **h.-fly,** mosca doméstica, *f*. **h. furnisher,** mueblista, *mf*. **h. painter,** pintor de brocha gorda, *m*. **h. party,** reunión en una casa de campo, *f*. **h.-physician,** médico (-ca) interno (-na). **h. porter,** portero, *m*. **h. property,** propiedad inmueble, *f*. **h.-room,** capacidad de una casa, *f*. **h. slipper,** zapatilla, *f*, pantuflo, *m*. **h.-surgeon,** cirujano interno, *m*. **h.-to-h.,** de casa en casa. **h.-warming,** reunión para colgar la cremallera, *f*
housebreaker *n* ladrón de casas, *m*
housebreaking *n* robo de una casa, *m*
houseful *n* casa, *f*
house furnishings *n pl* artefactos para el hogar, accesorios caseros, aparatos electrodomésticos, *m pl*
household *n* casa, *f*; familia, *f*; hogar, *m*. *a* de la casa; doméstico; del hogar. **to be a h. word,** andar en lenguas. **h. accounts,** cuentas de la casa, *f pl*. **h. duties,**

labores de la casa, *f pl.* **h. gods,** penates, *m pl.* **h. goods,** ajuar, mobiliario, *m.* **h. management,** gobierno de la casa, *m*
householder *n* padre de familia, *m;* dueño (-ña) (or inquilino (-na)) de una casa
house of ill repute *n* burdel, *m,* casa de citas, casa de zorras, casa pública, *f;* lupanar, *m*
housekeeper *n* ama de llaves, *f;* mujer de su casa, *f*
housekeeping *n* gobierno de la casa, *m;* economía doméstica, *f. a* doméstico. **to set up h.,** poner casa
housemaid *n* camarera, sirvienta, *f.* **housemaid's knee,** rodilla de fregona, *f*
housemaker *n* ama de casa, *f*
housetops *n* tejado, *m;* (flat roof) azotea, *f.* **to shout from the h.,** pregonar a los cuatro vientos
housewife *n* madre de familia, mujer de su casa, *f;* (sewing-bag) neceser de costura, *m*
housewifely *a* propio de una mujer de su casa; doméstico; (of a woman) hacendosa
housing *n* provisión de vivienda, *f;* (storage) almacenaje, *m;* alojamiento, *m; inf* casa, vivienda, *f.* **h. scheme,** urbanización, *f.* **h. shortage,** crisis de vivienda, *f,* déficit habitacional, *m*
hovel *n* casucha, *f*
hover *vi* revolotear; (of hawks, etc.) cernerse; estar suspendido; rondar; seguir de cerca, estar al lado (de); *fig* vacilar, dudar
hovering *n* revoloteo, *m;* (of birds of prey) calada, *f; fig* vacilación, *f. a* revolante, que revolotea; que se cierne (sobre); (menacing) que amenaza, inminente
how *adv* cómo; (by what means, in what manner) de qué modo; (at what price) a qué precio; qué; cuánto. *n* el cómo. **to know how,** saber. **For how long?** ¿Por cuánto tiempo? **How are you?** ¿Cómo está Vd.? *inf* ¿Qué tal? **How do you do!** ¡Mucho gusto (en conocerlo/conocerla/conocerlos/conocerlas)! **How old are you?** ¿Qué edad tiene Vd.? **How beautiful!** ¡Qué hermoso! **How big!** ¡Cuán grande! **How early?** ¿Cuán temprano?; ¿Cuándo a más tardar? **How far?** ¿A qué distancia? ¿Hasta qué punto? ¿Hasta dónde? **How fast?** ¿A qué velocidad? **How few!** ¡Qué pocos! **How little!** ¡Qué pequeño!; ¡Qué poco! **How long?** ¿Cuánto tiempo? **How many?** ¿Cuántos? *m pl;* ¿Cuántas? *f pl.* **How much is it?** ¿Cuánto vale? **How much cloth do you want?** ¿Cuánta tela quieres? **How often?** ¿Cuán a menudo? ¿Cuántas veces? **How would you like to go for a walk?** ¿Te gustaría pasearte? **How are you going to Lisbon?** ¿En qué vas a Lisboa?
however *adv* como quiera (que) (followed by subjunctive); por más que (followed by subjunctive); por . . . que (followed by subjunctive). *conjunc* (nevertheless) sin embargo, no obstante. **h. good it is,** por bueno que sea. **h. he does it,** como quiera que lo haga. **h. it may be,** sea como sea. **h. much,** por mucho que
howl *n* aullido, *m;* (groan) gemido, *m;* (cry) grito, *m;* (roar) rugido, bramido, *m;* lamento, *m. vi* aullar; gemir; gritar; rugir, bramar. *vt* chillar. **Each time he opened his mouth he was howled down,** Cada vez que abrió la boca se armó una bronca
howler *n* aullador (-ra); *zool* mono (-na) chillón (-ona); (blunder) coladura, plancha, *f.* **h. monkey** *Lat. Am.* araguato *m*
howling *a* aullante; gemidor; (crying) que llora; bramante, rugiente. *n* los aullidos; (groaning) el gemir, los gemidos; (crying) los gritos; (weeping) el lloro; (roaring) los bramidos, el rugir; los lamentos
hub *n* (of a wheel) cubo (de rueda) *m; fig* centro, *m.* **hub cap,** tapa de cubo, *f*
hubbub *n* algarada, barahúnda, *f*
huckster *n* revendedor (-ra). *vi* revender; (haggle) regatear
huddle *n* (heap) montón, *m;* colección, *f;* (group) corrillo, grupo, *m;* (mixture) mezcla, *f. vt* arrebujar, amontonar; acurrucar, arrebujar; (throw on) echarse. *vi* amontonarse; apiñarse; acurrucarse, arrebujarse
hue *n* color, *m;* matiz, tono, *m;* (of opinion) matiz, *m;* (clamor) clamor, *m,* gritería, *f.* **hue and cry,** alarma, *f*
huff *n* acceso de cólera, *m*
huffily *adv* malhumoradamente; petulantemente
huffiness *n* mal humor, *m;* petulancia, *f;* arrogancia, *f*
hug *n* abrazo, *m. vt* abrazar, apretujar; *fig* acariciar; *naut* navegar muy cerca de. **to hug oneself,** *fig* congratularse
huge *a* enorme, inmenso; gigante; vasto
hugely *adv* inmensamente, enormemente
hugeness *n* inmensidad, enormidad, *f;* vastedad, *f*
Huguenot *a* and *n* hugonote (-ta)
hulk *n* barco viejo, *m;* pontón, *m*
hulking *a* pesado, desgarbado
hull *n naut* casco (de un buque), *m;* (shell) cáscara, *f;* (pod) vaina, *f, vt* mondar
hullabaloo *n* alboroto, tumulto, *m;* vocerío, *m*
hullo *interj* See **hallo**
hum *n* zumbido, *m;* ruido confuso, *m. vi* (sing) canturrear; zumbar; (confused sound) zurrir; (hesitate) vacilar. *vt* (a tune) tararear
human *a* humano. **the h. touch,** el don de gentes. **h. being,** ser humano, hombre, *m*
humane *a* humanitario, humano
humanely *adv* humanitariamente
humaneness *n* humanidad, *f*
humanism *n* humanismo, *m*
humanist *n* humanista, *mf*
humanistic *a* humanista
humanitarian *a* humanitario
humanitarianism *n* humanitarismo, *m*
humanity *n* humanidad, *f;* raza humana, *f.* **the humanities,** las humanidades
humanize *vt* humanizar; (milk) maternizar. *vi* humanizarse
humanly *adv* humanamente
humble *a* humilde; modesto; (cringing) servil; sumiso; pobre. *vt* humillar; mortificar. **to h. oneself,** humillarse
humbleness *n* humildad, *f;* modestia, *f;* (abjectness) servilismo, *m;* sumisión, *f;* pobreza, *f;* (of birth, etc.) obscuridad, *f*
humbling *n* humillación, *f;* mortificación, *f*
humbly *adv* humildemente; modestamente; servilmente
humbug *n* (fraud) embuste, engaño, *m;* (nonsense) disparate, *m,* tontería, *f;* mentira, *f;* (person) farsante, charlatán, *m;* (sweetmeat) caramelo de menta, *m. vt* engañar, embaucar; burlarse de
humdrum *a* monótono; aburrido
humeral *a* humeral. *n ecc* velo humeral, *m*
humerus *n anat* húmero, *m*
humid *a* húmedo
humidity *n* humedad, *f*
humiliate *vt* humillar, mortificar. **to h. oneself,** humillarse
humiliating *a* humillante; degradante
humiliation *n* humillación, mortificación, *f;* degradación, *f*
humility *n* humildad, *f;* modestia, *f*
humming *n* zumbido, *m;* (of a tune) tarareo, *m. a* zumbador. **h.-bird,** pájaro mosca, colibrí, *m.* **h.-top,** trompa, *f*
humoresque *n mus* capricho musical, *m*
humorist *n* humorista, *mf*
humorous *a* humorístico; cómico, risible
humorously *adv* humorísticamente; cómicamente
humorousness *n* humorismo, *m;* lo cómico
humor *n* humor, *m;* humorismo, *m;* (temperament) disposición, *f,* carácter, *m;* (whim) capricho, *m. vt* seguir el humor (a), complacer; satisfacer, consentir en; (a lock, etc.) manejar. **in a good (bad) h.,** de buen (mal) humor. **I am not in the h. to . . .** No estoy de humor para . . . **sense of h.,** sentido de humor, *m*
humored *a* (in compounds) de humor . . . **good-h.,** de buen humor. **ill-h.,** malhumorado, de mal humor

humorless *a* sin sentido humorístico, sin sentido de humor
hump *n* joroba, giba, *f;* (hillock) montecillo, *m; inf* depresión, *f*
humpback *n* giba, joroba, *f;* (person) jorobado (-da), giboso (-sa)
humpbacked *a* jorobado, giboso, corcovado
humph *interj* ¡qué va!; ¡patrañas!
humus *n* humus, mantillo, *m*
hunch *n*: **I have a hunch that . . .** *Mexico* Me late que . . .
hunchback *n* joroba, giba, *f;* (person) jorobado (-da), corcovado (-da), giboso (-sa)
hunchbacked *a* jorobado, giboso, corcovado
hundred *n* ciento, *m;* centenar, *m,* centena, *f. a* ciento; (before nouns and adjectives, excluding numerals, with the exception of mil and millón) cien. **a h. thousand,** cien mil. **one h. and one,** ciento uno. **by the h.,** a centenares. **hundreds of people,** centenares de personas, *m pl.* **h.-millionth,** *a* and *n* cienmillonésimo *m.* **h.-thousandth,** *a* and *n* cienmilésimo *m.*
hundredfold *adv* cien veces. *n* céntuplo, *m*
hundredth *a* centésimo, céntimo. *n* centésimo, *m,* centésima parte, *f*
Hungary Hungría, *f*
Hungarian *a* and *n* húngaro (-ra); (language) húngaro, *m*
hunger *n* hambre, *f;* apetito, *m;* (craving) deseo, *m,* ansia, *f. vi* estar hambriento, tener hambre. **to h. for,** desear, ansiar. **h.-strike,** huelga de hambre, *f*
hungrily *adv* hambrientamente, con hambre; ansiosamente
hungry *a* hambriento; (of land) pobre; (anxious) deseoso. **to be h.,** tener hambre. **to make h.,** dar hambre
hunk *n* rebanada, *f,* pedazo, *m*
hunt *n* caza, cacería, montería, *f;* grupo de cazadores, *m;* (search) busca, *f;* (pursuit) persecución, *f. vt* cazar; cazar a caballo; (search) buscar; rebuscar, explorar; (pursue) perseguir. **to h. down,** perseguir. **to h. for,** buscar. **to h. out,** buscar; descubrir, desenterrar
hunter *n* cazador, *m;* caballo de caza, *m;* (watch) saboneta, *f*
hunting *n* caza, *f;* caza a caballo, *f;* persecución, *f. a* cazador, de caza. **to go h.,** ir a cazar. **h.-box,** pabellón de caza, *m.* **h.-cap,** gorra de montar, *f.* **h.-crop,** látigo para cazar, *m.* **h.-ground,** coto de caza, terreno de caza, *m.* **h.-horn,** cuerno de caza, *m,* corneta de monte, *f.* **h. party,** partido de caza, *m,* cacería, *f*
huntsman *n* cazador, montero, *m*
huntsmanship *n* montería, arte de cazar, *f*
hurdle *n* valla, *f;* zarzo, *m.* **h.-race,** carrera de obstáculos, *f;* carrera de vallas, *f*
hurdy-gurdy *n* organillo, *m*
hurl *vt* lanzar, tirar, arrojar, echar. **to h. oneself,** lanzarse. **to h. oneself against,** arrojarse a (or contra). **to h. oneself upon,** abalanzarse sobre
hurly-burly *n* alboroto, tumulto, *m*
hurrah *interj* ¡hurra! ¡viva! *n* vítor, *m.* **H. for . . . !** ¡Viva . . . !, ¡Vivan . . . ! **to shout h.,** vitorear
hurricane *n* huracán, *m.* **h.-lamp,** lámpara sorda, *f*
hurried *a* apresurado, precipitado; hecho a prisa; superficial
hurriedly *adv* apresuradamente, precipitadamente, con prisa; superficialmente; (of writing) a vuela pluma
hurry *n* prisa, *f;* precipitación, *f;* urgencia, *f;* confusión, *f;* alboroto, *m.* **in a h.,** aprisa. **in a great h.,** aprisa y corriendo. **to be in a h.,** llevar prisa, estar de prisa. **There is no h.,** No corre prisa, No hay prisa
hurry *vt* apresurar, dar prisa, *Lat. Am.* apurar (a); llevar aprisa; hacer andar aprisa; enviar apresuradamente; precipitar; acelerar. *vi* darse prisa; apresurarse. **to h. after,** correr detrás de, seguir apresuradamente. **to h. away,** *vi* marcharse aprisa, marcharse corriendo; huir; salir precipitadamente. *vt* hacer marcharse aprisa; llevar con prisa. **to h. back,** *vi* volver aprisa, apresurarse a volver. *vt* hacer volver aprisa. **to h. in,** *vi* entrar aprisa, entrar corriendo. *vt* hacer entrar aprisa. **to h. off.** See **to h. away. to h. on,** *vi* apresurarse. *vt* apresurar, precipitar. **to h. out,** salir rápidamente. **to h. over,** hacer rápidamente; concluir aprisa; despachar rápidamente; (travel over) atravesar aprisa; pasar rápidamente por. **to h. toward,** llevar rápidamente hacia; arrastrar hacia; impeler hacia. **to h. up,** *vi* darse prisa. *vt* apresurar, precipitar, *Lat. Am.* apurar; estimular
hurt *n* herida, *f;* (harm) daño, mal, *m;* perjuicio, *m. vt* (wound) herir; (cause pain) doler; hacer daño (a); hacer mal (a); (damage) perjudicar, estropear, *Lat. Am.* afectar; (offend) ofender; (the feelings) mortificar, lastimar, herir. *vi* doler; hacer mal; perjudicarse, estropearse. **I haven't h. myself,** No me he hecho daño. **Does it still h. you?** ¿Te duele todavía? **to h. deeply,** *fig* herir en el alma. **to h. a person's feelings,** herirle (a uno) el amor propio, lastimar, ofender
hurtful *a* nocivo, dañino; injurioso, pernicioso
hurtfulness *n* nocividad, *f;* perniciosidad, *f*
hurtle *vt* lanzar. *vi* lanzarse; volar; caer
husband *n* esposo, marido, *m. vt* economizar, ahorrar. **h. and wife,** los esposos, los cónyuges
husbandry *n* labor de los campos, agricultura, *f;* (thrift) frugalidad, parsimonia, *f*
hush *n* silencio, *m,* tranquilidad, *f. interj* ¡chitón! ¡calla! ¡silencio! *vt* silenciar, hacer callar, imponer silencio (a); (a baby) adormecer; *fig* sosegar, calmar. *vi* callarse, enmudecer. **to h. up,** mantener secreto, ocultar. **h.-h.,** secreto. **h. money,** so-borno, chantaje, *m*
hushaby *interj* ¡duerme!
husk *n* (of grain) cascabillo, *m;* zurrón, *m;* cáscara, *f;* (of chestnut) erizo, *m; vt Lat. Am.* deshojar (corn)
huskily *adv* roncamente
huskiness *n* ronquera, *f; inf* robustez, *f*
husky *a* (of voice) ronco; *bot* cascarudo; (Eskimo) esquimal; *inf* robusto, fuerte. *n* perro esquimal, *m*
hussy *n* pícara, bribona, *f*
hustle *vt* empujar, codear; *fig* precipitar; *inf* acelerar. *vi* codearse; andarse de prisa
hut *n* choza, cabaña, barraca, *f, Mexico* jacal, *elsewhere in Lat. Am.* bohío *m*
hutch *n* (chest) arca, *f,* cofre, *m;* (cage) jaula, *f;* (for rabbits) conejera, *f;* (for rats) ratonera, *f; inf* choza, *f*
hutment *n* campamento de chozas, *m*
hyacinth *n* jacinto, *m*
hybrid *a* híbrido; mestizo, mixto. *n* híbrido, *m*
hybridism *n* hibridismo, *m*
hybridization *n* hibridación, *f*
hybridize *vt* cruzar. *vi* producir (or generar) híbridos
hydrangea *n bot* hortensia, *f*
hydrant *n* boca de riego, *f*
hydrate *n chem* hidrato, *m. vt* hidratar
hydraulic *a* hidráulico. **h. engineering,** hidrotecnia, *f*
hydraulics *n* hidráulica, *f*
hydrocarbon *n chem* hidrocarburo, *m*
hydrochloric *a* clorhídrico. **h. acid,** ácido clorhídrico, *m*
hydrogen *n* hidrógeno, *m.* **h. peroxide,** agua oxigenada, *f*
hydrogenation *n* hidrogenación, *f*
hydrogenize *vt* hidrogenizar
hydrolysis *n* hidrólisis, *f*
hydromel *n* aguamiel, *f,* hidromel, *m*
hydropathic *a* hidropático. **h. establishment,** balneario, *m*
hydrophobia *n* hidrofobia, rabia, *f*
hydrophobic *a* hidrofóbico, rabioso
hydroplane *n* hidroplano, *m*
hydrotherapic *a* hidroterápico
hydrotherapy *n* hidroterapia, *f*
hyena *n* hiena, *f*
hygiene *n* higiene, *f.* **personal h.,** higiene privada, *f*
hygienic *a* higiénico

hymen *n anat* himen, *m*; himeneo, *m*
hymeneal *a* nupcial
hymn *n* himno, *m*. **h.-book,** himnario, *m*
hyperbole *n* hipérbole, *f*
hyperbolical *a* hiperbólico
hypercorrection *n* seudocultismo, supercultismo, *m*, ultracorrección, *f*
hypercritic *n* hipercrítico, *m*
hypercritical *a* hipercrítico, criticón
hypersensitive *a* vidrioso, quisquilloso
hypertrophy *n* hipertrofia, *f*. *vi* hipertrofiarse
hyphen *n* guión, *m*
hypnosis *n* hipnosis, *f*
hypnotic *a* hipnótico. *n* (person) hipnótico (-ca); (drug) hipnótico, narcótico, *m*
hypnotism *n* hipnotismo, *m*
hypnotist *n* hipnotizador (-ra)
hypnotization *n* hipnotización, *f*
hypnotize *vt* hipnotizar
hypo *n* (sodium hyposulphite) hiposulfito sólido, *m*
hypochondria *n* hipocondría, *f*
hypochondriac *n* hipocondríaco (-ca)
hypochondriacal *a* hipocondríaco
hypocrisy *n* hipocresía, *f*; mojigatería, gazmoñería, *f*
hypocrite *n* hipócrita, *mf*; mojigato (-ta). **to be a h.,** ser hipócrita
hypocritical *a* hipócrita; mojigato, gazmoño
hypocritically *adv* hipócritamente, con hipocresía
hypodermic *a* hipodérmico. **h. syringe,** jeringa de inyecciones, *f*
hypotenuse *n geom* hipotenusa, *f*
hypothesis *n* hipótesis, *f*
hypothetical *a* hipotético
hysterectomy *n surg* histerectomía, *f*
hysteria *n med* histerismo, *m*; histeria, *f*, ataque de nervios, *m*
hysterical *a* histérico. **to become h.,** tener un ataque de nervios. **hysterics,** *n pl* ataque de nervios, *m*

I

i *n* (letter) i. *1st pers pron* yo. **It is I,** Soy yo. Normally omitted, the verb alone being used except when **yo** is needed for emphasis, e.g. **Hablo a María,** I speak to Mary, *but* **Yo toco el violín, pero Juan toca el piano,** *I* play the violin, but *John* plays the piano
Iago Yago, *m*
Iberian Peninsula, the la Peninsula Ibérica
Iberian *a* ibero, ibérico. *n* ibero (-ra)
ibex *n zool* íbice, *m*
ice *n* hielo, *m*; (ice cream) helado, *m*. *vt* helar; cubrir de hielo; congelar, cuajar; (a cake, etc.) garapiñar, escarchar, alcorzar. **to ice up,** (*aer, aut*) helarse. **to be as cold as ice,** *inf* estar hecho un hielo. **His words cut no ice,** Sus palabras ni pinchan ni cortan. **ice-age,** edad del hielo, *f*. **ice-ax,** piolet, *m*. **ice-box,** nevera, *f*. **ice-cream,** helado, mantecado, *m*. **ice-cream cone,** cucurucho de helado, *m*. **ice-cream freezer,** heladora, *f*. **ice-cream vendor,** mantequero (-ra). **ice-field,** campo de hielo, *m*. **ice-floe,** témpano de hielo flotante, *m*. **ice hockey,** hockey sobre patines, *m*. **ice-pack,** bolsa para hielo, *f*. **ice-skates,** patines de cuchilla, *m pl*. **ice water,** agua helada, *f*
iceberg *n* iceberg, témpano de hielo, banco de hielo, *m*
icebound *a* aprisionado por el hielo; atascado en el hielo; (of roads, etc.) helado
iced *a* helado; congelado, cuajado; (cakes) garapiñado, escarchado; (of drinks) con hielo. **i. drink,** sorbete, *m*
Iceland Islandia, *f*
Icelander *n* islandés (-esa)
icelandic *a* islandes, islándico. *n* (language) islandés, *m*
icicle *n* carámbano, canelón, cerrión, *m*
icily *adv* fríamente; *fig* frígidamente, con indiferencia, con frialdad
iciness *n* frialdad, frigidez, *f*; *fig* indiferencia, frigidez, *f*
icing *n* helada, *f*, hielo, *m*; (on a cake, etc.) alcorza, capa de azúcar, *f*
icon *n* icono, *m*
iconoclast *n* iconoclasta, *mf*
iconoclastic *a* iconoclasta
iconography *n* iconografía, *f*
iconology *n* iconología, *f*
icy *a* helado; glacial, frío; *med* álgido; *fig* indiferente, desabrido; *poet* frígido, gélido
idea *n* idea, *f*, concepto, *m*; (opinion) juicio, *m*, opinión, *f*; (notion) impresión, noción, *f*; (plan) proyecto, plan, designio, *m*. **to form an i. of,** hacerse una idea de, formar un concepto de. **to have an i. of,** tener una idea de; tener nociones de. **An i. struck me,** Se me ocurrió una idea. **full of ideas,** preñado (or lleno) de ideas. **I had no i. that . . .** No tenía la menor idea de que . . . No sabía que . . . **What an i.!** ¡Qué idea!
ideal *a* ideal; excelente, perfecto; (utopian) utópico; (imaginary) imaginario, irreal, ficticio. *n* ideal, *m*; modelo, prototipo, *m*
idealism *n* idealismo, *m*
idealist *n* idealista, *mf*
idealistic *a* idealista
idealization *n* idealización, *f*
idealize *vt* idealizar
ideally *adv* idealmente
ideation *n phil* ideación, *f*
idem *adv* ídem
identical *a* idéntico, mismo, igual; muy parecido, semejante
identically *adv* idénticamente
identifiable *a* identificable
identification *n* identificación, *f*. **i. number,** placa de identidad, *f*
identify *vt* identificar. **to i. oneself with,** identificarse con
identity *n* identidad, *f*. **i. card,** cédula personal, *f*; carnet de identidad, *m*. **i. disc,** disco de identidad, *m*
ideogram, ideograph *n* ideograma, *m*
ideography *n* ideografía, *f*
ideological *a* ideológico
ideologist *n* ideólogo (-ga)
ideology *n* ideología, *f*
Ides *n pl* idus, *m pl*
idiocy *n* idiotez, imbecilidad, *f*; (foolishness) necedad, tontería, sandez, *f*
idiom *n* idiotismo, *m*; modismo, *m*, locución, *f*; (language) habla, *f*; lenguaje, *m*
idiomatic *a* idiomático
idiopathy *n med* idiopatía, *f*
idiosyncrasy *n* idiosincrasia, *f*
idiosyncratic *a* idiosincrásico
idiot *n* idiota, imbécil, *mf*; (fool) necio (-ia), tonto (-ta), mentecato (-ta)
idiotic *a* idiota, imbécil; (foolish) necio, tonto, sandío
idle *a* desocupado; indolente, ocioso; (unemployed) cesante, sin empleo; (lazy) perezoso, holgazán; (of machines) parado, inactivo; (useless) vano, inútil, sin efecto; (false) falso, mentiroso, infundado; (stupid) fútil, frívolo. *vi* holgar, estar ocioso; holgazanear, haraganear, gandulear. **to i. away,** malgastar, perder. **to i. away the time,** pasar el rato, matar el tiempo. **i. efforts,** vanos esfuerzos, *m pl*. **i. fancies,** ilusiones, fantasías, *f pl*, sueños, *m pl*. **i. hours,** horas desocupadas, *f pl*, ratos perdidos, *m pl*. **i. question,** pregunta ociosa, *f*. **i. tale,** cuento de viejas, *m*. **i. threat,** reto vacuo, *m*
idleness *n* ociosidad, indolencia, inacción, *f*; pereza, holgazanería, gandulería, *f*; (uselessness) inutilidad, futilidad, *f*

idler *n* ocioso (-sa); haragán (-ana); perezoso (-sa), holgazán (-ana), gandul (-la), *Lat. Am.* aplanacalles *mf*
idly *adv* ociosamente, perezosamente; (uselessly) vanamente
idol *n* ídolo, *m.* **a popular i.,** el ídolo de las masas, *m*
idolater *n* idólatra, *mf;* (admirer) amante, *mf* esclavo (-va), admirador (-ra)
idolatrous *a* idólatra, idolátrico
idolatrously *adv* idolatradamente, con idolatría
idolatry *n* idolatría, *f;* (devotion) adoración, pasión, *f*
idolization *n* idolatría, *f*
idolize *vt* idolatrar, adorar
idyll *n* idilio, *m*
idyllic *a* idílico
if *conjunc* si; (even if) aunque, aun cuando; (whenever) cuando, en caso de que; (whether) si. **as if,** como si (foll. by subjunc.). **If he comes, we shall tell him,** Si viene se lo diremos. **If he had not killed the tiger, she would be dead,** Si él no hubiera matado al tigre, ella estaría muerta. **If ever there was one,** Si alguna vez lo hubiera. **if necessary,** si fuese necesario. **if not,** si no, si no es que (e.g., **Poet and philosopher are twins, if not one and the same,** Poeta y filósofo son hermanos gemelos, si no es que la misma cosa). **If only!** ¡Ojalá que! (foll. by subjunc.)
igloo *n* iglú, *m*
igneous *a* ígneo
ignite *vt* encender, pegar fuego (a), incendiar. *vi* prender fuego, incendiarse; arder
ignition *n* ignición, *f; aut* encendido, *m.* **i. coil,** *aut* carrete de inducción del encendido, *m.* **i. key,** *aut* llave del contacto, *f*
ignoble *a* innoble, vil, indigno
ignobly *adv* bajamente, vilmente
ignominious *a* ignominioso
ignominiously *adv* ignominiosamente
ignominy *n* ignominia, deshonra, afrenta, *f*
ignoramus *n* ignorante, *mf*
ignorance *n* ignorancia, *f;* (unawareness) desconocimiento, *m.* **to plead i.,** pretender ignorancia
ignorant *a* ignorante; inculto. **He is an i. fellow,** Es un ignorante. **to be i. of,** no saber, ignorar. **to be very i.,** ser muy ignorante, *inf* ser muy burro
ignorantly *adv* ignorantemente, por ignorancia; neciamente
ignore *vt* no hacer caso de, desatender; (omit) pasar por alto de; *law* rechazar; (pretend not to recognize) hacer semblante de no reconocer; (not recognize) no reconocer
iguana *n zool* iguana, *f*
ileac *a anat* ilíaco
ileum *n anat* íleon, *m*
Iliad *n* Ilíada, *f*
ilium *n anat* ilion, *m*
ill *n* mal, *m. a* (sick) enfermo, malo; (bad) malo; (unfortunate) desdichado, funesto. *adv* mal. **to be ill,** estar malo. **to be taken ill,** caer enfermo. **ill-advised,** mal aconsejado; desacertado, imprudente. **ill-advisedly,** imprudentemente. **ill at ease,** incómodo. **ill-bred,** mal criado, mal educado, mal nacido. **ill-breeding,** mala crianza, mala educación, *f.* **ill-disposed,** malintencionado. **ill fame,** mala fama, *f.* **ill-fated,** malhadado, malaventurado, aciago, fatal. **ill-favored,** mal parecido, feúcho. **ill-feeling,** hostilidad, *f,* rencor, *m.* **ill-gotten,** maladquirido. **ill-humor,** mal humor, *m.* **ill-humored,** de mal humor, malhumorado. **ill-luck,** desdicha, mala suerte, malaventura, *f;* infortunio, *m.* **ill-mannered,** mal educado. **ill-natured,** malévolo, perverso. **ill-naturedly,** malignamente. **ill-omened,** nefasto. **ill-spent,** malgastado, perdido. **ill-spoken,** mal hablado. **ill-suited,** malavenido. **ill-timed,** inoportuno, intempestivo. **ill-treat,** maltratar, malparar, tratar mal. **ill-treated,** que ha sido tratado mal; maltrecho. **ill-treatment,** maltratamiento, *m,* crueldad, *f.* **ill-turn,** mala jugada, *f.* **to do an ill-turn,** hacer un flaco servicio. **ill will,** mala voluntad, *f;* rencor, *m,* ojeriza, *f.* **to bear a person ill will,** guardarle rencor
illegal *a* ilegal; indebido, ilícito
illegality *n* ilegalidad, *f*
illegally *adv* ilegalmente
illegibility *n* ilegibilidad, *f*
illegible *a* ilegible, indescrifrable
illegibly *adv* de un modo ilegible
illegitimacy *n* ilegitimidad, *f;* falsedad, *f*
illegitimate *a* ilegítimo, bastardo; falso; ilícito, desautorizado
illegitimately *adv* ilegítimamente
illiberal *a* iliberal; intolerante, estrecho de miras; (mean) avaro, tacaño, ruin
illiberality *n* iliberalidad, *f;* intolerancia, *f;* (avarice) tacañería, avaricia, ruindad, *f*
illiberally *adv* avariciosamente, ruinmente
illicit *a* ilícito, indebido, ilegal
illicitly *adv* ilícitamente, ilegalmente
illicitness *n* ilicitud, ilegalidad, *f*
illimitable *a* ilimitado, sin límites, infinito
illiteracy *n* analfabetismo, *m*
illiterate *a* and *n* analfabeto (-ta), iliterato (-ta)
illness *n* enfermedad, dolencia, *f,* mal, *m*
illogical *a* ilógico; absurdo, irracional
illogicality *n* falta de lógica, *f;* absurdo, *m,* irracionalidad, *f*
illuminant *a* iluminador, alumbrador
illuminate *vt* iluminar, alumbrar; *art* iluminar; (explain) aclarar, ilustrar
illuminated *a* iluminado, encendido; *art* iluminado. **i. sign,** letrero luminoso, *m*
illuminati *n pl* secta de los alumbrados, *f*
illuminating *a* iluminador; (explanatory) aclaratorio. *n art* iluminación, *f*
illumination *n* iluminación, *f,* alumbrado, *m;* (for decoration) luminaria, *f; art* iluminación, *f; fig* inspiración, *f*
illuminator *n art* iluminador (-ra)
illumine *vt* encender, alumbrar; *fig* inspirar
illusion *n* ilusión, *f,* engaño, *m;* (dream) esperanza, ilusión, *f,* ensueño, *m.* **to harbor illusions,** tener ilusiones
illusive *a* ilusivo, engañoso, falso
illusively *adv* falsamente, aparentemente
illusoriness *n* ilusión, falsedad, *f,* engaño, *m*
illusory *a* ilusorio, deceptivo, falso, irreal
illustrate *vt* ilustrar, aclarar, explicar, elucidar; *art* ilustrar; (prove) probar, demostrar
illustration *n* ejemplo, *m;* ilustración, *f; art* grabado, *m;* estampa, *f;* (explanation) elucidación, aclaración, *f*
illustrative *a* ilustrativo, ilustrador, explicativo, aclaratorio
illustrator *n* ilustrador (-ra), grabador (-ra)
illustrious *a* ilustre, famoso, renombrado, distinguido
illustriously *adv* ilustremente, noblemente
illustriousness *n* eminencia, *f,* renombre, *m,* grandeza, *f*
image *n* (optics) imagen, *f;* efigie, imagen, *f;* (religious) imagen, estatua, *f; art* figura, *f;* (metaphor) metáfora, expresión, *f;* (of a person) retrato, *m.* **to be the i. of,** ser el retrato de. **sharp i.,** imagen nítida, *f.* **i. breaker,** iconoclasta, *mf.* **i. vendor,** vendedor (-ra) de imágenes
imagery *n art* imaginería, *f;* (style) metáforas, *f pl*
imaginable *a* imaginable
imaginary *a* imaginario; fantástico, de ensueño
imagination *n* imaginación, *f;* imaginativa, fantasía, inventiva, *f,* ingenio, *m*
imaginative *a* imaginativo; fantástico
imagine *vt* imaginar, concebir; idear, proyectar, inventar; figurarse, suponer. **Just i.!** ¡Imagínese usted!
imam *n* imán, *m*
imbecile *a* imbécil; (foolish) necio, estúpido, tonto. *n* imbécil, *mf;* (fool) necio (-ia), tonto (-ta), estúpido (-da)
imbecility *n* imbecilidad, *f;* (folly) necedad, sandez, *f*

imbibe *vt* embeber, absorber; (drink) sorber, chupar; empaparse de
imbibing *n* imbibición, absorción, *f*
imbricate *a* (*zool, bot*) imbricado
imbroglio *n* embrollo, lío, *m*
imbue *vt* imbuir, calar, empapar; teñir. **to i. with,** infundir de
imitable *a* imitable
imitate *vt* imitar; copiar, reproducir; (counterfeit) contrahacer
imitation *n* imitación, *f*; copia, *f*; remedo, traslado, *m*. *a* imitado; falso, artificial
imitative *a* imitativo; imitador
imitativeness *n* facultad imitativa (or de imitacion), *f*
imitator *n* imitador (-ra); contrahacedor (-ra), falsificador (-ra)
immaculate *a* inmaculado, puro; (of dress) elegante. **I. Conception,** la Purísima Concepción
immaculately *adv* inmaculadamente; elegantemente
immaculateness *n* pureza, *f*; (of dress) elegancia, *f*
immanence *n* inmanencia, inherencia, *f*
immanent *a* inmanente; inherente
immaterial *a* inmaterial, incorpóreo; sin importancia. **It is i. to me,** Me es indiferente, No me importa, Me da lo mismo, Me da igual
immateriality *n* inmaterialidad, *f*
immature *a* inmaturo; precoz; (of fruit) verde
immaturity *n* falta de madurez, *f*; precocidad, *f*
immeasurability *n* inmensurabilidad, inmensidad, *f*
immeasurable *a* inmensurable, inmenso, imponderable
immeasurably *adv* inmensamente, enormemente
immediate *a* (of place) inmediato, cercano, contiguo; (of time) próximo, inmediato, directo; (of action) inmediato, perentorio; (on letters) urgente. **to take i. action,** tomar acción inmediata
immediately *adv* (of place) próximamente, contiguamente; (of time) luego, seguidamente, en el acto, ahora mismo, enseguida; directamente; (as soon as) así que
immemorial *a* inmemorial, inmemorable
immemorially *adv* desde tiempo inmemorial
immense *a* inmenso, enorme; vasto, extenso; infinito
immensely *adv* inmensamente, enormemente
immensity *n* inmensidad, *f*; extensión, vastedad, *f*
immerse *vt* sumergir, hundir en, zambullir; bautizar por sumersión. *fig* **to be immersed in,** estar absorto en
immersion *n* sumersion, *f*, hundimiento, *m*; *ast* inmersión, *f*
immigrant *a* and *n* inmigrante, *mf*
immigrate *vi* inmigrar
immigration *n* inmigración, *f*
imminence *n* inminencia, *f*
imminent *a* inminente
immobile *a* inmóvil, inmoble; impasible, imperturbable
immobility *n* inmovilidad, *f*; impasibilidad, imperturbabilidad, *f*
immobilization *n* inmovilización, *f*
immobilize *vt* inmovilizar
immoderate *a* inmoderado, excesivo, indebido
immoderately *adv* inmoderadamente, excesivamente
immoderateness *n* inmoderación, *f*, exceso, *m*
immodest *a* inmodesto; indecente, deshonesto; (pert) atrevido, descarado
immodestly *adv* impúdicamente, inmodestamente
immodesty *n* inmodestia, impudicia, *f*; deshonestidad, licencia, *f*; (forwardness) descaro, atrevimiento, *m*
immolate *vt* inmolar, sacrificar
immolation *n* inmolación, *f*, sacrificio, *m*
immolator *n* inmolador (-ra)
immoral *a* inmoral; licencioso, vicioso; incontinente
immorality *n* inmoralidad, *f*
immortal *a* inmortal; perenne, eterno, imperecedero. *n* inmortal, *mf*
immortality *n* inmortalidad, *f*; fama inmortal, *f*
immortalize *vt* inmortalizar, perpetuar
immortally *adv* inmortalmente, eternamente, para siempre
immovability *n* inamovibilidad, inmovilidad, *f*; (of purpose) inflexibilidad, tenacidad, constancia, *f*
immovable *a* inmoble, fijo, inmóvil; (of purpose) inconmovible, inalterable, constante. *n pl.* **immovables** *law* bienes inmuebles, *m pl*. *ecc* **i. feast,** fiesta fija, *f*
immovably *adv* inmóvilmente, fijamente
immune *a* inmune, libre; *med* inmune. **i. from,** exento de; libre de
immunity *n* inmunidad, libertad, *f*; exención, *f*; *med* inmunidad, *f*
immunization *n med* inmunización, *f*
immunize *vt* inmunizar
immure *vt* emparedar, recluir, encerrar
immutability *n* inmutabilidad, inalterabilidad, *f*
immutable *a* inmutable, inalterable, constante
immutably *adv* inmutablemente
imp *n* trasgo, diablillo, duende, *m*; (child) picaruelo (-la)
impact *n* impacto, *m*, impacción, *f*; choque, *m*, colisión, *f*
impair *vt* perjudicar, echar a perder, deteriorar, empeorar, desmejorar. **to be impaired,** deteriorarse, perjudicarse
impairment *n* deterioración, perjuicio, empeoramiento, *m*
impale *vt* (punishment) empalar; (with a sword) atravesar, espetar
impalement *n* (punishment) empalamiento, *m*; atravesamiento, *m*, transfixión, *f*
impalpability *n* impalpabilidad, intangibilidad, *f*
impalpable *a* impalpable, intangible; incorpóreo
impart *vt* comunicar, dar parte (de); conferir
impartial *a* imparcial, ecuánime
impartiality *n* imparcialidad, ecuanimidad, entereza, *f*, desinterés, *m*
impartially *adv* imparcialmente, con desinterés
impassability *n* impracticabilidad, *f*
impassable *a* intransitable, impracticable; (of water) invadeable
impasse *n* callejón sin salida, *m*
impassibility *n* impasibilidad, imperturbabilidad, indiferencia, *f*
impassible *a* impasible, insensible; indiferente, imperturbable
impassion *vt* apasionar, conmover
impassioned *a* apasionado, vehemente, ardiente
impassive *a* impasible, insensible; indiferente, imperturbable; apático
impassively *adv* indiferentemente
impassivity *n* impasibilidad, *f*; indiferencia, *f*; apatía, *f*
impatience *n* impaciencia, *f*
impatient *a* impaciente; intolerante. **to make i.,** impacientar. **to grow i.,** impacientarse, perder la paciencia. **to grow i. at,** impacientarse ante. **to grow i. to,** impacientarse a or por. **to grow i. under,** impacientarse bajo
impatiently *adv* con impaciencia, impacientemente
impeach *vt law* denunciar, delatar, acusar, hacer juicio político (Argentina); censurar, criticar, tachar
impeachable *a law* delatable, denunciable, acusable; censurable
impeacher *n* acusador (-ra), denunciador (-ra), delator (-ra)
impeachment *n law* acusación, denuncia, *f*; reproche, *m*, queja, *f*
impeccability *n* (perfection) impecabilidad, perfección, *f*; elegancia, *f*
impeccable *a* impecable, intachable, perfecto; elegante
impeccably *adv* perfectamente; elegantemente
impecuniosity *n* indigencia, probreza, *f*
impecunious *a* indigente, pobre

impede *vt* impedir, obstruir, estorbar; *fig* dificultar, embarazar
impediment *n* obstáculo, estorbo, *m*; *fig* dificultad, *f*; *law* impedimento, *m*. **to have an i. in one's speech,** tener una dificultad en el hablar
impel *vt* impulsar, impeler; *fig* estimular, obligar, mover, constreñir. **I felt impelled (to),** Me sentí obligado (a)
impend *vi* ser inminente, amenazar
impending *a* inminente, pendiente
impenetrability *n* impenetrabilidad, *f*; *fig* enigma, secreto, misterio, *m*
impenetrable *a* impenetrable; intransitable; denso, espeso; *fig* enigmático, insondable, secreto
impenetrably *adv* impenetrablemente, densamente
impenitence *n* impenitencia, *f*
impenitent *a* impenitente, incorregible
impenitently *adv* sin penitencia
imperative *a* imperioso, perentorio; *gram* imperativo; (necessary) esencial, urgente. *n* mandato, *m*, orden, *f*; *gram* imperativo, *m*. **in the i.,** en el imperativo
imperatively *adv* imperativamente
imperativeness *n* perentoriedad, *f*; urgencia, importancia, *f*
imperceptible *a* imperceptible, insensible
imperceptibly *adv* imperceptiblemente
imperceptive *a* insensible
imperfect *a* imperfecto; incompleto, defectuoso. *a* and *n gram* imperfecto *m*
imperfection *n* imperfección, *f*; defecto, desperfecto, *m*; falta, tacha, *f*
imperfectly *adv* imperfectamente
imperial *a* imperial, imperatorio. *n* (beard) pera, *f*. **i. preference,** preferencia dentro del Imperio, *f*
imperialism *n* imperialismo, *m*
imperialist *n* imperialista, *mf*
imperialistic *a* imperialista
imperial *vt* arriesgar, poner en peligro, aventurar
imperious *a* imperioso, altivo, arrogante; (pressing) urgente, apremiante
imperiously *adv* imperiosamente, con arrogancia
imperiousness *n* autoridad, arrogancia, altivez, *f*; necesidad, urgencia, *f*, apremio, *m*
imperishability *n* (immortality) inmortalidad, perennidad, *f*
imperishable *a* imperecedero, inmarchitable, perenne, eterno
impermanence *n* inestabilidad, interinidad, *f*; brevedad, fugacidad, *f*
impermanent *a* interino, no permanente
impermeability *n* impermeabilidad, *f*
impermeable *a* impermeable
impersonal *a* impersonal, objetivo; *gram* impersonal
impersonality *n* objetividad, *f*
impersonally *adv* impersonalmente
impersonate *vt* personificar, simbolizar; *theat* representar
impersonation *n* personificación, simbolización, *f*; *theat* representación, *f*
impertinence *n* impertinencia, majadería, insolencia, *f*; inoportunidad, *f*; despropósito, *m*
impertinent *a* impertinente, insolente; (unseasonable) intempestivo, inoportuno; (irrelevant) fuera de propósito
impertinently *adv* con insolencia, impertinentemente
imperturbability *n* imperturbabilidad, serenidad, impasibilidad, *f*; impavidez, *f*
imperturbable *a* imperturbable, impasible, sereno; impávido
imperturbably *adv* con serenidad, imperturbablemente
impervious *a* impermeable, impenetrable; *fig* insensible. **He is i. to arguments,** No hace caso de argumentos
imperviousness *n* impermeabilidad, impenetrabilidad, *f*; *fig* insensibilidad, *f*
impetigo *n med* impétigo, *m*
impetuosity *n* impetuosidad, temeridad, irreflexión, *f*
impetuous *a* impetuoso, temerario, irreflexivo; violento, vehemente
impetuously *adv* impetuosamente; con vehemencia
impetus *n mech* ímpetu, *m*, impulsión, *f*; *fig* incentivo, estímulo, impulso, *m*
impiety *n* impiedad, irreligión, irreligiosidad, *f*
impinge (upon) *vi* chocar con, tropezar con
impious *a* impío, irreligioso, sacrílego; (wicked) malvado, perverso, malo
impish *a* travieso, revoltoso, enredador
implacability *n* implacabilidad, *f*
implacable *a* implacable, inexorable, inflexible, riguroso
implacably *adv* implacablemente
implant *vt fig* implantar, inculcar, instilar
implantation *n fig* implantación, instilación, inculcación, *f*
implement *n* instrumento, utensilio, *m*, herramienta, *f*; (of war) elemento, *m*. *vt* cumplir, hacer efectivo; llevar a cabo
implicate *vt* enredar, envolver; (imply) implicar, contener, llevar en sí; (in a crime) comprometer. **to be implicated in a crime,** estar implicado en un crimen.
implication *n* implicación, inferencia, repercusión, sugestión, *f*; (in a crime) complicidad, *f*
implicit *a* implícito, virtual, tácito; (absolute) ciego, absoluto, implícito. **with i. faith,** con fe ciega
implicitness *n* carácter implícito, *m*, lo implícito
implied *a* tácito, implícito
implore *vt* implorar, suplicar
imploring *a* suplicante, implorante
imploringly *adv* con encarecimiento, a súplica, de un modo suplicante
imply *vt* implicar, indicar, presuponer; (mean) querer decir, significar; (hint) insinuar, sugerir
impolicy *n* indiscreción, imprudencia, impolítica, *f*
impolite *a* descortés, mal educado
impolitely *adv* con descortesía
impoliteness *n* descortesía, falta de urbanidad, *f*
impolitic *a* impolítico
imponderability *n* imponderabilidad, *f*
imponderable *a* imponderable
import *vt com* importar; (mean) significar, querer decir. *a com* importado, de importación. *n com* importación, *f*; (meaning) significado, sentido, *m*; (value) importe, valor, *m*; (contents) contenido, tenor, *m*; importancia, *f*. **i. duty,** derechos de importación derechos de entrada, *m pl*, gravamen a la importación, *m*. **i. licence,** permiso de importación, *m*. **i. trade,** negocios de importación, *m pl*
importable *a* importable, que se puede importar
importance *n* importancia, *f*; valor, alcance, *m*, magnitud, *f*; consideración, eminencia, *f*. **to be fully conscious of one's i.,** tener plena conciencia de su importancia
important *a* importante; distinguido; presuntuoso, vanidoso. **to be i.,** importar, ser importante. **i. person,** personaje, *m*, persona importante, *f*
importantly *adv* importantemente, con importancia
importation *n* importación, *f*; *com* introducción (or importación) de géneros extranjeros, *f*
importer *n* importador (-ra)
importunate *a* (of a demand) insistente, importuno; (of persons) impertinente, pesado
importunately *adv* importunadamente
importune *vt* importunar, asediar, perseguir
importuning *n* persecución, importunación, *f*
importunity *n* importunidad, insistencia, impertinencia, *f*
impose *vt* (on, upon) imponer, infligir, cargar; *print* imponer. *vi* (on, upon) (deceive) engañar, embaucar
imposing *a* imponente, impresionante; (of persons) majestuoso, importante
imposition *n* imposición, *f*; (burden) impuesto, tributo,

m, carga, *f*; (*print, etc.*) imposición, *f*; (trick) fraude, engaño, *m*, decepción, *f*

impossibility *n* imposibilidad, *f*

impossible *a* imposible. **Nothing is i.,** No hay nada imposible, *inf* De menos nos hizo Dios. **to do the i.,** hacer lo imposible

impostor *n* impostor (-ra), bribón (-ona), embustero (-ra)

imposture *n* impostura, *f*, engaño, fraude, *m*

impotence *n* impotencia, *f*

impotent *a* impotente

impound *vt* acorralar; (water) embalsar; (goods) confiscar

impoverish *vt* empobrecer, depauperar, arruinar; (health) debilitar; (land) agotar

impoverished *a* indigente, necesitado; (of land) agotado

impoverishment *n* empobrecimiento, *m*, ruina, *f*; (of land) agotamiento, *m*

impracticability *n* impracticabilidad, imposibilidad, *f*

impracticable *a* impracticable, no factible, imposible

imprecation *n* imprecación, maldición, *f*

imprecatory *a* imprecatorio, maldiciente

impregnable *a* inexpugnable, inconquistable

impregnate *vt* impregnar, empapar; *biol* fecundar. **to become impregnated,** impregnarse

impregnation *n* impregnación, *f*; *biol* fecundación, fertilización, *f*; *fig* inculcación, *f*

impresario *n* empresario, *m*

imprescriptible *a* imprescriptible, inalienable

impress *vt* imprimir; (on the mind) impresionar; inculcar, imbuir; (with respect) imponer; *mil* reclutar; (of goods) confiscar. *n* impresión, marca, señal, huella, *f*

impression *n* impresión, *f*; marca, señal, huella, *f*; *print* impresión, *f*; efecto, *m*; idea, noción, *f*. **He has the i. that they do not like him,** Sospecha que no les es simpático. **to be under the i.,** tener la impresión

impressionability *n* susceptibilidad, sensibilidad, *f*

impressionable *a* susceptible, impresionable, sensitivo

impressionism *n* impresionismo, *m*

impressionist *n* impresionista, *mf*

impressionistic *a* impresionista

impressive *a* impresionante; emocionante; imponente, majestuoso; enfático

impressively *adv* solemnemente, de modo impresionante; enfáticamente

impressiveness *n* efecto impresionante, *m*, *Lat. Am.* imponencia *f*; grandiosidad, pompa, *f*; majestuosidad, *f*; fuerza, *f*

imprint *n* impresión, señal, marca, huella, *f*; *print* pie de imprenta, *m*. *vt* imprimir; (on the mind) grabar, fijar

imprison *vt* encerrar, encarcelar, aprisionar

imprisonment *n* encarcelación, prisión, *f*, encierro, *m*

improbability *n* improbabilidad, *f*; inverosimilitud, *f*

improbable *a* improbable; inverosímil

improbity *n* improbidad, *f*

impromptu *a* indeliberado, impremeditado, espontáneo. *adv* de improviso, in promptu. *n* improvisación, *f*

improper *a* impropio, inadecuado; incorrecto; indebido; indecente, indecoroso. **i. fraction,** *math* quebrado impropio, *m*

improperly *adv* impropiamente, incorrectamente; indecorosamente

impropriety *n* inconveniencia, *f*; incorrección, *f*; (style) impropiedad, *f*; falta de decoro, *f*

improvable *a* mejorable, perfectible

improve *vt* mejorar; perfecionar; (beautify) embellecer, hermosear; (land) bonificar; *lit* corregir, enmendar; (cultivate) cultivar; (increase) aumentar; (an opportunity) aprovechar; (strengthen) fortificar; (business) sacar provecho de, explotar. *vi* mejorar; perfeccionarse; (progress) hacer progresos, progresar, adelantarse; *com* subir; (become beautiful) hacerse hermoso, embellecerse; (increase) aumentarse. **to i. upon,** mejorar, perfeccionar; pulir

improvement *n* mejora, *f*; perfeccionamiento, *m*; aumento, *m*; adelantamiento, progreso, *m*; (in health) mejoría, *f*; embellecimiento, *m*; cultivación, *f*; (of land) abono, *m*

improver *n* aprendiz (-za)

improvidence *n* imprevisión, *f*; improvidencia, *f*

improvident *a* impróvido, desprevenido

improvidently *adv* impróvidamente

improvisation *n* improvisación, *f*

improvise *vt* improvisar

improviser *n* improvisador (-ra)

imprudence *n* imprudencia, *f*; desacierto, *m*, indiscreción, *f*

imprudent *a* imprudente; desacertado, indiscreto, mal avisado, irreflexivo

imprudently *adv* imprudentemente; sin pensar

impudence *n* impudencia, *f*, descaro, *m*, insolencia, desvergüenza, *f*, atrevimiento, *m*

impudent *a* impudente, descarado, insolente, desvergonzado, atrevido, *Peru* lisurero

impudently *adv* descaradamente, con insolencia

impugn *vt* impugnar, contradecir, atacar

impugnable *a* impugnable, atacable

impugnment *n* impugnación, *f*

impulse *n* ímpetu, *m*, impulsión, *f*; impulso, estímulo, *m*; incitación, instigación, *f*; motivo, *m*; (fit) arranque, arrebato, acceso, *m*

impulsion *n* ímpetu, *m*, impulsión, *f*; empuje, *m*, arranque, *m*

impulsive *a* impelente; irreflexivo, impulsivo

impulsively *adv* por impulso

impulsiveness *n* irreflexión, *f*; carácter impulsivo, *m*

impunity *n* impunidad, *f*. **with i.,** impunemente

impure *a* impuro; adulterado, mezclado; (indecent) deshonesto, indecente; (dirty) turbio, sucio

impurity *n* impureza, *f*; adulteración, mezcla, *f*; deshonestidad, liviandad, *f*; suciedad, turbiedad, *f*

imputable *a* imputable, atribuible

imputation *n* imputación, atribución, *f*; (in a bad sense) acusación, *f*, reproche, *m*

impute *vt* imputar, achacar, atribuir; acusar, reprochar

imputer *n* imputador (-ra); recriminador (-ra), acusador (-ra)

in *prep* en; a; (of duration) durante, mientras; (with) con; (through) por; dentro de; (under) bajo; (following a superlative) de; (of specified time) dentro de, de aquí a; (with afternoon, etc.) por; (out of) sobre. **course in medieval Catalan literature,** curso de literatura catalana medioeval. **dressed in black,** vestido de negro. **in London,** en Londres. **in the morning,** por la mañana; (in the course of) durante la mañana. **in time,** a tiempo; dentro de algún tiempo. **in a week,** dentro de una semana. **in the best way,** del mejor modo. **in writing,** por escrito. **in anger,** con enojo. **in one's hand,** en la mano. **in addition to,** además de, a más de. **in case,** por si acaso, en caso de que. **in order to,** a fin de, para (foll. by infin.). **in order that,** para que (foll. by subjunc.). **in so far as,** en cuanto. **in spite of,** a pesar de. **in the distance,** a lo lejos, en lontananza. **in the meantime,** entre tanto. **in the middle of,** en el medio de; a la mitad de. **in the style of,** al modo de; a la manera de, a la (francesa, etc.)

in *adv* adentro, dentro; (at home) en casa; (of sun) escondido; (of fire) alumbrado; (in power) en el poder; (of harvest) cosechado; (of boats) entrado (with haber); (of trains) llegado (with haber). **to be in,** estar dentro; haber llegado; estar en casa. **to be in for,** estar expuesto a, correr el riesgo de. **to be in with a person,** ser muy amigo de, estar muy metido con. **Come in!** ¡Adelante!; ¡Pase usted! **ins and outs,** sinuosidades, *f pl*; (of river) meandros, *m pl*; (of an affair) pormenores, detalles, *m pl*. **in less time than you can say Jack Robinson,** en menos de Jesús, en un credo, en menos que canta un gallo, en menos que se persigna un cura loco. **in the middle of nowhere,**

donde Cristo dio las tres voces, (Western Hemisphere) donde el diablo perdió el poncho.
in *a* interno. **in-law** (of relations) político. **in-patient,** enfermo (-ma) de hospital
inability *n* incapacidad, inhabilidad, ineptitud, incompetencia, *f*; impotencia, *f*
inaccessibility *n* inaccesibilidad, *f*
inaccessible *a* inaccesible
inaccuracy *n* inexactitud, incorrección, *f*
inaccurate *a* inexacto, incorrecto
inaccurately *adv* inexactamente, erróneamente
inaction *n* inacción, *f*
inactive *a* inactivo, pasivo; (of things) inerte; (lazy) perezoso, indolente; (machinery) parado; (motionless) inmóvil; (at leisure) desocupado, sin empleo
inactivity *n* inactividad, pasividad, *f*; (of things) inercia, *f*; pereza, indolencia, *f*; (of machinery) paro, *m*; inmovilidad, *f*; (leisure) desocupación, *f*
inadaptable *a* inadaptable, no adaptable
inadequacy *n* insuficiencia, escasez, *f*; imperfección, *f*, defecto, *m*
inadequate *a* inadecuado, insuficiente, escaso; imperfecto, defectuoso
inadequately *adv* inadecuadamente
inadmissible *a* inadmisible, no admisible
inadvertence *n* inadvertencia, *f*; equivocación, *f*, descuido, *m*
inadvertent *a* inadvertido, accidental, casual; negligente
inadvertently *adv* inadvertidamente, sin querer
inalienability *n* inalienabilidad, *f*
inalienable *a* inajenable, inalienable
inalterability *n* inalterabilidad, *f*
inalterable *a* inalterable
inalterably *adv* inalterablemente, sin alteración
inane *a* lelo, fatuo, vacío, necio
inanimate *a* (of matter) inanimado; sin vida, exánime, muerto
inanition *n* inanición, *f*
inanity *n* vacuidad, fatuidad, necedad, *f*
inappeasable *a* implacable, riguroso
inapplicability *n* no aplicabilidad, *f*
inapplicable *a* inaplicable
inapposite *a* fuera de propósito, no pertinente, inoportuno
inappreciable *a* inapreciable, imperceptible
inappreciation *n* falta de apreciación, *f*
inappreciative *a* desagradecido, ingrato. **i. of,** insensible a, indiferente a
inapproachable *a* inaccesible, huraño, adusto
inappropriate *a* impropio, inconveniente, inadecuado, incongruente; inoportuno
inappropriately *adv* impropiamente; inoportunamente
inappropriateness *n* impropiedad, inconveniencia, incongruencia, *f*; inoportunidad, *f*
inapt *a* inepto, inhábil; impropio
inaptitude *n* ineptitud, inhabilidad, *f*; impropiedad, *f*
inarticulate *a* (of speech) inarticulado; (reticent) inexpresivo, reservado; indistinto; *anat* inarticulado
inarticulately *adv* indistintamente, de un modo inarticulado
inarticulateness *n* tartamudez, *f*; inexpresión, reserva, *f*; silencio, *m*
inartistic *a* antiartístico, antiestético
inartistically *adv* sin gusto (estético)
inasmuch (as) *adv* puesto que, visto que, dado que
inattention *n* desatención, inaplicación, abstracción, *f*; falta de solicitud, *f*
inattentive *a* desatento, distraído; poco solícito, no atento
inattentively *adv* sin atención, distraídamente
inaudibility *n* imposibilidad de oír, *f*
inaudible *a* inaudible, no audible, ininteligible
inaudibly *adv* indistintamente, de modo inaudible
inaugurate *vt* inaugurar; (open) estrenar, abrir, dedicar; (install) investir, instalar; (initiate) originar, iniciar, dar lugar (a)
inauguration *n* inauguración, *f*; (opening) estreno, *m*, apertura, *f*; (investiture) instalación, investidura, *f*
inauspicious *a* poco propicio, desfavorable; ominoso, triste, infeliz
inauspiciously *adv* en condiciones desfavorables, desfavorablemente; infelizmente, bajo malos auspicios
inauspiciousness *n* condiciones desfavorables, *f pl*; infelicidad, *f*; malos auspicios, *m pl*
inborn *a* innato, instintivo, inherente
inbred *a* innato, inherente, instintivo
Inca *a* incaico, de los incas, *Lat. Am. also* incásico. *n* inca, *m*
incalculability *n* imposibilidad de calcular, *f*; (of persons) volubilidad, veleidad, *f*; infinidad, immensidad, *f*
incalculable *a* incalculable, innumerable; (of persons) voluble, veleidoso, caprichoso; infinito, immenso
incalculably *adv* enormemente, infinitamente; caprichosamente
incandescence *n* incandescencia, candencia, *f*
incandescent *a* incandescente, candente. **i. light,** luz incandescente, *f*. **to make i.,** encandecer
incantation *n* hechizo, *m*, encantación, *f*, ensalmo, *m*
incapability *n* incapacidad, *f*; inhabilidad, ineptitud, incompetencia, *f*
incapable *a* incapaz; inhábil, incompetente; (physically) imposibilitado
incapacitate *vt* imposibilitar, incapacitar, inutilizar; (disqualify) inhabilitar, incapacitar
incapacitation *n* inhabilitación, *f*
incapacity *n* incapacidad, inhabilidad, *f*
incarcerate *vt* encarcelar
incarceration *n* encarcelación, prisión, *f*
incarnate *a* encarnado. *vt* encarnar
incarnation *n* encarnación, *f*
incautious *a* incauto, imprudente
incautiously *adv* incautamente
incautiousness *n* imprudencia, negligencia, falta de cautela, *f*
incendiary *a* incendiario. **i. bomb,** incendiaria, *f*
incense *n* incienso, *m*; *fig* adulación, *f*. *vt ecc* incensar; (annoy) irritar, exasperar, enojar. **i. burner,** incensario, *m*
incentive *n* incentivo, estímulo, motivo, *m*. *a* estimulador, incitativo
inception *n* comienzo, principio, *m*; inauguración, *f*
incertitude *n* incertidumbre, *f*
incessant *a* incesante, continuo, constante
incessantly *adv* incesantemente, sin cesar
incest *n* incesto, *m*
incestuous *a* incestuoso
inch *n* pulgada, *f*. **every i. a man,** hombre hecho y derecho. **Not an i.!** ¡Ni pizca! **within an i. of,** a dos dedos de. **i. by i.,** palmo a palmo, paso a paso. **i. tape,** cinta métrica, *f*
inchoate *a* rudimentario; imperfecto, incompleto
incidence *n* incidencia, *f*
incident *a* propio, característico, incidental. *n* incidente, acontecimiento, *m*, ocurrencia, *f*
incident of navigation *n* accidente de navegación, *m*
incidental *a* incidente, incidental; accidental, accesorio, no esencial. **i. expense,** gasto imprevisto, *m*
incidentally *adv* (secondarily) incidentalmente; (by the way) de propósito
incinerate *vt* incinerar
incineration *n* incineración, cremación, *f*
incinerator *n* incinerador, *m*
incipient *a* incipiente, naciente, rudimentario
incision *n* incisión, *f*; corte, tajo, *m*; *med* abscisión, *f*
incisive *a* (of mind) agudo, penetrante; (of words) mordaz, incisivo, punzante
incisively *adv* en pocas palabras; mordazmente, incisivamente
incisiveness *n* (of mind) agudeza, penetración, *f*; (of words) mordacidad, *f*, sarcasmo, *m*

incisor *n* diente incisivo, *m*
incite *vt* incitar, estimular, animar; provocar, tentar. **to i. to,** mover a, incitar a
incitement *n* incitación, instigación, *f*; estímulo, *m*; tentación, *f*; aliciente, *m*
incivility *n* incivilidad, descortesía, *f*
inclemency *n* inclemencia, *f*, rigor, *m*
inclement *a* inclemente, riguroso, borrascoso
inclination *n* inclinación, *f*; (slope) declive, *m*, pendiente, cuesta, *f*; (tendency) propensión, tendencia, *f*; (liking) afición, *f*; amor, *m*; (bow) reverencia, *f*; *geom* inclinación, *f*
incline *vt* inclinar, torcer; doblar; (cause) inclinar (a), hacer. *vi* inclinarse, torcerse; (tend) tender, propender, inclinarse; (colors) tirar (a). *n* declive, *m*, pendiente, cuesta, inclinación, *f*. **I am inclined to believe it,** Me inclino a creerlo. **I am inclined to do it,** Estoy por hacerlo, Creo que lo haré
inclined *a* torcido, inclinado, doblado; *fig* propenso, adicto. **i. plane,** plano inclinado, *m*
include *vt* incluir, contener, encerrar; comprender, abrazar
including *present part* incluso, inclusive. **not i.,** no comprendido
inclusion *n* inclusión, *f*
inclusive *a* inclusivo. **January 2 to January 12 i.,** del 2 al 12 de enero, ambos inclusivos. **not i. of,** sin contar, exclusivo de. **i. of,** que incluye. **i. terms,** todo incluido, todos los gastos incluidos
incognito *a* and *adv* and *n* incógnito, *m*.
incoherence *n* incoherencia, inconsecuencia, *f*
incoherent *a* incoherente, inconexo, inconsecuente. **an i. piece of writing,** un escrito sin pies ni cabeza
incoherently *adv* con incoherencia
incombustibility *n* incombustibilidad, *f*
incombustible *a* incombustible
income *n* renta, *f*, ingreso, *m*; *com* rédito, *m*. **i.-tax,** impuesto de utilidades, *m*. **i.-tax commissioners,** inspectores de impuestos de utilidades, *m pl*. **i.-tax return,** declaración de utilidades, *f*
incoming *a* entrante; nuevo. *n* entrada, llegada, *f*. *n pl* **incomings,** ingresos, *m pl*
incommensurability *n* inconmensurabilidad, *f*
incommensurable *a* inconmensurable, no conmensurable
incommensurate *a* desproporcionado, desmedido
incommode *vt* incomodar, molestar, fastidiar
incommodious *a* estrecho; incómodo, inconveniente
incommodiousness *n* estrechez, *f*; incomodidad, *f*
incommunicable *a* incommunicable, indecible, inexplicable
incommunicative *a* insociable, intratable, adusto, huraño
incomparable *a* incomparable; sin par, sin igual, excelente
incomparableness *n* excelencia, perfección, *f*
incomparably *adv* incomparablemente, con mucho
incompatibility *n* incompatibilidad, *f*
incompatible *a* incompatible
incompetence *n* incompetencia, ineptitud, inhabilidad, *f*; *law* incapacidad, *f*
incompetent *a* incompetente, incapaz, inepto, inhábil; *law* incapaz
incompetently *adv* inhábilmente
incomplete *a* incompleto; imperfecto, defectuoso; (unfinished) sin terminar, inacabado, inconcluso. **incomplete sentence,** frase que queda colgando, *f*
incompletely *adv* incompletamente; imperfectamente
incompleteness *n* estado incompleto, *m*; imperfección, *f*; inconclusión, *f*
incomprehensibility *n* incomprensibilidad, *f*
incomprehensible *a* incomprensible
incomprehension *n* incomprensión, falta de comprensión, *f*
inconceivable *a* inconcebible, inimaginable
inconclusive *a* inconcluyente, cuestionable, dudoso, no convincente
inconclusiveness *n* carácter inconcluso, *m*, falta de conclusiones, *f*
incongruity *n* incongruencia, desproporción, disonancia, *f*
incongruous *a* incongruente, incongruo; chocante, desproporcionado, disonante
incongruously *adv* incongruentemente, incongruamente
inconsequence *n* inconsecuencia, *f*
inconsequent, inconsequential *a* inconsecuente, ilógico; inconsistente
inconsiderable *a* insignificante
inconsiderate *a* desconsiderado, irreflexivo, irrespetuoso
inconsiderately *adv* sin consideración, desconsideradamente
inconsiderateness *n* desconsideración, falta de respeto, *f*
inconsistency *n* inconsistencia, inconsecuencia, incompatibilidad, contradicción, anomalía, *f*
inconsistent *a* inconsistente, inconsiguiente, incompatible, contradictorio, anómalo
inconsistently *adv* contradictoriamente
inconsolable *a* inconsolable, desconsolado. **to be i.,** estar inconsolable, (*inf* of a woman) estar hecha una Magdalena
inconsolably *adv* desconsoladamente
inconspicuous *a* que no llama la atención; insignificante, humilde, modesto
inconspicuously *adv* humildemente, modestamente
inconspicuousness *n* modestia, humildad, *f*
inconstancy *n* inconstancia, movilidad, *f*; mudanza, veleidad, *f*
inconstant *a* inconstante, mudable, variable; veleidoso, volátil, voluble
incontestable *a* incontestable, evidente, indisputable
incontinence *n* incontinencia, *f*
incontinent *a* incontinente
incontrollable *a* ingobernable, indomable
incontrovertible *a* incontrovertible, incontrastable
inconvenience *n* incomodidad, inconveniencia, *f*; (of time) inoportunidad, *f*. *vt* incomodar, causar inconvenientes (a)
inconvenient *a* incómodo, inconveniente, molesto, embarazoso; (of time) inoportuno. **at an i. time,** a deshora
inconveniently *adv* incómodamente; (of time) inoportunamente
incorporate *vt* incorporar, agregar; comprender, incluir, encerrar. *vi* asociarse, incorporarse. *a* incorpóreo, inmaterial; incorporado, asociado
incorporation *n* incorporación, agregación, *f*; asociación, *f*
incorporeal *a* incorpóreo, inmaterial
incorporeity *n* incorporeidad, inmaterialidad, *f*
incorrect *a* incorrecto; inexacto, erróneo, falso
incorrectness *n* incorrección, *f*
incorrigibility *n* incorregibilidad, *f*
incorrigible *a* incorregible, empecatado
incorrigibly *adv* incorregiblemente, obstinadamente
incorrupt *a* incorrupto; recto, honrado
incorruptibility *n* incorruptibilidad, *f*; honradez, probidad, *f*
incorruptible *a* incorrupto; honrado, incorruptible
incorruption *n* incorrupción, *f*
increase *vt* aumentar, acrecentar; (in numbers) multiplicar; (extend) ampliar, extender; (of price) encarecer, aumentar. *vi* aumentar, crecer; multiplicarse; extenderse; encarecerse, aumentar. *n* aumento, crecimiento, *m*; multiplicación, *f*; (in price) encarecimiento, *m*, alza, *f*; (of water) crecida, *f*; (of moon) creciente, *f*. **It is on the i.,** Va en aumento. **to i. and multiply,** crecer y multiplicar
increasingly *adv* más y más; en creciente, en aumento

incredibility *n* incredibilidad, *f*
incredible *a* increíble; fabuloso, extraordinario. **It seems i.,** Es increíble, *inf* Parece mentira
incredibly *adv* increíblemente
incredulity *n* incredulidad, *f*, escepticismo, *m*
incredulous *a* incrédulo, escéptico
incredulously *adv* con incredulidad, escépticamente
increment *n* aumento, incremento, *m*; adición, añadidura, *f*; *math* incremento, *m*. **unearned i.,** plusvalía, mayor valía, *f*
incriminate *vt* incriminar
incriminating *a* incriminante, acriminador
incrust *vt* incrustar, encostrar
incrustation *n* incrustación, *f*; (scab) costra, *f*
incubate *vt* empollar; *med* incubar
incubation *n* empolladura, incubación, *f*; *med* incubación, *f*
incubator *n* incubadora, *f*
incubus *n* íncubo, *m*; (burden) carga, *f*
inculcate *vt* inculcar, implantar, instilar
inculcation *n* inculcación, implantación, instilación, *f*
incumbency *n* posesión, duración de, posesión, duración (de cualquier puesto), *f*
incumbent *a* obligatorio. *n ecc* beneficiado, *m*. **to be i. on,** incumbir a, ser de su obligación
incur *vi* incurrir (en), incidir (en). **to i. an obligation,** contraer una obligación
incurability *n* incurabilidad, *f*
incurable *a* incurable, insanable; *fig* sin solución, irremediable. *n* incurable, *mf*
incurably *adv* incurablemente, irremediablemente
incurious *a* indiferente, sin interés; incurioso, negligente, descuidado
incursion *n* incursión, invasión, irrupción, *f*, acometimiento, *m*
indebted *a* empeñado, adeudado; (obliged) reconocido
indebtedness *n* deuda, *f*; (gratitude) obligación, *f*; agradecimiento, *m*
indecency *n* indecencia, *f*
indecent *a* indecente; obsceno, deshonesto
indecently *adv* torpemente, indecentemente
indecision *n* indecisión, vacilación, irresolución, *f*
indecisive *a* indeciso, irresoluto, vacilante
indeclinable *a* indeclinable
indecorous *a* indecoroso, indecente, indigno
indecorum *n* indecoro, *m*, indecencia, *f*; incorrección, *f*
indeed *adv* en efecto, de veras, a la verdad, realmente, por cierto, claro está. *interr* ¿de veras? ¿es posible? **I shall be very glad i.,** Estaré contento de veras. **It is i. an excellent book,** Es en efecto un libro excelente. **There are differences i. between this house and the other,** Hay diferencias, claro está, entre esta casa y la otra
indefatigability *n* resistencia, *f*, aguante, *m*, tenacidad, *f*
indefatigable *a* incansable, infatigable, resistente
indefatigably *adv* infatigablemente
indefensible *a* indefendible, insostenible
indefinable *a* indefinible
indefinite *a* indefinido, incierto; (delicate) sutil, delicado; *gram* indefinido; (vague) vago. *gram* **i. article,** artículo indefinido, *m*
indefinitely *adv* indefinidamente
indefiniteness *n* lo indefinido, el carácter indefinido, *m*; vaguedad, *f*
indelibility *n* resistencia, *f*, lo indeleble; *fig* duración, tenacidad, *f*
indelible *a* indeleble, imborrable; *fig* inolvidable
indelibly *adv* indeleblemente
indelicacy *n* falta de buen gusto, grosería, *f*; (tactlessness) indiscreción, falta de tacto, *f*
indelicate *a* grosero, descortés; indecoroso, inmodesto; (tactless) inoportuno, indiscreto
indemnification *n* indemnización, compensación, *f*
indemnify *vt* indemnizar, compensar
indemnity *n* indemnización, reparación, *f*
indent *vt* endentar, mellar; *print* sangrar
indentation *n* impresión, depresión, *f*; corte, *m*, mella, *f*; línea quebrada, *f*, zigzag, *m*
indenture *n* escritura, *f*, instrumento, *m*. *vt* escriturar
independence *n* independencia, libertad, *f*; (autonomy) autonomía, *f*. **I. Day,** Fiesta de la Independencia, *f*. **i. movement,** movimiento en favor de la independencia, *m*
independent *a* independiente; libre; (autonomous) autónomo; **i. of,** libre de; aparte de. **a person of i. means,** una persona acomodada
independently *adv* independientemente
indescribability *n* imposibilidad de describir, *f*, lo indescriptible
indescribable *a* indescriptible; indefinible, indecible, inexplicable; incalificable
indestructibility *n* indestructibilidad, *f*
indestructible *a* indestructible
indeterminable *a* indeterminable
indeterminate *a* indeterminado, indefinido, vago; *math* indeterminado
indetermination *n* irresolución, indecisión, duda, vacilación, *f*
index *n* (forefinger) dedo índice, *m*; (of book) tabla de materias, *f*, indice, *m*; (on instruments) manecilla, aguja, *f*; *math* índice, *m*; (sign) señal, indicación, *f*. *vt* poner índice (a); poner en el índice. **i. card,** ficha, *f*. **I. expurgatorius,** Indice expurgatorio, *m*
India *n* la India, *f*. **I. paper,** papel de China, *m*. **i.-rubber,** *bot* caucho, *m*; (eraser) goma de borrar, *f*. **i.-rubber tree,** yacio, *m*
Indian *a* and *n* indio (-ia). **I. chief,** cacique, *m*. **I. club,** maza, *f*. **I. corn,** maíz, *m*. **I. ink,** tinta china, *f*. **I. summer,** veranillo, veranillo de San Martín, *m*
Indian Ocean, the el Océano Indico, *m*
indicate *vt* indicar, señalar; (show) denotar, mostrar, anunciar
indication *n* indicación, *f*; señal, *f*, indicio, síntoma, *m*; prueba, *f*
indicative *a* indicador, indicativo, demostrativo; *gram* indicativo. *n gram* indicativo, *m*. **to be i. of,** indicar, señalar
indicator *n* indicador, señalador, *m*
indict *vt* acusar; *law* demandar, enjuiciar
indictable *a* procesable, denunciable, enjuiciable
indictment *n* acusación, *f*; *law* procesamiento, *m*
indifference *n* indiferencia, apatía, *f*, desinterés, desapego, *m*; imparcialidad, neutralidad, *f*; (coldness) frialdad, tibieza, *f*
indifferent *a* indiferente, apático; imparcial, neutral; frío; (ordinary) regular, ordinario, ni bien ni mal
indifferently *adv* con indiferencia; imparcialmente; friamente
indigence *n* indigencia, necesidad, penuria, *f*
indigenous *a* indígena, nativo, natural
indigent *a* indigente, necesitado, menesteroso
indigestible *a* indigesto
indigestion *n* indigestión, *f*, *Mexico* insulto *m*; *fig* empacho, ahíto, *m*
indignant *a* indignado. **to make i.,** indignar
indignantly *adv* con indignación
indignation *n* indignación, cólera, *f*
indignity *n* indignidad, *f*; ultraje, *m*
indigo *n* añil, índigo, *m*
indirect *a* indirecto; oblicuo; tortuoso; *gram* **i. case,** caso oblicuo, *m*
indirectness *n* (of route) rodeo, *m*, desviación, *f*; oblicuidad, *f*; (falsity) tortuosidad, *f*
indiscernible *a* imperceptible
indiscipline *n* indisciplina, falta de disciplina, *f*
indiscreet *a* indiscreto, imprudente, impolítico
indiscretion *n* indiscreción, imprudencia, *f*; (slip) desliz, *m*
indiscriminate *a* general, universal; indistinto, promiscuo
indiscriminately *adv* promiscuamente

indiscrimination *n* universalidad, indistinción, *f*
indispensability *n* indispensabilidad, precisión, necesidad, *f*
indispensable *a* imprescindible, indispensable, insustituible
indispensably *adv* forzosamente, indispensablemente
indispose *vt* indisponer. **to be indisposed,** estar indispuesto, indisponerse
indisposed *a* indispuesto, enfermo, destemplado; (reluctant) maldispuesto
indisposition *n* indisposición, enfermedad, *f*
indisputability *n* verdad manifiesta, certeza, evidencia, *f*
indisputable *a* innegable, incontestable; irrefutable, evidente
indisputably *adv* indisputablemente
indissolubility *n* indisolubilidad, *f*
indissoluble *a* indisoluble
indistinct *a* indistinto; indeterminado, confuso, vago
indistinctly *adv* indistintamente; confusamente, vagamente
indistinctness *n* incertidumbre, vaguedad, indistinción, indeterminación, *f*
indistinguishable *a* indistinguible
individual *a* (single) solo, único; individual, individuo, particular, propio; personal. *n* individuo, *m*, particular, *mf*
individualism *n* individualismo, *m*
individualist *n* individualist, *mf*
individualistic *a* individualista
individuality *n* individualidad, personalidad, *f*; carácter, *m*, naturaleza, *f*
individualize *vt* particularizar, individuar
individually *adv* individualmente, particularmente
indivisibility *n* indivisibilidad, *f*
indivisible *a* incompartible, impartible, indivisible
indivisibly *adv* indivisiblemente
Indo (in compounds) indo. **I.-Chinese,** *a* and *n* indochino (-na). **I.-European,** indoeuropeo. **I.-Germanic,** indogermánico
indocile *a* indócil, desobediente, rebelde
indocility *n* indocilidad, desobediencia, falta de docilidad, *f*
indolence *n* indolencia, pereza, desidia, *f*
indolent *a* indolente, perezoso, holgazán; *med* indoloro
indolently *adv* perezosamente
indomitable *a* indomable, indómito
indoor *a* de casa; de puertas adentro, interno. **i. swimming pool,** piscina bajo techo, *f*. **i. tennis,** tenis en pistas cubiertas, tenis bajo techo, *m*
indoors *adv* en casa; adentro, bajo techo
indorsee *n* endosatario (-ia)
indubitable *a* indudable
indubitably *adv* indudablemente, sin duda
induce *vt* inducir, mover; instigar, incitar; producir, ocasionar; *elec* inducir. **Nothing would i. me to do it,** Nada me induciría a hacerlo
inducement *n* incitamento, *m*; estímulo, *m*; aliciente, atractivo, *m*; tentación, *f*
induct *vt* instalar; introducir, iniciar
induction *n* instalación, *f*; iniciación, introducción, *f*; *phys* inducción, *f*. **i. coil,** carrete de inducción, *m*
inductive *a* (of reasoning) inductivo; *phys* inductor
indulge *vt* (children) consentir, mimar; (a desire) satisfacer, dar rienda suelta a; (with a gift) agasajar (con), dar gusto (con). **to i. in,** *vt* consentir en. *vi* entregarse a, permitirse, gustar de
indulgence *n* (of children) mimo, cariño excesivo, *m*; (of a desire) propensión (a), afición (a), *f*; (toward others) tolerancia, transigencia, *f*; *ecc* indulgencia, *f*
indulgent *a* indulgente; tolerante, transigente
indult *n ecc* indulto, *m*
industrial *a* industrial. **i. alcohol,** alcohol desnaturalizado, *m*. **i. school,** escuela de artes y oficios, *f*. *com* **i. shares,** valores industriales, *m pl*
industrialism *n* industrialismo, *m*
industrialist *n* industrial, *m*
industrialization *n* industrialización, *f*
industrialize *vt* industrializar
industrious *a* industrioso, aplicado, diligente
industriously *adv* industriosamente, diligentemente
industriousness *n* industria, laboriosidad, *f*
industry *n* diligencia, aplicación, *f*; (work) trabajo, *m*, labor, *f*; *com* industria, *f*
inebriate *a* borracho, ebrio. *n* borracho (-cha). *vt* embriagar, emborrachar
inebriation *n* embriaguez, borrachera, *f*
inedible *a* incomible, no comestible
inedited *a* inédito
ineffable *a* indecible, inefable
ineffaceable *a* imborrable, indeleble
ineffective *a* ineficaz; vano, fútil. **to be i.,** (of persons) no pinchar ni cortar. **to prove i.,** quedar sin efecto; no tener influencia
ineffectiveness *n* ineficacia, *f*; futilidad, *f*
inefficiency *n* ineficacia, incompetencia, ineptitud, *f*
inefficient *a* ineficaz, incapaz
inefficiently *adv* ineficazmente
inelastic *a* inelástico
inelegance *n* inelegancia, fealdad, vulgaridad, *f*
inelegant *a* inelegante, ordinario, de mal gusto
inelegantly *adv* sin elegancia
ineligibility *n* ineligibilidad, *f*
ineligible *a* inelegible
inept *a* inepto, inoportuno; absurdo, ridiculo; (of persons) incompetente, ineficaz
ineptitude *n* ineptitud, *f*; necedad, *f*; (of persons) incapacidad, incompetencia, *f*
ineptly *adv* ineptamente, neciamente
inequality *n* desigualdad, desemejanza, disparidad, *f*; (of surface) escabrosidad, aspereza, *f*; *fig* injusticia, *f*; (of opportunity) diferencia, *f*
inequitable *a* desigual, injusto
inequity *n* injusticia, desigualdad, *f*
ineradicable *a* indeleble, imborrable
ineradicably *adv* indeleblemente
inert *a* inerte, inactivo, pasivo; ocioso, flojo, perezoso
inertia *n* inercia, inacción, *f*; abulia, pereza, *f*; *phys* inercia, *f*
inertly *adv* indolentemente, sin mover, pasivamente
inescapable *a* ineludible, inevitable
inessential *a* no esencial
inestimable *a* inestimable
inevitability *n* fatalidad, necesidad, *f*; lo inevitable
inevitable *a* inevitable, necesario, fatal, forzoso, ineludible
inevitably *adv* inevitablemente, necesariamente, forzosamente
inexact *a* inexacto, incorrecto
inexactitude *n* inexactitud, *f*
inexcusable *a* imperdonable, inexcusable, irremisible
inexcusableness *n* enormidad, *f*; lo inexcusable
inexcusably *adv* inexcusablemente
inexhaustible *a* inagotable, inexhausto
inexorability *n* inflexibilidad, inexorabilidad, *f*
inexorable *a* inexorable, inflexible, duro
inexorably *adv* inexorablemente, implacablemente
inexpediency *n* inoportunidad, inconveniencia, imprudencia, *f*
inexpedient *a* inoportuno; inconveniente; impolítico, imprudente. **to deem i.,** creer inoportuno
inexpensive *a* poco costoso, barato
inexpensiveness *n* baratura, *f*, bajo precio, *m*
inexperience *n* inexperiencia, falta de experiencia, *f*
inexperienced *a* inexperto, novato
inexpert *a* inexperto, imperito
inexpertly *adv* sin habilidad
inexpertness *n* impericia, torpeza, *f*
inexpiable *a* inexpiable
inexplicable *a* inexplicable
inexplicit *a* no explícito
inexplosive *a* inexplosible

inexpressible *a* inexplicable, indecible, inefable
inexpressive *a* inexpresivo; (of persons) reservado, callado, poco expresivo, retraído
inexpressiveness *n* falta de expresión, *f*; (of persons) reserva, *f*, silencio, retraimiento, *m*
inexpugnable *a* inexpugnable
inextinguishable *a* inapagable, inextinguible
inextricable *a* inextricable, intrincado, enmarañado
inextricably *adv* intrincadamente
infallibility *n* infalibilidad, *f*
infallible *a* infalible
infamous *a* infame, torpe, vil, ignominioso; odioso, repugnante
infamously *adv* infamemente
infamy *n* infamia, torpeza, vileza, ignominia, *f*; deshonra, *f*
infancy *n* infancia, niñez, *f*; *law* minoridad, *f*
infant *n* criatura, *f*; crío (-ía), niño (-ña); *law* menor, *mf* **i. school,** escuela de párvulos, *f*
infanticidal *a* infanticida
infanticide *n* (act) infanticidio, *m*; (person) infanticida, *mf*
infantile *a* infantil. **i. paralysis,** parálisis infantil, *f*
infantry *n mil* infantería, *f*
infantryman *n mil* infante, peón, *m*
infatuate *vt* infatuar, embobar
infatuation *n* infatuación, *f*, encaprichamiento, *m*
infect *vt* infectar, contagiar; *fig* pegar, influir; (*fig* in a bad sense) corromper, pervertir, inficionar. **to become infected,** infectarse
infected *a* infecto
infection *n* infección, *f*, contagio, *m*; *fig* influencia, *f*; (*fig* in a bad sense) corrupción, perversión, *f*
infectious *a* infeccioso, contagioso; (*fig* in a bad sense) corruptor; *fig* contagioso
infectiousness *n* contagiosidad, *f*
infelicitous *a* poco apropiado, desacertado
infelicity *n* infelicidad, desdicha, *f*, infortunio, *m*; desacierto, *m*, inoportunidad, *f*
infer *vt* inferir, concluir, educir, deducir, implicar
inferable *a* deducible, demostrable
inference *n* inferencia, deducción, conclusión, *f*
inferential *a* ilativo, deductivo
inferior *a* inferior; (in rank) subordinado, subalterno; (of position) secundario. *n* inferior, *mf* subordinado (-da). **to be not i.,** no ser inferior, *inf* no quedarse en zaga
inferiority *n* inferioridad, *f*. **i. complex,** complejo de inferioridad, *m*
infernal *a* infernal; *poet* inferno, tartáreo
infernally *adv* infernalmente
inferno *n* infierno, *m*
infertile *a* infértil, infecundo, estéril
infertility *n* infertilidad, infecundidad, esterilidad, *f*
infest *vt* infestar. **to be infested with,** plagarse de
infestation *n* infestación, *f*
infidel *n* infiel, gentil, *mf* pagano (-na); (atheist) descreído (-da), ateo (-ea). *a* pagano; infiel, descreído, ateo
infidelity *n* infidelidad, alevosía, perfidia, *f*
infiltrate *vt* infiltrar. *vi* infiltrarse
infiltration *n* infiltración, *f*
infinite *a* infinito, ilimitado; inmenso, enorme; (of number) innumerable, infinito. *n* infinito, *m*
infinitely *adv* infinitamente
infinitesimal *a* infinitesimal. **i. calculus,** cálculo infinitesimal, *m*
infinitive *a* and *n gram* infinitivo, *m*.
infinitude, infinity *n* infinidad, infinitud, *f*; (extent) inmensidad, *f*; (of number) sinfín, *m*; *math* infinito, *m*
infirm *a* achacoso, enfermizo, enclenque; (shaky) inestable, inseguro; (of purpose) irresoluto, vacilante
infirmary *n* enfermería, *f*, hospital, *m*
infirmity *n* achaque, *m*, enfermedad, dolencia, *f*; (fault) flaqueza, falta, *f*
inflame *vt* encender; (excite) acalorar, irritar, provocar; *med* inflamar. *vi* encenderse, arder; acalorarse, irritarse; *med* inflamarse
inflammability *n* inflamabilidad, *f*
inflammable *a* inflamable
inflammation *n* inflamación, *f*
inflammatory *a* inflamador; *med* inflamatorio
inflate *vt* inflar, hinchar; (with pride) engreír, ensoberbecer
inflation *n* inflación, hinchazón, *f*; *com* inflación, *f*
inflationism *n* inflacionismo, *m*
inflator *n mech* bomba para inflar, *f*
inflect *vt* torcer; (voice) modular; *gram* conjugar, declinar
inflection *n* dobladura, *f*; (of voice) tono, acento, *m*, modulación, *f*; *gram* conjugación, declinación, *f*
inflexibility *n* inflexibilidad, dureza, rigidez, *f*
inflexible *a* inflexible, rígido; *fig* inexorable, inalterable
inflexibly *adv* inflexiblemente
inflict *vt* infligir, imponer
infliction *n* imposición, *f*; castigo, *m*
inflorescence *n bot* inflorescencia, *f*
inflow *n* afluencia, *f*, flujo, *m*
influence *n* influencia, *f*, influjo, *m*; ascendiente, *m*; (importance) influencia, importancia, *f*. *vt* influir, afectar; persuadir, inducir. **to have i. over,** (a person) tener ascendiente sobre. *law* **undue i.,** influencia indebida, *f*
influential *a* influyente; (of person) prestigioso, importante
influenza *n med* gripe, *f*, trancazo, *m*
influx *n* influjo, *m*; (of rivers) desembocadura, afluencia, *f*
inform *vt* (fill) infundir, llenar; (tell) informar, enterar, advertir; instruir; (with about) poner al corriente de, participar. *vi* (with against) delatar (a), denunciar. **to i. oneself,** informarse, enterarse. **to be informed about,** estar al corriente de
informal *a* irregular; sin ceremonia, de confianza; (meeting) no oficial, extraoficial
informality *n* irregularidad, *f*; falta de ceremonia, sencillez, *f*; intimidad, *f*
informally *adv* sin ceremonia
informant *n* informante, *mf*; informador (-ra)
information *n* información, instrucción, *f*; noticia, *f*, aviso, *m*; *law* denuncia, delación, *f*. **piece of i.,** información, *f*. **i. bureau,** oficina de información, *f*
informative *a* informativo
informer *n* delator (-ra), denunciador (-ra)
infrared *a phys* infrarrojo, ultrarrojo
infraction *n* contravención, infracción, transgresión, *f*
infrequency *n* infrecuencia, rareza, irregularidad, *f*
infrequent *a* infrecuente, raro, irregular
infrequently *adv* rara vez, infrecuentemente
infringe *vt* infringir, violar, contravenir, quebrantar
infringement *n* contravención, violación, infracción, *f*
infringer *n* infractor (-ra), contraventor (-ra), violador (-ra), transgresor (-ra)
infuriate *vt* enfurecer, enloquecer, enojar. **to be infuriated,** estar furioso
infuse *vt* vaciar, infiltrar; *fig* infundir, inculcar, instilar
infusible *a* infundible
infusion *n* infusión, *f*; *fig* instilación, inculcación, *f*
ingathering *n* cosecha, recolección, *f*
ingenious *a* ingenioso; mañoso, hábil
ingeniously *adv* ingeniosamente, hábilmente
ingenuity *n* ingeniosidad, inventiva, listeza, habilidad, *f*
ingenuous *a* ingenuo, franco, sincero, cándido, sencillo, inocente
ingenuousness *n* ingenuidad, franqueza, sinceridad, *f*; candor, *m*
ingest *vt* ingerir
ingestion *n* ingestión, *f*
inglorious *a* vergonzoso, ignominioso, deshonroso; desconocido, obscuro
ingloriously *adv* vergonzosamente, ignominiosamente; obscuramente

ingloriousness *n* deshonra, ignominia, *f*; obscuridad, *f*
ingoing *a* entrante, que entra. *n* ingreso, *m*, entrada, *f*; *com* **i. and outgoing,** entradas y salidas, *f pl*
ingot *n* pepita, *f*, lingote, *m*; (of any metal) barra, *f*
ingrained *a* innato, natural
ingratiate *vt* (oneself with) congraciarse con, captarse la buena voluntad de, insinuarse en el favor de
ingratiating *a* obsequioso
ingratitude *n* ingratitud, *f*, desagradecimiento, *m*
ingredient *n* ingrediente, *m*
ingress *n* ingreso, *m*; derecho de entrada, *m*
ingrowing *a* que crece hacia adentro. **i. nail,** uñero, *m*
inhabit *vt* habitar, ocupar, vivir en, residir en
inhabitable *a* habitable, vividero
inhabitant *n* habitante, residente, *m*; vecino (-na)
inhabited *a* habitado, poblado
inhalation *n* inspiración, *f*; *med* inhalación, *f*
inhale *vt* aspirar; *med* inhalar
inharmonious *a mus* disonante, inarmónico; desavenido, discorde, desconforme. **to be i.,** disonar; (of people) llevarse mal
inhere *vi* ser inherente; pertenecer (a), residir (en)
inherence *n* inherencia, *f*
inherent *a* inherente; innato, intrínseco, natural
inherently *adv* intrínsecamente
inherit *vt* heredar
inheritance *n* herencia, *f*; patrimonio, abolengo, *m*
inheritor *n* heredero, *m*
inhibit *vt* inhibir, impedir; *ecc* prohibir. **be inhibited, became inhibited,** cohibirse
inhibition *n* inhibición, *f*
inhibitory *a* inhibitorio
inhospitable *a* inhospitalario
inhospitably *adv* desabridamente
inhuman *a* inhumano; cruel, bárbaro
inhumanity *n* inhumanidad, crueldad, *f*
inhumanly *adv* inhumanamente, cruelmente
inhume *vt* inhumar, sepultar
inimical *a* enemigo, hostil, opuesto, contrario
inimically *adv* hostilmente
inimitable *a* inimitable
inimitably *adv* inimitablemente
iniquitous *a* inicuo, malvado, perverso, nefando; *inf* diabólico
iniquity *n* iniquidad, maldad, injusticia, *f*
initial *a* inicial. *n* inicial, letra inicial, *f*. *vt* firmar con las iniciales
initially *adv* al principio, en primer lugar
initiate *a* iniciado. *vt* iniciar, poner en pie, empezar, entablar; (a person) admitir
initiation *n* principio, *m*; (of a person) iniciación, admisión, *f*
initiative *n* iniciativa, *f*. **to take the i.,** tomar la iniciative
initiator *n* iniciador (-ra)
inject *vt* inyectar
injection *n* inyección, *f*. **i. syringe,** jeringa de inyecciones, *f*
injudicious *a* imprudente, indiscreto
injudiciously *adv* imprudentemente
injudiciousness *n* imprudencia, indiscreción, *f*
injunction *n* precepto, mandato, *m*; *law* embargo, *m*
injure *vt* perjudicar, dañar, *Lat. Am.* afectar; menoscabar, deteriorar; (hurt) lastimar, lisiar. **to i. oneself,** hacerse daño
injured *a* (physically) lisiado; (morally) ofendido
injurer *n* perjudicador (-ra)
injurious *a* dañoso, perjudicial, malo; ofensivo, injurioso
injuriously *adv* perjudicialmente
injury *n* perjuicio, daño, *m*; (physical) lesión, *Lat. Am. also* lastimadura *f*; (insult) agravio, insulto, *m*
injustice *n* injusticia, desigualdad, *f*. **You do him an i.,** Le juzgas mal
ink *n* tinta, *f*. *vt* entintar. **copying-ink,** tinta de copiar, *f*. **marking-ink,** tinta indeleble, *f*. **printer's ink,** tinta de imprenta, *f*. **ink-stand** or **ink-well,** tintero, *m*
inker *n print* rodillo, *m*
inkling *n* sospecha, noción, *f*
inky *a* manchado de tinta. **i. black,** negro como el betún
inland *n* el interior de un país, *a* interior, mediterráneo; del país, regional. *adv* tierra adentro. **to go i.,** internarse en un país. **I. Revenue,** delegación de contribuciones, *f*. **i. town,** ciudad del interior, *f*
inlay *vt* taracear, ataracear, embutir; incrustar. *n* taracea, *f*, embutido, *m*
inlet *n* entrada, admisión, *f*; *geog* ensenada, *f*. **i. valve,** válvula de admisión, *f*
inmate *n* residente, habitante, *m*; (of hospital) paciente, *mf*; enfermo (-ma); (of prison) prisionero
inmost. See **innermost**
inn *n* posada, fonda, venta, *f*, mesón, *m*. **Inns of Court,** Colegio de Abogados, *m*
innate *a* innato, inherente, instintivo, nativo
innately *adv* naturalmente, instintivamente
innavigable *a* innavegable
inner *a* interior, interno. **i. tube** *aut* cámara de neumatico, cámara de aire, *f*
innermost *a* más adentro; *fig* más íntimo, más hondo
innings *n* (sport) turno, *m*
innkeeper *n* fondista, *mf*; tabernero (-ra), mesonero (-ra), posadero (-ra)
innocence *n* inocencia, *f*; pureza, *f*; (guilelessness) simplicidad, *f*, candor, *m*
innocent *a* inocente, puro; (guiltless) inocente, inculpable; (foolish) simple, tonto, candoroso, inocentón; (harmless) innocuo. *n* inocente, *mf* **Holy Innocents,** Santos Inocentes, *m pl*
innoculator *n* inoculador, *m*
innocuous *a* innocuo, inofensivo
innocuousness *n* inocuidad, *f*
innovate *vt* innovar
innovation *n* innovación, *f*
innovator *n* innovador (-ra)
innuendo *n* indirecta, insinuación, *f*
innumerable *a* innumerable, incalculable. **i. things,** un sinfín de cosas
inobservance *n* inobservancia, *f*, incumplimiento, *m*
inoculate *vt* inocular
inoculation *n* inoculación, *f*
inodorous *a* inodoro
inoffensive *a* inofensivo, innocuo; (of people) pacífico, apacible, manso
inoffensively *adv* inofensivamente
inoffensiveness *n* inocuidad, *f*; (of people) mansedumbre, *f*
inoperable *a* inoperable
inoperative *a* ineficaz, impracticable, inútil
inopportune *a* inoportuno, intempestivo, inconveniente
inopportunely *adv* inoportunamente, a destiempo
inopportuneness *n* inoportunidad, inconveniencia, *f*
inordinate *a* desordenado, excesivo
inordinately *adv* desmedidamente
inorganic *a* inorgánico
inoxidizable *a* inoxidable
input *n* capacidad instalada, *f*, insumo, *m*
inquest *n law* indagación, investigación, *f*
inquietude *n* inquietud, *f*, desasosiego, *m*, agitación, preocupación, *f*
inquire *vt* and *vi* preguntar, averiguar, indagar. **to i. about,** (persons) preguntar por; (things) hacer preguntas sobre. **to i. into,** investigar, examinar, averiguar. **to i. of,** preguntar a. **"I. within,"** «Se dan informaciones»
inquirer *n* indagador (-ra), inquiridor (-ra)
inquiring *a* indagador, inquiridor
inquiringly *adv* interrogativamente
inquiry *n* interrogación, pregunta, *f*; indagación, pes-

quisa, investigación, *f*; examen, *m*. **i. office,** oficina de informaciones, *f*. **on i.,** al preguntar
inquisition *n* investigación, indagación, *f*; inquisición, *f*. **Holy I.,** Santo Oficio, *m*, Inquisición, *f*
inquisitive *a* curioso, inquiridor; preguntador, impertinente, mirón
inquisitively *adv* con curiosidad, impertinentemente
inquisitiveness *n* curiosidad, *f*; impertinencia, *f*
Inquisitor *n ecc* inquisidor, *m*
inquisitorial *a* inquisitorial, inquisidor
inroad *n* incursión, *f*
insalubrious *a* malsano, insalubre
insane *a* loco, demente, insano; (senseless) insensato, ridículo. **to become i.,** enloquecer, volverse loco, perder la razón. **to drive i.,** volver a uno el juicio, enloquecer, trastornar. **i. person,** demente, *mf*, loco (-ca)
insanely *adv* locamente
insanitary *a* antihigiénico, malsano
insanity *n* demencia, locura, *f*; enloquecimiento, *m*; (folly) insensatez, ridiculez, *f*
insatiability *n* insaciabilidad, *f*
insatiable *a* insaciable
insatiably *adv* insaciablemente
inscribe *vt* inscribir
inscription *n* inscripción, *f*; letrero, *m*; (of a book) dedicatoria, *f*; *com* inscripción, anotación, *f*, asiento, *m*
inscrutability *n* enigma, misterio, *m*; incomprensibilidad, *f*
inscrutable *a* enigmático, insondable, incomprensible, inescrutable
inscrutably *adv* incomprensiblemente, enigmáticamente
insect *n* insecto, *m*. **insects** *Lat. Am.* bichería *m*. **i. powder,** polvos insecticidas, *m pl*
insecticide *a* and *n* insecticida *m*.
insecure *a* inseguro, precario
insecurely *adv* inseguramente
insecurity *n* inseguridad, *f*; incertidumbre, inestabilidad, *f*
inseminate *vt fig* implantar; *med* fecundar
insemination *n fig* implantación, *f*; *med* fecundación, *f*
insensate *a* (unfeeling) insensible, insensitivo; (stupid) insensato, sin sentido, necio
insensibility *n* insensibilidad, inconsciencia, *f*; (stupor) sopor, letargo, *m*; impasibilidad, indiferencia, *f*
insensible *a* insensible, inconsciente; indiferente, impasible, duro de corazón; (scarcely noticeable) imperceptible. **to make i.,** (to sensations) hacer indiferente (a); insensibilizar
insensibly *adv* insensiblemente, imperceptiblemente
insensitive *a* insensible, insensitivo; (person) hecho un tronco, hecho un leño
insensitiveness *n* insensibilidad, *f*
insentient *a* insensible
inseparability *n* inseparabilidad, *f*
inseparable *a* inseparable
insert *vt* insertar, intercalar; (introduce) meter dentro, introducir, encajar; (in a newspaper) publicar
insertion *n* inserción, intercalación, *f*; (introduction) introducción, *f*; metimiento, encaje, *m*; *sew* entredós, *m*; (in a newspaper) publicación, *f*
inshore *a* cercano a la orilla. *adv* cerca de la orilla. **i. fishing,** pesca de arrastre, *f*
inside *a* interior, interno. *adv* adentro, dentro. *n* interior, *m*; (contents) contenido, *m*; (lining) forro, *m*; (*inf* stomach) entrañas, *f pl*. **to turn i. out,** volver al revés. **to walk on the i. of the pavement,** andar a la derecha de la acera. **from the i.,** desde el interior; por dentro. **on the i.,** por dentro, en el interior. **i. information,** información confidencial, *f*. **i. out,** al revés, de dentro afuera
insidious *a* insidioso, enganoso, traidor
insidiously *adv* insidiosamente
insidiousness *n* insidia, *f*; engaño, *m*, traición, *f*
insight *n* percepción, perspicacia, intuición, *f*, atisbo, *m*
insignia *n pl* insignias, *f pl*
insignificance *n* insignificancia, futilidad, pequeñez, *f*
insignificant *a* insignificante; fútil, trivial
insincere *a* insincero, hipócrita, falso
insincerely *adv* falsamente, hipócritamente
insincerity *n* insinceridad, hipocresía, falsedad, falta de sinceridad, doblez, *f*
insinuate *vt* insinuar, introducir; (hint) soltar una indirecta, sugerir; (oneself) insinuarse, introducirse con habilidad
insinuation *n* insinuación, introducción, *f*; (hint) indirecta, *f*
insipid *a* insípido, insulso; (dull) soso
insipidity *n* insipidez, insulsez, *f*, desabor, *m*; (dullness) sosería, *f*
insist *vi* insistir; persistir, obstinarse. **to i. on,** insistir en; obstinarse en, hacer hincapié en, aferrarse en (or a)
insistence *n* insistencia, *f*; obstinación, pertinacia, *f*
insistent *a* insistente; porfiado, obstinaz
insistently *adv* con insistencia; porfiadamente
insobriety *n* falta de sobriedad, *f*; embriaguez, ebriedad, *f*
insole *n* (of shoes) plantilla, *f*
insolence *n* insolencia, altanería, majadería, frescura, *f*, atrevimiento, descaro, *m*
insolent *a* insolente, arrogante, atrevido, descarado, desmesurado, fresco
insolently *adv* insolentemente, con descaro
insolubility *n* insolubilidad, *f*
insoluble *a* insoluble
insolvency *n* in olvencia, *f*
insolvent *a* insolvente
insomnia *n* insomnio, *m*
insomuch *adv* (gen. with as or that) de modo (que), así (que), de suerte (que)
inspect *vt* examinar, investigar, inspeccionar; (officially) registrar, reconocer
inspection *n* inspección, investigación, *f*; examen, *m*; (official) reconocimiento, registro, *m*
inspector *n* inspector, *m*, veedor, interventor, *m*
inspectorate *n* inspectorado, *m*; cargo de inspector, *m*
inspiration *n* (of breath) inspiración, aspiración, *f*; numen, *m*, inspiración, vena, *f*. **to find i. in,** inspirarse en.
inspire *vt* (inhale) aspirar, inspirar; (stimulate) animar, alentar, iluminar; (suggest) sugerir, inspirar; infundir. **to i. enthusiasm,** entusiasmar. **to i. hope,** dar esperanza, esperanzar
inspired *a* inspirado, intuitivo, iluminado; (of genius) genial
inspirer *n* inspirador (-ra)
inspiring *a* alentador, animador; inspirador
inspirit *vt* alentar, inspirar, estimular, animar
inspiriting *a* alentador, estimulador
instability *n* inestabilidad, mutabilidad, inconstancia, *f*
install *vt* (all meanings) instalar. **to i. oneself,** instalarse, establecerse
installation *n* (all meanings) instalación, *f*
installment *n* (of a story) entrega, *f*; *com* plazo, *m*, cuota, *f*. **by installments,** *com* a plazos. **i. plan,** pago a plazos, pago por cuotas, *m*
instance *n* ejemplo, caso, *m*; (request) solicitación, *f*, ruego, *m*; *law* instancia, *f*. *vt* citar como ejemplo, mencionar; demostrar, probar. **for i.,** por ejemplo, verbigracia. **in that i. . . .,** en el caso . . . **in the first i.,** en primer lugar, primero
instant *a* immediato, urgente; *com* corriente, actual. *n* instante, momento, *m*; *inf* tris, santiamén, *m*. *com* **the 2nd i.,** el 2° (segundo) del corriente. **this i.,** (immediately) en seguida
instantaneous *a* instantáneo. *phot* **i. exposure,** instantánea, *f*
instantaneously *adv* instantáneamente
instantaneousness *n* instantaneidad, *f*
instantly *adv* en seguida, al instante, inmediatamente
instead *adv* en cambio; (with of) en vez de, en lugar de
instep *n* empeine, *m*

instigate *vt* instigar, incitar, aguijar, animar, provocar; fomentar
instigating *a* instigador, provocador, fomentador
instigation *n* instigación, incitación, *f;* estímulo, *m*
instigator *n* instigador (-ra), provocador (-ra), fomentador (-ra)
instil *vt* instilar; (ideas) inculcar, infundir
instilment *n* inculcación, implantación, insinuación, *f*
instinct *n* instinto, *m.* **i. with,** imbuido de, lleno de. **by i.,** por instinto, movido por instinto
instinctive *a* instintivo, espontáneo
instinctively *adv* por instinto
institute *vt* instituir, fundar, establecer; (an inquiry) iniciar, empezar. *n* instituto, *m; pl* **institutes,** *law* instituta, *f*
institution *n* (creation) fundación, creación, *f;* institución, *f,* instituto, *m;* (beginning) comienzo, *m,* iniciación, *f;* (charitable) asilo, *m;* (custom) uso, *m,* costumbre, tradición, *f*
institutional *a* institucional
instruct *vt* (teach) instruir, enseñar; (order) mandar, dar orden (a)
instruction *n* (teaching) instrucción, enseñanza, *f; pl* **instructions,** (orders) instrucciones, f *pl* orden, *f,* mandato, *m*
instructive *a* instructivo, instructor, informativo
instructively *adv* instructivamente
instructiveness *n* el carácter informativo, lo instructivo
instructor *n* instructor, preceptor, *m*
instrument *n* instrumento, *m;* (tool) herramienta, *f,* utensilio, aparato, *m;* (agent) órgano, agente, medio, *m; law* instrumento, *m,* escritura, *f. vt mus* instrumentar. **percussion i.,** instrumento de percusión, *m.* **scientific i.,** instrumento científico, *m.* **stringed i.,** instrumento de cuerda, *m.* **wind i.,** instrumento de viento, *m*
instrumental *a* instrumental; influyente. **to be i. in,** contribuir a
instrumentalist *n mus* instrumentista, *m*
instrumentality *n* mediación, intervención, agencia, *f,* buenos oficios, *m pl*
instrumentation *n mus* instrumentación, *f;* mediación, *f*
insubordinate *a* insubordinado, rebelde, desobediente, refractario
insubordination *n* insubordinación, rebeldía, desobediencia, *f*
insubstantial *a* irreal; insubstancial
insubstantiality *n* irrealidad, *f;* insubstancialidad, *f*
insufferable. See **intolerable**
insufficiency *n* insuficiencia, falta, carestía, *f*
insufficient *a* insuficiente, falto. **"I. Postage,"** «Falta de franqueo»
insufficiently *adv* insuficientemente
insular *a* isleño, insular; (narrow-minded) intolerante, iliberal
insularity *n* carácter isleño, *m;* (narrow-mindedness) iliberalidad, intolerancia, *f*
insulate *vt* aislar
insulating *a* aislador. **i. tape,** *elec* cinta aisladora, *f*
insulation *n* aislamiento, *m*
insulator *n elec* aislador, *m*
insulin *n med* insulina, *f*
insult *n* insulto, agravio, ultraje, *m,* afrenta, ofensa, *f. vt* insultar, ofender, afrentar. **He was insulted,** Fue insultado; Se mostró ofendido
insulter *n* insultador (-ra)
insulting *a* insultante, injurioso, ofensivo. **He was very i. to them,** Les insultó, Les trató con menosprecio
insultingly *adv* con insolencia, ofensivamente
insuperability *n* dificultades insuperables, *f pl,* imposibilidad, *f,* lo insuperable
insuperable *a* insuperable, invencible
insuperably *adv* invenciblemente
insupportable *a* insoportable, inaguantable, intolerable, insufrible
insupportably *adv* insufriblemente, insoportablemente
insurable *a* asegurable
insurance *n* aseguramiento, *m; com* seguro, *m;* aseguración, *f.* **accident i.,** seguro contra accidentes, *m.* **fire-i.,** seguro contra incendio, *m.* **life i.,** seguro sobre la vida, *m.* **maritime i.,** seguro marítimo, *m.* **National I. Act,** Ley del Seguro Nacional Obligatorio, *f.* **i. broker,** corredor de seguros, *m.* **i. company,** compañía de seguros, *f.* **i. policy,** póliza de seguros, *f.* **i. premium,** prima de seguros, *f*
insure *vt com* asegurar. **to i. oneself,** asegurarse. **the insured,** (person) el asegurado
insurer *n* asegurador (-ra)
insurgent *a* insurgente, rebelde; (of sea) invasor. *n* rebelde, *mf* insurrecto (-ta)
insurmountable *a* insalvable, insuperable, invencible, intransitable
insurrection *n* insurrección, sublevación, *f,* levantamiento, *m*
insurrectionary *a* rebelde, amotinado, insurgente
insusceptible *a* no susceptible, indiferente, insensible
intact *a* intacto, íntegro, indemne
intake *n* (of a stocking) menguado, *m; mech* aspiración, *f;* válvula de admisión, *f; aer* admisión, toma, *f;* orificio de entrada, *m*
intangibility *n* intangibilidad, *f*
intangible *a* intangible; incomprensible
integer *n math* número entero, *m*
integral *a* íntegro, intrínseco, inherente; *math* entero. *n math* integral, *f.* **i. calculus,** cálculo integral, *m*
integrate *vt* integrar, completar; formar en un todo; *math* integrar
integrity *n* integridad, honradez, rectitud, entereza, *f*
intellect *n* intelecto, entendimiento, *m*
intellectual *a* intelectual, mental. *n* intelectual
intellectualism *n* intelectualismo, *m,* intelectualidad, *f*
intellectually *adv* intelectualmente, mentalmente
intelligence *n* inteligencia, comprensión, mente, *f;* (quickness of mind) agudeza, perspicacia, *f;* (news) noticia, *f,* conocimiento, informe, *m.* **the latest i.,** las últimas noticias. **i. quotient,** cociente de inteligencia, *m.* **I. Service,** Inteligencia, *f;* policía secreta, *f.* **i. test,** prueba de inteligencia, *f*
intelligent *a* inteligente
intelligentsia *n* clase intelectual, intelectualidad, *f, inf* masa cefálica, *f*
intelligibility *n* comprensibilidad, inteligibilidad, *f*
intelligible *a* inteligible, comprensible
intelligibly *adv* inteligiblemente
intemperance *n* intemperancia, inmoderación, *f;* exceso en la bebida, *m*
intemperate *a* intemperante, destemplado, descomedido; inmoderado; bebedor en exceso
intemperately *adv* inmoderadamente
intend *vt* intentar, proponerse, pensar; destinar, dedicar; (mean) querer decir. **to be intended,** estar destinado; tener por fin; querer decir
intendant *n* intendente, *m*
intended *a* pensado, deseado. *n inf* novio (-ia), futuro (-ra), prometido (-da)
intense *a* intenso, vivo, fuerte; (of emotions) profundo, hondo, vehemente; (of colors) subido, intenso; (great) extremado, sumo, muy grande
intensification *n* intensificación, *f;* aumento, *m*
intensify *vt* intensar, intensificar; aumentar
intensity *n* intensidad, fuerza, *f;* (of emotions) profundidad, vehemencia, violencia, *f;* (of colors) intensidad, *f*
intensive *a* intensivo
intensive-care unit *n* sala de terapia intensiva, unidad de cuidades intensivos, unidad de vigilancia intensiva, *f*
intent *n* intento, propósito, deseo, *m. a* atento; (ab-

sorbed) absorto, interesado; (on doing) resuelto a, decidido a. **to all intents and purposes,** en efecto, en realidad. **to be i. on,** (reading, etc.) estar absorto en, entregarse a. **with i. to defraud,** con el propósito deliberado de defraudar
intention *n* intención, voluntad, *f*, propósito, pensamiento, proyecto, *m*
intentional *a* intencional, deliberado, premeditado
intentionally *adv* a propósito, intencionalmente, de pensado
intentioned *a* intencionado
intently *adv* atentamente
inter *vt* enterrar, sepultar
inter *pref* inter, entre. **i.-allied,** interaliado, de los aliados. **i.-denominational,** intersectario. **i.-university,** interuniversitario. **i.-urban,** interurbano
interaction *n* interacción, acción recíproca, acción mutua, *f*
intercalate *vt* intercalar, interpolar
intercede *vi* interceder, mediar. **to i. for,** hablar por
intercept *vt* interceptar, detener; entrecoger, atajar
interception *n* interceptación, detención, *f*
intercession *n* mediación, intercesión, *f*
intercessor *n* intercesor (-ra), mediador (-ra)
interchange *n* intercambio, *m*; (of goods) comercio, tráfico, *m*. *vt* cambiar, trocar; alternar
interchangeable *a* intercambiable
intercom *n* teléfono interior, *m*
intercommunicate *vi* comunicarse
intercommunication *n* comunicación mutua, *f*; comercio, *m*
intercostal *a anat* intercostal
intercourse *n* (social) trato, *m*, relaciones, *f pl*; *com* comercio, tráfico, *m*; (of ideas) intercambio, *m*; (sexual) coito, trato sexual, *m*
interdependence *n* dependencia mutua, mutualidad, *f*
interdependent *a* mutuo
interdict *n* interdicto, veto, *m*, prohibición, *f*; *ecc* entredicho, *m*. *vt* interdecir, prohibir, privar; *ecc* poner entredicho
interdiction *n* interdicción, prohibición, *f*
interest *n* interés, *m*; provecho, *m*; *com* premio, rédito, interés, *m*; (in a firm) participación, *f*; (curiosity) interés, *m*; curiosidad, *f*; simpatía, *f*; (influence) influencia, *f*. *n pl* **interests,** (commercial undertakings) empresas, *f pl*, intereses, negocios, *m pl*. *vt* interesar. **to be interested in,** interesarse en, (on behalf of) por. **to be in one's own i.,** ser en provecho de uno, ser en su propio interés. **to bear eight per cent. i.,** dar interés del ocho por ciento. **to pay with i.,** pagar con creces. **to put out at i.,** dar a interés. **in the interests of,** en interés de. **compound i.,** interés compuesto, *m*. **simple i.,** interés sencillo, *m*. **vested interests,** intereses creados, *m pl*
interesting *a* interesante, curioso, atractivo
interestingly *adv* amenamente, de modo interesante
interfere *vi* intervenir, meterse, entremeterse, mezclarse; *inf* mangonear, meter las narices; (with) meterse con; (impede) estorbar, impedir
interference *n* intervención, *f*, entrometimiento, *m*; (obstacle) estorbo, obstáculo, *m*; *phys* interferencia, *f*; *rad* parásitos, *m pl*
interfering *a* entremetido, oficioso; *inf* mangoneador
interim *n* ínterin, intermedio, *Lat. Am. also* interregno *m*. *a* interino, provisional. **in the i.,** entre tanto, en el ínterin. *com* **i. dividend,** dividendo interino, *m*
interior *a* interior, interno; doméstico. *n* interior, *m*
interject *vt* interponer
interjection *n* exclamación, interjección, *f*; interposición, *f*
interlace *vt* entrelazar, entretejer
interleave *vt* interfoliar, interpaginar
interline *vt* entrerrenglonar, interlinear
interlinear *a* interlineal
interlineation *n* interlineación, *f*
interlining *n* entretela, *f*
interlock *vt* (of wheels, etc.). endentar; trabar; cerrar. *vi* endentarse; entrelazarse, unirse; cerrar
interlocutor *n* interlocutor (-ra)
interloper *n* intruso (-sa); *com* intérlope, *m*
interloping *a* intérlope
interlude *n* intervalo, intermedio, *m*; *mus* interludio, *m*; *theat* entremés, *m*
intermarriage *n* casamiento entre parientes próximos, entre razas distintas, o entre grupos étnicos distintos, *m*
intermarry *vi* contraer matrimonio entre parientes próximos, entre personas de razas distintas, o entre grupos étnicos distintos
intermediary *a* and *n* intermediario (-ia)
intermediate *a* intermedio, medio, medianero. *n* sustancia intermedia, *f*. *vi* intervenir, mediar
interment *n* entierro, *m*
intermezzo *n theat* intermedio, *m*; *mus* intermezzo, *m*
interminable *a* interminable, inacabable
interminably *adv* interminablemente, sin fin, sin cesar
intermingle *vt* entremezclar, entreverar. *vi* mezclarse
intermission *n* intermisión, interrupción, pausa, *f*; *theat* entreacto, *m*. **without i.,** sin pausa, sin tregua
intermittence *n* intermitencia, alternación, *f*
intermittent *a* intermitente, discontinuo; (of fever) intermitente
intermittently *adv* a intervalos, a ratos, a pausas
intern *n med* practicante de hospital *m*, interno (-na), interno de hospital, alumno interno, *m*. *vt* confinar, encerrar
internal *a* interno, interior; (of affairs) doméstico, civil; intrínseco; íntimo. **i.-combustion engine,** motor de combustión interna, *m*
internally *adv* interiormente
international *a* internacional. *n sport* un partido internacional. **i. law,** derecho internacional, *m*
internationalism *n* internacionalismo, *m*
internationalist *n* internacionalista, *mf*
internationalization *n* internacionalización, *f*
internationalize *vt* hacer internacional, poner bajo un control internacional
internecine *a* sanguinario, feroz
internee *n* internado (-da)
internment *n* internamiento, *m*. **i. camp,** campo de internamiento, *m*
interoceanic *a* interoceánico
interpolate *vt* interpolar, intercalar, interponer
interpolation *n* interpolación, inserción, añadidura, *f*
interpolator *n* interpolador (-ra)
interpose *vt* interponer; (a remark) interpolar. *vi* interponerse, intervenir; (interfere) entrometerse; interrumpir
interposition *n* interposición, *f*; entrometimiento, *m*
interpret *vt* interpretar; (translate) traducir; (explain) explicar, descifrar. *vi* interpretar.
interpretation *n* interpretación, *f*; (translation) traducción, *f*; (explanation) explicación, *f*
interpretative *a* interpretativo, interpretador
interpreter *n* intérprete, *mf*
interregnum *n* interregno, *m*
interrelation *n* relación mutua, *f*
interrogate *vt* interrogar, examinar, preguntar
interrogating *a* interrogante
interrogation *n* interrogación, *f*, examen, *m*; pregunta, *f*. **mark of i.,** punto de interrogación, *m*
interrogative *a* interrogativo. *n* palabra interrogativa, *f*
interrogatively *adv* interrogativamente
interrogator *n* examinador (-ra), interrogador (-ra)
interrogatory *a* interrogativo. *n* interrogatorio, *m*
interrupt *vt* interrumpir
interruptedly *adv* interrumpidamente
interrupter *n* interruptor (-ra); *elec* interruptor, *m*
interruption *n* interrupción, *f*
intersect *vt* cruzar. *vi* cruzarse, intersecarse
intersection *n* intersección, *f*; cruce, *m*, (of streets) bocacalle, *Lat. Am.* cruza *f*

intersperse *vt* diseminar, esparcir; interpolar, entremezclar
interstice *n* intervalo, intermedio, *m*; (chink) intersticio, *m*, hendedura, *f*
intertwine *vt* entretejer, entrelazar. *vi* entrelazarse
interval *n* intervalo, intermedio, *m*, pausa, *f*; *theat* entreacto, *m*, intermisión, *f*; (in schools) recreo, *m*. **at intervals,** a trechos, de vez en cuando. **lucid i.,** intervalo claro, intervalo lúcido, *m*
intervene *vi* intervenir, tomar parte (en), mediar; (occur) sobrevenir, acaecer; *law* interponerse
intervening *a* intermedio; interventor
intervention *n* intervención, mediación, *f*
interventionist *n pol* partidario (-ia) de la intervención
interview *n* entrevista, *f*, interviev, *m*. *vt* entrevistarse con
interviewer *n* interrogador (-ra); (reporter) reportero, periodista, *m*
interweave *vt* entretejer, entrelazar
interweaving *n* entretejimiento, *m*
intestacy *n* ausencia de un testamento, *f*
intestate *a* and *n* intestado (-da)
intestinal *a* intestinal, intestino. **i. worm,** lombriz intestinal, *f*
intestine *n* intestino, *m*. **large i.,** intestino grueso, *m*. **small i.,** intestino delgado, *m*
intimacy *n* intimidad, *f*, familiaridad, *f*; (of nobility and others) privanza, *f*
intimate *a* íntimo; (of relations) entrañable, estrecho; intrínseco, esencial; (of knowledge) profundo, completo, detallado. *n* amigo (-ga) de confianza. *vt* intimar, dar a entender, indicar. **to become i.,** intimarse. **to be on i. terms with,** tratar de tú (a), ser amigo íntimo de
intimately *adv* íntimamente, al fondo
intimation *n* intimación, indicación, *f*; (hint) insinuación, indirecta, *f*
intimidate *vt* intimidar, aterrar, infundir miedo (a), espantar, acobardar, amedrentar
intimidation *n* intimidación, *f*
intimidatory *a* aterrador, amenazador
into *prep* en; a, al, a la; dentro, adentro; (of transforming, forming, etc.) en. **Throw it i. the fire,** Échalo al (or en el) fuego. **She went i. the house,** Entró en la casa. **to look i.,** mirar dentro de; mirar hacia el interior (de); investigar
intolerable *a* intolerable, insufrible, inaguantable, insoportable, inllevable
intolerableness *n* intolerabilidad, *f*
intolerably *adv* intolerablemente, insufriblemente
intolerance *n* intolerancia, intransigencia, *f*
intolerant *a* intolerante, intransigente; *med* intolerante
intonation *n* entonación, *f*
intone *vt* entonar; *ecc* salmodiar
intoxicant *a* embriagador. *n* bebida alcohólica, *f*
intoxicate *vt* emborrachar, embriagar; *med* intoxicar, envenenar; (excite) embriagar, embelesar
intoxicated *a* borracho; (excited) ebrio, embriagado; *med* intoxicado
intoxicating *a* embriagador
intoxication *n* borrachera, embriaguez, *f*; *med* intoxicación, *f*, envenenamiento, *m*; (excitement) entusiasmo, *m*, ebriedad, *f*
intractability *n* insociabilidad, hurañería, *f*
intractable *a* intratable, insociable, huraño
intramural *adv* intramuros
intransigence *n* intransigencia, intolerancia, *f*
intransigent *a* intransigente, intolerante
intransitive *a* intransitivo, neutro
intrauterine *a med* intrauterino
intravenous *a med* intravenoso
intrepid *a* intrépido, osado, audaz
intrepidity *n* intrepidez, osadía, audacia, *f*
intrepidly *adv* intrépidamente, audazmente
intricacy *n* intrincación, complejidad, *f*
intricate *a* intrincado, complejo
intricately *adv* intrincadamente
intrigue *n* intriga, maquinación, *f*, enredo, *m*; (amorous) lío, *m*. *vi* intrigar, enredar; (amorous) tener un lío. *vt* (interest) atraer, interesar; (with) intrigar con. **to be intrigued** *Lat. Am.* intrigarse
intriguer *n* intrigante, *mf*, urdemalas, *m*, enredador (-ra)
intriguing *a* enredador; (attractive) atrayente, interesante, seductor
intrinsic *a* intrínseco, innato, inherente, esencial
intrinsically *adv* intrínsecamente, esencialmente
introduce *vt* introducir; hacer entrar; insertar, injerir; (a person) presentar; poner de moda, introducir; (a bill) presentar; (a person to a thing) llamar la atención sobre. **Permit me to i. my friend,** Permítame que le presente mi amigo
introduction *n* introducción, *f*; (of a book) prefacio, prólogo, *m*, advertencia, *f*; (of a person) presentación, *f*; inserción, *f*
introductory *a* introductor, preliminar, preparatorio
intromission *n* intromisión, *f*
introspection *n* introspección, *f*
introspective *a* introspectivo
introversion *n psy* introversión *f*
introvert *a* and *n psy* introverso (-sa)
intrude *vt* introducir, imponer. *vi* entremeterse, inmiscuirse. **Do I i.?** ¿Estorbo?
intruder *n* intruso (-sa)
intrusion *n* intrusión, *f*; *geol* intromisión, *f*
intrusive *a* intruso
intuition *n* intuición, *f*. **to know by i.,** intuir, saber por intuición
intuitive *a* intuitivo
inundate *vt* inundar, anegar; *fig* abrumar
inundation *n* inundación, anegación, *f*; *fig* diluvio, *m*, abundancia, *f*
inure *vt* endurecer, habituar
inurement *n* habituación, *f*
invade *vt* invadir, irrumpir, asaltar; *med* invadir
invader *n* invasor (-ra), acometedor (-ra), agresor (-ra)
invading *a* invasor, irruptor
invalid *a* inválido, nulo. **to become i.,** caducar
invalid *n* inválido (-da), enfermo (-ma). **to become an i.,** quedarse inválido. **to i. out of the army,** licenciar por invalidez. **i. carriage,** cochecillo de inválido, *m*
invalidate *vt* invalidar, anular
invalidation *n* invalidación, *f*
invalidity *n* invalidez, nulidad, *f*
invaluable *n* inestimable
invariability *n* invariabilidad, invariación, inalterabilidad, inmutabilidad, *f*
invariable *a* invariable, inmutable, inalterable
invariably *adv* invariablemente, inmutablemente
invariant *n math* invariante, *m*
invasion *n* invasión, irrupción, *f*; *med* invasión, *f*
invective *n* invectiva, diatriba, *f*
inveigh (against) *vi* desencadenarse (contra), prorrumpir en invectivas (contra)
inveigle *vt* seducir, engatusar, persuadir
invent *vt* inventar, descubrir, originar; (a falsehood) fingir; (create) idear, componer
invention *n* invención, *f*, invento, descubrimiento, *m*; (imagination) ingeniosidad, inventiva, *f*; (falsehood) ficción, mentira, *f*; (finding) invención, *f*, hallazgo, *m*
inventive *a* inventor, inventivo; ingenioso, despejado
inventiveness *n* inventiva, *f*
inventor *n* inventor (-ra), autor (-ra)
inventory *n* inventario, *m*; descripción, *f*. *vt* inventariar
inverse *a* inverso. **i. proportion,** razón inversa, *f*
inversely *adv* inversamente, a la inversa
inversion *n* inversión, *f*, trastrocamiento, *m*; *gram* hipérbaton, *m*
invert *vt* invertir, trastornar, trastrocar. **inverted commas,** comilla, *f*
invertebrate *a* and *n* invertebrado *m*.
invest *vt com* invertir; *mil* sitiar, cercar; (foll. by with) poner, cubrir con; (of qualities) conferir, otorgar, dar.

vi (with in) poner dinero en, echar caudal en; *inf* comprar
investigable *a* averiguable
investigate *vt* investigar, estudiar; examinar, averiguar; explorar. **to i. closely** *Lat. Am.* interiorizar
investigation *n* investigación, *f*, estudio, *m*; examen, *m*, averiguación, *f*; encuesta, pesquisa, *f*
investigator *n* investigador (-ra); averiguador (-ra)
investigatory *a* investigador
investiture *n* investidura, instalación, *f*
investment *n* (*com* of money) inversión, *f*, empleo, *m*; *mil* cerco, *m*; (investiture) instalación, *f*; *pl* **investments,** *com* acciones, *f pl*, fondos, *m pl*
investor *n* inversionista, *m*; accionista, *mf*, *Lat. Am.* inversor (-ra) *mf*
inveteracy *n* antigüedad, *f*, lo arraigado
inveterate *a* inveterado, antiguo, arraigado, incurable
invidious *a* odioso, repugnante, injusto
invidiousness *n* injusticia, *f*, lo odioso
invigorate *vt* vigorizar, dar fuerza (a), avivar
invigorating *a* fortaleciente, fortificador, vigorizador
invincibility *n* invencibilidad, *f*
invincible *a* invencible, indomable; *fig* insuperable
inviolability *n* inviolabilidad, *f*
inviolable *a* inviolable
inviolate *a* inviolado
invisibility *n* invisibilidad, *f*
invisible *a* invisible. **i. ink,** tinta simpática, *f*. **i. mending,** zurcido invisible, *m*
invitation *n* invitación, *f*; convite, *m*; (card) tarjeta de invitación, *f*
invite *vt* invitar, convidar; (request) pedir, rogar; (of things) incitar, tentar.
inviting *a* atrayente, incitante; (of food) apetitoso; (of looks) provocativo
invocation *n* invocación, *f*
invocatory *a* invocatorio, invocador
invoice *n com* factura, *f*. *vt* facturar. **proforma i.,** factura simulada, *f*. **shipping i.,** factura de expedición, *f*. **i. book,** libro de facturas, *m*
invoke *vt* invocar; suplicar, implorar; (*laws*) acogerse (a)
involuntarily *adv* sin querer, involuntariamente
involuntariness *n* involuntariedad, *f*
involuntary *a* involuntario; instintivo, inconsciente
involve *vt* (entangle) enredar, embrollar, enmarañar; (implicate) comprometer; (imply) implicar, ocasionar, suponer, traer consigo
involved *a* complejo, intrincado; (of style) confuso, obscuro
invulnerability *n* invulnerabilidad, *f*
invulnerable *a* invulnerable
inward *a* interior, interno; íntimo, espiritual. *adv* adentro
inwardly *adv* interiormente; para sí, entre sí
inwards *adv* hacia dentro; adentro
iodine *n* yodo, *m*. **i. poisoning,** yodismo, *m*
ion *n chem* ion, *m*
Ionian *a* and *n* jónico (-ca)
Ionic *a* jónico. **i. foot** *poet* jónico, *m*
iota *n* (letter) iota, *f*; jota, pizca, *f*, ápice, *m*. **not an i.,** ni pizca
I.O.U. *n com* abonaré, *m*
ipecacuanha *n* ipecacuana, *f*
Iranian *a* and *n* iranio (-ia)
irascibility *n* irascibilidad, iracundia, irritabilidad, *f*
irascible *a* irascible, iracundo, irritable
irate *a* airado, colérico, enojado
ire *n* ira, cólera, furia, *f*
Ireland Irlanda, *f*
iridescence *n* iridiscencia, *f*
iridescent *a* iridiscente. **to look i.,** irisar, tornasolarse
iridium *n chem* iridio, *m*
iris *n anat* iris, *m*; *bot* irídea, *f*
Irish *a* and *n* irlandés (-esa). **the I.,** los irlandeses
Irish Sea Mar de Irlanda, *f*
irksome *a* fastidioso, tedioso, aburrido
irksomeness *n* tedio, fastidio, aburrimiento, *m*
iron *n* hierro, *m*; (for clothes) plancha, *f*; (tool) utensilio, *m*, herramienta, *f*; (golf) hierro, *m*; *pl* **irons,** grillos, *m pl*, cadenas, *f pl*. *a* de hierro, férreo; *fig* duro, severo. *vt* (linen) planchar; (with out) allanar. **to have too many irons in the fire,** tener demasiados asuntos entre manos. **to put in irons,** echar grillos (a). **to strike while the i. is hot,** A hierro caliente batir de repente. **cast-i.,** hierro colado, *m*. **scrap i.,** hierro viejo, *m*. **sheet i.,** hierro en planchas, *m*. **wrought i.,** hierro dulce, *m*. **i. age,** edad de hierro, *f*. **i.-foundry,** fundición de hierro, *f*. **i. lung,** *med* pulmón de hierro, pulmón de acero, *m*. **i.-mold,** mancha de orín, *f*. **i. smelting furnace,** alto horno, *m*. **i. tonic,** *med* reconstituyente ferruginoso, *m*. **i. will,** voluntad de hierro, *f*
ironclad *a* blindado, acorazado. *n* buque de guerra blindado, acorazado, *m*
ironer *n* planchador (-ra)
ironical *a* irónico
ironically *adv* con ironía, irónicamente
ironing *n* planchado, *m*; ropa por planchar, *f*. *a* de planchar. **i. board,** tabla de planchar, *f*
ironist *n* ironista, *mf*
ironmonger *n* ferretero (-ra). **ironmonger's shop,** ferretería, *f*
ironmongery *n* ferretería, quincallería, *f*
iron sulphide sulfuro de hierro, *m*
ironwork *n* herraje, *m*; obra de hierro, *f*
ironworks *n* herrería, *f*
irony *n* ironía, *f*. *a* (like iron) ferrugiento
Iroquois *a* and *n* iroqués (-esa)
irradiate *vt* irradiar; *fig* iluminar, aclarar
irradiation *n* irradiación, *f*; *fig* iluminación, *f*
irrational *a* ilógico, ridículo, irracional
irrationality *n* irracionalidad, *f*
irreclaimable *a* irrecuperable, irredimible; (of land) inservible, improductivo; irreformable
irreconcilable *a* irreconciliable
irreconcilably *adv* irremediablemente
irrecoverable *a* irrecuperable, incobrable
irredeemable *a* irredimible, perdido. **i. government loan,** deuda perpetua, *f*
irredeemably *adv* perdidamente
irreducible *a* irreducible
irrefutability *n* verdad, *f*
irrefutable *a* irrefutable, indisputable, innegable, irrebatible
irregular *a* irregular; anormal; (of shape) disforme; desordenado; *gram* irregular; (of surface) desigual, escabroso
irregularity *n* irregularidad, *f*; anormalidad, *f*; (of shape) desproporción, irregularidad, *f*; (of surface) escabrosidad, desigualdad, *f*; exceso, *m*, demasía, *f*
irrelevance *n* inconexión, *f*; inoportunidad, *f*; futilidad, poca importancia, *f*; (stupidity) desatino, *m*, impertinencia, *f*
irrelevant *a* inaplicable, fuera de propósito; inoportuno; sin importancia, fútil; (stupid) impertinente
irreligion *n* irreligión, impiedad, *f*
irreligious *a* irreligioso, impío
irremediable *a* irremediable, irreparable
irremediably *adv* sin remedio, irremediablemente
irreparable *a* irreparable
irreplaceable *a* irreemplazable
irrepressible *a* incontrolable, indomable
irreproachable *a* irreprochable, intachable
irresistible *a* irresistible
irresistibleness *n* superioridad, *f*
irresolute *a* irresoluto, indeciso, vacilante
irresoluteness *n* irresolución, indecisión, *f*
irrespective *a* (with of) independiente de, aparte de, sin distinción de
irresponsibility *n* irresponsabilidad, *f*
irresponsible *a* irresponsable
irretrievable *a* irrecuperable

irretrievably *adv* irreparablemente, sin remedio
irreverence *n* irreverencia, *f*
irreverent *a* irreverente, irrespetuoso
irrevocability *n* irrevocabilidad, *f*
irrevocable *a* irrevocable; inquebrantable
irrigable *a* regadío
irrigate *vt agr* poner en regadío, regar; *med* irrigar
irrigation *n agr* riego, *m; med* irrigación, *f*. **i. channel,** cacera, acequia, *f*, canal de riego, *m*
irritability *n* irritabilidad, iracundia, *f*
irritable *a* irritable, irascible, iracundo
irritably *adv* con irritación, airadamente
irritant *a* irritante, irritador. *n* irritador, *m; med* medicamento irritante, *m*
irritate *vt* provocar, estimular; irritar, molestar, exasperar; *med* irritar
irritating *a* irritador, irritante
irritatingly *adv* de un modo irritante
irritation *n* irritación, *f*, enojo, *m; physiol* picazón, *f*, picor, *m*
irruption *n* irrupción, invasión, *f*
isinglass *n* cola de pescado, *f*
Islamic *a* islámico
Islamism *n* islamismo, *m*
Islamite *a* and *n* islamita *mf*
island *n* isla, *f*, *a* isleño
islander *n* isleño (-ña)
islet *n* isleta, *f*; isolote, *m*
isobaric *a* isobárico
isolate *vt* aislar, apartar
isolated *a* aislado, apartado, solitario; único, solo
isolation *n* aislamiento, apartamiento, *m*, soledad, *f*
isolationism *n pol* aislacionismo, aislamientismo, *m*
isolationist *a* and *n pol* aislacionista, aislamientista, *mf*
isomerism *n chem* isomería, *f*
isometric *a* isométrico
isosceles *a* isósceles
isotope *n* isotope, isotopo, *m*
Israelite *a* and *n* israelita *mf*
issue *n* salida, *f*; (result) resultado, *m*, consecuencia, *f*; (of a periodical) número, *m*; *print* edición, tirada, *f*; (offspring) prole, sucesión, *f*; (of notes, bonds) emisión, *f*; *med* flujo, *m*; cuestión, *f*, problema, *m*. *vi* salir, fluir, manar; nacer, originarse; resultar, terminarse. *vt* (an order) expedir, emitir, dictar; publicar, dar a luz; (of notes, bonds) poner en circulación, librar. **at i.,** en disputa, en cuestión. **to join i.,** llevar la contraria, oponer
isthmian *a* ístmico
isthmus *n* istmo, *m*
it *pron* (as subject) él, *m*; ella, *f*; (gen. omitted with all verbs in Sp.); (as object) lo, *m*; la, *f*; (as indirect object) le (se with an object in 3rd pers.); (meaning that thing, that affair) eso, ello. Sometimes omitted in other cases, e.g. **He has thought it necessary to stay at home,** Ha creído necesario de quedarse en casa. **We heard it said that . . .,** Oímos decir que . . . **to make it perfectly clear that . . .,** dejar bien claro que . . . *n* (slang) garbo, aquél, *m*; atractivos, *m pl*. **Is it not so?** ¿No es así? **That is it,** Eso es. **It's me,** Soy yo
Italy Italia, *f*
Italian *a* and *n* italiano (-na) (language) italiano, *m*. *art* **I. School,** escuela italiana, *f*
italic *a* (of Italy) itálico; *print* itálico, bastardillo. *n* letra bastardilla, bastardilla, letra itálica, *f*. **italics mine,** el subrayado es mío, los subrayados son míos
italicize *vt* imprimir en bastardilla; dar énfasis (a)
itch *n* sarna, *f*; *fig* picazón, *f*; prurito, capricho, *m*. *vi* picar; *fig* sentir picazón; (with to) rabiar por, suspirar por.
itching *n* picazón, *f*, picor, *m*. *a* sarnoso, picante; *med* pruriginoso. **to have an i. palm,** *fig* ser de la virgen del puño
item *n* ítem, artículo, *m*; *com* partida, *f*; punto, detalle, *m*; (of a program) número, *m*; asunto, *m*. *adv* ítem
iterative *a* iterativo
Ithaca Ítaca, *f*
itinerant *a* nómada, errante
itinerary *n* itinerario, *m*, ruta, *f*
its *poss a* su (with pl. obj.) sus. **a book and its pages,** un libro y sus páginas.
itself *pron* él mismo, *m*; ella misma, *f*; (with prep.) sí; (with reflex. verb) se; (with noun) el mismo, la misma; (meaning alone) solo. **in i.,** en sí
ivied *a* cubierto de hiedra
ivory *n* marfil, *m*. *a* ebúrneo, de marfil, marfileño. **vegetable i.,** marfil vegetal, *m*. **i. carving,** talla de marfil, *f*
ivory tower *n* torre de marfil, *f*
ivory-tower *a* de torre de marfil
ivy *n* hiedra, *f*

J

j *n* (letter) jota, *f*
jab *vt* (with a hypodermic needle, etc.) pinchar; introducir (en); clavar (con); (scrape) hurgar; (place) poner. *n* pinchazo, *m*; golpe, *m*. **He jabbed his pistol in my ribs,** Me puso la pistola en las costillas
jabber *vt* and *vi* chapurrear; (of monkeys) chillar
jabbering *n* chapurreo, *m*; (of monkeys) chillidos, *m pl*
Jack *n* Juan, *m*; (man) hombre, *m*; (sailor) marinero, *m*; (in cards) sota, *f*; (for raising weights) gato, *m*; (of a spit) torno, *m*; (of some animals) macho, *m*; (bowls) boliche, *m*. *vt* (with up) solevantar con gatos. **Union J.,** pabellón británico, *m*. **j.-boot,** bota de montar, *f*. **J.-in-office,** mandarín, funcionario impertinente, *m*. **J.-in-the-box,** faca, *f*. **j.-knife,** navaja, *f*. **J. of all trades,** hombre de muchos oficios, *m*. **jack of all trades, master of none,** aprendiz de todo, oficial de nada. **j.-rabbit,** liebre americana, *f*. **J.-tar,** marinero, *m*
jackal *n* chacal, adive, *m*
jackanapes *n* impertinente, *m*; mequetrefe, *m*
jackass *n* asno, *m*; (fool) tonto, asno, *m*. **laughing j.,** martín pescador, *m*
jacket *n* chaqueta, *f*; americana, *f*; (for boilers, etc.) camisa, *f*; (of a book) forro, *m*, sobrecubierta, *f*. **strait j.,** camisa de fuerza, *f*
jacks *n* (game) matatenas, *f pl*, cantillos, *m pl*
jade *n min* jade, *m*; (horse) rocín, *m*; (woman) mala pécora, *f*; (saucy wench) mozuela, picaruela, *f*
jaded *a* fatigado, agotado, rendido; (of the palate) saciado
jagged *a* dentado
jaguar *n* jaguar, *m*
jai alai *n Mexico* frontón, *m*
jail cárcel, prisión, *f*; encierro, *m*. *vt* encarcelar. *a* carcelario, carcelero.
jailbird malhechor; presidiario, *m*
jailer *n* carcelero (-ra)
jalopy carcacho, *m*, (Mexico), cafetera rusa, *f*, (Spain)
jalousie *n* celosía, *f*
jam *vt* (ram) apretar; apiñar; estrujar; (a machine) atascar; (radio) causar interferencia (a); (preserve) hacer confitura de. *vi* atascarse. *n* (of people) agolpamiento, *m*; (traffic) atasco, *m*; (preserve) confitura, mermelada, compota, *f*. **He jammed his hat on,** Se encasquetó el sombrero. **She suddenly jammed down on the brakes,** Frenó de repente. **jam-dish,** compotera, *f*. **jam-jar,** pote para confitura, *m*
Jamaican *a* jamaicano, *n* jamaicano (-na)
jamboree campamento, *m*
jamming *n rad* interferencias, *f pl*
jangle *vi* cencerrear; chocar; rechinar. *n* cencerreo, *m*; choque, *m*; rechinamiento, *m*

janissary *n* jenízaro, *m*
janitor *n* portero, *m*; (in a university, etc.) bedel, *m*
January *n* enero, *m*
Japan el Japón, *m*
japan *n* charol, *m*. *vt* charolar
Japanese *a* japonés. *n* japonés (-esa); (language) japonés, *m*
jar *n* chirrido, *m*; choque, *m*; sacudida, *f*; vibración, trepidación, *f*; (quarrel) riña, *f*; (receptacle) jarra, *f*; (for tobacco, honey, cosmetics, etc.) pote, *m*; (Leyden) botella (de Leyden), *f*. *vi* chirriar; vibrar, trepidar; chocar; (of sounds) ser discorde; (of colors) chillar. *vt* sacudir; hacer vibrar. **It jarred on my nerves,** Me atacaba los nervios. **It gave me a nasty jar,** *fig* Me hizo una impresión desagradable. **on the jar,** entreabierto
jardiniere *n* jardinera, *f*
jargon *n* jerga, jerigonza, *f*; monserga, *f*; (technical) lenguaje especial, *m*
jarring *a* discorde, disonante; en conflicto, opuesto; (to the nerves) que ataca a los nervios
jasmine *n* jazmín, *m*. **yellow j.,** jazmín amarillo, *m*
jasper *n min* jaspe, *m*
jaundice *n* ictericia, *f*
jaundiced *a* envidioso; desengañado, desilusionado
jaunt *n* excursión, *f*, *vi* ir de excursión
jauntily *adv* airosamente, con garbo
jauntiness *n* garbo, *m*, gentileza, ligereza, *f*
jaunty *a* garboso, airoso
Javanese *a* javanés. *n* javanés (-esa)
javelin *n* jabalina, *f*. **j. throwing,** lanzamiento de la jabalina, *m*
jaw *n* quijada, *f*; maxilar, *m*; *pl* **jaws,** boca, *f*; (of death, etc.) garras, *f pl*; *mech* quijada, *f*; (narrow entrance) boca, abertura, *f*. **jaw-bone,** mandíbula, *f*; *anat* hueso maxilar, *m*
jay *n* arrendajo, *m*
jazz *n* jazz, *m*. *vi* bailar el jazz. **j. band,** orquesta de jazz, *f*
jealous *a* celoso; envidioso. **to be j. of,** tener celos de. **to make j.,** dar celos (a)
jealously *adv* celosamente
jealousy *n* celos, *m pl*
jeans *n* vaqueros, *m pl*
jeep *n mil* yip, *m*
jeer *n* burla, mofa, *f*; insulto, *m*, *vi* burlarse; (with at) mofarse de
jeerer *n* mofador (-ra)
jeering *a* mofador. *n* burlas, *f pl*; insultos, *m pl*
jeeringly *adv* burlonamente
jellied *a* en gelatina
jelly *n* jalea, *f*; gelatina, *f*, *vi* solidificarse. **j.-bag,** manga, *f*. **j.-fish,** aguamala, aguaviva, malagna, medusa, *f*
jeopardize *vt* arriesgar, poner en juego; comprometer
jeopardy *n* peligro, *m*
jeremiad *n* jeremiada, *f*
jerk *n* sacudida, *f*. *vt* sacudir, dar una sacudida (a); lanzar bruscamente; (pull) tirar de; (push) empujar. *vi* moverse a sacudidas. **I jerked myself free,** Me libré de una sacudida
jerkily *adv* con sacudidas; espasmódicamente; nerviosamente
jerkin *n* justillo, *m*
jerky *a* espasmódico; nervioso (also of style)
jerry-built *a* mal construido, de pacotilla
jersey *n* jersey, *m*. *a* de jersey; de Jersey. **football j.,** camiseta de fútbol, *f*, jersey de fútbol, *m*. **J. cow,** vaca jerseysa, *f*
Jerusalem Jerusalén, *m*
jest *n* broma, chanza, *f*; (joke) chiste, *m*; (laughingstock) hazmerreír, *m*. *vi* bromear; burlarse (de). **in j.,** en broma, de guasa
jester *n* burlón (-ona); (practical joker, etc.) bromista, *mf*; (at a royal court) bufón, *m*
jesting *n* bromas, *f pl*; chistes, *m pl*; burlas, *f pl*. *a* de broma; burlón
jestingly *adv* en broma
Jesuit *n* Jesuita, *m*
Jesuitical *a* jesuítico
jet *n min* azabache, *m*; (stream) chorro, *m*; (pipe) surtidero, *m*; (burner) mechero, *m*, *vi* chorrear. **jet-black,** negro como el azabache, de azabache. **jet-propelled engine,** motor de retroacción, *m*. **jet-propelled plane,** aeroplano de reacción, *m*
jetsam *n* echazón, *f*; *fig* víctima, *f*
jettison *n* echazón, *f*. *vt* echar (mercancías) al mar; *fig* librarse de, abandonar
jetty *n* dique, malecón, *m*; (landing pier) embarcadero, muelle, *m*
Jew *n* judío, *m*. **Jew's harp,** birimbao, *m*
jewel *n* joya, alhaja, *f*; (of a watch) rubí, *m*; *fig* alhaja, *f*. *vt* enjoyar, adornar con piedras preciosas. **j.-box, -case,** joyero, *m*
jeweled *a* adornado con piedras preciosas, enjoyado; (of a watch) con rubíes
jeweler *n* joyero (-ra). **jeweler's shop,** joyería, *f*
jewelry *n* joyas, *f pl*; artículos de joyería, *m pl*
Jewess *n* judía, *f*
Jewish *a* judío
Jewry *n* judería, *f*
jib *n naut* foque, *m*. *vi* (of a horse) plantarse; (refuse) rehusar. **to jib at,** vacilar en; mostrarse desinclinado. **jib-boom,** *naut* botalón de foque, *m*
jiffy *n* instante, credo, *m*. **in a j.,** en un decir Jesús, en un credo, en un santiamén
jig *n* (dance) jiga, *f*. *vi* bailar una jiga; bailar, agitarse, sacudirse. *vt* agitar, sacudir; (sieve) cribar
jigger *n naut* cangreja de mesana, *f*; aparejo de mano, *m*; jigger, *m*
jigsaw puzzle *n* rompecabezas, *m*
jilt *vt* dar calabazas (a)
jingle *n* tintineo, *m*; ruido, *m*; verso, *m*; estribillo, *m*. *vi* tintinar; sonar; rimar
jingoism *n* jingoísmo, *m*
jitters, to have the no tenerlas todas consigo, no saber dónde meterse
job *n* tarea, *f*; trabajo, *m*; empleo, *m*; (affair) asunto, *m*; (thing) cosa, *f*; (unscrupulous transaction) intriga, *f*. **It is a good (bad) job that . . . ,** Es una buena (mala) cosa que . . . **He has done a good job,** Ha hecho un buen trabajo. **He has lost his job,** Ha perdido su empleo, Le han declarado cesante. **odd-job man,** factótum, *m*. **job-lot,** colección miscelánea, *f*; *com* saldo de mercancías, *m*
jobber *n* (workman) destajista, *m*; (in stocks) agiotista, *m*; *com* corredor, *m*
jobless *a* sin trabajo
jockey *n* jockey, *m*. *vt* engañar; (with into) persuadir, hacer; (with out of) quitar, robar. **j. cap,** gorra de jockey, *f*. **J. Club,** jockey-club, *m*
jocose *a* jocoso, gracioso, guasón
jocosity *n* jocosidad, *f*
jocular *a* gracioso, alegre; chistoso, zumbón
jocularity *n* alegría, jocosidad, *f*
jocularly *adv* en broma; alegremente
jocund *a* alegre, jovial; jocundo
jocundity *n* alegría, *f*; jocundidad, *f*
jog *vt* empujar; (the memory) refrescar. *vi* ir despacio; andar a trote corto. *n* empujón, *m*. **He jogged me with his elbow,** Me dio con el codo. **jog-trot,** trote corto, *m*
joie de vivre *n* goce de vivir, arregosto de vivir, *m*
join *vt* juntar; unir; añadir; (railway lines) empalmar; juntarse con; (meet) encontrarse (con); reunirse (con); (a club, etc.) hacerse miembro (de); (share) acompañar; (regiments, ships) volver (a). *vi* juntarse; unirse; asociarse. *n* unión, *f*; (railway) empalme, *m*; (roads) bifurcación, *f*. **At what time will you j. me?** ¿A qué hora me vendrás a buscar? **He has joined his ship,** Ha vuelto a su buque. **Will you j. me in a drink?** ¿Me quieres acompañar en una bebida? **to j. battle,** librar batalla. **to j. forces,** combinar; *inf* juntar meriendas. **to**

j. in, tomar parte en, participar en. **to j. together,** *vt* unir, juntar. *vi* juntarse; asociarse. **to j. up,** alistarse
joiner *n* carpintero, ensamblador, *m*,
joinery *n* ensambladuría, *f*; carpintería, *f*
joining *n* juntura, conjunción, *f*; (*carp* etc.) ensambladura, *f*; *fig* unión, *f*
joint *n* juntura, junta, *f*; *anat* coyuntura, articulación, *f*; (knuckle) nudillo, *m*; (of meat) cuarto, *m*; (hinge) bisagra, *f*; *bot* nudo, *m*, *a* unido; combinado; colectivo; mixto; mutuo; (in compounds) co. *vt* juntar; (meat) descuartizar. **out of j.,** dislocado; (of the times) fuera de compás. **j. account,** cuenta corriente mutua, *f*. **j.-heir,** coheredero, *m*. **j. stock company,** compañía por acciones, sociedad anónima, *f*
jointed *a* articulado; (foldable) plegadizo
jointly *adv* juntamente, en común, colectivamente
joist *n* sopanda, viga, *f*
joke *n* chiste, *m*; burla, broma, *f*. *vi* bromear, chancearse. *vt* burlarse (de). **Can he take a j.?** ¿Sabe aguantar una broma? **practical j.,** broma pesada, *f*. **to play a j.,** gastar una broma, hacer una burla
joker *n* bromista, *Argentina also* fomista, *mf*; (in cards) comodín, *m*
joking *n* chistes, *m pl*, bromas, *f pl*. *a* chistoso; cómico
jokingly *adv* en broma, de guasa
jollification *n* regocijo, *m*; festividades, fiestas, *f pl*
jollity *n* alegría, *f*, regocijo, *m*
jolly *a* alegre, jovial; (tipsy) achispado; (amusing) divertido; (nice) agradable. *adv* muy. **He is a j. good fellow,** Es un hombre estupendo. **I am j. glad,** Estoy contentísimo, Me alegro mucho
jolt *n* sacudida, *f*. *vt* sacudir. *vi* (of a vehicle) traquetear
jolting *n* sacudidas, *f pl*, sacudimiento, *m*; (of a vehicle) traqueteo, *m*
jonquil *n bot* junquillo, *m*
Jordan Jordania, *f*
joss *n* ídolo chino, *m*. **j.-stick,** pebete, *m*
jostle *vt* empujar, empellar. *vi* dar empujones, codear
jot *n* jota, pizca, *f*. *vt* (down) apuntar. **not a jot,** ni jota, ni pizca. **to be not worth a jot,** no valer un comino
jotter *n* taco para notas, *m*; (exercise book) cuaderno, *m*
jotting *n* apunte, *m*; observación, *f*
journal *n* (diary) diario, *m*; (ship's) diario de navegación, *m*; (newspaper) periódico, *m*; (review) revista, *f*
journalese *n* lenguaje periodistico, *m*
journalism *n* periodismo, *Lat. Am. also* diarismo, *m*
journalist *n* periodista, *mf*
journalistic *a* periodistico
journey *n* viaje, *m*; expedición, *f*; trayecto, *m*; camino, *m*. *vi* viajar. **j. by sea,** viaje por mar. **Pleasant j.!** ¡Buen viaje! ¡Feliz viaje! **outward j.,** viaje de ida, *m*. **return j.,** viaje de regreso, *m*
Jove *n* Júpiter, *m*. **By J.!** ¡Pardiez! ¡Caramba!
jovial *a* jovial
joviality *n* jovialidad, *f*
jowl *n* (cheek) carrillo, *m*; (of cattle, etc.) papada, *f*; (jaw) quijada, *f*
joy *n* alegría, *f*; felicidad, *f*; deleite, placer, *m*, *vi* alegrarse. **I wish you joy,** Te deseo la felicidad. **joy-ride,** excursión en coche, *f*; vuelo en avión, *m*. **joy-stick,** (of an airplane) palanca de gobierno, *f*
joyful *a* alegre
joyfulness *n* alegría, *f*
joyless *a* sin alegría, triste
joylessness *n* falta de alegría, tristeza, *f*
joyous. See **joyful**
jubilant *a* jubiloso; triunfante
jubilantly *adv* con júbilo, alegremente; triunfalmente
jubilation *n* júbilo, *m*, alegría, *f*; ruido triunfal, *m*
jubilee *n* jubileo, *m*
jubilee volume *n* libro de homenaje, libro jubilar, *m*
Judaic *a* judaico
Judaism *n* judaísmo, *m*
Judas *n* (traitor and hole) judas, *m*
Judezmo el judesmo, *m*
judge *n* juez, *m*; (connoisseur) conocedor (-ra) (de); (umpire) arbitrio, *m*. *vt* juzgar; considerar, tener por. *vi* servir como juez; juzgar. **judging by,** a juzgar por. **to be a good j. of,** ser buen juez de. **to j. for oneself,** formar su propia opinión
judgment, judgement *n law* fallo, *m*; sentencia, *f*; juicio, *m*; (understanding) entendimiento, discernimiento, *m*; (opinion) opinión, *f*, parecer, *m*. **In my j. . . . ,** Según mi parecer, . . . Según creo yo . . . **Last J.,** Juicio Final, *m*. **to pass j. on,** *law* pronunciar sentencia (en or sobre); dictaminar sobre; juzgar. **to sit in j. on,** ser juez de; juzgar. **j.-day,** Día del Juicio, *m*. **j.-seat,** tribunal, *m*
judicature *n* judicatura, *f*; (court) juzgado, *m*
judicial *a* judicial; legal; (of the mind) juicioso. **j. inquiry,** investigación judicial, *f*. **j. separation,** separación legal, *f*
judiciary *a* judicial. *n* judicatura, *f*
judicious *a* juicioso, prudente.
judiciously *adv* prudentemente, juiciosamente
judiciousness *n* juicio, *m*, prudencia, sensatez, *f*
judo *n* yudo, *m*
judoka *n* yudoca, *mf*
jug *n* jarro, *m*; cántaro, *m*; pote, *m*; (jail) *Argentina, Chile* capacha *f*. *vt cul* estofar. *vi* (of nightingale) trinar, cantar. **jugged hare,** *n* liebre en estofado, *f*
juggle *vi* hacer juegos malabares. **to j. out of,** (money, etc.) quitar con engaño, estafar. **to j. with,** *fig* (facts, etc.) tergiversar, falsificar; (person) engañar
juggler *n* malabarista, *mf*; (deceiver) estafador (-ra)
jugglery *n* prestidigitación, *f*; juegos malabares, *m pl*; (imposture) engaño, *m*, estafa, *f*; trampas, *f pl*
jugular *a anat* yugular. **j. vein,** yugular, *m*
juice *n* jugo, *m*; *fig* zumo, *m*. **digestive j.,** jugo digestivo, *m*
juiciness *n* jugosidad, *f*; suculencia, *f*
juicy *a* jugoso; suculento
jujube *n* pastilla, *f*
jukebox *n* tocadiscos, vitrola, sinfonola, *f*
July *n* julio, *m*
jumble *vt* mezclar, confundir. *n* mezcla confusa, colección miscelánea, confusión, *f*. **j. sale,** tómbola, *f*
jump *n* salto, *m*; (in prices, etc.) aumento, *m*. **at one j.,** de un salto. **high j.,** salto de altura, *m*. **long j.,** salto de longitud, *m*. **to be on the j.,** *inf* estar nervioso, tener los nervios en punta
jump *vi* saltar; dar un salto; brincar; (of tea-cups, etc.) bailar; (throb) pulsar. *vt* saltar; hacer saltar; (a child) brincar; (omit) pasar por alto de, omitir. **The train jumped the rails,** El tren se descarriló. **to j. out of bed,** saltar de la cama. **to j. to the conclusion that . . . ,** darse prisa a concluir que . . . **to j. about,** dar saltos, brincar; revolverse, moverse de un lado para otro. **to j. at,** saltar sobre; precipitarse sobre, abalanzarse hacia; (an offer) apresurarse a aceptar; (seize) coger con entusiasmo. **to j. down,** bajar de un salto. **to j. over,** saltar; saltar por encima de. **to j. up,** saltar; (on to a horse, etc.) montar rápidamente; levantarse apresuradamente. **to j. with,** (agree) convenir en, estar conforme con
jumper *n* saltador (-ra); (sailor's) blusa, *f*; jersey, suéter *m*, *Lat. Am.* chompa, *f*
jumping *n* saltos, *m pl*. *a* saltador. **j.-off place,** base avanzada, *f*; *fig* trampolín, *m*. **j.-pole,** pértiga, *f*
jumpiness *n* nerviosidad, *f*
jumpy *a* nervioso, agitado
junction *n* unión, *f*; (of roads) bifurcación, *f*; (railway) empalme, *m*; (connection) conexión, *f*
juncture *n* coyuntura, *f*; momento, *m*; crisis, *f*, momento crítico, *m*; (joint) junta, *f*
June *n* junio, *m*
jungle *n* selva, *f*. **j.-fever,** fiebre de los grandes bosques, *f*
junior *a* joven; hijo; más joven; menos antiguo; subordinado, segundo. *n* joven, *mf* **Carmen is my j. by three years,** Carmen es tres años más joven que yo.

James Thomson, Jr., James Thomson, hijo. **the j. school,** los pequeños. **j. partner,** socio menor, *m*
juniper *n bot* enebro, *m*
junk *n* trastos viejos, *m pl*; (nonsense) patrañas, *f pl*; *naut* junco, *m*; (salt meat) tasajo, *m*. **j.-shop,** tienda de trastos viejos, *f*
junk bond bono-basura, *m*
junketing *n* festividades, *f pl*
juridical *a* jurídico
jurisconsult *n* jurisconsulto, *m*
jurisdiction *n* jurisdicción, *f*; competencia, *f*
jurisprudence *n* jurisprudencia, *f*
jurist *n* jurista, legista, *mf*
juror *n* (miembro del) jurado, *m*
jury *n* jurado, *m*. **to be on the j.,** formar parte del jurado. **j.-box,** tribuna del jurado, *f*
juryman *n* miembro del jurado, *m*
just *a* justo; justiciero; exacto; fiel. **Peter the J.,** Pedro el justiciero
just *adv* justamente, exactamente; precisamente; (scarcely) apenas; (almost) casi; (entirely) completamente; (simply) meramente, solamente, tan sólo; (newly) recién (followed by past part.), recientemente. **He only j. missed being run over,** Por poco le atropellan. **It is j. near,** Está muy cerca. **It is j. the same to me,** Me es completamente igual. **J. as he was leaving,** Cuando estaba a punto de marcharse, En el momento de marcharse. **Just as you arrive in Spain, you must . . .** Nada más llegar a España, tienes que . . . **That's j. it!** ¡Eso es! ¡Exactamente! **to have j.,** acabar de. **They have j. dined,** Acaban de cenar. **J. as you wish,** Como Vd. quiera. **j. at that moment,** precisamente en aquel momento. **j. by,** muy cerca; al lado. **j. now,** ahora mismo; hace poco; pronto, dentro de poco. **j. yet,** todavía. **They will not come j. yet,** No vendrán todavía. **Just looking** (browser to shopkeeper) Estoy viendo, Estamos viendo
justice *n* justicia, *f*; (judge) juez, *m*; (magistrate) juez municipal, *m*. **to bring to j.,** llevar ante el juez (a). **to do j. to,** (a person) hacer justicia (a); (a meal) hacer honor (a). **to do oneself j.,** quedar bien
justifiable *a* justificable
justifiably *adv* con justicia, justificadamente
justification *n* justificación, *f*
justify *vt* justificar, vindicar; (excuse) disculpar; *print* justificar. **to be justified (in),** tener derecho (a), tener motivo (para), tener razón (en)
justly *adv* justamente; con justicia; con derecho; con razón; exactamente; debidamente
justness *n* justicia, *f*; exactitud, *f*
jut (out) *vi* salir, proyectar; sobresalir
jute *n* yute, *m*
juvenile *a* juvenil; de la juventud; para la juventud; joven; de niños; para niños. *n* joven, *mf*. **j. court,** tribunal de menores, *m*. **j. lead,** *theat* galancete, galán joven, *m*. **j. offender,** delincuente infantil, *m*
juxtapose *vt* yuxtaponer
juxtaposition *n* yuxtaposición, *f*

K

k *n* (letter) ka, *f*
kaiser *n* káiser, emperador, *m*. **the K.** el emperador alemán, *m*
kaleidoscope *n* calidoscopio, *m*
kaleidoscopic *a* calidoscópico
kangaroo *n* canguro, *m*
kaolin *n* caolín, *m*
kapok *n* miraguano, *m*
keel *n* quilla, *f*. *vt* carenar. **to k. over,** volcar; caer; *naut* zozobrar
keelson *n* sobrequilla, *f*
keen *a* (of edges) afilado; agudo; penetrante; vivo; sutil; ardiente; celoso, entusiasta; mordaz; (desirous) ansioso; (of appetite) grande, bueno. **He is a k. tennis player,** Es tenista entusiasta. **Joan has a very k. ear,** Juana tiene un oído muy agudo. **I'm not very k. on apples,** No me gustan mucho las manzanas
keenly *adv* agudamente; vivamente; (of feeling) hondamente; (of looking) atentamente
keenness *n* (of a blade) afiladura, *f*; agudeza, *f*; viveza, *f*; sutileza, *f*; perspicacia, *f*; (enthusiasm) entusiasmo, *m*, afición, *f*; (desire) ansia, *f*
keep *vt* guardar; tener; que darse con; retener; conservar; mantener; (a shop, hotel, etc.) dirigir, tener; (a school) ser director de; (a promise, etc.) cumplir; (the law, etc.) observar, guardar; (celebrate) solemnizar; (a secret) guardar; (books, accounts, a house, in step) llevar; (sheep, etc., one's bed) guardar; (a city, etc.) defender; (domestic animals, cars, etc.) tener; (lodge) alojar; (detain) detener; (reserve) reservar; (cause) hacer. **They had kept this room for me,** Me habían reservado este cuarto. **Dorothy has kept the blue dress,** Dorotea se ha quedado con el vestido azul. **The government could not k. order,** El gobierno no sabía mantener el orden. **I did not know how to k. their attention,** No sabía retener su atención. **Carmen kept quiet,** Carmen guardó silencio, Carmen se calló. **Can you k. a secret?** ¿Sabes guardar un secreto? **to k. an appointment,** acudir a una cita. **to k. in repair,** conservar en buen estado. **to k. someone from doing something,** evitar que uno haga algo. **to k. someone waiting,** hacer que espere uno. **to k. something from someone,** ocultar algo de uno. **We were kept at it night and day,** Nos hacían trabajar día y noche. **I always k. it by me,** Lo tengo siempre a mi lado (or conmigo). **to k. away,** alejar; mantener a distancia; no dejar venir. **to k. back,** (a crowd, etc.) detener; cortar el paso (a); no dejar avanzar; (retain) guardar, retener; reservar; (tears, words) reprimir, contener; (evidence, etc.) callar, suprimir. **to k. down,** no dejar subir (a); sujetar; (a nation, etc.) oprimir, subyugar; (emotions) dominar; (prices, expenses) mantener bajo; (check) moderar, reprimir. **to k. in,** (feelings) contener; reprimir; (the house) hacer quedarse en casa, no dejar salir; (imprison) encerrar; (school) hacer quedar en la escuela (a). **to k. off,** alejar; tener a distancia (a); cerrar el paso (a), no dejar avanzar; no andar sobre; no tocar; (a subject) no tratar de, no discutir, no tocar. **K. your hands off!** ¡No toques! **to k. on,** guardar; retener; (eyes) fijar en, poner en. **to k. out,** no dejar entrar; excluir. **It is difficult to k. him out of trouble,** Es difícil de evitar que se meta en líos. **to k. to,** seguir; limitarse a; adherirse a; **K. to the Left,** «Tome su izquierda», **K. to the right,** «Tome su derecha»; (a path, etc.) seguir por; (one's bed) guardar; (fulfil) cumplir; (oblige) hacer, obligar. **to k. under,** subyugar, oprimir; dominar; controlar. **to k. up,** mantener; (appearances) guardar; conservar; persistir en; (prices) sostener; (in good repair) conservar en buen estado; (go on doing) continuar. **He kept me up late last night,** Anoche me entretuvo hasta muy tarde; Ayer me hizo trasnochar; Anoche me hizo velar. **to k. one's end up,** volver por sí, hacerse fuerte. **to k. up one's spirits,** no desanimarse
keep *vi* quedar; (be) estar; (continue) seguir, continuar; mantenerse; (at home, etc.) quedarse, permanecer; (be accustomed) acostumbrar, soler; (persist) perseverar; (of food) conservarse fresco. **How is he keeping?** ¿Cómo está? **to k. in with someone,** cultivar a alguien. **to k. up with the times,** mantenerse al corriente. **to k. at,** seguir; persistir; perseverar; (pester) importunar. **John keeps at it,** Juan trabaja sin descansar. **to k. away,** mantenerse apartado; mantenerse a distancia; no acudir. **to k. back,** hacerse a un lado,

apartarse, alejarse. **to k. down,** quedarse tumbado; seguir acurrucado; no levantarse; esconderse. **to k. from,** (doing something) guardarse de. **to k. off,** mantenerse a distancia. **If the storm keeps off,** Si no estalla una tempestad. **If the rain keeps off,** Si no empieza a llover, Si no hay lluvia. **to k. on,** continuar; seguir. **to k. straight on,** seguir derecho. **I'm tired, but I still k. on,** Estoy cansado, pero sigo trabajando. **to k. out,** quedarse fuera. **to k. out of,** (quarrels, trouble, etc.) no meterse en, evitar. **to k. out of sight,** no dejarse ver, no mostrarse, mantenerse oculto. **to k. together,** quedarse juntos; reunirse

keep *n* (of a castle) mazmorra, *f;* (maintenance) subsistencia, *f;* comida, *f.* **for keeps,** para siempre jamás

keeper *n* guarda, *mf;* (in a park, zoo, of a lunatic) guardián, *m;* (of a museum, etc.) director, *m;* (of animals) criador (-ra); (gamekeeper) guardabosque, *m;* (of a boardinghouse, shop, etc.) dueño (-ña); (of accounts, books) tenedor, *m.* **Am I my brother's k.?** ¿Soy yo responsable por mi hermano?

keeping *n* guarda, *f;* conservación, *f;* protección, *f;* (of a rule) observación, *f;* (of an anniversary, etc.) celebración, *f;* (of a person) mantenimiento, *m.* **in k. with,** en armonía con; de acuerdo con. **out of k. with,** en desacuerdo con. **to be in safe k.,** estar en buenas manos; estar en un lugar seguro. **k. back,** retención, *f*

keepsake *n* recuerdo, *m*

keg *n* barrilete, *m*

ken *n* alcance de la vista, *m;* vista, *f;* comprensión, *f*

Kennedy Round, the la serie Kénnedy, *f*

kennel *n* (of a dog) perrera, *f;* (of hounds) jauría, *f;* (dwelling) cuchitril, *m;* (gutter) arroyo, *m.* **k. man,** perrero, *m*

kepi *n* quepis, *m*

Kepler Keplero

kerb, kerbstone See **curb**

kerchief *n* pañuelo, *m;* pañoleta, *f.* **brightly-colored k.,** pañuelo de hierbas, *m*

kernel *n* almendra, semilla, *f; fig* meollo, *m,* esencia, *f*

kerosene *n* petróleo de lámpara, *m;* kerosén, *m*

ketchup *n* salsa de tomate y setas, *f*

kettle *n* caldero, *m, Mexico* marmita, *f.* **pretty k. of fish,** olla de grillos, *f.* **k.-drum,** timbal, *m.* **k.-drum player,** timbalero, *m*

key *n* llave, *f;* (*fig arch, mus*) clave, *f;* (tone) tono, *m;* (of a piano, typewriter, etc.) tecla, *f; mech* chaveta, *f;* (of a wind instrument) pistón, *m;* (winged fruit) sámara, *f; elec* conmutador, *m.* **major (minor) key,** tono mayor (menor), *m.* **latch-key,** llave de la puerta, *f;* (Yale) llavín, *m.* **master key,** llave maestra, *f.* **skeleton key,** ganzúa, *f.* **He is all keyed up,** Tiene los nervios en punta. **key industry,** industria clave, *f.* **key man,** hombre indispensable, *m.* **key point,** punto estratégico, *m.* **key-ring,** llavero, *m.* **key signature,** *mus* clave, *f.* **key word,** palabra clave, *f*

keyboard *n* teclado, *m*

keyhole *n* ojo de la cerradura, *m.* **through the k.,** por el ojo de la cerradura

keynote *n mus* tónica, *f; fig* piedra clave, idea fundamental, *f*

keystone *n* piedra clave, *f*

khaki *n* caqui, *m*

kick *vt* dar un puntapié (a); golpear; (a goal) chutar. *vi* (of horses, etc.) dar coces, cocear; (of guns) recular. **to k. one's heels,** hacer tiempo. **to kick the bucket,** palmarla, *Lat. Am.* arrancarse. **to k. up a row,** hacer un ruido de mil diablos; (quarrel) armar camorra. **to k. about,** dar patadas (a). **to k. away,** quitar con el pie; lanzar con el pie. **to k. off,** quitar con el pie; lanzar; sacudirse. **k.-off,** *n* golpe de salida, puntapié inicial, saque, *m.* **to k. out,** echar a puntapiés

kick *n* puntapié, *m;* golpe, *m;* coz, *f;* (of guns) culatazo, *m.* **free k.,** golpe franco, *m*

kicking *n* coces, *f pl;* acoceamiento, *m;* pataleo, *m;* golpeamiento, *m*

kid *n* cabrito, *m,* chivo (-va); carne de cabrito, *f;* (leather) cabritilla, *f; inf* crío, *m.* **kid gloves,** guantes de cabritilla, *m pl*

kidnap *vt* secuestrar

kidnapper *n* secuestrador (-ra); ladrón (-ona) de niños

kidnapping *n* secuestro, *m*

kidney *n* riñón, *m; fig* especie, índole, *f.* **k.-bean,** (plant) judía, *f;* (fruit) habichuela, judía, *f,* fréjol, *Mexico* calamaco, *m*

Kidron Cedrón, *m*

kill *vt* matar; destruir; suprimir. **to k. off,** exterminar. **to k. time,** entretener el tiempo, pasarse las horas muertas. **to k. two birds with one stone,** matar dos pájaros de un tiro. **k.-joy,** aguafiestas, *mf*

killer *n* matador (-ra); (murderer) asesino, *mf*

killing *n* matanza, *f;* (murder) asesinato, *m. a* matador; destructivo; (comic) cómico; ridículo, absurdo; (ravishing) irresistible

kiln *n* horno de cerámica, horno, *m*

kilo *n* kilo, *m*

kilocycle *n elec* kilociclo, *m*

kilogram *n* kilogramo, *m*

kiloliter *n* kilolitro, *m*

kilometer *n* kilómetro, *m*

kilometric *a* kilométrico

kilowatt *n elec* kilovatio, *m*

kin *n* parientes, *m pl;* familia, *f;* clase, especie, *f.* **the next of kin,** los parientes próximos, la familia

kind *n* género, *m,* clase, *f;* especie, *f; inf* tipo, *m.* **He is a queer k. of person,** Es un tipo muy raro. **What k. of cloth is it?** ¿Qué clase de tela es? **Nothing of the k!** ¡Nada de eso! **payment in k.,** pago en especie, *m*

kind *a* bondadoso, bueno; cariñoso, tierno; amable; favorable, propicio. **Will you be so k. as to . . .** Tenga Vd. la bondad de . . . **With k. regards,** Con un saludo afectuoso. **You have been very k. to her,** Vd. ha sido muy bueno para ella. **k.-hearted,** bondadoso. **k.-heartedness,** bondad, benevolencia, *f*

kindergarten *n* jardín de la infancia, kindergarten, *m*

kindle *vt* encender; hacer arder; *fig* avivar. *vi* prender, empezar a arder; encenderse; *fig* inflamarse

kindliness *n* bondad, *f*

kindling *n* encendimiento (del fuego), *m;* (wood) leña menuda, *Lat. Am.* charamusca, *f*

kindly *a* bondadoso; bueno; benévolo; propicio, favorable; (of climate) benigno. *adv* con bondad, bondadosamente; fácilmente. **K. sit down,** Haga el favor de sentarse

kindness *n* bondad, *f;* benevolencia, *f;* amabilidad, *f;* cariño, *m;* favor, *m,* atención, *f*

kindred *n* parentesco, *m;* parientes, *m pl;* familia, *f;* afinidad, *f, a* emparentado; hermano

king *n* (ruler, important person, chess, cards) rey, *m;* (in draughts) dama, *f.* **king's evil,** escrófula, *f.* **k.-bolt,** perno real, *m.* **k.-craft,** arte de reinar, *m,* or *f.* **k.-cup,** *bot* botón de oro, *m.* **K.-of-Arms,** rey de armas, *m.* **k.-post,** pendolón, *m*

kingdom *n* reino, *m.* **animal k.,** reino animal, *m*

kingfisher *n* martín pescador, alción, *m*

kink *n* nudo, *m;* pliegue, *m;* (curl) rizo, *m; fig* peculiaridad, *f*

kinsfolk *n* parientes, *m pl,* familia, *f*

kinship *n* parentesco, *m;* afinidad, *f*

kinsman *n* pariente, deudo, *m*

kinswoman *n* parienta, *f*

kiosk *n* quiosco, *m*

kipper *n* arenque ahumado, *m. vt* ahumar

kiss *n* beso, *m;* (in billiards) pelo, *m. vt* besar; dar un beso (a); (of billiard balls) tocar. **to k. each other,** besarse. **k.-curl,** rizo de la sien, *m,* sortijilla, *f*

kit *n* (tub) cubo, *m;* (for tools, etc.) cajita, caja, *f;* (soldier's) equipo, *m.* **kit-bag,** mochila, *f*

kitchen *n* cocina, *f.* **k.-boy,** pinche (de cocina), *m.* **k.-garden,** huerta, *f.* **k.-maid,** fregona, *f.* **k.-range,** cocina económica, *f.* **k.-sink,** fregadero, *Chile, Mexico, also* lavaplatos, *m.* **k.-stove,** horno de cocina, *m.* **k. utensils,** batería de cocina, *f*

kitchenette *n* cocinilla, *f*
kite *n orn* milano, *m;* cometa, pájara, *f.* **to fly a k.,** hacer volar una cometa. **box-k.,** cometa celular, *f*
kith and kin *n pl* parientes y amigos, *m pl*
kitten *n* gatito (-ta). *vi* (of a cat) parir
kittenish *a* de gatito; juguetón
kitty *n* michito, *m;* (in card games) platillo, *m*
kleptomania *n* cleptomanía, *f*
kleptomaniac *a* cleptómano. *n* cleptómano (-na)
knack *n* destreza, *f;* talento, *m;* (trick) truco, *m*
knapsack *n* mochila, *f; mil* alforja, *f*
knave *n* bellaco, truhán, tunante, *m;* (at cards) sota, *f*
knavery *n* bellaquería, truhanería, *f*
knavish *a* de bribón; taimado, truhanesco
knead *vt* amasar; (massage) sobar; *fig* formar
kneading *n* amasijo, *m;* (massaging) soba, *f.* **k.-trough,** amasadera artesa *f*
knee *n* rodilla, *f; fig* ángulo, codillo, *m.* **on bended k.,** de hinojos. **on one's knees,** de rodillas, arrodillado. **to go down on one's knees,** arrodillarse, ponerse de rodillas. **k.-breeches,** calzón corto, *m;* calzón ceñido, *m;* (Elizabethan) gregüescos, *m pl.* **k.-cap,** rótula, *f.* **k.-deep,** hasta las rodillas. **k.-joint,** articulación de la rodilla, *f; mech* junta de codillo, *f.* **k.-pad,** rodillera, *f*
kneel (down) *vi* arrodillarse, hincarse de rodillas, ponerse de rodillas
kneeling *a* arrodillado, de rodillas
knell *n* toque de difuntos, tañido fúnebre, *m;* toque de campanas, *m; fig* muerte, *f. vi* tocar a muerto. *vt fig* anunciar, presagiar
knickerbockers *n pl* bragas, *f pl;* calzón corto, *m;* (women's) pantalones, *m pl*
knickknack *n* chuchería, *f*
knife *n* cuchillo, *m.* **to have one's k. in someone,** tener enemiga (a), querer mal (a). **war to the k.,** guerra a muerte, *f.* **k.-edge,** filo de cuchillo, *m;* fiel de soporte, *m.* **k. grinder,** amolador, *m.* **k.-handle,** mango de cuchillo, *m.* **k. thrust,** cuchillada, *f*
knife, fork, and spoon cuchara, tenedor, y cuchillo
knight *n* caballero, *m;* (chess) caballo, *m. vt* armar caballero, calzar la espuela; (in modern usage) dar el título de caballero. **untried k.,** caballero novel, *m.* **k. commander,** comendador, *m.* **k.-errant,** caballero andante, *m.* **k.-errantry,** caballería andante, *f.* **Knight of Labor,** Caballero del Trabajo *m.* **k. of the rueful countenance,** el caballero de la triste figura
knighthood *n* caballería, *f;* (in modern usage) título de caballero, *m*
knightly *a* caballeresco; de caballero; de caballería
knit *vt* and *vi* hacer calceta, hacer media; juntar, ligar; unir. **Isabel is knitting me a jumper,** Isabel me hace un jersey de punto de media. **to k. one's brows,** fruncir el ceño
knitted *a* de punto. **k. goods,** géneros de punto, *m pl*
knitter *n* calcetero (-ra); (machine) máquina de hacer calceta, *f*
knitting *n* acción de hacer calceta, *f;* trabajo de punto, *m,* labor de calceta, *f;* unión, *f.* **k.-machine,** máquina de hacer calceta, *f.* **k.-needle,** aguja de media, aguja de hacer calceta, *f*
knob *n* protuberancia, *f;* (of a door, etc.) perilla, borlita, *f;* (ornamental) bellota, *f;* (of sugar) terrón, *m;* (of a stick) puño, *m*
knock *n* golpe, *m;* choque, *m;* (with a knocker) aldabada, *f*
knock *vt* golpear; chocar (contra). *vi* llamar a la puerta; (of an engine) picar. **to k. one's head against,** chocar con la cabeza contra, dar con la cabeza contra. **to k. about,** *vt* pegar; aporrear. *vi* viajar; vagar, rodar; callejear. **to k. against,** golpear contra; chocar contra. **to k. down,** derribar; (of vehicles) atropellar, *Mexico* antellevar; (houses, etc.) demoler; (an argument, etc.) destruir; (a tender, etc.) rebajar; (of an auctioneer) rematar al mejor postor. **to k. in,** (nails, etc.) clavar. **to k. into one another,** toparse. **to k. off,** hacer caer; sacudir; quitar; (from price) descontar; (from speed, etc.) reducir; (finish) terminar pronto; (runs in cricket) hacer. **to k. out,** (remove) quitar; (boxing) dejar fuera de combate, noquear; (*fig* stun) atontar; (an idea, etc.) bosquejar. **to k. over,** volcar. **to k. up,** hacer saltar; (call) llamar; (runs at cricket) hacer; (tire) agotar, rendir; (building) construir toscamente. **to k. up against,** chocar contra; tropezar con. **k.-kneed,** *a* patiabierto. **k.-out,** "knock-out," *m*
knocker *n* (on a door) aldaba, *f.* **k.-up,** despertador, *m*
knocking *n* golpes, *m pl,* golpeo, *m;* (with a knocker) aldabeo, *m.* **k. over,** vuelco, *m;* (by a vehicle) atropello, *m*
knoll *n* altillo, otero, *m*
knot *n* nudo, *m;* (bow) lazo, *m;* (of hair) moño, *m; naut* nudo, *m,* milla náutica, *f;* (of people) corrillo, grupo, *m;* (on timber) nudo, *m. vt* anudar. *vi* hacer nudos; enmarañarse. **to tie a k.,** hacer un nudo
knotted *a* nudoso
knotty *a* nudoso; *fig* intrincado, difícil, complicado. **a k. problem,** problema espinoso
know *vt* conocer; saber; (understand) comprender; (recognize) reconocer. **I k. her very well by sight,** La conozco muy bien de vista. **John knows Latin,** Juan sabe latín. **How can I k.?** ¿Cómo lo voy a saber yo? **I knew you at once,** Te reconocí en seguida. **They always k. best,** Siempre tienen razón. **Did you k. about Philip?** ¿Has oído lo de Felipe? **to be in the k.,** estar bien informado, saber de buena tinta. **to get to k.,** (a person) llegar a conocer, trabar amistad con. **to make known,** dar a conocer; manifestar. **Who knows?** ¿Quién sabe? **to k. by heart,** saber de coro. **to k. how,** (to do something) saber. **to k. oneself,** conocerse a sí mismo. **k.-it-all,** sabelotodo, *mf,* marisabidilla, *f*
knowing *a* inteligente; malicioso; (of animals) sabio. **There is no k.,** No hay modo de saberlo. **worth k.,** digno de saberse
knowingly *adv* a sabiendas, de intento; conscientemente; (cleverly) hábilmente; (with look, etc.) de un aire malicioso
knowledge *n* conocimiento, *m.* **To the best of my k. the book does not exist,** El libro no existe que yo sepa. **He has a thorough k. of . . .,** Conoce a fondo . . . **lack of k.,** ignorancia, *f.* **He did it without my k.,** Lo hizo sin que lo supiera yo. **It is a matter of common k. that . . .** Es notorio que . . .
knowledgeable *a* sabedor
known *a* conocido
knuckle *n* (of a finger) nudillo, *m,* articulación del dedo, *f;* (of meat) jarrete, *m.* **He knuckled down to his work,** Se puso a trabajar con ahínco. **to k. under,** someterse. **k.-duster,** rompecabezas, *m*
kopeck *n* copec, *f*
Koran *n* Corán, Alcorán, *m*
Korea Corea, *f*
kosher *a* cosher; (slang) genuino
kowtow *vi* saludar humildemente; *fig* bajar la cerviz
Kremlin *n* Kremlín, *m*
kudos *n* prestigio, *m,* gloria, *f*
Kurdish *a* curdo
kyrie eleison *n* kirieleisón, *m*

L

l *n* (letter) ele, *f*
la *n mus* la, *m*
label *n* etiqueta, (on a garment), rótula, *m,* (on a can), *f;* (on a museum specimen, etc.) letrero, *m; fig* califica-

ción, *f.* *vt* poner etiqueta en; marcar, rotular; *fig* calificar, designar, clasificar

labial *a* labial. *n* letra labial, *f*

labor *n* trabajo, *m;* labor, *f;* fatiga, pena, *f;* clase obrera, *f;* (manual workers) mano de obra, *f;* (effort) esfuerzo, *m;* (of childbirth) dolores de parto, *m pl. vi* trabajar; (strive) esforzarse, afanarse; (struggle) forcejar, luchar; (try) procurar, tratar de; avanzar con dificultad; (in childbirth) estar de parto. *vt* elaborar; pulir, perfeccionar. **to l. under,** sufrir; tener que luchar contra. **hard l.,** trabajo arduo, *m; law* trabajos forzosos, *m pl,* presidio, *m.* **Ministry of L.,** Ministerio de Trabajo, *m.* **to be in l.,** estar de parto. **to l. in vain,** trabajar en balde, arar en el mar. **to l. under a delusion,** estar en el error, estar equivocado. **L. Exchange,** Bolsa de Trabajo, *f.* **l. leader,** dirigente sindical, *m.* **L. party,** partido laborista, partido obrero, *m.* **l. question,** cuestión obrera, *f;* (domestic) problema del servicio, *m.* **l.-saving,** *a* que ahorra trabajo. **l. union,** sindicato, *m*

laboratory *n* laboratorio, *m*

labored *a* (of style) premioso, artificial; forzado; (of breathing) fatigoso; (slow) torpe, lento

laborer *n* obrero, *m;* (on the land) labrador, labriego, *m;* (on the roads, etc.) peón, *m;* (by the day) jornalero, *m*

laborious *a* laborioso; arduo, difícil, penoso

laboriously *adv* laboriosamente; con dificultad, penosamente

laboriousness *n* laboriosidad, *f;* dificultad, *f*

Labrador dog *n* perro de Labrador, *m*

labyrinth *n* laberinto, *m*

labyrinthine *a* laberíntico; intrincado

lace *n* (of shoes, corsets, etc.) cordón, *m;* (tape) cinta, *f;* encaje, *m;* (narrow, for trimming) puntilla, *f;* (of gold or silver) galón, *m. vt* and *vi* (shoes, etc.) atarse los cordones; (trim) guarnecer con encajes, etc.; *fig* ornar; (a drink) echar (coñac, etc.) en. **blond l.,** blonda, *f.* **gold l.,** galón de oro, *m.* **point l.,** encaje de aguja, *m.* **l. curtain,** cortina de encaje, *f;* (of net) visillo, *m.* **l. maker** or **seller,** encajero (-ra), *mf.* **l. making,** obra de encaje, *f.* **l.-pillow,** almohadilla para encajes, *f.* **l. shoes,** zapatos con cordones, *m pl*

lacerate *vt* lacerar

laceration *n* laceración, *f*

lachrymal *a* lagrimal, lacrimal

lachrymose *a* lacrimoso

lack *n* falta, *f.* **l. of evidence,** falta de pruebas, *f;* carestía, escasez, *f;* (absence) ausencia, *f;* (need) necesidad, *f. vt* carecer de; no tener; necesitar. *vi* hacer falta; necesitarse. **to l. confidence in oneself,** no tener confianza en sí mismo, carecer de confianza en sí mismo. **l.-luster,** (of eyes) apagado, mortecino. **l. of evidence,** falta de pruebas, *f*

lackadaisical *a* lánguido; indiferente; (dreamy) ensimismado, distraído

lackey *n* lacayo, *m*

laconic *a* lacónico

lacquer *n* laca, *f, vt* dar laca (a), barnizar con laca. **gold l.,** sisa dorada, *f.* **l. work,** laca, *f*

lacquering *n* barnizado de laca, *m;* laca, capa de barniz de laca, *f*

lactate *n* lactato, *m, vi* lactar

lactation *n* lactancia, *f*

lacteal *a* lácteo

lactic *a* láctico

lactose *n* lactosa, *f*

lacuna *n* laguna, *f*

lacy *a* de encaje; parecido a encaje; *fig* transparente, etéreo

lad *n* muchacho, joven, mozalbete, *m;* zagal, *m;* (stable, etc.) mozo, *m.* **He's some l.!** ¡Qué tío que es! **l. of the village,** chulo, *m*

ladder *n* escalera de mano, *f; naut* escala, *f;* (in a stocking, etc.) carrera, *f.* **companion l.,** escala de toldilla, *f.* **to l. one's stocking,** escurrirse un punto de las medias

Ladies and gentlemen *n. pl* Señoras y señores, Señoras y caballeros. **ladies' man,** hombre de salón, Perico entre ellas, mujeriego, *m*

lading *n* flete, *m,* carga, *f*

ladle *n* cucharón, cazo, *m. vt* servir con cucharón; (a boat) achicar; *inf* distribuir, repartir

lady *n* dama, *f;* señora, *f;* (English title) milady, *f;* (woman) mujer, *f.* **to be a l.,** ser una señora. **leading l.,** *theat* dama primera, *f.* **Our L.,** Nuestra Señora. **young l.,** señorita, *f; inf* novia, *f.* **lady's maid,** doncella, *f.* **l. of the house,** señora de la casa, *f.* **l. bug,** *ent* catalina mariquita, vaca de San Antonio, *f.* **L. Chapel,** capilla de la Virgen, *f.* **L. Day,** día de la Anunciación (de Nuestra Señora), *m.* **l.-help,** asistenta, *f.* **l.-in-waiting,** dama de servicio, *f.* **l.-killer,** ladrón de corazones, castigador, tenorio, *m.* **l.-love,** querida, amada, *f.* **l. mayoress,** alcaldesa, *f*

ladylike *a* de dama; elegante; distinguido; bien educado; delicado; (of men) afeminado

ladyship *n* señoría, *f.* **Your L.,** Su Señoría

lag *vt* recubrir; aislar. *vi* retrasarse; quedarse atrás; ir (or andar) despacio; rezagarse; *naut* roncear. *n* retraso, *m; mech* retardación de movimiento, *f*

laggard *n* holgazán (-ana), haragán (-ana)

lagoon *n* laguna, *f*

laid *past part* of verb **to lay. l. up,** (ill) enfermo; *naut* inactivo; (of cars, etc.) fuera de circulación

lair *n* cubil, *m;* guarida, madriguera, *f*

laity *n* legos, *m pl*

lake *n* lago, *m;* (pigment) laca, *f.* **small l.,** laguna, *f.* **l. dwelling,** vivienda palustre, *f*

lama *n* lama, *m*

lamb *n* cordero (-ra). *vi* parir corderos. **lamb's wool,** lana de cordero. *f*

lambent *a* ondulante, vacilante; centelleante

lamblike *a* manso como un cordero; inocente

lambskin *n* corderina, piel de cordero, *f*

lame *a* estropeado, lisiado; (in the feet) cojo; (of meter) que cojea, malo; (of arguments) poco convincente; frívolo, flojo. *vt* lisiar; hacer cojo. **l. excuse,** pretexto frívolo. **to be l.,** (in the feet) (permanently) ser cojo; (temporarily) estar cojo

lamely *adv* cojeando, con cojera; *fig* sin convicción; mal

lameness *n* cojera, *f;* falta de convicción, *f*

lament *n* lamento, *m;* queja, lamentación, *f. vi* lamentarse; quejarse. *vt* lamentar, deplorar, llorar

lamentable *a* lamentable, deplorable; lastimero

lamentation *n* lamentación, *f,* lamento, *m.* **Book of Lamentations,** Libro de los lamentos, *m*

lamenting *n* lamentación, *f*

lamina *n* lámina, *f*

laminate *a* laminado, laminar. *vt* laminar

lamp *n* lámpara, *f;* (on vehicles, trains, ships and in the street) farol, *m;* luz, *f;* (oil) candil, *m,* lámpara de aceite, *f.* **safety-l.,** lámpara de seguridad, lámpara de los mineros, *f.* **street l.,** farol (de las calles), *m.* **l.-black,** negro de humo, *m.* **l.-chimney,** tubo de una lámpara, *m.* **l. factory** or **shop,** lamparería, *f.* **l.-holder,** portalámpara, *f.* **l.-lighter,** farolero, lamparero, *m.* **l.-post,** farola, *f.* **l.-shade,** pantalla (de lámpara,) *f.* **l. stand,** pie de lámpara, *m*

lamplight *n* luz de la lámpara, *f;* luz artificial, *f.* **in the l.,** a la luz de la lámpara; en luz artificial

lampoon *n* pasquinada, *f,* pasquín, *m, vt* pasquinar, satirizar

lampooner *n* escritor (-ra) de pasquinadas, libelista, *m*

lamprey *n* lamprea, *f*

lance *n* lanza, *f;* (soldier) lancero, *m. vt* alancear; *med* lancinar. **l. in rest,** lanza en ristre, *f.* **l. thrust,** lanzada, *f.* **l.-corporal,** soldado de primera clase, *m*

lancer *n mil* lancero, *m; pl* lancers, (dance and music) lanceros, *m pl*

lancet *n* apostemero, *m,* lanceta, *f.* **l. arch,** arco puntiagudo, *m*

land *n* tierra, *f;* terreno, *m;* (country) país, *m;* (region) región, *f;* territorio, *m;* (estate) bienes raíces, *m pl,* tierras, fincas, *f pl.* *vt* desembarcar; echar en tierra; (*fig* place) poner; *inf* dejar plantado (con); (obtain) obtener; (a fish) sacar del agua; (a blow) dar (un golpe); (leave) dejar. *vi* desembarcar; saltar en tierra; (of a plane) aterrizar; (arrive) llegar; (fall) caer. **to l. on water** *Lat. Am.* acuatizar. **cultivated l.,** tierras cultivadas, *f pl.* **dry l.,** (not sea) tierra firme, *f.* **native l.,** patria, *f;* suelo natal, *m.* **on l.,** en tierra. **to see how the l. lies,** *fig* tantear el terreno. **l. of milk and honey,** jauja, *f,* paraíso, *m.* **l. of promise,** tierra de promisión, *f.* **l. agent,** procurador de fincas, *m.* **l. breeze,** brisa de tierra, *f.* **l. forces,** fuerzas terrestres, *f pl.* **l. law,** leyes agrarias, *f pl.* **l.-locked,** cercado de tierra, mediterráneo **l.-lubber,** marinero de agua dulce, *m.* **l. mine,** mina terrestre, *f.* **l. surveying,** agrimensura, *f.* **l. surveyor,** agrimensor, *m.* **l. tax,** contribución territorial, *f*

landau *n* landó, *m*

landed *a* hacendado. **l. gentry,** hacendados, terratenientes, *m pl.* **l. property,** bienes raíces, *m pl*

landfall *n* derrumbamiento de tierras, *m*

landing *n* desembarque, desembarco, *m;* (landing place) desembarcadero, *m; aer* aterrizaje, *m;* (of steps) descanso, rellano, *m,* mesa, mesilla, *f.* **forced l.,** aterrizaje forzoso, *m.* **l. certificate,** *com* tornaguía, *f.* **l. craft,** barcaza de desembarco, *f.* **l. field,** campo de aterrizaje, *m,* pista de vuelo, *f.* **l.-net,** salabardo, *m.* **l. party,** trozo de abordaje, *m.* **l. signal,** *aer* señal de aterrizaje, *f.* **l.-stage,** desembarcadero, *m;* (jetty) atracadero, *m*

landlady *n* patrona, huéspeda, *f*

landlord *n* (of houses, land) propietario, *m;* hotelero, patrón, *m*

landmark *n* (of a hill or mountain) punto destacado, *m;* lugar conocido, *m;* característica, *f; fig* monumento, *m*

landmass *n* unidad territorial, *f*

landowner *n* hacendado, terrateniente, *m*

landscape *n* paisaje, *m;* perspectiva, *f.* **l. gardener,** arquitecto de jardines, *m.* **l. painter,** paisajista, *mf*

landslide *n* desprendimiento de tierras, *m; fig* cambio brusco de la opinión pública, *m*

landward *adv* hacia tierra

lane *n* vereda, senda, *f;* (of traffic) carril, *m, Argentina, Spain,* línea, *f*

language *n* lenguaje, *m;* lengua, *f,* idioma, *m.* **modern l.,** lengua viva, *f.* **strong l.,** palabras mayores, *f pl*

languid *a* lánguido

languidness *n* languidez, *f*

languish *vi* languidecer

languishing *a* lánguido; amoroso, sentimental

languishingly *adv* lánguidamente; amorosamente

languor *n* languidez, *f*

languorous *a* lánguido

languorously *adv* con langor

lank *a* flaco, descarnado, alto y delgado; (of hair) lacio

lankiness *n* flacura, *f*

lanky *a* larguirucho, descarnado, *Lat. Am.* largucho

lanoline *n* lanolina, *f*

lantern *n* linterna, *f;* (*naut* and of a lighthouse) farol, *m; arch* linterna, *f;* (small) farolillo, *m.* **dark l.,** linterna sorda, *f.* **magic l.,** linterna mágica, *f.* **l.-jawed,** carilargo. **l. maker,** farolero, *m.* **l. slide,** diapositiva, *f*

lap *n* regazo, *m;* falda, *f;* (knees) rodillas, *f pl;* (lick) lamedura, *f;* (of water) murmurio, susurro, *m;* (in a race) vuelta, *f;* (stage) etapa, *f.* *vt* (wrap) envolver; (cover) cubrir; (fold) plegar; (lick) lamer; (swallow) tragar. *vi* (overlap) traslaparse; estar replegado; (lick) lamer; (of water) murmurar, susurrar, besar. **l.-dog,** perro de faldas, perro faldero, *m*

lapel *n* solapa, *f*

lapidary *a* lapidario

lapidate *vt* lapidar

lapis lazuli *n* lapislázuli, *m*

Laplander *n* lapón (-ona)

lapping *n* (licking) lamedura, *f;* (of water) murmurio, susurro, chapaleteo, *m*

lapse *n* lapso, *m;* (fault) desliz, *m,* falta, *f;* (of time) transcurso, intervalo, *m;* (fall) caída, *f;* (*law* termination) caducidad, *f.* **lapse (into),** *vi* caer (en), recaer (en), reincidir (en); volver a, caer de nuevo (en); (*law* cease) caducar; (*law* pass to) pasar (a); dejar de existir, desaparecer. **after the l. of three days,** después de tres días, al cabo de tres días. **with the l. of years,** en el transcurso de los años

larceny *n* latrocinio, *m*

lard *n* manteca, *f;* lardo, *m.* *vt cul* lardear, mechar; *fig* sembrar (con), adornar (con)

larder *n* despensa, *f*

large *a* grande; grueso; amplio; vasto, extenso; (wide) ancho; considerable; (in number) numeroso; (main, chief) principal; liberal; magnánimo. **at l.,** en libertad, suelto. **on the l. side,** algo grande. **l.-headed,** cabezudo. **l.-hearted,** que tiene un gran corazón, magnánimo. **l. mouth,** boca grande, boca rasgada, *f.* **l.-nosed,** narigudo. **l. scale,** en gran escala. **l.-sized,** de gran tamaño. **l.-toothed,** dentudo, que tiene dientes grandes. **l. type,** letras grandes, *f pl*

largely *adv* grandemente; en gran manera; en so mayor parte, considerablemente; muy; ampliamente; liberalmente; extensamente

largeness *n* gran tamaño, *m;* (of persons) gran talle, *m;* amplitud, *f;* vastedad, extensión, *f;* (width) anchura, *f;* liberalidad, *f;* (generosity) magnanimidad, *f;* grandeza de ánimo, *f*

larger *a comp* más grande, etc. See **large. to grow l.,** crecer, aumentarse. **to make l.,** hacer más grande; aumentar

largesse *n* liberalidad, *f*

largo *n* and *adv mus* largo, *m*

lariat *n* lazo, *m*

lark *n* alondra, *f;* (spree) juerga, *f;* (joke) risa, *f.* **to rise with the l.,** levantarse con las gallinas

larva *n* larva, *f*

laryngeal *a* laríngeo

laryngitis *n* laringitis, *f*

larynx *n* laringe, *f*

lascivious *a* lascivo, lujurioso

lasciviousness *n* lujuria, lascivia, *f*

lash *n* (thong) tralla, *f;* (whip) látigo, *m;* (blow) latigazo, *m;* azote, *m;* (of the eye) pestaña, *f.* *vt* dar latigazos (a); azotar; (of waves) romper contra; (of hail, rain) azotar; (excite) provocar; (the tail) agitar (la cola); (scold) fustigar; (fasten) sujetar, atar; *naut* trincar. **to l. out,** (of horses, etc.) dar coces; (in words) prorrumpir (en)

lashing *n* (whipping) azotamiento, *m;* (tying) ligadura, atadura, *f;* amarradura, *f*

lass *n* muchacha, chica, mozuela, *f;* zagala, *f;* niña, *f*

lassitude *n* lasitud, *f*

lasso *n* lazo, *m,* mangana, *Argentina* armada, *f,* *vt* lazar, manganear, *Lat. Am.* lacear

last *vi* durar; subsistir, conservarse; continuar

last *a* último; (with month, week, etc.) pasado; (supreme) extremo, (el) mayor. *adv* al fin; finalmente; por último; después de todos; por última vez; la última vez. *n* el, *m,* (*f,* la) último (-ma); los últimos, *m pl,* (*f pl,* las últimas); (end) fin, *m;* (for shoes) horma, *f.* **at l.,** en fin; por fin, a la postre. **at the l. moment,** a última hora. **I have not been there these l. five years,** Hace cinco años que no voy allá. **John spoke l.,** Juan habló el último. **She came at l.,** Por fin llegó. **to the l.,** hasta el fin. **l. but one,** penúltimo (-ma). **l. hope,** última esperanza, *f;* último recurso, *m.* **l. kick,** *inf* último suspiro, *m.* **l. night,** anoche. **l. week,** la semana pasada

lasting *a* permanente, perdurable; duradero; constante; (of colours) sólido

lastly *adv* en conclusión, por fin, finalmente, por último

latch *n* pestillo, *m,* *vt* cerrar con pestillo. **l.-key,** llave de la puerta, *f;* (Yale) llavín, *m*

late *a* tarde; tardío; (advanced) avanzado; (last) último; reciente; (dead) difunto; (former) antiguo, ex . . . ; (new) nuevo. *adv* tarde. **Better l. than never,** Más vale tarde que nunca. **Helen arrived l.,** Elena llegó tarde. **The train arrived five minutes l.,** El tren llegó con cinco minutos de retraso. **He keeps l. hours,** Se acuesta muy tarde, Se acuesta a las altas horas de la noche (*inf* a las tantas). **of l.,** últimamente. **to grow l.,** hacerse tarde. **l.-eighteenth-century poetry,** la poesía de fines del siglo diez y ocho; llorado, malogrado (e.g. **the l. Mrs. Smith,** la llorada Sra. Smith, la malograda Sra. Smith);

lateen *a* latino. **l. sail,** vela latina, *f*

lately *adv* recientemente; últimamente, hace poco

latency *n* estado latente, *m*

lateness *n* lo tarde; lo avanzado; retraso, *m*. **the l. of the hour,** la hora avanzada

latent *a* latente

later *a* más tarde; posterior; más reciente. *adv* más tarde; (afterwards) luego, después; posteriormente. **sooner or l.,** tarde o temprano. **l. on,** más tarde

lateral *a* lateral, ladero

late registration *n* matrícula tardía, *f*

latest *a* and *adv sup* último; más reciente, etc. See **late. at the l.,** a lo más tarde, a más tardar. **l. fashion,** última moda, *f*. **l. news,** últimas noticias, *f pl*; novedad, *f*

latex *n* (*bot chem*) látex, *m*

lath *n* listón, *m*. **to be as thin as a l.,** no tener más que el pellejo, estar en los huesos

lathe *n* torno, *m*

lather *n* espuma de jabón, *f*, jabonaduras, *f pl*; (of sweat) espuma, *f*. *vt* enjabonar; *inf* zurrar. *vi* hacer espuma

lathering *n* jabonadura, *f*; *inf* tunda, zurra, *f*

Latin *n* latín, *m*, *a* latino. **Low L.,** bajo latín, *m*. **L.-American,** *a* latinoamericano. *n* latinoamericano (-na)

Latinism *n* latinismo, *m*

Latinist *n* latinista, *mf*

latitude *n* latitud, *f*; libertad, *f*

latitudinal *a* latitudinal

latrine *n* letrina, *f*

latter *a* más reciente; último, posterior; moderno. **the l.,** éste, *m*; ésta, *f*; esto, *neut*; éstos, *m pl*; éstas, *f pl*. **the l. half,** la segunda mitad. **toward the l. end of the year,** hacia fines del año. **L.-Day Saint,** santo de los últimos días *m*, santa de los últimos días, *f*

latterly *adv* recientemente, últimamente; en los últimos tiempos; hacia el fin

lattice *n* rejilla, *f*; celosía, reja, *f*. *vt* poner celosía (a); entrelazar. **l.-work,** enrejado, *m*

latticed *a* (of windows, etc.) con reja

Latvia Latvia, Letonia, *f*

Latvian *a* latvio. *n* latvio (-ia)

laud *n* alabanza, *f*; *pl*. **lauds,** *ecc* laudes, *f pl*. *vt* alabar, elogiar

laudability *n* mérito, *m*, lo meritorio

laudable *a* loable, meritorio

laudably *adv* laudablemente

laudatory *a* laudatorio

laugh *n* risa, *f*; carcajada, *f*. *vi* reír; (smile) sonreír; reírse. **loud l.,** risa estrepitosa, *f*. **to l. in a person's face,** reírsele a uno en las barbas. **to l. loudly,** reírse a carcajadas. **to l. to oneself,** reírse interiormente. **to l. to scorn,** poner en ridículo. **to l. at,** reírse de; burlarse de, ridiculizar

laughable *a* risible, irrisible, ridículo, absurdo

laughing *a* risueño, alegre; (absurd) risible, *n* risa, *f*. **to burst out l.,** reírse a carcajadas. **l.-gas,** gas hilarante, *m*. **l.-stock,** hazmerreír, *m*

laughingly *adv* riendo

laughter *n* risa, *f*; (in a report) risas, *f pl*. **burst of l.,** carcajada, *f*. **to burst into l.,** soltar el trapo, reírse a carcajadas, desternillarse de risa

launch *n* botadura (de un buque), *f*; lancha, *f*; bote, *m*; canoa, *f*. *vt* (throw) lanzar; (a blow) asestar; (a vessel) botar, echar al agua; (begin) iniciar, dar principio a; (make) hacer. **to l. an offensive,** *mil* emprender una ofensiva. **to l. into,** arrojarse en; entregarse a. **motor l.,** canoa automóvil, *f*. **steam l.,** bote de vapor, *m*

launching *n* botadura (de un buque), *f*; (throwing) lanzamiento, *m*; (beginning) iniciación, *f*; inauguración, *f*; (of a loan, etc.) emisión, *f*. **l. site,** rampa, *f*

launder *vt* lavar y planchar (ropa)

laundress *n* lavandera, *f*

laundromat *n* lavandería automática, *f*

laundry *n* lavadero, *m*, lavandería, *f*; (washing) colada, *f*; *inf* ropa lavada or ropa para lavar, *f*. **l.-man,** lavandero, *m*

laureate *a* laureado. *n* poeta laureado, *m*

laurel *n* laurel, cerezo, *m*, *a* láureo. **to crown with l.,** laurear. **l. wreath,** lauréola, *f*

Lausanne Lausana, Losana, *f*

lava *n* lava, *f*

lavabo *n* lavabo, *m*; *ecc* lavatorio, *m*

lavatory *n* lavabo, *m*; retrete, excusado, *m*

lavender *n* espliego, *m*, lavanda, *f*. **l.-water,** agua de lavanda, *f*

lavish *a* pródigo; profuso, abundante; (spender) *Mexico* disparador. *vt* prodigar

lavishly *adv* pródigamente; en profusión

lavishness *n* prodigalidad, *f*; profusión, abundancia, *f*

law *n* ley, *f*; derecho, *m*; jurisprudencia, *f*; código de leyes, *m*. **according to law,** según derecho. **canon law,** derecho civil, *m*. **constitutional law,** derecho político, *m*. **criminal law,** derecho penal, *m*. **in law,** por derecho, de acuerdo con la ley; desde el punto de vista legal. **international law,** derecho internacional, *m*. **maritime law,** código marítimo, *m*. **sumptuary law,** ley suntuaria, *f*. **to be the law,** ser la ley. **to go to law,** pleitear (sobre). **to sue at law,** pedir en juicio, poner pleito. **to take the law into one's own hands,** tomar la ley por su propia mano. **law-abiding,** observante de la ley; amigo del orden. **law-breaker,** transgresor (-ra). **law court,** tribunal de justicia, *m*; palacio de justicia, *m*. **law of nature,** ley natural, *f*. **law report,** revista de tribunales, *f*. **law school,** escuela de derecho, *f*. **law student,** estudiante de derecho, *mf*

lawful *a* legítimo; legal; lícito; válido

lawfully *adv* legalmente; legítimamente, lícitamente

lawfulness *n* legalidad, *f*; legitimidad, *f*

lawgiver *n* legislador (-ra)

lawless *a* ilegal; desordenado; ingobernable, rebelde

lawlessness *n* ilegalidad, *f*; desorden, *m*; rebeldía, *f*

lawn *n* césped, prado, *m*; (cloth) estopilla, *f*. **l.-mower,** cortacésped *m*, tundidora de césped, *f*, máquina segadora del césped, *f*. **l.-tennis,** tenis (en pista de hierba), *m*

lawsuit *n* pleito, litigio, *m*, causa, acción, *f*

lawyer *n* abogado (-da). **lawyer's office** or **practice,** bufete, *m*

lax *a* laxo; indisciplinado; vago; descuidado

laxative *n* laxante, *m*, purga, *f*, *a* laxativo

laxity *n* laxitud, *f*; descuido, *m*; indiferencia, *f*

lay *a* laico, seglar, lego; profano. *n* poema, *m*, trova, *f*; romance, *m*; (song) canción, *f*. **the lay of the land,** la configuración del terreno. **lay brother,** confeso, monigote, *m*. **lay figure,** maniquí, *m*. **lay sister,** (hermana) lega, *f*

lay *vt* and *vi* poner; colocar; dejar; (strike) tumbar; (demolish) derribar; (the dust) matar; (pipes, etc.) instalar; (hands on) asentar (la mano en); (deposit) depositar; (beat down corn, etc.) encamar, abatir; (eggs, keel) poner; (the table) cubrir, poner; (stretch) extender(se); (bury) depositar en el sepulcro; (a bet) hacer; (wager) apostar; (an accusation) acusar; (the wind, etc.) sosegar, amainar; (a ghost) exorcizar; (impute) atribuir, imputar; (impose) imponer; (prepare) prepara; (make) hacer; (open) abrir; (blame, etc.) echar; (claim) reclamar; (reveal) revelar. **Don't lay the blame on me!** ¡No me eches la culpa! **We laid our plans,** Hicimos nuestros planes; Hicimos nuestros preparativos. **to lay siege to,** asediar. **to lay the colors on too thick,** *fig* recargar las tintas. **to lay the foundations,** abrir los cimientos; *fig* crear, establecer; fundar. **to lay about one,** dar garrotazos de ciego. **to lay aside,** poner a un lado; arrinconar; (save) ahorrar;

(cast away) desechar; abandonar; (reserve) reservar; (a person) apartar de sí; (incapacitate) incapacitar. **lay something at somebody's feet,** embutir algo en el guante de fulano. **to lay before,** mostrar; presentar; poner a la vista; revelar. **to lay by,** See **to lay aside. to lay down,** acostar; depositar; (a burden) posar; (arms) rendir; (one's life); entregar; (give up) renunciar (a); (sketchout) trazar, dibujar; (plan) proyectar; (keep) guardar; (as a principle) establecer, sentar; (the law) dictar. **to lay oneself down,** echarse, tumbarse. **to lay in,** (a stock) proveerse de, hacer provisión de; (hoard) ahorrar; (buy) compara. **to lay off,** *naut* virar de bordo; *inf* quitarse de encima. **to lay on,** *vt* colocar sobre; (thrash) pegar; (blows) descargar; (paint, etc.) dar; (water, etc.) instalar; (impose) imponer; (exaggerate) exagerar. *vi* atacar. **to lay open,** abrir; descubrir, revelar; manifestar; exponer. **to lay oneself open to attack,** exponerse a ser atacado. **to lay out,** poner; arreglar; (the dead) amortajar; (one's money) invertir, emplear; (at interest) poner a rédito; (plan) planear; (knock down) derribar. **to lay oneself out to,** esforzarse a; tomarse la molestia de. **to lay over,** cubrir; sobreponer; extender sobre. **to lay to,** *vi naut* estar a la capa. **to lay up,** guardar, acumular, atesorar; poner a un lado; (a ship) desarmar; (a car) poner fuera de circulación; (a person) obligar a guardar cama, incapacitar

layabout = lazybones

layer *n* capa, *f*; *geol* estrato, *m*; *min* manto, *m*; (bird) gallina (pata, etc.) ponedera, *f*; (one who bets) apostador (-ra); *agr* acodo, *m*. *vt* (of plants) acodar

layette *n* canastilla, *f*

laying *n* colocación, *f*; puesta, *f*; (of an egg) postura, *f*. **l. down,** depósito, *m*; conservación, *f*; (explanation) exposición, *f*. **l. on of hands,** imposición de manos, *f*. **l. out,** tendedura, *f*; (of money) empleo, *m*; inversión, *f*; (arrangement) arreglo, *m*

layman *n* seglar, *mf*; profano (-na)

layout *n* plan, *m*; diagramación, disposición, *f*; distribución, *f*; esquema, *m*

laze *vi* holgazanear, gandulear, no hacer nada; encontrarse a sus anchas

lazily *adv* perezosamente; indolentemente; lentamente

laziness *n* pereza, holgazanería, *f*; indolencia, *f*; lentitud, *f*

lazy *a* perezoso, holgazán; indolente. **l.bones,** gandul (-la), *Lat. Am.* aplanacalles *mf*

lead *n* (metal) plomo, *m*; (in a pencil) mina, *f*; (plummet) sonda, *f*; *print* interlínea, *f*; *pl* **leads,** (roofs) tejados, *m pl*. *vt* emplomar; guarnecer con plomo; *print* interlinear. **black-l.,** grafito, *m*. **deep-sea l.,** *naut* escandallo, *m*. **white l.,** albayalde, *m*. **to heave the l.,** echar el escandallo, sondar. **l.-colored,** de color de plomo, plomizo. **l. mine,** mina de plomo, *f*. **l. poisoning,** saturnismo, *m*

lead *n* delantera, *f*; primer lugar, *m*; dirección, *f*, mando, *m*; (suggestion) indicación, *f*; (influence) influencia, *f*; (dog's) traílla, *f*; *theat* protagonista, *mf*; *theat* papel principal, *m*; (at cards) mano, *f*

lead *vt* and *vi* (conduct) conducir, llevar; guiar; (induce) mover, persuadir, inducir; inclinar; (cause) hacer, causar; (captain) capitanear, encabezar; dirigir; (channel) encauzar; (with life) llevar; (give) dar; (head) ir a la cabeza de; *mil* mandar; (at cards) salir; (at games) jugar en primer lugar; tomar la delantera; *fig* superar a los demás; (of roads) conducir. **to take the l.,** ir delante; ir a la cabeza, tomar la delantera; tomar la iniciativa. **to l. one to think,** hacer pensar. **to l. the way,** mostrar el camino; ir adelante. **to l. along,** llevar (por la mano, etc.), conducir; conducir por; guiar. **to l. astray,** descarriar; desviar (de), seducir (de). **to l. away,** conducir (a otra parte); llevarse (a). **to l. back,** conducir de nuevo; hacer volver. **This path leads back to the village,** Por esta senda se vuelve al pueblo. **to l. in, into,** conducir a (or ante); introducir en, hacer entrar en; invitar a entrar en; (of rooms) comunicarse con; (sin, etc.) inducir a. **to l. off,** *vi* ir adelante; (begin) empezar; (of rooms) comunicarse con. *vt* hacer marcharse, llevarse (a). **to l. on,** *vt* conducir; guiar; hacer pensar en; (make talk) dar cuerda (a). *vi* ir a la cabeza; tomar la delantera. **to l. out,** conducir afuera; (to dance) sacar. **to l. to,** conducir a; desembocar en, salir a; (cause) dar lugar a, causar; (make) hacer; (incline) inclinar. **This street leads to the square,** Por esta calle se va a la plaza, Esta calle conduce a la plaza. **to l. up to,** conducir a; (in conversation, etc.) preparar el terreno para; preparar; tener lugar antes de, ocurrir antes de

leaden *a* hecho de plomo, plúmbeo; (of skies, etc.) plomizo, de color de plomo, aplomado. **l.-footed,** pesado; lento

leader *n* conductor (-ra); guía, *mf*; jefe (-fa); general, *m*; director (-ra); (in a journal) artículo de fondo, *m*; (of an orchestra) primer violín, *m*. **follow-the-l.,** (game) juego de seguir la fila, *m*

leadership *n* dirección, *f*; jefatura, *f*; *mil* mando, *m*

lead-in *a rad* de entrada. *n rad* conductor de entrada, *m*

leading *n* (leadwork) emplomadura, *f*

leading *n* (guidance) dirección, *f*. *a* principal; primero; importante; eminente. **l. article,** artículo de fondo, *m*; editorial, *m*. **l. card,** primer naipe, *m*. **l. counsel,** abogado (-da) principal. **l. lady,** *theat* dama primera, primera actriz, *f*; (cinema) estrella (de la pantalla), *f*. **l. man,** *theat* primer galán, *m*. **l. question,** pregunta que sugiere la respuesta, *f*; cuestión importante, *f*. **l. strings,** andadores, *m pl*; *fig* tutelaje, *m*

leaf *n* (*bot* and of a page, door, window, table, screen, etc.) hoja, *f*; (petal) pétalo, *m*, *vi* echar hojas. **gold l.,** pan de oro, *m*. **to turn over a new l.,** volver la hoja, hacer libro nuevo, hacer vida nueva. **to turn over the leaves of a book,** hojear (un libro). **l.-bud,** yema, *f*. **l.-mold,** abono verde, *m*. **l. tobacco,** tabaco en hoja, *m*

leafiness *n* frondosidad, *f*

leafless *a* sin hojas

leaflet *n* hojuela, *f*; (pamphlet) folleto, *m*

leafy *a* frondoso

league *n* (measure) legua, *f*; liga, federación, sociedad, *f*; (football) liga, *f*. *vt* aliar; asociar. *vi* aliarse; asociarse, confederarse. **to be in l.,** *inf* estar de manga. **L. of Nations,** Sociedad de las Naciones, *f*

leak *n* (hole) agujero, *m*, grieta, *f*; *naut* vía de agua, *f*; (of gas, liquids, etc.) escape, *m*; (in a roof, etc.) gotera, *f*; *elec* resistencia de escape, *f*. *vi naut* hacer agua; (gas, liquids, etc.) escaparse, salirse; (drip) gotear. **to l. out,** (of news, etc.) trascender, saberse. **to spring a l.,** aparecer una vía de agua, hacer agua

leakage *n* (of gas, liquids) escape, *m*, fuga, *f*; derrame, *m*; pérdida, *f*; (of information) revelación, *f*

leaky *a naut* que hace agua; agujereado; poroso; que tiene goteras

lean *a* magro, seco, enjuto, delgado; (of meat) magro; *fig* pobre, estéril. *n* carne magra, *f*, magro, *m*. **to grow l.,** enflaquecer

lean *vi* inclinarse; apoyarse (en). *vt* apoyar (en); dejar arrimado (en). **to l. out of the window,** asomarse a la ventana. **to l. against,** apoyarse en, recostarse en (or contra). **to l. back,** echarse hacia atrás; recostarse. **to l. over,** inclinarse. **to l. upon,** apoyarse en; descansar sobre

leaning *n* inclinación, tendencia, *f*; predilección, afición, *f*

leanness *n* magrura, flaqueza, *f*; (of meat) magrez, *f*; *fig* pobreza, *f*

leap *n* salto, *m*; brinco, *m*; (caper) zapateta, *f*; *fig* salto, *m*. *vi* saltar, dar un salto; brincar. *vt* saltar; hacer saltar. **at one l.,** en un salto. **by leaps and bounds,** en saltos. **My heart leaped,** Mi corazón dio un salto. **to l. to the conclusion that . . . ,** saltar a la conclusión de que . . . **to l. to the eye,** saltar a la vista. **l. frog,** salto, salto de la muerte, *m*, pídola *f*. **l. year,** año bisiesto, *m*, salta cabrillas, *f pl*

leaping *a* saltador. *n* saltos, *m pl*

learn *vt* and *vi* aprender; instruirse; enterarse de. **to l. by heart,** aprender de memoria. **to l. from a reliable source,** saber de buena tinta. **to l. from experience,** aprender por experiencia

learned *a* sabio, docto; erudito; (of professions) liberal; versado (en), entendido (en). **a l. society,** una sociedad erudita

learner *n* aprendedor (-ra)

learning *n* saber, *m*; conocimientos, *m pl*; erudición, *f*; estudio, *m*; (literature) literatura, *f*

lease *n* arrendamiento, arriendo, *m*; contrato de arrendamiento, *m*. *vt* dar en arriendo, arrendar. **on l.,** en arriendo. **to take a new l. on life,** recobrar su vigor. **Lend L. Act,** ley de préstamo y arriendo, *f*

leaseholder *n* concesionario, *m*; arrendatario (-ia)

leash *n* (of a dog) traílla, *f*

least *a sup* **little,** mínimo; el (la, etc.) menor; más pequeño. *adv* menos. *n* lo menos. **at l.,** siquiera; por lo menos, al menos. **at the very l.,** a lo menos. **not in the l.,** de ninguna manera, nada. **to say the l. of,** sin exagerar, para no decir más

leather *n* cuero, *m*; piel, *f*, *a* de cuero; de piel. **patent l.,** charol, *m*. **Spanish l.,** cordobán, *m*. **tanned l.,** curtido, *m*. **l. apron,** mandil, *m*. **l. bag,** saco de cuero, *m*. **l. bottle,** bota, *f*. **l. breeches,** pantalón de montar, *m*. **l. jerkin,** coleto, *m*. **l. shield,** adarga, *f*. **l. strap,** correa, *f*. **l. trade,** comercio en cueros, *m*

leatherette *n* cartón cuero, *m*

leathery *a* de cuero; (of the skin) curtido por la intemperie; (tough) correoso

leave *n* (permission) permiso, *m*; (*mil* etc.) licencia, *f*; (farewell) despedida, *f*. *vt* and *vi* dejar; abandonar; salir (de), quitar, marcharse (de), *Lat. Am.* egresar (de . . .); (as surety) empeñar; (by will) legar, mandar; (an employment) darse de baja (de), dejar; (give into the keeping of) entregar; (bid farewell) despedirse (de). **By your l.,** Con permiso de Vd. (Vds.). Con la venia de Vd. (Vds.) **on l.,** de permiso. **l.-taking,** despedidas, *f pl*. **to be left,** quedar. **to be left over,** quedar; sobrar. **Two from four leaves two,** De cuatro a dos van dos. **to take French l.,** despedirse a la inglesa. **to take l. of,** despedirse de. **to take one's l.,** marcharse; despedirse. **to l. a deep impression,** *fig* impresionar mucho; quedar grabado (en). **to l. undone,** dejar de hacer, no hacer; dejar sin terminar. **to l. about,** *vt* dejar por todas partes. *vi* (of time) marcharse a eso de . . . **to l. ajar,** entreabrir, (when opening), entrecerrar (when closing), entornar. **to l. alone,** dejar a solas; dejar en paz; no molestar, no meterse con. **to l. aside,** omitir; prescindir de; olvidar. **to l. behind,** dejar atrás; olvidar. **l. much to be desired,** tener mucho que desear. **to l. off,** *vt* dejar de; abandonar; (garments) no ponerse, quitarse. *vi* terminar. **to l. out,** dejar fuera; dejar a un lado, descontar; omitir; pasar por; (be silent about) callar; suprimir. **to l. to,** dejar para; dejar hacer

leaven *n* levadura, *f*, fermento, *m*, *vt* fermentar; (*fig* permeate) penetrar (en), infiltrar en, imbuir; (a speech) salpimentar (con)

leaving *n* salida, partida, marcha, *f*, *Lat. Am.* egreso, *m*; *pl* **leavings,** sobras, *f pl*; desechos, *m pl*

lecherous *a* lascivo, lujurioso

lechery *n* lascivia, lujuria, *f*

lectern *n* atril, *m*; (in a church) facistol, *m*

lecture *n* conferencia, *f*; (in a university) lección, clase, *f*; discurso, *m*; (*inf* scolding) sermoneo, *m*. *vi* dar una conferencia; (in a university) dar clase. *vt* (*inf* scold) predicar, sermonear. **l. room,** sala de conferencias, *f*; (in a university) sala de clase, aula, *f*

lecturer *n* conferenciante, *Lat. Am.* conferencista, *mf*; (in a university) auxiliar, *m*; (professor) catedrático (-ca), profesor (-ra)

lectureship *n* auxiliaría, *f*

ledge *n* borde, *m*; capa, *f*; (of a window) alféizar, *m*; (shelf) anaquel, *m*

ledger *n* libro mayor, *m*

leech *n* sanguijuela, *f*

leek *n* puerro, *m*

leer *vi* mirar de soslayo; guiñar el ojo; mirar con los ojos llenos de deseo. *n* mirada de soslayo, *f*; mirada de lascivia, *f*

lees *n pl* heces, *f pl*; sedimento, *m*

leeward *n* sotavento, *m*. **on the l. side,** a sotavento

leeway *n naut* deriva, *f*; *fig* amplitud, margen de holgura, márgenes de maniobra, *f pl*

left *past part* dejado, etc. See **leave.** *a* izquierdo. *adv* a la izquierda; hacia la izquierda. *n* izquierda, *f*. **on the l.,** a la izquierda. **the L.,** *pol* las izquierdas. **the Left Bank (of Paris)** la Ribera izquierda, la Orilla izquierda **L. face!** ¡Izquierda! **l.-hand,** mano izquierda, *f*; izquierda, *f*. **l.-hand drive,** conducción a la izquierda, *f*. **l.-handed,** zurdo. **l. luggage office,** consigna, *f*. **l.-overs,** sobras, *f pl*, desperdicios, *m pl*

leg *n* pierna, *f*; (of animals, birds, furniture) pata, *f*; (of a triangle) cateto, *m*; (of a pair of compasses, trousers, lamb, veal) pierna, *f*; (of boots, stockings) caña, *f*; (of pork) pernil, *m*; (support) pie, *m*; (stage) etapa, *f*. **to be on one's last legs,** estar en las últimas; estar acabándose; estar sin recursos. **to pull a person's leg,** tomar el pelo (a). **leg-pull,** tomadura de pelo, *f*. **leg-of-mutton sleeve,** manga de pernil, *f*

legacy *n* legado, *m*, manda, *f*; herencia, *f*

legal *a* legal; de derecho; jurídico; (lawful, permissible) legítimo, lícito; (of a lawyer) de abogado. **l. expenses,** litisexpensas, *f pl*. **l. inquiry,** investigación jurídica, *f*

legalistics *n*. *Lat. Am.* abogaderas, abogaderías, *f pl*

legality *n* legalidad, *f*

legalization *n* legalización, *f*

legalize *vt* legalizar; autorizar, legitimar

legally *adv* según la ley; según derecho; legalmente

legal tender *n* moneda de curso liberatorio, *f*

legate *n* legado, *m*. **papal l.,** legado papal, *m*

legatee *n* legatario (-ia), *Lat. Am.* asignatario (-ia)

legation *n* legación, *f*

legend *n* leyenda, *f*

legendary *a* legendario

legerdemain *n* juegos de manos, *m pl*

legged *a* con piernas; de piernas . . . ; de patas . . . **a three-l. stool,** un taburete de tres patas. **long l.,** zancudo

leggings *n pl* polainas, *f pl*

legibility *n* legibilidad, *f*

legible *a* legible

legion *n* legión, *f*. **L. of Honor,** Legión de Honor, *f*

legionary *a* legionario. *n* legionario, *m*

legislate *vt* legislar

legislation *n* legislación, *f*

legislative *a* legislativo, legislador

legislator *n* legislador (-ra)

legislature *n* legislatura, *f*

legitimacy *n* legitimidad, *f*; justicia, *f*

legitimate *a* legítimo; justo

legitimation *n* legitimación, *f*

leisure *n* ocio, *m*, desocupación, *f*; tiempo libre, *m*. **at one's l.,** con sosiego, despacio. **You can do it at your l.,** Puedes hacerlo cuando tengas tiempo. **to be at l.,** estar desocupado, no tener nada que hacer. **l. moments,** ratos perdidos, momentos de ocio, *m pl*

leisured *a* desocupado, libre; sin ocupación; (wealthy) acomodado

leisurely *a* pausado, lento, deliberado; tardo

lemon *n* limón, *m*; (tree) limonero, *m*, *a* limonado, de color de limón; hecho o sazonado con limón. **l. drop,** pastilla de limón, *f*. **l.-grove,** limonar, *m*. **l.-squash,** limonada natural, *f*. **l.-squeezer,** exprime limones, *m*, exprimidera, *f*

lemonade *n* limonada, *f*. **l. powder,** limonada seca, *f*

lemur *n* lemur, *m*

lend *vt* prestar. **to l. an ear to,** prestar atención a. **It does not l. itself to . . . ,** No se presta a . . . **to l. a hand,** echar una mano, dar una mano

lender *n* el, *m*, (*f*, la) que presta; prestador (-ra); (of money) prestamista, *mf*; *com* mutuante, *mf*

lending *n* prestación, *f*, préstamo, *m*. **l.-library,** biblioteca circulante, *f*
length *n* largo, *m*; longitud, *f*; (of fabric) corte, *m*; (of a ship) eslora, *f*; (in racing) largo, *m*; distancia, *f*; (in time) duración, *f*; alcance, *m*. **at l.,** por fin, finalmente; (in full) extensamente, largamente. **by a l.,** por un largo. **full-l.,** de cuerpo entero. **three feet in l.,** tres pies de largo. **to go the l. of . . . ,** llegar al extremo de . . .
lengthen *vt* alargar; prolongar; extender. *vi* alargarse; prolongarse; extenderse; (of days) crecer
lengthening *n* alargamiento, *m*; prolongación, *f*; crecimiento, *m*
lengthily *adv* largamente
lengthiness *n* largueza, *f*; prolijidad, *f*
lengthy *a* largo; demasiado largo, larguísimo; (of speech) prolijo; verboso
lenience, leniency *n* lenidad, *f*; indulgencia, *f*
lenient *a* indulgente; poco severo
leniently *adv* con indulgencia
Leningrad Leningrado, *m*
lenitive *a* lenitivo. *n* lenitivo, *m*
lens *n* lente, *m*; (of the eye) cristalino, *m*
Lent *n* Cuaresma, *f*
Lenten *a* de Cuaresma, cuaresmal
lentil *n* lenteja, *f*
lentitude *n* lentitud, *f*
Leo *n* León, *m*
leonine *a* leonino
leopard *n* leopardo, *m*
leper *n* leproso (-sa). **l. colony,** colonia de leprosos, *f*
leprosy *n* lepra, *f*
leprous *a* leproso
lesbian *a* and *n* lesbiana
lesion *n* lesión, *f*
less *a* menor; más pequeño; menos; inferior. *adv* menos; sin. **l. than,** menos de (que). **more or l.,** poco más o menos. **no l.,** nada menos. **none the l.,** sin embargo. **to grow l.,** disminuir. **l. and l.,** cada vez menos
lessee *n* arrendatario (-ia); inquilino (-na)
lessen *vi* disminuir; reducirse. *vt* disminuir; reducir; (lower) rebajar; (disparage) menospreciar
lessening *n* disminución, *f*; reducción, *f*
lesser *a comp* menor; más pequeño. See **little**
lesson *n* lección, *f*. **to give a l.,** dar lección, dar clase; *fig* dar una lección (a). **to hear a l.,** tomar la lección
lessor *n* arrendador (-ra)
lest *conjunc* para que no; por miedo de (que), no sea que. **I did not do it l. they should not like it,** No lo hice por miedo de que no les gustase
let *vt* dejar, permitir; (lease) arrendar. *vi* alquilarse, ser alquilado. **Let** as an expression of the imperative is rendered in Spanish by the subjunctive or the imperative, e.g. **Let them go!** ¡Que se vayan! ¡Déjalos marchar! **He let them go,** Les dejó marchar. **to let fall,** dejar caer. **to let go,** dejar marchar; soltar; poner en libertad (a). **to let loose,** dar suelta a; *fig* desencadenar. **to let one know,** hacer saber, comunicar. **to let the cat out of the bag,** tirar de la manta. **to let th chance slip,** perder la ocasión. **to let alone,** (a thing) no tocar; (a person) dejar en paz, dejar tranquilo; (an affair) no meterse (en or con); (omit) no mencionar, omitir toda mención de. **to let down,** bajar; (by a rope) descolgar; (hair, etc.) dejar caer; (a dress, etc.) alargar; *naut* calar; (disappoint) dejar plantado. **to let in,** dejar entrar; hacer entrar; invitar a entrar; recibir; (insert) insertar. **to let into,** (initiate) iniciar en, admitir en; (a secret) revelar. Other meanings, see **to let in. to let off,** dejar salir; dejar en libertad; exonerar; perdonar; (a gun) disparar; (fireworks, etc.) hacer estallar. **to let out,** dejar salir; poner en libertad; (from a house) acompañar a la puerta; abrir la puerta; *sew* ensanchar; (hire) alquilar; (the fire, etc.) dejar extinguirse. **to let up,** dejar subir; (decrease) disminuir; (end) terminar
let *n* estorbo, impedimento, obstáculo, *m*. **without let or hindrance,** sin estorbo ni obstáculo
lethal *a* letal. **l. weapon,** instrumento de muerte, *m*
lethargic *a* aletargado; letárgico
lethargy *n* letargo, *m*; *med* letargía, *f*
letter *n* (of the alphabet) letra, *f*; (epistle) carta, *f*; *print* carácter, *m*; (lessor) arrendador (-ra); *pl* **letters,** letras, *fpl*; (correspondence) correo, *m*; correspondencia, *f*. *vt* inscribir; imprimir. **capital l.,** letra mayúscula, *f*. **first letters,** *fig* primeras letras, *fpl*. **registered l.,** carta certificada, *f*, certificado, *m*. **small l.,** letra minúscula, *f*. **the l. of the law,** la ley escrita. **to be l.-perfect,** saber de memoria. **to the l.,** *fig* a la letra. **letters patent,** patente, *f*; título de privilegio, *m*. **l.-balance,** pesacartas, *m*. **l.-book,** *com* libro copiador, *m*. **l.-box,** buzón de correos, *m*. **l.-card,** tarjeta postal del gobierno, *f*. **l. of credit,** carta de crédito, *f*. **l. of introduction,** carta de presentación, *f*. **l.-writer,** escritor (-ra) de cartas
lettered *a* culto, instruido; (printed) impreso
lettering *n* inscripción, *f*; letrero, rótulo, *m*
letterpress *n* imprenta, *f*; (not illustrations) texto, *m*
letting *n* (hiring) arrendamiento, *m*
lettuce *n* lechuga, *f*. **l. plant,** lechuguino, *m*. **l. seller,** lechuguero (-ra)
Leuven Lovaina, *f*
Levant, the el Levante, *m*
Levantine *a* and *n* levantino (-na)
levee *n* besamanos, *m*, recepción, *f*
level *n* nivel, *m*; ras, *m*, flor, *f*; llano, *m*; (plain) llanura, *f*; (instrument) nivel, *m*, *a* llano; igual; al nivel (de); uniforme; imparcial. *adv* a nivel; igualmente. *vt* nivelar; igualar; allanar; (a blow) asestar; (a gun) apuntar; (raze) arrasar, derribar; adaptar; hacer uniforme. **on the l.,** a nivel; *fig* de buena fe. **spirit l.,** nivel de burbuja, *m*. **to make l. again,** rellanar. **l. country,** campaña, llanura, *f*. **l. with the ground,** a ras de la tierra. **l. with the water,** a flor de agua. **l. crossing,** paso a nivel, *m*. **l.-headed,** sensato, cuerdo. **l. stretch,** rellano, *m*; llanura, *f*
leveler *n* nivelador (-ra)
leveling *a* nivelador; de nivelación; igualador. *n* nivelación, *f*; allanamiento, *m*; (to the ground) arrasamiento, *m*; igualación, *f*
levelness *n* nivel, *m*; planicie, *f*; igualdad, *f*
lever *n* palanca, *f*; (handle) manivela, *f*; escape de reloj, *m*; (excuse) pretexto, *m*; (means) modo, *m*. *vt* sopalancar. **control l.,** *aer* palanca de mando, *f*. **hand-l.,** palanca de mano, *f*
leverage *n* sistema de palancas, *m*; acción de palanca, *f*; *fig* influencia, fuerza, *f*, poder, *m*
Leviathan *n* leviatán, *m*
levitation *n* levitación, *f*
Levite *n* levita, *m*
Levitical *a* levítico
Leviticus *n* Levítico, *m*
levity *n* levedad, frivolidad, ligereza, *f*
levy *n* exacción (de tributos), *f*; impuesto, *m*; (of a fine) imposición, *f*; *mil* leva, *f*. *vt* (taxes) exigir; (a fine) imponer; (troops) reclutar, enganchar
levying *n* (of a tax) exacción (de tributos), *f*; (of a fine) imposición, *f*; (of troops) leva, *f*
lewd *a* lascivo, lujurioso, impúdico
lewdness *n* lascivia, lujuria, impudicia, *f*
lexicographer *n* lexicógrafo, *m*
lexicography *n* lexicografía, *f*
lexicon *n* léxico, *m*
liability *n* responsabilidad, obligación, *f*; tendencia, *f*; riesgo, *m*; *pl* **liabilities,** obligaciones, *fpl*; *com* pasivo, *m*
liable *a* responsable; propenso (a); expuesto (a); sujeto (a)
liaison *n* lío, *m*; coordinación, *f*. **l. officer,** oficial de coordinación, *m*
liar *n* mentiroso (-sa)
libation *n* libación, *f*
libel *n* libelo, *m*; difamación, *f*, *vt* difamar, calumniar
libeler *n* libelista, *mf* difamador (-ra)
libelous *a* difamatorio

liberal *a* liberal; generoso; abundante. *n* liberal, *mf* **l. profession,** carrera liberal, *f.* **l.-minded,** tolerante. **l.-mindedness,** tolerancia, *f*
liberalism *n* liberalismo, *m*
liberality *n* liberalidad, *f;* generosidad, *f*
liberalize *vt* liberalizar
liberate *vt* (a prisoner) poner en libertad; librar (de); (a gas, etc.) dejar escapar
liberation *n* liberación, *f;* (of a captive) redención, *f;* (of a slave) manumisión, *f*
liberator *n* libertador (-ra)
libertinage *n* libertinaje, *m*
libertine *n* libertino, *m*
libertinism *n* libertinaje, *m*
liberty *n* libertad, *f;* (familiarity) familiaridad, *f;* (right) privilegio, *m,* prerrogativa, *f;* (leave) permiso, *m.* **at l.,** en libertad; desocupado, libre. **I have taken the l. of giving them your name,** Me he tomado la libertad de darles su nombre. **to set at l.,** poner en libertad (a). **to take liberties with,** tratar con familiaridad; (a text) tergiversar. **l. of speech,** libertad de palabra, libertad de expresión, *f.* **l. of thought,** libertad de pensamiento, *f*
libidinous *a* libidinoso
Libra *n* Libra, *f*
librarian *n* bibliotecario (-ia)
librarianship *n* carrera *f,* or empleo *m,* de bibliotecario
library *n* biblioteca, *f;* (book shop) librería, *f.* **l. catalog,** catálogo de la biblioteca, *m*
librettist *n* libretista, *mf*
libretto *n* libreto, *m*
Libya Libia, *f*
Libyan *a* and *n* libio (-ia)
license *n* licencia, *f,* permiso, *m;* autorización, *f;* (driving) carnet de chófer, permiso de conducción, *m;* (of a car) permiso de circulación, *m;* (for a wireless, etc.) licencia, *f;* (marriage) licencia de casamiento, *f;* (excess) libertinaje, desenfreno, *m.* **import l.,** permiso de importación, *m.* **poetic l.,** licencia poética, *f.* **l. number,** (of a car) número de matriculación, *m.* *vt* licenciar; autorizar; (a car) sacar la licencia del automóvil
licensee *n* concesionario (-ia)
licentiate *n* licenciado (-da)
licentious *a* licencioso, disoluto
licentiousness *n* libertinaje, *m,* disipación, *f*
lichen *n* liquen, *m*
licit *a* lícito
lick *vt* lamer; (of waves) besar; (of flames) bailar; (thrash) azotar; (defeat) vencer. **to l. one's lips,** relamerse los labios, chuparse los dedos. **to l. the dust,** morder el polvo
licking *n* lamedura, *f;* (beating) paliza, tunda, *f;* (defeat) derrota, *f*
lid *n* cobertera, *f;* tapa, *f;* (of the eye) párpado, *m*
lie *n* mentira, *f;* invención, falsedad, *f;* mentís, *m, vi* mentir. **to give the lie to,** desmentir, dar el mentís. **to lie barefacedly,** mentir por la mitad de la barba. **white lie,** mentira oficiosa, *f*
lie *vi* estar tumbado, estar echado; estar recostado; descansar, reposar; (in the grave) yacer; (be) estar; (be situated) hallarse, estar situado; (stretch) extenderse; (sleep) dormir; (depend) depender; (consist) consistir, estribar; (as an obligation) incumbir. **Here lies . . . ,** Aquí descansa . . . , Aquí yace . . . **It does not lie in my power,** No depende de mí. **to let lie,** dejar; dejar en paz. **to lie at anchor,** estar anclado. **to lie fallow,** estar en barbecho; *fig* descansar. **to lie about,** estar esparcido por todas partes; estar en desorden. **to lie along,** estar tendido a lo largo de; *naut* dar a la banda. **to lie back,** recostarse; apoyarse (en). **to lie by,** estar acostado al lado de; (of things, places) estar cerca (de); descansar. **to lie down,** tenderse, tumbarse, echarse, acostarse; reposar. **Lie down!** (to a dog) ¡Echate! **to lie down under,** tenderse bajo; (an insult) tragar, sufrir. **to lie in,** consistir en; depender de; (of childbirth) estar de parto. **to lie open,** estar abierto; estar expuesto (a); estar al descubierto, estar a la vista. **to lie over,** (be postponed) quedar aplazado. **to lie to,** *naut* estarse a la capa, ponerse en facha. **to lie under,** estar bajo, hallarse bajo; estar bajo el peso de; (be exposed to) estar expuesto a. **to lie with,** dormir con; (concern) tocar (a); corresponder (a)
lie *n* configuración, *f;* disposición, *f;* posición, *f.* **the lie of the land,** la configuración del terreno
lieu *n* lugar, *m.* **in l. of,** en lugar de, en vez de
lieutenant *n* teniente, lugarteniente, *m;* (naval) alférez, *m.* **first l.,** (in the army) primer teniente, teniente, *m;* (in the navy) alférez de navío, *m.* **naval l.,** teniente de navío, *m.* **second l.,** (in the army) segundo teniente, *m;* (in the navy) alférez de fragata, *m.* **l.-colonel,** teniente coronel
life *n* vida, *f;* (being) ser, *m;* (society) mundo, *m,* sociedad, *f;* (vitality) vitalidad, *f;* vigor, *m, a* de vida; (of annuities, etc.) vitalicio; (life-saving) de salvamento. **for l.,** de por vida. **from l.,** del natural. **high l.,** gran mundo, *m,* alta sociedad, *f.* **low l.,** vida del hampa, vida de los barrios bajos, *f.* **to the l.,** al vivo. **to lay down one's l.,** entregar la vida. **to take one's l. in one's hands,** jugarse la vida. **l. annuity,** fondo vitalicio, *m.* **l.-belt,** (cinturón) salvavidas, *m.* **l.-blood,** sangre vital, *f; fig* nervio, *m;* vigor, *m.* **l.-boat,** (on a ship) bote salvavidas, *m;* (on the coast) lancha de salvamento, *f.* **l.-boat station,** estación de salvamento, *f.* **l.-giving,** vivificante, que da vida; tonificante. **l.-guard,** (soldier) guardia militar, *f;* Guardia de Corps, *f,* (at beach or swimming pool) guardavivas, *mf.* **l.-insurance,** seguro sobre la vida, *m.* **l.-interest,** usufructo, *m.* **l.-jacket,** chaleco salvavidas, *m.* **l.-like,** natural. **l.-line,** cable de salvamento, *m.* **l.-saving,** *a* de salvamento; curativo. **l.-saving apparatus,** aparato salvavidas, *m.* **l.-sized,** de tamaño natural
life cycle *n* ciclo vital, *m*
life imprisonment *n* reclusión perpetua, *f*
life jacket *n* chaleco salvavidas, *f*
lifeless *a* sin vida, muerto; inanimado; *fig* desanimado
lifelessness *n* falta de animación; inercia
lifelong *a* de toda la vida
lifetime *n* vida, *f*
lift *n* esfuerzo para levantar, *m;* acción de levantar, *f;* alza, *f;* (blow) golpe, *m;* (help) ayuda, *f;* (hitch, ride) *Mexico* aventón; *m,* (elevator) ascensor, *m;* (for goods) montacargas, *m; pl* **lifts,** *naut* balancines, *m pl.* **to give a l. to,** (help) ayudar; (hitchhiker etc.) dar un aventón.
lift *vt* levantar; alzar, elevar; (pick up) coger; (one's hat) quitarse; (steal) hurtar; exaltar. *vi* (of mist) disiparse; desaparecer. **to l. the elbow,** empinar el codo. **to l. down,** quitar (de); (a person) bajar en brazos. **to l. up,** alzar; erguir, levantar; levantar en brazos
lifting *n* acción de levantar, *f;* levantamiento, alzamiento, *m*
ligament *n* ligamento, *m*
ligature *n* (*surg mus*) ligadura, *f*
light *a* (not dark) claro, con mucha luz, bañado de luz; (of colors) claro; (not heavy, and of sleep, food, troops, movements) ligero; (of reading) de entretenimiento; (irresponsible) frívolo; (easy) fácil; (slight) leve; (of hair) rubio; (happy) alegre; (fickle) inconstante, liviano; (of complexion) blanco. *adv* ligero. **to be l.,** no pesar mucho; estar de día. **to grow l.,** (dawn) clarear; iluminarse. **to make l. of,** no tomar en serio; no preocuparse de; (suffering) sufrir sin quejarse. **l.-colored,** (de color) claro. **l.-fingeredness,** sutileza de manos, *f.* **l.-footed,** ligero de pies. **l.-haired,** de pelo rubio. **l.-headed,** casquivano, ligero de cascos; delirante. **l.-headedness,** ligereza de cascos, frivolidad, *f;* delirio, *m.* **l.-hearted,** alegre (de corazón). **l.-heartedness,** alegría, *f.* **l. horse,** *mil* caballería ligera, *f.* **l. troops,** tropas ligeras, *f pl.* **l.-weight,** *n* (*boxing*) peso ligero, *m, a* de peso ligero
light *n* luz., *f;* (day) día, *m;* (match) cerilla, *f;* (of a cigarette, etc.) fuego, *m;* (of a window) cristal, vidrio, *m;* (point of view) punto de vista, *m;* (in a picture) toque

de luz, *m*; *pl* **lights,** (offal) bofes, *m pl*. **against the l.,** al trasluz. **by the l. of,** a la luz de; según. **half-l.,** media luz, *f*. **high light(s),** *art* claros, *m pl*; *fig* momento culminante, *m*; acontecimiento de más interés, *m*. **to come to l.,** descubrirse. **to put a l. to the fire,** encender el fuego. **l.-year,** año de luz, *m*
light *vt* (a lamp, fire, etc.) encender; iluminar. *vi* encenderse; iluminarse; *fig* animarse; brillar. **to l. upon,** encontrar por casualidad; tropezar con
lighten *vt* (illuminate) iluminar; (of weight) aligerar; (cheer) alegrar; (mitigate) aliviar. *vi* (grow light) clarear; (of lightning) relampaguear; (become less heavy) disminuir de peso, aligerarse; volverse más alegre
lightening *n* aligeramiento, *m*; (easing) alivio, *m*; luz, *f*
lighter *n* (boat) lancha, barcaza, gabarra, *f*; (device) encendedor, *m*. **pocket l.,** encendedor de bolsillo, *m*. **l. man,** gabarrero, *m*
light-fingered *a* ligero de manos
lighthouse *n* faro, *m*. **l.-keeper,** guardafaro, *m*
lighting *n* iluminación, *f*; alumbrado, *m*. **flood l.,** iluminación intensiva, *f*. **l.-up time,** hora de encender los faros, *f*
lightly *adv* ligeramente; fácilmente; (slightly) levemente; ágilmente; sin seriedad. **l. wounded,** levemente herido
lightness *n* ligereza, *f*; poco peso, *m*; agilidad, *f*; (brightness) claridad, *f*; (inconstancy) liviandad, inconstancia, *f*; frivolidad, *f*
lightning *n* relámpago, rayo, *m*. **as quick as l.,** como un relámpago. **to be struck by l.,** ser herido por un relámpago. **l.-rod,** pararrayos, *m*
lightship *n* buque faro, *m*
ligneous *a* leñoso
lignite *n* lignito, *m*
likable *a* simpático
like *a* semejante; parecido; igual, mismo; (characteristic) típico, característico; (likely) probable; (equivalent) equivalente. *adv* como; igual (que); del mismo modo (que). *n* semejante, igual, *mf*; tal cosa, *f*; cosas semejantes, *f pl*. **Don't speak to me l. that,** No me hables así. **He was l. a fury,** Estaba hecho una furia. **They are very l. each other,** Se parecen mucho. **to be l.,** parecerse (a), semejar. **to look l.,** parecer ser (que); tener el aspecto de; (of persons) parecerse (a). **to return l. for l.,** pagar en la misma moneda
like *vt* gustar, agradar; estar aficionado (a), gustar de; (wish) querer. **As you l.,** Como te parezca bien, Como quieras. **If you l.,** Si quieres. **James likes painting,** Jaime está aficionado a la pintura. **Judith does not l. the north of England,** A Judit no le gusta el norte de Inglaterra. **I don't l. to do it,** No me gusta hacerlo. **I should l. him to go to Madrid,** Me gustaría que fuese a Madrid
likelihood *n* posibilidad, *f*; probabilidad, *f*
likely *a* probable; verosímil, creíble, plausible; posible; (suitable) satisfactorio, apropiado; (handsome) bien parecido. *adv* probablemente. **They are not l. to come,** No es probable que vengan
liken *vt* comparar
likeness *n* parecido, *m*, semejanza, *f*; (portrait) retrato, *m*
likewise *adv* igualmente, asimismo, también. *conjunc* además
liking *n* (for persons) simpatía, *f*, cariño, *m*; (for things) gusto, *m*, afición, *f*; (appreciation) aprecio, *m*. **I have a l. for old cities,** Me gustan (or me atraen) las viejas ciudades. **to take a l. to,** (things) aficionarse a; (persons) prendarse de, tomar cariño (a)
lilac *n* lila, *f*. **l. color,** color de lila, *m*
Lilliputian *a* liliputiense. *n* liliputiense, *mf*
lilt *n* canción, *f*; ritmo, *m*; armonía, *f*
lily *n* lirio, *m*, azucena, *f*; (of France) flor de lis, *f*. **l. of the valley,** lirio de los valles, muguete, *m*. **l.-white,** blanco como la azucena
limb *n anat* miembro, *m*; (of a tree) rama, *f*
limbless *a* mutilado
limbo *n* limbo, *m*
lime *n chem* cal, *f*; (for catching birds) liga, hisca, *f*; (linden tree) tilo, *m*; (tree like a lemon) limero, *m*; (fruit) lima, *f*. *vt* (whiten) encalar; *agr* abonar con cal. **slaked l.,** cal muerta, *f*. **l.-flower,** flor del tilo, tila, *f*; flor del limero, *f*. **l.-juice,** jugo de lima, *m*. **l.-kiln,** calera, *f*. **l.-pit,** pozo de cal, *m*. **l. tree** *Lat. Am.* limo, *m*
limelight *n* luz de calcio, *f*; *fig* centro de atención, *m*; publicidad, *f*. **to be in the l.,** ser el centro de atención, estar a la vista (de público)
limestone *n* piedra caliza, *f*. **l. deposit,** calar, *m*
limit *n* límite, *m*; confín, *m*; linde, *m*, or *f*; limitación, *f*. *vt* limitar; fijar; (restrict) restringir. **This is the l.!** ¡Este es el colmo! ¡No faltaba más!
limitation *n* limitación, *f*; restricción, *f*
limitative *a* restrictivo, limitativo
limited *a* limitado; restringido; escaso; (of persons) de cortos alcances; *com* anónimo. **l. company,** sociedad anónima, *f*
limited monarchy *n* monarquía moderada, *f*
limiting adjective *n* adjetivo determinativo, *m*
limitless *a* sin límites; ilimitado, inmenso
limousine *n* limousina, *f*, coche cerrado, *m*
limp *a* flojo; débil; fláccido; lánguido. *n* cojera, *f*. *vi* cojear. **to l. off,** marcharse cojeando. **to l. up,** acercarse cojeando; subir cojeando
limpid *a* límpido, cristalino, puro
limpidity *n* limpidez, *f*
limping *a* cojo
limply *adv* flojamente; débilmente; lánguidamente
limpness *n* flojedad, *f*; debilidad, *f*; languidez, *f*
linchpin *n* pezonera, *f*
linden *n* tilo, *m*
line *vt* (furrow) surcar; (troops, etc.) poner en fila; alinear; (clothes, nests, etc.) forrar; (building) revestir; (one's pocket) llenar. *vi* estar en línea, alinearse
line *n* (most meanings) línea, *f*; (cord) cuerda, *f*; *naut* cordel, *m*; (fishing) sedal, *m*; (railway) vía, *f*; (wrinkle) surco, *m*; arruga, *f*; (row) hilera, ringlera, fila, *f*; (of verse) verso, *m*; *print* renglón, *m*; (of business) ramo, *m*; profesión, *f*; (interest) especialidad, *f*. **bowling** or **serving l.,** línea de saque, *f*; **hard lines,** mala suerte, *f*; apuro, *m*, situación difícil, *f*. **in a l.,** en fila; en cola. **in direct l.,** (of descent) en línea recta. **It is not in my l.,** No es una especialidad mía; No es uno de mis intereses. **on the lines of,** conforme a; parecido a. **to cross the l.,** (equator) pasar la línea; (railway) cruzar la vía. **to drop a l.,** escribir unas líneas, poner unas líneas. **to read between the lines,** leer entre líneas. **l.-drawing,** dibujo de líneas, *m*. **l. of battle,** línea de batalla, *f*
lineage *n* linaje, *m*, familia, raza, *f*
lineal *a* lineal
lineament *n* lineamento, *m*; (of the face) facciones, *f pl*
linear *a* lineal. **l. equation,** ecuación de primer grado, *f*
lined *a* rayado, con líneas; (of the face) surcado, arrugado; (of gloves, etc.) forrado. **lined paper,** papel rayado, *m*
linen *n* lino, *m*; *inf* ropa blanca, *f*; *a* de lino. **clean l.,** ropa limpia, *f*. **dirty l.,** ropa sucia, *f*; ropa para lavar, *f*. **table-l.,** mantelería, *f*. **l. cupboard,** armario para ropa blanca, *m*. **l. draper,** lencero (-ra). **l.-draper's shop,** lencería, *f*. **l. room,** lencería, *f*. **l. tape,** trenzadera, *f*. **l. thread,** hilo de lino, *m*
liner *n* (ship) transatlántico, *m*; buque de vapor, *m*; *aer* avión de pasaje, *m*
linesman *n* soldado de línea, *m*; *sport* juez de línea, *m*
ling *n bot* brezo, *m*; *icht* especie de abadejo, *f*
linger *vi* (remain) quedarse; tardar en marcharse; ir lentamente; hacer algo despacio
lingerie *n* ropa blanca, *f*
lingering *a* lento; largo, prolongado; melancólico, triste
lingeringly *adv* lentamente; largamente; melancólicamente
linguist *n* lingüista, *mf*
linguistic *a* lingüístico

linguistics *n* lingüística, *f*
liniment *n* linimento, *m*
lining *n* (of a garment, etc.) forro, *m*; (building) revestimiento, *m*
link *n* (in a chain) eslabón, *m*; (of beads) sarta, *f*; *fig* enlace, *m*, cadena, *f*; conexión, *f*; *mech* corredera, *f*; (torch) hacha de viento, *f*. *vt* enlazar, unir; *fig* encadenar. **missing l.,** *fig* estabón perdido, *m*. **to l. arms,** cogerse del brazo
linking *n* encadenamiento, *m*; *fig* conexión, *f*
links *n pl* campo de golf, *m*
linoleum *n* linóleo, *m*
linotype *n* linotipia, *f*
linseed *n* linaza, *f*. **l. cake,** bagazo, *m*. **l.-oil,** aceite de linaza, *m*
lint *n med* hilas, *f pl*; (fluff) borra, *f*
lintel *n* dintel, *m*; (threshold) umbral, *m*
lion *n* león, *m*; *fig* celebridad, *f*. **l. cage** or **den,** leonera, *f*. **l.-hearted,** valeroso. **l.-hunter,** cazador (-ra) de leones. **l.-keeper,** leonero (-ra). **lion's mane,** melena, *f*. **l.-tamer,** domador (-ra) de leones
lioness *n* leona, *f*
lionize *vt* dar bombo (a), hacer la rueda (a), tratar como una celebridad (a)
lion's share *n* parte del león, tajada del león, *f*
lip *n* labio, *m*; (of a vessel) pico, *m*; (of a crater) borde, *m*; *fig* boca, *f*. **to open one's lips,** abrir la boca. **to smack one's lips,** chuparse los dedos. **lip reading,** lectura labial, *f*. **lip-service,** amor fingido, *m*; promesas hipócritas, *f pl*. **lip stick,** lápiz para los labios, *m*
lipped *a* (in compounds) con labios . . . , que tiene labios; (of vessels in compounds) con . . . picos
liquefaction *n* licuefacción, *f*
liquefiable *a* liquidable
liquefy *vt* liquidar. *vi* liquidarse
liqueur *n* licor, *m*. **l.-glass,** copita de licor, *f*. **l.-set,** licorera, *f*
liquid *n* líquido, *m*, *a* líquido; límpido. **l. air,** aire líquido, *m*. **l. measure,** medida para líquidos, *f*
liquidate *vt* liquidar; saldar (cuentas); *mil* soldar
liquidation *n* liquidación, *f*
liquidness *n* liquidez, *f*; fluidez, *f*
liquor *n* licor, *m*. **l. shop,** aguardentería, *f*. **l. traffic,** negocio de vinos y licores, *m*; contrabando, *m*
liquorice *n* regaliz, *m*
lira *n* lira, *f*
Lisbon Lisboa, *f*
lisp *n* ceceo, *m*; balbuceo, *m*, *vi* cecear; balbucir
lisping *a* ceceoso; balbuciente. *n* ceceo, *m*; (of a child, etc.) balbuceo, *m*
lissom *a* flexible; ágil
list *n* lista, *f*; catálogo, *m*; matrícula, *f*; *naut* recalcada, *f*; inclinación, *f*; (tournament) liza, *f*. *vt* hacer una lista de; catalogar; matricular, inscribir. *vi naut* recalcar; inclinarse a un lado. **to enter the lists,** entrar en liza. **l. of wines,** lista de vinos, *f*
listen *vi* escuchar; (attend) attender. **Don't you want to l. to the music?** ¿No quieres escuchar la música? **to l. in,** (to the radio) escuchar la radio; (eavesdrop) escuchar a hurtadillas
listener *n* oyente, *mf*; (to radio) radiooyente, *mf*
listless *a* lánguido, apático, indiferente
listlessly *adv* lánguidamente, indiferentemente
listlessness *n* apatía, languidez, indiferencia, inercia, *f*
litany *n* letanía, *f*
liter *n* litro, *m*
literal *a* literal. **l.-minded,** sin imaginación
literalness *n* literalidad, *f*
literary *a* literario
literary executor *n* depositario de la obra literaria, *m*
literate *a* and *n* literato (-ta)
literature *n* literatura, *f*
lithe *a* flexible; sinuoso y delgado; ágil
litheness *n* flexibilidad, *f*; sinuosidad, *f*; delgadez, *f*; agilidad, *f*
lithograph *n* litografía, *f*, *vt* litografiar
lithographer *n* litógrafo, *m*
lithographic *a* litográfico
lithography *n* litografía, *f*
Lithuania Lituania, *f*
Lithuanian *a* lituano, *n* lituano (-na); (language) lituano, *m*
litigant *n* litigante, *mf*
litigate *vi* and *vt* litigar, pleitear
litigation *n* litigación, *f*
litigious *a* litigioso
litmus *n* tornasol, *m*. **l. paper,** papel de tornasol, *m*
litter *n* litera, *f*; (stretcher) camilla, *f*; (bed) lecho, *m*; cama de paja, *f*; (brood) camada, cría, *f*; (rubbish) cosas en desorden, *f pl*; (papers) papeletas, *f pl*; (untidiness) desarreglo, desorden, *m*, confusión, *f*, *vt* poner en desorden
little *a* pequeño; poco; (scanty) escaso; insignificante; bajo, mezquino. *adv* poco. **a l.,** un poco (de); un tanto. **in l.,** en pequeño. **not a l.,** no poco; bastante. **l. by l.,** poco a poco. **l. or no,** poco o nada. **however l.,** por pequeño que. **as l. as possible,** lo menos posible. **to make l. of,** no dar importancia a; sacar poco en claro de, no comprender bien; no hacer caso de; (persons) acoger mal. **l. by l.,** poco a poco. **l. finger,** dedo meñique, *m*. **l. one,** pequeñuela, *f*, pequeñito, *m*
littleness *n* pequeñez, *f*; poquedad, *f*; mezquindad, *f*; trivialidad, *f*
littoral *a* and *n* litoral, *m*
liturgical *a* litúrgico. **l. calendar,** calendario litúrgico, *m*
liturgical vestment *n* paramento litúrgico, *m*
liturgy *n* liturgia, *f*
live *a* vivo, viviente; (alight) encendido; (of a wire, etc.) cargado de electricidad. **l. cartridge,** cartucho con bala, *m*. **l. coal,** ascua, *f*. **l.-stock,** ganadería, *f*. **l. wire,** conductor eléctrico, *m*; *fig* fuerza viva, *f*
live *vi* vivir; residir, habitar; (of ships) mantenerse a flote; salvarse; subsistir. *vt* (one's life) llevar, pasar. **Long l.!** ¡Viva! **to have enough to l. on,** tener de que vivir. **to l. together,** convivir. **to l. again,** volver a vivir. **to l. at,** vivir en, habitar. **to l. down,** sobrevivir a; (a fault) lograr borrar. **to l. on,** vivir de. **to l. up to,** vivir con arreglo a, vivir en conformidad con; estar al nivel de, merecer. **to l. up to one's income,** vivir al día, gastarse toda la renta
live broadcast *n* emisión en directo, *f*
livelihood *n* vida, subsistencia, *f*. **to make a l.,** ganarse la vida
liveliness *n* vivacidad, vida, *f*; animación, *f*; alegría, *f*
livelong *a* entero, todo; eterno. **all the l. day,** todo el santo día
lively *a* vivo; vivaracho; brioso, enérgico; alegre; bullicioso; animado; (fresh) fresco; (of colours) brilliante; intenso
liver *n* vividor (-ra), el, *m*, (*f*, la) que vive; habitante, *m*; *anat* hígado, *m*. **l. cancer,** cáncer del hígado, *m*. **l. complaint,** mal de hígado, *m*. **l. extract,** extracto de hígado, *m*
livery *n* librea, *f*; uniforme, *m*; *poet* vestiduras, *f pl*. **l. stables,** pensión de caballos, *f*; cochería de alquiler, *f*
livid *a* lívido; cárdeno, amoratado
lividness *n* lividez, *f*
living *a* viviente; vivo, vital. *n* vida, *f*; modo de vivir, *m*; beneficio eclesiástico, *m*. **the l.,** los vivos. **to make one's l.,** ganarse la vida. **l. memory,** memoria de personas vivientes, memoria de los que aún viven, *f*. **l.-room,** sala de estar, *f*. **l. soul,** ser viviente; *inf* bicho viviente, *m*. **l. wage,** jornal básico, *m*
lizard *n* lagarto (-ta). **giant l.,** dragón, *m*. **wall l.,** lagartija, *f*. **l. hole,** lagartera, *f*
llama *n* llama, *f*
load *n* carga, *f*; peso, *m*; (cart) carretada, *f*; *elec* carga, *f*; (quantity) cantidad, *f*. *vt* cargar (con); (with honors) llenar (de); (*fig* weigh down) agobiar (con); (a stick with lead) emplomar; (*elec* and of dice) cargar; (wine) mezclar vino con un narcótico. **to be loaded with**

fruit, estar cargado de fruta. **to l. oneself with,** cargarse de. **to l. the dice,** cargar los dados. **to l. again,** recargar

loader *n* cargador, *m*

loading *n* carga, *f*. **l. depot,** cargadero, *m*

loaf *n* pan, *m*; (French) barra de pan, *f*. *vi* golfear, vagabundear, gandulear. **l. sugar,** azúcar de pilón, *m*

loafer *n* vago (-ga); azotacalles, *mf*; gandul (-la); golfo (-fa)

loafing *n* gandulería, *f*, vagabundeo, *m*

loam *n* marga, *f*

loamy *a* margoso

loan *n* empréstito, *m*; (lending) prestación, *f*; préstamo, *m*. *vt* prestar. **l. fund,** caja de empréstitos, *f*. **l. company office,** casa de préstamos, *f*

loath *a* desinclinado, poco dispuesto

loathe *vt* abominar, detestar, odiar, aborrecer; repugnar

loather *n* el, *m*, (*f*, la) que odia; aborrecedor (-ra)

loathing *n* aborrecimiento, odio, *m*; repugnancia, aversión, *f*

loathsome *a* odioso, aborrecible; asqueroso; repugnante

loathsomeness *n* carácter repugnante, *m*; asquerosidad, *f*

lobby *n* pasillo, *m*; antecámara, *f*; (in a hotel, house) vestíbulo, recibidor, *m*; (waiting-room) sala de espera, *f*; (in Parliament) sala de los pasos perdidos, *f*. *vt* and *vi* cabildear

lobe *n bot* lobo, *m*; (*anat arch*) lóbulo, *m*

lobster *n* langosta, *f*; bogavante, *m*. **l.-pot,** cambín, *m*, nasa, *f*

local *a* local; de la localidad. **l. anesthetic,** anestésico local, *m*. **l. color,** color local, *m*

locale *n* local, *m*

locality *n* localidad, *f*; situación, *f*

localization *n* localización, *f*

localize *vt* localizar

locate *vt* situar; colocar; localizar. **to be located,** situarse; hallarse

location *n* colocación, *f*; emplazamiento, *m*; localidad, *f*; situación, posición, *f*

loch *n* lago, *m*

lock *n* cerradura (of a door, including a vehicle) *f*; (of a gun) cerrojo, *m*; (in wrestling) llave, *f*; (on rivers, canals) presa, *f*; (at a dock) esclusa, *f*; (of hair) mechón, *m*, guedeja, *f*; (ringlet) bucle, *m*; *pl* **locks,** (hair) cabellos, *m pl*, pelo, *m*. **spring l.,** cerradura de golpe, *f*. **to put a l. on,** poner cerradura a. **under l. and key,** bajo cuatro llaves. **l.-jaw,** trismo, *m*. **l. keeper,** esclusero (-ra) *mf*. **l.-out strike,** huelga patronal, *f*

lock *vt* cerrar con llave; *fig* encerrar; (embrace) abrazar estrechamente; (of wheels, etc.) trabar; (twine) entrelazar. *vi* cerrarse con llave. **to l. in,** cerrar con llave; encerrar. **to l. out,** cerrar la puerta (a); dejar en la calle (a). **to l. up,** encerrar; (imprison) encarcelar

locker *n* (drawer) cajón, *m*; (cupboard) armario, *m*; *naut* cajonada, *f*

locket *n* guardapelo, *m*; medallón, *m*

locksmith *n* cerrajero, *m*. **locksmith's trade,** cerrajería, *f*

locomotion *n* locomoción, *f*

locomotive *a* locomotor. *n* locomotora, *f*

locum tenens *n* interino (-na)

locust *n* langosta migratoria, *f*

locution *n* locución, *f*

lode *n* filón, *m*

lodestar *n* estrella polar, *f*; *fig* norte, *m*

lodge *n* casita, garita, *f*; casa de guarda, *f*; (freemason's) logia, *f*; (porter's) portería, *f*, *vi* hospedarse, alojarse, vivir, parar; penetrar; entrar (en); fijarse (en). *vt* hospedar, alojar; albergar; (a blow) asestar; (a complaint) hacer, dar; (money, etc.) depositar. **to l. an accusation against,** querellarse contra, quejarse de. **l.-keeper,** conserje, *m*

lodger *n* huésped (-eda), *Lat. Am.* alojado (-da)

lodging *n* hospedaje, alojamiento, *m*; (inn) posada, *f*; residencia, *f*; casa, *f*. **l.-house,** casa de huéspedes, *f*

loft *n* desván, sotabanco, *m*; pajar, *m*

loftily *adv* en alto; (proudly) con arrogancia, con altanería

loftiness *n* altura, *f*; sublimidad, *f*; nobleza, *f*; dignidad, *f*; (haughtiness) altanería, soberbia, *f*

lofty *a* alto; sublime; noble; eminente; (haughty) altanero, soberbio

log *n* madero, tronco, *m*; palo, *m*; leño, *m*; *naut*, diario de a bardo *m*, barquilla, *f*. **to lie like a log,** estar hecho un tronco. **log-book,** *naut* cuaderno de bitácora, *m*. **log-cabin,** cabañas de troncos, *m*. **log-wood,** palo campeche, *m*

logarithm *n* logaritmo, *m*

logarithmic *a* logarítmico

logic *n* lógica, *f*

logical *a* lógico

logician *n* lógico (-ca)

loin *n* ijar, *m*; (of meat) falda, *f*; *pl* **loins,** lomos, riñones *m pl*. **to gird up one's loins,** *fig* arremangarse los faldones. **l.-cloth,** taparrabo, *m*

loiter *vi* vagabundear, vagar, errar; haraganear; rezagarse

loiterer *n* haragán (-ana); vago (-ga); rezagado (-da)

loll *vi* recostarse (en), apoyarse (en). *vt* (the tongue) sacar

Lombardy-Venetia Lombardo-Véneto, *m*

London Londres, *m*

Londoner *n* londinense, *mf*

lone. See **lonely**

loneliness *n* soledad, *f*; aislamiento, *m*

lonely *a* solitario; solo; aislado, remoto; desierto

lonesome *a* solo, solitario

long *a* largo; prolongado; de largo; (extensive) extenso; (big) grande; (much) mucho. **a l. time,** mucho tiempo. **It is five feet l.,** Tiene cinco pies de largo. **l.-armed,** que tiene los brazos largos. **l.-boat,** falúa, *f*. **l. clothes,** (infant's) mantillas, *f pl*. **l.-distance call,** conferencia telefónica, *f*. **l.-distance race,** carrera de fondo, *f*. **l.-eared,** de orejas largas. **l.-faced,** de cara larga, carilargo. **l.-forgotten,** olvidado hace mucho tiempo. **l.-haired,** que tiene el pelo largo. **l.-headed,** dolicocéfalo; *fig* astuto, sagaz. **l.-legged,** zanquilargo, zancudo. **l.-lived,** que vive hasta una edad avanzada; longevo; duradero. **l.-lost,** perdido hace mucho tiempo. **l.-sighted,** présbita; previsor; sagaz. **l.-standing,** viejo, de muchos años. **l.-suffering,** sufrido, paciente. **l.-tailed,** de cola larga. **l.-waisted,** de talle largo. **l.-winded,** prolijo

long *adv* mucho tiempo; mucho; durante mucho tiempo. **as l. as,** mientras (que). **before l.,** dentro de poco. **the l. and the short of it,** en resumidas cuentas. **How l. has she been here?** ¿Cuánto tiempo hace que está aquí? **not l. before,** poco tiempo antes. **l. ago,** tiempo ha, muchos años ha

long *vi* anhelar, suspirar (por), desear con vehemencia

longanimity *n* longanimidad, *f*

longer *a comp* más largo. *adv comp* más tiempo. **How much l. must we wait?** ¿Cuánto tiempo más hemos de esperar? **He can no l. walk as he used,** Ya no puede andar como antes

longevity *n* longevidad, *f*

longing *a* anheloso, ansioso; de envidia. *n* anhelo, *m*, ansia, *f*; deseo vehemente, *m*; envidia, *f*

longingly *adv* con ansia; impacientemente; con envidia

longish *a* algo largo

longitude *n* longitud, *f*

longitudinal *a* longitudinal

long take *n cinema* toma larga, *f*

loofah *n* esponja vegetal, *f*

look *n* mirada, *f*; (glance) vistazo, *m*, ojeada, *f*; (air) semblante, aire, porte, *m*; (appearance) aspecto, *m*; apariencia, *f*. **good looks,** buen parecer, *m*; guapeza, *f*. **the new l.,** la nueva línea, la nueva silueta, la nueva moda. **to be on the l.-out,** andar a la mira

look *vi* and *vt* mirar; considerar, contemplar; (appear, seem) parecer; tener aire (de); tener aspecto (de); hacer el efecto (de); (show oneself) mostrarse; (of buildings, etc.) caer (a), dar (a); mirar (a).; (seem to be) revelar (e.g., **You don't l. thirty,** No revelas treinta años) **to l. alike,** parecerse. **to l. hopeful,** *fig* prometer bien. **to l. out of the corner of the eye,** mirar de reojo. **to l. (a person) up and down,** mirar de hito en hito. **to l. about one,** mirar a su alrededor; observar. **to l. after,** tener la mirada puesta en, mirar; (care for) cuidar; (watch) vigilar; mirar por. **to l. at,** mirar; considerar; examinar. **He looked at his watch,** Miró su reloj. **He looked at her,** La miró. **to l. away,** desviar los ojos, apartar la mirada. **to l. back,** mirar hacia atrás, volver la cabeza; (in thought) pensar en el pasado. **to l. down,** bajar los ojos; mirar el suelo; mirar hacia abajo. **to l. down upon,** dominar, mirar a; (scorn) despreciar; mirar de arriba para abajo. **to l. for,** buscar; buscar con los ojos; (await) aguardar; (expect) esperar. **to l. forward,** mirar hacia el porvenir; pensar en el futuro; esperar con ilusión. **to l. in,** entrar por un instante, hacer una visita corta. **to l. into,** mirar dentro de; mirar hacia el interior de; estudiar, investigar, *Lat. Am. also* interiorizar. **to l. on,** *vt* mirar; considerar; (of buildings, etc.) dar a. *vi* ser espectador. **to l. on to,** dar a, mirar a. **to l. out,** *vi* (be careful) tener cuidado; (look through) mirar por; asomarse a. *vt* (search) buscar; (find) hallar; (choose) escoger, elegir. **L. out!** ¡Atención! ¡Ojo!, *Mexico* ¡abusado! **to l. out for,** buscar; (await) aguardar, esperar; (be careful) tener cuidado con. **to l. out of,** mirar por; asomarse a. **to l. over,** mirar bien; (persons) mirar de hito en hito; examinar; visitar; (a house) inspeccionar; (a book) hojear; mirar superficialmente. **to l. round,** *vt* (a place) visitar. *vi* volver la cabeza, volverse; mirar hacia atrás. **to l. round for,** buscar con los ojos; buscar por todas partes. **to l. through,** mirar por; mirar a través de; examinar; (search) registrar; (understand) registrar. **to l. to,** (be careful of) tener cuidado de; (attend to) atender a; (care for) cuidar de; (count on) contar con; (resort to) acudir a; (await) esperar. **to l. toward,** mirar hacia, mirar en la dirección de; caer a. **to l. up,** *vi* mirar hacia arriba; (aspire) aspirar; (improve) mejorar. *vt* visitar, ir (or venir) a ver; (turn up) buscar; averiguar. **to l. upon,** mirar. Other meanings see **to l. on. They l. upon her as their daughter,** La miran como una hija suya. **to l. up to,** *fig* respetar

looking *a* (in compounds) de . . . aspecto, de . . . apariencia. **dirty-l.,** de aspecto sucio. **l.-glass,** espejo, *m*

lookout vigilancia, observación, *f*; (view) vista, *f*, panorama, *m*; (viewpoint) miradero, *m*; *mil* atalaya, *m*; *naut* gaviero, *m*; (*fig* prospect) perspectiva, *f*

loom *n* telar, *m*, *vi* asomar, aparecer

loop *n* (turn) vuelta, *f*; (in rivers, etc.) recodo, *m*, curva, *f*; (fold) pliegue, *m*; bucle, *m*; (fastening) fiador, *m*, presilla, *f*; *aer* rizo, *m*; (knot) nudo corredizo, *m*. **to l. the l.,** *aer* hacer el rizo, hacer rizos. **l.-line,** empalme de ferrocarril, *m*

loophole *n* saetera, aspillera, *f*; *fig* escapatoria, *f*; pretexto, *m*, excusa, *f*

loose *a* suelto; (free) libre; (slack) flojo; (of garments) holgado; (untied) desatado; (unfastened) desprendido; movible; (unchained) desencadenado; en libertad; (of the bowels) suelto (de vientre); (pendulous) colgante; (of a nail, tooth, etc.) inseguro; poco firme; que se mueve; (of knots, etc.) flojo; (of the mind, etc.) incoherente, ilógico; poco exacto; (of style, etc.) vago, impreciso; (of conduct) disoluto, vicioso; (careless) negligente, descuidado. *vt* (untie) desatar; desprender; soltar; aflojar; (of a priest) absolver; *fig* desencadenar. **to break l.,** desprenderse; soltarse; libertarse; escapar; *fig* desencadenarse. **to let l.,** desatar; aflojar; poner en libertad; soltar; *fig* desencadenar; (interject) lanzar. **to turn l.,** poner en libertad; dar salida (a); echar de casa, poner en la calle. **to work l.,** desprenderse; aflojarse; desvencijarse. **l.-box,** caballeriza, *f*. **l. change,** suelto, *m*. **l.-leaf notebook,** libreta de hojas sueltas, *f*

loosely *adv* flojamente; sueltamente; (vaguely) vagamente; incorrectamente; incoherentemente; (carelessly) negligentemente; (viciously) disolutamente

loosen *vt* (untie) desatar; aflojar; soltar; desasir; (the tongue) desatar; *fig* hacer menos riguroso, ablandar

looseness *n* flojedad, *f*; (of clothing) holgura, *f*; soltura, *f*; relajación, *f*; (of the bowels) diarrea, *f*; (viciousness) licencia, *f*, libertinaje, *m*; (vagueness) vaguedad, *f*; incoherencia, *f*

loosening *n* desprendimiento, *m*; desasimiento, *m*; aflojamiento, *m*

loot *n* botín, *m*, *vt* saquear

looter *n* saqueador (-ra)

looting *n* saqueo, pillaje, *m*, *a* saqueador

lop *vt* mochar; podar; destroncar; cortar de un golpe. *a* (of ears) gacho. **to lop off the ends,** cercenar. **to lop off the top,** desmochar. **lop-sided,** desproporcionado; desequilibrado

lopping *n* desmoche, *m*; poda, *f*

loquacious *a* locuaz, gárrulo

loquacity *n* locuacidad, garrulidad, *f*

lord *n* señor, *m*; (husband) esposo, *m*; (English title) lord, *m*, (*pl* lores); (Christ) Señor, *m*. **feudal l.,** señor de horca y cuchillo, *m*. **my l.,** milord. **my lords,** milores. **Our L.,** Nuestro Señor. **the Lord's Prayer,** el Padrenuestro. **to l. it over,** mandar como señor, mandar a la baqueta. **L. Chamberlain,** camarero mayor, *m*. **L. Chancellor,** gran canciller, *m*. **L. Chief Justice,** presidente del tribunal supremo, *m*. **L.-Lieutenant,** virrey, *m*. **L. Mayor,** alcalde, *m*. **L. Privy Seal,** guardasellos del rey, *m*

lordliness *n* suntuosidad, *f*; liberalidad, munificencia, *f*; dignidad, *f*; (haughtiness) altivez, arrogancia, *f*

lordly *a* señorial, señoril; altivo, arrogante

lordship *n* señoría, *f*; señorío, poder, *m*. **his l.,** su señoría

lore *n* saber, *m*; erudición, *f*; tradiciones, *f pl*

lorgnette *n* impertinentes, *m pl*

lose *vt* perder; hacer perder, quitar; (forget) olvidar. *vi* perder; (of clocks) atrasar. **to be lost in thought,** estar ensimismado, estar absorto. **to l. oneself (in)** perderse (en); abstraerse (en); entregarse (a). **to l. one's footing,** resbalar. **to l. one's way,** extraviarse, perder el camino. **to l. one's self-control,** perder el tino. **to l. one's head,** perder la cabeza. **to l. ground,** perder terreno. **to l. one's voice,** perder la voz. **to l. patience,** perder la paciencia, perder los estribos

loser *n* perdedor (-ra)

losing *a* perdedor. *n* pérdida, *f*

loss *n* pérdida, *f*. **at a l.,** *com* con pérdida; perplejo, dudoso. **heavy losses,** *mil* pérdidas cuantiosas, *f pl*. **loss of blood** *Lat. Am.* desangre *m*. **We are at a l. for words . . . ,** No tenemos palabras para . . .

lot *n* suerte, *f*; fortuna, *f*; lote, *m*; parte, porción, cuota, *f*; (for building) solar, *m*. **a lot of people,** muchas personas. **Our lot would have been very different,** Nuestra suerte hubiera sido muy distinta, Otro gallo nos cantara. **to draw lots,** echar suertes, sortear. **to take the lot,** *inf* alzarse con el santo y la limosna

lotion *n* loción, *f*

lottery *n* lotería, *f*. **l. ticket,** billete de la lotería, *m*

lotus *n* loto, *m*. **l.-eating,** lotofagía, *f*: *fig* indolencia, pereza, *f*

loud *a* fuerte; (noisy) ruidoso, estrepitoso; alto; (gaudy) chillón, llamativo, cursi, *Lat. Am. also* figuroso. *adv* ruidosamente. **l.-speaker,** *rad* altavoz, *Mexico* magnavoz. *m*

loudly *adv* en alta voz; fuertemente; ruidosamente, con estrépito

loudness *n* (noise) ruido, *m*; sonoridad, *f*; (force) fuerza, *f*; (of colors, etc.) mal gusto, *m*, vulgaridad, *f*

lounge *n* sala de estar, *f*; salón, *m*, *vi* reclinarse, ponerse a sus anchas; apoyarse (en); gandulear; vagar. **l. chair,**

poltrona, *f.* **l.-lizard,** *inf* pollo pera, *m.* **l.-suit,** traje americano, *m*
lounger *n* holgazán (-ana); golfo (-fa), azotacalles, *mf*
louse *n* piojo, *m*
lousy *a* piojoso
lout *n* patán, zamacuco, *m*
loutish *a* rústico
lovable *a* amable; simpático
lovableness *n* amabilidad, *f*
love *n* amor, *m;* (friendship) amistad, *f;* (enthusiasm, liking) afición, *f;* (in tennis) cero, *m, vt* querer, amar; gustar mucho; tener afición (a). *vi* estar enamorado. **I should l. to dine with you,** Me gustaría mucho cenar con Vds. **to be in l. with,** estar enamorado de. **to fall in l. with,** enamorarse de. **They l. each other,** Se quieren. **to make l. to,** hacer el amor (a), galantear. **l. affair,** amorío, lance de amor, *m.* **l.-bird,** periquito, *m.* **l.-letter,** carta amatoria, carta de amor, *f.* **l.-making,** galanteo, *m.* **l.-philtre,** filtro, *m.* **l.-song,** canción de amor, *f.* **l.-story,** historia de amor, *f.* **l.-token,** prenda de amor, *f*
loveless *a* sin amor
loveliness *n* hermosura, belleza, *f;* encanto, *m;* amabilidad, *f*
lovely *a* hermoso, bello; delicioso; amable; *inf* estupendo
lover *n* amante, *mf;* aficionado (-da)
lovesick *a* enfermo de amor, enamorado
loving *a* amoroso; cariñoso; (friendly) amistoso; de amor
low *a* bajo; de poca altura; (of dresses, etc.) escotado; (of musical notes) grave; (soft) suave; (feeble) débil; (depressed) deprimido, triste, abatido; (plain) sencillo; (of a fever) lento; (of a bow) profundo; pequeño; inferior; humilde; (ill) enfermo; (vile) vil, ruin; obsceno, escabroso. *adv* bajo; cerca de la tierra; en voz baja; (cheaply) barato, a bajo precio. **in a low voice,** en voz baja, paso. **to lay low,** (kill) tumbar; (knock down) derribar; incapacitar. **to lie low,** descansar; estar muerto; esconderse, agacharse; callar. **to run low,** escasear. **low-born,** de humilde cuna. **low-brow,** nada intelectual. **low comedy,** farsa, *f.* **low flying,** *n* bajo vuelo, *m, a* que vuela bajo; terrero, rastrero; que vuela a ras de tierra. **low frequency,** baja frecuencia, *f.* **low Latin,** bajo latín, *m.* **Low Mass,** misa rezada, *f.* **low neck,** escote, *m.* **low-necked,** escotado. **low-pitched,** grave. **low-spirited,** deprimido. **Low Sunday,** domingo de Cuasimodo, *m.* **low tension,** baja tensión, *f.* **low trick,** mala pasada, *f.* **low water,** marea baja, bajamar, *f;* (of rivers) estiaje, *m*
low *vi* berrear, mugir. *n* berrido, mugido, *m*
low-ceiling *a* bajo de techo.
lower *vt* bajar; descolgar; disminuir; (price) rebajar; (a boat, sails) arriar. *vi* (of persons) fruncir el ceño, mostrarse malhumorado; (of the sky) encapotarse, cargarse; (menace) amenazar. **to l. a boat,** arriar un bote. **to l. oneself,** (by a rope, etc.) descolgarse. **to l. the flag,** abatir la bandera
lower *a comp* más bajo; menos alto; bajo; inferior. **l. classes,** clase obrera, *f,* clases bajas, *f pl.* **l. down,** más abajo. **L. House,** Cámara de los Comunes, *f;* cámara baja, *f.* **l. jaw,** mandíbula inferior, *f.* **l. storey,** piso bajo, *m;* piso de abajo, *m*
Lower California Baja California, *f*
lowering *n* abajamiento, *m;* descenso, *m;* (of prices) baja, *f;* (of a boat) arriada, *f;* (of the flag) abatimiento, *m, a* (of persons) ceñudo; (of the sky) anublado, encapotado; (threatening) amenazador
lowest *a sup* el (la, etc.) más bajo; el (la, etc.) más profundo; ínfimo
lowing *n* berrido, mugido, *m*
lowland *n* tierra baja, *f.* **the Lowlands,** las tierras bajas de Escocia
lowliness *n* humildad, *f;* modestia, *f*
lowly *a* humilde
lowness *n* poca altura, *f;* situación poco elevada, *f;* pequeñez, *f;* (of musical notes) gravedad, *f;* (softness) suavidad, *f;* (feebleness) debilidad, *f;* (sadness) tristeza, *f,* abatimiento, *m;* (of price) baratura, *f;* inferioridad, *f;* humildad, *f;* (vileness) bajeza, *f;* obscenidad, *f*
loyal *a* leal, fiel
loyalist *n* realista, *mf;* defensor (-ra) del gobierno legítimo
loyalty *n* lealtad, fidelidad, *f*
loyalty oath *n* (approximate equivalent) certificado de adhesión, *m*
lozenge *n* pastilla, *f*
lubricant *a* and *n* lubricante *m*
lubricate *vt* lubricar, engrasar
lubricating oil *n* aceite lubricante, *m*
lubrication *n* lubricación, *f,* engrasado, *m*
lubricator *n* lubricador, *m;* engrasador, *m*
Lucerne Lucerna, *f*
lucid *a* lúcido; claro
lucidity *n* lucidez, *f;* claridad, *f*
lucidly *adv* claramente
luck *n* destino, azar, *m;* (good) buenaventura, suerte, *f.* **to bring bad l.,** traer mala suerte. **to try one's l.,** probar fortuna
luckily *adv* por fortuna, afortunadamente, felizmente
luckless *a* desdichado
lucky *a* afortunado; dichoso, venturoso, *Lat. Am. also* lechudo; feliz. **to be l.,** tener buena suerte
lucrative *a* lucrativo
lucre *n* lucro, *m*
lucubration *n* lucubración, *f*
ludicrous *a* absurdo, risible, ridículo
ludicrousness *n* ridiculez, *f*
lug *n* tirón, *m;* (ear and projection) oreja, *f, vt* tirar (de); arrastrar. **to lug about,** arrastrar (por); llevar con dificultad. **to lug in,** arrastrar adentro; introducir; hacer entrar. **to lug out,** arrastrar afuera; hacer salir
luggage *n* equipaje, *m.* **excess l.,** exceso de equipaje, *m.* **piece of l.,** bulto, *m.* **to register one's l.,** facturar el equipaje. **l. carrier,** (on buses, etc.) baca, *f;* (on a car) portaequipajes, *m.* **l. porter,** mozo de equipajes, *m.* **l. rack,** (on a car) portaequipajes, *m;* (in a train) rejilla para el equipaje, *f.* **l. receipt,** talón de equipaje, *m.* **l. room,** consigna, *f.* **l. van,** furgón de equipajes, *m*
lugubrious *a* lúgubre
lukewarm *a* tibio, templado; *fig* indiferente, frío
lukewarmness *n* tibieza, *f; fig* indiferencia, frialdad, *f*
lull *n* momento de calma, *m;* tregua, *f;* silencio, *m, vt* (a child) arrullar, adormecer; (soothe) sosegar, calmar; disminuir, mitigar
lullaby *n* canción de cuna, *f*
lumbago *n* lumbago, *m*
lumbar *a* lumbar
lumber *n* (wood) maderas de sierra, *f pl;* (rubbish) trastos viejos, *m pl. vt* amontonar trastos viejos; obstruir. *vi* andar pesadamente; avanzar ruidosamente, avanzar con ruido sordo. **l.-jack,** maderero, ganchero, *m.* **l.-room,** leonera, *f.* **l.-yard,** maderería, *f,* depósito de maderas, *m*
lumbering *a* pesado
luminary *n* lumbrera, *f*
luminosity *n* luminosidad, *f*
luminous *a* luminoso
lump *n* masa, *f;* bulto, *m;* pedazo, *m;* (of sugar) terrón *m;* (swelling) hinchazón, *f;* protuberancia, *f. vt* amontonar. **to l. together,** mezclar; incluir. **in the l.,** en la masa; en grueso. **Let him l. it!** ¡Que se rasque! **l. in one's throat,** nudo en la garganta, *m.* **l. of sugar,** terrón de azúcar, *m.* **l. sum,** cantidad gruesa, *f*
lumpishness *n* hobachonería, *f*
lunacy *n* locura, *f*
lunar *a* lunar
lunatic *n* loco (-ca); demente, *mf a* de locos; loco. **l. asylum,** manicomio, *m*
lunch, luncheon *n* almuerzo, *m, Mexico* fajina, *f;*

(snack) merienda, *f*. *vi* almorzar. **l. basket** or **pail,** fiambrera, *f*
lunch counter, luncheonette *Mexico* almuercería, *elsewhere in Lat. Am.* lonchería, *f*
lunette *n* (*arch mil*) luneta, *f*
lung *n* pulmón, *m*
lunge *n* (fencing) estocada, *f*; embestida, *f*. *vi* dar una estocada; abalanzarse sobre
lurch *n* sacudida, *f*; *naut* guiñada, *f*; tambaleo, *m*; movimiento brusco, *m*. *vi naut* guiñar; tambalearse; andar haciendo eses. **to leave in the l.,** dejar plantado
lure *n* añagaza, *f*; reclamo, *m*; aliciente, atractivo, *m*; seducción, *f*. *vt* atraer, tentar
lurid *a* misterioso, fantástico; cárdeno; ominoso; funesto, triste; (orange) anaranjado; (vicissitudinous) accidentado
lurk *vi* acechar, espiar; esconderse
lurking *a* (in ambush) en acecho; (of fear, etc.) vago
luscious *a* delicioso; suculento; meloso; atractivo, apetitoso; sensual
lusciousness *n* suculencia, *f*; melosidad, *f*; atractivo, *m*; sensualidad, *f*
lush *a* jugoso; fresco y lozano; maduro
lust *n* lujuria, lascivia, *f*; codicia, *f*; deseo, *m*. **l. for revenge,** deseo de venganza, *m*
lustful *a* lujurioso, lúbrico, lascivo
luster *n* lustre, brillo, *m*; brillantez, *f*
lusterless *a* sin brillo; mate, deslustrado; (of eyes) apagado
lustrous *a* lustroso
lusty *a* vigoroso, fuerte, lozano
lute *n* laúd, *m*, vihuela, *f*. **l.-player,** vihuelista, *mf*
Lutheran *a* luterano. *n* luterano (-na)
Lutheranism *n* luteranismo, *m*
luxation *n* luxación, *f*
luxuriance *n* lozanía, *f*; exuberancia, superabundancia, *f*
luxuriant *a* lozano; fértil; exuberante
luxuriate *vi* crecer con exuberancia; complacerse (en); disfrutar (de), gozar (de)
luxurious *a* lujoso
luxuriously *adv* lujosamente, con lujo
luxury *n* lujo, *m*. **l. goods,** artículos de lujo, *m pl*
lyceum *n* liceo, *m*
lye *n* lejía, *f*
lying *a* (recumbent) recostado; (untrue) mentiroso, falso. *n* mentiras, *f pl*. **l.-in,** parto, *m*
lymph *n* linfa, *f*; vacuna, *f*
lymphatic *a* linfático; flemático
lynch *vt* linchar
lynching *n* linchamiento, *m*
lynx *n* lince, *m*. **l.-eyed,** de ojos de lince
lyre *n* lira, *f*. **l.-bird,** pájaro lira, *m*
lyric *n* poesía lírica, *f*; poema lírico, *m*; letra (de una canción,) *f*
lyrical *a* lírico
lyricism *n* lirismo, *m*

M

m *n* (letter) eme, *f*
ma'am *n* señora, *f*
macabre *a* macabro
macadam *n* macadán, *m*, *a* de macadán
macadamize *vt* macadanizar
macaroni *n* macarrones, *m pl*
macaronic *a* macarrónico
macaroon *n* macarrón de almendras, *m*
macaw *n* macagua, *f*, guacamayo, *m*
mace *n* maza, *f*; *cul* macis, *f*. **m.-bearer,** macero, *m*
Macedonian *a* macedón, macedonio. *n* macedonio (-ia)
macerate *vt* macerar. *vi* macerarse
machete *n Mexico* alfanje, *elsewhere* machete, *m*
Machiavellian *a* maquiavélico
Machiavellism *n* maquiavelismo, *m*
machination *n* maquinación, *f*
machine *n* máquina, *f*; mecanismo, *m*; aparato, *m*; instrumento, *m*; organización, *f*, *vt* trabajar a máquina; *sew* coser a máquina. **m.-gun,** *n* ametralladora, *f*. *vt* ametrallar. **m.-gun carrier,** portametralladoras, *m*. **m.-gunner,** ametrallador, *m*. **m.-made,** hecho a máquina. **m.-oil,** aceite de motores, *m*. **m.-shop,** taller de maquinaria, *m*, *Lat. Am.* maestranza, *f*. **m.-tool,** máquina herramienta, *f*
machinery *n* maquinaria, *f*; mecanismo, *m*; organización, *f*; sistema, *m*
machinist *n* maquinista, *mf*; *sew* costurera a máquina, *f*
mackerel *n* caballa, *f*. **m. sky,** cielo aborregado, *m*
mackintosh *n* impermeable, *m*
macrocosm *n* macrocosmo, *m*
mad *a* loco; fuera de sí; (of a dog, etc.) rabioso; furioso. **as mad as a hatter,** loco como una cabra. **to drive mad,** volver loco (a). **to go mad,** volverse loco, enloquecer, perder el seso. **mad with joy (pain),** loco de alegría (dolor). **mad dog,** perro rabioso, *m*
madam *n* señora, *f*; (French form) madama, *f*. **Yes, m.,** Sí señora
madcap *n* locuelo (-la), *f*, botarate, *m*; tarambana, *mf*
madden *vt* enloquecer; enfurecer, exasperar
maddening *a* exasperante, irritador
madder *n bot* rubia, *f*
made *past part* and *a* hecho; formado. **self-m. man,** un hombre hecho y derecho. **m.-to-measure,** hecho a la medida. **m.-up,** compuesto; (of clothes) confeccionado, ya hecho; (of the face) pintado; (fictitious) inventado, ficticio; artificial
Madeira *n* vino de Madera, *m*, *a* de Madera
madhouse *n* casa de locos, *f*, manicomio, *m*
madly *adv* locamente; furiosamente
madman *n* loco, *m*
madness *n* locura, *f*; (of a dog, etc.) rabia, *f*; furia, *f*
Madonna *n* Madona, *f*
madrigal *n* madrigal, *m*
Madrilenian *a* madrileño, matritense. *n* madrileño (-ña)
madwoman *n* loca, *f*
Maecenas *n* mecenas, *m*
maelstrom *n* remolino, vórtice, *m*
magazine *n* (store) almacén, *m*; (for explosives) polvorín, *m*, santabárbara, *f*; (periodical) revista, *f*. **m. rifle,** rifle de repetición, *m*
Magdalen *n* magdalena, *f*
magenta *n* color magenta, *m*
maggot *n* gusano, *m*, cresa, *f*; *fig* manía, *f*, capricho, *m*
maggoty *a* gusanoso
Magi, the *n pl* los reyes magos
magic *n* magia, *f*; mágica, *f*; *fig* encanto, *m*, *a* mágico. **as if by m.,** por ensalmo. **m. lantern,** linterna mágica, *f*
magically *adv* por encanto
magician *n* mago, mágico, brujo, *m*; (conjurer) jugador de manos, *m*
magisterial *a* magistral
magistracy *n* magistratura, *f*
magistrate *n* magistrado, *m*; juez municipal, *m*
Magna Charta *n* Carta Magna, *f*
magnanimity *n* magnanimidad, generosidad, *f*
magnanimous *a* magnánimo, generoso
magnanimously *adv* magnánimamente
magnate *n* magnate, *m*
magnesia *n* magnesia, *f*
magnesium *n* magnesio, *m*. **m. light,** luz de magnesio, *f*
magnet *n* imán, *m*

magnetic *a* magnético; *fig* atractivo. **m. field,** campo magnético, *m.* **m. needle,** brújula, *f*
magnetics *n* la ciencia del magnetismo, *f*
magnetism *n* magnetismo, *m*
magnetization *n* imanación, magnetización, *f*
magnetize *vt* magnetizar, imanar; (hypnotize) magnetizar; *fig* atraer
magnification *n* (by a lens, etc.) aumento, *m*; exageración, *f*
magnificence *n* magnificencia, *f*
magnificent *a* magnífico
magnify *vt* (by lens) aumentar; exagerar; (praise) magnificar
magnifying *a* de aumento, vidrio de aumento. **m. glass,** lente de aumento, *m*
magniloquence *n* grandilocuencia, *f*
magniloquent *a* grandílocuo
magnitude *n* magnitud, *f*
magnolia *n* magnolia, *f*
magnum *n* botella de dos litros, *f*
magpie *n* marica, picaza, *f*
maharaja *n* maharajá, *m*
mahogany *n* caoba, *f*, *a* de caoba
Mahomedan. See **Mohammedan**
maid *n* doncella, muchacha, *f*; virgen, *f*; soltera, *f*; (servant) criada, *f*; (daily) asistenta, *f*. **old m.,** solterona, *f*. **m.-of-all-work,** criada para todo, *f*. **m.-of-honor,** dama de honor, *f*
maiden *n* doncella, joven, soltera, *f*; virgen, *f*; zagala, *f*. *a* de soltera; soltera *f*; virginal; (of speeches, voyages, etc.) primero. **m. lady,** dama soltera, *f*. **m.-name,** apellido de soltera, *m*. **m. speech,** primer discurso, *m*
maidenhood *n* doncellez, virginidad, *f*
maidenly *a* virginal; modesto, modoso; tímido
maidservant *n* criada, sirvienta, *f*
mail *n* mala, *f*; (bag) valija, *f*; correo, *m*; correspondencia, *f*; (armour) cota de malla, *f*. *vt* mandar por correo; armar con cota de malla. **coat of m.,** cota de malla, *f*. **royal m.,** malla real, *f*. **m.-bag,** valija de correo, *f*; portacartas, *m*. **m.-boat,** buque correo, *m*. **m.-cart,** ambulancia de correos, *f*. **m.-clad,** vestido de cota de malla; armado. **m.-coach,** coche correo, *m*, diligencia, *f*. **m.-order,** pedido postal, *m*. **m.-order business,** negocio de ventas por correo, *m*. **m.-plane,** avión postal, *m*. **m. service,** servicio de correos, *m*. **m. steamer,** vapor correo, *m*. **m. train,** tren correo, *m*. **m. van,** (on a train) furgón postal, *m*
mailed *a* de malla; armado. **m. fist,** *fig* puño de hierro, *m*
maim *vt* mancar; mutilar, tullir; estropear
maimed *a* manco; tullido, mutilado
main *a* mayor; principal; más importante, esencial; maestro. *n* (mainland) continente, *m*; (sea) océano, *m*; (pipe) cañería maestra, *f*. **by m. force,** por fuerza mayor. **in the m.,** en general, generalmente; en su mayoría. **m. beam,** viga maestra, *f*. **m. body,** (of a building) ala principal, *f*; (of a church) cuerpo (de iglesia), *m*; (of an army) cuerpo (del ejército), *m*; mayor parte, mayoría, *f*. **m. line,** línea principal, *f*. **m. mast,** palo mayor, *m*. **m. thing,** cosa principal, *f*, lo más importante. **m. wall,** pared maestra, *f*
mainland *n* continente, *m*; tierra firme, *f*
mainly *adv* principalmente; en su mayoría; generalmente
mainsail *n* vela mayor, *f*
mainspring *n* (of a watch) muelle real, *m*; motivo principal, *m*; origen, *m*
mainstay *n* estay mayor, *m*; *fig* sostén principal, *m*
maintain *vt* mantener; sostener; tener; guardar; afirmar
maintainable *a* sostenible; defendible
maintenance *n* mantenimiento, *m*; manutención, *f*, sustento, *m*; conservación, *f*, subsistencia, *f*
maize *n* maíz, *m*. **m. field,** maizal, *m*
majestic *a* majestuoso
majesty *n* majestad, *f*; majestuosidad, *f*. **His** or **Her M.,** Su Majestad
majolica *n* mayólica, *f*
major *a* mayor; principal. *n* mayor de edad, *m*; *mil* comandante. **anthropology major,** alumno con la especialidad en antropología *m*. **m.-domo,** mayordomo, *m*. **m.-general,** general de división, *m*. **m. road,** carretera, *f*; ruta de prioridad, *f*. **m. scale,** escala mayor, *f*
Majorca Mallorca, *f*
majority *n* mayoría, *f*; mayor número, *m*; generalidad, *f*. **to have attained one's m.,** ser mayor de edad
make *vt* hacer; crear, formar; (manufacture) fabricar, confeccionar; construir; (produce) producir; causar; (prepare) preparar; (a bed, a fire, a remark, poetry, friends, enemies, war, a curtsey) hacer; (earn, win) ganar; (a speech) pronunciar; (compel) obligar (a), forzar (a); inclinar (a); (arrive at) alcanzar, llegar (a); (calculate) calcular; (arrange) arreglar; deducir; (be) ser; (equal) ser igual a; (think) creer; (appoint as) constituir (en), hacer; (behave) portarse (como). *vi* (begin) ir (a), empezar (a); (make as though) hacer (como si); (of the tide) crecer; contribuir (a); tender (a). **He made as if to go,** Hizo como si de marchara. **to m. as though . . . ,** aparentar, fingir. **It made me ill,** Me hizo sentir mal. **They have made it up,** Han hecho las paces. **They m. a great deal of money,** Hacen (or ganan) mucho dinero. **You cannot m. me believe it,** No puedes hacerme creerlo. **He is making himself ridiculous,** Se está poniendo en ridículo. **to m. ready,** preparar. **to m. the tea,** hacer el té; preparar el té. **Two and two m. four,** Dos y dos son cuatro. **to m. oneself known,** darse a conocer. **to m. one of . . . ,** ser uno de . . . **to m. after,** seguir; correr detrás de. **to m. again,** hacer de nuevo, rehacer. **to m. angry** *Mexico.* amuinar, **to m. away with,** quitar; suprimir; destruir; (kill) matar; (squander) derrochar; (steal) llevarse; hurtar. **to m. away with oneself,** quitarse la vida, suicidarse. **to m. for,** encaminarse a, dirigirse a; (attack) abalanzarse sobre, atacar; (tend to) contribuir a, tender a. **to m. off,** marcharse corriendo, largarse; huir, escaparse. **to m. out,** (discern) distinguir; descifrar; (understand) comprender; (prove) probar, justificar; (draw up) redactar; (fill in a form) completar, llenar; (a check, etc.) extender; (an account) hacer; (get on, succeed or otherwise) ir (with bien or mal); (convey) dar la impresión de que; sugerir. **I cannot m. it out,** No lo puedo comprender. **How did you m. out** (get on)? ¿Cómo te fue? **to m. over,** hacer de nuevo, rehacer; (transfer) ceder, traspasar. **to m. up,** hacer; acabar; concluir; (clothes) confeccionar; fabricar; (the face) pintarse, maquillarse; (the fire) echar carbón, etc. a; *print* compaginar; (invent) inventar; (lies) fabricar; (compose) formar; (package) empaquetar; reparar; indemnizar; compensar; (an account) ajustar; preparar; arreglar; (conciliate) conciliar; enumerar; *theat* caracterizarse. **to m. up for,** reemplazar; compensar; (lost time, etc.) recobrar. **to m. up to,** compensar; indemnizar; (flatter) adular, halagar; procurar congraciarse con, procurar obtener el favor de; (court) galantear (con). **m. an impression (on),** dejar(le a fulano) una impresión
make *n* forma, *f*; hechura, *f*; estructura, *f*; confección, *f*; manufactura, *f*; producto, *m*; (trade name) marca, *f*; (character) carácter, temperamento, *m*. **m.-believe,** *n* artificio, pretexto, *m*, *a* fingido, *vi* fingir. **land of m.-believe,** reino de los sueños, *m*. **m.-up,** (for the face, etc.) maquillaje, *m*; *theat* caracterización, *f*; *print* imposición, *f*; (whole) conjunto, *m*; (character) carácter, modo de ser, *m*
maker *n* creador, *m*; autor (-ra); artífice, *mf*; (manufacturer) fabricante, *m*; constructor, *m*; (of clothes, etc.) confeccionador (-ra); (worker) obrero (-ra)
makeshift *n* expediente, *m*, *a* provisional
makeweight *n* añadidura (de peso), *f*, contrapeso, *m*; *fig* suplente, *m*

making *n* creación, *f*; hechura, *f*; (manufacture) fabricación, *f*; construcción, *f*; (of clothes, etc.) confección, *f*; formación, *f*; preparación, *f*; estructura, *f*; composición, *f*; *pl* **makings,** (profits) ganancias, *f pl*; (elements) elementos, *m pl*; germen, *m*; rasgos esenciales, *m pl*, características, *f. pl* **m.-up,** (of clothes) confección, *f*; *print* ajuste, *m*; (of the face) maquillaje, *m*; (invention) invención, *f*; fabricación, *f*

maladjustment *n* mal ajuste, *m*; inadaptación, *f*

maladministration *n* desgobierno, *m*, mala administración, *f*; (of funds) malversación, *f*

maladroit *a* torpe

maladroitness *n* torpeza, *f*

malady *n* enfermedad, *f*; mal, *m*

Malaga *n* vino de Málaga, *m*

malaria *n* paludismo, *m*

malarial *a* palúdico. **m. fever,** fiebre palúdica, *f*

Malaya Malasia, *f*, Archipiélago Malayo, *m*

Malayan *a* malayo. *n* malayo (-ya)

malcontent *n* malcontento (-ta). *a* descontento

Maldives Maldivas, *f pl*

male *a* macho; masculino. *n* macho, *m*; varón, *m*. **m. child,** niño, *m*; niño varón, *m*; (son) hijo varón, *m*. **m. flower,** flor masculina, *f*. **m. issue,** sucesión masculina, *f*. **m. nurse,** enfermero, *m*. **m. sex,** sexo masculino, *m*

malediction *n* maldición, *f*

malefactor *n* malhechor (-ra)

malefic *a* maléfico

malevolence *n* malevolencia, *f*

malevolent *a* malévolo, maligno

malformation *n* formación anormal, deformidad, deformación congénita, *f*

malice *n* malicia, *f*; *law* alevosía, *f*. **to bear m.,** guardar rencor

malicious *a* malicioso; maligno, rencoroso

maliciousness *n* malicia, mala intención, *f*

malign *vt* calumniar, difamar. *a* maligno; malévolo

malignancy *n* malignidad, *f*; malevolencia, *f*

malignant *a* maligno; malévolo; *med* maligno

malinger *vi* fingirse enfermo

malingerer *n* enfermo (-ma) fingido (-da)

malingering *n* enfermedad fingida, *f*

mallard *n* pato (-ta), silvestre

malleability *n* maleabilidad, *f*

malleable *a* maleable

mallet *n* mazo, *m*; (in croquet) pala, *f*, mazo, *m*; (in polo) maza (de polo), *f*

mallow *n* malva, *f*

malmsey *n* (wine) malvasía, *f*

malnutrition *n* desnutrición, alimentación deficiente, *f*

malodorous *a* de mal olor, hediondo, fétido

malpractice *n* (wrongdoing) maleficencia, *f*; (by a doctor) tratamiento equivocado, perjudicial o ilegal, *m*; (malversation) malversación, *f*; inmoralidad, *f*

malt *n* malta, *m*. *vt* preparar el malta. **m.-house,** fábrica de malta, *f*. **m. vinegar,** vinagre de malta, *m*

malted milk *n* leche malteada, *f*

malt shop *n* café-nevería, *m*

Maltese *a* maltés. *n* maltés (-esa). **M. cat,** gato maltés, *m*. **M. cross,** cruz de Malta, *f*. **M. dog,** perro maltés, *m*

Malthusian *a* maltusiano

Malthusianism *n* maltusianismo, *m*

maltose *n* maltosa, *f*

maltreat *vt* maltratar

maltreatment *n* maltrato, *m*,

mamma *n anat* mama, *f*; (mother) mamá, *f*

mammal *n* mamífero, *m*

mammalian *a* mamífero

mammary *a* mamario. **m. gland,** mama, teta, *f*

mammon *n* becerro de oro, *m*

mammoth *n* mamut, *m*, *a* gigantesco, enorme

man *n* hombre, *m*; varón, *m*; persona, *f*; (servant) criado, *m*; (workman) obrero, *m*; (soldier) soldado, *m*; (sailor) marinero, *m*; (humanity) raza humana, *f*; (husband) marido, *m*; (chess) peón, *m*; (checkers) dama, *f*; (a ship) buque, *m*. **no man,** nadie; ningún hombre. **young man,** joven, *m*. **to a man,** como un solo hombre. **to come to man's estate,** llegar a la edad viril. **Man overboard!** ¡Hombre al agua! **man and wife,** marido y mujer, *m*, cónyuges, esposos, *m pl*. **man about town,** hombre de mundo, señorito, *m*. **man-at-arms,** hombre de armas, *m*. **man-eater,** caníbal, *mf*; tigre, *m*. **man-eating,** *a* antropófago. **man hater,** misántropo, *m*; mujer que odia a los hombres, *f*. **man-hole,** pozo, *m*. **man-hunter,** caníbal, *mf*; (woman) castigadora, *f*. **man in charge,** encargado, *m*. **man in the moon,** mujer de la luna, *f*. **man in the street,** hombre de la calle, hombre medio, *m*. **man of letters,** hombre de letras, literato, *m*; **man of straw,** bausán, *m*; (figure-head) testaferro, *m*. **man of the world,** hombre del mundo, *m*. **man of war,** buque de guerra, *m*. **man-power,** mano de obra, *f*, brazos, *m pl*, (e.g. **lack of manpower,** falta de brazos, *f*). **man servant,** criado, *m*

man *vt* armar; *mil* poner guarnición (a); ocupar; *naut* tripular; dirigir; *fig* fortificar

manacle *n* manilla, *f*; *pl* **manacles,** esposas, *f pl*; grillos, *m pl*. *vt* poner esposas (a)

manage *vt* manejar; (animals) domar; dirigir; gobernar; administrar; (arrange) agenciar, arreglar; (work) explotar; (do) hacer; (eat) comer. *vi* arreglárselas (para); (get along) ir tirando; (know how) saber hacer; (succeed in) lograr; (do) hacer

manageability *n* lo manejable; flexibilidad, *f*; (of animals, persons) docilidad, mansedumbre, *f*

manageable *a* manejable; flexible; (of persons, animals) dócil

management *n* manejo, *m*; dirección, *f*; gobierno, *m*; administración, *f*; arreglo, *m*; (working) explotación, *f*; *com* gerencia, *f*; *theat* empresa, *f*; conducta, *f*; (economy) economía, *f*; (skill) habilidad, *f*; prudencia, *f*. **the m.,** la dirección, el cuerpo de directores. **domestic m.,** economía doméstica, *f*

manager *n* director, *m*; administrador, *m*; jefe, *m*; *theat* empresario, *m*; *com* gerente, *m*; regente, *m*. **She is not much of a m.,** No es muy mujer de su casa. **manager's office,** dirección, *f*

manageress *n* directora, *f*; administradora, *f*; jefa, *f*

managerial *a* directivo; administrativo. **m. board,** junta directiva, *f*

managership *n* puesto de director, *m*; jefatura, *f*

managing *a* directivo; (officious) mandón, dominante; (niggardly) tacaño

manatee *n* manatí, *m*

mandarin *n* mandarín, *m*; (language) mandarina, *f*. **m. orange,** mandarina, *f*

mandate *n* mandato, *m*. **mandated territory,** territorios bajo mandato, *m pl*

mandatory *a* obligatorio

mandible *n* mandíbula, *f*

mandolin *n* bandolín, *m*, bandurria, *f*

mandrake *n* mandrágora, *f*

mandrill *n* mandril, *m*

mane *n* melena, *f*; (of a horse) crines, *f pl*

maned *a* (in compounds) con melena . . . ; con crines . . .

maneuver *n* maniobra, *f*. *vi* maniobrar, hacer maniobras. *vt* hacer maniobrar; manipular

maneuvering *n* maniobras, *f pl*; maquinaciones, intrigas, *f pl*

manfully *adv* valientemente; vigorosamente

manganate *n* manganato, *m*

manganese *n* manganeso, *m*

mange *n* sarna, *f*; (in sheep) roña, *f*

manger *n* pesebre, *m*

manginess *n* estado sarnoso, *m*

mangle *n* (for clothes) exprimidor de la ropa, *m*. *vt* pasar por el exprimidor; (mutilate) mutilar, lacerar, magullar; (a text) mutilar

mangling *n* (mutilation) mutilación, laceración, *f*

mango *n* mango, *m*
mangy *a* sarnoso
manhandle *vt* maltratar
manhood *n* virilidad, *f;* edad viril, *f;* masculinidad, *f;* los hombres; (manliness) hombradía, *f,* valor, *m*
mania *n* manía, *f;* obsesión, *f;* capricho, *m,* chifladura, *f, Lat. Am.* barreno, *m*
maniac *n* maníaco (-ca). *a* maníaco, maniático
manicure *n* manicura, *f. vt* arreglar las uñas. **m.-set,** estuche de manicura, *m*
manicurist *n* manicuro (-ra)
manifest *n naut* manifiesto, *m. vt* mostrar; hacer patente, probar; manifestarse. *vi* publicar un manifiesto; (of spirits) manifestarse. *a* manifiesto, evidente, claro, patente. **to make m.,** poner de manifiesto
manifestation *n* manifestación, *f*
manifestly *adv* evidentemente, manifiestamente
manifesto *n* manifiesto, *m*
manifold *a* múltiple; numeroso; diverso, vario
manikin *n* enano, *m;* muñeco, *m; art* maniquí, *m*
Manilla *n* Manila, *f;* cigarro filipino, *m.* **M. hemp,** cáñamo de Manila, *m*
maniple *n* manípulo, *m*
manipulate *vt* manipular
manipulation *n* manipulación, *f*
manipulative *a* manipulador
mankind *n* humanidad, raza humana, *f,* género humano, *m*
manlike *a* de hombre, masculino; varonil; (of a woman) hombruno
manliness *n* masculinidad, hombradía, *f;* virilidad, *f;* valor, *m;* (of a woman) aire hombruno, *m*
manly *a* masculino, de hombre; varonil, viril; valiente; fuerte. **to be very m.,** ser muy hombre, ser todo un hombre
manna *n* maná, *m*
mannequin *n* manequín, modelo, *f.* **m. parade,** exposición de modelos, *f*
manner *n* manera, *f,* modo, *m;* aire, porte, *m;* conducta, *f;* (style) estilo, *m;* (sort) clase, *f; gram* modo, *m; pl* **manners,** modales, *m pl,* crianza, educación, *f;* (customs) costumbres, *f pl.* **after the m. of,** en (or según) el estilo de. **in a m. of speaking,** en cierto modo, para decirlo así. **in this m.,** de este modo. **to have bad (good) manners,** tener malos (buenos) modales, ser mal (bien) criado. **the novel of manners,** la novela de costumbres
mannered *a* amanerado; (in compounds) . . . educado, de . . . modales; de costumbres . . . **well-m.,** bien educado, de buenos modales
mannerism *n* amaneramiento, *m;* afectación, *f; theat* latiguillo, *m.* **to acquire mannerisms,** amanerarse
mannerliness *n* cortesía, buena educación, urbanidad, *f*
mannerly *a* cortés, bien educado, atento
mannish *a* (of a woman) hombruno; de hombre, masculino
manor *n* feudo, *m;* finca, hacienda, *f;* casa solariega, *f;* señorío, *m*
manorial *a* señorial
mansion *n* mansión, *f;* casa solariega, *f;* hotel, *m.* **m.-house,** casa solariega, *f;* residencia del alcalde de Londres, *f*
manslaughter *n* homicidio, *m; law* homicidio sin premeditación, *m*
mantelpiece *n* repisa de chimenea, *f*
mantilla *n* mantilla, *f*
mantle *n* capa, *f,* manto, *m; fig* cobertura, *f;* (gas) camiseta, *f,* manguito, *mf; zool* manto, *m. vt* cubrir; envolver; ocultar. *vi* extenderse; (of blushes) inundar, subirse (a las mejillas)
Mantuan *a* mantuano
manual *a* manual. *n* manual, *m; mus* teclado de órgano, *m.* **m. work,** trabajo manual, *m*
manufactory *n* fábrica, *f,* taller, *m*
manufacture *n* fabricación, *f;* manufactura, *f. vt* manufacturar, fabricar
manufacturer *n* fabricante, industrial, *m.* **manufacturer's price,** precio de fábrica, *m*
manufacturing *a* manufacturero, fabril. *n* fabricación, *f*
manure *n* estiércol, abono, *m. vt* estercolar, abonar. **m. heap,** estercolero, *m*
manuring *n* estercoladura, *f*
manuscript *n* manuscrito, *m, a* manuscrito
many *a* muchos (-as); numeroso; diversos (-as); varios (-as). *n* muchos (-as); la mayoría; las masas; muchedumbre, multitud, *f.* **a great m.,** muchísimos, *m pl,* muchísimas, *f pl;* un gran número. **as m. as . . . ,** tantos como . . . **How m. are there?** ¿Cuántos hay? ¿Cuántas hay? **m. a time,** muchas veces. **three too m.,** tres de más. **for m. long years,** por largos años. **m.-colored,** multicolor. **m.-headed,** con muchas cabezas. **m.-sided,** multilátero; polifacético; complicado
Maori *n* maorí, *m,* (*pl* maoríes)
map *n* mapa, *m;* plano, *m;* (chart) carta, *f. vt* hacer un mapa (or plano) de. **to map out,** *surv* apear; trazar; (plan) proyectar. **ordnance map,** mapa del estado mayor, *m.* **map of the world,** mapamundi, mapa del mundo, *m.* **map-making,** cartografía, *f*
maple *n* (tree) arce, *m;* (wood) madera de arce, *f.* **m.-syrup,** jarabe de arce, *m*
mapping *n* cartografía, *f*
maquiladora *n* maquiladora, *f*
mar *vt* estropear; desfigurar; (happiness) destruir, aguar; frustrar
maraca *n Lat. Am.* alfandoque, *m*
maraschino *n* marrasquino, *m.* **m. cherry,** cerezas en marrasquino, *f pl*
maraud *vi* merodear
marauder *n* merodeador, *m*
marauding *a* merodeador, *n* merodeo, *m*
marble *n* mármol, *m;* (for playing with) canica, *f, a* de marmol, marmóreo; *fig* insensible; (of paper, etc.) jaspeado. *vt* jaspear. **m. cutter,** marmolista, *m.* **m. works,** marmolería, *f*
marbled *a* jaspeado
March *n* marzo, *m.* **as mad as a M. hare,** loco como una cabra, loco de atar
march *n* marcha, *f;* (step) paso, *m; fig* marcha, *f,* progreso, *m.* **forced m.,** marcha forzada, *f.* **quick m.,** paso doble, *m.* **to steal a m. on,** tomar la delantera (a), ganar por la mano (a). **to strike up a m.,** batir la marcha. **m.-past,** desfile, *m*
march *vi* marchar; (of properties) lindar (con). *vt* hacer marchar, poner en marcha (a). **to m. back,** *vi* regresar (or volver) a pie. *vt* hacer volver a pie. **to m. in,** entrar (a pie) en. **to m. off,** marcharse. **to m. on,** seguir marchando; seguir adelante; avanzar. **to m. past,** desfilar ante
marching *n* marcha, *f. a* en marcha; de marcha. **to receive one's m. orders,** recibir la orden de marchar; *inf* ser despedido. **m. order,** orden de marcha, *m.* **m. song,** canción de marcha, *f*
mardi gras *n* martes de carnaval, *m*
mare *n* yegua, *f*
margarine *n* margarina, *f*
margin *n* borde, lado, *m,* orilla, *f;* (of a page) margen, *mf;* reserva, *f;* sobrante, *m.* **in the m.,** al margen
marginal *a* marginal. **m. note,** acotación, nota marginal, *f*
marigold *n* caléndula, maravilla, *f*
marihuana *n* marijuana, *f. Lat. Am.* cáñamo *m*
marine *a* marino, de mar; marítimo; naval. *n* (fleet) marina, *f;* (soldier) soldado de marina, *m.* **Tell that to the marines!** ¡Cuéntaselo a tu tía! **mercantile m.,** marina mercante, *f.* **m. forces,** infantería de marina, *f.* **m. insurance,** seguro marítimo, *m*
mariner *n* marinero, marino, *m.* **mariner's compass,** aguja de marear, brújula, *f*
marionette *n* marioneta, *f,* títere, *m*

marital *a* marital
maritime *a* marítimo
mark *n* marca, *f;* señal, *f;* mancha, *f;* impresión, *f;* (target) blanco, *m;* (standard) norma, *f;* (level) nivel, *m;* (distinction) importancia, distinción, *f;* (in examinations) nota, *f;* calificación, *f;* (signature) cruz, *f;* (coin) marco, *m. vt* marcar; señalar; (price) poner precio (a); (notice) observar, darse cuenta (de); (characterize) caracterizar. **trade-m.,** marca de fábrica, *f.* **to be beside the m.,** no dar en el blanco; errar el tiro; *fig* no tener nada que ver con; equivocarse. **to hit the m.,** dar en el blanco; *fig* dar en el clavo. **to make one's m.,** firmar con una cruz; distinguirse. **to m. time,** marcar el paso; *fig* hacer tiempo. **to m. down,** (a person) señalar; escoger; (in price) rebajar. **to m. out,** marcar; trazar; definir; (erase) borrar; (a person) escoger; destinar **m. somebody absent,** ponerle a fulano su ausencia. **m. somebody present,** ponerle a fulano su asistencia.
Mark *n* Marcos. **the Gospel according to St. M.,** el Evangelio de San Marcos
marked *a* marcado; señalado; notable; acentuado; particular, especial. **He speaks with a m. Galician accent,** Habla con marcado acento gallego
markedly *adv* marcadamente; notablemente; especialmente, particularmente
marker *n* (billiards) marcador, *m;* (football, etc.) tanteador, *m*
market *n* mercado, *m;* tráfico, *m;* venta, *f;* (price) precio, *m;* (shop) bazar, emporio, *m. vt* and *vi* comprar en un mercado; vender en un mercado. **black m.,** mercado negro, estraperlo, *m.* **open m.,** mercado al aire libre, *m; fig* mercado libre, *m.* **m. day,** día de mercado, *m.* **m. garden,** huerto, *m,* huerta, *f.* **m. gardener,** hortelano, *m.* **m.-place,** plaza de mercado, *f; fig* mercado, *m.* **m. price,** precio corriente, *m.* **m. stall,** tabanco, puesto de mercado, *m.* **m.-woman,** verdulera, *f*
marketable *a* comerciable, vendible; corriente
marketing *n* venta, *f;* compra en un mercado, *f;* mercado, *m.* **to go m.,** ir al mercado
marking *n* marca, *f;* (spot on animals, etc.) pinta, *f.* **m.-ink,** tinta de marcar, *f.* **m.-iron,** ferrete, hierro de marcar, *m*
marksman *n* tirador (-ra)
marksmanship *n* puntería, *f*
marl *n* marga, *f*
marmalade *n* mermelada de naranjas amargas, *f*
marmoset *n* tití, *m*
marmot *n zool* marmota, *f*
maroon *n* (color) marrón, *m;* (slave) cimarrón (-ona); (firework) petardo, *m. a* de marrón. *vt* abandonar, dejar
marquee *n* marquesina, *f*
marqueterie *n* marquetería, *f*
marquis *n* marqués, *m*
marriage *n* matrimonio, *m;* unión, *f;* (wedding) boda, *f,* casamiento, *m.* **by m.,** (of relationship) político. **She is an aunt by m.,** tía política. **m. articles,** capitulaciones (matrimoniales), *f pl.* **m. contract,** contrato matrimonial, *m.* **m. license,** licencia de casamiento, *f.* **m. portion,** dote, *mf.* **m. rate,** nupcialidad, *f.* **m. register,** acta matrimonial, *f.* **m. song,** epitalamio, *m*
marriageable *a* casadero
married *past part* and *a* casado; matrimonial, conyugal. **newly-m. couple,** los recién casados. **to get m. to,** casarse con. **m. couple,** matrimonio, *m,* cónyuges, *m pl.* **m. life,** vida conyugal, *f*
married name *n* nombre de casada, *f*
marrow *n* tuétano, *m,* médula, *f; fig* meollo, *m.* **to the m. of one's bones,** hasta los tuétanos.
marrowbone *n* hueso medular, *m.* **on one's marrowbones,** de rodillas
marry *vt* casarse con, contraer matrimonio con; casar; (of a priest) unir en matrimonio; *fig* juntar, unir. *vi* casarse. **to m. again,** volver a casarse
Marseillaise *n* marsellesa, *f*
Marseilles Marsella, *f*
marsh *n* marjal, pantano, *Central America* chagüe, *m.* **m.-mallow,** *bot* malvavisco, *m.* **m. marigold,** calta, *f*
marshal *n* mariscal, *m, vt* poner en orden, arreglar; dirigir. **field-m.,** capitán general de ejército, *m*
marshaling *n* ordenación, *f;* dirección, *f.* **m.-yard,** (railway) apartadero ferroviario, *m*
marshy *a* pantanoso
mart *n poet* plaza de mercado, *f;* mercado, *m;* emporio, *m;* (auction rooms) martillo, *m*
marten *n* marta, *f*
martial *a* militar; marcial, belicoso. **m. array,** orden de batalla, *m.* **m. law,** derecho militar, *m;* estado de guerra, *m.* **m. spirit,** marcialidad, *f,* espíritu belicoso, *m*
martially *adv* militarmente; marcialmente
Martian *a* marciano
martinet *n mil* ordenancista, *m;* rigorista, *mf*
Martinique Martinica, *f*
Martinmas *n* día de San Martín, *m*
martyr *n* mártir, *mf vt* martirizar
martyrdom *n* martirio, *m*
martyrize *vt* martirizar
marvel *n* maravilla, *f.* **to m. at,** maravillarse de, admirarse de
marvelous *a* maravilloso
marvelousness *n* maravilla, *f,* carácter maravilloso, *m,* lo maravilloso
Marxism *n* marxismo, *m*
Marxist *a* and *n* marxista, *mf*
marzipan *n* mazapán, *m*
mascot *n* mascota, *f*
masculine *a* masculino; varonil, macho; de hombre; (of a woman) hombruno. *n* masculino, *m*
masculinity *n* masculinidad, *f*
mash *n* mezcla, *f;* amasijo, *m;* pasta, *f,* puré, *m. vt* mezclar; amasar. **mashed potatoes,** puré de patatas (de papas), *m*
mask *n* máscara, *f;* antifaz, *m;* (death) mascarilla, *f;* (person) máscara, *mf. vt* enmascarar; *fig* encubrir, disimular. *vi* ponerse una máscara; disfrazarse. **masked ball,** *n* baile de máscaras, *m*
masker *n* máscara, *mf*
masochism *n* masoquismo, *m*
mason *n* albañil, *m;* (freemason) francmasón, masón, *m*
masonic *a* masónico. **m. lodge,** logia de francmasones, *f*
masonry *n* (trade) albañilería, *f;* mampostería, *f*
masque *n* mascarada, *f*
masquerade *n* mascarada, *f*
masquerader *n* máscara, *mf*
mass *n* misa, *f.* **to hear m.,** oír misa. **to say m.,** celebrar misa. **high m.,** misa mayor, *f.* **low m.,** misa rezada, *f.* **m. book,** libro de misa, *m*
mass *n* masa, *f;* (shape) bulto, *m;* (heap) montón, *m;* (great number) muchedumbre, *f;* (cloud of steam, etc.) nube, *f. vt* amasar; *mil* concentrar. *vi* congregarse en masa. **in a m.,** en masa; en conjunto. **the m. (of) . . . ,** la mayoría (de) . . . **the masses,** las masas, el vulgo, el pueblo. **m. formation,** columna cerrada, *f.* **m.-meeting,** mitin, mitin popular, *m.* **m.-production,** fabricación en serie, *f*
massacre *n* matanza, carnicería, *f, vt* hacer una carnicería (de)
massage *n* masaje, *m;* (friction) fricción, *f. vt* dar un masaje (a)
masseur, masseuse *n* masajista, *mf*
massive *a* macizo; sólido
massively *adv* macizamente; sólidamente
massiveness *n* macicez, *f;* solidez, *f*
mast *n naut* palo, árbol, *m;* (for wireless) mástil, *m;* poste, *m;* (beech) hayuco, *m;* (oak) bellota, *f. vt naut* arbolar. **at half-m.,** a media asta. **m.-head,** calcés, tope, *m*
masted *a* arbolado; (in compounds) de . . . palos

master *n* (of the house, etc.) señor, amo, *m;* maestro, *m; naut* patrón, *m;* (owner) dueño, *m;* (teacher) profesor, maestro, *m;* (young master and as address) señorito, *m;* director, *m;* jefe, *m;* (expert) perito, *m;* (of a military order) maestre, *m, a* maestro; superior. *vt* dominar; ser maestro en; dominar, conocer a fondo. **This picture is by an old m.,** Este cuadro es de un gran maestro antiguo. **to be m. of oneself,** ser dueño de sí. **to be one's own m.,** ser dueño de sí mismo; trabajar por su propia cuenta; ser independiente; estar libre. **m. builder,** maestro de obras, *m.* **m. hand,** mano maestra, *f.* **M. of Arts,** maestro (-tra) en artes. **M. of Ceremonies,** maestro de ceremonias, *m.* **M. of Foxhounds,** cazador mayor, *m.* **M. of the Horse,** caballerizo mayor del rey, *m.* **M. of the Rolls,** archivero mayor, *m.* **m.-key,** llave maestra, *f.* **m. mind,** águila, *f,* ingenio, *m.* **m. stroke,** golpe maestro, *m*

masterful *a* imperioso, dominante; autoritario, arbitrario

masterfulness *n* imperiosidad, *f;* arbitrariedad, *f*

masterless *a* sin amo

masterliness *n* maestría, *f;* excelencia, *f;* perfección, *f*

masterly *a* maestro; excelente; perfecto. **m. performance,** obra maestra, *f; theat* representación perfecta, *f;* ejecución excelente, *f*

masterpiece *n* obra maestra, *f*

master plan *n* plan regulador, *m*

masterstroke *n* golpe magistral, golpe de maestro, *m*

mastery *n* dominio, *m;* autoridad, *f;* poder, *m;* ventaja, *f;* superioridad, maestría, *f;* conocimiento profundo, *m.* **to gain the m. of,** hacerse el señor de; llegar a dominar

mastic *n* masilla, almáciga, *f*

masticate *vt* masticar, mascar

mastication *n* masticación, *f*

mastiff *n* mastín, alano, *m*

mastodon *n* mastodonte, *m*

mastoid *a* mastoides. *n* apófisis mastoides, *f*

masturbate *vi* masturbarse

masturbation *n* masturbación, *f*

mat *n* esterilla, *f;* alfombrilla, *f;* (on the table) tapete individual, *m. vt* (tangle) enmarañar, desgreñar. *vi* enmarañarse

match *n sport* partido, *m;* (wrestling, boxing) lucha, *f;* (fencing) asalto, *m;* (race) carrera, *f;* (contest) concurso, *m;* (equal) igual, *mf;* (pair) pareja, *f;* compañero (-ra); (marriage) boda, *f,* casamiento, *m;* (for lighting) cerilla, *f,* fósforo, *Mexico* cerillo, *m;* (for guns) mecha, *f. vt* competir con; (equal) igualar; ser igual (a); hacer juego con; emparejar, aparear; armonizar. *vi* ser igual; hacer juego; armonizarse. **good m.,** *inf* buen partido, *m.* **as thin as a m.,** más delgado que una cerilla. **to meet one's m.,** dar con la horma de su zapato. **to play a m.,** jugar un partido. **m.-box,** cajita de cerillas, fosforera, *f.* **m.-seller,** fosforero (-ra)

matchless *a* incomparable, sin igual, sin par

matchwood *n* madera para cerillas, *f*

mate *n* compañero, camarada, *m;* (spouse) compañero (-ra); pareja, *f;* (on merchant ships) piloto, *m;* (assistant) ayudante, *m;* (at chess) mate, *m. vt* (marry) casar, desposar; (animals, birds) aparear, acoplar; (chess) dar jaque mate (a). *vi* casarse; aparearse, acoplarse

maté *n* maté, té del Paraguay, *m*

materfamilias *n* madre de familia, *f*

material *a* material; importante, esencial; considerable; sensible, notable; grave. *n* material, *m;* materia, *f;* (fabric) tela, *f;* tejido, *m.* **raw materials,** materias primas, *f pl.* **writing materials,** utensilios de escritorio, *m pl;* papel de escribir, *m*

materialism *n* materialismo, *m*

materialist *n* materialista, *mf*

materialistic *a* materialista

materiality *n* materialidad, *f;* importancia, *f*

materialization *n* materialización, *f*

materialize *vt* materializar

maternal *a* materno, maternal. **m. grandparents,** abuelos maternos, *m pl*

maternity *n* maternidad, *f.* **m. center,** centro de maternidad, *m.* **m. hospital,** casa de maternidad, *f*

mathematical *a* matemático

mathematician *n* matemático, *m*

mathematics *n pl;* matemáticas, *f pl.* **applied m.,** matemáticas prácticas, *f pl.* **higher m.,** matemáticas superiores, *f pl.* **pure m.,** matemáticas teóricas, *f pl*

matinee *n* función de tarde, *f*

mating *n* (of animals) apareamiento, acoplamiento, *m;* unión, *f;* casamiento, *m*

matins *n pl ecc* maitines, *m pl*

matriarch *n* matriarca, *f*

matriarchal *a* matriarcal

matriarchy *n* matriarcado, *m*

matricide *n* (crime) matricidio, *m;* (person) matricida, *mf*

matriculate *vt* matricular. *vi* matricularse

matriculation *n* matriculación, *f*

matrimonial *a* matrimonial, de matrimonio; marital. **m. agency,** agencia de matrimonios, *f*

matrimony *n* matrimonio, *m*

matrix *n* matriz, *f*

matron *n* matrona, mujer casada, madre de familia, *f;* (of a hospital) matrona, *f;* (of a school) ama de llaves, *f;* directora, *f.* **m. of honor,** (at a wedding) madrina, *f*

matronly *a* de matrona, matronal; respetable; serio

matt *a* mate

matted *a* enmarañado, enredado

matter *n* materia, *f;* substancia, *f;* caso, *m;* cuestión, *f;* asunto, *m;* causa, *f;* (distance) distancia, *f;* (amount) cantidad, *f;* (duration) espacio de tiempo, *m;* (importance) importancia, *f; med* pus, *m; pl* **matters,** asuntos, *m pl,* etc.; situación, *f.* **as if nothing were the m.,** como si no hubiese pasado nada. **for that m.,** en cuanto a eso. **grey m.,** substancia gris, *f.* **in the m. of,** en el caso de. **It is a m. of taste,** Es cuestión de gusto. **printed m.,** impresos, *m pl.* **What is the m.?** ¿Qué pasa? ¿Qué hay? **What is the m. with him?** ¿Qué tiene? ¿Qué le pasa? **m.-of-course,** cosa natural, *f.* **m.-of-fact,** práctico; sin imaginación; positivista. **m. of fact,** *n* hecho positivo, *m,* realidad, *f.* **As a m. of fact . . . ,** En realidad . . . , El caso es que . . . **m. of form,** cuestión de fórmula, *f;* pura formalidad, *f*

matter *vi* importar; (discharge) supurar. **What does it m.?** ¿Qué importa? **It doesn't m.,** Es igual, No importa, Da lo mismo

Matterhorn, the el Matterhorn, *m*

matting *n* estera, *f*

mattress *n* colchón, *m.* **spring-m.,** colchón de muelles, *m.* **m.-maker,** colchonero, *m*

mature *a* maduro; *com* vencido. *vt* madurar. *vi* madurarse; *com* vencer

maturity *n* madurez, *f;* edad madura, *f;* (*com* of a bill) vencimiento, *m*

matutinal *a* matutino

maudlin *a* sensiblero; lacrimoso; (tipsy) calamocano

maul *vt* maltratar; herir

maundy *n* lavatorio, *m.* **M. Thursday,** Jueves Santo, *m*

Mauritius Mauricio, *m,* Isla de Francia, *f*

mausoleum *n* mausoleo, *m*

mauve *n* color purpúreo delicado, color de malva, *m, a* de color de malva

maw *n* (of a ruminant) cuajar, *m;* (of a bird) buche, *m; fig* abismo, *m*

mawkish *a* insípido, insulso; sensiblero; asqueroso

mawkishness *n* insipidez, insulsez, *f;* sensiblería, *f;* asquerosidad, *f*

maxilla *n* hueso maxilar, maxilar, *m*

maxillary *a* maxilar

maxim *n* máxima, *f*

maximum *a* máximo. *n* máximo, *m*

may *v aux* poder; ser posible; (expressing wish, hope) ojalá que . . . , Dios quiera que . . . , or the present subjunctive may be used, e.g. **May you live many**

years! ¡(qué) Viva Vd. muchos años! (to denote uncertainty, the future tense of the verb is often used, e.g. **You may perhaps remember the date,** Vd. quizás se acordará de la fecha. **Who may he be?** ¿Quién será?) **May God grant it!** ¡(que) Dios lo quiera! **It may be that . . . ,** Puede ser que . . . , Es posible que . . . , Quizás . . . **He may come on Saturday,** Es posible que venga el sábado; Puede venir el sábado. **May I come in?** ¿Puedo entrar? ¿Se puede entrar? **May I come and see you?** ¿Me das permiso para hacerte una visita? ¿Me dejas venir a verte? **May I go then?** ¿Puedo irme pues? ¿Tengo permiso para marcharme entonces?

May *n* mayo, *m; fig* abril, *m; bot* espina blanca, *f.* **May Day,** primero de mayo, *m.* **mayflower,** flor del cuclillo, *f.* **mayfly,** cachipolla, *f.* **May queen,** maya, *f*

maybe *adv* quizás, tal vez

mayonnaise *n* mayonesa, *f.* **m. sauce,** salsa mayonesa, *f*

mayor *n* alcalde, *Argentina* intendente, *m*

mayoral *a* de alcalde

mayoralty *n Argentina* intendencia, *f*

mayoress *n* alcaldesa, *f*

maypole *n* mayo, *m.* **m. dance,** danza de cintas, *f*

maze *n* laberinto, *m; fig* perplejidad, *f. vt* dejar perplejo, aturdir

mazurka *n* mazurca, *f*

me *pron* me; (after a preposition only) mí. **They sent it for me,** Lo mandaron para mí. **Dear me!** ¡Ay de mí!

meadow *n* prado, *m,* pradera, *f.* **m.-sweet,** reina de los prados, *f*

meager *a* magro, enjuto, flaco; (scanty) exiguo, escaso, insuficiente; pobre; *fig* árido

meagerness *n* exigüidad, escasez, *f;* pobreza, *f; fig* aridez, *f*

meal *n* comida, *f;* (flour) harina, *f.* **to have a good m.,** comer bien. **test m.,** *med* comida de prueba, *f.* **m.-time,** hora de comida, *f*

mealy *a* harinoso; (of the complexion) pastoso

mean *a* (middle) medianero; (average) mediano; (humble) humilde; pobre; inferior; bajo, vil, ruin; (avaricious) tacaño, mezquino, *Argentina* agalludo, *Chile, Peru* coñete, **m.-spirited,** vil, de alma ruin

mean *n* medio, *m;* medianía, *f; pl* **means,** medio, *m;* expediente, *m;* medios, *m pl;* (financial) recursos, *m pl;* modo, *m,* manera, *f.* **by all means,** por todos los medios; (certainly) ¡ya lo creo! ¡no faltaba más! ¡naturalmente! **by means of,** mediante, por medio de; con la ayuda de. **by no means,** de ningún modo; nada. **by some means,** de algún modo, de alguna manera

mean *vt* destinar (para); pretender, proponerse; intentar, pensar; querer decir, significar; importar; (wish) querer; (concern, speak about) tratarse (de). *vi* tener el propósito, tener la intención. **I did not m. to do it,** Lo hice sin querer. **What does this word m.?** ¿Qué significa esta palabra? **What do you m. by that?** ¿Qué quieres decir con eso? **This portrait is meant to be Joan,** Este retrato quiere ser Juana. **What do they m. to do?** ¿Qué piensan (or se proponen) hacer? **Do you really m. it?** ¿Lo dices en serio? **Charles always means well,** Carlos siempre tiene buenas intenciones

meander *n* meandro, serpenteo, *m;* camino tortuoso, *m, vi* serpentear; errar, vagar; (in talk) divagar

meandering *n* meandros, *m pl,* serpenteo, *m;* (in talk) divagaciones, *f pl, a* serpentino, tortuoso

meaning *n* intención, voluntad, *f;* significación, *f,* significado, *m;* (of words) acepción, *f;* (sense) sentido, *m;* (thought) pensamiento, *m. a* significante. **double m.,** doble intención, *f.* **He gave me a m. look,** Me miró con intención. **What is the m. of it?** ¿Qué significa? ¿Qué quiere decir?

meaningful *a* significante

meaningless *a* sin sentido; insensato; insignificante

meaningly *adv* significativamente; con intención

meanness *n* pobreza, *f;* inferioridad, *f;* mediocridad, *f;* bajeza, ruindad, *f;* (stinginess) mezquindad, tacañería, *Lat. Am. also* lechería, *f*

meantime, meanwhile *n* ínterin, *m, adv* entre tanto, mientras tanto, a todo esto. **in the m.,** mientras tanto, en el ínterin

measles *n* sarampión, *m.* **German m.,** rubéola, *f*

measurable *a* mensurable

measure *n* medida, *f;* capacidad, *f;* (for measuring) regla, *f;* número, *m;* proporción, *f;* (limit) límite, *m;* (*fig* step) medida, *f;* (metre) metro, *m; mus* compás, *m;* (degree) grado, *m;* manera, *f;* (parliamentary) proyecto (de ley), *m. vt* medir; proporcionar, distribuir; (water) aforar; (land) apear; (height of persons) tallar; (for clothes) tomar las medidas (a); (judge) juzgar; (test) probar; (*poet* traverse) recorrer. **a suit made to m.,** un traje hecho a medida. **in great m.,** en gran manera, en alto grado. **in some m.,** hasta cierto punto. **to m. one's length,** caer tendido. **to take a person's m.,** *fig* tomar las medidas (a). **to m. up to,** *fig* estar al nivel de, ser igual a

measured *a* mesurado, moderado; uniforme; limitado. **to walk with m. tread,** andar a pasos contados

measurement *n* medición, *f;* medida, *f;* dimensión, *f*

meat *n* carne, *f;* (food) alimento, *m;* (meal) comida, *f; fig* substancia, *f.* **to sit at m.,** estar a la mesa. **cold meats,** fiambres, *m pl.* **m.-ball,** albóndiga, *f.* **m.-chopper,** picador, *m.* **m.-dish,** fuente, *f.* **m.-eater,** comedor (-ra) de carne. **m. extract,** carne concentrada, *f.* **m.-market,** carnicería, *f.* **m.-pie,** pastel de carne, *m.* **m.-safe,** fresquera, *f*

meaty *a* carnoso; *fig* substancial

Mecca la Meca, *f*

mechanic *n* mecánico, *m*

mechanical *a* mecánico; maquinal

mechanically *adv* mecánicamente; maquinalmente

mechanical pencil *n* lapicero, *m*

mechanics *n* mecánica, *f*

mechanism *n* mecanismo, *m;* (philosophy) mecanicismo, *m*

mechanize *vt* convertir en máquina; (gen. *mil*) mecanizar; motorizar

medal *n* medalla, *f*

medallion *n* medallón, *m*

medallist *n* grabador de medallas, *m;* el, *m,* (*f,* la) que recibe una medalla

meddle *vi* tocar; meterse (con or en); entremeterse, inmiscuirse; intrigar

meddler *n* entremetido (-da); intrigante, *mf*

meddlesome *a* entremetido; oficioso; impertinente; enredador, intrigante. **to be very m.,** meterse en todo

meddlesomeness *n* entremetimiento, *m;* oficiosidad, *f;* impertinencia, *f;* intrigas, *f pl*

media, the los medios informativos, *m pl*

median *a* del medio

mediate *vi* intervenir, mediar, arbitrar; abogar (por). *a* medio; interpuesto

mediation *n* mediación, intervención, *f;* intercesión, *f;* interposición, *f*

mediator *n* mediador (-ra); arbitrador, *m;* intercesor (-ra)

mediatory *a* de mediador; intercesor

medical *a* médico; de medicina; de médico. *n inf* estudiante de medicina, *m.* **Army M. Service,** Servicio de Sanidad Militar, *m.* **m. books,** libros de medicina, *m pl.* **m. examination,** examen médico, *m,* exploración médica, *f.* **m. jurisprudence,** medicina legal, *f.* **m. knowledge,** conocimientos médicos, *m pl.* **m. practitioner,** médico (-ca). **m. school,** escuela de medicina, *f*

medicament *n* medicamento, *m*

medicate *vt* medicar; medicinar

medicated *a* medicado

medication *n* medicación, *f*

medicinal *a* medicinal

medicine *n* medicina, *f;* medicamento, *m;* (charm) ensalmo, hechizo, *m.* **patent m.,** específico far-

macéutico, *m*. **m. ball,** balón medical, *m*. **m. chest,** botiquín, *m*. **m. man,** hechizador, *m*
medico- *prefix* médico-. **m.-legal,** médicolegal
medieval *a* medieval
medievalism *n* afición a la edad media, *f*; espíritu medieval, *m*
mediocre *a* mediocre
mediocrity *n* mediocridad, *f*; medianía, *f*
meditate *vt* idear, proyectar, meditar. *vi* meditar, reflexionar; pensar, intentar
meditation *n* meditación, *f*
meditative *a* meditabundo, contemplativo; de meditación
meditatively *adv* reflexivamente
Mediterranean *a* mediterráneo. *n* Mar Mediterráneo, *m*
medium *n* medio, *m*; (cooking) término medio, a medio cocer, a medio asar, *m*; (environment) medio ambiente, *m*; (agency) intermediario, *m*; (spiritualism) médium, *m*; *art* medio, *m*, *a* mediano; regular; mediocre. **through the m. of,** por medio de. **m.-sized,** de tamaño regular
medlar *n* (fruit) níspola, *f*; (tree) níspero, *m*
medley *n* mezcla, *f*; miscelánea, *f*, *a* mezclado, mixto
medulla *n* medula, *f*
meek *a* dulce, manso; humilde; modesto; pacífico
meekly *adv* mansamente; humildemente; modestamente
meekness *n* mansedumbre, *f*; humildad, *f*; modestia, *f*
meet *vt* encontrar; encontrarse con; tropezar con; (by arrangement) reunirse con; (make the acquaintance of) conocer (a); (satisfy) satisfacer; cumplir (con); (a bill) pagar, saldar; (refute) refutar; (fight) batirse (con); (confront) hacer frente (a). *vi* juntarse; encontrarse; reunirse; verse; (of rivers) confluir. *n* montería, *f*, *a* conveniente. **I shall m. you at the station,** Te esperaré en la estación. **Until we m. again!** ¡Hasta la vista! **to go to m.,** ir al encuentro de. **to m. half-way,** encontrar a la mitad del camino; partir la diferencia con; hacer concesiones (a). **to m. the eye,** saltar a la vista. **to m. with,** encontrar; experimentar; sufrir
meeting *n* encuentro, *m*; reunión, *f*; (interview) entrevista, *f*; (of rivers, etc.) confluencia, *f*; (public, etc.) mitin, *m*; (council) concilio, *m*; concurso, *m*; (race) concurso de carreras de caballos, *m*. **creditors' m.,** concurso de acreedores, *m*. **m.-house,** templo de los Cuáqueros, *m*. **m.-place,** lugar de reunión, *m*; lugar de cita, *m*; centro, *m*. **to adjourn the m.,** levantar la sesión. **to call a m.,** convocar una sesión. **to open the m.,** abrir la sesión
megalomania *n* megalomanía, monomanía de grandezas, *f*
megalomaniac *n* megalómano (-na)
megaphone *n* megáfono, portavoz, *m*
Meknès Mequínez, *f*
melancholia *n* melancolía, *f*
melancholy *a* melancólico. *n* melancolía, *f*
mellifluence *n* melifluidad, *f*
mellifluous *a* melifluo; dulce
mellow *a* maduro; dulce; (of wine) rancio; blando; suave; (of sound) melodioso; (slang) alegre; (tipsy) entre dos luces. *vt* madurar; ablandar; suavizar. *vi* madurarse
mellowing *n* maduración, *f*
mellowness *n* madurez, *f*; dulzura, *f*; (of wine) ranciedad, *f*; blandura, *f*; suavidad, *f*; melodia, *f*
melodic *a* melódico
melodious *a* melodioso
melodiously *adv* melodiosamente
melodiousness *n* melodía, *f*
melodrama *n* melodrama, *m*
melodramatic *a* melodramático
melody *n* melodía, *f*
melon *n* melón, *m*; sandía, *f*. **slice of m.,** raja de melón, *f*. **m. bed,** sandiar, *m*. **m.-shaped,** amelonado
melt *vi* derretirse; deshacerse; disolverse; evaporarse; desaparecer; (of money, etc.) hacerse sal y agua; (relent) enternecerse, ablandarse. *vt* fundir; (snow, etc.) derretir; (*fig* soften) ablandar. **He melted away,** *inf* Se escurrió. **to m. into tears,** deshacerse en lágrimas. **to m. down,** fundir
melting *a* fundente; (forgiving) indulgente; (tender) de ternura; lánguido; dulce. *n* fusión, *f*; derretimiento, *m*. **m. point,** punto de fusión, *m*. **m. pot,** *met* crisol, *m*; *fig* caldera de razas, *f*, *m*
member *n* miembro, *m*; (of a club, etc.) socio (-ia). **M. of Parliament,** diputado a Cortes, *m*
membership *n* calidad de miembro, socio(-ia); número de miembros (*or* socios), *m*, composición, integración, *f*
membrane *n* membrana, *f*
membranous *a* membranoso
memento *n* recuerdo, *m*
memoir *n* memoria, *f*
memorable *a* memorable
memorably *adv* memorablemente
memorandum *n* memorándum, *m*
memorial *a* conmemorativo. *n* monumento conmemorativo, *m*; memorial, *m*
memorize *vt* aprender de memoria
memory *n* memoria, *f*; recuerdo, *m*. **from m.,** de memoria. **If my m. does not deceive me,** Si mal no me acuerdo. **in m. of,** en conmemoración de; en recuerdo de
memory span *n* retentiva memorística, *f*
menace *n* amenaza, *f*, *vt* amenazar
menacing *a* amenazador
menacingly *adv* con amenazas
menagerie *n* colección de fieras, *f*; casa de fieras, *f*
mend *vt* remendar; componer; reparar; (darn) zurcir; (rectify) remediar; reformar; enmendar; (a fire) echar carbón (or leña, etc.) a; (one's pace) avivar. *vi* (in health and of the weather) mejorar. *n* remiendo, *m*; (darn) zurcido, *m*. **to be on the m.,** ir mejorando. **to m. one's ways,** reformarse, enmendarse
mendacious *a* mendaz
mendacity *n* mendacidad, *f*
Mendelism *n* mendelismo, *m*
mender *n* componedor (-ra); (darner) zurcidor (-ra); reparador (-ra); (cobbler and tailor) remendón, *m*
mendicancy *n* mendicidad, *f*
mendicant *a* mendicante. *n* mendicante, *mf*. **m. friar,** fraile mendicante, *m*
mending *n* compostura, *f*; reparación, *f*; (darning) zurcidura, *f*; ropa por zurcir, *f*
menial *a* doméstico; servil; bajo, ruin. *n* criado (-da); lacayo, *m*
meningeal *a* meningeo
meningitis *n* meningitis, *f*
menopause *n* menopausia, *f*
menses *n* menstruación, *f*
menstrual *a* menstrual
menstruate *vi* menstruar
menstruation *n* menstruación, *f*,
mental *a* mental; intelectual. **m. derangement,** enajenación mental, *f*. **m. hospital,** manicomio, *m*
mentality *n* mentalidad, *f*
mentally *adv* mentalmente. **m. deficient,** anormal
menthol *n* mentol, *m*
mention *n* mención, *f*; alusión, *f*. *vt* hacer mención (de), mencionar, mentar, hablar (de); aludir (a); (quote) citar; (in dispatches) nombrar. **Don't m. it!** (keep silent) ¡No digas nada!; (you're welcome) ¡No hay de que!
mentor *n* mentor, *m*
menu *n* menú, *m*; lista de platos, *f*
meow *vi* maullar. *n* maullido, *m*
Mephistophelean *a* mefistofélico
mercantile *a* mercantil; mercante. **m. law,** derecho mercantil, *m*. **m. marine,** marina mercante, *f*
mercantilism *n* mercantilismo, *m*
mercenariness *n* lo mercenario
mercenary *a* mercenario. *n* (soldier) mercenario, *m*

mercer *n* mercero, *m*
mercerize *vt* mercerizar
mercery *n* mercería, *f*
merchandise *n* mercancía, *f*
merchant *n* traficante (en), *mf*, negociante (en), *m*; comerciante, *Lat. Am.* marchante (-ta), *mf* mercader, *m*. *a* mercante. **The M. of Venice,** El Mercader de Venecia. **m. navy, service,** marina mercante, *f*. **m. ship,** buque mercante, *m*
merchantman *n* buque mercante, *m*
merciful *a* misericordioso, piadoso; compasivo; clemente; indulgente
mercifully *adv* misericordiosamente; compasivamente; con indulgencia
mercifulness *n* misericordia, *f*; compasión, *f*; indulgencia, *f*
merciless *a* despiadado, inhumano
mercilessly *adv* sin piedad
mercilessness *n* inhumanidad, *f*; falta de compasión, *f*
mercurial *a* mercurial; (changeable) volátil; (lively) vivo
mercury *n* mercurio, *m*; (*ast* and *myth*) Mercurio, *m*. **Mercury's wand,** caduceo, *m*
mercy *n* misericordia, *f*; compasión, *f*; clemencia, *f*; indulgencia, *f*; merced, *f*. **at the m. of the elements,** a la intemperie. **to be at the m. of,** estar a la merced de
mere *a* mero; simple; no más que, solo. *n* lago, *m*
merely *adv* meramente, solamente; simplemente, sencillamente
meretricious *a* (archaic) meretricio; (flashy) de oropel; llamativo, charro
meretriciousness *n* mal gusto, *m*
merge *vt* fundir; *com* fusionar; mezclar. *vi* fundirse; *com* fusionarse; mezclarse
merger *n* combinación, *f*; *com* fusión, *f*
meridian *n* (*geog ast*) meridiano, *m*; (noon) mediodía, *m*; (peak) apogeo, *m*
meringue *n* merengue, *m*, *Lat. Am.* espumilla, *f*
merino *a* de merino; merino. *n* (fabric and sheep) merino, *m*
merit *n* mérito, *m*, *vt* merecer, ser digno de
meritorious *a* meritorio
meritoriously *adv* merecidamente
meritoriousness *n* mérito, *m*
merlon *n* merlón, *m*, almena, *f*
mermaid *n* sirena, *f*
merrily *adv* alegremente
merriment *n* alegría, *f*; júbilo, *m*; regocijo, *m*; diversión, *f*; juego, *m*
merriness *n* alegría, *f*; regocijo, *m*; *inf* ebriedad, *f*
merry *a* alegre; jovial; feliz; regocijado, divertido; (tipsy) calamocano. **to make m.,** divertirse. **to make m. over,** reírse de. **M. Christmas!** ¡Felices Navidades! **m.-andrew,** bufón, *m*. **m.-go-round,** caballitos, *m pl*, tiovivo, *m*, *Lat. Am.* calesita, *f*. **m.-making,** festividades, fiestas, *f pl*
meseta *n* meseta, *f*
mesh *n* malla, *f*; *mech* engranaje, *m*; (network) red, *f*; (snare) lazo, *m*. *vt* coger con red; *mech* endentar
mesmerism *n* mesmerismo, *m*
mesmerize *vt* hipnotizar
mess *n* (of food) plato de comida, *m*; porción, ración, *f*; rancho, *m*; (mixture) mezcla, *f*; (disorder) desorden, *m*; suciedad, *f*; (failure) fracaso, *m*. *vt* (dirty) ensuciar; desordenar; (mismanage) echar a perder. **to be in a m.,** *inf* estar aviado. **to get in a m.,** *inf* hacerse un lío. **to make a m. of,** ensuciar; desordenar; (spoil) echarlo todo a rodar
message *n* mensaje, *m*; recado, *m*; (telegraphic) parte, *m*. **I have to take a m.,** Tengo que hacer un recado
messenger *n* mensajero (-ra); (of telegrams) repartidor, *m*; heraldo, *m*; anuncio, *m*
Messiah *n* Mesías, *m*
Messianic *a* mesiánico
messrs. *n pl* (abbreviation) sres. (from señores), *m pl*
metabolism *n* metabolismo, *m*
metabolize *va* metabolizar
metal *n* metal, *m*; vidrio en fusión, *m*; (road) grava, *f*; *her* metal, *m*; (mettle) temple, temperamento, *m*; brío, fuego, *m*; *pl* metals, (of a railway) rieles, *m pl*. **m. engraver,** grabador en metal, *m*. **m. polish,** limpiametales, *m*. **m. shavings,** cizallas, *f pl*. **m. work,** metalistería, *f*. **m. worker,** metalario, *m*
metallic *a* metálico
metalloid *n* metaloide, *m*
metallurgic *a* metalúrgico
metallurgist *n* metalúrgico, *m*
metallurgy *n* metalurgia, *f*
metamorphosis *n* metamorfosis, *f*
metaphor *n* metáfora, *f*
metaphorical *a* metafórico
metaphysical *a* metafísico
metaphysician *n* metafísico, *m*
metaphysics *n* metafísica, *f*
metathesis *n* metátesis, *f*
mete (out) *vt* repartir, distribuir
metempsychosis *n* metempsicosis, *f*
meteor *n* meteoro, *m*
meteoric *a* meteórico
meteorite *n* meteorito, *m*
meteorological *a* meteorológico
meteorologist *n* meteorologista, *mf*
meteorology *n* meteorología, *f*
meter *n* (for gas, etc.) contador, *m*; (verse and measure) metro, *m*
methane *n* metano, *m*
method *n* método, *m*; técnica, *f*; táctica, *f*
methodical *a* metódico; ordenado, sistemático
Methodism *n* metodismo, *m*
Methodist *n* metodista, *mf*
methyl *n* metilo, *m*. **m. alcohol,** alcohol metílico, *m*
methylated spirit *n* alcohol desnaturalizado, *m*
meticulous *a* meticuloso; minucioso
meticulously *adv* con meticulosidad
meticulousness *n* meticulosidad, *f*; minuciosidad, *f*
metric *a* métrico. **m. system,** sistema métrico, *m*
metrics *n* métrica, *f*
metronome *n* metrónomo, *m*
metropolis *n* metrópoli, *f*; capital, *f*
metropolitan *a* metropolitano; de la capital. *n ecc* metropolitano, *m*
mettle *n* temple, temperamento, *m*; fuego, brío, *m*; valor, *m*. **You have put him on his m.,** Le has picado en el amor propio
mew *n* (gull) gaviota, *f*; (of a cat) maullido, *m*; (of sea-birds) alarido, *m*. *vi* (of a cat) maullar; (of sea-birds) dar alaridos. **to mew up,** encerrar
mews *n* establos, *m pl*, caballeriza, *f*
Mexican *a* mejicano. *n* mejicano (-na)
Mexico Méjico, *m*
mezzanine *n* entresuelo, *m*
mezzosoprano *n* mezzo-soprano
mi *n mus* mi, *m*
miaow *n* miau, *m*, *vi* maullar
miasma *n* miasma, *m*
miasmatic *a* miasmático
mica *n* mica, *f*
microbe *n* microbio, *m*
microbial *a* microbiano
microbiologist *n* microbiólogo, *m*
microbiology *n* microbiología, *f*
microcosm *n* microcosmo, *m*
microphone *n* micrófono, *m*
microscope *n* microscopio, *m*
microscopic *a* microscópico
microwave *n* microonda, *f*
mid *a* medio. *prep* entre; en medio de; a mediados de. **from mid May to August,** desde mediados de mayo hasta agosto. **a mid-fourteenth century castle,** un castillo de mediados del siglo catorce. **in mid air,** en medio del aire. **in mid channel,** en medio del canal. **in mid winter,** en medio del invierno

midday *n* mediodía, *m*, *a* del mediodía, meridional. **at m.,** a mediodía
midden *n* muladar, *m*
middle *a* medio; en medio de; del centro; intermedio; (average) mediano. *n* medio, *m*; mitad, *f*; centro, *m*; (waist) cintura, *f*. **in the m. of,** en medio de. **in the m. of nowhere,** donde Cristo dio las tres voces. **toward the m. of the month,** a mediados del mes. **m. age,** edad madura, *f*. **m.-aged,** de edad madura, de cierta edad. **M. Ages,** edad media, *f*. **m. class,** clase media, burguesía, *f*, *a* de la clase media, burgués. **m. distance,** término medio, *m*. **m. ear,** oído medio, *m*. **m. finger,** dedo de en medio (or del corazón), *m*. **m. way,** *fig* término medio, *m*. **m. weight,** peso medio, *m*
Middle East, the el Oriente Medio, el Levante, *m*
middleman *n* agente de negocios, *m*; (retailer) revendedor, *m*; intermediario, *m*
middling *a* mediano; mediocre; regular, así, así
midge *n* mosquito, *m*, mosca de agua, *f*
midget *n* enano (-na). **m. submarine,** submarino de bolsillo, *m*
midnight *n* medianoche, *f*. *a* de medianoche; nocturno. **at m.,** a medianoche. **to burn the m. oil,** quemarse las cejas. **m. mass,** misa del gallo, *f*
midriff *n* diafragma, *m*
midship *a* maestro. *n* medio del buque, *m*. **m. beam,** bao maestro, *m*. **m. gangway,** crujía, *f*
midshipman *n* guardiamarina, *m*
midst *n* medio, *m*; seno, *m*, *prep* entre. **in the m. of,** en medio de. **There is a traitor in our m.,** Hay un traidor entre nosotros (or en nuestra compañía)
midstream, *n* **in m.** *m*. en medio de la corriente
midsummer *n* pleno verano, *m*; solsticio estival, *m*; fiesta de San Juan, *f*. **A M. Night's Dream,** El Sueño de la Noche de San Juan
midway *a* and *adv* situado a medio camino; a medio camino, a la mitad del camino; entre. *n* mitad del camino, *f*; medio, *m*. **m. between . . . ,** equidistante de . . . , entre
midwife *n* comadrona, partera, *f*
midwifery *n* obstetricia, *f*
midwinter *n* medio del invierno, *m*
mien *n* aire, *m*; porte, semblante, *m*
might *vi* poder. **It m. or m. not be true,** Podría o no podría ser verdad. **How happy Mary m. have been!** ¡Qué feliz pudo haber sido María! **I thought that you m. have seen him in the theater,** Creí que pudieras haberle visto en el teatro. **That I m. . . . !** ¡Que yo pudiese . . . ! **This m. have been avoided if . . .** Esto podía haberse evitado si . . .
might *n* fuerza, *f*; poder, *m*. **with m. and main,** con todas sus fuerzas
mightily *adv* fuertemente; poderosamente; *inf* muchísimo, sumamente
mightiness *n* fuerza, *f*; poder, *m*; grandeza, *f*
mighty *a* fuerte, vigoroso; poderoso; grande; *inf* enorme; (proud) arrogante. *adv inf* enormemente, muy
migraine *n* migraña, jaqueca, *f*
migrant *a* migratorio, de paso. *n* ave migratoria, ave de paso, *f*
migrate *vi* emigrar
migration *n* migración, *f*
migratory *a* migratorio, de paso; (of people) nómada, pasajero
migratory worker *n* trabajador golondrino, *m*
Milanese *a* milanés. *n* milanés (-esa)
milch *a f*, (of cows) lechera
mild *a* apacible, pacífico; manso; dulce; suave; (of the weather) blando; *med* benigno; (light) leve; (of drinks) ligero; (weak) débil
mildew *n* mildiu, añublo, *m*; moho, *m*. *vt* anublar; enmohecer. *vi* anublarse; enmohecerse
mildly *adv* suavemente; dulcemente; con indulgencia
mildness *n* apacibilidad, *f*; mansedumbre, *f*; suavidad, *f*; (of weather) blandura, *f*; dulzura, *f*; indulgencia, *f*; (weakness) debilidad, *f*
mile *n* milla, *f*
mileage *n* distancia en millas, *f*; kilometraje, *m*
milestone *n* hito, *m*, piedra miliaria, *f*; mojón kilométrico, *m*
milfoil *n* milenrama, *f*
militancy *n* carácter militante, *m*; belicosidad, *f*
militant *a* militante, combatiente; belicoso; agresivo. *n* combatiente, *mf*
militarily *adv* militarmente
militariness *n* lo militar, el carácter militar
militarism *n* militarismo, *m*
militarist *n* militarista, *mf*
militaristic *a* militarista
militarization *n* militarización, *f*
militarize *vt* militarizar
military *a* militar; de guerra. **the m.,** los militares. **m. academy,** colegio militar, *m*. **m. camp,** campo militar, *m*. **m. law,** código militar, *m*. **m. man,** militar, *m*. **m. police,** policía militar, *f*. **m. service,** servicio militar, *m*
militate (against) *vi* militar contra
militia *n* milicia, *f*
militiaman *n* miliciano, *m*
milk *n* leche, *f*. *a* de leche; lácteo. *vt* ordeñar. *vi* dar leche. **to have m. and water in one's veins,** tener sangre de horchata. **condensed m.,** leche condensada, leche en lata, *f*. **m.-can,** lechera, *f*. **m.-cart,** carro de la leche, *m*. **m. chocolate,** chocolate con leche, *m*. **m. of magnesia,** leche de magnesia, *f*. **m.-pail,** ordeñadero, *m*. **m.-tooth,** diente de leche, *m*. **m.-white,** blanco como la leche
milkiness *n* lactescencia, *f*; carácter lechoso, *m*; (whiteness) blancura, *f*
milking *n* ordeño, *m*. **m.-machine,** máquina ordeñadora, *f*. **m.-stool,** taburete, banquillo, *m*
milkmaid *n* lechera, *f*
milkman *n* lechero, *m*
milksop *n* marica, *m*
milky *a* lechero; de leche; lechoso, como leche; *ast* lácteo. **the Milky Way** la Vía láctea *f*
mill *n* molino, *m*; (for coffee, etc.) molinillo, *m*; (factory) fábrica, *f*; taller, *m*; (textile) hilandería, *f*; fábrica de tejidos, *f*; (fight) riña a puñetazos, *f*; pugilato, *m*. *vt* (grind) moler; (coins) acordonar; (cloth) abatanar; (chocolate) batir. **cotton m.,** hilandería de algodón, *f*. **hand-m.,** molinillo, *m*. **paper-m.,** fábrica de papel, *f*. **saw-m.,** serrería, *f*. **spinning m.,** hilandería, *f*. **water m.,** molino de agua, *m*. **m.-course,** saetín, canal de molino, *m*. **m.-dam,** esclusa de molino, *f*. **m.-hand,** obrero (-ra). **m.-pond,** cubo, *m*. **m.-race,** caz, *m*. **m.-wheel,** rueda de molino, *f*
millennial *a* milenario
millennium *n* milenario, *m*
miller *n* molinero, *m*. **miller's wife,** molinera
millet *n* mijo, *m*
milligram *n* miligramo, *m*
milliliter *n* mililitro, *m*
millimeter *n* milímetro, *m*
milliner *n* sombrerero (-ra), modista, *mf* **milliner's shop,** sombrerería, tienda de modista, *f*
millinery *n* sombreros, *m pl*; modas, *f pl*; tienda de modista, *f*
milling *n* molienda, *f*; acuñación, *f*; (edge of coin) cordoncillo, *m*. **m. machine,** fresadora, *f*
million *n* millón, *m*. **the m.,** las masas
millionaire *a* millonario. *n* millonario, *m*
millionairess *n* millonaria, *f*
millionth *a* millonésimo
millstone *n* piedra de moler, muela, *f*
mime *n* (Greek farce and actor) mimo, *m*; (mimicry) mímica, *f*; pantomima, *f*. *vi* hacer en pantomima
mimetic *a* mímico, imitativo
mimic *a* mímico; (pretended) fingido. *n* imitador (-ra). *vt* imitar, contrahacer; *biol* imitar, adaptarse a
mimicry *n* mímica, imitación, *f*; *biol* mimetismo, *m*

minaret *n* minarete, *m;* (of a mosque) alminar, *m*
minatory *a* amenazador
mince *vt* desmenuzar; (meat) picar; (words) medir (las palabras). *vi* andar con pasos menuditos; andar o moverse con afectación; hacer remilgos. **m.-meat,** carne picada, *f;* (sweet) conserva de fruta y especias, *f*
mincing *a* afectado. *n* acción de picar carne, *f.* **m. machine,** máquina de picar carne, *f*
mincingly *adv* con afectación; con pasos menuditos
mind *n* inteligencia, *f;* espíritu ánimo, *m;* imaginación, *f;* alma, *f;* (memory) memoria, *f,* recuerdo, *m;* (understanding) entendimiento, *m;* (genius) ingenio, *m;* (cast of mind) mentalidad, *f;* (opinion) opinión, *f;* (liking) gusto, *m;* (thoughts) pensamiento, *m;* (intention) propósito, *m,* intención, *f;* (tendency) propensión, inclinación, *f.* **I have a good m. to go away,** Por poco me marcho; Tengo ganas de marcharme. **I have changed my m.,** He cambiado de opinión. **out of m.,** olvidado. **I shall give him a piece of my m.,** Le diré cuatro verdades. **It had quite gone out of my m.,** Lo había olvidado completamente. **I can see it in my mind's eye,** Está presente a mi imaginación. **I shall bear it in m.,** Lo tendré en cuenta. **I thought in my own m. that . . . ,** Pensé por mis adentros que . . . **We are both of the same m.,** Ambos somos de la misma opinión. **to be out of one's m.,** estar fuera de juicio. **to call to m.,** acordarse de. **to have something on one's m.,** estar preocupado. **to make up one's m. (to),** resolverse (a), decidirse (a), determinar; animarse (a). **m.-reader,** adivinador (-ra) del pensamiento
mind *vt* (remember) recordar, no olvidar; (heed) atender a; hacer caso de; tener cuidado de; (fear) tener miedo de; (obey) obedecer; preocuparse de; (object to) molestar; importar; (care for) cuidar. *vi* tener cuidado; molestar; (feel) sentir; (fear) tener miedo; (be the same thing) ser igual. **Do you m. being quiet a moment?** ¿Quieres hacer el favor de callarte un momento? **Do you m. if I smoke?** ¿Le molesta si fumo? **They don't m.,** No les importa, Les da igual. **Never m.!** ¡No se moleste!; ¡No se preocupe!; ¡No importa! ¡Vaya! **M. what you are doing!** ¡Cuidado con lo que haces! **M. your own business!** ¡No te metas donde no te llaman!
minded *a* dispuesto, inclinado; de . . . pensamientos; de . . . disposición
mindful *a* atento (a), cuidadoso (de); que se acuerda (de)
mine *a poss* mío, *m,* (mía, *f;* míos, *m pl;* mías, *f pl*); el mío, *m,* (la mía, *f;* lo mío, *neut;* los míos, *m pl;* las mías, *f pl*); mi (*pl* mis). **a friend of m.,** un amigo mío; uno de mis amigos
mine *n* mina, *f. vt* minar; extraer; sembrar minas en, colocar minas en. *vi* minar; hacer una mina; dedicarse a la minería. **drifting m.,** mina a la deriva, *f.* **land m.,** mina terrestre, *f.* **magnetic m.,** mina magnética, *f.* **to lay mines,** colocar (or sembrar) minas. **m.-sweeper,** dragaminas, buque barreminas, *m*
minefield *n* campo de minas, *m;* barrera de minas, *f*
minelayer *n* barca plantaminas, *f,* barco siembraminas, lanzaminas, *m*
miner *n* minero, *m; mil* zapador minador, *m*
mineral *n* mineral, *m, a* mineral. **m. baths,** baños, *m pl.* **m. water,** agua mineral, *f;* gaseosa, *f*
mineralogical *a* mineralógico
mineralogist *n* mineralogista, *m*
mineralogy *n* mineralogía, *f*
mingle *vt* mezclar; confundir. *vi* mezclarse; confundirse
mingling *n* mezcla, *f*
miniature *n* miniatura, *f. a* en miniatura. **m. edition,** edición diamante, *f*
miniature golf *n* minigolf, *m*
miniaturist *n* miniaturista, *mf*
minibus *n* micro, microbús, *Mexico* combi, *m*
minimize *vt* aminorar, reducir al mínimo; mitigar; (underrate) tener en menos, despreciar
minimum *n* mínimo, *m, a* mínimo
mining *n* minería, *f, a* minero; de mina; de minas; de minero. **m. engineer,** ingeniero de minas, *m*
minion *n* favorito (-ta); satélite, *m; print* miñona, *f*
minister *n* ministro, *m. vi* servir; suministrar, proveer de; (contribute) contribuir (a). **m. of health,** ministro de sanidad, *m.* **m. of war,** ministro de la guerra, *m*
ministration *n ecc* ministerio, *m;* servicio, *m;* agencia, *f*
ministry *n* ministerio, *m.* **m. of food,** Ministerio de Abastecimientos, *m*
mink *n* visón, *m*
minnow *n* pez pequeño de agua dulce, *m*
minor *a* menor. *n* menor de edad, *m;* (logic) menor, *f; mus* tono menor, *m; ecc* menor, *m.* **to be a m.,** ser menor de edad. **m. key,** tono menor, *m.* **m. orders,** *ecc* órdenes menores, *f pl.* **m. scale,** escala menor, *f*
Minorca Menorca, *f*
minority *n* minoría, *f;* (of age) minoridad, *f.* **in the m.,** en la minoría
minster *n* catedral, *f;* monasterio, *m*
minstrel *n* trovador, juglar, *m;* músico, *m;* cantante, *m*
minstrelsy *n* música, *f;* canto, *m;* arte del trovador, *m,* or *f;* gaya ciencia, *f*
mint *n bot* menta, hierbabuena, *f;* casa de moneda, casa de la moneda, ceca, *f; fig* mina, *f;* (source) origen, *m. vt* (money) acuñar; *fig* inventar, *a* (postage stamp) en estado nuevo
minter *n* acuñador, *m; fig* inventor (-ra)
minting *n* (of coins) acuñación, *f; fig* invención, *f*
minuet *n* minué, *m*
minus *a* menos; negativo; desprovisto de; sin. *n* signo menos, *m;* cantidad negativa, *f*
minute *a* menudo, diminuto; insignificante; minucioso
minute *n* minuto, *m;* momento, *m;* instante, *m;* (note) minuta, *f; pl* **minutes,** actas, *f pl.* **in a m.,** en un instante. **m.-book,** libro de actas, minutario, *m.* **m.-hand,** minutero, *m*
minutely *adv* minuciosamente; en detalle; exactamente
minuteness *n* suma pequeñez, *f;* minuciosidad, *f*
minx *n* picaruela, *f;* coqueta, *f*
miracle *n* milagro, *m.* **m.-monger,** milagrero (-ra). **m. play,** milagro, *m*
miraculous *a* milagroso
miraculously *adv* milagrosamente, por milagro
miraculousness *n* carácter milagroso, *m,* lo milagroso
mirage *n* espejismo, *m*
mire *n* fango, lodo, *m;* (miry place) lodazal, *m*
mirror *n* espejo, *m. vt* reflejar. **to look in the m.,** mirarse al espejo. **full-length m.,** espejo de cuerpo entero, *m.* **small m.,** espejuelo, *m*
mirth *n* alegría, *f,* júbilo, *m;* risa, *f;* hilaridad, *f*
mirthful *a* alegre
mirthless *a* sin alegría, triste
miry *a* lodoso, fangoso, cenagoso
misadventure *n* desgracia, *f;* accidente, *m*
misanthrope *n* misántropo, *m*
misanthropic *a* misantrópico
misanthropy *n* misantropía, *f*
misapplication *n* mala aplicación, *f;* mal uso, *m;* abuso, *m*
misapply *vt* aplicar mal; hacer mal uso de; abusar de
misapprehend *vt* comprender mal; equivocarse sobre
misapprehension *n* concepto erróneo, *m;* equivocación, *f,* error, *m*
misappropriate *vt* malversar
misappropriation *n* malversación, *f*
misbehave *vi* portarse mal; (of a child) ser malo
misbehavior *n* mala conducta, *f*
miscalculate *vt* calcular mal; engañarse (sobre)
miscalculation *n* mal cálculo, error, *m;* desacierto, *m*
miscall *vt* mal nombrar; llamar equivocadamente; (abuse) insultar
miscarriage *n med* aborto, *m;* (failure) malogro, fracaso, *m;* (of goods) extravío, *m*

miscarriage of justice *n* yerro en la administración de la justicia, *m*
miscarry *vi med* abortar, malparir; (fail) malograrse, frustrarse; (of goods) extraviarse
miscellaneous *a* misceláneo; vario, diverso
miscellany *n* miscelánea, *f*
mischance *n* mala suerte, *f;* infortunio, *m,* desgracia, *f;* accidente, *m*
mischief *n* daño, *m;* mal, *m;* (wilfulness) travesura, *f;* (person) diablillo, *m.* **m.-maker,** enredador (-ra), chismoso (-sa); alborotador, *m;* malicioso (-sa). **m.-making,** *a* enredador; chismoso; malicioso; alborotador
mischievous *a* dañino, perjudicial, malo; malicioso; chismoso; (wilful) travieso; juguetón; (of glances, etc.) malicioso
mischievously *adv* maliciosamente; con (or por) travesura
mischievousness *n* mal, *m;* malicia, *f;* maleficencia, *f;* travesura, *f*
misconceive *vt* formar un concepto erróneo de; concebir mal, juzgar mal
misconception *n* concepto erróneo, *m,* idea falsa, *f;* error, *m,* equivocación, *f;* engaño, *m*
misconduct *n* mala conducta, *f.* **to m. oneself,** portarse mal
misconstruction *n* mala interpretación, *f;* falsa interpretación, *f;* tergiversación, *f;* mala traducción, *f*
misconstrue *vt* interpretar mal; entender mal; tergiversar; traducir mal
miscount *vt* contar mal, equivocarse en la cuenta de; calcular mal. *n* error, *m;* yerro de cuenta, *m*
miscreant *n* malandrín, *m;* bribón, *m, a* vil, malandrín
misdeed *n* delito, malhecho, crimen, *m*
misdemeanor *n* mala conducta, *f; law* delito, *m;* ofensa, *f,* malhecho, *m*
misdirect *vt* informar mal (acerca del camino); (a letter) dirigir mal, poner unas señas incorrectas en
miser *n* avaro (-ra)
miserable *a* infeliz, desgraciado; miserable; despreciable; sin valor
miserably *adv* miserablemente
miserliness *n* avaricia, tacañería, *f*
miserly *a* avaro, tacaño
misery *n* miseria, *f;* sufrimiento, *m;* dolor, tormento, *m*
misfire *vi* no dar fuego; (of a motor-car, etc.) hacer falsas explosiones, errar el encendido
misfit *n* traje que no cae bien, *m;* zapato que no va bien, *m;* (person) inadaptado, *m*
misfortune *n* infortunio, *m,* mala suerte, adversidad, *f;* desdicha, desgracia, *f;* mal, *m*
misgive *vt* hacer temer; llenar de duda; hacer recelar; hacer presentir
misgiving *n* temor, *m;* duda, *f;* recelo, *m;* presentimiento, *m*
misgovern *vt* gobernar mal; administrar mal; dirigir mal
misgovernment *n* desgobierno, *m;* mala administración, *f*
misguided *a* mal dirigido; extraviado; engañado; (blind) ciego
misguidedly *adv* equivocadamente
mishap *n* desgracia, *f;* contratiempo, accidente, *m.* **to have a m.,** sufrir una desgracia; tener un accidente
misinform *vt* informar mal; dar informes erróneos (a)
misinformation *n* noticia falsa, *f;* información errónea, *f*
misinterpret *vt* interpretar mal; entender mal; torcer; tergiversar; traducir mal
misinterpretation *n* mala interpretación, *f;* interpretación falsa, *f;* tergiversación, *f;* mala traducción, *f*
misjudge *vt* juzgar mal; equivocarse (en or sobre); tener una idea falsa de
misjudgment *n* juicio errado, *m;* idea falsa, *f;* juicio injusto, *m*
mislay *vt* extraviar, perder
mislead *vt* extraviar; llevar a conclusiones erróneas, despistar; engañar
misleading *a* de falsas apariencias; erróneo, falso; engañoso
mismanage *vt* administrar mal; dirigir mal; echar a perder
mismanagement *n* mala administración, *f;* desgobierno, *m*
misname *vt* mal nombrar; llamar equivocadamente
misnomer *n* nombre equivocado, *m;* nombre inapropiado, *m*
misogynist *n* misógino, *m*
misogyny *n* misoginia, *f*
misplace *vt* colocar mal; poner fuera de lugar
misplaced *a* mal puesto; inoportuno; equivocado
misprint *n* error de imprenta, *m,* errata, *f, vt* imprimir con erratas
mispronounce *vt* pronunciar mal
mispronunciation *n* mala pronunciación, *f*
misquotation *n* cita errónea, *f*
misquote *vt* citar mal, citar erróneamente
misrepresent *vt* desfigurar; tergiversar; falsificar
misrepresentation *n* desfiguración, *f;* tergiversación, *f;* falsificación, *f*
misrule *vt* gobernar mal. *n* mal gobierno, desgobierno, *m;* confusión, *f*
miss *n* señorita, *f*
miss *vt* (one's aim) errar (el tiro, etc.); no acertar (a); (let fall) dejar caer; (lose a train, the post, etc., one's footing, an opportunity, etc.) perder; (fall short of) dejar de; no ver; no notar; pasar por alto de; omitir; echar de menos; notar la falta de; no encontrar. *vi* errar; (fail) salir mal, fracasar. **I m. you,** Te echo de menos. **to be missing,** faltar; estar ausente; haberse marchado; haber desaparecido. **to m. one's mark,** errar el blanco. **to m. out,** omitir, pasar por alto de. **She doesn't miss a beat,** (fig.) No se le escapa nada
missal *n* misal, *m*
misshapen *a* deforme
missile *n* arma arrojadiza, *f;* proyectil, *m*
missing *a* que falta; perdido; ausente; *mil* desaparecido
mission *n* misión, *f*
missionary *n* misionero, *m*
missionize *vi* misionar
missis *n* señora, *f; inf* mujer, *f*
Mississippi el Misisipí, *m*
missive *n* misiva, *f*
Missouri el Misuri, *m*
misspend *vt* malgastar; desperdiciar; perder
mist *n* bruma, neblina, *f;* vapor, *m;* (drizzle) llovizna, *f; fig* nube, *f. vt* anublar, empañar. *vi* lloviznar
mistakable *a* confundible
mistake *vt* comprender mal; equivocarse sobre; errar; (with for) confundir con, equivocarse con. *n* equivocación, *f;* error, *m;* inadvertencia, *f;* (in an exercise, etc.) falta, *f.* **And no m.!** *inf* Sin duda alguna. **by m.,** por equivocación; (involuntarily) sin querer. **If I am not mistaken,** Si no me engaño, Si no estoy equivocado. **to make a m.,** equivocarse
mistaken *a* (of persons and things) equivocado; (of things) erróneo; incorrecto
mistakenly *adv* equivocadamente; injustamente, falsamente
mister *n* señor, *m*
mistily *adv* a través de la neblina; obscuramente; indistintamente, vagamente
mistimed *a* intempestivo; inoportuno
mistiness *n* neblina, bruma, *f;* vaporosidad, *f;* obscuridad, *f*
mistletoe *n* muérdago, *m*
mistranslate *vt* traducir mal; interpretar mal
mistranslation *n* mala traducción, *f;* traducción inexacta, *f*
mistress *n* señora, *f;* maestra, *f;* (fiancée) prometida, *f;* (beloved) amada, dulce dueña, *f;* (concubine) amiga,

querida, *f*. **M. (Mrs.) Gómez,** Sra Gómez. **m. of the robes,** camarera mayor, *f*
mistrust *vt* desconfiar de, no tener confianza en; dudar de. *n* desconfianza, *f*; recelo, *m*, suspicacia, *f*; aprensión, *f*
mistrustful *a* desconfiado; receloso, suspicaz. **to be m. of,** recelarse de
misty *a* brumoso, nebuloso; vaporoso; (of the eyes) anublado; (of windows, etc.) empañado
misunderstand *vt* comprender mal; tomar en sentido erróneo; interpretar mal
misunderstanding *n* concepto erróneo, error, *m*; equivocación, *f*; (disagreement) desavenencia, *f*
misuse *vt* emplear mal; abusar de; (funds) malversar; (ill-treat) tratar mal. *n* abuso, *m*; (of funds) malversación, *f*
mite *n* (coin) ardite, *m*; (trifle) pizca, *f*; óbolo, *m*; *ent* ácaro, *m*
miter *n* mitra, *f*; *carp* inglete, *m*, *vt carp* cortar ingletes en
mitigate *vt* (pain) aliviar; mitigar; suavizar
mitigation *n* (of pain) alivio, *m*; mitigación, *f*
mitten *n* mitón, *m*
mix *vt* mezclar; (salad) aderezar; (concrete, etc.) amasar; combinar, unir; (sociably) alternar (con); (confuse) confundir. *vi* mezclarse; frecuentar la compañía (de); frecuentar; (get on well) llevarse bien
mixed *a* mezclado; vario, surtido; mixto; (confused) confuso. **m. doubles,** parejas mixtas, *f pl*. **m. up,** (in disorder) revuelto; confuso. **m. up with,** implicado en; asociado con
mixer *n* mezclador, *m*; (person) mezclador (-ra); *inf* persona sociable, *f*. **electric m.,** mezclador eléctrico, *m*
mixture *n* mezcla, *f*; (medicine) poción, medicina, *f*
mizzen *n* mesana, *f*. **m.-mast,** palo de mesana, *m*. **m.-sail,** vela de mesana, *f*. **m.-topsail,** sobremesana, *f*
mnemonics *n* mnemotecnia, *f*
Moabite *n* moabita, *mf*
moan *vt* lamentar; llorar. *vi* gemir; quejarse, lamentarse. *n* gemido, *m*; lamento, *m*; quejido, *m*
moaning *n* gemidos, *m pl*
moat *n* foso, *m*
mob *n* (crowd) muchedumbre, multitud, *f*; (rabble) populacho, *m*, gentuza, *f*. *vt* atropellar; atacar. **mob-cap,** cofia, *f*
mobile *a* móvil; ambulante; (fickle) voluble. **m. canteen,** cantina ambulante, *f*
mobility *n* movilidad, *f*
mobilization *n* movilización, *f*
mobilize *vt* movilizar. *vi* movilizarse
moccasin *n* mocasín, *m*
mocha *n* café de Moca, *m*
mock *vt* ridiculizar; burlarse (de), mofarse (de); (cause to fail) frustrar; (mimic) imitar; (delude) engañar. *vi* mofarse, burlarse, reírse. *a* cómico, burlesco; falso; fingido; imitado. **to make a m. of,** poner en ridículo; hacer absurdo; burlarse de. **m.-heroic,** heroicocómico. **m.-orange,** *bot* jeringuilla, *f*. **m.-turtle soup,** sopa hecha con cabeza de ternera a imitación de tortuga, *f*
mocker *n* mofador (-ra); el, *m*, (*f*, la) que se burla de
mockery *n* mofa, burla, *f*; ridículo, *m*; ilusión, apariencia, *f*. **to make a m. of,** mofarse de; hacer ridículo
mocking *a* burlón. **m. bird,** pájaro burlón, *m*
mockingly *adv* burlonamente
modality *n* modalidad, *f*
mode *n* modo, *m*; manera, *f*; (fashion) moda, *f*; uso, *m*, costumbre, *f*
model *n* modelo, *m*; (artist's) modelo vivo, *m*, *a* modelo; en miniatura. *vt* modelar; moldear; formar; hacer; planear. **m. display,** (hats, etc.) exposición de modelos, *f*. **m. railway,** ferrocarril en miniatura, *m*
modeler *n* modelador (-ra); disenador, *m*
modeling *n* modelado, *m*; modelo, *m*. **m. wax,** cera para moldear, *f*
moderate *a* moderado; (of prices, etc.) módico; (fair, medium) regular, mediano; razonable; mediocre. *n* moderado, *m*. *vt* moderar; modificar; calmar. *vi* moderarse; calmarse
moderately *adv* moderadamente; módicamente; medianamente; bastante; razonablemente; mediocremente
moderation *n* moderación, *f*. **in m.,** en moderación
moderator *n* moderador, *m*; (Church of Scotland) presidente, *m*; *univ* examinador, *m*; *univ* inspector de exámenes, *m*. **m. lamp,** lámpara de regulador, *f*
modern *a* moderno. *n* modernista, *mf*. **in the m. way,** a la moderna. **m. language,** lengua viva, *f*
modernism *n* modernismo, *m*
modernist *n* modernista, *mf*
modernistic *a* modernista
modernity *n* modernidad, *f*
modernization *n* modernización, *f*
modernize *vt* modernizar
modernness *n* modernidad, *f*
modest *a* modesto; (of a woman) púdico
modesty *n* modestia, *f*; (of a woman) pudor, *m*
modicum *n* porción pequeña, *f*; poco, *m*
modifiable *a* modificable
modification *n* modificación, *f*
modify *vt* modificar. **It has been much modified,** Se ha modificado mucho; Se han hecho muchas modificaciones
modifying *a* modificante, modificador
modish *a* de moda en boga; elegante
modishness *n* elegancia, *f*
modiste *n* modista, *mf*
modulate *vt* and *vi* modular
modulation *n* modulación, *f*
modus vivendi *n* modo de conveniencia, *m*
Mogul *a* mogol. *n* mogol (-la). **the Great M.,** el Gran Mogol
Mohammedan *a* mahometano, agareno
Mohammedanism *n* mahometismo, *m*
Mohican *n* mohican, *m*
moiety *n* mitad, *f*
moiré *n* muaré, *m*
moist *a* húmedo
moisten *vt* humedecer, mojar
moisture *n* humedad, *f*
molar *n* muela, *f*, *a* molar
molasses *n pl* melaza, *f*
mold *n* (fungus) moho, *m*; (humus) mantillo, *m*; (iron-mould) mancha de orín, *f*; (matrix) molde, *m*, matriz, *f*; *cul* cubilete, *m*; *naut* gálibo, *m*; (for jelly, etc.) molde, *m*; *arch* moldura, *f*; (temperament) temple, *m*, disposición, *f*. *vt* moldear; (cast) vaciar; *carp* moldurar; *naut* galibar; *fig* amoldar, formar; *agr* cubrir con mantillo. **to m. oneself on,** modelarse sobre. **m.-board,** (of a plough) orejera, *f*
Moldavian *a* moldavo. *n* moldavo (-va)
molder *n* moldeador, *m*; *fig* amolador (-ra); creador (-ra). *vi* desmoronarse, convertirse en polvo; *fig* decaer, desmoronarse; vegetar
moldiness *n* moho, *m*
molding *n* amoldamiento, *m*; vaciado, *m*; *arch* moldura, *f*; *fig* formación,
moldy *a* mohoso, enmohecido; *fig* anticuado
mole *n* (animal) topo, *m*; (spot) lunar, *m*; (breakwater) dique, malecón, *m*; muelle, *m*
molecular *a* molecular
molecule *n* molécula, *f*
molehill *n* topera, *f*
moleskin *n* piel de topo, *f*
molest *vt* molestar; perseguir, importunar; faltar al respeto (a)
molestation *n* importunidad, persecución, *f*; molestia, incomodidad, *f*
mollification *n* apaciguamiento, *m*; mitigación, *f*
mollify *vt* apaciguar, calmar; mitigar
mollusk *n* molusco, *m*
mollycoddle *n* alfeñique, mírame y no me toques, *m*; niño (-ña), mimado (-da)

Moloch *n* Moloc, *m*
molt *vi* mudar, *n* muda, *f*
molten *a* fundido; derretido
Moluccas, the las Malucas, *f pl*
moment *n* momento, *m*; instante *m*; (importance) importancia, *f*. **at this m.,** en este momento. **Do it this m.!** ¡Hazlo al instante (or en seguida)!
momentarily *adv* momentáneamente; cada momento
momentariness *n* momentaneidad, *f*
momentary *a* momentáneo
momentous *a* de suma importancia; crítico; grave
momentousness *n* importancia, *f*; gravedad, *f*
momentum *n* momento, *m*, velocidad adquirida *f*; *fig* ímpetu, *m*. **to gather m.,** cobrar velocidad, acelerar
monarch *n* monarca, *m*
monarchic *a* monárquico
monarchism *n* monarquismo, *m*
monarchist *n* monárquico (-ca)
monarchy *n* monarquía, *f*
monastery *n* monasterio, *m*
monastic *a* monástico. **m. life,** vida de clausura, *f*
monasticism *n* vida monástica, *f*
Monday *n* lunes, *m*
monetary *a* monetario
monetization *n* monetización, *f*
money *n* dinero, *m*; (coin) moneda, *f*; sistema monetario, *m*. **paper m.,** papel moneda, *m*. **ready m.,** dinero contante, *m*. **to make m.,** ganar (or hacer) dinero; enriquecerse. **M. talks,** Poderoso caballero es Don Dinero. **m.-bag,** talega, *f*; (person) ricacho (-cha). **m.-bags,** riqueza, *f*. **m.-box,** alcancía, hucha, *f*. **m.-changer,** cambista, *mf* **m.-lender,** prestamista, *mf* **m.-making,** *n* el hacer dinero; prosperidad, ganancia, *f*. *a* lucrativo, *Lat. Am.* libranza de correos, libranza postal, *f*. **m.-order,** giro postal, *m* (postal)
moneyed *a* adinerado; acomodado
mongoose *n* mangosta, *f*
mongrel *a* mestizo, atravesado. *n* perro mestizo, *m*; (in contempt) mestizo. *m*
monitor *n* monitor, *m*
monitory *a* monitorio. *n ecc* monitorio, *m*
monk *n* monje, *m*. **to become a m.,** hacerse monje, tomar el hábito. **monk's-hood,** acónito, *m*
monkey *n* mono (-na); (imp) diablillo, *m*; (of a piledriver) pilón de martinete, *m*; (in glass-making) crisol, *m*. **to m. with,** meterse con; entremeterse. **m. nut,** cacahuete, *m*. **m.-puzzle,** (tree) araucaria, *f*. **m. tricks,** monadas, travesuras, diabluras, *f pl*. **m.-wrench,** llave inglesa, *f*
monkish *a* monacal, de monje; monástico
monochromatic *a* monocromo
monochrome *n* monocromo, *m*
monocle *n* monóculo, *m*
monogamist *n* monógamo (-ma)
monogamous *a* monógamo
monogamy *n* monogamia, *f*
monogram *n* monograma, *m*
monograph *n* monografía, *f*, opúsculo, *m*
monolith *n* monolito, *m*
monolithic *a* monolítico
monologue *n* monólogo, *m*
monomania *n* monomanía, *f*
monomaniac *n* monomaníaco (-ca)
monomial *n* monomio, *m*, *a* de un solo término
monoplane *n* monoplano, *m*
monopolist *n* monopolista, *mf*; acaparador (-ra)
monopolization *n* monopolio, *m*
monopolize *vt* monopolizar
monopoly *n* monopolio, *m*
monotheism *n* monoteísmo, *m*
monotheist *n* monoteísta, *mf*
monotone *n* monotonía, *f*
monotonous *a* monótono
monotony *n* monotonía, *f*
monoxide *n* monóxido, *m*
Monroe doctrine *n* monroísmo, *m*
monseigneur *n* monseñor, *m*
monsoon *n* monzón, *mf*
monster *n* monstruo, *m*
monstrance *n* custodia, *f*
monstrosity *n* monstruosidad, *f*
monstrous *a* monstruoso; horrible, atroz; enorme
montage *n* montaje, *m*
month *n* mes, *m*. **He arrived a m. ago,** Llegó hace un mes. **a m. later** *Lat. Am.* al mes
monthly *a* mensual. *adv* mensualmente, cada mes. *n* revista (or publicación) mensual, *f*; *pl* **monthlies,** menstruación, regla, *f*. **m. salary** or **payment,** mensualidad, *f*
monument *n* monumento, *m*
monumental *a* monumental
moo *vi* (of cattle) mugir. *n* mugido, *m*
mood *n* humor, *m*; espíritu, *m*; *gram* modo, *m*
moodily *adv* taciturnamente; tristemente, pensativamente
moodiness *n* mal humor, *m*, taciturnidad, *f*; melancolía, tristeza, *f*
moody *a* taciturno, de mal humor; triste, melancólico, pensativo
mooing *n* (of cattle) mugido, *m*
moon *n* luna, *f*; satélite, *m*; mes lunar, *m*; luz de la luna, *f*. **full m.,** plenilunio, *m*; luna llena, *f*. **new m.,** novilunio, *m*, luna nueva, *f*
moonbeam *n* rayo de luna, *m*
moonless *a* sin luna
moonlight *n* luz de la luna, *f*. **in the m.,** a la luz de la luna. **to do a m. flit,** *inf* mudarse por el aire
moonlighting *n* el pluriempleo, *m*
moonlit *a* iluminado por la luna. **moonlit night,** noche de luna, *f*
moonshine *n* claridad de la luna, *f*; *fig* música celestial, ilusión, *f*
moonstone *n* adularia, *f*
moonstruck *a* lunático
Moor *n* moro (-ra)
moor *n* páramo, brezal, *m*; (marsh) pantano, *m*; (for game) coto, *m*. *vt* amarrar, aferrar; afirmar con anclas o cables. **m.-hen,** polla de agua, *f*
mooring *n* amarre, *m*. **m.-mast,** *aer* poste de amarre, *m*
moorings *n pl* amarradero, *m*
Moorish *a* moro; árabe. **M. architecture,** arquitectura árabe, *f*. **M. girl,** mora, *f*
moorland *n* páramo, brezal, *m*
moose *n* anta, *f*
moot *n* junta, *f*; ayuntamiento, *m*. *a* discutible. *vt* (bring up) suscitar; (discuss) discutir, debatir
mop *n* (implement) trapeador, *m*, *Ecuador*, escoba con fleco, *f*, *elsewhere in Lat. Am.* lampazo, *m*; (of hair) mata (de pelo), *f*. *vt* trapear *Ecuador*; (dry) enjugar, secar. **to mop up,** *inf* limpiar; *mil* acabar con (el enemigo)
mope *vi* replace by tristear. **to m. about,** vagar tristemente
moquette *n* moqueta, *f*
moral *a* moral; (chaste) casto, virtuoso; honrado. *n* (maxim) moraleja, *f*; *pl* **morals,** moralidad, *f*; ética, *f*; moral, *f*; (conduct) costumbres, *f pl*. **m. philosophy,** filosofía moral, *f*. **m. support,** apoyo moral, *m*. **m. tale,** apólogo, *m*
morale *n* moral, *f*
moralist *n* moralista, *m*
morality *n* moralidad, *f*; virtud, *f*; castidad, *f*. **m. play,** moralidad, *f*, drama alegórico, *m*
moralization *n* moralización, *f*
moralize *vt* and *vi* moralizar
moralizer *n* moralizador (-ra)
moralizing *a* moralizador
morally *adv* moralmente
morals. See **moral**
morass *n* marisma, ciénaga, *f*
moratorium *n* moratoria, *f*
Moravian *a* moravo. *n* moravo (-va)
morbid *a* mórbido, mórboso; (of the mind, etc.) insano

morbidezza *n* (*art* and *lit*) morbidez, *f*
morbidity *n* morbidez, *f*
mordacity *n* mordacidad, *f*
mordant *a* mordaz; (of acid) mordiente. *n* mordiente, *m*
more *a* and *adv* más. **The m. he earns, the less he saves,** Cuanto más gana, menos ahorra. **the m. the better,** cuanto más, tanto mejor. **without m. ado,** sin más ni más; sin decir nada. **Would you like some m.?** ¿Quiere Vd. más? (of food) ¿Quiere Vd. repetir? **no m.,** no más; (never) nunca más; (finished) se acabó. **once m.,** otra vez, una vez más. **m. and m.,** cada vez más, más y más. **m. or less,** más o menos; (about) poco más o menos
moreover *adv* además, también; por otra parte
morganatic *a* morganático
morgue *n* depósito de cadáveres, *m*
moribund *a* moribundo
Mormon *a* mormónico. *n* mormón (-ona)
Mormonism *n* mormonismo, *m*
morning *n* mañana, *f*, *a* matutino, de la mañana. **Good m.!** ¡Buenos días! **the next m.,** la mañana siguiente. **very early in the m.,** muy de mañana. **m. coat,** chaqué, *m*. **m. dew,** rocío de la mañana, *m*. **m. paper,** periódico de la mañana, *m*. **m. star,** lucero del alba, *m*. **m. suit,** chaqué, *m*
Moroccan *a* marroquí, marrueco. *n* marrueco (-ca), marroquí, *mf*
Morocco Marruecos, *m*
morocco *n* (leather) marroquí, tafilete, *m*
morose *a* sombrío, taciturno, malhumorado
morosely *adv* taciturnamente
moroseness *n* taciturnidad, *f*; mal humor, *m*
morphia, morphine *n* morfina, *f*. **m. addict,** morfinómano (-na)
morrow *n* mañana, *f*; día siguiente, *m*
Morse code *n* la clave telegráfica de Morse, *f*, el alfabeto de Morse, *m*
morsel *n* pedazo, *m*; (mouthful) bocado, *m*
mortal *a* mortal. *n* mortal, *mf*. **m. sin,** pecado mortal, pecado capital, *m*
mortality *n* mortalidad, *f*
mortally wounded *adv* herido de muerte
mortar *n* (for building) argamasa, *f*; (for mixing and *mil*) mortero, *m*. **m. and pestle,** mortero y majador, *m*. **m.-board,** (in building) cuezo, *m*; (academic cap) birrete, *m*
mortgage *n* hipoteca, *f*. *vt* hipotecar. *a* hipotecario. **to pay off a m.,** redimir una hipoteca
mortgageable *a* hipotecable
mortgaged debt *n* deuda garantizada con una hipoteca, *f*
mortgagee *n* acreedor (-ra) hipotecario (-ia)
mortgagor *n* deudor (-ra) hipotecario (-ia)
mortification *n* mortificación, *f*; humillación, *f*; *med* gangrena, *f*
mortify *vt* mortificar; humillar. *vi med* gangrenarse
mortifying *a* humillante
mortise *n* muesca, *f*. *vt* hacer muescas (en); ensamblar
mortuary *a* mortuorio. *n* depósito de cadáveres, *m*
Mosaic *a* mosaico
mosaic *n* mosaico, *m*
Moscow Moscú, *m*
mosque *n* mezquita, *f*
mosquito *n* mosquito, *m*. **m. net,** mosquitero, *m*
moss *n* musgo, *m*; moho, *m*; (swamp) marjal, *m*
mossgrown *a* musgoso, cubierto de musgo; *fig* anticuado
mossiness *n* estado musgoso, *m*
mossy *a* musgoso
most *a* el (la, los, etc.) más; la mayor parte de; la mayoría de; (el, etc.) mayor. *adv* más; el (la, etc.) más; (extremely) sumamente; (very) muy; (before adjectives sometimes expressed by superlative, e.g. **m. reverend,** reverendisimo, **m. holy,** santísimo, etc.). *n* (highest price) el mayor precio; la mayor parte; el mayor número; lo más. **m. of all,** sobre todo. **m. people,** la mayoría de la gente. **at the m.,** a lo más, a lo sumo. **for the m. part,** en su mayor parte; casi todos; generalmente, casi siempre. **to make the m. of,** sacar el mayor partido posible de; aprovechar bien; exagerar
mostly *adv* principalmente; en su mayoría; en su mayor parte; casi siempre; en general, generalmente
mote *n* átomo, *m*; mota, *f*. **to see the m. in our neighbor's eye and not the beam in our own,** ver la paja en el ojo del vecino y no la viga en el nuestro
moth *n* mariposa nocturna, *f*; polilla, *f*. **m.ball,** bola de naftalina, *f*. **m.-eaten,** apolillado
mother *n* madre, *f*; madre de familia, *f*; (of alcoholic beverages) madre, *f*. *vt* cuidar como una madre (a); servir de madre (a); (animals) ahijar. **M. Church,** madre iglesia, *f*; iglesia metropolitana, *f*. **m.-in-law,** suegra, *f*. **m. land,** (madre) patria, *f*. **m.-of-pearl,** *n* madreperla, *f*, nácar, *m*. *a* nacarado, nacáreo. **M. Superior,** (madre) superiora, *f*. **m. tongue,** lengua materna, *f*
motherhood *n* maternidad, *f*
motherless *a* huérfano de madre, sin madre
motherlike *a* de madre, como una madre
motherliness *n* cariño maternal, *m*
motherly *a* maternal
motif *n* motivo, *m*; tema, *m*; *sew* adorno, *m*
motion *n* movimiento, *m*; *mech* marcha, operación, *f*; mecanismo, *m*; (sign) seña, señal, *f*; (gesture) ademán, gesto, *m*; (carriage) aire, porte, *m*; (of the bowels) movimiento del vientre, *m*, deyección, *f*; (will) voluntad, *f*, deseo, *m*; (proposal in an assembly or debate) proposición, moción, *f*; *law* pedimento, *m*. *vt* hacer una señal (a). *vi* hacer señas. **to set in m.,** poner en marcha. **m. picture,** fotografía cinematográfica, película, *f*. **m.-picture theater,** cine, *m*
motionless *a* inmóvil
motivate *vt* motivar
motive *n* motivo, *m*. *a* motor; motivo. **with no m.,** sin motivo. **m. power,** fuerza motriz, *f*
motley *a* abigarrado, multicolor; (mixed) diverso, vario. *n* traje de colores, *m*, botarga, *f*
motor *n* motor, *m*; automóvil, *m*, *a* motor; movido por motor; con motor; (traveling) de viaje. *vi* ir en automóvil. *vt* llevar en automóvil (a). **m.boat,** lancha automóvil, *f*. **m.bus,** autobús, ómnibus, *m*. **m.car,** automóvil, *m*. **m.-coach,** autobús, *m*. **m.cycle,** motocicleta, *f*. **m.cyclist,** motociclista, *mf* **m.-launch,** canoa automóvil, *f*. **m.oil,** aceite para motores, *m*. **m.-road,** autopista, *f*. **m.-rug,** manta de viaje, *f*. **m.-scooter,** bicicleta con motor, *f*. **m.-spirit,** bencina, *f*
motoring *n* automovilismo, *m*
motorist *n* automovilista, motorista, *mf*
mottled *a* abigarrado; (of marble, etc.) jaspeado, esquizado; manchado (con), con manchas (de); pintado (con)
motto *n her* divisa, *f*; mote, *m*; (in a book, etc.) lema, *m*
mound *n* montón, *m*; (knoll) altozano, *m*; (for defence) baluarte, *m*; (for burial) túmulo, *m*
mount *n* (hill, and in palmistry) monte, *m*; (for riding) caballería, *f*; montadura, *f*; (for a picture) borde, *m*. *vt* subir; (machines, etc.) montar; (jewels) engastar; (a picture) poner un borde a; (a play) poner en escena; poner a caballo; proveer de caballo. *vi* montar; subir; (increase) aumentar. **to m. a horse,** subir a caballo, montar. **to m. guard,** *mil* montar la guardia. **to m. the throne,** subir al trono
mountain *n* montaña, *f*; (mound) montón, *m*. *a* de montaña(s); montañés; alpino, alpestre. **to make a m. out of a molehill,** convertir un grano de arena en una montaña. hacer de una pulga un camello, hacer de una pulga un elefante. **m.-chain,** cadena de montañas, *f*. **m. climber** *Lat. Am.* andinista, *mf*. **m. climbing** *Lat. Am.* andinismo, *m*. **m. dweller,** montañés (-esa). **m. railway,** ferrocárril de cremallera, *m*. **m.-side,** falda de una montaña, *f*
mountaineer *n* (inhabitant) montañés (-esa); (climber) alpinista, *mf*. *vi* hacer alpinismo

mountaineering *n* alpinismo, *m*
mountainous *a* montañoso; (huge) enorme
mountebank *n* saltabanco, *m*; charlatán, *m*
mounting *n* (ascent) subida, *f*; ascensión, *f*; (of machinery, etc.) armadura, *f*; montadura, *f*; (of a precious stone) engaste, *m*. **m.-block,** subidero, *m*
mourn *vi* afligirse, lamentarse; (wear mourning) estar de luto. *vt* llorar; lamentar; llevar luto por
mourner *n* lamentador (-ra); (paid) plañidera, *f*; el, *m*, (*f*, la) que acompaña al féretro
mournful *a* triste, acongojado; funesto, lúgubre; fúnebre; lamentable
mournfully *adv* tristemente
mournfulness *n* tristeza, *f*; melancolía, aflicción, *f*, pesar, *m*
mourning *n* aflicción, *f*; lamentación, *f*; luto, *m*. **deep m.,** luto riguroso, *m*. **half m.,** medio luto, *m*. **to be in m.,** estar de luto. **to be in m. for,** llevar luto por. **to come out of m.,** dejar el luto. **m.-band,** (on the hat) tira de gasa, *f*; (on the arm) brazal de luto, *m*. **m.-coach,** coche fúnebre, *m*
mouse *n* ratón (-na); *naut* barrilete, *m*. *vi* cazar ratones. **m.-coloured,** de color de rata. **m.-hole, m.-trap,** ratonera, *f*
mouser *n* gato ratonero, *m*
mousing *n* caza de ratones, *f*
moustache *n* bigote, mostacho, *m*
mousy *a* ratonesco, ratonil
mouth *n* (*anat* human being, of a bottle, cave) boca, *f*; entrada, *f*; (of a river) desembocadura, *f*; (of a channel) embocadero, *m*; (of a wind-instrument) boquilla, *f*. *vt* pronunciar con afectación; (chew) mascar. *vi* clamar a gritos, vociferar. **down in the m.,** *inf* con las orejas caídas. **It makes my m. water,** Se me hace la boca agua. **large m.,** boca rasgada, *f*. **m.-gag,** abrebocas, *m*. **m.-organ,** armónica, *f*. **m.-wash,** antiséptico bucal, *m* (Argentina), enjuague, *m*
mouthed *a* que tiene boca . . . ; de boca . . . **open-m.,** boquiabierto
mouthful *n* bocado, *m*; (of smoke, air) bocanada, *f*
mouthpiece *n* (of wind-instruments, tobacco-pipe, waterpipe) boquilla, *f*; (of a wineskin) brocal, *m*; (spokesman) portavoz, *m*; intérprete, *mf*
movable *a* movible; (of goods) mobiliario. **m. feast,** fiesta movible, *f*
movable type *n* tipos sueltos, *m pl*
movables *n pl* bienes muebles, efectos, *m pl*
move *n* movimiento, *m*; (of household effects) mudanza, *f*; (motion) marcha, *f*; (in a game) jugada, *f*; (*fig* step) paso, *m*; (device) maniobra, *f*. **Whose m. is it?** ¿A quién le toca jugar? **to be on the m.,** estar en movimiento; estar de viaje. **to be always on the m.,** *inf* parecer una lanzadera
move *vt* mover; poner en marcha; (furniture) trasladar; cambiar de lugar; (stir) remover; (shake) agitar, hacer temblar; (transport) transportar; (a piece in chess, etc.) jugar; (pull) arrancar; (impel) impulsar; (incline) inclinar, disponer; (affect emotionally) conmover, emocionar, enternecer; impresionar. *vi* moverse; ponerse en marcha; (walk) andar; ir; avanzar; (a step forward, etc.) dar; (move house) trasladarse; (act) entrar en acción; (in games) hacer una jugada; (progress) progresar; (shake) agitarse, temblar; removerse; (propose in an assembly) hacer una proposición; (in a court of law) hacer un pedimento; (grow) crecer. **to m. about,** pasearse; ir y venir; (of traffic) circular; (remove) trasladarse; (stir, tremble) agitarse. **to m. along,** caminar por; avanzar por. **to m. aside,** *vt* apartar; poner a un lado; (curtains) descorrer. *vi* ponerse a un lado; quitarse de en medio. **to m. away,** *vt* alejar. *vi* alejarse; marcharse; trasladarse; mudar de casa. **to m. back,** retroceder, volver hacia atrás. **to m. down,** bajar, descender. **to m. forward,** adelantarse; avanzar; progresar. **to m. in,** entrar (en); tomar posesión de una casa. **to m. off,** *vt* quitar. *vi* marcharse; ponerse en marcha; alejarse, apartarse. **to m. on,** avanzar; ponerse en marcha; circular; (of time) pasar, correr. **to m. out,** *vt* sacar, quitar. *vi* salir; (from a house) mudarse, abandonar (una casa, etc.). **to m. round,** dar vueltas, girar; (turn round) volverse. **to m. to,** (make) hacer, animar (a); causar. **to m. up,** *vt* montar, subir. *vi* montar; avanzar
movement *n* movimiento, *m*; *mech* mecanismo, *m*; (Stock Exchange) actividad, *f*. **encircling m.,** *mil* movimiento envolvente, *m*
mover *n* motor, *m*; móvil, *m*; promotor (-ra); (of a motion, proposer) autor (-ra) de una moción
movie *n inf* cine, *m*. **m. camera,** máquina de impresionar, *f*. **m. star,** estrella de la pantalla, *f*
moving *a* móvil; motor; (affecting) emocionante, conmovedor; impresionante; patético. *n* movimiento, *m*; traslado, *m*; cambio de domicilio, *m*. **m. picture,** fotografía cinematográfica, *f*. **m. staircase,** escalera móvil, *f*
movingly *adv* con emoción; patéticamente
mow *vt* segar. *vi* (grimace) hacer muecas
mowing *n* siega, *f*. **m.-machine,** segadora, *f*
Mr. See **mister**
Mrs. See **mistress**
much *a* mucho. *adv* mucho; (by far) con mucho; (with past part.) muy; (pretty nearly) casi, más o menos. **m. of a size,** más o menos del mismo tamaño. **I was m. angered,** Estuve muy enfadado. **as m. as,** tanto como. **as m. more,** otro tanto. **How m. is it?** ¿Cuánto es? ¿Cuánto cuesta? **however m. . . . ,** por mucho que . . . **not m.,** no mucho. **not to think m. of,** tener en poco (a). **so m. so that,** tanto que. **too m.,** demasiado. **to make m. of,** dar grande importancia a; (a person) apreciar, querer; agasajar; (a child) mimar, acariciar
mucilage *n* mucílago, *m*
muck *n* (dung) estiércol, *m*; (filth) porquería, inmundicia, *f*; suciedad, *f*; (rubbish, of a literary work, etc.) porquería, *n*. **to m. up,** ensuciar; (spoil) estropear por completo
mucky *a* muy sucio; puerco; asqueroso, repugnante
mucosity *n* mucosidad, *f*
mucous *a* mucoso. **m. membrane,** mucosa, *f*
mucus *n* mucosidad, *f*; (from the nose) moco, *m*
mud *n* lodo, barro, fango, *m*. **to stick in the mud,** (of a ship, etc.) embarrancarse. **mudbath,** baño de barro, *m*. **mud wall,** tapia, *f*
muddiness *n* estado fangoso, *m*; (of liquids) turbiedad, *f*; suciedad, *f*
muddle *vt* (bewilder) dejar perplejo, aturdir; (intoxicate) emborrachar; (stupefy) entontecer; (spoil) estropear; embarullar, dejar en desorden; hacer un lío de. *n* desorden, *m*; confusión, *f*; lío, embrollo, *m*. **in a m.,** en desorden; en confusión. **to make a m.,** armar un lío. **to m. away,** derrochar sin ton ni son
muddled *a* desordenado; confuso; estúpido; torpe; (drunk) borracho
muddy *a* fangoso, lodoso, barroso; cubierto de lodo; (of liquids, etc.) turbio; (of the complexion) cetrino. *vt* enlodar, cubrir de lodo; ensuciar; (liquids) enturbiar
mudguard *n* guardabarro, *m*
muezzin *n* almuecín, almuédano, *m*
muff *n* manguito, *m*; (for a car radiator) cubierta para radiador, *f*; (*inf* at games, etc.) maleta, *m*. *vt* dejar escapar (una pelota); (an opportunity) perder
muffin *n* mollete, *m*
muffle *vt* embozar, arrebozar; envolver; encubrir, ocultar, tapar; (stifle sound of) apagar; (oars, bells) envolver con tela para no hacer ruido; *fig* ahogar. **to m. oneself up,** embozarse
muffled *a* (of sound) sordo; confuso; apagado. **m. drum,** tambor enlutado, *m*
muffler *n* bufanda, tapaboca, *f*; (furnace) mufla, *f*; (of a car radiator) cubierta para radiador, *f*; (silencer) silencioso, *m*
mufti *n* mufti, *m*
mug *n* vaso, *m*; (tankard) pichel, tarro, *m*; (face) jeta, *f*; (dupe) primo, *m*; (at games, etc.) maleta, *m*

mulatto *a* mulato. *n* mulato (-ta). **m.-like,** amulatado
mulberry *n* (fruit) mora, *f.* (bush) morera, *f.* **m. plantation,** moreral, *m*
mule *n* mulo (-la); (slipper) mula, chinela, *f;* (spinning-jenny) huso mecánico, *m*
mulish *a* mular; terco como una mula
mulishness *n* terquedad de mula, *f*
mullet *n* (red) salmonete, *m,* trilla, *f;* (grey) mújol, *m*
multicolored *a* multicolor
multifarious *a* numeroso, mucho; diverso, vario
multiform *a* multiforme
multilateral *a* multilátero
multimillionaire *a* archimillonario, multimillonario, *n* multimillonario, *m*
multiple *a* múltiple, múltiplo. *n* múltiplo, *m*
multiple-choice question *n* pregunta optativa, *f*
multiplicand *n* multiplicando, *m*
multiplication *n* multiplicación, *f.* **m. table,** tabla de multiplicación, *f*
multiplicity *n* multiplicidad, *f*
multiplier *n math* multiplicador, *m;* máquina de multiplicar, *f*
multiply *vt* multiplicar. *vi* multiplicarse
multitude *n* multitud, *f.* **the m.,** las masas
multitudinous *a* muy numeroso
mumble *vi* and *vt* musitar, hablar entre dientes; refunfuñar; (chew) mascullar
mummer *n* momero (-ra); máscara, *mf*
mummery *n* momería, *f;* mascarada, *f*
mummification *n* momificación, *f*
mummify *vt* momificar. *vi* momificarse
mummy *n* momia, *f;* carne de momia, *f;* (*inf* mother) mama, *f.* **m. case,** sarcófago, *m*
mumps *n pl* parotiditis, papera, *f*
munch *vt* masticar, mascullar, mascar
mundane *a* mundano
municipal *a* municipal. **m. charter,** fuero municipal, *m.* **m. government,** gobierno municipal, *m*
municipality *n* municipio, *m*
munificence *n* munificencia, *f*
munificent *a* munífico, generoso
munition *n* munición, *f. vt* municionar. **m. dump,** depósito de municiones, *m.* **m. factory,** fábrica de municiones, *f.* **m. worker,** obrero (-ra) de una fábrica de municiones
mural *a* mural. *n* pintura mural, *f*
murder *n* asesinato, *m. vt* asesinar; dar muerte (a), matar; (a work, etc.) degollar. **He was murdered,** Fue asesinado. **willful m.,** homicidio premeditado, *m*
murderer *n* asesino, *m*
murderess *n* asesina, *f*
murderous *a* homicida; cruel, sanguinario; fatal; imposible, intolerable
murderously *adv* con intento de asesinar; (with look) con ojos asesinos; cruelmente
murkiness *n* obscuridad, lobreguez, *f,* tinieblas, *f pl*
murky *a* lóbrego, negro, obscuro; (of one's past, etc.) negro, accidentado
murmur *n* murmullo, *m;* rumor, *m;* susurro, *m;* (grumble) murmurio, *m. vi* murmurar, susurrar; (complain) murmurar, quejarse. *vt* murmurar, decir en voz baja
murmuring *n* murmurio, *m, a* que murmura, susurrante
muscatel *a* moscatel. *n* moscatel, *m.* **m. grape,** uva moscatel, *f*
muscle *n* músculo, *m*
Muscovite *a* moscovita. *n* moscovita, *mf*
muscular *a* muscular, musculoso; (brawny) membrudo, fornido. **m. pains,** (in the legs, etc.) agujetas, *f pl*
muscularity *n* fuerza muscular, *f*
musculature *n* musculatura, *f*
Muse *n* musa, *f*
muse *n* meditación, *f. vi* meditar, reflexionar, rumiar; mirar las musarañas, estar distraído. **to m. on,** meditar en (or sobre)
museum *n* museo, *m*
museum of arms *n* museo de armas, *m,* aploteca, *f*
mushroom *n* seta, *f. a* de setas; de forma de seta; (upstart) advenedizo; (ephemeral) efímero, de un día. **m.-bed,** setal, *m.* **m.-spawn,** esporas de setas, *f pl*
music *n* música, *f;* armonía, *f;* melodía, *f. a* de música. **to set to m.,** poner en música. **m.-hall,** teatro de variedades, *m;* salón de conciertos, *m.* **m. master,** profesor de música, *m.* **m. publisher,** editor de obras musicales, *m.* **m. stand,** atril, *m;* tablado para una orquesta, *m.* **m. stool,** taburete de piano, *m*
musical *a* musical; de música; armonioso, melodioso. **She is very m.,** Es muy aficionada a la música; Tiene mucho talento para la música. **m.-box,** caja de música, *f.* **m. comedy,** zarzuela, *f.* **m. instrument,** instrumento de música, *m*
musical chairs *n* escobas, *f pl,* el juego de sillas, *m sg*
musically *adv* musicalmente; melodiosamente
musician *n* músico (-ca)
musing *n* meditación, *f;* ensueños, *m pl, a* pensativo, meditabundo
musingly *adv* reflexivamente
musk *n* (substance) almizcle, *m;* perfume de almizcle, *m. a* de almizcle; almizclero; (of scents) almizcleño. **m.-deer,** almizclero, *m.* **m.-rat,** rata almizclera, *f*
musket *n* mosquete, *m*
musketeer *n* mosquetero, *m*
Muslim *a* musulmán, mahometano. *n* musulmán (-ana)
muslin *n* muselina, *f, a* de muselina
mussel *n* mejillón, *m.* **m.-bed,** criadero de mejillones, *m*
must *vi* haber de; tener que; deber; (expressing probability) deber de, ser. **This question m. be settled without delay,** Esta cuestión debe ser resuelta sin demora. **You m. do it at once,** Tienes que hacerlo en seguida. **I m. have seen him in the street sometime,** Debo haberle visto en la calle alguna vez. **One m. eat to live,** Se ha de comer para vivir. **Well, go if you m.,** Bueno, vete si no hay más remedio. **It m. be a difficult decision for him,** Debe ser una decisión difícil para él. **It m. have been about twelve o'clock when . . . ,** Serían las doce cuando . . .
must *n* mosto, zumo de la uva, *m;* (mould) moho, *m*
mustang *n* potro mesteño, *m*
mustard *n* mostaza, *f.* **m. gas,** iperita, *f.* **m. plaster,** sinapismo, *m.* **m. pot,** mostacera, *f.* **m. spoon,** cucharita para la mostaza, *f*
muster *n* lista, *f,* rol, *m;* revista, *f;* reunión, *f, vt* pasar lista (de); pasar revista (a); reunir. *vi* juntarse, reunirse. **to m. out,** (from the army) dar de baja (a). **to m. up sufficient courage,** cobrar ánimos suficientes. **to pass m.,** pasar revista; ser aceptado. **m.-roll,** *mil* muestra, *f; naut* rol de la tripulación, *m*
mustiness *n* moho, *m;* ranciedad, *f;* (of a room, etc.) olor de humedad, *m*
musty *a* mohoso; rancio; que huele a humedad. **to go m.,** enmohecerse
mutability *n* mutabilidad, *f;* inconstancia, inestabilidad, *f*
mutable *a* mudable; inconstante, inestable
mutation *n* mutación, *f*
mute *a* mudo; silencioso. *n* mudo (-da); *mus* sordina, *f;* (phonetics) letra muda, *f.* **deaf m.,** sordomudo (-da)
muted *a* (of sounds) sordo, apagado
mutely *adv* mudamente; en silencio
muteness *n* mudez, *f;* silencio, *m*
mutilate *vt* mutilar; estropear
mutilation *n* mutilación, *f*
mutineer *n* amotinador, rebelde, *m*
mutinous *a* amotinado; rebelde, sedicioso; turbulento
mutiny *n* motín, *m;* sublevación, insurrección, *f, vi* amotinarse, sublevarse
mutt *n* chucho, *m*

mutter *vt* and *vi* murmurar, musitar; mascullar, decir (or hablar) entre dientes; gruñir, refunfuñar; (of thunder, etc.) tronar, retumbar. *n* murmurio, *m*; rumor, *m*; retumbo, *m*
mutton *n* carnero, *m*, *a* de carnero. **m.-chop,** chuleta, *f*
mutual *a* mutuo, recíproco; común. **by m. consent,** de común acuerdo. **m. aid society,** sociedad de socorros mutuos, *f*. **m. insurance company,** sociedad de seguros mutuos, *f*
mutual fund *n* fondo de inversiones rentables, *m*
mutualism *n* mutualismo, *m*
mutuality *n* mutualidad, *f*
mutually *adv* mutuamente, recíprocamente
muzzle *n* (snout) hocico, *m*; (for a dog) bozal, *m*; (of a gun) boca, *f*. *vt* abozalar, poner un bozal (a); (*fig* gag) amordazar, imponer silencio (a)
muzzling *n* acción de abozalar, *f*; (*fig* gagging) amordazamiento, *m*
my *a poss* mi, *mf*; mis, *mf pl* **my relatives,** mis parientes. **My goodness!** ¡Dios mío!
myelitis *n* mielitis, *f*
myopia *n* miopía, *f*
myopic *a* miope
myriad *n* miríada, *f*
myrmidon *n* rufián, *m*; asesino, *m*; secuaz, *m*
myrrh *n* mirra, *f*
myrtle *n* mirto, arrayán, *m*
myself *pron* yo mismo; (as a reflexive with a preposition) mí; (with a reflexive verb) me. **I m. sent it,** yo mismo (-ma) lo mandé
mysterious *a* misterioso
mysteriousness *n* misterio, *m*, lo misterioso
mystery *n* misterio, *m*. **m. play,** (religious) misterio, drama litúrgico, *m*; (thriller) comedia de detectives, *f*. **m. story,** novela policíaca, *f*; novela de aventuras, *f*
mystic *a* místico
mysticism *n* misticismo, *m*
mystification *n* mistificación, *f*
mystify *vt* mistificar
myth *n* mito, *m*
mythical *a* mítico
mythologist *n* mitólogo, *m*
mythology *n* mitología, *f*

N

n *n* (letter) ene, *f*
nab *vt inf* atrapar, apresar, agazapar
nabob *n* nabab, *m*; ricacho, *m*
nacre *n* nácar, *m*, madreperla, *f*
nadir *n* nadir, *m*
nag *n* jaca, *f*; (wretched hack) rocín, jamelgo, penco, *m*. *vt* zaherir, echar en cara, regañar; (of one's conscience) remorder; *Lat. Am.* majaderear (pester) *vi* criticar, regañar
nagging *n* zaherimiento, *m*. *a* zaheridor, criticón; (pain) continuo, incesante, constante
naiad *n myth* náyade, *f*
nail *vt* clavar, enclavar; (for ornament) clavetear, tachonar, adornar con clavos. *n* uña, *f*; *mech* clavo, *m*; (animal's) garra, *f*. **to n. down,** sujetar (or cerrar) con clavos. **to n. to (on to),** clavar en. **to n. together,** fijar con clavos. *inf* **on the n.,** en el acto, en seguida. *inf* **to hit the n. on the head,** dar en el clavo. **brass-headed n.,** tachón, *m*. **French n.,** punta de París, *f*. **headless n.,** puntilla, *f*. **hob-n.,** clavo de herradura, *m*. **hook n.,** gancho, *m*. **round-headed n.,** bellota, *f*. **n.-brush,** cepillo para las (or de) uñas, *m*. **n.-file,** lima para las uñas, *f*. **n. head,** cabeza de un clavo, *f*. **n.-puller,** sacaclavos, arrancaclavos, botador, *m*. **n.-scissors,** tijeras para las uñas, *f pl*. **n. trade,** ferretería, *f*. **n. varnish,** barniz para las uñas, *m*
nailed *a* adornado con clavos, claveteado
nailer *n* fabricante de clavos, chapucero, *m*
nailing *n* enclavación, *f*
naive *a* ingenuo, candoroso, espontáneo
naively *adv* ingenuamente, espontáneamente
naiveté *n* ingenuidad, naturalidad, franqueza, *f*; candor, *m*
naked *a* desnudo, nudo, *Peru* calato, *elsewhere in Lat. Am.* encuerado; desabrigado, indefenso, desamparado; (birds) implume; calvo; (truth) simple, sencillo, puro; evidente, patente. **stark n.,** en cueros vivos, tal como le parió su madre. **with the n. sword,** con la espada desnuda. **n. eye,** simple vista, *f*. **n. light,** llama descubierta, *f*
nakedly *adv* nudamente; desabrigadamente; abiertamente, claramente
nakedness *n* desnudez, *f*; *fig* desabrigo, *m*, aridez, *f*; *fig* claridad, *f*. **the truth in all its n.,** la verdad desnuda
namby-pamby *a* soso, insípido, ñoño
name *n* nombre, *m*; título, *m*; fama, opinión, *f*; renombre, crédito, *m*; autoridad, *f*; apodo, mal nombre, *m*. *vt* nombrar, llamar, imponer el nombre de, apellidar; mencionar, señalar; (appoint) designar, elegir; (ships) bautizar. **by n.,** por nombre. **Christian n.,** nombre de pila, *m*. **in his n.,** en nombre de él, en nombre suyo; de parte de él. **in n. only,** nada más que en nombre. **to be named,** llamarse. **to call** (a person) **names,** poner como un trapo (a). **to go under the n. of,** vivir bajo el nombre de. **to have a good n.,** tener buena fama. **What is her n.?** ¿Cómo se llama? **n. day,** santo, *m*. **n. plate,** (machinery) placa de fábrica, *f*; (streets) rótulo, *m*; (professional) placa profesional, *f*
nameless *a* anónimo; desconocido; (inexpressible) vago, indecible
namely *adv* a saber, es decir
namesake *n* tocayo (-ya)
naming *n* bautizo, *m*; nombramiento, *m*; designación, *f*
nannygoat *n* cabra, *f*
nap *n* (cloth) pelusa, *f*, pelo, tamo, *m*; (plants) vello, *m*, pelusilla, *f*; (sleep) siesta, *f*, sueño, *m*; (cards) napolitana, *f*. **to take a nap,** *vi* dormitar, echar un sueño, echar una siesta. **to take an afternoon nap,** dormir la siesta. **to be caught napping,** estar desprevenido
nape *n* nuca, *f*, cogote, *m*; (animal's) testuz, *m*,
naphtha *n chem* nafta, *f*. **wood n.,** alcohol metílico, *m*
naphthalene *n chem* naftalina, *f*
napkin *n* (table) servilleta, *f*; (babies') pañal, *m*. **n.-ring,** servilletero, *m*
Naples Nápoles, *m*
Napoleonic *a* napoleónico
narcissism *n* narcisismo, *m*
narcissus *n* narciso, *m*
narcosis *n med* narcosis, *f*
narcotic *a med* narcótico, calmante, soporífero. *n med* narcótico, *m*, opiata, *f*
nard *n bot* nardo, *m*, tuberosa, *f*
narrate *vt* narrar, contar; referir, relatar
narration *n* narración, narrativa; relación, descripción, *f*, relato, *m*
narrative *a* narrador, narrativo, narratorio. *n* narrativa, *f*; descripción, *f*
narrator *n* narrador (-ra), relator (-ra), descriptor (-ra)
narrow *vt* estrechar, angostar; reducir, limitar. *vi* reducirse, hacerse más estrecho; (eyes) entornarse; (knitting) menguar. *a* estrecho, angosto; limitado, restringido, reducido, corto; (avaricious) ruin, avaro, mezquino; (ideas) intolerante, intransigente. **"Narrow Road,"** «Camino Estrecho». *n pl* **narrows,** *naut* estrecho, *m*; desfiladero, paso estrecho, *m*. **to have a n. escape,** escapar en una tabla. **n.-brimmed** (hats), de ala estrecha. **n. circumstances,** estrechez, escasez de

medios, *f.* **n.-gauge railway,** ferrocarril de vía estrecha (or de vía angosta), *m.* **n. life,** vida de horizontes estrechos, *f.* **n. majority,** escasa mayoría, *f.* **n.-minded,** cerrado al mundo, intolerante, intransigente. **n.-mindedness,** intolerancia, intransigencia, estrechez de miras, *f*
narrowing *n* estrechez, *f,* estrechamiento, *m;* reducción, limitación, *f;* (in knitting) menguado, *m*
narrowly *adv* estrechamente; por poco, con dificultad; atentamente, cuidadosamente. **I n. escaped being run over,** Por poco me atropellan
narrowness *n* estrechez, angostura, *f;* (of means) pobreza, miseria, *f;* (of ideas) intolerancia, intransigencia, *f*
nasal *a* nasal, gangoso. *n* letra nasal, *f*
nasally *adv* nasalmente. **to speak n.,** hablar por las narices, ganguear
nascent *a* naciente
nastily *adv* suciamente; ofensivamente, de un modo insultante; maliciosamente, con malignidad
nastiness *n* suciedad, inmundicia, porquería, *f;* (indecency) obscenidad, indecencia, *f;* (rudeness) insolencia, impertinencia, grosería, *f;* (difficulty) dificultad, *f,* lo malo
nasturtium *n* mastuerzo, *m,* capuchina, *f*
nasty *a* nauseabundo, repugnante; asqueroso, inmundo, sucio; (obscene) indecente, obsceno; desagradable, malo; (malicious) rencoroso, malicioso; violento; malévolo, amenazador; peligroso; difícil. *fig* **to be in a n. mess,** tener el agua al cuello. **to turn n.,** *inf* ponerse desagradable
nation *n* nación, *f,* estado, país, *m;* (people) pueblo, *m*
national *a* nacional; público; patriótico. *n* nacional, *mf.* **n. anthem,** himno nacional, *m.* **n. debt,** deuda pública, *f.* **n. schools,** escuelas públicas, *f pl.* **n. socialism,** nacionalsocialismo, *m.* **n. socialist,** *a* and *n* nacionalsocialista *mf.* **n. syndicalism,** *pol* nacionalsindicalismo, *m.* **n. syndicalist,** *a* and *n pol* nacionalsindicalista, *mf*
nationalism *n* nacionalismo, patriotismo, *m*
nationalist *a* and *n* nacionalista, *mf*
nationality *n* nacionalidad, *f;* nación, *f*
nationalization *n* nacionalización, *f*
nationalize *vt* nacionalizar, *Lat. Am. also* estatizar
National Labor Relations Board *n* Junta Nacional de Relaciones Laborales
nationally *adv* nacionalmente, como nación; del punto de vista nacional
native *a* (of a place) nativo, natal, oriundo; indígena; nacional, típico, del país; (vocabulary) patrimonial (as opposed to borrowed vocabulary); (of genius) natural, innato, instintivo; *min* nativo; (language) vernáculo. *n* nacional, *mf;* natural, *mf;* ciudadano (-na) indígena, aborigen (gen. pl.), *mf;* producto nacional, *m.* **He is a n. of Madrid,** Nació en Madrid, Es natural de Madrid, Es madrileño. **Native American commune** (in Peru) ayllu, *m.* **native informant,** sujeto, *m.* **n. land,** patria, tierra. **n. of the capital** *Lat. Am.* capitalino, n. of Rio de Janeiro carioca, *mf.* **n. place,** lugar natal, *m.* **n. region,** patria chica, *f.* **n. soil,** terruño, *m.* **n. tongue,** lengua materna, *f*
Native American *movement Lat. Am.* indigenismo, *m*
nativity *n* navidad, natividad, *f;* (manger) nacimiento, *m*
natty *a inf* chulo, majo; coquetón
natural *a* natural; (wild) virgen, salvaje; nativo; (of products) crudo; normal; (usual) acostumbrado, corriente, natural; (of likeness) fiel, verdadero; (illegitimate) ilegítimo, bastardo; (of qualities) innato, instintivo; físico; característico, propio; (of people) inafectado, sencillo, genuino; *mus* natural. *n mus* becuadro, *m; mus* nota natural, *f;* imbécil, *mf* **n. features,** geografía física, *f.* **n. history,** historia natural, *f.* **n. philosophy,** filosofía natural, *f.* **n. science,** ciencias naturales, *f pl.* **n. selection,** selección natural, *f.* **n. state,** estado virgen, *m*
natural child *n* hijo ilegítimo, *m*
naturalism *n* naturalismo, *m*
naturalist *n* (*lit* and *science*) naturalista, *mf*
naturalistic *a* naturalista
naturalization *n* naturalización, *f;* aclimatación, *f.* **n. papers,** carta de naturaleza, *f*
naturalize *vt* naturalizar; aclimatar. **to become naturalized,** naturalizarse
naturally *adv* naturalmente, por naturaleza; normalmente; sin afectación; instintivamente, por instinto; (without art) al natural. **n. curly hair** *Guatemala* colocho, *m*
naturalness *n* naturalidad, *f;* sencillez, desenvoltura, *f;* desembarazo, *m*
nature *n* naturaleza, *f;* (of people) carácter, fondo, temperamento, genio, natural, modo de ser, *m;* (kind) género, *m,* especie, *f;* (essence) condición, esencia, cualidad, *f, art* **from n.,** del natural. **good n.,** bondad natural, afabilidad, *f.* **ill n.,** mala índole, *f.* **nature cure,** naturismo, *m.* **n. curist,** naturista, *mf.* **n. study,** historia natural, *f.* **n. worship,** panteísmo, culto de la naturaleza, *m*
natured *a* de carácter, de índole, con un modo de ser, de condición
naught *n* nada, *f;* cero, *m. a* inútil, sin valor. **all for n.,** todo en balde. **to come to n.,** malograrse. **to set at n.,** tener en menos; despreciar
naughtily *adv* traviesamente; con picardía, con malicia
naughtiness *n* travesura, picardía, mala conducta, *f;* malicia, *f*
naughty *a* travieso, pícaro, revoltoso, malo; salado, escabroso, verde (stories, etc.). **to be n.,** (children) ser malo
nausea *n* náusea, *f,* bascas, *f pl,* mareo, *m; fig* asco, *m;* repugnancia, *f*
nauseate *vt* dar náuseas; *fig* repugnar, dar asco
nauseating *a* repugnante, horrible; asqueroso
nauseous *a* nauseabundo, asqueroso; *fig* repugnante
nauseousness *n* náusea, asquerosidad, *f; fig* repugnancia, *f,* asco, *m*
nautical *a* náutico, marítimo. **n. day, twenty-four hours,** singladura, *f*
naval *a* naval; de marina, marítimo. **n. base,** base naval, *f.* **n. engagement,** batalla naval, *f.* **n. hospital,** hospital de marina, *m.* **n. law,** código naval, *m.* **n. officer,** oficial de marina, *m.* **n. power,** poder marítimo, *m.* **n. reservist,** marinero de reserva, *m.* **n. yard,** arsenal, *m*
Navarre Navarra, *f*
nave *n arch* nave, *f;* (of wheels) cubo, *m*
navel *n* ombligo, *m.* **n. string,** cordón umbilical, *m*
navigability *n* navegación, practicabilidad de navegar, *f*
navigable *a* navegable, practicable
navigate *vt* navegar, marear, dirigir (unbuque); *fig* conducir, guiar. *vi* navegar
navigation *n* navegación, *f;* (science of) náutica, marina, *f.* **n. company,** empresa naviera, *f.* **n. laws,** derecho marítimo, *m.* **n. lights,** luces de navegación, *f pl*
navigator *n* navegador, navegante, *m;* piloto, *m*
navvy *n* peón, bracero, jornalero, *m; mech* máquina, excavadora, *f.* **road n.,** peón caminero, *m.* **to work like a n.,** estar hecho un azacán, sudar la gota gorda
navy *n* marina, *f;* armada, *f;* (color) azul marino, *m.* **n. board,** consejo de la armada, *m.* **n. department** ministerio de marina, *m.* **n. estimates,** presupuesto de marina, *m.* **n. list,** escalafón de marina, *m*
nay *adv* no; al contrario, más bien, mejor dicho. *n* negativa, *f,* voto contrario, *m*
Nazarene *a* and *n* nazareno (-na)
Nazareth Nazaret, *m*
Nazi *a* and *n* nacionalsocialista, naci, *mf*
Nazism *n* nacismo, *m*
n.d. (no date) *s.f.* (sin fecha)
Neapolitan *a* and *n* neapolitano (-na)
near *vi* acercarse, aproximarse. *a* cercano, immediato,

contiguo; (of time) inminente, próximo; (relationship) cercano, consanguíneo; (of friends) íntimo, entrañable; (mean) tacaño, avariento

near *prep* cerca de, junto a; hacia, en la dirección de; (of time) cerca de, casi. *adv* cerca, *Central America, Chile, Mexico* lueguito; (time) cerca, próximamente. **to be n. to,** estar cerca de. **to bring n.,** acercar, aproximar. **It was a n. thing,** Escapamos por un pelo. **n. at hand,** a la mano; (time) cerca, inminente. **n.-by,** *a* cercano, inmediato, *Central America, Chile, Mexico* lueguito. *adv* cerca. **n. side,** (of vehicles) lado de la acera, *m.* **n.-sighted,** corto de vista, miope. **n.-sightedness,** miopía, cortedad de vista, *f*

nearest *a comp* and *sup* más cercano, más cerca; más corto. **the n. way,** el camino más corto, el camino directo

nearly *adv* casi; cerca de, aproximadamente; estrechamente; íntimamente. **It touches me n.,** Me toca de cerca, Es de sumo interés para mí. **They n. killed me,** Por poco me matan. **to be n.,** (of age) frisar en, rayar en

nearness *n* (of place) cercanía, proximidad, contigüidad, *Argentina* adyacencia, *f;* (of time) inminencia, proximidad, *f;* (relationship) consanguinidad, *f;* (avarice) avaricia, tacañería, *f;* (dearness) intimidad, amistad estrecha, *f*

neat *a zool* vacuno; elegante, sencillo, de buen gusto; (of the body) bien hecho, airoso, esbelto; (clean) limpio, aseado; (of handwriting) legible, bien proporcionado; pulido, esmerado, acabado; hábil, astuto, diestro; (of liquor, spirits) puro, solo. **to make a n. job of,** hacer (algo) bien

neatly *adv* sencillamente, con elegancia, con primor; con aseo, limpiamente; bien (proporcionado); diestramente, hábilmente

neatness *n* aseo, *m,* limpieza, *f;* elegancia, sencillez, *f;* buen gusto, *m;* destreza, habilidad, *f;* (aptness) pertinencia, *f*

nebula *n ast* nebulosa, *f*

nebulosity *n* nebulosidad, *f; ast* nebulosa, *f;* vaguedad, imprecisión, *f*

nebulous *a* nebuloso; vago, impreciso, confuso

necessarily *adv* necesariamente; inevitablemente, sin duda

necessary *a* necesario, inevitable; imprescindible, preciso, indispensable, esencial; obligatorio, debido, forzoso. *n* requisito esencial, *m.* **if n.,** en caso de necesidad; si fuera necesario. **to be n.,** hacer falta; necesitarse

necessitate *vt* necesitar, exigir, requerir, obligar

necessitous *a* pobre, indigente, miserable, necesitado

necessity *n* necesidad, *f;* menester, *m,* (e.g., **an indispensable n.,** un menester imprescindible); consecuencia, *f,* resultado, efecto, *m;* inevitabilidad, fatalidad, *f;* (poverty) indigencia, pobreza, *f.* **Fire and clothing are necessities,** El fuego y el vestir son cosas necesarias. **from n.,** por necesidad. **in case of n.,** si fuese necesario, en caso de necesidad. **of n.,** de necesidad, sin remedio. **physical necessities,** menesteres físicos, *m pl.* **prime n.,** artículo de primera necesidad, *m.* **to be under the n. of,** tener que, tener la necesidad de

Necessity is the mother of invention La necesidad es una gran inventora, La necesidad aguza el ingenio

neck *n* cuello, *m,* garganta, *f;* (of bottles) gollete, cuello, *m;* (of animals) pescuezo, *m; geog* istmo, *m,* lengua de tierra, *f;* (of musical instruments) clavijero, mástil, *m; sew* escote, *m.* **low-necked,** (of dresses) escotado. **She fell on his n.,** Se colgó de su cuello. **He won by a n.,** Ganó por un cuello; *fig* Ganó por un tris. **to break anyone's n.,** romperle el pescuezo. **to wring the n. of,** torcer el pescuezo (a). **n. and n.,** parejos. **n. or nothing,** todo o nada, perdiz o no comerla. **n. stock,** alzacuello, *m*

neckband *n* tirilla de camisa, *f*

necklace *n* collar, *m*

necklet *n* collar, *m;* (of fur) cuello, *m*

necktie *n* corbata, *f*

necrological *a* necrológico

necrology *n* necrología, *f*

necropolis *n* necrópolis, *f*

nectar *n* néctar, *m*

nectarine *n bot* variedad de melocotón, *f*

need *vt* necesitar, haber menester, requerir, exigir. *vi* ser necesario, hacer falta, carecer; haber (de). **N. I obey?** ¿He de obedecer? **You need to write carefully,** Hay que escribir con cuidado. **The work n. not be done for tomorrow,** No es preciso hacer el trabajo para mañana

need *n* necesidad, *f;* cosa necesaria, *f;* falta; (poverty) indigencia, pobreza, *f;* urgencia, *f;* (shortage) escasez, carestía, *f.* **in case of n.,** en caso de necesidad, en caso de urgencia. **I have n. of two more books,** Me hacen falta dos libros más

needful *a* necesario, preciso; indispensable, esencial. **the n.,** lo necesario

needfulness *n* necesidad, falta, *f*

neediness *n* pobreza, penuria, miseria, estrechez, *f*

needle *n sew* aguja, *f;* (of compass) brújula, aguja imanada, *f;* (monument) obelisco, *m;* (of scales) field, *m,* lengüeta, *f;* (of phonograph) pría, *f,* (of measuring instruments) índice, *m; med* aguja de inyecciones, *f. inf* **to be as sharp as a n.,** no tener pelo de tonto. **pack n.,** aguja espartera, *f.* **n.-case,** alfiletero, agujero, *m.* **n. maker,** fabricante de agujas, *m.* **n.-shaped,** en forma de aguja, acicular. *vt Lat. Am.* engorrar

needle and thread hilo y aguja

needless *a* innecesario, supérfluo. **n. to say,** claro está que . . ., huelga decir que . . .

needlessly *adv* innecesariamente, inútilmente; en vano, de balde

needlessness *n* superfluidad, *f,* lo innecesario

needlewoman *n* (professional) cosedora, *f;* costurera, *f.* **She is a good n.,** Cose bien (or es una buena cosedora)

needlework *n* labor de aguja, labor blanca, costura, *f;* bordado, *m.* **to do n.,** hacer costura

needs *adv* necesariamente, sin remedio *n pl* necesidades, *f pl.* **if n. must,** si hace falta. **N. must when the devil drives,** A la fuerza ahorcan

needy *a* necesitado, menesteroso, corto de medios, pobre, apurado

ne'er-do-well *n* calavera, perdido, *m.* **to be a n.,** ser de mala madera

nefarious *a* nefario, vil, nefando

nefariously *adv* vilmente, nefariamente

negation *n* negación, *f*

negative *vt* negar, denegar; votar en contra (de), oponerse (a); (prevent) impedir, imposibilitar. *a* negativo. *n* negativa, negación, *f;* repulsa, denegación, *f; phot* negativo, *m,* prueba negativa, *f; elec* electricidad negativa, *f.* **to reply in the n.,** dar una respuesta negativa

negativeness *n* el carácter negativo, *m*

neglect *vt* descuidar, desatender; abandonar, dejar; (ignore) despreciar, no hacer caso (de); omitir, olvidar. *n* descuido, *m,* desatención, *f;* inobservancia, *f;* abandono, olvido, *m;* desdén, *m,* frialdad, *f.* **to fall into n.,** caer en desuso. **to n. one's obligations,** descuidar sus obligaciones

neglectful *a* negligente, descuidado, omiso

negligee *n* salto de cama, quimono, *m,* bata, *f*

negligence *n* negligencia, *f,* descuido, *m;* flojedad, pereza, *f;* (of dress) desaliño, *m*

negligent *a* negligente, descuidado; remiso, flojo, perezoso

negligently *adv* negligentemente; con indiferencia

negligible *a* insignificante, escaso, insuficiente; sin importancia, desdeñable

negotiable *a* negociable; (of a road) practicable, transitable

negotiate *vt* gestionar, agenciar, tratar; (a bend) tomar;

(an obstacle) salvar, franquear; *vi* negociar. **to n. a bill of exchange,** descontar una letra de cambio. **to n. for a contract,** tratar un contrato
negotiation *n* negociación, *f*; *com* gestión, transacción, *f*; (of a bend) toma, *f*; (of an obstacle) salto, *m*
negotiator *n* negociador (-ra)
neigh *vi* relinchar. *n* relincho, relinchido, *m*
neighbor *n* vecino (-na); (biblical) prójimo (-ma)
neighborhood *n* vecindad, *f*, vecindario, *m*; cercanía, *f*, afueras, *f pl*, alrededores, *m pl*; *a* de barrio (e.g. **neighborhood moviehouse,** cine del barrio)
neighboring *a* vecino; cercano, inmediato, adyacente
neighborliness *n* buena vecindad, *f*
neighborly *a* amistoso, sociable, bondadoso. **to be n.,** ser de buena vecindad.
neither *a* ningún; ninguno de los dos, e.g. **N. explanation is right,** Ninguna de las dos explicaciones es correcta. *conjunc* ni, tampoco, e.g. **N. Mary nor John,** Ni María ni Juan. **N. will he give it to her,** Tampoco se lo dará. *pron* ni uno ni otro, ninguno, e.g. **N. of them heard it,** Ni uno ni otro lo oyó.
nemesis *n* némesis, *f*; justicia, *f*
nenuphar *n bot* nenúfar, *m*
neo- *prefix* neo. **neo-Catholic,** *a* and *n* neo-católico (-ca). **neo-Platonic,** neoplatónico. **neo-Platonism,** neoplatonismo, *m*
neolithic *a* neolítico
neologism *n* neologismo, *m*
neon *n chem* neón, *m*
neon sign anuncio luminoso, *m*
neophyte *n* neófito (-ta); aspirante, *mf*
nephew *n* sobrino, *m*
nephritis *n med* nefritis, *f*
nepotism *n* nepotismo, *m*
nerve *n* (*anat bot*) nervio, *m*; valor, ánimo, *m*; vitalidad, *f*; *inf* descaro, *m*, desvergüenza, frescura, *f*. *vt* animar, alentar, envalentonar; esforzar; dar fuerza (a). *vi* animarse, esforzarse (a). **My nerves are all on edge,** Se me crispan los nervios. **n.-cell,** neurona, *f*. **to lose one's n.,** perder la cabeza; perder los nervios. **to strain every n.,** hacer un esfuerzo supremo. **n. center,** centro nervioso, *m*. **n.-racking,** espantoso, horripilante. **n. strain,** tensión nerviosa, *f*
nerveless *a* sin nervio; enervado
nerviness *n* nervosidad, *f*
nervous *a* nervioso, asustadizo, tímido; agitado, excitado; (of style) vigoroso. **n. breakdown,** crisis nerviosa, *f*. **n. system,** sistema nervioso, *m*
nervously *adv* nerviosamente; tímidamente
nervousness *n* nervosidad, timidez, *f*; agitación, *f*; (of style) vigor, *m*; energía, *f*
nervy *a* nervioso
nest *vi* anidar, hacerse un nido. *n* (bird's) nido, *m*; (animal's) madriguera, *f*; (of drawers) juego, *m*, serie, *f*; (of thieves) cueva, guarida, *f*; *inf* casita, *f*, hogar, *m*. **to feather one's n.,** hacer su agosto. **n.-egg,** *fig* nidal, *m*. **n. of eggs,** nidada de huevos, *f*
nestle *vt* apoyar. *vi* apiñarse, hacerse un ovillo. **to n. up to a person,** apretarse contra
nestling *n* pichón, pollo, *m*; pajarito, *m*
net *vt* coger con redes; obtener, coger; cubrir con redes. *vi* hacer redes. *n* red, *f*; (mesh) malla, *f*; (fabric) tul, *m*. **net making,** manufactura de redes, *f*
net *a com* líquido, neto, limpio; (of fabric) de tul. **net amount,** importe líquido, importe neto, *m*. **net balance,** saldo líquido, *m*. **net cost,** precio neto, *m*. **net profit,** beneficio neto (or líquido), *m*
nether *a* inferior, bajero, más bajo. **n. regions,** infierno, *m*
Netherland *a* neerlandés, holandés
Netherlander *n* neerlandés (-esa), holandés (-esa)
Netherlands, the los Países Bajos *m pl*
nethermost *a* lo más bajo, ínfimo, más hondo
netting *n* red, (obra de) malla, *f*; *naut* jareta, *f*; manufactura de redes, *f*; pesca con redes, *f*. **wire-n.,** tela metálica, malla de alambre, *f*
nettle *vt* picar; *fig* irritar, picar, fastidiar, disgustar. *n* ortiga, *f*. **n.-rash,** urticaria, *f*
network *n* red, malla, randa, *f*; (of communications) sistema, *m*, red, *f*
neuralgia *n* neuralgia, *f*
neuralgic *a* neurálgico
neurasthenia *n* neurastenia, *f*
neurasthenic *a* and *n* neurasténico (-ca)
neuritis *n* neuritis, *f*
neurologist *n* neurólogo, *m*
neurology *n* neurología, *f*
neuropath *n* neurópata, *m*
neuropathic *a* neuropático
neurosis *n* neurosis, *f*
neurosurgeon *n* neurocirujano, *m*
neurotic *a* and *n* neurótico (-ca)
neuter *a* neutro; (of verbs) intransitivo; (*zool bot*) sin sexo
neutral *a* neutral; (*chem mech*) neutro; (of colors) indeciso, indeterminado; (of persons) imparcial, indiferente. *n* neutral, *mf mech* **to go into n.,** pasar a marcha neutra
neutrality *n* neutralidad, *f*; indiferencia, *f*; imparcialidad, *f*
neutralization *n* neutralización, *f*
neutralize *vt* neutralizar
never *adv* nunca, jamás; de ningún modo, no; ni aun, ni siquiera. **Better late than n.,** Más vale tarde que nunca. **Never look a gift horse in the mouth,** A caballo regalado no se le mira el diente. **Were the hour n. so late,** Por más tarde que fuese la hora. **n. again,** nunca jamás. **n. a one,** ni siquiera uno. **n. a whit,** ni pizca. **N. mind!** ¡No importa! ¡No te preocupes! ¡No hagas caso! **n.-ceasing,** continuo, incesante. **n.-ending,** inacabable, eterno, sin fin. **n.-failing,** infalible. **n.-to-be-forgotten,** inolvidable
nevermore *adv* nunca jamás
nevertheless *adv* sin embargo, no obstante, con todo
new *a* nuevo; novel, fresco; distinto, diferente; moderno; (inexperienced) novato, no habituado; reciente. *adv* (in compounds) recién. **as good as new,** como nuevo. **brand-new,** flamante, nuevecito. **newborn,** recién nacido. **new-comer,** recién llegado (-da). **new-fashioned,** de última moda. **new-found,** recién hallado. **new-laid egg,** huevo fresco, *m*. **new moon,** luna nueva, *f*, novilunio, *m*. **new rich,** ricacho (-cha); indio, *m*. **new student,** alumno de nuevo ingreso. **New Testament,** Nuevo Testamento, *m*. **New World,** Nuevo Mundo, *m*. **New York (er),** *a* and *n* neoyorquino (-na). **New Zealand(er),** *a* and *n* neozelandés (-esa)
newel *n* (of stair) alma, *f*, árbol, nabo, *m*. **n.-post,** pilarote (de escalera), *m*
newest *a sup* novísimo; más reciente
Newfoundland Terranova, *f*. **N. dog,** perro de Terranova, *m*
newish *a* bastante nuevo
newly *adv* nuevamente; hace poco, recientemente. The abb. form **recién** is used only with past part, e.g. **the n. painted door,** la puerta recién pintada. **the n.-weds,** los desposados, los recién casados
newness *n* novedad, *f*; inexperiencia, falta de práctica, *f*; innovación, *f*
New Orleans Nueva Orleans, *f*
news *n pl* noticias, *f pl*; nueva, *f*; reporte, aviso, *m*; novedad, *f*. **No n. is good n.,** Falta de noticias, buena señal. **piece of n.,** noticia, *f*. **What's the n.?** ¿Qué hay de nuevo? **n. agency,** agencia de noticias, agencia periodística, *f*. **n.-agent,** agente de la prensa, *m*; vendedor (-ra) de periódicos. **n. bulletin,** *rad* boletín de noticias, *m*. *inf* **n.-hound,** gacetillero (-ra). **n. item,** noticia de actualidad, *f*. **n.-print,** papel para periódicos, *m*. **n.-room,** gabinete de lectura, *m*. **n. reel,** película noticiera, revista cinematográfica, *f*, noticiario cinematográfico, noticiero *m*, actualidades, *f pl*.

n.-stand, puesto de periódicos, quiosco de periódicos, *m.* **n. theater,** cine de actualidades, *m*
newsboy *n Lat. Am.* canillito, *m*
newscast *n* noticiario, *m*
newsgirl *n Lat. Am.* canillita, *f*
newsletter circular noticiera, relación de sucesos, *f*
newspaper *n* periódico, diario, noticiero, *m.* **n. clipping, n. cutting,** recorte de periódico, *m.* **n. paragraph,** suelto, *m.* **n. reporter,** reportero (-ra); periodista, *mf* **n. reporting,** reporterismo, *m.* **n. serial,** folletín, *m,* novela por entregas, *f.* **n. vendor,** vendedor (-ra) de periódicos, *n*
news report *n* reportaje, *m*
newsy *a inf* lleno de noticias, noticioso
newt *n* tritón, *m*
Newtonian *a* neutoniano
New York Nueva York, *f*
New Zealand Nueva Zelandia, *f*
next *a* (of place) siguiente, vecino, contiguo; (of time) próximo, siguiente. **on the n. page,** en la página siguiente. **the n. day,** el día siguiente. **the n.-door house,** la casa vecina. **the n. life,** la otra vida. **n. month (yesar),** el mes (año) próximo (or que viene). **n. time,** otra vez, la próxima vez
next *adv* (of time) luego, en seguida; (of place) inmediatamente después. **I come n.,** Ahora me toca a mí. **It is n. to a certainty that . . . ,** Es casi seguro que . . . **the n. best,** el segundo. **the n. of kin,** los pariente más cercarro, *m,* parientes más cercanos, *m pl.* **to wear n. to the skin,** llevar sobre la piel. **n. to,** al lado de, junto a; primero después de; casi. **n. to nothing,** casi nada, muy poco. **What n.?** ¿Qué más?; ¿Y ahora qué?
nib *n* punto, tajo (de una pluma), *m*
nibble *vt* mordiscar, mordisquear, roer; (horses) rozar; (fish) picar; *fig* considerar, tantear; *vi* picar. *n* mordisco, *m;* roedura, *f*
Nicaraguan *a* and *n* nicaragüeño (-ña)
Nice Niza, *f*
nice *a* escrupuloso, minucioso, exacto; (of persons) simpático, afable, amable; fino; (of things) agradable, bonito; bueno; sutil, delicado; (*inf iron*) bonito. **a n. point,** un punto delicado. **a n. view,** una vista agradable (or bonita). **n.-looking,** guapo. **n. people,** gente fina, *f;* gente simpática, *f*
nicely *adv* muy bien; con elegancia; primorosamente; con amabilidad, gentilmente; agradablemente
Nicene *a* niceno
niceness *n* exactitud, minuciosidad, *f;* (of persons) bondad, amabilidad, *f;* amenidad, hermosura, *f;* lo bonito; sutileza, *f;* refinamiento, *m*
nicety *n* exactitud, *f;* sutileza, *f,* refinamiento, *m.* **niceties,** *n pl* detalles, *m pl.* **to a n.,** con la mayor precisión; a la perfección
niche *n* nicho, templete, *m;* (vaulted) hornacina, *f, fig* **to find a n. for oneself,** encontrarse una buena posición; situarse
nick *vt* cortar en muescas, mellar, tarjar. *n* mella, muesca, *f.* **in the n. of time,** en el momento oportuno, a tiempo
nickel *n* níquel, *m; com* moneda de níquel, *f.* **n.-plated,** niquelado
nickname *vt* apodar, motejar, apellidar. *n* apodo, sobrenombre, mote, mal nombre, *m*
nicotine *n* nicotina, *f*
nicotinism *n* nicotismo, *m*
nictitating membrane *n anat* membrana nictitante, *f*
niece *n* sobrina, *f*
niggardliness *n* tacañería, avaricia, parsimonia, mezquindad, *f*
niggardly *a* tacaño, avaricioso, mezquino, ruin, miserable
niggling *a* nimio, meticuloso; escrupuloso, minucioso
nigh. See **near**
night *n* noche, *f; fig* oscuridad, *f,* tinieblas, *f pl.* **all n.,** toda la noche, la noche entera. **all n. service,** servicio nocturno permanente, *m.* **at** or **by n.,** de noche. **every n.,** todas las noches, cada noche. **Good n.!** ¡Buenas noches! **last n.,** ayer por la noche, anoche, la noche pasada. **restless n.,** noche mala, noche toledana, *f.* **the n. before last,** anteayer por la noche, *m.* **to-n.,** esta noche. **tomorrow n.,** mañana por la noche. **to be n.,** ser de noche. **to spend the n.,** pernoctar, pasar la noche. **n.-bird,** pájaro nocturno, *m; inf* trasnochador (-ra). **n.-blindness,** nictalopia, *f.* **n.-cap,** gorro de dormir, *m.* **n. clothes,** traje de dormir, *m.* **n. club,** cabaré *m.* **n. dew,** relente, sereno, *m.* **n. flying,** vuelo nocturno, *m.* **n.-jar,** *orn* chotacabras, *m.* **n.-light,** mariposa, lamparilla, *f.* **n. mail,** último correo, *m;* tren correo de la noche, *m.* **n. school,** escuela nocturna, *f.* **n. shift,** turno de noche, *m.* **n. table** *Mexico* buró, *m.* **n. watch,** ronda de noche, *f; naut* sonochada, *f.* **n. watchman,** (in the street) sereno, *m;* (of a building) vigilante nocturno, *m*
nightfall *n* anochecer, crepúsculo, atardecer, *m*
nightgown *n* camisa de noche, *f*
nightingale *n* ruiseñor, *m*
nightly *a* de noche; nocturno, nocturnal. *adv* todas las noches, cada noche
nightmare *n* pesadilla, *f*
nightmarish *a* de pesadilla, horrible
nightshade *n bot* hierba mora, *f,* solano, *m*
nihilism *n* nihilismo, *m*
nihilist *n* nihilista, *mf*
Nile, the el Nilo, *m*
nimble *a* ágil, activo, *Mexico* alacre; vivo, listo. **n.-fingered,** ligero de dedos. **n.-witted,** despierto, vivo
nimbleness *n* agilidad, actividad, *Mexico* alacridad, *f;* viveza, habilidad, *f*
nimbly *adv* ágilmente, ligeramente
nimbus *n* nimbo, *m,* aureola, *f*
nincompoop *n* papirote, *m,* papanatas, *mf* tonto (-ta)
nine *a* and *n* nueve, *m.* **He is n.,** Tiene nueve años. **the N.,** las nueve Musas. **n. o'clock,** las nueve. **to be dressed up to the nines,** estar hecho un brazo de mar
ninefold *a* and *adv* nueve veces
ninepins *n* juego de bolos, *m*
nineteen *a* and *n* diez y nueve, diecinueve *m*
nineteenth *a* décimonono. *n* (of month) el diez y nueve; (of monarchs) diez y nueve. **the n. century,** el siglo diez y nueve
ninetieth *a* nonagésimo, noventa
ninety *a* and *n* noventa *m.* **n.-one,** noventa y uno. **n.-two,** noventa y dos. **the n.-first chapter,** el capítulo noventa y uno
ninny *n* parapoco, chancleta, *mf;* mentecato (-ta)
ninth *a* noveno, nono. *n* nueve, *m;* (of the month) el nueve (of sovereigns) nono. **one n.,** un noveno
ninthly *adv* en noveno (or nono) lugar
nip *vt* pellizcar, pinchar; mordiscar, morder; (wither) marchitar; (freeze) helar; (run) correr. *vi* pinchar; picar (el viento). *n* pellizco, pinchazo, *m;* mordisco, *m;* (of spirits) trago, *m;* copita, *f;* (in the air) viento frío, hielo, *m.* **to nip in,** colarse dentro, deslizarse en. **to nip off,** pirarse, mudarse. *fig* **to nip in the bud,** cortar en flor
nippers *n pl* alicates, *m pl;* tenacillas, pinzas, *f pl*
nipping *n* pinchadura, *f;* mordedura, *f.* *a* punzante; helado, glacial, mordiente. **n. off,** (of a point) despuntadura, *f*
nipple *n* pezón, *m;* pezón artificial, *m*
nit *n ent* liendre, *f*
nitrate *n chem* nitrato, *m*
nitre *n* salitre, *m*
nitric *a* nítrico
nitrite *n chem* nitrito, *m*
nitro- *prefix chem* nitro. **n.-cellulose,** algodón pólvora, *m.* **n.-glycerine,** nitroglicerina, *f*
nitrogen *n chem* nitrógeno, *m*
no *a* ningún, ninguno, ninguna, e.g. **by no means,** de ningún modo. **No** is often not translated in Sp., e.g. **I have no time,** No tengo tiempo. *adv* no. *n* voto negativo, no, *m.* **to be of no account,** no tener impor-

tancia; no significar nada. **to be no good for,** no servir para. **to be of no use,** ser inútil. **to have no connection with,** no tener nada que ver con. **for no reason,** sin motivo alguno. **"No Admittance,"** «Entrada Prohibida.» **no, indeed,** Cierto que no. **no-man's land,** tierra de nadie, *f.* **no more,** no más. **No more of this!** ¡No hablemos más de eso! **no one,** nadie, ninguno. **no sooner,** no bien, tan pronto (como). **no such thing,** no tal. **"No Thoroughfare,"** «Prohibido el Paso.» **whether or not,** sea o no sea

Noah's Ark *n* arca de Noé, *f*

nobility *n* nobleza, *f;* (of rank) aristocracia, nobleza, *f;* (of conduct) caballerosidad, hidalguía, generosidad, bondad, *f;* (grandeur) grandeza, sublimidad, *f.* **the higher n.,** los nobles de primera clase

noble *a* noble; (in rank) aristocrático, noble, linajudo; (of conduct) caballeroso, generoso; (of buildings) sublime, magnífico. *n* noble, *m,* aristócrata, *mf* **to make n.,** ennoblecer. **n.-mindedness,** generosidad, grandeza de alma, *f.* **n. title,** título de nobleza, título del reino, *m*

noblewoman *n* dama noble, mujer noble, aristócrata, *f*

nobly *adv* noblemente, generosamente. **n. born,** noble de nacimiento

nobody *n* nadie, ninguno. **There was n. there,** No había nadie allí. *inf* **a n.,** un (una) cualquiera, una persona insignificante. **n. else,** nadie más, ningún otro

nocturnal *a* nocturno, nocherniego, nocturnal

nocturne *n mus* nocturno, *m*

nod *vt* inclinar la cabeza; hacer una señal (or señas) con la cabeza; *vi* dar cabezadas; cabecear; (of trees) mecerse, inclinarse; inclinar la cabeza. *n* señal (or seña) con la cabeza, *f;* inclinación de la cabeza, *f;* cabeceo, *m,* cabezada, *Lat. Am.* cabeceada, *f.* **A nod is as good as a wink,** A buen entendedor pocas palabras. **He nodded to me as he passed,** Me saludó con la cabeza al pasar. **He signed to me with a nod,** Me hizo una señal con la cabeza

nodding *a* que cabecea; *bot* colgante, inclinado; temblante. *n* cabeceo, *m;* saludo con la cabeza, *m*

noddle *n* mollera, *f*

node *n* (*bot med*) nudo, *m*

nodule *n* nódulo, *m;* nudillo, *m*

noise *n* ruido, son, *m;* tumulto, clamor, estruendo, alboroto, *Central America* embullo, *m.* **to make a n.,** hacer ruido. **to n. abroad,** divulgar, publicar

noiseless *a* silencioso, callado, sin ruido

noiselessness *n* silencio, *m,* falta de ruido, *f*

noisily *adv* ruidosamente

noisiness *n* ruido, estrépito, tumulto, clamor, *m;* (of voices) gritería, *f*

noisome *a* ofensivo; fétido, apestoso

noisy *a* ruidoso; estruendoso; estrepitoso, clamoroso

nomad *a* nómada, errante; (of flocks) trashumante. *n* nómada, *mf*

nomadism *n* nomadismo, *m*

nomenclature *n* nomenclatura, *f*

nominal *a* nominal; titular; insignificante, de poca importancia. **the n. head,** el director en nombre

nominalism *n* nominalismo, *m*

nominally *adv* nominalmente, en nombre

nominate *vt* nombrar, designar, elegir; fijar, señalar

nominating *a* nominador

nomination *n* nombramiento, *m,* nominación, *f;* señalamiento, *m*

nominator *n* nominador (-ra)

nominee *n* nómino propuesto, *m*

non *adv* non; des-; in-; falta de. **non-acceptance,** rechazo, *m.* **non-acquaintance,** ignorancia, *f.* **non-admission,** no admisión, *f;* denegación, *f,* rechazo, *m.* **non-aggression,** no agresión, *f.* **non-alcoholic,** no alcohólico. **non-appearance,** ausencia, *f; law* no comparecencia, contumacia, *f.* **non-arrival,** ausencia, *f;* falta de recibo, *f.* **non-attendance,** falta de asistencia, ausencia, *f.* **non-carbonated,** sin gas. **non-combatant,** no combatiente. **non-commissioned officer,** oficial subalterno, *m.* **non-committal,** evasivo, equívoco, ambiguo. **non-compliance,** falta de obediencia, *f.* **non-concurrence,** falta de acuerdo, *f.* **non-conducting,** no conductivo. **non-conductor,** mal conductor, *m; elec* aislador, *m.* **non-contagious,** no contagioso. **non-cooperation,** *pol* resistencia pasiva, *f;* no cooperación, *f.* **non-delivery,** falta de entrega, *f.* **non-essential,** no esencial, prescindible. **non-execution,** no cumplimiento, *m.* **non-existence,** no existencia, *f.* **non-existent,** inexistente, no existente. **non-intervention,** no intervención, *f.* **non-manufacturing,** no industrial. **non-member,** visitante, *mf* **non-observance,** incumplimiento, *m;* violación, *f.* **non-payment,** falta de pago, *f.* **non-performance,** falta de ejecución, *f.* **non-poisonous,** no venenoso, innocuo. **non-resistance,** falta de resistencia, *f;* obediencia pasiva, *f.* **non-skid,** antideslizante, antirresbaladizo. **non-smoking,** que no fuma; (of a railway compartment, etc.) para no fumadores. **non-stop,** continuo, incesante; directo, sin parar; *aer* sin escalas

nonagenarian *a* and *n* nonagenario (-ia)

non-aligned *a* no abanderado

non-alignment *n* no abanderamiento *m*

nonce word *n* palabra ocasional, *f*

nonchalance *n* aplomo, *m,* indiferencia, frialdad, calma, *f*

nonchalant *a* indiferente, frío, impasible

nonchalantly *adv* con indiferencia

nonconformist *a* and *n* disidente *mf; a* inconforme, *n,* inconformista, *mf*

nonconformity *n* disidencia, *f*

nondescript *a* indeterminado, indefinido, indeciso, mediocre

none *pron* nadie, ninguno; nada. *a* and *n* ninguno (-na). *adv* no; de ningún modo, de ninguna manera. **I have n.,** No lo tengo, No tengo ninguno. **We have n. of your things,** No tenemos ninguna de tus cosas. **I was n. the worse,** No me hallaba peor. **N. can read his account with pleasure,** Nadie puede leer su narración con gusto. **n. the less,** no menos; sin embargo

nonentity *n* persona sin importancia, medianía, *f,* cero, *m*

nones *n pl ecc* nona, *f;* (Roman Calendar) nonas, *f pl,*

nonplussed *a* cortado, perplejo, confuso

non-profit *a* sin fines de lucro, sin fines lucrativos

non-self-governing *a* no autónomo

nonsense *n* disparate, despropósito, desatino, *m,* absurdidad, *f; inf* galimatías, *m;* pamplina, patraña, *f.* **to talk n.,** hablar sin ton ni son. **N.!** ¡A otro perro con este hueso! ¡Patrañas!

nonsensical *a* absurdo, ridículo, disparatado

noodle *n cul* tallarín, *m; inf* mentecato (-ta), bobo (-ba)

nook *n* escondrijo, lugar retirado, rincón, *m*

noon *n* mediodía, *m; fig* punto culminante, apogeo, *m,* *a* de mediodía, meridional. **at n.,** a mediodía

noose *vt* coger con lazos. *n* lazo corredizo, dogal, *m*

nopal *n bot* nopal, *m*

No Parking «Se Prohibe Estacionar,» «Se Prohibe Estacionarse»

nor *conjunc* ni, no, tampoco. **He removed neither his coat nor his hat,** No se quitó ni el gabán ni el sombrero. **Nor was this the first time,** Y no fue ésta la primera vez. **Nor I,** Ni yo tampoco

Nordic *a* and *n* nórdico (-ca)

norm *n* modelo, *m,* norma, regla, pauta, *f;* (of size) marca, *f;* (*bot zool*) tipo, *m*

normal *a* normal; común, natural, corriente, regular; *math* perpendicular, normal. *n* condición normal, *f,* estado normal, *m; math* normal, *f.* **to become n.,** normalizarse, hacerse normal. **to make n.,** normalizar. **n. school,** escuela normal, *f*

normality *n* normalidad, *f*

normalization *n* normalización, *f*

normalize *vt* normalizar

normally *adv* normalmente

Norman *a* and *n* normando (-da)

Normandy Normandía, *f*
Norse *n* noruego (language), *m*, *a* escandinavo
Norseman *n* normando, viking (*pl* -os), hombre del norte, *m*
north *n* norte, *m*. *a* del norte, septentrional. **n. by west,** norte, cuarta noroeste. **n. of the city,** al norte de la ciudad. **N.-American,** *a* and *n* norte-americano (-na). **n.-east,** *a* and *n* nordeste *m*. **n.-easter,** viento del nordeste, *m*. **n.-easterly,** del nordeste (winds). **n.-eastern,** del nordeste (places). **n.-eastward,** hacia el nordeste. **n.-n.-east,** nornordeste, *m*. **n.-n.-west,** nornorueste, *m*. **n.-polar,** ártico. **N. Star,** estrella del norte, estrella polar, *f*. **n.-west,** noroeste, *m*. **n.-wester,** viento del noroeste, *m*. **n.-westerly,** del noroeste (winds). **n.-westerly gale,** temporal del noroeste, *m*. **n.-western,** del noroeste; situado al noroeste. **n.-westwards,** hacia el noroeste. **n. wind,** el viento del norte, el cierzo
North America, Norteamérica, América del Norte, *f*
northern *a* del norte, septentrional, norteño; (of races) nórdico. **N. Cross,** crucero, *m*. **n. lights,** aurora boreal, *f*
northerner *n* hombre del norte, *m*, habitante del norte, *mf*
northernmost *a sup* al extremo norte, más septentrional
northwards *adv* hacia el norte
Norway Noruega, *f*
Norwegian *a* and *n* noruego (-ga); (language) noruego, *m*
nose *n* nariz, *f*; (of animals) hocico, *m*; (sense of smell) olfato, *m*; (of ships) proa, *f*; (of jug) pico, *m*, boca, *f*; (projecting piece) cuerno, *m*, nariz, *f*; (of airplane) cabeza, *f*. *vt* acariciar con la nariz; avanzar lentamente. *vi* husmear, olfatear. **to n. into,** *inf* meter las narices, poner baza. **to n. out,** descubrir, averiguar. **to bleed at the n.,** echar sangre por las narices. **to blow one's n.,** sonar (or limpiarse) las narices. **to keep one's n. to the grindstone,** estar sobre el yunque, batir el cobre. *fig* **to lead by the n.,** tener a uno agarrado por las narices. **to pay through the n.,** costar un ojo de la cara. **to speak through the n.,** ganguear. **to turn up one's n.,** *fig* hacer gestos (a), volver la cara. **flat n.,** nariz chata, *f*. **snub n.,** nariz respingona, *f*. **well-shaped n.,** nariz perfilada, *f*. **under one's n.,** bajo las narices de uno. **n.-bag,** cebadera, mochila, *f*; morral, *m*. **n.-bleeding,** *med* epistaxis, *f*; hemorragia de las narices, *f*. **n.-dive,** *aer* descenso de cabeza, picado, *m*. *vi* picar. **n.-piece,** (of microscope) ocular, *m*. **n.-ring,** (of a bull, etc.) narigón, *m*
-nosed *a* de nariz . . . , con la nariz . . .
nosegay *n* ramillete, *m*
nosey Parker *n inf* mequetrefe, *m*; cócora, *Lat. Am.* averigüetas, *Argentina* hurguete, *mf*
No Smoking «Prohibido Fumar», Se Prohibe Fumar
nostalgia *n* nostalgia, añoranza, *f*
nostalgic *a* nostálgico
nostril *n* ventana de la nariz, *f*, *n pl* **nostrils,** narices, *f pl*
nostrum *n* panacea, *f*, curalotodo, *m*; medicina patentada, *f*
not *adv* no; sin; ni, ni siquiera. **Is it not true? We think not,** ¿No es verdad? No lo creemos. **You have seen Mary, have you not?** Vd. ha visto a María, ¿verdad? **not caring whether he came or not,** sin preocuparse de que viniese o no. **not that he will come,** no es decir que venga. **not at all,** de ningún modo; (courtesy) ¡de nada! **not even,** ni siquiera. **not guilty,** no culpable. **not one,** ni uno. **not so much as,** no tanto como; ni siquiera. **It is not so much that, as it is . . .** No es tanto eso, cuanto que . . . **not to say,** por no decir
notability *n* notabilidad, *f*; (person) notable, *mf* persona de importancia, *f*
notable *a* notable, señalado, memorable; digno de atención. *n* persona eminente, *f*, notable, *mf*
notably *adv* notablemente, señaladamente
notary *n* notario, escribano, *m*
notation *n* notación, *f*
notch *vt* cortar muescas (en); mellar, ranurar, entallar. *n* muesca, mella, ranura, entalladura, *f*
note *vt* notar, observar; anotar, apuntar; advertir, hacerse cuenta de. *n mus* nota, *f*; son, acento, *m*; (letter) recado, billete, *m*; anotación, glosa, *f*; apuntación, *f*, apunte, *m*, nota, *f*; (importance) importancia, distinción, *f*; *com* vale, abonaré, *m*; (sign) marca, señal, *f*. **to n. down,** anotar. **worthy of note,** digno de atención. **n.-book,** libro de apuntes, cuaderno, *m*, libreta, *f*. **n.-case,** cartera, *f*, *com* **n. of hand,** pagaré, *m*. **n.-paper,** papel de escribir, *m*. **n.-taker,** apuntador (-ra)
noted *a* célebre, famoso, ilustre, eminente, insigne
noteworthy *a* digno de nota, notable, digno de atención
nothing *n* nada, *f*; la nada; cero, *m*. *adv* en nada. **to come to n.,** anonadarse, fracasar. **to do n.,** no hacer nada. **to do n. but,** no hacer más que. **to have n. to do with,** no tener nada que ver con; *inf* no tener arte ni parte en. **There is n. else to do,** No hay nada más que hacer; No hay más remedio. **There is n. to fear,** No hay de que tener miedo. **We could make n. of the book,** No llegamos a comprender el libro. **for n.,** de balde, en vano; gratis. **next to n.,** casi nada. **n. else or more,** nada más. **n. like,** ni con mucho. **n. much,** poca cosa. **n. new,** nada nuevo. **n. similar,** nada semejante. **n. to speak of,** poca cosa
nothingness *n* nada, *f*
notice *vt* observar, reparar en, darse cuenta (de), marcar, caer en la cuenta (de), fijarse (en). *n* observación, atención, *f*; aviso, *m*, notificación, *f*; anuncio, *m*; (term) plazo, *m*; (review) crítica, *f*. **at short n.,** a corto aviso. **until further n.,** hasta nuevo aviso (or orden). **to attract n.,** atraer la atención. **I hadn't noticed,** No me había fijado. **to be beneath one's n.,** no merecer su atención. **to be under n.,** estar dimitido. **to bring to the n. of,** dar noticia de. **to escape n.,** pasar desapercibido. **to give n.,** hacer saber, informar; (of employer) despedir (a); (of employee) dimitir, dar la dimisión. **to take n. of,** notar, darse cuenta de; hacer caso, atender (a). **n. board,** letrero, tablero de anuncios, *m*. **n. to quit,** desahúcio, *m*
noticeable *a* perceptible, evidente; digno de observación, notable
noticeably *adv* perceptiblemente; notablemente
notifiable *a* declarable, notificable
notification *n* notificación, intimación, advertencia, *f*, aviso, *m*
notify *vt* notificar, comunicar, avisar, intimar, hacer saber
notion *n* noción, idea, *f*, concepto, *m*; (view) opinión, *f*, parecer, *m*; (novelty) novedad, *f*; artículo de fantasía, *m*. **I have a n. that . . . ,** Tengo la idea de que . . . , Sospecho que . . . **I haven't a n.,** No tengo idea
No Tipping «No Se Admiten Propinas»
notoriety *n* notoriedad, publicidad, *f*; escándalo, *m*; persona notoria, *f*
notorious *a* notorio, famoso, conocido; escandaloso, sensacional
notoriously *adv* notoriamente
notwithstanding *prep* a pesar de. *adv* sin embargo, no obstante. *conjunc* aunque, bien que, por más que
nougat *n* turrón, *m*
nought *n math* cero, *m*; nada, *f*
noun *n* substantivo, nombre, *m*
nourish *vt* sustentar, alimentar, nutrir; *fig* fomentar, favorecer
nourishing *a* nutritivo, alimenticio, nutricio
nourishment *n* nutrición, *f*; sustento, *m*; alimento, *m*; *fig* fomento, pasto, *m*
Nova Scotia Nueva Escocia, *f*

novel *a* nuevo, original, inacostumbrado. *n* novela, *f.* **n. of roguery,** novela picaresca, *f*
novelette *n* novela corta, *f*
novelist *n* novelista, *mf*
novelty *n* novedad, *f;* innovación, *f;* cambio, *m*
November *n* noviembre, *m*
novice *n ecc* novicio (-ia); comenzante, principiante, *mf,* aspirante, *m, Lat. Am.* advenedizo (-za)
novocain *n med* novocaína, *f*
now *adv* ahora, actualmente, al presente, a la fecha; en seguida, ahora, inmediatamente; poco ha, hace poco; pues bien. *interj* ¡A ver! ¡Vamos! *conjunc* pero, mas. *n* presente, *m,* actualidad, *f.* **before now,** antes, en otras ocasiones, ya, previamente. **just now,** ahora mismo, hace poco. **now . . . now,** ya . . . ya; sucesivamente, en turno. **now and then,** de vez en cuando, de tarde en tarde. **now that,** ya que, ahora que, dado que. **until now,** hasta el presente, hasta aquí, hasta ahora
nowadays *adv* hoy en día, actualmente, en nuestros días
nowhere *adv* en ninguna parte. **in the middle of n.,** donde Cristo dio las tres voces. **n. else,** en ninguna otra parte. *inf* **n. near,** ni con mucho; muy lejos (de)
nowise *adv* de ningún modo, en modo alguno, de ninguna manera
noxious *a* dañoso, nocivo; pestífero
noxiousness *n* nocividad, *f*
nozzle *n* (of a hose-pipe) boquilla, *f; mech* gollete, *m;* tubo de salida, *m,* tobera, *f;* inyector, *m*
n.p. (no place) s.l. (sin lugar)
nuance *n* matiz, *m,* gradación, sombra, *f*
nubile *a* núbil
nuclear *a* nuclear
nucleus *n* núcleo, *m;* centro, foco, *m*
nude *a* desnudo, nudo, *Peru* calato, *elsewhere in Lat. Am.* encuerado
nudge *vt* dar un codazo (a). *n* codazo, *m*
nudism *n* nudismo, *m*
nudist *n* nudista, *mf*
nudity *n* desnudez, *f*
nugget *n min* pepita, *f*
nuisance *n* molestia, incomodidad, *f,* fastidio, *m; inf* tostón, *m,* lata, *Lat. Am.* fregada, *Colombia* vaina, *f.* **to make a n. of oneself,** meterse donde no le llaman, ser un pelmazo. **What a n.!** ¡Qué lata! ¡Qué fastidio!, *Colombia* ¡Qué vaina!
null *a* nulo, inválido, sin fuerza legal. **n. and void,** nulo, írrito
nullification *n* anulación, invalidación, *f*
nullity *n* nulidad, *f*
numb *vt* entumecer, entorpecer. *a* entumecido; torpe, dormido; paralizado; *fig* insensible, pasmado. **n. with cold,** entumecido de frío
number *vt* numerar, contar; poner número (a); (pages of a book) foliar; ascender a. *n* número, *m;* (figure) cifra, *f;* (crowd) multitud, muchedumbre, *f;* cantidad, *f;* (of a periodical) ejemplar, *m; gram* número, *m; pl* versos, *m pl.* **Numbers,** (Bible) Números, *m pl;* **to be numbered among,** figurar entre. **among the n. of,** entre la muchedumbre de. **a n. of,** varios, muchos, una cantidad de. **in great n.,** en gran número; en su mayoría. **6 Peace Street,** Calle de la Paz n^{O} (número) 6. **one of their n.,** uno entre ellos. **n. board,** (racing) indicador, *m.* **n. plate,** *aut* chapa de identidad, placa de número, *f*
numbering *n* numeración, *f*
numberless *a* innumerable, sin número, sin fin, infinito
numbness *n* entumecimiento, entorpecimiento, *m; fig* insensibilidad, *f*
numeral *a* numeral. *n* número, *m,* cifra, *f; gram* nombre o adjetivo numeral, *m*
numerator *n* numerador
numerical *a* numérico
numerous *a* numeroso; nutrido, grande; muchos (-as)
numerousness *n* numerosidad, multitud, muchedumbre, *f*
numismatic *a* numismático. *n pl* **numismatics,** numismática, *f*
numismatist *n* numismático, *m*
numskull *n* zote, topo, *m*
nun *n* monja, religiosa, *f.* **to become a nun,** profesar, tomar el hábito, meterse monja
nuncio *n* nuncio, *m.* **acting n.,** pronuncio, *m*
nunnery *n* convento de monjas, *m*
nuptial *a* nupcial. *n pl* **nuptials,** nupcias, *f pl,* enlace, *m.* **n. mass,** *ecc* misa de velaciones, *f.* **n. song,** epitalamio, *m*
nurse *vt* criar; dar de mamar (a), amamantar; (the sick) cuidar, asistir; (fondle) acariciar, mecer; *fig* fomentar, promover. *vi* trabajar como enfermera. *n* (of the sick) enfermera, *f;* (wet) nodriza, ama de leche, *Lat. Am.* criandera, *f;* (children's) niñera, *f; fig* fomentador, *m.* **male n.,** enfermero, *m*
nursery *n agr* plantel, vivero semillero, criadero, *m;* (children's room) cuarto de los niños, *m; fig* sementera, *f;* semillero, *m.* **n. governess,** aya, *f.* **n. rhyme,** canción infantil, *f*
nurseryman *n* horticultor, *m;* jardinero, *m*
nursing *n* lactancia, crianza, *f;* (of the sick) asistencia, *f,* cuido, *m.* **n. home,** clínica, *f.* **n. mother,** madre lactante, *f*
nurture *vt* alimentar; criar, educar. *n* nutrición, alimentación, *f;* crianza, educación, *f*
nut *vi* coger nueces. *n bot* nuez, *f; mech* tuerca, hembra de tornillo, *f, inf* **to be a tough nut to crack,** ser un tío de cuidado. **to crack nuts,** cascar nueces. **to go nutting,** coger nueces. **cashew nut,** anacardo, *m.* **loose nut,** *mech* tuerca aflojada, *f.* **nut-brown,** castaño. **nut tree,** nogal, *m*
nutcrackers *n pl* cascanueces, quebrantanueces, *m*
nutmeg *n* nuez moscada, nuez de especia, *f*
nutria *n zool* nutria, *f*
nutriment *n* nutrimento, alimento, *m*
nutrition *n* nutrición, alimentación, *f*
nutritious, nutritive *a* nutritivo, alimenticio, alible
nutshell *n* cáscara de nuez, *f.* **to put in a n.,** decir en resumidas cuentas, decir en forma apastillada
nutty *a* de nuez
nuzzle *vt* acariciar con la nariz
nylon *n* nilón, nylon, *m.* **n. stockings,** medias de cristal (or de nilón), *f pl*
nymph *n* ninfa, *f; ent* crisálida, *f.* **n.-like,** como una ninfa; de ninfa
nymphomania *n* ninfomanía, *f,* furor uterino, *m*

o *n* (letter) o, *f, interj* ¡o! **O that . . . !** ¡Ojalá que!
oaf *n* zoquete, zamacuco, *m*
oafish *a* lerdo, torpe
oafishness *n* torpeza, estupidez, *f*
oak *n* (tree and wood) roble, *m, a* de roble. **carved oak,** roble tallado, *m.* **holm-oak,** encina, *f.* **oak-apple,** agalla, *f.* **oak grove,** robledo, *m*
oakum *n* estopa, *f*
oar *n* remo, *m.* **to lie on the oars,** cesar de remar. **to pull at the oars,** bogar, remar. **to put in one's oar,** *inf* meter baza. **to ship the oars,** armar los remos. **to unship the oars,** desarmar los remos. **oar-stroke,** palada, *f*
oarsman *n* remero, bogador, *m*

oarsmanship *n* arte de remar, *m*, or *f*
OAS (Organization of American States) OEA (Organización de los Estados Americanos)
oasis *n* oasis, *m*
oast *n* horno para secar el lúpulo, *m*
oat *n bot* avena, *f*. **wild oat,** avena silvestre, *f*. **to sow one's wild oats,** correrla, andarse a la flor del berro. **oat field,** avenal, *m*
oath *n* juramento, *m*; (curse) blasfemia, *f*, reniego, *m*. **on o.,** bajo juramento. **to break an o.,** violar el juramento. **to put on o.,** tomar juramento, hacer prestar juramento. **to take an o.,** prestar (or hacer) juramento. **to take the o. of allegiance,** jurar la bandera
oatmeal *n* harina de avena, *f*
obduracy *n* obduración, obstinación, terquedad, *f*
obdurate *a* obstinado, terco, porfiado. **He is o. to our requests,** Es sordo a nuestros ruegos
obedience *n* obediencia, sumisión, docilidad, *f*. **blind o.,** obediencia ciega, *f*. **in o. to,** conforme a, de acuerdo con
obedient *a* obediente, sumiso, dócil. **to be o. to,** ser obediente (a), obedecer (a)
obediently *adv* obedientemente, dócilmente. **Yours o.,** Su atento servidor (su att. s.)
obeisance *n* reverencia, cortesía, *f*, saludo, *m*; (homage) homenaje, *m*
obelisk *n* obelisco, *m*
obese *a* obeso, corpulento, grueso, gordo
obesity *n* obesidad, gordura, corpulencia, *f*
obey *vt* and *vi* obedecer. *vt* (carry out) cumplir, observar. **to be obeyed,** ser obedecido
obfuscate *vt* ofuscar, cegar
obfuscation *n* ofuscamiento, *m*, confusión, *f*
obituary *a* mortuorio, necrológico. *n* obituario, *m*, necrología, *f*. **o. column,** (in newspaper) sección necrológica, *f*. **o. notice,** esquela de defunción, *f*
object *n* objeto, artículo, *m*, cosa, *f*; (purpose) propósito, intento, *m*; (aim) fin, término, *m*; *gram* complemento, *m*; *inf* individuo, *m*. *vt* objetar, poner reparos (a). *vi* oponerse, poner objeciones. **I o. to that remark,** Protesto contra esa observación. **If you don't o.,** Si Vd. no tiene inconveniente. **o. finder,** objetivo, *m*. **o. lesson,** lección de cosas, *f*; lección práctica, *f*
objection *n* objeción, protesta, *f*, reparo, *m*; (obstacle) dificultad, *f*, inconveniente, *m*. **to have no o.,** no tener inconveniente. **to raise an o.,** hacer constar una protesta, poner una objeción
objectionable *a* censurable, reprensible; desagradable, molesto
objective *a* objetivo; *gram* acusativo. *n* objeto, propósito, *m*; destinación, *f*; *mil* objetivo, *m*, *gram* **o. case,** caso acusativo, *m*,
objectivism *n phil* objetivismo, *m*
objectivity *n* objetividad, *f*
objector *n* objetante, *mf*, impugnador (-ra). **conscientious o.,** (dissident) el, *m*, (*f*, la) que protesta contra; (pacifist) pacifista, *mf*
oblation *n* oblación, ofrenda, *f*
obligation *n* obligación, *f*; deber, *m*, precisión, *f*; compromiso, *m*. **of o.,** de deber; de precepto. **to be under an o.,** estar bajo una obligación; deber un favor. **to place under an o.,** poner bajo una obligación
obligatory *a* obligatorio, forzoso
oblige *vt* (insist on) obligar, hacer, forzar; (gratify) hacer un favor (a), complacer. **He obliged me with a match,** Me hizo el favor de una cerilla. **They are much obliged to you,** Le están muy reconocidos. **Much obliged!** ¡Se agradece!
obliging *a* atento, condescendiente, complaciente, servicial, *Lat. Am.* acomedido
obligingly *adv* cortésmente
obligingness *n* cortesía, amabilidad, bondad, *f*
oblique *a* oblicuo, sesgado; (indirect) indirecto, evasivo; *gram* oblicuo
obliquely *adv* oblicuamente, al sesgo, sesgadamente; indirectamente. **to place o.,** poner al sesgo
obliquity *n* oblicuidad, *f*, sesgo, *m*; (of conduct, etc.) tortuosidad, *f*
obliterate *vt* borrar; destruir, aniquilar. **to be obliterated,** borrarse; quedar destruido
obliteration *n* testación, *f*; destrucción, *f*. **o. raid,** bombardeo de saturación, *m*
oblivion *n* olvido, *m*. **to cast into o.,** echar al olvido
oblivious *a* olvidadizo, descuidago
oblong *a* oblongo, cuadrilongo, rectangular. *n* rectángulo, cuadrilongo, *m*
obloquy *n* infamia, maledicencia, deshonra, *f*
obnoxious *a* odioso, ofensivo, aborrecible
obnoxiously *adv* odicsamente
obnoxiousness *n* odiosidad, *f*
oboe *n mus* oboe, *m*. **o. player,** oboe, *m*
obol *n* óbolo, *m*
obscene *a* indecente, obsceno, escabroso
obscenely *adv* obscenamente, escabrosamente
obscenity *n* indecencia, obscenidad, *f*
obscurantism *n* obscurantismo, *m*
obscurantist *a* and *n* obscurantista *mf*
obscure *a* (indistinct) obscuro, indistinto; (dark) lóbrego, tenebroso; (remote) retirado, apartado; (puzzling) confuso; (unknown) desconocido; humilde; (difficult to understand) abstruso, obscuro; (vague) vago. *vt* obscurecer; (hide) esconder; (eclipse) eclipsar. **to o. the issue,** hacer perder de vista el problema
obscurely *adv* obscuramente; humildemente, retiradamente; confusamente; vagamente
obscurity *n* (darkness) obscuridad, lobreguez, *f*; (difficulty of meaning) ambigüedad, confusión, vaguedad, *f*; humildad, *f*
obsequies *n pl* exequias, *f pl*, ritos fúnebres, *m pl*
obsequious *a* servil, empalagoso, zalamero
obsequiously *adv* servilmente
obsequiousness *n* servilismo, *m*, sumisión, *f*
observable *a* observable, perceptible, visible; notable
observably *adv* notablemente
observance *n* observancia, *f*, cumplimiento, *m*; práctica, costumbre, *f*; (religious) rito, *m*
observant *a* observador; obediente, atento. **o. of,** observador de; atento a
observation *n* observación, *f*, examen, escrutinio, *m*; (experience) experiencia, *f*; (remark) advertencia, *f*, comento, *m*. **to escape o.,** no ser advertido. **o. car.,** vagón-mirador, *m*, **o. post,** puesto de observación, *m*
observatory *n* observatorio, *m*
observe *vt* (laws) cumplir; (holy days, etc.) guardar; (notice) observar, mirar, notar, ver, reparar en; (remark) decir, advertir; (examine) vigilar, atisbar, examinar; *ast* observar. *vi* ser observador. **to o. silence,** guardar silencio
observer *n* observador (-ra)
obsess *vt* obsesionar, obcecar
obsessed *a* obseso
obsession *n* obsesión, obcecación, idea fija, manía, *f*
obsidian *n min* obsidiana, *f*
obsolescent *a* que se hace antiguo, que cae en desuso
obsolete *a* obsoleto, anticuado; *biol* rudimentario, atrofiado
obstacle *n* obstáculo, impedimento, *m*; dificultad, *f*, inconveniente, *m*. **to put obstacles in the way of,** *fig* dificultar, hacer difícil. **o. race,** carrera de obstáculos, *f*
obstetric *a* obstétrico
obstetrician *n* obstétrico (-ea), médico (-ca) partero (-ra)
obstetrics *n* obstetricia, tocología, *f*
obstinacy *n* obstinación, terquedad, tenacidad, porfía, *f*, tesón, *m*; persistencia, *f*
obstinate *a* terco, porfiado, obstinado, tenaz; refractario; persistente, pertinaz. **to be o.,** ser terco; porfiar. **to be o. about,** obstinarse en.
obstinately *adv* tercamente
obstreperous *a* turbulento, ruidoso
obstruct *vt* obstruir: impedir; cerrar; (thwart) estorbar; (hinder) dificultar, embarazar; (the traffic) obstruir,

atascar. *vi* estorbar. **to become obstructed,** obstruirse, cerrarse
obstruction *n* obstrucción, *f*; estorbo, obstáculo, *m*. **to cause a street o.,** obstruir el tráfico
obstructionism *n* obstruccionismo, *m*
obstructionist *n* obstruccionista, *mf*
obstructive *a* estorbador, obstructor
obtain *vt* obtener, conseguir, lograr; recibir; (by threats) arrancar. *vi* estar en boga, estar en vigor, predominar. **to o. on false pretences,** conseguir por engaño
obtainable *a* asequible, alcanzable. **easily o.,** fácil a obtener
obtainer *n* conseguidor (-ra), adquisidor (-ra)
obtainment *n* obtención, *f*, logro, *m*
obtrude *vt* imponer
obtrusion *n* imposición, *f*; importunidad, *f*
obtrusive *a* importuno; entremetido; pretencioso
obtrusiveness *n* importunidad, *f*; entremetimiento, *m*
obtuse *a* (blunt) obtuso, romo; (stupid) estúpido, torpe, lerdo. **o. angle,** obtusángulo, *m*
obtuseness *n* (bluntness) embotamiento, *m*; (stupidity) estupidez, torpeza, *f*
obverse *a* del anverso. *n* anverso, *m*
obviate *vt* obviar, evitar
obvious *a* evidente, manifiesto, patente, obvio, aparente, transparente; poco sutil
obviously *adv* evidentemente, patentemente
obviousness *n* evidencia, transparencia, *f*
occasion *n* ocasión, *f*; oportunidad, *f*, momento oportuno, tiempo propicio, *m*; (reason) motivo, origen, *m*, causa, razón, *f*; (need) necesidad, *f*. *vt* ocasionar, causar, producir. **as o. demands,** cuando las circunstancias lo exigen, en caso necesario. **for the o.,** para la ocasión. **on one o.,** una vez. **on the o. of,** en la ocasión de. **on that o.,** en tal ocasión, en aquella ocasión. **He has given me no o. to say so,** No me ha dado motivos de decirlo. **There is no o. for it,** No hay necesidad para ello. **to have o. to,** haber de, tener que, necesitar. **to lose no o.,** no perder ripio (or oportunidad). **to rise to the o.,** estar al nivel de las circunstancias. **to take this o.,** aprovechar esta oportunidad
occasional *a* (occurring at times) de vez en cuando, intermitente; poco frecuente, infrecuente; (of verse) de ocasión. **o. table,** mesilla, *f*
occasionally *adv* de vez en cuando
occiput *n anat* occipucio, *m*
occlude *vt* obstruir, cerrar; *med* ocluir; *chem* absorber
occlusion *n* cerramiento, *m*; *med* oclusión, *f*; *chem* absorción de gases, *f*
occlusive *a* oclusivo
occult *a* oculto, escondido, misterioso; mágico. **o. sciences,** creencias ocultas, *f pl*
occultation *n ast* ocultación, *f*, eclipse, *m*
occultism *n* ocultismo, *m*
occultist *n* ocultista, *mf*
occupancy *n* ocupación, posesión, *f*; (tenancy) tenencia, *f*
occupant *n* habitante, *mf*; ocupante, *mf*; (tenant) inquilino (-na)
occupation *n* ocupación *f*; (tenure) inquilinato, *m*, tenencia, *f*; (work) trabajo, quehacer, *m*, labor, *f*; (employment) empleo, oficio, *m*; profesión, *f*
occupational *a* de oficio. **o. disease,** enfermedad profesional, *f*
occupier *n* ocupante, *mf*, inquilino (-na)
occupy *vt* ocupar; (live in) vivir en, habitar; (time) emplear, pasar; (take over) apoderarse de, ocupar. **to o. oneself in** or **with,** ocuparse en, ocuparse con. **to be occupied in** or **with,** estar ocupado con, ocuparse en
occur *vi* (happen) suceder, tener lugar, acaecer; (exist) encontrarse, existir; (of ideas) ocurrirse, venirse. **to o. to one's mind,** venírsele a las mientes. **to o. again,** volver a suceder, ocurrir de nuevo. **An idea occurred to her,** Se le ocurrió una idea
occurrence *n* ocurrencia, *f*; incidente, suceso, acontecimiento, *m*. **to be of frequent o.,** ocurrir con frecuencia, acontecer a menudo
ocean *n* océano, *m*; *fig* mar, abundancia, *f*. **o.-going vessel,** buque de alta mar, *m*
Oceania el Mundo Novísmo, *m*
oceanic *a* oceánico
oceanography *n* oceanografía, *f*
ocelot *n zool* ocelote, *m*
ocher *n* ocre, *m*
octagon *n* octágono, *m*
octagonal *a* octagonal
octave *n* (*ecc* metrics, *mus*) octava, *f*
octavo *n print* libro, etc. en octavo (8°), *m*. **in o.,** en octavo. **large o.,** octavo mayor, *m*. **small o.,** octavo menor, *m*
octet *n mus* octeto, *m*
October *n* octubre, *m*, 2 October 1996, el segundo (2°) de octubre de mil novecientos noventa y seis
octogenarian *a* and *n* octogenario (-ia)
octopus *n* pulpo, *m*
ocular *a* ocular, visual. *n* ocular, *m*
oculist *n* oculista, *mf*
odd *a* (of numbers) impar; (of volumes, etc.) suelto; (strange) raro, curioso, extraño, extravagante; (casual) casual, accidental; (extra) y pico, y tantos, sobrante; (of gloves, etc.) sin pareja. **at odd moments,** en momentos de ocio. **at odd times,** de vez en cuando. **thirty odd,** treinta y pico. **odd number,** número impare, *m*. **odd or even,** pares o impares. **odd trick,** (at cards) una baza más
oddity *n* excentricidad, rareza, extravagancia, *f*; (person) ente singular, *m*; (curio) objeto curioso, *m*, antigüedad, *f*
oddly *adv* singularmente
oddment *n* bagatela, baratija, *f*
oddness *n* singularidad, rareza, extravagancia, *f*
odds *n pl* diferencia, desigualdad, *f*; (superiority) ventaja, superioridad, *f*; (quarrel) disputa, riña, *f*. **The o. are that . . . ,** Lo más probable es que . . . **to fight against dreadful o.,** luchar contra fuerzas muy superiores. **o. and ends,** (remains) sobras y picos, *f pl*; (trifles) ñaques, *m pl*, chucherías, *f pl*
Odessa Odesa, *f*
odious *a* odioso, detestable, aborrecible, repugnante
odiousness *n* odiosidad, *f*
odium *n* odio, *m*
odor *n* olor, *m*, (fragrance) perfume, aroma, *m*, fragancia, *f*; *fig* sospecha, *f*. **in bad o.,** *fig* en disfavor. **o. of sanctity,** olor de santidad, *m*
odoriferous *a* odorífero; (perfumed) oloroso, perfumado
odorless *a* inodoro
odorous *a* fragante, oloroso
odyssey *n* odisea, *f*
of *prep* de. **of** has many idiomatic translations which are given as far as possible under the heading of the word concerned. It is also not translated. **I robbed him of his reward,** Le robé su recompensa. **I was thinking of you,** Pensaba en tí. **It was very good of you to . . . ,** Vd. ha tenido mucha bondad de . . . **Your naming of the child Mary,** El que Vd. haya dado el nombre de María al niño. **29th of Sept., 1936,** el 29 de septiembre de 1936. **Of course!** ¡Claro está! ¡Ya lo creo! ¡Naturalmente! **of late,** últimamente. **of the** (before *m, sing*) del; (before *f, sing*) de la; (before *m pl*) de los; (before *f pl*) de las. **to dream of,** soñar con. **to smell of,** oler a tener olor de. **to taste of, etc.,** saber a, tener gusto de.
off *prep* de; fuera de; cerca de; desde; *naut* a la altura de. **from off,** de. **Take your gloves off the table!** ¡Quítate los guantes de la mesa! **The wheel was off the car,** La rueda se había desprendido del coche. **to be off duty,** no estar de servicio; *mil* no estar de guardia. **to lunch off cold meat,** almorzar de carne fría. **off one's head,** chiflado
off *a* (contrasted with near) de la derecha, derecho; (un-

likely) improbable, remoto. *adv* (with intransitive verbs of motion) se (e.g. **He has gone off,** Se ha marchado); (contrasted with on) de (e.g. **He has fallen off the horse,** Ha caído del caballo); (of place at a distance) lejos, a distancia de; (of time) generally a verb is used (e.g. **The wedding is three months off,** Faltan tres meses para la boda); (completely) enteramente. **Off** is often not translated in Sp. (e.g. **to put off,** aplazar, **to cut off,** cortar). **day off,** día libre, día de asueto, *m.* **How far off is the house from here? The house is five miles off.** ¿Cuántas millas está la casa de aquí? La casa está a cinco millas de aquí. **His hat is off,** Está sin sombrero, Se ha quitado el sombrero. **The cover is off,** La cubierta está quitada. **The party is off,** Se ha anulado la reunión. **6% off,** un descuento de seis por ciento. *interj* **Off with you!** ¡Márchate! ¡Fuera! **off and on,** de vez en cuando, espasmódicamente. **off color,** (ill) malucho; (of jokes) verde. **off season,** estación muerta, *f.* **off-shore,** a vista de tierra. **off-stage,** entre bastidores

offal *n* (butchers') menudencias, *f pl,* asadura, *f,* menudos, despojos, *m pl;* desperdicio, *m*

offend *vt* ofender; agraviar, insultar; herir; desagradar, disgustar; *vi* ofender, pecar. **to be offended,** resentirse, insultarse. **This offends my sense of justice,** Esto ofende mi sentimiento de justicia. **to o. against,** pecar contra; violar

offender *n* delincuente, *mf;* agraviador (-ra), pecador (-ra), transgresor (-ra). **old o.,** *law* criminal inveterado, *m*

offense *n* ofensa, transgresión, violación, *f;* pecado, *m; law* delito, crimen, *m;* (insult) agravio, *m,* afrenta, *f.* **the first o.,** el primer delito, *m.* **fresh o.,** nuevo delito, *m.* **political o.,** crimen político, *m.* **technical o.,** *law* cuasidelito, *m.* **to commit an o. against,** ofender contra. **to take o.,** resentirse, darse por ofendido

offensive *a* ofensivo, desagradable, repugnante; (insulting) injurioso, agraviador, agresivo. *n mil* ofensiva, *f.* **to take the o.,** tomar la ofensiva

offensiveness *n* lo desagradable; (insult) ofensa, *f;* lo injurioso

offer *n* oferta, *f;* ofrecimiento, *m;* (of help) promesa, *f;* proposición, *f; com* oferta, *f. vt* ofrecer; prometer; (opportunities, etc.) deparar, brindar; tributar. *vi* ofrecerse, ocurrir, surgir. **to o. up,** ofrecer; inmolar, sacrificar. **He did not offer to go,** No hizo ademán de marcharse. **to o. resistance,** oponer resistencia. **o. of marriage,** oferta de matrimonio, *f*

offerer *n* ofrecedor (-ra)

offering *n* ofrecimiento, *m; ecc* ofrenda, oblación, *f,* sacrificio, *m;* regalo, don, *m,* dádiva, *f*

offhand *a* sin preparación, de repente; (casual) casual, despreocupado; (discourteous) brusco, descortés

offhandedly *adv* sin preparación, espontáneamente; negligentemente; bruscamente

office *n* oficina, *m;* (post) cargo, puesto, destino, *m;* (state department) ministerio, *m;* (of a Cabinet minister) cartera, *f;* (room) oficina, *f;* despacho, escritorio, *m;* (of a newspaper) redacción, *f;* (lawyer's) bufete, *m;* departamento, *m; ecc* oficio, *m pl.* **offices,** negocio, *m;* oficinas, *f pl;* (prayers) rezos, *m pl; ecc* oficios, *m pl.* **domestic offices,** dependencias, *f pl.* **good offices,** *fig* buenos oficios, *m pl.* **head o.,** casa central, oficina principal, *f.* **private o.,** despacho particular, *m.* **to be in o.,** estar en el poder. **o.-bearer,** miembro de la junta, *m;* funcionario, *m.* **o.-boy,** mozo de oficina, *m.* **o. employee,** oficinista, *mf.* **o. hours,** horas de oficina, *f pl;* (professions) horas de consulta, *f pl.* **o.-seeker,** aspirante, *m;* pretendiente, *m.* **o. work,** trabajo de oficina, *m*

officer *n* oficial, funcionario, *m;* (police) agente de policía, *m;* (of the Church) dignatario, *m;* (*mil nav aer*) oficial, *m. vt* mandar. **commissioned o.,** oficial, *m.* **non-commissioned o.,** oficial subalterno, *m.* **to be well officered,** tener buena oficialidad. **Officers' Training Corps,** Escuela de Oficiales, *f*

office worker *n* oficinista, *mf*

official *a* oficial; autorizado; ceremonioso, grave. *n* funcionario, *m;* oficial público, *m.* **high o.,** funcionario importante. *m.* **o. mourning,** duelo oficial, *m.* **o. receiver,** fiscal de quiebras, *m*

officialdom *n* funcionarismo, *m;* círculos oficiales, *m pl*

officiant *n* oficiante, *m*

officiate *vi* celebrar; oficiar, funcionar

officiating *a* oficiante; celebrante. **o. priest,** sacerdote oficiante, celebrante, *m*

officious *a* oficioso, entremetido

officiousness *n* oficiosidad, *f*

offing *n naut* mar afuera, *m.* **in the o.,** cerca

off season fuera de temporada

offset *n* compensación, *f, vt* compensar, neutralizar

offshoot *n* renuevo, vástago, *m*

offside *a* (of a car) del lado derecho (or izquierda); *sport* fuera de juego

offspring *n* vástago, *m;* descendiente, *mf;* prole, *f;* hijos, *m pl*

often *adv* a menudo, mucho, con frecuencia, frecuentemente, muchas veces. **as o. as,** tan a menudo como, siempre que. **as o. as not,** no pocas veces. **How o.?** ¿Cuántas veces? **It is not o. that . . . ,** No ocurre con frecuencia que . . . **so o.,** tantas veces, con frecuencia. **Do you go there o.?** ¿Va Vd. allí con frecuencia (or frecuentemente)? **Not o.,** Voy rara vez allá

ogival *a arch* ojival

ogive *n arch* ojiva, *f*

ogle *vt* and *vi* comer(se) con los ojos (a), ojear, guiñar el ojo (a). *n* ojeada, *f,* guiño, *m*

ogling *n* guiño, *m,* ojeada, *f*

ogre *n* ogro, *m*

oh! *interj* ¡o! **O no!** ¡Ca! ¡Claro que no!

ohm *n elec* ohmio, *m*

oil *n* aceite, *m;* petróleo, *m;* óleo, *m. vt* aceitar, engrasar, *Argentina* enaceitar; olear, ungir, untar; (bribe) sobornar, untar la mano; *fig* suavizar. *a* aceitero; petrolero. **to pour oil on troubled waters,** echar aceite sobre aguas turbulentas. **to strike oil,** encontrar un pozo de petróleo; *fig* encontrar un filón. **crude oil,** petróleo bruto, *m.* **heavy oil,** aceite pesado, *m.* **thin oil,** aceite ligero, *m. art* **in oils,** al óleo. **oil-bearing,** petrolífero. **oil-box,** engrasador, *m.* **oil-burner,** quemador de petróleo, *m.* **oil-can,** aceitera, *f.* **oil-colors,** pinturas al óleo, *f pl.* **oil field,** yacimiento petrolífero, campo de petróleo, *m.* **oil-filter,** separador de aceite, *m.* **oil-gauge,** nivel de aceite, *m.* **oil lamp,** velón, candil, quinqué, *m.* **oil of turpentine,** aceite de trementina, aguarrás, *m.* esencia de trementina, *f.* **oil-painting,** pintura al óleo, *f.* **oil pipeline,** oleoducto, *m.* **oil shop,** aceitería, *f.* **oil-silk,** encerado, *m.* **oil stove,** estufa de petróleo, *f.* **oil tanker,** *naut* petrolero, *m.* **oil-well,** pozo de petróleo, *m*

oilcake *n* bagazo, *m*

oilcloth *n* hule, *m;* linóleo, *m*

oiler *n* (can) aceitera, *f; naut* petrolero, *m;* lubricador, *m*

oiliness *n* oleaginosidad, untuosidad, *f*

oiling *n* engrasado, *m*

oilskin *n* encerado, *m*

oil seed *n* semilla oleaginosa, *f*

oily *a* aceitoso, grasiento

ointment *n* ungüento, *m,* pomada, *f*

old *a* viejo; antiguo, anciano; (of wines, etc.) añejo; (worn out) usado, gastado; (inveterate) arraigado, inveterado. **How old are you?** ¿Cuántos años tiene usted? **to be sixteen years old,** tener dieciséis años. **He is old enough to know his own mind,** Tiene bastante edad para saber lo que quiere. **to grow old,** envejecer. **to remain an old maid,** quedar soltera; *inf* quedarse para vestir imágenes. **of old,** antiguamente. **prematurely old,** revejido averiado. **old age,** vejez, senectud, *f.* **old bachelor,** solterón, *m.* **old clothes,** ropa vieja (or usada), ropa de segunda mano, *f.* **old-clothes dealer,** ropavejero (-ra). **old-clothes shop,** ropavejería, *f.* **old-established,** viejo. **old-fash-**

ioned, pasado de moda, viejo; (of people) chapado a la antigua. **old lady,** anciana, dama vieja, *f.* **old-looking,** de aspecto viejo, avejentado. **old maid,** solterona, *f.* **old-maidish,** remilgado. **old man,** viejo, *m; theat* barba, *m.* **old salt,** lobo de mar, *m.* **Old Testament,** Antiguo Testamento, *m.* **old wives' tale,** cuento de viejas, *m.* **old woman,** vieja, *f.* **Old World,** Viejo Mundo, mundo antiguo, *m*

old-age home *n* asilo de ancianos, *m*

olden *a* antiguo. **o. days,** días pasados, *m pl*

older *a comp* más viejo, mayor. **The older the madder,** A la vejez viruelas

old hat *n* viejo conocido

oldish *a* bastante viejo, de cierta edad

oldness *n* antigüedad, ancianidad, edad, *f*

oleaginous *a* oleaginoso

oleander *n bot* adelfa, *f*, baladre, *m*

olfactory *a* olfatorio, olfativo

oligarchic *a* oligárquico

oligarchy *n* oligarquía, *f*

olive *n* (tree) olivo, *m;* (fruit) aceituna, oliva, *f, a* aceitunado, *Lat. Am.* aceituno. **wild o. tree,** acebuche, *m.* **o.-complexioned,** con tez aceitunada. **o. green,** verde oliva, *m.* **o. grove,** olivar, *m.* **o. oil,** aceite de oliva, *m*

olympiad *n* olimpíada, *f*

olympian *a* olímpico

olympic *a* olímpico. **o. games,** juegos olímpicos, *m pl*

olympus *n* olimpo, *m*

omasum *n zool* librillo, libro, *m*

omber *n* tresillo, hombre, *m*

omega *n* omega, *f*

omelet *n* tortilla, *f.* **sweet o.,** tortilla dulce, *f*

omen *n* pronóstico, presagio, agüero, *m, vt* agorar, anunciar

ominous *a* ominoso, azaroso, siniestro, amenazante

ominously *adv* ominosamente, con amenazas

omission *n* omisión, *f;* olvido, descuido, *m;* supresión, *f*

omit *vt* omitir; olvidar, descuidar; (suppress) suprimir, excluir, callar, dejar a un lado

omitting *pres part* salvo, excepto

omnibus *n* ómnibus, autobús, *m.* **o. conductor,** cobrador de autobús, *m.* **o. driver,** conductor de autobús, *m.* **o. route,** trayecto de autobús, *m.* **o. service,** servicio de autobuses, *m.* **o. volume,** volumen de obras coleccionadas, *m*

omnipotence *n* omnipotencia, *f*

omnipotent *a* omnipotente, todopoderoso

omnipresence *n* omnipresencia, ubicuidad, *f*

omnipresent *a* ubicuo

omniscience *n* omnisciencia, *f*

omniscient *a* omniscio, omnisciente

omnivorous *a* omnívoro

on *prep* (upon) sobre, en, encima de; (concerning) de, acerca de, sobre; (against) contra; (after) después; (according to) según; (with gerund) en; (with infin.) al; (at) a; (connected with, employed in) de; (by means of) por, mediante; (near to) cerca de, sobre; (into) en. Untranslated before days of week, dates of month or time of day (e.g. **on Monday,** el lunes. **on Friday afternoons,** los viernes por la tarde). **She has a bracelet on her wrist,** Tiene una pulsera en la muñeca. **He will retire on a good income,** Se jubilará con una buena renta. **on my uncle's death,** después de la muerte (or a la muerte) de mi tío, al morir. **On seeing them, he stopped,** Al verles se paró. **on leave,** con licencia, en uso de licencia. **on the next page,** en la página siguiente. **on this occasion,** en esta ocasión. **on the other hand,** en cambio. **on second thoughts,** luego de pensarlo bien. **on the way,** en camino. **on one side,** a un lado. **on the left,** a la izquierda. **on time,** a tiempo. **on my honor,** bajo palabra de honor. **on pain of death,** so pena de muerte, bajo pena de muerte. **on an average,** por término medio. **on his part,** por su parte. **on and after,** desde, a partir de. **on credit,** de fiado. **on fire,** ardiendo, en llamas. **on foot,** a pie. **on purpose,** a propósito; con intención. **on,** *adv* puesto (e.g. **She has her gloves on,** Tiene los guantes puestos); (forward) adelante, hacia adelante; (continue, with a verb) seguir, continuar (e.g. **He went on talking,** Siguió hablando). Often **on** is included in Sp. verb (e.g. **The new play is on,** Se ha estrenado la nueva comedia. **The fight is on,** Ya ha empezado la lucha). **On!** *interj* ¡Adelante! **and so on,** y así sucesivamente. **to have on,** llevar puesto. **on and off,** de vez en cuando. **on and on,** sin cesar

onanism *n* onanismo, *m*

once *adv* una vez; (formerly) en otro tiempo, antiguamente; *conjunc* si (e.g. **O. you give him the opportunity,** Si le das la oportunidad). **all at o.,** todo junto, a un mismo tiempo; simultáneamente; (suddenly) súbitamente, de repente. **at o.,** en seguida, inmediatamente, *Lat. Am. also* lueguito. **for o.,** por una vez. **more than o.,** más de una vez. **not o.,** ni siquiera una vez. **o. before,** una vez antes. **o. and for all,** una vez para siempre; por última vez. **o. in a while,** de vez en cuando. **o. more,** otra vez. **o. or twice,** una vez o dos, algunas veces. **o. too often,** una vez demasiado. **O. upon a time,** En tiempos pasados, En tiempos de Maricastaña; (as beginning of a story) Érase una vez, Había una vez, Hubo una vez

once in a blue moon a cada muerte de un obispo

one *a* un, uno, una; (first) primero; (single) único, solo; (indifferent) igual, indiferente; (some, certain) algún, cierto, un (e.g. **one day,** cierto día). *n* uno; (hour) la una; (of age) un año. Often not translated in Sp. (e.g. **I shall take the blue one,** Tomaré el azul). *pron* se; uno. **one's,** su, de uno (e.g. **one's work,** el trabajo de uno). **I for one do not think so,** Yo por uno no lo creo. **It is all one,** Es igual, No hace diferencia alguna. **only one,** un solo. **that one,** ése, *m*, ésa, *f*, eso, *neut.* **this one,** éste, *m*, ésta, *f*, esto, *neut.* **these ones,** éstos, etc. **those ones,** ésos, etc. **the one,** el (que), *m*, la (que), *f.* **with one accord,** unánimemente. **one and all,** todos. **one another,** se, uno a otro, mutuamente. **one by one,** uno a uno. **one day,** un día; un día de éstos, algún día. **one-eyed,** tuerto. **one-handed,** manco. **one-sided,** parcial. **one-way street,** *Spain* calle de dirección única, *Argentina* calle de una sola mano, *Mexico* calle de un sentido, calle de una corrida, *f.* **one-way traffic,** tráfico en una sola dirección, *m*

oneiric *a* onírico

oneness *n* unidad, *f*

onerous *a* oneroso, pesado, molesto, gravoso

onerousness *n* pesadez, molestia, dificultad, inconveniencia, *f*

one-seater *n* avión de una plaza, *m*

oneself *pron* se, uno mismo (una misma); (after prep.) sí mismo, sí. **It must be done by o.,** Uno mismo ha de hacerlo

onion *n* cebolla, *f.* **string of onions,** ristra de cebollas, *f.* **young o.,** babosa, *f.* **o. bed,** cebollar, *m.* **o. seed,** cebollino, *m.* **o. seller,** cebollero (-ra)

on-line *a computers* lineal

onlooker *n* espectado (-ra), observador (-ra); testigo, *mf*

only *a* único, solo. *adv* únicamente, sólo; no . . . más (que), tan sólo; con la excepción de, salvo. *conjunc* pero, salvo (que), si no fuera (que). **I shall o. give you three,** No te daré más de tres. **The o. thing one can do,** Lo único que se puede hacer. **I o. wished to see her,** Quería verla nada más. **if o.,** ¡ojalá (que)! **not o. . . . ,** no sólo . . . **o.-begotten,** *a* unigénito. **o. child,** hijo (-ja) único (-ca)

onrush *n* asalto, ataque, acometimiento, *m*, acometida, embestida, *f;* (of water, etc.) acceso, *m;* torrente, *m*, corriente, *f*

onset *n* ataque, *m*, acometida, *f;* (beginning) principio, *m.* **at the first o.,** al primer ímpetu

onslaught *n* asalto, ataque, *m*

onus *n* responsabilidad, *f.* **o. of proof,** obligación de probar, *f*

onward *a* progresivo. *adv* adelante, hacia adelante; (as a command) ¡Adelante!
onyx *n* ónice, *m*
ooze *n* légamo, limo, fango, *m*, lama, *f*. *vi* exudar, rezumarse; manar; *vt* sudar. **to o. satisfaction,** caérsele (a uno) la baba. **to o. away,** (of money, etc.) desaparecer, volar. **to o. out,** (news) divulgarse
oozing *a* fangoso, legamoso, lamoso
opacity *n* opacidad, *f*
opal *n* ópalo, *m*
opalescence *n* opalescencia, *f*
opalescent *a* opalescente, iridiscente
opaline *a* opalino
opaque *a* opaco
opaqueness *n* opacidad, *f*
op. cit. (opere citato) obra cit. (obra citada)
open *vt* abrir; (a package) desempaquetar, desenvolver; (remove lid) destapar; *Lat. Am.* desenlatar (canned food); (unfold) desplegar; (inaugurate) inaugurar; iniciar, empezar; establecer; (an abscess) cortar; (with arms, heart, eyes) abrir; (with mind, thought) descubrir, revelar; (make accessible) franquear, hacer accesible; (tear) romper; *vi* abrirse; empezar, comenzar; (of a view, etc.) aparecer, extenderse; inaugurarse; (of a career, etc.) prepararse. **to o. fire against,** abrir el fuego contra. **to o. into,** comunicar con, salir a. **to o. into each other,** (of rooms) comunicarse. **to o. on,** mirar a, dar a, caer a. **to o. out,** *vt* abrir; desplegar; revelar. *vi* extenderse; revelarse. **to o. the eyes of,** *fig* desengañar, desilusionar. **to o. up,** abrir; explorar, hacer accessible; revelar; *fig inf* desabrocharse. **to o. with** or **by,** empezar con
open *a* abierto; descubierto; expuesto; (unfenced) descercado; (not private) público; libre; (unfolded) desplegado, extendido; (persuasible) receptivo; no resuelto, pendiente; (frank) franco, candoroso; (with sea) alto; (liberal) generoso, hospitalario; sin prejuicios; *com* abierto, pendiente; sin defensa; (of weather) despejado; (of a letter) sin sellar; (without a lid) destapado; (well-known) manifiesto, bien conocido. *n* aire libre, *m*. **in the o. air,** al aire libre, al raso, a cielo abierto. **to break o.,** forzar. **to cut o.,** abrir de un tajo, cortar. **to leave o.,** dejar abierto. **wide o.,** muy abierto; (of doors) de par en par. **o. boat,** barco descubierto, *m*. **o. car,** coche abierto, *m*. **o. carriage,** carruaje descubierto, *m*. **o. cast,** *min* roza abierta, *f*. **o.-eyed,** con los ojos abiertos. **o.-handed,** generoso, dadivoso, *Lat. Am. also* maniabierto. **o. letter,** carta abierta, *f*. **o.-minded,** imparcial. **o.-mouthed,** con la boca abierta, boquiabierto. **o. question,** cuestión por decidir, cuestión discutible, *f*. **o. secret,** secreto a voces, *m*. **o. sea,** alta mar, *f*. **o. town,** ciudad abierta, *f*. **o. tramcar,** jardinera, *f*. **o. truck,** vagoneta, *f*. **o.-work,** *sew* calado, enrejado, *m*
opener *n* abridor, *m*
opening *n* abertura, brecha, *f*; orificio, *m*; inauguración, apertura, *f*; principio, *m*; (chance) oportunidad, *f*; (employment) puesto, *m*. **o. price,** *com* (on Exchange) precio de apertura, *m*, primer curso *m*
openly *adv* abiertamente, francamente; públicamente
openness *n* situación expuesta, *f*; espaciosidad, *f*; franqueza, *f*, candor, *m*; imparcialidad, *f*
opera *n* ópera, *f*. **comic o.,** zarzuela, *f*. **o.-cloak,** abrigo de noche, *m*. **o.-glasses,** gemelos de teatro, *m pl*. **o.-hat,** clac, *m*. **o.-house,** teatro de la ópera, *m*. **o. singer,** cantante de ópera, operista, *mf*
operate *vi* funcionar, trabajar; obrar; (with on, upon) producir efecto sobre; influir; *surg* operar; (on Exchange) especular, jugar a la bolsa; *vt* hacer funcionar, manejar; mover, impulsar; dirigir
operatic *a* de ópera, operístico
operating *a* (of surgeons) operante; de operación. **o. table,** mesa de operaciones, *f*. **o. theater,** anfiteatro, *m*; sala de operaciones, *f*
operation *n* funcionamiento, *m*, acción, *f*; *surg* intervención quirúrgica, operación, *f*; (*mil naut*) maniobra, *f*; manipulación, *f*. **to come into o.,** ponerse en práctica; hacerse efectivo. **to continue in o.,** (*laws*) seguir en vigor. **to perform an o.,** *surg* operar, praticar una intervención quirúrgica; hacer una maniobra. **to put into o.,** poner en práctica
operative *a* operativo, activo. *n* operario (-ia), obrero (-ra). **to become o.,** tener efecto
operator *n* operario (-ia); (telephone) telefonista, *mf*; (machines, engines) maquinista, *mf*; *surg* operador, *m*
operetta *n* opereta, *f*
ophthalmologist *n* oftalmólogo, *m*
ophthalmology *n* oftalmología, *f*
opiate *n* opiata, *f*, narcótico, *m*, *a* opiado
opine *vi* and *vt* opinar, creer
opinion *n* opinión, *f*, parecer, juicio, *m*; concepto, *m*, idea, *f*. **in my o.,** según mi parecer. **to be of the o. that,** ser de la opinión que, opinar que. **to be of the same o.,** estar de acuerdo, concurrir. **public o.,** opinión (or voz) pública, *f*
opinionated *a* terco, obstinado
opium *n* opio, *m*. **o. addict,** opiónamo (-ma). **o. den,** fumadero de opio, *m*. **o. eater,** mascador de opio, opiófago, *m*. **o. smoker,** fumador (-ra) de opio
Oporto Oporto, Porto, *m*
opponent *n* antagonista, *mf*, enemigo (-ga); contrario (-ia), adversario (-ia), competidor (-ra)
opportune *a* oportuno, tempestivo, conveniente, a propósito. **to be o.,** venir al caso. **o. moment,** momento oportuno, *m*; hora propicia, *f*
opportunely *adv* oportunamente. **to come o.,** venir a pelo
opportuneness *n* oportunidad, tempestividad, conveniencia, *f*
opportunism *n* oportunismo, *m*
opportunist *n* oportunista, *Lat. Am. also* maromero (-ra), *mf*
opportunity *n* oportunidad, ocasión, posibilidad, *f*. **to give an o. for,** dar margen para. **to open new opportunities,** abrir nuevos horizontes. **to take the o.,** tomar la oportunidad
opposable *a* oponible
oppose *vt* (counterbalance) oponer, contrarrestar; combatir; hacer frente (a), contrariar, pugnar contra, oponerse (a)
opposed (to) *a* opuesto a, enemigo de, contra
opposing *a* opuesto; enemigo, contrario
opposite *a* (facing) de cara a, frente a, del otro lado de; opuesto; (antagonistic) contrario, antagónico; otro, diferente. *n* contraria, *f*, lo opuesto; antagonista, *mf*; adversario (-ia). **the o. sex,** el otro sexo. **o. leaves,** *bot* hojas opuestas, *f pl*. **o. to,** frente a; distinto de
opposition *n* oposición, *f*; (obstacle) estorbo, impedimento, *m*, dificultad, *f*; resistencia, hostilidad, *f*; (*ast pol*) oposición, *f*; (difference) contraste, *m*, diferencia, *f*. *a* de la oposición. **in o.,** en oposición; *pol* en la oposición. **to be in o.,** estar en oposición; *pol* ser de la oposición, estar en la oposición
oppress *vt* oprimir, tiranizar, sojuzgar, apremiar; (of moral causes) abrumar, agobiar, desanimar; (of heat, etc.) ahogar
oppression *n* opresión, tiranía, crueldad, *f*; (moral) agobio, sufrimiento, *m*, ansia, *f*; (difficulty in breathing) sofocación, *f*, ahogo, *m*
oppressive *a* opresivo, tiránico, cruel; (taxes, etc.) gravoso; (of heat) sofocante, asfixiante; agobiador, abrumador
oppressor *n* opresor (-ra), sojuzgador (-ra), tirano (-na)
opprobrious *a* oprobioso, vituperioso; infame
opprobrium *n* oprobio, *m*, ignominia, *f*
opt *vi* optar, escoger, elegir
optic, optical *a* óptico. **o. illusion,** ilusión óptica, *f*; engaño a la vista, trampantojo, *m*. **o. nerve,** nervio óptico, *m*
optician *n* óptico, *m*
optics *n* óptica, *f*
optimism *n* optimismo, *m*

optimist *n* optimista, *mf*
optimistic *a* optimista
optimum *n* lo óptimo; (used as adjective) óptimo
option *n* opción, *f*, (all meanings)
optional *a* discrecional, facultativo
opulence *n* opulencia, riqueza, magnificencia, *f*; (abundance) abundancia, copia, *f*
opulent *a* opulento, rico, acaudalado; abundante
opus *n* obra, composición, *f*
opuscule *n* opúsculo, *m*
or *conjunc* o; (before a word beginning with o or ho) u; (negative) ni. *n her* oro, *m*. **an hour or so,** una hora más o menos, alrededor de una hora. **either . . . or,** o . . . o. **or else,** o bien. **whether . . . or,** que . . . que, siquiera . . . siquiera, ya . . . ya. **without . . . or,** sin . . . ni
oracle *n* oráculo, *m*
oracular *a* profético, vatídico; ambiguo, misterioso, sibilino; dogmático, magistral
oral *a* verbal, hablado; *anat* oral, bucal
oral cavity *n* cavidad bucal, *f*
orange *n* (tree) naranjo, *m*; (fruit) naranja, *f*; **bitter o.,** naranja amarga, *f*. **blood o.,** naranja dulce, *f*. **tangerine o.,** naranja mandarina, *f*. **o. blossom,** azahar, *m*. **o. color,** color de naranja, *m*. **o.-colored,** de color de naranja, anaranjado. **o.-flower water,** agua de azahar, *f*. **o. grove,** naranjal, *m*. **o. grower** (or **seller**), naranjero (-ra). **o. peel,** piel de naranja, *f*. **o.-stick,** (for nails) limpiauñas, *m*
orangeade *n* naranjada, *f*; (mineral water) gaseosa, *f*
orangery *n* naranjal, *m*
orangoutan *n zool* orangután, *m*
oration *n* oración, declamación, *f*, discurso, *m*
orator *n* orador (-ra), declamador (-ra)
oratorical *a* oratorio, declamatorio, retórico
oratorio *n mus* oratorio, *m*
oratory *n* oratoria, elocuencia, *f*; *ecc* oratorio, *m*, capilla, *f*
orb *n* orbe, *m*; esfera, *f*, globo, *m*; astro, *m*; *poet* ojo, *m*
orbit *n ast* órbita, *f*; *anat* órbita, cuenca del ojo, *f*
orbital *a anat* orbital
orchard *n* huerto, vergel, *m*; (especially of apples) pomar, *m*
orchestra *n* orquesta, *f*. **with full o.,** con gran orquesta. *theat* **o. seat, o. stall,** butaca de piatea, *f*
orchestral *a* orquestal, instrumental
orchestrate *vt* orquestar, instrumentar
orchestration *n* orquestración, instrumentación, *f*
orchid *n* orquídea, *f*
orchitis *n med* orquitis, *f*
ordain *vt* mandar, disponer, decretar; *ecc* ordenar. **to be ordained as,** *ecc* ordenarse de
ordeal *n hist* ordalías, *f pl*; prueba severa, *f*
order *n* (most meanings) orden, *m*; (command) precepto, mandamiento, decreto, *m*; orden, *f*; (rule) regla, *f*; (for money) libranza postal, *f*; (for goods) pedido, encargo, *m*; (arrangement) método, arreglo, *m*, clasificación, *f*; (condition) estado, *m*; *arch* estilo, *m*; (*zool bot*) orden, *m*; (sort) clase, especie, *f*; (rank) clase social, *f*; *ecc* orden, *f*; (badge) condecoración, insignia, *f*; (association) sociedad, asociación, compañía, *f*; (to view a house, etc.) permiso, *m*; (series) serie, *f*. **His liver is out of o.,** No está bién del hígado. **in good o.,** en buen estado; arreglado. **in o.,** (alphabetical, etc.) en orden; arreglado; (parliamentary) en regla. **in o. that,** para que, a fin de que. **in o. to,** a fin de, para. **out of o.,** estropeado, descompuesto; (on a notice) No funciona; (parliamentary) fuera del orden del dia. **till further o.,** hasta nueva orden. **to o.,** *com* por encargo especial. **to give an o.,** dar una orden; *com* poner un pedido. **to go out of o.,** descomponerse. **to keep in o.,** mantener en orden. **to put in o.,** poner en orden, ordenar. **to take holy orders,** tomar órdenes sagradas. **O.!** ¡Orden! **O. in Council,** orden real, *f*. **o. of knighthood,** orden de caballería, *f*. **o. of the day,** orden del día, *f*. **o. paper,** orden del día, *f*; reglamento, *m*
order *vt* disponer; arreglar; (command) mandar, ordenar; (request) rogar, pedir; (direct) dirigir, gobernar; *com* encargar, cometer; (a meal, a taxi) encargar. **I ordered them to do it,** Les mandé hacerlo. **to o. about,** mandar. **to o. back,** hacer volver, mandar que vuelva. **to o. down,** hacer bajar, pedir (a uno) que baje. **to o. in,** mandar entrar. **to o. off,** despedir, decir (a uno) que se vaya. **to o. out,** mandar salir; (the troops) hacer salir la tropa; echar. **to o. up,** mandar subir, hacer subir
orderliness *n* orden, aseo, método, *m*; limpieza, *f*; buena conducta, formalidad, *f*; buena administración, *f*
orderly *a* bien arreglado, metódico; aseado, en orden; (of behaviour) formal, bien disciplinado. *n mil* ordenanza, *m*; ayudante de hospital *m*
ordinal *a* and *n* ordinal *m*
ordinance *n* ordenanza, *f*, reglamento, *m*; *arch* ordenación, *f*; *ecc* rito, *m*
ordinarily *adv* de ordinario, ordinariamente, comúnmente
ordinary *a* (usual) corriente, común, usual, ordinario, normal; (average) mediano, mediocre; (somewhat vulgar) ordinario, vulgar. *n ecc* ordinario, *m*. **out of the o.,** excepcional; poco común. **o. seaman,** marinero, *m*. **o. share,** *com* acción ordinaria, *f*
ordination *n ecc* ordenación, *f*
ordnance *n* artillería, *f*, cañones, *m pl*; pertrechos de guerra, *m pl*. **o. survey map,** mapa del estado mayor, *m*. **o. survey number,** acotación, *f*
ore *n min* mena, *f*, quijo, *Lat. Am.* llampo, *m*
organ *n* (all meanings) órgano, *m*. **barrel-o.,** organillo, órgano de manubrio, *m*. **o.-blower,** entonador (-ra). **o.-grinder,** organillero (-ra). **o.-loft,** tribuna del órgano, *f*. **o.-pipe,** cañón de órgano, *m*. **o.-stop,** registro de órgano, *m*
organdie *n* organdi, *m*
organic *a* orgánico. **o. chemistry,** química orgánica, *f*
organism *n* organismo, *m*
organist *n* organista, *mf*
organization *n* organización, *f*; grupo, *m*, asociación, sociedad, *f*; organismo, *m*
organize *vt* organizar; arreglar. *vi* organizarse; asociarse, constituirse
organizer *n* organizador (-ra)
organizing *a* organizador
orgasm *n med* orgasmo, *m*
orgiastic *a* orgiástico
orgy *n* orgía, *f*
oriel *n arch* mirador, *m*
orient *a poet* naciente, oriental. *n* Oriente, Este, *m*. **pearl of fine o.,** perla de hermoso oriente, *f*
oriental *a* and *n* oriental, *mf*
orientalism *n* orientalismo, *m*
orientalist *n* orientalista, *mf*
orientate *vt* orientar; dirigir, guiar. *vi* mirar (or caer) hacia el este; orientarse
orientation *n* orientación, *f*
orifice *n* orificio, *m*; abertura, boca, *f*
origin *n* origen, génesis, *m*; raíz, causa, *f*; principio, comienzo, *m*; (extraction) descendencia, procedencia, familia, *f*, nacimiento, *m*
original *a* original; primitivo, primero; ingenioso. *n* original, *m*; prototipo, modelo, *m*. **o. sin,** pecado original, *m*
originality *n* originalidad, *f*
originally *adv* originalmente; al principio; antiguamente
originate *vt* (produce) ocasionar, producir, suscitar, iniciar, engendrar; (create) inventar, crear. *vi* originarse, surgir, nacer. **to o. in,** tener su origen en, surgir de, emanar de, venir de
origination *n* origen, principio, génesis, *m*
originator *n* iniciador (-ra), fundador (-ra); autor (-ra), creador (-ra)
oriole *n orn* oropéndola, *f*
Orion *n ast* Orión, *m*

Orkneys, the las Orcades, *f pl*
ornament *n* adorno, *m;* decoración, *f; fig* ornamento, *m;* (trinket) chuchería, *f, n pl.* **ornaments,** *ecc* ornamentos, *m pl. vt* ornar, adornar, decorar, embellecer
ornamental *a* ornamental, decorativo
ornamentation *n* ornamentación, decoración, *f*
ornate *a* vistoso, ornado en demasía, barroco
ornateness *n* elegancia, vistosidad, magnificencia, *f*
ornithological *a* ornitológico
ornithologist *n* ornitólogo, *m*
ornithology *n* ornitología, *f*
orphan *a* and *n* huérfano (-na)
orphanage *n* orfanato, hospicio, *m*
orphanhood *n* orfandad, *f*
Orphean *a* órfico
orthodox *a* ortodoxo
orthodoxy *n* ortodoxia, *f*
orthographic *a* ortográfico
orthography *n* ortografía, *f*
orthopedic *a* ortopédico
orthopedics *n* ortopedia, *f*
orthopedist *n* ortopedista, *mf* ortopédico (-ca)
oscillate *vi* oscilar, fluctuar; (hesitate) dudar, vacilar. *vt* hacer oscilar
oscillation *n* oscilación, fluctuación, vibración, *f; elec* oscilación, *f*
oscillator *n* oscilador, *m*
oscillatory *a* oscilante
osculation *n* ósculo, *m*
osier *n bot* mimbre, *m,* or *f.* **o. bed,** mimbrera, *f*
osmic *a chem* ósmico
osmosis *n* (*phys chem*) ósmosis, *f*
osprey *n orn* quebrantahuesos, *m*
osseous *a* óseo
ossification *n* osificación, *f*
ossify *vt* osificar; *vi* osificarse
ossuary *n* osario, *m*
osteitis *n med* osteítis, *f*
Ostend Ostende, *m*
ostensible *a* ostensible; aparente, engañoso, ilusorio
ostensibly *adv* en apariencia, ostensiblemente
ostentation *n* ostentación, *f;* aparato, fausto, boato, alarde, *m,* soberbia, *f*
ostentatious *a* ostentoso; aparatoso, fastuoso, rumboso
ostentatiously *adv* con ostentación
osteology *n* osteología, *f*
osteomyelitis *n med* osteomielitis, *f*
osteopath *n* osteópata, *m*
osteopathy *n* osteopatía, *f*
osteoplasty *n surg* osteoplastia, *f*
ostler *n* mozo de cuadras, establero, *m*
ostracism *n* ostracismo, *m*
ostracize *vt* desterrar; excluir del trato, echar de la sociedad
ostrich *n* avestruz, *m.* **o. farm,** criadero de avestruces, *m*
otalgia *n med* otalgia, *f,* dolor de oídos, *m*
other *a* otro. *pron* el otro, *m;* la otra, *f;* lo otro, *neut adv* (with than) de otra manera que, de otro modo que; otra cosa que. **this hand, not the o.,** esta mano, no la otra. **every o. day,** un día sí y otro no, cada dos días. **no o.,** ningún otro, *m;* otra ninguna, *f.* **someone or o.,** alguien. **the others,** los (las) demás, *m, f pl;* los otros, *m pl;* las otras, *f pl.* **o. people,** otros, *m pl,* los demás
otherwise *adv* de otra manera, de otro modo, otramente; (in other respects) por lo demás, por otra parte; (if not) si no
otitis *n med* otitis, *f*
otologist *n* otólogo, *m*
otology *n* otología, *f*
otter *n zool* nutria, *f.* **o. hound,** perro para cazar la nutria
ottoman *a* otomano, turco. *n* otomana, *f*
ouch! *interj* ¡ax!, ¡huy!
ought *v aux* deber, tener la obligación (de); ser conveniente, convenir; ser necesario (que), tener que. **I o. to have done it yesterday,** Debía haberlo hecho ayer. **She o. not to come,** No debe (debiera, debería) venir. **He o. to see them tomorrow,** (should) Conviene que les vea mañana; Tiene la obligación de verles mañana; (must) Es necesario que les vea mañana, Tiene que verles mañana.
ounce *n* (animal and weight) onza, *f.* **He hasn't an o. of common sense,** No tiene pizca de sentido común
our *a* nuestro
ours *pron* nuestro, *m;* nuestra, *f;* nuestros, *m pl;* nuestras, *f pl;* de nosotros, *m pl;* de nosotras, *f pl;* el nuestro, *m;* la nuestra, *f;* lo nuestro, *neut;* los nuestros, *m pl;* las nuestras, *f pl.* **This book is ours,** Este libro es nuestro (or el nuestro)
ourselves *pron pl* nosotros mismos, *m pl;* nosotras mismas, *f pl*
oust *vt* despedir, desahuciar, expulsar, echar
out *adv* afuera; hacia fuera; (gone out) fuera, salido, ausente; (invested) puesto; (published) publicado, salido; (discovered) conocido, descubierto; (on strike) en huelga; (mistaken) en error, equivocado; (of journeys) de ida, (on ships) de navegación (e.g. **on the second day out,** al segundo día de navegación); (of fire, etc.) extinguido; (at sea) en el mar; (of girls in society) puesta de largo, que ha entrado en sociedad; (of fashion) fuera de moda; (of office) fuera del poder; (in holes) roto, agujereado, andrajoso; (exhausted) agotado; (expired) vencido; (of a watch) llevar . . . minutos (horas) de atraso or de adelanto; (unfriendly) reñido; (way out) salida, *f;* (sport) fuera de juego; (of flowers) abierto; (of chickens) empollado. **a scene out of one of Shakespeare's plays,** una escena de una de las comedias de Shakespeare. **I am out $6,** He perdido seis dólares. **I am out of tea,** Se me ha acabado el té. **to drink out of a glass,** beber de un vaso. **to read out of a book,** leer en un libro. **to speak out,** hablar claro. **Murder will out,** El asesinato se descubrirá. **out-and-out,** completo; (with rogue, etc.) redomado. **out of,** fuera de; (beyond) más allá de; (through, by) por; (with) con; (without) sin; (from among) entre; (in) en; (with a negative sense) no. **out of breath,** jadeante, sin aliento. **out of character,** impropio. **out of commission,** fuera de servicio. **out of danger,** fuera de peligro. **out of date,** anticuado. **out of hand,** en seguida; indisciplinado. **out of money,** sin dinero. **out of necessity,** por necesidad. **out of one's mind,** loco, demente. **out of order.** See **order. out of print,** agotado. **out of reach,** fuera de alcance, inasequible. **out of season,** fuera de temporada. **out of sight,** fuera del alcance de la vista; invisible. **Out of sight, out of mind,** Ojos que no ven, corazón que no siente. **out of sorts,** indispuesto. **out of temper,** de mal genio. **out of the question,** imposible. **out of the way,** *adv* (of work) terminado, hecho; (remote) fuera del camino; (put aside) arrinconado; donde no estorbe. **out-of-the-way,** *a* remoto, aislado; (unusual) extraordinario, singular. **out of this world,** lo máximo, lo último. **out of touch with,** alejado de; sin relaciones con; sin simpatía con. **out of work,** sin empleo, sin trabajo, en paro forzoso. **out-patient,** enfermo (-ma) de un dispensario. **Out!** *interj* ¡Fuera! ¡Fuera de aquí! ¡Márchate! **Out with it!** ¡Hable Vd.! sin rodeos! ¡Hablen claro!
outbalance *vt* exceder, sobrepujar
outbid *vt* pujar, mejorar
outbidding *n* puja, mejora, *f*
outbreak *n* (of war) declaración, *f;* comienzo, *m;* (of disease) epidemia, *f;* (of crimes, etc.) serie, *f*
outbuilding *n* dependencia, *f,* edificio accesorio, anexo, *m*
outburst *n* acceso, arranque, *m,* explosión, *f*
outcast *n* paria, *mf;* desterrado (-da), proscripto (-ta)
outclass *vt* aventajar, ser superior (a), exceder
outcome *n* consecuencia, *f,* resultado, *m*
outcry *n* clamor, grito, *m;* protesta, *f*
outdistance *vt* dejar atrás

outdo *vt* eclipsar, aventajar, sobrepujar
outdoor *a* externo; (of activities) al aire libre; fuera de casa
outdoors *adv* fuera de casa; al aire libre
outer *a* externo, exterior
outer space espacio extraatmosférico, espacio extraterreste, espacio exterior, espacio sideral, espacio sidéreo, espacio ultraterrestre, *m*
outermost *a sup* (el, etc.) más externo, más exterior; extremo, de más allá
outfit *n* equipo, *m;* (of clothes) traje, *m;* (of furniture or trousseau) ajuar, *m;* (gear) pertrechos, avíos, *m pl. vt* aviar equipar
outfitter *n* proveedor (-ra), abastecedor (-ra)
outflank *vt mil* flanquear; ser más listo (que)
outgoing *a* saliente, que sale; cesante. **outgoings,** *n pl* gastos, *m pl*
outgrow *vt* hacerse demasiado grande para; crecer más que; (ideas) perder; (illness) curarse de, curarse con la edad; pasar de la edad de, ser ya viejo para. **to o. one's clothes,** quedársele a uno chica la ropa. **to o. one's strength,** estar demasiado crecido para su edad
outgrowth *n* excrecencia, *f;* resultado, fruto, *m,* consecuencia, *f*
outhouse *n* edificio accesorio, *m*
outing *n* excursión, vuelta, *f,* paseo, *m*
outlandish *a* extraño, singular, raro; absurdo, ridículo
outlast *vt* durar más que; (outlive) sobrevivir a
outlaw *n* bandido, proscrito, *m, vt* proscribir
outlay *n* gasto, desembolso, *m*
outlet *n* salida, *f;* orificio de salida, *m;* (of drains, etc.) desagüe, *m;* (of streets, rivers) desembocadura, *f; fig* escape, *m,* válvula de seguridad, *f*
outline *n* perfil, contorno, *m;* (drawing) esbozo, bosquejo, *m;* idea general, *f;* plan general, *m, vt* esbozar, bosquejar. **in o.,** en esbozo; en perfil. **to be outlined** (against), dibujarse (contra), destacarse (contra)
outlive *vt* sobrevivir (a); (live down) hacer olvidar
outlook *n* (view) perspectiva, vista, *f;* (opinion) actitud, *f,* punto de vista, *m;* aspecto, *m,* apariencia, *f;* (for trade, etc.) perspectiva, *f,* posibilidades, *f pl.* **o. tower,** atalaya, *f*
outlying *a* remoto, lejano, distante
outmaneuver *vt* superar en estrategia
outmatch *vt* aventajar, superar
outmoded *a* anticuado, pasado de moda
outnumber *vt* ser más numerosos que, exceder en número
out-of-court settlement *n* arreglo pacífico, *m*
out-of-town *a* de las provincias
outpost *n mil* avanzada, *f,* puesto avanzado, *m*
outpouring *n* derramamiento, *m;* efusión, *f*
output *n* producción, *f.* **o. capacity,** capacidad de producción, *f*
outrage *n* barbaridad infamia, atrocidad, *f;* rapto, *m,* violación, *f. vt* ultrajar; violar; violentar
outrageous *a* atroz, terrible; desaforado, monstruoso; injurioso; ridiculo
outrageousness *n* lo atroz; violencia, furia, *f;* escándalo, *m;* enormidad, *f;* lo excesivo; lo horrible
outré *a* cursi, extravagante
outride *vt* cabalgar más a prisa que
outright *adv* (frankly) de plano (e.g. **to reject outright,** rechazar de plano), francamente, sin reserva; (immediately) en seguida, immediatamente. *a* categórico; completo; franco
outrival *vt* vencer, superar
outrun *vt* correr más que
outset *n* principio, comienzo, *m*
outshine *vt* brillar más que, eclipsar en brillantez; superar, eclipsar
outside *adv* afuera, fuera. *prep* fuera de, al otro lado de, al exterior de; (besides) aparte de, fuera de. *a* externo, exterior; (of labor, etc.) desde fuera; máximo; ajeno. *n* exterior, *m;* superficie, *f;* aspecto, *m,* apariencia, *f.* **at the o.,** a lo sumo, cuando más. **from the o.,** de (or desde) fuera. **on the o.,** (externally) por fuera. **o. the door,** a la puerta
outsider *n* forastero (-ra); desconocido (-da), *Argentina, Chile also* cuico (-ca); caballo desconocido, *m;* persona poco deseable, *f*
outsize *n* artículo de talla mayor que las corrientes, *m*
outskirts *n pl* alrededores, *m pl,* afueras, immediaciones, cercanías, *f pl*
outspoken *a* franco. **to be o.,** decir lo que se piensa, no tener pelos en la lengua
outspokenness *n* franqueza, *f,*
outspread *a* extendido; (of wings) desplegadas
outstanding *a* excelente; sobresaliente, conspicuo; *com* pendiente, sin pagar. **to be o.,** *com* estar pendiente; *fig* sobresalir. **o. account,** *com* cuenta pendiente, *f*
outstay *vt* quedarse más tiempo que. **to o. one's welcome,** pegársele la silla
outstretched *a* extendido
outstrip *vt* dejar atrás, pasar; aventajar, superar
outvote *vt* emitir más votos que; rechazar por votación
outward *a* exterior, externo; aparente, visible. *adv* exteriormente; hacia fuera; superficialmente. **o. bound,** con rumbo a . . . **o. voyage,** el viaje de ida
outwardly *adv* exteriormente; hacia fuera; en apariencia
outwear *vt* durar más que; gastar
outweigh *vt* exceder, valer más que
outwit *vt* ser más listo que; vencer
outworn *a* anticuado, ya viejo
oval *n* óvalo, *m, a* oval, ovalado, aovado
ovarian *a* (*bot zool*) ovárico
ovary *n* ovario, *m*
ovation *n* ovación, recepción entusiasta, *f*
oven *n* horno, *m.* **o. peel,** pala de horno, *f.* **o. rake,** hurgón, *m*
over *prep* (above, upon, over) sobre, encima de; (on the other side) al otro lado de; (across) allende, a través de; (more than) más de; (beyond) más allá de; (of rank) superior a; (during) durante; (in addition) además de; (through) por. *n* (cricket) serie de saques, *f, adv* encima; en; por encima; al otro lado; de un lado a otro; enfrente; al lado contrario; de un extremo a otro; (finished) terminado; (ruined) arruinado, perdido; (more) más; (excessively) demasiado, excesivamente; (covered) cubierto (de); (extra) en exceso; (completely) enteramente; (from head to foot) de pies a cabeza, de hito en hito; (of time) pasado. **over** is also used as a prefix. Indicating excess, it is generally translated by demasiado or excesivamente. In other meanings, it is either not translated or its meaning forms part of the verb, being translated as re-, super-, trans-, ultra. Very often a less literal translation is more successful than the employment of the above prefixes. **all o.,** (everywhere) en todas partes; (finished) todo acabado; (covered) cubierto (de); (up and down) de pies a cabeza. **all the world o.,** en todo el mundo. **embroidered all o.,** todo bordado. **He is o. in Germany,** Está en Alemania. **He trembled all o.,** Estaba todo tembloroso. **that which is o.,** el exceso, lo que queda. **to read o.,** leer, repasar. **o. again,** de nuevo. **o. and above,** por encima de, fuera de, en exceso de. **o. and o.,** repetidamente, muchas veces. **o. my signature,** bajo mi firma. **o. six months since . . . ,** más de seis meses desde que . . .
overabundance *n* sobreabundancia, *f*
overabundant *a* sobreabundante
overact *vt* exagerar (un papel)
overall *n* bata, *f;* guardapolvo, *m; a* deconjunto (e.g., **overall assessment,** evaluación de conjunto) *pl* **overalls,** mono, *m*
overanxious *a* demasiado ansioso; demasiado inquieto. **to be o.-a.,** preocuparse demasiado
overarch *vt* abovedar
overawe *vt* intimidar, acobardar
overbalance *vt* hacer perder el equilibrio. hacer caer; preponderar. *vi* perder el equilibrio, caer

overbalancing *n* pérdida del equilibrio, caída, *f;* preponderancia, *f*
overbearing *a* dominante, autoritario, imperioso
overboard *adv* al agua, al mar.
overburden *vt* sobrecargar, agobiar
overcast *a* anublado, cerrado, encapotado. *vt sew* sobrehilar. **to become o.,** anublarse
overcharge *n* recargo, *m;* (price) recargo de precio, precio excesivo, *m.* *vt* recargar, cobrar un precio excesivo; *elec* sobrecargar. *vi* cobrar demasiado
overcloud *vt* anublar; *fig* entristecer
overcoat *n* abrigo, sobretodo, gabán, *m*
overcome *vt* vencer, rendir, subyugar; (difficulties) triunfar de, allanar, dominar. *vi* saber vencer. *a* (by sleep, etc.) rendido; (at a loss) turbado, confundido; (by kindness) agradecidisimo
overconfidence *n* confianza excesiva, *f*
overcooked *a* recocido, demasiado cocido
overcrowd *vt* atestar, llenar de bote en bote; (over-populate) sobrepoblar
overcrowding *n* sobrepoblación, *f*
overdo *vt* exagerar; ir demasiado lejos, hacer demasiado; *cul* recocer; (overtire) fatigarse demasiado
overdose *n* dosis excesiva, *f*
overdraft *n com* giro en descubierto, *m*
overdraw *vt* and *vi com* girar en descubierto
over-dressed *a* que viste demasiado; cursi
overdue *a* atrasado; *com* vencido y no pagado
overeat *vi* comer demasiado, atracarse, *Lat. Am.* jambarse
overestimate *vt* estimar en valor excesivo; exagerar, sobreestimar, *n* presupuesto excesivo, *m;* estimación excesiva, *f*
overexcite *vt* sobreexcitar
overexposure *n phot* exceso deexposición, *m*
overfatigue *vt* fatigar demasiado. *n* cansancio excesivo, *m*
overfeeding *n* sobrealimentación, *f*
overflow *vt* inundar, derramarse por; *fig* cubrir, llenar; desbordarse. *vi* (with) rebosar de. *n* inundación, *f,* desbordamiento, derrame, *m; fig* residuo, resto, exceso, *m;* (plumbing) sumidero, vertedero, *m,* descarga, *f.* **The river overflowed its banks,** El río se desbordó, El río salió de cauce
overflowing *a* rebosante; superabundante; (its banks) *Lat. Am.* desbocado. **filled to o.,** lleno hasta los bordes. **o. with health,** rebosante de salud, vendiendo salud
overgrown *a* (gawky) talludo; (plants) exuberante, vicioso; frondoso, cubierto de verdura
overhang *vt* caer a, mirar a; colgar; *fig* amenazar. *vi* colgar, sobresalir; *fig* amenazar
overhanging *a* saledizo, sobresaliente; colgante, pendiente
overhaul *vt* examinar, investigar; componer, hacer una inspección general de; (of boats overtaking) alcanzar. *n* examen, *m,* investigación, *f; med* exploración general, *f*
overhead *adv* arriba, en lo alto, encima de la cabeza. *a* aéreo, elevado; general, fijo. **o. cable,** cable eléctrico, *m.* **o. expenses,** gastos generales, *m pl.* **o. railway,** ferrocarril aéreo (or elevado), *m*
overhear *vt* (accidentally) oír por casualidad, oír sin querer; (on purpose) alcanzar a oír, lograr oír
overheat *vt* acalorar, hacer demasiado caliente, recalentar. *vi* (in argument) acalorarse; hacerse demasiado caliente
overheating *n* recalentramiento, *m*
overindulge *vt* mimar demasiado; dedicarse a algo con exceso; tomar algo con exceso. *vi* darse demasiada buena vida
overjoyed *a* contentísimo, lleno de alegría, encantado
overland *adv* por tierra. *a* terrestre, trascontinental
overlap *vi* traslaparse; coincidir. *n* traslapo, *m*
overlay *vt* cubrir, dar una capa; (with silver) platear; (with gold) dorar. *n* capa, *f;* cubierta, *f*
overleaf *adv* a la vuelta
overload *vt* sobrecargar, recargar. *n* sobrecarga, *f*
overlook *vt* (face) dar a, mirar a, dominar; (supervise) vigilar, examinar, inspeccionar; (not notice) no notar, pasar por alto, no hacer, caso de, no fijarse en; (neglect) desdeñar; (ignore) no darse cuenta de, ignorar; (excuse) perdonar, tolerar, hacer la vista gorda
overlord *n* señor de horca y cuchillo, señor, jefe, *m*
overmuch *adv* demasiado, en exceso
overnight *adv* la noche pasada, durante la noche; toda la noche. *a* de la víspera, nocturno. **to stay o. with,** pasar la noche con
overpass *n* pasaje elevado, viaducto, *m*
overpay *vt* pagar demasiado
overpayment *n* pago excesivo, *m*
overpopulate *vt* sobrepoblar, become overpopulated recargarse de habitantes (with people), recargarse de animales (with animals)
overpower *vt* vencer, subyugar; (of scents, etc.) trastornar; rendir, dominar
overpowering *a* irresistible
overpraise *vt* encarecer, alabar mucho
overproduce *vt* and *vi* sobreproducir
overproduction *n* sobreproducción, *f*
overrate *vt* exagerar el valor de; (of property) sobrevalorar
overreach *vt* sobrealcanzar. **to o. oneself,** sobrepasarse, ir demasiado lejos
override *vt* (trample) pasar por encima (de); *fig* rechazar, poner a un lado; (bully) dominar; (a horse) fatigar, reventar
overripe *a* demasiado maduro
overrule *vt law* denegar, no admitir; vencer
overrun *vt* (flood) inundar; (ravage) invadir; (infest) plagar, infestar; desbordarse, derramarse
oversea *a* ultramarino, de ultramar. *adv* en ultramar, allende los mares
oversee *vt* vigilar, inspeccionar
overseer *n* capataz, mayoral, sobrestante, contramaestre, *m;* inspector (-ra), veedor (-ra)
oversell *vt* and *vi* vender en exceso
oversensitive *a* demasiado sensitivo; vidrioso; susceptible
oversew *vt* sobrecoser
overshadow *vt* sombrear; *fig* eclipsar, obscurecer; (sadden) entristecer
overshoe *n* chanclo, *m;* (for snow) galocha, *f*
overshoot *vt* tirar más allá del blanco; *fig* exceder, rebasar el límite conveniente, **overshoot the target** (fig.) ir más allá del blanco, ir más allá de lo razonable. **to o. oneself,** exagerar; propasarse, descomedirse
oversight *n* inadvertencia, omisión, equivocación, *f;* descuido, *m*
oversimplify *vt* simplificar en exceso
oversleep *vi* dormir demasiado; *inf* pegársele a uno las sábanas, levantarse demasiado tarde
overspend *vt* and *vi* gastar demasiado
overspread *vt* desparramar, salpicar, esparcir, sembrar; cubrir
overstate *vt* exagerar, encarecer, ponderar
overstatement *n* exageración, ponderación, *f*
overstep *vt* exceder, pasar, violar; rebasar, pasar más allá (de)
overstrain *vt* fatigar demasiado, agotar. *n* fatiga, *f.* **to o. oneself,** esforzarse demasiado, cansarse demasiado
overstrung *a* nervioso, excitable; (piano) de cuerdas cruzadas
oversubscribe *vt* subscribir en exceso
overt *a* abierto, público; manifiesto, evidente
overtake *vt* alcanzar, pasar, dejar atrás; adelantarse (a); (surprise) coger, sorprender; (overwhelm) vencer, dominar
overtax *vt* oprimir de tributos; agobiar, cansar demasiado
overthrow *vt* volcar, echar por tierra, derribar; *fig* vencer, destruir, destronar. *n* vuelco, derribo, *m; fig* destrucción, ruina, *f*
overtime *adv* fuera de las horas estipuladas. *n* horas ex-

traordinarias de trabajo, *fpl.* **to work o.,** trabajar horas extraordinarias
overtone *n mus* armónico, *m*
overtop *vt* dominar, sobresalir, elevarse encima de
overture *n mus* obertura, *f*
overturn *vt* volcar, derribar, echar a rodar, echar abajo; (upset) revolver, desordenar. *vi* volcar, venirse abajo, allanarse; estar revuelto
overturning *n* vuelco, salto de campana, *m*
overweening *a* arrogante, insolente, altivo
overweight *n* sobrepeso, exceso en el peso, *m.* **to be o.,** pesar más de lo debido
overwhelm *vt* (conquer) vencer, aplastar, derrotar; (of waves, etc.) sumergir, hundir, inundar, engolfar; (in argument) confundir, dejar confuso, avergonzar; (of grief, etc.) vencer, postrar, dominar; (of work) inundar
overwhelming *a* irresistible, invencible, abrumador, apabullante
overwind *vt* (a watch) dar demasiada cuerda a; romper la cuerda de
overwork *vt* hacer trabajar demasiado (or con exceso); esclavizar. *vi* trabajar demasiado. *n* exceso de trabajo, demasiado trabajo, *m*
overwrought *a* (overworked) agotado por el trabajo, rendido, muy cansado; nerviosísimo, sobreexcitado, exaltado, muy agitado
ovine *a* ovejuno
ovoid *a* ovoide
ovulation *n med* ovulación, *f*
owe *vt* deber, tener deudas (de); deber, estar agradecido (por), estar obligado (a). *vi* estar en deuda, estar endeudado, tener deudas. **He owes his tailor $30,** Le debe treinta dólares a su sastre. **I owe him thanks for his help,** Le estoy agradecido por su ayuda (*or* Le debo las gracias por . . .). **He owes his success to good fortune,** Su éxito se debe a la suerte
owing *a* sin pagar. **o. to,** debido a, a causa de, por. **We had to stay in o. to the rain,** Tuvimos que quedarnos en casa a causa de la lluvia. **What is o. to you now?** ¿Cuánto se le debe ahora?
owl *n* búho, mochuelo, *Peru* carancho, *m.* **barn** or **screech owl,** lechuza, *f.* **brown owl,** autillo, *m*
owlish *a* parecido a un búho, de búho
own *a* propio. *n* (dearest) bien, *m. vt* poseer, tener, ser dueño de; (recognize) reconocer; (admit) confesar. *vi* confesar. **my (thy, his, our, your) own,** mi (tu, su, nuestro, vuestro) propio, *m,* (*f,* propia); mis (tus, sus, nuestros, vuestros) propios, *m pl,* (*f pl,* propias); (when not placed before a noun) el mío (tuyo, suyo, nuestro, vuestro), la mía (tuya, etc.), los míos (tuyos, etc.), las mías (tuyas, etc.); (relations) los suyos. **in his own house,** en su propia casa. **my (thy, his, etc.) own self,** yo (tú, él) mismo, *m,* (*f,* misma, *m pl,* mismos, *f pl,* mismas). **a room of one's own,** un cuarto para sí (or para uno mismo). **to be on one's own,** ser independiente; estar a solas. **to hold one's own,** mantenerse en sus trece. **to own up,** confesar
owner *n* dueño (-ña), propietario (-ia), posesor (-ra)
ownerless *a* sin dueño, sin amo
ownership *n* posesión, *f,* dominio, *m;* propiedad, *f*
ox *n* buey (*pl* bueyes), *m.* **oxeye daisy,** margarita, *f.* **oxstall,** boyera, *f*
oxidation *n chem* oxidación, *f*
oxide *n chem* óxido, *m*
oxidization *n* oxidación, *f*
oxidize *vt chem* oxidar; *vi* oxidarse
oxygen *n* oxígeno, *m.* **o. mask,** máscara de oxígeno, *f.* **o. tent,** tienda de oxígeno, *f*
oxygenate *vt chem* oxigenar
oxygenation *n chem* oxigenación, *f*
oyez, oyez! *interj* ¡oíd!
oyster *n* ostra, *f.* **o. bed,** pescadero (or criadero) de ostras, *m.* **o. culture,** ostricultura, *f*
ozone *n* ozono, *m*

P

p *n* (letter) pe, *f.* **to mind one's p's and q's,** poner los puntos sobre las íes; ir con pies de plomo
pabulum *n* pábulo, *m;* sustento, *m*
pace *n* paso, *m;* (gait) andar, *m,* marcha, *f;* (of a horse) andadura, *f;* (speed) velocidad, *f. vi* pasear(se), andar; (of a horse) amblar. *vt* recorrer, andar por; marcar el paso para; (with out) medir a pasos. **at a good p.,** a un buen paso. **to keep p. with,** ajustarse al paso de, ir al mismo paso que; andar al paso de; (events) mantenerse al corriente de. **to p. up and down,** pasearse, dar vueltas. **p.-maker,** el que marca el paso
paced *a* de andar . . . ; (of a horse) de andadura . . . ; de paso . . .
pachyderm *n* paquidermo, *m*
Pacific, the el (Océano) Pacífico, *m*
pacific *a geog* pacífico; sosegado, tranquilo, pacífico. **He is of a p. disposition,** Es amigo de la paz
pacification *n* pacificación, *f*
pacificatory *a* pacificador
pacifier *n* pacificador (-ra)
pacifism *n* pacifismo, *m*
pacifist *a* pacifista. *n* pacifista, *mf*
pacify *vt* pacificar; calmar, tranquilizar; aplacar, conciliar
pack *n* (bundle) fardo, lío, *m;* paquete, *m;* (load) carga, *f;* (of hounds) jauría, *f;* (herd) hato, *m;* (of seals) manada, *f;* (of cards) baraja (de naipes), *f;* (of rogues) cuadrilla, *f;* (of lies, etc.) colección, *f;* masa, *f;* (of ice) témpanos flotantes, *m pl;* (Rugby football) delanteros, *m pl;* (for the face) compresa, *f.* **p.-horse,** caballo de carga, *m.* **p.-needle,** aguja espartera, *f.* **p.-saddle,** albarda, *f.* **p.-thread,** bramante, *m*
pack *vt* embalar; empaquetar; envasar; encajonar; (a suit-case, etc.) hacer; (cram) apretar; (crowd) atestar, llenar; (a pipe joint, etc.) empaquetar; (an animal) cargar. *vi* llenar; (one's luggage) hacer el equipaje, hacer el baúl, arreglar el equipaje. **packed like sardines,** como sardinas en banasta. **The train was packed,** El tren estababa lleno de bote en bote. **to p. off,** (a person) despachar; poner de partitas en la calle. **to p. up,** hacer el equipaje; empaquetar; embalar; *inf* liar el hato
package *n* paquete, *m;* bulto, *m;* (bundle) fardo, *m*
packer *n* embalador, *m;* envasador (-ra)
packet *n* paquete, *m;* (of cigarettes, etc.) cajetilla, *f;* (boat) paquebote, *m.* **to make one's p.,** *inf* hacer su pacotilla
packing *n* embalaje, *m;* envoltura, *f;* envase, *m;* (on a pipe, etc.) guarnición, *f.* **I must do my p.,** Tengo que hacer las maletas. **p.-case,** caja de embalaje, *f.* **p.-needle,** aguja espartera, *f*
pact *n* pacto, convenio, *m.* **to make a p.,** pactar
pad *n* almohadilla, *f,* cojinete, *m;* (on a bed, chair) colchoneta, *f;* (on a wound) cabezal, *m;* (for polishing) muñeca, *f;* (hockey) defensa, *f;* (cricket) espinillera, *f;* (writing) bloque, *m;* (of a calendar) taco, *m;* (blotting) secafirmas, *m;* (of a quadruped's foot) pulpejo, *m;* (of fox, hare) pata, *f;* (leaf) hoja grande, *f, vt* almohadillar; acolchar; rellenar, forrar; (out, a book, etc.) meter paja en. **inking-pad,** almohadilla de entintar, *f.* **padded cell,** celda acolchonada, *f.* **shoulder-pad,** (in a garment) hombrera, *f*
padding *n* relleno, *m,* almohadilla, *f;* (material) borra, *f,* algodón, *m; fig* paja, *f,* ripio, *m,*
paddle *n* (oar) canalete, zagual, *m;* paleta, *f;* (flipper) aleta, *f, vt* and *vi* remar con canalete; (dabble) chapotear. **double p.,** remo doble, *m.* **p.-steamer,** vapor de

ruedas, vapor de paleta, *m*. **p.-wheel,** rueda de paletas, *f*
paddler *n* remero (-ra); el, *m*, (*f*, la) que chapotea
paddling *n* chapoteo, chapaleo, *m*
paddock *n* prado, *m*, dehesa, *f*; parque, *m*; (near a racecourse) en silla dero, picadero, *m*; (toad) sapo, *m*
padlock *n* candado, *m*, *vt* cerrar con candado, acerrojar
Paduan *a* and *n* paduano (-na)
paean *n* himno de alegría, *m*
pagan *a* and *n* pagano (-na)
paganism *n* paganismo, *m*
page *n* (boy) paje, *m*; (squire) escudero, *m*; (of a book, etc.) página, *f*; *fig* hoja, *f*. *vt* compaginar; (a person) vocear. **on p. nine,** en la página nueve. **to turn the p.,** *fig* volver la hoja
pageant *n* espectáculo, *m*; (procession) desfile, *m*; representación teatral, *f*; fiesta, *f*; *fig* pompa, *f*, aparato, *m*
pageantry *n* pompa, *f*, aparato, *m*, magnificencia, *f*
paginate *vt* paginar
pagination *n* paginación, *f*
pagoda *n* pagoda, *f*
paid *a* pagado; (on a parcel) porte pagado. **p. mourner,** plañidera, *f*. **p.-up share,** acción liberada, *f*
pail *n* cubo, pozal, *m*, cubeta, *f*
pailful *n* cubo (de agua, etc.), *m*
pain *n* dolor, *m*; sufrimiento, *m*; (mental) tormento, *m*, angustia, *f*; *law* pena, *f*; *pl* **pains,** (effort) trabajo, esfuerzo, *m*. *vt* doler; atormentar, afligir. **dull p.,** dolor sordo, *m*. **I have a p. in my head,** Me duele la cabeza. **on p. of death,** so pena de muerte. **to be in great p.,** sufrir mucho. **to take pains,** tomarse trabajo, esforzarse, esmerarse
pained *a* dolorido; afligido; de angustia
painful *a* doloroso; angustioso; fatigoso; (troublesome) molesto; (embarrassing) embarazoso; difícil; (laborious) arduo
painfully *adv* dolorosamente; penosamente; fatigosamente; con angustia; laboriosamente
painfulness *n* dolor, *m*; angustia, aflicción, *f*; tormento, *m*; dificultad, *f*
painless *a* sin dolor, indoloro
painlessly *adv* sin dolor; sin sufrir
painlessness *n* falta de dolor, *f*
painstaking *a* concienzudo; diligente, industrioso; cuidadoso. *n* trabajo, *m*; diligencia, industria, *f*; cuidado, *m*
paint *n* pintura, *f*; (for preserving metal) pavón, *m*; (rouge) colorete, *m*. *vt* pintar. *vi* pintar; pintarse. **The door is painted blue,** La puerta está pintada de azul. **p.-box,** caja de pinturas, *f*. **p.-brush,** pincel, *m*; (for house painting) brocha, *f*
painter *n* pintor (-ra); (house) pintor de brocha gorda, pintor de casas, *m*; (of a boat) boza, *f*. **sign-p.,** pintor de muestras, *m*
painting *n* pintura, *f*; (picture) cuadro, *m*, pintura, *f*
pair *n* par, *m*; (of people) pareja, *f*; (of oxen) yunta, *f*. *vt* parear, emparejar; (persons) unir, casar; (animals) aparear. *vi* parearse; casarse; aparearse. **a carriage and p.,** un landó con dos caballos. **a p. of steps,** una escalera de mano. **a p. of pants a p. of trousers,** unos pantalones. **in pairs,** de dos en dos; por parejas. **to p. off,** *vi* formar pareja; *inf* casarse
pal *n* camarada, compinche, *mf*; amigote, *m*
palace *n* palacio, *m*
paladin *n* paladín, *m*
paleographer *n* paleógrafo, *m*
paleography *n* paleografía, *f*
paleolithic *a* paleolítico
paleology *n* paleología, *f*
paleontology *n* paleontología, *f*
palatable *a* sabroso, apetitoso; *fig* agradable, aceptable
palatableness *n* buen sabor, gusto agradable, *m*; *fig* lo agradable
palatably *adv* agradablemente
palatal *a* paladial. *n* letra paladial, *f*
palatalize *vt* palatizar
palate *n* paladar, *m*. **hard p.,** paladar, *m*. **soft p.,** velo del paladar, *m*
palatial *a* (of a palace) palaciego; (sumptuous) magnífico, suntuoso
pale *n* (stake) estaca, *f*; límite, *m*; *her* palo, *m*, *a* pálido; (wan) descolorido, *Lat. Am. also* lívido; (of colours) claro, desmayado; (of light) tenue, mortecino; (lustreless) sin brillo, muerto. *vi* palidecer, perder el color; *fig* eclipsarse
palely *adv* pálidamente; vagamente, indistintamente
paleness *n* palidez, *f*; (wanness) descoloramiento, *m*, amarillez, *f*; (of light) tenuidad, *f*
palette *n* paleta, *f*. **p.-knife,** espátula, *f*
palimpsest *n* palimpsesto, *m*
palindrome *n* capicúa *f*, (of numbers), palíndromo *m*
paling *n* palizada, estacada, valla, *f*
palisade *n* palenque, *m*, tranquera, palizada, *f*; *mil* estacada, *f*
palish *a* algo pálido; paliducho
pall *n* (on a coffin) paño mortuorio, *m*; (*fig* covering) manto, *m*, capa, *f*; *ecc* palio, *m*; (over a chalice) palia, *f*. *vi* perder el sabor, hacerse insípido; saciarse (de); aburrirse (de), cansarse (de). **The music of Bach never palls on me,** No me canso nunca de la música de Bach
palladium *n min* paladio, *m*; (safeguard) paladión, *m*
pallet *n* jergón, *m*; camilla, *f*; *mech* fiador de rueda, *m*; torno de alfarero, *m*
palliate *vt* (pain) paliar, aliviar; mitigar; (excuse) disculpar, excusar
palliation *n* paliación, *f*; mitigación, *f*; disculpa, *f*
palliative *a* paliativo; (extenuating) atenuante. *n* paliativo, *m*
pallid *a* pálido, *Lat. Am. also* lívido
pallidness *n* palidez, *f*
pallor *n* palidez, *f*
palm *n* (of the hand, and *fig*., victory) palma, *f*; (measurement) ancho de la mano, *m*; (tree) palmera, *f*. *vt* (a card, etc.) empalmar; (with off) defraudar (con); dar gato por liebre (a). **to bear away the p.,** llevar la palma. **p. branch,** palma, *f*. **p. grove,** palmar, *m*. **p.-oil,** aceite de palma, *m*; (bribe) soborno, *m*. **P. Sunday,** Domingo de Ramos, *m*. **p. tree,** palmera, *Lat. Am.* chonta, *f*
palmate *a* palmeado
palmer *n* peregrino, *m*; (caterpillar) oruga velluda, *f*
palming *n* (in conjuring, etc.) empalme, *m*
palmist *n* quiromántico (-ca)
palmistry *n* quiromancía, *f*
palmy *a* palmar; (flourishing) floreciente; (happy) dichoso, feliz; (prosperous) próspero; triunfante
Palmyra Palmira, *f*
palp *n* palpo, *m*
palpability *n* palpabilidad, *f*
palpable *a* palpable
palpate *vt* palpar
palpation *n* palpación, *f*
palpitate *vi* palpitar
palpitating *a* palpitante
palpitation *n* palpitación, *f*
palsied *a* paralítico
palsy *n* parálisis, *f*, *vt* paralizar
paltriness *n* mezquindad, pequeñez, *f*
paltry *a* mezquino, insignificante, pobre
paludism *n med* paludismo, *m*
pampas *n* pampa, *f*
pamper *vt* mimar, consentir demasiado; criar con mimos, regalar; alimentar demasiado bien
pampered *a* mimado, consentido; demasiado bien alimentado
pamphlet *n* folleto, *m*
pamphleteer *n* folletinista, *mf*
pan *n* (vessel) cazuela, *f*; cacerola, *f*; (brain) cráneo, *m*; (of a balance) platillo, *m*; (of a firelock) cazoleta, *f*, *cinem* toma panorámica *f*, *prefix* pan-. **to pan off,** separar el oro en una gamella. **to pan out,** dar oro; *fig* suceder. **Pan-Americanism,** panamericanismo, *m*

Pan *n* Pan, *m.* **pipes of Pan,** flauta de Pan, *f*
panacea *n* panacea, *f*
panache *n* penacho, *m*
panada *n cul* panetela, *f*
Panama el Panamá, *m*
Panama *a* panameño. (-ña). **P. hat,** sombrero de jipijapa, panamá *m*
pancake *n* fruta de sartén, hojuela, *f.* **p. landing,** *aer* aterrizaje brusco, *m.* **P. Tuesday,** martes de Carnaval, *m*
panchromatic *a* pancromático
pancreas *n* páncreas, *m*
pancreatic *a* pancreático
panda *n zool* panda, *mf*
pandemic *a* pandémico
pandemonium *n* pandemonio
pander *n* alcahuete, *m, vi* alcahuetear. **to p. to,** prestarse a; favorecer, ayudar
pandore *n mus* bandola, *f*
pane *n* hoja de vidrio, hoja de cristal, *f;* cuadro, *m*
panegyric *a* panegírico. *n* panegírico, *m*
panel *n* panel, entrepaño, *m; art* tabla, *f;* (in a dress) paño, *m;* (list) lista, *f,* registro, *m;* (jury) jurado, *m;* lista de jurados, *f, vt* labrar a entrepaños; artesonar. **p. doctor,** médico (-ca) de seguros
paneled *a* entrepañado; (of ceilings) artesonado. **p. ceiling,** artesonado, *m*
paneling *n* entrepaños, *m pl;* artesonado, *m*
panful *n* cazolada, *f*
pang *n* punzada (de dolor), *f,* dolor agudo, *m;* dolor, *m;* (anguish of mind) angustia, *f,* tormento, *m;* (of conscience) remordimiento, *m*
panic *n* pánico, *m;* pavor, espanto, *m;* terror súbito, *m, a* pánico. *vi* espantarse. **p.-monger,** alarmista, *mf* **p.-stricken,** aterrorizado, despavorido
panicky *a inf* lleno de pánico; nervioso
pannier *n* (basket) alforja, *f;* cesto, *m;* (bustle) caderillas, *f pl*
panoply *n* panoplia, *f*
panorama *n* panorama, *m*
panoramic *a* panorámico
pansy *n* pensamiento, *m,* trinitaria, *f*
pant *vi* jadear; (of dogs) hipar; resollar; (of the heart) palpitar. *n* jadeo, *m;* palpitación, *f.* **to p. after,** suspirar por
pantaloon *n* (trouser) pantalón, *m;* (Pantaloon) Pantalón, *m*
pantechnicon *n* almacén de muebles, *m;* (van) carro de mudanzas, *m*
pantheism *n* panteísmo, *m*
pantheist *n* panteísta, *mf*
pantheistic *a* panteísta
pantheon *n* panteón, *m*
panther *n* pantera, *f*
panties *n pl* pantalones, *m pl*
panting *a* jadeante, sin aliento. *n* jadeo, *m;* resuello, *m,* respiración difícil, *f;* palpitación, *f*
pantomime *n* pantomima, *f;* revista, *f.* **in p.,** en pantomima; por gestos
pantry *n* despensa, *f*
pants *n pl* calzoncillos, *m pl;* (trousers) pantalones, *m pl.* **p. buttoned down the sides** *Mexico* calzoneras, *f pl*
panzer division *n* división motorizada, *f*
pap *n* (nipple) pezón, *m;* (soft food) papilla, *f*
papa *n* papá, *m*
papacy *n* papado, pontificado, *m*
papal *a* papal, pontificio. **p. bull,** bula pontificia, *f.* **p. nuncio,** nuncio del Papa, nuncio apostólico, *m.* **p. see,** sede apostólica, *f*
papaya *n Cuba* fruta bomba, *f*
paper *n* papel, *m;* hoja de papel, *f;* documento, *m;* (lecture) comunicación, *f;* (newspaper) periódico, *m;* (journal) revista, *f;* (exam.) examen escrito, trabajo, *m;* ejercicio, *m; pl* **papers,** (credentials) documentación, *f,* credenciales, *f pl; com* valores negociables, *m pl;* (packet) paquete, *m, a* de papel; para papeles; parecido al papel. *vt* (a room) empapelar; (a parcel) envolver. **daily p.,** diario, *m.* **in p. covers,** (of books) en rústica. **slip of p.,** papeleta. *f.* **to send in one's papers,** entregar su dimisión. **p. bag,** saco de papel, *m.* **p.-chase,** rally-paper, *m.* **p. clip,** prendedero de oficina, **sujetapapeles,** *Central America* ataché, *elsewhere in Lat. Am.* broche, *m.* **p.-cutting machine,** guillotina, *f.* **p. folder,** plegadera, *f.* **p.-hanger,** empapelador, *m.* **p.-hanging,** empapelado, *m.* **p.-knife,** cortapapel, *m.* **p.-maker,** fabricante de papel, *m.* **p.-making,** manufactura de papel, *f.* **p.-mill,** fábrica de papel, *f.* **p.-money,** papel moneda, *m.* **p.-pulp,** pasta, *f.* **p.-streamer,** serpentina, *f.* **p.-weight,** pisapapeles, *m*
papering *n* (of a room) empapelado, *m*
papery *a* semejante al papel
papier-mâché *n* cartón piedra, *m*
papillary *a* papilar
paprika *n* pimienta húngara, *f*
papyrus *n* papiro, *m*
par *n* par, *f.* **at par,** *com* a la par. **above (below) par,** *com* por encima (*or* debajo) de la par. **He is a little below par,** No está muy bien de salud. **to be on par with,** ser el equivalente de; ser igual a. **par excellence,** por excelencia
parable *n* parábola, *f*
parabola *n geom* parábola, *f*
parachute *n* paracaídas, *m; bot* vilano, *m.* **to p. down,** lanzarse en paracaídas. **p. troops,** cuerpo de paracaidistas, *m*
parachutist *n* paracaidista, *mf*
parade *n* alarde, *m; mil* parada, revista, *f;* (procession) desfile, *m,* procesión, *f;* (promenade) paseo, *m. vt* (display) hacer alarde de, hacer gala de, ostentar; (troops) formar en parada; pasar revista (a); (patrol) recorrer. *vi mil* tomar parte en una parada; desfilar. **to p. up and down,** pasearse. **p.-ground,** campo de instrucción, *m;* plaza de armas, *f*
paradigm *n* paradigma, *m*
paradise *n* paraíso, edén, *m; fig* jauja, *f.* **bird of p.,** ave del paraíso, *f*
paradisiac *a* paradisíaco
paradox *n* paradoja, *f*
paradoxical *a* paradójico
paradoxicality *n* lo paradójico
paraffin *n* parafina, *f. vt* parafinar. **p.-oil,** parafina líquida, *f*
paragon *n* modelo perfecto, dechado, *m*
paragraph *n* párrafo, *m;* (in a newspaper) suelto, *m, vt* dividir en párrafos; escribir un suelto sobre. **new p.,** párrafo aparte, *m*
Paraguay el Paraguay, *m*
Paraguayan *a* and *n* paraguayo (-ya)
parakeet *n orn* perico, *m*
parallel *a* paralelo; igual; semejante, análogo. *n* línea paralela, *f;* paralelo, *m; mil* paralela, *f; geog* paralelo, *m; print* pleca, *f. vt* poner en paralelo; cotejar, comparar; igualar. **to run p. to,** ser paralelo a; ser conforme a. **p. bars,** paralelas, *f pl*
parallelism *n* paralelismo, *m*
parallelogram *n* paralelogramo, *m*
paralyse *vt* paralizar
paralysis *n* parálisis, *f*
paralytic *a* and *n* paralítico (-ca)
paramount *a* supremo, sumo
paramour *n* amante, querido, *m;* querida, amiga, *f*
paranoia *n* paranoia, *f*
paranoiac *n* paranoico, *m*
parapet *n* (*arch* and *mil*) parapeto, *m*
paraphernalia *n law* bienes parafernales, *m, p;* (finery) atavíos, adornos, *m pl;* equipo, *m;* arreos, *m pl;* insignias, *f pl*
paraphrase *n* paráfrasis, *f, vt* parafrasear
parasite *n* parásito, *m; inf* zángano, *m,* gorrista, *mf, Mexico* arrimado, *m*
parasitic *a* parásito, parasitario; *med* parasítico
parasitology *n* parasitología, *f*

parasol *n* parasol, quitasol, *m*
parathyroid *a* paratiroides. *n* paratiroides, *f pl*
paratroops *n pl* paracaidistas, *m pl*
paratyphoid *n* paratifoidea, *f*
parboil *vt* sancochar
parcel *n* paquete, *m*; fardo, *m*; (of land) parcela, *f*. **to p. out,** repartir, distribuir; dividir. **to p. up,** envolver, empaquetar. **p. post,** servicio de paquetes, *m*
parceling *n* empaque, *m*; (out) reparto, *m*, distribución, *f*; división, *f*
parch *vt* secar; abrasar, quemar; (roast) tostar. *vi* secarse; quemarse, abrasarse
parched *a* seco, sediento. **p. with thirst,** muerto de sed
parchedness *n* sequedad, aridez, *f*
parchment *n* pergamino, *m*; (of a drum) parche, *m*. **p.-like,** apergaminado
pardon *n* perdón, *m*; *ecc* indulgencia, *f*. *vt* perdonar; indultar, amnistiar. **a general p.,** una amnistia. **I beg your p.!** ¡Vd. dispense!; ¡Perdone Vd.! **to beg p.,** pedir perdón; disculparse. **P.?** ¿Cómo?
pardonable *a* perdonable, disculpable, excusable
pardonableness *n* disculpabilidad, *f*
pardonably *adv* disculpablemente, excusablemente
pardoner *n* vendedor de indulgencias, *m*; perdonador (-ra)
pardoning *n* perdón, *m*; remisión, *f*
pare *vt* (one's nails) cortar; (fruit) mondar; (potatoes, etc.) pelar; (remove) quitar; (reduce) reducir
parent *n* padre, *m*; madre, *f*; (ancestor) antepasado, *m*; (origin) origen, *m*, fuente, *f*; (cause) causa, *f*; (author) autor, *m*; autora, *f*; *pl* **parents,** padres, *m pl*. *a* madre, materno; principal
parentage *n* parentela, *f*; linaje, *m*, familia, alcurnia, *f*; procedencia, *f*, nacimiento, origen, *m*
parental *a* paternal; maternal, de madre
parentally *adv* como un padre; como una madre
parenthesis *n* paréntesis, *m*
parenthetical *a* entre paréntesis; de paréntesis
parenthood *n* paternidad, *f*; maternidad, *f*
pariah *n* paria, *mf*
parietal *a* parietal
paring *n* (act) raedura, *f*; peladura, mondadura, *f*; (shred) brizna, *f*; (refuse) desecho, desperdicio, *m*. **p.-knife,** trinchete, *m*
Paris París, *m*
parish *n* parroquia, *f*; feligresía, *f*, *a* parroquial. **p. church,** parroquia, *f*. **p. clerk,** sacristán de parroquia, *m*. **p. priest,** párroco, *m*. **p. register,** registro de la parroquia, *m*
parishioner *n* parroquiano (-na); feligrés (-esa)
Parisian *a* parisiense. *n* parisiense, *mf*
parity *n* paridad, *f*
park *n* parque, *m*; jardín, *m*. *vt* (vehicles) estacionar; (dump) depositar. **car p.,** parque de automóviles, *m*. **p.-keeper,** guardián del parque, *m*
parking *n* (of vehicles) estacionamiento, *m*; (dumping) depósito, *m*. **p. lights,** *aut* luces de estacionamiento, *f pl*. **p. place,** parque de estacionamiento, *m*
parking meter *n Mexico* estacionómetro, *m*, *Argentina, Spain* parquímetro, *m*, *elsewhere in Lat. Am.* parcómetro, *m*, *Spain* reloj de estacionamiento, *m*
parlance *n* lenguaje, *m*. **in common p.,** en lenguaje vulgar
parley *n* plática, conversación, *f*; discusión, *f*; *mil* parlamento, *m*. *vi mil* parlamentar; discutir; conversar. *vt* hablar
parliament *n* parlamento, *m*; cortes, *f pl*; cuerpo legislativo, *m*
parliamentarian *a* and *n* parlamentario; (of an academy) censor, *m*
parliamentarianism *n* parlamentarismo, *m*,
parliamentary *a* parlamentario. **p. immunity,** inviolabilidad parlamentaria, *f*
parlor *n* salón, gabinete, *m*; sala de recibo, *f*; (in a convent) locutorio, *m*. **p. games,** diversión de salón, *f*, juego de sociedad, *m*. **p.-maid,** camarera, *f*
parlous *a* crítico, malo. *adv* sumamente, muy
Parmesan *a* parmesano, de Parma. *n* parmesano (-na). **P. cheese,** queso de Parma, *m*
Parnassian *a* del parnaso; parnasiano. *n* parnasiano, *m*
Parnassus *n* Parnaso, *m*
parochial *a* parroquial, parroquiano; *fig* provincial
parochialism *n* provincialismo, *m*
parochially *adv* por parroquias
parodist *n* parodista, *mf*
parody *n* parodia, *f*, *vt* parodiar
parole *n* (of convict) libertad vigilada, *f*
paroxysm *n* paroxismo, *m*; ataque, acceso, *m*
parquet (floor) entarimado *m*; (of theater) platea, *f*
parricide *n* (act) parricidio, *m*; (person) parricida, *mf*
parrot *n* papagayo, loro, *m*, *Lat. Am.* cata, *f*
parry *vt* (a blow, and in fencing) parar; rechazar; evitar. *n* parada, *f*; (in fencing) quite, *m*, parada, *f*
parse *vt* analizar
Parsee *n* parsi, *m*
parsimonious *a* parsimonioso
parsimoniously *adv* con parsimonia
parsimony *n* parsimonia, *f*
parsley *n* perejil, *m*
parsnip *n* chirivía, *f*
parson *n* párroco, cura, *m*; (clergyman) clérigo, *m*
parsonage *n* rectoría, *f*
part *n* parte, *f*; porción, *f*; trozo, *m*; *mech* pieza, *f*; (*gram* and of a literary work) parte, *f*; (of a living organism) miembro, *m*; (duty) deber, *m*, obligación, *f*; *theat* papel, *m*; *mus* voz, *f*; *pl* **parts,** (region) partes, *f pl*, lugar, *m*; (talents) partes, dotes, *f pl*. **foreign parts,** países extranjeros, *m pl*, el extranjero. **For my p. . . . ,** Por lo que a mí toca, Por mi parte. **for the most p.,** en su mayoría. **from all parts,** de todas partes. **in p.,** en parte; parcialmente. **spare p.,** pieza de recambio, *f*. **The funny p. of it is . . . ,** Lo cómico del asunto es . . . **the latter p. of the month,** los últimos días del mes, la segunda quincena del mes. **to form p. of,** formar parte de. **to play a p.,** hacer un papel. **to take a person's p.,** apoyar a alguien, ser partidario de alguien. **to take in good p.,** tomar bien. **to take p. in,** tomar parte en, participar en. **p. of speech,** parte de la oración, *f*. **p.-owner,** copropietario (-ia). **p.-time job,** trabajo de unas cuantas horas, *m*
part *vt* distribuir, repartir; dividir; separar (de); (open) abrir. *vi* partir, marcharse; despedirse; (of roads, etc.) bifurcarse; dividirse; (open) abrirse. **to p. one's hair,** hacerse la raya. **to p. from,** (things) separarse de; (people) despedirse de. **to p. with,** separarse de; deshacerse de; perder; (dismiss) despedir (a)
partake *vt* participar de, compartir; tomar parte en. *vi* tomar algo (de comer, de beber). **to p. of,** comer (beber) de; tener rasgos de
partaker *n* partícipe, *mf*
Parthian *a* parto. *n* parto (-ta). **P. shot,** la flecha del parto
partial *a* parcial; (fond of) aficionado (a). **p. eclipse,** eclipse parcial, *m*
partiality *n* parcialidad, *f*; preferencia, predilección, *f*
partially *adv* en parte, parcialmente; (with bias) con parcialidad
participant *a* participante. *n* partícipe, *mf*
participate *vi* participar (de), compartir; tomar parte (en)
participation *n* participación, *f*
participial *a gram* participial
participle *n gram* participio, *m*. **past p.,** participio pasado (or pretérito or pasivo), *m*. **present p.,** participio activo (or presente), *m*
particle *n* partícula, *f*; *fig* átomo, grano, *m*, pizca, *f*; *gram* partícula, *f*
parti-colored *a* bicolor
particular *a* particular; especial; individual; singular; cierto; exacto; escrupuloso; difícil, exigente. *n* detalle,

pormenor, *m;* circunstancia, *f;* caso particular, *m; pl* **particulars,** informes, detalles, *m pl.* **further particulars,** más detalles. **in p.,** en particular; sobre todo. **He is very p. about . . . ,** Es muy exigente en cuanto a . . . ; Le es muy importante . . . , Le importa mucho . . .
particularize *vt* particularizar, detallar; especificar
particularly *adv* en particular; particularmente; sobre todo
parting *n* despedida, *f;* partida, *f;* separación, *f;* (of the hair) raya, crencha, *f;* (cross roads) bifurcación, *f. a* de despedida. **at p.,** al despedirse. **to reach the p. of the ways,** *fig* llegar al punto decisivo
partisan *n* partidario (-ia); (fighter) guerrillero, *m, a* partidario; de guerrilleros
partisanship *n* partidarismo, *m*
partition *n* partición, *f;* división, *f;* (wall) pared, *f,* tabique, *m.* **the p. of Ireland,** la división de Irlanda. *vt* **to p. off** *Lat. Am.* entabicar
partly *adv* en parte
partner *n* asociado (-da); *com* socio (-ia); (dancing) pareja, *f;* (in games, and companion) compañero (-ra); (spouse) consorte, *mf;* (in crime) codelincuente, *mf* **sleeping p.,** socio comanditario, *m.* **working p.,** socio industrial, *m*
partnership *n* asociación, *f; com* sociedad, compañía, *f.* **deed of p.,** artículos de sociedad, *m pl.* **to take into p.,** tomar como socio (a). **to form a p.,** asociarse
partridge *n orn* perdiz, *f.* **young p.,** perdigón, *m*
parturient *a f,* parturienta. *n* parturienta, *f*
parturition *n* parto, *m*
party *n* partido, *m;* grupo, *m;* (of pleasure, etc.) partida, *f;* reunión, fiesta, *f; mil* pelotón, destacamento, *m; law* parte, *f;* (person) interesado (-da); (accessory) cómplice, *mf.* **rescue p.,** pelotón de salvamento, *m.* **to be a p. to,** prestarse a; ser cómplice en. **to give a p.,** dar una fiesta, dar una reunión. **p.-spirit,** espíritu del partido, *m.* **p.-wall,** pared medianera, *f*
parvenu *n* advenedizo (-za)
parvis *n arch* atrio, *m*
Paschal *a* pascual
pass *n* (in an exam.) aprobación, *f;* (crisis) crisis, situación crítica, *f;* estado, *m;* (with the hands) pase, *m;* (permit) permiso, *m; mil* licencia, *f;* (safe-conduct) salvoconducto, *m;* (in football, etc.) pase, *m;* (membership card) carnet, *m;* (defile) desfiladero, paso, puerto, *m; naut* rebasadero, *m;* (fencing) estocada, *f.* **free p.,** billete de favor, *m.* **p.-book,** libreta de banco, *f.* **p. certificate,** (in exams.) aprobado, *m.* **p.-key,** llave maestra, *f*
pass *vi* pasar; (of time) correr, pasar, transcurrir; (happen) occurrir, tomar lugar; (end) cesar, desaparecer; (die) morir. *vt* pasar; hacer pasar; (the butter, etc.) dar, alargar; (in football, hockey) pasar; (excel) aventajar, exceder; (a Bill, an examination) aprobar; (sentence) fallar, pronunciar; (a remark) hacer; (transfer) traspasar; (tolerate) sufrir, tolerar; evacuar. **He passed in psychology,** Aprobó sicología. **to allow to p.,** ceder el paso (a). **to bring to p.,** ocasionar. **to come to p.,** suceder. **to let p.,** (put up with) dejar pasar; no hacer caso de; (forgive) perdonar. **to p. a vote of confidence,** votar una proposición de confianza. **to p. the buck,** *inf* echarle a uno el muerto. **pass the hat, pass the plate,** pasar la gorra. **to p. along,** pasar por; pasar. **to p. away,** pasar; desaparecer; (die) morir, fallecer; (of time) transcurrir. **to p. by,** pasar por, pasar delante de, pasar al lado de; (omit) pasar por alto de, omitir; (ignore) pasar sin hacer caso de. **to p. for,** pasar por. **to p. in,** entrar. **to p. in and out,** entrar y salir. **to p. off,** *vi* pasar; cesar, acabarse; desaparecer; evaporarse, disiparse; (of events) tener lugar. *vt* (oneself) darse por; dar por, hacer pasar por. **to p. a cat off as hare,** dar gato por liebre. **to p. on,** *vi* pasar; seguir su camino, continuar su marcha. *vt* pasar algo de uno a otro. **to p. out,** salir. **to p. over,** pasar por encima de; pasar; cruzar, atravesar; (transfer) traspasar; (disregard) pasar por alto de, dejar a un lado; omitir. **to p. over in silence,** pasar en silencio (por). **to p. round,** circular. **to p. through,** cruzar, atravesar, pasar por; (pierce) traspasar; *fig* experimentar
passable *a* transitable, pasadero; (fairly good) regular, mediano; tolerable
passably *adv* medianamente, pasaderamente, tolerablemente
passage *n* pasaje, *m;* paso, tránsito, *m;* (voyage) viaje, *m,* travesía, *f;* (corridor) pasillo, *m;* (entrance) entrada, *f;* (way) camino, *m;* (alley) callejón, *m;* (in a mine) galería, *f;* (of time) transcurso, *m;* (of birds) pasa, *f;* (in a book, and *mus*) pasaje, *m;* (occurrence) episodio, incidente, *m;* (of a Bill) aprobación, *f.* **p. money,** pasaje, *m.* **p. of arms,** lucha, *f,* combate, *m;* disputa, *f*
passementerie *n* pasamanería, *f*
passenger *n* viajero (-ra); (on foot) peatón, *m.* **by p. train,** en gran velocidad
passerby *n* transeúnte, paseante, *mf*
passing *a* pasajero; fugitivo; momentáneo. *adv* sumamente, extremadamente. *n* pasada, *f;* paso, *m;* (death) muerte, *f;* (disappearance) desaparición, *f;* (of a law) aprobación, *f.* **in p.,** de paso. **p.-bell,** toque de difuntos, *m*
passing grade *n* calificación mínima aprobatoria, *f*
passion *n* pasión, *f;* (Christ's) Pasión, *f;* (anger) cólera, *f.* **to fly into a p.,** montar en cólera. **p.-flower,** pasionaria, granadilla, *f.* **P. play,** drama de la Pasión, *m.* **P. Sunday,** Domingo de Pasión, *m.* **P. Week,** Semana Santa, *f*
passionate *a* apasionado; (quick-tempered) irascible, colérico; (fervid) vehemente, intenso, ardiente
passionately *adv* con pasión, apasionadamente; (irascibly) coléricamente; (fervidly) con vehemencia, ardientemente
passionless *a* sin pasión, frío; impasible; imparcial
passive *a* pasivo. *n gram* pasiva, *f.* **p. resistance,** resistencia pasiva, *f*
passiveness, passivity *n* pasividad, *f*
Passover *n* Pascua de los judíos, *f*
passport *n* pasaporte, *m*
password *n* contraseña, *f*
past *a* pasado; último; (expert) consumado; (former) antiguo, ex-. *n* pasado, *m;* historia, *f,* antecedentes, *m pl, prep* después de; (in front of) delante de; (next to) al lado de; (beyond) más allá de; (without) sin; fuera de; (of age) más de; (no longer able to) incapaz de. *adv* más allá. (The translation of **past** as an adverb is often either omitted, or included in the verb, e.g. **The years flew p.,** Los años transcurrieron. **for centuries p.,** durante siglos.) **I am p. caring,** Nada me importa ya. **It is a quarter p. ten,** Son las diez y cuarto. **It is p. four o'clock,** Son las siete pasadas, Son después de las cuatro. **what's p. is p.,** lo pasado, pasado. **p. doubt,** fuera de duda. **p. endurance,** insoportable. **p. help,** sin remedio, irremediable. **p. hope,** sin esperanza. **p.-master,** maestro, consumado, experto, *m.* **p. participle,** participio pasado, *m.* **p. president,** ex-presidente, *m.* **p. tense,** (tiempo) pasado, *m*
paste *n* pasta, *f;* (gloy) engrudo, *m. vt* (affix) pegar; (glue) engomar, engrudar
pasteboard *n* cartón, *m,* cartulina, *f, a* de cartón, de cartulina
pastel *n art* pastel, *m.* **p. drawing,** pintura al pastel, *f*
pastelist *n* pastelista, *mf*
pasteurization *n* pasteurización, *f*
pasteurize *vt* pasteurizar
pastille *n* pastilla, *f*
pastime *n* pasatiempo, entretenimiento, *m,* diversión, recreación, *f*
pastor *n* pastor, *m*
pastoral *a* pastoril; *ecc* pastoral. *n ecc* pastoral, *f;* (*poet mus*) pastorela, *f*
pastorate *n* pastoría, *f*
pastry *n* (dough) pasta, *f;* pastel, *m,* torta, *f;* pastelería, *f.* **p.-cook,** repostero, *m,* pastelero (-ra)

pasturage *n* (grass, etc.) pasto, *m;* pasturaje, *m;* pastoreo, *m*
pasture *n* (grass, etc.) pasto, herbaje, *m;* pasturaje, *m;* (field) prado, *m,* pradera, dehesa, *f. vi* pacer; pastar. *vt* apacentar, pastar, *Argentina* costear
pasty *a* pastoso; (pale) pálido. *n* empanada, *f*
pat *n* toque, *m;* caricia, *f;* (for butter) molde (de mantequilla), *m. vt* tocar; acariciar, pasar la mano (sobre). *adv* a propósito; oportunamente; fácilmente. **pat of butter,** pedacito de mantequilla, *m.* **pat on the back,** golpe en la espalda, *m; fig* elogio, *m*
Patagonian *a* and *n* patagón (-ona)
patch *n* (mend) remiendo, *m;* (piece) pedazo, *m;* (plaster and *aut.,* etc.) parche, *m;* (beauty spot) lunar postizo, *m;* (of ground) parcela, *f;* (of flowers, etc.) masa, *f;* (stain, and *fig*) mancha, *f. vt* (mend) remendar; poner remiendo (a); pegar; (roughly) chafallar; (the face) ponerse lunares postizos. **p. of blue sky,** pedazo de cielo azul. **patch of green grass,** mancha de hierba verde. **to be not a p. on,** no ser de la misma clase que; (of persons) no llegarle a los zancajos de. **to p. up a quarrel,** hacer las paces
patchwork *n* labor de retazos, obra de retacitos, *f; fig* mezcla, mezcolanza, *f.* **p. quilt,** centón, *m*
patchy *a* desigual; manchado
patella *n anat* rótula, *f*
patency *n* evidencia, claridad, *f*
patent *a* evidente, patente; patentado. *n* patente, *f. vt* patentar. **p. of nobility,** carta de hidalguía, ejecutoria, *f.* **"P. Applied For,"** «Patente Solicitada.» **Patent Pending** marca en trámite. **p. leather,** *n* charol, *m. a* de charol. **p. medicine,** específico farmacéutico, *m*
patentee *n* el, *m,* (*f,* la) que obtiene una patente; inventor (-ra)
patently *adv* evidentemente, claramente
paterfamilias *n* padre de familia, *m*
paternal *a* paterno, paternal
paternally *adv* paternalmente
paternity *n* paternidad, *f*
path *n* senda, vereda, *f,* sendero, *m;* camino, *m;* (track) pista, *f;* (traject) trayectoria, *f.* **the beaten p.,** el camino trillado
pathetic *a* patético
pathless *a* sin senda
pathogenic *a med* patógeno
pathological *a* patológico
pathologist *n* patólogo, *m*
pathology *n* patología, *f*
pathos *n* lo patético
patience *n* paciencia, *f.* **He tries my p. very much,** Me cuesta mucho no impacientarme con él. **to lose p.,** perder la paciencia; (grow angry) perder los estribos. **to play p.,** hacer solitarios
patient *a* paciente. *n* paciente, *mf;* (ill person) enfermo (-ma); (of a physician) cliente, *mf*
patiently *adv* con paciencia, pacientemente
patina *n* pátina, *f*
patriarch *n* patriarca, *m*
patriarchal *a* patriarcal
patriarchy *n* patriarcado, *m*
patrician *a* and *n* patricio (-ia)
patrimonial *a* patrimonial
patrimony *n* patrimonio, *m*
patriot *n* patriota, *mf*
patriotic *a* patriótico
patriotism *n* patriotismo, *m*
patrol *n* patrulla, *f;* ronda, *f, vi* and *vt* patrullar; rondar; recorrer. **p. boat,** lancha escampavía, *f.* **p. flight,** vuelo de patrulla, *m*
patron *n* (of a freed slave) patrono, *m;* (of the arts, etc.) mecenas, protector, *m;* (customer) parroquiano (-na), cliente, *mf.* **p. saint,** santo (-ta) patrón (-ona)
patronage *n* (protection) patrocinio, *m;* protección, *f; ecc* patronato, *m;* (regular custom) clientela, *f;* (of manner) superioridad, *f*
patroness *n* patrona, *f;* protectora, *f;* (of a charity, etc.) patrocinadora, *f;* (of a regiment, etc.) madrina, *f*
patronize *vt* patrocinar; proteger, favorecer; (a shop) ser parroquiano de; (treat arrogantly) tratar con superioridad
patronizing *a* (with air, behavior, etc.) de superioridad, de altivez
patten *n* zueco, chanclo, *m*
patter *n* (jargon) jerga, *f;* charla, *f;* (of rain) azotes, *m pl;* (of feet) son, *m;* golpecitos, *m pl. vt* (repeat) decir mecánicamente. *vi* (chatter) charlar; (of rain) azotar, bailar; correr ligeramente
pattern *n* modelo, *m;* (*sew* and dressmaking) patrón, *m;* (in founding) molde, *m;* (templet) escantillón, *m;* (of cloth, etc.) muestra, *f;* (design) dibujo, diseño, *m;* (example) ejemplar, *m. vt* diseñar; estampar. **p. book,** libro de muestras, *m*
patty *n* empanada, *f,* pastelillo, *m*
paucity *n* poquedad, *f;* corto número, *m;* insuficiencia, escasez, *f*
paunch *n* panza, barriga, *f*
pauper *n* pobre, *mf*
pauperism *n* pauperismo, *m*
pauperization *n* empobrecimiento, *m*
pauperize *vt* empobrecer, reducir a la miseria
pause *n* pausa, *f;* intervalo, *m;* silencio, *m;* interrupción, *f; mus* pausa, *f. vi* pausar, hacer una pausa; detenerse, interrumpirse; vacilar. **to give p. to,** hacer vacilar (a)
pave *vt* empedrar, enlosar. **to p. the way for,** facilitar el paso de, preparar el terreno para, abrir el camino de
pavement *n* pavimento, *m, Mexico* escarpa, *f;* (sidewalk) acera, *f.* **p.-artist,** pintor callejero, *m*
pavilion *n* pabellón, *m;* (for a band, etc.) quiosco, *m;* (tent) tienda de campaña, *f*
paving *n* pavimentación, *f;* empedrado, *m;* see **pavement. p.-stone,** losa, *f*
paw *n* pata, *f;* (with claws) garra, *f; inf* manaza, *f. vt* tocar con la pata; (scratch) arañar; (handle) manosear. *vi* (of a horse) piafar
pawing *n* (of a horse) el piafar; (handling) manoseo, *m*
pawn *n* (chess) peón (de ajedrez), *m;* empeño, *m; fig* prenda, *f. vt* empeñar, pignorar; dar en prenda. **p.-ticket,** papeleta de empeño, *f*
pawnbroker *n* prestamista, *mf*
pawnshop *n* casa de préstamos, casa de empeño, *f,* monte de piedad, *m*
pay *n* paga, *f;* (*mil nav*) soldada, *f;* salario, *m;* (of a workman) jornal, *m;* (reward) recompensa, compensación, *f;* (profit) beneficio, provecho, *m.* **pay-day,** día de paga, *m.* **pay-office,** pagaduría, *f.* **pay list, paysheet,** nómina, *Mexico* lista de raya, *f*
pay *vt* pagar; (a debt) satisfacer; (spend) gastar; (recompense) remunerar, recompensar; (hand over) entregar; (yield) producir; (a visit) hacer; (attention) prestar; (homage) rendir; (one's respects) presentar. *vi* pagar; producir ganancia; sacar provecho; ser una ventaja, ser provechoso. **It would not pay him to do it,** No le saldría a cuenta hacerlo. **This job doesn't pay,** Este trabajo no da dinero. **to pay a compliment (to),** cumplimentar, decir alabanzas (a), echar una flor (a). **to pay attention,** prestar atención; hacer caso. **to pay cash,** pagar al contado. **to pay in advance,** pagar adelantado, *Lat. Am.* aprontar. **to pay in full,** saldar. **to pay off old scores,** ajustar cuentas viejas. **to pay one's addresses to,** hacer la corte (a), pretender en matrimonio (a). **to pay the penalty,** sufrir el castigo, hacer penitencia. **to pay with interest,** *fig* pagar con creces. **to pay again,** volver a pagar, pagar de nuevo. **to pay back,** devolver, restituir; (money only) reembolsar; *fig* pagar en la misma moneda, vengarse (de). **to pay down,** pagar al contado. **to pay for,** pagar, costear; satisfacer. **to pay in,** ingresar. **to pay off,** (persons) despedir; (a debt) saldar; (a mortgage) cancelar, redimir. **to pay out,** (persons) vengarse de; (money) pagar; (ropes, etc.) arriar. **to pay up,** pagar; pagar por completo; (shares, etc.) redimir

payable *a* pagadero; a pagar; que puede ser pagado
payee *n* tenedor, *m*
payer *n* pagador (-ra)
paying *n*. See **payment**
paymaster *n* pagador, *m*; tesorero, *m*. **P.-General,** ordenador general de pagos, *m*
payment *n* pago, *m*, paga, *f*, *Lat. Am. also* entero, *m*; remuneración, *f*; *fig* recompensa, satisfacción, *f*; *fig* premio, *m*. **in p. of,** en pago de. **on p. of,** mediante el pago de. **p. in advance,** pago adelantado, anticipo, *m*
pea *n* guisante, *m*, *Lat. Am.* alverjana, arveja, *f*. **dry or split pea,** guisante seco, *m*. **sweet pea,** guisante de olor, *m*. **pea-flour,** harina de guisantes, *f*. **pea-green,** verde claro, *m*. **pea-jacket,** chaquetón de piloto, *m*. **pea-shooter,** cerbatana, *f*
peace *n* paz, *f*; tranquilidad, quietud, *f*, sosiego, *m*; *law* orden público, *m*. **P.!** ¡Silencio! **to hold one's p.,** callarse, guardar silencio. **to make p.,** hacer las paces. **P. be upon this house!** ¡Paz sea en esta casa! **p.-footing,** pie de paz, *m*. **p.-loving,** pacífico. **p.-offering,** sacrificio propiciatorio, *m*; satisfacción, oferta de paz, *f*
peaceable *a* pacífico; apacible; tranquilo, sosegado
peaceableness *n* paz, *f*; apacibilidad, *f*; tranquilidad, quietud, *f*, sosiego, *m*
peaceably *adv* pacíficamente; tranquilamente
peaceful *a* pacífico; tranquilo; silencioso. **to come with p. intentions,** venir de paz
peacefully *adv* en paz; pacíficamente; tranquilamente
peacefulness *n* paz, *f*; tranquilidad, calma, quietud, *f*; silencio, *m*; carácter pacífico, *m*
peacemaker *n* pacificador (-ra); conciliador (-ra)
peach *n* (fruit) melocotón, *m*; (tree) melocotonero, melocotón, *m*; (girl) breva, *f*. **p.-colour,** color de melocotón, *m*
peacock *n* pavo real, pavón, *m*. *vi* pavonearse; darse humos. **The p. spread its tail,** El pavo real hizo la rueda
peahen *n* pava real, *f*
peak *n* punta, *f*; (of a cap) visera, *f*; (of a mountain) peñasco, *m*, cumbre, cima, *f*; (mountain itself) pico, *m*; (*naut* of a hull) pico, *m*; *fig* auge, apogeo, *m*; punto más alto, *m*. *vi* consumirse, enflaquecer. **p. hours,** horas de mayor tráfico, *f pl*
peaked *a* en punta; puntiagudo; picudo; (of a cap) con visera; (wan) ojeroso; (thin) delgaducho, macilento, consumido
peal *n* toque (or repique) de campanas, *m*; campanillazo, *m*; carillón, *m*; (noise) estruendo, ruido, *m*; (of thunder) trueno, *m*; (of an organ) sonido, *m*. *vi* repicar; sonar. *vt* tañer, echar a vuelo (las campanas); (of a bell that one presses) hacer sonar, tocar. **a p. of laughter,** una carcajada
peanut *n* cacahuete, *m*. **p. butter,** mantequilla de cacahuete, *f*
pear *n* pera, *f*. **p.-shaped,** piriforme, de figura de pera. **p. tree,** peral, *m*
pearl *n* perla, *f*; (mother-of-pearl) nácar, *m*, *a* de perla; perlero. *vt* (dew) rociar, aljofarar. *vi* pescar perlas; formar perlas. **seed p.,** aljófar, *m*. **p.-ash,** carbonato potásico, *m*. **p.-barley,** cebada perlada, *f*. **p.-button,** botón de nácar, *m*. **p.-fisher,** pescador de perlas, *m*. **p.-fishery,** pescaduría de perlas, *f*. **p.-grey,** gris de perla, *m*
pearly *a* perlino; de perla; nacarado; (dewy) aljofarado
peasant *n* campesino (-na), labrador (-ra). *a* campesino
peasant movement *Mexico* agrarismo, *m*
peasantry *n* campesinos, *m pl*, gente del campo, *f*
peat *n* turba, *f*. **p.-bog,** turbera, *f*
pebble *n* guijarro, *m*, pedrezuela, guija, *f*; (gravel) guijo, *m*; cristal de roca, *m*; lente de cristal de roca, *m*
pebbled, pebbly *a* guijarroso, enguijarrado
peccadillo *n* pecadillo, *m*
peck *n* (of a bird) picotazo, *m*, picada, *f*; (kiss) besito, *m*; (large amount) montón, *m*; multitud, *f*. *vt* (of a bird) picotear; sacar (or coger) con el pico; (kiss) besar rápidamente. *vi* (with at) picotear; picar
pectoral *a* pectoral
peculiar *a* particular, peculiar, individual; propio, característico; (marked) especial; (unusual) extraño, raro, extraordinario
peculiarity *n* peculiaridad, particularidad, *f*; singularidad, *f*; (eccentricity) excentricidad, rareza, *f*
peculiarly *adv* particularmente, peculiarmente; especialmente; extrañamente
pecuniarily *adv* pecuniariamente
pecuniary *a* pecuniario
pedagogic *a* pedagógico
pedagogy *n* pedagogía, *f*
pedal *a zool* del pie. *n* pedal, *m*. *vi* pedalear
pedant *n* pedante, *mf*
pedantic *a* pedante
pedantically *adv* con pedantería, pedantescamente
pedantry *n* pedantería, *f*
peddle *vi* ser buhonero. *vt* revender
peddling *n* buhonería, *f*. *a* trivial, insignificante; mezquino
pedestal *n* pedestal, *m*; *fig* fundamento, *m*, base, *f*. **to put on a p.,** *fig* poner sobre un pedestal
pedestrian *n* peatón, peón, *m*, *a* pedestre; *fig* patoso. **p. traffic,** circulación de los peatones, *f*
pedestrian crosswalk, cruce peatonal *Argentina*, cruce de peatones, *m*
pediatrician *n* pediatra, *mf*
pedigree *n* genealogía, *f*; raza, *f*; (of words) etimología, *f*. *a* (of animals) de raza, de casta. **p. dog,** perro de casta, *m*
pediment *n arch* frontón, *m*
pedlar *n* buhonero (-ra), *Lat. Am.* marchante (-ta), *mf*
pedometer *n* pedómetro, cuentapasos, *m*
peel *n* (baker's) pala, *f*; (of fruit, etc.) piel, *f*, hollejo, *m*. *vt* pelar, mondar; (bark) descortezar; *Lat. Am.* deshojar (fruit). *vi* descascararse, desconcharse; (of the bark of a tree) descortezarse
peeling *n* (of fruit, etc.) peladura, monda, *f*; (of bark) descortezadura, *f*; (of paint, etc.) desconchadura, *f*
peep *vi* (of birds) piar; (of mice) chillar; (peer) atisbar, mirar a hurtadillas; (appear) asomar; mostrarse; (of the dawn) despuntar. *n* (of birds) pío, *m*; (of mice) chillido, *m*; (glimpse) vista, *f*; (glance) ojeada, mirada furtiva, *f*; **at the p. of day,** al despuntar el día. **p.-hole,** mirilla, *f*, atisbadero, *m*; escucha, *f*. **p.-show,** óptica, *f*
peeper (eye) avizón *m*
peer *n* par, *m*; igual, *mf*. *vi* atisbar; escudriñar; *fig* asomar, aparecer
peerage *n* nobleza, aristocracia, *f*; dignidad de par, *f*
peeress *n* paresa, *f*
peerless *a* sin par, incomparable, sin igual
peevish *a* displicente, malhumorado; picajoso, vidrioso, enojadizo
peevishness *n* displicencia, *f*, mal humor, *m*; impaciencia, *f*
peg *n* clavija, *f*; (of a tent) estaca, *f*; (of a barrel) estaquilla, *f*; (of a violin, etc.) clavija, *f*; (for coats, etc.) colgadero, *m*; (of whisky, etc.) trago, *m*; *fig* pretexto, *m*. *vt* clavar, enclavijar, empernar. **to take down a peg,** bajar los humos (a). **to peg away,** batirse el cobre. **to peg down,** fijar con clavijas; (a tent) sujetar con estacas; (prices) fijar
peignoir *n* peinador, salto de cama, *m*, bata, *f*
pekinese *n* perro (-rra) pequinés (-esa)
pelican *n* pelícano, *m*
pellagra *n med* pelagra, *f*
pellet *n* bolita, *f*; (pill) píldora, *f*; (shot) perdigón, *m*
pellmell *adv* a trochemoche; atropelladamente
pellucid *a* diáfano
Peloponesian *a* and *n* peloponense, *mf*
pelota *n* pelota vasca, *f*. **p. player,** pelotari, *m*
pelt *n* pellejo, *m*; cuero, *m*; (fur) piel, *f*; (blow) golpe, *m*. *vt* llover (piedras, etc.) sobre, arrojar . . . sobre; (questions) disparar; (throw) tirar. *vi* (of rrain) azotar, diluviar
pelvic *a* pélvico, pelviano

pelvis *n* pelvis, *f*
pen *n* (for sheep, etc.) aprisco, *m*; corral, *m*; (paddock) parque, *m*; (for hens) pollera, *f*; (for writing and *fig.*, author, etc.) pluma, *f*. *vt* (shut up) acorralar; encerrar; (write) escribir (con pluma). **pen-and-ink drawing,** dibujo a la pluma, *m*. **pen-holder,** portaplumas, *m*. **pen-name,** seudónimo, *m*. **pen-wiper,** limpiaplumas, *m*
penal *a* penal. **p. code,** código penal, *m*. **p. colony,** colonia penal, *f*. **p. servitude,** trabajos forzados (or forzosos), *m pl*. **p. servitude for life,** cadena perpetua, *f*
penalization *n* castigo, *m*
penalize *vt* penar, imponer pena (a); castigar
penalty *n law* penalidad, *f*; castigo, *m*; (fine) multa, *f*; (risk) riesgo, *m*; *sport* sancíon, *m*. **the p. of,** la desventaja de. **under p. of,** so pena de. **p. kick,** (football) penalty, *m*
penance *n* penitencia, *f*. **to do p.,** hacer penitencia
penchant *n* tendencia, *f*; inclinación, *f*
pencil *n* lápiz, *m*; (automatic) lapicero, *m*. *vt* escribir (or dibujar or marcar) con lápiz. **p.-case,** estuche para lápices, *m*. **p.-holder,** lapicero, *m*. **p.-sharpener,** cortalápices, afilalápices, *m*
pendant *n* (jewel) pendiente, *m*; *arch* culo de lámpara, *m*; (*naut* rope) amantillo, *m*; (flag) gallardete, *m*
pending *a* pendiente. *prep* durante. **to be p.,** pender; amenazar
pendulous *a* péndulo; colgante; oscilante
pendulum *n* péndola, *f*, péndulo, *m*
penetrability *n* penetrabilidad, *f*
penetrable *a* penetrable
penetrate *vt* and *vi* penetrar
penetrating *a* penetrante
penetration *n* penetración, *f*
penguin *n* pingüino, pájaro bobo, *m*
penicillin *n* penicilina, *f*
peninsula *n* península, *f*
peninsular *a* peninsular. **P. War,** Guerra de la Independencia, *f*
penis *n* pene, *m*
penitence *n* penitencia, *f*
penitent *a* penitente. *n* penitente, *mf*
penitential *a* penitencial
penitentiary *n ecc* penitenciaria, *f*; casa de corrección, *f*; penitenciaria, *f*, presidio, *m*; cárcel modelo, *f*, *a* penitenciario
penknife *n* cortaplumas, *m*
penmanship *n* caligrafía, *f*
pennant *n naut* gallardete, *m*; banderola, *f*; (ensign) insignia, bandera, *f*
penniless *a* sin un penique, sin blanca; indigente, pobre de solemnidad, *Peru* calato. **to leave p.,** dejar en la miseria; *inf* dejar sin camisa
pennilessness *n* falta de dinero, extrema pobreza, *f*
penning *n* escritura, *f*; (drawing up) redacción, *f*; (of bulls, etc.) acorralamiento, *m*
pennon *n* pendón, *m*, banderola, *f*; (ensign) bandera, insignia, *f*
Pennsylvanian *a* and *n* pensilvano (-na)
penny *n* de un centavo, penique, *m*; perra gorda, *f*. *a* de un penique. **p.-a-liner,** gacetillero, *m*. **p. dreadful,** folletín, *m*, novela por entregas, *f*. **p.-in-the-slot machine,** tragaperras, *m*
pennyworth *n* penique, valor de un penique, *m*
pension *n* pensión, *f*; *mil* retiro, *m*; (grant) beca, *f*; (boardinghouse) pensión de familia, *f*. *vt* pensionar, dar una pensión (a); (with off) jubilar. **old age p.,** pensión para la vejez, *f*. **retirement p.,** pensión vitalicia, *f*
pensioner *n* pensionista, *mf*; (*mil* and *nav*) inválido, *m*
pensive *a* pensativo, meditabundo; cabizbajo, triste
pensively *adv* pensativamente; tristemente
pensiveness *n* reflexión, meditación profunda, *f*; tristeza, melancolía, *f*
pentagon *n* pentágono, *m*
Pentateuch *n* pentateuco, *m*
Pentecost *n* Pentecostés, *m*, Pascua, *f*
pentecostal *a* de Pentecostés, pascual
penthouse *n* cobertizo, tinglado, *m*, tejavana, *f*
pent-up *a* encerrado; enjaulado; (of emotion) reprimido
penultimate *a* penúltimo. *n* penúltimo, *m*
penurious *a* pobre; escaso; (stingy) tacaño, avaro
penury *n* penuria, *f*
peony *n* peonía, *f*, saltaojos, *m*, rosa albardera, rosa montés, *f*
people *n* pueblo, *m*; nación, *f*; gente, *f*; personas, *f pl*; (used disparagingly, mob) populacho, vulgo, *m*; (inhabitants) habitantes, *m pl*; (subjects) súbditos, *m pl*; (relations) parientes, *m pl*; familia, *f*. *vt* poblar. **little p.,** (children) gente menuda, *f*. **respectable p.,** gente de bien, *f*. **the p. of Burgos,** los habitantes de Burgos. **P. say,** Se dice, La gente dice. **Very few p. think as you do,** Hay muy pocas personas que opinan como Vd. **How are your p.** (family)? ¿Cómo están los de tu casa? ¿Cómo está tu familia? **"People Working"** «Trabajadores»
peopling *n* población, *f*; colonización, *f*
pep *n inf* energía, *f*, ánimo, *m*. **p. talk**, discurso estimulante, *m*. **p. up**, animar
Pepin the Short Pipino el Breve
peplum *n* peplo, *m*
pepper *n* pimienta, *f*; (plant) pimentero, pimiento, *m*, *vt* sazonar con pimienta; (pelt) acribillar; (with questions) disparar; (a literary work with quotations, etc.) salpimentar. **black p.,** pimienta negra, *f*. **red p.,** pimiento, *m*; (cayenne) pimentón, *m*. **p.-castor,** pimentero, *m*
peppercorn *n* grano de pimienta, *m*
peppermint *n* menta, *f*. **p. drop,** pastilla de menta, *f*
peppery *a* picante; (irascible) colérico, irascible
pepsin *n chem* pepsina, *f*
peptic *a* péptico
per *prep* por. **ninety miles per hour,** noventa millas por hora. **ten pesetas per dozen,** diez pesetas la docena. **$60 per annum,** sesenta dólares al año. **per cent.,** por ciento
perambulate *vt* recorrer
perambulator *n* cochecito para niños, *m*
percale *n* percal, *m*
percaline *n* percalina, *f*
perceive *vt* percibir, comprender, darse cuenta de; percibir, discernir
percentage *n* tanto por ciento, *m*; porcentaje, *m*
perceptible *a* perceptible, visible; sensible
perceptibly *adv* visiblemente; sensiblemente
perception *n* percepción, *f*; sensibilidad, *f*
perceptive *a* perceptivo
perch *n icht* perca, *f*; (for birds) percha, *f*; (measure) pértiga, *f*. *vi* posarse (en or sobre). *vt* posar (en or sobre)
percolate *vi* filtrar; *fig* penetrar. *vt* filtrar, colar
percolation *n* filtración, *f*
percolator *n* filtro, *m*. **coffee p.,** colador de café, *m*
percussion *n* percusión, *f*; choque, *m*. **p. cap,** fulminante, *m*. **p. instrument,** instrumento de percusión, *m*
perdition *n* perdición, *f*; ruina, *f*
peregrination *n* peregrinación, *f*
peremptorily *adv* perentoriamente
peremptoriness *n* perentoriedad, *f*
peremptory *a* perentorio; (of manner, etc.) imperioso, autoritario
perennial *a bot* vivaz; perenne; eterno, perpetuo. *n* planta vivaz, *f*
perennially *adv* perennemente
perfect *a* perfecto; (of a work) acabado; completo. *n gram* (tiempo) perfecto, *m*. *vt* perfeccionar; (oneself) perfeccionarse. **to have a p. knowledge of . . . ,** conocer a fondo . . . **They are p. strangers to me,** Me son completamente desconocidos
perfectible *a* perfectible
perfecting *n* perfeccionamiento, *m*; terminación, *f*

perfection *n* perfección, *f*; excelencia, *f*. **to p.,** a la perfección, a las mil maravillas
perfectionist *n* perfeccionista, *mf*
perfidious *a* pérfido
perfidy *n* perfidia, *f*
perforate *vt* perforar, agujerear
perforating *a* perforador
perforation *n* perforación, *f*; agujero, *m*
perforce *adv* a la fuerza, forzosamente
perform *vt* hacer; poner por obra, llevar a cabo; desempeñar, cumplir; ejercer; (a piece of music, etc.) ejecutar; realizar; (a play) representar, dar; (a part in a play) desempeñar (el papel de . . .); (Divine Service) oficiar. *vi theat* trabajar, representar un papel; (a musical instrument) tocar; (sing) cantar; (of animals) hacer trucos
performable *a* hacedero, practicable, ejecutable; *theat* que puede representarse; *mus* tocable
performance *n* ejecución, realización, *f*; desempeño, ejercicio, *m*; cumplimiento, *m*; acción, *f*; hazaña, *f*; (work) obra, *f*; *theat* función, representación, *f*; (*theat* acting of a part) interpretación, *f*; *mus* ejecución, *f*; *mech* potencia, *f*. **first p.,** *theat* estreno, *m*
performer *n mus* ejecutante, *mf*, músico, *m*; *theat* actor (-triz), representante, *mf*; artista, *mf*
performing *a* (of animals) sabio. **p. dog,** perro sabio, *m*
perfume *n* perfume, *m*; fragancia, *f*; aroma, *m*. *vt* perfumar; embalsamar, aromatizar, llenar con fragancia. **p. burner,** perfumador, *m*
perfumer *n* perfumista, *mf*
perfumery *n* perfumería, *f*
perfuming *n* acción de perfumar, *f*, *a* que perfuma
perfunctorily *adv* perfunctoriamente, sin cuidado; superficialmente
perfunctoriness *n* descuido, *m*, negligencia, *f*; superficialidad, *f*
perfunctory *a* perfunctorio, negligente; superficial; ligero, de cumplido
pergola *n* emparrado, cenador, *m*
perhaps *adv* quizá, quizás(s), tal vez
peril *n* peligro, *m*; riesgo, *m*. *vt* poner en peligro; arriesgar. **at one's p.,** a su riesgo. **in p.,** en peligro
perilous *a* peligroso, arriesgado
perimeter *n* perímetro, *m*
perineum *n anat* perineo, *m*
period *n* período, *m*; época, *f*; edad, *f*, tiempo, *m*; duración, *f*; término, plazo, *m*; *gram* período, *m*; (full stop) punto final, *m*; *med* menstruación, regla, *f*. **p. furniture,** muebles de época, *m pl*
periodic *a* periódico
periodical *a* periódico. *n* publicación periódica, revista, *f*
periodicity *n* periodicidad, *f*
peripatetic *a* peripatético
peripheral *a* periférico
periphery *n* periferia, *f*
periphrastic *a* perifrástico
periscope *n* periscopio, *m*
perish *vi* perecer; marchitarse; desaparecer, acabar. **to be perished with cold,** estar muerto de frío
perishable *a* perecedero, frágil
peritoneum *n* peritoneo, *m*
peritonitis *n* peritonitis, *f*
periwig *n* peluca, *f*
periwinkle *n zool* caracol marino, *m*; *bot* vincapervinca, *f*
perjure *vt* perjurar. **to p. oneself,** perjurarse
perjurer *n* perjuro (-ra); perjurador (-ra)
perjury *n* perjurio, *m*. **to commit p.,** jurar en falso, perjurar
perk (up) *vi* levantar la cabeza; recobrar sus bríos, alzar la cabeza; sacar la cabeza
perkiness *n* desenvoltura, gallardía, *f*, despejo, *m*
perky *a* desenvuelto, gallardo; coquetón; atrevido; (gay) alegre
permanence *n* permanencia, *f*; estabilidad, *f*
permanent *a* permanente; estable; (of posts, etc.) fijo. **p. wave,** ondulación permanente, *f*. **p. way,** *rw* vía, *f*
permanganate *n* permanganato, *m*
permeability *n* permeabilidad, *f*
permeable *a* permeable
permeate *vt* penetrar; impregnar; *fig* infiltrar (en)
permeation *n* penetración, *f*; impregnación, *f*; *fig* infiltración, *f*
permissible *a* permisible, admisible; lícito
permission *n* permiso, *m*, licencia, *f*
permissive *a* permisivo, tolerado; (optional) facultativo
permit *vt* permitir; dar permiso (a), dejar; tolerar, sufrir; admitir. *n* permiso, *m*; licencia, *f*; pase, *m*. **Will you p. me to smoke?** ¿Me permites fumar?
permutation *n* permutación, *f*
permute *vt* permutar
pernicious *a* pernicioso. **p. anemia,** anemia perniciosa, *f*
perniciousness *n* perniciosidad, *f*
pernickety *a* tiquismiquis
peroration *n* peroración, *f*
peroxide *n* peróxido, *m*
perpendicular *a* perpendicular. *n* perpendicular, *f*
perpendicularity *n* perpendicularidad, *f*
perpendicularly *adv* perpendicularmente
perpetrate *vt law* perpetrar; cometer
perpetration *n law* perpetración, *f*; comisión, *f*
perpetrator *n* el, *m*, (*f*, la) que comete; *law* autor (-ra); perpetrador (-ra)
perpetual *a* perpetuo, perdurable, eterno; incesante, constante; (life-long) perpetuo
perpetually *adv* perpetuamente; sin cesar; continuamente; constantemente
perpetuate *vt* perpetuar, eternizar; inmortalizar
perpetuation *n* perpetuación, *f*
perpetuity *n* perpetuidad, *f*. **in p.,** para siempre
perplex *vt* dejar perplejo, aturdir, confundir; embrollar
perplexed *a* perplejo, irresoluto; confuso; (of questions, etc.) complicado, intrincado
perplexedly *adv* perplejamente
perplexing *a* difícil; complicado; confuso
perplexity *n* perplejidad, *f*; confusión, *f*
perquisites *n pl* emolumentos, *m pl*; gajes, percances, *m pl*; (tips) propinas, *f pl*
persecute *vt* perseguir; importunar, molestar
persecution *n* persecución, *f*
persecutor *n* perseguidor (-ra)
perseverance *n* perseverancia, *f*
persevere *vi* perseverar
persevering *a* perseverante
perseveringly *adv* con perseverancia, perseverantemente
Persia (la) Persia, *f*
Persian *a* persa; de Persia; pérsico. *n* persa, *mf*; (language) persa, *m*. **P. blinds,** persianas, *f pl*. **P. cat,** gato (-ta) de Angora
persiennes *n pl* persianas, *f pl*
persist *vi* persistir; persistir (en), empeñarse (en), obstinarse (en)
persistence *n* persistencia, *f*
persistent *a* persistente
persistently *adv* con persistencia, persistentemente
person *n* persona, *f*. **first p.,** *gram* primera persona, *f*. **in p.,** en persona. **no p.,** nadie
personable *a* bien parecido
personage *n* personaje, *m*
personal *a* personal; íntimo; particular; en persona; (movable) mueble. **He is to make a p. appearance,** Va a estar presente en persona. **p. column,** (in a newspaper) columna de los suspiros, *f*. **p. equation,** ecuación personal, *f*. **p. estate,** (goods) bienes muebles, *m pl*
personality *n* personalidad, *f*; (insult) personalismo, *m*. **dual p.,** conciencia doble, *f*

personate *vt* (in a play) hacer el papel de; (impersonate) hacerse pasar por
personification *n* personificación, *f*
personify *vt* personificar
personnel *n* personal, *m*
perspective *n* perspectiva, *f*, *a* en perspectiva
perspicacious *a* perspicaz, clarividente, sagaz
perspicacity *n* perspicacia, clarividencia, sagacidad, *f*
perspicuity *n* perspicuidad, claridad, lucidez, *f*
perspicuous *a* perspicuo, claro
perspiration *n* sudor, *m*
perspire *vi* sudar, transpirar
persuadable *a* persuasible
persuade *vt* persuadir; inducir (a), instar (a), mover (a), inclinar (a)
persuasion *n* persuasión, *f*; persuasiva, *f*; opinión, *f*; creencia, *f*; religión, *f*; secta, *f*
persuasive *a* persuasivo. *n* persuasión, *f*; aliciente, atractivo, *m*
persuasively *adv* de un modo persuasivo, persuasivamente
persuasiveness *n* persuasiva, *f*
pert *a* petulante; respondón, desparpajado
pertain *vi* pertenecer (a); tocar (a), incumbir (a), convenir (a); estar relacionado (con)
pertinacious *a* pertinaz
pertinaciously *adv* con pertinacia
pertinacity *n* pertinacia, *f*
pertinence *n* pertinencia, *f*
pertinent *a* pertinente, atinado
pertinently *adv* atinadamente
pertly *adv* con petulancia; con descaro
pertness *n* petulancia, *f*; desparpajo, descaro, *m*
perturb *vt* perturbar, agitar, turbar, inquietar
perturbation *n* perturbación, agitación, inquietud, *f*; confusión, *f*; desorden, *m*
perturbed *a* perturbado, agitado, ansioso, intranquilo
perturbing *a* perturbador, inquietador
Peru el Perú
peruke *n* peluca, *f*
perusal *n* lectura, *f*; examen, *m*
peruse *vt* leer con cuidado, estudiar, examinar
Peruvian *a* and *n* peruano (-na)
pervade *vt* penetrar; llenar, saturar; difundirse por; reinar en
pervasion *n* penetración, *f*
pervasive *a* penetrante
perverse *a* (wicked) perverso, depravado; obstinado; travieso; intratable
perversion *n* perversión, *f*
perversity *n* (wickedness) perversidad, *f*; obstinacia, *f*; travesura, *f*
perversive *a* perversivo
pervert *vt* pervertir; (words, etc.) torcer, tergiversar
pervious *a* penetrable; permeable
pessimism *n* pesimismo, *m*
pessimist *n* pesimista, *mf*
pessimistic *a* pesimista
pessimistically *adv* con pesimismo
pest *n* insecto nocivo, *m*; animal dañino, *m*; parásito, *m*; (pestilence) peste, *f*; *fig* plaga, *f*; (person) mosca, *f*
pester *vt* importunar, molestar, incomodar, *Lat. Am.* acatorrar, cargosear, majaderear. **to p. constantly,** *inf* no dejar a sol ni a sombra
pestering *n* importunaciones, *f pl*; *a* = **annoying**
pestilence *n* pestilencia, peste, *f*; plaga, *f*
pestilential *a* pestilente, pestífero; pernicioso
pestle *n* mano de mortero, *f*, *vt* pistar, machacar, majar
pet *n* animal doméstico, *m*; niño (-ña) mimado (-da); favorito (-ta); (dear) querido (-da); (peevishness) despecho, malhumor, *m*. *vt* acariciar; (spoil) mimar. **to be a great pet,** ser un gran favorito
petal *n* pétalo, *m*, hoja, *f*
Peter *n* Pedro, *m*. **blue P.,** bandera de salida, *f*. **Peter's pence,** los diezmos de San Pedro
peter (out) *vi* desaparecer; agotarse
petition *n* petición, *f*; súplica, *f*; instancia, solicitud, *f*; memorial, *m*. *vt* suplicar; pedir, demandar; dirigir un memorial (a). **to file a p.,** elevar una instancia
petitioner *n* peticionario (-ia)
pet peeve *Lat. Am.* barreno, *m*
Petrarchan *a* petrarquista
petrifaction *n* petrificación, *f*
petrify *vt* petrificar; *inf* dejar seco. **to become petrified,** petrificarse
petrol *n* bencina, gasolina, *f*. *a* de gasolina, de bencina. **to run out of p.,** tener una pana de bencina. **p. gauge,** indicador del nivel de gasolina, *m*. **p. pump,** surtidor de gasolina, *m*. **p. station,** puesto de bencina, *m*, estación de servicio, *f*. **p. tank,** depósito de bencina, *m*
petroleum *n* petróleo, *m*. *a* petrolero; de petróleo. **p. works,** refinería de petróleo, *f*
petrology *n* petrografía, *f*
petrous *a* pétreo
petticoat *n* enagua, *f*; *pl* **petticoats,** (slang) faldas, *f pl*. *a* de faldas, de mujeres; de mujer
pettifogger *n* (lawyer) picapleitos, *m*, rábula, *mf*; (quibbler) sofista, *mf*
pettifogging *a* charlatán, mezquino, trivial
pettiness *n* trivialidad, insignificancia, *f*; pequeñez, *f*; mezquindad, *f*; ruindad, bajeza, *f*
petty *a* trivial, sin importancia, insignificante; inferior; pequeño; mezquino; ruin; bajo. **p. cash,** gastos menores de caja, *m pl*. **p. expense,** gasto menudo, *m*. **p. officer,** suboficial, *m*. **p. thief,** ratero (-ra)
petulance *n* mal humor, *m*, displicencia, irritabilidad, *f*
petulant *a* malhumorado, displicente, enojadizo, irritable
petulantly *adv* displicentemente, con mal humor
petunia *n* petunia, *f*
pew *n* banco (de iglesia), *m*. **p.-opener,** sacristán, *m*
pewter *n* peltre, *m*, *a* de peltre
phalange *n* falange, *f*
phalanx *n* falange, *f*
phallic *a* fálico
phallus *n* falo, *m*
phantasmagoria *n* fantasmagoría, *f*
phantasmagoric *a* fantasmagórico
phantom *n* fantasma, espectro, *m*; sombra, ficción, *f*; visión, *f*
Pharisaical *a* farisaico
Pharisee *n* fariseo, *m*
pharmaceutical *a* farmacéutico; *n* producto farmacéutico, *m*
pharmacist *n* farmacéutico, *m*
pharmacological *a* farmacológico
pharmacologist *n* farmacólogo, *m*
pharmacology *n* farmacología, *f*
pharmacopeia *n* farmacopea, *f*
pharmacy *n* farmacia, *f*
pharyngeal *a* faríngeo
pharyngitis *n* faringitis, *f*
pharynx *n* faringe, *f*
phase *n* fase, *f*; aspecto, *m*; *ast* fase, *f*
pheasant *n* faisán, *m*. **hen p.,** faisana, *f*. **p. shooting,** caza de faisanes, *f*
phenic *a* fénico
phenol *n* fenol, *m*
phenomenal *a* fenomenal
phenomenon *n* fenómeno, *m*
phial *n* redoma, *f*
philander *vi* galantear
philanderer *n* Tenorio, galanteador, *m*
philandering *n* galanteo, *m*
philanthropic *a* filantrópico
philanthropist *n* filántropo, *m*
philanthropy *n* filantropía, *f*
philatelic *a* filatélico
philatelist *n* filatelista, *mf*
philately *n* filatelia, *f*
philharmonic *a* filarmónico

philippic *n* filípica, *f*
Philippine *a* and *n* filipino (-na)
Philippines, the las (Islas) Filipinas, *f pl*
Philistine *a* and *n* filisteo (-ea)
philological *a* filológico
philologist *n* filólogo, *m*
philology *n* filología, *f*
philosopher *n* filósofo, *m*. **philosopher's stone,** piedra filosofal, *f*
philosophic(al) *a* filosófico
philosophize *vi* filosofar
philosophy *n* filosofía, *f*. **moral p.,** filosofía moral, *f*. **natural p.,** filosofía natural, *f*
philter *n* filtro, *m*
phlebitis *n* flebitis, *f*
phlebotomist *n* sangrador, flebotomiano, *m*
phlebotomy *n* flebotomía, *f*
phlegm *n* flema, *f*, *Lat. Am.* desgarro, *m*
phlegmatic *a* flemático
phlox *n* flox, *m*
Phoenician *a* and *n* fenicio (-ia)
phoenix *n* fénix, *f*
phoenitic *a* fonético
phoneticist *n* fonetista, *mf*
phonetics *n* fonética, *f*
phonograph *n* fonógrafo, *m*
phonological *a* fonológico
phonology *n* fonología, *f*
phony *a* falso; espurio. **p. war,** guerra tonta, guerra falsa, *f*
phosphate *n* fosfato, *m*
phosphoresce *vi* fosforecer, ser fosforescente
phosphorescence *n* fosforescencia, *f*
phosphorescent *a* fosforescente
phosphoric *a* fosfórico
phosphorus *n* fósforo, *m*
photo *n* foto, *f*
photochemistry *n* fotoquímica, *f*
photogenic *a* fotogénico
photograph *n* fotografía, *f*. *vt* fotografiar, retratar. **to have one's p. taken,** hacerse retratar
photographer *n* fotógrafo, *m*
photographic *a* fotográfico
photography *n* fotografía, *f*
photogravure *n* fotograbado, *m*
photostat *n* fotostato, *m*
photosynthesis *n* fotosíntesis, *f*
phrase *n* frase, *f*; *mus* frase musical, *f*. *vt* expresar, frasear; redactar. **p.-book,** libro de frases, *m*
phraseology *n* fraseología, *f*
phrasing *n* (drawing up) redacción, *f*; (style) estilo, *m*; *mus* frases, *f pl*
phrenetic *a* frenético
Phrygian *a* and *n* frigio (-ia)
Phrygian cap *n* gorro frigio, *m*
phthisis *n* tisis, *f*
phylactery *n* filactria, *f*
phylloxera *n* filoxera, *f*
physical *a* físico. **p. fitness,** buen estado físico, *m*. **p. geography,** geografía física, *f*. **p. jerks,** ejercicios físicos, *m pl*. **p. sciences,** ciencias físicas, *f pl*. **p. training,** educación física, *f*
physician *n* médico (-ca)
physicist *n* físico, *m*
physics *n* física, *f*
physiognomist *n* fisonomista, *mf*
physiognomy *n* fisonomía, *f*
physiological *a* fisiológico
physiologist *n* fisiólogo, *m*
physiology *n* fisiología, *f*
physiotherapy *n* fisioterapia, *f*
physique *n* físico, *m*
pianist *n* pianista, *mf*
piano, pianoforte *n* piano, *m*. **baby grand p.,** piano de media cola, *m*. **grand p.,** piano de cola, *m*. **upright p.,** piano vertical, *m*. **p. maker,** fabricante de pianos, *m*. **p. stool,** taburete de piano, *m*. **p. tuner,** afinador de pianos, *m*
pianola *n* piano mecánico, *m*
picaresque *a* picaresco
piccolo *n* flautín, *m*
pick *n* (tool) pico, zapapico, *m*; (mattock) piqueta, *f*; (choice) selección, *f*; derecho de elección, *m*; (best) lo mejor, lo más escogido; (*fig* cream) flor, nata, *f*. **tooth-p.,** mondadientes, *m*. **p.-a-back,** sobre los hombros, a cuestas. **p.-ax,** zapapico, *m*, alcotana, *f*. **p.-me-up,** tónico, *m*; trago, *m*
pick *vt* (with a pick-ax, make a hole) picar; (pluck, pick up) coger; (remove) sacar; (clean) limpiar; (one's teeth) mondarse (los dientes); (one's nose) hurgarse (las narices); (a bone) roer; (a lock) abrir con ganzúa; (a pocket) bolsear, robar del bolsillo; (peck) picotear; (choose) escoger; (a quarrel) buscar. *vi* (steal) hurtar, robar; (nibble) picar. **I have a bone to p. with you,** Tengo que ajustar unas cuentas contigo. **Take your p.!** ¡Escoja! **to p. and choose,** mostrarse difícil. **to p. to pieces,** *fig* criticar severamente. **to p. one's way through,** abrirse camino entre; andar con precaución por; andar a tientas por. **to p. off,** coger; arrancar; quitar; (shoot) disparar; fusilar. **to p. out,** entresacar; escoger; (recognize) reconocer; (understand) llegar a comprender; (a tune) tocar de oídas; (a song) cantar de oídas; (of colours) contrastar, resaltar. **to p. up,** *vt* (ground, etc.) romper con pico; coger; tomar; recoger; (raise) levantar, alzar; (information, etc.) cobrar, adquirir; (a living) ganar; (make friends with) trabar amistad con; (recover) recobrar; (find) encontrar, hallar; (buy) comprar; (learn) aprender; (a wireless message) interceptar; (a radio station) oír, tener. *vi* recobrar la salud; reponerse; mejorar. *n mech* recobro, *m*
picket *n* estaca, *f*; (*mil* and during strikes) piquete, *m*. *vt* cercar con estacas; poner piquetes ante (or alrededor de); poner de guardia; estacionar
picking *n* (gathering) recolección, *f*; (choosing) selección, *f*; (pilfering) robo, *m*; *pl* **pickings,** desperdicios, *m pl*; (perquisites) gajes, *m pl*; ganancias, *f pl*
pickle *n* (solution) escabeche, *m*; (vegetable, etc.) encurtido, *m*; (plight) apuro, *m*; (child) diablillo, *m*. *vt* encurtir, escabechar
picklock *n* (thief and instrument) ganzúa, *f*
pickpocket *n* carterista, *mf* ratero (-ra)
picnic *n* partida de campo, jira, *f*, picnic, *m*. *vi* llevar la merienda al campo, hacer un picnic
picnicker *n* excursionista, *mf*
pictorial *a* pictórico; ilustrado. *n* revista ilustrada, *f*
pictorially *adv* pictóricamente; en grabados; por imágenes
picture *n* cuadro, *m*; (of a person) retrato, *m*; imagen, *f*; (illustration) grabado, *m*, lámina, *f*; fotografía, *f*; (outlook) perspectiva, *f*; idea, *f*. *vt* pintar; describir; imaginar. **to go to the pictures,** ir al cine. **motion p.,** película, *f*. **talking p.,** película sonora, *f*. **p. book,** libro con láminas, *m*. **p. frame,** marco, *m*. **p. gallery,** museo de pinturas, *m*; galería de pinturas, *f*. **p. hat,** pamela, *f*. **p. palace,** cine, *m*. **p. postcard,** tarjeta postal, *f*. **p. restorer,** restaurador de cuadros, *m*. **p. writing,** pictografía, *f*
picturesque *a* pintoresco
picturesqueness *n* carácter pintoresco, *m*, lo pintoresco; pintoresquismo, *m*
pie *n* (savoury) empanada, *f*; (sweet) pastel, *m*, torta, *f*; (of meat) pastelón, *m*; *print* pastel, *m*. **apple pie,** torta de manzanas, *f*. **to eat humble pie,** bajar las orejas. **to have a finger in the pie,** meter baza
piebald *a* pío; tordo
piece *n* pedazo, *m*; trozo, *m*; parte, porción, *f*; (literary, artistic work, coin, of fabric, at chess, etc. and slang) pieza, *f*; (of luggage) bulto, *m*; (of paper) hoja, *f*; (of ground) parcela, *f*; (of money) moneda, *f*, *vt* remendar; unir, juntar. **a p. of advice,** un consejo. **a p. of bread,** un pedazo de pan; una rebanada de pan. **a p. of folly,** un acto de locura. **a p. of furniture,** un mueble. **a p.**

of insolence, una insolencia. **a p. of news,** una noticia. **a p. of paper,** un papel, una hoja de papel, una cuartilla. **a p. of poetry,** una poesía. **Peter has a five-shilling p.,** Pedro tiene una moneda de cinco chelines. **to break in pieces,** *vt* hacer pedazos, romper. *vi* hacerse pedazos, romperse. **to come or fall to pieces,** deshacerse; (of machines) desarmarse. **to cut in pieces,** cortar en pedazos; (an army) destrozar. **to give a p. of one's mind (to),** decir cuatro verdades (a), decir cuántas son cinco (a). **to go to pieces,** (of persons) hacerse pedazos. **to take to pieces,** (a machine) desmontar; deshacer. **to tear or pull to pieces,** hacer pedazos, despedazar; desgarrar. **p. goods,** géneros en piezas, *m pl.* **p.-work,** trabajo a destajo, *m.* **to do p.-work,** trabajar a destajo. **p.-worker,** destajista, *mf*

piecemeal *adv* en pedazos; a remiendos; en detalle; poco a poco

piecrust *n* pasta, *f*

pied *a* bicolor; abigarrado, de varios colores

pier *n* (jetty) dique, *m;* embarcadero, *m;* malecón, *m;* (of a bridge) pila, *f;* (pillar) columna, *f;* (between windows, etc.) entrepaño, *m.* **p.-glass,** espejo de cuerpo entero, *m.* **p. head,** punta del dique, *f.* **p. table,** consola, *f*

pierce *vt* penetrar; (of sorrow, etc.) traspasar, herir; (bore) agujerear, taladrar. *vi* penetrar

pierced ear *n* oreja perforada, *f*

piercing *a* penetrante; (of the wind, etc.) cortante; (of the voice, etc.) agudo. *n* penetración, *f*

piercingly *adv* de un modo penetrante, agudamente

pietism *n* pietismo, *m*

pietist *n* pietista, *mf*

pietistic *a* pietista

piety *n* piedad, devoción, *f*

piezometer *n* piezómetro, *m*

piffle *n* patrañas, tonterías, *f pl*

pig *n* puerco, cerdo, *Lat. Am.* chancho, *m; inf* cochino, *m;* (metal) lingote, *m.* **to buy a p. in a poke,** cerrar un trato a ciegas. **p.-eyed,** de ojos de cerdo. **p.-iron,** arrabio; hierro colado en barras, lingote de fundición, *m*

pigeon *n* paloma, *f,* palomo, *m; inf* primo, *m. vt* embaucar, engañar. **carrier p.,** paloma mensajera, *f.* **clay p.,** pichón de barro, platillo de arcilla, *m.* **male p.,** pichón, *m.* **pouter p.,** paloma buchona, *f.* **young p.,** palomino, *m.* **p. fancier,** palomero, *m.* **p.-hole,** casilla, *f. vt* encasillar. **set of p.-holes,** encasillado, *m.* **p.-shooting,** tiro de pichón, *m.* **p.-toed,** patituerto

piggy bank *n* alcancía, *f*

pigheaded *a* terco, testarudo, *Lat. Am.* empecinado

pigheadedness *n* terquedad, testarudez, *f*

piglet *n* cerdito, *m*

pigment *n* pigmento, *m*

pigmentation *n* pigmentación, *f*

pigskin *n* piel de cerdo, *f*

pigsty *n* pocilga, *f*

pigtail *n* coleta, *f*

pike *n mil* pica, *f,* chuzo, *m;* (peak) pico, *m*

pilaster *n* pilastra, *f*

pile *n* estaca, *f;* poste, *m;* (engineering) pilote, *m;* (heap) pila, *f,* montón, *m;* (pyre) pira, *f;* (building) edificio grande, *m; elec* pila, *f;* (hair) pelo, *m;* (nap) pelusa, *f; pl* **piles,** *med* almorranas, *f pl. vt* clavar pilotes en; apoyar con pilotes; (heap) amontonar; (load) cargar. **to make one's p.,** *inf* hacer su pacotilla. **to p. arms,** poner los fusiles en pabellón. **to p. on,** (coal, etc.) echar; (increase) aumentar. **to p. it on,** exagerar, intensificar; (a table) cargar. **to p. up,** *vi* amontonarse; acumularse; *vt Lat. Am.* empilonar; (of a ship) encallar. **p.-driver,** máquina, *f;* martinete, *m.* **p. dwelling,** vivienda palustre, sostenida por pilares, *f*

pilfer *vt* sisar, sonsacar, hurtar, ratear, *Mexico* chalequear

pilferer *n* sisador (-ra), ratero (-ra)

pilfering *n* sisa, ratería, *f*

pilgrim *n* peregrino (-na). **pilgrim's staff,** bordón, *m*

pilgrimage *n* peregrinación, *f;* romería, *f.* **to make a p.,** hacer una peregrinación, peregrinar; ir en romería

piling *n* amontonamiento, *m;* (of buildings) pilotaje, *m*

pill *n* píldora, *f.* **to gild the p.,** *fig* dorar la píldora. **p.-box,** caja de píldoras, *f;* casamata, *f, mil* nido de ametralladoras, *m*

pillage *vt* pillar, saquear. *n* saqueo, *m*

pillager *n* saqueador (-ra)

pillaging *n* pillaje, *m, a* pillador, saqueador

pillar *n* pilar, *m,* columna, *f;* (person) sostén, soporte, *m.* **from p. to post,** de Ceca en Meca. **p. of salt,** estatua de sal, *f.* **the Pillars of Hercules,** las Columnas de Hércules. **to be a p. of strength,** *inf* ser una roca. **p.-box,** buzón, *m*

pillared *a* con columnas, sostenido por columnas; en columnas

pillion *n* (on a horse, etc.) grupera, *f;* (on a motorcycle) grupa, *f.* **to ride p.,** ir a la grupa

pillory *n* picota, argolla, *f. vt* empicotar; *fig* poner en ridículo; censurar duramente

pillow *n* almohada, *f;* (for lace-making) cojín, *m;* (of a machine) cojinete, *m. vt* apoyar; reposar; servir como almohada. **to take counsel of one's p.,** consultar con la almohada. **p.-case,** funda de almohada, *f*

pilot *n* piloto, *m; naut* práctico, piloto (de puerto), *m. vt* guiar, conducir; (*naut aer*) pilotar, pilotear. **p. boat,** vaporcito del práctico, *m.* **p. jacket,** chaquetón de piloto, *m.* **p. officer,** oficial de aviación, *m*

pilotage *n* pilotaje, *m; naut* practicaje, *m*

pilotless *a* sin piloto

pimento *n* pimiento, *m*

pimp *n* rufián, alcahuete, *m, vi* alcahuetear

pimple *n* grano, *m*

pimply *a* con granos

pin *n* alfiler, *m;* prendedor, *m;* clavija, *f;* clavo, *m,* chaveta, *f;* (bolt) perno, *m. vt* prender con alfileres; (with a peg) enclavijar; fijar; sujetar. **to pin up,** sujetar con alfileres; (the hair) sujetar con horquillas. **I don't care a pin,** No me importa un bledo. **to be on pins,** estar en ascuas. **to suffer from pins and needles,** tener aguijones. **pin-head,** cabeza de alfiler, *f.* **pin-money,** alfileres, *m pl.* **pin-oak,** *bot* pincarrasco, *m,* carrasca, *f.* **pin point,** punta de alfiler, *f.* **pin-prick,** alfilerazo, *m*

pinafore *n* delantal de niño, *m*

pince-nez *n* quevedos, *m pl*

pincers *n pl* pinzas, tenazas, *f pl,* alicates, *m pl;* (of crustaceans) pinzas, *f pl.* **p. movement,** movimiento de pinzas, *m*

pinch *vt* pellizcar; (crush) estrujar; aplastar; apretar; (of the cold) helar; (steal) hurtar, birlar; (arrest) coger, prender. *n* pellizco, torniscón, *m;* pulgarada, *f;* (of snuff) polvo, *m;* (distress) miseria, *f;* (pain) dolor, *m,* angustia. *f.* **at a p.,** en caso de apuro. **to know where the shoe pinches,** saber dónde le aprieta el zapato

pinched *a* (by the cold) helado; (wan) marchito, descolorido

pincushion *n* acerico, *m*

Pindaric *a* pindárico

pine *n bot* pino, *m. vi* languidecer, marchitarse, consumirse. **to p. for,** anhelar, suspirar por, perecer por. **pitch-p.,** pino de tea, *m.* **p.-apple,** piña de las Indias, *f,* ananás, *m.* **p. cone,** piña, *f.* **p. kernel,** piñón, *m.* **p. needle,** pinocha, *f.* **p. wood,** pinar, *m,* pineda, *f*

pineal *a* en figura de piña; *anat* pineal

ping *n* silbido de una bala, *m;* zumbido, *m.* **p. pong,** tenis de mesa, pingpong, *m*

pinion *n* (wing) ala, *f;* (small feather) piñón, *m;* (in carving) alón, *m;* (wheel) piñón, *m. vt* atar las alas de; cortar un piñón de; (a person) atar; (the arms of) trincar, asegurar

pink *n bot* clavel, *m;* color de rosa, *m;* (perfection) modelo, *m;* colmo, *m;* (hunting) color rojo, *m;* levitín rojo de caza, *m. a* de color de rosa, rosado. *vt sew* picar; (pierce) penecrar, atravesar. *vi* (of an engine) picar

pinking *n sew* picadura, *f*

pinkish *a* rosáceo
pinnacle *n naut* pinaza, *f*
pinnacle *n* pináculo, *m*
pinpoint *vt* precisar
pint *n* (measure) pinta, *f*
pintle *n* (pin) perno, *m*
pioneer *n* pionero, explorador, *m*; introductor, *m*. **to be a p. in . . . ,** ser el primero en (or a) . . . **pioneering role,** papel de iniciador (e.g. **She played a pioneering role,** jugó un papel de iniciadora)
pious *a* pío, devoto, piadoso
piously *adv* piadosamente, devotamente
pip *n* (of fruit) pepita, *f*; (on cards, dice) punto, *m*; (disease) moquillo, *m*; (of an army, etc., officer) insignia, *f*
pipe *n* (for tobacco) pipa (de fumar) *Argentina* cachimba, *f*; *mus* caramillo, *m*; (boatswain's) pito, *m*; (of a bird) trino, *m*; (voice) voz aguda, *f*; tubo, *m*; (for water, etc.) cañería, *f*; (of a hose) manga, *f*; (of an organ) cañón, *m*; (of wine) pipa, *f*; *pl* **pipes,** *mus* gaita, *f*. *vi* tocar el caramillo (or la gaita); empezar a cantar; silbar; (of birds) trinar. *vt* (a tune) tocar; (sing) cantar; (whistle) llamar con pito; conducir con cañerías; instalar cañerías en. **He smokes a p.,** Fuma una pipa. **I smoked a p.** (of tobacco) **before I went to bed,** Fumé una pipa antes de acostarme. **Put that in your p. and smoke it!** ¡Chúpate eso! **p. clay,** blanquizal, *m*. **p. cleaner,** limpiapipas, *m*. **p. layer,** cañero, fontanero, *m*. **p. laying,** instalación de cañerías, *f*. **p.-line,** cañería, *f*; (oil) oleoducto, *m*. **p. tobacco,** tabaco de pipa, *m*
pipeful *n* pipa, *f*
piper *n* (bagpiper) gaitero, *m*; flautista, *mf*
pipette *n chem* pipeta, *f*
piping *n* sonido del caramillo, *m*; música de la flauta, etc., *f*; (of birds) trinos, *m pl*; voz aguda, *f*; (for water, etc.) cañería, tubería, *f*; *sew* cordoncillo, *m*. **p.-hot,** hirviente
pipkin *n* ollita de barro, *f*
pippin *n* (apple) camuesa, *f*
piquancy *n* picante, *m*
piquant *a* picante
pique *n* (resentment, and score in game) pique, *m*. **to p. oneself upon,** preciarse de, jactarse de. **to be piqued,** estar enojado; *inf* amoscarse
piquet *n* juego de los cientos, *m*
piracy *n* piratería, *f*
pirate *n* pirata, *mf*. *vi* piratear. *vt* publicar una edición furtiva de. **p. edition,** edición furtiva, *f*
piratical *a* pirata, pirático; de pirata, de piratas
pirouette *n* pirueta, *f*
Pisces *n pl* peces, *m pl*
pisciculture *n* piscicultura, *f*
Pisgah Fasga, *f*
pistachio *n* pistacho, *m*
pistil *n bot* pistilo, *m*
pistol *n* pistola, *f*. **p. belt,** charpa, *f*, cinto de pistolas, *m*. **p. case,** pistolera, *f*. **p. shot,** pistoletazo, *m*
piston *n mech* émbolo, pistón, *m*; *mus* pistón, *m*, llave, *f*. **p. ring,** anillo de émbolo, segmento de émbolo, *m*. **p. rod,** biela, *f*. **p. stroke,** carrera del émbolo, *f*
pit *n* hoyo, *m*; foso, *m*; (in a garage) foso de reparación, *m*; *theat* platea, *f*; (trap) trampa, *f*; (scar) hoyo, *m*; precipicio, *m*; (hell) infierno, *m*. *vt* (with smallpox) marcar con viruelas; (against) competir con. **pithead,** boca de mina, *f*. **pit of the stomach,** boca del estómago, *f*. **pit stall,** butaca de platea, *f*
pitch *n chem* pez, brea, *f*, alquitrán, *m*; (place) puesto, *m*; (throwing) lanzamiento, *m*; (distance thrown) alcance, *m*; (for cricket) cancha, *f*; (bowling) saque, *m*; (slope) pendiente, inclinación, *f*; (height) elevación, *f*; *mus* tono, *m*; (*fig* degree) grado, extremo, *m*; (*naut aer*) cabeceo, *m*; (of threads of a screw, etc.) paso, *m*. *vt* (camp) asentar; (a tent, etc.) colocar, poner; (throw) lanzar, arrojar, tirar; (cricket, etc.) lanzar; (fix in) clavar; *mus* graduar el tono de; (tell) narrar. *vi* (fall) caer; *naut* cabecear, zozobrar; *aer* cabecear. **to paint with p.,** embrear. **to p. into,** (attack) acometer, atacar; (scold) desatarse contra; (food) engullir. **p.-black,** negro como la pez; oscuro como boca de lobo. **p.-pine,** pino de tea, *m*. **p.-pipe,** diapasón vocal, *m*
pitched battle *n* batalla campal, *f*
pitcher *n* jarro, cántaro, *m*; (in baseball) lanzador de pelota, *m*
pitcherful *n* jarro (de), *m*
pitchfork *n* horquilla, *f*, aventador, *m*. *vt* levantar con horquilla; *fig* lanzar
pitching *n* (pavement) adoquinado, *m*; (of a ship) socollada, *f*; cabeceo, *m*
piteous *a* lastimero; triste; plañidero; compasivo, tierno
piteousness *n* estado lastimero, *m*; tristeza, *f*; compasión, ternura, *f*
pitfall *n* trampa, *f*; *fig* añagaza, *f*, lazo, peligro, *m*
pith *n bot* médula, *f*; médula espinal, *f*; *fig* meollo, *m*; fuerza, *f*, vigor, *m*; substancia, *f*; quinta esencia, *f*; importancia, *f*
pithiness *n* jugosidad, *f*; fuerza, *f*, vigor, *m*
pithy *a* meduloso; *fig* jugoso; enérgico, vigoroso
pitiable *a* lastimoso, digno de compasión; (paltry) despreciable
pitiful *a* piadoso, compasivo; conmovedor, doloroso, lastimero; (contemptible) miserable
pitifully *adv* lastimosamente
pitiless *a* sin piedad, despiadado
pitilessness *n* crueldad, inhumanidad, *f*
pitman *n* minero, *m*; aserrador de foso, *m*
pittance *n* pitanza, *f*; pequeña porción, *f*; ración de hambre, *f*
pitted *a* picoso
pituitary *a* pituitario
pity *n* piedad, compasión, *f*; lástima, *f*. *vt* compadecerse de, tener lástima (a); compadecer. **It is a p. that . . . ,** Es lástima que . . . **Have p.!** ¡Ten piedad! **to take p. on,** tener lástima (de). **to move to p.,** dar lástima (a), enternecer
pityingly *adv* con lástima
pivot *n* pivote, *m*; eje, *m*; *fig* punto de partida, *m*, *vi* girar sobre un pivote o eje
pivotal *a fig* cardinal, principal, fundamental
pixy *n* duende, *m*. **p. hood,** caperuza, *f*
pizzicato *a* pichigato
placability *n* placabilidad, *f*
placable *a* aplacable, placable
placard *n* cartel, *m*. *vt* fijar carteles (en); publicar por carteles
placate *vt* aplacar, ablandar, apaciguar
placatory *a* placativo
place *n* lugar, *m*; sitio, *m*; (position) puesto, *m*; (seat) asiento, *m*; (laid at table) cubierto, *m*; (square) plaza, *f*; (house) residencia, *f*; (in the country) casa de campo, finca, *f*; (in a book) pasaje, *m*; (in an examination) calificación, *f*; (rank) posición, *f*, rango, *m*; situación, *f*; (employment) empleo, *m*, colocación, *f*. *vt* poner; colocar; (in employment) dar empleo (a); (appoint) nombrar; (an order) dar; (money) invertir; (remember) recordar, traer a la memoria; (size up) fijar; (confidence) poner. **in p.,** en su lugar; apropiado. **in p. of,** en vez de, en lugar de. **in the first p.,** en primer lugar, primero. **in the next p.,** luego, después. **out of p.,** fuera de lugar; inoportuno. **It is not my p. to . . . ,** No me toca a mí de . . . **to give p. to,** ceder el paso (a); ceder (a). **to take p.,** verificarse, tener lugar, ocurrir. **p. of business,** establecimiento, local de negocios, *m*. **p. of worship,** edificio de culto, *m*
placenta *n* placenta, *f*
placid *a* plácido, apacible; calmoso; sereno, sosegado; dulce
placidity *n* placidez, *f*; serenidad, tranquilidad, *f*, sosiego, *m*
placidly *adv* plácidamente
placing *n* colocación, *f*; posición, *f*; localización, *f*
placket *n* abertura (en una falda), *f*
plagiarism *n* plagio, *m*

plagiarist *n* plagiario (-ia)
plagiarize *vt* plagiar, hurtar
plague *n* plaga, *f;* peste, pestilencia, *f. vt* importunar, atormentar; plagar
plaice *n* (nearest equivalent) platija, *f*
plaid *n* manta escocesa, *f;* género de cuadros, *m, a* a cuadros
plain *a* claro; evidente; (simple) sencillo; llano; sin adorno; (flat) liso, igual; (candid) franco; (with truth, etc.) desnudo; mero; puro, sin mezcla; (of words) redondo; (ugly) feo. *adv* claramente; llanamente; sencillamente; francamente. *n* llanura, *f,* llano, *m.* **the p. truth,** la pura verdad. **p. clothes,** traje de paisano, *m.* **p. clothes man,** detective, *m.* **p. cooking,** cocina sencilla, cocina casera, *f.* **p. dealing,** buena fe, sinceridad, *f.* **p. dweller,** llanero (-ra). **p. living,** vida sencilla, *f.* **p. people,** gente sencilla, *f.* **p. sailing,** *fig* camino fácil, *m.* **p. sewing,** costura, *f.* **p.-song,** canto llano, *m.* **p. speaking,** franqueza, *f.* **p.-spoken,** franco. **in p. English,** sin rodeos, en cristiano (e.g. **Speak in p. English!** Habla sin rodeos! Habla en cristiano!)
plainly *adv* claramente; sencillamente; llanamente; francamente; rotundamente
plainness *n* claridad, *f;* sencillez, *f;* llaneza, *f;* franqueza, *f;* (ugliness) fealdad, *f*
plainsman *n* hombre de las llanuras, *m*
plaint *n* queja, *f,* lamento, *m; law* demanda, querella, *f*
plaintiff *n* demandante, *mf,* actor, *m,* parte actora, actora, *f*
plaintive *a* quejumbroso, dolorido; patético
plaintively *adv* quejumbrosamente
plaintiveness *n* melancolía, tristeza, *f;* voz quejumbrosa, *f*
plait *n* trenza, *f. vt* trenzar; tejer. **in plaits,** (of hair) en trenzas
plan *n* plan, *m;* (map) plano, *m;* proyecto, *m. vt* planear; proyectar; proponerse. **the Marshall P.,** el Plan Marshall. **to make a p. of,** trazar un plano de. **to make plans,** hacer planes
planchette *n* mesa giratoria, *f*
plane *n* (tree) plátano, *m;* (tool) cepillo, *m; geom* plano, *m;* (level) nivel, *m; aer* avión, *m,* plano. *vt carp* acepillar, alisar. *vi aer* planear
planet *n* planeta, *m*
planetarium *n* planetario, *m*
planetary *a* planetario
planing *n* acepilladura, alisadura, *f,*
plank *n* tabla, *f; fig* fundamento, principio, *m; pl* **planks,** tablazón, *f. vt* entablar, enmaderar
planking *n* entablado, *m,* tablazón, *f*
plankton *n* plancton, *m*
planned *a* proyectado, planeado; dirigido. **p. economy,** economía dirigida, *f*
planner *n* proyectista, *mf;* autor (-ra) de un plan
planning *n* proyecto, *m;* concepción, *f*
plant *n bot* planta, *f;* instalación, *f,* material, *m. vt* plantar; (place) colocar; fijar; (a blow) asestar; (people) establecer; (instil) inculcar, imbuir (con); (conceal) esconder. **p. pot,** florero, *m.* **p. stand,** jardinera, *f*
plantain *n bot* llantén, *m*
plantation *n* plantación, *f;* plantío, *m; fig* colonia, *f;* introducción, *f,* establecimiento, *m*
planter *n* plantador, cultivador, *m*
planting *n* plantación, *f; fig* colonia, *f;* introducción, *f.* **p. out,** trasplante, *m*
plantlike *a* como una planta; de planta
plaque *n* placa, *f;* medalla, *f*
plash *n* (puddle) charco, *m;* (sound) chapaleteo, *m. vt* and *vi* chapotear, chapalear
plasma *n* plasma, *m*
plaster *n* (for walls, etc.) argamasa, *f;* yeso, *m; med* parche, emplasto, *m. vt* (walls, etc.) enlucir, enyesar; poner emplastos (a or en); (daub) embadurnar manchar; (cover) cubrir. **p. cast,** vaciado, yeso, *m.* **p. of Paris,** escayola, *f*
plasterer *n* yesero, *m*
plastering *n* revoque, enyesado, guarnecido, *m.* **p. trowel,** fratás, *m*
plastic *a* plástico. *n* plástica, *f; pl* **plastics,** materias plásticas, *f pl.* **p. surgery,** cirugía plástica, cirugía estética, *f*
plasticine *n* plasticina, *f*
plasticity *n* plasticidad, *f*
plate *n* plancha, chapa, *f;* (engraving and *phot.,* of a doctor, etc.) placa, *f;* (illustration) lámina, *f;* (cutlery, etc.) vajilla, *f;* (for eating) plato, *m;* (for money) platillo, *m;* electrotipo, *m;* (dental) dentadura postiza, *f. vt* (with armor) blindar; (with metal) planchear; (silver) platear; (electro-plate) niquelar. **silver p.,** vajilla de plata, plata, *f.* **p.-armor,** armadura, *f;* (of a ship) blindaje, *m.* **p.-draining rack,** escurreplatos, *m.* **p.-glass,** vidrio plano, *m.* **p.-rack,** escurridero para platos, *m.* **p. warmer,** calientaplatos, *m*
plateau *n* meseta, altiplanicie, *f, Lat. Am.* altiplano, *m*
plateful *n* plato (de), *m*
plater *n* plateador, *m;* platero, *m*
plateresque *a arch* plateresco
platform *n* plataforma, *f;* (railway) andén, *m.* **p. ticket,** billete de andén, *m*
plating *n* niquelado, *m;* electrogalvanización, *f;* (with armor) blindaje, *m*
platinum *n* platino, *m.* **p. blonde,** rubia platino, *f*
platitude *n* perogrullada, *f,* lugar común, *m;* trivialidad, vulgaridad, *f*
platitudinous *a* lleno de perogrulladas; trivial
platonic *a* platónico
Platonism *n* platonismo, *m*
Platonist *n* platonista, *mf*
platoon *n mil* pelotón, *m*
platter *n* fuente, *f,* trinchero, *m;* plato, *m*
plaudit *n* aplauso, *m,* aclamación, *f;* (praise) elogio, *m,* alabanza, *f*
plausibility *n* plausibilidad, *f*
plausible *a* plausible
plausibly *adv* plausiblemente
play *vi* jugar; (frolic) juguetear, retozar; recrearse, divertirse; *mech* moverse; (on a musical instrument) tocar; (wave) ondear, flotar; *theat* representar; (behave) conducirse. *vt* jugar; (of a searchlight, etc.) enfocar; (direct) dirigir; (a fish) agotar; (a joke, etc.) hacer; (a piece in a game) mover; (a musical instrument or music) tocar; (a string instrument) tañer; (a character in a play) hacer el papel de; (a drama, etc.) representar, poner en escena. **to p. a joke,** gastar una broma, hacer una burla. **to p. fair,** jugar limpio. **to p. false,** jugar sucio, engañar. **to p. the fool,** hacerse el tonto, hacerse el payaso. **to p. at,** jugar a; (pretend) fingir; hacer sin entusiasmo. **to p. off,** confrontar, contraponer. **to p. on.** See **to p. upon. to p. on the . . . ,** (of musical instruments) tocar. **to p. to,** (a person) tocar para. **to p. upon,** tocar; (a person's fears, etc.) explotar. **to p. up to,** (a person) adular, hacer la rueda (a). **to p. with,** jugar con; burlarse de; (an idea) acariciar play, *n* juego, *m;* diversión, *f,* recreo, *m;* (reflection) reflejo, *m;* movimiento libre, *m;* (to the imagination, etc.) rienda suelta, *f; mech* holgura, *f; lit* pieza dramática, comedia, *f;* (performance) función, representación, *f;* (*theater*) teatro, *m.* **fair p.,** juego limpio, *m.* **foul p.,** juego sucio, *m;* traición, perfidia, *f.* **to bring into p.,** poner en juego. **to come into p.,** entrar en juego. **to give p. to,** dar rienda a. **p. on words,** juego de palabras, *m.* **p.-pen,** cuadro enrejado, *m*
playact *vi* hacer la comedia
playbill *n* cartel, *m;* programa, *m*
played-out *a* agotado; viejo
player *n* jugador (-ra); *theat* actor (-triz), representante, *mf; mus* músico (-ca), tocador (-ra)
playfellow *n* camarada, *mf;* compañero (-ra) de juego, compañero de juegos
playful *a* juguetón; travieso; alegre
playfully *adv* en juego, de broma; alegremente

playfulness *n* carácter juguetón, *m*; travesuras, *f pl*; alegría, *f*
playgoer *n* persona que frecuenta los teatros, *f*; espectador de comedias, *m*
playground *n* patio de recreo, *m*
playing *n* juego, *m*. **p.-cards,** naipes, *m pl*, cartas, *f pl*. **p.-field,** campo de deportes, *m*
playlet *n* comedia corta, *f*
playmate. See **playfellow**
plaything *n* juguete, *m*
playtime *n* recreación, *f*; (in schools) hora de recreo, *f*, recreo, *m*
playwright *n* dramaturgo, *m*, autor (-ra) de comedias
plea *n law* informe, *m*; declaración, *f*; *law* acción, *f*, proceso, *m*; (excuse) pretexto, *m*, excusa, *f*; (entreaty) súplica, *f*. **under p. of,** bajo pretexto de, con excusa de
plead *vi law* pleitear; *law* declarar; suplicar; (of counsel, etc.) abogar (por); interceder (por). *vt* defender en juicio; aducir, alegar; pretender. **to p. guilty,** confesarse culpable. **to p. not guilty,** negar la acusación. **to p. ignorance,** pretender ignorancia
pleading *n* súplicas, *f pl*; *law* defensa, *f*; *pl* **pleadings,** alegatos, *m pl*, *a* implorante
pleasant *a* agradable; placentero; ameno; encantador; dulce; alegre; (of persons) simpático, amable; bueno; divertido
pleasantly *adv* agradablemente; de un modo muy amable; alegremente
pleasantness *n* agrado, *m*; placer, *m*; amabilidad, *f*; alegría, *f*
pleasantry *n* jocosidad, *f*; broma, chanza, *f*
please *vi* dar placer, gustar, dar gusto, agradar; parecer bien, querer, servirse; tener a bien, placer. *vt* deleitar, agradar, gustar; halagar; contentar, satisfacer. **I will do what I p.,** Haré lo que me parezca bien. **If you p.,** Si te parece bien; Con tu permiso. **She is very easy to p.,** Es muy fácil de darle placer. **When you p.,** Cuando Vd. quiera, Cuando a Vd. le venga bien Cuando Vd. guste. **"Please Do Not Disturb,"** «No Molesten.» **P. sit down!** ¡Haga el favor de sentarse! ¡Sírvase de sentarse! **P. God!** ¡Plegue a Dios!
pleased *a* contento (de or con); encantado (de); alegre (de); satisfecho (de or con). **I am p. with my new house,** Estoy contento con mi nueva casa. **I'm p. to meet you,** Mucho gusto (en conocerle), Mucho gusto (en conocerla). **to be p.,** estar contento; complacerse en
pleasing *a* agradable, grato; placentero; halagüeño
pleasurable *a* agradable; divertido, entretenido
pleasure *n* placer, *m*; gusto, *m*; satisfacción, *f*; (will) voluntad, *f*; recreo, *m*; diversión, distracción, *f*. **to give p. (to),** dar placer (a); deleitar, agradar; complacer. **to take p. in,** gustar de, disfrutar de; complacerse en. **I shall do it with great p.,** Lo haré con mucho gusto, Lo haré con mucho placer. **p.-boat,** barco de recreo, *m*. **p.-ground,** parque de atracciones, *m*. **p.-seeking,** amigo de placeres, frívolo. **p. trip,** viaje de recreo, *m*; excursión, *f*
pleasure craft *n* barco de recreo, *m*, (one vessel); barcas de recreo (collectively), *m pl*
pleat *n* pliegue, *m*, *vt* plegar, hacer pliegues en
pleating *n* plegado, *m*
plebeian *a* plebeyo. *n* plebeyo (-ya)
plebiscite *n* plebiscito, *m*. **to take a p.,** hacer un plebiscito
plectrum *n* plectro, *m*
pledge *n* prenda, *f*; empeño, *m*; garantía, *f*; (hostage) rehén, *m*; (toast) brindis, *m*. *vt* empeñar, dar en prenda; garantizar; brindar por; prometer. **to p. oneself,** comprometerse. **to p. support for,** prometer apoyo para
Pleiades *n pl* pléyades, *f pl*
plenary *a* pleno; plenario. **p. indulgence,** indulgencia plenaria, *f*. **p. session,** sesión plenaria, *f*
plenipotentiary *a* plenipotenciario. *n* plenipotenciario, *m*
plenitude *n* plenitud, *f*
plenteous, plentiful *a* copioso, abundante. **to be p.,** abundar
plentifully *adv* en abundancia
plenty *n* abundancia, *f*; en abundancia; de sobra; mucho. *adv inf* bastante. **There is p. of food,** Hay comida en abundancia. **We have p. of time,** Tenemos tiempo de sobra
pleonasm *n* pleonasmo, *m*
plethora *n* plétora, *f*
pleurisy *n* pleuresía, *f*
plexus *n* plexo, *m*
pliability *n* flexibilidad, *f*; docilidad, *f*
pliable, pliant *a* flexible; dócil
pliers *n pl* pinzas, *f pl*, alicates, *m pl*, tenazas, *f pl*
plight *vt* (one's word) empeñar, dar; prometer en matrimonio. *n* (fix) aprieto, apuro, *m*. **to p. one's troth,** dar palabra de matrimonio
plinth *n arch* plinto, *m*
Pliny the Elder Plinio el Antiguo, Plinio el Mayor
Pliny the Younger Plinio el Menor
plod *vi* andar despacio, caminar con trabajo; *fig* trabajar con ahínco
plodder *n* trabajador lento y concienzudo, *m*; (student) empollón (-ona)
plot *n* (of land) parcela, *f*; terreno, solar, *m*; (plan) proyecto, *m*; estratagema, *m*; (literary) intriga, trama, *f*; (story) argumento, *m*; (conspiracy) conjuración, *f*, complot, *m*. *vt* trazar (un plano, etc.); urdir, tramar. *vi* conspirar, intrigar
plotter *n* conspirador (-ra conjurado (-da)
plotting *n* trazado (de un plano, una gráfica), *m*; (conspiracy) conspiración, *f*; maquinaciones, *f pl*; (hatching) trama, *f*
plover *n* ave fría, *f*, chorlito, *m*
plow *n* arado, *m*; *ast* el Carro, la Osa Mayor; (in an examination) escabechina, *f*. *vt* and *vi* arar; *fig* surcar; (in examinations) escabechar, dar calabazas (a), suspender. **plow the sands,** arar en el mar. **p. handle,** esteva, *f*. **to p. up,** roturar
plowman *n* arador, surcador, *m*; (peasant) labrador, *m*
plowshare *n* reja de arado, *f*
pluck *vt* (pick) coger; (a bird) desplumar; *mus* puntear; (in an examination) calabacear escabechar. *vi* tirar (de). *n* (tug) tirón, *m*; (of an animal) asadura, *f*; (courage) coraje, *m*. **to p. up courage,** tomar coraje, sacar ánimos. **to p. off,** quitar. **to p. out,** arrancar; quitar
pluckily *adv* valientemente
pluckiness *n* coraje, valor, *m*
plucky *a* valiente, esforzado, resuelto, animoso
plug *n* tapón, tarugo, *m*; (in building) nudillo, *m*; (of a switchboard) clave, *f*; *elec* enchufe, *m*; (of a w.c.) tirador, *m*; (of a bath, etc.) tapón, *m*; (of tobacco) rollo, *m*. *vt* atarugar, taponar, obturar; (in building) rellenar. *vi* (with away) batirse el cobre, sudar la gota gorda. **to p. in,** enchufar
plum *n* (tree) ciruelo, *m*; (fruit) ciruela, *f*; (raisin) pasa, *f*; (*inf* prize) breva, golosina, *f*. **p. cake,** pastel de fruta, *m*
plumage *n* plumaje, *m*
plumb *n* plomada, *f*; (sounding-lead) escandallo, *m*. *a* perpendiculo; recto; completo. *adv* a plomo, verticalmente; exactamente. *vt* aplomar; *naut* sondar; (*fig* pierce) penetrar; (understand) comprender. *vi* trabajar como plomero. **p.-line,** plomada, *f*
plumbago *n* plombagina, *f*
plumber *n* plomero, fontanero, *m*; instalador de cañerías, *m*
plumbic *a chem* plúmbico
plumbing *n* plomería, fontanería, *f*; instalación de cañerías, *f*
plumbless *a poet* insondable
plume *n* pluma, *f*; penacho, *m*. *vt* adornar con plumas; desplumar; **to p. itself,** (of a bird) limpiarse las plumas. **to p. oneself on,** echárselas de, hacer alarde de; jactarse de
plumed *a* plumado; con plumas; empenachado

plumelet *n* agujas, *f pl*
plummet *n* plomada, *f*; (weight) plomo, *m*; (sounding-lead) sonda, *f*
plump *a* gordito, llenito; rollizo; hinchado. *adv* de golpe; claramente. *vt* (swell) hinchar, rellenar; (make fall) hacer (or dejar) caer. *vi* (swell) hincharse; engordar; (fall) caer a plomo; dejarse caer. **to p. for,** escoger, dar apoyo (a); votar por. **p.-cheeked,** mofletudo
plumpness *n* gordura, *f*; lo rollizo
plumy *a* como una pluma; plumado
plunder *vt* saquear; pillar; despojar. *n* saqueo, pillaje, *m*; (booty) botín, despojo, *m*
plunderer *n* saqueador (-ra); ladrón (-ona)
plundering *n* saqueo, *m*; despojo, *m*. *a* saqueador
plunge *vt* chapuzar; sumergir; hundir; meter. *vi* sumergirse; (into water) zambullirse; (rush) precipitarse, lanzarse; *naut* zozobrar; (of a horse) encabritarse; (gamble) jugarse el todo. *n* sumersión, *f*; zambullida, *f*; chapuz, *m*; (rush) salto, *m*; (*fig* step) paso, *m*
plunger *n mech* émbolo, *m*
plunging *n* (of a ship) zozobra, *f*; (of a horse) cabriolas, *f pl*; saltos, *m pl*, For other meanings, see **plunge**
plural *a* plural. *n* plural, *m*. **in the p.,** en el plural. **to make p.,** poner en plural
plurality *n* pluralidad, *f*
pluralize *vt* pluralizar
plus *prep* and *a* más; (*math elec*) positivo. *n* signo más, *m*; *math* cantidad positiva, *f*. **p. fours,** pantalones de golf, *m pl*
plush *n* felpa, *f*; velludo, *m*
plushy *a* felpudo; de felpa
Pluto *n* Plutón, *m*; (pipe-line) oleoducto, *m*
plutocracy *n* plutocracia, *f*
plutocrat *n* plutócrata, *mf*
plutocratic *a* plutocrático
pluviometer *n* pluviómetro, *m*
ply *n* cabo, *m*. *vt* emplear, usar; manejar; ejercer; ofrecer, servir (con); importunar (con). *vi* hacer el trayecto; hacer el servicio; ir y venir; hacer viajes. **to ply for hire,** tomar viajeros; ofrecerse para ser alquilado
plywood *n* madera contrachapada, *f*
pneumatic *a* neumático. *n* (tire) neumático, *m*. **p. drill,** barreno neumático, *m*
pneumococcus *n* neumococo, *m*
pneumonia *n* pulmonía, *f*. **double p.,** pulmonía doble, *f*
poach *vi* cazar (or pescar) en vedado. *vt* robar caza de un vedado; *fig* invadir; (*fig* steal) hurtar; (eggs) escalfar. **to p. upon another's preserves,** meterse en los asuntos de otro
poacher *n* cazador furtivo, *m*
poaching *n* caza (or pesca) furtiva, *f*
pock *n* pústula, *f*. **p.-mark,** hoyo, *m*. **p.-marked,** picado de viruelas
pocket *n* bolsillo, *m*; bolsillo del reloj, *m*; faltriquera, *f*; *min* bolsa, *f*, depósito, *m*; *fig* bolsa, *f*; (in billiards) tronera, *f*. *vt* meter (or poner) en el bolsillo; (an insult) tragarse; (in billiards) entronerar; (a profit) ganar; apropiarse. **air-p.,** bolsa de aire, *f*. **to be out of p.,** haber perdido, tener una pérdida. **to have a person in one's p.,** calzarse a una persona. **to p. one's pride,** olvidarse de su orgullo. **p. battleship,** acorazado de bolsillo, *m*. **p.-book,** cartera, *f*. **p. dictionary,** diccionario de bolsillo, *m*. **p.-flap,** portezuela, *f*. **p.-handkerchief,** pañuelo (de bolsillo), *m*. **p.-knife,** cortaplumas, *m*. **p.-lighter,** encendedor de bolsillo, *m*. **p.-money,** alfileres, *m pl*, dinero del bosillo, *m*. **p. picking,** ratería de carterista, *f*
pocketful *n* bolsillo lleno (de), *m*; lo que cabe en un bolsillo
pocket of resistance *n* foco de resistencia, *m*
pod *n bot* vaina, *f*; (of a silkworm) capullo, *m*. *vt* desvainar; mondar. *vi* hincharse, llenarse
podgy *a* gordo, grueso
poem *n* poema, *m*; *pl* **poems,** poesías, *f pl*, versos, *m pl*
poet *n* poeta, *m*. **p. laureate,** poeta laureado, *m*
poetaster *n* poetastro, *m*
poetess *n* poetisa, *f*
poetic *a* poético. **p. licence,** licencia poética, *f*
poeticize *vt* poetizar; hacer un poema (de)
poetics *n* poética, *f*
poetry *n* poesía, *f*; versos, poemas, *m pl*
pogrom *n* pogrom, *m*
poignancy *n* (of emotions) profundidad, violencia, *f*, lo patético; (of a retort, etc.) mordacidad, acerbidad, *f*
poignant *a* (moving) conmovedor, hondo, agudo; patético; (mordant) mordaz, agudo
poignantly *adv* de un modo conmovedor, patéticamente; mordazmente
poinsettia *n* flor de nochebuena, *f*
point *n* (usual meanings and *ast.*, *math.*, in cards, in a speech, etc.) punto, *m*; característica, *f*; cualidad, *f*; (purpose) motivo, fin, *m*; (question) cuestión, *f*; asunto, *m*; (wit) agudeza, *f*; (significance) significación, *f*; (detail) detalle, *m*; (in rationing) cupón, *m*; (sharp end) punta, *f*; (of a shawl, etc.) pico, *m*; (of land) promontorio, cabo, *m*; (engraving) buril, *m*; (railway) aguja, *f*; (of horses) cabo, *m*. **Mary has many good points,** María tiene muchas cualidades buenas. **There is no p. in being angry,** No hay para que enfadarse. **in p.,** en cuestión; a propósito. **in p. of fact,** en efecto, en verdad. **on the p. of,** a punto de. **to be to the p.,** venir al caso; ser apropiado. **to carry one's p.,** salir con la suya. **to come to the p.,** ir al grano, ir al caso, ir al mollo del asunto. **to make a p. of,** insistir en; tener por principio. **to win on points,** (boxing) ganar por puntos. **p. at issue,** cuestión bajo consideración, *f*, punto en cuestión, *m*. **p.-blank,** a boca de jarro. **p.-duty,** regulación de tráfico, *f*. **p. lace,** encaje de aguja, *m*. **p. of honor,** punto de honor, *m*; cuestión de honor, *f*. **p. or order,** cuestión de orden, *f*. **p. of view,** punto de vista, *m*. **What's your p.?** ¿A dónde quieres llegar con esto?
point *vt* sacar punta (a), afilar; (a moral, etc.) inculcar; (in building) rejuntar; *gram* puntuar; (of dogs) mostrar la caza. **He pointed his gun at them,** Les apuntó con su fusil. **The hands of the clock pointed to seven o'clock,** Las agujas del reloj marcaban las siete. **to p. with the finger,** señalar con el dedo. **to p. at,** señalar, indicar; (with a gun) apuntar; dirigir. **to p. out,** señalar, indicar; enseñar, mostrar; advertir
pointed *a* (sharpened) afilado; (in shape) puntiagudo; picudo; *arch* ojival; *fig* mordaz; satírico; (of a remark, etc.) directo; personal; aparente, evidente
pointedly *adv* explícitamente, categóricamente; mordazmente; directamente; satíricamente
pointedness *n* forma puntiaguda, *f*; (incisiveness) mordacidad, aspereza, *f*; claridad, *f*
pointer *n* (of a clock, weighing-machine, etc.) aguja, *f*; (of a balance) fiel, *m*; (wand) puntero, *m*; *fig* índice, *m*; (dog) perro de muestra, *m*
pointillisme *n art* puntillismo, *m*
pointing *n* (in building) rejuntado, *m*; (of a gun) puntería, *f*
pointless *a* sin motivo, innecesario; fútil; sin importancia
pointlessly *adv* sin motivo, sin necesidad; fútilmente
pointsman *n* (railway) guardagujas, *m*; (policeman) guardia del tráfico, *m*
poise *vt* balancear; pesar. *vi* balancearse; posar, estar suspendido. *n* equilibrio, *m*; (of mind) serenidad de ánimo, sangre fría, *f*; aplomo, *m*; (bearing) porte, aire, *m*
poison *n* veneno, *m*; *fig* ponzoña, *f*, veneno, *m*. *vt* envenenar; intoxicar; *fig* emponzoñar. **p. gas,** gas asfixiante, *m*
poisoner *n* envenenador (-ra); *fig* corruptor (-ra)
poisoning *n* envenenamiento, *m*; intoxicación, *f*
poisonous *a* venenoso; tóxico; *fig* ponzoñoso, pernicioso. **p. snake,** serpiente venenosa

poisonousness *n* venenosidad, *f;* toxicidad, *f; fig* veneno, *m,* ponzoña, *f*

poke *vt* (thrust) clavar; (make) hacer; (the fire) atizar; hurgar; (push) empujar; (put away) arrinconar. *vi* andar a tientas; meterse. **Don't p. your nose into other people's business!** ¡No te metas donde no te llaman! **They poked his eyes out,** Le saltaron los ojos. **to p. fun at,** burlarse de, mofarse de. **to p. the fire,** atizar la lumbre (or el fuego). **to p. about for,** buscar a tientas. **p.-bonnet,** capelina, *f*

poker *n* (game) póker, *m;* (for the fire) hurgón, atizador, *m.* **p. work,** pirograbado, *m*

poky *a* estrecho, ahogado, pequeño; miserable

Poland Polonia, *f*

polar *a* polar. **p. bear,** oso (-sa) blanco (-ca). **p. lights,** aurora boreal, *f*

polarimeter *n* polarímetro, *m*

polarity *n* polaridad, *f*

polarization *n* polarización, *f*

polarize *vt* polarizar

pole *n* palo largo, *m;* poste, *m;* (of a tent) mástil, *m;* (of a cart) pértiga, *f; sport* pértiga, garrocha, *f;* (measurement) percha, *f;* (*ast geog biol math elec*) polo, *m. vt* (a punt) impeler con pértiga. **from p. to p.,** de polo a polo. **greasy p.,** cucaña, *f.* **under bare poles,** *naut* a palo seco. **p.-ax,** hachuela de mano, *f;* hacha de marinero, *f;* (butcher's) mazo, *m.* **p. jumping,** salto de pértiga, salto a la garrocha, *m.* **p.-star,** estrella polar, *f*

Pole *n* polaco (-ca)

polemic *n* polémica, *f*

polemical *a* polémico

police *n* policía, *f. vt* mantener servicio de policía en; mantener el orden público en; administrar, regular. **mounted p.,** policía montada, *f.* **p. constable,** (agente de) policía, guardia urbano, *m.* **p. court,** tribunal de la policía, *m.* **p. dog,** perro de policía, *m.* **p. force,** cuerpo de policía, *m,* policía, *f.* **p. magistrate,** juez municipal, *m.* **p. station,** comisaría de policía, *f.* **p. trap,** puesto oculto de la policía del tráfico, *m.* **p. woman,** policía, *f*

policeman *n* policía, guardia, *Lat. Am.* cívico, *m*

policy *n* política, *f;* táctica, *f;* sistema, *m;* norma de conducta, *f;* ideas, *f pl,* principios, *m pl;* prudencia, *f;* (insurance) póliza, *f.* **fixed premium p.,** póliza a prima fija, *f.* **p.-holder,** asegurado (-da), tenedor (de una póliza), *m*

poliomyelitis *n* poliomielitis, *f*

polish *vt* (metals and wood) pulir; (furniture and shoes) dar brillo (a); (*lit* works) pulir, limar; (persons) descortezar, civilizar. *n* (shine) brillo, *m;* (furniture) cera para los muebles, *f;* (metal, silver) líquido para limpiar metales, *m;* (for shoes) betún para zapatos, *m;* (varnish) barniz, *m;* (of *lit.* works) pulidez, elegancia, *f;* (of persons) urbanidad, cultura, *f.* **to p. off,** terminar a prisa; (a person) acabar con; (food) engullir

Polish *a* polaco, polonés. *n* (language) polaco, *m*

polished *a* (of verses, etc.) pulido, elegante; (of person) culto, distinguido; (of manners) fino, cortés

polisher *n* (machine) pulidor, *m;* lustrador, *m.* **floor-p.,** lustrador de piso, *m.* **French p.,** barnizador, *m*

polite *a* cortés, bien educado; atento; elegante

politely *adv* cortésmente; atentamente

politeness *n* cortesía, *f.* **for p. sake,** por cortesía

politic *a* político

political *a* político. **p. agent,** agente político, *m.* **p. economist,** hacendista, *mf* **p. economy,** economía política, *f*

politically *adv* políticamente

politician *n* político (-ca)

politics *n* política, *f.* **to dabble in p.,** meterse en política

polity *n* forma de gobierno, constitución política, *f*

polka *n* polca, *f*

polka-dot *a* con puntos

poll *n* (head of person) cabeza, *f;* (voters' register) lista electoral, *f;* (voting) votación, *f;* (polling booth) colegio electoral, *m;* (counting of votes) escrutinio, *m. vt* (trees) desmochar; (vote) votar, dar su voto (a); (obtain votes) obtener, recibir; (count votes) escrutar. **p.-tax,** capitación, *f*

pollard *vt* desmochar. *n* (tree) árbol desmochado, *m*

pollen *n* polen, *m*

pollinate *vt* fecundar con polen

pollination *n* polinización, *f*

polling *n* votación, *f.* **p. booth,** colegio electoral, *m*

pollute *vt* contaminar; ensuciar; profanar; (corrupt morally) corromper

polluter *n* profanador (-ra), corruptor (-ra)

pollution *n* contaminación, *f;* profanación, *f;* corrupción, *f*

polo *n* polo, *m.* **p. mallet,** maza de polo, *f.* **p. player,** jugador de polo, *m,* polista, *mf*

polonaise *n* polonesa, *f*

poltroon *n* cobarde, *m*

polychrome *a* policromo

polygamist *n* polígamo (-ma)

polygamous *a* polígamo

polygamy *n* poligamia, *f*

polygenesis *n* poligenismo, *m*

polyglot *n* poligloto (-ta). **p. Bible,** poliglota, *f*

polygon *n* polígono, *m*

Polynesia Polinesia, *f*

polyp *n* pólipo, *m*

polyphonic *a* polifónico

polyphony *n* polifonía, *f*

polytechnic *a* politécnico

polytheism *n* politeísmo, *m*

polytheistic *a* politeísta

pomade *n* pomada, *f*

pomegranate *n* granada, *f*

Pomeranian *a* pomerano. **P. dog,** perro pomerano, *m*

pommel *n* pomo, *m, vt* aporrear

pomp *n* pompa, magnificencia, *f,* fausto, aparato, *m;* ostentación, *f*

Pompeii Pompeya, *f*

pompom *n* pompón, *m*

pomposity *n* pomposidad, presunción, *f;* (of language) ampulosidad, *f*

pompous *a* pomposo, ostentoso; (of style) ampuloso, hinchado; importante. **to be p.,** (of persons) darse tono

pond *n* charca, *f,* estanque, *m*

ponder *vt* ponderar, estudiar, considerar. *vi* meditar (sobre), reflexionar (sobre)

ponderable *a* ponderable

ponderous *a* pesado; macizo, abultado; grave; (dull) pesado, aburrido

ponderously *adv* pesadamente; gravemente

ponderousness *n* pesadez, *f;* gravedad, importancia, *f*

poniard *n* puñal, *m, vt* apuñalar

pontiff *n* pontífice, *m*

pontifical *a* pontificio

pontificate *n* pontificado, *m*

pontoneer *n* pontonero, *m*

pontoon *n* pontón, *m.* **p. bridge,** puente de pontones, *m*

pony *n* jaca, *f*

poodle *n* perro (-rra) de aguas, perro de lanas, perro lanudo

pooh-pooh *vt* despreciar, desdeñar. **Pooh!** ¡Bah!

pool *n* (in a river) rebalsa, *f;* charca, *f,* estanque, *m;* (of blood, etc.) charco, *m;* (swimming) *Spain* piscina, *Lat. Am.* alberca, *f;* (in cards) baceta, *f; com* asociación, *f; fig* fuente, *f; pl* **pools,** (football) apuestas benéficas de fútbol, *f pl. vt* (resources, etc.) combinar; juntar

poop *n* popa, *f.* **p. lantern,** fanal, *m*

poor *a* pobre; malo; (insignificant or unfortunate) infeliz, desgraciado. **the p.,** los pobres. **to be in p. health,** estar mal de salud. **to be p. stuff,** ser de pacotilla. **to be poorer than a church mouse,** ser más pobre que las ratas. **to have a p. opinion of,** tener en poco (a). **P. me!** ¡Ay de mí! ¡Pecador de mí! **p.-box,**

cepillo, *m*. **p.-law,** ley de asistencia pública, *f*. **p.-spirited,** apocado
poorhouse *n* asilo, *m*
poorly *adv* pobremente; mal. *a* indispuesto, malo
poorness *n* pobreza, *f*; mala calidad, *f*; (lack) carestía, *f*; (of soil) infertilidad, *f*; (of character) mezquindad, *f*
pop *n* (of a cork) taponazo, *m*; (of a gun) detonación, *f*; (drink) gaseosa, *f*, *adv* ¡pum! *vi* (of a cork) saltar; (of guns) detonar. *vt* (corks) hacer saltar; (a gun, a question, etc.) disparar. **popgun,** escopeta de aire comprimido, *f*. **to pop down,** bajar a presuradamente. **to pop in,** (visit) dejarse caer; entrar rápidamente. **to pop off,** marcharse a prisa; (die) estirar la pata, *Lat. Am.* arrancarse. **to pop up,** subir corriendo; aparecer de pronto
popcorn *nsg* palomitas (de maíz), rosetas (de maíz) *fpl* (Spain), cabritos *mpl* (Chile), alborotos *mpl* (Argentina, Central America, Peru), cabritas *fpl* (elsewhere)
pope *n* Papa, *m*
poplar *n* (black) chopo, álamo, *m*; (white) álamo blanco, *m*. **p. grove,** alameda, *f*
poplin *n* popelina, *f*
poppy *n* amapola, adormidera, *f*
populace *n* pueblo, *m*; (scornful) populacho, *m*
popular *a* popular; en boga, de moda; cómun. **He is a p. hero,** Es un héroe popular
popularity *n* popularidad, *f*
popularization *n* vulgarización, *f*
popularize *vt* popularizar, vulgarizar
popularly *adv* popularmente
populate *vt* poblar
population *n* población, *f*
populous *a* populoso; muy poblado
porcelain *n* porcelana, *f*
porch *n* pórtico, *m*; (of a house) portal, *m*
porcine *a* porcino, porcuno
porcupine *n* puerco espín, *m*
pore *n* poro, *m*. **to p. over,** estar absorto en; examinar cuidadosamente
pork *n* carne de cerdo, *f*. **salt p.,** tocino, *m*. **p. butcher,** tocinero, *m*. **p. pie,** pastel de carne de cerdo, *m*
pornographic *a* pornográfico
pornography *n* pornografía, *f*
porosity *n* porosidad, *f*
porous *a* poroso
porphyry *n* pórfido, *m*
porpoise *n* marsopa, *f*, puerco marino, *m*
porridge *n* gachas, *f pl*, *m*
port *n* puerto, *m*; (in a ship) porta, *f*; (larboard) babor, *m*; (wine) vino de Oporto, *m*; (mien) porte, *m*, presencia, *f*. *vt* (the helm) poner a babor; *mil* llevar un fusil terciado. **to put into p.,** tomar puerto. **to stop at a p.,** hacer escala en un puerto. **p. dues,** derechos de puerto, *m pl*
portable *a* portátil; móvil. **p. typewriter,** máquina de escribir portátil (or de viaje), *f*. **p. wireless,** radio portátil, *f*
portal *n* portal, *m*
portcullis *n* rastrillo, *m*
portend *vt* presagiar, anunciar
portent *n* augurio, presagio, *m*; portento, *m*
portentous *a* ominoso; portentoso; importante
porter *n* (messenger) mozo de cordel, *m*; (of a university, hotel) portero, *m*; (of a block of flats) conserje, *m*; (railway) mozo de estación, *Argentina* changador, *m*; (drink) cerveza negra, *f*. **porter's lodge,** portería, *f*; conserjería, *f*
porterage *n* porte, *m*
portfolio *n* carpeta, *f*; (*pol* of a minister) cartera, *f*; (*pol* ministry) ministerio, *m*
porthole *n* tronera, *f*
portico *n* pórtico, *m*
portion *n* porción, *f*; parte, *f*; (marriage) dote, *mf*; (piece) pedazo, *m*; (in a restaurant) ración, *f*; (in life) fortuna, *f*. *vt* dividir; repartir; (dower) dotar
portliness *n* corpulencia, *f*
portly *a* corpulento, grueso
portmanteau *n* maleta, *f*
portmanteau word *n* palabra de acarreo, *f*
portrait *n* retrato, *m*. **p. painter,** pintor (-ra) de retratos
portraiture *n* retratos, *m pl*; descripción, pintura, *f*
portray *vt* retratar; pintar, representar; (in words) describir, pintar
portrayal *n* pintura, *f*; retrato, *m*; (in words) descripción, *f*
portrayer *n* retratista, *mf*, pintor (-ra)
portress *n* portera, *f*; (in a convent) tornera, *f*
Portuguese *a* portugués. *n* portugués (-esa); (language) portugués, *m*
pose *vt* colocar; (a problem, etc.) plantear; (a question) hacer; *vi* colocarse; (with as) echárselas de, dárselas de, fingir ser; hacerse pasar por. *n* actitud, postura, *f*; (affected) pose, *f*; (deception) engaño, *m*
poser *n* problema difícil, *m*; (in an examination) pega, *f*; pregunta embarazosa, *f*
position *n* posición, *f*; situación, *f*; actitud, postura, *f*; condición, *f*, estado, *m*; (post) puesto, empleo, *m*. **He is not in a p. to . . . ,** No está en condiciones de . . . , No está para . . . **to place in p.,** poner en posición, colocar
positive *a* positivo; absoluto; (convinced) convencido, seguro; (downright) categórico; *inf* completo. *n* realidad, *f*; *phot* (prueba) positiva, *f*
positively *adv* positivamente; categóricamente
positiveness *n* certitud, seguridad, *f*; terquedad, obstinacia, *f*
positivism *n* positivismo, *m*
posse *n* pelotón, *m*; multitud, muchedumbre, *f*
possess *vt* poseer; gozar (de); (of ideas, etc.) dominar. **to p. oneself of,** apoderarse de, apropiarse. **What possessed you to do it?** ¿Qué te hizo hacerlo?
possession *n* posesión, *f*. **to take p. of,** tomar posesión de; hacerse dueño de, apoderarse de; (a house, etc.) entrar en, ocupar
possessive *a* posesivo. *n* posesivo, *m*
possessor *n* poseedor (-ra); dueño (-ña); propietario (-ia)
possibility *n* posibilidad, *f*
possible *a* posible. **as soon as p.,** cuanto antes, lo más pronto posible. **to make p.,** hacer posible, posibilitar
possibly *adv* posiblemente; (perhaps) quizás. **I shall come as soon as I p. can,** Vendré lo más pronto posible
post *n* (pole) poste, *m*; (of a sentry, etc.) puesto, *m*; (employment) empleo, *m*; (mail) correo, *m*; *mil* toque, *m*. *vt* (a notice) fijar; anunciar; (to an appointment) destinar; (letters, etc.) echar al correo; *com* pasar al libro mayor; (inform) tener al corriente. *vi* viajar en posta. **"P. no bills!"** «Se prohibe fijar carteles.» **registered p.,** correo certificado, *m*. **p. card,** postal, *f*. **p.-chaise,** silla de posta, *f*. **p.-date,** posfecha, *f*. **p.-free,** franco de porte. **p.-haste,** con gran celeridad. **p.-horse,** caballo de posta, *m*. **p.-impressionism,** post-impresionismo, *m*. **p.-mortem,** *n* autopsia, *f*. **p.-natal,** post-natal. **p.-nuptial,** postnupcial. **p. office,** correo, *m*, correos, *m pl*; (on a train) ambulancia de correos, *f*. **p. office box,** *Spain* apartado de correos, *m*, *Lat. Am.* casilla, *f*. **p. office savings bank,** caja postal de ahorros, *f*. **p.-paid,** porte pagado; franco. **p.-war,** *n* postguerra, *f*. *a* de la postguerra
postage *n* porte de correos, franqueo, *m*. **p. stamp,** sello postal, *m*, *Mexico* timbre, m, *elsewhere in Lat. Am.* estampilla, *f*
postage meter *n* franqueadora, *f*
postal *a* postal. **p. money order** *Spain* giro postal, *m*, *Lat. Am.* libranza de correos, libranza postal, *f*. **p. order,** orden postal de pago, *f*. **p. packet,** paquete postal, *m*
poster *n* cartel, *m*. *vt* fijar carteles (a or en); anunciar por carteles. **bill-p.,** fijador de carteles, *m*
poste restante *n* lista de correos, *f*
posterior *a* posterior. *n* trasero, *m*, asentaderas, *f pl*

posteriority *n* posterioridad, *f*
posterity *n* posteridad, *f*
postgraduate *n* estudiante graduado que hace estudios avanzados, *m. a* avanzado; para estudiantes graduados
posthumous *a* póstumo
posthumously *adv* después de la muerte
postman *n* cartero, *m*
postmark *n* matasellos, *m, vt* poner matasellos (a)
postmaster *n* administrador de correos, *m*
postmistress *n* administradora de correos, *f*
postpone *vt* aplazar, diferir; retrasar; (subordinate) postergar
postponement *n* aplazamiento, *m*; tardanza, *f*
postscript *n* posdata, *f, Mexico* aumento, *m*
postulate *n* postulado, *m, vt* postular
posture *n* postura, actitud, *f*; (of affairs) estado, *m*, situación, *f. vi* tomar una postura
posy *n* (nosegay) ramillete de flores, *m*; flor, *f*; (motto) mote, *m*
pot *n* pote, *m*; tarro, *m*; (flower-) tiesto, *m*; (for cooking) olla marmita, *f*; jarro, *m. vt* plantar en tiestos; conservar en potes. **pot-bellied,** panzudo. **pot-boiler,** obra literaria escrita con el sólo propósito de ganar dinero, *f.* **pot-herb,** hierba que se emplea para sazonar, hortaliza, *f.* **pot-hole,** bache, **pot-luck,** comida ordinaria, *f.* **pot-shot,** tiro fácil, *m*; tiro al azar, *m*
potage *n* potaje, *m*
potash *n* potasa, *f.* **caustic p.,** potasa cáustica, *f*
potassium *n* potasio, *m*
potato *n* patata, *f.* **sweet p.,** batata, *f.* **p. beetle,** coleóptero de la patata, *m.* **p. omelet,** tortilla a la española, *f.* **p. patch,** patatal, *m.* **p. peeler,** pelapatatas, *m*
potency *n* potencia, *f*; fuerza, eficacia, *f*
potent *a* potente, fuerte; eficaz
potentate *n* potentado, *m*
potential *a* potencial; virtual; (*phys gram*) potencial, *n* poder, *m*; *gram* modo potencial, *m*; *phys* energía potencial, *f*; *elec* tensión potencial, *f*
potentiality *n* potencialidad, *f*
pothook *n* garabato de cocina, *m*; palote, *m*; (scrawl) garabato, *m*
potion *n* poción, *f*,
potpourri *n* popurrí, *m*
potter *n* alfarero, *m. vi* gandulear. *vt* perder. **potter's clay,** barro de alfarero, *m.* **potter's wheel,** tabanque, *m.* **potter's workshop,** alfar, *m*
pottery *n* alfarería, *f*; (china) loza, porcelana, *f*
pouch *n* bolsa, *f*; *zool* bolsa marsupial, *f*; (for tobacco) tabaquera, *f*; (for cartridges) cartuchera, *f. vt* embolsar. *vi* bolsear
poulterer *n* pollero (-ra)
poultice *n* apósito, emplasto, *m, vt* poner emplastos (a or en)
poultry *n* volatería, *f.* **p. dealer,** gallinero (-ra) vendedor (-ra) de volatería. **p. manure** *Mexico* cuitla, *f.* **p. yard,** gallinero, *m*
poultry farming *n* avicultura, *f*
pounce *n* (swoop) calada, *f. vi* (swoop) calarse; saltar (sobre); agarrar, hacer presa (en); *fig* atacar; descubrir, hacer patente
pound *n* (weight and currency) libra, *f*; (for cattle) corral de concejo, *m*; (thump) golpe, *m. vt* (break up) machacar, pistar; (beat) batir; (thump) golpear, aporrear. **p. sterling,** libra esterlina, *f.* **p. troy,** libra medicinal, *f*
pounding *n* machucamiento, *m*; batimiento, *m*
pour *vt* vaciar, verter; derramar. *vi* correr; (of rain) diluviar, llover a cántaros; (fill) llenar; (of crowds, words, etc.) derramarse. **to p. out the tea,** servir el té. **The crowd poured in,** La multitud entró en tropel
pouring *a* (of rain) torrencial
pout *vi* torcer el gesto; hacer pucheritos
poverty *n* pobreza, *f.* **p.-stricken,** menesteroso, indigente, necesitado
powder *n* polvo, *m*; (face) polvos de arroz, *m pl*; (gun) pólvora, *f. vt* polvorear; (crush) reducir a polvo, pulverizar. *vi* ponerse polvos. **p.-flash,** fogonazo, *m.* **p.-flask,** polvorín, *m.* **p.-magazine,** santabárbara, *f.* **p.-mill,** fábrica de pólvora, *f.* **p.-puff,** polvera, borla de empolvarse, *f*
powdered *a* en polvo
powdery *a* polvoriento; friable
power *n* poder, *m*; facultad, capacidad, *f*; vigor, *m*, fuerza, *f*; (*pol* and *math*) potencia, *f*; *mech* fuerza, *f*; influencia, *f.* **as far as lies within my p.,** en cuanto me sea posible. **It does not lie within my p.,** No está dentro de mis posibilidades, No está en mi poder. **the Great Powers,** las grandes potencias. **the powers that be,** los que mandan. **to be in p.,** estar en el poder. **p.-house, p.-station,** central eléctrica, *f.* **p. of attorney,** poderes, *m pl*, procuración, *f.* **to grant p. of attorney (to),** dar poderes (a)
powerful *a* poderoso; fuerte; eficaz; potente; (of arguments, etc.) convincente
powerfully *adv* poderosamente; fuertemente
powerless *a* impotente
power steering *n* dirección asistida *f* (Spain), servo dirección *f*
powwow *n* conferencia, *f*; conversación, *f*
pox *n* sífilis, *f*; (smallpox) viruelas, *f pl*; (chicken-pox) viruelas falsas, *f pl*
practicability *n* factibilidad, *f*
practicable *a* practicable, factible, posible; viable, transitable
practical *a* (doable) factible; práctico; virtual. **p. joke,** burla de consecuencias
practically *adv* prácticamente; en práctica; virtualmente; (in fact) en efecto. **p. nothing,** casi nada
practicalness *n* carácter práctico, *m*
practice *n* (custom) costumbre, *f*; práctica, *f*; ejercicio, *m*; (of a doctor, etc.) clientela, *f*; profesión, *f*; (religious) rito, *m*, ceremonias, *f pl*; (experience) experiencia, *f.* **It is not his p. to . . . ,** No es su costumbre de . . . **to be out of p.,** estar desentrenado. **to put into p.,** poner en práctica. **P. makes perfect,** El ejercicio hace maestro. *vt* tener la costumbre de; practicar; (a profession) ejercer; (a game) entrenarse en; (work at) estudiar; (a musical instrument) tocar; (accustom) acostumbrar. **to p. what one preaches,** predicar con el ejemplo
practiced *a* experimentado; experto
practitioner *n* médico (-ca). **general p.,** médico (-ca) general
pragmatic *a* pragmatista; (historical) pragmático; práctico
pragmatism *n* pragmatismo, *m*
pragmatist *n* pragmatista, *mf*
Prague Praga, *f*
prairie *n* pradera, sabana, pampa, *f, a* de la pradera, etc.
praise *vt* alabar; ensalzar, glorificar; elogiar. *n* alabanza, *f*; elogio, *m*; glorificación, *f*, ensalzamiento, *m.* **to p. to the skies,** poner en los cuernos de la luna poner por las nubes, poner sobre las estrellas hacerse lenguas de
praiseworthiness *n* mérito, *m*
praiseworthy *a* digno de alabanza, laudable
prance *vi* (of a horse) caracolear, encabritarse, cabriolar; saltar; andar airosamente. *n* corveta, cabriola, *f*; salto, *m*
prank *n* travesura, diablura, *f.* **to play pranks,** hacer diabluras
prate, prattle *vi* charlar, chacharear; (lisp) balbucir; (of brooks, etc.) murmurar, susurrar. *vt* divulgar. *n* charla, cháchara, *f*; balbuceo, *m*
prattler *n* parlanchín (-ina); (gossip) chismoso (-sa); (child) niño (-ña)
prattling *n* charla, *f*; (lisping) balbuceo, *m*; (of brooks, etc.) murmullo, susurro, ruido armonioso, *m. a* charlatán, gárrulo; balbuciente; (of brooks, etc.) parlero
prawn *n* camarón, *m*
pray *vt* and *vi* suplicar; implorar; rezar, orar. **P. be seated,** Haga el favor de sentarse
prayer *n* rezo, *m*, plegaria, oración, *f*; súplica, *f*; *law* petición, *f.* **p. book,** libro de devociones, devocionario, *m.*

p.-meeting, reunión para rezar, *f.* **p.-rug,** alfombra de rezo, *f*
praying *n* rezo, *m;* suplicación, *f*
pre- *prefix* de antes de (e.g. **pre-World-War-1 publications,** publicaciones de antes de la Primera Guerra Mundial)
preach *vt* and *vi* predicar
preacher *n* predicador (-ra). **to turn p.,** meterse a predicar
preaching *n* predicación, *f, a* predicador
preamble *n* preámbulo, *m*
prearrange *vt* preparar de antemano, predisponer
precarious *a* precario; inseguro; incierto, arriesgado
precariousness *n* condición precaria, *f;* inseguridad, *f;* incertidumbre, *f*
precaution *n* precaución, *f.* **to take precautions,** tomar precauciones
precautionary *a* de precaución; preventivo
precede *vt* preceder (a), anteceder (a); tomar precedencia (a), exceder en importancia (a). *vi* ir delante; tener la precedencia
precedence *n* precedencia, *f;* prioridad, *f;* superioridad, *f.* **to take p. over,** tomar precedencia (a), preceder (a)
precedent *n* precedente, *m, a* precedente. **without p.,** sin precedente
preceding *a* anterior, precedente
precept *n* precepto, *m*
preceptor *n* preceptor, *m*
precinct *n* (police station) *Argentina* comisaría de sección, *Mexico* delegación, *f*
precincts *n pl* recinto, *m;* ámbito, *m;* distrito, barrio, *m*
preciosity *n* afectación, *f*
precious *a* precioso; de gran valor; hermoso; amado; muy querido; (with rogue, etc.) redomado; completo. **p. little,** muy poco. **p. nearly,** casi, por poco . . . **p. stone,** piedra preciosa, *f*
preciousness *n* preciosidad, *f;* gran valor, *m*
precipice *n* precipicio, *m*
precipitancy *n* precipitación, *f*
precipitant *a* precipitado
precipitate *vt* precipitar, despeñar, arrojar; acelerar; *chem* precipitar. *vi* precipitarse. *n* precipitado, *m. a* precipitado, súbito. **to p. oneself,** tirarse, lanzarse
precipitately *adv* precipitadamente
precipitation *n chem* precipitación, *f; chem* precipitado, *m;* (rain, etc.) precipitación pluvial, *f*
precipitous *a* precipitoso, escarpado, acantilado
precipitously *adv* en precipicio
precise *a* preciso; exacto; justo; puntual; escrupuloso; formal; claro; pedante, afectado; ceremonioso
precisely *adv* precisamente; exactamente; puntualmente; escrupulosamente; claramente; con afectación; ceremoniosamente. **at six o'clock p.,** a las seis en punto
precision *n* precisión, *f;* exactitud, *f;* puntualidad, *f;* escrupulosidad, *f;* claridad, *f;* afectación, *f;* ceremonia, *f*
preclude *vt* excluir; impedir, hacer imposible
preclusion *n* exclusión, *f;* imposibilidad, *f*
precocious *a* precoz
precocity *n* precocidad, *f*
preconceived *a* preconcebido
preconception *n* idea preconcebida, *f;* (prejudice) prejuicio, *m*
preconcerted *a* concertado de antemano
precursor *n* precursor (-ra)
precursory *a* precursor
predatory *a* rapaz; de rapiña; voraz
predecease *vt* morir antes (de or que); *law* premorir. *n law* premuerto, *m*
predecessor *n* predecesor (-ra); (ancestor) antepasado, *m*
predestination *n* predestinación, *f*
predestine *vt* predestinar
predetermination *n* predeterminación, *f*
predetermine *vt* predeterminar
predicament *n* (logic) predicamento, *m;* situación, *f;* (fix) apuro, *m; pl* **predicaments,** categorías, *f pl*
predicate *vt* afirmar. *n* (logic, *gram*) predicado, *m*
predict *vt* predecir, pronosticar, profetizar
prediction *n* predicción, *f;* pronóstico, vaticinio, *m,* profecía, *f*
predilection *n* predilección, *f*
predispose *vt* predisponer
predisposition *n* predisposición, *f*
predominance *n* predominio, *m*
predominant *a* predominante
predominate *vi* predominar
preeminence *n* preeminencia, *f;* primacia, superioridad, *f*
preeminent *a* preeminente; superior; extraordinario
preeminently *adv* preeminentemente; extraordinariamente; por excelencia; entre todos
preen *vt* (of birds) limpiarse; (of people) darse humos, jactarse
preexist *vi* preexistir
preexistence *n* preexistencia, *f*
prefabricated *a* prefabricado
preface *n* prólogo, *m; ecc* prefacio, *m;* introducción, *f. vt* dar principio (a), empezar. **He prefaced his remarks by . . . ,** Dijo a modo de introducción
prefatory *a* preliminar, introductorio; a manera de prólogo
prefect *n* prefecto, *m*
prefecture *n* prefectura, *f*
prefer *vt* preferir, gustar más (a); (promote) ascender, elevar; (a charge, etc.) presentar. **to p. a charge against,** pedir en juicio (a). **I p. oranges to apples,** Me gustan más las naranjas que las manzanas, Prefiero las naranjas a las manzanas
preferability *n* preferencia, ventaja, *f*
preferable *a* preferible
preferably *adv* preferiblemente, con preferencia
preference *n* preferencia, *f;* privilegio, *m.* **p. share,** acción privilegiada, acción preferente, *f*
preferential *a* preferente
preferment *n* promoción, *f,* ascenso, *m;* puesto eminente, *m*
preferred *a* preferente; favorito, predilecto. **p. share,** acción preferente, *f*
prefix *vt* anteponer, prefijar; (to a word) poner prefijo (a). *n* prefijo, *m*
pregnancy *n* embarazo, *m,* preñez, *f*
pregnant *a* embarazada, encinta, preñada, *f; fig* fértil; *fig* preñado
prehensile *a* prensil
prehistoric *a* prehistórico
prehistory *n* prehistoria, *f*
prejudge *vt* prejuzgar
prejudice *n* prejuicio, *m; law* perjuicio, *m. vt* influir, predisponer; (damage) perjudicar. **without p.,** sin perjuicio
prejudiced *a* parcial; con prejuicios
prejudicial *a* perjudicial
prelacy *n* prelacía, *f;* episcopado, *m*
prelate *n* prelado, *m*
preliminarily *adv* preliminarmente
preliminary *a* preliminar. *n* preliminar, *m*
prelude (to) *n* preludio (de) *m;* presagio (de) *m, vt* and *vi* preludiar
premature *a* prematuro
prematurely *adv* prematuramente
prematureness *n* lo prematuro
premeditate *vt* premeditar
premeditatedly *adv* premeditadamente, con premeditación
premeditation *n* premeditación, *f*
premier *a* primero, principal. *n* primer ministro, *m;* (in Spain) presidente del Consejo de Ministros, *m*
premiere *n* estreno, *m*
premiership *n* puesto de primer ministro, *m; in Spain* presidencia del Consejo de Ministros, *f*
premise *n* (logic) premisa, *f; pl* **premises,** local, *m;*

recinto, *m*; establecimiento, *m*; propiedad, *f*; tierras, *f pl*. **on the premises,** en el local; en el establecimiento
premium *n* (prize) premio, *m*, recompensa, *f*; *com* prima, *f*; precio, *m*. **at a p.,** a premio; a una prima; (of shares) sobre la par; *fig* en boga, muy solicitado, en gran demanda
premonition *n* presentimiento, presagio, *m*
premonitory *a* premonitorio
prenatal *a* prenatal, antenatal
preoccupation *n* preocupación, *f*
preoccupied *a* preocupado; abstraído, absorto
preoccupy *vt* preocupar
prepaid *a* porte pagado, franco de porte
preparation *n* preparación, *f*; preparativo, *m*, disposición, *f*; (patent food) preparado, *m*. **I have made all my preparations,** He hecho todos mis preparativos. **The book is in p.,** El libro está en preparación
preparative *a* preparativo. *n* preparativo, *m*
preparatory *a* preparatorio, preparativo; preliminar. **p. school,** escuela preparatoria, *f*, *m*. **p. to,** como preparación para; antes de
prepare *vt* preparar; aparejar, aviar; equipar; (cloth) aprestar. *vi* prepararse; hacer preparativos
preparedness *n* estado de preparación, *m*; preparación, *f*, apercibimiento, *m*
prepay *vt* pagar adelantado, *Lat. Am.* aprontar; (a letter, etc.) franquear
prepayment *n* pago adelantado, *m*; (of a letter, etc.) franqueo, *m*
preponderance *n* preponderancia, *f*
preponderant *a* preponderante, predominante
preponderantly *adv* predominantemente; en su mayoría
preponderate *vi* preponderar; prevalecer (sobre), predominar (sobre)
preposition *n* preposición, *f*
prepossess *vt* predisponer; causar buena impresión (a)
prepossessing *a* atractivo
preposterous *a* ridículo, absurdo
preposterously *adv* absurdamente
preposterousness *n* ridiculez, *f*
Prep School *n* preparatoria, *f*
prepuce *n* prepucio, *m*
Pre-Raphaelite *a* and *n* prerrafaelista, *mf*
prerequisite *n* requisito necesario, esencial, *m*, *a* previamente necesario, esencial
prerogative *n* prerrogativa, *f*
presage *n* presagio, *m*; anuncio, *m*. *vt* presagiar; anunciar
Presbyterian *a* and *n* presbiteriano (-na)
prescience *n* presciencia, previsión, *f*
prescient *a* presciente
prescind *vt* prescindir (de); separar (de). *vi* separarse
prescribe *vt* and *vi* prescribir; *med* recetar; dar leyes; *law* prescribir
prescription *n* prescripción, *f*; *med* receta, *f*
presence *n* presencia, *f*; (ghost) aparición, *f*. **in the p. of,** en presencia de, delante; a vista de. **p. of mind,** presencia de ánimo, serenidad de ánimo, *f*
present *a* presente; actual; (with month) corriente; *gram* presente. **at p.,** al presente, actualmente. **at the p. day,** a la fecha, en la actualidad, hoy día. **P. company excepted!** ¡Mejorando lo presente! **the present writer,** el que suscribe, el que esto escribe, el que estas líneas traza. **to be p. at,** presenciar, ser testigo de; asistir a, acudir a; hallarse en. **p.-day,** de hoy, actual. **p. tense,** *gram* tiempo presente, *m*
present *n* (time) presente, *m*; actualidad, *f*; *gram* tiempo presente, *m*; (gift) regalo, *m*, dádiva, *f*. **By these presents . . . ,** *law* Por estas presentes . . . **to make a p. of,** regalar. **Jane made me a p. of a watch,** Juana me regaló un reloj
present *vt* presentar; ofrecer; manifestar; (a gift) regalar, dar; (*ecc mil*) presentar. **New problems presented themselves,** Nuevos problemas surgieron. **to p. arms,** presentar las armas. **He presented himself in the office,** Se presentó en la oficina. **He presented his friend Mr. Moreno to me,** Me presentó a su amigo el Sr. Moreno
presentable *a* presentable
presentation *n* presentación, *f*; homenaje, *m*; (exhibition) exposición, *f*. **on p.,** *com* a presentación
presentiment *n* presentimiento, *m*, corazonada, *f*. **I had a p. that . . . ,** Tuve el presentimiento de que . . . , Tuve una corazonada que . . . **to have a p. about,** presentir
presently *adv* pronto; en seguida; dentro de poco
preservation *n* conservación, *f*; (from harm) preservación, *f*
preservative *a* preservativo. *n* preservativo, *m*
preserve *vt* preservar (de); guardar; proteger; conservar; *cul* hacer conservas de; (in syrup) almibarar. *n cul* conserva, *f*; (of fruit) compota, confitura, *f*; (covert) coto, *m*. **preserved fruit,** dulce de almíbar, *m*. **p. dish,** compotera, *f*
preserver *n* conservador (-ra); (saviour) salvador (-ra); (benefactor) bienhechor (-ra)
preserving *n* (from harm) preservación, *f*; conservación, *f*. **p. pan,** cazuela para conservas, *f*
preside *vi* (over) presidir; dirigir, gobernar. **He presided at the meeting,** Presidio la reunión
presidency *n* presidencia, *f*
president *n* presidente, *m*; (of a college) rector, *m*. **lady p.,** presidenta, *f*
presidential *a* presidencial
presidentship *n* presidencia, *f*
press *vt* prensar; (juice out of) exprimir; (clothes) planchar; (a bell, a hand, and of a shoe, etc.) apretar, *Mexico* apachurrar; (embrace) dar un abrazo (a); (a stamp, a kiss, etc.) imprimir; (an enemy) hostigar, acosar; (in a game) apretar; (crowd upon) oprimir; (emphasize) insistir en; (urge) instar, instigar; (compel) obligar; apremiar; (oppress) abrumar, agobiar; (paper) satinar; (an advantage) aprovecharse de. **Lola pressed his hand,** Lola le apretó la mano. **Time presses,** El tiempo es breve. **I did not p. the point,** No insistí. **to p. against,** pegar(se) contra. **to p. down,** comprimir; *fig* agobiar. **to p. for,** exigir, reclamar. **to p. forward, on,** avanzar; seguir el camino, continuar la marcha; (hurry) apretar el paso
press *n* (pressure) apretón, *m*; (push) golpe, *m*; (throng) muchedumbre, *f*; (of business, etc.) urgencia, *f*; (apparatus) prensa, *f*; (printing press and publishing firm) imprenta, *f*; (cupboard) armario, *m*. **Associated P.,** Prensa Asociada, *f*. **freedom of the p.,** libertad de la prensa, *f*. **in p., in the p.,** en prensa. **in the p. of battle,** en lo más reñido de la batalla. **to go to p.,** entrar en prensa. **p.-agent,** agente de publicidad, *m*. **p.-box,** tribuna de la prensa, *f*. **p. clipping, p.-cutting,** recorte de prensa, *m*. **p.-gallery,** tribuna de la prensa, *f*. **p.-gang,** ronda de enganche, *f*. **p.-mark,** número de catálogo, *m*. **p. proof,** prueba de imprenta, *f*. **p.-room,** taller de imprenta, *m*. **p.-stud,** botón automático, *m*. **p. conference,** rueda de prensa, entrevista de prensa, conferencia de pensa, *f*
pressing *a* urgente, apremiante; importuno. *n* prensado, *m*, prensadura, *f*; expresión, *f*; (of a garment) planchado, *m*
pressingly *adv* urgentemente, con urgencia; importunamente
pressman *n* tirador, *m*; (journalist) periodista, *m*
pressure *n* presión, *f*; (of the hand) apretón, *m*; apremio, *m*; opresión, *f*; (weight) peso, *m*; (force) fuerza, *f*; urgencia, *f*. **p.-cooker,** cazuela de presión, olla de presión, *f*, presto, *m*. **p.-gauge,** manómetro, *m*
prestidigitation *n* prestidigitación, *f*, juegos de manos, *m pl*
prestige *n* prestigio, *m*
prestigious *a* prestigiado
presumable *a* presumible
presume *vt* presumir; suponer, sospechar; (attempt) pretender. *vi* presumir; tomarse libertades; abusar (de)

presumption *n* presunción, *f;* suposición, *f;* (effrontery) atrevimiento, *m;* insolencia, *f*
presumptive *a* presuntivo; (with heir, etc.) presunto
presumptuous *a* presumido, insolente, presuntuoso; atrevido
presumptuously *adv* presuntuosamente
presumptuousness *n* presunción, presuntuosidad, *f;* atrevimiento, *m*
presuppose *vt* presuponer
presupposition *n* presuposición, *f*
pretence *n* (claim) pretensión, *f;* afectación, *f;* (simulation) fingimiento, *m;* pretexto, *m.* **false pretences,** apariencias fingidas, *f pl;* engaño, *m,* estafa, *f.* **to make a p. of,** fingir. **under p. of,** bajo pretexto de
pretend *vt* dar como pretexto de; aparentar, fingir, simular, hacer el papel (de). *vi* pretender (a); tener pretensiones (de); ser pretendiente (a); fingir
pretended *a* supuesto, fingido; falso
pretender *n* pretendiente, *m;* hipócrita, *mf*
pretension *n* pretensión, *f;* afectación, simulación, *f*
pretentious *a* pretencioso; (of persons) presumido
pretentiousness *n* pretensiones, *f pl,* lo pretencioso
preterite *n* (tiempo) pretérito, *m, a* pretérito, pasado
pretext *n* pretexto, *m. vt* pretextar. **under p. of,** bajo pretexto de, so color de
prettily *adv* lindamente; con gracia; agradablemente
prettiness *n* lo bonito; elegancia, *f;* gracia, *f*
pretty *a* bonito; (of women, children) guapo, mono; (of men) lindo; elegante; excelente; *iron* bueno. *adv* bastante; medianamente; (very) muy; (almost) casi. **p. good,** bastante bueno. **p.-p.,** de muñeca; mono. *n* chuchería, *f,* guapos, *m pl.* **p. ways,** monerías, *f pl*
prevail *vi* prevalecer, predominar; ser la costumbre. **to p. against or over,** triunfar de, vencer (a). **to p. on, upon,** inducir, convencer, persuadir. **to be prevailed upon to,** dejarse persuadir a
prevailing *a* prevaleciente; dominante; predominante, reinante; general; común; (fashionable) en boga
prevalence *n* predominio, *m;* existencia, *f;* (habit) costumbre, *f;* (fashion) boga, *f*
prevalent *a* prevaleciente; predominante; general; común; corriente; (fashionable) en boga
prevaricate *vi* tergiversar; *law* prevaricar
prevarication *n* tergiversación, *f,* equívoco, *m*
prevaricator *n* tergiversador (-ra)
prevent *vt* evitar; (hinder) impedir (a)
preventable *a* evitable
prevention *n* prevención, *f;* (preventive) estorbo, obstáculo, *m*
preventive *a* preventivo. *n* preservativo, *m*
preview *n* vista de antemano, *f;* (of a film) avances, *m pl* (Cuba, Mexico), colas, *f pl* (Argentina), cortos *m pl* (Venezuela), sinopsis, *f* (Uruguay), tráiler, *m* (Spain)
previous *a* previo, anterior. **p. to,** antes de
previously *adv* anteriormente, antes, previamente
previousness *n* anterioridad, *f;* inoportunidad, *f*
prevision *n* previsión, *f*
prewar *a* de antes de la guerra
prey *n* presa, *f; fig* víctima, *f;* (booty) botín, *m. vi* (of animals) devorar; (plunder) robar, pillar; (of sorrow, etc.) hacer presa (de); agobiar, consumir; (sponge on) vivir a costa de. **to fall a p. to,** ser víctima de
price *n* precio, *m;* valor, *m;* costa, *f. vt* evaluar, tasar; poner precio a; preguntar el precio de; fijar el precio de. **at any p.,** a cualquier precio; (whatever the cost) cueste lo que cueste. **at a reduced p.,** a precio reducido. **fixed p.,** precio fijo, *m.* **p. ceiling,** precio máximo, precio tope, *m.* **p. control,** control de precios, *m.* **price list,** lista de precios, *f;* tarifa, *f;* (of shares, etc.) boletín de cotización, *m.* **Prices are subject to change without notice,** Los precios están sujetos a variación sin previo aviso.
priceless *a* sin precio; (amusing) divertidisimo. **These jewels are p.,** Estas joyas no tienen precio
prick *n* pinchazo, *m;* picadura, *f;* punzada, *f;* (prickle) espina, *f;* (with a goad) aguijonazo, *m;* (with a pin) alfilerazo, *m;* (with a spur) espolada, *f;* (of conscience) remordimiento, escrúpulo, *m. vt* pinchar, punzar; picar; (with remorse) atormentar, causar remordimiento (a); (urge on) incitar. **to p. the ears,** aguzar las orejas
pricking *n* picadura, *f;* punzada, *f.* **prickings of conscience,** remordimientos, *m pl*
prickle *n* espina, *f;* (irritation) escozor, *m*
prickly *a* espinoso; erizado. **p. heat,** salpullido causado por exceso de calor, *m.* **p. pear,** higo chumbo, *m,* chumbera, *f*
pride *n* orgullo, *m;* arrogancia, *f;* (splendour) pompa, *f,* fausto, aparato, *m;* belleza, *f;* vigor, *m;* (of lions) manada, *f.* **to take p. in,** estar orgulloso de. **to p. oneself,** sentirse orgulloso, ufanarse. **to p. oneself upon,** jactarse de, preciarse de
prie-dieu *n* reclinatorio, *m*
prier *n* espía, *mf;* curioso (-sa)
priest *n* sacerdote, *m;* cura, *m.* **high-p.,** sumo sacerdote, *m.* **p.-ridden,** dominado por el clero
priestess *n* sacerdotisa, *f*
priesthood *n* sacerdocio, *m*
priestly *a* sacerdotal
prig *n* fatuo (-ua), mojigato (-ta)
priggish *a* fatuo, gazmoño
priggishness *n* gazmoñería, fatuidad, *f*
prim *a* almidonado, etiquetero; peripuesto; afectado
primacy *n* primacía, *f*
prima donna *n* cantatriz, *f*
primarily *adv* en primer lugar principalmente
primary *a* primario; primitivo; principal. **p. education,** enseñanza primaria, *f.* **p. color,** color primario, *m.* **p. school,** escuela primaria, *f.* **p. election,** elección interna (dentro de un partido), *f*
primate *n* primado, *m*
prime *a* primero; principal; excelente; de primera calidad; de primera clase. *n* (spring) primavera, *f;* (of life, etc.) flor, *f,* vigor, *m;* (best) nata, crema, *f; ecc* prima, *f;* (number) número primo, *m. vt* preparar, aprestar; (fire-arms) cebar. **p. the pump**, cebar la bomba; (with paint, etc.) imprimar; (instruct) dar instrucciones (a), informar. **in his p.,** en la flor de su edad. **of p. quality,** de primera calidad. **P. Minister,** Primer Ministro, *m.* **p. necessity,** artículo de primera necesidad, *m*
primer *n* cartilla, *f,* abecedario, *m;* libro de lectura, *m;* (prayer book) devocionario, *m*
primeval *a* primevo, primitivo
priming *n* preparación, *f;* (of fire-arms) cebo, *m;* (of paint, etc.) imprimación, *f;* instrución, *f*
primitive *a* primitivo; anticuado. *n* primitivo, *m*
primitiveness *n* lo primitivo; carácter primitivo, *m*
primly *adv* afectadamente, con afectación; gravemente
primness *n* afectación, *f;* gravedad, *f*
primogeniture *n* primogenitura, *f*
primordial *a* primordial
primrose *n* primavera, *f;* color amarillo pálido, *m*
prince *n* príncipe, *m.* **P. Consort,** príncipe consorte, *m.* **P. of Wales,** (Britain) príncipe heredero, *m;* (Spanish equivalent) Príncipe de Asturias, *m.* **p. regent,** príncipe regente, *m.* **P. Charming,** el Príncipe Azul, *m*
princeliness *n* magnificencia, *f;* nobleza, *f*
princely *a* principesco; magnífico; noble
princess *n* princesa, *f*
principal *a* principal; fundamental; mayor. *n* principal, jefe, *m;* (of a university) rector, *m;* (of a school) director (-ra); *law* causante, *m; com* capital, *m*
principality *n* principado, *m*
principally *adv* principalmente
principle *n* principio, *m.* **in p.,** en principio
principled *a* de principios . . .
print *n* (mark) impresión, marca, *f;* (type) letra de molde, *f,* tipo, *m;* (of books) imprenta, *f;* (fabric) estampado, *m;* (picture) grabado, *m;* (photograph) positiva impresa, *f;* (mold) molde, *m. vt* marcar; imprimir; (on the mind) grabar; *print* tirar, hacer una tirada (de); (in photography) tirar una prueba (de); (publish) sacar a

luz, publicar; (fabrics) estampar. **in p.,** impreso; publicado; **He likes to see his name in print,** Le gusta ver su nombre en letras de molde; (available) existente. **to be out of p.,** estar agotado. **p. dress,** vestido estampado, *m*

printed *a* impreso. **p. fabric,** estampado, *m*. **p. matter,** impresos, *m pl*

printer *n* impresor, *m*; tipógrafo, *m*. **printer's devil,** aprendiz de impresor, *m*. **printer's ink,** tinta de imprenta, tinta tipográfica, *f*. **printer's mark,** pie de imprenta, *m*

printing *n* imprenta, *f*; impresión, *f*; (of fabrics) estampación, *f*; (art of) tipografía, *f*. **p. house,** imprenta, *f*. **p. machine,** máquina de imprimir, *f*. **p. press,** prensa tipográfica, *f*. **p. types,** caracteres de imprenta, *m pl*

prior *n* prior, *m*, *a* anterior, previo. **p. to,** anterior a, antes de

prioress *n* priora, *f*

priority *n* prioridad, *f*

prism *n* prisma, *m*; espectro solar, *m*

prismatic *a* prismático

prison *n* prisión, cárcel, *f*. **p.-breaking,** huida de la prisión, *f*. **p. camp,** campo de prisioneros, *m*. **p. van,** coche celular, *m*. **p. yard,** patio de la prisión, *m*

prisoner *n* prisionero (-ra), preso (-sa). **to take p.,** prender, hacer prisionero (a)

pristine *a* pristino, original

privacy *n* soledad, *f*, aislamiento, retiro, *m*; intimidad, *f*; secreto, *m*

private *a* particular; privado; secreto; confidencial; reservado; íntimo; personal; doméstico; (of hearings, etc.) a puertas cerradas, secreto; (own) propio. *n* (soldier) soldado raso, *m*. **in p.,** en secreto; confidencialmente, de persona a persona. **They wish to be p.,** Quieren estar a solas. **p. company,** sociedad en comandita, *f*. **p. hotel,** pensión, *f*. **p. house,** casa particular, *f*. **p. individual,** particular, *mf*. **p. interview,** entrevista privada, *f*. **p. life,** vida privada, *f*. **p. office,** despacho particular, *m*. **p. secretary,** secretario (-ia) particular. **p. viewing, (of a film)** función privada, *f*; **(of an exhibition)** día de inauguración, *m*

privateer *n* corsario, *m*

privately *adv* privadamente; en secreto; personalmente; confidencialmente; (of hearings) a puertas cerradas

privation *n* privación, *f*; carencia, escasez, *f*

privet *n* alheña, *f*

privilege *n* privilegio, *m*; derecho, *m*; inmunidad, *f*. *vt* privilegiar

privileged *a* privilegiado; confidencial

privy *a* privado; cómplice; enterado; personal, particular. *n* (latrine) retrete, *m*. **p. council,** consejo privado, *m*

prize *n* premio, *m*; recompensa, *f*, galardón, *m*; (capture) presa, *f*. *a* que ha ganado un premio; premiado; (huge) enorme; (complete) de primer orden. *vt* estimar, apreciar. **to p. open,** abrir con una palanca. **to carry off the p.,** ganar el premio. **cash p.,** premio en metálico, *m*. **first p.,** primer premio, *m*; (in a lottery) premio gordo, *m*. **p. court,** tribunal de presas, *m*. **p. fight,** partido de boxeo, *m*. **p. fighter,** boxeador, *m*. **p. giving,** distribución de premios, *f*. **p. money,** premio en metálico, *m*; (boxing) bolsa, *f*

pro *prep* pro. **pro forma invoice,** factura simulada, *f*

probability *n* probabilidad, *f*

probable *a* probable

probably *adv* probablemente

probate *n* verificación de un testamento, *f*

probation *n* probación, *f*; *law* libertad vigilada, *f*

probationary *a* de probación; de prueba

probationer *n* novicio, *m*; estudiante de enfermera, *f*; candidato, *m*; aspirante, *m*

probe *n surg* sonda, cala, tienta, *f*. *vt surg* tentar; escudriñar

probing *n* sondeo, *m*

probity *n* probidad, integridad, *f*

problem *n* problema, *m*; cuestión, *f*. **p. play,** drama de tesis, *m*

problematic *a* problemático

problem child *n* niño problemático, *m* (male), niña problemática, *f* (female)

proboscis *n* (of an elephant) trompa, *f*; (of an insect) trompetilla, *f*

Probus Probo, *m*

procedure *n* procedimiento, *m*

proceed *vi* seguir el camino, continuar la marcha; avanzar, seguir adelante; ir; proceder; ponerse (a); empezar (a); (say) proseguir; (come to) llegar a, ir a; (of a play, etc.) desarrollarse. **Before we p. any further . . .** Antes de ir más lejos . . . **to p. to blows,** llegar a las manos. **to p. against,** proceder contra, procesar. **to p. from,** venir de. **to p. with,** proseguir; poner por obra; usar

proceeding *n* modo de obrar, *m*; conducta, *f*; procedimiento, *m*; transacción, *f*; *pl* **proceedings,** (measures) medidas, *f pl*, actos, *m pl*; (of a learned society or a conference) actas, *f pl*. **to take proceedings against,** *law* procesar

proceeds *n pl* producto, *m*; ganancias, *f pl*; beneficios, *m pl*. **net p.,** producto neto, *m*

process *n* proceso, *m*; (method) procedimiento, *m*; (course) curso, *m*; marcha, *f*; (*law zool*) proceso, *m*. *vt* beneficiar (ore), trasformar, elaborar. **in p. of,** en curso de. **in the p. of time,** con el tiempo marchando el tiempo

processing industry *n* industria de trasformación, industria de elaboración, *f*

procession *n* desfile, *m*; cortejo, *m*; (religious) procesión, *f*. **funeral p.,** cortejo fúnebre, *m*. **to walk in p.,** desfilar

processional *a* procesional

proclaim *vt* proclamar; publicar, pregonar; anunciar; (reveal) revelar; (outlaw) denunciar

proclamation *n* proclamación, *f*; proclama, *f*, anuncio, *m*; declaración, *f*

proclivity *n* proclividad, propensión, *f*

procrastinate *vi* tardar (en decidirse), aplazar su decisión; vacilar; perder el tiempo

procrastination *n* dilación, tardanza, *f*; vacilación, *f*; pereza, *f*

procrastinator *n* perezoso (-sa)

procreate *vt* procrear

procreation *n* procreación, *f*

procreator *n* procreador (-ra)

proctor *n* procurador, *m*; *univ* censor, *m*

procurable *a* procurable; asequible

procure *vt* obtener, conseguir, lograr

procurement *n* obtención, *f*, logro, *m*

procurer *n* alcahuete, *m*

procuress *n* alcahueta, celestina, trotaconventos, *f*

prod *n* (with a bayonet, etc.) punzada, *f*; *fig* pinchazo, *m*. *vt* punzar; (in the ribs, etc.) clavar; *fig* pinchar

prodigal *a* and *n* pródigo (-ga)

prodigality *n* prodigalidad, *f*

prodigally *adv* pródigamente

prodigious *a* prodigioso

prodigiousness *n* prodigiosidad, *f*; enormidad, *f*

prodigy *n* prodigio, *m*; portento, *m*. **child p.,** niño prodigio

produce *vt* producir; dar frutos; (show) mostrar, presentar; (take out) sacar; (occasion) causar, traer consigo, ocasionar; (goods) fabricar, manufacturar; (of shares, etc.) rendir; *geom* prolongar; (a play) poner en escena. *n* producto, *m*; víveres, comestibles, *m pl*

producer *n* productor (-ra); *theat* director de escena, *m*

product *n* producto, *m*; (result) fruto, resultado, *m*, consecuencia, *f*; *math* producto, *m*

production *n* producción, *f*; producto, *m*; *geom* prolongación, *f*; (of a play) dirección escénica, *f*; (performance) producción, *f*. **p. cost,** coste de producción, *m*

productive *a* productivo

productivity *n* productividad, *f*

profanation *n* profanación, *f*
profane *a* profano; sacrílego, blasfemo. *vt* profanar
profaner *n* profanador (-ra)
profanity *n* profanidad, *f*; blasfemia, *f*
profess *vt* (assert) afirmar, manifestar; declarar; (a faith, a profession, teach) profesar; (feign) fingir; (pretend) tener pretensiones de. *vi* (as a monk or nun) tomar estado, entrar en religión. **He professed himself surprised,** Se declaró sorprendido
professed *a* declarado; *ecc* profeso; ostensible, fingido
profession *n* profesión, *f*; carrera, *f*; declaración, *f*. **p. of faith,** profesión de fe, *f*. **the learned professions,** las carreras liberales
professional *a* profesional; de la profesión; de profesión; de carrera. **p. diplomat,** diplomático (-ca) de carrera. **p. etiquette,** etiqueta profesional, *f*. **p. man,** hombre profesional, *m*; hombre de carrera liberal, *m*
professor *n* catedrático (-ca), profesor (-ra)
professorate *n* profesorado, *m*
professorial *a* de catedrático; de profesor
professorship *n* cátedra, *f*
proffer *vt* proponer; ofrecer. *n* oferta, *f*
proficiency *n* pericia, habilidad, *f*
proficient *a* proficiente, experto, adepto, perito
profile *n* perfil, *m*. *vt* perfilar. **in p.,** de perfil
profit *n* provecho, *m*; utilidad, *f*; ventaja, *f*; *com* ganancia, *f*, *vt* aprovechar. *vi* ganar; *com* sacar ganancia. **to p. by,** aprovechar. **gross p.,** ganancia total, *f*. **p. and loss,** ganancias y pérdidas, *f pl*. **p. sharing,** participación en las ganancias, participación de utilidades, *f*
profitable *a* provechoso, útil, ventajoso; lucrativo. **p. use,** aprovechamiento, *m*
profitably *adv* con provecho, provechosamente; lucrativamente
profiteer *n* estraperlista, *mf*
profit incentive *n* acicate del lucro, *m*
profitless *a* sin provecho, infructuoso, inútil
profligacy *n* libertinaje, *m*
profligate *a* licencioso, disoluto. *n* libertino, *m*
profound *a* profundo
profundity *n* profundidad, *f*
profuse *a* profuso; pródigo; lujoso
profusely *adv* profusamente; pródigamente; lujosamente
profusion *n* profusión, abundancia, *f*; prodigalidad, *f*; exceso, *m*
progenitor *n* progenitor, *m*; (ancestor) antepasado, *m*
progeny *n* prole, *f*
prognosis *n* prognosis, *f*; presagio, *m*; *med* pronóstico, *m*
prognosticate *vt* pronosticar, presagiar
prognostication *n* pronosticación, *f*; pronóstico, presagio, augurio, *m*
program *n* programa, *m*
progress *n* progreso, *m*; avance, *m*; (betterment) mejora, *f*; (of events) marcha, *f*. *vi* avanzar, marchar; (improve) progresar, adelantar; mejorar. **to make p.,** adelantarse; hacer progresos
progression *n* progresión, *f*
progressive *a* progresivo; avanzado; *pol* progresista. *n pol* progresista, *mf*
progressiveness *n* carácter progresivo, *m*
prohibit *vt* prohibir; defender; (prevent) impedir, privar. **His health prohibited him from doing it,** Su salud le impidió hacerlo
prohibition *n* prohibición, *f*; interdicción, *f*; (of alcohol) prohibicionismo, *m*
prohibitionist *n* prohibicionista, *mf*
prohibitive *a* prohibitivo, prohibitorio
project *vt* (all meanings) proyectar. *vi* sobresalir; destacarse. *n* proyectil, plan, *m*
projectile *n* proyectil, *m*, *a* arrojadizo
projecting *a* saliente; (of teeth) saltón
projection *n* (hurling) lanzamiento, *m*; prominencia, protuberancia, *f*; (other meanings) proyección, *f*
projector *n* proyectista, *mf*; proyector, *m*
proletarian *a* proletario
proletariate *n* proletariado, *m*
prolific *a* prolífico; fecundo, fértil
prolix *a* prolijo
prolixity *n* prolijidad, *f*
prolog *n* prólogo, *m*, *vt* prologar
prolong *vt* prolongar
prolongation *n* prolongación, *f*
promenade *n* paseo, *m*; bulevar, *m*; avenida, *f*. *vi* pasearse. *vt* recorrer, andar por, pasearse por. **p. deck,** cubierta de paseo, *f*
Promethean *a* de Prometeo
prominence *n* prominencia, *f*; protuberancia, *f*; eminencia, *f*; importancia, *f*
prominent *a* prominente, saliente; (of eyes, teeth) saltón; (distinguished) eminente, distinguido. **They placed the vase in a p. position,** Pusieron el florero muy a la vista. **to play a p. part,** desempeñar un papel importante. **p. eyes, ojos** saltones, *m pl*
promiscuous *a* promiscuo
promiscuousness *n* promiscuidad, *f*
promise *n* promesa, *f*; (hope) esperanza, *f*; (word) palabra, *f*; (future) porvenir, *m*. *vt* and *vi* prometer. **a young man of p.,** un joven de porvenir. **to break one's p.,** faltar a su palabra; no cumplir una promesa. **to keep one's p.,** guardar su palabra; cumplir su promesa. **to p. and do nothing,** apuntar y no dar. **under p. of,** bajo palabra de. **p. of marriage,** palabra de matrimonio, *f*
promised *a* prometido. **P. Land,** Tierra de promisión, *f*
promising *a* que promete bien, que promete mucho; prometedor; (of the future, etc.) halagüeño; (of persons) que llegará
promissory *a* promisorio. **p. note,** pagaré, abonaré, *m*
promontory *n* promontorio, *m*
promote *vt* fomentar, promover; provocar; (aid) favorecer, proteger; avanzar; estimular; (to a post) ascender; (an act bill) promover; *com* negociar
promoter *n* promotor (-ra); instigador (-ra); (*theat* etc.) empresario, *m*
promotion *n* (encouragement) fomento, *m*; (furtherance) adelanto, *m*; protección, *f*, favorecimiento, *m*; (in employment, etc.) promoción, *f*, ascenso, *m*; (of a company, etc.) creación, *f*
prompt *a* pronto; diligente; presuroso; puntual; rápido; *com* inmediato. *vt* impulsar, incitar, mover; dictar; insinuar; *theat* apuntar; (remind) recordar. **He came at five o'clock p.,** Vino a las cinco en punto. **p. book,** libro del traspunte, *m*. **p. box,** concha (del apuntador), *f*
prompter *n theat* apuntador, (in the wings) traspunte, *m*
prompting *n* sugestión, *f*; instigación, *f*; *pl* **promptings,** impulso, *m*; (of the heart, etc.) dictados, *m pl*
promptitude *n* prontitud, presteza, *f*; prisa, expedición, *f*; puntualidad, *f*
promptly *adv* inmediatamente, en seguida; con prontitud, con celeridad; puntualmente
promptness *n* See **promptitude**
promulgate *vt* promulgar; divulgar, diseminar
promulgation *n* promulgación, *f*; divulgación, diseminación, *f*
prone *a* postrado; inclinado, propenso
proneness *n* postración, *f*; inclinación, tendencia, propensión, *f*
prong *n* (pitchfork) horquilla, *f*; (of a fork) diente, *m*, púa, *f*
pronged *a* dentado, con púas
pronoun *n* pronombre, *m*
pronounce *vt* pronunciar; declarar; articular
pronounced *a* marcado; perceptible; bien definido
pronouncement *n* pronunciamiento, *m*
pronunciation *n* pronunciación, *f*; articulación, *f*
proof *n* prueba, *f*; demostración, *f*; ensayo, *m*; *law* testimonio, *m*; (*phot print*) prueba, *f*; *math* comprobación, *f*, *a* hecho a prueba (de); impenetrable (a); *fig* insensible

(a). *vt* (raincoats, etc.) impermeabilizar. **in p. whereof,** en fe de lo cual. **p. against bombs,** a prueba de bombas. **p. reading,** corrección de pruebas, *f*
prop *n* apoyo, puntal, estribadero, *m;* (for a tree) horca, *f,* rodrigón, *m; naut* escora, *f; fig* báculo, *m,* columna, *f,* apoyo, *m. vt* apoyar; apuntalar; (a tree) ahorquillar; (a building) acodalar; *naut* escorar; *fig* sostener. **He propped himself against the wall,** Se apoyó en el muro, Se arrimó al muro
propaganda *n* propaganda, *f*
propagandist *n* propagandista, *mf*
propagate *vt* propagar. *vi* propagarse
propagation *n* propagación, *f*
propagator *n* propagador (-ra)
propel *vt* propulsar, empujar, mover
propeller *n* propulsor, *m; mech* hélice, *f*
propelling *n* propulsión, *f.* **p. pencil,** lapicero, *m*
propensity *n* propensión, tendencia, inclinación, *f*
proper *a* propio; apropiado; correcto; decente; (prim) afectado; serio, formal; (exact) justo, exacto; (suitable (for)) bueno (para), apto (para); (true) verdadero; (characteristic) peculiar; *her* natural; (with rascal, etc.) redomado; (handsome) guapo. **If you think it p.,** Si te parece bien. **p. noun,** nombre propio, *m*
properly *adv* decentemente; correctamente; propiamente; bien. **to do (a thing) p.,** hacer algo bien. **p. speaking,** propiamente dicho, hablando con propiedad
propertied *a* propietario, hacendado; (rich) pudiente, adinerado
property *n* propiedad, *f;* (belongings) bienes, *m pl;* posesiones, *f pl;* (estate) hacienda, *f;* (quality) cualidad, *f; pl* **properties,** *theat* accesorios, *m pl.* **personal p.,** bienes muebles, *m pl;* cosas personales, *f pl.* **real p.,** bienes raíces, *m pl.* **p. man,** *theat* encargado de los accesorios, *m.* **p. owner,** propietario (-ia). **p. tax,** contribución sobre la propiedad, *f*
prophecy *n* profecía, *f;* predicción, *f*
prophesier *n* See **prophet**
prophesy *vt* profetizar; presagiar, predecir. *vi* hacer profecías
prophet *n* profeta, *m*
prophetess *n* profetisa, *f*
prophetic *a* profético
prophylactic *a* and *n* profiláctico, *m*
propinquity *n* propincuidad, proximidad, *f;* (relationship) parentesco, *m*
propitiate *vt* propiciar; apaciguar, conciliar
propitiation *n* propiciación, *f*
propitiator *n* propiciador (-ra)
propitiatory *a* propiciador
propitious *a* propicio, favorable
propitiousness *n* lo propicio
proportion *n* proporción, *f;* parte, *f;* porción, *f; pl* **proportions,** proporciones, *f pl;* dimensiones, *f pl. vt* proporcionar; repartir, distribuir. **in p.,** en proporción; conforme (a), según; *com* a prorrata. **in p. as,** a medida que. **out of p.,** desproporcionado. **He has lost all , sense of p.,** Ha perdido su equilibrio (mental)
proportional *a* proporcional; en proporción (a); proporcionado (a). **p. representation,** representación proporcional, *f*
proportionally *adv* proporcionalmente, en proporción
proportionate *a* proporcionado; proporcional. *vt* proporcionar
proportionately *adv* See **proportionally**
proposal *n* proposición, *f;* oferta, *f;* (plan) propósito, proyecto, *m.* **p. of marriage,** oferta de matrimonio, *f*
propose *vt* proponer; ofrecer; (a toast) dar, brindar. *vi* pretender, intentar, tener la intención de; pensar; (marriage) declararse
proposer *n* proponente, *m;* (of a motion) autor (-ra) de una proposición
proposition *n* proposición, *f;* (plan) proyecto, propósito, *m*
propound *vt* proponer; plantear, presentar
proprietary *a* propietario; de propiedad
proprietor *n* propietario, *m;* dueño, *m*
proprietorship *n* propiedad, pertenencia, *f*
proprietress *n* propietaria, *f;* dueña, *f*
propriety *n* decoro, *m;* conveniencia, *f;* corrección, *f*
propulsion *n* propulsión, *f*
propulsive *a* propulsor
prorogation *n* prorrogación, *f*
prorogue *vt* prorrogar, suspender (la sesión de una asamblea legislativa)
pros and cons el pro y el contra
prosaic *a* prosaico
proscenium *n* proscenio, *m*
proscribe *vt* proscribir
proscription *n* proscripción, *f*
prose *n* prosa, *f.* **p. writer,** prosista, *mf*
prosecute *vt* proseguir, llevar adelante; (*law* a person) procesar; (*law* a claim) pedir en juicio
prosecution *n* prosecución, *f;* cumplimiento, *m; law* acusación, *f;* (*law* party) parte actora, *f.* **in the p. of his duty,** en el cumplimiento de su deber
prosecutor *n* demandante, actor, *m.* **public p.,** fiscal, *m*
proselyte *n* prosélito, *m*
proselytism *n* proselitismo, *m*
prose writer *n* prosador, *m*
prosody *n* prosodia, *f*
prospect *n* perspectiva, *f;* esperanza, *f;* probabilidad, *f;* (in mining) indicio de filón, *m;* criadero (de oro, etc.), *m. vi* explorar; (of a mine) prometer (bien), dar buenas esperanzas. *vt* explorar, inspeccionar; examinar. **He is a man with good prospects,** Es un hombre de porvenir
prospecting *n* la prospección, *f*
prospective *a* en expectativa, futuro; previsor
prospector *n* explorador, operador, *m*
prospectus *n* prospecto, programa, *m*
prosper *vi* prosperar. *vt* favorecer, prosperar
prosperity *n* prosperidad, *f*
prosperous *a* próspero; favorable
prostate *n* próstata, *f*
prostitute *n* prostituta, *f, vt* prostituir
prostitution *n* prostitución, *f*
prostrate *a* tendido; postrado; abatido. *vt* derribar; arruinar; (by grief, etc.) postrar; (oneself) postrarse
prostration *n* postración, *f;* abatimiento, *m.* **nervous p.,** neurastenia, *f*
prosy *a* aburrido, árido; pedestre, prosaico; verboso, prolijo
protagonist *n* protagonista, *mf*
protean *a* proteico
protect *vt* proteger
protection *n* protección, *f;* defensa, *f;* garantía, *f;* abrigo, *m;* refugio, *m;* (passport) salvoconducto, *m; pol* proteccionismo, *m*
protectionism *n* proteccionismo, *m*
protectionist *n* proteccionista, *mf*
protective *a* protector; *pol* proteccionista
protector *n* protector, *m*
protectorate *n* protectorado, *m*
protectress *n* protectriz, *f*
protein *n* proteína, *f*
protest *vt* protestar; *law* hacer el protesto de una letra de cambio. *vi* declarar; insistir (en); hacer una protesta. *n* protesta, *f; law* protesto, *m.* **under p.,** bajo protesta. **to p. against,** protestar contra
Protestant *a* and *n* protestante, *mf*
Protestantism *n* protestantismo, *m*
protestation *n* protestación, *f*
protester *n* el, *m,* (*f,* la) que protesta
protest literature *n* literatura de denuncia, *f*
protocol *n* protocolo, *m, vt* protocolizar
protoplasm *n* protoplasma, *m*
prototype *n* prototipo, *m*
protract *vt* prolongar; dilatar
protracted *a* prolongado; largo
protraction *n* prolongación, *f*

protractor *n* (*geom* and *surv*) transportador, *m*. **p. muscle,** músculo extensor, *m*
protrude *vt* sacar fuera. *vi* salir fuera; sobresalir
protuberance *n* protuberancia, *f*
protuberant *a* protuberante, prominente
proud *a* orgulloso; arrogante; noble; glorioso; magnífico; soberbio, *Mexico* alzado. **to be p.,** enorgullecerse. **to make p.,** enorgullecer; hacer orgulloso. **to be p. of,** ser orgulloso de, pagarse de, gloriarse en. **p. flesh,** carnosidad, *f*, bezo, *m*
proudly *adv* con orgullo, orgullosamente
provable *a* demostrable
prove *vt* probar; demostrar; (experience) experimentar, sufrir; poner a prueba; (a will) verificar; (show) mostrar; confirmar. *vi* resultar, salir (bien or mal)
provenance *n* origen, *m*
Provençal *a* provenzal. *n* provenzal, *mf*; (language) provenzal, *m*
Provence Provenza, *f*
provender *n* forraje, *m*; *inf* provisiones, *f pl*
proverb *n* refrán, *m*; proverbio, *m*. **collection of proverbs,** refranero, *m*. **Book of Proverbs,** Proverbios, *m pl*
proverbial *a* proverbial
proverbially *adv* proverbialmente
provide *vt* proporcionar, dar; proveer, surtir, suplir; (stipulate) estipular; preparar (por); tomar precauciones (contra); sufragar los gastos (de); proporcionar medios de vida (a); señalar una pensión (a). **to p. oneself with,** proveerse de
provided (that) *conjunc* si; a condición de que, siempre que, con tal que
providence *n* providencia, *f*
provident *a* próvido, previsor, prudente; económico
providential *a* providencial
providentially *adv* providencialmente
providently *adv* próvidamente, prudentemente
provider *n* proveedor (-ra)
province *n* provincia, *f*; esfera, *f*; función, incumbencia, *f*
provincial *a* provincial, de provincia; provinciano. *n* provinciano (-na); *ecc* provincial, *m*
provincialism *n* provincialismo, *m*
provision *n* provisión, *f*; (stipulation) estipulación, *f*; *pl* **provisions,** provisiones, *f pl*; víveres, comestibles, *m pl*. *vt* abastecer, aprovisionar. **to make p. for,** hacer provisión para, proveer de. **to make p. for one's family,** asegurar el porvenir de su familia. **p. merchant,** vendedor (-ra) de comestibles
provisional *a* provisional, interino
provisioning *n* aprovisionamiento, abastecimiento, *m*
proviso *n* condición, estipulación, disposición, *f*
provisory *a* provisional; condicional
provocation *n* provocación, *f*
provocative *a* provocativo, provocador
provocatively *adv* de un modo provocativo
provoke *vt* provocar; suscitar; incitar, excitar; (irritate) sacar de madre (a), indignar
provoker *n* provocador (-ra); instigador (-ra)
provoking *a* provocativo; (irritating) enojoso, irritante
provost *n* preboste, *m*; (of a college) director, *m*; (in Scotland) alcalde, *m*. **p.-marshal,** capitán preboste, *m*
prow *n* proa, *f*
prowess *n* valor, *m*, destreza, *f*; proeza, *f*
prowl *vi* and *vt* rondar; cazar al acecho
prowler *n* rondador (-ra); ladrón (-ona)
proximity *n* proximidad, *Argentina* adyacencia, *f*
proximo *adv* en (or del) mes próximo
proxy *n* poder, *m*; delegación, *f*; apoderado, *m*; delegado (-da); substituto (-ta). **to be married by p.,** casarse por poderes
prude *n* mojigata, beata, *f*
prudence *n* prudencia, *f*
prudent *a* prudente
prudently *adv* con prudencia
prudery *n* mojigatería, beatería, damería, gazmoñería, *f*
prudish *a* mojigato, gazmoño, remilgado
prune *n* ciruela pasa, *f*; color de ciruela, *m*. *vt* podar; (cut) cortar; reducir
pruning *n* poda, *f*; reducción, *f*. **p. knife,** podadera, *f*
prurient *a* lascivo, lujurioso, salaz
Prussia Prusia, *f*
Prussian *a* and *n* prusiano (-na). **P. blue,** azul de Prusia, *m*
prussic acid *n* acido prúsico, *m*
pry *vi* escudriñar; acechar, espiar, fisgonear; (meddle) entremeterse, meterse donde no le llaman. *vt* See **prize**
prying *n* fisgoneo, *m*; curiosidad, *f*. *a* fisgón, curioso
psalm *n* salmo, *m*. **to sing psalms,** salmodiar
psalmist *n* salmista, *m*
psaltery *n* salterio, *m*
pseudo- *a* seudo. **p.-learned,** erudito a la violeta
pseudonym *n* seudónimo, *m*
psychiatrist *n* siquiatra, *m*
psychiatry *n* siquiatría, *f*
psychic *a* síquico
psychoanalysis *n* sicoanálisis, *mf*
psychoanalyst *n* sicoanalista, *mf*
psychoanalyze *vt* sicoanalizar
psychological *a* sicológico
psychologist *n* sicólogo (-ga)
psychology *n* sicología, *f*
psychopathic *a* sicopático
psychosis *n* sicosis, *f*
psychotherapy *n* sicoterapia, *f*
ptomaine poisoning *n* intoxicación por tomaínas, *f*
puberty *n* pubertad, *f*
pubescent *a* púber
pubic *a* púbico
pubis *n* pubis, *m*
public *a* and *n* público *m*. **in p.,** en público. **p. assistance,** asistencia pública, *f*. **p. funds,** hacienda pública, *f*. **p. health,** higiene pública, *f*. **p.-house,** taberna, *f*. **p. opinion,** opinión pública, *f*. *inf* el qué dirán. **p.-spirited,** patriótico. **p. thoroughfare,** vía pública, *f*. **p. works,** obras públicas, *f pl*
publican *n* tabernero, *m*
publication *n* publicación, *f*
publicist *n* publicista, *mf*
publicity *n* publicidad, *f*
publicity agent *n* publicista, *mf*
publish *vt* publicar, divulgar, difundir; (a book, etc.) dar a luz, dar a la prensa, publicar; (of a publisher) editar. **to p. abroad,** pregonar a los cuatro vientos. **to p. banns of marriage,** correr las amonestaciones
publisher *n* publicador (-ra); (of books) editor (-ra)
publishing *n* publicación, *f*. **p. house,** casa editorial, *f*. **the p. world,** el mundo de la edición, *m*
puck *n* trasgo, *m*; diablillo, picaruelo, *m*
pucker *vt* (one's brow, etc.) fruncir; (crease) arrugar. *vi* arrugarse. *n* frunce, *m*; arruga, *f*; (fold) bolsa, *f*
puckering *n* fruncido, *m*; arrugas, *f pl*
puckish *a* travieso
pudding *n* pudín, budín, *m*. **black p.,** morcilla, *f*
puddle *n* charco, *m*
puerile *a* pueril
puerperal *a* puerperal. **p. fever,** fiebre puerperal, *f*
Puerto Rican *a* and *n* puertorriqueño (-ña), *a* boricua, *n* borinqueño (-ña)
puff *vt* and *vi* (blow) soplar; (at a pipe, etc.) chupar; (smoke) lanzar bocanadas de humo; (make pant) hacer jadear; (advertise) dar bombo (a); (distend) hinchar; (make conceited) envanecerse; (of a train, etc.) bufar; resoplar. *n* soplo, *m*; (of smoke, etc.) bocanada, *f*; (of an engine, etc.) resoplido, bufido, *m*; (for powder) borla (para polvos), *f*; (pastry) bollo, *m*; (advertisement) bombo, *m*. **to be puffed up,** *fig* hincharse, inflarse. **p. of wind,** ráfaga de aire, *f*. **p.-ball,** bejín, *m*.

p.-pastry, hojaldre, *m*, or *f*. **p.-sleeve,** manga de bullón, *f*
puffiness *n* hinchazón, *f*
puffy *a* (of the wind) a ráfagas; (panting) jadeante; (swollen) hinchado
pug *n* (dog) doguino, *m*. **p.-nosed,** de nariz respingona
pugilism *n* boxeo, pugilato, *m*
pugilist *n* pugilista, *mf*, boxeador, *m*
pugnacious *a* pugnaz, belicoso
pugnacity *n* pugnacidad, belicosidad, *f*
pull *n* tirón, *m*; sacudida, *f*; golpe, *m*; (row) paseo en barco, *m*; (with the oars) golpe (de remos), *m*; (at a bell) tirón, *m*; (bell-rope) tirador, *m*; (at a bottle) trago, *m*; (strain) fuerza, *f*; atracción, *f*; (struggle) lucha, *f*; (advantage) ventaja, *f*; (influence) influencia, *f*, *Central America, Mexico* arranque *m*. **to give a p.,** tirar (de), dar un tirón (a). **to have plenty of p.,** *inf* tener buenas aldabas
pull *vt* tirar (de); (drag) arrastrar; (extract) sacar; (a boat) remar; (gather) coger; *print* imprimir. **He pulled the trigger (of his gun),** Apretó el gatillo. **He was sitting by the fire pulling at his pipe,** Estaba sentado cerca del fuego fumando su pipa. **to p. a hat well down on the head,** calarse el sombrero. **to p. a person's leg,** tomar el pelo (a). **to p. oneself together,** componer el semblante, serenarse; recobrar el aplomo; (tidy oneself) arreglarse. **to p. apart,** *vt* separar; romper en dos. *vi* separarse; romperse en dos. **to p. away,** *vt* arrancar; quitar. *vi* tirar con esfuerzo. **to p. back,** tirar hacia atrás; hacer retroceder (a); retener. **to p. down,** hacer bajar, obligar a bajar; (objects) bajar; (buildings) derribar, demoler; (humble) humillar; degradar; (weaken) debilitar. **to p. in,** tirar hacia dentro; hacer entrar; (a horse) enfrenar; (expenditure) reducir. **to p. off,** arrancar; (clothes) quitarse; (a deal) cerrar (un trato), concluir con éxito; (win) ganar. **to p. on,** *vt* (gloves, etc.) meterse, ponerse. *vi* seguir remando. **to p. open,** abrir; abrir rápidamente. **to p. out,** hacer salir; obligar a salir; (teeth, daggers, etc.) sacar; (hair) arrancar. **to p. round, through,** *vt* ayudar a reponerse (a); sacar de un aprieto. *vi* restablecerse; reponerse, cobrar la salud, sanar. **to p. together,** obrar de acuerdo; (get on) llevarse (bien or mal). **He pulled himself together very quickly,** Se repuso muy pronto. **to p. up,** *vt* montar, subir; (a horse) sofrenar; (stop) parar; (by the root) desarraigar, extirpar; (interrupt) interrumpir; (scold) reñir. *vi* parar(se); (restrain oneself) reprimirse, contenerse
pullet *n* polla, *f*
pulley *n* polea, *f*; *naut* garrucha, *f*. **p. wheel,** roldana, *f*
pulling *n* tracción, *f*; tirada, *f*; arranque, *m*
pullover *n* jersey, *m*, *Lat. Am.* chompa, *f*
pullulate *vi* pulular
pulmonary *a* pulmonar
pulp *n* pulpa, *f*; (of fruit) carne, *f*; (paper) pasta, *f*; (of teeth) bulbo dentario, *m*. *vt* reducir a pulpa; deshacer (el papel). **to beat to a p.,** *inf* poner como un pulpo
pulpit *n* púlpito, *m*
pulpy *a* pulposo; *bot* carnoso
pulsate *vi* pulsar, latir
pulsation *n* pulsación, *f*, latido, *m*
pulsatory *a* pulsante, pulsativo, latiente
pulse *n* pulso, *m*; pulsación, *f*, latido, *m*; vibración, *f*; (vegetable) legumbre, *f*, *vi* pulsar, latir; vibrar. **to take a person's p.,** tomar el pulso (a)
pulverization *n* pulverización, *f*
pulverize *vt* pulverizar
puma *n* puma, *f*, *Lat. Am.* león, *m*
pumice *n* piedra pómez, *f*
pummel *vt* aporrear
pump *n* *mech* bomba, *f*; (for water, etc.) aguatocha, *f*; *naut* pompa, *f*; (slipper) escarpín, *m*, *vt* bombear, extraer por medio de una bomba; (inflate) inflar; (for information) sondear, sonsacar. **hand-p.,** bomba de mano, *f*. **to work a p.,** darle a la bomba
pumpkin *n* calabaza, *f*, *Central America* ayote, *m*, *Chile* zapallo, *m*; (plant) calabacera, *f*
pun *n* retruécano, *m*
punch *n* (drink) ponche, *m*; (blow) puñetazo, golpe, *m*; *mech* punzón, *m*; (for tickets, etc.) taladro, *m*; *inf* fuerza, *f*. *vt* (perforate) taladrar, punzar; estampar; (hit) dar un puñetazo (a). **p.-ball,** pelota de boxeo, *f*. **p.-bowl,** ponchera, *f*
Punchinello *n* Polichinela, *m*. **Punch and Judy show,** títeres, *m pl*
punctilious *a* formal, puntual, puntilloso
punctiliousness *n* formalidad, punctualidad, *f*
punctual *a* puntual
punctually *adv* puntualmente
punctuate *vt* puntuar
punctuation *n* puntuación, *f*
puncture *n* pinchazo, *m*; perforación, *f*; *surg* punción, *f*. *vt* pinchar; perforar; punzar. **We have a p. in the right tire,** Tenemos un pinchazo en el neumático derecho
pungency *n* picante, *m*; acerbidad, mordacidad, *f*
pungent *a* picante; acerbo, mordaz
Punic *a* púnico, cartaginés
punish *vt* castigar; maltratar
punishable *a* punible
punishment *n* castigo, *m*; pena, *f*; maltrato, *m*
punitive *a* punitivo
punt *n* batea, *f*. *vt* impeler una batea con una pértiga; ir en batea; (a ball) golpear, dar un puntapié (a)
puny *a* débil, encanijado; insignificante; pequeño
pup *n* cachorro (-rra). *vi* parir la perra
pupa *n* crisálida, *f*
pupil *n* alumno (-na), discípulo (-la); (of the eye) pupila, niña (del ojo), *f*; *law* pupilo (-la). *a* escolar. **day p.,** alumno (-na) externo (-na). **p. teacher,** maestro (-tra) alumno (-na)
puppet *n* títere, *m*, marioneta, *f*; muñeca, *f*; (person) maniquí, *m*. **p. show,** función de títeres, *f*. **p. showman,** titiritero, titerero, *m*
puppy *n* perrito (-ta), cachorro (-rra)
purblind *a* ciego; (short-sighted and *fig*) miope
purchasable *a* comprable, que puede comprarse; *fig* sobornable
purchase *vt* comprar; adquirir; *fig* lograr, conseguir. *n* compra, *f*; adquisición, *f*; *mech* apalancamiento, *m*; fuerza, *f*; (lever) palanca, *f*, aparejo, *m*; *fig* influencia, *f*. **p. tax,** impuesto de lujo, *m*
purchaser *n* comprador (-ra)
purchasing *n* See **purchase. p. power,** poder de adquisición, *m*
pure *a* puro. **p.-bred,** de raza
purgation *n* purgación, *f*
purgative *a* purgativo. *n* purga, *f*
purgatorial *a* del purgatorio; (expiatory) purgatorio
purgatory *n* purgatorio, *m*
purge *n* purgación, *f*; (laxative) purga, *f*; *pol* depuración, *f*; purificación, *f*. *vt* purgar; *pol* depurar; purificar; expurgar
purging *n* purgación, *f*; *pol* depuración, *f*; *fig* purificación, *f*
purification *n* purificación, *f*
purificatory *a* purificador, purificatorio, que purifica
purifier *n* purificador (-ra)
purify *vt* purificar; (metals) acrisolar; refinar; depurar; (purge) purgar
purist *n* purista, *mf*
puritan *a* and *n* puritano (-na)
Puritanism *n* puritanismo, *m*
purity *n* pureza, *f*
purl *vi* (of a stream, etc.) murmurar, susurrar. *n* (of a stream, etc.) susurro, murmullo, *m*
purlieu *n* límite, *m*; *pl* **purlieus,** alrededores, *m pl*, inmediaciones, *f pl*; (slums) barrios bajos, *m pl*
purling *a* murmurante, que susurra, parlero. *n* murmullo, susurro, *m*
purloin *vt* hurtar, robar

purple *n* púrpura, *f*, *a* purpúreo. *vt* purpurar, teñir de púrpura. *vi* purpurear

purplish *a* purpurino, algo purpúreo

purport *vt* dar a entender, querer decir; significar; indicar; parecer; tener el objeto de; pretender. *n* importe, *m*; sentido, significado, *m*; objeto, *m*

purpose *n* objeto, *m*; propósito, fin, *m*; intención, *f*; proyecto, *m*; designio, *m*; determinación, voluntad, *f*; efecto, *m*; ventaja, utilidad, *f*, *vi* and *vt* proponerse; pensar, tener el propósito (de), intentar. **It will serve my p.,** Servirá para lo que yo quiero. **for the p. of . . . ,** con el propósito de . . . , con el fin de . . . for purposes of . . . para efectos de . . . **on p.,** de propósito, expresamente, *Central America* adifés. **to no p.,** inútilmente; en vano

purposeful *a* resuelto; de substancia

purposeless *a* irresoluto, vacilante, vago; sin objeto; inútil

purposely *adv* expresamente, de intento

purr *vi* ronronear. *n* ronroneo, *m*

purse *n* bolsa, *f*; monedero, portamonedas, *m*. **to p. one's lips,** apretar los labios

purser *n naut* contador, sobrecargo, *Argentina* comisario, *m*. **purser's office,** contaduría, *f*

pursuance *n* cumplimiento, desempeño, *m*, prosecución, *f*. **in p. of,** en cumplimiento de; en consecuencia de

pursuant *a* and *adv* según; conforme (a), de acuerdo (con); en consecuencia (de)

pursue *vt* perseguir; seguir; (search) buscar; (hunt) cazar; (a submarine, etc.) dar caza (a); (continue) proseguir, continuar; (an occupation) dedicarse (a), ejercer

pursuer *n* perseguidor (-ra)

pursuit *n* perseguimiento, *m*; (search) busca, *f*; (hunt) caza, *f*; (performance) prosecución, *f*, desempeño, *m*; (employment) ocupación, *f*. **in p. of,** en busca de. **p. plane,** avión de caza, *m*

purulence *n* purulencia, *f*

purulent *a* purulento

purvey *vt* proveer, surtir, suministrar; abastecer; procurar

purveyance *n* suministro, abastecimiento, *m*; provisión, *f*

purveyor *n* suministrador (-ra), proveedor (-ra), bastecedor (-ra)

pus *n* pus, *m*

push *n* empujón, *m*; empellón, *m*; impulso, *m*; (of a person) empuje, *m*, energía, *f*; (attack) ataque, *m*; ofensiva, *f*; (effort) esfuerzo, *m*; crisis, *f*, momento crítico, *m*. **at a push,** *inf* en caso de necesidad; en un aprieto, si llegara el caso. **to give the p. to,** *inf* despedir (a). **p.-bicycle,** bicicleta, *f*. **p.-button,** botón, *m*; botón de llamada, *m*. **p.-cart,** carretilla de mano, *f*; (child's) cochecito de niño, *m*

push *vt* empujar; (jostle) empellar, dar empellones (a); (a finger in one's eye, etc.) clavar; (a button) apretar; (*fig* a person) proteger, ayudar; dar publicidad (a); (a claim, etc.) insistir en; (compel) obligar. *vi* empujar; dar empujones, empellar. **I am pushed for time,** Me falta tiempo. **He is pushed for money,** Está apurado por dinero. **I have pushed my finger in my eye,** Me he clavado el dedo en el ojo. **to p. against,** empujar contra; lanzarse contra; empellar, dar empellones (a). **to p. aside, away,** apartar con la mano; rechazar, alejar. **to p. back,** (hair, etc.) echar hacia atrás; (people) hacer retroceder; rechazar. **to p. by,** pasar. **to p. down,** hacer bajar; hacer caer; (demolish) derribar. **to p. forward,** *vt* empujar hacia delante, hacer avanzar; (a plan, etc.) llevar adelante. *vi* adelantarse a empujones; avanzar; seguir el camino. **to p. oneself forward,** *fig* abrirse camino; entremeterse; darse importancia. **to p. in,** *vt* empujar; hacer entrar; clavar, hincar. *vi* entrar a la fuerza; entremeterse. **to p. off,** *vt* apartar con la mano (a); *inf* quitar de encima (a). *vi naut* desatracar; *inf* ponerse en camino. **to p. open,** empujar, abrir. **to p. out,** *vt* empujar hacia fuera; hacer salir; echar. *vi naut* zarpar. **to p. through,** *vt* (business, etc.) despachar rápidamente; (a crowd) abrirse camino por. *vi* aparecer, mostrarse. **to p. to,** cerrar. **to p. up,** empujar; hacer subir; (windows, etc.) levantar. **be pushing up the daises,** mirar los árboles de raíz

pushing *a* enérgico, emprendedor; ambicioso; agresivo. **by p. and shoving,** a empellones, a empujones

pusillanimity *n* pusilanimidad, *f*

pusillanimous *a* pusilánime

puss *n* micho (-cha). **P.! P.!** ¡Miz, Miz!

pustule *n* pústula, *f*

put *vt* poner; colocar; (pour out) echar; aplicar; emplear; (estimate) calcular; presentar; (ask) preguntar; (say) decir; (express) expresar; (a question) hacer; (a problem) plantear; (the weight) lanzar; (rank) estimar. **As the Spanish put it,** Como dicen los españoles. **If I may put it so,** Si puedo expresarlo así, Por así decirlo. **hard put to it,** en dificultades, apurado. **How will you put it to her?** ¿Cómo se lo vas a explicar a ella? **to put ashore,** echar en tierra (a). **to put a child to bed,** acostar a un niño. **to put in order,** arreglar; ordenar, *Lat. Am.* acotejar. **to put out of joint,** dislocar. **to put out of order,** estropear. **to put to death,** matar; (judicially) ajusticiar. **to put about,** *vt* (a rumor) diseminar, divulgar; (worry) preocupar. *vi naut* virar, cambiar de rumbo **to put a roof on** =**roof** *vt*. **to put aside,** poner a un lado; descartar; (omit) omitir, pasar por alto de; (fears, etc.) desechar. **to put away,** quitar; guardar; poner en salvo; arrinconar; (thoughts) desechar, ahuyentar; (save) ahorrar; (banish) despedir, alejar; (a wife) repudiar, divorciar; (food) tragar. **to put back,** *vt* echar hacia atrás; hacer retroceder; (replace) devolver, restituir; (the clock) retrasar; (retard) retardar, atrasar. *vi* volver; *naut* volver a puerto. **to put down,** depositar; poner en el suelo; (the blinds) bajar; (an umbrella) cerrar; (a rebellion) sofocar; (gambling, etc.) suprimir; (humble) abatir, humillar; degradar; (silence) hacer callar; (reduce) reducir, disminuir; (write) apuntar, anotar; (a name) inscribir; (to an account) poner a la cuenta de; (estimate) juzgar, creer; (impute) atribuir. **The book is so interesting that it's hard to put down,** El libro es tan interesante que es difícil dejarlo. **to put forth,** (leaves, flowers, sun's rays) echar; (a book) publicar, dar a luz; (a hand) alargar; (an arm) extender; (show) manifestar, mostrar; (strength, etc.) desplegar; (use) emplear. **to put forward,** avanzar; (a clock) adelantar; (a suggestion, etc.) hacer; (propose) proponer; (a case) presentar. **to put oneself forward,** ponerse en evidencia. **to put in,** poner dentro; (a hand, etc.) introducir; (liquids) echar en; (a government) poner en el poder; (an employment) nombrar, colocar; (insert) insertar; (a claim) presentar; (say) decir. **I shall put in two hours' work before bedtime,** Trabajaré por dos horas antes de acostarme. **He put in a good word for you,** Habló en tu favor. **to put in writing,** poner por escrito. **to put in for,** (an employment) solicitar (un empleo); (as a candidate) presentarse como candidato para. **to put into,** meter dentro (de); (words) expresar; (port) arribar, hacer escala en (un puerto). **to put off,** desechar; (garments) quitarse, despojarse (de); (postpone) diferir, aplazar; (evade) evadir, entretener; quitarse de encima (a), desembarazarse (de); (confuse) desconcertar; (discourage) desanimar; quitar el apetito (a). **to put on,** poner sobre; (clothes) ponerse; (pretend) fingir, afectar; poner; (a play) poner en escena; (the hands of a clock) adelantar; (weight) engordar, poner carnes; (add) añadir; (*sport* score) hacer; (bet) apostar; (the light) encender; (assume) tomar; (the brake) frenar; (abuse) abusar (de). engañar. **He put the kettle on the fire,** Puso la tetera en el fuego. **to put on airs and graces,** darse humos. **to put on probation,** dar el azul a, poner a prueba a. **to put on more trains,** poner más trenes. **put one's foot down,** ponerle a fulano el alto. **to put out,** *vt* (eject) echar, expulsar; hacer salir; poner en la calle; (a tenant) desahuciar; (one's hand) alargar; (one's arm) extender; (one's tongue) sacar; (eyes) saltar; (fire, light) apagar, extinguir; (leaves, etc.) echar; (horns) sacar; (head) asomar, sacar; (use) emplear; (give) entregar, dar; (at interest) dar a interés; (finish) terminar; (dislocate) dislocar; (worry) desconcertar; turbar; poner los nervios en punta (a); (anger) enojar; (inconvenience) incomodar; (a book) publicar; (a boat) echar al mar. *vi* (of a ship) hacerse a la vela, zarpar. **to put out to grass,** mandar a pacer. **We put out to sea,** Nos hicimos a la mar. **to put the cart before the horse,** poner la carreta por delante de los bueyes. **to put through,** (perform) desempeñar; concluir, terminar; (thrust) meter; (subject to) someter a; (exercise) ejercitar; (on the telephone) poner en comunicación (con). **to put together,** juntar; (a machine, etc.) montar, armar. **to put two and two together,** atar cabos. **to put up,** *vt* (sails, a flag) izar; (raise a window) levantar, cerrar; (open a window, or an umbrella) abrir; (one's hands, etc.) poner en alto; (one's fists) alzar; (a prayer) ofrecer, hacer; (as a candidate) nombrar; (for sale) poner (a la venta); (the price) aumentar; (a prescription) preparar; (food) conservar; (pack) empaquetar; (a sword) envainar; (lodge) alojar; (a petition) presentar; (build) construir; *mech* montar; (*inf* plan) arreglar. *vi* alojarse. **to put upon,** abusar (de); oprimir; (accuse) imputar, acusar (de). **to put up to,** incitar (a), instigar (a); dar informaciones sobre; poner al corriente (de). **to put up with,** tolerar, soportar, aguantar; resignarse a; contentarse con, conformarse con

putative *a* supuesto; (of relationship) putativo

putrefaction *n* putrefacción, *f*

putrefy *vt* pudrir. *vt* pudrirse, descomponerse

putrid *a* pútrido; *inf* apestoso

putt *vt* and *vi* patear.

putting *n* acción de poner, *f*; colocación, *f*. **p. forward of the clock,** adelanto de la hora, *m*. **p. off,** tardanza, dilación, *f*. **p. the weight,** lanzamiento del peso, *m*. **p. up,** (for office) candidatura, *f*. **p. green,** pista de golf en miniatura, *f*

putty *n* masilla, *f*, *vt* enmasillar, rellenar con masilla

puzzle *vt* dejar perplejo; desconcertar; confundir; embrollar. *n* problema, *m*; dificultad, *f*; enigma, *m*; (perplexity) perplejidad, *f*; (game) rompecabezas, *m*. **to p. out,** procurar resolver; encontrar la solución de. **to p. over,** pensar en, meditar sobre. **I am puzzled by . . . ,** Me trae (or tiene) perplejo . . . . **to be puzzled** *Lat. Am.* intrigarse

pygmy *a* and *n* pigmeo (-ea)

pyjamas *n* pijama, *m*

pylon *n* pilón, *m*; poste, *m*; (at an airport) poste de señales, *m*

pylorus *n* píloro, *m*

pyorrhœa *n* piorrea, *f*

pyramid *n* pirámide, *f*

pyramidal *a* piramidal

pyre *n* pira, *f*

Pyrenean *a* pirineo, pirenaico

Pyrenees, the los Pirineos, *m pl*

pyromancy *n* piromancia, *f*

pyrotechnic *a* pirotécnico

pyrotechnics *n* pirotecnia, *f*

pyrotechnist *n* pirotécnico, *m*

Pyrrhic *a* pírrico

Pythagorean *a* and *n* pitagórico (-ca)

Pythian *a* pitio

python *n* pitón, *m*

pythoness *n* pitonisa, *f*

Q

q *n* (letter) cu, *f*

quack *vi* (of a duck) graznar. *n* (of a duck) graznido, *m*; (charlatan) charlatán, farsante, *m*; curandero, *m*. **q. doctor,** matasanos, medicastro, curandero, *m*. **q. medicine,** curanderismo, *m*

quackery *n* charlatanería, *f*, charlatanismo, *m*

quadrangle *n* cuadrángulo, *m*; (courtyard) patio, *m*

quadrangular *a* cuadrangular

quadratic *a* cuadrático. **q. equation,** cuadrática, ecuación de segundo grado, *f*

quadrature *n* (*math ast*) cuadratura, *f*

quadrennial *a* cuadrienal

quadrilateral *a* and *n* cuadrilátero *m*

quadrille *n* cuadrilla, *f*; (card game) cuatrillo, *m*

quadruped *a* and *n* cuadrúpedo *m*

quadruple *a* cuádruple. *vt* cuadruplicar. *n* cuádruplo, *m*

quadruplet *n* serie de cuatro cosas, *f*; bicicleta de cuatro asientos, *f*; uno (una) de cuatro niños (-as) gemelos (-as)

quadruplication *n* cuadruplicación, *f*

quaff *vt* beber a grandes tragos, vaciar de un trago

quagmire *n* tremedal, pantano, *m*; *fig* cenagal, *m*

quail *n* codorniz, *f*; (U.S.A.) parpayuela, *f*. *vi* cejar, retroceder; temblar, acobardarse

quaint *a* pintoresco; curioso, raro; (eccentric) excéntrico, extravagante

quaintly *adv* de un modo pintoresco; curiosamente; con extravagancia

quaintness *n* lo pintoresco; rareza, singularidad, *f*; (eccentricity) extravagancia, *f*

quake *vi* estremecerse, vibrar; temblar. *n* estremecimiento, *m*; (of the earth) terremoto, *m*. **to q. with fear,** temblar de miedo

Quaker *n* cuáquero (-ra)

quaking *a* temblón; tembloroso. *n* temblor, *m*; estremecimiento, *m*. **q. ash,** álamo temblón, *m*

qualifiable *a* calificable

qualification *n* calificación, *f*; requisito, *m*; capacidad, aptitud, *f*; (reservation) reservación, salvedad, *f*

qualified *a* apto, competente; (of professions) con título universitario; habilitado; limitado

qualify *vt* habilitar; calificar; modificar; suavizar; *vi* habilitarse; prepararse; llenar los requisitos

qualifying *a gram* calificativo

qualitative *a* cualitativo

quality *n* cualidad, *f*; calidad, *f*; propiedad, *f*. **This cloth is of good q.,** Esta tela es de buena calidad. **the q.,** la alta sociedad, la aristocracia

qualm *n* náusea, *f*; mareo, desmayo, *m*; (of conscience) escrúpulo, remordimiento, *m*

quandary *n* incertidumbre, perplejidad, *f*; dilema, apuro, *m*. **to be in a q.,** estar perplejo

quantitative *a* cuantitativo

quantity *n* cantidad, *f*; gran cantidad, *f*. **unknown q.,** incógnita, *f*

quantum *n* cantidad, *f*; tanto, *m*. **q. theory,** teoría de la quanta, *f*

quarantine *n* cuarentena, *f*, *vt* someter a cuarentena

quarrel *vi* pelear, disputar; (scold) reñir; (find fault) criticar. *n* pelea, disputa, *Argentina* arenga, *f*; (glazier's) diamante de vidriero, *m*. **to pick a q. with,** armar pleito con, reñir con, *Chile, Peru* cruzar. **to q. with,** reñir con, romper con; quejarse de

quarreller *n* reñidor (-ra)

quarrelling *n* disputas, altercaciones, *f pl*

quarrelsome *a* pendenciero, peleador, belicoso

quarrelsomeness *n* belicosidad, pugnacidad, *f*

quarry *n* cantera, *f*; *fig* mina, *f*; (prey) presa, *f*; víctima, *f*. *vt* explotar una cantera; examinar

quarrying *n* explotación de canteras, *f*; cantería, *f*

quarryman *n* cantero, *m*

quart *n* cuarto de galón, *m*

quartan *a* cuartanal. *n* (fever) cuartana, *f*
quarter *n* (fourth part) cuarta parte, *f*, cuarto, *m*; (of a year) trimestre, *m*; (of an hour, the moon, a ton, an animal, etc.) cuarto, *m*; (of the compass) cuarta, *f*; *naut* cuartelada, *f*; (of a town) barrio, *m*; (mercy) cuartel, *m*; *her* cuartel, *m*; dirección, *f*; origen, *m*, fuente, *f*; *pl* **quarters,** vivienda, *f*; alojamiento, *m*; (barracks) cuartel, *m*. *vt* cuartear; (a body) descuartizar, hacer cuartos (a); (troops) alojar; (in barracks) acuartelar; *her* cuartelar. **a q. of an hour,** un cuarto de hora. **at close quarters,** de cerca. **hind quarters,** cuartos traseros, *m pl*. **It is a q. to four,** Son las cuatro menos cuarto. **It is a q. past four,** Son las cuatro y cuarto. **q.-day,** primer día de un trimestre, *m*. **q.-deck,** alcázar, *m*; cuerpo de oficiales de un buque, *m*. **q.-mile,** cuarto de milla, *m*. **q.-plate,** cuarto de placa, *m*. **q.-sessions,** sesión trimestral de los juzgados municipales, *f*. **q.-staff,** barra, *f*. **q.-tone,** cuarto de tono, *m*
quartering *n* (punishment) descuartizamiento, *m*; *her* cantón, *m*
quarterly *a* trimestral, trimestre. *n* publicación trimestral, *f*, *adv* trimestralmente
quartermaster *n* *mil* cabo furriel, *m*; *nav* maestre de víveres, cabo de mar, *m*. **q.-general,** intendente de ejército, *m*
quartet *n* cuarteto, *m*
quarto *n* papel en cuarto, *m*; libro en cuarto, *m*. **in q.,** en cuarto
quartz *n* cuarzo, *m*
quash *vt* *law* anular, derogar; *inf* sofocar, reprimir
quasi *a* and *adv* cuasi
quasimodo *n* cuasimodo, *m*
quatrain *n* cuarteta, *f*
quaver *vi* vibrar; temblar; (trill) trinar, hacer quiebros. *vt* decir con voz temblorosa. *n* vibración, *f*; trémolo, *m*; (trill) trino, *m*; (musical note) corchea, *f*
quaveringly *adv* con voz temblorosa
quavery *a* trémulo, tembloroso
quay *n* muelle, *m*
queasiness *n* náusea, *f*; escrupulosidad, *f*
queasy *a* propenso a la náusea; nauseabundo; delicado, escrupuloso
queen *n* reina, *f*; (in a Spanish pack of cards) caballo, *m*; (in a French or English pack and in chess) reina, *f*. **to q. it,** conducirse como una reina; mandar. **q. bee,** maestra, abeja reina, *f*. **q. cell,** maestril, *m*. **q. mother,** reina madre, *f*. **q. regent,** reina regente, *f*
queenliness *n* majestad de reina, *f*
queenly *a* de reina; regio
queer *a* raro; extraño, singular; ridículo; (shady) sospechoso; (ill) malucho, algo enfermo; (mad) chiflado
queerly *adv* extrañamente; ridiculamente
queerness *n* rareza, extrañeza, singularidad, *f*; ridiculez, *f*
quell *vt* subyugar; reprimir; apaciguar, calmar
quench *vt* apagar; calmar; satisfacer. **to q. one's thirst,** apagar la sed
quenching *n* apagamiento, *m*; satisfacción, *f*
querulous *a* quejumbroso
querulousness *n* hábito de quejarse, *m*; quejumbre, *f*
query *n* pregunta, *f*; duda, *f*; punto de interrogación, *m*. *vt* preguntar; dudar (de); poner en duda. *vi* hacer una pregunta; expresar una duda
quest *n* busca, *f*; (adventure) demanda, *f*. **in q. of,** en busca de
question *n* pregunta, *f*; problema, *m*; asunto, *m*; cuestión, *f*; (discussion) debate, *m*, discusión, *f*. *vt* and *vi* interrogar; examinar; poner en duda, dudar de; preguntarse; hacer preguntas. **beyond q.,** fuera de duda. **to ask a q.,** hacer una pregunta. **without q.,** sin duda. **It is out of the q.,** Es completamente imposible. **It is a q. of whether . . . ,** Se trata de si . . . **q.-mark,** punto interrogante, *m*
questionable *a* cuestionable, discutible, dudoso; equívoco, sospechoso
questionableness *n* lo discutible; carácter dudoso, *m*; carácter sospechoso, *m*
questioner *n* preguntador (-ra); interrogador (-ra)
questioning *n* preguntas, *f pl*; interrogatorio, *m*
questioningly *adv* interrogativamente
questionnaire *n* cuestionario, *m*
quetzal *n* (money and *orn*) quetzal, *m*
queue *n* coleta, *f*; cola, *f*, *vi* formar cola; hacer cola
quibble *n* equívoco, subterfugio, *m*; sutileza, *f*; (pun) retruécano, *m*. *vi* hacer uso de subterfugios; sutilizar
quibbler *n* sofista, *mf*
quibbling *n* sofistería, *f*, sofismas, *m pl*, sutilezas, *f pl*
quick *a* vivo; agudo; penetrante; sagaz; rápido, veloz; (ready) pronto; ágil, activo; (light) ligero. *adv* rápidamente; (soon) pronto. *n* carne viva, *f*; *fig* lo vivo. **Be q.!** ¡Date prisa! **He was very q.,** Lo hizo muy aprisa; Volvió (or Fue, according to sense) rápidamente. **the q. and the dead,** los vivos y los muertos. **to cut to the q.,** herir en lo más vivo. **q. march,** paso doble, *m*. **q.-sighted,** de vista aguda; perspicaz. **q. step,** paso rápido, *m*. **q.-tempered,** de genio vivo, colérico. **q. time,** compás rápido, *m*; *mil* paso doble, *m*. **q.-witted,** de ingenio agudo
quicken *vt* vivificar; animar; acelerar; excitar, avivar. *vi* vivificarse; despertarse; renovarse; acelerarse; (stir) moverse. **to q. one's step,** acelerar el paso
quicklime *n* cal viva, *f*
quickly *adv* rápidamente; (soon) pronto; (immediately) en seguida; (promptly) con presteza; vivamente
quickness *n* viveza, *f*; (of wit, etc.) agudeza, *f*; rapidez, velocidad, *f*; (promptness) prontitud, *f*; agilidad, *f*; (lightness) ligereza, *f*; (understanding) penetración, sagacidad, *f*
quicksand *n* arena movediza, *f*; *fig* cenagal, *m*
quicksilver *n* azogue, mercurio, *m*, *vt* azogar
quiescence *n* reposo, *m*; quietud, tranquilidad, *f*; inactividad, *f*; pasividad, *f*
quiescent *a* quieto; inactivo; pasivo
quiet *a* tranquilo; quieto; silencioso; quedo; monótono; inactivo; (informal) sin ceremonia; (simple) sencillo; (of the mind) sereno; (of colours, etc.) suave. *n* tranquilidad, quietud, *f*; silencio, *m*; paz, *f*; (of mind) serenidad, *f*. *vt* tranquilizar, sosegar; calmar. **to be q.,** callarse; no hacer ruido. **Be q.!** ¡Estate quieto! ¡A callar!
quietism *n* quietismo, *m*
quietist *n* quietista, *mf*
quietistic *a* quietista
quietly *adv* tranquilamente; en silencio; sin ruido; en calma; (simply) sencillamente; dulcemente
quietness *n* tranquilidad, quietud, *f*; calma, *f*; paz, *f*; silencio, *m*
quietus *n* (quittance) quitanza, *f*, finiquito, *m*; golpe de gracia, *m*; muerte, *f*
quill *n* pluma de ave, *f*; (of a feather) cañón, *m*; (pen) pluma, *f*; (of a porcupine) púa, *f*. **q.-driver,** cagatintas, *mf*
quilt *n* colcha, *f*, edredón, *m*. *vt* acolchar. **q. maker,** colchero, *m*
quilting *n* acolchamiento, *m*; colchadura, *f*
quince *n* (tree and fruit) membrillo, *m*. **q. cheese,** carne de membrillo, *f*. **q. jelly,** jalea de membrillo, *f*
quincentenary *n* quinto centenario, *m*
quinine *n* quinina, *f*
quinsy *n* angina, *f*
quintessence *n* quinta esencia, *f*
quintessential *a* quintaesenciado
quintet *n* quinteto, *m*
quintuple *a* quíntuplo
quintuplet *n* quintupleto, *m*; uno (una) de cinco niños (-as) gemelos (-as)
quip *n* agudeza, salida, *f*; (hint) indirecta, *f*; donaire, *m*, chanza, burla, *f*
quire *n* (of paper) mano (de papel), *f*
quirk *n* (quip) agudeza, salida, *f*; (quibble) sutileza, evasiva, *f*, (gesture) gesto, *m*

quit *vt* abandonar; dejar; renunciar (a). *vi* marcharse, *inf* tomar las de Villadiego, poner pies en polvorosa; (slang) dejar de, cesar de. **notice to q.,** aviso de desahúcio, *m*
quite *adv* completamente, enteramente; totalmente; del todo; (very) muy; (fairly) bastante. **It is not q. the thing to do,** Esto es algo que no se hace. **Q. so!** ¡Claro!; ¡Eso es! Se comprende. **It is not q. so good as we hoped,** No es tan bueno como esperábamos. **Peter is q. grown-up,** Pedro está hecho un hombre (*or* es todo un hombre)
quits *adv* quito, descargado. **be q.,** estar en paz
quittance *n* quitanza, *f;* recibo, *m;* recompensa, *f*
quitter *n* desertor (-ra); cobarde, *mf*
quiver *vi* temblar; vibrar; estremecerse; palpitar; (of light) titilar. *n* (for arrows) aljaba, *f,* carcaj, *m.* See also **quivering**
quivering *a* tremulante; vibrante; palpitante. *n* temblor, *m;* estremecimiento, *m*
quixotic *a* quijotesco
quixotism *n* quijotismo, *m*
quiz *n* examen parcial, *m. vt* tomar el pelo (a); burlarse (de); (stare) mirar de hito en hito (a)
quizzical *a* burlón; cómico; estrafalario
quizzically *adv* burlonamente; cómicamente
quoin *n* piedra angular, *f;* ángulo, *m;* (wedge) cuña, *f. vt* meter cuñas (a)
quoit *n* tejo, *m; pl* **quoits,** juego de tejos, *m*
quondam *a* antiguo
quorum *n* quórum, *m.* **to form a q.,** hacer un quórum
quota *n* cuota, *f*
quotable *a* citable; (Stock Exchange) cotizable
quota system *n* tablas diferenciales, *f pl*
quotation *n* citación, *f;* cita, *f; com* cotización, *f.* **q. mark,** comilla, *f*
quote *vt* citar; *com* cotizar. *n inf* comilla, *f*
quoth *vt* **q. I,** dije yo. **q. he,** dijo él
quotient *n* cociente, *m.* **intelligence q.,** cociente intelectual, *m*

R

r *n* (letter) erre, *f*
rabbet *n* ranura, *f,* rebajo, *m. vt* ensamblar a rebajo. **r.-joint,** junta a rebajo, *f*
rabbi *n* rabí, rabino, *m.* **grand r.,** gran rabino, *m*
rabbinical *a* rabínico
rabbinism *n* rabinismo, *m*
rabbit *n* conejo (-ja). *a* conejuno, de conejo. *vi* cazar conejos. **young r.,** gazapo, *m.* **r.-hutch,** jaula para conejos, *f.* **r.-warren,** conejera, *f*
rabble *n* populacho, vulgo, *m,* plebe, *f*
Rabelaisian *a* rabelasiano
rabid *a* rabioso; fanático; furioso, violento
rabies *n* rabia, hidrofobia, *f*
raccoon *n* mapache, *m*
race *n* carrera, *f;* (current) corriente, *f;* (prize) premio, *m;* (breed) raza, *f;* casta, estirpe, *f;* (family) linaje, *m,* familia, *f;* (scornful) ralea, *f;* (struggle) lucha, *f. vi* tomar parte en una carrera; correr de prisa; asistir a concursos de carreras de caballos; (of a machine) dispararse. *vt* (hacer) correr; competir en una carrera (con); desafiar a una carrera. **flat r.,** carrera llana, *f.* **mill-r.,** caz, *m.* **to run a r.,** tomar parte en una carrera; *fig* hacer una carrera. **r.-card,** programa de carreras de caballos, *m.* **r. hatred,** odio de razas, *m.* **r.-meeting,** concurso de carreras de caballos, *m.* **r. suicide,** suicidio de la raza, *m.* **r.-track,** pista, *f*
racecourse hipódromo, *m;* estadio, *m*
racehorse *n* caballo de carrera, *m*
racer *n* (horse) caballo de carreras, *m;* (person) carrerista, *mf;* (car) coche de carreras, *m;* (boat) yate de carreras, *m;* (bicycle) bicicleta de carreras, *f*
rachitic *a* raquítico
racial *a* racial, de raza
racialism *n* rivalidad de razas, *f*
raciness *n* sabor, *m;* savia, *f,* picante, *m*
racing *n* carreras, *f pl; mech* disparo, *m, a* de carreras; hípico. **r. calendar,** calendario de concursos de carreras de caballos, *m.* **r. car,** coche de carreras, *m.* **r. cycle,** bicicleta de carreras, *f*
rack *n* (for hay) percha (del pesebre), *f;* (in a railway compartment) rejilla, *f;* (for billiard cues) taquera, *f;* (for clothes) percha, *f;* (for torture) potro, *m; mech* cremallera, *f. vt* poner en el potro, torturar; atormentar. **to be on the r.,** estar en el potro **to r. one's brains,** devanarse los sesos, quebrarse la cabeza. **r. and ruin,** ruina total, *f.* **r. railway,** ferrocarril de cremallera, *m,*
racket *n sport* raqueta, *f;* (din) barahúnda, *f;* ruido, estrépito, *m;* confusión, *f;* (bustle) bullicio, *m,* agitación, *f;* (swindle) estafa, *f;* (binge) parranda, *f.* **to play rackets,** jugar a la raqueta
racking *n* tortura, *f;* (of wine) trasiego, *m, a* torturante; (of a pain or cough) persistente
racoon *n* mapache, *m*
racquet *n* See **racket**
racy *a* picante; sabroso
radar *n* radar, *m*
raddled *a* pintado de almagre; mal pintado
radial *a* radial
radiance *n* resplandor, brillo, *m,* luminosidad, *f*
radiant *a* radiante; brillante, luminoso. *n geom* línea radial, *f.* **r. heat,** calor radiante, *m*
radiantly *adv* con resplandor; brillantemente; con alegría
radiate *vi* radiar. *vt* irradiar
radiation *n* irradiación, *f; geom* radiación, *f*
radiator *n* (for central heating and of a car) radiador, *m;* (stove) calorífero, *m*
radical *a* radical. *n* (*math chem*) radical, *m; pol* radical, *mf*
radicalism *n* radicalismo, *m*
radio *n* radio, *f;* radiocomunicación, *f.* **r. amateur, r. enthusiast,** radioaficionado (-da). **r. announcer,** locutor (-ra). **r. broadcast,** radioemisión, radiodifusión, *f.* **r. listener,** radiooyente, *mf* **r. receiver,** (technical) radiorreceptor, *m;* (usual word) aparato de radio, *m.* **r. transmitter,** radiotransmisor, *m*
radioactive *a* radiactivo
radioactive fallout *n* caída radiactiva, llovizna radiactiva, precipitación radiactiva, *f*
radioactivity *n* radiactividad, *f*
radiofrequency *n* radiofrecuencia, *f*
radiolocation *n* radiolocación, *f*
radiologist *n* radiólogo, *m*
radiology *n* radiología, *f*
radiometer *n* radiómetro, *m*
radiometry *n* radiometría, *f*
radioscopy *n* radioscopia, *f*
radiotherapeutics, radiotherapy *n* radioterapia, *f*
radish *n* rábano, *m.* **horse-r.,** rábano picante, *m*
radium *n* radio, *m*
radius *n* (*geom anat*) radio, *m;* (of a wheel) rayo, *m;* (scope) alcance, *m*
raffia *n* rafia, *f*
raffish *a* disoluto, libertino
raffle *n* rifa, *f,* sorteo, *m;* lotería, *f. vt* rifar, sortear
raffling *n* sorteo, *m,* rifa, *f*
raft *n* balsa, *f;* (timber) armadía, *f. vt* transportar en balsa; cruzar en balsa
rafter *n* (of a roof) viga, traviesa, *f;* (raftsman) balsero, *m*
raftered *a* con vigas
rag *n* jirón, guiñapo, *m;* (for cleaning) paño, trapo, *m;*

(for papermaking) estraza, *f;* (of smoke, etc.) penacho, *m;* (newspaper) papelucho, *m; pl* **rags,** harapos, *m pl; inf* viejos hábitos, *m pl. vt* (tease) tomar el pelo (a); burlarse de; hacer una broma pesada (a). **r.-and-bone-man, ragpicker,** andrajero, trapero (Mexico), pepinador, *m.* **r. doll,** muñeca de trapo, *f*
ragamuffin *n* galopín, *m*
rage *n* (anger) cólera, rabia, ira, *f;* (of the elements) furia, violencia, *f;* (ardour) entusiasmo, ardor, *m;* (fashion) boga, moda, *f;* (craze) manía, *f;* (of the poet) furor, *m. vi* (be angry) rabiar, estar furioso; (of the sea) encresparse, alborotarse, enfurecerse; (of wind, fire, animals) bramar, rugir; (of pain) rabiar; (be prevalent) prevalecer, desencadenarse. **to r. against,** protestar furiosamente contra; culpar amargamente (de). **to be all the r.,** *inf* ser la ultima moda. **to fly into a r.,** montar en cólera. **to put into a r.,** hacer rabiar
ragged *a* harapiento, andrajoso; roto; (uneven) desigual; (rugged) peñascoso, áspero, escabroso; (serrated) serrado; dentellado; (of a coastline) accidentado; (unfinished) inacabado, sin terminar; (of style) descuidado, sin pulir
raggedness *n* harapos, *m pl;* estado andrajoso, *m;* aspereza, escabrosidad, *f;* lo serrado; lo accidentado; (of style) falta de elegancia, tosquedad, *f*
raging *a* furioso, rabioso; violento; (roaring) bramante; (of the sea) bravío; intenso. *n* furia, *f;* violencia, *f;* intensidad, *f*
raglan *n* raglán, *m.* **r. sleeve,** manga raglán, *f*
ragout *n* estofado, *m*
ragpicker *n* trapero (-ra)
ragtime *n* música sincopada, *f*
raid *n* incursión, correría, *f;* asalto, ataque, *m;* (by the police) razzia, *f;* (by aircraft) bombardeo, *m, vt* invadir; atacar, asaltar; apoderarse de; hacer una razzia en; (by aircraft) bombear, bombardear; (pillage) pillar, saquear. **obliteration r.,** hombardeo de saturación, *m*
raider *n* corsario, *m;* atacador, asaltador, *m;* (aircraft) avión enemigo, *m*
rail *n* barra, *f;* antepecho, *m;* (of a staircase) barandilla, *f,* pasamano, *m;* (track) riel, *m;* (railway) ferrocarril, *m;* (of a ship) barandilla, *f;* (of a chair) travesaño, *m pl.* **rails,** (fence) cerca, barrera, palizada, *f. vt* cercar con una palizada, poner cerca a; mandar por ferrocarril. **by r.,** por ferrocarril. **to run off the rails,** descarrilar. **to r. at,** protestar contra; prorrumpir en invectivas contra, injuriar de palabra (a)
railing *n* barandilla, *f;* antepecho, *m,* enrejado, *m;* (grille) reja, *f;* (jeers) burlas, *f pl;* insultos, *m pl,* injurias, *f pl;* quejas, *f pl*
raillery *n* jocosidad, tomadura de pelo, *f;* sátiras, *f pl*
railway *n* ferrocarril, *m;* vía férrea, *f,* camino de hierro, *m, a* de ferrocarril, ferroviario. **elevated r.,** ferrocarril aéreo, *m.* **narrow gauge r.,** ferrocarril de vía estrecha, *m.* **r. buffet,** fonda, *f,* (or restaurante, *m*) de estación. **r. carriage,** departamento de tren, *m.* **r. company,** compañía de ferrocarriles, *f.* **r. crossing,** paso a nivel, *m.* **r. engine,** locomotora, *f.* **r. guard,** jefe del tren, *m.* **r. guide,** guía de ferrocarriles, *f.* **r. line,** vía férrea, *f.* **r. marshalling yard,** apartadero ferroviario, *m.* **r. passenger,** viajero (-ra) en un tren. **r. platform,** andén, *m.* **r. porter,** mozo de estación, *m.* **r. siding,** vía muerta, *f.* **r. signal,** disco de señales, *m.* **r. station,** estación (de ferrocarril), *f.* **r. system,** sistema ferroviario, *m.* **r. ticket,** billete de tren, *m*
railwayman *n* ferroviario, empleado de los ferrocarriles, *m*
raiment *n* ropa, *f; poet* hábitos, *m pl*
rain *n* lluvia, *f. vi* and *vt* llover. **a r. of arrows,** una lluvia de flechas. **fine r.,** llovizna, *f.* **to r. cats and dogs,** llover a cántaros. **to r. hard,** diluviar. **r. cloud,** nubarrón, *m.* **r.-gauge,** pluviómetro, *m*
rainbow *n* arco iris, arco de San Martín, *m*
raincoat *n* abrigo impermeable, *m*
raindrop *n* gota de lluvia, *f*
rainfall *n* cantidad llovida, *f;* (shower) aguacero, *m*
rainless *a* sin lluvia, seco
rainstorm *n* chaparrón, *m,* tempestad de lluvia, *f*
rainwater *n* lluvia, *f;* agua lluvia, *f*
rainy *a* lluvioso. **r. day,** día de lluvia, *m; fig* tiempo de escasez, *m*
raise *vt* levantar; alzar; (the hat) quitar; solevantar; (dough) fermentar; (erect) erigir, edificar; (dust) levantar; elevar; (promote) ascender; (increase) aumentar; hacer subir; (spirits, memories) evocar; (the dead) resucitar; (cause) causar; dar lugar (a); hacer concebir; (a question, a point) hacer; plantear; (breed or educate) criar; (a crop) cultivar; (an army) alistar; (gather together) juntar; (a subscription) hacer; (money, etc.) obtener, hallar; (a siege, etc.) levantar, alzar; (a laugh, a protest, etc.) suscitar, provocar; (utter) poner, dar; (a fund) abrir. **to r. oneself,** incorporarse. **He succeeded in raising himself,** Logró alzarse; Logró mejorar su posición. **He raised their hopes unduly,** Les hizo concebir esperanzas desmesuradas. **to r. an objection (to),** poner objeción (a). **to r. an outcry,** armar un alboroto. **to r. a point,** hacer una observación; plantear una cuestión. **to r. a siege,** levantar un sitio. **to r. Cain,** armar lo de Dios es Cristo. **to r. one's voice,** alzar la voz
raised *a* (in relief) en relieve; (embossed) de realce
raiser *n* (breeder) criador (-ra); (cultivator) cultivador (-ra); (educator) educador (-ra); autor (-ra); fundador (-ra); (of objections, etc.) suscitador (-ra)
raisin *n* pasa, *f*
raising *n* levantamiento, *m;* alzamiento, *m;* (of a building, monument) erección, *f;* elevación, *f;* (increase) aumento, *m;* provocación, *f;* fundación, *f;* (breeding or education) crianza, *f;* (of spirits) evocación, *f;* (of the dead) resucitación, *f;* producción, *f;* (of crops) cultivo, *m*
rake *n agr* rastrillo, *m,* rastra, *f;* (for the fire) hurgón, *m;* (croupier's) raqueta, *f;* (of a mast, funnel) inclinación, *f;* (person) tenorio, calavera, *m. vt agr* rastrillar; (a fire, etc.) hurgar; (sweep) barrer; recoger; (ransack) buscar (en); (with fire) enfilar, tirar a lo largo de; (scan) escudriñar. *vi* trabajar con el rastrillo; (slope) inclinarse. **r. off,** tajada, *f.* **to r. together,** juntar con el rastrillo; amontonar; ahorrar. **to r. up,** (revive) resucitar, desenterrar
raking *n* rastrillaje, *m;* (the fire, etc.) hurgonada, *f*
rakish *a* (of a ship) de palos muy inclinados, (dissolute) disoluto, libertino; (dashing) elegante
rakishly *adv* disolutamente; elegantemente
rakishness *n* (licentiousness) libertinaje, *m,* disipación, disolución, *f;* (elegance) elegancia, *f*
rally *vt* reunir; *mil* rehacer; (faculties) concentrar; (tease) tomar el pelo (a). *vi* reunirse; *mil* rehacerse; (revive) mejorar, recobrar las fuerzas; (of markets, etc.) mejorar *n* reunión, *f*
rallying *n* reunión, *f;* (of faculties, etc.) concentración, *f;* (recovery) mejora, *f.* **r. point,** punto de reunión, *m*
ram *n zool* carnero, morueco, *m; ast* Aries, Carnero, *m;* (*mil* etc.) ariete, *m;* (tool) pisón, *m; nav* espolón, *m, vt* golpear con ariete o espolón; (of a gun) atacar; apisonar; meter a la fuerza; hacer tragar a la fuerza; (squeeze) apretar; (crowd) atestar
Ramadan *n* ramadán, *m*
ramble *vi* vagar, vagabundear; hacer una excursión. *vt* errar por
rambler *n* excursionista, *mf;* paseante, *mf; bot* rosa trepante, *f*
rambling *a* (of houses) encantado; laberíntico; (straggly) disperso; (of thought, etc.) incoherente, inconexo. *n* vagabundeo, *m;* excursiones, *f pl;* paseo, *m;* (digression) digresiones, *f pl;* (delirium) desvaríos, *m pl*
ramification *n* ramificación, *f*
ramify *vi* ramificarse, tener ramificaciones. *vt* ramificar; dividir en ramales
rammer *n* pisón de empedrador, *m;* baqueta (de fusil), *f;* (of a ship) espolón, *m*

ramp *n* rampa, *f*; (swindle) estafa, *f*; (storm, commotion) tormenta, *f*
rampage *vi* alborotarse; bramar
rampant *a* salvaje; *her* rampante; (of persons) impaciente, furioso; (of plants, growth) lozano, exuberante; desenfrenado; (rife) prevaleciente, predominante
rampart *n* muralla, *f*; terraplén, *m*; *fig* baluarte, *m*. *vt* abaluartar, abastionar
ramrod *n* baqueta, *f*
ramshackle *a* destartalado, ruinoso; desvencijado; (badly made) mal hecho
ranch *n* rancho, *m*, hacienda (de ganado), *Lat. Am.* estancia, *f*
rancher *n* ranchero (-ra), *Lat. Am.* estanciero (-ra) *mf*
rancid *a* rancio
rancorous *a* rencoroso
rancor *n* rencor, encono, *m*
random *n* azar, *m*, *a* fortuito, al azar; sin orden ni concierto. **at r.,** a la ventura, al azar; sin pensar; (of shooting) sin apuntar. **to talk at r.,** hablar a trochemoche
range *n* línea, hilera, *f*; (of mountains) cadena, *f*; serie, *f*; clase, *f*; variedad, *f*; (of goods) surtido, *m*; (of a gun, voice, vision, etc.) alcance, *m*; (area) extensión, área, *f*; esfera de actividad, *f*; (scope) alcance, *m*; (of voice, musical instrument) compás, *m*; (of colors) gama, *f*; (for shooting) campo de tiro, *m*; (for cooking) cocina económica, *f*. **at close r.,** de cerca. **out of r.,** fuera de alcance. **within r.,** al alcance. **r.-finder,** (of guns, cameras) telémetro, *m*. **r. of mountains,** cadena de montañas, *f*; sierra, *f*
range *vt poet* arreglar; alinear; ordenar; clasificar; (a gun, etc.) apuntar; (place oneself) ponerse; sumarse (a); (roam) recorrer; (scan) escudriñar. *vi* extenderse; (roam) vagar; (of plants) crecer (en); variar, fluctuar; oscilar, vacilar; (of guns, etc.) alcanzar; (of the mind) pasar (por); (include) incluir
ranger *n* (wanderer) vagabundo, *m*; (keeper) guardabosque, *m*; *mil* batidor, *m*
ranging *n* arreglo, *m*; alineación, *f*; ordenación, *f*; clasificación, *f*; (roving) vida errante, *f*
rank *n* línea, *f*; fila, *f*; grado, *m*; clase, *f*; rango, *m*; categoría, *f*; posición, *f*; calidad, *f*; distinción, *f*. *vt* ordenar; clasificar; (estimate) estimar; poner (entre). *vi* ocupar un puesto; tener un grado, rango, etc.; estar al nivel (de); ser igual (a); contarse (entre). *a* (luxuriant) lozano, exuberante; fértil; (thick) espeso; (rancid) rancio; (complete) consumado; completo; (foul-smelling) fétido; *fig* repugnante, aborrecible; (very) muy. **of the first r.,** de primera calidad; de primera clase; de distinción. **the r. and file,** los soldados, la tropa; las masas, hombres de filas, *m pl*, mujeres de fila, *f pl*, la mayoría; los socios ordinarios (de un club, etc.). **to break ranks,** *mil* romper filas. **to rise from the ranks,** ascender de las filas. **to r. high,** ocupar alta posición; ser de los mejores (de). **to r. with,** estar al nivel de; (be numbered among) contarse entre, figurar entre
rankle *vi fig* irritar, molestar; envenenarse la vida, hacerse odioso
rankly *adv* ranciamente; lozanamente; con exuberancia; abundantemente; groseramente
rankness *n* rancidez, *f*; olor rancio, *m*; fertilidad, lozanía, *f*; exuberancia, *f*, vigor, *m*; enormidad, *f*
ransack *vt* (search) registrar; (pillage) saquear; *fig* buscar en
ransacking *n* (searching) registro, *m*; (sacking) saqueo, *m*
ransom *n* rescate, *m*, redención, *f*; liberación, *f*. *vt* rescatar, redimir
ransomer *n* rescatador (-ra)
ransoming *n* redención, *f*; liberación, *f*
rant *vi* declamar a gritos, vociferar; despotricar (contra); desvariar; hablar por hablar, hablar sin ton ni son. *n* declamación, vociferación, *f*; desvarío, *m*
ranter *n* declamador (-ra); agitador populachero, *m*; predicador chillón, *m*
rap *n* golpecito, *m*; toque, *m*; (with the knocker) aldabada, *f*; (worthless trifle) ardite, maravedí, *m*. *vt* and *vi* golpear; tocar. **He doesn't care a rap,** No le importa un ardite. **to rap at the door,** tocar a la puerta. **to rap with the knuckles,** golpear con los nudillos. **to rap out an oath,** proferir una blasfemia
rapacious *a* rapaz
rapacity *n* rapacidad, *f*
rape *n* (carrying off) rapto, *m*. **the Rape of the Sabine Women,** el Rapto de las Sabinas, *m*; *law* estupro, *m*; violación, *f*; *bot* nabo silvestre, *m*. *vt* (carry off) raptar, robar; violar, forzar
rapid *a* rápido. *n* rápido, *m*. **r. combustion,** combustión activa, *f*
rapidity *n* rapidez, *f*
rapidly *adv* rápidamente, con rapidez
rapids *npl Argentina* correntada, *f sg*
rapier *n* estoque, *m*; espadín, *m*
rapine *n* rapiña, *f*
rapping *n* golpecitos, *m pl*; golpeo, *m*; toques, *m pl*; (of the knocker) aldabeo, *m*
rapscallion *n* bribón, *m*
rapt *past part* and *a* arrebatado; absorto; extático, extasiado
rapture *n* arrebato, *m*; éxtasis, *m*; transporte, *m*; embriaguez, *f*; entusiasmo, *m*
rapturous *a* embelesado; extático; entusiasta
rapturously *adv* extáticamente; con entusiasmo
rare *a* raro; extraordinario; exótico; infrecuente
raree show *n* barracón de los fenómenos, barracón de las atracciones, *m*
rarefaction *n* rarefacción, *f*
rarefy *vt* rarefacer. *vi* rarefacerse
rareness *n* rareza, *f*; singularidad, *f*; infrecuencia, *f*
rarity *n* raridad, *f*; (uncommonness and rare object) rareza, *f*
rascal *n* sinvergüenza, *m*; truhán, bribón, pícaro, *m*; (affectionately) picaruelo, *m*
rascality *n* bellaquería, truhanería, *f*
rascally *a* redomado; vil, ruin, canallesco
rash *a* temerario, precipitado; imprudente. *n* erupción, *f*, salpullido, *m*
rasher *n* magra, *f*; (of bacon) torrezno, *m*
rashly *adv* temerariamente, precipitadamente; imprudentemente, con imprudencia
rashness *n* temeridad, precipitación, *f*; imprudencia, *f*
rasp *n* escofina, *f*, rallo, *m*; sonido áspero, *m*. *vt* raspar, escofinar; (get on one's nerves) poner los nervios en punta (a)
raspberry *n* frambuesa, *f*. **r.-cane,** frambueso, *m*. **r. jam,** mermelada de frambuesa, *f*
rasping *a* (of the voice) áspero, estridente
rat *n* rata, *f*; desertor, *m*; (black leg) esquirol, *m*. *vi* cazar ratas; ser desertor; ser esquirol. **rat-catcher,** cazador de ratas, *m*. **rat poison,** matarratas, *m*, raticida, *f*. **rat-trap,** ratonera, *f*
ratable *a* sujeto a contribución; imponible; valuable
ratafia *n* ratafía, *f*
rataplan *n* rataplán, *m*
ratchet *n mech* trinquete, *m*; (of a watch) disparador, *m*. **r.-drill,** carraca, *f*. **r.-wheel,** rueda dentada con trinquete, *f*
rate *n* velocidad, *f*; razón, proporción, *f*; (of exchange) tipo, *m*; tanto, *m*; precio, *m*; clase, *f*; modo, *m*, manera, *f*; *naut* clasificación, *f*; (tax) contribución, *f*, impuesto, *m*; *pl* **rates,** (of a house) inquilinato, *m*. *vt* tasar; estimar; fijar el precio (a); *naut* clasificar; imponer una contribución (de); (scold) reñir. **at a great r.,** rápidamente, velozmente. **at a r. of,** a razón de; a una velocidad de. **at any r.,** de todos modos; por lo menos; sea como fuere. **at this r.,** de este modo; a este paso; a esa cuenta; en esta proporción; (with seguir) así. **first-r.,** de primera clase. **rates and taxes,** contribuciones e impuestos, *f pl*. **r. of climb,** *aer* velocidad ascensional,

f. **r. of exchange,** tipo de cambio, *m.* **r.-payer,** contribuyente, *mf*
rather *adv* más bien; antes; (more willingly) de mejor gana; (somewhat) algo, un poco; (perhaps) quizás; mejor dicho; (fairly) bastante; (very) muy; mucho; al contrario. **R.!** ¡Ya lo creo! **or r.,** o más bien. **anything r. than . . . ,** todo menos . . . **He had r.,** Preferiría. **r. than,** antes que, en vez de
ratification *n* ratificación, *f;* (of a bill) aprobación, *f*
ratifier *n* ratificador (-ra)
ratify *vt* ratificar
ratifying *n* ratificación, *f, a* ratificatorio
rating *n* tasación, *f;* valuación, *f;* clasificación, *f;* impuesto, *m,* contribución, *f;* repartición de impuestos, *f;* (of a ship's company) graduación, *f;* (scolding) reprensión, *f*
ratio *n* razón, *f;* proporción, *f.* **in direct r.,** en razón directa
ratiocinate *vi* raciocinar
ratiocination *n* raciocinación, *f*
ration *n* ración, *f. vt* racionar. **r.-book,** cartilla de racionamiento, *f*
rational *a* racional; razonable, juicioso. *n* ser racional, *m*
rationalism *n* racionalismo, *m*
rationalist *n* racionalista, *mf*
rationalistic *a* racionalista
rationality *n* racionalidad, *f;* justicia, *f*
rationalization *n* racionalización, *f;* justificación, *f*
rationalize *vt* hacer racional; concebir racionalmente; *math* quitar los radicales (a); justificar
rationing *n* racionamiento, *m*
rattan *n* rota, *f,* bejuco, *m;* junquillo, *m*
ratteen *n* ratina, *f*
ratter *n* perro ratonero, *m;* gato que caza ratas, *m*
ratting *n* caza de ratas, *f;* deserción, *f*
rattle *vi* hacer ruido; rechinar, crujir; (of loose windows, etc.) zangolotearse; (knock) golpear; tocar; (patter) bailar; sonar; (of the dying) dar un estertor. *vt* (shake) sacudir; hacer vibrar; (jolt) traquetear; (do rapidly) acabar rápidamente; (confuse) aturdir, hacer perder la cabeza (a); desconcertar. **to r. along,** deslizarse (or correr) rápidamente. **to r. off,** (repeat) decir rápidamente; terminar apresuradamente. **to r. on about,** charlar mucho de, hablar sin cesar sobre
rattle *n* rechinamiento, crujido, *m;* zangoloteo, *m;* ruido, *m;* son (de la lluvia, etc.), *m;* (in the throat) estertor, *m;* (of a rattlesnake) cascabel, *m;* (child's) sonajero, *m;* matraca, *f;* carraca, *f;* (chatter) charla, *f.* **r.-headed,** de cabeza de chorlito, casquivano
rattlesnake *n* serpiente de cascabel, *f,* crótalo, *m*
rattling *n* See **rattle**
raucous *a* ronco, estridente
raucousness *n* ronquedad, *f,* estridor, *m*
ravage *vt* devastar; (pillage) saquear; destruir; (spoil) estropear. *n* devastación, *f;* destrucción, *f;* estrago, *m*
ravager *n* devastador (-ra); saqueador (-ra)
rave *vi* desvariar, delirar; (of the elements) bramar, rugir. **to r. about,** hablar con entusiasmo de; delirar por. **to r. against,** vociferar contra, despotricarse contra
ravel *vt* deshilar, destejer; *fig* enredar. **to r. out,** deshilarse; *fig* desenredarse, desenmarañarse
raven *n* cuervo, *m, a* negro como el azabache
ravening *a* rapaz, salvaje
Ravenna Rávena, *f*
ravenous *a* voraz
ravenously *adv* vorazmente
ravenousness *n* voracidad, *f*
ravine *n* cañada, *f,* barranco, cañón, *m*
raving *n* delirio, *m,* desvaríos, *m pl. a* delirante; violento; bravío
ravioli *n pl* ravioles, *m pl*
ravish *vt* (carry off) arrebatar, raptar; extasiar, encantar; (rape) violar, forzar
ravisher *n* raptador, *m;* violador, *m*
ravishing *n* violación, *f, a* encantador
ravishment *n* violación, *f;* arrobamiento, *m;* transporte, éxstasis, *m*
raw *a* (of meat, etc., silk, leather, weather) crudo; bruto; (inexpert) bisoño; (of flesh) vivo; *com* en bruto. **raw-boned,** huesudo. **raw hand,** novato (-ta). **raw material,** primera materia, *f.* **raw materials,** materias primas, *f pl.* **raw score,** puntuación bruta, *f.* **raw silk,** seda cruda, seda en rama, *f.* **raw sugar,** azúcar bruto, *m*
rawhide *a* de cuero crudo
rawness *n* crudeza, *f;* inexperiencia, *f;* (of weather) humedad, *f*
ray *n* rayo, *m;* (line) raya, *f;* (radius) radio, *m;* (fish) raya, *f.* **cathode rays,** rayos catódicos, *m pl*
rayon *n* rayón, *m*
raze *vt* arrasar, asolar; demoler; (erase) borrar, tachar
razor *n* navaja, *f.* **electric r.,** máquina de afeitar eléctrica, *f.* **safety r.,** máquina de afeitar, *f.* **slash with a r.,** navajada, *f.* **r. blade,** hoja de afeitar, *f.* **r. case,** navajero, *m.* **r. strop,** suavizador, *m*
re *n mus* re, *m; prep law* causa, *f; com* concerniente a
re *prefix* (attached to verb) re-; (after the verb) de nuevo; (followed by infin.) volver a . . . **to re-count,** volver a contar, contar de nuevo, recontar
reabsorb *vt* resorber
reabsorption *n* reabsorción, resorción, *f*
reach *vt* (stretch out) alargar; extender; alcanzar; llegar hasta; (arrive at) llegar a; (achieve) lograr, obtener. *vi* extenderse; alcanzar; penetrar. *n* alcance, *m;* extensión, *f;* poder, *m;* capacidad, *f;* (of a river) tabla, *f.* **as far as the eye could r.,** hasta donde alcanzaba la vista. **He reached home very soon,** Llegó muy pronto a casa. **out of r.,** fuera de alcance. **to r. a deadlock,** llegar a un punto muerto. **within r.,** al alcance. **within easy r.,** de fácil acceso; a corta distancia. **to r. after,** procurar alcanzar; hacer esfuerzos para obtener. **to r. back,** (of time) remontarse. **to r. down,** bajar. **r.-me-downs,** ropa hecha, *f*
react *vi* reaccionar. *vt* hacer de nuevo; *theat* volver a representar
reaction *n* reacción, *f*
reactionary *a* and *n* reaccionario (-ia)
reactive *a* reactivo
read *vt* leer; (a riddle, etc.) adivinar; descifrar; interpretar; (study) estudiar; (the Burial Service, etc.) decir; (correct) corregir; (of thermometers, etc.) marcar. *vi* leer; estudiar; (be written) estar escrito, decir. **The play acts better than it reads,** La comedia es mejor representada que leída. **to r. aloud,** leer en voz alta. **to r. between the lines,** leer entre líneas. **to r. proofs,** corregir pruebas. **to r. to oneself,** leer para sí. **to r. about,** leer; (learn) enterarse de. **to r. again,** volver a leer, leer otra vez. **to r. on,** continuar leyendo. **to r. out,** leer en alta voz. **to r. over,** leer; leerlo todo. **to r. over and over again,** leer muchas veces, leer y releer.
read *past part* leído, etc. **well-r.,** releído; instruido, culto
readability *n* legibilidad, *f;* interés, *m,* amenidad, *f*
readable *a* legible; interesante
readdress *vt* dirigir de nuevo (una carta, etc.); poner la nueva dirección en (una carta, etc.)
reader *n* lector (-ra); *ecc* lector, *m;* (proof) corrector de pruebas, *m;* (citation collector for a dictionary) cedulista, *mf;* (university) profesor (-ra) auxiliar a cátedra; (book) libro de lectura, *m.* **to be a great r.,** leer mucho. **the Spanish r.** (reader of Spanish books) el lector de español
readily *adv* fácilmente; en seguida, inmediatamente; de buena gana, con placer
readiness *n* prontitud, expedición, *f;* buena voluntad, *f;* (of speech, etc.) facilidad, *f.* **in r.,** preparado. **r. of wit,** viveza de ingenio, *f*
reading *n* lectura, *Lat. Am. also* leída, *f;* (erudition) conocimientos, *m pl;* (recital) declamación, *f;* (lecture) conferencia, *f;* (study) estudio, *m;* interpretación, *f;* (of a thermometer, etc.) registro, *m;* (of a will) apertura, *f.* **at one reading** *Lat. Am.* de una leída. **r.-book,** libro

de lectura, *m*. **r.-desk,** atril, *m*. **r.-glass,** lente para leer, *m*, carlita, *f*. **r.-lamp,** lámpara de sobremesa, *f*. **r.-matter,** material de lectura, *m*. **r.-room,** gabinete de lectura, *m*, sala de lectura, *f*
readjourn *vt* (a meeting) suspender (la sesión) de nuevo
readjust *vt* reajustar, reacomdar; *vi* reacomodarse
readjustment *n* reajuste, *m*, reacomodación, *f*
readmission *n* readmisión, *f*
ready *a* listo, preparado; dispuesto; pronto; (on the point of) a punto de; (easy) fácil; (near at hand) a la mano; (with money) contante; (with wit, etc.) vivo; (available) disponible; (nimble) ágil, ligero. **I am r. to do it,** Estoy dispuesto a hacerlo. **in r. cash,** en dinero contante. **to get r.,** prepararse; (dress) vestirse. **to make r.,** *vt* preparar; aprestar; *print* imponer. *vi* prepararse, disponerse. **r.-made,** hecho; confeccionado. **r.-made clothing,** ropa hecha, *f*. **r. money,** dinero contante, *m*. **r.-witted,** de ingenio vivo
reaffirm *vt* afirmar de nuevo; reiterar, volver a repetir
reaffirmation *n* reiteración, *f*
reafforestation *n* nuevas plantaciones, *f pl*
reagent *n* reactivo, *m*
real *a* real; verdadero; efectivo; (with silk, etc.) puro; sincero. **r. estate, r. property,** bienes raíces, *m pl*
realism *n* realismo, *m*
realist *n* realista, *mf*
realistic *a* realista
reality *n* realidad, *f*; verdad, *f*
realizable *a* realizable; factible
realization *n* realización, *f*; comprensión, *f*
realize *vt* (understand) darse cuenta de, hacerse cargo de; realizar; (make real) dar vida (a); (accomplish) llevar a cabo; *com* realizar; (gain) adquirir
really *adv* realmente; en verdad; en realidad; en efecto; (frankly) francamente. **R.?** ¿De veras?
realm *n* reino, *m*, dominios, *m pl*; *fig* esfera, *f*
realty *n* bienes raíces, *m pl*
ream *n* resma, *f*
reanimate *vt* reanimar
reap *vt* segar; *fig* cosechar, recoger
reaper *n* segador (-ra); (machine) segadora mecánica, *f*
reaping *n* siega, *f*; *fig* cosecha, *f*. **r.-machine,** segadora mecánica, *f*
reappear *vi* reaparecer
reappearance *n* reaparición, *f*
reapplication *n* nueva aplicación, *f*; (of paint, etc.) otra capa, *f*; (for a post, etc.) neuva solicitud, *f*
reapply *vt* aplicar de nuevo; (paint, etc.) dar otra capa (de); (for a post, etc.) mandar una nueva solicitud
reappoint *vt* designar de nuevo
rear *vt* (lift) alzar, levantar; (breed, educate) criar; (build) erigir, construir. *vi* (of horses) encabritarse, corcovear
rear *n* cola, *f*; parte de atrás, *f*; parte posterior, *f*; última fila, *f*; (background) fondo, *m*; *inf* trasera, *f*; *mil* retaguardia, *f*. *a* de atrás; trasero; último; posterior; de última fila; *mil* de retaguardia. **in the r.,** por detrás; a la cola; a retaguardia. **to bring up the r.,** cerrar la marcha. **r.-admiral,** contra almirante, *m*. **r.-axle,** eje trasero, *m*. **r.-guard,** retaguardia, *f*. **r. lamp,** faro trasero, *m*. **r. rank,** última fila, *f*. **r. view,** vista por detrás, *f*; vista posterior, *f*
rearing *n* (breeding) cría, *f*; (education) crianza, *f*
rearm *vt* rearmar. *vi* rearmarse
rearmament *n* rearmamento, *m*
rearrange *vt* volver a arreglar; arreglar de otra manera; (a literary work) refundir, adaptar
rearrangement *n* nuevo arroglo, *m*; (of a literary work) refundición, adaptación, *f*
reascend *vi* and *vt* subir de nuevo, subir otra vez; montar de nuevo (sobre)
reason *n* razón, *f*. **I have plenty of r. to . . .** No me faltarían motivos para . . . *vi* and *vt* razonar. **to r. out of,** disuadir de. **by r. of,** a causa de, con motivo de; en virtud de. **for this r.,** por esto, por esta razón. **out of all r.,** fuera de razón. **to stand to r.,** ser lógico, estar puesto en razón. **with r.,** con razón. **r. of state,** razón de estado, *f*
reasonable *a* razonable; racional
reasonableness *n* lo razonable; moderación, *f*; justicia, *f*; racionalidad, *f*
reasonably *adv* razonablemente; con razón; bastante
reasoning *n* razonamiento, *m*
reassemble *vt* reunir otra vez. *vi* juntarse de nuevo
reassert *vt* afirmar de nuevo, reiterar
reassertion *n* reiteración, *f*
reassess *vt* tasar de nuevo; repartir de nuevo; (a work of art) hacer una nueva apreciación (de)
reassessment *n* nueva tasación, *f*; nuevo repartimiento, *m*; (of a work of art) nueva estimación, *f*
reassume *vt* reasumir
reassumption *n* reasunción, *f*
reassurance *n* afirmación repetida, *f*; confianza restablecida, *f*
reassure *vt* asegurar de nuevo; tranquilizar, confortar
reassuring *a* tranquilizador, consolador
rebate *n* rebaja, *f*, descuento, *m*; reducción, *f*. *vt* rebajar, descontar; reducir. **to r. pro rata,** ratear
rebec *n mus* rabel, *m*
rebel *n* rebelde, *mf*, insurrecto (-ta). *vi* rebelarse, sublevarse. **r. leader,** cabecilla, *m*
rebellion *n* rebelión, *f*
rebellious *a* rebelde; revoltoso; refractario
rebelliousness *n* rebeldía, *f*
rebind *vt* atar de nuevo; (a book) reencuadernar
rebirth *n* renacimiento, *m*
rebore *vt* (an engine) descarbonizar
reboring *n* (of an engine) descarburación, *f*
reborn, to be *vi* renacer; ser reincarnado
rebound *a* (of books) reencuadernado. *vi* rebotar; repercutir; (revive) reavivarse. *n* rebote, resalto, *m*; reacción, *f*, rechazo, *m*
rebuff *n* repulsa, *f*, desaire, *m*; contrariedad, *f*. *vt* rechazar; contrariar
rebuild *vt* reedificar
rebuilding *n* reedificación, *f*
rebuke *n* reconvención, reprensión, censura, *f*, reproche, *m*, *vt* reprender, censurar, reprochar
rebukingly *adv* en tono de censura; con reprensión, con reprobación
rebut *vt* refutar
rebuttal *n* refutación, *f*
recalcitrance *n* terquedad, obstinacia, *f*; rebeldía, *f*
recalcitrant *a* reacio, recalcitrante
recall *vt* llamar; hacer volver; (dismiss) destituir; (ambassador, etc.) retirar; (remind or remember) recordar; (revoke) revocar. *n* llamada, *f*; *mil* toque de llamada, *m*; (of ambassadors, etc.) retirada, *f*; (dismissal) destitución, *f*. **beyond r.,** irrevocable; (forgotten) olvidado
recant *vt* retractar, retirar. *vi* desdecirse (de), retractarse
recantation *n* recantación, *f*
recapitulate *vt* recapitular, resumir
recapitulation *n* recapitulación, *f*
recapture *vt* volver a prender, hacer prisionero nuevamente; (a place) volver a tomar; (a ship) represar
recast *vt* (metals, a literary work) refundir; (alter) cambiar; (reckon) volver a calcular
recasting *n* (metals, a literary work) refundición, *f*
recede *vi* retroceder; alejarse (de), separarse (de); desviarse (de); retirarse; desaparecer; (diminish) disminuir; (of prices) bajar
receding *a* que retrocede, etc.
receipt *n* recibo, *m*; (for money) recibí, *m*; (recipe) receta, *f*; *pl* **receipts,** ingresos, *m pl*. *vt* firmar (or extender) recibo. **on r. of,** al recibir. **to acknowledge the r. of,** acusar recibo de. **r. book,** libro talonario, *m*
receive *vt* and *vi* recibir; admitir, aceptar; acoger; (money) percibir, cobrar; (lodge) hospedar, alojar; (contain) contener. **to r. one's degree** *Lat. Am.* diplomarse. **to be well received,** tener buena acogida
receiver *n* recibidor (-ra); (of stolen goods) receptador

(-ra); (in bankruptcies) síndico, *m*; (for other legal business) receptor, *m*; (of a telephone) auricular, *m*; *elec* receptor, *m*; *rad* radiorreceptor, *m*. **to hang up (the r.),** colgar (el auricular)
receivership *n* sindicatura, *f*; receptoría, *f*
receiving *n* recibimiento, *m*; (of money, etc.) cobranza, *f*, percibo, *m*; (of stolen goods) encubrimiento, *m*. *a* que recibe; recipiente; de recepción. **r. set,** aparato de radio, *m*
recency *n* lo reciente; novedad, *f*
recent *a* reciente; nuevo. **in r. years,** en estos últimos años
recently *adv* recientemente; (before past participles) recién. **until r.,** hasta hace poco. **r. painted,** recién pintado
receptacle *n* receptáculo, recipiente, *m*; *bot* receptáculo, *m*
reception *n* recepción, *f*; recibo, *m*; (welcome) acogida, *f*; (of evidence) recepción, *f*. **r. room,** pieza de recibo, *f*, gabinete, *m*
receptive *a* receptivo; susceptible
receptiveness *n* sensibilidad, susceptibilidad, *f*
recess *n* (holiday) vacaciones, *f pl*; (during school hours) hora de recreo, *f*; (*fig* heart) seno, *m*, entrañas, *f pl*; (of the soul, heart) hondón, *m*; (in a coastline, etc.) depresión, *f*; (in a wall) nicho, *m*; (alcove) alcoba, *f*. **parliamentary r.,** interregno parlamentario, *m*
recessional *n* himno que se canta mientras se retiran los eclesiásticos y el coro, *m*
recharge *vt* (a gun, etc.) recargar; acusar de nuevo
recipe *n* receta, *f*
recipient *n* recibidor (-ra); el, *m*, (*f*, la) que recibe. *a* recipiente; receptivo
reciprocal *a* recíproco
reciprocate *vt* reciprocar; *mech* producir movimiento de vaivén. *vi mech* oscilar, tener movimiento alternativo; corresponder; ser recíproco
reciprocation *n* reciprocación, *f*; reciprocidad, correspondencia, *f*
reciprocity *n* reciprocidad, *f*
recital *n* narración, relación, *f*; enumeración, *f*; recitación, *f*; *mus* recital, *m*
recitation *n* recitación, *f*
recitative *n* recitado, *m*
recite *vt* recitar, repetir; narrar; declamar. *vi* decir una recitación
reciter *n* recitador (-ra); declamador (-ra)
reckless *a* temerario, audaz; precipitado; descuidado (de); indiferente (a); excesivo; imprudente
recklessly *adv* temerariamente; descuidadamente; imprudentemente
recklessness *n* temeridad, audacia, *f*; descuido, *m*; imprudencia, *f*; indiferencia, *f*
reckon *vt* calcular, computar; contar; enumerar; (believe) considerar, juzgar; (attribute) atribuir; (think) creer (que). **to r. up,** echar cuentas, calcular. **to r. with,** contar con; tomar en serio
reckoner *n* calculador (-ra). **ready r.,** tablas matemáticas, *f pl*
reckoning *n* cálculo, *m*, calculación, *f*; cuenta, *f*; *fig* retribución, *f*, castigo, *m*; *naut* estima, *f*. **the day of r.,** el día de ajuste de cuentas; el día del juicio final. **to be out in one's r.,** equivocarse en el cálculo; engañarse en el juicio
reclaim *vt* (land) entarquinar; (reform) reformar; (tame) domesticar; (claim) reclamar; (restore) restaurar
reclamation *n* (of land) entarquinamiento, *m*; cultivo, *m*; (reform) reformación, *f*; (restoration) restauración, *f*; (claiming) reclamación, *f*
recline *vt* apoyar; recostar; reclinar; descansar, reposar. *vi* recostarse, reclinarse; estar tumbado; apoyarse; descansar
reclining *n* reclinación, *f*. *a* inclinado; acostado; (of statues) yacente
recluse *a* solitario. *n* recluso (-sa); solitario (-ia); ermitaño, *m*, anacoreta, *mf*
recognition *n* reconocimiento, *m*
recognizable *a* que puede reconocerse; identificable
recognizance *n* reconocimiento, *m*; *law* obligación, *f*
recognize *vt* reconocer; confesar
recoil *n* reculada, *f*; (of a gun) culatazo, *m*; (refusal) rechazo, *m*; (result) repercusión, *f*; (repugnance) aversión, repugnancia, *f*. *vi* recular; retroceder; repercutir; sentir repugnancia
recoin *vt* acuñar de nuevo
recollect *vt* acordarse de, recordar. **to r. oneself,** reponerse, recobrarse
recollection *n* recuerdo, *m*, memoria, *f*
recommence *vt* and *vi* empezar de nuevo
recommend *vt* recomendar; aconsejar; encargar
recommendable *a* recomendable
recommendation *n* recomendación, *f*
recommendatory *a* recomendatario
recommender *n* el, *m*, (*f*, la) que recomienda
recompense *n* recompensa, *f*, *vt* recompensar
recomposition *n* recomposición, *f*
reconcilability *n* posibilidad de reconciliación, *f*; compatibilidad, *f*
reconcilable *a* reconciliable; compatible; conciliable
reconcile *vt* reconciliar; (quarrels) componer, ajustar; (opposing theories, etc.) conciliar. **to r. oneself (to),** aceptar; acostumbrarse (a); resignarse (a)
reconciler *n* reconciliador (-ra)
reconciliation *n* reconciliación, *f*; (of theories, etc.) conciliación, *f*
reconciliatory *a* reconciliador
recondite *a* recóndito
recondition *vt* recondicionar
reconnaissance *n* reconocimiento, *m*; exploración, *f*. **r. flight,** vuelo de reconocimiento, *m*. **r. plane,** avión de reconocimiento, *m*
reconnoiter *vt mil* reconocer; explorar. *vi mil* practicar un reconocimiento; correr la campaña
reconnoitering *n* reconocimiento, *m*, *a* de reconocimiento
reconquer *vt* reconquistar
reconquest *n* reconquista, *f*
reconsecrate *vt* consagrar de nuevo
reconsider *vt* considerar de nuevo, volver a considerar; volver a discutir
reconsideration *n* nueva consideración, *f*; nueva discusión, *f*
reconstitute *vt* reconstituir
reconstitution *n* reconstitución, *f*
reconstruct *vt* reconstruir
reconstruction *n* reconstrucción, *f*
reconversion *n* reconversión, *f*
recopy *vt* copiar de nuevo
record *vt* apuntar; inscribir; (recount) contar, escribir; recordar; registrar; (of thermometers, etc.) marcar, registrar; hacer un disco de gramófono de; (radio, cinema) impresionar. *n* relación, *f*; crónica, *f*; historia, *f*; (soldier's) hoja de servicios, *f*; (past) antecedentes, *m pl*; documento, *m*; inscripción, *f*; (entry) partida, *f*; testimonio, *m*; (memory) recuerdo, *m*; registro, *m*; (gramophone) disco de gramófono, *m*; *sport* record, *m*, plusmarca, *f*; *pl* **records,** *m pl*; (notes) notas, *f pl*; (facts) datos, *m pl*; anales, *m pl*. **keeper of the records,** archivero, *m*. **off the r.,** confidencialmente. **on r.,** escrito; registrado; inscrito en los anales de la historia. **to break a r.,** supremar precedentes. **r.-holder,** plusmarquista, *mf*
recorder *n* registrador, *m*; archivero, *m*; *law* juez, *m*; (historian) historiador, *m*; *mus* caramillo, *m*; *mech* contador, indicador, *m*; (scientific) aparato registrador, *m*
recording *a* registrador. **r. apparatus,** (cinema, radio, gramophone) máquina de impresionar, *f*; (scientific) aparato registrador, *m*. **r. van,** carro de sonido, *m*
recount *vt* contar de nuevo; (tell) referir, narrar, contar
recoup *vt* compensar, indemnizar; recobrar, desquitarse de
recourse *n* recurso, *m*. **to have r. to,** recurrir, *a*

recover *vt* (regain) recobrar; *fig* reconquistar; (retrieve) rescatar; *law* reivindicar. *vi* reponerse; (in health) recobrar la salud, sanar, curarse; *law* ganar un pleito. **to r. consciousness,** volver en sí
recoverable *a* recuperable
recovery *n* (regaining) recobro, *m,* recuperación, *f;* (of money) cobranza, *f;* (retrieval) rescate, *m; fig* reconquista, *f;* (from illness) mejoría, convalecencia, *f;* restablecimiento, *m; law* reivindicación, *f*
recreant *a* traidor, falso, desleal. *n* apóstata, *mf* traidor (-ra)
recreate *vt* recrear
recreation *n* recreación, *f;* (break in schools) recreo, *m.* **r. hall,** sala de recreo, *f*
recreative *a* recreativo
recriminate *vi* recriminar
recrimination *n* recriminación, reconvención, *f*
recriminator *n* recriminador (-ra)
recriminatory *a* recriminador
recross *vt* volver a cruzar, cruzar de nuevo
recrudesce *vi* recrudecer
recrudescence *n* recrudescencia, *f*
recrudescent *a* recrudescente
recruit *n* recluta, *m. vt* reclutar; (restore) reponer
recruiting *n* reclutamiento, *m.* **r. office,** caja de reclutamiento, *f*
rectal *a* rectal
rectangle *n* rectángulo, *m*
rectangular *a* rectangular
rectifiable *a* rectificable
rectification *n* rectificación, *f*
rectifier *n* rectificador, *m*
rectify *vt* rectificar
rectilinear *a* rectilíneo
rectitude *n* rectitud, *f*
rector *n* (of a university or school) rector, *m;* (priest) párroco, *m*
rectorship *n* rectorado, *m*
rectory *n* rectoral, rectoría, *f*
rectum *n* recto, *m*
recumbent *a* recostado, reclinado; (of a statue) yacente
recuperable *a* recuperable
recuperate *vt* recuperar, recobrar. *vi* restablecerse, reponerse; recuperarse
recuperation *n* recuperación, *f*
recuperative *a* recuperativo
recur *vi* presentarse a la imaginación; volver (sobre); presentarse de nuevo, aparecer otra vez; repetirse; reproducirse
recurrence *n* reaparición, *f;* repetición, *f*
recurrent *a* periódico; *med* recurrente
red *a* rojo; (of wine) tinto. *n* color rojo, *m;* (in billiards) mingo, *m,* bola roja, *f; pol* rojo, *m.* **to catch red-handed,** coger con el hurto en las manos; coger con las manos en la masa, coger en el acto. **to grow red,** enrojecerse, ponerse rojo; volverse rojo. **red-berried,** con bayas rojas. **red cabbage,** lombarda, *f.* **red cedar,** cedro dulce, *m.* **red corpuscle,** glóbulo rojo, *m.* **Red Cross,** Cruz Roja, *f.* **red currant,** grosella, *f.* **red currant bush,** grosellero, *m.* **red-eyed,** con los ojos inyectados. **red fir,** pino silvestre, *m.* **red flush,** (in the sky) arrebol, *m.* **red-gold,** bermejo; (of hair, etc.) rojo. **red-haired,** pelirrojo, de pelo rojo. **red-handed,** con las manos ensangrentadas; *fig* en el acto. **red-head** (person) pelirrojo (-ja). **red-heat,** incandescencia, *f.* **red-hot,** candente. *m.* **red-lead,** minio, *m.* **red-letter,** de fiesta; extraordinario. **red-letter day,** día de fiesta, *m;* día extraordinario, *m.* **red mullet,** salmonete, *m,* trilla, *f.* **red ocher,** almagre, *m.* **red pepper,** pimiento, *m;* (cayenne) pimentón, *Lat. Am.* ají, *m,* **Red Sea,** mar Rojo, mar Bermejo, *m.* **red tape,** balduque, *m;* formulismo, *m;* burocracia, *f.* **red wine,** vino tinto, *m*
redbreast *n* petirrojo, *m*
redden *vt* rojear, enrojecer; pintar de rojo. *vi* enrojecerse, ponerse rojo; volverse rojo
reddish *a* rojizo
redeem *vt* (a mortgage, bonds, etc.) amortizar; (from pawn) desempeñar; (a promise, etc.) cumplir; libertar; redimir; compensar; (a fault) expiar; (reform) reformar; (rescue) rescatar
redeemable *a* redimible; amortizable
redeemer *n* rescatador (-ra); salvador (-ra); *theol* Redentor, *m*
redeeming *a* redentor; compensatorio. **r. feature,** compensación, *f;* rasgo bueno, *m.* **There is no r. feature in his work,** No hay nada bueno en su obra
redemption *n* (of a mortgage, etc.) amortización, *f;* (from pawn) desempeño, *m;* (of a promise, etc.) cumplimiento, *m;* (ransom, etc.) rescate, *m; theol* redención, *f;* compensación, *f;* (of a fault) expiación, *f;* reformación, *f*
redemptive *a* redentor
redescend *vi* bajar de nuevo
rediscovery *n* nuevo descubrimiento, *m*
redistribute *vt* distribuir de nuevo, volver a distribuir
redistribution *n* nueva distribución, *f*
redness *n* rojez, *f,* color rojo, *m*
redolent *a* fragante, oloroso; *fig* evocador (de)
redouble *vt* redoblar. *vi* redoblarse
redoubling *n* redoblamiento, *m*
redoubt *n* reducto, *m*
redoubtable *a* formidable, terrible; valiente
redound *vi* redundar (en)
redress *vt* rectificar; reparar; remediar; hacer justicia (a); corregir
reduce *vt* reducir; disminuir; (in price) rebajar; abreviar; (exhaust, weaken) agotar; (impoverish) empobrecer; (degrade) degradar. **to r. to the ranks,** *mil* volver a las filas; degradar. **to be in reduced circumstances,** estar en la indigencia
reducible *a* reducible
reduction *n* reducción, *f;* (in price) rebaja, *f*
redundance *n* redundancia, *f*
redundant *a* redundante; superfluo, excesivo
reduplicate *vt* reduplicar
reduplication *n* reduplicación, *f*
reecho *vt* repetir; devolver el son de, hacer reverberar. *vi* repercutirse, reverberar
reed *n bot* caña, *f;* (arrow) saeta, *f;* (pipe) caramillo, *m;* (in wind-instruments) lengüeta, *f; arch* junquillo, *m;* (in a loom) peine, *m;* (pastoral poetry) poesía bucólica, *f. vt* (thatch) bardar con cañas
reedit *vt* reeditar, volver a editar
reedy *a* juncoso, lleno de cañas; (of the voice) silbante
reef *n* arrecife, escollo, encalladero, *m; min* filón, *m; naut* rizo, *m. vt naut* arrizar. **to take in reefs,** *naut* hacer el rizo. **r.-knot,** nudo de marino, *m*
reek *n* humo, *m;* olor, *m. vi* humear; oler (de); *fig* recordar, hacer pensar (en)
reeky *a* humoso
reel *n* carrete, *m;* devanadera, *f;* (of a fishing rod) carrete, carretel, *m;* (cinema) cinta, *f;* (dance) baile escocés, *m. vt* devanar. *vi* tambalear, titubear; (of ships, etc.) cabecear; temblar; oscilar. **to r. about drunkenly,** (of persons) andar haciendo eses, arrimarse a las paredes. **to r. off,** recitar; enumerar; decir rápidamente
reelect *vt* reelegir
reelection *n* reelección, *f*
reeligible *a* reelegible
reeling *n* tambaleo, *m;* andar vacilante, *m;* (of a ship, etc.) cabeceo, *m;* oscilación, *f*
reembarcation *n* reembarque, *m*
reembark *vt* reembarcar. *vi* reembarcarse
reemerge *vi* reaparecer
reemergence *n* reaparición, *f*
reenact *vt* revalidar (una ley); decretar de nuevo
reenactment *n* revalidación (de una ley), *f;* nuevo decreto, *m*
reengage *vt* contratar de nuevo
reengagement *n* nuevo contrato, *m*

reenlist *vt* and *vi* alistar(se) de nuevo
reenlistment *n* reenganche, *m*
reenter *vt* volver a entrar (en); reingresar (en)
reentry *n* segunda entrada, *f*, reingreso, *m*
reequip *vt* equipar de nuevo
reestablish *vt* restablecer; restaurar
reestablishment *n* restablecimiento, *m*; restauración, *f*
reeve *vt naut* laborear, guarnir
reexamination *n* reexaminación, *f*; nuevo examen, *m*; *law* nuevo interrogatorio, *m*
reexamine *vt* reexaminar; *law* interrogar de nuevo
reexport *vt* reexportar
reexportation *n* reexportación, *f*
refashion *vt* volver a hacer; formar de nuevo
refection *n* refección, *f*
refectory *n* refectorio, *m*
refer *vt* atribuir (a); (send) enviar, remitir; (assign) referir (a), relacionar (con). *vi* referirse (a); aludir (a); hablar (de)
referee *n* árbitro, *m*; *law* juez arbitrador, *m*; (reference) garante, *mf* fiador (-ra). *vi* servir de árbitro
reference *n* referencia, *f*; consulta, *f*; mención, *f*; alusión, *f*; (relation) relación, *f*; *pl* **references,** *com* referencias, *f pl*. **for r.,** para consulta. **in r. to,** con referencia a, respecto a, en cuanto a. **terms of r.,** puntos de consulta, *m pl*. **work of r.,** libro de consulta, *m*
reference book *n* libro de consulta, *m*
referendum *n* referéndum, *m*
refill *vt* rellenar; rehenchir; (pen) llenar de nuevo con tinta. *n* (for a pencil) mina de recambio, *f*
refine *vt* refinar; (metals) acrisolar; (fats) clarificar; *fig* perfeccionar, pulir, refinar
refined *a* refinado; fino; culto; cortés; elegante; delicado; (subtle) sutil; (affected) afectado
refinement *n* refinamiento, *m*; finura, *f*; cultura, *f*; cortesía, *f*; elegancia, *f*; delicadeza, *f*; (subtlety) sutileza, *f*; (affectation) afectación, *f*
refiner *n* refinador, *m*
refinery *n* refinería, *f*
refining *n* refinación, *f*; *fig* refinamiento, *m*
refit *vt* reparar; *naut* embonar
refitting *n* reparación, *f*; *naut* embonada, *f*
reflect *vt* reflejar; reflexionar. *vi* reflejar; reflexionar (sobre), pensar (en), meditar (sobre). **This offer reflects credit on him,** Esta oferta le hace honor. **to r. on, upon,** reflexionar sobre; (disparage) desacreditar; (affect unfavorably) perjudicar
reflecting *a* reflector
reflection *n phys* reflexión, *f*; reflejo, *m*; consideración, *f*, pensamiento, *m*; (aspersion) censura, *f*, reproche, *m*. **upon mature r.,** después de pensarlo bien
reflective *a phys* reflector; reflexivo, pensativo, meditabundo
reflectively *adv* reflexivamente
reflector *n* reflector, *m*; (shade) pantalla, *f*
reflex *a* reflejo. *n* reflejo, *m*; acción refleja, *f*. **r. action,** acción refleja, *f*
refloat *vt* (a ship) poner otra vex a flote, desvarar
reflux *n* reflujo, *m*
reform *n* reforma, *f*. *a* de reforma; reformista. *vt* reformar; formar de nuevo. *vi* reformarse
reformation *n* reformación, *f*; **Reformation,** Reforma, *f*
reformatory *a* reformatorio, reformador. *n* reformatorio, *m*, casa de corrección, *f*
reformer *n* reformador (-ra), reformista, *mf*
refract *vt* refractar
refraction *n* refracción, *f*
refractive *a* refringente
refractoriness *n* terquedad, obstinacia, *f*; rebeldía, indocilidad, *f*
refractory *a* (of substances) refractario; recalcitrante, intratable, rebelde
refrain *n* estribillo, estrambote, *m*
refrain *vi* abstenerse (de), evitar
refresh *vt* refrescar
refreshing *a* refrescante; atractivo; estimulante; interesante
refreshment *n* (solace) solaz, reposo, *m*; recreación, *f*, deleite, *m*; (food and (or) drink) refresco, *m*. **r.-room,** (at a station) fonda, *f*. **r. stand** *Mexico* fresquería, *f*
refrigerate *vt* refrigerar; enfriar; refrescar
refrigeration *n* refrigeración, *f*; enfriamiento, *m*. **r. chamber,** cámara frigorífica, *f*
refrigerative *a* refrigerante, frigorífico
refrigerator *n* refrigerador, *m*, nevera, *f*
refringent *a* refringente
refuel *vt* (a furnace) cargar con carbón, etc.; (of a ship) tomar carbón; (of an airplane, motor vehicle) tomar bencina
refuge *n* refugio, *m*; asilo, *m*; (resort) recurso, *m*; subterfugio, *m*; (traffic island) refugio para peatones, *m*. **to take r.,** refugiarse; resguardarse (de)
refugee *a* refugiado. *n* refugiado (-da)
refulgence *n* refulgencia, *f*
refulgent *a* refulgente
refund *vt* reembolsar; devolver
refunding *n* reembolso, *m*; devolución, *f*
refurbish *vt* restaurar; renovar; (a literary work) refundir
refurnish *vt* amueblar de nuevo
refusal *n* negativa, *f*; (rejection) rechazo, *m*; (option) opción, *f*; preferencia, *f*
refuse *vt* negar; (reject) rechazar. *vi* negarse (a), rehusar; (of a horse) resistirse a saltar
refuse *n* desecho, *m*; desperdicios, *m pl*; residuo, *m*; basura, *f*. *a* de desecho. **r. dump,** muladar, *m*
refutable *a* refutable
refutation *n* refutación, *f*
refute *vt* refutar
regain *vt* recobrar, recuperar; cobrar; ganar de nuevo; *fig* reconquistar. **to r. one's breath,** cobrar aliento. **to r. consciousness,** volver en sí
regal *a* regio, real
regale *vt* regalar, agasajar; recrear, deleitar
regalia *n* regalía, *f*; insignias reales, *f pl*; distintivos, *m pl*, insignias, *f pl*
regally *adv* regiamente
regard *vt* mirar; observar; considerar; (respect) respetar; (concern) importar, concernir; relacionarse con. *n* mirada, *f*; atención, *f*; (esteem) aprecio, *m*, estimación, *f*; respeto, *m*; veneración, *f*; (relation) referencia, *f*; *pl* **regards,** recuerdos, saludos, *m pl*. **He has little r. for their feelings,** Le importan poco sus susceptibilidades. **With kindest regards,** Con mis saludos más afectuosos. **as regards, with r. to,** con referencia a, respecto a, en cuanto a
regardful *a* atento (a), cuidadoso (de); que se preocupa (de)
regarding *prep* tocante a, en cuanto a, respecto de
regardless *a* negligente (de); indiferente (a), insensible (a); que no se interesa (en); que no se inqueta (por); sin preocuparse (de)
regatta *n* regata, *f*
regency *n* regencia, *f*
regeneracy *n* regeneración, *f*
regenerate *vt* regenerar. *a* regenerado
regeneration *n* regeneración, *f*
regenerative *a* regenerador
regenerator *n* regenerador (-ra)
regent *n* regente, *mf*
régime *n* régimen, *m*
regimen *n* (*gram med*) régimen, *m*,
regiment *n* regimiento, *m*. *vt* regimentar. **r. of the line,** tropa de línea, *f*
regimental *a* de (un) regimiento, perteneciente a un regimiento
regimentation *n* regimentación, *f*
region *n* región, *f*
regional *a* regional
regionalism *n* regionalismo, *m*
regionalist *n* regionalista, *mf*

regionalistic *a* regionalista
register *n* (record and *mech mus print*) registro, *m;* (of ships, etc.) matrícula, *f;* lista, *f. vt* registrar; matricular; (a ship) abanderar; inscribir; (one's child in a school) anotar (Argentina), inscribir; (of thermometers, etc.) marcar; (letters) certificar; (luggage) facturar; (in one's mind) grabar; (emotion) mostrar, manifestar. *vi* (at a hotel, etc.) registrarse; *print* estar en registro. **cash r.,** caja registradora, *f.* **r. of births, marriages and deaths,** registro civil, *m*
registered letter *n* carta certificada, *f*
registrar *n* registrador, *m;* archivero, *m;* secretario, *m;* (of a school) jefe de inscripciones, secretario general (the latter has many more duties). **r. of births, marriages and deaths,** secretario del registro civil, *m.* **registrar's office,** oficina del registro civil, *f*
registration *n* registro, *m;* inscripción, *f;* (of a vehicle, etc.) matrícula, *f; naut* abanderamiento, *m;* (of a letter, etc.) certificación, *f.* **r. number,** número de matrícula, *m*
registry *n* registro, *m;* inscripción, *f;* matrícula, *f.* **r. office,** oficina del registro civil, *f;* (for servants) agencia doméstica, *f*
regression *n* regresión, *f,* retroceso, *m*
regret *vt* sentir; lamentar, pesar; arrepentirse (de); (miss) echar de menos (a). *n* sentimiento, pesar, *m;* (remorse) remordimiento, *m.* **I r. very much that . . . ,** Me pesa mucho que . . . , Siento mucho que . . . **to send one's regrets,** mandar sus excusas
regretful *a* lleno de pesar; arrepentido; lamentable, deplorable. **He was most r. that . . . ,** Lamentaba mucho que . . .
regretfully *adv* con pesar
regrettable *a* lamentable, deplorable; doloroso; (with loss, etc.) sensible
regrettably *adv* lamentablemente; sensiblemente
regroup *vt* arreglar de nuevo; formar de nuevo; reorganizar
regular *a* regular; normal; (ordinary) corriente, común; (in order) en regla; (*gram bot ecc mil geom*) regular. *n ecc* regular, *m;* (soldier) soldado de línea, *m;* (officer) militar de carrera, *m;* (client) parroquiano habitual, *m*
regularity *n* regularidad,
regularization *n* regularización, *f*
regularize *vt* regularizar
regularly *adv* regularmente
regulate *vt* regular; ajustar, arreglar; (direct) dirigir; reglamentar
regulation *n* regulación, *f;* arreglo, *m;* (rule) reglamento, *m, a* de reglamento; normal
regulative *a* regulador
regulator *n mech* regulador, *m*
regurgitate *vt* and *vi* regurgitar
regurgitation *n* regurgitación, *f*
rehabilitate *vt* rehabilitar
rehabilitation *n* rehabilitación, *f*
rehash *vt* (a literary work, etc.) refundir
rehearing *n* nueva audición, *f,* (of a case) revisión, *f*
rehearsal *n theat* ensayo, *m;* recitación, *f;* relación, narración, *f.* **dress r.,** ensayo general, *m*
rehearse *vt theat* ensayar; recitar; (narrate) narrar; enumerar
reheat *vt* recalentar
reign *n* reinado, *m. vi* reinar; predominar
reigning *a* reinante; predominante
reimburse *vt* reembolsar
reimbursement *n* reembolso, *m*
reimport *vt* importar de nuevo, reimportar, *n* reimporte, *m*
reimportation *n* reimportación, *f*
reimpose *vt* reimponer
reimposition *n* reimposición, *f*
reimprison *vt* encarcelar de nuevo, reencarcelar
reimprisonment *n* reencarcelamiento, *m*
rein *n* rienda, *f. vt* llevar las riendas (de); (hold back) refrenar. **to give r. to,** *fig* dar rienda suelta (a)
reincarnation *n* reencarnación, *f*
reincorporate *vt* reincorporar
reincorporation *n* reincorporación, *f*
reindeer *n* reno, *m*
reinforce *vt* reforzar; (concrete) armar; fortalecer. **reinforced concrete,** *n* hormigón armado, *m*
reinforcement *n* reforzamiento, *m;* (*mil nav fig*) refuerzo, *m*
reins. *n* See **rein**
reinsert *vt* volver a insertar
reinstall *vt* reinstalar; rehabilitar
reinstalment *n* reinstalación, *f;* rehabilitación, *f;* restablecimiento, *m*
reinstate *vt* reponer, restablecer; reinstalar; rehabilitar
reinstatement *n* restablecimiento, *m;* rehabilitación, *f*
reinsurance *n* reaseguro, *m*
reinsure *vt* reasegurar
reintegrate *vt* reintegrar
reintegration *n* reintegración, *f*
reinter *vt* enterrar de nuevo
reinvest *vt* reinvertir
reinvestment *n* reinversión, *f*
reinvigorate *vt* reanimar, dar nuevo vigor (a)
reinvite *vt* invitar de nuevo (a)
reissue *n* nueva emisión, *f;* (of a book, etc.) nueva edición, reimpresión, *f. vt* hacer una nueva emisión (de); reeditar, publicar de nuevo
reiterate *vt* reiterar, repetir
reiteration *n* reiteración, *f*
reiterative *a* reiterativo
reject *vt* rechazar, rehusar; repudiar; repulsar; desechar
rejection *n* rechazamiento, *m;* repudiación, refutación, *f;* repulsa, *f*
rejoice *vt* alegrar, regocijar. *vi* alegrarse (de), regocijarse (de), gloriarse (en)
rejoicing *n* regocijo, júbilo, *m,* alegría, *f;* algazara, *f,* fiestas, *f pl*
rejoin *vt* and *vi* juntar de nuevo; volver a; reunirse con; (reply) contestar, replicar
rejoinder *n* contestación, respuesta, *f*
rejuvenate *vt* rejuvenecer
rejuvenation *n* rejuvenecimiento, *m*
rekindle *vt* encender de nuevo; despertar, reavivar. *vi* encenderse de nuevo; reavivarse
relapse *n* reincidencia, recaída, *f; med* recidiva, *f. vi* reincidir (en); *med* recaer
relapsed *a* relapso
relate *vt* (recount) relatar, narrar; relacionar; unir; (of kinship) emparentar. *vi* ajustarse (a); referirse (a). **The first fact is not related to the second,** El primer hecho no tiene nada que ver con el segundo
related *a* relacionado; (by kinship) emparentado. **John is well-r.,** Juan es de buena familia; Juan es de familia influyente; Juan tiene buenas relaciones
relater *n* narrador (-ra)
relation *n* (narrative) relación, narración, *f;* conexión, *f;* relación, *f;* (kinship) parentesco, *m;* (person) pariente (-ta). **in r. to,** con relación a, en cuanto a
relationship *n* parentesco, *m;* conexión, relación, *Lat. Am.* atingencia, *f*
relative *a* relativo. *n* pariente (-ta); *pl* **relatives,** parientes, *m pl,* parentela, *f*
relativism *n* relativismo, *m*
relativity *n* relatividad, *f*
relax *vt* relajar; aflojar; soltar; (make less severe) ablandar; (decrease) mitigar. *vi* relajarse; aflojar; (rest) descansar
relaxation *n* relajación, *f;* aflojamiento, *m;* ablandamiento, *m;* mitigación, *f;* (rest) descanso, reposo, *m;* (pastime) pasatiempo, *m;* (amusement) diversión, *f*
relaxing *a* relajante; (of climate) enervante
relay *n* (of horses) parada, *f;* (shift) tanda, *f;* relevo, *m; elec* relais, *m; rad* redifusión, *f. vt* enviar por posta; *elec* reemitir; *rad* retransmitir; (lay again) colocar de nuevo. **r. race,** carrera de equipo, carrera de relevos, *f*
release *vt* soltar; (hurl) lanzar; (set free) poner en liber-

tad (a); librar (de); absolver; (surrender) renunciar (a); dar al público, poner en circulación; (lease again) realquilar. *n* soltura, *f*; lanzamiento, *m*; liberación, *f*; (from pain) alivio, *m*; remisión, *f*; exoneración, *f*; publicación, *f*; (of films) representación, *f*; *law* soltura, *f*
relegate *vt* relegar
relegation *n* relegación, *f*
relent *vi* ablandarse, enternecerse; ceder
relenting *n* enternecimiento, desenojo, *m*
relentless *a* implacable, inexorable; despiadado
relentlessly *adv* inexorablemente; sin piedad
relentlessness *n* inexorabilidad, *f*; falta de piedad, *f*
relet *vt* realquilar
relevance *n* conexión, *f*; pertinencia, *f*; aplicabilidad, *f*
relevant *a* relativo; pertinente, a propósito, oportuno; aplicable
reliability *n* seguridad, *f*; formalidad, *f*; confianza, *f*; exactitud, *f*; veracidad, *f*
reliable *a* seguro; formal; digno de crédito, de confianza, solvente digno de confianza; exacto; veraz
reliably *adv* seguramente; de una manera digna de confianza; exactamente
reliance *n* confianza, *f*. **to place r. on,** tener confianza en
reliant *a* confiado
relic *n* vestigio, rastro, *m*; *ecc* reliquia, *f*
relict *n* viuda, *f*
relief *n* (alleviation) alivio, *m*; desahogo, *m*; (help) socorro, *m*, ayuda, *f*; beneficencia, *f*; *mil* relevo, *m*; (pleasure) placer, *m*, satisfacción, *f*; (consolation) consuelo, *m*; *law* remisión, *f*; *art* relieve, *m*. **high r.,** alto relieve, *m*. **low r.,** bajo relieve, *m*. **r. map,** mapa en relieve, *m*. **r. train,** tren de socorro, *m*
relieve *vt* aliviar; aligerar, suavizar; mitigar; (one's feelings, etc.) desahogar; (*mil* and to take the place of) relevar; (free) librar; (dismiss) destituir; (remove) quitar; (rob) robar; (help) socorrer, remediar; (redeem) redimir; (ornament) adornar; (from a wrong) hacer justicia (a)
relieving *n* alivio, *m*; aligeramiento, *m*; mitigación, *f*; (of the feelings) desahogo, *m*; *mil* relevo, *m*; (help) socorro, *m*. **r. arch,** sobrearco, *m*
relight *vt* volver a encender. *vi* encenderse de nuevo
religion *n* religión, *f*
religiosity *n* religiosidad, *f*
religious *a* religioso; en religión; piadoso, crevente; devoto. *n* religioso (-sa). **r. orders,** órdenes religiosas, *f pl*. **r. toleration,** libertad de cultos, *f*
religiousness *n* religiosidad, *f*
relinquish *vt* abandonar; (one's grip) soltar; renunciar; desistir (de), dejar (de); (a post) dimitir (de)
relinquishment *n* abandono, *m*; renuncia, *f*; dejamiento, *m*; (of a post) dimisión, *f*
reliquary *n* relicario, *m*
relish *n* gusto, *m*; sabor, *m*; (touch, smack) dejo, *m*; condimento, *m*; apetito, *m*, gana, *f*. *vt* gustar de; comer con apetito; saborear, paladear; *fig* seducir, atraer, gustar. *vi* tener gusto (de). **I do not much r. the idea,** No me seduce la idea
relishing *n* saboreo, *m*; (enjoyment) goce, *m*, fruición, *f*; consideración, *f*
relive *vt* vivir de nuevo, volver a vivir
reload *vt* recargar
reluctance *n* repugnancia, desgana, *f*. **with r.,** a regañadientes, de mala gana
reluctant *a* poco dispuesto (a), que tiene repugnancia a (hacer algo), sin gana; (forced) forzado; artificial; (hesitating) vacilante
reluctantly *adv* de mala gana, con repugnancia, a disgusto
rely on *vi* contar con, confiar en, depender de
remain *vi* quedar; permanecer; (be left over) sobrar; continuar. **I r. yours faithfully . . . ,** (in a letter) Queda de Vd. su att. s.s. . . . **It remains to be written,** Queda por escribir
remainder *n* resto, *m*; restos, *m pl*, sobras, *f pl*; residuo, *m*. **The r. of the people went away,** Los demás se marcharon
remaining *pres. part* and *a* que queda; sobrante. **r. to be paid** *Lat. Am.* impago
remains *n pl* restos, *m pl*; sobras, *f pl*, desperdicios, *m pl*; ruinas, *f pl*
remake *vt* rehacer; reformar
remand *vt law* reencarcelar. *n law* reencarcelamiento, *m*
remark *n* observación, *f*; nota, *f*; comentario, *m*. *vt* and *vi* observar; notar. **to r. on,** comentar, hacer una observación sobre
remarkable *a* notable, singular, extraordinario
remarkably *adv* singularmente
remarriage *n* segundas nupcias, *f pl*, segundo casamiento, *m*
remarry *vt* volver a casar (a). *vi* casarse en segundas nupcias; volver a casarse
remediable *a* remediable
remedial *a* remediador; curativo, terapéutico
remedy *n* remedio, *m*; recurso, *m*, *vt* remediar; curar
remember *vt* recordar; tener presente; acordarse de. *vi* acordarse; no olvidarse. **R. me to your mother,** Dale recuerdos míos a tu madre. **If I r. rightly . . . ,** Si bien me acuerdo . . . **And r. that I shall do no more!** ¡Y no olvides que no haré más!
remembrance *n* recuerdo, *m*; memoria, *f*; *pl* **remembrances,** recuerdos, *m pl*
remind *vt* recordar
reminder *n* recuerdo, *m*; (warning) advertencia, *f*. **a gentle r.,** una indirecta, una insinuación
reminisce *vi inf* recordar viejas historias
reminiscence *n* reminiscencia, *f*, recuerdo, *m*
reminiscent *a* evocador, que recuerda; de reminiscencia; que piensa en el pasado. **to be r. of,** recordar; *inf* oler a
reminiscently *adv* evocadoramente, como si recordara
remiss *a* negligente, descuidado
remission *n* remisión, *f*
remissly *adv* negligentemente
remissness *n* negligencia, *f*, descuido, *m*
remit *vt* remitir; *com* remesar, enviar. *vi* (pay) pagar
remittance *n* remesa, *f*, envío, *m*
remitter *n* remitente, *mf*
remnant *n* resto, *m*; (of fabric) retal, retazo, *m*; (relic) vestigio, *m*, reliquia, *f*. **r. sale,** saldo, *m*
remodel *vt* rehacer; reformar; modelar de nuevo; (a play, etc.) refundir
remodeling *n* reformación, *f*; (of a play, etc.) refundición, *f*
remonstrance *n* protesta, *f*; reconvención, *f*
remonstrate *vi* protestar, objetar. **to r. with,** reprochar, reconvenir
remorse *n* remordimiento, *m*
remorseful *a* lleno de remordimientos; penitente, arrepentido
remorsefully *adv* con remordimiento
remorseless *a* sin conciencia, sin remordimientos; despiadado, inflexible
remorselessness *n* inexorabilidad, crueldad, dureza, *f*
remote *a* distante, lejano; remoto; aislado; ajeno; (slight) leve, vago. **r. control,** mando a distancia, *m*
remotely *adv* remotamente
remoteness *n* distancia, *f*; aislamiento, *m*; alejamiento, *m*; (vagueness) vaguedad, *f*
remount *vt* subir de nuevo, montar de nuevo; *mil* remontar. *vi* (go back to) remontar (a), derivarse (de). *n mil* remonta, *f*
removable *a* que puede quitarse; (of collars, etc.) de quita y pon; transportable; (of officials, etc.) amovible
removal *n* acción de quitar o levantar, *f*; sacamiento, *m*; separación, *f*; eliminación, *f*; alejamiento, *m*; traslado, *m*; (from office, etc.) deposición, *f*; supresión, *f*; asesinato, *m*. **r. van,** carro de mudanzas, *m*
remove *vt* quitar; retirar; levantar; sacar; apartar; separar; eliminar; trasladar; (from office) destituir; su-

primir; asesinar. *vi* trasladarse. *n* grado, *m*; distancia, *f*; (departure) partida, *f*. **to r. oneself,** quitarse de en medio. **to r. one's hat,** descubrirse. **first cousin once removed,** hijo de primo carnal, primo hermano del padre, primo hermano de la madre, *m*
remunerate *vt* remunerar
remuneration *n* remuneración, *f*
remunerative *a* remunerador
renaissance *n* renacimiento, *m*, *a* renacentista
Renaissance man *n* hombre del Renacimiento, *m*
Renaissance woman *n* mujer del Renacimiento, *f*
renal *a* renal
rename *vt* poner otro nombre (a)
renascent *a* renaciente, que renace
rend *vt* desgarrar, rasgar; *fig* lacerar; (split) hender; *fig* dividir. **to r. from,** arrancar (a). **to r. the air,** (with cries, etc.) llenar el aire
render *vt* (return) devolver; dar; rendir; (make) hacer; (help, service) prestar; interpretar; (translate) traducir; (fat) derretir y clarificar
rendering *n* versión, *f*; interpretación, *f*
rendezvous *n* cita, *f*; lugar de cita, *m*; reunión, *f*. *vi* reunirse
rending *n* desgarro, *m*; hendimiento, *m*
renegade *a* renegado. *n* renegado (-da)
renew *vt* renovar; (resume) reanudar; (a lease, etc.) prorrogar
renewable *a* renovable
renewal *n* renovación, *f*; (resumption) reanudación, *f*; (of a lease, etc.) prorrogación, *f*
renewed *a* renovado; nuevo
rennet *n* cuajo, *m*
renounce *vt* renunciar; (a throne) abdicar; renegar (de), repudiar; abandonar. *vi law* desistir; (cards) renunciar
renouncement *n* renuncia, *f*; (of a throne) abdicación, *f*; repudiación, *f*
renovate *vt* renovar; limpiar; restaurar
renovation *n* renovación, *f*; limpiadura, *f*; restauración, *f*
renovator *n* renovador (-ra)
renown *n* renombre, *m*, fama, *f*
renowned *a* renombrado, famoso
rent *n* (tear) rasgadura, *f*; desgarro, *m*; abertura, *f*; raja hendedura, *f*; (discord) división, *f*; (hire) alquiler, *m*; arrendamiento, *m*. *vt* arrendar, alquilar. **r.-free,** sin pagar alquiler
rentable *a* alquilable, arrendable
rental. See **rent**
renter *n* arrendador (-ra)
rentier *n* rentista, *mf*
renting *n* alquiler, arrendamiento, *m*
renumber *vt* numerar de nuevo
renunciation *n* renunciación, renuncia, *f*
reoccupy *vt* volver a ocupar, ocupar otra vez
reopen *vt* abrir de nuevo, volver a abrir. *vi* abrirse nuevamente, abrirse otra vez
reopening *n* reapertura, *f*
reorder *vt* ordenar de nuevo, *com* volver a pedir. *n com* nuevo pedido, *m*
reorganization *n* reorganización, *f*
reorganize *vt* reorganizar
reorganizing *a* reorganizador
repack *vt* reembalar; reenvasar; volver a hacer (una maleta)
repaint *vt* pintar de nuevo
repainting *n* nueva pintura, *f*
repair *vt* arreglar (e.g. a machine) componer, remendar; reparar; restaurar; rehacer. *vi* (with to) dirigirse a, ir a; acudir a. *n* arreglo *m*, reparación, *f*; compostura, *f*; restauración, *f*. **to keep in r.,** conservar en buen estado
repairable *a* que se puede componer
repairer *n* componedor (-ra); restaurador (-ra)
repairing *a* reparador
reparable *a* reparable; remediable
reparation *n* reparación, *f*
repartee *n* respuestas, agudezas, *f pl*; *inf* dimes y diretes, *m pl*
repast *n* comida, *f*; (light) colación, *f*
repatriate *vt* repatriar
repatriation *n* repatriación, *f*
repay *vt* reembolsar; recompensar, pagar; pagar en la misma moneda. *vi* pagar. **It well repays a visit,** Vale la pena de visitarse
repayable *a* reembolsable
repayment *n* reembolso, *m*; pago, retorno, *m*
repeal *n* abrogación, revocación, *f*, *vt* abrogar, rescindir, revocar
repeat *vt* repetir; reiterar; (renew) renovar; duplicar. *n* repetición, *f*
repeated *a* reiterado; redoblado
repeatedly *adv* reiteradamente, repetidamente
repeater *n* repetidor (-ra); reloj de repetición, *m*; arma de repetición, *f*
repel *vt* repeler; ahuyentar; (spurn) rechazar; *phys* resistir; repugnar
repellent *a* repulsivo
repent *vt* arrepentirse de. *vi* arrepentirse
repentance *n* arrepentimiento, *m*, penitencia, *f*
repentant *a* arrepentido, penitente, contrito
repentantly *adv* arrepentidamente, con contrición
repeople *vt* repoblar
repeopling *n* repoblación, *f*
repercuss *vt* repercutir (en)
repercussion *n* repercusión, *f*
repercussive *a* repercusivo
repertory *n* repertorio, *m*
repetition *n* repetición, *f*; recitación, *f*
repetitive *a* iterativo
repine *vi* afligirse (de); quejarse (de); padecer nostalgia
repining *n* pesares, *m pl*; quejas, *f pl*, descontento, *m*; nostalgia, *f*
replace *vt* (put back) reponer, colocar de nuevo; restituir, devolver; (renew) renovar; (in a post, etc.) reemplazar, substituir
replaceable *a* restituible; renovable; reemplazable
replacement *n* reposición, *f*; restitución, devolución, *f*; renovación, *f*; reemplazo, *m*
replant *vt* replantar
replanting *n* replantación, *f*
replenish *vt* rellenar
replenishment *n* relleno, *m*
replete *a* repleto
repletion *n* repleción, *f*
replica *n* réplica, *f*
reply *n* respuesta, contestación, *f*, *vi* responder, contestar. **Awaiting your r.,** En espera de sus noticias. **in his r.,** en su respuesta
repolish *vt* repulir
repopulate *vt* repoblar
repopulation *n* repoblación, *f*
report *n* (rumor) voz, *f*, rumor, *m*; (reputation) fama, *f*; (news) noticia, *f*; (journalistic) reportaje, *m*; (*mil nav* and from school) parte, *f*; (weather) boletín, *m*; (proceedings) actas, *f pl*; (statement) informe, *m*; relación, *f*; (of a gun, etc.) detonación, *f*; explosión, *f*. *vt* dar cuenta de, relatar; informar; (measure) registrar; (*mil nav*) dar parte de; comunicar; (journalistic) hacer un reportaje de; (transcribe) transcribir; (accuse) denunciar; quejarse de. *vi* presentar informe; ser reportero; (present oneself) presentarse, comparecer. **It is reported that . . . ,** Se informa que . . .
report card *n* boletín de calificaciones, *m*
reporter *n* reportero (-ra); *law* relator, *m*
reporting *n* reporterismo, *m*
repose *n* reposo, *m*; quietud, *f*; tranquilidad, serenidad, *f*. *vt* reposar, descansar; reclinar; (place) poner. *vi* reposar; tener confianza (en); basarse (en)
repository *n* repositorio, depósito, *m*; almacén, *m*; (furniture) guardamuebles, *m*; (person) depositario (-ia)
repoussé (work) *n* repujado, *m*. **to work in r.,** repujar

reprehend *vt* reprender, reprobar
reprehensible *a* reprensible
reprehension *n* reprensión, *f*
represent *vt* representar; significar
representation *n* representación, *f*
representational *a art* realista
representative *a* que representa; representativo. *n* representante, *mf*
repress *vt* reprimir
repression *n* represión, *f*
repressive *a* represivo
reprieve *vt law* aplazar la ejecución (de); *fig* dar una tregua (a)
reprimand *n* reprimenda, *f*, *vt* reprender
reprint *n* reimpresión, tirada aparte, separata, *f*, *vt* reimprimir
reprinting *n* reimpresión, *f*
reprisal *n* represalia, *f*. **to take reprisals,** tomar represalias
reproach *n* reproche, *m*; censura, *f*; (shame) vergüenza, *f*. *vt* reprochar; censurar, echar en cara, afear
reproachful *a* severo; lleno de reproches; de censura; (shameful) vergonzoso
reproachfully *adv* con reprobación, con reprensión, severamente
reproachfulness *n* severidad, *f*. **the r. of my gaze,** mi mirada llena de reproches
reprobate *n* réprobo (-ba)
reproduce *vt* reproducir. *vi* reproducirse
reproducible *a* reproductible
reproduction *n* reproducción, *f*
reproductive *a* reproductor; de reproducción
reproof *n* reconvención, *f*
reprove *vt* censurar, culpar; reprender
reprovingly. See **rebukingly**
reptile *a* and *n* reptil, *m*
republic *n* república, *f*. **the r. of letters,** la república de las letras
republican *a* and *n* republicano (-na)
republicanism *n* republicanismo, *m*
republish *vt* publicar de nuevo; volver a editar
repudiate *vt* repudiar; negar, rechazar
repudiation *n* repudiación, *f*
repugnance *n* repugnacia, *f*
repugnant *a* repugnante; contrario; opuesto. **to be r. to,** repugnar (a)
repulse *vt* repulsar, repeler; rebatir, refutar; (refuse) rechazar, *n* repulsa, *f*; refutación, *f*; rechazo, *m*
repulsion *n phys* repulsión, *f*; repugnancia, aversión, *f*
repulsive *a* repulsivo, repugnante, repelente
repulsiveness *n* carácter repulsivo, *m*; aspecto repugnante, *m*
reputable *a* honrado, respetable, formal
reputation *n* reputación, *f*; fama, *f*, renombre, *m*. **to have the r. of,** ser reputado como, pasar por
reputed *a* supuesto; putativo
reputedly *adv* según la opinión común, según dice la gente
request *n* ruego, *m*, petición, *f*; instancia, *f*; solicitud, *f*; *com* demanda, *f*. *vt* pedir, rogar; suplicar; solicitar. **in r.,** en boga; solicitado; en demanda, **on r.,** a solicitud. **r. stop,** (for buses) parada discrecional, *f*
requiem *n* réquiem, *m*. **r. mass,** misa de difuntos, *f*
require *vt* exigir, requerir; necesitar; (wish) desear; invitar. *vi* ser necesario
required *a* necesario; obligatorio
requirement *n* deseo, *m*; requisito, *m*; formalidad, *f*; estipulación, *f*; necesidad, *f*
requisite *n* requisito, *m*. *a* necesario, requisito, preciso. **to be r.,** ser necesario, ser menester hacer falta
requisition *vt mil* requisar
requisitioning *n* requisa, *f*
requital *n* recompensa, *f*; compensación, satisfacción, *f*
requite *vt* pagar, recompensar; (affection) corresponder a
reread *vt* releer
reredos *n* retablo, *m*
resale *n* reventa, *f*
rescind *vt* rescindir
rescission *n* rescisión, *f*
rescue *vt* salvar; librar; *mil* rescatar. *n* socorro, *m*; salvamento, *m*; *mil* rescate, *m*. **to go to the r. of,** ir al socorro de. **r. party,** expedición de salvamento, *f*; *mil* expedición de rescate, *f*
rescuer *n* salvador (-ra)
reseal *vt* resellar
research *n* investigación, *f*, *vt* investigar
researcher *n* investigador (-ra)
reseda *n bot* reseda, *f*
resell *vt* revender
resemblance *n* parecido, *m*, semejanza, *f*. **The two sisters bear a strong r. to each other,** Las dos hermanas se parecen mucho
resemble *vt* parecerse (a). **Mary doesn't r. her mother,** María no se parece a su madre
resent *vt* resentirse de; ofenderse por, indignarse por; tomar a mal
resentful *a* resentido; ofendido, indignado, agraviado; vengativo
resentfully *adv* con resentimiento; con indignación
resentment *n* resentimiento, *m*
reservation *n* reservación, *f*; reserva, *f*; territorio reservado, *m*; santuario, *m*. **mental r.,** reserva mental, *f*
reserve *n* reserva, *f*. *vt* reservar. *a* de reserva. **without r.,** sin reserva
reserved *a* reservado; callado, taciturno. **r. compartment,** reservado, *m*. **r. list,** (*mil nav*) sección de reserva, *f*
reservedly *adv* con reserva
reservist *n* reservista, *mf*
reservoir *n* depósito, *m*; cisterna, *f*, aljibe, tanque, *m*
reset *vt* montar de nuevo
resettle *vt* repoblar; rehabilitar; (a dispute) llegar a un nuevo acuerdo sobre
resettlement *n* repoblación, *f*; rehabilitación, *f*; (of a dispute) nuevo acuerdo, *m*
reshape *vt* reformar
reship *vt* reembarcar
reshipment *n* reembarque, *m*
reshuffle *vt* volver a barajar; *fig* cambiar
reside *vi* residir, habitar; vivir
residence *n* residencia, *f*; permanencia, estada, *f*; domicilio, *m*
resident *a* residente; (of a servant) que duerme en casa; interno. *n* residente, *mf*; (diplomacy) residente, *m*. **r. of the capital** *Lat. Am.* capitalino (-na) *mf*. **r. of Rio de Janeiro** carioca, *mf*
residential *a* residencial
residue *n* resto, *m*; (*law, chem*) residuo, *m*
residuum *n* residuo, *m*
resign *vt* renunciar (a); ceder; resignar. *vi* dimitir. **to r. oneself,** resignarse
resignation *n* resignación, *f*; (from a post) dimisión, *f*. **to send in one's r.,** dimitir
resigned *a* resignado
resignedly *adv* con resignación
resilience *n* elasticidad, *f*
resilient *a* elástico
resin *n* resina, *f*, *Central America, Mexico* copal, *m*; (solid, for violin bows, etc.) colofonia, *f*
resinous *a* resinoso
resist *vt* and *vi* (bear) aguantar; (impede) impedir; (repel, ward off) resistir; rechazar; hacer frente (a); oponerse (a); negarse (a)
resistance *n* resistencia, *f*; aguante, *m*, tenacidad, *f*; oposición, *f*; repugnancia, *f*. **passive r.,** resistencia pasiva, *f*. **r. coil,** *elec* resistencia, *f*. **r. movement,** movimiento de resistencia, *m*
resistant *a* resistente
resister *n* el, *m*, (*f*, la) que resiste
resole *vt* remontar
resolute *a* resuelto, decidido

resolutely *adv* resueltamente
resolution *n* resolución, *f;* (proposal placed before a legislative body, etc.) proposición, *f;* propósito, *m*
resolve *vt* resolver; desarrollar, deshacer (an abbreviation, acronym, or initialism). *vi* resolverse. *n* propósito, *m;* (of character) resolución, firmeza, *f*
resonance *n* resonancia, *f;* sonoridad, *f*
resonant *a* resonante; reverberante, sonoro
resort *n* recurso, *m;* punto de reunión. *m;* (frequentation) frecuentación, *f;* (gathering) concurrencia, *f;* reunión, *f. vi* acudir (a), acogerse (a); hacer uso (de); pasar (a); (frequent) frecuentar, concurrir. **health r.,** balneario, *m.* **holiday r.,** playa de verano, *f;* pueblo de veraneo, *m.* **in the last r.,** en último recurso
resound *vi* resonar, retumbar, retronar; *fig* tener fama, ser celebrado. *vt* hacer reverberar; *fig* celebrar
resounding *a* retumbante, resonante
resource *n* recurso, *m;* (of character) inventiva, *f; pl* **resources**; recursos, fondos, *m pl*
resourceful *a* ingenioso
resourcefulness *n* ingeniosidad, *f*
respect *n* respeto, *m;* consideración, *f;* (reference, regard) respecto, *m; pl* **respects,** (greetings) saludos, *m pl;* homenaje, *m. vt* respetar; honrar; (concern, regard) concernir, tocar (a). **in other respects,** por lo demás. **in r. of,** tocante a, respecto a. **in some respects,** desde algunos puntos de vista. **out of r. for,** por consideración a
respectability *n* respetabilidad, *f*
respectable *a* respetable; pasable; considerable
respectably *adv* respetablemente
respected *a* and *part* respetado; apreciado, estimado; digno de respeto, honrado
respectful *a* respetuoso
respectfully *adv* respetuosamente
respectfulness *n* aire respetuoso, *m;* conducta respetuosa, *f*
respecting *prep* con respecto a, en cuanto a, tocante a; a propósito de
respective *a* respectivo; relativo
respectively *adv* respectivamente
respiration *n* respiración, *f*
respirator *n* respirador, *m*
respiratory *a* respiratorio
respire *vt* and *vi* respirar; exhalar; descansar
respite *n* tregua, pausa, *f;* respiro, *m; law* espera, *f. vt* dar tregua (a); (postpone) aplazar; (relieve) aliviar
resplendence *n* resplandor, *m,* refulgencia, *f,* esplendor, fulgor, *m*
resplendent *a* resplandeciente, refulgente, relumbrante. **He was r. in a new uniform,** Lucía (or Ostentaba) un nuevo uniforme. **to be r.,** ser resplandeciente; relumbrar, refulgir
resplendently *adv* esplendorosamente
respond *vi* responder; contestar; (obey) obedecer; reaccionar
respondent *n* (in a suit) demandado (-da)
response *n* respuesta, *f; ecc* responso, *m*
responsibility *n* responsabilidad, *f*
responsible *a* responsable
responsive *a* simpático; sensible, sensitivo
responsiveness *n* simpatía, *f;* sensibilidad, *f*
rest *n* descanso, *m;* reposo, *m;* (the grave) última morada, *f;* tranquilidad, paz, *f;* inacción, *f;* (prop) soporte, apoyo, *m;* base, *f;* (for a lance) ristre, *m;* (for a rifle) apoyo, *m; mus* silencio, *m,* pausa, *f;* (in verse) cesura, *f.* **in r.,** en ristre. **the r.,** el resto; los demás, los otros. **to set at r.,** calmar, tranquilizar; (remove) quitar. **r.-cure,** cura de reposo, *f.* **r.-house,** hospedería, *f;* refugio, *m.* **r.-room, lounge,** sala de descanso, *f;* (toilet) excusado, retrete, *m;* (in theaters) saloncillo, *m*
rest *vi* reposar, descansar; (lie down) acostarse, echarse; (stop) cesar, parar; estar en paz; apoyarse (en); descansar (sobre); posar; depender (de); (remain) quedar. *vt* descansar; dar un descanso (a); (lean) apoyar; basar (en). **It rests with them,** Depende de ellos. **These valuable documents now rest in the Library of Congress,** Estos valiosos documentos han parado en la Biblioteca del Congresso. **May he r. in peace!** ¡Que en paz descanse! **to r. assured,** estar seguro. **to r. on one's oars,** cesar de remar; descansar
restate *vt* repetir, afirmar de nuevo
restatement *n* repetición, *f*
restaurant *n* restaurante, restorán, *m.* **r.-car,** coche-comedor, *m*
restful *a* descansado; tranquilo, sosegado
resting *n* reposo, *m.* **last r.-place,** última morada, *f.* **r.-place,** descansadero, *m;* refugio, *m*
restitution *n* restitución, *f*
restive *a* (of a horse) repropio, ingobernable; inquieto, agitado; impaciente
restiveness *n* inquietud, agitación, *f;* impaciencia, *f*
restless *a* agitado; inquieto, intranquilo; turbulento; sin reposo; (wakeful) desvelado; (ceaseless) incesante. **r. night,** noche desvelada, noche intranquila, *inf* noche toledana, *f*
restlessly *adv* agitadamente; con inquietud; turbulentamente; incesantemente
restlessness *n* agitación, *f;* inquietud, intranquilidad, *f;* turbulencia, *f;* falta de reposo, *f;* (wakefulness) desvelo, *m;* movimiento incesante, *m*
restock *vt* (with goods) surtir de nuevo; proveer de nuevo; restablecer; repoblar
restoration *n* restauración, *f;* renovación, *f;* restablecimiento, *m;* (returning) restitución, *f*
restorative *a* and *n* restaurativo *m*
restore *vt* restaurar; restituir; devolver; restablecer; reponer; (repair) reformar, reparar; reconstruir; (to former rank, etc.) rehabilitar. **He restored the book to its place,** Devolvió el libro a su sitio
restorer *n* restaurador (-ra)
restrain *vt* refrenar; reprimir; (restrict) limitar, restringir; (prevent) impedir; desviar; (detain) recluir. **to r. oneself,** contenerse
restrained *a* moderado, mesurado; sobrio; (of emotion) contenido
restraining *a* restrictivo; moderador, calmante
restraint *n* freno, *m;* restricción, *f;* limitación, *f;* prohibición, *f;* compulsión, *f;* (reserve) reserva, *f;* moderación, *f*
restrict *vt* restringir; limitar
restriction *n* restricción, *f;* limitación, *f*
restrictive *a* restrictivo
result *n* resultado, *m;* consecuencia, resulta, *f;* solución, *f. vi* resultar. **as the r. of,** de resultas de
resultant *a* resultante; consecuente. *n* resultado, *m; mech* resultante, *f*
resume *vt* reasumir; (continue) reanudar, continuar; (summarize) resumir
résumé *n* resumen, *m,* recapitulación, *f*
resummon *vt* convocar de nuevo (a); citar de nuevo (a)
resumption *n* (renewal) reanudación, *f;* reasunción, *f*
resurgence *n* resurgimiento, *m*
resurrect *vt inf* desenterrar; resucitar
resurrection *n* resurrección, *f*
resuscitate *vt* and *vi* resucitar
resuscitation *n* resurrección, *f;* renovación, *f;* renacimiento, *m*
retail *n* venta al por menor, reventa, *f. adv* al por menor. *vt* (goods) vender al por menor, revender; (tell) contar; repetir. **r. trade,** comercio al por menor, *m*
retailer *n* vendedor (-ra) al por menor; (of a story) narrador (-ra); el, *m,* (*f,* la) que cuenta algo
retain *vt* retener; guardar; conservar; (a barrister) ajustar; (hire) contratar
retainer *n* (dependent) criado, dependiente, *m;* partidario, adherente, *m;* (fee) honorario, *m; pl* **retainers,** séquito, *m,* adherentes, *m pl,* gente, *f*
retaining wall *n* muro de contención, *m*
retake *vt* volver a tomar; reconquistar
retaking *n* reconquista, *f*

retaliate *vt* vengarse de, desquitarse de. *vi* vengarse, tomar represalias
retaliation *n* represalias, *f pl*; desquite, *m*, satisfacción, *f*. **law of r.,** talión, *m*,
retaliatory *a* de represalias; de desquite
retard *vt* retardar
retch *vi* tener náuseas, procurar vomitar
retching *n* náusea, basca, *f*
retell *vt* repetir, volver a contar
retention *n* retención, *f*; conservación, *f*
retentive *a* retentivo
retentiveness *n* poder de retención, *m*; (memory) retentiva, *f*
reticence *n* reticencia, reserva, *f*
reticent *a* reservado, inexpresivo, taciturno
retina *n* retina, *f*
retinue *n* séquito, acompañamiento, *m*, comitiva, *f*
retire *vi* retirarse; (to bed) recogerse, acostarse; (from a post) jubilarse. *vt* retirar; jubilar. **to r. from a post,** *mil* rendir el puesto
retired *a* retirado; (remote) apartado, aislado; (hidden) escondido; (former) antiguo; (from employment, etc.) jubilado; (of an officer) retirado. **to place on the r. list,** jubilar; (*mil nav*) dar el retiro (a)
retirement *n* retirada, *f*; (solitude) apartamiento, aislamiento, *m*; retiro, *m*; (superannuation) jubilación, *f*
retiring *a* que se retira; (from a post) dimitente; (with pension, etc.) de jubilación; (reserved) reservado; modesto
retort *vi* replicar. *vt* retorcer; devolver (una acusación, etc.). *n* réplica, *f*; contestación, *f*; *chem* retorta, *f*
retouch *vt* retocar
retrace *vt* volver a trazar; volver a andar (un camino); (one's steps) volver sobre sus pasos, volver atrás; (in memory) rememorar, recordar; buscar el origen (de); (recount) narrar, contar
retract *vt* retractar, retirar; (draw back) retraer. *vi* retractarse
retraction *n* retracción, *f*
retranslate *vt* hacer una nueva traducción (de)
retransmission *n* retransmisión, *f*
retread *vt* pisar de nuevo; (tires) recauchetear
retreat *n* retirada, *f*; (*mil* signal) retreta, *f*; (refuge and *ecc*) retiro, *m*. *vi* retirarse; retroceder; refugiarse
retreat house *n* casa de ejercicios, *f*
retreating *a* que se retira; que retrocede; *mil* que se bate en retirada
retrench *vt* reducir; disminuir; *vi* economizar, hacer economías
retrenchment *n* disminución, reducción, *f*; economías, *f pl*
retrial *n* (of a person) nuevo proceso, *m*; (of a case) revisión, *f*
retribution *n* retribución, *f*; justo castigo, *m*, pena merecida, *f*
retrievable *a* recuperable, que puede recobrarse; reparable
retrieval *n* recuperación, *f*; reparación, *f*; (of game) cobra, *f*; (of one's character) rehabilitación, *f*
retrieve *vt* (game, of dogs) cobrar; (regain) recobrar, recuperar; restaurar; reparar; restablecer; (one's character) rehabilitar. *vi* cobrar la caza
retriever *n* (dog) perdiguero (-ra)
retroactive *a* retroactivo
retrocede *vi* retroceder
retrograde *a* retrógrado
retrogression *n* retrogradación, regresión, *f*; *med* retroceso, *m*
retrogressive *a* retrógrado
retrospect *n* mirada retrospectiva, *f*, examen del pasado, *m*. **in r.,** retrospectivamente
retrospection *n* retrospección, *f*
retrospective *a* retrospectivo
retrospectively *adv* retrospectivamente
retry *vt* (a case) rever; (a person) procesar de nuevo
return *vi* regresar, *Lat. Am.* devolverse; volver; reaparecer; presentarse de nuevo; *law* revertir; (answer) contestar, responder. *vt* (give back or put back) devolver; (a ball) restar; (a kindness, visit) pagar; restituir; (reciprocate) corresponder (a); recompensar; contestar (a); dar; rendir; (yield) producir; (a verdict) fallar, pronunciar; (report) dar parte de; anunciar; (exchange) cambiar; (elect) elegir. *n* regreso, *m*; vuelta, *f*; (giving or putting back) devolución, *f*; pago, *m*; restitución, *f*; correspondencia, *f*; recompensa, *f*; (reply) respuesta, *f*; (reappearance) reaparición, *f*; reinstalación, *f*; repetición, *f*; (gain) ganancia, *f*, provecho, *m*; rendimiento, *m*; (exchange) cambio, *m*; (report) parte oficial, *f*; informe, *m*; lista, *f*; (election) elección, *f*; *pl* **returns,** tablas estadisticas, *f pl*; (of an election) resultados, *m pl*. **Many happy returns!** ¡Feliz cumpleaños! **by return mail,** a vuelta de correo. **on my (his, etc.) r.,** a la vuelta, cuando vuelva. **to r. like for like,** pagar en la misma moneda. **r. journey, r. trip,** viaje de vuelta, *m*. **r. match,** partido de vuelta, *m*. **r. ticket,** billete de ida y vuelta, *m*; billete de vuelta, *m*
returnable *a* restituible; susceptible a ser devuelto; (on approval) a prueba; *law* devolutivo
returning *a* que vuelve. *n* See **return**
"Return to Sender" «Al remitente»
reunion *n* reunión, *f*
reunite *vt* reunir. *vi* reunirse
revaccinate *vt* revacunar
revaccination *n* revacunación, *f*
reveal *vt* revelar; descubrir
revealer *n* revelador (-ra)
revealing *a* revelador. *n* revelación, *f*; descubrimiento, *m*
reveille *n mil* diana, *f*
revel *vi* divertirse; regocijarse (en), gozarse (en); entregarse (a); (carouse) ir de parranda; emborracharse. *n* algazara, jarana, *f*; *pl* **revels,** fiestas, festividades, *f pl*
revelation *n* revelación, *f*; descubrimiento, *m*; (in the Bible) Apocalipsis, *m*
reveler *n* convidado alegre, *m*; (at night) trasnochador (-ra); (drunk) borracho (-cha); (masked) máscara, *mf*
revelry *n* festividades, *f pl*, regocijo, *m*; orgías, *f pl*, *Central America* embullo, *m*
revenge *n* venganza, *f*. *vt* vengarse de; desquitarse de
revengeful *a* vengativo
revengefully *adv* vengativamente
revengefulness *n* deseo de venganza, *m*; carácter vengativo, *m*
revenger *n* vengador (-ra)
revenue *n* rentas públicas, *f pl*; (treasury) fisco, *m*; *com* rédito, *m*, ingresos, *m pl*; beneficio, *m*. **Inland R.,** delegación de contribuciones, *f*. **r. officer,** agente fiscal, *m*
reverberate *vt* and *vi* (of sound) retumbar, resonar; (of light, etc.) reverberar
reverberation *n* (reflection) reverberación, *f*; (of sound) retumbo, eco, *m*
revere *vt* reverenciar, venerar, honrar
reverence *n* reverencia, *f*, *vt* reverenciar
reverend *a* reverendo
reverent *a* reverente
reverie *n* ensueño, *m*
reversal *n* inversión, *f*; (of a verdict) revocación, *f*
reverse *vt* invertir; (a steam engine) dar contra vapor (a); (a vehicle) poner en marcha atrás; (arms) llevar a la funerala; (a judgment, etc.) revocar, derogar. *vi* (dancing) dar vueltas al revés. *n* lo contrario, lo opuesto; (back) dorso, revés, *m*; (change) cambio, *m*; (check) revés, *m*, vicisitud, *f*; (loss) pérdida, *f*; (defeat) derrota, *f*; *mech* marcha atrás, *f*, *a* inverso; contrario, opuesto. **quite the r.,** todo el contrario. **r. turn,** (of an engine) cambio de dirección, *m*; (in dancing) vuelta al revés, *f*
reversible *a* reversible
reversion *n* reversión, *f*; *biol* atavismo, *m*; (of offices) futura, *f*; (of property) reversión, *f*
revert *vi law* revertir; volver (a)

review *n* examen, análisis, *m*; juicio crítico, *m*; (journal and *mil*) revista, *f*; (criticism) revista, reseña, *f*; *law* revisión, *f*. *vt* examinar, analizar; (*mil* etc.) pasar revista (a); revisar; repasar; (a book, etc.) reseñar; *law* revisar. *vi* escribir revistas
review article *n* artículo de reseña, *m*
reviewer *n* revistero (-ra), crítico, *m*
revile *vt* injuriar, maldecir, difamar
reviler *n* maldiciente, *m*, insultador (-ra)
reviling *n* insultos, *m pl*, injurias, *f pl*
revisal *n* revisión, *f*
revise *vt* revisar; repasar; corregir; (change) cambiar
reviser *n* revisor, *m*; corrector de pruebas, *m*
revision *n* revisión, *f*; repaso, *m*; corrección de pruebas, *f*
revisit *vt* volver a visitar, visitar de nuevo
revival *n* resurgimiento, *m*; renovación, *f*; (awakening) despertamiento, *m*; restablecimiento, *m*; resurrección, *f*; (of learning) renacimiento, *m*; *theat* reposición, *f*; (religious) despertar religioso, *m*
revive *vi* reponerse; restablecerse; resucitar; renovarse; renacer; cobrar fuerzas; (recover consciousness) volver en sí. *vt* hacer revivir; resucitar; restablecer; renovar; restaurar; despertar; (fire, colours) avivar
reviver *n* resucitador (-ra)
revivification *n* revivificación, *f*
revivify *vt* revivificar
revocable *a* revocable
revocation *n* revocación, *f*
revoke *vt* revocar, anular, derogar; (wills) quebrantar. *vi* revocar, anular; (at cards) renunciar. *n* (cards) renuncio, *m*
revolt *n* rebelión, *f*, *vi* rebelarse, sublevarse. *vt* repugnar, indignar, dar asco (a)
revolting *a* repugnante, asqueroso; (rebellious) rebelde
revolution *n* revolución, *f*; (turn) vuelta, *f*, giro, *m*
revolutionary *a* and *n* revolucionario (-ia)
revolutionize *vt* revolucionar
revolve *vi* dar vueltas, girar; suceder periódicamente. *vt* hacer girar; (ponder) revolver, discurrir
revolver *n* revólver, *m*
revolving *a* giratorio; que vuelve; periódico. **r. chair,** silla giratoria, *f*. **r. door,** puerta giratoria, *f*. **r. stage,** escenario giratorio, *m*
revue *n theat* revista, *f*
revulsion *n* revulsión, *f*
revulsive *a med* revulsivo
rev up *vt* (an engine) calentar
reward *n* recompensa, *f*; retribución, *f*. *vt* recompensar; satisfacer, premiar
rewarding *a* premiador; que recompensa. *n* recompensación, *f*. **a rewarding experience,** una experiencia compensadora, *f*
rewrite *vt* escribir de nuevo; volver a escribir; redactar otra vez
rhapsody *n* rapsodia, *f*
rheostat *n* reóstato, *m*
rhetoric *n* retórica, *f*
rhetorical *a* retórico; declamatorio
rhetorician *n* retórico (-ca)
rheumatic *a* reumático. **r. fever,** reumatismo poliarticular agudo, *m*
rheumatism *n* reumatismo, reuma, *m*
rheumy *a* catarroso; (of the eyes) legañoso
Rhine, the el Rin, *m*
rhinestone circón, *m*
rhinoceros *n* rinoceronte, *m*
Rhodes Rodas, *f*
rhododendron *n* rododendro, *m*
rhubarb *n* ruibarbo, *m*
rhyme *n* rima, *f*; verso, *m*. *vi* and *vt* rimar. **without r. or reason,** sin ton ni son; a tontas y a locas
rhymer *n* rimador (-ra)
rhyming *a* rimador
rhythm *n* ritmo, *m*
rhythmic *a* rítmico
rib *n* (*anat, bot, aer, naut, arch*) costilla, *f*; (of an umbrella or fan) varilla, *f*; (in cloth) cordoncillo, *m*, lista, *f*
ribald *a* escabroso, ribaldo, indecente
ribaldry *n* ribaldería, escabrosidad, indecencia, *f*
ribbed *a* con costillas; (of cloth) listado, con listas
ribbon *n* cinta, *f*; tira, *f*; (tatter) jirón, *m*. **to tear to ribbons,** hacer jirones
rice *n* arroz, *m*. *a* de arroz; con arroz. **r. field,** arrozal, *m*. **r.-paper,** papel de paja de arroz, *m*. **r.-pudding,** arroz con leche, *m*
rich *a* rico; opulento; (happy) dichoso; (of land, etc.) fértil; abundante; (of objects) magnífico, suntuoso, hermoso; precioso; (of food) exquisito; suculento; (highly seasoned) muy sazonado; (creamy) con mucha nata; (of colours) brillante, vivo. **new r.,** ricacho (-cha). **newly-r.,** advenedizo. **to grow r.,** enriquecerse, *Lat. Am. also* fondearse
riches *n* riqueza, *f*
richly *adv* ricamente; abundantemente; magníficamente; bien
richness *n* riqueza, *f*; opulencia, *f*; (of land, etc.) fertilidad, *f*; abundancia, *f*; (of objects) magnificencia, suntuosidad, hermosura, *f*; preciosidad, *f*; (of food) gusto exquisito, *m*; suculencia, *f*; (piquancy) gusto picante, *m*; (of colours) viveza, *f*
rickets *n* raquitismo, *m*
rickety *a med* raquítico; destartalado, desvencijado; (unsteady) tambaleante; cojo
rickshaw *n* riksha, *m*
ricochet *n* rebote, *m*, *vi* rebotar
rid *vt* librar (de). **to get rid of,** librarse de; quitarse de encima (a); perder, quitarse; (dismiss) despedir. **to rid oneself of,** librarse de, deshacerse de
riddance *n* libramiento, *m*
riddle *n* acertijo, *m*; enigma, problema, *m*; misterio, *m*; (sieve) tamiz de alambre, *m*; *vt* (guess) adivinar; (sift) cribar; (with holes) acribillar
ride *vi* (a horse) montar a caballo, cabalgar; pasear a caballo; (a mule, a bicycle) montar en, pasear en; (a vehicle, train) ir en; (a carriage, car) andar en, pasear en; (float) flotar; (on the wind) dejarse llevar por el viento; ser llevado por el viento; (go) ir; (come) venir; (a distance) hacer . . . a caballo, en coche, etc.; *naut* estar al ancla; *mech* tener juego. *vt* (a horse, mule, bicycle) montar; ir montado sobre; manejar; (a race) hacer; (float) flotar en; (cleave, the sea, etc.) surcar. *n* paseo (a caballo, en bicicleta, en coche, etc.), *m*; viaje (en un autobús, de tren, etc.), *m*; (bridle path) camino de herradura, *m*; cabalgata, *f*, desfile a caballo, *m*; (hitch, lift) *Mexico* aventón, *m*. **a r. on horseback,** un paseo a caballo. **They gave me a r. in their car,** (e.g. to see the sights) Me llevaron a paseo en su auto, (a lift to a certain place) Me dieron un aventón. **ride at anchor,** estar fondeado. **to r. a bicycle,** montar en bicicleta. **to r. rough-shod over,** mandar a la baqueta (a), mandar a puntapiés (a). **to r. sidesaddle,** cabalgar a mujeriegas. **to r. at,** embestir con. **to r. away,** marcharse, alejarse; marcharse a caballo, etc. **to r. back,** volver; volver a caballo, en bicicleta, etc. **to r. behind,** seguir a caballo; ir inmediatamente detrás (de); (on the back seat) ocupar el asiento de atrás; (on the same animal) cabalgar en la grupa. **to r. down,** atropellar; (trample) pisotear, pasar por encima de. **to r. on,** seguir su camino. **to r. out,** salir a paseo en caballo, etc.; irse a paseo en coche, etc.; (a storm) hacer frente a, luchar con. **to r. over,** pasar por encima de; recorrer. **to r. up,** *vi* llegar, acercarse; (of a tie, etc.) subir. *vt* montar
rider *n* cabalgador (-ra); jinete, *m*; persona que va en coche, etc., *f*; (on a bicycle) ciclista, *mf*; (on a motorcycle) motociclista, *mf*; (horsebreaker) domador de caballos, *m*; (clause) añadidura, *f*; corolario, *m*
ridge *n* cumbre, cima, *f*; (of mountains) cordillera, sierra, *f*; (of a roof, of a nose) caballete, *m*; *agr* lomo, caballón, *m*; (wrinkle) arruga, *f*; (on coins) cordoncillo, *m*. *vt* surcar; formar lomos (en); (wrinkle) arrugar

ridicule *n* ridículo, *m*, *vt* poner en ridículo, ridiculizar, burlarse (de), mofarse (de)
ridiculous *a* ridículo, absurdo
riding *a* cabalgante; que va a caballo; montado (a, en, sobre); *naut* al ancla; (in compounds) de equitación; de montar. *n* equitación, *f*; paseo a caballo; en bicicleta, etc., *m*; acción de ir a caballo, etc., *f*; (district) comarca, *f*. **r.-boots,** botas de montar, *f pl*. **r.-habit,** traje de montar, *m*; (woman's) amazona, *f*. **r.-master,** profesor de equitación, *m*. **r.-saddle,** silla de montar, *f*. **r.-school,** escuela de equitación, *f*
rife *a* común; corriente; frecuente; prevalente; abundante; general. **r. with,** abundante en; lleno de
riffraff *n* desperdicios, *m pl*; (rabble) gentuza, canalla, *f*
rifle *n* rifle, fusil rayado, *m*. *vt* robar; (a suitcase, etc.) desvalijar; (a gun) rayar. **r.-case,** *Mexico* carcaj, *m*. **r.-range,** campo de tiro, *m*. **r.-sling,** portafusil, *m*. **r.-shot,** fusilazo, *m*
rifleman *n* fusilero, *m*
rifler *n* saqueador (-ra)
rifling *n* (robbing) saqueo, robo, *m*; (of a suitcase, etc.) desvalijamiento, *m*
rift *n* hendedura, abertura, *f*; grieta, *f*
rig *n naut* aparejo, *m*; *inf* atavío, *m*. *vt* (a ship) aparejar; equipar; (elections) falsificar. **to rig out,** proveer de; equipar con; ataviar. **to rig up,** arreglar; armar, construir
rigging *n* (of a ship) aparejo, *m*
right *a* recto; correcto; conveniente, debido; apropiado; exacto; (opposite of left hand) derecho; (straight) directo; en línea recta; razonable; (true) verdadero, genuino, legítimo; (just) justo; (prudent) prudente; (in health) sano. **All r.!** ¡Está bien! **I feel all r.,** Me siento perfectamente bien, Estoy bien. **He is the r. man for the job,** Él es el hombre que hace falta para el puesto. **It is the r. word,** Es la palabra apropiada. **on the r.,** a la derecha. **to be r.,** (of persons) tener razón. **to make r.,** poner en orden; arreglar. **r.-angle,** ángulo recto, *m*. **r.-angled,** rectangular. **r.-angled triangle,** triángulo rectángulo, *m*. **the R. Bank (of Paris),** la Orilla derecha, la Ribera derecha, *f*. **r. hand,** *n* (mano) derecha, diestra, *f*; derecha, *f*; (person) brazo derecho, *m*. *a* de la mano derecha; de la derecha; a la derecha. **r.-handed,** derecho; diestro, hábil. **r. mind,** entero juicio, *m*. **r.-minded,** juicioso, prudente; honrado. **r.-of-way,** derecho a la vía, *m*
right *adv* directamente; inmediatamente; derechamente; correctamente; debidamente; exactamente; bien; (quite, thoroughly) completamente; honradamente; (very) muy. **r. on,** adelante; en frente. **R. about face!** ¡Media vuelta a la derecha! **r. at the bottom,** al fondo; al final; el último (de la clase, etc.). **r. at the end of his speech,** al fin de su discurso. **r. away, r. now** en seguida, inmediatamente, *Mexico* ahorita, *elsewhere in Lat. Am.* lueguito
right *n* razón, *f*; verdad, *f*; justicia, *f*; (good) bien, *m*; derecho, *m*; (not left side) derecha, *f*; (of political parties) derechas, *f pl*. **r. and wrong,** el bien y el mal. **"All rights reserved,"** «Derechos reservados.» **by rights,** por derecho. **It is on the r.,** Está a la derecha. **to exercise one's r.,** usar de su derecho. **r. of association,** derecho de asociación, *m*. **r. of way,** derecho de paso, *m*. **to be in the r.,** tener razón; estar en su derecho
right *vt* enderezar; rectificar; corregir; poner en orden; *naut* enderezar; hacer justicia (a). **to r. wrongs,** deshacer agravios
righteous *a* recto, virtuoso, justo; justificado
righteously *adv* virtuosamente; justamente
righteousness *n* rectitud, integridad, virtud, *f*; justicia, *f*
rightful *a* justo; legítimo; verdadero
rightfully *adv* justamente; legitimamente; verdaderamente
rightfulness *n* justicia, *f*; legitimidad, *f*; verdad, *f*
rightly *adv* justamente; debidamente; correctamente; bien. **r. or wrongly,** mal que bien
rightness *n* rectitud, *f*; derechura, *f*; justicia, *f*; exactitud, *f*
rigid *a* rígido; inflexible; severo, riguroso
rigidity *n* rigidez, *f*; inflexibilidad, *f*; severidad, *f*
rigmarole *n* monserga, *f*, galimatías, *m*, jerigonza, *f*
rigor *n* rigor, *m*
rigorous *a* riguroso
rigor *n* rigor, *m*
rile *vt inf* irritar, sacar de tino (a)
rim *n* borde, *m*; orilla, *f*; (of a wheel) llanta, *f*, aro, *m*
rime *n* escarcha, *f*, *vt* cubrir con escarcha. See also **rhyme**
rind *n* (of fruit) cáscara, corteza, *f*; (of cheese) costra, *f*; (of bacon) piel, *f*
ring *n* círculo, *m*; (round the eyes) ojera, *f*; (for curtains, etc.) anilla, *f*; (for the finger) anillo, *m*, sortija, *f*; (for children's games, etc.) corro, *m*; (for the ears) arete, *m*; (of smoke and for the nose) anillo, *m*; (for hitching, etc.) argolla, *f*; (for boxing) cuadrilátero, *m*; (on a racecourse) picadero, *m*; (at a circus, bull-fight) ruedo, redondel, *m*; *fig* arena, *f*; (group) camarilla, *f*, grupo, *m*; (metallic sound) sonido metálico, *m*; resonancia, *f*; (tinkle) tintín, *m*; (of a bell) repique, tañido, son (de la campana), *m*; (of bells) juego de campanas, *m*; (of laughter, etc.) ruido, *m*; (of truth, etc.) apariencia, *f*. **r.-bolt,** *naut* cáncamo, *m*. **r. finger,** dedo anular, *m*. **r.-master,** director de circo, *m*
ring *vt* (surround) cercar, rodear; (a bull, etc.) poner un anillo (a); (sound) hacer sonar; sonar; (a door bell, etc.) tocar, apretar; (bells) echar a vuelo; (announce by pealing the bells) anunciar, proclamar; sonar, tañer. *vi* (of bells) sonar; (re-echo) resonar; (of the ears) zumbar; (tinkle) tintinar. **to r. the bell,** tocar la campana; tocar el timbre. **to r. off,** colgar el teléfono. **to r. up,** llamar por teléfono, telefonear
ringing *n* acción de tocar las campanas o el timbre, *f*; toque, *m*; repique, *m*; campanilleo, *m*; (in the ears) zumbido, *m*. *a* resonante, sonoro. **r. signal,** señal de llamada, *f*. **the r. of the bells,** el son de las campanas
ringleader *n* cabecilla, *m*
ringlet *n* rizo, bucle, *m*
ringworm *n* tiña, *f*
rink *n* pista, *f*. **skating-r.,** sala de patinar, *f*; pista de patinar, *f*
rinse *n* enjuague, *m*; enjuagadura, *f*; (of clothes) aclarado, *m*. *vt* enjuagar; (clothes) aclarar; lavar
rinsing *n* See **rinse;** *pl* **rinsings,** lavazas, *f pl*, *a* de aclarar
Rio de Janeiro *n* Rio de Janeiro, *f*; *a* carioca, *formal* fluminense, *mf*
riot *n* motín, *m*; tumulto, *m*; desorden, *m*; exceso, *m*; orgía, *f*; disipación, *f*. *vi* amotinarse; alborotarse; entregarse a la disipación (or al placer); (enjoy) gozar, disfrutar. **to run r.,** hacer excesos; perder el freno; desmandarse; *fig* extenderse por todas partes; crecer en abundancia, cubrir todo
rioter *n* amotinador (-ra); alborotador (-ra)
riotous *a* sedicioso; bullicioso; disoluto; desordenado; desenfrenado
riotousness *n* sedición, *f*; disolución, *f*; excesos, *m pl*, desenfreno, *m*; desorden, *m*
rip *vt* rasgar; (unsew) descoser; (wood, etc.) partir; (make) hacer. *vi* rasgarse. *n* rasgón, *m*; rasgadura, *f*; desgarro, *m*; (libertine) calavera, *m*. **to rip off,** arrancar; quitar. **to rip open,** abrir; (an animal) abrir en canal
riparian *a* and *n* ribereño (-ña)
ripe *a* maduro; preparado; perfecto, acabado
ripen *vt* and *vi* madurar
ripeness *n* madurez, *f*
ripening *n* maduración, *f*
ripping *n* rasgadura, *f*; (unstitching) deshiladura, *f*. *a inf* estupendo

ripple *n* rizo, *m*; onda, *f*; (of sound) murmullo, *m*. *vt* rizar. *vi* rizarse; murmurar
rippling *n* rizado, *m*; murmullo, *m*
rise *vi* ascender; subir; levantarse; ponerse de pie; (of a meeting) suspenderse; (from the dead) resucitar; (grow) crecer; (swell) hincharse; (of sun, moon) salir; (of sound, gradient, price, stock exchange quotations) subir; (of river source) nacer; (in revolt) sublevarse, rebelarse; (to the mind) presentarse, surgir; (appear) aparecer; (of buildings, etc.) elevarse, alzarse; (in the world) mejorar de posición; (originate) originarse (en), proceder (de); (of mercury) alzarse; (of fish) picar. **He has risen in my estimation,** Ha ganado en mi estimación. **She rose early,** Se levantó temprano. **The color rose in her cheeks,** Se le subieron los colores a la cara. **to r. to the occasion,** estar al nivel de las circunstancias. **to r. to one's feet,** ponerse de pie. **to r. to the bait,** morder el anzuelo. **to r. again,** levantarse de nuevo; resucitar; renovarse, suscitarse otra vez. **to r. above,** alzarse por encima de; mostrarse superior a
rise *n* ascensión, *f*; subida, *f*; levantamiento, *m*; (in price, temperature) alza, *f*; (increase) aumento, *m*; (of the sun, moon) salida, *f*; (of a river) nacimiento, *m*; (origin) origen, *m*; (growth, development) desarrollo, crecimiento, *m*; (promotion) ascenso, *m*; (slope) cuesta, *f*; pendiente, *f*; (high ground) eminencia, altura, *f*. **to give r. to,** dar lugar a, causar. **r. and fall,** subida y baja, *f*; (of the voice) ritmo, *m*; (of music) cadencia, *f*; (of institutions) grandeza y decadencia, *f*. **r. to power,** subida al poder, *f*
riser *n* el, *m*, (*f*, la) que se levanta; (of a step) contrahuella, *f*. **early r.,** madrugador (-ra). **late r.,** el, *m*, (*f*, la) que se levanta tarde
risibility *n* risibilidad, *f*
risible *a* risible
rising *n* subida, *f*; (of the source of rivers) nacimiento, *m*; (overflowing of rivers) crecimiento, *m*; (of sun, moon) salida, *f*; (from the dead) resurrección, *f*; (rebellion) sublevación, insurrección, *f*; (of the tide) crecida, *f*; (of bread) levadura, *f*; (of an assembly) suspensión, *f*; (of a theater curtain) subida, *f*; (literary) renacimiento, *m*, *a* creciente; naciente; saliente; (promising) de porvenir; (young) joven. **the r. generation,** los jóvenes, la generación joven. **He is r. forty,** Raya en los cuarenta. **He likes early r.,** Le gusta madrugar. **On the r. of the curtain . . . ,** Al levantarse el telón . . . **the r. of the moon,** la salida de la luna, *f*. **the r. tide,** la marea creciente
risk *n* riesgo, *m*; peligro, *m*. *vt* arriesgar; atreverse (a), osar. **at the r. of,** al riesgo de. **to take a r.,** tomar un riesgo; correr peligro. **to r. everything on the outcome,** jugar el todo por el todo
risk capital *n* capital-riesgo, *m*
riskiness *n* peligro, *m*
risky *a* arriesgado, peligroso
rissole *n* risol, *m*, (*pl* risoles)
rite *n* rito, *m*
rite of passage *n* rito de tránsito, *m*
ritual *a* ritual. *n* rito, *m*, ceremonia, *f*
ritualist *n* ritualista, *mf*
ritualistic *a* ritualista
rival *n* rival, *mf a* competidor; rival. *vt* rivalizar con, competir con
rivalry *n* rivalidad, *f*
river *n* río, *m*. *a* del río; fluvial. **r.-basin,** cuenca de un río, *f*. **r.-bed,** lecho, cauce (de un río), *m*. **r. civilization,** civilización fluvial, *f*. **r.-god,** dios de los ríos, *m*. **r.-mouth,** ría, *f*. **r. port,** puerto fluvial, *m*
riverside *n* ribera, orilla de un río, *f*. *a* de la(s) orilla(s) de un río; situado a la orilla de un río; ribereño
rivet *n* remache, roblón, *m*. *vt* remachar; clavar; *fig* fijar, concentrar; *fig* cautivar, absorber
Riviera, the la Riviera, *f*
riveter *n* remachador, *m*
riveting *n* remachado, remache, *m*; *fig* fijación, concentración, *f*; *fig* absorción, *f*. **r. machine,** remachadora, *f*
rivulet *n* riachuelo, arroyo, *m*
road *n* camino, *m*; carretera, *f*; ruta, *f*; *pl* **roads,** *naut* rada, *f*. **high r.,** camino real, *m*. **main r.,** carretera, *f*. **secondary r.,** carretera de segunda clase, *f*. **on the r. to . . . ,** en el camino de . . . **to get out of the r.,** *inf* quitarse de en medio. **to go by r.,** ir por carretera. **"R. up!"** «Carretera en reparaciones.» **r.-book,** guía de carreteras, *f*. **r. house,** albergue de carretera, *m*. **r. maker,** constructor de caminos, *m*; (navvy) peón caminero, *m*. **r. making,** construcción de caminos, *f*. **r. map,** mapa de carreteras, *m*. **r. sign,** señal de carretera, señal de tránsito, señal vial, *f*, poste indicador, *m*. **The r. to hell is paved with good intentions,** El camino del infierno está empedrado de buenas intenciones. **"R. Repairs,"** «Camino en Reparación»
roadmender *n* peón caminero, *m*
roadside *n* borde del camino, *m*, *a* al lado del camino
roadstead *n* rada, *f*
roadster *n* automóvil de turismo, *m*; bicicleta de carreras, *f*; caballo de aguante, *m*; buque fondeado en rada, *m*
roadway *n* calzada, carretera, *f*
roam *vi* vagar, vagabundear, andar errante. *vt* errar por
roamer *n* vagabundo (-da), hombre errante, *m*
roaming *n* vagabundeo, *m*; excursiones, *f pl*, paseos, *m pl*; *a* errante, vagabundo; nómada
roan *a* roano, sabino. *n* caballo roano, *m*
roar *vi* rugir; (of a bull, of the wind, of a person in anger) bramar; dar voces; (of the fire) crepitar; (of cannon) retumbar; (of thunder) estallar. *vt* gritar. *n* rugido, bramido, *m*; (shout) grito, *m*; (of the fire) crepitación, *f*; (of cannon, thunder) estallido, *m*; (noise) ruido, *m*. **to r. with laughter,** reírse a carcajadas
roaring *n* (of horses) asma de los caballos, *f*, For other meanings, see under **roar.** *a* rugiente, bramante; *inf* magnífico. **to do a r. trade,** hacer un buen negocio
roast *n* asado, *m*, carne asada, *f*. *a* asado; tostado. *vt* asar; (coffee and to warm one's feet, etc.) tostar; (metals) calcinar; (scold) desollar vivo (a). *vi* asarse; tostarse. **r. beef,** rosbif, *m*
roaster *n* asador, *m*; (for coffee or peanuts) tostador, *m*; (for chestnuts, etc.) tambor, *m*
roasting *n* asación, *f*; (of coffee) tostado, *m*; (of metals) calcinación, *f*. **r. spit,** asador, *m*
rob *vt* robar; quitar, privar (de). **They have robbed her of her pocketbook,** Le han robado la cartera
robber *n* ladrón (-ona); (footpad) salteador de caminos, *m*; (brigand) bandido, *m*
robbery *n* robo, *m*. **It's daylight r.!** ¡Es un desuello! **to commit a r.,** cometer un robo. **r. with violence,** robo armado, *m*
robe *n* traje talar, *m*, toga, *f*; (of a monk, nun) hábito, *m*; (of a priest, etc.) sotana, *f*; *poet* manto, *m*; (infant's) mantillas, *f pl*; *pl* **robes,** traje de ceremonia, *m*. *vt* vestir; cubrir, revestir (de). *vi* vestirse. **bath r.,** albornoz, *m*
robin *n* petirrojo, *m*
roble *n* rublo, *m*
robot *n* hombre mecánico, *m*; *aer* piloto mecánico, *m*. **traffic r.,** torre del tráfico, *f*, aparato automático, *m*. **r. plane,** avión sin piloto, *m*
robust *a* robusto; fuerte, vigoroso. **to make r.,** robustecer
robustness *n* robustez, *f*; vigor, *m*, fuerza, *f*
rock *n* roca, *f*; (in the sea) abrojo, escollo, *m*; peña, *f*, peñasco, *m*. **as firm as a r.,** como una roca. **to be on the rocks,** *inf* estar a la cuarta pregunta. **r. bottom,** *n* fondo, *m*. *a* mínimo, más bajo. **r. crystal,** cuarzo, *m*. **r.-garden,** jardincito rocoso, jardin alpestre, *m*. **r.-plant,** planta alpestre, *f*. **r.-rose,** heliantemo, *m*. **r.-salt,** sal gema, *f*
rock *vt* mecer; (shake) hacer temblar, sacudir; (to sleep) arrullar. *vi* mecerse, balancearse; tambalearse; agitarse; temblar
rocker *n* (of a chair, cradle) balancín, *m*; (chair) mecedora, *f*
rockery *n* jardincito rocoso, *m*

rocket *n* cohete, volador, *m*. *vi* lanzarse. **r.-launching aircraft,** caza lanzacohetes, *f*
rockiness *n* abundancia de rocas, *f*; fragosidad, escabrosidad, *f*
rocking *n* balanceo, *m*; (staggering) tambaleo, *m*; oscilación, *f*; (of an infant) arrullo, *m*. **r.-chair,** mecedora, *f*. **r.-horse,** caballo balancín, caballo mecedor, *m*
rocky *a* rocoso; de roca; roqueño; (rough) fragoso, escabroso; (rugged) peñascoso, escarpado. **the R. Mountains,** las Montañas Rocosas, *f pl*
rococo *n* rococó, *m*
rod *n* vara, *f*; bastón de mando, *m*; (for fishing) caña, *f*; (measure) pértiga, *f*; (surveying) jalón, *m*; palo, *m*; (for punishment) vergajo, *m*; *mech* vástago, *m*. **connecting rod,** biela, *f*. **to fish with rod and line,** pescar con caña
rodent *a* and *n* roedor, *m*
roe *n* (deer) corzo (-za); (of fish) hueva, *f*. **soft roes,** lechas, *f pl*
rogue *n* bribón (-ona), pícaro (-ra), pillo (-lla), *Argentina* farabute, *mf*; *law* vago, *m*; (affectionate) picaruelo (-la)
roguery *n* truhanería, picardía, *f*; (knaves) pícaros, *m pl*; (mischief) travesuras, *f pl*. **novel of r.,** novela picaresca, *f*
roguish *a* picaresco, bellaco; (mischievous) travieso, juguetón; malicioso
roguishly *adv* como un pícaro; con malicia
roguishness *n* picardía, bribonería, bellaquería, *f*; (mischievousness) travesuras, *f pl*; malicia, *f*
role *n* papel, *m*
roll *n* rollo, *m*; (list) rol, *m*, lista, *f*; (of bread) panecillo, *Mexico* bolillo, *m*; (of a drum) redoble, *m*; (of thunder) tronido, *m*; (of cloth) pieza, *f*; (of tobacco) rollo, *m*; (of meat, etc.) pastel, *m*; (of a ship) balanceo, *m*; *pl* **rolls,** (records) archivos, *m pl*. **He has a nautical r.,** Tiene un andar de marinero. **to call the r.,** pasar lista. **r. film,** película fotográfica, *f*. **r. of honour,** lista de honor, *f*. **r.-on corset,** faja elástica, *f*, corsé de goma, *m*. **r.-top desk,** buró de cierre enrollable, *m*
roll *vi* rodar; dar vueltas; (wallow) revolcarse; (of a ship) balancearse, bambolearse; (in money, etc.) nadar; (flow) correr, fluir; (*fig* of time) pasar tranquilamente; (of vehicle) rodar; pasar rodando; (of country) ondular; (of the sea) ondear; (of drums) redoblar; (of thunder) retumbar. *vt* hacer rodar; arrollar; (a cigarette) liar; (metals) laminar; (move) mover; (the eyes) guiñar (los ojos); (the ground) apisonar; (pastry) aplanar; (of an organ) sonar; (a drum) redoblar. **Mary rolled her eyes heavenwards,** María puso los ojos en blanco. **to r. away,** alejarse; desaparecer; (of time) pasar. **to r. back,** volver, retirarse; desaparecer. **to r. by,** pasar rodando; desaparecer. **to r. down,** bajar rodando, rodar por. **to r. in,** llegar en gran cantidad (or en gran número). **to r. off,** caer de. **to r. on,** seguir su marcha; fluir sin cesar; seguir su curso; (of time) avanzar. **to r. out,** (metal) laminar; (pastry) aplanar; (bring out) sacar; desenrollar. **to r. over,** *vt* volcar; tumbar; dar la vuelta (a). *vi* dar la vuelta; volverse al otro lado. **to r. up,** arrollar; envolver; (of hedgehogs, etc.) enroscarse, hacerse un ovillo
roll-call vote *n* votación nominal, *f*
roller *n* rodillo, *m*; cilindro, *m*; (wheel, castor) rueda, *f*; (for flattening the ground) apisonadora, *f*; *print* rodillo, *m*; (wave) ola grande, *f*. **r.-bandage,** venda, *f*. **r. canary,** canario de raza flauta, *m*. **r.-skate,** patín de ruedas, *m*. **r.-skating,** patinaje de ruedas, *m*. **r.-towel,** toalla continua, *f*
rollicking *a* alegre, jovial; juguetón
rolling *a* rodante; (of landscape) ondulante, quebrado. *n* rodadura, *f*; (wallowing) revuelco, *m*; (of metals) laminación, *f*; (of a ship) balanceo, *m*; (rolling up) enrollamiento, *m*. **r.-pin,** rollo, rodillo de pastelero, *m*. **r.-stock,** material móvil ferroviario, *m*
Roman *a* romano, de los romanos; (of noses and *print*) romano. *n* romano (-na). **in R. fashion,** a la romana. **R. Catholic,** *a* católico; católico apostólico romano. *n* el católico (-ca). **R. Catholicism,** catolicismo, *m*. **R. figures,** números romanos, *m pl*. **R. nose,** nariz romana, *f*. **R. road,** vía romana, *f*. **R. type,** *print* tipo romano, *m*
Romance *a* (of languages) romance. *n* (language) romance, *m*
romance *n* novela de caballería, *f*; romance, *m*; aventura, *f*; cuento, *m*, novela, *f*; romanticismo, *m*; *mus* romanza, *f*. *vi* inventar ficciones; exagerar
romancer *n* romancerista, *mf*; mentiroso (-sa), embustero (-ra)
Romanesque *a* románico; romanesco
romantic *a* and *n* romántico (-ca)
romantically *adv* románticamente; de un modo romántico
romanticism *n* romanticismo, *m*
romanticist *n* romántico (-ca)
Rome Roma, *f*
romp *vi* juguetear, brincar, retozar, loquear; correr rápidamente. *n* locuelo (-la), saltaparedes, *mf*; (game) retozo, *m*. **The horse romped home easily,** El caballo ganó la carrera fácilmente
rompers *n* mono, *m*
romping *n* juegos, *m pl*, travesuras, *f pl*
rondo *n* rondó, *m*
rood *n* cruz, *f*; crucifijo, *m*; cuarto de acre, *m*. **By the r.!** ¡Por mi santiguada!
roof *n* tejado, techado, *m*; (of a motor-car, bus) tejadillo, *m*; (of coaches, etc.) imperial, *f*; cubierta, *f*; (of the mouth) paladar, *m*; (bower) enramada, *f*; (of heaven) bóveda (del cielo), *f*. *vt* techar, tejar, *Lat. Am.* entechar; (shelter) abrigar. **r.-garden,** azotea, *f*. **r.-gutter,** canalera, *f*
roofer *n* techador, *m*; constructor de tejados, *m*
rook *n* chova, *f*, grajo, *m*; (chess) torre, *f*. *vt* engañar, estafar; (overcharge) desollar vivo (a)
rookery *n* manada de grajos, *f*; colonia de grajos, aves marinas or focas, *f*
room *n* (in a house) habitación, *f*, cuarto, *m*; sala, *f*; cámara, *f*; (behind a shop) trastienda, *f*; (space) sitio, espacio, *m*; lugar, *m*; (opportunity) oportunidad, *f*; (cause) motivo, *m*, causa, *f*. *vi* alojarse. **bath-r.,** cuarto de baño, *m*. **dining-r.,** comedor, *m*. **drawing-r.,** salón, *m*. **There is no r. for us in this car,** No cabemos en este coche. **There is still r. for improvement,** Se puede mejorar todavía. **There isn't r. for anything else,** No cabe más. **to be r.,** caber, haber sitio. **to make r.,** hacer sitio
roomed *a* (in compounds) de . . . habitaciones; de . . . salas
roominess *n* espaciosidad, amplitud, amplitud de habitación, *f*; (of garments) holgura, *f*
rooming house *n* casa de huéspedes, *f*
roommate *n* compañero de cuarto, compañero de pieza, *m*
roomy *a* espacioso, amplio; (of garments) holgado
roost *n* percha de gallinero, *f*, *Lat. Am.* dormidero, *m*. *vi* dormir en una percha; recogerse. **to rule the r.,** ser el amo del cotarro
rooster *n* gallo, *m*,
root *n* raíz, *f*; *gram* radical, *m*; *mus* base, *f*; origen, *m*; explicación, *f*. *vt* arraigar; *fig* fijar, clavar. *vi* echar raíces; *fig* arraigarse; (of pigs, etc.) hozar, escarbar; revolver. **to r. out,** arrancar de raíz; *fig* desarraigar; (destroy) extirpar. **cubed r.,** raíz cúbica, *f*. **from the r.,** (entirely) de raíz. **square r.,** raíz cuadrada, *f*. **to cut close to the r.,** cortar a raíz
rooted *a* (in compounds) de raíces . . . ; arraigado
rope *n* soga, cuerda, *f*; (hawser) maroma, *f*; *naut* cabo, *m*; (tight-rope) cable, *m*, cuerda de volatinero, *f*; (string) ristra, sarta, *f*; hilo, *m*; *pl* **ropes,** (boxing) cuerdas del cuadrilátero, *f pl*. *vt* encordelar, atar con cuerdas. **to r. in,** encerrar; (a person) enganchar, coger. **a r. of pearls,** una sarta de perlas. **to give a person plenty of r.,** dar mucha latitud (a). **to know the ropes,** conocer todos los trucos. **r.-ladder,** escala de

cuerda, *f*. **r.-maker,** cordelero (-ra), soguero, *m*. **r.-making,** cordelería, soguería, *f*. **r.-trick,** truco de la cuerda, *m*. **r.-walk,** cordelería, *f*. **r.-yarn,** *naut* filástica, *f*

rosary *n* rosario, *m*. **to say the r.,** rezar el rosario

rose *n* rosa, *f*; color de rosa, *m*; (rosette) roseta, *f*; *arch* rosetón, *m*; (of watering-can) pomo, *m*, roseta, *f*. *a* de rosa, rosado. **to see the world through r.-colored spectacles,** ver las cosas en color de rosa. **to turn to r.,** volverse color de rosa, rosear. **r.-bay,** *bot* rododafne, adelfa, *f*. **r.-bush,** rosal, *m*. **r.-color,** color de rosa, rosa, *m*. **r.-colored,** de color de rosa, rosado. **r.-garden,** rosalera, rosaleda, *f*. **r. grower,** cultivador (-ra) de rosas. **r. hip,** escaramujo, *m*. **r. leaf,** hoja de rosa, *f*; pétalo de rosa, *m*. **r.-like,** como una rosa, de rosa. **r.-red,** de color de rosa; como una rosa. **climbing r.-tree,** rosal trepador, *m*. **dwarf r.-tree,** rosal bajo, *m*. **standard r.-tree,** rosal de tallo, *m*. **r.-water,** agua de rosas, *f*. **r.-window,** rosetón, *m*, rosa, *f*. **r.-wood,** palo de rosa, *m*

rosé *a* (of wines) rosado

rosebud *n* capullo de rosa, *m*

rosemary *n* romero, *m*

rosin *n* (solid, for violin-bows, etc.) colofonia, *f*; resina, *f*. *vt* dar con colofonia; dar con resina

rosiness *n* color de rosa, *m*

roster *n* lista, *f*; registro, *m*, matrícula, *f*

rostrum *n* tribuna, *f*; *zool* pico, *m*; (of a ship) espolón, *m*

rosy *a* róseo, rosado; sonrosado; *fig* de color de rosa, halagüeño; optimista. **r.-cheeked,** con (de) mejillas sonrosadas

rot *n* putrefacción, podredumbre, *f*; (in trees) caries, *f*; (in sheep) comalía, *f*; (slang) patrañas, *f pl*, disparates, *m pl*, *vi* pudrirse; descomponerse; *fig* echarse a perder; (slang) decir disparates. *vt* pudrir; *fig* corromper; (slang) tomar el pelo (a)

rota *n* lista, *f*; orden del día, *m*

rotary *a* rotativo. **r. printing press,** rotativa, *f*

rotary telephone *n* teléfono de discado, *m*

rotate *vi* girar, dar vueltas; alternarse. *vt* hacer girar

rotating *a* rotativo; giratorio

rotation *n* rotación, *f*; turno, *m*. **in r.,** por turnos. **r. of crops,** rotación de cultivos, *f*

rotatory *a* rotatorio

rote, to learn by *vt* aprender de memoria, aprender por repetición, aprender de cotorra

rotogravure *n* rotograbado, *m*

rotten *a* putrefacto; podrido; (of bones, teeth) cariado; dañado, echado a perder; *fig* corrompido; (slang) pésimo. **to smell r.,** oler a podredumbre; apestar

rottenness *n* putrefacción, podredumbre, *f*; *fig* corrupción, *f*

rotter *n* (slang) perdido, *m*

rotting *n* pudrición, *f*, *a* que se pudre

rotund *a* rotundo

rotunda *n* rotonda, *f*

rotundity *n* redondez, *f*; rotundidad, *f*

roué *n* calavera, libertino, *m*

rouge *n* colorete, *m*, *vt* and *vi* pintar de rojo, poner(se) colorete

rough *a* áspero; duro; (of country) fragoso, escabroso; (uneven) desigual; (stormy) borrascoso, tempestuoso; (of the sea) encrespado, bravo; (of movement) violento; (bristling) erizado; (of the hair) despeinado; (unpolished) tosco; basto; (unskilled, clumsy) torpe; (of sounds, tastes) áspero; (of persons) rudo, inculto; (severe) severo; (of behavior) brutal; (of manners) brusco; (rude) grosero; (approximate) aproximado. *adv* duramente, mal. *n* estado tosco, *m*; (person) matón, *m*. **in the r.,** en bruto; (roughed out) bosquejado. **to grow r.,** (of the sea) encresparse, embravecerse. **to take the r. with the smooth,** *fig* aceptar la realidad; tomar lo bueno con lo malo. **to r. it,** luchar contra las dificultades, pasar apuros; llevar una vida sencilla; vivir mal. **to r. out,** bosquejar. **r. and ready,** improvisado; provisional. **r. and tumble,** *n* camorra, pendencia, *f*. **r.-cast,** *vt* dar una primera capa de mezcla gruesa (a); bosquejar. **r. diamond,** diamante bruto (or en bruto), *m*. **r.-draft,** borrador, *m*; bosquejo, *m*. **r.-haired,** (of a dog) de pelo crespo. **r.-hewn,** modelado toscamente; desbastado; *fig* cerril, tosco. **r.-house,** jarana, *f*. **r.-rider,** domador (de caballos), *m*. **r. sketch,** bosquejo, esbozo, *m*. **r.-spoken,** malhablado

roughen *vt* poner áspero. *vi* ponerse áspero

roughly *adv* rudamente, toscamente; duramente; brutalmente; bruscamente; (of tastes, sounds) ásperamente; (approximately) aproximadamente, más o menos

roughness *n* aspereza, *f*; dureza, *f*; tosquedad, *f*; rudeza. *f*; (of the sea, wind) braveza, *f*; violencia, *f*; (of manner) brusquedad, *f*; brutalidad, *f*; (vulgarity) grosería, *f*. **the r. of the way,** la aspereza del camino

roulette *n* ruleta, *f*

round *a* redondo; (plump) rollizo; rotundo, categórico; sonoro. **a r. sum,** una cantidad redonda; un número redondo. **to walk at a r. pace,** andar a un buen paso. **r. dance,** baile en ruedo, *m*. **r.-faced,** carilleno, de cara redonda. **r.-house,** cuerpo de guardia, *m*; *naut* tumbadillo, *m*. **r.-shouldered,** cargado de espaldas. **r. table,** mesa redonda, *f*; (of King Arthur) Tabla Redonda, *f*. **r. trip,** viaje redondo, viaje de ida y vuelta, *m*. **r.-up,** rodeo de ganado, *m*; arresto, *m*

round *n* círculo, *m*; esfera, *f*; redondez, *f*; (slice) rodaja, *f*; (of a ladder) peldaño, *m*; (patrol and *mil*) ronda, *f*; circuito, *m*; vuelta, *f*, giro, *m*; serie, *f*; rutina, *f*; (of ammunition) andanada, descarga, *f*; (of cartridge) cartucho con bala, *m*; (of applause, etc.) salva, *f*; (of golf) partido, *m*; (in a fight) asalto, *m*; *sport* vuelta, *f*; (of drinks) ronda, *f*; (doctor's) visitas, *f pl*

round *vt* redondear; (*fig* complete) acabar, perfeccionar; (go round, e.g. a corner) dar vuleta (a), doblar, trasponer; rodear, cercar; (of a ship) doblar. *vi* redondearse. **to r. off,** redondear; terminar; coronar. **to r. up,** (cattle) rodear. **to r. upon,** volverse contra

round *adv* alrededor, en derredor; por todos lados; a la redonda, en torno; en circunferencia; en conjunto (**r.** is not translated in Spanish, e.g. **I shall come r. to your house,** Vendré a tu casa). *prep* alrededor de. **all the year r.,** todo el año, el año entero. **r. about,** a la redonda de, al derredor de; (nearly) cerca de; (of time by the clock) a eso de. **The road is closed and we shall have to go r.,** El camino está cerrado y tendremos que dar una vuelta. **to come r.,** volver; dejarse persuadir; recobrar su buen humor. **to go r.,** (spin) dar vueltas; (of the wind) cambiar. **There is enough to go r.,** Hay bastante para todos

roundabout *a* indirecto; desviado; vago. *n* tiovivo, *m*; (traffic) redondel, *m*. **He spoke in a r. way,** Hablaba con circunloquios. **We went there by a r. way,** Fuimos dando un rodeo

roundly *adv* en redondo; rotundamente, claramente

roundness *n* redondez, *f*; rotundidad, *f*

rouse *vt* despertar; animar; excitar; suscitar, provocar. **to r. oneself,** despertarse; animarse (a hacer algo)

rousing *a* que despierta; (moving) emocionante; (enthusiastic) entusiasta; grande, bueno

rout *n* (rabble) chusma, *f*; (party) sarao, *m*; (defeat) derrota, *f*; (meeting) reunión, *f*. *vt* derrotar, poner en fuga; vencer

route *n* ruta, *f*; camino, *m*; itinerario, *m*. **r. march,** marcha de maniobras, *f*

routine *n* rutina, *f*, *a* rutinario, de rutina

rove *vi* vagar, errar

rover *n* vagabundo (-da); pirata, *m*

roving *a* vagabundo, errante; ambulante

row *n* (line) hilera, fila, hila, *f*; (in a theater, etc.) fila, *f*; (string) ristra, *f*; (in a boat) paseo en bote, *m*; (commotion) alboroto, *m*; (noise) ruido, *m*; (shindy) gresca, camorra, *f*; (scolding) regaño, *m*, *vi* (a boat) remar, bogar. *vt* conducir remando; (scold) regañar. **to be a**

row, (shindy) haber la de San Quintín. **to start a row,** (shindy) armar camorra.
rowboat *n* bote de remos, *m*
rowdiness *n* alboroto, *m*
rowdy *a* alborotador. *n* trafalmejas, *mf* rufián, *m*. **rowdy party** *Lat. Am.* fandango, *m*
rower *n* remero (-ra), bogador (-ra)
rowing *a* que rema; de remos. *n* deporte del remo, *m*; paseo en bote, *m*. **r.-boat,** bote de remos, *m*. **r.-club,** club náutico, *m*. **r.-seat,** bancada, *f*. **r.-stroke,** bogada, *f*
royal *a* real; regio. *n naut* sobrejuanete, *m*. **r. academy,** real academia, *f*. **r. eagle,** águila real, *f*. **R. Highness,** Alteza Real, *f*. **r. letters patent,** cédula real, *f*. **R. Mail,** mala real, *f*. **R. Standard,** estandarte real, *m*
royalist *a* and *n* realista, *mf*
royally *adv* realmente; regiamente
royalty *n* realeza, *f*; miembro de la familia real, *m*; tanto por ciento de los ingresos, *m*; derechos de autor, *m pl*
R.R. (abbrev. of *railroad*) F.R. (abbrev. of *ferrocarril*)
rub *vt* frotar, estregar; fregar; rozar; friccionar; (make sore) raspar. **to rub one's hands together,** frotarse las manos. **to rub the wrong way,** frotar a contrapelo. **to rub against,** rozar. **to rub along,** *inf* ir tirando. **to rub down,** (a horse) bruzar; limpiar; (dry) secar; (wear down) desgastar. **to rub in,** dar fricciones con; frotar con; (an idea, etc.) machacar. **to rub off,** *vt* quitar (frotando); borrar. *vi* borrarse; separarse (de). **to rub out,** *vt* borrar. *vi* borrarse. **to rub up,** (polish) limpiar; *fig* refrescar
rub *n* frotación, *f*; roce, *m*; fricción, *f*; *fig* obstáculo, *m*; dificultad, *f*. **to give a rub,** frotar, etc. **rub-a-dub,** rataplán, *m*
rubber *a* de caucho, de goma. *n* caucho, *m*, goma, *f*; (for erasing) goma de borrar, *f*; (masseur) masajista, *mf*; (at whist, etc.) partida, *f*; *pl* **rubbers,** zapatos de goma, chanclos, *m pl*. **synthetic r.,** caucho artificial, *m*. **r. band,** goma, banda de goma, *f*. **r. belt,** *mech* correa de transmisión de caucho, *f*. **r.-plant, tree,** cauchera, *f*, *Central America, Mexico* hule, *m*. **r. plantation,** cauchal, *m*. **r.-plantation worker** cauchero (-a) *mf*. **r. planter,** cauchero, *m*. **r. stamp,** estampilla, *f*
rubbing *n* frotación, *f*; fricción, *f*; roce, *m*; (of floors, dishes, etc.) fregado, *m*
rubbish *n* basura, *f*; desperdicios, *m pl*, desecho, *m*; (of goods) pacotilla, *f*; (nonsense) pamplinas, patrañas, *f pl*, disparates, *m pl*. **r. cart,** carro del basurero, *m*
rubbishy *a* sin valor, malo; (of goods) de pacotilla, de calidad inferior
rubble *n* escombros, *m pl*; cascote, *m*; piedra bruta, *f*
rubicund *a* rubicundo
rubric *n* rúbrica, *f*
ruby *n* rubí, *m*. *a* de rubíes; de rubí. **r. lips,** labios de rubí, *m pl*
rucksack *n* mochila, *f*
rudder *n* timón, gobernalle, *m*
ruddiness *n* rubicundez, *f*; rojez, *f*; frescura, *f*
ruddy *a* rubicundo; rojo; frescote; (of animals) barcino
rude *a* rudo; tosco; vigoroso; grosero, descortés
rudely *adv* toscamente; groseramente
rudeness *n* rudeza, *f*; tosquedad, *f*; grosería, incivilidad, descortesía, *f*
rudiment *n* rudimento, *m*
rudimentary *a* rudimentario
rue *vt* lamentar, llorar. *n bot* ruda, *f*
rueful *a* triste, melancólico; lamentable
ruefulness *n* tristeza, *f*
ruff *n* golilla, lechuguilla, *f*; (of a bird) collarín de plumas, *m*; (of an animal) collarín de pelo, *m*
ruffian *n* rufián, *m*
ruffle *n sew* volante fruncido, *m*; (of a bird) collarin de plumas, *m*; (of an animal) collarín de pelo, *m*; (ripple) rizo, *m*; (annoyance) irritación, *f*. *vt* (ripple) rizar; (pleat) fruncir; (feathers) erizar; (hair) despeinar; agitar; (annoy) irritar, incomodar
ruffling *n* (rippling) rizado, *m*; (pleating) fruncido, *m*; (of the temper) irritación, *f*
rug *n* (floor) alfombra, *f*; manta de viaje, *f*. **rug strap,** portamantas, *m*
rugged *a* áspero, escabroso; escarpado, abrupto; (wrinkled) arrugado; tosco; (harsh) duro, severo; inculto; rudo; mal acabado; vigoroso
ruggedness *n* aspereza, escabrosidad, *f*; lo escarpado; dureza, severidad, *f*; rudeza, *f*; vigor, *m*
ruin *n* ruina, *f*. *vt* arruinar; echar a perder, estropear por completo; (a woman) perder
ruination *n* ruina, perdición, *f*
ruined *a* arruinado; en ruinas
ruinous *a* ruinoso; en ruinas
rule *n* regla, *f*; gobierno, *m*; autoridad, *f*, mando, *m*; administración, *f*; (reign) reinado, *m*; (of a court, etc.) orden, *f*; (for measuring) regla, *f*; *print* regleta, *f*; *pl* **rules,** reglas, *f pl*; reglamento, *m*. *vt* gobernar; regentar, regir; (control) dominar; (of a chairman, etc.) disponer, decidir; (guide) guiar; (lines) reglar. *vi* gobernar; (of a monarch) reinar; (of prices) mantenerse; estar en boga, prevalecer. **as a r.,** por regla general, en general. **slide-r.,** regla de cálculo, *f*. **to make it a r.,** tener por regla; tener por costumbre; tener por máxima. **to r. out,** excluir; *law* no admitir. **to r. over,** (of a king, etc.) reinar sobre. **r. of the road,** reglamento del tráfico, *m*. **r. of thumb,** regla empírica, *f*; rutina, *f*
ruler *n* gobernador (-ra); soberano (-na); (master) amo (ama); (for ruling lines) regla, *f*
ruling *a* regente; dominante; (current) vigente. *n* gobierno, *m*; *law* decisión, *f*, fallo, *m*; (with lines) rayado, *m*. **r. pen,** tiralíneas, *m*
rum *n* ron, *m*
Rumanian *a* rumano. *n* rumano (-na); (language) rumano, *m*
rumble *vi* retumbar, tronar; (of vehicles) rugir; crujir. *n* retumbo, trueno, *m*; rugido, *m*; ruido sordo, *m*; rumor, *m*; crujido, *m*
rumbling *a* que retumba, etc. *n* ruido sordo, *m*; retumbo, *m*; crujido, *m*; (in the bowels) rugido, *m*
ruminant *a* and *n* rumiante, *mf*
ruminate *vi* and *vt* rumiar
rumination *n* rumia, *f*; meditación, reflexión, *f*
rummage *vt* revolver, desordenar, trastornar; explorar. **to r. out,** desenterrar
rumor *n* rumor, *m*, fama, *f*. **It is rumored that . . . ,** Hay rumores de que . . . , La voz corre que . . . , Se dice que . . .
rump *n* (of an animal) nalgas, ancas, *f pl*; cuarto trasero, *m*; (of a bird) rabadilla, *f*; (scornful) culo, *m*, posaderas, *f pl*. **r.-steak,** solomillo, *m*
rumple *vt* arrugar; desordenar
run *vi* correr; acudir; (flee) huir; (rush) precipitarse, lanzarse; (in a race) tomar parte en una carrera; competir; (pass over) deslizarse (por); (of machines) andar, marchar; (of traffic) circular; (leave, of trains, ships, etc.) salir; (ply between) hacer el trayecto entre . . . y . . . ; (flow) fluir, correr; (into the sea, of rivers) desembocar (en); (spurt) chorrear, manar; (drip) gotear; (leak) dejar fugar (el agua, etc.); (of colors) correrse; caer; (of tears) correr; derramarse; (of eyes) llorar; (melt) derretirse; (of a sore) supurar; (travel or go) ir; moverse; (work) trabajar; funcionar; (of editions of a book) agotarse; (of a play) representarse; (cross) cruzar; (elapse) correr; transcurrir, pasar; (become) hacerse; (of wording) decir; (be current) correr; (for parliament, etc.) hacerse candidato; (navigate) navegar; (spread) extenderse; (be) estar; ser; (of thoughts) pasar; (last) durar; (tend) tender (a). *vt* (a race, a horse) correr; (drive) conducir; (a business, etc.) administrar; dirigir; (govern) gobernar, regir; (hunt) cazar; perseguir; (water, etc.) hacer correr; (pierce) clavar; introducir; (push) empujar; (one's hand, eye, etc.) pasar; (risks, etc.) correr; (possess) tener; establecer un servicio de (autobuses, etc.); (smuggle) hacer contrabando de. **The ship ran aground,** El barco encalló. **to run dry,** se-

carse; agotarse. **to run in the family,** estar en la familia. **to run into debt,** endeudarse, contraer deudas. **to run to seed,** granar; agotarse. **Steamers run daily between Barcelona and Mallorca,** Hay servicio diario de vapores entre Barcelona y Mallorca. **A stab of pain ran up his leg,** Sintió un dolor agudo en la pierna. **Feeling was running high,** Los ánimos estaban excitados. **My arrangements ran smoothly,** Mis planes marchaban bien. **Funds are running low,** El dinero escasea. **The tune runs in my head,** Tengo la canción metida en la cabeza. **The message runs like this,** El mensaje reza así, El mensaje dice así. **He ran his fingers through his hair,** Se mesaba los cabellos. **to run about,** andar de un lado a otro, correr por todas partes; (gad) corretear. **to run across,** cruzar corriendo; (meet) topar con, tropezar con. **to run after,** correr detrás (de); perseguir; buscar. **to run against,** (collide with) dar contra; (meet) tropezar con. **to run at,** abalanzarse hacia, precipitarse sobre; atacar. **to run away,** huir, escaparse; (slip away) escurrirse; (of a horse) dispararse, desbocarse. **to run away with,** huir con, fugarse con; (carry off) arrebatar; (steal) llevarse; (imagine) imaginarse, figurarse; (of temper, etc.) dominar, poseer. **to run back,** volver corriendo; llegar corriendo; retroceder rápidamente, correr hacia atrás. **to run backwards,** correr hacia atrás; **to run backwards and forwards,** ir y venir. **to run behind,** correr detrás (de); quedarse atrás; (be late) estar atrasado. **to run down,** *vi* bajar corriendo; descender, bajar; (of a clock) parar; (of a battery) gastarse; (of liquids) correr; fluir; (drop by drop) destilar. *vt* (capture) coger; alcanzar; (a person by a vehicle) atropellar; (a ship) echar a pique; (disparage) hablar mal de. **run-down,** (in health) agotado; (of a clock) parado. **to run for,** buscar corriendo; correr para coger (el autobús, etc.); (president, etc.) ser candidato para. **to run in,** *vi* entrar corriendo. *vt* arrestar; hacer prisionero; *print* encerrar. **to run into,** tropezar con; chocar con; (plunge into) meterse de cabeza en; (of sums of money, etc.) ascender a; (of streets, rivers, etc.) desembocar en. **to run off,** *vi* escaparse corriendo; marcharse corriendo. *vt* deslizarse por; (drain) vaciar; *print* imprimir; (compose) componer. **to run off with,** huir con. **to run on,** correr delante; continuar; (of the mind) pensar en, entregarse a; hablar sin cesar; *print* recorrer. **to run out,** *vi* salir corriendo; (of liquids) derramarse; salir; (end) acabarse; agotarse; (project) sobresalir. *vt* (cricket) coger al lanzador fuera de la línea de saque. **to run out of,** no tener más de, haber terminado. **to run over,** *vi* rebosar; derramarse. *vt* (of a vehicle) atropellar, pasar por encima de, *Mexico* antellevar; (peruse) repasar; revisar. **run pell-mell,** salir pitando, salir volando, salvarse por pies. **to run through,** correr por; pasar por; recorrer; (go directly) ir directamente (a); (pierce) traspasar, pasar de parte a parte; (squander) derrochar, malbaratar; (read) hojear, leer por encima. **to run up,** *vt* (hoist) izar; hacer de prisa; construir rápidamente; (incur) incurrir. *vi* subir corriendo; (of plants) trepar (por); (shrink) encogerse; (of expenses) aumentar. **to run up to time,** llegar a su hora. **to run up against,** tropezar con; (opposition, etc.) encontrar.

run *n* carrera, corrida, *f*; (excursion) visita, excursión, *f*; (cricket) carrera, *f*; (walk) paseo, *m*; (by train or sea) viaje, *m*; (by bus, tram) trayecto, *m*; (sea crossing) travesía, *f*; (distance run) recorrido, *m*; (of events, etc.) curso, *m*; marcha, *f*; (of markets, etc.) tendencia, *f*; (rhythm) ritmo, *m*; dirección, *f*; distancia, *f*; *mus* serie de notas, *f*; serie, *f*; duración, *f*; *theat* serie de representaciones, *f*; (freedom to use) libre uso, *m*; (majority) mayoría, *f*; (on a bank) asedio, *m*; (on a book, etc.) demanda, *f*; (for sheep, etc.) terreno de pasto, *m*; (for fowls) gallinero, *m* (in a stocking) *Lat. Am.* acarraladura, *f*, *m*. **a run of bad luck,** una temporada de mala suerte. **at a run,** corriendo. **in the long run,** a la larga, al fin y al cabo. **on the run,** en fuga; ocupado. **Prices came down with a run,** Los precios bajaron de golpe. **take-off run,** *aer* recorrido de despegue, *m*

runaway *a* fugitivo; (of a horse) desbocado

rung *n* (of a ladder) peldaño, *m*; (of a chair) travesaño, *m*; (lath) listón, *m*

runner *n* corredor (-ra); (carrier of sedan chair, etc.) silletero, *mf*; (smuggler) contrabandista, *m*; (courier) estafeta, *f*; (messenger) mensajero, *m*; (ring) anillo movible, pasador corredizo, *m*; rueda móvil, *f*; (of a sledge) patín, *m*; *bot* tallo rastrero, *m*. **r.-up,** el segundo

running *a* corredor; (of water, bank accounts) corriente; (of a knot) corredizo; (of a sore) supurante; (continuous) continuo; (consecutive) consecutivo. *n* carrera, *f*; marcha, *f*; funcionamiento, *m*; administración, *f*; gobierno, *m*; dirección, *f*; (flowing) derrame, *m*; (of trains, buses, etc.) servicio, *m*; (smuggling) contrabando, *m*; (of a sore) supuración, *f*. **six times r.,** seis veces consecutivas. **The car is in r. order,** El auto está en buen estado. **r. away,** fuga, *f*. **r.-board,** (of a car, etc.) estribo, *m*; (of a locomotive) plataforma, *f*. **r. costs,** gastos de mantenimiento, *m pl*; (railway) gastos de tracción, *m pl*. **r. fight,** acción de retirada, *f*. **r.-knot,** lazo corredizo, *m*. **r. title,** *print* título de la columna, *m*

run-off match *n* desempate, *m*

runway *n* (for launching a ship) grada, *f*; (of an airfield) pista de aterrizaje, *f*

rupee *n* rupia, *f*

rupestrian *a* rupestre

rupture *n* rompimiento, *m*, rotura, *f*; ruptura, *f*; *med* hernia, *f*

ruptured *a med* herniado, quebrado

rupturing *n* ruptura, *f*

rural *a* rural, campestre, del campo; agrario

ruse *n* artimaña, treta, ardid, *f*

rush *n bot* junco, *m*; acometida, *f*; ataque, *m*; (of water) torrente, *m*; (bustle) bullicio, *m*; (speed) prisa, *f*; precipitación, *f*; acceso, *m*; (crowd) tropel, *m*, masa, *f*; (struggle) lucha, *f*; furia, *f*. *vi* precipitarse, lanzarse; agolparse. *vt* llevar rápidamente (a); despachar rápidamente; precipitar; (attack) asaltar, atacar; (capture) tomar, capturar; hacer de prisa; (a bill) hacer aprobar de prisa. **to r. upon,** abalanzarse hacia; embestir. **in a r.,** en tropel, en masa; de prisa. **to r. to a conclusion,** precipitarse a una conclusión. **r.-bottomed,** con asiento de enea. **r. hour,** hora de mayor circulación, *f*, hora de aglomeración, hora-pico (Argentina), hora brava (Argentina, informal). **r. order,** pedido urgente, *m*

rushy *a* juncoso

russet *a* rojizo; rojo. **r. apple,** manzana asperiega, *f*

Russia Rusia, *f*

Russian *a* ruso. *n* ruso (-sa); (language) ruso, *m*. **R. leather,** piel de Rusia, *f*

rust *n* herrumbre, *f*, orín, *m*; moho, *m*; (disease) añublo, tizón, *m*. *vt* aherrumbrar; enmohecer. *vi* aherrumbrarse; enmohecerse

rustic *a* rústico; campesino, aldeano; (scornful) palurdo, grosero. *n* aldeano, *m*; (scornful) patán, *m*

rusticate *vi* rusticar, vivir en el campo. *vt* enviar al campo

rustication *n* rusticación, *f*

rusticity *n* rusticidad, *f*

rustiness *n* herrumbre, *f*; enmohecimiento, *m*; color rojizo, *m*; *fig* falta de práctica, *f*

rustle *n* susurro, *m*; murmurio, *m*; (of silk, a dress, etc.) frufru, *m*; (of paper, etc.) crujido, *m*. *vi* susurrar; murmurar; crujir. *vt* (a paper) hacer crujir

rustless *a* inoxidable

rustling *n* see **rustle**

rusty *a* herrumbroso; enmohecido, mohoso; (red) rojizo, (worn out) usado, viejo; (out of practice) desacostumbrado; (forgotten) empolvorado, oxidado (e.g. **My Portuguese is rusty,** Mi portugués está empolvorado)

rut *n* rodera, *f*, bache, surco, *m*; *fig* sendero trillado, *m*; *fig* rutina, *f*; (sexual appetite) celo, *m*, *vi* estar en celo
ruthless *a* inhumano, insensible, despiadado; inexorable, inflexible
ruthlessly *adv* inhumanamente; inflexiblemente, inexorablemente
ruthlessness *n* inhumanidad, *f*; inflexibilidad, inexorabilidad, *f*
rye *n* centeno, *m*. **rye field,** centenar, *m*

S

s *n* (letter) ese, *f*
sabbatarian *a* sabatario
Sabbath *n* (Jewish) sábado, *m*; (Christian) domingo, *m*
sabbatical *a* sabático
sable *n* (animal and fur) marta, *f*; *her* sable, *m*. *a her* sable; *poet* negro
sabotage *n* sabotaje, *m*, *vt* cometer un acto de sabotaje en
saboteur *n* saboteador, *m*
sabre *n* sable, *m*; (soldier) jinete, *m*. *vt* dar sablazos (a), acuchillar. **s. cut, thrust,** sablazo, *m*
sac *n biol* saco, *m*
saccharin *n* sacarina, *f*
sachet *n* sachet, *m*; bolsa, *f*. **handkerchief s.,** bolsa para pañuelos, *f*
sack *n* (bag) saco, *m*; *mil* saqueo, saqueamiento, saco, *m*. *vt* meter en sacos; (dismiss) dar pasaporte (a), despedir; *mil* saquear. **to get the s.,** recibir el pasaporte. **to give the s.,** dar el pasaporte (a), poner de patitas en la calle (a). **s. coat,** saco, *m*
sackcloth *n* harpillera, *f*. **to repent in s. and ashes,** ponerse cenizas en la cabeza
sacking *n* harpillera, *f*; *mil* saqueo, *m*
sacrament *n* sacramento, *m*; Eucaristía, *f*. **the Blessed S.,** el Santísimo Sacramento. **to receive the Holy S.,** comulgar. **to receive the last sacraments,** recibir los sacramentos, recibir la Extremaunción
sacramental *a* sacramental
sacramentalist *n* sacramentario (-ia)
sacred *a* sagrado; sacro, santo; consagrado. **Nothing is s. to them,** No hay nada sagrado para ellos, No respetan nada. **the S. Heart of Jesus,** el Sagrado Corazón (de Jesús). **S. to the memory of . . .** Consagrado a la memoria de . . . **s. music,** música sagrada, *f*
sacredness *n* carácter sagrado, *m*; santidad, *f*; inviolabilidad, *f*
sacrifice *n* sacrificio, *m*. *vt* and *vi* sacrificar. **s. of the mass,** sacrificio del altar, *m*
sacrificial *a* sacrificador; del sacrificio
sacrilege *n* sacrilegio, *m*
sacrilegious *a* sacrílego
sacristan *n* sacristán, *m*
sacristy *n* sacristía, *f*
sacrosanct *a* sacrosanto
sacrum *n anat* sacro, *m*
sad *a* triste; melancólico; (of a mistake) deplorable, funesto; *inf* redomado; (pensive) pensativo. **How s.!** ¡Qué lástima! ¡Qué triste! **It made me s.,** Me entristeció
sadden *vt* entristecer, acongojar, afligir
saddle *n* (riding) silla de montar, *Lat. Am.* albarda, *f*; (of a bicycle, etc.) sillín, *m*; *mech* silla, *f*; *anat* espalda, *f*. *vt* ensillar. **to s. with the responsibility of,** echar la responsabilidad de (a). **s. of mutton,** lomo de carnero, *m*. **s.-bag,** alforja, *Lat. Am.* buchaca, *f*. **s.-cloth,** mantilla de silla, *f*. **s.-tree,** arzón, *m*
saddler *n* sillero, guarnicionero, *m*
Sadducee *n* saduceo (-ea)
sadism *n* sadismo, *m*
sadist *n* sadista, *mf*
sadistic *a* sadístico
sadly *adv* tristemente; (very) muy
sadness *n* tristeza, melancolía, *f*
safe *a* al abrigo (de); seguro; salvo; (certain) cierto; prudente; digno de confianza. *n* caja de caudales, *f*; (for food) alacena, *f*. **I stood beneath a tree s. from the rain,** Estaba de pie bajo un árbol, al abrigo de la lluvia. **to put something in a s. place,** poner algo en salvo; poner algo en un lugar seguro. **s. and sound,** sano y salvo. **s.-conduct,** salvoconducto, *m*. **s.-keeping,** lugar seguro, *m*; (of a person) buenas manos, *f pl*
safeguard *n* protección, garantía, *f*; precaución, *f*. *vt* proteger, guardar; tomar precauciones (contra)
safely *adv* seguramente; sin accidente, sin novedad, sano y salvo; sin peligro. **You may s. tell him,** Puedes decírselo con toda seguridad. **to put** (something) **away s.,** poner (algo) en un lugar seguro
safety *n* seguridad, *f*. *a* de seguridad; (of locks) de golpe. **a place of s.,** un lugar seguro. **in s.,** en salvo, en seguro; con seguridad. **to believe in s. first,** poner la seguridad en primer lugar. **to play for s.,** jugar seguro. **with complete s.,** con toda seguridad. **s.-belt,** (cinto) salvavidas, *m*. **s.-catch,** fiador, *m*. **s.-curtain,** telón de seguridad, telón contra incendios, *m*. **s.-fuse,** espoleta de seguridad, *f*. **s.-glass,** vidrio inastillable, *m*. **s.-island,** refugio para peatones, *m*. **s.-lamp,** lámpara de seguridad, *f*. **s.-latch,** pestillo de golpe, *m*. **s.-lock,** (of fire-arms) seguro, *m*; (of doors, etc.) cerradura de seguridad, *f*. **s.-pin,** imperdible, *m*. **s.-razor,** máquina de afeitar, *f*. **s.-valve,** válvula de seguridad, *f*
saffron *n* azafrán, *m*, *a* azafranado, de color de azafrán.
sag *vi* doblegarse, ceder; inclinarse; *naut* caer a sotavento; (of prices) bajar; (of spirits, etc.) flaquear
saga *n* saga, *f*; epopeya, *f*
sagacious *a* sagaz, perspicaz; (of animals) sabio
sagacity *n* sagacidad, perspicacia, *f*; (of animals) sagacidad, *f*
sage *n* sabio, *m*; *bot* salvia, *f*. *a* sabio; sagaz; cuerdo
Sagittarius *n* Sagitario, *m*
Sahara, the el Sáhara, *m*
said *a* antedicho; tal dicho. **No sooner s. than done,** Dicho y hecho. **the s. Mr. Martínez,** el tal Sr. Martínez
sail *n* (of a ship) vela, *f*; (sailing-ship) velero, *m*; (of a windmill) aspa, *f*; *mech* ala, *f*; (trip) paseo en barco, *m*. *vi* navegar; ir en barco; dar un paseo en barco; (leave) salir en barco; zarpar; (of swans, etc.) deslizarse; (of clouds, etc.) flotar. *vt* (a ship) gobernar; (the sea) navegar por. **She sailed into the room,** Entró majestuosamente en la sala. **The ship sailed at eight knots,** El buque navegaba a ocho nudos. **to go for a s.,** dar un paseo en barco. **to s. round the world,** dar la vuelta al mundo. **to s. the seas,** navegar por los mares. **to set s.,** darse a la vela, zarpar. **to take in the sails,** amainar. **s.-maker,** velero, *m*. **to s. into,** entrar en. **to s. round,** (the Cape, etc.) doblar. **to s. up,** subir en barco; (of a boat) ir río arriba
sailcloth *n* lona, *f*
sailing *n* navegación, *f*; (departure) salida, *f*. **It's all plain s.,** Todo va viento en popa. **s.-boat,** bote de vela, *m*. **s.-ship,** buque de vela, velero, *m*
sailor *n* marinero, *m*. **John is a bad s.,** Juan se marea fácilmente. **to be a good s.,** no marearse. **s.-blouse,** marinera, *f*. **s.-suit,** traje de marinero, *m*
saint *n* santo (-ta); (before masculine names of Sts., excluding Sts. Dominic and Thomas) San; *inf* ángel, *m*. **All Saints' Day,** el día de Todos los Santos. **saint's day,** fiesta de un santo (or de una santa), *f*; (of a person) santo, *m*. **St. Bernard dog,** perro de San Bernardo, *m*. **St. John the Baptist,** San Juan Bautista. **St. Martin's summer,** el veranillo de San Martín. **St. Vitus's dance,** el baile de San Vito

sainthood *n* santidad, *f*
saintliness *n* santidad, *f*
saintly *a* de santo; de santa; santo; *inf* angelical
Saint Petersburg San Petersburgo, *m*
sake *n* amor, *m*; causa, *f*. **for God's s.,** por el amor de Dios. **for the s. of,** para; por amor de. **to talk for talking's s.,** hablar por hablar
salable *a* vendible
salaciousness *n* salacidad, *f*
salad *n* ensalada, *f*; (lettuce) lechuga, *f*. **fruit s.,** macedonia de frutas, *f*. **s.-bowl,** ensaladera, *f*. **s.-dressing,** aderezo, aliño, *m*, salsa para ensalada, *f*. **s.-oil,** aceite para ensaladas, *m*
salamander *n* salamandra, *f*
salaried *a* a sueldo; (of posts) retribuido
salary *n* sueldo, salario, *m*
sale *n* venta, *f*; (auction) almoneda, subasta pública, *f*. **(clearance) s.,** liquidación, *f*, saldo, *m*, *Mexico* barata, *f*. **to be on s.,** estar de venta. **"Piano for s.,"** «Se vende un piano.» **s. price,** precio de venta, *m*; precio de saldo, *m*
sales contract *n* contrato de compraventa, *m*
salesman *n* dependiente de tienda, *m*; (traveller) viajante, *m*
salesmanship *n* arte de vender, *mf*
salesroom *n* salón de ventas, *m*
saleswoman *n* dependiente de tienda, vendedera, *f*
salient *a* saliente; *fig* prominente, conspicuo, notable, *n* saliente, *m*. **s. angle,** ángulo saliente, *m*
saline *a* salino. *n* (marsh) saladar, *m*; *med* salino, *m*
saliva *n* saliva, *f*
salivary *a* salival
salivate *vi* salivar
salivation *n* salivación, *f*
sallow *a* cetrino, oliváceo, lívido
sallowness *n* amarillez, lividez, *f*; palidez, *f*
sally *n* (*mil* etc.) salida, *f*; (quip) ocurrencia, salida, *f*. *vi* hacer una salida, salir. **to s. forth,** ponerse en camino
salmon *n* salmón, *m*; color de salmón, *m*. **s.-net,** salmonera, *f*. **s. trout,** trucha asalmonada, *f*
salon *n* salón, *m*
Salonika Salónica, *f*
saloon *n* sala, *f*; (of a steamer) cámara, *f*, salón, *m*; (on train, for sleeping) departamento de coche cama, *m*; (on train, for dining) coche comedor, *m*; *aut* coche cerrado, *m*. **billiard s.,** salón de billares, *m*. **dancing s.,** salón de baile, *m*. **hair-dresser's s.,** salón de peluquero, *m*. **s. bar,** bar, *m*
salsify *n bot* salsifí, *m*
salt *n* sal, *f*; (spice) sabor, *m*; (wit) sal, agudeza, *f*. *a* salobre, salino; salado; (of land) salitroso. *vt* (season) poner sal en; (cure) salar. **kitchen s.,** sal de cocina, *f*. **old s.,** *inf* lobo de mar, *m*. **rock s.,** sal gema, *f*. **sea s.,** sal marina, *f*. **to be not worth one's s.,** no merecer el pan que se come. **to take with a pinch of s.,** tomar con su grano de sal. **s.-cellar,** salero, *m*. **s. lagoon,** albufera, *f*. **s. lake,** lago salado, *m*. **s. marsh,** saladar, *m*. **s. meat,** carne salada, cecina, *f*. **s. merchant,** salinero, *m*. **s.-mine,** mina de sal, *f*. **s.-spoon,** cucharita de sal, *f*. **s. water,** agua salada, *f*; agua de mar, *f*. **s.-water fish,** pez de mar, *m*. **s.-works,** salinas, *f pl*
saltiness *n* sabor de sal, *m*; salobridad, *f*
salting *n* saladura, *f*; (salt marsh) saladar, *m*
saltless *a* sin sal, soso, insípido; *fig* soso
saltpeter *n* salitre, *m*. **s. bed,** salitral, *m*. **s. works,** salitrería, *f*
salty *a* salado; salobre
salubrious *a* salubre, saludable, sano
salubriousness *n* salubridad, *f*
salutary *a* saludable, beneficioso
salutation *n* salutación, *f*, saludo, *m*
salute *vt* and *vi* saludar. *n* saludo, *m*; (of guns) salva, *f*. **to fire a s.,** hacer salvas, saludar con . . . salvas. **The soldier saluted them,** El soldado les saludó. **to take the s.,** tomar el saludo. **saluting base,** puesto de mando, *m*
Salvadoran, Salvadorian *a* and *n* salvadoreño (-ña)
salvage *n* salvamento, *m*, *vt* salvar
salvation *n* salvación, *f*. **to work out one's own s.,** salvar el alma. **the S. Army,** el Ejército de la Salvación, *m*
salve *n* pomada, *f*; *fig* bálsamo, *m*. *vt* curar; (overcome) vencer; (soothe) tranquilizar; *naut* salvar. **to s. one's conscience,** tranquilizar la conciencia
salver *n* salva, bandeja, *f*
salvo *n* (of guns or applause) salva, *f*; (reservation) salvedad, reservación, *f*. **s. of applause,** salva de aplausos, *f*
Samaritan *a* and *n* samaritano (-na)
same *a* mismo; igual; parecido; idéntico. *adv* lo mismo; del mismo modo. **all the s.,** sin embargo; con todo, a pesar de eso. **at the s. time,** al mismo tiempo; a la vez. **just the s.,** igual; (nevertheless) sin embargo. **He bowed deeply and I did the s.,** Él hizo una profunda reverencia y yo hice lo mismo. **They do not look at things the s. as we do,** No ven las cosas del mismo modo que nosotros. **If it is the s. to her,** Si le da igual. **It's all the s.,** Es igual, Lo mismo da, Es todo uno. **Ávila, capital of the province of the s. name,** Ávila, capital de la provincia de su nombre
"Same-Day Service" «En el día» (Argentina)
sameness *n* identidad, *f*; semejanza, *f*, parecido, *m*; monotonía, *f*
samovar *n* samovar, *m*
sampan *n* (boat) champán, *m*
sample *n* muestra, *f*; prueba, *f*; ejemplo, *m*. *vt* sacar una muestra de; (try) probar. **s. book,** muestrario, *m*
sampler *n* probador, *m*; (of wines) catador, *m*; *sew* dechado, *m*
sanatorium *n* sanatorio, *m*
sanctification *n* santificación, *f*; consagración, *f*
sanctify *vt* santificar; consagrar
sanctimonious *a* santurrón, mojigato, beato
sanctimoniousness *n* beatería, mojigatería, santurronería, *f*
sanction *n* sanción, *f*. *vt* sancionar; autorizar. **to apply sanctions,** *pol* aplicar sanciones
sanctity *n* santidad, *f*; lo sagrado; inviolabilidad, *f*. **odor of s.,** olor de santidad, *f*
sanctuary *n* santuario, *m*; (historical) sagrado, sagrado asilo, *m*; refugio, asilo, *m*. **to take s.,** acogerse a sagrado; refugiarse
sand *n* arena, *f*; (for drying writing) arenilla, *f*; granos de arena, *m pl*; *pl* **sands,** playa, *f*; (of life) horas de la vida, *f pl*. *vt* arenar. **to plough the s.,** arar en el mar. **s.-bag,** *n* saco de arena, *m*. *vt* (a building) proteger con sacos de arena; (a person) golpear con un saco de arena. **s.-bank,** banco de arena, *m*, barra, *f*. **to run on a s.-bank,** encallar. **s.-colored,** de color de arena. **s.-dune,** médano, *m*. **s.-paper,** *n* papel de lija, *m*. *vt* pulir con papel de lija, lijar. **s.-pit,** arenal, *m*. **s. shoes,** alpargatas, *f pl*
sandal *n* sandalia, *f*, *Central America* caite, *m*; (rope-soled) alpargata, *f*. **s.-wood,** sándalo, *m*
sandiness *n* naturaleza arenosa, *f*; (of hair) color bermejo, *m*
sandstone *n* arenisca, *f*
sandstorm *n* tempestad de arena, *f*; simún, *m*
sandwich *n* emparedado, bocadillo, *m*. *vt* insertar. **I found myself sandwiched between two fat men,** Me encontré aplastado entre dos hombres gordos. **s.-man,** hombre sándwich, *m*
sandy *a* arenoso; sabuloso; (of hair) rojo, rufo, bermejo. **a s. beach,** una playa arenosa
sane *a* de juicio sano; razonable, prudente; sesudo. **He is a very s. person,** Es un hombre con mucho sentido común. **to be s.,** estar en su juicio; (of a policy, etc.) ser prudente, ser razonable
sangfroid *n* sangre fría, *f*; aplomo, *m*
sanguinary *a* sanguinario
sanguine *a* (of complexion) rubicundo; sanguíneo; optimista, confiado. *n* (drawing) sanguina, *f*. **to be s.**

about the future, ser optimista acerca del porvenir, tener confianza en el porvenir
sanhedrin *n* sanedrín, *m*
sanitary *a* sanitario; higiénico. **s. inspector,** inspector de sanidad, *m*. **s. napkin, s. towel,** servilleta higiénica, toalla sanitaria, *mf*, paño higiénico, *m*
sanitation *n* higiene, *f*; sanidad pública, *f*; (apparatus) instalación sanitaria, *f*
sanity *n* juicio sano, *m*; prudencia, *f*; (common sense) sentido común, *m*, sensatez, *f*
Santa Claus *n* (Spanish equivalent) los Reyes Magos, *m pl*
São Paulo San Pablo, *m*
sap *n* (*bot* and *fig*) savia, *f*; *mil* zapa, *f*. *vt* (undermine) debilitar, agotar; *mil* zapar
sapidity *n* sapidez, *f*
sapling *n* arbolillo, *m*
sapper *n mil* zapador, *m*
Sapphic *a* sáfico. **S. verse,** verso sáfico, *m*
sapphire *n* zafiro, *m*. *a* de zafiros; cerúleo, de zafiro
Saracen *a* and *n* sarraceno (-na)
Saragossa Zaragoza, *f*
sarcasm *n* sarcasmo, *m*
sarcastic *a* sarcástico
sarcastically *adv* con sarcasmo, sarcásticamente
sarcophagus *n* sarcófago, *m*
sardine *n* sardina, *f*. **packed like sardines,** como sardinas en banasta. **s.-net,** sardinal, *m*
Sardinia Cerdeña, *f*
Sardinian *a* and *n* sardo (-da)
sardonic *a* sardónico
sarsaparilla *n* zarzaparrilla, *f*
sash *n* (with uniform) faja, *f*; (belt) cinto, cinturón, *m*; (of a window) cerco, *m*. **s. window,** ventana de guillotina, *f*
Satan *n* Satanás, *m*
satanic *a* satánico
satchel *n* saquito de mano, *m*, bolsa, *f*; (school) vademécum, *m*; cartapacio, *m*, cartera, *f*
sate *vt* saciar, hartar; satisfacer
sateen *n* satén, *m*
satellite *n* satélite, *m*
satiable *a* saciable
satiate *vt* saciar, hartar; satisfacer. *a* harto; repleto
satiety *n* saciedad, *f*
satin *n* raso, *m*. *a* de raso; (glossy) lustroso, terso. *vt* (paper) satinar
satiny *a* arrasado; lustroso, brillante
satire *n* sátira, *f*
satiric *a* satírico
satirist *n* escritor (-ra) satírico (-ca)
satirize *vt* satirizar
satisfaction *n* satisfacción, *f*; (contentment) contento, *m*, satisfacción, *f*; (for sin) expiación, *f*; (of a debt) pago, *m*; desquite, *m*; recompensa, *f*. **to demand s.,** pedir satisfacción. **to give** (someone) **s.,** dar contento (a), alegrar
satisfactorily *adv* satisfactoriamente
satisfactoriness *n* carácter satisfactorio, *m*, lo satisfactorio
satisfactory *a* satisfactorio; (for sin) expiatorio
satisfy *vt* satisfacer; (convince) convencer; (allay) tranquilizar, apaciguar. **I am satisfied with him,** Estoy satisfecho (Estoy contento) con él. **The explanation did not s. me,** La explicación no me convenció. **to s. oneself that . . . ,** asegurarse de que . . . **to s. one's thirst,** apagar la sed
satisfying *a* que satisface; satisfactorio; (of food) nutritivo
satrap *n* sátrapa, *m*
saturate *vt* saturar (de), empapar (de); *chem* saturar; *fig* imbuir; *fig* empapar. **to s. oneself in,** (a subject) empaparse en
saturation *n* saturación, *f*. **s. point,** (*chem* etc.) punto de saturación, *m*
Saturday *n* sábado, *m*
Saturn *n* Saturno, *m*
saturnine *a* saturnino, taciturno
satyr *n* sátiro, *m*
sauce *n* salsa, *f*; (thick fruit) compota, *f*; *inf* insolencia, *f*. **s.-boat,** salsera, *f*
saucepan *n* cazuela, cacerola, *f*. **double s.,** baño de María, *m*
saucer *n* platillo, *m*. **flying s.,** platillo volante, *m*. **s.-eyed,** con ojos redondos
sauciness *n* impertinencia, insolencia, *f*
saucy *a* respondón, descarado; (cheerful) alegre; (of hats, etc.) coquetón, majo
sauerkraut *n* chucruta, *f*
saunter *vi* pasearse, vagar, *n* paseo, *m*, vuelta, *f*
sausage *n* chorizo, *m*; salchicha, *f*. **s.-balloon,** globo cautivo, *m*. **s.-curl,** bucle, *m*. **s.-machine,** choricera, *f*. **s.-maker,** choricero (-ra)
savage *a* salvaje; feroz; (cruel) inhumano, cruel; (furious) furioso. *n* salvaje, *mf*
savagely *adv* bárbaramente; ferozmente; furiosamente
savagery *n* salvajismo, *m*; ferocidad, *f*; brutalidad, crueldad, *f*
savannah *n* sabana, *f*. **s. dweller,** sabanero (-ra)
save *vt* salvar; (keep) guardar; conservar; reservar; (money, one's clothes, etc.) ahorrar; (time) ganar; (avoid) evitar. *vi* salvar; hacer economías; ahorrar. **He saved my life,** Me salvó la vida. **They have saved a room for me,** Me han reservado una habitación. **to s. appearances,** guardar las apariencias. **to s. oneself trouble,** ahorrarse molestias. **to s. the situation,** estar al nivel de las circunstancias
save *prep* salvo, excepto, menos. *conjunc* sino, a menos que; con la excepción de. **all s. one,** todos menos uno. **all the conspirators s. he,** todos los conspiradores con la excepción de él
saving *a* frugal, económico; (stingy) tacaño, avaricioso; (clause) condicional. *n* salvación, *f*; (of money, time, etc.) ahorro, *m*, economía, *f*; *pl* **savings,** ahorros, *m pl*. *prep* salvo, excepto, fuera de. *conjunc* con excepción de que, fuera de que. **s. grace,** único mérito, *m*. **savings bank,** caja de ahorros, *f*. **savings fund,** montepío, *m*
savior *n* salvador (-ra). **the S.,** el Salvador, el Redentor
savor *n* sabor, gusto, *m*; (aftertaste) dejo, *m*; (zest) salsa, *f*. *vi* saber (a), tener sabor (de); *fig* oler (a). *vt* saborear, paladear; (flavor) sazonar
savoriness *n* buen sabor, *m*; (of a district) respetabilidad, *f*
savory *a* sabroso, apetitoso; (not sweet) no dulce; (of places) respetable; (of reputation, etc.) bueno. *n* entremés salado, *m*. **s. omelette,** tortilla, *f*
Savoy Saboya, *f*
saw *n* (maxim) sentencia, *f*; (proverb) refrán, decir, *m*; (tool) sierra, *f*. *vt* aserrar, *Lat. Am.* aserruchar; (the air) cortar. *vi* usar una sierra. **two-handled saw,** tronzador, *m*. **saw-fish,** pez sierra, *m*. **saw-mill,** molino de aserrar, *m*. **saw-pit,** aserradero, *m*
sawdust *n* aserrín, *m*
sawinghorse *n* caballete de aserrar, *m*
sawyer *n* aserrador, *m*
Saxon *a* and *n* sajón (-ona)
Saxony Sajonia, *f*
saxophone *n* saxófono, saxofón *m*
say *vt* decir; recitar. *vi* decir. **Let us say that the house is worth $100,000,** Pongamos por ejemplo que la casa vale cien mil dólares. **He has no say in the matter,** No entra ni sale en el asunto. **I have said my say,** He dicho lo que quería. **They say,** Se dice, Dicen, La gente dice. **You don't say!** ¡Calle! ¿De veras? ¡Imposible! **that is to say . . . ,** es decir . . . ; esto es . . . , a saber . . . **to say one's prayers,** rezar, decir sus oraciones. **to say again,** volver a decir; decir otra vez, repetir. **to say over and over again,** repetir muchas veces, decir repetidamente. **What do you say to that?** ¿Qué dices a esto?
saying *n* decir, *m*; (proverb) refrán, *m*; (maxim) sentencia, *f*. **As the s. is,** Como suele decirse; Según el

refrán. **It goes without s.,** Huelga decir. **It's only a s.,** Es un decir, nada más

scab *n* (of a wound) costra, *f;* (disease) escabro, *m;* (blackleg) esquirol, *m*

scabbard *n* vaina (de espada), *f*

scabby *a* costroso; (diseased) roñoso, sarnoso

scabies *n* sarna, *f.* **s. mite,** arador de la sarna, *m*

scaffold *n* (in building) andamio, *m;* (for execution) cadalso, patíbulo, *m.* **to go to the s.,** ir al patíbulo; acabar en el patíbulo

scaffolding *n* andamiada, *f;* (building, scaffold) andamio, *m*

scald *vt* escaldar; quemar; (instruments) esterilizar. *n* quemadura, escaldadura, *f.* **to s. oneself,** escaldarse. **scalding hot,** hirviendo

scale *n* (of a balance) platillo, *m; zool* escama, *f; bot* bráctea, *f; bot* hojuela, *f;* (flake) laminita, *f;* (*mus, math*) escala, *f;* (of charges, etc.) tarifa, *f;* (of salaries) escalafón, *m;* (of a thermometer) escala, *f.* *vt* escalar; (fish) escamar. **major s.,** escala mayor, *f.* **minor s.,** escala menor, *f.* **on a grand s.,** en gran escala. **on a small s.,** en pequeña escala. **pair of scales,** balanza, *f;* (for heavy weights) báscula, *f.* **social s.,** escala social, *f.* **The Scales,** *ast* Libra, *f.* **to draw to s.,** dibujar a escala. **to turn the scales,** pesar; *fig* inclinar la balanza. **to s. down,** (*art* and of charges) reducir

scaling *n* (of fish) escamadura, *f;* (of buildings) desconchadura, *f;* (ascent) escalamiento, *m*

scallop *n* (*icht* and badge) venera, *f;* concha, *f; sew* onda, *f,* festón, *m.* *vt cul* guisar en conchas; *sew* ondear, festonear

scalp *n anat* pericráneo, *m;* cuero cabelludo, *m; fig* trofeo, *m.* *vt* escalpar. **s.-hunter,** cazador de cabelleras, *m*

scalpel *n* escalpelo, *m*

scaly *a* escamoso, conchado; (of boilers) incrustado

scamp *n* bribón, granuja, *m,* *vt* (work) frangollar

scamper *vi* retozar, brincar; correr. *n* carrerita, *f.* **to s. off,** salvarse por los pies, huir; marcharse corriendo

scan *vt* (verse) medir, escandir; (examine) escudriñar, examinar; (glance at) dar un vistazo (a)

scandal *n* escándalo, *m;* maledicencia, *f;* (slander) calumnia, *f.* **to talk s.,** murmurar

scandalize *vt* escandalizar

scandalous *a* escandaloso; infame; calumnioso

scandalously *adv* escandalosamente

scandalousness *n* carácter escandaloso, *m*

Scandinavia Escandinavia, *f*

Scandinavian *a* escandinavo. *n* escandinavo (-va);

scant *a* escaso; insuficiente

scantily *adv* insuficientemente

scantiness *n* escasez, *f;* insuficiencia, *f*

scanty *a* insuficiente; escaso; (of hair) ralo; (of crops, etc.) pobre

scapegoat *n* víctima propiciatoria, *f;* cabeza de turco, *f.* **to be a s. for,** pagar el pato por

scapegrace *n* bribón, *m*

scapula *n anat* escápula, *f*

scapulary *n ecc* escapulario, *m*

scar *n* cicatriz, *f; fig* señal, *f.* *vt* marcar con una cicatriz. **to s. over,** cicatrizarse

scarab *n* escarabajo, *m;* escarabajo sagrado, *m*

scarce *a* escaso; insuficiente; raro. *adv poet* apenas. **to make oneself s.,** largarse, pirarse, escabullirse; ausentarse, esconderse

scarcely *adv* apenas; no bien; casi; (with difficulty) a duras penas, con dificultad. **It is s. likely he said that,** No es muy probable que lo hubiese dicho. **There were s. twenty people in the building,** Había apenas veinte personas en el edificio. **S. anyone likes his pictures,** Sus cuadros no le gustan a casi nadie

scarcity *n* escasez, insuficiencia, *f;* (famine) carestía, *f;* (rarity) rareza, *f*

scare *vt* asustar, espantar, llenar de miedo (a), *Lat. Am. also* julepear; intimidar. *n* susto, pánico, *m;* alarma, *f.* **What a s. I got!** ¡Qué susto me he llevado! **to s. away,** ahuyentar. **to be scared** *Lat. Am.* julepearse

scarecrow *n* espantapájaros, *m; inf* estantigua, *f,* mamarracho, espantajo, *m*

scaremonger *n* alarmista, *mf*

scarf *n* bufanda, *f;* (tie) corbata, *f; mil* faja, *f*

scarlatina *n med* escarlatina, *f*

scarlet *n* escarlata, *f.* *a* de color escarlata. **to turn s.,** (of persons) enrojecerse. **s. fever,** escarlatina, *f.* **s. hat,** *ecc* capelo (cardenalicio), *m.* **s. runner,** *bot* judía verde, *f*

scatheless *a* ileso, sano y salvo

scathing *a* mordaz, cáustico

scatter *vt* esparcir, sembrar con; (benefits, etc.) derramar; (put to flight) derrotar; dispersar; disipar; *fig* frustrar; (squander) derrochar, desparramar. *vi* dispersarse. **The crowd scattered,** La muchedumbre se dispersó. **s.-brained,** de cabeza de chorlito, atolondrado

scattered *a* disperso; esparcido

scattered showers *n* lluvias aisladas, *f pl*

scattering *n* dispersión, *f;* (defeat) derrota, *f;* esparcimiento, *m;* (small number) número pequeño, *m*

scavenge *vt* (streets) recoger la basura de, barrer

scavenger *n* (of the streets) barrendero, *m;* (dustman) basurero, *m; zool* animal que se alimenta de carne muerta, *m;* insecto que se alimenta de estiércol, *m.* *vt* See **scavenge**

scenario *n* escenario, *m*

scene *n* escena, *f;* teatro, lugar, *m;* espectáculo, *m;* (*theat* décor) decoración, *f;* (of a play) escena, *f;* (view) vista, perspectiva, *f.* **behind the scenes,** entre bastidores. **The s. is laid . . . ,** La acción pasa . . . **to come on the s.,** entrar en escena. **to make a s.,** hacer una escena. **s.-painter,** *n* escenógrafo (-fa). **s.-shifter,** tramoyista, *mf*

scenery *n theat* decorado, *m;* (landscape) paisaje, *m*

scenic *a* dramático; escénico; pintoresco. **s. railway,** montaña rusa, *f*

scenography *n* escenografía, *f*

scent *vt* perfumar; (smell) oler; (out) husmear, olfatear; (suspect) sospechar. *n* perfume, *m;* fragancia, *f,* aroma, *m;* (smell) olor, *m;* (of hounds) viento, *m;* (of game, etc.) rastro, viento, *m;* (*fig* of person) nariz, *f;* (trail) pista, *f.* **to lose the s.,** perder la pista. **to s. danger,** oler el peligro. **to throw off the s.,** despistar. **s.-bottle,** frasco de perfume, *m.* **s.-spray,** pulverizador, *m*

scented *a* perfumado; (of roses, etc.) de olor, oloroso; (in compounds) de . . . olfato. **s. sweet pea,** guisante de olor, *m*

scentless *a* sin olor; inodoro

scepter *n* cetro, *m*

sceptic *n* escéptico (-ca)

sceptical *a* escéptico

scepticism *n* escepticismo, *m*

schedule *n* lista, *m;* programa, *m;* (of taxes) clase, *f;* (of trains, etc.) horario, *m.* *vt* poner en una lista; inventariar

scheme *n* plan, *m;* proyecto, *m;* diagrama, esquema, *m;* (summary) resumen, *m;* (of colors, etc.) combinación, *f;* (plot) intriga, maquinación, *f.* *vt* proyectar. *vi* planear, formar planes; (intrigue) intrigar, conspirar. **color s.,** combinación de colores, *f*

schemer *n* (plotter) intrigante, *mf*

scheming *a* intrigante; astuto. *n* planes, proyectos, *m pl;* intrigas, maquinaciones, *f pl*

schism *n* cisma, *mf*

schismatic *a* cismático. *n* cismático (-ca)

scholar *n* (at school) colegial (-la); (disciple) alumno (-na); (student) estudiante, *mf;* (learned person) erudito (-ta), hombre de letras, *m;* (scholarship holder) becario, *m.* **to be a poor s.,** *fig* ser analfabeto

scholarly *a* de sabio, de hombre de letras; erudito

scholarship *n* erudición, *f;* saber, *m;* (exhibition) beca, *f.* **s. holder,** becario, *m*

scholastic *a* escolar, escolástico; pedante; (medieval) escolástico. *n* escolástico, *m.* **the s. profession,** el magisterio

school *n* escuela, *f;* colegio, *m;* academia, *f; univ* departamento, *m;* (faculty) facultad, *f;* (of fish) banco, *m. vt* enseñar, instruir; formar; disciplinar. **in s.,** en clase. **day s.,** escuela, *f,* colegio, *m.* **the Florentine s.,** (of painting) la escuela florentina. **the lower s.,** los alumnos del preparatorio. **private s.,** colegio particular, *m.* **s.-bag,** vademécum, *m.* **s.-book,** libro escolar, *m.* **s.-days,** los días de escuela; los años de colegio. **in his s.-days,** cuando él iba a la escuela. **s.-fees,** gastos de la enseñanza, *m pl,* cuota escolar, *f,*
schoolboy *n* muchacho de escuela, colegial, *m*
school district *n* sector escolar, *m*
schoolfellow *n* compañero de colegio, condiscípulo, *m*
schoolgirl *n* colegiala, *f*
schooling *n* educación, enseñanza, *f*
schoolmaster *n* maestro de escuela, professor, *Mexico* escuelante, *m*
schoolmistress *n* maestra de escuela, profesora, *f*
school of hard knocks *n* universidad sin tejados, *f*
schoolroom *n* aula, sala de clase, salón de clase, *m*
sciatic *a* ciático
sciatica *n* ciática, *f*
science *n* ciencia, *f*
scientific *a* científico; exacto, sistemático
scientist *n* hombre de ciencia, *m,* científico (-ca)
scimitar *n* cimitarra, *f*
scintilla *n fig* átomo, vestigio, *m*
scintillate *vi* centellear, lucir, chispear; (of persons) brillar
scion *n* (sucker) acodo, *m;* (shoot) vástago, renuevo, *m;* (human) descendiente, *mf.* **s. of a noble race,** vástago de una raza noble, *m*
scissors *n pl* tijeras, *f pl, Argentina* cortante, *msg.* **s.-sharpener,** amolador, *m*
sclerosis *n med* esclerosis, *f*
sclerotic *n anat* esclerótica, *f*
scoff *n* burla, mofa, *f. vi* burlarse. **to s. at,** burlarse de, mofarse de
scoffer *n* mofador (-ra); (at religion, etc.) incrédulo (-la)
scoffing *a* burlón. *n* mofas, burlas, *f pl*
scold *n* virago, *f, vt* reñir, reprender
scolding *n* reprensión, increpación, *f*
sconce *n* cubo de candelero, *m;* candelabro de pared, *m;* cornucopia, *f*
scone *n* bollo, *m*
scoop *n* pala de mano, *f;* cuchara de draga, *f;* (boat) achicador, *m;* (financial) golpe, *m;* (journalistic) éxito periodistico, *m. vt* sacar con pala (de); sacar con cuchara (de); (shares, etc.) comprar, obtener. **to s. out,** vaciar; excavar; (bail) achicar
scooter *n* (child's) patinete, patín del diablo, *m;* monopatín, *m*
scope *n* alcance, *m;* esfera de acción, *f;* lugar, *m.* **to give full s. to,** dar rienda suelta a. **to have full s.,** tener plena oportunidad; tener todas las facilidades. **within the s. of,** dentro del alcance de
scorbutic *a med* escorbútico
scorch *vt* chamuscar; (the skin) tostar; (of the sun) abrasar, quemar; (wither) agostar. **to s. along,** ir como un relámpago. **scorching,** *a* abrasador, ardiente; *fig* mordaz
score *n* (scratch) rasguño, *m;* señal, *f;* (crossing out) raya, *f;* (reckoning) cuenta, *f,* escote, *m;* (notch) muesca, *f; sport* tanteo, *m,* puntuación, *Lat. Am.* anotación, *f;* (point) punto, tanto, *m;* (twenty) veintena, *f;* (reason) motivo, *m,* causa, *f;* respecto, *m; mus* partitura, *f. vt* marcar; rayar; (erase) tachar, borrar; (cricket runs, etc.) hacer; (goals) marcar; (points) ganar; (reckon) apuntar. **s. a triumph,** apuntarse un triunfo; *mus* instrumentar; (for orchestra) orquestar. *vi* (be fortunate) llevar la ventaja. **to pay off old scores,** ajustar cuentas viejas. **to s. off someone,** ganar un punto (a), triunfar de. **upon that s.,** a ese respecto; por esa causa. **Upon what s.?** ¿Con qué motivo? **s.-board,** marcador, *m*
scorer *n* (of a goal, etc.) tanteador, *m;* (keeper of score) marcador, *m*
scoria *n* escoria, *f*
scorn *n* desprecio, desdén, *m. vt* despreciar, desdeñar; reírse de. **to s. to do,** no dignarse hacer
scornful *a* desdeñoso, despreciativo
scornfully *adv* desdeñosamente, con desprecio
Scorpion *n* Escorpión, *m*
scorpion *n* escorpión, alacrán, *m; ast* Escorpión, *m*
Scot *n* escocés, *m*
scotch *vt* (kill) matar; (thwart) frustrar; (a wheel) calzar
Scotland Escocia, *f*
Scotswoman *n* escocesa, *f*
Scottish *a* escocés
scoundrel *n* canalla, sinvergüenza, *mf*
scour *vt* (traverse) recorrer, batir; (pans, etc.) fregar, estregar; (free from) limpiar (de); (of water) arrastrar
scourge *vt* azotar, flagelar; castigar, mortificar. *n* disciplinas, *f pl; fig* verdugo, *m,* plaga, *f*
scout *n mil* batidor, explorador, *m. vi mil* explorar, reconocer. *vt* (flout) rechazar a mano airada, rechazar con desdén. **boy s.,** muchacho explorador, *m*
scowl *vi* fruncir el ceño. *n* ceño, *m.* **to s. at,** mirar con ceño
scowling *a* amenazador
scragginess *n* magrez, flaqueza, *f*
scraggy *a* flaco, magro, descarnado
scramble *vi* trepar. *vt* (throw) arrojar; (eggs) revolver. **scrambled eggs,** huevos revueltos, *m pl.* **to s. for,** andar a la rebatiña por; (for coins, etc.) luchar para. **to s. up,** escalar; subir a gatas
scrap *n* pedazo, *m;* fragmento, *m;* pizca, brizna, *f;* (shindy) suiza, camorra, *f;* (boxing) combate de boxeo, *m; pl* **scraps,** desperdicios, *m pl;* (food) restos de la comida, *m pl. vt* desechar; (expunge) borrar; *vi* (fight) armar camorra. **a few scraps of news,** algunas noticias. **Do you mind not coming? Not a s.,** ¿Te importa no venir? Ni pizca. **s.-book,** álbum de recortes, *m;* **s.-heap,** depósito de basura, *m; fig* olvido, *m.* **s. iron,** chatarra, *f,* hierro viejo, *m*
scrape *vt* raspar, rascar, raer; (one's shoes) restregar; (a musical instrument) rascar. *n* rasguño, *m;* ruido de raspar, *m;* (predicament) lío, apuro, *m;* dificultad, *f.* **to s. acquaintance with,** trabar amistad con. **to s. along,** *inf* ir tirando. **to s. away,** rascar; quitar. **to s. through,** (an examination) aprobar justo. **to s. together,** amontonar poco a poco
scrappy *a* escaso; fragmentario; (incoherent) descosido. **a s. meal,** una comida escasa
scratch *vt* arañar; (the earth) escarbar; (rub) rascar; (a hole) hacer; (sketch) dibujar, trazar; (a horse) retirar de una carrera. *vi* arañar; rascar; escarbar; (of a pen) rasguear; (back out) retirarse. *n* arañazo, *m;* (of a pen) rasgueo, *m;* (in a race) línea de salida, *f;* (in games) cero, *m. a* improvisado. **The dog scratched at the door,** El perro arañó la puerta. **to come up to s.,** estar al nivel de las circunstancias. **to s. one's head,** rascarse la cabeza. **to s. a person's eyes out,** sacar los ojos con las uñas (a). **to s. the surface of,** (a subject) tratar superficialmente. **to s. out,** tachar
scrawl *vi* hacer garabatos. *vt* garabatear, garrapatear. *n* garabato, *m*
scream *vt* and *vi* chillar. *n* chillido, *m.* **It was a perfect s.** Era para morirse de risa. **to s. with laughter,** reírse a carcajadas, morirse de risa
screaming *n* chillidos, *m pl. a* chillador; (piercing) penetrante, agudo; (funny) divertidisimo
screech *vi* chillar; (of owls, etc.) ulular; graznar. *n* chillido, *m,* ululación, *f;* graznido, *m.* **s.-owl,** úlula, *f*
screed *n* arenga, *f;* cita larga, *f*
screen *n* biombo, *m;* (wire) tela metálica, *f;* (nonfolding) mampara, *f;* (*eco*) cancel, *m;* (cinema, television) pantalla, *f;* (of trees, etc., and *mil*) cortina, *f;* (*fig* protection) abrigo, *m. vt* proteger; (shelter) abrigar; (hide) esconder, ocultar; (a light) proteger con pantalla; (a film) proyectar; (sieve) cribar, cerner; (examine) investigar.

to s. from view, ocultar la vista (de), esconder. **s. star,** estrella de la pantalla, *f*
screw *n* tornillo, *m*; (propeller) hélice, *f*; vuelta de tornillo, *f*; presión, *f*; (miser) tacaño, *m*; (salary) salario, *m*. *vt* atornillar; torcer; apretar, oprimir. **He has a s. loose,** Le falta un tornillo. **to s. down,** sujetar con tornillos. **to s. up,** cerrar con tornillos. **to s. up one's courage,** tomar coraje. **to s. up one's eyes,** desojarse, entornar los ojos. **s.-driver,** destornillador, *Mexico* desarmador, *m*
scribble *vt* escribir de prisa, *vi* garabatear, garrapatear; escribir, ser autor. *n* garabato, garrapato, *m*; mala letra, letra ilegible, *f*; (note) billete, *m*
scribbler *n* el, *m*, (*f*, la) que tiene mala letra; (author) autor (-ra) malo (-la)
scribbling *n* garabateo, *m*. **s.-block,** bloque de papel, *m*
scribe *n* escribiente, copista, *mf*; (Jewish history) escriba, *m*
scrimmage *n* reyerta, pelea, camorra, *f*; (Rugby) mêlée, *f*
script *n* letra cursiva, *f*; *print* plumilla, *f*; manuscrito, *m*; *law* escritura, *f*; examen escrito, *m*; (film) escenario, *m*
scriptural *a* bíblico
Scripture *n* Sagrada Escritura, *f*. **Scriptures,** Escrituras, *f pl*; (of non-Christian religions) los libros sagrados
scrofula *n* escrófula, *f*
scrofulous *a* escrofuloso
scroll *n* (of paper, etc.) rollo, *m*; pergamino, *m*; (flourish) rúbrica, *f*; (of an Ionic capital) voluta, *f*. **s. of fame,** lista de la fama, *f*
scrotum *n anat* escroto, *m*
scrounge *vi* sablear. *vt* dar un sablazo (a); hurtar
scrounger *n* sablista, *mf*, *Mexico* lapa, *f*
scrub *vt* fregar; limpiar; restregar. *n* fregado, *m*; limpieza, *f*; fricción, *f*; (brushwood) matorral, breñal, *m*, maleza, *f*
scrubbing *n* fregado, *m*. **s.-brush,** cepillo para el suelo, *m*
scrubby *a* (of plants) anémico; (of persons) insignificante, pobre; (of land) cubierto de maleza
scruff *n* nuca, *f*, pescuezo, *m*
scruple *n* escrúpulo, *m*. *vi* tener escrúpulos. **to have no scruples,** no tener escrúpulos
scrupulous *a* escrupuloso; exacto, meticuloso
scrupulously *adv* escrupulosamente; meticulosamente
scrupulousness *n* escrupulosidad, *f*; meticulosidad, *f*
scrutinize *vt* escudriñar, examinar, *Lat. Am. also* interiorizar; (votes) escrutar
scrutinizer *n* escudriñador (-ra); (of votes) escrutador (-ra)
scrutinizing *a* escrutador
scrutiny *n* escrutinio, *m*
scud *vi* correr; deslizarse; flotar. **to s. before the wind,** ir viento en popa
scuffle *vi* pelear, forcejear, andar a la rebatiña. *n* refriega, pelea, sarracina, arrebatiña, *f*
scull *n* remo, *m*, *vi* remar
scullery *n* fregadero, *m*. **s. maid,** fregona, *f*
sculptor *n* escultor, *m*, escultora, *f*
sculptural *a* escultural, escultórico
sculpture *n* escultura, *f*, *vt* esculpir
scum *n* espuma, *f*; (dregs) heces, *f pl*. *vt* espumar. **s. of the earth,** las heces de la sociedad
scupper *n naut* clava, *f*. *vt* abrir las clavas (de); (frustrate) frustrar, destruir
scurrility *n* grosería, indecencia, *f*
scurrilous *a* grosero, indecente
scurry *vi* echar a correr. *n* fuga precipitada, *f*; (of rain) chaparrón, *m*; (of snow) remolino, *m*. **to s. off,** escabullirse. **to s. through,** hacer de prisa, terminar rápidamente
scurvy *a* tiñoso, vil, ruin. *n* escorbuto, *Mexico* berbén, *m*. **a s. trick,** una mala pasada
scuttle *n* (trap-door) escotillón, *m*; *naut* escotilla, *f*; (for coal) carbonera, *f*; (flight) huida precipitada, *f*. *vt* (a boat) echar a pique, *vi* (run away) escabullirse, apretar a correr
scythe *n* dalle, *m*, guadaña, *f*, *vt* dallar, segar
sea *n* mar, *m*, or *f*; ola, *f*; multitud, *f*. **Black Sea,** Mar Negro. **Mediteranean Sea,** (Mar) Mediterráneo, *m*. **at sea,** en el mar; perplejo. **beyond the seas,** allende los mares. **by sea,** por mar. **by the sea,** a la orilla del mar. **high seas,** alta mar, *f*. **the seven seas,** todos los mares del mundo. **to go to sea,** hacerse marinero. **to put to sea,** hacerse a la mar, hacerse a la vela. **sea-anemone,** anémone de mar. *f*. **sea-bathing,** baños de mar, *m pl*. **sea-breeze,** brisa de mar, *f*. **sea captain,** capitán de mar, *m*. **sea chart,** carta de marear, *f*. **sea-coast,** litoral, *m*, costa marítima, *f*. **sea-cow,** manatí, *m*. **sea dog,** lobo de mar, *m*. **sea-fight,** combate naval, *m*. **sea-foam,** espuma de mar, *f*. **sea-girt,** rodeado por el mar. **sea-going,** de altura; navegante. **sea-going craft,** embarcación de alta mar, *f*. **sea-green,** verdemar, *m*. **sea-gull,** gaviota, *f*. **sea-horse,** caballo marino, *m*. **sea-legs,** piernas de marino, *f pl*. **sea-level,** nivel del mar, *m*. **sea-lion,** león marino, *m*. **sea-mist,** bruma, *f*. **sea-nymph,** nereida, *f*. **sea-power,** potencia naval, *f*. **sea-serpent,** serpiente de mar, *f*. **sea-sick,** mareado. **to be sea-sick,** marearse. **sea-sickness,** mal de mar, *m*. **sea-trip,** viaje por mar, *m*. **sea-urchin,** erizo de mar, *m*. **sea-wall,** dique de mar, *m*
seafarer *n* (traveller) viajero (-ra) por mar; (sailor) marinero, *m*
seafaring *a* marinero, marino. *n* viajes por mar, *m pl*; vida del marinero, *f*
seal *n zool* foca, *f*, lobo marino, *m*; piel de foca, *f*; sello, *m*; (stamp) estampillo, timbre, *m*; *vt* sellar; (stamp) estampar; (letters, etc.) cerrar; *vi* cazar focas. **His fate is sealed,** Su suerte está determinada. **His lips were sealed,** Sus labios estaban cerrados. **under my hand and s.,** firmado y sellado por mí. **s.-ring,** sortija de sello, *f*
sealing wax *n* lacre, *m*
sealskin *n* piel de foca, *f*
seam *n sew* costura, *f*; *naut* costura de los tablones, *f*; *anat* sutura, *f*; *surg* cicatriz, *f*; (wrinkle) arruga, *f*, surco, *m*; *geol* capa, *f*, yacimiento, *m*; *min* vena, *f*, filón, *m*. *vt* coser; juntar; (a face) surcar, arrugar
seaman *n* marinero, *m*; hombre de mar, *m*; navegante, *m*. **able-bodied s.,** marinero práctico, *m*
seamanlike *a* de marinero, marino; de buen marinero
seamanship *n* marinería, *f*; náutica, *f*
seamstress *n* costurera, *f*
seamy *a* con costuras. **the s. side of life,** el lado peor de la vida
seance *n* sesión, junta, *f*; sesión de espiritistas, *f*
seaplane *n* hidroavión, hidroplano, *m*
seaport *n* puerto de mar, *m*
sear *a* marchito. *vt* agostar, secar; (a wound) cauterizar; marchitar, ajar; (a conscience) endurecer
search *vt* registrar; (a wound) explorar; examinar; escudriñar; investigar. *vi* buscar. *n* busca, *f*; (of luggage, etc.) reconocimiento, *m*. **in s. of,** en busca de. **to s. after, for,** buscar; ir al encuentro de. **to s. out,** ir en busca de; preguntar por. **right of s.,** (international law) derecho de visita, *m*. **s.-party,** pelotón de salvamento, *m*. **s.-warrant,** auto de reconocimiento, auto de registro domiciliario, orden de allanamiento, orden de cateo, *m*
searching *a* escrutador; penetrante; minucioso. **a s. look,** una mirada penetrante. **a s. wind,** un viento penetrante. **a s. question,** una pregunta perspicaz
searchlight *n* reflector, proyector, *m*
seashore *n* playa, *f*; orilla del mar, *f*
seaside *n* orilla del mar, *f*; playa, *f*. **to go to the s.,** ir al mar, ir a la playa
season *n* estación, *f*; sazón, *f*; temporada, *f*; tiempo, *m*. *vt* (food) sazonar; (wood, wine) madurar; (accustom) acostumbrar, aclimatar; (with wit, etc.) salpimentar; (temper) templar, moderar. *vi* madurarse. **at that s.,** a

la sazón. **close s.,** veda, *f.* **in s.,** en sazón; a su tiempo. **out of s.,** fuera de sazón; fuera de tiempo, inoportuno. **the dead s.,** la estación muerta. **the autumn s.,** el otoño; (for social functions, etc.) la temporada de otoño. **s.-ticket,** billete de abono, *m*
seasonable *a* de estación; tempestivo, oportuno
seasonably *adv* en sazón; oportunamente
seasonal *a* estacional; de temporada
seasonal worker *n* trabajador por temporada, *m*
seasoned *a* (of food) sazonado; (of wood, etc.) maduro. **highly-s.,** (of a dish) picante, con muchas especies
seasoning *n cul* condimento, *m;* madurez, *f;* aclimatación, *f; fig* salsa, sal, *f*
seat *n* asiento, *m;* (bench) banco, *m;* (chair) silla, *f;* (in a cinema, etc.) localidad, *f;* (*theat* etc., ticket) entrada, *f;* (of a person) trasero, *m,* asentaderas, *f pl;* (of trousers) fondillos, *m pl;* (of government, etc.) sede, capital, *f;* (of war, etc.) teatro, *m;* (place) sitio, lugar, *m;* (house) casa solar, *f. vt* sentar; poner en una silla (a); encontrar sitio; (of buildings) tener . . . asientos; (a chair) poner asiento (a). **The hall seats a thousand,** La sala tiene mil asientos, Hay mil asientos en la sala. **Please be seated!** ¡Haga el favor de sentarse! **to be seated,** estar sentado; sentarse. **to have a good s.,** (on a horse) caer bien a caballo. **to hold a s. in parliament,** ser diputado a Cortes. **to keep one's s.,** permanecer sentado. **to take a s.,** tomar asiento, sentarse. **s.-back,** respaldo, *m;* **s. belt,** cinturón de seguridad, *m*
seater *n* de . . . asientos. **four-s.,** automóvil de cuatro asientos, *m*
seaweed *n* alga marina, *f;* (edible) *Lat. Am.* cochayuyo, *m*
seaworthy *a* (of a ship) en buen estado; marinero
sebaceous *a* sebáceo
secede *vi* retirarse (de); separarse (de)
secessionist *n* secesionista, *mf; pol* separatista, *mf. a* secesionista; *pol* separatista
secluded *a* apartado, retirado; solitario
seclusion *n* reclusión, *f;* apartamiento, retiro, *m;* soledad, *f*
second *a* segundo; otro; igual. *adv* en segundo lugar; después. *n* segundo, *m;* (in a duel) padrino, *m;* (helper) ayudante, *m;* (boxing) segundo, *m;* (railway compartment) departamento de segunda (clase), *m; mus* segunda, *f;* (of time) segundo, *m;* (moment) instante, momento, *m. vt* secundar; (a motion) apoyar; *mil* ayudar. **the s. of May,** el dos de mayo. **James the S.,** Jaime el segundo. **on s. thoughts,** después de pensarlo bien. **every s. day,** cada dos días. **They live on the s. floor,** Viven en el primer piso (since the ground floor is not counted separately in Spanish speaking areas, the American second floor = the Spanish **primer piso**). **the s. largest,** el más grande menos uno. **to be s. to none,** no ser inferior a ninguno; (of persons) no ser inferior a nadie; no ceder a nadie. **to come off s.,** llegar el segundo; ser vencido. **seconds hand,** (of watch) segundero, *m.* **s.-in-command,** segundo, *m;* subjefe, *m.* **s.-best,** segundo. **My s.-best hat,** Mi sombrero número dos. **to come off s.-best,** salir mal parado, ser vencido. **s. class,** segunda clase, *f.* **s.-class,** de segunda clase; de calidad inferior; mediocre. **s. cousin,** primo (-ma) segundo (-a). **s. gear,** segunda velocidad, *f.* **s.-hand,** *a* usado; de ocasión; no nuevo. *adv* de segunda mano. **s.-hand car,** un coche de segunda mano. **s.-hand clothing,** ropa usada, *f.* **s.-hand shop** *Lat. Am.* cambalache *m.* **s. lieutenant,** *mil* subteniente, segundo teniente, *m; nav* alférez de fragata, *m.* **s.-rate,** *a* inferior, mediocre. **s. sight,** doble vista, *f*
secondary *a* secundario; subordinado; accesorio; poco importante. **s. school** colegio, liceo. **s. education,** enseñanza secundaria, *f*
seconder *n* ayudante, *m;* el, *m,* (*f,* la) que apoya una proposición
secondly *adv* en segundo lugar
secrecy *n* secreto, *m;* reserva, *f,* silencio, *m.* **in the s. of one's own heart,** en lo más íntimo de su corazón
secret *a* secreto; clandestino; (of persons) reservado, taciturno; (secluded) remoto, apartado; oculto; misterioso. *n* secreto, *m;* (key) clave, *f.* **a s. code,** un código secreto. **in s.,** en secreto, secretamente. **open s.,** secreto a voces. **to keep a s.,** guardar un secreto. **to keep s.,** tener secreto, ocultar. **s. drawer,** secreto, *m.* **S. Service,** servicio de espionaje, *m*
secretaire *n* secreter, escritorio, *m*
secretarial *a* de secretario. **s. college,** academia comercial, *f*
secretariat *n* secretaría, *f*
secretary *n* secretario (-ia). **private s.,** secretario (-ia) particular. **S. of State,** ministro, *m;* Ministro de Estado, *m*
secrete *vt* esconder, ocultar; *med* secretar
secretion *n* escondimiento, *m; med* secreción, *f*
secretive *a* reservado, callado
secretly *adv* en secreto, secretamente; ocultamente, a escondidas
sect *n* secta, *f*
sectarian *a* and *n* sectario (-ia)
section *n* sección, *f;* porción, *f;* subdivisión, *f;* (of a law) artículo, *m. vt* seccionar. **conic s.,** sección cónica, *f*
sectional *a* en secciones. **s. bookcase,** biblioteca desmontable, *f*
sector *n* sector, *m*
secular *a* (very old) secular; (lay) seglar; laico; profano. **s. music,** música profana, *f.* **s. school,** escuela laica, *f*
secularization *n* secularización, *f*
secularize *vt* secularizar
secure *a* seguro; (certain) asegurado; (safe) en seguridad; sano y salvo; (firm) firme; fijo; (confident (in)) confiado (en). *vt* asegurar; (insure) garantizar; (lock) cerrar; (confine) prender; (acquire) adquirir, obtener; lograr, conseguir
securely *adv* seguramente; en seguridad, sin peligro; con confianza; (firmly) firmemente
security *n* seguridad, *f;* protección, defensa, *f;* garantía, *f;* (faith) confianza, *f; com* fianza, *f;* (person) fiador, *m; pl* **securities,** valores, títulos, *m pl.* **government securities,** papel del Estado, *m.* **to give s.,** *com* dar fianza. **to stand s. for,** *com* salir fiador de
sedan-chair *n* silla de manos, *f*
sedate *a* tranquilo, sosegado; formal, serio, grave
sedately *adv* sosegadamente; seriamente
sedateness *n* sosiego, *m,* tranquilidad, *f;* formalidad, compostura, *f*
sedative *a* and *n* sedativo, calmante *m*
sedentary *a* sedentario
sediment *n* sedimento, *Lat. Am.* concho, *m*
sedimentation *n* sedimentación, *f*
sedition *n* sedición, *f*
seditious *a* sedicioso
seduce *vt* seducir
seducer *n* seductor, *m*
seduction *n* seducción, *f*
seductive *a* seductivo, atractivo; persuasivo
sedulous *a* asiduo, diligente
see *n* sede, *f.* **The Holy S.,** la Santa Sede, *f*
see *vt* and *vi* ver; mirar; (understand) comprender; (visit) visitar; (attend to) atender a; ocuparse de. **He sees the matter quite differently,** Él mira el asunto de un modo completamente distinto, Su punto de vista sobre el asunto es completamente distinto. **You are not fit to be seen,** No eres nada presentable. **See you next Tuesday!** ¡Hasta el miércoles que viene! **I see!** ¡Ya! ¡Ahora comprendo! **Let's see!** ¡Vamos a ver! **Shall I see you home?** ¿Quieres que te acompañe a casa? **to go and see,** ir a ver. **to see red,** echar chispas. **to see the sights,** visitar los monumentos. **to see life,** ver mundo. **to see service,** servir (en el ejército, etc.). **to see about,** atender a; pensar en; ocuparse de. **to see after,** cuidar de; atender (a); ocuparse de. **to see again,** volver a ver. **to see into,** investigar, examinar.

to see off, (at the station, etc.) ir a despedir; acompañar. **to see out,** (a person) acompañar a la puerta; (a play, etc.) quedarse hasta el fin (de); no dejar el puesto. **to see over,** inspeccionar. **to see through,** (a house, etc.) inspeccionar; (a person) calarle las intenciones; (a mystery) penetrar; (a person through trouble) ayudar. **to see it through,** llevarlo al cabo; quedarse hasta el fin. **to see to,** atender a; ocuparse de; encargarse de. **to see to everything,** encargarse de todo

seed *n* semilla, *f*; simiente, *f*; (of fruit) pepita, *f*, grano, *m*; *fig* germen, *m*; (offspring) prole, descendencia, *f*. *vi* granar. *vt* sembrar. **s.-bed,** almáciga, *f*, semillero, *m*. **s.-pearl,** aljófar, *m*. **s.-plot,** sementera, *f*; *fig* semillero, *m*. **s.-time,** tiempo de sembrar, *m*

seedling *n* planta de semilla, *f*

seedsman *n* tratante en semillas, *m*

seedy *a* granado; (of clothes) raído, roto; (of persons) andrajoso, desharrapado; infeliz, desgraciado; (ill) indispuesto, malucho

seeing *n* vista, *f*; visión, *f*. **It is worth s.,** Vale la pena de verse. **s. that . . . ,** visto que, dado que, como que. **S. is believing,** Ver es creer

seek *vt* buscar; solicitar, pretender; (demand) pedir; (investigate) investigar; (to do something) procurar, tratar de. **They are much sought after,** Son muy populares, Están en demanda. **to s. after,** buscar; perseguir. **to s. for,** buscar

seeker *n* el, *m*, (*f*, la) que busca; investigador (-ra)

seem *vi* parecer. **He seemed honest,** Parecía honrado. **It seemed to me,** Me pareció a mí. **It seems that they were both at home last night,** Parece ser que ambos estaban en casa anoche

seeming *a* aparente; supuesto

seemingly *adv* aparentemente; en apariencia

seemliness *n* decoro, *m*

seemly *a* decoroso, decente

seep *vi* filtrar; rezumarse

seer *n* profeta, *m*

seesaw *n* columpio, *m*; vaivén, *m*. *vi* columpiarse; balancearse, oscilar. *a* de vaivén, oscilante

seethe *vi* hervir; *fig* bullir

segment *n* segmento, *m*

segregate *vt* segregar. *vi* segregarse. *a* segregado

segregation *n* segregación, *f*

Seine, the el Sena, *m*

seismic *a* sísmico

seismograph *n* sismógrafo, *m*

seismological *a* sismológico

seismology *n* sismología, *f*

seize *vt law* embargar; apoderarse de; asir; (a person) prender; coger; (a meaning) comprender; (an occasion, etc.) aprovecharse de; (of emotions) dominar; (of illnesses) atacar. *vi mech* atascarse. **He was seized by fear,** Le dominó el miedo. **to s. the opportunity,** aprovecharse de la oportunidad. **to s. upon a pretext,** valerse de un pretexto

seizure *n* asimiento, *m*; (of property) embargo, secuestro, *m*; (of a person) captura, *f*; arresto, *m*; *med* ataque, *m*

seldom *adv* rara vez, raramente; pocas veces

select *a* escogido, selecto; exclusivista. *vt* escoger

selection *n* selección, *f*. **selections from Cervantes,** trozos escogidos de Cervantes, *m pl*. **to make a s. from,** escoger entre. **s. committee,** comité de selección, *m*

selective *a* selectivo

self *n* mismo (-a), propio (-a); sí mismo (-a), se; personalidad, *f*; ser, *m*. **all by one's s.,** sin ayuda de nadie; solo; *inf* solito. **my other s.,** mi otro yo. **my better s.,** mi mejor parte. **the s.,** el yo. **s.-abasement,** humillación de sí mismo, *f*. **s.-acting,** automático. **s.-apparent,** evidente, patente. **s.-appointed,** nombrado por uno mismo. **s.-assertion,** presunción, *f*. **s.-assertive,** presumido. **s.-assurance,** confianza en sí mismo, *f*; aplomo, *m*; (impertinence) cara dura, frescura, *f*. **s.-centered,** egocéntrico. **s.-colored,** del mismo color; de su color natural. **s.-command,** dominio de sí mismo, *m*; sangre fría, ecuanimidad, *f*. **s.-complacent,** satisfecho de sí mismo. **s.-conceit,** vanidad, arrogancia, petulancia, *f*. **s.-confidence,** confianza en sí mismo, *f*; aplomo, *m*. **s.-confident,** seguro de sí mismo, lleno de confianza en sí mismo. **s.-conscious,** turbado, confuso, apocado. **s.-consciousness,** turbación, confusión, *f*, apocamiento, azoramiento, *m*. **s.-contained,** (of a person) reservado, poco comunicativo; dueño de sí mismo; (of things) completo; (of flats, etc.) independiente; con entrada independiente. **s.-contradictory,** contradictorio. **s.-control,** dominio de sí mismo, *m*; ecuanimidad, serenidad, sangre fría, *f*. **s.-controlled,** dueño de sí mismo; ecuánime, sereno. **s.-deception,** engaño de sí mismo, *m*; ilusiones, *f pl*. **s.-defense,** defensa propia, *f*. **s.-denial,** abnegación, *f*; renunciación, *f*; frugalidad, *f*. **s.-destruction,** suicidio, *m*. **s.-determination,** libre albedrío, *m*; (of peoples) autonomía, *f*; independencia, *f*. **s.-educating,** autodidacto. **s.-esteem,** respeto para uno mismo, *m*; amor propio, *m*. **s.-evident,** aparente, que salta a la vista. **s.-explanatory,** que se explica a sí mismo; evidente. **s.-generating,** autógeno. **s.-government,** (of a person) dominio de sí mismo, *m*; (of a state) autonomía, *f*. **s.-importance,** presunción, petulancia, *f*. **s.-important,** pagado de sí mismo. **to be s.-important,** darse importancia, darse tono. **s.-indulgence,** indulgencia con sí mismo, *f*; (of food, drink, etc.) excesos, *m pl*, falta de moderación, *f*. **s.-indulgent,** indulgente con sí mismo; dado a los placeres, sibarita. **s.-interest,** propio interés, *m*. **s.-knowledge,** conocimiento de sí mismo, *m*. **s.-love,** egolatría, *f*. **s.-made man,** hombre que ha llegado a su posición actual por sus propios esfuerzos, *m*. **self-medication,** automedicación, *f*. **s.-opinionated,** terco, obstinaz. **s.-portrait,** autorretrato, *m*. **s.-possessed,** dueño de sí mismo; reservado; de sangre fría. **s.-possession,** aplomo, *m*, sangre fría, serenidad, *f*. **s.-preservation,** protección de sí mismo, *f*. **s.-reliance,** independencia, *f*; confianza en sí mismo, *f*. **s.-reliant,** independiente; confiado en sí mismo. **s.-reproach,** remordimiento, *m*. **s.-respect,** respeto de sí mismo, *m*; amor propio, *m*, dignidad, *f*. **s.-respecting,** que se respeta; que tiene amor propio **s.-restraint,** dominio de sí mismo, *m*; moderación, *f*. **s.-righteous,** farisaico. **s.-sacrifice,** abnegación, *f*. **s.-sacrificing,** abnegado. **s.-same,** mismo, idéntico. **s.-satisfaction,** satisfacción de sí mismo, *f*; vanidad, *f*; (of desires, etc.) satisfacción, indulgencia, *f*. **s.-satisfied,** satisfecho de sí mismo, pagado de sí mismo. **s.-seeking,** *a* egoísta, interesado. *n* egoísmo, *m*. **s.-starter,** *mech* arranque automático, *m*. **s.-styled,** autodenominado, autotitulado, llamado por sí mismo. **s.-sufficiency,** suficiencia, *f*; presunción, *f*. **s.-sufficient,** que basta a sí mismo; contento de sí mismo. **s.-supporting,** que vive de su propio trabajo; (of an institution, business) independiente. **s.-taught,** autodidacto. **s.-willed,** voluntarioso

selfish *a* egoísta, interesado

selfishly *adv* interesadamente; por egoísmo

selfishness *n* egoísmo, *m*

sell *vt* vender. *vi* vender; venderse. **They sold him to his enemies,** Le vendieron a sus enemigos. **House to s.,** «Se vende una casa.» **to s. at a loss,** malvender, vender con pérdida. **to s. for cash,** vender al contado. **to s. retail,** vender al por menor. **to s. wholesale,** vender al por mayor. **to s. one's life dearly,** vender cara la vida. **They sold the chair for $10,** Vendieron la silla por diez dólares. **to s. off,** (goods) liquidar, saldar. **to s. out,** vender; agotar. **The best edition is sold out,** La mejor edición está agotada. **All the nylons have been sold out,** Se han vendido todas las medias de nilón (de cristal). **to s. up,** vender

seller *n* vendedor (-ra); comerciante (en), *m*

selling *n* venta, *f*. **s. off,** liquidación, *f*. **s. price,** precio de venta, *m*

selvage *n* (in cloth) orillo, *m*

semantics *n* semántica, *f*
semaphore *n* semáforo, *m*, *vt* and *vi* hacer señales semafóricas (a)
semaphoric *a* semafórico
semblance *n* apariencia, *f*. **to put on a s. of woe,** aparentar ser triste
semen *n* semen, *m*, esperma, *f*
semester *n* semestre, *m*
semi *prefix* semi; medio. **s.-conscious,** medio consciente. **s.-detached house,** casa doble, *f*
semicircle *n* semicírculo, *m*
semicircular *a* semicircular
semicolon *n* punto y coma, *m*
semidetached *a* (house) apartado
semiformal *a* de media ceremonia
seminarist *n* seminarista, *mf*
seminary *n* seminario, *m*; (for girls) colegio interno, *m*
Semite *n* semita, *mf*
Semitic *a* semítico, semita
Semitism *n* semitismo, *m*
semolina *n* sémola, *f*
senate *n* senado, *m*
senator *n* senador, *m*
senatorial *a* senatorio
send *vt* enviar, mandar; *com* remitir; (a ball) lanzar; (grant) conceder; permitir; (inflict) afligir (con). **I sent Jane for it,** Envié a Juana a buscarlo. **He sent us word that he could not come,** Nos mandó un recado diciéndonos que no podía venir. **to s. mad,** hacer enloquecer. **to s. packing,** mandar a paseo. **to s. again,** volver a mandar. **to s. away,** *vt* enviar; (dismiss) destituir; despedir; (scare off) ahuyentar, *vi* enviar a otra parte. **to s. back,** (goods) devolver; (persons) volver. **to s. down,** hacer bajar; (rain, etc.) mandar, derramar; (a student) suspender, expulsar. **to s. in,** mandar; (persons) hacer entrar, introducir; (food) servir; (a bill) presentar; (one's name) dar. **Please s. him in!** ¡Sírvase de invitarle a entrar! **to s. in one's resignation,** mandar su dimisión. **to s. off,** enviar, mandar; (goods) despachar; (persons) destituir; (scare) ahuyentar. **s.-off,** *n* despedida, *f*. **a good s.-off,** una despedida afectuosa. **to s. on,** (a letter) hacer seguir; (instructions) trasmitir. **to s. out,** hacer salir; mandar; (emit) despedir, dar; (new shoots, etc.) echar. **to s. round,** (the hat, etc.) hacer circular. **to s. up,** enviar arriba; mandar subir, hacer subir; mandar, enviar; (a ball) lanzar
sender *n* remitente, *mf*; *elec* transmisor, *m*
sending *n* envío, *m*
Senegal Senegal, *m*
Senegalese *a* and *n* senegalés (-esa)
senile *a* senil
senility *n* senilidad, *f*
senior *a* mayor, de mayor edad; más antiguo. **Martinez s.,** Martínez padre. **Charles is Mary's s. by five years,** Carlos es cinco años mayor que María. **s. member,** decano, *m*
seniority *n* ancianidad, *f*; antigüedad, *f*
senna *n bot* sena, *f*
sensation *n* sensación, *f*; sentimiento, *m*; impresión, *f*. **to create a s.,** causar una sensación
sensational *a* sensacional
sensationalism *n phil* sensualismo, *m*; efectismo, *m*
sensationalist *n phil* sensualista, *mf*; efectista, *mf*
sense *n* sentido, *m*. *vt* sentir. **in a s.,** hasta cierto punto; desde un punto de vista. **in the full s. of the word,** en toda la extensión de la palabra. **common s.,** sentido común, *m*. **He has no s. of smell,** No tiene olfato. **the five senses,** los cinco sentidos. **to be out of one's senses,** estar fuera de sí, estar trastornado. **You must be out of your senses!** ¡Debes de haber perdido el juicio! ¡Estás loco! **to come to one's senses,** (after unconsciousness) volver en sí; (after folly) recobrar el sentido común. **to talk s.,** hablar con sentido común, hablar razonablemente. **s. organ,** órgano de los sentidos, *m*. **have a good s. of direction,** saber orientarse, tener buena orientación. **have no s. of smell,** ser incapaz de percibir olores. **have no s. of taste,** ser incapaz de distinguir gustos
senseless *a* (unconscious) sin sentido, insensible; desmayado; (silly) necio, estúpido. **to knock s.,** derribar, tumbar
senselessness *n* falta de sentido común, *f*; locura, absurdidad, *f*
sensibility *n* sensibilidad, *f*
sensible *a* sensible; (conscious) consciente (de); sesudo. **to be s. of,** estar consciente de; estar persuadido de
sensibly *adv* sensiblemente; sesudamente, cuerdamente
sensitive *a* sensitivo; susceptible (a); impresionable. **s. plant,** sensitiva, *f*
sensitivity *n* sensibilidad, *f*; susceptibilidad, *f*; delicadeza, *f*
sensitize *vt phot* sensibilizar
sensory *a* sensorio
sensual *a* sensual; voluptuoso
sensualism *n* sensualismo, *m*
sensualist *n* sensualista, *mf*
sensuality *n* sensualidad, *f*
sensually *adv* sensualmente
sensuous *a* sensorio
sensuousness *n* sensualidad, *f*
sentence *n law* sentencia, *f*; (penalty) pena, *f*; *gram* frase, *f*; (maxim) máxima, sentencia, *f*. *vt* sentenciar, condenar. **to pass s.,** pronunciar sentencia, fallar. **under s. of,** bajo pena de
sententious *a* sentencioso
sentient *a* sensible
sentiment *n* sentimiento, *m*; (sentimentality) sentimentalismo, *m*; opinión, *f*
sentimental *a* sentimental; (mawkish) sensiblero
sentimentalist *n* romántico (-ca), persona sentimental, *f*
sentimentality *n* sentimentalismo, *m*, sensiblería, *f*
sentimentalize *vt* idealizar
sentimentally *adv* sentimentalmente
sentinel *n* centinela, *mf*
sentry *n* centinela, *m*. **to be on s. duty,** estar de guardia. **s.-box,** garita de centinela, *f*
separable *a* separable
separate *a* separado; distinto; independiente. *vt* separar; dividir. *vi* separarse; (of husband and wife) separarse de bienes y de cuerpos
separately *adv* separadamente; aparte
separation *n* separación, *f*; *law* separación de bienes y de cuerpos, *f*
separatism *n* separatismo, *m*
separatist *a* and *n* separatista *mf*
Sephardic *a* Sefaradí
sepia *n* (color and fish) sepia, *f*
September *n* setiembre, septiembre, *m*
septic *a* séptico
septicemia *n* septicemia, *f*
septuagenarian *n* setentón (-ona); septuagenario (-ia)
septum septo, tabique, *m*
sepulcher *n* sepulcro, *m*
sepulchral *a* sepulcral
sequel *n* (of a story, etc.) continuación, *f*; consecuencia, *f*; resultado, *m*
sequence *n* sucesión, *f*; serie, *f*; orden, *mf*; (at cards) serie, *f*; *gram* correspondencia, *f*; (*ecc* and cinema) secuencia, *f*. **s. of tenses,** correspondencia de los tiempos, *f*
sequestered *a* aislado, remoto
sequestrate *vt* secuestrar
sequestration *n* secuestro, *m*,
sequin *n* lentejuela, *f*
seraglio *n* serrallo, *m*
seraph *n* serafín, *m*
seraphic *a* seráfico
seraphim *n* serafín, *m*
Serbia Servia, *f*

Serbian *a* servio. *n* servio (-ia); (language) servio, *m*
serenade *n* serenata, *f*, *vt* dar una serenata (a)
serene *a* sereno. **His S. Highness,** Su Alteza Serenísima
serenity *n* serenidad, *f*; tranquilidad, *f*
serf *n* siervo (-va)
serfdom *n* servidumbre, *f*
serge *n* estameña, *f*; (silk) sarga, *f*
sergeant *n mil* sargento, *m*; (police) sargento de policía, *m*. **s.-at-arms,** macero, *m*. **s.-major,** sargento instructor, *m*
serial *a* en serie; (of a story) por entregas. *n* novela por entregas, *f*. **s. number,** número de serie, *m*
sericulture *n* sericultura, *f*
series *n* serie, *f*; cadena, *f*; *math* serie, progresión, *f*. **in s.,** en serie
serious *a* serio; sincero; verdadero; (of illness, etc.) grave; importante. **He was s.** (not laughing) **when he said it,** Lo dijo en serio. **He is very s. about it,** Lo toma muy en serio. **to grow s.,** (of persons) ponerse serio; (of events) hacerse grave
seriously *adv* seriamente; en serio; gravemente. **to take** (something) **s.,** tomar (algo) en serio. **to take oneself s.,** tomarse muy en serio
seriousness *n* seriedad, *f*; gravedad, *f*. **in all s.,** en serio, seriamente
sermon *n* sermón, *m*
sermonize *vt* and *vi* sermonear
serpent *n* serpiente, *f*; *mus* serpentón, *m*
serpentine *a* serpentino; (of character) tortuoso. *n min* serpentina, *f*
serrated *a* serrado; dentellado
serried *a* apretado, apiñado
serum *n* suero, *m*
servant *n* servidor (-ra); (domestic) criado (-da); (employee) empleado (-da); (slave and *fig*) siervo (-va); *pl* **servants,** (domestic) servidumbre, *f*, servicio, *m*. **I remain your obedient s.,** Quedo de Vd. atento y seguro servidor (att. y s.s.). **civil s.,** empleado del estado, *m*. **general s.,** criada para todo, *f*. **man s.,** criado, *m*. **the s. problem,** el problema del servicio. **Your s., sir,** Servidor de Vd., señor. **s.-girl,** criada, *f*
serve *vt* servir (a); ser útil (a); satisfacer; (in a shop) despachar; (an apprenticeship, etc.) hacer; (a prison sentence) cumplir; (treat) tratar; (of stallion) cubrir; (a warrant, etc.) ejecutar; (a notice) entregar; (a ball) servir; (on a jury, etc.) formar parte de; *naut* aforrar. *vi* servir; (*mil*, *nav*) hacer el servicio. *n sport* saque, *m*. **It serves you right!** ¡Lo tienes merecido! **to s. at table,** servir a la mesa. **to s. as,** servir de. **to s. out,** distribuir; servir. **Serves 8,** (recipe) Da 8 porciones
server *n ecc* acólito, *m*; *sport* saque, *m*; (tray) bandeja, *f*; (for fish, etc.) pala, *f*
service *n* servicio, *m*; *ecc* oficio, *m*; servicio de mesa, *m*; (of a writ) entrega, *f*; *sport* saque, *m*. **coffee s.,** juego de café, *m*. **diplomatic s.,** cuerpo diplomático, *m*. **At your s.,** Para servir a Vd., A su disposición. **on active s.,** en acto de servicio; en el campo de batalla. **to go into s.,** (of servants) ir a servir. **to render s.,** prestar servicios. **s. tree,** serbal, *m*
serviceable *a* (of persons) servicial; (of things) servible, utilizable; útil; práctico; (lasting) duradero
service road *n* vía de servicio, *f*
serviette *n* servilleta, *f*. **s. ring,** servilletero, *m*
servile *a* servil, *Lat. Am. also* incondicional
servility *n* servilismo, *m*
serving *a* sirviente; al servicio (de). **s. maid,** criada, *f*. **s. table,** trinchero, *m*
servitude *n* servidumbre, esclavitud, *f*. **penal s.,** cadena perpetua, *f*
session *n* sesión, *f*; junta, *f*. **petty sessions,** tribunal de primera instancia, *m*
set *vt* poner; colocar; fijar; (seeds, etc.) plantar; (bones) reducir, componer; (gems) engastar, montar; (a clock) regular; (sails) desplegar; (the teeth of a saw) trabar, triscar; (congeal) hacer coagular; (a trap) armar; (a snare) tender; (a razor) afilar; (make ready) preparar; (type) componer; (cause) hacer; *mus* poner en música; *mus* adaptar; (order) mandar; (prescribe) dar, asignar; (estimate) estimar, evaluar; (an example, etc.) dar; (establish) establecer, crear. *vi* (of the sun, etc.) ponerse; (solidify) coagularse; solidificarse; (of tides) fluir; (of the wind) soplar; (of dogs) hacer punta. **The joke set him laughing,** El chiste le hizo reír. **set an example,** dar ejemplo, dar el ejemplo. **set a precedent,** sentar precedente. **to set a person's mind at rest,** tranquilizar, sosegar. **to set a trap,** armar lazo. **to set at ease,** poner a sus anchas (a), hacer cómodo (a). **to set at naught,** despreciar. **to set eyes on,** poner los ojos en. **to set fire to,** pegar fuego a, incendiar. **to set free,** poner en libertad, librar (de). **to set in motion,** poner en marcha. **to set one's teeth,** apretar los dientes. **to set people talking,** dar que hablar a la gente. **to set the fashion,** fijar la moda; poner de moda. **to set the alarm at seven o'clock,** poner el despertador a las siete. **to set the table,** poner la mesa. **to set to work,** ponerse a trabajar. **to set about,** *vi* (begin) ponerse (a); empezar; (undertake) emprender. *vt* (a rumour, etc.) divulgar. **They set about each other,** Empezaron a golpearse, Vinieron a las manos. **to set against,** indisponer (con), enemistar (con); hacer el enemigo (de), ser hostil (a); (balance) oponer, balancear. **to set oneself against,** oponerse a; atacar, luchar contra. **to set aside,** poner a un lado; apartar; (discard) desechar; (omit) omitir, pasar por alto de; dejar aparte, excluir; (keep) reservar; (money, etc.) ahorrar; (reject) rechazar; (quash) anular. **to set back,** retrasar; hacer retroceder. **set-back,** *n* revés, *m*; contrariedad, *f*. **to set before,** poner ante; (facts) exponer; (introduce) presentar. **to set down,** poner en tierra; depositar; (of a bus, etc.) dejar; (in writing) poner por escrito; anotar, apuntar; narrar, contar; (attribute) atribuir; (fix) fijar, formular; (believe to be) creer. **Passengers are set down at . . . ,** Los viajeros pueden apearse en . . . **to set forth,** *vt* (one's opinions, etc.) exponer; publicar; (display) exhibir, mostrar; (make) hacer. *vi* ponerse en camino. **to set going,** poner en marcha; echar a andar. **to set in,** empezar; (of the tide) fluir. **A reaction has set in,** Se ha hecho sentir una reacción. **to set off,** *vt* (explode) hacer estallar; (cause) hacer; (heighten) realzar; hacer resaltar; (counterbalance) contraponer. *vi* partir; ponerse en camino. **set-off,** *n* contraste, *m*, contraposición, *f*. **to set off against,** contraponer. **to set on,** *vt* (a dog) azuzar; (incite) instigar, incitar. *vi* atacar. **to set out,** *vt* (state) exponer, manifestar; (embellish) realzar; (display) arreglar, disponer. *vi* ponerse en camino, partir. **to set over,** (rule) tener autoridad sobre, gobernar. **to set to,** (begin to) ponerse a, empezar a; (work) ponerse a trabajar. **set-to,** *n* lucha, *f*; (boxing) asalto, *m*; (quarrel) pelea, riña, *f*. **to set up,** *vt* (a monument, etc.) erigir, levantar; (fix) fijar; (apparatus, machinery) montar; (exalt) exaltar; (found) establecer, *Lat. Am. also* instaurar; crear; (propound) exponer; (a howl, etc.) dar; (equip with) proveer de; instalar; (make strong) robustecer; fortificar; (type) componer; (raise) alzar. *vi* establecerse; dárselas de. **He sets himself up as a painter,** Se las da de pintor. **to set** (a person) **up as a model,** poner como modelo (a). **to set up house,** poner casa. **to set up a business,** establecer un comercio. **set-up,** *n* establecimiento, *m*; arreglo, *m*. **to set upon,** atacar
set *n* (of sun, etc.) puesta, *f*, ocaso, *m*; (of the head, etc.) porte, *m*; (of a garment) corte, *m*; (of the tide, etc.) dirección, *f*; (slant) inclinación, *f*; (*fig* drift) tendencia, *f*, movimiento, *m*; (of the teeth of a saw) triscamiento, *m*; (of men, houses, etc.) grupo, *m*; (of tools, golf clubs, china, etc.) juego, *m*; (gang) pandilla, camarilla, *f*; clase, *f*; (*dance*) tanda, *f*; (tennis) partido, *f*; *theat* decoración, *f*; *rad* aparato de radio, *m*, radio, *f*. **coffee set,** juego de café, *m*. **all-mains set,** radio de corriente eléctrica, *f*. **battery set,** radio de batería, *f*. **portable**

set, radio portátil, *f*. **the smart set,** el mundo elegante. **to have a shampoo and set,** hacerse lavar y marcar (el pelo). **to make a set,** hacer juego. **to make a dead set at,** hacer un ataque vigoroso (a), atacar resueltamente; procurar insinuarse en el favor de. **set of teeth,** dentadura, *f*

set *a* fijo; inmóvil; (of a smile) forzado; (of a task) asignado; (of times) señalado, fijo; (prescribed) prescrito, establecido; (firm) firme; (resolved) resuelto; (well-known) consabido; (obstinate) terco, nada adaptable. **well set-up,** apuesto, bien plantado. **He is set on doing it,** Se empeña en hacerlo. **to be dead set against,** estar completamente opuesto a. **set phrase,** frase hecha, *f*. **set-square,** cartabón, *m*

setter *n* (perro) séter, perdiguero, *m*. **s.-on,** instigador (-ra)

setting *n* (of the sun, etc.) puesta, *f*; (of mortar, etc.) fraguado, *m*; (of a jelly) solidificación, *f*; (of jewels) engaste, *m*, montadura, *f*; (of bones) aliño, *m*; (of teeth of saw) traba, *f*; (of razor) afiladura, *f*; (of a trap) armadura, *f*; (of a machine, etc.) ajuste, *m*; (frame) marco, *m*; *mus* arreglo, *m*; *theat* decorado, *m*; (emplacement) lecho, *m*. **the s. sun,** el sol poniente. **s. free,** liberación, *f*. **s. off,** partida, salida, *f*. **s. out,** ida, marcha, *f*; principio, *m*. **s.-up,** creación, institución, *f*, establecimiento, *m*; (of a machine) montaje, *m*; *print* composición, *f*

settle *vt* colocar; asegurar, afirmar; (a country) colonizar; (live in) establecer (en); (populate) poblar; (in a profession, etc.) dar; (install) instalar; (the imagination, etc.) sosegar, calmar; (resolve) resolver; (arrange) disponer, arreglar; (differences) componer, concertar; (an opponent, etc.) confundir; (a bill) saldar, pagar; (a claim) satisfacer; (clarify) depositar, clarificar; (end) poner fin (a). *vi* establecerse; (of weather) serenarse; (to work, etc.) empezar a, ponerse a; aplicarse a; (decide) decidirse; (alight) posarse; (of foundations, etc.) asentarse; (of a ship) zozobrar; (of sediment) depositarse; (of liquid) clarificarse. **to s. accounts with,** *fig* ajustar cuentas con. **to s. down,** establecerse, arraigarse; adaptarse (a); (become calm) sosegarse, calmarse; sentar el juicio; (of foundations) asentarse; (of a ship) zozobrar; (of sediment) depositarse. **to s. in,** *vt* instalar. *vi* instalarse. **to s. on,** (choose) escoger; (decide on) decidirse (a). **to s. a pension on,** señalar pensión (a). **to s. up,** *vt* (one's affairs) poner en orden; (bill) pagar, saldar. *vi* llegar a un acuerdo; pagar cuentas

settled *a* fijo; permanente; invariable; (of countries) colonizado; (of weather) sereno

settlement *n* (of a country) colonización, *f*; (of a dispute) arreglo, ajuste, *m*; (of a question) solución, *f*; decisión, *f*; (of a bill) saldo, pago, *m*, liquidación, *f*; (of an obligation) satisfacción, *f*; (colony) colonia, *f*; (creation) creación, institución, *f*; establecimiento, arraigo, *m*. **deed of s.,** escritura de donación, *f*. **marriage s.,** contrato matrimonial, *m*; **s. out of court,** arreglo pacífico, *m*

settler *n* colono, *m*; colonizador (-ra)

seven *a* and *n* siete *m*. **It is s. o'clock,** Son las siete. **the s. deadly sins,** los siete pecados capitales

seventeen *a* diecisiete, diez y siete. *n* diecisiete, *m*. **She is just s.,** Acaba de cumplir los diez y siete años

seventeenth *a* décimoséptimo; (of monarchs and of the month) diez y siete. *n* décimoséptimo, *m*. **Louis the S.,** Luis diez y siete. **the s. of June,** el diez y siete de junio

seventh *a* séptimo; (of the month) siete. *n* séptimo, *m*; séptima parte, *f*; *mus* séptima, *f*. **Edward the S.,** Eduardo séptimo. **the s. of August,** el siete de agosto

seventieth *a* septuagésimo, setentavo. *n* setentavo, *m*

seventy *a* and *n* setenta, *m*

sever *vt* separar; romper; dividir

several *a* distinto, diferente; respectivo; varios, *m pl*, (*f pl*, varias); algunos, *m pl*, (*f pl*, algunas)

severally *adv* separadamente; individualmente; independientemente

severance *n* separación, *f*; (of friendship, etc.) ruptura, *f*

severe *a* severo; riguroso; fuerte; duro; (of style) austero; (of pain) agudo; (of illness) grave

severely *adv* severamente; intensamente; gravemente

severity *n* severidad, *f*; intensidad, *f*; (of weather) inclemencia, *f*; (of illness) gravedad, *f*

sew *vt* and *vi* coser, *Lat. Am.* costurar, costurear. **to sew on,** coser, pegar

sewage *n* aguas residuales, *f pl*. **s. system,** alcantarillado, *m*

sewer *n* alcantarilla, cloaca, *f*, albañal, *m*

sewing *n* costura, *f*. **s. bag,** costurero, *m*. **s. cotton,** hilo de coser, *m*. **s.-machine,** máquina de coser, *f*. **s. silk,** torzal, *m*

sex *n* sexo, *m*. **the fair sex,** el bello sexo. **the weaker sex,** el sexo débil. **sex appeal,** atractivo, *m*

sexagenarian *n* sexagenario (-ia)

sexless *a* neutro; frígido

sexologist *n* sexólogo (-ga)

sexology *n* sexología, *f*

sextant *n* sextante, *m*

sexton *n* sacristán, *m*; sepulturero, *m*; (bell-ringer) campanero, *m*

sexual *a* sexual

sexuality *n* sexualidad, *f*

Sforza Esforcia, *f*

sh! *interj* ¡Chitón! ¡Chis!

shabbily *adv* (of dressing) pobremente; (of treatment) mezquinamente

shabbiness *n* pobreza, *f*; estado andrajoso, *m*; (of behavior) mezquindad, ruindad, *f*

shabby *a* (of persons) desharrapado, andrajoso, *Lat. Am.* maltraído; (of garments) raído, roto; (of a neighborhood, etc.) pobre; (mean) ruin, mezquino

shack *n* choza, *f*, *Mexico* jacal, *elsewhere in Lat. Am.* bohío *m*

shackle *n* traba, *f*; *pl* **shackles,** grillos, *m pl*, esposas, *f pl*; *fig* cadenas, *f pl*. *vt* poner esposas (a), encadenar; (a horse) apear; *fig* atar; (impede) estorbar

shad *n* sábalo, *m*

shade *n* sombra, *f*; (in a picture) toque de obscuro, *m*; (for the eyes) visera, *f*; (of a lamp) pantalla, *f*; (ghost) espectro, fantasma, *m*; (of color) matiz, *m*; (tinge) dejo, *m*. *vt* sombrear, dar sombra (a); (the face, etc.) proteger, resguardar; (a drawing) esfumar. **in the s.,** a la sombra. **80° in the s.,** ochenta grados a la sombra. **to put** (a person) **in the s.,** eclipsar

shadiness *n* sombra, *f*

shading *n* sombra, *f*; *art* degradación, *f*

shadow *n* sombra, *f*; obscuridad, *f*; (in a picture) toque de obscuro, *m*. *vt* sombrear; obscurecer; (a person) seguir **to cast a s.,** proyectar una sombra. **to s. forth,** indicar; simbolizar. **s. show,** sombras chinescas, *f pl*

shadowy *a* umbroso; vago, indistinto, indefinido

shady *a* sombreado, umbrío; sombrío; (of persons, etc.) sospechoso. **It was s. in the wood,** Hacía sombra en el bosque

shaft *n* fuste, *m*; (arrow) flecha, saeta, *f*, dardo, *m*; (of a golf club, etc.) mango, *m*; (of a cart) vara, *f*; *mech* árbol, eje, *m*; (of a column and a feather) cañón, *m*; (of light) rayo, *m*; (of a mine) pozo, tiro, *m*; (air-shaft) conducto de aire, ventilador, *m*. **cam-s.,** árbol de levas, *m*. **driving s.,** árbol motor, *m*

shaggy *a* peludo; lanudo

shagreen *n* chagrén, *m*

shah *n* cha, *m*

shake *vt* sacudir; agitar; hacer temblar; (weaken) debilitar, hacer flaquear. *vi* estremecerse; temblar; (trill) trinar. **He managed to s. himself free,** Consiguió librarse por una sacudida. **to s. hands,** darse la mano, estrecharse la mano. **to s. one's finger at,** señalar con el dedo (a). **to s. one's fist at,** amenazar con el puño (a). **to s. one's head,** mover la cabeza; negar con la cabeza. **to s. one's sides,** (with laughter) reírse a carcajadas. **to s. with fear,** temblar de miedo. **to s. down,** sacudir, hacer caer. **s.-down,** *n* cama improvisada, *f.* **to s. off,** sacudirse; librarse (de), perder; quitar de encima (a). **to s. out,** (unfurl) desplegar; sacudir. **to s. up,** agitar; sacudir, remover

shake *n* sacudida, *f;* (of the head) movimiento (de la cabeza), *m;* (of the hand) apretón (de manos), *m;* temblor, *m; mus* trino, gorjeo, *m.* **in two shakes,** *inf* en un periquete. **to give a person a good s.,** sacudir violentamente (a)

Shakespearean *a* shakespeariano

shakiness *n* inestabilidad, *f;* poca firmeza, *f;* temblor, *m;* lo dudoso. **the s. of his voice,** su voz trémula

shaking *n* sacudimiento, *m;* temblor, *m;* (of windows, etc.) zangoloteo, *m*

shaky *a* inestable; poco firme; (of hands, etc.) tembloroso; (of the voice) trémulo; (of gait) vacilante; dudoso

shale *n* esquisto, *m*

shall *v aux* (expressing simple future) **I s. arrive tomorrow,** Llegaré mañana. **S. we go to the sea next week?** ¿Iremos al mar la semana próxima?; (expressing obligation, compulsion) **You s. not go out,** No has de salir, No quiero que salgas. **He s. see her immediately,** Tiene que verla en seguida; (as a polite formula) **S. I go?** ¿Quiere Vd. que vaya? **S. we buy the soap?** ¿Quiere Vd. que compremos el jabón? ¿Compraremos el jabón?

shallot *n bot* chalote, *m,* ascalonia, *f*

shallow *a* poco profundo; (of a receptacle) llano; (of persons) superficial, frívolo; (of knowledge, etc.) superficial, ligero, somero. *n* bajío, *m*

shallowness *n* poca profundidad, *f;* superficialidad, *f*

sham *vt* fingir, simular. *n* farsa, *f;* imitación, *f;* engaño, *m;* (person) farsante, *m. a* fingido; falso; espurio. **to s. illness,** fingirse enfermo. **to s. dead,** hacer la mortecina. **You're just a s.,** Eres un farsante

sham battle *n mil* simulacro de combate, simulacro guerrero, *m*

shamble *vi* andar arrastrándose. *n* andar pesado, *m; pl* **shambles,** matadero, *m; fig* carnicería, *f*

shambling *a* pesado, lento

shame *n* vergüenza, *f;* ignominia, *f;* deshonra, *f. vt* avergonzar; deshonrar. **For s.!** ¡Qué vergüenza! **What a s.!** ¡Qué lástima! **to put to s.,** avergonzar

shamefaced *a* (bashful) vergonzoso, tímido; (ashamed) avergonzado

shamefacedly *adv* vergonzosamente, tímidamente; con vergüenza

shameful *a* vergonzoso, escandaloso; indecente

shamefully *adv* escandalosamente

shameless *a* desvergonzado; impúdico, indecente

shamelessly *adv* desvergonzadamente

shamelessness *n* desvergüenza, poca vergüenza, *f;* impudicia, deshonestidad, *f*

shampoo *n* champú, *m. vt* dar un champú (a); dar un masaje (a). **dry s.,** champú seco, *m*

shank *n* zanca, *f; mech* pierna, *f;* (handle) mango, *m;* (of a button) rabo, *m,* cola, *f.* **go on Shank's mare, ride on Shank's mare,** caminar en coche de San Francisco, ir en boricua de Villadiego

shanty *n* choza, *f*

shanty town *n* barriada (Peru), callampa, población, población, callampa (Chile), *f,* rancho (Venezuela), *m,* villa-miseria (Argentina), *f*

shape *n* forma, *f;* bulto, *m;* fantasma, *m;* (of a garment) corte, *m;* (of a person) talle, *m; cul* molde, *m;* (of a hat) forma, *f. vt* formar; (a garment) cortar; (ideas) dar forma (a); adaptar; (stone, etc.) labrar; (one's life) dominar. *vi* (of events) desarrollarse. **to go out of s.,** perder la forma. **to take s.,** tomar forma. **to s. one's course,** dirigirse (hacia, a); *naut* dar el rumbo. **to s. well,** prometer bien

shaped *a* de forma de . . . , que tiene figura de . . . **pear-s.,** piriforme

shapeless *a* informe; disforme

shapelessness *n* informidad, *f;* deformidad, *f*

shapeliness *n* belleza de forma, *f;* simetría, *f*

shapely *a* bien formado; simétrico

share *n* porción, *f;* parte, *f;* cuota, *f;* contribución, *f;* (part ownership) interés, *m;* (in a company) acción, *f. vt* distribuir; compartir; dividir; tomar parte en. *vi* participar (de); tomar parte (en). **to fall to one's s.,** tocar, corresponder. **to go shares with,** dividir con, compartir con. **to take a s. in the conversation,** tomar parte en la conversación. **paid-up s.,** *com* acción liberada, *f.* **to s. out,** repartir, distribui

sharecropper *Lat. Am.* agregado (-da), *mf*

shareholder *n* accionista, *mf*

sharer *n* partícipe, *mf*

shark *n icht* tiburón, *m; inf* caimán, *m*

sharp *a* (of edges) afilado, cortante, *Lat. Am. also* filoso, filudo; (of points) punzante, puntiagudo; (of features, etc.) anguloso; (of bends, etc.) brusco; (of outlines, etc.) definido, distinto; (of pain, sound) agudo; (marked) marcado; (intense) intenso; (of winds, glance, etc.) penetrante; (of hearing) fino; (of appetite) bueno; (of showers) fuerte; (quick) rápido; (clever, etc.) vivo, listo; perspicaz; (of children) despierto, precoz; (unscrupulous) astuto, sin escrúpulos; (of criticism, remarks) mordaz; (of rebukes, sentences, etc.) severo; (of winters, etc.) riguroso; (of fighting) encarnizado; (of taste) picante; (sour) ácido; *mus* sostenido. *adv* en punto; puntualmente. *n mus* sostenido, *m.* **at five o'clock s.,** a las cinco en punto. **Look s.!** ¡Date prisa! **s.-edged,** afilado. **s.-eyed,** con ojos de lince; de mirada penetrante. **s.-featured,** de facciones angulosas. **s.-nosed,** de nariz puntiaguda. **s.-pointed,** puntiagudo. **s. practice,** procedimientos poco honrados, *m pl.* **s.-tongued,** de lengua áspera. **s. turn,** curva brusca, curva cerrada, *f.* **s.-witted,** de inteligencia viva, listo

sharpen *vt* (knives) afilar, amolar; (pencils, etc.) sacar punta (a); (wits, etc.) despabilar; (appetite) abrir. **This walk has sharpened my appetite,** Este paseo me ha abierto el apetito. **to s. one's claws,** afilarse las uñas

sharper *n inf* caballero de industria, timador, *m;* (at cards) fullero, *m*

sharply *adv* claramente; bruscamente; severamente; ásperamente

sharpness *n* (of cold, etc.) intensidad, *f;* severidad, *f;* (cleverness) agudeza, perspicacia, *f;* (of a child) precocidad, *f;* (sarcasm, etc.) mordacidad, *f;* aspereza, *f;* brusquedad, *f*

sharpshooter *n* franco tirador, *m*

sharpsighted *a* de vista penetrante, listo, perspicaz

shatter *vt* romper, quebrantar; hacer añicos; *fig* destrozar. **You have shattered my illusions,** Has destrozado todas mis ilusiones

shave *vt* afeitar, rasurar; (wood, etc.) acepillar. *vi* afeitarse; (of razors) afeitar. *n* afeitada, *f.* **to have a s.,** hacerse afeitar. **to have a close s.,** *inf* escapar por un pelo

shaving *n* afeitada, *f;* (of wood, etc.) viruta, acepilladura, *f.* **s.-bowl,** bacía, *f.* **s.-brush,** brocha de afeitar, *f.* **s.-glass,** espejo de afeitar, *m.* **s.-soap,** jabón de afeitar, *m.* **s.-stick,** barra de jabón de afeitar, *f*

shawl *n* chal, mantón, rebozo, *m*

she *pers pron* ella; la; (female) hembra, *f;* (translated by fem. ending in the case of animals, etc., e.g. **she bear,** osa, **she cat,** gata). **It is her,** Es ella. **she who is dancing,** la que baila

sheaf *n* (of corn, etc.) gavilla, garba, *f;* (of arrows) haz, *m;* (of papers, etc.) paquete, atado, *m.* **to bind in sheaves,** agavillar

shear *vt* (sheep) esquilar, trasquilar; tonsurar; cortar; (cloth) tundir

shearer *n* (of sheep) esquilador, *m*

shearing *n* (of sheep) esquileo, *m,* tonsura, *f;* (of cloth) tunda, *f.* **s. machine,** esquiladora, *f.* **s. season,** esquileo, *m*

shears *n pl* tijeras grandes, *f pl,* cizalla, *f*

sheath *n* vaina, *f*. **s.-knife,** cuchillo de monte, *m*
sheathe *vt* envainar; *naut* aforrar
shed *vt* derramar; (skin, etc.) mudar; perder; (remove) quitarse, desprenderse de; (get rid of) deshacerse de. *n* cobertizo, sotechado, *m*; cabaña, *f*. **to s. light on,** echar luz sobre, iluminar
sheen *n* lustre, *m*; brillo, *m*
sheep *n* oveja, *f*; carnero, *m*; ganado lanar, *m*. **He is the black s. of the family,** Es el garbanzo negro de la familia. **to cast sheep's eyes at,** lanzar miradas de carnero degollado. **s. breeder,** ganadero, *m*. **s.-dip,** desinfectante para ganado, *m*. **s.-dog,** perro de pastor, *m*. **s.-like,** ovejuno, de oveja. **s.-shearing,** esquileo, *m*
sheepfold *n* aprisco, redil, *m*
sheepish *a* tímido, vergonzoso; estúpido
sheepishly *adv* tímidamente
sheepishness *n* timidez, cortedad, *f*; estupidez, *f*
sheepskin *n* piel de carnero, *f*. **s. jacket,** zamarra, *f*
sheer *a* puro; completo, absoluto; (steep) escarpado, acantilado; a pico; (of fabrics) transparente; ligero, fino. *adv* completamente; de un golpe; (perpendicularly) a pico. **to s. off,** desviarse; largarse, marcharse
sheet *n* (bed) sábana, *f*; (shroud) mortaja, *f*; (of paper) hoja, *f*; cuartilla, *f*; (pamphlet) folleto, *m*; (news) periódico, *m*, hoja, *f*; (of metal, etc.) lámina, plancha, *f*; (of water, etc.) extensión, *f*; *naut* escota, *f*. *vt* poner sábanas en; envolver en sábanas; (a corpse) amortajar. **to be as white as a s.,** estar pálido como un muerto. **s. bend,** (knot) nudo de tejedor, *m*. **s. glass,** vidrio en lámina, *m*. **s. iron,** hierro en planchas, *m*
sheik *n* jeque, *m*
shekel *n* (coin) siclo, *m*; *pl* **shekels,** dinero, *m*
shelf *n* estante, anaquel, *m*; (reef) banco de arena, bajío, *m*; (of rock) escalón, *m*. **to be on the s.,** *inf* quedarse para tía, quedarse para vestir imágenes
shell *n* (of small shellfish) concha, *f*; (of tortoise) coraza, *f*; (of insects, lobsters, etc.) caparazón, *m*; (of a nut) cáscara, *f*; (of an egg) cascarón, *m*; (of peas, beans) vaina, *f*; (*com* and *mus*) concha, *f*; (of a building) casco, *m*; (outside) exterior, *m*; (empty form) apariencia, *f*; *mil* granada, *f*. *vt* pelar; (nuts) descascarar; (beans, etc.) desvainar; *mil* bombardear. **to be under s.-fire,** sufrir un bombardeo. **s. shock,** neurosis de guerra, *f*
shellfish *n* crustáceo, *m*; (as food) marisco, *m*
shelling *n mil* bombardeo, *m*
shelter *n* abrigo, amparo, *m*; refugio, *m*; asilo, *m*. *vt* dar asilo (a); abrigar; (defend) amparar, proteger; (hide) esconder. *vi* refugiarse; resguardarse; esconderse
sheltered *a* abrigado
sheltering *a* protector
shelve *vt* (books) poner en un estante; (persons) destituir; (questions, etc.) aplazar, arrinconar; proveer de estantes, *vi* (slope) inclinarse, formar declive; (of sea bed) formar escalones
shelving *a* inclinado; (of ocean bed) acantilado
shepherd *n* pastor, *m*. *vt* guardar; guiar, conducir. **s. boy,** zagal, *m*. **shepherd's pouch,** zurrón, *m*
shepherdess *n* pastora, *f*
sherbet *n* sorbete, *m*
sheriff *n* (in U.K.) sheriff, *m*; (U.S.A.) jefe de la policía, *m*
sherry *n* (vino de) jerez, *m*. **dry s.,** jerez seco, *m*
shield *n* escudo, *m*; (round) rodela, *f*; *her* escudo de armas, *m*; *fig* defensa, *f*, amparo, *m*. *vt* proteger, amparar. **to s. a person,** proteger a una persona. **to s. one's eyes from the sun,** proteger los ojos del sol. **s.-bearer,** escudero, *m*
shift *vt* mover; trasladar; quitar, librarse de; cambiar. *vi* moverse; (of the wind) girar; cambiar. *n* cambio, *m*; (expedient) recurso, expediente, *m*; (dodge) artificio, *m*, trampa, *f*; (of workmen) tanda, *f*, turno, *m*. **to make s.,** arreglárselas (para hacer algo); procurar (hacer algo); (manage) ir tirando. **to s. for oneself,** componérselas, arreglárselas. **to s. the scenes,** *theat* cambiar de decoración. **to s. the helm,** *naut* cambiar el timón. **to work in shifts,** trabajar por turnos
shiftiness *n* falta de honradez, informalidad, *f*; astucia, *f*
shifting *a* (of light, etc.) cambiante; (of sand, etc.) movedizo; (of wind) mudable; (of moods) voluble. **s. sand,** arena movediza, *f*
shiftless *a* perezoso; sin energía, ineficaz
shiftlessness *n* pereza, *f*; falta de energía, *f*
shifty *a* (tricky) tramposo, astuto; (dishonest) informal, falso; (of gaze) furtivo. **s.-eyed,** *a* de mirada furtiva
Shiite *a* and *n* chiita
shilling *n* chelín, *m*. **nine shillings in the £,** nueve chelines por libra. **to cut off with a s.,** desheredar
shilly shally *n* irresolución, vacilación, *f*, *vi* estar irresoluto, titubear, no saber qué hacer
shimmer *vi* rielar; relucir. *n* luz trémula, *f*; resplandor, *m*; viso, *m*
shin *n* espinilla, *f*; (of beef) corvejón, *m*. **to s. up,** trepar
shindy *n* suiza, reyerta, tasquera, *f*. **to kick up a s.,** armar camorra
shine *vi* brillar; resplandecer, relucir, relumbrar. *vt* (shoes) dar lustre (a). *n* brillo, *m*; lustre, *m*; (shoeshine) *Mexico* bola, *f*. **in rain or s.,** en buen o mal tiempo. **to s. with happiness,** radiar felicidad. **to take the s. out of,** eclipsar
shingle *n* (pebbles) guijarros, *m pl*; cascajo, *m*; *carp* barda, *f*; (hair) pelo a la garçonne, *m*; *pl* **shingles,** *med* zona, *f*, herpe zóster, *m*. *vt* (the hair) cortar a la garçonne
shining *a* resplandeciente, brillante, reluciente; radiante. **s. with happiness,** radiante de felicidad. **s. example,** ejemplo notable, *m*
shintoism *n* sintoísmo, *m*
shiny *a* brillante; lustroso, terso; (of trousers, etc.) reluciente; (of paper) glaseado
ship *n* buque, barco, *m*; (sailing) velero, *m*. *vt* embarcar; (oars) armar. *vi* embarcar; (as a member of crew) embarcarse. **on board s.,** a bordo. **to s. a sea,** embarcar agua. **to take s.,** embarcar. **to s. off,** mandar. **ship's boat,** lancha, *f*. **ship's boy,** grumete, *m*. **ship's carpenter,** carpintero de ribera, *m*. **ship's company,** tripulación, *f*. **s.-breaker,** desguazador, *m*. **s.-canal,** canal de navegación, *m*. **s.-load,** cargamento, *m*
shipbuilder *n* constructor de buques, arquitecto naval, *m*
shipbuilding *n* construcción naval, *f*
shipment *n* embarque, *m*; despacho por mar, *m*; (consignment) remesa, *f*
shipowner *n* naviero, *m*
shipper *n* naviero, *m*; importador, *m*; exportador, *m*
shipping *n* embarque, *m*; buques, barcos, *m pl*; (of a country) marina, *f*. **s. agent,** consignatario de buques, *m*. **s. company,** compañía de navegación, *f*. **s. offices,** oficinas de una compañía de navegación, *f pl*
shipshape *a* en buen orden; bien arreglado
shipwreck *n* naufragio, *m*, *vt* hacer naufragar, echar a pique
shipwrecked person *n* náufrago (-ga). **to be shipwrecked,** naufragar
shipyard *n* astillero, varadero, *m*
shire *n* condado, *m*
shirk *vt* eludir, esquivar; desentenderse de. *vi* faltar al deber
shirker *n* gandul (-la); persona que no cumple con su deber, *f*
shirr *vt* fruncir
shirt *n* camisa, *f*. **dress s.,** camisa de pechera dura, *f*. **hair-s.,** cilicio, *m*. **in one's s.-sleeves,** en mangas de camisa. **s.-blouse,** blusa sencilla, *f*. **s.-collar,** cuello de camisa, *m*. **s. factory** or **shop,** camisería, *f*. **shirt-front,** pechera, *f*. **s.-maker,** camisero (-ra)
shirting *n* tela para camisas, *f*
shiver *vi* temblar, tiritar; dar diente con diente; (of a boat) zozobrar. *vt* (break) hacer añicos, romper; (sails) sacudir. *n* temblor, estremecimiento, *m*; escalofrío, *m*; (of glass, etc.) fragmento, *m*, astilla, *f*. **You give me the shivers,** Me das escalofríos

shivery *a* tembloroso; friolero. **I feel s.,** Tengo escalofríos
shoal *n* (of fish) banco, *m;* gran cantidad, *f;* (of people) multitud, muchedumbre, *f;* (water) bajo fondo, *m;* (sand-bank) banco, bajío, *m, a* poco profundo. **I know shoals of people in Valencia,** Conozco a muchísima gente de Valencia
shock *n* choque, *m; elec* conmoción, *f; med* shock, *m;* (*med* stroke) conmoción cerebral, *f;* (fright) sobresalto, susto, *m. vt* sacudir, dar una sacudida (a); chocar; escandalizar, horrorizar. *vi* chocar. **electric s.,** conmoción eléctrica, *f.* **She is easily shocked,** Ella se escandaliza fácilmente. **s. of hair,** mata de pelo, *f.* **s. absorber,** *mech* amortiguador, *m; aut* amortiguador (de los muelles), *m.* **s. troops,** tropas de asalto, *f pl,* elementos de choque, *m pl*
shocking *a* escandaloso; repugnante, horrible; espantoso. **How s.!** ¡Qué horror! **s. bad,** malísimo
shockingly *adv* horriblemente
shod *a* calzado; (of horses) herrado
shoddy *n* pacotilla, *f. a* de pacotilla; espurio, falso
shoe *n* zapato, *m;* (horse) herradura, *f;* (*naut mech*) zapata, *f. vt* (horses) herrar. **I should not like to be in his shoes,** No me gustaría estar en su pellejo. **That is quite another pair of shoes,** Eso es harina de otro costal. **to cast a s.,** (of horses) desherrarse, perder una herradura. **to put on one's shoes,** ponerse los zapatos, calzarse. **to remove one's shoes,** quitarse los zapatos, descalzarse. **wooden shoes,** zuecos, *m pl.* **s.-buckle,** hebilla de zapato, *f.* **s.-lace,** cordón de zapato, *m.* **s.-leather,** cuero para zapatos, *m;* calzado, *m.* **s.-scraper,** limpiabarros, *m,* estregadera, *f.* **s.-shop,** zapatería, *f*
shoeblack *n* betún, *m;* (person) limpiabotas, *m*
shoehorn *n* calzador, *m*
shoemaker *n* zapatero (-ra)
shoemaking *n* fabricación de calzado, zapatería, *f*
shoeshine *n Mexico* bola, *f*
shoo! *interj* ¡fuera!; ¡zape! *vt* ahuyentar
shoot *vt* (throw) lanzar; precipitar; (empty) vaciar; (a rapid) salvar; (rays, etc.) echar; (an arrow, a gun, etc.) disparar; (a person, etc.) pegar un tiro (a); *sport* tirar; *mil* fusilar, pasar por las armas, *Lat. Am.* afusilar; (a film) hacer, impresionar. *vi* lanzarse, precipitarse; (of pain) latir; (sprout) brotar; disparar; tirar; (at football) tirar a gol, chutar. **to s. a glance at,** lanzar una mirada (a). **I was shot in the foot,** Una bala me hirió en el pie. **to s. the sun,** *naut* tomar el sol. **to s. ahead,** tomar la delantera. **to s. at,** tirar a, *Lat. Am.* abalear. **to s. at** *Central America, Mexico* balacear. **to s. by,** pasar como una bala. **to s. down,** *aer* derribar; matar de un tiro. **to s. up,** (of children) espigarse; (of prices) subir mucho; (of cliffs, etc.) elevarse
shoot *n* partida de caza, *f;* tiro, *m; bot* renuevo, retoño, *m*
shooting *n* tiro, *m;* caza con escopeta, *f;* (of guns) tiroteo, *m;* (of an arrow) disparo, *m;* (of a film) rodaje, *m.* **to go s.,** ir a cazar con escopeta. **s.-box,** pabellón de caza, *m.* **s. butts,** tiradero, *m.* **s. dog,** perro de caza, *m.* **s.-gallery,** tiro al blanco, *m.* **s. match,** concurso de tiro, *m.* **s. pain,** punzada de dolor, *f.* **s. party,** partida de caza, *f.* **s. practice,** ejercicios de tiro, *m pl.* **s.-range,** campo de tiro, *m.* **s. star,** estrella fugaz, *f*
shop *n* tienda, *f;* (workshop) taller, *m. vi* ir de compras, ir de tiendas; comprar. **to talk s.,** hablar de negocios. **s.-assistant,** dependiente (-ta). **s.-soiled,** deslucido. **s.-steward,** representante de los obreros de una fábrica o taller, *m.* **s. window,** escaparate, *Mexico* aparador, *m*
shopkeeper *n* tendero (-ra), *Chile* despachero (-ra)
shoplifter *n* ladrón (-ona) de tiendas, ratero (-ra) de las tiendas
shoplifting *n* ratería en las tiendas, *f*
shopper *n* comprador (-ra)
shopping *n* compra, *f;* compras, *f pl.* **to go s.,** ir de compras. **s. basket,** cesta para compras, *f.* **s. center,** centro comercial, *m*
shopwalker *n* jefe de recepción, *m*
shore *n* orilla, ribera, *f;* costa, *f;* (sands) playa, *f.* **off s.,** en alta mar. **on s.,** en tierra. **to come on s.,** desembarcar. **to s. up,** apuntalar, acodalar; *fig* apoyar
short *a* corto; (of persons) bajo; breve; (of temper) vivo; insuficiente; distante (de); (brusque) seco; (of money) alcanzado. *adv* súbitamente; brevemente. *n* (vowel) vocal breve, *m; pl* **shorts,** calzones cortos, *m pl.* **for s.,** para mayor brevedad. **for a s. time,** por poco tiempo. **in a s. time,** dentro de poco. **in s.,** en breve, en resumen, en pocas palabras. **on s. notice,** con poco tiempo de aviso. **s. of,** con la excepción de, menos. **to be s.,** faltar, ser escaso. **to be s. with someone,** tratar con sequedad (a). **to fall s. of expectations,** no cumplir las esperanzas. **to go s. of,** pasarse sin. **to grow s.,** escasear. **s.-circuit,** corto circuito, *m.* **s. cut,** atajo, *Lat. Am.* desecho, *m.* **s.-haired,** pelicorto. **s.-handed,** falto de mano de obra. **s.-lived,** de vida corta; efímero, fugaz. **to be short-lived,** tener vida corta. **s.-sighted,** corto de vista. **s.-sightedness,** miopía, cortedad de vista, *f.* **s. story,** cuento, *m.* **s.-tempered,** irascible, irritable, de genio vivo. **s.-waisted,** corto de talle. **s.-winded,** corto de resuello; asmático
shortage *n* falta, escasez, *f;* carestía, *f.* **water s.,** carestía de agua, *f*
shortcoming *n* defecto, *m;* imperfección, *f*
shorten *vt* acortar; reducir, disminuir; abreviar. *vi* acortarse
shorthand *n* taquigrafía, estenografía, *f. a* taquigráfico, estenográfico
shortly *adv* dentro de poco, pronto; brevemente, en resumen, en pocas palabras; (curtly) bruscamente, secamente
shortness *n* cortedad, *f;* brevedad, *f;* (of a person) pequeñez, *f;* (lack) falta, *f;* (of memory, sight) cortedad, *f;* brusqueness) sequedad, brusquedad, *f.* **s. of breath,** falta de aliento, respiración difícil, *f*
shot *n* perdigón, *m; inf* perdigones, *m pl;* bala, *f;* (firing) tiro, *m;* (person) tirador (-ra); (stroke, etc.) golpe, *m,* tirada, *f;* (cinema) fotograma, *m. a* (of silk) tornasolado. **at one s.,** de un tiro. **like a s.,** *fig* como una bala. **to exchange shots,** tirotearse. **to fire a s.,** disparar un tiro. **to have a s. at,** probar suerte. **s.-gun,** escopeta, *f.* **s. silk,** seda tornasolada, *f*
should *v aux* (expressing future) **I s. like to go to the sea,** Me gustaría ir al mar; (expressing conditional) **I s. like to see them if I could,** Me gustaría verlos si pudiera; (expressing obligation) **You s. go at once,** Debes ir en seguida; (expressing probability) **They s. arrive tomorrow,** Seguramente llegarán mañana; (expressing doubt) **If the moment s. be opportune,** Si el momento fuera oportuno. **I s. just think so!** ¡Ya lo creo! ¡No lo dudo!
shoulder *n* hombro, *m;* (of mutton) espalda, *f;* (of a hill) falda, *f. vt* echar al hombro, echar sobre sí; (a responsibility) cargar con, hacerse responsable para; (jostle) dar codazos (a). **s. to s.,** hombro a hombro. **S. arms!** ¡Armas al hombro! **s.-blade,** omoplato, *m.* **s.-knot,** charretera, *f.* **s.-pad,** hombrera, *f.* **s.-strap,** *mil* dragona, *f;* (of a dress, etc.) tirante, *m;* (of a water carrier, etc.) correón, *m*
shouldered *a* de hombros . . . , de espaldas . . . **round-s.,** cargado de espaldas
shout *vi* gritar, hablar a gritos. *vt* gritar. *n* grito, *m.* **shouts of applause,** aclamaciones, *f pl,* aplausos, *m pl.* **to s. from the housetops,** pregonar a los cuatro vientos. **to s. with laughter,** reírse a carcajadas. **to s. down,** silbar. **to s. out,** gritar
shouting *n* gritos, *m pl,* vocerío, clamor, *m;* (applause) aclamaciones, *f pl*
shove *vt* empujar; poner. *n* empujón, *m.* **to s. along,** empujar. **to s. aside,** empujar a un lado; apartar a codazos. **to s. away,** rechazar. **to s. back,** hacer retroceder. **to s. forward,** hacer avanzar, empujar hacia

adelante. **to s. off,** (a boat) echar afuera. **to s. out,** empujar hacia fuera

shovel *n* pala, *f. vt* traspalar. **s. hat,** sombrero de teja, *m*

show *vt* mostrar; hacer ver; (disclose) descubrir; revelar; (exhibit) exhibir; (indicate) indicar; (prove) demostrar, probar; (conduct) conducir, llevar, guiar; (explain) explicar; (oneself) presentarse. *vi* mostrarse; verse; parecer. **to s. cause,** mostrar causa. **to s. fight,** ofrecer resistencia. **s. signs of,** dar señales de. **to s. itself,** declararse, asomarse, surgir. **to s. to the door,** acompañar a la puerta. **to s. in,** (a person) hacer entrar, introducir (en). **to s. off,** *vt* exhibir; realzar; (new clothes, etc.) lucir. *vi* darse importancia; pavonearse. **to s. out,** (a person) acompañar a la puerta; (in anger) poner de patitas en la calle. **to s. through,** *vi* trasparentarse. *vt* conducir por. **to s. up,** *vt* invitar a subir; (a fraud, etc.) descubrir; (a swindler) desenmascarar; (defects) revelar. *vi* (stand out) destacarse; (be present) asomarse, asistir

show *n* (exhibition) exposición, *f*; espectáculo, *m*; (sign) indicio, *m*, señal, *f*; (ostentation) pompa, *f*, aparato, *m*, ostentación, *f*; (appearance) apariencia, *f*; (affair) negocio, *m*. **to give the s. away,** echar los títeres a rodar. **to make a s. of,** hacer gala de. **s.-case,** escaparate, *m*, vitrina, *f*. **s. of hands,** votación por manos levantadas, *f*. **s.-room,** salón de muestras, *m*

showdown *n* cartas boca arriba, *m*

shower *n* chaparrón, chubasco, *m*; (of spray, etc.) chorro, *m*; (of stones, arrows, etc.) lluvia, *f*; (of honors) cosecha, *f*, (bridal) despedida de soltera, despedida de soltería, *f*. *vt* derramar; rociar; mojar; llover. *vi* chaparrear, llover. **shower (bath)** ducha, *f*, *Argentina* baño de China, *f*

shower cap *n* gorro de ducha, *m*

showery *a* lluvioso

showily *adv* aparatosamente, con ostentación

showiness *n* ostentación, *f*; esplendor, *m*, magnificencia, *f*

showman *n* director de un espectáculo de feria, *m*; titiritero, *m*; pregonero, *m*

showy *a* vistoso; ostentoso, *Lat. Am. also* figuroso

shrapnel *n* granada, *m*, granada de metralla, *f*

shred *n* fragmento, *m*; (of cloth) jirón, *m*; brizna, *f*; *fig* pizca, *f*. *vt* desmenuzar. **to tear in shreds,** hacer pedazos

shrew *n zool* musaraña, *f*; (woman) fiera, *f*

shrewd *a* sagaz, perspicaz; prudente; (of the wind) penetrante; (pain) punzante. **to have a s. idea of,** tener una buena idea de. **a s. diplomat,** un fino diplomático

shrewdly *adv* sagazmente, con perspicacia; prudentemente

shrewdness *n* sagacidad, perspicacia, *f*; prudencia, *f*

shrewish *a* regañón

shrewishness *n* mal genio, *m*

shriek *vi* chillar, gritar. *vt* decir a voces, gritar. *n* chillido, *m*; grito agudo, *m*. **shrieks of laughter,** carcajadas, *f pl*

shrieking *n* gritos, chillidos, *m pl*

shrift to give short, enviar normala (a), enviar a paseo (a)

shrill *a* estridente, agudo

shrillness *n* estridencia, *f*

shrimp *n* camarón, *m*, gamba, *f*, *vi* pescar camarones

shrine *n* relicario, *m*; sepulcro de santo, *m*; templete, *m*, capilla, *f*; santuario, *m*

shrink *vi* encogerse; contraerse; disminuir, reducirse. *vt* encoger; reducir, disminuir; desaparecer; disiparse. **I shrank from doing it,** Me repugnaba hacerlo. **to s. away from,** retroceder ante; recular ante; huir de. **to s. back,** recular (ante)

shrinkage *n* encogimiento, *m*; contracción, *f*; reducción, disminución, *f*

shrinking *a* tímido

shrive *vt* confesar

shrivel *vi* avellanarse; (of persons, through old age) acartonarse, apergaminarse; (wither) marchitarse; arrugarse. *vt* arrugar; secar, marchitar

shroud *n* sudario, *m*, mortaja, *f*; *naut* obenque, *m*. **to wrap in a s.,** amortajar

Shrove Tuesday *n* martes de carnaval, *m*

shrub *n* arbusto, *m*; matajo, *m*

shrubbery *n* arbustos, *m pl*, maleza, *f*; bosquecillo, *m*

shrug *vi* encogerse de hombros. *n* encogimiento de hombros, *m*

shrunken *a* contraído; acartonado, apergaminado; seco, marchito. **shrunken head,** cabeza reducida, *f*

shudder *vi* estremecerse; vibrar. *n* estremecimiento, *m*; escalofrío, *m*; (of an engine, etc.) vibración, *f*

shuffle *vt* (the feet) arrastrar; (scrape) restregar; (cards) barajar; (papers) mezclar. *vi* arrastrar los pies, arrastrarse; (cards) barajar; *fig* tergiversar. *n* (of the cards) barajadura, *f*; *fig* evasiva, *f*; embuste, *m*. **to s. along,** andar arrastrando los pies

shuffling *n* el arrastrar, *m*, (e.g. **the shuffling of chairs,** el arrastrar de sillas)

shun *vt* evitar, rehuir, esquivar

shunt *vt rw* apartar; *elec* shuntar. *vi rw* hacer maniobras

shunting *n* (of trains) maniobras, *f pl*

shut *vt* and *vi* cerrar. **to s. again,** volver a cerrar. **to s. down,** *vt* cerrar; (a machine) parar. *vi* (of factories, etc.) cerrar. **to s. in,** encerrar; (surround) cercar, rodear. **to s. off,** (water, etc.) cortar; (isolate) aislar (de). **to s. out,** excluir; obstruir, impedir; negar la entrada (a). **to s. up,** *vt* cerrar; encerrar; *inf* hacer callar (a); *vi inf* callarse, cerrar la boca. **to s. oneself up,** encerrarse

shutter *n* (window) contraventana, *f*, postigo, *m*; (of a camera) obturador, *m*; (of a fireplace) campana (de hogar), *f*. *vt* poner contraventanas (a); cerrar los postigos de

shuttle *n* (weaver's, and sewing-machine) lanzadera, *f*, (airplane service) puente aéreo, *m*. **s.-cock,** volante, gallito, *m*

shy *a* (of animals) tímido, salvaje; (of persons) huraño, tímido; vergonzoso. *vi* (of a horse) respingar; (of persons) asustarse (de). *vt* (a ball, etc.) lanzar. *n* (of a horse) respingo, *m*; (of a ball) lanzamiento, *m*; (try) prueba, tentativa, *f*. **to fight shy of,** procurar evitar. **to have a shy at,** probar

shyly *adv* tímidamente; con vergüenza, vergonzosamente

shyness *n* timidez, *f*; hurañía, *f*; vergüenza, *f*

Siamese *a* siamés. *n* siamés (-esa); (language) siamés, *m*. **S. cat,** gato siamés, *m*

sic *vt* atacar; abijar, azuzar (a dog); *adv* así (in academic prose)

Sicilian *a* and *n* siciliano (-na)

Sicily Sicilia, *f*

sick *a* enfermo; mareado. **the s.,** los enfermos. **to be s.,** vomitar; estar enfermo. **to be s. of,** estar harto de. **to feel s.,** sentirse mareado. **to be on the s.-list,** estar enfermo. **s.-bed,** lecho de dolor, *m*. **s.-headache,** jaqueca, con náuseas, *f*. **s.-leave,** *mil* permiso por enfermedad, *m*. **s.-nurse,** enfermera, *f*

sicken *vi* caer enfermo, enfermar; (feel sick) marearse; (recoil from) repugnar; (weary of) cansarse (de), aburrirse (de). *vt* marear; dar asco (a), repugnar; cansar, aburrir. **It sickens me,** Me da asco. **He is sickening for measles,** Muestra síntomas de sarampión

sickening *a* nauseabundo; repugnante; (tedious) fastidioso

sickle *n* hoz, segadera, *f*

sickliness *n* falta de salud, *f*; náusea, *f*; (paleness) palidez, *f*

sickly *a* enfermizo, achacoso, malucho, *Lat. Am.* farruto, *Central America, Mexico* fifiriche; (of places, etc.) malsano; (pale) pálido; débil; (of a smell) nauseabundo; (mawkish) empalagoso

sickness *n* enfermedad, *f*; mal, *m*; náusea, *f*, mareo, *m*

side *n* lado, *m*; (hand) mano, *f*; (of a river, etc.) orilla, *f*, margen, *m*; (of a person) costado, *m*; (of an animal) ijada, *f*; (of a hill) falda, pendiente, ladera, *f*; (of a ship) banda, *f*, costado, *m*; (aspect) aspecto, *m*; punto de vista, *m*; (party) partido, grupo, *m*; (team) equipo, *m*; (of descent) lado, *m*. *a* lateral, de lado; oblicuo. **on all sides,** por todas partes. **on both sides,** por ambos lados. **s. by s.,** lado a lado. **the other s. of the picture,** el revés de la medalla. **to change sides,** cambiar de partido. **to pick sides,** escoger el equipo. **to put on s.,** darse tono, alzar el gallo. **to split one's sides,** desternillarse de risa, reírse a carcajadas. **to s. with,** declararse por, ponerse al lado de, tomar el partido de. **wrong s. out,** al revés. **s.-car,** sidecar, asiento lateral, *m*. **s.-chain,** *chem* cadena lateral, *f*. **s.-dish,** entremés, *m*. **s. door,** puerta lateral, *f*. **s.-face,** *a* de perfil. *n* perfil, *m*. **s.-glance,** mirada de soslayo, *f*. **s.-issue,** cuestión secundaria, *f*. **s.-line,** negocio accesorio, *m*; ocupación secundaria, *f*; *rw* vía secundaria, *f*. **s.-saddle,** silla de señora, silla de montar de lado, *f*. **s.-show,** (at a fair) barraca, *f*, puesto de feria, *m*; exhibición secundaria, *f*; función secundaria, *f*. **s.-table,** trinchero, *m*. **s.-track,** *n rw* apartadero, *m*. *vt* desviar (de), apartar (de). **s.-view,** perfil, *m*. **s.-walk,** acera, *f Mexico* banqueta *f*, *elsewhere in Lat. Am.* andén *m*, vereda *f*. **s.-whiskers,** patillas, *f pl*

sidelight *n* luz lateral, *f*; (on a ship) ojo de buey, *m*; *fig* información incidental, *f*

sidelong *adv* de lado, lateralmente; (of glances) de soslayo. *a* oblicuo

side road *n* camino lateral, *m*

sideways *adv* oblicuamente, de lado; (edgewise) de soslayo. *a* de soslayo

siding *n rw* apartadero, *m*

sidle *vi* andar (or ir) de lado. **to s. up to,** acercarse servilmente a; arrimarse (a)

siege *n* asedio, sitio, cerco, *m*. **to lay s. to,** poner cerco (a), sitiar, asediar cercar. **to raise a s.,** levantar un sitio

sienna *n* tierra de siena natural, *f*. **burnt s.,** tierra de siena tostada, *f*

sieve *n* cedazo, tamiz, *m*, criba, *f*, *Lat. Am.* arnero, *m*, *vt* tamizar, cerner, cribar

sift *vt* (sieve) cerner, cribar; (sugar, etc.) salpicar (con); (a question) escudriñar, examinar minuciosamente

sifting *n* cribado, *m*; (of a question) investigación minuciosa, *f*; *pl* **siftings,** cerniduras, *f pl*

sigh *vi* suspirar; (of the wind) susurrar. *n* suspiro, *m*; (of the wind) susurro, *m*. **to s. for,** suspirar por; lamentar

sighing *n* suspiros, *m pl*; (of the wind) susurro, *m*

sight *n* vista, *f*; visión, *f*; espectáculo, *m*; (fright) estantigua, *f*. *vt* ver, divisar; (aim) apuntar. **front s.,** (of guns) alza, *f*. **short s.,** (of eyes) vista corta, *f*. **at first s.,** a primera vista. **in s.,** a la vista. **in s. of,** a vista de. **out of s.,** que no está a la vista; perdido de vista. **Out of s., out of mind,** Ojos que no ven, corazón que no siente. **to be lost to s.,** perderse de vista. **to lose s. of,** perder de vista (a). **to catch a s. of,** vislumbrar. **to come in s.,** aparecer, asomarse. **to know by s.,** conocer de vista (a). **s.-reading,** lectura a primera vista, *f*

sightly *a* hermoso; deleitable

sightseeing *n* turismo, *m*. **to go s.**, visitar los monumentos, ver los puntos de interés

sightseer *n* curioso (-sa); turista, *mf*

sign *n* señal, *f*; seña, *f*; indicio, *m*; (of the zodiac and *mus*) signo, *m*; marca, *f*; *ecc* símbolo, *m*; (of a shop, etc.) muestra, *f*, rótulo, *m*; (symptom) síntoma, *m*. *vt* firmar; indicar; *ecc* persignar. **as a s. of,** en señal de. **to converse by signs,** hablar por señas. **to make the s. of the cross over,** santiguar. **to show signs (of),** dar señas (de); indicar. **s.-painter,** pintor de muestras, *m*

signal *n* señal, *f*. *vt* señalar; hacer señas (a). *vi* hacer señales. *a* insigne, notable. **fog-s.,** señal de niebla, *f*. **landing s.,** *aer* señal de aterrizaje, *f*. **to give the s. for,** dar la señal para. **s.-box,** garita de señales, *f*. **s. code,** *naut* código de señales, *m*

signalize *vt* señalar, distinguir

signaler *n* señalador, *m*

signalman *n rw* guardavía, *m*

signatory *a* and *n* signatario (-ia)

signature *n* firma, *f*; (*mus* and *print*) signatura, *f*

signboard *n* letrero, *m*, muestra, *f*

signet *n* sello, *m*. **s.-ring,** anillo de sello, *m*

significance *n* significación, *f*, significado, *m*; importancia, *f*

significant *a* significativo, significante; expresivo; importante

significantly *adv* significativamente; expresivamente

signify *vt* significar; querer decir; importar. *vi* significar, tener importancia; importar

signpost *n* indicador de dirección, *m*

silage *n* forraje conservado en silo, *m*

silence *n* silencio, *m*, *interj* ¡silencio! *vt* hacer callar, imponer silencio (a); silenciar. **to keep s.,** guardar silencio, callarse. **to pass over in s.,** pasar en silencio (por), pasar por alto de. **S. gives consent,** Quien calla otorga

silencer *n* (of fire-arms) silencioso, *m*; *aut* silenciador, silencioso, *m*

silent *a* silencioso. **to become s.,** enmudecer; callar. **to remain s.,** callarse, guardar silencio; permanecer silencioso. **s. partner,** *n* socio (-ia) comanditario (-ia)

silent film, silent movie *n* película muda, *f*

silently *adv* silenciosamente, en silencio

silhouette *n* silueta, *f*. *vt* representar en silueta; destacar. **in s.,** en silueta. **to be silhouetted against the sky,** destacarse contra el sielo

silica *n* sílice, *f*

silk *n* seda, *f*, *a* de seda. **artificial s.,** seda artificial, *f*. **floss s.,** seda ocal, *f*. **sewing s.,** seda de coser, *f*. **twist s.,** seda cordelada, *f*. **as smooth as s.,** como una seda. **s. growing,** sericultura, *f*. **s. hat,** sombrero de copa, *m*. **s. merchandise,** sedería, *f*. **s. stocking,** media de seda, *f*

silken *a* de seda; sedoso

silkiness *n* carácter sedoso, *m*; suavidad, *f*

silk-screen process *n* imprenta por tamiz, imprenta serigráfica, imprenta tamigráfica, impresión con estarcido de seda, *f*, proceso tamigráfico, *m*, serigrafía, tamigrafía, *f*

silkworm *n* gusano de seda, *m*

silky *a* sedoso; (of wine) suave

sill *n* (of a window) alféizar, antepecho, *m*; (of a door) umbral, *m*

silliness *n* tontería, estupidez, *f*

silly *a* tonto, estúpido; imbécil, *Central America also* azurumbado. *n* tonto (-ta). **You are a s. ass,** Eres un imbécil

silo *n* silo, *m*

silt *n* aluvión, *m*, sedimentación, *f*. **to s. up,** *vt* cegar (or obstruir) con aluvión. *vi* cegarse con aluvión

silver *n* plata, *f*. *a* de plata; argénteo; (of the voice, etc.) argentino. *vt* platear; (mirrors) azogar; (hair) blanquear. **s. birch,** abedul, *m*. **s. fox,** zorro plateado, *m*. **s.-gry,** gris perla, *m*. **s.-haired,** de pelo entrecano. **s.-paper,** papel de estaño, *m*. **s.-plate,** *n* vajilla de plata, *f*. *vt* platear. **s.-tongued,** de pico de oro; de voz argentina. **s. wedding,** bodas de plata, *f pl*

silversmith *n* platero, *m*. **silversmith's shop,** platería, *f*

silvery *a* plateado, argentado; (of sounds) argentino

simian *a* símico

similar *a* parecido (a), semejante (a); similar; *geom* semejante. **to be s. to,** asemejarse (a), parecerse (a)

similarity *n* parecido, *m*, semejanza, similitud, *f*

similarly *adv* de un modo parecido, asimismo

simile *n* símil, *m*

simmer *vi* hervir a fuego lento; *fig* estar a punto de estallar. **to s. down,** *fig* moderarse poco a poco. **to s. over,** *fig* estallar

simper *vi* sonreírse bobamente

simpering *n* sonrisilla tonta, *f*

simperingly *adv* con sonrisa necia

simple *a* sencillo; simple; ingenuo, inocente; crédulo; (humble) humilde; (mere) mero. **s.-hearted,** ino-

cente, cándido, sin malicia. **s.-minded,** ingenuo; crédulo. **s.-mindedness,** ingenuidad, *f*; credulidad, *f*
simpleton *n* primo (-ma); papanatas, *m*, tonto (-ta)
simplicity *n* sencillez, *f*; simplicidad, candidez, *f*
simplifiable *a* simplificable
simplification *n* simplificación, *f*
simplify *vt* simplificar
simply *adv* sencillamente; simplemente, meramente; absolutamente
simulacrum *n* simulacro, *m*
simulate *vt* fingir, aparentar, simular
simulation *n* simulación, *f*, fingimiento, *m*
simultaneous *a* simultáneo
simultaneously *adv* simultáneamente; al mismo tiempo (que)
simultaneousness *n* simultaneidad, *f*
sin *n* pecado, *m*, *vi* pecar; faltar (a)
since *adv* desde entonces, desde (que). *prep* desde. *conjunc* desde que; ya que, puesto que. **a long time s.,** hace mucho. **not long s.,** hace poco. **How long is it s. . . . ?** ¿Cuánto tiempo hace que . . . ? **s. then,** desde entonces
sincere *a* sincero
sincerely *adv* sinceramente. **Yours s.,** Su afectísimo . . .
sincerity *n* sinceridad, *f*
sine *n math* seno, *m*
sinecure *n* canonjía, sinecura, *f*, empleo de aviador (Mexican slang), *m*
sinew *n* tendón, *m*; *pl* **sinews,** nervio, *m*, fuerza, *f*
sinewy *a* (stringy) fibroso; musculoso, nervudo
sinful *a* (of persons) pecador; (of thoughts, acts) pecaminoso
sinfulness *n* pecado, *m*; culpabilidad, perversidad, maldad, *f*
sing *vi* cantar; (of the ears) zumbar; (of wind, water) murmurar, susurrar; (of a cat) ronronear. *vt* cantar. **to s. a child to sleep,** dormir a un niño cantando. **to s. another song,** *inf* bajar el tono. **to s. small,** hacerse el chiquito. **to s. the praises of,** hacer las alabanzas de. **to s. out,** vocear, gritar. **s.-song,** *n* canturía, *f*; concierto improvisado, *m*. *a* monótono
Singapore Singapur, *m*
singe *vt* chamuscar; (a fowl) aperdigar; (hair) quemar las puntas de los cabellos
singer *n* cantor (-ra); (professional) cantante, *mf*; (bird) ave cantora, *f*
singing *n* canto, *m*; (of the ears) zumbido, *m*. *a* cantante. **s.-bird,** ave cantora, *f*. **s.-master,** maestro de cantar, *m*
single *a* único; sencillo; solo; simple; (individual) particular; individual; (unmarried) soltero. *n* (tennis) juego sencillo, individual, *m*. **in s. file,** de reata. **to s. out,** escoger; singularizar. **s. bed,** cama de monja, *f*. **s. bedroom,** habitación individual, habitación con una sola cama, *f*. **s.-breasted,** (of coats) recto. **s. combat,** combate singular, *m*. **s. entry,** *com* partida simple, *f*. **s.-handed,** de una mano; para una sola persona; sin ayuda, solo, en solitario. **s.-minded,** sin doblez, sincero de una sola idea. **s. ticket,** billete sencillo, *m*
singleness *n* celibato, *m*, soltería, *f*. **with s. of purpose,** con un solo objeto
single room *Mexico* cuarto sencillo, *m*
singlet *n* camiseta, *f*
singly *adv* separadamente, uno a uno; a solas, solo; sin ayuda
singular *a* and *n* singular, *m*
singularity *n* singularidad, *f*
singularly *adv* singularmente
sinister *a* siniestro
sink *vi* ir al fondo; bajar; hundirse; (of ships) irse a pique, naufragar; sumergirse; disminuir; caer (en); penetrar; (of persons, fires) morir; (of the sun, etc.) ponerse. *vt* (a ship) echar a pique; sumergir; hundir; dejar caer; bajar; (wells) cavar; reducir, disminuir; (invest) invertir; (one's identity, etc.) tener secreto; (differences) olvidar; (engrave) grabar. **My heart sank,** Se me cayeron las alas del corazón. **He sank to his knees,** Cayó de rodillas. **He is sinking fast,** Está en las últimas. **Their words began to s. in,** Sus palabras empezaban a tener efecto (or hacer mella). **I found her sunk in thought,** La encontré ensimismada. **to s. one's voice,** bajar la voz. **to s. down on a chair,** dejarse caer en una silla. **to s. into misery,** caer en la miseria. **to s. under,** (a responsibility, etc.) estar agobiado bajo
sink *n* (kitchen) fregadero, *Chile, Mexico also* lavaplatos, *m*; sumidero, *m*, sentina, *f*. **s. of iniquity,** sentina, *f*
sinker *n* (engraver) grabador (-ra); (of a fishing line) plomada, *f*
sinking *n* hundimiento, *m*; (of the sun) puesta, *f*; (of wells) cavadura, *f*; sumergimiento, *m*. **the s. of a boat,** el hundimiento de un buque. **with s. heart,** con la muerte en el alma. **s. fund,** fondo de amortización, *m*
sinless *a* sin pecado, inocente, puro
sinner *n* pecador (-ra)
sinuous *a* sinuoso, tortuoso; flexible, ágil
sinus *n* (*anat* etc.) seno, *m*
sip *vt* sorber; (wine) saborear, paladear. *n* sorbo, *m*
siphon *n* sifón, *m*, *vt* sacar con sifón
sir *n* señor, *m*; (British title) sir. **Dear s.,** Muy Señor mío
sire *n* (to a monarch) Señor, *m*; (father) padre, *m*; (stallion) semental, *m*. *vt* procrear, engendrar
siren *n* sirena, *f*. **s. suit,** mono, *m*
sirloin *n* solomillo, *Mexico* diezmillo, *m*
sirocco *n* siroco, *m*
sister *n* hermana, *f*; (before nun's christian name) Sor; (hospital) hermana del hospital, *f*; enfermera, *f*. **s. language,** lengua hermana, *f*. **s. ship,** buque gemelo, *m*. **s.-in-law,** cuñada, hermana política, *f*. **S. of Mercy,** Hermana de la Caridad, *f*
sisterhood *n* hermandad, *f*; comunidad de monjas, *f*
sisterly *a* de hermana
sit *vi* sentarse; estar sentado; (of birds) posarse; (of hens) empollar; (in Parliament, etc.) ser diputado; (of a committee, etc.) celebrar sesión; (on a committee, etc.) formar parte de; (function) funcionar; (of garments, food, and *fig*) sentar. **to sit a horse,** mantenerse a caballo; montar a caballo. **to sit oneself,** sentarse, tomar asiento. **to sit by,** (a person) sentarse (or estar sentado) al lado de. **to sit for** (a portrait) servir de modelo para; hacerse retratar. **to sit tight,** no moverse. **to sit down,** sentarse; (besiege) sitiar. **to sit on,** sentarse (en or sobre); (eggs) empollar; (a committee, etc.) formar parte de; (investigate) investigar; (snub) dejar aplastado (a). **to sit out,** quedarse hasta el fin (de). **to sit out a dance,** conversar un baile. **to sit up,** incorporarse en la cama; tenerse derecho; (at night) velar; (of dogs, etc.) pedir. **to sit up and take notice,** abrir los ojos. **to sit up in bed,** incorporarse en la cama. **to sit up late,** estar de pie hasta muy tarde
sit-down strike *n* huelga de brazos caídos, huelga de sentados, *f*
site *n* sitio, local, *m*; (for building) solar, *m*
sitting *n* asentada, *f*; (of Parliament, etc.) sesión, *f*; (for a portrait) estadia, *f*; (of eggs) nidada, *f*. **at a s.,** de una asentada. **s.-room,** sala de estar, *f*
situated *a* situado. **How is he s.?** ¿Cómo está situado? ¿Cuál es su situación?
situation *n* situación, *f*; (job) empleo, *m*
six *a* and *n* seis, *m*. **It is six o'clock,** Son las seis. **Everything is at sixes and sevens,** Todo está en desorden. **six-foot,** de seis pies. **six hundred,** seiscientos (-as)
sixfold *a* séxtuplo
sixteen *a* and *n* diez y seis, dieciséis, *m*. **John is s.,** Juan tiene dieciséis años
sixteenth *a* décimosexto; (of the month) (el) diez y seis; (of monarch) diez y seis. *n* dieciseisavo, *m*
sixth *a* sexto; (of the month) (el) seis; (of monarchs) sexto. *n* seisavo, *m*; sexta parte, *f*; *mus* sexta, *f*. **Henry the S.,** Enrique sexto. **May the s.,** el seis de mayo

sixtieth *a* sexagésimo. *n* sesentavo, *m*; sexagésima parte, *f*
sixty *a* and *n* sesenta *m*. **John has turned s.,** Juan ha pasado los sesenta
sizable *a* bastante grande
size *n* tamaño, *m*; dimensión, *f*; (height) altura, *f*; (measurement) medida, *f*; talle, *m*; (in gloves, etc.) número, *m*; (glue) cola, *f*. *vt* clasificar por tamaños; (glaze, etc.) encolar. **to s. up,** tomar las medidas (a).
sizzle *vi* chisporrotear, chirriar. *n* chisporroteo, chirrido, *m*
skate *n* patín, *m*; *icht* raya, *f*, *vi* patinar
skater *n* patinador (-ra)
skating *n* patinaje, *m*. **s. rink,** sala de patinar, *f*; pista de hielo, pista de patinar, *f*, patinadero, *m*
skein *n* madeja, *f*
skeleton *n* esqueleto, *m*; (of a building) armadura, *f*; (of a literary work) esquema, *m*. **s. key,** ganzúa, *f*
sketch *n* croquis, apunte, *m*; (for a literary work) esbozo, esquema, *m*; (article) cuadro, artículo, *m*; descripción, *f*; *theat* entremés, sainete, *m*. *vt* dibujar; esbozar, bosquejar; trazar; describir. **s.-book,** álbum de croquis, *m*
sketchily *adv* incompletamente
sketching *n* arte de dibujar, *mf*. **He likes s.,** Le gusta dibujar
sketchy *a* bosquejado; incompleto; escaso
skewer *n* broqueta, *f*, *vt* espetar
ski *n* esquí, *m*, *vi* esquiar
skid *n* (of a vehicle) patinazo, *m*, *vi* patinar
skidding *n* patinaje, *m*
skier *n* esquiador (-ra), *mf*
skiff *n* esquife, *m*
skiing *n* patinaje sobre la nieve, *m*, el esquiar. **to go s.,** ir a esquiar
skill *n* habilidad, *f*
skilled *a* hábil; experto
skilled worker *n* obrero calificado, *m*
skillful *a* hábil
skim *vt* espumar; (milk) desnatar, *Lat. Am.* descremar; (touch lightly) deslizarse sobre, rozar; (a book) hojear
skimp *vt* escatimar; escasear; (work) frangollar. *vi* ser parsimonioso
skimpy *a* escaso
skin *n* tez, *f*, cutis, *m*; piel, *f*; (of fruit) pellejo, *m*, piel, *f*; (for wine) odre, pellejo, *m*; (on milk) espuma, *f*. *vt* despellejar; pelar, mondar; (graze) hacerse daño (a); *inf* desollar. **next to one's s.,** sobre la piel. **to s. over,** cicatrizarse. **to have a thin s.,** *fig* ser muy susceptible. **to save one's s.,** salvar el pellejo. **s.-deep,** superficial. **s.-tight,** escurrido, muy ajustado
skinflint *n* avaro (-ra)
skinny *a* flaco, descarnado, magro
skip *vi* retozar, brincar, saltar; saltar a la comba; (bolt) largarse, escaparse. *vt* saltar; (a book) hojear; (omit) omitir; pasar por alto de. *n* brinco, pequeño salto, *m*
skipper *n* *naut* patrón, *m*; (*inf* and *sport*) capitán, *m*
skirmish *vi* escaramuzar. *n* escaramuza, *f*
skirt *n* falda, *f*; (edge) margen, borde, *m*, orilla, *f*; (of a jacket, etc.) faldón, *m*. *vt* ladear; (hug) rodear, ceñir
skit *n* sátira, *f*; parodia, *f*
skittish *a* (of a horse) retozón; (of persons) frívolo; caprichoso
skittle *n* bolo, *m*; *pl* **skittles,** juego de bolos, *m*. **s. alley,** pista de bolos, bolera, *f*
skulk *vi* estar en acecho; esconderse; rondar
skull *n* cráneo, *m*; calavera, *f*. **s.-cap,** gorro, casquete, *m*; (for ecclesiastics) solideo, *m*
skunk *n* *zool* mofeta, *f*, chingue, mapurite, yaguré, zorrillo, zorrino, zorro hediondo, *m*
sky *n* cielo, *m*. **to praise to the skies,** poner en los cuernos de la luna. **s.-blue,** *n* azul celeste, *m*. *a* de color azul celeste, cerúleo. **s.-high,** hasta las nubes, hasta el cielo. **s.-line,** horizonte, *m*. **s.-scraper,** rascacielos, *m*. **s.-sign,** anuncio luminoso, *m*
skylight *n* claraboya, *f*, tragaluz, *m*
slab *n* bloque, *m*; losa, *f*, *Lat. Am. also* laja; plancha, *f*
slack *a* lento; flojo; (lazy) perezoso; negligente, descuidado; *com* encalmado; débil. *vi* ser perezoso. **the s. season,** la estación muerta. **to be s. in one's work,** ser negligente en el trabajo. **to s. off,** disminuir sus esfuerzos; dejar de trabajar
slacken *vt* and *vi* aflojar; disminuir, reducir. **The wind slackened,** El viento amainaba, El viento aflojaba. **to s. one's efforts,** disminuir sus esfuerzos. **to s. speed,** disminuir la velocidad
slackening *n* aflojamiento, *m*; disminución, *f*
slacker *n* gandul (-la)
slackness *n* flojedad, *f*; pereza, falta de energía, *f*; negligencia, *f*; *com* desanimación, *f*
slacks *n pl* pantalones, *m pl*
slake *vt* (one's thirst and lime) apagar; satisfacer
slam *vt* cerrar de golpe; golpear. *n* (of a door) portazo, *m*; golpe, *m*; (cards) capote, *m*. **He went out and slammed the door,** Salió dando un portazo
slander *n* calumnia, *f*, *vt* calumniar
slanderer *n* calumniador (-ra)
slanderous *a* calumnioso
slang *n* argot, *m*, jerga, *f*, *vt* poner como un trapo (a), llenar de insultos
slant *vi* estar al sesgo; inclinarse; ser oblicuo. *vt* inclinar. *n* inclinación, *f*; oblicuidad, *f*. **on the s.,** inclinado; oblicuo
slanting *a* al sesgo, inclinado; oblicuo
slap *vt* pegar con la mano. *n* bofetada, *f*; palmada, *Lat. Am.* cachetada, *f*. **to s. on the back,** golpear en la espalda. **s.-dash,** (of persons) irresponsable, descuidado; (of work) chapucero, sin cuidado.
slash *vt* (gash, also sleeves, etc.) acuchillar; cortar; (with a whip) dar latigazos (a). *n* cuchillada, *f*; corte, *m*; latigazo, *m*
slashing *a* mordaz, severo
slat *n* tablilla, *f*, *vi* (of sails) dar zapatazos, zapatear
slate *n* pizarra, *f*, esquisto, *m*; (for roofs and for writing) pizarra, *f*, *vt* (a roof) empizarrar; (censure) criticar severamente, censurar. **s.-colored,** apizarrado. **s. pencil,** pizarrín, *m*. **s. quarry,** pizarrería, *f*, pizarral, *m*
slater *n* pizarrero, *m*
slating *n* empizarrado, *m*; (criticism) crítica severa, censura, *f*; (scolding) peluca, *f*
slattern *n* pazpuerca, *f*
slatternly *a* desgarbado, desaliñado
slaughter *n* matanza, *f*; carnicería, *f*. *vt* (animals) sacrificar, matar; matar, hacer una carnicería de. **s.-house,** matadero, *m*
slaughterer *n* jifero, carnicero, *m*
Slav *a* and *n* eslavo (-va)
slave *n* esclavo (-va). *vi* trabajar como un negro. **white s. traffic,** trata de blancas, *f*. **s.-bangle,** esclava, *f*. **s.-driver,** capataz de esclavos, negrero, *m*; *fig* negrero, sayón de esclavos, *m*. **s.-trade,** trata de esclavos, *f*
slaver *n* negrero, *m*
slaver *vi* babear. *n* baba, *f*
slavering *a* baboso
slavery *n* esclavitud, *f*; trabajo muy arduo, *m*
slavish *a* de esclavo; servil
slavishly *adv* como esclava; servilmente
Slavonic *a* eslavo. *n* (language) eslavo, *m*, lengua eslava, *f*
slay *vt* matar; asesinar
slayer *n* matador (-ra); asesino, *mf*
slaying *n* matanza, *f*; asesinato, *m*
sledge *n* trineo, *m*. *vi* ir en trineo. *vt* transportar por trineo. **s.-hammer,** acotillo, *m*
sleek *a* liso, lustroso; (of general appearance) pulcro, bien aseado, elegante; (of manner) obsequioso
sleekness *n* lustre, *m*, lisura, *f*; (of an animal) gordura, *f*; elegancia, *f*
sleep *n* sueño, *m*. *vi* dormir; reposar, descansar. *vt* dormir. **a deep s.,** un sueño pesado. **He walks in his s.,** Es un sonámbulo. **to court s.,** conciliar el sueño. **to go to s.,** dormirse; entumecerse. **My foot has gone to s.,**

Se me ha dormido (*or* Se me ha entumecido) el pie. **to send a person to s.,** adormecer. **to s. like a top,** dormir como un lirón. **to s. oneself sober,** dormir la mona. **to s. in,** dormir tarde; dormir en casa. **to s. off,** (a cold, etc.) curarse . . . durmiendo; (drunkenness) dormirla. **to s. on,** *vt* (consider) dormir sobre, consultar con la almohada. *vi* seguir durmiendo. **to s. out,** dormir fuera de casa; dormir al aire libre

sleeper *n* durmiente, *mf*; *rw* traviesa, *f*; (on a train) coche cama, *m*. **to be a bad s.,** dormir mal. **to be a good s.,** dormir bien.

sleepily *adv* soñolientamente

sleepiness *n* somnolencia, *f*; letargo, *m*

sleeping *a* durmiente. *n* el dormir. **between s. and waking,** entre duerme y vela. **s.-bag,** saco-cama, *m*. **s.-car,** coche camas, *m*. **s.-draught,** narcótico, *m*. **s. partner,** *n* socio (-ia) comanditario (-ia). **s. sickness,** enfermedad del sueño, *f*

sleepless *a* (of persons) insomne, desvelado; (unremitting) incansable; (of the sea, etc.) en perpetuo movimiento. **to spend a s. night,** pasar una noche en vela, pasar una noche toledana, pasar una noche sin dormir

sleeplessness *n* insomnio, *m*

sleepwalker *n* sonámbulo (-la)

sleepwalking *n* sonambulismo, *m*

sleepy *a* soñoliento; letárgico. **to be s.,** tener sueño. **s.-head,** lirón, *m*, marmota, *f*

sleet *n* aguanieve, cellisca, nevisca, *f*, *vi* caer aguanieve, cellisquear, neviscar

sleeve *n* manga, *f*; (of a hose pipe, etc.) manguera, *f*; *mech* manguito, *m*. **to have something up one's s.,** traer algo en la manga

sleeved *a* con mangas . . . ; de . . . manga(s)

sleeveless *a* sin manga. **s. shirt** *Lat. Am.* cusma, *f*

sleigh *n* trineo, *m*, *vi* ir en trineo

sleight of hand *n* prestidigitación, *f*; juego de manos, *m*

slender *a* delgado; esbelto; tenue; escaso; pequeño; ligero. **Their means are very s.,** Sus recursos son muy escasos. **It is a very s. hope,** Es una esperanza muy remota

slenderness *n* delgadez, *f*; esbeltez, *f*; tenuidad, *f*; escasez, *f*

sleuth *n* (dog) sabueso, *m*; *inf* detective, *m*

slice *n* lonja, tajada, *f*; (of fruit) raja, *f*; (of bread, etc.) rebanada, *f*; (share) parte, porción, *f*; (for fish, etc.) pala, *f*. *vt* cortar en tajadas, etc.; rajar; cortar

slick *a* hábil, diestro

slide *vi* deslizarse, resbalar; (over a question) pasar por alto de; (into a habit, etc.) caer (en). *n* resbalón, *m*; pista de hielo, *f*; (chute) tobogán, *m*; (of a microscope) portaobjetos, *m*; (lantern) diapositiva, *f*; (for the hair) pasador, *m*; (of rock, etc.) desprendimiento, *m*; *mech* guía, *f*. **to let things s.,** dejar rodar la bola. **s.-rule,** regla de cálculo, *f*

sliding *a* resbaladizo; corredizo; movible. **s.-door,** puerta corrediza, puerta de corradera, *f*. **s.-roof,** techo corredizo, *m*. **s.-scale,** escala graduada, *f*. **s.-seat,** asiento movible, *m*; (in a rowing-boat) bancada corrediza, *f*

slight *a* delgado; débil, frágil; ligero; (small) pequeño; escaso; (trivial) insignificante, poco importante. *vt* desairar, despreciar, *Mexico* descolar. *n* desaire, desprecio, *m*; falta de respeto, *f*

slighting *a* despreciativo, de desprecio

slightingly *adv* con desprecio

slightly *adv* ligeramente; poco. **I only know her s.,** La conozco muy poco. **s. built,** de talle delgado

slightness *n* (slimness) delgadez, *f*; ligereza, *f*; (triviality) poca importancia, insignificancia, *f*

slim *a* delgado; escaso. *vi* adelgazarse. **He has very s. chances of success,** Tiene muy pocas posibilidades de conseguir el éxito

slime *n* légamo, limo, lodo, cieno, *m*; (of a snail) limazo, *m*; *fig* cieno, *m*

sliminess *n* limosidad, *f*; viscosidad, *f*

slimness *n* delgadez, *f*; escasez, *f*

slimy *a* limoso, legamoso; pecinoso, viscoso; (of persons) rastrero, servil

sling *vt* arrojar, lanzar; tirar con honda; (a sword, etc.) suspender; (lift) embragar; (a limb) poner en cabestrillo. *n* (for missiles) honda, *f*; *naut* balso, *m*; (for a limb) cabestrillo, *m*, charpa, *f*

slink *vi* (away, off) escurrirse, escabullirse

slip *vi* resbalar, deslizar; (stumble) resbalar, tropezar; (fall) caer; (out of place) salirse; (become untied) desatarse; (steal away) escabullirse; (glide) deslizarse; (of years) correr, pasar; (skid) patinar. *vt* deslizar; (garments, shoes) ponerse; (dogs, cables) soltar; (an arm round, etc.) pasar; *rw* desacoplar; (escape) escaparse de; (free oneself of) librarse de. *n* resbalón, *m*; (skid) patinazo, *m*; (stumble) tropezón, traspié, *m*; (oversight) inadvertencia, *f*; (mistake) falta, equivocación, *f*; (moral lapse) desliz, *m*; (petticoat) combinación, *f*; (cover) funda, *f*; *bot* vástago, *m*; *print* galerada, *f*; (of paper) papeleta, *f*; *pl* **slips,** *naut* anguilas, *f pl*. **It slipped my memory,** Se me fue de la memoria. **There's many a s. 'twixt the cup and the lip,** Del dicho al hecho hay muy gran trecho, De la mano a la boca desaparece la sopa. **to give** (someone) **the slip,** escaparse de. **You ought not to let the opportunity s.,** No debes perder la oportunidad. **to let s. a secret,** revelar un secreto. **to let s. an exclamation,** soltar (dar) una exclamación. **to s. into,** colarse en, deslizarse en. **to s. into,** colarse en, deslizarse en. **to s. into one's clothes,** vestirse rápidamente. **to s. on,** (a garment) ponerse. **to s. out,** salir a hurtadillas; escaparse; (of information) divulgarse. **s. of a boy,** mozalbete, joven imberbe, *m*. **s. of the tongue,** error de lengua, *m*. **s.-knot,** nudo corredizo, *m*

slipcover *n* cubierta, cubierta para muebles, funda, funda para muebles, *f*

slipper *n* babucha, chinela, *f*, pantuflo, *m*; (heelless) chancleta, *f*; (dancing) zapatilla de baile, *f*. **s.-shaped,** achinelado

slippered *a* en zapatillas

slippery *a* resbaladizo; poco firme, inestable; (of persons) informal, sin escrúpulos

slipshod *a* descuidado, negligente; poco correcto

slit *vt* cortar; hender, rajar; (the throat) degollar. *n* cortadura, *f*; resquicio, *m*. **to s. open,** abrir de un tajo

slither *vi* resbalar; deslizarse

sliver *n* raja, *f*; (of wood) astilla, *f*; (of cloth) tira, *f*

slobber *vi* babear; (blubber) gimotear, *n* baba, *f*

sloe *n* (fruit) endrina, *f*; (tree) endrino, *m*. **s.-colored,** endrino. **s.-eyed,** con ojos de mora

slog *vt* golpear duramente. **to s. away,** batirse el cobre, trabajar como un negro

slogan *n* grito de batalla, *m*; reclamo, *m*; frase hecha, *f*; mote, *m*

slop *n* charco, *m*; *pl* **slops,** agua sucia, *f*; alimentos líquidos, *m pl*. *vi* derramarse, verterse. *vt* verter, derramar

slope *n* inclinación, *f*; pendiente, *f*; (of a mountain, etc.) falda, ladera, cuesta, *f*; vertiente, *mf*. *vi* inclinarse; estar en declive; bajar (hacia). **to s. down,** declinar

sloping *a* inclinado; en declive; (of shoulders) caídos, *m pl*

sloppy *a* casi líquido; (muddy) lodoso, lleno de barro; (of work) chapucero; (of persons) baboso, sobón. **s. sentiment,** sensiblería, *f*

slot *n* ranura, muesca, *f*. **s.-machine,** máquina expendedora, *f*, expendedor, *m*; (in amusement arcades, etc.) tragaperras, *m*

sloth *n* pereza, indolencia, *f*; *zool* perezoso, *m*

slothful *a* perezoso, indolente

slouch *n* inclinación del cuerpo, *f*. *vi* andar cabizbajo, andar arrastrando los pies. **to s. about,** vagar, golfear. **s.-hat,** sombrero gacho, *m*

slough *n* (bog) cenagal, pantano, *m*, marisma, *f*; (of a snake) camisa, *f*. *vt* (a skin) mudar; (prejudices, etc.) desechar

Slovak *n* eslovaco (-ca)

Slovakian *a* eslovaco

sloven *n* puerco, *m*; (at work) chapucero, *m*
Slovene *a* and *n* esloveno (-na)
slovenliness *n* desaseo, desaliño, *m*; (carelessness) descuido, *m*, negligencia, *f*; (of work) chapucería, *f*
slovenly *a* desgarbado, desaseado, *Central America* descacharrado, *Lat. Am.* distraído; (careless) descuidado, negligente; (of work) chapucero
slow *a* despacio; lento, *Lat. Am.* demorón; (stupid) torpe; tardo; (of clocks) atrasado; (boring) aburrido; (inactive) flojo. *adv* despacio, lentamente. **I was not s. to . . . ,** No tardé en . . . , *Lat. Am.* No dilaté en . . . **The clock is ten minutes s.,** El reloj lleva diez minutos de atraso. **to s. down,** aflojar el paso; ir más despacio. **s.-motion,** velocidad reducida, *f*. **s. train,** tren ómnibus, *m*. **s.-witted,** lerdo tardo
"Slow Down" «Moderar Su Velocidad»
slow learner *n* alumno de lento aprendizaje, *m*
slowly *adv* despacio, lentamente; poco a poco
slowness *n* lentitud, *f*; (delay) tardanza, *f*; (stupidity) torpeza, estupidez, *f*
slug *n* babosa, *f*
sluggard *n* gandul (-la), perezoso (-a)
sluggish *a* perezoso; (of the market) flojo; (of temperament, etc.) calmoso, flemático; (slow) lento
sluggishness *n* pereza, *f*; (of the market) flojedad, *f*; (slowness) lentitud, *f*
sluice *n* esclusa, *f*; canal, *m*, acequia, *f*. **to s. down,** lavar; echar agua sobre; (a person) dar una ducha (a), dar un baño (a). **s.-gate,** compuerta de esclusa, *f*; tajaderas, *f pl*, tablacho, *m*
slum *nsg* (inner-city slum) barrio bajo (understood everywhere), arrabales *mpl* (Argentina, Uruguay), banda de miseria *fsg* (Argentina), barracas *fpl* (Mexico), barriada *fsg* (Peru), callampa *fsg* (Chile), cantegriles *mpl* (Spain, Uruguay), chabolas *fpl* (Spain), clandestinos *mpl* (Colombia), morenales *mpl* (Honduras), orillas *fpl* (Mexico), población *fsg* (Chile), pueblo joven *msg* (Peru), ranchos *mpl* (Venezuela), tugurios *mpl* (Colombia), villa-miseria *fsg* (Argentina), rancherío *msg*, ribera *fpl*, villorio *msg* (elsewhere in Lat. Am.); (in Brazil) favelas *fpl*; (slum on the outskirs of an urban area) suburbio *msg*
slumber *vi* dormir; (go to sleep) dormirse, caer dormido; (be latent) estar latente. *n* sueño, *m*
slump *n com* baja repentina, *f*; *fig* baja, racha mala, *f*. *vi com* bajar repentinamente. **the s.,** la crisis económica. **to s. into an armchair,** dejarse caer en un sillón
slur *vt* (words) comerse sílabas o letras (de); (in writing) unir (las palabras); (*mus* of notes) ligar. **to cast a s. on,** difamar, manchar. **to s. over,** pasar por alto de, omitir, suprimir
slush *n* lodo, *m*; agua nieve, *f*; (sentimentality) ñoñería, *f*
sly *a* astuto, taimado, socarrón, *Lat. Am.* macuco; disimulado; (arch) malicioso. **on the sly,** a hurtadillas. **sly person** *Mexico* fistol, *m*
slyness *n* astucia, socarronería, *f*; disimulo, *m*; malicia, *f*
smack *n* (taste) sabor, gusto, *m*; (tinge) dejo, *m*; (blow) golpe, *m*; (with the hand) bofetada, palmada, *f*; (with a whip) latigazo, *m*; (crack of whip) restallido, chasquido, *m*; (kiss) beso sonado, *m*; (boat) lancha de pescar, *f*. *vi* (taste of) tener gusto de, saber a; (be tinged with) oler a. *vt* (a whip) hacer restallar; (slap) pegar con la mano. **to s. one's lips over,** chuparse los dedos
small *a* pequeño; menudo; menor; poco; (petty) mezquino, vulgar. *n* parte estrecha, *f*. **a s. number,** un pequeño número. **to make a person look s.,** humillar. **to make oneself s.,** hacerse chiquito. **s.-arms,** armas portátiles, *f pl*. **s. change,** suelto, *m*. **s. craft,** embarcaciones menores, *f pl*. **s. farm** *Lat. Am.* chacra, *Central America* labor, *f*. **s. fry,** pececillos, *m pl*; (children) gente menuda, *f*; gente sin importancia, *f*. **s. hours,** altas horas de la noche, *f pl*. **s.-minded,** adocenado, de cortos alcances. **s.-talk,** trivialidades, *f pl*, charla frívola, *f*
smallholding *n Lat. Am.* chacra, *f*
smallish *a* bastante pequeño; más bien pequeño que grande
smallpox *n* viruelas, *f pl*
smart *vi* picar; dolerse (de). *n* escozor, *m*; dolor, *m*. *a* severo; vivo; rápido; pronto; (competent) hábil; (clever) listo; (unscrupulous) cuco, astuto; (of personal appearance) majo; elegante, distinguido, *Lat. Am. also* fachoso; (neat) aseado; (fashionable, etc.) de moda; de buen tono. **to s. for,** ser castigado por. **to s. under,** sufrir
smarten *vt* embellecer. *vi* (up) ponerse elegante; mejorar. **I must go and s. myself up a little,** Tengo que arreglarme un poco
smartness *n* viveza, *f*; prontitud, rapidez, *f*; (cleverness) despejo, *m*, habilidad, *f*; (wittiness) agudeza, *f*; (astuteness) cuquería, astucia, *f*; (of dress, etc.) elegancia, *f*; buen tono, *m*
smash *vt* romper, quebrar; (a ball, etc.) golpear; (annihilate) destruir; (an opponent) aplastar. *vi* romperse, quebrarse; hacerse pedazos; (collide) chocar (con, contra); estallarse (contra); (financially) hacer bancarrota. *n* rotura, *f*; quebrantamiento, *m*; estruendo, *m*; (financial) quiebra, ruina, *f*; (car, etc.) accidente, *m*; desastre, *m*, catástrofe, *f*. **to s. to atoms,** hacer trizas. **to s. up,** hacer pedazos. **s. and grab raid,** atraco a mano armada, *m*
smash hit *n* éxito arrollador, éxito rotundo, *m*
smattering *n* conocimiento superficial, *m*, tintura, *f*, barniz, *m*
smear *n* mancha, *f*; *biol* frotis, *m*. *vt* embadurnar (de); manchar (con), ensuciar (con); (oneself) untarse; (blur) borrar
smell *n* (sense of) olfato, *m*; (odor) olor, *m*. *vt* oler. *vi* oler; tener olor; (disagreeably) oler mal, tener mal olor; (stink) apestar. **How good it smells!** ¡Qué bien huele! **to s. of,** oler a. **to s. out,** husmear
smelling *n* olfateo, *m*. **s.-bottle,** frasco de sales, *m*. **s.-salts,** sales (inglesas), *f pl*
smelt *vt* fundir. *n icht* eperlano, *m*
smelter *n* fundidor, *m*
smelting *n* fundición, *f*. **s. furnace,** horno de fundición, *m*
smile *vi* sonreír; reírse. *vt* expresar con una sonrisa. *n* sonrisa, *f*. **Mary smiled her thanks,** María dio las gracias con una sonrisa. **smile at adversity,** ponerse buena cara a mal tiempo. **to s. at threats,** reírse de las amenazas
smiling *a* sonriente, risueño
smilingly *adv* sonriendo, con una sonrisa, con cara risueña
smirch *vt* manchar. *n* mancha, *f*
smirk *vi* sonreír con afectación; hacer visajes. *n* sonrisa afectada, *f*
smirking *a* afectado; sonriente
smite *vt* golpear; (kill) matar; (punish) castigar; (pain) doler; (of bright light, sounds, etc.) herir; (cause remorse) remorder. **My conscience smites me,** Tengo remordimientos de conciencia. **to be smitten by,** *inf* estar prendado de. **I was smitten by a desire to smoke,** Me entraron deseos de fumar
smith *n* herrero, *m*. **smith's hammer,** destajador, *m*
smithereens *n pl* añicos, *m pl*
smithy *n* herrería, *f*
smock *n* blusa, *f*; (child's) delantal, *m*
smoke *n* humo, *m*. *vi* humear, echar humo; (tobacco) fumar. *vt* ahumar; ennegrecer; (tobacco) fumar. **smoked glasses,** gafas ahumadas, *f pl*. **s. helmet,** casco respiratorio, *m*. **s.-screen,** cortina de humo, *f*. **s. signal,** ahumada, *f*. **s.-stack,** chimenea, *f*
smokeless *a* sin humo
smoker *n* fumador (-ra)
smoking *a* humeante. *n* el fumar. **"S. Prohibited,"** «Se prohibe fumar.» **non-s. compartment,** *rw* departamento de no fumadores, *m*. **s.-carriage,** *rw* departamento para fumadores, *m*. **s.-room,** fumadero, *m*
smoky *a* humeante; lleno de humo; (black) ahumado

smooth *a* liso; igual; (of the skin, etc.) suave; (of water) calmo, tranquilo; (flattering, etc.) lisonjero; obsequioso; afable. *vt* allanar; (hair, etc.) alisar; (paths, etc.) igualar. **to s. down,** (a person) tranquilizar, calmar. **to s. over,** (faults) exculpar. **to s. the way for,** allanar el camino para. **s.-faced,** barbilampiño, lampiño, bien afeitado, todo afeitado; *fig* obsequioso, untuoso. **s.-haired,** de pelo liso. **s.-spoken,** de palabras lisonjeras; obsequioso
smoothly *adv* lisamente; (of speech) afablemente; con lisonjeras. **Everything was going s.,** Todo iba viento en popa
smoothness *n* igualdad, *f;* lisura, *f;* (of skin, etc.) suavidad, *f;* (of water) calma, tranquilidad, *f;* (of manner, etc.) afabilidad, *f*
smother *vt* ahogar, sofocar; (a fire) apagar; (cover) envolver, cubrir
smoulder *vi* arder sin llama, arder lentamente; (of passions, etc.) arder; estar latente
smouldering *a* que arde lentamente; *fig* latente
smudge *vt* manchar, ensuciar; (blur) borrar. *n* mancha, *f*
smug *a* satisfecho de sí mismo, pagado de sí mismo; farisaico
smuggle *vt* pasar de contrabando. *vi* hacer contrabando
smuggler *n* contrabandista, *mf*
smuggling *n* contrabando, *m*
smugly *adv* con presunción, de un aire satisfecho
smugness *n* satisfacción de sí mismo, *f;* fariseísmo, *m*
smut *n* copo de hollín, *m;* mancha, *f;* (disease) tizón, *m*
smutty *a* tiznado; ahumado; *inf* verde
snack *n* tentempié, piscolabis, bocado, *Lat. Am.* botana, *f.* **to take a s.,** tomar un piscolabis
snack bar *n* merendero, *m, Lat. Am.* lonchería, *f*
snaffle *n* filete, *m. vt* (a horse) refrenar. **s.-bridle,** bridón, *m*
snag *n* (of a tree) tocón, *m;* (of a tooth) raigón, *m;* (problem) busilis, *m;* obstáculo inesperado, *m*
snail *n* caracol, *m.* **at a snail's pace,** a paso de tortuga
snake *n* serpiente, *f.* **s.-charmer,** encantador de serpientes, *m*
snakelike *a* de serpiente; serpentino
snap *vt* morder; (break) romper; (one's fingers) castañetear; (a whip) chasquear; (down a lid, etc.) cerrar de golpe; (beaks, etc.) cerrar ruidosamente; *phot* sacar una instantánea de. *vi* partirse; quebrarse; hablar bruscamente. *n* (bite) mordedura, *f;* golpe seco, *m;* chasquido, *m;* rotura, *f;* (clasp) cierre, *m;* (of weather) temporada, *f;* (spirit) vigor, brío, *m; phot* instantánea, *f.* **to s. at,** procurar morder; (an invitation, etc.) aceptar gustoso. **to s. one's fingers at,** *fig* burlarse de. **to s. up,** coger, agarrar; (a person) cortar la palabra (a), interrumpir. **s.-fastener,** botón de presión, *m*
snapdragon *n* dragón, *m,* becerra, boca de dragón, *f*
snappily *adv* irritablemente
snappishness *n* irritabilidad, *f*
snappy *a* irritable; vigoroso
snapshot *n* instantánea, foto, *f*
snare *n* cepo, lazo, *m,* trampa, *f; fig* red, *f. vt* coger en el lazo; *fig* enredar
snarl *vi* (of dogs) regañar; (cats, etc.) gruñir. *n* regañamiento, *m;* gruñido, *m*
snarling *n* regañamiento, *m;* gruñidos, *m pl, a* gruñidor
snatch *vt* asir; agarrar; (enjoy) disfrutar; (an opportunity) tomar, aprovecharse de. *n* asimiento, agarro, *m;* (of time) rato, *m;* instante, *m;* (of song) fragmento, *m.* **to make a s. at,** procurar agarrar; alargar la mano hacia. **to s. a hurried meal,** comer aprisa. **to s. away,** arrebatar, quitar; (carry off) robar. **to s. up,** coger rápidamente; coger en brazos
sneak *vi* deslizarse (en), colarse (en); (lurk) rondar; (inform) acusar. *n* mandilón, *m;* (accuser) acusón (-ona). **to s. off,** escabullirse, irse a hurtadillas. **s.-thief,** *n* garduño (-ña)
sneaker *n* (shoe) zapatilla de tenis, *f*
sneaking *a* furtivo, ruin, mezquino; secreto
sneer *vi* sonreír irónicamente; burlarse, mofarse. *n* sonrisa sardónica, sonrisa de desprecio, *f;* burla, mofa, *f.* **to s. at,** mofarse de, burlarse de; hablar con desprecio de
sneering *a* mofador, burlón
sneeringly *adv* con una sonrisa sardónica; burlonamente
sneeze *vi* estornudar. *n* estornudo, *m.* **It's not to be sneezed at,** No es moco de pavo
sniff *vi* respirar fuertemente; resollar. *vt* oler, olfatear; aspirar. **to s. at,** oler. **to s. out,** *inf* husmear
snigger *vi* reírse por lo bajo, reírse disimuladamente. *n* risa disimulada, *f*
snip *vt* cortar con tijeras; cortar, quitar. *n* tijeretada, *f;* (of cloth, etc.) recorte, pedacito, *m*
sniper *n mil* paco, *m*
snippet *n* pedacito, fragmento, *m;* (of prose, etc.) trocito, *m;* (of news) noticia, *f*
snivel *vi* lloriquear, gimotear
sniveling *n* lloriqueo, gimoteo, *m. a* llorón; mocoso
snob *n* esnob, *mf*
snobbery *n* snobismo, *m*
snobbish *a* esnob
snood *n* (for the hair) redecilla, *f;* (turkey's) moco (de pavo), *m;* (fishing) cendal, *m*
snoop *vi* espiar; entremeterse
snooper *n Lat. Am.* averigüetas, *mf*
snooze *vi* dormitar, echar un sueño. *n* sueñecito, *m;* (afternoon) siesta, *f*
snore *vi* roncar. *n* ronquido, *m*
snoring *n* ronquidos, *m pl*
snort *vi* bufar; resoplar. *n* bufido, *m;* resoplido, *m*
snout *n* hocico, *m;* (of a pig) jeta, *f*
snow *n* nieve, *f. vi* nevar. *vt* nevar; *fig* inundar. **to s. under** (with), inundar con. **to be snowed up,** estar aprisionado por la nieve. **s.-blindness,** deslumbramiento causado por la nieve, *m.* **s.-boot,** bota para la nieve, *f.* **s.-bound,** aprisionado por la nieve; bloqueado por la nieve. **s.-capped,** coronado de nieve. **s.-clad,** cubierto de nieve. **s.-drift,** acumulación de nieve, *f.* **s.-field,** ventisquero, *m.* **s.-goggles,** gafas ahumadas, *f pl.* **s.-line,** límite de las nieves perpetuas, *m.* **s.-man,** figura de nieve, *f.* **s.-plough,** quitanieve, *m.* **s.-shoe,** raqueta de nieve, *f.* **s.-white,** blanco como la nieve
snowball *n* bola de nieves, *f; bot* bola de nieve, *f*
snowdrop *n* campanilla de invierno, violeta de febrero, *f*
snowfall *n* nevada, *f*
snowflake *n* copo de nieve, *m*
snowstorm *n* ventisca, *f*
snowy *a* nevoso; de nieve
snub *vt* repulsar; desairar, tratar con desdén, *Mexico* descolar. *n* repulsa, *f,* desaire, *m;* (nose) nariz respingona, *f.* **s.-nosed,** de nariz respingona
snuff *vt* (breathe) oler, olfatear; inhalar; (a candle) atizar, despabilar. *n* (of a candle) moco, *m,* despabiladura, *f;* (tobacco) rapé, *m.* **to take s.,** tomar rapé. **to s. out,** extinguir. **s.-box,** caja de rapé, tabaquera, *f*
snuffers *n pl* tenacillas, despabiladeras, *f pl*
snuffle *vi* hacer ruido con la nariz; respirar fuerte; (in speaking) ganguear
snuffling *a* mocoso; (of the voice) gangoso
snug *a* caliente; cómodo; (hidden) escondido, **to have a s. income,** tener el riñón bien cubierto, ser acomodado
snuggle *vi* hacerse un ovillo; acomodarse; ponerse cómodo. **to s. up to,** arrimarse a, apretarse contra
snugly *adv* cómodamente
snugness *n* comodidad, *f*
so *adv* así; de este modo, de esta manera; por lo tanto; tanto; (before adjs. and advs. but not before **más, mejor, menos, peor,** where **tanto** is used) tan; (in the same way) del mismo modo, de igual modo; (therefore) de modo que, de manera que; (also) también; (approximately) más o menos, aproximadamente. **Is that so?** ¿De veras? **if so . . . ,** si así es

. . . **He has not yet done so,** no lo ha hecho todavía. **I told you so!** ¡Ya te lo dije yo! **So be it!** ¡Así sea! **so far,** hasta aquí; hasta ahora. **so forth,** etcétera. **So long!** ¡Nos vemos! **so much,** tanto. **So much the worse for them,** Tanto peor para ellos. **so to speak . . . ,** por decirlo así. **so as to,** a fin de, para. **so long as,** con tal que, a condición de que. **so on,** etcétera. **so soon as,** tan pronto como. **so that,** de suerte que, de modo que, para que; con que. **so-and-so,** *n* fulano (-na); mengano (-na). **so-called.** así llamado, supuesto. **so-so,** así-así, regular

soak *vt* remojar; empapar; (skins) abrevar. *vi* estar en remojo. *n* remojo, *m;* (rain) diluvio, *m;* (booze) borrachera, *f.* **to s. into,** filtrar en; penetrar. **to s. through,** penetrar; filtrar **so-called,** así llamado, supuesto. **so-so,** así, regular

soaked *a* remojado. **He is s. to the skin,** Está calado hasta los huesos

soaking *n* remojo, *m;* empapamiento, *m,*

soap *n* jabón, *m. vt* jabonar; (flatter) enjabonar. **a tablet of s.,** una pastilla de jabón. **soft s.,** jabón blando, *m.* **toilet s.,** jabón de tocador, jaboncillo, *m.* **s.-bubble,** burbuja de jabón, *f.* **s. dish,** jabonera, *f.* **s. factory,** jabonería, *f.* **s.-flakes,** copos de jabón, *m pl*

soapbark tree *n* quillay, palo de jabón, *m*

soap box *n lit* caja de jabón, *f; fig* tribuna callejera, *f*

soap opera *n* radionovela (on radio), telenovela (on television), *f,* serial lacrimógeno (derogatory), *m*

soapsuds *n pl* jabonaduras, *f pl*

soapy *a* cubierto de jabón; jabonoso

soar *vi* remontarse; *fig* elevarse; (of prices, etc.) subir de golpe

soaring *n* remonte, vuelo, *m; fig* aspiración, *f;* (of prices, etc.) subida repentina, *f*

sob *vi* sollozar. *n* sollozo, *m.* **to sob one's heart out,** llorar a lágrima viva. **to sob out,** decir sollozando, decir entre sollozos

s.o.b. *n* (son of a bitch) hache de pe (hijo de puta)

sobbing *n* sollozos, *m pl, a* sollozante

sober *a* sobrio; moderado; (of colors) obscuro. **s.-minded,** serio; reflexivo

sobriety *n* sobriedad, *f;* moderación, *f;* seriedad, *f;* calma, tranquilidad, *f*

sobriquet *n* apodo, *m*

soccer *n* fútbol (Asociación), *m*

sociability *n* sociabilidad, *f*

sociable *a* sociable; amistoso

sociably *adv* sociablemente; amistosamente

social *a* social; sociable. *n* reunión, velada, *f.* **s.-democrat,** *a* and *n* socialdemócrata, *mf.* **s. event,** acontecimiento social, *m.* **s. insurance,** previsión social, *f.* **s. services,** servicios sociales, *m pl.* **s. work,** asistencia social, *f*

socialism *n* socialismo, *m*

socialist *a* socialista, laborista. *n* socialista, *mf*

socialization *n* socialización, *f*

socialize *vt* socializar

socially *adv* socialmente

society *n* sociedad, *f;* (fashionable) mundo elegante, *m,* alta sociedad, *f;* compañía, *f.* **to go into s.,** (of girls) ponerse de largo; entrar en el mundo elegante. **s. hostess,** dama de sociedad, *f.* **society for the prevention of cruelty to animals,** sociedad protectora de animales, *f.* **s. news,** noticias de sociedad, *f pl*

sociological *a* sociológico

sociologist *n* sociólogo (-ga)

sociology *n* sociología, *f*

sock *n* calcetín, *m;* (for a shoe) plantilla, *f*

socket *n mech* encaje, cubo, ojo, *m;* (of a lamp, and *elec*) enchufe, *m;* (of the eye) órbita, cuenca, *f;* (of a tooth) alvéolo, *m;* (of a joint) fosa, *f.* **His eyes started out of their sockets,** Sus ojos estaban fuera de su órbita

Socratic *a* socrático

sod *n* césped, *m;* (cut) tepe, *m*

soda *n* sosa, *f.* **caustic s.,** sosa cáustica, *f.* **s.-ash,** carbonato sódico, *m.* **s.-fountain,** aparato de aguas gaseosas, *m.* **s.-water,** sifón, *m*

sodden *a* saturado, empapado

sodium *n* sodio, *m*

Sodomite *n* sodomita, *mf*

sodomy *n* sodomía, *f*

sofa *n* sofá, *m*

soft *a* blando; suave; muelle; (flabby) flojo; (of disposition, etc.) dulce; (effeminate) muelle, afeminado; (lenient) indulgente; (easy) fácil; (silly) tonto. **to have a s. spot for,** (a person) tener una debilidad para. **s. coal,** carbón bituminoso, *m.* **s. drink,** bebida no alcohólica, *f.* **s. felt hat,** sombrero flexible, *m.* **s. fruit,** fruta blanda, *f.* **s.-boiled,** (of eggs) pasado por agua; (of persons) inocente, ingenuo. **s.-hearted,** de buen corazón; compasivo, bondadoso. **s.-heartedness,** buen corazón, *m,* bondad, *f.* **s.-spoken,** de voz suave; que habla con dulzura, meloso. **s. water,** agua blanda, *f*

soften *vt* ablandar, reblandecer) (weaken) debilitar; (mitigate; mitigar, suavizar; (the heart, etc.) enternecer. *vi* reblandecerse; enternecerse

softening *n* reblandecimiento, *m;* (relenting) enternecimiento, *m*

softly *adv* suavemente; dulcemente, tiernamente; sin ruido, silenciosamente

softness *n* blandura, *f;* suavidad, *f;* (sweetness, etc.) dulzura, *f;* (of character) debilidad de carácter, *f;* (silliness) necedad, estupidez, *f*

soggy *a* empapado de agua; saturado

soil *n* tierra, *f;* (country) país, *m,* tierra, *f. vt* ensuciar; *fig* manchar. **my native s.,** mi tierra, mi patria

soiled *a* sucio. **s. linen,** ropa sucia, *f*

soiree *n* velada, *f*

sojourn *vi* morar, residir, permanecer. *n* residencia, permanencia, *f*

sojourner *n* morador (-ra), residente, *mf*

sol *n mus* sol, *m.* **sol-fa,** *n* solfa, *f,* solfeo, *m. vt* solfear

solace *n* consuelo, solaz, *m. vt* consolar; solazar

solar *a* solar. **s. plexus,** *anat* plexo solar, *m.* **s. system,** sistema solar, *m*

solder *n* soldadura, *f, vt* soldar

soldering *n* soldadura, *f*

soldier *n* soldado, *m;* militar, *m.* **He wants to be a s.,** Quiere ser militar

soldierly *a* militar; marcial

soldiery *n* soldadesca, *f*

sole *n* (of a foot) planta, *f;* (of a shoe) suela, *f;* (of a plough) cepa, *f; icht* lenguado, *m,* suela, *f. vt* (shoes) solar, poner suela (a). *a* solo, único; exclusivo. **s. right,** exclusiva, *f,* derecho exclusivo, *m*

solecism *n* solecismo, *m*

solely *adv* sólo; únicamente, puramente; meramente

solemn *a* solemne; grave; serio; (sacred) sagrado. **Why do you look so s.?** ¿Por qué estás tan serio?

solemnity *n* solemnidad, *f*

solemnization *n* solemnización, celebración, *f*

solemnize *vt* solemnizar

solemnly *adv* solemnemente; gravemente

solicit *vt* solicitar; implorar, rogar encarecidamente

solicitation *n* solicitación, *f*

solicitor *n* abogado (-da)

solicitous *a* ansioso (de), deseoso (de); solícito, atento; (worried) preocupado

solicitude *n* solicitud, *f,* cuidado, *m;* (anxiety) preocupación, *f*

solid *a* sólido; macizo; (of persons) serio, formal; (unanimous) unánime. *n* sólido, *m.* **a s. meal,** una comida fuerte. **He slept for ten s. hours,** Durmió por diez horas seguidas. **solid-colored material,** tela lisa, *f.* **s. food,** alimentos sólidos, *m pl.* **s. geometry,** geometría del espacio, *f.* **solid gold,** oro de ley, *m.* **s. tire,** llanta de goma maciza, *f*

solidarity *n* solidaridad, *f*

solidification *n* solidificación, *f*

solidify *vt* solidificar. *vi* solidificarse; congelarse

solidity *n* solidez, *f*; unanimidad, *f*
solidly *adv* sólidamente
soliloquize *vi* soliloquiar, hablar a solas
soliloquy *n* soliloquio, *m*
solitaire *n* (diamond and game) solitario, *m*
solitary *a* solitario; solo, aislado, único. **He was in s. confinement for three months,** Estuvo incomunicado durante tres meses. **There is not a s. one,** No hay ni uno
solitude *n* soledad, *f*
solo *n* (performance and cards) solo, *m*. **to sing a s.,** cantar un solo. **It was his first s. flight,** Era su primer vuelo a solas
soloist *n* solista, *mf*
solstice *n* solsticio, *m*. **summer s.,** solsticio vernal, *m*. **winter s.,** solsticio hiemal, *m*
solubility *n* solubilidad, *f*
soluble *a* soluble
solution *n* solución, *f*
solvable *a* que se puede resolver, soluble
solve *vt* resolver, hallar la solución de
solvency *n* solvencia, *f*
solvent *a com* solvente; (*chem* and *fig*) disolvente. *n* disolvente, *m*
somatic *a* somático
somber *a* sombrío
somberly *adv* sombríamente
somberness *n* lo sombrío; sobriedad, *f*; melancolía, *f*
some *a* alguno (-a), algunos (-as); (before a masculine sing. noun) algún; unos (-as); un poco de, algo de; (as a partitive, often not translated, e.g. **Give me s. wine,** Dame vino); (approximately) aproximadamente, unos (-as). *pron* algunos (-as), unos (-as); algo, un poco. **I should like s. strawberries,** Me gustaría comer unas fresas. **s. day,** algún día. **S. say yes, others no,** Algunos dicen que sí, otros que no. **There are s. sixty people in the garden,** Hay unas sesenta personas en el jardín
somebody, someone *n* alguien, *mf*. **s. else,** otro (-a), otra persona, *f*. **S. or other said that the book is worth reading,** No sé quién dijo que el libro vale la pena de leerse. **to be s.,** *inf* ser un personaje
somehow *adv* de un modo u otro, de alguna manera. **S. I don't like them,** No sé por qué, pero no me gustan
somersault *n* salto mortal, *m*, *vi* dar un salto mortal
something *n* algo, *m*, alguna cosa, *f*. *adv* algún tanto. **Would you like s. else?** ¿Quiere Vd. otra cosa? **He left s. like fifty thousand pounds,** Dejó algo así como cincuenta mil libras. **He has s. to live for,** Tiene para que vivir
sometime *adv* algún día, alguna vez; en algún tiempo. *a* ex-. **Come and see me s. soon,** Ven a verme algún día de estos. **He will have to go abroad s. or another,** Tarde o temprano, tiene que ir al extranjero. **s. last month,** durante el mes pasado
sometimes *adv* algunas veces, a veces. **s. happy, s. sad,** algunas veces feliz y otras triste, ora feliz ora triste
somewhat *adv* algo; algún tanto, un tanto; un poco. **I am s. busy,** Estoy algo ocupado. **He is s. of a ladykiller,** Tiene sus puntos de castigador, Tiene algo de castigador
somewhere *adv* en alguna parte. **s. about,** por ahí. **s. else,** en otra parte
somnambulism *n* somnambulismo, *m*
somnambulist *n* somnámbulo (-la)
somnolence *n* somnolencia, *f*
somnolent *a* soñoliento; soporifero
son *n* hijo, *m*. **son-in-law,** yerno, hijo político, *m*
sonata *n* sonata, *f*
song *n* canto, *m*; canción, *f*; (poem) poema, verso, *m*. **It's nothing to make a s. about,** No es para tanto. **to break into s.,** ponerse a cantar. **to be not worth an old s.,** no valer un pito. **the S. of Songs,** Cantar de los Cantares, *m*. **s.-bird,** ave canora, *f*. **s.-book,** libro de canciones, *m*. **s.-writer,** compositor (-ra) de canciones
sonic *adj* sónico. **sonic boom,** estampido sónico, *m*
sonnet *n* soneto, *m*
sonorous *a* sonoro
sonorousness *n* sonoridad, *f*
soon *adv* pronto; dentro de poco, luego. **as s. as,** así que, en cuanto, luego que, no bien . . . **as s. as possible,** lo antes posible, lo más pronto posible, con la mayor antelación posible, cuanto antes. **s. after,** poco después (de). **See you s.!** ¡Hasta pronto! **sooner or later,** tarde o temprano. **the sooner the better,** cuanto antes mejor. **No sooner had he left the house, when . . .** Apenas hubo dejado la casa, cuando . . . **Emily would sooner go to London,** Emilia preferiría ir a Londres (A Emilia le gustaría más ir a Londres)
soot *n* hollín, *m*, *vt* cubrir de hollín
soothe *vt* tranquilizar, calmar, (pain) aliviar, mitigar
soothing *a* calmante, tranquilizador, sosegador; (of powders, etc.) calmante
soothingly *adv* con dulzura; suavemente; como un consuelo
soothsayer *n* adivino (-na), adivinador (-ra)
soothsaying *n* adivinanza, *f*
sooty *a* cubierto de hollín; negro como el hollín
sop *n* sopa, *f*; (bribe) soborno, *m*
sophism *n* sofisma, *m*
sophist *n hist* sofista, *m*; (quibbler) sofista, *mf*
sophistic *a phil* sofista; (of persons, arguments) sofístico
sophisticated *a* nada ingenuo; mundano; (cultured) culto
sophistication *n* falta de simplicidad, *f*; mundanería, *f*; cultura, *f*
sophistry *n* sofistería, *f*
Sophoclean *a* sofocleo
soporific *a* soporífico
sopping *a* muy mojado. **s. wet,** hecho una sopa
soprano *n* (voice and part) soprano, *m*; (singer) soprano, tiple, *mf*
sorcerer *n* encantador, mago, brujo, *m*
sorceress *n* hechicera, bruja, *f*
sorcery *n* sortilegio, *m*, hechicería, brujería, *f*; encanto, *m*
sordid *a* sórdido; (of motives, etc.) ruin, vil
sordidness *n* sordidez, *f*; (of motives, etc.) vileza, bajeza, *f*
sordine *n mus* sordina, *f*
sore *a* doloroso, malo; (sad) triste; (annoyed) enojado; (with need, etc.) extremo. *n* llaga, *Lat. Am. also* lacra, *f*; (on horses, etc., caused by girths) matadura, *f*; *fig* herida, *f*; recuerdo doloroso, *m*. **to open an old s.,** *fig* renovar la herida. **running s.,** úlcera, *f*. **s. throat,** dolor de garganta, *m*
sorely *adv* grandemente; muy; urgentemente. **He was s. tempted,** Tuvo grandes tentaciones
soreness *n* dolor, *m*; (resentment) amargura, *f*, resentimiento, *m*; (ill-feeling) rencor, *m*
sorrel *a* alazán. *n* (horse) alazán, *m*; *bot* acedera, *f*
sorrow *n* pesar, *m*, aflicción, pesadumbre, *f*; tristeza, *f*. *vi* afligirse; entristecerse. **To my great s.,** Con gran pesar mío. **s.-stricken,** afligido, agobiado de pena
sorrowful *a* afligido, angustiado; triste
sorrowfully *adv* con pena, tristemente
sorrowing *a* afligido. *n* aflicción, *f*; lamentación, *f*
sort *n* especie, *f*; clase, *f*; tipo, *m*. *vt* separar (de); clasificar. **a s. of hat,** una especie de sombrero. **all sorts of,** toda clase de. **He is a good s.,** Es buen chico. **He is a queer s.,** Es un tipo raro. **in some s.,** hasta cierto punto. **I am out of sorts,** Estoy destemplado. **Nothing of the s.!** ¡Nada de eso!
sorter *n* oficial de correos, *m*; clasificador (-ra)
sorting *n* clasificación, *f*
sotto voce *adv* a sovoz, en voz baja
soul *n* alma, *f*; espíritu, *m*; (departed) ánima, *f*; (being) ser, *m*; (life) vida, *f*; (heart) corazón, *m*. **All Souls' Day,** Día de los Difuntos, *m*. **He is a good s.!** ¡Es un bendito! **She is a simple s.,** Ella es una alma de Dios. **without seeing a living s.,** sin ver un bicho viviente. **Upon my s.!** ¡Por mi vida! **s. in purgatory,** alma en pena, *f*. **s.-stirring,** emocionante

soulful *a* sentimental, emocional; espiritual; romántico
soulless *a* sin alma; mecánico
sound *n* sonido, *m*; son, *m*; ruido, *m*; (strait) estrecho, *m*. *vi* sonar; hacer ruido; resonar; (seem) parecer. *vt* sonar; (the horn, the alarm, musical instrument) tocar; (express) expresar; proclamar; (praise) celebrar; *naut* hondear; *med* tentar; (the chest) auscultar; (try to discover) tentar, sondar; (experience) experimentar. **to the s. of,** al son de. **s.-box,** (of a gramophone) diafragma, *m*. **s.-detector,** fonolocalización de aviones, *f*. **s.-film,** película sonora, *f*. **s.-proof,** (of radio studios, etc.) aislado de todo sonido. **s.-track,** guía sonora, banda sonora, *f*. **s.-wave,** onda sonora, *f*
sound *a* sano; (of a person) perspicaz; (reasonable) lógico, razonable; (of a policy, etc.) prudente; (of an argument, etc.) válido; (of an investment) seguro; (solvent) solvente; (good) bueno; (deep) profundo. *adv* profundamente, bien
sounding *n naut* sondeo, *m*; *pl* **soundings,** sondas, *f pl*. *a* sonoro. **to take soundings,** sondar, echar la plomada. **s.-board,** tabla de armonía, *f*
soundless *a* sin ruido, silencioso
soundly *adv* sanamente; juiciosamente, prudentemente; bien; (deeply) profundamente
soundness *n* (of a person) perspicacia, *f*; (of a policy, etc.) prudencia, *f*; (of an argument, etc.) validez, fuerza, *f*; (financial) solvencia, *f*
soup *n* sopa, *f*. **clear s.,** consommé, *m*. **thick s.,** puré, *m*. **to be in the s.,** *inf* estar aviado. **s.-ladle,** cucharón, *m*. **s.-plate,** plato sopero, *m*. **s.-tureen,** sopera, *f*
sour *a* ácido, agrio; (of milk) agrio; (of persons, etc.) agrio, desabrido. *vt* agriar. **to go s.,** volverse agrio. **S. grapes!** ¡Están verdes!
source *n* (of a river, etc.) nacimiento, *m*; fuente, *f*; (of infection) foco, *m*. **to know from a good s.,** saber de buena tinta
sourly *adv* agriamente
sourness *n* acidez, agrura, *f*; acrimonia, *f*
south *n* sur, *m*; mediodía, *m*. *a* del sur. *adv* hacia el sur. **S. African,** *a* and *n* sudafricano (-na). **S. American,** *a* and *n* sudamericano (-na). **s.-east,** *n* sudeste, *m*. *a* del sudeste. *adv* hacia el sudeste. **s.-easter,** viento del sudeste, *m*. **s.-easterly,** *a* del sudeste; al sudeste. *adv* hacia el sudeste. **s.-eastern,** del sudeste. **s.-s.-east,** *n* sudsudeste, *m*. **s.-s.-west,** sudsudoeste, *m*. **s.-west,** *n* sudoeste, *m*. *a* del sudoeste. *adv* hacia el sudoeste. **s.-west wind,** viento sudoeste, ábrego, *m*. **s.-westerly,** *a* del sudoeste. *adv* hacia el sudoeste. **s.-western,** *a* del sudoeste
South Africa República Sudafricana, *f*
South America América del Sur, *f*
southerly *a* del sur; hacia el sur. **The house has a s. aspect,** La casa está orientada al sur
southern *a* del sur; del mediodía; meridional. **S. Cross,** Cruz, *f*, Crucero, *m*. **s. express,** sudexpreso, *m*
southerner *n* habitante del sur, *m*
South Sea Mar del Sur, Mar del Pacífico, *m*
southward *a* del sur; al sur. *adv* hacia el sur
souvenir *n* recuerdo, *m*
sovereign *a* soberano. *n* soberano (-na); (coin) soberano, *m*
sovereignty *n* soberanía, *f*
soviet *n* soviet, *m*, *a* soviético
Soviet Union, the la Unión Soviética, *f*
sow *n* cerda, puerca, marrana, *f*; (of a wild boar) jabalina, *f*; (of iron) galápago, *m*
sow *vt* sembrar; esparcir; diseminar
sower *n* sembrador (-ra)
sowing *n* sembradura, siembra, *f*. **s. machine,** sembradera, *f*. **s. time,** tiempo de la siembra, *m*
soya bean *n* soja, *f*
spa *n* balneario, *m*; (spring) manantial mineral, *m*, caldas, *f pl*
space *n* espacio, *m*; (of time) temporada, *f*; intervalo, *m*; (*print, mus*) espacio, *m*. *vt* espaciar. **blank s.,** blanco, *m*. **s.-bar,** tecla de espacios, *f*, espaciador, *m*
spacious *a* espacioso; amplio
spaciousness *n* espaciosidad, *f*; amplitud, *f*
spade *n* pala, azada, *f*; (cards) espada, *f*. **to call a s. a s.,** llamar al pan pan y al vino vino, llamar a las cosas por su nombre. **s.-work,** trabajo preparatorio, *m*, labor de pala, *f*
spaghetti *n* fideos, macarrones, *m pl*
Spain España, *f*
span *vt* medir a palmos; rodear; medir; (cross) atravesar, cruzar. *n* palmo, *m*; espacio, *m*, duración, *f*; (of a bridge) vano, *m*; (of wing, *aer, zool*) envergadura, *f*; (distance) distancia, *f*. **single-s. bridge,** puente de vano único. **the brief s. of human life,** la corta duración de la vida humana
spangle *n* lentejuela, *f*; (tinsel) oropel, *m*. *vt* adornar con lentejuelas; sembrar (de), esparcir (de). **spangled with stars,** sembrado de estrellas
Spaniard *n* español (-la). **a young S.,** un joven español
spaniel *n* perro de aguas, perro sabueso español *m*; (cocker) sabueso, *m*
Spanish *a* español. *n* (language) español, castellano, *m*. **a S. girl,** una muchacha española. **in S. fashion,** a la española. **S. American,** *a* and *n* hispanoamericano (-na). **S. broom,** retama de olor, *f*. **S. fly,** cantárida, *f*
Spanish America Hispanoamérica, *f*
spank *vt* pegar con la mano, azotar. *n* azotazo, *m*. **to s. along,** correr rápidamente; (of a horse) galopar
spanking *n* azotamiento, vapuleo, *m*
spanner *n* llave inglesa, llave de tuercas, *f*
spar *n naut* mastel, *m*; *min* espato, *m*; (boxing) boxeo, *m*; (quarrel) disputa, *f*. *vi* boxear; (argue) disputar
spare *a* (meager) frugal, escaso; (of persons) enjuto, flaco; (available) disponible; (extra) de repuesto. *n* recambio, *m*. **s. part,** pieza de recambio, pieza de repuesto, *f*. **s. room,** cuarto de amigos, *m*. **s. time,** ratos de ocio, *m pl*, tiempo disponible, *m*. **s. tire** *Mexico* llanta de refación, *f*. **s. wheel,** rueda de repuesto, *f*
spare *vt* (expense, etc.) escatimar; ahorrar; (do without) pasarse sin; (give) dar; (a life, etc.) perdonar; (avoid) evitar; dispensar de; (grant) hacer gracia de; (time) dedicar. **I cannot s. her,** No puedo estar sin ella. **They have no money to s.,** No tienen dinero de sobra. **to be sparing of,** ser avaro de
sparingly *adv* frugalmente; escasamente. **to eat s.,** comer con frugalidad
spark *n* chispa, *f*; (gallant) pisaverde, *m*. *vi* chispear, echar chispas
sparking *a* chispeante. *n* emisión de chispas, *f*. **s.-plug,** bujía de encendido, *f*
sparkle *vi* centellear, rutilar, destellar; *fig* brillar; (of wines) ser espumoso. *n* centelleo, destello, *m*; *fig* brillo, *m*
sparkling *a* rutilante, centelleante, reluciente; *fig* brillante, chispeante; (of wines) espumante
sparring match *n* combate de boxeo amistoso, *m*
sparrow *n* gorrión, *m*. **s.-hawk,** gavilán, esparaván, *m*
sparse *a* claro, ralo; esparcido
sparsely *adv* escasamente
Sparta Esparta, *f*
Spartan *a* and *n* espartano (-na)
spasm *n* espasmo, *m*; ataque, *m*; acceso, *m*
spasmodic *a* espasmódico; intermitente
spasmodically *adv* espasmódicamente
spat *n* (gaiter) polaina de tela, *f*
spate *n* crecida, *f*; *fig* torrente, *m*. **in s.,** crecido
spatter *vt* salpicar; (*fig* smirch) manchar. *vi* rociar. *n* salpicadura, *f*; rociada, *f*
spatula *n* espátula, *f*
spawn *vt* and *vi* desovar; engendrar. *n* huevas, *f pl*, freza, *f*; (offspring) producto, *m*
speak *vi* hablar; pronunciar un discurso; (sound) sonar. *vt* decir; (French, etc.) hablar. **She never spoke to him again,** Nunca volvió a dirigirle la palabra. **roughly speaking,** aproximadamente, más o menos. **Speaking for myself,** En cuanto a mí, Por mi parte. **without speaking,** sin decir nada, sin hablar. **to s.**

for, (a person) hablar por. **to s. for itself,** hablar por sí mismo, ser evidente. **to s. one's mind,** decir lo que se piensa. **to s. of,** hablar de. **to s. out,** hablar claro; hablar alto. **to s. up for,** (a person) hablar en favor de (alguien)

speaker *n* el, *m*, (*f*, la) que habla; (public) orador (-ra). **the S.,** el Presidente de la Cámara de los Comunes

speaking *a* hablante; para hablar; elocuente, expresivo. *n* habla, *f*, discurso, *m*. **They are not on s. terms,** No se hablan. **within s. distance,** al habla. **s.-trumpet,** portavoz, *m*. **s.-tube,** tubo acústico, *m*

spear *n* lanza, *f*; (javelin) venablo, *m*; (harpoon) arpón, *m*. *vt* herir con lanza, alancear; (fish) arponear. **s.-head,** punta de la lanza, *f*. **s.-thrust,** lanzada, *f*

special *a* especial; particular; extraordinario. *n* (train) tren extraordinario, *m*. **s. correspondent,** corresponsal extraordinario, *m*. **s. friend,** amigo (-ga) del alma, amigo intimo

specialist *n* especialista, *mf*

speciality *n* particularidad, *f*; especialidad, *f*

specialization *n* especialización, *f*

specialize *vt* especializar. *vi* especializarse

specially *adv* especialmente; particularmente; sobre todo

species *n* especie, *f*; raza, *f*

specific *a* específico; explícito. *n* específico, *m*. **s. gravity,** peso específico, *m*, densidad, *f*

specifically *adv* específicamente; explícitamente

specification *n* especificación, *f*

specify *vt* especificar

specimen *n* espécimen, *m*; ejemplo, *m*; *inf* tipo, *m*

specious *a* especioso. **s. arguments** *Lat. Am.* abogaderas, abogaderías, *fpl*

speciousness *n* plausibilidad, *f*; apariencia engañosa, *f*

speck *n* pequeña mancha, *f*; punto, *m*; átomo, *m*; (on fruit) maca, *f*

speckle *vt* motear, manchar

speckled *a* abigarrado; con manchas . . .

spectacle *n* espectáculo, *m*; escena, *f*; *pl* **spectacles,** gafas, *f pl*, anteojos, *m pl*. **s.-case,** cajita para las gafas, *f*

spectacled *a* con gafas, que lleva gafas

spectacular *a* espectacular

spectator *n* espectador (-ra)

spectral *a* espectral

specter *n* espectro, fantasma, *m*

spectrum *n phys* espectro, *m*

speculate *vi* especular (sobre, acerca de); *com* especular (en)

speculation *n* especulación, *f*

speculative *a* especulativo

speculator *n* especulador (-ra)

speech *n* habla, *f*; palabra, *f*; (idiom) lenguaje, *m*; (language) idioma, *m*; *gram* oración, *f*; (address) discurso, *m*; disertación, *f*. **part of s.,** parte de la oración, *f*. **to make a s.,** pronunciar un discurso. **s.maker,** orador (-ra)

speechless *a* mudo; sin habla; desconcertado, turbado

speed *n* prisa, rapidez, *f*; velocidad, *f*. *vt* dar la bienvenida (a); conceder éxito (a); (accelerate) acelerar. *vi* darse prisa; correr a toda prisa; (of arrows) volar. **at full s.,** a toda prisa; a toda velocidad; a todo correr. **maximum s.,** velocidad máxima, *f*. **with all s.,** a toda prisa. **s. of impact,** velocidad del choque, *f*. **s.-boat,** lancha de carrera, *f*. **s.-limit,** velocidad máxima, *f*, límite de velocidad, *m*

speedily *adv* aprisa, rápidamente; prontamente

speediness *n* rapidez, prisa, celeridad, *f*; prontitud, *f*

speeding *n* exceso de velocidad, *m*. **s. up,** aceleración, *f*

speedometer *n* cuentakilómetros, *m*

speedway *n* autódromo, *m*, pista de ceniza, *f*

speedy *a* rápido; pronto

spell *n* ensalmo, hechizo, *m*; encanto, *m*; (bout) turno, *m*; (interval) rato, *m*; temporada, *f*. *vt* (a word) deletrear; (a word in writing) escribir; (mean) significar; (be) ser. **a s. of good weather,** una temporada de buen tiempo. **by spells,** a ratos. **to learn to s.,** aprender la ortografía. **s.-bound,** encantado, fascinado; asombrado

spelling *n* deletreo, *m*; ortografía, *f*. **s.-book,** silabario, *m*; **s. mistake,** falta de ortografía, *f*

spelling bee *n* certamen de deletreo, *m*

spend *vt* gastar; (time, etc.) pasar; perder; consumir, agotar. *vi* gastar, hacer gastos. **to s. lavishly** *Mexico* disparar. **to s. oneself,** agotarse

spendthrift *n* derrochador (-ra), manirroto (-ta). *a* despilfarrado, pródigo

spent *a* agotado, rendido. **The night is far s.,** La noche está avanzada. **s. bullet,** bala fría, *f*

sperm *n biol* esperma, *f*; (whale) cachalote, *m*

spermaceti *n* esperma de ballena, *f*

sphere *n* esfera, *f*. **s. of influence,** zona de influencia, *f*

spherical *a* esférico

sphinx *n* esfinge, *f*. **s.-like,** de esfinge

spice *n* especia, *f*; *fig* sabor, *m*; (trace) dejo, *m*. *vt* especiar. **s. cupboard,** especiero, *m*

spick and span *a* limpio como una patena; (brand-new) flamante; (of persons) muy compuesto

spicy *a* especiado; aromático; *fig* picante

spider *n* araña, *f*. **spider's web,** telaraña, *f*

spidery *a* de araña; lleno de arañas. **s. writing,** letra de patas de araña, *f*

spigot *n* espiche, *m*

spike *n* punta (de hierro, etc.), *f*; escarpia, *f*; (for boots) clavo, *m*; *bot* espiga, *f*. *vt* clavetear; (a cannon) clavar

spill *vt* derramar. *n* (fall) caída, *f*

spilling *n* derramamiento, derrame, *m*

spin *vt* hilar; (a cocoon) tejer; (a top) bailar; (a ball) tornear; (a coin) lanzar. *vi* hilar; girar, bailar. *n* vuelta, *f*; paseo, *m*. **to send spinning downstairs,** hacer rodar por la escalera (a). **to s. a yarn,** contar un cuento. **to s. out,** prolongar

spinach *n* espinaca, *f*

spinal *a* espinal. **s. anaesthesia,** raquianestesia, *f*. **s. column,** columna vertebral, *f*

spindle *n* huso, *m*; *mech* eje, *m*. **s.-shaped,** ahusado

spine *n anat* espinazo, *m*, columna vertebral, *f*; *bot* espina, *f*; (of a porcupine, etc.) púa, *f*

spineless *a zool* invertebrado; *fig* débil

spinet *n* espineta, *f*

spinner *n* hilandero (-ra); máquina de hilar, *f*

spinney *n* arboleda, *f*; bosquecillo, *m*

spinning *n* hilado, *m*; hilandería, *f*. **s.-machine,** máquina de hilar, *f*. **s.-top,** trompo, *m*, peonza, *f*. **s.-wheel,** rueca, *f*

spinster *n* soltera, *f*. **confirmed s.,** solterona, *f*

spiny *a* con púas; espinoso

spiral *a* espiral; en espiral. *n* espiral, *f*

spirally *adv* en espiral

spire *n* (of a church) aguja, *f*; espira, *f*

spirit *n* espíritu, *m*; alma, *f*; (ghost) aparecido, fantasma, *m*; (outstanding person) ingenio, *m*, inteligencia, *f*; (disposition) ánimo, *m*; (courage) valor, espíritu, *m*; (for a lamp, etc.) alcohol, *m*. **the Holy S.,** El Espíritu Santo. **to be in high spirits,** no caber de contento, saltar de alegría. **to be in low spirits,** estar desalentado, estar deprimido. **to be full of spirits,** ser bullicioso, tener mucha energía. **to keep up one's spirits,** sostener el valor. **to s. away,** quitar secretamente, hacer desaparecer; (kidnap) secuestrar. **s.-level,** nivel de burbuja, *m*. **s.-stove,** cocinilla, *f*

spirited *a* animado, vigoroso; fogoso, animoso, brioso

spiritless *a* sin espíritu, apático; flojo, débil; (depressed) abatido, desalentado; (cowardly) sin valor, cobarde

spiritual *a* espiritual

spiritualism *n* espiritismo, *m*; *phil* espiritualismo, *m*

spiritualist *n* espiritista, *mf*; *phil* espiritualista, *mf*

spiritualistic *a* espiritista; *phil* espiritualista. **s. séance,** sesión espiritista, *f*

spirituality *n* espiritualidad, *f*

spiritually *adv* espiritualmente

spirituous *a* espiritoso
spirt *vi, vt, n.* See **spurt**
spit *n* (for roasting) espetón, asador, *m*; (sand-bank) banco de arena, *m*; (of land) lengua de tierra, *f*; (spittle) saliva, *f*. **the spit of, the spit and image of, the spitting image of,** la imagen viva de, la segunda edición de, *f*. *vt* (skewer) espetar; (saliva, etc.) escupir; (curses, etc.) vomitar. *vi* escupir, expectorar; (of a cat) fufear, decir fu; (sputter) chisporrotear; (rain) lloviznar
spite *n* malevolencia, mala voluntad, hostilidad, *f*; rencor, *m*, ojeriza, *f*. *vt* contrariar, hacer daño (a). **He has a s. against them,** Les tiene rencor. **in s. of,** a pesar de; a despecho de
spiteful *a* rencoroso, malévolo
spitefully *adv* malévolamente; con rencor; por maldad; por despecho
spitefulness *n* malevolencia, *f*; rencor, *m*
spitfire *n* cascarrabias, *mf*, furia, *f*
spittle *n* saliva, *f*
splash *vt* salpicar (de); manchar (con). *vi* derramarse, esparcirse; chapotear, chapalear. *n* chapoteo, *m*; (of rain, etc.) chapaleteo, *m*; (stain or patch) mancha, *f*. **John was splashing about in the sea,** Juan chapoteaba en el mar. **to make a s.,** *fig* causar una sensación. **s.-board,** alero, *m*
spleen *n anat* bazo, *m*; esplín, *m*
splendid *a* espléndido; magnífico; glorioso; excelente
splendidly *adv* espléndidamente; magníficamente; excelentemente
splendor *n* resplandor, *m*; magnificencia, *f*; (of exploits, etc.) esplendor, brillo, *m*
splice *vt* (ropes, timbers) empalmar; (marry) unir, casar. *n* empalme, *m*
splint *n surg* férula, *f*. **to put in a s.,** entablar
splinter *vt* astillar, hacer astillas. *vi* hacerse astillas
splintery *a* astilloso
split *vi* henderse; resquebrajarse; (of seams) nacerse; abrirse; dividirse. *vt* hender; partir; dividir; abrir; (the atom) escindir. *n* hendedura, *f*; grieta, *f*; división, *f*; (in fabric) rasgón, *m*; (quarrel) ruptura, *f*. **to s. hairs,** andar en quisquillas, pararse en pelillos, sutilizar. **I have a splitting headache,** Tengo un dolor de cabeza que me trae loco. **to s. one's sides,** reírse a carcajadas, desternillarse de risa. **to s. on a rock,** estrellarse contra una roca. **to s. the difference,** partir la diferencia. **The blow s. his head open,** El golpe le abrió la cabeza. **to s. on,** *inf* delatar, denunciar
splodge *n* mancha, *f*, borrón, *m*
splutter *vi* chisporrotear; (of a person) balbucir. *n* chisporroteo, *m*. **to s. out,** decir tartamudeando
spoil *n* botín, despojo, *m*; (of war) trofeo, *m*. *vt* estropear; echar a perder; (diminish) mitigar; (a child) mimar; (injure) dañar; (destroy) arruinar, destruir. *vi* estropearse; echarse a perder. **to be spoiling for a fight,** tener ganas de pelearse. **You have spoilt my fun,** Me has aguado la fiesta. **s.-sport,** aguafiestas, *mf*
spoilt *a* (of a child, etc.) mimado, consentido, malacostumbrado
spoke *n* (of a wheel) rayo, *m*; (of a ladder) travesaño, peldaño, *m*; *naut* cabilla (de la rueda del timón), *f*
spoken *a* hablado. **well-s.,** bien hablado; cortés
spokesman *n* portavoz, *m*. **to be s.,** llevar la palabra
spoliation *n* expoliación, *f*; despojo, *m*
sponge *n* esponja, *f*; (cadger) gorrón (-ona); (cake) bizcocho, *m*. *vt* limpiar con esponja. **to s.,** *inf* vivir de gorra. **s.-holder,** esponjera, *f*
sponger *n* gorrón (-ona), vividor, *m*, sablista, *mf*
sponginess *n* esponjosidad, *f*
sponging *n* esponjadura, *f*; *inf* sablazo, *m*
spongy *a* esponjoso
sponsor *n* garante, *mf*; valedor (-ra), patron (-na); (godfather) padrino, *m*; (godmother) madrina, *f*, (radio and TV) auspiciador, patrocinador, *m*
spontaneity *n* espontaneidad, *f*
spontaneous *a* espontáneo. **s. combustion,** combustión espontánea, *f*
spontaneously *adv* espontáneamente
spook *n* fantasma, espectro, *m*
spool *n* (for thread) bobina, *f*, carrete, *m*; (in a sewing machine) canilla, *f*; (of a fishing rod) carrete, *m*
spoon *n* cuchara, *f*. *vt* sacar con cuchara. *vi* (slang) besuquearse. **to s.-feed,** dar de comer con cuchara (a); tratar como un niño (a)
spoonful *n* cucharada, *f*
spoor *n* pista, huella de animal, *f*; rastro, *m*
sporadic *a* esporádico
spore *n bot* espora, *f*; *zool* germen, *m*
sport *n* deporte, sport, *m*; deportismo, *m*; (jest) broma, *f*; (game) juego, *m*; (plaything) juguete, *m*; (pastime) pasatiempo, *m*. *vi* jugar; recrearse, divertirse. *vt* llevar; ostentar, lucir. **He is a s.,** Es un buen chico. **to make s. of,** burlarse de. **sports car,** coche de deporte, *m*. **sports ground,** campo de recreo, *m*. **sports jacket,** chaqueta de deporte, americana, *f*. **sports shirt,** camisa corta, *f*
sporting *a* deportista; caballeroso. **I think there is a s. chance,** Me parece que hay una posibilidad de éxito
sporting goods *n* artículos de deporte, efectos de deportes, *m pl*
sportive *a* juguetón; bromista
sportsman *n* deportista, *m*; aficionado al sport, *m*; *fig* caballero, señor, *m*; buen chico, *m*
sportsmanlike *a* de deportista; caballeroso
sportsmanship *n* deportividad, *f*
spot *n* mancha, *f*; pinta, *f*; (on the face, etc.) peca, *f*; grano, *m*; (place) sitio, *m*; lugar, *m*; (of liquor) trago, *m*; (of food) bocado, *m*; (of rain) gota, *f*. *vt* manchar; motear; (recognize) reconocer; (understand) darse cuenta de, comprender. **a tender s.,** *fig* debilidad, *f*. **on the s.,** en el acto. **s. ball,** (billiards) pinta, *f*. **s. cash,** dinero contante, *m*
spotless *a* saltando de limpio; sin mancha; inmaculado; puro; virgen
spotlight *n* luz del proyector, *f*; proyector, *m*
spotted *a* (stained) manchado; (of animals, etc.) con manchas; (of garments, etc.) con pintas
spotty *a* lleno de manchas; moteado; (pimply) con granos
spouse *n* esposo, *m*; esposa, *f*
spout *vi* chorrear; *inf* hablar incesantemente. *vt* arrojar; vomitar; *inf* declamar, recitar. *n* (of a jug, etc.) pico, *m*; (for water, etc.) tubo, *m*, cañería, *f*; canalón, *m*; (gust) ráfaga, nube, *f*. **down s.,** tubo de bajada, *m*
spouting *n* chorreo, *m*; *inf* declamación, *f*
sprachgefühl *n* sentido del idioma, *m*
sprain *vt* dislocar, torcer. *n* dislocación, *f*, esguince, *m*. **Victoria has sprained her foot,** Victoria se ha torcido el pie
sprat *n* sardineta, *f*
sprawl *vi* recostarse (en); extenderse; (of plants) trepar. **He went sprawling,** Cayó cuan largo era
spray *n* (branch) ramo, *m*; (of water, etc.) rocío, *m*; (of the sea) espuma, *f*; (mechanical device) pulverizador, *m*. *vt* pulverizar; rociar; regar; (the throat) jeringar
spread *vt* tender; cubrir (de); poner; (stretch out) extender; (open out) desplegar; (of disease, etc.) propagar; diseminar; divulgar, difundir. *vi* extenderse; propagarse; difundirse; divulgarse; (become general) generalizarse. *n* extensión, *f*; expansión, *f*; propagación, *f*; divulgación, *f*; (*aer* and of birds) envergadura, *f*. **Carmen s. her hands to the fire,** Carmen extendió las manos al fuego. **The peacock s. its tail,** El pavo real hizo la rueda. **The dove s. its wings,** La paloma desplegó sus alas. **to s. out,** *vt* extender; desplegar; (scatter) esparcir, *vi* extenderse. **spread like wildfire,** correr como pólvora en reguero, propagarse como un reguero de pólvora, ser un reguero de pólvora
spreading *n* (of a disease) propagación, *f*; (of knowledge, etc.) divulgación, *f*; expansión, *f*; extensión, *f*
spree *n* juerga, parranda, *f*; excursión, *f*. **to go on the s.,** ir de juerga, ir de picos pardos

sprig *n* ramita, *f;* (of heather, etc.) espiga, *f;* (scion) vástago, *m*
sprightliness *n* vivacidad, *f,* despejo, *m;* energía, *f*
sprightly *a* vivaracho, despierto; enérgico
spring *vi* saltar, brincar; (become) hacerse; (seek) buscar; (of plants, water) brotar; (of tears) arrasar, llenar; (from) originarse (en), ser causado (por); inspirarse (en). *vt* (a mine) volar; (a trap) soltar. **to s. a surprise,** dar una sorpresa. **to s. a surprise on a person,** coger a la imprevista (a). **to s. at a person,** precipitarse sobre. **to s. to one's feet,** ponerse de pie de un salto. **to s. back,** saltar hacia atrás; recular; volver a su sitio. **to s. open,** abrirse súbitamente. **to s. up,** (of plants) brotar, crecer; (of difficulties, etc.) surgir, asomarse
spring *n* (jump) salto, brinco, *m;* (of water) fuente, *f,* manantial, *m;* (season) primavera, *f;* (of a watch, etc.) resorte, *m;* (of a mattress, etc.) muelle, *m. a* primaveral. *vi* saltar, brincar. **at one s.,** en un salto. **to give a s.,** dar un salto. **s.-board,** trampolín, *m.* **s.-mattress,** colchón de muelles, *m.* **s.-tide,** marea viva, *f*
springiness *n* elasticidad, *f*
springlike *a* primaveral
springtime *n* primavera, *f*
sprinkle *vt* esparcir; salpicar; rociar
sprinkling *n* salpicadura, *f;* rociadura, *f;* pequeño número, *m.* **a s. of snow,** una nevada ligera
sprint *vi* sprintar. *n* sprint, *m*
sprite *n* trasgo, *m;* hada, *f*
sprout *vi* brotar, despuntar, retoñar, tallecer; germinar. *vt* salir. *n* brote, retoño, pimpollo, *m;* germen, *m.* **Brussels sprouts,** coles de Bruselas, *f pl*
spruce *a* peripuesto, muy aseado, pulido; elegante, *n bot* pícea, *f.* **to s. oneself up,** arreglarse, ponerse elegante
spruceness *n* aseo, buen parecer, *m,* elegancia, *f*
spry *a* activo, ágil
spur *n* espuela, *f;* aguijada, *f;* (of a bird) espólon, *m; bot* espuela, *f;* (of a mountain range) espolón, estribo, *m; fig* estímulo, *m. vt* espolear, picar con la espuela; calzarse las espuelas; *fig* estimular, incitar, *Lat. Am.* espuelar. **on the s. of the moment,** bajo el impulso del momento
spurious *a* espurio; falso
spurn *vt* rechazar; tratar con desprecio; menospreciar
spurt *vi* (gush) chorrear, borbotar; brotar, surgir; (in racing, etc.) hacer un esfuerzo supremo. *vt* hacer chorrear; lanzar. *n* (jet) chorro, *m;* esfuerzo supremo, *m*
sputter *vi* chisporrotear; crepitar; (of a pen) escupir; (of a person) balbucir
sputtering *n* chisporroteo, *m;* crepitación, *f;* (of a person) balbuceo, *m*
sputum *n* esputo, *m*
spy *vt* observar, discernir. *vi* espiar, ser espía. *n* espía, *mf.* **to spy out the land,** explorar el terreno. **to spy upon, espiar;** seguir los pasos (a). **spy-glass,** catalejo, *m*
spying *n* espionaje, *m*
squabble *n* disputa, *f;* riña, *f. vi* pelearse; disputar
squabbling *n* riñas, querellas, *f pl;* disputas, *f pl*
squad *n* escuadra, *f;* pelotón, *m*
squadron *n mil* escuadrón, *m; nav* escuadra, *f; aer* escuadrilla, *f;* (of persons) pelotón, *m.* **s.-leader,** comandante, *m*
squalid *a* escuálido; (of quarrels, etc.) sórdido, mezquino
squall *vi* berrear; chillar. *n* berrido, *m;* chillido, *m;* (storm) chubasco, turbión, *m;* (storm) chubasco, turbión, *m; fig* tormenta, tempestad, *f*
squalor *n* escualidez, *f;* sordidez, mezquindad, *f*
squander *vt* derrochar, tirar, desperdiciar; (time, etc.) malgastar
squanderer *n* derrochador (-ra)
squandering *n* derroche, desperdicio, dispendio, *m;* (of time, etc.) pérdida, *f,* desperdicio, *m*
square *n math* cuadrado, *m;* rectángulo, *m;* (of a chessboard) escaque, *m;* (of a draughtboard and of graph paper) casilla, *f;* (in a town) plaza, *f;* (of troops) cuadro, *m, a* cuadrado; justo; igual; (honest) honrado, formal; (unambiguous) redondo, categórico; *math* cuadrado. **She wore a silk s. on her head,** Llevaba un pañuelo de seda en la cabeza. **five s. feet,** cinco pies cuadrados. **nine feet s.,** nueve pies en cuadro. **on the s.,** honradamente. **a s. dance,** contradanza, *f.* **a s. meal,** una buena comida. **s. dealing,** trato limpio, *m.* **The account is s.,** La cuenta está justa. **to get s. with,** desquitarse (de), vengarse de. **s. measure,** medida de superficie, *f.* **s. root,** raíz cuadrada, *f.* **s.-shouldered,** de hombros cuadrados
square *vt* cuadrar; *carp* escuadrar; (arrange) arreglar; (bribe) sobornar; (reconcile) acomodar; *math* cuadrar. *vi* conformarse (con), cuadrar (con). **to s. the circle,** cuadrar el círculo. **to s. one's shoulders,** enderezarse. **to s. accounts with,** saldar cuentas con. **to s. up to,** (a person) avanzar belicosamente hacia
squarely *adv* en cuadro; directamente; sin ambigüedades, rotundamente; (honestly) de buena fe, honradamente
squareness *n* cuadratura, *f;* (honesty) honradez, buena fe, *f*
squash *vt* aplastar. *vi* aplastarse; apretarse. *n* aplastamiento, *m;* (of fruit, etc.) pulpa, *f;* (of people) agolpamiento, *m;* muchedumbre, *f;* (drink) refresco (de limón, etc.), *m,* (sport) frontón con raqueta, *m*
squashy *a* blando y húmedo
squat *vi* acuclillarse, agacharse, agazaparse ponerse en cuclillas; estar en cuclillas; (on land, etc.) apropiarse sin derecho. *a* rechoncho
squatter *n* intruso (-sa); colono usurpador, *m*
squatter town *n.* See **shanty town**
squawk *vi* graznar; lanzar gritos agudos. *n* graznido, *m;* grito agudo, *m*
squeak *vi* (of carts, etc.) chirriar, rechinar; (of shoes) crujir; (of persons, mice, etc.) chillar; (slang) cantar. *n* chirrido, crujido, *m;* chillido, *m.* **to have a narrow s.,** escapar por un pelo
squeaking *n* chirrido, rechinamiento, *m;* crujido, *m;* (of humans, mice, etc.) chillidos, *m pl*
squeal *vi* lanzar gritos agudos, chillar; (complain) quejarse; (slang) cantar. *n* grito agudo, chillido, *m*
squealing *n* gritos agudos, chillidos, *m pl*
squeamish *a* que se marea fácilmente; mareado; (nauseated) asqueado; delicado; remilgado
squeamishness *n* tendencia a marearse, *f;* delicadeza, *f;* remilgos, *m pl*
squeeze *vt* apretar; estrujar; (fruit) exprimir; (extort) arrancar; (money from) sangrar. *n* (of the hand, etc.) apretón, *m;* estrujón, *m;* (of fruit juice) algunas gotas (de). **It was a tight s. in the car,** Íbamos muy apretados en el coche. **He was in a tight s.,** Se encontraba en un aprieto. **to s. one's way through the crowd,** abrirse camino a codazos por la muchedumbre. **to s. in,** *vt* hacer sitio para. *vi* introducirse con dificultad (en)
squelch *vi* gorgotear, chapotear. *vt* aplastar
squib *n* (firework) rapapiés, buscapiés, *m;* (lampoon) pasquinada, *f*
squid *n* calamar, *m*
squint *n* estrabismo, *m;* mirada furtiva, *f; inf* vistazo, *m,* mirada, *f. vi* ser bizco; bizcar. **to s. at,** mirar de soslayo. **s.-eyed,** bizco. **to be s.-eyed,** mirar contra el gobierno
squire *n* escudero, *m;* hacendado, *m. vt* escoltar, acompañar
squirm *vi* retorcerse; (with embarrassment) no saber dónde meterse. *n* retorcimiento, *m.* **to s. along the ground,** arrastrarse por el suelo
squirrel *n* ardilla, *f*
squirt *vt* (liquids) lanzar. *vi* chorrear, salir a chorros. *n* chorro, *m;* (syringe) jeringa, *f*
stab *vt* apuñalar, dar de puñaladas (a); herir. *n* puñalada, *f;* herida, *f;* (of pain, and *fig*) pinchzo, *m.* **a s. in the back,** una puñalada por la espalda
stability *n* estabilidad, *f;* solidez, firmeza, *f*
stabilize *vt* estabilizar

stable *a* estable; fijo, firme. *n* cuadra, caballeriza, *f*; (for cows, etc.) establo, *m*. *vt* poner en la cuadra; alojar. **s.-boy,** mozo de cuadra, *m*
stack *n* (of hay) niara, *f*, almiar, *m*; (heap) montón, *m*; (of rifles) pabellón, *m*; (of a chimney) cañón, *m*. *vt agr* hacinar; amontonar; *mil* poner (las armas) en pabellón
stacked *a* (woman) abultada de pechera
stadium *n* estadio, *m*
staff *n* vara, *f*; (bishop's, and *fig*) báculo, *m*; (pilgrim's) bordón, *m*; (pole) palo, *m*; (flagstaff) asta, *f*; (of an office, etc.) personal, *m*; (editorial) redacción, *f*; (corps) cuerpo, *m*; *mil* plana mayor, *f*, estado mayor, *m*; *mus* pentagrama, *m*. *vt* proveer de personal. **general s.,** estado mayor general, *m*. **s. officer,** *mil* oficial de estado mayor, *m*
stag *n* ciervo, *m*. **s.-beetle,** ciervo volante, *m*. **s.-hunting,** caza del ciervo, *f*
stage *n* (for workmen) andamio, *m*; (of a microscope) portaobjetos, *m*; *theat* escena, *f*, tablas, *f pl*; teatro, *m*; (of development, etc.) etapa, *f*; fase, *f*. *vt theat* escenificar, poner en escena; *theat* representar; (a demonstration, etc.) arreglar. **by easy stages,** poco a poco; (of a journey) a pequeñas etapas. **to come on the s.,** salir a la escena. **to go on the s.,** hacerse actor (actriz), dedicarse al teatro. **s. carpenter,** tramoyista, *m*. **s.-coach,** diligencia, *f*. **s.-craft,** arte de escribir para el teatro, *f*; arte escénica, *f*. **s.-direction,** acotación, *f*. **s.-door,** entrada de los artistas, *f*. **s.-effect,** efecto escénico, *m*. **s.-fright,** miedo al público, *m*. **s.-hand,** tramoyista, sacasillas, metesillas y sacamuertos, *m*. **s. manager,** director de escena, *m*. **s.-whisper,** aparte, *m*
stager, old *n* veterano, *m*
stagger *vi* tambalear; andar haciendo eses; (hesitate) titubear, vacilar. *vt* desconcertar. *n* titubeo, tambaleo, *m*; *aer* decalaje, *m*. **staggered working hours,** horas de trabajo escalonadas, *f pl*
staggering *a* tambaleante; (surprising) asombroso, sorprendente; (dreadful) espantoso. **a s. blow,** un golpe que derriba
staging *n* (scaffolding) andamio, *m*; *theat* producción, *f*; representación, *f*; decorado, *m*
stagnancy *n* (of water) estancación, *f*; (inactivity) estagnación, *f*; paralización, *f*
stagnant *a* estancado; paralizado. **to be s.,** estar estancado. **s. water,** agua estancada, *f*
stagnate *vi* estancarse; estar estancado; (of persons) vegetar
stagnation *n* (of water) estancación, *f*; estagnación, *f*; parálisis, *f*
staid *a* serio, formal, juicioso
staidness *n* seriedad, formalidad, *f*
stain *vt* manchar; (dye) teñir. *n* mancha, *f*; colorante, *m*. **without a s.,** *fig* sin mancha. **stained glass,** vidrio de color, *m*. **s.-remover,** quitamanchas, *m*
stainless *a* sin mancha; inmaculado, puro
stair *n* escalón, peldaño, *m*; escalera, *f*; *pl* **stairs,** escalera, *f*. **a flight of stairs,** una escalera; un tramo de escaleras. **below stairs,** escalera abajo. **s.-carpet,** alfombra de escalera, *f*. **s.-rod,** varilla para alfombra de escalera, *f*
staircase *n* escalera, *f*. **spiral s.,** escalera de caracol, *f*
stake *n* estaca, *f*; (for plants) rodrigón, *m*; (gaming) envite, *m*, apuesta, *f*; (in an undertaking) interés, *m*; *pl* **stakes,** (prize) premio, *m*; (race) carrera, *f*. *vt* estacar; (plants) rodrigar; (bet) jugar. **at s.,** en juego; en peligro. **to be burnt at the s.,** morir en la hoguera. **to s. one's all,** jugarse el todo por el todo. **to s. a claim,** hacer una reclamación. **to s. out,** jalonar
stalactite *n* estalactita, *f*
stalagmite *n* estalagmita, *f*
stale *a* no fresco; (of bread, etc.) duro, seco; (of air) viciado; viejo; pasado de moda; (tired) cansado
stalemate *n* (chess, checkers) tablas, *f pl*; *fig* punto muerto, *m*. **to reach a s.,** llegar a un punto muerto
staleness *n* rancidez, *f*; (of bread, etc.) dureza, *f*; (of news, etc.) falta de novedad, *f*
stalk *n bot* tallo, *m*; *bot* pedúnculo, *m*; (of a glass) pie, *m*. *vi* andar majestuosamente; *fig* rondar. *vt* (game) cazar al acecho; (a person) seguir los pasos (a)
stalking horse *n* boezuelo, *m*; *fig* pretexto, disfraz, *m*
stall *n* (in a stable) puesto (individual), *m*; (stable) establo, *m*; (choir) silla de coro, *f*; (in a fair, etc.) barraca, *f*, puesto, *m*; *theat* butaca, *f*; (finger-stall) dedal, *m*. *vt* (an engine) cortar accidentalmente. *vi aut* pararse de pronto; *aer* perder velocidad; (of a cart, etc.) atascarse. **pit s.,** *theat* butaca de platea, *f*
stalling *n aut* parada accidental, *f*; *aer* pérdida de velocidad, *f*. **Stop s.!** ¡Déjate de rodeos!
stallion *n* semental, *m*
stalwart *a* robusto, fornido; leal; valiente
stalwartness *n* robustez, *f*; lealtad, *f*; valor, *m*
stamina *n* resistencia, *f*
stammer *vi* tartamudear; (hesitate in speaking) titubear, balbucir. *n* tartamudez, *f*; titubeo, balbuceo, *m*
stammerer *n* tartamudo (-da)
stammering *a* tartamudo; balbuciente. *n* tartamudeo, *m*; balbuceo, *m*
stamp *vt* estampar; imprimir; (documents) timbrar; pegar el sello de correo (a); (characterize) sellar; (*fig* engrave) grabar; (coins) acuñar; (press) apisonar; (with the foot) golpear con los pies, patear; (in dancing) zapatear. *n* (with the foot) patada, *f*, golpe con los pies, *m*; (mark, etc.) marca, *f*; (rubber, etc.) estampilla, *f*; matasellos, *m*; cuño, *m*; (for documents) póliza, *f*; timbre, *m*; (for letters) sello, *m*; *Mexico* timbre, *m*, *elsewhere in Lat. Am.* estampilla, *f*, (machine) punzón, *m*; mano de mortero, *f*; (*fig* sign) sello, *m*; (kind) temple, *m*, clase, *f*. **The events of that day are stamped on my memory,** Los acontecimientos de aquel día están grabados en mi memoria. **to s. out,** (a fire, etc.) extinguir, apagar; (resistance, etc.) vencer; destruir. **postage-s.,** sello de correos, *m*. **s.-album,** álbum de sellos, *m*. **s.-duty,** impuesto del timbre, *m*. **s.-machine,** expendedor automático de sellos de correo, *m*
stampede *n* fuga precipitada, *f*; pánico, *m*. *vi* huir precipitadamente; (of animals) salir de estampía; huir en desorden. *vt* hacer perder la cabeza (a), sembrar el pánico entre
stamping *n* selladura, *f*; (of documents) timbrado, *m*; (of fabrics, etc.) estampado, *m*; (with the feet) pataleo, *m*; (in dancing) zapateo, *m*
stance *n* posición de los pies, *f*; postura, *f*
stanch *vt* restañar
stand *vi* estar de pie; ponerse de pie, incorporarse; estar; hallarse; sostenerse; ser; ponerse; (halt) parar; (remain) permanecer, quedar. *vt* poner; (endure) resistir; tolerar; sufrir; (entertain) convidar. **S.!** ¡Alto! **as things s.,** tal como están las cosas. **I cannot s. any more,** No puedo más. **I cannot s. him,** No le puedo ver. **Nothing stands between them and ruin,** No hay nada entre ellos y la ruina. **I stood him a drink,** Le convidé a un trago. **How do we s.?** ¿Cómo estamos? **It stands to reason that . . . ,** Es lógico que . . . **Edward stands six feet,** Eduardo tiene seis pies de altura. **to s. accused of,** ser acusado de. **to s. godfather** (or **godmother**) **to,** sacar de pila (a). **to s. in need (of),** necesitar, tener necesidad (de). **to s. on end,** (of hair) ponerse de punta, despeluzarse. **to s. one in good stead,** ser útil, ser ventajoso. **to s. one's ground,** no ceder, tenerse fuerte. **to s. to attention,** cuadrarse, permanecer en posición de firmes. **to s. well with,** tener buenas relaciones con, ser estimado de. **to s. aside,** tenerse a un lado; apartarse; (in favor of someone) retirarse. **to s. back,** quedarse atrás; recular, retroceder. **to s. by,** estar de pie cerca de; estar al lado de; estar presente (sin intervenir); ser espectador; estar preparado; (one's friends) ayudar, proteger; (a promise, etc.) atenerse (a); ser fiel (a); (of a ship) mantenerse listo. **s.-by,** *n* recurso, *m*. **to s. for,** representar; simbolizar; (mean) significar; (Parliament, etc.) presentarse como candidato; (put up with) tolerar, sufrir. **to s. in,** colaborar. **to s. in with,** estar de acuerdo con,

ser partidario de; compartir. **to s. off,** mantenerse a distancia. **to s. out,** (in relief, and *fig.* of persons) destacarse; (be firm) resistir, mantenerse firme; *naut* gobernar más afuera. **S. out of the way!** ¡Quítate del medio! **to s. over,** (be postponed) quedar aplazado. **to s. up,** estar de pie; ponerse de pie, incorporarse; tenerse derecho. **to s. up against,** resistir; oponerse a. **to s. up for,** defender; volverpor. **to s. up to,** hacer cara a

stand *n* puesto, *m;* posición, actitud, *f;* (for taxis, etc.) punto, *m;* (in a market, etc.) puesto, *m; sport* tribuna, *f;* (for a band) quiosco, *m;* (of a dish, etc.) pie, *m; mech* sostén, *m;* (opposition) resistencia, oposición, *f.* **to make a s. against,** oponerse resueltamente (a); ofrecer resistencia (a). **to take one's s.,** fundarse (en), apoyarse (en). **to take up one's s. by the fire,** ponerse cerca del fuego

standard *n* (flag) estandarte, *m,* bandera, *f;* (for gold, weights, etc.) marco, *m;* norma, *f;* convención, regla, *f;* (of a lamp) pie, *m;* (pole) poste, *m;* columna, *f;* (level) nivel, *m. a* corriente; normal; típico; clásico. **It is a s. type,** Es un tipo corriente. **gold s.,** patrón de oro, *m.* **s. author,** autor clásico, *m.* **s. formula,** fórmula clásica, *f.* **s. of living,** nivel de vida, *m.* **s.-bearer,** abanderado, *m.* **s.-lamp,** lámpara vertical, *f*

standardization *n* (of armaments, etc.) unificación de tipos, *f;* (of dyestuffs, medicinals, etc.) control, *m,* estandardización, *f*

standardize *vt* hacer uniforme; controlar

standing *a* de pie, derecho; permanente, fijo; constante. *n* posición, *f;* reputación, *f;* importancia, *f;* antigüedad, *f.* **It is a quarrel of long s.,** Es una riña antigua. **s. committee,** comisión permanente, *f.* **s. room,** sitio para estar de pie, *m.* **s. water,** agua estancada, *f.* **standoffish,** frío, etiquetero; altanero. **standoffishness,** frialdad, *f;* altanería, *f.* **standpoint,** punto de vista, *m*

standstill *n* parada, *f;* pausa, *f.* **at a s.,** parado; (of industry) paralizado

stanza *n* estrofa, estancia, *f*

staple *n* (fastener) grapa, *f;* (of wool, etc.) hebra, fibra, *f;* producto principal (de un pais), *m;* (raw material) materia prima, *f; a* principal; más importante; corriente

stapler, (device) cosepapeles, engrapador, *m,* atrochadora (Argentina), *f*

star *n* (all meanings) estrella, *f;* (asterisk) asterisco, *m. vt* estrellar, sembrar de estrellas; marcar con asterisco. *vi* (*theat* cinema) presentarse como estrella, ser estrella. **stars and stripes,** las barras y las estrellas. **to be born under a lucky s.,** tener estrella. **to see stars,** ver estrellas. **s.-gazing,** observación de las estrellas, *f;* ensimismamiento, *m.* **s.-spangled,** estrellado, tachonado de estrellas, sembrado de estrellas. **s.-turn,** gran atracción, *f*

starboard *n naut* estribor, *m*

starch *n* almidón, *m,* las harinas, *f pl, vt* almidonar

starchy *a* almidonado; (of food) feculento; *fig* tieso, entonado, etiquetero

stare *vi* mirar fijamente; abrir mucho los ojos. *n* mirada fija, *f.* **stony s.,** mirada dura, *f.* **to s. at,** (a person) clavar la mirada en; mirar de hito en hito (a). **The explanation stares one in the face,** La explicación salta a la vista (or está evidente). **to s. into space,** mirar las telarañas. **to s. out of countenance,** avergonzar con la mirada

starfish *n* estrella de mar, *f*

staring *a* (of colors) chillón, llamativo, encendido. **s. eyes,** ojos saltones, *m pl;* ojos espantados, *m pl*

stark *a* rígido; *poet* poderoso; absoluto. **s. staring mad,** loco de atar. **s.-naked,** en cueros vivos, en pelota

starless *a* sin estrellas

starlight *n* luz de las estrellas, *f, a* estrellado

starry *a* estrellado, sembrado de estrellas

start *vi* estremecerse, asustarse; saltar; (set out) salir; ponerse en camino; (of a train, a race) arrancar; ponerse en marcha; *aer* despegar; (begin) empezar; (of timbers) combarse. *vt* empezar; (a car, etc.) poner en marcha; (a race) dar la señal de partida; (a hare, etc.) levantar; (cause) provocar, causar; (a discussion, etc.) abrir; iniciar. *n* (fright) susto, *m;* (setting out) partida, salida, *f;* (beginning) principio, comienzo, *m;* (starting-point of a race) arrancadero, *m; aer* despegue, *m;* (advantage) ventaja, *f.* **at the s.,** al principio. **for a s.,** para empezar. **from s. to finish,** desde el principio hasta el fin. **She started to cry,** Se puso a llorar. **He has started his journey to Canada,** Ha empezado su viaje al Canadá. **I started up the engine,** Puse el motor en marcha. **to get a s.,** asustarse; tomar la delantera. **to give** (a person) **a s.,** asustar, dar un susto (a); dar la ventaja (a). **to give** (a person) **a s. in life,** ayudar a alguien a situarse en la vida. **to make a fresh s. (in life),** hacer vida nueva, empezar la vida de nuevo. **to s. after,** lanzarse en busca de; salir tras. **to s. back,** retroceder; emprender el viaje de regreso; marcharse. **to s. off,** salir, partir; ponerse en camino. **to s. up,** *vi* incorporarse bruscamente, ponerse de pie de un salto; (appear) surgir, aparecer. *vt* (an engine) poner en marcha

starter *n* iniciador (-ra); (for a race) starter, juez de salida, *m;* (competitor in a race) corredor, *m;* (of a car, etc.) arranque, *m*

starting *n* (setting out) salida, partida, *f;* (beginning) principio, *m;* (fear) estremecimiento, *m;* susto, *m.* **s.-gear,** palanca de arranque, *f.* **s.-handle,** manivela de arranque, *f.* **s.-point,** punto de partida, *m; fig* arrancadero, punto de arranque, *m.* **s.-post,** puesto de salida, *m*

startle *vt* asustar, sobresaltar, alarmar. **The news startled him out of his indifference,** Las noticias le hicieron salir de su indiferencia

startling *a* alarmante; (of dress, etc.) exagerado; (of colors) chillón

starvation *n* hambre, *f; med* inanición, *f.* **s. diet,** régimen de hambre, *m.* **s. wage,** ración de hambre, *f*

starve *vi* morir de hambre; pasar hambre, no tener bastante que comer; no comer. *vt* matar de hambre; privar de alimentos (a). **I am simply starving,** Tengo una hambre canina, Me muero de hambre. **to s. with cold,** *vi* morir de frío. *vt* matar de frío

starved *a* muerto de hambre, hambriento. **s. of affection,** hambriento de cariño

starving *a* que muere de hambre, hambriento

state *n* estado, *m;* condición, *f;* (anxiety) agitación, ansiedad, *f;* (social) rango, *m;* (pomp) magnificencia, pompa, *f;* (government, etc.) Estado, *m;* nación, *f. a* de Estado; de gala, de ceremonia. **the married s.,** el estado matrimonial. **s. of war,** estado de guerra. **in s.,** con gran pompa. **to lie in s.,** (of a body) estar expuesto. **s. apartments,** habitaciones de gala, *f pl.* **s. banquet,** comida de gala, *f.* **s. coach,** coche de gala, *m.* **s. control,** control por el Estado, *m.* **S. Department,** Ministerio de Estado, *m.* **s. education,** instrucción pública, *f.* **State of the Union message,** Mensaje al Congreso, *m.* **s. papers,** documentos de Estado, *m pl*

state *vt* decir (que), afirmar (que); (one's case, etc.) exponer; explicar; *math* proponer

statecraft *n* arte de gobernar, *m*

stated *a* arreglado, indicado; fijo. **the s. date,** la fecha indicada. **at s. intervals,** a intervalos fijos

statehood *n* estadidad, *f*

stateliness *n* dignidad, *f;* majestad, *f*

stately *a* majestuoso; imponente; noble; digno

statement *n* afirmación, declaración, *f;* resumen, *m;* exposición, *f; law* deposición, *f; com* estado de cuenta, *m.* **to make a s.,** hacer una declaración

stateroom *n* sala de recepción, *f;* (on a ship) camarote, *m*

statesman *n* hombre de estado, *m*

statesmanlike *a* de hombre de estado

statesmanship *n* arte de gobernar, *m*

static *a* estático

statics *n* estática, *f*

station *n* (place) puesto, sitio, *m;* (*rw* and *ecc*) estación,

f; (social) posición social, *f*; *naut* apostadero, *m*; *surv* punto de marca, *m*. *vt* estacionar, colocar, poner. **to s. oneself,** colocarse. **Stations of the Cross,** Estaciones, *f pl*. **s.-master,** jefe de la estación, *m*
stationary *a* estacionario; inmóvil; *ast* estacional
stationer *n* papelero (-ra). **stationer's shop,** papelería, *f*
stationery *n* papelería, *f*, efectos de escritorio, *m pl*; papel de escribir, *m*
station wagon *n* pisicorre, coche camioneta, coche rural, *m*
statistical *a* estadístico
statistician *n* estadista, *m*
statistics *n* estadística, *f*
statuary *a* estatuario. *n* estatuaria, *f*; estatuas, *f pl*; (sculptor) estatuario, *m*
statue *n* estatua, *f*; imagen, *f*
statuesque *a* escultural
statuette *n* figurilla, *f*
stature *n* estatura, *f*; (moral, etc.) valor, *m*
status *n* (*law* etc.) estado, *m*; posición, *f*; rango, *m*. **What is his s. as a physicist?** ¿Cómo se le considera entre los físicos? **social s.,** posición social, *f*; rango social, *m*
statute *n* ley, *f*; acto legislativo, *m*; estatuto, *m*; regla, *f*. **s. book,** código legal, *m*
statutory *a* establecido; reglamentario; estatutario
staunch *a* leal, fiel; firme, constante. *vt* restañar
staunchness *n* lealtad, fidelidad, *f*; firmeza, *f*
stave *n* (of a barrel, etc.) duela, *f*; (of a ladder) peldaño, *m*; (stanza) estrofa, *f*; *mus* pentagrama, *m*. **to s. in,** abrir boquete en; romper a golpes; quebrar. **to s. off,** apartar, alejar; (delay) aplazar, diferir; (avoid) evitar; (thirst, etc.) dominar
stay *vt* detener; (a judgment, etc.) suspender. *vi* permanecer; quedarse; detenerse; (of weather, etc.) durar; (lodge) hospedarse, vivir. **to come to s.,** venir a ser permanente. **to s. a person's hand,** detenerle a fulano el brazo. **to s. at home,** quedarse en casa. **s.-at-home,** *a* casero. *n* persona casera, *f*. **to s. the course,** terminar la carrera. **S.! Say no more!** ¡Calle! ¡No diga más! **to s. away,** ausontarse. **to s. up,** no acostarse; velar. **to s. with,** quedarse con; alojarse con; quedarse en casa de, vivir con
stay *n* estancia, permanencia, *f*; residencia, *f*; (restraint) freno, *m*; *law* suspensión, *f*; (endurance) aguante, *m*, resistencia, *f*; *naut* estay, *m*; (prop) puntal, *m*; *fig* apoyo, soporte, *m*; *pl* **stays,** corsé, *m*
stead *n* lugar, *m*. **in the s. of,** en el lugar de, como substituto de. **It has stood me in good s.,** Me ha sido muy útil
steadfast *a* fijo; constante; firme; tenaz. **s. gaze,** mirada fija, *f*
steadfastly *adv* fijamente; con constancia; firmemente; tenazmente
steadfastness *n* fijeza, *f*; constancia, *f*; firmeza, *f*; tenacidad, *f*
steadily *adv* firmemente; (without stopping) sin parar; continuamente; (assiduously) diligentemente; (uniformly) uniformemente. **Prices have gone up s.,** Los precios no han dejado de subir. **He looked at it s.,** Lo miraba sin pestañear (or fijamente)
steadiness *n* estabilidad, *f*; firmeza, *f*; constancia, *f*; (of persons) seriedad, formalidad, *f*; (of workers) diligencia, asiduidad, *f*
steady *a* firme; seguro; fijo; constante; uniforme; continuo; estacionario; (of persons) serio, formal, juicioso; (of workers) diligente, asiduo. *vt* afirmar; (persons) hacer más serio (a); (nerves, etc.) calmar, fortificar. **a s. job,** un empleo seguro. **S.!** ¡Calma!; *naut* ¡Seguro! **He steadied himself against the table,** Se apoyó en la mesa
steak *n* tajada, *f*; biftec, *Argentina* bife, *m*
steal *vt* robar, hurtar; tomar. *vi* robar, ser ladrón; (glide) deslizarse; (overwhelm) dominar, ganar insensiblemente (a). **to s. a kiss,** robar un beso. **to s. a look at,** mirar de soslayo (or de lado). **to s. away,** escurrirse, escabullirse; marcharse a hurtadillas. **to s. in,** deslizarse en, colarse en
stealthily *adv* a hurtadillas; a escondidas, furtivamente
stealthiness *n* carácter furtivo, *m*
stealthy *a* furtivo; cauteloso
steam *n* vapor, *m*. *a* de vapor. *vi* echar vapor. *vt cul* cocer al vapor; (clothes) mojar; (windows, etc.) empañar. **to have the s. up,** estar bajo presión. **The windows are steamed,** Los cristales están empañados. **s.-boiler,** caldera de vapor, *f*. **s.-engine,** máquina de vapor, *f*. **s.-hammer,** maza de fragua, *f*. **s.-heat,** calefacción por vapor, *f*. **s.-roller,** *lit* apisonadora, *fig* fuerza arrolladora, *f*
steamboat *n* vapor, *m*
steamer *n cul* marmita al vacío, *f*; *naut* buque de vapor, *m*
steamship *n* buque de vapor, piróscafo, *m*
steamy *a* lleno de vapor
steed *n* corcel, *m*
steel *n* (metal, and *poet* sword) acero, *m*; (for sharpening) afilón, *m*. *a* de acero; acerado. *vt* acerar; *fig* endurecer. **to be made of s.,** *fig* ser de bronce. **He cannot s. himself to do it,** No puede persuadirse a hacerlo. **to s. one's heart,** hacerse duro de corazón. **cold s.,** arma blanca, *f*. **stainless s.,** acero inoxidable, *m*. **s.-engraving,** grabado en acero, *m*
steel mill *n* fábrica de acero, *f*
steep *a* acantilado, escarpado; precipitoso; (of stairs, etc.) empinado; (of price) exorbitante. *vt* (soak) remojar, empapar; *fig* absorber; (in a subject) empaparse (en). *n* remojo, *m*. **It's a bit s.!** *inf* ¡Es un poco demasiado!
steeping *n* remojo, *m*, maceración, *f*
steeple *n* campanario, *m*, torre, *f*; aguja, *f*
steeplechase *n* steeplechase, *m*, carrera de obstáculos, *f*
steepness *n* carácter escarpado, *m*, lo precipitoso
steer *vt naut* gobernar; (a car, etc.) conducir; *fig* guiar, conducir. *vi naut* timonear; *naut* navegar; *aut* conducir. *n zool* novillo, *m*. **to s. clear of,** evitar. **to s. one's way through the crowd,** abrirse paso entre la muchedumbre
steerage *n* gobierno, *m*; (stern) popa, *f*; (quarters) entrepuente, *m*. **to go s.,** viajar en tercera clase
steering *n naut* gobierno, *m*; (tiller, etc.) gobernalle, timón, *m*; (of a vehicle) conducción, *f*. **s.-column,** barra de dirección, *f*. **s.-wheel,** *aut* volante de dirección, *m*; *naut* rueda del timón, *f*
stellar *a* estelar
stem *n* (of a tree) tronco, *m*; (of a plant) tallo, *m*; (of a glass, etc.) pie, *m*; (*mus* of a note) rabo, *m*; (of a pipe) tubo, *m*; (of a word) radical, *m*. *vt* (check) contener; (the tide) ir contra; (the current) vencer; (dam) estancar. **from s. to stern,** de proa a popa
stench *n* tufo, hedor, *m*, hediondez, *Lat. Am. also* fortaleza, *f*
stencil *n* patrón para estarcir, *m*; estarcido, *m*. *vt* estarcir
stenographer *n* estenógrafo (-fa), taquígrafo (-fa)
stenography *n* estenografía, taquigrafía, *f*
stentorian *a* estentóreo
step *n* paso, *m*; (footprint) huella, *f*; (measure) medida, *f*; (of a stair, etc.) escalón, peldaño, *m*, grada, *f*; (of a ladder) peldaño, *m*; (of vehicles) estribo, *m*; (grade) escalón, *m*; *mus* intervalo, *m*. **at every s.,** a cada paso. **flight of steps,** escalera, *f*; (before a building, etc.) escalinata, *f*. **in steps,** en escalones. **to bend one's steps towards,** dirigirse hacia. **to keep in s.,** llevar el paso. **to take a s.,** dar un paso. **to take steps,** tomar medidas. **s. by s.,** paso a paso; poco a poco. **s.-dance,** baile típico, *m*. **s.-ladder,** escalera de tijera, *f*
step *vi* dar un paso; pisar; andar. **Please s. in!** Sírvase de entrar. **Will you s. this way, please?** ¡Haga el favor de venir por aquí! **to s. aside,** ponerse a un lado; desviarse; *fig* retirarse (en favor de). **to s. in,** entrar; intervenir (en); (meddle) entrometerse. **He stepped**

into the train, Subió al tren. to s. on, pisar. to s. on board, *naut* ir a bordo. to s. out, salir; (from a vehicle) bajar; (a dance) bailar. **He stepped out a moment ago,** Salió hace un instante

stepbrother *n* hermanastro, medio hermano, *m*

stepchild *n* hijastro (-ra)

stepdaughter *n* hijastra, *f*

stepfather *n* padrastro, *m*

stepmother *n* madrastra, *f*

steppingstone *n* pasadera, *f*; *fig* escabel, escalón, *m*

stepsister *n* hermanastra, media hermana, *f*

stepson *n* hijastro, *m*

stereotype *n* estereotipia, *f*, clisé, *m*, *vt* (*print* and *fig*) estereotipar

sterile *a* estéril; árido

sterility *n* esterilidad, *f*; aridez, *f*

sterilization *n* esterilización, *f*

sterilize *vt* esterilizar

sterilizer *n* esterilizador, *m*

sterling *a* esterlina *f*; *fig* genuino. **pound s.,** libra esterlina, *f*

stern *a* severo, austero; duro. *n naut* popa, *f*

sternly *adv* con severidad, severamente, duramente

sternness *n* severidad, *f*; dureza, *f*

sternum *n anat* esternón, *m*

stethoscope *n* estetoscopio, *m*

stevedore *n* estibador, *m*

stew *vt* guisar a la cazuela, estofar; (mutton, etc.) hervir; (fruit) cocer. *n* estofado, *m*; *inf* agitación, *f*. **to be in a s.,** *inf* sudar la gota gorda. **stewed fruit,** compota de frutas, *f*. **s.-pot,** cazuela, olla, *f*, puchero, *m*

steward *n* administrador, *m*; mayordomo, *m*; (provision) despensero, *m*; *naut* camarero, *m*

stewardess *n naut* camarera, *f*

stick *vt* clavar (en), hundir (en); (put) poner; sacar; (stamps, etc.) pegar; fijar; (endure) resistir; tolerar. *vi* clavarse, hundirse; estar clavado; pegarse; (remain) quedar; (in the mud, etc.) atascarse, embarrancarse, (on a reef) encallarse; (in the throat, etc.) atravesarse; (stop) detenerse. **It sticks in my throat,** *inf* No lo puedo tragar. **Friends always s. together,** Los amigos no se abandonan. **The nickname stuck to him,** El apodo se le quedó. **to s. at,** persistir en; desistir (ante); pararse (ante); tener escrúpulos sobre. **to s. at nothing,** no tener escrúpulos. **He stuck at his work,** Siguió trabajando. **to s. down,** pegar. **to s. one's nose into other people's business** *Mexico* entrucharse. **to s. out,** *vi* proyectar; sobresalir. *vt* (one's chest) inflar; (one's tongue) sacar. **His ears s. out,** Tiene las orejas salientes. **to s. to,** (one's job) no dejar; (one's plans) adherirse (a); (one's principles) ser fiel (a); (one's friends) no abandonar; (one's word, etc.) cumplir; atenerse a. **to s. up,** *vi* (of hair) erizarse, ponerse de punta; salirse. *vt* clavar; (a notice) fijar. **to s. up for,** (a person) defender

stick *n* estaca, *f*; (for the fire) leña, *f*; (walking-s.) bastón, *m*; (of office) vara, *f*; (of sealing-wax, etc.) barra, *f*; palo, *m*; (baton) batuta, *f*; (of celery) tallo, *m*. **in a cleft s.,** entre la espada y la pared. **to give** (a person) **the s.,** dar palo (a)

stickiness *n* viscosidad, *f*

stickingplaster *n* esparadrapo, *m*

stick-in-the-mud *n* chapado a la antigua, *m*

stickler *n* rigorista, *mf*. **to be a s. for etiquette,** ser etiquetero

sticky *a* pegajoso, viscoso; *fig* difícil

stiff *a* rígido; inflexible; tieso; (of paste, etc.) espeso; (of manner) distante; (of a bow, etc.) frío; (of a person) almidonado, etiquetero; severo; (of examinations, etc.) difícil; (strong) fuerte; (of price, etc.) alto, exorbitante; (of a shirt front, etc.) duro. **s. with cold,** aterido de frío. **s. neck,** torticolis, *m*. **s.-necked,** terco, obstinaz

stiffen *vt* reforzar; atiesar; (paste, etc.) hacer más espeso; (*fig* strengthen) robustecer; (make more obstinate) hacer más tenaz. *vi* atiesarse; endurecerse; (straighten oneself) enderezarse; (of manner) volverse menos cordial; (become firmer) robustecerse; (become more obstinate) hacerse más tenaz. **The breeze stiffened,** Refrescó el viento

stiffly *adv* tiesamente; rígidamente; obstinadamente

stiffness *n* rigidez, *f*; tiesura, *f*; dureza, *f*; (of manner) frialdad, *f*; (obstinacy) terquedad, obstinación, *f*; (of an examination, etc.) dificultad, *f*

stifle *vt* ahogar, sofocar; apagar; suprimir

stifling *a* sofocante, bochornoso

stigma *n* estigma, *m*

stigmatize *vt* estigmatizar

stile *n* (nearest equivalent) portilla con escalones, *f*

still *a* tranquilo; inmóvil; quedo; silencioso; (of wine) no espumoso. *n* silencio, *m*. **in the s. of the night,** en el silencio de la noche. **Keep s.!** ¡Estate quieto! **to keep s.,** quedarse inmóvil, no moverse. **s.-birth,** nacimiento de un niño muerto, *m*. **s.-born,** nacido muerto. **s. life,** *art* bodegón, *m*, naturaleza muerta, *f*

still *vt* hacer callar, acallar; calmar, tranquilizar; apaciguar; (pain) aliviar

still *adv* todavía, aún; (nevertheless) sin embargo, no obstante; (always) siempre. **I think she s. visits them every week,** Me parece que sigue visitándoles cada semana. **s. and all,** con todo y eso. **s. more,** aún más. **s. to be paid** *Lat. Am.* impago

still *n* alambique, *m*. **salt water s.,** adrazo, *m*

stillness *n* quietud, tranquilidad, *f*; silencio, *m*. **in the s. of the night,** en el silencio de la noche

stilt *n* zanco, *m*

stilted *a* ampuloso, campanudo, hinchado

stimulant *a* and *n* estimulante, *m*

stimulate *vt* estimular; incitar (a), excitar (a)

stimulating *a* estimulante; (encouraging) alentador; (inspiring) sugestivo, inspirador

stimulation *n* excitación, *f*; (stimulus) estímulo, *m*

stimulus *n* estímulo, *m*; *med* estimulante, *m*; (incentive) impulso, incentivo, *m*; acicate, aguijón, *m*

sting *vt* picar, pinchar; (of snakes, etc.) morder; (of hot dishes) resquemar; (of hail, etc.) azotar; (pain) atormentar; (provoke) provocar (a), incitar (a). *n* (*zool* organ) aguijón, *m*; *bot* púa, *f*; (of a scorpion) uña, *f*; (of a serpent) colmillo, *m*; (pain and wound) pinchazo, *m*; (serpent's) mordedura, *f*; (stimulus) acicate, estímulo, *m*; (torment) tormento, dolor, *m*

stingily *adv* avaramente, tacañamente

stinginess *n* tacañería, avaricia, *f*

stinging *a* picante; *fig* mordaz; (of blows) que duele

stingy *a* tacaño, avaro, mezquino, *Argentina* agalludo, *Chile, Peru* coñete

stink *vi* apestar, heder, oler mal. *n* tufo, *m*, hediondez, *Lat. Am. also* fortaleza, *f*

stinking *a* apestoso, hediondo, fétido, mal oliente

stint *vt* escatimar; limitar. *n* límite, *m*, restricción, *f*. **without s.,** sin límite; sin restricción.

stipend *n* estipendio, salario, *m*

stipple *vt art* puntear. *n* punteado, *m*

stipulate *vi* estipular, poner como condición. *vt* estipular, especificar. **They stipulated for a five-day week,** Pusieron como condición (*or* Estipularon) que trabajasen cinco días por semana

stipulation *n* estipulación, *f*; condición, *f*

stir *vt* agitar; revolver; (the fire) atizar; (move) mover; (emotionally) conmover, impresionar; (the imagination) estimular. *vi* moverse. *n* movimiento, *m*; conmoción, *f*; (bustle) bullicio, *m*; sensación, *f*. **to make a s.,** causar una sensación. **to s. one's coffee,** revolver el café. **to s. up discontent,** fomentar el descontento

stirring *a* conmovedor, emocionante, impresionante; (of times, etc.) turbulento, agitado

stirrup *n* estribo, *m*. **s.-cup,** última copa, *f*. **s.-pump,** bomba de mano (para líquidos), *f*

stitch *n* (action) puntada, *f*; (result) punto, *m*; *surg* punto de sutura, *m*; (pain) punzada, *f*, pinchazo, *m*. *vt* coser; *surg* suturar

stoat *n* armiño, *m*; (weasel) comadreja, *f*

stock *n* (of a tree) tronco, *m;* (of a rifle) culata, *f;* (handle) mango, *m;* (of a horse's tail) nabo, *m;* (stem for grafting etc.) injerto, *m;* (race) raza, *f;* (lineage) linaje, *m,* estirpe, *f;* (supply) provisión, *f;* reserva, *f;* (of merchandise) surtido, *m; cul* caldo, *m;* (collar) alzacuello, *m; bot* alhelí, *m;* (government) papel del estado, *m,* valores públicos, *m pl;* (financial) valores, *m pl,* (of a company) capital, *m; pl* **stocks,** *hist* cepo, *m;* (of goods) existencias, *f pl,* stock, *m, a* corriente; del repertorio. **in s.** en existencia. **lives.,** ganado *m.* **rolling-s.,** *rw* materia móvil ferroviario, *m.* **s. phrase** frase hecha, *f.* **s. size,** talla corriente, *f.* **to lay in a s. of,** hacer provisión de, almacenar, **to stand s.-still,** quedarse completamente inmóvil. **to take s.,** *com* hacer inventario. **to take s. of,** inventariar; examinar, considerar. **s.-breeder,** ganadero, *m.* **s.-broker,** corredor de bolsa, bolsista, *m.* **s. exchange,** bolsa, *f.* **s.-in-hand,** *com* existencias, *f pl.* **s.-in-trade** (*com* etc.) capital, *m.* **s.-raising,** cría de ganados, ganadería, *f.* **s.-taking,** *com* inventario, *m*

stock *vt* proveer (de), abastecer (de); (of shops) tener existencia de

stockade *n* estacada, empalizada, *f, vt* empalizar

stocking *n* media, *f.* **nylon stockings,** medias de cristal (or de nilón), *f pl*

stocky *a* rechoncho, doblado, achaparrado

stodgy *a* (of food) indigesto; (of style, etc.) pesado, amazacotado

stoic *a* and *n* estoico (-ca)

stoical *a* estoico

stoke *vt* (a furnace, etc.) cargar, alimentar; (a fire) echar carbón, etc., en. **s.-hole,** cuarto de fogoneros, *m; naut* cámara de calderas, *f*

stoker *n* fogonero, *m;* (mechanical) cargador, *m*

stole *n* (*ecc* and of fur, etc.) estola, *f*

stolid *a* impasible, imperturbable

stolidly *adv* imperturbablemente

stomach *n* estómago, vientre, *m;* apetito, estómago, *m;* (courage) corazón, valor, *m. vt* digerir; (tolerate) tragar, sufrir. **s.ache,** dolor de estómago, *m*

stone *n* piedra, *f;* (gem) piedra preciosa, *f;* (of cherries, etc.) hueso, *m;* (of grapes, etc.) pepita, *f; med* cálculo, *m. a* de piedra. *vt* apedrear; (a wall, etc.) revestir de piedra; (fruit) deshuesar. **to pave with stones,** empedrar. **to leave no s. unturned,** no dejar piedra sin remover. **within a stone's throw,** a corta distancia, a un paso. **S. Age,** edad de piedra, *f.* **s.-breaker,** cantero, picapedrero, *m.* **s.-cold,** muy frío, completamente frío **s.-deaf,** *a* completamente sordo. **s.-fruit,** fruta de hueso, *f.* **s.-mason,** mazonero, albañil, *m;* picapedrero, *m.* **s.-quarry,** pedrera, cantera, *f*

stonily *adv* fríamente; fijamente, sin pestañear

stoniness *n* lo pedregoso; (of hearts, etc.) dureza, *f;* (of stares, etc.) fijeza, inmovilidad, *f*

stoning *n* apedreamiento, *m,* lapidación, *f*

stony *a* pedregoso; (of hearts, etc.) duro, insensible, empedernido; (of a stare, etc.) fijo, duro

stool *n* banquillo, taburete, *m;* (feces) excremento, *m*

stoop *vi* inclinarse, doblarse; encorvarse; ser cargado de espaldas; andar encorvado; (demean oneself) rebajarse (a). *vt* inclinar, doblar. *n* inclinación, *f;* cargazón de espaldas, *f*

stooping *a* inclinado, doblado; (of shoulders) cargado

stop *vt* (a hole) obstruir, atascar; (a leak) cegar, tapar; (a tooth) empastar; (stanch) restañar; (the traffic, etc.) parar; detener; (prevent) evitar; (discontinue) cesar (de), dejarse de; (cut off) cortar; (end) poner fin (a), acabar con; (payment) suspender. *vi* parar; detenerse; cesar; terminar; (stay) quedarse, permanecer. **I stopped myself from saying what I thought,** Me abstuve de decir lo que pensaba, Me mordí la lengua. **They stopped the food-supply,** Cortaron las provisiones. **to s. beating about the bush,** dejarse de historias. **to s. one's ears,** *fig* taparse los oídos. **to s. payments,** suspender pagos

stop *n* parada, *f;* pausa, *f;* interrupción, *f;* cesación, *f;* (of an organ) registro, *m.* **"Stop,"** (road sign) «Alto.» **full s.,** *gram* punto, *m.* **tram s.,** parada de tranvía, *f.* **to come to a full s.,** pararse de golpe; cesar súbitamente. **to put a s. to,** poner fin a, poner coto a, acabar con. *f pl.* **s.-watch,** cronógrafo, *m*

stopgap *n* (person) tapagujeros, *m;* substituto, *m*

stoppage *n* parada, *f;* cesación, *f;* suspensión, *f;* interrupción, *f;* pausa, *f;* (obstruction) impedimento, *m;* obstrucción, *f.* **s. of work,** suspensión de trabajo, *f*

stopper *n* tapón, *m;* obturador, *m, vt* cerrar con tapón, taponar

stopping *n* parada, *f;* cesación, *f;* suspensión, *f;* (of a tooth) empaste, *m.* **without s.,** sin parar. **without s. to draw breath,** de un aliento. **s.-place,** paradero, *m;* (of buses, etc.) parada, *f.* **s. train,** tren ómnibus, *m.* **s. up,** obturación, *f*

storage *n* almacenamiento, *m;* (charge) almacenaje, *m;* (place) depósito, *m.* **cold s.,** cámara frigorífica, *f.* **s. battery,** acumulador, *m*

store *n* provisión, *f;* abundancia, *f;* reserva, *f;* (of knowledge, etc.) tesoro, *m;* (for furniture, etc.) depósito, almacén, *m; pl* **stores,** (shop) almacenes, *m pl;* (food) provisiones, *f pl;* (*mil* etc.) pertrechos, *m pl. vt* proveer; guardar, acumular; tener en reserva; (furniture, etc.) almacenar; (hold) caber en, tomar. **in s.,** en reserva; en depósito, en almacén. **to set s. by,** estimar en mucho; dar importancia a. **to set little s. by,** estimar en poco; conceder poca importancia a. **s.-room,** despensa, *f*

storehouse *n* almacén, *m; fig* mina, *f,* tesoro, *m*

storekeeper = shopkeeper

storied *a* de . . . pisos. **two-s.,** de dos pisos

stork *n* cigüeña, *f*

storm *n* tempestad, tormenta, *f,* temporal, *m; fig* tempestad, *f; mil* asalto, *m. vt mil* tomar por asalto, asaltar. *vi* (of persons) bramar de cólera. **to take by s.,** tomar por asalto; *fig* cautivar, conquistar. **s. cloud,** nubarrón, *m.* **s.-signal,** señal de temporal, *f.* **s.-tossed,** *a* sacudido por la tempestad. **s. troops,** tropas de asalto, *f pl.* **s. window,** contravidriera, *f*

stormily *adv* tempestuosamente; con tormenta

storming *n* (*mil* etc.) asalto, *m;* violencia, *f.* **s.-party,** pelotón de asalto, *m*

stormy *a* tempestuoso; de tormenta; (of life, etc.) borrascoso; (of meetings, etc.) tempestuoso

story *n* historia, *f;* cuento, *m;* anécdota, *f;* (funny) chiste, *m;* (plot) argumento, enredo, *m;* (fib) mentira, *f;* (floor) piso *m.* **It's always the same old s.,** Es siempre la misma canción (or historia). **That is quite another s.,** Eso es harina de otro costal, *Argentina, Peru* esas son otras cuarenta. **short s.,** cuento, *m.* **s. book,** libro de cuentos, *m.* **s. teller,** cuentista, *mf;* (fibber) mentiroso (-sa)

stout *a* fuerte; (brave) intrépido, indómito; (fat) gordo, grueso; (firm) sólido, firme; (decided) resuelto; vigoroso. *n* (drink) cerveza negra, *f.* **s.-hearted,** valiente, intrépido

stove *n* estufa, *f;* (open, for cooking) cocina económica, *f;* (gas, etc., for cooking) cocina, *f,* fogón, *m.* **s. dealer; s. maker** *Argentina* fumista, *mf;* **s. pipe,** tubo de la chimenea, *m*

stow *vt* meter, poner; colocar; (hide) esconder; (cargo) estibar, arrimar

stowaway *n* polizón, llovido, *m, vi* embarcarse secretamente

straddle *vi* (*nav* etc.) graduar el tiro. *vt* montar a horcajadas en. **s.-legged,** patiabierto

strafe *vt* bombardear concentradamente; castigar; reñir

straggle *vi* rezagarse; vagar en desorden; dispersarse; estar esparcido; extenderse.

straggler *n* rezagado (-da)

straight *a* derecho; recto; (of hair) lacio; directo; (tidy) en orden; (frank) franco; (honest) honrado. *adv* derecho; en línea recta; directamente. **Keep s. on!** ¡Siga Vd. derecho! **to go s. to the point,** dejarse de rodeos, ir al grano. **to look s. in the eyes,** mirar derecho en

los ojos. **s. away,** inmediatamente, en seguida. **s. out,** sin rodeos
straighten *vt* enderezar; poner derecho; poner en orden; arreglar. *vi* ponerse derecho; enderezarse. **to s. one's face,** componer el semblante. **to s. the line,** *mil* rectificar el frente. **to s. out,** poner en orden; *fig* desenredar. **to s. oneself up,** erguirse
straightforward *a* honrado, sincero; franco; (simple) sencillo. **s. answer,** respuesta directa, *f*
straightforwardly *adv* honradamente; francamente
straightforwardness *n* honradez, integridad, *f*; franqueza, *f*; (simplicity) sencillez, *f*
straightness *n* derechura, rectitud, *f*; (of persons) honradez, probidad, *f*
straightway *adv* al instante, inmediatamente
strain *vt* estirar; forzar; esforzar; (one's eyes) quebrarse; (one's ears) aguzar (el oído); (a muscle, etc.) torcer; (a friendship) pedir demasiado (a), exigir demasiado (de); (a person's patience, etc.) abusar (de); (words) tergiversar; (embrace) abrazar estrechamente (a); (filter) filtrar; *cul* colar. *vi* hacer un gran esfuerzo, esforzarse (para). *n* tirantez, *f*; tensión, *f*; (effort) esfuerzo, *m*; (sprain) torcedura, *f*; (nervous) tensión nerviosa, *f*; *mech* esfuerzo, *m*; (breed) raza, *f*; *biol* cepa, *f*; (tendency) tendencia, *f*; (heredity) herencia, *f*; rasgo, *m*, vena, *f*; (style) estilo, *m*; *mus* melodia, *f*; (of mirth, etc.) son, ruido, *m*; (poetry) poesía, *f*. **to s. a point,** hacer una excepción. **to s. after effect,** buscar demasiado el efecto
strained *a* tenso; (of muscles, etc.) torcido; (of smiles, etc.) forzado. **s. relations,** *pol* estado de tirantez, *m*
strainer *n* filtro, *m*; coladero, *m*
strait *n geog* estrecho, *m*. **to be in great straits,** estar en un apuro. **s. laced,** *fig* de manga estrecha.
straiten *vt* estrechar; limitar, **in straitened circumstances,** en la necesidad
Strait of Magellan Estrecho de Magallanes, *m*
Straits Settlements Establecimientos del Estrecho, *m pl*
strand *n* (shore) playa, *f*; (of a river) ribera, orilla, *f*; (of rope) cabo, ramal, *m*; (of thread, etc.) hebra, *f*; (of hair) trenza, *f*. *vt* and *vi* (a ship) encallar, varar. **to be stranded,** hallarse abandonado; (by missing a train, etc.) quedarse colgado. **to leave stranded,** abandonar, dejar plantado (a)
strange *a* (unknown) desconocido; nuevo; (exotic, etc.) extraño, singular; extraordinario; raro; exótico. **I felt very s. in a s. country,** Me sentía muy solo en un país desconocido. **He is a very s. person,** Es una persona muy rara
strangely *adv* extrañamente, singularmente; de un modo raro
strangeness *n* novedad, *f*; singularidad, *f*; rareza, *f*
stranger *n* desconocido (-da); (from a foreign country) extranjero (-ra); (from another region, etc.) forastero (-ra).
strangle *vt* estrangular; (a sob, etc.) ahogar
stranglehold *n* collar de fuerza, *m*. **to have a s. (on),** tener asido por la garganta; paralizar
strap *n* correa, *f*; tirante de botas, *m*, *vt* atar con correas
strapping *a* rozagante, robusto
Strasburg Estrasburgo, *m*
stratagem *n* estratagema, *f*, ardid, *m*
strategic *a* estratégico
strategist *n* estratego, *m*
strategy *n* estrategia, *f*
stratification *n* estratificación, *f*
stratosphere *n* estratosfera, *f*
stratum *n geol* estrato, *m*, capa, *f*; (social, etc.) estrato, *m*
straw *n* paja, *f*. **I don't care a s.,** No se me da un bledo. **to be not worth a s.,** no valer un ardite. **to be the last s.,** ser el colmo. **to drink through a s.,** sorber con una paja. **s. hat,** sombrero de paja, *m*. **s.-colored,** pajizo
strawberry *n* (plant and fruit, especially small or wild) fresa, *f*; (large cultivated) fresón, *m*. **s. bed,** fresal, *m*. **s. ice,** helado de fresa, *m*
stray *vi* errar, vagar; perderse; (from a path, etc., also *fig*) descarriarse. *n* animal perdido, *m*; niño (-ña) sin hogar. *a* descarriado, perdido; errante; (sporadic) esporádico
stray bullet *n* bala perdida, *f*
streak *n* raya, *f*; (in wood and stone) vena, *f*; (of light) rayo, *m*; (of humor, etc.) rasgo, *m*. *vt* rayar. **like a s. of lightning,** como un relámpago
streaky *a* rayado; (of bacon) entreverado
stream *n* arroyo, riachuelo, *m*; río, *m*; (current) corriente, *f*; (of words, etc.) torrente, *m*. *vi* correr, fluir; manar, brotar; (float) flotar, ondear. *vt* (blood, etc.) manar, echar. **The tears streamed down Jean's cheeks,** Las lágrimas corrían por las mejillas de Juana. **s.-lined,** fuselado
stream-of-consciousness *n* escritura automática, *f*, fluir de la conciencia, *m*, flujo de la subconciencia, monólogo interior, *m*
streamer *n* gallardete, *m*, serpentina, *f*; (on a hat, etc.) cinta colgante, *f*, siguemepollo, *m*
street *n* calle, *f*. **the man in the s.,** el hombre medio. **at s. level,** a ras de suelo. **s. arab,** golfo, *m*. **s. cries,** gritos de vendedores ambulantes, *m pl*. **s. entertainer,** saltabanco, *m*. **s. brawl, s. fight,** algarada callejera, *f*. **s. fighting,** luchas en las calles, *f pl*. **s. musician,** músico ambulante, *m*. **s.-sweeper,** barrendero, *m*. **s.-walker,** buscona, prostituta, *f*
strength *n* fuerza, *f*; (of colors, etc.) intensidad, *f*; (of character) firmeza (de carácter), *f*; (of will) resolución, decisión, *f*; *mil* complemento, *m*. **The enemy is in s.,** El enemigo está presente en gran número. **by sheer s.,** a viva fuerza. **on the s. of,** confiando en, en razón de
strengthen *vt* fortificar; consolidar; reforzar. *vi* fortificarse; consolidarse; reforzarse
strengthening *a* fortificante; tonificante. *n* refuerzo, *m*; fortificación, *f*; consolidación, *f*
strenuous *a* activo, enérgico; vigoroso; (arduous) arduo
strenuously *adv* enérgicamente, vigorosamente
strenuousness *n* energía, *f*; vigor, *m*; (arduousness) arduidad, *f*
streptococcus *n med* estreptococo, *m*
streptomycine *n med* estreptomicina, *f*
stress *n* tensión, *f*; impulso, *m*; importancia, *f*, énfasis, *m*; *gram* acento (tónico), *m*; acentuación, *f*; *mech* esfuerzo, *m*. *vt* acentuar; poner énfasis en, insistir en. **under s. of circumstance,** impulsado por las circunstancias. **times of s.,** tiempos turbulentos, *m pl*. **to lay great s. on,** insistir mucho en; dar gran importancia a
stretch *vt* (make bigger) ensanchar; (pull) estirar; (one's hand, etc.) alargar, extender; (knock down) tumbar. *vi* ensancharse; dar de sí; ceder; extenderse. **to s. oneself,** estirarse, desperezarse. **to s. as far as,** llegar hasta, extenderse hasta. **to s. a point,** hacer una concesión. **to s. one's legs,** estirar las piernas
stretch *n* estirón, *m*; tensión, *f*; (of country, etc.) extensión, *f*; (scope) alcance, *m*. **by a s. of the imagination,** con un esfuerzo de imaginación. **He can sleep for hours at a s.,** Puede dormir durante horas enteras
stretcher *n* (for gloves) ensanchador, *m*; dilatador, *m*; (for canvas) bastidor, *m*; (for wounded, etc.) camilla, *f*. **s.-bearer,** camillero, *m*
strew *vt* esparcir; derramar
stricken *a* (wounded) herido; (ill) enfermo; (with grief) afligido, agobiado de dolor. **s. in years,** entrado en años
strict *a* exacto; estricto; escrupuloso; severo
strictly *adv* exactamente; estrictamente; severamente, con severidad. **s. speaking,** en rigor, en realidad
strictness *n* exactitud, *f*; escrupulosidad, *f*; rigor, *m*; severidad, *f*
stricture *n fig* crítica severa, censura, *f*. **to pass strictures on,** criticar severamente
stride *vi* andar a pasos largos, dar zancadas; cruzar a

grandes trancos. *vt* cruzar de un tranco; poner una pierna en cada lado de. *n* zancada, *f*, paso largo, tranco, *m*. **to s. up and down,** dar zancadas

strident *a* estridente; (of colors) chillón

strife *n* lucha, *f*, conflicto, *m*

strike *vt* golpear; pegar, dar una bofetada (a); (wound) herir; (a coin) acuñar; (a light) encender; (of a snake) morder; (a blow) asestar, dar; (of ships, a rock, etc.) chocar contra; estrellarse contra; (flags) bajar, arriar; (a tent) desmontar; (camp) levantar; (come upon) llegar a; (discover) encontrar por casualidad, tropezar con; hallar, descubrir; (seem) parecer; (impress) impresionar; (of ideas) ocurrirse; (an attitude) tomar, adoptar; (of a clock) dar; (a balance) hacer; (a bargain) cerrar, llegar a; (level) nivelar; (cuttings) enraciar. *vi* golpear; (of a clock) dar la hora; (of a ship) encallar; (go) ir; (penetrate) penetrar; (of a cutting) arraigar; (sound) sonar. **He struck the table with his fist,** Golpeó la mesa con el puño. **I was very much struck by the city's beauty,** La belleza de la ciudad me impresionó mucho. **The news struck fear into their hearts,** La noticia les llenó el corazón de miedo. **The clock struck three,** El reloj dio las tres. **The hour has struck,** *fig* Ha llegado la hora. **How did the house s. you?** ¿Qué te pareció la casa? **to s. a bargain,** cerrar un trato. **to s. a blow,** asestar un golpe. **to s. across country,** ir a campo traviesa. **to s. an attitude,** tomar una actitud. **to s. home,** dar en el blanco; herir; herir en lo más vivo; hacerse sentir. **to s. at,** asestar un golpe (a); acometer, embestir; atacar. **to s. down,** derribar; (of illness) acometer. **to s. off,** (a head, etc.) cortar; (a name) borrar, tachar; (print) imprimir. **to s. out,** *vi* asestar un golpe (a); (of a swimmer) nadar; echarse, lanzarse. *vt* (a word, etc.) borrar, rayar; (begin) iniciar. **to s. through,** (cross out) rayar, tachar; (of the sun's rays, etc.) penetrar. **to s. up,** *vt* tocar; empezar a cantar; (a friendship) trabar. *vi* empezar a tocar. **to s. up a march,** *mil* batir la marcha

strike *n* huelga, *f*. *vi* declararse en huelga. **go-slow s.,** tortuguismo, *m*. **lock-out s.,** huelga patronal, *f*. **sit-down s.,** huelga de brazos caídos, *f*. **to go on s.,** declararse en huelga. **s.-breaker,** esquirol, *m*. **s.-pay,** subsidio de huelga, *m*

striker *n* huelguista, *mf*

striking *a* notable, sorprendente; (impressive) impresionante; que llama la atención; llamativo

string *n* bramante, *m*; cuerda, *f*; (ribbon) cinta, *f*; (of beads, etc.) sarta, *f*; (of onions) ristra, *f*; (of horses, etc.) reata, *f*; hilera, *f*; (of a bridge) cable, *m*; (of oaths, lies) sarta, serie, *f*; (of beans) fibra, *f*. *vt* encordar; (beads, etc.) ensartar; (beans) quitar las fibras (de). **He is all strung up,** Se le crispan los nervios. **the strings,** los instrumentos de cuerda. **a s. of pearls,** un collar de perlas. **for strings,** *mus* para arco. **to pull strings,** *fig* manejar los hilos. **to s. up,** (an instrument) templar; (a person) pender, ahorcar. **s. bean,** judía verde, *f*, *Central America, Mexico* ejote, *m*

stringed *a* (of musical instruments) de cuerda. **s. instrument,** instrumento de cuerda, *m*

stringent *a* estricto, severo

stringy *a* fibroso; filamentoso; correoso; arrugado

strip *vt* desnudar; despojar (de), quitar; robar; (a cow) ordeñar hasta agotar la leche. *vi* desnudarse. *n* (tatter) jirón, *m*; tira, lista, *f*; (of wood) listón, *m*; (of earth) pedazo, *m*; (*geog* of land) zona, *f*. **to s. off,** *vt* quitar; (bark from a tree) descortezar; (one's clothes) despojarse de. *vi* desprenderse, separarse. **to s. the leaves from, to s. the petals from** *Lat. Am.* deshojar

stripe *n* raya, lista, *f*; (*mil* etc.) galón, *m*; (lash) azote, *m*. *vt* rayar. **the stripes of the tiger,** las rayas del tigre

striped *a* listado, a rayas; con rayas. **s. trousers,** pantalón de corte, *m*

stripling *n* joven imberbe, pollo, mancebo, *m*

strive *vi* esforzarse (a); pugnar (por, para); trabajar (por); (fight against) luchar contra; pelear con. **He was striving to understand,** Pugnaba por (or Se esforzaba a) comprender

stroke *n* (blow) golpe, *m*; (of the oars) golpe del remo, *m*, remada, *f*; (at billards) tacada, *f*; (in golf) tirada, *f*; (in swimming) braza, *f*; (of a clock) campanada, *f*; (of a pen) rasgo de la pluma, *m*; (of a brush) pincelada, *f*; *mech* golpe de émbolo, *m*; (caress) caricia con la mano, *f*. *vt* acariciar con la mano. **on the s. of six,** al acabar de dar las seis. **to have a s.,** tener un ataque de apoplejía. **s. of genius,** rasgo de ingenio, *m*. **s. of good luck,** racha de buena suerte, *f*

stroll *vi* pasearse, vagar. *n* vuelta, *f*, paseo, *m*. **to go for a s.,** dar una vuelta

stroller *n* paseante, *mf*

strolling *a* errante; ambulante. **s. player,** *n* cómico (-ca) ambulante

strong *a* fuerte; vigoroso; robusto; *Argentina* alentado; enérgico; firme; poderoso; (of colours) intenso, vivo; (of tea, coffee) cargado; *gram* fuerte. **The government took s. measures,** El gobierno tomó medidas enérgicas. **They gave very s. reasons,** Alegaron unas razones muy poderosas. **Grammar is not his s. point,** La gramática no es su punto fuerte. **The enemy is s. in numbers,** El enemigo es numéricamente fuerte. **The society is four thousand s.,** La sociedad tiene cuatro mil miembros. **s. box,** caja de caudales, *f*. **s. man,** hombre fuerte, *m*; (in a circus) hércules, *m*. **s.-minded,** de espíritu fuerte; independiente. **s. room,** cámara acorazada, *f*

stronghold *n* fortaleza, *f*; refugio, *m*

strongly *adv* vigorosamente; fuertemente; firmemente

strop *n* (razor) suavizador, *m*, *vt* suavizar

structural *a* estructural

structure *n* estructura, *f*; edificio, *m*; construcción, *f*

struggle *vi* luchar; pelear; disputarse, *Lat. Am.* abrocharse (con . . .); *n* lucha, *f*; combate, *m*; conflicto, *m*. **to s. to one's feet,** luchar por levantarse. **without a s.,** sin luchar

struggling *a* pobre, indigente, que lucha para vivir

strum *vt* (a stringed instrument) rascar; tocar mal

strut *vi* pavonearse. *vt* (prop) apuntalar. *n* pavonada, *f*; (prop) puntal, *m*. **to s. out,** salir de un paso majestuoso

stub *n* (of a tree) tocón, *m*; (of a pencil, candle, etc.) cabo, *m*; pedazo, fragmento, *m*; (of a cigarette or cigar) colilla, *f*. **s.-book,** talonario, *m*

stubborn *a* inquebrantable, tenaz; persistente; (pig-headed) terco, testarudo, *Lat. Am.* empecinado

stubbornness *n* tenacidad, *f*; terquedad, testarudez, *f*

stucco *n* estuco, *m*, *vt* estucar

stuck past part. of **stick. be stuck** (for an answer) = **be stumped**

stuck-up *a* = **haughty**

stud *n* (of horses) caballeriza, *f*; (nail) tachón, *m*; (for collars) pasador para camisas, *m*. *vt* tachonar; sembrar. **dress s.,** botón de la pechera, *m*. **s.-farm,** potrero, *m*

student *n* estudiante, *mf*. *a* estudiantil. **students** (as a body) *Lat. Am.* estudiantado, *msg*.

student body *n Lat. Am.* estudiantado, *m*

studied *a* estudiado; calculado; (of style) cerebral, reflexivo; (intentional) deliberado

studio *n* estudio, *m*. **broadcasting s.,** estudio de emisión, *m*

studious *a* estudioso, aplicado; (deliberate) intencional, deliberate; (eager) solícito, ansioso

studiously *adv* estudiosamente; con intención, deliberadamente; solícitamente

study *n* estudio, *m*; solicitud, *f*, cuidado, *m*; investigación, *f*; (room) gabinete, cuarto de trabajo, *m*. *vt* ocuparse de, cuidar de, atender a; considerar; estudiar; examinar; (the stars) observar; (try) procurar. *vi* estudiar. **in a brown s.,** en Babia. **to make a s. of,** hacer un estudio de, estudiar. **to s. for an examination,** prepararse para un examen

stuff *n* substancia, materia, *f*; (fabric) tela, *f*, paño, *m*; (rubbish) cachivaches, *m pl*, cosas, *f pl*. *a* de estofa. *vt* henchir; llenar; *cul* rellenar; (with food) ahitar (de);

(cram) atestar, apretar; (furniture) rehenchir; (an animal, bird) disecar; (put) meter, poner. **S. and nonsense!** ¡Patrañas! **to be poor s.,** ser de pacotilla; no valer para nada
stuffed animal *n* animal disecado, *m*
stuffiness *n* mala ventilación, *f;* falta de aire, *f;* calor, *m*
stuffing *n* (of furniture) rehenchimiento, *m; cul* relleno, *m*
stuffy *a* mal ventilado, poco aireado, ahogado
stumble *vi* tropezar; dar un traspié; (in speaking) tartamudear. *n* tropezón, *m;* traspié, *m.* **to s. through a speech,** pronunciar un discurso a tropezones. **to s. against,** tropezar contra. **to s. upon, across,** tropezar con; encontrar por casualidad
stumblingblock *n* tropiezo, impedimento, *m*
stump *n* (of a tree) tocón, *m;* (of an arm, leg) muñón, *m;* (of a pencil, candle) cabo, *m;* (of a tooth) raigón, *m;* (of a cigar) colilla, *f;* (cricket) poste, montante, *m; art* esfumino, *m;* (leg) pata, *f. vt* (disconcert) desconcertar; *art* esfumar; recorrer. **to s. up,** *inf* pagar. **be stumped** (for an answer) *Mexico* atrojarse
stun *vt* dejar sin sentido (a); aturdir de un golpe (a); (astound) pasmar
stunning *a* aturdidor; que pasma; *inf* estupendo
stunt *vt* impedir el crecimiento de; encanijar. *n* (advertising) anuncio de reclamo, *m;* recurso (para conseguir algo), *m;* proeza, *f*
stunted *a* (of trees, etc.) enano; (of children) encanijado; (of intelligence) inmaduro
stupefy *vt* atontar, embrutecer; causar estupor (a), asombrar
stupendous *a* asombroso; enorme
stupid *a* (with sleep, etc.) atontado; (silly) estúpido, tonto, *Lat. Am.* baboso, *Central America* azurumbado. *n* tonto (-ta)
stupidity *n* estupidez, *f;* tontería, *f*
stupor *n* estupor, *m*
sturdiness *n* robustez, *f,* vigor, *m;* firmeza, tenacidad, *f*
sturdy *a* robusto, vigoroso, fuerte; firme, tenaz
sturgeon *n icht* esturión, *m*
stutter *vi* tartamudear. *vt* balbucir. *n* tartamudeo, *m*
stutterer *n* tartamudo (-da)
stuttering *a* tartamudo; balbuciente. *n* tartamudeo, *m*
sty *n* (pig) pocilga, *f; med* orzuelo, *m*
Stygian *a* estigio
style *n* (for etching) buril, *m;* (*lit, art, arch,* etc.) estilo, *m;* (fashion) moda, *f;* (model) modelo, *m;* (behavior, etc.) tono, *m;* elegancia, *f;* (kind) especie, clase, *f;* (designation) tratamiento, *m; vt* llamar, nombrar. **the latest styles from Madrid,** los últimos modelos de Madrid. **He has a very individual s.,** Su estilo es muy personal. **They live in great s.,** Viven en gran lujo
stylet *n* estilete, *m*
stylish *a* elegante
stylishness *n* elegancia, *f*
stylist *n* estilista, *mf*
stylize *vt* estilizar
suasion *n* persuasión, *f*
suasive *a* suasorio, persuasivo
suave *a* afable, cortés, urbano; (of wine) suave
suavity *n* afabilidad, urbanidad, *f*
subaltern *n mil* subalterno, *m, a* subalterno, subordinado
subcommittee *n* subcomisión, *f*
subconscious *a* subconsciente. **the s.,** la subconsciencia
subconsciously *adv* subconscientemente
subcutaneous *a* subcutáneo
subdivide *vt* subdividir. *vi* subdividirse
subdivision *n* subdivisión, *f*
subdominant *n mus* subdominante, *f*
subdue *vt* subyugar, sojuzgar, vencer; (one's passions) dominar; (colors, voices) suavizar; (lessen) mitigar; apagar
subdued *a* (of colors) apagado; (of persons) sumiso; (depressed) deprimido, melancólico. **in a s. voice,** en voz baja
subheading *n* subtítulo, *m*
subhuman *a* subhumano
subject *a* sujeto; sometido (a); expuesto (a). *n* (of a country) súbdito (-ta); sujeto, *m;* (of study) asignatura, materia, *f;* (theme) tema, *m;* (*gram, phil*) sujeto, *m. vt* subyugar; someter. **It can only be done s. to his consent,** Podrá hacerse únicamente si él lo consiente. **He is a British s.,** Es súbdito británico. **to change the s.,** cambiar de conversación. **to s. to criticism,** criticar (a). **s.-matter,** materia, *f;* (of a letter) contenido, *m*
subjection *n* sujeción, *f;* sometimiento, *m.* **He was in a state of complete s.,** Estaba completamente sumiso. **to bring into s.,** subyugar
subjective *a* subjetivo
subjectiveness *n* subjetividad, *f*
subjectivism *n* subjetivismo, *m*
subjoin *vt* añadir, adjuntar
subjugate *vt* subyugar, someter
subjugation *n* subyugación, *f*
subjunctive *a* and *n* subjuntivo *m*
sublet *vt* subarrendar. *n* subarriendo, *m*
sublimate *vt* sublimar. *n* sublimado, *m*
sublimation *n* sublimación, *f*
sublime *a* sublime; absoluto, completo; extremo. **the s.,** lo sublime
sublimely *adv* sublimemente; completamente
submachine gun *n* pistola ametralladora, metralleta, *f,* subfusil ametrallador, *m*
submarine *a* submarino. *n* submarino, *m.* **midget s.,** submarino enano, submarino de bolsillo, *m.* **s. chaser,** cazasubmarino, *m*
submerge *vt* sumergir; inundar. *vi* sumergirse. **The submarine submerged,** El submarino se sumergió
submergence *n* sumergimiento, *m,* sumersión, *f;* hundimiento, *m*
submersible *a* sumergible
submersion *n* sumersión, *f;* hundimiento, *m*
submission *n* sometimiento, *m;* sumisión, resignación, *f;* docilidad, *f*
submissive *a* sumiso, dócil, manso
submissively *adv* sumisamente, con docilidad
submissiveness *n* sumisión, docilidad, *f*
submit *vt* someterse (a); doblarse ante; (a scheme, etc.) someter; presentar; (urge) proponer. *vi* someterse; resignarse; (surrender) rendirse, entregarse. **to s. to arbitration,** someter a arbitraje
subnormal *a* anormal
subordinate *a* subordinado; subalterno, inferior; secundario. *n* subordinado (-da). *vt* subordinar
subordination *n* subordinación, *f*
suborn *vt* sobornar, cohechar
subpena *n* citación, *f, vt* citar
subplot *n* intriga secundaria, trama secundaria, *f*
subscribe *vt* and *vi* subscribir; (to a periodical, etc.) abonarse (a)
subscriber *n* subscriptor (-ra); abonado (-da)
subscription *n* subscripción, *f;* (to a periodical, series of concerts, etc.) abono, *m;* (to a club) cuota, *f*
subsection *n* subsección, *f*
subsequent *a* subsiguiente, subsecuente; posterior. **s. to,** después de, posterior a. **s. upon,** de resultas de
subsequently *adv* más tarde; subsiguientemente; posteriormente
subservience *n* servilidad, *f;* utilidad, *f*
subservient *a* servil; subordinado; útil
subside *vi* (of water) bajar; (of ground) hundirse; (of foundations) asentarse; disminuir; calmarse; (be quiet) callarse. **to s. into a chair,** dejarse caer en un sillón
subsidence *n* hundimiento, *m;* desplome, derrumbamiento, *m;* (of floods) bajada, *f;* (of anger, etc.) apaciguamiento, *m*
subsidiary *a* subsidiario
subsidize *vt* subvencionar
subsidy *n* subvención, *f,* subsidio, *m;* prima, *f*

subsist *vi* subsistir
subsistence *n* subsistencia, *f*
subsoil *n* subsuelo, *m*
substance *n* substancia, *f*
substantial *a* substancial; sólido; importante
substantially *adv* substancialmente; sólidamente
substantiate *vt* establecer, verificar; justificar
substantiation *n* comprobación, verificación, *f*; justificación, *f*
substantive *a* real, independiente; *gram* substantivo. *n gram* substantivo, *m*
substitute *n* substituto (-ta); (material) substituto, *m*. *vt* substituir, reemplazar. **to be a s. for,** hacer las veces de
substitution *n* substitución, *f*, reemplazo, *m*
substratum *n* substrato, *m*
subterfuge *n* subterfugio, *m*; evasiva, *f*
subterranean *a* subterráneo
subtitle *n* subtítulo, *m*; (on films) guión, *m*
subtle *a* sutil; delicado; penetrante; (crafty) astuto
subtlety *n* sutileza, *f*; delicadeza, *f*; (craftiness) astucia, *f*
subtly *adv* sutilmente; con delicadeza
subtract *vt* restar, substraer
subtraction *n* resta, substracción, *f*
suburb *n* suburbio, *m*; *pl* **suburbs,** las afueras, *f pl* los arrabales, *m pl*
suburban *a* suburbano
subvention *n* subvención, *f*
subversion *n* subversión, *f*
subversive *a* subversivo
subvert *vt* subvertir
subway *n* (passageway) pasaje subterráneo, *m*; (underground railway) metro (Spain, Puerto Rico), subte (Argentina), *m*
succeed *vt* seguir (a); suceder (a); heredar. *vi* seguir (a); suceder (a); (be successful) tener éxito. **I did not s. in doing it,** No logré hacerlo. **to s. to the throne,** subir al trono
succeeding *a* subsiguiente; futuro; consecutivo; sucesivo
success *n* éxito, *m*; triunfo, *m*. **to be a s.,** tener éxito. **The film was a great s.,** La película tuvo mucho éxito
successful *a* que tiene éxito; afortunado, venturoso; próspero, *Lat. Am.* exitoso
successfully *adv* con éxito; prósperamente
succession *n* sucesión, *f*; (series) serie, *f*; (inheritance) herencia, *f*; (descendants) descendencia, *f*. **in s.,** sucesivamente
successive *a* sucesivo
successor *n* sucesor (-ra)
succinct *a* sucinto, conciso
succinctly *adv* sucintamente, brevemente, en pocas palabras
succor *vt* socorrer, auxiliar. *n* socorro, *m*, ayuda, *f*
succulence *n* suculencia, *f*
succulent *a* suculento
succumb *vi* sucumbir; someterse, ceder
such *a* tal; parecido, semejante; así; tanto; (before an adjective, adverb) tan. *n* el, *m*, (*f*, la) que, los, *m pl*, (*f pl*, las) que; tal. **s. men,** tales hombres. **I have never seen s. magnificence,** Nunca no he visto tanta magnificencia. **s. an important man,** un hombre tan importante. **s. pictures as these,** cuadros como estos. **S. is life!** ¡Así es la vida! **science as s.,** la ciencia como tal. **s.-and-s.,** tal y tal
suchlike *a* parecido, semejante; de esta clase
suck *vt* chupar; (the breast) mamar; sorber; (of a vacuum cleaner, etc.) aspirar. *n* chupada, *f*; succión, *f*. **to s. down,** tragar. **to s. up,** aspirar; absorber
sucker *n zool* ventosa, *f*; *bot* acodo, mugrón, *m*; (greenhorn) primo, *m*; (pig) lechón, *m*
suckingpig *n* lechón, cochinillo, *m*
suckle *vt* amamantar, dar el pecho (a)
suction *n* succión, *f*; aspiración, *f*. **s.-pump,** bomba aspirante, *f*
Sudan, the el Sudán, *m*
Sudanese *a* and *n* sudanés (-esa)
sudden *a* súbito; (unexpected) inesperado, impensado; (of bends) brusco. **all of a s.,** de repente; súbitamente
suddenly *adv* súbitamente; de pronto, de repente
suddenness *n* carácter repentino, *m*; (of a bend, etc.) brusquedad, *f*
suds *n pl* jabonaduras, *f pl*; espuma, *f*
sue *vt law* proceder contra, pedir en juicio; *law* demandar; (beg) suplicar. **to sue for peace,** pedir la paz
suede *n* ante, *m*. **s. glove,** guante de ante, *m*
suet *n* sebo, *m*
Suez Canal, the el Canal de Suez, *m*
suffer *vt* sufrir, padecer; pasar, experimentar; (tolerate) tolerar, sufrir; (allow) permitir. *vi* sufrir. **She suffers from her environment,** es la víctima de su medio ambiente
sufferance *n* tolerancia, *f*. **on s.,** por tolerancia
sufferer *n* enfermo (-ma); víctima, *f*
suffering *n* sufrimiento, padecimiento, *m*; dolor, *m*. *a* sufriente
suffice *vi* ser suficiente, bastar. *vt* satisfacer
sufficiency *n* suficiencia, *f*; (of money) subsistencia, *f*
sufficient *a* suficiente, bastante. **to be s.,** bastar, ser suficiente
sufficiently *adv* suficientemente, bastante
suffix *n gram* sufijo, *m*
suffocate *vt* ahogar, sofocar, asfixiar. *vi* sofocarse, asfixiarse
suffocating *a* sofocante, asfixiante
suffocation *n* sofocación, asfixia, *f*; ahogo, *m*
suffrage *n* sufragio, *m*; voto, *m*. **universal s.,** sufragio universal, *m*
suffragette *n* sufragista, *f*
suffuse *vt* bañar, inundar, cubrir
sugar *n* azúcar, *m*. *vt* azucarar. **brown s.,** azúcar moreno, *m*. **loaf s.,** azúcar de pilón, *m*. **white s.,** azúcar blanco, *m*. **to s. the pill,** dorar la píldora. **s.-almond,** peladilla, *f*. **s.-basin,** azucarera, *f*. **s.-beet,** remolacha, *f*. **s.-candy,** azúcar candi, *m*. **s.-cane,** caña de azúcar, *f*. **s.-cane syrup,** miel de caña, *f*. **s.-paste,** alfeñique, *m*, alcorza, *f*. **s.-refinery,** fábrica de azúcar, *f*. **s.-tongs,** tenacillas para azúcar, *f pl*
sugary *a* azucarado; *fig* meloso, almibarado
suggest *vt* implicar; indicar, dar a entender; sugerir; (advise) aconsejar; (hint) insinuar; (evoke) evocar. **I suggested they should go to London,** Les aconsejé que fueran a Londres. **An idea suggested itself to him,** Se le ocurrió una idea
suggestion *n* sugestión, *f*; insinuación, *f*
suggestive *a* sugestivo; estimulante
suicidal *a* suicida. **s. tendency,** tendencia suicida, tendencia al suicidio, *f*
suicide *n* (act) suicidio, *m*; (person) suicida, *mf*. **to commit s.,** darse la muerte, quitarse la vida suicidarse
suit *n* (request) petición, súplica, *f*; oferta de matrimonio, *f*; *law* pleito, *m*; (of clothes) traje, *Colombia, Venezuela* flus, *m*; (cards) palo, *m*; (of cards held) serie, *f*, *vt* convenir; sentar; ir bien (a); venir bien (a); (adapt) adaptar. **S. yourself!** ¡Haz lo que quieras! **The arrangement suits me very well,** El arreglo me viene muy bien. **The climate doesn't s. me,** El clima no me sienta bien. **The color does not s. you,** El color no te va bien. **to follow s.,** seguir el ejemplo (de); (cards) jugar el mismo palo. **s.-case,** maleta, *f*
suitability *n* conveniencia, *f*; aptitud, *f*
suitable *a* conveniente; apropiado; apto; a propósito. **Not s. for children,** No apto para menores. **to make s. for,** adaptar a las necesidades de
suitably *adv* convenientemente; apropiadamente
suite *n* (of retainers, etc.) séquito, acompañamiento, *m*; (of furniture, etc.) juego, *m*; *mus* suite, *f*. **private s.,** habitaciones particulares, *f pl*. **s. of rooms,** apartamiento, *m*
suitor *n law* demandante, *m*; pretendiente, *m*
sulk *vi* ponerse malhumorado, ser mohíno
sulkiness *n* mohína, *f*, mal humor, *m*

sulky *a* mohíno, malhumorado
sullen *a* taciturno, hosco; malhumorado, sombrío; (of a landscape, etc.) triste, sombrío
sullenly *adv* taciturnamente, hoscamente
sullenness *n* taciturnidad, hosquedad, *f*, mal humor, *m*
sully *vt* desdorar, empañar; manchar
sulphur *n* azufre, *m*
sulphuric *a* sulfúrico
sulphurous *a* sulfuroso
sultan *n* sultán, *m*
sultriness *n* bochorno, calor sofocante, *m*
sultry *a* bochornoso, sofocante
sum *n* suma, *f*; total, *m*; cantidad, *f*; (in arithmetic) problema (de aritmética), *m*. *vt* sumar, calcular. **in sum,** en suma; en resumen. **to sum up,** recapitular; resumir; (a person) tomar las medidas (a)
summarily *adv* someramente; *law* sumariamente
summarize *vt* resumir brevemente; compendiar
summary *a* somero; *law* sumario. *n* resumen, sumario, compendio, *m*. **summary records,** actas resumidas, *f pl*
summer *n* verano, estío, *m*. **to spend the s.,** veranear. **s.-house,** cenador, *m*. **s.-time,** verano, *m*; hora de verano, *f*. **s. wheat,** trigo tremesino, *m*
summing-up *n* recapitulación, *f*
summit *n* cima, cumbre, *f*; *fig* apogeo, *m*
summitry *n* diplomacia en la cumbre, *f*
summon *vt* llamar, hacer venir; mandar, requerir; *law* citar. **to s. up one's courage,** cobrar ánimos
summons *n* llamamiento, *m*; *mil* intimación, *f*; *law* citación, *f*. *vt law* citar
sump *n* (of a motor-car) pozo colector, *m*; *min* sumidero, *m*
sumptuous *a* suntuoso, lujoso, magnífico
sumptuousness *n* suntuosidad, magnificencia, *f*
sun *n* sol, *m*. **The sun was shining,** Hacía sol, El sol brillaba. **to bask in the sun,** tomar el sol. **sun-bathing,** baños de sol, *m pl*. **sun-blind,** toldo para el sol, *m*. **sun-bonnet,** capelina, *f*. **sun-glasses,** gafas ahumadas, *f pl*. **sun-helmet,** casco colonial, *m*. **sun-spot,** *ast* mancha del sol, *f*; (freckle) peca, *f*. **sun-worship,** adoración del sol, *f*
sunbeam *n* rayo de sol, *m*
sunburn *n* quemadura del sol, *f*; bronceado, *m*
sunburnt *a* quemado por el sol; bronceado, tostado por el sol
sundae *n* helado de frutas, *m*
Sunday *n* domingo, *m*. **in his S. best,** en su traje dominguero, endomingado. **S. school,** escuela dominical, *f*
Sunday's child *n* niño nacido de pies, niño nacido un domingo, niño mimado de la fortuna
sunder *vt* dividir en dos, hender; separar
sundial *n* reloj de sol, reloj solar, *m*
sundown *n* puesta del sol, *f*
sundry *a* varios (-as). *n pl* **sundries,** artículos diversos, *m pl*; *com* varios, *m pl*. **all and s.,** todo el mundo, todos y cada uno
sunflower *n* girasol, tornasol, *m*, trompeta de amor, *f*
sunken *a* (of eyes, etc.) hundido
sun letter *n* letra solar, *f*
sunless *a* sin sol
sunlight *n* luz del sol, *f*, rayos del sol, *m pl*. **artificial s.,** sol artificial, *m*. **in the s.,** al sol
sunny *a* de sol; bañado de sol; asoleado; expuesto al sol; (face) risueño; (of disposition, etc.) alegre. **to be s.,** hacer sol
sunrise *n* salida del sol, *f*. **from s. to sunset,** de sol a sol
sunset *n* puesta del sol, *f*. **at s.,** a la caída (or puesta) del sol
sunshade *n* parasol, quitasol, *m*, sombrilla, *f*
sunshine *n* luz del sol, *f*. **in the s.,** al sol
sunstroke *n* insolación, *f*
sup *vt* sorber. *vi* cenar. *n* sorbo, *m*
super *n* (actor) comparsa, *mf*; (film) superproducción, *f*; (of a beehive) alza, *f*
superabundance *n* superabundancia, sobreabundancia, *f*
superabundant *a* superabundante, sobreabundante. **to be s.,** sobreabundar
superannuate *vt* (retire) jubilar
superannuated *a* (retired) jubilado; (out-of-date) anticuado
superannuation *n* (retirement and pension) jubilación, *f*
superb *a* magnífico, espléndido
superbly *adv* magníficamente
supercargo *n naut* sobrecargo, *m*
supercharger *n* (*aut, aer*) compresor, *m*
supercilious *a* altanero, altivo, orgulloso; desdeñoso
superciliousness *n* altanería, altivez, *f*, orgullo, *m*; desdén, *m*
superficial *a* superficial
superficiality *n* superficialidad, *f*
superficially *adv* superficialmente
superfine *a* superfino
superfluity *n* superfluidad, *f*
superfluous *a* superfluo. **to be s.,** sobrar
superfortress *n aer* superfortaleza volante, *f*
superhuman *a* sobrehumano
superimpose *vt* sobreponer
superintend *vt* superentender, dirigir
superintendent *n* superintendente, *mf*; director (-ra); (school) inspector; (police) subjefe de la policía, *m*
superior *a* superior; (in number) mayor; (smug) desdeñoso. *n* superior (-ra). **Mother S.,** (madre) superiora, *f*. **s. to,** superior a; encima de
superiority *n* superioridad, *f*
superlative *a* extremo, supremo; *gram* superlativo. *n gram* superlativo, *m*
superlatively *adv* en sumo grado, superlativamente
superman *n* superhombre, *m*
supernatural *a* sobrenatural
supernumerary *a* and *n* supernumerario (-ia)
superposition *n* superposición, *f*
superscribe *vt* sobrescribir; poner el sobrescrito (a)
superscription *n* (on letters, documents) sobrescrito, *m*; leyenda, *f*
supersede *vt* reemplazar; suplantar
supersensible *a* suprasensible
superstition *n* superstición, *f*
superstitious *a* supersticioso
supertax *n* impuesto suplementario, *m*
supervene *vi* sobrevenir
supervise *vt* superentender, vigilar; dirigir
supervision *n* superintendencia, *f*; dirección, *f*
supervisor *n* superintendente, *mf*; inspector (-ra); director (-ra)
supine *a* supino; indolente, negligente. *n gram* supino, *m*
supper *n* cena, *f*. **the Last S.,** la Última Cena. **to have s.,** cenar. **s.-time,** hora de cenar, *f*
supplant *vt* suplantar; usurpar; reemplazar
supplanter *n* suplantador (-ra)
supple *a* flexible; dócil, manso; (fawning) adulador, servil, lisonjero
supplement *n* suplemento, *m*; (of a book) apéndice, *m*
supplementary *a* suplementario; adicional
suppleness *n* flexibilidad, *f*; docilidad, *f*; servilidad, *f*
suppliant *a* and *n* suplicante, *mf*
supplicate *vt* and *vi* suplicar
supplication *n* suplicación, *f*; súplica, *f*
supply *vt* proveer (de); suministrar; proporcionar, dar; (a deficiency) suplir; (a post) llenar; (a post temporarily) reemplazar. *n* suministro, surtimiento, *m*; provisión, *f*; (of electricity, etc.) suministro, *m*; *com* oferta, *f*; (person) substituto (-ta); *pl* **supplies,** *com* existencias, *f pl*; *mil* pertrechos, *m pl*; víveres, *m pl*, provisiones, *f pl*. **s. and demand,** oferta y demanda, *f*
support *vt* apoyar, sostener; mantener; (endure) soportar; (a cause) apoyar, defender; (corroborate) confirmar, vindicar. *n* apoyo, *m*; sostén, *m*; soporte, *m*. **to**

speak in s. of, defender, abogar por. **to s. oneself,** ganarse la vida, mantenerse
supporter *n* apoyo, *m;* defensor (-ra); partidario (-ia)
suppose *vt* suponer; imaginar(se); creer. **always supposing,** dado que, en el caso de que. **Supposing he had gone out?** ¿Y si hubiera salido? **I don't s. they will go to Spain,** No creo que vayan a España. **He is supposed to be clever,** Tiene fama de listo
supposed *a* supuesto; que se llama a sí mismo
supposition *n* suposición, hipótesis, *f*
suppress *vt* reprimir; (yawns, etc.) ahogar; contener; (heresies, rebellions, books, etc.) suprimir; (dissemble) disimular, esconder; (a heckler, etc.) hacer callar
suppressed *a* reprimido; contenido; disimulado
suppression *n* represión, *f;* supresión, *f;* disimulación, *f*
suppurate *vi* supurar
suppuration *n* supuración, *f*
supremacy *n* supremacía, *f*
supreme *a* supremo; sumo. **with s. indifference,** con suma indiferencia. **s. court,** tribunal supremo, *m*
surcharge *n* sobrecarga, *f*
sure *a* seguro; cierto. *adv* seguramente. **Be s. to . . . !** ¡Ten cuidado de . . . ! ¡No dejes de . . . ! **to be s.,** seguramente, sin duda; ¡claro!; (fancy!) ¡no me digas!; ¡qué sorpresa! **I am not so s. of that,** No diría yo tanto. **Come on Thursday for s.,** Venga el jueves sin falta. **It is s. to rain tomorrow,** Seguramente va a llover mañana. **to make s. of,** asegurarse de. **to be (or feel) s.,** estar seguro. **s.-footed,** de pie firme, seguro
surely *adv* seguramente; sin duda, ciertamente; por supuesto
sureness *n* seguridad, *f;* certeza, *f*
surety *n* garantía, fianza, *f;* (person) garante, *mf.* **to go s. for,** ser fiador (de), salir garante (por)
surf *n* resaca, *f;* rompiente, *m;* oleaje, *m.* **s.-board,** aquaplano, *m.* **s.-riding,** patinaje sobre las olas, *m*
surface *n* superficie, *f;* exterior, *m. a* superficial. *vi* (of a submarine) salir a la superficie. **on the s.,** en apariencia
surface mail *n* correo por vía ordinaria, servicio ordinario, servicio per vía de superficie, *m*
surfeit *n* exceso, *m,* superabundancia, *f;* saciedad, *f. vt* hartar; saciar
surge *vi* (of waves) embravecerse, hincharse; (of crowds) agitarse, bullir; (of emotions) despertarse. *n* (of sea, crowd, blood) oleada, *f;* (of anger) ola, *f.* **The blood surged into his face,** La sangre se le subió a las mejillas
surgeon *n* cirujano, *m;* (*nav, mil*) médico, *m*
surgery *n* cirugía, *f;* (doctor's) consultorio, *m;* (dispensary) dispensario, *m*
surgical *a* quirúrgico
surliness *n* mal genio, *m,* taciturnidad, *f;* brusquedad, *f*
surly *a* taciturno, huraño, malhumorado; brusco
surmise *n* conjetura, suposición, *f. vt* conjeturar, adivinar; imaginar, suponer. *vi* hacer conjeturas
surmount *vt* superar, vencer; coronar
surname *n* apellido, *m, vt* denominar, nombrar
surpass *vt* superar, exceder; aventajarse (a); eclipsar
surpassing *a* sin par, incomparable
surplus *n* exceso, sobrante, *m;* (*com* of accounts) superávit, *m.* **sale of s. stock,** liquidación de saldos, *f*
surplusage *n* material de desecho, *m*
surprise *n* sorpresa, *f;* asombro, *m. vt* sorprender; asombrar. **to s.** (someone) **in the act,** coger en el acto. **to take** (a person) **by s.,** sorprender (a). **He was surprised into admitting it,** Cogido a la imprevista, lo confesó
surprising *a* sorprendente
surrealism *n* surrealismo, *m*
surrealist *a* and *n* surrealista, *mf*
surrender *vt* rendir, entregar; (goods) ceder, renunciar (a). *vi* rendirse, entregarse; abandonarse. *n* rendición, capitulación, *f;* entrega, *f;* (of goods) cesión, *f;* (of an insurance policy) rescate, *m.* **to s. oneself to remorse,** abandonarse (or entregarse) al remordimiento. **to s. unconditionally,** entregarse a discreción
surreptitious *a* subrepticio
surreptitiously *adv* subrepticiamente, a hurtadillas
surround *vt* rodear; cercar; *mil* asediar, sitiar. *n* borde, *m.* **Peter was surrounded by his friends,** Pedro estaba rodeado por sus amigos
surrounding *a* (que está) alrededor de; vecino. **the s. country,** los alrededores
surroundings *n pl* cercanías, *f pl,* alrededores, *m pl;* (environment) medio, *m;* (medio) ambiente, *m*
surtax *n* impuesto suplementario, *m*
surveillance *n* vigilancia, *f*
survey *vt* contemplar, mirar; (events, etc.) pasar en revista; estudiar; (land, etc.) apear; (a house, etc.) inspeccionar. *n* vista general, *f;* inspección, *f;* (of facts, etc.) examen, *m;* estudio, *m;* (of land, etc.) apeo, *m;* (of literature, etc.) bosquejo, breve panorama, *m*
surveying *n* agrimensura, *f*
surveyor *n* agrimensor, *m;* (superintendent) inspector, *m;* superintendente, *m*
survival *n* supervivencia, *f.* **s. of the fittest,** supervivencia de los más aptos, *f*
survive *vt* sobrevivir a. *vi* sobrevivir; (of customs) subsistir, durar
survivor *n* sobreviviente, *mf*
susceptibility *n* susceptibilidad, *f;* tendencia, *f; pl* **susceptibilities,** sensibilidad, *f*
susceptible *a* susceptible; impresionable; sensible; (to love) enamoradizo. **He is s. to bronchitis,** Es susceptible a la bronquitis
suspect *a* and *n* sospechoso (-sa). *vt* sospechar; dudar; imaginar, suponer. *vi* tener sospechas
suspend *vt* suspender. **suspended animation,** muerte aparente, *f*
suspender *n* liga, *f; pl* **suspenders,** (braces) tirantes del pantalón, *m pl.* **s.-belt,** faja, *f*
suspense *n* incertidumbre, *f.* **to keep** (a person) **in s.,** dejar en la incertidumbre (a)
suspension *n* suspensión, *f.* **s.-bridge,** puente colgante, *m.* **s. of payments,** suspensión de pagos, *f,*
suspicion *n* sospecha, *f;* (touch) dejo, *m;* cantidad muy pequeña, *f.* **to be above s.,** estar por encima de toda sospecha. **to be under s.,** estar bajo sospecha. **I had no suspicions . . . ,** No sospechaba . . .
suspicious *a* (by nature) suspicaz; sospechoso. **to make s.,** hacer sospechar
suspiciously *adv* suspicazmente, desconfiadamente; de un modo sospechoso. **It seems s. like . . . ,** Tiene toda la apariencia de . . .
suspiciousness *n* carácter sospechoso, *m,* lo sospechoso; suspicacia, *f*
sustain *vt* sostener; mantener; sustentar; apoyar; corroborar, confirmar; (a note) prolongar. **to s. injuries,** recibir heridas
sustenance *n* mantenimiento, *m;* sustento, *m,* alimentos, *m pl*
suture *n* sutura, *f*
svarabhakti *adj* esvarabático
svelte *a* esbelto, gentil
swab *vt naut* lampacear; limpiar con lampazo; *surg* tamponar. *n* lampazo, *m; surg* torunda, *f,* tampón, *m*
swaddle *vt* envolver; (infants) fajar
swaddling clothes *n pl* pañales, *m pl.* **to be still in s. clothes,** *fig* estar en mantillas, estar en pañales
swagger *vi* fanfarronear, pavonearse; darse importancia. *n* pavoneo, *m;* aire importante, *m;* (coat) tonto, *m. a* majo; de última moda
swaggering *a* fanfarrón, jactancioso; importante
Swahili suaili; *n* suaili, *m*
swain *n* zagal, *m;* enamorado, *m;* pretendiente, amante, *m*
swallow *vt* tragar, engullir. *n* trago, *m;* sorbo, *m; orn* golondrina, *f.* **to s. an insult (a story),** tragar un insulto (una historia). **to s. one's words,** retractarse. **to**

s. one's pride, bajar la cerviz, humillarse. **to s. up,** tragar; absorber. **s.-tailed coat,** frac, *m*

swamp *n* pantano, *m*, marisma, *f*, *Argentina* fachinal, *f*, *Central America* chagüe, *m*. *vt* sumergir; (a boat) echar a pique, hundir; (inundate) inundar

swampy *a* pantanoso

swan *n* cisne, *m*. **swan's down,** plumón de cisne, *m*. **s.-song,** canto del cisne, *m*

swank *n* pretensiones, *f pl*, *vi* darse humos

sward *n* césped, *m*, hierba, *f*

swarm *n* enjambre, *m*; (of people) muchedumbre, multitud, *f*; tropel, *m*. *vi* (of bees) enjambrar; (of other insects) pulular; (of people) hormiguear, bullir, pulular. *vt* (climb) trepar. **to s. with,** estar infestado de

swarthiness *n* tez morena, *f*; color moreno, *m*

swarthy *a* moreno

swashbuckler *n* perdonavidas, matasiete, *m*

swashbuckling *a* matamoros, valentón, fanfarrón

swastika *n* esvástica, cruz gamada, *f*

swathe *vt* envolver; fajar; (with bandages) vendar

swathing *n* envoltura, *f*; (bandages) vendas, *f pl*

sway *vi* balancearse; oscilar; (stagger, of persons) bambolearse; (totter, of things) tambalearse; (of carriages) cabecear; (gracefully, in walking) cimbrarse. *vt* balancear, mecer; oscilar; hacer tambalear; (influence) influir, inclinar; (govern) regir, gobernar. *n* balanceo, *m*; oscilación, *f*; vaivén, *m*; tambaleo, *m*; (influence) ascendiente, dominio, *m*, influencia, *f*; (rule) imperio, poder, *m*. **to hold s. over,** gobernar, regir

swear *vt* jurar; (*law* etc.) declarar bajo juramento. *vi* jurar; (curse) echar pestes, blasfemar. **to s. at,** maldecir. **to s. by,** jurar por; poner fe implícita en. **to be sworn in,** prestar juramento. **to s. in,** tomar juramento (a). **to s. to,** atestiguar

sweat *n* sudor, *m*; *inf* trabajo arduo, *m*. *vi* sudar. *vt* sudar; hacer sudar; (workers) explotar. **by the s. of one's brow,** con el sudor de la frente, con el sudor del rostro. **s.-gland,** glándula sudorípara, *f*

sweated *a* (of persons) explotado; (of labor) mal retribuido

sweater *n* suéter, jersey, *m*

sweating *n* transpiración, *f*; (of workers) explotación, *f*

sweaty *a* sudoroso

Swede *n* sueco (-ca); (vegetable) naba, *f*

Sweden Suecia, *f*

sweep *vi* extenderse (por); (cleave) surcar; pasar rápidamente (por); invadir; dominar; andar majestuosamente; (with a brush) barrer. *vt* barrer; pasar (por); (the strings of a musical instrument) rasguear; (the sea) navegar por; (mines) barrer; (the horizon, etc.) examinar; (a chimney) deshollinar; (with a brush) barrer; (remove) arrebatar; quitar; llevarse; (abolish) suprimir. **to s. along,** *vt* (of the current, crowds, etc.) arrastrar. *vi* pasar majestuosamente; correr rápidamente (por). **to s. aside,** apartar con la mano; abandonar; (a protest) desoír, no hacer caso de. **to s. away,** barrer; (remove) llevarse; destruir; suprimir. **to s. down,** *vt* barrer; (carry) arrastrar. *vi* (of cliffs, etc.) bajar; (of an enemy) abalanzarse (sobre); lanzarse (por). **to s. off,** barrer; (a person) llevarse sin perder tiempo; arrebatar con violencia (a). **to be swept off one's feet,** ser arrastrado (por); perder el balance; (of emotion) ser dominado por. **to s. on,** seguir su avance inexorable; seguir su marcha. **to s. up,** recoger, barrer

sweep *n* barredura, *f*; (of a chimney) deshollinador, *m*; (of the tide) curso, *m*; (of a scythe, etc.) golpe, *m*; (range) alcance, *m*; (fold) pliegue, *m*; (curve) curva, *f*; (of water, etc.) extensión, *f*; (of wings) envergadura, *f*. **with a s. of the arm,** con un gesto del brazo. **to make a clean s. of,** hacer tabla rasa de

sweeping *a* completo; comprensivo; demasiado general; radical. **a s. judgment,** un juicio demasiado general. **s. change,** cambio radicale, *m pl*. **s. brush,** escoba, *f*

sweepings *n pl* barreduras, *f pl*; residuos, *m pl*; (of society) heces, *f pl*

sweepstake *n* lotería, *f*

sweet *a* dulce; (of scents) oloroso, fragante; (of sounds) melodioso, dulce; (charming) encantador; amable; (pretty) bonito. *n* bombón, *m*; golosina, *f*; (at a meal) (plato) dulce, *m*; dulzura, *f*; (beloved) amor, *m*, querido (-da). **How s. it smells!** ¡Qué buen olor tiene! **the sweets of life,** las dulzuras de la vida. **s.-pea,** guisante de olor, *m*, haba de las Indias, *f*. **s.-potato,** batata, *f*, *Lat. Am.* boniato, camote, *m*. **s.-scented,** perfumado, fragante. **s.-tempered,** amable, de carácter dulce. **s.-toothed,** goloso. **s.-william,** *bot* clavel de la China, clavel de ramillete, clavel de San Isidro, ramillete de Constantinopla, *m*, minutisa, *f*

sweetbread *n* lechecillas, *f pl*

sweeten *vt* azucarar; endulzar. **Cervantes sweetens one's bitter moments,** Cervantes endulza los momentos ásperos

sweetheart *n* amante, *mf*, amado (-da); (as address) querido (-da)

sweetish *a* algo dulce

sweetly *adv* dulcemente; (of scents) olorosamente; (of sounds) melodiosamente; (of behaviour, etc.) amablemente

sweetness *n* dulzura, *f*; (of scents) buen olor, *m*, fragancia, *f*; (of sounds) melodía, dulzura, *f*; (of character) bondad, amabilidad, *f*

sweet potato *n* batata, *f*, boniato, buniato, camote, *m*

sweet sixteen *n* (age) los dieciséis abriles, *m pl*; (party) quinceañera (at age fifteen) *f*

sweet turnip *Central America* jícama, *f*

swell *vi* hincharse; (of the sea) entumecerse; crecer; aumentarse. *vt* hinchar; aumentar. *n* (of the sea) oleada, *f*, oleaje, *m*; (of the ground) ondulación, *f*; (of sound) crescendo, *m*; (increase) aumento, *m*; (dandy) pisaverde, elegante, *m*; (important person) pájaro gordo, *m*; (at games, etc.) espada, *m*. *a* estupendo; elegantísimo; de primera, excelente. **to suffer from swelled head,** tener humos, darse importancia. **This foot is swollen,** Este pie está hinchado (or tumefacto). **The refugees have swelled the population,** Los refugiados han aumentado la población. **eyes swollen with tears,** ojos arrasados de lágrimas. **to s. with pride,** hincharse de orgullo

swelling *n* hinchazón, *f*; *med* tumefacción, *f*; (bruise, etc.) chichón, *m*

swelter *vi* abrasarse; arder. *n* bochorno, calor sofocante, *m*

swerve *vi* desviarse; apartarse (de); torcerse. *n* desvío, *m*

swift *a* rápido, veloz; pronto. *adv* velozmente, rápidamente. *n orn* vencejo, *m*. **s.-flowing,** (of rivers, etc.) de corriente rápida. **s.-footed,** de pies ligeros

swiftly *adv* rápidamente, velozmente

swiftness *n* rapidez, velocidad, *f*; prontitud, *f*

swim *vi* nadar; flotar; (glide) deslizarse; (fill) inundarse. *vt* (a horse) hacer nadar; pasar a nado; nadar. *n* natación, *f*. **eyes swimming with tears,** ojos inundados de lágrimas. **He enjoys a s.,** Le gusta nadar. **My head swims,** Se me va la cabeza. **Everything swam before my eyes,** Todo parecía bailar ante mis ojos. **to be in the s.,** formar parte (de), ser (de); (be up to date) estar al corriente. **to s. the Channel,** atravesar el canal de la Mancha a nado. **to s. with the tide,** ir con la corriente

swimmer *n* nadador (-ra). **He is a bad s.,** Nada mal

swimming *n* natación, *f*; (of the head) vértigo, *m*. **s.-bath,** piscina, *f*. **s.-costume,** traje de baño, *m*. **s.-pool,** piscina, *Lat. Am.* alberca, *f*

swindle *vt* engañar, estafar; defraudar (de). *n* estafa, *f*, timo, *m*; engaño, *m*; impostura, *f*, *Lat. Am.* cambullón, *Argentina* forro, *m*

swindler *n* estafador (-ra), trampeador (-ra); engañador (-ra)

swine *n* cerdo, puerco, *m*; (person) cochino (-na). **a herd of s.,** una manada de cerdos

swineherd *n* porquero, *m*
swing *vi* balancearse; oscilar; (hang) colgar, pender; columpiarse; girar; dar la vuelta; (of a boat) bornear. *vt* balancear; (hang) colgar; (rock) mecer; (in a swing, etc.) columpiar; hacer oscilar; (raise) subir. *n* oscilación, *f*; vaivén, *m*; balanceo, *m*; (rhythm) ritmo, *m*; (seat, etc.) columpio, *m*; (reach) alcance, *m*. **The door swung open,** La puerta se abrió silenciosamente. **He swung the car round,** Dio la vuelta al auto. **He swung himself into the saddle,** Montó de un salto. **to be in full s.,** estar a toda marcha. **to go with a s.,** tener mucho éxito. **s.-boat,** columpio, *m*. **s.-bridge,** puente giratorio, *m*. **s.-door,** puerta giratoria, *f*
swinging *a* oscilante; pendiente; rítmico. *n* balanceo, *m*; oscilación, *f*; vaivén, *m*; ritmo, *m*. **s. stride,** andar rítmico, *m*
swinish *a* porcuno, de cerdo; cochino, sucio
swipe *vt* golpear duro; aplastar; (steal) *Mexico* chalequear. *n* golpe fuerte, *m*
swirl *vi* arremolinarse. *n* remolino, *m*
swish *vt* (of an animal's tail) agitar, mover, menear; (of a cane) blandir; (thrash) azotar. *vi* silbar; (of water) susurrar; (of a dress, etc.) crujir. *n* silbo, *m*; (of water) susurro, murmullo, *m*; (of a dress, etc.) crujido, *m*
Swiss *a* and *n* suizo (-za)
switch *n* vara, *f*; (riding) látigo, *m*; (of hair) trenza, *f*; *elec* interruptor, *m*; *rw* aguja, *f*; (*rw* siding) desviadero, *m*. *vt* azotar; (a train) desviar; *elec* interrumpir; (transfer) trasladar; (of an animal, its tail) remover, mover rápidamente. **to s. off,** (*elec* and telephone) cortar; (*rad* and *aut*) desconectar. **to s. on,** conectar; (a light) poner (la luz); (a radio) encender
switchboard *n* cuadro de distribución, *m*
Switzerland Suiza, *f*
swivel *n* torniquete, *m*; anillo móvil, *m*; pivote, *m*. *vi* girar sobre un eje; dar una vuelta. **s.-chair,** silla giratoria, *f*. **s.-door,** puerta giratoria, *f*
swoon *vi* desvanecerse, desmayarse. *n* desmayo, desvanecimiento, *m*
swoop *vi* calarse, abatirse; (of robbers, etc.) abalanzarse (sobre). *n* calada, *f*. **at one fell s.,** de un solo golpe
sword *n* espada, *f*; sable, *m*. **to measure swords with,** cruzar espadas con. **to put to the s.,** pasar a cuchillo (a). **s.-arm,** brazo derecho, *m*. **s.-belt,** talabarte, *m*. **s.-cut,** sablazo, *m*. **s.-dance,** danza de espadas, *f*. **s.-fish,** pez espada, pez sierra, espadarte, *m*, jifia, *f*. **s.-play,** esgrima, *f*; manejo de la espada, *m*. **s.-stick,** bastón de estoque, *m*. **s.-thrust,** golpe de espada, *m*; estocada, *f*
swordsman *n* espadachín, *m*; esgrimidor, *m*
swordsmanship *n* manejo de la espada, *m*; esgrima, *f*
sybarite *a* and *n* sibarita, *mf*
sybaritic *a* sibarítico, sibarita
sycamore *n* sicomoro, *m*; falso plátano, *m*
sycophancy *n* servilismo, *m*
sycophant *n* sicofanta, *m*
syllabic *a* silábico
syllable *n* sílaba, *f*
syllabus *n* programa, *m*; compendio, *m*
syllogism *n* silogismo, *m*
sylph *n* sílfide, *f*, silfo, *m*; (woman) sílfide, *f*; (humming-bird) colibrí, *m*. **s.-like,** de sílfide; como una sílfide
sylvan *a* selvático, silvestre; rústico
symbiosis *n* simbiosis, *f*
symbol *n* símbolo, emblema, *m*; *math* símbolo, *m*; (of rank, etc.) insignia, *f*
symbolical *a* simbólico
symbolism *n* simbolismo, *m*
symbolist *n* simbolista, *mf*
symbolize *vt* simbolizar
symmetrical *a* simétrico
symmetry *n* simetría, *f*
sympathetic *a* simpático; compasivo; (of the public, etc.) bien dispuesto. *n anat* gran simpático, *m*. **s. words,** palabras de simpatía, *f pl*. **s. ink,** tinta simpática, *f*
sympathetically *adv* simpáticamente; con compasión
sympathize *vi* simpatizar (con); (understand) comprender; (condole) compadecerse (de), condolerse (de); dar el pésame
sympathizer *n* partidario (-ia)
sympathy *n* simpatía, *f*; compasión, *f*. **Paul is in s. with their aims,** Pablo está de acuerdo con sus objetos. **Please accept my s.,** (on a bereavement) Le acompaño a Vd. en su sentimiento
symphonic *a* sinfónico
symphony *n* sinfonía, *f*
symposium *n* colección de artículos, *f*
symptom *n* síntoma, *m*; señal, *f*, indicio, *m*. **to show symptoms of,** dar indicios de
symptomatic *a* sintomático
synagogue *n* sinagoga, *f*
synchronization *n* sincronización, *f*
synchronize *vi* coincidir, tener lugar simultáneamente; sincronizarse. *vt* sincronizar
synchronous *a* sincrónico
syncopate *vt* (*gram mus*) sincopar
syncopation *n mus* síncopa, *f*
syncope *n* (*med gram*) síncope, *m*
syndical *a* sindical
syndicalism *n* sindicalismo, *m*
syndicalist *n* sindicalista, *mf*
syndicate *n* sindicato, *m*, *vt* sindicar
syndication *n* sindicación, *f*
synod *n ecc* sínodo, *m*
synonym *n* sinónimo, *m*
synonymous *a* sinónimo
synopsis *n* sinopsis, *f*
synoptic *a* sinóptico
syntax *n* sintaxis, *f*
synthesis *n* síntesis, *f*
synthetic *a* sintético
synthetize *vt* sintetizar
syphilis *n* sífilis, *f*
syphilitic *a* and *n* sifilítico (-ca)
Syracuse Siracusa, *f*
syren *n*. See **siren**
Syria Siria, *f*
Syrian *a* and *n* siríaco (-ca), sirio (-ia)
syringe *n* jeringa, *f*, *vt* jeringar
syrup *n* jarabe, *m*; (for bottling fruit, etc.) almíbar, *m*
syrup cake *Argentina* chancaca, *f*
syrupy *a* siroposo
system *n* sistema, *m*; régimen, *m*; método, *m*; (body) organismo, *m*. **He has no s. in his work,** No tiene método en su trabajo. **the nervous s.,** el sistema nervioso. **the feudal s.,** el feudalismo, el sistema feudal
systematic *a* sistemático, metódico
systematically *adv* sistemáticamente, metódicamente
systematization *n* sistematización, *f*
systematize *vt* sistematizar
systole *n med* sístole, *f*

T

t *n* (letter) te, *f*. *a* en T, en forma de T. **T bandage,** vendaje en T, *m*. **T square,** regla T, *f*
tab *n* oreja, *f*
tabby *n* gato romano, *m*; (female) gata, *f*; *inf* vieja chismosa, *f*
tabernacle *n* tabernáculo, *m*; templo, *m*; *arch* templete, *m*; *ecc* custodia, *f*
tabes *n med* tabes, *f*
table *n* mesa, *f*; (food) comida, mesa, *f*; (of the law, weights, measures, contents, etc.) tabla, *f*; (of land) meseta, *f*; (of prices) lista, tarifa, *f*. *vt* (parliament) poner sobre la mesa; enumerar, apuntar, hacer una lista de. **to clear the t.,** alzar (or levantar) la mesa. **to lay the t.,** cubrir (or poner) la mesa. **to have a t.-d'hôte meal,** tomar el menú. **to rise from t.,** levantarse de la mesa. **to sit down to t.,** ponerse a la mesa. **The tables are turned,** Se volvió la tortilla. **side t.,** aparador, trinchero, *m*. **small t.,** mesilla, *f*. **t. of contents,** tabla de materias, *f*, índice, índice de materias, índice general, *m*. **t.-centrepiece,** centro de mesa, *m*. **t.-cloth,** mantel, *m*. **t.-companion,** comensal, *mf* **t.-knife,** cuchillo de mesa, *m*. **t.-lamp,** quinqué, *m*; lampara de mesa, *f*. **t.-land,** meseta, *f*. **t.-leg,** pata de una mesa, *f*. **t.-linen,** mantelería, *f*. **t.-napkin,** servilleta, *f*. **t.-runner,** camino de mesa, *m*. **t.-spoon,** cuchara para los legumbres, *f*. **t.-talk,** conversación de sobremesa, *f*. **t.-turning,** mesas que dan vueltas, *f pl*. **t.-ware,** artículos para la mesa, *m pl*
table d'hôte *n Spain* el menú, *m*, *Mexico* comida corrida *f*
tableau *n* cuadro, *m*. **tableaux vivants,** cuadros vivos, *m pl*
tablespoonful *n* cucharada, *f*
tablet *n* tabla, *f*; (with inscription) tarjeta, losa, lápida, *f*; *med* comprimido, *m*, tableta, *f*; (of soap, chocolate) pastilla, *f*. **writing t.,** taco de papel, *m*
tabloid *n* comprimido, *m*, pastilla, *f*
taboo *n* tabú, *m*. *a* prohibido, tabú. *vt* declarar tabú, prohibir
tabor *n mus* tamboril, tamborín, *m*. **t. player,** tamborilero, *m*
tabouret *n* (stool) taburete, *m*; (for embroidery) tambor de bordar, *m*; *mus* tamborilete, *m*
tabulate *vt* resumir en tablas; hacer una lista de, catalogar
tabulation *n* distribución en tablas, *f*
tacit *a* tácito
taciturn *a* taciturno, sombrío, reservado, de pocas palabras
tack *n* (nail) tachuela, puntilla, *f*; *sew* hilván, embaste, *m*; *naut* amura, *f*; *naut* puño de amura, *m*; *naut* bordada, *f*; *fig* cambio de política, *m*. *vt* clavar con tachuelas; *sew* hilvanar, embastar; *fig* añadir. *vi naut* virar; *fig* cambiar de política, adoptar un nuevo plan de acción. **t. puller,** sacabrocas, *m*
tackle *n* aparejo, *m*; maniobra, *f*; *naut* cuadernal, *m*, jarcia, *f*; (gear) aparejos, avíos, *m pl*; (football) carga, *f*. *vt* agarrar, asir; *fig* atacar, abordar; (football) cargar; (undertake) emprender; (a problem) luchar con. **t.-block,** polea, *f*
tacky *a* pegajoso, viscoso
tact *n* tacto, *m*, discreción, diplomacia, delicadeza, *f*
tactful *a* lleno de tacto, diplomático, discreto
tactfully *adv* discretamente, diplomáticamente
tactical *a* táctico
tactically *adv* según la táctica; del punto de vista táctico
tactician *n* táctico, *m*
tactics *n pl* táctica, *f*
tactile *a* táctil; tangible
tactless *a* que no tiene tacto, sin tacto alguno, indiscreto
tactlessly *adv* impolíticamente, indiscretamente
tactlessness *n* falta de tacto, *f*
tadpole *n* renacuajo, *m*
taffeta *n* tafetán, *m*
tag *n* herrete, *m*; (label) marbete, *m*, etiqueta, *f*; (of tail) punta del rabo, *f*; (of boot) tirador de bota, *m*; (game) marro, *m*; (rag) arrapiezo, *m*; (quotation) cita bien conocida, *f*; (of song, poem) refrán, *m*. **to play t.,** jugar al marro
Tagus el Tajo, *m*
tail *n* cola, *f*, rabo, *m*; (plait) trenza, *f*; (wisp of hair) mechón, *m*; (of a comet) cola, cabellera, *f*; (of a note in music) rabito, *m*; (of a coat) faldon, *m*; (of a kite) cola, *f*; (of the eye), rabo, *m*; (retinue) séquito, *m*, banda, *f*; (of an aeroplane) cola, *f*; (end) fin, *m*; (of coin) cruz, *f*; (line) fila, cola, *f*. *vt* seguir de cerca, pisarle (a uno) los talones. **to t. after,** seguir de cerca. **to t. away,** disminuir; desaparecer, perderse de vista. **to t. on,** unir, juntar. **to turn t.,** volver la espalda, poner los pies en polvorosa. **with the t. between the legs,** con el rabo entre piernas. **t.-board,** (of a cart) escalera, *f*. **t.-coat,** frac, *m*. **t.-end,** extremo, *m*; fin, *m*; lo último. **t.-feather,** pena, *f*. **t.-fin,** aleta caudal, *f*; *aer* timón de dirección, *m*. **t.-light,** farol trasero, *m*, *Mexico* calavera, *f*. **t.-piece,** (of a violin, etc.) cola, *f*; *print* marmosete, culo de lámpara, *m*. **t. spin** *aer* barrena de cola, *f*. **t. wind,** viento de cola, *m*
tailed *a* de rabo. **big-t.,** rabudo, de cola grande. **long-t.,** rabilargo. **short-t.,** rabicorto
tailless *a* rabón, sin rabo
tailor *n* sastre, *m*. **t.-made,** *n* traje sastre, *m*, *a* de hechura de sastre. **tailor's shop,** sastrería, *f*
tailoress *n* sastra, *f*
tailoring *n* sastrería, *f*; (work) corte, *m*
taint *n* corrupción, *f*; infección, *f*; (blemish) mancha, *f*; (tinge) dejo, *m*. *vt* corromper, pervertir; inficionar; (meat) corromper. *vi* corromperse, inficionarse; (meat) corromperse
take *vt* tomar; (receive) aceptar; (remove) quitar; (pick up) coger; (grab) asir, agarrar; *math* restar; (carry) llevar; (a person) traer, llevar; (guide) conducir, guiar; (win) ganar; (earn) cobrar, percibir; obtener; (make prisoner) hacer prisionero, prender; (a town, etc.) tomar, rendir, conquistar; (appropriate) apoderarse de, apropiarse; (steal) robar, hurtar; (ensnare) coger, cazar con trampas; (fish) pescar, coger; (a trick, in cards) hacer (una baza); (an illness) contraer, coger; (by surprise) sorprender, coger desprevenido (a); (attract) atraer; (drink) beber; (a meal) tomar; (select) escoger; (hire) alquilar; (suppose) suponer; (a journal) estar abonado a; (use) emplear, usar; (impers., require) necesitarse, hacer falta; (purchase) comprar; (assume) adoptar, asumir; (a leap) dar (un salto); (a walk) dar (un paseo); (a look) echar (un vistazo); (measures) tomar (medidas); (the chair) presidir; (understand) comprender; (a photograph) sacar (una fotografía); (believe) creer; (consider) considerar; (a note) apuntar; (jump over) saltar; (time) tomar, emplear. **I t. size three in shoes,** Calzo el número tres. **to t. to be,** (believe) suponer; (mistake) creer quivocadamente. **to t. (a thing) badly,** tomarlo (or llevarlo) a mal. **The book took me two hours to read,** Necesité dos horas para leer el libro, Leí el libro en dos horas. **And this, I t. it, is Mary?** ¿Y supongo que ésta será María? **to be taken with,** ser entusiasta de; (of persons) estar prendado de. **to t. aback,** desconcertar, coger desprevenido (a). **to t. again,** volver a tomar; llevar otra vez; (a photograph) retratar otra vez. **to t. along,** llevar; traer. **to t. a long time,** tardar, *Lat. Am.* dilatar. **to t. away,** quitar; llevarse. **to t. back,** devolver; (retract) retractar; (receive) recibir (algo) devuelto. **to t. down,**

bajar; (a building) derribar; (machinery) desmontar; (hair) deshacerse (el cabello); (swallow) tragar; (in writing) apuntar; (humble) quitar los humos (a), humillar. **to t. for,** creer, imaginar; (a walk, etc.) llevar a; (mistake) creer erróneamente; tomar por. **Whom do you t. me for?** ¿Por quién me tomas? **to. t. for granted (assume),** dar por descontado, dar por lecho, dar por sentado, dar por supuesto; (underestimate) no hacer caso de, tratar con indiferencia. **t. the lion's share (of),** llevarse la parte del león (de), llevarse la tajada del león (de). **t. shape,** cobrar perfiles más nítidos, estructurarse con más nitidez, ir adquiriendo consistencia, tomar forma. **t. the law into one's own hands,** tomar la justicia por la mano. **to t. from,** privar, quitar de; (subtract) restar; substraer de. **to t. in,** (believe) tragar, creer; (sail) acortar las velas; (deceive) engañar; (lead in) hacer entrar; (accept) recibir, aceptar. **to t. off,** quitar; (surgically) amputar; (one's hat, etc.) quitarse (el sombrero); (eyes) sacar; (take away) llevarse; (mimic) imitar; (ridicule) ridiculizar; (unstick) despegar; (discount) descontar. **to t. on,** emprender; aceptar; (at sports) jugar. **to t. on oneself,** encargarse de, tomar por su cuenta, asumir. **to t. out,** sacar; extraer; (remove) quitar; (outside) llevar fuera; (for a walk) llevar a paseo; (obtain) obtener, sacar; (tire) agotar, rendir. **to t. over,** tomar posesión de; asumir; (show) mostrar, conducir por. **t. the bull by the horns,** ir al toro por los cuernos. **take seriously,** tomar en serio. **to t. up,** subir; (pick up) recoger; tomar; (a challenge, etc.) aceptar; (a dress, etc.) acortar; (absorb) absorber; (of space) ocupar; (of time) ocupar, hacer perder; (buy) comprar; (adopt) dedicarse a; (arrest) arrestar, prender; (criticize) censurar, criticar; (begin) empezar; (resume) continuar

take *vi* tomar; (be successful) tener éxito; (of vaccination, etc.) prender; (a good (bad) photograph) salir bien (mal). **to t. after,** salir a, parecerse a; (of conduct) seguir el ejemplo de; **to t. off,** salir; *aer* despegar. **to t. on,** *inf* lamentarse. **to t. to,** dedicarse a; darse a; (of persons) tomar cariño a; (grow accustomed) acostumbrarse a. **to t. up with,** hacerse amigo de

take *n* toma, *f*; cogida, *f*; *print* tomada, *f*; *theat* taquilla, *f*. **t.-in,** engaño, *m*. **t.-off,** *aer* (recorrido de) despegue, *m*; caricatura, *f*; sátira, *f*

taking *n* toma, *f*; secuestro, *m*, *n pl* **takings,** ingresos, *m pl*; *theat* taquilla, entrada, *f*. *a* atractivo, encantador; simpático; (of disease) contagioso

talc *n min* talco, *m*

talcum powder *n* talco, polvo de talco, *m*

tale *n* (recital) narración, historia, *f*; relato, *m*; cuento, *m*; leyenda, historia, fábula, *f*; (number) cuenta, *f*, número, *m*; (gossip) chisme, *m*. **old wives' t.,** cuento de viejas, *m*. **to tell a t.,** contar una historia. **to tell tales,** contar cuentos; revelar secretos, chismear

talebearer *n* correveidile, *mf*; chismoso (-sa), soplón (-ona)

talebearing *n* el chismear, *m*

talent *n* (coin) talento, *m*; (ability) ingenio, *m*; habilidad, *f*. **the best t. in Spain,** la flor de la cultura española

talented *a* talentoso, ingenioso

talisman *n* talismán, *m*

talit taled, *m*

talk *vi* and *vt* hablar, decir. **to t. business,** hablar de negocios. **to t. for talking's sake,** hablar por hablar. **to t. French,** hablar francés. **to t. nonsense,** decir disparates. **to t. too much,** hablar demasiado; *inf* hablar por los codos, irse (a uno) la lengua. **to t. about,** hablar de; conversar sobre. **to t. at,** decir algo a alguien para que lo entienda otro. **Are you talking at me?** ¿Lo dices por mí? **to t. away,** seguir hablando; disipar. **to t. into,** persuadir, inducir (a). **to t. of,** hablar de; charlar sobre. **to t. on,** hablar acerca de (or sobre); (continue) seguir hablando. **to t. out of,** disuadir de. **to t. out of turn,** meterse donde no le llaman, meter la pata. **to t. over,** hablar de; discutir, considerar. **to t. round,** persuadir. **to t. to,** (address) hablar a; (consult) hablar con; (scold) reprender. **to t. to each other,** hablarse. **to t. up,** hablar claro

talk *n* conversación, *f*; (informal lecture) charla, *f*; (empty words) palabras, *f pl*; (notoriety) escándalo, *m*; rumor, *m*. **There is t. of . . . ,** Se dice que . . . ; Se habla de que. **to give a t.,** dar una charla. **to indulge in small t.,** hablar de cosas sin importancia, hablar de naderías

talkative *a* locuaz, gárrulo, hablador, decidor. **to be very t.,** ser muy locuaz; *inf* tener mucha lengua

talkativeness *n* locuacidad, garrulidad, *f*

talker *n* hablador (-ra), conversador (-ra); (lecturer) orador (-ra); (in a derogatory sense) fanfarrón (-ona), charlatán (-ana). **to be a good t.,** hablar bien, ser buen conversacionista

talking *a* que habla, hablante; (of birds, dolls, etc.) parlero. **to give a good t. to,** dar una peluca (a). **t.-film,** película sonora, *f*. **t.-machine,** fonógrafo, *m*

tall *a* alto; (of stories) exagerado. **five feet tall,** de cinco pies de altura

tallboy *n* cómoda alta, *f*

tallness *n* altura, *f*; estatura, talla, *f*; (of stories) lo exagerado

tallow *n* sebo, *m*. **t. candle,** vela de sebo, *f*. **t. chandler,** velero (-ra). **t.-faced,** con cara de color de cera

tallowy *a* seboso

tall tale *Peru* bacho, *m*

tally *n* tarja, tara, *f*; cuenta, *f*. *vt* llevar la cuenta (de). *vi* estar conforme, cuadrar

Talmud *n* Talmud, *m*

Talmudic *a* talmúdico

tamable *a* domable, domesticable

tambour *n mus* tambor, *m*; (for embroidery) tambor (or bastidor) para bordar, *m*

tambourine *n* pandereta, *f*

tame *a* domesticado, manso; (spiritless) sumiso; (dull) aburrido, soso. *vt* domar, domesticar; (curb) reprimir, gobernar, domar, suavizar. **to grow t.,** domesticarse

tamer *n* domador (-ra)

taming *n* domadura, *f*. **The T. of the Shrew,** La Fierecilla Domada

tamp *vt* apisonar; (in blasting) atacar (un barreno)

tamper *vi* (with) descomponer, estropear; (meddle with) meterse con; (witnesses) sobornar; (documents) falsificar

tampon *n surg* tampón, tapón, *m*, *vt* taponar

tan *vt* curtir, adobar; (of sun) tostar, quemar; (slang) zurrar. *vi* tostarse por el sol. *n* color café claro, *m*; bronceado, cutis tostado, *m*. *a* de color café claro

tandem *n* tándem, *m*

tang *n* (of sword, etc.) espiga, *f*; (flavor) fuerte sabor, *m*; (sound) retintín, *m*

tangent *a* and *n* tangente *f*. **to fly off at a t.,** *fig* salir por la tangente

tangerine *a* and *n* tangerino (-na). **t. orange,** naranja mandarina, *f*

tangible *a* tangible; *fig* real

Tangier Tánger, *m*

tangle *n* embrollo, enredo, nudo, *m*; (of streets) laberinto, *m*; *fig* confusión, *f*. *vt* embrollar, enmarañar; (entangle) enredar; *fig* poner en confusión, complicar. *vi* enmarañarse

tank *n* tanque, depósito (de agua, etc.), *m*; cisterna, *f*; (as a reservoir) aljibe, estanque, *m*; *mil* tanque, carro de asalto, *m*. **t. up** (get drunk) *Argentina* acatarrarse

tankard *n* pichel, bock, *m*

tanker *n* petrolero, *m*

tanned *a* bronceado, quemado por el sol, dorado por el sol

tanner *n* curtidor, *m*; (slang) medio chelín, *m*. **tanner's scraper,** descarnador, *m*. **tanner's vat,** noque, *m*

tannery *n* curtiduría, *f*

tannic *a chem* tánico. **t. acid,** ácido tánico, *m*

tannin *n chem* tanino, *m*

tanning *n* curtido, adobamiento, *m*

tantalize *vt* tentar, atormentar, provocar
tantalizing *a* tentador, atormentador; provocativo
tantamount *a* equivalente, igual. **to be t. to,** ser equivalente a
tantrum *n* pataleta, rabieta, *f,* berrinche, *m*
taoism *n* taoísmo, *m*
taoist *n* taoísta, *mf*
tap *n* (blow) pequeño golpe, toque ligero, *m;* palmadita, *f;* (for drawing water, etc.) grifo, *m,* llave, *f;* (of a barrel) canilla, *f;* (brew of liquor) clase de vino, *f;* (tap-room) bar con mostrador, *m;* (tool) macho de terraja, *m;* (piece of leather on shoe) tapa, *f; pl* **taps,** *mil* toque de apagar las luces, *m. vt* (strike) golpear ligeramente, dar una palmadita a; (pierce) horadar; (a barrel) decentar; *surg* hacer una puntura en; (trees) sangrar; *elec* derivar (una corriente); (of water, current) tomar; (information) descubrir; (telephone) escuchar las conversaciones telefónicas. *vi* golpear ligeramente. **to tap at the door,** llamar suavemente a la puerta. **on tap,** en tonel. **screw-tap,** terraja, *f.* **tap-dance,** claqué, *m.* **tap-root,** raíz pivotante, *f*
tape *n* (linen) cinta de hilo, *f;* (cotton) cinta de algodón, *f;* (telegraph machine) cinta de papel, *f;* (surveying) cinta para medir, *f.* **adhesive t.,** cinta adhesiva, *f.* **red t.,** balduque, *m; fig* burocracia, *f;* formulismo, *m.* **t.-machine,** telégrafo de cotizaciones, bancarias, *m.* **t.-measure,** cinta métrica, *f*
taper *n* bujía, cerilla, *f; ecc* cirio, *m. vi* ahusarse, rematar en punta. *vt* afilar
tapering *a* cónico, piramidal; (of fingers) afilado
tapestried *a* cubierto de tapices, tapizado
tapestry *n* tapiz, *m.* **t. weaver,** tapicero, *m*
tapeworm *n* tenia, lombriz solitaria, *f*
tapioca *n* tapioca, *f*
tapir *n zool* danta, *f*
tapis, to be on the estar sobre el tapete
tar *n* alquitrán, *m,* brea, *f. vt* embrear, alquitranar. **to tar and feather,** emplumar. **coal t.,** alquitrán mineral, *m*
tarantella *n* tarantela, *f*
tarantula *n* tarántula, *f*
tardily *adv* tardíamente; lentamente
tardiness *n* tardanza, lentitud, *f*
tardy *a* (late) tardío; (slow) lento; (reluctant) desinclinado
tare *n bot* yero, *m;* (in the Bible) cizaña, *f; com* tara, *f;* (of a vehicle) peso en vacío, *m*
target *n* blanco (de tiro), *m;* (shield) rodela, tarja, *f.* **t. practice,** tiro al blanco, *m*
tariff *n* tarifa, *f.* **to put a t. on,** tarifar
tarlatan *n* tarlatana, *f*
tarmac *n* alquitranado, *m*
tarn *n* lago de montaña, *m*
tarnish *n* deslustre, *m. vt* deslustrar, empañar; *fig* obscurecer, manchar. *vi* deslustrarse
tarpaulin *n* alquitranado, encerado, *m*
tarred *a* alquitranado, embreado
tarring *n* embreadura, *f*
tarry *vi* tardar, detenerse
tart *a* ácido, acerbo, agridulce; *fig* áspero. *n* tarta, *f;* pastelillo de fruta, *m*
tartan *n naut* tartana, *f;* (plaid) tartán, *m*
tartar *n chem* tártaro, *m;* (in teeth) sarro, tártaro, *m;* **cream of t.,** (cremor) tártaro, *m.* **t. emetic,** tártaro emético, *m.* **Tartar,** *a* and *n* tártaro (-ra)
Tartary Tartaria, *f*
tartly *adv* ásperamente, agriamente
tartness *n* acidez, *f; fig* aspereza, *f*
task *n* tarea, labor, *f;* empresa, *f;* misión, *f.* **to take to t.,** regañar, censurar. **t.-force,** (naval or military) contingente, *m*
taskmaster *n* el que señala una tarea; amo, *m*
tassel *n* borla, *f;* (of corn) panoja, espiga, *f*
taste *n* gusto, *m;* (flavor) sabor, *m;* (specimen) ejemplo, *m,* idea, *f;* (small quantity) un poco, muy poco; (liking) afición, inclinación, *f;* (of drink) sorbo, trago, *m;* (tinge) dejo, *m. vt* (appraise) probar; gustar, percibir el gusto de; (experience) experimentar, conocer. *vi* tener gusto, tener sabor. **a matter of t.,** cuestión de gusto. **Each to his own t.,** Entre gustos no hay disputa. **He had not tasted a bite,** No había probado bocado. **in bad (good) t.,** de mal (buen) gusto; de mal (buen) tono. **to have a t. for,** ser aficionado a, gustar de. **to t.,** *cul* a gusto, a sabor. **to t. of,** tener gusto de, saber a
tasted *a* (in compounds) de sabor . . .
tasteful *a* de buen gusto
tastefully *adv* con buen gusto
tastefulness *n* buen gusto, *m*
tasteless *a* insípido, soso, insulso; de mal gusto
tastelessness *n* insipidez, insulsez, *f;* mal gusto, *m*
taster *n* catador, *m;* (vessel) catavino, *m*
tasting *n* saboreo, *m,* gustación, *f, a* (in compounds) de sabor . . .
tasty *a* apetitoso, sabroso
tatter *n* andrajo, harapo, *m;* jirón, *m.* **to tear in tatters,** hacer jirones
tattered *a* andrajoso, haraposo
tatting *n* frivolité, *m*
tattoo *n* tatuaje, *m; mil* retreta, *f;* (display) parada militar, *f. vt* tatuar
tattooing *n* tatuaje, *m;* tamboreo, *m*
taunt *n* mofa, *f,* insulto, escarnio, *m. vt* insultar, atormentar. **to t. with,** echar en cara
taunting *a* insultante, burlón, insolente
tauntingly *adv* burlonamente, insolentemente
Taurus *n* tauro, toro, *m*
taut *a* tieso, tirante, tenso; en regla; *naut* **to make t.,** tesar
tauten *vt* tesar; poner tieso
tautness *n* tensión, *f*
tautological *a* tautológico
tautology *n* tautología, *f*
tavern *n* taberna, *f;* (inn) mesón, *m,* posada, *f.* **t.-keeper,** tabernero, *m*
tawdrily *adv* llamativamente, de un modo cursi
tawdriness *n* charrería, *f*
tawdry *a* chillón, charro, cursi
tawny *a* leonado
tax *n* contribución, gabela, imposición, *f; fig* carga, *f; vt* imponer contribuciones (a); *law* tasar; *fig* cargar, abrumar. **to tax with,** tachar (de), acusar (de). **direct (indirect) tax,** contribución directa (indirecta), *f.* **tax-collector,** recaudador de contribuciones, *m.* **tax-free,** libre de impuestos. **tax-rate,** tarifa de impuestos, *f,* cupo, *m.* **tax-register,** lista de contribuyentes, *f*
taxable *a* imponible, sujeto a impuestos
taxation *n* imposición de contribuciones (or impuestos), *f*
tax evasion *n* evasión tributaria, *f*
taxi *n* taxi, *Mexico* libre, *m. vi* ir en un taxi; *aer* correr por tierra. **t. driver,** chófer de un taxi, taxista, *m.* **t. rank, taxi stand,** parada de taxis, *f*
taxidermist *n* taxidermista, *mf*
taxidermy *n* taxidermia, *f*
taximeter *n* taxímetro, *m*
taxpayer *n* contribuyente, *mf*
taxpaying *a* tributario, que paga contribuciones
tax reform *n* reforma impositiva, reforma tributaria, *f*
tea *n* (liquid) té, *m;* (meal) merienda, *f.* **to have tea,** tomar el té, merendar. **tea-caddy,** bote para té, *m.* **tea-chest,** caja para té, *f.* **tea-cosy,** cubretetera, *m.* **tea-cup,** taza para té, *f.* **tea-dance,** té baile, *m.* **tea-kettle** or **tea-pot,** tetera, *f.* **tea-leaf,** hoja de té, *f.* **tea-party,** reunión para tomar el té, *f.* **tea-room,** salón de té, *m.* **tea-rose,** rosa de té, *f.* **tea-set,** juego de té, *m.* **tea-strainer,** colador de té, *m.* **tea-time,** hora de té, *f.* **tea-urn,** samowar, *m,* tetera para hacer té, *f.* **tea-wagon,** carrito para el té, *m*
teach *vt* (a person) enseñar, instruir; (a subject) enseñar; (to lecture on) ser profesor de; (a lesson) dar una lección (de). *vi* (be a teacher) dedicarse a la enseñanza. **to teach at . . . ,** desempeñor una cátedra en . . . **to t.**

a person Spanish, enseñar el castellano a alguien. **to t. how to,** enseñar a (followed by infin.)
teachability *n* docilidad, *f*
teachable *a* educable; dócil
teacher *n* preceptor, *m*; profesor, maestro, *m*. **woman t.,** profesora, maestra, *f*
teaching *n* enseñanza, *f*; (belief) doctrina, *f*, *a* docente. **t. profession,** magisterio, *m*
teaching method *n* método didáctico, *f*
teak *n bot* teca, *f*; (wood) madera de teca, *f*
team *n* (of horses) tiro, *m*; (of oxen, mules) par, *m*, pareja, yunta, *f*; *sport* partido, equipo, *m*; compañía, *f*, grupo, *m*. *vt* enganchar, uncir. **t.-work,** cooperación, *f*
teamster *n* gañán, *m*
tear *vt* rasgar; romper; lacerar; (in pieces) hacer pedazos, despedazar; (scratch) arañar; *fig* atormentar. **to t. asunder,** romper; desmembrar. **to t. away,** arrancar, quitar violentamente. **to t. down,** derribar, echar abajo. **to t. off,** arrancar; desgajar. **to t. oneself away,** arrancarse, desgarrarse. **to t. one's hair,** arrancarse los pelos, mesarse. **to t. open,** abrir apresuradamente. **to t. up,** hacer pedazos; (uproot) arrancar, desarraigar.
tear *vi* rasgarse; romper; correr precipitadamente. **to t. along,** correr rápidamente (por). **to t. away,** marcharse corriendo. **to t. down,** bajar corriendo. **to t. into,** entrar corriendo en. **to t. off,** irse precipitadamente, marcharse corriendo. **to t. up,** subir corriendo; llegar corriendo; atravesar rápidamente
tear *n* lágrima, *f*; (drop) gota, *f*. **with tears in one's eyes,** con lágrimas en los ojos. **to shed tears,** llorar, lagrimear. **to wipe away one's tears,** secarse las lágrimas. **t.-drop,** lágrima, *f*. **t.-duct,** conductor lacrimal, *m*. **t.-gas,** gas lacrimante, *m*. **t.-stained,** mojado de lágrimas
tear *n* (rent) rasgón, *m*
tearful *a* lloroso, lacrimoso
tearfully *adv* con lágrimas en los ojos
tearing *n* rasgadura, *f*, desgarro, *m*
tearjerker *n* drama lacrimón, *m*
tease *vt* (card) cardar; (annoy) fastidiar, irritar, molestar; (chaff) tomar el pelo (a), embromar; (pester) importunar. *n* bromista, *mf*
teasel *n bot* cardencha, *f*, *vt* cardar
teaser *n* (problem) rompecabezas, *m*; (person) bromista, *mf*
teaspoon *n* cucharita, *f*
teaspoonful *n* cucharadita, *f*
teat *n* pezón, *m*; (of animals) teta, *f*
technical *a* técnico. **t. offence,** *law* cuasidelito, *m*. **t. school,** escuela industrial, *f*
technicality *n* carácter técnico, *m*; tecnicismo, *m*; detalle técnico, *m*
technician *n* técnico, *m*
technicolor *n* tecnicolor, *m*
technique *n* técnica, *f*; ejecución, *f*; mecanismo, *m*
technological *a* tecnológico
technologist *n* tecnólogo, *m*
technology *n* tecnología, *f*
teddy bear *n* osito de trapo, *m*
tedious *a* aburrido, tedioso, pesado
tediously *adv* aburridamente
tediousness *n* aburrimiento, *m*, pesadez, *f*
tedium *n* tedio, *m*, monotonía, *f*
tee *n sport* meta, *f*; (golf) tee, *m*; (letter) te, *f*; cosa en forma de te, *f*. *vt* (golf) colocar la pelota en el tee
teem *vi* rebosar (de), abundar (en); pulular, hormiguear, estar lleno (de); (with rain) diluviar
teeming *a* prolífico, fecundo. **t. with,** abundante en, lleno de
teens *n pl* números y años desde trece hasta diez y nueve; edad de trece a diez y nueve años de edad. **to be still in one's t.,** no haber cumplido aún los veinte
teeter *vi* balancearse, columpiarse
teethe *vi* endentecer, echar los dientes
teething *n* dentición, *f*. **t.-ring,** chupador, *m*
teetotal *a* abstemio
teetotalism *n* abstinencia completa de bebidas alcohólicas, *f*
teetotaller *n* abstemio (-ia)
teetotum *n* perinola, *f*
telecast *vt* telefundir
telecommunication *n* telecomunicación, *f*
telegram *n* telegrama, *m*
telegraph *n* telégrafo, *m*. *vi* telegrafiar; *fig* hacer señas. *vt* telegrafiar, enviar por telégrafo. **t. line,** línea telegráfica, *f*. **t. office,** central de telégrafos, *f*. **t. pole,** poste telegráfico, *m*. **t. wire,** hilo telegráfico, *m*
telegraphic *a* telegráfico
telegraphist *n* telegrafista, *mf*
telegraphy *n* telegrafía, *f*. **wireless t.,** telegrafía sin hilos, *f*
telemetry *n* telemetría, *f*
teleology *n* teleología, *f*
telepathic *a* telepático
telepathy *n* telepatía, *f*
telephone *n* teléfono, *m*. *vi* telefonear. *vt* telefonear, llamar por teléfono. **to be on the t.,** (speaking) estar communicando; (of subscribers) tener teléfono. **dial t.,** teléfono automático, *m*. **t. call,** comunicación telefónica, *f*; conversación telefónica, *f*. **t. call box,** teléfono público, *m*. **t. directory,** guía de teléfonos, *f*. **t. exchange,** central telefónica, *f*. **t. number,** número de teléfono, *m*. **t. operator,** telefonista, *mf* **t. receiver,** receptor telefónico, *m*. **t. wire,** hilo telefónico, *m*
telephonic *a* telefónico
telephonist *n* telefonista, *mf*
telephony *n* telefonía, *f*. **wireless t.,** telefonía sin hilos, *f*
teleprinter *n* teletipo, *m*
telescope *n* telescopio, catalejo, *m*. *vt* enchufar. *vi* enchufarse, meterse una cosa dentro de otra
telescopic *a* telescópico; de enchufe
televise *vt* trasmitir por televisión
television *n* televisión, *f*. **on television,** por televisión. **I saw her on television,** La vi por televisión
television series *n* serie televisiva, *f*
tell *vt* contar, narrar; decir; revelar; expresar; (the time, of clocks) marcar; (inform) comunicar, informar; (show) indicar, manifestar; (explain) explicar; distinguir; (order) mandar; (compute) contar. *vi* decir; (have effect) producir efecto. **We cannot t.,** No sabemos. **Who can t.?** ¿Quién sabe? **T. that to the marines!;** Cuéntaselo a tu tía! **to t. its own tale,** hacer ver por sí mismo lo que hay. **to t. again,** volver a decir; contar otra vez. **to t. off,** regañar, reñir; (on a mission) despachar, mandar. **to t. on,** delatar. **to t. upon,** afectar
teller *n* narrador (-ra); (of votes) escrutador (-ra) de votos; (payer) pagador; (bank) cajero (-ra), *m*
telling *a* notable, significante. *n* narración, *f*
telltale *n* chismoso (-sa), soplón (-ona); (informer) acusón (-ona); *fig* indicio, *m*, señal, *f*, *a* revelador
temerity *n* temeridad, *f*
temper *n* (of metals) temple, *m*; (nature) naturaleza, *f*, carácter, *m*; espíritu, *m*; (mood) humor, *m*; (anger) mal genio, *m*. *vt* (of metals) templar; moderar, mitigar; mezclar. *vi* templarse. **bad (good) t.,** mal (buen) humor. **to keep one's t.,** no enojarse, no impacientarse. **to lose one's t.,** enojarse, perder la paciencia
tempera *n art* templa, *f*. **in t.,** al temple, *m*
temperament *n* temperamento, *m*; modo de ser, natural, *m*, naturaleza, índole, *f*; *mus* temple, *m*
temperamental *a* natural, innato; caprichoso
temperamentally *adv* por naturaleza
temperance *n* moderación, templanza, *f*; sobriedad, abstinencia, *f*
temperate *a* moderado; sobrio; (of regions) templado. **t. zone,** zona templada, *f*
temperately *adv* sobriamente
temperateness *n* moderación, sobriedad, mesura, *f*; (of regions) templanza, *f*
temperature *n* temperatura, *f*. **to have a t.,** tener fiebre

tempered *a* de humor . . . , de genio . . . **to be good (bad) t.,** ser de buen (mal) humor
tempering *n* temperación, *f*
tempest *n* tempestad, borrasca, *f*, temporal, *m*; *fig* tormenta, *f*
tempest in a teapot borrasca en un vaso de agua, *m*
tempestuous *a* tempestuoso, borrascoso; *fig* impetuoso, violento
tempestuousness *n* lo tempestuoso; *fig* impetuosidad, violencia, *f*
temple *n* templo, *m*; *anat* sien, *f*
tempo *n mus* tiempo, *m*
temporal *a* temporal; (transient) transitorio, fugaz; *anat* temporal. *n anat* hueso temporal, *m*
temporality *n* temporalidad, *f*
temporarily *adv* provisionalmente
temporariness *n* interinidad, *f*
temporary *a* provisional, interino
temporize *vi* ganar tiempo; contemporizar
temporizing *n* contemporización, *f*, *a* contemporizador
tempt *vt* tentar; atraer, seducir
temptation *n* tentación, *f*; aliciente, atractivo, *m*
tempter *n* tentador (-ra)
tempting *a* tentador, atrayente; seductor
ten *a* diez; (of the clock) las diez, *f pl*; (of age) diez años, *m pl*, *n* diez, *m*; (a round number) decena, *f*; **ten-millionth,** *a* and *n* diezmillonésimo *m*. **ten months old,** diezmesino. **ten syllable,** decasílabo. **ten thousand,** *a* and *n* diez mil *m*. **There are ten thousand soldiers,** Hay diez mil soldados. **ten-thousandth,** *a* and *n* diezmilésimo *m*
tenable *a* sostenible, defendible
tenacious *a* tenaz; (stubborn) porfiado, obstinaz, terco; (sticky) adhesivo. **to be t. of life,** estar muy apegado a la vida
tenaciously *adv* tenazmente; porfiadamente
tenacity *n* tenacidad, *f*; porfía, *f*; tesón, *m*
tenancy *n* inquilinato, *m*; tenencia, *f*
tenant *n* arrendatario (-ia), inquilino (-na); habitante, *m*; morador (-ra). **t. farmer** *Chile* inquilino (-na), *mf*
tench *n icht* tenca, *f*
tend *vt* cuidar, atender; guardar; vigilar. *vi* tender; inclinarse (a), propender (a)
tendency *n* tendencia, inclinación, propensión, *f*; proclividad, *f*
tendentious *a* tendencioso
tender *n* guardián, *m*; *com* oferta, propuesta, *f*; *naut* falúa, *f*; (of a railway engine) ténder, *m*. **legal t.,** moneda corriente, *f*
tender *a* tierno; delicado; (of conscience) escrupuloso; (of a subject) espinoso; compasivo, afectuoso, sensible; muelle, blando. **t.-hearted,** compasivo, tierno de corazón
tender *vt* ofrecer; dar; presentar. *vi* hacer una oferta. **to t. condolences,** dar el pésame. **to t. one's resignation,** presentar la dimisión. **to t. thanks,** dar las gracias
tenderly *adv* tiernamente
tenderness *n* ternura, *f*; sensibilidad, *f*; delicadeza, *f*; dulzura, *f*; indulgencia, *f*; compasividad, benevolencia, *f*; escrupulosidad, *f*; mimo, cariño, *m*
tendon *n anat* tendón, *m*. **t. of Achilles,** tendón de Aquiles, *m*
tenement *n* casa de vecindad, *f*; vivienda, *f*, *Lat. Am.* conventillo, *m*; *poet* morada, *f*
Teneriffe Tenerife, *f*
tenet *n* principio, dogma, *m*, doctrina, *f*
tenfold *a* décuplo. *adv* diez veces
tennis *n* tenis, *m*. **to play t.,** jugar al tenis. **t. ball,** pelota de tenis, *f*. **t. court,** campo de tenis, *m*, cancha de tenis, pista de tenis, *f*. **tennis club,** club de tenis, *m*. **t. racket,** raqueta de tenis, *f*; **tennis shoe,** zapatilla de tenis, *f*
tenon *n carp* espiga, *f*, *vt* espigar
tenor *n* curso, *m*; tenor, contenido, *m*; *mus* tenor, *m*; *mus* alto, *m*; (mus. instrument) viola, *f*. *a mus* de tenor
tense *n gram* tiempo, *m*. *a* tirante, estirado, tieso; tenso
tenseness *n* tirantez, *f*; tensión, *f*
tensile *a* tensor; extensible
tension *n* tensión, *f*; *elec* voltaje, *m*, tensión, *f*; (of sewing-machine) tensahílo, *m*. **state of t.,** (diplomatic) estado de tirantez, *m*
tent *n* tienda (de campaña), *Lat. Am.* carpa, *f*; (bell) pabellón, *m*; *surg* tienda, *f*. **oxygen t.,** tienda oxígena, *f*. **to pitch tents,** armar las tiendas de campaña; acamparse. **to strike tents,** plegar tiendas. **t. fly,** toldo de tienda, *m*. **t. maker,** tendero, *m*. **t. peg,** clave que sujeta las cuerdas de una tienda, *f*. **t. pole,** mástil (or montante) de tienda, *m*
tentacle *n* tentáculo, *m*
tentative *a* tentativo, interino, provisional, de prueba, *n* tentativa, *f*, ensayo, *m*
tentatively *adv* por vía de ensayo, experimentalmente
tenth *a* décimo; (of monarchs) diez; (of the month) (el) diez. *n* décimo, *m*; (part) décima parte, *f*; *mus* decena, *f*
tenthly *adv* en décimo lugar
tenuity *n* tenuidad, *f*; sutilidad, *f*; delgadez, *f*
tenuous *a* tenue; sutil; delgado; fino
tenure *n* tenencia, posesión, *f*; (duration) duración, *f*; (of office) administración, *f*
tepid *a* tibio
tepidity *n* tibieza, *f*
tercentenary *n* tercer centenario, *m*
tercet *n* terceto, *m*
term *n* (limit) límite, fin, *m*; (period) plazo, tiempo, período, *m*; (schools, universities) trimestre, *m*; (*math, law, logic*) término, *m*; (word) expresión, palabra, *f pl*. **terms,** (conditions) condiciones, *f pl*; (charges) precios, *m pl*, tarifa, *f*; (words) términos, *m pl*, palabras, *f pl*. *vt* llamar, calificar. **for a t. of years,** por un plazo de años. **in plain terms,** en palabras claras. **on equal terms,** en condiciones iguales. **to be on bad (good) terms with,** estar en (or tener) malas (buenas) relaciones con. **to come to terms,** llegar a un acuerdo; hacer las paces. **What are your terms?** ¿Cuáles son sus condiciones? (price) ¿Cuáles son sus precios? **terms of sale,** condiciones de venta, *f pl*
termagant *n* arpía, fiera, *f*
terminable *a* terminable
terminal *a* terminal, final; (of schools, universities) trimestre. *n* término, *m*; *elec* borne, *m*; (schools, universities) examen de fin de trimestre, *m*; (railway) estación terminal, *f*; (*arch* and figure) término, *m*; *arch* remate, *m*
terminate *vt* limitar; terminar, concluir, poner fin (a). *vi* terminarse, concluirse (por); cesar
termination *n* terminación, conclusión, *f*; fin, *m*; *gram* terminación, *f*; cabo, remate, *m*
terminology *n* nomenclatura, terminología, *f*
terminus *n* (railway) estación terminal, *f*; (*arch* and figure) término, *m*; *arch* remate, *m*; *myth* Término
termite *n ent* termita, *m*
term paper *n* trabajo de examen, *m*
terms of trade *n* relación de los precios de intercambio, *f*
terrace *n* terraza, *f*, *vt* terraplenar
terraced *a* en terrazas; con terrazas
terracotta *n* terracota, *f*
terrain *n* terreno, campo, *m*, región, *f*
terrapin *n* tortuga de agua dulce, *f*
terrestrial *a* terrestre, terrenal
terrible *a* terrible, pavoroso, espantoso; *inf* tremendo
terribleness *n* terribilidad, *f*, lo horrible
terrier *n* terrier, *m*; *inf* soldado del ejército territorial, *m*
terrific *a* espantoso, terrible; *inf* atroz, tremendo
terrify *vt* aterrorizar, espantar, horrorizar, *Lat. Am. also* julepear. **to be terrified** *Lat. Am.* julepearse
terrifying *a* aterrador, espantoso
territorial *a* territorial. *n* soldado del ejército territorial, *m*
territoriality *n* territorialidad, *f*
territory *n* región, comarca, *f*; (state) territorio, *m*; ju-

risdicción, *f.* **mandated territory,** territorio bajo mandato, *m pl*

terror *n* terror, pavor, espanto, *m.* **the Reign of T.,** el Reinado del Terror, *m.* **t.-stricken,** espantado, muerto de miedo

terrorism *n* terrorismo, *m*

terrorist *n* terrorista, *m*

terrorization *n* aterramiento, *m*

terrorize *vt* aterrorizar

terse *a* conciso, sucinto; seco, brusco

tersely *adv* concisamente; secamente

terseness *n* concisión, *f*; brusquedad, *f*

tertiary *a* tercero; *geol* terciario. *n ecc* terciario, *m*

tessera *n* tesela, *f*

test *n* (proof) prueba, *f*; examen, *m*; investigación, *f*; (standard) criterio, *m*, piedra de toque, *f*; *chem* análisis, *m*; (trial) ensayo, *m*; *zool* concha, *f.* *vt chem* ensayar; probar, poner a prueba; examinar; (eyes) graduar (la vista). **to put to the t.,** poner a prueba. **to stand the t.,** soportar la prueba. **t. match,** partido internacional de cricket, *m.* **t. meal,** *med* comida de prueba, *f.* **t. pilot,** *aer* piloto de pruebas, *m.* **t. tube,** tubo de ensayo, *m*

testament *n* testamento, *m.* **the New T.,** el Nuevo Testamento, *m.* **the Old T.,** el Antiguo Testamento, *m*

testamentary *a* testamentario

testate *a* testado

testator *n* testador, *m*, (**testatrix,** testadora, *f*)

testicle *n* testículo, *m*

testification *n* testificación, *f*

testify *vt* and *vi* declarar, atestar; *law* atestiguar, testificar, dar fe

testily *adv* malhumoradamente

testimonial *n* recomendación, *f*; certificado, *m*; (tribute) homenaje, *m*

testimony *n* testimonio, *m*, declaración, *f*; (proof) prueba, *f.* **in t. whereof,** en fe de lo cual. **to bear t.,** atestar

testiness *n* mal humor, *m*, irritación, *f*

testing grounds *n* campo de experimentación, campo de pruebas, *m*

testy *a* enojadizo, irritable, irascible, quisquilloso

tetanus *n* tétano, *m*

tether *n* traba, atadura, maniota, *f.* *vt* atar con una correa. **to be at the end of one's t.,** acabarse la resistencia; acabarse la paciencia

Teutonic *a* teutónico

text *n* texto, *m*; (subject) tema, *m*; (motto) lema, *m*; (of a musical composition) letra, *f.* **t.-book,** libro de texto, *m*

textile *a* textil, de tejer. *n* textil, *m*, materia textil, *f*; tejido, *m*

textual *a* textual

texture *n* (material and *biol*) tejido, *m*; textura, *f*

Thailand Tailandia, *f*

thalamus *n* (*anat, bot*) tálamo, *m*

Thames, the *n* el Támesis, *m.* **to set the T. on fire,** descubrir la pólvora

than *conjunc* que; (between **more, less,** or **fewer** and a number) de; (in comparisons of inequality) que, but que becomes *a* del (de la, de los, de las) que if the point of comparison is a noun in the principal clause, which has to be supplied mentally to fill up the ellipsis; (*b*) de lo que if there is no noun to act as a point of comparison, e.g. **He was older than I thought,** Era más viejo de lo que yo pensaba. **They have less than they deserve,** Tienen menos de lo que merecen. **They lose more money than** (**the money**) **they earn,** Pierden más dinero del que ganan. **He will meet with more opposition than he thought,** Va a encontrar más oposición de la que pensaba. **I have more books than you,** Tengo más libros que tú. **She has fewer than nine and more than five,** Ella tiene menos de nueve y más de cinco

thank *vt* agradecer, dar las gracias (a). **to t. for,** agradecer. **I will t. you to be more polite,** Le agradecería que fuese más cortés. **He has himself to t. for it,** Él mismo tiene la culpa de ello. **No, t. you,** No, muchas gracias. **T. goodness!** ¡Gracias a Dios!

thank *n* (now in pl. only, **thanks**) gracias, *f pl.* **a vote of thanks,** un voto de gracias. **Many thanks!** ¡Muchas gracias! **to return thanks,** dar las gracias. **thanks to,** merced a, debido a. **thanks to you,** gracias a tí. **t.-offering,** ofrecimiento en acción de gracias, *m*

thankful *a* agradecido. **I am t. to see,** Me alegro de ver, Me es grato ver

thankfully *adv* con gratitud, agradecido

thankfulness *n* agradecimiento, *m*; gratitud, *f*

thankless *a* ingrato; desagradecido; desagradable

thanksgiving *n* acción de gracias, *f.* **t. service,** servicio de acción de gracias, *m.* **Thanksgiving** (**Day**), *n* día de acción de dar gracias, día de gracias, *m*

that *dem a* ese, *m*; esa, *f*; aquel, *m*; aquella, *f*, *dem. pron* ése, *m*; ésa, *f*; eso, *neut*; aquél, *m*; aquélla, *f*; aquello, *neut*; (standing for a noun) el, *m*; la, *f*; lo, *neut* **All t. there is,** Todo lo que hay. **His temperament is t. of his mother,** Su temperamento es el de su madre. **We have not come to t. yet,** Todavía no hemos llegado a ese punto. **T. is what I want to know,** Eso es lo que quiero saber. **with t.,** con eso; (thereupon) en eso. **Go t. way,** Vaya Vd. por allí; Tome Vd. aquel camino. **T. is to say . . . ,** Es decir . . . **What do you mean by t.?** ¿Qué quieres decir con eso? **The novel is not as bad as all t.,** La novela no es tan mala como tú piensas (*or* como dicen, etc.)

that *pron. rel* que; el cual, *m*; la cual, *f*; lo cual, *neut*; (of persons) a quien, *mf*; a quienes, *mf pl*; (with from) de quien, *mf*; de quienes, *mf pl*; (of place) donde. **The letter t. I sent you,** la carta que te mandé. **The box t. John put them in,** la caja en la cual los puso Juan. **The last time t. I saw her,** La última vez que la vi

that *conjunc* que; (of purpose) para que; afin de que; (before infin.) para; (because) porque. **O t. he would come!** ¡Ojalá que viniese! **so t.,** para que; (before infin.) para; (as a result) de manera que; de modo que. **It is better t. he should not come,** Es mejor que no venga. **now t.,** ahora que

thatch *n* barda, *f*, *vt* bardar

thaw *n* deshielo, *m.* *vt* deshelar; derretir. *vi* deshelarse; derretirse

the *def art.* el, *m*; la, *f*; lo, *neut*; los, *m pl*; las, *f pl*; (before feminine sing. noun beginning with stressed a or ha) el; (untranslated between the name and number of a monarch, pope, ruler, e.g. **Charles the Tenth,** Carlos diez). *adv* (before a comparative) cuanto, tanto más. **at the** or **to the,** al, *m*, (also before feminine sing. noun beginning with a or ha); a la, *f*; a lo, *neut*; a los, *m pl*; a las, *f pl.* **from the** or **of the,** del, *m*, (also before feminine sing. noun beginning with stressed a or ha); de la, *f*; de lo, *neut*; de los, *m pl*; de las, *f pl.* **the one,** see **one.** **The sooner the better,** Cuanto antes mejor. **The room will be all the warmer,** El cuarto estará tanto más caliente

theater *n* teatro, *m*; (lecture) anfiteatro, *m*; (drama) teatro, *m*, obra dramática, *f*; (scene) teatro, *m*, escena, *f.* **t. attendant,** acomodador (-ra)

theater-in-the-round *n* teatro circular, teatro en círculo, *m*

theatin *a* and *n ecc* teatino *m*

theatrical *a* teatral. *n pl* **theatricals,** funciones teatrales, *f pl.* **amateur theatricals,** función de aficionados, *f.* **t. company,** compañía de teatro, *f.* **t. costumier,** mascarero (-ra), alquilador (-ra) de disfraces. **t. manager,** empresario de teatro, *m*

theatricality *n* teatralidad, *f*

theban *a* and *n* tebeo (-ea), tebano (-na)

Thebes Tebas, *f*

thee *pers pron* te; (after prep.) tí. **with t.,** contigo

theft *n* robo, hurto, *m*

their *poss a* su, *mf sing*; sus, *pl*; de ellos, *m pl*; de ellas, *f pl.* **They have t. books,** Tienen sus libros. **I have t. books,** Tengo los libros de ellos

theirs *poss pron* (el) suyo, *m*; (la) suya, *f*; (los) suyos, *m*

pl; (las) suyas, *f pl;* de ellos, *m pl;* de ellas, *f pl.* **These hats are t.,** Estos sombreros son los suyos
them *pers pron* ellos, *m pl;* ellas, *f pl;* (as object of a verb) los, *m pl;* las, *f pl;* (to them) les
thematic *a* temático
theme *n* tema, asunto, *m;* tesis, *f; mus* tema, motivo, *m*
themselves *pers pron pl* ellos mismos, *m pl;* ellas mismas, *f pl, reflexive pron* sí; sí mismos; (with a reflexive verb) se. **They t. told me about it,** Ellos mismos me lo dijeron. **They left it for t.,** Lo dejaron para sí (mismos)
then *adv* (of future time) entonces; (of past time) a la sazón, en aquella época, entonces; (next, afterwards) luego, después, en seguida; (in that case) en este caso, entonces; (therefore) por consiguiente. *a* de entonces. *n* entonces, *m. conjunc* (moreover) además; pues. **And what t.?** ¿Y qué pasó después?; ¿Y qué pasará ahora?; ¿Y qué más? **by t.,** por entonces. **now and t.,** de vez en cuando. **now . . . t.,** ya . . . ya, ora . . . ora. **since t.,** desde aquel tiempo; desde entonces; desde aquella ocasión. **until t.,** hasta entonces; hasta aquella época. **well t.,** bien, pues. **t. and there,** en el acto, en seguida; allí mismo
thence *adv* desde allí, de allí; (therefore) por eso, por esa razón, por consiguiente
thenceforth *adv* de allí en adelante, desde entonces
theocracy *n* teocracia, *f*
theocratic *a* teocrático
theologian *n* teólogo, *m*
theological *a* teológico, teologal
theologize *vi* teologizar
theology *n* teología, *f*
theorem *n* teorema, *m*
theoretical *a* teórico
theoretically *adv* teóricamente, en teoría
theorist *n* teórico, *m*
theorize *vi* teorizar
theory *n* teoría, *f*
theosophical *a* teosófico
theosophist *n* teósofo, *m*
theosophy *n* teosofía, *f*
therapeutic *a* terapéutico. *n* **therapeutics,** terapéutica, *f*
therapeutist *n* terapeuta, *mf*
therapy *suffix* terapia, *f*
there *adv* allí; ahí, allá; (at that point) en eso; (used pronominally as subject of verb) haber, e.g. **T. was once a king,** Hubo una vez un rey; **What is t. to do here?** ¿Qué hay que hacer aquí? *interj* ¡vaya!; (I told you so!) ¡ya ves! ¡ya te lo dije yo!; (in surprise) ¡toma! **about t.,** cerca de allí. **down t.,** allí abajo. **in t.,** allí dentro. **out t.,** allí fuera. **over t.,** ahí; allá a lo lejos. **up t.,** allí arriba. **T. came a time when . . . ,** Llegó la hora cuando . . . **T. it is!** ¡Allí está! **t. is** or **t. are,** hay. **t. was** or **t. were,** había, hubo. **t. may be,** puede haber, quizás habrá. **t. must be,** tiene que haber. **t. will be,** habrá. **T., t.!** (to a child, etc.) ¡Vamos!
thereabouts *adv* (near to a place) cerca de allí, por ahí, allí cerca; (approximately) approximadamente, cerca de
thereafter *adv* después, después de eso
thereby *adv* (near to that place) por allí cerca; (by that means) con lo cual, de este modo
therefore *adv* por lo tanto, por eso, así, por consiguiente; por esta razón
therein *adv* (inside) allí dentro; (in this, that particular) en estre, en eso, en ese particular
thereinafter *adv* posteriormente, más adelante
thereupon *adv* (in consequence) por consiguiente, por lo tanto; (at that point) luego, en eso; (immediately afterwards) inmediatamente después, en seguida
thermal *a* termal. **t. springs,** aguas termales, termas, *f pl*
thermodynamics *n* termodinámica, *f*
thermoelectric *a* termoeléctrico
thermometer *n* termómetro, *m*
Thermopylae Termópilas, *f*
thermos flask *n* termos, *m*
thermostat *n* termostato, *m*
thermostatic *a* termostático
thesaurus *n* tesoro, tesauro, *m*
these *dem pron pl* of **this,** éstos, *m pl;* éstas, *f pl, dem a* estos, *m pl;* estas, *f pl.* **Are not t. your flowers?** ¿No son éstas tus flores? **T. pictures have been sold,** Estos cuadros han se han vendito
thesis *n* tesis, *f*
Thespian *a* dramático
Thessaly Tesalia, *f*
they *pers pron pl* ellos, *m pl;* ellas, *f pl;* (people) se (followed by sing. verb). **T. say,** Dicen, Se dice
thick *a* espeso; (big) grueso, (wall) grueso, (string, cord) gordo; (vapors) denso; (muddy) turbio; (dense, close) tupido apretado; (numerous) numeroso, repetido, continuo; (full of) lleno (de); (of voice) velado, indistinto; (obtuse) estúpido, lerdo; (friendly) íntimo. *adv* densamente; continuamente, sin cesar. **three feet t.,** de tres pies de espesor. **That's a bit t.!** ¡Eso es un poco demasiado! **to be as t. as thieves,** estar unidos como los dedos de la mano. **t.-lipped,** con labios gruesos, bezudo. **t.-headed,** estúpido, lerdo. **t.-skinned,** de piel gruesa; *zool* paquidermo; *fig* sin vergüenza, insensible. **t. stroke,** (of letters) grueso, *m*
thick *n* espesor, *m;* parte gruesa, *f;* lo más denso; (of a fight) lo más reñido; centro, *m.* **in the t. of,** en el centro (de), en medio de
thicken *vt* espesar; (increase) aumentar, multiplicar; *cul* espesar. *vi* espesarse; condensar; aumentar, multiplicarse; (of a mystery, etc.) complicarse; hacerse más denso; *cul* espesarse
thickening *n* hinchamiento, *m;* gordura, *f;* (*cul* and of paints) espesante, *m*
thicket *n* matorral, soto, *m,* maleza, *f;* (grove) boscaje, *m*
thickly *adv* densamente; espesamente; continuamente, sin cesar; (of speech) indistintamente
thickness *n* espesor, *m;* grueso, *m;* densidad, *f;* (of liquids) consistencia, *f;* (layer) capa, *f;* (of speech) dificultad (en el hablar), *f*
thickset *a* doblado
thief *n* ladrón (-ona); (in a candle) moco de vela, *m.* **Stop t.!** ¡Ladrones! **thieves' den,** *fig* cueva de ladrones, *f*
thieve *vi* hurtar, robar. *vt* robar
thievish *a* ladrón
thigh *n* muslo, *m.* **t.-bone,** fémur, *m*
thimble *n* dedal, *m*
thimbleful *n* lo que cabe en un dedal; *fig* dedada, *f*
thin *a* delgado; (lean) flaco; (small) pequeño; delicado; fino; (of air, light) tenue, sutil; (clothes) ligero; (sparse) escaso; transparente; (watery) aguado; (of wine) bautizado; (not close) claro; (of arguments) flojo. *vt* adelgazar; aclarar; *agr* limpiar; reducir. *vi* adelgazarse; afilarse; reducirse. **somewhat t.,** (of persons) delgaducho, algo flaco. **to grow t.,** enflaquecer; afilarse. **to make t.,** hacer adelgazar volver flaco. **t.-clad,** ligero de ropa; mal vestido. **t.-faced,** de cara delgada. **t.-lipped,** de labios apretados. **t.-skinned,** de piel fina; *fig* sensitivo, sensible
thine. See **theirs.** *poss pron* (el) tuyo, *m;* (la) tuya, *f;* (los) tuyos, *m pl;* (las) tuyas, *f pl;* tu, *mf;* tus, *mf pl;* de tí. **The fault is t.,** La culpa es tuya, La culpa es de tí
thing *n* cosa, *f;* objeto, artículo, *m;* (affair) asunto, *m;* (contemptuous) sujeto, tipo, *m;* (creature) ser, *m,* criatura, *f; pl* **things,** (belongings) efectos, trastos, *m pl;* (luggage) equipaje, *m;* (clothes) trapitos, *m pl;* (circumstances) circunstancias, condiciones, *f pl.* **above all things,** ante todo, sobre todo. **a very pretty little t.,** (child) una pequeña muy mona. **as things are,** tal como están las cosas. **for one t.,** en primer lugar. **Her behavior is not quite the t.,** La conducta de ella no está bien vista. **It is a bad t. that . . . ,** Lo malo es que . . . **It is a good t. that . . . ,** Menos mal que . . . ; Lo

bueno es que . . . **No such t.!** ¡No hay tal!; ¡Nada de eso! **Poor t.!** ¡Pobrecito!; (woman) ¡Pobre mujer!; (man) ¡Pobre hombre! **to be just the t.,** venir al pelo. **with one t. and another,** entre unas cosas y otras. **I like things Spanish,** Me gusta lo español

think *vt* and *vi* pensar; (believe) creer; (deem) considerar, juzgar; imaginar; (suspect) sospechar; (opine) ser de opinión (que). **And to t. that . . . !** ¡Y pensar que . . . ! **As you t. fit,** Como usted quiera, Como a usted le parezca bien. **He thought as much,** Se lo figuraba. **He little thought that . . . !** ¡Cuán lejos estaba de pensar que . . . ! **He thinks nothing of . . . ,** No le importa . . . ; Desprecia, Tiene una opinión bastante mala de. **I don't t. so,** No lo creo. **I should just t. not!** ¡Claro que no! ¡Eso sí que no! **I should just t. so!** ¡Claro! ¡Ya lo creo! **It makes me t. of . . . ,** Me hace pensar en . . . **One might t.,** Podría creerse . . . **to t. better of something,** cambiar de opinión, considerar mejor. **to t. highly (badly) of,** tener buen (mal) concepto sobre. **to t. over carefully,** pensarlo bien, considerar detenidamente; *inf* consultar con la almohada. **to t. proper,** creer conveniente. **to t. to oneself,** pensar para sí (or entre sí). **to t. too much of oneself,** pensar demasiado en sí; tener demasiada buena opinión de sí mismo; tener humos. **What do you t. about it?** ¿Qué te parece? **to t. about,** (of persons) pensar en; (of things) pensar de (or sobre); meditar, considerar, reflexionar sobre. **to t. for,** pensar por. **to t. of,** pensar en; pensar de (or sobre). **What do you t. of this?** ¿Qué te parece esto? **to t. out,** idear, proyectar, hacer planes para; (a problem) resolver. **to t. over,** pensar; reflexionar sobre, meditar sobre. **I shall t. it over,** Lo pensaré.

thinker *n* pensador, *m*

thinking *n* pensamiento, *m*, reflexión, meditación, *f*; juicio, *m*; opinión, *f*, parecer, *m*. *a* pensador; inteligente; racional; serio. **To my way of t.,** Según pienso yo, A mi parecer. **way of t.,** modo de pensar, *m*

thinly *adv* delgadamente; esparcidamente; (lightly) ligeramente; poco numeroso

thinness *n* delgadez, *f*; (leanness) flaqueza, *f*; sutileza, tenuidad, *f*; (lack) escasez, *f*; pequeño número, *m*; poca consistencia, *f*

third *a* tercero (tercer before *m*, *sing* noun); (of monarchs) tercero; (of the month) (el) tres. *n* tercio, *m*, tercera parte, *f*; *mus* tercera, *f*. **T. time lucky!** ¡A la tercera va la vencida! **t. class,** *n* tercera clase, *f*. *a* de tercera clase. **t. party,** tercera persona, *f*. **t.-party insurance,** seguro contra tercera persona, *m*. **t. person,** tercero (-ra); *gram* tercera persona, *f*. **t.-rate,** de tercera clase

thirdly *adv* en tercer lugar

thirst *n* sed, *f*; *fig* deseo, *m*, ansia, *f*; entusiasmo, *m*. **to satisfy one's t.,** apagar (or matar) la sed

thirsty *a* sediento. **to be t.,** tener sed. **to make t.,** dar sed.

thirteen *a* and *n* trece *m*. **t. hundred,** *a* and *n* mil trescientos *m*

thirteenth *a* décimotercio; (of monarchs) trece; (of month) (el) trece, *m*, *n* décimotercio, trezavo, *m*

thirtieth *a* trigésimo; (of month) (el) treinta, *m*. *n* treintavo, *m*

thirty *a* and *n* treinta, *m*. **t.-first,** treinta y uno

this *dem a* este, *m*; esta, *f*, *dem pron* éste, *m*; ésta, *f*; esto, *neut* **by t. time,** a esta hora, ya. **like t.,** de este modo, así. **T. is Wednesday,** Hoy es miércoles. **What is all t.?** ¿Qué es todo esto?

thistle *n* cardo, *m*. **t.-down,** papo de cardo, vilano de cardo, *m*

thither *adv* allá, hacia allá; a ese fin. *a* más remoto

thong *n* correa, tira, *f*

thoracic *a* torácico

thorax *n* tórax, *m*

thorn *n* espina, *f*; (tree) espino, *m*; *fig* abrojo, *m*, espina, *f*. **to be a t. in the flesh of,** ser una espina en el costado de. **t. brake,** espinar, *m*

thornless *a* sin espinas

thorny *a* espinoso; *fig* difícil, arduo

thorough *a* completo; perfecto; (conscientious) concienzudo; (careful) cuidadoso. **t.-bred,** (of animals) de pura raza, de casta; (of persons) bien nacido. **t.-paced,** cabal, consumado

thoroughfare *n* vía pública, *f*. **"No t.,"** «Prohibido el paso», Calle cerrada

thoroughly *adv* completamente; (of knowing a subject) a fondo; concienzudamente

thoroughness *n* perfección, *f*; minuciosidad, *f*

those *dem a pl* of **that,** esos, *m pl*; esas, *f pl*; aquellos, *m pl*; aquellas, *f pl*, *dem pron* ésos, *m pl*; ésas, *f pl*; aquéllos, *m pl*; aquéllas, *f pl*; (standing for a noun) los, *m pl*; las, *f pl*. **t. who,** quienes, *mf pl*; los que, *m pl*; las que, *f pl*. **t. that** or **which,** los que, *m pl*; las que, *f pl*. **Your eyes are t. of your mother,** Tus ojos son los de tu madre

thou *pers pron* tú

though *conjunc* (followed by subjunc. when doubt is implied or uncertain future time) aunque, bien que; (nevertheless) sin embargo, no obstante; (in spite of) a pesar de que; (but) pero. **as t.,** como si (followed by subjunc.). **even t.,** aunque (followed by subjunc.)

thought *n* pensamiento, *m*; meditación, reflexión, *f*. **some thoughts on . . .** algunas reflexiones sobre . . . ; opinión, *f*; consideración, *f*; idea, *f*, propósito, *m*; (care) cuidado, *m*, solicitud, *f*; *inf* pizca, *f*. **on second thought,** después de pensarlo bien. **The t. struck him,** Se le ocurrió la idea. **to collect one's thoughts,** orientarse; informarse (de). **t.-reading,** adivinación del pensamiento, *f*. **t.-transference,** telepatía, transmisión del pensamiento, *f*

thoughtful *a* pensativo, meditabundo; serio; especulativo; (provident) previsor; (kind) atento, solícito; cuidadoso; (anxious) inquieto, intranquilo

thoughtfully *adv* pensativamente; seriamente; (providently) con previsión; (kindly) atentamente, solícitamente

thoughtfulness *n* natural reflexivo, *m*, seriedad, *f*; (kindness) solicitud, atención, *f*; (forethought) previsión, *f*

thoughtless *a* irreflexivo; (careless) descuidado, negligente; (unkind) inconsiderado; (silly) necio, estúpido

thoughtlessly *adv* sin pensar, irreflexivamente; negligentemente

thoughtlessness *n* irreflexión, *f*; descuido, *m*, negligencia, *f*; (unkindness) inconsideración, *f*; (silliness) neciedad, *f*

thousand *a* mil. *n* mil, *m*; millar, *m*. **one t.,** mil, *m*. **one t. three hundred,** *a* mil trescientos, *m pl*; mil trescientas, *f pl*. *n* mil trescientos, *m pl*. **two (three) t.,** dos (tres) mil. **by thousands,** por millares; por miles. **t.-fold,** mil veces más

thousandth *a* and *n* milésimo *m*

Thrace Tracia, *f*

thrall *n* esclavo (-va); esclavitud, *f*

thrash *vt* azotar, apalear *Mexico* festejar, *Lat. Am.* humear; *agr* trillar, desgranar; *inf* triunfar sobre, derrotar. *vi*, *agr* trillar el grano; arrojarse, agitarse. *fig* **to t. out,** ventilar

thrashing *n* apaleamiento, *m*, paliza, *Lat. Am. also* azotera, *f*; *agr* See **threshing**

thread *n* hilo, *m*; (fibre) hebra, fibra, *f*, filamento, *m*; (of a screw) filete, *m*; *fig* hilo, *m*, *a* de hilo. *vt* (a needle) enhebrar; (beads) ensartar; (make one's way) colarse a través de, atravesar; pasar por. **to hang by a t.,** pender de un hilo. **to lose the t. of,** *fig* perder el hilo de

threadbare *a* raído; muy usado; *fig* trivial, viejo

threadlike *a* como un hilo, filiforme

threadworm *n m*, lombriz intestinal, *f*

threat *n* amenaza, *f*

threaten *vt* and *vi* amenazar. **to t. with,** amenazar con

threatening *a* amenazador. *n* amenazas, *f pl*

threateningly *adv* con amenazas

three *a* and *n* tres *m*; (of the clock) las tres, *f pl*; (of one's age) tres años, *m pl*. **t.-color process,** tricromía, *f*.

t.-colored, tricolor. **t.-cornered,** triangular; (of hats) de tres picos, tricornio. **t.-cornered hat,** sombrero de tres picos, tricornio, *m.* **t. decker,** *naut* navío de tres puentes, *m*; novela larga, *f.* **t. deep,** en tres hileras. **t. hundred,** *a* and *n* trescientos *m.* **t.-hundredth,** *a* and *n* tricentésimo *m.* **t.-legged,** de tres patas. **t.-legged stool,** banqueta, *f.* **t.-per-cents,** accion al tres por ciento (3%), *f.* **t.-phase,** *elec* trifásico. **t.-ply,** (of yarn) triple; (of wood) de tres capas. **t.-quarter,** de tres cuartos. **t. quarters of an hour,** tres cuartos de hora, *m pl.* **t.-sided,** trilátero. **t. speed gear box,** cambio de marcha de tres velocidades, *m.* **t.-stringed,** *mus* de tres cuerdos. **t. thousand,** *a* tres mil, *mf pl;* *n* tres mil, *m*

threefold *a* triple

Three Musketeers, the los Tres Mosqueteros

threescore *a* and *n* sesenta, *m pl*

threesome *n* partido de tres, *m*

thresh *vt* trillar, desgranar. *vi* trillar el grano. **to t. out,** ventilar

threshing *n* trilla, *f.* **t. floor,** era, *f.* **t. machine,** trilladora, *f*

threshold *n* umbral, *Lat. Am. also* dintel, *m*; *psy* limen, *m*; *fig* comienzo, principio, *m*; (entrance) entrada, *f.* **to cross the t.,** atravesar (or pisar) los umbrales

thrice *adv* tres veces

thrift *n* frugalidad, parsimonia, *f*

thriftless *a* malgastador, manirroto

thrifty *a* frugal, económico

thrill *n* estremecimiento, *m*; emoción, *f.* *vt* conmover, emocionar; penetrar. *vi* estremecerse, emocionarse

thriller *n* libro, *m*, (or comedia, *f*) sensacional; (detective novel) novela policíaca, *f*

thrilling *a* sensacional, espeluznante; (moving) emocionante, conmovedor

thrive *vi* prosperar, medrar; enriquecerse, tener éxito; (grow) desarrollarse, robustecerse; florecer; (of plants) acertar

thriving *a* próspero; floreciente; robusto, vigoroso

throat *n* garganta, *f*; orificio, *m*; (narrow entry) paso, *m.* **sore t.,** dolor de garganta, *m.* **to cut one's t.,** cortarse la garganta. **to take by the t.,** asir (or agarrar) por la garganta

throat cancer *n* cáncer de la garganta, *m*

throaty *a* indistinto, ronco

throb *n* latido, *m*; pulsación, *f*; vibración, *f*; *fig* estremecimiento, *m.* *vi* palpitar, latir; vibrar

throbbing *n* pulsación, *f*; vibración, *f.* *a* palpitante; vibrante. **t. pain,** dolor pungente, *m*

throe *n* dolor, *m*, agonía, angustia, *f.* **in the throes of,** en medio de; luchando con; en las garras de. **throes of childbirth,** dolores de parto, *m pl.* **throes of death,** agonía de la muerte, *f*

thrombosis *n med* trombosis, *f*

throne *n* trono, *m*; (royal power) corona, *f*, poder real, *m.* *vt* elevar al trono. **speech from the t.,** el discurso de la corona, *m*

throng *n* muchedumbre, multitud, *f.* *vi* apiñarse remolinarse, acudir. *vt* atestar, llenar de bote en bote

throttle *n mech* regulador, *m*; *aut* estrangulador, *m*; *inf* garganta, *f.* *vt* estrangular; *fig* ahogar, suprimir. **to open (close) the t.,** abrir (cerrar) el estrangulador

throttling *n* estrangulación, *f*

through *prep* por; al través de; de un lado a otro de; por medio de; (between) entre; por causa de; gracias a. *adv* al través; de un lado a otro; (whole) entero, todo; (from beginning to end) desde el principio hasta el fin; (to the end) hasta el fin. *a* (of passages, etc.) que va desde . . . hasta . . . ; (of trains) directo. **to look t. the window,** mirar por la ventana, asomarse a la ventana. **to be wet t.,** estar calado hasta los huesos; estar muy mojado. **to carry t.,** llevar a cabo. **to fall t.,** caer por; (fail) fracasar. **to sleep the whole night t.,** dormir durante toda la noche, dormir la noche entera. **t. and t.,** completamente. **through the length and breadth of,** a lo largo y a lo ancho de, hasta los últimos rincones de. **t. traffic,** tráfico directo, *m.* **t. train,** tren directo, *m*

throughout *prep* por todo; durante todo. *adv* completamente; (from beginning to end) desde el principio hasta el fin; (everywhere) en todas partes

throw *vt* arrojar, lanzar, echar; (fire) disparar; (pottery) plasmar; (knock down) derribar; (slough) mudar (la piel); (cast off) despojarse de; (a rider) desmontar; (a glance) echar, dirigir (una mirada, etc.); (silk) torcer; (dice) echar; (light) dirigir, enfocar. **to t. oneself at the head of,** echarse a la cabeza de. **to t. open,** abrir de par en par; abrir. **to t. overboard,** *naut* echar al mar; desechar; (desert) abandonar. **to t. about,** esparcir, desparramar; derrochar. **to t. aside,** echar a un lado, desechar; abandonar, dejar. **to t. away,** tirar; desechar, *Lat. Am.* botar; (spend) malgastar, derrochar; (waste) sacrificar; (of opportunities) malograr, perder. **to t. back,** devolver; echar hacia atrás. **to t. down,** derribar, dar en el suelo con; echar abajo; (arms) rendir. **to t. down the glove,** arrojar el guante. **to t. oneself down,** tumbarse, echarse; (descend) echarse abajo. **to t. oneself down from,** arrojarse de. **to t. in,** echar dentro; (give extra) añadir; (the clutch) embragar; insertar; (a remark) hacer (una observación). **to t. off,** despojarse de; quitarse; (refuse) rechazar; sacudirse; (get rid of) despedir; (renounce) renunciar; (exhale) emitir, despedir; (verses) improvisar. **to t. on,** echar sobre; (garments) ponerse. **to t. oneself upon,** lanzarse sobre. **to t. out,** expeler; hacer salir; plantar en la calle; (utter) proferir, soltar; (one's chest) inflar; (discard) tirar, desechar, *Lat. Am.* botar; **to t. over,** (desert) abandonar, dejar. **to t. up,** (build) levantar; lanzar en el aire; (a post, etc.) renunciar (a), abandonar; vomitar, *Central America, Mexico* deponer

throw *n* echada, *f*; tiro, *m*; (at dice) lance, *m*; jugada, *f*; (wrestling) derribo, *m.* **within a stone's t.,** a tiro de piedra. **t.-back,** retroceso, *m*; *biol* atavismo, *m*

thrower *n* tirador (-ra), lanzador (-ra)

throwing *n* lanzamiento, *m*, lanzada, *f.* **t. the hammer,** lanzamiento del martillo, *m*

thrum *vt* and *vi* tocar mal; (of keyed instruments) teclear; (of stringed instruments) rascar las cuerdas (de)

thrust *n* empujón, *m*; (with a sword) estocada, *f*; (fencing) golpe, *m*; (with a lance) bote, *m*; ataque, *m*; asalto, *m.* *vt* empujar; (put) meter; (insert) introducir; (pierce) atravesar; (out, through, of the head, etc.) asomar. *vi* acometer, atacar, embestir; meterse, introducirse; (intrude) entrometerse; (fencing) dar un golpe. **to t. aside,** empujar a un lado; (proposals) rechazar. **to t. back,** hacer retroceder, empujar hacia atrás; (words) tragarse; (thoughts) apartar, rechazar. **to t. down,** empujar hacia abajo; hacer bajar; *fig* reprimir. **to t. forward,** empujar hacia delante; hacer seguir. **to t. oneself forward,** adelantarse; *fig* ponerse delante de los otros, darse importancia. **to t. in,** introducir; (stick) hincar; (insert) intercalar. **to t. on,** hacer seguir; empujar sobre; (garments) ponerse rápidamente. **to t. oneself in,** introducirse; entrometerse. **to t. out,** echar fuera; hacer salir, echar; expulsar; (the tongue) sacar (la lengua); (the head, etc.) asomar. **to t. through,** atravesar; (pierce) traspasar. **to t. one's way through,** abrirse paso por. **to t. upon,** imponer, hacer aceptar

thud *n* sonido sordo, *m*; golpe sordo, *m*

thug *n* asesino, criminal, *m*

thumb *n* pulgar, *m.* *vt* hojear; ensuciar con los dedos. **under the t. of,** *fig* en el poder de. **t. index,** índice pulgar, *m.* **t.-mark,** huella del dedo, *f.* **t.-screw,** tornillo de orejas, *m*, **t.-stall,** dedil, *m.* **t.-tack,** chinche, *m*

thump *n* golpe, porrazo, *m.* *vt* and *vi* golpear, aporrear; (the ground, of rabbits) zapatear

thunder *n* trueno, *m*; (of hooves, etc.) estampido, *m*; estruendo, *m.* *vi* tronar; retumbar; *fig* fulminar. *vt* gritar en una voz de trueno, rugir. **to t. along,** avanzar como el trueno; galopar ruidosamente. **t.-clap,** trueno, *m.* **t.-cloud,** nube de tormenta, *f*, nubarrón, *m.* **t.-storm,**

tronada, *f*. **t. struck,** muerto, estupefacto. **to be thunderstruck,** quedarse frío
thunderbolt *n* rayo, *m*
thunderer *n* fulminador, *m*. **the Thunderer,** Júpiter tonante, Júpiter tronante, *m*; el «Times» londinense, *m*
Thuringia Turingia, *f*
Thursday *n* jueves, *m*. **Holy T.,** Jueves Santo, *m*
thus *adv* así; de este modo; en estos términos; hasta este punto. **t. far,** hasta ahora; hasta este punto; hasta aquí. **Thus it is that . . . ,** Así es que . . .
thwack *n* golpe, *m*; *vt* golpear
thwart *vt* frustrar, impedir
thy *poss a* tu, *mf*; tus, *m pl*, and *f pl*
thyme *n bot* tomillo, *m*
thymus *n anat* timo, *m*
thyroid *a* tiroideo. **t. gland,** tiroides, *f*
thyself *poss pron* tu mismo, *m*; tu misma, *f*; (with prep.) tí mismo, *m*; tí misma, *f*; (in a reflexive verb) te
tiara *n* tiara, *f*
Tiberias Tiberíades, *f*
Tibetan *a* and *n* tibetano (-na); (language) tibetano, *m*
tibia *n anat* tibia, *f*
tic *n* (twitch) tic nervioso, *m*
tick *n ent* ácaro, *m*; (sound) tictac, *m*; (cover) funda de colchón, *f*; *inf* fiado, crédito, *m*; (mark) marca, *f vi* hacer tictac. *vt* poner una marca contra. **on t.,** *inf* al fiado. **to t. off,** poner una marca contra; *inf* reñir. **to t. over,** *aut* andar, marchar
ticket *n* billete, *Lat. Am.* boleto, *m*; (for an entertainment) entrada, localidad, *f*; (label) etiqueta, *f*; (pawn) papeleta de empeño, *f*; (for luggage) talón, *m*; (*pol* U.S.A.) candidatura, *f*, *vt* marcar. **to take one's t.,** sacar el billete (or for entertainment) la entrada, *f*). **excursion t.,** billete de excursión, *m*. **return t.,** billete de ida y vuelta, *m*. **season t.,** billete de abono, *m*. **single t.,** billete sencillo, *m*. **t. agency,** (for travel) agencia de viajes, *f*; (for entertainments) agencia de teatros, *f*. **t. collector or inspector,** revisor, *m*. **t. holder,** tenedor de billete, *m*; abonado (-da). **t. office,** (railway) despacho de billetes, *m*; taquilla, *Lat. Am.* boletería, *f*. **t.-of-leave,** libertad condicional, *f*. **t. punch,** sacabocados, *m*; (on tramcars) clasificador de billetes, *m*
ticking *n* (sound) tictac, *m*; (cloth) cotí, *m*
tickle *vt* hacer cosquillas (a), cosquillear; irritar; (gratify) halagar; (amuse) divertir. *vi* tener cosquillas; hacer cosquillas; ser irritante
ticklish *a* cosquilloso; (of persons) difícil, vidrioso; (of affairs) espinoso, delicado
tidal *a* de marea. **t. wave,** marejada, *f*; *fig* ola popular, *f*
tidbit *n* See **titbit**
tiddlywinks *n* juego de la pulga, *m*
tide *n* marea, *f*; (season) tiempo, *m*, estación, *f*; (trend) corriente, *f*; (progress) curso, *m*; marcha, *f*. *vi* (with over) vencer, superar; aguardar la ocasión. **to go against the t.,** ir contra la corriente. **to go with the t.,** seguir la corriente. **high t.,** marea alta, *f*. **low t.,** marea baja, *f*, bajamar, *m*. **neap t.,** marea muerta, *f*. **t. mark,** lengua del agua, *f*
tidily *adv* aseadamente; en orden, metódicamente
tidiness *n* aseo, *m*; buen orden, *m*
tidings *n pl* noticias, nuevas, *f pl*
tidy *a* aseado; metódico, en orden; pulcro; *inf* considerable. *vt* poner en orden, asear; limpiar; (oneself) arreglarse
tie *n* lazo, *m*, atadura, *f*; (knot) nudo, *m*; (for the neck) corbata, *f*; *sport* empate, *m*; *mus* ligado, *m*; *arch* tirante, *m*; (spiritual bond) lazo, *m*; (burden) carga, responsabilidad, **tie clasp,** pisa corbata, *mf*. **tie-pin,** alfiler de corbata, *Mexico* fistol, *m*. **tie seller,** corbatero (-ra)
tie *vt* atar; (bind) ligar; (lace) lacear; (a knot) hacer; (with a knot) anudar; (unite) unir; (*fig* bind) constreñir, obligar; (limit) limitar, restringir; (occupy) ocupar, entretener; (hamper) estorbar, impedir. *vi* atarse; *sport* empatar. **to tie one's tie,** hacer la corbata. **to tie down,** atar a; limitar; obligar. **They tied him down to a chair,** Le ataron a una silla. **to tie together,** enlazar, ligar; unir. **to tie up,** liar, atar; (wrap) envolver; recoger; *naut* amarrar, atracar; (restrict) limitar, restringir; (invest) invertir
tie-breaker *n* desempate, *m*
tier *n* fila, hilera, *f*. **in tiers,** en gradas; (of a dress) en volantes
tiff *n* disgusto, *m*
tiger *n* tigre, *m*. **t.-cat,** gato (-ta) atigrado (-da). **t.-lily,** tigridia, *f*
tigerish *a* atigrado, de tigre; salvaje, feroz
tight *a* apretado; (not leaky) hermético, impermeable; (taut) tieso, tirante; (narrow) estrecho; (trim) compacto; (of clothes) muy ajustado; (shut) bien cerrado; *naut* estanco; (risky) peligroso, difícil; (miserly) tacaño, *Argentina* agalludo; (of money, goods) escaso; (tipsy) borracho, *Mexico* abombado. **become t., get t.** (get tipsy) *Mexico* abombarse. **to be t.-fisted,** ser como un puño. **to hold t.,** agarrar fuerte. **t. corner,** *fig* aprieto, lance apretado, *m*. **t.-rope,** cuerda de volatinero, cuerda floja, *Lat. Am.* maroma, *f*. **t.-rope walker,** alambrista, equilibrista, *mf*; volatinero (-ra), bailarín de la cuerda floja, *m*, *Lat. Am.* maromero (-ra), *mf*. **t.-rope walker's pole,** balancín, *m*
tighten *vt* estrechar, apretar, *Lat. Am.* atesar; (stretch) estirar; (of saddle girths) cinchar. *vi* estrecharse; estirarse. **t. up** *Lat. Am.* atesar
tightly *adv* estrechamente
tightness *n* estrechez, *f*; tirantez, tensión, *f*; (feeling of constriction) opresión, *f*; (drunkenness) emborrachamiento, *m*
tights *n pl* mallas, *f pl*
tile *n* teja, *f*; (for flooring) baldosa, losa, *f*; (ornamental) azulejo, *m*; (hat) chistera, *f*. *vt* tejar; embaldosar. **t. floor,** enlosado, embaldosado, *m*. **t. manufacturer,** tejero, *m*. **t. works** or **yard,** tejar, *m*, (Colombia) galpón *m*
tiler *n* solador, *m*; tejero, *m*
till *n* (for money) cajón, *m*. *vt agr* cultivar, labrar. *prep* hasta. *conjunc* hasta que
tillable *a* laborable
tiller *n agr* labrador, *m*; *bot* mugrón, renuevo, vástago, *m*; *naut* caña del timón, *f*
tilling *n agr* cultivo, laboreo, *m*
tilt *n* inclinación, *f*; ladeo, *m*; (fight) torneo, *m*, justa, *f*. *vt* inclinar; ladear; (a drinking vessel) empinar. *vi* inclinarse; ladearse; (fight) justar. **to t. against,** *fig* arremeter contra, atacar. **at full t.,** a todo correr. **t. hammer,** martinete de báscula, *m*. **t.-yard,** palestra, *f*
tilting *n* incinación, *f*; (fighting) justas, *f pl*. *a* inclinado
timber *n* madera de construcción, *f*; (trees) árboles de monte, *m pl*; bosque, *m*; (beam) viga, *f*; *naut* cuaderna, *f*. *vt* enmaderar. **t. line,** límite del bosque maderable, *m*. **t. merchant,** maderero, *m*. **t. wolf,** lobo gris, *m*. **t. work,** maderaje, *m*. **t. yard,** maderería, *f*, corral de madera, *m*
timbered *a* enmaderado; (with trees) arbolado
timbre *n mus* timbre, *m*
timbrel *n mus* tamborete, tamboril, *m*
time *n* (in general) tiempo, *m*; (epoch) época, edad, *f*; tiempos, *m pl*; (of the year) estación, *f*; (by the clock) hora, *f*; (lifetime) vida, *f*; (particular moment of time) momento, *m*; (occasion) sazón, ocasión, *f*; (day) día, *m*; (time allowed) plazo, *m*; (in repetition) vez, *f*; *mus* compás, *m*; *mil* paso, *m*. *vt* ajustar al tiempo; hacer con oportunidad; (regulate) regular; calcular el tiempo que se emplea en hacer una cosa; (a blow) calcular. **all the t.,** todo el tiempo; continuamente, sin cesar. **a long t.,** mucho tiempo. **a long t. ago,** mucho tiempo ha, hace mucho tiempo. **at a t.,** a la vez, al mismo tiempo; (of period) en una época. **at any t.,** a cualquier hora; en cualquier momento; (when you like) cuando gustes. **at no t.,** jamás, nunca. **at some t.,** alguna vez; en alguna época. **at some t. or another,** un día u otro; en una u otra ocasión; en alguna época. **at that t.,** en aquella época; en la sazón; en aquel instante. **at the**

one t., de una vez. **at the present t.,** en la actualidad, al presente. **at the proper t.,** a su debido tiempo; a la hora señalada; a la hora conveniente. **at the same t.,** al mismo tiempo. **at the same t. as,** mientras, a medida que; al mismo instante que, **at times,** a veces, en ocasiones. **behind the times,** *fig* atrasado de noticias; pasado de moda. **behind t.,** atrasado. **by that t.,** para entonces. **every t.,** cada vez; siempre. **for some t.,** durante algún tiempo. **for some t. past,** de algún tiempo a esta parte. **for the t. being,** de momento, por ahora, por lo pronto. **from this t.,** desde hoy; desde esta fecha. **from this t. forward,** de hoy en adelante. **from t. to t.,** de vez en cuando, de cuando en cuando, de tarde en tarde. **in a month's t.,** en un mes. **in a short t.,** en breve, dentro de poco. **in good t.,** puntualmente; temprano. **in my t.,** en mis días, en mis tiempos. **in olden times,** antiguamente, en otros tiempos. **in the course of t.,** andando el tiempo, en el transcurso de los años. **in the t. of,** en la época de. **in t.,** (promptly) a tiempo; con el tiempo. **in t. to come,** en el porvenir. **It is t. to . . . ,** Es hora de . . . **many times,** frecuentemente, muchas veces. **Once upon a t.,** Érase una vez, Una vez había, Érase que érase. Érase que se era. **Since t. out of mind,** Desde tiempo inmemorial. **the last (next) t.,** la última (próxima) vez. **this t. of year,** esta estación del año. **T. hangs heavy on his hands,** El tiempo se le hace interminable. **T. flies,** El tiempo vuela. **T. will tell!** ¡El tiempo lo dirá! ¡Veremos lo que veremos! **What t. is it?** ¿Qué hora es? **The t. is . . . ,** La hora es . . . **within a given t.,** dentro de un plazo dado. **to be out of t.,** estar fuera de compás. **to gain t.,** ganar tiempo. **to have a good t.,** pasarlo bien, divertirse. **to have a bad t.,** pasarlo mal; *inf* tener un mal cuarto de hora. **to have no t. to,** no tener tiempo para + noun or pronoun, no tener tiempo de + infinitive. **to keep t.,** guardar el compás. **to kill t.,** engañar (or entretener) el tiempo. **to mark t.,** marcar el paso; *fig* hacer tiempo. **to pass the t.,** pasar el rato; pasar el tiempo. **to pass the t. of day,** saludar. **to serve one's t.,** (to a trade) servir el aprendizaje; (in prison) cumplir su condena; *mil* hacer el servicio militar. **to take t. to,** tomar tiempo para. **to take t. by the forelock,** asir la ocasión por la melena. **to waste t.,** perder el tiempo. **t. exposure,** pose, *f.* **t. fuse,** espoleta de tiempo, espoleta graduada, *f.* **t.-honored,** tradicional, consagrado por el tiempo. **t.-keeper,** capataz, *m;* reloj, *m.* **t.-saving,** que ahorra el tiempo. **t.-server,** lameculos, *mf* **t.-signal,** señales horarias, *f pl.* **t.-table,** horario, *m;* itinerario, programa, *m;* (railway) guía de ferrocarriles, *f.* **t. to come,** porvenir, *m,* lo venidero

timed *a* calculado; (**ill-**) intempestivo; (**well-**) oportuno

timeless *a* eterno

timeliness *n* tempestividad, oportunidad, *f*

timely *a* oportuno

timepiece *n* reloj, *m*

time zone *n* huso esférico, huso horario, *m*

timid *a* tímido, asustadizo, medroso; (shy) vergonzoso

timidity *n* timidez, *f;* vergüenza, *f*

timing *n* medida del tiempo, *f; mech* regulación, *f;* (timetable) horario, *m*

timorous *a* timorato, apocado, asustadizo

timorousness *n* encogimiento, *m,* timidez, *f*

tin *n* (metal) estaño, *m;* (container) lata, *f;* (sheet) hojalata, *f;* (money) plata, *f. vt* estañar; (place in tins) envasar en lata; cubrir con hojalata, hoja de aluminio, *f.* **tin-foil,** papel de estaño, *m.* **tin hat,** casco de acero, *m.* **tin opener,** abrelatas, abridor de latas, *m.* **tin-plate,** hojalata, *f.* **tin soldier,** soldado de plomo, *m.* **tin ware,** hojalatería, *f*

tincture *n* tintura, *f,* tinte, *m; med* tintura, *f;* (trace) dejo, *m;* (veneer) capa, *f. vt* teñir, tinturar

tinder *n* yesca, *f.* **t. box,** yescas, lumbres, *f pl*

tinge *n* tinte, matiz, *m; fig* dejo, toque, *m. vt* matizar, tinturar; *fig* tocar

tingle *n* picazón, comezón, *f;* (thrill) estremecimiento, *m. vi* picar; (of ears) zumbar; (thrill) estremecerse (de); vibrar

tingling *n* picazón, *f;* (of the ears) zumbido, *m;* (thrill) estremecimiento, *m*

tinker *n* calderero remendón, *m. vt* remendar. *vi* chafallar. **to t. with,** jugar con

tinkle *n* tilín, retintín, *m;* campanilleo, *m;* cencerreo, *m. vi* tintinar. *vt* hacer tintinar

tinkling *n* retintín, tintineo, *m;* campanilleo, *m*

tinned *a* (of food) en lata, en conserva

tinsel *n* oropel, *m;* (cloth) lama de oro o plata, *f,* brocadillo, *m; fig* oropel, *m. a* de oropel; de brocadillo; *fig* charro. *vt* adornar con oropel

tinsmith *n* hojalatero, estañador, *m*

tint *n* tinta, *f,* color, *m;* matiz, *m;* tinte, *m. vt* colorar, teñir; matizar

tinting *n* tintura, *f,* teñido, *m*

tiny *a* diminuto, minúsculo, menudo, chiquito

tip *n* punta, *f;* cabo, *m,* extremidad, *f;* (of an umbrella, etc.) regatón, *m;* (of a lance) borne, *m;* (of a cigarette) boquilla, *f;* (of a shoe) puntera, *f;* (of a finger) yema, *f;* (for rubbish) depósito de basura, *m;* (gratuity) propina, *f;* (information) informe oportuno, *m;* (tap) golpecito, *m.* **to have on the tip of one's tongue,** tener en la punta de la lengua. **tip-cart,** volquete, *m.* **tip-up seat,** asiento plegable, *m*

tip *vt* inclinar; volcar, voltear; (drinking vessel) empinar; poner regatón, etc. (a); *poet* tocar, golpear ligeramente; (reward) dar propina (a). *vi* inclinarse; (topple) tambalearse; (reward) dar propina. **to tip the wink,** guiñar el ojo (a). **to tip off,** (liquids) echar; hacer caer; (inform) decir en secreto; informar oportunamente. **to tip over,** *vt* volcar; hacer caer. *vi* volcarse; caer; (of a boat) zozobrar. **to tip up,** *vt* (a seat) levantar; (money) proporcionar (el dinero); (upset) volcar; hacer perder el equilibrio. *vi* volcarse; (of a seat) levantarse; (lose the balance) perder el equilibrio

tipple *n* bebida, *f. vt* beber, sorber. *vi* empinar el codo

tippler *n* borracho (-cha)

tipsily *adv* como borracho

tipsy *a* achispado, algo borracho, *Lat. Am.* mamado. **to be t.,** estar entre dos luces, estar entre dos velas

tiptoe (on) *adv* de puntillas; *fig* excitado, ansioso. **to stand on t.,** ponerse de puntillas, empinarse

tirade *n* diatriba, *f*

tire *n* (of a cart, etc.) llanta, *f; aut* neumático, *Lat. Am.* caucho, *m;* (of a perambulator, etc.) rueda de goma, *f.* **balloon t.,** neumático balón, *m.* **pneumatic t.,** neumático, *m.* **slack t.,** neumático desinflado, *m.* **solid t.,** neumático macizo, *m.* **spare t.,** neumático de recambio (or de repuesto), *m.* **t. burst,** estallido de un neumático, *m.* **t. valve,** válvula de cámara (del neumático), *f*

tire *vt* cansar, fatigar; (bore) aburrir. *vi* cansarse, fatigarse; aburrirse. **to be tired of,** estar cansado de. **to grow tired,** empezar a cansarse. **to t. out,** rendir de cansancio

tired *a* cansado, fatigado. **to be sick and t. of,** estar hasta la coronilla (de), (of persons) con. **t. of,** cansado de; disgustado de

tiredness *n* cansancio, *m,* fatiga, *f;* aburrimiento, *m*

tireless *a* infatigable, incansable

tiresome *a* fastidioso, molesto, pesado; (dull) aburrido

tiresomeness *n* pesadez, *f,* fastidio, *m;* tedio, aburrimiento, *m*

tiring *a* fatigoso

tissue *n* (cloth) tisú, *m,* lama, *f;* (paper) pañuelito *m; biol* tejido, *m;* (series) serie, sarta, *f.* **t. paper,** papel de seda, *m*

tit *n orn* paro, *m.* **tit for tat,** tal para cual

Titan *n* titán, *m*

titanic *a* titánico

titbit *n* golosina, *f*

tithe *n* décima, *f;* fracción, pequeña parte, *f, vt* diezmar. **t. gatherer,** diezmero (-ra)

titillate *vt* titilar, estimular

titivate *vi* arreglarse
title *n* título, *m*; (right) derecho, *m*; documento, *m*. **to give a t. to,** intitular; ennoblecer. **t. deed,** títulos de propiedad, *m*. **t. page,** portada, *f*. **t. role,** papel principal, *m*
titter *vi* reírse disimuladamente. *n* risa disimulada, *f*
tittle *n* adarme, tilde, ápice, *m*
titular *a* titular; nominal
to *prep* a; (as far as) hasta; (in the direction of) en dirección a, hacia; (with indirect object) a; (until) hasta; (compared with) en comparación con, comparado con; (against) contra; (according to) según; (as) como; (in) en; (so that, in order to, for the purpose of) para; (indicating possession) a, de; (of time by the clock) menos; (by) por; (before verbs of motion or which imply motion) a (sometimes para); (before some other verbs) de; en; (before verbs of beginning, inviting, exhorting, obliging) a; (indicating indirect object) a; (before a subjunctive or infinitive indicating future action or obligation) que. **To** is often not translated. With most Spanish infinitives no separate translation is necessary, e.g. leer, decir, to read, to speak. Some verbs are always followed by a preposition (e.g. **to begin to speak,** empezar a hablar, etc.). *adv* (shut) cerrado. **to come to,** volver en sí. **to lie to,** *naut* ponerse a la capa. **to and from,** de un lado a otro. **face to face,** cara a cara. **He has been a good friend to them,** Ha sido un buen amigo para ellos. **That is new to me,** Eso es nuevo para mí. **He went to London,** Se fue a Londres. **to go to France (Canada),** ir a Francia (al Canadá). **the road to Madrid,** la carretera de Madrid. **She kept the secret to herself,** Guardó el secreto para sí. **to go to the dentist,** ir al dentista. **We give it to them,** Se lo damos a ellos. **It belongs to me,** Pertenece a mí. **What does it matter to you?** ¿Qué te importa a tí? **I wish to see him,** Quiero verle. **They did it to help us,** Lo hicieron para ayudarnos. **I have to go to see her,** Tengo que ir a verla. **to this day,** hasta hoy, hasta el presente. **It is a quarter to six,** Son las seis menos cuarto. **to the house of . . ., to . . .'s** a casa de, *Lat. Am. also* donde (e.g. **My wife went to her friend's house** Mi mujer fue a casa de su amiga, Mi mujer fue donde su amiga). **to the last shilling,** hasta el último chelín. **the next to me,** el que me sigue. **closed to the public,** cerrado para el público
toad *n* sapo, *m*
toady *n* lameculos, *mf* adulador (-ra). *vt* lamer el culo (a), adular
toast *n cul* tostada, *f*; (drink) brindis, *m*. *vt* tostar; brindar, beber a la salud de. *vi* brindar. **buttered t.,** mantecada, *f*. **t.-rack,** portatostadas, *m*
toaster *n* (device) tostador, *m*; (person) brindador, *m*
toasting *n* tostadura, *f*, tueste, *m*, *a* de tostar. **t.-fork,** tostadera, *f*
tobacco *n* tabaco, *m*. *a* tabacalero. **black** or **cut t.,** picadura, *f*. **leaf t.,** tabaco de hoja, *m*. **mild t.,** tobaco flojo, *m*. **pipe t.,** tabaco de pipa, *m*. **plug t.,** tabaco para mascar, *m*. **strong t.,** tabaco fuerte, *m*. **Turkish t.,** tabaco turco, *m*. **Virginian t.,** tabaco rubio, *m*. **t.-pipe,** pipa (de tabaco), *f*. **t.-pipe cleaner,** escobillón para limpiar pipas, *m*. **t. plantation,** tabacal, *m*. **t. planter,** tabacalero (-ra). **t. poisoning,** tabaquismo, *m*. **t.-pouch** or **jar,** tabaquera, *f*
tobacconist *n* tabaquero (-ra). **tobacconist's shop,** tabaquería, *Lat. Am.* cigarrería, *f*, expendio, *m*
toboggan *n* tobogán, *m*. *vi* ir en tobogán. **t. run,** pista de tobogán, *f*
tocsin *n* rebato, *m*
today *adv* hoy; ahora, actualmente, al presente, hoy día. *n* el día de hoy. **from t.,** desde hoy. **from t. forward,** de hoy en adelante
toddle *vi* hacer pinos, empezar a andar; (stroll) dar una vuelta; (leave) marcharse
toddy *n* ponche, *m*
toe *n* dedo del pie, *m*; (cloven) pezuña, *f*; uña, *f*; (of furniture) base, *f*, pie, *m*; (of stockings, shoes) punta, *f*. **He stepped on my toe,** Me pisó el dedo del pie. **big toe,** dedo pulgar del pie, dedo gordo del pie, *m*. **little toe,** dedo pequeño del pie, *m*. **to toe the line,** ponerse en la raya; *fig* cumplir con su deber. **toe-cap,** puntera, *f*. **toe-dancing,** baile de puntillas, *m*. **toe-nail,** uña del dedo del pie, *f*
toffee *n* caramelo, *m*
toga *n* toga, *f*
together *adv* junto; (uninterruptedly) sin interrupción; (in concert) simultáneamente, a la vez, al mismo tiempo; (consecutively) seguido. **t. with,** con; junto con; en compañía de; (simultaneously) a la vez que
toil *n* labor, *f*, trabajo, *m pl*. **toils,** lazos, *m pl*; *fig* redes, *f pl*. *vi* trabajar, afanarse. **to t. along,** caminar penosamente (por); adelantar con dificultad. **to t. up,** subir penosamente
toiler *n* trabajador (-ra)
toilet *n* tocado, *m*; atavío, *m*; vestido, *m*; (w.c.) retrete, excusado, *m*; (for ladies) tocador, *m*. **to make one's t.,** arreglarse. **t. case,** neceser, *m*. **t.-paper,** papel higiénico, *m*. **t.-powder,** polvos de arroz, *m pl*. **t. roll,** rollo de papel higiénico, *m*. **t.-set,** juego de tocador, *m*. **t. soap,** jabón de olor, jabón de tocador, *m*
toiling *n* trabajo duro, *m*, *a* laborioso, trabajador
token *n* señal, muestra, *f*; prueba, *f*; (presage) síntoma, indicio, *m*; (remembrance) recuerdo, *m*. **as a t. of,** en señal de; como recuerdo de
Tokyo Tokio, *m*
tolerable *a* tolerable, soportable, llevadero; (fairly good) mediano, mediocre, regular
tolerably *adv* bastante
tolerance *n* tolerancia, *f*; paciencia, indulgencia, *f*
tolerant *a* tolerante; indulgente
tolerate *vt* tolerar, sufrir, soportar; permitir
toleration *n* tolerancia, *f*; indulgencia, paciencia, *f*. **religious t.,** libertad de cultos, *f*
toll *n* (of a bell) tañido, doble, *m*; (for passage) peaje, portazgo, *m*; (for grinding) derecho de molienda, *m*. *vt* and *vi* doblar, tañer. **to t. the hour,** dar la hora. **t. call,** conferencia telefónica interurbana, llamada a larga distancia, *f*. **t. gate,** barrera de peaje, *f*. **t. house,** oficina de portazgos, *f*
toll booth *n* caseta de pago, *f*
tolling *n* tañido, clamor (de las campanas), *m*
Tom *n* Tomás, *m*; (cat) gato, *m*. **Tom, Dick and Harry,** Fulano, Zutano y Mengano
tomahawk *n* hacha de guerra de los indios, *f*
tomato *n* tomate, jitomate (Mexico) *m*. **t. plant,** tomatera, *f*. **t. sauce,** salsa de tomate, *f*
tomb *n* tumba, *f*, sepulcro, *m*
tombac *n* tombac, *m*, tumbaga, *f*
tomboy *n* muchachote, torbellino, *m*
tombstone *n* piedra mortuoria, *f*, monumento funerario, *m*
tome *n* tomo, volumen, *m*
tomfoolery *n* necedad, tontería, *f*; payasada, *f*
tommy gun *n* pistola automática
tomorrow *adv* and *n* mañana, *f*. **a fortnight t.,** mañana en quince. **the day after t.,** pasado mañana. **t. afternoon (morning),** mañana por la tarde (mañana). **T. is Friday,** Mañana es viernes
ton *n* tonelada, *f*
tonality *n* tonalidad, *f*
tone *n* tono, *m*; (*mus, med, art*) tono, *m*; (of the voice) acento, *m*, entonación, *f*; (of musical instruments) sonido, *m*; (shade) matiz, *m*. *vt* entonar; *phot* virar. **to t. down,** *vt* (*art, mus*) amortiguar; *fig* suavizar, modificar. *vi* (*art, mus*) amortiguarse; *fig* suavizarse, modificarse. **to t. in with,** (of colors) *vt* armonizar con. *vi* armonizarse, corresponder en tono o matiz. **to t. up,** *vt* subir de color, intensificar el color de; *med* entonar, robustecer. **t. poem,** poema sinfónico, *m*
tonelessly *adv* sin tono; apáticamente
tongs *n pl* tenazas, *f pl*; tenacillas, *f pl*. **curling t.,** tenacillas para el pelo, *f pl*. **sugar t.,** tenacillas para azúcar, *f pl*

tongue *n anat* lengua, *f;* (language) idioma, *m,* lengua, *f;* (speech) modo de hablar, *m,* habla, *f; mus* lengüeta, *f;* (of buckle) diente, *m;* (of shoe) oreja, *f;* (of land) lengua, *f;* (of a bell) badajo, *m;* (flame) lengua, *f.* **My t. ran away with me,** *inf* Se me fue la mula. **to give t.,** ladrar. **to hold one's t.,** cerrar el pico, tener la boca. **t. of fire,** lengua de fuego, *f.* **t. tied,** con impedimento en el habla; turbado, confuso; mudo. **t.-twister,** trabalenguas, *m*

-tongued *a* de voz . . .

tonic *a* tónico. *n med* tónico, reconstituyente, *m; mus* tónica, *f*

tonight *adv* and *n* esta noche

tonnage *n* tonelaje, porte, *m;* (duty) derecho de tonelaje, *m*

tonner *n naut* de . . . toneladas

tonsil *n* amígdala, *f*

tonsillitis *n* amigdalitis, *f*

tonsure *n ecc* tonsura, *f, vt* tonsurar

tonsured *a* tonsurado

too *adv* demasiado; (very) muy; también; además. **too hard,** demasiado difícil, demasiado rígido; (of persons) demasiado duro. **too much,** demasiado. **too often,** con demasiada frecuencia

tool *n* herramienta, *f;* utensilio, *m;* instrumento, *m;* (person) criatura, *f. vt* labrar con herramienta; (a book) estampar en seco. **t.-bag,** capacho, *m.* **t. box,** caja de herramientas, *f*

tooling *n* (of books) estampación en seco, *f*

toot *n* sonido de bocina, *m, vi* sonar una bocina

tooth *n* diente, *m;* muela, *f;* (of comb) púa, *f;* (taste) gusto, paladar, *m;* (cog) diente de rueda, *m;* (of saw) diente, *m. vt* dentar; mellar. *vi mech* engranar. **armed to the teeth,** armado hasta los dientes. **double t.,** muela, *f.* **false teeth,** dentadura postiza, *f.* **set of teeth,** dentadura, *f.* **to cut one's teeth,** echar los dientes. **to have a sweet t.,** ser muy goloso. **to show one's teeth,** enseñar los dientes. **t.-brush,** cepillo para los dientes, *m.* **t. drawing,** extracción de un diente, *f.* **t.-paste,** pasta dentífrica, *f*

toothache *n* dolor de muelas, *m*

toothed *a* con dientes; dentado

toothless *a* desdentado, sin dientes; (of combs) sin púas

toothpick *n* mondadientes, *m*

top *n* (summit) cima, cumbre, *f;* (of a tree) copa, *f;* (of the head) coronilla, *f;* (of a page) cabeza, *f;* (crest) copete, *m,* cresta, *f;* (surface) superficie, *f;* (of a wall) coronamiento, *m;* (tip) punta, *f;* (point) ápice, *m;* (of a tram, bus) imperial, baca, *f;* (of a wave) cresta, *f;* (acme) auge, *m;* (of a class) primero (de la clase), *m;* (highest rank) último grado, *m;* (of a plant) hojas, *f pl;* (of a piano) cima, *f; naut* cofa, *f;* (head of a bed, etc.) cabeza, *f;* (lid) tapadera, *f;* (toy) trompo, peón, *m;* (humming) trompa, *f, a* más alto; máximo; (chief) principal, primero. *vt* (cover) cubrir de; (cut off) desmochar; (come level with) llegar a la cima de; (rise above) elevarse por encima (de), coronar, dominar; (be superior to) exceder, aventajar; (golf) topear. **at the top,** a la cabeza; a la cumbre. **from top to bottom,** de arriba abajo. **on top of,** encima de; (besides) en adición a, además de. **to be top-dog,** ser un gallito. **to sleep like a top,** dormir como un lirón. **top boots,** botas de campaña, *f pl.* **top-dog,** vencedor, *m;* poderoso, *m.* **top-hat,** sombrero de copa, *m.* **top-heavy,** más pesado por arriba que por abajo

topaz *n* topacio, jacinto occidental, *m*

topcoat *n* sobretodo, gabán, *m*

top floor *n* piso alto, *m*

topic *n* asunto, tema, *m*

topical *a* tópico; actual

topknot *n* cresta, *f,* penacho, *m;* (of birds) moño, *m;* copete, *m*

topmast *n* mastelero, *m*

topmost *a* más alto; más importante

topographer *n* topógrafo, *m*

topographical *a* topográfico

topography *n* topografía, *f*

topple *vi* tambalearse, estar al punto de caer. **to t. down,** volcarse; derribarse; caer. **to t. over,** *vi* venirse abajo; perder el equilibrio. *vt* derribar, hacer caer

topsail *n* gavia, *f*

topsyturvy *a* desordenado. *adv* en desorden, patas arriba, de arriba abajo

toque *n* toca, *f*

torch *n* antorcha, hacha, tea, *f.* **electric t.,** lamparilla eléctrica, *f.* **t.-bearer,** hachero, *m*

torchlight *n* luz de antorcha, *f.* **by t.,** a la luz de las antorchas

torment *n* tormento, *m,* angustia, *f;* (torture) tortura, *f;* suplicio, *m;* mortificación, *f;* disgusto, *m. vt* atormentar, martirizar; (torture) torturar; molestar

tormentor *n* atormentador (-ra)

tornado *n* tornado, *m*

torpedo *n* torpedo, *m; icht* pez torpedo, *m. vt* torpedear. **self-propelling t.,** torpedo automóvil, *m.* **t.-boat,** torpedero, *m.* **t.-boat destroyer,** cazatorpedero, contratorpedero, *m.* **t. netting,** red contra torpedos, *f.* **t. station,** base de torpederos, *f.* **t. tube,** tubo lanzatorpedos, *m*

torpedoing *n* torpedeamiento, torpedeo, *m*

torpid *a* aletargado, entorpecido; (of the mind) torpe, tardo, apático

torpidity, torpor *n* letargo, *m;* apatía, *f*

torrent *n* torrente, *m*

torrential *a* torrencial

torrid *a* tórrido. **t. zone,** zona tórrida, *f*

torsion *n* torsión, *f*

torso *n* torso, *m*

tort *n law* tuerto, *m*

tortoise *n* tortuga, *f.* **t.-shell,** carey, *m. a* de carey

tortuous *a* tortuoso

tortuousness *n* tortuosidad, *f*

torture *n* tortura, *f,* tormento, *m;* angustia, *f. vt* torturar, dar tormento (a); martirizar

torturer *n* atormentador (-ra)

torturing *a* torturador, atormentador; angustioso

toss *n* sacudimiento, *m,* sacudidad, *f;* (of the head) movimiento (de cabeza), *m;* (bull fighting) cogida, *f;* (from a horse) caída de caballo, *f. vt* echar, lanzar; agitar, sacudir; (of bulls) acornear. *vi* agitarse; (of plumes, etc.) ondear; (in a boat) balancearse a la merced de las olas; jugar a cara o cruz. **to t. a coin** *Mexico* echar un volado. **to t. in a blanket,** mantear, dar una manta (a). **to t. aside,** echar a un lado; abandonar. **to t. off,** beber de un trago. **to t. up,** jugar a cara o cruz

tot *n* (child) nene (-na), crío (-ía); (of drink) vaso pequeño, *m.* **to tot up,** sumar

total *a* total; absoluto, completo, entero. *n* total, *m,* suma, *f. vt* sumar. *vi* ascender (a). **t. employment,** ocupación total, *f.* **t. war,** guerra total, *f*

totalitarian *a* totalitario

totality *n* totalidad, *f*

totally *adv* totalmente, completamente

totem *n* tótem, *m*

totemism *n* totemismo, *m*

totter *vi* (of persons) bambolearse; tambalear, estar al punto de caer; *fig* aproximarse a su fin

tottering *a* vacilante; tambaleante. *n* bamboleo, *m;* tambaleo, *m*

toucan *n orn* tucán, *m*

touch *vt* tocar; (brush against) rozar; (reach) alcanzar; (musical instruments) tocar; (move) emocionar, enternecer; (spur on) aguijar; (food) tomar; (affect) influir, afectar; (arouse) despertar, estimular; (equal) compararse con, igualar; (consider) tratar ligeramente (de); (money) dar un sablazo (a). *vi* tocarse; imponer las manos para curar. **I have not touched a bite,** No he probado un bocado. **This touches me nearly,** Esto me toca de cerca. **to t. at,** hacer escala en, tocar en (un puerto). **to t. down on water** *Lat. Am.* acuatizar. **to t. off,** descargar. **to t. up,** retocar; corregir. **to t. upon,**

(a subject) tratar superficialmente de, tratar ligeramente de; hablar de; considerar

touch *n* (sense of) tacto, *m;* (contact) toque, contacto, *m;* (brushing) roce, *m;* (tap) golpe ligero, *m;* palmadita, *f;* (of an illness) ataque ligero, *m; mus* dedeo, *m;* (little) dejo, *m;* (test) prueba, *f,* toque, *m; art* toque, *m,* pincelada, *f.* **by the t.,** a tiento. **in t. with,** en relaciones con; en comunicación con; al corriente de. **to give the finishing t.,** dar la última pincelada; dar el último toque. **t.-line,** (football) línea de toque, línea lateral, *f.* **t.-me-not,** *inf* erizo, *m.* **t.-stone,** piedra de toque, *f*

touched *a* emocionado, conmovido

touchiness *n* susceptibilidad, *f, Argentina* acometividad, *f*

touching *a* patético, conmovedor. *prep* tocante a, acerca de. *n* tocamiento, *m*

touchy *a* susceptible, quisquilloso, vidrioso

tough *a* (hard) duro; vigoroso, fuerte, robusto; resistente; (of character) tenaz, firme; (of a job) difícil; espinoso. *n* chulo, *m*

toughen *vt* endurecer. *vi* endurecerse

toughness *n* dureza, *f;* vigor, *m,* fuerza, *f;* resistencia, *f;* tenacidad, firmeza, *f;* dificultad, *f*

toupee *n* tupé, *m*

tour *n* viaje, *m,* excursión, *f. vi* viajar. *vt* viajar por. **circular t.,** viaje redondo, *m.* **on t.,** *theat* en tour, de gira

touring *a* de turismo. *n* turismo, *m;* viaje, *m.* **t. car,** coche de turismo, *m*

tourist *n* turista, *mf;* viajero (-ra). **t. agency,** agencia de turismo, *f,* patronato de turismo, *m.* **t. ticket,** billete kilométrico, *m*

tournament *n* torneo, *m,* justa, *f;* (of games) concurso, *m*

tourniquet *n* torniquete, *m*

tousle *vt* despeinar; desordenar el pelo

tout *n* buhonero, *m.* **to t. for,** pescar, solicitar

tow *n* remolque, *m;* (rope) estopa, *f. vt* (*naut, aut*) remolcar. **on tow,** a remolque. **tow-path,** camino de sirga, *m.* **tow rope,** cable de remolque, *m*

towage *n* remolque, *m;* (fee) derechos de remolque, *m pl*

towards *prep* hacia, en dirección a; (of time) sobre, cerca de; (concerning) tocante a; (with persons) para, con

towel *n* toalla, *f. Lat. Am. also* limpiamanos, *m.* **roller t.,** toalla continua, *f.* **t. rail,** toallero, *m*

toweling *n* tela para toallas, *f*

tower *n* torre, *f;* (fortress) fortaleza, *f;* (belfry) campanario, *m;* (large) torreón, *m. vi* elevarse. **to t. above,** destacarse sobre, sobresalir; *fig* sobrepujar, superar

towered *a* torreado; de las . . . torres. **high t.,** de las altas torres

towering *a* elevado; dominante; orgulloso; *fig* violento, terrible

town *n* población, *f,* pueblo, *m;* ciudad, *f.* **t. clerk,** secretario de ayuntamiento, *m.* **t. council,** concejo municipal, *m.* **t. councilor,** concejero municipal, *m.* **t. crier,** pregonero, *m.* **t. hall,** (casa de) ayuntamiento, casa consistorial, *f.* **t. house,** casa de ciudad, *f.* **t. planning,** urbanismo, *m;* reforma urbana, *f.* **t. wall,** muralla, *f*

"Town Ahead" «Poblado Próximo»

townsman *n* ciudadano, *m*

town worthy *n* persona principal de la ciudad, *f*

toxic *a* tóxico

toxicological *a* toxicológico

toxicologist *n* toxicólogo, *m*

toxicology *n* toxicología, *f*

toxin *n* toxina, *f*

toy *n* juguete, *m. vi* (with) jugar con; acariciar. **toy maker,** fabricante de juguetes, *m*

toyshop *n* juguetería, tienda de juguetes, *f*

trace huella, pista, *f,* rastro, *m;* vestigio, *m;* indicio, *m,* evidencia, *f;* (of a harness) tirante, *m;* (touch) dejo, *m;* (of fear, etc.) sombra, *f. vt* trazar; (through transparent paper) calcar; seguir la pista (de); (write) escribir; (discern) distinguir; investigar; descubrir; determinar; (walk) atravesar, recorrer. **to t. back,** (of ancestry, etc.) hacer remontar (a)

traceable *a* que se puede trazar; atribuible

tracer *n* trazador (-ra). **t. bullet,** bala luminosa, *f*

tracery *n* tracería, *f*

trachea *n anat* tráquea, *f*

trachoma *n med* tracoma, *f*

tracing *n* calco, *m;* trazo, *m;* seguimiento, *m.* **t.-paper,** papel de calcar, *m*

track *n* huella, *f,* rastro, *m;* (for racing, etc.) pista, *f;* (of wheels) rodada, *f;* (railway) vía, *f;* (of a boat) estela, *f;* (path) senda, vereda, *f;* (sign) señal, evidencia, *f;* (course) ruta, *f. vt* rastrear, seguir la pista (de); *naut* sirgar. **to t. down,** seguir y capturar. **double t.,** vía doble, *f.* **off the t.,** extraviado; (of a train) descarrilado; *fig* por los cerros de Úbeda. **side t.,** desviadero, *m.* **to keep t. of,** *inf* no perder de vista (a); seguir las fortunas de

trackless *a* sin camino; sin huella; (of trams, etc.) sin rieles; (untrodden) no pisado

tract *n* tracto, *m;* región, *f; anat* vía, *f;* (written) tratado, *m*

tractability *n* docilidad, *f*

tractable *a* dócil

traction *n* tracción, *f.* **t.-engine,** máquina de arrastre (or de tracción), *f*

tractor *n* máquina de arrastre, *f;* tractor, *m*

trade *n* comercio, *m;* tráfico, *m;* negocio, *m;* industria, *f;* (calling) oficio, *m,* profesión, *f;* (dealers) comerciantes, *mf pl. vi* comerciar, traficar. *vt* cambiar. **to t. on,** explotar, aprovecharse de. **by t.,** de oficio, por profesión. **t.-mark,** marca de fábrica, *f.* **t.-name,** razón social, *f.* **t. price,** precio para el comerciante, *m.* **t. union,** sindicato, *m.* **T. Union Congress,** Congreso de Sindicatos, *m.* **t. unionism,** sistema de sindicatos obreros, *m.* **t.-winds,** vientos alisios, *m pl*

trader *n* comerciante, traficante, *mf;* mercader, *m;* (boat) buque mercante, *m*

tradesman *n* tendero, *m.* **tradesmen's entrance,** puerta de servicio, *f*

trading *n* comercio, tráfico, *m. a* mercantil, comerciante, mercante. **t. ship,** buque mercante, *m.* **t. station,** factoría, *f*

tradition *n* tradición, *f*

traditional *a* tradicional; del lugar

traditionalism *n* tradicionalismo, *m*

traditionalist *n* tradicionalista, *mf*

traditionally *adv* según la tradición, tradicionalmente

traduce *vt* calumniar, denigrar, vituperar

traducer *n* calumniador (-ra)

traffic *n* comercio, negocio, tráfico, *m;* (in transit) transporte, *m;* (in movement) circulación, *f. vi* comerciar, traficar, negociar. **to cause a block in the t.,** interrumpir la circulación. **t. block,** obstrución del tráfico, *f,* atasco en la circulación, *m.* **t. indicator,** (on a car) indicador de dirección, *m.* **t. island,** refugio para peatones, salvavidas, *m.* **t. light,** disco, *m,* luz (de tráfico), *f,* semáforo, *m.* **t. roundabout,** redondel, *m*

trafficker *n* traficante, *mf*

tragedian *n* trágico, *m*

tragedy *n* tragedia, *f*

tragic *a* trágico

tragicomedy *n* tragicomedia, *f*

tragicomic *a* tragicómico

trail *n* rastro, *m,* pista, huella, *f;* (path) sendero, *m;* (of a comet) cola, cabellera, *f. vt* rastrear, seguir el rastro de; (drag) arrastrar; (the anchor) garrar. *vi* arrastrar; (of plants) trepar. **on the t. of,** en busca de; siguiendo el rastro de; **put somebody on the t. of . . .** darle a fulano la pista de . . .

trailer *n* cazador (-ra); perseguidor (-ra); *aut* remolque, *m;* (cinema) anuncio de próximas atracciones, *m; bot* talle rastrero, *m*

train *n* (railway) tren, *m;* (of a dress) cola, *f;* (retinue) séquito, *m;* (procession) desfile, *m,* comitiva, *f;* (series) serie, sucesión, *f*; (of gunpowder) reguero de pólvora, *m*. **down t.,** tren descendente, *m*. **excursion t.,** tren de excursionistas, *m*. **express t.,** exprés, tren expreso, *m*. **fast t.,** rápido, *m*. **goods t.,** tren de mercancías, *m*. **mail t.,** tren correo, *m*. **next t.,** próximo tren, *m*. **passenger t.,** tren de pasajeros, *m*. **stopping t.,** tren ómnibus, *m*. **through t.,** tren directo, *m*. **up t.,** tren ascendente, *m*. **t.-bearer,** paje que lleva la cola, *m*; dama de honor, *f*; (of a cardinal, etc.) caudatario, *m*. **t.-ferry,** buque transbordador, *m*. **t.-oil,** aceite de ballena, *m*. **t. service,** servicio de trenes, *m*

train *vt* educar; adiestrar; enseñar; *sport* entrenar; (firearms) apuntar; (plants) guiar; (accustom) habituar, acostumbrar; (a horse for racing) entrenar; (circus) amaestrar. *vi* educarse; adiestrarse; *sport* entrenarse

trainer *n* (of men and racehorses) entrenador, *m*; (of performing animals) domador, *m*

training *n* educación, *f*; enseñanza, instrucción, *f*; *sport* entrenamiento, *m*. **t.-college,** escuela normal, *f*. **t.-ship,** buque escuela, *m*

trait *n* rasgo, *m*, característica, *f*

traitor *n* traidor, *m*

traitress *n* traidora, *f*

trajectory *n* trayectoria, *f*

tram *n* tranvía, *m*. *a* tranviario. **t. conductor,** cobrador de tranvía, *m*. **t. depot,** cochera de tranvías, *f*. **t. stop,** parada de tranvía, *f*

trammel *n* (of a horse) traba, *f*; *fig* obstáculo, estorbo, *m*. *vt* travar; *fig* estorbar, impedir

tramp *n* (person) vagabundo (-da); vago (-ga); (walk) caminata, *f*, paseo largo, *m*; ruido de pasos, *m*; *naut* vapor volandero, *m*. *vi* ir a pie; patear; vagabundear. *vt* vagar por

trample *n* pisoteo, *m*; (of feet) ruido de pasos, *m*. *vt* pisotear, pisar, hollar. *vi* pisar fuerte. **to t. on,** *fig* atropellar humillar

trance *n* rapto, arrobamiento, *m*; *med* catalepsia, *f*

tranquil *a* tranquilo, apacible; sereno, sosegado

tranquilizer *n* calmante, *m*

tranquility *n* tranquilidad, paz, quietud, *f*; serenidad, *f*, sosiego, *m*; calma, *f*

tranquilize *vt* tranquilizar, sosegar, calmar

tranquilizing *a* sosegador, tranquilizador

trans *prefix* trans-. **t.-Pyrenean,** *a* traspirenaico. **to t.-ship,** trasbordar. **t.-shipment,** trasbordo, *m*. **t.-Siberian,** trasiberiano

transact *vt* despachar, hacer. *vi* despachar un negocio

transaction *n* desempeño, *m*; negocio, *m*; transacción, operación, *f*; *pl* **transactions** (of a society) actas, *f pl*

transatlantic *a* transatlántico. **t. liner,** transatlántico, *m*

transcend *vt* exceder, superar, rebasar. *vi* trascender

transcendence *n* superioridad, *f*; trascendencia, *f*

transcendental *a* trascendental

transcontinental *a* transcontinental

transcribe *vt* trascribir, copiar; *mus* trascribir, adaptar

transcriber *n* copiador (-ra); *mus* adaptador (-ra)

transcript *n* traslado, trasunto, *m*; (student's) certificado de estudios, certificado de materias aprobadas, *m*, constancia de estudios, copia del expediente académico, hoja de estudios, *f*

transcription *n* trascripción, copia, *f*, trasunto, *m*; *mus* trascripción, adaptación, *f*, arreglo, *m*

transept *n arch* transepto, crucero, *m*

transfer *n* traslado, *m*; trasferencia, *f*, traspaso, *m*; *law* cesión, enajenación, *f*; (picture) calcomanía, *f*. *vt* trasladar; trasferir; pasar; *law* enajenar, ceder; estampar; calcografiar. *vi* trasbordarse. **deed of t.,** escritura de cesión, *f*. **t.-paper,** papel de calcar, *m*

transferable *a* trasferible

transferee *n* cesionario (-ia)

transference *n* traslado, *m*; transferencia, *f*; *law* cesión, enajenación, *f*

transferor *n* cesionista, *mf*

transfiguration *n* trasfiguración, *f*

transfigure *vt* trasfigurar, trasformar

transfix *vt* traspasar; *fig* paralizar

transfixion *n* trasfixión, *f*

transform *vt* trasformar; convertir, cambiar. **It is completely transformed,** Está completamente trasformado

transformation *n* trasformación, *f*; conversión, *f*, cambio, *m*

transformative *a* trasformador

transformer *n elec* trasformador, *m*

transfuse *vt* trasfundir

transfusion *n* trasfusión, *f*. **blood t.,** trasfusión de sangre, *f*

transgress *vt* exceder, sobrepasar; (violate) contravenir, violar, pecar contra. *vi* pecar

transgression *n* contravención, trasgresión, *f*; pecado, *m*

transgressor *n* trasgresor (-ra), pecador (-ra)

transient *a* transitorio, fugaz, pasajero; perecedero

transiently *adv* pasajeramente

transit *n* tránsito, paso, *m*; trasporte, *m*; *ast* tránsito, *m*. **in t.,** de tránsito

transition *n* transición, *f*; cambio, *m*; tránsito, paso, *m*

transitional *a* de transición, transitorio

transitive *a gram* transitivo, activo. **t. verb,** verbo transitivo, verbo activo, *m*

transitively *adv* transitivamente

transitorily *adv* transitoriamente; provisionalmente

transitoriness *n* brevedad, *f*, lo fugaz

transitory *a* transitorio, fugaz, pasajero, breve

translatable *a* traducible

translate *vt* traducir; interpretar; (transfer) trasladar

translation *n* traducción, *f*; versión, *f*; traslado, *m*

translator *n* traductor (-ra)

translucence *n* traslucidez, *f*

translucent *a* traslúcido, trasparente

transmigrate *vi* trasmigrar

transmigration *n* trasmigración, *f*

transmissibility *n* trasmisibilidad, *f*

transmissible *a* trasmisible

transmission *n* trasmisión, *f*

transmit *vt* trasmitir; remitir, dar

transmitter *n* trasmisor (-ra); *rad* radiotrasmisor, *m*; *elec* trasmisor, *m*

transmutable *a* trasmutable

transmutation *n* trasmutación, *f*

transmute *vt* trasmutar

transoceanic *a* transoceánico

transom *n carp* travesaño, *m*; *naut* yugo de popa, *m*

transpacific *a* traspacífico

transparency *n* trasparencia; diafanidad, *f*; (picture) trasparente, *m*

transparent *a* trasparente; diáfano; (of style) claro, limpio

transpiration *n* traspiración, *f*

transpire *vi* traspirar; rezumarse; hacerse público; *inf* acontecer. *vt* exhalar

transplant *vt* trasplantar

transplantation *n* trasplante, *m*, trasplantación, *f*,

transport *n* trasporte, *m*; *naut* navío de trasporte, *m*; *aer* avión de trasporte, *m*; (fit) acceso, paroxismo, *m*. *vt* trasportar; (convicts) deportar; *fig* (joy) colmar; (rage) llenar

transportable *a* trasportable

transportation *n* trasporte, *m*; (convicts) deportación, *f*

transporter *n* trasportador (-ra)

transpose *vt* trasponer; *mus* trasportar

transposition *n* trasposición, *f*

transversal *a* and *n* trasversal, *m*

transverse *a* trasverso, trasversal

transversely *adv* trasversalmente

trap *n* trampa, *f*; cepo, *m*; (net) lazo, *m*, red, *f*; (for mice, rats) ratonera, *f*; *mech* sifón de depósito, *m*; pequeño carruaje de dos ruedas, *m*; (door) puerta caediza, *f*; *theat* escotillón, *m*; *pl* **traps,** trastos, *m pl*; equipaje, *m*. *vt* coger con trampa; hacer caer en el lazo; *fig* tender el

lazo. *vi* armar una trampa; armar lazo. **to fall into a t.,** *fig* caer en la trampa. **to pack one's traps,** liar el hato
trapeze *n* trapecio (de gimnasia), *m*
trapper *n* cazador de animales de piel, *m*
trappings *n pl* arneses, jaeces, *m pl*; arreos, aderezos, *m pl*, galas, *f pl*
trash *n* paja, hojarasca, *f*; (of sugar, etc.) bagazo, *m*; trastos viejos, *m pl*; cachivaches, *m pl*; (literary) paja, *f*
trashy *a* de ningún valor, inútil, despreciable
traumatic *a med* traumático
traumatism *n med* traumatismo, *m*
travail *n* dolores de parto, *m pl*. *vi* estar de parto; trabajar
travel *n* el viajar, viajes, *m pl*. *vi* viajar; ver mundo; (of traffic) circular, pasar, ir. *vt* viajar por; recorrer; (with number of miles) hacer. **to t. over,** viajar por; recorrer. **t. worn,** fatigado por el viaje
travel agent *n* agente de viajes, *mf*
traveled *a* que ha viajado, que ha visto muchas partes
traveler *n* viajero (-ra); pasajero (-ra). **commercial t.,** viajante, *mf* **traveler's check,** cheque de viajeros, *m*. **traveler's joy,** *bot* clemátide, *f*
traveling *n* viajes, *m pl*. *a* viajero; para (or de) viajar; (itinerant) ambulante. **t. crane,** grúa móvil, *f*. **t. expenses,** gastos de viaje, *m pl*. **t. requisites,** objetos de viaje, *m pl*. **t. rug,** manta, *f*. **t. show,** circo ambulante, *m*
traversable *a* atravesable, transitable, practicable
traverse *n carp* travesaño, *m*; *law* negación, *f*; (*mil arch*) través, *m*; (crossing) travesía, *f*, *a* transversal. *adv* transversalmente. *vt* atravesar, cruzar; *law* negar
travesty *n* parodia, *f*, *vt* parodiar
trawl *vt* rastrear. *vi* pescar a la rastra. **t.-net,** red de arrastre, *f*
trawler *n* barco barredero, *m*; pescador a la rastra, *m*
trawling *n* pesca a la rastra, *f*
tray *n* bandeja, *f*; (of a balance) platillo, *m*; (in a wardrobe, etc.) cajón, *m*; (trough) artesa, *f*
treacherous *a* traidor, falso, pérfido, fementido; (of memory) infiel; engañoso; (of ice, etc.) peligroso
treacherously *adv* traidoramente, a traición
treachery *n* perfidia, traición, falsedad, *f*
treacle *n* melado, *m*
tread *n* pisada, *f*; paso, *m*; (of a stair) peldaño, *m*; (of tire) pastilla, *f*; (walk) andar, porte, *m*, *vi* pisar; (trample) pisotear; hollar; (oppress) oprimir. *vt* hollar; (a path) abrir; recorrer; caminar por; bailar. **to t. the grapes,** pisar las uvas. **to t. the stage,** pisar las tablas. **to t. under foot,** hollar; pisotear. **to t. on,** pisar. **to t. on one's heels,** pisarle los talones a uno; seguir de cerca. **to t. out,** (a measure) bailar
treading *n* pisoteo, *m*
treadle *n* pedal, *m*; (of a loom) cárcola, *f*
treadmill *n* molino de rueda de escalones, *m*; *fig* rueda, *f*
treason *n* traición, *f*. **high t.,** alta traición, lesa majestad, *f*
treasonable *a* desleal, traidor
treasonably *adv* traidoramente
treasure *n* tesoro, *m*; riqueza, *f*, caudal, *m*; *fig* perla, *f*. *vt* atesorar; acumular (or guardar) riquezas; (a memory) guardar. **t. trove,** tesoro hallado, *m*
treasurer *n* tesorero (-ra)
treasury *n* tesorería, *f*; (government department) Ministerio de Hacienda, *m*; (anthology) tesoro, *m*. **t. bench,** banco del Gobierno, *m*
treat *n* (pleasure) gusto, placer, *m*; (present) obsequio, *m*; (entertainment) fiesta, *f*. *vt* tratar; *med* tratar, curar; (regale) obsequiar. *vi* (stand host) convidar; (of) tratar de, versar sobre; (with) negociar con
treatise *n* tesis, monografía, disertación, *f*, tratado, *m*
treatment *n* tratamiento, *m*; (of persons) conducta hacia, *f*, modo de obrar con, *m*; *med* tratamiento, *m*; (*lit, art*) procedimiento, *m*, técnica, *f*
treaty *n* tratado, pacto, *m*; (bargain) contrato, *m*
treble *n mus* tiple, *m*; voz de tiple, *f*. *a* triple; *mus* sobreagudo. *vt* triplicar; *vi* triplicarse. **t. clef,** clave de sol, *f*
trebling *n* triplicación, *f*
tree *n* árbol, *m*; (for shoes) horma, *f*; (of a saddle) arzón, *m*. **breadfruit t.,** árbol del pan, *m*. **Judas t.,** árbol de amor, *m*. **t. of knowledge,** árbol de la ciencia, *m*. **t.-covered,** arbolado. **t.-frog,** rana de San Antonio, *f*
treeless *a* sin árboles
trefoil *n* trébol, trifolio, *m*
trek *vi* caminar, andar
trellis *n* enrejado, *m*; (for plants) espaldera, *f*. *vt* cercar con un enrejado; construir espalderas
tremble *vi* temblar; estremecerse; trepidar; vibrar; (sway) oscilar; (of flags) ondear; agitarse; ser tembloroso. **His fate trembled in the balance,** Su suerte estaba en la balanza. **to t. all over,** temblar de pies a cabeza
trembling *n* temblor, *m*; estremecimiento, *m*; trepidación, *f*; vibración, *f*; (fear) agitación, ansiedad, *f*; temor, *m*. *a* tembloroso; trémulo
tremendous *a* terrible, espantoso; formidable; grande; importante; *inf* tremendo; enorme
tremendously *adv* terriblemente; *inf* enormemente
tremor *n* temblor, movimento sísmico, *m*; (thrill) estremecimiento, *m*; vibración, *f*
tremulous *a* trémulo, tembloroso; vacilante; tímido
tremulously *adv* trémulamente; tímidamente
tremulousness *n* lo tembloroso; vacilación, *f*; timidez, *f*
trench *n* zanja, *f*, foso, *m*; (for irrigation) acequia, *f*; *mil* trinchera, *f*. *vt* hacer zanjas (en); acequiar; *mil* atrincherar. **t.-fever,** tifus exantemático, *m*. **t.-foot,** pie de trinchera, *m*. **t.-mortar,** mortero de trinchera, *m*
trenchant *a* mordaz
trencher *n* trinchero, *m*
trend *n* curso, rumbo, *m*; *fig* tendencia, *f*; dirección, *f*. *vi fig* tender
trepan *vt surg* trepanar
trepanning *n surg* trepanación, *f*
trepidation *n* trepidación, *f*
trespass *n* violación de propiedad, *f*; ofensa, *f*; pecado, *m*; (in the Lord's Prayer) deuda, *f*. *vi* (on land) entrar sin derecho, violar la propiedad; (upon) entrar sin permiso en; (with patience, etc.) abusar de; (against) pecar contra, infringir
trespasser *n* violador (-ra) de la ley de propiedad. **"Trespassers will be prosecuted,"** «Entrada prohibida,» «Prohibido el paso»
tress *n* (plait) trenza, *f*; rizo, bucle, *m*; *pl* **tresses,** cabellera, *f*
trestle *n* caballete, *m*; armazón, *m*. **trestle-table,** mesa de caballete, *f*
triad *n* terna, *f*; *mus* acorde, *m*
trial *n* prueba, *f*, ensayo, *m*; examen, *m*; (experiment) tentativa, *f*, experimento, *m*; (misfortune) desgracia, pena, *f*; (nuisance) molestia, *f*; *law* vista de una causa, *f*. **on t.,** a prueba; *law* en proceso. **to bring to t.,** procesar. **to stand one's t.,** ser procesado. **t. run,** marcha de ensayo, *f*. **t. trip,** *naut* viaje de ensayo, *m*
trial and error *n* tanteos, *m*. **by trial and error,** por tanteos.
triangle *n* triángulo, *m*. **acute-angled t.,** triángulo acutángulo, *m*. **obtuse-angled t.,** triángulo obtusángulo, *m*. **right-angled t.,** triángulo rectángulo, *m*. **the eternal t.,** el eterno triángulo
triangular *a* triangular, triángulo
triangulation *n* (in surveying) triangulación, *f*
tribal *a* tribal
tribe *n* tribu, *f*
tribesman *n* miembro de una tribu, *m*
tribulation *n* tribulación, *f*; pena, aflicción, desgracia, *f*
tribunal *n* (seat) tribunal, *m*; (court) juzgado, *m*; (confessional) confesionario, *m*
tribunary *a* tribúnico
tribunate *n* tribunado, *m*
tribune *n* (person) tribuno, *m*; tribuna, *f*

tributary *a* and *n* tributario *m*
tribute *n* tributo, *m;* contribución, imposición, *f*
trice *n* tris, soplo, *m.* **in a t.,** en un periquete, en un avemaría, en dos trancos
tricentennial *a* de trescientos años; *n* tercer centenario, tricentenario, *m*
trick *n* (swindle) estafa, *f,* engaño, *m;* (ruse) truco, *m,* estratagema, ardid, *f;* (mischief) travesura, *f;* burla, *f;* (illusion) ilusión, *f;* (habit) costumbre, *f;* (affectation) afectación, *f;* (jugglery) juego de manos, *m;* (knack) talento, *m;* (at cards) baza, *f. vt* engañar, estafar; (with out) adornar, ataviar; (with into) inducir fraudulentamente. *vi* trampear. **dirty t.,** *inf* mala pasada, perrada, *f.* **His memory plays him tricks,** La memoria le engaña. **to play a t. on,** gastar una broma (a). **to play tricks,** hacer travesuras. **t. riding,** acrobacia ecuestre, *f*
trickery *n* maullería, superchería, *f;* fraude, engaño, *m*
trickle *n* chorrito, hilo (de agua, etc.) *m. vi* gotear. **to t. down,** deslizar por, correr por, escurrir por
trickling *n* goteo, *m;* (sound) murmullo, *m*
trickster *n* embustero (-ra), trampeador (-ra). **to be a t.,** ser buena maula
tricky *a* informal, maullero; (of things) difícil; complicado; (clever) ingenioso; (person) = **crafty**
tricolor *a* tricolor
tricycle *n* triciclo, *m*
tried *a* probado
triennial *a* trienal
trifle *n* (object) baratija, fruslería, *f;* pequeñez, tontería, bagatela, *f; cul, f;* (small amount) pequeña cantidad, *f,* muy poco (de); (adverbially) algo. *vi* entretenerse, jugar. *vt* (away) malgastar. **to t. with,** jugar con
trifler *n* persona frívola, *f;* (with affections) seductor (-ra)
trifling *a* insignificante, sin importancia, trivial
trigger *n* (of a fire-arm) gatillo, *m; mech* tirador, *m*
trigonometric *a* trigonométrico
trigonometry *n* trigonometría, *f*
trilingual *a* trilingüe
trill *n* trino, *m, vi* trinar
trillion *n* trillón, *m*
trilogy *n* trilogía, *f*
trim *a* aseado; bien arreglado; bien ajustado; elegante; bonito; (of sail) orientado. **She has a t. waist,** *inf* Tiene un talle juncal. *n* orden, *m;* buen estado, *m;* buena condición, *f;* (toilet) atavío, *m. vt* arreglar; (tidy) asear; pulir; (ornament) ornar, adornar; (adapt) ajustar, adaptar; *sew* guarnecer; (lamps) despabilar; (a fire) atizar; (hair, moustache) atusar, recortar; (trees) mondar, atusar; *carp* alisar; (sails) templar, orientar; (distribute weight in a boat) equilibrar; (of quill pens) tajar. *vi* (waver) nadar entre dos aguas. **to t. oneself up,** arreglarse
trimly *adv* aseadamente; lindamente
trimmer *n* guarnecedor (-ra); contemporizador (-ra)
trimming *n* arreglo, *m;* guarnición, *f;* (on a dress) pasamanería, *f;* adorno, *m; agr* poda, *f;* adaptación, *f,* ajuste, *m; pl* **trimmings,** accesorios, *m pl*
trimness *n* aseo, buen orden, *m;* buen estado, *m;* elegancia, lindeza, *f;* (slimness) esbeltez, *f*
Trinidad and Tobago Trinidad, *f,* y Tobago, *m*
Trinidadian *n* and *a* trinitario
Trinity *n* Trinidad, *f*
trinket *n* joya, alhaja, *f;* dije, *m,* chuchería, baratija, *f*
trinomial *a math* de tres términos. *n math* trinomio, *m*
trio *n* trío, *m*
trip *n* excursión, *f;* viaje, *m;* (slip) traspié, tropiezo, *m;* (in wrestling) zancadilla, *f;* (mistake) desliz, *m. vi* (stumble) tropezar, caer; (move nimbly) andar airosamente, ir (or correr) ligeramente; (frolic) bailar, saltar; (wrestling, games) echar la zancadilla; (err) equivocarse; cometer un desliz. *vt* (up) hacer caer; echar la zancadilla (a); coger en una falta; hacer desdecirse; coger en un desliz; *naut* levantar (el ancla)
tripartite *a* tripartito
tripartition *n* tripartición, *f*
tripe *n* callos, *m pl*
triple *a* triple. *vt* triplicar. *vi* triplicarse
triplet *n poet* terceto, *m; mus* tresillo, *m;* cada uno (una) de tres hermanos (hermanas) gemelos (-as)
triplicate *a* triplicado. *vt* triplicar
triplication *n* triplicación, *f*
tripod *n* trípode, *m*
Tripoli Trípoli, *m*
tripper *n* turista, excursionista, *mf*
tripping *a* ligero, ágil
trippingly *adv* ligeramente
triptych *n* tríptico, *m*
trite *a* vulgar, trivial
triteness *n* trivialidad, vulgaridad, *f*
triumph *n* triunfo, *m. vi* triunfar; (over) triunfar de, vencer
triumphal *a* triunfal. **t. arch,** arco de triunfo, *m*
triumphant *a* triunfante, victorioso
triumvirate *n* triunvirato, *m*
trivet *n* trébedes, *f pl,* trípode, *m*
trivial *a* trivial, frívolo; insignificante, sin importancia
triviality *n* trivialidad, frivolidad, *f;* insignificancia, *f*
trochlea *n anat* tróclea, *f*
trodden *a* trillado, batido
troglodyte *a* and *n* troglodita, *mf*
Trojan *a* and *n* troyano (-na). **the T. War,** la guerra de Troya, *f*
trolley *n elec* trole, *m;* (for children) carretón, *m.* **t.-bus,** trolebús, *m. n* **trolley car** tranvía, *m.* **t.-pole,** trole, *m*
trollop *n* tarasca, ramera, *f*
trombone *n* trombón, *m.* **t. player,** trombón, *m*
troop *n* banda, muchedumbre, *f; theat* compañía, *f;* (of cavalry) escuadrón, *m; pl* **troops,** *mil* tropas, *f pl;* ejército, *m. vi* ir en tropel, congregarse; (with away) marcharse en tropel, retirarse; (with out) salir en masa. **fresh troops,** tropas frescas, *f pl.* **storm troops,** tropas de asalto, *f pl.* **t.-ship,** transporte de guerra, *m*
trooper *n* soldado de caballería, *m*
trope *n* tropo, *m*
trophy *n* trofeo, *m*
tropic *a* and *n* trópico, *m*
tropical *a* tropical; (figurative) figurativo
tropism *n* tropismo, *m*
trot *n* trote, *m. vi* trotar. *vt* hacer trotar. **to t. out,** *inf* sacar a relucir
troth *n* fe, *f;* palabra, *f.* **to plight one's t.,** dar palabra de matrimonio, desposarse
trotting *a* trotón. *n* trote, *m*
troubadour *n* trovador, *m, a* trovadoresco
trouble *n* (grief) aflicción, angustia, *f;* (difficulty) dificultad, *f;* (effort) esfuerzo, *m;* pena, desgracia, *f;* (annoyance) disgusto, sinsabor, *m;* (unrest) confusión, *f,* disturbio, *m;* (illness) enfermedad, *f;* mal, *m;* (disagreement) desavenencia, *f.* **The t. is . . . ,** Lo malo es; La dificultad está en que . . . **to be in t.,** estar afligido; estar en un apuro, estar entre la espada y la pared. **to be not worth the t.,** no valer la pena. **to stir up t.,** revolver el ajo; armar un lío. **to take the t. to,** tomarse la molestia de.
trouble *vt* turbar; agitar; afligir, inquietar; (badger) importunar; (annoy) molestar; (cost an effort) costar trabajo (e.g., **Learning Spanish did not t. him much,** No le costó mucho trabajo aprender el castellano). *vi* preocuparse; darse la molestia; inquietarse
troubled *a* agitado; inquieto; preocupado; (of life) accidentado, borrascoso. **to fish in t. waters,** pescar en agua turbia, pescar en río revuelto
troublemaker *n Lat. Am.* buscapleitos, *mf*
troublesome *a* dificultoso; molesto; inconveniente; importuno; fastidioso
trough *n* gamella, *f;* (for kneading bread) artesa, *f;* (of the waves) seno, *m;* (meteorological) mínimo, *m.* **drinking t.,** abrevadero, *m.* **stone t.,** pila, *f*
trounce *vt* zurrar, apalear; *fig* fustigar
troupe *n* compañía, *f*

trousers *n pl* pantalones, *m pl.* **plus four t.,** pantalones de golf, *m pl.* **striped t.,** pantalón de corte, *m.* **t. pocket,** bolsillo del pantalón, *m.* **t. press,** prensa para pantalones, *f*
trousseau *n* ajuar de novia, *m*
trout *n* trucha, *f*
trowel *n agr* almocafre, *m;* (mason's) paleta, *f,* palustre, *m*
troy weight *n* peso de joyería, *m*
truant *n* novillero, *m;* haragán (-ana). *a* haragán, perezoso. **to play t.,** (from school) hacer novillos; ausentarse
truce *n* tregua, *f;* suspensión, cesación, *f*
truck *n* (lorry) camión, *m;* carretilla de mano, *f;* (railway) vagón de carga, *m;* (intercourse) relaciones, *f pl;* (trash) cachivaches, *m pl,* cosas sin valor, *f pl*
truckage *n* camionaje, *m;* acarreo, *m*
truckle *vi* humillarse, no levantar los ojos. **t. bed,** carriola, *f*
truculence *n* truculencia, agresividad, *f*
truculent *a* truculento, agresivo
trudge *vi* caminar a pie; andar con dificultad, caminar lentamente, andar trabajosamente, *n* caminata, *f*
true *a* verdadero; real; leal, sincero; fiel; exacto; honesto; genuino; auténtico; alineado, a plomo. **That is t. of . . .** Es propio de . . . *adv* realmente; exactamente. **t.-bred,** de casta legítima. **t.-hearted,** leal, fiel, sincero
truffle *n* trufa, *f.* **to stuff with truffles,** trufar
truism *n* perogrullada, *f*
truly *adv* lealmente; realmente, verdaderamente; en efecto, por cierto; sinceramente, de buena fe. **Yours t.,** su seguro servidor (su s.s.)
trump *n* (cards) triunfo, *m;* son de la trompeta, *m; inf* gran persona, joya, *f. vt* ganar con el triunfo. **to t. up,** inventar. **t.-card,** naipe de triunfo, *m*
trumpery *a* de pacotilla; ineficaz. *n* oropel, *m*
trumpet *n* trompeta, *f. vt* trompetear; *fig* pregonar. *vi* (of elephant) barritar. **ear.-t.,** trompetilla (acústica), *f.* **speaking t.,** portavoz, *m.* **t. blast,** trompetazo, *m.* **t. shaped,** en trompeta
trumpeter *n* trompetero, trompeta, *m*
trumpeting *n* trompeteo, *m;* (of elephant) barrito, *m*
truncate *a* truncado. *vt* truncar
truncheon *n* porra (de goma), *f;* bastón de mando, *m.* **blow with a t.,** porrazo, *m*
trunk *n* (*anat bot*) tronco, *m;* (elephant's) trompa, *f;* (railway) línea principal, *f;* baúl, *m;* cofre, *m;* (of a car) *Lat. Am.* baúl *m; pl* **trunks,** (Elizabethan, etc.) trusas, *f pl;* calzoncillos cortos, *m pl.* **wardrobe t.,** baúl mundo, *m.* **t.-call,** conferencia telefónica, *f.* **t.-line,** tronco, *m.* **t.-road,** carretera de primera clase, carretera mayor, *f*
truss *n med* braguero, *m;* (of straw, etc.) haz, *m;* (of blossom) racimo, *m;* (framework) armazón, *f. vt* atar; *cul* espetar; (a building) apuntalar
trust *n* fe, confianza, *f;* deber, *m; law* fideicomiso, *m;* (credit) crédito, *m;* esperanza, expectación, *f; com* trust, *m. vt* tener confianza en; confiar en; esperar; creer; *com* dar crédito (a). *vi* confiar; *com* dar crédito. **in t.,** en confianza; en administración, en depósito. **on t.,** al fiado
trustee *n* guardián, *m; law* fideicomisario, depositario, consignatario, *m*
trustful *a* confiado
trusting *a Lat. Am.* creído
trustingly *adv* confiadamente
trust release *n* extinción de fideicomiso, *f*
trustworthiness *n* honradez, probidad, integridad, *f;* (of statements) exactitud, *f*
trustworthy *a* digno de confianza, honrado; fidedigno, seguro; exacto
trusty *a* leal, fiel; firme, seguro
truth *n* verdad, *f;* realidad, *f;* exactitud, *f.* **the plain t.,** la pura verdad. **to tell the t.,** decir la verdad
truthful *a* veraz; exacto, verdadero
truthfulness *n* veracidad, *f;* exactitud, *f*
try *vt* and *vi* procurar, tratar de; (test) probar, ensayar; (a case, *law*) ver (el pleito); (strain) poner a prueba; (tire) cansar, fatigar; (annoy) molestar, exasperar; (afflict) hacer sufrir, afligir; (attempt) intentar; (judge) juzgar; (the weight of) tomar a pulso; (assay) refinar. *n* tentativa, *f;* (football) tiro, *m.* **Try as he would . . . ,** Por más que hizo . . . **to try hard to,** hacer un gran esfuerzo para. **to try one's luck,** probar fortuna. **to try on,** (clothes) probarse (un vestido, etc.). **to try out,** poner a prueba, probar. **to try to,** tratar de, procurar
trying *a* molesto; fatigoso; irritante; (painful) angustioso, penoso
tryst *n* cita, *f;* lugar de cita, *m. vt* citar. *vi* citarse
tsar *n* zar, *m*
tsarina *n* zarina, *f*
tsetse fly *n* mosca tsetsé, *f*
tub *n* cuba, *f,* artesón, *m;* cubeta, *f. vi* bañarse. **tub thumper,** *inf* gerundio, *m*
tuba *n mus* tuba, *f*
tube *n* tubo, *m;* (railway) metro, ferrocarril subterráneo, *m;* tubo, *m; anat* trompa, *f.* **Eustachian t.,** *anat* trompa de Eustaquio, *f.* **Fallopian t.,** trompa de Falopio, *f.* **inner t.,** *aut* cámara de aire, *f.* **speaking t.,** tubo acústico, *m.* **test t.,** tubo de ensayo, *m*
tuber *n* tubérculo, *m.* **kind of tuber resembling a sweet potato** *Central America* malanga, *f*
tubercular *a* tuberculoso
tuberculosis *n* tuberculosis, *f*
tuberose *n* nardo, *m,* tuberosa, *f*
tubing *n* tubería, *f*
tuck *n sew* alforzar, *f;* pliegue, *m. vt* recoger; *sew* alforzar. *vi* hacer alforzas. **to t. in,** (in bed) arropar; *inf* tragar. **to t. under,** poner debajo; doblar. **to t. up,** (in bed) arropar; (skirt) sofaldar; (sleeves) arremangar
tucker *n* camisolín, *m*
Tuesday *n* martes, *m.* **Shrove T.,** martes de carnaval, *m*
tuft *n* (bunch) manojo, *m;* (on the head) copete, moño, *m,* cresta, *f;* (tassel) borla, *f;* mechón, *m*
tufted *a Lat. Am.* copetudo
tug *n* tirón, *m;* sacudida, *f;* (boat) remolcador, *m. vt* tirar de; halar; sacudir. *vi* tirar con fuerza. **to give a tug,** dar una sacudida. **tug of war,** *lit* lucha de la cuerda, *f; fig* estira y afloja, *msg*
tuition *n* (teaching) instrucción, enseñanza, *f;* lecciones, *f pl;* (fee) cuota, *f*
tulip *n* tulipán, *m.* **t. wood,** palo de rosa, *m*
tulle *n* tul, *m*
tumble *n* caída, *f;* (somersault) tumbo, *m;* voltereta, *f. vi* caer; (acrobats) voltear, dar saltos. *vt* hacer caer; desarreglar. **to t. down,** venirse abajo; caer por. **t. down,** ruinoso, destartalado. **to t. off,** caer de. **to t. out,** *vt* hacer salir; arrojar. *vi* salir apresuradamente. **to t. over,** *vt* tropezar con. *vi* volcarse. **to t. to,** *inf* caer en la cuenta
tumbler *n* (acrobat) volteador (-ra); vaso para beber, *m*
tumefaction *n* tumefacción, *f*
tumor *n* tumor, *m*
tumult *n* alboroto, tumulto, *m;* conmoción, agitación, *f;* confusión, *f*
tumultuous *a* tumultuoso, alborotado; ruidoso; confuso; turbulento, violento
tumulus *n* túmulo, *m*
tun *n* tonel, *m,* cuba, *f, vt* entonelar, embarrilar
tune *n* melodía, *f;* son, *m;* armonía, *f; fig* tono, *m; inf* suma, *f. vt mus* afinar, templar; *rad* sintonizar; (up, an engine) ajustar (un motor). *vi* (in) sintonizar el receptor; (up, *mus*) templar (afinar) los instrumentos. **in t.,** *mus* afinado, templado; *fig* armonioso; (agreement) de acuerdo, conforme. **out of t.,** *mus* desafinado, destemplado. **to be out of t.,** desentonar, discordar; *fig* no armonizar, no estar en armonía. **to go out of t.,** desafinar. **to put out of t.,** destemplar. **to change one's t.,** *inf* bajar el tono
tuneful *a* melodioso
tunefully *adv* melodiosamente, armoniosamente
tunefulness *n* melodía, *f*

tuneless *a* disonante, discordante
tuner *n* afinador, templador, *m*; *rad* sintonizador, *m*
tungsten *n* tungsteno, *m*
tunic *n* túnica, *Lat. Am. also* cusma, *f*
tuning *n* afinación, *f*; *rad* sintonización, *f*. **t. fork,** diapasón normal, *m*. **t. key,** templador, *m*
Tunis Túnez, *m*
Tunisian *a* and *n* tunecino (-na)
tunnel *n* túnel, *m*. *vt* hacer (or construir) un túnel por. *vi* hacer un túnel
tunneling *n* construcción de túneles, *f*; horadación, *f*
tunny *n* atún, *m*. **striped t.,** bonito, *m*. **t. fishery,** almadraba, *f*
turban *n* turbante, *m*
turbid *a* turbio; *fig* confuso, **to make t.,** enturbiar
turbine *n* turbina, *f*
turbulence *n* turbulencia, *f*; desorden, *m*; agitación, *f*
turbulent *a* turbulento; alborotado; (stormy) borrascoso; agitado
tureen *n* sopera, *f*
turf *n* césped, *m*; (fuel) turba, *f*; (racing) carreras de caballos, *f pl*
turgid *a* turgente, hinchado; (of style) pomposo
turgidity *n* turgencia, *f*; pomposidad, *f*
Turk *n* turco (-ca). **Turk's head,** (duster) deshollinador, *m*; *naut* cabeza de turco, *f*
Turkey Turquía, *f*
turkey *n* (cock) pavo, *m*; (hen) pava, *f*; **t. red,** rojo turco, *m*
Turkish *a* turco. *n* (language) turco, idioma turco, *m*. **T. bath,** baño turco, *m*. **T. slipper,** babucha, *f*. **T. towel,** toalla rusa, *f*
turmeric *n* cúrcuma, *f*. **t. paper,** papel de cúrcuma, *m*
turmoil *n* alboroto, tumulto, desorden, *m*
turn *n* turno, *m*; (twist) torcimiento, *m*; (bend) recodo, *m*, vuelta, *f*; (in a river) meandro, *m*; (in a road) viraje, *m*; (revolution) vuelta, revolución, *f*; (direction) dirección, *f*; (in spiral stair) espira, *f*; *theat* número, *m*; (change) cambio, *m*; vicisitud, *f*; (appearance) aspecto, *m*; (service) servicio, *m*; (nature) índole, naturaleza, *f*; (of phrase) giro, *m*, expresión, *f*; (walk) vuelta, *f*, paseo, *m*; (talent) talento, *m*. **a sharp t.,** (in a road) un viraje rápido. **at every t.,** a cada instante; en todas partes. **bad t.,** flaco servicio, *m*. **by turns,** por turnos. **good t.,** servicio, favor, *m*. **in its t.,** a su vez. **in t.,** sucesivamente. **Now it's my t.,** Ahora me toca a mí. **The affair has taken a new t.,** El asunto ha cambiado de aspecto. **turn of the century,** vuelta del siglo, *f*; **turn of the millenium,** vuelta del milenio, *f*. **to a t.,** *cul* a la perfección. **to have a t. for,** tener talento para. **to take turns at,** alternar en. **t.-table,** (railway) plataforma, *f*; (of a gramophone) disco giratorio, *m*. **t. up,** barahúnda, conmoción, *f*; (of trousers) dobladillo (del pantalón), *m*
turn *vt* (on a lathe) tornear; (revolve) dar vueltas a, girar; (a key, door handle, etc.) torcer; (the leaves of a book) hojear; (the brain) trastornar; (a screw) enroscar; (the stomach) revolver (el estómago), marear; (go round) doblar, dar la vuelta a; (change) cambiar, mudar; (translate) traducir, verter; (dissuade) disuadir; (deflect) desviar; (apply) adaptar; (direct, move) volver; (concentrate) dirigir; concentrar; (turn over) volver del revés al derecho; (upside-down) volver lo de arriba abajo; (make) hacer, volver; (make sour) volver agrio; (transform) transformar convertir; *mil* envolver. **He has turned thirty,** Ha cumplido los treinta. **He said it without turning a hair,** Lo dijo sin pestañear. **He turned his head,** Volvió la cabeza. **They have turned the corner,** Han doblado la esquina; *fig* Han pasado la crisis. **"Please t. over,"** «A la vuelta (de la página).» **to t. a deaf ear to,** no dar oídos a, no hacer caso de. **to t. one's hand to,** aplicarse a. **to t. to account,** sacar ventaja (de). **to t. adrift,** dejar a la merced de las olas; echar de casa, poner en la calle; abandonar. **to t. against,** causar aversión, hacer hostil. **to t. aside,** desviar. **to t. away,** despedir; rechazar; (the head, etc.) volver; desviar. **to t. back,** hacer volver; enviar de nuevo; (raise) alzar; (fold) doblar; (the clock) retrasar. **to t. down,** doblar; (gas) bajar; (a glass, etc.) poner boca abajo; (reject) rechazar; (a suitor) dar calabazas (a). **to t. from,** alejar de, desviar de. **to t. in,** doblar hacia dentro; entregar. **to t. in one's toes,** ser patizambo. **to t. inside out,** volver al revés. **to t. into,** (enter) entrar en; (change) cambiar en, transformar en; convertir en; (translate) traducir a. **to t. off,** (dismiss) despedir; (from) desviarse de, dejar; (light) apagar; (water) cortar; *mech* cerrar; (disconnect) desconectar; (avoid) evitar; (refuse) rechazar. **to t. off the tap,** (water, gas) cerrar la llave (del agua, del gas). **to t. on,** (light) encender; (water, gas, etc.) abrir la llave (del agua, del gas); (steam) dar (vapor); (electric current) establecer (la corriente eléctrica); (eyes) fijar. **to t. out,** (expel) expeler, echar; (dismiss) despedir; (animals) echar al campo; (produce) producir; (dress) vestir; (equip) equipar, guarnecer; (a light) apagar. **to t. over,** (the page) volver (la hoja); (transfer) ceder, traspasar; revolver; (upset) volcar; considerar, pensar. **to t. round,** dar vuelta (a); girar; (empty) descargar. **to t. up,** levantar; apuntar; hacia arriba; (the earth) labrar, cavar; (a glass) poner boca arriba; (one's sleeves, skirt) arremangar; (fold) doblar. **to t. up one's nose at,** mirar con desprecio. **to t. upon,** atacar, volverse contra, acometer; depender de, estribar en. **to t. upside down,** volver lo de arriba abajo; revolver; revolcar
turn *vi* (in a lathe) tornear; (revolve) girar, dar vueltas; (depend) depender (de); torcer; volverse; dar la vuelta; girar sobre los talones; dirigirse (a, hacia); (move) mudar de posición; (deviate) desviarse (de); (be changed) convertirse (en); (become) hacerse, venir a ser; (begin) meterse (a); (take to) dedicarse a; (seek help) acudir; (change behavior) enmendarse, corregirse; (the stomach) revolver (el estómago); (go sour) agriarse, avinagrarse; (rebel) sublevarse. **He turned to the left,** Dio la vuelta a la izquierda; Torció hacia la izquierda. **My head turns,** (with giddiness) Se me va la cabeza. **to t. about,** voltearse, dar la vuelta. **to t. against,** coger aversión (a), disgustarse con; volverse hostil (a). **to t. aside,** desviarse; dejar el camino. **to t. away,** volver la cabeza; apartarse; alejarse. **to t. back,** volver atrás; volver de nuevo; retroceder; volver sobre sus pasos. **to t. down,** doblarse; reducirse. **to t. from,** alejarse de; apartarse de, huir de. **to t. in,** doblarse hacia dentro; (retire) acostarse. **to t. into,** transformarse en; convertirse en. **to t. off,** (depart from) desviarse (de); (fork) torcer, bifurcarse. **to t. out,** estar vuelto hacia fuera; (leave home) salir de casa; (rise) levantarse (de la cama); (arrive) llegar, presentarse; (attend) asistir, acudir; (result) resultar. **to t. over,** mudar (or cambiar) de posición, revolverse; (upset) voltearse, volcarse. **to t. round,** girar; volverse; cambiar de frente; cambiar de dirección, dar la vuelta; (*aut, aer*) virar; (change views) cambiar de opinión; (change sides) cambiar de partido. **to t. round and round,** dar vueltas, girar. **to t. to,** (apply to) acudir a; (begin) ponerse a; (become) convertirse en; (face) dirigirse hacia; (address) dirigirse a. **to t. up,** (crop up), surgir, aparecer; (arrive) llegar; (happen) acontecer; (be found again) volver a hallarse, reaparecer; (cards) venir; (of hats) levantar el ala; (of hair, etc.) doblarse. **His nose turns up,** Tiene la nariz respingona
turncoat *n* desertor (-ra), renegado (-da). **to become a t.,** volver la casaca
turned-up *a* (of hats) con el ala levantada; (of noses) respingona
turner *n* (craftsman) tornero, torneador, *m*
turnery *n* tornería, *f*
turning *n* (bend) vuelta, *f*; (turnery) tornería, *f*; (of milk, etc.) agrura, *f*; *pl* **turnings,** *sew* ensanche, *m*. **t.-point,** punto decisivo, *m*, crisis, *f*. **t. yellow** *Lat. Am.* amarilloso
turnip *n* nabo, *m*. **t. field,** nabar, *m*

turnover *n com* ventas, *f pl; cul* pastelillo, *m*
turnpike *n* barrera de portazgo, *f*
turnstile *n* torniquete, *m*
turpentine *n* aguarrás, *m*, trementina, *f*
turpitude *n* infamia, maldad, *f*
turquoise *n* turquesa, *f*
turret *n* torrecilla, almenilla, *f; naut* torre blindada, *f*
turreted *a* con torres, guarnecido de torres; en forma de torre
turtle *n* (dove) tórtolo (-la); (sea) tortuga de mar, *f.* **to turn t.,** voltearse patas arriba; *naut* zozobrar. **t. soup,** sopa de tortuga, *f*
Tuscan *a* and *n* toscano (-na)
Tuscany Toscana, *f*
tusk *n* colmillo, *m*
tussle *n* lucha, *f;* agarrada, *f. vi* luchar, pelear; tener una agarrada
tutelage *n* tutela, *f*
tutelar *a* tutelar
tutor *n* (private) ayo, *m;* profesor (-ra); (Roman law) tutor, *m;* (supervisor of studies) preceptor. *vt* enseñar, instruir. *vi* ser profesor, dar clases
tutorial *n* (university) seminario, *m;* (private) clase particular, *f*
tutoring *n* enseñanza, instrucción, *f*
TWA la TWA, *f,* (pronounced as if written *túa*)
twaddle *n* disparates, *m pl,* tonterías, patrañas, *f pl*
twain *a* and *n* dos, *m*
twang *n* punteado de una cuerda, *m;* (of a guitar) zumbido, *m;* (in speech) gangueo, *m. vt* puntear; (las cuerdas de un instrumento) rasguear. *vi* zumbar. **to speak with a t.,** hablar con una voz gangosa
tweak *n* pellizco, *m;* sacudida, *f,* tirón, *m. vt* pellizcar; sacudir, tirar
tweed *n* mezcla, *f,* cheviot, *m*
tweezers *n pl* pinzas, tenacillas, *f pl*
twelfth *a* duodécimo; (of the month) (el) doce; (of monarchs) doce. *n* duodécimo, *m;* (part) dozavo, *m,* duodécima parte, *f.* **T.-night,** Día de Reyes, *m,* Epifanía, *f*
twelve *a* and *n* doce *m;* (of age) doce años, *m pl.* **t. o'clock,** las doce; (mid-day) mediodía, *m;* (midnight) media noche, *f,* las doce de la noche. **t.-syllabled,** dodecasílabo
twentieth *a* vigésimo; (of the month) (el) veinte; (of monarchs) veinte, *n* vigésimo, *m;* (part) vientavo, *m,* vigésima parte, *f*
twenty *a* veinte; (of age) veinte años, *m pl, n* veinte, *m;* (score) veintena, *f.* **t.-first,** vigésimo primero; (of date) (el) veintiuno, *m,* (In modern Spanish the ordinals above *décimo* "tenth" are generally replaced by the cardinals, e.g. **the twenty-ninth chapter,** el capítulo veintinueve.)
twice *adv* dos veces. **t. as many** or **as much,** el doble
twiddle *vt* jugar con; hacer girar. *vi* girar; vibrar. *n* vuelta, *f.* **to t. one's thumbs,** dar vuelta a los pulgares, estar mano sobre mano
twig *n* ramita, pequeña rama, *f*
twilight *n* crepúsculo, *m;* media luz, *f. a* crepuscular. **in the t.,** en el crepúsculo; en la media luz. **t. sleep,** parto sin dolor, *m*
twin *a* gemelo, mellizo; doble. *n* gemelo (-la), mellizo (-za); (of objects) pareja, *f,* par, *m.* **t.-engined,** bimotor. **t. screw,** (*naut aer*) de dos hélices
twine *n* bramante, cordel, *m;* guita, *f. vt* enroscar; (weave) tejer; (encircle) ceñir; (round, about) abrazar. *vi* (of plants) trepar; entrelazarse; (wind) serpentear
twinge *n* punzada, *f,* dolor agudo, *m; fig* remordimiento, tormento, *m. vi* causar un dolor agudo
twining *a bot* trepante, voluble. **t. plant,** planta enredadera (or trepante), *f*
twinkle *vi* centellear, chispear, titilar; (of eyes) brillar; (of feet) moverse rápidamente, bailar. *n* (in the eye) chispa, *f*
twinkling *n* centelleo, *m;* titilación, *f;* (of the eye) brillo, *m;* (glimpse) vislumbre, *m; fig* instante, momento, *m. a* titilante, centelleador. **in a t.,** en un dos por tres. **in the t. of an eye,** en un abrir y cerrar de ojos
twin-tailed comet *n* ceratias, *m*
twirl *n* rotación, vuelta, *f;* pirueta, *f. vi* hacer girar; voltear; torcer; (a stick, etc.) dar vueltas (a). *vi* girar, dar vueltas; dar piruetas
twirp *n inf* renacuajo, *m*
twist *n* (skein) mecha, *f;* trenza, *f;* (yarn) torzal, *m;* (of tobacco) rollo, *m;* (of bread) rosca de pan, *f;* (act of twisting) torcimiento, *m,* torsión, *f;* (in a road, etc.) recodo, *m,* curva, vuelta, *f;* (pull) sacudida, *f;* (contortion) regate, esguince, *m;* (in a winding stair) espira, *f;* (in ball games) efecto, *m;* (in a person's nature) peculiaridad, *f;* falta de franqueza, *f;* (to words) interpretación, *f. vt* torcer; enroscar; (plait) trenzar; (wring) estrujar; (weave) tejer; (encircle) ceñir; (a stick, etc.) dar vueltas a; (of hands) crispar; (distort) interpretar mal, torcer. *vi* torcerse; enroscarse; (wind) serpentear; dar vueltas; (coil) ensortijarse; (writhe) undular, retorcerse; (of a stair) dar vueltas
twisted *a* torcido, *Mexico* chueco; (of persons) contrahecho
twisting *n* torcimiento, *m;* torcedura, *f;* serpenteo, *m;* (interlacing) entrelazamiento, *m. a* sinuoso, serpenteado
twitch *n* sacudida, *f,* tirón, *m;* (nervous) contracción nerviosa, *f. vt* tirar bruscamente, quitar rápidamente; agarrar; (ears, etc.) mover; (hands) crispar, retorcer. *vi* crisparse; (of ears, nose) moverse
twitching *n* sacudida, *f;* (contraction) crispamiento, *m,* contracción nerviosa, *f;* (pain) punzada, *f;* (of conscience) remordimiento, *m*
twitter *n* piada, *f,* gorjeo, *m. vi* piar, gorjear
two *a* and *n* dos, *m;* (of the clock) (las) dos, *f pl;* (of age) dos años, *m pl. a* de dos. **in two,** en dos partes. **in two's,** de dos en dos. **one or two,** uno o dos; algunos, *m pl;* algunas, *f pl.* **two against two,** dos a dos. **two by two,** de dos en dos, a pares. **Two can live as cheaply as one,** Donde come uno comen dos. **to put two and two together,** atar cabos. **two-edged,** de dos filos. **two-faced,** de dos caras; *fig* de dos haces. **to be two-faced,** hacer a dos caras. **two-headed,** de dos cabezas; bicéfalo. **two hundred,** *a* and *n* doscientos, *m.* **two hundredth,** *a* ducentésimo. *n* ducentésima parte, *f;* doscientos, *m.* **two-legged,** bípedo. **two-ply,** de dos hilos. **two-seater,** *a* de dos asientos. **two-speed gear box,** cambio de marcha de dos velocidades, *m.* **two-step,** paso doble, *m.* **two of a kind,** (well-matched) tal para cual. **two-way switch,** *elec* interruptor de dos direcciones, *m*
twofold *a* doble. *adv* doblemente, dos veces
twosome *n* partido de dos, *m*
two swords' theory *n* teoría de los dos gladios, *f*
tying *n* ligadura, *f;* atadura, *f*
tympanum *n* (*anat, arch*) tímpano, *m*
type *n* tipo, *m; print* carácter, *m,* letra de imprenta, *f,* tipo, *m. vt* and *vi* escribir a máquina. **t. case,** caja de imprenta, *f.* **t. founder,** fundidor de letras de imprenta, *m.* **t. foundry,** fundición de tipos, *f.* **t.-setter,** cajista, *mf* **t.-setting,** composición tipográfica, *f*
typewrite *vt* and *vi* escribir a máquina
typewriter *n* máquina de escribir, *f*
typewriting *n* mecanografía, *f, a* mecanográfico
typewritten *a* escrito a máquina
typhoid *n* tifoidea, fiebre tifoidea, *f*
typhoon *n* tifón, *m*
typhus *n* tifus, tabardillo pintado, *m*
typical *a* típico, característico; simbólico. **t. Mexican dish** (of food) antojito, *m*
typify *vt* simbolizar, representar; ser ejemplo de
typist *n* mecanografista, *mf;* mecanógrafo (-fa)
typographic *a* tipográfico
typography *n* tipografía, *f*
typographer *n* tipógrafo, *m*
tyrannical *a* tiránico, despótico

tyrannization *n* tiranización, *f*
tyrannize *vi* tiranizar
tyranny *n* tiranía, *f*, despotismo, *m*
tyrant *n* déspota, *m*, tirano (-na)
Tyre Tiro, *m*
tyro *n* novicio (-cia), tirón (-ona), advenedizo (-za), *mf*
Tyrol, the el Tirol
Tyrolese *a* and *n* tirolés (-esa)

U

U *n* (letter) u, *f*. **U-boat,** submarino, *m*. **u-shaped,** en forma de U
ubiquitous *a* ubicuo, omnipresente
ubiquity *n* ubicuidad, omnipresencia, *f*
udder *n* ubre, teta, mama, *f*
ugh *interj* ¡uf!
ugliness *n* fealdad, *f*; (moral) perversidad, *f*; (of a situation) peligro, *m*, lo difícil
ugly *a* feo, *Lat. Am. also* feroz; (morally) repugnante, asqueroso, perverso; (of a situation) peligroso, difícil; (of a wound) grave, profundo; (of a look) amenazador; *inf* desagradable; (of weather) borrascoso. **to make u.,** afear, hacer feo
Ukraine Ucrania, *f*
Ukrainian *a* and *n* ucranio (-ia)
ukulele *n mus* ucelele, *m*
ulcer *n* úlcera, *f*, *Lat. Am. also* lacra
ulcerate *vt* ulcerar. *vi* ulcerarse
ulceration *n* ulceración, *f*
ulcerous *a* ulceroso
ulterior *a* (of place) ulterior; (of time) posterior, ulterior; (of motives) interesado, oculto; **ulterior motive,** segunda intención, *f*
ultimate *a* último; fundamental, esencial
ultimately *adv* por fin, al final; esencialmente
ultimatum *n* ultimátum, *m*
ultimo *adv* del mes anterior
ultra *a* exagerado, extremo. *prefix* ultra-. **u-red,** ultrarrojo. **u.-violet,** ultravioleta
ultramarine *a* ultramarino. *n* azul de ultramar, *m*
ultramontane *a* ultramontano
ululation *n* ululación, *f*, ululato, *m*
umbilical *a* umbilical
umbilicus *n* ombligo, *m*
umbra *n ast* cono de sombra, *m*
umbrage *n poet* sombra, *f*; resentimiento, enfado, *m*. **to take u.,** ofenderse, resentirse
umbrella *n* paraguas, *m*. **u. maker,** paragüero (-ra). **u. shop,** paragüería, *f*. **u. stand,** paragüero, *m*
umpire *n sport* árbitro, *m*; *law* juez arbitrador, tercero en discordia, *m*. *vt* arbitrar
un- *prefix* Used before adjectives, adverbs, abstract nouns, verbs and translated in Spanish by **in-, des-, nada, no, poco, sin,** as well as in other ways
unabashed *a* desvergonzado, descarado, insolente; (calm) sereno, sosegado
unabashedly *adv* sin rubor
unabated *a* no disminuido; cabal, entero
unabbreviated *a* íntegro, sin abreviar
unable *a* incapaz, impotente; (physical defect) imposibilitado. **to be u. to,** no poder, serle a uno imposible. **to be u. to control,** no poder controlar
unabridged *a*. See **unabbreviated**
unaccented *a* sin acento
unacceptability *n* lo inaceptable
unacceptable *a* inaceptable
unaccepted *a* rechazado, no aceptado
unaccommodating *a* poco complaciente, nada servicial
unaccompanied *a* solo, sin compañía; *mus* sin acompañamiento
unaccomplished *a* incompleto, sin terminar, inacabado; (not clever) sin talento
unaccountability *n* lo inexplicable; falta de responsabilidad, irresponsabilidad, *f*
unaccountable *a* inexplicable; irresponsable
unaccountably *adv* inexplicablemente, extrañamente
unaccredited *a* no acreditado, extraoficial
unaccustomed *a* no habituado; (unusual) desacostumbrado, insólito, inusitado
unacknowledged *a* no reconocido; (of letter) sin contestación, por contestar; no correspondido, sin devolver; (of crimes, etc.) inconfeso, no declarado
unacquainted *a* que no conoce; que desconoce, que ignora; no habituado. **to be u. with,** no conocer; ignorar; no estar acostumbrado a
unadaptable *a* inadaptable (also of persons)
unadorned *a* sin adorno sencillo, que no tiene adornos
unadulterated *a* sin mezcla, no adulterado, natural; genuino, verdadero; puro
unadventurous *a* nada aventurero, que no busca aventuras, tímido; tranquilo, sin incidente
unadvisability *n* imprudencia, *f*; inoportunidad, *f*
unadvisable *a* imprudente; inoportuno, no conveniente
unadvisedly *adv* imprudentemente
unesthetic *a* antiestético
unaffected *a* natural, llano, sin melindres; impasible; genuino, sincero. **u. by,** no afectado por
unaffectedly *adv* sin afectación
unaffectedness *n* naturalidad, sencillez, *f*; sinceridad, franqueza, *f*
unaffiliated *a* no afiliado
unafraid *a* sin temor
unaided *a* sin ayuda, solo a solas
unaired *a* sin ventilar, no ventilado; húmedo, sin airear
unalloyed *a* sin mezcla, puro
unalterability *n* lo inalterable; constancia, *f*
unalterable *a* inalterable; invariable, constante
unambiguous *a* no ambiguo, nada dudoso, claro
unambitious *a* sin ambición; modesto
unamusing *a* nada divertido
unanimity *n* unanimidad, *f*
unanimous *a* unánime
unanimously *adv* unánimemente, por unanimidad. **carried u.,** adoptado por unanimidad
unanswerability *n* imposibilidad de negar, *f*; lo irrefutable
unanswerable *a* incontestable, incontrovertible, incontrastable, irrefutable
unanswered *a* no contestado, sin contestar; (unrequited) no correspondido
unapparent *a* no aparente
unappealable *a* inapelable
unappeasable *a* implacable
unappeased *a* no satisfecho; implacable
unappetizing *a* no apetitoso; (unattractive) repugnante, feo
unappreciated *a* desestimado, no apreciado, tenido en poco; (misunderstood) mal comprendido
unapproachable *a* inaccesible
unapproachableness *n* inaccesibilidad, *f*
unappropriated *a* no concedido; libre
unapproved *a* sin aprobar, no aprobado
unarm *vt* desarmar. *vi* desarmarse, quitarse las armas
unarmed *a* desarmado; indefenso; (*zool, bot*) inerme
unarranged *a* no arreglado, sin clasificar; (accidental) fortuito, casual
unartistic *a* no artístico
unascertainable *a* no verificable
unashamed *a* sin vergüenza; tranquilo, sereno; insolente, descarado
unasked *a* sin pedir; no solicitado; espontáneo; (uninvited) no convidado

unassailable *a* inexpugnable; irrefutable; incontestable
unassisted *a*. See **unaided**
unassuming *a* modesto, sin pretensiones
unattached *a* suelto; *law* no embargado; *mil* de reemplazo; independiente
unattainable *a* inasequible, irrealizable
unattainableness *n* imposibilidad de alcanzar (or realizar), *f*; inaccesibilidad
unattended *a* solo, sin acompañamiento; (of ill person) sin tratamiento; (of entertainment, etc.) no concurrido
unattested *a* sin atestación
unattractive *a* poco atrayente, desagradable, antipático, feo
unattractiveness *n* fealdad, falta de hermosura, *f*; lo desagradable
unauthentic *a* no auténtico, sin autenticidad; apócrifo
unauthorized *a* no autorizado
unavailable *a* inaprovechable
unavailing *a* inútil, vano
unavenged *a* no vengado, sin castigo
unavoidable *a* inevitable, preciso, necesario. **to be u.,** no poder evitarse, no tener remedio
unavoidableness *n* inevitabilidad, necesidad, *f*
unavoidably *adv* irremediablemente
unaware *a* ignorante; inconsciente. **to be u. of,** ignorar, desconocer; no darse cuenta de
unawareness *n* ignorancia, *f*, desconocimiento, *m*; inconsciencia, *f*
unawares *adv* (by mistake) sin querer, inadvertidamente; (unprepared) de sobresalto, de improviso, inopinadamente. **He caught me u.,** Me cogió desprevenido
unbalance *vt* desequilibrar, hacer perder el equilibrio; *fig* trastornar
unbalanced *a* desequilibrado; *fig* trastornado; *com* no balanceado
unbaptized *a* no bautizado, sin bautizar
unbar *vt* desatrancar; *fig* abrir
unbearable *a* intolerable, insufrible, inaguantable, inllevable, insoportable
unbearably *adv* insoportablemente
unbeatable *a* inmejorable
unbeaten *a* (of paths) no frecuentado, no pisado; (of armies) no derrotado, no batido; invicto
unbecoming *a* impropio, inapropiado, inconveniente; indecoroso, indigno; indecente; (of clothes) que no va bien, que sienta mal
unbelief *n* incredulidad, *f*
unbelievable *a* increíble
unbelievably *adv* increíblemente
unbeliever *n* incrédulo (-la), descreído (-da)
unbeloved *a* no amado
unbend *vt* desencorvar, enderezar; entretenerse, descansar; (*naut* of sails) desenvergar; (*naut* of cables) desamarrar. *vi* enderezarse; mostrarse afable
unbending *a* inflexible, rígido, tieso; *fig* inexorable, inflexible, duro, terco; (amiable) afable, jovial
unbiased *a* imparcial, ecuánime
unbidden *a* espontáneo; (uninvited) no convidado, no invitado
unbind *vt* desligar, desatar; (bandages) desvendar; (books) desencuadernar
unbleached *a* crudo, sin blanquear
unblemished *a* no manchado; (pure) sin mancha, inmaculado, puro
unblessed *a* no bendecido, no consagrado; (accursed) maldito; (unhappy) desdichado
unblushing *a* desvergonzado, insolente
unbolt *vt* descerrojar, desempernar
unborn *a* sin nacer, no nacido todavía; venidero
unbosom *vt* confesar, declarar. **to u. oneself,** abrir su pecho (a) or (con)
unbought *a* no comprado; gratuito, libre; (not bribed) no sobornado
unbound *a* suelto, libre; (of books) en rama, no encuadernado
unbounded *a* ilimitado, infinito; inmenso
unbowed *a* erguido; no encorvado; (undefeated) invicto
unbreakable *a* irrompible, inquebrantable
unbridled *a* desenfrenado, violento; licencioso
unbroken *a* no quebrantado, intacto, entero; continuo, incesante; no interrumpido; (of soil) virgen; (of a horse) indomado; inviolado; (of the spirit) indómito; (of a record) no batido
unbrotherly *a* poco fraternal, indigno de hermanos
unbuckle *vt* deshebillar
unburden *vt* descargar; aliviar. **to u. oneself,** (express one's feelings) desahogarse
unburied *a* insepulto
unburnt *a* no quemado; incombusto
unbusinesslike *a* informal; poco comercial, descuidado
unbutton *vt* desabrochar, desabotonar
uncalled *a* no llamado, no invitado. **u.-for,** impertinente; innecesario
uncannily *adv* misteriosamente
uncanniness *n* lo misterioso
uncanny *a* misterioso, horroroso, pavoroso
uncared-for *a* abandonado, desatendido, desamparado
uncarpeted *a* sin alfombra
uncaught *a* no prendido, libre
unceasing *a* continuo, incesante, sin cesar, constante
unceasingly *adv* incesantemente, sin cesar
uncensored *a* no censurado
unceremonious *a* sin ceremonia, familiar; descortés, brusco
unceremoniousness *n* falta de ceremonia, familiaridad, *f*; incivilidad, descortesía, *f*
uncertain *a* incierto, dudoso; inseguro; precario; (hesitant) indeciso, vacilante, irresoluto
uncertainly *adv* inciertamente
uncertainty *n* incertidumbre, duda, *f*; inseguridad, *f*; irresolución, *f*
uncertificated *a* sin certificado (of teachers, etc.) sin título
uncertified *a* sin garantía; no garantizado; (of lunatics) sin certificar
unchain *vt* desencadenar
unchallenged *a* incontestable
unchangeable *a* invariable, inalterable, inmutable
unchangeableness *n* invariabilidad, inalterabilidad, *f*
unchanging *a* inmutable, invariable
uncharitable *a* nada caritativo, duro; intolerante, intransigente
uncharitableness *n* falta de caridad, *f*; intolerancia, intransigencia
uncharitably *adv* sin caridad; con intolerancia
unchaste *a* incasto, incontinente; deshonesto, impuro, lascivo
unchecked *a* desenfrenado; (unproved) no comprobado; *com* no confrontado
unchivalrous *a* nada galante, nada caballeroso
unchristened *a* no bautizado, sin bautizar
unchristian *a* (heathen) pagano; poco cristiano, indigno de un cristiano, nada caritativo
uncircumcised *a* incircunciso
uncircumscribed *a* incircunscripto
uncivil *a* descortés, incivil
uncivilizable *a* reacio a la civilización
uncivilized *a* no civilizado, bárbaro, salvaje, inculto
uncivilly *adv* descortésmente
unclad *a* sin vestir; desnudo
unclasp *vt* (jewelery) desengarzar; desabrochar; (of hands) soltar, separar
unclassifiable *a* inclasificable
unclassified *a* sin clasificar
uncle *n* tío, *m*; (pawnbroker) prestamista, *m*
unclean *a* sucio, puerco, inmundo; desaseado; impuro, obsceno; (ritually) poluto
uncleanliness *n* suciedad, porquería, *f*; desaseo, *m*; falta de limpieza, *f*

uncleanly *a* sucio, puerco; desaseado
uncleanness *n* suciedad, *f;* impureza, obscenidad, inmoralidad, *f*
unclench *vt* (of hands) abrir
Uncle Tom's Cabin La Cabaña del Tío Tom
unclouded *a* sin nubes, despejado, claro
uncoil *vt* desarrollar. *vi* desovillarse; (of snakes) desanillarse
uncollected *a* disperso; no cobrado; (in confusion) confuso, desordenado
uncolored *a* incoloro; *fig* imparcial, objetivo, sencillo
uncombed *a* despeinado, sin peinar
uncomfortable *a* incómodo; (anxious) intranquilo, inquieto, desasosegado, preocupado; (awkward) molesto, difícil, desagradable. **to be u.,** (people) estar incómodo; (anxious) estar preocupado; (of things) ser incómodo
uncomfortableness *n* incomodidad, *f;* malestar, *m;* intranquilidad, preocupación, *f;* dificultad, *f;* lo desagradable
uncomfortably *adv* incómodamente; intranquilamente; desagradablemente
uncomforted *a* desconsolado, sin consuelo
uncommercial *a* no comercial
uncommon *a* poco común, extraordinario, singular, raro, extraño; infrecuente; insólito
uncommonly *adv* extraordinariamente, muy; infrecuentemente, raramente
uncommonness *n* infrecuencia, rareza, *f;* singularidad, *f*
uncommunicative *a* reservado, poco expresivo
uncommunicativeness *n* reserva, *f*
uncomplaining *a* resignado, que no se queja
uncomplainingly *adv* con resignación
uncompliant *a* sordo, inflexible
uncomplicated *a* sencillo, sin complicaciones
uncomplimentary *a* descortés, poco halagüeño, ofensivo
uncompromising *a* inflexible, estricto, intolerante; irreconciliable
unconcealed *a* no oculto; abierto
unconcern *n* indiferencia, frialdad, *f,* desapego, *m;* (lack of interest) apatía, despreocupación, *f;* (nonchalance) desenfado, *m,* frescura, *f*
unconcerned *a* indiferente, frío, despegado; apático, despreocupado; desenfadado, fresco
unconcernedly *adv* con indiferencia; sin preocuparse; con desenfado
unconditional *a* incondicional, absoluto. **u. surrender,** rendición incondicional, *f*
unconditionally *adv* incondicionalmente; *mil* a discreción
unconfessed *a* inconfeso
unconfined *a* suelto, libre; ilimitado; sin estorbo
unconfirmed *a* no confirmado; (report) sin confirmar
uncongenial *a* incompatible, antipático; desagradable, repugnante
uncongeniality *n* incompatibilidad, antipatía, *f;* repugnancia, *f;* lo desagradable
unconnected *a* inconexo; *mech* desconectado; (relationship) sin parentesco; (confused) incoherente
unconquerable *a* invencible, indomable, inconquistable
unconquered *a* no vencido
unconscientious *a* poco concienzudo
unconscionable *a* excesivo, desmedido; sin conciencia
unconscious *a* inconsciente; (senseless) insensible, sin sentido; espontáneo; (unaware) ignorante. **to be u. of,** ignorar; perder la consciencia de. **to become u.,** perder el sentido
unconsciously *adv* inconscientemente, involuntariamente
unconsciousness *n* inconsciencia, *f;* (hypnosis, swoon) insensibilidad, *f;* (unawareness) ignorancia, falta de conocimiento, *f*
unconsecrated *a* no consagrado
unconsidered *a* indeliberado; sin importancia, trivial
unconstitutional *a* anticonstitucional, inconstitucional
unconstitutionally *adv* inconstitucionalmente
unconstrained *a* libre; voluntario; sin freno
uncontaminated *a* incontaminado; puro, sin mancha, impoluto
uncontested *a* sin oposición
uncontradicted *a* sin contradicción; incontestable
uncontrollable *a* irrefrenable, incontrolable, inmanejable; (temper) ingobernable; indomable
uncontrolled *a* libre, no controlado; desenfrenado, desgobernado
unconventional *n* poco convencional; bohemio, excéntrico, extravagante; original
unconventionality *a* excentricidad, extravagancia, independencia de ideas, *f;* (of a design) originalidad, *f*
unconversant *a* poco familiar, poco versado (en)
unconverted *a* no convertido; sin transformar
unconvinced *a* no convencido
unconvincing *a* no convincente, poco convincente, que no me (nos, etc.) convence; frívolo
uncooked *a* crudo, no cocido, sin cocer
uncork *vt* destapar, descorchar, quitar el corcho
uncorrected *a* sin corregir, no corregido
uncorroborated *a* no confirmado, sin confirmar
uncorrupted *a* incorrupto; puro, no pervertido; (unbribed) no sobornado, honrado
uncorruptible *a* incorruptible
uncountable *a* innumerable
uncounted *a* no contado, sin cuenta
uncouple *vt* soltar; desenganchar, desconectar
uncouth *a* grosero, chabacano, tosco, patán
uncouthness *n* grosería, tosquedad, patanería, *f*
uncover *vt* descubrir; (remove lid of) destapar; (remove coverings of) desabrigar, desarropar; (leave unprotected) desamparar; (disclose) revelar, dejar al descubierto. *vi* descubrirse, quitar el sombrero
uncovered *a* descubierto; desnudo; sin cubierta
uncreated *a* increado
uncritical *a* sin sentido crítico, poco juicioso
uncross *vt* (of legs) descruzar
uncrossed *a* (of check) sin cruzar
uncrowned *a* antes de ser coronado; sin corona
unction *n* unción, *f;* untadura, *f,* untamiento, *m;* (unguent) ungüento, *m;* (zeal) fervor, *m;* (flattery) insinceridad, hipocresía, *f;* (relish) gusto, entusiasmo, *m.* **extreme u.,** extremaunción, *f*
unctuous *a* untuoso, craso; insincero, zalamero
uncultivable *a* incultivable
uncultivated *a* inculto, yermo; (barbarous) salvaje, bárbaro; (uncultured) inculto, tosco; no cultivado
uncultured *a* inculto, iletrado
uncurbed *a* sin freno; *fig* desenfrenado
uncurl *vt* desrizar *vi* desrizarse; desovillarse
uncurtained *a* sin cortinas; con las cortinas recogidas
uncut *a* sin cortar, no cortado; (of gems) sin labrar
undamaged *a* indemne, sin daño
undated *a* sin fecha
undaunted *a* intrépido, atrevido
undeceive *vt* desengañar, desilusionar
undecided *a* (of question) pendiente, indeciso; dudoso; vacilante, irresoluto
undecipherable *a* indescifrable; ilegible
undeclared *a* no declarado
undefended *a* indefenso
undeferable *a* inaplazable
undefiled *a* impoluto, incontaminado; puro
undefinable *a* indefinible; inefable, vago
undefined *a* indefinido; indeterminado
undelivered *a* no recibido; (speech) no pronunciado; (not sent) no enviado
undemonstrative *a* poco expresivo, reservado
undeniable *a* incontestable, innegable, indudable; excelente; inequívoco, evidente
undeniably *adv* indudablemente

undenominational *a* sin denominación
undependable *a* indigno de confianza
under *prep* debajo de; bajo; (in) en; (less than) menos de, menos que; (at the orders of) a las órdenes de, al mando de; (in less time than) en menos de; (under the weight of) bajo el peso de; (at the foot of) al abrigo de; (for less than) por menos de; (at the time of) en la época de, en tiempos de; (according to) según, conforme a, en virtud de (e.g. **under the law,** en virtud de la ley); (of monarchs) bajo (or durante) el reinado de; (of rank) inferior a; (in virtue of) en virtud de; (of age) menor de; (with penalty, pretext, etc.) so; en; a (see below for examples); (*agr* of fields) plantado de, sembrado de. **u. arms,** bajo las armas. **u. contract,** bajo contrato. **u. cover,** al abrigo, bajo cubierto. **u. cover of,** bajo pretexto de, so color de. **u. fire,** bajo fuego. **u. oath,** bajo juramento. **u. pain of,** so pena de. **u. sail,** a la vela. **u. separate cover,** bajo cubierta separada, en sobre apartado, por separado. **u. steam,** al vapor. **u. way,** en camino; en marcha; en preparación. **to be u. an obligation,** deber favores; (to) tener obligacion de; estar obligado a
under *a* inferior; (of rank) subalterno, subordinado; bajo, bajero. *adv* debajo; abajo; más abajo; menos; (for less) para menos; (ill) mal; (insufficient) insuficiente. **to bring u.,** someter. **to keep u.,** dominar, subyugar
underact *vt* hacer un papel sin fogosidad
underarm *n* sobaco, *m. a* sobacal; (of bowling) de debajo del brazo. **to serve u.,** sacar por debajo
underbid *vt* ofrecer menos que
underbred *a* mal criado, mal educado
undercharge *vt* cobrar menos de lo debido
underclothes *n* ropa interior, *f*, paños menores, *m pl*
undercurrent *n* corriente submarina, *f; fig* tendencia oculta, *f*
undercut *n* (of meat) filete, *m*
underdeveloped *a* de desarrollo atrasado; *phot* no revelado lo suficiente
underdog *n* víctima, *f;* débil, paciente, *m.* **underdogs,** los de abajo, *m pl*
underdone *a* (of meat) crudo, medio asado
underdress *vt* and *vi* vestir(se) sin bastante elegancia
underestimate *vt* tasar en menos; desestimar, menospreciar
underfeed *vt* alimentar insuficientemente
underfoot *adv* debajo de los pies, en el suelo
undergo *vt* sufrir, padecer, pasar por. **undergo surgery,** someterse a la cirugía
undergraduate *n* estudiante no graduado, *m*
underground *a* subterráneo; *fig* oculto, secreto. *adv* bajo tierra, debajo de la tierra; *fig* en secreto, ocultamente. *n* sótano, *m*; metro, ferrocarril subterráneo, *m*
undergrown *a* enclenque
undergrowth *n* maleza, *f*
underhand *adv fig* bajo mano, ocultamente, a escondidas. *a fig* secreto, oculto
underlie *vt* estar debajo de; servir de base a, caracterizar
underline *vt* subrayar
underling *n* subordinado (-da)
underlying *a* fundamental, básico, esencial
undermentioned *a* abajo citado
undermine *vt* socavar, excavar; minar, destruir poco a poco
undermining *n* socava, excavación, *f;* destrucción, *f, a* minador
underneath *adv* debajo. *prep* bajo, debajo de
undernourished *a* mal alimentado
undernourishment *n* desnutrición, *f*
underpaid *a* insuficientemente retribuido, mal pagado
underpass *n* pasaje por debajo, *m*
underpay *vt* pagar mal, remunerar (or retribuir) deficientemente
underpayment *n* retribución mezquina, *f*, pago insuficiente, *m*
underpin *vt* apuntalar, socalzar
underpopulated *a* con baja densidad de población
underprivileged *a* menesteroso, pobre, necesitado
underrate *vt* tasar en menos; tener en poco, desestimar, menospreciar
underripe *a* verde
undersecretary *n* subsecretario (-ia)
undersell *vt* vender a un precio más bajo que
undershirt *n Spain* camiseta, *Lat. Am.* franela, *f*
underside *n* revés, envés, *m*
undersigned *a* infrascrito, suscrito. **the u.,** el abajo firmado, el infrascrito
undersized *a* muy pequeño, enclenque, enano
underskirt *n* enagua, *f;* refajo, *m*
underslung *a aut* con bajo centro de gravedad
understand *vt* comprender, entender; (know) saber; (be acquainted with) conocer; (hear) oír, tener entendido; (mean) sobrentender. *vi* comprender, entender; oír, tener entendido. **to u. each other,** comprenderse. **It being understood that . . .,** Bien entendido que . . .
understandable *a* comprensible; inteligible. **It is very u. why he does not wish to come,** Se comprende muy bien por qué no quiere venir
understanding *n* (intelligence) entendimiento, *m*, inteligencia, *f;* (agreement) acuerdo, *m;* (knowledge) conocimiento, *m;* (wisdom) comprensión, sabiduría, *f. a* inteligente; sabio; (sympathetic) comprensivo, simpático. **to come to an u.,** ponerse de acuerdo
understandingly *adv* con inteligencia; con conocimiento (de); con simpatía
understate *vt* decir menos que, rebajar, describir sin énfasis
understatement *n* moderación, *f*
understudy *n* sobresaliente, *mf. vt* sustituir
undertake *vt* comprometerse a, encargarse de; emprender, abarcar, acometer
undertaker *n* empresario, director de pompas fúnebres, *m*
undertaking *n* empresa, tarea, *f;* garantía, promesa, *f;* (funerals) funeraria, *f*
undertone *n* voz baja, *f; art* color tenue (or apagado), *m.* **in an u.,** en voz baja
undervalue *vt* tasar en menos; tener en poco, despreciar
underwater *a* subacuático, submarino. **underwater flipper,** aleta de bucear
underweight *a* de bajo peso, que pesa menos de lo debido, flaco
underworld *n* (hell) infierno, averno, *m;* (slums) hampa, *f*, fondos bajos de la sociedad, *m pl;* heces de la sociedad, *f pl.* **u. slang** *Peru* cantuja *f*
underwrite *vt com* asegurar contra riesgos; reasegurar; obligarse a comprar todas las acciones de una compañía no subscritas por el público, mediante un pago convenido
underwriter *n* asegurador, *m;* reasegurador, *m*
underwriting *n* aseguro, *m;* reaseguro, *m*
undeserved *a* inmerecido, no merecido
undeserving *a* indigno, desmerecedor; que no merece
undesirable *a* no deseable; nocivo, pernicioso; (unsuitable) inconveniente
undesired *a* no deseado; no solicitado, no buscado
undesirous *a* no deseoso
undestroyed *a* sin destruir, no destruido, intacto
undetected *a* no descubierto
undeveloped *a* no desarrollado; rudimentario; inmaturo; (of a country) no explotado, virgen; *phot* no revelado; (of land) sin cultivar
undeviating *a* directo; constante, persistente
undigested *a* no digerido, indigesto
undignified *a* sin dignidad; poco serio; indecoroso
undiluted *a* sin diluir, puro
undiminished *a* no disminuido, sin disminuir, cabal, íntegro
undimmed *a* no obscurecido, brillante
undiplomatic *a* impolítico, indiscreto
undirected *a* sin dirección; (of letters) sin señas

undiscernible *a* imperceptible, invisible
undiscerning *a* sin percepción, obtuso, sin discernimiento
undisciplined *a* indisciplinado
undisclosed *a* no revelado, secreto
undiscouraged *a* animoso, sin flaquear, sin desaliento
undiscovered *a* no descubierto, ignoto
undiscriminating *a* sin distinción; sin sentido crítico
undisguised *a* sin disfraz; abierto, claro
undismayed *a* intrépido, impávido; sin desaliento
undisposed *a* desinclinado; (of property) no enajenado, no invertido
undisputed *a* incontestable, indisputable
undistinguishable *a* indistinguible
undistinguished *a* (of writers) poco conocido; indistinto; sin distinción
undisturbed *a* sin tocar; tranquilo, sereno, impasible
undivided *a* indiviso, íntegro; junto; completo, entero
undo *vt* anular; reparar; desatar, deshacer; desasir; abrir
undoing *n* anulación, *f*; (reparation) reparación, *f*; (opening) abrir, *m*; ruina, *f*
undomesticated *a* salvaje, no domesticado; poco casero
undone *a* and *part* sin hacer; deshecho; arruinado, perdido. **I am undone!** ¡Estoy perdido! **to come u.,** desatarse. **to leave u.,** dejar sin hacer
undoubted *a* indudable, evidente, incontestable
undoubtedly *adv* sin duda
undramatic *a* no dramático
undreamed *a* no soñado. **u. of,** inopinado, no imaginado
undress *vt* desnudar, desvestir, *Peru* calatear. *vi* desnudarse. *n* traje de casa, *m*; paños menores, *m pl*; *mil* traje de cuartel, *m*
undressed *a* desnudo; en paños menores; (of wounds) sin curar; *com* en rama, en bruto
undrinkable *a* impotable
undue *a* excesivo, indebido; injusto; impropio; (of a bill of exchange) por vencer
undulant *a* ondulante. **u. fever,** fiebre mediterránea, fiebre de Malta, *f*
undulate *vi* ondular, ondear
undulating *a* ondulante
undulation *n* ondulación, undulación, *f*, ondeo, *m*; fluctuación, *f*
undulatory *a* ondulatorio, undoso
unduly *adv* excesivamente, demasiado, indebidamente; injustamente
undutiful *a* desobediente, irrespetuoso
undutifulness *n* desobediencia, falta de respeto, *f*
undying *a* inmortal, imperecedero; eterno
unearned *a* no ganado; inmerecido
unearth *vt* desenterrar; *fig* descubrir, sacar a luz
unearthing *n* desenterramiento, *m*; *fig* descubrimiento, *m*, revelación, *f*
unearthly *a* sobrenatural; misterioso, aterrador, espantoso, *Lat. Am. also* extraterrenal
uneasily *adv* con dificultad; incómodamente; inquietamente
uneasiness *n* malestar, *m*; (discomfort) incomodidad, *f*; (anxiety) inquietud, intranquilidad, *f*, desasosiego, *m*
uneasy *a* incómodo; inseguro; inquieto, intranquilo, desasosegado; aturdido, turbado. **to become u.,** inquietarse
uneatable *a* incomible
uneaten *a* no comido
uneconomical *a* poco económico, costoso, caro
unedifying *a* poco edificante
unedited *a* inédito
uneducated *a* ignorante; ineducado, inculto, indocto
unembarrassed *a* sereno, tranquilo, imperturbable; (financially) sin deudas, acomodado
unemotional *a* frío, impasible
unemployable *a* sin uso, inservible; (of persons) inútil para el trabajo
unemployed *a* sin empleo; (out of work) sin trabajo, parado; desocupado, ocioso; inactivo. *n* paro obrero, *m*. **the u.,** los sin trabajo, los cesantes, los desocupados
unemployment *n* paro forzoso, *m*. **u. benefit,** subvención contra el paro obrero, *f*. **u. insurance,** seguro contra el paro obrero, *m*,
unencumbered *a* libre, independiente; (of estates) libre de gravamen; (untaxable) saneado
unending *a* perpetuo, eterno, sin fin; inacabable, constante, continuo, incesante
unendurable *a* insoportable, insufrible, intolerable
unenlightened *a* ignorante
unenterprising *a* poco emprendedor, tímido
unenthusiastic *a* sin entusiasmo, tibio
unenviable *a* no envidiable
unequal *a* desigual; inferior; (out of proportion) desproporcionado; injusto; insuficiente; incapaz; (of ground) escabroso. **to be u. to the task,** ser incapaz de la tarea; no tener fuerzas para la tarea
unequalled *a* sin igual, incomparable, sin par, único
unequally *adv* desigualmente
unequivocal *a* inequívoco; redondo, claro, franco
unerring *a* infalible; seguro
unerringly *adv* infaliblemente; sin equivocarse
unessential *a* no esencial
uneven *a* desigual; (of roads) escabroso, quebrado; (of numbers) impar; irregular
unevenly *adv* desigualmente
unevenness *n* desigualdad, *f*; desnivel, *m*, irregularidad, *f*. **the unevenness of the terrain,** lo desigual del terreno, lo accidentado del terreno, *m*
uneventful *a* sin incidentes, sin acontecimientos notables; tranquilo
unexaggerated *a* nada exagerado
unexamined *a* no examinado, sin examinar
unexampled *a* sin igual, sin par
unexceptionable *a* intachable, irreprensible; correcto; impecable, perfecto
unexhausted *a* no agotado; inexhausto
unexpected *a* inesperado, imprevisto, inopinado, impensado; repentino, súbito
unexpectedly *adv* inesperadamente; de repente
unexpectedness *n* lo inesperado
unexpired *a* (of bill of exchange) no vencido; (of lease) no caducado
unexplored *a* inexplorado
unexpressed *a* no expresado; tácito, sobrentendido
unexpurgated *a* sin expurgar, completo
unfading *a* inmarcesible, inmarchitable; eterno, inmortal
unfailing *a* inagotable; inexhausto; seguro; indefectible
unfailingly *adv* siempre, constantemente; sin faltar
unfair *a* injusto; vil, bajo, soez; de mala fe, engañoso; (of play) sucio
unfairly *adv* injustamente; de mala fe
unfairness *n* injusticia, *f*; mala fe, *f*
unfaithful *a* infiel; desleal; inexacto, incorrecto. **to be u. to,** ser infiel a; faltar a
unfaithfulness *n* infidelidad, *f*; deslealtad, *f*; inexactitud, *f*
unfaltering *a* sin vacilar; resuelto, firme
unfamiliar *a* poco familiar; desconocido. **to be u. with,** ser ignorante de
unfashionable *a* pasado de moda, fuera de moda; poco elegante
unfashionableness *n* falta de elegancia, *f*
unfashionably *adv* contra la tendencia de la moda; sin elegancia
unfasten *vt* desatar; desabrochar, desenganchar; abrir; aflojar; soltar
unfathomable *a* insondable; impenetrable, inescrutable
unfavorable *a* desfavorable, adverso, contrario
unfavorably *adv* desfavorablemente
unfeathered *a* implume, sin plumas
unfeeling *a* insensible, impasible, frío; duro, cruel
unfeigned *a* sincero, natural, verdadero

unfenced *a* descercado, sin tapia; abierto
unfermented *a* no fermentado;
unfetter *vt* desencadenar, destrabar; poner en libertad, librar
unfilial *a* poco filial, desobediente
unfinished *a* incompleto, inacabado; sin acabar; imperfecto
unfit *a* incapaz; incompetente, inepto; (unsuitable) impropio; (useless) inservible, inadecuado; (unworthy) indigno; (ill) enfermo, malo. *vt* inhabilitar, incapacitar. **u. for human consumption,** impropio para el consumo humano
unfitness *n* incapacidad, *f*; incompetencia, ineptitud, *f*; impropiedad, *f*; falta de mérito, *f*; falta de salud, *f*
unfix *vt* desprender, despegar, descomponer; soltar. **to come unfixed,** desprenderse
unflagging *a* incansable, infatigable; persistente, constante
unflattering *a* poco halagüeño
unflinching *a* inconmovible, resuelto, firme
unfold *vt* desplegar, desdoblar; tender; abrir; (plans) revelar, descubrir; contar, manifestar. *vi* abrirse
unfolding *a* que se abre. *n* despliegue, *m*; revelación, *f*; narración, *f*
unforced *a* libre; espontáneo; fácil; natural
unforeseen *a* imprevisto, inesperado
unforgettable *a* involvidable
unforgivable *a* inexcusable, imperdonable
unforgiving *a* implacable, que no perdona, inexorable
unforgotten *a* no olvidado
unformed *a* informe; rudimentario; inmaturo; (inexperienced) inexperto, sin experiencia
unfortunate *a* desdichado, infortunado, desgraciado, desventurado. *n* desdichado (-da); pobre, *mf*; (prostitute) perdida, *f*
unfortunately *adv* por desdicha, desgraciadamente
unfounded *a* infundado, inmotivado, sin fundamento, injustificado
unframed *a* sin marco
unfrequented *a* poco frecuentado, solitario, retirado, aislado
unfriendliness *n* hostilidad, falta de amistad, frialdad, *f*; hurañía, insociabilidad, *f*
unfriendly *a* hostil, enemigo; (of things, events) perjudicial; huraño, insociable
unfrock *vt* degradar, exclaustrar
unfruitful *a* estéril, infecundo; infructuoso, improductivo, vano
unfulfilled *a* incumplido, sin cumplir; malogrado
unfurl *vt* desplegar; *naut* izar (las velas)
unfurnished *a* desamueblado, sin muebles; desprovisto (de), sin
ungainliness *n* falta de gracia, torpeza, *f*, desgarbo, *m*
ungainly *a* desgarbado
ungallant *a* poco caballeroso, nada galante
ungenerous *a* poco generoso; avaro, tacaño, mezquino; injusto
ungentlemanly *a* poco caballeroso, indigno de un caballero
unglazed *a* sin vidriar; (paper) sin satinar; deslustrado
ungloved *a* sin guante(s)
unglue *vt* desencolar, despegar
ungodliness *n* impiedad, *f*
ungodly *a* impío, irreligioso
ungovernable *a* ingobernable, indomable; irrefrenable
ungraceful *a* desagraciado, desgarbado, sin gracia
ungracious *a* desagradable, poco cortés, desdeñoso
ungraciousness *n* descortesía, aspereza, inurbanidad, *f*
ungrammatical *a* antigramatical, incorrecto
ungrateful *a* ingrato, desagradecido; desagradable, odioso
ungratefulness *n* ingratitud, *f*; lo desagradable
ungrounded *a* infundado; sin motivo
ungrudging *a* no avaro, liberal; generoso, magnánimo
ungrudgingly *adv* de buena gana
unguarded *a* indefenso, sin protección; descuidado; indiscreto, imprudente; sin reflexión
unguided *a* sin guía
unhallowed *a* impío, profano
unhampered *a* desembarazado, libre
unhappily *adv* desafortunadamente, por desgracia
unhappiness *n* infelicidad, desgracia, desdicha, tristeza, *f*
unhappy *a* infeliz, desgraciado, desdichado, triste; (ill-fated) aciago, funesto, malhadado; (remark) inoportuno, inapropiado
unharmed *a* ileso, sano y salvo; (of things) indemne, sin daño
unharness *vt* desaparejar; desenganchar; desarmar
unhealthiness *n* falta de salud, *f*; (of place) insalubridad, *f*
unhealthy *a* enfermizo; malsano, insalubre
unheard *a* no oído; sin ser escuchado; desconocido. **u.-of,** inaudito, no imaginado
unheeding *a* distraído; desatento, sin prestar atención (a); descuidado
unhelpful *a* poco servicial; inútil
unhesitating *a* resuelto, decidido; pronto, inmediato
unhesitatingly *adv* sin vacilar
unhinge *vt* desgoznar, desquiciar; (of the mind) trastornar
unhitch *vt* desenganchar; descolgar
unholy *a* impío, sacrílego
unhonored *a* sin que se reconociese sus méritos; despreciado; (check) protestado
unhook *vt* desenganchar; desabrochar; descolgar
unhoped-for *a* inesperado
unhurt *a* ileso, incólume, sano y salvo; (of things) sin daño
unicellular *a* unicelular
unicolored *a* unicolor
unicorn *n* unicornio, *m*
unidentified *a* no reconocido, no identificado
unification *n* unificación, *f*
uniform *a* uniforme; igual, constante, invariable; homogéneo. *n* uniforme, *m*. **in full u.,** de gran uniforme. **to make u.,** uniformar, igualar, hacer uniforme
uniformity *n* uniformidad, igualdad, *f*
uniformly *adv* uniformemente
unify *vt* unificar; unir
unilateral *a* unilateral
unimaginable *a* inimaginable, no imaginable
unimaginative *a* sin imaginación
unimpaired *a* no disminuido; sin alteración; intacto, entero; sin menoscabo
unimpeachable *a* irreprochable, intachable
unimportance *n* no importancia, insignificancia, trivialidad, *f*
unimportant *a* sin importancia, nada importante, insignificante, trivial, *Lat. Am. also* intrascendente
unimpressive *a* poco impresionante; nada conmovedor; (of persons) insignificante
uninflammable *a* no inflamable, incombustible
uninfluenced *a* no afectado (por), libre (de)
uninformed *a* ignorante
uninhabitable *a* inhabitable
uninhabited *a* deshabitado, inhabitado, vacío, desierto
uninjured *a* ileso; sin daño
uninspired *a* sin inspiración; pedestre, mediocre
uninstructive *a* nada instructivo
uninsured *a* no asegurado
unintelligent *a* nada inteligente, corto de alcances, tonto
unintelligibility *n* incomprensibilidad, *f*, lo ininteligible
unintelligible *a* ininteligible, incomprensible
unintentional *a* involuntario, inadvertido
unintentionally *adv* sin querer, involuntariamente
uninterested *a* no interesado, despreocupado
uninteresting *a* sin interés, poco interesante, soso

uninterrupted *a* ininterrum pido, sin interrupción; continuo, incesante
uninvited *a* no invitado, no convidado, sin invitación; (unlooked-for) no buscado
uninviting *a* poco atrayente; inhospitalario
union *n* unión, *f*; *mech* manguito de unión, *m*; conexión, *f*; (poverty) asociación, *f*; (of trade) gremio de oficios, *m*; sindicato (obrero), *m*; (workhouse) asilo, *m*; (U.S.A.) Estados Unidos de América, *m pl*
unionism *n* unionismo, *m*
unionist *n pol* unionista, *mf*
unique *a* único, sin igual, sin par
uniqueness *n* unicidad, *f*; lo singular
unisexual *a* unisexual
unison *n* unisonancia, *f*. **in u.,** al unísono
unit *n* unidad, *f*. **u. bookcase,** librería en secciones, *f*
Unitarian *a* and *n* unitario (-ia)
Unitarianism *n* unitarismo, *m*
unite *vt* unir, juntar; combinar, incorporar; (of countries) unificar; (of energies, etc.) reunir. *vi* unirse, juntarse; reunirse, concertarse; convenirse
united *a* unido; junto. **the U. Nations,** las Naciones Unidas, *f pl*
unitedly *adv* unidamente; armoniosamente, de acuerdo
United States of America los Estados Unidos de Norteamérica, *m pl*
unity *n* unidad, *f*; *math* la unidad; unión, *f*; conformidad, armonía, *f*. **the three unities,** las tres unidades
universal *a* universal; general; común. **to make u.,** universalizar, generalizar. **u. joint,** junta universal, *f*; *aut* cardán, *m*
universalize *vt* universalizar
universe *n* universo, *m*; creación, *f*, mundo, *m*
university *n* universidad, *f*. *a* universitario. **u. degree,** grado universitario, *m*
unjust *a* injusto
unjustifiable *a* injustificable, indisculpable, inexcusable
unjustifiably *adv* injustificadamente, inexcusablemente
unjustly *adv* injustamente, sin razón
unkempt *a* despeinado; desaseado, sucio
unkind *a* nada bondadoso, nada amable; poco complaciente; duro, cruel; desfavorable, nada propicio
unkindly *adv* sin bondad; con dureza, cruelmente
unkindness *n* falta de bondad, *f*; severidad, crueldad, dureza, *f*, rigor, *m*; acto de crueldad, *m*
unknowable *a* impenetrable, incomprehensible, insondable
unknowingly *adv* sin querer, involuntariamente; sin saberlo; insensiblemente
unknown *a* ignoto, desconocido; *math* incógnito. *n* lo desconocido, misterio, *m*; *math* incógnita, *f*; (person) desconocido (-da), forastero (-ra). *math* **u. quantity,** incógnita, *f*
unlabeled *a* sin etiqueta
unlace *vt* desenlazar; desatar
unladylike *a* indigno (or impropio) de una dama; vulgar, ordinario, cursi
unlamented *a* no llorado, no lamentado
unlatch *vt* alzar el pestillo de, abrir
unlawful *a* ilegal, ilícito
unlawfulness *n* ilegalidad, *f*
unlearn *vt* olvidar, desaprender
unleash *vt* soltar
unleavened *a* ázimo, sin levadura
unless *conjunc* a no ser que, a menos que, como no, si no (all followed by subjunc.); salvo, excepto, con excepción de
unlicensed *a* no autorizado, sin licencia
unlike *a* disímil, desemejante; distinto, diferente. *prep* a distinción de, a diferencia de, al contrario de. **They are quite u.,** No se parecen nada
unlikeliness *n* improbabilidad, *f*
unlikely *a* improbable, inverosímil; arriesgado
unlikeness *n* desemejanza, diferencia, *f*
unlimited *a* ilimitado, infinito, inmenso; sin restricción; excesivo, exagerado. **unlimited telephone,** teléfono no medido (Argentina)
unlined *a* no forrado, sin forro; sin rayas; (of face) sin arrugas
unlit *a* no iluminado, oscuro, sin luz
unload *vt* descargar; aligerar; *naut* hondear; (of shares) deshacerse de. *vi* descargar
unloading *n* descarga, *f*, descargue, *m*
unlock *vt* desencerrar, abrir; *fig* revelar, descubrir
unlooked-for *a* inopinado, inesperado
unloose *vt* desatar; soltar; poner en libertad
unlovable *a* indigno del querer; antipático, poco amable; repugnante
unloveliness *n* falta de hermosura, fealdad, *f*
unlovely *a* nada hermoso, feo; desagradable
unluckily *adv* desafortunadamente, por desgracia
unluckiness *n* mala suerte, *f*; (unsuitability) inoportunidad, *f*; lo nefasto, lo malo
unlucky *a* de mala suerte; desdichado, desgraciado, infeliz; (ill-omened) funesto, nefasto, fatal; inoportuno, inconveniente
unmanageable *a* indomable, indócil; ingobernable, inmanejable; (unwieldy) difícil de manejar, pesado
unmannerliness *n* mala crianza, descortesía, *f*
unmannerly *a* mal educado, descortés
unmarketable *a* invendible
unmarriageable *a* incasable
unmarried *a* soltero, célibe
unmask *vt* desenmascarar; *fig* quitar la careta (a). *vi* quitarse la máscara; *fig* quitarse la careta, descubrirse
unmeaning *a* sin sentido, vacío, sin significación
unmelodious *a* sin melodía, discorde
unmendable *a* incomponible
unmentionable *a* que no se puede mencionar; indigno de mencionarse
unmerciful *a* sin piedad, sin compasión; cruel, despiadado, duro
unmerited *a* inmerecido, desmerecido
unmethodical *a* poco metódico
unmindful *a* olvidadizo; desatento; negligente. **u. of,** sin pensar en, olvidando
unmistakable *a* inequívoco; manifiesto, evidente, indudable
unmistakably *adv* indudablemente
unmitigated *a* no mitigado; completo, absoluto; (of rogue) redomado
unmixed *a* sin mezcla; puro, sencillo; (free) limpio
unmoor *vt* desamarrar
unmoral *a* amoral, no moral; sin fin didáctico
unmounted *a* desmontado
unmoved *a* fijo; (unemotional) impasible, frío; (determined) firme, inflexible, inexorable
unmuffle *vt* desembozar, descubrir
unmusical *a* sin afición a la música; sin oído (para la música); inarmónico
unnamable *a* que no se puede nombrar, innominable
unnatural *a* desnaturalizado; (of vices, etc.) contra natural; innatural; (of style) rebuscado; artificial; inhumano, cruel
unnaturalness *n* lo monstruoso; lo innatural; artificialidad, *f*; inhumanidad, *f*
unnavigable *a* innavegable, no navegable
unnecessarily *adv* inútilmente, innecesariamente, sin necesidad
unnecessariness *n* inutilidad, *f*; superfluidad, *f*; lo innecesario
unnecessary *a* innecesario, superfluo, inútil
unneighborly *a* de mala vecindad, impropio de vecinos, poco servicial
unnerve *vt* acobardar quitar el valor, desanimar
unnoticed *a* inadvertido, no observado
unobjectionable *a* *Lat. Am.* inobjetable
unobliging *a* nada servicial

unobservable *a* inobservable
unobservant *a* inobservante
unobserved *a* sin ser notado, desapercibido
unobtainable *a* inalcanzable, inasequible
unobstructed *a* no obstruido; sin obstáculos; libre
unobtrusive *a* discreto, modesto
unobtrusiveness *n* discreción, modestia, *f*
unoccupied *a* (at leisure) desocupado, ocioso, sin ocupación; vacío, vacante, libre; (untenanted) deshabitado
unofficial *a* no oficial
unopened *a* sin abrir, cerrado; (of exhibitions, etc.) no inaugurado
unopposed *a* sin oposición
unorganized *a* inorganizado; *biol* inorgánico
unoriginal *a* poco original
unorthodox *a* heterodoxo
unostentatious *a* sencillo, modesto, sin ostentación
unostentatiousness *n* sencillez, modestia, falta de ostentación, *f*
unpack *vt* desempaquetar; (trunks) vaciar; (bales) desembalar. *vi* desempaquetar; deshacer las maletas
unpacking *n* desembalaje, *m*
unpaid *a* sin pagar, no pagado, *Lat. Am. also* impago
unpalatable *a* de mal sabor; desagradable
unparalleled *a* sin paralelo, sin par, sin igual
unpardonable *a* imperdonable, inexcusable, irremisible
unparliamentary *a* poco parliamentario
unpatriotic *a* antipatriótico
unpaved *a* sin empedrar
unperceived *a* inadvertido, sin ser notado
unperturbed *a* impasible, sin alterarse, sereno
unpleasant *a* desagradable, desapacible; ofensivo; (troublesome) enfadoso, molesto
unpleasantly *adv* desagradablemente
unpleasantness *n* lo desagradable; disgusto, sinsabor, *m*; (disagreement) disputa, riña, *f*
unpleasing *a* nada placentero; desagradable, sin atractivos
unplug *vt* desenchufar
unpolished *a* sin pulir, tosco, mate; *fig* inculto, cerril. **u. diamond,** diamante en bruto, *m*
unpolluted *a* impoluto, incontaminado; puro, sin pervertir
unpopular *a* impopular
unpopularity *n* impopularidad, *f*
unpractical *a* impracticable, imposible; (of persons) sin sentido práctico
unpracticed *a* no practicado; inexperto, inhábil
unpraiseworthy *a* inmeritorio
unprecedented *a* sin precedente, inaudito
unprejudiced *a* sin prejuicios, imparcial
unpremeditated *a* sin premeditación, indeliberado, impremeditado
unprepared *a* sin preparación, no preparado; desprevenido; desapercibido (unready)
unpreparedness *n* falta de preparación, imprevisión, *f*, desapercibimiento, *m*
unprepossessing *a* poco atrayente, antipático
unpresentable *a* impresentable
unpretentious *a* sin pretensiones, modesto
unpriced *a* sin precio
unprincipled *a* sin consciencia, sin escrúpulos
unprinted *a* sin imprimir, no impreso
unprocurable *a* inalcanzable, inasequible
unproductive *a* improductivo; infructuoso, estéril
unproductiveness *n* infructuosidad, *f*; esterilidad, *f*
unprofessional *a* sin profesión; contrario a la ética profesional
unprofitable *a* improductivo, infructuoso; sin provecho; inútil; nada lucrativo
unprogressive *a* reaccionario
unpromising *a* poco halagüeño
unpronounceable *a* impronunciable
unpropitious *a* desfavorable, nada propicio, nada halagüeño
unprosperous *a* impróspero
unprotected *a* sin protección; (of persons) indefenso, desválido
unproved *a* no probado, sin demostrar
unprovided *a* desapercibido, desprovisto. **u. for,** sin provisión (para); sin medios de vida, desamparado
unprovoked *a* no provocado, sin provocación; sin motivo
unpublished *a* inédito, no publicado, sin publicar
unpunctual *a* no puntual, retrasado
unpunctuality *n* falta de puntualidad, *f*, retraso, *m*
unpunctually *adv* sin puntualidad, tarde, con retraso
unpunishable *a* no punible
unpunished *a* impune, sin castigo
unpurchasable *a* que no puede comprarse
unqualified *a* incapaz, incompetente; (with professions) sin título; (downright) incondicional, absoluto
unquenchable *a* inextinguible, inapagable; insaciable
unquestionable *a* indiscutible, indudable, indubitable
unquestionably *adv* indudablemente
unquiet *a* inquieto, intranquilo; agitado
unravel *vt* deshilar; destejer; (a mystery, etc.) desentrañar, desembrollar, descifrar
unraveling *n* deshiladura, *f*; aclaración, *f*
unreadable *a* ilegible
unreadiness *n* falta de preparación, *f*, desapercibimiento, *m*; lentitud, *f*
unready *a* desapercibido, desprevenido; lento
unreal *a* irreal; falso, imaginario, ilusorio; ficticio; artificial; insincero, hipócrita; ideal; incorpóreo
unreality *n* irrealidad, *f*; falsedad, *f*; artificialidad, *f*; lo quimérico
unreasonable *a* irrazonable, irracional; disparatado, extravagante; (with price, etc.) exorbitante, excesivo
unreasonableness *n* irracionalidad, *f*; exorbitancia, *f*
unreasonably *adv* irracionalmente
unreasoning *a* irracional; sin motivo, sin causa
unreceipted *a* sin recibo
unrecognizable *a* que no puede reconocerse; imposible de reconocer
unrecognized *a* no reconocido
unreconciled *a* no resignado, no reconciliado
unrectified *a* no corregido, sin rectificar
unredeemed *a* no redimido; no mitigado; (of pledges) sin desempeñar
unrefined *a* no refinado, impuro; inculto, grosero
unreformed *a* no reformado
unrefuted *a* no refutado
unregenerate *a* no regenerado
unregretted *a* no llorado, sin lamentar
unrehearsed *a* sin preparación; *theat* sin ensayar; (extempore) improvisado
unrelated *a* inconexo; (of persons) sin parentesco
unrelenting *a* implacable, inflexible, inexorable
unreliability *n* incertidumbre, *f*; el no poder confiar en, informalidad, inestabilidad, *f*
unreliable *a* incierto, dudoso, indigno de confianza; (of persons) informal
unrelieved *a* no aliviado; absoluto, complete, total
unremitting *a* incansable
unremunerative *a* sin remuneración, no remunerado
unrepealed *a* vigente
unrepentant *a* impenitente
unrepresentative *a* poco representativo
unrepresented *a* sin representación
unrequited *a* no correspondido
unreserved *a* no reservado; expresivo, comunicativo, expansivo, franco
unreservedly *adv* sin reserva; con toda franqueza
unresisting *a* sin oponer resistencia
unresolved *a* sin resolverse, vacilante; incierto, dudoso, inseguro; sin solución
unresponsive *a* flemático; insensible, sordo
unresponsiveness *n* flema, *f*; insensibilidad, *f*

unrest *n* desasosiego, *m*, agitación, inquietud, *f*
unrestful *a* agitado, inquieto, intranquilo
unrestrained *a* desenfrenado; ilimitado, sin límites; sin reserva
unrestricted *a* sin restricción; ilimitado
unrevealed *a* no revelado, por descubrir, no descubierto
unrewarded *a* sin premio, no recompensado
unrighteous *a* injusto, malo, perverso
unrighteousness *n* injusticia, *f*; maldad, perversidad, *f*
unripe *a* verde, inmaturo
unripeness *n* falta de madurez, *f*
unrivaled *a* sin igual, sin par
unroll *vt* desarrollar. *vi* desarrollarse; (unfold) desplegarse (a la vista)
unromantic *a* poco (or nada) romántico
unruffled *a* sereno, plácido, ecuánime; no arrugado; (of hair) liso
unruliness *n* turbulencia, indisciplina, *f*; insubordinación, rebeldía, *f*
unruly *a* ingobernable, revoltoso; refractario, rebelde; (of hair) indomable
unsaddle *vt* desensillar; derribar (del caballo, etc.)
unsafe *a* inseguro; peligroso; arriesgado; (to eat) nocivo
unsafeness *n* inseguridad, *f*; peligro, riesgo, *m*
unsaid *a* sin decir, no dicho
unsalable *a* invendible
unsalaried *a* no asalariado
unsalted *a* soso, sin sal
unsanitary *a* antihigiénico
unsatisfactoriness *n* lo insatisfactorio
unsatisfactory *a* poco (or nada) satisfactorio; no aceptable
unsatisfied *a* no satisfecho; descontento; no convencido; (hungry) no harto; *com* no saldado
unsatisfying *a* que no satisface
unsavoriness *n* insipidez, *f*, mal sabor, *m*; lo desagradable; sordidez, suciedad, *f*
unsavory *a* insípido, de mal sabor; desagradable; sórdido, sucio
unscalable *a* inascendible, virgen
unscathed *a* sin daño, ileso
unscented *a* sin perfume, sin olor, no fragante
unscholarly *a* nada erudito; indigno de un erudito
unscientific *a* no científico
unscrew *vt* destornillar, *Lat. Am.* desenroscar. *vi* destornillarse
unscrewing *n* destornillamiento, *m*
unscrupulous *a* sin escrúpulos, poco escrupuloso, desaprensivo
unscrupulousness *n* falta de escrúpulos, desaprensión, *f*
unseal *vt* desellar, romper (*or* quitar) el sello (de)
unseasonable *a* intempestivo, fuera de sazón; inoportuno, inconveniente. **at an u. hour,** a una hora inconveniente, a deshora
unseasonableness *n* lo intempestivo, inoportunidad, *f*
unseasonably *adv* intempestivamente; a deshora; inoportunamente
unseasoned *a cul* sin sazonar, soso; (wood) verde; no maduro, sin madurar
unseat *vt* (from horse) tirar, echar al suelo; *pol* desituir
unseaworthy *a* innavegable
unseemliness *n* falta de decoro, *f*; indecencia, *f*
unseemly *a* indecoroso, indigno; indecente; impropio
unseen *a* no visto, invisible; inadvertido; secreto, oculto. *n* versión al libro abierto, *f*. **the u.,** lo invisible
unselfish *a* desinteresado, abnegado, nada egoísta; generoso
unselfishness *n* abnegación, *f*; desinterés, *m*; generosidad, *f*
unsentimental *a* no sentimental
unserviceable *a* inservible, inútil, que no sirve para nada, sin utilidad.
unsettle *vt* desarreglar; desorganizar; hacer inseguro; agitar, perturbar
unsettled *a* inconstante, variable; *com* pendiente, sin pagar; incierto; sin resolver; (of estates) sin solucionar
unshackle *vt* desencadenar
unshakable *a* inconmovible, firme
unshapely *a* desproporcionado
unshaven *a* sin afeitar
unsheathe *vt* desenvainar, sacar
unsheltered *a* desabrigado, desamparado; no protegido, sin protección; (of places) sin abrigo, expuesto; (from) sin defensa contra
unship *vt* desembarcar; (the oars) desarmar
unshod *a* descalzo; (of a horse) sin herraduras
unshorn *a* sin esquilar; intonso
unshrinkable *a* que no se encoge
unshrinking *a* intrépido; resoluto, sin vacilar
unsightly *a* feo, horrible, repugnante, antiestético
unsinkable *a* insumergible
unskilled *a* inexperto, inhábil, imperito, torpe
unsmokable *a* (of tobacco) infumable
unsociability *n* insociabilidad, hurañía, esquivez, *f*
unsociable *a* insociable, huraño, esquivo, arisco
unsocial *a* insocial, antisocial
unsold *a* no vendido, sin vender
unsolder *vt* desoldar, desestañar
unsoldierly *a* indigno de un soldado; poco marcial
unsophisticated *a* ingenuo, inocente, cándido
unsought *a* no solicitado; no buscado
unsound *a* enfermo; defectuoso; (rotten) podrido; (fallacious) erróneo, poco convincente; (of persons) informal, indigno de confianza; (of religious views) heterodoxo. **of u. mind,** insano
unsoundness *n* lo defectuoso; mal estado, *m*; falsedad, *f*; informalidad, *f*; heterodoxia, *f*
unsparing *a* severo, implacable; generoso, pródigo
unspeakable *a* indecible, inefable; que no puede mencionarse, horrible
unspecified *a* no especificado
unspoilt *a* intacto; ileso, indemne; no corrompido; no estropeado; (of children) no mimado
unspoken *a* no pronunciado
unsportsmanlike *a* indigno de un cazador; indigno de un deportista; nada caballeroso. **to play in an u. way,** jugar sucio
unstable *a* inestable; variable; inconstante; vacilante, irresoluto
unstained *a* no manchado; no teñido; inmaculado, sin mancha
unstamped *a* sin sello; no sellado
unstatesmanlike *a* impropio (*or* indigno) de un hombre de estado
unsteadiness *n* inestabilidad, falta de firmeza, *f*; inconstancia, *f*
unsteady *a* inestable, inseguro; inconstante
unstick *vt* desapegar
unstitch *vt* desapuntar
unstressed *a* sin énfasis; (of syllables) sin acento
unstudied *a* no estudiado; natural, espontáneo
unsubstantial *a* insubstancial; ligero; irreal, imaginario; incorpóreo; aparente
unsuccessful *a* sin éxito; infructuoso. **to be u.,** no tener éxito
unsuccessfully *adv* en vano, sin éxito
unsuitability *n* impropiedad, *f*; inconveniencia, incongruencia, *f*; incapacidad, *f*; inoportunidad, *f*
unsuitable *a* inapropiado; inconveniente; impropio; inservible; incapaz; inoportuno
unsung *a* no cantado; no celebrado en verso
unsupported *a* sin apoyo; sin defensa; no favorecido
unsurmountable *a* insuperable, infranqueable
unsurpassable *a* inmejorable, insuperable
unsurpassed *a* sin par
unsuspecting *a* no suspicaz, confiado, no receloso
unswerving *a* directo; sin vacilar, constante
unsymmetrical *a* asimétrico
unsympathetic *a* indiferente, incompasivo; antipático
unsystematic *a* sin sistema, asistemático, no metódico

untalented *a* sin talento
untamed *a* indomado, cerril, bravío, no domesticado; desenfrenado, violento. **u. horse** *Lat. Am.* bellaco, *m*
unteach *vt* desenseñar
untenable *a* insostenible
untenanted *a* desalquilado, deshabitado; vacío, desierto
unthankful *a* ingrato, desagradecido
unthinkable *a* inconcebible; imposible
unthinking *a* sin reflexión; desatento; indiscreto
unthinkingly *adv* sin pensar
unthread *vt* deshebrar
untidily *adv* en desorden, sin aseo
untidiness *n* desorden, *m*; desaseo, desaliño, *m*; falta de pulcritud, *f*
untidy *a* desarreglado; desaseado; abandonado; en desorden, sin concierto
untie *vt* desatar, desanudar; (knots) deshacer
until *prep* hasta. *conjunc* hasta que. (The subjunc. is required in clauses referring to future time, e.g. **No venga usted hasta que le avise yo,** Don't come until I tell you. In clauses referring to past or present time the indicative is generally used, e.g. **No la reconocí hasta que se volvió,** I didn't recognize her until she turned round)
untilled *a* sin cultivar
untimeliness *n* inoportunidad, *f*; lo prematuro
untimely *a* inoportuno, intempestivo; prematuro
untiring *a* incansable, infatigable
unto *prep* hacia
untold *a* no revelado; no narrado; sin decir, no dicho; incalculable
untouchable *a* que no puede tocarse, intangible; (of castes) intocable
untouched *a* sin tocar; intacto, incólume
untrained *a* indisciplinado; inexperto; no adiestrado
untranslatable *a* intraducible
untraveled *a* no frecuentado; (of persons) provinciano
untried *a* no experimentado. **u. knight,** caballero novel, *m*
untrodden *a* no hollado, no frecuentado; inexplorado, virgen
untroubled *a* tranquilo, sosegado
untrue *a* mentiroso, falso, engañoso; ficticio, imaginario; traidor, desleal; infiel
untrustworthiness *n* incertidumbre, inseguridad, *f*; (of persons) informalidad, *f*
untrustworthy *a* indigno de confianza; incierto, dudoso; desleal
untruth *n* mentira, falsedad, *f*; ficción, *f*
untruthful *a* mentiroso; falso
untruthfulness *n* falsedad, *f*
untwist *vt* destorcer
unused *a* no empleado; desacostumbrado; inusitado; (postage stamp) sin sellar
unusual *a* fuera de lo común, desacostumbrado; extraño, raro, peregrino, extraordinario
unusually *adv* excepcionalmente; infrecuentemente
unusualness *n* lo insólito; rareza, *f*
unutterable *a* indecible, inexpresable
unvarnished *a* sin barnizar; *fig* sencillo
unvarying *a* invariable, constante, uniforme
unveil *vt* quitar el velo; (memorial) descubrir; *fig* revelar. *vi* quitarse el velo; revelarse, quitarse la careta
unventilated *a* sin ventilación; sin aire, ahogado; (of topics) no discutido
unverifiable *a* que no puede verificarse
unverified *a* sin verificar
unvisited *a* no visitado; no frecuentado
unvoiced *a* no expresado
unwanted *a* no deseado; superfluo, de más
unwarlike *a* nada marcial, pacífico
unwarranted *a* sin garantía; inexcusable, injustificable
unwary *a* incauto, imprudente
unwashed *a* sin lavar; sucio
unwatched *a* no vigilado
unwavering *a* resuelto, firme; inexorable; (gaze) fijo
unwaveringly *adv* sin vacilar; inexorablemente
unwearied *a* incansable; infatigable
unwelcome *a* mal acogido; inoportuno; desagradable
unwell *a* indispuesto
unwholesome *a* malsano, nocivo, insalubre
unwholesomeness *n* insalubridad, *f*
unwieldiness *n* pesadez, dificultad de manejarse, *f*
unwieldy *a* pesado, abultado, difícil de manejar
unwilling *a* desinclinado, reluctante
unwillingly *adv* de mala gana
unwillingness *n* falta de inclinación, repugnancia, *f*
unwind *vt* desenvolver; (thread) desdevanar, desovillar. *vi* desarrollarse; desdevanarse
unwise *a* imprudente, indiscreto, incauto; (lacking wisdom) tonto
unwisely *adv* imprudentemente, indiscretamente
unwitting *a* inconsciente
unwittingly *adv* sin darse cuenta
unwomanly *a* poco femenino
unwonted *a* insólito, inusitado
unworkable *a* impráctico
unworkmanlike *a* chapucero, charanguero
unworldly *a* poco, mundano, espiritual
unworn *a* sin llevar, nuevo
unworthiness *n* indignidad, *f*
unworthy *a* indigno
unwounded *a* no herido, sin herida, ileso
unwrap *vt* desenvolver, desempapelar
unwritten *a* no escrito. **u. law,** ley consuetudinaria, *f*
unyielding *a* duro, firme; (of persons) inflexible, terco, resuelto, obstinado
unyoke *vt* desuncir, quitar el yugo
up *adv* (high) arriba, en alto; (higher) hacia arriba; (out of bed) levantado; (standing) de pie; (finished) concluido, terminado; (of time) llegado; (excited) agitado; (rebellious) sublevado; (of sun, etc.) salido; (come or gone up) subido; (of universities) en residencia; (for discussion) bajo consideración; (abreast of) al lado, al nivel; (incapable) incapaz, incompetente; (ill) enfermo, indispuesto. **"Up,"** (on elevators) «Para subir.» (For various idiomatic uses of **up** after verbs, see verbs themselves.) *a* (in a few expressions only) ascendente. *prep* en lo alto de; hacia arriba de; a lo largo de; (with country) en el interior de; (with current) contra. **to be up in arms,** sublevarse, rebelarse. **to be very hard up,** ser muy pobre, estar a la cuarta pregunta. **to drink up,** beberlo todo. **to go or come up,** subir. **to lay up,** acumular. **to speak up,** hablar en voz alta. **He has something up his sleeve,** Tiene algo en la manga. **It is all up,** Todo se acabó, Mi gozo en el pozo. **It is not up to much,** Vale muy poco; No es muy fuerte. **It is up to you,** Tú dirás, Tú harás lo que te parezca. **What is he up to?** ¿Qué está tramando? **What's up?** ¿Qué pasa? ¿Qué hay? **up and down,** *adv* bajando y subiendo, de arriba abajo; de un lado a otro; por todas partes. **up-and-down,** *a* fluctuante; (of roads) undulante; (of life) accidentado, borrascoso. **ups and downs,** vicisitudes, *f pl,* altibajos, *m pl.* **upgrade,** subida, *f.* **up in,** versado en, perito en. **well up in,** fuerte en. **up North,** al norte; en el norte; hacia el norte. **up there,** allí arriba, allí en lo alto. **up to,** hasta; (aware) al corriente de, informado de. **up to date,** *adv* hasta la fechą. **up-to-date,** *a* de última moda; al día. **up to now,** hasta ahora. **up train,** tren ascendente. **Up with . . . !** ¡Arriba! **Up you go!** (to children) ¡Upa!
upbraid *vt* reprender, echar en cara
upbringing *n* crianza, educación, *f*
upcountry *n* tierra adentro, *f*; lo interior (de un país). *a* de tierra adentro, del interior. *adv* tierra adentro, hacia el interior
update *vt* actualizar, poner al día
upheaval *n* solevantamiento, *m*; trastorno, *m*
uphill *a* ascendente; penoso, fatigoso, difícil. *adv* cuesta arriba, pecho arriba
uphold *vt* sostener, apoyar; (help) ayudar, consolar;

(protect) defender; (countenance) aprobar; *law* confirmar
upholder *n* sostenedor (-ra), defensor (-ra)
upholster *vt* entapizar, tapizar
upholsterer *n* tapicero, *m*
upholstery *n* tapicería, *f*; (of car) almohadillado, *m*
upkeep *n* mantenimiento, *m*, conservación, *f*
upland *n* tierra alta, *f*, *a* alto, elevado
uplift *vt* elevar. *n* elevación, *f*; *inf* fervor, *m*
upon *prep*. See **on**
upper *a comp* superior; alto; de arriba. *n* (of shoe) pala, *f*, *sport* **u.-cut,** golpe de abajo arriba, upper-cut, *m*. **U. Egypt,** Alto Egipto, *m*. **u. hand,** dominio, *m*; superioridad, ventaja, *f*. **u. house,** cámara alta, *f*; senado, *m*. **u. ten,** los diez primeros
upper classes *a* clases altas, capas altas, *f pl*
uppermost *a* más alto, más elevado; predominante, principal; más fuerte. *adv* en primer lugar; en lo más alto. **to be u.,** predominar
upright *a* recto, derecho; vertical; (honorable) honrado, digno, recto. *n* (stanchion) mástil, soporte, palo derecho, montante, *m*. *adv* en pie; derecho
uprightly *adv* rectamente, honradamente
uprightness *n* rectitud, honradez, probidad, *f*
uprising *n* insurrección, sublevación, *f*
uproar *n* alboroto, tumulto, estrépito, *m*, conmoción, *f*
uproarious *a* tumultuoso, estrepitoso
uproot *vt* desarraigar, *Lat. Am.* destroncar; *fig* arrancar; (destroy) extirpar
uprooting *n* desarraigo, *m*; arranque, *m*; extirpación, *f*
upset *vt* volcar; (overthrow) derribar, echar abajo; (frustrate) contrariar; desarreglar; (distress) trastornar, turbar; (of food) hacer mal. *vi* volcarse. *n* vuelco, *m*; trastorno, *m*. **u. price,** tipo de subasta, *m*
upsetting *a* turbante, inquietante
upshot *n* resultado, *m*; consecuencia, *f*
upside *n* lado superior, *m*; parte superior, *f*; (of trains) andén ascendente, *m*. **u. down,** al revés, de arriba abajo; en desorden
upstairs *adv* arriba, en el piso de arriba; (with go or come) al piso de arriba
upstanding *a* gallardo, guapo. **an u. young man (woman),** un buen mozo (una buena moza)
upstart *n* arribista, *mf*; advenedizo (-za), insolente, *mf*; presuntuoso (-sa)
upstream *a* and *adv* contra la corriente, agua arriba, río arriba
upturned *a* (of noses) respingada
upward *a* ascendente, hacia arriba
upwards *adv* hacia arriba; en adelante. **u. of,** más de
Urals, the los Urales, *m pl*
uranium *n min* uranio, *m*
Uranus *n ast* Urano, *m*
urban *a* urbano, ciudadano
urban renewal *n* renovación urbana, renovación urbanística, *f*
urbane *a* cortés, urbano, fino
urbanity *n* urbanidad, cortesía, finura, *f*
urbanization *n* urbanización, *f*
urbanize *vt* urbanizar
urchin *n* galopín, granuja, pilluelo, *m*
ureter *n anat* uréter, *m*
urethra *n anat* uretra, *f*
urge *vt* empujar, impeler; incitar, estimular, azuzar, animar; pedir con urgencia, recomendar con ahínco, instar, insistir (en). *n* instinto, impulso, *m*; deseo, *m*; ambición, *f*
urgency *n* urgencia, *f*; importancia, perentoriedad, *f*
urgent *a* urgente; importante, apremiante, perentorio. **to be u.,** urgir
urgently *adv* urgentemente
uric *a* úrico
urinal *n* orinal, urinario, *m*
urinalysis *n* análisis de orina, urinálisis, *m*
urinary *a* urinario
urinary tract *n* conducto urinario, *m*, vías urinarias, *f pl*
urinate *vi* orinar
urine *n* orín, *m*
urn *n* urna, *f*; (for coffee) cafetera, *f*; (for tea) tetera, *f*
Ursa *n ast* osa, *f*. **U. Major,** osa mayor, *f*. **U. Minor,** osa menor, *f*
urticaria *n med* urticaria, *f*
Uruguayan *a* and *n* uruguayo (-ya)
us *pron* nos; (with prep.) nosotros. **He came toward us,** Vino hacia nosotros
usable *a* aprovechable, servible
usage *n* (handling) tratamiento, *m*; uso, *m*, costumbre, *f*
use *n* uso, *m*; manejo, empleo, *m*; (custom) costumbre práctica, *f*; (need) necesidad, *f*; (usefulness) aprovechamiento, *m*; *law* usufructo, *m*. **directions for use,** direcciones para el uso, *f pl*, **for the use of . . .,** para uso de . . . **in use,** en uso. **out of use,** anticuado; fuera de moda. **to be of no use,** no servir; ser inútil. **to have no use for,** no tener necesidad de; *inf* tener en poco. **to make use of,** servirse de, aprovechar; *law* ejercer. **to put to use,** poner en uso, poner en servicio
use *vt* usar; (employ) emplear; (utilize) servirse de, utilizar; (handle) manejar; hacer uso de; (consume) gastar, consumir; (treat) tratar; practicar. **to use up,** agotar, acabar con; consumir. *vi impers* acostumbrar, soler (e.g. **It used to happen that . . . ,** Solía ocurrir que . . .). (**Used to** and the verb which follows are often translated simply by the imperfect tense of the following verb, e.g. **I used to see her every day,** La veía todos los días. Use of the verbs **acostumbrar** or **soler** to translate used to adds emphasis to the statement)
used *a* and *past part* acostumbrado, habituado; empleado; (clothes) usado; (postage stamp) sellado. **to become u. to,** acostumbrarse a
useful *a* útil; provechoso; servicial
usefully *adv* útilmente; con provecho
usefulness *n* utilidad, *f*; valor, *m*
useless *a* inútil; vano, infructuoso. **to render u.,** inutilizar
uselessness *n* inutilidad, *f*
user *n* el, *m*, (*f*, la) que usa, comprador (-ra)
usher *n* ujier, *m*; (in a theater) acomodador (-ra). *vt* introducir, anunciar; acomodar
usual *a* usual, acostumbrado, habitual; normal, común. **as u.,** como siempre. **in the u. form,** *com* al usado; como de costumbre. **with their usual courtesy,** con la cortesía que les es característica
usually *adv* por lo general, ordinariamente. **We u. go out on Sundays,** Acostumbramos salir los domingos
usurer *n* usurero (-ra)
usurious *a* usurario
usurp *vt* usurpar; asumir, arrogarse
usurpation *n* usurpación, *f*; arrogación, *f*
usurper *n* usurpador (-ra)
usurping *a* usurpador
usury *n* usura, *f*. **to practice u.,** usurear, dar (or tomar) a usura
utensil *n* utensilio, instrumento, *m*; herramienta, *f*. **kitchen utensils,** batería de cocina, *f*
uterine *a med* uterino
uterus *n* útero, *m*
utilitarian *a* utilitario
utilitarianism *n* utilitarismo, *m*
utility *n* utilidad, *f*; ventaja, *f*, beneficio, provecho, *m*. **u. goods,** artículos fabricados bajo la autorizacion del gobierno, *m pl*
utilizable *a* utilizable, aprovechable
utilization *n* empleo, aprovechamiento, *m*
utilize *vt* utilizar, servirse de; aprovechar
utmost *a* (outermost) extremo; (farthest) más remoto, más distante; (greatest) mayor, más grande. *n* lo más; todo lo posible. **to do one's u.,** hacer todo lo posible, hacer todo lo que uno pueda
utopian *a* utópico

utter *a* completo, total; terminate, absoluto; sumo, extremo. **He is an u. fool,** Es un tonto de capirote
utter *vt* pronunciar, proferir, decir, hablar; (a sigh, cry, etc.) dar; (express) manifestar, expresar, explicar; (coin) poner en circulación; (a libel) publicar; (disclose) revelar, descubrir
utterance *n* expresión, manifestación, *f;* pronunciación, *f;* (style) lenguaje, *m*
utterly *adv* enteramente, completamente
uttermost *a.* See **utmost**
uvula *n anat* úvula, *f*
uxorious *a* uxorio

V

v *n* (letter) ve, *f;* pieza en forma de V, *f*
vacancy *n* vacío, *m;* vacancia, *f;* (mental) vacuidad, *f;* (of offices, posts) vacante, *f;* (leisure) desocupación, ociosidad, *f;* (gap, blank) vacío, *m,* laguna, *f*
vacant *a* vacío; despoblado, deshabitado; (free) libre; (of offices, etc.) vacante; (leisured) ocioso; (absent-minded) distraído; (vague) vago; (foolish) estúpido, estólido
vacantly *adv* distraídamente; estúpidamente
vacate *vt* dejar vacío; (a post) dejar; (a throne) renunciar a; dejar vacante; *mil* evacuar; *law* anular, rescindir
vacation *n* (of offices) vacante, *f;* (holiday) vacaciones, *f pl, f.* **the long v.,** las vacaciones de verano. **to be on a v.,** estar de vacaciones
vaccinate *vt* vacunar
vaccination *n* vacunación, *f*
vaccine *n* vacuna, *f*
vacillate *vi* (sway) oscilar; (hesitate) vacilar, titubear, dudar
vacillating *a* vacilante
vacillation *n* vacilación, *f*
vacuity *n* vacuidad, *f*
vacuous *a* desocupado, ocioso; estúpido, vacío
vacuum *n* vacío, *m.* **v. brake,** freno al vacío, *m.* **v. cleaner,** aspirador de polvo, *m.* **v. flask,** termos, *m.* **v. pump,** bomba neumática, *f.* **vacuum-shelf dryer,** secador al vacío, *m*
vade mecum *n* vademécum, *m*
vagabond *n* vagabundo (-da); vago, *m;* (beggar) mendigo (-ga). *a* vagabundo, errante
vagabondage *n* vagabundeo, *m,* vagancia, *f*
vagary *n* (whim) capricho, antojo, *m,* extravagancia, *f;* (of the mind) divagación, *f*
vagina *n* vagina, *f*
vaginal *a* vaginal
vagrancy *n* vagancia, *f*
vagrant *n* vago, *m, a* vagabundo, errante
vague *a* vago; indistinto; equívoco, ambiguo; (uncertain) incierto
vaguely *adv* vagamente
vagueness *n* vaguedad, *f*
vain *a* vano; (fruitless) infructuoso; (useless) inútil; (unsubstantial) fútil, insubstancial; fantástico; (empty) vacío; (worthless) despreciable; (conceited) vanidoso, presumido. **in v.,** en vano, en balde, inútilmente. **v. about,** orgulloso de
vainglorious *a* vanaglorioso
vaingloriousness *n* vanagloria, *f*
vainly *adv* vanamente; inútilmente; (conceitedly) vanidosamente, con vanidad
valance *n* cenefa, *f*
vale *n* (valley) valle, *m. interj* ¡adiós! *n* (good-bye) vale, *m*
valediction *n* despedida, *f;* vale, *m*
valedictory *a* de despedida
Valencian *a* and *n* valenciano (-na)
valency *n chem* valencia, *f*
valet *n* criado, *m.* **v. de chambre,** ayuda de cámara, *m*
valetudinarian *a* valetudinario
Valhalla *n* el Valhala, *m*
valiant *a* valiente, esforzado, animoso, bravo
valiantly *adv* valientemente
valid *a* válido, valedero; (of laws in force) vigente
validate *vt* validar
validation *n* validación, *f*
validity *n* validez, *f*
validly *adv* válidamente
valise *n* valija, *f,* saco de viaje, *m*
Valkyrie *n* Valquiria, *f*
valley *n* valle, *m*
valor *n* valor, *m,* valentía, *f*
valorous *a* valoroso, esforzudo, intrépido
valse *n* vals, *m*
valuable *a* valioso; costoso; precioso; estimable; excelente. *n pl* **valuables,** objetos de valor, *m pl*
valuableness *n* valor, *m*
valuation *n* valuación, tasación, *f;* estimación, *f*
valuator *n* tasador, *m*
value *n* valor, *m;* precio, *m;* estimación, *f;* importancia, *f;* (*gram mus*) valor, *m; pl* **values,** valores morales, principios, *m pl. vt* tasar, valorar; estimar; apreciar; tener en mucho; hacer caso de; considerar. **to be of v.,** ser de valor
valued *a* apreciado, estimado; precioso
valueless *a* sin valor; insignificante
valuer *n* tasador, *m*
valve *n* (*elec, mech, anat*) válvula, *f;* (*bot, zool*) valva, *f*
valved *a* con válvulas; (in compounds) de . . . válvulas
valvular *a* valvular
vamp *n* (of a shoe) pala (de zapato), *f;* (patch) remiendo, *m; mus* acompañamiento improvisado, *m; inf* aventurera, *f. vt* (of shoes) poner palas (a); (patch) remendar; *mus* improvisar un acompañamiento; (of a woman) fascinar, engatusar
vampire *n* vampiro, *m*
van *n* (*mil, nav, fig*) vanguardia, *f;* camión, *m;* (for delivery) camión de reparto, *m;* (for furniture) conductora de muebles, *f;* (removal) carro de mudanzas, *m;* (mail) camión postal, *m;* (for bathing) caseta de baño, *f;* (for guard on trains) furgón de equipajes, *m;* (railroad car) vagón, *m*
vandal *a* and *n* vándalo (-la); bárbaro (-ra)
vandalism *n* vandalismo, *m*
Vandyke *n* cuadro de Vandyke, *m.* **V. beard,** perilla, *f.* **V. collar,** cuello de encaje, *m*
vane *n* (weathercock) veleta, *f;* (of a windmill) aspa, *f;* (of a propeller) paleta, *f;* (of a feather) barba, *f;* (of a surveying instrument) pínula, *f*
vanguard *n* vanguardia, *f.* **in the v.,** a vanguardia; *fig* en la vanguardia
vanilla *n* vainilla, *f*
vanish *vi* desaparecer; desvanecerse; disiparse
vanishing *n* desaparición, *f;* disipación, *f.* **v. cream,** crema desvanecedora, *f.* **v. point,** punto de la vista, *m*
vanity *n* vanidad, *f.* **v. case,** polvera de bolsillo, *f*
vanquish *vt* vencer, derrotar
vanquisher *n* vencedor (-ra)
vantage *n* ventaja (also in tennis), *f.* **v.-ground,** posición ventajosa, *f,* sitial de privilegio, *m*
vapid *a* insípido, insulso; (of speeches, etc.) soso, aburrido, insípido
vapidity *n* insipidez, sosería, *f*
vapor *n* vapor, *m; pl* **vapors,** (hysteria) vapores, *m pl. vi* (boast) jactarse, baladronear; decir disparates. **v. bath,** baño de vapor, *m*
vaporizable *a* vaporizable
vaporization *n* vaporización, *f*
vaporize *vt* vaporizar. *vi* vaporizarse
vaporizer *n* vaporizador, *m*
vaporous *a* vaporoso
variability *n* variabilidad, *f*

variable *a* variable. *n math* variable, *f*
variably *adv* variablemente
variance *n* variación, *f*, cambio, *m*; desacuerdo, *m*, disensión, *f*; diferencia, contradicción, *f*. **at v.,** en desacuerdo, reñidos; hostil (a), opuesto (a); (of things) distinto (de), en contradicción (con)
variant *n* variante, *f*
variation *n* variación, *f*; cambio, *m*; variedad, *f*; diferencia, *f*; (*mus* magnetism) variación, *f*
varicose *a* varicoso
varied success éxito vario, *m*
variegate *vt* abigarrar, matizar, salpicar
variegated *a* abigarrado; variado; mezclado
variegation *n* abigarramiento, *m*; diversidad de colores, *f*
variety *n* variedad, *f*; diversidad, *f*; (choice) surtido, *m*. **v. show,** función de variedades, *f*
various *a* vario, diverso; diferente
variously *adv* diversamente
varix *n* várice, *f*
varnish *n* barniz, *m*. *vt* barnizar; (pottery) vidriar; (conceal) disimular. **copal v.,** barniz copal, *m*. **japan v.,** charol japonés, *m*. **lacquer v.,** laca, *f*. **v. remover,** (for nails) quitaesmalte, *m*
varnishing *n* barnizado, *m*; (of pottery) vidriado, *m*
vary *vt* variar; cambiar; diversificar; modificar. *vi* variar; cambiar; (be different) ser distinto (de); (deviate) desviarse (de); (disagree) estar en desacuerdo, distar, estar en contradicción. **to v. directly (indirectly),** *math* variar en razón directa (inversa)
varying *a* variante, cambiante, diverso
vascular *a* vascular
vase *n* vaso, jarrón, *m*; urna, *f*
vaseline *n* vaselina, *f*
vassal *n* vasallo (-lla); esclavo (-va), siervo (-va). *a* tributario
vast *a* vasto, extenso; enorme; grande. *n* vastedad, inmensidad, *f*
vastly *adv* enormemente; muy; con mucho
vastness *n* vastedad, extensión, *f*; inmensidad, *f*; enormidad, *f*, gran tamaño, *m*; grandeza, *f*
vat *n* cuba, tina, *f*; alberca, *f*, estanque, *m*. **dyeing vat,** cuba de tintorero, *f*. **tanning vat,** noque, *m*. **wine vat,** lagar, *m*
Vatican *a* and *n* Vaticano, *m*
vaticinate *vt* and *vi* vaticinar, profetizar
vaticination *n* vaticinio, *m*, predicción, *f*
vaudeville *n* vodevil, *m*, zarzuela cómica, *f*
vault *n arch* bóveda, *f*; caverna, *f*; (for wine) bodega, cueva, *f*; (in a bank) cámara acorazada, *f*; (in a church) cripta, *f*; sepultura, *f*; (of the sky) bóveda celeste, *f*; (leap) salto, *m*; voltereta, *f*. *vi* (jump) saltar; (with a pole) saltar con pértiga; saltar por encima de; voltear. *vt arch* abovedar; saltar
vaulted *a* abovedado
vaulter *n* saltador (-ra)
vaulting *n* construcción de bóvedas, *f*; bóvedas, *f pl*; edificio abovedado, *m*; (jumping) salto, *m*. **v.-horse,** potro de madera, *m*
vaunt *vi* jactarse (de), hacer gala (de); triunfar (sobre). *vt* ostentar, sacar a relucir; (praise) alabar. *n* jactancia, *f*
veal *n* ternera, *f*. **v.-cutlet,** chuleta de ternera, *f*
vector *n* vector, *m*
Veda *n* Veda, *m*
veer *vi* (of the wind) girar; (of a ship) virar; *fig* cambiar (de opinión, etc.). *vt* virar
vegetable *n* vegetal, *m*; legumbre, *f*; *pl* **vegetables,** (green and generally cooked) verduras, *f pl*; (raw green) hortalizas, *f pl*. **v. dish,** fuente de legumbres, *f*. **v. garden,** huerto de legumbres, *m*; **v. ivory,** marfil vegetal, *m*. **v. kingdom,** reino vegetal, *m*. **v. soup,** sopa de hortelano, *f*
vegetal *a* vegetal
vegetarian *a* and *n* vegetariano (-na)
vegetarianism *n* vegetarianismo, *m*
vegetate *vi* vegetar
vegetation *n* vegetación, *f*
vehemence *n* vehemencia, *f*; violencia, *f*; impetuosidad, *f*; pasión, *f*, ardor, *m*
vehement *a* vehemente; violento; impetuoso; apasionado
vehemently *adv* con vehemencia; violentamente; con impetuosidad; apasionadamente
vehicle *n* vehículo, *m*; (means) medio, *m*; instrumento, *m*
vehicular *a* vehicular, de los vehículos; de los coches. **v. traffic,** circulación de los coches, *f*; los vehículos
veil *n* velo, *m*; (curtain) cortina, *f*; (disguise) disfraz, *m*; (excuse) pretexto, *m*; (appearance) apariencia, *f*. *vt* velar; cubrir con un velo; (hide) tapar, encubrir; (dissemble) disimular; (disguise) disfrazar. **to take the v.,** tomar el velo, profesar
vein *n* (*anat, bot*) vena, *f*; (*geol, min*) veta, *f*, filón, *m*; (in wood) fibra, hebra, *f*; (*fig* streak) rasgo, *m*; (inspiration) vena, *f*; (mood) humor, *m*
veined, veiny *a* venoso; de venas; veteado
velar *a* velar
vellum *n* vitela, *f*
velocity *n* velocidad, *f*; rapidez, *f*
velodrome *n* velódromo, *m*
velours *n* terciopelo, *m*
velvet *n* terciopelo, *m*, *a* hecho de terciopelo; aterciopelado
velveteen *n* pana, *f*, velludillo, *m*
velvety *a* aterciopelado
venal *a* venal
venality *n* venalidad, *f*
vend *vt* vender
vendor *n* vendedor (-ra)
veneer *vt* chapear, taracear; (conceal) disimular, disfrazar. *n* taraceado, chapeado, *m*; (plate) chapa, hoja para chapear, *f*; (*fig* gloss) barniz, *m*, apariencia, *f*
venerability *n* venerabilidad, respetabilidad, *f*
venerable *a* venerable
venerate *vt* venerar, reverenciar
veneration *n* veneración, *f*
venerator *n* venerador (-ra)
venereal *a* venéreo. **v. disease,** enfermedad venérea, *f*
Venetian *a* and *n* veneciano (-na). **v. blinds,** persianas, celosías, *f pl*
Venezuelan *a* and *n* venezolano (-na)
vengeance *n* venganza, *f*
vengeful *a* vengativo
venial *a* venial
veniality *n* venialidad, *f*
Venice Venecia, *f*
venison *n* venado, *m*
venom *n* veneno, *m*
venomous *a* venenoso; maligno, malicioso
venomously *adv* con malignidad, maliciosamente
venomousness *n* venenosidad, *f*; malignidad, *f*
venous *a* venoso
vent *n* abertura, *f*; salida, *f*; (air-hole) respiradero, *m*; (in pipes) ventosa, *f*; (in fire-arms) oído, *m*; *anat* ano, *m*; (*fig* outlet) desahogo, *m*; expresión, *f*. *vt* dejar escapar; (pierce) agujerear; (discharge) emitir, vomitar; (relieve) desahogar; expresar, dar expresión (a), dar rienda suelta (a)
venter *n law* vientre, *m*
ventilate *vt* ventilar; discutir
ventilation *n* ventilación, *f*
ventilator *n* ventilador, *m*
ventricle *n* ventrículo, *m*
ventriloquism *n* ventriloquia, *f*
ventriloquist *n* ventrílocuo (-ua)
venture *n* ventura, *f*; riesgo, *m*; aventura, *f*; especulación, *f*. *vt* arriesgar, aventurar; (stake) jugar; (state) expresar. *vi* aventurarse; (dare) atreverse, osar; permitirse. **at a v.,** a la ventura. **to v. on,** arriesgarse a; probar ventura con; lanzarse a; (a remark) permitirse. **to v. out,** atreverse a salir

venturesome *a* atrevido, audaz; (dangerous) arriesgado, peligroso
venturesomeness *n* atrevimiento, *m*, temeridad, *f*; (risk) riesgo, peligro, *m*
Venus *n* (planet) Venus, *m*; (woman) venus, *f*
veracious *a* veraz, verídico; verdadero
veracity *n* veracidad, *f*; verdad, *f*
veranda *n* veranda, *f*
verb *n* verbo, *m*. **auxiliary v.,** verbo auxiliar, *m*. **intransitive v.,** verbo intransitivo (neutro), *m*. **reflexive v.,** verbo reflexivo, *m*. **transitive v.,** verbo transitivo, *m*
verbal *a* verbal
verbally *adv* de palabra, verbalmente
verbatim *a* textual. *adv* textualmente, palabra por palabra
verbiage *n* verbosidad, palabrería, *f*
verbose *a* verboso, prolijo
verbosity *n* verbosidad, *f*
verdancy *n* verdura, *f*, verdor, *m*
verdant *a* verde
verdict *n law* veredicto, fallo, *m*, sentencia, *f*; opinión, *f*, juicio, *m*. **to bring in a v.,** fallar sentencia.
verdigris *n* cardenillo, verdin, *m*
verdure *n* verdura, *f*, verdor, *m*; *fig* lozanía, *f*
verge *n* (wand) vara, *f*; (edge) margen, borde, *m*; (of a lake, etc.) orilla, *f*; (horizon) horizonte, *m*; *fig* víspera, *f*, punto, *m*. **on the v. of,** al margen de, a la orilla de. **to be on the v. of,** *fig* estar a punto de; estar en vísperas de
verger *n* macero, *m*; (in a church) pertiguero, *m*
verifiable *a* verificable
verification *n* verificación, *f*
verifier *n* verificador (-ra)
verify *vt* verificar, confirmar; probar
verily *adv* de veras, en verdad
verisimilitude *n* verosimilitud, *f*
veritable *a* verdadero
veritably *adv* verdaderamente
verity *n* verdad, *f*
vermicelli *n* fideos, *m pl*
vermilion *n* bermellón, *m*
vermin *n* bichos dañinos, *m pl*; (insects) parásitos, *m pl*
vermouth *n* vermut, *m*
vernacular *a* vernáculo; nativo; vulgar. *n* lengua popular, *f*; lenguaje vulgar, *m*
versatile *a zool* versátil; inconstante, voluble; (clever) de muchos talentos; de muchos intereses; adaptable; completo, cabal
versatility *n* (cleverness) muchos talentos, *m pl*; adaptabilidad, *f*
verse *n* verso, *m*; (stanza) estrofa, *f*; (in the Bible) versículo, *m*; (poetry) poesía, *f*, versos, *m pl*. **to make verses,** escribir versos
versed *a* versado, experimentado
versicle *n* versículo, *m*
versification *n* versificación, *f*
versifier *n* versificador (-ra)
versify *vt* and *vi* versificar
version *n* versión, *f*; traducción, *f*; interpretación, *f*
versus *prep* contra
vertebra *n* vértebra, *f*
vertebral *a* vertebral
vertebrate *n* vertebrado, *m*
vertex *n* (*geom, anat*) vértice, *m*; *ast* cenit, *m*; cumbre, *f*
vertical *a* vertical
verticality *n* verticalidad, *f*
vertiginous *a* vertiginoso
vertigo *n* vértigo, *m*
verve *n* brío, *m*, fogosidad, *f*
very *a* mismo; (mere) mero; (true) verdadero; (with adjective and comparative) más grande; *inf* mismísimo; (complete) perfecto, completo. **The v. thought of it made him laugh,** Sólo con pensarlo se rió (*or* La mera idea le hizo reír). **this v. minute,** este mismísimo instante. **the v. day,** el mismo día
very *adv* muy; mucho; demasiado; (exactly) exactamente; completamente; absolutamente. **He is v. worried,** Está muy preocupado. **He is not v. well,** (i.e. rather ill) Está bastante bien. **This cloth is the v. best,** Esta tela es la mejor que hay. **I like it v. much,** Me gusta muchísimo. **He is v. much pleased,** Está muy contento. **so v. little,** tan poco; tan pequeño. **v. well,** muy bien
vesicle *n* vesícula, *f*
vesper *n* estrella vespertina, *f*, héspero, *m*; *pl* **vespers,** *ecc* vísperas, *f pl*
vessel *n* vasija, *f*, recipiente, *m*; (boat) barco, buque, *m*; (*anat, bot*) vaso, *m*
vest *n* camiseta, *f*; (waistcoat) chaleco, *m*. *vt* vestir; (with authority, etc.) revestir de; (property, etc.) hacer entrega de, ceder. *vi* tener validez; (dress) vestirse. **vested interests,** intereses creados, *m pl*. **v.-pocket,** bolsillo del chaleco, *m*. **v.-pocket camera,** cámara de bolsillo, *f*
vestal *a* vestal; virgen, casto. *n* vestal, *f*; virgen, *f*
vestibule *n* vestíbulo, *m*; (anteroom) antecámara, *f*; (of a theatre box) antepalco, *m*; *anat* vestíbulo, *m*
vestige *n* vestigio, rastro, *m*; sombra, *f*; *biol* rudimento, *m*
vestment *n* hábito, *m*; *ecc* vestidura, *f*
vestry *n* vestuario, *m*, sacristía, *f*
vesture *n* traje, hábito, *m*, vestidura, *f*
Vesuvius Vesubio, *m*
veteran *a* veterano; de los veteranos; aguerrido; anciano; experimentado. *n* veterano (-na)
veterinary *a* veterinario. **v. science,** veterinaria, *f*. **v. surgeon,** veterinario, *m*
veto *n* veto, *m*; prohibición, *f*. *vt* poner el veto; prohibir
vex *vt* contrariar, irritar; enojar; (make impatient) impacientar; fastidiar; (afflict) afligir, acongojar; (worry) inquietar
vexation *n* contrariedad, irritación, *f*; enojo, enfado, *m*; (impatience) impaciencia, *f*; fastidio, *m*; aflicción, *f*; inquietud, *f*; disgusto, *m*
vexatious *a* irritante; enojoso, enfadoso; fastidioso, molesto
vexatiousness *n* fastidio, *m*, molestia, *f*; incomodidad, *f*; contrariedad, *f*
vexed *a* discutido; contencioso; (thorny) espinoso, difícil
vexing *a* irritante; molesto; enfadoso
via *n* vía, *f*, *prep* por, por la vía de
viability *n* viabilidad, *f*
viable *a* viable
viaduct *n* viaducto, *m*
vial *n* frasco, *m*, ampolleta, *f*
vibrant *a* vibrante
vibrate *vi* vibrar; (of machines) trepidar; oscilar. *vt* hacer vibrar, vibrar
vibration *n* vibración, *f*; trepidación, *f*; oscilación, *f*, *Lat. Am.* cimbrón, *m*
vibrator *n elec* vibrador, *m*; *rad* oscilador, *m*
vicar *n* vicario, *m*; (of a parish) cura, *m*. **v.-general,** vicario general, *m*
vicarious *a* vicario; sufrido por otro; experimentado por otro
vicariously *adv* por delegación; por substitución. **I know it only vicariously,** Lo conozco sólo por referencia
vice *n* vicio, *m*; defecto, *m*; (in a horse) vicio, resabio, *m*; (tool) tornillo de banco, *m*, *prefix* vice. **v.-admiral,** vicealmirante, *m*. **v.-chairman,** vice-presidente (-ta). **v.-chancellor,** vicecanciller, *m*. **v.-consul,** vice-cónsul, *m*. **v.-consulate,** vice-consulado, *m*. **v.-president,** vicepresidente (-ta)
viceroy *n* virrey, *m*
viceversa *adv* viceversa
vicinity *n* vecindad, *f*; (nearness) cercanía, proximidad, *f*. **to be in the v. of,** estar en la vecindad de
vicious *a* vicioso. **v. circle,** círculo vicioso, *m*
viciousness *n* viciosidad, *f*; (in a horse) resabios, *m pl*

vicissitude *n* vicisitud, *f*
vicissitudinous *a* accidentado, vicisitudinario
victim *n* víctima, *f*
victimization *n* sacrificio, *m*; tormento, *m*
victimize *vt* hacer víctima (de); sacrificar; ser víctima (de), sufrir; (cheat) estafar, engañar
victor *n* víctor, vencedor, *m*
victoria *n* victoria, *f*
Victorian *a* victoriano
victorious *a* victorioso, triunfante. **to be v.,** triunfar, salir victorioso
victoriously *adv* victoriosamente, triunfalmente
victory *n* victoria, *f*
victress *n* vencedora, *f*
victual *n* vitualla, vianda, *f*; *pl* **victuals,** víveres, *m pl*, provisiones, *f pl*. *vt* avituallar; abastecer. *vi* tomar provisiones
victualler *n* abastecedor (-ra), proveedor (-ra)
victualling *n* abastecimiento, *m*
vide *Latin imperative* véase, véanse
videlicet *adv* a saber
video, *n* vídeo, *m*
videotape *n* videograbación, videocinta, *f*
vie *vi* (with) competir con; rivalizar con; (with a person for) disputar; luchar con
Vienna Viena, *f*
Viennese *a* and *n* vienés (-esa)
view *n* vista, *f*; perspectiva, *f*, panorama, *m*; (landscape) paisaje, *m*; escena, *f*; inspección, *f*; (judgment) opinión, *f*, parecer, *m*; consideración, *f*; (appearance) apariencia, *f*; aspecto, *m*; (purpose) propósito, *m*, intención, *f*; (sight) alcance de la vista, *m*; (show) exposición, *f*. *vt* examinar; inspeccionar; (look at) mirar; (see) ver, contemplar; considerar. **in v. of,** en vista de. **in my v.,** en mi opinión, segun creo yo. **on v.,** a la vista. **to keep in v.,** no perder de vista; *fig* no olvidar, tener presente. **to take a different v.,** pensar de un modo distinto. **to v. a house,** inspeccionar una casa. **with a v. to,** con el propósito de. **v.-finder,** enfocador, *m*. **v.-point,** punto de vista, *m*
viewer *n* espectador (-ra); examinador (-ra)
viewing *n* inspección, *f*, examen, *m*
vigil *n* vela, vigilia, *f*; *ecc* vigilia, *f*
vigilance *n* vigilancia, *f*, desvelo, *m*
vigilant *a* vigilante, desvelado
vigilantly *adv* vigilantemente
vignette *n* viñeta, *f*
vigorous *a* vigoroso, enérgico, fuerte; *Argentina* alentado
vigorously *adv* con vigor
vigor *n* vigor, *m*, fuerza, *f*
Viking *n* vikingo, *m*
vile *a* vil; bajo; despreciable; infame; *inf* horrible
vilely *adv* vilmente; *inf* mal, horriblemente
vileness *n* vileza, *f*; bajeza, *f*; infamia, *f*
vilification *n* vilipendio, *m*, difamación, *f*
vilifier *n* difamador (-ra)
vilify *vt* vilipendiar, difamar
villa *n* villa, torre, casa de campo, *f*; hotel, *m*
village *n* aldea, *f*, pueblo, *m*. **v. shop** *Lat. Am.* esquina, *f*
villager *n* aldeano (-na)
villain *n hist* villano, *m*; malvado, *m*
villainous *a* malvado; infame; vil
villainously *adv* vilmente
villainy *n* vileza, infamia, maldad, *f*
vindicate *vt* vindicar, justificar; defender
vindication *n* vindicación, justificación, *f*; defensa, *f*
vindicative *a* vindicativo, vindicador, justificativo
vindicator *n* vindicador (-ra)
vindictive *a* vengativo; rencoroso
vindictively *adv* vengativamente; rencorosamente
vindictiveness *n* deseo de venganza, *m*; rencor, *m*
vine *n* vid, parra, *f*; (twining plant) enredadera, *f*. **v.-arbor,** emparrado, *m*. **v.-branch,** sarmiento, *m*. **v.-clad,** cubierto de parras. **v.-grower,** vinicultor, *m*. **v.-growing,** vinicultura, *f*. **v.-leaf,** hoja de parra, *f*. **v.-pest,** filoxera, *f*. **v.-stock,** cepa, *f*
vinegar *n* vinagre, *m*. **v.-cruet,** vinagrera, *f*. **v.-sauce,** vinagreta, *f*
vinegary *a* vinagroso
vineyard *n* viña, *f*, viñedo, *m*. **v.-keeper,** viñador, *m*
vinification *n* vinificación, *f*
vinosity *n* vinosidad, *f*
vinous *a* vinoso
vintage *n* vendimia, *f*; (of wine) cosecha (de vino), *f*
vintner *n* vinatero, *m*
viola *n* (*mus, bot*) viola, *f*. **v. player,** viola, *mf*
violate *vt* (desecrate) profanar; (infringe) contravenir, infringir; (break) romper; (ravish) violar
violation *n* profanación, *f*; (infringement) contravención, *f*; (rape) violación, *f*
violator *n* violador (-ra); (ravisher) violador, *m*
violence *n* violencia, *f*
violent *a* violento
violently *adv* con violencia
violet *n* violeta, *f*. *a* violado, **v. color,** violeta, color violado, *m*
violin *n* violín, *m*
violinist *n* violinista, *mf*
violoncellist *n* violoncelista, *mf*
violoncello *n* violoncelo, *m*
viper *n* víbora, *f*
viperish *a* viperino
virago *n* virago, *f*,
Virgilian *a* virgiliano
virgin *n* virgen, *f*; (sign of the zodiac) Virgo, *m*. *a* virginal; (untouched) virgen. **the V.,** la Virgen. **v. soil,** tierra virgen, *f*
virginal *a* virginal
virginity *n* virginidad, *f*
Virgo *n* Virgo, *m*
virile *a* viril
virility *n* virilidad, *f*
virtual *a* virtual
virtue *n* virtud, *f*
virtuosity *n* virtuosidad, *f*
virtuoso *n* virtuoso (-sa)
virtuous *a* virtuoso
virulence *n* virulencia, *f*
virulent *a* virulento
virulently *adv* con virulencia
virus *n* virus, *m*
visa *n* visado, *m*
visage *n* cara, *f*, rostro, *m*; semblante, aspecto, *m*
viscera *n* víscera, *f*
visceral *a* visceral
viscid *a* viscoso
viscosity *n* viscosidad, *f*
viscount *n* vizconde, *m*
viscountess *n* vizcondesa, *f*
viscous *a* viscoso
visé *n* visado, *m*, *vt* visar
visibility *n* visibilidad, *f*. **poor v.,** mala visibilidad, *f*
visible *a* visible; aparente, evidente
visibly *adv* visiblemente; a ojos vistas
Visigoth *n* visigodo (-da)
Visigothic *a* visigodo, visigótico
vision *n* visión, *f*; (eyesight) vista, *f*. **field of v.,** campo visual, *m*
visionary *a* and *n* visionario (-ia)
visit *n* visita, *f*; (inspection) inspección, *f*; (doctor's) visita de médico, *f*. *vt* visitar; hacer una visita (a); ir a ver; inspeccionar; (frequent) frecuentar; (Biblical) visitar. **to be visited by an epidemic,** sufrir una epidemia. **to go visiting,** ir de visita. **to pay a v.,** hacer una visita
visitation *n* visita, *f*; *ecc* visitación, *f*; (inspection) inspección, *f*; (punishment) castigo, *m*
visiting *a* de visita. **v. card,** tarjeta de visita, *f*. **v. card case,** tarjetero, *m*. **visiting hours,** horas de visita, *f pl*
visitor *n* visita, *f*; (official) visitador, *m*

visor *n* visera, *f*
vista *n* vista, perspectiva, *f*
visual *a* visual. **the v. arts,** las artes visuales
visualize *vt* and *vi* imaginarse, ver mentalmente
vital *a* vital; esencial; trascendental
vitalism *n* vitalismo, *m*
vitality *n* vitalidad, *f*
vitalize *vt* vitalizar, vivificar; reanimar
vitals *n pl* partes vitales, *f pl*; *fig* entrañas, *f pl*
vitamin *n* vitamina, *f*
vitiate *vt* viciar; corromper, contaminar
viticultural *a* vitícola
viticulture *n* viticultura, *f*
vitreous *a* vítreo, vidrioso
vitrification *n* vitrificación, *f*
vitrify *vt* vitrificar. *vi* vitrificarse
vitriol *n* vitriolo, ácido sulfúrico, *m*
vitriolic *a* vitriólico
Vitruvius Vitrubio, *m*
vituperable *a* vituperable
vituperate *vt* vituperar
vituperation *n* vituperio, *m*
vituperative *a* vituperador
vivacious *a* animado, vivaracho
vivaciously *adv* animadamente
vivacity *n* vivacidad, animación, *f*
viva voce *a* oral. *n* examen oral, *m*
vivid *a* vivo; brillante; intenso; (of descriptions, etc.) gráfico
vividly *adv* vivamente; brillantemente
vividness *n* vivacidad, *f*; intensidad, *f*; (strength) fuerza, *f*
vivification *n* vivificación, *f*
vivify *vt* vivificar, avivar
vivifying *a* vivificante
vivisection *n* vivisección, *f*
vixen *n* raposa, zorra, *f*; (woman) arpía, *f*
viz *adv* a saber
vizier *n* visir, *m*. **grand v.,** gran visir, *m*
vocabulary *n* vocabulario, *m*
vocal *a* vocal. **v. cords,** cuerdas vocales, *f pl*
vocalist *n* cantante, *mf*, voz, *f*
vocalization *n* vocalización, *f*
vocalize *vt* vocalizar
vocation *n* vocación, *f*; oficio, *m*; empleo, *m*; profesión, *f*
vocational *a* profesional; práctico. **vocational guidance,** guía vocacional, orientación profesional, *f*. **v. training,** instrucción práctica, *f*; enseñanza de oficio, *f*
vociferate *vt* gritar. *vi* vociferar, vocear
vociferation *n* vociferación, *f*
vociferous *a* (noisy) ruidoso; vocinglero, clamoroso
vociferously *adv* ruidosamente; a gritos
vodka *n* vodca, *m*
vogue *n* moda, *f*. **in v.,** en boga, de moda
voice *n* voz, *f*. *vt* expresar, interpretar, hacerse eco de; hablar. **in a loud v.,** en voz alta. **in a low v.,** en voz baja
voiced *a* (in compounds) de voz . . . ; hablado
void *a* (empty) vacío; (vacant) vacante; deshabitado; (lacking in) privado (de), desprovisto (de); (without) sin; *law* inválido, nulo; sin valor. *n* vacío, *m*. *vt* evacuar; *law* anular; invalidar
voile *n* espumilla, *f*
volatile *a* volátil; (light) ligero; (changeable) voluble, inconstante
volatility *n* volatilidad, *f*; ligereza, *f*; volubilidad, *f*
volatilization *n* volatilización, *f*
volatilize *vt* volatilizar. *vi* volatilizarse
volcanic *a* volcánico
volcano *n* volcán, *m*. **extinct v.,** volcán extinto, *m*
volition *n* volición, *f*; voluntad, *f*
volley *n* (of stones, etc.) lluvia, *f*; (of fire-arms) descarga, *f*; (of cannon, naval guns) andanada, *f*; *sport* voleo, *m*; (of words, etc.) torrente, *m*; (of applause and as a salute) salva, *f*. *vt sport* volear; (abuse, etc.) dirigir. *vi* lanzar una descarga, hacer una descarga
volt *n elec* voltío, *m*; (of a horse and in fencing) vuelta, *f*. **v.-ampere,** voltamperio, *m*
voltage *n* voltaje, *m*. **v. control,** mando del voltaje, *m*
voltaic *a* voltaico
Voltairian *a* volteriano
voltmeter *n* voltímetro, *m*
volubility *n* garrulidad, locuacidad, *f*
voluble *a* gárrulo, locuaz
volume *n* (book) tomo, *m*; (amount, size, space) volumen, *m*; (of water) caudal (de río), *m*; (mass) masa, *f*; (of smoke) humareda, *f*, nubes de humo, *f pl*
volumed *a* (in compounds) en . . . volúmenes, de . . . tomos
volumetric *a* volumétrico
voluminous *a* voluminoso
voluminousness *n* lo voluminoso
voluntarily *adv* voluntariamente
voluntariness *n* carácter voluntario, *m*
voluntary *a* voluntario; espontáneo; libre; (charitable) benéfico; (intentional) intencional, deliberado. *n* solo de órgano, *m*
volunteer *n mil* voluntario (-ia). *a* de voluntarios. *vt* ofrecer; contribuir; expresar. *vi* ofrecerse para hacer algo; *mil* alistarse, ofrecerse a servir como voluntario
volunteering *n* voluntariado, *m*
voluptuary *n* voluptuoso (-sa); sibarita, *mf*
voluptuous *a* voluptuoso
voluptuously *adv* voluptuosamente
voluptuousness *n* voluptuosidad, *f*; sensualidad, *f*
volute *n arch* voluta, *f*
vomit *vt* and *vi* vomitar; arrojar, devolver, *Central America, Mexico* deponer. *n* vómito, *m*
vomiting *n* vómito, *m*
voodoo *n* vudú, *m*
voracious *a* voraz
voracity *n* voracidad, *f*
vortex *n* torbellino, *m*, vorágine, *f*; *fig* vórtice, *m*
votaress, votary *n* devoto (-ta), adorante, *mf*; partidario (-ia)
vote *n* voto, *m*; (voting) votación, *f*; (suffrage) sufragio, *m*; (election) elección, *f*. *vt* votar; asignar; nombrar; elegir; (consider) tener por. *vi* votar, dar el voto. **casting v.,** voto de calidad, *m*. **to put to the v.,** poner a votación. **to v. down,** desechar, rechazar. **v. of confidence,** voto de confianza, *m*. **v. of thanks,** voto de gracias, *m*
voter *n* votante, *mf*, votador (-ra); elector (-ra)
voting *n* votación, *f*; elección, *f*. *a* de votar; electoral. **v. paper,** papeleta de votación, *f*
votive *a* votivo. **v. offering,** exvoto, *m*
vouch *vi* atestiguar, afirmar; garantizar; responder (de)
voucher *n* (guarantor) fiador (-ra); (guarantee) garantía, *f*; (receipt) recibo, *m*; (proof) prueba, *f*; documento justificativo, *m*; vale, bono, *m*
vouchsafe *vt* conceder, otorgar
vouchsafement *n* concesión, *f*, otorgamiento, *m*
vow *n* voto, *m*; promesa solemne, *f*. *vt* hacer voto (de), hacer promesa solemne (de); jurar. **to take a vow,** hacer un voto
vowel *n* vocal, *f*
voyage *n* viaje (por mar), *m*; travesía, *f*. *vi* viajar por mar. **Good v.!** ¡Buen viaje!, Feliz viaje!
voyager *n* viajero (-ra)
vulcanite *n* ebonita, *f*
vulcanization *n* vulcanización, *f*
vulcanize *vt* vulcanizar
vulgar *a* vulgar; (ill-bred) ordinario, cursi; (in bad taste) de mal gusto; trivial; adocenado; (coarse) grosero. *n* vulgo, populacho, *m*. **v. fraction,** fracción común, *f*
vulgarism *n* vulgarismo, *m*; vulgaridad, *f*
vulgarity *n* vulgaridad, *f*; grosería, *f*; mal tono, *m*, cursilería, *f*
vulgarize *vt* vulgarizar; popularizar
vulgarly *adv* vulgarmente; comúnmente; groseramente

Vulgate *n* Vulgata, *f*
vulnerability *n* vulnerabilidad, *f*
vulnerable *a* vulnerable
vulpine *a* vulpino; astuto
vulture *n* buitre, *Argentina* carancho, *m*
vulva *n* vulva, *f*

w *n* ve doble, *f*
wabble *vi.* See **wobble**
wad *n* (of straw, etc.) atado, *m;* (of notes, etc.) rollo, *m;* (in a gun) taco, *m. vt sew* acolchar; (furniture) emborrar; (guns) atacar; (stuff) rellenar
wadding *n* borra, *f;* (lining) entretela, *f;* (for guns) taco, *m;* (stuffing) relleno, *m*
waddle *n* anadeo, *m, vi* anadear
waddling *a* patojo, que anadea
wade *vi* and *vt* andar (en el agua, etc.); vadear; (paddle) chapotear. **to w. in,** entrar en (el agua, etc.); *fig* meterse en. **to w. through,** (a book) leer con dificultad; estudiar detenidamente; ir por
wader *n* el, *m,* (*f,* la) que vadea; (bird) ave zancuda, *f; pl* **waders,** botas de vadear, *f pl*
wafer *n* (host) hostia, *f;* (for sealing) oblea, *f;* (for ices) barquillo, *m*
waffle *n cul* fruta de sartén, *f*
waft *vt* llevar por el aire o encima del agua; hacer flotar; (stir) mecer; (of the wind) traer. *n* (fragrance) ráfaga de olor, *f*
wag *n* (of the tail) coleada, *f;* movimiento, *m;* meneo, *m;* (jester) bromista, *mf. vt* mover ligeramente; agitar; (of the tail) menear (la cola), colear. *vi* menearse; moverse; oscilar; (of the world) ir. **And thus the world wags,** Y así va el mundo
wage, wages *n* salario, *m; fig* premio, galardón, *m.* **minimum wage,** salario mínimo, *m.* **wages clerk,** pagador (-ra). **wage-earner,** asalariado (-da); (worker) trabajador (-ra)
wage *vt* emprender; sostener; hacer. **to w. war,** hacer guerra
wager *n* (bet) apuesta, *f;* (test) prueba, *f, vt* (bet) apostar; (pledge) empeñar. **to lay a w.,** hacer una apuesta
wages *n pl.* See **wage**
waggish *a* zumbón, jocoso; cómico
waggishness *n* jocosidad, *f*
waggle *vt* menear; mover; agitar; oscilar. *vi* menearse; moverse; agitarse; oscilar. *n* meneo, movimiento, *m;* oscilación, *f*
wagon *n* carro, *m;* carreta, *f;* (railway) vagón, *m.* **w.-lit,** coche cama, *m.* **w.-load,** carretada, *f;* vagón, *m*
wagoner *n* carretero, *m*
Wagnerian *a* wagneriano
waif *n* niño (-ña) sin hogar; animal perdido o abandonado, *m;* objeto extraviado, *m;* objeto sin dueño, *m.* **waifs and strays,** niños abandonados, *m pl*
wail *n* lamento, gemido, *m;* (complaint) queja, *f. vi* lamentarse, gemir; quejarse (de). *vt* lamentar, deplorar
wailer *n* lamentador (-ra)
wailing *n* lamentaciones, *f pl,* gemidos, *m pl, a* lamentador, gemidor
wainscot *n* entablado de madera, *m. vt* enmaderar; poner friso de madera (a)
waist *n* cintura, *f;* (blouse) blusa, *f;* (belt) cinturón, *m;* (bodice) corpiño, *m;* (narrowest portion) cuello, *m,* garganta, *f; naut* combés, *m.* **w.-band,** pretina, *f.* **w.-deep,** hasta la cintura. **w.-line,** cintura, *f.* **w. measurement,** medida de la cintura, *f.* **w.-coat,** chaleco, *m.* **w. strap,** trincha, *f*
wait *vi* and *vt* esperar, aguardar; (serve) servir. **to keep waiting,** hacer esperar. **to w. at table,** servir a la mesa. **to w. on oneself,** servirse a sí mismo; cuidarse a sí mismo; hacer las cosas por sí solo. **to w. one's time,** aguardar la ocasión. **to w. for,** (until) esperar hasta que; (of persons) esperar (a), aguardar (a); (in ambush) acechar. **to w. upon,** (serve) servir (a); (visit) visitar; presentar sus respetos (a); (*fig* accompany) acompañar; (follow) seguir a
wait *n* espera, *f;* (pause) pausa, *f,* intervalo, *m;* (ambush) asechanza, *f; pl* **waits,** coro de nochebuena, *m.* **to lie in w. for,** estar en acecho para
waiter *n* camarero, mozo, *m;* (tray) bandeja, *f*
waiting *n* espera, *f. a* que espera; de espera; de servicio. **lady-in-w.,** dama de servicio, *f.* **w.-maid,** camarera, doncella, *f.* **w.-room,** (of a bus station, etc.) sala de espera, *f;* (of an office) antesala, *f*
waitress *n* camarera, *f*
waive *vt* renunciar (a); desistir (de)
wake *vi* estar despierto; despertarse; (watch) velar. *vt* despertar; (a corpse) velar (a). *n* vela, *f;* vigilia, *f;* (of a corpse) velatorio, *m;* (holiday) fiesta, *f;* (of a ship) estela, *f.* **in the w. of,** *naut* en la estela de; después de; seguido por
wakeful *a* vigilante; (awake) despierto. **to be w.,** pasar la noche en vela
wakefulness *n* vigilancia, *f;* (sleeplessness) insomnia, *f*
waken *vi* despertarse. *vt* despertar; (call) llamar
waking *a* despierto; de vela. *n* despertar, *m;* (watching) vela, *f*
wale *n* (weal) verdugo, *m,* huella de azote, *f, vt* azotar
Wales (País de) Gales, *m*
walk *n* (pace) paso, *m;* (modo de) andar, *m;* (journey on foot) paseo, *m,* vuelta, *f;* (long) caminata, *f;* (promenade) paseo, *m,* avenida, *f;* (path) senda, *f;* (rank) clase social, *f;* esfera, *f;* profesión, *f;* ocupación, *f.* **quick w.,** paseo rápido, *m;* (pace) andar rápido, *m.* **to go for a w.,** ir de paseo. **to take a w.,** dar un paseo (or una vuelta), pasear. **to take for a w.,** llevar a paseo, sacar a paseo. **w.-out,** (strike) huelga, *f.* **w.-over,** triunfo, *m,* (or victoria, *f*) fácil. **w. past,** desfile, *m*
walk *vi* andar; caminar; ir a pie; (take a walk) pasear, dar un paseo; (of ghosts) aparecer; (behave) conducirse. *vt* hacer andar; (take for a walk) sacar a paseo; andar de una parte a otra (de), recorrer; (a specified distance) hacer a pie, andar; (a horse) llevar al paso. **to w. abroad,** dar un paseo; salir. **to w. arm in arm,** ir de bracero. **to w. past,** pasar; (in procession) desfilar. **to w. quickly,** andar de prisa. **to w. slowly,** andar despacio, andar lentamente. **to w. the hospitals,** estudiar en los hospitales. **to w. the streets,** recorrer las calles; vagar por las calles. **to w. about,** pasearse; ir y venir. **to w. after,** seguir (a), ir detrás de. **to w. along,** andar por; recorrer. **to w. away,** marcharse, irse. **to w. away with,** (win) ganar, llevarse; (steal) quitar, tomar, alzarse con. **to w. back,** volver; volver a pie, regresar a pie. **to w. down,** bajar; bajar a pie; andar por. **to w. in,** entrar en; entrar a pie en; (walk about) pasearse en. **to w. on,** seguir andando; (step on) pisar. **to w. out,** salir. **to w. over,** andar por; llevar la victoria (a); triunfar fácilmente sobre. **to w. round,** dar la vuelta a. **to w. round and round,** dar vueltas. **to w. up,** subir andando; subir. **to w. up and down,** dar vueltas, ir y venir
walker *n* (pedestrian) peatón, *m;* andador (-ra); (promenader) paseante, *mf*
walking *n* el andar; (excursion on foot) paseo, *m. a* andante; de andar; a pie; ambulante. **at a w. pace,** a un paso de andadura. **w. encyclopedia,** enciclopedia ambulante, *f.* **w. match,** marcha atlética, *f.* **w.-stick,** bastón, *m.* **w. tour,** excursión a pie, *f*
Walkyrie *n* valquiria, *f*
wall *n* muro, *m;* (rampart) muralla, *f;* (*fig* and of an organ, cavity, etc.) pared, *f.* **partition w.,** tabique, *m.*

Walls have ears, Las paredes oyen. **w. lizard,** lagartija, *f.* **w. map,** mapa mural, *m.* **w.-painting,** pintura mural, *f.* **w.-paper,** papel pintado, *m.* **w. socket,** *elec* enchufe, *m*
wall *vt* cercar con un muro; amurallar. **to w. in,** murar. **to w. up,** tapiar, tabicar
wallet *n* cartera, *f*; bolsa de cuero, *f*
wallflower *n* alhelí, *m*
Walloon *a* and *n* valón (-ona)
wallop *n* golpe, *m*, *vt* tundir, zurrar
wallow *vi* revolcarse; encenagarse; (in riches, etc.) nadar (en). *n* revuelco, *m*
walnut *n* (tree and wood) nogal, *m*; (nut) nuez de nogal, *f*
walrus *n* morsa, *f*
waltz *n* vals, *m*, *vi* valsar
wan *a* ojeroso, descolorido; (of the sky, etc.) pálido, sin color
wand *n* vara, *f*; (conductor's) batuta, *f*. **magic w.,** varita mágica, *f*
wander *vi* errar, vagar; (deviate) extraviarse; (from the subject) desviarse del asunto; divagar; (be delirious) delirar. *vt* vagar por, errar por, recorrer
wanderer *n* vagabundo (-da); hombre, *m*, (*f*, mujer) errante; (traveler) viajero (-ra)
wandering *a* errante; vagabundo; nómada; (traveling) viajero; (delirious) delirante; (of thoughts, the mind) distraído; (of cells, kidneys, etc.) flotante. *n* vagancia, *f*; viaje, *m*; (delirium) delirio, *m*; (digression) divagación, *f*; (of a river, etc.) meandro, *m*. **the w. Jew,** el judío errante
wane *vi* (of the moon, etc.) menguar; (decrease) disminuir; (*fig* decay) decaer. *n* (of the moon) menguante de la luna, *f*; mengua, *f*; disminución, *f*; decadencia, *f*
waning *a* menguante
wanly *adv* pálidamente; *fig* tristemente
wanness *n* palidez, *f*; *fig* tristeza, *f*
want *vt* (lack) carecer de, faltar; (need) necesitar, haber menester de; (require or wish) querer, desear; (demand) exigir; (ought) deber; (do without) pasarse sin. *vi* hacer falta; carecer (de); (be poor) estar necesitado. **I don't w. to,** No quiero, No me da la gana. **to be wanted,** hacer falta; (called) ser llamado. **You are wanted on the telephone,** Te llaman por teléfono
wanted se necesita; (advertisement) demanda, *f*. **Estelle wants me to write a letter,** Estrella quiere que escriba una carta. **What do you w. me to do?** ¿Qué quiere Vd. que haga?; ¿En qué puedo servirle? **What does Paul w.?** ¿Qué quiere Pablo?; (require) ¿Qué necesita Pablo? **He wants (needs) a holiday,** Le hacen falta unas vacaciones, Necesita unas vacaciones
want *n* (lack) falta, *f*; escasez, carestía, *f*; (need) necesidad, *f*; (poverty) pobreza, indigencia, *f*; (absence) ausencia, *f*; (wish) deseo, *m*; exigencia, *f*. **in w. of,** por falta de; en la ausencia de. **to be in w.,** estar en la necesidad, ser indigente
wanting *a* deficiente (en); falto (de); (scarce) escaso; ausente; (in intelligence) menguado. *prep* (less) menos; (without) sin. **to be w.,** faltar. **to be w. in,** carecer de
wanton *a* (playful) juguetón; (wilful) travieso; (loose) suelto, libre; (unrestrained) desenfrenado; extravagante; excesivo; caprichoso; (dishevelled) en desorden; (reckless) indiscreto; (of vegetation) lozano; (purposeless) inútil; imperdonable; frívolo; (unchaste) disoluto; lascivo. *n* mujer disoluta, *f*; ramera, *f*; (child) niño (-ña) juguetón (-ona)
wantonly *adv* innecesariamente; sin motivo; excesivamente; lascivamente
war *n* guerra, *f*. *a* de guerra; guerrero. *vi* guerrear. **at war with,** en guerra con. **cold war,** guerra tonta, *f*. **on a war footing,** en pie de guerra. **We are at war,** Estamos en guerra. **to be on the war-path,** *fig inf* buscar pendencia, tratar de armarla. **to declare war on,** declarar la guerra (a). **to make war on,** hacer la guerra (a). **war to the death,** guerra a muerte, *f*. **war correspondent,** corresponsal en el teatro de guerra, *m*. **war-cry,** alarido de guerra, grito de combate, grito de guerra *m*. **war-dance,** danza guerrera, *f*. **war horse,** caballo de batalla, *m*. **war loan,** empréstito de guerra, *m*. **war-lord,** adalid, caudillo, jefe militar, *m*. **war material,** pertrechos de guerra, *m pl*; municiones, *f pl*. **war memorial,** monumento a los caídos, *m*. **war minister,** Ministro de la Guerra, *m*. **war neurosis,** neurosis de guerra, *f*. **War Office,** Ministerio de la Guerra, *m*. **war plane,** avión de guerra, *m*. **war-ship,** barco (or buque) de guerra, *m*. **war-wearied,** agotado por la guerra
warble *vt* and *vi* trinar; gorjear; murmurar. *n* trino, *m*; gorjeo, *m*; murmurio, *m*
ward *n* protección, *f*; (of a minor) pupilo (-la); (of locks, keys) guarda, *f*; (of a city) barrio, distrito, *m*; (of a hospital, etc.) sala, *f*; (of a prison) celda, *f*; (fencing) guardia, *f*. **w.-room,** cuarto de los oficiales, *m*. **w. sister,** hermana de una sala de hospital, *f*
ward *vt* proteger, defender. **to w. off,** desviar; evitar
warden *n* guardián, *m*; director (-ra); (of a prison) alcaide, *m*; (of a church) mayordomo de la iglesia, *m*; (of a port) capitán, *m*
warder *n* (gaoler) guardián, *m*; alabardero, guardia, *m*
Wardour-Street English *n* inglés arcaizante de magüerista, *m*
wardress *n* guardiana, *f*
wardrobe *n* guardarropa, ropero, *m*; (clothes) ropa, *f*; *theat* vestuario, *m*. **w. trunk,** baúl mundo, *m*
ware *n* mercadería, *f*; (pottery) loza, *f*; *pl* **wares,** mercancías, *f pl*
war effort *n* esfuerzo bélico, esfuerzo de guerra, esfuerzo guerrero, *m*
warehouse *n* almacén, *m*, *vt* almacenar
warehouseman *n* almacenero, *m*
warfare *n* guerra, *f*; lucha, *f*; arte militar, *m*, or *f*. **chemical w.,** guerra química, *f*
war head *n* (of torpedo) cabeza de combate, punto de combate, *f*; (of missile) detonante, *m*
war heroe *n* héroe de guerra, *m*
war heroine *n* heroína de guerra, *f*
warily *adv* con cautela, cautelosamente; prudentemente
wariness *n* cautela *f*; prudencia, *f*
warlike *a* belicoso, guerrero; militar, de guerra; marcial. **war-spirit,** espíritu belicoso, *m*, marcialidad, *f*
warm *a* caliente; (lukewarm) tibio; (hot) caluroso; (affectionate) cordial, cariñoso, afectuoso; (angry) acalorado; (enthusiastic) entusiasta, ardiente; (art) cálido; (of coats, etc.) de abrigo; (fresh) fresco, reciente; *inf* adinerado. *vt* calentar; *fig* encender; entusiasmar. *vi* calentarse; *fig* entusiasmarse (con). **to have a w. at the fire,** calentarse al lado del fuego. **to be w.,** (of things) estar caliente; (of coats, etc.) ser de abrigo; (of the weather) hacer calor; (of people) tener calor. **to grow w.,** calentarse; (grow angry) excitarse, agitarse; (of a discussion) hacerse acalorado. **to keep w.,** conservar caliente; calentar. **to keep oneself w.,** estar caliente, no enfriarse. **to w. up,** calentar. **w.-blooded,** de sangre caliente; ardiente. **w.-hearted,** de buen corazón; generoso; afectuoso, cordial. **w.-heartedness,** buen corazón, *m*; generosidad, *f*; cordialidad, *f*
warming *n* calentamiento, *m*; calefacción, *f*. *a* calentador; para calentar. **w.-pan,** calentador, *m*
warmly *adv* (affectionately) cordialmente, afectuosamente; con entusiasmo; (angrily) acaloradamente. **to be w. wrapped up,** estar bien abrigado
warmonger *n* atizador de guerra, belicista, fautor de guerra, fomentador de guerra, propagador (-ra) de guerra
warmth *n* calor, *m*
warn *vt* advertir; prevenir; amonestar; (inform) avisar
warning *n* advertencia, *f*; aviso, *m*; amonestación, *f*; (lesson) lección, *f*, escarmiento, *m*; alarma, *f*. *a* amonestador; de alarma. **to give w.,** prevenir, advertir; (dismiss) despedir. **to take w.,** escarmentar

warningly *adv* indicando el peligro; con alarma; con amenaza

warp *vt* torcer; combar; *naut* espiar; (the mind) pervertir. *vi* torcerse; combarse, bornearse; *naut* espiarse. *n* (in a fabric) urdimbre, *f;* (in wood) comba, *f,* torcimiento, *m;* *naut* espía, *f.* **w. and woof,** trama y urdimbre, *f*

warping *n* (of wood) combadura, *f;* (weaving) urdidura, *f;* *naut* espía, *f;* (of the mind) perversión, *f.* **w. frame,** urdidera, *f*

warrant *n* autoridad, *f;* justificación, *f;* autorización, *f;* garantía, *f;* decreto de prisión, *m;* orden, *f;* *com* orden de pago, *f;* *mil* nombramiento, *m;* motivo, *m,* razón, *f.* *vt* justificar; autorizar; garantizar, responder por; asegurar. **pay w.,** boletín de pago, *m*

warrantable *a* justificable

warrantor *n* garante, *mf*

warranty *n* autorización, *f;* justificación, *f;* *law* garantía, *f*

warren *n* (for hunting) vedado, *m;* (rabbit) conejera, *f;* vivar, *m,* madriguera, *f*

warrior *n* guerrero, *m;* soldado, *m*

Warsaw Varsovia, *f*

wart *n* verruga, *f*

wary *a* cauto, cauteloso; prudente

wash *vt* lavar; (dishes) fregar; (lave) bañar; (clean) limpiar; (furrow) surcar; (wet) regar, humedecer; (with paint) dar una capa de color o de metal. *vi* lavarse; lavar ropa. **Two of the crew were washed overboard,** El mar arrastró a dos de los tripulantes. **Will this material w.?** ¿Se puede lavar esta tela? ¿Es lavable esta tela? **to w. ashore,** echar a la playa. **w. away,** (remove by washing) quitar lavando; derrubiar; (water or waves) arrastrar, llevarse. **to w. one's hands,** lavarse las manos. **to look washed out,** estar ojeroso. **to w. down,** lavar; limpiar; (remove) llevarse; (accompany with drink) regar. **to w. off,** *vt* quitar lavando; hacer desaparecer; borrar; (of waves, etc.) llevarse; (of color) desteñir. *vi* borrarse; desteñirse. **to w. up,** lavar los platos, fregar la vajilla; (cast up) desechar. **w. one's dirty laundry in public,** sacar los más sucios trapillos a la colada

wash *n* lavadura, *f,* lavado, *m;* baño, *m;* (clothes) ropa para lavar, ropa sucia, *f;* colada, *f;* (of the waves) chapoteo, *m;* (lotion) loción, *f;* (coating) capa, *f;* (silt) aluvión, *m.* **w.-basin,** palangana, *f;* lavabo, *m.* **w.-board,** tabla de lavar, *f.* **w.-house,** lavadero, *m.* **w.-leather,** gamuza, badana, *f.* **w.-out,** fracaso, *m.* **w.-stand,** aguamanil, lavabo, *m.* **w.-tub,** cuba de lavar, *f*

washable *a* lavable

washer *n* lavador (-ra); (washerwoman) lavandera, *f;* (machine) lavadora, *f;* *mech* arandela, *f*

washerwoman *n* lavandera, *f*

washing *n* lavamiento, *m;* ropa sucia, ropa para lavar, *f;* ropa limpia, *f;* ropa, *f;* (bleaching) blanqueadura, *f;* (toilet) abluciones, *f pl;* *ecc* lavatorio, *m;* *pl* **washings,** lavazas, *f pl.* **There is a lot of w. to be done,** Hay mucha ropa que lavar. **w.-board,** tabla de lavar, *f.* **w.-day,** día de colada, *m.* **w.-machine,** lavadora, máquina de lavar, *f.* **w.-soda,** carbonato sódico, *m.* **w.-up,** lavado de los platos, *m.* **w.-up machine,** fregador mecánico de platos, *m*

wasp *n* avispa, *f,* *Lat. Am. also* jicote, *m.* **wasp's nest,** avispero, *m.* **w.-waisted,** (of clothes) ceñido, muy ajustado

waspish *a* enojadizo, irascible; malicioso; mordaz

waste *vt* desperdiciar, derrochar, malgastar; (time) perder; consumir; corroer; (devastate) asolar, devastar; echar a perder; malograr; disipar; agotar. *vi* gastarse; consumirse; perderse. **to w. time,** perder el tiempo. **to w. away,** (of persons) demacrarse, consumirse

waste *n* (wilderness) yermo, desierto, *m;* (vastness) inmensidad, vastedad, *f;* (loss) pérdida, *f;* (squandering) despilfarro, derroche, *m;* disminución, *f;* (refuse) desechos, *m pl;* (of cotton, etc.) borra, *f;* disipación, *f.* *a* (of land) sin cultivar; yermo; inútil; desechado, de desecho; superfluo. **to lay w.,** devastar. **w. land,** yermo, *m;* tierras sin cultivar, *f pl.* **w. paper,** papel usado, papel de desecho, *m.* **w.-paper basket,** cesto para papeles, *m.* **w.-pipe,** desaguadero, tubo de desagüe, *m*

wasteful *a* pródigo, derrochador, manirroto; antieconómico; ruinoso; inútil

wastefully *adv* pródigamente; antieconómicamente; inútilmente

wastefulness *n* prodigalidad, *f,* despilfarro, *m;* pérdida, *f;* gasto inútil, *m;* falta de economía, *f*

waster *n* gastador (-ra); disipador (-ra); (loafer) golfo, *m*

watch *vi* velar; mirar. *vt* mirar; observar; guardar; (await) esperar; (spy upon) espiar, acechar. **to w. for,** buscar aguardar. **to w. over,** vigilar, guardar; (care for) cuidar; proteger. **watch out!** *Mexico* ¡abusado!

watch *n* (at night) vela, *f;* (wakefulness) desvelo, *m;* observación, vigilancia, *f;* (*mil naut*) guardia, *f;* (sentinel) centinela, *m;* (watchman) sereno, vigilante, *m;* (guard) ronda, *f;* (timepiece) reloj de bolsillo, *m.* **to be on the w.,** estar al acecho, estar al alerta, estar a la mira. **to keep w.,** vigilar. **dog w.,** media guardia, *f.* **pocket w.,** reloj de bolsillo, *m.* **wrist w.,** reloj de pulsera, *m.* **w.-case,** caja de reloj, relojera, *f.* **w.-chain,** cadena de reloj, leontina, *f.* **w.-dog,** perro guardián, *m.* **w.-glass,** cristal de reloj, *m.* **w.-making,** relojería, *f.* **w.-night,** noche vieja, *f.* **w.-spring,** muelle de reloj, *m,* espiral, *f.*

watcher *n* observador (-ra); espectador (-ra); (at a sick bed) el, *m,* (*f,* la) que vela a un enfermo

watchful *a* vigilante, alerto; observador; atento, cuidadoso

watchfully *adv* vigilantemente; atentamente

watchfulness *n* vigilancia, *f;* cuidado, *m;* desvelo, *m*

watching *n* observación, *f;* (vigil) vela, *f*

watchmaker *n* relojero (-ra). **watchmaker's shop,** relojería, *f*

watchman *n* vigilante, sereno, *m;* guardián, *m*

watchword *n* (password) consigna, contraseña, *f;* (motto) lema, *m*

water *n* agua, *f;* (tide) marea, *f;* (of precious stones) aguas, *f pl;* (urine) orina, *f;* (quality) calidad, clase, *f.* *a* de agua; por agua; acuático; hidráulico. **fresh w.,** (not salt) agua dulce, *f;* agua fresca, *f.* **hard w.,** agua cruda, *f.* **high w.,** marea alta, *f.* **low w.,** marea baja, *f.* **of the first w.,** de primera clase. **running w.,** agua corriente, *f.* **soft w.,** agua blanda, *f.* **to make w.,** *naut* hacer agua; orinar. **to take the waters,** tomar las aguas. **under w.,** *adv* debajo del agua. *a* acuático. **w.-bird,** ave acuática, *f.* **w. blister,** ampolla, *f.* **w.-boatman,** chinche de agua, *f.* **w.-borne,** flotante. **w.-bottle,** cantimplora, *f.* **w.-brash,** acedia, *f.* **w.-butt,** barril, *m,* pipa, *f.* **w.-carrier,** aguador (-ra). **w.-cart,** carro de regar, *m.* **w.-closet,** retrete, excusado, *m.* **w.-color,** acuarela, *f.* **w.-color painting,** pintura a la acuarela, *f.* **w.-colorist,** acuarelista, *mf* **w.-cooled,** enfriado por agua. **w.-cooler,** cantimplora, *f.* **w.-finder,** zahorí, *m.* **w. front,** (wharf) muelle, *m;* puerto, *m;* litoral, *m.* **w.-gauge,** indicador de nivel de agua, *m,* vara de aforar, *f.* **w.-glass,** vidrio soluble, silicato de sosa, *m.* **w. heater,** calentador de agua, *m.* **w.-ice,** helado, *m.* **w.-level,** nivel de las aguas, *m.* **w.-lily,** nenúfar, *m,* azucena de agua, *f.* **w.-line,** lengua de agua, *f;* (of a ship) línea de flotación, *f.* **w.-logged,** anegado en agua. **w.-main,** cañería maestra de agua, *f.* **w. man,** barquero, *m.* **w.-melon,** sandía, *f.* **w. mill,** aceña, *f.* **w.-nymph,** náyade, *f.* **w.-pipe,** cañería del agua, *f.* **w. pitcher,** jarro, *m.* **w. plant,** planta acuática, *f.* **w.-polo,** polo acuático, *m.* **w.-power,** fuerza hidráulica, *f.* **w.-rate,** cupo del consumo de agua, *m.* **w. snake,** culebra de agua, *f.* **w. softener,** generador de agua dulce, *m;* purificador de agua, *m.* **w. spaniel,** perro (-rra) de aguas. **w. sprite,** ondina, *f.* **w.-supply,** abastecimiento de agua, *m;* traída de aguas, *f.* **w. tank,** depósito para agua, *m.* **w. tower,** arca de agua, *f.* **w. wave,** ondulado al agua, *m.* **w.-way,** canal, río, *m,* o vía *f,* navegable. **w.-wheel,** rueda hidráulica, *f,* azud, *m;* (for irrigation) aceña, *f.* **w. wings,** nadaderas, *f pl*

water *vt* (irrigate, sprinkle) regar; (moisten) mojar; (cattle, etc.) abrevar; (wine, etc.) aguar; diluir con agua; (bathe) bañar. *vi* (of animals) beber agua; (of engines, etc.) tomar agua; (of the eyes, mouth) hacerse agua. **My mouth waters,** Se me hace agua la boca

watercourse *n* corriente de agua, *f;* cauce, *m;* lecho de un río, *m*

watercress *n* berro, mastuerzo, *m*

watered *a* regado, abundante en agua; (of silk) tornasolado

watered-down *fig* pasado por agua

waterfall *n* salto de agua, *m,* cascada, catarata, *f*

wateriness *n* humedad, *f;* acuosidad, *f*

watering *n* riego, *m;* irrigación, *f;* (of eyes) lagrimeo, *m;* (of cattle, etc.) el abrevar (a); *naut* aguada, *f.* **w.-can,** regadera, *f.* **w.-cart,** carro de regar, *m.* **w.-place,** (for animals) aguadero, *m;* (for cattle) abrevadero, *m;* (spa) balneario, *m;* (by the sea) playa de veraneo, *f*

watermark *n* (in paper) filigrana, *f;* nivel del agua, *m. vt* filigranar

waterproof *a* impermeable; a prueba de agua. *n* impermeable, *m. vt* hacer impermeable, impermeabilizar

water-repellent *a* repelente al agua

watershed *n* vertiente, *f;* línea divisoria de las aguas, *f;* (river-basin) cuenca, *f*

waterspout *n* bomba marina, manga, trompa, *f*

watertight *a* impermeable, estanco; a prueba de agua; (of arguments, etc.) irrefutable

watertightness *n* impermeabilidad, *f*

waterworks *n* establecimiento para la distribución de las aguas, *m;* obras hidráulicas, *f pl*

watery *a* (wet) húmedo; acuoso; (of the sky) de lluvia; (of eyes) lagrimoso, lloroso; (sodden) mojado; (of soup, etc.) claro; insípido

watt *n* vatio, *m.* **w. hour,** vatio hora, *m.* **w.-meter,** vatímetro, *m*

wattage *n* vatiaje, *m*

wattle *n* zarzo, *m;* (of turkey) barba, *f;* (of fish) barbilla, *f*

wave *vi* ondear; ondular; flotar; hacer señales. *vt* (brandish) blandir; agitar; (the hair) ondular; ondear; hacer señales (de). **They waved goodby to him,** Le hicieron adiós con la mano; Le hicieron señas de despedida; Se despidieron de él agitando el pañuelo

wave *n* (of the sea) ola, *f; phys* onda, *f;* (in hair or a surface) ondulación, *f;* (movement) movimiento, *m;* (of anger, etc.) ráfaga, *f.* **long w.,** onda larga, *f.* **medium w.,** onda media, *f.* **short w.,** onda corta, *f.* **sound w.,** onda sonora, *f.* **to have one's hair waved,** hacerse ondular el pelo. **w. band,** franja undosa, escala de longitudes de onda, *f.* **w. crest,** cresta de la ola, cabrilla, *f.* **w.-length,** longitud de onda, *f*

wavelet *n* pequeña ola, olita, *f;* (ripple) rizo (del agua), *m*

wave of immigration una imigración, *f*

waver *vi* ondear; oscilar; (hesitate) vacilar, titubear; (totter) tambalearse; (weaken) flaquear

waverer *n* irresoluto (-ta), vacilante, *m*

wavering *n* vacilación, irresolución, *f. a* oscilante; vacilante, irresoluto; flotante

waving *n* ondulación, *f;* oscilación, *f;* agitación, *f;* movimiento, *m. a* ondulante; oscilante; que se balancea

wavy *a* ondulado; flotante

wax *n* cera, *f;* (cobblers') cerote, *m;* (in the ear) cerilla, *f. a* de cera. *vt* encerar. *vi* crecer; hacerse; ponerse. **to wax enthusiastic,** entusiasmarse. **waxed paper,** papel encerado, *m.* **wax chandler,** cerero, *m.* **wax doll,** muñeca de cera, *f.* **wax modeling,** modelado en cera, *m,* ceroplástica, *f.* **wax taper,** blandón, *m*

waxen *a* de cera; como la cera; de color de cera

waxing *n* enceramiento, *m;* (of the moon) crecimiento, *m;* aumento, *m*

wax museum *n* museo de cera, *m*

waxwork *n* figura de cera, *f*

waxy *a.* See **waxen**

way *n* camino, *m;* senda, *f;* paso, *m;* ruta, *f;* (railway, etc.) vía, *f;* dirección, *f;* rumbo, *m;* distancia, *f;* (journey) viaje, *m;* (sea crossing) travesía, *f;* avance, progreso, *m;* (*naut* etc.) marcha, *f;* método, *m;* modo, *m;* (means) medio, *m;* manera, *f;* (habit) costumbre, *f;* (behavior) conducta, *f,* modo de obrar, *m;* (line of business, etc.) ramo, *m;* (state) estado, *m,* condición, *f;* (course) curso, *m;* (respect) punto de vista, *m;* (particular kind) género, *m;* (scale) escala, *f.* **a long way off,** a gran distancia, a lo lejos. **a short way off,** a poca distancia, no muy lejos. **by way of,** pasando por; por vía de; como; por medio de; a modo de. **by the way,** de paso; durante el viaje; durante la travesía; a propósito, entre paréntesis. **in a small way,** en pequeña escala. **in a way,** hasta cierto punto; desde cierto punto de vista. **in many ways,** de muchos modos; por muchas cosas. **in no way,** de ningún modo; nada. **in the way,** en el medio. **in the way of,** en cuanto a, tocante a; en materia de. **I went out of my way to,** Dejé el camino para; Me di la molestia de. **Is this the way to . . . ?** ¿Es este el camino a . . . ? **Make way!** ¡Calle! **Milky Way,** vía láctea, *f.* **on the way,** en camino; al paso; durante el viaje. **out of the way,** puesto a un lado; arrinconado; apartado, alejado; (imprisoned) en prisión; fuera del camino; remoto; (unusual) original. **over the way,** en frente; al otro lado (de la calle, etc.). **right of w.,** derecho de paso, *m.* **The ship left on its way to . . . ,** El barco zarpó con rumbo a . . . **the Way of the Cross,** vía crucis, *f.* **This way!** ¡Por aquí!; De este modo, Así. **this way and that,** en todas direcciones, por todos lados. **"This way to . . . ,"** «Dirección a . . .» A . . . **under way,** en camino; en marcha; en preparación. **to bar the way,** cerrar el paso. **to be in the way,** estorbar. **to be out of the way of doing,** haber perdido la costumbre de hacer (algo). **to clear the way,** abrir paso, abrir calle; *fig* preparar el terreno. **to force one's way through,** abrirse paso por. **to find a way,** encontrar un camino; *fig* encontrar medios. **to find one's way,** hallar el camino; orientarse. **to get into the way of,** contraer la costumbre de. **to get under way,** *naut* zarpar, hacerse a la vela; ponerse en marcha. **to give way,** ceder; (break) romper. **to go a long way,** ir lejos; contribuir mucho (a). **to have one's own way,** salir con la suya. **to keep out of the way,** *vt* and *vi* esconder(se); mantener(se) alejado; mantener(se) apartado. **to lose one's way,** perder el camino; desorientarse; *fig* extraviarse. **to make one's way,** abrirse paso. **to make one's way down,** bajar. **to make one's way round,** dar la vuelta a. **to make one's way up,** subir. **to make way,** hacer lugar; hacer sitio; dar paso (a). **to pay one's way,** ganarse la vida; pagar lo que se debe. **to prepare the way for,** preparar el terreno para. **to put out of the way,** poner a un lado; apartar; (kill) matar; (imprison) poner en la cárcel; hacer cautivo (a). **to see one's way,** poder ver el camino; poder orientarse; ver el modo de hacer algo; ver cómo se puede hacer algo. **ways and means,** medios y arbitrios, *m pl.* **way back,** camino de regreso, *m;* vuelta, *f.* **way down,** bajada, *f.* **way in,** entrada, *f.* **way out,** salida, *f.* **way round,** camino alrededor, *m;* solución, *f;* modo de evitar . . . , *m.* **way through,** paso, *m.* **way up,** subida, *f*

wayfarer *n* transeúnte, *mf;* viajero (-ra)

wayfaring *a* que va de viaje; errante, ambulante

waylay *vt* asechar, salir al paso (de)

wayside *n* borde del camino, *m. a* (of flowers) silvestre; (by the side of the road) en la carretera

wayward *a* caprichoso; desobediente; voluntarioso; travieso; rebelde

waywardness *n* desobediencia, indocilidad, *f;* voluntariedad, *f;* travesura, *f;* rebeldía, *f*

we *pron* nosotros, *m pl;* nosotras, *f pl,* (Usually omitted except for emphasis or for clarity.) **We are in the garden,** Estamos en el jardín. **We have come, but they are not here,** Nosotros hemos venido pero ellos no están aquí

weak *a* débil; flojo; frágil; delicado; (insecure) inseguro;

(of arguments) poco convincente; (of prices, markets, etc.) flojo, en baja; (sickly) *Lat. Am.* farruto, *Central America, Mexico* fifiriche. **w.-eyed,** de vista floja. **w.-kneed,** débil de rodillas; *fig* sin voluntad. **w.-minded,** sin carácter; pusilánime; **w. spot,** debilidad, *f*; flaco, *m*; lado débil, *m*; desventaja, *f*

weaken *vt* debilitar; (diminish) disminuir. *vi* debilitarse; flaquear, desfallecer; (give way) ceder

weakening *n* debilitación, *f*. *a* debilitante; enervante

weaker *a comp* más débil. **the w. sex,** el sexo débil

weakling *n* ser delicado, *m*, persona débil, *f*; cobarde, *m*; *inf* alfeñique, *m*

weakly *a* enfermizo, delicado, enclenque. *adv* débilmente

weakness *n* debilidad, *f*; imperfección, *f*

weal *n* bienestar, *m*; prosperidad, *f*; (blow) verdugo, *m*

wealth *n* riqueza, *f*; abundancia, *f*; bienes, *m pl*

wealthy *a* rico, adinerado, acaudalado; abundante (en)

wean *vt* destetar, ablactar; separar (de); privar (de); enajenar el afecto de; (of ideas) desaferrar (de)

weaning *n* ablactación, *f*, destete, *m*

weapon *n* arma, *f*; *pl* **weapons,** (*zool, bot*) medios de defensa, *m pl*. **steel w.,** arma blanca, *f*

wear *n* uso, *m*; gasto, *m*; deterioro, *m*; (fashion) moda, boga, *f*. **for hard w.,** para todo uso. **for one's own w.,** para su propio uso. **for evening w.,** para llevar de noche. **for summer w.,** para llevar en verano. **w. and tear,** uso y desgaste, *m*; deterioro natural, *m*

wear *vt* llevar; llevar puesto; traer; usar; (have) tener; (exhibit) mostrar; (be clad in) vestir; (waste) gastar; deteriorar; (make) hacer; (exhaust) agotar, cansar, consumir. *vi* (last) durar; (of persons) conservar(se); (of time) correr; avanzar. **She wears well,** Está bien conservada. **to w. one's heart on one's sleeve,** tener el corazón en la mano. **to w. the trousers,** *fig inf* llevar los pantalones. **to w. well,** durar mucho. **to w. away,** *vt* gastar, roer; (rub out) borrar; consumir. *vi* (of time) pasar lentamente, transcurrir despacio. **to w. down,** gastar; consumir; reducir; agotar las fuerzas de; destruir; (tire) fatigar. **to w. off,** *vt* destruir; borrar. *vi* quitarse; borrarse; *fig* desaparecer, pasar. **to w. on,** (of time) transcurrir, correr, pasar. **to w. out,** *vt* usar; romper con el uso; consumir, acabar con; (exhaust) agotar; (tire) rendir. *vi* usarse; romperse con el uso; consumirse

wearable *a* que se puede llevar

wearer *n* el, *m*, (*f*, la) que lleva alguna cosa

weariness *n* cansancio, *m*, fatiga, lasitud, *f*; aburrimiento, *m*; aversión, repugnancia, *f*

wearing *n* uso, *m*; desgaste, *m*. *a* (tiring) agotador; cansado. **w. apparel,** ropa, *f*

wearisome *a* cansado; laborioso; aburrido, tedioso, pesado

wearisomeness *n* cansancio, *m*; aburrimiento, tedio, hastío, *m*

weary *a* cansado, fatigado; aburrido; hastiado; impaciente; tedioso, enfadoso. *vt* cansar, fatigar; aburrir; hastiar; molestar. *vi* cansarse, fatigarse; aburrirse. **to w. for,** anhelar, suspirar por; (miss) echar de menos (a). **to w. of,** aburrirse de; (things) impacientarse de; (people) impacientarse con

weasel *n* comadreja, *f*

weather *n* tiempo, *m*; intemperie, *f*; (storm) tempestad, *f*. *a naut* del lado del viento; de barlovento. *vt* (of rain, etc.) desgastar; curtir; secar al aire; *naut* pasar a barlovento; (bear) aguantar, capear; (survive) sobrevivir a; luchar con. *vi* curtirse a la intemperie. **Andrew is a little under the w.,** Andrés está algo destemplado; (with drink) Andrés tiene una mona; (depressed) Andrés está melancólico. **to be bad (good) w.,** hacer mal (buen) tiempo. **What is the w. like?** ¿Qué tiempo hace? ¿Cómo está el tiempo? **w.-beaten,** curtido por la intemperie. **w. chart,** carta meteorológica, *f*. **w. conditions,** condiciones meteorológicas, *f pl*. **w. forecast,** pronóstico del tiempo, *m*. **w.-hardened,** endurecido a la intemperie. **w. prophet,** meteorologista, *mf* **w. report,** boletín meteorológico, *m*. **w.-worn,** gastado por la intemperie; curtido por la intemperie

weathercock *n* veleta, *f*

weathering *n* desintegración por la acción atmosférica, *f*

weather-resistant *a* resistente a la intemperie

weave *vt* tejer; trenzar; entrelazar; *fig* tejer. *vi* tejer. *n* tejido, *m*; textura, *f*

weaver *n* tejedor (-ra)

weaving *n* tejido, *m*; tejeduría, *f*. **w. machine,** telar, *m*

web *n* tejido, *m*; tela, *f*; (network) red, *f*; (spider's) telaraña, *f*; (of a feather) barba, *f*; (of birds, etc.) membrana interdigital, *f*; (of intrigue) red, *f*; (snarl) lazo, *m*, trampa, *f*. **web-foot,** pie palmado, *m*. **web-footed,** palmípedo.

webbed *a* (of feet) unido por una membrana

wed *vt* casarse con; (join in marriage, cause to marry) casar; *fig* unir. *vi* estar casado; casarse

wedded *a* casado; matrimonial, conyugal; *fig* unido (a); aficionado (a), entusiasta (de), devoto (de); aferrado (a). **to be w. to one's own opinion,** estar aferrado a su propia opinión

wedding *n* boda, *f*, casamiento, *m*; (with golden, etc.) bodas, *f pl*; (union) enlace, *m*, *a* de boda, nupcial, matrimonial, conyugal; de novios, de la novia. **golden w.,** bodas de oro, *f pl*. **silver w.,** bodas de plata, *f pl*. **w. bouquet,** ramo de la novia, *m*. **w.-breakfast,** banquete de bodas, *m*. **w.-cake,** torta de la boda, *f*, pan de la boda, *m*. **w.-day,** día de la boda, *m*. **w.-march,** marcha nupcial, *f*. **w.-present,** regalo de boda, regalo de la boda, *m*. **w.-ring,** anillo de la boda, *m*, *Lat. Am.* argolla, *f*. **w. trip,** viaje de novios, *m*

wedge *n* cuña, *f*; (under a wheel) calza, alzaprima, *f*; *mil* cuña, mella, *f*; (of cheese) pedazo, *m*. *vt* acuñar, meter cuñas; (a wheel) calzar; (fix) sujetar. **to be the thin end of the w.,** ser el principio, ser el primer paso. **to drive a w.,** *mil* hacer mella, practicar una cuña. **to w. oneself in,** introducirse con dificultad (en). **w.-shaped,** cuneiforme

wedlock *n* matrimonio, *m*

Wednesday *n* miércoles, *m*

wee *a* pequeñito, chiquito. **a wee bit,** un poquito

weed *n* mala hierba, *f*; tabaco, *m*; (cigar) cigarro, *m*; (person) madeja, *f*; (*fig* evil) cizaña, *f*. *vt* carpir, desherbar, sachar, sallar, escardar. *Lat. Am.* desmalezar; *fig* extirpar, arrancar. **w.-grown,** cubierto de malas hierbas. **to w. out,** extirpar; quitar

weeder *n* (person) escardador (-ra); (implement) sacho, *m*

weedy *a* lleno de malas hierbas; *fig* raquítico

week *n* semana, *f*. **in a w.,** de hoy en ocho (días); en una semana; después de una semana. **once a w.,** una vez por semana. **a w. ago,** hace una semana. **a w. later** *Lat. Am.* a la semana. **Michael will come a w. from today,** Miguel llegará hoy en ocho. **w. in, w. out,** semana tras semana. **w.-day,** día de trabajo, día laborable, día de la semana que no sea el domingo. **on weekdays,** entre semana, *m*. **w.-end,** fin de semana, *m*. **w.-end case,** saco de noche, *m*

weekly *a* semanal, semanario; de cada semana. *adv* semanalmente, cada semana. *n* semanario, *m*, revista semanal, *f*

weep *vt* and *vi* llorar. **to w. for,** (a person) llorar (a); (on account of) llorar por; (with happiness, etc.) llorar de. **They wept for joy,** Lloraron de alegría

weeping *n* lloro, llanto, *m*, lágrimas, *f pl*. *a* lloroso, que llora; (of trees) llorón. **w.-willow,** sauce llorón, *m*

weevil *n* gorgojo, *m*

weigh *vt* pesar; (consider) considerar, ponderar, tomar en cuenta; comparar; (the anchor) levar. *vi* pesar; ser de importancia. **to w. anchor,** zarpar, levar el ancla, hacerse a la vela. **to w. down,** pesar sobre; sobrecargar; hacer inclinarse bajo; *fig* agobiar. **to be weighed down,** hundirse por su propio peso; *fig* estar agobiado. **to w. out,** pesar. **to w. with,** influir (en). **w.-bridge,** báscula, *f*

weighing *n* pesada, *f*; (weight) peso, *m*; (of the anchor) leva, *f*; (consideration) ponderación, consideración, *f*. **w.-machine,** báscula, *f*

weight *n* peso, *m*; (heaviness) pesantez, *f*; cargo, *m*; (of a clock and as part of a system) pesa, *f*; *fig* peso, *m*, importancia, *f*. *vt* cargar; (a stick) emplomar; aumentar el peso (de); poner un peso (a). **gross w.,** peso bruto, *m*. **heavy w.,** peso pesado, *m*. **light w.,** peso ligero, *m*. **middle w.,** peso medio, *m*. **net w.,** peso neto, *m*. **to lose w.,** adelgazar. **loss of w.,** (of a person) adelgazamiento, *m*. **to put on w.,** cobrar carnes, hacerse más gordo. **to put the w.,** *sport* lanzar el peso. **to throw one's w. about,** *inf* darse importancia. **to try the w. of,** sopesar. **weights and measures,** pesas y medidas, *f pl*. **weightlifting,** halterofilia, *f*

weighty *a* pesado; (influential) influyente; importante, de peso; grave

weir *n* presa, esclusa, *f*; (for fish) cañal, *m*

weird *a* misterioso, sobrenatural; fantástico; mágico; (queer) raro, extraño. **the W. Sisters,** las Parcas

weirdly *adv* misteriosamente; fantásticamente; (queerly) de un modo raro, extrañamente

weirdness *n* misterio, *m*; cualidad fantástica, *f*; lo sobrenatural; (queerness) rareza, *f*

welcome *a* bienvenido; (pleasant) grato, agradable. *n* bienvenida, *f*; buena acogida, *f*; (reception) acogida, *f*. *vt* dar la bienvenida (a); acoger con alegría, acoger con entusiasmo; agasajar, festejar; (receive) acoger, recibir; recibir con gusto. **W.!** ¡Bienvenido! **to bid w.,** dar la bienvenida (a). **You are w.,** Estás bienvenido. **You are w. to it,** Está a su disposición

welcoming *a* acogedor, cordial, amistoso

weld *vt* soldar; combinar; unificar

welder *n* soldador, *m*

welding *n* soldadura, *f*; unión, fusión, *f*

welfare *n* bienestar, bien, *m*; (health) salud, *f*; prosperidad, *f*; intereses, *m pl*. **w. state,** estado benefactor, estado de beneficencia, estado socializante, *m*. **w. work,** trabajo social, *m*

well *a* bien; bien de salud; bueno; conveniente; (advantageous) provechoso; favorable; (happy) feliz; (healed) curado; (recovered) repuesto. **I am very w.,** Estoy muy bien. **to get w.,** ponerse bien. **to make w.,** curar. **w. enough,** bastante bien

well *adv* bien; (very) muy; favorablemente; convenientemente; (easily) sin dificultad. **as w.,** también. **as w. as,** tan bien como; además de. **That is all very w. but . . . ,** Todo eso está muy bien pero . . . **to be w. up in,** estar versado en. **to get on w. with,** llevarse bien con. **Very w.!** ¡Está bien!; Muy bien. **w. and good,** bien está. **w. now,** ahora bien. **w. then,** conque; pues bien. **w.-advised,** bien aconsejado; prudente. **w.-aimed,** certero. **w.-appointed,** bien provisto; (furnished) bien amueblado. **w.-attended,** concurrido. **w.-balanced,** bien equilibrado. **w.-behaved,** bien educado; (of animals) manso. **w.-being,** bienestar, *m*; felicidad, *f*. **w.-born,** bien nacido, de buena familia. **w.-bred,** bien criado, bien educado; (of animals) de pura raza. **w.-chosen,** bien escogido. **w.-defined,** bien definido. **w.-deserved,** bien merecido. **w.-disposed,** bien dispuesto; favorable; bien intencionado. **w.-doing,** *n* el obrar bien; obras de caridad, *f pl*, *a* bondadoso, caritativo. **w.-done,** *a* bien hecho. *interj* ¡bravo! **w.-educated,** instruido, culto. **w.-favored,** guapo, de buen parecer. **w.-founded,** bien fundado. **w.-groomed,** elegante. **w.-grounded,** bien fundado; bien instruido. **w.-informed,** instruido; culto, ilustrado. **w.-intentioned,** bien intencionado. **w.-known,** bien conocido, notorio, *Lat. Am.* connotado. **w.-meaning,** bien intencionado. **w.-modulated,** armonioso. **w.-off,** acomodado, adinerado; feliz. **w.-read,** culto, instruido. **w.-shaped,** bien hecho; bien formado. **w.-shaped nose,** nariz perfilada, *f*. **w.-spent,** bien empleado. **w.-spoken,** bien hablado; bien dicho. **w.-stocked,** bien provisto. **w.-suited,** apropiado. **w.-timed,** oportuno. **w.-to-do,** acomodado, rico. **w.-wisher,** amigo (-ga). **w.-worn,** raído; (of paths) trillado

well *n* pozo, *m*; (of a stair) caja, *f*; cañón de escalera, *m*; (fountain) fuente, *f*, manantial, *m*; (of a fishing boat) vivar, *m*; (of a ship) sentina, *f*. **w.-sinker,** pocero, *m*

well *vi* chorrear, manar, brotar, fluir

Welsh *a* galés, de Gales. *n* (language) galés, *m*. **the W.,** los galeses

Welshman *n* galés, *m*

Welshwoman *n* galesa, *f*

welt *n* (of shoe) vira, *f*, cerquillo, *m*; (in knitting) ribete, *m*; (weal) verdugo, *m*

Weltanschauung *n* cosmovisión, postura de vida, *f*

welter *vi* revolcarse; bañarse (en), nadar (en). *n* confusión, *f*, tumulto, *m*; mezcla, *f*. **w.-weight,** peso welter, *m*

wench *n* mozuela, muchacha, *f*

wend *vt* dirigir, encaminar. *vi* ir. **to w. one's way,** dirigir sus pasos, seguir su camino

west *n* oeste, *m*; poniente, *m*; occidente, *m*. *a* del oeste; occidental. *adv* hacia el oeste, a poniente; al occidente. **W. Indian,** de las Antillas, de las Indias Occidentales. **w.-north-w.,** oesnorueste, *m*. **w.-south-w.,** oessudueste, *m*. **w. wind,** viento del oeste, poniente, *m*

westerly *a* del oeste; hacia el oeste; occidental

western *a* occidental; del oeste. *n* (novel) novela caballista, *f*; (film) película del oeste, *f*

Western Hemispheric americano

westernized *a* influido por el occidente

westernmost *a* más al oeste

West Indies Indias Occidentales, *f pl*

westward *a* que está al oeste. *adv* hacia el oeste; hacia el occidente

wet *a* mojado; húmedo; (rainy) lluvioso. *vt* mojar; humedecer. *n* (rain) lluvia, *f*. **"Mind the wet paint!"** «¡Cuidado, recién pintado!» **to be wet,** estar mojado; (of the weather) llover. **to get wet,** mojarse. **wet blanket,** *fig* aguafiestas, *mf* **wet through,** (of persons) calado, hecho una sopa. **wet-nurse,** nodriza, *Lat. Am.* criandera, *f*

wetting *n* mojada, *f*; humectación, *f*; (soaking) remojo, *m*

whack *n* golpe, *m*; (try) tentativa, *f*; (portion) porción, parte, *f*. *vt* golpear, aporrear, pegar

whale *n* ballena, *f*. **sperm w.,** cachalote, *m*. **w.-oil,** aceite de ballena, *m*

whalebone *n* barbas de ballena, *f pl*, ballena, *f*

whaler *n* (man) ballenero, pescador de ballenas, *m*; (boat) buque ballenero, *m*

whaling *a* ballenero. *n* pesca de ballenas, *f*. **w.-gun,** cañón arponero, *m*

wharf *n* muelle, embarcadero, descargadero, *m*, *vt* amarrar al muelle

what *a pron* (interrogative and exclamatory) qué; cómo; (relative) que; el que, *m*; la que, *f*; lo que, *neut*; los que, *m pl*; las que, *f pl*; (which, interrogative) cuál, *mf*; cuáles, *mf pl*; (how many) cuantos, *m pl*; cuantas, *f pl*; (interrogative and exclamatory) cuántos, *m pl*; cuántas, *f pl*; (how much, interrogative and exclamatory) cuánto, *m*; cuánta, *f*. **And w. not,** Y qué sé yo qué más. **Make w. changes you will,** Haz los cambios que quieras. **W. confidence he had . . . ,** La confianza que tenía . . . **W. is this called?** ¿Cómo se llama esto? **W. did they go there for?** ¿Por qué fueron? **W. do you take me for?** ¿Por quién me tomas? **That was not w. he said,** No fue eso lo que dijo. **to know what's w.,** saber cuántas son cinco. **You have heard the latest news, w.?** Has oído las últimas noticias, ¿verdad? **W. a pity!** ¡Qué lástima! **W., do you really believe it?** ¿Lo crees de veras? **W. else?** ¿Qué más? **W. for?** ¿Para qué? **what's-his-name,** fulano (-na) de tal, *m*. **W. ho!** ¡Hola! **W. if . . . ?** ¿Qué será si . . . ? **W. is the matter?** ¿Qué pasa? ¿Qué hay? **w. though . . . ,** aun cuando . . . ; ¿Qué importa qué? **w. with one thing, w. with another,** entre una cosa y otra. **What's more, . . .** Es más, . . .

whatever *a pron* cuanto; todo lo que; cualquier cosa que; cualquier. **W. sacrifice is necessary,** Cualquier sacrificio que sea necesario. **W. I have is yours,** Todo lo que tenga es vuestro. **W. happens,** Venga lo que venga. **It is of no use w.,** No sirve absolutamente para nada

wheal *n.* See **weal**

wheat *n* trigo, *m. a* de trigo. **summer w.,** trigo tremesino, *m.* **whole w.,** *a* de trigo entero. **w.-ear,** espiga de trigo, *f.* **w.-field,** trigal, *m.* **w.-sheaf,** gavilla de trigo, *f*

wheedle *vt* lagotear, engatusar, *Lat. Am. also* engaratusar; (flatter) halagar; (with out) sacar con mimos

wheedling *a* zalamero, mimoso; marrullero. *n* lagotería, *f,* mimos, *m pl;* (flattery) halagos, *m pl;* marrullería, *f*

wheel *n* rueda, *f;* (bicycle) bicicleta, *f;* (for steering a ship) timón, *m;* rueda del timón, *f;* (for steering a car) volante, *m;* (for spinning) rueca, *f;* (potter's) rueda de alfarero, *f;* (of birds) vuelo, *m;* (turn) vuelta, *f; mil* conversión, *f.* **Catherine w.,** (firework) rueda de Santa Catalina, *f.* **back w.,** rueda trasera, *f.* **front w.,** rueda delantera, *f.* **to break on the w.,** enrodar. **to go on wheels,** ir en ruedas; *fig* ir viento en popa. **to take the w.,** (in a ship) tomar el timón; tomar el volante. **w. of fortune,** rueda de la fortuna, *f.* **w.-chair,** silla de ruedas, *f.* **w.-house,** timonera, *f.* **w.-mark,** rodada, *f*

wheel *vt* hacer rodar; (push) empujar; (drive) conducir; transportar; llevar; pasear; (turn) hacer girar. *vi* girar; dar vueltas; ir en bicicleta. **to w. about,** cambiar de frente; volverse; cambiar de rumbo

wheelbarrow *n* carretilla, *f*

wheeled *a* de . . . ruedas; con ruedas. **w. chair,** silla de ruedas, *f*

wheeler-dealer *n Lat. Am.* ardilla, *f*

wheeling *n* rodaje, *m; mil* conversión, *f;* (of birds) vuelos, *m pl,* vueltas, *f pl.* **free-w.,** rueda libre, *f*

wheelwright *n* carpintero de carretas, ruedero, *m*

wheeze *vi* ser asmático, jadear, respirar fatigosamente, resollar

wheezing *n* resuello, jadeo, *m;* respiración fatigada, *f*

whelp *n* cachorro (-rra). *vi* and *vt* parir

when *adv* cuando (interrogative, cuándo); (as soon as) tan pronto como, en cuanto; (meaning 'and then') y luego, y entonces; (although) aunque. **I will see you w. I return,** Te veré cuando vuelva. **W. he came to see me he was already ill,** Cuando vino a verme estaba enfermo ya. **We returned a week ago, since w. I have not been out,** Volvimos hace ocho días y desde entonces no he salido. **Since w.?** ¿Desde cuándo?

whence *adv* de donde (*interrogative,* de dónde); a donde (*interrogative* a dónde); por donde, de que; por lo que. **W. does he come?** ¿De dónde viene? **W. comes it that?** ¿Cómo es que . . . ?

whenever *adv* cuando quiera que, siempre que; cada vez que, todas las veces que; cuando

where *adv pron* donde (*interrogative,* dónde); en donde; en que (*interrogative,* en qué); (to where with verbs of motion) a donde (*interrogative,* a dónde); (from where with verbs of motion) de donde (*interrogative,* de dónde). **W. are you going to?** ¿A dónde va Vd.? **This is w. we get out,** (of a bus, etc.) Nos apeamos aquí

whereabouts *adv* (*interrogative*) dónde; (relative) donde. *n* paradero, *m*

whereas *conjunc* (inasmuch as) visto que, ya que; (although) mientras (que)

whereat *adv* por lo cual; a lo cual

whereby *adv* cómo; por qué; por el cual, con el cual

wherefore *adv* (why) por qué; por lo cual. *n* porqué, *m*

wherein *adv* en donde (*interrogative,* en dónde); en que (*interrogative,* en qué)

whereinto *adv* en donde; dentro del cual; en lo cual

whereof *adv* de que; (whose) cuyo

whereon *adv* sobre que; en qué

whereto *adv* adonde; a lo que

whereupon *adv* dónde; sobre lo cual, con lo cual; en consecuencia de lo cual

wherever *adv* dondequiera (que), en cualquier sitio; adondequiera (que). **Sit w. you like,** Siéntate donde te parezca bien

wherewith *adv* con que (*interrogative,* con qué)

wherewithal *n* lo necesario; dinero necesario, *m*

whet *vt* (knives, etc.) afilar, amolar, aguzar; (curiosity, etc.) excitar, estimular

whether *conjunc* si; que; sea que, ya que. **W. he will or no,** Que quiera, que no quiera. **w. or not,** si o no

whetstone *n* afiladera, amoladera, piedra de amolar, *f*

whetting *n* aguzadura, amoladura, *f;* (of curiosity, etc.) estimulación, excitación, *f*

whey *n* suero (de la leche), *m*

which *a* and *pron* cuál, *mf;* cuáles, *mf pl;* que (interrogative, qué); el cual, *m;* la cual, *f;* lo cual, *neut;* los cuales, *m pl;* las cuales, *f pl;* el que, *m;* la que, *f;* lo que, *neut;* los que, *m pl;* las que, *f pl;* (who) quien. **all of w.,** todo lo cual, etc. **in w.,** en donde, en el que; donde. **the w.,** el cual, la cual, etc. **W. would you like?** ¿Cuál quieres? **The documents w. I have seen,** Los documentos que he visto. **W. way have we to go?** ¿Por dónde hemos de ir?

whichever *a* and *pron* cualquiera (que), *mf;* cualesquiera, *mf pl;* el que, *m;* la que, *f;* (of persons only) quienquiera (que), *mf;* quienesquiera (que), *mf pl* **Give me w. you like,** Dame el que quieras. **I shall take w. of you would like to come,** Me llevaré a cualquiera de Vds. que guste de venir

whiff *n* (of air) soplo, *m;* vaho, *m;* fragancia, *f*

while *n* rato, *m;* momento, *m;* tiempo, *m.* **after a w.,** al cabo de algún tiempo, después de algún tiempo. **a little w. ago,** hace poco. **all this w.,** en todo este tiempo. **at whiles,** a ratos, de vez en cuando. **between whiles,** de cuando en cuando; entre tanto. **It is worth your w. to do it,** Vale la pena de hacerse. **Mary smiled the w.,** María mientras tanto se sonreía. **once in a w.,** de vez en cuando; en ocasiones

while *conjunc* mientras (que); al (followed by an infinitive); al mismo tiempo que; a medida que; (although) aunque; si bien. **w. I was walking down the street,** mientras andaba por la calle, al andar yo por la calle. *vt* **to w. (away),** pasar, entretener. **to w. away the time,** pasar el rato

whim *n* capricho, antojo, *m;* manía, *f;* extravagancia, *f;* fantasía, *f*

whimper *n* quejido, sollozo, gemido, *m, vi* lloriquear, quejarse, sollozar, gemir

whimpering *n* lloriqueo, llanto, *m, a* que lloriquea

whimsical *a* antojadizo, caprichoso; fantástico

whimsicality *n* capricho, *m,* extravagancia, *f;* fantasía, *f*

whimsically *adv* caprichosamente; fantásticamente

whine *vi* gimotear, lloriquear; quejarse

whining *n* gimoteo, lloriqueo, *m;* quejumbres, *f pl. a* que lloriquea; quejumbroso

whinny *n* relincho, hin, *m, vi* relinchar

whip *vt* azotar; pegar; *cul* batir; *sew* sobrecoser; (ropes, etc.) ligar; (defeat) vencer. *vi* moverse rápidamente. **to w. down,** *vi* bajar volando, bajar corriendo. *vt* arrebatar (de). **to w. in,** entrar precipitadamente (en), penetrar apresuradamente (en). **to w. off,** cazar a latigazos, despachar a golpes; (remove) quitar rápidamente; (persons) llevar corriendo, llevar aprisa. **to w. open,** abrir rápidamente. **to w. out,** *vt* (draw) sacar rápidamente; (utter) saltar diciendo (que); proferir. *vi* escabullirse, escaparse, salir apresuradamente. **to w. round,** volverse de repente. **to w. up,** *vt* (horses, etc.) avivar con el látigo; (snatch) coger de repente agarrar; (gather) reunir. *vi* (mount) subir corriendo

whip *n* azote, zurriago, *Lat. Am.* chicote, *m;* (riding) látigo, *m.* **blow with a w.,** latigazo, *m.* **to have the w.-hand,** mandar, tener la sartén por el mango; tener la ventaja. **w.-cord,** tralla del látigo, *f*

whippet *n* especie de perro (-rra) lebrero (-ra)

whipping *n* paliza, *f*, vapuleo, azotamiento, *m*. **w. post,** picota, *f*. **w. top,** trompo, *m*, peonza, *f*
whirl *n* vuelta, *f*, giro, *m*; rotación, *f*; *fig* torbellino, *m*. *vi* girar; dar vueltas; (dance) bailar, danzar. *vt* hacer girar; dar vueltas (a); (carry) llevar rápidamente. **to w. along,** volar (por), pasar aprisa (por); dejar atrás los vientos, correr velozmente. **to w. past,** pasar volando (por); pasar como una exhalación. **to w. through,** atravesar rápidamente, cruzar volando
whirligig *n* perinola, *f*; (merry-go-round) tiovivo, *m*
whirlpool *n* vórtice, remolino, *m*; *fig* vorágine, *f*
whirlwind *n* torbellino, *m*, manga de viento, *f*
whirr *n* zumbido, *m*; (of wings) ruido (de las alas), *m*. *vi* girar; zumbar
whirring *n* zumbido, *m*; ruido, *m*. *a* que gira; que zumba
whisk *n* cepillo, *m*; *cul* batidor, *m*; (movement) movimiento rápido, *m*. *vt cul* batir; (wag) menear, mover rápidamente; (with off, away) quitar rápidamente; sacudirse; arrebatar; (take away a person) llevarse (a). *vi* moverse rápidamente; andar rápidamente
whiskers *n pl* mostacho, *m*, patillas, barbas, *f pl*; (of a feline) bigotes, *m pl*
whiskered *a* bigotudo
whisky *n* güísqui, *m*
whisper *n* cuchicheo, *m*; (rumour) voz, *f*; (of leaves, etc.) susurro, murmullo, *m*. *vi* and *vt* cuchichear, hablar al oído; (of leaves, etc.) susurrar; (of rumors) murmurar. **in a w.,** al oído, en un susurro
whisperer *n* cuchicheador (-ra); (gossip) murmurador (-ra)
whispering *n* cuchicheo, *m*; susurro, *m*; (gossip) murmurio, *m*. **w. gallery,** galería de los murmullos, *f*. *inf* sala de los secretos, *f*
whistle *n* (sound) silbido, silbo, *m*; (instrument) pito, silbato, *m*; *inf* gaznate, *m*. *vi* and *vt* silbar. **blast on the w.,** pitido, *m*. **to w. for,** llamar silbando; *inf* esperar sentado, buscar en vano
whistler *n* silbador (-ra)
whistling *n* silbido, *m*, *a* silbador
whit *n* pizca, *f*, bledo, *m*. **not a w.,** ni pizca
Whit, Whitsun *a* de Pentecostés. **W. Monday,** lunes de Pentecostés, *m*
white *a* blanco; pálido; puro. *n* color blanco, blanco, *m*; (pigment) pintura blanca, *f*; (whiteness) blancura, *f*; (of egg) clara (del huevo), *f*; (person) blanco, *m*. **Elizabeth went w.,** Isabel se puso pálida. **the w.,** (billiards) la blanca. **the w. of the eye,** lo blanco del ojo. **w. ant,** hormiga blanca, termita, *f*. **w. cabbage,** repollo, *m*. **w. caps,** (of waves) cabrillas, *f pl*; (of mountains) picos blancos, *m pl*. **w. clover,** trébol blanco, *m*. **w. corpuscle,** glóbulo blanco, *m*. **w. currant,** grosella blanca, *f*. **w. elephant,** elefante (-ta) blanco (-ca). **w. ensign,** pabellón blanco, *m*. **w.-faced,** de cara pálida. **w. fish,** pescado blanco, *m*. **w. flag,** bandera blanca, *f*. **w.-haired,** de pelo blanco. **w. heat,** calor blanco, *m*, candencia, *f*; ardor, *m*. **w. horses,** cabrillas, palomas, *f pl*. **w.-hot,** incandescente. **W. House, the,** la Casa Blanca, *f*. **w. lead,** albayalde, *m*. **w. lie,** mentira inocente, mentira oficiosa, mentira piadosa, la mentirilla, *f*. **w. man,** blanco, hombre de raza blanca, *m*. **the white man's burden,** la misión sagrada de la civilización blanca, *f*. **w. meat,** carne blanca, pechuga, *f*. **w. paper,** libro blanco, *m*. **w. sauce,** salsa blanca, *f*. **w. slave,** víctima de la trata de blancas, *f*. **w. slavery,** trata de blancas, *f*. **w. sugar,** azúcar blanco, azúcar de flor, *m*. **w. woman,** mujer de raza blanca, *f*
whiten *vt* blanquear. *vi* blanquearse
whiteness *n* blancura, *f*; palidez, *f*; pureza, *f*; *poet* nieve, *f*
whitening *n* blanqueo, *m*; blanco de España, *m*; blanco para los zapatos, *m*
whitewash *vt* blanquear, jalbegar, encalar; (*fig* of faults) disculpar, justificar
whitewashing *n* blanqueo, *m*, encaladura, *f*
whither *adv* (interrogative) adónde; (with a clause) adonde
whithersoever *adv* adondequiera
whiting *n* blanco de España, *m*; blanco para los zapatos, *m*; (fish) pescadilla, *f*, merlango, *m*
whitish *a* blanquecino
whitlow *n* panadizo, *m*
Whitsunday *n* domingo de Pentecostés, *m*
Whitsuntide *n* pascua de Pentecostés, *f*
whittle *n* navaja, *f*. *vt* cercenar, cortar; (sharpen) afilar, sacar punta (a); tallar; *fig* reducir. **to w. away, down,** *fig* reducir a nada
whizz *n* silbido, zumbido, *m*, *vi* silbar, zumbar
whizzing *n* silbido, *m*, *a* que zumba
who *pron* (interrogative) quién, *mf*; quiénes, *mf pl*; (relative) quien, *mf*; quienes, *mf pl*; que; (in elliptical constructions the person that, etc.) el que, *m*; la que, *f*; los que, *m pl*; las que, *f pl*
whoa *interj* ¡so!
whoever *pron* quienquiera (que); cualquiera (que); quien. **Give it to w. you like,** Dáselo a quien te parezca bien
whole *a* (healthy) sano; (uninjured) ileso, entero; todo. *n* todo, *m*; total, *m*; totalidad, *f*; conjunto, *m*. **on the w.,** por regla general, en general; en conjunto. **the w. week,** la semana entera, toda la semana. **w.-hearted,** sincero, genuino; entusiasta. **w.-heartedly,** de todo corazón. **w.-heartedness,** sinceridad, *f*; entusiasmo, *m*. **w. length,** *a* de cuerpo entero. **w. number,** número entero, *m*
wholemeal *n* harina de trigo entero, *f*, *a* de trigo entero
wholeness *n* totalidad, *f*; integridad, *f*; todo, *m*
wholesale *a com* al por mayor; en grueso; *fig* general; en masa. *n* venta al por mayor, *f*. **w. price,** precio al por mayor, *m*. **w. trade,** comercio al por mayor, *m*
wholesaler *n* comerciante al por mayor, *mf* mercader de grueso, *m*
wholesome *a* sano; saludable; (edifying) edificante
wholesomeness *n* sanidad, *f*; lo sano; lo saludable
wholly *adv* completamente, enteramente, totalmente; integralmente; del todo
whom *pron* quien; a quien, *mf*; a quienes, *mf pl*; (interrogative) a quién, *mf*; a quiénes, *mf pl*; al que, *m*; a la que, *f*; a los que, *m pl*; a las que, *f pl*. **from w.,** de quien; (interrogative) de quién. **the man w. you saw,** el hombre a quien viste
whoop *n* alarido, grito, *m*; estertor de la tos ferina, *m*. *vi* dar gritos, chillar; (whooping-cough) toser
whooping cough *n* tos ferina, coqueluche, *f*
whore *n* puta, ramera, *f*, *Lat. Am. also* araña, *f*
whorl *n* (of a shell) espira, *f*; *bot* verticilo, *m*; (of a spindle) tortera, *f*
whorled *a bot* verticilado; (of shells) en espira
whose *pron* cuyo, *m*; cuya, *f*; cuyos, *m pl*; cuyas, *f pl*; de quien, *mf*; de quienes, *mf pl*; (*interrogative*) de quién, de quiénes; **W. daughter is she?** ¿De quién es ella la hija? **This is the writer w. name I always forget,** Este es el autor cuyo nombre siempre olvido
whosoever *pron*. See **whoever**
why *adv* (*interrogative*) por qué; (on account of which) por el cual, *m*; por la cual, *f*; por lo cual, *neut*; por los cuales, *m pl*; por las cuales, *f pl*; (how) cómo. *n* ni porqué, *m*, *interj* ¡qué!; ¡cómo!; ¡toma!; si. **not to know the why or wherefore,** no saber ni el porqué ni el cómo, no saber ni el qué ni el por qué. **Why! I have just come,** ¡Si no hago más de llegar! **Why not?** ¿Por qué no? ¡Cómo no!
wick *n* mecha, torcida, *f*
wicked *a* malo; malvado, perverso; pecaminoso; malicioso; (mischievous) travieso
wickedly *adv* mal; perversamente; maliciosamente
wickedness *n* maldad, *f*; perversidad, *f*; pecado, *m*; (mischievousness) travesura, *f*
wicker *n* mimbre, *m*, *a* de mimbre
wicket *n* postigo, portillo, *m*; (half-door) media puerta, *f*; (at cricket) meta, *f*. **w.-keeper,** guardameta, *m*

wide *a* ancho; (in measurements) de ancho; vasto; extenso; grande; amplio; (loose) holgado; (distant) lejos; liberal; general, comprensivo. *adv* lejos; completamente. **far and w.,** por todas partes. **to be too w.,** ser muy ancho; estar muy ancho; (of garments) venir muy ancho. **two feet w.,** dos pies de ancho. **w.-awake,** muy despierto; despabilado; vigilante. **w.-eyed,** con los ojos muy abiertos; asombrado. **w.-open,** abierto de par en par

widely *adv* extensamente; generalmente; (very) muy

widen *vt* ensanchar; extender. *vi* ensancharse; extenderse

widening *n* ensanche, *m*; extensión, *f*

widespread *a* universal, generalizado; extenso; esparcido. **to become w.,** generalizarse

widow *n* viuda, *f*. *vt* dejar viuda; dejar viudo; *fig* privar. **to be a grass w.,** estar viuda. **to become a w.,** enviudar, perder al esposo. **widow's pension,** viudedad, *f*. **widow's weeds,** luto de viuda, *m*

widowed *a* viudo

widower *n* viudo, *m*. **to become a w.,** perder a la esposa, enviudar

widowerhood, widowhood *n* viudez, *f*

width *n* anchura, *f*; (of cloth) ancho, *m*; (of mind) liberalismo, *m*. **double w.,** (cloth) doble ancho, *m*

wield *vt* (a scepter) empuñar; (power, etc.) ejercer; (a pen, sword) manejar

wife *n* esposa, mujer, *f*; mujer, *f*; comadre, *f*. **husband and w.,** los cónyuges, los esposos. **old wives' tale,** cuento de viejas, *m*. **The Merry Wives of Windsor,** Las alegres comadres de Windsor. **to take to w.,** contraer matrimonio con, tomar como esposa (a)

wifely *a* de esposa, de mujer casada; de mujer de su casa; conyugal

wig *n* peluca, *f*; (hair) cabellera, *f*. **top wig,** peluquín, *m*. **wigmaker,** peluquero, *m*

wigged *a* con peluca, de peluca

wigging *n* (scolding) peluca, *f*

wigwam *n* tienda de indios, *f*

wild *a* (of animals, men, land) salvaje; (barren) desierto, yermo; (mountainous) riscoso, montañoso; (of plants, birds) silvestre; montés; (disarranged) en desorden, desarreglado; (complete) absoluto, completo; (dissipated) disipado; vicioso; (foolish) alocado; (of the sea) bravío; (of weather, etc.) borrascoso; (mad with delight, etc.) loco; (frantic, mad) frenético, loco; (with 'talk,' etc.) extravagante; insensato, desatinado; (shy) arisco; (incoherent) inconexo, incoherente; (frightened) alarmado, espantado; (wilful) travieso, indomable. *n* tierra virgen, *f*; desierto, *m*; soledad, *f*. **It made me w.,** (angry) Me hizo rabiar. **to run w.,** volver al estado silvestre; (of persons) llevar una vida de salvajes; volverse loco. **to shoot w.,** errar el tiro. **to spread like w. fire,** propagarse como el fuego. **w. beast,** fiera, *f*. **w. boar,** jabalí, *m*. **w. cat,** gato montés, *Lat. Am.* lince, *m*. **w. duck,** pato silvestre, *m*. **w. goat,** cabra montesa, *f*. **w.-goose chase,** caza infructuosa, *f*; empresa quimérica, *f*. **w. oats,** avenas locas, *f pl*; *fig* indiscreciones de la juventud, *f pl*. **to sow one's w. oats,** andarse a la flor del berro

wilderness *n* desierto, *m*; yermo, páramo, despoblado, *m*; soledad, *f*; (jungle) selva, *f*; (maze) laberinto, *m*; infinidad, *f*

wildly *adv* en un estado salvaje; sin cultivo; (rashly) desatinadamente; sin reflexión, sin pensar; (incoherently) incoherentemente; (stupidly, of looking, etc.) tontamente; (in panic) con ojos espantados, con terror en los ojos, alarmado

wildness *n* salvajez, *f*; estado silvestre, *m*; naturaleza silvestre, *f*; (ferocity) ferocidad, *f*; (of the wind, sea) braveza, *f*; (of the wind) violencia, *f*; (impetuosity) impetuosidad, *f*; (of statements, etc.) extravagancia, *f*; (incoherence) incoherencia, *f*; (disorder) desorden, *m*; (wilfulness, of children) travesuras, *f pl*; (of the expression) gesto espantado, *m*

wile *n* estratagema, *f*, engaño, *m*, ardid, *f*

wilily *adv* astutamente

wiliness *n* astucia, *f*

will *n* voluntad, *f*; albedrío, *m*; (wish) deseo, *m*; (pleasure) discreción, *f*, placer, *m*; (legal document) testamento, *m*. **against my w.,** contra mi voluntad. **at w.,** a voluntad; a gusto; a discreción. **free w.,** libre albedrío, *m*. **of one's own free w.,** por su propia voluntad. **iron w.,** voluntad de hierro, *f*. **last w. and testament,** última disposición, última voluntad, *f*. **to do with a w.,** hacer con toda el alma, hacer con entusiasmo. **to make one's w.,** otorgar (hacer) su testamento. **w.-power,** fuerza de voluntad, *f*

will *vt* querer; disponer, ordenar; (bequeath) legar, dejar en testamento, mandar; (oblige) sugestionar (a una persona) para que haga algo; hipnotizar. *vi aux.* querer; (As a sign of the future it is not translated separately in Spanish) **I w. come tomorrow,** Vendré mañana. **John does not approve, but I w. go,** Juan no lo aprueba pero yo quiero ir. **Do what you w.,** Haga lo que a Vd. le parezca bien, Haga lo que Vd. quiera; Haga lo que haga. **Boys w. be boys,** Los niños son siempre niños. **He w. not (won't) do it,** No lo hará; No quiere hacerlo

willful *a* rebelde, voluntarioso; (of children) travieso; (of crimes, etc.) premeditado

willfully *adv* voluntariosamente; intencionadamente; (of committing crimes) con premeditación

willfulness *n* rebeldía, *f*; (obstinacy) terquedad, obstinación, *f*

William the Silent Guillermo el Taciturno

willing *a* dispuesto, inclinado; (serviceable) servicial; deseoso; espontáneo; complaciente; gustoso; (willingly) de buena gana. **to be w.,** estar dispuesto (a), querer; consentir (en)

willingly *adv* de buena gana, con gusto

willingness *n* buena voluntad, *f*; deseo de servir, *m*; complacencia, *f*; (consent) consentimiento, *m*

will-o'-the-wisp *n* fuego fatuo, *m*

willow *n* sauce, *m*. **weeping w.,** sauce llorón, *m*. **w.-pattern china,** porcelana de estilo chino, *f*. **w. tree,** sauce, *m*

willowy *a* lleno de sauces; (slim) cimbreño, esbelto, alto y delgado

willy nilly *adv* de buen o mal grado, mal que bien

wilt *vi* (of plants) marchitarse, secarse; *fig* languidecer; ajarse. *vt* marchitar; *fig* ajar; hacer languidecer

wily *a* astuto, chuzón

wimple *n* toca, *f*

win *vt* ganar; (reach) alcanzar, lograr; (a victory, etc.) llevarse; conquistar. *vi* ganar; triunfar. *n* triunfo, *m*. **to win back,** volver a ganar; recobrar

wince *vi* retroceder, recular; (flinch) quejarse; (of a horse) respingar. *n* respingo, *m*. **without wincing,** sin quejarse; estoicamente

winch *n* cabria, *f*; (handle) manubrio, *m*

wind *n* viento, *m*; aire, *m*; (flatulence) flatulencia, *f*; (breath) respiración, *f*, aliento, *m*; (idle talk) paja, *f*. **breath of w.,** soplo de viento, *m*. **following w.,** viento en popa, *m*. **high w.,** viento alto, viento fuerte, *m*. **land w.,** viento terrenal, *m*. **It's an ill w. that blows nobody good,** No hay mal que por bien no venga. **There is something in the w.,** Hay algo en el aire, Se trama algo. **to get w. of,** husmear. **to sail before the w.,** navegar de viento en popa. **The w. stiffened,** Refrescó el viento. **You took the w. out of his sails,** Le deshinchaste las velas. **w.-instrument,** instrumento de viento, *m*. **w.-proof,** a prueba del viento. **w.-swept,** expuesto a todos los vientos. **w. storm,** ventarrón, *m*

wind *vi* serpentear; desfilar lentamente; torcerse. *vt* (turn) dar vueltas (a); (a handle) manejar, mover; (a watch) dar cuerda (a); (wool, etc.) devanar, ovillar; (wrap) envolver; (of arms, embrace) rodear (con); (a horn) tocar. **to w. off,** devanar; desenrollar. **to w. round,** (wrap) envolver; (skirt) rodear; (embrace) ceñir con (los brazos); (pass by) pasar por; deslizarse

por; (of snakes) enroscarse. **to w. up,** (a watch) dar cuerda (a); (thread) devanar; (conclude) concluir; *com* liquidar; (excite) agitar, emocionar
windbag *n* pandero, *m*, sacamuelas, *mf*
winder *n* (person) devanador (-ra); (machine) devanadera, *f*; (of a clock) llave, *f*
windfall *n* fruta caída del árbol, *f*; (good luck) breva, *f*; ganancia inesperada, lotería, *f*
windiness *n* tiempo ventoso, *m*; situación expuesta a todos los vientos, *f*; (of speech) pomposidad, verbosidad, *f*
winding *a* tortuoso; (e.g., road) sinuoso; serpentino; en espiral. *n* tortuosidad, *f*; meandro, recoveco, *m*, vuelta, curva, *f*. **w. sheet,** mortaja, *f*, sudario, *m*. **w. stair,** escalera de caracol, *f*. **w.-up,** conclusión, *f*; *com* liquidación, *f*
windlass *n* torno, *m*
windless *a* sin viento
windmill *n* molino de viento, *m*
window *n* ventana, *f*; (of a shop) escaparate, *Mexico* aparador, *m*; (in a train, car, bank, etc.) ventanilla, *f*; (booking office) taquilla, *f*; (of a church) vidriera, *f*. **casement w.,** ventana, *f*. **sash w.,** ventana de guillotina, *f*. **small w.,** ventanilla, *f*. **stained glass w.,** vidriera, *f*. **to lean out of the w.,** asomarse a la ventana. **to look out of the w.,** mirar por la ventana. **w. blind,** (Venetian) persiana, *f*; transparente, *m*; (against the sun) toldo, *m*. **w.-dresser,** decorador (-ra) de escaparates. **w. frame,** marco de ventana, *m*. **w.-pane,** cristal (de ventana), *m*. **w.-shutter,** contraventana, *f*. **w.-sill,** repisa de la ventana, *f*, alféizar, *m*
windpipe *n* tráquea, *f*
windscreen *n* parabrisas, guardabrisa, *m*. **w.-wiper,** limpiaparabrisas, limpiavidrios, *m*
windward *n* barlovento, *m*. *a* de barlovento. *adv* a barlovento
windy *a* ventoso; expuesto al viento; (of style) hinchado, pomposo. **It is w.,** Hace viento
wine *n* vino, *m*; zumo fermentado (de algunas frutas), *m*. *a* de vino; de vinos; para vino. **in w.,** *cul* en vino; (drunk) ebrio, borracho. **heavy w.,** vino fuerte, *m*. **light w.,** vino ligero, *m*. **local w.,** vino del país, *m*, **matured w.,** vino generoso, *m*. **red w.,** vino tinto, *m*. **thin w.,** vinillo, *m*. **white w.,** vino blanco, *m*. **w.-cellar,** bodega, cueva, *f*. **w.-colored,** de color de vino. **w.-cooler,** cubo para enfriar vinos, *m*. **w. country,** tierra de vino, *f*. **w. decanter,** garrafa para vino, *f*. **w.-grower,** vinicultor (-ra). **w.-growing,** *n* vinicultura, *f*. *a* vinícola. **w. lees,** zupia, *f*. **w. merchant,** comerciante en vinos, *mf*. vinatero, *m*. **w.-press,** lagar, *m*. **w.-taster,** catavinos, *m*. **w. waiter,** bodeguero, *m*
wineskin *n* bota, *f*, odre, pellejo, *m*
wing *n* (of a bird and *zool, arch, aer, mil, bot*) ala, *f*; (flight) vuelo, *m*; *theat* bastidor, *m*; *fig* protección, *f*. *vt* dar alas (a); llevar sobre las alas; (wound) herir en el ala; herir en el brazo; volar por. *vi* volar. **beating of wings,** batir de alas, aleteo, *m*. **in the wings,** *theat* entre bastidores. **on the w.,** al vuelo. **to clip a (person's) wings,** cortar (*or* quebrar) las alas (a). **under his w.,** bajo su protección. **w.-case,** élitro (de un insecto), *m*. **w. chair,** sillón con orejas, *m*. **w.-commander,** teniente coronel de aviación, *m*. **w.-span,** (*zool* and *aer*) envergadura, *f*. **w.-spread,** extensión del ala, *f*. **w.-tip,** punta del ala, *f*
winged *a* alado, con alas; (in compounds) de alas . . .; (swift) alado; (of style) elevado, alado
wink *vi* (blink) pestañear; (as a signal, etc.) guiñar; (of stars, etc.) titilar, parpadear, centellear. *vt* guiñar (el ojo). *n* pestañeo, *m*; guiño, *m*. **not to sleep a w.,** no pegar los ojos. **to take forty winks,** echar una siesta. **to w. at,** guiñar el ojo (a); (ignore) hacer la vista gorda
winking *n* (blinking) parpadeo, *m*; (as a signal) guiños, *m pl*; (of stars, etc.) titilación, *f*, pestañeo, *m*. *a* (of stars, etc.) titilante. **like w.,** en un abrir y cerrar de ojos.
winner *n* ganador (-ra); vencedor (-ra)
winning *a* ganador; vencedor; (attractive) encantador. *n* ganancia, *f*. **w. number,** número galardonado, número premiado, número vencedor, *m*. **w.-post,** meta, *f*. **w. side,** *sport* equipo vencedor, *m*; (politics, etc.) partido vencedor, *m*
winnings *n* ganancias, *f pl*
winnow *vt* aventar, abalear; *fig* separar
winnower *n* aventador (-ra)
winnowing *n* abaleo, aventamiento, *m*; *fig* separación, *f*. **w. fork,** bieldo, *m*. **w. machine,** aventador mecánico, *m*
winsome *a* sandunguero; dulce, encantador
winsomeness *n* sandunga, *f*; encanto, *m*, dulzura, *f*
winter *n* invierno, *m*. *a* de invierno; hiemal. *vi* pasar el invierno, invernar. *vt* (of cattle, etc.) guardar en invierno. **in w.,** en invierno, durante el invierno. **w. clothes,** ropa de invierno, *f*. **w. palace,** palacio de invierno, *m*. **w. pasture** *Lat. Am.* invernada, *f*. **w. quarters,** invernadero, *m*. **w. season,** invierno, *m*; temporada de invierno, *f*. **w. sleep,** invernada, *f*. **w. solstice,** solsticio hiemal, *m*. **w. sports,** deportes de nieve, *m pl*. **w. wheat,** trigo de invierno, *m*
wintry *a* de invierno; invernal; (of a smile, etc.) glacial
wipe *vt* limpiar; (rub) frotar; (dry) secar; (remove) quitar. *n* limpión, *m*; (blow) golpe de lado, *m*. **to w. one's eyes,** enjugarse las lagrimas. **to w. off, out,** limpiar; (remove) quitar; (erase) borrar; (kill) destruir completamente, exterminar; (a military force) destrozar; (a debt) cancelar
wire *n* alambre, *m*; hilo metálico, *m*; telégrafo (eléctrico), *m*; *inf* telegrama, *m*. *vt* atar con alambre; (fence) alambrar; (snare) coger con lazo de alambre; (of electrical equipment, etc.) instalar; (telegraph) telegrafiar. *vi* (telegraph) telegrafiar. **barbed w.,** alambre espinoso, *m*. **live w.,** alambre cargado (de electricidad), *m*; (person) fuerza viva, *f*. **w.-cutters,** cortaalambres, *m pl*. **w.-entanglement,** *mil* alambrada, *f*. **w. fence,** alambrera, *f*, cercado de alambre, *m*. **w. gauze,** tela metálica, *f*. **w. nail,** punta de París, *f*. **w.-netting,** malla de alambre, *f*; alambrado, *m*. **w.-pulling,** influencias secretas, *f pl*; intrigas políticas, *f pl*
wiredraw *vt* estirar (alambre), tirar (el hilo de hierro, plata, etc.); (arguments, etc.) sutilizar
wiredrawer *n* estirador, *m*
wireless *a* sin hilos; (of a message) radiotelegráfico; por radio. *n* telegrafía sin hilos, *f*; radiotelefonía, *f*; (telegram) radiocomunicación, *f*; (broadcasting) radio, *f*. *vt* radiotelegrafiar. **Let's listen to the w.,** Vamos a escuchar la radio. **portable w.,** radio portátil, *f*. **w. engineer,** ingeniero radio-telegrafista, *m*. **w. enthusiast,** radioaficionado (-da). **w. licence,** permiso de radiorreceptor, *m*. **w. operator,** radiotelegrafista, *mf*. **w. room,** cuarto de telegrafía sin hilos, *m*. **w. set,** aparato de radio, *m*. **w. station,** estación de radiotelegrafía, *f*; (broadcasting) radioemisora, *f*. **w. telegraph,** telégrafo sin hilos, *m*. **w. telegraphy,** telegrafía sin hilos, radiotelegrafía, *f*. **w. telephony,** telefonía sin hilos, *f*. **w. transmission,** radioemisión, *f*
wiretap *vi* poner escucha. *vt* poner escucha a
wiring *n* instalación de alambres eléctricos, *f*
wiry *a* semejante a un alambre; (of persons) nervudo
wisdom *n* sabiduría, *f*; (learning) saber, *m*; (judgment) juicio, *m*. **Book of W.,** Libro de la Sabiduría, *m*. **w.-tooth,** muela del juicio, *f*
wise *a* sabio; juicioso, prudente; (informed) enterado, informado. **a w. man,** un sabio. **in no w.,** de ningún modo. **the W. Men of the East,** los magos. **w. guy,** *inf* toro corrido, *m*
wisely *adv* sabiamente; prudentemente, con prudencia
wish *n* deseo, *m*. **Best wishes for the New Year,** Los mejores deseos para el Año Nuevo. **w.-bone,** espoleta, *f*
wish *vt* querer; desear; ansiar; (with 'good morning', etc.) dar. **I w. he were here!** ¡Ojalá que estuviera aquí! **Theresa wishes us to go,** Teresa quiere que vayamos. **I w. it had happened otherwise,** Quisiera que las cosas hubiesen pasado de otra manera. **I w.**

you would make less noise, Me gustaría que hicieses menos ruido. **I only w. one thing,** Solamente deseo una cosa. **I w. you good luck,** Te deseo mucha suerte. **I wished him a merry Christmas,** Le deseé unas Pascuas muy felices, Le felicité las Pascuas. **to w. a prosperous New Year,** desear un próspero Año Nuevo. **to w. good-by,** despedirse (de). **to w. good day,** dar los buenos días. **to w. for,** desear

wisher *n* el que, *m,* (*f,* la que) desea, deseador (-ra)

wishful *a* deseoso; ansioso; ávido. **w. thinking,** ilusiones, *f pl;* optimismo injustificado, optimismo exagerado, *m*

wisp *n* mechón, *m;* jirón, *m;* trozo, pedazo, *m*

wistaria *n* vistaria, *f*

wistful *a* ansioso; triste; patético; (envious) envidioso; (regretful) de pesar; (remorseful) de remordimiento; (thoughtful) pensativo

wistfully *adv* con ansia; tristemente; patéticamente; con envidia; con pesar; con remordimiento; pensativo

wistfulness *n* ansia, *f;* tristeza, *f;* (envy) envidia, *f;* (regret) pesar, *m;* (remorse) remordimiento, *m;* (thoughtfulness) lo pensativo, lo distraído

wit, to *adv* a saber

wit *n* (reason) juicio, *m;* agudeza, gracia, *f,* rasgo de ingenio, *m;* ingenio, *m;* inteligencia, *f,* talento, *m;* (person) hombre de ingenio, *m;* mujer de ingenio, *f.* **my five wits,** mis cinco sentidos. **to be at one's wits' end,** no saber qué hacer. **to live by one's wits,** ser caballero de industria. **to lose one's wits,** perder el juicio

witch *n* bruja, *f.* **witches' sabbath,** aquelarre, *m.* **w.-doctor,** hechizador, mago, *m.* **witch-hazel,** carpe, *m;* loción de carpe, *f*

witchcraft *n* brujería, *f;* sortilegio, encantamiento, *m*

witchery *n* brujería, *f; fig* encanto, *m,* magia, *f*

with *prep* con; en compañia de; en casa de; (against) contra; (among) entre; en; (by) por; (towards) hacia; para con; (according to) según; (notwithstanding) a pesar de; a; (concerning) con respecto a; en el caso de. **Rose is w. Antony,** Rosa está con Antonio. **He was w. his dog,** Estaba acompañado por su perro. **He pulled at it w. both hands,** Lo tiró con las dos manos. **filled w. fear,** lleno de miedo. **to shiver w. cold,** temblarse de frío. **the girl w. golden hair,** la muchacha del pelo dorado. **They killed it w. one blow,** Lo mataron de un solo golpe. **It rests w. you to decide,** Tú tienes que decidirlo; Te toca a tí decidirlo. **to begin w.,** *adv* para empezar; *v* empezar por. **w. all speed,** a toda prisa. **to part w.,** desprenderse de; (of people) despedirse de; separarse de. **w. that . . .,** (at once) en esto . . . (disease and poverty, etc.) **are still with us,** están todavía en el mundo

withal *adv* además; al mismo tiempo. *prep* con

withdraw *vt* retirar; (words) retractar; (remove) quitar, privar (de); (a legal action) apartar. *vi* retirarse; retroceder; apartarse; irse

withdrawal *n* retirada, *f;* (retirement) retiro, *m;* apartamiento, *m*

withdrawn *a* (abstracted) ensimismado, meditabundo

wither *vi* marchitarse, secarse, ajarse. *vt* marchitar, secar, ajar; *fig* hacer languidecer, matar; (snub) avergonzar

withered *a* marchito, mustio; muerto; (of persons) acartonado, seco

witheredness *n* marchitez, *f;* sequedad, *f*

withering *a* que marchita; (scorching) abrasador, ardiente; (scornful) despreciativo, desdeñoso; (biting) mordaz, cáustico

withers *n* cruz, *f*

withhold *vt* retener; detener; (restrain) refrenar; apartar; (refuse) negar; abstenerse de; (refuse to reveal) ocultar

withholding *n* detención, *f;* (refusal) negación, *f*

within *adv* dentro, adentro; en el interior; en casa; *fig* en su interior. **He stayed w.,** Se quedó dentro. **Is Mrs. González w.?** ¿Está en casa la Sra. González?

within *prep* dentro de; el interior de; en; entre; (within range of) al alcance de; a la distancia de; (near) cerca de; a poco de; (of time) en el espacio de, en; dentro de; (almost) por poco, casi. **He was w. an ace of being killed,** Por poco le matan. **to be w. hearing,** estar al alcance de la voz. **seen from w.,** visto desde dentro. **twice w. a fortnight,** dos veces en quince días. **w. himself,** por sus adentros, entre sí. **w. an inch of,** *fig* a dos dedos de. **w. a few miles of Edinburgh,** a unas millas de Edimburgo. **w. a short distance,** en una corta distancia; a poca distancia

without *prep* sin; falto de; (outside) fuera de; (beyond) más allá de. *adv* exteriormente; por fuera; hacia afuera; fuera. **It goes w. saying,** No hay que decir. **w. more ado,** sin más ni más. **w. my knowledge,** sin que yo lo supiese. **w. regard for,** sin miramentos por. **w. saying more,** sin decir más. **without batting an eyelash,** sin sobresaltos

withstand *vt* resistir, oponerse (a); soportar

withstanding *n* resistencia, oposición (a), *f*

witless *a* sin seso, tonto, necio

witness *n* (evidence) testimonio, *m;* (person) testigo, *mf;* espectador (-ra). **in w. whereof,** en fe de lo cual. **to bear w.,** atestiguar, dar testimonio. **to bring forward witnesses,** hacer testigos. **w. my hand,** en fe de lo cual, firmo. **w.-box,** puesto de los testigos, *m.* **w. for the defence,** testigo de descargo, *mf.* **w. for the prosecution,** testigo de cargo, *mf*

witness *vt* (show) mostrar, señalar; (see) ser testigo de, ver, presenciar; *law* atestiguar. *vi* dar testimonio; servir de testigo

witticism *n* rasgo de ingenio, donaire, *m,* agudeza, *f*

wittily *adv* ingeniosamente, donairosamente, agudamente

wittiness *n* viveza de ingenio, donosura, *f*

witty *a* salado, gracioso. **w. sally,** agudeza, *f*

wizard *n* mago, hechicero, *m*

wizardry *n* magia, *f*

wizened *a* seco, arrugado; (of persons) acartonado

wobble *vi* tambalearse, balancearse; (quiver) temblar; oscilar; *mech* galopar; (stagger) titubear; *fig* vacilar

wobbly *a* que se bambolea; inestable; *fig* vacilante

woe *n* dolor, *m;* congoja, aflicción, *f;* mal, desastre, infortunio, *m.* **Woe is me!** ¡Ay de mí! ¡Desdichado de mí!

woebegone *a* angustiado

woeful *a* triste; doloroso; funesto

woefully *adv* tristemente; dolorosamente

wolf *n* lobo (-ba). **a w. in sheep's clothing,** un lobo en piel de cordero. **to cry w.,** gritar «el lobo!» **to keep the w. from the door,** ponerse a cubierto del hambre. **w.-cub,** lobezno, *m.* **w.-hound,** perro lobo, *m.* **w. pack,** manada de lobos, *f*

wolfish *a* lobuno, de lobo

wolfram *n* volframio, *m*

woman *n* mujer, *f;* hembra, *f;* (lady-in-waiting) dama de servicio, *f.* **a fine figure of a w.,** una real hembra. **w. doctor,** médica, *f.* **w.-hater,** misógino, *m.* **w. of the town,** mujer de la vida airada, *f.* **w. of the world,** mujer de mundo, *f*

womanhood *n* feminidad, *f;* sexo feminino, *m*

womanish *a* afeminado

womankind *n* el sexo femenino, las mujeres

womanliness *n* feminidad, *f;* carácter femenino, *m*

womanly *a* femenino, de mujer

womb *n* útero, *m,* matriz, *f; fig* seno, *m*

women's dormitory *n* residencia para señoritas, *f*

wonder *n* maravilla, *f;* prodigio, *m;* portento, milagro, *m;* (surprise) sorpresa, *f;* admiración, *f;* asombro, *m;* (problem) enigma, *m;* misterio, *m. vi* admirarse, asombrarse, maravillarse; sorprenderse. *vt* (ask oneself) preguntarse; desear saber. **I wondered what the answer would be,** Me preguntaba qué sería la respuesta. **It is no w. that . . .,** No es mucho que . . ., No es sorprendente que . . . **It is one of the wonders of the world,** Es una de las maravillas del mundo. **to**

work wonders, hacer milagros. **to w. at,** asombrarse de, maravillarse de; sorprenderse de. **w.-working,** milagroso
wonderful *a* maravilloso; magnífico; asombroso; *inf* estupendo
wonderfully *adv* maravillosamente; admirablemente
wondering *a* de asombro, sorprendido; perplejo
wonderingly *adv* con asombro
wonderland *n* mundo fantástico, *m;* reino de las hadas, *m;* país de las maravillas, *m.* **"Alice in W.,"** Alicia en el país de las maravillas
wonderment *n.* See **wonder**
wondrous *a* maravilloso. *adv* extraordinariamente
wont *n* costumbre, *f. vi* soler. **as he was w.,** Como solía
won't. See **will not**
wonted *a* sólito, acostumbrado
woo *vt* galantear; hacer la corte (a), solicitar amores a; cortejar, *Lat. Am.* afilar. *fig* solicitar; perseguir
wood *n* bosque, *m;* madera, *f;* (for the fire, etc.) leña, *f;* (cask) barril, *m. a* de madera; (of the woods) selvático. **dead w.,** ramas muertas, *f pl; fig* paja, *f.* **w. alcohol,** alcohol metílico, *m.* **w.-anemone,** anémona de los bosques, *f.* **w.-block floor,** entarimado, *m.* **w.-borer,** xiló-fago, *m.* **w.-carver,** tallista, *mf* **w.-carving,** talla en madera, *f.* **w.-craft,** conocimiento del campo, *m.* **w.-cut,** grabado en madera, *m.* **w.-cutter,** leñador, *m.* **w.-engraver,** grabador (-ra) en madera. **w.-engraving,** grabado al boj, *m.* **w.-fibre,** fibra de madera, *f.* **w.-louse,** cochinilla, *f.* **w.-nymph,** ninfa de los bosques, *f.* **w.-pigeon,** paloma torcaz, *f.* **w.-pile,** pila de leña, leñera, *f.* **w.-pulp,** pulpa de madera, *f.* **w.-shaving,** acepilladura, *f.* **w.-splinter,** tasquil, *m,* astilla, *f.* **w.-wind,** *mus* madera, *f.* **w.-worm,** carcoma, *f*
wooded *a* provisto de árboles, plantado de árboles, arbolado
wooden *a* de madera; de palo; (of smiles) mecánico; (stiff) indiferente, sin emoción; (clumsy) torpe; (of character) inflexible. **He has a w. leg,** Tiene una pata de palo. **w. beam,** madero, *m;* viga de madera, *f.* **w. bridge,** pontón, *m.* **w. galley,** *print* galerín, *m*
woodland *n* bosques, *m pl. a* de bosque; silvestre
woodpecker *n* pájaro carpintero, picamaderos, *m*
woodshed *n* leñera, *f*
woodwork *n* maderaje, *m;* molduras, *f pl;* carpintería, *f*
woody *a* leñoso; arbolado, con árboles. **w. tissue,** tejido leñoso, *m*
wooer *n* pretendiente, galanteador, *m*
woof *n* trama, *f*
wooing *n* galanteo, *m*
wool *n* lana, *f. a* de lana; lanar. **to go w.-gathering,** estar distraído. **to pull the w. over a person's eyes,** engañar como a un chino. **w.-bearing,** lanar. **w.-carding,** cardadura de lana, *f.* **w.-growing,** cría de ganado lanar, *f.* **w. merchant,** comerciante en lanas, *mf,* lanero, *m.* **w.-pack,** fardo de lana, *m.* **w. trade,** comercio de lana, *m*
woollen *a* de lana; lanar. *n* paño de lana, *m;* género de punta de lana, *m*
woolliness *n* lanosidad, *f*
woolly *a* lanudo, lanoso; de lana; *bot* velloso; (of hair) lanoso, crespo. *n* género de punta de lana, *m;* (sweater) jersey, *m*
word *n* palabra, *f; gram* vocablo, *m; theol* verbo, *m;* (maxim) sentencia, *f,* dicho, *m;* (message) recado, *m;* (news) aviso, *m,* noticias, *f pl;* (*mil* command) voz de mando, *f;* (order) orden, *f;* (password) contraseña, *f;* (term) término, *m. vt* expresar; formular; (draw up) redactar; escribir. **He was as good as his w.,** Fue hombre de palabra. **I do not know how to w. this letter,** No sé cómo redactar esta carta. **in a w.,** en una palabra; en resumidas cuentas. **by w. of mouth,** de palabra. **I give you my w. for it,** Le doy mi palabra de honor. **in other words,** en otros términos; en efecto. **the W. (of God),** el Verbo (de Dios). **to have a w. with,** hablar con; conversar con; entablar conversación con. **to leave w.,** dejar recado. **to have words with,** tener palabras con. **to keep one's w.,** cumplir su palabra
word index *n* índice de vocablos, *m*
wordiness *n* palabrería, verbosidad, *f*
wording *n* fraseología, *f;* expresión, *f;* estilo, *m;* (terms) términos, *m pl;* (drawing up) redacción, *f*
wordy *a* verboso, prolijo
work *n* trabajo, *m;* (sewing) labor, *f;* (literary, artistic production and theological) obra, *f;* (behavior) acción, *f,* acto, *m;* (employment) empleo, *m;* (business affairs) negocios, *m pl; pl* **works,** obras, fortificaciones, *f, pl;* obras públicas, *f pl;* construcciones, *f pl;* (of a machine) mecanismo, *m;* motor, *m;* (factory) fábrica, *f,* taller, *m.* **w. of art,** obra de arte. **w. accident,** accidente del trabajo, *m.* **w.-bag,** bolsa de costura, *f,* saco de labor, *m.* **w.-box,** (on legs) costurero, *m;* (small) neceser de costura, *m.* **w.-people,** obreros (-as). **w.-room,** taller, *m;* (study) estudio, *m;* (for sewing) cuarto de costura, *m.* **w.-table,** banco de taller, *m;* (for writing) mesa de escribir, *f*
work *vi* trabajar, *Central America also* laborar; *sew* hacer labor de aguja, coser; (embroider) bordar; *mech* funcionar, marchar; (succeed) tener éxito; ser eficaz; (be busy) estar ocupado; (be employed) tener empleo; (of the face) demudarse, torcerse; (ferment) fermentar; (operate) obrar *vt* trabajar; operar, hacer funcionar; mover; (control) manejar; (a mine) explotar; (embroider) bordar; (wood) tallar; (a problem) resolver; calcular; (iron, etc.) labrar; (the soil) cultivar; (a ship) maniobrar; (do) hacer; (bring about) efectuar; traer consigo; producir; (agitate oneself) agitarse, emocionarse, excitarse. **to w. in repoussé,** repujar. **to w. loose,** desprenderse. **to w. one's passage,** trabajar por el pasaje. **to w. overtime,** trabajar horas extraordinarias. **to w. two ways,** ser espada de dos filos. **to w. at,** trabajar en; ocuparse en; dedicarse a; elaborar. **to w. in,** *vt* introducir; insinuar. *vi* combinarse. **to w. into,** penetrar en. **to w. off,** usar, emplear; (get rid of) deshacerse de, librarse de. **to w. on, upon,** influir en; obrar sobre; estar ocupado en. **to w. out,** *vt* calcular; resolver; (a mine, topic, etc.) agotar; (develop) elaborar, desarrollar; trazar, planear; (find) encontrar. *vi* llegar (a); resultar; venir a ser. **to w. up,** crear; (promote) fomentar; producir; (excite) agitar, excitar; (fashion) dar forma (a), labrar; (finish) terminar
workable *a* laborable; factible, practicable; (of a mine) explotable
workableness *n* practicabilidad, *f*
workaday *a* de todos los días; prosaico
workbench banco de mecánico, *f,* banco de taller, banco de trabajo, *m,* mesa de trabajo, *f*
workday *n* día de trabajo, día laborable, *m*
worker *n* trabajador (-ra); (manual) obrero (-ra); (of a machine) operario (-ia). **w.-ant,** hormiga obrera, *f.* **w.-bee,** abeja obrera, *f*
workhouse *n* asilo, *m*
working *a* de trabajo; (of capital) de explotación; trabajador, que trabaja; obrero. *n* trabajo, *m;* (of a machine, organism, institution) funcionamiento, *m;* explotación, *f;* (of a mine) laboreo, *m;* (of a ship) maniobra, *f;* (of metal, stone, wood) labra, *f;* operación, *f;* (result) efecto, resultado, *m;* (calculation) cálculo, *m.* **"Not w.,"** «No funciona.» **to be in w. order,** funcionar bien. **w.-class,** clase obrera, *f;* pueblo, *m.* **w.-clothes,** ropa de trabajo, *f.* **w.-day,** día de trabajo, *m.* **w.-hours,** horas de trabajo, horas hábiles, *f pl.* **w. hypothesis,** postulado, *m.* **w.-man,** obrero, *m;* trabajador, *m.* **w.-out,** elaboración, *f;* ensayo, *m.* **w.-plan,** plan de trabajo, *m.* **w.-woman,** obrera, *f;* trabajadora, *f*
workless *a* sin trabajo
workman *n* obrero, *m;* (agricultural) labrador, *m*
workmanlike *a* bien hecho, bien acabado; (clever) hábil

workmanship *n* trabajo, *m;* manufactura, *f;* hechura, *f;* (cleverness) habilidad, *f*
workshop *n* taller, *m*
world *n* mundo, *m.* **For all the w. as if . . . ,** Exactamente como si . . . **to see the w.,** ver mundo. **to treat the w. as one's oyster,** ponerse el mundo por montera. **w. without end,** por los siglos de los siglos. **w.-power,** potencia mundial, gran potencia, *f.* **w.-wide,** mundial, universal
world almanac *n* compendio mundial, *m*
worldliness *n* mundanería, *f,* conocimiento del mundo, *m;* frivolidad, vanidad mundana, *f;* egoísmo, *m;* prudencia, *f*
worldly *a* de este mundo; mundano; humano; profano; frívolo. **to be w.-wise,** tener mucho mundo
worm *n* gusano, *m;* lombriz, *f; chem* serpentín, *m;* (of a screw) tornillo sinfin, *m;* (person) gusano, *m; fig* gusano roedor, remordimiento, *m.* **intestinal w.,** lombriz intestinal, *f,* gusano de la conciencia. **w.-eaten,** carcomido. **w.-hole,** picadura de gusano, lombriguera, *f.* **w.-powder,** polvos antihelmínticos, *m pl.* **w.-shaped,** vermiforme. **having worms, suffering from worms** *Lat. Am.* lombriciento
worm *vt* (a dog) dar un vermífugo (a). *vi* arrastrarse como un gusano. **to w. one's way into,** deslizarse en; *fig* insinuarse en, introducirse en. **to w. out,** (secrets, information) sonsacar
wormwood *n* ajenjo, *m*
wormy *a* gusanoso, lleno de gusanos
worn *a* (of garments) raído; estropeado; gastado; (of paths) trillado; (of the face) arrugado, cansado. **w. out,** acabado; muy usado; (tired) rendido; (exhausted) agotado
worrier *n* inquietador (-ra); receloso (-sa); aprensivo (-va)
worry *n* preocupación, inquietud, ansiedad, *f;* problema, cuidado, *m. vt* (prey) zamarrear; preocupar, inquietar; molestar; importunar. *vi* estar preocupado, estar intranquilo, inquietarse. **Don't worry,** Pierda cuidado, No pase cuidado
worrying *a* inquietante, perturbador; molesto
worse *a comp* peor; inferior. *adv* peor; menos. *n* lo peor. **so much the w.,** tanto peor. **to be w. off,** estar peor; estar en peores circunstancias; ser menos feliz. **to be the w. for wear,** ser muy usado; estar ajado; ser ya viejo. **to grow w.,** empeorarse; (of an ill person) ponerse peor. **w. and w.,** de mal en peor, peor que peor. **w. than ever,** peor que nunca
worsen *vt* agravar, hacer peor; exasperar. *vi* agravarse, empeorarse; exasperarse
worsening *n* agravación, *f,* empeoramiento, *m;* exasperación, *f*
worship *n* culto, *m;* adoración, *f;* veneración, *f. vt* adorar; reverenciar. *vi* adorar; rezar; dar culto (a). **place of w.,** edificio de culto, *m.* **Your W.,** vuestra merced
worshipful *a* venerable, respetable
worshipper *n* adorador (-ra); *pl* **worshippers,** (in a church, etc.) fieles, *m pl,* congregación, *f*
worshipping *n* adoración, *f,* culto, *m*
worst *a* el (la, etc.) peor; más malo. *adv* el (la, etc.) peor. *n* el (la, etc.) peor; lo peor. *vt* vencer, derrotar; triunfar sobre **If the w. comes to the w.,** En el peor de los casos. **The w. of it is that . . . ,** Lo peor es que . . . **to have the w. of it,** salir perdiendo, llevar la peor parte
worsted *n* estambre, *m, a* de estambre
worth *n* valor, *m;* precio, *m;* mérito, *m, a* (que) vale; de precio de; cuyo valor es de; equivalente a; (que) merece; digno de. **He bought six hundred pesetas w. of sweets,** Compró seiscientas pesetas de dulces. **He sang for all he was w.,** Cantó con toda su alma. **It is w. seeing,** Es digno de verse, Vale la pena de verse. **to be w.,** valer. **to be w. while,** valer la pena, merecer la pena
worthily *adv* dignamente
worthiness *n* mérito, valor, *m*
worthless *a* sin valor; sin mérito; inútil; malo; (of persons) vil, despreciable, indigno
worthlessness *n* falta de valor, *f;* falta de mérito, *f;* inutilidad, *f;* (of persons) bajeze, vileza, *f*
worthy *a* digno de respeto, benemérito, respetable; digno, merecedor; meritorio. *n* varón ilustre, hombre célebre, *m;* héroe, *m;* (*inf iron*) tío, *m.* **to be w. of,** ser digno de, merecer
would *preterite* and *subjunctive* of **will.** (indicating a conditional tense) **They w. come if . . . ,** Vendrían si . . . ; (indicating an imperfect tense) **Often he w. sing,** Muchas veces cantaba, **Now and then a blackbird w. whistle,** De vez en cuando silbó un mirlo; (expressing wish, desire) **What w. they?** ¿Qué quieren? **The place where I w. be,** El lugar donde quisiera estar. **W. I were at home!** ¡Ojalá que estuviese en casa! **I thought that I w. tell you,** Se me ocurrió la idea de decírselo. **It w. seem that . . . ,** Parece ser que . . . , Según parece . . . ; Se diría que . . . **He said that he w. never have done it,** Dijo que no lo hubiera hecho nunca. **They w. have been killed if he had not rescued them,** Habrían sido matados si él no los hubiese salvado. **He w. go,** Se empeñó en ir. **He w. not do it,** Rehusó hacerlo, Se resistió a hacerlo; No quiso hacerlo. **This w. probably be the house,** Sin duda esta sería la casa. **W. you be good enough to . . . ,** Tenga Vd. la bondad de . . . , Haga el favor de . . .
would-be *a* supuesto; llamado; aspirante (a); en esperanza de (followed by infin.); (frustrated) frustrado, malogrado
wound *n* herida, lesión, *Lat. Am. also,* lastimadura, *f. vt* herir; (the feelings) lastimar, lacerar. **deep w.,** herida penetrante, *f.* **the wounded,** los heridos.
wounding *n* herida, *f, a fig* lastimador
wraith *n* fantasma, espectro, *m,* sombra, *f*
wrangle *vi* discutir; altercar, disputar acaloradamente; reñir; (bargain) regatear. *n* argumento, *m;* disputa, *f,* altercado, *m;* riña, *f*
wrangler *n* disputador (-ra); (Cambridge University) laureado en matemáticas, *m*
wrangling *n* disputas, *f pl,* altercación, *f;* (bargaining) regateo, *m*
wrap *vt* envolver; arrollar; cubrir; abrigar; (conceal) ocultar. *n* envoltorio, *m;* abrigo, *m; pl* **wraps,** abrigos y mantas de viaje, *m pl.* **W. yourself up well!** ¡Abrígate bien! **to be wrapped up in,** estar envuelto en; *fig* estar entregado a, estar absorto en; (a person) estar embelesado con
wrapper *n* envoltura, *f;* embalaje, *m;* (of a newspaper) faja, *f;* (of a book) sobrecubierta, *f;* (dressing-gown) bata, *f,* salto de cama, *m*
wrapping *n* envoltura, cubierta, *f.* **w.-paper,** papel de envolver, *m*
wrath *n* ira, *f*
wrathful *a* airado
wreak *vt* ejecutar; (anger, etc.) descargar. **to w. one's vengeance,** vengarse
wreath *n* guirnalda, *f;* corona, *f;* trenza, *f.* **funeral w.,** corona funeraria, *f*
wreathe *vt* trenzar; (entwine) entrelazar (de); (garland) coronar (de), enguirnaldar (con); (encircle) ceñir, rodear; (a face in smiles) iluminar
wreck *n* naufragio, *m;* buque naufragado, *m;* destrucción, *f; fig* ruina, *f;* (remains) restos, *m pl;* (person) sombra, *f. vt* hacer naufragar; destruir; *fig* arruinar; hacer fracasar. **I am a complete w.,** *inf* Estoy hecho una ruina. **to be wrecked,** irse a pique, naufragar; *fig* arruinarse; frustrarse
wreckage *n* naufragio, *m;* restos de naufragio, *m pl;* ruinas, *f pl;* (of a car, plane, etc.) restos, *m pl;* accidente, *m*
wrecked *a* naufragado
wrecker *n* destructor (-ra); (of ships) raquero, *m*
wrench *n* (jerk) arranque, *m;* (pull) tirón, *m;* (sprain) torcedura, *f;* (tool) llave, *f;* (pain) dolor, *m. vt* arrancar;

forzar; torcer, dislocar. **He has wrenched his arm,** Se ha torcido el brazo

wrest *vt* arrebatar, arrancar

wrestle *vi* luchar. *n* lucha grecorromana, *f*; *fig* lucha, *f*. **to w. with,** *fig* luchar con; luchar contra, *Lat. Am.* abrocharse (con . . .)

wrestler *n* luchador, *m*

wrestling *n* lucha grecorromana, *f*. **all-in-w.,** lucha libre, *f*. **w.-match,** lucha, *f*

wretch *n* infeliz, *mf*; (ruffian) infame, *m*; (playful) picaruelo (-la). **a poor w.,** un pobre diablo

wretched *a* (unhappy) infeliz, desdichado; miserable; pobre; (ill) enfermo; horrible; malo; mezquino; despreciable; lamentable

wretchedly *adv* tristemente; pobremente; muy mal; ruinmente

wretchedness *n* infelicidad, desdicha, *f*; miseria, pobreza, *f*; escualidez, *f*; ruindad, *f*

wriggle *vi* agitarse, moverse; menearse; serpear, culebrear; retorcerse. *n* See under **wriggling. to w. into,** insinuarse en, deslizarse dentro (de). **to w. out,** escaparse. **to w. out of a difficulty,** extricarse de una dificultad

wriggling *n* meneo, *m*; retorcimiento, *m*; serpenteo, culebreo, *m*

wring *vt* torcer; estrujar; exprimir; arrancar; (force) forzar. **to w. one's hands,** restregarse las manos. **to w. the neck of,** torcer el pescuezo (a). **to w. out,** exprimir; estrujar

wringer *n* torcedor (-ra); (for clothes) exprimidor de ropa, *m*

wringing *n* torsión, *f*. **w.-machine,** exprimidor de ropa, *m*

wrinkle *n* arruga, *f*; pliegue, *m*; *inf* noción, *f*. *vt* arrugar. *vi* arrugarse. **to w. one's brow,** (frown) fruncir el ceño; (in perplexity) arrugar la frente

wrinkling *n* arrugamiento, *m*

wrinkly *a* arrugado

wrist *n* muñeca, *f*. **w.-band,** tira del puño de la camisa, *f*. **w. bandage,** pulsera, *f*

wristlet *n* pulsera, *f*; manguito elástico, *m*. **w. watch,** reloj de pulsera, *m*

writ *n* escritura, *f*; *law* decreto judicial, mandamiento, *m*; orden, *f*; título ejecutorio, *m*; hábeas corpus, *m*. **Holy W.,** la Sagrada Escritura. **to issue a w.,** dar orden. **to serve a w.,** notificar una orden. **w. of privilege,** auto de excarcelación, *m*

write *vt* and *vi* escribir; *fig* mostrar. **He writes a good hand,** Tiene buena letra. **I shall w. to them for a list,** Les escribiré pidiendo una lista. **to w. back,** contestar por escrito; contestar a una carta. **to w. down,** poner por escrito; anotar, apuntar; describir. **to w. for,** escribir para; escribir para pedir algo; escribir algo en vez de otra persona. **to w. off,** escribir; escribir rápidamente; cancelar. **to w. on,** seguir escribiendo; escribir sobre. **to w. out,** copiar; redactar. **to w. over again,** escribir de nuevo, escribir otra vez, volver a escribir. **to w. up,** redactar; *com* poner al día; (praise) escribir alabando

writer *n* escritor (-ra); autor (-ra). **the present w.,** el que, *m*, (*f*, la que) esto escribe. **writer's cramp,** calambre del escribiente, *m*

writhe *vi* retorcerse

writhing *n* retorsión, *f*

writing *n* escritura, *f*; (work) escrito, *m*; inscripción, *f*; documento, *m*; (style) estilo, *m*; (hand) letra, *f*; el arte de escribir; trabajo literario, *m*. **in one's own w.,** de su propia letra. **in w.,** por escrito. **w.-case,** escribanía, *f*. **w.-desk,** escritorio, *m*. **w.-pad,** taco de papel, *m*. **w.-paper,** papel de escribir, *m*. **w.-table,** mesa de escribir, *f*

written *a* escrito

wrong *a* injusto; mal; equivocado, erróneo; inexacto; falso; incorrecto; desacertado; inoportuno. **It is the w. one,** No es el que hacía falta; No es el que quería. **to be in the w. place,** estar mal situado; estar mal colocado. **to be w.,** estar mal; no tener razón; (mistaken) estar equivocado; (of deeds or things) estar mal hecho; (be unjust) ser injusto; (of clocks) andar mal. **to do w.,** hacer mal; obrar mal. **to get out of bed on the w. side,** levantarse del izquierdo. **to go w.,** (of persons) descarriarse; (of affairs) ir mal; salir mal; frustrarse; (of apparatus) estropearse, no funcionar. **We have taken the w. road,** Nos hemos equivocado de camino. **You were very w. to . . . ,** Has hecho muy mal en . . . **w.-headed,** terco, obstinado; disparatado. **w.-headedness,** terquedad, obstinación, *f*. **w. number,** (telephone) número errado, *m*. **w. side,** revés, *m*; lado malo, *m*. **w. side out,** al envés; al revés

wrong *adv* mal; injustamente; sin razón; incorrectamente; equivocadamente; (inside out) al revés. **to get it w.,** (a sum) calcular mal; (misunderstand) comprender mal

wrong *n* mal, *m*; injusticia, *f*; perjuicio, *m*; ofensa, *f*, agravio, *m*; culpa, *f*; error, *m*. **to be in the w.,** no tener razon; haber hecho mal. **to put one in the w.,** echar la culpa (a), hacer responsable (de)

wrong *vt* hacer mal (a); perjudicar; ser injusto con; ofender

wrongdoer *n* malhechor (-ra); pecador (-ra); perverso (-sa)

wrongdoing *n* maldad, maleficencia, *f*; pecado, *m*; injusticia, *f*

wrongful *a* injusto; perjudicial; falso

wrongfully *adv* injustamente; falsamente

wrongly *adv* injustamente; erróneamente, equivocadamente; perversamente; mal

wrongness *n* mal, *m*; injusticia, *f*; falsedad, *f*; inexactitud, *f*, error, *m*

wrought *a* forjado; labrado; (hammered) batido; trabajado. **w. iron,** hierro dulce, hierro forjado, *m*. **w. up,** muy excitado, muy agitado, muy nervioso

wry *a* torcido; tuerto; triste; pesimista; desilusionado; irónico. **wry face,** mueca *f*, de desengaño, de ironía, de disgusto, etc. **make a wry face,** torcer el gesto, *Mexico* engestarse. **wry neck,** *orn* torcecuello, *m*

wryly *adv* tristemente; irónicamente

Wuthering Heights Cumbres borrascosas

wye *n* (letter) ye, i griega, *f*; horquilla, cosa en forma de Y, *f*

x *n* equis, *f*

x-ray *vt* tomar una radiografía (de). **x-ray,** rayo x, *m pl*. **x-ray examination,** examen con rayos x, *m*. **x-ray photograph,** radiografía, *f*

xylophone *n* xilófono, *m*

Y

y *n* (letter) i griega, ye, *f*
yacht *n* yate, *m.* **y. club,** club marítimo, *m.* **y. race,** regata de yates, *f*
yachting *n* navegación en yate, *f,* paseo en yate, *m*
yachtsman *n* deportista náutico, balandrista, balandrismo, *m*
yam *n* batata, *f, Lat. Am.* boniato, camote, *m*
yank *n* tirón, *m,* sacudida, *f. vt* dar un tirón (a); sacar de un tirón
Yankee *a* and *n* yanqui, *mf*
yap *vi* ladrar. *n* ladrido, *m*
yapper *n* (yapping dog) gozque, gozquejo, *m*
yapping *n* ladridos, *m pl, a* que ladra
yard *n* (measure) yarda, *f; naut* verga, *f;* corral, *m;* (courtyard) patio, *m. vt* acorralar. **goods y.,** estación de mercancías, *f.* **y.-arm,** penol (de la verga), *m.* **y.-stick,** vara de medir de una yarda, *f*
yarn *n* hilaza, *f;* hilo, *m;* (story) historia, *f,* cuento, *m.* **to spin a y.,** contar una historia
yaw *vi naut* guiñar; *aer* serpentear. *n naut* guiñada, *f; aer* serpenteo, *m*
yawn *vi* bostezar; quedarse con la boca abierta; (of chasms, etc.) abrirse. *n* bostezo, *m.* **to stifle a y.,** ahogar un bostezo
yawning *a* abierto. *n* bostezos, *m pl*
yea *adv* en verdad, ciertamente; y aun . . . no sólo . . . sino. *n* si, *m*
year *n* año, *m; pl* **years,** años, *m pl,* edad, *f.* **We are getting on in years,** Nos vamos haciendo viejos. **He is five years old,** Tiene cinco años. **all the y. round,** todo el año, el año entero. **by the y.,** al año. **every other y.,** cada dos años, un año sí y otro no. **in after years,** en años posteriores. **last y.,** el año pasado. **next y.,** el año próximo. el año que viene. **y. after y.,** año tras año. **New Y.,** Año Nuevo, *m.* **to see the New Y. in,** ver empezar el Año Nuevo. **New Year's Day,** día de Año Nuevo, *m.* **(A) Happy New Y.!** ¡Feliz Año Nuevo! **y.-book,** anuario, *m.* **a y. later** *Lat. Am.* al año
yearling calf *n* becerra *f*
yearly *a* anual. *adv* anualmente, cada año; una vez al año
yearn *vi* anhelar, suspirar (por); desear vivamente
yearning *n* sed, ansia, *f;* anhelo, deseo vehemente, *m. a* ansioso; anhelante; (tender) tierno
yeast *n* levadura, *f*
yell *vi* and *vt* chillar; gritar. *n* chillido, *m;* grito, *m*
yelling *n* chillidos, *m pl;* gritos, *m pl,* gritería, *f*
yellow *a* amarillo; (of hair) rubio; (cowardly) cobarde; (newspaper) amarillista, sensacionalista. **to turn y.,** *vi* ponerse amarillo; amarillear. *vt* volver amarillo. **y. fever,** fiebre amarilla, *f.* **y.-hammer,** *orn* emberizo, *m*
yellowing *n* amarilleo, *m*
yellowish *a* amarillento, *Lat. Am.* amarilloso
yellowness *n* amarillez, *f*
yellow pages *n* páginas amarillas, páginas doradas, *f pl*
yelp *vi* gañir. *n* gañido, *m*
yelping *n* gañidos, *m pl*
yen *n* (currency) yen, *m;* (desire) deseo vivo, *m*
yeoman *n* pequeño propietario rural, *m;* soldado de caballería, *m.* **Y. of the Guard,** alabardero de la Casa Real, *m*
yes *adv* sí. **Yes?** ¿De verdad? ¿Y qué pasó después? ¿Y entonces? **to say yes,** decir que sí; dar el sí. **yes-man,** amenista, sacristán de amén, *m*
yesterday *adv* ayer. *n* ayer, *m.* **the day before y.,** anteayer
yet *adv* aún, todavía. **as yet,** hasta ahora; todavía. **He has not come yet,** No ha venido todavía. **yet again,** otra vez
yet *conjunc* sin embargo, no obstante, con todo; pero. **The book is well written and yet I do not like it,** El libro está bien escrito, y sin embargo no me gusta
yew *n* tejo, *m;* madera de tejo, *f*
Yiddish *n* yídis, yídish, yídico, *m; a* yídico
yield *vt* producir; dar; (grant) otorgar; (afford) ofrecer; (surrender) ceder. *vi* producir; (submit) rendirse, someterse; (of disease) responder; (give way) flaquear, doblegarse; dar de sí; (consent) consentir (en); (to circumstances, etc.) ceder (a), sucumbir (a). *n* producción, *f,* producto, *m; com* rédito, *m;* (crop) cosecha, *f.* **to y. to temptation,** ceder a la tentación. **to y. up,** entregar; devolver
yielding *a* flexible; (soft) blando; dócil, sumiso; fácil; condescendiente
yogurt *n* yogur, *m*
yoke *n* yugo, *m;* (of oxen) yunta, *f;* (for pails) balancín, *m;* (of a garment) canesú, *m; fig* férula, *f,* yugo, *m. vt* uncir, acoplar. **to throw off the y.,** sacudir el yugo
yokel *n* patán, rústico, *m*
yolk *n* (of an egg) yema, *f*
yonder *a* aquel, *m;* aquella, *f;* aquellos, *m pl;* aquellas, *f pl. adv* allí; allí a lo lejos
yore *n* **in days of y.,** antaño; en otro tiempo
you *pers pron nominative* (polite form) usted (Vd.), *mf;* ustedes (Vds.), *mf pl;* (familiar form) *sing* tu, *mf;* (*plural*) vosotros, *m pl;* vosotras, *f pl;* (one) uno, *m;* una, *f;* se (followed by 3rd pers. sing. of verb). *pers pron accusative* (polite form) le, *m;* la, *f;* les, *m pl;* las, *f pl;* a usted, a ustedes; (informal form) te, *mf,* os, *mf pl;* (after most prepositions) ti, *mf;* vosotros, *m pl;* vosotras, *f pl.* **Are you there?** (telephone) ¡Oiga! **I gave the parcel to you,** Te (os) di el paquete; Di el paquete a usted (a ustedes). **I shall wait for you in the garden,** Te (os) esperaré en el jardín; Esperaré a Vds. (a Vd.) en el jardín. **This present is for you,** Este regalo es para tí (para vosotros, para Vd. (Vds.)). **Away with you!** ¡Vete! ¡Marchaos! **Between you and me,** Entre tú y yo. **you can't eat your cake and have it too,** no hay rosa sin espinas. **You never can tell,** No se sabe nunca, Uno no sabe nunca
young *a* joven; nuevo, reciente; inexperto; poco avanzado. *n* cría, *f,* hijuelos, *m pl.* **y. blood,** *inf* pollo pera, *m.* **y. girl,** jovencita, *f.* **y. man** joven, *m.* **y. people,** jóvenes, *m pl.* **in his y. days,** en su juventud. **The night is y.,** La noche está poca avanzada. **to grow y. again,** rejuvenecer. **with y.,** (of animals) preñada *f*
younger *a* más joven; menor. **Peter is his y. brother,** Pedro es su hermano menor. **to look y.,** parecer más joven
youngish *a* bastante joven
youngster *n* jovencito, chico, muchacho, *m;* niño, *m*
your *a poss* (polite form) su (*pl* sus), de usted (Vd.), (*pl* de ustedes (Vds.)); (familiar form) tu (*pl* vuestro). **I have y. papers,** Tengo tus (vuestros) papeles; Tengo los papeles de Vd. (*or* de Vds.). **How is y. mother?** ¿Cómo está su (tu) madre? **It is y. turn,** Te toca a ti, Le toca a Vd.
yours *pron poss* (polite form) (el) suyo, *m;* (la) suya, *f;* (los) suyos, *m pl;* (las) suyas, *f pl;* el, *m;* la, *f;* lo, *neut;* los, *m pl;* las, *f pl;* de usted (Vd.), *mf sing* or de ustedes (Vds.), *mf pl;* (familiar form) (el) tuyo, *m;* (la) tuya, *f;* (los) tuyos, *m pl;* (las) tuyas, *f pl;* (el) vuestro, *m;* (la) vuestra, *f;* (los) vuestros, *m pl;* (las) vuestras, *f pl.* **This is a picture of y.,** (addressing one person), Este es uno de los cuadros de usted (Vd.), Este es uno de tus cuadros. **This hat is mine, it is not y.,** Este sombrero es el mío, no es el tuyo. **The horse is y.,** El caballo es tuyo (de Vd.). **Y. affectionately,** Un abrazo de tu amigo . . . **Y. faithfully,** Queda de Vd. su att. (atentísimo) s.s. (seguro servidor). **Y. sincerely,** Queda de Vd. su aff. (afectuoso)

yourself *pron pers* (familiar form *sing*) tú mismo, *m*; tú misma, *f*; (after a preposition) tí, *mf*; (polite form) usted (Vd.) mismo, *m*; usted misma, *f*; *pl* **yourselves,** (familiar form) vosotros mismos, *m pl*; vosotras mismas, *f pl*; (polite form) ustedes (Vds.) mismos, *m pl*; ustedes mismas, *f pl*. **This is for y.,** Esto es para ti; Esto es para Vd.
youth *n* juventud, *f*; (man) joven, chico, mozalbete, *m*; (collectively) jóvenes, *m pl*, juventud, *f*
youthful *a* joven, juvenil; de la juventud
yowl *n* gañido, aullido, *m*. *vi* gañir, aullar
Yucatan *a* yucateco
yucca *n bot* yuca, *f*
Yugoslav *n* yugoeslavo (-va). *a* yugoeslavo
Yugoslavia Yugoeslavia, *f*
Yukon, the el Yukón, *m*
Yule *n* Navidad, *f*. **y.-log,** leño de Navidad, *m*. **y-tide,** Navidades, *f pl*

Z

z *n* (letter) zeda, zeta, *f*
zeal *n* celo, entusiasmo, *m*; ardor, fervor, *m*
zealot *n* fanático (-ca)
zealous *a* celoso, entusiasta
zealously *adv* con entusiasmo
zebra *n* cebra, *f*
zenith *n* cenit, *m*; *fig* apogeo, punto culminante, *m*
zephyr *n* céfiro, *m*, brisa, *f*
zero *n* cero, *m*. **below z.,** bajo cero. **z. hour,** hora cero, *f*
zest *n* sabor, gusto, *m*; entusiasmo, *m*. **to eat with z.,** comer con buen apetito. **to enter on with z.,** emprender con entusiasmo
zigzag *n* zigzag, *m*. *a* and *adv* en zigzag. *vi* zigzaguear, hacer zigzags, serpentear; (of persons) andar haciendo eses
Zimbabwe Zimbabue
zinc *n* cinc, *m*. **z. oxide,** óxido de cinc, *m*
Zion *n* Sión, *m*
Zionism *n* sionismo, *m*
Zionist *n* and *a* sionista
zip *n* (of a bullet) silbido, *m*; *inf* energía, *f*. **zip fastener,** cierre de cremallera, *m*
zip code *n* código postal, *m*
zipper *n* cremallera, *f*, cierre relámpago, cierre, cerrador, *m*
zircon *n* circón, *m*
zither *n* cítara, *f*
zodiac *n* zodiaco, *m*
zone *n* zona, *f*; faja, *f*
zoo *n* jardín zoológico, *m*
zoological *a* zoológico. **Z. garden,** jardín zoológico, *m*
zoologist *n* zoólogo, *m*
zoology *n* zoología, *f*
zoom *n* zumbido, *m*. *vi* zumbar; *aer* empinarse
Zulu *a* and *n* zulú *mf*
Zuyder Zee, the el Zuyderzée, *m*

Numbers/Números

Cardinal/Cardinales

one	1	uno, una
two	2	dos
three	3	tres
four	4	cuatro
five	5	cinco
six	6	seis
seven	7	siete
eight	8	ocho
nine	9	nueve
ten	10	diez
eleven	11	once
twelve	12	doce
thirteen	13	trece
fourteen	14	catorce
fifteen	15	quince
sixteen	16	dieciséis
seventeen	17	diecisiete
eighteen	18	dieciocho
nineteen	19	diecinueve
twenty	20	veinte
twenty-one	21	veintiuno
twenty-two	22	veintidós
thirty	30	treinta
thirty-one	31	treinta y uno
thirty-two	32	treinta y dos
forty	40	cuarenta
fifty	50	cincuenta
sixty	60	sesenta
seventy	70	setenta
eighty	80	ochenta
ninety	90	noventa
one hundred	100	cien
one hundred one	101	ciento uno
one hundred two	102	ciento dos
two hundred	200	doscientos, -as
three hundred	300	trescientos, -as
four hundred	400	cuatrocientos, -as
five hundred	500	quinientos, -as
six hundred	600	seiscientos, -as
seven hundred	700	setecientos, -as
eight hundred	800	ochocientos, -as
nine hundred	900	novecientos, -as
one thousand	1,000	mil
two thousand	2,000	dos mil
one hundred thousand	100,000	cien mil
one million	1,000,000	un millón
two million	2,000,000	dos millones

Ordinal/Ordinales*

first	1st / 1°	primero
second	2nd / 2°	segundo
third	3rd / 3°	tercero
fourth	4th / 4°	cuarto
fifth	5th / 5°	quinto
sixth	6th / 6°	sexto
seventh	7th / 7°	séptimo
eighth	8th / 8°	octavo
ninth	9th / 9°	noveno
tenth	10th / 10°	décimo

*Spanish ordinal numbers are used as adjectives: el primer hombre, los primeros hombres, la primera mujer, las primeras mujeres, etc.

Weights and Measures/Pesos y Medidas

1 centímetro	=	.3937 inches	1 kilolitro	=	264.18 gallons
1 metro	=	39.37 inches	1 inch	=	2.54 centímetros
1 kilómetro	=	.621 mile	1 foot	=	.305 metros
1 centigramo	=	.1543 grain	1 mile	=	1.61 kilómetros
1 gramo	=	15.432 grains	1 grain	=	.065 gramos
1 kilogramo	=	2.2046 pounds	1 pound	=	.455 kilogramos
1 tonelada	=	2.204 pounds	1 ton	=	.907 toneladas
1 centilitro	=	.338 ounces	1 ounce	=	2.96 centilitros
1 litro	=	1.0567 quart (liquid);	1 quart	=	1.13 litros
		.908 quart (dry)	1 gallon	=	4.52 litros

Signs/Señales

Caution	Precaución	**No smoking**	Prohibido fumar
Danger	Peligro	**No admittance**	Entrada prohibida
Exit	Salida	**One way**	Dirección única
Entrance	Entrada	**No entry**	Dirección prohibida
Stop	Alto	**Women**	Señoras or Mujeres or Damas
Closed	Cerrado	**Men**	Señores or Hombres or Caballeros
Open	Abierto	**Ladies' Room**	Cuarto de Damas
Slow	Despacio	**Men's Room**	Servicio

Days of the Week/Días de la Semana

Sunday	domingo	Thursday	jueves
Monday	lunes	Friday	viernes
Tuesday	martes	Saturday	sábado
Wednesday	miércoles		

Months/Meses

January	enero	October	octubre
February	febrero	November	noviembre
March	marzo	December	diciembre
April	abril		
May	mayo		
June	junio		
July	julio		
August	agosto		
September	septiembre		

Useful Phrases/Locuciones Útiles

Good day or Good morning! ¡Buenos días!
Good afternoon! ¡Buenas tardes!
Good night or Good evening! ¡Buenas noches!
Hello! ¡Hola!
Welcome! ¡Bienvenido!
See you later! ¡Hasta luego!
Goodbye! ¡Adiós!
How are you? ¿Cómo está usted?
I am fine, thank you. Estoy bien, gracias.
I am pleased to meet you. Mucho gusto en conocerle.
May I introduce . . . Quisiera presentar . . .
Thank you very much. Muchas gracias.
You're welcome. De nada *or* No hay de qué.
Please. Por favor.
Excuse me. Con permiso.
Good luck! ¡Buena suerte!
To your health! ¡Salud!

Please help me. Ayúdeme, por favor.
I don't know. No sé.
I don't understand. No entiendo.
Do you understand? ¿Entiende usted?
I don't speak Spanish. No hablo español.
Do you speak English? ¿Habla usted inglés?
How do you say . . . in Spanish? ¿Cómo se dice . . . en español?
What do you call this? ¿Cómo se llama esto?
Speak slowly, please. Hable despacio, por favor.
Please repeat. Repita, por favor.
I don't like it. No me gusta.
I am lost. Ando perdido or Me he extraviado.

What is your name? ¿Cómo se llama usted?
My name is . . . Me llamo . . .
I am an American. Soy norteamericano.
Where are you from? ¿De dónde es usted?
I'm from . . . Soy de . . .

How is the weather? ¿Qué tiempo hace?
It's cold (hot) today. Hace frío (calor) hoy.
What time is it? ¿Qué hora es?

How much is it? ¿Cuánto es?
It is too much. Es mucho.
What do you wish? ¿Qué desea usted?
I want to buy . . . Quiero comprar . . .
May I see something better? ¿Podría ver algo mejor?
May I see something cheaper? ¿Podría ver algo menos caro?
It is not exactly what I want. No es precisamente lo que quiero.

I am hungry. Tengo hambre.
I am thirsty. Tengo sed.
Where is there a restaurant? ¿Dónde hay restaurante?
I have a reservation. Tengo reservación.
I would like . . . Quisiera . . . ; Me gustaría . . .
Please give me . . . Me da . . .
Please bring me . . . Me trae . . .
May I see the menu? ¿Se puede ver el menú?
The bill, please. La cuenta, por favor.
Is service included in the bill? ¿El servicio está incluido en la cuenta?
Where is there a hotel? ¿Dónde hay hotel?
Where is the post office? ¿Dónde está el correo?
Is there any mail for me? ¿Tengo correo?
Where can I mail this letter? ¿Dónde se puede echar esta carta?

Take me to . . . Lléveme a . . .
I believe I am ill. Creo que estoy enfermo.
Please call a doctor. Por favor, llame al médico.

Please call the police. Por favor, llame a la policía.
I want to send a telegram. Quiero poner telegrama.
As soon as possible. Cuanto antes.
What is the postage? ¿Cuánto es el franqueo?
Where is the nearest drugstore? ¿Dónde está la farmacia más cercana?

Round trip. Ida y vuelta.
Please help me with my luggage. Por favor, ayúdeme con el equipaje.

Where can I get a taxi? ¿Dónde hay taxi?
What is the fare to . . . ¿Cuánto es el pasaje hasta . . . ?
Please take me to this address. Por favor, lléveme a esta dirección.
Where can I change my money? ¿Dónde se puede cambiar dinero?
Where is the nearest bank? ¿Dónde está el banco más cercano?
Can you accept my check? ¿Aceptará cheque?
Do you accept traveler's checks? ¿Aceptan cheques de viaje?
Where is the men's (women's) room? ¿Dónde está el servicio de caballeros (de señoras)?
Please let me off at . . . Por favor, déjeme bajar en . . .

Right away! ¡Pronto!
Help! ¡Socorro!
Who is it? ¿Quién es?
Just a minute! ¡Un momento no más!
Come in! ¡Pase usted!
Pardon me. Dispense usted.
Stop! ¡Pare!
Look out! ¡Cuidado!
Hurry! ¡De prisa! *or* ¡Dése prisa!
Go on! ¡Siga!
To (on, at) the right. A la derecha.
To (on, at) the left. A la izquierda.
Straight ahead. Adelante.